AUSTRALIAN
INTEGRATED
COMPACT
DICTIONARY
& THESAURUS

AUSTRALIAN INTEGRATED COMPACT DICTIONARY & THESAURUS

Compiled by
Anne Knight

To obtain access to the
Oxford Australian Online Dictionary & Thesaurus
visit **www.oup.com.au/adt**
and enter password: **oxforddictionaries**

OXFORD
UNIVERSITY PRESS
AUSTRALIA & NEW ZEALAND

OXFORD
UNIVERSITY PRESS

Oxford University Press is a department of the University of Oxford. It furthers the University's objective of excellence in research, scholarship, and education by publishing worldwide. Oxford is a registered trademark of Oxford University Press in the UK and in certain other countries.

Published in Australia by
Oxford University Press
253 Normanby Road, South Melbourne, Victoria 3205, Australia

© Oxford University Press 2005

The moral rights of the author have been asserted

First published 2005
Reprinted 2008, 2010, 2011

This dictionary is based on the *Australian School Dictionary* (second edition) and the *Australian School Thesaurus* compiled by Anne Knight.

National Library of Australia Cataloguing-in-Publication data

The Australian integrated compact dictionary and thesaurus.

ISBN 978 0 19 555020 7.

1. English language—Australia—Dictionaries. 2. English language—Australia—Synonyms and antonyms—Dictionaries. 3. English Language—Dictionaries. 4. English language— Synonyms and antonyms—Dictionaries. I. Knight, Anne.

423

OWLS
OXFORD DICTIONARY WORD AND LANGUAGE SERVICE

Do you have a query about words, their origin, meaning, use, spelling, or pronunciation, or any other aspect of international English? Then write to OWLS at the Australian National Dictionary Centre, Australian National University, Canberra ACT 0200 (email ANDC@anu.edu.au). All queries will be answered using the full resources of *The Australian National Dictionary* and *The Oxford English Dictionary*.

The Australian National Dictionary Centre and Oxford University Press also produce *Ozwords*, a biannual newsletter that contains interesting items about Australian words and language. Subscription is free—please contact the *Ozwords* subscription manager at Oxford University Press, GPO Box 2784, Melbourne, VIC 3001, or ozwords.au@oup.com

Typeset by Promptset Pty Ltd
Printed in Hong Kong by Sheck Wah Tong Printing Press Ltd

Preface

The Australian Integrated Compact Dictionary and Thesaurus is a handy reference book combining a dictionary and a thesaurus in a single easy-to-use volume. The top section of each page contains the dictionary text, while the lower section contains corresponding thesaurus entries for approximately two-thirds of the words covered by the dictionary.

The dictionary text offers clear definitions for more than 15,000 headwords, with many examples to clarify meaning and notes providing guidance on points of grammar and usage. Pronunciations are indicated when not obvious using a simple respelling system. Plurals of nouns, comparatives and superlatives of adjectives and adverbs, and derived forms of verbs are given where they are irregular or there might be doubt about their spelling. Etymologies are included where they shed light on a word's meaning or help with recognising word elements.

The thesaurus text provides lists of synonyms (words with the same or similar meaning) for more than 10,000 entries in the dictionary text. Within thesaurus entries the synonyms are grouped and numbered to match the dictionary senses, with the individual lists arranged in alphabetical order.

Like other Australian dictionaries published by Oxford University Press, the *Australian Integrated Compact Dictionary and Thesaurus* draws its ultimate authority from the vast resources of the *Oxford English Dictionary* and its continually updated database. Australian material is drawn from the *Australian National Dictionary* and the database of Australian English maintained by the Australian National Dictionary Centre in Canberra.

Guide to dictionary entries

Headword: the word being defined in the entry. Entries are arranged in alphabetical order of headwords.

Plural: the plural form of the headword.

Raised numbers: distinguish words with the same spelling that have separate entries for different parts of speech or unrelated meanings.

Compound: a word formed from the headword plus one or more other words.

Derivative: a word derived from the headword whose meaning can be worked out from the meaning of the headword.

Verb forms: the first form is the past tense, the second the past participle, and the third the present participle.

Phrase: a set phrase whose main word is the headword of the entry.

Verb forms: the first form is the past tense and past participle; the second is the present participle.

amnesia (*say* am-**nee**-zee-a) *noun* loss of memory. [from Greek *a-* = without, + *-mnesis* = memory]

formal *adjective* strictly following the accepted rules or customs; ceremonious. **formally** *adverb*

kilo *noun* (*plural* **kilos**) a kilogram.

kind¹ *noun* a class of similar things or animals; a sort or type.
payment in kind payment in goods not in money.

Usage Correct use is *this kind of thing* or *these kinds of things* (not 'these kind of things').

kind² *adjective* friendly and helpful; considerate. **kind-hearted** *adjective*, **kindness** *noun*

kindy *noun* (*Australian informal*) kindergarten.

king *noun* **1** a man who is the ruler of a country through inheriting the position. **2** a person or thing regarded as supreme, *the lion is the king of beasts.* **3** the most important piece in chess. **4** a playing card with a picture of a king. **kingly** *adjective*, **kingship** *noun*

opt *verb* choose.
opt out decide not to join in. [from Latin *optare* = wish for]

weapon *noun* something used to do harm in a battle or fight. **weaponry** *noun*

wear¹ *verb* (**wore, worn, wearing**) **1** have something on your body as clothes, ornaments, etc. **2** damage something by rubbing or using it often; become damaged in this way, *The carpet has worn thin.* **3** last while in use, *It has worn well.* **wearable** *adjective*, **wearer** *noun*
wear off be removed by wear or use; become less intense.
wear on pass gradually, *The night wore on.*
wear out use or be used until it becomes weak or useless; exhaust.

wear² *noun* **1** clothes, *formal wear.* **2** damage resulting from ordinary use, *wear and tear.*

weary¹ *adjective* (**wearier, weariest**) **1** tired. **2** tiring, *It's weary work.* **wearily** *adverb*, **weariness** *noun*

weary² *verb* (**wearied, wearying**) tire.

worn¹ *past participle* of **wear¹**.

Pronunciation: where it is not obvious we show how to say the word. (See also p. vi.)

Etymology: the origin of the headword.

Definition: the meaning of the headword.

Usage note: a note explaining correct usage.

Usage label: indicates the word belongs to Australian English and is normally used informally. (See p. vi for more information on usage labels.)

Part of speech: describes the grammatical use of a word as a *noun*, *verb*, *adverb*, *adjective*, etc.

Numbers: used for different senses of the headword.

Example: shows how the word is used and helps to clarify the meaning.

Adjective forms: the comparative and superlative forms of the headword.

Cross-reference: refers the reader to another entry for more information.

Guide to thesaurus entries

Headword: the word for which synonyms are given in the entry. Entries are arranged in alphabetical order of headwords.

Raised number: identifies the particular headword in the dictionary section with the same raised number.

Cross-reference: refers the reader to another entry for a list of synonyms.

Plural: the form of the headword for which synonyms are given.

Phrase: a set phrase whose main word is the headword of the entry. Synonyms are offered for the whole phrase.

Part of speech: describes the grammatical use of a word as a *noun, verb, adverb, adjective,* etc.

Derivative: a word derived from the headword for which synonyms are offered.

formal *adjective* (*a formal occasion*) ceremonial, official, solemn, stately; (*a formal manner*) ceremonious, conventional, dignified, pompous, prim, proper, punctilious, reserved, starchy, stiff, stilted, strait-laced.

kind¹ *noun* brand, breed, category, class, classification, form, genre, genus, ilk (*informal*), make, nature, order, set, sort, species, strain, style, type, variety.

kind² *adjective* affectionate, altruistic, amiable, attentive, avuncular, benevolent, benign, big-hearted, caring, charitable, compassionate, considerate, fatherly, friendly, generous, genial, gentle, good, good-natured, gracious, helpful, hospitable, humane, kind-hearted, kindly, lenient, loving, merciful, motherly, neighbourly, nice, obliging, philanthropic, soft-hearted, sympathetic, tender-hearted, thoughtful, understanding, unselfish, warm-hearted, well-meaning.

king *noun* **1** monarch, ruler, sovereign; see also RULER.

opt *verb* (*opt for*) choose, decide on, go for, pick, select, settle on, vote for.

weapon *noun* (*weapons*) armaments, arms, munitions, weaponry.

wear¹ *verb* **1** be attired in, clothe yourself in, don, dress in, have on, put on, sport. **2** abrade, corrode, eat away, erode, grind down, rub away, scuff, wear away, wear down. **3** endure, last, stand up, survive.
wear off decrease, diminish, dwindle, fade, lessen, subside.
wear out 1 become shabby, become threadbare, fray, wear thin. **2** drain, exhaust, fatigue, tire out, weary.

wear² *noun* **1** apparel (*formal*), attire (*formal*), clobber (*slang*), clothes, clothing, dress, garb, garments, gear (*informal*), raiment (*old use*). **2** damage, deterioration, disrepair, wear and tear.

weary¹ *adjective* **1** all in (*informal*), beat (*slang*), dog-tired, done in (*informal*), drained, drowsy, exhausted, fagged out (*informal*), fatigued, jaded, knackered (*slang*), pooped (*informal*), sleepy, spent, tired, whacked (*informal*), worn out, zonked (*slang*).
weariness *noun* exhaustion, fatigue, languor, lassitude, lethargy, listlessness, tiredness.

weary² *verb* drain, exhaust, fatigue, sap, tire, wear out.

Example: shows the context for which the following synonyms are suitable.

Synonyms: arranged in alphabetical order for each sense of the headword.

Verb plus preposition: synonyms are substitutable for the phrase.

Number: identifies the particular dictionary sense of the headword for which synonyms are given. Synonyms are not always offered for every dictionary sense, and in some cases a single list of synonyms is applicable to several senses.

Usage label: indicates a restricted use of a synonym. In the thesaurus the label is found in brackets after the synonym it qualifies. (See p. vi for more information on usage labels.)

Spelling

Many verbs ending in **-ise** (such as *realise*) and their corresponding nouns ending in **-isation** (such as *realisation*) may also be spelt with *z* instead of *s*. However, only **-ise** should be used in *advertise, advise, apprise, arise, chastise, comprise, compromise, demise, despise, devise, enfranchise, enterprise, excise, exercise, franchise, improvise, incise, merchandise, practise, promise, revise, rise, supervise, surmise, surprise, televise*, and in verbs ending in *-aise, -oise*, and *-uise*.

Pronunciation

Help is given with pronunciation when the word is difficult to pronounce, or when two words with the same spelling are pronounced differently. The pronunciation is given in brackets with *say*, e.g.

chaos (*say* **kay**-oss) *noun*

Words are broken up into small units (usually of one syllable), and the syllable that is spoken with most stress is shown in bold type, like **this**. In the pronunciation guide note the following distinctions:

oo	shows	the	sound	as in	*soon*
uu	"	"	"	"	" *book*
th	"	"	"	"	" *thin*
th	"	"	"	"	" *this*
zh	"	"	"	"	" *vision*

Usage labels

If the use of a word is restricted in any way this is indicated by a label printed in italics. Some words or senses may be restricted to a particular region or subject area, while others may be classed as *informal, slang, formal, derogatory,* and so on. Words labelled *formal* are normally restricted to formal (especially written) English, whereas those labelled *informal* are normally used only in speaking or informal writing. Words marked *slang* are generally used very informally, or restricted to a particular social group. Those marked *derogatory* are normally used to express a low opinion or to be deliberately insulting.

Proprietary terms

This dictionary includes some words which are, or are asserted to be, proprietary names or trade marks. Their inclusion does not imply that they have acquired for legal purposes a non-proprietary or general significance, nor is any other judgement implied concerning their legal status. In cases where the editor has some evidence that a word is used as a proprietary name or trade mark this is indicated by the label *trade mark*, but no judgement concerning the legal status of such words is made or implied thereby.

► Aa ◄

a *adjective* (called the *indefinite article* and changing to **an** before most vowel sounds) **1** one (but not any special one), *Can you lend me a book?* **2** each; per, *We can see it once a day or once an hour.*

a-¹ *prefix* **1** on; to; towards (as in *afoot, ashore, aside*). **2** in the process of (as in *a-hunting*).

a-² *prefix* (**an-** is used before a vowel sound) not; without (as in *asymmetrical, anarchy*). [from Greek *a-* = not]

ab- *prefix* (changing to **abs-** before *c* and *t*) away; from (as in *abduct, abnormal, abstract*). [from Latin *ab* = away]

aback *adverb* **taken aback** surprised.

abacus (*say* **ab**-a-kus) *noun* (*plural* **abacuses**) a frame used for counting with beads sliding on wires.

abandon¹ *verb* **1** give up. **2** leave a person, thing, or place without intending to return, *Abandon ship!* **abandonment** *noun*

abandon² *noun* a casual and careless manner, *dancing with great abandon.*

abase *verb* (**abased, abasing**) humiliate.

abashed *adjective* embarrassed.

abate *verb* (**abated, abating**) make or become less; die down, *The storm had abated.* **abatement** *noun*

abattoir (*say* **ab**-at-wahr) *noun* a slaughterhouse. [French]

abbey *noun* (*plural* **abbeys**) **1** a monastery or convent. **2** a church that was once part of a monastery, *Westminster Abbey.*

abbot *noun* the head of an abbey.

abbreviate *verb* (**abbreviated, abbreviating**) shorten something.

abbreviation *noun* **1** a shortened form of a word or words, such as maths, St., USA. **2** abbreviating something.

abdicate *verb* (**abdicated, abdicating**) resign from a throne; give up an important responsibility. **abdication** *noun*

abdomen (*say* **ab**-dom-en) *noun* **1** the lower front part of a person's or animal's body, containing the stomach, intestines, and other digestive organs. **2** the rear section of an insect's body. **abdominal** (*say* ab-**dom**-in-al) *adjective*

abduct *verb* take a person away illegally; kidnap. **abduction** *noun*, **abductor** *noun* [from *ab-*, + Latin *ductum* = led]

abet *verb* (**abetted, abetting**) help or encourage someone to commit a crime.

abeyance (*say* ab-**ay**-ans) *noun* **in abeyance** suspended or postponed.

abhor *verb* (**abhorred, abhorring**) detest. **abhorrent** *adjective*, **abhorrence** *noun* [from Latin *abhorrere* = shrink in fear]

►►► THESAURUS ◄◄◄

abandon¹ *verb* **1** abdicate, cancel, chuck in (*informal*), discontinue, drop, forgo, give up, quit, resign, scrap, surrender, throw in (*informal*), waive, yield. **2** (*abandon a person*) desert, ditch (*informal*), forsake, jilt, leave, leave in the lurch, run out on (*informal*), walk out on (*informal*); (*abandon a place*) evacuate, leave, quit, vacate.

abate *verb* decrease, die down, ease, moderate, subside, weaken.

abbey *noun* **1** convent, friary, monastery, nunnery, priory, religious house.

abbreviate *verb* abridge, contract, cut, reduce, shorten, truncate.

abbreviation *noun* **1** acronym, contraction, shortening.

abdicate *verb* quit, resign, stand down, step down; see also RENOUNCE.

abdomen *noun* **1** belly, gut (*informal*), insides (*informal*), intestines, paunch, stomach, tummy (*informal*).

abduct *verb* carry off, kidnap, seize, snatch (*informal*).

abet *verb* aid, assist, encourage, help, incite, support.

abhor *verb* abominate, detest, hate, loathe, recoil from, shrink from.
abhorrent *adjective* abominable, detestable, disgusting, hateful, horrid, loathsome, odious, repugnant, repulsive, revolting.

1

▶▶DICTIONARY◀◀

abide *verb* (**abided, abiding**) **1** (*old use*; *past tense* **abode**) remain; dwell. **2** bear; tolerate, *I can't abide flies*.
abide by keep a promise etc.

abiding *adjective* lasting; permanent.

ability *noun* (*plural* **abilities**) **1** being able to do something. **2** cleverness; talent.

abject (*say* **ab**-jekt) *adjective* **1** wretched; miserable, *living in abject poverty*. **2** humble, *an abject apology*. [from *ab-* + Latin *-jectum* = thrown]

able *adjective* **1** having the power or skill or opportunity to do something. **2** skilful; clever.
ably *adverb*

abnormal *adjective* not normal; unusual.
abnormally *adverb*, **abnormality** *noun*

aboard *adverb & preposition* on or into a ship or aircraft or train.

abode *noun* (*old use*) the place where someone lives.

abolish *verb* put an end to a law or custom etc.
abolition (*say* ab-ol-**ish**-on) *noun*

abominable *adjective* very bad; detestable.
abominably *adverb*

abominate *verb* (**abominated, abominating**) detest. **abomination** *noun*

aborigines (*say* ab-er-**ij**-in-eez) *plural noun* the original inhabitants of a country; **Aborigines** the original inhabitants of Australia. **aboriginal, Aboriginal** *adjective & noun*. **Aboriginality** *noun* awareness of being an Australian Aboriginal, Aboriginal culture. [from Latin *ab origine* = from the beginning]

abort *verb* put an end to something before it has been completed, *They aborted the space flight because of problems.*

abortion *noun* removal of a foetus from the womb before it has developed enough to survive.

abortive *adjective* unsuccessful, *an abortive attempt.*

abound *verb* **1** be plentiful or abundant, *Fish abound in the river.* **2** have something in great quantities, *The river abounds in fish.*

about¹ *preposition* **1** near in amount or size or time etc., *It costs about $5. Come about two o'clock.* **2** on the subject of; in connection with, *Tell me about your holiday.* **3** all round; in various parts of, *They ran about the playground.*

▶▶THESAURUS◀◀

abide *verb* **1** dwell, live, remain, reside, stay. **2** bear, endure, put up with, stand, stomach, suffer, take, tolerate.
abide by accept, adhere to, agree to, comply with, conform to, follow, keep to, obey, observe, stick to.

abiding *adjective* endless, enduring, eternal, everlasting, lasting, permanent, steadfast, unending.

ability *noun* **1** capability, capacity, potential, power, strength. **2** aptitude, capability, capacity, cleverness, competence, expertise, facility, flair, genius, gift, knack, know-how, potential, proficiency, prowess, skill, talent.

able *adjective* **1** allowed, authorised, available, eligible, fit, free, permitted. **2** accomplished, adept, adroit, capable, clever, competent, gifted, intelligent, proficient, qualified, skilful, talented.

abnormal *adjective* anomalous, atypical, bizarre, curious, deviant, eccentric, exceptional, extraordinary, freakish, irregular, odd, peculiar, queer, rare, singular, strange, uncommon, unconventional, unnatural, unusual, weird.

abnormality *noun* anomaly, deformity, irregularity, malformation, peculiarity.

abolish *verb* cancel, do away with, eliminate, end, eradicate, extinguish, get rid of, put an end to, remove, stamp out, wipe out.
abolition *noun* cancellation, elimination, ending, eradication, removal.

abominable *adjective* abhorrent, appalling, atrocious, base, contemptible, despicable, detestable, disgusting, execrable, foul, hateful, heinous, horrible, loathsome, obnoxious, odious, repugnant, repulsive, terrible, vile.

abominate *verb* abhor, detest, hate, loathe.

aboriginal *adjective* earliest, first, indigenous, native, original.

abortion *noun* (*when spontaneous*) miscarriage, (*when induced*) termination.

abortive *adjective* failed, fruitless, futile, ineffective, unsuccessful, vain.

abound *verb* **1** be abundant, be plentiful, flourish, proliferate, thrive. **2** be full, overflow, swarm, teem.

about¹ *preposition* **1** around, close to, near. **2** concerning, connected with, dealing with, involving, on, regarding, relating to.

▶▶ D I C T I O N A R Y ◀◀

about² *adverb* **1** approximately. **2** in various directions, *They were running about.* **3** not far away, *He is somewhere about.*
be about to be going to do something.

above¹ *preposition* **1** higher than. **2** more than.

above² *adverb* **1** at or to a higher place. **2** earlier in a book etc.

above board *adjective* & *adverb* honest; without deception.

abrade *verb* (**abraded**, **abrading**) scrape or wear something away by rubbing it. **abrasion** *noun*

abrasive¹ *adjective* **1** that abrades things. **2** harsh, *an abrasive manner.*

abrasive² *noun* a rough substance used for rubbing or polishing things.

abreast *adverb* **1** side by side. **2** keeping up with something.

abridge *verb* (**abridged**, **abridging**) shorten a book etc. by using fewer words, *an abridged edition.* **abridgement** *noun* [from Old French *abregier* = shorten]

abroad *adverb* in or to another country.

abrupt *adjective* **1** sudden; hasty. **2** brief and rude. **abruptly** *adverb*, **abruptness** *noun* [from *ab-*, + Latin *ruptum* = broken]

abs- *prefix* see **ab-**.

abscess (*say* **ab**-sis) *noun* (*plural* **abscesses**) an inflamed place where pus has formed in the body.

abscond *verb* go away secretly, *The cashier had absconded with the money.*

absence *noun* **1** being away; the period of this. **2** a lack of something.

absent¹ *adjective* not here; not present, *absent from school.*

absent² (*say* ab-**sent**) *verb* **absent yourself** stay away.

absentee *noun* a person who is absent. **absenteeism** *noun*

absent-minded *adjective* having your mind on other things, forgetful.

absolute *adjective* **1** complete. **2** not restricted. [same origin as *absolve*]

absolutely *adverb* **1** completely. **2** (*informal*) yes, I agree.

absolution *noun* a priest's formal declaration that people's sins are forgiven.

absolve *verb* (**absolved**, **absolving**) **1** clear a person of blame or guilt. **2** release from a promise or obligation. [from *ab-*, + Latin *solvere* = set free]

absorb *verb* **1** soak up; take in. **2** receive something and reduce its effects. *The buffers*

▶▶ T H E S A U R U S ◀◀

about² *adverb* **1** almost, approximately, around, more or less, nearly, roughly. **3** around, hereabouts, near, nearby.
be about to be going to, be on the brink of, be on the point of, be on the verge of, be ready to.

above¹ *preposition* **1** higher than, on top of, over, superior to. **2** beyond, exceeding, greater than, higher than, more than, over.

above² *adverb* **1** on high, overhead, upstairs. **2** before, earlier, previously.

above board *adjective* clean, fair, honest, honourable, legal, legitimate, open, straight.

abrasion *noun* graze, lesion, scrape, scratch.

abridge *verb* abbreviate, condense, cut, edit, reduce, shorten, trim.

abroad *adverb* overseas.

abrupt *adjective* **1** hasty, precipitate, quick, rapid, sharp, sudden, swift, unexpected. **2** blunt, brisk, brusque, curt, gruff, impolite, rude, short.

abscond *verb* bolt, disappear, do a bunk (*slang*), escape, flee, make off, nick off (*Australian slang*), run off, shoot through (*Australian informal*).

absence *noun* **1** absenteeism, non-attendance, truancy. **2** dearth, deficiency, lack, want.

absent¹ *adjective* away, elsewhere, missing, off.

absent² *verb* **absent yourself** play hookey (*informal*), play truant, skive off (*informal*), stay away, wag (*informal*).

absent-minded *adjective* abstracted, daydreaming, distracted, dreamy, far-away, forgetful, inattentive, oblivious, preoccupied, scatterbrained, scatty (*informal*).

absolute *adjective* **1** complete, downright, out-and-out, outright, perfect, positive, pure, sheer, thorough, total, unmitigated, unqualified, utter. **2** autocratic, complete, omnipotent, sovereign, supreme, total, unconditional, unlimited, unqualified, unrestricted.

absolution *noun* forgiveness, pardon, remission.

absolve *verb* **1** acquit, clear, exonerate, forgive, pardon, vindicate. **2** discharge, excuse, exempt, free, release, set free.

absorb *verb* **1** (*absorb liquid*) draw up, mop up, soak up, suck up, take up; (*absorb information*) assimilate, digest, take in. **3** captivate, capture, engage, engross, interest, monopolise, occupy, preoccupy.
absorbing *adjective* captivating, engrossing, fascinating, gripping, interesting, riveting.

▶▶ D I C T I O N A R Y ◀◀

absorbed most of the shock. **3** take up a person's attention or time. **absorbent** *adjective*, **absorption** *noun*

abstain *verb* keep yourself from doing something (e.g. from voting); refrain. **abstainer** *noun*, **abstention** *noun*

abstemious (*say* ab-**steem**-ee-us) *adjective* eating or drinking only small amounts; not greedy. **abstemiously** *adverb*, **abstemiousness** *noun*

abstinence *noun* abstaining, especially from alcohol. **abstinent** *adjective*

abstract¹ (*say* **ab**-strakt) *adjective* **1** concerned with ideas, not with objects, *Truth is abstract.* **2** (of a painting or sculpture) showing the artist's ideas or feelings, not showing a recognisable person or thing.

abstract² (*say* ab-**strakt**) *verb* take out; remove, *He abstracted some cards from the pack.* **abstraction** *noun*

abstract³ (*say* **ab**-strakt) *noun* a summary. [from *abs-*, + Latin *tractum* = pulled]

abstracted *adjective* with your mind on other things; not paying attention.

abstruse (*say* ab-**strooss**) *adjective* hard to understand; obscure.

absurd *adjective* ridiculous; foolish. **absurdly** *adverb*, **absurdity** *noun* [from Latin *absurdus* = out of tune]

abundance *noun* plenty.

abundant *adjective* plentiful. **abundantly** *adverb*

abuse¹ (*say* ab-**yooz**) *verb* (**abused, abusing**) **1** use badly or wrongly; misuse. **2** ill-treat. **3** say unpleasant things to a person or thing.

abuse² (*say* ab-**yooss**) *noun* **1** a misuse. **2** ill-treatment. **3** words abusing a person or thing; insults. **abusive** *adjective* [from *ab-* + *use*]

abut *verb* (**abutted, abutting**) end against something, *Their shed abuts against ours.* **abutment** *noun*

abysmal (*say* ab-**iz**-mal) *adjective* extremely bad, *abysmal ignorance.*

abyss (*say* ab-**iss**) *noun* (*plural* **abysses**) an extremely deep pit.

ac- *prefix* see **ad-**.

academic *adjective* **1** of a school or college or university. **2** scholarly. **3** theoretical; having no practical application.

academy *noun* (*plural* **academies**) **1** a school or college, especially for specialised training. **2** a society of scholars, *The Australian Academy of Science.*

accede (*say* ak-**seed**) *verb* agree to what is asked or suggested, *accede to a request.* [from *ac-*, + Latin *cedere* = go]

accelerate *verb* (**accelerated, accelerating**) **1** make or become quicker. **2** happen or cause to happen earlier or more quickly. **acceleration** *noun* [from *ac-*, + Latin *celer* = swift]

▶▶ T H E S A U R U S ◀◀

abstain *verb* (**abstain from**) avoid, decline, desist from, do without, forgo, go without, refrain from.

abstinence *noun* non-indulgence, self-denial, sobriety, teetotalism, temperance.

abstract¹ *adjective* **1** academic, conceptual, intangible, intellectual, theoretical.

abstract³ *noun* outline, précis, résumé, summary, synopsis.

absurd *adjective* comic, crazy, farcical, foolish, funny, illogical, inane, laughable, ludicrous, mad, nonsensical, outrageous, preposterous, ridiculous, senseless, silly, strange, stupid, unreasonable, zany.

abundance *noun* heaps (*informal*), lashings (*informal*), loads (*informal*), lots (*informal*), oodles (*informal*), plenty, stacks (*informal*), tons (*informal*), wealth.

abundant *adjective* ample, bountiful, copious, generous, lavish, liberal, overflowing, plentiful, profuse, teeming.

abuse¹ *verb* **1** exploit, misuse. **2** assault, damage, harm, hurt, ill-treat, maltreat, mistreat, molest. **3** attack, be rude to, curse, denigrate, disparage, insult, revile, slander, swear at.

abuse² *noun* **2** assault, exploitation, ill-treatment, maltreatment, mistreatment. **3** calumny, curses, denigration, insults, invective, obscenities, revilement, slander, swearing, vilification, vituperation.

abusive *adjective* derogatory, disparaging, foul-mouthed, impolite, insulting, obscene, offensive, pejorative, rude, scornful, scurrilous, slanderous.

abyss *noun* bottomless pit, chasm, hole.

academic *adjective* **1** educational, pedagogic, scholastic. **2** bookish, erudite, highbrow, intellectual, learned, scholarly, studious. **3** abstract, hypothetical, speculative, theoretical.

accelerate *verb* **1** go faster, quicken, speed up, step on it (*informal*). **2** expedite, hasten, speed up, step up.

▶▶ D I C T I O N A R Y ◀◀

accelerator *noun* something that speeds things up; the pedal that a driver presses to make a motor vehicle go faster.

accent¹ (*say* **ak**-sent) *noun* **1** the way a person pronounces words, *She has a French accent.* **2** emphasis; accenting part of a word, *In 'action', the accent is on 'ac-'.* **3** a mark placed over a letter to show its pronunciation, e.g. on *café.*

accent² (*say* ak-**sent**) *verb* pronounce part of a word more strongly than the other parts; emphasise.

accentuate (*say* ak-**sent**-yoo-ayt) *verb* (**accentuated, accentuating**) emphasise; accent. **accentuation** *noun*

accept *verb* **1** take a thing that is offered or presented. **2** say yes to an invitation etc. **acceptance** *noun*

acceptable *adjective* worth accepting; pleasing. **acceptably** *adverb*, **acceptability** *noun*

access¹ (*say* **ak**-sess) *noun* a way in; a way to reach something.

access² *verb* find information that has been stored in a computer.

accessible *adjective* able to be reached. **accessibly** *adverb*, **accessibility** *noun*

accession *noun* **1** acceding; reaching a rank or position. **2** an addition, *recent accessions to our library.*

accessory (*say* ak-**sess**-er-ee) *noun* (*plural* **accessories**) **1** an extra thing that goes with something. **2** a person who helps another with a crime.

accident *noun* an unexpected happening, especially one causing injury or damage.
by accident by chance; without its being arranged in advance. [from *ac-*, + Latin *cadens* = falling]

accidental *adjective* happening or done by accident. **accidentally** *adverb*

acclaim *verb* welcome or applaud. **acclaim** *noun*, **acclamation** *noun* [from *ac-*, + Latin *clamare* = to shout]

acclimatise *verb* (**acclimatised, acclimatising**) make or become used to a new climate or new conditions. **acclimatisation** *noun*

accolade (*say* ak-ol-**ayd**) *noun* **1** praise. **2** the ceremonial conferring of a knighthood by tapping a person on the shoulders with a sword.

accommodate *verb* (**accommodated, accommodating**) **1** provide room or lodging for somebody. **2** help by providing something, *We can accommodate you with skis.*

accommodation *noun* somewhere to live; lodgings.

▶▶ T H E S A U R U S ◀◀

accent¹ *noun* **1** brogue, dialect, intonation, pronunciation. **2** emphasis, prominence, stress.

accent² *verb* accentuate, emphasise, stress.

accentuate *verb* accent, draw attention to, emphasise, highlight, stress, underline.

accept *verb* **1** get, receive, take. **2** agree to, consent to, go along with, put up with, reconcile yourself to, resign yourself to, take, tolerate, welcome.

acceptable *adjective* adequate, admissible, appropriate, passable, pleasing, proper, satisfactory, seemly, suitable, tolerable.

access¹ *noun* admission, admittance, approach, entrance, entry, way in.

access² *verb* retrieve.

accessible *adjective* attainable, available, handy, obtainable, retrievable.

accessory *noun* **1** attachment, extension, extra, fitting. **2** abetter, accomplice, assistant, associate, confederate, partner.

accident *noun* calamity, catastrophe, disaster, misadventure, misfortune, mishap; (*a car accident*) collision, crash, pile-up (*informal*), prang (*slang*), smash.

accidental *adjective* chance, coincidental, fluky, fortuitous, inadvertent, serendipitous, unexpected, unforeseen, unintentional, unplanned.

acclaim *verb* applaud, cheer, clap, hail, praise, salute, welcome.
acclaim *noun* acclamation, applause, approval, commendation, ovation, praise, welcome.

acclimatise *verb* adapt, adjust, become accustomed, become inured, get used.

accolade *noun* **1** acclaim, compliment, honour, praise, tribute.

accommodate *verb* **1** billet, board, house, put up, take in. **2** furnish, grant, provide, supply.

accommodation *noun* billet, digs (*informal*), home, house, housing, lodgings, premises, quarters, residence.

accompanist *noun* a person who plays a musical accompaniment.

accompany *verb* (**accompanied, accompanying**) **1** go somewhere with somebody. **2** be present with something, *Thunder accompanied the storm.* **3** play music that supports a singer or another player etc. **accompaniment** *noun*

accomplice (*say* a-**kum**-pliss) *noun* a person who helps another in a crime etc.

accomplish *verb* do something successfully. **accomplishment** *noun*

accomplished *adjective* skilled.

accord[1] *noun* **1** agreement; consent. **2** a formal agreement or treaty.
of your own accord voluntarily; without being asked or compelled.

accord[2] *verb* **1** be consistent with something. **2** (*formal*) give, *He was accorded this privilege.*

accordance *noun* **in accordance with** in agreement with, *This is done in accordance with the rules.*

according *adverb* **according to** as stated by, *According to him, we are stupid*; in a way that suits, *Price the apples according to their size.* **accordingly** *adverb*

accordion *noun* a portable musical instrument like a large concertina.

accost *verb* approach and speak to a person.

account[1] *noun* **1** a statement of money owed, spent, or received; a bill. **2** an arrangement to keep money in a bank etc. **3** a description; a report.
on account of because of.
on no account certainly not.
take into account consider.

account[2] *verb* **account for** make it clear why something happens.

accountable *adjective* responsible; having to explain why you have done something. **accountability** *noun*

accountant *noun* a keeper or inspector of financial accounts. **accountancy** *noun*

accounting *noun* keeping financial accounts.

accoutrements (*say* a-**koo**-trim-ents) *plural noun* equipment. [French]

accredited *adjective* officially recognised, *our accredited agent.*

accretion (*say* a-**kree**-shon) *noun* a growth or increase in which things are added gradually.

accrue (*say* a-**kroo**) *verb* (**accrued, accruing**) accumulate. **accrual** *noun*

accumulate *verb* (**accumulated, accumulating**) **1** collect; pile up. **2** grow numerous; increase. **accumulation** *noun* [from *ac-*, + Latin *cumulus* = heap]

accumulator *noun* a storage battery.

accompany *verb* **1** attend, be with, chaperone, escort, go with, partner, tag along with, travel with. **3** back up, play with, support.
accompaniment *noun* background, backing, support.

accomplice *noun* abetter, accessory, assistant, collaborator, helper, partner, sidekick (*informal*).

accomplish *verb* achieve, attain, bring off, carry out, complete, do, effect, execute, finish, fulfil, perform, succeed in.
accomplishment *noun* ability, achievement, attainment, deed, exploit, feat, gift, skill, talent.

accomplished *adjective* able, adept, brilliant, consummate, experienced, expert, gifted, proficient, skilful, skilled, talented.

accord[1] *noun* **2** agreement, compact, pact, treaty.
of your own accord off your own bat, of your own free will, of your own volition, spontaneously, unasked, voluntarily, willingly.

accord[2] *verb* **1** agree, be consistent, coincide, concur, correspond, harmonise, tally.

accordingly *adverb* consequently, hence, so, therefore, thus.

accost *verb* bail up (*Australian*), buttonhole, confront, hail, stop, waylay.

account[1] *noun* **1** bill, invoice, receipt, statement. **3** chronicle, description, explanation, history, log, narrative, record, report, story, tale.
take into account allow for, consider, take into consideration.

account[2] *verb* **account for** excuse, explain, give grounds for, justify.

accountable *adjective* answerable, liable, responsible.

accumulate *verb* **1** acquire, amass, collect, gather, hoard, pile up, stockpile, store up. **2** accrue, build up, grow, increase, multiply, pile up.
accumulation *noun* build-up, collection, heap, hoard, mass, pile, stack, stockpile, store.

▶▶ D I C T I O N A R Y ◀◀

accurate *adjective* correct; exact. **accurately** *adverb*, **accuracy** *noun*

accusation *noun* accusing someone; a statement accusing a person of a fault or crime etc.

accuse *verb* (**accused, accusing**) say that a person (whom you name) has committed a crime etc.; blame. **accuser** *noun*

accustom *verb* make a person become used to something. [from *ac-* + *custom*]

accustomed *adjective* customary, usual.

ace *noun* **1** a playing card with one spot. **2** a very skilful person or thing.

acetylene (*say* a-**set**-il-een) *noun* a gas that burns with a bright flame, used in cutting and welding metal.

ache[1] *noun* **1** a dull continuous pain. **2** mental distress.

ache[2] *verb* (**ached, aching**) have an ache.

achieve *verb* (**achieved, achieving**) succeed in doing or producing something; accomplish. **achievable** *adjective*, **achievement** *noun* [from Old French *a chief* = to a head]

acid[1] *noun* a chemical substance that contains hydrogen and neutralises alkalis. **acidic** *adjective*, **acidity** *noun*

acid[2] *adjective* **1** sharp-tasting; sour. **2** looking or sounding bitter, *an acid reply*. **acidly** *adverb*

acid rain rain made acid by mixing with waste gases from factories etc.

acknowledge *verb* (**acknowledged, acknowledging**) **1** admit that something is true. **2** state that you have received or noticed something, *Acknowledge this letter*. **3** express thanks or appreciation for something. **acknowledgement** *noun*

acme (*say* **ak**-mee) *noun* the highest degree of something, *the acme of perfection*. [from Greek *akme* = highest point]

acne (*say* **ak**-nee) *noun* inflamed red pimples on the face and neck.

acorn *noun* the seed of the oak-tree.

acoustic (*say* a-**koo**-stik) *adjective* **1** of sound or hearing. **2** (of a musical instrument) not electronic, *an acoustic guitar*. **acoustically** *adverb* [from Greek *akouein* = hear]

acoustics (*say* a-**koo**-stiks) *plural noun* **1** the qualities of a hall etc. that make it good or bad for carrying sound. **2** the properties of sound.

acquaint *verb* tell somebody about something, *Acquaint him with the facts*. **be acquainted with** know slightly.

acquaintance *noun* **1** a person you know slightly. **2** being acquainted.

▶▶ T H E S A U R U S ◀◀

accurate *adjective* careful, correct, exact, factual, faithful, meticulous, perfect, precise, right, spot on (*informal*), true.
accuracy *noun* correctness, exactitude, exactness, faithfulness, fidelity, meticulousness, precision, truth.

accusation *noun* allegation, charge, imputation, indictment.

accuse *verb* blame, charge, denounce, impeach, incriminate, indict, point the finger at (*informal*).

accustom *verb* (*accustom to*) acclimatise to, adjust to, familiarise with, habituate to, inure to, make used to.

accustomed *adjective* customary, established, expected, familiar, fixed, habitual, normal, regular, set, usual.

ace *noun* **2** champion, expert, master, star, winner.

ache[1] *noun* **1** discomfort, hurt, pain, pang, soreness. **2** agony, anguish, distress, grief, misery, pain, sorrow, suffering.

ache[2] *verb* be painful, be sore, hurt, pound, throb.

achieve *verb* accomplish, attain, carry out, fulfil, reach, realise, succeed in.
achievement *noun* accomplishment, attainment, deed, feat; see also SUCCESS.

acid[2] *adjective* **1** acidic, sharp, sour, tangy, tart, vinegary. **2** acerbic, bitter, caustic, cutting, sarcastic, sharp, stinging.

acknowledge *verb* **1** accept, admit, agree, allow, concede, confess, grant, recognise. **2** answer, reply to, respond to.
acknowledgement *noun* **1** acceptance, admission, confession. **2** answer, reply, response. **3** appreciation, credit, notice, recognition, reward, thanks.

acme *noun* apex, climax, culmination, height, peak, pinnacle, summit, top, zenith.

acquaint *verb* (*acquaint with*) advise of, enlighten about, familiarise with, fill in on (*informal*), inform of, make aware of, tell.
be acquainted with be aware of, be familiar with, be versed in, know.

acquaintance *noun* **1** associate, colleague, contact.

▶▶ DICTIONARY ◀◀

acquiesce (*say* ak-wee-**ess**) *verb* (**acquiesced,** **acquiescing**) agree to something. **acquiescent** *adjective*, **acquiescence** *noun*

acquire *verb* (**acquired, acquiring**) obtain. **acquisition** *noun* [from *ac-*, + Latin *quaerere* = seek]

acquisitive (*say* a-**kwiz**-it-iv) *adjective* eager to acquire things.

acquit *verb* (**acquitted, acquitting**) decide that somebody is not guilty. **acquittal** *noun*

acre (*say* **ay**-ker) *noun* an area of land measuring about 0.405 hectares. **acreage** *noun*

acrid *adjective* bitter, *an acrid smell.*

acrimonious (*say* ak-rim-**oh**-nee-us) *adjective* (of a person's manner or words) sharp and bad-tempered or bitter. **acrimony** (*say* **ak**-rim-on-ee) *noun*

acrobat *noun* a person who performs spectacular gymnastic stunts for entertainment. **acrobatic** *adjective*, **acrobatics** *plural noun* [from Greek *akrobatos* = walking on tiptoe]

acronym (*say* **ak**-ron-im) *noun* a word or name formed from the initial letters of other words, *ASEAN is an acronym of Association of South East Asian Nations.* [from Greek *akros* = top, + *onyma* = name]

across *preposition & adverb* **1** from one side to the other, *Swim across the river. Are you across yet?* **2** on the opposite side, *the house across the street.*

acrostic *noun* a word-puzzle or poem in which the first or last letters of each line form a word or words.

acrylic (*say* a-**kril**-ik) *noun* a kind of fibre, plastic, or resin made from an organic acid.

act¹ *noun* **1** an action. **2** a law passed by a parliament. **3** one of the main divisions of a play or opera. **4** a short performance in a programme of entertainment, *a juggling act.* **5** (*informal*) a pretence, *She is only putting on an act.*

act² *verb* **1** do something; behave; perform actions. **2** perform a part in a play or film etc. **3** function; have an effect. **4** pretend. [from Latin *actum* = done]

acting *adjective* serving temporarily, especially as a substitute, *the acting principal.*

action *noun* **1** doing something. **2** something done. **3** a battle; fighting, *He was killed in action.* **4** a lawsuit. **5** a series of events in a play etc.; exciting activity.
out of action not functioning.
take action do something.

activate *verb* (**activated, activating**) start something working. **activation** *noun*, **activator** *noun*

active *adjective* **1** doing things; moving about; taking part in activities. **2** functioning; in operation, *an active volcano.* **3** radioactive. **4** (of a form of a verb) used when the subject of the verb is performing the action. In 'Tom *washed* the car' the verb is active; in 'The car *was washed* by Tom' the verb is passive. **actively** *adverb*, **activeness** *noun*

▶▶ THESAURUS ◀◀

acquire *verb* buy, collect, come by, gain, get, obtain, pick up, procure, purchase, secure.
acquisition *noun* accession, possession, purchase.

acquit *verb* absolve, clear, exonerate, let off, release, vindicate.

acrimonious *adjective* bitter, cutting, embittered, hostile, nasty, spiteful, tart, virulent.

acrobat *noun* gymnast, tightrope walker, trapeze artist.

across *preposition* **1** over, through, throughout.

act¹ *noun* **1** accomplishment, achievement, action, deed, exploit, feat, undertaking. **2** decree, edict, law, statute. **4** performance, routine, show, sketch, skit. **5** deception, front, hoax, pretence, sham, show.

act² *verb* **1** behave, conduct yourself. **2** appear, impersonate, perform, play, portray. **3** function,

have an effect, operate, work. **4** fake, feign, make believe, pretend, sham.

acting *adjective* deputy, interim, provisional, substitute, temporary.

action *noun* **1** activity, motion, operation, performance, practice, work. **2** act, deed, effort, endeavour, exploit, feat, move, step, undertaking. **3** battle, combat, conflict, fighting, warfare. **4** lawsuit, litigation, proceedings, prosecution. **5** activity, adventure, drama, events, excitement, happenings, incidents.

activate *verb* actuate, set off, start, switch on, trigger, turn on.

active *adjective* **1** busy, diligent, dynamic, energetic, full of beans (*informal*), hardworking, hyperactive, industrious, involved, lively, occupied, participating, sprightly, spry, strenuous, vigorous, vivacious. **2** functioning, operative, working.

▶▶ D I C T I O N A R Y ◀◀

activist *noun* a person who believes in vigorous action, especially in politics.

activity *noun* (*plural* **activities**) **1** an action or occupation, *outdoor activities*. **2** being active or lively.

actor *noun* a performer in a play or film.

actress *noun* a female actor.

actual *adjective* real. **actually** *adverb*, **actuality** *noun*

actuate *verb* (**actuated**, **actuating**) activate. **actuation** *noun*

acumen (*say* **ak**-yoo-men) *noun* sharpness of mind. [Latin, = a point]

acupuncture (*say* **ak**-yoo-punk-cher) *noun* pricking parts of the body with needles to relieve pain or cure disease. **acupuncturist** *noun* [from Latin *acu* = with a needle, + *puncture*]

acute *adjective* **1** sharp; strong, *acute pain*. **2** having a sharp mind. **acutely** *adverb*, **acuteness** *noun*
acute accent a mark over a vowel, as over *e* in *café*.
acute angle an angle of less than 90°.

AD *abbreviation* Anno Domini (Latin = in the year of Our Lord), used in dates counted from the birth of Jesus Christ.

ad- *prefix* (changing to **ac-, af-, ag-, al-, an-, ap-, ar-, as-, at-** before certain consonants) to; towards (as in *adapt, admit*). [from Latin *ad* = to]

adamant (*say* **ad**-am-ant) *adjective* firm and not giving way to requests.

Adam's apple the lump at the front of a man's neck.

adapt *verb* make or become suitable for a new purpose or situation. **adaptable** *adjective*, **adaptation** *noun* [from *ad-*, + Latin *aptus* = fitted]

adaptor *noun* a device to connect pieces of electrical or other equipment.

add *verb* **1** put one thing with another. **2** make another remark.
add to increase.
add up make or find a total; (*informal*) make sense; seem reasonable.

addendum *noun* (*plural* **addenda**) a thing added at the end of a book. [Latin, = thing to be added]

adder *noun* a small poisonous snake. [originally called *a nadder*, which became *an adder*]

addict *noun* a person who does or uses something that he or she cannot give up. **addicted** *adjective*, **addiction** *noun* [from Latin *addictus* = person given as a servant to someone to whom he owes money]

addictive *adjective* causing people to become addicts.

▶▶ T H E S A U R U S ◀◀

activist *noun* agitator, campaigner, crusader, firebrand, lobbyist, militant, protester, stirrer.

activity *noun* **1** enterprise, hobby, occupation, pastime, project, pursuit, undertaking, venture. **2** action, bustle, exercise, exertion, hurly-burly, hustle, industry, liveliness, movement.

actor *noun* actress, performer, player, star, trouper; (*group of actors*) cast, company, troupe.

actual *adjective* authentic, confirmed, factual, genuine, real, true, verified.

actually *adverb* genuinely, indeed, in fact, really, truly.

acute *adjective* **1** excruciating, extreme, intense, keen, piercing, severe, sharp, shooting, stabbing. **2** astute, canny, clever, discerning, discriminating, incisive, keen, penetrating, perceptive, sharp, shrewd, subtle.

adamant *adjective* determined, firm, immovable, inflexible, intransigent, resolute, resolved, stubborn, unyielding.

adapt *verb* adjust, alter, change, convert, edit, modify, remake, rewrite, transform; (*adapt to*) acclimatise to, accustom to, adjust to, become accustomed to, get used to.
adaptable *adjective* accommodating, amenable, easygoing, flexible, malleable, versatile.

add *verb* **1** affix, append, attach, combine, join, tack on.
add to augment, enlarge, increase, swell.
add up calculate, compute, count, reckon, sum, total, tot up (*informal*), work out.
add up to amount to, come to, make, total.

addendum *noun* appendix, postscript, supplement.

addict *noun* (*a TV addict*) devotee, enthusiast, fan, fanatic, freak (*informal*), lover, nut (*informal*); (*a drug addict*) druggie (*informal*), junkie (*slang*), user (*informal*).
addicted *adjective* dependent on, hooked on (*slang*).
addiction *noun* dependence, habit, obsession.

▶▶ D I C T I O N A R Y ◀◀

addition *noun* **1** the process of adding. **2** something added. **additional** *adjective*, **additionally** *adverb*
in addition also; as an extra thing.

additive *noun* a substance added to another in small amounts for a special purpose, e.g. as a flavouring.

addled *adjective* (of eggs) rotted and producing no chick after being brooded.

address¹ *noun* **1** the details of the place where someone lives or where letters etc. should be delivered to a person or firm. **2** a speech to an audience.

address² *verb* **1** write an address on a parcel etc. **2** make a speech or remark etc. to somebody. **3** give your attention to something.

addressee *noun* the person to whom a letter etc. is addressed.

adenoids *plural noun* thick spongy flesh at the back of the nose and throat, which may hinder breathing.

adept (*say* **ad**-ept) *adjective* very skilful.

adequate *adjective* enough; good enough. **adequately** *adverb*, **adequacy** *noun*

adhere *verb* (**adhered**, **adhering**) **1** stick to something. **2** keep to, *We adhered to the rules.* **adhesion** *noun* [from *ad*-, + Latin *haerere* = to stick]

adherent (*say* ad-**heer**-ent) *noun* a person who supports a certain group or theory etc. **adherence** *noun*

adhesive¹ *adjective* causing things to stick together.

adhesive² *noun* a substance used to stick things together; glue.

adieu (*say* a-**dew**) *interjection* goodbye. [from French *à* = to, + *Dieu* = God]

adjacent *adjective* near; next. [from *ad*-, + Latin *jacens* = lying]

adjective *noun* a word that describes a noun or adds to its meaning, e.g. *big, honest, strange, our.* **adjectival** *adjective*, **adjectivally** *adverb*

adjoin *verb* be next or nearest to something.

adjourn (*say* a-**jern**) *verb* **1** break off a meeting etc. until a later time. **2** break off and go somewhere else, *They adjourned to the library.* **adjournment** *noun* [from Latin, = to another day]

adjudge *verb* (**adjudged**, **adjudging**) judge; give a decision, *He was adjudged to be guilty.*

adjudicate (*say* a-**joo**-dik-ayt) *verb* (**adjudicated**, **adjudicating**) act as judge in a competition etc. **adjudication** *noun*, **adjudicator** *noun* [from *ad*-, + Latin *judicare* = to judge]

adjunct (*say* **aj**-unkt) *noun* something added that is useful but not essential. [from *ad*-, + Latin *junctum* = joined]

adjust *verb* **1** put a thing into its proper position or order. **2** alter so as to fit. **3** make oneself used to new circumstances. **adjustable** *adjective*, **adjustment** *noun*

▶▶ T H E S A U R U S ◀◀

addition *noun* **1** calculation, computation, totalling, totting up (*informal*). **2** (*an addition to a document*) appendix, attachment, codicil, postscript, rider, supplement; (*an addition to a building*) annexe, extension, wing.
additional *adjective* added, backup, extra, further, more, new, other, supplementary.

address¹ *noun* **1** abode (*old use*), domicile, location, residence. **2** discourse, lecture, oration, sermon, speech, talk.

address² *verb* **2** lecture, speak to, talk to. **3** apply yourself to, attend to, devote yourself to, focus on, tackle, turn to.

adept *adjective* accomplished, capable, competent, expert, masterful, masterly, proficient, skilful, skilled, talented.

adequate *adjective* acceptable, all right, enough, fair, OK (*informal*), passable, satisfactory, sufficient, tolerable.

adhere *verb* **1** attach, cling, hold fast, stick. **2** (*adhere to*) abide by, comply with, follow, keep to, stick to.

adhesive¹ *adjective* gummed, sticky.

adhesive² *noun* cement, fixative, glue, gum, paste.

adjacent *adjective* adjoining, bordering, contiguous, neighbouring, next-door.

adjoin *verb* abut on, be adjacent to, be next to, border on.

adjourn *verb* **1** break off, defer, discontinue, interrupt, postpone, put off, suspend.

adjudicate *verb* arbitrate, judge, referee, umpire.
adjudicator *noun* arbitrator, judge, referee, umpire.

adjust *verb* **1** arrange, regulate, set, tune. **2** adapt, alter, change, fit, modify, reshape, tailor. **3** acclimatise, adapt, become accustomed, get used, reconcile yourself.

ad lib¹ *adverb* as you like; freely.

ad lib² *verb* (**ad libbed, ad libbing**) say or do something without any rehearsal or preparation. [from Latin *ad libitum* = according to pleasure]

administer *verb* **1** give; provide, *He administered a rebuke.* **2** manage business affairs; administrate.

administration *noun* **1** administering. **2** the management of public or business affairs. **3** the people who manage an organisation etc.; the government. **administrator** *noun*, **administrative** *adjective*

admirable *adjective* worth admiring; excellent. **admirably** *adverb*

admiral *noun* a naval officer of high rank. [from Arabic *amir* = commander]

admire *verb* (**admired, admiring**) **1** look at something and enjoy it. **2** think that someone or something is very good. **admiration** *noun*, **admirer** *noun* [from *ad-*, + Latin *mirari* = wonder at]

admissible *adjective* able to be admitted or allowed.

admission *noun* **1** admitting. **2** the charge for being allowed to go in. **3** a statement admitting something; a confession.

admit *verb* (**admitted, admitting**) **1** allow someone or something to come in. **2** state reluctantly that something is true; confess, *We admit that the task is difficult. He admitted his crime.* [from *ad-*, + Lattin *mittere* = send]

admittance *noun* being allowed to go in, especially to a private place.

admittedly *adverb* as an agreed fact; without denying it.

admonish *verb* advise or warn firmly but mildly. **admonition** *noun*

ado *noun* fuss; excitement. [originally in *much ado* = much to do]

adolescence (*say* ad-ol-**ess**-ens) *noun* the time between being a child and being an adult. **adolescent** *adjective* & *noun*

adopt *verb* **1** take someone into your family as your own child. **2** accept something; take and use, *They adopted new methods of working.* **adoption** *noun* [from *ad-*, + Latin *optare* = choose]

adore *verb* (**adored, adoring**) **1** love very much. **2** worship. **adorable** *adjective*, **adoration** *noun* [from *ad-*, + Latin *orare* = pray]

▶▶ THESAURUS ◀◀

ad lib¹ *adverb* extempore, impromptu, off the cuff, off the top of your head (*informal*).

ad lib² *verb* extemporise, improvise, play it by ear (*informal*).

administer *verb* **1** carry out, deal out, dispense, give, hand out, mete out, provide. **2** conduct, control, direct, govern, look after, manage, operate, oversee, run, supervise.

administration *noun* **1** control, direction, management, running, supervision. **3** government, ministry, regime.
administrator *noun* chief, controller, director, executive, governor, head, manager, superintendent.

admirable *adjective* commendable, excellent, exemplary, honourable, laudable, praiseworthy, worthy.

admire *verb* **2** appreciate, approve of, esteem, idolise, look up to, praise, regard highly, respect, revere, think highly of, venerate.
admiration *noun* approval, commendation, praise, respect, veneration.
admirer *noun* (*a woman's admirer*) beau, boyfriend, lover, suitor, sweetheart; (*an actor's admirer*) devotee, fan, follower, supporter.

admission *noun* **1** access, admittance, entrance, entry. **3** acceptance, acknowledgement, confession, declaration, disclosure, statement.

admit *verb* **1** allow in, let in, permit entry, take in. **2** accept, acknowledge, concede, confess, grant, own up.

admittance *noun* access, admission, entrance, entry.

admonish *verb* chide (*old use*), rebuke, reprimand, reproach, reprove, scold, tell off (*informal*), tick off (*informal*).

ado *noun* bother, commotion, fuss, kerfuffle (*informal*), to-do, trouble.

adolescence *noun* puberty, teens, youth.
adolescent *adjective* teenage, youthful.
adolescent *noun* minor, teenager, youngster, youth.

adopt *verb* **2** accept, approve, assume, choose, embrace, endorse, espouse, ratify, take up, use.

adore *verb* **1** cherish, dote on, idolise, love. **2** exalt, extol, glorify, hallow, honour, laud (*formal*), magnify (*old use*), praise, revere, venerate, worship.
adorable *adjective* appealing, cute (*informal*), darling, dear, delightful, irresistible, likeable, lovable, lovely, sweet (*informal*).

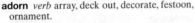
DICTIONARY

adorn *verb* decorate. **adornment** *noun*

adrenalin (*say* a-**dren**-al-in) *noun* a hormone that stimulates the nervous system.

adrift *adjective & adverb* drifting.

adroit (*say* a-**droit**) *adjective* skilful. [from French *à droit* = according to right]

adulation *noun* very great flattery.

adult (*say* **ad**-ult) *noun* a fully grown or mature person. **adult** *adjective*

adulterate *verb* (**adulterated, adulterating**) make a thing impure or less good by adding something to it. **adulteration** *noun* [from Latin *adulterare* = corrupt]

adultery *noun* being unfaithful to your wife or husband by having sexual intercourse with someone else. **adulterer** *noun*, **adulterous** *adjective*

advance¹ *noun* **1** a forward movement; progress. **2** an increase. **3** a loan; payment made before it is due.
in advance beforehand; ahead.

advance² *verb* (**advanced, advancing**) **1** move forward; make progress. **2** lend or pay money ahead of the proper time, *Advance her a month's salary*. **advancement** *noun*

advanced *adjective* **1** far on in progress. **2** not elementary. **3** ahead of the times.

advantage *noun* **1** something useful or helpful. **2** the next point won after deuce in tennis.

take advantage of use profitably or unfairly.
to advantage making a good effect, *The painting shows to advantage here.*
to your advantage profitable or helpful to you.

advantageous (*say* ad-van-**tay**-jus) *adjective* giving an advantage; beneficial.

Advent *noun* the period before Christmas, when Christians commemorate the coming of Christ.

advent *noun* the arrival of a new person or thing, *the advent of computers*. [from *ad-*, + Latin *ventum* = arrived]

adventure *noun* **1** an exciting or dangerous experience. **2** willingness to take risks. **3** danger; taking risks. **adventurer** *noun*, **adventurous** *adjective*

adverb *noun* a word that adds to the meaning of a verb or adjective or another adverb and tells how, when, or where something happens, e.g. *gently*, *soon* and *upstairs*. **adverbial** *adjective*, **adverbially** *adverb* [from *ad-*, + Latin *verbum* = word]

adversary (*say* **ad**-ver-ser-ee) *noun* (*plural* **adversaries**) an opponent, an enemy.

adverse *adjective* unfavourable; harmful, *adverse effects*. **adversely** *adverb*, **adversity** *noun* [from Latin *adversus* = opposite (*ad* = to, *versus* = turned)]

THESAURUS

adorn *verb* array, deck out, decorate, festoon, ornament.

adult *noun* grown-up.
adult *adjective* developed, full-sized, fully grown, grown-up, mature.

adulterate *verb* contaminate, dilute, pollute, water down, weaken.

adultery *noun* infidelity, unfaithfulness.

advance¹ *noun* **1** breakthrough, development, headway, improvement, progress. **2** addition, gain, increase, rise. **3** loan, prepayment.
in advance ahead, beforehand, up front.

advance² *verb* **1** approach, go ahead, go forward, go on, make headway, move forward, proceed, progress. **2** lend, prepay.

advanced *adjective* **2** complicated, difficult, hard, higher. **3** avant-garde, innovative, modern, new, progressive, revolutionary, sophisticated, up to date.

advantage *noun* **1** asset, benefit, blessing, bonus, boon, gain, help, plus.
take advantage of capitalise on, cash in on, exploit, make the most of, make use of, use.

advantageous *adjective* beneficial, favourable, good, helpful, profitable, useful, valuable.

advent *noun* appearance, arrival, coming, dawn.

adventure *noun* **1** escapade, experience, exploit, incident. **3** danger, excitement, risk, uncertainty.
adventurous *adjective* bold, brave, daring, enterprising, intrepid, venturesome.

adversary *noun* enemy, foe, opponent, rival.

adverse *adjective* bad, detrimental, harmful, ill, injurious, unfavourable, untoward.
adversity *noun* affliction, calamity, catastrophe, disaster, distress, hardship, misfortune, trouble.

advertise *verb* (**advertised, advertising**) **1** make something publicly known, *advertise a meeting*. **2** praise goods etc. in order to encourage people to buy or use them. **3** ask or offer by a public notice, *advertise for a secretary*. **advertisement** *noun*, **advertiser** *noun*

advice *noun* **1** a statement telling a person what you think he or she should do. **2** a piece of information, *We received advice that the goods had been dispatched.*

advisable *adjective* that is the wise thing to do. **advisability** *noun*

advise *verb* (**advised, advising**) **1** give somebody advice; recommend. **2** inform. **adviser** *noun*, **advisory** *adjective*

advocate¹ (*say* **ad**-vok-ayt) *verb* (**advocated, advocating**) speak in favour of something; recommend, *We advocate reform.*

advocate² (*say* **ad**-vok-at) *noun* **1** a person who advocates a policy etc., *She is an advocate of reform*. **2** a lawyer presenting someone's case in a lawcourt.

aegis (*say* **ee**-jiss) *noun* protection; sponsorship, *The scheme is under the aegis of the Scout Association*. [from Greek *aigis* = magical shield of the God Zeus]

aerate (*say* **air**-ayt) *verb* (**aerated, aerating**) **1** add air to something. **2** add carbon dioxide to a liquid, *aerated water.*

aerial¹ *adjective* **1** of or in or from the air. **2** of or by aircraft.
aerial ping-pong a joking name for Australian National Football.

aerial² *noun* a wire or rod etc. for receiving or transmitting radio or television signals.

aero- *prefix* of air or aircraft (as in *aeronautics*). [from Greek *aer* = air]

aerobatics *plural noun* spectacular performances by flying aircraft, **aerobatic** *adjective* [from *aero-* + *acrobatics*]

aerobics *plural noun* exercises to stimulate breathing and strengthen the heart and lungs. **aerobic** *adjective*

aerodrome *noun* an airfield. [from *aero-*, + Greek *dromos* = running-track]

aeronautics *noun* the study of aircraft and flying. **aeronautic** *adjective*, **aeronautical** *adjective* [from *aero-* + *nautical*]

aeroplane *noun* a flying machine with wings. [from *aero-* + *plane¹*]

aerosol *noun* a device for producing a fine spray of a substance. [from *aero-* + *solution*]

aerospace *noun* the earth's atmosphere and space beyond it.

aesthetic (*say* iss-**thet**-ik) *adjective* of or showing appreciation of beautiful things. [from Greek, = perceiving]

af- *prefix* see **ad-**.

afar *adverb* far away, *The din was heard from afar.*

affable *adjective* polite and friendly. **affably** *adverb*, **affability** *noun*

affair *noun* **1** a thing; a matter; an event. **2** a temporary sexual relationship between two people who are not married to each other. [from French *à faire* = to do]

advertise *verb* **1** announce, make known, proclaim, publicise. **2** market, plug (*informal*), promote, push (*informal*), tout.
advertisement *noun* ad (*informal*), advert (*informal*), announcement, blurb, commercial, notice, plug (*informal*), promotion, publicity, trailer.

advice *noun* **1** counsel, guidance, opinion, recommendation, suggestion, tip. **2** information, news, notification, word.

advisable *adjective* expedient, judicious, politic, prudent, recommended, sensible, wise.

advise *verb* **1** counsel, recommend, suggest, urge, warn. **2** acquaint (with), inform, notify, tell.
adviser *noun* consultant, counsellor, guide, mentor.

advocate¹ *verb* be in favour of, champion, endorse, favour, recommend, support.

advocate² *noun* **1** backer, champion, promoter, proponent, supporter. **2** attorney (*American*), barrister, counsel, lawyer.

aegis *noun* auspices, patronage, protection, sponsorship.

aerial¹ *adjective* **1** bird's-eye, overhead.

aerial² *noun* antenna.

aeroplane *noun* see AIRCRAFT.

afar *adverb* far away, far off.

affable *adjective* amiable, amicable, congenial, cordial, courteous, easygoing, friendly, genial, good-tempered, kindly, pleasant.

affair *noun* **1** activity, business, case, concern, episode, event, happening, incident, interest, matter, occurrence, operation, thing, undertaking. **2** fling, liaison, love affair, relationship, romance.

▶▶ D I C T I O N A R Y ◀◀

affect *verb* **1** have an effect on. **2** (of a disease etc.) attack. **3** arouse sympathy or sadness in a person. **4** pretend, *She affected ignorance.*

affectation *noun* a pretence; behaviour that is put on for show and not natural.

affected *adjective* pretended; unnatural.

affection *noun* love; a liking.

affectionate *adjective* showing affection; loving. **affectionately** *adverb*

affidavit (*say* af-id-**ay**-vit) *noun* a statement written down and sworn to be true, for use as legal evidence. [Latin, = he or she has stated on oath]

affiliated *adjective* officially connected with a larger organisation. [from Latin *affiliatum* = adopted (from *af-*, + *filius* = son)]

affinity *noun* (*plural* **affinities**) **1** a strong attraction. **2** a relationship or similarity to each other, *There are many affinities between the two languages.*

affirm *verb* state definitely or firmly. **affirmation** *noun*

affirmative *adjective* that says 'yes', *an affirmative reply.* (Compare *negative.*)

affix[1] (*say* a-**fiks**) *verb* attach; add in writing, *affix a stamp; affix your signature.*

affix[2] (*say* **aff**-iks) *noun* a prefix or suffix.

afflict *verb* cause somebody distress. **affliction** *noun* [from *af-* + Latin *flictum* = struck]

affluent (*say* **af**-loo-ent) *adjective* rich. **affluence** *noun* [from Latin *affluens* = overflowing (see *fluent*)]

afford *verb* **1** have enough money to pay for something. **2** have enough time or resources etc. to do something.

afforestation *noun* the planting of trees to form a forest.

affray *noun* fighting or rioting in public.

affront[1] *verb* insult; offend; embarrass.

affront[2] *noun* an insult.

afield *adverb* at or to a distance; away from home, *travelling far afield.*

aflame *adjective* & *adverb* in flames; glowing.

afloat *adjective* & *adverb* floating; on the sea.

afoot *adjective* happening, *Great changes are afoot.*

aforesaid *adjective* mentioned previously.

afraid *adjective* frightened; alarmed. **be afraid** regret, *I'm afraid I'm late.*

afresh *adverb* again; in a new way, *We must start afresh.*

African[1] *adjective* of Africa or its people.

African[2] *noun* an African person.

Afrikaans (*say* af-rik-**ahns**) *noun* a language developed from Dutch, used in South Africa. [from Dutch, = African]

Afrikaner (*say* af-rik-**ah**-ner) *noun* a White person in South Africa whose language is Afrikaans.

▶▶ T H E S A U R U S ◀◀

affect *verb* **1** concern, have an effect on, have an impact on, impinge on, touch. **2** attack, damage, infect, strike. **3** disturb, move, stir, touch, upset.

affected *adjective* artificial, fake, feigned, insincere, phoney (*informal*), pretended, sham, studied, unnatural.

affection *noun* caring, fondness, liking, love, tenderness, warmth.

affectionate *adjective* caring, devoted, doting, fond, kind, loving, tender-hearted, warm-hearted.

affiliated *adjective* allied, associated, connected.

affinity *noun* **1** attraction, fondness, liking, rapport, sympathy. **2** closeness, connection, correspondence, likeness, relationship, resemblance, similarity.

affirm *verb* assert, confirm, declare, state, swear.

affirmative *adjective* agreeing, assenting, favourable, positive.

affix[1] *verb* add, append, attach, fasten, join, stick, tack.

afflict *verb* affect, distress, oppress, plague, strike, torment, trouble. **affliction** *noun* adversity, distress, hardship, illness, misery, misfortune, pain, sickness, suffering, trouble.

affluent *adjective* moneyed, opulent, prosperous, rich, wealthy, well-heeled (*informal*), well off, well-to-do.

afford *verb* **1** bear the expense of, manage, pay for, spare.

affront[1] *verb* insult, offend, outrage, scandalise.

affront[2] *noun* insult, offence, slap in the face (*informal*), slight, snub.

afraid *adjective* alarmed, anxious, apprehensive, fearful, frightened, nervous, panic-stricken, scared, terrified, timid, worried. **be afraid** be apologetic, be regretful, be sorry, regret.

▶▶ D I C T I O N A R Y ◀◀

Afro- *prefix* African.

aft *adverb* at or towards the back of a ship or aircraft.

after[1] *preposition* **1** later than, *Come after tea.* **2** behind in place or order, *Which letter comes after H?* **3** trying to catch; pursuing, *Run after him.* **4** in spite of, *We can come after all.* **5** in imitation or honour of, *She is named after her aunt.* **6** about; concerning, *He asked after you.*

after[2] *adverb* **1** behind, *Jill came tumbling after.* **2** later, *It came a week after.*

after[3] *adjective* coming or done afterwards, *in after years; the after-effects.*

aftermath *noun* the conditions after something, *the aftermath of war.* [from *after* + *math* = mowing (i.e. new grass that grows after a mowing)]

afternoon *noun* the time from noon or lunchtime to evening.

afterthought *noun* something thought of or added later.

afterwards *adverb* at a later time.

ag- *prefix* see **ad-**.

again *adverb* **1** another time; once more, *try again.* **2** as before, *You will soon be well again.* **3** besides; moreover.

against *preposition* **1** touching; hitting, *He leant against the wall.* **2** in opposition to; not in favour of, *They voted against the proposal.* **3** in preparation for, *Protect them against the cold.*

age[1] *noun* **1** the length of time a person has lived or a thing has existed. **2** a special period of history or geology, *the ice age.*

ages *plural noun* (*informal*) a very long time, *We've been waiting for ages.*

come of age reach the age at which you have an adult's legal rights and obligations (now at 18 years; formerly 21).

age[2] *verb* (**aged, ageing**) make or become old.

aged *adjective* **1** (*say* ayjd) having the age of, *a girl aged 9.* **2** (*say* **ay**-jid) very old, *an aged man.*

age-group *noun* people who are all of the same age.

agency *noun* (*plural* **agencies**) **1** the office or business of an agent, *a travel agency.* **2** the means by which something is done, *Flowers are pollinated by the agency of bees.*

agenda (*say* a-**jen**-da) *noun* (*plural* **agendas**) a list of things to be done or discussed, *The agenda is rather long.* [from Latin, = things to be done]

agent *noun* **1** a person who organises things for other people. **2** a spy, *a secret agent.* [from Latin *agens* = doing things]

agglomeration *noun* a mass of things collected together. [from *ag-*, + Latin *glomus* = mass]

aggravate *verb* (**aggravated, aggravating**) **1** make a thing worse or more serious. **2** (*informal*) annoy. **aggravation** *noun* (from *ag-*, + Latin *gravare* = load heavily]

aggregate (*say* **ag**-rig-at) *adjective* combined; total, *the aggregate amount.* [from *ag-*, + Latin *gregatum* = herded together]

aggression *noun* starting an attack or war etc.; aggressive behaviour. [from *ag-* against, + Latin *gressum* = gone]

▶▶ T H E S A U R U S ◀◀

aftermath *noun* after-effects, consequences, follow-up, outcome, sequel, upshot, wake.

afterwards *adverb* after, later, next, subsequently.

again *adverb* **1** afresh, anew, another time, once more. **3** also, besides, furthermore, in addition, moreover.

against *preposition* **2** anti, averse to, in opposition to, opposed to, opposing, versus.

age[1] *noun* **2** days, epoch, era, period, time.
ages *plural noun* an eternity (*informal*), donkey's years (*informal*), yonks (*slang*).

age[2] *verb* develop, grow older, mature, mellow, ripen.

aged *adjective* **2** elderly, old, retired.

agency *noun* **1** bureau, business, company, firm, office, organisation.

agenda *noun* list, plan, programme, schedule.

agent *noun* **1** broker, delegate, envoy, go-between, intermediary, middleman, negotiator, proxy, representative, spokesperson. **2** intelligence officer, mole (*informal*), spy.

aggravate *verb* **1** compound, exacerbate, inflame, intensify, worsen. **2** annoy, bother, exasperate, get on someone's nerves, irritate, provoke, rile (*informal*), vex.

aggregate *adjective* combined, cumulative, total, whole.

▶▶ D I C T I O N A R Y ◀◀

aggressive *adjective* **1** likely to attack people. **2** forceful. **aggressively** *adverb*, **aggressiveness** *noun*

aggressor *noun* the person or nation that started an attack or war etc.

aggrieved (*say* a-**greevd**) *adjective* resentful because of being treated unfairly.

aghast *adjective* horrified.

agile *adjective* moving quickly or easily. **agilely** *adverb*, **agility** *noun*

agitate *verb* (**agitated**, **agitating**) **1** make someone feel upset or anxious. **2** stir up public interest or concern; campaign, *They agitated for a new bypass.* **3** shake something about. **agitation** *noun*, **agitator** *noun* [from Latin *agitare* = shake]

aglow *adjective* glowing.

agnostic (*say* ag-**nost**-ik) *noun* a person who believes that it is impossible to know whether God exists. **agnosticism** *noun* [from *a-* = not, + Greek *gnostikos* = knowing]

ago *adverb* in the past, *long ago.* [from an old word *agone* = gone by]

agog *adjective* eager and excited.

agony *noun* (*plural* **agonies**) extremely great pain or suffering. **agonising** *adjective* [from Greek *agon* = a struggle]

agoraphobia (*say* ag-er-a-**foh**-bee-a) *noun* abnormal fear of being in open spaces. [from Greek *agora* = market-place, + *phobia*]

agrarian (*say* a-**grair**-ee-an) *adjective* of farm land or its cultivation. [from Latin *ager* = field]

agree *verb* (**agreed**, **agreeing**) **1** think or say the same as another person etc. **2** consent, *She agreed to come; She agreed to the plan.* **3** suit a person's health or digestion, *Curry doesn't agree with me.* **4** correspond in grammatical number, gender, or person. In 'They were good teachers', *they* agrees with *teachers* (both are plural forms) and *were* agrees with *they*; *was* would be incorrect because it is singular. **5** be in harmony, *Their answers agree.*

agreeable *adjective* **1** willing, *We shall go if you are agreeable.* **2** pleasant, *an agreeable place.* **agreeably** *adverb*

agreement *noun* **1** agreeing. **2** an arrangement that people have agreed on.

agriculture *noun* the process of cultivating land on a large scale and rearing livestock; farming. [from Latin *agric* = of a field, + *culture*]

aground *adverb* & *adjective* stranded on the bottom in shallow water.

ah *interjection* an exclamation of surprise, pity, admiration, etc.

ahead *adverb* **1** further forward; in front. **2** forwards, *Full steam ahead!*

ahoy *interjection* an exclamation used by seamen to call attention.

▶▶ T H E S A U R U S ◀◀

aggressive *adjective* **1** attacking, bellicose, belligerent, combative, hostile, militant, pugnacious, warlike. **2** assertive, forceful, insistent, persistent, pushy, self-assertive, zealous.

aghast *adjective* appalled, dismayed, horrified, shocked, stunned.

agile *adjective* flexible, limber, lissom, lithe, nimble, quick-moving, sprightly, spry, supple.

agitate *verb* **1** disturb, excite, fluster, perturb, ruffle, stir up, trouble, unsettle, upset, work up, worry. **2** campaign, lobby, protest, stir. **3** beat, churn, shake, stir, toss, whisk.
agitator *noun* activist, campaigner, demagogue, firebrand, lobbyist, protester, rabble-rouser, stirrer.

agony *noun* anguish, distress, pain, suffering, torment, torture.
agonising *adjective* acute, excruciating, harrowing, intolerable, painful, severe, unbearable.

agree *verb* **1** be of the same mind, be unanimous, concur, see eye to eye. **2** (*agree to come*) consent, promise, undertake; (*agree to a plan*) accede to, accept, acquiesce in, allow, approve, assent to, back, consent to, endorse, grant, OK (*informal*), support. **5** accord, be consistent, be in harmony, coincide, conform, correspond, fit, harmonise, match, suit, tally.

agreeable *adjective* **1** amenable, in accord, in agreement, in favour, willing. **2** amiable, congenial, friendly, likeable, nice, pleasant.

agreement *noun* **1** accord, concord, consensus, harmony, unanimity. **2** accord, arrangement, bargain, compact, contract, covenant, deal, pact, settlement, treaty.

agriculture *noun* agribusiness, farming.

aground *adverb* & *adjective* beached, grounded, marooned, shipwrecked, stranded.

ahead *adverb* **1** in advance, in front, in the lead. **2** forwards, on, onwards.

▶▶ DICTIONARY ◀◀

aid[1] *noun* **1** help. **2** something that helps, *a hearing aid*. **3** money, food, etc. sent to another country to help it, *overseas aid*.
in aid of for the purpose of; to help something.

aid[2] *verb* help.

aide *noun* an assistant. [French]

Aids *noun* a disease that greatly weakens a person's ability to resist infections. [from the initial letters of 'acquired immune deficiency syndrome']

ail *verb* (*old use*) be ill; make a person ill.

ailing *adjective* ill; unwell.

ailment *noun* a slight illness.

aim[1] *verb* **1** point a gun etc. **2** throw or kick in a particular direction. **3** try or intend to do something.

aim[2] *noun* **1** aiming a gun etc. **2** purpose; intention.

aimless *adjective* without a purpose. **aimlessly** *adverb*

air[1] *noun* **1** the mixture of gases that surrounds the earth and which everyone breathes. **2** the open space above the earth. **3** a breeze or light wind. **4** a tune; a melody. **5** an appearance or impression of something, *an air of mystery*. **6** an impressive or haughty manner, *He puts on airs*.
by air in or by aircraft.
on the air on radio or television.

air[2] *verb* **1** put clothes etc. in a warm place to finish drying. **2** ventilate a room. **3** express, *He aired his opinions*.

airborne *adjective* **1** (of an aircraft) in flight. **2** carried by the air or by aircraft.

air-conditioning *noun* a system for controlling the temperature, purity, etc. of a room or building. **air-conditioned** *adjective*

aircraft *noun* (*plural* **aircraft**) an aeroplane, glider, or helicopter etc.

aircraft-carrier *noun* a large ship with a long deck where aircraft can take off and land.

airfield *noun* an area equipped with runways etc. where aircraft can take off and land.

air force the part of a country's armed forces that is equipped with aircraft.

airgun *noun* a gun in which compressed air shoots a pellet or dart.

airlift *noun* the emergency transport of supplies by air.

airline *noun* a company that provides a regular service of transport by aircraft.

airliner *noun* a large aircraft for carrying passengers.

airlock *noun* **1** a compartment with an airtight door at each end, through which people can go in and out of a pressurised chamber. **2** a bubble of air that stops liquid flowing through a pipe.

airmail *noun* mail carried by air.

airman *noun* (*plural* **airmen**) a man who is a member of an air force or of the crew of an aircraft.

airport *noun* an airfield for aircraft carrying passengers and goods.

▶▶ THESAURUS ◀◀

aid[1] *noun* **1** assistance, backing, collaboration, cooperation, encouragement, help, succour, support. **3** charity, contribution, donation, funding, grant, relief, sponsorship, subsidy, support.

aid[2] *verb* abet, assist, back, collaborate with, contribute to, cooperate with, encourage, facilitate, give to, help, lend a hand to, promote, relieve, subsidise, succour, support.

aide *noun* assistant, helper.

ailing *adjective* crook (*Australian informal*), ill, indisposed, infirm, poorly, sick, unwell.

ailment *noun* affliction, complaint, condition, disease, disorder, illness, indisposition, infection, infirmity, malady, sickness, trouble.

aim[1] *verb* **1** direct, focus, level, point, train. **3** aspire, endeavour, intend, plan, purpose, seek, strive, try.

aim[2] *noun* **2** ambition, design, end, goal, intention, object, objective, plan, point, purpose, target.

aimless *adjective* drifting, goalless, pointless, purposeless.

air[1] *noun* **2** aerospace, atmosphere, sky. **3** breeze, draught, wind. **4** melody, strain, tune. **5** ambience, appearance, atmosphere, aura, feeling, impression, look, mood.

air[2] *verb* **2** freshen, open up, ventilate. **3** express, get off your chest, make known, reveal, say, tell, vent, voice.

aircraft *noun* (*kinds of aircraft*) aeroplane, airliner, airship, biplane, bomber, fighter, glider, helicopter, jet, jumbo jet, jump jet, microlight, monoplane, plane, seaplane, turbojet.

airport *noun* aerodrome, airfield, airstrip, landing strip.

▶▶ D I C T I O N A R Y ◀◀

air raid an attack by aircraft.

airship *noun* a large balloon with engines, designed to carry passengers or goods.

airstrip *noun* a strip of ground prepared for aircraft to land and take off.

airtight *adjective* not letting air in or out.

airworthy *adjective* (of an aircraft) fit to fly. **airworthiness** *noun*

airy *adjective* 1 with plenty of fresh air. 2 light as air. 3 light-hearted; insincere, *airy promises*. **airily** *adverb*

aisle (*say* I'll) *noun* 1 a passage between or beside rows of seats or pews. 2 a side part of a church.

ajar *adverb* & *adjective* slightly open, *Leave the door ajar*.

akimbo *adverb* **arms akimbo** with hands on hips and elbows out.

akin *adjective* related; similar.

al- *prefix* see **ad-**.

alabaster (*say* **al**-a-bast-er) *noun* a kind of hard stone, usually white.

alacrity *noun* speed and willingness, *She accepted with alacrity*.

alarm¹ *noun* 1 a warning sound or signal; an apparatus for giving this. 2 being alarmed. 3 an alarm clock.
alarm clock a clock that can be set to make a sound at a fixed time to wake a sleeping person.

alarm² *verb* make someone frightened or anxious. [from Italian *all'arme!* = to arms!]

alarmist *noun* a person who raises unnecessary alarm.

alas *interjection* an exclamation of sorrow.

albatross *noun* (*plural* **albatrosses**) a large sea-bird with very long wings.

albino (*say* al-**been**-oh) *noun* (*plural* **albinos**) a person or animal with no colour in the skin and hair (which are white). [from Latin *albus* = white]

album *noun* 1 a book with blank pages in which to keep a collection of photographs, stamps, autographs, etc. 2 a long-playing record; a set of records. [Latin, = white piece of stone etc. on which to write things]

albumen (*say* **al**-bew-min) *noun* white of egg. [from Latin *albus* = white]

alchemy (*say* **al**-kim-ee) *noun* an early form of chemistry, the chief aim of which was to turn ordinary metals into gold. **alchemist** *noun* [from Arabic *alkimiya* = the art of changing metals]

alcheringa (*say* al-cher-**ring**-ga) *noun* the Dreamtime. [from Aranda (an Aboriginal language)]

alcohol *noun* 1 a colourless liquid made by fermenting sugar or starch. 2 an intoxicating drink containing this liquid (e.g. wine, beer, whisky). [from Arabic *al-kuhl*]

alcoholic¹ *adjective* of alcohol; containing alcohol.

alcoholic² *noun* a person who is seriously addicted to alcohol. **alcoholism** *noun*

alcove *noun* a section of a room etc. that is set back from the main part; a recess. [from Arabic *al-kubba* = the arch]

alder *noun* a kind of tree, often growing in marshy places.

alderman (*say* **awl**-der-man) *noun* (*plural* **aldermen**) a local government councillor in some Australian states and in England. [from Old English *aldor* = older, + *man*]

ale *noun* beer.

alert¹ *adjective* watching for something; ready to act. **alertly** *adverb*, **alertness** *noun*

▶▶ T H E S A U R U S ◀◀

airtight *adjective* hermetically sealed, impermeable.

airy *adjective* 1 breezy, draughty, fresh, ventilated, well-ventilated.

aisle *noun* 1 corridor, gangway, gap, passage, passageway, path.

alarm¹ *noun* 1 alert, bell, signal, siren, tocsin, warning. 2 anxiety, apprehension, consternation, dismay, dread, fear, fright, panic, terror, trepidation, worry.

alarm² *verb* agitate, dismay, disturb, frighten, panic, perturb, petrify, put the wind up (*informal*), scare, startle, terrify, unnerve.

album *noun* 1 book, display book. 2 collection, compilation, disc, record, recording.

alcohol *noun* 2 booze (*informal*), drink, grog (*Australian informal*), liquor, spirits, wine.

alcoholic¹ *adjective* intoxicating, spirituous.

alcoholic² *noun* boozer (*informal*), dipsomaniac, drunk, drunkard, soak (*informal*), sot, wino (*informal*).

alcove *noun* bay, niche, nook, recess.

alert¹ *adjective* attentive, awake, aware, careful, observant, on the ball (*informal*), on the lookout, on your guard, on your toes, ready, vigilant, wary, watchful.

▶▶ DICTIONARY ◀◀

alert² *noun* a warning or alarm.
on the alert on the lookout; watchful.

alert³ *verb* warn of danger etc.; make someone aware of something. [from Italian *all'erta!* = to the watch-tower!]

alga (*say* al-ga) *noun* (*plural* **algae**, *say* (**al**-jee) a kind of plant that grows in water, with no true stems or leaves.

algebra (*say* **al**-jib-ra) *noun* mathematics in which letters and symbols are used to represent quantities. **algebraic** (*say* al-jib-**ray**-ik) *adjective* [from Arabic *al-jabr* = putting together broken parts]

alias¹ (*say* **ay**-lee-as) *noun* (*plural* **aliases**) a false or different name.

alias² *adverb* also named, *Robert Zimmerman, alias Bob Dylan.* [Latin, = at another time]

alibi (*say* **al**-ib-I) *noun* (*plural* **alibis**) evidence that a person accused of a crime was somewhere else when it was committed. [Latin, = at another place]

Usage It is incorrect to use this word as if it meant simply 'an excuse'.

alien¹ (*say* **ay**-lee-en) *noun* **1** a person who is not a citizen of the country where he or she is living; a foreigner. **2** a being from another world.

alien² *adjective* **1** foreign. **2** unnatural, *Cruelty is alien to her nature.* [from Latin *alius* = another]

alienate (*say* **ay**-lee-an-ayt) *verb* (**alienated**, **alienating**) make a person become unfriendly or hostile. **alienation** *noun*

alight¹ *adjective* **1** on fire. **2** lit up. [from *a-¹* + *light¹*]

alight² *verb* **1** get out of a vehicle or down from a horse etc. **2** fly down and settle, *The bird alighted on a branch.* [from *a-¹* + *light²*]

align (*say* al-**I'n**) *verb* **1** arrange in a line. **2** join as an ally. *They aligned themselves with the Germans.* **alignment** *noun* [from French *à ligne* = into line]

alike *adjective & adverb* like one another; in the same way, *The twins are very alike. Treat them alike.*

alimentary canal the tube along which food passes from the mouth to the anus in the process of being digested and absorbed by the body. [from Latin *alimentum* = food]

alive *adjective* **1** living. **2** alert, *Be alive to the possible dangers.* **3** swarming with; full of, *The place was alive with tourists.*

alkali (*say* **alk**-al-I) *noun* (*plural* **alkalis**) a substance that neutralises acids. **alkaline** *adjective* [from Arabic *al-kily* = the ashes]

all¹ *adjective* the whole number or amount of, *All my books are here; all day.*

all² *noun* **1** everything, *That is all I know.* **2** everybody, *All are agreed.*

all³ *adverb* **1** completely. *She was dressed all in white.* **2** to each team or competitor, *The score is fifteen all.*

all-clear *noun* a signal that a danger has passed.

all in (*informal*) exhausted, *I'm all in.*

all-in *adjective* including or allowing everything, *an all-in price.*

all right satisfactory; in good condition; as desired; yes, I consent.

all-round *adjective* general; not specialist, *an all-round athlete.* **all-rounder** *noun*

▶▶ THESAURUS ◀◀

alert² *noun* alarm, signal, siren, warning.

alert³ *verb* caution, forewarn, prepare, warn.

alias¹ *noun* assumed name, false name, nickname, nom de plume, pen-name, pseudonym, stage name.

alien¹ *noun* **1** foreigner, outsider, stranger. **2** extraterrestrial.

alien² *adjective* **1** exotic, foreign, outlandish, strange, unfamiliar. **2** contrary, foreign, inconsistent, uncharacteristic.

alienate *verb* antagonise, estrange, turn away, turn off.

alight¹ *adjective* **1** ablaze, blazing, burning, on fire.

alight² *verb* **1** descend, disembark, get down, get off. **2** land, perch, settle.

align *verb* **1** line up, straighten up. **2** affiliate, ally, associate, join, side.

alike *adjective* akin, comparable, equivalent, identical, indistinguishable, similar, synonymous.

alive *adjective* **1** animate, breathing, existing, live, living, quick (*old use*), surviving. **2** (*alive to*) alert to, aware of, conscious of, mindful of, sensitive to. **3** (*alive with*) crawling with (*informal*), full of, packed with, swarming with, teeming with.

all³ *adverb* **all right 1** acceptable, fine, OK (*informal*), passable, satisfactory. **2** fine, OK (*informal*), safe, safe and sound, unharmed, uninjured, unscathed.

all there (*informal*) having an alert mind.

all the same in spite of this; making no difference, *I like him, all the same*.

Allah the Muslim name of God.

allay (*say* a-**lay**) *verb* (**allayed, allaying**) calm, *to allay their fears*.

allegation (*say* al-ig-**ay**-shon) *noun* a statement made without proof.

allege (*say* a-**lej**) *verb* (**alleged, alleging**) say something without being able to prove it, *He alleged that I had cheated*. **allegedly** (*say* a-**lej**-id-lee) *adverb*

allegiance (*say* a-**lee**-jans) *noun* loyalty. [compare *liege*]

allegory (*say* **al**-ig-er-ee) *noun* (*plural* **allegories**) a story in which the characters and events represent or symbolise an underlying meaning. **allegorical** (*say* al-ig-**o**-rik-al) *adjective*

alleluia *interjection* praise to God. [from Hebrew]

allergic *adjective* very sensitive to something that may make you ill, *He is allergic to pollen, which gives him hay fever*. **allergy** (*say* **al**-er-jee) *noun*

alleviate (*say* a-**lee**-vee-ayt) *verb* (**alleviated, alleviating**) make a thing less severe, *to alleviate pain*. **alleviation** *noun* [from *al*-, + Latin *levis* = light]

alley *noun* (*plural* **alleys**) **1** a narrow street or passage. **2** a place where you can play skittles or tenpin bowling. [from French *aller* = go]

alliance *noun* an association formed by countries or groups who wish to support each other.

allied *adjective* **1** joined as allies. **2** of the same kind.

alligator *noun* a kind of crocodile. [from Spanish *el lagarto* = the lizard]

alliteration *noun* having the same letter or sound at the beginning of several words, e.g. in *Sit in solemn silence*. [from *al*, + Latin *littera* = letter]

allocate *verb* (**allocated, allocating**) allot; set aside for a particular purpose. **allocation** *noun* [from *al*-, + Latin *locus* = a place]

allot *verb* (**allotted, allotting**) distribute portions, jobs, etc. to different people.

allotment *noun* **1** a piece of public land used for growing vegetables, fruit, or flowers, for pasture or building. **2** allotting; the amount allotted.

allow *verb* **1** permit, *Smoking is not allowed*. **2** permit someone to have something; provide with, *She was allowed $20 for books*. **3** agree, *I allow that you have been patient*. **allowable** *adjective*

allowance *noun* **1** allowing something. **2** what is allowed, *an allowance of $20 for books*.
make allowances be considerate; excuse, *Make allowances for his age*.

alloy *noun* a metal formed by mixing two or more metals etc.

allay *verb* alleviate, calm, diminish, ease, lessen, quell, reduce, subdue.

allegation *noun* accusation, assertion, charge, claim, statement.

allege *verb* affirm, assert, avow, claim, declare, profess, state.

allegiance *noun* devotion, duty, faithfulness, fidelity, loyalty.

allegory *noun* fable, parable.

allergy *noun* reaction, sensitivity.

alleviate *verb* assuage, diminish, ease, lessen, mitigate, moderate, reduce, relieve, soften.

alley *noun* **1** back street, lane, passage, passageway, path.

alliance *noun* affiliation, association, coalition, confederation, league, partnership, union.

allocation *noun* allotment, allowance, cut

(*informal*), lot, portion, quota, ration, share, slice (*informal*).

allot *verb* allocate, apportion, assign, dispense, distribute, dole out, give out, mete out, ration, share out.

allotment *noun* **1** block, lot, plot, section (*Australian historical*). **2** allocation, allowance, quota, ration, share.

allow *verb* **1** approve, authorise, enable, let, permit. **2** allocate, allot, assign, give, grant, permit, provide.

allowance *noun* **2** allocation, allotment, annuity, benefit, dole, endowment, grant, payment, pension, pocket money, portion, quota, ration, stipend, subsidy.
make allowances for allow for, bear in mind, make concessions for, take into account, take into consideration; see also EXCUSE[1].

▶▶ DICTIONARY ◀◀

allude *verb* (**alluded**, **alluding**) mention something briefly or indirectly, *He alluded to his wealth.* **allusion** *noun*

allure *verb* (**allured**, **alluring**) entice; attract. **allurement** *noun* [from French *à* = to, + *lure*]

alluvium (*say* a-**loo**-vee-um) *noun* sand and soil etc. deposited by a river or flood, in Australia especially of alluvium containing gold. **alluvial** *adjective*

ally[1] *noun* (*plural* **allies**) **1** a country in alliance with another. **2** a person who cooperates with another.

ally[2] *verb* (**allied**, **allying**) form an alliance.

almanac *noun* an annual publication containing a calendar and other information.

almighty *adjective* **1** having complete power. **2** (*informal*) very great, *an almighty din.*

almond (*say* **ah**-mond) *noun* an oval edible nut.

almost *adverb* near to being something but not quite, *almost ready.*

alms (*say* ahmz) *noun* (*old use*) money and gifts given to the poor.

almshouse *noun* a house founded by charity for poor people.

aloft *adverb* high up; up in the air.

alone *adjective* without any other people or things; without help. [from *all one*]

along[1] *preposition* following the length of something, *Walk along the path.*

along[2] *adverb* **1** on; onwards, *Push it along.* **2** accompanying somebody, *I've brought my brother along.*

alongside *preposition* & *adverb* next to something; beside.

aloof[1] *adverb* apart; not taking part, *We stayed aloof from their quarrels.*

aloof[2] *adjective* distant and not friendly in manner, *She seemed aloof.*

aloud *adverb* in a voice that can be heard.

alpha *noun* the first letter of the Greek alphabet, = a.

alphabet *noun* the letters used in a language, usually arranged in a set order. **alphabetical** *adjective*, **alphabetically** *adverb* [from *alpha*, *beta*, the first two letters of the Greek alphabet]

alpine *adjective* of high mountains. [from the Alps, mountains in Switzerland]

already *adverb* by now; before now.

Alsatian (*say* al-**say**-shan) *noun* a large strong dog, often used by the police.

also *adverb* as an extra person or thing; besides; as well.

altar *noun* a table or similar structure used in religious ceremonies.

alter *verb* make or become different; change. **alteration** *noun* [from Latin *alter* = other]

altercation (*say* ol-ter-**kay**-shon) *noun* a noisy argument or quarrel.

alternate[1] (*say* ol-**tern**-at) *adjective* happening or arriving in turns; first the one and then the other. **alternately** *adverb*

Usage See the note on *alternative.*

▶▶ THESAURUS ◀◀

allude *verb* (*allude to*) hint at, mention, refer to, touch on.
  allusion *noun* hint, intimation, mention, reference.

alluring *adjective* attractive, beguiling, captivating, charming, enchanting, fascinating.

ally[1] *noun* **2** associate, colleague, confederate, friend, partner.

ally[2] *verb* affiliate, band together, combine, join forces, side, team up, unite.

almighty *adjective* **1** all-powerful, omnipotent, sovereign, supreme.

almost *adverb* all but, approximately, close to, nearly, not quite, practically, virtually, wellnigh.

alone *adjective* apart, by yourself, isolated, on your own, separate, single, solitary, solo,

unaccompanied, unaided, unassisted; see also LONELY.

alongside *preposition* adjacent to, beside, close to, next to.

aloof[2] *adjective* cool, distant, remote, standoffish, unapproachable, unfriendly, unsociable, unsympathetic.

aloud *adverb* audibly, out loud.

also *adverb* additionally, as well, besides, furthermore, in addition, moreover, too.

alter *verb* adapt, adjust, amend, change, convert, modify, remodel, reshape, revise, transform, vary.

altercation *noun* argument, barney (*informal*), clash, disagreement, dispute, fight, quarrel, row, scrap (*informal*), set-to, squabble.

alternate[1] *adjective* every other, every second.

►► DICTIONARY ◄◄

alternate² (*say* **ol**-tern-ayt) *verb* (**alternated**, **alternating**) use or come alternately. **alternation** *noun*
  alternating current electric current that keeps reversing its direction at regular intervals. **alternator** *noun*

alternative¹ *adjective* **1** available instead of something else. **2** unconventional, *alternative medicine.* **alternatively** *adverb*

> **Usage** Do not confuse *alternative* with *alternate.* If there are *alternative colours* it means that there is a choice of two or more colours, but *alternate colours* means that there is first one colour and then the other.

alternative² *noun* one of two or more possibilities.
  no alternative no choice.

although *conjunction* though.

altimeter *noun* an instrument used in aircraft etc. for showing the height above sea-level. [from Latin *altus* = high, + *meter*]

altitude *noun* the height of something, especially above sea-level. [from Latin *altus* = high]

alto *noun* (*plural* **altos**) **1** an adult male singer with a very high voice. **2** a contralto. [Italian, = high]

altogether *adverb* **1** with all included; in total, *The outfit costs $40 altogether.* **2** completely, *The creek dries up altogether in summer.* **3** on the whole, *Altogether, it was a good concert.*

> **Usage** Do not confuse *altogether* and *all together.*

altruistic (*say* al-troo-**ist**-ik) *adjective* unselfish; thinking of other people's welfare. **altruist** *noun* **altruism** *noun* [from Italian *altrui* = somebody else]

aluminium *noun* a lightweight silver-coloured metal.

always *adverb* **1** at all times. **2** often, *You are always crying.* **3** whatever happens, *You can always sleep on the floor.*

a.m. *abbreviation* ante meridiem (Latin, = before noon).

amalgam *noun* **1** an alloy of mercury. **2** a soft mixture.

amalgamate *verb* (**amalgamated**, **amalgamating**) mix; combine. **amalgamation** *noun*

amass *verb* heap up; collect.

amateur (*say* **am**-at-er) *noun* a person who does something as a hobby, not as a professional. **amateurish** *adjective* [from Latin *amator* = lover)

amaze *verb* (**amazed**, **amazing**) surprise somebody greatly; fill with wonder. **amazement** *noun*

ambassador *noun* a person sent to a foreign country to represent his or her own government.

amber *noun* **1** a hard clear yellowish substance used for making ornaments. **2** a yellow traffic-light shown as a signal for caution, placed between red (= stop) and green (= go).

ambi- *prefix* both; on both sides (as in *ambidextrous*). [from Latin *ambo* = both]

ambidextrous *adjective* able to use either the left hand or the right hand equally well. [from *ambi-*, + Latin *dexter* = right-handed]

►► THESAURUS ◄◄

alternate² *verb* change, interchange, oscillate, rotate, swing, switch, take turns, vary.

alternative¹ *adjective* **1** different, other, second. **2** non-conventional, unconventional.

alternative² *noun* choice, option, possibility.

altitude *noun* elevation, height.

altogether *adverb* **1** all told, in all, in total, in toto. **2** absolutely, completely, entirely, perfectly, quite, thoroughly, totally, utterly, wholly.

always *adverb* **1** consistently, every time, invariably, regularly. **2** constantly, continually, continuously, eternally, forever, perpetually, repeatedly. **3** in any case, in any event, whatever happens.

amalgamate *verb* blend, combine, incorporate, integrate, join, merge, mix, unite.

amass *verb* accumulate, collect, gather, heap up, hoard, pile up, stock up, store up.

amateur *noun* dabbler, dilettante, layman, layperson, non-professional.
  amateurish *adjective* clumsy, incompetent, inexpert, unprofessional, unskilful.

amaze *verb* astonish, astound, bewilder, confound, dumbfound, flabbergast, nonplus, overwhelm, shock, stagger, startle, stun, stupefy, surprise, take aback.
  amazement *noun* astonishment, bewilderment, shock, stupefaction, surprise, wonder.

ambassador *noun* attaché, consul, diplomat, envoy, legate, plenipotentiary, representative.

▶▶DICTIONARY◀◀

ambiguous *adjective* having more than one possible meaning; unclear. **ambiguously** *adverb*, **ambiguity** *noun*

ambition *noun* **1** a strong desire to achieve something. **2** the thing desired.

ambitious *adjective* **1** full of ambition. **2** showing or requiring ambition, *an ambitious project.*

ambivalent (*say* am-**biv**-al-ent) *adjective* having mixed feelings about something (e.g. liking and disliking it). **ambivalence** *noun* [from *ambi-*, + Latin *valens* = strong]

amble *verb* (**ambled, ambling**) walk at a slow easy pace. [from Latin *ambulare* = walk]

ambrosia (*say* am-**broh**-zee-a) *noun* something delicious. [in Greek mythology, ambrosia was the food of the gods]

ambulance *noun* a vehicle equipped to carry sick or injured people.

ambush[1] *noun* (*plural* **ambushes**) a surprise attack from troops etc. who have concealed themselves.

ambush[2] *verb* lie in wait for someone; attack from an ambush.

ameliorate (*say* a-**mee**-lee-er-ayt) *verb* (**ameliorated, ameliorating**) make or become better; improve. **amelioration** *noun* [from *ad-*, + Latin *melior* = better]

amen *interjection* a word used at the end of a prayer or hymn, meaning 'may it be so'. [from Hebrew, = certainly]

amenable (*say* a-**meen**-a-bul) *adjective* willing to be guided or controlled by something, *He is not amenable to discipline.* [from French *amener* = to lead]

amend *verb* alter something so as to improve it. **amendment** *noun*
make amends make up for having done something wrong; atone.

amenity (*say* a-**men**-it-ee or a-**meen**-it-ee) *noun* (*plural* **amenities**) a pleasant or useful feature of a place etc., *The town has many amenities.*

American *adjective* **1** of the continent of America. **2** of the United States of America. **American** *noun*

amethyst *noun* a purple precious stone.

amiable *adjective* friendly; good-tempered. **amiably** *adverb*

amicable *adjective* friendly. **amicably** *adverb* [from Latin *amicus* = friend]

amid or **amidst** *preposition* in the middle of; among.

amino acid (*say* a-**meen**-oh) an acid found in proteins.

amir (*say* a-**meer**) *noun* an emir. [Arabic, = a ruler]

amiss[1] *adjective* wrong; faulty, *There is nothing amiss with the engine.*

amiss[2] *adverb* wrongly; faultily.
take amiss be offended by, *Don't take his criticism amiss.*

ammonia *noun* a colourless gas or liquid with a strong smell.

ammunition *noun* a supply of bullets, shells, grenades, etc. for use in fighting. [from French *la munition*, wrongly taken as *l'ammunition*]

▶▶THESAURUS◀◀

ambiguous *adjective* equivocal, imprecise, indefinite, uncertain, unclear, vague.

ambition *noun* **1** drive, enterprise, enthusiasm, get-up-and-go (*informal*), motivation, push, zeal. **2** aim, aspiration, desire, dream, goal, intention, object, objective, purpose.

ambitious *adjective* **1** aspiring, eager, enterprising, go-ahead, high-flying, keen, pushy, zealous. **2** bold, challenging, daring, difficult, formidable, grandiose.

amble *verb* & *noun* dawdle, ramble, saunter, stroll, walk, wander.

ambush[1] *noun* snare, trap.

ambush[2] *verb* attack, ensnare, lie in wait for, pounce on, swoop on, trap, waylay.

ameliorate *verb* enhance, improve, make better, upgrade.

amend *verb* adapt, adjust, alter, change, correct, edit, improve, modify, rectify, revise.
make amends for atone for, compensate for, expiate, make reparation for, make restitution for.

amenity *noun* convenience, facility, feature.

amiable *adjective* affable, agreeable, amicable, friendly, genial, good-natured, kind, kindly, pleasant.

amicable *adjective* cordial, friendly, harmonious, peaceful.

amiss[1] *adjective* awry, defective, faulty, incorrect, out of order, wrong.

ammunition *noun* bullets, cartridges, grenades, missiles, projectiles, rounds, shells, shot, shrapnel.

▶▶▶ DICTIONARY ◀◀◀

amnesia (*say* am-**nee**-zee-a) *noun* loss of memory. [from Greek *a-* = without, + *-mnesis* = memory]

amnesty *noun* (*plural* **amnesties**) a general pardon for people who have committed a crime.

amoeba (*say* a-**mee**-ba) *noun* (*plural* **amoebas**) a microscopic creature consisting of a single cell which constantly changes shape.

amok *adverb* **run amok** rush about in a destructive or murderous frenzy. [from Malay, = fighting mad]

among or **amongst** *preposition* **1** surrounded by; in, *There were weeds among the flowers.* **2** between, *Divide the sweets among the children.* [from Old English *ongemang* = in a crowd]

amoral (*say* ay-**mor**-al) *adjective* not based on moral standards; neither moral nor immoral. [from *a-²* = not, + *moral*]

amorous *adjective* showing love, *amorous glances.* [from Latin *amor* = love]

amorphous (*say* a-**mor**-fus) *adjective* shapeless, *an amorphous mass.* [from *a-²* = not, + Greek *morphe* = form]

amount¹ *noun* **1** a quantity. **2** a total.

amount² *verb* **amount to** add up to; be equivalent to, *Their reply amounts to a refusal.* [from Latin *ad montem* = to the mountain, upwards]

amp *noun* **1** an ampere. **2** (*informal*) an amplifier.

ampere (*say* **am**-pair) *noun* a unit for measuring electric current. [named after the French scientist A.M. Ampère]

ampersand *noun* the symbol & (= and).

amphi- *prefix* both; on both sides; in both places (as in *amphibian*). [from Greek *amphi* = around]

amphibian *noun* **1** an amphibious animal; an animal (e.g. a frog) that at first (as a tadpole) has gills and lives in water but later develops lungs and breathes air. **2** an amphibious aircraft or tank etc. [from *amphi-*, + Greek *bios* = life]

amphibious *adjective* able to live or move both on land and in water.

amphitheatre *noun* an oval or circular unroofed building with tiers of seats round a central arena. [from Greek *amphi* = all round, + *theatre*]

Usage This word does not mean 'an ancient theatre'; Greek and Roman *theatres* were semicircular.

ample *adjective* **1** quite enough, *ample provisions.* **2** large. **amply** *adverb*

amplifier *noun* a device for making something louder.

amplify *verb* (**amplified, amplifying**) **1** make louder or stronger, *to amplify sound.* **2** give more details about something. [from Latin *amplificare* = make more ample]

amplitude *noun* **1** breadth. **2** largeness; abundance.

amputate *verb* (**amputated, amputating**) cut off by a surgical operation. **amputation** *noun*

amuse *verb* (**amused, amusing**) **1** make a person laugh or smile. **2** make time pass pleasantly for someone. **amusing** *adjective* [from French *amuser* = distract]

amusement *noun* **1** amusing; being amused. **2** something that amuses.

▶▶▶ THESAURUS ◀◀◀

amnesty *noun* pardon, reprieve.

among *preposition* **1** amid, amidst, amongst, in the middle of, in the midst of, surrounded by.

amorous *adjective* affectionate, loving, passionate, tender.

amount¹ *noun* extent, lot (*informal*), mass, measure, quantity, sum, total, volume.

amount² *verb* **amount to** add up to, come to, equal, make, total.

ample *adjective* **1** abundant, bountiful, copious, enough, generous, lavish, liberal, plentiful, profuse, sufficient. **2** big, large, stout.

amplify *verb* **1** boost, enhance, increase, intensify, magnify, strengthen. **2** add to, develop, elaborate on, enlarge upon, expand, fill out, supplement.

amputate *verb* chop off, cut off, remove.

amuse *verb* cheer up, delight, divert, entertain. **amusing** *adjective* comical, diverting, droll, entertaining, farcical, funny, hilarious, humorous, laughable, ludicrous, priceless (*informal*), ridiculous, witty, zany.

amusement *noun* **1** delight, enjoyment, entertainment, fun, hilarity, merriment, mirth, pleasure, recreation. **2** distraction, diversion, entertainment, game, hobby, interest, pastime, sport.

▶▶DICTIONARY◀◀

an *adjective* see **a**.

an-¹ *prefix* see **a-²**.

an-² *prefix* see **ad-**.

ana- *prefix* up; back (as in *analysis*). [from Greek *ana* = up]

anabranch *noun* an arm of a river leaving and later rejoining it.

anachronism (*say* an-**ak**-ron-izm) *noun* something wrongly placed in a particular historical period, or regarded as out of date, *Bows and arrows would be an anachronism in modern warfare*. [from *ana-*, + Greek *chronos* = time]

anaemia (*say* a-**nee**-mee-a) *noun* a poor condition of the blood that makes a person pale. **anaemic** *adjective* [from *an-¹* = without, + Greek *haima* = blood]

anaesthetic (*say* an-iss-**thet**-ik) *noun* a substance or gas that makes you unable to feel pain. **anaesthesia** *noun* [from *an-¹* = without, + Greek *aisthesis* = sensation]

anaesthetist (*say* an-**ees**-thet-ist) *noun* a person trained to give anaesthetics. **anaesthetise** *verb*

anagram *noun* a word or phrase made by rearranging the letters of another, *'Trap' is an anagram of 'part'*. [from *ana-*, + Greek *gramma* = letter.]

anal (*say* **ay**-nal) *adjective* of the anus.

analgesic (*say* an-al-**jee**-sik) *noun* a substance that relieves pain. [from *an-¹* = without, + Greek *algesis* = pain]

analogy (*say* a-**nal**-oj-ee) *noun* (*plural* **analogies**) a partial likeness between two things that are compared, *the analogy between the human heart and a pump*. **analogous** *adjective*

analyse *verb* (**analysed, analysing**) **1** separate something into its parts. **2** examine and interpret something, *analyse the causes*. **analysis** *noun*, **analytic** *adjective*, **analytical** *adjective* [from *ana-*, + Greek *lysis* = loosening]

analyst *noun* a person who analyses things.

anarchist (*say* **an**-er-kist) *noun* a person who believes that all forms of government are bad and should be abolished.

anarchy (*say* **an**-er-kee) *noun* **1** lack of government or control, resulting in lawlessness. **2** disorder. [from *an-¹* = without, + Greek *arche* = rule]

anatomy (*say* an-**at**-om-ee) *noun* the study of how the body is constituted. **anatomical** *adjective*, **anatomist** *noun* [from *ana-*, + Greek *tome* = cutting]

ancestor *noun* anyone from whom a person is descended. **ancestral** *adjective*, **ancestry** *noun*

anchor¹ *noun* a heavy object joined to a ship by a chain or rope and dropped to the bottom of the sea to stop the ship from moving. **anchorage** *noun*

anchor² *verb* **1** fix or be fixed by an anchor. **2** fix firmly.

anchovy *noun* (*plural* **anchovies**) a small fish with a strong flavour.

ancient *adjective* **1** very old. **2** of times long past, *ancient history*.

ancillary (*say* an-**sil**-er-ee) *adjective* helping people to do something, *ancillary services*. [from Latin *ancilla* = servant]

and *conjunction* **1** together with; in addition to, *We had cakes and buns*. **2** so that; with this result, *Work hard and you will pass*. **3** to, *Go and buy a pen*.

▶▶THESAURUS◀◀

anaemic *adjective* colourless, pale, pallid, pasty, sickly, wan, white.

analogy *noun* comparison, likeness, metaphor, parallel, resemblance, similarity.
analogous *adjective* akin, comparable, corresponding, like, parallel, similar.

analyse *verb* **1** break down, dissect, divide, separate, take apart. **2** examine, interpret, investigate, study.
analysis *noun* breakdown, examination, interpretation, investigation, study.

anarchy *noun* chaos, confusion, disorder, lawlessness.

ancestor *noun* forebear, forefather, predecessor, progenitor.
ancestry *noun* ancestors, blood, descent, extraction, forebears, genealogy, lineage, origin, pedigree, roots, stock.

anchor² *verb* fasten, moor, secure, tie up.

ancient *adjective* **1** antiquated, antique, archaic, obsolete, old, old-fashioned, out-of-date. **2** bygone, early, former, old, olden, prehistoric, primeval, primitive, primordial.

ancillary *adjective* auxiliary, subordinate, subsidiary, support, supporting.

► ► D I C T I O N A R Y ◄ ◄

anecdote *noun* a short amusing or interesting story about a real person or thing.

anemone (*say* a-**nem**-on-ee) *noun* a plant with cup-shaped red, purple, or white flowers. [from Greek, = wind-flower]

anew *adverb* again; in a new or different way, *begin anew*.

angel *noun* **1** an attendant or messenger of God. **2** a very kind or beautiful person. **angelic** (*say* an-**jel**-ik) *adjective* [from Greek *angelos* = messenger]

angelica *noun* a fragrant plant whose crystallised stalks are used in cookery as a decoration.

anger¹ *noun* a strong feeling that makes you want to quarrel or fight.

anger² *verb* make a person angry.

angle¹ *noun* **1** the space between two lines or surfaces that meet; the amount by which a line or surface must be turned to make it lie along another. **2** a point of view.

angle² *verb* (**angled, angling**) **1** put something in a slanting position. **2** present news etc. from one point of view.

angler *noun* a person who fishes with a fishing-rod and line. **angling** *noun*

Anglican *adjective* of the Church of England. **Anglican** *noun*

Anglo- *prefix* English or British, *an Anglo-French agreement*. [from the *Angles*, a Germanic tribe who came to England in the 5th century and eventually gave their name to it]

Anglo-Celtic *adjective* of or from the British Isles.

Anglo-Saxon *noun* **1** an English person, especially of the time before the Norman conquest in 1066. **2** the English language from about 700 to 1150, also called *Old English*.

angry *adjective* (**angrier, angriest**) feeling anger. **angrily** *adverb*

anguish *noun* severe suffering, great sorrow or pain. **anguished** *adjective*

angular *adjective* **1** having angles or sharp corners. **2** (of a person) bony, not plump.

animal *noun* **1** a living thing that can feel and usually move about, *Horses, birds, fish, bees, and people are all animals.* **2** a brutish person; someone not worthy of being called human. [from Latin *animalis* = having breath]

animate¹ *adjective* having life.

animate² *verb* (**animated, animating**) **1** make a thing lively. **2** produce something as an animated cartoon. **animation** *noun*, **animator** *noun*

animated cartoon a film made by photographing a series of drawings.

► ► T H E S A U R U S ◄ ◄

anecdote *noun* narrative, story, tale, yarn (*informal*).

angel *noun* **1** archangel, cherub, messenger of God, seraph.
angelic *adjective* **1** celestial, cherubic, heavenly, seraphic. **2** good, innocent, kind, pure.

anger¹ *noun* annoyance, displeasure, exasperation, fury, indignation, ire, irritation, outrage, pique, rage, temper, vexation, wrath.

anger² *verb* annoy, bug (*informal*), displease, enrage, exasperate, gall, incense, infuriate, irritate, madden, outrage, pique, provoke, rile (*informal*), vex.

angle¹ *noun* **1** bend, corner. **2** approach, outlook, perspective, point of view, position, slant, standpoint, viewpoint.

angle² *verb* **1** slant, slope, tilt, turn, twist.

angry *adjective* annoyed, bad-tempered, cross, displeased, enraged, exasperated, furious, hot under the collar (*informal*), incensed, indignant, infuriated, irascible, irate, irritated, livid (*informal*), mad (*informal*), outraged, resentful, riled (*informal*), ropeable (*Australian informal*), shirty (*informal*), snaky (*Australian informal*), up in arms, wild, wrathful.

be angry, become angry blow your stack (*informal*), blow your top (*informal*), do your block (*Australian informal*), do your lolly (*informal*), explode, flare up, flip your lid (*informal*), fly off the handle (*informal*), freak (out) (*informal*), fume, get steamed up (*informal*), go crook (*Australian informal*), go off the deep end (*informal*), hit the roof (*informal*), lose your temper, rage, rave, seethe.

anguish *noun* agony, distress, grief, misery, pain, sorrow, suffering, torment, torture, woe.

animal *noun* **1** beast, brute, creature; (*animals*) fauna, livestock, wildlife.

animate¹ *adjective* alive, breathing, live, living, sentient.

animate² *verb* **1** buck up (*informal*), energise, enliven, excite, fire up, galvanise, inspire, liven up, motivate, perk up (*informal*), rouse, stimulate.
animated *adjective* active, bright, energetic, enthusiastic, excited, exuberant, lively, passionate, spirited, vigorous, vivacious.
animation *noun* dynamism, energy, enthusiasm, excitement, liveliness, spirit, verve, vigour, vitality, vivacity, zest.

▶▶ DICTIONARY ◀◀

animosity (*say* an-im-**oss**-it-ee) *noun* a feeling of hostility.

aniseed *noun* a sweet-smelling seed used for flavouring things.

ankle *noun* the part of the leg where it joins the foot.

annals *plural noun* a history of events, especially when written year by year. [from Latin *annales* = yearly books]

annex *verb* 1 take possession of something and add it to what you have already. 2 add or join a thing to something else. [from *an-*², + Latin *nexum* = tied]

annexe *noun* a building added to a larger or more important building.

annihilate (*say* an-**I**-il-ayt) *verb* (**annihilated, annihilating**) destroy completely. **annihilation** *noun* [from *an-*², + Latin *nihil* = nothing]

anniversary *noun* (*plural* **anniversaries**) a day when you remember something special that happened on the same day in a previous year. [from Latin *annus* = year, + *versum* = turned]

annotate (*say* **an**-oh-tayt) *verb* (**annotated, annotation**) add notes of explanation to something written or printed. **annotation** *noun*

announce *verb* (**announced, announcing**) make something known, especially by saying it publicly or to an audience. **announcement**

noun [from *an-*², + Latin *nuntius* = messenger]

announcer *noun* a person who announces items in a broadcast.

annoy *verb* 1 make a person slightly angry. 2 be troublesome to someone. **annoyance** *noun* [from Latin *in odio* = hateful]

annual¹ *adjective* 1 happening or done once a year, *her annual visit*. 2 of one year; reckoned by the year, *our annual income*. 3 living for one year or one season, *an annual plant*. **annually** *adverb*

annual² *noun* 1 a book that comes out once a year. 2 an annual plant. [from Latin *annus* = year]

annuity (*say* a-**new**-it-ee) *noun* (*plural* **annuities**) a fixed annual allowance of money, especially from a kind of investment. [same origin as *annual*]

annul *verb* (**annulled, annulling**) cancel a law or contract; end something legally, *Their marriage was annulled*. **annulment** *noun* [from *an-*², + Latin *nullus* = none]

Annunciation *noun* the Christian festival (on 25 March) commemorating the announcement by the angel to the Virgin Mary that she was to be the mother of Jesus Christ.

anode *noun* the electrode by which electric current enters a device. (Compare *cathode*.) [from *ana-* = up, + Greek *hodos* = way]

▶▶ THESAURUS ◀◀

animosity *noun* acrimony, antagonism, antipathy, bitterness, enmity, hatred, hostility, ill will, malevolence, malice, rancour, resentment.

annex *verb* 1 conquer, occupy, seize, take over, take possession of.

annexe *noun* addition, extension, wing.

annihilate *verb* destroy, eliminate, eradicate, exterminate, extinguish, get rid of, kill, liquidate, murder, obliterate, slaughter, wipe out.

anniversary *noun* birthday, jubilee.

annotation *noun* comment, explanation, footnote, note.

announce *verb* advertise, broadcast, declare, disclose, divulge, make known, proclaim, promulgate, publicise, publish, report, reveal, tell.

announcement *noun* advertisement, bulletin, communiqué, declaration, disclosure, notice, notification, proclamation, pronouncement, publication, report, statement.

announcer *noun* broadcaster, compère, disc jockey, DJ, herald, master of ceremonies, MC, newsreader, presenter.

annoy *verb* aggravate (*informal*), anger, badger, bother, bug (*informal*), distress, drive someone mad (*informal*), drive someone up the wall (*informal*), exasperate, gall, get on someone's nerves, get under someone's skin (*informal*), get up someone's nose (*informal*), harass, hassle, infuriate, irk, irritate, madden, nark (*informal*), needle (*informal*), pester, pique, plague, provoke, rankle, rile (*informal*), rub someone up the wrong way (*informal*), trouble, try, upset, vex, worry.

annoyed *adjective* angry, cheesed off (*slang*), cranky, crook (*Australian informal*), cross, displeased, exasperated, fed up (*informal*), irritated, mad, miffed (*informal*), narked (*informal*), needled (*informal*), peeved (*informal*), put out, riled (*informal*), shirty (*informal*), upset, vexed.

annual¹ *adjective* 1, 2 yearly.

annul *verb* abolish, cancel, invalidate, nullify, rescind, revoke, void.

▶▶ DICTIONARY ◀◀

anoint *verb* put oil or ointment on something, especially in a religious ceremony.

anomaly (*say* an-**om**-al-ee) *noun* (*plural* **anomalies**) something that does not follow the general rule or that is unlike the usual or normal kind. [from *an-*¹ = not, + Greek *homalos* = even]

anon *adverb* (*old use*) soon, *I will say more about this anon.*

anon. *abbreviation* anonymous.

anonymous (*say* an-**on**-im-us) *adjective* of or by a person whose name is not known or not made public, *an anonymous donor.* **anonymously** *adverb.* **anonymity** (*say* an-on-**im**-it-ee) *noun* [from *an-*¹ = not, + Greek *onyma* = name]

anorak *noun* a thick warm jacket with a hood. [from an Eskimo word]

anorexia (*say* an-er-**eks**-ee-a) *noun* an illness that makes a person unwilling to eat. **anorexic** *adjective* [from *an-*¹ = not, + Greek *orexis* = appetite]

another *adjective* **1** additional; one more. **2** different. **another** *pronoun*

answer¹ *noun* **1** a reply. **2** the solution to a problem.

answer² *verb* **1** give or find an answer to; reply. **2** respond to a signal, *Answer the telephone.* **answer back** reply cheekily. **answer for** be responsible for. **answer to** correspond to, *This answers to the description of the stolen bag.*

answerable *adjective* **1** able to be answered. **2** having to be responsible for something.

ant *noun* a very small insect that lives as one of an organised group.

ant- *prefix* see **anti-**.

antagonise *verb* (**antagonised**, **antagonising**) cause a person to feel antagonism.

antagonism (*say* an-**tag**-on-izm) *noun* an unfriendly feeling; hostility. **antagonist** *noun*, **antagonistic** *adjective* [from *ant-*, + Greek *agon* = struggle]

Antarctic *adjective* of the regions round the South Pole.

ante- *prefix* before (as in *ante-room*). [from Latin]

ant-eater *noun* an animal that feeds on ants and termites, in Australia an echidna or numbat.

antediluvian (*say* an-tee-dil-**oo**-vee-an) *adjective* **1** of the time before Noah's Flood in the Old Testament. **2** (*informal*) very old or out of date. [from *ante-*, + Latin *diluvium* = deluge]

antelope *noun* (*plural* **antelope** or **antelopes**) an animal like a deer.

antenatal (*say* an-tee-**nay**-tal) *adjective* before birth; during pregnancy.

antenna *noun* **1** (*plural* **antennae**) a feeler on the head of an insect or crustacean. **2** (*plural* **antennas**) an aerial.

anterior *adjective* **1** situated at the front or the head. (The opposite is *posterior*.) **2** earlier. [Latin, = further forward]

ante-room *noun* a room leading to a more important room.

anthem *noun* a religious or patriotic song, usually sung by a choir or group of people.

anther *noun* the part of a flower's stamen that bears pollen.

anthill *noun* a mound over an ants' nest.

anthology *noun* a collection of poems, stories, songs, etc. in one book. [from Greek *anthos* = flower, + *-logia* = collection]

anthracite *noun* a kind of hard coal.

anthrax *noun* a disease of sheep and cattle that can also infect people.

▶▶ THESAURUS ◀◀

anoint *verb* grease, oil, rub, smear.

anomaly *noun* abnormality, deviation, inconsistency, irregularity, oddity, peculiarity.

anonymous *adjective* incognito, nameless, unidentified, unknown, unnamed.

another *adjective* **1** additional, extra, further, second. **2** alternative, different.

answer¹ *noun* **1** acknowledgement, rejoinder, reply, response, retort, riposte. **2** explanation, solution.

answer² *verb* **1** acknowledge, rejoin, reply, respond, retort.

answer back argue, be cheeky, contradict, disagree, talk back.

answer to conform to, correspond to, fit, match.

answerable *adjective* **2** accountable, liable, responsible.

antagonism *noun* animosity, antipathy, conflict, discord, friction, hatred, hostility, opposition, rivalry.

anthem *noun* canticle, chorale, hymn, psalm.

anthology *noun* collection, compendium, compilation, miscellany, selection, treasury.

▶▶ DICTIONARY ◀◀

anthropoid *adjective* resembling a human being, *Gorillas are anthropoid apes.* [from Greek *anthropos* = human being]

anthropology *noun* the study of human beings and their customs. **anthropological** *adjective*, **anthropologist** *noun* [from Greek *anthropos* = human being, + *-logy*]

anti- *prefix* (changing to **ant-** before a vowel) against; preventing (as in *antifreeze*). [from Greek *anti* = against]

anti-aircraft *adjective* used against enemy aircraft.

antibiotic *noun* a substance (e.g. penicillin) that destroys bacteria or prevents them from growing. [from *anti-*, + Greek *bios* = life]

antibody *noun* (*plural* **antibodies**) a protein that forms in the blood as a defence against certain substances which it then attacks and destroys.

anticipate *verb* (**anticipated, anticipating**) **1** do something before the proper time or before someone else, *Others may have anticipated Columbus in discovering America.* **2** foresee, *They had anticipated our needs.* **3** expect, *We anticipate that it will rain.* **anticipation** *noun*, **anticipatory** *adjective* [from *ante-*, + Latin *capere* = take]

Usage Many people regard the use in sense 3 as incorrect; it is best to avoid it and use 'expect'.

anticlimax *noun* a disappointing ending or result where something exciting had been expected.

anticlockwise *adverb* & *adjective* moving in the direction opposite to clockwise.

antics *plural noun* comical or foolish actions.

anticyclone *noun* an area where air pressure is high, usually producing fine settled weather.

antidote *noun* something that acts against the effects of a poison or disease. [from *anti-*, + Greek *dotos* = given]

antifreeze *noun* a liquid added to water to make it less likely to freeze.

antihistamine *noun* a substance that protects people against unpleasant effects when they are allergic to something.

antimony *noun* a brittle silvery metal.

antipathy (*say* an-**tip**-ath-ee) *noun* a strong dislike. [from *anti-*, + Greek *pathos* = feeling]

antipodes (*say* an-**tip**-od-eez) *plural noun* places on opposite sides of the earth. **antipodean** *adjective*
the Antipodes Australia, New Zealand, and the areas near them, which are almost exactly opposite Europe. [from Greek, = having the feet opposite (*pod-* = foot)]

antiquarian (*say* anti-**kwair**-ee-an) *adjective* of the study of antiques.

antiquated *adjective* old-fashioned.

antique¹ (*say* an-**teek**) *adjective* very old; belonging to the distant past.

antique² *noun* something that is valuable because it is very old. [from Latin *antiquus* = ancient]

antiquity (*say* an-**tik**-wit-ee) *noun* ancient times.
antiquities *plural noun* objects that were made in ancient times.

anti-Semitic (*say* anti-sim-**it**-ik) *adjective* unfriendly or hostile towards Jews. **anti-Semitism** (*say* anti-**sem**-it-izm) *noun*

antiseptic¹ *adjective* **1** able to destroy bacteria, especially those that cause things to become septic or to decay. **2** thoroughly clean and free from germs.

antiseptic² *noun* a substance with an antiseptic effect.

▶▶ THESAURUS ◀◀

anticipate *verb* **1** forestall, pre-empt. **3** expect, forecast, foresee, predict.

anticlimax *noun* comedown, disappointment, flop (*informal*), let-down.

antics *plural noun* capers, fooling around, mischief, pranks, shenanigans (*informal*), tomfoolery, tricks.

antidote *noun* antitoxin, antivenene, corrective, countermeasure, cure, remedy.

antipathy *noun* abhorrence, aversion, detestation, dislike, hatred, hostility, loathing, revulsion.

antiquated *adjective* ancient, antediluvian (*informal*), antique, archaic, behind the times, obsolete, old, old-fashioned, outdated, outmoded, out of date, prehistoric, primitive, quaint, unfashionable.

antique¹ *adjective* ancient, antiquated, archaic, old, old-fashioned, veteran, vintage.

antique² *noun* collectable, collector's item, heirloom, relic.

antiseptic² *noun* bactericide, disinfectant, germicide.

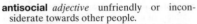

antisocial *adjective* unfriendly or inconsiderate towards other people.

antistatic *adjective* counteracting the effects of static electricity. .

antithesis (*say* an-**tith**-iss-iss) *noun* (*plural* **antitheses**) **1** the direct opposite of something, *Slavery is the antithesis of freedom.* **2** contrast of ideas. [from *anti-,* + Greek *thesis* = placing]

antitoxin *noun* a substance that neutralises a toxin and prevents it from having a harmful effect. **antitoxic** *adjective*

antivivisectionist *noun* a person who is opposed to experiments on live animals.

antler *noun* the branching horn of a deer.

antonym (*say* **ant**-on-im) *noun* a word that is opposite in meaning to another, *'Soft' is an antonym of 'hard'.* [from *ant-,* + Greek *onyma* = name]

anus (*say* **ay**-nus) *noun* the opening at the lower end of the alimentary canal, through which solid waste matter is passed out of the body.

anvil *noun* a large block of iron on which a blacksmith hammers metal into shape. [from Old English *an* = on, + *filt-* = beat]

anxious *adjective* **1** worried. **2** eager, *She is anxious to please us.* **anxiously** *adverb,* **anxiety** *noun*

any[1] *adjective & pronoun* **1** one or some, *Have you any wool? There isn't any.* **2** no matter which, *Come any day you like.* **3** every, *Any fool knows that!*

any[2] *adverb* at all; in some degree, *Is that any better?*

anybody *noun & pronoun* any person.

anyhow *adverb* **1** anyway. **2** (*informal*) carelessly, *He does his work anyhow.*

anything *noun & pronoun* any thing.

anyway *adverb* whatever happens; whatever the situation may be.

anywhere[1] *adverb* in or to any place.

anywhere[2] *pronoun* any place, *Anywhere will do.*

Anzac *noun* a member of the Australian and New Zealand Army Corps (1914–1918).
Anzac Day 25 April, commemorating the landing on Gallipoli, 1915, and all Australian war dead. [initials]

aorta (*say* ay-**or**-ta) *noun* the great artery carrying blood away from the left side of the heart.

ap-[1] *prefix* see **ad-**.

ap-[2] *prefix* see **apo-**.

apace *adverb* quickly.

apart *adverb* **1** away from each other; separately, *Keep your desks apart.* **2** into pieces, *It fell apart.* **3** excluded, *Joking apart, what do you think of it?* [from French *à* = to, + *part* = side]

apartheid (*say* a-**part**-hayt) *noun* the former policy in South Africa of keeping people of different races apart. [Afrikaans, = being apart]

apartment *noun* **1** a set of rooms. **2** a flat.

apathy (*say* **ap**-ath-ee) *noun* lack of interest or concern. **apathetic** (*say* ap-a-**thet**-ik) *adjective* [from *a-*[2] = without, + Greek *pathos* = feeling]

ape[1] *noun* any of the four kinds of monkey (gorillas, chimpanzees, orang-utans, gibbons) that do not have a tail.

ape[2] *verb* (**aped, aping**) imitate; mimic.

aperient (*say* a-**peer**-ee-ent) *noun* a laxative. [from Latin *aperiens* = opening]

aperitif (*say* a-**perri**-teef) *noun* an alcoholic drink taken before a meal to stimulate the appetite. [French]

antisocial *adjective* inconsiderate, offensive, unfriendly.

antonym *noun* opposite.

anxious *adjective* **1** afraid, apprehensive, concerned, fearful, nervous, tense, troubled, uneasy, uptight (*informal*), worried. **2** desirous, desperate, eager, keen, longing, wanting.
anxiety *noun* apprehension, concern, dismay, disquiet, dread, foreboding, fear, misgiving, nervousness, stress, tension, trepidation, uneasiness, worry.

apart *adverb* **1** independently, separately. **2** asunder, into pieces.

apart from aside from, except, excluding, not counting, not including, other than, save.

apartment *noun* **2** bedsit (*British*), condominium (*American*), flat, home unit (*Australian*), penthouse, unit (*Australian*).

apathy *noun* coolness, impassivity, indifference, listlessness, passivity, unconcern.
apathetic *adjective* impassive, indifferent, listless, passive, unconcerned, unemotional, uninterested, unmoved, unresponsive.

ape[2] *verb* copy, imitate, mimic.

►► D I C T I O N A R Y ◄◄

aperture *noun* an opening. [from Latin *aperire* = to open]

apex (*say* **ay**-peks) *noun* (*plural* **apexes**) the tip or highest point.

aphid (*say* **ay**-fid) *noun* (*plural* **aphids**) a tiny insect (e.g. a greenfly) that sucks the juices from plants.

aphis (*say* **ay**-fiss) *noun* (*plural* **aphides**, *say* **ay**-fid-eez) an aphid.

aphorism (*say* **af**-er-izm) *noun* a short witty saying.

apiary (*say* **ay**-pee-er-ee) *noun* (*plural* **apiaries**) a place with a number of hives where bees are kept. **apiarist** *noun* [from Latin *apis* = bee]

apiece *adverb* to, for, or by each, *They cost fifty cents apiece.*

aplomb (*say* a-**plom**) *noun* dignity and confidence. [from French, = straight as a plumb-line]

apo- *prefix* (changing to **ap-** before a vowel or h) from; out or away (as in *Apostle*). [from Greek *apo* = away from]

apocryphal (*say* a-**pok**-rif-al) *adjective* untrue; invented, *This account of his travels is apocryphal.* [from the *Apocrypha*, books of the Old Testament that were not accepted by the Jews as part of the Hebrew Scriptures]

apologetic *adjective* making an apology. **apologetically** *adverb*

apologise *verb* (**apologised**, **apologising**) make an apology.

apology *noun* (*plural* **apologies**) 1 a statement saying that you are sorry for having done something wrong or badly. 2 a poor specimen, *this feeble apology for a meal.* [from Greek *apologia* = a speech in your own defence]

apoplexy (*say* **ap**-op-lek-see) *noun* sudden loss of the ability to feel and move, caused by the blocking or breaking of a blood-vessel in the brain. **apoplectic** *adjective* [from Greek, = a stroke]

Apostle *noun* any of the twelve men sent out by Christ to preach the Gospel. [from Greek *apostellein* = send out]

apostrophe (*say* a-**poss**-trof-ee) *noun* the punctuation mark ' used to show that letters have been missed out (as in *I can't* = I cannot) or to show possession (as in *the boy's book; the boys' books*). [from *apo-*, + Greek *strophe* = turning]

apothecary (*say* a-**poth**-ik-er-ee) *noun* (*plural* **apothecaries**) (*old use*) a chemist who prepares medicines.

appal *verb* (**appalled**, **appalling**) fill with horror; shock somebody very much. [from Old French *apalir* = become pale]

apparatus *noun* the equipment for a particular experiment or job etc.

apparel *noun* (*formal*) clothing.

apparent *adjective* 1 clear; obvious. 2 seeming; appearing to be true but not really so. **apparently** *adverb* [same origin as *appear*]

apparition *noun* 1 a ghost. 2 something strange or surprising that appears.

appeal¹ *verb* 1 ask for something earnestly or formally, *They appealed for funds.* 2 ask for a decision to be changed, *He appealed against the prison sentence.* 3 seem attractive or interesting, *Cricket doesn't appeal to me.*

appeal² *noun* 1 the action of appealing for something or about a decision; an earnest or formal request. 2 attraction; interest.

►►► T H E S A U R U S ◄◄

aperture *noun* crack, gap, hole, opening, slit.

apex *noun* acme, crest, height, peak, pinnacle, summit, tip, top, vertex, zenith.

apologetic *adjective* contrite, penitent, regretful, remorseful, repentant, sorry.

apologise *verb* beg pardon, express regret, repent, say sorry.

apostle *noun* evangelist, messenger, missionary.

appal *verb* disgust, dismay, horrify, outrage, shock, sicken, terrify.
appalling *adjective* abominable, atrocious, awful, dire, dreadful, frightful, ghastly, hideous, horrendous, horrible, outrageous, repulsive, shocking, sickening, terrible.

apparatus *noun* appliance, contraption, device, equipment, gear, instrument, machine, machinery, tool.

apparent *adjective* 1 clear, conspicuous, discernible, evident, manifest, obvious, patent, plain, unmistakable, visible. 2 ostensible, outward, seeming, superficial.

apparition *noun* 1 ghost, hallucination, phantom, spectre, spirit, spook (*informal*), vision.

appeal¹ *verb* 1 apply, ask, beg, entreat, implore, petition, plead, request, solicit. 3 attract, entice, fascinate, interest, lure, tempt.

appeal² *noun* 1 call, entreaty, petition, plea, request. 2 attraction, charm, fascination, interest, temptation.

appear *verb* **1** come into sight. **2** seem. **3** take part in a play, film, or show etc.

appearance *noun* **1** appearing. **2** what somebody looks like. **3** what something appears to be.

appease *verb* (**appeased, appeasing**) calm or pacify someone, especially by giving in to demands. **appeasement** *noun* [from French *à* = to, + *paix* = peace]

appellation *noun* a name or title.

append *verb* add at the end; attach. [from *ap-*, + Latin *pendere* = hang]

appendage *noun* something added or attached; a thing that forms a natural part of something larger.

appendicitis *noun* inflammation of the appendix.

appendix *noun* **1** (*plural* **appendixes**) a small tube leading off from the intestine. **2** (*plural* **appendices**) a section added at the end of a book. [same origin as *append*]

appetising *adjective* stimulating the appetite. **appetiser** *noun*

appetite *noun* a desire, especially for food. [from *ap-*, + Latin *petere* = seek]

applaud *verb* show that you like something, especially by clapping your hands. **applause** *noun* [from *ap-*, + Latin *plaudere* = clap hands]

apple *noun* a round fruit with a red, yellow, or green skin.
the apple of your eye a person or thing that you love and are proud of.
She's apples (*Australian slang*) everything is in order.

appliance *noun* a device, *electrical appliances*.

applicable (*say* **ap**-lik-a-bul) *adjective* able to be applied; suitable; relevant.

applicant *noun* a person who applies for something.

application *noun* **1** the action of applying. **2** a formal request. **3** the ability to apply yourself.

applied *adjective* put to practical use, *applied science*.

appliqué (*say* a-**plee**-kay) *noun* needlework in which cut-out pieces of material are sewn or fixed ornamentally on another piece. [French, = put on]

apply *verb* (**applied, applying**) **1** put one thing on another. **2** start using something. **3** concern; be relevant, *This rule does not apply to you.* **4** make a formal request, *apply for a job.*
apply yourself give all your attention to a job; work diligently.

appoint *verb* **1** choose a person for a job. **2** arrange officially, *They appointed a time for the meeting.*

appear *verb* **1** arrive, attend, be present, come, emerge, front up (*informal*), materialise, show up, surface, turn up. **2** give an impression of being, look, seem. **3** act, perform, play, star, take the part of.

appearance *noun* **1** advent, arrival, coming. **2** air, aspect, demeanour, expression, look, manner, mien. **3** front, guise, illusion, impression, pretence, semblance, show.

appease *verb* calm, mollify, pacify, placate, quiet, quieten, soothe, tranquillise.

appendix *noun* **2** addendum, addition, attachment, supplement.

appetising *adjective* appealing, delicious, mouth-watering, palatable, tasty, tempting.
appetiser *noun* aperitif, hors d'oeuvre, starter.

appetite *noun* craving, desire, fondness, hunger, inclination, keenness, liking, longing, passion, relish, stomach, taste, thirst.

applaud *verb* acclaim, approve, clap, commend, compliment, congratulate, give someone a big hand (*informal*), give someone an ovation, praise.

applause *noun* clapping, hand (*informal*), ovation, plaudits; see also APPROVAL.

appliance *noun* apparatus, contraption, device, equipment, gadget, implement, instrument, machine, utensil.

applicable *adjective* apposite, appropriate, fitting, germane, pertinent, relevant, suitable.

applicant *noun* candidate, competitor, entrant, interviewee, job-seeker.

application *noun* **2** appeal, claim, petition, request, submission. **3** assiduity, commitment, dedication, diligence, effort, industry, perseverance, persistence.

apply *verb* **1** put on, smear, spread. **2** administer, employ, enforce, exercise, put into effect, use, utilise. **3** be relevant, concern, pertain, refer, relate. **4** (*apply for*) ask for, audition for, put in for, register for, request, seek, solicit.

appoint *verb* **1** choose, designate, elect, name, nominate, select. **2** arrange, assign, decide on, determine, establish, fix, organise, settle on.

▶▶ D I C T I O N A R Y ◀◀

appointment *noun* **1** an arrangement to meet or visit somebody at a particular time. **2** choosing somebody for a job. **3** a job or position.

apportion *verb* divide into shares; allot. **apportionment** *noun*

apposite (*say* **ap**-o-zit) *adjective* (of a remark) suitable; relevant.

apposition *noun* placing things together, especially nouns and phrases in a grammatical relationship. In *We visited Canberra, the capital of Australia* 'the capital of Australia' is in apposition to 'Canberra'. [from *ap-* + *position*]

appraise *verb* (**appraised, appraising**) estimate the value or quality of a person or thing. **appraisal** *noun*

appreciable *adjective* enough to be noticed or felt; perceptible. **appreciably** *adverb*

appreciate *verb* (**appreciated, appreciating**) **1** enjoy; value. **2** understand. **3** increase in value. **appreciation** *noun*, **appreciative** *adjective* [from *ap-*, + Latin *pretium* = price]

apprehend *verb* **1** seize; arrest. **2** understand. **3** expect something with fear or worry. [from *ap-*, + Latin *prehendere* = to grasp]

apprehension *noun* **1** fear. **2** understanding. **3** arrest. **apprehensive** *adjective*

apprentice¹ *noun* a person who is learning a trade or craft by a legal agreement with an employer. **apprenticeship** *noun*

apprentice² *verb* (**apprenticed, apprenticing**) place a person as an apprentice. [from French *apprendre* = learn]

approach¹ *verb* **1** come near. **2** go to someone with a request or offer, *They approached me for help.* **3** set about doing something or tackling a problem. **approachable** *adjective*

approach² *noun* (*plural* **approaches**) **1** approaching. **2** a way or road. **3** a way of doing or tackling something.

approbation *noun* approval.

appropriate¹ (*say* a-**proh**-pree-at) *adjective* suitable. **appropriately** *adverb*

appropriate² (*say* a-**proh**-pree-ayt) *verb* (**appropriated, appropriating**) take something and use it as your own. **appropriation** *noun*

approval *noun* **1** approving somebody or something. **2** permission; consent.
on approval received by a customer to examine before deciding to buy.

▶▶ T H E S A U R U S ◀◀

appointment *noun* **1** arrangement, assignation, date, engagement, interview, meeting, rendezvous. **2** choice, election, selection. **3** job, office, position, post, situation.

appreciable *adjective* considerable, noticeable, perceptible, significant, substantial.

appreciate *verb* **1** be grateful for, be thankful for, cherish, prize, think highly of, treasure, value. **2** acknowledge, comprehend, realise, recognise, understand. **3** escalate, gain, go up, improve, increase, inflate, mount, rise.
appreciative *adjective* grateful, obliged, thankful.

apprehend *verb* **1** arrest, capture, catch, detain, nab (*informal*), nail, nick (*slang*), seize, take into custody. **2** comprehend, grasp, perceive, realise, understand.

apprehension *noun* **1** anxiety, concern, dread, fear, foreboding, nervousness, trepidation, uneasiness, worry. **2** appreciation, comprehension, realisation, recognition, understanding. **3** arrest, capture, seizure.
apprehensive *adjective* afraid, anxious, edgy (*informal*), fearful, frightened, nervous, troubled, uneasy, worried.

apprentice¹ *noun* beginner, cadet, learner, novice, probationer, pupil, tiro, trainee.

approach¹ *verb* **1** advance, come near, draw near, loom, near. **2** appeal to, apply to, ask. **3** go about, handle, set about, tackle.
approachable *adjective* accessible, affable, easygoing, friendly.

approach² *noun* **1** advance, advent, arrival, coming, nearing. **2** access, entry, way, way in. **3** attitude, manner, method, procedure, style, technique, way.

appropriate¹ *adjective* applicable, apposite, apropos, apt, befitting, fitting, pertinent, proper, relevant, right, seemly, suitable, timely.

appropriate² *verb* commandeer, confiscate, requisition, seize, take; see also STEAL.

approval *noun* **1** acclaim, acclamation, admiration, applause, appreciation, approbation, commendation, favour, praise. **2** acceptance, agreement, assent, authorisation, blessing, consent, endorsement, go-ahead, OK (*informal*), permission, ratification, sanction, support, validation.

▶▶ D I C T I O N A R Y ◀◀

approve *verb* (**approved, approving**) **1** say or think that a person or thing is good or suitable. **2** agree to.

approximate¹ (*say* a-**proks**-im-at) *adjective* almost exact or correct but not completely so. **approximately** *adverb*

approximate² (*say* a-**proks**-im-ayt) *verb* (**approximated, approximating**) make or be almost the same as something. [from *ap*-, + Latin *proximus* = very near]

apricot *noun* a juicy orange-coloured fruit with a stone in it.

apron *noun* **1** a garment worn over the front of the body, especially to protect other clothes. **2** a hard-surfaced area on an airfield where aircraft are loaded and unloaded.

apron stage a part of a theatre stage in front of the curtain. [originally *a naperon*, from French *nappe* = tablecloth]

apropos (*say* ap-rop-**oh**) *adverb* concerning. *Apropos of tennis, who is the new champion?* [from French *à propos* = to the purpose]

apse *noun* a semicircular part projecting from a church or other building.

apt *adjective* **1** likely, *He is apt to be careless.* **2** suitable, *an apt quotation.* **3** quick at learning, *an apt pupil.* **aptly** *adverb*, **aptness** *noun* [from Latin *aptus* = fitted]

aptitude *noun* a talent or skill.

aqualung *noun* a diver's portable breathing-apparatus, with cylinders of compressed air connected to a face-mask. [from Latin *aqua* = water, + *lung*]

aquamarine *noun* a bluish-green precious stone. [from Latin *aqua marina* = sea-water]

aquarium *noun* (*plural* **aquariums**) a tank or building in which live fish and other water animals are displayed. [from Latin *aquarius* = of water]

aquatic *adjective* of, on, or in water, *aquatic sports.* [from Latin *aqua* = water]

aquatint *noun* an etching made on copper by using nitric acid.

aqueduct *noun* a bridge carrying a water-channel across low ground or a valley. [from Latin *aqua* = water, + *ducere* = to lead]

aquiline (*say* **ak**-wil-I'n) *adjective* hooked like an eagle's beak, *an aquiline nose.* [from Latin *aquila* = eagle]

ar- *prefix* see **ad-**.

Arab *noun* a member of a people living in Arabia and other parts of the Middle East and North Africa. **Arabian** *adjective*

arabesque (*say* a-rab-**esk**) *noun* **1** (in dancing) a position with one leg stretched backwards in the air. **2** an ornamental design of leaves and branches.

Arabic¹ *adjective* of the Arabs or their language.

arabic figures the symbols 1, 2, 3, 4, etc.

Arabic² *noun* the language of the Arabs.

arable *adjective* suitable for ploughing or growing crops on, *arable land.* [from Latin *arare* = to plough]

arachnid (*say* a-**rak**-nid) *noun* a member of the group of animals that includes spiders and scorpions. [from Greek *arachne* = spider]

arbiter *noun* a person who has the power to decide what shall be done or used etc.

arbitrary (*say* **ar**-bit-rer-ee) *adjective* chosen or done on an impulse, not according to a rule or law, *an arbitrary decision.* **arbitrarily** *adverb*

arbitration *noun* settling a dispute by calling in a person or persons from outside to make a decision. **arbitrate** *verb*, **arbitrator** *noun* [from Latin *arbitrari* = to judge]

Arbitration Court a tribunal for settling industrial disputes and making award rates for industry.

arboreal (*say* ar-**bor**-ee-al) *adjective* of trees; living in trees. [from Latin *arbor* = tree]

▶▶ T H E S A U R U S ◀◀

approve *verb* **1** (*approve of*) acclaim, admire, applaud, be pleased with, commend, favour, like, praise. **2** agree to, allow, assent to, authorise, back, consent to, endorse, pass, permit, ratify, sanction, support, validate.

approximate¹ *adjective* ballpark (*informal*), close, estimated, inexact, rough.

approximately *adverb* about, almost, approaching, around, circa, close to, nearly, roughly.

apron *noun* **1** pinafore.

apt *adjective* **1** inclined, liable, likely, tending. **2** applicable, apposite, appropriate, apropos, felicitous, fitting, relevant, suitable. **3** bright, clever, intelligent, quick, sharp, smart.

aptitude *noun* ability, capability, capacity, facility, flair, gift, knack, skill, talent.

arbitrary *adjective* capricious, chance, indiscriminate, random, subjective, unreasoned, whimsical.

arbitrator *noun* adjudicator, arbiter, judge, referee, umpire.

►►DICTIONARY◄◄

arboretum (*say* ar-ber-**ee**-tum) *noun* a place where trees are grown for study and display. [from Latin *arbor* = tree]

arbour (*say* **ar**-ber) *noun* a shady place among trees.

arc *noun* **1** a curve; part of the circumference of a circle. **2** a luminous electric current passing between two electrodes.
arc lamp or **arc light** a light using an electric arc. [same origin as *archer*]

arcade *noun* a covered passage or area, especially for shopping.

arcane *adjective* secret; mysterious.

arch¹ *noun* (*plural* **arches**) **1** a curved structure that helps to support a bridge or other building etc. **2** something shaped like this.

arch² *verb* form into an arch; curve. [same origin as *arc*]

arch³ *adjective* pretending to be playful, *an arch smile*. **archly** *adverb*

arch- *prefix* chief; principal (as in *arch-enemy*).

archaeology (*say* ar-kee-**ol**-oj-ee) *noun* the study of the remains of ancient civilisations. **archaeological** *adjective*, **archaeologist** *noun* [from Greek *archaios* = old, + -*logy*]

archaic (*say* ar-**kay**-ik) *adjective* belonging to former or ancient times. [from Greek *arche* = beginning]

archangel *noun* an angel of the highest rank.

archbishop *noun* the chief bishop of a province of the Church.

archdeacon *noun* a senior priest ranking next below a bishop.

arch-enemy *noun* the chief enemy.

archer *noun* a person who shoots with a bow and arrows. **archery** *noun* [from Latin *arcus* = a bow or curve]

archetype (*say* **ark**-i-typ) *noun* the original form or model from which others are copies. [from *arch-* + *type*]

archipelago (*say* ark-i-**pel**-ag-oh) *noun* (*plural* **archipelagos**) a large group of islands, or the sea containing these. [from *arch-*, + Greek *pelagos* = sea]

architect (*say* **ark**-i-tekt) *noun* a person who designs buildings. [from *arch-*, + Greek *tekton* = builder]

architecture *noun* **1** the process of designing buildings. **2** a particular style of building. **architectural** *adjective*

archives (*say* **ark**-I'vz) *plural noun* the historical documents etc. of an organisation or community. [from Greek *archeia* = public records]

archivist (*say* **ar**-kiv-ist) *noun* a person trained to deal with archives.

archway *noun* an arched passage or entrance.

arctic *adjective* very cold, *The weather was arctic*. [from the Arctic, the area round the North Pole]

ardent *adjective* full of ardour; enthusiastic. **ardently** *adverb* [from Latin *ardens* = burning]

ardour (*say* **ar**-der) *noun* great warmth of feeling.

arduous *adjective* needing much effort; laborious. **arduously** *adverb* [from Latin *arduus* = steep]

area *noun* **1** the extent or measurement of a surface. **2** a particular region. **3** a space set aside for a specific purpose, *a picnic area*.

►►THESAURUS◄◄

arc *noun* **1** arch, bend, bow, crescent, curve.

arcade *noun* cloister, colonnade, gallery, mall, passage, portico, walk.

arcane *adjective* abstruse, esoteric, inscrutable, mysterious, obscure, secret.

arch¹ *noun* **1** archway, span, vault. **2** arc, bow, curve, semicircle.

arch² *verb* bend, bow, curve, hump.

arch³ *adjective* mischievous, playful, roguish, saucy, teasing.

archaic *adjective* ancient, antiquated, antique, obsolete, old, olden, old-fashioned, outmoded, out of date.

archetype *noun* model, original, pattern, prototype, standard.

archives *plural noun* annals, chronicles, documents, papers, records, registers.

ardent *adjective* avid, eager, earnest, enthusiastic, fervent, impassioned, keen, passionate, vehement, zealous.

ardour *noun* eagerness, earnestness, enthusiasm, fervour, keenness, passion, warmth, zeal.

arduous *adjective* difficult, exacting, exhausting, formidable, gruelling, hard, herculean, laborious, onerous, strenuous, taxing, tough.

area *noun* **1** extent, measurement, size. **2** district, locality, neighbourhood, precinct, quarter, region, territory, vicinity, zone. **3** place, space, spot.

▶▶ DICTIONARY ◀◀

area school a primary and secondary school formed by amalgamating several small rural schools.

arena (*say* a-**reen**-a) *noun* the level area in the centre of an amphitheatre or sports stadium. [Latin, = sand]

aren't (*mainly spoken*) are not.
aren't I? (*informal*) am I not?

argosy *noun* (*plural* **argosies**) (*poetic*) a large merchant ship; a fleet of ships.

arguable *adjective* **1** able to be asserted; likely to be correct. **2** able to be doubted; not certain. **arguably** *adverb*

argue *verb* (**argued, arguing**) **1** say that you disagree; exchange angry comments. **2** state that something is true and give reasons.

argument *noun* **1** a disagreement; a quarrel. **2** a reason put forward; a series of reasons.

argumentative *adjective* fond of arguing.

aria (*say* **ar**-ee-a) *noun* a solo in an opera or oratorio. [Italian]

arid *adjective* dry and barren.

arise *verb* (**arose, arisen, arising**) **1** come into existence; come to people's notice, *Problems arose.* **2** (*old use*) rise; stand up, *Arise, Sir Francis.*

aristocracy (*say* a-ris-**tok**-ra-see) *noun* people of the highest social rank; members of the nobility. [from Greek *aristos* = best, + *-cracy*]

aristocrat (*say* **a**-ris-tok-rat) *noun* a member of the aristocracy. **aristocratic** *adjective*

arithmetic *noun* the science or study of numbers; calculating with numbers. **arithmetical** *adjective* [from Greek *arithmos* = number]

ark *noun* **1** the ship in which Noah and his family escaped the Flood. **2** a wooden box in which the writings of the Jewish Law were kept. [from Latin *arca* = box]

arm[1] *noun* **1** either of the two upper limbs of the body, between the shoulder and the hand. **2** a sleeve. **3** something shaped like an arm or jutting out from a main part; the raised side part of a chair. **armful** *noun* [Old English]

arm[2] *verb* **1** supply with weapons. **2** prepare for war.
armed forces or **armed services** a country's military forces; the army, navy, and air force. [from Latin *arma* = weapons]

armada (*say* ar-**mah**-da) *noun* a fleet of warships.
the Armada or **Spanish Armada** the warships sent by Spain to invade England in 1588. [Spanish, = navy]

armadillo *noun* (*plural* **armadillos**) a small burrowing South American animal whose body is covered with a shell of bony plates.

armaments *plural noun* the weapons of an army etc.

armature *noun* **1** the current-carrying part of a dynamo or electric motor. **2** the 'keeper' of a magnet.

armchair *noun* a chair with arms.

▶▶ THESAURUS ◀◀

arena *noun* amphitheatre, field, ground, pitch, ring, stadium.

arguable *adjective* **2** contentious, controversial, debatable, disputable, doubtful, moot, uncertain.

argue *verb* **1** barney (*informal*), bicker, debate, differ, disagree, dispute, feud, fight, haggle, have words, quarrel, quibble, row (*informal*), spar, squabble, wrangle. **2** assert, claim, contend, declare, maintain, reason, show.

argument *noun* **1** altercation, barney (*informal*), blue (*Australian informal*), clash, controversy, debate, disagreement, dispute, feud, fight, quarrel, row (*informal*), spat (*informal*), squabble, tiff, wrangle. **2** case, defence, grounds, justification, reason, reasoning.

argumentative *adjective* belligerent, contentious, contrary, disputatious, pugnacious, quarrelsome.

arid *adjective* barren, desert, dry, infertile,

lifeless, parched, unproductive, waste, waterless.

arise *verb* **1** appear, come up, crop up, emerge, occur, originate, present itself. **2** get up, rise, stand up.

aristocracy *noun* elite, gentry, nobility, peerage, upper class.

aristocrat *noun* grandee, lady, lord, noble, nobleman, noblewoman, peer, peeress.
aristocratic *adjective* blue-blooded, courtly, high-born, noble, titled, upper-class.

arm[1] *noun* **1** appendage, forelimb, limb, tentacle (*of an octopus*). **3** (*arm of a tree*) bough, branch, limb.

arm[2] *verb* **1** equip, furnish, provide, supply.
armed forces air force, armed services, army, defence forces, forces, marines, military, navy, services, troops.

armada *noun* convoy, fleet, flotilla, navy, squadron.

▶▶DICTIONARY◀◀

armistice *noun* an agreement to stop fighting in a war or battle. [from Latin *arma* = weapons, + *sistere* = stop]

armour *noun* 1 a protective covering for the body, formerly worn in fighting. 2 a metal covering on a warship, tank, or car to protect it from missiles. **armoured** *adjective* [same origin as *arm²*]

armoury *noun* a place where weapons and ammunition are stored.

armpit *noun* the hollow underneath the top of the arm, below the shoulder.

arms *plural noun* 1 weapons. 2 a coat of arms (see *coat*).
arms race competition between nations in building up supplies of weapons.
up in arms protesting vigorously. [same origin as *arm²*]

army *noun* (*plural* **armies**) 1 a large number of people trained to fight on land. 2 a large group.

aroma (*say* a-**roh**-ma) *noun* a smell, especially a pleasant one. **aromatic** (*say* a-ro-**mat**-ik) *adjective*

around *adverb* & *preposition* all round; about.

arouse *verb* (**aroused, arousing**) rouse.

arpeggio (*say* ar-**pej**-ee-oh) *noun* (*plural* **arpeggios**) the notes of a musical chord played one after the other instead of together. [from Italian *arpa* = harp]

arrange *verb* (**arranged, arranging**) 1 put into a certain order; adjust. 2 form plans for something, *We arranged to be there.* 3 prepare music for a particular purpose. **arrangement** *noun*

arrant *adjective* thorough and obvious, *Arrant nonsense!*

array¹ *noun* 1 a display. 2 an orderly arrangement.

array² *verb* (**arrayed, arraying**) 1 arrange in order. 2 clothe; adorn. [from *ar-*, + old form of *ready*]

arrears *plural noun* 1 money that is owing and ought to have been paid earlier. 2 a backlog of work etc.
in arrears behindhand.

arrest¹ *verb* 1 seize a person by authority of the law. 2 stop a process or movement.

arrest² *noun* 1 arresting somebody. 2 stopping something.

arrive *verb* (**arrived, arriving**) 1 reach the end of a journey or a point on it. 2 come, *The great day arrived.* **arrival** *noun*

▶▶THESAURUS◀◀

armistice *noun* ceasefire, peace, peace treaty, truce.

armour *noun* 1 chain mail, mail, protective covering.

arms *plural noun* 1 armaments, firearms, weapons. 2 coat of arms, crest, emblem, insignia, shield.

army *noun* 1 armed forces, armed services, military, soldiers, troops. 2 crowd, horde, host, mob, multitude, throng.

aroma *noun* bouquet, fragrance, odour, perfume, savour, scent, smell.
aromatic *adjective* fragrant, pungent, spicy, strong-smelling.

around *adverb* & *preposition* 1 (*travel around*) about, all round, here and there, hither and thither. 2 (*stay around*) about, at hand, close by, in the vicinity, near, nearby. 3 (*around 500*) about, approximately, circa, close to, nearly, roughly. 4 (*a screen around the bed*) encircling, on all sides of, round, surrounding.

arouse *verb* awake, awaken, excite, inspire, provoke, rouse, stimulate, stir up, waken, wake up.

arrange *verb* 1 array, categorise, classify, display, dispose, group, lay out, line up, order, organise, position, put in order, rank, set out, sort. 2 contrive, fix, organise, plan, prepare, schedule, settle, set up, wangle (*slang*). 3 adapt, orchestrate, score, set.

arrangement *noun* 1 array, categorisation, classification, display, grouping, layout, line-up, order, organisation, set-up, system. 2 agreement, bargain, contract, deal, plan, provision, settlement, understanding. 3 adaptation, orchestration, setting, version.

array¹ *noun* arrangement, collection, display, exhibit, line-up, series, show.

array² *verb* 2 adorn, attire, clothe, deck, dress, garb, robe.

arrears *plural noun* 1 back pay, debt, outstanding amount. 2 accumulation, backlog, build-up, pile-up.
in arrears behind, behindhand, late, overdue.

arrest¹ *verb* 1 apprehend, capture, catch, collar (*informal*), detain, nab (*informal*), nail, nick (*slang*), seize, take into custody. 2 block, check, curb, halt, inhibit, prevent, retard, stem, stop.

arrive *verb* 1 appear, come, disembark, enter, get in, land, roll up (*informal*), show up, touch down, turn up; (*arrive at*) come to, get to, hit, make, reach.
arrival *noun* advent, appearance, approach, coming, entrance, entry.

►►► DICTIONARY ◄◄

arrogant *adjective* proud and dictatorial in manner. **arrogantly** *adverb*, **arrogance** *noun*

arrow *noun* **1** a pointed stick to be shot from a bow. **2** a sign with an outward-pointing V at the end, used to show direction or position. **arrowhead** *noun*

arsenal *noun* a place where weapons and ammunition are stored or manufactured. [from Arabic, = workshop]

arsenic *noun* a very poisonous metallic substance. [from Persian *zar* = gold]

arson *noun* the crime of deliberately setting fire to a house or building etc. **arsonist** *noun*

art *noun* **1** producing something beautiful, especially by painting or drawing; things produced in this way. **2** a skill, *the art of sailing*.
arts *plural noun* subjects (e.g. languages, literature, history) in which opinion and understanding are very important, as opposed to sciences where measurements and calculations are used.
the arts painting, music, and writing etc. considered together.
art union (*Australian*) a lottery.

artefact *noun* a man-made object. [from Latin *arte* = by art, + *factum* = made]

artery *noun* (*plural* **arteries**) **1** any of the tubes that carry blood away from the heart to all parts of the body. (Compare *vein*.) **2** an important road or route. **arterial** (*say* ar-**teer**-ee-al) *adjective*

artesian well a well that is bored straight down into a place where water will rise easily to the surface.

artful *adjective* crafty. **artfully** *adverb*

arthritis (*say* arth-**ry**-tiss) *noun* a disease that makes joints in the body stiff and painful. **arthritic** (*say* arth-**rit**-ik) *adjective* [from Greek *arthron* = joint]

arthropod *noun* an animal of the group that includes insects, spiders, crabs, and centipedes. [from Greek *arthron* = joint, + *podos* = of a foot]

artichoke *noun* a kind of plant with a flower-head used as a vegetable.

article *noun* **1** a piece of writing published in a newspaper or magazine. **2** an object.
definite article the word 'the'.
indefinite article the word 'a' or 'an'.

articulate[1] *adjective* able to express things clearly and fluently.

articulate[2] *verb* (**articulated**, **articulating**) **1** say or speak clearly. **2** connect by a joint. **articulation** *noun*
articulated vehicle a vehicle that has sections connected by a flexible joint.

artifice *noun* a piece of trickery; a clever device. [same origin as *artificial*]

artificial *adjective* **1** not natural; made by human beings in imitation of a natural thing. **2** insincere. **artificially** *adverb*, **artificiality** *noun*
artificial respiration helping somebody to start breathing again after their breathing has stopped. [from Latin *ars* = art, + *facere* = make]

artillery *noun* **1** large guns. **2** the part of the army that uses large guns.

artisan (*say* art-iz-**an**) *noun* a skilled worker.

►►► THESAURUS ◄◄

arrogant *adjective* cocky, conceited, condescending, contemptuous, disdainful, egotistic, haughty, high and mighty, lofty, overbearing, presumptuous, proud, scornful, self-important, snobbish, snooty (*informal*), stuck-up (*informal*), supercilious, vain.

arsenal *noun* ammunition dump, armoury, arms depot, magazine, ordnance depot, store.

arsonist *noun* firebug (*informal*), pyromaniac.

art *noun* **2** craft, flair, gift, knack, skill, talent, technique, trick.

artful *adjective* astute, clever, crafty, cunning, deceitful, ingenious, scheming, shifty, shrewd, sly, tricky, wily.

article *noun* **1** essay, feature, item, piece, report, story, write-up. **2** item, object, piece, thing.

articulate[1] *adjective* clear, coherent, comprehensible, eloquent, fluent, intelligible, lucid, understandable.

articulate[2] *verb* **1** enunciate, pronounce, say, speak, utter.

artifice *noun* dodge (*informal*), ruse, stratagem, subterfuge, trick, wile.

artificial *adjective* **1** bogus, counterfeit, fake, false, imitation, man-made, manufactured, mock, phoney (*informal*), pseudo, sham, synthetic. **2** affected, false, feigned, forced, hollow, insincere, phoney (*informal*), pretended, simulated, skin-deep, superficial.

artisan *noun* craftsman, craftswoman, technician, tradesman, tradeswoman.

▶▶ DICTIONARY ◀◀

artist *noun* **1** a person who produces works of art, especially a painter. **2** an entertainer. **artistry** *noun*

artistic *adjective* **1** of art or artists. **2** showing skill and good taste. **artistically** *adverb*

artless *adjective* simple and natural; not artful. **artlessly** *adverb*

arvo *noun* (*Australian slang*) afternoon.

as¹ *adverb* equally; similarly, *This is just as easy.*

as² *preposition* in the character or function etc. of, *Use it as a handle.*

as³ *conjunction* **1** when; while, *She slipped as she got off the bus.* **2** because, *As he was late, we missed the train.* **3** in the way that, *Leave it as it is.*
as for with regard to, *As for you, I despise you.*
as it were in some way, *She became, as it were, her own enemy.*
as well also.

as- *prefix* see **ad-**.

asbestos *noun* a soft fireproof material.

ascend *verb* go up.
ascend the throne become king or queen. [from Latin *ascendere* = climb up]

ascendancy *noun* being in control, *They gained ascendancy over others.*

ascendant *adjective* rising.
in the ascendant rising, especially in power or influence.

ascension *noun* ascending.
Ascension Day the 40th day after Easter, when Christians commemorate the ascension of Christ into heaven.

ascent *noun* **1** ascending. **2** a way up; an upward path or slope.

ascertain (*say* as-er-**tayn**) *verb* find out by asking. **ascertainable** *adjective*

ascetic¹ (*say* a-**set**-ik) *adjective* not allowing yourself pleasure and luxuries. **asceticism** *noun*

ascetic² *noun* a person who leads an ascetic life, often for religious reasons. [from Greek *asketes* = hermit]

ascribe *verb* (**ascribed, ascribing**) attribute.

aseptic (*say* ay-**sep**-tik) *adjective* clean and free from bacteria that cause things to become septic. [from *a-²* = not, + *septic*]

asexual *adjective* (in biology, of reproduction) by other than sexual methods. [from *a-²* = not, + *sexual*]

ash¹ *noun* (*plural* **ashes**) the powder that is left after something has been burned. **ashen** *adjective*, **ashy** *adjective*
Ash Wednesday the first day of Lent.
the Ashes the trophy for which England and Australia play each other at cricket.

ash² *noun* (*plural* **ashes**) a tree with silvery-grey bark.

ashamed *adjective* feeling shame.

ashore *adverb* to or on the shore.

ashtray *noun* a small bowl for tobacco ash.

Asian¹ *adjective* of Asia or its people.

Asian² *noun* an Asian person.

Asiatic *adjective* of Asia.

aside¹ *adverb* **1** to or at one side, *pull it aside.* **2** away; in reserve.
aside from other than.

aside² *noun* words spoken so that only certain people will hear.

asinine (*say* **ass**-in-I'n) *adjective* silly; stupid. [same origin as *ass*]

▶▶ THESAURUS ◀◀

artist *noun* **1** (*kinds of artist*) cartoonist, engraver, graphic designer, illustrator, painter, photographer, sculptor. **2** artiste, entertainer, musician, performer.

artistic *adjective* **2** aesthetic, attractive, beautiful, creative, decorative, imaginative, tasteful.

artless *adjective* genuine, guileless, honest, ingenuous, innocent, natural, open, simple, sincere, straightforward, unaffected, unsophisticated.

ascend *verb* climb, go up, mount, rise, scale, soar.

ascent *noun* **2** climb, gradient, hill, incline, rise, slope.

ascertain *verb* confirm, determine, discover, establish, find out, identify, learn, uncover, verify, work out.

ascetic¹ *adjective* abstemious, austere, frugal, harsh, puritanical, self-disciplined, spartan, strict, temperate.

ascribe *verb* attribute, impute, put down.

ash¹ *noun* (*ashes*) cinders, embers, remains.

ashamed *adjective* abashed, embarrassed, humiliated, mortified, red-faced, shame-faced, sheepish.

aside¹ *adverb* **1** away, out of the way, to one side, to the side.
aside from apart from, besides, in addition to, other than.

▶▶ D I C T I O N A R Y ◀◀

ask *verb* **1** speak so as to find out something. **2** seek to obtain from someone. **3** invite, *Ask her to the party*.

askance (*say* a-**skanss**) *adverb* **look askance at** regard with distrust or disapproval.

askew *adverb* & *adjective* crooked; not straight or level.

asleep *adverb* & *adjective* sleeping.

asp *noun* a small poisonous snake.

asparagus *noun* a plant whose young shoots are eaten as a vegetable.

aspect *noun* **1** one part of a problem or situation, *Violence was the worst aspect of the crime*. **2** a person's or thing's appearance, *The forest had a sinister aspect*. **3** the direction a house etc. faces, *This room has a southern aspect*. [from *as-*, + Latin *specere* = to look]

aspen *noun* a tree with leaves that move in the slightest wind.

asperity *noun* harshness; severity. [from Latin *asper* = rough]

aspersions *plural noun* an attack on someone's reputation, *He cast aspersions on his rivals*.

asphalt (*say* **ass**-falt) *noun* a sticky black substance like tar, often mixed with gravel to surface roads, etc.

asphyxia (*say* ass-**fiks**-ee-a) *noun* suffocation. [Greek, = stopping of the pulse]

asphyxiate (*say* ass-**fiks**-ee-ayt) *verb* (**asphyxiated, asphyxiating**) suffocate. **asphyxiation** *noun* [from *asphyxia*]

aspic *noun* a savoury jelly containing meats, eggs, etc.

aspidistra *noun* a house-plant with broad leaves. [from Greek *aspis* = a shield]

aspirant (*say* **asp**-er-ant) *noun* a person who aspires to something.

aspirate (*say* **asp**-er-at) *noun* the sound of 'h'. [same origin as *aspire*]

aspiration *noun* ambition; strong desire.

aspire *verb* (**aspired, aspiring**) have a high ambition, *He aspired to become a champion*. [from *ad-* = to, + Latin *spirare* = breathe]

aspirin *noun* a medicinal drug used to relieve pain or reduce fever.

ass *noun* (*plural* **asses**) **1** a donkey. **2** (*informal*) a stupid person. [from Latin *asinus* = donkey]

assail *verb* attack. **assailant** *noun* [from Latin *assilire* = leap upon]

assassin *noun* a person who assassinates somebody. [from Arabic, = hashish-takers, fanatics who murdered people during the time of the Crusades]

assassinate *verb* (**assassinated, assassinating**) kill an important person deliberately and violently, especially for political reasons. **assassination** *noun*

assault[1] *noun* a violent or illegal attack.

assault[2] *verb* make an assault on someone. [same origin as *assail*]

assay (*say* a-**say**) *noun* a test made on metal or ore to discover its quality. [from French *essai* = trial]

▶▶ T H E S A U R U S ◀◀

ask *verb* **1** enquire of, inquire of, interrogate, query, question, quiz. **2** appeal, apply, beg, beseech, demand, entreat, implore, petition, plead, pray, request, seek, solicit, supplicate. **3** invite, summon.

askew *adjective* awry, cock-eyed (*informal*), crooked, lopsided, on an angle, out of line, slanting.

asleep *adverb* & *adjective* dormant, dozing, hibernating, napping, resting, sleeping, slumbering, snoozing.
fall asleep doze off, drop off, flake out (*informal*), go to sleep, nod off.

aspect *noun* **1** angle, detail, facet, feature, side. **3** orientation, outlook, prospect, view.

aspiration *noun* aim, ambition, desire, dream, goal, hope, longing, objective, wish, yearning.

aspire *verb* (*aspire to*) aim for, desire, hanker after, hope for, long for, set your sights on, wish for, yearn for.

ass *noun* **1** donkey, jackass (*male*), jenny (*female*). **2** see FOOL[1].

assail *verb* assault, attack, bombard, lay into, set upon.
assailant *noun* assaulter, attacker, mugger.

assassin *noun* executioner, hit man (*slang*), killer, murderer.

assassinate *verb* execute, kill, murder, slay.

assault[1] *noun* attack, blitz, charge, incursion, offensive, onslaught, raid, strike.

assault[2] *verb* assail, attack, beat up, hit, molest, mug, rape, set upon, strike.

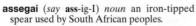

assegai (*say* **ass**-ig-I) *noun* an iron-tipped spear used by South African peoples.

assemble *verb* (**assembled, assembling**) **1** bring or come together. **2** fit or put together. **assemblage** *noun*

assembly *noun* (*plural* **assemblies**) **1** assembling. **2** a regular meeting, such as when everybody in a school meets together. **3** people who regularly meet for a special purpose; a parliament.
assembly line a series of workers and machines along which a product passes to be assembled part by part.

assent[1] *verb* consent; say you agree.

assent[2] *noun* consent; approval.

assert *verb* state firmly. **assertion** *noun*
assert yourself use firmness or authority.

assertive *adjective* asserting yourself.

assess *verb* decide or estimate the value or quality of a person or thing. **assessment** *noun*, **assessor** *noun* [from Latin *assessor* = an assistant judge]

asset *noun* something useful.
assets *plural noun* a person's or firm's property, reckoned as having value.

assiduous (*say* a-**sid**-yoo-us) *adjective* working hard; persevering. **assiduously** *adverb*, **assiduity** *noun*

assign *verb* **1** allot; give. **2** appoint a person to perform a task. [from *as-*, + Latin *signare* = mark out]

assignation (*say* ass-ig-**nay**-shon) *noun* **1** assigning something. **2** an arrangement to meet someone.

assignment *noun* **1** assigning. **2** something assigned; a task given to someone.

assimilate *verb* (**assimilated, assimilating**) take in and absorb something, e.g. nourishment into the body or knowledge into the mind. **assimilation** *noun*

assist *verb* help. **assistance** *noun* [from Latin *assistere* = stand by]

assistant[1] *noun* **1** a person who assists another; a helper. **2** a person who serves customers in a shop.

assistant[2] *adjective* helping a person and ranking next below him or her, *the assistant manager.*

associate[1] *verb* (**associated, associating**) **1** to put or go naturally or regularly together. **2** work together; have frequent dealings.

assemble *verb* **1** accumulate, bring together, collect, come together, congregate, flock, gather, group, marshal, meet, mobilise, muster, rally, round up, swarm, throng. **2** build, construct, erect, fabricate, fit together, make up, manufacture, put together.

assembly *noun* **3** conference, congregation, congress, convention, council, crowd, gathering, group, meeting, mob, multitude, rally, synod, throng.

assent[1] *verb* accede, accept, acquiesce, agree, approve, consent, permit, sanction.

assent[2] *noun* acceptance, accord, acquiescence, agreement, approval, consent, permission, sanction.

assert *verb* allege, argue, attest, claim, contend, declare, insist, maintain, proclaim, state, swear.

assertive *adjective* aggressive, authoritative, bold, dogmatic, forceful, insistent, pushy, self-assertive, strong-willed.

assess *verb* appraise, calculate, compute, estimate, evaluate, gauge, grade, judge, mark, rate, reckon, value, work out.

asset *noun* advantage, benefit, blessing, boon, help, strength.

assets *plural noun* capital, holdings, means, possessions, property, resources, securities, wealth.

assiduous *adjective* diligent, hard-working, indefatigable, industrious, persevering.

assign *verb* **1** allocate, allot, deal out, dispense, distribute, give out. **2** appoint, delegate, designate, nominate, select.

assignment *noun* **2** homework, job, project, task, work.

assimilate *verb* absorb, digest, take in; see also LEARN.

assist *verb* abet, advance, aid, back, collaborate with, cooperate with, help, lend a hand, relieve, serve, succour, support.
assistance *noun* aid, backing, backup, collaboration, cooperation, help, reinforcement, relief, service, succour, support.

assistant[1] *noun* **1** abetter, accessory, accomplice, aide, auxiliary, deputy, helper, offsider (*Australian*), sidekick (*informal*), subordinate, underling.

associate[1] *verb* **1** connect, identify, link, relate. **2** consort, fraternise, hang around (*informal*), hang out (*informal*), hobnob, keep company, mix, socialise.

associate² *noun* a colleague or companion; a partner. **associate** *adjective* [from *as-*, + Latin *socius* = an ally]

association *noun* **1** an organisation of people; a society. **2** associating. **3** something associated.

Association football (*British*) soccer.

assonance (*say* **ass**-on-ans) *noun* similarity of vowel sounds, e.g. in *vermin* and *furnish*. [from *as-*, + Latin *sonus* = sound]

assorted *adjective* of various sorts put together; mixed. **assortment** *noun*

assuage (*say* a-**swayj**) *verb* (**assuaged, assuaging**) soothe; make less severe, *We drank to assuage our thirst*. [from *as-*, + Latin *suavis* = pleasant]

assume *verb* (**assumed, assuming**) **1** accept (without proof or question) that something is true or sure to happen. **2** take on; undertake, *She assumed the extra responsibility.* **3** put on, *He assumed an innocent expression.* **assumption** *noun*

assumed name a false name. [from *as-*, + Latin *sumere* = take]

assurance *noun* **1** a promise or guarantee that something is true or will happen. **2** life insurance. **3** self-confidence.

assure *verb* (**assured, assuring**) **1** tell somebody confidently; promise. **2** make certain.

aster *noun* a garden plant with daisy-like flowers in various colours. [from Greek *aster* = star]

asterisk *noun* a star-shaped sign * used to draw attention to something. [from Greek *asteriskos* = little star]

astern *adverb* **1** at the back of a ship or aircraft. **2** backwards, *Full speed astern!*

asteroid *noun* one of the small planets found mainly between the orbits of Mars and Jupiter. [same origin as *aster*]

asthma (*say* **ass**-ma) *noun* a disease that makes breathing difficult. **asthmatic** *adjective & noun*

astigmatism (*say* a-**stig**-mat-izm) *noun* a defect that prevents an eye or lens from focusing properly. **astigmatic** *adjective* [from *a-²* = not, + Greek *stigma* = a point]

astir *adverb & adjective* in motion; moving.

astonish *verb* surprise somebody greatly. **astonishment** *noun*

astound *verb* astonish; shock greatly.

astral *adjective* of the stars. [same origin as *aster*]

astray *adverb & adjective* away from the right path or place or course of action.

astride *adverb & preposition* with one leg on each side of something.

astringent *adjective* **1** causing skin or body tissue to contract. **2** harsh; severe, *astringent criticism.* [from *as-*, + Latin *stringere* = bind tightly]

astrology *noun* the study of how the stars may affect people's lives. **astrologer** *noun*, **astrological** *adjective* [from Greek *astron* = star, + *-logy*]

associate² *noun* colleague, co-worker, fellow-worker, partner, workmate; see also COMPANION.

association *noun* **1** alliance, body, club, federation, group, league, organisation, society, union. **2** connection, link, relation, relationship, tie-up.

assorted *adjective* different, diverse, miscellaneous, mixed, sundry, varied.
assortment *noun* array, collection, hotchpotch, medley, miscellany, mixture, potpourri, range, selection, variety.

assuage *verb* alleviate, appease, ease, quench, relieve, slake, soothe.

assume *verb* **1** believe, expect, guess, imagine, presume, presuppose, suppose, surmise, think. **2** accept, adopt, take on, undertake. **3** acquire, adopt, affect, put on.
assumption *noun* guess, hypothesis, presump-tion, presupposition, supposition, surmise, theory.

assurance *noun* **1** commitment, guarantee, oath, pledge, promise, undertaking. **3** aplomb, confidence, poise, self-assurance, self-confidence.

assure *verb* **1** declare, give your word, guarantee, pledge, promise, swear, vow. **2** ensure, guarantee, make sure of, secure.
assured *adjective* bold, cocksure, confident, cool, self-assured, self-confident, unafraid.

astonish *verb* amaze, astound, confound, dumbfound, flabbergast, nonplus, shock, stagger, startle, stun, stupefy, surprise, take aback.
astonishment *noun* amazement, surprise, wonder.

astray *adverb* **go astray** be lost, be mislaid, be misplaced, go missing, go walkabout (*informal*).

▶▶ DICTIONARY ◀◀

astronaut *noun* a person who travels in a spacecraft. **astronautics** *noun* [from Greek *astron* = star, + *nautes* = sailor]

astronomy *noun* the study of the stars and planets and their movements. **astronomer** *noun* **astronomical** *adjective* [from Greek *astron* = star, + *-nomia* = arrangement]

astute *adjective* clever; shrewd. **astutely** *adverb*, **astuteness** *noun*

asunder *adverb* apart; into pieces.

asylum *noun* **1** refuge and safety; a place of refuge, *The defeated rebels sought political asylum in another country.* **2** (*old use*) a mental hospital. [from Greek, = refuge]

asymmetrical (*say* ay-sim-**et**-rik-al) *adjective* not symmetrical. **asymmetrically** *adverb*

at *preposition* This word is used to show (**1**) position (*at the top*), (**2**) time (*at midnight*), (**3**) condition (*stand at ease*), (**4**) direction towards something (*Aim at the target*), (**5**) level or price etc. (*Sell them at $1 each*), (**6**) cause (*We were annoyed at his failure*).
at all in any way; of any kind.
at it doing or working at something.
at once immediately; at the same time, *It all came out at once.*

at- *prefix* see **ad-**.

atheist (*say* **ay**th-ee-ist) *noun* a person who believes that there is no God. **atheism** *noun* [from *a-²* = not, + Greek *theos* = god]

athlete *noun* a person who is good at athletics.

athletic *adjective* **1** physically strong and active. **2** of athletes. **athletically** *adverb*

athletics *plural noun* physical exercises and sports, e.g. running and jumping.

atlas *noun* (*plural* **atlases**) a book of maps. [named after Atlas, a giant in Greek mythology, who was made to support the universe]

ATM *abbreviation* automated teller machine.

atmosphere *noun* **1** the air round the earth. **2** a feeling given by surroundings, *the happy atmosphere of the showground.* **atmospheric** *adjective* [from Greek *atmos* = vapour, + *sphere*]

atoll *noun* a ring-shaped coral reef.

atom *noun* the smallest particle of a substance. **atomic** *adjective*
atomic energy energy created by splitting the nuclei of certain atoms. [from Greek *atomos* = indivisible]

atomiser *noun* a device for making a liquid into a fine spray.

atone *verb* (**atoned**, **atoning**) make amends; make up for having done something wrong. **atonement** *noun* [from *at one*]

atrocious (*say* a-**troh**-shus) *adjective* extremely bad or wicked. **atrociously** *adverb* [from Latin *atrox* = cruel]

atrocity (*say* a-**tross**-it-ee) *noun* (*plural* **atrocities**) something extremely bad or wicked; wickedness.

attach *verb* **1** fix or join to something else. **2** regard as belonging to something, *We attach great importance to neatness.* **attachment** *noun*
attached to fond of.

▶▶ THESAURUS ◀◀

astronaut *noun* cosmonaut, spaceman, spacewoman.

astronomical *adjective* colossal, enormous, exorbitant, huge, incredible (*informal*), massive, unbelievable, vast.

astute *adjective* canny, clever, discerning, intelligent, knowing, observant, perceptive, quick, sharp, shrewd, sly.

asylum *noun* **1** protection, refuge, safety, sanctuary, shelter. **2** lunatic asylum (*old use*), mental home, mental hospital, mental institution, psychiatric hospital.

asymmetrical *adjective* irregular, lopsided, unbalanced, uneven.

atheist *noun* see NON-BELIEVER.

athletic *adjective* **1** active, brawny, husky, muscular, robust, sporty (*informal*), strapping, strong.

athletics *plural noun* games, races, sport, sports, track and field events.

atmosphere *noun* **1** aerospace, air, heavens, sky. **2** air, ambience, aura, climate, environment, feeling, mood, tone, vibes (*informal*).

atone *verb* (*atone for*) compensate for, expiate, make amends for, make up for, pay for, pay the penalty for.

atrocious *adjective* (*an atrocious crime*) abominable, appalling, barbaric, brutal, cruel, despicable, evil, heinous, horrific, monstrous, savage, vicious, wicked; (*atrocious weather*) bad, dreadful (*informal*), foul, shocking (*informal*), terrible (*informal*), unpleasant.

atrocity *noun* crime, cruelty, evil, horror, offence, outrage.

attach *verb* **1** affix, append, bind, connect, couple, fasten, fix, glue, join, link, pin, secure, staple, stick, tack, tie.
attachment *noun* accessory, appendage, extra, fitting.
attached to close to, devoted to, fond of.

attaché (*say* a-**tash**-ay) *noun* a special assistant to an ambassador, *our military attaché.*
attaché case a small case in which documents etc. may be carried. [French, = attached]

attack¹ *noun* **1** a violent attempt to hurt or overcome somebody. **2** a piece of strong criticism. **3** sudden illness or pain.

attack² *verb* make an attack. **attacker** *noun*

attain *verb* accomplish; succeed in doing or getting something. **attainable** *adjective*, **attainment** *noun*

attempt¹ *verb* make an effort to do something; try.

attempt² *noun* an effort to do something; a try. [from *at-*, + Latin *temptare* = try]

attend *verb* **1** give care and thought to something; look and listen, *Why don't you attend to your teacher?* **2** be present somewhere; go regularly to a meeting etc. **3** look after someone; be an attendant. **4** accompany. **attendance** *noun*

attendant *noun* a person who helps or accompanies someone.

attention *noun* **1** attending to someone or something. **2** a position in which a soldier etc.

stands with feet together and arms straight downwards.

attentive *adjective* giving attention. **attentively** *adverb*, **attentiveness** *noun*

attenuate *verb* (**attenuated**, **attenuating**) make a thing thinner or weaker. **attenuation** *noun*

attest *verb* declare or prove that something is true or genuine. **attestation** *noun* [from *at-*, + Latin *testari* be a witness]

attic *noun* a room in the roof of a house.

attire¹ *noun* (*formal*) clothes.

attire² *verb* (**attired**, **attiring**) (*formal*) clothe.

attitude *noun* **1** the position of the body or its parts; posture. **2** a way of thinking or behaving.

attorney *noun* (*plural* **attorneys**) **1** a person who is appointed to act on behalf of another in business matters. **2** (*American*) a lawyer.
Attorney-General *noun* the chief legal officer of the country.

attract *verb* **1** get someone's attention or interest; seem pleasant to someone. **2** pull something by an invisible force, *Magnets attract metal pins.* **attractive** *adjective*, **attractively** *adverb*, **attractiveness** *noun* [from *at-*, + Latin *tractum* = pulled]

attack¹ *noun* **1** ambush, assault, blitz, bombardment, charge, foray, incursion, invasion, offensive, onslaught, raid, rush, sortie, strike. **3** bout, fit, outbreak, seizure, spell.

attack² *verb* **1** ambush, assail, assault, beat up, besiege, bombard, fall upon, invade, molest, mug, pounce on, raid, set about (*informal*), set upon, storm, strike. **2** condemn, criticise, denounce, knock (*informal*), malign, pan (*informal*), revile, slam (*informal*), slate (*informal*), vilify.
attacker *noun* aggressor, assailant, assaulter, mugger.

attain *verb* accomplish, achieve, arrive at, gain, obtain, reach.

attempt¹ *verb* endeavour, strive, try, venture.

attempt² *noun* bid, effort, endeavour, go, try.

attend *verb* **1** (*attend to a problem*) deal with, handle, see to, take care of; (*attend to the teacher*) heed, listen to, pay attention to, take notice of. **2** appear at, be present at, go to, show up at (*informal*), turn up at, visit. **3** care for, look after, take care of, tend, wait on. **4** accompany, chaperone, escort, guard.

attendant *noun* aide, assistant, chaperone, companion, escort, helper, servant, steward, usher.

attention *noun* **1** care, concentration, concern, heed, notice, regard, thought.
pay attention attend, concentrate, listen, pay heed, watch.

attentive *adjective* alert, awake, aware, careful, diligent, mindful, observant, vigilant, watchful; see also CONSIDERATE.

attest *verb* affirm, assert, certify, confirm, swear to, testify to, verify, vouch for.

attic *noun* garret, loft.

attire¹ *noun* apparel (*formal*), clothes, clothing, costume, dress, garb, garments, gear (*informal*), outfit, raiment (*old use*), wear.

attitude *noun* **2** demeanour, disposition, feeling, frame of mind, manner, mien, mood, opinion, outlook, position, stance, stand, standpoint, thoughts, view, viewpoint.

attract *verb* **1** allure, appeal to, draw, entice, fascinate, interest, lure, pull.
attractive *adjective* alluring, appealing, beautiful, bonny (*Scottish*), captivating, charming, comely, enchanting, enticing, fascinating, fetching, good-looking, handsome, interesting, inviting, irresistible, lovely, nice, pleasant, pleasing, pretty, striking, stunning, sweet (*informal*), tempting, winsome.

▶▶DICTIONARY◀◀

attraction *noun* **1** attracting. **2** something that attracts interest.

attribute¹ (*say* a-**trib**-yoot) *verb* (**attributed, attributing**) regard as belonging to or created by, *We attribute his success to hard work.* **attribution** *noun*

attribute² (*say* **at**-rib-yoot) *noun* a quality or characteristic, *Kindness is one of his attributes.* [from *at-*, + Latin *tribuere* = allot]

attributive (*say* a-**trib**-yoo-tiv) *adjective* expressing an attribute and placed before the word it describes, e.g. *old* in *the old dog.* (Compare *predicative*.) **attributively** *adverb*

attrition (*say* a-**trish**-on) *noun* wearing something away gradually.

attune *verb* (**attuned, attuning**) bring into harmony.

aubergine (*say* **oh**-ber-*zh*een) *noun* the deep-purple fruit of the eggplant.

auburn *adjective* (of hair) reddish-brown.

auction¹ *noun* a public sale where things are sold to the person who offers the most money for them.

auction² *verb* sell by auction. **auctioneer** *noun* [from Latin *auctum* = increased]

audacious (*say* aw-**day**-shus) *adjective* bold; daring. **audaciously** *adverb*, **audacity** *noun* [from Latin *audax* = bold]

audible *adjective* loud enough to be heard. **audibly** *adverb*, **audibility** *noun* [from Latin *audire* = hear]

audience *noun* **1** people who have gathered to hear or watch something. **2** a formal interview with an eminent person. [from Latin *audire* = hear]

audio *noun* reproduced sounds.
audio typist a person who types from dictation that has been recorded.

audiovisual *adjective* using both sound and pictures to give information.

audit¹ *noun* an official examination of financial accounts to see that they are correct.

audit² *verb* (**audited, auditing**) make an audit of accounts. **auditor** *noun*

audition *noun* a test to see if a performer is suitable for a job. **audition** *verb* [same origin as *audience*]

auditorium *noun* (*plural* **auditoriums**) the part of a building where the audience sits.

augment *verb* increase or add to something. **augmentation** *noun* [from Latin *augere* = increase]

augur (*say* **awg**-er) *verb* be a sign of what is to come, *These exam results augur well.* [from Latin *augur* = prophet]

august (*say* aw-**gust**) *adjective* majestic; imposing. [from Latin *augustus* = majestic]

auk *noun* a kind of sea-bird.

aunt *noun* the sister of your father or mother; your uncle's wife.

auntie or **aunty** *noun* (*informal*) aunt.

au pair (*say* oh **pair**) a young person from overseas who works for a time in someone's home. [French]

aura (*say* **or**-a) *noun* a general feeling surrounding a person or thing, *an aura of happiness.* [Greek, = breeze]

▶▶THESAURUS◀◀

attraction *noun* **1** allure, appeal, attractiveness, charm, enticement, fascination, lure, pull. **2** crowd-pleaser, drawcard, feature, interest.

attribute¹ *verb* ascribe, credit, impute, put down to.

attribute² *noun* characteristic, feature, property, quality, trait, virtue.

audacious *adjective* adventurous, bold, brave, confident, courageous, daredevil, daring, fearless, game, heroic, intrepid, plucky, reckless, venturesome.
audacity *noun* boldness, cheek, effrontery, gall (*slang*), hide (*informal*), impertinence, impudence, insolence, nerve, temerity.

audible *adjective* clear, discernible, distinct, perceptible.

audience *noun* **1** congregation, crowd, listeners, spectators, viewers.

audit¹ *noun* check, examination, inspection, review, scrutiny.

audit² *verb* check, examine, go over, inspect, review, scrutinise.

audition *noun* screen test, test, trial, try-out.

auditorium *noun* hall, theatre.

augment *verb* add to, boost, eke out, increase, supplement, swell.

augur *verb* be a sign of, bode, foreshadow, portend, presage, promise.

august *adjective* dignified, grand, imposing, impressive, majestic, noble, venerable.

aura *noun* air, ambience, atmosphere, feeling, mood, spirit, vibes (*informal*).

aural (*say* **or**-al) *adjective* of the ear; of hearing. **aurally** *adverb* [from Latin *auris* = ear]

Usage Do not confuse *aural* with *oral*.

aurora (*say* aw-**raw**-ra) *noun* bands of coloured light appearing in the sky at night, the **aurora borealis** (*say* bor-ee-**ah**-liss) in the northern hemisphere and the **aurora australis** (*say* os-**trah**-liss) in the southern hemisphere. [from Latin *aurora* = dawn]

auspices (*say* **aw**-spiss-eez) *plural noun* protection; sponsorship, *under the auspices of the Red Cross.*

auspicious (*say* aw-**spish**-us) *adjective* fortunate; favourable, *an auspicious start.*

Aussie[1] (*say* **oz**-ee) *noun* (*informal*) **1** Australia. **2** an Australian, *He's a dinkum Aussie.*

Aussie[2] (*say* **oz**-ee) *adjective* (*informal*) Australian.

Aussie Rules (*informal*) Australian Rules.

austere (*say* os-**teer**) *adjective* very simple and plain, without luxuries. **austerely** *adverb*, **austerity** *noun* [from Greek, = severe]

Australasian *adjective* of Australasia, a region consisting of Australia, New Zealand, New Guinea, and neighbouring islands in the South Pacific.

Australia Day a public holiday on 26 January commemorating the beginning of British settlement at Sydney Cove.

Australian[1] *noun* a native or inhabitant of Australia.

Australian[2] *adjective* of Australia, *Australian English.*

Australian Rules a game of football originating in Victoria played by 18 a side with an oval football.

aut- *prefix* see **auto-**.

authentic *adjective* genuine, *an authentic signature.* **authentically** *adverb*, **authenticity** *noun*

authenticate *verb* (**authenticated**, **authenticating**) confirm something as being authentic. **authentication** *noun*

author *noun* the writer of a book, play, poem, etc. **authorship** *noun* [from Latin *auctor* = originator]

authorise *verb* (**authorised**, **authorising**) give official permission for something. **authorisation** *noun*

authoritarian *adjective* believing that people should be completely obedient to those in authority.

authoritative *adjective* having proper authority or expert knowledge; official.

authority *noun* (*plural* **authorities**) **1** the right or power to give orders to other people. **2** a person or organisation with the right to give orders. **3** an expert; a book etc. that gives reliable information, *an authority on spiders.* [same origin as *author*]

autistic (*say* aw-**tist**-ik) *adjective* unable to communicate with people or respond to surroundings. [from *auto-*]

auto- *prefix* (changing to **aut-** before a vowel) self-; of or by yourself or itself (as in *autograph, automatic*). [from Greek *autos* = self]

autobiography *noun* (*plural* **auto-biographies**) the story of a person's life written by himself or herself. **autobiographical** *adjective* [from *auto-* + *biography*]

auspices *plural noun* aegis, authority, control, patronage, protection, sponsorship.

auspicious *adjective* favourable, promising, propitious.

austere *adjective* abstemious, ascetic, frugal, hard, harsh, plain, puritanical, restrained, rigorous, self-denying, self-disciplined, severe, simple, spartan, strict.

authentic *adjective* actual, dinkum (*Australian informal*), genuine, real, true, trustworthy.

authenticate *verb* certify, confirm, endorse, prove, substantiate, validate, verify, vouch for.

author *noun* biographer, composer, creator, dramatist, essayist, novelist, playwright, poet, writer.

authorise *verb* allow, approve, commission, empower, entitle, give permission for, OK (*informal*), license, permit, sanction.

authoritarian *adjective* autocratic, bossy, dictatorial, dogmatic, domineering, severe, strict.

authority *noun* **1** command, control, dominion, influence, jurisdiction, power, right, sovereignty, supremacy. **3** arbiter, connoisseur, expert, judge, pundit, scholar, specialist.

▶▶ DICTIONARY ◀◀

autocracy (*say* aw-**tok**-ra-see) *noun* (*plural* **autocracies**) despotism; rule by a person with unlimited power. [from *auto-* + *-cracy*]

autocrat *noun* a person with unlimited power; a dictatorial person. **autocratic** *adjective*, **autocratically** *adverb*

autograph¹ *noun* a person's signature.

autograph² *verb* sign your name on or in a book etc. [from *auto-* + *-graph*]

automate *verb* (**automated**, **automating**) work something by automation.

automatic *adjective* **1** working on its own without continuous attention or control by people. **2** done without thinking. **automatically** *adverb* [from Greek *automatos* = self-operating]

automation *noun* making processes automatic; using machines instead of people to do jobs.

automaton (*say* aw-**tom**-at-on) *noun* a robot; a person who seems to act mechanically without thinking.

automobile *noun* (*American*) a motor car. [from *auto-* + *mobile*]

autonomy (*say* aw-**ton**-om-ee) *noun* self-government. **autonomous** *adjective* [from *auto-*, + Greek *-nomia* = arrangement]

autopsy (*say* **aw**-top-see) *noun* (*plural* **autopsies**) a post-mortem. [from Greek *autopsia* = seeing with your own eyes]

autumn *noun* the season between summer and winter. **autumnal** *adjective*

auxiliary¹ *adjective* giving help and support, *auxiliary services*.

auxiliary verb a verb used in forming tenses etc. of other verbs, e.g. *have* in *I have finished*.

auxiliary² *noun* (*plural* **auxiliaries**) a helper. [from Latin *auxilium* = help]

avail¹ *noun* usefulness; help, *Their pleas were of no avail.*

avail² *verb* be useful or helpful, *Nothing availed against the storm.*
avail yourself of make use of something. [from Latin *valere* = be strong]

available *adjective* ready or able to be used; obtainable. **availability** *noun*

avalanche *noun* a mass of snow or rock falling down the side of a mountain. [French, from *avaler* = descend]

avarice (*say* **av**-er-iss) *noun* greed for gain. **avaricious** *adjective* [from Latin *avarus* = greedy]

avenge *verb* (**avenged**, **avenging**) take vengeance for something done to harm you. **avenger** *noun*

avenue *noun* **1** a wide street. **2** a road with trees along both sides.

average¹ *noun* **1** the value obtained by adding several quantities together and dividing by the number of quantities. **2** the usual or ordinary standard.

average² *adjective* **1** worked out as an average, *Their average age is ten.* **2** of the usual or ordinary standard; mediocre.

average³ *verb* (**averaged**, **averaging**) work out, produce, or amount to as an average.

averse *adjective* unwilling; feeling opposed to something. [same origin as *avert*]

aversion *noun* a strong dislike.

▶▶ THESAURUS ◀◀

autocratic *adjective* absolute, despotic, dictatorial, domineering, high-handed, imperious, tyrannical.

automatic *adjective* **1** automated, computerised, electronic, mechanised, programmed, pushbutton, self-operating, self-regulating. **2** instinctive, involuntary, mechanical, reflex, spontaneous, unconscious, unthinking.

autonomous *adjective* free, independent, self-governing.

autopsy *noun* necropsy, post-mortem.

autumn *noun* fall (*American*).

auxiliary¹ *adjective* ancillary, assisting, backup, helping, reserve, supplementary, support, supporting.

auxiliary² *noun* aide, assistant, helper.

available *adjective* accessible, at hand, at your disposal, free, handy, obtainable, ready, usable.

avalanche *noun* deluge, flood, inundation, torrent.

avenge *verb* get even for, get your own back for (*informal*), repay, take revenge for; see also RETALIATE.

average² *adjective* **1** mean. **2** intermediate, mediocre, medium, middling, normal, ordinary, regular, standard, usual.

averse *adjective* disinclined, loath, opposed, reluctant, unwilling.

aversion *noun* antipathy, dislike, hatred, hostility, loathing, revulsion.

▶▶ D I C T I O N A R Y ◀◀

avert *verb* **1** turn something away, *People averted their eyes from the accident.* **2** prevent, *We averted a disaster.* [from *ab-* = away, + Latin *vertere* = turn]

aviary *noun* (*plural* **aviaries**) a large cage or building for keeping birds. [from Latin *avis* = bird]

aviation *noun* the flying of aircraft. **aviator** *noun* [from Latin *avis* = bird]

avid (*say* **av**-id) *adjective* eager, *an avid reader.* **avidly** *adverb*, **avidity** *noun*

avocado (*say* av-ok-**ah**-doh) *noun* (*plural* **avocados**) a pear-shaped tropical fruit with a leathery skin.

avoid *verb* **1** keep yourself away from someone or something. **2** keep yourself from doing something. **3** refrain from, *Avoid rash promises.* **avoidable** *adjective*, **avoidance** *noun*

avoirdupois (*say* av-er-dew-**poiz**) *noun* a system of weights using the unit of 16 ounces = 1 pound. [from French, = goods of weight]

avuncular *adjective* like a kindly uncle.

await *verb* wait for.

awake¹ *verb* (**awoke**, **awoken**, **awaking**) wake up.

awake² *adjective* not asleep.

awaken *verb* awake. **awakening** *noun*

award¹ *verb* give something officially as a prize, payment, or penalty.

award² *noun* something awarded.
award rate a wage settled by an industrial tribunal as the minimum legal payment for work.

aware *adjective* knowing; realising, *Were you aware of the danger?* **awareness** *noun*

awash *adjective* with waves or water flooding over it.

away¹ *adverb* **1** to or at a distance; not at the usual place. **2** out of existence, *The water had boiled away.* **3** continuously; persistently, *We worked away at it.*

away² *adjective* played on an opponent's ground, *an away match.*

awe *noun* fearful or reverent wonder. **awed** *adjective*, **awe-inspiring** *adjective*, **awestricken** *adjective*, **awestruck** *adjective*

aweigh *adverb* hanging just clear of the sea-bottom, *The anchor is aweigh.*

awesome *adjective* causing awe.

awful *adjective* **1** very bad, *an awful accident.* **2** (*informal*) very great, *That's an awful lot of money.* **3** causing awe or fear. **awfully** *adverb* [from *awe* + *-ful*]

awhile *adverb* for a short time.

▶▶ T H E S A U R U S ◀◀

avert *verb* **1** turn away. **2** fend off, prevent, stave off, ward off.

aviator *noun* airman, airwoman, aviatrix (*female, old use*), flyer, pilot.

avid *adjective* eager, enthusiastic, fervent, keen, passionate, zealous.

avoid *verb* **1** cold-shoulder, elude, give a wide berth to, ignore, keep away from, leave alone, shun, steer clear of. **2** bypass, circumvent, dodge, escape, evade, get out of, shirk, sidestep, skirt. **3** abstain from, eschew, keep off, refrain from.

awake¹ *verb* arouse, awaken, rouse, stir, wake, wake up.

awake² *adjective* conscious, open-eyed, sleepless, wakeful, wide awake.

award¹ *verb* accord, allot, assign, bestow, confer, give, grant, present.

award² *noun* badge, colours, cup, decoration, honour, medal, prize, scholarship, trophy.

aware *adjective* (*aware of*) acquainted with, alert to, alive to, conscious of, familiar with, informed about, mindful of, sensible of.

awe *noun* admiration, amazement, fear, respect, reverence, veneration, wonder.

awe-inspiring *adjective* amazing, astonishing, awesome, breathtaking, impressive, magnificent, marvellous, stupendous, wonderful, wondrous (*poetical*).

awesome *adjective* daunting, fearsome, formidable, intimidating, overwhelming, terrible.

awful *adjective* **1** abominable, appalling, atrocious, bad, deplorable, disgusting, dreadful, foul, frightful, ghastly, horrible, lousy (*informal*), nasty, rotten (*informal*), shocking, terrible, unpleasant. **2** big, excessive, huge, impressive, inordinate, large, tremendous.
awfully *adverb* **1** abominably, appallingly, atrociously, badly, deplorably, dreadfully, frightfully, horribly, lousily (*informal*), nastily, poorly, reprehensibly, shockingly, terribly, unpleasantly. **2** exceedingly, extremely, really, terribly (*informal*), very.

▶▶ DICTIONARY ◀◀

awkward *adjective* **1** difficult to use or deal with; not convenient. **2** clumsy; not skilful. **3** embarrassed. **awkwardly** *adverb*, **awkwardness** *noun*

awl *noun* a small pointed tool for making holes in leather, wood, etc.

awning *noun* a roof-like shelter made of canvas etc.

awry *adverb & adjective* **1** twisted to one side; crooked. **2** wrong, *plans went awry*.

axe¹ *noun* **1** a tool for chopping things. **2** (*informal*) being axed.
have an axe to grind have a personal interest in something and want to take care of it.

axe² *verb* (**axed**, **axing**) remove; reduce; abolish.

axiom *noun* an established general truth or principle. **axiomatic** *adjective*

axis *noun* (*plural* **axes**) **1** a line through the centre of a spinning object. **2** a line dividing a thing in half. [Latin, = axle]

axle *noun* the rod through the centre of a wheel, on which the wheel turns.

ayatollah (*say* I-a-**tol**-a) *noun* a Muslim religious leader in Iran. [Persian, = token of God]

aye (*say as* I) *adverb* yes.

azalea (*say* a-**zay**-lee-a) *noun* a kind of flowering shrub.

azure *adjective & noun* sky-blue.

▶▶ THESAURUS ◀◀

awkward *adjective* **1** cumbersome, difficult, hard, inconvenient, ticklish, tricky, troublesome, unmanageable, unwieldy. **2** bumbling, bungling, clumsy, gauche, gawky, ham-fisted (*informal*), maladroit, uncoordinated, ungainly. **3** embarrassed, ill at ease, self-conscious, uncomfortable, uneasy.

awry *adverb* **1** askew, crookedly, on an angle, out of line, unevenly. **2** amiss, wrong.

axe¹ *noun* **1** adze, battleaxe, chopper, cleaver, hatchet, mogo, tomahawk.

axe² *verb* abolish, cancel, discontinue, do away with, eliminate, get rid of, give the chop (*informal*), remove, scrap, terminate, wind up.

axiom *noun* fundamental, principle, truth; see also PROVERB.

axle *noun* arbor, rod, shaft, spindle.

► Bb ◄

baa *noun* the cry of a sheep or lamb.

babble *verb* (**babbled, babbling**) 1 talk in a meaningless way. 2 make a murmuring sound. **babble** *noun*, **babbler** *noun*

babe *noun* a baby.

baboon *noun* a kind of large monkey.

baby *noun* (*plural* **babies**) a very young child or animal. **babyish** *adjective*

babysitter *noun* someone who looks after a child while its parents are out.

bachelor *noun* a man who has not married. **Bachelor of Arts** or **Science** a person who has taken a first degree in arts or science.

bacillus (*say* ba-**sil**-us) *noun* (*plural* **bacilli**) a rod-shaped bacterium.

back¹ *noun* 1 the part furthest from the front. 2 the back part of the body from the shoulders to the buttocks. 3 the part of a chair etc. that your back rests against. 4 a defending player near the goal in football, hockey, etc.

back² *adjective* 1 placed at or near the back. 2 of the back.
backblocks a settlement far from towns or cities.
back yard an enclosed area behind a house.

back³ *adverb* 1 to or towards the back. 2 to the place you have come from, *Go back home.* 3 to an earlier time or condition or position, *Put the clocks back one hour.*

back⁴ *verb* 1 move backwards. 2 give support or help to someone. 3 bet on something. 4 cover the back of something, *Back the rug with canvas.* **backer** *noun*
back down withdraw a claim or argument.
back out refuse to do what was agreed.
back up give support or help to a person or thing. **back-up** *noun*

backbiting *noun* spiteful talk.

backbone *noun* 1 the column of small bones down the centre of the back. 2 strength of character.

backdrop *noun* a painted curtain at the back of a stage.

backfire *verb* (**backfired, backfiring**) 1 make an explosion when fuel burns too soon in an engine or ignites in the exhaust system. 2 produce an unwanted effect, *Their plans backfired.*

backgammon *noun* a game played on a board with draughts and dice. [from *back* + Old English *gamen* = game]

►► THESAURUS ◄◄

babble *verb* 1 chatter, gabble, gibber, jabber, mumble, yabber (*Australian informal*). 2 burble, gurgle, murmur.

baby *noun* babe, bairn (*Scottish*), child, infant, toddler, tot.
babyish *adjective* childish, immature, infantile, juvenile, sooky (*Australian informal*).

babysitter *noun* carer, childminder, minder, nanny, sitter.

back¹ *noun* 1 end, rear, tail; (*of a ship*) poop, stern. 2 backbone, spinal column, spine, vertebral column.

back² *adjective* 2 dorsal, hind, rear.
backblocks back of beyond, backwoods, bush (*Australian*), interior, never-never (*Australian*), outback (*Australian*), the sticks (*Australian informal*), up country, Woop Woop (*Australian informal*).

back⁴ *verb* 1 move backwards, reverse. 2 aid, assist, encourage, endorse, help, promote, sponsor, subsidise, support, underwrite. 3 bet on, gamble on.
backer *noun* benefactor, patron, promoter, sponsor, supporter, underwriter.
back away move backwards, pull back, recoil, retire, retreat, withdraw.
back down back-pedal, backtrack, concede, give in, submit, surrender, yield.
back out of escape from, get out of, go back on, renege on, withdraw from, wriggle out of.
back up affirm, confirm, corroborate, document, reinforce, second, substantiate, support, verify.

backbone *noun* 1 spinal column, spine, vertebral column. 2 courage, determination, fortitude, grit, guts (*informal*), pluck, resolve.

backfire *verb* 2 boomerang, fail, rebound, recoil.

▶▶ DICTIONARY ◀◀

background *noun* **1** the back part of a scene or view etc. **2** the conditions influencing something. **3** a person's experience and education etc.

backhand *noun* a stroke made in tennis etc. with the back of the hand turned outwards. **backhanded** *adjective*

backing *noun* **1** support. **2** material that forms a support or lines the back of something. **3** musical accompaniment.

backlash *noun* (*plural* **backlashes**) a violent reaction to an event etc.

backlog *noun* an amount of work that should have been finished but is still waiting to be done.

backpack *noun* a bag carried on the back by schoolchildren, hikers, etc.

backpacker *noun* a tourist or traveller with a backpack.

backside *noun* (*informal*) the buttocks.

backstroke *noun* a way of swimming on your back.

backward[1] *adjective* **1** going backwards. **2** having made less than the normal progress. **backwardness** *noun*

backward[2] *adverb* backwards.

backwards *adverb* **1** to or towards the back. **2** with the back end going first. **3** in reverse order, *Count backwards*.
backwards and forwards in each direction alternately; to and fro.

backwater *noun* **1** a branch of a river that comes to a dead end with stagnant water. **2** a place that is not affected by progress or new ideas.

bacon *noun* smoked or salted meat from the back or sides of a pig.

bacterium *noun* (*plural* **bacteria**) a microscopic organism. **bacterial** *adjective*

bad *adjective* (**worse, worst**) **1** not having the right qualities; not good. **2** wicked; evil. **3** serious, *a bad accident*. **4** ill; unhealthy; diseased. **5** harmful, *Sweets are bad for your teeth*. **6** decayed, *This meat has gone bad*.
badness *noun*
not bad quite good.

bade *old past tense* of **bid**[3].

badge *noun* a thing that you wear on your clothes to show people who you are or what school or club etc. you belong to.

▶▶ THESAURUS ◀◀

background *noun* **1** backcloth, backdrop, setting. **2** circumstances, context, environment, setting. **3** education, experience, history, training, upbringing.

backing *noun* **1** aid, approval, assistance, endorsement, funding, help, patronage, sponsorship, subsidy, support.

backlash *noun* counteraction, reaction.

backlog *noun* accumulation, arrears, build-up, stockpile.

backpack *noun* haversack, knapsack, pack, rucksack.

backward[1] *adjective* **1** rearward, regressive, retrograde, retrogressive, reverse. **2** handicapped, retarded, slow, underdeveloped, undeveloped.

backwards *adverb* **2** in reverse, rearwards.
backwards and forwards back and forth, hither and thither, to and fro.

bacterium *noun* bug (*informal*), germ, microbe, micro-organism.

bad *adjective* **1** defective, deficient, faulty, inadequate, incompetent, inferior, poor, shoddy, substandard, unacceptable, unsatisfactory, unsound. **2** abhorrent, abominable, atrocious, awful, base, beastly, corrupt, criminal, cruel, deplorable, depraved, despicable, detestable, disgraceful, dishonest, dishonourable, evil, hateful, immoral, infamous, loathsome, malevolent, malicious, mean, nasty, naughty, notorious, reprehensible, sinful, ungodly, unrighteous, unworthy, vile, villainous, wicked. **3** appalling, awful, dire, disastrous, dreadful, frightful, ghastly, grave, hideous, horrendous, horrible, horrific, nasty, serious, severe, shocking, terrible. **4** ailing, crook (*Australian informal*), diseased, ill, indisposed, off colour, poorly, sick, unhealthy, unwell. **5** damaging, dangerous, deleterious, destructive, detrimental, harmful, hurtful, injurious, ruinous, unhealthy. **6** decayed, foul, mildewed, mouldy, nauseating, noxious, obnoxious, off, offensive, on the nose (*Australian informal*), putrid, rancid, repulsive, revolting, rotten, spoiled, stinking, tainted, vile.
bad-tempered *adjective* angry, cantankerous, crabby, cranky, cross, crotchety, grouchy, gruff, grumpy, hot-tempered, ill-tempered, irascible, irritable, moody, peevish, petulant, quarrelsome, shirty (*informal*), short-tempered, snaky (*Australian informal*), snappy (*informal*), stroppy (*informal*), sullen, surly, testy.

badge *noun* crest, emblem, insignia, logo, medal, shield, sign, symbol.

▶▶ DICTIONARY ◀◀

badger¹ *noun* a grey burrowing animal with a white patch on its head.

badger² *verb* pester. [named after the old sport of tormenting badgers]

badly *adverb* (**worse, worst**) **1** in a bad way; not well. **2** severely; so as to cause much injury, *He was badly wounded.* **3** very much, *She badly wanted to win.*

badminton *noun* a game in which a light object called a shuttlecock is hit to and fro with racquets across a high net. [named after Badminton in England, where it was invented in about 1870]

baffle *verb* (**baffled, baffling**) **1** puzzle or perplex somebody. **2** frustrate, *We baffled their attempts to capture us.* **bafflement** *noun*

bag¹ *noun* a flexible container for holding or carrying things.
bags (*informal*) plenty, *bags of room.*

bag² *verb* (**bagged, bagging**) **1** (*informal*) seize; catch. **2** put into a bag or bags. **3** (*informal*) claim or demand, *I bags sitting up front.*

bagatelle *noun* **1** a game played on a board with small balls struck into holes. **2** a trifle, a negligible amount. **3** a short slight piece of music.

baggage *noun* luggage.

baggy *adjective* hanging loosely.

bagpipes *plural noun* a musical instrument in which air is squeezed out of a bag into pipes.

baht *noun* the unit of money in Thailand.

bail¹ *noun* money paid or promised as a guarantee that a person accused of a crime will return for trial if released temporarily.

bail² *verb* provide bail for a person.
bail out rescue a person from a difficulty.

bail³ *noun* one of the two small pieces of wood placed on top of the stumps in cricket.

bail⁴ *verb* scoop out water that has entered a boat. [from French *baille* = bucket]

bail⁵ *verb* (*Australian*) **bail up** drive a cow into a stall in a milking shed; hold up and rob a traveller; buttonhole somebody.

bailey *noun* the courtyard of a castle; the wall round this courtyard.

bailiff *noun* a law officer who helps a sheriff by serving writs and performing arrests.

Bairam (*say* by-**rahm**) *noun* either of two Muslim festivals, one in the tenth month and one in the twelfth month of the Islamic year.

bairn *noun* (*Scottish*) a child.

bait¹ *noun* food put on a hook or in a trap to catch fish or animals.

bait² *verb* **1** put bait on a hook or in a trap. **2** torment or tease by jeering.

baize *noun* thick green cloth used chiefly for covering snooker tables.

bake *verb* (**baked, baking**) **1** cook in an oven. **2** make or become very hot. **3** make a thing hard by heating it.
baked beans cooked white beans, usually tinned with tomato sauce.

baker *noun* a person who bakes and sells bread or cakes. **bakery** *noun*

balaclava a hood covering the head and neck and part of the face. [named after the Battle of Balaclava (1854) in the Crimean War]

balance¹ *noun* **1** a steady position; having the weight or amount evenly distributed. **2** an apparatus for weighing things, with two containers hanging from a bar. **3** the difference between money paid into an account and money taken out of it. **4** the money left after something has been paid for.

▶▶ THESAURUS ◀◀

badger² *verb* bully, harass, hassle (*informal*), hound, nag, pester.

baffle *verb* **1** bamboozle (*informal*), bewilder, confound, confuse, flummox (*informal*), mystify, perplex, puzzle, stump.

bag¹ *noun* receptacle; (*kinds of bag*) attaché case, backpack, briefcase, carpet bag, carry bag, case, dilly bag (*Australian*), duffel bag, grip, handbag, haversack, holdall, kitbag, knapsack, pack, port (*Australian*), pouch, purse (*American*), rucksack, sack, satchel, schoolbag, shopping bag, shoulder bag, suitcase, swag (*Australian*), travelling bag, tucker bag (*Australian informal*).

baggage *noun* bags, cases, luggage, suitcases, trunks.

baggy *adjective* floppy, loose, roomy, shapeless.

bail¹ *noun* bond, guarantee, security, surety.

bail² *verb* **bail out** assist, help, relieve, rescue.

bail⁵ *verb* **bail up 1** hold up, rob, stick up (*informal*). **2** buttonhole, corner, detain, waylay.

bait¹ *noun* attraction, decoy, enticement, lure, temptation.

bait² *verb* **2** badger, goad, provoke, tantalise, tease, torment.

bake *verb* **1** cook, roast. **3** fire, harden.

balance¹ *noun* **1** equilibrium, poise, stability, steadiness. **2** scales, weighing machine. **4** difference, excess, leftovers, remainder, residue, rest, surplus.

▶▶ DICTIONARY ◀◀

balance² *verb* (**balanced, balancing**) make or be steady or equal. [from Latin *bilanx* = having two scale-pans]

balcony *noun* (*plural* **balconies**) **1** a platform projecting from an outside wall in a building. **2** the upstairs part of a theatre or cinema.

bald *adjective* **1** without hair on the top of the head. **2** with no details; blunt, *a bald statement*. **baldly** *adverb*, **baldness** *noun*

bale¹ *noun* a large bundle of hay, straw, cotton, etc., usually tied up tightly.

bale² *verb* (**baled, baling**) **bale out** jump out of an aircraft with a parachute.

baleful *adjective* bringing harm or evil; menacing, *a baleful frown*. **balefully** *adverb* [from Old English *balu* = evil]

ball¹ *noun* **1** a round object used in many games. **2** a solid or hollow sphere; a round mass, *a ball of string*.
ball of muscle (*Australian*) someone who is very fit.

ball² *noun* a grand gathering where people dance. [same origin as *ballet*]

ballad *noun* a simple song or poem telling a story.

ballast (*say* **bal**-ast) *noun* heavy material carried in a ship to keep it steady.

ball-bearings *plural noun* small steel balls rolling in a groove on which parts can move easily in machinery.

ballcock *noun* a floating device controlling the water-level in a cistern.

ballerina (*say* bal-er-**een**-a) *noun* a female ballet-dancer.

ballet (*say* **bal**-ay) *noun* a stage entertainment telling a story or expressing an idea in dancing and mime. [from Old French *baler* = to dance]

ballistic (*say* bal-**ist**-ik) *adjective* of projectiles such as bullets and missiles. [from Greek *ballein* = to throw]

balloon *noun* **1** an inflatable rubber pouch with a neck, used as a toy or decoration. **2** a large round bag inflated with hot air or light gases to make it rise in the air. **3** an outline round spoken words in a strip cartoon. **balloon** *verb*

ballot¹ *noun* **1** a secret method of voting by means of papers or tokens. **2** a piece of paper on which a vote is made.

ballot² *verb* (**balloted, balloting**) vote or allow people to vote by a ballot. [from Italian *ballotta* = little ball (because originally this voting was by dropping balls into a box)]

ballpoint pen a pen with a tiny ball round which the ink flows.

ballroom *noun* a large room where dances are held.

balm *noun* **1** a sweet-scented ointment. **2** a soothing influence.

balmy *adjective* **1** sweet-scented like balm. **2** soft and warm. **3** (*slang*) barmy.

balsa *noun* a kind of very lightweight wood.

balsam *noun* **1** a kind of gum produced by certain trees. **2** a tree producing balsam. **3** a kind of flowering plant.

balustrade *noun* a row of short posts or pillars supporting a rail or strip of stonework round a balcony or terrace.

bamboo *noun* **1** a tall plant with hard hollow stems. **2** a stem of the bamboo plant. [from a Malay word]

bamboozle *verb* (**bamboozled, bamboozling**) (*informal*) cheat or mystify someone.

ban¹ *verb* (**banned, banning**) forbid something officially.

ban² *noun* an order that bans something.

▶▶ THESAURUS ◀◀

balance² *verb* cancel out, counteract, counterbalance, equalise, even out, level, neutralise, offset.
balanced *adjective* even-handed, fair, impartial, unbiased.

balcony *noun* **1** deck, terrace, veranda. **2** gallery, the gods (*informal*), upper dress circle.

bald *adjective* **1** hairless, shaved.

bale¹ *noun* bundle, pack, package, parcel, truss.

bale² *verb* **bale out** eject, jump out, parachute.

ball¹ *noun* **2** bead, drop, globe, orb, pellet, sphere.

ball² *noun* dance, formal, social.

ballerina *noun* ballet-dancer, dancer.

balloon *verb* billow, bulge, puff out, swell.

ballot¹ *noun* **1** election, plebiscite, poll, referendum, vote.

balm *noun* **1** balsam, embrocation, liniment, ointment, salve.

balmy *adjective* **2** gentle, mild, pleasant, warm.

bamboozle *verb* baffle, bewilder, cheat, con (*informal*), confound, deceive, dupe, fool, hoax, hoodwink, mislead, mystify, perplex, puzzle, take in, trick.

ban¹ *verb* forbid, outlaw, prohibit, proscribe.

ban² *noun* boycott, embargo, moratorium, prohibition, proscription, veto.

▶▶ DICTIONARY ◀◀

banal (*say* ban-**ahl**) *adjective* ordinary and uninteresting. **banality** *noun*

banana *noun* a finger-shaped yellow or green fruit.

band¹ *noun* **1** a strip or loop of something. **2** a range of values, wavelengths, etc.

band² *noun* **1** an organised group doing something together, *a band of robbers.* **2** a set of people playing music together.

band³ *verb* form an organised group.

bandage *noun* a strip of material for binding up a wound. **bandage** *verb*

bandicoot *noun* a rat-like Australian marsupial.

bandit *noun* a member of a band of robbers. [from Italian *bandito* = outlawed or banned]

bandstand *noun* a platform for a band playing music outdoors.

bandwagon *noun* a wagon for a band playing music in a parade.
jump or **climb on the bandwagon** join in something that is successful.

bandy¹ *adjective* having legs that curve outwards at the knees.

bandy² *verb* (**bandied, bandying**) pass to and fro, *The story was bandied about.*

bane *noun* a cause of trouble or worry etc., *Exams are the bane of our lives!* **baneful** *adjective*, **banefully** *adverb*

bang¹ *noun* **1** a sudden loud noise like that of an explosion. **2** a sharp blow or knock.

bang² *verb* **1** hit or shut noisily. **2** make a sudden loud noise.

bang³ *adverb* **1** with a bang; suddenly. **2** (*informal*) exactly, *bang in the middle.*

banger *noun* **1** a firework made to explode noisily. **2** (*slang*) a sausage. **3** (*slang*) a noisy old car.

bangle *noun* a stiff bracelet. [from Hindi *bangri*]

banish *verb* punish a person by sending him or her away. **banishment** *noun*

banisters *plural noun* a handrail with upright supports beside a staircase.

banjo *noun* (*plural* **banjos**) **1** an instrument like a guitar with a round body. **2** (*Australian slang*) a shovel.

bank¹ *noun* **1** a slope. **2** a long piled-up mass of sand, snow, cloud, etc. **3** a row of lights or switches etc.

bank² *verb* **1** build or form a bank. **2** tilt sideways while changing direction, *The plane banked as it prepared to land.*

bank³ *noun* **1** a business that looks after people's money. **2** a reserve supply, *a blood bank.*

bank⁴ *verb* put money in a bank.
bank on rely on.

▶▶ THESAURUS ◀◀

banal *adjective* clichéd, commonplace, hackneyed, humdrum, trite, unimaginative, uninteresting, unoriginal.

band¹ *noun* **1** belt, circle, cord, elastic, hoop, ligature, line, loop, ribbon, ring, strap, string, strip, stripe, tie.

band² *noun* **1** body, bunch, clique, company, gang, group, mob, pack, party, push (*Australian old use*). **2** ensemble, group, orchestra.

band³ *verb* affiliate, ally, associate, gather, group, join, team up, unite.

bandage *noun* dressing, gauze, plaster, tourniquet.

bandit *noun* brigand, buccaneer, bushranger, criminal, crook (*informal*), desperado, gangster, highwayman, outlaw, pirate, robber, thief.

bandstand *noun* platform, rotunda, stage.

bandy¹ *adjective* bandy-legged, bow-legged.

bandy² *verb* circulate, pass, spread.

bane *noun* curse, plague, scourge, trial, woe.

bang¹ *noun* **1** blast, boom, clap, clatter, crash, detonation, explosion, pop, report, shot, thud. **2** blow, bump, hit, knock, punch, whack.

bang² *verb* **1** bash, hammer, hit, knock, pound, punch, slam, strike, thump. **2** blast, boom, crash, detonate, explode, pop.

bangle *noun* anklet, armlet, bracelet.

banish *verb* cast out, deport, dismiss, drive out, excommunicate (*from a church*), exile, expatriate, expel, oust, remove, send away, transport.

banisters *plural noun* handrail, railing, stair-rail.

bank¹ *noun* **1** brink, edge, embankment, shore, side, slope, verge. **2** mass, mound, pile. **3** group, row, series, set.

bank² *verb* **1** accumulate, amass, collect, heap, pile, stack. **2** incline, lean, list, pitch, tilt.

bank³ *noun* **2** kitty, pool, reserve, store.

bank⁴ *verb* deposit, invest, put aside, save.
bank on bargain on, count on, depend on, pin your hopes on, rely on.

▶▶ DICTIONARY ◀◀

banker¹ *noun* a person who runs a bank.

banker² *noun* (*Australian*) a river flowing as high as its banks, *The river's running a banker.*

banknote *noun* a piece of paper money issued by a bank.

bankrupt *adjective* unable to pay debts. **bankruptcy** *noun* [from *bank³*, + Latin *ruptum* = broken]

banksia *noun* an Australian shrub with yellowish cylindrical heads of flowers. [from Sir Joseph Banks, English naturalist (1743–1820)]

banner *noun* **1** a flag. **2** a strip of cloth with a design or slogan, carried on a pole or two poles in a procession etc.

banns *plural noun* an announcement in a church that the two people named are going to marry each other. [from *ban* = proclamation]

banquet *noun* a formal public meal. **banqueting** *noun* [from Old French *banquet* = little bench]

bantam *noun* a kind of small fowl. [named after Bantan, in Java]

banter *noun* playful teasing or joking.

Bantu *noun* (*plural* **Bantu** or **Bantus**) a member of a group of Black African peoples. [Bantu word = people]

baobab (*say* **bay**-o-bab) *noun* a tree with a massive trunk and edible pulpy fruit.

baptise *verb* (**baptised, baptising**) receive a person into the Christian Church in a ceremony in which he or she is sprinkled with or dipped in water, and usually given a name or names. [from Greek *baptisein* = to dip]

baptism *noun* baptising.

Baptist *noun* a member of a group of Christians who believe that a person should

not be baptised until old enough to understand what baptism means.

bar¹ *noun* **1** a long piece of hard substance. **2** a counter or room where refreshments, especially alcoholic drinks, are served. **3** a barrier; an obstruction. **4** one of the small equal sections into which music is divided, *three beats to the bar.*
the Bar barristers.

bar² *verb* (**barred, barring**) **1** fasten with a bar or bars. **2** block; obstruct, *A man with a dog barred the way.* **3** forbid; ban.

barb *noun* the backward-pointing part of a spear or fish-hook etc. [from Latin *barba* = beard]

barbarian *noun* an uncivilised or brutal person. **barbaric** *adjective*, **barbarous** *adjective*, **barbarity** *noun*, **barbarism** *noun* [from Greek *barbaros* = babbling, not speaking Greek]

barbecue *noun* **1** a metal frame for grilling food over an open fire outdoors. **2** a party where food is cooked in this way.

barbed *adjective* having a barb or barbs.
barbed wire wire with small spikes in it, used to make fences.

barber *noun* a men's hairdresser. [from Latin *barba* = beard]

barbie *noun* (*Australian informal*) a barbecue.

bard *noun* (*formal*) a poet or minstrel.

bardie *noun* a Western Australian name for an edible grub found in the bark of some trees. [from Nyungar, a Western Australian language]

bare¹ *adjective* **1** without clothing or covering. **2** unfurnished; empty of stores etc., *The cupboard was bare.* **3** plain; without details, *the bare facts.* **4** only just enough, *the bare necessities of life.* **barely** *adverb*, **bareness** *noun*

▶▶ THESAURUS ◀◀

bankrupt *adjective* broke (*informal*), bust (*informal*), failed, in liquidation, insolvent, ruined.

banner *noun* **1** flag, pennant, standard. **2** placard, sign.

banquet *noun* dinner, feast, meal, repast (*formal*).

banter *noun* badinage, chiacking (*Australian informal*), jesting, joking, kidding (*informal*), raillery, repartee, ribbing (*informal*), teasing.

baptise *verb* christen; see also NAME².

bar¹ *noun* **1** (*a wooden or metal bar*) bail, batten, beam, block, girder, pole, rail, rod, stake, stick; (*a bar of soap*) block, cake, hunk, lump, piece, slab. **2** counter, saloon. **3** barrier,

block, hindrance, impediment, obstacle, obstruction, restriction.

bar² *verb* **2** block, impede, obstruct. **3** ban, exclude, forbid, keep out, outlaw, prevent, prohibit.

barbaric *adjective* **1** barbarian, barbarous, primitive, savage, uncivilised, uncultivated, uncultured, wild. **2** barbarous, brutal, cruel, inhuman, rough, savage, vicious.

barber *noun* haircutter, hairdresser.

bard *noun* minstrel, musician, poet, troubadour.

bare¹ *adjective* **1** denuded, exposed, naked, nude, stripped, unclothed, uncovered, undressed. **2** empty, unfurnished, uninhabited,

▶▶DICTIONARY◀◀

bare² *verb* (**bared, baring**) uncover; reveal, *The dog bared its teeth in a snarl.*

bareback *adjective* & *adverb* riding on a horse without a saddle.

barefaced *adjective* shameless; bold and unconcealed, *It's barefaced robbery!*

bargain¹ *noun* 1 an agreement about buying or selling or exchanging something. 2 something bought cheaply.

bargain² *verb* argue over the price to be paid or what you will do in return for something.
bargain for be prepared for; expect, *He got more than he bargained for.*

barge¹ *noun* a long flat-bottomed boat.

barge² *verb* (**barged, barging**) move clumsily or heavily.
barge in intrude.

baritone *noun* a male singer with a voice between a tenor and a bass. [from Greek *barys* = heavy, + *tone*]

barium (*say* **bair**-ee-um) *noun* a soft silvery-white metal.

bark¹ *noun* the short harsh sound made by a dog or fox. **bark** *verb*

bark² *noun* the outer covering of a tree's branches or trunk.
bark painting a picture painted on bark, originally as ceremonial art in Arnhem Land.

bark³ *verb* scrape your skin accidentally.

barley *noun* a cereal plant from which malt is made.
barley sugar a sweet made from boiled sugar.

bar mitzvah a religious ceremony for Jewish boys aged 13. [Hebrew, = son of the commandment]

barmy *adjective* (*slang*) crazy.

barn *noun* a building for storing hay or grain etc. on a farm. **barnyard** *noun*
barn dance a kind of country dance; an informal gathering for dancing. [from Old English *bere ern* = barley-house]

barnacle *noun* a shellfish that attaches itself to rocks and the bottoms of ships.

barney *noun* (*slang*) a noisy dispute.

barometer (*say* ba-**rom**-it-er) *noun* an instrument that measures air pressure, used in forecasting the weather. [from Greek *baros* = weight, + *meter*]

baron *noun* 1 a member of the lowest rank of noblemen. 2 an important owner of an industry or business, *a newspaper baron.* **baroness** *noun*, **barony** *noun*, **baronial** *adjective*

baronet *noun* a nobleman ranking below a baron but above a knight. **baronetcy** *noun*

baroque (*say* ba-**rok**) *noun* an elaborately decorated style of architecture used in the 17th and 18th centuries.

barrack *verb* 1 tease or jeer at, *the newly wed had some barracking to put up with.* 2 (*Australian*) encourage or cheer on, *we were there to barrack for the home team.*

barracks *noun* a large building or group of buildings for soldiers to live in. [from Spanish *barraca* = a soldier's tent]

barracouta (*say* ba-ra-**koo**-ta) *noun* a long narrow Australian fish.

barrage (*say* **ba**-rahzh) *noun* 1 an artificial barrier; a dam. 2 heavy gunfire. [from French *barre* = a bar]

barramundi (*say* ba-ra-**mun**-dee) *noun* a large freshwater Australian fish.

▶▶THESAURUS◀◀

unoccupied, vacant. 3 bald, plain, unadorned, unembellished, unvarnished. 4 basic, meagre, mere, scant.
barely *adverb* hardly, only just, scarcely.

bare² *verb* expose, reveal, show.

barefaced *adjective* blatant, brazen, downright, flagrant, shameless, unconcealed, undisguised.

bargain¹ *noun* 1 accord, agreement, compact, contract, covenant, deal, pact. 2 give-away (*informal*), good buy, snip (*informal*), special, steal (*informal*).

bargain² *verb* barter, discuss terms, haggle, negotiate.
bargain for anticipate, be prepared for, envisage, expect, foresee.

barge² *verb* bump, collide, crash, knock, lurch, slam.
barge in burst in, butt in, interrupt, intrude.

bark¹ *noun* bay, bow-wow, growl, woof, yap, yelp.
bark *verb* bay, growl, woof, yap, yelp.

barn *noun* outbuilding, outhouse, shed.

barney *noun* altercation, argument, fight, quarrel, row, squabble.

barrack *verb* 2 (*barrack for*) cheer on, egg on, encourage, support.

barracks *noun* billet, camp, garrison, quarters.

barrage *noun* 1 barrier, dam, wall. 2 battery, bombardment, fusillade, gunfire, hail, onslaught, salvo, volley.

▶▶ D I C T I O N A R Y ◀◀

barrel *noun* **1** a large rounded container with flat ends. **2** the metal tube of a gun, through which the shot is fired.

barrel-organ *noun* a musical instrument from which you produce tunes by turning a handle.

barren *adjective* **1** not producing any fruit, seeds, etc.; not fertile, *barren land*. **2** unable to have young, *a barren couple*. **barrenness** *noun*

barricade[1] *noun* a barrier, especially one put up hastily across a street etc.

barricade[2] *verb* (**barricaded, barricading**) block or defend with a barricade.

barrier *noun* **1** something that prevents people or things from getting past. **2** an obstacle.

barrister *noun* a lawyer who represents people in the higher lawcourts.

barrow *noun* **1** a wheelbarrow. **2** a small cart pushed or pulled by hand. [from Old English *bearwe* = carrying]

barter[1] *verb* trade by exchanging goods for other goods, not for money.

barter[2] *noun* the system of bartering.

basalt (*say* **bas**-awlt) *noun* a kind of dark volcanic rock.

base[1] *noun* **1** the lowest part of something; the part on which a thing stands. **2** a basis. **3** a headquarters. **4** each of the four corners that must be reached by a runner in baseball. **5** a substance that can combine with an acid to form a salt.

base[2] *verb* (**based, basing**) use something as a basis, *The story is based on facts*. [from Greek *basis* = stepping]

base[3] *adjective* **1** dishonourable, *base motives*. **2** not of great value, *base metals*. **basely** *adverb*, **baseness** *noun* [from French *bas* = low]

baseball *noun* an American ball game rather like rounders.

basement *noun* a room or rooms below ground level.

bash[1] *verb* hit hard; attack violently.

bash[2] *noun* (*plural* **bashes**) **1** a hard hit. **2** (*informal*) a try, *Have a bash at it*.

bashful *adjective* shy and self-conscious. **bashfully** *adverb* [from *abash*]

Basic *noun* a computer language designed to be easy to learn. [from the initials of *Beginners' all-purpose symbolic instruction code*]

basic *adjective* forming a basis or starting-point; very important, *Bread is a basic food*. **basically** *adverb* [from *base*[1]]

basilica (*say* ba-**zil**-ik-a) *noun* a large oblong hall or church with two rows of columns and an apse at one end.

basilisk (*say* **baz**-il-isk) *noun* a mythical reptile said to cause death by its glance or breath.

basin *noun* **1** a deep bowl. **2** a washbasin. **3** an enclosed area of water. **4** the area from which water drains into a river, *the Amazon basin*.

▶▶ T H E S A U R U S ◀◀

barrel *noun* **1** butt, cask, drum, hogshead, keg, tun.

barren *adjective* **1** arid, bare, desert, infertile, lifeless, unproductive, waste. **2** childless, infertile, sterile.

barricade[1] *noun* barrier, blockade, fence.

barricade[2] *verb* block off, fence off, obstruct, shut off.

barrier *noun* **1** bar, barricade, boom, fence, gate, obstruction, partition, rail, screen, wall. **2** bar, block, hindrance, impediment, obstacle, restriction, stumbling block.

barrister *noun* advocate, attorney (*American*), counsel; see also LAWYER.

barrow *noun* **1** wheelbarrow. **2** cart, handcart.

barter[1] *verb* exchange, swap, trade.

base[1] *noun* **1** bottom, foot, foundation, pedestal, plinth, stand, support. **3** camp, depot, headquarters, installation, post, station.

base[2] *verb* build, establish, found, ground, root.

base[3] *adjective* **1** bad, contemptible, cowardly, despicable, dishonourable, evil, ignoble, immoral, low, mean, selfish, shabby, sordid, underhand, wicked.

basement *noun* cellar, crypt, vault.

bash[1] *verb* assault, attack, batter, beat, clout, hit, mug, punch, strike, thump.

bash[2] *noun* **1** blow, hit, knock, punch, thump.

bashful *adjective* coy, demure, diffident, reserved, reticent, self-conscious, sheepish, shy.

basic *adjective* central, elementary, essential, fundamental, key, necessary, primary, radical, root, rudimentary, underlying.
basically *adverb* at bottom, at heart, essentially, for the most part, fundamentally.

basin *noun* **1** bowl, container, dish, font. **2** sink, washbasin, washbowl.

▶▶ DICTIONARY ◀◀

basis *noun* (*plural* **bases**) something to start from or add to; the main principle or ingredient. [same origin as *base¹*]

bask *verb* sit or lie comfortably warming yourself.

basket *noun* a container for holding or carrying things, made of interwoven strips of flexible material or wire.

basketball *noun* a game rather like netball.

bass¹ (*say* bayss) *adjective* deep-sounding; of the lowest notes in music.

bass² *noun* (*plural* **basses**) **1** a male singer with a very deep voice. **2** a bass instrument or part. [from *base¹*]

bass³ (*say* bas) *noun* (*plural* **bass**) a fish of the perch family.

basset *noun* a short-legged dog used for hunting hares. [from French *bas* = low]

bassoon *noun* a bass woodwind instrument.

bastard *noun* **1** an illegitimate child. **2** (*slang*) a person; an unpleasant or difficult person or thing. **bastardy** *noun*

baste *verb* (**basted, basting**) **1** moisten meat with fat while it is cooking. **2** tack material or a hem.

bastion *noun* **1** a projecting part of a fortified building. **2** a centre of support for a cause.

bat¹ *noun* **1** a wooden implement used to hit the ball in cricket, baseball, etc. **2** a batsman, *their opening bat.*
off your own bat without help from other people.

bat² *verb* (**batted, batting**) **1** use a bat in cricket etc. **2** hit.

bat³ *noun* a flying animal that looks like a mouse with wings.

batch¹ *noun* (*plural* **batches**) a set of things or people dealt with together.

batch² *verb* (*Australian*) live alone without conveniences.

bated *adjective* **with bated breath** anxiously; hardly daring to speak. [from *abate*]

bath¹ *noun* **1** washing your whole body while sitting in water. **2** a large container for water in which to wash your whole body; this water, *Your bath is getting cold.* **3** a liquid in which something is placed, *an acid bath.*

bath² *verb* wash in a bath.

bathe *verb* (**bathed, bathing**) **1** go swimming. **2** wash something gently. **bathe** *noun*, **bather** *noun*, **bathing-suit** *noun*

bathers *noun* (*Australian*) a swimming costume.

bathroom *noun* a room usually containing a bath.

baths *plural noun* **1** a building with rooms where people can bath. **2** a public swimming-bath.

baton *noun* a short stick, e.g. one used to conduct an orchestra.

batsman *noun* (*plural* **batsmen**) a player who uses a bat in cricket etc.

battalion *noun* an army unit containing two or more companies. [from Italian *battaglia* = battle]

batten¹ *noun* a strip of wood or metal holding something in place.

batten² *verb* feed or grow fat on something, *Pigeons battened on the crops.*

batter¹ *verb* hit hard and often.

batter² *noun* **1** a beaten mixture of flour, eggs, and milk, used for making pancakes etc. **2** a batsman in baseball. [from Latin *battuere* = to beat]

battering-ram *noun* a heavy pole used to break down walls or gates.

▶▶ THESAURUS ◀◀

basis *noun* base, beginning, footing, foundation, grounds, premise, principle, starting point, support.

bask *verb* sunbake, sunbathe, sun yourself, warm yourself.

basket *noun* carrier, hamper, pannier, punnet.

bass¹ *adjective* deep, low, sonorous.

bat¹ *noun* **1** club, racquet, stick.

batch¹ *noun* bunch, collection, group, lot, number, set.

bathe *verb* **1** bogey (*Australian*), paddle, swim, take a dip. **2** clean, cleanse, rinse, wash.

bathers *plural noun* bathing costume, bathing suit, bikini, cossie (*Australian informal*), one-piece, swimmers (*Australian informal*), swimming costume, swimsuit, togs (*Australian informal*), trunks, two-piece.

baton *noun* cane, rod, staff, stick, truncheon, wand.

batter¹ *verb* abuse, assault, bash, beat, belt (*slang*), clobber (*slang*), hit, pound, pummel, strike, thump, wallop (*slang*), whack.

▶▶ D I C T I O N A R Y ◀◀

battery *noun* (*plural* **batteries**) **1** a portable device for storing and supplying electricity. **2** a set of similar pieces of equipment; a group of large guns. **3** a series of cages in which poultry or animals are kept close together. [same origin as *batter*]

battle¹ *noun* **1** a fight between large organised forces. **2** a struggle. **battlefield** *noun*, **battleground** *noun*

battle² *verb* (**battled, battling**) fight; struggle. [same origin as *batter*]

battlements *plural noun* the top of a castle wall, often with gaps from which the defenders could fire at the enemy.

battler *noun* (*Australian*) someone who struggles against difficulties and does not give up.

battleship *noun* a heavily armed warship.

batty *adjective* (*slang*) crazy. [from *bat³*]

bauble *noun* a showy but valueless thing.

baulk *verb* **1** shirk or jib at something; stop and refuse to go on, *The horse baulked at the fence.* **2** frustrate; prevent from doing or getting something.

bauxite *noun* the clay-like substance from which aluminium is obtained.

bawdy *adjective* (**bawdier, bawdiest**) funny but vulgar. **bawdiness** *noun*

bawl *verb* **1** shout. **2** cry noisily.

bay¹ *noun* **1** a place where the shore curves inwards. **2** an alcove.
bay window a window projecting from the main wall of a house.

bay² *noun* a kind of laurel-tree.

bay³ *noun* the long deep cry of a hunting hound or other large dog.

at bay cornered but defiantly facing attackers, *a stag at bay*; prevented from coming near or causing harm, *We need laws to keep poverty at bay.*

bay⁴ *adjective* reddish-brown.

bayonet *noun* a stabbing-blade attached to a rifle. [named after *Bayonne* in France, where it was first made]

bazaar *noun* **1** a set of shops or stalls in an Oriental country. **2** a sale to raise money for a charity etc. [from Persian *bazar*]

bazooka *noun* a portable weapon for firing anti-tank rockets. [the word originally meant a musical instrument rather like a trombone]

BC *abbreviation* before Christ (used of dates reckoned back from the birth of Jesus Christ).

be *verb* (**am, are, is; was, were; been, being**) **1** exist. **2** occupy a position, *The shop is on the corner.* **3** happen; take place, *The wedding is tomorrow.*
This verb is also used (**1**) to join subject and predicate (*He is my teacher*), (**2**) to form parts of other verbs (*It is raining. He was killed*).
have been have gone or come as a visitor etc., *We have been to Fiji.*

be- *prefix* used to form verbs (as in *befriend, belittle*) or strengthen their meaning (as in *begrudge*).

beach *noun* (*plural* **beaches**) the part of the seashore nearest to the water.

beacon *noun* a light (or formerly a fire) used as a signal.

bead *noun* **1** a small piece of a hard substance with a hole in it for threading with others on a string or wire, e.g. to make a necklace. **2** a drop of liquid.

▶▶ T H E S A U R U S ◀◀

battery *noun* **2** group, sequence, series, set.

battle¹ *noun* **1** action, affray, campaign, clash, combat, conflict, confrontation, crusade, encounter, engagement, fight, fighting, fray, hostilities, offensive, skirmish, strife, war, warfare.

battle² *verb* see FIGHT².

battler *noun* fighter, struggler, toiler, worker.

battleship *noun* see WARSHIP.

bauble *noun* decoration, ornament, trinket.

baulk *verb* **1** hesitate, jib, prop, pull up, shy, stop.

bawl *verb* **1** bellow, cry out, roar, shout, yell. **2** cry, howl, sob, wail, weep.

bay¹ *noun* **1** bight, cove, estuary, gulf, inlet. **2** alcove, compartment, niche, nook, recess.

bay³ *noun* bark, cry, howl, yelp.
keep at bay see WARD OFF (at WARD²).

bazaar *noun* **2** charity sale, fair, fête, flea market (*informal*), garage sale, jumble sale, trash and treasure market.

be *verb* **1** be alive, dwell, exist, live, remain, reside. **2** be found, be located, be situated, sit. **3** fall, happen, occur, take place.

beach *noun* coast, sands, seashore, seaside, shore, strand.

beacon *noun* flare, lighthouse, signal fire, signal light, signal station.

bead *noun* **1** (*beads*) necklace, necklet, rosary. **2** bubble, drop, droplet.

▶▶▶ D I C T I O N A R Y ◀◀◀

beadle *noun* (*old use*) an official of a parish.

beady *adjective* like beads; small and bright, *beady eyes*.

beagle *noun* a small hound used for hunting hares. **beagling** *noun*

beak *noun* the hard horny part of a bird's mouth.

beaker *noun* 1 a tall drinking-mug, often without a handle. 2 a glass container used for pouring liquids in a laboratory.

beam¹ *noun* 1 a long thick bar of wood or metal. 2 a ray or stream of light or other radiation. 3 a bright look on someone's face; a happy smile.

beam² *verb* 1 smile happily. 2 send out a beam of light or other radiation.

bean *noun* 1 a kind of plant with seeds growing in pods. 2 its seed or pod eaten as food. 3 the seed of coffee etc.

bear¹ *noun* a large heavy animal with thick fur.
native bear (*old use*) koala.

bear² *verb* (**bore, borne, bearing**) 1 carry; bring or take. 2 support. 3 have a mark etc., *She still bears the scar.* 4 endure; tolerate, *I can't bear this pain.* 5 produce; give birth to, *She bore him two sons.* **bearer** *noun*

bearable *adjective* able to be borne; tolerable.

beard¹ *noun* hair on and around a man's chin.
bearded *adjective*

beard² *verb* come face to face with a person and challenge him or her boldly.

bearing *noun* 1 the way a person stands, walks, behaves, etc. 2 relevance, *It has no bearing on this problem.* 3 the direction or position of one thing in relation to another. 4 a device for preventing friction in a machine, *ball-bearings.*
get your bearings work out where you are in relation to things.

beast *noun* 1 any large four-footed animal. 2 (*informal*) a person you dislike. **beastly** *adjective*

beat¹ *verb* (**beat, beaten, beating**) 1 hit often, especially with a stick. 2 shape or flatten something by beating it. 3 stir vigorously. 4 make repeated movements, *The heart beats.* 5 do better than somebody; overcome. **beater** *noun*

beat² *noun* 1 a regular rhythm or stroke, *the beat of your heart.* 2 emphasis in rhythm; the strong rhythm of pop music. 3 a policeman's regular route.

beatific (*say* bee-a-**tif**-ik) *adjective* showing great happiness, *a beatific smile.*

beatify (*say* bee-**at**-i-fy) *verb* (**beatified, beatifying**) (in the Roman Catholic Church)

▶▶▶ T H E S A U R U S ◀◀◀

beaker *noun* 1 cup, glass, tumbler.

beam¹ *noun* 1 board, girder, joist, plank, rafter, support, timber. 2 gleam, ray, shaft, streak, stream.

beam² *verb* 1 grin, smile. 2 broadcast, emit, radiate, send out, transmit.

bear² *verb* 1 bring, carry, convey, deliver, take, transport. 2 carry, hold up, support, sustain, take. 3 have, possess, show, wear. 4 abide, cope with, endure, put up with, stand, stomach, suffer, take, tolerate. 5 bring forth, give birth to, have, produce.

bearable *adjective* acceptable, endurable, sustainable, tolerable.

beard¹ *noun* facial hair, goatee, whiskers, ziff (*Australian slang*).

bearing *noun* 1 air, behaviour, carriage, demeanour, deportment, manner, mien, posture, stance. 2 connection, relation, relationship, relevance. 3 (*bearings*) location, orientation, position, whereabouts.

beast *noun* 1 animal, brute, creature, quadruped. 2 brute, fiend, monster, savage.
beastly *adjective* 1 animal, bestial. 2 (*informal*) abominable, awful, disgusting, hateful, horrible, mean, nasty, rotten, unpleasant.

beat¹ *verb* 1 bash, baste, batter, belt (*slang*), cane, clobber (*slang*), clout (*informal*), club, cudgel, drub, flog, hit, knock, lash, lay into (*informal*), pound, quilt (*Australian slang*), slap, smack, smite, spank, stoush (*Australian slang*), strike, thrash, thump, thwack, trounce, wallop (*slang*), whack, whip. 3 agitate, mix, stir, whip, whisk. 4 flutter, palpitate, pound, pulsate, throb, thump. 5 clobber (*slang*), conquer, crush, defeat, euchre, get the better of, lick (*informal*), outdo, outstrip, outwit, overcome, overwhelm, prevail over, pulverise, rout, slaughter, stonker (*Australian slang*), surpass, thrash, triumph over, trounce, vanquish, win against.
beat up assault, attack, bash up, batter, mug, thrash.

beat² *noun* 1 accent, pulse, rhythm, stress. 3 circuit, course, path, round, route.

▶▶ D I C T I O N A R Y ◀◀

honour a person who has died by declaring that he or she is among the Blessed, as a step towards declaring that person a saint. **beatification** *noun* [from Latin *beatus* = blessed]

beaut¹ *adjective* (*Australian informal*) excellent.

beaut² *noun* (*Australian informal*) an excellent thing.

beautiful *adjective* having beauty. **beautifully** *adverb*

beautify *verb* (**beautified, beautifying**) make beautiful. **beautification** *noun*

beauty *noun* (*plural* **beauties**) 1 a quality that gives pleasure to your senses or your mind. 2 a person or thing that has beauty.

beaver¹ *noun* an amphibious animal with soft brown fur and strong teeth.

beaver² *verb* work hard, *beavering away*.

becalmed *adjective* (in sailing) unable to move because there is no wind.

because *conjunction* for the reason that. **because of** for the reason of, *He limped because of his bad leg.*

beck *noun* **at someone's beck and call** always ready and waiting to do what he or she asks. [from *beckon*]

beckon *verb* make a sign to a person asking him or her to come.

become *verb* (**became, become, becoming**) 1 come or grow to be; start being, *It became*

dark. 2 be suitable for; make a person look attractive. **become of** happen to, *What became of that friend you had?*

bed *noun* 1 a thing to sleep or rest on; a piece of furniture with a mattress and coverings. 2 a piece of a garden where plants are grown. 3 the bottom of the sea or of a river. 4 a flat base; a foundation. 5 a layer of rock or soil.

bedclothes *plural noun* sheets, blankets, etc.

bedding *noun* mattresses and bedclothes.

bedlam *noun* uproar. [from 'Bedlam', the popular name of the Hospital of St Mary of Bethlehem, a London mental hospital in the 14th century]

Bedouin (*say* **bed**-oo-in) *noun* (*plural* **Bedouin**) a member of an Arab people living in tents in the desert. [from Arabic *badawi* = desert-dweller]

bedpan *noun* a container for use as a lavatory by a bedridden person.

bedraggled (*say* bid-**rag**-eld) *adjective* very untidy; wet and dirty.

bedridden *adjective* too weak to get out of bed.

bedrock *noun* solid rock beneath soil.

bedroom *noun* a room for sleeping in.

bedsitter *noun* a room used for both living and sleeping in.

bedspread *noun* a covering spread over a bed during the day.

bedstead *noun* the framework of a bed.

▶▶ T H E S A U R U S ◀◀

beautiful *adjective* appealing, attractive, bonny (*Scottish*), captivating, charming, comely, delightful, exquisite, fair (*old use*), fetching, fine, glorious, good-looking, gorgeous, handsome, irresistible, lovely, pleasing, pretty, radiant, stunning.

beautify *verb* adorn, decorate, embellish, enhance, improve, prettify, smarten up, titivate (*informal*), tizzy up (*Australian*).

beauty *noun* 1 attractiveness, elegance, glamour, glory, good looks, handsomeness, loveliness, magnificence, prettiness, radiance, splendour.

because *conjunction* as, for, since. **because of** as a result of, by reason of, on account of, owing to, thanks to.

beckon *verb* gesture, motion, signal.

become *verb* 1 change into, develop into, grow into, turn into. 2 befit, be right for, flatter, look good on, suit.

becoming see ATTRACTIVE (at ATTRACT), SUITABLE. **become of** befall (*formal*), happen to.

bed *noun* 1 (*kinds of bed*) berth, bunk, camp bed, cot, cradle, crib, divan, folding bed, four-poster, futon, hammock, sofa bed, stretcher, trundle bed, waterbed. 2 border, patch, plot, strip. 3 bottom, channel, course. 4 base, bottom, foundation.

bedclothes *plural noun* bedding, bed linen, bedspread, blankets, covers, linen, pillows, quilt, sheets.

bedlam *noun* chaos, confusion, madhouse (*informal*), mayhem, pandemonium, rumpus, uproar.

bedraggled *adjective* dishevelled, messy, ruffled, scruffy, unkempt, untidy, wet.

bedroom *noun* chamber (*old use*), dormitory.

▶▶ D I C T I O N A R Y ◀◀

bedtime *noun* the time for going to bed.

bee *noun* a stinging insect with four wings that makes honey.

beech *noun* (*plural* **beeches**) a tree with smooth bark and glossy leaves.

beef *noun* meat from an ox, bull, or cow.
beef road (*Australian*) an all-weather road for trucking cattle from remote areas.

beefeater *noun* a guard at the Tower of London, wearing Tudor dress as uniform.

beefy *adjective* having a solid muscular body. **beefiness** *noun*

beehive *noun* a box or other container for bees to live in.

beeline *noun* **make a beeline for** go straight or quickly towards something.

beer *noun* an alcoholic drink made from malt and hops. **beery** *adjective*

beeswax *noun* a yellow substance produced by bees, used for polishing wood.

beet *noun* (*plural* **beet** or **beets**) a plant with a thick root used as a vegetable or for making sugar.

beetle *noun* an insect with hard shiny wing-covers.

beetling *adjective* prominent; overhanging, *beetling brows*.

beetroot *noun* (*plural* **beetroot**) the crimson root of beet used as a vegetable.

befall *verb* (**befell, befallen, befalling**) (*formal*) happen; happen to someone.

befitting *adjective* suitable.

before¹ *adverb* at an earlier time, *Have you been here before?*

before² *preposition* & *conjunction* **1** earlier than, *I was here before you!* **2** ahead of; in front of, *leg before wicket.*

beforehand *adverb* earlier; in readiness.

befriend *verb* act as a friend to someone.

beg *verb* (**begged, begging**) **1** ask to be given money, food, etc. **2** ask earnestly or humbly or formally.
beg the question argue in an illogical way by relying on the result that you are trying to prove.
go begging be available.
I beg your pardon I apologise; I did not hear what you said.
beg-pardon (*Australian*) apology, *The land-lady threw him out with no beg-pardons.*

beget *verb* (**begot, begotten, begetting**) (*old use*) **1** be the father of someone. **2** produce, *War begets misery.*

beggar *noun* **1** a person who lives by begging. **2** (*informal*) a person, *You lucky beggar!* **beggary** *noun*

begin *verb* (**began, begun, beginning**) **1** do the earliest or first part of something; start speaking. **2** come into existence, *The problem began last year.* **3** have something as its first element, *The word begins with B.*

beginner *noun* a person who is just beginning to learn a subject.

▶▶ T H E S A U R U S ◀◀

bee *noun* bumble-bee, drone, honey bee, queen, worker.
bee-keeper *noun* apiarist.

beefy *adjective* brawny, burly, hefty, muscular, nuggety (*Australian*), solid, stocky, strapping, strong, sturdy, thickset.

beer *noun* ale, bitter, lager, stout.

befall *verb* come about, come to pass, crop up, eventuate, happen, occur, take place.

befitting *adjective* appropriate, becoming, fitting, proper, right, seemly, suitable.

before¹ *adverb* beforehand, earlier, formerly, hitherto, in the past, previously.

before² *preposition* **1** earlier than, prior to. **2** ahead of, in front of.

beforehand *adverb* ahead, earlier, in advance, in anticipation, in readiness.

befriend *verb* look after, make a friend of, take care of, welcome.

beg *verb* **1** cadge, scrounge, sponge. **2** ask, beseech, entreat, implore, plead, pray, request.

beget *verb* **1** father, procreate, sire. **2** breed, bring about, cause, create, engender, generate, give rise to, produce, result in.

beggar *noun* **1** cadger, down-and-out, mendicant, scrounger, sponger, tramp. **2** fellow, person, rascal, wretch (*informal*).

begin *verb* **1** commence, create, embark on, establish, found, get going, get under way, inaugurate, initiate, introduce, kick off (*informal*), launch, open, originate, set up, start. **2** appear, arise, commence, crop up, emerge, originate, spring up, start.

beginner *noun* apprentice, learner, new chum (*Australian informal*), novice, recruit, starter, tiro, trainee.

►► DICTIONARY ◄◄

beginning *noun* **1** the starting point; a source or origin. **2** the first part.

begone *verb* (*old use*) go away immediately, *Begone dull care!*

begonia (*say* big-**oh**-nee-a) *noun* a garden plant with brightly coloured flowers.

begot *past tense* of **beget**.

begrudge *verb* (**begrudged**, **begrudging**) grudge.

beguile (*say* big-**I**'ll) *verb* (**beguiled**, **beguiling**) **1** amuse. **2** deceive.

behalf *noun* **on behalf of** for a person; done to help a person or charity etc.

behave *verb* (**behaved**, **behaving**) **1** act or function in a particular way, *They behaved badly.* **2** show good manners, *Behave yourself!* **behaviour** *noun*, **behavioural** *adjective*

behead *verb* cut the head from; execute a person in this way.

behest *noun* (*formal*) a command.

behind[1] *adverb* **1** at or to the back; at a place people have left, *Don't leave it behind.* **2** not making good progress; late, *I'm behind with my rent.*

behind[2] *preposition* **1** at or to the back of; on the further side of. **2** having made less progress than, *He is behind the others in French.* **3** supporting; causing, *What is behind all this trouble?*

behind a person's back kept secret from him or her deceitfully.

behind the times out of date.

behind[3] *noun* **1** (*informal*) a person's bottom. **2** in Australian Rules Football a score of one point when a ball is sent over a line between a goal-post and an outer post.

behindhand *adverb* & *adjective* **1** late. **2** out of date.

behold *verb* (**beheld**, **beholding**) (*old use*) see. **beholder** *noun*

beholden *adjective* owing thanks; indebted, *We are greatly beholden to you.*

behove *verb* (**behoved**, **behoving**) be a person's duty, *It behoves you to be loyal.*

beige (*say* bay*zh*) *noun* & *adjective* light fawn colour.

being *noun* **1** existence. **2** a creature.

belated *adjective* coming very late or too late. **belatedly** *adverb*

belay *verb* (**belayed**, **belaying**) fasten a rope by winding it round a peg or spike.

belch *verb* **1** send out wind from your stomach through your mouth noisily. **2** send out fire or smoke etc. from an opening. **belch** *noun*

beleaguered (*say* bil-**eeg**-erd) *adjective* besieged; oppressed. [from Dutch *belegeren* = camp round]

belfry *noun* (*plural* **belfries**) a tower or part of a tower in which bells hang.

belief *noun* **1** believing. **2** something a person believes.

►► THESAURUS ◄◄

beginning *noun* **1** birth, commencement, creation, dawn, founding, genesis, inception, introduction, onset, opening, origin, outset, rise, root, source, start, starting point. **2** introduction, opening, preamble, preface, prelude, prologue.

begrudge *verb* envy, grudge, mind, object to, resent.

behalf *noun* **on behalf of** as a representative of, for, representing.

behave *verb* **1** (*of a person*) act, conduct yourself, react; (*of a machine*) function, operate, perform, run, work. **2** be polite, be well-mannered, mind your manners.
behaviour *noun* actions, conduct, demeanour, deportment, manners.

behead *verb* decapitate, guillotine.

behind[1] *adverb* **1** at the back, at the rear, in the back, in the rear. **2** in arrears, behindhand, late, overdue.

behind[2] *preposition* **1** after, at the back of, at the rear of, beyond, following, on the far side of, on the other side of. **2** less advanced than, trailing. **3** at the bottom of, underlying.
behind a person's back covertly, deceitfully, in secret, secretly, slyly, sneakily, surreptitiously.
behind the times antediluvian, antiquated, obsolete, old-fashioned, outdated, outmoded, out of date.

behold *verb* observe, see, survey, view, witness.

beige *adjective* biscuit, buff, coffee, fawn, neutral.

being *noun* **1** existence, life. **2** animal, creature, entity, individual, living thing, mortal, person.

belch *verb* **1** bring up wind, burp (*informal*). **2** discharge, emit, give off, send out, spew.

belief *noun* **1** confidence, credence, faith, reliance, trust. **2** conviction, credo, creed, doctrine, dogma, faith, ideology, opinion, persuasion, philosophy, religion, view.

▶▶ D I C T I O N A R Y ◀◀

believe *verb* (**believed**, **believing**) think that something is true or that someone is telling the truth. **believable** *adjective*, **believer** *noun* **believe in** think that something exists or is good or can be relied on.

belittle *verb* (**belittled**, **belittling**) make something seem of little value, *Do not belittle their success.* **belittlement** *noun*

bell *noun* 1 a cup-shaped metal instrument that makes a ringing sound when struck by the clapper hanging inside it; any device that makes a ringing or buzzing sound to attract attention. 2 a bell-shaped object.

bellbird *noun* a bird with a clear ringing note.

belle *noun* a beautiful woman. [French]

bellicose (*say* **bel**-ik-ohs) *adjective* eager to fight. [from Latin *bellum* = war]

belligerent (*say* bil-**ij**-er-ent) *adjective* 1 aggressive; eager to fight. 2 fighting; engaged in a war. **belligerently** *adverb*, **belligerence** *noun* [from Latin *bellum* = war, *gerens* = waging]

bellow¹ *noun* 1 the loud deep sound made by a bull or other large animal. 2 a deep shout.

bellow² *verb* give a bellow; shout.

bellows *plural noun* a device for pumping air into a fire, organ-pipes, etc.

belly *noun* (*plural* **bellies**) the abdomen; the stomach.

belong *verb* have a proper place, *The pans belong in the kitchen.* **belong to** be the property of; be a member of, *We belong to the same club.*

belongings *plural noun* a person's possessions.

beloved *adjective* dearly loved.

below¹ *adverb* at or to a lower position; underneath, *There's fire down below.*

below² *preposition* lower than; under, *The temperature was ten degrees below zero.*

belt¹ *noun* 1 a strip of cloth or leather etc. worn round the waist. 2 a band of flexible material used in machinery. 3 a long narrow area, *a belt of rain.*

belt² *verb* 1 put a belt round something. 2 (*slang*) hit. 3 (*slang*) rush along.

bemused *adjective* 1 bewildered. 2 lost in thought.

bench *noun* (*plural* **benches**) 1 a long seat. 2 a long table for working at. 3 the seat where judges or magistrates sit; the judges or magistrates hearing a lawsuit.

bend¹ *verb* (**bent**, **bending**) 1 change from being straight. 2 turn downwards; stoop, *She bent to pick it up.*

bend² *noun* a place where something bends; a curve or turn.

▶▶ T H E S A U R U S ◀◀

believe *verb* accept, be certain of, be convinced of, be sure of, credit, have faith in, rely on, trust. **believable** *adjective* acceptable, convincing, credible, plausible. **believer** *noun* adherent, convert, disciple, follower, supporter, zealot.

belittle *verb* denigrate, depreciate, disparage, knock (*informal*), put down, run down, sling off at (*Australian informal*).

bell *noun* 1 alarm, carillon, chime, knell, peal, ring, signal, tocsin.

belligerent *adjective* 1 aggressive, argumentative, bellicose, hostile, provocative, pugnacious, quarrelsome, truculent. 2 fighting, militant, warmongering, warring.

bellow² *verb* bawl, roar, scream, shout, yell.

belly *noun* abdomen, guts (*informal*), paunch, stomach, tummy (*informal*).

belong *verb* go, have a place. **belong to** 1 be owned by, be the property of. 2 be a member of, be a part of, be associated with.

belongings *plural noun* chattels, effects, gear (*informal*), goods, possessions, property, stuff (*informal*), things (*informal*).

beloved *adjective* adored, cherished, darling, dear, loved, precious, treasured.

below¹ *adverb* beneath, downstairs, downstream, underneath.

below² *preposition* beneath, less than, lower than, under, underneath.

belt¹ *noun* 1 band, cummerbund, girdle, sash, strap. 3 area, district, region, strip, zone.

belt² *verb* 2 beat, flog, hit, lash, strap, thrash, whip.

bemused *adjective* 1 bewildered, confused, perplexed, puzzled.

bench *noun* 1 form, pew, seat, settle. 2 counter, table, work surface, worktop. 3 judges, magistrates.

bend¹ *verb* 1 angle, arch, bow, buckle, contort, curl, curve, distort, flex, kink, loop, turn, twist, veer, warp, wind. 2 bow, crouch, duck, hunch, incline, kneel, lean, stoop.

bend² *noun* angle, arc, corner, crook, curve, kink, loop, turn, twist.

►►DICTIONARY◄◄

bend³ *noun* a kind of knot.

bene- (*say* ben-ee) *prefix* well (as in *benefit, benevolent*). [from Latin *bene* = well]

beneath¹ *preposition* **1** under. **2** unworthy of, *Cheating is beneath you.*

beneath² *adverb* underneath.

benediction *noun* a blessing. [from *bene-* + Latin *dicere* = to say]

benefactor *noun* a person who gives money or other help. [from *bene-*, + Latin *factor* = doer]

beneficial *adjective* having a good or helpful effect; advantageous.

beneficiary (*say* ben-if-**ish**-er-ee) *noun* (*plural* **beneficiaries**) a person who receives benefits, especially from a will.

benefit¹ *noun* **1** something that is helpful or profitable. **2** a payment to which a person is entitled from government funds or from an insurance policy.

benefit² *verb* (**benefited, benefiting**) **1** do good to a person or thing. **2** receive a benefit. [from *bene-*, + Latin *facere* = do]

benevolent *adjective* **1** kind and helpful. **2** formed for charitable purposes, *a benevolent fund.* **benevolently** *adverb*, **benevolence** *noun* [from *bene-*, + Latin *volens* = wishing]

benign (*say* bin-**I**'n) *adjective* **1** kindly. **2** favourable. **3** (of a disease) mild, not malignant. **benignly** *adverb* [from Latin *benignus* = kind-hearted]

benignant (*say* bin-**ig**-nant) *adjective* kindly.

bent¹ *adjective* curved; crooked. **bent on** intending to do something.

bent² *noun* a talent for something.

benzene *noun* a substance obtained from coal-tar and used as a solvent, motor fuel, and in the manufacture of plastics.

benzine *noun* a spirit obtained from petroleum and used in dry cleaning.

bequeath *verb* leave something to a person, especially in a will.

bequest *noun* something bequeathed.

bereaved *adjective* deprived of a relative or friend who has died. **bereavement** *noun* [from *reave* = take forcibly]

bereft *adjective* deprived of something.

beret (*say* **bair**-ay) *noun* a round flat cap.

beriberi (*say as* berry-berry) *noun* a tropical disease caused by a vitamin deficiency. [from a Sinhalese word]

berley *noun* (*Australian*) bait thrown into fishing ground to attract fish.

berry *noun* (*plural* **berries**) any small round juicy fruit without a stone.

berserk (*say* ber-**serk**) *adjective* **go berserk** become uncontrollably violent. [from Icelandic *berserkr* = wild warrior (*ber-* = bear, *serkr* = coat)]

►►THESAURUS◄◄

beneath¹ *preposition* **1** below, under, underneath. **2** unbefitting, unfit for, unworthy of.

benefactor *noun* backer, donor, patron, philanthropist, sponsor, supporter.

beneficial *adjective* advantageous, constructive, favourable, good, helpful, positive, profitable, rewarding, useful, valuable.

beneficiary *noun* heir, heiress, inheritor, legatee, recipient.

benefit¹ *noun* **1** advantage, asset, blessing, boon, help, profit, use. **2** allowance, assistance, dole (*informal*), handout (*informal*), income support, payment.

benefit² *verb* **1** advance, aid, assist, further, help, serve. **2** gain, profit.

benevolent *adjective* **1** benign, caring, charitable, compassionate, friendly, generous, good, gracious, helpful, humane, humanitarian, kind, kindly, liberal, magnanimous, merciful, philanthropic, warm-hearted.

benign *adjective* **1** benevolent, caring, compassionate, genial, gentle, good, gracious, humane, kind, kind-hearted, kindly, lenient, merciful, soft-hearted, sympathetic, tender-hearted, warm-hearted. **3** harmless, non-malignant.

bent¹ *adjective* arched, bowed, contorted, crooked, curved, distorted, hunched, twisted, warped.
bent on determined on, intent on, set on.

bent² *noun* ability, aptitude, flair, gift, inclination, leaning, liking, skill, talent.

bequeath *verb* hand down, leave, make over, pass on, will.

bequest *noun* endowment, gift, inheritance, legacy, settlement.

bereaved *adjective* orphaned, widowed.

bereft *adjective* (*bereft of*) deprived of, devoid of, lacking, robbed of, without.

berserk *adjective* beside yourself, crazy, demented, deranged, frantic, frenzied, insane, mad, maniacal, manic, wild.

▶▶ DICTIONARY ◀◀

berth¹ *noun* **1** a sleeping-place on a ship or train. **2** a place where a ship can moor.
give a wide berth keep at a safe distance from a person or thing.

berth² *verb* moor in a berth.

beryl *noun* a pale-green precious stone.

beseech *verb* (**besought, beseeching**) ask earnestly; implore. [from *be-* + *seek*]

beset *verb* (**beset, besetting**) surround, *They are beset with problems.*

beside *preposition* **1** by the side of; near. **2** compared with.
be beside himself or **herself** etc. be very excited or upset.
beside the point not relevant.

besides *preposition & adverb* in addition to; also, *Who came besides you? And besides, it's the wrong colour.*

besiege *verb* (**besieged, besieging**) **1** surround a place with troops in order to capture it. **2** crowd round, *Fans besieged the pop star after the concert.*

besotted *adjective* infatuated.

besought *past tense of* **beseech**.

best¹ *adjective* most excellent.
best man the bridegroom's chief attendant at a wedding.

best² *adverb* **1** in the best way; most. **2** most usefully; most wisely, *We had best go.*

bestial (*say* **best**-ee-al) *adjective* of or like a beast; cruel. **bestiality** *noun* [from Latin *bestia* = beast]

bestow *verb* present. **bestowal** *noun*

bet¹ *noun* **1** an agreement that you will pay money etc. if you are wrong in forecasting the result of a race etc. **2** the money that you agree to pay in this way.

bet² *verb* (**bet** or **betted, betting**) **1** make a bet. **2** (*informal*) think most likely; predict, *I bet he will forget.*

beta (*say* **beet**-a) *noun* the second letter of the Greek alphabet, = b.

betide *verb* **woe betide you** trouble will come to you. [from *be-*, + an old word *tide* = befall]

betoken *verb* be a sign of.

betray *verb* **1** be disloyal to a person or country etc. **2** reveal something that should have been kept secret. **betrayal** *noun*, **betrayer** *noun* [from *be-*, + Latin *tradere* = hand over]

betrothed *adjective* (*formal*) engaged to be married. **betroth** *verb*, **betrothal** *noun*

better¹ *adjective* **1** more excellent; more satisfactory. **2** recovered from illness.

better² *adverb* **1** in a better way; more. **2** more usefully; more wisely, *We had better go.*

better³ *verb* **1** improve something. **2** do better than. **betterment** *noun*

▶▶ THESAURUS ◀◀

berth¹ *noun* **1** bed, bunk. **2** anchorage, dock, landing stage, moorings, pier, quay, wharf.

berth² *verb* anchor, dock, land, moor, tie up.

beseech *verb* appeal to, ask, beg, entreat, implore, plead with, pray, supplicate.

beside *preposition* **1** alongside, close to, near to, next to.
beside the point immaterial, irrelevant, unconnected.

besides *preposition* apart from, aside from, as well as, excluding, in addition to, not counting.
besides *adverb* also, anyway, furthermore, in addition, in any case, moreover, too.

besiege *verb* **1** blockade, encircle, encompass, lay siege to, surround. **2** assail, badger, beleaguer, beset, harass, hound, pester.

besotted *adjective* enamoured, infatuated, smitten (*informal*).

best¹ *adjective* finest, first-rate, foremost, greatest, leading, optimal, optimum, pre-eminent, superlative, supreme, top, top-notch (*informal*), unequalled, unrivalled, unsurpassed.

bestial *adjective* animal, beastly, brutish, depraved, inhuman, savage, wild.

bestow *verb* award, confer, give, grant, present.

bet¹ *noun* **1** flutter (*informal*), gamble, punt, risk, wager. **2** stake, wager.

bet² *verb* **1** gamble, punt, risk, stake, venture, wager. **2** be certain, be convinced, be sure, predict.

betray *verb* **1** be disloyal to, denounce, dob in (*Australian informal*), double-cross, grass (on) (*slang*), inform on, rat on (*informal*), shop (*informal*), tell on (*informal*). **2** blab, disclose, divulge, expose, give away, let slip, reveal, tell. **betrayal** *noun* denunciation, disloyalty, perfidy, treachery, treason, unfaithfulness.

better¹ *adjective* **1** finer, greater, superior. **2** cured, fitter, healed, healthier, improved, on the mend (*informal*), recovered, stronger, well.
get better convalesce, improve, rally, recover, recuperate.
get the better of beat, conquer, defeat, outdo, outwit, overcome.

better³ *verb* **2** beat, do better than, exceed, improve on, surpass, top.

▶▶ DICTIONARY ◀◀

bettong *noun* (*Australian*) a short-nosed rat-kangaroo.

between *preposition & adverb* **1** within two or more given limits, *between the walls*. **2** connecting two or more people, places, or things, *The train runs between Sydney and Perth*. **3** shared by, *Divide this money between you*. **4** separating; comparing, *Can you tell the difference between them?*

Usage The preposition *between* needs the objective form of a pronoun (*me*, *her*, *him*, *them*, or *us*) after it. The expression 'between you and I' is incorrect; say *between you and me*.

betwixt *preposition & adverb* (*old use*) between.

bevel *verb* (**bevelled**, **bevelling**) give a sloping edge to something.

beverage *noun* any kind of drink.

bevy *noun* (*plural* **bevies**) a large group.

bewail *verb* mourn for something.

beware *verb* be careful, *Beware of pickpockets*. [from *be-*, + *ware* = wary]

bewilder *verb* puzzle someone hopelessly. **bewilderment** *noun* [from *be-*, + an old word *wilder* = lose your way]

bewitch *verb* **1** put a magic spell on someone. **2** delight someone very much.

beyond *preposition & adverb* **1** further than; further on, *Don't go beyond the boundary*. **2** outside the range of; too difficult for, *The problem is beyond me*.

bi- *prefix* two (as in *bicycle*); twice (as in *biannual*). [from Latin *bis* = twice]

biannual *adjective* happening twice a year. **biannually** *adverb*

Usage Do not confuse this word with *biennial*.

bias *noun* (*plural* **biases**) **1** a feeling or influence for or against someone or something; a prejudice. **2** a tendency to swerve. **3** a slanting direction. **biased** *adjective*

bib *noun* **1** a cloth or covering put under a baby's chin during meals. **2** the part of an apron above the waist.

Bible *noun* the sacred book of the Jews (the Old Testament) and of the Christians (the Old and New Testament). [from Greek *biblia* = books (originally = rolls of papyrus from Byblos, a port now in Lebanon)]

biblical *adjective* of or in the Bible.

bibliography (*say* bib-lee-**og**-ra-fee) *noun* (*plural* **bibliographies**) **1** a list of books about a subject or by a particular author. **2** the study of books and their history. **bibliographical** *adjective* [from Greek *biblion* = book, + *graphy*]

bicentenary (*say* by-sen-**teen**-er-ee) *noun* a 200th anniversary. **bicentennial** (*say* by-sen-**ten**-ee-al) *adjective*

biceps (*say* **by**-seps) *noun* the large muscle at the front of the arm above the elbow. [Latin, = two-headed (because its end is attached at two points)]

bicker *verb* quarrel over unimportant things; squabble.

bicuspid *noun* a tooth with two points. [from *bi-*, + Latin *cuspis* = sharp point]

bicycle *noun* a two-wheeled vehicle driven by pedals. **bicyclist** *noun*

bid¹ *noun* **1** the offer of an amount you are willing to pay for something, especially at an auction. **2** an attempt.

▶▶ THESAURUS ◀◀

beverage *noun* drink, liquid, refreshment.

bevy *noun* collection, company, gathering, group, mob (*Australian*).

beware *verb* be careful, be cautious, be on your guard, be wary, look out, mind, take heed, watch out.

bewilder *verb* baffle, bamboozle (*informal*), confound, confuse, nonplus, perplex, puzzle, stump.

bewitch *verb* **1** cast a spell on, jinx (*informal*), point the bone at (*Australian*). **2** beguile, captivate, charm, delight, enchant, enthral, entrance, fascinate, spellbind.

beyond *preposition* **1** farther than, further than, over, past.

bias *noun* **1** favouritism, inclination, leaning, partiality, prejudice, slant. **3** angle, cross, diagonal, slant. **biased** *adjective* distorted, one-sided, partial, prejudiced, slanted, unbalanced, unfair.

Bible *noun* Holy Writ, Scripture, the Scriptures, the Word of God.

bicycle *noun* bike (*informal*), cycle, push-bike (*informal*), two-wheeler (*informal*); (*kinds of bicycle*) BMX, moped, mountain bike, penny farthing, racing bike, tandem.

bid¹ *noun* **1** offer, proposal, submission, tender. **2** attempt, effort, try.

▶▶ DICTIONARY ◀◀

bid² *verb* (**bid**, **bidding**) make a bid. **bidder** *noun*

bid³ *verb* (**bid** (or *old use* **bade**), **bid** or **bidden**, **bidding**) **1** command, *Do as you are bid* or *bidden.* **2** say as a greeting or farewell, *bidding them good night.*

bidding *noun* a command.

bide *verb* (**bided**, **biding**) wait.

bidet (*say* **bee**-day) *noun* a low washbasin to sit on for washing the lower part of the body. [from French *bidet* = a pony]

biennial¹ (*say* by-**en**-ee-al) *adjective* **1** lasting for two years. **2** happening every second year. **biennially** *adverb*

biennial² *noun* a plant that lives for two years, flowering and dying in the second year. [from *bi-*, + Latin *annus* = year]

bier (*say as* beer) *noun* a movable stand on which a coffin or a dead body is placed before it is buried.

bifocal (*say* by-**foh**-kal) *adjective* (of spectacle lenses) made in two sections, with the upper part for looking at distant objects and the lower part for reading.

bifocals *plural noun* bifocal spectacles.

big *adjective* (**bigger**, **biggest**) **1** large. **2** important, *the big match.* **3** more grown-up; elder, *my big sister.*

big smoke (*originally Aboriginal pidgin*) a central town or city.

bigamy (*say* **big**-a-mee) *noun* the crime of marrying a person when you are already married to someone else. **bigamous** *adjective*, **bigamist** *noun* [from *bi-*, + Greek *gamos* = marriage]

bight *noun* **1** a loop of rope. **2** a long inward curve in a coast.

big-note *verb* (*Australian*) exalt (oneself), *Don't believe all he says; he's just big-noting himself.*

bigot *noun* a bigoted person.

bigoted *adjective* narrow-minded and intolerant. **bigotry** *noun*

bike *noun* (*informal*) a bicycle or motorcycle.

bikie *noun* (*Australian slang*) a motorcyclist, especially one of a gang.

bikini *noun* (*plural* **bikinis**) a woman's very small two-piece swim-suit. [named after the island of Bikini in the Pacific Ocean, which was laid bare by an atomic bomb test in 1946]

bikkies *plural noun* (*Australian slang*) money, *big bikkies.* [from *biscuit*]

bilateral *adjective* **1** of or on two sides. **2** of two people or groups, *a bilateral agreement.* [from *bi-* + *lateral*]

bilberry *noun* (*plural* **bilberries**) a small dark-blue edible berry.

bilby *noun* an Australian nocturnal burrowing marsupial with blue-grey fur.

bile *noun* a bitter liquid produced by the liver, helping to digest fats.

bilge *noun* **1** the bottom of a ship; the water that collects there. **2** (*slang*) nonsense; worthless ideas.

bilingual (*say* by-**ling**-gwal) *adjective* **1** written in two languages. **2** able to speak two languages. [from *bi-*, + Latin *lingua* = language]

bilious *adjective* feeling sick; sickly. **biliousness** *noun* [from *bile*]

bilk *verb* cheat someone by not paying them what you owe; defraud.

bill¹ *noun* **1** a written statement of charges for goods or services that have been supplied. **2** a poster. **3** a list; a programme of entertainment. **4** the draft of a proposed law to be discussed by Parliament. **5** (*American*) a banknote.
bill of fare a menu.

bill² *noun* a bird's beak.

billabong *noun* (in Australia) a backwater.

▶▶ THESAURUS ◀◀

bid² *verb* offer, proffer, propose, tender.

bid³ *verb* **1** ask, command, instruct, invite, order, tell. **2** say, tell, wish.

big *adjective* **1** ample, astronomical, broad, bulky, colossal, considerable, enormous, fat, gargantuan, giant, gigantic, ginormous (*slang*), great, hefty, huge, hulking, humungous (*slang*), immeasurable, immense, incalculable, jumbo (*informal*), king-sized, large, lofty, mammoth, massive, mighty, monstrous, monumental, outsize, prodigious, sizeable, spacious, stag-

gering, stupendous, substantial, tall, tidy (*sum*), tremendous, vast. **2** critical, grand, great, important, major, momentous, significant, vital. **3** elder, grown-up, older.

bigoted *adjective* biased, dogmatic, intolerant, narrow-minded, opinionated, prejudiced.

bilious *adjective* ill, nauseous, queasy, sick.

bill¹ *noun* **1** account, invoice, statement, tab (*informal*). **2** advertisement, flyer, notice, placard, poster. **4** draft legislation, proposed legislation. **5** banknote, note.

▶▶ DICTIONARY ◀◀

billet¹ *noun* a lodging for troops, conference delegates or sports teams, especially in a private house.

billet² *verb* (**billeted, billeting**) house someone in a billet.

billiards *noun* a game in which three balls are struck with cues on a cloth-covered table (**billiard-table**). [from French *billard* = cue]

billion *noun* **1** a thousand million (1,000,000,000). **2** a million million. **billionth** *adjective* & *noun* [from *bi-* + *million*]

Usage Although the word originally meant a million million, nowadays it usually means a thousand million.

---

billow¹ *noun* a huge wave.

billow² *verb* rise or roll like waves.

billy *noun* (*plural* **billies**) a pot with a lid, used by campers etc. as a kettle or cooking-pot. **billycan** *noun*

billycart *noun* (*Australian*) a go-cart, a home-made children's vehicle of planks and a box on wheels. [from *billy-goat* and *cart*]

billy-goat *noun* a male goat. (Compare *nanny-goat*.) [from the name *Billy*]

bin *noun* a large or deep container.

binary (*say* **by**-ner-ee) *adjective* involving sets of two; consisting of two parts.
binary digit either of the two digits (0 and 1) used in the system of numbers known as binary notation or the binary scale. [from Latin *binarius* = two together]

bind¹ *verb* (**bound, binding**) **1** fasten material round something. **2** fasten the pages of a book into a cover. **3** tie up; tie together. **4** make somebody agree to do something; oblige. **binder** *noun*
bind a person over make him or her agree not to break the law.

bind² *noun* (*slang*) a nuisance; a bore.

bine *noun* the flexible stem of the hop plant.

binge *noun* (*slang*) an uncontrolled outing or feast.

bingo *noun* a game using cards on which numbered squares are covered up as the numbers are called out at random.

binoculars *plural noun* a device with lenses for both eyes, making distant objects seem nearer. [from Latin *bini* = two together, + *oculus* = eye]

bio- *prefix* life (as in *biology*). [from Greek *bios* = life]

biochemistry *noun* the study of the chemical composition and processes of living things. **biochemical** *adjective*, **biochemist** *noun*

biography (*say* by-**og**-ra-fee) *noun* the story of a person's life. **biographical** *adjective*, **biographer** *noun* [from *bio-* + *-graphy*]

biology *noun* the study of the life and structure of living things. **biological** *adjective*, **biologist** *noun* [from *bio-* + *-logy*]

bionic (*say* by-**on**-ik) *adjective* (of a person or parts of the body) operated by electronic devices. [from *bio-* + electro*nic*]

biopsy (*say* **by**-op-see) *noun* (*plural* **biopsies**) examination of tissue from a living body. [from *bio-* + auto*psy*]

bipartite *adjective* having two parts; involving two groups, *a bipartite agreement*.

biped (*say* **by**-ped) *noun* a two-footed animal. [from *bi-*, + Latin *pedis* = of a foot]

biplane *noun* an aeroplane with two sets of wings, one above the other.

birch *noun* (*plural* **birches**) **1** a deciduous tree with slender branches. **2** a bundle of birch branches for flogging people.

bird *noun* **1** an animal with feathers, two wings, and two legs. **2** (*slang*) a person. **3** (*slang*) a young woman.
bird's-eye view a view from above.

birdie *noun* **1** (*informal*) a bird. **2** a score of one stroke under par for a hole at golf.

▶▶ THESAURUS ◀◀

billet² *verb* accommodate, house, lodge, put up.

billow² *verb* balloon, puff out, rise, roll, surge, swell.

billycart *noun* go-cart, hill trolley.

bin *noun* can, container, crate, receptacle, skip, tin.

bind¹ *verb* **1** bandage, cover, dress, swathe, wrap. **3** attach, connect, fasten, hold together, join, link, secure, strap, tie, truss. **4** compel, constrain, force, oblige, require.
binder *noun* cover, file, folder.

bind² *noun* difficulty, dilemma, fix, jam (*informal*), predicament, quandary, spot (*informal*).

binge *noun* bender (*slang*), fling, orgy, spree.

binoculars *plural noun* field glasses, opera glasses.

biography *noun* life story, memoirs, profile, reminiscences.

bird *noun* **1** birdie (*informal*), chick, cock, fledgeling, fowl, hen, nestling.
bird's-eye view aerial view, overhead view.

►►DICTIONARY◄◄

Biro *noun* (*plural* **Biros**) (*trade mark*) a kind of ballpoint pen. [named after its Hungarian inventor L. Biro]

birth *noun* **1** the process by which a baby or young animal comes out from its mother's body. **2** origin; beginning. **3** parentage, *He is of noble birth.*
birth control ways of avoiding conceiving a baby.
birth rate the number of children born in one year for every 1,000 people.

birthday *noun* the anniversary of the day a person was born.

birthmark *noun* a coloured mark that has been on a person's skin since birth.

birthright *noun* a right or privilege to which a person is entitled through being born into a particular family (especially as the eldest son) or country.

biscuit *noun* a small flat piece of pastry baked crisp. [from Latin *bis* = twice, + *coctus* = cooked]

bisect (*say* by-**sekt**) *verb* divide into two equal parts. **bisection** *noun*, **bisector** *noun* [from *bi*-, + Latin *sectum* = cut]

bishop *noun* **1** an important member of the clergy in charge of all the churches in a city or district. **2** a chess piece shaped like a bishop's mitre.

bishopric *noun* the position or diocese of a bishop.

bismuth *noun* **1** a greyish-white metal. **2** a compound of this used in medicine.

bison (*say* **by**-son) *noun* (*plural* **bison**) a wild ox found in North America and Europe, with a large shaggy head.

bistro *noun* a small restaurant.

bit¹ *noun* **1** a small piece or amount of something. **2** the metal part of a horse's bridle that is put into its mouth. **3** the part of a tool that cuts or grips things when twisted. **4** a short distance or time, *Wait a bit.*
bit by bit gradually.

bit² *past tense* of **bite**.

bit³ *noun* (in computers) a unit of information expressed as a choice between two possibilities. [from *bi*nary dig*it*]

bitch *noun* (*plural* **bitches**) **1** a female dog, fox, or wolf. **2** (*informal*) a spiteful woman. **bitchy** *adjective*

bite¹ *verb* (**bit**, **bitten**, **biting**) **1** cut or take with your teeth. **2** penetrate; sting. **3** accept bait, *The fish are biting.*
bite the dust fall wounded and die.

bite² *noun* **1** biting. **2** a mark or spot made by biting, *an insect bite.* **3** a snack.
put the bite on (*Australian slang*) cadge from someone, scrounge money or food.

bitter *adjective* **1** tasting sharp, not sweet. **2** feeling or causing mental pain or resentment, *a bitter disappointment.* **3** very cold. **bitterly** *adverb*, **bitterness** *noun*

bittern *noun* a marsh bird, the male of which makes a booming cry.

bitumen (*say* **bit**-yoo-min) *noun* **1** a black substance used for covering roads etc. **2** (*Australian*) a tarred road. **bituminous** (*say* bit-**yoo**-min-us) *adjective*

bivalve *noun* a shellfish (e.g. an oyster) that has a shell with two hinged parts.

bivouac¹ (*say* **biv**-oo-ak) *noun* a temporary camp without tents.

bivouac² *verb* (**bivouacked**, **bivouacking**) camp in a bivouac.

►►THESAURUS◄◄

birth *noun* **1** childbirth, confinement, delivery, labour, nativity. **2** beginning, creation, founding, genesis, origin, start. **3** ancestry, blood, descent, extraction, lineage, origin, parentage, pedigree, stock.
give birth to bear, bring forth, deliver, produce, reproduce.

biscuit *noun* bickie (*informal*), cookie, cracker, wafer.

bisect *verb* cut in half, halve.

bistro *noun* bar, brasserie, café, restaurant.

bit¹ *noun* **1** chip, crumb, fragment, iota, jot, morsel, particle, piece, portion, scrap, segment, skerrick (*Australian informal*), slice, speck. **4** jiffy (*informal*), minute, moment, second, tick (*informal*).

bit by bit by degrees, gradually, little by little, progressively.

bitchy *adjective* catty (*informal*), malicious, mean, nasty, spiteful, vindictive.

bite¹ *verb* **1** champ, crunch, gnaw, munch, nibble. **2** nip, sting, wound.

bite² *noun* **2** nip, sting, wound. **3** morsel, mouthful, piece.

bitter *adjective* **1** acrid, harsh, sharp. **2** (*bitter memories*) distressing, galling, heartbreaking, painful, poignant, sad, sorrowful, unpleasant; (*bitter comments*) acrimonious, embittered, hostile, rancorous, resentful, spiteful, vicious, virulent. **3** biting, cold, freezing, harsh, piercing, sharp.

▶▶ D I C T I O N A R Y ◀◀

bizarre (*say* biz-**ar**) *adjective* very odd in appearance or effect.

blab *verb* (**blabbed, blabbing**) tell tales; let out a secret.

Black *noun* a person with a very dark or black skin; an Aboriginal. **Black** *adjective*

black¹ *noun* the very darkest colour, like coal or soot.

black² *adjective* **1** of the colour black. **2** very dirty. **3** dismal; not hopeful, *The outlook is black*. **4** hostile; disapproving, *He gave me a black look*. **blackly** *adverb*, **blackness** *noun*
black coffee coffee without milk.
black economy employment in which payments are concealed to avoid tax.
black eye an eye with a bruise round it.
black hole a region in outer space with such a strong gravitational field that no matter or radiation can escape from it.
black magic evil magic.
black market illegal trading.
black sheep one bad character in a well-behaved group.
black spot a dangerous place.
black stump (*Australian*) a distant edge of settlement.

black³ *verb* make a thing black.
black out cover windows etc. so that no light can penetrate; faint, lose consciousness. **blackout** *noun*

blackberry *noun* (*plural* **blackberries**) a sweet black berry.

blackbird *noun* a European songbird, the male of which is black.

blackboard *noun* a dark board for writing on with chalk.

blacken *verb* **1** make or become black. **2** speak evil of, *blacken someone's character*.

blackguard (*say* **blag**-erd) *noun* a scoundrel.

blackhead *noun* a small black spot in the skin.

blackleg *noun* a person who works while fellow workers are on strike.

blacklist *verb* put someone on a list of those who are disapproved of.

blackmail *verb* demand money etc. from someone by threats. **blackmail** *noun*, **blackmailer** *noun*

blacksmith *noun* a person who makes and repairs iron things, especially one who makes and fits horseshoes.

bladder *noun* **1** the bag-like part of the body in which urine collects. **2** the inflatable bag inside a football.

blade *noun* **1** the flat cutting-part of a knife, sword, axe, etc. **2** the flat wide part of an oar, spade, propeller, etc. **3** a flat narrow leaf, *blades of grass*. **4** a broad flat bone, *shoulder-blade*.

blame¹ *verb* (**blamed, blaming**) **1** say that somebody or something has caused what is wrong, *They blamed me*. **2** find fault with someone, *We can't blame them for wanting a holiday*.

blame² *noun* blaming; responsibility for what is wrong.

blameless *adjective* deserving no blame; innocent.

▶▶ T H E S A U R U S ◀◀

bizarre *adjective* curious, eccentric, fantastic, grotesque, odd, outlandish, peculiar, strange, unusual, weird.

blab *verb* **1** disclose, divulge, let out, reveal. **2** blow the gaff (*slang*), let the cat out of the bag (*informal*), spill the beans (*slang*), squeal (*slang*), tattle, tell, tell tales, tittle-tattle.

black² *adjective* **1** dark, dusky, ebony, inky, jet-black, moonless, pitch-black, raven, sable, sooty, starless, swarthy. **2** blackened, dirty, filthy, grimy, grubby, sooty. **3** depressed, dismal, gloomy, glum, lugubrious, melancholy, sad, sombre. **4** angry, furious, glowering, hostile, menacing, sullen, threatening.

black³ *verb* **black out** collapse, faint, flake out (*informal*), lose consciousness, pass out (*informal*), swoon.

blacken *verb* **1** darken, dirty, soil, stain. **2** defame, denigrate, discredit, libel, malign, slander, smear, speak ill of, sully, tarnish.

blackguard *noun* knave (*old use*), miscreant, rascal, rogue, scoundrel, villain.

blacklist *verb* ban, bar, blackball, boycott, debar, exclude, ostracise, veto.

blackmail *verb* hold to ransom, threaten. **blackmail** *noun* extortion.

blade *noun* **1** cutting edge, edge. **3** frond, leaf, shoot.

blame¹ *verb* **1** accuse, charge, condemn, criticise, find guilty, hold responsible, make accountable, reproach, reprove.

blame² *noun* censure, criticism, culpability, fault, guilt, liability, rap (*informal*), reprimand, reproach, reproof, responsibility.

blameless *adjective* guiltless, innocent, irreproachable, unimpeachable.

▶▶ D I C T I O N A R Y ◀◀

blanch *verb* make or become white or pale, *He blanched with fear.*

blancmange (*say* bla-**monj**) *noun* a jelly-like pudding made with milk. [from French *blanc* = white, + *mange* = eat]

bland *adjective* **1** having a mild flavour not a strong one. **2** gentle and casual; not irritating or stimulating, *a bland manner.* **blandly** *adverb*, **blandness** *noun* [from Latin *blandus* = soothing]

blandishments *plural noun* flattering or coaxing words. [same origin as *bland*]

blank¹ *adjective* **1** not written or printed on; unmarked. **2** without interest or expression, *a blank look.* **3** without an opening, *a blank wall.* **blankly** *adverb*, **blankness** *noun*
blank cartridge a cartridge that makes a noise but does not fire a bullet.
blank cheque a signed cheque with the amount not yet filled in.
blank verse poetry without rhymes.

blank² *noun* **1** an empty space. **2** a blank cartridge. [from French *blanc* = white]

blanket¹ *noun* **1** a warm cloth covering used on a bed etc. **2** any thick soft covering, *a blanket of snow.*

blanket² *adjective* covering a wide range of conditions etc., *a blanket agreement.*

blare *verb* (**blared, blaring**) make a loud harsh sound. **blare** *noun*

blasé (*say* **blah**-zay) *adjective* bored or unimpressed by things because you are used to them. [French]

blaspheme (*say* blas-**feem**) *verb* (**blasphemed, blaspheming**) utter blasphemies. [from Greek *blasphemos* = evil-speaking]

blasphemy (*say* **blas**-fim-ee) *noun* (*plural* **blasphemies**) irreverent talk about sacred things. **blasphemous** *adjective*

blast¹ *noun* **1** a strong rush of wind or air. **2** an explosion. **3** a loud noise, *the blast of the trumpets.*

blast² *verb* blow up with explosives.
blast off launch by the firing of rockets.
blast-off *noun*

blast-furnace *noun* a furnace for smelting ore, with hot air driven in.

blatant (*say* **blay**-tant) *adjective* very obvious, *a blatant lie.* **blatantly** *adverb* [from an old word meaning 'noisy']

blaze¹ *noun* a very bright flame, fire, or light.

blaze² *verb* (**blazed, blazing**) **1** burn or shine brightly. **2** show great feeling, *He was blazing with anger.*

blaze³ *noun* **1** a white mark on an animal's face. **2** a mark chipped in the bark of a tree to show a route.

blaze⁴ *verb* (**blazed, blazing**) mark a tree or route by cutting blazes.
blaze a trail show the way for others to follow.

blazer *noun* a kind of jacket, often with a badge or in the colours of a school or team etc. [from *blaze²*]

bleach¹ *verb* make or become white.

bleach² *noun* (*plural* **bleaches**) a substance used to bleach things.

bleak *adjective* **1** bare and cold, *a bleak hillside.* **2** dreary; miserable, *a bleak future.* **bleakly** *adverb*, **bleakness** *noun*

▶▶ T H E S A U R U S ◀◀

bland *adjective* **1** flavourless, insipid, mild, plain, tasteless, uninteresting, wishy-washy.

blank¹ *adjective* **1** clean, empty, plain, unfilled, unmarked, unused. **2** deadpan, emotionless, expressionless, impassive, poker-faced, vacant, vacuous.

blank² *noun* **1** gap, space, void.

blanket¹ *noun* **1** cover, covering, rug. **2** cloak, covering, layer, mantle, sheet.

blanket² *adjective* comprehensive, general, inclusive, overall.

blare *verb* blast, boom, resound, roar, sound, trumpet.

blasé *adjective* bored, indifferent, nonchalant, unexcited, unimpressed, uninterested.

blasphemy *noun* disrespect, impiety, irreverence, profanity, sacrilege.

blasphemous *adjective* disrespectful, impious, irreligious, irreverent, profane, sacrilegious, ungodly.

blast¹ *noun* **1** draught, gust, rush. **2** detonation, discharge, explosion. **3** blare, boom, honk, toot.

blast² *verb* blow up, destroy, detonate, explode.
blast-off *noun* launch, lift-off, take-off.

blatant *adjective* barefaced, flagrant, obvious, open, overt, unashamed, unconcealed.

blaze¹ *noun* conflagration, fire, flames, inferno.

blaze² *verb* **1** burn, flame, flare, glow, shine.

blazer *noun* coat, jacket.

bleach¹ *verb* blanch, fade, lighten, peroxide, whiten.

bleak *adjective* **1** bare, barren, chilly, cold, desolate, windswept, wintry. **2** black, depressing, dismal, dreary, gloomy, grim, hopeless, unpromising.

▶▶▶ DICTIONARY ◀◀

bleary *adjective* watery and not seeing clearly, *bleary eyes.* **blearily** *adverb*

bleat[1] *noun* the cry of a lamb, goat, or calf.

bleat[2] *verb* make a bleat.

bleed *verb* (**bled, bleeding**) **1** lose blood. **2** draw blood or fluid from.

bleep *noun* a short high sound used as a signal. **bleep** *verb*

blemish *noun* (*plural* **blemishes**) a flaw, a mark that spoils a thing's appearance. **blemish** *verb*

blench *verb* flinch.

blend[1] *verb* mix smoothly or easily. **blender** *noun*

blend[2] *noun* a mixture.

bless *verb* **1** make sacred or holy. **2** bring God's favour on a person or thing.

blessing *noun* **1** a prayer that blesses a person or thing; being blessed. **2** something that people are glad of. **3** approval.

blight[1] *noun* **1** a disease that withers plants. **2** a bad or evil influence.

blight[2] *verb* **1** affect with blight. **2** spoil something.

blind[1] *adjective* **1** without the ability to see. **2** without any thought or understanding, *blind obedience.* **3** (of bulbs) not producing a flower. **4** (in cookery) without a filling, *bake*

the pastry cases blind. **5** (of a passage, or road) closed at one end. **blindly** *adverb*, **blindness** *noun*

blind[2] *verb* make a person blind.

blind[3] *noun* **1** a screen for a window. **2** a deception; something used to hide the truth, *His journey was a blind.*

blindfold *verb* cover someone's eyes with a cloth etc.

blink *verb* shut and open your eyes rapidly. **blink** *noun*

blinkers *plural noun* leather pieces fixed on a bridle to prevent a horse from seeing sideways. **blinkered** *adjective*

bliss *noun* perfect happiness. **blissful** *adjective*, **blissfully** *adverb*

blister *noun* a swelling like a bubble, especially on skin. **blister** *verb*

blithe *adjective* casual and carefree. **blithely** *adverb*

blitz *noun* (*plural* **blitzes**) a sudden violent attack; the bombing of London in 1940. [short for German *blitzkrieg* (*blitz* = lightning, *krieg* = war)]

blizzard *noun* a severe snowstorm.

bloated *adjective* swollen by fat, gas, or liquid.

bloater *noun* a salted smoked herring.

▶▶▶ THESAURUS ◀◀

bleary *adjective* blurred, cloudy, filmy, fuzzy, misty, watery.

bleed *verb* **1** haemorrhage, lose blood.

bleep *noun & verb* beep, signal.

blemish *noun* blotch, defect, discoloration, disfigurement, fault, flaw, imperfection, mark, scar, spot, stain.

blend[1] *verb* combine, fuse, incorporate, integrate, mingle, mix, synthesise.

blend[2] *noun* amalgam, combination, composite, compound, fusion, mix, mixture, synthesis.

bless *verb* **1** consecrate, dedicate, hallow, sanctify.
   blessed *adjective* **1** beatified, consecrated, hallowed, holy, revered, sacred, sanctified. **2** fortunate, happy.

blessing *noun* **1** benediction, grace, prayer, thanksgiving. **2** asset, boon, gift, godsend, help. **3** approval, consent, favour, OK (*informal*), sanction, support.

blight[1] *noun* **1** disease, fungus, mildew, pestilence, rust. **2** affliction, bane, curse, plague, scourge.

blight[2] *verb* **2** damage, dash, frustrate, mar, ruin, spoil, wreck.

blind[1] *adjective* **1** sightless, unsighted, visually impaired. **2** mindless, uncritical, unreasoning, unthinking.
   blind alley cul-de-sac, dead end, no through road.

blind[2] *verb* see DAZZLE.

blind[3] *noun* **1** holland blind, screen, shade, shutter, venetian blind, vertical blind.

blink *verb* flash, flicker, glimmer, shimmer, sparkle, twinkle, wink.

bliss *noun* delight, ecstasy, euphoria, happiness, heaven, joy, paradise, pleasure, rapture.
   blissful *adjective* delightful, happy, heavenly, joyous, rapturous, wonderful.

blister *noun* bubble, swelling.

blithe *adjective* carefree, careless, c⌐ cheerful, gay, happy, heedless, i⌐ joyous, light-hearted, merry, n⌐

blitz *noun* attack, ca⌐ (*informal*), offensiv⌐

bloated *adjecti⌐ puffed u⌐

blob *noun* a small round mass of something, *blobs of paint.*

block¹ *noun* **1** a solid piece of something. **2** an obstruction. **3** a large building divided into flats or offices. **4** a group of buildings. **5** (*Australian*) an area of land divided for settlement. **6** (*Australian*) a plot of land for residential building.
block letters plain capital letters.

block² *verb* obstruct; prevent from moving or being used. **blockage** *noun*

blockade¹ *noun* the blocking of a city or port etc. in order to prevent people and goods from going in or out.

blockade² *verb* (**blockaded, blockading**) set up a blockade of a place.

bloke *noun* (*slang*) a man.

blond or **blonde¹** *adjective* fair-haired; fair. [from Latin *blondus* = yellow]

blonde² *noun* a fair-haired girl or woman.

blood *noun* **1** the red liquid that flows through veins and arteries. **2** family relationship; ancestry, *He is of royal blood.*
in cold blood deliberately and cruelly.

bloodbath *noun* a massacre.

blood-curdling *adjective* horrifying.

bloodhound *noun* a large dog formerly used to track people by their scent.

bloodshed *noun* the killing or wounding of people.

bloodshot *adjective* (of eyes) streaked with red.

bloodthirsty *adjective* eager for bloodshed.

blood-vessel *noun* a tube carrying blood in the body; an artery, vein, or capillary.

bloody *adjective* (**bloodier, bloodiest**) **1** blood-stained. **2** with much bloodshed. **3** (*in strong language*) damned, very great, *Don't be a bloody fool.*
bloody-minded *adjective* deliberately awkward and not helpful.

bloom¹ *noun* **1** a flower. **2** the fine powder on fresh ripe grapes etc.

bloom² *verb* produce flowers.

blossom¹ *noun* a flower or mass of flowers, especially on a fruit-tree.

blossom² *verb* **1** produce flowers. **2** develop into something, *She blossomed into a fine singer.*

blot¹ *noun* **1** a spot of ink. **2** a flaw or fault; something ugly, *a blot on the landscape.*

blot² *verb* (**blotted, blotting**) **1** make a blot or blots on something. **2** dry with blotting-paper.
blot out cross out thickly; obscure, *Fog blotted out the view.*

blotch *noun* (*plural* **blotches**) an untidy patch of colour. **blotchy** *adjective*

blob *noun* bead, dollop, drop, globule, splash, splotch, spot.

block¹ *noun* **1** bar, brick, cake, chock, chunk, cube, hunk, ingot, slab, wedge. **2** barrier, blockade, obstacle, obstruction. **5,6** acreage, allotment, plot, section (*Australian historical*).

block² *verb* bar, blockade, bung up, choke, clog, fill up, halt, hamper, hinder, hold back, impede, jam, obstruct, stop, stop up.
blockage *noun* barrier, block, blockade, bottleneck, impediment, jam, obstacle, obstruction, stoppage.

blockade¹ *noun* barricade, barrier, block, siege.

bloke *noun* boy, chap (*informal*), character, fellow (*informal*), guy (*informal*), man.

blond, blonde¹ *adjective* fair, flaxen, golden, light, tow-coloured.

blood *noun* **1** gore. **2** ancestry, birth, descent, family, kindred, kith and kin, line, lineage, parentage, race, relations, relatives, stock.

blood-curdling *adjective* chilling, frightening, hair-raising, horrific, horrifying, spine-chilling, ᵗ⌐rrifying.

bloodshed *noun* carnage, killing, massacre, murder, slaughter, slaying, wounding.

bloodthirsty *adjective* brutal, ferocious, fierce, homicidal, murderous, sanguinary, savage, vicious.

bloody *adjective* **1** bleeding, bloodstained. **2** cruel, gory, sanguinary, violent.

bloom¹ *noun* **1** blossom, bud, flower.

bloom² *verb* blossom, burgeon, flower.

blossom¹ *noun* bloom, flower.

blossom² *verb* **1** bloom, burgeon, flower. **2** bloom, develop, flourish, grow, thrive.

blot¹ *noun* **1** blotch, mark, smudge, splotch, spot, stain. **2** blemish, defect, eyesore, fault, stain.

blot² *verb* **1** smudge, spot, stain. **2** absorb, dry, soak up.
blot out cover, efface, mask, obliterate, obscure, wipe out.

blotch *noun* blemish, blot, mark, patch, spot.

▶▶ D I C T I O N A R Y ◀◀

blotter *noun* a pad of blotting-paper; a holder for blotting-paper.

blotting-paper *noun* absorbent paper for soaking up ink from writing.

blouse *noun* a garment like a shirt.

blow¹ *verb* (**blew**, **blown**, **blowing**) **1** send out a current of air. **2** (of the wind) move along. **3** move in or with a current of air, *His hat blew off.* **4** make or sound something by blowing, *blow bubbles*; *blow the whistle.* **5** melt with too strong an electric current, *A fuse has blown.* **6** (*slang*) damn, *Blow you!*
blow in (*informal*) arrive unexpectedly. **blow-in** *noun* (*Australian*)
blow up inflate; exaggerate; explode; shatter by an explosion.

blow² *noun* the action of blowing.

blow³ *noun* **1** a hard knock or hit. **2** a shock; a disaster.

blowlamp *noun* a portable device for directing a very hot flame at something.

blowpipe *noun* a tube for sending out a dart or pellet by blowing.

blubber *noun* the fat of whales.

bludge *verb* (*Australian informal*) **1** avoid work or responsibility. **2** impose on other people. **bludge** *noun*, **bludger** *noun*

bludgeon (*say* **bluj**-on) *noun* a short stick with a thickened end, used as a weapon.

blue¹ *noun* the colour of a cloudless sky.
out of the blue unexpectedly.

blue² *adjective* **1** of the colour blue. **2** unhappy; depressed. **3** indecent; obscene, *blue films.* **blueness** *noun*
blue blood aristocratic family.

bluebell *noun* a plant with blue bell-shaped flowers.

bluebottle *noun* **1** a large bluish fly. **2** (*Australian*) a jellyfish with a painful sting.

blueprint *noun* a detailed plan.

blues *noun* a slow sad jazz song or tune.
the blues a very sad feeling; depression.

bluestone *noun* (*Australian*) a building stone.

blue-tongue *noun* an Australian lizard with a cobalt-blue tongue.

bluey *noun* (*Australian*) a bushman's swag.

bluff¹ *verb* deceive someone, especially by pretending to be able to do something.

bluff² *noun* bluffing; a threat that you make but do not intend to carry out. [from Dutch *bluffen* = boast]

bluff³ *adjective* frank and hearty in manner. **bluffness** *noun*

bluff⁴ *noun* a cliff with a broad steep front.

bluish *adjective* rather blue.

blunder¹ *noun* a stupid mistake.

▶▶ T H E S A U R U S ◀◀

blouse *noun* shirt.

blow¹ *verb* **1** breathe out, exhale, puff. **2** blast, bluster, gust, roar, whistle. **3** carry, convey, drive, move, send, sweep, waft. **4** blare, blast, play, sound, toot.
blow out extinguish, put out, snuff.
blow up 1 enlarge, expand, fill, inflate, pump up, swell. **2** exaggerate, magnify, overstate. **3** detonate, explode, go off. **4** blast, bomb, burst apart, destroy, shatter.

blow³ *noun* **1** bang, bash, belt (*slang*), box, buffet, clout (*informal*), hit, king-hit (*Australian informal*), knock, punch, rap, slap, smack, stroke, thump, thwack, wallop (*slang*), whack. **2** body blow, bombshell, calamity, disappointment, disaster, misfortune, setback, shock, upset.

blubber *noun* fat, flab (*informal*).

bludge *verb* **1** idle, loaf, skive (*informal*), slack, take it easy. **2** borrow, cadge, scab (*Australian slang*), scrounge, sponge.
bludger *noun* freeloader (*informal*), hanger-on, idler, layabout, loafer, parasite, shirker, slacker, sponger.

bludgeon *noun* see CLUB¹.

blue² *adjective* **1** aqua, aquamarine, azure, cobalt, indigo, navy (blue), powder blue, Prussian blue, royal blue, sapphire, sky blue, turquoise, ultramarine. **2** depressed, despondent, downcast, down in the dumps (*informal*), gloomy, low, melancholy, sad, unhappy. **3** bawdy, coarse, dirty, indecent, lewd, obscene, risqué, rude.

blueprint *noun* design, outline, pattern, plan, scheme.

bluey *noun* drum (*Australian*), matilda (*Australian*), shiralee (*Australian*), swag (*Australian*).

bluff¹ *verb* deceive, dupe, fake, feign, fool, hoodwink, mislead, pretend, sham, take in, trick.

bluff² *noun* deception, pretence, sham, trick.

bluff⁴ *noun* cliff, escarpment, headland, precipice, scarp.

blunder¹ *noun* blue (*Australian informal*), booboo (*slang*), bungle, clanger (*informal*), gaffe, howler (*informal*), mistake, slip-up (*informal*).

▶▶ D I C T I O N A R Y ◀◀

blunder² *verb* **1** make a blunder. **2** move clumsily and uncertainly.

blunderbuss *noun* an old type of gun that fired many balls in one shot. [from Dutch *donderbus* = thunder-gun]

blunt¹ *adjective* **1** not sharp. **2** speaking in plain terms; straightforward, *a blunt refusal*. **bluntly** *adverb*, **bluntness** *noun*

blunt² *verb* make a thing blunt.

blur¹ *verb* (**blurred, blurring**) make or become indistinct or smeared. **blurred** *adjective*, **blurry** *adjective*

blur² *noun* an indistinct appearance; a smear.

blurt *verb* say something suddenly or tactlessly, *He blurted it out.*

blush¹ *verb* become red in the face because you are ashamed or embarrassed.

blush² *noun* (*plural* **blushes**) reddening in the face.

bluster *verb* **1** blow in gusts; be windy. **2** talk threateningly. **blustery** *adjective*

BMX *abbreviation* a kind of bicycle for use in racing on a dirt track.

boa (*say* **boh**-a) *noun* (also **boa constrictor**) a large South American snake that squeezes its prey so as to suffocate it.

boab *noun* a baobab.

boar *noun* **1** a wild pig. **2** a male pig.

board¹ *noun* **1** a flat piece of wood. **2** a flat piece of stiff material, e.g. a chessboard. **3** daily meals supplied in return for payment or work, *board and lodging*. **4** a committee. **5** (*Australian*) the part of the floor of a shearing-shed where the shearers work. **on board** on or in a ship, aircraft, etc.

board² *verb* **1** go on board a ship, etc. **2** give or get meals and accommodation. **board up** block with fixed boards.

boarder *noun* **1** a pupil who lives at a boarding-school during the term. **2** a lodger who receives meals.

boarding house a house where people obtain board and lodging for payment.

boarding school a school where pupils live during the term.

boast¹ *verb* **1** speak with great pride and try to impress people. **2** have something to be proud of, *The town boasts a fine park*. **boaster** *noun*, **boastful** *adjective*, **boastfully** *adverb*

boast² *noun* a boastful statement.

boat *noun* a hollow structure built to travel on water and carry people etc. **in the same boat** in the same situation; suffering the same difficulties.

boater *noun* a hard flat straw hat.

boating *noun* going out in a boat (especially a rowing-boat) for pleasure.

boatswain (*say* **boh**-sun) *noun* a ship's officer in charge of rigging, boats, anchors, etc.

bob *verb* (**bobbed, bobbing**) move quickly, especially up and down. **bob up** appear suddenly.

bobbin *noun* a small spool holding thread or wire in a machine.

▶▶ T H E S A U R U S ◀◀

blunder² *verb* **2** lumber, lurch, stagger, stumble.

blunt¹ *adjective* **1** dull, unsharpened. **2** abrupt, candid, curt, direct, frank, open, outspoken, upfront (*informal*).

blunt² *verb* dull.

blurred *adjective* blurry, confused, dim, distorted, foggy, fuzzy, hazy, indistinct, misty, out of focus, unclear.

blurt *verb* (**blurt out**) blab, burst out with, call out, utter.

blush¹ *verb* colour, flush, glow, go red, redden.

blustery *adjective* blowy, gusty, rough, squally, stormy, wild, windy.

board¹ *noun* **1** beam, plank, sheet, slat, timber. **4** committee, council, panel.

board² *verb* **1** catch, embark, get on, go on board. **2** live, lodge, reside.

boast¹ *verb* **1** be conceited, blow your own trumpet, brag, congratulate yourself, crow, have tickets on yourself (*Australian informal*), show off, skite (*Australian informal*), swagger, swank (*informal*), talk big (*informal*). **boaster** *noun* braggart, show-off, skite (*Australian informal*). **boastful** *adjective* bragging, cocky (*informal*), conceited, egotistical, proud, swaggering, swanky (*informal*), vain.

boat *noun* craft, vessel; (*various boats*) barge, canoe, catamaran, cutter, dinghy, ferry, gondola, houseboat, hydrofoil, junk, kayak, ketch, launch, lifeboat, motor boat, pontoon, punt, raft, rowing boat, sailing boat, sampan, skiff, sloop, speedboat, trawler, tug, yacht, yawl; see also SHIP¹.

bob *verb* bounce, curtsy, duck, jerk, jig, jump, leap, nod. **bob up** appear, come up, show up, turn up.

bobbin *noun* reel, spool.

▶▶ DICTIONARY ◀◀

bobble *noun* a small round ornament, often made of wool.

bob-sleigh or **bob-sled** *noun* a sledge with two sets of runners.

bode *verb* (**boded, boding**) be a sign or omen of what is to come, *It bodes well.*

bodice *noun* the upper part of a dress.

bodkin *noun* a thick blunt needle for drawing tape etc. through a hem.

body *noun* (*plural* **bodies**) **1** the structure consisting of bones and flesh etc. of a person or animal. **2** the main part of this apart from the head and limbs. **3** a corpse. **4** the main part of something, *a car body.* **5** a group or quantity regarded as a unit, *the school's governing body.* **6** a distinct object or piece of matter, *Stars and planets are heavenly bodies.*
bodily *adjective & adverb*
body surfing surf-riding without a surfboard.

bodyguard *noun* a guard to protect a person's life.

Boer (*say* **boh**-er) *noun* **1** an Afrikaner. **2** (in history) an early Dutch inhabitant of South Africa. [from Dutch, = farmer]

bog *noun* an area of wet spongy ground. **boggy** *adjective*
bogged down stuck and unable to make any progress.

bogey *noun* (*Australian*) a swim or bathe; a swimming hole.

boggle *verb* (**boggled, boggling**) hesitate in fear or doubt, *Our minds boggled at the idea.* [from dialect *bogle* = bogy]

bogus *adjective* not real; sham.

bogy *noun* (*plural* **bogies**) **1** an evil spirit. **2** something that frightens people. **bogyman** *noun* [originally *Old Bogey* = the Devil]

boil[1] *verb* **1** make or become hot enough to bubble and give off steam. **2** cook or wash something in boiling water. **3** be very hot.

boil[2] *noun* **1** an inflamed swelling under the skin. **2** boiling-point, *Bring the milk to the boil.* [from Latin *bulla* = a bubble]

boiler *noun* a container in which water is heated or clothes are boiled.

boisterous *adjective* noisy and lively.

bold *adjective* **1** brave; courageous. **2** impudent. **3** (of colours) strong and vivid. **boldly** *adverb*, **boldness** *noun*

bole *noun* the trunk of a tree.

bollard *noun* **1** a short thick post to which a ship's mooring-rope may be tied. **2** a short post for directing traffic or keeping off a pavement etc.

bolster[1] *noun* a long pillow for placing across a bed under other pillows.

bolster[2] *verb* add extra support.

bolt[1] *noun* **1** a sliding bar for fastening a door. **2** a thick metal pin for fastening things together. **3** a sliding bar that opens and closes the breech of a rifle. **4** a shaft of lightning. **5** an arrow shot from a crossbow. **6** the action of bolting.
a bolt from the blue a surprise, usually an unpleasant one.
bolt upright quite upright.

▶▶ THESAURUS ◀◀

bode *verb* augur, indicate, portend, presage, promise.

body *noun* **1** anatomy, figure, form, frame, physique, shape. **2** torso, trunk. **3** cadaver, carcass, corpse, remains. **4** fuselage, hull, shell. **5** see GROUP[1]. **6** object, thing.
bodily *adjective* corporal, physical.

bodyguard *noun* escort, guard, minder, protector.

bog *noun* fen, marsh, mire, morass, mudflat, quagmire, quicksand, slough, swamp, wetlands.
boggy *adjective* marshy, miry, muddy, spongy, swampy, wet.
bogged down immobilised, impeded, stuck, trapped.

bogus *adjective* counterfeit, fake, false, forged, imitation, phoney (*informal*), sham.

bogyman *noun* bogy, devil, evil spirit, goblin.

boil[1] *verb* **1** bubble, heat, seethe, simmer. **2** cook, simmer, stew.

boil[2] *noun* **1** abscess, carbuncle, gumboil, inflammation, pustule.

boisterous *adjective* active, energetic, exuberant, high-spirited, lively, noisy, rough, rowdy, unruly, vivacious, wild.

bold *adjective* **1** brave, confident, courageous, daring, fearless, game, heroic, intrepid, unafraid, undaunted. **2** assertive, audacious, brazen, cheeky, forward, immodest, impudent, presumptuous, shameless. **3** bright, conspicuous, showy, striking, strong, vibrant, vivid.

bolster[1] *noun* cushion, pillow, support.

bolster[2] *verb* boost, encourage, prop up, reinforce, shore up, strengthen, support.

bolt[1] *noun* **1** bar, catch, latch, lock, snib. **4** flash, shaft.
a bolt from the blue bombshell, shock, surprise, thunderbolt.
bolt upright erect, straight.

▶▶ DICTIONARY ◀◀

bolt² *verb* **1** fasten with a bolt or bolts. **2** run away; (of a horse) run off out of control. **3** swallow food quickly.

bomb¹ *noun* **1** an explosive device. **2** (*Australian slang*) a dilapidated old car.
the bomb an atomic or hydrogen bomb.

bomb² *verb* attack with bombs. **bomber** *noun* [from Greek *bombos* = loud humming]

bombard *verb* **1** attack with gunfire or many missiles. **2** direct a large number of questions or comments etc. at somebody. **bombardment** *noun*

bombastic (*say* bom-**bast**-ik) *adjective* using pompous words.

bombshell *noun* a great shock.

bonanza (*say* bon-**an**-za) *noun* sudden great wealth or luck.

bond¹ *noun* **1** something that binds, restrains, or unites people or things. **2** a document stating an agreement.

bond² *verb* connect or unite with a bond.

bondage *noun* slavery; captivity.

bone¹ *noun* one of the hard parts of a person's or animal's body (excluding teeth, nails, horns, and cartilage).

bone² *verb* (**boned**, **boning**) remove the bones from meat or fish.

bone-dry *adjective* quite dry.

bonfire *noun* an outdoor fire to burn rubbish or celebrate something. [originally *bone fire*, = a fire to dispose of people's or animals' bones]

bonnet *noun* **1** a hat with strings that tie under the chin. **2** a Scottish beret. **3** the hinged cover over a car engine.

bonny *adjective* (**bonnier**, **bonniest**) **1** healthy-looking. **2** (*Scottish*) good-looking. [from French *bon* = good]

bonus (*say* **boh**-nus) *noun* (*plural* **bonuses**) an extra payment or benefit. [from Latin *bonus* = good]

bony *adjective* **1** with large bones; having bones with little flesh on them. **2** full of bones. **3** like bones.

bonzer *adjective* (*Australian slang*) excellent.

boo *verb* shout 'boo' in disapproval.

boobook *noun* a small brown Australian owl with a spotted back and wings.

booby *noun* (*plural* **boobies**) a babyish or stupid person.
booby prize a prize given as a joke to someone who comes last in a contest.
booby trap something designed to hit or injure someone unexpectedly.

book¹ *noun* a set of sheets of paper, usually with printing or writing on them, fastened together inside a cover. **bookseller** *noun*, **bookshop** *noun*, **bookstall** *noun*

▶▶ THESAURUS ◀◀

bolt² *verb* **1** fasten, latch, lock, secure, snib. **2** dart off, dash off, escape, run away, run off, scarper, take off, tear off. **3** gobble, gulp, guzzle, shovel in, wolf.

bomb¹ *noun* **1** device (*euphemism*), explosive, grenade, incendiary, missile. **2** heap (*informal*), jalopy (*informal*), rattletrap (*informal*), rust bucket (*informal*), wreck.

bomb² *verb* attack, blitz, blow up, bombard, shell.

bombard *verb* **1** attack, besiege, blitz, bomb, fire at, pelt, shell. **2** assail, attack, besiege, hound.

bombastic *adjective* extravagant, grandiloquent, grandiose, high-flown, inflated, ostentatious, pompous.

bombshell *noun* bolt from the blue, jolt, shock, surprise.

bonanza *noun* bonus, godsend, windfall.

bond¹ *noun* **1** attachment, connection, link, relationship, tie. **2** agreement, bargain, contract, deal, guarantee.
bonds *plural noun* chains, fetters, handcuffs, manacles, ropes, shackles.

bond² *verb* adhere, bind, cement, connect, fasten, fuse, join, link, stick, tie.

bondage *noun* captivity, enslavement, serfdom, servitude, slavery.

bone² *verb* fillet.

bonnet *noun* **1** cap, hat. **3** hood (*American*).

bonus *noun* addition, bounty, extra, gratuity, perk (*informal*), plus, premium, reward, supplement, tip.

bony *adjective* **1** angular, emaciated, gaunt, lean, raw-boned, scrawny, skinny, thin.

boo *verb* heckle, hoot, jeer, scoff.

book¹ *noun* publication, tome, volume, work; (*kinds of book*) almanac, annual, anthology, atlas, concordance, dictionary, digest, directory, encyclopedia, guidebook, handbook, hymnal, manual, missal, novel, omnibus, primer, textbook, thesaurus, yearbook; (*a book for writing or drawing in*) account book, album, daybook, diary, exercise book, journal, ledger, logbook, memo book, notebook, passbook, pocketbook, scrapbook, sketchbook.

▶▶ DICTIONARY ◀◀

book² *verb* **1** reserve a place in a theatre, hotel, train, etc. **2** write something down in a book or list; enter in a police record, *The police booked him for speeding.*

bookcase *noun* a piece of furniture with shelves for books.

bookkeeping *noun* recording details of buying, selling, etc. **bookkeeper** *noun*

booklet *noun* a small thin book.

bookmaker *noun* a person whose business is taking bets.

bookmark *noun* something to mark a place in a book.

bookworm *noun* **1** a grub that eats holes in books. **2** a person who loves reading.

boom¹ *verb* **1** make a deep hollow sound. **2** be growing and prospering, *Business is booming.*

boom² *noun* **1** a booming sound. **2** prosperity; growth.

boom³ *noun* **1** a long pole at the bottom of a sail to keep it stretched. **2** a long pole carrying a microphone etc. **3** a chain or floating barrier that can be placed across a river or a harbour entrance.

boomerang¹ *noun* a curved wooden missile used by Australian Aborigines, especially one that can be thrown so that it returns to the thrower if it fails to hit anything.

boomerang² *verb* (of a plan) backfire.

boon *noun* a benefit. [from Old Norse *bon* = prayer]

boon companion a friendly companion. [from French *bon* = good]

boor *noun* an ill-mannered person. **boorish** *adjective*

boost¹ *verb* **1** increase the strength, value, or reputation of a person or thing. **2** push something upwards. **booster** *noun*

boost² *noun* **1** an increase. **2** an upward push.

boot *noun* **1** a shoe that covers the foot and ankle or leg. **2** the compartment for luggage in a car. **booted** *adjective*

bootee *noun* a baby's knitted boot.

booth *noun* a small stall or enclosure.

booty *noun* loot.

booze¹ *verb* (**boozed, boozing**) (*slang*) drink alcohol.

booze² *noun* (*slang*) alcoholic drink.

bora *noun* an Aboriginal boys' initiation ceremony.

borak *noun* (*Australian old use*) rubbish. **poke borak at** mock or taunt.

borax *noun* a soluble white powder used in making glass, detergents, etc.

border¹ *noun* **1** the boundary of a country; the part near this. **2** an edge. **3** something placed round an edge to strengthen or decorate it. **4** a strip of ground round a garden or part of it.

border² *verb* put or be a border to something.

borderline¹ *noun* a boundary.

borderline² *adjective* on the boundary between two different groups or kinds of things, *a borderline case.*

▶▶ THESAURUS ◀◀

book² *verb* **1** order, reserve. **2** charge, fine.

booklet *noun* brochure, handbook, handout, leaflet, pamphlet.

boom¹ *verb* **1** echo, resonate, resound, reverberate. **2** expand, flourish, grow, prosper, thrive.

boom² *noun* **1** bang, blast, reverberation, roar, rumble, thunder. **2** expansion, growth, improvement, upturn.

boomerang² *verb* backfire, rebound, recoil.

boon *noun* advantage, asset, benefit, blessing, help.

boost¹ *verb* **1** assist, bolster, encourage, heighten, improve, increase, lift, raise, strengthen. **2** hoist, lift, push, raise.
booster *noun* immunisation, injection, inoculation, jab (*informal*), shot, vaccination.

boost² *noun* assistance, encouragement, help, impetus, shot in the arm, stimulus.

boot *noun* **1** gumboot, wellington; see also SHOE¹. **2** trunk (*American*).

booth *noun* **1** kiosk, stall, stand. **2** box, compartment, cubicle, enclosure.

booty *noun* gains, haul, loot, pickings, plunder, spoils, swag (*informal*), takings.

booze² *noun* alcohol, drink, grog (*Australian*), liquor.

border¹ *noun* **1** boundary, frontier, limit. **2** brink, circumference, edge, margin, perimeter, periphery, rim, verge. **3** binding, edge, edging, frame, frieze, fringe, hem, margin, mount, strip, surround.

border² *verb* abut on, adjoin, be next to, flank.

borderline¹ *noun* boundary, dividing line, limit, threshold.

borderline² *adjective* doubtful, line-ball (*Australian*), marginal, touch-and-go, uncertain.

▶▶ D I C T I O N A R Y ◀◀

bore¹ *verb* (**bored, boring**) **1** drill a hole. **2** get through by pushing.

bore² *noun* **1** the internal width of a gun-barrel. **2** a hole made by boring. **3** (*Australian*) an artesian well.

bore³ *verb* (**bored, boring**) make somebody feel uninterested by being dull.

bore⁴ *noun* a boring person or thing. **boredom** *noun*

bore⁵ *noun* a tidal wave with a steep front that moves up some estuaries.

bore⁶ *past tense* of **bear²**.

born *adjective* **1** have come into existence by birth. (See the note on *borne*) **2** having a certain natural quality or ability, *a born leader*.

borne *past participle* of **bear²**.

> **Usage** The word *borne* is used before *by* or after *have*, *has*, or *had*, e.g. *children borne by Eve; she had borne him a son*. The word *born* is used e.g. in *a son was born*.

boronia *noun* an aromatic Australian shrub. [from Francesco *Borone*, Italian botanist]

borough (*say* **bu**rra) *noun* an important town or district. [from Old English *burg* = fortress or fortified town]

borrow *verb* **1** get something to use for a time, with a promise to give it back afterwards. **2** obtain money as a loan. **borrower** *noun*

bosom *noun* a person's breast.

boss¹ *noun* (*plural* **bosses**) (*informal*) a manager; a person whose job is to give orders to workers etc.

boss² *verb* (*slang*) order someone about. [from Dutch *baas* = master]

boss³ *noun* a round raised knob or stud.

bossy *adjective* (*informal*) fond of ordering people about. **bossiness** *noun*

bot *verb* (*Australian slang*) cadge. **bot on** impose on.

botany *noun* the study of plants. **botanical** *adjective*, **botanist** *noun* [from Greek *botane* = a plant]

botch *verb* spoil something by poor or clumsy work. **botch** *noun*

both¹ *adjective & pronoun* the two; not only one, *Are both films good? Both are old*.

both² *adverb* **both . . . and** not only . . . but also, *The house is both small and ugly*.

bother¹ *verb* **1** cause somebody trouble or worry; pester. **2** take trouble; feel concern, *Don't bother to reply*.

bother² *noun* trouble; worry.

bottle¹ *noun* **1** a narrow-necked container for liquids. **2** (*slang*) courage.

bottle² *verb* (**bottled, bottling**) put or store in bottles. **bottle up** conceal or restrain feelings, etc.

bottlebrush *noun* **1** a cylindrical brush for washing bottles. **2** an Australian plant with flowers resembling a bottlebrush.

▶▶ T H E S A U R U S ◀◀

bore¹ *verb* **1** drill, gouge, penetrate, perforate, pierce.

bore² *noun* **1** calibre, diameter, gauge.

bore³ *verb* send to sleep, tire, weary. **bored** *adjective* blasé, fed up, jack (*Australian slang*), jaded, tired. **boring** *adjective* dreary, dull, monotonous, repetitious, routine, soul-destroying, tedious, tiresome, unexciting, uninteresting.

boredom *noun* apathy, dreariness, dullness, monotony, tedium.

borrow *verb* be lent, have the loan of; see also CADGE.

bosom *noun* breasts, bust, chest.

boss¹ *noun* administrator, chief, director, employer, foreman, governor (*slang*), head, leader, manager, master, overseer, proprietor, superintendent, supervisor.

boss² *verb* control, give orders to, order about, push around, tell what to do.

bossy *adjective* autocratic, despotic, dictatorial, domineering, imperious, masterful, officious, overbearing, tyrannical.

botch *verb* bungle, make a hash of (*informal*), make a mess of, mess up, muck up (*informal*), muff (*informal*), ruin, spoil, wreck.

bother¹ *verb* **1** annoy, concern, disconcert, distress, disturb, harass, hassle (*informal*), hound, irritate, nag, perturb, pester, plague, put out (*informal*), trouble, upset, worry. **2** care, concern yourself, take the time, take the trouble, trouble yourself.

bother² *noun* difficulty, fuss, hassle (*informal*), inconvenience, irritation, nuisance, pest, problem, to-do, trouble, worry.

bottle¹ *noun* **1** carafe, container, cruet, decanter, flagon, flask, magnum, phial, vial.

bottle² *verb* **bottle up** conceal, hide, keep back, suppress.

▶▶ D I C T I O N A R Y ◀◀

bottleneck *noun* a narrow place where something (especially traffic) cannot flow freely.

bottler *noun* (*Australian slang*) an admirable or unusual person or thing.

bottom[1] *noun* **1** the lowest part; the base. **2** the part furthest away, *the bottom of the garden.* **3** a person's buttocks.

bottom[2] *adjective* lowest, *the bottom shelf.*

bottomless *adjective* extremely deep.

boudoir (*say* **boo**-dwar) *noun* a woman's private room. [from French, = place to sulk in]

bough *noun* a large branch coming from the trunk of a tree.

boulder *noun* a very large smooth stone.

boulevard (*say* **bool**-ev-ard) *noun* a wide street, often with trees. [French]

bounce[1] *verb* (**bounced, bouncing**) **1** spring back when thrown against something. **2** cause a ball etc. to bounce. **3** (*slang,* of a cheque) be sent back by the bank as worthless. **4** jump suddenly; move in a lively manner. **bouncer** *noun*

bounce[2] *noun* **1** the action or power of bouncing. **2** a lively confident manner, *full of bounce.* **bouncy** *adjective*

bound[1] *verb* jump or spring; run with jumping movements, *bounding along.*

bound[2] *noun* a bounding movement.

bound[3] *past tense* of **bind**.

bound[4] *adjective* obstructed or hindered by something, *We were fog-bound.*
bound to certain to, *He is bound to fail.*
bound up with closely connected with, *Happiness is bound up with success.*

bound[5] *adjective* going towards something, *We are bound for Spain.*

bound[6] *verb* limit; be the boundary of, *Their land is bounded by the river.*

boundary *noun* (*plural* **boundaries**) **1** a line that marks a limit. **2** a hit to the boundary of a cricket field. [from *bound*[6]]

bounden *adjective* obligatory, *your bounden duty.* [from *bind*[1]]

boundless *adjective* unlimited.

bounds *plural noun* limits. [from *bound*[6]]
out of bounds where you are not allowed to go.

bountiful *adjective* **1** plentiful; abundant, *bountiful harvest.* **2** giving generously.

bounty *noun* (*plural* **bounties**) **1** a generous gift. **2** generosity in giving things. **3** a reward for doing something. [from Latin *bonitas* = goodness]

bouquet (*say* boh-**kay**) *noun* a bunch of flowers. [French, = group of trees]

bout *noun* **1** a boxing or wrestling contest. **2** a period of exercise or work or illness, *a bout of flu.*

▶▶ T H E S A U R U S ◀◀

bottleneck *noun* blockage, hold-up, jam, obstruction.

bottom[1] *noun* **1** base, bed, depths, floor, foot, foundation, pedestal, support, underneath, underside. **3** backside (*informal*), behind (*informal*), bum (*slang*), butt (*slang*), buttocks, posterior, rear (*informal*), rump, seat.

bottom[2] *adjective* base, ground, lowest.

bottomless *adjective* deep, inexhaustible, infinite.

bough *noun* branch, limb.

boulder *noun* gibber (*Australian*), rock, stone.

boulevard *noun* avenue, parade, road, street.

bounce[1] *verb* **1** rebound, recoil, ricochet. **4** bob, bound, hop, jump, leap, spring.

bouncy *adjective* elastic, resilient, springy.

bound[1] *verb* bob, bounce, gallop, hurdle, jump, leap, lope, spring, vault.

bound[2] *noun* bob, bounce, gallop, hurdle, jump, leap, lope, spring, vault.

bound[4] *adjective* confined, restricted, tied.
bound to certain to, destined to, sure to.

bound[5] *adjective* (*bound for*) destined for, en route for, heading for, off to, travelling to.

bound[6] *verb* border, circumscribe, enclose, limit, surround.

boundary *noun* **1** border, borderline, bounds, circumference, confines, demarcation, edge, fringes, frontier, limit, margin, perimeter, threshold.

boundless *adjective* endless, infinite, limitless, unbounded, unlimited, vast.

bounds *plural noun* boundaries, limitations, limits.
out of bounds off limits.

bountiful *adjective* **1** abundant, ample, copious, lavish, plentiful, prolific. **2** generous, lavish, liberal, munificent, open-handed, unstinting.

bounty *noun* **2** benevolence, charity, generosity, goodness, kindness, largesse, liberality, philanthropy. **3** gift, gratuity, premium, reward.

bouquet *noun* bunch, corsage, posy, spray.

bout *noun* **1** competition, contest, fight, match, round. **2** attack, fit, period, session, spell, stint, stretch, turn.

boutique (*say* boo-**teek**) *noun* a small shop selling fashionable clothes. [French]

bovine (*say* **boh**-vyn) *adjective* of or like oxen. [from Latin *bovis* = of an ox]

bow¹ (*rhymes with* go) *noun* **1** a strip of wood curved by a tight string joining its ends, used for shooting arrows. **2** a wooden rod with horsehair stretched between its ends, used for playing a violin etc. **3** a knot made with loops. **bow-legged** *adjective* bandy.
bow-tie *noun* a man's necktie tied into a bow.
bow-window *noun* a curved window.

bow² (*rhymes with* cow) *verb* **1** bend your body forwards to show respect or as a greeting. **2** bend downwards, *bowed by the weight*.

bow³ *noun* bowing your body.

bow⁴ (*rhymes with* cow) *noun* the front part of a ship.

bowel *noun* the intestine. [from Latin *botellus* = little sausage]

bower *noun* a leafy shelter; a summer house.

bowerbird *noun* **1** an Australian bird which decorates its nest with feathers, shells, etc. **2** someone who collects and hoards things.

bowl¹ *noun* **1** a rounded usually deep container for food or liquid. **2** the rounded part of a spoon or tobacco-pipe etc.

bowl² *noun* a ball used in the game of **bowls** or in bowling, when heavy balls are rolled towards a target.

bowl³ *verb* **1** send a ball to be played by a batsman; get a batsman out by bowling. **2** send a ball etc. rolling.

bowler¹ *noun* a person who bowls.

bowler² *noun* (also **bowler hat**) a man's stiff felt hat with a rounded top.

bowyang *noun* (*Australian*) a string or narrow strap tied round a trouser leg below the knee.

box¹ *noun* (*plural* **boxes**) **1** a container made of wood, cardboard, etc., usually with a top or lid. **2** a compartment in a theatre, lawcourt, etc., *witness-box*. **3** a hut or shelter, *sentry-box*. **4** a small evergreen shrub. **5** an Australian tree with similar hard wood.
box number the number of a pigeonhole to which letters may be addressed in a newspaper office or post office.
out of the box (*Australian*) excellent.
the box (*informal*) television.

box² *verb* put something into a box.

box³ *verb* **1** fight with the fists. **2** slap, *box someone's ears*.

boxer *noun* **1** a person who boxes. **2** a dog that looks like a bulldog.

Boxing Day the day after Christmas Day. [from the old custom of giving presents (*Christmas boxes*) to tradesmen and servants on that day]

box-office *noun* an office for booking seats at a theatre or cinema etc.

boy *noun* **1** a male child. **2** a young man.
boyhood *noun*, **boyish** *adjective*

boycott *verb* refuse to use or have anything to do with, *They boycotted the buses when the fares went up*. **boycott** *noun* [from the name of Captain Boycott, a harsh landlord in Ireland whose tenants in 1880 refused to deal with him]

bow² *verb* **1** bend, bob, curtsy, genuflect, kneel, nod, salaam, stoop.

bow⁴ *noun* fore, front, prow.

bowel *noun* (*bowels*) entrails, guts, innards (*informal*), insides (*informal*), intestines, viscera.

bower *noun* arbour, gazebo, pavilion, pergola, shelter, summer house.

bowl¹ *noun* **1** basin, dish, tureen.

bowl³ *verb* **1** deliver, fling, hurl, lob, pitch, throw, toss.
bowl over flabbergast, floor, overwhelm, stun, surprise.

box¹ *noun* **1** carton, case, chest, coffer, container, crate, pack, package, receptacle, trunk. **2** compartment, stall, stand. **3** booth, cabin, cubicle, hut, shelter.

box² *verb* **box in** box up, confine, coop up, enclose, hem in, shut in, surround.

box³ *verb* **1** fight, spar. **2** clout (*informal*), cuff, punch, slap, thump; see also HIT¹.

boxer *noun* **1** fighter, prizefighter, pugilist, sparring partner.

boy *noun* child, fellow, guy (*informal*), kid (*informal*), lad, male, schoolboy, youngster, youth.
boyish *adjective* childish, childlike, immature, juvenile, young, youthful.

boycott *verb* avoid, ban, blacklist, ostracise, shun, stay away from.
boycott *noun* ban, blacklist, embargo, prohibition.

▶▶ D I C T I O N A R Y ◀◀

boyfriend *noun* a boy that a girl regularly goes out with.

bra *noun* a brassière.

brace¹ *noun* **1** a device for holding things in place. **2** a pair, *a brace of pheasants*.

brace² *verb* (**braced, bracing**) support; make a thing firm against something. [from Latin *bracchia* = arms]

bracelet *noun* an ornament worn round the wrist. [same origin as *brace*]

braces *plural noun* straps to hold trousers up, passing over the shoulders.

bracing *adjective* invigorating.

bracken *noun* **1** a large fern. **2** a mass of ferns.

bracket¹ *noun* **1** a mark used in pairs to enclose words or figures, *There are round brackets ( ) and square brackets [ ]*. **2** a support attached to a wall etc. **3** a group or range between certain limits, *a high income bracket*.

bracket² *verb* (**bracketed, bracketing**) **1** enclose in brackets. **2** put things together because they are similar.

brackish *adjective* (of water) slightly salt.

bract *noun* a leaf-like part of a plant that is often coloured like a petal.

bradawl *noun* a small tool for boring holes.

brae (*say* bray) *noun* (*Scottish*) a hillside.

brag *verb* (**bragged, bragging**) boast.

braggart *noun* a person who brags.

brahmin *noun* a member of the highest Hindu class, originally priests. [from Sanskrit *brahman* = priest]

braid¹ *noun* **1** a plait of hair. **2** a strip of cloth with a woven decorative pattern, used as trimming.

braid² *verb* **1** plait. **2** trim with braid.

Braille *noun* a system of representing letters etc. by raised dots which blind people can read by feeling them. [named after Louis Braille, a blind French teacher who invented it in about 1830]

brain *noun* **1** the organ inside the top of the head that controls the body. **2** the mind; intelligence.

brainwash *verb* force a person to give up one set of ideas or beliefs and accept new ones; indoctrinate.

brainwave *noun* a sudden bright idea.

brainy *adjective* clever; intelligent.

braise *verb* (**braised, braising**) cook slowly in a little liquid in a closed container. [from French *braise* = burning coals]

brake¹ *noun* a device for slowing or stopping something.

brake² *verb* (**braked, braking**) use a brake.

bramble *noun* a blackberry bush or a prickly bush like it.

bran *noun* ground-up husks of grain.

branch¹ *noun* (*plural* **branches**) **1** a woody arm-like part of a tree or shrub. **2** a part of a railway, road, or river etc. that leads off from the main part. **3** a shop or office etc. that belongs to a large organisation.

branch² *verb* form a branch.
  branch out start something new. [from Latin *branca* = a paw]

▶▶ T H E S A U R U S ◀◀

boyfriend *noun* admirer, beau, date (*informal*), escort, fellow, male companion, suitor, swain (*poetical*).

brace¹ *noun* **1** bracket, buttress, calliper, prop, splint, stay, strut, support. **2** couple, pair.

brace² *verb* reinforce, shore up, strengthen, support, tighten.
  brace yourself prepare yourself, steady yourself, steel yourself.

bracelet *noun* armlet, bangle, wristlet.

braces *plural noun* straps, suspenders (*American*).

bracing *adjective* invigorating, refreshing, stimulating.

bracket¹ *noun* **1** brace, parenthesis. **2** shelf, support. **3** category, class, division, group, range, set.

brackish *adjective* briny, slightly saline, slightly salty.

brag *verb* blow your own trumpet (*informal*), boast, crow, show off, skite (*Australian informal*), swagger, swank (*informal*).

braid¹ *noun* **1** plait. **2** ribbon, trimming.

brain *noun* **2** intellect, intelligence, mind, reason, sense, wit.

brainwash *verb* condition, indoctrinate.

brainwave *noun* brainstorm, idea, inspiration, thought.

brainy *adjective* bright, brilliant, clever, gifted, intellectual, intelligent, smart, studious.

brake² *verb* halt, pull up, slow down, stop.

branch¹ *noun* **1** bough, limb, offshoot. **2** (*of a river*) anabranch, arm, billabong, distributary. **3** arm, department, division, office, part, section, subdivision.

branch² *verb* divide, fork, split, subdivide.
  branch out diversify, expand, extend, open out, spread.

► ► DICTIONARY ◄ ◄

brand¹ *noun* **1** a particular make of goods. **2** a mark made by branding. **3** a piece of burning wood.

brand² *verb* **1** mark cattle or sheep etc. with a hot iron to identify them. **2** sell goods under a particular trade mark.

brandish *verb* wave something about.

brand-new *adjective* completely new.

brandy *noun* (*plural* **brandies**) a strong alcoholic drink. [from Dutch *brandewijn* = burnt (distilled) wine]

brash *adjective* **1** impudent. **2** reckless.

brass *noun* (*plural* **brasses**) **1** a metal that is an alloy of copper and zinc. **2** wind instruments made of brass, e.g. trumpets and trombones. **brass** *adjective*, **brassy** *adjective*

brassière (*say* **bras**-ee-air) *noun* a piece of underwear worn by women to support their breasts. [French]

brat *noun* (*contemptuous*) a child.

bravado (*say* brav-**ah**-doh) *noun* a display of boldness. [from Spanish *bravata*]

brave¹ *adjective* **1** having or showing courage. **2** spectacular, *a brave show of poppies*. **bravely** *adverb*, **bravery** *noun*

brave² *noun* an American-Indian warrior.

brave³ *verb* (**braved, braving**) face and endure something bravely.

bravo (*say* **brah**-voh) *interjection* well done!

brawl¹ *noun* a noisy quarrel or fight.

brawl² *verb* take part in a brawl.

brawn *noun* **1** muscular strength. **2** cold boiled pork or veal pressed in a mould.

brawny *adjective* strong and muscular.

bray *noun* the loud harsh cry of a donkey. **bray** *verb*

brazen¹ *adjective* **1** made of brass. **2** shameless, *brazen impudence*.

brazen² *verb* **brazen it out** behave as if there is nothing to be ashamed of when you know you have done wrong.

brazier (*say* **bray**-zee-er) *noun* a metal framework for holding burning coals.

breach¹ *noun* (*plural* **breaches**) **1** the breaking of an agreement or rule etc. **2** a broken place; a gap.

breach² *verb* break through; make a gap.

bread *noun* a food made by baking flour and water, usually with yeast. **breadcrumbs** *noun*

breadth *noun* width; broadness.

breadwinner *noun* the member of a family who earns money to support the others.

break¹ *verb* (**broke, broken, breaking**) **1** divide or fall into pieces by hitting or pressing. **2** fail to keep a promise or law etc. **3** stop for a time; end, *She broke her silence*. **4** change, *the weather broke*. **5** damage; stop working

► ► THESAURUS ◄ ◄

brand¹ *noun* **1** make, marque, sort, trade mark, type.

brand² *verb* **1** identify, label, mark, stamp.

brandish *verb* flourish, swing, wave.

brash *adjective* **1** arrogant, audacious, bold, brazen, bumptious, cocky (*informal*), impertinent, impudent, self-assertive.

bravado *noun* boldness, daring, front, show, showing off.

brave¹ *adjective* **1** bold, courageous, daring, dauntless, fearless, gallant, game, heroic, intrepid, lion-hearted, plucky, undaunted, valiant.
bravery *noun* boldness, courage, daring, fearlessness, fortitude, gallantry, grit (*informal*), guts (*informal*), heroism, intrepidity, mettle, nerve, pluck, prowess, valour.

brave² *noun* fighter, warrior.

brave³ *verb* defy, endure, face, weather, withstand.

brawl¹ *noun* clash, confrontation, fight, fisticuffs, free-for-all, mêlée, punch-up

(*informal*), quarrel, row, scrap (*informal*), scuffle, set-to (*informal*), skirmish, stoush (*Australian slang*), struggle, tussle.

brawny *adjective* beefy, burly, hefty, muscular, nuggety (*Australian*), sinewy, stocky, strong, sturdy, thickset.

bray *noun* hee-haw, neigh, whinny.

brazen¹ *adjective* **2** audacious, bold, cheeky, forward, impertinent, impudent, insolent, saucy, shameless, unashamed.

breach¹ *noun* **1** breaking, contravention, infringement, transgression, violation. **2** aperture, break, crack, fissure, gap, hole, opening, space, split.

breadth *noun* broadness, extent, magnitude, range, scope, span, spread, thickness, width.

break¹ *verb* **1** burst, bust (*informal*), collapse, come apart, crack, crash, crumble, damage, demolish, destroy, disintegrate, fall apart, fracture, fragment, ruin, shatter, smash, snap, splinter, split, wreck; see also DIVIDE. **2** breach, contravene, disobey, flout, go back on, infringe,

▶▶ D I C T I O N A R Y ◀◀

properly. **6** (of waves) fall in foam. **7** go suddenly or with force, *They broke through*. **8** appear suddenly, *Dawn had broken*. **9** do better than, *break a record*. **breakage** *noun*

break down stop working properly; collapse.

break in force one's way into a building; accustom to a new routine. **break-in** *noun*

break out begin suddenly; escape.

break the news make something known.

break up break into small parts; separate at the end of a school term; (of a couple) separate. **break-up** *noun*

break² *noun* **1** a broken place; a gap. **2** an escape; a sudden dash. **3** a short rest from work. **4** a number of points scored continuously in snooker etc. **5** (*informal*) a piece of luck; an opportunity.

break of day dawn.

breakable *adjective* able to be broken.

breakdown *noun* **1** breaking down; failure. **2** collapse of mental or physical health. **3** an analysis of accounts or statistics.

breaker *noun* a large wave breaking on the shore.

breakfast *noun* the first meal of the day. [from *break + fast³*]

breakneck *adjective* dangerously fast.

breakthrough *noun* an important advance or achievement.

breakwater *noun* a wall built out into the sea to protect a coast from heavy waves.

breakwind *noun* (*Australian*) a shelter, a wind-break.

bream *noun* (*plural* **bream**) a kind of fish with an arched back.

breast *noun* **1** one of the two parts on the upper front of a woman's body that produce milk to feed a baby. **2** a person's or animal's chest.

breastbone *noun* the flat bone down the centre of the chest or breast.

breastplate *noun* a piece of armour covering the chest.

breath (*say* breth) *noun* **1** air drawn into the lungs and sent out again. **2** a gentle blowing, *a breath of wind*.

out of breath panting.

take your breath away surprise or delight you greatly.

under your breath in a whisper.

breathalyser *noun* a device for measuring the amount of alcohol in a person's breath. **breathalyse** *verb* [from *breath + analyse*]

breathe (*say* bree*th*) *verb* (**breathed, breathing**) **1** take air into the body and send it out again. **2** speak; utter, *Don't breathe a word of this*.

breather (*say* **bree**-ther) *noun* a pause for rest, *Let's take a breather*.

breathless *adjective* out of breath.

▶▶ T H E S A U R U S ◀◀

renege on, transgress, violate. **3** adjourn, discontinue, interrupt, pause, stop. **9** beat, exceed, outdo, outstrip, surpass.

break down 1 conk out (*informal*), fail, go bung (*Australian informal*), go on the blink (*informal*), malfunction, pack up (*informal*), seize up, stop working. **2** burst into tears, collapse, crack up (*informal*), cry, go to pieces (*informal*), weep.

break in 1 barge in, burst in, butt in, interrupt, intrude. **2** discipline, tame, train.

break-in *noun* burglary, forced entry, robbery.

break out 1 begin, commence, erupt, start. **2** bolt, escape, flee, get away, take flight.

break up divorce, part, separate, split up.

break-up *noun* breakdown, collapse, dissolution, failure, separation, split-up.

break² *noun* **1** breach, breakage, burst, chink, cleft, crack, discontinuity, fissure, fracture, gap, gash, hole, leak, opening, rent, rift, rupture, slit, smash, space, split, tear. **2** bolt, dash, escape, run. **3** breather, hiatus, interlude, intermission, interruption, interval, let-up (*informal*), lull, pause, playtime, recess, respite, rest, smoko

(*Australian informal*), spell (*Australian*); see also HOLIDAY. **5** chance, opening, opportunity.

breakable *adjective* brittle, delicate, flimsy, fragile, weak.

breakdown *noun* **1** collapse, crash (*Computing*), failure, hitch, malfunction, stoppage. **3** analysis, dissection, itemisation, run-down.

breakneck *adjective* dangerous, fast, headlong, reckless.

breakthrough *noun* advance, development, discovery, progress.

breakwater *noun* jetty, mole, pier.

breast *noun* **2** bosom, bust, chest.

breath *noun* **1** exhalation, gasp, inhalation, pant, puff, respiration.

breathe *verb* **1** exhale, inhale, pant, puff, respire. **2** let out, utter, whisper.

breather *noun* break, interval, pause, recess, rest, spell (*Australian*).

breathless *adjective* gasping, out of breath, panting, puffed, short of breath, winded.

breathtaking *adjective* very surprising or delightful.

breech *noun* (*plural* **breeches**) the back part of a gun-barrel, where the bullets are put in.

breeches (*say* **brich**-iz) *plural noun* trousers reaching to just below the knees.

breed¹ *verb* (**bred, breeding**) **1** produce young creatures. **2** keep animals so as to produce young ones from them. **3** bring up; train. **4** create; produce, *Poverty breeds illness.* **breeder** *noun*

breed² *noun* a variety of animals with qualities inherited from their parents.

breeze *noun* a wind. **breezy** *adjective*

breeze-block *noun* a lightweight building-block made of cinders and cement.

brethren *plural noun* (*old use*) brothers.

breve (*say* breev) *noun* a note in music, equal to two semibreves in length.

brevity *noun* shortness; briefness.

brew¹ *verb* **1** make beer or tea. **2** develop, *Trouble is brewing.*

brew² *noun* a brewed drink.

brewer *noun* a person who brews beer for sale.

brewery *noun* (*plural* **breweries**) a place where beer is brewed.

briar *noun* a brier.

bribe¹ *noun* money or a gift offered to a person to influence him or her.

bribe² *verb* (**bribed, bribing**) give someone a bribe. **bribery** *noun*

brick¹ *noun* **1** a small hard block of baked clay etc. used to build walls. **2** a rectangular block of something.

brick² *verb* close something with bricks, *We bricked up the gap in the wall.*

bricklayer *noun* a worker who builds with bricks.

bride *noun* a woman on her wedding-day. **bridal** *adjective* [from Old English *bryd*]

bridegroom *noun* a man on his wedding-day.

bridesmaid *noun* a girl or unmarried woman who attends the bride at a wedding.

bridge¹ *noun* **1** a structure built over and across a river, railway, or road etc. to allow people to cross it. **2** a high platform above a ship's deck, for the officer in charge. **3** the bony upper part of the nose. **4** something that connects things. **5** a card game rather like whist.

bridge² *verb* (**bridged, bridging**) make or form a bridge over something.

bridle *noun* the part of a horse's harness that fits over its head.

bridle-path or **bridle-road** *noun* a road suitable for horses but not for vehicles.

brief¹ *adjective* short. **briefly** *adverb*, **briefness** *noun*
in brief in a few words.

brief² *noun* instructions and information given to someone, especially to a barrister.

breathtaking *adjective* amazing, astounding, awe-inspiring, exciting, overwhelming, spectacular, stupendous.

breed¹ *verb* **1** bear young, multiply, procreate, produce young, reproduce. **2** propagate, raise, rear. **3** bring up, develop, educate, nurture, raise, rear, train. **4** create, engender, generate, give rise to, lead to, produce, result in, yield.

breed² *noun* kind, sort, strain, type, variety.

breeze *noun* draught, wind, zephyr.
breezy *adjective* airy, blowy, draughty, fresh, windy.

brevity *noun* briefness, conciseness, curtness, shortness, succinctness, terseness.

brew¹ *verb* **1** (*brew tea*) infuse, prepare; (*brew beer*) ferment, make. **2** develop, fester, gather force, hatch.

bribe¹ *noun* backhander (*informal*), carrot, enticement, graft (*informal*), hush money, incentive, inducement, kickback (*informal*), pay-off (*informal*), sling (*Australian informal*), sweetener (*informal*).

bribe² *verb* buy, buy off, corrupt, grease someone's palm (*slang*), influence, pervert, sling (*Australian informal*), tempt.

bridal *adjective* marriage, matrimonial, nuptial, wedding.

bridge¹ *noun* **1** crossing, span; (*kinds of bridge*) aqueduct, drawbridge, flyover, footbridge, overpass, pontoon bridge, suspension bridge, swing bridge, viaduct. **4** bond, connection, link, tie.

bridge² *verb* cross, extend across, span, straddle, traverse.

brief¹ *adjective* (*a brief report*) abridged, concise, short, succinct, terse; (*brief happiness*) ephemeral, fleeting, momentary, passing, short-lived, temporary, transient, transitory.
in brief briefly, concisely, in a nutshell, in short, in summary, succinctly.

brief² *noun* directions, guidelines, instructions.

DICTIONARY

brief³ *verb* **1** to give a brief to a barrister. **2** instruct or inform someone concisely in advance. [from Latin *brevis* = short]

briefcase *noun* a flat case for carrying documents etc.

briefing *noun* a meeting to give someone concise instructions or information.

briefs *plural noun* very short knickers or underpants.

brier *noun* **1** a thorny bush, especially the wild rose. **2** a hard root used especially for making tobacco-pipes.

brigade *noun* **1** a large unit of an army. **2** a group of people organised for a special purpose, *the fire brigade*. [from Italian *brigata* = a troop]

brigadier *noun* a brigade-commander.

brigand *noun* a member of a band of robbers.

bright *adjective* **1** giving a strong light; shining. **2** (of colour) intense, strong. **3** sunny. **4** clever. **5** cheerful. **brightly** *adverb*, **brightness** *noun*

brighten *verb* **1** make or become brighter. **2** make or become more cheerful.

brilliant *adjective* **1** very bright; sparkling. **2** very clever. **brilliantly** *adverb*, **brilliance** *noun* [from Italian *brillare* = shine]

brim¹ *noun* **1** the edge of a cup etc. **2** the projecting edge of a hat.
brim-full *adjective* completely full.

brim² *verb* (**brimmed, brimming**) be full to the brim.
brim over overflow.

brimstone *noun* (*old use*) sulphur.

brine *noun* salt water. **briny** *adjective*

bring *verb* (**brought, bringing**) **1** cause a person or thing to come; lead; carry. **2** cause; result in.
bring about cause to happen.
bring off achieve; do something successfully.
bring up look after and train growing children; mention a subject; vomit; cause to stop suddenly.

brink *noun* **1** the edge of a steep place or of a stretch of water. **2** the point beyond which something will happen, *We were on the brink of war*.

brisk *adjective* quick and lively. **briskly** *adverb*, **briskness** *noun*

bristle¹ *noun* **1** a short stiff hair. **2** one of the still pieces of hair, wire, or plastic etc. in a brush. **bristly** *adjective*

bristle² *verb* (**bristled, bristling**) **1** (of an animal) raise its bristles in anger or fear. **2** show indignation.

THESAURUS

brief³ *verb* **2** advise, fill in (*informal*), inform, instruct, prepare, put in the picture (*informal*).

briefs *plural noun* drawers (*old use*), jocks (*informal*), knickers, panties, pants, trunks, underpants.

brigade *noun* **2** band, corps, crew, force, group, squad, team.

brigand *noun* bandit, buccaneer, bushranger, desperado, gangster, highwayman, outlaw, pirate, robber, thief.

bright *adjective* **1** beaming, blazing, dazzling, glaring, gleaming, glistening, glittering, glowing, incandescent, luminous, lustrous, radiant, resplendent, shining, sparkling. **2** bold, brilliant, flashy, gaudy, intense, showy, strong, vivid. **3** clear, cloudless, fair, fine, sunny. **4** able, astute, brainy, brilliant, clever, gifted, ingenious, intelligent, quick-witted, sharp, smart, talented. **5** animated, cheerful, gay, happy, jolly, light-hearted, lively, merry, sparkling, vivacious.

brighten *verb* **1** illuminate, lighten, light up. **2** animate, buck up (*informal*), buoy up, cheer up, enliven, liven up, perk up.

brilliant *adjective* **1** blazing, bright, dazzling, glaring, gleaming, radiant, resplendent, scintillating, shining, sparkling. **2** brainy, bright,

clever, exceptional, gifted, ingenious, intelligent, outstanding, smart, talented.

brim¹ *noun* **1** brink, edge, lip, rim.

brim² *verb* **brim over** overflow, pour over, run over, slop over, spill over.

bring *verb* **1** accompany, bear, carry, conduct, convey, deliver, escort, fetch, lead, take, transport, usher. **2** cause, create, generate, give rise to, lead to, produce, result in, yield.
bring about accomplish, achieve, cause, effect, produce.
bring in 1 initiate, institute, introduce, start. **2** earn, net, produce, realise, yield.
bring off accomplish, achieve, carry off, pull off, succeed in.
bring out 1 draw attention to, emphasise, highlight, point out, point up, reveal, show. **2** issue, produce, publish, release.
bring up 1 care for, look after, nurture, raise, rear, train. **2** broach, introduce, mention, raise. **3** see VOMIT.

brink *noun* **1** bank, border, brim, edge, margin, perimeter, threshold, verge.

brisk *adjective* bustling, energetic, fast, keen, lively, quick, rapid, snappy, spanking (*informal*), vigorous.

bristle¹ *noun* **1** hair, stubble, whisker.

bristle with be full of, *The plan bristled with problems.*

brittle *adjective* hard but easy to break or snap. **brittleness** *noun*

broach *verb* 1 make a hole in something and draw out liquid. 2 start a discussion of something, *They broached the subject.*

broad *adjective* 1 large across; wide. 2 full and complete, *broad daylight.* 3 in general terms; not detailed, *We are in broad agreement.* 4 strong and unmistakable, *a broad hint; a broad accent.* **broadly** *adverb,* **broadness** *noun*
broad bean a bean with large flat seeds.

broadcast¹ *noun* a programme sent out on the radio or on television.

broadcast² *verb* (**broadcast, broadcasting**) send out or take part in a broadcast. **broadcaster** *noun*

broaden *verb* make or become broader.

broad-minded *adjective* tolerant; not easily shocked.

broadside *noun* 1 firing by all guns on one side of a ship. 2 a verbal attack.
broadside on sideways on.

brocade *noun* material woven with raised patterns.

broccoli *noun* (*plural* **broccoli**) a kind of cauliflower with greenish flower-heads. [Italian, = cabbage-heads]

brochure (*say* **broh**-shoor) *noun* a booklet or pamphlet containing information. [from French, = stitching]

brogue (*rhymes with* rogue) *noun* 1 a strong kind of shoe. 2 a strong accent, *He spoke with an Irish brogue.*

broil *verb* 1 cook on a fire or gridiron. 2 make or be very hot. [from French *brûler* = to burn]

broke *adjective* (*informal*) having spent all your money; bankrupt.

broken-hearted *adjective* overwhelmed with grief.

broken home a family lacking one parent through divorce or separation.

broker *noun* a person who buys and sells things for other people.

brolga *noun* a large grey Australian crane with a red patch on the head.

bromide *noun* a substance used in medicine to calm the nerves.

bronchial (*say* **bronk**-ee-al) *adjective* of the tubes that lead from the windpipe to the lungs. [from Greek *bronchos* = windpipe]

bronchitis (*say* bronk-**I**-tiss) *noun* a disease with bronchial inflammation.

brontosaurus *noun* (*plural* **brontosauruses**) a large dinosaur that fed on plants, recently renamed apatosaurus. [from Greek *bronte* = thunder, + *sauros* = lizard]

bronze *noun* 1 a metal that is an alloy of copper and tin. 2 something made of bronze; a bronze medal, usually given as third prize. 3 yellowish-brown. **bronze** *adjective*
Bronze Age the time when tools and weapons were made of bronze.

bronze-wing *noun* an Australian pigeon with bronze markings on the wings.

brooch *noun* (*plural* **brooches**) an ornament with a hinged pin for fastening it on to clothes.

brood¹ *noun* young birds that were hatched together.

brittle *adjective* breakable, crisp, fragile, hard.

broach *verb* 2 bring up, introduce, mention, raise.

broad *adjective* 1 big, expansive, extensive, great, large, sweeping, vast, wide. 3 basic, general, overall, sweeping, vague. 4 clear, explicit, marked, obvious, strong, unmistakable.

broadcast¹ *noun* programme, show, telecast, transmission.

broadcast² *verb* air, relay, screen, send out, telecast, televise, transmit.

broaden *verb* enlarge, expand, extend, open out, spread out, widen.

broad-minded *adjective* flexible, liberal, open-minded, permissive, tolerant, understanding, unprejudiced.

brochure *noun* booklet, catalogue, flyer, handout, leaflet, pamphlet, prospectus.

brogue *noun* 2 accent, dialect.

broke *adjective* bankrupt, destitute, penniless, skint (*informal*), stony-broke (*slang*), strapped for cash (*informal*); see also POOR.

broken-hearted *adjective* desolate, devastated, disconsolate, forlorn, grief-stricken, heartbroken, woebegone, wretched.

broker *noun* agent, dealer, intermediary, middleman, negotiator.

brooch *noun* badge, clasp, pin.

brood¹ *noun* clutch, family, litter, offspring, young.

▶▶DICTIONARY◀◀

brood² *verb* **1** sit on eggs to hatch them. **2** keep thinking about something, especially with resentment.

broody *adjective* **1** (of a hen) wanting to sit on eggs. **2** thoughtful; brooding.

brook¹ *noun* a small stream.

brook² *verb* tolerate, *brook no delay*.

broom *noun* **1** a brush with a long handle, for sweeping. **2** a shrub with yellow, white, or pink flowers.

broomstick *noun* a broom-handle.

broth *noun* a kind of thin soup.

brothel *noun* a house in which women work as prostitutes.

brother *noun* **1** a son of the same parents as another person. **2** a man who is a fellow member of a Church, trade union, etc. **brotherhood** *noun*, **brotherly** *adjective* [from Old English *brothor*]

brother-in-law *noun* (*plural* **brothers-in-law**) the brother of a married person's husband or wife; the husband of a person's sister.

brow *noun* **1** an eyebrow. **2** the forehead. **3** the ridge at the top of a hill; the edge of a cliff.

brown¹ *noun* a colour between orange and black.

brown² *adjective* **1** of the colour brown. **2** having a brown skin; suntanned.

brown³ *verb* make or become brown.

Brownie *noun* a member of a junior branch of the Guides.

browse *verb* (**browsed, browsing**) **1** feed on grass or leaves. **2** read or look at something casually.

bruise¹ *noun* a dark mark made on the skin by hitting it.

bruise² *verb* (**bruised, bruising**) give or get a bruise or bruises.

brumby *noun* (*Australian*) a wild or partly tamed horse.

brunette *noun* a woman with dark-brown hair. [from French *brun* = brown]

brunt *noun* the chief impact or strain, *They bore the brunt of the attack.*

brush¹ *noun* (*plural* **brushes**) **1** an implement used for cleaning or painting things or for smoothing the hair, usually with pieces of hair, wire, or plastic etc. set in a solid base. **2** a fox's bushy tail. **3** brushing, *Give it a good brush.* **4** a short fight, *They had a brush with the enemy.* **5** (*Australian*) dense forest.

brush² *verb* **1** use a brush on something. **2** touch gently in passing. **brush aside** dismiss a person or idea lightly. **brush up** revise a subject.

brusque (*say* bruusk) *adjective* curt and offhand in manner. **brusquely** *adverb* [from Italian *brusco* = sour]

▶▶THESAURUS◀◀

brood² *verb* **2** dwell (on), fret, meditate, mull, ponder, reflect, stew (*informal*), sulk, think, worry.

broody *adjective* **2** depressed, gloomy, pensive, thoughtful.

brook¹ *noun* creek (*Australian*), rill, rivulet, stream, watercourse.

brook² *verb* allow, endure, permit, put up with, stand, tolerate.

broth *noun* bouillon, consommé, soup, stock.

brother *noun* **1** male sibling. **2** associate, colleague, comrade, fellow, fellow member, friend, mate.
brotherhood *noun* association, community, fraternity, order, society.
brotherly *adjective* fraternal; see also FRIENDLY.

brown² *adjective* **1** auburn, bay, beige, biscuit, bronze, buff, camel, chestnut, chocolate, coffee, copper, fawn, hazel, khaki, mocha, ochre, rust, sepia, tan, tawny, umber, walnut. **2** bronzed, dark-skinned, suntanned, tanned.
brown-haired *adjective* brunette, dark-haired.

brown³ *verb* (*brown the meat etc.*) cook, fry, grill, sauté, seal, sear, toast; (*brown one's skin*) bronze, suntan, tan.

browse *verb* **1** feed, graze. **2** flick through, flip through, glance through, leaf through, look through, scan, skim (through), thumb through.

bruise¹ *noun* contusion, discoloration, shiner (*informal*).

bruise² *verb* blacken, damage, discolour, injure, mark.

brumby *noun* bronco, mustang, warrigal (*Australian*), wild horse.

brunt *noun* force, impact, strain, stress.

brush¹ *noun* **4** clash, confrontation, dealings, encounter, skirmish.

brush² *verb* **1** clean, dust, polish, scrub, smooth, sweep, tidy. **2** graze, touch.
brush aside dismiss, disregard, ignore, reject, sweep aside.
brush up on bone up on (*informal*), go over, revise, study.

brusque *adjective* abrupt, blunt, curt, offhand, short, terse.

▶▶ D I C T I O N A R Y ◀◀

Brussels sprouts the edible buds of a kind of cabbage. [named after Brussels, the capital of Belgium]

brutal *adjective* very cruel. **brutally** *adverb*, **brutality** *noun*

brute *noun* **1** a brutal person. **2** an animal. **brutish** *adjective* [from Latin *brutus* = stupid]

B.Sc. *abbreviation* Bachelor of Science.

bubble[1] *noun* **1** a thin transparent ball of liquid filled with air or gas. **2** a small ball of air in something.
bubble gum chewing-gum that can be blown into large bubbles.

bubble[2] *verb* (**bubbled, bubbling**) **1** send up bubbles; rise in bubbles. **2** show great liveliness.

bubbler *noun* (*Australian*) a drinking fountain.

bubbly *adjective* **1** full of bubbles. **2** lively, *a bubbly personality*.

buccaneer *noun* a pirate.

buck[1] *noun* a male deer, rabbit, or hare.

buck[2] *verb* **1** (of a horse) jump with its back arched. **2** oppose, resist.
buck up (*slang*) hurry; cheer up.

buck[3] *noun* an object used in the game of poker to show whose turn it is.
pass the buck (*slang*) pass the responsibility for something to another person. **buck-passing** *noun*

bucket[1] *noun* **1** a container with a handle, for carrying liquids etc. **2** (*Australian*) a carton for ice-cream, chips, etc. **bucketful** *noun*

bucket[2] *verb* (*Australian*) condemn, criticise.

buckle[1] *noun* a device through which a belt or strap is threaded to fasten it.

buckle[2] *verb* (**buckled, buckling**) **1** fasten with a buckle. **2** bend or crumple.
buckle down to start working hard at.

buckler *noun* a small round shield.

Buckley's chance (*Australian*) no chance at all.

bucolic (*say* bew-**kol**-ik) *adjective* of country life. [from Greek *boukolos* = herdsman]

bud *noun* a flower or leaf before it opens.

Buddhism (*say* **buud**-izm) *noun* a faith that started in Asia and follows the teachings of the Indian philosopher Gautama Buddha, who lived in the 5th century BC. **Buddhist** *noun* [from Sanskrit *Buddha* = enlightened one]

budding *adjective* beginning to develop.

buddy *noun* (*plural* **buddies**) (*informal*) a friend.

budge *verb* (**budged, budging**) move slightly.

budgerigar *noun* an Australian bird often kept as a pet in a cage.

budget[1] *noun* **1** a plan for spending money wisely. **2** an amount of money set aside for a purpose. **budgetary** *adjective*
the Budget estimates of government income and expenditure presented to Parliament.

budget[2] *verb* (**budgeted, budgeting**) plan a budget.

budgie *noun* (*informal*) a budgerigar.

▶▶ T H E S A U R U S ◀◀

brutal *adjective* atrocious, barbarous, beastly, bloodthirsty, callous, cruel, ferocious, inhuman, inhumane, merciless, ruthless, sadistic, savage, vicious.

brute *noun* **1** beast, bully, monster, ogre, sadist. **2** animal, beast, creature.

bubble[2] *verb* **1** boil, effervesce, fizz, foam, froth, seethe, simmer.

bubbly *adjective* **1** aerated, carbonated, effervescent, fizzy, foamy, frothy, sparkling. **2** animated, buoyant, exuberant, lively, sparkling, vivacious.

buccaneer *noun* adventurer, brigand, corsair (*old use*), marauder, pirate, privateer.

buck[2] *verb* **1** jump, leap, start. **2** fight, oppose, resist.
buck up 1 get a move on (*informal*), hasten, hurry up, make haste, rush. **2** brighten, cheer up, liven up, perk up.

bucket[1] *noun* **1** pail, scuttle.

buckle[1] *noun* catch, clasp, clip, fastening.

buckle[2] *verb* **1** do up, fasten. **2** bend, cave in, collapse, contort, crumple, distort, give way, twist, warp.

Buckley's chance Buckley's (*Australian informal*), no chance, no hope, no show (*informal*).

bud *noun* shoot, sprout.

budding *adjective* burgeoning, developing, growing, promising, up-and-coming.

buddy *noun* chum (*informal*), cobber (*Australian informal*), companion, comrade, confidant, confidante, crony, friend, mate, pal (*informal*).

budge *verb* move, shift, stir.

budget[1] *noun* **1** estimate, plan. **2** allocation, allowance.

budget[2] *verb* allocate, allow, estimate, plan, set aside.

▶▶DICTIONARY◀◀

buff¹ *adjective* of a dull yellow colour.

buff² *verb* polish with soft material. [from *buff leather* = leather of buffalo hide]

buffalo *noun* (*plural* **buffalo** or **buffaloes**) a large ox. Different kinds are found in Asia, Africa, and North America (where they are also called *bison*).

buffer *noun* something that softens a blow, especially a device on a railway engine or wagon or at the end of a track.
buffer state a small country between two powerful ones, thought to reduce the chance of these two attacking each other.

buffet¹ (*say* **buf**-ay) *noun* **1** a refreshment counter. **2** a meal where guests serve themselves. [from French, = stool]

buffet² (*say* **buf**-it) *noun* a hit, especially with the hand.

buffet³ *verb* (**buffeted, buffeting**) hit, knock, *Strong winds buffeted the aircraft.* [from Old French *buffe* = a blow]

buffoon *noun* a clown; a person who plays the fool. **buffoonery** *noun* [from Latin *buffo* = clown]

bug¹ *noun* **1** an insect. **2** (*informal*) a germ or microbe. **3** (*informal*) a secret hidden microphone.

bug² *verb* (**bugged, bugging**) (*informal*) **1** fit with a 'bug'. **2** annoy.

bugbear *noun* something you fear or dislike. [from an old word *bug* = bogy]

buggy *noun* (*plural* **buggies**) **1** (*old use*) a light horse-drawn carriage. **2** a small strong vehicle.

bugle *noun* a brass instrument like a small trumpet, used for sounding military signals. **bugler** *noun*

build¹ *verb* (**built, building**) make something by putting parts together.
build in include. **built-in** *adjective*
build up establish gradually; accumulate; cover an area with buildings; increase; make stronger or more famous, *build up a reputation.* **built-up** *adjective*

build² *noun* the shape of someone's body, *of slender build.*

builder *noun* someone who puts up buildings.

building *noun* **1** the process of constructing houses etc. **2** a permanent built structure that people can go into.
building society an organisation that accepts deposits of money and lends to people who want to buy houses etc.

bulb *noun* **1** a thick rounded part of a plant from which a stem grows up and roots grow down. **2** a rounded part of something, *the bulb of a thermometer.* **3** a glass globe that produces electric light. **bulbous** *adjective*

bulge¹ *noun* a rounded swelling; an outward curve. **bulgy** *adjective*

bulge² *verb* (**bulged, bulging**) form or cause to form a bulge.

bulimia (*say* bu-**lim**-ee-a) *noun* abnormal hunger especially alternating with vomiting.

bulk¹ *noun* **1** the size of something, especially when it is large. **2** the greater portion; the majority, *The bulk of the population voted for it.*
in bulk in large amounts.

bulk² *verb* increase the size or thickness of something, *bulk it out.*

bulky *adjective* (**bulkier, bulkiest**) taking up much space. **bulkiness** *noun*

▶▶THESAURUS◀◀

buffer *noun* cushion, damper, guard, pad, shield.

buffet¹ *noun* **1** café, cafeteria, counter, snack bar.

buffet³ *verb* batter, hit, knock, pound, strike.

buffoon *noun* clown, comic, fool, jester, wag.

bug¹ *noun* **1** insect, mite. **2** bacterium, germ, infection, microbe, micro-organism, virus, wog (*Australian informal*).

bug² *verb* **1** eavesdrop on, listen in on, tap. **2** annoy, bother, exasperate, irritate, trouble.

bugbear *noun* bogy, dread, nightmare, pet hate.

buggy *noun* **1** carriage, gig, trap.

build¹ *verb* assemble, construct, erect, fabricate, form, make, put together, put up, raise.

build up 1 develop, enlarge, establish, expand. **2** accrue, accumulate, amass, grow. **3** escalate, grow, increase, intensify, rise, strengthen.

build² *noun* figure, frame, physique, shape.

building *noun* **2** construction, edifice, premises, structure.

bulge¹ *noun* bump, curve, hump, lump, protrusion, protuberance, swelling.

bulge² *verb* bloat, distend, enlarge, expand, protrude, stick out, swell.

bulk¹ *noun* **1** magnitude, mass, size, volume, weight. **2** best part, greater part, lion's share, majority, most.
in bulk in quantity, in volume, wholesale.

bulky *adjective* big, cumbersome, heavy, huge, large, massive, unwieldy, voluminous.

bull[1] *noun* the fully-grown male of cattle or of certain other large animals (e.g. elephant, whale, seal).

bull[2] *noun* an edict issued by the pope.

bullbar *noun* (*Australian*) a heavy metal grid on the front of a vehicle to reduce damage if colliding with a kangaroo etc.

bulldog *noun* a dog of a powerful courageous breed with a short thick neck.

bulldoze *verb* (**bulldozed, bulldozing**) clear with a bulldozer.

bulldozer *noun* a powerful tractor with a wide metal blade or scoop in front, used for shifting soil or clearing ground.

bulldust *noun* (*Australian*) **1** fine dust on outback roads. **2** (*slang*) nonsense.

bullet *noun* a small lump of metal shot from a rifle or revolver.

bulletin *noun* a public statement giving news.

bullet-proof *adjective* able to keep out bullets.

bullfight *noun* a public entertainment in which bulls are tormented and killed in an arena. **bullfighter** *noun*

bullfinch *noun* a bird with a strong beak and a pink breast.

bullion *noun* bars of gold or silver.

bullock *noun* a castrated bull.

bullocky *noun* (*Australian informal*) a bullock-driver.
bullocky's joy treacle or golden syrup.

bullroarer *noun* a flat strip of wood on a string making a whirring sound when whirled around, used especially in Aboriginal religious rites.

bull's-eye *noun* **1** the centre of a target. **2** a hard shiny peppermint sweet.

bully[1] *verb* (**bullied, bullying**) **1** use strength or power to hurt or frighten a weaker person. **2** start play in hockey, when two opponents tap the ground and each other's stick, *bully off*.

bully[2] *noun* (*plural* **bullies**) someone who bullies people.

bulrush *noun* (*plural* **bulrushes**) a tall rush with a thick velvety head.

bulwark *noun* a wall of earth built as a defence; a protection.
bulwarks *plural noun* a ship's side above the level of the deck.

bum *noun* (*slang*) a person's bottom.

bumble *verb* (**bumbled, bumbling**) **1** move or behave clumsily. **2** speak in a rambling way.

bumble-bee *noun* a large bee with a loud hum.

bump[1] *verb* **1** knock against something. **2** move along with jolts.
bump into (*informal*) meet by chance.
bump off (*slang*) kill.

bump[2] *noun* **1** the action or sound of bumping. **2** a swelling or lump. **bumpy** *adjective*

bumper[1] *noun* **1** a bar along the front or back of a motor vehicle to protect it in collisions. **2** a ball in cricket that bounces high.

bumper[2] *adjective* unusually large or plentiful, *a bumper crop*.

bumpkin *noun* a country person with awkward manners.

bumptious (*say* **bump**-shus) *adjective* conceited. **bumptiousness** *noun*

bulldoze *verb* clear, demolish, flatten, level, raze.

bulletin *noun* announcement, broadcast, communiqué, dispatch, message, newsletter, notice, report, statement.

bullfighter *noun* matador, picador, toreador.

bull's-eye *noun* **1** bull, centre, middle.

bully[1] *verb* **1** cow, frighten, harass, hector, intimidate, oppress, persecute, pick on, push around (*informal*), stand over, terrorise, threaten, torment, tyrannise.

bully[2] *noun* intimidator, persecutor, ruffian, tormentor, tough, tyrant.

bulwark *noun* barrier, buffer, defence, earth-work, fortification, protection, rampart, wall.

bumble *verb* **1** blunder, flounder, lumber, lurch, stumble. **2** babble, mumble, mutter, ramble.

bump[1] *verb* **1** hit, hurt, injure, knock. **2** bounce, bucket, jerk, jolt, shake.
bump into come across, meet, run into, see.
bump off see KILL[1].

bump[2] *noun* **1** bang, collision, crash, knock, thud, thump. **2** bulge, hump, lump, protrusion, protuberance, swelling.
bumpy *adjective* (*a bumpy road*) corrugated, potholed, rough, uneven; (*a bumpy ride*) bouncy, jarring, jolting, rough.

bumpkin *noun* hick (*informal*), hill-billy (*American informal*), peasant, rustic, yokel.

bumptious *adjective* arrogant, brash, cocky (*informal*), conceited, overbearing, self-assertive, self-important.

bun *noun* **1** a small round sweet cake. **2** hair twisted into a rounded bunch at the back of the head.

bunch *noun* (*plural* **bunches**) **1** a number of things joined or fastened together. **2** (*informal*) a group; a gang.

bundle¹ *noun* a number of things tied or wrapped together.

bundle² *verb* (**bundled, bundling**) **1** make into a bundle. **2** push hurriedly or carelessly, *They bundled him into a taxi.*

bung¹ *noun* a stopper for closing a hole in a barrel or jar.

bung² *verb* (*slang*) throw, *Bung it here.*
  bunged up (*informal*) blocked.

bung³ *adjective* (*Australian slang*) injured, useless.
  go bung break down, go bankrupt.

bungalow *noun* a house without any upstairs rooms. [from Hindi *bangla* = of Bengal]

bungle *verb* (**bungled, bungling**) do something unsuccessfully; spoil by being clumsy. **bungle** *noun,* **bungler** *noun*

bunion *noun* a swelling at the side of the joint where the big toe joins the foot.

bunk¹ *noun* a bed built like a shelf.

bunk² *noun* **do a bunk** (*slang*) run away. **bunk** *verb*

bunker *noun* **1** a container for storing fuel. **2** a sandy hollow built as an obstacle on a golf-course. **3** an underground shelter.

bunny *noun* (*plural* **bunnies**) (*informal*) a rabbit. [from dialect *bun* = rabbit]

bunting¹ *noun* a kind of small bird.

bunting² *noun* strips of cloth hung up to decorate streets and buildings.

bunyip *noun* a mythical Australian monster in swamps and billabongs.

buoy¹ (*say* boi) *noun* (*plural* **buoys**) a floating object anchored to mark a channel or underwater rocks etc.

buoy² *verb* **1** keep something afloat. **2** hearten; cheer, *They were buoyed up with new hope.*

buoyant (*say* **boi**-ant) *noun* **1** able to float. **2** light-hearted; cheerful. **buoyantly** *adverb,* **buoyancy** *noun*

bur *noun* a plant's seed-case or flower that clings to hair or clothes.

burble *verb* (**burbled, burbling**) make a gentle murmuring sound. **burble** *noun*

burden¹ *noun* **1** something carried; a heavy load. **2** something troublesome that you have to bear, *Exams are a burden.* **burdensome** *adjective*

burden² *verb* put a burden on a person etc.

bureau (*say* bewr-oh) *noun* (*plural* **bureaux**) **1** a writing-desk. **2** a business office, *They will tell you at the Information Bureau.* [French, = desk]

bunch *noun* **1** batch, bundle, cluster, collection, lot, pack, quantity, set, sheaf, wad; (*a bunch of flowers*) bouquet, corsage, nosegay, posy, spray. **2** band, crowd, gang, group, lot, mob, team.

bundle¹ *noun* bale, bunch, collection, package, parcel, set, sheaf, swag (*Australian*).

bundle² *verb* **1** pack, package, tie, wrap. **2** pack off, push, shove, thrust.

bung¹ *noun* cork, plug, stopper.

bung² *verb* put, shove, stick (*informal*), throw, toss.
  bunged up blocked (up), clogged up, congested, stuffed up.

bung³ *adjective* **go bung** be on the blink (*informal*), be out of order, break down, conk out (*informal*), fail, go kaput (*informal*), pack up (*informal*), seize up.

bungle *verb* botch, fluff (*slang*), foul up (*informal*), goof (*slang*), mess up, mismanage, muff (*informal*), ruin, spoil, wreck.

bungle *noun* blunder, botch, mess, mistake, mix-up.

bunk¹ *noun* bed, berth.

bunk² *noun* **do a bunk** abscond, bolt, escape, flee, make off, nick off (*Australian slang*), run off, scarper (*informal*), shoot through (*Australian informal*), vanish.

buoy¹ *noun* float, marker.

buoy² *verb* **2** (*buoy up*) boost, cheer, encourage, hearten, sustain, uplift.

buoyant *adjective* **1** floating, light. **2** bouncy, carefree, cheerful, light-hearted, lively, resilient.

burden¹ *noun* **1** load, weight. **2** care, concern, problem, strain, trial, trouble, worry.

burden² *verb* encumber, load, lumber, oppress, saddle, weigh down, worry.

bureau *noun* **1** desk, writing-desk. **2** agency, branch, department, division, office.

▶▶ D I C T I O N A R Y ◀◀

bureaucracy (*say* bewr-**ok**-ra-see) *noun* (*plural* **bureaucracies**) **1** government by officials, not by elected representatives. **2** too much official routine. **bureaucratic** (*say* bewr-ok-**rat**-ik) *adjective* [from *bureau* + *-cracy*]

bureaucrat (*say* **bewr**-ok-rat) *noun* an official of a bureaucracy.

burgeon (*say* **ber**-jon) *verb* grow rapidly.

burger *noun* a hamburger.

burglar *noun* a person who enters a building illegally, especially in order to steal things. **burglary** *noun*

burgle *verb* (**burgled, burgling**) rob a place as a burglar.

burgundy *noun* a rich red or white wine. [originally made in Burgundy in France]

burial *noun* burying somebody.

burlesque (*say* ber-**lesk**) *noun* a comical imitation.

burly *adjective* (**burlier, burliest**) with a strong heavy body; sturdy.

burn¹ *verb* (**burned** or **burnt, burning**) **1** blaze or glow with fire; produce heat or light by combustion. **2** damage or destroy something by fire, heat, or chemicals. **3** be damaged or destroyed by fire etc. **4** feel very hot.

Usage The word *burnt* (not *burned*) is always used when an adjective is required, e.g. in *burnt wood*. As parts of the verb, either *burned* or *burnt* may be used, e.g. *the wood had burned* or *had burnt completely*.

burn² *noun* **1** a mark or injury made by burning. **2** the firing of a spacecraft's rockets.

burn³ *noun* (*Scottish*) a brook.

burner *noun* the part of a lamp or cooker that gives out the flame.

burning *adjective* **1** intense, *a burning ambition*. **2** very important; hotly discussed, *a burning question*.

burnish *verb* polish by rubbing.

burp *verb* bring up wind from the stomach through the mouth.

burr *noun* **1** a bur. **2** a whirring sound. **3** a soft country accent.

burrow¹ *noun* a hole or tunnel dug by a rabbit or fox etc. as a dwelling.

burrow² *verb* **1** dig a burrow. **2** push your way through or into something; search deeply, *She burrowed in her handbag.*

bursar *noun* a person who manages the finances and other business of a school or college. [from Latin *bursa* = a bag]

bursary *noun* a grant given to a student.

burst¹ *verb* (**burst, bursting**) **1** break or force apart. **2** come or start suddenly, *It burst into flame. They burst out laughing.* **3** be very full, *bursting with energy.*

▶▶ T H E S A U R U S ◀◀

bureaucracy *noun* **1** administration, official-dom, public service. **2** formalities, paperwork, red tape, regulations.

bureaucrat *noun* administrator, functionary, official, public servant.

burglar *noun* housebreaker, intruder, robber, thief.
  burglary *noun* break-in, breaking and entering, larceny, robbery, stealing, theft.

burial *noun* entombment, funeral, interment. **burial ground** see CEMETERY.

burlesque *noun* caricature, imitation, mockery, parody, send-up (*informal*), spoof (*informal*), take-off (*informal*).

burly *adjective* beefy, brawny, hefty, husky, muscular, nuggety (*Australian*), stocky, stout, strapping, strong, sturdy, thickset, tough.

burn¹ *verb* **1** be ablaze, be alight, be on fire, blaze, catch fire, flame, flare, smoulder. **2** blacken, brown, char, cremate (*a corpse*), ignite, incinerate, kindle, scald, scorch, sear, set

alight, set fire to, set on fire, singe, toast. **4** feel hot, flush, redden.

burning *adjective* **1** ardent, deep, fervent, intense, passionate, strong. **2** crucial, important, pressing, urgent, vital.

burnish *verb* buff, polish, rub, shine.

burp *verb* belch, bring up wind.

burrow¹ *noun* den, hole, lair, tunnel, warren.

burrow² *verb* **1** dig, excavate, tunnel. **2** delve, fossick (*Australian informal*), rummage, search.

bursar *noun* accountant, financial controller, treasurer.

bursary *noun* allowance, endowment, grant, scholarship.

burst¹ *verb* **1** blow out, break, bust (*informal*), disintegrate, explode, pop, puncture, rip, rupture, split, tear. **2** (*burst into a room*) barge, fly, run, rush; (*burst into tears*) break, collapse, dissolve, erupt.
  bursting *adjective* see FULL¹.

▶▶ D I C T I O N A R Y ◀◀

burst² *noun* **1** bursting; a split. **2** something short and forceful, *a burst of gunfire*.

bury *verb* (**buried, burying**) **1** place a dead body in the earth, a tomb, or the sea. **2** put underground; cover up.
bury the hatchet agree to stop quarrelling or fighting.

bus *noun* (*plural* **buses**) a large vehicle for passengers to travel in. [short for *omnibus*]

busby *noun* (*plural* **busbies**) a tall fur cap worn by the Hussars at ceremonies.

bush *noun* (*plural* **bushes**) **1** a shrub. **2** wild uncultivated land, especially in Africa and Australia. **bushy** *adjective*
bush telegraph unofficial circulation of news, grapevine.
the bush (*Australian*) the country, not the city.

bushel *noun* a measure for grain and fruit.

bushfire *noun* (*Australian*) a dangerous outbreak of fire in uncleared or forest land.

bushranger *noun* (*Australian*) in the past a person who committed armed robbery, escaping into, or living in the bush.

bushwalker *noun* a person hiking in the bush.
bushwalking *noun*

busily *adverb* in a busy way.

business (*say* **biz**-niss) *noun* (*plural* **businesses**) **1** a person's concern or responsibilities, *Mind your own business*. **2** a person's occupation. **3** an affair or subject, *I'm tired of the whole business*. **4** a shop or firm. **5** buying and selling things; trade.

businesslike *adjective* practical; well-organised.

busker *noun* a person who entertains people in the street. **busking** *noun* [from an old word *busk* = be a pedlar]

bust¹ *noun* **1** a sculpture of a person's head, shoulders, and chest. **2** the upper front part of a woman's body.

bust² *verb* (**bust, busting**) (*informal*) burst.

bustard *noun* a large bird that can run very swiftly.

bustle¹ *verb* (**bustled, bustling**) hurry in a busy or excited way.

bustle² *noun* hurried or excited activity.

bustle³ *noun* padding used to puff out the top of a long skirt at the back.

busy¹ *adjective* (**busier, busiest**) **1** having much to do; occupied. **2** full of activity. **busily** *adverb*, **busyness** *noun*

busy² *verb* (**busied, busying**) **busy yourself** occupy yourself; keep busy.

▶▶ T H E S A U R U S ◀◀

burst² *noun* **2** blaze, explosion, fusillade, outbreak, outburst, round, rush, spurt, volley.

bury *verb* **1** entomb, inter, lay to rest. **2** conceal, cover up, hide, submerge.

bus *noun* coach, minibus, omnibus.

bush *noun* **1** plant, shrub. **2** brush, forest, scrub, woodland, woods.
bushy *adjective* **1** scrubby, shrubby. **2** (*a bushy tail*) bristly, fluffy, fuzzy, hairy, shaggy, thick, woolly.
the bush backblocks (*Australian*), country, donga (*Australian*), inland, interior, mallee (*Australian*), mulga (*Australian*), outback (*Australian*), sticks (*Australian informal*).

bushfire *noun* blaze, conflagration, fire.

bushranger *noun* bandit, brigand, escapee, highwayman, outlaw, robber.

bushwalker *noun* hiker, rambler, trekker, walker.

business *noun* **1** concern, duty, function, job, province, responsibility, task, work. **2** calling, career, employment, field, industry, job, line, occupation, profession, trade, vocation, work. **3** affair, concern, issue, matter, situation, subject, topic. **4** company, concern, corporation, enterprise, establishment, firm, outfit (*informal*), practice, undertaking, venture. **5** buying and selling, commerce, trade, trading.

businesslike *adjective* efficient, methodical, organised, practical, professional, systematic.

businessman, businesswoman *noun* entrepreneur, executive, industrialist, magnate, merchant, trader, tycoon.

busker *noun* street entertainer, street performer.

bust¹ *noun* **1** sculpture. **2** bosom, breast, chest.

bust² *verb* break, burst, collapse, crack.
go bust fail, go bankrupt, go broke (*informal*).

bustle¹ *verb* dash, hasten, hurry, hustle, rush, tear.

bustle² *noun* activity, busyness, commotion, excitement, hurly-burly, hurry, hustle.

busy¹ *adjective* **1** active, employed, engaged, industrious, involved, occupied, on the go (*informal*), snowed under (*informal*), working. **2** active, bustling, frenetic, frenzied, full, hectic, lively.

▶▶ DICTIONARY ◀◀

busybody *noun* (*plural* **busybodies**) a person who interferes.

but¹ *conjunction* however; nevertheless, *I wanted to go, but I couldn't.*

but² *preposition* except, *There is no one here but me.*

but³ *adverb* only; no more than, *We can but try.*

butcher¹ *noun* **1** a person who cuts up meat and sells it. **2** a person who kills cruelly or needlessly. **butchery** *noun*

butcher² *verb* kill cruelly or needlessly.

butler *noun* the chief manservant of a household, in charge of the wine-cellar. [from Old French *bouteillier* = bottler]

butt¹ *noun* **1** the thicker end of a weapon or tool. **2** a stub, *cigarette butts.* [from Dutch *bot* = stumpy]

butt² *noun* a large cask or barrel. [from Latin *buttis* = cask]

butt³ *noun* **1** a person or thing that is a target for ridicule or teasing, *He was the butt of their jokes.* **2** a mound of earth behind the targets on a shooting-range.
butts *plural noun* a shooting-range. [from Old French *but* = goal]

butt⁴ *verb* **1** push or hit with the head as a ram or goat does. **2** place the edges of things together.
butt in interrupt; intrude; meddle. [from Old French *buter* = hit]

butter *noun* a soft fatty food made by churning cream. **buttery** *adjective*

buttercup *noun* a wild plant with bright yellow cup-shaped flowers.

butter-fingers *noun* a person who often drops things.

butterfly *noun* (*plural* **butterflies**) **1** an insect with large white or coloured wings. **2** a swimming-stroke in which both arms are lifted at the same time.

buttermilk *noun* the liquid that is left after butter has been made.

butternut *noun* a pear-shaped pumpkin.

butterscotch *noun* a kind of hard toffee.

buttock *noun* either of the two fleshy rounded parts at the lower end of the back.

button¹ *noun* **1** a knob or disc sewn on clothes as a fastening or ornament. **2** a small knob, *Press the button.*

button² *verb* fasten with a button or buttons.

buttonhole¹ *noun* **1** a slit through which a button passes to fasten clothes. **2** a flower worn on a lapel.

buttonhole² *verb* (**buttonholed, buttonholing**) stop somebody so that you can talk to him or her.

buttress *noun* (*plural* **buttresses**) a support built against a wall. **buttress** *verb* [same origin as *butt⁴*]

buy¹ *verb* (**bought, buying**) get something by paying for it. **buyer** *noun*

buy² *noun* something bought; a purchase.

buzz¹ *noun* (*plural* **buzzes**) a vibrating humming sound.

buzz² *verb* **1** make a buzz. **2** threaten an aircraft by deliberately flying close to it.

▶▶ THESAURUS ◀◀

busybody *noun* interferer, meddler, mischief-maker, Nosy Parker (*informal*), snooper (*informal*), stickybeak (*Australian informal*).

but¹ *conjunction* however, nevertheless, still, yet.

but² *preposition* apart from, aside from, except, other than, save.

butcher² *verb* kill, massacre, murder, slaughter, slay.

butt¹ *noun* **1** handle, shaft, stock. **2** end, remnant, stub; (*cheque butt*) counterfoil.

butt² *noun* barrel, cask, hogshead, tun.

butt³ *noun* **1** object, subject, target, victim.

butt⁴ *verb* **1** bump, knock, poke, prod, push, ram.
butt in chip in (*informal*), interfere, interrupt, intervene, meddle, poke your nose in (*informal*).

buttocks *plural noun* backside (*informal*), behind (*informal*), bottom, bum (*slang*), butt (*slang*), haunches, posterior, rear (*informal*), rump, seat.

button¹ *noun* **2** control, knob, switch.

button² *verb* do up, fasten.

buttonhole² *verb* accost, bail up (*Australian*), corner, detain, waylay.

buttress *noun* prop, reinforcement, stay, support.
buttress *verb* brace, prop up, reinforce, shore up, support.

buy¹ *verb* acquire, come by, gain, get, obtain, pay for, procure, purchase.
buyer *noun* client, consumer, customer, patron, purchaser, shopper.

buy² *noun* acquisition, deal, purchase.

buzz¹ *noun* burr, drone, hum, vibration, whirr.

buzz² *verb* **1** burr, drone, hum, throb, whirr.

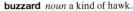 DICTIONARY ◄◄

buzzard *noun* a kind of hawk.

buzzer *noun* a device that makes a buzzing sound as a signal.

by[1] *preposition* This word is used to show (**1**) closeness (*Sit by me*), (**2**) direction or route (*We got here by a short cut*), (**3**) time (*They came by night*), (**4**) manner or method (*cooking by gas*), (**5**) amount (*You missed it by centimetres*).
by the way incidentally.
by yourself alone; without help.

by[2] *adverb* **1** past, *I can't get by*. **2** in reserve; for future use, *Put it by*.
by and by soon; later on.
by and large on the whole.

bye *noun* **1** a run scored in cricket when the ball goes past the batsman without being touched. **2** having no opponent for one round in a tournament.

bye-bye *interjection* goodbye.

by-election *noun* an election to replace a Member of Parliament who has died or resigned.

bygone *adjective* belonging to the past.
let bygones be bygones forgive and forget.

by-law *noun* a law that applies only to a particular town or district.

bypass[1] *noun* (*plural* **bypasses**) **1** a road taking traffic past a city etc. **2** a channel that allows something to flow when the main route is blocked.

bypass[2] *verb* avoid by means of a bypass.

by-product *noun* something produced while something else is being made.

bystander *noun* a person standing near but not taking part in something.

byte *noun* a fixed number of bits (= binary digits) in a computer, often representing a single character.

byway *noun* a minor road.

byword *noun* **1** a person or thing spoken of as a famous example, *Their firm became a byword for quality*. **2** a proverb.

 THESAURUS ◄◄

by[1] *preposition* **1** alongside, beside, close to, near, next to. **2** along, through, via. **3** at, during.
by yourself alone, single-handed, unaccompanied, unaided, unassisted.

by[2] *adverb* **1** past. **2** aside, away, in reserve.
by and by before long, presently, soon.
by and large all things considered, generally speaking, on the whole.

bygone *adjective* ancient, former, olden, past.

bypass[1] *noun* **1** detour, deviation, diversion, ring road, ring route.

bypass[2] *verb* (*bypass a city*) avoid, go round; (*bypass a problem*) avoid, circumvent, dodge, evade, ignore, sidestep, skirt.

by-product *noun* consequence, offshoot, repercussion, side benefit, side effect, spin-off.

bystander *noun* eyewitness, observer, onlooker, passer-by, spectator, witness.

byword *noun* **1** example, model, symbol. **2** adage, catchphrase, maxim, motto, proverb, saying, slogan.

cab *noun* **1** a taxi. **2** a compartment for the driver of a truck, train, bus, or crane.
first cab off the rank (*Australian informal*) the first person to do or get something.

cabaret (*say* **kab**-er-ay) *noun* an entertainment, especially one provided for the customers in a restaurant or nightclub. [French, = tavern]

cabbage *noun* a vegetable with green or purple leaves.

cabbage-tree *noun* an Australian palm with large fan-shaped leaves.
cabbage-tree hat a shady hat made from plaited leaves of the cabbage-tree.

caber *noun* a tree-trunk used in the sport of 'tossing the caber'.

cabin *noun* **1** a hut or shelter. **2** a compartment in a ship, aircraft, or spacecraft. **3** a driver's cab.

cabinet *noun* a cupboard or container with drawers or shelves.

Cabinet *noun* the group of chief ministers, chosen by the Prime Minister, who meet to decide government policy.

cable *noun* **1** a thick rope of fibre or wire; a thick chain. **2** a telegram sent overseas.

cacao (*say* ka-**kay**-oh) *noun* (*plural* **cacaos**) a tropical tree with a seed from which cocoa and chocolate are made.

cache (*say* kash) *noun* **1** hidden stores of treasure. **2** a hiding-place for treasure or stores. [from French *cacher* = hide]

cackle *noun* **1** the loud clucking noise a hen makes. **2** a loud silly laugh. **3** noisy chatter.
cackle *verb*

cacophony (*say* kak-**off**-on-ee) *noun* a loud harsh unpleasant sound. [from Greek *kakos* = bad, + *phone* = sound]

cactus *noun* (*plural* **cacti**) a fleshy plant, usually with prickles, from a hot dry climate.

cad *noun* a dishonourable person.

cadaverous (*say* kad-**av**-er-us) *adjective* pale and gaunt. [from Latin *cadaver* = corpse]

caddy *noun* (*plural* **caddies**) a small box for holding tea.

cadence (*say* **kay**-denss) *noun* **1** rhythm; the rise and fall of the voice in speaking. **2** the final notes of a musical phrase.

cadenza (*say* ka-**den**-za) *noun* an elaborate passage for a solo instrument or singer, to show the performer's skill.

cadet *noun* a young person being trained for the armed forces or the police.

cadge *verb* (**cadged, cadging**) get something by begging for it. **cadger** *noun*

cadmium *noun* a metal that looks like tin.

Caesarean section (*say* siz-**air**-ee-an) a surgical operation for taking a baby alive out of the mother's womb. [so called because Julius Caesar is said to have been born in this way]

café (*say* **kaf**-ay) *noun* a small restaurant. [French, = coffee]

cafeteria (*say* kaf-it-**eer**-ee-a) *noun* a self-service café.

caffeine (*say* **kaf**-een) *noun* a stimulant substance found in tea and coffee.

caftan *noun* a long loose coat or dress.

cage *noun* **1** a container with bars or wires, in which birds or animals are kept. **2** the enclosed platform of a lift. **caged** *adjective*

► ► T H E S A U R U S ◄ ◄

cabin *noun* **1** chalet, hut, lodge, shack, shanty, shelter. **2** berth, compartment, room.

cabinet *noun* buffet, case, chest, closet, console, cupboard, locker, sideboard, wall unit.

cable *noun* **1** chain, cord, flex, guy, hawser, lead, line, rope, wire. **2** telegram, wire (*informal*).

cache *noun* **1** hoard, reserve, stash (*informal*), stockpile, store, supply. **2** depot, hiding place, repository.

cackle *verb* **1** cluck, squawk. **2** see LAUGH[1].

cadet *noun* learner, novice, recruit, trainee.

cadge *verb* beg, bludge (*Australian informal*), bot (*Australian slang*), hum (*Australian slang*), put the bite on (*Australian informal*), scab (*Australian slang*), scrounge, sponge.

café *noun* bistro, brasserie, buffet, cafeteria, coffee shop, eatery (*informal*), milk bar, restaurant, snack bar, tea room.

cage *noun* **1** aviary, coop, enclosure, hutch, pen. **caged** *adjective* confined, cooped up, locked up, penned, shut in.

cagoule (*say* kag-**ool**) *noun* a waterproof jacket.

cairn *noun* a pile of loose stones set up as a landmark or monument.

cajole *verb* (**cajoled, cajoling**) coax.

cake *noun* **1** a baked food made from a mixture of flour, fat, eggs, sugar, etc. **2** a shaped or hardened mass, *a cake of soap*; *fish cakes*.

caked *adjective* covered with dried mud etc.

calamine *noun* a pink powder used to make a soothing lotion for the skin.

calamity *noun* (*plural* **calamities**) a disaster. **calamitous** *adjective*

calcium *noun* a chemical substance found in teeth, bones, and lime. [from Latin *calcis* = of lime]

calculate *verb* (**calculated, calculating**) **1** find out by using mathematics; count. **2** plan something deliberately; intend. **calculable** *adjective*, **calculating** *adjective*, **calculation** *noun*

calculator *noun* a small electronic device for making calculations.

calculus *noun* mathematics for working out problems about rates of change. [from Latin *calculus* = small stone (used on an abacus)]

calendar *noun* something that shows the dates of the month or year.

calf¹ *noun* (*plural* **calves**) a young cow, whale, seal, etc.

calf² *noun* (*plural* **calves**) the fleshy back part of the leg below the knee.

calibre (*say* kal-ib-er) *noun* **1** the diameter of a tube or gun-barrel, or of a bullet etc. **2** ability; importance, *someone of your calibre*. [from Arabic *kalib* = mould]

calico *noun* a kind of cotton cloth. [from Calicut, a town in India]

caliph (*say* **kal**-if or **kay**-lif) *noun* the former title of the ruler in certain Muslim countries. [from Arabic *khalifa* = successor of Muhammad]

call¹ *noun* **1** a shout or cry. **2** a visit. **3** a summons. **4** telephoning somebody.

call² *verb* **1** shout or speak loudly, e.g. to attract someone's attention; utter a call. **2** tell somebody to come to you; summon. **3** wake a person up. **4** telephone somebody. **5** make a short visit. **6** name a person or thing. **7** (*Australian*) describe a race for a broadcast. **caller** *noun*

call a person's bluff challenge a person to do what was threatened, and expose the fact that it was a bluff.

call for come and collect; require, *The scandal calls for investigation*.

call up summon to join the armed forces.

calligraphy (*say* kal-**ig**-raf-ee) *noun* beautiful handwriting. [from Greek *kalos* = beautiful, + *-graphy*]

calling *noun* an occupation; a profession or trade.

cajole *verb* beguile, coax, entice, persuade, seduce, sweet-talk (*informal*), wheedle.

cake *noun* **1** baba, bun, cheesecake, cupcake, doughnut, éclair, flan, gateau, lamington, muffin, pastry, scone, sponge, tart, torte. **2** (*a cake of soap*) bar, block, hunk, lump, piece, slab; (*a fish cake*) croquette, patty.

caked *adjective* coated, covered, encrusted.

calamity *noun* accident, catastrophe, disaster, misadventure, misfortune, mishap, tragedy.

calculate *verb* **1** add up, assess, compute, count, determine, estimate, figure out, reckon, total, tot up (*informal*), work out. **2** aim, design, intend, mean, plan.
calculating *adjective* crafty, cunning, designing, devious, plotting, scheming, shrewd, sly, wily.
calculation *noun* answer, computation, estimate, forecast, result, sum.

calendar *noun* daybook, diary, programme, schedule, timetable.

calf¹ *noun* heifer, mickey (*Australian*), poddy (*Australian*).

call¹ *noun* **1** bellow, cooee (*informal*), cry, exclamation, roar, scream, shout, shriek, signal, yell. **2** stay, stop, visit. **3** appeal, invitation, plea, request, summons. **4** bell (*informal*), buzz (*informal*), phone call, ring, telephone call.

call² *verb* **1** bellow, cooee (*informal*), cry, cry out, exclaim, roar, scream, shout, shriek, yell. **2** ask, bid, command, fetch, invite, order, page, send for, summon. **3** arouse, awaken, rouse, waken. **4** contact, phone, ring, telephone. **5** drop in, look in, pay a visit, visit. **6** address as, baptise, christen, describe as, designate, dub, label, name, nickname, term.
call for 1 collect, fetch, get, pick up. **2** demand, deserve, justify, necessitate, occasion, require, warrant.
call up conscript, draft (*American*), recruit, summon.

calling *noun* career, employment, job, mission, niche, occupation, profession, trade, vocation.

▶▶ D I C T I O N A R Y ◀◀

calliper *noun* a support for a weak or injured leg.

callipers *plural noun* compasses for measuring the width of tubes or of round objects.

callous (*say* **kal**-us) *adjective* hard-hearted; unsympathetic. **callously** *adverb*, **callousness** *noun*

callow *adjective* immature and inexperienced. **callowly** *adverb*, **callowness** *noun*

callus *noun* (*plural* **calluses**) a small patch of skin that has become thick and hard through being continually pressed or rubbed.

calm¹ *adjective* **1** quiet and still; not windy. **2** not excited or agitated. **calm** *noun*, **calmly** *adverb*, **calmness** *noun*

calm² *verb* make or become calm.

calorie *noun* a unit for measuring an amount of heat or the energy produced by food. **calorific** *adjective* [from Latin *calor* = heat]

calumny (*say* **kal**-um-nee) *noun* (*plural* **calumnies**) slander.

calve *verb* (**calved, calving**) give birth to a calf.

calypso *noun* (*plural* **calypsos**) a West Indian song about current happenings.

calyx (*say* **kay**-liks) *noun* (*plural* **calyces**) a ring of leaves (*sepals*) forming the outer case of a bud.

camaraderie (*say* kam-er-**ah**-der-ee) *noun* comradeship. [French]

camber *noun* a slight upward curve or arch, e.g. on a road to allow drainage.

cambric *noun* thin linen or cotton cloth.

camel *noun* a large animal with a long neck and either one or two humps on its back, used in desert countries for riding and for carrying goods.

camellia *noun* a kind of evergreen flowering shrub.

cameo (*say* **kam**-ee-oh) *noun* (*plural* **cameos**) **1** a small hard piece of stone carved with a raised design in its upper layer. **2** a short well-performed part in a play etc.

camera *noun* a device for taking photographs, films, or television pictures. **cameraman** *noun* **in camera** in a judge's private room; in private.

camomile *noun* a plant with sweet-smelling daisy-like flowers.

camouflage¹ (*say* **kam**-off-lah*zh*) *noun* a way of hiding things by making them look like part of their surroundings.

camouflage² *verb* (**camouflaged, camouflaging**) hide by camouflage. [from French *camoufler* = disguise]

camp¹ *noun* a place where people live in tents or huts etc. **campsite** *noun*

camp² *verb* make a camp; live in a camp. **camper** *noun* [same origin as *campus*]

campaign¹ *noun* **1** a series of battles in one area or with one purpose. **2** a planned series of actions, *an advertising campaign.*

campaign² *verb* take part in a campaign. **campaigner** *noun*

camphor *noun* a strong-smelling white substance used in medicine and mothballs and in making plastics. **camphorated** *adjective*

campion *noun* a wild plant with pink or white flowers.

campus *noun* (*plural* **campuses**) the grounds of a university or college. [Latin, = field]

▶▶ T H E S A U R U S ◀◀

callous *adjective* cold-hearted, cruel, hard-hearted, harsh, heartless, insensitive, merciless, pitiless, ruthless, thick-skinned, uncaring, unfeeling, unsympathetic.

calm¹ *adjective* **1** (*a calm day*) balmy, halcyon, mild, quiet, still; (*calm seas*) even, flat, motionless, quiet, smooth, steady, still. **2** collected, composed, cool, imperturbable, level-headed, nonchalant, peaceful, phlegmatic, placid, relaxed, sedate, self-possessed, serene, stoical, tranquil, unexcited, unfazed (*informal*), unflappable (*informal*), unruffled. **calm** *noun* calmness, lull, peace, quietness, repose, serenity, stillness, tranquillity.

calmness *noun* calm, composure, coolness, equanimity, imperturbability, nonchalance, poise, presence of mind, serenity.

calm² *verb* allay, alleviate, appease, lull, mollify, pacify, quell, quieten, relieve, soothe, still, subdue.

calm down collect yourself, compose yourself, cool off, relax, settle, simmer down.

camouflage² *verb* conceal, cover up, disguise, hide, mask, screen.

camp¹ *noun* base, bivouac, encampment, tent.

camp² *verb* encamp, pitch your tent.

campaign¹ *noun* **1** action, battle, blitz, crusade, fight, manoeuvre, offensive, operation, war. **2** crusade, drive, offensive, strategy.

campaign² *verb* agitate, battle, canvass, crusade, fight, lobby, press, push, strive, work.

campus *noun* grounds, property, site.

▶▶ DICTIONARY ◀◀

can¹ *noun* **1** a metal or plastic container for liquids. **2** a sealed tin in which food or drink is preserved.

can² *verb* (**canned, canning**) preserve in a sealed can. **canner** *noun*

can³ *auxiliary verb* (*past tense* **could**) **1** be able to, *He can play the violin.* **2** have the right or permission to, *You can go.* [from an old word meaning 'know']

Usage In sense 2 it is more formal to say *You may go.*

canal *noun* **1** an artificial river cut through land so that boats can sail along it or so that it can drain or irrigate an area. **2** a tube through which something passes in the body, *the alimentary canal.* [same origin as *channel*]

canary *noun* (*plural* **canaries**) a small yellow bird that sings.

cancan *noun* a lively dance in which the legs are kicked very high.

cancel *verb* (**cancelled, cancelling**) **1** say that something planned will not be done or will not take place. **2** stop an order or instruction for something. **3** mark a stamp or ticket etc. so that it cannot be used again. **cancellation** *noun*
cancel out stop each other's effect, *The good and harm cancel each other out.*

cancer *noun* **1** a disease in which harmful growths form in the body. **2** a tumour, especially a harmful one. **cancerous** *adjective* [from Latin *cancer* = crab]

candelabrum (*say* kan-dil-**ab**-rum) *noun* (*plural* **candelabra**) a candlestick with several branches for holding candles. [from Latin *candela* = candle]

candid *adjective* frank. **candidly** *adverb*, **candidness** *noun* [from Latin *candidus* = white]

candidate *noun* **1** a person who wants to be elected or chosen for a particular job or position etc. **2** a person taking an examination. **candidacy** *noun*, **candidature** *noun* [from Latin *candidus* = white (because Roman candidates for office had to wear a pure white toga)]

candied *adjective* coated or preserved in sugar.
candied peel bits of the peel of citrus fruits candied for use in cooking. [from *candy*]

candle *noun* a stick of wax with a wick through it, giving light when burning. **candlelight** *noun*

candlestick *noun* a holder for a candle or candles.

candour (*say* **kan**-der) *noun* being candid; frankness.

candy *noun* (*plural* **candies**) (*American*) sweets; a sweet. [from Arabic *kand* = sugar]

cane¹ *noun* **1** the stem of a reed or tall grass etc. **2** a thin stick.
cane toad a large toad introduced into Queensland to control insects in sugar-cane plantations but spreading more widely.

cane² *verb* (**caned, caning**) beat with a cane.

canine¹ (*say* **kayn**-I'n) *adjective* of dogs.
canine tooth a pointed tooth.

canine² *noun* **1** a dog. **2** a canine tooth. [from Latin *canis* = dog]

canister *noun* a metal container.

canker *noun* a disease that rots the wood of trees and plants or causes ulcers and sores on animals.

cannabis *noun* hemp, especially when smoked as a drug. [from *Cannabis*, the Latin name of the hemp plant]

cannibal *noun* **1** a person who eats human flesh. **2** an animal that eats animals of its own kind. **cannibalism** *noun* [named after the

▶▶ THESAURUS ◀◀

can¹ *noun* caddy, canister, tin.

can² *verb* preserve, tin.

canal *noun* **1** channel, watercourse, waterway. **2** duct, passage, tube.

cancel *verb* **1** abandon, call off, scrap, scrub (*informal*), stop, wash out (*informal*); see also DISCONTINUE. **2** abolish, annul, countermand, quash, repeal, rescind, retract, revoke. **3** cross out, delete, erase, obliterate, scratch out, wipe out.
cancel out balance out, counteract, counterbalance, negate, neutralise, nullify, offset, undo.

cancer *noun* **2** carcinoma, growth, malignancy, melanoma, tumour.

candid *adjective* blunt, direct, forthright, frank, honest, open, outspoken, plain, sincere, straight, straightforward, upfront (*informal*).

candidate *noun* **1** applicant, competitor, contender, contestant, entrant, interviewee, nominee, runner. **2** entrant, examinee.

cane¹ *noun* **2** rod, staff, stick, walking-stick.

cane² *verb* beat, hit, flog, lash, strike, thrash, whack.

canister *noun* caddy, can, tin.

▶▶ D I C T I O N A R Y ◀◀

Caribs, a former man-eating tribe in the West Indies]

cannibalise *verb* (**cannibalised, cannibalising**) take a machine etc. apart to provide spare parts for others. **cannibalisation** *noun*

cannon¹ *noun* 1 (*plural* **cannon**) a large heavy gun. 2 the hitting of two balls in billiards by the third ball.

cannon² *verb* (**cannoned, cannoning**) bump into something heavily.

cannon-ball *noun* a large solid ball fired from a cannon.

cannot can not.

canny *adjective* (**cannier, canniest**) shrewd. **cannily** *adverb*

canoe¹ *noun* a narrow lightweight boat.

canoe² *verb* (**canoed, canoeing**) travel in a canoe. **canoeist** *noun*

canon *noun* 1 a member of the clergy who is part of a cathedral chapter. 2 a general principle; a rule.

canonise *verb* (**canonised, canonising**) declare officially that someone is a saint. **canonisation** *noun*

canopy *noun* (*plural* **canopies**) 1 a hanging cover forming a shelter above a throne, bed, or person etc. 2 the part of a parachute that spreads in the air.

cant¹ *verb* slope; tilt. [from a Dutch word meaning 'edge']

cant² *noun* 1 insincere talk. 2 jargon. [from Latin *cantare* = sing]

can't (*mainly spoken*) cannot.

cantaloupe *noun* a small round orange-coloured melon; a rockmelon.

cantankerous *adjective* bad-tempered.

cantata (*say* kant-**ah**-ta) *noun* a musical composition for singers, like an oratorio but shorter. [from Italian *cantare* = sing]

canteen *noun* 1 a restaurant for workers in a factory, office, etc. 2 a case or box containing a set of cutlery. 3 a soldier's or camper's water-flask.

canter¹ *noun* a gentle gallop.

canter² *verb* go or ride at a canter. [short for 'Canterbury gallop', the gentle pace at which pilgrims were said to travel to Canterbury in the Middle Ages]

canticle *noun* a religious song with words taken from the Bible, e.g. the Magnificat. [from Latin, = little song]

cantilever *noun* a projecting beam or girder supporting a bridge etc.

canton *noun* each of the districts into which Switzerland is divided.

canvas *noun* (*plural* **canvases**) 1 a kind of strong coarse cloth. 2 a piece of canvas for painting on; a painting. [from Latin *Cannabis* = hemp, from whose fibres cloth was made]

canvass *verb* visit people to ask for votes, opinions, etc. **canvasser** *noun*

canyon *noun* a deep valley, usually with a river running through it. [from Spanish *cañon* = tube]

cap¹ *noun* 1 a soft hat without a brim but often with a peak. 2 a special head-dress, e.g. that worn by a nurse; an academic mortar-board; a cap showing membership of a sports team. 3 a cap-like cover or top. 4 something that makes a bang when fired in a toy pistol.

cap² *verb* (**capped, capping**) 1 put a cap or cover on something; cover. 2 award a sports cap to a person chosen as a member of a team. 3 do better than something, *Can you cap that joke?*

capable *adjective* able to do something. **capably** *adverb*, **capability** *noun*

capacious (*say* ka-**pay**-shus) *adjective* roomy; able to hold a large amount.

▶▶ T H E S A U R U S ◀◀

canoe¹ *noun* dugout, kayak.

canopy *noun* 1 awning, cover, covering, tester.

canteen *noun* 1 cafeteria, dining room, refectory, restaurant, snack bar, tuckshop.

canvass *verb* campaign, electioneer, solicit votes.

canyon *noun* chasm, defile, gorge, gully, pass, ravine, valley.

cap¹ *noun* 1,2 hat, head-covering, headgear; (*kinds of cap*) beanie, beret, bonnet, busby, deerstalker, fez, mob cap, mortarboard, nightcap, skullcap, yarmulke. 3 cover, lid, top.

capable *adjective* able, accomplished, adept, clever, competent, effective, efficient, expert, gifted, proficient, skilful, skilled, smart, talented.

capability *noun* ability, aptitude, calibre, capacity, competence, potential, proficiency, prowess, skill, talent.

▶▶ DICTIONARY ◀◀

capacity *noun* (*plural* **capacities**) **1** the amount that something can hold. **2** ability; capability. **3** the position that someone occupies, *In my capacity as your guardian I am responsible for you.*

cape¹ *noun* a cloak.

cape² *noun* a promontory on the coast.

caper¹ *verb* jump or run about playfully.

caper² *noun* **1** capering. **2** (*slang*) an activity; an adventure.

caper³ *noun* a bud of a prickly shrub, pickled for use in sauces etc.

capillary¹ (*say* ka-**pil**-er-ee) *noun* (*plural* **capillaries**) any of the very fine blood-vessels that connect veins and arteries.

capillary² *adjective* of or occurring in a very narrow tube; of a capillary. [from Latin *capillus* = hair]

capital¹ *adjective* **1** important. **2** (*informal*) excellent.

capital city the most important city in a country.

capital letter a large letter of the kind used at the start of a name or sentence.

capital punishment punishing criminals by putting them to death.

capital² *noun* **1** a capital city. **2** a capital letter. **3** the top part of a pillar. **4** money or property that can be used to produce more wealth. [from Latin *caput* = head]

capitalise (*say* **kap**-it-al-I'z) *verb* (**capitalised, capitalising**) **1** write or print as a capital letter. **2** change something into capital; provide with capital (= money). **capitalisation** *noun*

capitalise on profit by something; use it to your own advantage, *You could capitalise on your skill at drawing.*

capitalism (*say* **kap**-it-al-izm) *noun* a system in which trade and industry are controlled by private owners for profit. (Compare *Communism.*)

capitalist (*say* **kap**-it-al-ist) *noun* **1** a person who has much money or property being used to make more wealth; a very rich person. **2** a person who is in favour of capitalism.

capitulate *verb* (**capitulated, capitulating**) admit that you are defeated and surrender. **capitulation** *noun*

caprice (*say* ka-**preess**) *noun* a capricious action or impulse; a whim.

capricious (*say* ka-**prish**-us) *adjective* deciding or changing your mind in an impulsive way. **capriciously** *adverb*, **capriciousness** *noun*

capsize *verb* (**capsized, capsizing**) overturn, *the boat capsized.*

capstan *noun* a thick post that can be turned to pull in a rope or cable etc. that winds round it as it turns.

capsule *noun* **1** a hollow pill containing medicine. **2** a plant's seed-case that splits open when ripe. **3** a compartment that can be separated from the rest of a spacecraft.

captain¹ *noun* **1** a person in command of a ship, aircraft, sports team, etc. **2** an army officer ranking next below a major; a naval officer ranking next below a commodore. **captaincy** *noun*

captain² *verb* be the captain of a sports team etc. [same origin as *capital*]

▶▶ THESAURUS ◀◀

capacity *noun* **1** dimensions, magnitude, size, volume. **2** ability, aptitude, capability, competence, gift, potential, power, skill, talent. **3** duty, function, office, position, post, role.

cape¹ *noun* cloak, cope, mantle, poncho, shawl, stole, wrap.

cape² *noun* head, headland, point, promontory.

caper¹ *verb* bound, cavort, dance, frisk, frolic, gambol, hop, jump, leap, play, prance, romp, scamper, skip.

capital¹ *adjective* **1** chief, foremost, important, leading, main, major, principal.

capital letter block letter, upper-case letter.

capital² *noun* **4** assets, cash, finance, funds, means, money, principal, resources, stock, wealth.

capitalise *verb* **capitalise on** cash in on, exploit, make the most of, profit from, take advantage of.

capitalism *noun* free enterprise, private enterprise.

capitulate *verb* cave in, give in, give up, submit, succumb, surrender, throw in the towel, yield.

capricious *adjective* changeable, erratic, fickle, flighty, impulsive, inconstant, mercurial, temperamental, unpredictable, unreliable, variable, volatile, whimsical.

capsize *verb* flip over, invert, keel over, overturn, tip over, turn over, turn turtle.

capsule *noun* **1** pill, tablet.

captain¹ *noun* **1** commander, master, skipper; see also CHIEF¹.

▶▶ D I C T I O N A R Y ◀◀

caption *noun* **1** the words printed with a picture to describe it. **2** a short title or heading in a newspaper or magazine.

captious (*say* **kap**-shus) *adjective* pointing out small mistakes or faults.

captivate *verb* (**captivated, captivating**) charm or delight someone. **captivation** *noun*

captive[1] *noun* someone taken prisoner.

captive[2] *adjective* taken prisoner; unable to escape. **captivity** *noun*

captor *noun* someone who has captured a person or animal.

capture[1] *verb* (**captured, capturing**) **1** seize; make a prisoner of someone. **2** take or obtain by force, trickery, skill, or attraction, *He captured her heart.*

capture[2] *noun* **1** capturing. **2** a person or thing captured. [from Latin *capere* = take]

car *noun* **1** a motor car. **2** a carriage, *dining-car.* [from Latin *carrus* = wagon]

carafe (*say* ka-**raf**) *noun* a glass bottle holding wine or water for pouring out at the table. [from Arabic *gharrafa*]

caramel *noun* **1** a kind of toffee tasting like burnt sugar. **2** burnt sugar used for colouring and flavouring food.

carapace (*say* **ka**-ra-payss) *noun* the shell on the back of a tortoise or crustacean.

carat *noun* **1** a measure of weight for precious stones. **2** a measure of the purity of gold, *Pure gold is 24 carats.*

caravan *noun* **1** an enclosed carriage equipped for living in, able to be towed by a motor vehicle or a horse. **2** a group of people travelling together across desert country. **caravanning** *noun* [from Persian *karwan*]

caraway *noun* a plant with spicy seeds that are used for flavouring food.

carbohydrate *noun* a compound of carbon, oxygen, and hydrogen (e.g. sugar).

carbolic *noun* a kind of disinfectant.

carbon *noun* **1** a substance that is present in all living things and that occurs in its pure form as diamond and graphite. **2** carbon paper. **3** a carbon copy.
carbon copy a copy made with carbon paper; an exact copy.
carbon dioxide a gas formed when things burn, or breathed out by animals.
carbon paper thin paper with a coloured coating, placed between sheets of paper to make copies of what is written or typed on the top sheet.

carbonate *noun* a compound that gives off carbon dioxide when mixed with acid.

carbonated *adjective* with carbon dioxide added, *Carbonated drinks are fizzy.*

carboniferous *adjective* producing coal. [from *carbon*, + Latin *ferre* = to bear]

carbuncle *noun* **1** a bad abscess in the skin. **2** a bright-red gem.

carburettor *noun* a device for mixing fuel and air in an engine.

carcass *noun* (*plural* **carcasses**) **1** the dead body of an animal. **2** the bony part of a bird's body before or after it is cooked. **3** a framework, e.g. of a tyre.

card[1] *noun* **1** a small usually oblong piece of stiff paper or of plastic. **2** a playing card. **3** cardboard.
cards *plural noun* a game using playing cards.
on the cards likely; possible.

▶▶ T H E S A U R U S ◀◀

caption *noun* heading, headline, subtitle, surtitle, title.

captivate *verb* attract, beguile, bewitch, capture, charm, delight, enchant, enthral, entrance, fascinate, mesmerise, seduce.

captive[1] *noun* convict, detainee, hostage, prisoner.

captivity *noun* bondage, confinement, custody, detention, imprisonment, incarceration, internment, servitude, slavery.

captor *noun* abductor, kidnapper.

capture[1] *verb* **1** apprehend, arrest, catch, collar (*informal*), nab (*informal*), nail, nick (*slang*), seize. **2** catch, hold, take, win.

capture[2] *noun* **1** apprehension, arrest, seizure.

car *noun* **1** auto (*informal*), automobile (*American*), motor, motor car, motor vehicle, vehicle, wheels (*slang*); (*an old or dilapidated car*) banger, bomb (*Australian*), heap, jalopy, rattletrap, rust bucket, wreck; (*kinds of car*) convertible, coupé, fastback, four-wheel drive, hatchback, hearse, hot rod, limousine, panel van (*Australian*), saloon, sedan, soft-top, sports car, station wagon (*Australian*), ute (*Australian informal*), utility (*Australian*), van, wagon (*informal*).

caravan *noun* **1** camper, campervan, mobile home, trailer (*American*), van.

carcass *noun* **1** body, cadaver, corpse, remains.

▶▶▶ D I C T I O N A R Y ◀◀◀

card² *verb* clean and disentangle wool-fibres with a wire brush or toothed instrument called a *card*.

cardboard *noun* a kind of thin board made of layers of paper or wood-fibre.

cardiac (*say* **kard**-ee-ak) *adjective* of the heart. [from Greek *kardia* = heart]

cardigan *noun* a knitted jacket. [named after the Earl of Cardigan, who led the Charge of the Light Brigade in the Crimean War (1854)]

cardinal¹ *noun* a senior priest in the Roman Catholic Church.

cardinal² *adjective* 1 chief; most important, *the cardinal features of our plan*. 2 deep scarlet (like a cardinal's cassock).
cardinal numbers the whole numbers one, two, three, etc. (Compare *ordinal*.)
cardinal points the four main points of the compass (North, East, South, West).

cardiology *noun* the study of the structure and diseases of the heart. **cardiological** *adjective*, **cardiologist** *noun* [from Greek *kardia* = heart, + *-logy*]

care¹ *noun* 1 serious attention and thought, *Plan your holiday with care*. 2 caution to avoid damage or loss, *Glass—handle with care*. 3 protection; supervision, *Leave the child in my care*. 4 worry; anxiety, *freedom from care*. [from Old English *caru* = sorrow]

care² *verb* (**cared, caring**) 1 feel interested or concerned. 2 feel affection.
care for have in your care; be fond of.

career¹ *noun* 1 progress through life, especially in work. 2 an occupation with opportunities for promotion.

career² *verb* rush along wildly.

carefree *adjective* without worries or responsibilities.

careful *adjective* 1 giving serious thought and attention to something. 2 avoiding damage or danger etc.; cautious. **carefully** *adverb*, **carefulness** *noun*

careless *adjective* 1 not taking care or paying attention. 2 done without care. 3 unthinking, insensitive. **carelessly** *adverb*, **carelessness** *noun*

caress¹ *noun* a gentle loving touch.

caress² *verb* touch lovingly.

caret *noun* a mark (^ or ⅄) showing where something is to be inserted in writing or printing. [Latin, = it is lacking]

caretaker *noun* a person employed to look after a school, block of flats, etc.

cargo *noun* (*plural* **cargoes**) goods carried in a ship or aircraft.

▶▶▶ T H E S A U R U S ◀◀◀

care¹ *noun* 1,2 attention, carefulness, caution, circumspection, concentration, diligence, meticulousness, precision, thoroughness, thought. 3 charge, control, custody, guardianship, hands, keeping, protection, responsibility, supervision. 4 anxiety, bother, burden, concern, problem, trouble, woe, worry.
take care be careful, be cautious, beware, be wary, look out, take heed, take pains, watch out.
take care of 1 keep an eye on, look after, mind, supervise, take charge of, watch over. 2 attend to, deal with, take charge of.

care² *verb* 1 be concerned, be interested, bother, concern yourself, mind, worry.
care for 1 attend to, look after, mind, mother, nurse, take care of, tend, watch over. 2 be fond of, be keen on, cherish, like, love.

career¹ *noun* 2 calling, employment, job, occupation, profession, trade, vocation, work.

career² *verb* hurtle, run, rush, shoot, speed.

carefree *adjective* blithe, breezy, casual, cheerful, contented, easygoing, footloose, happy-go-lucky, laid-back (*informal*), light-hearted, nonchalant, relaxed, untroubled.

careful *adjective* 1 accurate, conscientious, diligent, fastidious, methodical, meticulous, neat, organised, painstaking, pernickety (*informal*), precise, punctilious, rigorous, scrupulous, systematic, thorough. 2 alert, attentive, cautious, chary, circumspect, guarded, mindful, on guard, prudent, vigilant, wary, watchful.

careless *adjective* 1 absent-minded, inattentive, incautious, irresponsible, lax, negligent, rash, reckless, slack. 2 cursory, disorganised, hasty, hit-or-miss, imprecise, inaccurate, inexact, lax, messy, perfunctory, shoddy, slapdash, slipshod, sloppy, slovenly, untidy. 3 imprudent, inconsiderate, indiscreet, insensitive, tactless, thoughtless, uncaring, unguarded, unthinking.

caress² *verb* cuddle, embrace, fondle, hug, kiss, pat, pet, stroke, touch.

caretaker *noun* curator, custodian, janitor, keeper, sexton, steward, verger, warden.

cargo *noun* consignment, freight, goods, load, shipment.

▶▶ D I C T I O N A R Y ◀◀

Caribbean *adjective* of or from the Caribbean Sea, a part of the Atlantic Ocean east of Central America.

caribou (*say* **ka**-rib-oo) *noun* (*plural* **caribou**) a North American reindeer.

caricature *noun* an amusing or exaggerated picture of someone. [from Italian *caricare* = exaggerate]

caries (*say* **kair**-eez) *noun* (*plural* **caries**) decay in teeth or bones. [Latin]

carmine *adjective* & *noun* deep red.

carnage *noun* the killing of many people.

carnal *adjective* of the body as opposed to the spirit; not spiritual. [from Latin *carnis* = of flesh]

carnation *noun* a garden flower with a sweet smell.

carnival *noun* a festival, often with a procession in fancy dress. [originally this meant the festivities before Lent when meat (Latin *carnis* = of flesh) was given up until Easter]

carnivorous (*say* kar-**niv**-er-us) *adjective* meat-eating. (Compare *herbivorous*.) **carnivore** *noun* [from Latin *carnis* = of flesh, + *vorare* = devour]

carol *noun* a joyful song; a Christmas hymn. **caroller** *noun*, **carolling** *noun*

carouse *verb* (**caroused, carousing**) drink and be merry.

carousel (*say* ka-roo-**sel**) *noun* **1** (*American*) a merry-go-round. **2** a rotating conveyor, e.g. for baggage at an airport.

carp¹ *noun* an edible freshwater fish.

carp² *verb* keep finding fault.

carpenter *noun* a person who makes things out of wood. **carpentry** *noun*

carpet *noun* a thick soft covering for a floor. **carpeted** *adjective*, **carpeting** *noun*

carport *noun* a shelter for a car.

carriage *noun* **1** one of the separate parts of a train, where passengers sit. **2** a passenger vehicle pulled by horses. **3** carrying goods from one place to another; the cost of carrying goods, *Carriage is extra.* **4** a moving part carrying or holding something in a machine.

carriageway *noun* the part of a road on which vehicles travel.

carrier *noun* a person or thing that carries something.

carrion *noun* dead and decaying flesh. [same origin as *carnal*]

carrot *noun* a plant with a thick orange-coloured root used as a vegetable.

carry *verb* (**carried, carrying**) **1** take something from one place to another. **2** support the weight of something. **3** travel clearly, *Sound carries in the mountains.* **4** win; approve, *The motion was carried by ten votes to six.* **be carried away** be very excited. **carry on** continue; manage; (*informal*) behave excitedly; (*informal*) complain. **carry out** put into practice. [same origin as *car*]

cart¹ *noun* an open vehicle for carrying loads.

cart² *verb* **1** carry in a cart. **2** (*informal*) carry something heavy or tiring, *I've carted these books all round the school.*

cart-horse *noun* a large strong horse used for pulling heavy loads.

cartilage *noun* tough white flexible tissue attached to a bone.

▶▶ T H E S A U R U S ◀◀

caricature *noun* burlesque, cartoon, parody, satire, send-up (*informal*), spoof (*informal*), take-off (*informal*).

carnage *noun* bloodbath, bloodshed, butchery, holocaust, killing, massacre, murder, slaughter.

carnival *noun* celebration, fair, festival, fête, fiesta, gala, jamboree, Mardi Gras, pageant, show.

carol *noun* canticle, hymn, song.

carpentry *noun* cabinetmaking, joinery, woodwork.

carpet *noun* floor covering, mat, rug, runner.

carriage *noun* **1** car, coach. **2** brougham, buggy, chaise, chariot, coach, curricle, gig, hansom, landau, phaeton, post-chaise, stagecoach, sulky, trap, wagon.

carrier *noun* **1** carter, courier, dispatch rider, haulier, messenger. **2** basket, container, holder, pannier, receptacle.

carry *verb* **1** bear, bring, cart, convey, ferry, fetch, freight, haul, lift, lug, move, remove, ship, take, transfer, transport. **2** bear, hold up, support, sustain, take. **carry on 1** continue, go on, keep on, persevere, persist, remain. **2** conduct, manage, operate, run. **3** complain, go on, rant, rave, spout. **carry out** accomplish, complete, conduct, discharge, do, execute, finish, fulfil, perform, undertake.

cart¹ *noun* barrow, billycart, dray, float, go-cart, handcart, trolley, tumbrel, wagon, wheelbarrow.

▶▶ DICTIONARY ◀◀

cartography *noun* drawing maps. **carto-grapher** *noun*, **cartographic** *adjective* [from French *carte* = map, + *-graphy*]

carton *noun* a cardboard or plastic container.

cartoon *noun* 1 an amusing drawing. 2 a comic strip (see *comic*). 3 an animated film. **cartoonist** *noun*

cartridge *noun* 1 a case containing the explosive for a bullet or shell. 2 a container holding film for a camera, ink for a pen, etc. 3 the device that holds the stylus of a record-player.

cartwheel *noun* 1 the wheel of a cart. 2 a handstand balancing on each hand in turn with arms and legs spread like spokes of a wheel.

carve *verb* (**carved, carving**) 1 make by cutting wood or stone etc. 2 cut designs or letters etc. in wood or stone etc. 3 cut cooked meat into slices. **carver** *noun*

cascade¹ *noun* a waterfall.

cascade² *verb* (**cascaded, cascading**) fall like a cascade.

case¹ *noun* 1 a container. 2 a suitcase. [from Latin *capsa* = box]

case² *noun* 1 an example of something existing or occurring; a situation, *In every case we found that someone had cheated.* 2 something investigated by police etc. or by a lawcourt, *a murder case.* 3 a set of facts or arguments to support something, *She put forward a good case for equality.* 4 the form of a word that shows how it is related to other words. *Fred's* is the possessive case of *Fred; him* is the objective case of *he*. **in any case** anyway.

in case because something may happen; lest. [from Latin *casus* = occasion]

casement *noun* a window that opens on hinges at its side.

cash¹ *noun* 1 money in coin or notes. 2 immediate payment for goods etc. **cash register** a device that registers the amount of money put in, used in a shop.

cash² *verb* change a cheque etc. for cash. **cash in on** (*informal*) profit from something.

cashew *noun* a kind of small nut.

cashier *noun* a person who takes in and pays out money in a bank or takes payments in a shop.

cashmere *noun* very fine soft wool. [first made from the hair of goats from Kashmir in Asia]

casing *noun* a protective covering.

casino *noun* (*plural* **casinos**) a public building or room for gambling.

cask *noun* 1 a barrel. 2 (*Australian*) a box with plastic or foil lining for storing and serving wine or juice.

casket *noun* a small box for jewellery etc.

cassava *noun* a tropical plant with starchy roots that are an important source of food in tropical countries.

casserole *noun* 1 a covered dish in which food is cooked and served. 2 food cooked in a casserole. [from Greek, = little cup]

cassette *noun* a small sealed case containing recording tape, film, etc. [French, = little case]

cassock *noun* a long garment worn by clergy and members of a church choir.

▶▶ THESAURUS ◀◀

carton *noun* box, case, container, pack, package, packet.

cartoon *noun* 1 caricature, drawing. 2 comic, comic strip. 3 animated film, animation.

carve *verb* 1 chip, chisel, fashion, hew, sculpt (*informal*), sculpture, shape, whittle. 2 engrave, etch, inscribe. 3 cut, slice.

cascade¹ *noun* cataract, falls, rapids, waterfall.

case¹ *noun* 1 box, cabinet, canteen (*of cutlery*), capsule, carton, cartridge, casing, casket, chest, coffer, container, covering, crate, envelope, holder, holster, housing, jacket, pack, packaging, receptacle, sheath, shell, skin, sleeve, wrapper. 2 attaché case, bag, briefcase, holdall, port (*Australian*), portmanteau, suitcase, trunk; (*cases*) baggage, luggage.

case² *noun* 1 example, illustration, instance, occasion, occurrence, situation. 2 action, dispute, hearing, lawsuit, proceedings, suit, trial. 3 arguments, facts.

cash¹ *noun* 1 banknotes, change, coins, currency, dosh (*slang*), dough (*slang*), funds, money, notes, paper money, ready money, wherewithal (*informal*).

cash² *verb* redeem, turn into cash. **cash in on** capitalise on, exploit, make the most of, profit from, take advantage of.

cask *noun* 1 barrel, butt, hogshead, keg, tub, tun, vat.

casket *noun* box, case, chest, coffer, container.

casserole *noun* 2 cassoulet, fricassee, goulash, hotpot, ragout, stew.

cast¹ *verb* (**cast, casting**) **1** throw. **2** shed or throw off. **3** make a vote. **4** make something of metal or plaster in a mould. **5** choose performers for a play or film etc.
casting vote the vote that decides which group wins when the votes on each side are equal.
cast iron a hard alloy of iron made by casting it in a mould.

cast² *noun* **1** a shape made by pouring liquid metal or plaster into a mould. **2** all the performers in a play or film.

castanets *plural noun* two pieces of wood, ivory, etc. held in one hand and clapped together to make a clicking sound, usually for dancing. [from Spanish *castañetas* = little chestnuts]

castaway *noun* a shipwrecked person.

caste *noun* (in India) one of the social classes into which Hindus are born. [from Spanish *casta* = descent from ancestors]

caster sugar finely ground white sugar.

castigate *verb* (**castigated, castigating**) punish or rebuke severely. **castigation** *noun* [from Latin *castigare* = punish]

castle *noun* **1** a large old fortified building. **2** a piece in chess, also called a rook.
castles in the air day-dreams. [from Latin *castellum* = fort]

castor *noun* **1** a small wheel on the leg of a table, chair, etc. **2** a container with holes for sprinkling sugar. [from *cast*]

castor oil oil from the seeds of a tropical plant, used as a laxative.

castrate *verb* (**castrated, castrating**) remove the testicles of a male animal; geld. (Compare *spay*.) **castration** *noun*

casual *adjective* **1** happening by chance; not planned. **2** not careful; not methodical. **3** informal; suitable for informal occasions, *casual clothes*. **4** not permanent, *casual work*. **casually** *adverb*, **casualness** *noun*

casualty *noun* (*plural* **casualties**) a person who is killed or injured in war or in an accident.

casuarina (*say* kas-yoo-a-**ree**-na) *noun* a tree with jointed branches that resemble gigantic horse-tails.

cat *noun* **1** a small furry domestic animal. **2** an animal of the same family as the domestic cat, *Lions and tigers are cats*. **3** (*informal*) a spiteful girl or woman.
let the cat out of the bag reveal a secret.

cata- *prefix* (becoming **cat-** before a vowel; combining with an *h* to become **cath-**) **1** down (as in *catapult*). **2** thoroughly (as in *catalogue*). [from Greek *kata* = down]

cataclysm (*say* **kat**-a-klizm) *noun* a violent upheaval or disaster.

catacombs (*say* **kat**-a-koomz) *plural noun* underground passages with compartments for tombs.

catafalque (*say* **kat**-a-falk) *noun* a decorated platform for a person's coffin.

catalogue¹ *noun* **1** a list of things (e.g. of books in a library), usually arranged in order. **2** a book containing a list of things available, *Christmas catalogue*.

catalogue² *verb* (**catalogued, cataloguing**) enter something in a catalogue. [from Greek *katalogos* = list]

cast¹ *verb* **1** chuck (*informal*), drop, eject, fling, heave, hurl, launch, pitch, shy, sling, throw, toss. **2** discard, get rid of, shed, slough, throw off. **4** fashion, form, model, mould, sculpt, shape.

cast² *noun* **1** form, mould, shape. **2** actors, company, performers, players, troupe.

caste *noun* class, level, order, rank, standing, station, stratum.

castigate *verb* admonish, censure, chastise, chide (*old use*), criticise, haul over the coals, punish, rebuke, reprimand, reproach, reprove, scold, tear strips off (*informal*), tell off (*informal*), tick off (*informal*).

castle *noun* **1** château, citadel, fort, fortress, mansion, palace, stronghold.

casual *adjective* **1** accidental, chance, fortuitous, random, serendipitous, unexpected, unforeseen, unintentional, unplanned. **2** apathetic, blasé, carefree, careless, easygoing, happy-go-lucky, lackadaisical, laid-back (*informal*), lax, light-hearted, nonchalant, offhand, relaxed, slap-happy (*informal*), unconcerned, unthinking. **3** informal, leisure, sports. **4** erratic, irregular, occasional, temporary.

casualty *noun* fatality, victim.

cat *noun* **1** feline, kitten, moggie (*informal*), puss, pussy (*informal*), tom, tomcat.

catalogue¹ *noun* **1** directory, file, index, inventory, list, register.

catalogue² *verb* index, list, record, register.

▶▶DICTIONARY◀◀

catalyst (*say* **kat**-a-list) *noun* something that starts or speeds up a change or reaction. [from *cata*-, + Greek *lysis* = loosening]

catamaran *noun* a boat with twin hulls. [from Tamil *kattumaram* = tied wood]

catapult¹ *noun* **1** a device with elastic for shooting small stones. **2** an ancient military device for hurling stones etc.

catapult² *verb* hurl or rush violently. [from *cata*-, + Greek *pellein* = throw]

cataract *noun* **1** a large waterfall or rush of water. **2** a cloudy area that forms in the eye and prevents a person from seeing clearly.

catarrh (*say* ka-**tar**) *noun* inflammation in your nose that makes it drip a watery fluid. [from Greek, = flow down]

catastrophe (*say* ka-**tass**-trof-ee) *noun* a sudden great disaster. **catastrophic** (*say* kat-a-**strof**-ik) *adjective*, **catastrophically** *adverb*

catch¹ *verb* (**caught, catching**) **1** take and hold something. **2** capture. **3** overtake. **4** be in time to get on a bus or train etc. **5** become infected with an illness. **6** hear, *I didn't catch what he said.* **7** surprise or detect somebody, *caught in the act.* **8** trick somebody. **9** make or become fixed or unable to move; snag; entangle, *I caught my dress on a nail.* **10** hit; strike, *The blow caught him on the nose.*
catch fire start burning.
catch it (*informal*) be scolded or punished.

catch on (*informal*) become popular; understand.

catch² *noun* (*plural* **catches**) **1** catching something. **2** something caught or worth catching. **3** a hidden difficulty. **4** a device for fastening something.

catching *adjective* infectious.

catchment area **1** the whole area from which water drains into a river etc. **2** the area from which a school takes pupils or a hospital takes patients.

catchphrase *noun* a popular phrase.

catchy *adjective* easy to remember, soon becoming popular, *a catchy tune.*

catechism (*say* **kat**-ik-izm) *noun* a set of questions and answers that give the basic beliefs of a religion.

categorical (*say* kat-ig-o-rik-al) *adjective* definite and absolute, *a categorical refusal.* **categorically** *adverb*

category *noun* (*plural* **categories**) a set of people or things classified as being similar to each other.

cater *verb* provide food etc. **caterer** *noun*

caterpillar *noun* the creeping worm-like creature that will turn into a butterfly or moth. [from Old French *chatepelose* = hairy cat]

cath- *prefix* see **cata-**.

▶▶THESAURUS◀◀

catapult¹ *noun* **1** ging (*Australian informal*), shanghai (*Australian*), sling, slingshot.

catapult² *verb* fling, hurl, propel, throw.

cataract *noun* **1** cascade, falls, waterfall.

catastrophe *noun* accident, blow, calamity, disaster, misadventure, misfortune, mishap, tragedy.
catastrophic *adjective* calamitous, devastating, dire, disastrous.

catch¹ *verb* **1** clutch, grab, grasp, grip, hang on to, hold on to, seize, snatch. **2** (*catch a thief*) apprehend, arrest, capture, collar (*informal*), cop (*informal*), corner, intercept, nab (*informal*), nail, nick (*slang*), pick up, seize; (*catch a fish, wild animal, etc.*) bag, capture, ensnare, gaff, hook, land, net, snare, trap. **3** catch up with, draw level with, overtake, reach. **5** become infected with, come down with, contract, get. **7** detect, discover, find, spot, surprise. **9** entangle, jam, snag, stick.

catch on 1 become fashionable, become popular, take off. **2** comprehend, cotton on (*informal*), get it (*informal*), latch on (*informal*), learn, understand.

catch² *noun* **2** bag, booty, haul, prize, take. **3** difficulty, disadvantage, drawback, hitch, problem, snag, trap. **4** bolt, clasp, clip, fastener, hasp, hook, latch, lock.

catching *adjective* communicable, contagious, infectious, transmissible.

catchphrase *noun* byword, catchword, motto, proverb, slogan, watchword.

catchy *adjective* attractive, haunting, memorable, popular, tuneful.

categorical *adjective* absolute, definite, emphatic, explicit, express, unambiguous, unequivocal, unqualified, unreserved.

category *noun* class, classification, division, group, grouping, kind, rank, set, sort, type.

cater *verb* provide food, supply food.
cater to indulge, pander to, satisfy.

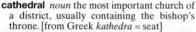

cathedral *noun* the most important church of a district, usually containing the bishop's throne. [from Greek *kathedra* = seat]

Catherine wheel a firework that spins round. [named after St Catherine, who was martyred on a spiked wheel]

cathode *noun* the electrode by which electric current leaves a device. (Compare *anode*.) [from *cata-* = down, + Greek *hodos* = way]

Catholic¹ *adjective* **1** of all Christians, *the Holy Catholic Church*. **2** Roman Catholic (see *Roman*). **Catholicism** *noun*

Catholic² *noun* a Roman Catholic.

catholic *adjective* including most things, *Her taste in literature is catholic*. [from Greek *katholikos* = universal]

catkin *noun* a spike of small soft flowers on trees such as hazel and willow. [from Dutch *katteken* = kitten]

catnap *noun* a short sleep.

Catseye *noun* (*trade mark*) one of a line of reflecting studs marking the centre or edge of a road.

cattle *plural noun* animals with horns and hoofs, kept by farmers for their milk and beef.

catty *adjective* (**cattier, cattiest**) speaking or spoken spitefully.

caucus *adjective* (*plural* **caucuses**) (*in Australia*) the parliamentary members of a political party.

cauldron *noun* a large deep pot for boiling things in. [from Latin *caldarium* = hot bath]

cauliflower *noun* a cabbage with a large head of white flowers. [from French *chou fleuri* = flowered cabbage]

cause¹ *noun* **1** a person or thing that makes something happen or produces an effect. **2** a reason, *There is no cause for worry*. **3** a purpose for which people work; an organisation or charity.

cause² *verb* (**caused, causing**) be the cause of; make something happen.

causeway *noun* a raised road across low or marshy ground.

caustic *adjective* **1** able to burn or wear things away by chemical action. **2** sarcastic. **caustically** *adverb* [from Greek *kaustikos* = capable of burning]

cauterise *verb* (**cauterised, cauterising**) burn the surface of flesh to destroy infection or stop bleeding. **cauterisation** *noun* [from Greek *kauterion* = branding-iron]

caution¹ *noun* **1** care taken so as to avoid danger etc. **2** a warning.

caution² *verb* warn someone.

cautionary *adjective* giving a warning.

cautious *adjective* showing caution. **cautiously** *adverb*, **cautiousness** *noun*

cavalcade *noun* a procession. [from Italian *cavalcare* = ride]

cavalry *noun* soldiers who fight on horseback or in armoured vehicles. (Compare *infantry*.) [from Latin *caballus* = horse]

cave¹ *noun* a large hollow place in the side of a hill or cliff, or underground.

cave² *verb* (**caved, caving**) **cave in** fall inwards; give way in an argument. [from Latin *cavus* = hollow]

caveat (*say* kav-ee-at) *noun* a warning. [Latin, = let a person beware]

catholic *adjective* all-embracing, broad, comprehensive, eclectic, liberal, universal, varied, wide.

cattle *plural noun* bullocks, bulls, calves, cows, heifers, livestock, oxen, steers, stock.

catty *adjective* bitchy (*informal*), malicious, mean, nasty, sly, spiteful, vicious.

cause¹ *noun* **1** beginning, genesis, origin, root, source. **2** basis, call, grounds, justification, need, occasion, reason. **3** aim, end, goal, object, principle, purpose.

cause² *verb* bring about, create, effect, generate, give rise to, induce, lead to, occasion, precipitate, produce, provoke, result in, spark off.

caustic *adjective* **1** burning, corrosive. **2** acrimonious, biting, bitter, cutting, sarcastic, scathing, sharp, stinging, virulent.

caution¹ *noun* **1** alertness, attention, attentiveness, care, carefulness, circumspection, discretion, heed, prudence, vigilance, wariness. **2** admonition, warning.

caution² *verb* admonish, advise, alert, counsel, forewarn, warn.

cautious *adjective* alert, attentive, careful, chary, circumspect, discreet, guarded, heedful, mindful, prudent, vigilant, wary, watchful.

cave¹ *noun* cavern, cavity, den, dugout, grotto, hole, hollow, pothole.

cave² *verb* **cave in 1** collapse, fall in, subside. **2** capitulate, give in, submit, surrender, yield.

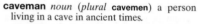

caveman *noun* (*plural* **cavemen**) a person living in a cave in ancient times.

cavern *noun* a large cave. **cavernous** *adjective*

caviar (*say* **kav**-ee-ar) *noun* the pickled roe of sturgeon or other large fish.

cavil *verb* (**cavilled, cavilling**) raise petty objections.

caving *noun* exploring caves.

cavity *noun* (*plural* **cavities**) a hollow or hole. [same origin as *cave*]

cavort (*say* ka-**vort**) *verb* caper about.

caw *noun* the harsh cry of a crow etc.

cc *abbreviation* cubic centimetre(s).

CD *abbreviation* compact disc.

CD-ROM *noun* a compact disc storing data that can be read but not altered by a computer.

cease[1] *verb* (**ceased, ceasing**) stop; end.

cease[2] *noun* **without cease** not ceasing.

ceasefire *noun* a signal to stop firing.

ceaseless *adjective* not ceasing.

cedar *noun* an evergreen tree with hard fragrant wood. **cedarwood** *noun*

cede (*say* seed) *verb* (**ceded, ceding**) give up your rights to something; surrender, *They had to cede some of their territory.* [from Latin *cedere* = yield]

cedilla (*say* sid-**il**-a) *noun* a mark under c in certain languages to show that it is pronounced as *s*, e.g. in *façade*. [from Spanish, = a little *z*]

ceiling *noun* **1** the flat surface under the top of a room. **2** the highest limit that something can reach.

celebrate *verb* (**celebrated, celebrating**) **1** do something special or enjoyable to show that a day or event is important. **2** make merry. **3** perform a religious ceremony. **celebrant** *noun*, **celebration** *noun*

celebrated *adjective* famous.

celebrity *noun* (*plural* **celebrities**) **1** a famous person. **2** fame; being famous.

celery *noun* a vegetable with crisp white or green stems.

celestial (*say* sil-**est**-ee-al) *adjective* **1** of the sky. **2** of heaven; divine.
celestial bodies stars etc.

celibate (*say* **sel**-ib-at) *adjective* remaining unmarried, especially for religious reasons. **celibacy** *noun*

cell *noun* **1** a very small room, e.g. in a monastery or a prison. **2** a microscopic unit of living matter. **3** a compartment of a honeycomb. **4** a device for producing electric current chemically. **5** a small group or unit in an organisation etc. [from Latin *cella* = store-room]

cellar *noun* an underground room. [same origin as *cell*]

cello (*say* **chel**-oh) *noun* a musical instrument like a large violin, placed between the knees of a player. **cellist** *noun* [short for *violoncello* (same origin as *violin*)]

cavity *noun* cave, crater, gap, hole, hollow, pit, pocket.

cease[1] *verb* break off, conclude, cut out, desist, die away, discontinue, end, finish, halt, knock off (*informal*), leave off, peter out, quit, refrain from, stop, suspend, terminate.

ceasefire *noun* armistice, truce.

ceaseless *adjective* constant, continual, continuous, endless, eternal, everlasting, incessant, interminable, non-stop, permanent, perpetual, persistent, relentless.

cede *verb* give up, grant, hand over, relinquish, surrender, yield.

ceiling *noun* **2** cap, limit, upper limit.

celebrate *verb* **1** commemorate, keep, mark, observe, remember. **2** make merry, party, rejoice, revel. **3** officiate at, perform, solemnise.
celebration *noun* carnival, commemoration, festival, festivity, gala, jamboree, jollification,

jubilee, merrymaking, observance, party, revelry, solemnisation.

celebrated *adjective* acclaimed, distinguished, eminent, famous, illustrious, notable, noted, popular, prominent, renowned, respected, well-known.

celebrity *noun* **1** big name, identity (*Australian informal*), luminary, notable, personage, personality, star. **2** eminence, fame, popularity, prestige, prominence, renown, stardom.

celestial *adjective* **1** astral, heavenly, stellar. **2** angelic, beatific, divine, heavenly, spiritual, sublime.

celibate *adjective* chaste, single, unmarried, unwed, virginal.

cell *noun* **1** compartment, cubicle, den, dungeon, room. **3** cavity, compartment, hole.

cellar *noun* basement, crypt, dugout, vault.

▶▶ DICTIONARY ◀◀

cellular *adjective* **1** of or containing cells. **2** with an open mesh, *cellular blankets*.

celluloid *noun* a kind of plastic.

cellulose *noun* **1** tissue that forms the main part of all plants and trees. **2** paint made from cellulose.

Celsius (*say* **sel**-see-us) *adjective* (of a temperature scale) measuring temperature on a scale using 100 degrees, where water freezes at 0° and boils at 100°. [named after A. Celsius, a Swedish astronomer]

Celtic *adjective* of the languages or inhabitants of ancient Britain and France before the Romans came, or of their descendants, e.g. Irish, Welsh, Gaelic.

cement¹ *noun* **1** a mixture of lime and clay used in building, to join bricks together, etc. **2** a strong glue.

cement² *verb* **1** put cement on something. **2** join firmly; strengthen.

cemetery (*say* **sem**-et-ree) *noun* (*plural* **cemeteries**) a place where people are buried. [from Greek *koimeterion* = dormitory]

cenotaph (*say* **sen**-o-taf) *noun* a monument, especially as a war memorial, to people who are buried elsewhere. [from Greek *kenos* = empty, + *taphos* = tomb]

censer *noun* a container in which incense is burnt. [same origin as *incense*]

censor *noun* a person who examines films, books, letters, etc. and removes or bans anything that seems harmful. **censor** *verb*, **censorship** *noun* [Latin, = a magistrate with power to ban unsuitable people from ceremonies]

censorious (*say* sen-**sor**-ee-us) *adjective* criticising something strongly.

censure (*say* **sen**-sher) *noun* strong criticism or disapproval of something. **censure** *verb*

census *noun* (*plural* **censuses**) an official count or survey of population, traffic, etc. [Latin, from *censere* = estimate]

cent *noun* a coin worth one-hundredth of a dollar. [from Latin *centum* = 100]

centenarian (*say* sent-in-**air**-ee-an) *noun* a person who is 100 years old or more.

centenary (*say* sen-**teen**-er-ee) *noun* a 100th anniversary. **centennial** (*say* sen-**ten**-ee-al) *adjective*

centi- *prefix* **1** one hundred (as in *centipede*). **2** one-hundredth (as in *centimetre*). [from Latin *centum* = 100]

centigrade *adjective* Celsius. [from *centi-*, + Latin *gradus* = step]

centimetre *noun* one-hundredth of a metre, about four-tenths of an inch.

centipede *noun* a small crawling creature with a long body and many legs. [from *centi-*, + Latin *pedes* = feet]

central *adjective* **1** of or at the centre. **2** most important. **centrally** *adverb*
central heating a system of heating a building from one source by circulating hot water or hot air or steam in pipes or by linked radiators.

centralise *verb* (**centralised, centralising**) bring under a central authority's control. **centralisation** *noun*

centre¹ *noun* **1** the middle point or part. **2** an important place, e.g. from which things are organised; a place where certain things happen, *shopping centre*.

centre² *verb* (**centred, centring**) place something in or at the centre. [from Greek *kentron* = sharp point]

centrifugal *adjective* moving away from the centre; using centrifugal force.
centrifugal force a force that makes a thing that is travelling round a central point fly outwards off its circular path. [from Latin *centrum* = centre, + *fugere* = flee]

▶▶ THESAURUS ◀◀

cement² *verb* **2** bond, braze, fuse, glue, join, paste, solder, stick, unite, weld.

cemetery *noun* burial ground, churchyard, graveyard, necropolis.

censor *verb* ban, bowdlerise, cut out, delete, expurgate, remove.

censure *noun* condemnation, criticism, disapproval, rebuke, reprimand, reproach, reproof.
censure *verb* castigate, chide (*old use*), condemn, criticise, rap over the knuckles, rebuke, reprimand, reproach, reprove, scold, upbraid.

central *adjective* **1** innermost, medial, median, mid, middle. **2** cardinal, chief, core, essential, foremost, fundamental, key, main, major, paramount, primary, principal.

centre¹ *noun* **1** bull's-eye, core, heart, hub, middle, midpoint, nucleus. **2** focus, headquarters, heart, hub, nucleus.

centre² *verb* concentrate, focus, home in.

▶▶ DICTIONARY ◀◀

centurion (*say* sent-**yoor**-ee-on) *noun* an officer in the ancient Roman army. [originally he was in charge of 100 men (Latin *centum* = 100)]

century *noun* (*plural* **centuries**) **1** a period of one hundred years. **2** a hundred runs scored by a batsman in an innings at cricket. [from Latin *centum* = 100]

cephalopod (*say* **sef**-al-o-pod) *noun* a mollusc (such as an octopus) that has a head with a ring of tentacles round the mouth. [from Greek *kephale* = head, + *podos* = of a foot]

ceramic *adjective* of pottery.

ceramics *plural noun* pottery-making.

cereal *noun* **1** a grass producing seeds which are used as food, e.g. wheat, barley, rice. **2** a breakfast food made from these seeds. [from the name of Ceres, Roman goddess of the corn]

cerebral (*say* se-rib-ral) *adjective* of the brain. **cerebral palsy** a condition involving muscle spasms and involuntary movements. [from Latin *cerebrum* = brain]

ceremonial *adjective* of or used in a ceremony; formal. **ceremonially** *adverb*

ceremonious *adjective* full of ceremony; elaborately performed.

ceremony *noun* (*plural* **ceremonies**) **1** a formal religious or public occasion, *a wedding ceremony*; *an opening ceremony*. **2** the formal actions carried out on an important occasion.

certain *adjective* **1** feeling sure, convinced. **2** known for sure; without doubt. **3** able to be relied on to happen, *Victory was certain*; *It is certain to rain*. **4** unfailing, reliable, *a certain cure*. **5** particular but not named, *a certain person*.

certainly *adverb* **1** for certain. **2** yes.

certainty *noun* (*plural* **certainties**) **1** something that is sure to happen. **2** being sure.

certificate *noun* an official written or printed statement giving information about a person etc., *a birth certificate*.

certify *verb* (**certified**, **certifying**) declare something formally; show on a certificate. **certification** *noun*, **certified** *adjective*

certitude *noun* a feeling of certainty.

cervix *noun* **1** the neck. **2** the neck of the womb. **cervical** *adjective* [Latin, = neck]

cessation *noun* ceasing.

cession *noun* ceding something.

cesspit or **cesspool** *noun* a covered pit where liquid waste or sewage is stored temporarily.

chafe *verb* (**chafed**, **chafing**) **1** rub a person's skin to make it warm again. **2** make or become sore by rubbing. **3** become irritated or impatient, *We chafed at the delay*. [from French *chauffer* = make warm]

chaff[1] *noun* **1** husks of grain, separated from the seed. **2** teasing; joking.

chaff[2] *verb* tease; joke.

chaffinch *noun* (*plural* **chaffinches**) a kind of finch.

▶▶ THESAURUS ◀◀

ceremonial *adjective* formal, ritual, ritualistic, solemn, stately.

ceremonious *adjective* dignified, formal, overpolite, pompous, prim, proper, punctilious, solemn, starchy, stiff.

ceremony *noun* **1** celebration, event, function, observance, occasion, rite, ritual, sacrament, service. **2** decorum, formality, pageantry, pomp, protocol, ritual.

certain *adjective* **1** assured, confident, convinced, definite, positive, sure. **2** definite, indisputable, indubitable, irrefutable, plain, undeniable, undoubted, unquestionable. **3** destined, fated, guaranteed, inescapable, inevitable, sure, unavoidable; (*certain to*) bound to, sure to. **4** dependable, fail-safe, guaranteed, infallible, reliable, sure, sure-fire (*informal*), trustworthy, unfailing. **5** particular, specific.

certainly *adverb* **1** assuredly, clearly, definitely, indubitably, surely, undoubtedly, without doubt. **2** absolutely, by all means, of course, yes.

certainty *noun* **1** cert (*slang*), cinch (*informal*), foregone conclusion, moral certainty, sure thing (*informal*). **2** assurance, certitude, confidence, conviction.

certificate *noun* award, credentials, degree, diploma, document, licence, paper, qualification.

certify *verb* affirm, attest, bear witness, confirm, declare, endorse, guarantee, testify, verify, vouch, warrant. **certified** *adjective* accredited, authorised, chartered, licensed, official, qualified.

chafe *verb* **2** abrade, fret, gall, rub.

▶▶ D I C T I O N A R Y ◀◀

chagrin (*say* **shag**-rin) *noun* a feeling of being annoyed and embarrassed or disappointed. [French]

chain[1] *noun* **1** a row of metal rings linked together. **2** a connected series of things, *a chain of mountains; a chain of events*.
chain-letter *noun* a letter that you are asked to copy and send to several other people.
chain reaction a series of happenings in which each causes the next.
chain store one of a number of similar shops owned by the same firm.

chain[2] *verb* fasten with a chain or chains.

chair[1] *noun* **1** a movable seat, with a back, for one person. **2** a position of authority at a meeting, *Mr Bloggs was in the chair*.

chair[2] *verb* be the chairman of, *Who will chair this meeting?*

chairman *noun* (*plural* **chairmen**) the person who is in control of a meeting. **chairmanship** *noun*, **chairwoman** *noun* (*plural* **chairwomen**), **chairperson** *noun*

Usage The word *chairman* may be used of a man or of a woman; they are addressed formally as *Mr Chairman* and *Madam Chairman*.

chalet (*say* **shal**-ay) *noun* **1** a Swiss hut or cottage. **2** a hut in a holiday camp etc.

chalice *noun* a large goblet for holding wine, especially one used at Holy Communion. [from Latin *calix* = cup]

chalk *noun* **1** a soft white or coloured stick used for writing on blackboards or for drawing. **2** soft white limestone. **chalky** *adjective*

chalkie *noun* (*Australian slang*) a school-teacher.

challenge[1] *noun* a demand to have a contest, do something difficult, say who you are, etc.

challenge[2] *verb* (**challenged, challenging**) **1** make a challenge to someone. **2** question whether something is true or correct. **challenger** *noun*

challenging *adjective* demanding, testing, *challenging work*.

chamber *noun* **1** (*old use*) a room. **2** a hall used for meetings of a parliament etc.; the members of the group using it. **3** a compartment in machinery etc.
chamber music music for a small group of players.
chamber-pot *noun* a receptacle for urine etc., used in a bedroom.

chamberlain *noun* an official who manages the household of a sovereign or great noble.

chambermaid *noun* a woman employed to clean bedrooms at a hotel etc.

chameleon (*say* kam-**ee**-lee-on) *noun* a small lizard that can change its colour to that of its surroundings.

chamois *noun* (*plural* **chamois**) **1** (*say* **sham**-wa) a small wild antelope living in the mountains. **2** (*say* **sham**-ee) a piece of soft yellow leather used for washing and polishing things. [French]

champ *verb* munch or bite something noisily.

champagne (*say* sham-**payn**) *noun* a bubbly white wine from Champagne in France.

champion[1] *noun* **1** a person or thing that has defeated all the others in a sport or competition etc. **2** someone who supports a

▶▶ T H E S A U R U S ◀◀

chain[1] *noun* **1** (*chains*) bonds, fetters, handcuffs, irons, manacles, shackles. **2** combination, line, progression, range (*of mountains*), row, sequence, series, set, string, succession, train.

chain[2] *verb* bind, fasten, fetter, handcuff, join, link, secure, tie.

chair[1] *noun* **1** place, seat; (*kinds of chair*) armchair, banana chair, chaise longue, deckchair, dining chair, easy chair, high chair, recliner chair, rocking chair, throne, wheelchair.

chair[2] *verb* conduct, direct, lead, preside over, run.

chairman *noun* chair, chairperson, chairwoman, moderator, president, speaker (*in a legislative assembly*).

challenge[1] *noun* dare, invitation, provocation, summons, trial.

challenge[2] *verb* **1** dare, defy, invite, provoke, summon. **2** contest, dispute, object to, protest against, query, question.

challenging *adjective* demanding, inspiring, stimulating, taxing, testing, thought-provoking.

chamber *noun* **1** bedroom, boudoir, hall, office, room. **2** assembly, council, house, legislative body.

champion[1] *noun* **1** ace, conqueror, hero, title-holder, victor, winner. **2** advocate, backer, defender, guardian, patron, protector, supporter, upholder.
championship *noun* competition, contest, match, tournament.

▶▶▶ DICTIONARY ◀◀◀

cause by fighting, speaking, etc. **championship** *noun*

champion² *verb* support a cause by fighting or speaking for it.

chance¹ *noun* **1** a possibility. **2** an opportunity, *Now is your chance to escape.* **3** the way things happen without being planned, *I met her by chance.*
take a chance take a risk.

chance² *verb* (**chanced, chancing**) **1** happen by chance, *I chanced to meet her.* **2** (*informal*) risk, *Let's chance it.*

chance³ *adjective* happening by chance; accidental.

chancel *noun* the part of a church nearest to the altar.

chancellor *noun* an important official in a State or university.

chancy *adjective* risky.

chandelier (*say* shand-il-**eer**) *noun* a hanging support for several lights. [from French *chandelle* = candle]

change¹ *verb* (**changed, changing**) **1** make or become different. **2** exchange. **3** put on fresh clothes or coverings etc. **4** go from one train or bus etc. to another.

change² *noun* **1** changing; alteration. **2** coins or notes of small values. **3** money given back to the payer when the price is less than the amount handed over. **4** a fresh set of clothes. **5** a variation in routine, *Let's walk home for a change.* **6** an exchange.

changeable *adjective* likely to change; changing frequently.

changeling *noun* a child believed to have been substituted secretly for another, especially by fairies.

channel¹ *noun* **1** a stretch of water connecting two seas. **2** a way for water to flow along. **3** the part of a river or sea etc. that is deep enough for ships. **4** a broadcasting wavelength.

channel² *verb* (**channelled, channelling**) **1** make a channel in something. **2** direct something through a channel or other route. [from Latin *canalis* = canal]

chant¹ *noun* **1** a tune to which words with no regular rhythm are fitted, e.g. one used in singing psalms. **2** a rhythmic call or shout.

chant² *verb* **1** sing. **2** call out words in a rhythm. [from Latin *cantare* = sing]

chaos (*say* **kay**-oss) *noun* great disorder. **chaotic** *adjective*, **chaotically** *adverb* [Greek, = bottomless pit]

▶▶▶ THESAURUS ◀◀◀

chance¹ *noun* **1** likelihood, possibility, probability, prospect, risk. **2** break (*informal*), look-in (*informal*), occasion, opening, opportunity, turn. **3** accident, coincidence, destiny, fate, fluke, fortune, luck.

chance³ *adjective* accidental, casual, co-incidental, fortuitous, lucky, unexpected, unintentional, unplanned.

chancy *adjective* dangerous, dicey (*slang*), hazardous, perilous, precarious, risky, uncertain.

change¹ *verb* **1** adapt, adjust, affect, alter, amend, be transformed, chop and change, convert, develop, evolve, fluctuate, have an effect on, have an impact on, influence, metamorphose, modify, mutate, rearrange, reform, reorganise, revise, revolutionise, shift, swing, transfigure, transform, transmute, vary. **2** exchange, interchange, replace, substitute, swap, switch, trade.

change² *noun* **1** about-turn, adaptation, adjustment, alteration, amendment, conversion, development, deviation, difference, fluctuation, innovation, metamorphosis, modification, mutation, rearrangement, reform, reorganisation, reversal, revision, revolution,

shift, swing, transfiguration, transformation, transition, transmutation, U-turn, variation, variety. **2** coins, coppers, silver. **6** exchange, interchange, replacement, substitution, swap, switch.

changeable *adjective* capricious, erratic, fickle, fitful, flighty, inconsistent, inconstant, mercurial, moody, temperamental, unpredictable, unreliable, unsteady, variable, volatile.

channel¹ *noun* **1** narrows, passage, strait. **2** aqueduct, canal, conduit, culvert, ditch, drain, duct, dyke, furrow, groove, gully, gutter, outlet, sluice, trench, trough, watercourse, waterway. **4** band, frequency, station, wavelength.

channel² *verb* **2** direct, guide, lead, steer.

chant¹ *noun* **1** canticle, psalm, song.

chant² *verb* intone, recite, sing.

chaos *noun* anarchy, bedlam, confusion, disarray, disorder, havoc, mayhem, mess, muddle, pandemonium, tumult, turmoil, upheaval.
chaotic *adjective* confused, disorderly, disorganised, haphazard, haywire (*informal*), jumbled, messy, muddled, out of control, topsy-turvy, uncontrolled, unruly.

▶▶ D I C T I O N A R Y ◀◀

chap *noun* (*informal*) a man. [short for *chapman*, an old word for a pedlar]

chapel *noun* **1** a place used for Christian worship, other than a cathedral or parish church; a religious service in this. **2** a section of a large church, with its own altar.

chaperone (*say* **shap**-er-ohn) *noun* an older woman in charge of a young one on social occasions. **chaperone** *verb*

chaplain *noun* a member of the clergy who looks after a college or hospital or regiment etc.

chapped *adjective* with skin split or cracked from cold etc.

chapter *noun* **1** a division of a book. **2** the clergy of a cathedral or members of a monastery. The room where they meet is called a **chapter house**.

char *verb* (**charred, charring**) make or become black by burning. [from *charcoal*]

character *noun* **1** a person in a story or play etc. **2** all the qualities that make a person or thing what he, she, or it is. **3** (*informal*) a person. **4** (*informal*) an eccentric or interesting person. **5** a letter of the alphabet; a symbol or digit.

characterise *verb* (**characterised, characterising**) **1** be a characteristic of. **2** describe the character of. **characterisation** *noun*

characteristic[1] *noun* a quality that forms part of a person's or thing's character.

characteristic[2] *adjective* typical of a person or thing. **characteristically** *adverb*

charade (*say* sha-**rahd**) *noun* **1** a scene in the game of *charades*, in which people try to guess a word from other people's acting. **2** a pretence.

charcoal *noun* a black substance made by burning wood slowly.

charge[1] *noun* **1** the price asked for something. **2** a rushing attack. **3** the amount of explosive needed to fire a gun etc. **4** electricity in something. **5** an accusation of having committed a crime. **6** care, custody; a person or thing in someone's care.
in charge in control; deciding what shall happen to a person or thing.

charge[2] *verb* (**charged, charging**) **1** ask a particular price. **2** rush forward in an attack. **3** give an electric charge to something. **4** accuse someone of committing a crime. **5** entrust someone with a responsibility or task.

charger *noun* (*old use*) a cavalry horse.

chariot *noun* a horse-drawn vehicle with two wheels, used in ancient times for fighting, racing, etc. **charioteer** *noun*

charisma (*say* ka-**riz**-ma) *noun* the special quality that makes a person popular, influential, etc. [Greek, = divine favour]

charismatic (*say* ka-riz-**mat**-ik) *adjective* having charisma.

charity *noun* (*plural* **charities**) **1** an organisation set up to help people who are poor or have suffered a disaster. **2** giving money or help etc. to the needy. **3** loving

▶▶ T H E S A U R U S ◀◀

chap *noun* bloke (*informal*), boy, fellow, guy (*informal*), lad (*informal*), man, person.

chaperone *noun* companion, escort, protector. **chaperone** *verb* accompany, escort, protect, watch over.

chaplain *noun* clergyman, clergywoman, minister, padre, pastor, priest.

chapter *noun* **1** division, part, section, subdivision.

char *verb* blacken, brown, scorch, sear, singe, toast.

character *noun* **1** part, persona, role. **2** attributes, characteristics, disposition, features, flavour, make-up, manner, nature, peculiarities, personality, qualities, spirit, temperament, traits. **3** chap (*informal*), fellow, human being, individual, person, specimen, type (*informal*). **4** card (*informal*), eccentric, individual, oddball (*informal*), oddity, weirdo (*informal*). **5** figure, letter, sign, symbol.

characteristic[1] *noun* aspect, attribute, feature, hallmark, mark, peculiarity, property, quality, trait.

characteristic[2] *adjective* distinctive, idiosyncratic, individual, particular, peculiar, recognisable, singular, special, typical, unique.

charade *noun* **2** farce, mockery, pretence, sham.

charge[1] *noun* **1** cost, expense, fare, fee, levy, payment, price, rate, tariff, terms, toll. **5** accusation, allegation, complaint, imputation, indictment. **6** care, command, control, custody, keeping, protection, responsibility, supervision.

charge[2] *verb* **1** ask, debit, demand, levy, require. **2** assault, attack, rush, storm. **4** accuse, blame, book, impeach, indict. **5** burden, encumber, entrust, give, saddle.

charity *noun* **1** fund, good cause, institution. **2** alms (*old use*), assistance, contributions, donations, financial assistance, handouts. **3**

►►► DICTIONARY ◄◄

kindness towards others; being unwilling to think badly of people. **charitable** *adjective*, **charitably** *adverb* [from Latin *caritas* = love]

charlatan (*say* **shar**-la-tan) *noun* a person who falsely claims to be an expert. [from Italian, = babbler]

charm¹ *noun* **1** the power to please or delight people; attractiveness. **2** a magic spell; a small object believed to bring good luck. **3** an ornament worn on a bracelet etc.

charm² *verb* **1** give pleasure or delight to people. **2** put a spell on; bewitch. **charmer** *noun* [from Latin *carmen* = song or spell]

charnel-house *noun* a place in which the bodies or bones of the dead are kept.

chart¹ *noun* **1** a map for people sailing ships or flying aircraft. **2** an outline map showing special information, *a weather chart*. **3** a diagram or list etc. giving information in an orderly way.
the charts a list of the records that are most popular.

chart² *verb* make a chart of something; map. [from Latin *charta* = card]

charter¹ *noun* **1** an official document giving somebody certain rights etc. **2** chartering an aircraft, ship, or vehicle.

charter² *verb* **1** hire an aircraft, ship, or vehicle. **2** give a charter to someone.

chartered accountant an accountant who is qualified according to the rules of an association that has a royal charter.

chary (*say* **chair**-ee) *adjective* cautious about doing or giving something.

chase *verb* (**chased, chasing**) go quickly after a person or thing in order to capture or catch them up or drive them away. **chase** *noun*

chasm (*say* kazm) *noun* a deep opening in the ground. [Greek, = wide hollow]

chassis (*say* **shas**-ee) *noun* (*plural* **chassis**) the framework under a car etc., on which other parts are mounted.

chaste *adjective* not having sexual intercourse at all, or only with the person to whom you are married. **chastity** *noun* [from Latin *castus* = pure]

chasten (*say* **chay**-sen) *verb* discipline a person by punishing them; make someone feel subdued.

chastise *verb* (**chastised, chastising**) punish severely. **chastisement** *noun*

chat¹ *noun* a friendly conversation.

chat² *verb* (**chatted, chatting**) have a chat. [from *chatter*]

château (*say* **shat**-oh) *noun* (*plural* **châteaux**) a large country house in France. [French]

►►► THESAURUS ◄◄

altruism, benevolence, compassion, generosity, goodwill, humanity, kindness, love, philanthropy, sympathy.
charitable *adjective* see GENEROUS.

charlatan *noun* cheat, con man (*informal*), fake, fraud, humbug, impostor, phoney (*informal*), quack, swindler, trickster.

charm¹ *noun* **1** allure, appeal, attractiveness, charisma, magnetism. **2** incantation, magic, sorcery, spell, witchcraft, witchery, wizardry. **3** amulet, mascot, talisman, trinket.

charm² *verb* allure, attract, beguile, bewitch, captivate, delight, enchant, enthral, entrance, fascinate, hold spellbound, hypnotise, mesmerise, seduce.
charming *adjective* appealing, attractive, beguiling, captivating, delightful, enchanting, enthralling, fascinating, likeable, pleasant, pleasing, sweet (*informal*).

chart¹ *noun* **1** map, plan. **3** diagram, graph, histogram, table, tabulation.

chart² *verb* graph, map, plot, record, register.

charter² *verb* **1** hire, lease, rent.

chase *verb* follow, hound, hunt, pursue, run after, track, trail.

chasm *noun* abyss, breach, canyon, cavity, cleft, crack, crevasse, fissure, gap, gorge, hole, opening, ravine, rift.

chassis *noun* frame, framework, skeleton, substructure.

chaste *adjective* celibate, pure, virginal, virtuous.
chastity *noun* celibacy, purity, sexual abstinence, virginity, virtue.

chastise *verb* beat, castigate, censure, chasten, chide (*old use*), discipline, flog, lash, punish, rebuke, reprimand, reproach, reprove, scold, tell off (*informal*), thrash, upbraid.

chat¹ *noun* chinwag (*informal*), conversation, gossip, natter (*informal*), talk, yabber (*Australian informal*), yak (*informal*).

chat² *verb* chatter, converse, gossip, have a word, mag (*Australian informal*), natter (*informal*), prattle, talk, yabber (*Australian informal*), yak (*informal*).

▶▶DICTIONARY◀◀

chattel *noun* something you own that can be moved from place to place (distinguished from a house or land).

chatter¹ *verb* **1** talk quickly about unimportant things; keep on talking. **2** make a rattling sound. **chatterer** *noun*

chatter² *noun* chattering talk or sound.

chatterbox *noun* a talkative person.

chauffeur (*say* **shoh**-fer) *noun* a person employed to drive a car. [French, = stoker]

chauvinism (*say* **shoh**-vin-izm) *noun* prejudiced belief that your own group or country etc. is superior to others. **chauvinist** *noun*, **chauvinistic** *adjective* [from the name of Nicolas Chauvin, a French soldier under Napoleon, noted for his extreme patriotism]

cheap *adjective* **1** low in price; not expensive. **2** of poor quality; of low value. **cheaply** *adverb*, **cheapness** *noun* [from Old English *ceap* = a bargain]

cheapen *verb* make or become cheap.

cheat¹ *verb* **1** trick or deceive somebody. **2** try to do well in an examination or game etc. by breaking the rules.

cheat² *noun* a person who cheats.

check¹ *verb* **1** make sure that something is correct or in good condition. **2** make something stop or go slower.

check² *noun* **1** checking something. **2** stopping or slowing; a pause. **3** (*American*) a bill in a restaurant. **4** the situation in chess when a king may be captured. [from Persian *shah* = king]

check³ *noun* a pattern of squares. **checked** *adjective* [from *chequered*]

checkmate *noun* the winning situation in chess. **checkmate** *verb* [from Persian *shah mat* = the king is dead]

check-out *noun* a place where goods are paid for in a self-service shop.

cheek *noun* **1** the side of the face below the eye. **2** impudence.

cheeky *adjective* impudent. **cheekily** *adverb*, **cheekiness** *noun*

cheer¹ *noun* **1** a shout of praise or pleasure or encouragement, especially 'hurray'. **2** cheerfulness, *full of good cheer.*

cheer² *verb* **1** give a cheer. **2** gladden or encourage somebody.

cheer up make or become cheerful.

▶▶THESAURUS◀◀

chatter¹ *verb* **1** babble, chat, gabble, gossip, jabber, natter (*informal*), prattle, talk, yak (*informal*).

chatter² *noun* chit-chat, gossip, talk, tattle, tittle-tattle.

chatterbox *noun* chatterer, gasbag (*informal*), magpie, windbag (*informal*).

cheap *adjective* **1** bargain, budget, competitive, cut-price, discount, economical, inexpensive, keen, low, reasonable, reduced, sale. **2** gimcrack, inferior, poor, rubbishy, second-rate, shoddy, tacky (*informal*), tinny, tinpot, trashy, worthless.

cheat¹ *verb* **1** bamboozle (*informal*), bilk, bluff, con (*informal*), deceive, defraud, diddle (*informal*), double-cross, dupe, fleece, have on (*informal*), hoax, hoodwink, outwit, rip off (*informal*), rob, rook, rort (*Australian slang*), short-change, swindle, take for a ride (*informal*), trick, welsh on. **2** break the rules, copy, crib (*informal*).

cheat² *noun* charlatan, con man (*informal*), crook (*informal*), embezzler, extortioner, fraud, racketeer, rogue, shark, sharp (*informal*), sharper, shicer (*Australian slang*), shyster (*informal*), swindler, trickster, welsher.

check¹ *verb* **1** audit, check on, check out, check up, correct, double-check, examine, inspect, investigate, look over, mark, monitor, screen, scrutinise, suss out (*informal*), test, verify, vet. **2** curb, frustrate, hamper, hinder, hold back, impede, inhibit, limit, restrict, retard, slow down, stop, stunt, thwart.

check² *noun* **1** check-up, examination, going-over (*informal*), inspection, investigation, once-over (*informal*), probe, scrutiny, search, test. **2** brake, constraint, control, curb, limitation, restraint, restriction.

cheek *noun* **1** chap, jowl. **2** audacity, boldness, effrontery, front, gall (*slang*), hide (*informal*), impertinence, impudence, insolence, nerve, presumption, temerity.

cheeky *adjective* arrogant, audacious, bold, brazen, discourteous, disrespectful, forward, fresh (*informal*), impertinent, impolite, impudent, insolent, pert, presumptuous, rude, saucy, shameless.

cheer¹ *noun* **2** cheerfulness, gaiety, gladness, glee, good spirits, happiness, jollity, joy, merriment, mirth, pleasure.

cheer² *verb* **1** applaud, barrack for (*Australian*), clap, encourage, shout for, support. **2** brighten, buck up (*informal*), buoy up, comfort, console, divert, encourage, gladden, hearten, perk up, uplift.

▶▶ D I C T I O N A R Y ◀◀

cheerful *adjective* **1** looking or sounding happy. **2** pleasantly bright. **cheerfully** *adverb*, **cheerfulness** *noun*

cheerio *interjection* (*informal*) goodbye.

cheerless *adjective* gloomy; dreary.

cheery *adjective* bright and cheerful.

cheese *noun* a solid food made from milk.

cheetah *noun* a kind of leopard.

chef (*say* shef) *noun* the cook in a hotel or restaurant. [French, = chief]

chemical[1] *adjective* of or produced by chemistry.

chemical[2] *noun* a substance obtained by or used in chemistry.

chemist *noun* **1** a person who makes or sells medicines. **2** an expert in chemistry.

chemistry *noun* **1** the way that substances combine and react with one another. **2** study of substances and their reactions etc. [same origin as *alchemy*]

cheque *noun* a printed form on which you write instructions to a bank to pay out money from your account. [from *check*[2]]

chequered *adjective* marked with a pattern of squares.

cherish *verb* **1** look after a person or thing lovingly. **2** be fond of. [from French *cher* = dear]

cherry *noun* (*plural* **cherries**) a small soft round fruit with a stone.

cherub *noun* (*plural* **cherubim** or **cherubs**) an angel, often pictured as a chubby child with wings. **cherubic** (*say* che-**roo**-bik) *adjective* [from Hebrew]

chess *noun* a game for two players with sixteen pieces each (called **chessmen**) on a

board of 64 squares (a **chessboard**). [same origin as *check*[2]]

chest *noun* **1** the front part of the body between the neck and the waist. **2** a large strong box for storing things in.

chest of drawers a piece of furniture with drawers for storing clothes etc.

chestnut *noun* **1** a tree that produces hard brown nuts. **2** the nut of this tree. **3** an old joke or story.

chevron (*say* **shev**-ron) *noun* a V-shaped stripe.

chew *verb* grind food between the teeth. **chewy** *adjective*

chewing-gum *noun* a sticky flavoured substance for chewing.

chiack (*say* **chy**-ack) *verb* (*Australian slang*) tease, jeer at.

chic (*say* sheek) *adjective* stylish and elegant. [French]

chicanery (*say* shik-**ayn**-er-ee) *noun* trickery. [from French *chicaner* = quibble]

chick *noun* a very young bird.

chicken[1] *noun* **1** a young bird, especially of the domestic fowl. **2** the flesh of a domestic fowl as food.

chicken[2] *adjective* (*slang*) afraid to do something; cowardly.

chicken[3] *verb* **chicken out** (*slang*) withdraw because you are afraid.

chickenpox *noun* a disease that produces red spots on the skin.

chicory *noun* a plant whose leaves are used as salad.

chide *verb* (**chided, chidden, chiding**) (*old use*) scold.

▶▶ T H E S A U R U S ◀◀

cheerful *adjective* **1** blithe, bright, buoyant, carefree, cheery, chirpy, contented, elated, exhilarated, exuberant, gay, glad, gleeful, good-humoured, happy, happy-go-lucky, jaunty, jolly, jovial, joyful, joyous, jubilant, light-hearted, lively, merry, optimistic, perky, positive, radiant, upbeat (*informal*).

chemist *noun* **1** apothecary (*old use*), dispenser, druggist, pharmacist.

chequered *adjective* check, checked, chequerboard, criss-cross, plaid, tartan.

cherish *verb* **1** care for, foster, look after, nurse, nurture, protect. **2** adore, be fond of, dote on, hold dear, love, prize, treasure, value.

chest *noun* **1** bosom, breast, bust, ribcage, thorax. **2** ark, box, case, casket, coffer, crate, ottoman, strongbox, trunk.

chest of drawers bureau, chest, dresser, lowboy, tallboy.

chew *verb* champ, chomp, crunch, gnaw, grind, masticate, munch, nibble.

chic *adjective* classy (*informal*), elegant, fashionable, smart, sophisticated, stylish.

chick *noun* fledgeling, nestling.

chicken[1] *noun* **1** chook (*Australian informal*), fowl, hen, rooster.

chicken[3] *verb* **chicken out** back out, opt out, pike out (*Australian informal*), pull out, withdraw.

chief¹ *noun* a person with the highest rank or authority.

chief² *adjective* most important; main. **chiefly** *adverb*

chieftain *noun* the chief of a tribe, band of robbers, etc.

chiffon (*say* **shif**-on) *noun* a very thin almost transparent fabric. [French]

chilblain *noun* a sore swollen place, usually on a hand or foot, caused by cold weather. [from *chill + blain* = a sore]

child *noun* (*plural* **children**) **1** a young person; a boy or girl. **2** someone's son or daughter.

childhood *noun* the time when a person is a child.

childish *adjective* like a child; unsuitable for a grown person. **childishly** *adverb*

childless *adjective* having no children.

childlike *adjective* innocent, frank, etc., like a child.

chill¹ *noun* **1** unpleasant coldness. **2** an illness that makes you shiver.

chill² *verb* make a person or thing cold.

chilli *noun* (*plural* **chillies**) the hot-tasting pod of a red pepper.

chilly *adjective* **1** rather cold. **2** unfriendly. **chilliness** *noun*

chime¹ *noun* a series of notes sounded by a set of bells each making a different musical sound.

chime² *verb* (**chimed, chiming**) make a chime.

chimney *noun* (*plural* **chimneys**) a tall pipe or structure that carries away smoke from a fire.

chimney-pot *noun* a pipe fitted to the top of a chimney.

chimney-sweep *noun* a person who cleans soot from inside chimneys.

chimpanzee *noun* an African ape, smaller than a gorilla.

chin *noun* the lower part of the face below the mouth.

china *noun* thin delicate pottery.

chink¹ *noun* **1** a narrow opening, *a chink in the curtains*. **2** a chinking sound.

chink² *verb* make a sound like glasses or coins being struck together.

chintz *noun* a shiny cotton cloth used for making curtains etc. [from Hindi]

chip¹ *noun* **1** a thin piece cut or broken off something hard. **2** a fried oblong strip of potato. **3** a place where a small piece has been knocked off something. **4** a small counter used in games. **5** a microchip.

chip heater (*Australian*) a domestic water heater using small pieces of wood as fuel.

a chip off the old block a child who is very like his or her father.

have a chip on your shoulder have a grievance and feel bitter or resentful.

chip² *verb* (**chipped, chipping**) **1** knock small pieces off something. **2** cut a potato into chips.

chief¹ *noun* boss, captain, chieftain, commander, director, employer, governor, head, leader, manager, master, overseer, president, principal, ruler, superintendent, supervisor.

chief² *adjective* basic, cardinal, central, dominant, essential, first, foremost, fundamental, greatest, head, highest, key, leading, main, major, overriding, paramount, predominant, primary, prime, principal, supreme.
chiefly *adverb* especially, for the most part, generally, in the main, mainly, mostly, particularly, primarily, principally.

child *noun* **1** babe, baby, bairn (*Scottish*), boy, girl, infant, juvenile, kid (*informal*), lad, lass, minor, piccaninny, toddler, tot, youngster, youth. **2** daughter, descendant, offspring, son.

childhood *noun* boyhood, girlhood, infancy, youth.

childish *adjective* babyish, immature, infantile, juvenile, naïve, puerile, silly.

childlike *adjective* artless, guileless, ingenuous, innocent, naïve, simple, trusting, youthful.

chill¹ *noun* **1** chilliness, coldness, crispness, iciness, nip.

chill² *verb* cool, refrigerate.

chilly *adjective* **1** cold, crisp, freezing, frosty, icy, nippy (*informal*), raw, wintry. **2** aloof, cold, cool, frosty, hostile, icy, stony, unfriendly, unwelcoming.

chime² *verb* ding, dong, peal, ring, sound, strike, toll.

china *noun* crockery, dinner service, porcelain, pottery, tableware.

chink¹ *noun* **1** aperture, breach, cleft, crack, cranny, fissure, gap, hole, opening, rift, slit, split.

chip¹ *noun* **1** bit, flake, fragment, piece, shard, shaving, sliver, splinter. **2** crisp, French fry.

chip² *verb* **1** break, damage, nick, splinter.

▶▶ D I C T I O N A R Y ◀◀

chipboard *noun* board made from chips of wood pressed and stuck together.

chipolata *noun* a small spicy sausage.

chiropody (*say* ki-**rop**-od-ee) *noun* treatment of ailments of the feet, e.g. corns. **chiropodist** *noun* [from Greek *cheir* = hand, + *pod-* = foot]

chirp *verb* make short sharp sounds like a small bird. **chirp** *noun*

chirpy *adjective* lively and cheerful.

chisel¹ *noun* a tool with a sharp end for shaping wood, stone, etc.

chisel² *verb* (**chiselled**, **chiselling**) shape or cut with a chisel.

chivalrous (*say* **shiv**-al-rus) *adjective* being considerate and helpful towards people less strong than yourself. **chivalry** *noun* [= like a perfect knight (same origin as *Cavalier*)]

chive *noun* a small herb with leaves that taste like onions.

chivvy *verb* (**chivvied**, **chivvying**) try to make someone hurry.

chlorinate *verb* (**chlorinated**, **chlorinating**) put chlorine into something. **chlorination** *noun*

chlorine (*say* **klor**-een) *noun* a greenish-yellow gas used to disinfect water etc. [from Greek *chloros* = green]

chloroform (*say* **klo**-ro-form) *noun* a liquid that gives off a vapour that makes people unconscious.

chlorophyll (*say* **klo**-ro-fil) *noun* the substance that makes plants green. [from Greek *chloros* = green, + *phyllon* = leaf]

chock *noun* a block or wedge used to prevent something from moving.

chock-a-block *adjective* crammed or crowded together.

chock-full *adjective* crammed full.

chocolate *noun* **1** a solid brown food or powder made from roasted cacao seeds. **2** a drink made with this powder. **3** a sweet made of or covered with chocolate. [from Mexican *chocolatl*]

choice¹ *noun* **1** choosing; the power to choose between things. **2** a variety from which someone can choose, *There is a wide choice of holidays.* **3** a person or thing chosen, *This is my choice.*

choice² *adjective* of the best quality, *choice bananas.*

choir *noun* a group of people trained to sing together, especially in a church. [from Latin *chorus* = choir]

choke¹ *verb* (**choked**, **choking**) **1** cause somebody to stop breathing properly. **2** be unable to breathe properly. **3** clog.

choke² *noun* a device controlling the flow of air into the engine of a motor vehicle.

choko *noun* a green pear-shaped vegetable.

cholera (*say* **kol**-er-a) *noun* an infectious disease that is often fatal. [from Greek *chole* = bile]

cholesterol (*say* kol-**est**-er-ol) *noun* a fatty substance that can clog the arteries. [from Greek *chole* = bile, + *stereos* = stiff]

chook *noun* (*Australian informal*) a chicken or a fowl.

choose *verb* (**chose**, **chosen**, **choosing**) take one or more from among a number of people or things; select. **choosy** *adjective*

▶▶ T H E S A U R U S ◀◀

chirp *verb* cheep, chirrup, peep, tweet, twitter.

chirpy *adjective* bright, cheerful, happy, light-hearted, lively, perky, vivacious.

chivalrous *adjective* considerate, courteous, courtly, gallant, gentlemanly, heroic, honourable, noble, polite.

chock *noun* block, wedge.

chock-a-block *adjective* chockers (*informal*), chock-full, crammed, crowded, full, jam-packed (*informal*), packed.

choice¹ *noun* **1** alternative, option. **2** array, assortment, collection, range, selection, variety. **3** decision, election, pick, preference, selection.

choice² *adjective* excellent, fine, first-class, first-rate, prime, prize, select, superior.

choir *noun* choral group, choristers, chorus, ensemble, singers.

choke¹ *verb* **1** asphyxiate, smother, stifle, strangle, suffocate, throttle. **2** gag, gasp. **3** block, clog, congest, crowd, jam, obstruct, pack.

chook *noun* chicken, fowl, poultry.

choose *verb* adopt, appoint, decide on, draw lots for, elect, name, nominate, opt for, pick, plump for, prefer, select, settle on, single out, vote for.

choosy *adjective* fastidious, finicky, fussy, particular, pernickety (*informal*), picky (*informal*), selective.

▶▶ DICTIONARY ◀◀

chop¹ *verb* (**chopped, chopping**) cut or hit something with a heavy blow.

chop² *noun* **1** a chopping blow. **2** a small thick slice of meat, usually on a rib.

chopper *noun* **1** a chopping tool; a small axe. **2** (*slang*) a helicopter.

choppy *adjective* (**choppier, choppiest**) not smooth; full of small waves, *a choppy sea*. **choppiness** *noun*

chopsticks *plural noun* a pair of thin sticks used for lifting Chinese and Japanese food to your mouth.

choral *adjective* of or for or sung by a choir or chorus.

chorale (*say* kor-**ahl**) *noun* a choral composition using the words of a hymn.

chord¹ (*say* kord) *noun* a number of musical notes sounded together. [from *accord*]

chord² (*say* kord) *noun* a straight line joining two points on a curve. [from *cord*]

chore (*say* chor) *noun* a regular or dull task.

choreography (*say* ko-ree-**og**-ra-fee) *noun* the composition of ballets or stage dances. **choreographer** *noun* [from Greek *choreia* = dance, + -*graphy*]

chorister (*say* **ko**-rist-er) *noun* a member of a choir.

chortle *noun* a loud chuckle. [a mixture of *chuckle* and *snort*]

chorus¹ *noun* (*plural* **choruses**) **1** the words repeated after each verse of a song or poem. **2** music sung by a group of people. **3** a group singing together.

chorus² *verb* (**chorused, chorusing**) sing or speak in chorus. [from Greek]

christen *verb* **1** baptise. **2** give a name or nickname to a person or thing. **christening** *noun*

Christian¹ *noun* a person who believes in Jesus Christ and his teachings.

Christian² *adjective* of Christians or their beliefs. **Christianity** *noun*

Christian name a name given to a person at his or her christening.

Christmas *noun* (*plural* **Christmases**) the day (25 December) when Christians commemorate the birth of Jesus Christ; the days round it.
Christmas pudding a dark pudding containing dried fruit etc., eaten at Christmas.
Christmas tree an evergreen or artificial tree decorated at Christmas. [from *Christ* + *mass³*]

chromatic (*say* krom-**at**-ik) *adjective* of colours.
chromatic scale a musical scale going up or down in semitones. [from Greek *chroma* = colour]

chrome (*say* krohm) *noun* chromium. [from Greek *chroma* = colour (because its compounds have brilliant colours)]

chromium (*say* **kroh**-mee-um) *noun* a shiny silvery metal. [from *chrome*]

chromosome (*say* **kroh**-mos-ohm) *noun* a tiny thread-like part of an animal cell or plant cell, carrying genes. [from Greek *chroma* = colour, + *soma* = body]

chronic *adjective* lasting for a long time, *a chronic illness*. **chronically** *adverb* [from Greek *chronikos* = of time]

chronicle *noun* a record of events in the order of their happening. [same origin as *chronic*]

chronological *adjective* arranged in the order of happening. **chronologically** *adverb*

chronology (*say* kron-**ol**-oh-jee) *noun* the arrangement of events in the order in which they happened, e.g. in history or geology. [from Greek *chronos* = time, + -*logy*]

chronometer (*say* kron-**om**-it-er) *noun* a very exact device for measuring time. [from Greek *chronos* = time, + *meter*]

chrysalis *noun* (*plural* **chrysalises**) a caterpillar that is changing into a butterfly or moth. [from Greek *chrysos* = gold (the colour of its covering)]

▶▶ THESAURUS ◀◀

chop¹ *verb* cleave, cut, fell, hack, hew, split; (*chop up*) chip, cube, cut, dice, mince.

chopper *noun* **1** axe, cleaver, hatchet, tomahawk.

choppy *adjective* rough, stormy, turbulent.

chore *noun* duty, errand, job, task, work.

chorus¹ *noun* **1** jingle, refrain. **3** choir, choral group, ensemble, singers.

christen *verb* **1** baptise. **2** call, dub, name, nickname.
christening *noun* baptism.

Christmas *noun* Xmas, yule (*old use*), yuletide (*old use*).

chronic *adjective* ceaseless, constant, continuing, continuous, lifelong, lingering, long-standing, perennial, permanent, persistent, unending.

▶▶ DICTIONARY ◀◀

chrysanthemum *noun* a garden flower that blooms in autumn. [from Greek *chrysos* = gold, + *anthemon* = flower]

chubby *adjective* (**chubbier, chubbiest**) plump. **chubbiness** *noun*

chuck[1] *verb* (*informal*) throw.
chuck in give up, *He chucked in his job.*
chuck out throw away; force a person to leave a place.

chuck[2] *noun* **1** the gripping-part of a lathe. **2** the part of a drill that holds the bit.

chuckle *verb* (**chuckled, chuckling**) laugh quietly. **chuckle** *noun*

chug *verb* (**chugged, chugging**) make the sound of an engine.

chum *noun* (*informal*) a friend. **chummy** *adjective*

chunk *noun* a thick piece of something. **chunky** *adjective*

chupatty (*say* chup-**at**-ee) *noun* (*plural* **chupatties**) a small flat piece of a kind of bread. [from Hindi]

church *noun* (*plural* **churches**) **1** a public building for Christian worship. **2** a religious service in a church, *I will see you after church.*
the church all Christians; a group of these. [from Greek *kuriakon* = Lord's house]

churchyard *noun* the ground round a church, often used as a graveyard.

churlish *adjective* ill-mannered; surly.

churn[1] *noun* **1** a large can in which milk is carried from a farm. **2** a machine in which milk is beaten to make butter.

churn[2] *verb* **1** make butter in a churn. **2** stir or swirl vigorously.
churn out produce in large quantities.

chute (*say* shoot) *noun* a steep channel for people or things to slide down. [French, = a fall]

chutney *noun* a strong-tasting mixture of fruit, peppers, etc., eaten with meat. [from Hindi *catni*]

cider *noun* an alcoholic drink from apples.

cigar *noun* a roll of compressed tobacco-leaves for smoking. [from Spanish *cigarro*]

cigarette *noun* a small roll of shredded tobacco in thin paper for smoking. [French, = little cigar]

cinder *noun* a small piece of partly burnt coal or wood.

cine-camera (*say* **sin**-ee) *noun* a camera used for taking moving pictures.

cinema *noun* **1** a place where films are shown. **2** films in general. [from Greek *kinema* = movement]

cinnamon (*say* **sin**-a-mon) *noun* a yellowish-brown spice.

cipher (*say* **sy**-fer) *noun* **1** the symbol 0, representing nought or zero. **2** a kind of code. [from Arabic *sifr* = nought]

circle[1] *noun* **1** a perfectly round flat shape or thing. **2** a circular route. **3** a number of people with similar interests. **4** the balcony of a cinema or theatre.

▶▶ THESAURUS ◀◀

chubby *adjective* dumpy, fat, obese, overweight, plump, podgy, rotund, round, stout, tubby.

chuck[1] *verb* cast, fling, heave, hurl, pitch, sling, throw, toss.
chuck in give up, jack in (*slang*), leave, pack in (*informal*), quit, resign, throw in, toss in (*informal*).
chuck out boot out (*slang*), cast out, discard, ditch (*informal*), expel, get rid of, kick out (*informal*), throw away, throw out.

chuckle *verb & noun* chortle, giggle, laugh, snigger, titter.

chum *noun* buddy (*informal*), cobber (*Australian informal*), companion, comrade, confidant(e), crony, friend, mate, pal (*informal*).

chunk *noun* hunk, lump, mass, piece, slab, wedge, wodge.

church *noun* **1** abbey, basilica, cathedral, chapel, minster, sanctuary, shrine, tabernacle, temple. **2** devotions, divine service, service, worship.

churlish *adjective* bad-tempered, boorish, ill-bred, ill-mannered, impolite, mean, rude, surly, uncivil, unfriendly, unsociable.

churn[2] *verb* **1** agitate, beat, stir, whip, whisk. **2** foam, heave, seethe, swirl, toss.

cigarette *noun* ciggy (*informal*), fag (*slang*), smoke (*informal*).

cinder *noun* (*cinders*) ashes, clinker, embers.

cinema *noun* **2** films, flicks (*informal*), motion pictures, movies (*informal*), pictures (*informal*), the screen.

circle[1] *noun* **1** band, disc, halo, hoop, loop, ring, round. **2** circuit, circumnavigation, lap, loop, orbit, revolution. **3** clique, company, group, set, sphere, world.

▶▶ D I C T I O N A R Y ◀◀

circle² *verb* (**circled, circling**) move in a circle; go round something.

circuit (*say* **ser**-kit) *noun* **1** a circular line or journey. **2** a motor-racing track. **3** the path of an electric current. [from Latin *circum* = round, + *itum* = gone]

circuitous (*say* ser-**kew**-it-us) *adjective* going a long way round, not direct.

circular¹ *adjective* **1** shaped like a circle; round. **2** moving round a circle. **circularity** *noun*

circular² *noun* a letter or advertisement etc. sent to a number of people.

circulate *verb* (**circulated, circulating**) **1** go round something continuously, *Blood circulates in the body*. **2** pass from place to place. **3** send round; send to a number of people. **circulation** *noun*

circum- *prefix* around (as in *circumference*). [from Latin *circum* = around]

circumcise *verb* (**circumcised, circumcising**) cut off the fold of skin at the tip of the penis. **circumcision** *noun* [from *circum-*, + Latin *caedere* = cut]

circumference *noun* the distance round something, especially round a circle. [from *circum-*, + Latin *ferens* = carrying]

circumflex accent a mark over a vowel, as over *e* in *fête*.

circumlocution *noun* a roundabout expression, using many words where a few would do, e.g. 'at this moment in time' for 'now'.

circumnavigate *verb* (**circumnavigated, circumnavigating**) sail completely round something. **circumnavigation** *noun* [from *circum-* + *navigate*]

circumscribe *verb* (**circumscribed, circumscribing**) **1** draw a line round something. **2**

limit; restrict, *Her powers are circumscribed by many regulations*. [from *circum-*, + Latin *scribere* = write]

circumspect *adjective* cautious and watchful. **circumspection** *noun* [from *circum-*, + Latin *specere* = to look]

circumstance *noun* a fact or condition connected with an event or person or action. [from *circum-*, + Latin *stans* = standing]

circumstantial (*say* ser-kum-**stan**-shal) *adjective* **1** giving full details, *a circumstantial account of her journey*. **2** consisting of facts that strongly suggest something but do not actually prove it, *circumstantial evidence*.

circumvent *verb* find a way of avoiding, *We managed to circumvent the rules*. **circumvention** *noun* [from *circum-*, + Latin *ventum* = come]

circus *noun* (*plural* **circuses**) a travelling show with clowns, acrobats, animals, etc. [Latin, = ring]

cistern *noun* a tank for storing water.

citadel *noun* a fortress protecting a city.

cite (*say as* sight) *verb* (**cited, citing**) quote as an example. **citation** *noun*

citizen *noun* a person belonging to a particular city or country and having certain rights and duties because of this. **citizenship** *noun* [same origin as *city*]

citizenry *noun* all the citizens.

citrus fruit a lemon, orange, etc.

city *noun* (*plural* **cities**) a large important town, usually with special rights given by a charter. [from Latin *civitas* = city]

civic *adjective* of a city or town; of citizens. [from Latin *civis* = citizen]

civics *noun* the study of the way citizens and towns are governed and of the rights and duties of citizens.

▶▶ T H E S A U R U S ◀◀

circle² *verb* circumnavigate, circumscribe, encircle, go round, orbit, ring, tour.

circuit *noun* **1** circle, lap, loop, orbit, revolution. **2** course, ring, track.

circular¹ *adjective* **1** discoid, round.

circular² *noun* bulletin, flyer, leaflet, memorandum, newsletter, notice.

circulate *verb* **1** flow, go round, move round. **2,3** distribute, issue, pass round, release, send round.

circumference *noun* boundary, edge, limit, margin, perimeter.

circumstance *noun* background, condition, context, detail, event, fact, particular, position, situation.

citadel *noun* acropolis, bastion, castle, fort, fortress, garrison, stronghold.

cite *verb* adduce, mention, name, put forward, quote, refer to, specify.

citizen *noun* denizen, dweller, inhabitant, national, native, resident.

city *noun* big smoke (*slang*), metropolis, town.

civic *adjective* citizen's, communal, community, local, municipal, public.

►►DICTIONARY◄◄

civil *adjective* **1** of citizens. **2** of civilians; not military, *civil aviation*. **3** polite. **civilly** *adverb*
civil defence protection of civilians in an air raid etc.
civil rights the rights of citizens, especially to have freedom, equality, and the right to vote.
civil war war between groups of people of the same country.

civilian *noun* a person who is not serving in the armed forces.

civilisation *noun* **1** a civilised condition or society. **2** making or becoming civilised.

civilise *verb* (**civilised, civilising**) bring culture and education etc. to a primitive community.
civilised *adjective*

civility *noun* (*plural* **civilities**) politeness; a polite act.

clad *adjective* clothed.

claim¹ *verb* **1** ask for something to which you believe you have a right. **2** declare; state something without being able to prove it.
claimant *noun*

claim² *noun* **1** claiming. **2** something claimed. **3** a piece of ground claimed or assigned to someone for mining etc. **4** a right or title to something. [same origin as *clamour²*]

clairvoyant *noun* a person who is said to be able to perceive future events or things that are happening out of sight. **clairvoyance** *noun* [from French *clair* = clear, + *voyant* = seeing]

clam *noun* a large shellfish.

clamber *verb* climb with difficulty.

clammy *adjective* damp and slimy.

clamour¹ *noun* **1** a loud confused noise. **2** an outcry; a loud protest or demand. **clamorous** *adjective*

clamour² *verb* make a loud protest or demand. [from Latin *clamare* = call out]

clamp¹ *noun* a device for holding things tightly.

clamp² *verb* fix with a clamp; fix firmly.
clamp down on become stricter about something; put a stop to it.

clan *noun* a group sharing the same ancestor, especially in Scotland.

clandestine (*say* klan-**dest**-in) *adjective* done secretly; kept secret.

clang *noun* a loud ringing sound. **clang** *verb*

clangour *noun* a clanging noise.

clank *noun* a sound like heavy pieces of metal banging together. **clank** *verb*

clap¹ *verb* (**clapped, clapping**) **1** strike the palms of the hands together loudly, especially as applause. **2** slap in a friendly way, *clapped him on the shoulder*. **3** put quickly, *They clapped him into gaol*.

clap² *noun* **1** a sudden sharp noise, *a clap of thunder*. **2** clapping; applause. **3** a friendly slap.

clapper *noun* the tongue or hanging piece inside a bell that strikes against the bell to make it sound.

claptrap *noun* insincere talk.

claret *noun* a kind of red wine.

clarify *verb* (**clarified, clarifying**) make or become clear or easier to understand. **clarification** *noun* [from Latin *clarus* = clear]

►►THESAURUS◄◄

civil *adjective* **1** citizen's, civic. **2** civilian, non-military. **3** cordial, courteous, obliging, polite, respectful, well-mannered.

civilised *adjective* cultivated, cultured, developed, educated, enlightened, refined, sophisticated.

clad *adjective* attired, clothed, dressed.

claim¹ *verb* **1** ask for, bags (*informal*), demand, lay claim to, request, require. **2** allege, assert, contend, declare, insist, maintain, make out, pretend, profess, state.

claim² *noun* **1** application, call, demand, request. **4** entitlement, right, title.

clairvoyance *noun* ESP, extrasensory perception, second sight, sixth sense.

clamber *verb* climb, crawl, scramble, shin.

clammy *adjective* damp, dank, humid, moist, sticky, sweaty, wet.

clamour¹ *noun* commotion, din, hubbub, hullabaloo, noise, outcry, racket, row, rumpus, shouting, uproar.

clamour² *verb* call, cry out, demand, protest, shout.

clamp¹ *noun* brace, clasp, clip, fastener, grip, support, vice.

clamp² *verb* clasp, clip, fasten, grip, secure.

clan *noun* family, group, line, tribe.

clang *noun* chime, clangour, clank, clash, clink, jangle, peal, ringing.

clank *noun* clang, clash, clatter, clunk, jangle, rattle.

clap¹ *verb* **1** applaud.

clap² *noun* **1** bang, burst, crack, crash, explosion, peal. **2** applause, hand (*informal*).

clarify *verb* clear up, elucidate, explain, make clear, shed light on, spell out.

▶▶ DICTIONARY ◀◀

clarinet *noun* a woodwind instrument.
clarinettist *noun*

clarion *noun* an old type of trumpet.

clarity *noun* clearness.

clash *verb* 1 make a loud sound like that of cymbals banging together. 2 conflict. 3 happen inconveniently at the same time. 4 (of colours) look unpleasant together. **clash** *noun*

clasp¹ *noun* 1 a device for fastening things, with interlocking parts. 2 a grasp.

clasp² *verb* 1 grasp or hold tightly. 2 fasten with a clasp.

class¹ *noun* (*plural* **classes**) 1 a group of children, students, etc. who are taught together. 2 a group of similar people, animals, or things. 3 people of the same social or economic level. 4 level of quality, *first class*.

class² *verb* 1 classify. 2 (*Australian*) grade fleeces in a shearing shed. **classer** *noun* [from Latin *classis* = a social division of the Roman people]

classic¹ *adjective* 1 generally agreed to be excellent or important. 2 very typical, *a classic case*. 3 having enduring worth.

classic² *noun* a classic book, film, writer, etc. [from Latin *classicus* = of the highest class]

classical *adjective* 1 of ancient Greek or Roman literature, art, etc. 2 serious or conventional in style, *classical music*.

classics *noun* the study of ancient Greek and Latin languages and literature etc.

classified *adjective* 1 put into classes or groups. 2 (of information) declared officially to be secret and available only to certain people.

classify *verb* (**classified**, **classifying**) arrange things in classes or groups. **classification** *noun*, **classificatory** *adjective*

classmate *noun* someone in the same class at school etc.

classroom *noun* a room where a class of children or students is taught.

clatter *verb* & *noun* rattle.

clause *noun* 1 a single part of a treaty, law, or contract. 2 part of a complex sentence, with its own verb, *There are two clauses in 'We choose what we want'*.

claustrophobia *noun* fear of being inside something. [from Latin *claustrum* = enclosed space, + *phobia*]

claw¹ *noun* 1 a sharp nail on a bird's or animal's foot. 2 a claw-like part or device used for grasping things.

claw² *verb* grasp, pull, or scratch with a claw or hand.

clay *noun* a kind of stiff sticky earth that becomes hard when baked, used for making bricks and pottery. **clayey** *adjective*

▶▶ THESAURUS ◀◀

clarity *noun* clearness, limpidity, purity, transparency.

clash *verb* 1 bang, clang, clank, clatter, crash, jangle. 2 argue, battle, be opposed, conflict, contend, disagree, dispute, feud, fight, quarrel, squabble, wrangle.
clash *noun* 1 bang, clang, clangour, clank, clatter, crash, jangle. 2 altercation, battle, combat, conflict, confrontation, contest, disagreement, fight, skirmish. 3 discord, disharmony, incompatibility, mismatch.

clasp¹ *noun* 1 brooch, buckle, catch, clip, fastener, hook, lock.

clasp² *verb* 1 clutch, embrace, enfold, grasp, grip, hold, hug, squeeze. 2 clip, fasten, join, secure.

class¹ *noun* 1 form, grade, group, set, year. 2 category, classification, division, family, genre, genus, group, kind, league, order, set, sort, species, subset, type, variety. 3 caste, level, order, rank, station, stratum.

class² *verb* 1 arrange, categorise, classify, grade, group, label, rank, sort.

classic¹ *adjective* 1 excellent, exemplary, first-class, first-rate, outstanding. 2 archetypal, characteristic, model, standard, typical. 3 abiding, ageless, enduring, established, immortal, lasting, time-honoured, traditional.

classical *adjective* 1 Greek, Latin, Roman. 2 ageless, conventional, enduring, serious, standard, traditional.

classify *verb* arrange, categorise, class, grade, group, label, order, organise, pigeon-hole, rank, sort.

clatter *noun* banging, clack, clang, clangour, clank, jangle, rattle.

clause *noun* 1 article, condition, paragraph, provision, proviso, section, stipulation.

claw¹ *noun* 1 nail, nipper, pincer, talon.

claw² *verb* lacerate, maul, scratch, slash, tear.

▶▶ DICTIONARY ◀◀

clean¹ *adjective* **1** without any dirt or marks or stains. **2** fresh; not yet used. **3** honourable; not unfair, *a clean fight*. **4** not indecent. **cleanness** *noun*

clean² *verb* make a thing clean.

clean³ *adverb* completely, *I clean forgot.*

cleaner *noun* **1** a person who cleans things, especially rooms etc. **2** something used for cleaning things.

cleanly¹ (*say* **kleen**-lee) *adverb* in a clean way.

cleanly² (*say* **klen**-lee) *adjective* taking care to be clean, *cleanly habits*. **cleanliness** *noun*

cleanse (*say* klenz) *verb* (**cleansed, cleansing**) **1** clean. **2** make pure. **cleanser** *noun*

cleanskin *noun* (*Australian*) an unbranded animal.

clear¹ *adjective* **1** transparent; not muddy or cloudy. **2** easy to see or hear or understand; distinct. **3** free from obstacles or unwanted things. **4** free from guilt, *a clear conscience*. **5** complete, *Give three clear days' notice*. **clearly** *adverb*, **clearness** *noun*

clear² *adverb* **1** distinctly; clearly, *We heard you loud and clear*. **2** completely, *He got clear away*. **3** apart; not in contact, *Stand clear of the doors*.

clear³ *verb* **1** make or become clear. **2** show that someone is innocent or reliable. **3** jump over something without touching it. **4** get approval or authorisation for something, *Clear this with the headmaster*.

clear away remove used plates etc.

clear off or **out** (*informal*) go away.

clear up make things tidy; become better or brighter; solve, *clear up the mystery*. [from Latin *clarus* = clear]

clearance *noun* **1** clearing something. **2** getting rid of unwanted goods. **3** the space between two things.

clearing *noun* an open space in a forest.

clearway *noun* a road on which vehicles must not stop between certain hours.

cleave¹ *verb* (*past tense* **cleaved, clove**, or **cleft**; *past participle* **cleft** or **cloven**; *present participle* **cleaving**) **1** divide by chopping; split. **2** make a way through, *cleaving the waves*. **cleavage** *noun*

cleave² *verb* (**cleaved, cleaving**) (*old use*) cling to something.

cleaver *noun* a butcher's chopper.

clef *noun* a symbol on a stave in music, showing the pitch of the notes, *treble clef; bass clef*. [French, = key]

cleft¹ *past tense* of **cleave¹**.

cleft² *noun* a split; a separation.

clemency *noun* mildness; mercy.

clench *verb* close teeth or fingers tightly.

▶▶ THESAURUS ◀◀

clean¹ *adjective* **1** cleansed, disinfected, fresh, hygienic, immaculate, laundered, sanitary, sanitised, scoured, scrubbed, spick and span, spotless, sterilised, unsoiled, washed. **2** (*clean air*) clear, fresh, pure, purified, uncontaminated, unpolluted; (*a clean page*) blank, fresh, new, unmarked, unused. **3** above board, fair, honest, honourable, sporting, sportsmanlike. **4** decent, innocent, inoffensive, respectable.

clean² *verb* bath, bathe, brush, cleanse, decontaminate, disinfect, dry-clean, dust, groom, launder, mop, purge, purify, rinse, sanitise, scour, scrub, shampoo, shower, sponge, sterilise, swab, sweep, swill, tidy (up), vacuum, wash, wipe.

cleanser *noun* antiseptic, bactericide, detergent, disinfectant, germicide, sanitiser, soap, steriliser.

clear¹ *adjective* **1** (*a clear liquid*) clean, crystal-clear, crystalline, limpid, pure, see-through, transparent; (*clear skies*) bright, cloudless, fair, starry, sunny, unclouded. **2** apparent, blatant, clear-cut, coherent, comprehensible, crystal-clear, definite, distinct, evident, glaring, intelligible, lucid, manifest, marked, noticeable, obvious, palpable, patent, plain, pronounced, straightforward, unambiguous, understandable, unequivocal, unmistakable, visible. **3** empty, free, open, passable, unimpeded, unobstructed. **4** blameless, easy, guilt-free, guiltless, untroubled.

clear³ *verb* **1** clean, empty, evacuate, free, unblock, unclog. **2** absolve, acquit, exonerate, vindicate. **3** bound over, jump over, leap over, spring over, vault. **4** approve, authorise, OK (*informal*), pass, sanction.

clear off see LEAVE¹.

clear up 1 clean up, sort out, straighten up, tidy up. **2** clarify, explain, resolve, settle, sort out.

clearing *noun* gap, glade, opening, space.

cleaver *noun* chopper, hatchet, meat-axe; see also KNIFE¹.

clench *verb* clamp together, close, grit, set.

▶▶ D I C T I O N A R Y ◀◀

clergy *noun* the people who have been ordained as priests or ministers of the Christian Church.

clerical *adjective* **1** of clerks or their work. **2** of the clergy.

clerk (*say* klark) *noun* a person employed to keep records or accounts, deal with papers in an office, etc.

clever *adjective* quick at learning and understanding things; skilful. **cleverly** *adverb*, **cleverness** *noun*

cliché (*say* **klee**-shay) *noun* a phrase or idea that is used too often. [French, = stereotyped]

click *noun* a short sharp sound. **click** *verb*

client *noun* a person who gets help from a lawyer, architect, or professional person other than a doctor; a customer.

clientele (*say* klee-on-**tel**) *noun* clients.

cliff *noun* a steep rock-face, especially on a coast.

climate *noun* the regular weather conditions of an area. **climatic** (*say* kly-**mat**-ik) *adjective*

climax *noun* (*plural* **climaxes**) the most interesting or important point of a story,

series of events, etc. [from Greek *klimax* = ladder]

climb *verb* **1** go up or over or down something. **2** grow upwards. **3** go higher. **climb** *noun*, **climber** *noun*
climb down admit that you have been wrong.

clinch *verb* **1** fasten securely. **2** settle definitely, *clinch the deal*. **3** (in boxing) be clasping each other. **clinch** *noun* [from *clench*]

cling *verb* (**clung**, **clinging**) hold on tightly.

clinic *noun* a place where people see doctors etc. for treatment or advice. **clinical** *adjective* [from Greek *klinikos* = of a bed]

clink *noun* a thin sharp sound like glasses being struck together. **clink** *verb*

clinker *noun* a piece of rough stony material left after coal has burned.

clip¹ *noun* a fastener for keeping things together, usually worked by a spring.

clip² *verb* (**clipped**, **clipping**) fasten with a clip.

clip³ *verb* (**clipped**, **clipping**) **1** cut with shears or scissors etc. **2** (*informal*) hit.

clip⁴ *noun* **1** clipping something; a piece clipped off or out. **2** a sequence taken from a film. **3** the wool cut from a sheep or flock at one shearing.

▶▶ T H E S A U R U S ◀◀

clergy *noun* ministry, priesthood; (*various members of the clergy*) archbishop, archdeacon, bishop, canon, cardinal, chaplain, churchman, churchwoman, clergyman, clergywoman, cleric, curate, deacon, deaconess, dean, minister, padre, parson, pastor, preacher, prelate, priest, primate, rector, vicar.

clerical *adjective* **1** book, bookkeeping, office, paper, secretarial, stenographic, white-collar. **2** ecclesiastical, ministerial, priestly, sacerdotal.

clerk *noun* bookkeeper, office worker, record-keeper, secretary.

clever *adjective* able, accomplished, adept, adroit, artful, astute, brainy, bright, brilliant, canny, crafty, cunning, deft, dexterous, expert, gifted, ingenious, intelligent, inventive, nifty (*informal*), perceptive, quick-witted, resourceful, sharp-witted, shrewd, skilful, slick, sly, smart, talented, wily, wise, witty.
cleverness *noun* ability, adroitness, astuteness, brains, brilliance, cunning, dexterity, expertise, ingenuity, intelligence, mastery, quickness, resourcefulness, shrewdness, skill, smartness, talent, wit, wizardry.

cliché *noun* banality, commonplace, hackneyed phrase, platitude.

click *noun* crack, snap, tick.

client *noun* consumer, customer, patron, shopper, user.

cliff *noun* bluff, crag, escarpment, precipice, rock face, scarp.

climate *noun* clime (*literary*), weather.

climax *noun* apex, crisis, culmination, highlight, peak, pinnacle, summit, zenith.

climb *verb* **1** clamber over, go over, mount, scale, shin. **3** ascend, go up, rise, soar.

clinch *verb* **2** close, conclude, finalise, secure, settle, sew up (*informal*).

cling *verb* adhere, attach, stick; (*cling to*) clasp, cleave to (*old use*), clutch, embrace, grasp, grip, hang on to, hold on to, hug.

clinic *noun* health centre, hospital, infirmary, medical centre, surgery.

clink *verb* jangle, jingle, ring, tinkle.

clip¹ *noun* clasp, fastener, grip, hook.

clip² *verb* attach, fasten, fix, join, pin, secure, staple.

clip³ *verb* **1** bob, crop, cut, prune, shear, shorten, snip, trim.

clip⁴ *noun* **2** excerpt, extract, segment, snippet, trailer.

▶▶ D I C T I O N A R Y ◀◀

clipper *noun* an old type of fast sailing-ship.

clippers *plural noun* an instrument for cutting hair.

clique (*say* kleek) *noun* a small group of people who stick together and keep others out.

cloak[1] *noun* a sleeveless garment that hangs loosely from the shoulders.

cloak[2] *verb* cover; conceal.

cloakroom *noun* a place where people can leave outdoor clothes, luggage, etc.

clobber *verb* (*slang*) **1** hit hard again and again. **2** defeat completely.

cloche (*say* klosh) *noun* a glass or plastic cover to protect outdoor plants. [French, = bell]

clock[1] *noun* **1** a device (other than a watch) that shows what the time is. **2** a measuring device with a dial or showing figures. [from Latin *clocca* = bell]

clock[2] *verb* **clock in** or **out** register the time you arrive at work or leave work.
clock up achieve a certain speed.

clockwise *adverb* & *adjective* moving round a circle in the same direction as a clock's hands. [from *clock* + *wise*[2]]

clockwork *noun* a mechanism with a spring that has to be wound up.
like clockwork very regularly.

clod *noun* a lump of earth or clay.

clog[1] *noun* a shoe with a wooden sole.

clog[2] *verb* (**clogged, clogging**) block up.

cloister *noun* a covered path along the side of a church or monastery etc., round a

courtyard. [from Latin *claustrum* = enclosed place]

clone *noun* an animal or plant made from the cells of another animal or plant and therefore exactly like it. **clone** *verb*

close[1] (*say* klohss) *adjective* **1** near. **2** dear to each other, *close friends*. **3** detailed; concentrated, *with close attention*. **4** tight; with little empty space, *a close fit*. **5** in which competitors are nearly equal, *a close contest*. **6** stuffy. **closely** *adverb*, **closeness** *noun*

close[2] *adverb* closely, *close behind*.

close[3] *noun* a cul-de-sac.

close[4] (*say* klohz) *verb* (**closed, closing**) **1** shut. **2** end.
close in get nearer; get shorter.

close[5] *noun* end, *at the close of play*. [from Latin *clausum* = shut]

closet[1] *noun* a cupboard; a small room; a storeroom.

closet[2] *verb* (**closeted, closeting**) shut away in a private room.

closure *noun* closing.

clot[1] *noun* **1** a small mass of blood, cream, etc. that has become solid. **2** (*slang*) a stupid person.

clot[2] *verb* (**clotted, clotting**) form clots.
clotted cream cream thickened by being scalded.

cloth *noun* **1** woven material or felt. **2** a piece of this material. **3** a tablecloth.

clothe *verb* (**clothed, clothing**) put clothes on someone.

▶▶ T H E S A U R U S ◀◀

clippers *plural noun* cutters, scissors, secateurs, shears, snips.

clique *noun* circle, crowd, faction, group, mob, set.

cloak[1] *noun* burnous, cape, coat, cope, mantle, poncho, shroud, wrap.

clock[1] *noun* **1** chronometer, timepiece.

clog[2] *verb* block, bung up, choke, jam, obstruct, stop up.

close[1] *adjective* **1** accessible, adjacent, at hand, near, neighbouring; see also IMPENDING. **2** affectionate, attached, dear, devoted, familiar, fond, inseparable, intimate. **3** alert, attentive, careful, concentrated, detailed, minute, searching, thorough. **4** cramped, narrow, tight.

5 even, level-pegging, narrow, neck and neck, tight. **6** airless, humid, muggy, oppressive, stale, stifling, stuffy, sultry.

close[2] *adverb* alongside, close by, near, nigh (*old use*), within cooee (*Australian informal*).

close[4] *verb* **1** bar, block, bolt, cork, fasten, latch, lock, plug, seal, secure, shut, slam, stop. **2** conclude, end, finish, stop, terminate, wind up.

close[5] *noun* completion, conclusion, culmination, end, finale, finish, halt, stop, termination.

closet[1] *noun* cupboard, wardrobe.

clot[2] *verb* coagulate, solidify, thicken.

cloth *noun* **1** fabric, material, stuff, textile.

clothe *verb* array, attire, deck, dress, garb, robe.

▶▶▶ D I C T I O N A R Y ◀◀◀

clothes *plural noun* things worn to cover the body. [originally the plural of *cloth*]

clothing *noun* clothes.

cloud[1] *noun* **1** a mass of condensed water-vapour floating in the sky. **2** a mass of smoke, dust, etc., in the air.

cloud[2] *verb* fill or obscure with clouds.

cloudburst *noun* a sudden violent rainstorm.

cloudless *adjective* without clouds.

cloudy *adjective* (**cloudier, cloudiest**) **1** full of clouds. **2** not transparent, *The liquid became cloudy.* **cloudiness** *noun*

clout *verb & noun* (*informal*) hit.

clove[1] *noun* the dried bud of a tropical tree, used as a spice.

clove[2] *noun* one of the small bulbs in a compound bulb, *a clove of garlic.*

clove[3] *past tense* of **cleave**[1].
clove hitch a kind of knot.

cloven *past participle* of **cleave**[1].
cloven hoof a hoof that is divided, like those of cows and sheep.

clover *noun* a small plant usually with three leaves on each stalk.
in clover in ease and luxury.

clown[1] *noun* **1** a performer who does comical tricks and actions, especially in a circus. **2** a person who clowns.

clown[2] *verb* behave comically.

cloying *adjective* sickeningly sweet.

club[1] *noun* **1** a heavy stick used as a weapon. **2** a stick with a shaped head used to hit the ball in golf. **3** a group of people who meet because they are interested in the same thing; the premises where they meet. **4** a playing card with black clover-leaves on it.

club[2] *verb* (**clubbed, clubbing**) hit with a heavy stick.
club together join with other people in subscribing, *club together to buy a boat.*

cluck *verb* make a hen's throaty cry. **cluck** *noun*

clue *noun* something that helps a person to solve a puzzle or a mystery.
not have a clue (*informal*) be stupid or helpless.

clump[1] *noun* **1** a cluster or mass of things. **2** a clumping sound.

clump[2] *verb* **1** form a cluster or mass. **2** walk with a heavy tread.

clumsy *adjective* (**clumsier, clumsiest**) **1** heavy and ungraceful; likely to knock things over or drop things. **2** not skilful; not tactful, *a clumsy apology.* **clumsily** *adverb*, **clumsiness** *noun*

cluster[1] *noun* a small close group.

cluster[2] *verb* form a cluster.

clutch[1] *verb* grasp tightly.

clutch[2] *noun* (*plural* **clutches**) **1** a tight grasp. **2** a device for connecting and disconnecting the engine of a motor vehicle from its gears.

clutch[3] *noun* (*plural* **clutches**) a set of eggs for hatching.

clutter[1] *noun* things lying about untidily.

▶▶▶ T H E S A U R U S ◀◀◀

clothes *plural noun* apparel (*formal*), attire (*formal*), clobber (*slang*), clothing, costume, dress, finery, garb, garments, gear (*informal*), get-up (*informal*), kit, outfit, raiment (*old use*), rig (*informal*), togs (*informal*), uniform, vestments, wardrobe, wear.

cloud[1] *noun* **1** fog, haze, mist, vapour.

cloud[2] *verb* blur, darken, dim, fog, grow overcast, muddy, obscure.

cloudless *adjective* blue, bright, clear, fair, starlit, starry, sunny, unclouded.

cloudy *adjective* **1** dull, gloomy, grey, heavy, leaden, louring, overcast. **2** hazy, milky, muddy, murky, opaque.

clown[1] *noun* buffoon, comedian, comic, fool, jester, joker, wag, zany.

club[1] *noun* **1** bat, baton, bludgeon, cudgel, nulla-nulla, stick, truncheon, waddy. **3** alliance, association, fellowship, group, guild, league, organisation, society, union.

club[2] *verb* batter, beat, bludgeon, clobber, cudgel, hit, strike, wallop.

clue *noun* cue, guide, hint, idea, indication, inkling, key, lead, pointer, sign, suggestion, tip.

clump[1] *noun* **1** bunch, cluster, group, mass, tuft.

clumsy *adjective* **1** awkward, blundering, bungling, fumbling, gawky, ham-fisted (*informal*), heavy-handed, inept, maladroit, unco (*informal*), uncoordinated, ungainly, unskilful.

cluster[1] *noun* assembly, batch, bunch, collection, congregation, crowd, gathering, group, herd, hive, huddle, swarm, throng.

cluster[2] *verb* assemble, bunch, collect, congregate, crowd, flock, gather, group, herd, huddle, throng.

clutch[1] *verb* clasp, cling to, grasp, grip, hang on to, hold, hug.

clutter[1] *noun* jumble, litter, mess, muddle.

▶▶ D I C T I O N A R Y ◀◀

clutter² *verb* fill with clutter.

Co. *abbreviation* Company.

c/o *abbreviation* care of.

co- *prefix* together, jointly (as in *coexistence, cooperate*); joint (as in *co-pilot*). [from *com-*]

coach¹ *noun* (*plural* **coaches**) **1** a bus used for long journeys. **2** a carriage of a railway train. **3** a large horse-drawn carriage with four wheels. **4** an instructor in sports. **5** a teacher giving private specialised tuition.

coach² *verb* instruct or train somebody, especially in sports.

coachwood *noun* an Australian tree with light tough wood used in motorbody work, furniture, etc.

coagulate *verb* (**coagulated, coagulating**) change from liquid to semi-solid; clot. **coagulant** *noun*, **coagulation** *noun*

coal *noun* a hard black mineral substance used for burning to supply heat; a piece of this. **coalfield** *noun*

coalesce (*say* koh-a-**less**) *verb* combine and form one whole thing. **coalescence** *noun*, **coalescent** *adjective*

coalition *noun* an alliance.

coarse *adjective* **1** not smooth, not delicate; rough. **2** composed of large particles; not fine. **3** not refined; vulgar. **coarsely** *adverb*, **coarseness** *noun*

coarsen *verb* make or become coarse.

coast¹ *noun* the seashore; the land close to it. **coastal** *adjective*, **coastline** *noun*

the coast is clear there is no chance of being seen or hindered.

coast² *verb* ride without using power.

coastguard *noun* a person whose job is to keep watch on the coast, detect or prevent smuggling, etc.

coat¹ *noun* **1** an outdoor garment with sleeves. **2** the hair or fur on an animal's body. **3** a coating, *a coat of paint*.
coat of arms a design on a shield, used as an emblem by a family, city, etc.

coat² *verb* cover with a coating.

coating *noun* a covering layer.

coax *verb* persuade gently or patiently.

cob *noun* **1** the central part of an ear of maize, on which the corn grows. **2** a sturdy horse for riding. **3** a male swan. (The female is a *pen*.)

cobalt *noun* a hard silvery-white metal.

cobber *noun* (*Australian informal*) a friend, mate.

cobble¹ *noun* a rounded stone used for paving streets etc. **cobbled** *adjective*

cobble² *verb* (**cobbled, cobbling**) make or mend roughly.

cobbler *noun* a shoe repairer.

cobra (*say* **koh**-bra) *noun* a poisonous snake that can rear up.

cobweb *noun* the thin sticky net made by a spider to trap insects. [from an old word *coppe* = spider, + *web*]

cocaine *noun* a drug made from the leaves of a tropical plant called *coca*.

▶▶ T H E S A U R U S ◀◀

clutter² *verb* crowd, litter, mess up, scatter, strew.

coach¹ *noun* **1** bus, omnibus (*formal*). **3** carriage, stagecoach. **4,5** instructor, teacher, trainer, tutor.

coach² *verb* drill, instruct, teach, train, tutor.

coagulate *verb* clot, congeal, curdle, solidify, stiffen, thicken.

coalition *noun* alliance, amalgamation, association, bloc, partnership, union.

coarse *adjective* **1** harsh, loose-weave, prickly, rough, scratchy. **3** boorish, common, crude, foul, impolite, improper, indecent, low, offensive, rough, rude, uncouth, unrefined, vulgar.

coast¹ *noun* beach, coastline, foreshore, seaboard, seashore, seaside, shore.

coast² *verb* cruise, drift, freewheel, glide.

coat¹ *noun* **1** (*kinds of coat*) anorak, blazer, cagoule, dinner-jacket, doublet, duffel coat, greatcoat, jacket, mackintosh, overcoat, parka, raincoat, tailcoat, topcoat, trench coat, tuxedo, waistcoat, windcheater, wrap. **2** fleece, fur, hair, hide, pelt, skin. **3** coating, cover, film, layer, overlay.
coat of arms blazon, crest, emblem, heraldic device, shield.

coat² *verb* cover, daub, encase, encrust, laminate, paint, plaster, protect, seal, smear, spread, veneer.

coating *noun* coat, cover, covering, film, glaze, layer, outside, overlay, sealant, skin, surface, veneer.

coax *verb* beguile, cajole, charm, entice, induce, inveigle, persuade, sweet-talk (*informal*), talk into, tempt.

cobber *noun* buddy (*informal*), chum (*informal*), companion, comrade, confidant, confidante, crony, friend, mate, pal (*informal*).

cobbler *noun* shoemaker, shoe repairer.

▶▶ D I C T I O N A R Y ◀◀

cock¹ *noun* **1** a male bird; a male fowl. **2** a stopcock. **3** a lever in a gun.

cock² *verb* **1** make a gun ready to fire by raising the cock. **2** turn something upwards or in a particular direction, *The dog cocked its ears.*

cockatoo *noun* a crested parrot.

cocked hat a triangular hat worn with some uniforms.

cockerel *noun* a young male fowl.

cocker spaniel a kind of small spaniel.

cock-eyed *adjective* (*slang*) **1** crooked; not straight. **2** absurd.

cockle *noun* an edible shellfish.

cockney *noun* (*plural* **cockneys**) **1** a person born in the East End of London. **2** the dialect or accent of cockneys.

cockpit *noun* the compartment where the pilot of an aircraft sits.

cockroach *noun* (*plural* **cockroaches**) a beetle-like insect.

cocksure *adjective* very sure; too confident.

cocktail *noun* **1** a mixed alcoholic drink. **2** a food containing shellfish or fruit.

cocky¹ *adjective* (**cockier, cockiest**) (*informal*) conceited. **cockiness** *noun*

cocky² *noun* (*Australian informal*) a farmer with a small property, usually a dairy farm.

cocoa *noun* **1** a hot drink made from a powder of crushed cacao seeds. **2** this powder. [an alteration of *cacao*]

coconut *noun* **1** a large round nut that grows on a kind of palm-tree. **2** its white lining, used in sweets and cookery. [from Spanish *coco* = grinning face (the base of the nut looks like a monkey's face)]

cocoon¹ *noun* **1** the covering round a chrysalis. **2** a protective wrapping.

cocoon² *verb* protect by wrapping.

cod *noun* (*plural* **cod**) a large edible sea-fish.

coddle *verb* (**coddled, coddling**) cherish and protect carefully.

code¹ *noun* **1** a word or phrase used to represent a message in order to keep its meaning secret. **2** a set of signs used in sending messages by machine etc., *the Morse code.* **3** a set of laws or rules, *a code of practice.*

code² *verb* (**coded, coding**) put into code.

codicil *noun* an addition to a will.

codify *verb* (**codified, codifying**) arrange laws or rules into a code or system. **codification** *noun*

coeducation *noun* educating boys and girls together. **coeducational** *adjective*

coefficient *noun* a number by which another number is multiplied; a factor.

coerce (*say* koh-**erss**) *verb* (**coerced, coercing**) compel someone by using threats or force. **coercion** *noun*

coexist *verb* exist together. **coexistence** *noun*, **coexistent** *adjective*

coffee *noun* **1** a hot drink made from the roasted ground seeds (*coffee-beans*) of a tropical plant. **2** these seeds. [from Arabic *kahwa*]

coffer *noun* a large strong box for holding money and valuables.

coffin *noun* a long box in which a body is buried or cremated.

cog *noun* one of a number of projections round the edge of a wheel, fitting into and pushing those on another wheel.

cog-wheel *noun* a wheel with cogs.

cogent (*say* **koh**-jent) *adjective* convincing, *a cogent argument.*

cogitate *verb* (**cogitated, cogitating**) think deeply. **cogitation** *noun*

cognac (*say* **kon**-yak) *noun* brandy, especially from Cognac in France.

cohere *verb* (**cohered, cohering**) stick to each other in a mass. **cohesion** *noun*, **cohesive** *adjective* [from *co-*, + Latin *haerere* = to stick]

▶▶ T H E S A U R U S ◀◀

cock¹ *noun* **1** cockerel, rooster.

cock² *verb* **2** prick up, raise, tilt, tip.

cock-eyed *adjective* **1** askew, awry, crooked, lopsided. **2** absurd, crazy, foolish, hare-brained, ludicrous, mad, stupid, wild.

cocky¹ *adjective* arrogant, brash, bumptious, cocksure, conceited, impudent, opinionated, overconfident, self-assured, self-confident, vain.

code¹ *noun* **1** cipher. **3** laws, principles, regulations, rules, system.

code² *verb* encode, encrypt.

codicil *noun* addendum, appendix, postscript, rider, supplement.

coerce *verb* bludgeon, browbeat, bulldoze (*informal*), bully, compel, constrain, dragoon, force, intimidate, lean on (*informal*), press, pressure, railroad.

coffin *noun* box, casket, sarcophagus.

►►► D I C T I O N A R Y ◄◄

coherent (*say* koh-**heer**-ent) *adjective* **1** cohering. **2** clear and reasonable; not incoherent. **coherently** *adverb*

coil¹ *noun* something wound into a spiral.

coil² *verb* wind into a coil.

coin¹ *noun* a shaped piece of metal used to buy things.

coin² *verb* **1** manufacture coins. **2** (*informal*) make a lot of money as profit. **3** invent a word or phrase.

coinage *noun* **1** coining. **2** coins; a system of money. **3** a new word or phrase.

coincide *verb* (**coincided**, **coinciding**) **1** happen at the same time as something else. **2** be in the same place. **3** be the same, *My opinion coincided with hers.* [from *co-,* + Latin *incidere* = fall on]

coincidence *noun* the happening of similar events at the same time by chance. **coincidental** *adjective*

coke *noun* the solid fuel left when gas and tar have been extracted from coal.

col- *prefix* see **com-**.

colander *noun* a bowl-shaped container with holes for straining water from vegetables etc. after cooking.

cold¹ *adjective* **1** having or at a low temperature; not warm. **2** not friendly or loving; not enthusiastic. **coldly** *adverb*, **coldness** *noun*
cold shoulder deliberate unfriendliness.
cold-shoulder *verb*
cold war a situation where nations are enemies without actually fighting.
get cold feet feel afraid or reluctant to do something.

cold² *noun* **1** lack of warmth; low temperature; cold weather. **2** an infectious illness that makes your nose run, your throat sore, etc.

cold-blooded *adjective* **1** having a body temperature that changes according to the surroundings. **2** callous; deliberately cruel.

colic *noun* stomach-ache.

collaborate *verb* (**collaborated**, **collaborating**) work together on a job. **collaboration** *noun*, **collaborator** *noun* [from *col-,* + Latin *laborare* = to work]

collage (*say* kol-**ahzh**) *noun* a picture made by fixing small objects to a surface. [French, = gluing]

collapse¹ *verb* (**collapsed**, **collapsing**) **1** fall down or inwards suddenly; break. **2** become very weak or ill. **3** break down; fail. **4** fold up.

collapse² *noun* collapsing; a breakdown. [from *col-,* + Latin *lapsum* = slipped]

►►► T H E S A U R U S ◄◄

coherent *adjective* **2** articulate, clear, connected, consistent, intelligible, logical, lucid, rational, structured, systematic, understandable.

coil¹ *noun* circle, convolution, curl, helix, kink, loop, ring, spiral, twist, whorl.

coil² *verb* bend, curl, entwine, kink, loop, roll, turn, twine, twirl, twist, wind, wrap.

coin¹ *noun* cash, change, copper, money, silver.

coin² *verb* **1** mint, strike. **3** create, devise, invent, make up, originate.

coincide *verb* **1** be concurrent, clash, happen simultaneously, happen together, synchronise. **3** accord, agree, be the same, concur, correspond, match, square, tally.

coincidence *noun* accident, chance, fluke, luck.
coincidental *adjective* accidental, chance, fortuitous, unintentional, unplanned.

cold¹ *adjective* **1** biting, bitter, bleak, chill, chilly, cool, crisp, freezing, frigid, frosty, glacial, icy, nippy (*informal*), perishing (*informal*), raw, subzero, wintry. **2** aloof, callous, clinical, cold-hearted, cool, distant, frigid, frosty, hard-hearted, heartless, hostile, indifferent, inhuman, insensitive, severe, stand-offish, stony, uncaring, undemonstrative, unemotional, unenthusiastic, unfeeling, unfriendly, unkind, unsympathetic.
cold-shoulder *verb* freeze out (*informal*), ostracise, rebuff, send to Coventry, snub.

cold-blooded *adjective* **2** brutal, callous, cold-hearted, cruel, hard-hearted, heartless, inhuman, inhumane, merciless, pitiless, ruthless, savage, unemotional, unfeeling.

collaborate *verb* cooperate, join forces, team up, work together.
collaborator *noun* **1** ally, assistant, associate, colleague, co-worker, fellow worker, helper, partner. **2** fraterniser, quisling, traitor.

collapse¹ *verb* **1** break, buckle, cave in, crumble, crumple, disintegrate, drop, fall down, give way, subside, tumble down. **2** faint, fall down, flop, keel over, pass out, sink, slump, swoon. **3** break down, fail, fold, founder, go bung (*Australian informal*), go bust (*informal*).

collapse² *noun* breakdown, cave-in, destruction, disintegration, downfall, failure, fall, ruin, subsidence.

collapsible *adjective* able to be folded up.

collar[1] *noun* **1** an upright or turned-over band round the neck of a garment etc. **2** a band that goes round the neck of a dog, cat, horse, etc.

collar[2] *verb* (*informal*) seize. [from Latin *collum* = neck]

collate *verb* (**collated, collating**) bring together and compare lists, books, etc. **collation** *noun*

collateral *adjective* **1** parallel to something. **2** additional but less important.

colleague *noun* a person you work with.

collect[1] (*say* kol-**ekt**) *verb* **1** bring people or things together from various places. **2** obtain examples of things as a hobby, *She collects stamps.* **3** come together. **4** ask for money or contributions etc. from people. **5** fetch, *Collect your coat from the cleaners.* **collector** *noun*

collect[2] (*say* **kol**-ekt) *noun* a short prayer.

collection *noun* **1** collecting. **2** things collected. **3** money collected for a charity etc.

collective *adjective* of a group taken as a whole, *our collective opinion.*
collective noun a noun that is singular in form but refers to many individuals taken as a unit, e.g. *army, herd.*

college *noun* **1** a place where people can continue learning something after they have left school. **2** a school.

collide *verb* (**collided, colliding**) crash into something. **collision** *noun*

collie *noun* a dog with a long pointed face.

colliery *noun* (*plural* **collieries**) a coal-mine and its buildings. [from *coal*]

colloquial (*say* col-**oh**-kwee-al) *adjective* suitable for conversation but not for formal speech or writing. **colloquially** *adverb*, **colloquialism** *noun* [from *col-* + Latin *loqui* = speak]

collusion *noun* a secret agreement between two or more people who are trying to deceive or cheat someone. [from *col-*, + Latin *ludere* = to play]

cologne (*say* kol-**ohn**) *noun* eau de Cologne or a similar liquid.

colon[1] *noun* a punctuation mark (:), often used to introduce lists.

colon[2] *noun* the largest part of the intestine.

colonel (*say* **ker**-nel) *noun* an army officer in charge of a regiment. [from French]

colonial *adjective* of a colony.

colonialism *noun* the policy of acquiring and keeping colonies.

colonise *verb* (**colonised, colonising**) establish a colony in a country. **colonisation** *noun*, **colonist** *noun*

colonnade *noun* a row of columns.

colony *noun* (*plural* **colonies**) **1** an area of land that the people of another country settle in and control. **2** the people of a colony. **3** a group of people or animals of the same kind living close together.

coloration *noun* colouring.

collate *verb* arrange, collect, sort, systematise.

colleague *noun* associate, collaborator, co-worker, fellow worker, partner, workmate.

collect[1] *verb* **1** accumulate, acquire, amass, garner, gather, heap up, hoard, pile up, save, stockpile, store. **3** assemble, cluster, come together, congregate, convene, flock, gather, group, herd, rally, swarm, throng. **4** obtain, raise, receive, solicit. **5** bring, fetch, get, obtain, pick up.

collection *noun* **2** (*of things*) accumulation, anthology, arrangement, array, assortment, batch, bundle, compendium, compilation, conglomeration, corpus, group, heap, hoard, jumble, library, mass, medley, miscellany, mixture, pile, selection, series, set, stack, stockpile, store, storehouse, swag (*Australian*), treasury, variety; (*of people*) assembly, band, bevy, body, bunch, cluster, company,

congregation, crowd, flock, gathering, group, herd, horde, host, mass, mob, multitude, pack, swarm, throng. **3** alms (*old use*), contributions, donations, gifts, offering, offertory.

college *noun* **1** academy, conservatorium, institute, school, seminary, university.

collide *verb* (*collide with*) bump into, cannon into, crash into, hit, knock into, ram into, run into, slam into, smash into, strike.
collision *noun* bingle (*Australian informal*), crash, impact, pile-up (*informal*), prang (*informal*), smash.

colloquial *adjective* casual, chatty, conversational, everyday, familiar, informal, vernacular.

colonise *verb* occupy, people, populate, settle.
colonist *noun* immigrant, pioneer, settler.

colony *noun* **1** dependency, dominion, possession, province, settlement, territory. **3** community, group.

►► DICTIONARY ◄◄

colossal *adjective* immense; enormous.

colossus *noun* (*plural* **colossi**) **1** a huge statue. **2** a person of immense importance. [from the bronze statue of Apollo at Rhodes, the *Colossus of Rhodes*]

colour¹ *noun* **1** the effect produced by waves of light of a particular wavelength. **2** the use of various colours, not only black and white. **3** the colour of someone's skin. **4** a substance used to colour things. **5** the special flag of a ship or regiment.
colours *plural noun* an award given to the best members of a sports team.

colour² *verb* **1** put colour on; paint or stain. **2** blush. **3** influence what someone says or believes. **colouring** *noun*

colour-blind *adjective* unable to see the difference between certain colours.

coloured *adjective* **1** having colour. **2** having a dark skin; Black.

colourful *adjective* **1** full of colour. **2** lively; with vivid details.

colourless *adjective* **1** without colour. **2** lacking interest.

colt *noun* a young male horse.

column *noun* **1** a pillar. **2** something long or tall and narrow, *a column of smoke; a column of trucks*. **3** a vertical section of a page, *There are four columns on this page*. **4** a regular article in a newspaper. **columnist** *noun*

com- *prefix* (becoming **col-** before *l*, **cor-** before *r*, **con-** before many other consonants) with; together (as in *combine, connect*). [from Latin *cum* = with]

coma (*say* **koh**-ma) *noun* a state of deep unconsciousness, especially in someone who is ill or injured. [from Greek, = deep sleep]

comb¹ *noun* **1** a strip of wood or plastic etc. with teeth, used to tidy hair or hold it in place. **2** something like this, e.g. to separate strands of wool. **3** the red crest on a fowl's head. **4** a honeycomb.

comb² *verb* **1** tidy with a comb. **2** search thoroughly.

combat *noun & verb* (**combated, combating**) fight. **combatant** (*say* **kom**-ba-tant) *noun*

combination *noun* **1** combining. **2** a number of people or things that are combined. **3** a series of numbers or letters used to open a combination lock.
combination lock a lock that can be opened only by setting a dial or dials to positions shown by numbers or letters.

combine¹ (*say* komb-**I**'n) *verb* (**combined, combining**) join or mix together.

combine² (*say* **komb**-I'n) *noun* a group of people or firms combining in business.
combine harvester a machine that both reaps and threshes grain. [from *com-*, + Latin *bini* = pair]

►► THESAURUS ◄◄

colossal *adjective* big, enormous, extensive, gargantuan, giant, gigantic, ginormous (*slang*), great, huge, humungous (*slang*), immense, large, mammoth, massive, mighty, monstrous, monumental, prodigious, stupendous, towering, tremendous, vast, whopping (*slang*).

colour¹ *noun* **1** hue, shade, tinge, tint, tone. **4** dye, paint, pigment, stain, tint.

colour² *verb* **1** dye, paint, stain, tinge, tint. **2** blush, flush, glow, redden. **3** affect, bias, distort, influence, prejudice, taint.

colourful *adjective* **1** bright, brilliant, flashy, gaudy, gay, loud, multicoloured, showy, vibrant, vivid. **2** descriptive, graphic, interesting, lively, picturesque, vivid.

colourless *adjective* **1** anaemic, ashen, pale, pallid, pasty, sickly, wan, washed out, waxen, white. **2** boring, drab, dreary, dull, insipid, lacklustre, lifeless, monotonous, nondescript, ordinary, tame, unexciting, unimaginative, wishy-washy.

column *noun* **1** pile, pillar, pole, post, shaft, support, upright. **2** file, line, procession, queue, row, string, train. **4** article, feature, leader, piece.

comb² *verb* **1** groom, tidy. **2** fossick through (*Australian informal*), ransack, rummage through, scour, search.

combat *noun* action, battle, clash, conflict, confrontation, contest, duel, engagement, fight, hostility, skirmish, struggle, war.
combat *verb* battle, counter, fight, oppose, resist, tackle.

combination *noun* **1,2** alliance, amalgam, amalgamation, association, blend, coalition, composite, conjunction, fusion, marriage, merger, mix, mixture, partnership, synthesis, union.

combine¹ *verb* ally, amalgamate, associate, band together, bind, blend, coalesce, compound, consolidate, federate, fuse, incorporate, integrate, join forces, lump together, marry, merge, mix, put together, synthesise, team up, unite.

▶▶ D I C T I O N A R Y ◀◀

combustible *adjective* able to be set on fire and burn.

combustion *noun* the process of burning, a chemical process (accompanied by heat) in which substances combine with oxygen in air.

come *verb* (**came, come, coming**) This word is used to show (**1**) movement towards somewhere (*Come here!*), (**2**) arrival, reaching a place or condition or result (*They came to a city. We came to a decision*), (**3**) happening (*How did you come to lose it?*), (**4**) occurring (*It comes on the next page*), (**5**) resulting (*That's what comes of being careless*).
come about happen.
come across find or meet by chance.
come by obtain.
come in for receive a share of.
come out become known; be published; (of stains etc.) be removed; (of a problem) be solved.
come to amount to; become conscious again.
come to pass happen.
come up come to higher place or position; arise, *A problem came up*.
come up with produce an idea etc.

comedian *noun* someone who entertains people by making them laugh.

comedy *noun* (*plural* **comedies**) **1** a play or film etc. that makes people laugh. **2** humour.

[from Greek *komos* = merry-making, + *oide* = song]

comely *adjective* good-looking.

comet *noun* an object moving across the sky with a bright tail of light. [from Greek *kometes* = long-haired]

comfort¹ *noun* **1** a comfortable feeling or condition. **2** soothing somebody who is unhappy or in pain. **3** a person or thing that gives comfort.

comfort² *verb* make a person less unhappy; soothe.

comfortable *adjective* **1** free from worry or pain. **2** making someone feel comfortable; not tight or harsh. **comfortably** *adverb*

comfy *adjective* (*informal*) comfortable.

comic¹ *adjective* making people laugh. **comical** *adjective*, **comically** *adverb*
comic strip a series of drawings telling a comic story or a serial.

comic² *noun* **1** a paper full of comic strips. **2** a comedian.

comma *noun* a punctuation mark (,) used to mark a pause in a sentence or to separate items in a list. [from Greek *komma* = clause]

command¹ *noun* **1** a statement telling somebody to do something; an order. **2** authority; control. **3** ability to use something; mastery, *She has a good command of Spanish*.

▶▶ T H E S A U R U S ◀◀

come *verb* **1** advance, approach, draw near. **2** appear, arrive, blow in (*informal*), drop in, lob in (*Australian slang*), materialise, reach, roll up (*informal*), show up, turn up. **3** happen, occur, take place.
come about arise, come to pass, happen, occur, take place.
come across chance upon, come upon, discover, find, happen on, stumble on.
come back reappear, recur, resurface, return.
come down descend, drop, fall, land, nosedive, plunge.
come out appear, become known, be published, be revealed, emerge, leak out.
come to 1 add up to, amount to, equal, tot up to. **2** come round, rally, recover, regain consciousness, revive.
come up 1 ascend, pop up, rise, surface. **2** arise, crop up, happen, occur.
come up with contribute, produce, propose, put forward, submit, suggest.

comedian *noun* comic, humorist, jester, joker, wag, wit.

comedy *noun* **2** farce, fun, hilarity, humour, joking, satire, slapstick.

comfort¹ *noun* **1** contentment, ease, luxury, opulence, well-being. **2** commiseration, condolence, consolation, reassurance, relief, solace, support, sympathy.

comfort² *verb* cheer, console, encourage, gladden, reassure, relieve, solace, soothe, sympathise with.

comfortable *adjective* **1** at ease, at home, contented, relaxed. **2** comfy (*informal*), cosy, easy, luxurious, pleasant, relaxing, restful, snug, soft.

comical *adjective* absurd, amusing, comic, droll, farcical, funny, hilarious, humorous, laughable, ludicrous, nonsensical, ridiculous, silly, zany.

command¹ *noun* **1** bidding, commandment, decree, dictate, direction, directive, edict, injunction, instruction, order, precept, summons. **2** authority, charge, control, leadership, power, rule. **3** control, grasp, mastery, understanding.

►► D I C T I O N A R Y ◄◄

command² *verb* **1** give a command to somebody; order. **2** have authority over. **3** deserve and get, *They command our respect.* **commander** *noun*

commandant (*say* **kom**-an-dant) *noun* a military officer in charge of a fortress etc.

commandeer *verb* take or seize something for military purposes or for your own use.

commandment *noun* a sacred command, especially one of the Ten Commandments given to Moses.

commando *noun* (*plural* **commandos**) a soldier trained for making dangerous raids.

commemorate *verb* (**commemorated, commemorating**) be a celebration or reminder of some past event or person etc. **commemoration** *noun*, **commemorative** *adjective* [compare *memory*]

commence *verb* (**commenced, commencing**) begin. **commencement** *noun*

commend *verb* **1** praise, *He was commended for bravery.* **2** entrust, *We commend him to your care.* **commendation** *noun*

commendable *adjective* deserving praise.

comment¹ *noun* an opinion given about an event etc. or to explain something.

comment² *verb* make a comment.

commentary *verb* (*plural* **commentaries**) a set of comments, especially describing an event while it is happening. **commentate** *verb*, **commentator** *noun*

commerce *noun* trade and the services that assist it, e.g. banking and insurance. [from *com*-, + Latin *merx* = merchandise]

commercial¹ *adjective* **1** of commerce. **2** paid for by firms etc. whose advertisements are included, *commercial radio.* **3** profitable. **commercially** *adverb*

commercial² *noun* a broadcast advertisement.

commercialised *adjective* altered in order to become profitable, *a commercialised resort.* **commercialisation** *noun*

commiserate *verb* (**commiserated, commiserating**) sympathise. **commiseration** *noun* [from *com*-, + Latin *miserari* = to pity]

commission¹ *noun* **1** committing something. **2** authorisation to do something; the task etc. authorised, *a commission to paint a portrait.* **3** an appointment to be an officer in the armed forces. **4** a group of people given authority to do or investigate something. **5** payment to someone for selling your goods etc.

commission² *verb* give a commission to a person or for a task etc.

commissionaire *noun* an attendant in uniform at the entrance to a theatre, large shop, offices, etc.

commissioner *noun* **1** an official appointed by commission. **2** a member of a commission (see *commission¹* 4).

►► T H E S A U R U S ◄◄

command² *verb* **1** bid, call upon, charge, decree, direct, instruct, order, prescribe, require, summon, tell. **2** be in charge of, control, direct, govern, head, lead, manage, rule, supervise. **3** compel, deserve, earn, get.

commandment *noun* command, law, order, precept, principle, rule.

commemorate *verb* celebrate, mark, observe, remember.

commence *verb* begin, embark on, enter upon, get going, get under way, inaugurate, initiate, kick off (*informal*), launch, open, start. **commencement** *noun* beginning, birth, dawn, founding, genesis, inauguration, inception, onset, opening, origin, outset, start.

commend *verb* **1** acclaim, applaud, approve, extol, laud (*formal*), praise, recommend.

commendable *adjective* admirable, laudable, meritorious, praiseworthy, worthy.

comment¹ *noun* annotation, note, observation, opinion, reference, reflection, remark, statement.

comment² *verb* mention, observe, remark, say.

commentary *noun* account, description, narration, report, voice-over. **commentator** *noun* broadcaster, commenter, journalist, narrator, presenter, reporter.

commerce *noun* business, trade.

commercial¹ *adjective* **1** business, mercantile, trade, trading. **3** economic, money-making, profitable, profit-making.

commercial² *noun* ad (*informal*), advert (*informal*), advertisement, plug (*informal*).

commission¹ *noun* **2** assignment, authority, duty, job, mission, order, task, warrant. **4** board, committee, council, panel. **5** brokerage, cut (*informal*), fee, percentage, share.

▶▶ DICTIONARY ◀◀

commit *verb* (**committed, committing**) **1** do; perform, *commit a crime*. **2** place in someone's care or custody; consign, *He was committed to prison*. **3** pledge; assign, *Don't commit all your spare time to helping him*.

commitment *noun* **1** an engagement or obligation. **2** a pledge or promise. **3** dedication; loyalty.

committal *noun* **1** committing a person to prison etc. **2** giving a body ceremonially for burial or cremation.

committee *noun* a group of people appointed to deal with something.

commode *noun* a box or chair into which a chamber-pot is fitted. [same origin as *commodity*]

commodious *adjective* roomy.

commodity *noun* (*plural* **commodities**) a useful thing; a product. [from Latin *commodus* = convenient]

commodore *noun* **1** a naval officer ranking next below a rear admiral. **2** the commander of part of a fleet.

common¹ *adjective* **1** ordinary; usual; occurring frequently, *a common weed*. **2** of all or most people, *They worked for the common good*. **3** shared, *Music is their common interest*. **4** vulgar. **commonly** *adverb*, **commonness** *noun*

common sense normal good sense in thinking or behaviour.

in common shared by two or more people or things.

common² *noun* (chiefly in Britain) a piece of land that everyone can use. [from Latin *communis* = common]

commoner *noun* a member of the ordinary people, not of the nobility.

commonplace *adjective* ordinary; usual.

Commonwealth *noun* **1** an association of countries, *The Commonwealth consists of Britain and various other countries, including Canada, Australia, and New Zealand*. **2** a federal association of States, *the Commonwealth of Australia*.

commotion *noun* an uproar; a fuss.

communal (*say* **kom**-yoo-nal) *adjective* shared by several people. **communally** *adverb* [same origin as *common*]

commune¹ (*say* **kom**-yoon) *noun* **1** a group of people sharing a home, food, etc. **2** a district of local government in France and some other countries.

commune² *verb* (**communed, communing**) talk together.

communicant *noun* **1** a person who communicates with someone. **2** a person who receives Holy Communion.

communicate *verb* (**communicated, communicating**) **1** pass news, information, etc. to other people. **2** have social dealings. **3** (of rooms etc.) open into each other; connect.

▶▶ THESAURUS ◀◀

commit *verb* **1** carry out, do, perform, perpetrate. **2** commend, consign, entrust, hand over. **3** bind, pledge, promise.

commitment *noun* **1** duty, engagement, obligation, responsibility, task, tie. **2** pledge, promise, undertaking, vow, word. **3** allegiance, dedication, devotion, loyalty.

committee *noun* board, cabinet, council, panel, working party.

commodity *noun* article, item, product; (*commodities*) goods, merchandise, produce, wares.

common¹ *adjective* **1** common or garden (*informal*), commonplace, conventional, customary, everyday, familiar, frequent, general, habitual, normal, ordinary, plain, prevalent, regular, routine, simple, standard, typical, universal, usual, well-known, widespread. **2** general, popular, public, universal. **3** communal, joint, mutual (*informal*), shared. **4** boorish, coarse, crude,

ill-bred, low, plebeian, rude, uncouth, unrefined, vulgar.

common sense gumption (*informal*), intelligence, judgement, nous (*informal*), sense.

commonplace *adjective* common, customary, everyday, familiar, mundane, normal, ordinary, regular, routine, usual.

commotion *noun* ado, ballyhoo, clamour, din, disturbance, fracas, furore, fuss, hubbub, hullabaloo, kerfuffle (*informal*), noise, pandemonium, racket, riot, rumpus, shindy (*informal*), stir, to-do, tumult, turmoil, unrest, uproar.

communal *adjective* common, joint, public, shared.

communicate *verb* **1** announce, broadcast, convey, declare, disclose, disseminate, divulge, express, impart, indicate, make known, pass on, promulgate, relate, relay, report, reveal, say, show, signal, speak, state, voice. **2** commune, confer, converse, correspond, get in touch, make contact, speak, talk, write.

▶▶ D I C T I O N A R Y ◀◀

communication *noun* **1** communicating. **2** something communicated; a message. **communications** *plural noun* links between places (e.g. roads, railways, telephones, radio).

communicative *adjective* willing to talk.

communion *noun* religious fellowship.
Communion or **Holy Communion** the Christian ceremony in which consecrated bread and wine are given to worshippers.

communiqué (*say* ko-**mew**-nik-ay) *noun* an official message giving a report. [French, = communicated]

communism *noun* a system where property is shared by the community.

Communism *noun* a political system where the State controls property, production, trade, etc. (Compare *capitalism.*) **Communist** *noun* [from French *commun* = common]

community *noun* (*plural* **communities**) **1** the people living in one area. **2** a group with similar interests or origins.

commute *verb* (**commuted, commuting**) **1** travel a fairly long way by train, bus, or car to and from your daily work. **2** exchange; alter a punishment to something less severe. [from *com-*, + Latin *mutare* = change]

commuter *noun* a person who commutes to and from work.

compact¹ *noun* an agreement; a contract. [from *com-* + *pact*]

compact² *adjective* **1** closely or neatly packed together. **2** concise. **compactly** *adverb*, **compactness** *noun*
compact disc a small disc from which recorded sound etc. is reproduced by means of a laser beam.

compact³ *noun* a small flat container for face-powder.

compact⁴ *verb* join or press firmly together or into a small space. [from Latin *compactum* = put together]

companion *noun* **1** a person who accompanies another. **2** one of a matching pair of things. **3** (in book-titles) a guidebook or reference book, *The Oxford Companion to Music.* **companionship** *noun* [from *com-*, + Latin *panis* = bread, = 'person who eats bread with another']

companionable *adjective* sociable.

company *noun* (*plural* **companies**) **1** a number of people together. **2** a business firm. **3** having people with you; companionship. **4** visitors, *We've got company.* **5** a section of a battalion.

comparable (*say* **kom**-per-a-bul) *adjective* similar. **comparably** *adverb*

comparative *adjective* of comparisons; comparing a thing with something else, *They live in comparative comfort.* **comparatively** *adverb*

comparative *noun* the form of an adjective or adverb that expresses 'more', *The comparative of 'big' is 'bigger'.*

▶▶ T H E S A U R U S ◀◀

communication *noun* **1** contact, conversation, correspondence, dialogue, speaking, writing. **2** advice, announcement, bulletin, communiqué, dispatch, information, letter, memorandum, message, news, note, notice, notification, report, statement.

communicative *adjective* chatty, forthcoming, garrulous, informative, loquacious, open, talkative.

Communion *noun* Eucharist, Holy Communion, Lord's Supper, Mass.

communiqué *noun* announcement, bulletin, communication, dispatch, message, report, statement.

community *noun* **1** citizens, nation, people, populace, public, residents, society; see also DISTRICT. **2** group, people, sector, set.

compact² *adjective* **1** little, neat, small. **2** brief, concise, condensed, laconic, pithy, succinct, terse.

companion *noun* **1** assistant, associate, attendant, buddy (*informal*), chaperone, chum (*informal*), cobber (*Australian informal*), comrade, consort, crony, escort, friend, mate, pal (*informal*), partner, playmate, sidekick (*informal*).

company *noun* **1** assembly, audience, congregation, crew, crowd, gathering, group, mob, party, throng, troop, troupe (*of actors*). **2** business, concern, corporation, establishment, firm, institution, organisation. **3** companionship, fellowship, friendship, society. **4** callers, guests, visitors.

comparable *adjective* analogous, corresponding, equivalent, like, parallel, similar.

compare *verb* (**compared, comparing**) **1** put things together so as to tell in what ways they are similar or different. **2** liken. **3** form the comparative and superlative of an adjective or adverb.
compare notes share information.
compare with be similar to; be as good as, *Our football oval cannot compare with the Melbourne Cricket Ground.* [from Latin *comparare* = match with each other]

comparison *noun* **1** comparing. **2** similarity.

compartment *noun* one of the spaces into which something is divided; a separate room or enclosed space. [from *com-*, + Latin *partiri* = to share]

compass *noun* (*plural* **compasses**) a device with a pointer that points north.
compasses or **pair of compasses** a device for drawing circles, usually with two rods hinged together at one end.

compassion *noun* pity; mercy. **compassionate** *adjective*, **compassionately** *adverb* [from *com-*, + Latin *passum* = suffered]

compatible *adjective* **1** able to exist or be used together. **2** consistent; not incompatible. **compatibly** *adverb*, **compatibility** *noun*

compel *verb* (**compelled, compelling**) force somebody to do something. [from *com-*, + Latin *pellere* = to drive]

compendious *adjective* giving much information concisely.

compendium *noun* a package of notepaper and envelopes, or of games. [Latin, = a saving]

compensate *verb* (**compensated, compensating**) **1** give a person money etc. to make up for a loss or injury. **2** have a balancing effect, *This victory compensates for our earlier defeats.* **compensation** *noun*, **compensatory** *adjective*

compère (*say* kom-pair) *noun* a person who introduces the performers in a show or broadcast. **compère** *verb* [French, = godfather]

compete *verb* (**competed, competing**) **1** take part in a competition. **2** try to win or gain something.

competent *adjective* able to do a particular thing. **competently** *adverb*, **competence** *noun*

competition *noun* **1** a game or race or other contest in which people try to win. **2** competing. **3** the people competing with yourself. **competitive** *adjective*

competitor *noun* someone who competes; a rival.

compile *verb* (**compiled, compiling**) put things together into a list or collection, e.g. to form a book. **compiler** *noun* **compilation** *noun*

compare *verb* **1** contrast, juxtapose, weigh up. **2** liken.
compare with approach, be on a par with, be similar to, compete with, match, rival.

comparison *noun* **1** contrast, juxtaposition. **2** analogy, likeness, parallel, resemblance, similarity.

compartment *noun* area, bay, booth, box, carrel, cell, chamber, cubby hole, cubicle, division, niche, part, pigeon-hole, pocket, recess, section, slot, space, stall.

compassion *noun* concern, feeling, humanity, mercy, pity, sympathy, tenderness.
compassionate *adjective* humane, kind-hearted, lenient, merciful, soft-hearted, sympathetic, tender-hearted, warm-hearted.

compatible *adjective* **1** harmonious, like-minded, well-matched, well-suited. **2** consistent, in accord, in agreement, reconcilable.

compel *verb* coerce, constrain, drive, force, impel, make, oblige, press, pressure, push, require.

compensate *verb* **1** indemnify, make amends, make up, recompense, reimburse, repay. **2** cancel out, counterbalance, make up for, neutralise, offset.

compensation *noun* compo (*Australian informal*), damages, indemnity, recompense, redress, reparation, restitution.

compère *noun* anchorperson, announcer, host, master of ceremonies, MC, presenter.

compete *verb* **1** enter, participate, take part. **2** contend, contest, fight, rival, strive, struggle, vie.

competent *adjective* able, adept, capable, effective, efficient, handy, practical, proficient, qualified, skilful, skilled, trained.

competition *noun* **1** challenge, championship, contest, game, match, meet, quiz, rally, tournament. **2** opposition, rivalry.

competitor *noun* adversary, candidate, challenger, contender, contestant, entrant, opponent, participant, player, rival.

compile *verb* accumulate, assemble, collate, collect, gather, organise, put together.

▶▶ D I C T I O N A R Y ◀◀

complacent *adjective* self-satisfied. **complacently** *adverb*, **complacency** *noun* [from *com-*, + Latin *placens* = pleasing]

complain *verb* say that you are annoyed or unhappy about something. **complainer** *noun*

complaint *noun* **1** a statement complaining about something. **2** an illness.

complement¹ *noun* **1** the quantity needed to fill or complete something, *The ship had its full complement of sailors.* **2** the word or words used after verbs such as *be* and *become* to complete the sense. In *She was brave* and *He became king of England*, the complements are *brave* and *king of England*.

complement² *verb* make a thing complete, *The hat complements the outfit.* [same origin as *complete*]

Usage Do not confuse with *compliment*.

complementary *adjective* completing; forming a complement.
complementary angles angles that add up to 90°.

Usage Do not confuse with *complimentary*.

complete¹ *adjective* **1** having all its parts. **2** finished. **3** thorough; in every way, *a complete stranger.* **completely** *adverb*, **completeness** *noun*

complete² *verb* (**completed**, **completing**) make a thing complete; add what is needed. **completion** *noun* [from Latin *completum* = filled up]

complex¹ *adjective* **1** made up of parts. **2** complicated. **complexity** *noun*

complex² *noun* **1** a complex whole; a set of buildings. **2** a group of feelings or ideas that influence a person's behaviour etc., *a persecution complex.* **3** (*informal*) an obsessive concern. [from Latin *complexum* = embraced, plaited]

complexion *noun* **1** the natural colour and appearance of the skin of the face. **2** the way things seem, *That puts a different complexion on the matter.*

compliant *adjective* complying; obedient. **compliance** *noun*

complicate *verb* (**complicated**, **complicating**) make a thing complex or complicated. [from *com-*, + Latin *plicare* = to fold]

complicated *adjective* **1** made up of many parts. **2** difficult through being complex.

complication *noun* **1** something that complicates things or adds difficulties. **2** a complicated condition.

complicity *noun* being involved in a crime etc.

▶▶ T H E S A U R U S ◀◀

complacent *adjective* content, pleased with yourself, self-satisfied, smug.

complain *verb* beef (*slang*), bitch (*informal*), carp, gripe (*informal*), grizzle (*informal*), groan, grumble, moan, object, protest, rail, wail, whine, whinge (*informal*).
complainer *noun* grizzler (*informal*), grouch (*informal*), grumbler, malcontent, moaner, objector, protester, whinger (*informal*).

complaint *noun* **1** beef (*slang*), criticism, grievance, gripe (*informal*), grizzle (*informal*), grumble, objection, protest. **2** affliction, ailment, disease, disorder, illness, malady, sickness.

complement² *verb* complete, round off, set off.

complete¹ *adjective* **1** comprehensive, entire, full, intact, total, unabridged, unbroken, uncut, whole. **2** accomplished, concluded, done, ended, finished. **3** absolute, downright, out-and-out, outright, perfect, positive, proper, pure, sheer, thorough, total, utter.

completely *adverb* absolutely, altogether, entirely, fully, perfectly, quite, thoroughly, totally, utterly, wholly.

complete² *verb* accomplish, achieve, carry out, conclude, end, finalise, finish, fulfil, round off, wind up, wrap up (*informal*); (*complete a form*) fill in, fill out.

complex¹ *adjective* **1** composite, compound, multiple. **2** complicated, elaborate, intricate, involved, sophisticated.

complex² *noun* **3** fixation, hang-up (*informal*), obsession, preoccupation, thing (*informal*).

complexion *noun* **1** colour, skin, tone.

compliant *adjective* biddable, deferential, docile, obedient, submissive, tractable, yielding.

complicated *adjective* **1** complex, elaborate, intricate, sophisticated. **2** complex, difficult, intricate, involved, knotty, messy, problematical, tricky.

complication *noun* **1** difficulty, hitch, obstacle, problem, setback, snag, stumbling block.

▶▶ DICTIONARY ◀◀

compliment¹ *noun* something said or done to show that you approve of a person or thing, *pay compliments*.
compliments *plural noun* formal greetings given in a message.
compliment² *verb* pay someone a compliment; congratulate.

Usage Do not confuse with *complement*.

complimentary *adjective* **1** expressing a compliment. **2** given free of charge.

Usage Do not confuse with *complementary*.

comply *verb* (**complied, complying**) obey laws or rules.
compo *noun* (*Australian informal*) a payment made under a workers' compensation scheme, *Dad was on compo after his injury last year*.
component *noun* each of the parts of which a thing is composed.
compose *verb* (**composed, composing**) **1** form; make up, *The class is composed of 20 students*. **2** write music or poetry etc. **3** arrange in good order. **4** make calm, *compose yourself*. [from Latin *compositum* = put together]
composed *adjective* calm, *a composed manner*. **composedly** *adverb*
composer *noun* a person who composes music etc.

composite (*say* **kom**-poz-it) *adjective* made up of a number of parts or different styles. [same origin as *compose*]
composition *noun* **1** composing. **2** something composed, especially a piece of music. **3** an essay or story written as a school exercise. **4** the parts that make something, *the composition of the soil*.
compost *noun* **1** decayed leaves and grass etc. used as a fertiliser. **2** a soil-like mixture for growing seedlings, cuttings, etc. [same origin as *compose*]
composure *noun* calmness of manner.
compound¹ *adjective* made of two or more parts or ingredients.
compound² *noun* a compound substance.
compound³ *verb* put together; combine. [from Latin *componere* = put together]
compound⁴ *noun* a fenced area containing buildings. [from Malay *kampong* = enclosure]
comprehend *verb* **1** understand. **2** include. **comprehension** *noun*
comprehensible *adjective* understandable.
comprehensive *adjective* including all or many kinds of people or things.
compress¹ (*say* kom-**press**) *verb* press together or into a smaller space. **compression** *noun*, **compressor** *noun*

▶▶ THESAURUS ◀◀

compliment¹ *noun* acclamation, accolade, bouquet, commendation, congratulations, flattery, honour, plaudits, praise, tribute.
compliment² *verb* applaud, commend, congratulate, flatter, pay tribute to, praise.
complimentary *adjective* **1** admiring, approving, commendatory, congratulatory, favourable, flattering, positive. **2** free, free of charge, gratis, on the house (*informal*).
comply *verb* (*comply with*) accord with, conform to, follow, fulfil, meet, obey, satisfy.
component *noun* bit, constituent, element, ingredient, module, part, piece, unit.
compose *verb* **1** constitute, form, make up. **2** compile, concoct, construct, create, devise, fashion, formulate, invent, make up, produce, put together, write.
composed *adjective* calm, collected, controlled, cool, nonchalant, placid, sedate, self-controlled, serene, stoical, tranquil, unruffled.

composition *noun* **2** creation, opus, piece, work. **3** article, essay, paper, story. **4** constitution, make-up, structure.
composure *noun* calmness, control, cool (*informal*), coolness, equanimity, poise, self-control, serenity.
compound¹ *adjective* complex, composite, multiple.
compound² *noun* alloy, amalgam, blend, combination, composite, mixture, synthesis.
compound⁴ *noun* enclosure, pen, pound, yard.
comprehend *verb* **1** appreciate, conceive, fathom, follow, grasp, perceive, realise, see, take in, understand.
comprehension *noun* conception, grasp, insight, perception, realisation, understanding.
comprehensive *adjective* all-inclusive, broad, complete, detailed, exhaustive, extensive, full, inclusive, sweeping, thorough.
compress¹ *verb* compact, condense, cram, crush, pack down, press, squash, squeeze.

▶▶ DICTIONARY ◀◀

compress² (*say* **kom**-press) *noun* a soft pad or cloth pressed on the body to stop bleeding or cool inflammation etc.

comprise *verb* (**comprised**, **comprising**) include; consist of, *The pentathlon comprises five events.*

Usage Do not use *comprise* with *of*. It is incorrect to say 'The group was comprised of 20 men'; correct usage is 'was composed of'.

compromise¹ (*say* **kom**-prom-I'z) *noun* settling a dispute by each side accepting less than it asked for.

compromise² *verb* (**compromised**, **compromising**) 1 settle by a compromise. 2 expose to danger or suspicion etc., *His confession compromises his sister.*

compulsion *noun* compelling.

compulsive *adjective* having or resulting from an uncontrollable urge, *a compulsive gambler; a compulsive desire.*

compulsory *adjective* that must be done; not optional.

compunction *noun* a guilty feeling, *She felt no compunction about hitting the burglar.* [from *com-*, + Latin *punctum* = pricked (by conscience)]

compute *verb* (**computed**, **computing**) calculate. **computation** *noun*

computer *noun* an electronic machine for making calculations, storing and analysing information put into it, or controlling machinery automatically.

computerise *verb* (**computerised**, **computerising**) equip with computers, perform or produce by computer. **computerisation** *noun*

computing *noun* the use of computers.

comrade *noun* a companion who shares in your activities. **comradeship** *noun* [from Spanish *camarada* = room-mate]

con¹ *noun* (*slang*) a confidence trick. **con man** a person using confidence tricks.

con² *verb* (**conned**, **conning**) (*slang*) swindle.

con³ *noun* a reason against something, *There are pros and cons.* [from Latin *contra* = against]

con- *prefix* see **com-**.

concave *adjective* curved like the inside of a ball or circle. (The opposite is *convex*.) **concavity** *noun* [from *con-*, + Latin *cavus* = hollow]

conceal *verb* hide; keep something secret. **concealment** *noun*

concede *verb* (**conceded**, **conceding**) 1 admit that something is true. 2 grant; allow, *They conceded us the right to cross their land.* 3 admit that you have been defeated.

conceit *noun* being too proud of yourself; vanity. **conceited** *adjective*

conceivable *adjective* able to be imagined or believed. **conceivably** *adverb*

▶▶ THESAURUS ◀◀

comprise *verb* be composed of, be made up of, consist of, contain, include.

compromise¹ *noun* bargain, deal, happy medium, middle course, trade-off.

compromise² *verb* 1 come to terms, give and take, make a deal, make concessions, meet halfway, strike a bargain.

compulsive *adjective* (*a compulsive gambler*) addicted, habitual, incorrigible, obsessive; (*a compulsive desire*) compelling, driving, irresistible, overpowering, uncontrollable.

compulsory *adjective* mandatory, necessary, obligatory, prescribed, required, unavoidable.

compute *verb* add up, calculate, reckon, total, tot up, work out.

comrade *noun* ally, associate, buddy (*informal*), chum (*informal*), cobber (*Australian informal*), colleague, companion, crony, fellow, friend, mate, pal (*informal*), partner.

con¹ *noun* confidence trick, deception, hoax, swindle, swizz (*informal*), trick. **con man** charlatan, cheat, confidence man, fraud, humbug, illywhacker (*Australian informal*), impostor, phoney (*informal*), quack, swindler, trickster.

con² *verb* cheat, deceive, have (*slang*), hoax, hoodwink, mislead, rip off (*informal*), swindle, trick.

conceal *verb* bury, camouflage, cover up, disguise, hide, keep secret, mask, obscure, plant, screen, secrete.

concede *verb* 1 accept, acknowledge, admit, confess. 2 allow, give, grant, yield. 3 admit defeat, give in, give up, resign, surrender.

conceit *noun* arrogance, boastfulness, egotism, pride, vanity.

conceited *adjective* arrogant, boastful, bumptious, cocky, egotistical, haughty, immodest, proud, self-important, self-satisfied, smug, stuck-up (*informal*), swollen-headed (*informal*), vain.

▶▶ DICTIONARY ◀◀

conceive *verb* (**conceived**, **conceiving**) **1** become pregnant; form a baby in the womb. **2** form an idea or plan; imagine, *I can't conceive why you want to come.*

concentrate *verb* (**concentrated**, **concentrating**) **1** give your full attention or effort to something. **2** bring or come together in one place. **3** make a liquid etc. less dilute. [from *con-* + *centre*]

concentration *noun* concentrating.
concentration camp a place where political prisoners etc. are brought together and confined.

concentric *adjective* having the same centre, *concentric circles.*

concept *noun* an idea.

conception *noun* **1** conceiving. **2** an idea.

concern[1] *verb* **1** be important to or affect somebody. **2** worry somebody. **3** be about; have as its subject, *The story concerns a group of rabbits.*

concern[2] *noun* **1** something that concerns you; a responsibility. **2** worry. **3** a business.

concerned *adjective* **1** worried. **2** involved in or affected by something.

concerning *preposition* on the subject of; about, *laws concerning seat-belts.*

concert *noun* a musical entertainment.

concerted *adjective* done in cooperation with others, *We made a concerted effort.*

concertina *noun* a portable musical instrument with bellows, played by squeezing.

concerto (*say* kon-**chert**-oh) *noun* (*plural* **concertos**) a piece of music for a solo instrument and an orchestra. [Italian]

concession *noun* **1** conceding. **2** something conceded. **concessionary** *adjective*

conciliate *verb* (**conciliated**, **conciliating**) **1** win over an angry or hostile person by friendliness. **2** reconcile people who disagree. **conciliation** *noun*

concise *adjective* brief; giving much information in a few words. **concisely** *adverb*, **conciseness** *noun*

conclave *noun* a private meeting.

conclude *verb* (**concluded**, **concluding**) **1** bring or come to an end. **2** decide; form an opinion by reasoning, *The jury concluded that he was guilty.* [from *con-*, + Latin *claudere* = shut]

conclusion *noun* **1** an ending. **2** an opinion formed by reasoning.

conclusive *adjective* putting an end to all doubt. **conclusively** *adverb*

▶▶▶ THESAURUS ◀◀◀

conceive *verb* **2** contrive, create, devise, dream up, envisage, formulate, hatch, imagine, plan, think up.

concentrate *verb* **1** (*concentrate on*) apply yourself to, attend to, be absorbed in, focus on, pay attention to, put your mind to. **3** boil down, condense, reduce.

concept *noun* belief, idea, notion, principle, thought.

conception *noun* **1** beginning, birth, creation, formulation, genesis, inception, origin, outset, start. **2** concept, idea, image, impression, notion, picture, understanding, vision.

concern[1] *verb* **1** affect, apply to, be important to, interest, matter to, relate to, touch. **2** bother, disturb, perturb, trouble, worry. **3** be about, deal with, have to do with, involve, refer to, surround.

concern[2] *noun* **1** affair, business, responsibility. **2** anxiety, burden, care, problem, trouble, worry. **3** business, company, corporation, enterprise, establishment, firm, organisation.

concerned *adjective* **1** anxious, caring, distressed, solicitous, troubled, uneasy, worried. **2** interested, involved.

concerning *preposition* about, re, regarding, relating to, with reference to, with regard to.

concert *noun* gig (*informal*), performance, recital, show.

concerted *adjective* collaborative, combined, cooperative, coordinated, joint, united.

concession *noun* **2** discount, privilege, reduction, right.

concise *adjective* abridged, brief, compact, condensed, pithy, short, succinct, summary, terse.

conclude *verb* **1** bring to an end, cease, close, complete, come to an end, end, finish, round off, stop, terminate, wind up. **2** decide, deduce, gather, infer, judge, reason.

conclusion *noun* **1** close, completion, end, ending, finish, termination. **2** decision, deduction, finding, inference, judgement, verdict.

conclusive *adjective* absolute, convincing, decisive, definitive, incontrovertible, indisputable, unequivocal.

concoct *verb* **1** make something by putting ingredients together. **2** invent, *concoct an excuse.* **concoction** *noun* [from *con-*, + Latin *coctum* = cooked]

concord *noun* friendly agreement or harmony. [from *con-*, + Latin *cor* = heart]

concordance *noun* **1** agreement. **2** an index of the words used in a book or an author's works.

concourse *noun* **1** a crowd. **2** an open area through which people pass, e.g. at an airport. [same origin as *concur*]

concrete¹ *noun* cement mixed with sand and gravel, used in building.

concrete² *adjective* **1** able to be touched and felt; not abstract. **2** definite, *We need concrete evidence, not theories.*

concur *verb* (**concurred, concurring**) **1** agree. **2** happen together; coincide. **concurrence** *noun*, **concurrent** *adjective* [from *con-*, + Latin *currere* = run]

concussion *noun* a temporary injury to the brain caused by a hard knock. **concussed** *adjective* [from Latin *concussum* = shaken violently]

condemn *verb* **1** say that you strongly disapprove of something. **2** convict or sentence a criminal. **3** destine to something unhappy, *condemned to a lonely life.* **4** declare that houses etc. are not fit to be used. **condemnation** *noun* [from *con-*, + Latin *damnare* = damn]

condense *verb* (**condensed, condensing**) **1** make a liquid denser or more compact. **2** put something into fewer words. **3** change from gas or vapour to liquid, *Steam condenses on windows.* **condensation** *noun*, **condenser** *noun*

condescend *verb* **1** behave in a way which shows that you feel superior. **2** allow yourself to do something that seems unsuitable for a person of your high rank. **condescending** *adjective*, **condescension** *noun*

condiment *noun* a seasoning (e.g. salt or pepper) for food.

condition¹ *noun* **1** the state or fitness of a person or thing, *This bicycle is in good condition.* **2** the situation or surroundings etc. that affect something, *working conditions.* **3** something required as part of an agreement. **on condition that** only if; on the understanding that something will be done.

condition² *verb* **1** put something into a proper condition. **2** train; accustom.

conditional *adjective* containing a condition (see *condition¹* 3); depending. **conditionally** *adverb*

condole *verb* (**condoled, condoling**) express sympathy. **condolence** *noun* [from *con-*, + Latin *dolere* = grieve]

condom *noun* a sheath for the penis.

condone *verb* (**condoned, condoning**) forgive or ignore wrongdoing, *Do not condone violence.* **condonation** *noun*

condor *noun* a kind of large vulture.

conducive *adjective* helping to cause or produce something, *Noisy surroundings are not conducive to work.*

concoct *verb* **1** cook, make, prepare, put together. **2** cook up, create, devise, fabricate, invent, make up, put together, think up.
concoction *noun* blend, confection, creation, mixture, preparation.

concord *noun* accord, agreement, harmony, peace, unity.

concrete² *adjective* actual, definite, factual, material, objective, palpable, physical, real, solid, specific, substantial, tangible.

concur *verb* **1** accord, agree, assent, be of the same mind, see eye to eye.
concurrent *adjective* coexistent, coincident, parallel, simultaneous.

condemn *verb* **1** blame, censure, criticise, denounce, disapprove of, rebuke. **2** convict, declare guilty, sentence.

condense *verb* **1** boil down, concentrate, reduce, thicken. **2** abbreviate, abridge, compress, cut, précis, reduce, shorten, summarise.

condescending *adjective* disdainful, haughty, high and mighty, hoity-toity, patronising, snobbish, snooty (*informal*), supercilious, superior.

condition¹ *noun* **1** fettle, fitness, form, health, nick (*informal*), order, repair, shape, state, trim. **2** (*conditions*) circumstances, environment, situation, surroundings. **3** prerequisite, provision, proviso, qualification, requirement, stipulation, term.

condition² *verb* **2** accustom, teach, train.

condolence *noun* commiseration, pity, sympathy.

condone *verb* connive at, disregard, forgive, ignore, overlook, tolerate, turn a blind eye to.

▶▶ DICTIONARY ◀◀

conduct¹ (*say* kon-**dukt**) *verb* **1** lead or guide. **2** be the conductor of an orchestra or choir. **3** manage or direct something, *conduct an experiment*. **4** allow heat, light, sound, or electricity to pass along or through. **5** behave, *They conducted themselves with dignity*.

conduct² (*say* **kon**-dukt) *noun* behaviour. [from *con-*, + Latin *ducere* = to lead]

conduction *noun* the conducting of heat or electricity etc. (see *conduct¹* 4).

conductor *noun* **1** a person who directs the performance of an orchestra or choir by movements of the arms. **2** a person who collects the fares on a bus etc. **3** something that conducts heat or electricity etc.

conduit (*say* **kon**-joot) *noun* **1** a pipe or channel for liquid. **2** a tube protecting electric wire.

cone *noun* **1** an object that is circular at one end and narrows to a point at the other end. **2** the dry cone-shaped fruit of a pine, fir, or cedar tree.

confection *noun* something made of various things, especially sweet ones, put together.

confectioner *noun* someone who makes or sells sweets. **confectionery** *noun*

confederacy *noun* (*plural* **confederacies**) a union of States; a confederation.

confederate¹ *adjective* allied; joined by an agreement or treaty.

confederate² *noun* **1** a member of a confederacy. **2** an ally; an accomplice. [from *con-*, + Latin *foederatum* = allied]

confederation *noun* **1** the process of joining in an alliance. **2** a group of people, organisations, or States joined together by an agreement or treaty.

confer *verb* (**conferred, conferring**) **1** grant; bestow. **2** hold a discussion.

conference *noun* a meeting for holding a discussion.

confess *verb* state openly that you have done something wrong or have a weakness; admit. **confession** *noun*

confessional *noun* an enclosed stall where a priest hears confessions.

confessor *noun* a priest who hears confessions.

confetti *noun* tiny pieces of coloured paper thrown by wedding guests at the bride and bridegroom. [Italian]

confidant *noun* (**confidante** is used of a woman) a person in whom someone confides.

confide *verb* (**confided, confiding**) **1** tell confidentially, *confide a secret to someone* or *confide in someone*. **2** entrust. [from *con-*, + Latin *fidere* = to trust]

confidence *noun* **1** firm trust. **2** a feeling of certainty or boldness; being sure that you can do something. **3** something told confidentially.
confidence trick swindling a person after persuading him or her to trust you.
in confidence as a secret.
in a person's confidence trusted with his or her secrets.

confident *adjective* **1** showing or feeling confidence; bold. **2** feeling certain. **confidently** *adverb*

confidential *adjective* **1** that should be kept secret. **2** trusted to keep secrets, *a confidential secretary*. **confidentially** *adverb*, **confidentiality** *noun*

▶▶ THESAURUS ◀◀

conduct¹ *verb* **1** direct, escort, guide, lead, pilot, show, steer, take, usher. **3** administer, be in charge of, chair, control, direct, lead, manage, organise, preside over, run, supervise. **5** (*conduct yourself*) acquit yourself, act, behave.

conduct² *noun* actions, behaviour, deportment, manners.

conductor *noun* **1** director, maestro.

confer *verb* **1** award, bestow, give, grant, present. **2** consult, converse, discuss, speak, talk.

conference *noun* assembly, congress, convention, forum, gathering, meeting, symposium.

confess *verb* acknowledge, admit, declare, disclose, own up.

confide *verb* **1** confess, disclose, divulge, impart, tell, trust.

confidence *noun* **1** belief, faith, reliance, trust. **2** aplomb, assurance, boldness, certainty, conviction, coolness, courage, self-assurance, self-confidence, self-reliance.
confidence trick con (*slang*), deception, hoax, swindle, swizz (*informal*), trick.

confident *adjective* **1** bold, cocksure, daring, fearless, self-assured, self-confident. **2** certain, convinced, positive, sure.

confidential *adjective* **1** classified, hush-hush (*informal*), intimate, off the record, personal, private, secret.

configuration *noun*   **1**   a   method   of arrangement of parts etc. **2** a shape.

confine *verb* (**confined, confining**) **1** keep within limits; restrict, *Please confine your remarks to the subject being discussed.* **2** keep somebody in a place. [from *con-*, + Latin *finis* = limit, end]

confined *adjective* narrow; restricted, *a confined space.*

confinement *noun* **1** confining. **2** the time of giving birth to a baby.

confines (*say* **kon**-fynz) *plural noun* the limits or boundaries of an area.

confirm *verb* **1** prove that something is true or correct. **2** make a thing definite, *Please write to confirm your booking.* **3** make a person a full member of the Christian Church. **confirmation** *noun*, **confirmatory** *adjective*

confiscate *verb* (**confiscated, confiscating**) take something away as a punishment. **confiscation** *noun*

conflagration *noun* a great and destructive fire. [same origin as *flagrant*]

conflict[1] (*say* **kon**-flikt) *noun* **1** a fight or struggle. **2** disagreement.

conflict[2] (*say* kon-**flikt**) *verb* have a conflict; differ or disagree. [from *con-* = together, + Latin *flictum* = struck]

confluence *noun* the place where two rivers unite. [from *con-*, + Latin *fluens* = flowing]

conform *verb* keep to accepted rules or customs etc. **conformist** *noun*, **conformity** *noun* [from Latin *conformare* = shape evenly]

confound *verb* **1** astonish or puzzle someone. **2** confuse.

confront *verb* **1** come or bring face to face, especially in a hostile way. **2** be present and have to be dealt with, *Problems confront us.* **confrontation** *noun*

confuse *verb* (**confused, confusing**) **1** make a person puzzled or muddled. **2** mistake one thing for another. **confusion** *noun*

confute *verb* (**confuted, confuting**) prove a person or statement to be wrong. **confutation** *noun*

congeal (*say* kon-**jeel**) *verb* become jellylike instead of liquid, especially in cooling. [from Latin *congelare* = freeze]

confine *verb* **1** contain, keep, limit, localise, restrict. **2** box in, coop up, enclose, hold captive, imprison, intern, jail, keep, lock up, pen, shut in, shut up.

confirm *verb* **1** attest to, authenticate, back up, bear out, corroborate, establish, prove, reinforce, substantiate, support, validate, verify, witness to.

confiscate *verb* appropriate, commandeer, impound, seize, take away.

conflict[1] *noun* **1** action, battle, clash, combat, encounter, engagement, fight, fray, strife, struggle, war. **2** antagonism, confrontation, contention, difference, disagreement, discord, dispute, dissension, friction, hostility, opposition, strife.

conflict[2] *verb* be at odds, be at variance, be incompatible, clash, contradict, differ, disagree.

conform *verb* comply, fit in, toe the line (*informal*); (*conform to*) abide by, accord with, comply with, correspond to, fit, follow, keep to, match, obey.

conformity *noun* accord, accordance, agreement, compliance, harmony, keeping.

confound *verb* astonish, astound, baffle, bewilder, confuse, disconcert, flummox (*informal*), mystify, nonplus, perplex, puzzle, surprise.

confront *verb* **1** accost, brave, challenge, defy, encounter, face, face up to, meet, oppose, stand up to, take on.

confuse *verb* **1** baffle, bewilder, confound, disconcert, disorientate, flummox (*informal*), fluster, mislead, mix up, mystify, nonplus, perplex, puzzle, rattle (*informal*). **2** mistake, mix up, muddle.

confused *adjective* **1** baffled, bemused, bewildered, bushed (*Australian informal*), disoriented, flummoxed (*informal*), flustered, hazy, mixed-up, muddled, perplexed. **2** chaotic, disorganised, garbled, higgledy-piggledy, incoherent, jumbled, messy, muddled, topsy-turvy, unclear.

confusion *noun* **1** anarchy, bedlam, chaos, commotion, disorder, disorganisation, havoc, jumble, mayhem, mess, muddle, pandemonium, riot, shambles, tumult, turmoil, upheaval, uproar. **2** misunderstanding, mix-up, muddle.

congeal *adjective* coagulate, set, solidify, thicken.

►► D I C T I O N A R Y ◄◄

congenial *adjective* pleasant through being similar to yourself or suiting your tastes; agreeable, *a congenial companion.* **congenially** *adverb*

congenital (*say* kon-**jen**-it-al) *adjective* existing in a person from birth. **congenitally** *adverb* [from *con-*, + Latin *genitus* = born]

congested *adjective* crowded; too full of something. **congestion** *noun*

conglomeration *noun* a mass of different things put together. [from *con-*, + Latin *glomus* = mass]

congratulate *verb* (**congratulated, congratulating**) tell a person that you are pleased about his or her success or good fortune. **congratulation** *noun*, **congratulatory** *adjective* [from *con-*, + Latin *gratulari* = show joy]

congregate *verb* (**congregated, congregating**) assemble; flock together. [from *con-*, + Latin *gregatum* = herded]

congregation *noun* a group who have gathered to take part in worship.

congress *noun* a conference.

Congress *noun* the parliament of the USA. [from *con-*, + Latin *-gressus* = going]

congruent *adjective* **1** suitable; consistent. **2** (of geometrical figures) having exactly the same shape and size. **congruence** *noun*

conic *adjective* of a cone.

conical *adjective* cone-shaped. **conically** *adverb*

conifer (*say* **kon**-if-er) *noun* an evergreen tree with cones. **coniferous** *adjective* [from *cone* + Latin *ferens* = bearing]

conjecture *noun* a guess. **conjecture** *verb*, **conjectural** *adjective*

conjugal (*say* **kon**-jug-al) *adjective* of a husband and wife.

conjunction *noun* **1** a word that joins words or phrases or sentences, e.g. *and, but.* **2** combination, *The four armies acted in conjunction.* [from Latin *conjunctum* = yoked together]

conjure *verb* (**conjured, conjuring**) perform puzzling tricks. **conjuror** *noun* **conjure up** produce, *Mention of the Arctic conjures up visions of snow.*

connect *verb* **1** join together; link. **2** think of as being associated with each other. **connection** *noun*, **connective** *adjective*, **connector** *noun* [from *con-*. + Latin *nectere* = bind]

conning-tower *noun* a projecting part on top of a submarine, containing the periscope.

connive (*say* kon-**I'v**) *verb* (**connived, conniving**) **connive at** take no notice of wrongdoing that ought to be reported or punished. **connivance** *noun* [from Latin *connivere* = shut the eyes]

connoisseur (*say* kon-a-**ser**) *noun* a person with great experience and appreciation of something, *a connoisseur of wine.* [French, = one who knows]

►► T H E S A U R U S ◄◄

congenial *adjective* agreeable, amiable, compatible, friendly, genial, nice, pleasant, sympathetic.

congenital *adjective* inborn, innate.

congested *adjective* blocked, chock-a-block, choked, clogged up, crowded, jammed, overcrowded, packed, stuffed up.

congratulate *verb* applaud, commend, compliment, praise.
congratulations *plural noun* compliments, felicitations, good wishes, greetings.

congregate *verb* assemble, cluster, collect, converge, crowd, flock, gather, group, herd, huddle, mass, meet, muster, rally, swarm, throng.

congregation *noun* flock, parishioners.

congress *noun* assembly, conference, convention, council, gathering, meeting, symposium, synod.

conjecture *noun* assumption, guess, hunch, hypothesis, speculation, supposition, surmise, suspicion, theory.
conjecture *verb* assume, guess, hypothesise, speculate, suppose, surmise, suspect, theorise.

conjure *verb* **conjure up** bring to mind, call up, evoke, produce.

conjuring *noun* legerdemain, magic, sleight of hand, tricks.

connect *verb* **1** attach, couple, fasten, hitch, interlock, join, link, secure, tie, unite. **2** associate, bracket together, correlate, link, relate.
connection *noun* **1** bond, hook-up, join, joint, junction, link. **2** association, correlation, correspondence, interconnection, link, relation, relationship, tie-up.

connive *verb* **connive at** condone, ignore, overlook, turn a blind eye to, wink at.

connoisseur *noun* authority, buff (*informal*), expert, specialist.

▶▶ DICTIONARY ◀◀

conquer *verb* defeat; overcome. **conqueror** *noun*.

conquest *noun* 1 conquering. 2 conquered territory.

conscience (*say* kon-shens) *noun* knowing what is right and wrong, especially in your own actions. [from *con-*, + Latin *sciens* = knowing]

conscientious (*say* kon-shee-**en**-shus) *adjective* careful and honest, *conscientious workers*. **conscientiously** *adverb*
conscientious objector a person who refuses to serve in the armed forces because he or she believes it is wrong.

conscious (*say* **kon**-shus) *adjective* awake; aware of what is happening. **consciously** *adverb*, **consciousness** *noun*

conscript¹ (*say* kon-**skript**) *verb* make a person join the armed forces. **conscription** *noun*

conscript² (*say* **kon**-skript) *noun* a conscripted person. [from *con-*, + Latin *scriptus* = written in a list, enlisted]

consecrate *verb* (**consecrated, consecrating**) make a thing sacred; dedicate to God. **consecration** *noun*

consecutive *adjective* following one after another. **consecutively** *adverb* [from Latin *consecutum* = following]

consensus *noun* (*plural* **consensuses**) general agreement; the opinion of most people. [same origin as *consent*]

consent¹ *noun* agreement to what someone wishes; permission.

consent² *verb* say that you are willing to do or allow what someone wishes. [from *con-*, + Latin *sentire* = feel]

consequence *noun* 1 something that happens as the result of an event or action. 2 importance, *It is of no consequence.*

consequent *adjective* happening as a result. **consequently** *adverb* [same origin as *consecutive*]

consequential *adjective* consequent.

conservation *noun* conserving; preservation, especially of the natural environment. **conservationist** *noun*

conservative *adjective* 1 liking traditional ways and disliking changes. 2 (of an estimate) moderate; low. **conservatively** *adverb*, **conservatism** *noun*

conservatorium *noun* (*Australian*) a school of music.

conservatory *noun* a greenhouse.

▶▶ THESAURUS ◀◀

conquer *verb* beat, crush, defeat, get the better of, lick (*informal*), master, overcome, overpower, overthrow, prevail over, rout, stonker (*Australian slang*), subdue, subjugate, surmount, thrash, triumph over, trounce, vanquish.
conqueror *noun* champion, vanquisher, victor, winner.

conquest *noun* 1 annexation, capture, defeat, invasion, occupation, subjugation, takeover.

conscience *noun* ethics, morals, principles, scruples.

conscientious *adjective* careful, dedicated, diligent, dutiful, hard-working, honest, meticulous, painstaking, particular, punctilious, responsible, rigorous, scrupulous, thorough.

conscious *adjective* alert, awake, aware.

conscript¹ *verb* call up, draft (*American*).

consecrate *verb* bless, dedicate, hallow, sanctify.

consecutive *adjective* in a row, straight, successive, uninterrupted.

consensus *noun* agreement, harmony, unanimity.

consent¹ *noun* acceptance, acquiescence, agreement, approval, assent, authorisation, concurrence, endorsement, go-ahead, leave, OK (*informal*), permission, sanction.

consent² *verb* accede, acquiesce, agree, allow, approve, authorise, concur, permit.

consequence *noun* 1 aftermath, effect, outcome, ramification, repercussion, result, sequel, upshot. 2 account, gravity, import, importance, moment, seriousness, significance.

consequent *adjective* consequential, ensuing, following, resultant, resulting.
consequently *adverb* accordingly, as a result, hence, so, therefore, thus.

conservation *noun* maintenance, preservation, protection, safe keeping, saving.
conservationist *noun* environmentalist, green (*informal*), greenie (*Australian informal*), preservationist.

conservative *adjective* 1 conventional, hidebound, middle-of-the-road, old-fashioned, orthodox, reactionary, traditional. 2 cautious, low, moderate, understated.

conservatory *noun* glasshouse, greenhouse, hothouse.

▶▶ DICTIONARY ◀◀

conserve *verb* (**conserved, conserving**) prevent something valuable from being changed, spoilt, or wasted. [from *con-*, + Latin *servare* = keep safe]

consider *verb* **1** think carefully about or give attention to something, especially in order to make a decision. **2** allow for. **3** have an opinion; think to be, *Consider yourself lucky*.

considerable *adjective* fairly great, *a considerable amount* . **considerably** *adverb*

considerate *adjective* taking care not to inconvenience or hurt others. **considerately** *adverb*

consideration *noun* **1** being considerate. **2** careful thought or attention. **3** a fact that must be kept in mind. **4** payment given as a reward.

take into consideration allow for.

considering *preposition* taking something into consideration, *The car runs well considering its age.*

consign *verb* hand something over formally; entrust.

consignment *noun* **1** consigning. **2** a batch of goods etc. sent to someone.

consist *verb* be made up or composed of, *The flat consists of three rooms.*

consistency *noun* (*plural* **consistencies**) **1** being consistent. **2** thickness or stiffness, especially of a liquid.

consistent *adjective* **1** keeping to a regular pattern or style; not changing. **2** not contradictory. **consistently** *adverb*

consolation *noun* **1** consoling. **2** something that consoles someone.

consolation prize a prize given to a competitor who has just missed winning one of the main prizes.

console¹ (*say* kon-**sohl**) *verb* (**consoled, consoling**) comfort someone who is unhappy or disappointed. [from *con-*, + Latin *solari* = to comfort]

console² (*say* **kon**-sohl) *noun* **1** a frame containing the keyboard and stops etc. of an organ. **2** a panel holding the controls of equipment. **3** a cabinet for a radio or television set. [French]

consolidate *verb* (**consolidated, consolidating**) **1** make or become secure and strong. **2** combine two or more organisations, funds, etc. into one. **consolidation** *noun* [from *con-* + *solid*]

consonant *noun* a letter that is not a vowel, *B, c, d, f, etc. are consonants.* [from *con-*, + Latin *sonans* = sounding]

consort¹ (*say* **kon**-sort) *noun* a husband or wife, especially of a monarch.

consort² (*say* kon-**sort**) *verb* be in someone's company, *consort with criminals.* [from Latin *consors* = sharer]

consortium *noun* (*plural* **consortia**) a combination of countries, companies, or other groups acting together.

conspicuous *adjective* **1** easily seen; noticeable. **2** remarkable. **conspicuously** *adverb*, **conspicuousness** *noun*

▶▶ THESAURUS ◀◀

conserve *verb* hold on to, husband, keep, maintain, preserve, save.

consider *verb* **1** contemplate, deliberate over, examine, look at, meditate on, mull over, ponder, reflect on, ruminate over, study, think about, weigh. **2** allow for, bear in mind, pay heed to, respect, take into account. **3** believe, deem, judge, rate, reckon, regard, think.

considerable *adjective* appreciable, big, decent, extensive, fair, goodly, large, noticeable, respectable, significant, sizeable, substantial, tidy (*informal*).

considerate *adjective* attentive, helpful, kind, neighbourly, obliging, polite, sensitive, solicitous, thoughtful, unselfish.

consignment *noun* **2** batch, cargo, delivery, load, shipment.

consist *verb* (*consist of*) be composed of, comprise, contain, include.

consistency *noun* **1** agreement, compatibility, conformity, congruence, correspondence, uniformity. **2** density, firmness, solidity, stiffness, texture, thickness, viscosity.

consistent *adjective* **1** constant, dependable, invariable, predictable, reliable, stable, steady, unchanging, uniform. **2** compatible, corresponding, in accordance, in agreement, in keeping.

console¹ *verb* cheer, comfort, encourage, relieve, solace, soothe.

consolidate *verb* **1** fortify, reinforce, strengthen. **2** amalgamate, combine, incorporate, join, merge, unite.

conspicuous *adjective* **1** apparent, blatant, clear, evident, flagrant, glaring, manifest, noticeable, obtrusive, obvious, ostentatious, patent, prominent, pronounced, showy, unconcealed, visible. **2** distinguished, impressive, notable, outstanding, remarkable, striking.

►►► DICTIONARY ◄◄

conspiracy *noun* (*plural* **conspiracies**) planning with others to do something illegal; a plot.

conspire *verb* (**conspired, conspiring**) take part in a conspiracy. **conspirator** *noun*, **conspiratorial** *adjective* [from *con-*, + Latin *spirare* = breathe]

constable *noun* a police officer of the lowest rank. [from Latin, originally = officer in charge of the stable]

constabulary *noun* a police force.

constant *adjective* **1** not changing. **2** happening all the time. **3** faithful; loyal. **constantly** *adverb*, **constancy** *noun* [from *con-*, + Latin *stans* = standing]

constellation *noun* a group of stars. [from *con-*, + Latin *stella* = star]

consternation *noun* anxiety or dismay.

constipated *adjective* unable to empty the bowels easily or regularly. **constipation** *noun*

constituency *noun* (*plural* **constituencies**) (*British*) electorate (sense 2).

constituent *noun* one of the parts that form a whole thing. **constituent** *adjective*

constitute *verb* (**constituted, constituting**) make up or form something, *Twelve months constitute a year.* [from *con-*, + Latin *statuere* = set up]

constitution *noun* **1** the group of laws or principles that state how a country is to be organised and governed. **2** the nature of the body in regard to healthiness, *She has a strong constitution.* **3** constituting. **4** the composition of something. **constitutional** *adjective*

constrain *verb* compel; oblige.

constraint *noun* **1** constraining; compulsion. **2** a restriction. **3** a strained manner caused by holding back feelings.

constrict *verb* squeeze or tighten something by making it narrower. **constriction** *noun* [from *con-*, + Latin *strictum* = bound]

construct *verb* make something by placing parts together; build. **constructor** *noun* [from *con-*, + Latin *structum* = built]

construction *noun* **1** constructing. **2** something constructed; a building. **3** two or more words put together to form a phrase or clause or sentence. **4** an explanation or interpretation, *They put a bad construction on our refusal.*

constructive *adjective* constructing; being helpful, *constructive suggestions.*

construe *verb* (**construed, construing**) interpret; explain.

consul *noun* **1** a government official appointed to live in a foreign city to help people from his or her own country who visit there. **2** either of the two chief magistrates in ancient Rome. **consular** *adjective* [Latin]

consulate *noun* the building where a consul works.

consult *verb* go to a person or book etc. for information or advice. **consultation** *noun*

►►► THESAURUS ◄◄

conspiracy *noun* collusion, intrigue, plot, scheme.

conspire *verb* collaborate, collude, connive, intrigue, plot, scheme.

constant *adjective* **1** even, fixed, invariable, level, stable, steady, unchanging, uniform, unvarying. **2** ceaseless, chronic, continual, continuous, endless, everlasting, incessant, never-ending, non-stop, perennial, permanent, perpetual, persistent, regular, repeated, unending. **3** dependable, devoted, faithful, firm, loyal, reliable, steadfast, true, trustworthy.

consternation *noun* alarm, anxiety, dismay, fear, panic, shock, terror.

constituent *noun* component, element, ingredient, material, part, unit.

constitute *verb* compose, form, make up.

constitution *noun* **1** charter, laws, principles, rules. **2** health, physique. **4** composition, make-up, structure.

constrain *verb* bind, compel, force, make, oblige, press, pressure, urge.

constraint *noun* **1** compulsion, force, obligation, pressure. **2** check, curb, limitation, restriction.

constrict *verb* compress, cramp, pinch, squeeze.

construct *verb* assemble, build, create, erect, fabricate, fashion, form, make, manufacture, produce, put together.

construction *noun* **2** building, edifice, structure.

constructive *adjective* beneficial, helpful, positive, practical, productive, useful, valuable.

consult *verb* confer with, discuss with, refer to, speak to, talk with.
consultation *noun* conference, discussion, hearing, interview, meeting, talk.

▶▶ D I C T I O N A R Y ◀◀

consultant *noun* a person who is qualified to give expert advice.

consultative *adjective* for consultation, *a consultative committee.*

consume *verb* (**consumed, consuming**) 1 eat or drink something. 2 use up, *Much time was consumed in waiting.* 3 destroy, *Fire consumed the building.* [from *con-*, + Latin *sumere* = take up]

consumer *noun* a person who buys or uses goods or services.

consummate¹ (*say* **kon**-sum-ayt) *verb* accomplish; make complete. **consummation** *noun*

consummate² (*say* kon-**sum**-at) *adjective* perfect; highly skilled, *a consummate artist.* [from *con-*, + Latin *summus* = highest]

consumption *noun* 1 consuming. 2 (*old use*) tuberculosis of the lungs.

contact¹ *noun* 1 touching. 2 being in touch; communication. 3 a person to communicate with when you need information or help.

contact lens a tiny lens worn against the eyeball instead of spectacles.

contact² *verb* get in touch with a person. [from *con-*, + Latin *tactum* = touched]

contagion *noun* a contagious disease.

contagious *adjective* spreading by contact with an infected person, *a contagious disease.*

contain *verb* 1 have inside, *The box contains chocolates.* 2 consist of, *A centimetre contains 10 millimetres.* 3 restrain; hold back, *Try to contain your laughter.* [from *con-*, + Latin *tenere* = hold]

container *noun* 1 a box or bottle etc. designed to contain something. 2 a large box-like object of standard design in which goods are transported.

contaminate *verb* (**contaminated, contaminating**) make a thing dirty or impure or diseased etc.; pollute. **contamination** *noun*

contemplate *verb* (**contemplated, contemplating**) 1 look at something thoughtfully. 2 consider or think about something, *We are contemplating a visit to England.* **contemplation** *noun*, **contemplative** *adjective*

contemporary¹ *adjective* 1 belonging to the same period, *Dickens was contemporary with Thackeray.* 2 modern, *contemporary furniture.*

contemporary² *noun* (*plural* **contemporaries**) a person who is contemporary with another or who is about the same age, *She was my contemporary at college.* [from *con-*, + Latin *tempus* = time]

contempt *noun* a feeling of despising a person or thing.

contemptible *adjective* deserving contempt.

contemptuous *adjective* feeling or showing contempt. **contemptuously** *adverb*

▶▶ T H E S A U R U S ◀◀

consultant *noun* adviser, expert, specialist.

consume *verb* 1 devour, eat up, gobble up, guzzle, knock back, swallow. 2 deplete, drain, eat into, exhaust, expend, take up, use up, utilise. 3 burn, demolish, destroy, devastate, gut, ravage, raze.

consumer *noun* buyer, client, customer, end-user, patron, purchaser, user.

contact¹ *noun* 2 communication, connection, touch.

contact² *verb* communicate with, correspond with, get hold of, get in touch with, reach, speak to, talk to, write to.

contagious *adjective* catching, communicable, infectious, transmittable.

contain *verb* 1 enclose, hold, house. 2 be composed of, consist of, include, incorporate. 3 control, curb, hold back, keep in, repress, restrain, stifle, suppress.

container *noun* 1 holder, receptacle, repository, vessel; (*various containers*) bag, barrel, basket, bin, bottle, box, bucket, caddy, can, canister, carton, cartridge, case, cask, casket, chest, coffer, crate, cup, dish, drum, jar, keg, packet, pot, pouch, punnet, sachet, sack, skip, tank, tin, trunk, tub, vat.

contaminate *verb* adulterate, defile, foul, infect, poison, pollute, spoil, taint.

contemplate *verb* 1 eye, gaze at, look at, observe, regard, stare at, study, survey, view, watch. 2 cogitate on, consider, deliberate over, meditate on, mull over, ponder, reflect on, ruminate on, think over; see also ENVISAGE.

contemporary¹ *adjective* 2 current, latest, modern, new, present-day, recent, trendy (*informal*), up to date, up to the minute.

contempt *noun* disdain, disgust, dislike, disrespect, hatred, loathing, scorn.

contemptible *adjective* abominable, base, dastardly, despicable, detestable, hateful, loathsome, low, mean, miserable, odious, pitiful, shabby, shameful, vile, worthless.

contemptuous *adjective* derisive, disdainful, haughty, insolent, scornful, sneering, snooty (*informal*), supercilious.

▶▶DICTIONARY◀◀

contend *verb* **1** struggle in a battle etc. or against difficulties. **2** compete. **3** assert; declare in an argument etc., *We contend that he is innocent.* **contender** *noun* [from *con-*, + Latin *tendere* = strive]

content¹ (*say* kon-**tent**) *adjective* contented.

content² *noun* contentment.

content³ *verb* make a person contented. [from Latin *contentum* = restrained]

content⁴ (*say* **kon**-tent) *noun* (also **contents** *plural noun*) what something contains. [from Latin *contenta* = things contained]

contented *adjective* happy with what you have; satisfied. **contentedly** *adverb*

contention *noun* **1** contending; arguing. **2** an assertion put forward.

contentment *noun* a contented state.

contest¹ (*say* **kon**-test) *noun* a competition; a struggle in which rivals try to obtain something or to do best.

contest² (*say* kon-**test**) *verb* **1** compete for or in, *contest an election.* **2** dispute; argue that something is wrong or not legal.

contestant *noun* a person taking part in a contest; a competitor.

context *noun* the words that come before and after a particular word or phrase and help to fix its meaning. [from *con-*, + Latin *textum* = woven]

contiguous *adjective* adjoining.

continent *noun* one of the main masses of land in the world, *The continents are Europe,* *Asia, Africa, North America, South America, Australia, and Antarctica.* **continental** *adjective*

the Continent the mainland of Europe, not including the British Isles. [from Latin, = continuous land]

contingency *noun* (*plural* **contingencies**) something that may happen but is not intended.

contingent¹ *adjective* **1** depending, *His future is contingent on success in this exam.* **2** possible but not certain, *other contingent events.*

contingent² *noun* a group contributed to a larger group or gathering.

continual *adjective* continuing for a long time without stopping or with only short breaks, *Stop this continual quarrelling!* **continually** *adverb*

continuance *noun* continuing.

continue *verb* (**continued**, **continuing**) **1** do something without stopping. **2** begin again after stopping, *The game will continue after lunch.* **continuation** *noun* [same origin as *contain*]

continuous *adjective* continuing; without a break. **continuously** *adverb*, **continuity** *noun*

contort *verb* twist or force out of the usual shape. **contorted** *adjective*, **contortion** *noun* [from *con-*, + Latin *tortum* = twisted]

contortionist *noun* a person who can twist his or her body into unusual postures.

▶▶THESAURUS◀◀

contend *verb* **1,2** battle, clash, compete, contest, fight, grapple, strive, struggle, vie. **3** allege, argue, assert, claim, declare, insist, maintain.

content¹ *adjective* contented, fulfilled, gratified, happy, pleased, satisfied.

content³ *verb* gratify, please, satisfy.

content⁴ *noun* **contents** components, constituents, elements, ingredients, parts.

contest¹ *noun* battle, bout, challenge, championship, combat, competition, conflict, duel, fight, game, match, race, rally, struggle, tournament.

contest² *verb* **1** battle for, compete for, contend for, fight for, struggle for, vie for. **2** argue, challenge, debate, dispute, question.

contestant *noun* candidate, challenger, competitor, contender, entrant, opponent, participant, player, rival.

context *noun* background, circumstances, environment, setting, situation, surroundings.

continual *adjective* constant, endless, everlasting, frequent, habitual, incessant, perpetual, persistent, recurrent, regular, repeated.

continue *verb* **1** carry on, endure, extend, go on, keep going, keep on, last, maintain, persevere, persist, proceed, prolong, protract, remain, stay, survive. **2** pick up, recommence, resume, take up.

continuation *noun* extension, postscript, resumption, sequel, supplement.

continuous *adjective* ceaseless, constant, endless, everlasting, incessant, interminable, never-ending, non-stop, permanent, perpetual, persistent, relentless, solid, steady, unbroken, unceasing, uninterrupted, unrelieved.

contort *verb* bend, buckle, deform, distort, twist, warp.

contorted *adjective* bent, buckled, deformed, distorted, misshapen, twisted, warped, wry.

contour *noun* **1** a line (on a map) joining the points that are the same height above sea-level. **2** an outline.

contra- *prefix* against. [Latin]

contraband *noun* smuggled goods. [from *contra-*, + Italian *banda* = a ban]

contraception *noun* preventing conception; birth-control. [from *contra-* + *conception*]

contraceptive *noun* a substance or device that prevents conception.

contract¹ (*say* **kon**-trakt) *noun* **1** a formal agreement to do something. **2** a document stating the terms of an agreement.

contract² (*say* kon-**trakt**) *verb* **1** make or become smaller. **2** make a contract. **3** get an illness, *She contracted measles.* [from *con-*, + Latin *tractum* = pulled]

contraction *noun* **1** contracting. **2** a shortened form of a word or words, *Can't* is a contraction of *cannot*.

contractor *noun* a person who makes a contract, especially for building.

contradict *verb* **1** say that something said is not true or that someone is wrong. **2** say the opposite of, *These rumours contradict previous ones.* **contradiction** *noun*, **contradictory** *adjective* [from *contra-*, + Latin *dicere* = say]

contralto *noun* (*plural* **contraltos**) a female singer with a low voice. [Italian, from *contra- + alto*]

contraption *noun* a strange-looking device or machine.

contrary¹ *adjective* **1** (*say* **kon**-tra-ree) of the opposite kind or direction etc.; opposed; unfavourable. **2** (*say* kon-**trair**-ee) awkward and obstinate.

contrary² (*say* **kon**-tra-ree) *noun* the opposite. **on the contrary** the opposite is true. [from Latin *contra* = against]

contrast¹ *noun* **1** a difference clearly seen when things are compared. **2** something showing a clear difference.

contrast² *verb* **1** compare or oppose two things so as to show that they are clearly different. **2** be clearly different when compared. [from *contra-*, + Latin *stare* = to stand]

contravene *verb* (**contravened, contravening**) act against a rule or law. **contravention** *noun* [from *contra-*, + Latin *venire* = come]

contretemps (*say* **kawn**-tre-tahn) *noun* an unfortunate happening. [French, = out of time (in music)]

contribute *verb* (**contributed, contributing**) **1** give money or help etc. when others are doing the same. **2** write something for a newspaper or magazine etc. **3** help to cause something. **contribution** *noun*, **contributor** *noun*, **contributory** *adjective* [from *con-*, + Latin *tribuere* = bestow]

contrite *adjective* penitent.

contrivance *noun* a device.

contour *noun* **2** form, lines, outline, profile, shape.

contract¹ *noun* agreement, bargain, bond, charter, compact, covenant, deal, deed, pact, policy, treaty, understanding, undertaking.

contract² *verb* **1** become smaller, shrink, tighten. **2** agree, arrange, negotiate, undertake. **3** acquire, catch, come down with, develop, get, pick up.

contradict *verb* **1** counter, deny, gainsay (*formal*), oppose.
contradictory *adjective* conflicting, incompatible, inconsistent, irreconcilable, opposing.

contraption *noun* apparatus, appliance, device, gadget, gizmo (*informal*), implement, machine, tool.

contrary¹ *adjective* **1** conflicting, contradictory, converse, opposing, opposite. **2** cantankerous, defiant, disobedient, headstrong, intractable, obstinate, perverse, pigheaded, rebellious,

recalcitrant, refractory, stroppy (*informal*), stubborn, unreasonable, wayward, wilful.

contrary² *noun* antithesis, converse, opposite, reverse.

contrast¹ *noun* **1** comparison, difference, disparity, dissimilarity, distinction.

contrast² *verb* **1** compare, differentiate, distinguish, set against each other. **2** differ, disagree.

contribute *verb* **1** chip in (*informal*), donate, fork out (*slang*), give, pitch in (*informal*), provide, put in, subscribe, supply. **3** (*contribute to*) advance, have a hand in, lead to, play a part in, promote.
contribution *noun* donation, gift, grant, handout, help, input, offering, offertory, subscription.

contrite *adjective* penitent, regretful, remorseful, repentant, sorry.

▶▶ DICTIONARY ◀◀

contrive *verb* (**contrived, contriving**) plan cleverly; find a way of doing or making something.

control¹ *verb* (**controlled, controlling**) have the power to give orders or to restrain something. **controller** *noun*

control² *noun* controlling a person or thing; authority.

controversial *adjective* causing controversy.

controversy (*say* kon-tro-ver-see or kon-**trov**-er-see) *noun* a long argument or disagreement. [from *contra-*, + Latin *versum* = turned]

contusion *noun* a bruise.

conundrum *noun* a riddle; a hard question.

conurbation *noun* a large urban area where towns have spread into each other. [from *con-*, + Latin *urbs* = city]

convalesce *verb* (**convalesced, convalescing**) be recovering from an illness. **convalescence** *noun*, **convalescent** *adjective* & *noun* [from *con-*, + Latin *valescere* = grow strong]

convection *noun* the passing on of heat within liquid, air, or gas by circulation of the warmed parts. [from *con-*, + Latin *vectum* = carried]

convector *noun* a device that circulates warmed air.

convene *verb* (**convened, convening**) summon or assemble for a meeting etc. **convener** *noun* [from *con-*, + Latin *venire* = come]

convenience *noun* **1** being convenient. **2** something that is convenient. **3** a public toilet.

at your convenience whenever you find convenient; as it suits you.

convenient *adjective* **1** easy to use or deal with. **2** easy to reach. **conveniently** *adverb* [from Latin *convenire* = to suit]

convent *noun* a place where nuns live and work. [same origin as *convene*]

convention *noun* **1** an accepted way of doing things. **2** a formal assembly.

conventional *adjective* **1** done or doing things in the accepted way; traditional. **2** (of weapons) not nuclear. **conventionally** *adverb*, **conventionality** *noun*

converge *verb* (**converged, converging**) come to or towards the same point from different directions. **convergence** *noun*, **convergent** *adjective* [from *con-*, + Latin *vergere* = turn]

conversant *adjective* familiar with something, *Are you conversant with the rules of this game?* [from *converse¹*]

conversation *noun* talk between people. **conversational** *adjective*

converse¹ (*say* kon-**verss**) *verb* (**conversed, conversing**) hold a conversation. [from Latin, = keep company]

converse² (*say* **kon**-verss) *adjective* opposite; contrary. **conversely** *adverb*

▶▶ THESAURUS ◀◀

contrive *verb* arrange, engineer, manage, plan, plot, scheme, wangle (*slang*).

control¹ *verb* (*control an organisation*) administer, command, direct, dominate, govern, head, lead, manage, oversee, preside over, regulate, rule, supervise; (*control your temper*) bridle, check, contain, curb, hold back, master, repress, restrain, subdue.

control² *noun* authority, charge, command, direction, domination, influence, jurisdiction, leadership, management, mastery, power, rule, supervision, sway.

controversial *adjective* contentious, debatable, disputable, moot.

controversy *noun* argument, debate, disagreement, dispute, quarrel, row (*informal*), wrangle.

convalesce *verb* get better, improve, mend, recover, recuperate.

convenient *adjective* **1** handy, helpful, practical, suitable, timely, useful, well-timed. **2** accessible, handy, nearby.

convent *noun* abbey, cloister, nunnery, priory, religious community.

convention *noun* **1** custom, etiquette, formality, practice, protocol, rule, tradition. **2** assembly, conference, congress, council, gathering, jamboree, meeting, rally, synod.

conventional *adjective* **1** accepted, accustomed, customary, established, mainstream, normal, ordinary, orthodox, regular, standard, traditional, usual.

converge *verb* come together, intersect, join, meet, merge.

conversation *noun* chat, chatter, chinwag (*informal*), confabulation, dialogue, discourse, discussion, gossip, natter (*informal*), talk, tête-à-tête, yabber (*Australian informal*), yak (*informal*).

converse¹ *verb* chat, chatter, gossip, natter (*informal*), prattle, speak, talk, yabber (*Australian informal*), yak (*informal*).

▶▶ DICTIONARY ◀◀

converse³ *noun* an opposite idea or statement etc. [same origin as *convert*]

conversion *noun* converting.

convert (*say* kon-**vert**) *verb* **1** change. **2** cause a person to change his or her beliefs. **3** kick a goal after scoring a try at Rugby football. **converter** *noun* [from *con-*, + Latin *vertere* = turn]

convertible *adjective* able to be converted. **convertibility** *noun*

convex *adjective* curved like the outside of a ball or circle. (The opposite is *concave*.) **convexity** *noun*

convey *verb* **1** transport. **2** communicate a message or idea etc. **conveyor** *noun*

conveyance *noun* **1** conveying. **2** a vehicle for transporting people.

conveyancing *noun* transferring the legal ownership of land etc. from one person to another.

conveyor belt a continuous moving belt for conveying objects.

convict¹ (*say* kon-**vikt**) *verb* prove or declare that a certain person is guilty of a crime.

convict² (*say* **kon**-vikt) *noun* a convicted person who is in prison; in Australia used especially of convicts transported to Australia in the late eighteenth and nineteenth centuries. [from *con-*, + Latin *victum* = conquered]

conviction *noun* **1** convicting or being convicted of a crime. **2** being convinced. **3** a firm opinion or belief. **carry conviction** be convincing.

convince *verb* (**convinced, convincing**) make a person feel certain that something is true. [from *con-*, + Latin *vincere* = conquer]

convivial *adjective* sociable and lively. [from Latin *convivium* = feast]

convoke *verb* (**convoked, convoking**) summon people to an assembly or meeting. **convocation** *noun* [from *con-*, + Latin *vocare* = to call]

convoluted *adjective* **1** coiled; twisted. **2** complicated. **convolution** *noun* [from *con-*, + Latin *volutum* = rolled]

convoy *noun* a group of ships or trucks travelling together.

convulse *verb* (**convulse, convulsing**) cause violent movements or convulsions. **convulsive** *adjective* [from *con-*, + Latin *vulsum* = pulled]

convulsion *noun* **1** a violent movement of the body. **2** a violent upheaval.

coo *verb* (**cooed, cooing**) make a dove's soft murmuring sound. **coo** *noun*

cooee *interjection* an Australian bush cry to attract attention, originally Aboriginal. **within cooee of** near.

cook¹ *verb* make food ready to eat by heating it. **cook up** (*informal*) concoct; invent.

cook² *noun* a person who cooks.

cooker *noun* a stove for cooking food.

cookery *noun* the action or skill of cooking food.

▶▶ THESAURUS ◀◀

converse³ *noun* antithesis, contrary, opposite, reverse.

convert *verb* **1** adapt, change, modify, switch, transform, turn.

convey *verb* **1** bear, bring, carry, conduct, deliver, fetch, haul, shift, take, transfer, transport. **2** communicate, impart, make known, put across, tell, transmit.

convict¹ *verb* condemn, declare guilty.

convict² *noun* criminal, felon, lag (*slang*), prisoner.

conviction *noun* **2** assurance, certainty, confidence, earnestness, fervour. **3** belief, creed, faith, opinion, persuasion, tenet, view.

convince *verb* assure, persuade, prove to, satisfy, sway, win over.

convinced *adjective* certain, confident, definite, positive, sure.

convincing *adjective* cogent, compelling, forceful, irresistible, persuasive, powerful, sound, strong, telling.

convoy *noun* armada, company, fleet, flotilla, group.

convulsion *noun* **1** fit, paroxysm, seizure, spasm.

cook¹ *verb* make, prepare, put together; (*various ways to cook*) bake, barbecue, boil, braise, broil, casserole, flambé, fry, grill, parboil, poach, roast, sauté, simmer, steam, stew, toast. **cook up** concoct, devise, fabricate, invent, make up, plan, plot.

cookery *noun* cooking, cuisine.

▶▶DICTIONARY◀◀

cool¹ *adjective* **1** fairly cold; not hot or warm. **2** calm. **3** not enthusiastic. **4** *(informal)* excellent; fashionable. **coolly** *adverb*, **coolness** *noun*

cool² *verb* make or become cool. **cooler** *noun*

coolamon (*say* **kool**-a-mon) *noun* (*Australian*) a wooden or bark dish for carrying water.

coolibah (*say* **kool**-i-bah) *noun* an Australian eucalyptus tree that grows along rivers.

coolie *noun* an unskilled labourer in countries of eastern Asia.

coop¹ *noun* a cage for poultry.

coop² *verb* **coop up** confine or shut in.

cooperate *verb* (**cooperated, cooperating**) work helpfully with other people. **cooperation** *noun*, **cooperative** *adjective*

co-opt *verb* invite someone to become a member of a committee etc. [from *co-,* + Latin *optare* = choose]

coordinate¹ *verb* (**coordinated, coordinating**) organise people or things to work properly together. **coordination** *noun*, **coordinator** *noun*

coordinate² *noun* **1** a coordinated thing. **2** a quantity used to fix the position of something. [from *co-,* + Latin *ordinare* = arrange]

coot *noun* a water-bird with a horny white patch on its forehead.

Cootamundra wattle (*say* koot-a-**mun**-dra) *noun* a graceful wattle tree with bluish grey foliage. [from a town in New South Wales]

cop¹ *verb* (**copped, copping**) (*slang*) catch, *You'll cop it!*

cop² *noun* (*slang*) **1** a police officer. **2** capture; arrest, *It's a fair cop!*

cope¹ *verb* (**coped, coping**) manage or deal with something successfully.

cope² *noun* a long loose cloak worn by clergy in ceremonies etc.

copier *noun* a device for copying things.

coping *noun* the top row of stones or bricks in a wall, usually slanted so that rainwater will run off. [from *cope²*]

copious *adjective* plentiful; in large amounts. **copiously** *adverb*

copper¹ *noun* **1** a reddish-brown metal used to make wire, coins, etc. **2** a reddish-brown colour. **3** a coin made of copper or metal of this colour. **copper** *adjective* [from Latin *cuprum* = Cyprus metal (because the Romans got most of their copper from Cyprus)]

copper² *noun* (*slang*) a policeman. [from *cop*]

copperplate *noun* neat handwriting.

coppice *noun* a group of small trees.

copra *noun* dried coconut-kernels.

copse *noun* a coppice.

copulate *verb* (**copulated, copulating**) have sexual intercourse with someone. **copulation** *noun*

copy¹ *noun* (*plural* **copies**) **1** a thing made to look like another. **2** something written or typed out again from its original form. **3** one of a number of specimens of the same book or newspaper etc.

copy² *verb* (**copied, copying**) **1** make a copy of something. **2** do the same as someone else; imitate. **copyist** *noun*

▶▶THESAURUS◀◀

cool¹ *adjective* **1** chilly, cold, nippy (*informal*). **2** calm, collected, composed, laid-back (*informal*), level-headed, nonchalant, relaxed, sedate, self-possessed, serene, unemotional, unexcited, unflappable (*informal*), unflustered, unruffled. **3** cold, frosty, half-hearted, hostile, icy, indifferent, lukewarm, offhand, unenthusiastic, unfriendly, unwelcoming. **4** see EXCELLENT, TRENDY.

cool² *verb* chill, freeze, refrigerate.

coop¹ *noun* cage, enclosure, pen.

coop² *verb* **coop up** box in, cage in, confine, imprison, keep, lock up, pen in, shut up.

cooperate *verb* assist, collaborate, help, join forces, pull together, unite, work together. **cooperation** *noun* assistance, collaboration, contribution, help, involvement, participation, support, teamwork.

cooperative *adjective* accommodating, helpful, obliging, willing.

coordinate¹ *verb* integrate, orchestrate, organise, synchronise. **coordinator** *noun* controller, director, manager, organiser.

cope¹ *verb* (**cope with**) contend with, deal with, endure, face, handle, manage, withstand.

copious *adjective* abundant, ample, bountiful, generous, lavish, liberal, plentiful, profuse.

copy¹ *noun* **1** carbon copy, counterfeit, double, duplicate, facsimile, fake, forgery, imitation, likeness, photocopy, print, replica, reproduction, twin.

copy² *verb* **1** counterfeit, crib, duplicate, forge, photocopy, plagiarise, print, reproduce. **2** ape, imitate, mimic, parody, take off (*informal*).

▶▶ DICTIONARY ◀◀

copyright *noun* the legal right to print a book, reproduce a picture, record a piece of music, etc.

coquette (*say* ko-**ket**) *noun* a woman who flirts. **coquettish** *adjective* [French]

cor- *prefix* see **com-**.

coral *noun* **1** a hard red, pink, or white substance formed by the skeletons of tiny sea-creatures massed together. **2** a pink colour.

corbel *noun* a piece of stone or wood projecting from a roof to support something.

cord *noun* **1** a long thin flexible strip of twisted threads or strands. **2** a piece of flex. **3** a cord-like structure in the body, *the spinal cord.* **4** corduroy.

cordial¹ *noun* a fruit-flavoured drink.

cordial² *adjective* warm and friendly. **cordially** *adverb*, **cordiality** *noun* [from Latin *cordis* = of the heart]

cordon¹ *noun* a line of people, ships, fortifications, etc. placed round an area to guard or enclose it.

cordon² *verb* surround with a cordon.

corduroy *noun* cotton cloth with velvety ridges.

corduroy road (*Australian*) a path made with logs or slats laid side by side.

core *noun* **1** the hard central part of an apple or pear etc., containing the seeds. **2** the central or most important part of something.

corella (*say* ko-**rel**-a) *noun* a white Australian cockatoo.

corgi *noun* (*plural* **corgis**) a small dog with short legs and upright ears.

cork¹ *noun* **1** the lightweight bark of a kind of oak-tree. **2** a stopper for a bottle, made of cork or other material.

cork² *verb* close with a cork.

corkscrew *noun* **1** a device for removing corks from bottles. **2** a spiral.

corm *noun* a part of a plant rather like a bulb.

cormorant *noun* a large black sea-bird.

corn¹ *noun* **1** the seed of wheat and similar plants. **2** a plant (such as wheat) grown for its grain. **3** maize.

corn² *noun* a small hard lump on the foot.

cornea *noun* the transparent covering over the pupil of the eye. **corneal** *adjective*

corned *adjective* preserved with salt, *corned beef.*

corner¹ *noun* **1** the angle or area where two lines or sides or walls meet or where two streets join. **2** a free hit or kick from the corner of a hockey or football field. **3** a region, *a quiet corner of the world.*

corner² *verb* **1** drive someone into a corner or other position from which it is difficult to escape. **2** travel round a corner. **3** obtain possession of all or most of something, *corner the market.*

cornerstone *noun* **1** a stone built into the corner at the base of a building. **2** something that is a vital foundation.

cornet *noun* a musical instrument rather like a trumpet. [from Latin *cornu* = horn, trumpet]

cornflakes *plural noun* toasted maize flakes eaten for breakfast.

cornflour *noun* flour made from maize or rice, used in sauces, milk puddings, etc.

cornflower *noun* a plant with blue flowers that grows wild in fields of corn.

cornice *noun* a band or ornamental moulding on walls just below a ceiling or at the top of a building.

cornucopia *noun* a horn-shaped container overflowing with fruit and flowers; a plentiful supply. [from Latin *cornu* = horn, + *copiae* = of plenty]

corny *adjective* (**cornier**, **corniest**) (*informal*) **1** repeated so often that people are bored, *corny jokes.* **2** sentimental. [from *corn¹*]

▶▶ THESAURUS ◀◀

cord *noun* **1** cable, lace, line, rope, string, twine.

cordial² *adjective* affable, amiable, amicable, friendly, genial, heartfelt, kind, sincere, warm.

cordon¹ *noun* chain, circle, line, ring.

cordon² *verb* **cordon off** close off, enclose, seal off, shut off, surround.

core *noun* **1** centre, heart, inside, middle. **2** centre, crux, essence, gist, heart, kernel, nitty-gritty (*informal*), nub, nucleus.

cork¹ *noun* **2** bung, plug, stopper.

corkscrew *noun* **2** helix, spiral.

corner¹ *noun* **1** angle, bend, crossroads, curve, intersection, junction, turn.

corner² *verb* **1** bail up (*Australian*), buttonhole, capture, catch, trap. **3** control, dominate, monopolise.

corny *adjective* **1** banal, feeble, hackneyed, outworn, trite, weak. **2** mawkish, old-fashioned, over-sentimental, schmaltzy, soppy (*informal*).

▶▶▶ DICTIONARY ◀◀

corollary (*say* ker-**ol**-er-ee) *noun* (*plural* **corollaries**) a fact etc. that logically accompanies another, *The work is difficult and, as a corollary, tiring.*

corona (*say* kor-**oh**-na) *noun* a circle of light round something. [Latin, = crown]

coronary *noun* short for **coronary thrombosis**, blockage of an artery carrying blood to the heart.

coronation *noun* the crowning of a king or queen. [same origin as *corona*]

coroner *noun* an official who holds an inquiry into the cause of a death thought to be from unnatural causes.

coronet *noun* a small crown.

corporal[1] *noun* a soldier ranking next below a sergeant.

corporal[2] *adjective* of the body. [from Latin *corpus* = body]
corporal punishment punishment by being whipped or beaten.

corporate *adjective* shared by members of a group, *corporate responsibility.*

corporation *noun* 1 a group of people elected to govern a town. 2 a group of people legally authorised to act as an individual in business etc.

corps (*say* kor) *noun* (*plural* **corps**, *say* korz) 1 a special army unit, *the Medical Corps.* 2 a large group of soldiers. 3 a set of people engaged in the same activity, *the diplomatic corps.*

corpse *noun* a dead body. [from Latin *corpus* = body]

corpulent *adjective* having a bulky body; fat. **corpulence** *noun*

corpuscle *noun* one of the red or white cells in blood. [from Latin, = little body]

corral (*say* kor-**ahl**) *noun* (*American*) an enclosure for horses, cattle, etc.

correct[1] *adjective* 1 true; accurate; without any mistakes. 2 proper; done or said in an approved way. **correctly** *adverb*, **correctness** *noun*

correct[2] *verb* 1 make a thing correct by altering or adjusting it. 2 mark the mistakes in something. 3 point out or punish a person's faults. **correction** *noun*, **corrective** *adjective*, **corrector** *noun* [from cor-, + Latin *rectus* = straight]

correlate *verb* (**correlated**, **correlating**) compare or connect things systematically. **correlation** *noun* [from cor- + *relate*]

correspond *verb* 1 write letters to each other. 2 agree; match, *Your story corresponds with his.* 3 be similar or equivalent, *Their assembly corresponds to our parliament.* [from cor- + *respond*]

correspondence *noun* 1 letters; writing letters. 2 similarity; agreement.

correspondent *noun* 1 a person who writes letters to another. 2 a person employed to gather news and send reports to a newspaper or radio station etc.

corridor *noun* a passage in a building.

corroborate *verb* (**corroborated**, **corroborating**) help to confirm a statement etc. **corroboration** *noun*

corroboree (*say* ko-**rob**-o-ree) *noun* an Aboriginal dance ceremony with song and rhythmical music.

▶▶▶ THESAURUS ◀◀

corollary *noun* consequence, result, upshot.

coronation *noun* crowning, enthronement.

corporal[2] *adjective* bodily, physical.

corporation *noun* 1 council. 2 company, firm, organisation.

corpse *noun* body, cadaver, carcass, remains.

correct[1] *adjective* 1 accurate, exact, faultless, flawless, perfect, precise, proper, right, spot on (*informal*), true. 2 acceptable, appropriate, conventional, decent, decorous, fitting, impeccable, proper, right, seemly, suitable.

correct[2] *verb* 1 adjust, alter, amend, cure, fix, improve, mend, put right, rectify, remedy, repair, revise. 2 assess, check, mark. 3 admonish, censure, chasten, chastise, discipline, rebuke, reprimand, reprove, scold.

correlation *noun* connection, correspondence, interdependence, link, relationship, tie-up.

correspond *verb* 1 communicate, exchange letters, keep in touch, send letters, write. 2 accord, agree, be consistent, coincide, concur, conform, fit, match, square, tally.
corresponding *adjective* analogous, equivalent, homologous, like, matching, parallel, similar.

correspondence *noun* 1 communications, letters, mail, messages.

correspondent *noun* 2 journalist, reporter, writer.

corridor *noun* hall, hallway, lobby, passage, passageway.

corroborate *verb* back up, bear out, confirm, substantiate, support, validate, verify.

▶▶ D I C T I O N A R Y ◀◀

corrode *verb* (**corroded, corroding**) destroy metal gradually by chemical action. **corrosion** *noun*, **corrosive** *adjective* [from *cor-*, + Latin *rodere* = gnaw]

corrugated *adjective* shaped into alternate ridges and grooves, *corrugated iron*. [from *cor-*, + Latin *ruga* = wrinkle]

corrupt¹ *adjective* **1** dishonest; accepting bribes. **2** wicked. **3** decaying.

corrupt² *verb* **1** cause to become dishonest or wicked. **2** spoil; taint. **corruption** *noun*, **corruptible** *adjective* [from *cor-*, + Latin *ruptum* = broken]

corsair *noun* a pirate ship; a pirate.

corset *noun* a piece of underwear worn to shape or support the body.

cortège (*say* kort-**ayzh**) *noun* a funeral procession. [French]

cosh *noun* a heavy weapon for hitting people.

cosine *noun* (in a right-angled triangle) the ratio of the length of a side adjacent to one of the acute angles to the length of the hypotenuse. (Compare *sine*.)

cosmetic *noun* a substance (e.g. face-powder, lipstick) put on the skin to make it look more attractive.

cosmic *adjective* **1** of the universe. **2** of outer space, *cosmic rays*. [from *cosmos*]

cosmonaut *noun* a Russian astronaut. [from *cosmos* + *astronaut*]

cosmopolitan *adjective* **1** of or from many countries; containing people from many countries. **2** free from national prejudices. [from *cosmos* + Greek *polites* = citizen]

cosmos (*say* **koz**-moss) *noun* the universe. [from Greek, = the world]

Cossack *noun* a member of a people of south Russia, famous as horsemen.

cosset *verb* (**cosseted, cosseting**) pamper; cherish lovingly.

cossie (*say* **koz**-ee) *noun* (*Australian informal*) a swimming costume.

cost¹ *noun* the price of something.

cost² *verb* (**cost, costing**) **1** have a certain price. **2** (*past tense* is **costed**) estimate the cost of something.

costermonger *noun* a person who sells fruit etc. from a barrow in the street. [from old words *costard* = large apple, + *monger* = trader]

costly *adjective* (**costlier, costliest**) expensive. **costliness** *noun*

costume *noun* clothes, especially for a particular purpose or of a particular place or period.

cosy¹ *adjective* (**cosier, cosiest**) warm and comfortable. **cosily** *adverb*, **cosiness** *noun*

cosy² *noun* (*plural* **cosies**) a cover placed over a teapot or boiled egg to keep it hot.

cot *noun* a baby's bed with high sides. [from Hindi *khat* = bedstead]

▶▶ T H E S A U R U S ◀◀

corrode *verb* consume, destroy, eat away, erode, oxidise, rot, rust, wear away.

corrugated *adjective* fluted, furrowed, grooved, ribbed, ridged, wrinkled.

corrupt¹ *adjective* **1** bent (*slang*), crooked, dishonest, shady, shonky (*Australian informal*), unscrupulous, venal. **2** decadent, degenerate, depraved, dissolute, evil, immoral, iniquitous, perverted, sinful, wicked.

corrupt² *verb* **1** bribe, buy off, influence, lead astray, pervert, tempt. **2** (*corrupt a text*) alter, spoil, tamper with.

corruption *noun* bribery, decadence, degeneracy, depravity, dishonesty, fraud, graft, immorality, perversion, sinfulness, unscrupulousness, venality, vice, wickedness.

cortège *noun* procession, train.

cosmetic *noun* (*cosmetics*) beauty products, make-up.

cosmonaut *noun* astronaut, space traveller.

cosmopolitan *adjective* **1** international, multi-cultural, multiracial. **2** broad-minded, liberal, sophisticated, urbane, worldly.

cosmos *noun* universe, world.

cost¹ *noun* charge, expenditure, expense, fare, fee, outlay, overheads, payment, price, rate, tariff, toll.

cost² *verb* **1** be priced at, be worth, fetch, sell for. **2** estimate, price, value.

costly *adjective* dear, exorbitant, expensive, extravagant, precious, pricey (*informal*), valuable.

costume *noun* apparel (*formal*), attire (*formal*), clothes, clothing, dress, garb, garments, gear (*informal*), livery, outfit, raiment, regalia, uniform, vestments.

cosy¹ *adjective* comfortable, comfy (*informal*), friendly, homely, relaxing, secure, snug, warm.

cot *noun* cradle, crib.

▶▶ D I C T I O N A R Y ◀◀

cottage *noun* a small simple house, especially in the country.
cottage cheese soft white cheese made from curds without pressing.

cotton *noun* **1** a soft white substance covering the seeds of a tropical plant; the plant itself. **2** thread made from this substance. **3** cloth made from cotton thread.
cotton wool soft fluffy wadding originally made from cotton.

couch¹ *noun* (*plural* **couches**) **1** a long soft seat like a sofa but with only one end raised. **2** a sofa or settee.

couch² *verb* **1** express in words of a certain kind, *The request was couched in polite terms.* **2** lie in a lair etc. or in ambush.

cougar (*say* **koo**-ger) *noun* (*American*) a puma.

cough¹ (*say* kof) *verb* send out air from the lungs with a sudden sharp sound.

cough² *noun* **1** the act or sound of coughing. **2** an illness that makes you cough.

could *past tense* of **can³**.

couldn't (*mainly spoken*) could not.

council *noun* a group of people chosen or elected to discuss or discuss something, especially those elected to organise the affairs of a town or local government area. [from Latin *concilium* = assembly]

councillor *noun* a member of a council.

counsel¹ *noun* **1** advice, *give counsel.* **2** a barrister or group of barristers representing someone in a lawsuit.
take counsel with consult. [from Latin *consulere* = consult]

counsel² *verb* (**counselled, counselling**) give advice to someone; recommend.

counsellor *noun* an adviser.

count¹ *verb* **1** say numbers in their proper order. **2** find the total of something by using numbers. **3** include in a total, *There are six of us, counting the dog.* **4** be important, *It's what you do that counts.* **5** regard; consider, *I should count it an honour to be invited.*
count on rely on.

count² *noun* **1** counting. **2** a number reached by counting a total. **3** any of the points being considered, e.g. in accusing someone of crimes, *guilty on all counts.*

count³ *noun* a European nobleman.

countdown *noun* counting numbers backwards to zero before an event.

countenance¹ *noun* a person's face; the expression on the face.

countenance² *verb* (**countenanced, countenancing**) give approval to; allow, *Will they countenance this plan?*

counter¹ *noun* **1** a flat-topped fitment over which customers are served in a shop, bank, etc. **2** a small round token used for keeping accounts or scores in certain games. **3** a device for counting things.
under the counter sold or obtained in an underhand way.

counter² *verb* **1** counteract. **2** counter-attack; return an opponent's blow by hitting back.

counter³ *adverb* contrary to something, *This is counter to what we really want.*

counter- *prefix* **1** against; opposing; done in return (as in *counter-attack*). **2** corresponding (as in *countersign*). [from Latin *contra* = against]

▶▶ T H E S A U R U S ◀◀

cottage *noun* cabin, chalet, hut, lodge, shack, weekender (*Australian*).

cotton *noun* **2** thread, yarn.

couch¹ *noun* chaise longue, chesterfield, divan, ottoman, settee, sofa.

council *noun* assembly, board, committee, conference, congress, corporation, synod.

counsel¹ *noun* **1** advice, direction, guidance, recommendation.

counsel² *verb* advise, direct, guide, recommend.

counsellor *noun* adviser, guide, mentor.

count¹ *verb* **2** add up, calculate, compute, enumerate, number, sum up, tally, total, tot up (*informal*). **3** consider, include, reckon with, take into account. **4** be important, carry weight, matter, rate highly, signify. **5** consider, deem, judge, look upon, rate, reckon, regard, think.
count on assume, bank on, depend on, expect, reckon on, rely on.

count² *noun* **1** census, poll, stocktaking. **2** aggregate, amount, figure, number, reckoning, tally, total. **3** charge, point.

counter¹ *noun* **1** bar, checkout, stand. **2** chip, disc, piece, token.

counter² *verb* **2** contradict, counter-attack, fight back, hit back, oppose, parry, rebut, retaliate.

counteract *verb* act against something and reduce or prevent its effects. **counteraction** *noun*

counter-attack *verb* attack to oppose or return an enemy's attack. **counter-attack** *noun*

counterbalance *noun* a weight or influence that balances another. **counterbalance** *verb*

counterfeit (*say* **kownt**-er-feet) *adjective, noun,* & *verb* fake. [from Old French *countrefait* = made in opposition]

counterfoil *noun* a section of a cheque or receipt etc. that is detached and kept as a record.

countermand *verb* cancel a command or instruction that has been given.

counterpane *noun* a bedspread.

counterpart *noun* a person or thing that corresponds to another, *Their President is the counterpart of our Prime Minister.*

counterpoint *noun* a method of combining melodies in harmony.

counterpoise *noun* & *verb* counterbalance.

countersign¹ *noun* a password or signal that has to be given in response to something.

countersign² *verb* add another signature to a document to give it authority.

counterweight *noun* & *verb* counterbalance.

countess *noun* (*plural* **countesses**) the wife or widow of a count or earl; a female count.

countless *adjective* too many to count.

countrified *adjective* like the country.

country *noun* (*plural* **countries**) **1** the land occupied by a nation. **2** all the people of a country. **3** less densely settled districts outside cities. **4** an area of land, *rugged country.* **country** *adjective*
country dance a folk-dance.

countryman *noun* (*plural* **countrymen**) **1** a man who lives in the countryside. **2** a man who belongs to the same country as yourself. **countrywoman** *noun* (*plural* **countrywomen**)

countryside *noun* country areas; land in the country.

county *noun* (*plural* **counties**) a territorial division in some countries for local government purposes. [originally = the land of a count (*count³*)]

coup (*say* koo) *noun* a sudden action taken to win power; a clever victory. [French, = a blow]

couple¹ *noun* two people or things considered together; a pair.

couple² *verb* (**coupled, coupling**) fasten or link together.

couplet *noun* a pair of lines in rhyming verse.

coupon *noun* a piece of paper that gives you the right to receive or do something. [French, = piece cut off]

courage *noun* the ability to face danger or difficulty or pain even when you are afraid; bravery. **courageous** *adjective* [from Latin *cor* = heart]

counteract *verb* cancel out, counter, counterbalance, negate, neutralise, offset, oppose, undo.

counterfeit *adjective* bogus, dud (*informal*), fake, forged, imitation, phoney (*informal*), sham, spurious.
counterfeit *verb* copy, fake, forge, imitate, reproduce.

counterpart *noun* equivalent, opposite number, parallel.

countless *adjective* endless, frequent, incalculable, innumerable, many, myriad, numerous.

country *noun* **1** commonwealth, democracy, duchy, emirate, kingdom, land, monarchy, nation, principality, realm, republic, state, territory. **2** citizens, community, inhabitants, nation, people, populace, population, public. **3** backblocks (*Australian*), backwoods, bush (*Australian*), inland, interior, outback (*Australian*), rural district, sticks (*informal*). **4**

countryside, land, landscape, region, scenery, terrain, territory.
country *adjective* agricultural, bucolic, farming, pastoral, provincial, rural, rustic.

countryman, countrywoman *noun* **1** bushie (*Australian informal*), farmer, rustic. **2** compatriot.

couple¹ *noun* brace, duo, pair, twosome.

couple² *verb* connect, fasten, hitch, join, link, tie, yoke.

coupon *noun* entry form, form, ticket, token, voucher.

courage *noun* boldness, bottle (*slang*), bravery, daring, determination, fearlessness, fortitude, gallantry, grit, guts (*informal*), heroism, mettle, nerve, pluck, prowess, spirit, spunk (*informal*), valour.

courageous *adjective* bold, brave, daring, dauntless, determined, fearless, gallant, game, heroic, intrepid, lion-hearted, mettlesome, plucky, resolute, spirited, stoical, stout-hearted, unafraid, undaunted, valiant.

▶▶ D I C T I O N A R Y ◀◀

courgette (*say* koor-zh**et**) *noun* a kind of small vegetable marrow, a zucchini.

courier (*say* **koor**-ee-er) *noun* **1** a messenger. **2** a person employed to guide and help a group of tourists. [from Latin *currere* = to run]

course¹ *noun* **1** an onward movement or progression, *in the ordinary course of events.* **2** the direction in which something goes; a route, *the ship's course.* **3** a series of events or actions etc., *Your best course is to start again.* **4** a series of lessons, exercises, etc. **5** part of a meal, *the meat course.* **6** a racecourse. **7** a golf-course.
of course without a doubt; as we expected.

course² *verb* (**coursed, coursing**) move or flow freely, *Tears coursed down his cheeks.* [from Latin *cursus* = running]

court¹ *noun* **1** a royal household. **2** a lawcourt; the judges etc. in a lawcourt. **3** an enclosed area for games such as tennis or netball. **4** a courtyard.

court² *verb* try to win somebody's love or support. **courtship** *noun*

courteous (*say* **ker**-tee-us) *adjective* polite. **courteously** *adverb*, **courtesy** *noun*

courtier *noun* (*old use*) one of a king's or queen's companions at court.

courtly *adjective* dignified and polite.

court martial (*plural* **courts martial**) **1** a court for trying people who have broken military law. **2** a trial in this court.

court-martial *verb* (**court-martialled, court-martialling**) try a person by a court martial.

courtyard *noun* a space surrounded by walls or buildings.

cousin *noun* a child of your uncle or aunt.

cove¹ *noun* a small bay.

cove² *noun* (*slang*) a fellow, a chap; (in early Australia) a manager or overseer.

coven (*say* **kuv**-en) *noun* a group of witches.

covenant (*say* **kuv**-en-ant) *noun* a formal agreement; a contract.

Coventry *place-name* **send a person to Coventry** refuse to speak to him or her.

cover¹ *verb* **1** place one thing over or round another; conceal. **2** travel a certain distance, *We covered fifteen kilometres a day.* **3** aim a gun at somebody, *I've got you covered.* **4** protect by insurance or a guarantee, *These goods are covered against fire or theft.* **5** be enough money to pay for something, *$5 will cover my fare.* **6** deal with or include, *The book covers all kinds of farming.* **coverage** *noun*
cover up conceal facts etc.

cover² *noun* **1** a thing used for covering something else; a lid, wrapper, envelope, etc. **2** the binding of a book. **3** something that hides or shelters or protects you.

▶▶ T H E S A U R U S ◀◀

courier *noun* **1** carrier, dispatch rider, messenger, runner.

course¹ *noun* **1** development, flow, march, passage, progression, sequence, succession, unfolding. **2** direction, line, orbit, path, route, track. **4** classes, curriculum, lessons, programme, series. **6** circuit, racecourse, track.
of course by all means, certainly, naturally, obviously, without a doubt.

court¹ *noun* **1** attendants, courtiers (*old use*), entourage, household, retinue, train. **2** bar, bench, lawcourt, tribunal.

court² *verb* date (*informal*), go out with, woo (*old use*).

courteous *adjective* chivalrous, civil, considerate, diplomatic, gallant, gracious, polite, proper, respectful, tactful, thoughtful, well-behaved, well-bred, well-mannered.
courtesy *noun* chivalry, civility, consideration, deference, diplomacy, gallantry, good manners, politeness, respect, tact, thoughtfulness.

courtyard *noun* court, forecourt, patio, quad (*informal*), quadrangle, yard.

cove¹ *noun* bay, inlet.

covenant *noun* agreement, bargain, compact, contract, deal, pact, pledge, promise, undertaking.

cover¹ *verb* **1** bandage, bind, blot out, bury, camouflage, cloak, clothe, cloud, coat, conceal, drape, dress, encase, enclose, encrust, envelop, hide, mask, obscure, overlay, plaster, protect, screen, shield, shroud, surround, swaddle, swathe, veil, wrap. **2** travel, traverse. **4** indemnify, insure, protect. **6** deal with, encompass, include, survey, take in.
cover up conceal, hide, hush up, suppress, whitewash.

cover² *noun* **1** armour, binder, binding, canopy, cap, case, casing, cladding, coating, cocoon, covering, cowl, envelope, folder, hood, housing, jacket, lid, mantle, mask, outside, overlay, pall, roof, screen, sheath, shell, shield, shroud, skin, sleeve, slip, surface, top, veneer, wrapper, wrapping. **3** camouflage, disguise, façade, front, hiding place, protection, refuge, sanctuary, screen, shelter, smokescreen.

▶▶ D I C T I O N A R Y ◀◀

coverlet *noun* a bedspread.

covert[1] (*say* **kuv**-ert) *noun* an area of thick bushes etc. in which birds and animals hide.

covert[2] *adjective* stealthy; done secretly.

covet (*say* **kuv**-it) *verb* (**coveted, coveting**) wish to have something, especially a thing that belongs to someone else. **covetous** *adjective*

cow[1] *noun* the fully-grown female of cattle or of certain other large animals (e.g. elephant, whale, seal).

cow[2] *verb* intimidate; subdue someone by bullying.

coward *noun* a person who shows fear in a shameful way, or who attacks people who cannot defend themselves. **cowardice** *noun*, **cowardly** *adjective*

cowboy *noun* 1 a man in charge of grazing cattle on a ranch in the USA. 2 (*slang*) a reckless financier.

cower *verb* crouch or shrink back in fear.

cowl *noun* 1 a monk's hood. 2 a hood-shaped covering, e.g. on a chimney.

cowshed *noun* a shed for cattle.

cowslip *noun* a wild plant with small yellow flowers in spring.

cox *noun* (*plural* **coxes**) a coxswain.

coxswain (*say* **kok**-swayn or **kok**-sun) *noun* 1 a person who steers a rowing-boat. 2 a sailor with special duties.

coy *adjective* pretending to be shy or modest; bashful. **coyly** *adverb*, **coyness** *noun*

crab *noun* a shellfish with ten legs.

crab-apple *noun* a small sour apple.

crabhole *noun* (*Australian*) a hole or shallow depression in the ground.

crack[1] *noun* 1 a line on the surface of something where it has broken but not come completely apart. 2 a narrow gap. 3 a sudden sharp noise. 4 a knock, *a crack on the head*. 5 (*informal*) a joke; a wisecrack. 6 a drug made from cocaine.

crack[2] *adjective* (*informal*) first-class, *He is a crack shot*.

crack[3] *verb* 1 make or get a crack; split. 2 make a sudden sharp noise. 3 break down, *He cracked under the strain*.
crack a joke tell a joke.
crack down on (*informal*) stop something that is illegal or against rules.
get cracking (*informal*) get busy.

cracker *noun* 1 a paper tube that bangs when pulled apart. 2 a firework that explodes with a crack. 3 a thin biscuit.

crackle *verb* (**crackled, crackling**) make small cracking sounds. **crackle** *noun*

crackling *noun* crisp skin on roast pork.

-cracy *suffix* forming nouns meaning 'ruling' or 'government' (e.g. *democracy*). [from Greek *-kratia* = rule]

cradle[1] *noun* 1 a small cot for a baby. 2 a supporting framework.

cradle[2] *verb* (**cradled, cradling**) hold gently.

craft *noun* 1 a job that needs skill, especially with the hands. 2 skill. 3 cunning; trickery. 4 (*plural* **craft**) a ship or boat; an aircraft or spacecraft.

craftsman, craftswoman *noun* a person who is good at a craft. **craftsmanship** *noun*

▶▶ T H E S A U R U S ◀◀

covert[2] *adjective* clandestine, concealed, disguised, furtive, hidden, secret, secretive, surreptitious.

covet *verb* crave, desire, fancy, hanker after, long for, want, yearn for.
covetous *adjective* avaricious, desirous, envious, grasping, greedy.

coward *noun* baby, chicken (*informal*), crybaby, scaredy-cat (*informal*), sissy, sook (*Australian informal*), wimp (*informal*).
cowardly *adjective* chicken-hearted, craven, dastardly, faint-hearted, fearful, gutless (*informal*), lily-livered, pusillanimous, spineless, timid, timorous, yellow (*informal*).

cower *verb* cringe, crouch, draw back, flinch, quail, recoil, shrink.

coy *adjective* bashful, demure, diffident, modest, self-conscious, sheepish, shy, timid, underconfident.

crack[1] *noun* 1,2 breach, break, chink, cleft, cranny, crevasse, crevice, fissure, fracture, gap, opening, rift, rupture, slit, split. 3 crackle, pop, snap.

crack[3] *verb* 1 break, chip, cleave, fracture, shatter, splinter, split. 2 clap, crackle, strike. 3 break down, collapse, crack up, fall apart, give way, go to pieces.

cradle[1] *noun* 1 basket, bassinet, cot, crib.

craft *noun* 1 handicraft, trade. 2 art, craftsmanship, skill, technique. 4 aircraft, boat, raft, ship, spacecraft, vessel.

craftsman, craftswoman *noun* artisan, artist, maker, smith, technician.
craftsmanship *noun* artistry, expertise, handiwork, skill, workmanship.

▶▶DICTIONARY◀◀

crafty *adjective* (**craftier, craftiest**) cunning. **craftily** *adverb*, **craftiness** *noun*

crag *noun* a steep piece of rough rock. **craggy** *adjective*, **cragginess** *noun*

cram *verb* (**crammed, cramming**) 1 push many things into a space. 2 fill very full.

cramp¹ *noun* pain caused by a muscle tightening suddenly.

cramp² *verb* 1 keep in a very small space. 2 hinder someone's freedom or growth etc. **cramped** *adjective*

cranberry *noun* (*plural* **cranberries**) a small sour red berry used for making jelly and sauce.

crane¹ *noun* 1 a machine for lifting and moving heavy objects. 2 a large wading bird with long legs and neck.

crane² *verb* (**craned, craning**) stretch your neck to try and see something.

crane-fly *noun* a flying insect with very long thin legs.

cranium *noun* the skull.

crank¹ *noun* 1 an L-shaped part used for changing the direction of movement in machinery. 2 a person with strange or fanatical ideas.

crank² *verb* move by means of a crank.

cranky *adjective* 1 bad-tempered. 2 eccentric; strange.

cranny *noun* (*plural* **crannies**) a crevice.

crash¹ *noun* 1 the loud noise of something breaking or colliding. 2 a violent collision or fall. 3 a sudden drop or failure.

crash² *verb* 1 make a loud smashing noise. 2 have a crash; cause to crash. 3 move with a crash.

crash³ *adjective* intensive, *a crash course.*

crash-helmet *noun* a padded helmet worn to protect the head in a crash.

crash-landing *noun* an emergency landing of an aircraft, which usually damages it.

crass *adjective* 1 very obvious or shocking; gross, *crass ignorance.* 2 very stupid. [from Latin *crassus* = thick]

crate *noun* 1 a packing case made of strips of wood. 2 an open container with compartments for carrying bottles.

crater *noun* 1 a bowl-shaped cavity or hollow. 2 the mouth of a volcano.

cravat *noun* 1 a short scarf. 2 a wide necktie.

crave *verb* (**craved, craving**) 1 desire strongly. 2 (*formal*) beg for something.

craven *adjective* cowardly.

craving *noun* a strong desire; a longing.

crawl¹ *verb* 1 move with the body close to the ground or other surface, or on hands and knees. 2 move slowly. 3 be covered with crawling things. 4 (*informal*) flatter someone in the hope of winning favour. **crawler** *noun*

▶▶THESAURUS◀◀

crafty *adjective* artful, astute, calculating, canny, clever, cunning, deceitful, devious, foxy, guileful, knowing, machiavellian, shifty (*informal*), shrewd, sly, sneaky, subtle, tricky, underhand, wily.

crag *noun* bluff, cliff, precipice, rock, scarp.

cram *verb* 1 force, jam, pack, push, ram, squash, squeeze, stuff. 2 crowd, fill, overfill, pack.

cramp² *verb* 2 hamper, hinder, impede, inhibit, limit, restrict, stunt, thwart. **cramped** *adjective* confined, crowded, narrow, poky, tight.

crane¹ *noun* 1 cherry picker, davit, derrick, hoist.

crank¹ *noun* 2 eccentric, fanatic, freak (*informal*), maniac, nut (*informal*), weirdo (*informal*).

cranky *adjective* 1 bad-tempered, cantankerous, crabby, cross, crotchety, grouchy (*informal*), ill-tempered, irritable, peevish, snaky (*Australian informal*), surly. 2 bizarre, eccentric, odd, peculiar, quirky, strange, weird.

crash¹ *noun* 1 bang, boom, clang, clangour, clank, clatter, smash, wham. 2 accident, bingle (*Australian informal*), collision, pile-up (*informal*), prang (*slang*), smash. 3 collapse, failure.

crash² *verb* 2 fall, nosedive, plummet, plunge, shatter, smash, topple, tumble; (*crash into*) bang into, bump into, collide with, knock into, plough into, ram into, run into, slam into, smash into.

crate *noun* 1 box, carton, case, packing case, tea chest.

crater *noun* 1 cavity, hole, hollow, pit.

crave *verb* 1 desire, hanker after, hunger for, long for, pine for, thirst for, want, wish for, yearn for.

craving *noun* desire, fancy, hankering, hunger, longing, thirst, wish, yearning, yen.

crawl¹ *verb* 1 creep, move on all fours, slither, squirm, worm your way, wriggle, writhe. 2 edge forward, go at a snail's pace, inch forward, move slowly. 4 fawn, grovel, kowtow, lick someone's boots, suck up (*informal*), toady.

▶▶ D I C T I O N A R Y ◀◀

crawl² *noun* **1** a crawling movement. **2** a very slow pace. **3** an overarm swimming stroke.

crayfish *noun* (*plural* **crayfish**) **1** a freshwater crustacean. **2** (*Australian informal*) a marine lobster (**rock lobster**).

crayon *noun* a stick or pencil of coloured wax etc. for drawing.

craze *noun* a temporary enthusiasm.

crazed *adjective* driven insane.

crazy *adjective* (**crazier**, **craziest**) **1** insane. **2** very foolish, *this crazy idea.* **crazily** *adverb*, **craziness** *noun*

creak¹ *noun* a harsh squeak like that of a stiff door-hinge. **creaky** *adjective*

creak² *verb* make a creak.

cream¹ *noun* **1** the fatty part of milk. **2** a yellowish-white colour. **3** a food containing or looking like cream, *chocolate cream.* **4** a soft substance, *hand cream.* **5** the best part. **creamy** *adjective*

cream² *verb* make creamy; beat butter etc. until it is soft like cream.

cream off remove the best part of something.

crease¹ *noun* **1** a line made in something by folding, pressing, or crushing it. **2** a line on a cricket pitch marking a batsman's or bowler's position.

crease² *verb* (**creased**, **creasing**) make a crease or creases in something.

create *verb* (**created**, **creating**) **1** bring into existence; make or produce, especially something that no one has made before. **2** (*slang*) make a fuss; grumble. **creation** *noun*, **creative** *adjective*, **creativity** *noun*

creator *noun* a person who creates something. **the Creator** God.

creature *noun* a person or animal.

crèche *noun* a place where babies and young children are looked after while their parents are at work. [French]

credence *noun* belief, *Don't give it any credence.* [from Latin *credere* = believe]

credentials *plural noun* documents showing a person's identity, qualifications, etc. [same origin as *credit*]

credible *adjective* able to be believed; convincing. **credibly** *adverb*. **credibility** *noun* [same origin as *credit*]

credit¹ *noun* **1** honour; acknowledgement. **2** an arrangement trusting a person to pay for something later on. **3** an amount of money in someone's account at a bank etc., or entered in an account-book as paid in. (Compare *debit.*) **4** belief; trust, *I put no credit in this rumour.*

credit card a card authorising a person to buy on credit.

credits a list of people who have helped to produce a film or television programme.

▶▶ T H E S A U R U S ◀◀

craze *noun* enthusiasm, fad, fashion, mania, passion, rage, thing (*informal*), vogue.

crazy *adjective* **1** barmy (*slang*), batty (*slang*), berserk, bonkers (*slang*), crackers (*slang*), crazed, cuckoo (*informal*), daft (*informal*), demented, deranged, dotty (*informal*), flaky (*slang*), insane, loony (*informal*), loopy (*informal*), mad, mental (*informal*), nuts (*informal*), nutty (*informal*), off your head, out of your mind, potty (*informal*), round the bend (*informal*), screwy (*informal*), troppo (*Australian slang*), unbalanced, unhinged, wacky (*slang*). **2** absurd, cock-eyed (*informal*), crackpot (*informal*), daft (*informal*), foolish, half-baked (*informal*), hare-brained, idiotic, impractical, imprudent, inane, lunatic, mad, outrageous, preposterous, ridiculous, senseless, silly, stupid, unwise, unworkable, zany.

cream¹ *noun* **4** emollient, lotion, ointment, salve.

crease¹ *noun* **1** corrugation, crinkle, crumple, fold, furrow, groove, line, pucker, ridge, ruck, wrinkle.

crease² *verb* crimp, crinkle, crumple, fold, furrow, pleat, pucker, ruck, rumple, wrinkle.

create *verb* **1** beget, bring into being, compose, conceive, construct, design, devise, engender, establish, fashion, form, found, generate, give rise to, initiate, institute, invent, lead to, make, originate, pioneer, produce, set up, think up. **creation** *noun* beginning, birth, formation, foundation, genesis, invention, making, origin. **creative** *adjective* fertile, imaginative, ingenious, inventive, original, productive, resourceful.

creator *noun* architect, author, designer, inventor, maker, originator, producer.

creature *noun* animal, beast, being, living thing, organism.

crèche *noun* child care centre, nursery, preschool.

credible *adjective* believable, conceivable, plausible, reasonable.

credit¹ *noun* **1** acclaim, acknowledgement, distinction, esteem, glory, honour, merit, praise, recognition, reputation.

credit² *verb* (**credited, crediting**) **1** believe. **2** attribute; say that a person has done or achieved something, *Columbus is credited with the discovery of America.* **3** enter something as a credit in an account-book. (Compare *debit.*) [from Latin *credere* = believe, trust]

creditable *adjective* deserving praise. **creditably** *adverb*

creditor *noun* a person to whom money is owed.

credulous *adjective* too ready to believe things; gullible.

creed *noun* a set or formal statement of beliefs. [from Latin *credi* = I believe]

creek *noun* **1** a small stream, especially an intermittent one. **2** (in the UK) a narrow inlet.
up the creek (*slang*) in difficulties.

creep¹ *verb* (**crept, creeping**) **1** move along close to the ground. **2** move quietly or secretly. **3** come gradually. **4** prickle with fear, *It makes my flesh creep.*

creep² *noun* **1** a creeping movement. **2** (*slang*) an unpleasant person, especially one who seeks to win favour.
the creeps (*informal*) a nervous feeling caused by fear or dislike.

creeper *noun* a plant that grows along the ground or up a wall etc.

creepy *adjective* (**creepier, creepiest**) making people's flesh creep.

cremate *verb* (**cremated, cremating**) burn a dead body to ashes. **cremation** *noun*

crematorium *noun* (*plural* **crematoria**) a place where corpses are cremated.

creosote *noun* an oily brown liquid used to prevent wood from rotting. [from Greek, = flesh-preserver]

crêpe (*say* krayp) *noun* cloth, paper, or rubber with a wrinkled surface.

crescendo (*say* krish-**end**-oh) *noun* (*plural* **crescendos**) a gradual increase in loudness. [Italian]

crescent *noun* **1** a narrow curved shape (e.g. the new moon) coming to a point at each end. **2** a curved street. [from Latin *crescens* = growing]

cress *noun* a plant with hot-tasting leaves, used in salads and sandwiches.

crest *noun* **1** a tuft of hair, skin, or feathers on an animal's or bird's head. **2** the top of a hill or wave etc. **3** a design used on notepaper etc. **crested** *adjective*

crestfallen *adjective* disappointed; dejected.

cretin (*say* **kret**-in) *noun* a person who is mentally undeveloped through lack of certain hormones.

crevasse (*say* kri-**vass**) *noun* a deep open crack, especially in a glacier.

crevice *noun* a narrow opening, especially in a rock or wall.

crew¹ *noun* **1** the people working in a ship or aircraft. **2** a group working together, *the camera crew.* **3** (*informal*) a group of people.

crew² *past tense* of **crow²**

crib¹ *noun* **1** a baby's cot. **2** a framework holding fodder for animals. **3** a model representing the Nativity of Jesus Christ. **4** something cribbed. **5** a translation for use by students. **6** (*Australian*) a worker's packed lunch.

crib² *verb* (**cribbed, cribbing**) copy someone else's work.

cribbage *noun* a card game.

crick *noun* painful stiffness in the neck or back.

on credit by instalments, on hire purchase, on the never-never (*informal*), on the slate (*informal*), on tick (*informal*).

creditable *adjective* admirable, commendable, honourable, laudable, meritorious, praise-worthy, respectable, worthy.

creed *noun* belief(s), conviction(s), doctrine, dogma, faith, principles, religion, tenets.

creek *noun* **1** brook, rill, river, rivulet, stream, tributary, watercourse.

creep¹ *verb* **1** crawl, move on all fours, slither, squirm, worm your way, wriggle, writhe. **2** edge, inch, slink, slip, sneak, steal, tiptoe.

creepy *adjective* disturbing, eerie, frightening, hair-raising, scary, sinister, spooky (*informal*), terrifying, uncanny, weird.

crest *noun* **1** comb, topknot, tuft. **2** apex, brow, crown, peak, pinnacle, summit, top. **3** badge, emblem, insignia, symbol.

crevice *noun* chink, cleft, crack, cranny, fissure, gap, opening, rift, split.

crew¹ *noun* **1,2** company, corps, party, personnel, squad, staff, team, workforce. **3** band, bunch, crowd, gang, group, mob, troop.

crib¹ *noun* **1** cot, cradle.

crib² *verb* cheat, copy, lift (*informal*), plagiarise.

▶▶ DICTIONARY ◀◀

cricket¹ *noun* a game played outdoors between teams with a ball, bats, and two wickets. **cricketer** *noun*

cricket² *noun* an insect like a grasshopper.

crime *noun* **1** an action that breaks the law. **2** law-breaking.

criminal *noun* a person who has committed a crime or crimes. **criminal** *adjective*, **criminally** *adverb*

criminology *noun* the study of crime. [from Latin *crimen* offence, + *-logy*]

crimp *verb* press into small ridges.

crimson *adjective* & *noun* deep-red.

cringe *verb* (**cringed**, **cringing**) shrink back in fear, cower.

crinkle *verb* (**crinkled**, **crinkling**) make or become wrinkled. **crinkly** *adjective*

crinoline *noun* a long skirt worn over a framework that makes it stand out.

cripple¹ *noun* a person who is permanently lame.

cripple² *verb* (**crippled**, **crippling**) **1** make a person a cripple. **2** weaken or damage something seriously.

crisis *noun* (*plural* **crises**) an important and dangerous or difficult situation; a decisive moment.

crisp¹ *adjective* **1** very dry so that it breaks with a snap. **2** fresh and stiff, *a crisp $10 note*. **3** cold and dry, *a crisp morning*. **4** brisk and sharp, *a crisp manner*. **crisply** *adverb*, **crispness** *noun*

crisp² *noun* a very thin fried slice of potato (usually sold in packets).

criss-cross *adjective* & *adverb* with crossing lines.

criterion (*say* kry-**teer**-ee-on) *noun* (*plural* **criteria**) a standard by which something is judged. [from Greek, = means of judging]

Usage Note that *criteria* is a plural. It is incorrect to say 'a criteria' or 'this criteria'; correct usage is *this criterion, these criteria.*

critic *noun* **1** a person who gives opinions on books, plays, films, music, etc. **2** a person who criticises. [from Greek *krites* = judge]

critical *adjective* **1** criticising. **2** of critics or criticism. **3** of or at a crisis; very serious. **critically** *adverb*

criticise *verb* (**criticised**, **criticising**) say that a person or thing has faults.

criticism *noun* **1** criticising; pointing out faults. **2** the work of a critic.

▶▶ THESAURUS ◀◀

crime *noun* felony (*old use*), misdeed, misdemeanour, offence, wrong, wrongdoing; see also SIN¹.

criminal *noun* baddy (*informal*), convict, crim (*Australian informal*), crook (*informal*), culprit, delinquent, desperado, felon, jailbird, lawbreaker, malefactor, miscreant, offender, outlaw, transgressor, villain, wrongdoer.
criminal *adjective* corrupt, crooked, dishonest, illegal, illicit, lawless, shady, unlawful, wrong.

cringe *verb* cower, crouch, draw back, flinch, quail, recoil, shrink back, wince.

crinkle *verb* crease, crimp, crumple, furrow, pucker, rumple, wrinkle.

cripple² *verb* **1** debilitate, disable, incapacitate, lame, maim, paralyse, weaken. **2** bring to a standstill, damage, hamstring, hurt, immobilise, paralyse.

crisis *noun* climax, crunch (*informal*), crux, danger period, emergency, height, turning point.

crisp¹ *adjective* **1** brittle, crispy, crunchy, crusty. **3** bracing, chilly, cold, cool, fresh, nippy (*informal*). **4** abrupt, brisk, brusque, curt, sharp, snappy (*informal*), terse.

criterion *noun* benchmark, measure, principle, rule, standard, touchstone, yardstick.

critic *noun* **1** evaluator, judge, reviewer. **2** attacker, detractor, fault-finder, knocker (*informal*), objector, opponent.

critical *adjective* **1** captious, censorious, disapproving, disparaging, judgemental, nit-picking (*informal*), uncomplimentary. **3** (*of critical importance*) crucial, decisive, key, momentous, pivotal, vital; (*in a critical condition*) dangerous, grave, perilous, precarious, risky, serious.

criticise *verb* bag (*Australian informal*), belittle, censure, condemn, decry, denounce, disparage, find fault with, knock (*informal*), object to, pan (*informal*), pick holes in, rebuke, reprimand, rubbish, slam (*informal*), slate (*informal*), tell off (*informal*), tick off (*informal*).

criticism *noun* **1** censure, condemnation, disapproval, disparagement, fault-finding, flak (*informal*), nit-picking (*informal*), reproach. **2** analysis, appraisal, commentary, critique, evaluation, review.

croak *noun* a deep hoarse sound like that of a frog. **croak** *verb*, **croaky** *adjective*

crochet (*say* **kroh**-shay) *noun* a kind of needlework done by using a hooked needle to loop a thread into patterns. **crochet** *verb* (**crocheted, crocheting**)

crock¹ *noun* a piece of crockery.

crock² *noun* (*informal*) a decrepit person or thing.

crockery *noun* household china.

crocodile *noun* **1** a large tropical reptile with a thick skin, long tail, and huge jaws. **2** a long line of schoolchildren walking in pairs.

crocodile tears sorrow that is not sincere (so called because the crocodile was said to weep while it ate its victim).

crocus *noun* (*plural* **crocuses**) a small plant with yellow, purple, or white flowers.

croissant (*say* **krwah**-sahn) *noun* a flaky crescent-shaped bread roll. [French, = crescent]

crone *noun* a very old woman.

crony *noun* (*plural* **cronies**) a close friend or companion.

crook¹ *noun* **1** a shepherd's stick with a curved end. **2** something bent or curved. **3** (*informal*) a person who makes a living dishonestly.

crook² *verb* bend, *She crooked her finger.*

crook³ *adjective* (*Australian informal*) **1** bad or unpleasant, *a crook job; The weather's crook.* **2** ill, *feeling crook.* **3** angry.

go crook become angry.

crooked *adjective* **1** bent; twisted; not straight. **2** dishonest.

croon *verb* sing softly and gently.

crop¹ *noun* **1** something grown for food, *a good crop of wheat.* **2** a whip with a loop instead of a lash. **3** part of a bird's throat. **4** a very short haircut.

crop² *verb* (**cropped, cropping**) **1** (of animals) bite off, *sheep were cropping the grass.* **2** cut very short. **3** produce a crop.

crop up happen unexpectedly.

cropper *noun* **come a cropper** (*slang*) fall heavily; fall badly.

croquet (*say* **kroh**-kay) *noun* a game played with wooden balls and mallets.

crosier (*say* **kroh**-zee-er) *noun* a bishop's staff shaped like a shepherd's crook.

cross¹ *noun* **1** a mark or shape made like + or x. **2** an upright post with another piece of wood across it, used in ancient times for crucifixion. **3** a mixture of two different things.

the Cross the cross on which Christ was crucified, used as a symbol of Christianity.

cross² *verb* **1** go across something. **2** draw a line or lines across something. **3** make the sign of shape of a cross, *Cross your fingers for luck.* **4** produce something from two different kinds.

cross out draw a line across something because it is unwanted, wrong, etc.

cross³ *adjective* **1** going from one side to another. **2** annoyed; bad-tempered. **crossly** *adverb*, **crossness** *noun*

croaky *adjective* hoarse, husky, rasping, rough, throaty.

crockery *noun* china, dishes, earthenware, plates, pottery, tableware.

crook¹ *noun* **1** crosier, staff, stick. **3** baddy (*informal*), cheat, criminal, knave (*old use*), lawbreaker, malefactor, rogue, scoundrel, swindler, thief, villain, wrongdoer.

crook³ *adjective* **1** bad, inferior, poor, shoddy, slipshod, unsatisfactory. **2** ailing, ill, indisposed, lousy (*informal*), poorly, rotten (*informal*), sick, unwell.

go crook see BECOME ANGRY (at ANGRY).

crooked *adjective* **1** askew, awry, bent, bowed, cock-eyed (*informal*), contorted, crippled, curved, deformed, lopsided, off-centre, serpentine, sinuous, slanting, tortuous, twisted, uneven, winding, zigzag. **2** bent (*slang*), corrupt, criminal, dishonest, fraudulent, shady, shifty, shonky (*Australian informal*), underhand, unscrupulous, untrustworthy.

crop¹ *noun* **1** harvest, produce, vintage, yield.

crop² *verb* **1** browse, eat, graze, nibble. **2** bob, clip, cut, shear, snip, trim.

crop up appear, arise, come up, emerge, happen, occur, turn up.

cross¹ *noun* **2** crucifix, rood. **3** bitser (*Australian informal*), blend, combination, cross-breed, hybrid, mixture, mongrel.

cross² *verb* **1** cut across, extend across, go across, pass over, span, straddle, traverse. **2** criss-cross, intersect. **4** cross-breed, interbreed, mate.

cross out cancel, delete, obliterate, scratch out, strike out.

cross³ *adjective* **2** angry, annoyed, bad-tempered, cantankerous, crabby, cranky, crotchety, disagreeable, fractious, grouchy (*informal*), grumpy, ill-tempered, impatient, irascible, irate, irritable, maggoty (*Australian informal*), peevish, petulant, shirty (*informal*), snaky (*Australian informal*), surly, testy, tetchy.

▶▶ D I C T I O N A R Y ◀◀

cross- *prefix* **1** across; crossing something (as in *crossbar*). **2** from two different kinds (as in *cross-breed*).

crossbar *noun* a horizontal bar, especially between two uprights.

crossbow *noun* a powerful bow with mechanism for pulling and releasing the string.

cross-breed *verb* (**cross-bred**, **cross-breeding**) breed by mating an animal with one of a different kind. **cross-breed** *noun* (Compare *hybrid*.)

crosse *noun* a hooked stick with a net across it, used in lacrosse.

cross-examine *verb* cross-question someone, especially in a lawcourt. **cross-examination** *noun*

cross-eyed *adjective* with eyes that look or seem to look towards the nose.

crossfire *noun* lines of gunfire that cross each other.

crossing *noun* a place where people can cross a road, railway, etc.

cross-legged *adjective* & *adverb* with ankles crossed and knees spread apart.

crosspatch *noun* a bad-tempered person.

cross-question *verb* question someone carefully in order to test answers given to previous questions.

cross-reference *noun* a note telling people to look at another part of a book etc. for more information.

crossroads *noun* a place where two or more roads cross one another.

cross-section *noun* **1** a drawing of something as if it has been cut through. **2** a typical sample.

crosswise *adverb* & *adjective* with one thing crossing another.

crossword *noun* short for **crossword puzzle**, a puzzle in which words have to be guessed from clues and then written into the blank squares in a diagram.

crotch *noun* the part between the legs where they join the body; a similar angle in a forked part.

crotchet *noun* a note in music, lasting half as long as a minim (written ♩).

crotchety *adjective* peevish.

crouch *verb* lower your body, with your arms and legs bent.

croup (*say* kroop) *noun* a disease causing a hard cough and difficulty in breathing.

crow¹ *noun* a large black bird.
  as the crow flies in a straight line.
  crow's nest a lookout platform high up on a ship's mast.

crow² *verb* (**crowed** or **crew**, **crowing**) **1** make a shrill cry as a cock does. **2** boast; be triumphant. **crow** *noun*

crowbar *noun* an iron bar used as a lever.

crowd¹ *noun* a large number of people in one place.

crowd² *verb* **1** come together in a crowd. **2** cram; fill uncomfortably full.

crown¹ *noun* **1** an ornamental head-dress worn by a king or queen. **2** (often **Crown**) the sovereign, *This land belongs to the Crown.* **3** the highest part, *the crown of the road.* **4** a former coin worth 5 shillings (50 cents).
  crown of thorns a shiny starfish that destroys coral reefs.

crown² *verb* **1** place a crown on as a symbol of royal power or victory. **2** form or cover or decorate the top of something. **3** reward;

▶▶ T H E S A U R U S ◀◀

cross-examine *verb* cross-question, examine, grill, interrogate, question.
  cross-examination *noun* examination, interrogation, questioning.

crosspatch *noun* curmudgeon, grouch (*informal*), grump, malcontent, sourpuss (*informal*).

crossroads *noun* crossing, interchange, intersection, junction.

crouch *verb* bend, cower, duck, huddle, hunch, squat, stoop.

crow² *verb* **2** blow your own trumpet, boast, brag, gloat, show off, skite (*Australian informal*), swagger, swank (*informal*).

crowd¹ *noun* assembly, company, congregation, crush, flock, gathering, herd, horde, host, mass, mob, multitude, pack, rabble, swarm, throng.

crowd² *verb* **1** assemble, cluster, collect, congregate, flock, gather, herd, mill, swarm, throng. **2** cram, huddle, jam, pack, pile, press, shove, squash, squeeze, stuff.
  crowded *adjective* congested, full, jam-packed, overflowing, over-populated, packed, populous.

crown¹ *noun* **1** coronet, diadem, tiara. **3** apex, brow, crest, peak, pinnacle, summit, top.

crown² *verb* **1** enthrone, install, invest. **3** cap, complete, consummate, round off, top off.
  crowning *noun* coronation, enthronement.

▶▶DICTIONARY◀◀

make a successful end to something, *Our efforts were crowned with victory.* **4** (*slang*) hit on the head. [from Latin *corona* = garland or crown]

crucial (*say* **kroo**-shal) *adjective* most important. **crucially** *adverb* [from Latin *crucis* = of a cross]

crucible *noun* a melting-pot for metals.

crucifix *noun* (*plural* **crucifixes**) a model of the Cross or of Jesus Christ on the Cross. [from Latin, = fixed to a cross]

crucify *verb* (**crucified**, **crucifying**) put a person to death by nailing or binding the hands and feet to a cross. **crucifixion** *noun*

crude *adjective* **1** in a natural state; not yet refined, *crude oil.* **2** not well finished; rough, *a crude carving.* **3** vulgar. **crudely** *adverb*, **crudity** *noun* [from Latin *crudus* = raw, rough]

cruel *adjective* (**crueller**, **cruellest**) causing pain or suffering. **cruelly** *adverb*, **cruelty** *noun*

cruet *noun* a set of small containers for salt, pepper, oil, etc. for use at the table.

cruise[1] *noun* a pleasure-trip in a ship.

cruise[2] *verb* (**cruised**, **cruising**) **1** sail or travel at a moderate speed. **2** have a cruise.

cruiser *noun* **1** a fast warship. **2** a large motor boat.

crumb *noun* a tiny piece of bread, etc.

crumble *verb* (**crumbled**, **crumbling**) break or fall into small fragments. **crumbly** *adjective*

crumpet *noun* a soft flat cake made with yeast, eaten toasted with butter.

crumple *verb* (**crumpled**, **crumpling**) **1** crush or become crushed into creases. **2** collapse loosely.

crunch[1] *verb* **1** crush something noisily between the teeth. **2** make a sound like crunching.

crunch[2] *noun* crunching; a crunching sound. **crunchy** *adjective* **the crunch** (*informal*) a crucial event.

Crusade *noun* a military expedition made by Christians in the Middle Ages to recover Palestine from the Muslims who had conquered it. **Crusader** *noun*

crusade *noun* a campaign against something bad.

crush[1] *verb* **1** press something so that it gets broken or harmed. **2** crease or crumple. **3** defeat.

crush[2] *noun* (*plural* **crushes**) **1** a crowd of people pressed together. **2** a drink made with crushed fruit.

crust *noun* **1** the hard outer layer of something, especially bread. **2** the rocky outer layer of the earth.

▶▶THESAURUS◀◀

crucial *adjective* critical, decisive, important, key, momentous, pivotal, serious, significant, vital.

crude *adjective* **1** natural, raw, unprocessed, unrefined. **2** improvised, makeshift, primitive, rough, rudimentary, simple, unsophisticated. **3** blue, coarse, improper, indecent, lewd, obscene, ribald, rude, vulgar.

cruel *adjective* atrocious, barbaric, beastly, bloodthirsty, brutal, callous, cold-blooded, ferocious, fiendish, hard-hearted, harsh, heartless, inhuman, inhumane, mean, merciless, monstrous, pitiless, ruthless, sadistic, savage, severe, tyrannical, unkind, vicious, violent.

cruelty *noun* atrocity, barbarity, bestiality, brutality, callousness, ferocity, fiendishness, hard-heartedness, harshness, heartlessness, inhumanity, meanness, mercilessness, monstrousness, pitilessness, ruthlessness, sadism, savagery, severity, tyranny, unkindness, viciousness, violence.

cruise[1] *noun* journey, sail, trip, voyage.

cruise[2] *verb* **2** sail, voyage.

crumb *noun* bit, fragment, morsel, particle, piece, scrap, speck.

crumble *verb* break up, crush, decompose, disintegrate, fall apart, go to pieces, grind, powder, pulverise. **crumbly** *adjective* friable.

crumple *verb* **1** crease, crinkle, crush, rumple, screw up, wrinkle. **2** collapse, fall down, flop.

crunch[1] *verb* **1** chew, chomp, gnaw, masticate, munch.

crunch[2] *noun* **the crunch** acid test, moment of truth, showdown, test.

crusade *noun* campaign, drive, movement, push, struggle, war.

crush[1] *verb* **1** compress, crumble, crunch, grind, mangle, mash, pound, press, pulp, pulverise, shatter, smash, squash, squeeze. **2** crease, crinkle, crumple, rumple, scrunch, wrinkle. **3** conquer, defeat, overcome, overpower, overthrow, overwhelm, rout, subdue, suppress, thrash, trounce, vanquish.

crust *noun* **1** coating, incrustation, outside, rind, scab, skin.

▶▶ D I C T I O N A R Y ◀◀

crustacean (*say* krust-**ay**-shon) *noun* an animal with a shell, e.g. a crab.

crusty *adjective* (**crustier, crustiest**) 1 having a crisp crust. 2 having a harsh or irritable manner. **crustiness** *noun*

crutch *noun* (*plural* **crutches**) a support like a long walking stick for helping a lame person to walk.

cry[1] *noun* (*plural* **cries**) 1 a loud wordless sound expressing pain, grief, joy, etc. 2 a shout. 3 crying, *Have a good cry*.

cry[2] *verb* (**cried, crying**) 1 shed tears; weep. 2 call out loudly.

crypt *noun* a room under a church.

cryptic *adjective* hiding its meaning in a puzzling way. **cryptically** *adverb* [from Greek *kryptos* = hidden]

cryptogram *noun* something written in cipher. [from Greek *kryptos* = hidden, + *-gram*]

crystal *noun* 1 a transparent colourless mineral rather like glass. 2 very clear high-quality glass. 3 a small solid piece of certain substances, *crystals of snow and ice*. **crystalline** *adjective*

crystallise *verb* (**crystallised, crystallising**) 1 form into crystals. 2 become definite in form. **crystallisation** *noun*
crystallised fruit fruit preserved in sugar.

cub *noun* a young lion, tiger, fox, bear, etc.

Cub or **Cub Scout** a member of the junior branch of the Scout Association.

cubby hole a small compartment.

cube[1] *noun* 1 something that has six equal square sides. 2 the number produced by multiplying something by itself twice, *The cube of 3 is 3x3x3=27*.
cube root the number that gives a particular number if it is multiplied by itself twice, *The cube root of 27 is 3*.

cube[2] *verb* (**cubed, cubing**) 1 multiply a number by itself twice, *4 cubed is 4x4x4=64*. 2 cut into small cubes.

cubic *adjective* three-dimensional.
cubic foot, cubic metre, etc., the volume of a cube with sides that are one foot or one metre etc. long.

cubicle *noun* a compartment of a room.

cuckoo *noun* a bird that makes a sound like 'cuck-oo'.

cucumber *noun* a usually long green-skinned vegetable eaten raw or pickled.

cud *noun* half-digested food that a cow etc. brings back from its first stomach to chew again.

cuddle *verb* (**cuddled, cuddling**) put your arms closely round a person or animal that you love. **cuddly** *adjective*

cudgel[1] *noun* a short thick stick used as a weapon.

cudgel[2] *verb* (**cudgelled, cudgelling**) beat with a cudgel.
cudgel your brains think hard about a problem.

cue[1] *noun* something said or done that acts as a signal for an actor etc. to say or do something. [origin unknown]

cue[2] *noun* a long rod for striking the ball in billiards or snooker. [from *queue*]

cuff[1] *noun* 1 the end of a sleeve that fits round the wrist. 2 hitting somebody with your hand; a slap.

cuff[2] *verb* hit somebody with your hand.

cuisine (*say* kwiz-**een**) *noun* a style of cooking. [French, = kitchen]

cul-de-sac *noun* (*plural* **culs-de-sac**) a street with an opening at one end only; a dead end. [French, = bottom of a sack]

culinary *adjective* of cooking; for cooking.

▶▶ T H E S A U R U S ◀◀

crutch *noun* prop, support.

cry[1] *noun* 1,2 bellow, call, exclamation, howl, scream, screech, shout, shriek, squawk, squeak, squeal, wail, whimper, whine, whoop, yell, yelp, yowl.

cry[2] *verb* 1 bawl, blubber, break down, grizzle, howl, shed tears, snivel, sob, wail, weep, whimper. 2 bellow, call out, exclaim, roar, scream, shout, yell.

crypt *noun* undercroft, vault.

cryptic *adjective* baffling, coded, enigmatic, hidden, inscrutable, mysterious, obscure, perplexing, puzzling.

crystallise *verb* 2 take form, take shape.

cubby hole carrel, compartment, cubicle, niche, nook, pigeon-hole.

cube[2] *verb* 2 chop, cut, dice.

cubicle *noun* booth, carrel, compartment, cubby hole, stall.

cuddle *verb* caress, clasp, embrace, fondle, hug, nurse, squeeze.

cue[1] *noun* hint, prompt, reminder, sign, signal.

cul-de-sac *noun* blind alley, close, dead end.

cull *verb* **1** pick, *culling fruit.* **2** select and use, *culling lines from several poems.* **3** pick out and kill surplus animals from a flock. **cull** *noun*

culminate *verb* (**culminated, culminating**) reach its highest or last point. **culmination** *noun* [from Latin *culmen* = summit]

culpable *adjective* deserving blame. [from Latin *culpare* = to blame]

culprit *noun* the person who has done something wrong.

cult *noun* a religion; devotion to a person or thing.

cultivate *verb* (**cultivated, cultivating**) **1** use land to grow crops. **2** grow crops. **3** develop things by looking after them. **cultivation** *noun*, **cultivator** *noun*

culture *noun* **1** appreciation and understanding of literature, art, music, etc. **2** customs and traditions, *West Indian culture.* **3** improvement by care and training, *physical culture.* **4** cultivating things. **cultural** *adjective*

cultured *adjective* educated to appreciate literature, art, music, etc.

cultured pearl a pearl formed by an oyster when a speck of grit etc. is put into its shell.

culvert *noun* a drain that passes under a road or railway etc.

cumbersome *adjective* clumsy to carry or manage. (Compare *encumber.*)

cummerbund *noun* a broad sash.

cumulative *adjective* accumulating; increasing by continuous additions. [from Latin *cumulus* = heap]

cunning[1] *adjective* **1** clever at deceiving people. **2** cleverly designed or planned.

cunning[2] *noun* being cunning.

cup[1] *noun* **1** a small bowl-shaped container for drinking from. **2** anything shaped like a cup. **3** a goblet-shaped ornament given as a prize. **cupful** *noun*

cup[2] *verb* (**cupped, cupping**) form into the shape of a cup, *cup your hands.*

cupboard *noun* a recess or piece of furniture with a door, for storing things.

cupcake *noun* a small cake baked in a cup-shaped container.

cupidity (*say* kew-**pid**-it-ee) *noun* greed for gain. [from Latin *cupido* = desire]

cupola (*say* **kew**-pol-a) *noun* a small dome on a roof.

cur *noun* a scruffy or bad-tempered dog.

curable *adjective* able to be cured.

curate *noun* a member of the clergy who helps a vicar. [same origin as *cure*]

curative (*say* **kewr**-at-iv) *adjective* helping to cure illness.

curator (*say* kewr-**ay**-ter) *noun* a person in charge of a museum or other collection. [same origin as *cure*]

curb[1] *verb* restrain, *curb your impatience.*

curb[2] *noun* a restraint, *Put a curb on spending.* [from Latin *curvare* = to curve]

curd *noun* (also called **curds**) a thick substance formed when milk turns sour.

culminate *verb* climax, close, conclude, end up, finish, terminate, wind up.

culprit *noun* lawbreaker, malefactor, miscreant, offender, troublemaker, wrongdoer.

cult *noun* religion, sect.

cultivate *verb* **1** farm, till, work. **2** grow, produce, raise, tend. **3** develop, foster, nurture, refine, work on.

culture *noun* **2** art, arts, civilisation, customs, literature, music, society, traditions. **3** development, education, training.

cultured *adjective* civilised, cultivated, educated, enlightened, highbrow, intellectual, refined, sophisticated, well-bred.

cumbersome *adjective* awkward, bulky, clumsy, heavy, inconvenient, ponderous, unwieldy, weighty.

cumulative *adjective* accumulated, aggregate, combined.

cunning[1] *adjective* **1** artful, astute, calculating, clever, crafty, deceitful, devious, dodgy (*informal*), foxy, guileful, ingenious, knowing, machiavellian, scheming, sharp, shifty, shrewd, sly, sneaky, subtle, tricky, underhand, wily.

cunning[2] *noun* cleverness, craftiness, deceitfulness, deviousness, guile, ingenuity, shrewdness, slyness, subtlety, trickery, wiliness.

cup[1] *noun* **1** beaker, chalice, goblet, mug, tankard, teacup. **3** award, prize, trophy.

cupboard *noun* (*kinds of cupboard*) buffet, built-in, cabinet, chest, chiffonier, closet, dresser, larder, linen press, locker, pantry, safe, sideboard, wardrobe.

curator *noun* conservator, custodian, keeper, manager.

curb[1] *verb* check, contain, control, curtail, hold back, limit, moderate, rein in, restrain, restrict, slow down.

▶▶ D I C T I O N A R Y ◀◀

curdle *verb* (**curdled, curdling**) form into curds. **make someone's blood curdle** horrify or terrify him or her.

cure¹ *verb* (**cured, curing**) **1** get rid of someone's illness. **2** stop something bad. **3** treat something so as to preserve it, *Fish can be cured in smoke.*

cure² *noun* **1** something that cures a person or thing; a remedy. **2** curing; being cured, *We cannot promise a cure.* [from Latin *curare* = take care of something]

curfew *noun* a time or signal after which people must remain indoors until the next day.

curio *noun* (*plural* **curios**) an object that is a curiosity.

curiosity *noun* (*plural* **curiosities**) **1** being curious. **2** something unusual and interesting.

curious *adjective* **1** wanting to find out about things; inquisitive. **2** strange; unusual. **curiously** *adverb* [from Latin, = careful (compare *cure*)]

curl¹ *noun* a curve or coil, e.g. of hair.

curl² *verb* form into curls. **curl up** sit or lie with knees drawn up.

curler *noun* a device for curling the hair.

curlew *noun* a wading bird with a long curved bill.

curling *noun* a game played on ice with large flat stones.

curly *adjective* full of curls; curling.

currant *noun* **1** a small black dried grape used in cookery. **2** a small round red, black, or white berry.

currawong *noun* an Australian bird like a crow with a loud ringing call.

currency *noun* (*plural* **currencies**) **1** the money in use in a country. **2** the general use of something, *Some words have no currency now.* [from *current*]

current¹ *adjective* happening now; used now. **currently** *adverb*

current² *noun* **1** water or air etc. moving in one direction. **2** the flow of electricity along a wire etc. or through something. [from Latin *currens* = running]

curricle *noun* an old type of lightweight carriage drawn by two horses.

curriculum *noun* (*plural* **curricula**) a course of study.

curry¹ *noun* (*plural* **curries**) food cooked with spices that taste hot. **curried** *adjective* [from Tamil *kari* = sauce]

curry² *verb* (**curried, currying**) groom a horse with a rubber or plastic pad (called a **currycomb**). **curry favour** seek to win favour by flattering someone.

curse¹ *noun* **1** a call or prayer for a person or thing to be harmed; the evil produced by this. **2** something very unpleasant. **3** an angry word or words.

curse² *verb* (**cursed, cursing**) **1** make a curse. **2** use a curse against a person or thing. **be cursed with something** suffer from it.

cursor *noun* a movable indicator (usually a flashing light) on a VDU screen. [Latin, = runner (compare *current*)]

▶▶ T H E S A U R U S ◀◀

cure¹ *verb* **1** heal, make better, remedy. **2** correct, fix, mend, put right, rectify, remedy, repair.

cure² *noun* **1** antidote, corrective, medicine, remedy, restorative, therapy, treatment.

curiosity *noun* **1** inquisitiveness, interest, nosiness (*informal*), prying, snooping (*informal*). **2** curio, novelty, oddity, rarity.

curious *adjective* **1** inquiring, inquisitive, interested, nosy (*informal*), prying, snoopy (*informal*). **2** abnormal, bizarre, extraordinary, funny, mysterious, odd, peculiar, queer, strange, unusual, weird.

curl¹ *noun* dreadlock, kink, ringlet, wave.

curl² *verb* bend, coil, curve, loop, spiral, turn, twist, wind; (*curl hair*) crimp, frizz, perm, wave.

curly *adjective* crimped, frizzed, frizzy, permed, wavy.

currency *noun* **1** cash, coinage, legal tender, money.

current¹ *adjective* actual, contemporary, existing, latest, modern, present, present-day, prevailing, prevalent, up to date.

current² *noun* **1** flow, stream, tide.

curse¹ *noun* **1** evil spell, hex, jinx (*informal*), malediction. **3** blasphemy, expletive, oath, obscenity, profanity, swear-word.

curse² *verb* **1** damn, revile, swear at. **be cursed with** be afflicted with, be blighted with, be plagued with, be troubled with, suffer from.

▶▶ DICTIONARY ◀◀

cursory *adjective* hasty and not thorough, *a cursory inspection*. **cursorily** *adverb* [from Latin, = of a runner]

curt *adjective* brief and hasty or rude, *a curt reply*. **curtly** *adverb*, **curtness** *noun*

curtail *verb* **1** cut short, *The lesson was curtailed*. **2** reduce, *We must curtail our spending*. **curtailment** *noun*

curtain *noun* **1** a piece of material hung at a window or door. **2** the large cloth screen hung at the front of a stage.

curtsy[1] *noun* (*plural* **curtsies**) a movement of respect made by women and girls, putting one foot behind the other and bending the knees.

curtsy[2] *verb* (**curtsied**, **curtsying**) make a curtsy. [= *courtesy*]

curvature *noun* curving; a curved shape.

curve[1] *verb* (**curved**, **curving**) bend smoothly.

curve[2] *noun* a curved line or shape. **curvy** *adjective*

cushion[1] *noun* **1** a bag, usually of cloth, filled with soft material so that it is comfortable to sit on or lean against. **2** anything soft or springy that protects or supports something, *The hovercraft travels on a cushion of air*.

cushion[2] *verb* **1** supply with cushions, *cushioned seats*. **2** protect from the effects of a knock or shock etc., *His fur hat cushioned the blow*.

cushy *adjective* (*informal*) pleasant and easy, *a cushy job*. [from Hindi *khus* = pleasant]

cusp *noun* a pointed end where two curves meet, e.g. a tip of a crescent moon. [from Latin *cuspis* = point]

custard *noun* **1** a sweet yellow sauce made with milk. **2** a pudding made with beaten eggs and milk.

custodian *noun* a person who has custody of something; a keeper.

custody *noun* **1** care and supervision; guardianship. **2** imprisonment.
take into custody arrest. [from Latin *custos* = guardian]

custom *noun* **1** the usual way of behaving or doing something. **2** regular business from customers.
customs *plural noun* taxes charged on goods brought into a country; the place at a port or airport where officials examine your luggage.

customary *adjective* according to custom; usual. **customarily** *adverb*

custom-built *adjective* made according to a customer's order.

customer *noun* a person who uses a shop, bank, or other business.

cut[1] *verb* (**cut**, **cutting**) **1** divide or wound or separate something by using a knife, axe, scissors, etc. **2** make a thing shorter or smaller; remove part of something, *They are*

▶▶ THESAURUS ◀◀

cursory *adjective* brief, hasty, hurried, perfunctory, quick, slapdash, superficial.

curt *adjective* abrupt, blunt, brief, brusque, gruff, offhand, short, snappy (*informal*), terse.

curtail *verb* **1** abbreviate, abridge, cut short, shorten, truncate. **2** curb, cut back, decrease, reduce, restrain, restrict, trim.

curtain *noun* **1** drape, hanging, screen.

curtsy[1] *noun* bob, bow, obeisance.

curtsy[2] *verb* bob, bow, genuflect.

curve[1] *verb* arc, arch, bend, bow, circle, coil, kink, loop, spiral, turn, twist, wind.
curved *adjective* arched, bent, bowed, concave, convex, crescent-shaped, crooked, humped, looped, rounded, serpentine, sinuous, spiral, tortuous, twisting, winding.

curve[2] *noun* arc, arch, bend, bow, crescent, crook, curl, curvature, kink, loop, spiral, turn, twist.

cushion[1] *noun* **1** bolster, hassock, kneeler, pad, pillow.

cushion[2] *verb* **2** absorb, buffer, damp, dampen, deaden, lessen, reduce, soften.

cushy *adjective* easy, pleasant, soft (*informal*), undemanding.

custodian *noun* caretaker, curator, guardian, keeper, steward, warden.

custody *noun* **1** care, charge, guardianship, hands, keeping. **2** detention, imprisonment, jail, prison.

custom *noun* **1** convention, habit, practice, routine, tradition, way, wont. **2** business, patronage, support, trade.
customs *noun* duty, import tax, levy, tariff.

customary *adjective* accustomed, habitual, normal, ordinary, regular, routine, standard, traditional, typical, usual, wonted.

customer *noun* buyer, client, consumer, patron, purchaser, shopper.

cut[1] *verb* **1** amputate, bisect, carve, chip, chisel, chop, cleave, clip, crop, cube, detach, dice, dissect, divide, dock, engrave, fell, gash, gouge, guillotine, hack, hew, incise, knife, lacerate,

cutting all their prices. **3** divide a pack of playing cards. **4** hit a ball with a chopping movement. **5** go through or across something. **6** stay away from something deliberately, *She cut her music lesson.* **7** make a sound-recording. **8** switch off electrical power or an engine etc.

cut a corner pass round it very closely.

cut and dried already decided.

cut back reduce. **cutback** *noun*

cut in interrupt.

cut lunch (*Australian*) a packed lunch, usually sandwiches.

cut off interrupt; prevent from continuing; isolate.

cut out omit; shape by cutting; (*informal*) stop doing or using something.

cut² *noun* **1** cutting; the result of cutting. **2** a small wound. **3** a reduction. **4** (*informal*) a share.

be a cut above something be superior.

cute *adjective* (*informal*) **1** clever. **2** attractive. **cutely** *adverb*, **cuteness** *noun* [from *acute*]

cuticle (*say* **kew**-tik-ul) *noun* the skin at the base of a nail.

cutlass *noun* (*plural* **cutlasses**) a short sword with a broad curved blade.

cutlery *noun* knives, forks, and spoons.

cutlet *noun* a thick slice of meat for cooking.

cut-out *noun* a shape cut out of paper, cardboard, etc.

cutter *noun* **1** a person or thing that cuts. **2** a small fast sailing-ship.

cutting *noun* **1** a steep-sided passage cut through high ground for a road or railway.

2 a clipping. **3** a piece cut from a plant to form a new plant.

cuttlefish *noun* (*plural* **cuttlefish**) a sea creature that sends out a black liquid when attacked.

cyanide *noun* a very poisonous chemical.

cyber- *prefix* relating to computers and electronic communication (as in *cyberspace*).

cycle¹ *noun* **1** a bicycle or motorcycle. **2** a series of events that are regularly repeated in the same order. **cyclic** *adjective*, **cyclical** *adjective*

cycle² *verb* (**cycled, cycling**) ride a bicycle etc. **cyclist** *noun* [from Greek *kyklos* = circle]

cyclone *noun* a wind that rotates round a calm central area. **cyclonic** *adjective*

cygnet *noun* (*say* **sig**-nit) a young swan.

cylinder *noun* an object with straight sides and circular ends. **cylindrical** *adjective* [from Greek *kylindein* = to roll]

cymbal *noun* a percussion instrument consisting of a metal plate that is hit to make a ringing sound.

cynic (*say* **sin**-ik) *noun* a person who believes that people's reasons for doing things are selfish or bad, and shows this by sneering at them. **cynical** *adjective*, **cynically** *adverb*, **cynicism** *noun*

cypress *noun* (*plural* **cypresses**) an evergreen tree with dark leaves.

cyst (*say* sist) *noun* an abnormal swelling containing fluid or soft matter.

czar (*say* zar) *noun* a tsar.

lance, lop, mangle, mince, mow, mutilate, nick, notch, pare, pierce, pink, prune, reap, remove, saw, score, scythe, sever, shave, shear, shred, slash, slice, slit, snick, snip, split, stab, trim, truncate, whittle, wound. **2** abbreviate, abridge, condense, curtail, reduce, shorten. **5** cross, go across, intersect.

cut back downsize (*informal*), economise, rationalise, reduce, retrench.

cutback *noun* cut, economy, rationalisation, reduction, retrenchment.

cut in break in, butt in, interrupt, intervene.

cut off 1 disconnect, discontinue, halt, stop, suspend. **2** isolate, maroon, separate.

cut out censor, delete, eliminate, excise, exclude, leave out, omit, remove.

cut² *noun* **2** gash, groove, incision, indentation, laceration, nick, notch, slash, slit, snick, wound.

3 decline, decrease, fall, lowering, reduction. **4** commission, percentage, portion, share, slice.

cute *adjective* **2** adorable, attractive, pretty, sweet (*informal*).

cutting *noun* **2** clipping, extract, piece, section. **3** slip.

cycle¹ *noun* **1** bicycle, moped, motorcycle, motor scooter, penny farthing, scooter, tandem, tricycle. **2** repetition, revolution, rotation, round, sequence, series.

cycle² *verb* pedal, ride.

cyclone *noun* hurricane, tropical cyclone, typhoon.

cynical *adjective* jaundiced, sardonic, sceptical, scoffing, sneering, suspicious.

▶ Dd ◀

dab¹ *noun* **1** a quick gentle touch. **2** a small lump, *a dab of butter.*

dab² *verb* (**dabbed, dabbing**) touch quickly and gently.

dabble *verb* (**dabbled, dabbling**) **1** splash something about in water. **2** do something as a hobby, *dabble in chemistry.*

dachshund (*say* **daks**-huund) *noun* a small dog with a long body and very short legs. [German, = badger-dog]

dad or **daddy** *noun* (*plural* **daddies**) (*informal*) father.

daddy-long-legs *noun* (*plural* **daddy-long-legs**) a spider with long thin legs.

daffodil *noun* a yellow flower that grows from a bulb.

daft *adjective* (*informal*) silly; crazy.

dag *noun* (*Australian*) **1** a lock of wool clotted with dung on a sheep. **2** (*informal*) a socially awkward adolescent.

dagger *noun* a pointed knife with two sharp edges, used as a weapon.

daggy *adjective* (*Australian informal*) unfashionable.

dahlia (*say* **day**-lee-a) *noun* a garden plant with brightly-coloured flowers. [named after a Swedish botanist, A. Dahl]

daily *adverb* & *adjective* every day.

dainty *adjective* (**daintier, daintiest**) small, delicate, and pretty. **daintily** *adverb*, **daintiness** *noun*

dairy *noun* (*plural* **dairies**) a place where milk, butter, etc. are produced or sold.

dais (*say* **day**-iss) *noun* a low platform, especially at the end of a room.

daisy *noun* (*plural* **daisies**) a small flower with white petals and a yellow centre. [from *day's eye*]

dale *noun* a valley.

dally *verb* (**dallied, dallying**) dawdle.

dam¹ *noun* **1** a wall built to hold water back. **2** (*Australian*) an artificial pond with earth walls.

dam² *verb* (**dammed, damming**) hold water back with a dam.

dam³ *noun* the mother of a horse or dog etc. (Compare *sire*.) [from *dame*]

damage¹ *noun* something that reduces the value or spoils the appearance of a thing or spoils its appearance.

damage² *verb* (**damaged, damaging**) cause damage to something.

damages *plural noun* money paid as compensation for an injury or loss.

Dame *noun* the title of a lady who has been given the equivalent of a knighthood.

dame *noun* a comic middle-aged woman in a pantomime, usually played by a man. [from Latin *domina* = lady]

damn *verb* curse. [from Latin *damnare* = condemn]

damnation *noun* being damned or condemned to hell.

▶▶THESAURUS◀◀

dab¹ *noun* **1** pat, touch.

dab² *verb* apply, daub, pat.

dabble *verb* **1** dip, paddle, splash. **2** play, potter, tinker.

dagger *noun* dirk, knife, kris, stiletto.

daily *adjective* day-to-day, diurnal, everyday.

dainty *adjective* delicate, dinky (*informal*), exquisite, fine, pretty, small.

dais *noun* platform, podium, rostrum, stage.

dally *verb* dawdle, delay, dilly-dally (*informal*), hang about, linger, loiter, take your time, tarry.

dam¹ *noun* **1** bank, barrage, barrier, embankment, wall, weir. **2** pond, reservoir, tank (*Australian*).

damage¹ *noun* destruction, devastation, harm, havoc, hurt, injury, loss, mutilation, ruin.

damage² *verb* blemish, blight, break, bruise, bust (*informal*), chip, cripple, dent, destroy, devastate, flaw, harm, hurt, impair, injure, mangle, mar, mutilate, ravage, ruin, sabotage, scar, scratch, spoil, vandalise, wound, wreck.

damages *plural noun* compensation, costs, indemnity, reparations, restitution.

damnation *noun* eternal punishment, hell, perdition.

▶▶ D I C T I O N A R Y ◀◀

damp[1] *adjective* slightly wet; not quite dry. **damply** *adverb*, **dampness** *noun*

damp[2] *noun* moisture in the air or on a surface or all through something.
damp course a layer of material built into a wall to prevent dampness in the ground from rising.

damp[3] *verb* 1 make damp; moisten. 2 reduce the strength of something, *The defeat damped their enthusiasm.*

dampen *verb* damp.

damper *noun* 1 a metal plate that can be moved to increase or decrease the movement of air flowing into a fire or furnace etc. 2 something that reduces sound or enthusiasm etc. 3 (*Australian*) a simple kind of bread baked in ashes.

damsel *noun* (*old use*) a young woman.

damson *noun* a small dark-purple plum.

dance[1] *verb* (**danced**, **dancing**) move about in time to music.

dance[2] *noun* 1 a set of movements used in dancing. 2 a piece of music for dancing to. 3 a party or gathering where people dance.
dancer *noun*

dandelion *noun* a yellow wild flower with jagged leaves. [from French *dent-de-lion* = tooth of a lion]

dandruff *noun* tiny white flakes of dead skin in a person's hair.

dandy *noun* (*plural* **dandies**) 1 a man who likes to look very smart. 2 (*Australian*) an ice-cream bucket.

danger *noun* something dangerous.

dangerous *adjective* likely to kill or do great harm. **dangerously** *adverb*

dangle *verb* (**dangled**, **dangling**) hang or swing loosely.

dank *adjective* damp and chilly.

dapper *adjective* dressed neatly and smartly.

dappled *adjective* marked with patches of a different colour.

dare[1] *verb* (**dared**, **daring**) 1 be brave or bold enough to do something. 2 challenge a person to do something risky.

dare[2] *noun* a challenge to do something risky.

daredevil *noun* a person who is very bold and reckless.

daring[1] *noun* boldness; courage.

daring[2] *adjective* bold; willing to take risks.

dark[1] *adjective* 1 with little or no light. 2 not light in colour, *a dark suit.* 3 having dark hair. 4 secret, *Keep it dark!* **darkly** *adverb*, **darkness** *noun*

dark[2] *noun* 1 absence of light, *Cats can see in the dark.* 2 the time when darkness has come, *She went out after dark.*

darken *verb* make or become dark.

▶▶ T H E S A U R U S ◀◀

damp[1] *adjective* clammy, dank, humid, moist, muggy, sodden, soggy, steamy, sticky, wet.

damp[3] *verb* 1 dampen, moisten, sprinkle, wet. 2 cool, dampen, dash, discourage, dull, restrain.

dance[1] *verb* bob, caper, cavort, frolic, gambol, jig, jump, leap, pirouette, prance, romp, skip, trip, twirl.

dance[2] *noun* 3 ball, disco (*informal*), formal, prom (*American*), social.

danger *noun* hazard, jeopardy, peril, pitfall, risk, snare, threat, trouble.

dangerous *adjective* (*a dangerous undertaking*) chancy, dicey (*slang*), dodgy (*informal*), hairy (*slang*), hazardous, perilous, precarious, risky, tricky, uncertain, unsafe; (*a dangerous criminal, animal, etc.*) desperate, destructive, ferocious, menacing, savage, threatening, treacherous, vicious, violent, wild.

dangle *verb* hang, sway, swing.

dapper *adjective* chic, natty (*informal*), neat, smart, snazzy (*informal*), spruce, trim, well-dressed.

dappled *adjective* mottled, piebald, pied, skewbald, spotted.

dare[1] *verb* 1 be bold enough, be game, have the nerve, presume, venture. 2 challenge, defy, taunt.

daring[1] *noun* boldness, bravery, courage, intrepidity, nerve, pluck, prowess, valour.

daring[2] *adjective* adventurous, audacious, bold, brave, courageous, fearless, game, heroic, intrepid, plucky, reckless, valiant, venturesome.

dark[1] *adjective* 1 black, dim, dingy, dull, dusky, gloomy, moonless, murky, overcast, pitch-dark, shadowy, shady, starless, unlit. 2 (*dark skin*) black, brown, dusky, swarthy, tanned. 3 black, brown, brunette. 4 confidential, hidden, hush-hush (*informal*), secret.

dark[2] *noun* 1 blackness, darkness, dimness, gloom. 2 dusk, evening, gloaming, night, nightfall, night-time, sunset, twilight.

darken *verb* become overcast, blacken, cloud over.

▶▶▶ D I C T I O N A R Y ◀◀◀

dark-room *noun* a room kept dark for developing and printing photographs.

darling *noun* someone who is loved very much. [from Old English *dearling* = little dear]

darn¹ *verb* mend a hole by weaving threads across it.

darn² *noun* a place that has been darned.

dart¹ *noun* 1 an object with a sharp point thrown at a target. 2 a darting movement. 3 a tapering tuck stitched in something to make it fit.

dart² *verb* run suddenly and quickly.

darts *noun* a game in which darts are thrown at a circular board (**dartboard**).

dash¹ *verb* 1 run quickly; rush. 2 throw a thing violently against something, *The storm dashed the ship against the rocks.*

dash² *noun* (*plural* **dashes**) 1 a short quick run; a rush. 2 energy; liveliness. 3 a small amount, *Add a dash of brandy.* 4 a short line (–) used in writing or printing.

dashboard *noun* a panel with dials and controls in front of the driver of a car etc.

dashing *adjective* lively and showy.

dastardly *adjective* contemptible and cowardly.

data (*say* **day**-ta) *plural noun* pieces of information. **databank** *noun*, **database** *noun*

Usage It is best to use this word as a plural (e.g. *Here are the data*) because it is really a Latin plural meaning 'things given'. (The singular is *datum*.)

date¹ *noun* 1 the time when something happens or happened or was written, stated as the day, month and year (or any of these). 2 an appointment to meet. 3 (*informal*) a person with whom one has a social engagement.

date² *verb* (**dated**, **dating**) 1 give a date to something. 2 have existed from a particular time, *The church dates from 1895.* 3 seem old-fashioned. [from Latin *data* = given (at a certain time)]

date³ *noun* a small sweet brown fruit that grows on a kind of palm-tree.

daub *verb* paint or smear something clumsily. **daub** *noun*

daughter *noun* a girl or woman who is someone's child.

daughter-in-law *noun* (*plural* **daughters-in-law**) a son's wife.

daunt *verb* make somebody afraid or discouraged. **daunting** *adjective*

dauntless *adjective* brave; not to be daunted. **dauntlessly** *adverb*

dawdle *verb* (**dawdled**, **dawdling**) go slowly and lazily. **dawdler** *noun*

▶▶▶ T H E S A U R U S ◀◀◀

darling *noun* beloved, dear, love, pet, sweet, sweetheart.

darn¹ *verb* mend, repair, sew.

dart¹ *noun* 1 arrow, missile, projectile, shaft.

dart² *verb* bolt, dash, jump, leap, race, run, scoot, shoot, spring, streak, tear, zip.

dash¹ *verb* 1 bolt, dart, fly, gallop, hasten, hurry, hurtle, hustle, race, run, rush, scoot, shoot, speed, sprint, stampede, streak, sweep, tear, whiz, zip, zoom. 2 fling, hurl, knock, shatter, smash, strike, throw.

dash² *noun* 1 bolt, run, rush, sprint, spurt. 2 energy, flair, gusto, liveliness, panache, pizazz (*informal*), spirit, style, verve, vigour, vivacity, zest. 3 drop, hint, splash, sprinkling, suggestion, touch.

dashing *adjective* bold, debonair, gallant, plucky, smart, spirited, stylish.

data *plural noun* evidence, facts, figures, information, material.

date¹ *noun* 1 age, epoch, era, period, time, vintage. 2 appointment, arrangement, assignation, booking, commitment, engagement, meeting, rendezvous. 3 boyfriend, companion, escort, girlfriend, partner.

date² *verb* 2 (*date from*) come from, have existed from, originate in.

daub *verb* paint, plaster, slap, slop, smear.

daunt *verb* alarm, discourage, dishearten, dismay, frighten, intimidate, perturb, put off, scare, unnerve.
daunting *adjective* awesome, fearsome, forbidding, formidable, frightening, overwhelming.

dauntless *adjective* bold, brave, courageous, fearless, gallant, game, heroic, intrepid, plucky, unafraid, undaunted, valiant.

dawdle *verb* dally, delay, dilly-dally (*informal*), hang about, lag behind, linger, loiter, straggle, take your time.
dawdler *noun* laggard, slowcoach, sluggard, straggler.

▶▶▶DICTIONARY◀◀◀

dawn¹ *noun* **1** the time when the sun rises. **2** the beginning.

dawn² *verb* **1** begin to grow light in the morning. **2** begin to be realised, *The truth dawned on them.*

day *noun* **1** the 24 hours between midnight and the next midnight. **2** the light part of this time. **3** a particular day, *sports day.* **4** a period of time, *in Queen Victoria's day.*

daybreak *noun* dawn.

daydream¹ *noun* pleasant thoughts of something you would like to happen.

daydream² *verb* have daydreams.

daylight *noun* **1** the light of day. **2** dawn.

dazed *adjective* unable to think or see clearly. **daze** *noun*

dazzle *verb* (**dazzled, dazzling**) **1** make a person unable to see clearly because of too much bright light. **2** amaze or impress a person by a splendid display.

de- *prefix* **1** removing (as in *defrost*). **2** down, away (as in *descend*). **3** completely (as in *denude*). (from Latin *de* = away from]

deacon *noun* **1** a member of the clergy ranking below bishops and priests. **2** (in some Churches) a church officer who is not a member of the clergy. **deaconess** *noun* [from Greek *diakonos* = servant]

dead *adjective* **1** no longer alive. **2** not lively. **3** not functioning; no longer in use. **4** exact; complete, *a dead loss.*

dead end a road or passage with one end closed; a situation where there is no chance of making progress.

dead heat a race in which two or more winners finish exactly together.

deaden *verb* make pain or noise etc. weaker.

deadline *noun* a time limit. [originally this meant a line round an American military prison; if a prisoner went beyond it he could be shot]

deadlock *noun* a situation in which no progress can be made.

deadly *adjective* (**deadlier, deadliest**) likely to kill.

deaf *adjective* **1** unable to hear. **2** unwilling to hear. **deafness** *noun*

deafen *verb* make somebody become deaf, especially by a very loud noise.

deal¹ *verb* (**dealt, dealing**) **1** hand something out; give. **2** give out cards for a card-game. **3** do business; trade, *He deals in scrap metal.* **dealer** *noun*

deal with be concerned with, *This book deals with words and meanings*; do what is needed, *deal with the problem.*

▶▶▶THESAURUS◀◀◀

dawn¹ *noun* **1** break of day, cock-crow, crack of dawn, daybreak, first light, sunrise, sun-up. **2** beginning, birth, inception, onset, origin, start, threshold.

dawn² *verb* **2** (*dawn on*) occur to, strike.

day *noun* **2** daylight, daytime. **4** age, epoch, era, period, time.

daydream¹ *noun* castle in the air, dream, fantasy, illusion, pipe dream, reverie.

daydream² *verb* dream, fantasise, muse.

daylight *noun* **1** daytime, light, sunlight, sunshine. **2** break of day, dawn, morning, sunrise.

dazed *adjective* bewildered, confused, stunned, stupefied. **daze** *noun* bewilderment, confusion, muddle, shock, stupor, trance.

dazzle *verb* **1** blind, daze. **2** amaze, awe, blind, confuse, impress, overawe, stun. **dazzling** *adjective* blinding, brilliant, radiant, resplendent, sparkling.

dead *adjective* **1** deceased, departed, late, lifeless. **2** dormant, inactive, inert, quiet, slow, sluggish, stagnant, static. **3** defunct, disused,

extinct, obsolete. **4** absolute, complete, thorough, total, utter.

dead end blind alley, close, cul-de-sac.

dead heat draw, tie.

deaden *verb* (*deaden pain*) anaesthetise, dull, kill, numb, subdue; (*deaden noise*) damp, muffle, mute, quieten, soften, stifle, suppress.

deadline *noun* time limit.

deadlock *noun* halt, impasse, stalemate, stand-off, standstill.

deadly *adjective* fatal, lethal, mortal, terminal.

deaf *adjective* **1** hard of hearing, hearing-impaired, stone-deaf.

deal¹ *verb* **1** allocate, allot, apportion, distribute, divide, dole out, give out, hand out, share out. **3** do business, handle, market, sell, trade, traffic. **dealer** *noun* distributor, merchant, peddler (*of drugs*), retailer, salesperson, seller, shop-keeper, stockist, supplier, trader, trafficker, vendor, wholesaler. **deal with 1** be about, be concerned with, consider, cover, touch on, treat. **2** attend to, cope with, grapple with, handle, look after, manage, see to, sort out, tackle, take care of, treat.

▶▶ D I C T I O N A R Y ◀◀

deal² *noun* **1** an agreement or bargain. **2** someone's turn to deal at cards.
a good deal or **a great deal** a large amount.

deal³ *noun* sawn fir or pine wood.

dean *noun* **1** an important member of the clergy in a cathedral etc. **2** a college or university official; the head of a university faculty etc. **deanery** *noun*

dear *adjective* **1** loved very much. **2** a polite greeting in letters, *Dear Sir*. **3** expensive. **dearly** *adverb*, **dearness** *noun*

dearth (*say* derth) *noun* a scarcity.

death *noun* dying; the end of life.

deathly *adjective* & *adverb* like death.

death-trap *noun* a dangerous place, vehicle etc.

debar *verb* (**debarred, debarring**) forbid; ban, *He was debarred from the contest.*

debase *verb* (**debased, debasing**) reduce the quality or value of something. **debasement** *noun*

debatable *adjective* questionable; that can be argued against.

debate¹ *noun* a formal discussion.

debate² *verb* (**debated, debating**) hold a debate. **debater** *noun*

debilitate *verb* make weak.

debility (*say* dib-**il**-it-ee) *noun* weakness.

debit¹ *noun* an entry in an account-book showing how much money is owed. (Compare *credit*.)

debit² *verb* (**debited, debiting**) enter something as a debit in an account-book. [from Latin *debitum* = what is owed]

debonair (*say* deb-on-**air**) *adjective* cheerful and confident. [from French *de bon air* = of good disposition]

debris (*say* **deb**-ree) *noun* scattered broken pieces of something; rubbish left behind. [from French *débris* = broken down]

debt (*say* det) *noun* something that you owe someone.
in debt owing money etc. [same origin as *debit*]

debtor (*say* **det**-or) *noun* a person who owes money to someone.

debut (*say* **day**-bew) *noun* someone's first public appearance. [from French *débuter* = begin]

deca- *prefix* ten (as in *decathlon*). [from Greek *deka* = ten]

decade (*say* **dek**-ayd) *noun* a period of ten years.

decadent (*say* **dek**-a-dent) *adjective* becoming less good than it was. **decadence** *noun* [same origin as *decay*]

decamp *verb* **1** pack up and leave a camp. **2** go away suddenly or secretly.

decant (*say* dik-**ant**) *verb* pour wine etc. gently from one container into another.

decanter (*say* dik-**ant**-er) *noun* a decorative glass bottle into which wine etc. is poured for serving.

decapitate *verb* (**decapitated, decapitating**) behead. **decapitation** *noun* [from *de-*, + Latin *caput* = head]

decathlon *noun* an athletic contest in which each competitor takes part in ten events. [from *deca-*, + Greek *athlon* = contest]

▶▶ T H E S A U R U S ◀◀

deal² *noun* **1** agreement, arrangement, bargain, contract, pact, settlement, transaction.
a good deal see LOT.

dear *adjective* **1** beloved, cherished, close, darling, loved, precious, treasured, valued. **3** costly, exorbitant, expensive, extortionate, pricey (*informal*).

dearth *noun* absence, deficiency, lack, paucity, scarcity, shortage, want.

death *noun* decease (*formal*), demise (*formal*), dying, end, passing.
put to death execute, kill, slay.

deathly *adjective* ashen, cadaverous, deathlike, ghostly, pale.

debatable *adjective* arguable, contentious, controversial, disputable, dubious, moot, questionable.

debate¹ *noun* argument, conference, controversy, discussion, dispute, wrangle.

debate² *verb* argue, contest, discuss, dispute, wrangle over.

debilitate *verb* cripple, disable, enervate, enfeeble, incapacitate, weaken.

debris *noun* detritus, flotsam, fragments, litter, remains, rubbish, rubble, wreckage.

debt *noun* due, liability, obligation.

decadent *adjective* corrupt, debased, degenerate, depraved, immoral.

decapitate *verb* behead, guillotine.

▶▶ D I C T I O N A R Y ◀◀

decay *verb* **1** go bad; rot. **2** become less good or less strong. **decay** *noun*

decease (*say* dis-**eess**) *noun* death.

deceased *adjective* dead.

deceit (*say* dis-**eet**) *noun* deceiving; a deception. **deceitful** *adjective*, **deceitfully** *adverb*

deceive *verb* (**deceived**, **deceiving**) cause a person to believe something that is not true. **deceiver** *noun*

decent *adjective* **1** respectable; proper; suitable. **2** (*informal*) kind. **decently** *adverb*, **decency** *noun*

deception *noun* deceiving someone; a trick. **deceptive** *adjective*, **deceptively** *adverb*

deci- (*say* **dess**-ee) *prefix* one-tenth (as in *decimetre*). [same origin as *decimal*]

decibel (*say* **dess**-ib-el) *noun* a unit for measuring the loudness of sound. [originally one-tenth of the unit called a *bel*]

decide *verb* (**decided**, **deciding**) **1** make up your mind; make a choice. **2** settle a contest or argument. **decider** *noun*

decided *adjective* **1** having clear and definite opinions. **2** noticeable, *a decided difference*. **decidedly** *adverb*

deciduous (*say* dis-**id**-yoo-us) *adjective* losing its leaves in autumn, *a deciduous tree, not an evergreen tree*. [from Latin *decidere* = fall off]

decimal¹ *adjective* using tens or tenths. **decimal fraction** a fraction with tenths shown as numbers after a dot (³⁄₁₀ is 0.3; 1½ is 1.5). **decimal point** the dot in a decimal fraction.

decimal² *noun* a decimal fraction. [from Latin *decimus* = tenth]

decimalise *verb* (**decimalised**, **decimalising**) express something as a decimal. **decimalisation** *noun*

decimate (*say* **dess**-im-ayt) *verb* (**decimated**, **decimating**) **1** destroy one-tenth of. **2** (loosely) destroy a large part of, *The famine decimated the population*. [from Latin *decimare* = kill every tenth man (this was the ancient Roman punishment for an army guilty of mutiny or other serious crime)]

decipher (*say* dis-**I**-fer) *verb* **1** decode. **2** work out the meaning of something written badly. **decipherment** *noun*

decision *noun* **1** deciding; what you have decided. **2** determination.

decisive (*say* dis-**I**-siv) *adjective* **1** that settles or ends something, *a decisive battle*. **2** full of determination; resolute. **decisively** *adverb*, **decisiveness** *noun*

deck¹ *noun* **1** a floor on a ship or bus. **2** a level surface in various devices.

▶▶ T H E S A U R U S ◀◀

decay *verb* **1** break down, decompose, deteriorate, disintegrate, go bad, go off, go rotten, moulder, perish, putrefy, rot, spoil.

deceased *adjective* dead, departed, late.

deceit *noun* artifice, cheating, chicanery, cunning, deceitfulness, deception, dishonesty, double-dealing, duplicity, fraud, guile, humbug, hypocrisy, lies, misrepresentation, pretence, skulduggery (*informal*), treachery, trickery, untruthfulness, wiliness.

deceitful *adjective* crafty, crooked, cunning, devious, dishonest, false, hypocritical, lying, machiavellian, phoney (*informal*), shifty, sneaky, treacherous, tricky, two-faced, underhand, unfaithful, untrustworthy.

deceive *verb* bamboozle (*informal*), beguile, bluff, cheat, con (*informal*), defraud, delude, diddle (*informal*), double-cross, dupe, fool, have (*slang*), have on (*informal*), hoax, hoodwink, kid (*informal*), mislead, rip off (*informal*), string along (*informal*), suck in (*informal*), swindle, take for a ride (*informal*), take in, trick.

decent *adjective* **1** acceptable, appropriate, becoming, correct, decorous, honourable, law-abiding, polite, proper, respectable, seemly, suitable, upright. **2** civil, considerate, fair, generous, good, kind, obliging, sporting.

deception *noun* bluff, con (*informal*), fraud, hoax, lie, pretence, ruse, sham, subterfuge, swindle, swizz (*informal*), trick; see also DECEIT.

deceptive *adjective* deceiving, false, illusory, misleading, specious, unreliable.

decide *verb* **1** choose, elect, opt for, pick, plump for, select. **2** adjudicate, conclude, determine, judge, resolve, rule, settle.

decided *adjective* **1** adamant, determined, firm, fixed, resolute. **2** clear, clear-cut, definite, distinct, marked, noticeable, obvious, pronounced, unmistakable.

decipher *verb* crack, decode, figure out, interpret, make out, read, translate, work out.

decision *noun* **1** adjudication, conclusion, determination, finding, judgement, resolution, ruling, sentence, verdict; see also CHOICE¹.

decisive *adjective* **1** conclusive, critical, crucial, deciding, significant. **2** decided, determined, firm, resolute, unhesitating.

deck¹ *noun* **1** floor, level, platform, storey.

►►DICTIONARY◄◄

deck² *verb* decorate with something.

deckchair *noun* a folding chair with a canvas or plastic seat.

declaim *verb* make a speech etc. loudly and dramatically. **declamation** *noun* [from *de-*, + Latin *clamare* = to shout]

declare *verb* (**declared, declaring**) **1** say something clearly or firmly. **2** tell customs officials that you have goods on which you ought to pay duty. **3** end a cricket innings before all the batsmen are out. **declaration** *noun*
declare war announce that you are starting a war against someone. [from *de-*, + Latin *clarare* = make clear]

decline¹ *verb* (**declined, declining**) **1** refuse. **2** become weaker or smaller. **3** slope downwards.

decline² *noun* a gradual decrease or loss of strength. [from *de-*, + Latin *clinare* = bend]

decode *verb* (**decoded, decoding**) find the meaning of something written in code. **decoder** *noun*

decompose *verb* (**decomposed, decomposing**) decay. **decomposition** *noun*

decompression *noun* reducing air-pressure.

decontamination *noun* getting rid of the harmful effects caused by poisonous chemicals or radioactive material.

décor (*say* **day**-kor) *noun* the style of furnishings and decorations used in a room etc. [French (compare *decorate*)]

decorate *verb* (**decorated, decorating**) **1** make something look more beautiful or colourful. **2** put fresh paint or paper on walls. **3** give somebody an award. **decoration** *noun*, **decorator** *noun*, **decorative** *adjective* [from Latin *decor* = beauty]

decorous (*say* **dek**-er-us) *adjective* polite and dignified. **decorously** *adverb*

decorum (*say* dik-**or**-um) *noun* decorous behaviour.

decoy¹ (*say* **dee**-koi) *noun* something used to tempt a person or animal into a trap or into danger.

decoy² (*say* dik-**oi**) *verb* tempt into a trap etc.

decrease¹ *verb* (**decreased, decreasing**) make or become smaller or fewer.

decrease² *noun* decreasing; the amount by which something decreased. [from *de-*, + Latin *crescere* = grow]

decree¹ *noun* **1** an official order. **2** a judgement or decision.

►►THESAURUS◄◄

deck² *verb* adorn, decorate, festoon, trim.

declare *verb* **1** affirm, announce, assert, avow, confess, contend, disclose, make known, proclaim, profess, pronounce, reveal, state, testify, voice.
declaration *noun* affirmation, announcement, assertion, attestation, avowal, confession, proclamation, profession, pronouncement, protestation, statement, testimony.

decline¹ *verb* **1** pass up, refuse, reject, turn down. **2** decrease, deteriorate, diminish, dwindle, ebb, fall off, flag, go downhill, go to the pack (*Australian informal*), sink, slip, slump, wane, weaken, worsen.

decline² *noun* decrease, deterioration, downturn, drop, falling off, recession, slump, wane.

decode *verb* crack, decipher, figure out, interpret, make out, read, translate.

decompose *verb* decay, disintegrate, go bad, go off, go rotten, moulder, perish, putrefy, rot, spoil.

decorate *verb* **1** adorn, deck, dress, embellish, festoon, ornament, tizzy (*Australian informal*),

trim. **2** do up (*informal*), paint, paper, refurbish, renovate.
decoration *noun* **1** adornment, ornament, trimming. **2** award, badge, medal, medallion.
decorative *adjective* fancy, ornamental, ornate, pretty.

decorous *adjective* becoming, correct, decent, honourable, polite, proper, refined, respectable, seemly.

decorum *noun* correctness, decency, dignity, politeness, propriety, respectability, seemliness.

decoy¹ *noun* bait, enticement, lure, stoolpigeon, trap.

decoy² *verb* allure, bait, entice, lure, trap.

decrease¹ *verb* abate, contract, cut, cut back, decline, diminish, drop (off), dwindle, ease off, ebb, fall, lessen, lower, reduce, shorten, shrink, slacken, subside, taper off, wane.

decrease² *noun* contraction, cut, cutback, decline, drop, ebb, fall, reduction.

decree¹ *noun* **1** command, commandment, dictate, direction, directive, edict, instruction, law, order, ordinance, proclamation, statute. **2** decision, judgement, ruling, verdict.

▶▶ DICTIONARY ◀◀

decree² *verb* (**decreed, decreeing**) make a decree.

decrepit (*say* dik-**rep**-it) *adjective* old and weak; dilapidated. **decrepitude** *noun* [from Latin, = creaking]

dedicate *verb* (**dedicated, dedicating**) 1 devote to a special use, *She dedicated herself to her work.* 2 name a person as a mark of respect, e.g. at the beginning of a book. **dedication** *noun*

deduce *verb* (**deduced, deducing**) work something out by reasoning. **deducible** *adjective* [from *de-*, + Latin *ducere* = to lead]

deduct *verb* subtract part of something.

deductible *adjective* able to be deducted.

deduction *noun* 1 deducting; something deducted. 2 deducing; something deduced.

deed *noun* 1 something that someone has done; an act. 2 a legal document.

deem *verb* (*formal*) consider, *I should deem it an honour to be invited.*

deep *adjective* 1 going a long way down or back or in, *a deep well; deep cupboards.* 2 measured from top to bottom or front to back, *a hole a metre deep.* 3 intense; strong, *deep colours; deep feelings.* 4 low-pitched, not shrill, *a deep voice.* **deeply** *adverb*, **deepness** *noun*

deepen *verb* make or become deeper.

deep-freeze *noun* a freezer.

deer *noun* (*plural* **deer**) a fast-running graceful animal, the male of which usually has antlers.

deface *verb* (**defaced, defacing**) spoil the surface of something, e.g. by scribbling on it. **defacement** *noun*

defame *verb* (**defamed, defaming**) attack a person's good reputation; slander, libel. **defamation** (*say* def-a-**may**-shon) *noun*, **defamatory** (*say* dif-**am**-a-ter-ee) *adjective*

default¹ *verb* fail to do what you have agreed to do. **defaulter** *noun*

default² *noun* failure to do something.

defeat¹ *verb* 1 win a victory over someone. 2 baffle; be too difficult for someone.

defeat² *noun* 1 defeating someone. 2 being defeated; a lost game or battle.

defeatist *noun* a person who expects to be defeated. **defeatism** *noun*

defecate (*say* **dee**-fik-ayt) *verb* (**defecated, defecating**) get rid of faeces from your body. **defecation** *noun*

defect¹ (*say* dif-**ekt** or **dee**-fekt) *noun* a flaw.

▶▶ THESAURUS ◀◀

decree² *verb* command, decide, declare, dictate, direct, enact, ordain, order, prescribe, proclaim, rule.

decrepit *adjective* battered, derelict, dilapidated, ramshackle, rickety, run-down, tumbledown.

dedicate *verb* 1 commit, consecrate, devote, give, pledge. 2 address, inscribe.

deduce *verb* conclude, gather, infer, reason, suss out (*informal*), work out.

deduct *verb* knock off (*informal*), remove, subtract, take away, take off.

deduction *noun* 1 discount, rebate, removal, subtraction. 2 conclusion, inference, reasoning.

deed *noun* 1 accomplishment, achievement, act, action, exploit, feat, work. 2 contract, document, paper.

deem *verb* consider, count, judge, rate, reckon, regard, think.

deep *adjective* 1 bottomless, cavernous, profound, unfathomed. 3 (*deep colours*) dark, intense, rich, strong, vivid; (*deep feelings*) burning, earnest, extreme, fervent, heartfelt,

intense, keen, profound, serious, strong. 4 bass, booming, low, resonant, sonorous.

deer *noun* (*male deer*) buck, hart, stag; (*female deer*) doe, hind; (*young deer*) fawn.

deface *verb* damage, disfigure, mar, spoil.

defame *verb* blacken, denigrate, discredit, disparage, libel, malign, slander, smear, vilify.

defeat¹ *verb* 1 beat, clobber (*slang*), conquer, crush, euchre, get the better of, lick (*informal*), outclass, outdo, outwit, overcome, overpower, overthrow, overwhelm, paste (*slang*), prevail over, pulverise (*informal*), rout, slaughter (*informal*), stonker (*Australian slang*), surpass, thrash, triumph over, trounce, vanquish. 2 baffle, beat, confound, frustrate, perplex, puzzle.

defeat² *noun* beating, conquest, downfall, drubbing, failure, licking (*informal*), loss, overthrow, pasting (*informal*), reverse, thrashing.

defect¹ *noun* blemish, bug (*informal*), fault, flaw, imperfection, mark, spot, stain; see also DEFICIENCY.

▶▶▷ DICTIONARY ◁◀◀

defect² (say dif-**ekt**) verb desert your own country etc. and join the enemy. **defection** noun, **defector** noun

defective adjective having defects; incomplete. **defectiveness** noun

defence noun **1** defending something. **2** something that defends or protects. **3** a reply put forward by a defendant.

defenceless adjective having no defences.

defend verb **1** protect, especially against an attack. **2** try to prove that a statement is true or that an accused person is not guilty. **defender** noun

defendant noun a person accused of something in a lawcourt.

defensible adjective able to be defended. **defensibility** noun

defensive adjective used or done for defence; protective. **defensively** adverb
on the defensive ready to defend yourself.

defer¹ verb (**deferred, deferring**) postpone. **deferment** noun, **deferral** noun [same origin as differ]

defer² verb (**deferred, deferring**) give way to a person's wishes or authority; yield. [from Latin deferre = to grant]

deference (say **def**-er-ens) noun polite respect. **deferential** (say def-er-**en**-shal) adjective, **deferentially** adverb

defiant adjective defying; openly disobedient. **defiantly** adverb, **defiance** noun

deficiency noun (plural **deficiencies**) **1** a lack; a shortage. **2** a defect. **deficient** adjective

deficit (say **def**-iss-it) noun **1** the amount by which a total is smaller than what is required. **2** the amount by which spending is greater than income.

defile verb (**defiled, defiling**) **1** make a thing dirty or impure. **2** profane. **defilement** noun [from an old word defoul]

define verb (**defined, defining**) **1** explain what a word or phrase means. **2** show clearly what something is; specify. **3** show a thing's outline. **definable** adjective [from de-, + Latin finis = limit]

definite adjective **1** clearly stated; exact, Fix a definite time. **2** certain; settled, Is it definite that we are to move? **definitely** adverb
definite article the word 'the'.

definition noun **1** a statement of what a word or phrase means or of what a thing is. **2** being distinct; clearness of outline (e.g. in a photograph).

definitive (say dif-**in**-it-iv) adjective finally settling something; conclusive, a definitive victory.

▶▶▷ THESAURUS ◁◀◀

defect² verb change sides, desert, go over.
defector noun apostate, deserter, renegade, traitor, turncoat.

defective adjective crook (Australian informal), deficient, dud (informal), faulty, imperfect, malfunctioning, on the blink (informal), out of order.

defence noun **1** preservation, protection, security. **2** buffer, bulwark, cover, fortification, guard, protection, safeguard, shield. **3** excuse, explanation, justification, plea.

defenceless adjective helpless, powerless, vulnerable, weak.

defend verb **1** fortify, guard, preserve, protect, safeguard, secure, shelter, shield. **2** champion, justify, stand up for, support, uphold, vindicate.

defer¹ verb adjourn, delay, hold over, postpone, put off, shelve.

defer² verb bow, give in, give way, submit, yield.

deferential adjective courteous, dutiful, meek, obsequious, polite, respectful, submissive.

defiant adjective contrary, disobedient, insubordinate, mutinous, obstinate, rebellious, recalcitrant, refractory, truculent.

deficiency noun **1** absence, dearth, deficit, insufficiency, lack, shortage, want. **2** defect, failing, fault, flaw, imperfection, shortcoming, weakness.
deficient adjective **1** insufficient, lacking, light on (Australian informal), short, wanting. **2** defective, faulty, imperfect, inadequate, unsatisfactory.

deficit noun **1** deficiency, shortfall.

defile verb **1** contaminate, dirty, poison, pollute, soil, taint. **2** corrupt, desecrate, dishonour, profane, violate.

define verb **1** clarify, explain. **2** delineate, describe, detail, set out, specify, spell out, state.

definite adjective **1** clear, defined, distinct, exact, explicit, fixed, particular, precise, specific. **2** assured, certain, decided, fixed, positive, settled, sure.

definition noun **1** description, elucidation, explanation, interpretation.

deflate *verb* (**deflated, deflating**) **1** let out air from a tyre or balloon etc. **2** make someone feel less proud or less confident. **3** reduce or reverse inflation. **deflation** *noun*, **deflationary** *adjective* [from *de-* + *inflate*]

deflect *verb* make something turn aside. **deflection** *noun*, **deflector** *noun* [from *de-*, + Latin *flectere* = to bend]

deforest *verb* clear away the trees from an area. **deforestation** *noun*

deform *verb* spoil a thing's shape or appearance. **deformation** *noun*

deformed *adjective* badly or abnormally shaped. **deformity** *noun*

defraud *verb* take something from a person by fraud; cheat, swindle.

defray *verb* (**defrayed, defraying**) provide money to pay costs or expenses. **defrayal** *noun*

defrost *verb* thaw out something frozen.

deft *adjective* skilful and quick. **deftly** *adverb*, **deftness** *noun*

defunct *adjective* dead.

defuse *verb* (**defused, defusing**) **1** remove the fuse from a bomb etc. **2** make a situation less dangerous.

defy *verb* (**defied, defying**) **1** resist something openly; refuse to obey, *They defied the law*. **2** challenge a person to do something you believe cannot be done, *I defy you to prove*

this. **3** prevent something being done, *The door defied all efforts to open it.*

degenerate¹ *verb* (**degenerated, degenerating**) become worse; lose good qualities. **degeneration** *noun*

degenerate² *adjective* having degenerated. **degeneracy** *noun*

degrade *verb* (**degraded, degrading**) **1** humiliate; disgrace. **2** decompose. **degradation** (*say* deg-ra-**day**-shon) *noun*

degree *noun* **1** a unit for measuring temperature. **2** a unit for measuring angles. **3** extent, *to some degree*. **4** a stage in a scale or series. **5** an award to someone at a university or college who has successfully finished a course.

dehydrated *adjective* dried up, with its moisture removed. **dehydration** *noun* [from *de-*, + Greek *hydor* = water]

deign (*say* dayn) *verb* condescend, be gracious enough to do something.

deity (*say* **dee**-it-ee) *noun* (*plural* **deities**) a god or goddess. [from Latin *deux* = god]

dejected *adjective* sad; gloomy; downcast. **dejectedly** *adverb*, **dejection** *noun* [from *de-*, + Latin *-jectum* = cast]

delay¹ *verb* (**delayed, delaying**) **1** make someone or something late; hinder. **2** postpone. **3** wait; linger.

delay² *noun* delaying; the time for which something is delayed, *a two-hour delay*.

deflect *verb* avert, divert, parry, turn aside.

deformed *adjective* contorted, crooked, disfigured, distorted, grotesque, lopsided, malformed, misshapen, twisted, warped. **deformity** *noun* contortion, disfigurement, distortion, malformation.

defraud *verb* bilk, cheat, con (*informal*), deceive, diddle (*informal*), dupe, fleece, have (*slang*), hoodwink, rip off (*informal*), rook, swindle, take for a ride (*informal*), trick.

defrost *verb* de-ice, melt, thaw, unfreeze.

deft *adjective* adept, adroit, agile, dexterous, expert, neat, nimble, proficient, skilful.

defunct *adjective* dead, extinct, obsolete.

defy *verb* **1** confront, disobey, flout, oppose, resist, stand up to. **2** challenge, dare.

degenerate¹ *verb* decline, deteriorate, regress, retrogress, sink, worsen.

degrade *verb* **1** abase, cheapen, debase, demean, disgrace, humiliate, lower.

degrading *adjective* demeaning, humiliating, menial, undignified.

degree *noun* **4** grade, level, order, rank, stage, step.

dehydrated *adjective* desiccated, dried.

deign *verb* condescend, lower yourself, stoop, vouchsafe.

deity *noun* divinity, god, goddess.

dejected *adjective* crestfallen, depressed, despondent, disconsolate, discouraged, disheartened, dispirited, doleful, downcast, down-hearted, forlorn, gloomy, glum, heavy-hearted, melancholy, miserable, morose, sad, sorrowful.

delay¹ *verb* **1** detain, hamper, hinder, hold up, impede, inhibit, obstruct, retard, slow. **2** defer, postpone, put off, shelve. **3** dilly-dally (*informal*), hang back, hesitate, linger, pause, procrastinate, stall, temporise, wait.

delay² *noun* hold-up, interruption, lull, pause, postponement, setback, wait.

▶▶ DICTIONARY ◀◀

delectable *adjective* delightful. **delectably** *adverb*

delegate¹ (*say* **del**-ig-at) *noun* a person who represents others and acts on their instructions.

delegate² (*say* **del**-ig-ayt) *verb* (**delegated, delegating**) **1** appoint as a delegate, *We delegated Jones to represent us.* **2** entrust, *We delegated the work to Jones.* [from Latin *delegare* = entrust]

delegation (*say* del-ig-**ay**-shon) *noun* **1** delegating. **2** a group of delegates.

delete (*say* dil-**eet**) *verb* (**deleted, deleting**) strike out something written or printed. **deletion** *noun*

deli *noun* **1** a delicatessen. **2** a local shop selling sandwiches, drinks, confectionery, newspapers, etc.

deliberate¹ (*say* dil-**ib**-er-at) *adjective* **1** done on purpose, intentional. **2** slow and careful. **deliberately** *adverb*

deliberate² (*say* dil-**ib**-er-ayt) *verb* (**deliberated, deliberating**) discuss or think carefully. **deliberation** *noun*

delicacy *noun* (*plural* **delicacies**) **1** being delicate. **2** a delicious food.

delicate *adjective* **1** fine; soft; fragile. **2** pleasant and not strong or intense. **3** becoming ill easily. **4** needing great care, *a delicate situation.* **5** taking great care to avoid offence, *The situation requires delicate handling.* **delicately** *adverb*, **delicateness** *noun*

delicatessen *noun* a shop that sells cooked meats, cheeses, salads, etc. [from German, = delicacies to eat]

delicious *adjective* tasting or smelling very pleasant. **deliciously** *adverb*

delight¹ *verb* **1** please someone greatly. **2** feel great pleasure.

delight² *noun* great pleasure. **delightful** *adjective*, **delightfully** *adverb*

delinquent (*say* dil-**ing**-kwent) *noun* someone who breaks the law or commits an offence. **delinquent** *adjective*, **delinquency** *noun*

delirium (*say* dil-**irri**-um) *noun* **1** a state of mental confusion. and agitation during a feverish illness. **2** wild excitement. **delirious** *adjective*, **deliriously** *adverb*

deliver *verb* **1** take letters or goods etc. to someone's house or place of work. **2** give a speech or lecture etc. **3** help with the birth of a baby. **4** aim or strike a blow or an attack. **5** rescue; set free. **deliverer** *noun*, **deliverance** *noun*, **delivery** *noun* [from *de-*, + Latin *liberare* = set free]

▶▶ THESAURUS ◀◀

delegate¹ *noun* agent, ambassador, deputy, emissary, envoy, proxy, representative, spokesperson.

delegate² *verb* **1** appoint, authorise, commission, depute, designate, empower, nominate. **2** assign, depute, entrust, hand over, transfer.

delete *verb* cancel, cross out, cut out, edit out, efface, erase, expunge, obliterate, remove, rub out, strike out, take out, wipe out.

deliberate¹ *adjective* **1** calculated, conscious, intended, intentional, planned, premeditated, studied, wilful. **2** careful, cautious, measured, painstaking, slow, unhurried.

deliberate² *verb* cogitate, confer about, consider, debate, discuss, meditate, mull over, muse, ponder, reflect, ruminate, think.

delicate *adjective* **1** breakable, dainty, exquisite, filmy, fine, flimsy, fragile, intricate, lacy, light, sheer, thin. **2** faint, gentle, mild, muted, pale, pastel, soft, subdued, subtle. **3** feeble, frail, infirm, sickly, tender, unhealthy, weak. **4** awkward, hazardous, precarious, sensitive, ticklish, touchy, tricky. **5** careful, diplomatic, discreet, sensitive, skilful, tactful.

delicious *adjective* appetising, delectable, luscious, mouth-watering, palatable, scrumptious (*informal*), tasty, yummy (*informal*).

delight¹ *verb* **1** amuse, captivate, charm, divert, enchant, enrapture, entertain, entrance, fascinate, please, thrill. **2** (*delight in*) adore, appreciate, be fond of, be keen on, enjoy, like, love, luxuriate in, relish, revel in, savour, take pleasure in.

delight² *noun* bliss, ecstasy, enjoyment, gratification, happiness, joy, pleasure, satisfaction. **delightful** *adjective* adorable, agreeable, attractive, beautiful, charming, delectable, enchanting, enjoyable, heavenly, lovable, lovely, nice, pleasant, pleasurable, wonderful.

delinquent *noun* criminal, hooligan, lawbreaker, miscreant, offender, troublemaker, wrongdoer.

delirious *adjective* **1** demented, deranged, frantic, frenzied, hysterical, incoherent, lightheaded, mad, raving. **2** ecstatic, euphoric, excited, wild.

deliver *verb* **1** bear, bring, carry, convey, distribute, give out, hand over, take, transport. **2** give, make, present, utter. **4** aim, deal, inflict,

▶▶▶ D I C T I O N A R Y ◀◀

dell *noun* a small valley with trees.

delphinium *noun* a garden plant with tall spikes of flowers, usually blue.

delta *noun* a triangular area at the mouth of a river where it spreads into branches. [shaped like the Greek letter delta (= D), written Δ]

delude *verb* (**deluded, deluding**) deceive.

deluge[1] *noun* **1** a large flood. **2** a heavy fall of rain. **3** something coming in great numbers, *a deluge of questions*.

deluge[2] *verb* (**deluged, deluging**) overwhelm by a deluge.

delusion *noun* a false belief.

de luxe of very high quality. [French, = of luxury]

delve *verb* (**delved, delving**) search deeply, e.g. for information, *delving into history*. [the original meaning was *dig*]

demagogue (*say* **dem**-a-gog) *noun* a leader who wins support by making emotional speeches rather than by careful reasoning. [from Greek *demos* = people, + *agogos* = leading]

demand[1] *verb* **1** ask for something firmly or forcefully. **2** need, *It demands skill.*

demand[2] *noun* **1** a firm or forceful request. **2** a desire to have something, *There is a great demand for computers.*
in demand wanted; desired. [from *de-*, + Latin *mandare* = to order]

demarcation (*say* dee-mar-**kay**-shon) *noun* marking the boundary of something.

demean *verb* lower a person's dignity, *I wouldn't demean myself to ask for it!*

demeanour (*say* dim-**een**-er) *noun* a person's behaviour or manner.

demented *adjective* driven mad; crazy. [from *de-*, + Latin *mentis* = of the mind]

demerara (*say* dem-er-**air**-a) *noun* light-brown cane sugar. [named after Demerara in South America]

demerit *noun* a fault; a defect.

demi- *prefix* half (as in *demisemiquaver*).

demigod *noun* a partly divine being.

demise (*say* dim-**I'z**) *noun* (*formal*) death.

demisemiquaver *noun* a note in music, equal to half a semiquaver.

demist *verb* remove misty condensation from a windscreen etc. **demister** *noun*

demo *noun* (*plural* **demos**) (*informal*) a demonstration.

democracy *noun* (*plural* **democracies**) **1** government of a country by representatives elected by the whole people. **2** a country governed in this way. **democrat** *noun*, **democratic** *adjective*, **democratically** *adverb* [from Greek *demos* = people, + *cracy*]

Democrat *noun* a member of a political party with *Democrat*(ic) in its title, e.g. the Australian Democrats.

demolish *verb* knock something down and break it up. **demolition** *noun* [from *de-*, + Latin *moliri* = build]

▶▶▶ T H E S A U R U S ◀◀

strike. **5** emancipate, free, liberate, release, rescue, save, set free.
delivery *noun* **1** consignment, conveyance, dispatch, distribution, shipment, transport. **2** childbirth.

delude *verb* beguile, bluff, con (*informal*), deceive, dupe, fool, have on (*informal*), hoax, hoodwink, kid (*informal*), mislead, trick.

deluge[1] *noun* **1** flood, inundation, spate. **2** cloudburst, downpour, rain, torrent. **3** flood, rush, shower, spate, stream, torrent.

deluge[2] *verb* flood, inundate, overrun, overwhelm, swamp.

delusion *noun* fantasy, illusion, misbelief, misconception.

de luxe elegant, first-class, grand, luxurious, posh (*informal*), superior, upmarket.

delve *verb* dig, examine, investigate, probe, research, search.

demand[1] *verb* **1** ask for, claim, clamour for, insist on, order, press for, request, require. **2** call for, need, require.
demanding *adjective* arduous, challenging, difficult, exacting, hard, onerous, strenuous, taxing, tough.

demand[2] *noun* **1** command, order, request, summons. **2** call, need, requirement, want.

demean *verb* debase, degrade, humble, humiliate, lower.

demeanour *noun* bearing, behaviour, conduct, deportment, manner, mien.

demented *adjective* berserk, bonkers (*slang*), crazy, deranged, insane, lunatic, mad, nutty (*informal*), out of your mind, potty (*informal*), screwy (*informal*), unbalanced, unhinged.

democratic *adjective* elected, popular, representative.

demolish *verb* destroy, dismantle, knock down, level, pull down, raze, tear down, wreck.

demon *noun* **1** a devil; an evil spirit. **2** a fierce or forceful person. **demonic** (*say* dim-**on**-ik) *adjective* [from Greek *daimon* = a spirit]

demonstrable (*say* **dem**-on-strab-ul) *adjective* able to be shown or proved. **demonstrably** *adverb*

demonstrate *verb* (**demonstrated**, **demonstrating**) **1** show; prove. **2** describe and explain. **3** take part in a demonstration. **demonstrator** *noun*

demonstration *noun* **1** demonstrating; showing how to do or work something. **2** a meeting or procession etc. held to show everyone what you think about something.

demonstrative (*say* dim-**on**-strat-iv) *adjective* **1** showing or proving something. **2** showing feelings or affections openly. **3** (in grammar) pointing out the person or thing referred to, *This, that, these*, and *those* are demonstrative adjectives or pronouns. **demonstratively** *adverb*, **demonstrativeness** *noun*

demoralise *verb* (**demoralised**, **demoralising**) dishearten someone; weaken someone's confidence or morale. **demoralisation** *noun*

demote *verb* (**demoted**, **demoting**) reduce to a lower position or rank. **demotion** *noun* [from *de-* + *promote*]

demur[1] (*say* dim-**er**) *verb* (**demurred**, **demurring**) raise objections.

demur[2] *noun* an objection raised.

demure *adjective* quiet and serious. **demurely** *adverb*, **demureness** *noun*

den *noun* **1** a lair. **2** a person's private room. **3** a place where something illegal happens, *a gambling den*.

deniable *adjective* able to be denied.

denial *noun* denying or refusing something.

denier (*say* **den**-yer) *noun* a unit for measuring the fineness of silk, rayon, or nylon thread.

denim *noun* a kind of strong cotton cloth. [from *serge de Nim* = fabric of Nîmes (a town in southern France)]

denizen (*say* **den**-iz-en) *noun* an inhabitant, *Monkeys are denizens of the jungle.*

denomination *noun* **1** a name or title. **2** a religious group with a special name, *Baptists, Anglicans and other denominations*. **3** a unit of weight or of money, *coins of small denomination*.

denominator *noun* the number below the line in a fraction, showing how many parts the whole is divided into, e.g. 4 in ¼. (Compare *numerator*.)

denote *verb* (**denoted**, **denoting**) mean; indicate, *In road signs, P denotes a car park*. **denotation** *noun*

dénouement (*say* day-**noo**-mahn) *noun* the final outcome of a plot or story, revealed at the end. [French, = unravelling]

denounce *verb* (**denounced**, **denouncing**) **1** speak strongly against something. **2** accuse, *They denounced him as a spy*. **denunciation** *noun* [from *de-*, + Latin *nuntiare* = announce]

dense *adjective* **1** thick; packed close together. **2** stupid. **densely** *adverb*

density *noun* (*plural* **densities**) **1** thickness. **2** (in physics) the proportion of weight to volume.

dent[1] *noun* a hollow left in a surface where something has pressed or hit it.

demon *noun* **1** bogy, devil, evil spirit, fiend, goblin, hobgoblin, imp.
demonic *adjective* devilish, diabolical, evil, fiendish, satanic, wicked.

demonstrate *verb* **1** display, establish, exhibit, present, prove, show. **2** describe, explain, illustrate, show, teach. **3** march, parade, protest, rally.

demonstration *noun* **1** display, exhibition, presentation, show. **2** demo (*informal*), march, parade, protest, rally, sit-in.

demoralise *verb* crush, depress, discourage, dishearten.

demure *adjective* bashful, coy, diffident, modest, prim, quiet, reserved, shy, unassuming.

den *noun* **1** burrow, hole, lair, nest. **2** hideaway, hide-out (*informal*), retreat, sanctum, study.

denial *noun* contradiction, disclaimer, negation, refusal, rejection, repudiation.

denomination *noun* **2** church, persuasion, sect.

denote *verb* express, indicate, mean, represent, signal, signify, stand for, symbolise.

denounce *verb* **1** attack, censure, condemn, criticise, decry, object to. **2** accuse, betray, dob in (*Australian informal*), incriminate, inform against, report.

dense *adjective* **1** close, compact, heavy, impenetrable, packed, solid, thick. **2** bovine, dim (*informal*), dull, dumb (*informal*), feeble-minded, foolish, obtuse, slow, stupid, thick, unintelligent.

dent[1] *noun* depression, dimple, dint, hollow, indentation.

▶▶ D I C T I O N A R Y ◀◀

dent² *verb* make a dent in something.

dental *adjective* of or for the teeth; of dentistry. [from Latin *dentis* = of a tooth]

dentist *noun* a person who is trained to treat teeth, fill or extract them, fit false ones, etc. **dentistry** *noun*

denture *noun* a set of false teeth.

denude *verb* (**denuded, denuding**) make bare or naked; strip something away. **denudation** *noun*

denunciation *noun* denouncing.

deny *verb* (**denied, denying**) **1** say that something is not true. **2** refuse to give or allow something, *deny a request.*

deodorant (*say* dee-**oh**-der-ant) *noun* a substance that removes smells.

deodorise *verb* (**deodorised, deodorising**) remove smells. **deodorisation** *noun* [from *de-*, + Latin *odor* = a smell]

depart *verb* go away; leave.

department *noun* one part of a large organisation. **departmental** *adjective*

departure *noun* departing.

depend *verb* **depend on** rely on, *We depend on your help*; be controlled by something else, *Whether we can picnic depends on the weather.* [from *de-*, + Latin *pendere* = hang]

dependable *adjective* reliable.

dependant *noun* a person who depends on another, *She has two dependants.*

Usage Note that the spelling ends in *-ant* for this noun but *-ent* for the adjective *dependent.*

dependency *noun* (*plural* **dependencies**) **1** dependence. **2** a country that is controlled by another.

dependent *adjective* **1** depending, *She has two dependent children; they are dependent on her.* **2** unable to do without, *dependent on drugs.* **dependence** *noun*

depict *verb* **1** show in a painting or drawing etc. **2** describe. **depiction** *noun* [from *de-*, + Latin *pictum* = painted]

deplete (*say* dip-**leet**) *verb* (**depleted, depleting**) reduce the amount of something by using up large amounts. **depletion** *noun* [from *de-*, + Latin *-pletum* = filled]

deplore *verb* (**deplored, deploring**) **1** regret something, *We deplore his death.* **2** find something extremely bad, *She deplores waste.* **deplorable** *adjective*, **deplorably** *adverb* [from *de-*, + Latin *plorare* = weep]

deploy *verb* spread out; place troops etc. in good positions. **deployment** *noun*

deport *verb* send an unwanted person out of a country. **deportation** *noun* [from *de-*, + Latin *portare* = carry]

deportment *noun* a person's manner of standing, walking, and behaving.

depose *verb* (**deposed, deposing**) **1** remove a person from power. **2** make a sworn statement. **deposition** *noun*

▶▶ T H E S A U R U S ◀◀

deny *verb* **1** contradict, disclaim, gainsay (*formal*), negate, reject, repudiate. **2** deprive of, disallow, refuse, withhold.

depart *verb* clear off (*informal*), decamp, embark, emigrate, escape, exit, go away, leave, make off, make tracks (*informal*), nick off (*Australian slang*), push off (*informal*), quit, retire, run away, run off, scarper (*informal*), scram (*informal*), set off, set out, shoot through (*Australian informal*), skedaddle (*informal*), take your leave, withdraw.

department *noun* branch, bureau, division, office, part, section, unit.

departure *noun* exit, exodus, going away, leaving, retreat, withdrawal.

depend *verb* **depend on 1** bank on, count on, need, reckon on, rely on. **2** hang on, hinge on, rest on, turn on.

dependable *adjective* consistent, constant, faithful, loyal, reliable, stalwart, steadfast, steady, true, trustworthy.

dependent *adjective* **2** addicted, hooked (*slang*), reliant.

depict *verb* **1** draw, illustrate, paint, picture, portray, represent, show, sketch. **2** describe, narrate, outline, record, relate.

deplore *verb* **1** bewail, grieve over, lament, mourn, regret. **2** abhor, condemn, deprecate, disapprove of.
deplorable *adjective* abominable, appalling, awful, bad, dire, disgraceful, dreadful, lamentable, pathetic, regrettable, reprehensible, shameful, shocking, wretched.

deploy *verb* arrange, dispose, organise, position, spread out.

deport *verb* banish, exile, expatriate, expel, send away, transport.

deportment *noun* bearing, behaviour, carriage, conduct, demeanour, manner, mien.

depose *verb* **1** dethrone, get rid of, oust, remove.

▶▶ D I C T I O N A R Y ◀◀

deposit¹ *noun* **1** an amount of money paid into a bank etc. **2** money paid as a first instalment. **3** a layer of matter deposited or accumulated naturally.

deposit² *verb* (**deposited, depositing**) **1** put down. **2** pay money as a deposit. **depositor** *noun* [from *de-*, + Latin *positum* = placed]

depot (*say* **dep**-oh) *noun* **1** a place where things are stored. **2** a headquarters. **3** a place where buses, trams, trains, etc. are kept. [same origin as *deposit*]

depraved *adjective* behaving wickedly; of bad character. **depravity** *noun*

deprecate (*say* **dep**-rik-ayt) *verb* (**deprecated, deprecating**) say that you disapprove of something. **deprecation** *noun* [from Latin *deprecari* = keep away misfortune by prayer]

depreciate (*say* dip-**ree**-shee-ayt) *verb* (**depreciated, depreciating**) make or become lower in value. [from *de-*, + Latin *pretium* = price]

depredation (*say* dep-rid-**ay**-shon) *noun* the act of plundering or damaging something. (Compare *predator*.)

depress *verb* **1** make somebody sad. **2** lower the value of something, *Threat of war depressed prices.* **3** press down, *Depress the lever.* **depressed** *adjective*, **depressive** *adjective*

depression *noun* **1** a great sadness or feeling of hopelessness. **2** a long period when trade is very slack because people cannot afford to buy things. **3** a shallow hollow in the ground or on a surface. **4** an area of low air-pressure which may bring rain. **5** pressing something down.

deprive *verb* (**deprived, depriving**) take or keep something away from somebody. **deprival** *noun*, **deprivation** *noun* [from *de-*, + Latin *privare* = rob]

depth *noun* **1** being deep; how deep something is. **2** the deepest or lowest part.
in depth thoroughly.
out of your depth in water that is too deep to stand in; trying to do something that is too hard for you.

deputation *noun* group of people sent as representatives of others.

depute (*say* dip-**yoot**) *verb* (**deputed, deputing**) **1** appoint a person to do something, *We deputed John to take the message.* **2** assign or delegate a task to someone, *We deputed the task to him.*

deputise *verb* (**deputised, deputising**) act as someone's deputy.

deputy *noun* (*plural* **deputies**) a person appointed to act as a substitute for another.

derail *verb* cause a train to leave the rails. **derailment** *noun*

▶▶ T H E S A U R U S ◀◀

deposit¹ *noun* **2** down payment, first instalment. **3** alluvium, crust, dregs, lees, precipitate, sediment, silt.

deposit² *verb* **1** drop, dump, lay, leave, park (*informal*), place, put down, set down. **2** bank, pay in, save.

depot *noun* **1** cache, repository, store, storehouse, warehouse. **2** base, headquarters. **3** garage, station, terminal, terminus.

depraved *adjective* base, corrupt, degenerate, dissolute, evil, immoral, perverted, vile, wicked.

depreciate *verb* decrease, devalue, drop, go down, lower, reduce.

depress *verb* **1** dishearten, oppress, sadden, weigh down. **3** lower, press down, push down. **depressed** *adjective* blue, dejected, desolate, despondent, disconsolate, disheartened, dismal, dispirited, down, downcast, downhearted, down in the dumps, gloomy, glum, heavy-hearted, hopeless, in the doldrums, low, melancholy, miserable, morose, out of sorts,

pessimistic, sad, unhappy, woebegone, wretched.

depression *noun* **1** the blues, dejection, despair, despondency, gloom, hopelessness, low spirits, melancholy, pessimism, sadness, unhappiness, wretchedness. **2** decline, downturn, recession, slump. **3** basin, cavity, crabhole (*Australian*), crater, dent, dip, gilgai (*Australian*), hole, hollow, indentation, pit, trough. **4** cyclone, low, trough.

deprive *verb* (*deprive of*) deny, dispossess of, refuse, rob of, take away.

depth *noun* **1** deepness, intensity, profundity, strength.
in depth comprehensively, extensively, in detail, intensively, thoroughly.

deputise *verb* (*deputise for*) fill in for, hold the fort for, stand in for, substitute for, take the place of.

deputy *noun* assistant, delegate, lieutenant, locum, offsider (*Australian*), proxy, relief, replacement, representative, reserve, stand-in, substitute, surrogate, understudy.

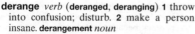

▶▶▷ DICTIONARY ◁◀◀

derange *verb* (**deranged, deranging**) **1** throw into confusion; disturb. **2** make a person insane. **derangement** *noun*

derelict (*say* **d**erri-likt) *adjective* abandoned and left to fall into ruin. **dereliction** *noun* [from *de-* = completely, + Latin *relictum* = left behind]

deride *verb* (**derided, deriding**) laugh at with contempt or scorn; ridicule. [from *de-*, + Latin *ridere* = to laugh]

derision *noun* scorn; ridicule. **derisive** (*say* dir-**I**-siv) *adjective*, **derisively** *adverb*, **derisory** *adjective*

derivation *noun* **1** deriving. **2** the origin of a word from another language or from a simple word to which a prefix or suffix is added; etymology.

derivative *adjective* derived from something. **derivative** *noun*

derive *verb* (**derived, deriving**) **1** obtain from a source, *She derived great enjoyment from music.* **2** form or originate from something, *Some English words are derived from Latin words.* [from *de-*, + Latin *rivus* = a stream]

dermatology *noun* the study of the skin and its diseases. **dermatologist** *noun* [from Greek *derma* = skin, + *-logy*]

dermis *noun* the layer of skin below the epidermis.

derogatory (*say* dir-**og**-at-er-ee) *adjective* contemptuous; disparaging.

derrick *noun* **1** a kind of crane for lifting things. **2** a tall framework holding the machinery used in drilling an oil-well etc. [this word originally meant 'a gallows', named after Derrick, a London hangman in about 1600]

dervish *noun* (*plural* **dervishes**) a member of a Muslim religious group who vowed to live a life of poverty. [from Persian *darvish* = poor]

descant *noun* a tune sung or played above the main tune. [from *dis-*, + Latin *cantus* = song]

descend *verb* go down. [from Latin *descendere* = climb down]
be descended from have as an ancestor; come by birth from a certain person or family.
descendant *noun*

descent *noun* **1** descending. **2** a downward slope. **3** family origin.

describe *verb* (**described, describing**) **1** say what someone or something is like. **2** draw in outline; move in a pattern. **description** *noun*, **descriptive** *adjective* [from *de-*, + Latin *scribere* = writer]

desecrate (*say* **dess**-ik-rayt) *verb* (**desecrated, desecrating**) treat a sacred thing irreverently. **desecration** *noun* [from *de-* + *consecrate*]

desert[1] (*say* **dez**-ert) *noun* a large area of dry often sandy land. **desert** *adjective*
desert island an uninhabited island.

▶▶▷ THESAURUS ◁◀◀

deranged *adjective* berserk, crazy, demented, insane, irrational, lunatic, mad, unbalanced, unhinged.

derelict *adjective* abandoned, decrepit, deserted, dilapidated, forsaken, neglected, run-down, tumbledown.

deride *verb* jeer at, laugh at, make fun of, mock, poke borak at (*Australian informal*), poke fun at, ridicule, satirise, scoff at, sneer at, take the mickey out of (*informal*), taunt, tease.

derision *noun* contempt, disdain, mockery, ridicule, sarcasm, scorn.

derivation *noun* **2** etymology, origin, root, source.

derive *verb* **1** draw, gain, get, glean, obtain, receive. **2** come, originate, stem.

derogatory *adjective* belittling, contemptuous, disparaging, insulting, pejorative, uncomplimentary.

descend *verb* climb down, come down, drop, fall, go down, nosedive, plummet, plunge, sink, swoop down.

descendant *noun* child, heir, scion; (*descendants*) issue, offspring, progeny, seed (*old use*).

descent *noun* **1** coming down, dive, drop, fall, plunge. **3** ancestry, birth, blood, extraction, genealogy, lineage, origin, parentage, stock, strain.

describe *verb* **1** characterise, depict, detail, elaborate, explain, express, narrate, outline, portray, recount, relate, represent, tell (about). **description** *noun* account, characterisation, commentary, depiction, explanation, outline, picture, portrait, portrayal, profile, record, report, representation, sketch, story.

desecrate *verb* debase, defile, degrade, profane, violate.

desert[1] *noun* wasteland, wilderness.
desert *adjective* arid, barren, desolate, dry, infertile, uncultivated, uninhabited, waste, wild.

▶▶ D I C T I O N A R Y ◀◀

desert² (*say* diz-**ert**) *verb* **1** abandon; leave without intending to return. **2** run away from military service. **deserter** *noun*, **desertion** *noun*

deserts (*say* diz-**erts**) *plural noun* what a person deserves, *He got his deserts.* [from *deserve*]

deserve *verb* (**deserved**, **deserving**) have a right to something; be worthy of something. **deservedly** *adverb*

desiccated *adjective* dried.

design¹ *noun* **1** a drawing that shows how something is to be made. **2** the way something is made or arranged. **3** lines and shapes that form a decoration; a pattern. **4** a mental plan or scheme.
have designs on plan to get hold of.

design² *verb* **1** draw a design for something. **2** plan or intend something for a special purpose. **designer** *noun* [from *de-*, + Latin *signare* = mark out]

designate¹ *verb* (**designated**, **designating**) **1** mark or describe as something particular, *They designated the river as the boundary.* **2** appoint someone to a job. **designation** *noun*

designate² *adjective* appointed to a job but not yet doing it, *the bishop designate.* [same origin as *design*]

desirable *adjective* **1** causing people to desire it; worth having. **2** worth doing; advisable. **desirability** *noun*

desire¹ *noun* a feeling of wanting something very much. **desirous** *adjective*

desire² *verb* (**desired**, **desiring**) have a desire for something.

desist (*say* diz-**ist**) *verb* cease.

desk *noun* **1** a piece of furniture with a flat top and often drawers, used when writing or reading etc. **2** a counter at which a cashier or receptionist sits.

desolate *adjective* **1** lonely; sad. **2** uninhabited. **desolation** *noun*

despair¹ *noun* a feeling of hopelessness.

despair² *verb* feel despair. [from *de-*, + Latin *sperare* = to hope]

despatch *noun* & *verb* dispatch.

desperado (*say* dess-per-**ah**-doh) *noun* (*plural* **desperadoes**) a reckless criminal.

desperate *adjective* **1** extremely serious; hopeless, *a desperate situation.* **2** reckless and ready to do anything. **desperately** *adverb*, **desperation** *noun* [same origin as *despair*]

▶▶ T H E S A U R U S ◀◀

desert² *verb* **1** abandon, ditch (*informal*), dump (*informal*), forsake, jilt, leave, leave in the lurch, walk out on. **2** abscond, defect, run away.

deserter *noun* absconder, defector, escapee, fugitive, runaway.

deserts *plural noun* come-uppance (*informal*), due, nemesis, punishment, retribution, reward.

deserve *verb* be entitled to, be worthy of, command, earn, justify, merit, warrant.

design¹ *noun* **1** blueprint, diagram, draft, drawing, model, outline, pattern, plan, sketch. **2** arrangement, composition, configuration, form, layout, style. **3** motif, pattern.

design² *verb* **1** conceive, draft, draw, lay out, plan, sketch, visualise. **2** aim, calculate, intend, mean, plan, tailor.
designer *noun* architect, couturier, creator, inventor, originator, planner.

designate¹ *verb* **1** identify, indicate, mark, specify, stipulate. **2** appoint, choose, name, nominate, select.
designation *noun* epithet, name, title.

desirable *adjective* **1** alluring, appealing, attractive, popular, sought-after, worthwhile. **2** advisable, preferable, recommended.

desire¹ *noun* ambition, appetite, aspiration, craving, fancy, hunger, itch, longing, lust, passion, thirst, urge, wish, yen.

desire² *verb* covet, crave, fancy, hanker after, hope for, hunger for, long for, lust after, set your heart on, thirst for, want, wish for, yearn for.

desist *verb* cease, discontinue, leave off, refrain, stop.

desolate *adjective* **1** dejected, depressed, despondent, disconsolate, forlorn, forsaken, glum, heavy-hearted, lonely, melancholy, miserable, unhappy, wretched. **2** barren, bleak, deserted, dismal, dreary, empty, inhospitable, isolated, lonely, remote, stark, uninhabited, wild, windswept.

despair¹ *noun* depression, desperation, despondency, hopelessness.

despair² *verb* give up, lose hope.

desperate *adjective* **1** acute, bad, critical, dire, grave, hopeless, serious, urgent. **2** dangerous, daring, foolhardy, impetuous, rash, reckless, violent, wild.

▶▶ D I C T I O N A R Y ◀◀

despicable *adjective* deserving to be despised; contemptible.

despise *verb* (**despised, despising**) think someone or something is inferior or worthless. [from *de-*, + Latin *-spicere* = to look]

despite *preposition* in spite of.

despondent *adjective* sad; gloomy. **despondently** *adverb*, **despondency** *noun*

despot (*say* **dess**-pot) *noun* a tyrant. **despotism** *noun*, **despotic** (*say* dis-**pot**-ik) *adjective*

dessert (*say* diz-**ert**) *noun* fruit or a sweet food as the last course of a meal. [from French *desservir* = clear the table]

dessertspoon *noun* a medium-sized spoon used for eating desserts etc.

destination *noun* the place to which a person or thing is travelling.

destined *adjective* having as a destiny; intended.

destiny *noun* (*plural* **destinies**) fate.

destitute *adjective* left without anything; living in extreme poverty. **destitution** *noun*

destroy *verb* ruin or put an end to something. **destruction** *noun*, **destructive** *adjective* [from *de-*, + Latin *struere* = build]

destroyer *noun* a fast warship.

desultory (*say* **dess**-ul-ter-ee) *adjective* casual and disconnected, *desultory talk*.

detach *verb* unfasten; separate. **detachable** *adjective*, **detachment** *noun*

detached *adjective* **1** separated. **2** not prejudiced; not involved in something.

detail *noun* **1** a very small part of a design or plan or decoration etc. **2** a small piece of information. **detailed** *adjective*

detain *verb* **1** keep someone waiting. **2** keep someone at a place. [from *de-*, + Latin *tenere* = hold]

detainee *noun* a person who is officially detained or kept in custody.

▶▶ T H E S A U R U S ◀◀

despicable *adjective* abominable, bad, base, contemptible, detestable, evil, hateful, loathsome, low, mean, odious, outrageous, reprehensible, rotten, shameful, vile, wicked.

despise *verb* detest, disdain, dislike, feel contempt for, hate, loathe, look down on, scorn, spurn.

despondent *adjective* dejected, depressed, discouraged, disheartened, dispirited, doleful, down, downcast, down-hearted, forlorn, gloomy, glum, heavy-hearted, melancholy, miserable, morose, sad, sorrowful, unhappy, wretched.

despot *noun* autocrat, dictator, tyrant.

despotic *adjective* absolute, authoritarian, autocratic, dictatorial, domineering, imperious, oppressive, tyrannical.

dessert *noun* afters (*informal*), pudding, sweet.

destination *noun* end, goal, objective, target.

destined *adjective* doomed, fated, intended, meant, ordained, predestined.

destiny *noun* doom, fate, fortune, karma, kismet, lot, portion.

destitute *adjective* bankrupt, broke (*informal*), down and out, hard up (*informal*), impecunious, impoverished, insolvent, needy, penniless, penurious, poor, poverty-stricken.

destroy *verb* annihilate, blow up, break, bust (*informal*), crush, demolish, devastate, dismantle, eliminate, exterminate, extinguish, knock down, lay waste, level, mutilate, ob- literate, pull down, pull to pieces, put an end to, ravage, raze, ruin, sabotage, shatter, smash, spoil, tear down, undermine, vandalise, wipe out, wreck, zap (*slang*); see also KILL[1].

destruction *noun* annihilation, damage, demolition, devastation, elimination, extermination, extinction, havoc, holocaust, killing, massacre, ruin, sabotage, slaughter, vandalism, wreckage.

destructive *adjective* adverse, baleful, damaging, dangerous, deleterious, detrimental, devastating, disastrous, harmful, injurious, malign, malignant, negative, pernicious, ruinous.

detach *verb* disconnect, disengage, part, pull off, release, remove, separate, slip off, take off, undo, unfasten.

detached *adjective* **1** free-standing, separate. **2** aloof, disinterested, impartial, neutral, objective, unbiased, uninvolved, unprejudiced.

detail *noun* **2** aspect, circumstance, element, fact, factor, feature, item, particular, point, respect.

detailed *adjective* blow-by-blow, comprehensive, elaborate, exact, exhaustive, full, graphic, in-depth, itemised, minute, rigorous, thorough.

detain *verb* **1** bail up (*Australian*), buttonhole, delay, hinder, hold up, impede, keep, waylay. **2** arrest, capture, confine, hold in custody, imprison, jail.

▶▶ DICTIONARY ◀◀

detect *verb* discover. **detection** *noun*, **detector** *noun* [from *de-*, + Latin *tectum* = covered]

detective *noun* a person who investigates crime.

detention *noun* detaining; being detained; being made to stay late in school as a punishment.

deter *verb* (**deterred, deterring**) discourage or prevent a person from doing something. **determent** *noun* [from *de-*, + Latin *terrere* = to frighten]

detergent *noun* a substance used for cleaning or washing things.

deteriorate (*say* dit-**eer**-ee-er-ayt) *verb* (**deteriorated, deteriorating**) become worse. **deterioration** *noun* [from Latin *deterior* = worse]

determination *noun* **1** strong intention; having decided firmly. **2** determining or deciding something.

determine *verb* (**determined, determining**) **1** decide, *determine what is to be done.* **2** find out; calculate, *determine the height of the mountain.* [from *de-*, + Latin *terminare* = set a limit]

determined *adjective* full of determination; with your mind firmly made up.

determiner *noun* a word (such as *a, the, many*) that modifies a noun.

deterrent *noun* something that may deter people; a nuclear weapon that deters countries from making war on the one that has it. **deterrence** *noun*

detest *verb* dislike very much; loathe. **detestable** *adjective*, **detestation** *noun*

detonate (*say* **det**-on-ayt) *verb* (**detonated, detonating**) explode; cause something to explode. **detonation** *noun*, **detonator** *noun* [from *de-* = thoroughly, + Latin *tonare* = to thunder]

detour (*say* **dee**-toor) *noun* a roundabout route instead of the normal one. [from French *détourner* = turn away]

detract *verb* lessen the amount or value, *It will not detract from our pleasure.* **detraction** *noun* [from *de-*, + Latin *tractum* = pulled]

detriment (*say* **det**-rim-ent) *noun* harm; damage, *She worked long hours, to the detriment of her health.*

detrimental (*say* det-rim-**en**-tal) *adjective* harmful. **detrimentally** *adverb*

deuce *noun* a score in tennis where both sides have 40 points and must gain two consecutive points to win.

devalue *verb* (**devalued, devaluing**) reduce a thing's value. **devaluation** *noun*

devastate *verb* (**devastated, devastating**) ruin or cause great destruction to something. **devastation** *noun*

▶▶ THESAURUS ◀◀

detect *verb* discern, discover, find, identify, locate, note, notice, observe, perceive, see, sense, spot, track down, uncover.

detective *noun* cop (*slang*), investigator, policeman, police officer, policewoman, private eye (*informal*), sleuth.

detention *noun* captivity, confinement, custody, imprisonment.

deter *verb* daunt, discourage, dissuade, hinder, impede, obstruct, prevent, put off, scare off.

deteriorate *verb* decline, degenerate, diminish, go backwards, go downhill, go to the dogs (*informal*), go to the pack (*Australian informal*), retrogress, sink, slip, wane, weaken, worsen.

determination *noun* **1** backbone, courage, doggedness, fortitude, grit, guts (*informal*), perseverance, persistence, pertinacity, resolve, spirit, tenacity, will-power.

determine *verb* **1** agree on, decide, fix on, resolve, settle. **2** ascertain, calculate, discover, establish, find out, work out.

determined *adjective* adamant, dogged, firm, headstrong, intransigent, persistent, pertinacious, purposeful, resolute, single-minded, steadfast, strong-willed, stubborn, tenacious.

detest *verb* abhor, abominate, despise, dislike, hate, loathe.

detestable *adjective* abhorrent, abominable, atrocious, contemptible, deplorable, despicable, disgusting, hateful, horrid, intolerable, loathsome, objectionable, obnoxious, odious, repugnant, repulsive, revolting, vile.

detonate *verb* discharge, explode, let off, set off.

detour *noun* bypass, deviation, diversion.

detract *verb* (*detract from*) diminish, lessen, reduce, take away from.

detrimental *adjective* adverse, damaging, deleterious, destructive, harmful, injurious, pernicious, prejudicial.

devastate *verb* damage, demolish, destroy, lay waste, level, ravage, raze, ruin, wreck.

▶▶ DICTIONARY ◀◀

devastated *adjective* overwhelmed with shock or grief.

develop *verb* (**developed, developing**) **1** make or become bigger or better. **2** come gradually into existence, *Storms developed.* **3** begin to have or use, *They developed bad habits.* **4** use an area of land for building houses, shops, factories, etc. **5** treat photographic film with chemicals so that pictures appear. **developer** *noun*, **development** *noun*

deviate (*say* **dee**-vee-ayt) *verb* (**deviated, deviating**) turn aside from a course or from what is usual or true. **deviation** *noun* [from *de-*, + Latin *via* = way]

device *noun* **1** something made for a particular purpose, *a device for opening tins.* **2** a design used as a decoration or emblem. **leave them to their own devices** leave them to do as they wish.

devil *noun* **1** an evil spirit. **2** a wicked, cruel, or annoying person. **devilish** *adjective*, **devilry** *noun*

devilment *noun* mischief.

devious (*say* **dee**-vee-us) *adjective* **1** roundabout; not direct, *a devious route.* **2** not straightforward; underhand. **deviously** *adverb*, **deviousness** *noun*

devise *verb* (**devised, devising**) invent; plan.

devoid *adjective* lacking or without something, *His work is devoid of merit.*

devolution *noun* devolving; giving authority to another person etc.; handing over responsibility for government.

devolve *verb* (**devolved, devolving**) pass or be passed to a deputy or successor.

devote *verb* (**devoted, devoting**) give completely, *He devoted his time to sport.*

devoted *adjective* very loving or loyal.

devotee (*say* dev-o-**tee**) *noun* a person who is devoted to something; an enthusiast.

devotion *noun* great love or loyalty; being devoted.

devotions *plural noun* prayers.

devour *verb* eat or swallow something hungrily or greedily. [from *de-*, = completely, + Latin *vorare* = to swallow]

devout *adjective* earnestly religious or sincere. **devoutly** *adverb*, **devoutness** *noun*

dew *noun* tiny drops of water that form during the night on surfaces of things in the open air. **dewdrop** *noun*, **dewy** *adjective*

▶▶ THESAURUS ◀◀

devastated *adjective* dismayed, overcome, overwhelmed, shattered, shocked, traumatised.

develop *verb* **1** advance, blossom, build up, cultivate, diversify, enlarge, evolve, expand, flourish, grow, improve, increase, mature, mushroom, progress. **3** acquire, contract, get, pick up.

development *noun* advance, building, enlargement, evolution, expansion, growth, improvement, increase, progress, spread.

deviate *verb* depart, digress, diverge, stray, turn aside.

device *noun* **1** apparatus, appliance, contraption (*informal*), gadget, implement, instrument, invention, machine, tool, utensil.

devil *noun* **1** bogy, demon, evil spirit, fiend. **2** monster, rascal, rogue, scamp, scoundrel. **the Devil** Lucifer, Old Nick, Satan.

devilish *adjective* demonic, diabolical, evil, fiendish, hellish, infernal, satanic, ungodly, villainous, wicked.

devious *adjective* **1** circuitous, indirect, roundabout, tortuous, winding. **2** calculating, crafty, cunning, deceitful, dishonest, sly, sneaky, underhand, wily.

devise *verb* conceive, concoct, contrive, cook up (*informal*), create, design, dream up, formulate, hatch, invent, make up, plan, plot, produce, think up, work out.

devoid *adjective* (*devoid of*) bereft of, free from, lacking, without.

devote *verb* commit, consecrate, dedicate, give, set aside.

devoted *adjective* close, committed, constant, dedicated, enthusiastic, faithful, loving, loyal, reliable, staunch, true.

devotee *noun* aficionado, buff (*informal*), enthusiast, fan, fanatic, follower, lover, supporter.

devotion *noun* affection, allegiance, attachment, commitment, dedication, fervour, fondness, love, loyalty, zeal.

devotions *plural noun* prayers, worship.

devour *verb* bolt, consume, demolish (*informal*), eat, gobble, gorge, gulp down, guzzle, knock back, scoff (*informal*), swallow, wolf.

devout *adjective* ardent, committed, dedicated, devoted, earnest, fervent, genuine, godly, holy, pious, religious, sincere, staunch.

dexterity (*say* deks-**terri**-tee) *noun* skill in handling things. **dexterous** *adjective* [from Latin *dexter* = on the right-hand side]

di-¹ *prefix* two; double (as in *dioxide*). [from Greek *dis* = twice]

di-² *prefix* see **dis-**.

dia- *prefix* through (as in *diarrhoea*); across (as in *diagonal*). [from Greek *dia* = through]

diabetes (*say* dy-a-**bee**-teez) *noun* a disease in which there is too much sugar in a person's blood. **diabetic** (*say* dy-a-**bet**-ik) *adjective* & *noun*

diabolical *adjective* **1** like a devil; very wicked. **2** very clever or annoying.

diadem (*say* **dy**-a-dem) *noun* a crown or headband worn by a royal person.

diagnose *verb* (**diagnosed**, **diagnosing**) find out what disease a person has or what is wrong. **diagnosis** *noun*, **diagnostic** *adjective*

diagonal (*say* dy-**ag**-on-al) *noun* a straight line joining opposite corners. **diagonal** *adjective*, **diagonally** *adverb* [from *dia-*, + Greek *gonia* = angle]

diagram *noun* a kind of drawing or picture that shows the parts of something or how it works. [from *dia-* + -*gram*]

dial¹ *noun* a circular object with numbers or letters round it.

dial² *verb* (**dialled**, **dialling**) telephone a number by turning a telephone dial or pressing numbered buttons.

dialect *noun* the words and pronunciations used by people in one district but not in the rest of a country.

dialogue *noun* a conversation.

dialysis (*say* dy-**al**-iss-iss) *noun* a way of removing harmful substances from the blood by letting it flow through a machine. [from *dia-*, + Greek *lysis* = loosening]

diameter (*say* dy-**am**-it-er) *noun* **1** a line drawn straight across a circle or sphere and passing through its centre. **2** the length of this line. [from Greek, = measuring across]

diametrically *adverb* completely, *diametrically opposite*.

diamond *noun* **1** a very hard precious stone that looks like clear glass. **2** a shape with four equal sides and four angles that are not right angles. **3** a playing card with red diamond shapes on it. [from Greek *adamas* = adamant (= a very hard stone)]

diaper *noun* a baby's nappy.

diaphanous (*say* dy-**af**-an-us) *adjective* (of fabric) almost transparent.

diaphragm (*say* **dy**-a-fram) *noun* **1** the muscular partition inside the body that separates the chest from the abdomen and is used in breathing. **2** a hole that can be altered in size to control the amount of light that passes through a camera lens.

diarist *noun* a person who keeps a diary.

diarrhoea (*say* dy-a-**ree**-a) *noun* too frequent and too watery emptying of the bowels. [from *dia-*, + Greek *rhoia* = a flow]

diary *noun* (*plural* **diaries**) a book in which someone writes down what happens each day. [from Latin *dies* = day]

diatribe *noun* a strong verbal attack.

dice¹ *noun* (strictly this is the plural of **die²**, but it is often used as a singular, *plural* **dice**) a small cube marked with dots (1 to 6) on its sides, used in games.

dice² *verb* (**diced**, **dicing**) **1** play gambling games using dice. **2** cut into small cubes.

dictate *verb* (**dictated**, **dictating**) **1** speak or read something aloud for someone else to write down. **2** give orders in an officious way. **dictation** *noun* [from Latin *dictare* = keep saying]

dictates (*say* **dik**-tayts) *plural noun* orders, commands.

dexterous *adjective* adept, adroit, agile, deft, nimble, skilful.

diabolical *adjective* **1** devilish, evil, fiendish, hellish, infernal, inhuman, satanic, ungodly, villainous, wicked.

diagnose *verb* detect, determine, identify, name, recognise.

diagonal *adjective* oblique, slanting, sloping.

diagram *noun* chart, drawing, figure, graph, illustration, outline, picture, plan, representation, sketch.

dial² *verb* call, phone, ring, telephone.

dialect *noun* accent, brogue, idiom, lingo (*informal*), patois, variety, vernacular; see also LANGUAGE.

dialogue *noun* communication, conference, conversation, discourse, discussion, talk.

diameter *noun* **2** bore, calibre, thickness, width.

diary *noun* chronicle, journal, log, record.

dictate *verb* **2** command, decree, lay down the law, ordain, order, prescribe.

▶▶ D I C T I O N A R Y ◀◀

dictator *noun* a ruler who has unlimited power. **dictatorial** (*say* dik-ta-**tor**-ee-al) *adjective*, **dictatorship** *noun*

diction *noun* a person's way of speaking words, *clear diction.*

dictionary *noun* (*plural* **dictionaries**) a book that contains words in alphabetical order so that you can find out how to spell them and what they mean. [from Latin *dictio* = word]

didactic (*say* dy-**dak**-tik) *adjective* having the manner of someone who is lecturing people. **didactically** *adverb* [from Greek *didaktikos* = teaching]

diddle *verb* (**diddled, diddling**) (*slang*) cheat; swindle.

didgeridoo (*say* dij-er-i-**doo**) *noun* an Aboriginal musical instrument in the form of a long wooden tube.

didn't (*mainly spoken*) did not.

die¹ *verb* (**died, dying**) 1 stop living or existing. 2 stop burning or functioning, *The engine died.*
die down become less loud or strong.
die out cease to exist.

die² *noun* singular of **dice.**

die³ *noun* a device that stamps a design on coins etc. or that cuts or moulds metal.

die-hard *noun* a person who obstinately refuses to give up old ideas or policies.

diesel (*say* **dee**-zel) *noun* 1 an engine that works by burning oil in compressed air. 2 fuel for this kind of engine. [named after a German engineer, R. Diesel]

diet¹ *noun* 1 special meals that someone eats in order to be healthy or to become less fat. 2 the sort of foods usually eaten by a person or animal.

diet² *verb* (**dieted, dieting**) keep to a diet. [from Greek *diaita* = way of life]

diet³ *noun* the parliament of certain countries (e.g. Japan). [from Latin *dieta* = day's business]

dietitian (*say* dy-it-**ish**-an) *noun* an expert in diet and nutrition.

dif- *prefix* see **dis-.**

differ *verb* 1 be different. 2 disagree. [from *dif-* = apart, + Latin *ferre* = carry]

difference *noun* 1 being different; the way in which things differ. 2 the remainder left after one number is subtracted from another, *The difference between 8 and 3 is 5.* 3 a disagreement.

different *adjective* 1 unlike; not the same. 2 separate; distinct. **differently** *adverb*

Usage *Different from* is the preferred phrase; *different to* is acceptable in informal use; *different than* is common in American use.

differential *noun* 1 a difference in wages between one group of workers and another. 2 a differential gear.
differential gear a system of gears that makes a vehicle's driving wheels revolve at different speeds when going round corners.

differentiate *verb* (**differentiated, differentiating**) 1 make different, *These things differentiate one breed from another.* 2 distinguish; recognise differences, *We do not differentiate between them.* **differentiation** *noun*

▶▶ T H E S A U R U S ◀◀

dictator *noun* autocrat, despot, tyrant.
dictatorial *adjective* authoritarian, autocratic, bossy, despotic, domineering, imperious, overbearing, peremptory, totalitarian, tyrannical.
dictatorship *noun* autocracy, despotism, tyranny.

dictionary *noun* glossary, lexicon, phrase book, thesaurus, vocabulary.

die¹ *verb* 1 bite the dust (*slang*), breathe one's last, croak (*slang*), depart this world, expire, fall (*in war*), go to glory (*slang*), kick the bucket (*slang*), lose one's life, pass away, pass on, perish, snuff it (*slang*). 2 break down, conk out (*informal*), fail.
die down decline, decrease, diminish, ebb, fade, fizzle out, lessen, peter out, subside, taper off, wane.
die out cease, disappear, end, pass, vanish.

diet¹ *noun* 2 fare, food intake, nourishment, nutrition.

differ *verb* 1 be different, be dissimilar, be distinguishable, be poles apart, be unlike, contrast. 2 be at odds, clash, conflict, disagree, quarrel.

difference *noun* 1 contrast, deviation, disparity, dissimilarity, distinction, divergence, nuance, variation; see also CHANGE². 2 balance, deficit, gap. 3 argument, conflict, disagreement, dispute, quarrel, strife, tiff.

different *adjective* 1 altered, alternative, changed, conflicting, contradictory, contrary, contrasting, disparate, dissimilar, divergent, diverse, other, unlike. 2 discrete, distinct, individual, separate.

differentiate *verb* 2 contrast, discriminate, distinguish, separate, set apart, tell apart.

▶▶▶ D I C T I O N A R Y ◀◀

difficult *adjective* **1** needing much effort or skill. **2** not easy to deal with; troublesome.

difficulty *noun* (*plural* **difficulties**) **1** being difficult. **2** a difficult thing; a problem or hindrance.

diffident (*say* **dif**-id-ent) *adjective* shy and not self-confident; hesitating to put yourself or your ideas forward. **diffidently** *adverb*, **diffidence** *noun* [from *dif-* = not, + Latin *fidere* = to trust]

diffract *verb* break up a beam of light etc. **diffraction** *noun* [from *dif-* = apart, + Latin *fractum* = broken]

diffuse¹ *verb* (**diffused, diffusing**) **1** spread something widely or thinly, *diffused lighting.* **2** mix slowly, *diffusing gases.* **diffusion** *noun*

diffuse² *adjective* **1** diffused; spread widely; not concentrated. **2** using many words; not concise. **diffusely** *adverb*, **diffuseness** *noun* [from *dif-* = apart, + Latin *fusum* = poured]

dig¹ *verb* (**dug, digging**) **1** break up soil and move it; make a hole or tunnel by moving soil. **2** poke; push, *Dig a knife into it.* **3** seek or discover by investigating, *We dug up some facts.*

dig² *noun* **1** a piece of digging. **2** a poke.

digest¹ (*say* dy-**jest**) *verb* **1** soften and change food in the stomach etc. so that the body can absorb it. **2** take information into your mind and think it over. **digestible** *adjective*, **digestion** *noun*

digest² (*say* **dy**-jest) *noun* a summary of news, information, etc.

digestive *adjective* of digestion; digesting, *the digestive system.*

digger *noun* **1** someone who digs. **2** a prospector for gold. **3** (*Australian*) a soldier, especially in the trenches.

digit (*say* **dij**-it) *noun* **1** any of the numerals from 0 to 9. **2** a finger or toe. [from Latin *digitus* = finger or toe]

digital *adjective* of or using digits. **digital clock** or **watch** one that shows the time with a row of figures.

dignified *adjective* having dignity.

dignitary *noun* (*plural* **dignitaries**) an important official.

dignity *noun* **1** a calm and serious manner. **2** a high rank. [from Latin *dignus* = worthy]

▶▶▶ T H E S A U R U S ◀◀

difficult *adjective* **1** (*a difficult task*) arduous, demanding, exacting, exhausting, formidable, gruelling, hard, herculean, laborious, onerous, strenuous, taxing, tiring, tough, uphill; (*a difficult problem*) abstruse, baffling, challenging, complex, complicated, confusing, hard, knotty, perplexing, problematical, puzzling, thorny, ticklish, tough, tricky. **2** awkward, demanding, fussy, intractable, obstreperous, recalcitrant, refractory, stroppy (*informal*), stubborn, troublesome, trying, uncooperative.

difficulty *noun* **2** adversity, complication, hang-up (*informal*), hardship, hassle (*informal*), hindrance, hitch, hurdle, impediment, obstacle, ordeal, pitfall, pressure, problem, snag, stumbling block, trouble.
in difficulties in a bind (*informal*), in a fix, in a jam (*informal*), in a mess, in a pickle (*informal*), in a plight, in a predicament, in a quandary, in a spot (*informal*), in dire straits, in hot water (*informal*), in strife (*Australian informal*), in the soup (*informal*), in trouble, up the creek (*informal*).

diffident *adjective* bashful, coy, hesitant, meek, modest, reserved, reticent, shy, tentative, timid, timorous, unassertive.

diffuse¹ *verb* **1** circulate, disperse, spread.

diffuse² *adjective* **1** dispersed, scattered, spread out. **2** long-winded, rambling, verbose, wordy.

dig¹ *verb* **1** burrow, delve (*old use*), excavate, gouge, hollow, scoop, tunnel. **2** jab, plunge, poke, prod, stab, thrust. **3** (*dig up*) discover, dredge up, ferret out, find, fossick out (*Australian informal*), root out, seek, uncover, unearth.

dig² *noun* **1** excavation. **2** nudge, poke, prod, thrust.

digest¹ *verb* **2** absorb, assimilate, comprehend, grasp, take in, understand.

digit *noun* **1** figure, integer, number, numeral.

dignified *adjective* calm, decorous, elegant, formal, grand, honourable, imposing, majestic, noble, proper, sedate, serious, sober, solemn, staid, stately.

dignitary *noun* celebrity, luminary, personage, VIP, worthy.

dignity *noun* **1** decorum, formality, gravity, majesty, nobility, poise, propriety, self-respect, solemnity, stateliness. **2** position, rank, standing, station, status.

▶▶DICTIONARY◀◀

digress *verb* stray from the main subject. **digression** *noun* [from *di-*² = away, + Latin *gressum* = gone]

dike *noun* a dyke.

dilapidated *adjective* falling to pieces. **dilapidation** *noun*

dilate *verb* (**dilated, dilating**) make or become wider or larger. [from *di-*² = apart, + Latin *latus* = wide]

dilatory (*say* dil-at-er-ee) *adjective* slow in doing something; not prompt.

dilemma (*say* dil-**em**-a) *noun* a situation where someone has to choose between two possible actions, each of which will bring difficulties. [from Greek, = double proposal]

diligent (*say* **dil**-ij-ent) *adjective* working hard. **diligently** *adverb*, **diligence** *noun* [from Latin *diligens* = conscientious]

dill *noun* (*Australian slang*) a fool or simpleton.

dilly-bag *noun* (*Australian*) a small bag, originally of plaited grass or fibre.

dilute¹ *verb* (**diluted, diluting**) make a liquid weaker by adding water or other liquid. **dilution** *noun*

dilute² *adjective* diluted, *a dilute acid.*

dim¹ *adjective* (**dimmer, dimmest**) **1** not bright or clear; only faintly lit. **2** (*informal*) stupid. **dimly** *adverb*, **dimness** *noun*

dim² *verb* (**dimmed, dimming**) make or become dim. **dimmer** *noun*

dimension *noun* **1** a measurement such as length, width, area, or volume. **2** size; extent. **dimensional** *adjective*

diminish *verb* make or become smaller. **diminution** *noun*

diminutive (*say* dim-**in**-yoo-tiv) *adjective* very small.

dimple *noun* a small hollow or dent, especially in the skin. **dimpled** *adjective*

din¹ *noun* a loud annoying noise.

din² *verb* (**dinned, dinning**) **1** make a din. **2** force a person to learn something by continually repeating it, *Din it into him.*

dine *verb* (**dined, dining**) have dinner. **diner** *noun*

ding-dong *noun* the sound of a bell or alternate strokes of two bells.

dinghy (*say* **ding**-gee) *noun* (*plural* **dinghies**) a kind of small boat. [from Hindi, = Indian river-boat]

dingo *noun* (*plural* **dingoes**) an Australian wild dog.

dingy (*say* **din**-jee) *adjective* dirty-looking. **dingily** *adverb*, **dinginess** *noun*

dink *verb* (*Australian slang*) give someone a ride on the bar of a bicycle.

dinkum *adjective* (*Australian informal*) genuine, true, *a dinkum Aussie.*

dinner *noun* the main meal of the day, either at midday or in the evening.

▶▶THESAURUS◀◀

digress *verb* deviate, diverge, drift, ramble, stray, wander.

dilapidated *adjective* battered, broken down, decrepit, derelict, ramshackle, rickety, ruined, run-down, tumbledown.

dilate *verb* broaden, distend, enlarge, expand, swell, widen.

dilemma *noun* bind (*informal*), catch-22 (*informal*), difficulty, fix, hole (*informal*), jam (*informal*), mess, plight, predicament, problem, quandary, spot (*informal*).

diligent *adjective* assiduous, attentive, careful, conscientious, earnest, hard-working, indefatigable, industrious, meticulous, painstaking, persevering, scrupulous, sedulous, steady, studious, thorough.

dilute¹ *verb* adulterate, thin, water down, weaken.

dim¹ *adjective* **1** blurred, cloudy, dark, dingy, dull, dusky, faint, fuzzy, gloomy, hazy, indistinct, murky, obscure, pale, shadowy, vague, weak. **2** see STUPID.

dimension *noun* **1** area, breadth, capacity, depth, height, length, measurement, proportion, thickness, volume, width. **2** extent, magnitude, scale, scope, size.

diminish *verb* abate, contract, decline, decrease, dwindle, fade, lessen, reduce, shrink, subside, wane.

din¹ *noun* bedlam, clamour, clatter, commotion, hubbub, hullabaloo, noise, pandemonium, racket, row (*informal*), rumpus, shindy (*informal*), tumult, uproar.

dine *verb* eat, feast, have dinner, sup.

dingy *adjective* dark, dirty, dismal, drab, dreary, dull, gloomy, shabby.

dinkum *adjective* authentic, bona fide, dinky-di (*Australian informal*), genuine, honest-to-goodness (*informal*), real, true, veritable.

dinner *noun* banquet, feast, meal, repast (*formal*), supper, tea.

▶▶▶ D I C T I O N A R Y ◀◀

dinosaur (*say* **dy**-noss-or) *noun* a prehistoric lizard-like animal, often of enormous size. [from Greek *deinos* = terrible, + *sauros* = lizard]

dint *noun* a dent.
by dint of by means of.

diocese (*say* **dy**-oss-iss) *noun* a district under the care of a bishop. **diocesan** (*say* dy-**oss**-iss-an) *adjective*

dioxide *noun* an oxide with two atoms of oxygen to one of another element, *carbon dioxide*. [from *di*-¹ + *oxide*]

dip¹ *verb* (**dipped, dipping**) **1** put down into a liquid. **2** go down. **3** lower.

dip² *noun* **1** dipping. **2** a downward slope or hollow. **3** a quick swim. **4** a substance into which things are dipped.

diphtheria (*say* dif-**theer**-ee-a) *noun* a serious disease that causes inflammation in the throat. [from Greek, = leather (because a tough skin forms)]

diphthong (*say* **dif**-thong) *noun* a compound vowel-sound made up of two sounds, e.g. *oi* in *point* (made up of 'aw' + 'ee') or *ou* in *loud* ('ah' + 'oo'). [from *di*-¹, + Greek *phthongos* = sound]

diploma *noun* a certificate awarded by a college etc. for skill in a particular subject. [from Greek, = folded paper]

diplomacy *noun* keeping friendly with other nations or other people.

diplomat *noun* **1** a person employed in diplomacy on behalf of his or her country. **2** a tactful person.

diplomatic *adjective* **1** of diplomats or diplomacy. **2** tactful. **diplomatically** *adverb*

dire *adjective* dreadful; serious, *dire need*.

direct¹ *adjective* **1** as straight as possible. **2** going straight to the point; frank. **3** exact, *the direct opposite*. **directly** *adverb & conjunction*, **directness** *noun*

direct current electric current flowing only in one direction.

direct object the word that receives the action of the verb. In '*she hit him*', 'him' is the direct object.

direct² *verb* **1** tell someone the way. **2** guide or aim in a certain direction. **3** control; manage. **4** order, *He directed his troops to advance*. **director** *noun* [from Latin *directum* = kept straight]

direction *noun* **1** directing. **2** the line along which something moves or faces. **directional** *adjective*

directions *plural noun* information on how to use or do something.

directive *noun* a command.

directory *noun* (*plural* **directories**) a book containing a list of people with their telephone numbers, addresses, etc.

dirge *noun* a slow mournful song.

dirk *noun* a kind of dagger.

▶▶▶ T H E S A U R U S ◀◀

dip¹ *verb* **1** dunk, immerse, plunge, sink, steep, submerge, wet. **2** decline, descend, drop, go down, slope downwards.

dip² *noun* **2** depression, hollow. **3** bathe, bogey (*Australian*), plunge, swim.

diploma *noun* award, certificate, qualification.

diplomacy *noun* courtesy, delicacy, discretion, tact, tactfulness.

diplomat *noun* **1** ambassador, attaché, consul, envoy, representative.

diplomatic *adjective* **2** courteous, delicate, discreet, judicious, polite, politic, sensitive, tactful.

dire *adjective* (*dire consequences*) appalling, calamitous, catastrophic, disastrous, dreadful, gloomy, grave, grim, horrible, terrible; (*dire need*) critical, desperate, drastic, extreme, pressing, serious, urgent.

direct¹ *adjective* **1** straight, unswerving. **2** blunt, candid, explicit, forthright, frank, honest, open, outspoken, plain, straight, straightforward, to the point. **3** absolute, complete, diametrical, exact, polar.

direct² *verb* **1** conduct, guide, lead, navigate, point, show, steer, usher. **2** aim, level, point, target, train, turn. **3** administer, command, control, govern, head, lead, manage, mastermind, oversee, preside over, regulate, run, superintend, supervise. **4** bid, command, instruct, order, tell.

director *noun* administrator, boss, captain, chairperson, chief, commander, conductor, coordinator, executive, governor, head, leader, manager, superintendent, supervisor.

direction *noun* **1** administration, charge, command, control, guidance, leadership, management, supervision. **2** course, line, route, tack, way.

directions *plural noun* guidelines, instructions, orders, recipe, rules.

directory *noun* index, list, register.

dirge *noun* elegy, keen, lament.

▶▶▶ D I C T I O N A R Y ◀◀◀

dirt *noun* **1** earth, soil. **2** anything that is not clean.

dirty¹ *adjective* (**dirtier**, **dirtiest**) **1** not clean; soiled. **2** unfair; dishonourable, *a dirty trick*. **3** indecent; obscene. **dirtily** *adverb*, **dirtiness** *noun*

dirty² *verb* (**dirtied**, **dirtying**) make or become dirty.

dis- *prefix* (changing to **dif-** before words beginning with *f*, and to **di-** before some consonants) **1** not; the reverse of (as in *dishonest*). **2** apart; separated (as in *disarm*, *disperse*). [from Latin, = not; away]

disabled *adjective* made unable to do something because of illness or injury. **disability** *noun*, **disablement** *noun*

disadvantage *noun* something that hinders or is unhelpful. **disadvantaged** *adjective*, **disadvantageous** *adjective*

disagree *verb* (**disagreed**, **disagreeing**) **1** have or express a different opinion from someone. **2** have a bad effect, *Rich food disagrees with me*. **disagreement** *noun*

disagreeable *adjective* **1** unpleasant. **2** bad-tempered.

disappear *verb* stop being visible; vanish. **disappearance** *noun*

disappoint *verb* fail to do what someone hopes for. **disappointment** *noun*

disapprobation *noun* disapproval.

disapprove *verb* (**disapproved**, **disapproving**) have or show an unfavourable opinion; not approve. **disapproval** *noun*

disarm *verb* **1** reduce the size of armed forces. **2** take away someone's weapons. **3** overcome a person's anger or doubt, *Her friendliness disarmed their suspicions*. **disarmament** *noun*

disarray *noun* disorder, confusion.

▶▶▶ T H E S A U R U S ◀◀◀

dirt *noun* **1** clay, earth, loam, soil. **2** dust, filth, grime, mire, muck, mud, soot.

dirty¹ *adjective* **1** blackened, dingy, dusty, filthy, foul, grimy, grotty (*slang*), grubby, insanitary, messy, muddy, soiled, sooty, sordid, squalid, stained, unclean, unwashed. **2** base, contemptible, despicable, dishonest, dishonourable, low, low-down, mean, nasty, shabby, underhand, unfair, unsporting. **3** bawdy, blue, coarse, crude, filthy, improper, indecent, lewd, obscene, offensive, pornographic, rude, smutty, tasteless, vulgar.

dirty² *verb* blacken, foul, muddy, pollute, soil, stain, sully, tarnish.

disabled *adjective* crippled, handicapped, incapacitated, lame, maimed.
disability *noun* handicap, impairment, incapacity.

disadvantage *noun* drawback, handicap, hindrance, impediment, inconvenience, liability, minus.
disadvantaged *adjective* deprived, under-privileged.

disagree *verb* **1** argue, be at loggerheads, be at odds, be at variance, be incompatible, clash, conflict, contrast, differ, dissent, diverge, quarrel, squabble, wrangle.
disagreement *noun* altercation, argument, clash, conflict, controversy, difference, dispute, dissension, dissent, quarrel, row, squabble, tiff, wrangle.

disagreeable *adjective* **1** disgusting, distasteful, nasty, objectionable, obnoxious, offensive, repugnant, repulsive, revolting, unpleasant. **2** bad-tempered, crabby, cross, crotchety, fractious, grouchy (*informal*), grumpy, irritable, shirty (*informal*), snaky (*Australian informal*), stroppy (*informal*), surly, unfriendly.

disappear *verb* clear, dissipate, evaporate, fade, melt away, pass, vanish; see also RUN AWAY (at RUN¹).

disappoint *verb* dash the hopes of, discourage, disenchant, dishearten, disillusion, dissatisfy, frustrate, let down, sadden, thwart.
disappointment *noun* **1** chagrin, discontent, disenchantment, disillusionment, dissatisfaction, frustration, regret, sadness, unhappiness. **2** anticlimax, comedown, damp squib, failure, fiasco, fizzer (*Australian informal*), flop (*informal*), let-down, non-event, swizz (*informal*), wash-out (*informal*).

disapprove *verb* (**disapprove of**) censure, condemn, criticise, denounce, deplore, deprecate, frown on, object to, take a dim view of (*informal*).
disapproval *noun* censure, condemnation, criticism, disapprobation, disfavour, dissatisfaction, objection, opposition.

disarray *noun* chaos, confusion, disorder, havoc, mess, muddle, shambles.

▶▶DICTIONARY◀◀

disaster *noun* **1** a very bad accident or misfortune. **2** a complete failure. **disastrous** *adjective*, **disastrously** *adverb* [literally 'an unlucky star', from *dis-*, + Latin *astrum* = star]

disband *verb* break up a group.

disbelieve *verb* be unable or unwilling to believe something. **disbelief** *noun*

disburse *verb* (**disbursed, disbursing**) pay out money. **disbursement** *noun*

disc *noun* **1** any round flat object. **2** a gramophone record. **3** (in computers, usually **disk**) a storage device consisting of magnetically coated plates.
disc jockey a person who introduces and plays records. [from Latin *discus* = disc]

discard *verb* throw away; put something aside as being useless or unwanted.

discern (*say* dis-**sern**) *verb* perceive; see or recognise clearly. **discernible** *adjective*, **discernment** *noun*

discerning *adjective* perceptive; showing good judgement.

discharge¹ *verb* (**discharged, discharging**) **1** release a person. **2** dismiss from employment. **3** send something out, *discharge smoke*. **4** fire a gun or missile. **5** pay or do what was agreed, *discharge the debt*.

discharge² *noun* **1** discharging. **2** something that is discharged.

disciple *noun* a person who accepts the teachings of another whom he or she regards as a leader; any of the original followers of Jesus Christ. [from Latin *discipulus* = learner]

disciplinarian *noun* a person who believes in strict discipline.

discipline¹ *noun* orderly and obedient behaviour. **disciplinary** (*say* **dis**-ip-lin-er-ee) *adjective*

discipline² *verb* (**disciplined, disciplining**) **1** train to be orderly and obedient. **2** punish. [from Latin *disciplina* = training]

disclaim *verb* disown; say that you are not responsible for something.

disclose *verb* (**disclosed, disclosing**) reveal. **disclosure** *noun*

disco *noun* (*plural* **discos**) (*informal*) a discothèque.

discolour *verb* spoil a thing's colour; stain. **discoloration** *noun*

discomfit *verb* (**discomfited, discomfiting**) disconcert; dismay. **discomfiture** *noun*

discomfort *noun* being uncomfortable.

▶▶THESAURUS◀◀

disaster *noun* **1** accident, adversity, calamity, cataclysm, catastrophe, misfortune, mishap, reverse, tragedy. **2** failure, fiasco, fizzer (*Australian informal*), flop (*informal*), wash-out (*informal*).
disastrous *adjective* appalling, calamitous, cataclysmic, catastrophic, devastating, dire, dreadful, ruinous, terrible, tragic.

disband *verb* break up, disperse, dissolve, separate, split up.

disbelieve *verb* distrust, doubt, mistrust, question.

discard *verb* cast off, chuck out (*informal*), dice (*Australian informal*), dispose of, ditch (*informal*), dump, get rid of, jettison, reject, scrap, shed, throw away.

discern *verb* detect, make out, notice, observe, perceive, recognise, see, sense.

discerning *adjective* critical, discriminating, intelligent, judicious, perceptive, sharp, shrewd, wise.

discharge¹ *verb* **1** free, liberate, release. **2** dismiss, fire, kick out (*informal*), sack (*informal*). **3** belch, eject, emit, empty out, expel, exude, give out, leak, ooze, pour out,

release, secrete, send out, spurt. **4** detonate, explode, fire, let off, set off, shoot, trigger. **5** clear, meet, pay, settle, square.

disciple *noun* adherent, apprentice, devotee, follower, pupil, supporter.

disciplinarian *noun* authoritarian, hard-liner, martinet, stickler, taskmaster.

discipline¹ *noun* control, order, routine, system.

discipline² *verb* **1** coach, drill, educate, indoctrinate, instruct, train. **2** chastise, correct, penalise, punish, rebuke, reprimand.

disclaim *verb* deny, disown, refuse, reject, repudiate.

disclose *verb* air, betray, blab, blow (*slang*), bring to light, divulge, expose, give away, impart, leak, let out, let slip, make known, make public, publish, reveal, tell, uncover.

disco *noun* club, discothèque, nightclub.

discolour *verb* bleach, fade, scorch, stain, tarnish, tinge.

discomfort *noun* ache, affliction, distress, hardship, irritation, misery, pain, soreness, suffering, uneasiness.

disconcert (*say* dis-kon-**sert**) *verb* make a person feel uneasy.

disconnect *verb* break a connection; detach. **disconnection** *noun*

disconnected *adjective* not having a connection between its parts.

disconsolate (*say* dis-**kon**-sol-at) *adjective* disappointed.

discontent *noun* lack of contentment; dissatisfaction. **discontented** *adjective*, **discontentment** *noun*

discontinue *verb* (**discontinued, discontinuing**) put an end to something.

discord *noun* **1** disagreement; quarrelling. **2** musical notes sounded together and producing a harsh or unpleasant sound. **discordant** *adjective* [from *dis-* = not, + Latin *cordis* = of the heart]

discothèque (*say* **dis**-ko-tek) *noun* **1** a place or party where records are playing for dancing. **2** the equipment for playing records for dancing. [French, = record-library]

discount[1] *noun* an amount by which a price is reduced.

discount[2] *verb* ignore; disregard, *We cannot discount the possibility.*

discourage *verb* (**discouraged, discouraging**) **1** take away someone's enthusiasm or confidence. **2** try to persuade someone not to do something; dissuade; deter. **discouragement** *noun*

discourse[1] *noun* **1** a formal speech or piece of writing about something. **2** a conversation.

discourse[2] *verb* (**discoursed, discoursing**) speak or write at length about something.

discourteous *adjective* not courteous; rude. **discourteously** *adverb*, **discourtesy** *noun*

discover *verb* **1** find. **2** be the first person to find something. **discoverer** *noun*, **discovery** *noun* [from *dis-* = apart, + *cover*]

discredit[1] *verb* (**discredited, discrediting**) **1** destroy people's confidence in a person or thing; disgrace. **2** distrust.

discredit[2] *noun* **1** disgrace. **2** distrust. **discreditable** *adjective*

discreet *adjective* **1** not giving away secrets. **2** not showy. **discreetly** *adverb*

Usage Do not confuse with *discrete*.

disconcert *verb* agitate, confuse, discomfit, disturb, faze (*informal*), fluster, perturb, put off, rattle (*informal*), ruffle, throw (*informal*), trouble, unnerve, upset, worry.

disconnect *verb* cut off, detach, disengage, switch off, turn off, uncouple, undo, unplug.

disconnected *adjective* disjointed, disorganised, garbled, haphazard, incoherent, jumbled, rambling, random, unsystematic.

discontent *noun* disenchantment, displeasure, disquiet, dissatisfaction, misery, regret, resentment, restlessness, unhappiness. **discontented** *adjective* browned off (*slang*), cheesed off (*slang*), disenchanted, disgruntled, displeased, dissatisfied, fed up (*informal*), miserable, unhappy.

discontinue *verb* abandon, break off, cancel, cease, cut, end, finish, interrupt, stop, suspend, terminate.

discord *noun* **1** argument, conflict, disagreement, disharmony, dissension, disunity, friction, quarrelling, strife. **discordant** *adjective* cacophonous, dissonant, grating, harsh, jarring, strident.

discount[1] *noun* concession, cut, deduction, rebate, reduction.

discourage *verb* **1** daunt, demoralise, depress, dishearten, dismay, intimidate. **2** deter, dissuade, put off, talk out of.

discourse[1] *noun* **1** address, dissertation, essay, lecture, monograph, oration, paper, sermon, speech, talk, thesis, treatise. **2** see CONVERSATION.

discourteous *adjective* bad-mannered, boorish, cheeky, disrespectful, ill-mannered, impertinent, impolite, impudent, insolent, insulting, rude, uncivil, uncouth.

discover *verb* **1** come across, come upon, detect, dig up, ferret out, find, find out, hear of, hit on, identify, learn, light on, locate, perceive, read of, realise, spot, stumble on, suss out (*informal*), track down, uncover, unearth, work out. **discoverer** *noun* creator, explorer, inventor, pioneer.

discredit[1] *verb* **1** (*discredit a person*) blacken, defame, denigrate, disgrace, disparage, malign, slander, smear, sully, vilify; (*discredit an idea*) challenge, debunk (*informal*), disprove, explode, invalidate, question.

discreet *adjective* **1** careful, cautious, chary, circumspect, diplomatic, guarded, judicious, prudent, tactful, wary.

▶▶DICTIONARY◀◀

discrepancy (*say* dis-**krep**-an-see) *noun* (*plural* **discrepancies**) difference; lack of agreement, *There are several discrepancies in the two accounts.* **discrepant** *adjective* [from Latin, = discord]

discrete *adjective* separate; distinct from each other.

Usage Do not confuse with *discreet*.

discretion (*say* dis-**kresh**-on) *noun* **1** being discreet; keeping secrets. **2** power to take action according to your own judgement, *The treasurer has full discretion.*

discriminate *verb* (**discriminated, discriminating**) **1** notice the differences between things; distinguish; prefer one thing to another. **2** treat people differently or unfairly, e.g. because of their race, sex, or religion. **discrimination** *noun* [from Latin *discrimen* = separator]

Usage Note that these words have both a 'good' sense and a 'bad' sense. A *discriminating* person can mean someone who judges carefully and well, but it can also mean someone who judges unfairly.

discus *noun* (*plural* **discuses**) a thick heavy disc thrown in athletic contests.

discuss *verb* talk with other people about a subject. **discussion** *noun*

disdain[1] *noun* scorn; contempt. **disdainful** *adjective*, **disdainfully** *adverb*

disdain[2] *verb* **1** regard or treat with disdain. **2** not do something because of disdain, *She disdained to reply.* [from *dis-* = not, + Latin *dignus* = worthy]

disease *noun* an unhealthy condition; an illness. **diseased** *adjective* [from *dis-* = not, + *ease*]

disembark *verb* put or go ashore. **disembarkation** *noun*

disembodied *adjective* freed from the body, *a disembodied spirit.*

disembowel *verb* (**disembowelled, disembowelling**) take out the bowels or inside parts of something.

disengage *verb* (**disengaged, disengaging**) disconnect; detach.

disentangle *verb* (**disentangled, disentangling**) free from tangles or confusion.

disfavour *noun* disapproval; dislike.

disfigure *verb* (**disfigured, disfiguring**) spoil a person's or thing's appearance. **disfigurement** *noun*

disgorge *verb* (**disgorged, disgorging**) pour or send out, *The pipe disgorged its contents.* [from *dis-* + *gorge* = throat]

disgrace[1] *noun* **1** shame; loss of approval or respect. **2** something that causes shame. **disgraceful** *adjective*, **disgracefully** *adverb*

disgrace[2] *verb* (**disgraced, disgracing**) bring disgrace upon someone.

▶▶THESAURUS◀◀

discrepancy *noun* difference, disagreement, disparity, inconsistency.

discrete *adjective* disconnected, distinct, separate.

discretion *noun* **1** care, discernment, judgement, prudence, sense, sensitivity, tact, wisdom.

discriminate *verb* **1** differentiate, distinguish, tell apart.
discrimination *noun* bias, favouritism, inequity, intolerance, prejudice, unfairness.

discuss *verb* argue, confer on, consider, converse about, debate, deliberate, examine, have out, speak about, talk about, thrash out.
discussion *noun* argument, conference, consultation, conversation, debate, deliberation, dialogue, examination, exchange, talk.

disdain[1] *noun* contempt, derision, scorn.
disdainful *adjective* arrogant, contemptuous, derisive, haughty, hoity-toity, proud, scornful, sneering, snobbish, snooty (*informal*), supercilious, superior.

disdain[2] *verb* **1** despise, look down on, rebuff, reject, scorn, sneer at, spurn.

disease *noun* affliction, ailment, bug (*informal*), complaint, condition, disorder, illness, infection, malady, plague, sickness.

disembark *verb* alight, get off, get out, go ashore, land.

disentangle *verb* detach, extricate, free, liberate, sort out, straighten out, unravel, untangle, untie, untwist.

disfigure *verb* damage, deface, deform, mar, mutilate, ruin, scar, spoil.

disgrace[1] *noun* **1** discredit, dishonour, disrepute, humiliation, ignominy, reproach, scandal, shame, stigma.
disgraceful *adjective* contemptible, degrading, discreditable, dishonourable, ignominious, outrageous, scandalous, shameful, unbecoming, unseemly.

disgrace[2] *verb* bring dishonour to, bring shame on, degrade, embarrass, humiliate, let down.

▶▶ D I C T I O N A R Y ◀◀

disgruntled *adjective* discontented; resentful.

disguise¹ *verb* (**disguised, disguising**) make a person or thing look different so as to deceive people.

disguise² *noun* something used for disguising.

disgust¹ *noun* a feeling that something is very unpleasant or disgraceful.

disgust² *verb* cause disgust. **disgusted** *adjective*, **disgusting** *adjective* [from *dis-* = not, + Latin *gustare* = to taste]

dish¹ *noun* (*plural* **dishes**) **1** a plate or bowl for food. **2** food served on a dish.

dish² *verb* (*informal*) ruin; spoil people's hopes, *It had dished our chances.*

dishcloth *noun* a cloth for washing dishes.

dishearten *verb* cause a person to lose hope or confidence.

dishevelled (*say* dish-**ev**-eld) *adjective* ruffled and untidy. **dishevelment** *noun* [from *dis-* = apart, + Old French *chevel* = hair]

dishonest *adjective* not honest. **dishonestly** *adverb*, **dishonesty** *noun*

dishonour *noun* & *verb* disgrace. **dishonourable** *adjective*

dishwasher *noun* a machine for washing dishes etc. automatically.

disillusion *verb* get rid of someone's pleasant but wrong beliefs. **disillusionment** *noun*

disincentive *noun* something that discourages an action or effort.

disinclination *noun* unwillingness.

disinclined *adjective* unwilling to do something.

disinfect *verb* destroy the germs in something. **disinfection** *noun*

disinfectant *noun* a substance used for disinfecting things.

disinherit *verb* deprive a person of the right to inherit something.

disintegrate *verb* (**disintegrated, disintegrating**) break up into small parts or pieces. **disintegration** *noun*

disinter *verb* (**disinterred, disinterring**) dig up something buried; unearth.

▶▶▶ T H E S A U R U S ◀◀◀

disgruntled *adjective* browned off (*slang*), cheesed off (*slang*), cross, discontented, displeased, dissatisfied, fed up (*informal*), unhappy.

disguise¹ *verb* camouflage, conceal, cover up, dress up, hide, mask, masquerade, veil.

disguise² *noun* camouflage, costume, cover, mask, masquerade.

disgust¹ *noun* abhorrence, antipathy, aversion, contempt, dislike, distaste, hatred, loathing, nausea, repugnance, repulsion, revulsion.

disgust² *verb* appal, horrify, nauseate, offend, repel, revolt, shock, sicken, turn someone's stomach.
  disgusting *adjective* appalling, detestable, distasteful, dreadful, filthy, foul, gross (*informal*), loathsome, nauseating, objectionable, obnoxious, offensive, off-putting, repellent, repugnant, repulsive, revolting, shocking, sickening, unpleasant, vile, yucky (*informal*).

dish¹ *noun* **1** basin, bowl, casserole, container, coolamon (*Australian*), plate, platter, ramekin, receptacle, tureen; (*dishes*) crockery.

dishearten *verb* demoralise, depress, discourage, dismay, sadden.

dishevelled *adjective* bedraggled, messy, ruffled, scruffy, tangled, tousled, unkempt, untidy.

dishonest *adjective* bent (*slang*), corrupt, criminal, crooked, deceitful, deceptive, dodgy (*informal*), false, fraudulent, hypocritical, insincere, lying, mendacious, misleading, shady, shonky (*Australian informal*), two-faced, underhand, unscrupulous, untrustworthy, untruthful.

dishonour *noun* discredit, disgrace, disrepute, humiliation, ignominy, reproach, scandal, shame, stigma.
  dishonourable *adjective* base, despicable, discreditable, disgraceful, disreputable, ignominious, improper, low, opprobrious, reprehensible, shabby, shameful, unprincipled.

disillusion *verb* disabuse, disappoint, disenchant, enlighten, undeceive.

disincentive *noun* deterrent, discouragement.

disinfect *verb* clean, cleanse, fumigate, purify, sanitise, sterilise.

disinfectant *noun* antiseptic, bactericide, germicide, sanitiser, steriliser.

disintegrate *verb* break up, collapse, crumble, decay, decompose, deteriorate, fall apart, perish, rot, shatter.

▶▶ DICTIONARY ◀◀

disinterested *adjective* impartial; not biased; not influenced by hope of gaining something yourself, *She gave us some disinterested advice.*

Usage Do not use this word as if it meant 'not interested' or 'bored' (the word for this is *uninterested*).

disjointed *adjective* disconnected.

disk *noun* a disc.

dislike[1] *noun* a feeling of not liking somebody or something.

dislike[2] *verb* (**disliked, disliking**) not to like somebody or something.

dislocate *verb* (**dislocated, dislocating**) 1 dislodge a bone from its proper position in one of the joints. 2 disrupt, *Fog dislocated the traffic.* **dislocation** *noun*

dislodge *verb* (**dislodged, dislodging**) move or force something from its place.

disloyal *adjective* not loyal. **disloyally** *adverb*, **disloyalty** *noun*

dismal *adjective* gloomy. **dismally** *adverb* [from Latin *dies mali* = unlucky days]

dismantle *verb* (**dismantled, dismantling**) take something to pieces.

dismay *noun* a feeling of surprise and discouragement. **dismay** *verb*

dismiss *verb* 1 send someone away; disband. 2 tell a person that you will no longer employ him or her. 3 stop considering an idea etc. 4 get a batsman or side out. **dismissal** *noun*, **dismissive** *adjective* [from *dis-*, + Latin *missum* = sent]

dismount *verb* get off a horse or bicycle.

disobedient *adjective* not obedient. **disobediently** *adverb*, **disobedience** *noun*

disobey *verb* (**disobeyed, disobeying**) not to obey; disregard orders.

disorder *noun* 1 untidiness. 2 a disturbance. 3 an illness. **disorderly** *adjective*

disorganise *verb* (**disorganised, disorganising**) throw into confusion. **disorganisation** *noun*

▶▶ THESAURUS ◀◀

disinterested *adjective* detached, dispassionate, impartial, neutral, objective, unbiased, uninvolved, unprejudiced.

disjointed *adjective* desultory, disconnected, disorganised, fragmented, incoherent, jumbled, mixed up, rambling.

dislike[1] *noun* abhorrence, animosity, antipathy, aversion, contempt, detestation, disgust, distaste, hatred, horror, hostility, loathing, repugnance, resentment, revulsion.

dislike[2] *verb* abominate, despise, detest, hate, have an aversion to, loathe, object to, resent, take exception to.

disloyal *adjective* faithless, false, perfidious, treacherous, two-faced, unfaithful, untrue. **disloyalty** *noun* betrayal, infidelity, perfidy, treachery, treason, unfaithfulness.

dismal *adjective* black, bleak, cheerless, depressing, dreary, funereal, gloomy, grim, lugubrious, melancholy, miserable, mournful, sad, sombre.

dismantle *verb* demolish, knock down, pull to pieces, take apart, take down, undo.

dismay *noun* agitation, alarm, anxiety, apprehension, consternation, discouragement, dread, fear, horror, shock, terror, trepidation. **dismay** *verb* alarm, appal, daunt, depress, disconcert, discourage, dishearten, distress, frighten, horrify, scare, shock, terrify, unnerve.

dismiss *verb* 1 disband, let go, release, send away. 2 discharge, fire, get rid of, give notice to, give the boot to (*slang*), give the sack to (*informal*), kick out (*informal*), lay off, make redundant, pension off, remove, sack (*informal*). 3 discard, give up, pooh-pooh (*informal*), reject, set aside, spurn.

dismount *verb* alight, descend, get down, get off.

disobedient *adjective* contrary, defiant, insubordinate, intractable, mutinous, naughty, obstreperous, perverse, rebellious, recalcitrant, refractory, unmanageable, unruly, wayward.

disobey *verb* break, contravene, defy, disregard, flout, ignore, infringe, transgress, violate.

disorder *noun* 1 chaos, confusion, disarray, mess, muddle, shambles, untidiness. 2 anarchy, bedlam, chaos, commotion, confusion, disturbance, havoc, lawlessness, mayhem, pandemonium, rioting, trouble, turmoil, unrest, uproar. 3 ailment, complaint, condition, disease, illness, malady, sickness. **disorderly** *adjective* 1 chaotic, confused, disorganised, higgledy-piggledy, jumbled, messy, muddled, topsy-turvy, unsystematic, untidy. 2 badly-behaved, boisterous, lawless, obstreperous, riotous, rowdy, turbulent, undisciplined, unruly, wild.

disorganised *adjective* careless, confused, disorderly, haphazard, messy, slipshod, sloppy, unmethodical, unsystematic.

▶▶ D I C T I O N A R Y ◀◀

disown *verb* refuse to acknowledge that a person or thing has any connection with you.

disparage (*say* dis-**pa**-rij) *verb* (**disparaged**, **disparaging**) belittle; declare that something is small or unimportant. **disparagement** *noun*

disparity *noun* (*plural* **disparities**) difference; inequality.

dispassionate *adjective* calm and impartial. **dispassionately** *adverb*

dispatch[1] *verb* **1** send off to a destination. **2** kill.

dispatch[2] *noun* **1** dispatching. **2** a report or message sent. **3** promptness; speed.

dispel *verb* (**dispelled**, **dispelling**) drive away; scatter, *Wind dispels fog.* [from *dis-* = apart, + Latin *pellere* = to drive]

dispensary *noun* (*plural* **dispensaries**) a place where medicines are dispensed.

dispense *verb* (**dispensed**, **dispensing**) **1** distribute; deal out. **2** prepare medicine according to prescriptions. **dispensation** *noun*, **dispenser** *noun*
dispense with do without something. [from *dis-* = separately, + Latin *pensum* = weighed]

disperse *verb* (**dispersed**, **dispersing**) scatter. **dispersal** *noun*, **dispersion** *noun* [from Latin *dispersum* = scattered]

displace *verb* (**displaced**, **displacing**) **1** shift from its place. **2** take a person's or thing's place. **displacement** *noun*

display[1] *verb* show; arrange something so that it can be clearly seen.

display[2] *noun* **1** the displaying of something; an exhibition. **2** something displayed. [from *dis-* = separately, + Latin *plicare* = to fold]

displease *verb* (**displeased**, **displeasing**) annoy or not please someone. **displeasure** *noun*

disposable *adjective* made to be thrown away after it has been used.

disposal *noun* getting rid of something.
at your disposal for you to use; ready for you.

dispose *verb* (**disposed**, **disposing**) **1** place in position; arrange, *Dispose your troops in two lines.* **2** make a person ready or willing to do something, *I feel disposed to help him.*
be well disposed be friendly.
dispose of get rid of. [from *dis-* = away, + French *poser* = to place]

disposition *noun* **1** a person's nature or qualities. **2** arrangement.

disproportionate *adjective* out of proportion; too large or too small.

disprove *verb* (**disproved**, **disproving**) show that something is not true.

▶▶ T H E S A U R U S ◀◀

disown *verb* cast off, deny, disclaim, ostracise, reject, renounce, repudiate.

disparage *verb* bag (*Australian informal*), belittle, criticise, depreciate, knock (*informal*), rubbish, run down, talk down.
disparaging *adjective* critical, derogatory, insulting, pejorative, uncomplimentary.

disparity *noun* contrast, difference, discrepancy, gap, inequality.

dispassionate *adjective* calm, clinical, composed, disinterested, impartial, neutral, objective, unbiased, unemotional, uninvolved, unprejudiced.

dispatch[1] *verb* **1** consign, convey, deliver, forward, mail, post, send, transmit. **2** see KILL[1].

dispatch[2] *noun* **2** bulletin, communication, communiqué, letter, message, report.

dispel *verb* allay, banish, drive away, remove, scatter.

dispense *verb* **1** allocate, allot, apportion, deal out, dish out (*informal*), distribute, dole out, give out, hand out, issue, mete out. **2** make up, prepare, provide, supply.
dispense with dispose of, do without, forgo, get rid of, relinquish.

disperse *verb* break up, disband, scatter, spread out.

displace *verb* **2** oust, replace, supersede, supplant.

display[1] *verb* demonstrate, exhibit, flaunt, manifest, parade, present, reveal, show.

display[2] *noun* **2** array, demonstration, exhibition, exposition, pageant, presentation, show, spectacle.

displease *verb* anger, annoy, exasperate, irk, irritate, offend, trouble, upset, vex, worry.
displeasure *noun* anger, annoyance, chagrin, disapproval, disfavour, exasperation, indignation, irritation, wrath.

disposable *adjective* discardable, throw-away.

dispose *verb* **1** arrange, array, group, marshal, order, organise, place, set out.
dispose of discard, dispatch, ditch (*informal*), dump, get rid of, give away, scrap, sell, throw away, throw out.

disposition *noun* **1** attitude, character, make-up, nature, personality, spirit, temperament.

disprove *verb* confute, debunk (*informal*), discredit, explode, negate, rebut, refute.

►►►DICTIONARY◄◄

disputation *noun* a debate; an argument.

dispute¹ *verb* (**disputed, disputing**) **1** argue; debate. **2** quarrel. **3** raise an objection to, *We dispute their claim.*

dispute² *noun* **1** an argument; a debate. **2** a quarrel.
in dispute being argued about. [from *dis-* = apart, + Latin *putare* = consider]

disqualify *verb* (**disqualified, disqualifying**) bar someone from a competition etc. because he or she has broken the rules or is not properly qualified to take part. **disqualification** *noun*

disquiet *noun* anxiety; worry. **disquieting** *adjective*

disregard¹ *verb* ignore.

disregard² *noun* the act of ignoring something.

disrepair *noun* bad condition caused by not doing repairs.

disreputable *adjective* not respectable.

disrepute *noun* discredit; bad reputation.

disrespect *noun* lack of respect; rudeness.
disrespectful *adjective*, **disrespectfully** *adverb*

disrupt *verb* put into disorder; interrupt a continuous flow, *Fog disrupted traffic.* **disruption** *noun*, **disruptive** *adjective* [from *dis-* = apart, + Latin *ruptum* = broken]

dissatisfied *adjective* not satisfied. **dissatisfaction** *noun*

dissect (*say* dis-**sekt**) *verb* cut something up so as to examine it. **dissection** *noun* [from *dis-* = apart, + Latin *sectum* = cut]

disseminate *verb* (**disseminated, disseminating**) spread ideas etc. widely. **dissemination** *noun* [from *dis-* = apart, + Latin *seminare* = sow (scatter seeds)]

dissent¹ *noun* disagreement.

dissent² *verb* disagree. [from *dis-* = apart, + Latin *sentire* = feel]

dissertation *noun* a discourse.

disservice *noun* a harmful action done by someone who was intending to help.

dissident *noun* a person who disagrees; someone who opposes the authorities. **dissident** *adjective*, **dissidence** *noun*

dissipate *verb* (**dissipated, dissipating**) **1** dispel; disperse. **2** squander; waste; fritter away. **dissipation** *noun* [from Latin *dissipare* = scatter]

dissociate *verb* (**dissociated, dissociating**) separate something in your thoughts. **dissociation** *noun*

dissolute *adjective* living a frivolous and selfish life.

dissolution *noun* dissolving.

►►►THESAURUS◄◄

dispute¹ *verb* **1,2** argue, bicker, clash, debate, disagree, haggle, quarrel, squabble, wrangle. **3** challenge, contest, doubt, query, question.

dispute² *noun* altercation, argument, battle, conflict, controversy, debate, disagreement, feud, quarrel, row, squabble, wrangle.

disqualify *verb* ban, bar, debar, outlaw, preclude, prohibit.

disregard¹ *verb* brush aside, forget, ignore, neglect, overlook, pay no attention to; see also DISOBEY.

disrepair *noun* decay, dilapidation, neglect, ruin.

disreputable *adjective* (*a disreputable company*) discreditable, dishonourable, dodgy (*informal*), dubious, notorious, shady, shonky (*Australian informal*), suspect, untrustworthy; (*a disreputable appearance*) dirty, scruffy, seedy, shabby, sleazy, slovenly, unkempt, untidy.

disrespect *noun* contempt, impiety, impoliteness, insolence, irreverence, rudeness.

disrespectful *adjective* cheeky, contemptuous, discourteous, impertinent, impolite, impudent, insolent, irreverent, offensive, rude, uncivil.

disrupt *verb* break up, cut into, disturb, interfere with, interrupt, obstruct, upset.

dissatisfied *adjective* browned off (*slang*), cheesed off (*slang*), disappointed, discontented, disenchanted, disgruntled, displeased, fed up (*informal*), frustrated, unhappy.

dissect *verb* cut up, dismember.

disseminate *verb* broadcast, circulate, distribute, promulgate, publicise, publish, spread.

dissent² *verb* differ, disagree, object, protest.

disservice *noun* bad turn, injury, injustice, unkindness, wrong.

dissident *noun* apostate, dissenter, nonconformist, objector, protester, rebel.

dissipate *verb* **1** clear, disappear, dispel, disperse, evaporate, scatter. **2** blow (*slang*), fritter away, squander, waste.

dissociate *verb* cut off, detach, distance, divorce, isolate, separate.

dissolve *verb* (**dissolved,** **dissolving**) **1** mix something with a liquid so that it becomes part of the liquid. **2** make or become liquid; melt. **3** put an end to a marriage or partnership etc. **4** dismiss an assembly, *Parliament was dissolved and a general election was held.* [from *dis-* = separate, + Latin *solvere* = loosen]

dissuade *verb* (**dissuaded,** **dissuading**) persuade somebody not to do something. **dissuasion** *noun* [from *dis-* = apart, + Latin *suadere* = advise]

distaff *noun* a stick holding raw wool etc. for spinning into yarn.

distance *noun* the amount of space between two places.
in the distance far away.

distant *adjective* **1** far away. **2** not friendly; not sociable. **distantly** *adverb* [from *dis-* = apart, + Latin *stans* = standing]

distaste *noun* dislike.

distasteful *adjective* unpleasant.

distemper *noun* **1** a disease of dogs and certain other animals. **2** a kind of paint.

distend *verb* make or become swollen because of pressure from inside. **distension** *noun* [from *dis-* = apart, + Latin *tendere* = stretch]

distil *verb* (**distilled, distilling**) purify a liquid by boiling it and condensing the vapour. **distillation** *noun* [from *dis-* = apart, + Latin *stillare* = drip down]

distiller *noun* a person who makes alcoholic liquors by distillation. **distillery** *noun*

distinct *adjective* **1** easily heard or seen; noticeable. **2** clearly separate or different. **distinctly** *adverb*, **distinctness** *noun*

Usage See *distinctive.*

distinction *noun* **1** a difference. **2** distinguishing; making a difference. **3** excellence; honour. **4** an award for excellence; a high mark in an examination.

distinctive *adjective* that distinguishes one thing from another or others, *The school has a distinctive uniform.* **distinctively** *adverb.*

Usage Do not confuse this word with *distinct.* A *distinct* mark is a clear mark; a *distinctive* mark is one that is not found anywhere else.

distinguish *verb* **1** make or notice differences between things. **2** see or hear something clearly. **3** bring honour to, *He distinguished himself by his bravery.* **distinguishable** *adjective* [from Latin *distinguere* = to separate]

distinguished *adjective* excellent; famous.

distort *verb* **1** pull or twist out of its normal shape. **2** misrepresent; give a false account of something, *distort the truth.* **distortion** *noun* [from *dis-* = apart, + Latin *tortum* = twisted]

distract *verb* take a person's attention away from something. [from *dis-* = apart, + Latin *tractum* = pulled]

dissolve *verb* **2** liquefy, melt. **3** annul, break up, cancel, end, sever, terminate, wind up.

dissuade *verb* (**dissuade from**) advise against, deter from, discourage from, put off.

distance *noun* gap, haul, interval, length, range, space, span, stretch.

distant *adjective* **1** far, far-away, far-flung, far-off, outlying, remote. **2** aloof, cold, cool, detached, estranged, formal, offhand, remote, reserved, stand-offish, unfriendly, withdrawn.

distasteful *adjective* detestable, disagreeable, disgusting, loathsome, nauseating, objectionable, offensive, off-putting, repugnant, repulsive, revolting, sickening, unpalatable, unpleasant, vile.

distend *verb* bloat, bulge, enlarge, expand, puff up, swell up.

distinct *adjective* **1** clear, clear-cut, definite, marked, noticeable, obvious, plain, pronounced, sharp, strong, unmistakable. **2** different, discrete, individual, separate, unconnected.

distinction *noun* **1** contrast, difference. **3** class, eminence, excellence, fame, merit, note, prestige, prominence, quality, renown, superiority, worth.

distinctive *adjective* characteristic, different, distinguishing, idiosyncratic, individual, peculiar, personal, singular, special, specific, unique.

distinguish *verb* **1** characterise, differentiate, discriminate, identify, mark, separate, set apart, single out, tell apart. **2** discern, identify, make out, perceive, pick out, recognise.

distinguished *adjective* celebrated, eminent, famed, famous, great, illustrious, important, legendary, notable, noted, outstanding, preeminent, prominent, renowned, respected, well-known.

distort *verb* **1** bend, buckle, contort, deform, skew, twist, warp. **2** colour, falsify, garble, misrepresent, pervert, slant, twist.

distract *verb* divert, draw away, sidetrack.

distracted *adjective* distraught.

distraction *noun* **1** something that distracts a person's attention. **2** an amusement. **3** great worry or distress.

distraught (*say* dis-**trawt**) *adjective* greatly upset by worry or distress.

distress[1] *noun* great sorrow, pain, or trouble.

distress[2] *verb* cause distress to a person.

distribute *verb* (**distributed, distributing**) **1** deal or share out. **2** spread or scatter. **distribution** *noun*, **distributor** *noun* [from *dis-* = separate, + Latin *tributum* = given]

district *noun* part of a town or country, *wine-growing district*.

distrust[1] *noun* lack of trust; suspicion. **distrustful** *adjective*

distrust[2] *verb* not to trust.

disturb *verb* **1** spoil someone's peace or rest. **2** cause someone to worry. **3** move a thing from its position. **disturbance** *noun* [from *dis-* = thoroughly, + Latin *turbare* = confuse, upset]

disuse *noun* the state of not being used.

disused *adjective* no longer used.

ditch[1] *noun* (*plural* **ditches**) a trench dug to hold water or carry it away, or to serve as a boundary.

ditch[2] *verb* **1** (*informal*) bring an aircraft down in a forced landing on the sea. **2** (*informal*) abandon; discard.

dither *verb* **1** tremble. **2** hesitate nervously.

ditto *noun* (used in lists) the same again.

ditty *noun* (*plural* **ditties**) a short song.

divan *noun* a bed or couch without a raised back or sides. [Persian, = cushioned bench]

dive *verb* (**dived, diving**) **1** go under water, especially head first. **2** move down quickly. **dive** *noun*

diver *noun* **1** someone who dives. **2** a person who works under water in a special suit with an air supply. **3** a bird that dives for its food.

diverge *verb* (**diverged, diverging**) go aside or in different directions. **divergent** *adjective*, **divergence** *noun* [from *di-*[2] = apart, + Latin *vergere* = to slope]

divers (*say* **dy**-verz) *adjective* (*old use*) various.

distraction *noun* **2** amusement, diversion, entertainment, escape, pastime, recreation.

distraught *adjective* agitated, distressed, frantic, hysterical, overwrought, upset.

distress[1] *noun* adversity, affliction, agony, anguish, danger, difficulty, discomfort, misery, pain, sorrow, suffering, torment, torture, trouble, woe.

distress[2] *verb* afflict, bother, dismay, disturb, grieve, hurt, pain, perturb, sadden, shake, shock, torment, torture, trouble, upset, worry. **distressing** *adjective* appalling, disturbing, grievous, harrowing, heartbreaking, heart-rending, horrific, painful, pathetic, poignant, sad, terrible, tragic, traumatic, upsetting.

distribute *verb* **1** allocate, allot, apportion, assign, circulate, deal out, deliver, dish out (*informal*), dispense, divide up, dole out, give out, hand out, issue, mete out, pass round, serve, share out.

district *noun* area, community, electorate (*Australian*), locality, municipality, neighbourhood, place, precinct, province, quarter, region, sector, shire, suburb, territory, vicinity, ward, zone.

distrust[1] *noun* doubt, mistrust, scepticism, suspicion.

distrustful *adjective* chary, mistrustful, paranoid, sceptical, suspicious, wary.

distrust[2] *verb* be wary of, doubt, have misgivings about, mistrust, question, suspect.

disturb *verb* **1** annoy, bother, disrupt, hassle (*informal*), interrupt, pester. **2** agitate, alarm, churn up, discomfit, disconcert, distress, fluster, perturb, rattle (*informal*), ruffle, shake, startle, trouble, unsettle, upset, worry. **disturbance** *noun* commotion, fracas, hullabaloo, kerfuffle (*informal*), racket, riot, row, rumpus, stir, to-do, trouble, tumult, turmoil, unrest, uproar.

disused *adjective* abandoned, idle, neglected, obsolete.

ditch[1] *noun* channel, drain, dyke, gutter, moat, trench.

ditch[2] *verb* **2** abandon, dice (*Australian informal*), discard, drop, dump (*informal*), get rid of, reject.

dither *verb* **2** hesitate, hum and haw, shilly-shally, vacillate, waver.

dive *verb* **1** dip, plunge, submerge. **2** descend, drop, nosedive, pitch, plummet, plunge, swoop. **dive** *noun* header, nosedive, plunge.

diverge *verb* **1** branch, divide, fork, separate, split. **2** depart, deviate, digress, stray, turn aside.

►►DICTIONARY◄◄

diverse (*say* dy-**verss**) *adjective* varied; of several different kinds. **diversity** *noun*

diversify *verb* (**diversified**, **diversifying**) make or become varied; involve yourself in different kinds of things. **diversification** *noun*

diversion *noun* 1 diverting something from its course; an alternative route for traffic when a road is closed. 2 a recreation; an entertainment. **diversionary** *adjective*

divert *verb* 1 turn something aside from its course. 2 entertain; amuse. [from *di-²* = apart, + Latin *vertere* = to turn]

divest *verb* 1 strip of clothes, *He divested himself of his robes.* 2 take away; deprive, *They divested him of power.*

divide *verb* (**divided**, **dividing**) 1 separate from something or into smaller parts; split up. 2 distribute. 3 arrange in separate groups. 4 find how many times one number is contained in another, *Divide six by three* (6 ÷ 3 = 2). **divider** *noun*

dividend *noun* 1 a share of a business's profit. 2 a number that is to be divided by another. (Compare *divisor*.)

dividers *plural noun* a pair of compasses for measuring distances.

divine¹ *adjective* 1 of God; coming from God. 2 like a god. 3 (*informal*) excellent; beautiful. **divinely** *adverb*

divine² *verb* (**divined**, **divining**) prophesy or guess what is about to happen. [from Latin *divus* = god]

division *noun* 1 dividing. 2 a dividing line; a partition. 3 one of the parts into which

something is divided. 4 (in Parliament) separation of members into two sections for counting votes. **divisional** *adjective*

divisive (*say* div-**I**-siv) *adjective* causing disagreement within a group.

divisor *noun* a number by which another is to be divided. (Compare *dividend* 2.)

divorce¹ *noun* the legal ending of a marriage.

divorce² *verb* (**divorced**, **divorcing**) 1 end a marriage by divorce. 2 separate; think of things separately.

divulge *verb* (**divulged**, **divulging**) reveal information. **divulgence** *noun*

Diwali (*say* di-**wah**-lee) *noun* a Hindu religious festival at which lamps are lit, held in October or November. [from Sanskrit, = row of lamps]

dixie *noun* (*Australian*) an ice-cream carton, dandy, bucket.

DIY *abbreviation* do-it-yourself.

dizzy *adjective* (**dizzier**, **dizziest**) giddy. **dizzily** *adverb*, **dizziness** *noun*

DJ *abbreviation* disc jockey.

DNA *abbreviation* deoxyribonucleic acid, a substance in chromosomes that stores genetic information.

do¹ *verb* (**did**, **done**, **doing**) This word has many uses, including (**1**) perform or carry out a job, duty, etc., (**2**) produce or make (*do an extra copy*), (**3**) deal with, attend to (*do your hair; do the dishes*), (**4**) solve (*do a puzzle*), (**5**) act or proceed (*do as I say*), (**6**) fare, get on (*She is doing well at school*), (**7**) be suitable or enough (*This will do*), (**8**) be the cause of (*do*

►►THESAURUS◄◄

diverse *adjective* assorted, different, heterogeneous, miscellaneous, mixed, motley, varied, various.

diversion *noun* 1 bypass, detour, deviation. 2 amusement, distraction, entertainment, escape, game, hobby, pastime, recreation, sport.

divert *verb* 1 deflect, redirect, shunt, sidetrack, switch, turn aside. 2 amuse, cheer up, distract, entertain, interest, occupy.

divide *verb* 1 bifurcate, branch, break up, carve up, cut up, diverge, fork, joint, part, partition, separate, split, subdivide. 2 allot, apportion, deal out, dish out (*informal*), distribute, dole out, parcel out, share. 3 arrange, categorise, class, classify, group, sort.

divine¹ *adjective* 1 celestial, godlike, heavenly, holy, sacred, spiritual, superhuman, supernatural.

division *noun* 1 allocation, distribution, partition, separation, sharing, splitting. 3 branch, compartment, department, part, section, sector, segment, subdivision.

divorce¹ *verb* 1 break up, part, separate, split up.

divulge *verb* betray, blab, blow (*slang*), disclose, expose, give away, impart, leak, let out, let slip, make known, publish, reveal, tell.

dizzy *adjective* faint, giddy, light-headed, reeling, unsteady, woozy (*informal*). **dizziness** *noun* faintness, giddiness, light-headedness, vertigo.

do¹ *verb* 1 accomplish, carry out, complete, execute, fulfil, perform, undertake. 2 make, prepare, produce, turn out. 3 attend to, deal with, handle, look after, manage, see to. 4 answer, solve, work out. 5 act, behave, conduct yourself, practise. 6 fare, get on, make out. 7 be

►►►DICTIONARY◄◄◄

a lot of harm), (**9**) cover a distance in travelling (*do 500 kilometres a day*). The verb is also used with other verbs (**1**) in questions (*Do you want this?*), (**2**) in statements with 'not' (*He does not want it*), (**3**) for emphasis (*I do like nuts*), (**4**) to avoid repeating a verb that has just been used (*We work as hard as they do*).
do away with get rid of.
do up fasten, *Do your coat up*; repair or redecorate, *Do up the spare room*.

do² *noun* (*plural* **dos**) (*informal*) a party; an entertainment.

dob *verb* (**dobbed, dobbing**) **dob in** (*Australian slang*) inform on.

docile (*say* **doh**-syl) *adjective* willing to obey. **docilely** *adverb*, **docility** *noun* [from Latin *docilis* = easily taught]

dock¹ *noun* a place where ships are loaded, unloaded, or repaired.

dock² *verb* **1** bring or come into a dock. **2** (of spacecraft) join together in space.

dock³ *noun* an enclosure for the prisoner on trial in a lawcourt. [from Flemish *dok* = cage]

dock⁴ *noun* a weed with broad leaves.

dock⁵ *verb* **1** cut short an animal's tail. **2** reduce or take away part of someone's wages or supplies etc.

docker *noun* a labourer who loads and unloads ships.

docket *noun* a document or label listing the contents of a package.

dockyard *noun* an open area with docks and equipment for building or repairing ships.

doctor *noun* **1** a person who is trained to treat sick or injured people. **2** a person who holds an advanced degree (a **doctorate**) at a university, *Doctor of Music*. [from Latin *doctor* = teacher]

doctrine *noun* a belief held by a religious, political, or other group. **doctrinal** *adjective* [same origin as *doctor*]

document *noun* a written or printed paper giving information or evidence about something. **documentation** *noun*

documentary¹ *adjective* **1** consisting of documents, *documentary evidence*. **2** showing real events or situations.

documentary² *noun* (*plural* **documentaries**) a film giving an account of something, often showing real events etc.

dodder *verb* totter. **doddery** *adjective*

dodge¹ *verb* (**dodged, dodging**) move quickly to avoid someone or something.

dodge² *noun* **1** a dodging movement. **2** (*informal*) a trick; a clever way of doing something.

dodgem *noun* a small electrically-driven car at a fair etc. in which each driver tries to bump some cars and dodge others.

dodgy *adjective* (*informal*) tricky; awkward.

►►►THESAURUS◄◄◄

acceptable, be adequate, be enough, be satisfactory, be sufficient, be suitable, suffice.
do away with abolish, axe, discard, get rid of, scrap, stop.
do up 1 buckle, fasten, lace up, zip. **2** redecorate, refurbish, renovate, repair, restore.
do without abstain from, dispense with, forgo, go without.

do² *noun* event, function, occasion, party, reception.

dob *verb* **dob in** blow the whistle on, denounce, grass (on) (*slang*), inform on, report, shelf (*Australian slang*), shop (*slang*), split on (*slang*), tell on.

docile *adjective* biddable, compliant, gentle, manageable, meek, mild, obedient, passive, submissive, tame, tractable.

dock¹ *noun* berth, jetty, landing stage, pier, quay, slipway, wharf; (*docks*) dockyard, harbour, marina, port, shipyard.

dock² *verb* **1** berth, moor, put in.

docker *noun* longshoreman, stevedore, watersider (*Australian*), waterside worker, wharfie (*Australian informal*), wharf labourer.

docket *noun* invoice, receipt.

doctor *noun* **1** consultant, general practitioner, GP, intern, locum, medical practitioner, medico (*informal*), physician, quack (*slang*), registrar, specialist, surgeon.

doctrine *noun* belief, conviction, credo, creed, dogma, philosophy, precept, principle, teaching, tenet.

document *noun* certificate, charter, contract, deed, form, instrument, licence, paper, policy, record, report.

doddery *adjective* decrepit, frail, infirm, shaky, tottering, trembling, unsteady.

dodge¹ *verb* avoid, bob, duck, escape, evade, sidestep, skirt round, swerve, veer.

dodge² *noun* **2** lurk (*Australian informal*), racket, rort (*Australian slang*), ruse, scam (*slang*), scheme, trick.

▶▶ D I C T I O N A R Y ◀◀

dodo *noun* (*plural* **dodos**) a large heavy bird that used to live on an island in the Indian Ocean but has been extinct for over 200 years. [from Portuguese *doudo* = fool]

doe *noun* a female deer, rabbit, or hare.

doer *noun* a person who does things.

doesn't (*mainly spoken*) does not.

doff *verb* take off, *He doffed his hat.* [from *do off*; compare *don*]

dog¹ *noun* a four-legged animal that barks, often kept as a pet.
dog fence a fence to keep out dingoes.

dog² *verb* (**dogged, dogging**) follow closely or persistently, *Reporters dogged his footsteps.*

doge (*say* dohj) *noun* the elected ruler of the former republics of Venice and Genoa. [from Latin *dux* = leader]

dog-eared *adjective* (of a book) having the corners of the pages bent from constant use.

dogfish *noun* (*plural* **dogfish**) a kind of small shark.

dogged (*say* **dog**-id) *adjective* persistent; obstinate. **doggedly** *adverb*

doggerel *noun* bad verse.

dogma *noun* a belief or principle that a Church or other authority declares is true and must be accepted.

dogman *noun* (*plural* **dogmen**) (*Australian*) a person directing the operation of a crane, often while riding on its load.

dogmatic *adjective* expressing ideas in a very firm authoritative way. **dogmatically** *adverb* [from *dogma*]

doh *noun* a name for the keynote of a scale in music, or the note C.

doily *noun* (*plural* **doilies**) a small ornamental table-mat.

do-it-yourself *adjective* suitable for an amateur to make or use.

doldrums *plural noun* **1** the ocean regions near the equator where there is little or no wind. **2** a time of depression or inactivity.

dole¹ *verb* (**doled, doling**) distribute.

dole² *noun* (*informal*) money paid by the State to unemployed people.

doleful *adjective* mournful. **dolefully** *adverb* [from an old word *dole* = grief]

doll *noun* a toy model of a person.

dollar *noun* a unit of money in Australia, New Zealand, the USA, and some other countries. [from German *thaler* = a silver coin]

dolly *noun* (*plural* **dollies**) (*informal*) a doll.

dolphin *noun* a sea animal like a small whale with a beak-like snout.

domain (*say* dom-**ayn**) *noun* realm.

dome *noun* a roof shaped like the top half of a ball. **domed** *adjective*

domestic *adjective* **1** of the home or household. **2** (of animals) kept by people, not wild. **domestically** *adverb*, **domesticated** *adjective* [from Latin *domus* = home]

domicile (*say* **dom**-iss-syl) *noun* a residence; home. **domiciled** *adjective*

dominate *verb* (**dominated, dominating**) **1** control by being stronger or more powerful. **2** be conspicuous or prominent, *The mountain dominated the whole landscape.* **dominant** *adjective*, **dominance** *noun*, **domination** *noun* [from Latin *dominus* = master]

▶▶ T H E S A U R U S ◀◀

dog¹ *noun* bitch (*female*), cur, hound, mongrel, mutt (*informal*), pooch (*slang*), pup, puppy, whelp.

dogged *adjective* determined, firm, obstinate, patient, persistent, pertinacious, resolute, single-minded, stubborn, tenacious, unwavering.

dogma *noun* belief, credo, creed, doctrine, principle, teaching, tenet.

dogmatic *adjective* assertive, authoritative, categorical, cocksure, dictatorial, opinionated, peremptory.

dole¹ *verb* (*dole out*) allocate, allot, apportion, deal out, deliver, dish out (*informal*), dispense, distribute, give out, hand out, issue, mete out, share out.

dole² *noun* benefit, social security, unemployment benefit.

doleful *adjective* dismal, down in the dumps (*informal*), gloomy, glum, lugubrious, melancholy, mournful, rueful, sad, sorrowful, unhappy, woebegone.

domain *noun* dominion, empire, kingdom, land, province, realm, territory.

dome *noun* cupola.

domestic *adjective* **1** family, home, household. **2** domesticated, house-trained, pet, tame.

domicile *noun* abode (*old use*), accommodation, address, dwelling, habitation, home, house, residence.

dominate *verb* **1** control, govern, monopolise, rule.
dominant *adjective* chief, commanding, controlling, influential, leading, main, outstanding, paramount, predominant, prevailing, principal, ruling.

domineer *verb* behave in a dominating way. **domineering** *adjective*

dominion *noun* **1** authority to rule others; control. **2** an area over which someone rules; a domain.

domino *noun* (*plural* **dominoes**) a small flat oblong piece of wood or plastic with dots (usually 1 to 6) or a blank space at each end, used in the game of dominoes.

don *verb* (**donned, donning**) put on, *don a cloak*. [from *do on*; compare *doff*]

donate *verb* (**donated, donating**) present money or a gift to a fund or institution etc. **donation** *noun*

donkey *noun* (*plural* **donkeys**) an animal that looks like a small horse with long ears.

donor *noun* someone who gives something, *a blood donor*.

don't (*mainly spoken*) do not.

doodle *verb* (**doodled, doodling**) scribble or draw absent-mindedly. **doodle** *noun*

doom¹ *noun* a grim fate; death; ruin.

doom² *verb* destine to a grim fate.

doomsday *noun* the day of the Last Judgement; the end of the world.

Doona *noun* (*trade mark*) a thick soft quilt used instead of blankets.

door *noun* a movable barrier on hinges (or one that slides or revolves), used to open or close an entrance. **doorknob** *noun*, **doormat** *noun*

doorstep *noun* the step or piece of ground just outside a door.

doorway *noun* the opening into which a door fits.

dope¹ *noun* **1** (*informal*) a drug, especially one taken or given illegally. **2** (*slang*) a stupid person. **dopey** *adjective*

dope² *verb* (**doped, doping**) (*informal*) give a drug to a person or animal. [from Dutch *doop* = sauce]

dormant *adjective* **1** sleeping. **2** living or existing but not active; not extinct, *a dormant volcano*. [from French, = sleeping]

dormitory *noun* (*plural* **dormitories**) a room for several people to sleep in, especially in a school or institution. [from Latin *dormire* = to sleep]

dormitory town or **suburb** a place from which people travel to work elsewhere.

dormouse *noun* (*plural* **dormice**) an animal like a large mouse that hibernates in winter.

dorsal *adjective* of or on the back, *Some fish have a dorsal fin*. [from Latin *dorsum* = the back]

dosage *noun* **1** the giving of medicine in doses. **2** the size of a dose.

dose¹ *noun* an amount of medicine etc. taken at one time.

dose² *verb* (**dosed, dosing**) give a dose of medicine to a person or animal.

dossier (*say* **doss**-ee-er or **doss**-ee-ay) *noun* a set of documents containing information about a person or event.

domineering *adjective* authoritarian, bossy, dictatorial, imperious, masterful, overbearing, peremptory, tyrannical.

dominion *noun* **1** ascendancy, authority, control, jurisdiction, power, rule, sovereignty, supremacy, sway. **2** domain, empire, kingdom, realm, state, territory.

donate *verb* bequeath, bestow, chip in (*informal*), contribute, fork out (*slang*), give, grant, present, provide, subscribe.
donation *noun* alms (*old use*), bequest, contribution, gift, handout, offering, present, subscription.

donkey *noun* ass, jackass (*male*), jenny (*female*).

donor *noun* benefactor, contributor, giver, provider, sponsor.

doom¹ *noun* death, destiny, destruction, end, fate, fortune, lot, ruin.

doom² *verb* condemn, destine, fate, ordain, predestine.

door *noun* doorway, entrance, entry, exit, gate, hatch, portal, trapdoor.

doorstep *noun* step, threshold.

dope¹ *noun* **1** drug, narcotic, opiate. **2** ass (*informal*), clot (*informal*), fool, idiot (*informal*), imbecile, mug (*informal*), nincompoop, twit (*slang*).
dopey *adjective* **1** groggy, half asleep, sleepy, somnolent. **2** dumb (*informal*), foolish, idiotic, imprudent, reckless, senseless, silly, stupid, unwise.

dope² *verb* anaesthetise, drug, sedate.

dormant *adjective* **1** asleep, comatose, hibernating, resting, sleeping. **2** inactive, inert, latent, quiescent.

dose¹ *noun* amount, dosage, measure, portion, quantity.

dossier *noun* file, records.

►►DICTIONARY◄◄

dot¹ *noun* a tiny spot.

dot² *verb* (**dotted, dotting**) mark with dots.

dotage (*say* **doh**-tij) *noun* a condition of weakness of mind caused by old age, *He is in his dotage.*

dote *verb* (**doted, doting**) **dote on** be very fond of.

dotty *adjective* (**dottier, dottiest**) (*informal*) crazy; silly. **dottiness** *noun*

double¹ *adjective* **1** twice as much; twice as many. **2** having two things or parts that form a pair, *a double-barrelled gun.* **3** suitable for two people, *a double bed.* **doubly** *adverb*

double² *noun* **1** a double quantity or thing. **2** a person or thing that looks exactly like another.

double³ *verb* (**doubled, doubling**) **1** make or become twice as much or as many. **2** bend or fold in two. **3** turn back sharply, *The fox doubled back on its tracks.* **4** dink.

double-bass *noun* a musical instrument with strings, like a large cello.

double-cross *verb* deceive or cheat a trusting friend.

double-decker *noun* a bus with two decks.

doublet *noun* a man's close-fitting jacket worn in the 15th-17th centuries.

doubt¹ *noun* a feeling of not being sure about something.

doubt² *verb* feel doubt. **doubter** *noun* [from Latin *dubitore* = hesitate]

doubtful *adjective* **1** feeling doubt. **2** casting doubt. **doubtfully** *adverb*

doubtless *adverb* certainly.

dough *noun* **1** a thick mixture of flour and water used for making bread, pastry, etc. **2** (*slang*) money. **doughy** *adjective*

doughnut *noun* a round or ring-shaped bun that has been fried and covered in sugar.

doughty (*say* **dow**-tee) *adjective* valiant.

dour (*say* **doo**-er) *adjective* stern and gloomy-looking. **dourly** *adverb* [from Gaelic *dur* = dull, obstinate]

douse *verb* (**doused, dousing**) **1** put into water; pour water over something. **2** put out, *douse the light.*

dove *noun* a kind of pigeon.

dovetail¹ *noun* a wedge-shaped joint used to join two pieces of wood.

dovetail² *verb* **1** join pieces of wood with a dovetail. **2** fit neatly together, *My plans dovetailed with hers.*

dowager *noun* a woman who holds a title or property after her husband has died, *the dowager duchess.*

dowdy *adjective* (**dowdier, dowdiest**) shabby; unfashionable. **dowdily** *adverb*

dowel *noun* a headless wooden or metal pin for holding together two pieces of wood, stone, etc. **dowelling** *noun*

down¹ *adverb* **1** to or in a lower place or position or level, *It fell down.* **2** to a source or place etc., *Track them down.* **3** in writing, *Take down these instructions.* **4** as a payment, *We will pay $5 down and the rest later.*
be down on disapprove of, *She is down on smoking.*
down under in Australia or New Zealand.

down² *preposition* downwards through or along or into, *Pour it down the drain.*

►►THESAURUS◄◄

dot¹ *noun* fleck, mark, point, speck, speckle, spot.

dot² *verb* fleck, speckle, spot, stipple.

dote *verb* **dote on** adore, cherish, idolise, love, treasure, worship.

double¹ *adjective* **2** dual, duplicate, paired, twin, twofold.

double² *noun* **2** clone, copy, dead spit, duplicate, look-alike, ringer (*informal*), spitting image, twin.

double³ *verb* **4** dink (*Australian*), dinky (*Australian*), donkey (*Australian*), double-bank (*Australian*), double-dink (*Australian*).

double-cross *verb* betray, cheat, deceive, trick.

doubt¹ *noun* disbelief, distrust, hesitation, incredulity, misgiving, mistrust, qualm, question, reservation, scepticism, suspicion, uncertainty.

doubt² *verb* distrust, mistrust, question, suspect.

doubtful *adjective* **1** distrustful, dubious, hesitant, mistrustful, sceptical, suspicious, uncertain, undecided, unsure.

dour *adjective* forbidding, gloomy, grim, harsh, morose, severe, stern, sullen, unfriendly.

douse *verb* **1** drench, immerse, saturate, soak, submerge, wet.

dowdy *adjective* daggy (*Australian informal*), drab, dull, frumpish, old-fashioned, shabby, sloppy, unattractive, unfashionable.

▶▶ D I C T I O N A R Y ◀◀

down³ *noun* (*Australian*) **have a down on** have a prejudice or grudge against.

down⁴ *noun* very fine soft feathers or hair. **downy** *adjective*

down⁵ *noun* a grass-covered hill, *Darling Downs.*

downcast *adjective* **1** looking downwards, *downcast eyes.* **2** dejected.

downfall *noun* **1** a fall from power or prosperity. **2** a heavy fall of rain or snow.

downhill *adverb* & *adjective* down a slope.

download *verb* transfer (data) from a central storage device to another.

downpour *noun* a great fall of rain.

downright *adjective* **1** frank; straightforward. **2** thorough; complete, *a downright lie.*

downstairs *adverb* & *adjective* to or on a lower floor.

downstream *adjective* & *adverb* in the direction in which a stream flows.

downward *adjective* & *adverb* going towards what is lower. **downwards** *adverb*

dowry *noun* (*plural* **dowries**) property or money brought by a bride to her husband when she marries him.

doze¹ *verb* (**dozed, dozing**) sleep lightly.

doze² *noun* a light sleep. **dozy** *adjective*

dozen *noun* a set of twelve.

Usage Correct use is *ten dozen* (not *ten dozens*).

drab *adjective* (**drabber, drabbest**) **1** not colourful. **2** dull; uninteresting, *a drab life.* **drably** *adverb*, **drabness** *noun*

drack *adjective* (*Australian*) dreary, unattractive.

Draconian (*say* drak-**oh**-nee-an) *adjective* very harsh, *Draconian laws.* [named after Draco, who established very severe laws in ancient Athens]

draft¹ *noun* **1** a rough sketch or plan. **2** a written order for a bank to pay out money.

draft² *verb* **1** prepare a draft. **2** select for a special duty, *She was drafted to our office in Paris.* **3.** (*Australian*) separate sheep or cattle from a flock or herd for some special purpose. **4** (*American*) conscript.

Usage This is also the American spelling of *draught.*

drag¹ *verb* (**dragged, dragging**) **1** pull something heavy along. **2** search a river or lake etc. with nets and hooks. **3** continue slowly and dully.
    drag out make something last longer than necessary.

drag² *noun* **1** a hindrance; something boring. **2** (*slang*) women's clothes worn by men.

dragon *noun* **1** a mythological monster, usually with wings and able to breathe out fire. **2** a fierce person. [from Greek *drakon* = serpent]

dragonfly *noun* (*plural* **dragonflies**) an insect with a long thin body and two pairs of transparent wings.

dragoon¹ *noun* a member of certain cavalry regiments.

dragoon² *verb* force someone into doing something.

drain¹ *noun* **1** a pipe or ditch etc. for taking away water or other liquid. **2** something that takes away strength or resources. **drainpipe** *noun*

▶▶ T H E S A U R U S ◀◀

down⁴ *noun* feathers, fluff, plumage.

downcast *adjective* **2** blue, crestfallen, dejected, depressed, despondent, disconsolate, discouraged, disheartened, dispirited, down, down-hearted, down in the dumps, gloomy, heavy-hearted, low, melancholy, miserable, sad, unhappy, wretched.

downfall *noun* **1** collapse, destruction, fall, ruin, undoing.

downpour *noun* cloudburst, deluge, rainstorm, shower, storm.

downright *adjective* **2** absolute, arrant, complete, out-and-out, outright, pure, sheer, thorough, utter.

doze¹ *verb* drop off, kip (*slang*), nap, nod off, sleep, slumber, snooze.

drab *adjective* **1** cheerless, colourless, dingy, dismal, dreary, dull, sombre, unattractive.

draft¹ *noun* **1** outline, plan, sketch.

draft² *verb* **1** draw up, frame, outline, plan. **4** call up, conscript.

drag¹ *verb* **1** draw, haul, lug, pull, tow, tug.
    drag out draw out, extend, prolong, protract, spin out.

drag² *noun* **1** bind (*informal*), bore, nuisance, pain in the neck (*informal*), strain.

drain¹ *noun* **1** channel, conduit, culvert, ditch, gutter, outlet, pipe, sewer, trench.

▶▶ D I C T I O N A R Y ◀◀

drain² *verb* **1** take away water etc. through a drain. **2** flow or trickle away. **3** empty liquid out of a container. **4** take away strength etc.; exhaust. **drainage** *noun*.

drake *noun* a male duck.

drama *noun* **1** a play. **2** writing or performing plays. **3** a series of exciting events.

dramatic *adjective* **1** of drama. **2** exciting; impressive, *a dramatic change*. **dramatics** *plural noun*, **dramatically** *adverb*

dramatise *verb* (**dramatised**, **dramatising**) **1** make a story etc. into a play. **2** make something seem exciting. **dramatisation** *noun*

dramatist *noun* a person who writes plays.

drape *verb* (**draped**, **draping**) hang cloth etc. loosely over something.

draper *noun* a shopkeeper who sells cloth or clothes.

drapery *noun* (*plural* **draperies**) **1** a draper's stock. **2** cloth arranged in loose folds.

drastic *adjective* having a strong or violent effect. **drastically** *adverb*

draught (*say* drahft) *noun* **1** a current of usually cold air indoors. **2** a haul of fish in a net. **3** the depth of water needed to float a ship. **4** a swallow of liquid. **draughty** *adjective*

draughts *noun* a game played with 24 round pieces on a chessboard.

draughtsman *noun* (*plural* **draughtsmen**) **1** a person who makes drawings. **2** a piece used in the game of draughts.

draw¹ *verb* (**drew**, **drawn**, **drawing**) **1** produce a picture or outline by making marks on a surface. **2** pull. **3** take out, *draw water*. **4** attract, *The show drew large crowds*. **5** end a game or contest with the same score on both sides. **6** move; come, *The ship drew nearer*. **7** make out by thinking, *draw conclusions*. **8** write out a cheque to be cashed.
draw back move back.
draw out make something last longer.
draw up come to a halt; prepare a document etc.

draw² *noun* **1** the drawing of lots (see *lot*). **2** the drawing out of a gun etc., *He was quick on the draw*. **3** an attraction. **4** a drawn game.

drawback *noun* a disadvantage.

drawbridge *noun* a bridge over a moat, hinged at one end so that it can be raised or lowered.

drawer *noun* **1** a sliding box-like compartment in a piece of furniture. **2** a person who draws something. **3** someone who draws (= writes out) a cheque.

drawing *noun* a picture or outline drawn.

drawing pin a short pin with a flat top to be pressed with your thumb, used for fastening paper etc. to a surface.

drawing room a sitting room.

drawl¹ *verb* speak very slowly or lazily.

drawl² *noun* a drawling way of speaking.

dray *noun* a strong low flat cart for carrying heavy loads.

dread¹ *noun* great fear.

▶▶ T H E S A U R U S ◀◀

drain² *verb* **1** draw off, empty, pour off, remove, siphon off. **2** discharge, empty, flow out, seep out, trickle away. **4** consume, deplete, exhaust, sap, spend, use up.

drama *noun* **1** play, show. **2** acting, dramatics, stagecraft, theatre. **3** action, excitement, suspense.

dramatic *adjective* **1** stage, theatrical. **2** impressive, marked, noticeable, radical, spectacular, startling, striking.

dramatist *noun* playwright, screenwriter, scriptwriter.

drastic *adjective* desperate, dire, extreme, radical, severe, strong.

draught *noun* **1** breeze, wind.

draw¹ *verb* **1** delineate, depict, doodle, illustrate, outline, picture, portray, represent, scribble, sketch, trace. **2** drag, haul, lug, pull, tow, tug. **3** extract, remove, pull out, take out. **4** attract, bring in, entice, lure, pull. **5** be equal, tie. **7** deduce, gather, infer, make out, work out.

draw back cringe, recoil, retreat, shrink back, withdraw.
draw out drag out, extend, lengthen, prolong, protract, spin out.
draw up 1 come to a halt, come to a stop, halt, pull up, stop. **2** compose, draft, formulate, prepare, write out.

draw² *noun* **3** attraction, drawcard, enticement, lure. **4** dead heat, deadlock, stalemate, tie.

drawback *noun* catch, disadvantage, handicap, hindrance, inconvenience, liability, minus, shortcoming.

drawing *noun* cartoon, chart, design, diagram, illustration, pattern, picture, plan, portrait, sketch.

drawing room parlour (*old use*), reception room, salon, sitting room.

dread¹ *noun* alarm, anxiety, apprehension, consternation, dismay, fear, foreboding, horror, panic, terror, trepidation.

▶▶ DICTIONARY ◀◀

dread² *verb* fear greatly.

dreadful *adjective* **1** terrible. **2** (*informal*) very bad, *dreadful weather*. **dreadfully** *adverb*

dreadlocks *plural noun* hair worn in many ringlets or plaits.

dream¹ *noun* **1** things a person seems to see while sleeping. **2** something imagined; an ambition or ideal. **dreamy** *adjective*, **dreamily** *adverb*

dream² *verb* (**dreamt** or **dreamed**, **dreaming**) **1** have a dream or dreams. **2** have an ambition. **3** think something might happen, *I never dreamt she would leave*. **dreamer** *noun*

dreamtime *noun* (also called *dreaming*) a translation of *alcheringa*, in Aboriginal belief, events beyond living memory which shaped the physical, spiritual and moral world.

dreary *adjective* (**drearier**, **dreariest**) **1** dull; boring. **2** gloomy. **drearily** *adverb*, **dreariness** *noun*

dredge *verb* (**dredged**, **dredging**) drag something up, especially by scooping at the bottom of a river or the sea. **dredger** *noun*

dregs *plural noun* worthless bits that sink to the bottom of a liquid.

drench *verb* make wet all through.

dress¹ *noun* (*plural* **dresses**) **1** a woman's or girl's garment with a bodice and skirt. **2** clothes; costume, *fancy dress*.

dress rehearsal a rehearsal at which the cast wear their costumes.

dress² *verb* **1** put clothes on. **2** arrange a display in a window etc.; decorate, *dress the shop windows*. **3** prepare food for cooking or eating. **4** put a dressing on a wound. **dresser** *noun*

dressage (*say* **dress**-ah*zh*) *noun* management of a horse to show its obedience and style. [French, = training]

dresser *noun* a sideboard with shelves at the top for dishes etc.

dressing *noun* **1** a bandage, plaster, or ointment etc. for a wound. **2** a sauce of oil, vinegar, etc. for a salad. **3** manure or other fertiliser for spreading on the soil.

dressing gown a loose garment for wearing when you are not fully dressed.

dressmaker *noun* a maker of women's clothes. **dressmaking** *noun*

dribble *verb* (**dribbled**, **dribbling**) **1** let saliva trickle out of your mouth. **2** move the ball forward in football or hockey with slight touches of your feet or stick.

dried *past tense* of **dry²**.

drier *noun* a device for drying hair, laundry, etc.

drift¹ *verb* **1** be carried gently along by water or air. **2** move slowly and casually; live casually with no definite objective. **drifter** *noun*

▶▶ THESAURUS ◀◀

dread² *verb* be afraid of, be scared of, fear.

dreadful *adjective* **1** appalling, awful, calamitous, catastrophic, dire, disastrous, fearful, frightful, ghastly, grisly, hideous, horrendous, horrible, horrific, shocking, terrible, tragic. **2** see BAD.

dream¹ *noun* **1** daydream, fantasy, hallucination, illusion, nightmare, reverie, trance, vision. **2** ambition, aspiration, desire, goal, hope, wish.

dream² *verb* **1** daydream, fancy, fantasise, hallucinate, imagine.
dream up conceive, concoct, create, devise, hatch, imagine, invent, think up.

dreary *adjective* **1** boring, deadly (*informal*), dull, humdrum, lacklustre, lifeless, monotonous, mundane, stodgy, tedious, tiresome, uninteresting. **2** bleak, cheerless, colourless, depressing, dingy, dismal, drab, dull, gloomy, miserable, sombre.

dregs *plural noun* deposit, grounds, lees, remains, residue, sediment.

drench *verb* douse, saturate, soak, souse, wet.

dress¹ *noun* **1** frock, gown, kimono, robe, sari. **2** apparel (*formal*), attire (*formal*), clobber (*slang*), clothes, clothing, costume, garb, garments, gear (*informal*), get-up (*informal*), outfit, raiment, rig (*informal*), togs (*informal*), vestments, wear.

dress² *verb* **1** array, attire, clothe, deck out, doll up (*informal*), robe. **4** bandage, bind.

dresser *noun* buffet, cupboard, sideboard.

dressing *noun* **1** bandage, plaster, poultice. **2** mayonnaise, sauce, vinaigrette.

dressing gown bath robe, brunch coat, housecoat, negligée, robe, wrapper.

dressmaker *noun* couturier, couturière, seamstress, tailor.

dribble *verb* **1** drool, salivate, slaver, slobber.

dried *adjective* dehydrated, desiccated.

drift¹ *verb* **1** coast, float, waft. **2** meander, mosey (*slang*), ramble, roam, rove, saunter, stray, wander.

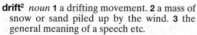

▶▶ D I C T I O N A R Y ◀◀

drift² *noun* **1** a drifting movement. **2** a mass of snow or sand piled up by the wind. **3** the general meaning of a speech etc.

driftwood *noun* wood floating on the sea or washed ashore by it.

drill¹ *noun* **1** a tool for making holes; a machine for boring holes or wells. **2** repeated exercises in gymnastics, military training, etc.

drill² *verb* **1** make a hole etc. with a drill. **2** do repeated exercises; make people do exercises.

drily *adverb* in a dry way.

drink¹ *verb* (**drank, drunk, drinking**) **1** swallow liquid. **2** drink a lot of alcoholic drinks. **drinker** *noun*

drink² *noun* **1** a liquid for drinking. **2** an amount of liquid swallowed. **3** an alcoholic drink.

drip¹ *verb* (**dripped, dripping**) fall or let something fall in drops.

drip² *noun* **1** liquid falling in drops; the sound it makes. **2** an apparatus for dripping liquid into the veins of a sick person.

drip-dry *adjective* made of material that dries easily and does not need ironing.

dripping *noun* fat melted from roasted meat and allowed to set.

drive¹ *verb* (**drove, driven, driving**) **1** make something or someone move. **2** operate a motor vehicle or a train etc. **3** cause; compel, *Hunger drove them to steal.* **4** force someone into a state, *She is driving me crazy.* **5** rush; move rapidly, *Rain drove against the window.* **driver** *noun*

drive² *noun* **1** a journey in a vehicle. **2** a hard stroke in cricket or golf etc. **3** the transmitting of power to machinery, *four-wheel drive.* **4** energy; enthusiasm. **5** an organised effort, *a sales drive.* **6** a track for vehicles through the grounds of a house.

drive-in *adjective* that you can use without getting out of your car.

drivel *noun* silly talk; nonsense.

drizzle *noun* very fine rain. **drizzly** *adjective*

droll *adjective* amusing in an odd way.

dromedary *noun* (*plural* **dromedaries**) a camel with one hump, bred for riding on. [from Greek *dromas* = runner]

drone¹ *verb* (**droned, droning**) **1** make a deep humming sound. **2** talk in a boring voice.

drone² *noun* **1** a droning sound. **2** a male bee.

drongo *noun* (*plural* **drongos**) (*Australian slang*) a fool or simpleton.

drool *verb* dribble.
drool over be very emotional about liking something.

droop *verb* hang down weakly.

drop¹ *noun* **1** a tiny amount of liquid. **2** a small round sweet. **3** a hanging ornament. **4** a fall; a decrease. **5** a descent.

▶▶ T H E S A U R U S ◀◀

drift² *noun* **1** movement, shift, tide. **3** gist, meaning, point, tenor, trend.

drill¹ *noun* **2** exercises, practice, training.

drill² *verb* **1** bore, penetrate, pierce. **2** coach, instruct, teach, train.

drink¹ *verb* **1** down, drain, gulp, guzzle, lap, quaff, sip, swallow, swig (*informal*), swill.

drink² *noun* **1** beverage, liquid, refreshment. **2** gulp, mouthful, sip, swallow, swig (*informal*). **3** alcohol, booze (*informal*), grog (*Australian*), liquor.

drip¹ *verb* dribble, drizzle, filter, leak, sprinkle, trickle.

drip² *noun* **1** drop, droplet, splash.

drive¹ *verb* **1** herd, propel, push, send, urge. **2** control, guide, handle, operate, pilot, steer. **3** compel, constrain, force, impel, motivate, oblige, pressure, push, spur.
driver *noun* chauffeur, motorist.

drive² *noun* **1** excursion, jaunt, journey, outing, run, spin, trip. **4** ambition, determination, energy, enterprise, enthusiasm, go, initiative, motivation, push, vigour, zeal. **5** campaign, crusade, push.

drizzly *adjective* damp, misty, rainy, showery, wet.

droll *adjective* see FUNNY.

drone¹ *verb* **1** buzz, hum, purr, whirr.

drool *verb* dribble, salivate, slaver, slobber.

droop *verb* dangle, flop, hang down, sag, wilt, wither.

drop¹ *noun* **1** bead, drip, droplet, globule, spot, splash, sprinkling; see also DASH². **4** cut, decline, decrease, fall, reduction, slump. **5** descent, precipice, slope.

▶▶ DICTIONARY ◀◀

drop² *verb* (**dropped, dropping**) **1** fall. **2** let something fall. **3** put down a passenger etc., *Drop me at the station.* **4** lower; become lower. **5** omit. **6** abandon; give up.
  drop in visit someone casually.
  drop off fall asleep.
  drop out stop taking part in something.
  drop-out *noun*

droplet *noun* a small drop.

drought (*say* drout) *noun* a long period of dry weather.

drove *noun* a moving herd, flock, or crowd, *droves of people.*

drover *noun* someone who drives a herd or flock, especially over a long distance.

drown *verb* **1** die or kill by suffocation under water. **2** flood; drench. **3** make so much noise that another sound cannot be heard.

drowsy *adjective* sleepy. **drowsily** *adverb*, **drowsiness** *noun*

drubbing *noun* a beating; a severe defeat.

drudge *noun* a person who does dull work.
  drudgery *noun*

drug¹ *noun* **1** a substance used in medicine. **2** a substance that affects your senses or your mind, *a drug addict.*

drug² *verb* (**drugged, drugging**) give a drug to someone, especially to make them unconscious.

Druid (*say* **droo**-id) *noun* a priest of an ancient Celtic religion in Britain and France.

drum¹ *noun* **1** a musical instrument made of a cylinder with a skin or parchment stretched over one or both ends. **2** a cylindrical object or container, *an oil drum.* **3** (*Australian*) a swagman's bundle of possessions. **4** (*Australian*) a reliable piece of information.

drum² *verb* (**drummed, drumming**) **1** play a drum or drums. **2** tap or thrum on something.
  drummer *noun*

drumstick *noun* **1** a stick for beating a drum. **2** the lower part of a cooked bird's leg.

drunk¹ *adjective* excited or helpless through drinking too much alcohol.

drunk² *noun* a person who is drunk.

drunkard *noun* a person who is often drunk.

drunken *adjective* **1** drunk, *a drunken man.* **2** caused by drinking alcohol.

dry¹ *adjective* (**drier, driest**) **1** without water or moisture. **2** thirsty. **3** boring; dull. **4** (of remarks or humour) said in a matter-of-fact or ironical way, *dry wit.* **drily** *adverb*, **dryness** *noun*
  dry cleaning a method of cleaning clothes etc. by a liquid that evaporates quickly.
  dry dock a dock that can be emptied of water so that ships can float in and then be repaired.

▶▶ THESAURUS ◀◀

drop² *verb* **1** collapse, descend, dive, fall, nosedive, plummet, plunge, sink, slump, tumble. **2** let fall, let go of, release. **4** decline, decrease, diminish, lower, reduce. **5** eliminate, exclude, leave out, omit. **6** abandon, desert, discard, ditch (*informal*), dump, forsake, give up, jilt, leave, reject, scrap.
  drop in call in, look in, pop in, visit.
  drop off doze, drowse, fall asleep, kip (*slang*), nap, nod off, sleep, snooze.

drove *noun* crowd, flock, herd, horde, mob, swarm.

drown *verb* **2** drench, engulf, flood, inundate, submerge, swamp.

drowsy *adjective* dopey (*informal*), dozy, lethargic, sleepy, somnolent, tired, weary.

drudge *noun* dogsbody (*informal*), hack, labourer, menial, servant, worker.

drug¹ *noun* **1** medicament, medication, medicine, pill.

drug² *verb* anaesthetise, dope, knock out (*informal*), sedate, stupefy.

drum¹ *noun* **1** bongo, kettledrum, side drum, snare drum, tabor, tambour, timpano, tom-tom. **2** barrel, cask, container, cylinder, keg, tub. **3** bluey (*Australian*), matilda (*Australian*), shiralee (*Australian*), swag (*Australian*).

drum² *verb* **2** beat, pound, rap, tap, thump.
  drummer *noun* timpanist.

drunk¹ *adjective* drunken, full (*slang*), full as a goog (*Australian slang*), happy (*informal*), inebriated, intoxicated, jolly (*informal*), legless (*slang*), merry (*informal*), paralytic (*informal*), pickled (*slang*), plastered (*slang*), shickered (*Australian slang*), sloshed (*slang*), smashed (*slang*), sozzled (*slang*), tanked (*slang*), tiddly (*informal*), tipsy, under the influence (*informal*), under the weather.

drunkard *noun* alcoholic, boozer (*informal*), dipsomaniac, drunk, inebriate, soak (*informal*), sot, tippler, wino (*informal*).

dry¹ *adjective* **1** arid, bone-dry, dehydrated, desiccated, parched, scorched, waterless. **2** dehydrated, parched, thirsty. **3** boring, dull, prosaic, tedious, uninteresting. **4** ironic, laconic, subtle, wry.

▶▶ D I C T I O N A R Y ◀◀

dry² *verb* (**dried, drying**) make or become dry.

dryad *noun* a wood-nymph.

dual *adjective* composed of two parts; double. **dual carriageway** a road with a dividing strip between lanes of traffic in opposite directions. [from Latin *duo* = two]

dub¹ *verb* (**dubbed, dubbing**) **1** make someone a knight by touching him on the shoulder with a sword. **2** give a person or thing a nickname. [from an old French word, = knight a person]

dub² *verb* (**dubbed, dubbing**) **1** change or add new sound to the sound-track of a film or magnetic tape. **2** copy a recording. [short for *double*]

dubbin *noun* thick grease used to soften leather and make it waterproof.

dubious (*say* **dew**-bee-us) *adjective* **1** doubtful. **2** questionable, unreliable. **dubiously** *adverb* [from Latin *dubium* = doubt]

ducat (*say* **duk**-at) *noun* a former gold coin used in Europe.

duchess *noun* (*plural* **duchesses**) a duke's wife or widow.

duchy *noun* (*plural* **duchies**) the territory of a duke.

duck¹ *noun* **1** a swimming bird with a flat beak; the female of this. **2** a batsman's score of nought at cricket. **3** a ducking movement.

duck² *verb* **1** bend down quickly to avoid something. **2** go or push quickly under water. **3** dodge; avoid doing something.

duckling *noun* a young duck.

duck-shove *verb* (*Australian*) evade responsibility. **duck-shover** *noun*

duct *noun* a tube or channel through which liquid, gas, air, or cables can pass. [from Latin *ductum* = conveyed]

ductile *adjective* (of metal) able to be drawn out into fine strands.

dud *noun* (*informal*) something that is useless or a fake or fails to work. **dud** *adjective*

dudgeon (*say* **duj**-on) *noun* indignation.

due¹ *adjective* **1** expected; scheduled to do something or to arrive, *The train is due in ten minutes.* **2** owing; needing to be paid. **3** that ought to be given; rightful, *Treat her with due respect.* **due to** caused by.

Usage Correct use is as in *His lateness was due to an accident.* Many people dislike the use of 'due to' without a preceding noun (e.g. 'lateness') to which it refers. It is best to avoid uses such as 'He was late, due to an accident' where there is no such noun. (Use *because of* or *owing to* instead.)

due² *adverb* exactly, *We sailed due east.*

due³ *noun* **1** a person's right; something deserved; proper respect, *Give him his due.* **2** a fee, *harbour dues.*

duel *noun* a fight between two people, especially with pistols or swords. **duelling** *noun*, **duellist** *noun*

Usage Do not confuse this word with *dual.*

duet *noun* a piece of music for two players or singers. [from Latin *duo* = two]

duff *verb* (*Australian*) steal horses or cattle, *cattle duffing.* (compare *rustle 2.*)

duffel coat a thick overcoat with a hood, fastened with toggles. [named after Duffel, a town in Belgium]

duffer *noun* **1** a person who is stupid or not good at doing something. **2** (*Australian*) a cattle-thief or horse-thief.

▶▶ T H E S A U R U S ◀◀

dry² *verb* dehydrate, desiccate, shrivel, wilt, wither.

dual *adjective* binary, double, twin, twofold.

dub¹ *verb* **2** christen, name, nickname, rename.

dubious *adjective* **1** disbelieving, distrustful, doubtful, mistrustful, sceptical, suspicious, uncertain, unsure. **2** dodgy (*informal*), fishy (*informal*), questionable, shady, suspect, suspicious, unreliable, untrustworthy.

duck¹ *noun* **1** drake (*male*), duckling (*young*).

duck² *verb* **1** bend down, bob down, crouch, stoop. **2** bob, dip, dive, plunge, submerge. **3** avoid, dodge, evade, get out of, shirk, sidestep.

duct *noun* canal, channel, conduit, pipe, tube.

dud *adjective* bung (*Australian informal*), defective, inoperative, unusable, useless, worthless.

due¹ *adjective* **1** expected, scheduled. **2** outstanding, owed, owing, payable, unpaid. **3** adequate, appropriate, deserved, fitting, merited, proper, rightful, suitable.

due³ *noun* **1** deserts, entitlement, right. **2** (*dues*) fee, levy, sub (*informal*), subscription.

duel *noun* combat, contest, fight.

duffer *noun* **1** clot (*informal*), fool, goose (*informal*), idiot, mug (*informal*), muggins (*informal*), nincompoop, nitwit (*informal*), silly, twit (*slang*).

▶▶ DICTIONARY ◀◀

dug-out *noun* **1** an underground shelter. **2** a canoe made by hollowing out a tree-trunk.

duke *noun* a member of the highest rank of noblemen. **dukedom** *noun* [from Latin *dux* = leader]

dulcet (*say* **dul**-sit) *adjective* sweet-sounding. [from Latin *dulcis* = sweet]

dulcimer *noun* a musical instrument with strings that are struck by two hammers.

dull *adjective* **1** not bright or clear, *dull weather.* **2** stupid. **3** boring, *a dull concert.* **4** not sharp, *a dull pain; a dull thud.* **dull** *verb*, **dully** *adverb*, **dullness** *noun*

dullard *noun* a stupid person.

duly *adverb* in the due or proper way.

dumb *adjective* **1** unable to speak; silent. **2** (*informal*) stupid. **dumbly** *adverb*, **dumbness** *noun*

dumbfound *verb* astonish; strike a person dumb with surprise. [from *dumb* + *confound*]

dummy *noun* (*plural* **dummies**) **1** something made to look like a person or thing. **2** an imitation teat given to a baby to suck. [from *dumb*]

dump[1] *noun* **1** a place where something (especially rubbish) is left or stored. **2** (*informal*) a dull or unattractive place.

dump[2] *verb* **1** get rid of something that is not wanted. **2** put down carelessly.

dumpling *noun* a lump of dough cooked in a stew etc. or baked with fruit inside.

dumps *plural noun* (*informal*) low spirits, *in the dumps.*

dumpy *adjective* short and fat.

dunce *noun* a person who is slow at learning. [from Duns Scotus, a Scottish philosopher in the Middle Ages, whose followers were said by their opponents to be unable to understand new ideas]

dune *noun* a mound of loose sand shaped by the wind.

dung *noun* solid waste matter excreted by an animal.

dungarees *plural noun* overalls made of thick strong cloth. [from Hindi *dungri*]

dungeon (*say* **dun**-jon) *noun* an underground cell for prisoners.

dunk *verb* dip something into liquid.

dunny *noun* (*Australian slang*) a toilet, especially one detached from a residence.

duodenum (*say* dew-o-**deen**-um) *noun* the part of the small intestine that is just below the stomach. **duodenal** *adjective*

dupe *verb* (**duped, duping**) deceive.

duplicate[1] *noun* **1** something that is exactly the same as something else. **2** an exact copy.

▶▶ THESAURUS ◀◀

dull *adjective* **1** cloudy, dismal, gloomy, grey, overcast, sunless; (*dull colours*) dark, dingy, drab, dreary, faded, flat, matt, sombre, subdued, tarnished. **2** bovine, dense, dim, dumb (*informal*), obtuse, slow, stupid, thick. **3** bland, boring, dreary, dry, humdrum, lacklustre, lifeless, monotonous, mundane, ordinary, prosaic, routine, stodgy, tedious, tiresome, unimaginative, uninteresting, vapid. **4** (*a dull knife*) blunt, blunted; (*a dull sound*) deadened, indistinct, muffled, muted.
dull *verb* deaden, numb, relieve, soothe, subdue.

dumb *adjective* **1** mute, silent, speechless, tongue-tied. **2** dense, dim (*informal*), foolish, obtuse, slow, stupid, thick, unintelligent.

dumbfounded *adjective* amazed, astonished, astounded, confounded, flabbergasted, nonplussed, speechless, staggered, stunned, surprised, thunderstruck.

dummy *noun* **1** lay figure, mannequin, model. **2** pacifier.

dump[1] *noun* **1** garbage dump, garbage tip, rubbish tip, scrap heap, tip.

dump[2] *verb* **1** chuck out (*informal*), discard, dispose of, ditch (*informal*), get rid of, offload, scrap, throw out. **2** deposit, drop, place, plonk, put down, set down, throw down, unload.

dumpy *adjective* chubby, fat, plump, podgy, pudgy, rotund, squat, stout, tubby.

dunce *noun* blockhead, bonehead, clot (*informal*), dill (*Australian informal*), dimwit (*informal*), dolt, dope (*informal*), dullard, dummy (*informal*), dunderhead, fool, half-wit, idiot, ignoramus, imbecile, moron (*informal*), nincompoop, nitwit (*informal*), nong (*Australian informal*), simpleton, twit (*slang*).

dung *noun* droppings, excrement, faeces, manure, muck.

dungeon *noun* cell, lock-up, prison.

dunk *verb* dip, immerse, sop.

dupe *verb* bluff, cheat, con (*informal*), deceive, delude, fool, hoax, hoodwink, kid (*informal*), mislead, string along (*informal*), suck in (*informal*), swindle, take in, trick.

duplicate[1] *noun* clone, copy, double, facsimile, photocopy, replica, reproduction, twin.

▶▶ DICTIONARY ◀◀

duplicate² *verb* (**duplicated, duplicating**) make or be a duplicate. **duplication** *noun* **duplicator** *noun* [from Latin *duplex* = double]

duplicity (*say* dew-**plis**-it-ee) *noun* deceitfulness. [from Latin *duplex* = double]

durable *adjective* strong and likely to last. **durably** *adverb*, **durability** *noun* [from Latin *durare* = endure]

duration *noun* the time something lasts.

duress (*say* dewr-**ess**) *noun* the use of force or threats to get what you want.

during *preposition* while something else is going on.

dusk *noun* twilight in the evening.

dusky *adjective* dark; shadowy.

dust¹ *noun* tiny particles of earth or other solid material.

dust² *verb* **1** wipe away dust. **2** sprinkle with dust or something powdery.

duster *noun* a cloth for dusting things.

dustpan *noun* a pan into which dust is brushed from a floor.

dust storm a storm with clouds of dust gathered in the air.

dust-up *noun* a fight, a disturbance.

dusty *adjective* (**dustier, dustiest**) **1** covered with dust. **2** like dust.

dutiful *adjective* doing your duty; obedient. **dutifully** *adverb* [from *duty* + *-full*]

duty *noun* (*plural* **duties**) **1** what you ought to do or must do. **2** a task that must be done. **3** a tax charged on imports and on certain other goods.
on duty actually doing what is your regular work.

dux *noun* the top student in a class or school.

dwarf¹ *noun* (*plural* **dwarfs**) a very small person or thing.

dwarf² *verb* make something seem small by contrast, *The ocean liner dwarfed the tugs that were towing it.*

dwell *verb* (**dwelt, dwelling**) live somewhere. **dweller** *noun*
dwell on think or talk about something for a long time.

dwelling *noun* a house etc. to live in.

dwindle *verb* (**dwindled, dwindling**) get smaller gradually.

dye¹ *verb* (**dyed, dyeing**) colour something by putting it into a liquid. **dyer** *noun*

dye² *noun* a substance used to dye things.

dyke *noun* **1** a long wall or embankment to hold back water and prevent flooding. **2** a ditch for draining water from land.

dynamic *adjective* energetic; active. **dynamically** *adverb* [from Greek *dynamis* = power]

▶▶ THESAURUS ◀◀

duplicate² *verb* copy, photocopy, replicate, reproduce.

durable *adjective* hard-wearing, indestructible, long-lasting, serviceable, solid, stout, strong, sturdy, tough.

duration *noun* length, period, span, term, time.

duress *noun* coercion, compulsion, force, pressure, threat.

dusk *noun* evening, gloaming, nightfall, sundown, sunset, twilight.

dust¹ *noun* bulldust (*Australian*), dirt, grime, grit, powder, sawdust, soot.

dust² *verb* **1** brush, clean, wipe. **2** dredge, sprinkle.

dust storm Darling shower (*Australian*), dust devil, sandstorm, willy willy (*Australian*).

dutiful *adjective* compliant, conscientious, devoted, diligent, faithful, loyal, obedient, reliable, responsible.

duty *noun* **1** allegiance, loyalty, obligation, responsibility. **2** assignment, charge, chore, function, job, office, role, task. **3** customs, excise, levy, tariff, tax, toll.

dwarf¹ *noun* elf, gnome, leprechaun, midget, pygmy, troll.

dwarf² *verb* dominate, overshadow, tower over.

dwell *verb* abide (*old use*), live, reside; see also INHABIT.
dwell on concentrate on, focus on, harp on, linger over.

dwelling *noun* abode (*old use*), domicile, habitation, home, house, lodging, residence; see also FLAT³, HOUSE¹.

dwindle *verb* contract, decline, decrease, diminish, lessen, reduce, shrink, wane.

dye¹ *verb* colour, paint, stain, tint.

dye² *noun* colour, colouring, pigment, stain, tint.

dyke *noun* **1** embankment, levee, stopbank, wall. **2** canal, channel, ditch, furrow, gutter, watercourse.

dynamic *adjective* active, energetic, forceful, go-ahead, high-powered, lively, powerful, progressive, vigorous.

dynamite *noun* **1** a powerful explosive. **2** something likely to make people very excited or angry. [same origin as *dynamic*]

dynamo *noun* (*plural* **dynamos**) a machine that makes electricity.

dynasty (*say* **din**-a-stee) *noun* (*plural* **dynasties**) a succession of rulers all from the same family. **dynastic** *adjective* [same origin as *dynamic*]

dys- *prefix* bad; difficult. [from Greek]

dysentery (*say* **dis**-en-tree) *noun* a disease causing severe diarrhoea. [from *dys-*, + Greek *entera* = bowels]

dyslexia (*say* dis-**leks**-ee-a) *noun* unusually great difficulty in being able to read and spell. **dyslexic** *adjective* [from *dys-*, + Greek *lexis* = speech]

dyspepsia (*say* dis-**pep**-see-a) *noun* indigestion. **dyspeptic** *adjective* [from *dys-*, + Greek *peptikos* = able to digest]

dystrophy (*say* **dis**-trof-ee) *noun* a disease that weakens the muscles. [from *dys-*, + Greek *-trophia* = nourishment]

dynasty *noun* family, house, line, lineage.

► Ee ◄

E. *abbreviation* east; eastern.

e- *prefix* see **ex-**.

each *adjective & pronoun* every; every one, *each child*; *each of you*.

eager *adjective* strongly wanting to do something; enthusiastic. **eagerly** *adverb*, **eagerness** *noun*

eagle *noun* a large bird of prey with very strong sight.

ear¹ *noun* **1** the organ of the body that is used for hearing. **2** hearing-ability, *She has a good ear for music.*

ear² *noun* the spike of seeds at the top of a stalk of wheat, etc.

earache *noun* pain in the ear.

eardrum *noun* a membrane in the ear that vibrates when sounds reach it.

earl *noun* a British nobleman. **earldom** *noun*

early *adjective & adverb* (**earlier**, **earliest**) **1** before the usual or expected time. **2** near the beginning, *early in the book*. **earliness** *noun*

earmark *verb* put aside for a particular purpose. [from the custom of marking an animal's ear to identify it]

earn *verb* get something by working or in return for what you have done.

earnest *adjective* showing serious feelings or intentions. **earnestly** *adverb*, **earnestness** *noun*

earnings *plural noun* money earned.

earphone *noun* a listening device that fits over the ear.

earring *noun* an ornament worn on the ear.

earshot *noun* the distance within which a sound can be heard.

earth¹ *noun* **1** the planet (*Earth*) that we live on. **2** its surface; the ground; soil. **3** the hole where a fox or badger lives. **4** connection to the ground to complete an electrical circuit.

earth² *verb* connect an electrical circuit to the ground.

earthenware *noun* pottery made of coarse baked clay.

earthly *adjective* of this earth or our life on it.

earthquake *noun* a violent movement of part of the earth's surface.

earthworm *noun* a worm that lives in the soil.

earthy *adjective* like earth or soil.

earwig *noun* a crawling insect with pincers at the end of its body.

ease¹ *noun* **1** absence of effort. **2** freedom from trouble or pain.

►► THESAURUS ◄◄

eager *adjective* ardent, avid, bursting, desirous, earnest, enthusiastic, fervent, impatient, interested, itching, keen, longing, motivated, passionate, raring (*informal*), willing, yearning, zealous.

eagerness *noun* alacrity, ardour, desire, earnestness, enthusiasm, fervour, hunger, impatience, keenness, longing, readiness, yearning, zeal.

early *adjective* **1** premature. **2** beginning, first, initial, preliminary.

early *adverb* ahead of time, prematurely, too soon.

earmark *verb* assign, designate, reserve, set aside, specify, tag.

earn *verb* **1** bring in, clear, collect, draw, get, gross, make, net, obtain, rake in (*informal*), receive, take home, work for. **2** be entitled to, be worthy of, deserve, gain, merit, win.

earnest *adjective* ardent, conscientious, determined, diligent, fervent, grave, heartfelt, impassioned, intense, passionate, serious, sincere, sober, solemn, staid, strong, thoughtful, wholehearted, zealous.

earnings *plural noun* income, pay, remuneration, salary, wages.

earth¹ *noun* **1** globe, planet, world. **2** clay, dirt, ground, land, loam, soil.

earthenware *noun* ceramics, crockery, pottery, terracotta.

earthly *adjective* mortal, mundane, physical, secular, terrestrial, worldly.

earthquake *noun* quake (*informal*), shock, tremor.

ease¹ *noun* **1** deftness, dexterity, effortlessness, facility, simplicity. **2** comfort, contentment, leisure, luxury, prosperity, relaxation, repose, rest.

DICTIONARY

ease² *verb* (**eased, easing**) **1** make less painful or less tight or troublesome. **2** move gently or gradually, *ease it in*. **3** become less severe, *The pressure eased.*

easel *noun* a stand for supporting a blackboard or a painting. [from Dutch *ezel* = donkey (which carries a load)]

easily *adverb* **1** without difficulty; with ease. **2** by far, *easily the best*. **3** very likely, *He could easily be lying.*

east¹ *noun* **1** the direction where the sun rises. **2** the eastern part of a country, city, etc.

east² *adjective & adverb* towards or in the east; coming from the east. **easterly** *adjective*, **eastern** *adjective*, **easterner** *noun*, **easternmost** *adjective*
Eastern States *plural noun* the Australian states on the east coast, sometimes including South Australia.

Easter *noun* the Sunday (in March or April) when Christians commemorate the resurrection of Christ; the days around it.

eastward *adjective & adverb* towards the east. **eastwards** *adverb*

easy¹ *adjective* (**easier, easiest**) **1** able to be done or used or understood without trouble. **2** free from pain, trouble or anxiety. **easiness** *noun*
easy chair a comfortable armchair.

easy² *adverb* in an easy way; with ease; comfortably, *Take it easy!*

easygoing *adjective* relaxed and tolerant.

eat *verb* (**ate, eaten, eating**) **1** chew and swallow as food. **2** have a meal, *When do we eat?* **3** use up; destroy gradually, *Extra expenses ate up our savings*; *Acid ate into the metal.*

eatable *adjective* fit to be eaten.

eau de Cologne (*say* oh-de-kol-**ohn**) *noun* a perfume first made at Cologne.

eaves *plural noun* the overhanging edges of a roof.

eavesdrop *verb* (**eavesdropped, eavesdropping**) listen secretly to a private conversation. **eavesdropper** *noun* [as if outside a wall, where water drops from the eaves]

ebb¹ *noun* **1** the movement of the tide when it is going out, away from the land. **2** a low point, *Our courage was at a low ebb.*

ebb² *verb* **1** flow away from the land. **2** weaken; become less, *strength ebbed.*

ebony *noun* a hard black wood.

eccentric (*say* ik-**sen**-trik) *adjective* behaving strangely. **eccentric** *noun*, **eccentrically** *adverb*, **eccentricity** (*say* ek-sen-**triss**-it-ee) *noun* [from Greek *ekkentros* = away from the centre]

ecclesiastical (*say* ik-lee-zee-**ast**-ik-al) *adjective* of the Church or the clergy. [from Greek *ekklesia* = church]

echidna (*say* e-**kid**-na) *noun* an Australian egg-laying mammal that feeds on ants and termites.

THESAURUS

ease² *verb* **1** allay, alleviate, assuage, calm, lessen, lighten, mitigate, pacify, palliate, quell, quieten, reduce, relax, relieve, soothe, still, subdue. **3** abate, diminish, let up, moderate, slacken.

easy¹ *adjective* **1** effortless, elementary, foolproof, light, painless, simple, straightforward, uncomplicated, undemanding, user-friendly. **2** carefree, comfortable, cosy, cushy (*informal*), leisurely, peaceful, relaxed, restful, soft (*informal*), tranquil, untroubled.

easygoing *adjective* calm, carefree, casual, even-tempered, happy-go-lucky, indulgent, laid-back (*informal*), lenient, liberal, nonchalant, open-minded, permissive, placid, relaxed, soft, tolerant, unflappable (*informal*).

eat *verb* **1** bite, bolt, chew, chomp, consume, devour, feast on, feed on, gnaw, gobble, gorge, gulp, guzzle, ingest, knock back (*informal*), masticate, munch, nibble, partake of, peck, pick at, polish off, scoff, stuff, swallow, tuck in (*informal*), wolf. **2** breakfast, dine, lunch, snack, sup. **3** consume, corrode, destroy, erode, make a hole in, rot, use up, wear away.

eatable *adjective* digestible, edible.

eavesdrop *verb* bug (*informal*), listen in, monitor, overhear, tap.

ebb² *verb* **1** flow back, go out, recede, retreat, subside. **2** decline, decrease, diminish, dwindle, fade, wane, weaken.

eccentric *adjective* abnormal, bizarre, cranky, dotty (*informal*), freakish, idiosyncratic, irregular, nutty (*informal*), odd, offbeat, outlandish, peculiar, queer, singular, strange, unconventional, unusual, way-out, weird, zany. **eccentric** *noun* character, crackpot (*informal*), crank, dag (*Australian informal*), dingbat (*informal*), freak, hard case (*Australian informal*), nonconformist, nut (*informal*), oddball (*informal*), oddity, screwball (*informal*), weirdo (*informal*).

▶▶ D I C T I O N A R Y ◀◀

echo¹ *noun* (*plural* **echoes**) a sound that is heard again as it is reflected off something.

echo² *verb* (**echoed, echoing**) **1** make an echo. **2** repeat a sound or saying.

éclair (*say* ay-**klair**) *noun* a finger-shaped cake of pastry with a creamy filling.

eclipse¹ *noun* the blocking of the sun's or moon's light when the moon or the earth is in the way.

eclipse² *verb* (**eclipsed, eclipsing**) **1** block the light and cause an eclipse. **2** outshine, seem better or more important, *Her performance eclipsed all the others.*

ecology (*say* ee-**kol**-o-jee) *noun* the study of living things in relation to each other and to where they live. **ecological** *adjective*, **ecologically** *adverb*, **ecologist** *noun* [from Greek *oikos* = house, + *-logy*]

economic (*say* ee-kon-**om**-ik) *adjective* **1** of economy or economics. **2** profitable.

economical *adjective* using as little as possible. **economically** *adverb*

economics *noun* the study of how money is used and how goods and services are provided and used. **economist** *noun*

economise *verb* (**economised, economising**) be economical; use or spend less.

economy *noun* (*plural* **economies**) **1** a country's or household's income (e.g. from what it sells or earns) and the way this is spent (e.g. on goods and services). **2** being economical. **3** a saving, *We made economies.* [from Greek *oikos* = house, + *-nomia* = management]

ecstasy (*say* **ek**-sta-see) *noun* a feeling of great delight. **ecstatic** (*say* ik-**stat**-ik) *adjective*, **ecstatically** *adverb* [from Greek, = standing outside yourself]

eczema (*say* **eks**-im-a) *noun* a skin disease causing rough itching patches.

eddy¹ *noun* (*plural* **eddies**) a swirling patch of water or air or smoke etc.

eddy² *verb* (**eddied, eddying**) swirl.

edge¹ *noun* **1** the part along the side or end of something. **2** the sharp part of a knife or axe or other cutting-instrument.
be on edge be tense and irritable.

edge² *verb* (**edged, edging**) **1** be the edge or border of something. **2** put a border on. **3** move gradually, *He edged away.*

edgeways *adverb* with the edge forwards or outwards.

edgy *adjective* tense and irritable. **edginess** *noun*

edible *adjective* suitable for eating, not poisonous, *edible fruits.*

edict (*say* **ee**-dikt) *noun* an official command. [from *e-*, + Latin *dictum* = said]

edifice (*say* **ed**-if-iss) *noun* a large building.

edify *verb* (**edified, edifying**) be an improving influence on a person's mind. **edification** *noun*

edit *verb* (**edited, editing**) **1** be the editor of a newspaper or other publication. **2** make written material ready for publishing. **3** choose and put the parts of a film or tape-recording etc. into order.

▶▶ T H E S A U R U S ◀◀

echo¹ *noun* resonance, reverberation.

echo² *verb* **1** reflect, resound, reverberate. **2** ape, copy, imitate, mimic, parrot, repeat, reproduce.

eclipse¹ *noun* blocking out, covering, darkening, obscuring, shadowing.

eclipse² *verb* **2** exceed, outshine, overshadow, surpass.

economic *adjective* **1** budgetary, financial, fiscal, monetary, trade. **2** cost-effective, profitable.

economical *adjective* careful, frugal, provident, sparing, thrifty.

economise *verb* be economical, conserve, cut back, cut costs, retrench, save, scrimp, skimp, stint, tighten your belt.

ecstasy *noun* bliss, delight, elation, euphoria, happiness, joy, rapture.

ecstatic *adjective* blissful, delighted, elated, euphoric, exultant, happy, joyful, overjoyed, over the moon, rapt, rapturous.

eddy¹ *noun* swirl, vortex, whirl, whirlpool.

edge¹ *noun* **1** border, boundary, brim, brink, circumference, end, extremity, fringe, kerb, limit, lip, margin, outskirts, perimeter, periphery, rim, selvedge, side, verge.

edge² *verb* **1** bind, border, fringe, hem, trim. **3** crawl, creep, inch, sidle, slink, steal, worm.

edgy *adjective* anxious, irritable, jittery (*informal*), jumpy, nervous, nervy, on edge, on tenterhooks, tense, uptight (*informal*).

edible *adjective* digestible, eatable.

edifice *noun* building, construction, structure.

edify *verb* see EDUCATE.

edit *verb* **2** adapt, adjust, alter, assemble, check, collate, compile, correct, modify, polish, put together, revise, rewrite.

►►DICTIONARY◄◄

edition *noun* **1** the form in which something is published, *a paperback edition*. **2** all the copies of a book etc. issued at the same time, *the first edition*.

editor *noun* **1** the person in charge of a newspaper or a section of it. **2** a person who edits something.

editorial[1] *adjective* of editing or editors.

editorial[2] *noun* a newspaper article giving the editor's comments on something.

educate *verb* (**educated, educating**) provide with education. **educative** *adjective*, **educator** *noun* [from Latin *educare* = bring up, train]

education *noun* the process of training people's minds and abilities so that they acquire knowledge and develop skills. **educational** *adjective*, **educationally** *adverb*, **educationist** *noun*

eel *noun* a long fish that looks like a snake.

eerie *adjective* (**eerier, eeriest**) strange in a frightening or mysterious way. **eerily** *adverb*, **eeriness** *noun*

ef- *prefix* see **ex-**.

efface *verb* (**effaced, effacing**) wipe or rub out. **effacement** *noun*

effect[1] *noun* **1** a change produced by an action or cause; a result. **2** an impression produced, *a cheerful effect*.

effect[2] *verb* cause; produce, *We want to effect a change*. [from *ef-*, + Latin *-fectum* = done]

Usage Do not confuse with *affect*.

effective *adjective* **1** producing an effect. **2** impressive. **effectively** *adverb*, **effectiveness** *noun*

effectual *adjective* producing the result desired. **effectually** *adverb*

effeminate *adjective* (of a man) having qualities that are thought to be feminine. **effeminacy** *noun*

effervesce (*say* ef-er-**vess**) *verb* (**effervesced, effervescing**) give off bubbles of gas; fizz. **effervescent** *adjective*, **effervescence** *noun* [from Latin, = bubble over (compare *fervent*)]

efficacious (*say* ef-ik-**ay**-shus) *adjective* able to produce the result desired. **efficacy** (*say* **ef**-ik-a-see) *noun*

efficient *adjective* doing work well; effective. **efficiently** *adverb*, **efficiency** *noun* [same origin as *effect*]

effigy *noun* (*plural* **effigies**) a model or sculptured figure.

effort *noun* **1** the use of energy; the energy used. **2** something difficult or tiring. **3** an attempt, *This painting is a good effort*.

effortless *adjective* done with little or no effort. **effortlessly** *adverb*

►►THESAURUS◄◄

edition *noun* **1** copy, form, version. **2** issue, number, publication.

educate *verb* bring up, coach, edify, enlighten, indoctrinate, inform, instruct, nurture, rear, school, teach, train, tutor.
  educated *adjective* cultivated, cultured, enlightened, erudite, informed, knowledgeable, learned, literate, scholarly.

education *noun* cultivation, development, edification, enlightenment, instruction, schooling, teaching, training, tuition, upbringing.
  educational *adjective* **1** academic, pedagogical, scholastic. **2** edifying, educative, enlightening, informative, instructive.

eerie *adjective* creepy, frightening, ghostly, mysterious, scary, spooky (*informal*), uncanny, weird.

efface *verb* delete, erase, expunge, obliterate, rub out, wipe out.

effect[1] *noun* **1** consequence, impact, outcome, repercussion, result, upshot. **2** illusion, impression, sensation.

effect[2] *verb* accomplish, achieve, bring about, cause, perform, produce.

effective *adjective* **1** capable, competent, effectual, efficient, productive, strong, successful. **2** compelling, convincing, forceful, impressive, persuasive, potent, powerful, striking, successful.

effeminate *adjective* camp, unmanly, womanish.

effervescent *adjective* aerated, bubbly, carbonated, fizzy, foaming, gassy, sparkling.

efficient *adjective* businesslike, capable, competent, effective, effectual, organised, productive, proficient, skilful.

effigy *noun* dummy, figure, guy, image, likeness, model, puppet, statue.

effort *noun* **1** elbow grease, energy, exertion, labour, pains, strain, struggle, toil, trouble, work. **3** attempt, endeavour, try.

effortless *adjective* cushy (*informal*), easy, painless, simple, undemanding.

▶▶ DICTIONARY ◀◀

effusive *adjective* making a great show of affection or enthusiasm. **effusively** *adverb*, **effusiveness** *noun*

e.g. *abbreviation* for example. [short for Latin *exempli gratia* = for the sake of an example]

egalitarian (*say* ig-al-it-**air**-ee-an) *adjective* believing that everybody is equal and that nobody should be given special privileges. [from French *égal* = equal]

egg¹ *noun* **1** a more or less round object produced by the female of birds, fishes, reptiles and insects, which may develop into a new individual if fertilised. **2** a hen's or duck's egg used as food.

egg² *verb* encourage with taunts or dares etc., *We egged him on.*

eggplant *noun* a plant with dark-purple fruit (*aubergine*) used as a vegetable.

ego (*say* **eeg**-oh) *noun* (*plural* **egos**) a person's self or self-respect. [Latin, = I]

egotist (*say* **eg**-oh-tist) *noun* a conceited person who is always talking about himself or herself. **egotism** *noun*, **egotistic** *adjective*

eiderdown *noun* a quilt stuffed with soft material. [originally the soft down of the *eider*, a kind of Arctic duck]

eight *noun* & *adjective* the number 8; one more than seven. **eighth** *adjective* & *noun*

eighteen *noun* & *adjective* the number 18; one more than seventeen. **eighteenth** *adjective* & *noun*

eighty *noun* & *adjective* (*plural* **eighties**) the number 80; eight times ten. **eightieth** *adjective* & *noun*

eisteddfod (*say* I-ste*th*-vod) *noun* an annual gathering of poets and musicians for competitions. [Welsh]

either¹ *adjective* & *pronoun* **1** one or the other of two, *Either team can win; either of them.* **2** both of two, *There are paths on either side of the river.*

either² *adverb* also; similarly, *If you won't go, I won't either.*

either³ *conjunction* (used with *or*) the first of two possibilities, *He is either ill or drunk. Either come right in or go away.*

eject *verb* **1** send out forcefully. **2** expel; compel to leave. **ejection** *noun*, **ejector** *noun* [from *e-*, + Latin *-jectum* = thrown]

eke (*say* eek) *verb* (**eked**, **eking**) **eke out** manage to make (a living) with difficulty.

elaborate¹ (*say* il-**ab**-er-at) *adjective* having many parts or details; complicated. **elaborately** *adverb*, **elaborateness** *noun*

elaborate² (*say* il-**ab**-er-ayt) *verb* (**elaborated**, **elaborating**) describe or work out in detail. **elaboration** *noun* [from *e-*, + Latin *laborare* = to work]

elapse *verb* (**elapsed**, **elapsing**) (of time) pass. [from *e-*, + Latin *lapsum* = slipped]

elastic¹ *noun* cord or material woven with strands of rubber etc. so that it can stretch.

elastic² *adjective* able to be stretched or squeezed and then go back to its original length or shape. **elasticity** *noun*

elated *adjective* with raised spirits, feeling very pleased. **elation** *noun* [from *e-*, + Latin *latum* = carried]

elbow¹ *noun* the joint in the middle of the arm.

elbow² *verb* push with the elbow.

elder¹ *adjective* older, *my elder brother.*

elder² *noun* **1** an older person, *Respect your elders!* **2** an official in certain Churches. [an old form of *older*]

▶▶ THESAURUS ◀◀

egg² *verb* (*egg on*) encourage, goad, incite, prompt, push, sool on (*Australian informal*), spur on, urge.

egotistic *adjective* conceited, egocentric, egotistical, narcissistic, proud, self-centred, self-important, vain.

eiderdown *noun* continental quilt, Doona (*trade mark*), duvet, quilt.

eject *verb* **1** discharge, emit, expel, send out, spew, spit out (*informal*). **2** banish, chuck out (*informal*), evict, expel, get rid of, kick out (*informal*), oust, remove, throw out, turf out (*informal*), turn out.

elaborate¹ *adjective* busy, complex, complicated, detailed, fancy, fussy, intricate, involved, ornate, showy, sophisticated.

elaborate² *verb* enlarge on, expand (on), flesh out, work out.

elapse *verb* go by, pass, roll by, slip by.

elastic² *adjective* expandable, resilient, rubbery, springy, stretchy.

elated *adjective* chuffed (*slang*), delighted, ecstatic, enraptured, euphoric, exhilarated, exultant, happy, joyful, jubilant, overjoyed, over the moon, rapt, rapturous, thrilled.

elbow² *verb* jostle, nudge, push, shove, thrust.

elder² *noun* **1** senior.

▶▶ DICTIONARY ◀◀

elder³ *noun* a tree with white flowers and black berries. **elderberry** *noun*

elderly *adjective* rather old.

eldest *adjective* oldest. [an old form of *oldest*]

elect *verb* 1 choose by voting. 2 choose to do something; decide. [from *e-*, + Latin *lectum* = chosen]

election *noun* electing; the process of electing Members of Parliament.

elector *noun* a person who has the right to vote in an election. **electoral** *adjective*

electorate *noun* 1 all the electors. 2 (*Australian*) a district represented by a Member of Parliament elected by the people who live there.

electric *adjective* 1 of or worked by electricity. 2 causing sudden excitement, *The news had an electric effect.* **electrical** *adjective*, **electrically** *adverb* [from Greek *elektron* = amber (which is easily given a charge of static electricity)]

electrician *noun* a person whose job is to deal with electrical equipment.

electricity *noun* a form of energy carried by certain particles of matter (electrons and protons) used for lighting and heating and for making machines work.

electrify *verb* (**electrified, electrifying**) 1 give an electric charge to something. 2 supply with electric power; cause to work with electricity. 3 thrill with sudden excitement. **electrification** *noun*

electro- *prefix* of or using electricity.

electrocute *verb* (**electrocuted, electrocuting**) kill by electricity. **electrocution** *noun*

electrode *noun* a solid conductor through which electricity enters or leaves a vacuum tube. [from *electro-*, + Greek *hodos* = way]

electromagnet *noun* a magnet worked by electricity. **electromagnetic** *adjective*

electron *noun* a particle of matter with a negative electric charge. [see *electric*]

electronic *adjective* produced or worked by a flow of electrons. **electronically** *adverb* **electronic mail** messages distributed by a computer system, email.

electronics *noun* the use or study of electronic devices.

elegant *adjective* graceful and dignified. **elegantly** *adverb*, **elegance** *noun*

elegy (*say* **el**-ij-ee) *noun* (*plural* **elegies**) a sorrowful or serious poem.

element *noun* 1 each of the parts that make up a whole thing. 2 each of about 100 substances composed of atoms that have the same number of protons. 3 a basic or elementary principle, *the elements of algebra.* 4 a wire or coil that gives out heat in an electric fire or cooker etc. 5 a suitable or satisfying environment, *in one's element.* **the elements** the forces of weather, such as rain, wind and cold.

elementary *adjective* dealing with the simplest stages of something; easy.

elephant *noun* a very large animal with a trunk and tusks. [from Greek *elephas* = ivory (the material of its tusks)]

elephantine (*say* el-if-**ant**-I'n) *adjective* very large; clumsy.

elevate *verb* (**elevated, elevating**) lift up; put high up. **elevation** *noun* [from *e-*, + Latin *levare* = to lift]

elevator *noun* 1 something that raises things. 2 (*American*) a lift.

eleven *adjective* & *noun* the number 11; one more than ten. **eleventh** *adjective* & *noun*

elf *noun* (*plural* **elves**) (in fairy-tales) a small being with magic powers. **elfin** *adjective*

▶▶ THESAURUS ◀◀

elderly *adjective* aged, ageing, old, oldish, retired, senior.

eldest *adjective* first-born, oldest.

elect *verb* 1 appoint, choose, opt for, pick, select, vote for.

election *noun* ballot, poll, vote.

electorate *noun* 1 constituents, electors, people, voters. 2 constituency, seat.

elegant *adjective* chic, dignified, fashionable, graceful, gracious, grand, handsome, luxurious, opulent, plush, posh (*informal*), refined, smart, stately, stylish, sumptuous, tasteful.

elegy *noun* dirge, lament, requiem.

element *noun* 1 component, constituent, factor, ingredient, member, part, unit. 3 (*elements*) basics, essentials, fundamentals, principles, rudiments.

elementary *adjective* basic, fundamental, introductory, primary, rudimentary, simple.

elevate *verb* boost, exalt, lift, promote, raise, upgrade, uplift. **elevation** *noun* altitude, height.

elf *noun* fairy, gnome, goblin, gremlin (*informal*), hobgoblin, imp, leprechaun, pixie, spirit, sprite.

▶▶ D I C T I O N A R Y ◀◀

elicit (*say* ill-**iss**-it) *verb* draw out information by reasoning or questioning.

eligible (*say* **el**-ij-ib-ul) *adjective* qualified or suitable for something. **eligibility** *noun*

eliminate *verb* (**eliminated, eliminating**) get rid of; remove. **elimination** *noun* [from Latin *e-* = out, + *limen* = entrance]

elision (*say* il-**li**zh-on) *noun* omitting part of a word in pronouncing it, e.g. in saying *I'm* for *I am.*

elite (*say* ay-**leet**) *noun* a group of people given privileges which are not given to others. [from Old French *élit* = chosen]

elixir (*say* il-**iks**-er) *noun* a sweetened and flavoured liquid medicine. [from Arabic *al-iksir* = substance that would cure illness and change metals into gold]

Elizabethan (*say* il-iz-a-**beeth**-an) *adjective* of the time of Queen Elizabeth I (1558–1603). **Elizabethan** *noun*

elk *noun* a large kind of deer.

ellipse (*say* il-**ips**) *noun* an oval shape.

elliptical (*say* il-**ip**-tik-al) *adjective* **1** shaped like an ellipse. **2** with some words omitted, *an elliptical phrase.* **elliptically** *adverb*

elm *noun* a tall tree with rough leaves.

El Niño (*say* el **nin**-yoh) an irregular warming of the southern Pacific Ocean surface that causes far-reaching changes in weather. [from Spanish *El Niño de Navidad* = the Christmas Child]

elocution (*say* el-o-**kew**-shon) *noun* speaking clearly. [same origin as *eloquent*]

elongated *adjective* made longer; lengthened. **elongation** *noun*

elope *verb* (**eloped, eloping**) run away secretly with a lover. **elopement** *noun*

eloquent *adjective* speaking fluently and expressing ideas vividly. **eloquently** *adverb*. **eloquence** *noun* [from *e-*, + Latin *loqui* = speak]

else *adverb* **1** besides; other, *Nobody else knows.* **2** otherwise; if not, *Run or else you'll be late.*

elsewhere *adverb* somewhere else.

elucidate (*say* il-**oo**-sid-ayt) *verb* (**elucidated, elucidating**) make something clear by explaining it. **elucidation** *noun* [compare *lucid*]

elude (*say* ill-**ood**) *verb* (**eluded, eluding**) avoid being caught by someone, *The fox eluded the hounds.* **elusive** *adjective*

em- *prefix* see **en-**.

emaciated (*say* im-**ay**-see-ay-tid) *adjective* very thin from illness or starvation. **emaciation** *noun*

email[1] *noun* electronic mail.

email[2] *verb* send by email.

emanate (*say* **em**-an-ayt) *verb* (**emanated, emanating**) come from a source.

emancipate (*say* im-**an**-sip-ayt) *verb* (**emancipated, emancipating**) set free from slavery or other restraints. **emancipation** *noun*

embalm *verb* preserve a corpse from decay by using spices or chemicals.

embankment *noun* a long bank of earth or stone to hold back water or support a road or railway.

embargo *noun* (*plural* **embargoes**) a ban. [from Spanish *embargar* = restrain]

embark *verb* put or go on board a ship or aircraft. **embarkation** *noun*
embark on begin, *They embarked on a dangerous exercise.*

▶▶ T H E S A U R U S ◀◀

elicit *verb* call forth, draw out, evoke, extract, get, obtain.

eligible *adjective* acceptable, allowed, authorised, entitled, qualified, suitable.

eliminate *verb* abolish, cut out, delete, destroy, do away with, eradicate, exclude, exterminate, get rid of, omit, remove, root out, stamp out, weed out.

elite *noun* best, choice, chosen, cream, pick.

ellipse *noun* oval.

elocution *noun* articulation, delivery, diction, enunciation, oratory, public speaking, speech.

elongated *adjective* drawn out, extended, lengthened, protracted, stretched out.

eloquent *adjective* articulate, expressive, fluent, forceful, persuasive, powerful.

elude *verb* avoid, dodge, escape from, evade, give the slip to, shake off.
elusive *adjective* fugitive, indefinable, intangible, subtle, transient.

emaciated *adjective* cadaverous, gaunt, scrawny, skinny, thin.

emanate *verb* come, flow, issue, originate, proceed, spring, stem.

emancipate *verb* deliver, free, liberate, release, set free.

embankment *noun* bank, levee, stopbank.

embark *verb* board ship, get on, go aboard.
embark on begin, commence, enter on, start, undertake.

embarrass *verb* make someone feel awkward or ashamed. **embarrassment** *noun*

embassy *noun* (*plural* **embassies**) **1** an ambassador and his or her staff. **2** the building where they work.

embed *verb* (**embedded, embedding**) fix firmly in something solid.

embellish *verb* **1** ornament something. **2** add details to a story etc. **embellishment** *noun*

embers *plural noun* small pieces of glowing coal or wood in a dying fire.

embezzle *verb* (**embezzled, embezzling**) take dishonestly money that was left in your care. **embezzlement** *noun*

emblazon *verb* ornament with heraldic or other emblems.

emblem *noun* a symbol; a device representing something, *The crown is a royal emblem*. **emblematic** *adjective*

embody *verb* (**embodied, embodying**) **1** express principles or ideas in a visible form, *The house embodies our idea of a modern home*. **2** incorporate; include, *Parts of the old treaty are embodied in the new one*. **embodiment** *noun*

emboss *verb* decorate with a raised design.

embrace[1] *verb* (**embraced, embracing**) hold closely in your arms.

embrace[2] *noun* embracing; a hug. [from *em-*, + Latin *bracchium* = an arm]

embrocation *noun* a lotion for rubbing on parts of the body that ache.

embroider *verb* **1** ornament cloth with needlework. **2** add made-up details to a story to make it more interesting. **embroidery** *noun*

embroil *verb* involve in an argument or quarrel.

embryo (*say* **em**-bree-oh) *noun* (*plural* **embryos**) **1** a baby or young animal as it starts to grow in the womb; a young bird growing in an egg. **2** anything in its earliest stages of development. **embryonic** (*say* em-bree-**on**-ik) *adjective* [from *em-*, + Greek *bryein* = grow]

emerald *noun* **1** a bright-green precious stone. **2** its colour.

emerge *verb* (**emerged, emerging**) **1** come out; appear. **2** (of facts) become known. **emergence** *noun*, **emergent** *adjective*

emergency *noun* (*plural* **emergencies**) a sudden serious happening needing prompt action.

emery-paper *noun* paper with a gritty coating like sandpaper.

emetic (*say* im-**et**-ik) *noun* a medicine used to make a person vomit.

emigrate *verb* (**emigrated, emigrating**) leave your own country and go and live in another. **emigration** *noun*, **emigrant** *noun* [from *e-* + *migrate*]

Usage People are *emigrants* from the country they leave and *immigrants* in the country where they settle.

embarrass *verb* abash, chagrin, discomfit, disconcert, distress, humiliate, mortify, shame. **embarrassed** *adjective* abashed, ashamed, awkward, chagrined, discomfited, disconcerted, distressed, humiliated, mortified, self-conscious, shamefaced, sheepish, uncomfortable.

embed *verb* fix, implant, insert, lodge, set, stick.

embellish *verb* **1** adorn, beautify, decorate, dress up, enhance, ornament, prettify, tizzy (*Australian*). **2** embroider, enhance, exaggerate, improve upon.

embers *plural noun* cinders, coals.

embezzle *verb* misappropriate, steal.

emblem *noun* badge, coat of arms, crest, device, hallmark, insignia, logo, seal, sign, symbol.

embody *verb* **1** exemplify, express, represent. **2** contain, include, incorporate, integrate.

embodiment *noun* epitome, model, personification, quintessence, soul.

embrace[1] *verb* clasp, cuddle, enfold, hold, hug.

embroider *verb* **1** sew, stitch, work. **2** embellish, enhance, improve upon. **embroidery** *noun* needlework, sewing.

embroil *verb* entangle, involve, mix up.

embryonic *adjective* early, immature, incipient, rudimentary, undeveloped.

emerge *verb* **1** appear, come out, materialise, peep out, show up, surface. **2** become apparent, become known, be revealed, come out, come to light, transpire, turn out.

emergency *noun* crisis, danger, difficulty, predicament.

emigrate *verb* depart, leave, migrate, move, quit, relocate. **emigrant** *noun* émigré, expatriate, refugee, settler.

▶▶▶ D I C T I O N A R Y ◀◀◀

eminence *noun* **1** being eminent; distinction. **2** a piece of ground; a hill.
His Eminence a cardinal's title.

eminent *adjective* famous; distinguished; outstanding. **eminently** *adverb*

emir (*say* em-**eer**) *noun* a Muslim ruler. [from Arabic *amir* = ruler]

emit *verb* (**emitted, emitting**) send out (light, heat, fumes, etc.) **emission** *noun*, **emitter** *noun* [from *e-*, + Latin *mittere* = send]

emolument (*say* im-**ol**-yoo-ment) *noun* payment for work; a salary.

emotion *noun* a strong feeling in the mind, such as love or hate. **emotional** *adjective*, **emotionally** *adverb*

emotive *adjective* causing emotion.

empathy *noun* identifying yourself mentally with another person and understanding him or her. [from *em-*, + Greek *pathos* = feeling]

emperor *noun* a man who rules an empire.

emphasis (*say* **em**-fa-sis) *noun* special importance given to something.

emphasise *verb* (**emphasised, emphasising**) put emphasis on something.

emphatic (*say* im-**fat**-ik) *adjective* using emphasis. **emphatically** *adverb*

empire *noun* **1** a group of countries controlled by one person or government. **2** a set of shops or firms under one control.

employ *verb* **1** pay a person to work for you. **2** make use of, *Our doctor employs the most modern methods.* **employer** *noun*, **employment** *noun*

employee *noun* a person employed by someone (who is the *employer*).

emporium (*say* em-**por**-ee-um) *noun* a large shop.

empower *verb* give someone the power to do something; authorise.

empress *noun* (*plural* **empresses**) **1** a woman who rules an empire. **2** an emperor's wife.

empty[1] *adjective* **1** with nothing in it. **2** with nobody in it. **3** with no meaning or no effect, *empty promises.* **emptily** *adverb*, **emptiness** *noun*

empty[2] *verb* (**emptied, emptying**) make or become empty.

emu *noun* (*plural* **emus**) a large long-legged Australian bird which cannot fly.

emulate *verb* (**emulated, emulating**) try to do as well as someone or something, especially by imitating them, *He is emulating his father.* **emulation** *noun*

▶▶▶ T H E S A U R U S ◀◀◀

eminence *noun* **1** celebrity, distinction, fame, importance, note, pre-eminence, prominence, renown, repute, standing, stature.

eminent *adjective* celebrated, distinguished, famous, great, illustrious, important, notable, noted, outstanding, pre-eminent, prominent, renowned, respected, well-known.

emit *verb* beam, discharge, expel, exude, give off, give out, issue, leak, ooze, pour forth, radiate, send out, shed, transmit.

emotion *noun* feeling, passion, sentiment.
emotional *adjective* ardent, demonstrative, excitable, fervent, passionate, sensitive, sentimental, temperamental.

emotive *adjective* emotional, impassioned, moving, passionate, poignant, sentimental, stirring, touching.

emperor *noun* Caesar, czar, head of state, kaiser, mikado, monarch, ruler, sovereign, tsar.

emphasis *noun* accent, attention, importance, priority, prominence, stress, weight.

emphasise *verb* accent, accentuate, draw attention to, highlight, impress, insist on, point up, stress, underline.

emphatic *adjective* categorical, decisive, definite, forceful, strong, unequivocal, vigorous.

empire *noun* **1** domain, dominion, kingdom, realm, territory.

employ *verb* **1** appoint, contract, engage, give work to, hire, sign up, take on. **2** apply, make use of, use, utilise.
employer *noun* **1** boss, chief, manager, master, proprietor. **2** business, company, corporation, establishment, firm, organisation.
employment *noun* business, calling, career, job, occupation, profession, pursuit, trade, vocation, work.

employee *noun* hand, wage-earner, worker; (*employees*) human resources, labour, personnel, staff, workforce.

empower *verb* authorise, commission, enable, equip, give power to, license.

empty[1] *adjective* **1** bare, blank, clean, clear, hollow, unfilled, unfurnished, unused, void. **2** deserted, uninhabited, unoccupied, vacant. **3** hollow, idle, insincere, insubstantial, meaningless, vain.

empty[2] *verb* clear, drain, evacuate, pour out, remove, tip out.

emulsion *noun* **1** a creamy or slightly oily liquid. **2** the coating on photographic film which is sensitive to light.

en- *prefix* (changing to **em-** before words beginning with *b*, *m*, or *p*) in; into; on. [from Latin or Greek, = in]

enable *verb* (**enabled**, **enabling**) give the means or ability to do something.

enact *verb* **1** make into a law by a formal process, *Parliament enacted new laws against drugs.* **2** perform, *enact a play.* **enactment** *noun*

enamel[1] *noun* **1** a shiny substance for coating metal. **2** paint that dries hard and shiny. **3** the shiny surface of teeth.

enamel[2] *verb* (**enamelled**, **enamelling**) coat or decorate with enamel.

enamoured (*say* in-**am**-erd) *adjective* in love with someone. [from *en-*, + French *amour* = love]

encamp *verb* settle in a camp.

encampment *noun* a camp.

encase *verb* (**encased**, **encasing**) enclose in a case.

enchant *verb* **1** put under a magic spell. **2** fill with intense delight. **enchanter** *noun*, **enchantment** *noun*, **enchantress** *noun*

encircle *verb* (**encircled**, **encircling**) surround. **encirclement** *noun*

enclose *verb* (**enclosed**, **enclosing**) **1** put a wall or fence round; shut in on all sides. **2** put into a box or envelope etc.

enclosure *noun* **1** enclosing. **2** an enclosed area. **3** something enclosed with a letter or parcel.

encompass *verb* **1** surround. **2** contain.

encore (*say* **on**-kor) *noun* an extra item performed at a concert etc. after previous items have been applauded. [French, = again]

encounter[1] *verb* **1** meet someone unexpectedly. **2** experience, *We encountered some difficulties.*

encounter[2] *noun* **1** an unexpected meeting. **2** a battle.

encourage *verb* (**encouraged**, **encouraging**) **1** give confidence or hope; hearten. **2** try to persuade; urge. **3** stimulate; help to develop, *Encourage healthy eating.* **encouragement** *noun*

encroach *verb* intrude upon someone's rights; go further than the proper limits, *The extra work would encroach on their free time.* **encroachment** *noun*

encrust *verb* cover with a crust or layer. **encrustation** *noun*

encumber *verb* be a burden to; hamper. **encumbrance** *noun*

enable *verb* allow, assist, authorise, entitle, facilitate, let, license, permit, qualify.

enact *verb* **1** decree, legislate, ordain, pass. **2** act out, perform, play.

enchant *verb* bewitch, captivate, charm, delight, enrapture, enthral, entrance, fascinate, hold spellbound, hypnotise, mesmerise, thrill. **enchanter** *noun* magician, sorcerer, warlock, wizard.
enchantress *noun* magician, siren, sorceress, witch.

encircle *verb* besiege, circle, enclose, encompass, hem in, ring, surround.

enclose *verb* **1** box in, circle, close in, confine, cordon off, encircle, encompass, fence in, pen, restrict, ring, shut in, surround, wall in. **2** include, insert, send with.

enclosure *noun* **2** cage, compound, coop, corral, fold, hutch, paddock, pen, pound, run, stall, sty, yard.

encompass *verb* **1** circle, encircle, enclose, ring, surround. **2** contain, cover, embrace, include, incorporate.

encounter[1] *verb* **1** bump into (*informal*), chance upon, meet, run into. **2** be faced with, come up against, confront, contend with, experience, face, grapple with, meet with, run into.

encounter[2] *noun* **1** meeting. **2** battle, brush, clash, conflict, confrontation, fight, run-in.

encourage *verb* **1** buck up (*informal*), build up, buoy up, cheer up, comfort, hearten, inspire, reassure. **2** egg on, exhort, persuade, spur, urge. **3** aid, assist, boost, foster, further, help, promote, stimulate.
encouragement *noun* boost, incentive, inspiration, reassurance, shot in the arm, stimulus, support.

encroach *verb* impinge, infringe, intrude, invade, make inroads, poach, trespass.

encumber *verb* burden, hamper, load down, lumber, saddle, weigh down.

encyclopedia *noun* a book or set of books containing all kinds of information. **encyclopedic** *adjective* [from Greek, = general education]

end[1] *noun* 1 the limit of something. 2 an extreme point or part. 3 the part furthest from the front. 4 a remnant. 5 the finish or final part of something. 6 the half of a sports field or court defended or occupied by one team or player. 7 destruction; death. 8 purpose, *She did it to gain her own ends.*

end[2] *verb* bring or come to an end.

endanger *verb* cause danger to.

endear *verb* cause to be loved, *She endeared herself to us all.* **endearing** *adjective*

endeavour[1] (*say* in-**dev**-er) *verb* attempt.

endeavour[2] *noun* an attempt.

endemic (*say* en-**dem**-ik) *adjective* (of a disease) often found in a certain area or group of people. [from *en-*, + Greek *demos* = people]

ending *noun* the last part.

endless *adjective* 1 never stopping. 2 with the ends joined to make a continuous strip for use in machinery etc., *an endless belt.* **endlessly** *adverb*

endorse *verb* (**endorsed, endorsing**) 1 sign your name on the back of a cheque or document. 2 make an official entry on a licence about an offence committed by its holder. 3 confirm or give your approval to something. **endorsement** *noun* [from Latin *in dorsum* = on the back]

endow *verb* 1 provide a source of income to establish something, *She endowed a scholarship.* 2 provide with an ability or quality, *He was endowed with great talent.* **endowment** *noun*

endure *verb* (**endured, enduring**) 1 suffer or put up with pain or hardship etc. 2 continue to exist; last. **endurable** *adjective*, **endurance** *noun*

enemy *noun* (*plural* **enemies**) 1 one who hates and opposes or seeks to harm another. 2 a nation or army etc. at war with another.

energetic *adjective* full of energy. **energetically** *adverb*

encyclopedic *adjective* comprehensive, extensive, vast, wide-ranging.

end[1] *noun* 1 boundary, limit, terminus. 2 extremity, point, tip. 3 back, rear, tail. 4 butt, remains, remnant, stub. 5 breakup, cessation, close, completion, conclusion, culmination, ending, expiration, expiry, finale, finish, termination. 7 death, demise (*formal*), destruction, downfall, extinction, fall, passing, ruin. 8 aim, design, goal, intention, object, objective, purpose.

in the end eventually, finally, in the long run, ultimately.

end[2] *verb* abolish, break off, bring to an end, cease, close, come to an end, complete, conclude, cut off, discontinue, dissolve, eliminate, eradicate, expire, finish, get rid of, halt, peter out, put an end to, put a stop to, round off, run out, stamp out, stop, terminate, wind up, wipe out.

endanger *verb* imperil, jeopardise, put at risk, threaten.

endearing *adjective* appealing, attractive, charming, disarming, engaging, likeable, lovable, winsome.

endeavour[1] *verb* aim, attempt, make an effort, strive, try.

endeavour[2] *noun* attempt, effort, try.

ending *noun* conclusion, denouement, end, finale, finish, resolution, termination.

endless *adjective* 1 abiding, boundless, ceaseless, constant, continual, continuous, eternal, everlasting, immeasurable, incessant, inexhaustible, infinite, interminable, limitless, never-ending, non-stop, ongoing, permanent, perpetual, persistent, unending.

endorse *verb* 1 countersign, sign. 3 agree with, approve, assent to, back, confirm, OK (*informal*), ratify, sanction, second, subscribe to, support, vouch for.

endow *verb* 2 bestow, bless, favour, provide, supply.

endure *verb* 1 abide, bear, brave, brook, cope with, experience, put up with, stand, stomach, suffer, tolerate, undergo, weather, withstand. 2 carry on, continue, last, live on, persist, prevail, remain, stay, survive.

endurance *noun* fortitude, hardiness, patience, perseverance, persistence, stamina, staying power, strength, tenacity.

enemy *noun* adversary, antagonist, foe, opponent, opposition, rival.

energetic *adjective* active, animated, brisk, dynamic, forceful, full of beans (*informal*), go-ahead, hard-working, high-powered, indefatigable, industrious, lively, perky, spirited, sprightly, spry, strenuous, tireless, vibrant, vigorous, zippy.

▶▶▶ **DICTIONARY** ◀◀

energy *noun* **1** strength to do things, liveliness. **2** the ability of matter or radiation to do work, *electrical energy*. [from *en-*, + Greek *ergon* = work]

enfold *verb* **1** wrap up. **2** clasp.

enforce *verb* (**enforced**, **enforcing**) compel people to obey a law or rule. **enforcement** *noun*, **enforceable** *adjective*

enfranchise *verb* (**enfranchised**, **enfranchising**) give the right to vote in elections. **enfranchisement** *noun*

engage *verb* (**engaged**, **engaging**) **1** arrange to employ or use, *Engage a typist*. **2** occupy the attention of, *They engaged her in conversation*. **3** promise. **4** begin a battle with, *We engaged the enemy*.

engaged *adjective* **1** having promised to marry somebody. **2** in use; occupied.

engagement *noun* **1** engaging something. **2** a promise to marry somebody. **3** an arrangement to meet somebody or do something. **4** a battle.

engaging *adjective* attractive; charming.

engine *noun* **1** a machine that provides power. **2** a vehicle that pulls a railway train, a locomotive. [from Latin *ingenium* = clever invention (compare *ingenious*)]

engineer[1] *noun* an expert in engineering.

engineer[2] *verb* plan and construct or cause to happen, *He engineered a meeting between them*.

engineering *noun* the design and building or control of machinery or of structures such as roads and bridges.

engrave *verb* (**engraved**, **engraving**) carve words or lines etc. on a surface. **engraver** *noun*, **engraving** *noun*

engross *verb* occupy a person's whole attention, *He was engrossed in his book*.

engulf *verb* flow over and cover; swamp.

enhance *verb* (**enhanced**, **enhancing**) make a thing more attractive; increase its value. **enhancement** *noun*

enigma (*say* in-**ig**-ma) *noun* something very difficult to understand, a puzzle.

enigmatic (*say* en-ig-**mat**-ik) *adjective* mysterious and puzzling. **enigmatically** *adverb*

enjoy *verb* get pleasure from something. **enjoyable** *adjective*, **enjoyment** *noun*

enlarge *verb* (**enlarged**, **enlarging**) make or become bigger. **enlargement** *noun*

enlighten *verb* give knowledge to a person, inform. **enlightenment** *noun*

▶▶▶ **THESAURUS** ◀◀

energy *noun* **1** drive, enthusiasm, force, go, gusto, liveliness, oomph (*informal*), pep, power, stamina, steam, verve, vigour, vim (*informal*), vitality, vivacity, zeal, zest, zing (*informal*), zip.

enforce *verb* administer, apply, carry out, implement, impose, insist on.

engage *verb* **1** appoint, employ, hire, recruit, take on. **2** absorb, engross, involve, occupy.

engaged *adjective* **1** affianced (*formal*), betrothed (*formal*). **2** busy, in use, occupied.

engagement *noun* **2** betrothal. **3** appointment, arrangement, assignation, booking, commitment, date (*informal*), meeting, rendezvous.

engaging *adjective* appealing, attractive, charming, delightful, disarming, enchanting, endearing, likeable, lovable, winning, winsome.

engineer[2] *verb* arrange, bring about, contrive, fix, mastermind, orchestrate, organise, plan, rig, wangle (*slang*).

engrave *verb* carve, chisel, cut, etch, incise, inscribe.

engrossed *adjective* absorbed, immersed, involved, lost, occupied, preoccupied.

engulf *verb* cover, flood, inundate, overrun, overwhelm, submerge, swallow up, swamp.

enhance *verb* boost, enrich, heighten, improve, increase, intensify, strengthen.

enigma *noun* conundrum, mystery, problem, puzzle, riddle, secret.

enigmatic *adjective* arcane, baffling, cryptic, inscrutable, mysterious, obscure, perplexing, puzzling, unfathomable.

enjoy *verb* appreciate, bask in, be fond of, be keen on, delight in, fancy, lap up, like, love, luxuriate in, relish, revel in, savour, wallow in. **enjoy yourself** be happy, have a ball (*informal*), have a good time, have fun.

enjoyable *adjective* agreeable, cool (*informal*), delightful, good, lovely (*informal*), nice, pleasant, pleasurable, satisfying.

enjoyment *noun* amusement, delectation, delight, entertainment, fun, happiness, joy, kick (*informal*), pleasure, recreation, satisfaction, thrill, zest.

enlarge *verb* add to, blow up (*informal*), broaden, bulge, distend, expand, extend, fill out, grow, lengthen, magnify, stretch, swell, widen.

enlighten *verb* edify, educate, inform, instruct, teach.

▶▶ DICTIONARY ◀◀

enlist *verb* **1** take into or join the armed forces. **2** obtain someone's support or services etc., *enlist their help.* **enlistment** *noun*

enliven *verb* make more lively. **enlivenment** *noun*

enmity *noun* being somebody's enemy; hostility.

enormity *noun* (*plural* **enormities**) **1** great wickedness, *the enormity of this crime.* **2** great size; hugeness, *the enormity of their task.*

Usage Many people regard the use in sense 2 as incorrect. It is best to avoid it and use *magnitude.*

enormous *adjective* very large; huge. **enormously** *adverb*, **enormousness** *noun* [from *e-*, + Latin *norma* = standard]

enough *adjective* (e.g. 'enough food'). *noun* (e.g. 'I have had enough'), & *adverb* (e.g. 'Are you warm enough?') as much or as many as necessary.

enquire *verb* (**enquired, enquiring**) ask, *He enquired if I was well.* **enquiry** *noun*

Usage See the note under *inquire.*

enrage *verb* (**enraged, enraging**) make very angry.

enrapture *verb* (**enraptured, enrapturing**) fill with intense delight.

enrich *verb* make richer. **enrichment** *noun*

enrol *verb* (**enrolled, enrolling**) **1** become a member of a society etc. **2** make into a member. **enrolment** *noun*

ensconce *verb* (**ensconced, ensconcing**) settle comfortably, *ensconced in a chair.*

ensemble (*say* on-**somb**l) *noun* **1** a group of things that go together. **2** a group of musicians. [French]

enshrine *verb* (**enshrined, enshrining**) keep as if in a shrine, *His memory is enshrined in our hearts.*

ensign *noun* a military or naval flag. [the word is related to *insignia*]

enslave *verb* (**enslaved, enslaving**) make a slave of; force into slavery. **enslavement** *noun*

ensue *verb* (**ensued, ensuing**) happen afterwards or as a result.

ensure *verb* (**ensured, ensuring**) make certain of; guarantee, *Good food will ensure good health.*

Usage Do not confuse with *insure.*

entail *verb* make necessary, involve, *This plan entails danger.* **entailment** *noun*

entangle *verb* (**entangled, entangling**) tangle. **entanglement** *noun*

entente (*say* on-**tont**) *noun* a friendly understanding between countries. [French]

enter *verb* **1** come in; go in. **2** put into a list or book. **3** register as a competitor.

▶▶ THESAURUS ◀◀

enlist *verb* **1** call up, conscript, draft (*American*), enrol, join up, recruit, register, sign on, volunteer. **2** drum up, gather, get, mobilise, muster, obtain, secure.

enmity *noun* acrimony, animosity, antagonism, antipathy, bitterness, hatred, hostility, ill will, malevolence, opposition, rancour.

enormous *adjective* astronomical, big, colossal, gargantuan, giant, gigantic, ginormous (*slang*), great, huge, humungous (*slang*), immeasurable, immense, incalculable, jumbo, king-sized, large, mammoth, massive, mighty, monstrous, monumental, outsize, prodigious, spacious, staggering, stupendous, sweeping, tremendous, vast.

enough *adjective* adequate, ample, sufficient.

enquire *verb* ask, inquire, query, question. **enquiry** *noun* inquiry, query, question.

enrage *verb* anger, annoy, exasperate, incense, infuriate, irritate, madden, outrage, provoke, rile (*informal*).

enrol *verb* **1** enlist, join up, register, sign on. **2** accept, admit, enlist, recruit, take on.

ensemble *noun* **2** band, group, orchestra.

ensign *noun* banner, flag, jack, standard.

ensue *verb* follow, result. **ensuing** *adjective* following, next, subsequent, succeeding.

ensure *verb* guarantee, make certain, make sure, secure.

entail *verb* call for, involve, mean, necessitate, require.

entangle *verb* catch up, ensnare, entwine, interlace, intertwine, mat, mix up, ravel, snarl, tangle, trap, twist.

enter *verb* **1** come in, go in, infiltrate, intrude in, invade, penetrate. **2** inscribe, jot, list, note, record, register, write. **3** compete in, go in, participate in, register for, sign up for, take part in.

▶▶ D I C T I O N A R Y ◀◀

enterprise *noun* **1** being enterprising; adventurous spirit. **2** an undertaking or project. **3** business activity, *private enterprise*.

enterprising *adjective* willing to undertake new or adventurous projects.

entertain *verb* **1** amuse. **2** have people as guests and give them food and drink. **3** consider, *He refused to entertain the idea.* **entertainer** *noun*

entertainment *noun* **1** entertaining; being entertained. **2** something performed before an audience to amuse or interest them.

enthral (*say* in-**thrawl**) *verb* (**enthralled**, **enthralling**) hold spellbound; fascinate.

enthusiasm *noun* a strong liking, interest, or excitement. **enthusiast** *noun*

enthusiastic *adjective* full of enthusiasm. **enthusiastically** *adverb*

entice *verb* (**enticed**, **enticing**) attract or persuade by offering something pleasant. **enticement** *noun*

entire *adjective* whole, complete. **entirely** *adverb*

entirety (*say* int-**I**-rit-ee) *noun* completeness; the total.
in its entirety in its complete form.

entitle *verb* (**entitled**, **entitling**) give the right to have something, *This coupon entitles you to a ticket.* **entitlement** *noun*

entitled *adjective* having as a title.

entomb (*say* in-**toom**) *verb* place in a tomb. **entombment** *noun*

entomology (*say* en-tom-**ol**-ojee) *noun* the study of insects. **entomologist** *noun* [from Greek *entomon* = insect, + *-logy*]

entrails *plural noun* the intestines.

entrance[1] (*say* **en**-trans) *noun* **1** the way into a place. **2** entering, *Her entrance is the signal for applause.* **3** the right to enter. [from *enter*]

entrance[2] (*say* in-**trahns**) *verb* (**entranced**, **entrancing**) fill with intense delight; enchant. [from *en-* + *trance*]

entrant *noun* someone who enters for an examination or contest etc.

▶▶ T H E S A U R U S ◀◀

enterprise *noun* **1** drive, get-up-and-go, initiative, push, resourcefulness. **2** endeavour, mission, operation, project, undertaking, venture. **3** business, company, concern, corporation, establishment, firm, operation, organisation.

enterprising *adjective* adventurous, bold, daring, energetic, go-ahead, imaginative, industrious, intrepid, resourceful, venturesome.

entertain *verb* **1** amuse, delight, divert, please. **2** play host to, receive, regale, welcome, wine and dine. **3** consider, contemplate, harbour, think about.

entertainer *noun* artist, artiste, performer, player; (*various entertainers*) actor, actress, busker, clown, comedian, comic, conjuror, dancer, instrumentalist, jester, juggler, magician, minstrel, musician, singer, vocalist.

entertainment *noun* **1** amusement, distraction, diversion, enjoyment, fun, pastime, pleasure, recreation, sport. **2** extravaganza, performance, presentation, production, show, spectacle.

enthral *verb* beguile, bewitch, captivate, charm, enchant, enrapture, entrance, fascinate, hold spellbound, hypnotise, mesmerise.

enthusiasm *noun* ardour, eagerness, excitement, exuberance, fervour, gusto, keenness, passion, relish, verve, zeal, zest.

enthusiast *noun* addict, aficionado, buff (*informal*), devotee, fan, fanatic, follower, freak (*informal*), lover, nut (*informal*), supporter, zealot.

enthusiastic *adjective* ardent, avid, committed, eager, excited, exuberant, fervent, hearty, keen, passionate, warm, wholehearted, zealous.

entice *verb* allure, attract, bribe, cajole, coax, decoy, inveigle, lure, persuade, seduce, tempt.

entire *adjective* complete, full, intact, total, unbroken, whole.
entirely *adverb* absolutely, altogether, completely, fully, one hundred per cent, perfectly, quite, totally, utterly, wholly.

entitle *verb* allow, authorise, permit, qualify. **entitlement** *noun* claim, eligibility, prerogative, right.

entitled *adjective* called, named, titled.

entrance[1] *noun* **1** access, door, doorway, entry, foyer, gate, gateway, opening, passage, porch, portal, postern, threshold, way in. **2** appearance, arrival, entry. **3** admission, admittance, entry.

entrance[2] *verb* beguile, bewitch, captivate, charm, delight, enchant, enrapture, enthral, fascinate, hold spellbound, hypnotise, mesmerise, transport.

entrant *noun* applicant, candidate, competitor, contestant, participant.

▶▶▶ D I C T I O N A R Y ◀◀

entreat *verb* request earnestly; beg.

entreaty *noun* an earnest request.

entrench *verb* **1** fix or establish firmly, *These ideas are entrenched in his mind.* **2** settle in a well-defended position. **entrenchment** *noun*

entrust *verb* place a person or thing in someone's care.

entry *noun* (*plural* **entries**) **1** an entrance. **2** something entered in a list or in a diary etc.

entwine *verb* (**entwined, entwining**) twine round.

enumerate *verb* (**enumerated, enumerating**) count; list one by one. [from *e-*, + Latin *numerare* = to number]

envelop (*say* en-**vel**-op) *verb* (**enveloped, enveloping**) wrap thoroughly.

envelope (*say* **en**-vel-ohp) *noun* a wrapper or covering, especially a folded cover for a letter.

enviable *adjective* likely to be envied.

envious *adjective* feeling envy. **enviously** *adverb*

environment *noun* surroundings, especially as they affect people's lives. **environmental** *adjective*

environmentalist *noun* a person who wishes to protect or improve the environment.

environs (*say* in-**vy**-ronz) *plural noun* the surrounding districts, *They all lived in the environs of Adelaide.*

envisage (*say* in-**viz**-ij) *verb* (**envisaged, envisaging**) picture in the mind; imagine as

being possible, *It is difficult to envisage such a change.*

envoy *noun* an official representative, especially one sent by one government to another. [from French *envoyé* = sent]

envy[1] *noun* **1** a feeling of discontent aroused when someone possesses things that others would like to have for themselves. **2** something causing this, *Their car is the envy of all their friends.*

envy[2] *verb* (**envied, envying**) feel envy towards someone.

enzyme *noun* a kind of substance that assists chemical processes.

epaulette (*say* **ep**-al-et) *noun* an ornamental flap on the shoulder of a coat.

ephemeral (*say* if-**em**-er-al) *adjective* lasting only a very short time.

epi- *prefix* on; above; in addition. [from Greek *epi* = on]

epic *noun* **1** a long poem or story about heroic deeds or history. **2** a spectacular film.

epicentre *noun* the point where an earthquake reaches the earth's surface.

epidemic *noun* an outbreak of a disease that spreads quickly among the people of an area. [from *epi-*, + Greek *demos* = people]

epidermis *noun* the outer layer of the skin. [from *epi-*, + Greek *derma* = skin]

epigram *noun* a short witty saying. [from *epi- + -gram*]

▶▶▶ T H E S A U R U S ◀◀

entreat *verb* appeal to, beg, beseech, implore, plead with, pray, request, supplicate.

entrench *verb* **1** establish, fix, root, settle.

entrust *verb* assign, charge, commend, commit, consign, delegate, hand over, trust.

entry *noun* **1** access, approach, door, doorway, entrance, gate, gateway, opening, way in. **2** item, jotting, note, record.

entwine *verb* entangle, intertwine, interweave, snarl, tangle, twine, twist, weave.

envelop *verb* cocoon, cover, shroud, surround, swaddle, swathe, wrap.

envelope *noun* case, cover, covering, holder, jacket, pocket, sheath, wrapper.

envious *adjective* covetous, green, grudging, jealous, resentful.

environment *noun* ambience, atmosphere, circumstances, conditions, context, ecosystem, element, environs, habitat, medium, milieu, setting, situation, surroundings.

environmentalist *noun* conservationist, ecologist, green, greenie (*Australian informal*).

environs *noun* district, neighbourhood, outskirts, surroundings, vicinity.

envisage *verb* conceive of, contemplate, foresee, imagine, picture, predict, visualise.

envoy *noun* agent, ambassador, delegate, diplomat, emissary, messenger, representative.

envy[1] *noun* **1** covetousness, jealousy, resentment.

envy[2] *verb* begrudge, be jealous of, covet, grudge, resent.

ephemeral *adjective* brief, fleeting, impermanent, momentary, passing, short-lived, temporary, transient, transitory.

epidemic *noun* outbreak, pestilence, plague.

epigram *noun* aphorism, pun, quip, saying, witticism.

▶▶▶ D I C T I O N A R Y ◀◀◀

epilepsy *noun* a disease of the nervous system, causing convulsions. **epileptic** *adjective* & *noun*

epilogue (*say* **ep**-il-og) *noun* a short section at the end of a book or play etc. [from *epi-*, + Greek *logos* = speech]

Epiphany (*say* ip-**if**-an-ee) *noun* a Christian festival on 6 January, commemorating the showing of the infant Christ to the 'wise men' from the East.

episcopal (*say* ip-**iss**-kop-al) *adjective* **1** of a bishop or bishops. **2** (of a Church) governed by bishops.

episode *noun* **1** one event in a series of happenings. **2** one programme in a radio or television serial.

epistle *noun* a letter, especially one forming part of the New Testament.

epitaph *noun* words written on a tomb or describing a person who has died. [from *epi-*, + Greek *taphos* = womb]

epithet *noun* an adjective; words expressing something special about a person or thing, e.g. 'the Great' in *Alfred the Great*.

epoch (*say* **ee**-pok) *noun* an era. **epoch-making** *adjective* very important.

equable (*say* **ek**-wa-bul) *adjective* steady; calm, *She has an equable manner.*

equal[1] *adjective* **1** the same in amount, size, or value etc. **2** having the necessary strength, courage, or ability etc., *She was equal to the task.* **equally** *adverb*

equal[2] *noun* a person or thing that is equal to another, *She has no equal.*

equal[3] *verb* (**equalled**, **equalling**) be the same in amount, size or value etc.

equalise *verb* (**equalised**, **equalising**) make things equal. **equalisation** *noun*

equaliser *noun* a goal or point that makes the score equal.

equality *noun* being equal.

equanimity (*say* ekwa-**nim**-it-ee) *noun* calmness of mind or temper. [from *equi-*, + Latin *animus* = mind]

equate *verb* (**equated**, **equating**) say things are equal or equivalent.

equation *noun* a statement that two amounts etc. are equal, e.g. $3 + 4 = 2 + 5$.

equator *noun* an imaginary line round the earth at an equal distance from the North and South Poles.

equatorial (*say* ek-wa-**tor**-ee-al) *adjective* of or near the equator.

equestrian (*say* ik-**wes**-tree-an) *adjective* of horse-riding. [from Latin *equus* = horse]

equi- *prefix* equal; equally. [from Latin *aequus* = equal]

equilateral (*say* ee-kwi-**lat**-er-al) *adjective* (of a triangle) having all sides equal. [from *equi-* + *lateral*]

equilibrium (*say* ee-kwi-**lib**-ree-um) *noun* balance, being balanced. [from *equi-*, + Latin *libra* = balance]

equine (*say* **ek**-wyn) *noun* of or like a horse. [from Latin *equus* = horse]

equinox (*say* **ek**-win-oks) *noun* (*plural* **equinoxes**) the times of year when day and night are equal in length. **equinoctial** *adjective* [from *equi-*, + Latin *nox* = night]

equip *verb* (**equipped**, **equipping**) supply with what is needed.

equipment *noun* the things needed for a particular purpose.

equity (*say* **ek**-wit-ee) *noun* fairness, justice. **equitable** *adjective*

▶▶▶ T H E S A U R U S ◀◀◀

epilogue *noun* conclusion, postscript.

episode *noun* **1** affair (*informal*), event, happening, incident, occasion, occurrence. **2** chapter, instalment, part, scene, section.

epistle *noun* communication, letter, note.

epoch *noun* age, era, period, time.

equal[1] *adjective* **1** equivalent, even, identical, level, like, matching, parallel, same, uniform.

equal[2] *noun* match, parallel, peer, rival.

equal[3] *verb* add up to, amount to, be equivalent to, come up to, draw with, match, tie with.

equality *noun* egalitarianism, equivalence, evenness, parity, sameness, uniformity.

equilibrium *noun* balance, poise, stability, steadiness.

equip *verb* arm, fit out, furnish, kit out, prepare, provide, rig out, stock, supply.

equipment *noun* apparatus, appliances, gear, hardware, implements, instruments, kit, machinery, materials, outfit, paraphernalia, plant, rig, supplies, tackle, tools.

equity *noun* even-handedness, fairness, impartiality, justice. **equitable** *adjective* even-handed, fair, impartial, just, open-minded, proper, reasonable, right, unbiased.

▶▶ D I C T I O N A R Y ◀◀

equivalent *adjective* equal in importance, meaning, value, etc. **equivalence** *noun* [from *equi-*, + Latin *valens* = worth]

equivocal (*say* ik-**wiv**-ok-al) *adjective* **1** able to be interpreted in two ways, ambiguous. **2** questionable, suspicious, *an equivocal character*. **equivocally** *adverb* [from *equi-*, + Latin *vocare* = to call]

era (*say* **eer**-a) *noun* a period of history.

eradicate *verb* (**eradicated**, **eradicating**) get rid of something; remove all traces of it. **eradication** *noun* [from Latin, = root out (*e-* = out, *radix* = a root)]

erase *verb* (**erased**, **erasing**) **1** rub out. **2** remove a recording on magnetic tape. **eraser** *noun* [from *e-*, + Latin *rasum* = scraped]

erasure *noun* **1** erasing. **2** the place where something has been erased.

ere (*say as* air) *preposition & conjunction* (*old use*) before.

erect¹ *adjective* standing on end; upright.

erect² *verb* set up; build. **erection** *noun*, **erector** *noun*

ermine *noun* **1** a kind of weasel with brown fur that turns white in winter. **2** this valuable white fur.

erode *verb* (**eroded**, **eroding**) wear away, *Water eroded the rocks*. **erosion** *noun* [from *e-*, + Latin *rodere* = gnaw]

erotic *adjective* arousing sexual feelings. **erotically** *adverb*

err (*say* er) *verb* **1** make a mistake. (Compare *error*.) **2** do wrong. [from Latin *errare* = wander]

errand *noun* a short journey to take a message or fetch goods etc.

errant (*say* **e**-rant) *adjective* **1** misbehaving. **2** wandering; travelling in search of adventure, *a knight errant*. [same origin as *err*]

erratic (*say* ir-**at**-ik) *adjective* not reliable; not regular. **erratically** *adverb*

erroneous (*say* ir-**oh**-nee-us) *adjective* incorrect. **erroneously** *adverb*

error *noun* a mistake. [same origin as *err*]

erudite (*say* **e**-rew-dyt) *adjective* having great knowledge or learning. **eruditely** *adverb*, **erudition** *noun*

erupt *verb* **1** burst out. **2** (of a volcano) shoot out lava. **eruption** *noun* [from *e-*, + Latin *ruptum* = burst]

escalate *verb* (**escalated**, **escalating**) make or become greater or more serious, *The riots escalated into a war*. **escalation** *noun*

escalator *noun* a staircase with an endless line of steps moving up or down.

escapade (*say* eska-**payd**) *noun* a reckless adventure; a piece of mischief.

▶▶ T H E S A U R U S ◀◀

equivalent *adjective* commensurate, comparable, corresponding, equal, identical, interchangeable, matching, same, tantamount.

equivocal *adjective* **1** ambiguous, imprecise, indefinite, obscure, uncertain, unclear, vague.

era *noun* age, day, epoch, period, time.

eradicate *verb* annihilate, destroy, eliminate, exterminate, get rid of, obliterate, remove, root out, uproot, weed out, wipe out.

erase *verb* **1** blot out, cancel, delete, efface, expunge, obliterate, remove, rub out, wipe out.

erect¹ *adjective* bolt upright, perpendicular, standing, upright, vertical.

erect² *verb* build, construct, pitch (*a tent*), put up, raise, set up.

erode *verb* abrade, corrode, destroy, eat away, grind down, rub away, wear away, weather. **erosion** *noun* abrasion, corrosion, eating away, wearing away, weathering.

erotic *adjective* seductive, sensual, sexy, suggestive, titillating.

err *verb* **1** be incorrect, go wrong, make a mistake, miscalculate, slip up. **2** do wrong, go astray, sin, transgress, trespass (*old use*).

errand *noun* chore, job, mission, task.

erratic *adjective* capricious, changeable, fickle, inconsistent, irregular, spasmodic, uneven, unpredictable, variable.

error *noun* bloomer (*slang*), blue (*Australian informal*), blunder, booboo (*slang*), clanger (*informal*), fault, flaw, gaffe, howler (*informal*), inaccuracy, lapse, miscalculation, misprint, mistake, oversight, slip, slip-up (*informal*), typo (*informal*).

erupt *verb* **1** belch, burst out, discharge, gush out, issue, pour out, shoot forth, spew, spurt out.

escalate *verb* blow up, heighten, increase, intensify, jump, mount, multiply, rise, skyrocket, soar, step up, worsen.

escapade *noun* adventure, caper, exploit, lark, prank, scrape.

▶▶▶ DICTIONARY ◀◀◀

escape[1] *verb* (**escaped, escaping**) **1** get yourself free; get out or away. **2** avoid something, *He escaped punishment.*

escape[2] *noun* **1** escaping. **2** a way to escape.

escapee *noun* a person who has escaped.

escapist *noun* a person who likes to avoid thinking about serious matters by occupying his or her mind in entertainments, daydreams, etc. **escapism** *noun*

escarpment *noun* a steep slope at the edge of some high level ground.

escort[1] (*say* **ess**-kort) *noun* **1** a person or group accompanying a person or thing, especially as a protection. **2** a companion for a social event.

escort[2] (*say* iss-**kort**) *verb* act as an escort to somebody or something.

Eskimo *noun* (*plural* **Eskimos** or **Eskimo**) a member of a people living near the Arctic coast of North America, Greenland, and Siberia. [from an American Indian word, = 'eaters of raw flesh']

Usage The people themselves prefer the name *Inuit.*

especial *adjective* special.

especially *adverb* **1** specially. **2** more than anything else.

espionage (*say* **ess**-pee-on-ah*z*h) *noun* spying. [from French *espion* = spy]

esplanade *noun* a flat open area used as a promenade, especially by the sea.

espresso *noun* (*plural* **espressos**) coffee made by forcing steam through ground coffee-beans. [Italian, = pressed out]

espy *verb* (**espied, espying**) catch sight of.

Esq. *abbreviation* (short for **Esquire**) a title written after a man's surname where no title is used before his name. (Latin *scutarius* = shield-bearer)

essay[1] (*say* **ess**-ay) *noun* **1** a short piece of writing in prose. **2** an attempt.

essay[2] (*say* ess-**ay**) *verb* attempt.

essence *noun* **1** the most important quality or element of something. **2** a concentrated liquid. [from Latin *esse* = to be]

essential[1] *adjective* **1** not able to be done without. **2** fundamental. **essentially** *adverb*

essential[2] *noun* an essential thing.

establish *verb* **1** set up a business, government, or relationship etc. on a firm basis. **2** show to be true; prove, *He established his innocence.*

establishment *noun* **1** establishing something. **2** a business firm or other institution. **the Establishment** people who are established in positions of power and influence.

estate *noun* **1** an area of land with a set of houses or factories on it. **2** a large area of land owned by one person. **3** all that a person owns when he or she dies. **4** (*old use*) a condition or status, *the holy estate of matrimony.* **estate agent** a person whose business is selling or letting houses and land. **estate car** (*British*) a station wagon.

▶▶▶ THESAURUS ◀◀◀

escape[1] *verb* **1** abscond, bolt, break free, break out, flee, get away, get out, run away, scarper, slip away, take flight. **2** avoid, dodge, elude, evade, get out of, wriggle out of.

escape[2] *noun* **1** breakout, flight, getaway. **2** exit, outlet, way out.

escapee *noun* absconder, bolter, escaper, fugitive, runaway.

escort[1] *noun* **1** bodyguard, chaperone, convoy, guard, minder, protector. **2** companion, date (*informal*), partner.

escort[2] *verb* accompany, chaperone, conduct, guide, lead, take, usher.

especially *adverb* **1** chiefly, expressly, particularly, primarily, specially, specifically. **2** exceptionally, extraordinarily, outstandingly, particularly.

essay[1] *noun* **1** article, composition, critique, dissertation, paper, thesis.

essence *noun* **1** core, crux, gist, heart, kernel, nub, pith, quintessence, substance. **2** concentrate, extract.

essential[1] *adjective* **1** imperative, indispensable, necessary, requisite, vital. **2** basic, central, chief, fundamental, inherent, intrinsic, key, main, primary, principal.

essential[2] *noun* must, necessity, prerequisite, requirement, requisite.

establish *verb* **1** begin, build, construct, create, found, inaugurate, initiate, institute, introduce, originate, pioneer, set up, start. **2** confirm, demonstrate, prove, show, substantiate, verify.

establishment *noun* **2** business, company, concern, corporation, enterprise, firm, institution, organisation, plant.

estate *noun* **1** area, development. **3** assets, fortune, money, property, wealth.

esteem¹ *verb* think that a person or thing is excellent.

esteem² *noun* respect and admiration. [the word is related to *estimate*]

ester *noun* a kind of chemical compound.

estimable *adjective* worthy of esteem.

estimate¹ (*say* **ess**-tim-at) *noun* a calculation or guess about amount or value.

estimate² (*say* **ess**-tim-ayt) *verb* (**estimated, estimating**) make an estimate. **estimation** *noun*

estranged *adjective* unfriendly after having been friendly or loving. **estrangement** *noun*

estuary (*say* **ess**-tew-er-ee) *noun* (*plural* **estuaries**) the mouth of a river where it reaches the sea and the tide flows in and out. [from Latin *aestus* = tide]

etc. *abbreviation* (short for **et cetera**) and other similar things; and so on. [from Latin *et* = and, + *cetera* = the other things]

etch *verb* 1 engrave a picture with acid on a metal plate, especially for printing. 2 cut or impress deeply, *The scene is etched on my memory.* **etcher** *noun*

etching *noun* a picture printed from an etched metal plate.

eternal *adjective* lasting for ever; not ending or changing. **eternally** *adverb*, **eternity** *noun*

ether (*say* **ee**-ther) *noun* 1 a colourless liquid that evaporates easily into fumes that are used as an anaesthetic. 2 the upper air.

ethereal (*say* ith-**eer**-ee-al) *adjective* light and delicate. **ethereally** *adverb*

ethical (*say* **eth**-ik-al) *adjective* 1 of ethics. 2 morally right; honourable. **ethically** *adverb*

ethics (*say* **eth**-iks) *plural noun* standards of right behaviour; moral principles. [from Greek *ethos* = character]

ethnic *adjective* belonging to a particular racial group within a larger set of people. [from Greek *ethnos* = nation]

etiquette (*say* **et**-ik-et) *noun* the rules of correct behaviour.

etymology (*say* et-im-**ol**-oj-ee) *noun* (*plural* **etymologies**) 1 an account of the origin of a word and its meaning. 2 the study of the origins of words. **etymological** *adjective* [from Greek *etymon* = original word, + *-logy*]

EU *abbreviation* European Union.

eu- (*say* yoo) *prefix* well. [from Greek]

eucalypt (*say* **yoo**-kal-ipt) *noun* a eucalyptus tree.

eucalyptus (*say* yoo-kal-**ip**-tus) *noun* (*plural* **eucalyptuses**) 1 a kind of evergreen tree. 2 a strong-smelling oil obtained from its leaves.

Eucharist (*say* **yoo**-ker-ist) *noun* the Christian sacrament in which bread and wine are consecrated and swallowed commemorating the Last Supper of Christ and his disciples. [from Greek, = thanksgiving]

eulogy (*say* **yoo**-loj-ee) *noun* a piece of praise for a person or thing. [from *eu-*, + Greek *-logia* = speaking]

euphemism (*say* **yoo**-fim-izm) *noun* a mild word or phrase used instead of an offensive or frank one. *'To pass away' is a euphemism for 'to die'.* **euphemistic** *adjective*, **euphemistically** *adverb* [from *eu-*, + Greek *pheme* = speech]

euphonium (*say* yoof-**oh**-nee-um) *noun* a large brass wind instrument. [from *eu-*, + Greek *phone* = sound]

euphoria (*say* yoo-**for**-ee-a) *noun* a feeling of general happiness. [from *eu-*, + Greek *phoros* = bearing]

esteem² *noun* admiration, appreciation, approval, estimation, regard, respect, reverence, veneration.

estimate¹ *noun* appraisal, approximation, assessment, calculation, evaluation, guesstimate (*informal*), judgement, opinion, valuation.

estimate² *verb* appraise, assess, calculate, evaluate, guess, judge, put, rate, reckon, size up, value.

estranged *adjective* alienated, driven apart.

estuary *noun* firth, inlet, mouth.

etch *verb* 2 carve, engrave, impress, imprint, inscribe, stamp.

eternal *adjective* see EVERLASTING.

ethical *adjective* 2 above board, correct, honourable, moral, principled, proper, right, righteous, upright, virtuous.

ethics *plural noun* moral code, morality, morals, principles, scruples.

ethnic *adjective* cultural, national, racial.

etiquette *noun* code of behaviour, conventions, decorum, form, manners, proprieties, protocol, rules.

Eucharist *noun* Holy Communion, Lord's Supper, Mass.

▶▶ D I C T I O N A R Y ◀◀

Eurasian *adjective* having European and Asian parents or ancestors. **Eurasian** *noun* [from *Euro*pean + *Asian*]

euro¹ *noun* (*plural* **euros**) a kind of large kangaroo.

euro² *noun* the unit of money in most countries of the European Union.

European *adjective* of Europe or its people. **European** *noun*

euthanasia (*say* yooth-an-**ay**-zee-a) *noun* the act of causing somebody to die gently and without pain, especially when they are suffering from a painful incurable disease. [from *eu-*, + Greek *thanatos* = death]

evacuate *verb* (**evacuated, evacuating**) **1** move people away from a dangerous place. **2** make a thing empty of air or other contents. **evacuation** *noun* [from *e-*, + Latin *vacuus* = empty]

evacuee *noun* a person who has been evacuated.

evade *verb* (**evaded, evading**) avoid a person or thing by cleverness or trickery. [from *e-*, + Latin *vadere* = go]

evaluate *verb* (**evaluated, evaluating**) estimate the value of something; assess. **evaluation** *noun*

Evangelist *noun* any of the writers (Matthew, Mark, Luke, John) of the four Gospels.

evangelist *noun* a person who preaches the Christian faith enthusiastically. **evangelism** *noun*, **evangelical** *adjective* [from Greek, = announce good news (*eu-* = well, *angelos* = messenger)]

evaporate *verb* (**evaporated, evaporating**) **1** change from liquid into steam or vapour. **2** cease to exist, *Their enthusiasm had evaporated.* **evaporation** *noun* [from *e-* = out, + Latin *vapor* = steam]

evasion *noun* **1** evading. **2** an evasive answer or excuse.

evasive *adjective* evading something; not frank or straightforward. **evasively** *adverb*, **evasiveness** *noun*

eve *noun* **1** the day or evening before an important day or event, *Christmas Eve.* **2** (*old use*) evening.

even¹ *adjective* **1** level; smooth. **2** not varying. **3** calm; not easily upset, *an even temper.* **4** equal, *Our scores were even.* **5** able to be divided exactly by two, *Six and fourteen are even numbers.* (Compare *odd.*) **evenly** *adverb*, **evenness** *noun*

even² *verb* make or become even.

even³ *adverb* (used to emphasise a word or statement) *She ran even faster.* **even so** although that is correct.

even⁴ *noun* (*old use*) evening.

evening *noun* the time at the end of the day before most people go to bed.

evensong *noun* the service of evening prayer in the Anglican Church.

event *noun* **1** something that happens, especially something important. **2** an item in a sports contest. [from *e-*, + Latin *ventum* = come]

eventful *adjective* full of happenings.

▶▶ T H E S A U R U S ◀◀

evacuate *verb* **1** move out, relocate, remove, send away. **2** clear, empty.

evade *verb* avoid, dodge, duck, elude, escape from, shirk, shun, sidestep, steer clear of.

evaluate *verb* appraise, assess, calculate, compute, judge, review, size up, value, weigh up.

evangelist *noun* missionary, preacher.

evaporate *verb* **1** dry up, vaporise. **2** disappear, fade away, melt away, vanish.

evasive *adjective* ambiguous, devious, equivocal, non-committal, oblique, roundabout, shifty.

even¹ *adjective* **1** flat, flush, level, plane, smooth, straight. **2** consistent, constant, regular, steady, unchanging, uniform, unvarying. **4** balanced,

drawn, equal, identical, level, neck and neck, square, the same, tied.
even-tempered *adjective* calm, easygoing, equable, imperturbable, placid, serene, steady, tranquil, unfazed (*informal*), unflappable (*informal*).

even² *verb* balance, equalise, level, straighten, tie.

evening *noun* dusk, eventide (*old use*), gloaming, night, nightfall, sundown, sunset, twilight.

event *noun* **1** affair, circumstance, episode, eventuality, experience, happening, incident, occasion, occurrence. **2** competition, contest, item, race.

eventful *adjective* action-packed, busy, exciting, full, memorable, momentous, unforgettable.

► ► D I C T I O N A R Y ◄ ◄

eventual *adjective* happening at last, *his eventual success.* **eventually** *adverb*

eventuality (*say* iv-en-tew-**al**-it-ee) *noun* (*plural* **eventualities**) something that may happen.

ever *adverb* **1** at any time, *the best thing I ever did.* **2** always, *ever hopeful.* **3** (*informal*, used for emphasis), *Why ever didn't you tell me?*

evergreen *adjective* having green leaves all the year. **evergreen** *noun*

everlasting *adjective* **1** lasting for ever. **2** lasting for a very long time, *an everlasting problem.*

every *adjective* each without any exceptions, *We enjoyed every minute.*
  every one each one, *Every one of them is growing.*
  every other day or **week** etc., each alternate one; every second one.

everybody *pronoun* every person.

everyday *adjective* ordinary; usual, *everyday clothes.*

everyone *pronoun* everybody.

everything *pronoun* **1** all things; all. **2** the only or most important thing, *Beauty is not everything.*

everywhere *adverb* in every place.

evict *verb* make people move out from where they are living. **eviction** *noun* [from Latin *evictum* = expelled]

evidence *noun* **1** anything that gives people reason to believe something. **2** statements made or objects produced in a lawcourt to prove something.

evident *adjective* obvious; clearly seen. **evidently** *adverb*

evil¹ *adjective* wicked; harmful. **evilly** *adverb*

evil² *noun* something evil; a sin.

evoke *verb* (**evoked, evoking**) produce or inspire a memory or feelings etc., *The photographs evoked happy memories.* **evocation** *noun*, **evocative** *adjective* [from *e-* = out, + Latin *vocare* = call]

evolution (*say* ee-vol-**oo**-shon) *noun* **1** evolving; gradual change into something different. **2** the development of animals and plants from earlier or simpler forms. **evolutionary** *adjective*

evolve *verb* (**evolved, evolving**) develop gradually or naturally. [from *e-*, + Latin *volvere* = to roll]

ewe (*say* yoo) *noun* a female sheep.

ewer (*say* **yoo**-er) *noun* a large water-jug.

ex- *prefix* (changing to **ef-** before words beginning with *f*; shortened to **e-** before many consonants) **1** out; away (as in *extract*). **2** up, upwards; thoroughly (as in *extol*). **3** formerly (as in *ex-president*). [from Latin *ex* = out of]

► ► T H E S A U R U S ◄ ◄

eventuality *noun* contingency, possibility; see also EVENT.

eventually *adverb* at last, finally, in the end, ultimately.

everlasting *adjective* **1** endless, eternal, immortal, infinite, limitless, never-ending, timeless, unending, unlimited. **2** abiding, ceaseless, chronic, constant, continual, continuous, endless, eternal, incessant, interminable, nonstop, perennial, permanent, perpetual, persistent, recurrent, repeated.

everybody *pronoun* all, all and sundry, everyone, one and all, the world.

everyday *adjective* common, commonplace, customary, daily, day-to-day, familiar, mundane, normal, ordinary, regular, routine, usual.

everywhere *adverb* extensively, far and wide, globally, high and low, near and far, ubiquitously, universally.

evict *verb* chuck out (*informal*), drive out, eject, expel, get rid of, kick out (*informal*), remove, throw out, turf out (*informal*), turn out.

evidence *noun* **1** data, documentation, facts, grounds, indication, manifestation, proof, sign, symptom, token. **2** affidavit, deposition, statement, testimony.

evident *adjective* apparent, clear, manifest, noticeable, obvious, patent, plain, undeniable, unmistakable.

evil¹ *adjective* abominable, atrocious, bad, base, beastly, corrupt, demonic, depraved, despicable, detestable, diabolical, foul, hateful, heinous, immoral, infamous, iniquitous, loathsome, malevolent, malicious, nefarious, satanic, sinful, sinister, ungodly, unrighteous, vicious, vile, villainous, wicked.

evil² *noun* corruption, depravity, immorality, iniquity, sin, turpitude, ungodliness, vice, wickedness, wrong, wrongdoing.

evoke *verb* arouse, awaken, call up, conjure up, elicit, inspire, rouse, stimulate, stir up, suggest.

evolve *verb* develop, grow, unfold.

▶▶ DICTIONARY ◀◀

exacerbate (*say* eks-**ass**-er-bayt) *verb* (**exacerbated, exacerbating**) make a pain or disease or other problem worse.

exact¹ *adjective* **1** correct. **2** clearly stated; giving all details, *exact instructions*. **exactly** *adverb*, **exactness** *noun*

exact² *verb* insist on something and obtain it, *He exacted obedience from the recruits*. **exaction** *noun* [from *ex-* = out, + Latin *actum* = performed]

exacting *adjective* making great demands, *an exacting task*.

exactitude *noun* exactness.

exaggerate *verb* (**exaggerated, exaggerating**) make something seem bigger, better, or worse etc. than it really is. **exaggeration** *noun* [from *ex-* = upwards, + Latin *agger* = heap]

exalt (*say* ig-**zawlt**) *verb* **1** raise in rank or status etc. **2** praise highly. **exaltation** *noun* [from *ex-* = up, + Latin *altus* = high]

exam *noun* (*informal*) an examination.

examination *noun* **1** a test of a person's knowledge or skill. **2** examining something; an inspection.

examine *verb* (**examined, examining**) **1** test a person's knowledge or skill. **2** inspect; look at something closely. **examiner** *noun*

examinee *noun* a person being tested in an examination.

example *noun* **1** anything that shows what others of the same kind are like or how they work. **2** a person or thing good enough to be worth imitating.

exasperate *verb* (**exasperated, exasperating**) annoy someone greatly. **exasperation** *noun* [from *ex-* = thoroughly, + Latin *asper* = rough]

excavate *verb* (**excavated, excavating**) **1** dig out. **2** uncover by digging. **excavation** *noun*, **excavator** *noun* [from *ex-* = out, + Latin *cavus* = hollow]

exceed *verb* **1** be greater than, surpass. **2** do more than you need or ought to do; go beyond a thing's limits, *He has exceeded his authority*. [from *ex-* = out, beyond, + Latin *cedere* = go]

exceedingly *adverb* very; extremely.

excel *verb* (**excelled, excelling**) be better than others at doing something. [from *ex-*, + Latin *celsus* = lofty]

Excellency *noun* the title of high officials such as ambassadors and governors.

▶▶ THESAURUS ◀◀

exact¹ *adjective* **1** accurate, correct, literal, perfect, precise, right, spot-on (*informal*), true. **2** careful, detailed, explicit, fastidious, meticulous, minute, painstaking, particular, precise, punctilious, rigorous, scrupulous, specific, strict.

exact² *verb* claim, demand, extort, extract, insist on.

exacting *adjective* arduous, demanding, difficult, hard, onerous, stiff, taxing, tough.

exaggerate *verb* inflate, lay it on thick (*informal*), magnify, make a mountain out of a molehill, overdo, overestimate, overstate, pile it on (*informal*).
exaggeration *noun* hyperbole, magnification, overstatement.

exalt *verb* **1** advance, elevate, promote, raise, upgrade. **2** adore, extol, glorify, hallow, honour, laud (*formal*), magnify (*old use*), praise, revere, venerate, worship.

examination *noun* **1** exam (*informal*), oral (*informal*), quiz, test; see also CROSS-EXAMINATION (at CROSS-EXAMINE). **2** analysis, audit, check, inspection, investigation,

observation, perusal, probe, review, scrutiny, study, survey.

examine *verb* **1** question, quiz, sound out, test; see also CROSS-EXAMINE. **2** analyse, audit, check, consider, go over, inquire into, inspect, investigate, look at, look over, peruse, pore over, probe, research, review, scan, scrutinise, sift, study, survey, vet.

example *noun* **1** case, illustration, instance, model, precedent, prototype, sample, specimen. **2** model, paragon, pattern, standard.

exasperate *verb* anger, annoy, bug (*informal*), enrage, get on someone's nerves, infuriate, irk, irritate, madden, needle (*informal*), peeve (*informal*), provoke, rile (*informal*), vex.

excavate *verb* **1** burrow, dig, hollow out, mine, scoop out, shovel out, tunnel. **2** dig up, exhume, uncover, unearth.

exceed *verb* **1** beat, better, excel, outdo, outnumber, overtake, pass, surpass, top, transcend. **2** go beyond, go over, overstep.

excel *verb* be outstanding, shine, stand out.

►►► DICTIONARY ◄◄◄

excellent *adjective* extremely good. **excellently** *adverb*, **excellence** *noun*

except¹ *preposition* excluding; not including, *They all left except me.*

except² *verb* exclude; leave out, *I blame you all, no one is excepted.* [from *ex-* = out, + Latin *-ceptum* = taken]

excepting *preposition* except.

exception *noun* **1** a person or thing that is left out or does not follow the general rule. **2** exclusion; excepting, *All were pardoned with the exception of traitors.*
take exception raise objections to something.

exceptional *adjective* **1** forming an exception; very unusual. **2** outstandingly good. **exceptionally** *adverb*

excerpt (*say* **ek**-serpt) *noun* a passage taken from a book or speech or film etc.

excess *noun* (*plural* **excesses**) too much of something. [from *exceed*]

excessive *adjective* too much; too great. **excessively** *adverb*

exchange¹ *verb* (**exchanged**, **exchanging**) give something and receive something else for it. **exchangeable** *adjective*

exchange² *noun* **1** exchanging. **2** a place where things (especially stocks and shares) are bought and sold, *a stock exchange.* **3** a place where telephone lines are connected to each other when a call is made.

exchequer *noun* a national treasury into which public funds (such as taxes) are paid. [the word refers to the table, covered with a cloth divided into squares (a *chequered* pattern), on which the accounts of the Norman kings were kept by means of counters]

excise¹ (*say* **eks**-I'z) *noun* a tax charged on certain goods and licences etc. [from a Dutch word meaning 'tax']

excise² (*say* iks-**I'z**) *verb* (**excised**, **excising**) remove something by cutting it away, *The surgeon excised the tumour.* [from *ex-* = out, + Latin *caesum* = cut]

excitable *adjective* easily excited.

excite *verb* (**excited**, **exciting**) **1** rouse a person's feelings; make eager, *The thought of finding gold excited them.* **2** cause a feeling; arouse, *The invention excited great interest.* **excitedly** *adverb* [from *ex-* = out, + Latin *citare* = wake]

excitement *noun* a strong feeling of eagerness or pleasure.

►►► THESAURUS ◄◄◄

excellent *adjective* ace (*informal*), admirable, awesome (*informal*), beaut (*Australian informal*), brilliant (*informal*), capital, choice, classic, cool (*informal*), exceptional, fabulous, fantastic, far-out (*informal*), fine, first-class, first-rate, great, groovy (*slang*), impressive, magnificent, marvellous, masterly, matchless, meritorious, model, out of the box (*Australian informal*), outstanding, peerless, perfect, prize, remarkable, select, sensational, splendid, sterling, super (*informal*), superb, superior, superlative, supreme, swell (*informal*), terrific (*informal*), top-notch (*informal*), tremendous, wicked (*slang*), wizard (*informal*), wonderful. **excellence** *noun* greatness, merit, perfection, pre-eminence, quality, superiority.

except¹ *preposition* apart from, bar, besides, but, excluding, other than, save.

exception *noun* **1** anomaly, departure, deviation, inconsistency, irregularity. **2** exclusion, omission.

exceptional *adjective* **1** abnormal, anomalous, atypical, extraordinary, odd, phenomenal, rare, remarkable, singular, special, uncommon, unusual. **2** see EXCELLENT.

excerpt *noun* citation, clip, extract, passage, quotation, selection, trailer.

excess *noun* glut, over-abundance, overflow, oversupply, superfluity, surfeit, surplus.

excessive *adjective* exaggerated, exorbitant, extortionate, extravagant, extreme, fulsome, immoderate, inordinate, intemperate, outrageous, overdone, profuse, steep, superfluous, unreasonable.

exchange¹ *verb* barter, change, interchange, substitute, swap, trade.

excitable *adjective* emotional, highly-strung, hotheaded, mercurial, nervous, temperamental, volatile.

excite *verb* **1** agitate, animate, arouse, disturb, fluster, rouse, stir up, thrill, upset, wind up (*informal*), work up. **2** arouse, awaken, generate, incite, inspire, kindle, provoke, stimulate, whet.
exciting *adjective* breathtaking, electrifying, exhilarating, gripping, heady, moving, riveting, rousing, sensational, spectacular, stimulating, stirring, suspenseful, thrilling.

excitement *noun* action, activity, ado, adventure, agitation, ferment, flurry, frenzy, furore, fuss, kerfuffle, kicks (*informal*), sensation, stir, thrill, to-do, unrest.

►DICTIONARY◄

exclaim *verb* shout or cry out in eagerness or surprise. [from *ex-* = out, + Latin *clamare* = cry]

exclamation *noun* 1 exclaiming. 2 a word or words exclaimed expressing joy or pain or surprise etc.
exclamation mark the punctuation mark ! placed after an exclamation.

exclude *verb* (**excluded**, **excluding**) 1 keep somebody or something out. 2 leave out, *Do not exclude the possibility of drought.* **exclusion** *noun* [from *ex-* = out, + Latin *claudere* = shut]

exclusive *adjective* 1 allowing only certain people to be members etc., *an exclusive club.* 2 not shared with others, *This newspaper has an exclusive report.* **exclusively** *adverb*, **exclusiveness** *noun*
exclusive of excluding, not including, *This is the price exclusive of meals.* [same origin as *exclude*]

excommunicate *verb* (**excommunicated**, **excommunicating**) cut off a person from membership of a Church. **excommunication** *noun* [from Latin, = put out of the community]

excrement (*say* **eks**-krim-ent) *noun* waste matter excreted from the bowels, dung.

excrescence (*say* iks-**kress**-ens) *noun* 1 an outgrowth on a plant or animal's body. 2 an ugly addition or part. [from *ex-* = out, + Latin *crescens* = growing]

excrete *verb* (**excreted**, **excreting**) expel waste matter from the body. **excretion** *noun*, **excretory** *adjective* [from *ex-* = out, + Latin *cretum* = separated]

excruciating (*say* iks-**kroo**-shee-ayt-ing) *adjective* extremely painful; agonising. **excruciatingly** *adverb* [from *ex-* = thoroughly, + Latin *cruciatum* = tortured]

exculpate (*say* **eks**-kul-payt) *verb* (**exculpated**, **exculpating**) clear a person from blame. **exculpation** *noun* [from *ex-* = away, + Latin *culpa* = blame]

excursion *noun* a short journey made for pleasure. [from *ex-* = out, + Latin *cursus* = course]

excusable *adjective* able to be excused. **excusably** *adverb*

excuse¹ (*say* iks-**kewz**) *verb* (**excused**, **excusing**) 1 forgive. 2 allow someone not to do something or to leave a room etc., *Please may I be excused from swimming?*

excuse² (*say* iks-**kewss**) *noun* a reason given to explain why something wrong has been done. [from *ex-* = away, + Latin *causa* = accusation]

execrable (*say* **eks**-ik-rab-ul) *adjective* very bad; abominable.

execute *verb* (**executed**, **executing**) 1 put someone to death as a punishment. 2 perform or produce something, *She executed the somersault perfectly.* **execution** *noun* [from *ex-* = out, + Latin *sequi* = follow]

executioner *noun* an official who executes a condemned person.

executive¹ (*say* ig-**zek**-yoo-tiv) *noun* a senior person with authority in a business or government organisation.

executive² *adjective* having the authority to carry out plans or laws.

►►THESAURUS◄◄

exclaim *verb* bawl, bellow, call out, cry out, shout, yell.

exclude *verb* 1 ban, bar, debar, expel, forbid, keep out, leave out, ostracise, oust, prohibit, shut out. 2 eliminate, omit, preclude, reject, rule out.

exclusive *adjective* 1 closed, private, restricted, select. 2 complete, full, sole, undivided, unique.

excrete *verb* defecate, urinate, void.

excruciating *adjective* acute, agonising, insufferable, intolerable, painful, severe, unbearable.

excursion *noun* drive, expedition, hike, holiday, jaunt, journey, outing, pleasure-trip, ramble, ride, run, tour, trek, trip, walk.

excusable *adjective* forgivable, pardonable, venial.

excuse¹ *verb* 1 (*excuse a person*) exonerate, forgive, let off, make allowances for, pardon; (*excuse an action*) condone, explain, justify, mitigate, vindicate, warrant. 2 exempt, free, let off, release.

excuse² *noun* defence, explanation, justification, plod (*Australian informal*), pretext, reason.

execute *verb* 1 kill, put to death, slay; (*various ways to execute*) behead, crucify, electrocute, garrotte, gas, guillotine, hang, lynch, shoot, stone. 2 accomplish, carry out, complete, do, effect, fulfil, implement, perform.

executive¹ *noun* administrator, chief, director, manager.

▶▶ DICTIONARY ◀◀

executor (*say* ig-**zek**-yoo-ter) *noun* a person appointed to carry out the instructions in someone's will.

exemplary (*say* ig-**zem**-pler-ee) *adjective* very good; being an example to others, *His conduct was exemplary.*

exemplify *verb* (**exemplified, exemplifying**) be an example of something.

exempt¹ *adjective* not having to do something that others have to do, *Charities are exempt from paying tax.*

exempt² *verb* make someone or something exempt. **exemption** *noun* [from *ex-* = out, + Latin *emptum* = taken]

exercise¹ *noun* **1** using your body to make it strong and healthy. **2** a piece of work done for practice.

exercise² *verb* (**exercised, exercising**) **1** do exercises. **2** give exercise to an animal etc. **3** use, *exercise patience.* [from Latin *exercere* = keep someone working]

exert *verb* use power or influence etc., *He exerted all his strength.* **exertion** *noun*
exert yourself make an effort.

exhale *verb* (**exhaled, exhaling**) breathe out. **exhalation** *noun* [from *ex-*, + Latin *halare* = breathe]

exhaust¹ *verb* **1** make somebody very tired. **2** use up something completely. **exhaustion** *noun*

exhaust² *noun* **1** the waste gases or steam from an engine. **2** the pipe etc. through which they are sent out. [from *ex-* = out, + Latin *haustum* = drained]

exhaustive *adjective* thorough; trying everything possible, *We made an exhaustive search.* **exhaustively** *adverb*

exhibit¹ *verb* (**exhibited, exhibiting**) show in public. **exhibitor** *noun*

exhibit² *noun* something exhibited.

exhibition *noun* a collection of things arranged for people to look at.

exhibitionist *noun* a person who behaves in a way that is meant to attract attention. **exhibitionism** *noun*

exhilarate (*say* ig-**zil**-er-ayt) *verb* (**exhilarated, exhilarating**) make someone very happy; elate. **exhilaration** *noun* [from *ex-* = thoroughly, + Latin *hilaris* = cheerful (compare *hilarious*)]

exhort (*say* ig-**zort**) *verb* urge someone earnestly. **exhortation** *noun* [from *ex-*, + Latin *hortari* = encourage]

▶▶ THESAURUS ◀◀

exemplify *verb* embody, epitomise, illustrate, personify, represent, typify.

exempt¹ *adjective* excused, freed, immune, released, relieved, spared.

exempt² *verb* excuse, free, let off, release, relieve, spare.
exemption *noun* dispensation, immunity, privilege.

exercise¹ *noun* **1** activity, aerobics, callisthenics, exertion, games, gymnastics, PE, physical education, physical training, PT, sport. **2** drill, manoeuvres, movements, practice, training.

exercise² *verb* **1** limber up, loosen up, practise, train, work out. **3** apply, employ, exert, use, utilise, wield.

exert *verb* apply, employ, exercise, use, utilise, wield.
exertion *noun* effort, exercise, labour, strain, toil, work.

exhale *verb* blow, breathe out, expire, pant, puff.

exhaust¹ *verb* **1** drain, fatigue, tire out, weaken, wear out, weary. **2** blow (*slang*), consume, deplete, dissipate, expend, spend, use up.

exhausted *adjective* all in (*informal*), burnt out, bushed (*informal*), dog-tired, done in (*informal*), drained, fagged out (*informal*), fatigued, knackered (*slang*), played out, pooped (*informal*), run down, sapped, spent, tired out, washed out, weak, weary, whacked (*informal*), worn out, zapped (*slang*), zonked (*slang*).

exhausting *adjective* arduous, difficult, gruelling, hard, heavy, laborious, strenuous, tiring.

exhaust² *noun* **1** emissions, fumes, gases, smoke.

exhaustive *adjective* complete, comprehensive, detailed, full, in-depth, intensive, minute, thorough.

exhibit¹ *verb* display, present, show.

exhibition *noun* demonstration, display, expo, exposition, fair, presentation, show.

exhilarated *adjective* cheerful, delighted, ecstatic, elated, euphoric, excited, happy, joyful, overjoyed, thrilled.

exhort *verb* advise, appeal to, beseech, encourage, entreat, implore, plead with, urge.

▶▶ D I C T I O N A R Y ◀◀

exhume (*say* iks-**hume**) *verb* (**exhumed, exhuming**) dig up something that has been buried. **exhumation** *noun* [from *ex-* = out, + Latin *humare* = bury]

exile¹ *verb* (**exiled, exiling**) banish.

exile² *noun* **1** a banished person. **2** having to live away from your own country, *He was in exile for ten years.*

exist *verb* **1** have a place as part of what is real, *Do ghosts exist?* **2** stay alive, *We cannot exist without food.* **existence** *noun*, **existent** *adjective* [from *ex-*, + Latin *sistere* = stand]

exit¹ *verb* leave the stage.

exit² *noun* **1** the way out of a building. **2** going off the stage, *The actress made her exit.* [Latin, = he or she goes out]

exodus *noun* (*plural* **exoduses**) the departure of many people. [from Greek, = a way out (*ex* = out, *hodos* = way)]

exonerate *verb* (**exonerated, exonerating**) declare or prove that a person is not to blame for something. **exoneration** *noun* [from *ex-* = out, + Latin *oneris* = of a burden]

exorbitant *adjective* much too great; excessive, *exorbitant prices.* [from *ex-* = out, + Latin *orbita* = orbit]

exorcise *verb* (**exorcised, exorcising**) get rid of an evil spirit. **exorcism** *noun*, **exorcist** *noun*

exotic *adjective* **1** very unusual, *exotic clothes.* **2** from another part of the world, *exotic plants.* **exotically** *adverb* [from Greek *exo* = outside]

expand *verb* **1** make or become larger or fuller. **2** give more details about something, *He expanded on his initial description.* **expansion** *noun*, **expansive** *adjective* [from *ex-* = out, + Latin *pandere* = spread]

expanse *noun* a wide area.

expatriate (*say* eks-**pat**-ree-at) *noun* a person living away from his or her own country. [from *ex-* = away, + Latin *patria* = native land]

expect *verb* **1** think or believe that something will happen or that someone will come. **2** think that something ought to happen, *She expects obedience.* [from *ex-* = out, + Latin *spectare* = to look]

expectant *adjective* expecting something to happen; hopeful. **expectantly** *adverb*, **expectancy** *noun*
expectant mother a woman who is pregnant.

expectation *noun* **1** expecting something; being hopeful. **2** something you expect to happen or get.

expedient¹ (*say* iks-**pee**-dee-ent) *adjective* **1** suitable, convenient. **2** useful and practical though perhaps unfair. **expediently** *adverb*, **expediency** *noun*

expedient² *noun* a means of doing something, especially when in difficulty.

expedite (*say* **eks**-pid-dyt) *verb* (**expedited, expediting**) make something happen more quickly.

expedition *noun* **1** a journey made in order to do something. **2** speed; promptness. **expeditionary** *adjective*

▶▶ T H E S A U R U S ◀◀

exile¹ *verb* banish, deport, expatriate, expel, send away.

exile² *noun* **1** deportee, expatriate, outcast, refugee. **2** banishment, deportation, expatriation, expulsion.

exist *verb* **1** be, be real, live, occur. **2** keep going, live, subsist, survive.
existence *noun* being, life, subsistence, survival.

exit¹ *verb* see LEAVE¹.

exit² *noun* **1** door, outlet, way out. **2** departure, escape, retreat.

exonerate *verb* absolve, acquit, clear, free, pardon, vindicate.

exorbitant *adjective* excessive, expensive, extortionate, high, inordinate, outrageous, preposterous, steep, unreasonable.

exotic *adjective* **1** bizarre, curious, different, extraordinary, odd, outlandish, peculiar, rare, singular, strange, unfamiliar, unusual, weird. **2** alien, foreign, imported.

expand *verb* **1** bloat, broaden, build up, develop, distend, enlarge, extend, fatten, grow, increase, open out, spread (out), stretch (out), swell, unfurl, widen. **2** (*expand on*) amplify, elaborate upon, enlarge upon, expatiate on, flesh out, pad out.

expanse *noun* area, extent, sea, stretch, sweep, tract.

expect *verb* **1** anticipate, bargain for, contemplate, envisage, forecast, foresee, predict. **2** count on, demand, insist on, rely on, require.

expectant *adjective* eager, hopeful, ready, waiting, watchful.

expectation *noun* **2** anticipation, hope, likelihood, outlook, probability, prospect.

expedition *noun* **1** excursion, exploration, journey, mission, outing, safari, tour, trek, trip, voyage.

►►► DICTIONARY ◄◄

expeditious (*say* eks-pid-**ish**-us) *adjective* quick and efficient. **expeditiously** *adverb*

expel *verb* (**expelled, expelling**) 1 send or force something out, *This fan expels stale air.* 2 make a person leave a school or country etc. **expulsion** *noun* [from *ex*- = out, + Latin *pellere* = drive]

expend *verb* spend; use up.

expendable *adjective* 1 able to be expended. 2 able to be sacrificed in order to gain something.

expenditure *noun* expending; the spending of money or effort etc.

expense *noun* the cost of doing something.

expensive *adjective* costing a lot. **expensively** *adverb*, **expensiveness** *noun*

experience¹ *noun* 1 what you learn from doing or seeing things. 2 something that has happened to you.

experience² *verb* (**experienced, experiencing**) have something happen to you. [same origin as *experiment*]

experienced *adjective* having great skill or knowledge from much experience.

experiment¹ *noun* a test made in order to find out what happens or to prove something. **experimental** *adjective*, **experimentally** *adverb*

experiment² *verb* carry out an experiment. **experimentation** *noun* [from Latin *experiri* = to test]

expert¹ *noun* a person with great knowledge or skill in something.

expert² *adjective* having great knowledge or skill. **expertly** *adverb*, **expertness** *noun*

expertise (*say* eks-per-**teez**) *noun* expert ability.

expiate (*say* **eks**-pee-ayt) *verb* (**expiated, expiating**) atone for; make amends for wrongdoing. **expiation** *noun*

expire *verb* (**expired, expiring**) 1 come to an end; stop being usable, *Your season ticket has expired.* 2 die. 3 breathe out air. **expiration** *noun*, **expiry** *noun* [from *ex*-, + Latin *spirare* = breathe]

explain *verb* 1 make something clear to somebody else; show its meaning. 2 account for something, *That explains his absence.* **explanation** *noun* [from *ex*-, + Latin *planare* = make level or plain]

explanatory (*say* iks-**plan**-at-er-ee) *adjective* giving an explanation.

explicit (*say* iks-**pliss**-it) *adjective* stated or stating something openly and exactly. (Compare *implicit*.) **explicitly** *adverb* [from Latin, = unfolded]

►►► THESAURUS ◄◄

expel *verb* 2 banish, chuck out (*informal*), deport, discharge, dismiss, drive out, eject, evict, exile, get rid of, kick out (*informal*), remove, send away, throw out, turf out (*informal*).

expenditure *noun* expenses, outgoings, outlay, overheads, spending.

expense *noun* charge, cost, fee, payment, price; see also EXPENDITURE.

expensive *adjective* costly, dear, exorbitant, extravagant, luxurious, precious, priceless, pricey (*informal*), valuable.

experience¹ *noun* 1 background, familiarity, involvement, practice. 2 adventure, episode, event, happening, incident, occurrence, ordeal.

experience² *verb* bear, encounter, endure, face, feel, go through, know, meet with, suffer, sustain, undergo.

experienced *adjective* accomplished, competent, expert, fully-fledged, practised, proficient, seasoned, skilled, veteran, well-versed.

experiment¹ *noun* investigation, test, trial. **experimental** *adjective* pilot, test, trial.

experiment² *verb* investigate, research, test, try.

expert¹ *noun* ace, adept, authority, buff (*informal*), connoisseur, consultant, dab hand (*informal*), genius, know-all (*informal*), maestro, master, old hand, past master, pro (*informal*), professional, pundit, scholar, specialist, virtuoso, whiz (*informal*).

expert² *adjective* accomplished, capable, competent, experienced, knowledgeable, practised, professional, proficient, qualified, skilful, skilled, talented.

expertise *noun* know-how, knowledge, mastery, proficiency, skill.

expire *verb* 1 cease, end, finish, lapse, run out, stop, terminate. 2 breathe your last, die, pass away, perish. 3 breathe out, exhale.

explain *verb* 1 clarify, clear up, decipher, define, demonstrate, describe, detail, elaborate, elucidate, expound, illustrate, interpret, show, spell out, teach. 2 account for, excuse, justify. **explanation** *noun* 1 account, clarification, commentary, definition, description, elucidation, interpretation, key. 2 excuse, justification, reason.

explicit *adjective* categorical, clear, definite, exact, express, particular, plain, positive, precise, specific, unambiguous, unequivocal.

▶▶▶ D I C T I O N A R Y ◀◀

explode *verb* (**exploded, exploding**) **1** burst or suddenly release energy with a loud noise. **2** cause a bomb to go off. **3** increase suddenly or quickly. [from *ex-* = out, + Latin *plaudere* = clap the hands (originally said of the audience clapping or hissing to drive a player off the stage)]

exploit¹ (*say* **eks**-ploit) *noun* a brave or exciting deed.

exploit² (*say* iks-**ploit**) *verb* **1** use or develop resources. **2** use selfishly. **exploitation** *noun*

exploratory (*say* iks-**plorra**-ter-ee) *adjective* for the purpose of exploring.

explore *verb* (**explored, exploring**) **1** travel through a country etc. in order to learn about it. **2** examine something, investigate, *We explored the possibilities.* **exploration** *noun*, **explorer** *noun* [from Latin, = search out]

explosion *noun* **1** the exploding of a bomb etc.; the noise made by exploding. **2** a sudden great increase.

explosive¹ *adjective* able to explode.

explosive² *noun* an explosive substance.

exponent *noun* **1** a person who expounds something. **2** someone who uses a certain technique. **3** the raised number etc. written to the right of another (e.g. 3 in 2^3) showing how many times the first one is to be multiplied by itself.

export¹ *verb* send goods abroad to be sold. **exportation** *noun*, **exporter** *noun*

export² *noun* **1** exporting things. **2** something exported. [from *ex-* = away, + Latin *portare* = carry]

expose *verb* (**exposed, exposing**) **1** reveal, uncover. **2** allow light to reach a photographic film so as to take a picture. **exposure** *noun* [from *ex-* = out, + Latin *positum* = put]

expostulate *verb* (**expostulated, expostulating**) make a protest. **expostulation** *noun*

expound *verb* explain in detail.

express¹ *adjective* **1** going or sent quickly. **2** expressed; clearly stated, *This was done against my express orders.*

express² *noun* (*plural* **expresses**) a fast train stopping at only a few stations.

express³ *verb* **1** put ideas etc. into words; make your feelings known. **2** press or squeeze out, *Express the juice.*

expression *noun* **1** the look on a person's face that shows his or her feelings. **2** a word or phrase etc. **3** a way of speaking or of playing music etc. so as to show feeling for its meaning. **4** expressing, *this expression of opinion.* **expressionless** *adjective*

expressive *adjective* full of expression.

expressly *adverb* **1** clearly; plainly, *This was expressly forbidden.* **2** specially, *designed expressly for children.*

expressway *noun* a multi-laned highway for high-speed traffic.

▶▶▶ T H E S A U R U S ◀◀

explode *verb* **1** blast, blow up, burst, detonate, erupt, go off. **2** detonate, discharge, let off, set off.

exploit¹ *noun* achievement, act, adventure, deed, escapade, feat.

exploit² *verb* **1** capitalise on, cash in on, make the most of, profit from, take advantage of, use, utilise. **2** abuse, misuse, take advantage of, use.

explore *verb* **1** inspect, look around, prospect, reconnoitre, scout, survey, tour, travel about. **2** analyse, examine, inquire into, investigate, look into, probe, research, study, survey.
explorer *noun* discoverer, pioneer, prospector, surveyor, trailblazer, traveller.

explosion *noun* **1** bang, blast, boom, burst, detonation, discharge, eruption, outburst, pop, report, shot.

explosive¹ *adjective* charged, dangerous, dicey (*slang*), precarious, tense, unstable, volatile.

explosive² *noun* dynamite, gelignite, gunpowder, jelly (*slang*), nitroglycerine, TNT.

expose *verb* **1** bare, betray, disclose, display, divulge, lay bare, leak, let out, make known, reveal, show, uncover.

express¹ *adjective* **1** direct, expeditious, fast, hasty, high-speed, non-stop, prompt, quick, rapid, speedy, swift. **2** clear, definite, exact, explicit, particular, plain, precise, specific, unequivocal.

express³ *verb* **1** air, communicate, convey, disclose, indicate, put into words, reveal, speak, state, utter, vent, verbalise, voice.

expression *noun* **1** air, appearance, aspect, countenance, face, look, mien. **2** idiom, phrase, saying, term, word. **3** eloquence, emotion, feeling, intonation, meaning, sensitivity.
expressionless *adjective* blank, deadpan, empty, poker-faced, vacant, vacuous, wooden.

expressive *adjective* eloquent, meaningful, revealing, significant, telling.

▶▶▶ DICTIONARY ◀◀◀

expulsion *noun* expelling; being expelled. **expulsive** *adjective*

expunge *verb* (**expunged, expunging**) erase; wipe out.

exquisite (*say* **eks**-kwiz-it) *adjective* very beautiful. **exquisitely** *adverb* [from *ex-* = out, + Latin *quaesitum* = sought]

extemporise *verb* (**extemporised, extemporising**) speak or produce or do something without advance preparation. **extemporisation** *noun* [from Latin *ex tempore* = impromptu (literally 'out of the time')]

extend *verb* 1 stretch out. 2 make something become longer or larger. 3 offer; give, *Extend a warm welcome to our friends*. **extendible** *adjective*, **extensible** *adjective* [from *ex-* = out, + Latin *tendere* = stretch]

extension *noun* 1 extending; being extended. 2 something added on; an addition to a building. 3 one of a set of telephones in an office or house etc.

extensive *adjective* covering a large area or range, *extensive gardens*; *extensive knowledge*. **extensively** *adverb*, **extensiveness** *noun*

extent *noun* 1 the area or length over which something extends. 2 the amount, level, or scope of something, *the full extent of his power*.

extenuating *adjective* making a crime seem less great by providing a partial excuse, *There were extenuating circumstances*. **extenuation** *noun*

exterior[1] *adjective* outer.

exterior[2] *noun* the outside of something. [Latin, = further out]

exterminate *verb* (**exterminated, exterminating**) destroy or kill all the members or examples. **extermination** *noun*, **exterminator** *noun* [from *ex-* = out, + Latin *terminus* = boundary]

external *adjective* outside. **externally** *adverb*

extinct *adjective* 1 not existing any more, *The dodo is an extinct bird*. 2 not burning; not active, *an extinct volcano*. [same origin as *extinguish*]

extinction *noun* 1 making or becoming extinct. 2 extinguishing; being extinguished.

extinguish *verb* 1 put out a fire or light. 2 put an end to; nullify; destroy, *Our hopes of victory were extinguished*. [from Latin *extinguere* = quench]

extinguisher *noun* a portable device for sending out water, chemicals, or gases to extinguish a fire.

extol *verb* (**extolled, extolling**) praise.

extort *verb* obtain something by force or threats. **extortion** *noun* (from *ex-* = out, + Latin *tortum* = twisted]

extortionate *adjective* charging or demanding far too much.

extra[1] *adjective* additional; more than is usual, *extra strength*.

▶▶▶ THESAURUS ◀◀◀

expulsion *noun* banishment, eviction, exclusion, removal.

exquisite *adjective* beautiful, dainty, delicate, elegant, fine, lovely, perfect.

extend *verb* 1 hold out, reach out, stick out, straighten out, stretch out. 2 carry on, continue, drag out, elongate, enlarge, lengthen, prolong, protract, spin out, stretch. 3 accord, bestow, confer, give, grant, impart, offer, proffer.

extension *noun* 2 addition, annexe, wing.

extensive *adjective* big, broad, comprehensive, far-reaching, huge, immense, large, spacious, sweeping, thorough, vast, wholesale, wide, wide-ranging, widespread.

extent *noun* 1 area, breadth, expanse, length, size, spread, stretch, width. 2 amount, degree, limit, range, scale, scope.

extenuating *adjective* mitigating.

exterior[1] *adjective* external, outer, outside, outward, superficial.

exterior[2] *noun* façade, face, outside, shell, surface.

exterminate *verb* annihilate, destroy, eliminate, eradicate, get rid of, kill, liquidate, murder, root out, slaughter, wipe out.

external *adjective* exterior, outer, outside, outward, superficial.

extinct *adjective* 1 dead, died out. 2 burnt out, extinguished, inactive.

extinguish *verb* 1 douse, put out, quench, smother, snuff out.

extort *verb* exact, extract, squeeze, wring.

extortionate *adjective* excessive, exorbitant, immoderate, inordinate, outrageous, preposterous, steep, unreasonable.

extra[1] *adjective* additional, auxiliary, excess, further, more, other, reserve, spare, superfluous, supplementary, surplus.

▶▶ D I C T I O N A R Y ◀◀

extra² *adverb* more than usually, *extra strong.*

extra³ *noun* **1** an extra person or thing. **2** a person acting as part of a crowd in a film or play. [Latin, = outside]

extra- *prefix* outside; beyond (as in *extraterrestrial*). [from Latin, = outside]

extract¹ (*say* iks-**trakt**) *verb* take out, remove. **extractor** *noun*

extract² (*say* **eks**-trakt) *noun* **1** a passage taken from a book, speech, film, etc.; an excerpt. **2** a substance separated or obtained from another. [from *ex-* = out, + Latin *tractum* = pulled]

extraction *noun* **1** extracting. **2** descent; ancestry, *He is of Chinese extraction.*

extradite *verb* (**extradited, extraditing**) **1** hand over an accused person to the jurisdiction where the crime was committed. **2** obtain such a person for trial or punishment. **extradition** (*say* eks-tra-**dish**-on) *noun* [from *ex-*, + Latin *tradere* = hand over]

extraneous (*say* iks-**tray**-nee-us) *adjective* **1** added from outside. **2** not belonging to the matter in hand; irrelevant.

extraordinary *adjective* very unusual or strange. **extraordinarily** *adverb*

extrasensory *adjective* outside the range of the known human senses.

extravagant *adjective* spending or using too much. **extravagantly** *adverb*, **extravagance** *noun* [from *extra-*, + Latin *vagans* = wandering]

extravaganza *noun* a very spectacular show.

extreme¹ *adjective* **1** very great or intense, *extreme cold.* **2** furthest away, *the extreme north.* **3** going to great lengths in actions or opinions; not moderate. **extremely** *adverb*

extreme² *noun* **1** something extreme. **2** either end of something. [from Latin, = furthest outside]

extremist *noun* a person who holds extreme (not moderate) opinions in political or other matters.

extremity (*say* iks-**trem**-it-ee) *noun* (*plural* **extremities**) **1** an extreme point; the very end. **2** an extreme need or feeling or danger etc.

extricate (*say* **eks**-trik-ayt) *verb* (**extricated, extricating**) release from a difficult position. **extrication** *noun* [from *ex-*, + Latin *tricae* = entanglements]

extrovert *noun* a person who is generally friendly and likes company. (The opposite is *introvert.*) **extroverted** *adjective* [from *extro-* = outside, + Latin *vertere* = to turn]

extrude *verb* (**extruded, extruding**) push or squeeze out. **extrusion** *noun* [from *ex-*, + Latin *trudere* = to push]

exuberant (*say* ig-**zew**-ber-ant) *adjective* very lively. **exuberantly** *adverb*, **exuberance** *noun*

exude *verb* (**exuded, exuding**) **1** give off like sweat or a smell etc. **2** ooze out.

▶▶ T H E S A U R U S ◀◀

extra² *adverb* especially, exceptionally, extremely, particularly, unusually.

extra³ *noun* **1** accessory, addition, add-on, attachment, bonus, luxury, supplement.

extract¹ *verb* draw out, pull out, remove, take out.

extract² *noun* **1** citation, clip, clipping, cutting, excerpt, passage, quotation, snippet, trailer. **2** concentrate, distillate, essence.

extraordinary *adjective* abnormal, amazing, astonishing, bizarre, curious, exceptional, incredible, miraculous, odd, outstanding, peculiar, phenomenal, rare, remarkable, singular, special, strange, striking, uncommon, unusual, weird.

extravagant *adjective* improvident, lavish, munificent, over-generous, prodigal, profligate, spendthrift, wasteful.

extreme¹ *adjective* **1** acute, excessive, great, intense, severe. **2** farthest, furthermost, furthest, utmost, uttermost. **3** Draconian, drastic, fanatical, hard-line, harsh, immoderate, intemperate, radical, severe, stiff, stringent, uncompromising, unreasonable.
extremely *adverb* awfully (*informal*), especially, exceedingly, exceptionally, extraordinarily, remarkably, terribly (*informal*), very.

extreme² *noun* **2** boundary, end, extremity, limit, maximum, minimum, pole.

extroverted *adjective* gregarious, outgoing, sociable.

exuberant *adjective* animated, boisterous, energetic, excited, exhilarated, full of beans (*informal*), high-spirited, irrepressible, lively, spirited, vivacious.

exude *verb* drip, emanate, ooze, secrete, seep.

▶▶ D I C T I O N A R Y ◀◀

exult *verb* rejoice greatly. **exultant** *adjective*, **exultation** *noun*

eye¹ *noun* **1** the organ of the body that is used for seeing. **2** the power of seeing, *She has sharp eyes.* **3** the small hole in a needle. **4** a spot or leaf-bud that seems like an eye. **5** the centre of a storm.

eye² *verb* (**eyed, eyeing**) look at; watch.

eyeball *noun* the ball-shaped part of the eye inside the eyelids.

eyebrow *noun* the fringe of hair growing on the face above the eye.

eyelash *noun* (*plural* **eyelashes**) one of the short hairs that grow on an eyelid.

eyelid *noun* either of the two folds of skin that can close over the eyeball.

eyepiece *noun* the lens of a telescope or microscope etc. that you put to your eye.

eyesight *noun* the ability to see.

eyesore *noun* something that is ugly to look at.

eyewitness *noun* (*plural* **eyewitnesses**) a person who actually saw an accident or crime etc.

eyrie (*say* **I**-ree) *noun* the nest of an eagle or other bird of prey.

▶▶ T H E S A U R U S ◀◀

exult *verb* crow, gloat, glory, rejoice, revel. **exultant** *adjective* delighted, ecstatic, elated, gleeful, jubilant, overjoyed, triumphant.

eye² *verb* behold (*old use*), contemplate, gaze at, look at, observe, ogle, peer at, stare at, study, view, watch.

eyesight *noun* sight, vision.

eyesore *noun* blight, blot, monstrosity.

eyewitness *noun* bystander, looker-on, observer, onlooker, spectator, witness.

►Ff

fable *noun* a short story that teaches about behaviour, often with animals as characters. [from Latin *fabula* = story]

fabric *noun* 1 cloth. 2 the framework of a building (walls, floors, and roof).

fabricate *verb* (**fabricated, fabricating**) 1 construct; manufacture. 2 invent, *fabricate an excuse*. **fabrication** *noun*

fabulous *adjective* 1 (*informal*) wonderful. 2 incredibly great, *fabulous wealth*. 3 told of in fables. **fabulously** *adverb*

façade (*say* fas-**ahd**) *noun* 1 the front of a building. 2 an outward appearance, especially a deceptive one. [French (same origin as *face*)]

face¹ *noun* 1 the front part of the head. 2 the expression on a person's face. 3 the front or upper side of something. 4 a surface, *A cube has six faces*.

face² *verb* (**faced, facing**) 1 look or have the front towards something, *Our room faced the sea*. 2 meet and have to deal with something; encounter, *Explorers face many dangers*. 3 cover a surface with a layer of different material. [from Latin *facies* = appearance]

facet (*say* **fas**-it) *noun* 1 one of the many sides of a cut stone or jewel. 2 one aspect of a situation or problem.

facetious (*say* fas-**ee**-shus) *adjective* trying to be funny at an unsuitable time, *facetious remarks*. **facetiously** *adverb*

facial (*say* **fay**-shal) *adjective* of the face.

facile (*say* **fas**-I'll) *adjective* done or produced easily or with little thought or care. [from Latin *facilis* = easy]

facilitate (*say* fas-**il**-it-ayt) *verb* (**facilitated, facilitating**) make easy or easier. **facilitation** *noun*

facility (*say* fas-**il**-it-ee) *noun* (*plural* **facilities**) 1 something that provides you with the means to do things, *There are sports facilities*. 2 easiness.

facsimile (*say* fak-**sim**-il-ee) *noun* an exact reproduction of a document etc. [from Latin *fac* = make, + *simile* = a likeness]

fact *noun* 1 something that is certainly true. 2 an item of information. [from Latin *factum* = thing done]

faction *noun* a small united group within a larger one, especially in politics.

factor *noun* 1 something that helps to bring about a result, *Hard work was a factor in her success*. 2 a number by which a larger number can be divided exactly, *2 and 3 are factors of 6*.

►►►THESAURUS◄◄◄

fable *noun* allegory, legend, myth, parable, story, tale.

fabric *noun* 1 cloth, material, stuff, textile.

fabricate *verb* 1 assemble, build, construct, make, manufacture, produce. 2 concoct, devise, hatch, invent, make up, manufacture.

fabulous *adjective* 1 see EXCELLENT. 2 extraordinary, great, inconceivable, incredible, mind-boggling (*informal*), phenomenal, prodigious, stupendous, tremendous, unbelievable. 3 fabled, fanciful, fictional, fictitious, imaginary, legendary, mythical.

façade *noun* 1 exterior, face, front, frontage, outside. 2 appearance, exterior, front, mask, pretence, show, veneer.

face¹ *noun* 2 air, countenance, expression, look, physiognomy, visage. 3 façade, front, side, surface.

face² *verb* 1 front on, lie opposite, look out on, overlook. 2 brave, confront, cope with, deal

with, encounter, experience, meet, weather, withstand.

facet *noun* 2 aspect, face, feature, side.

facetious *adjective* amusing, comical, flippant, funny, humorous, jocular, joking, witty.

facilitate *verb* aid, assist, ease, expedite, help, simplify.

facility *noun* 1 amenity, convenience, resource. 2 competence, ease, effortlessness, fluency, proficiency, skill.

facsimile *noun* copy, duplicate, photocopy, replica, reproduction.

fact *noun* 1 actuality, certainty, reality, truth. 2 circumstance, detail, particular; (*facts*) data, evidence, information, low-down (*slang*).

faction *noun* camp, clique, division, group, lobby, set, wing.

factor *noun* 1 aspect, circumstance, component, element, influence, ingredient, part.

▶▶▶ D I C T I O N A R Y ◀◀

factory *noun* (*plural* **factories**) a large building where machines are used to make things. [from Latin *facere* = make or do]

factotum (*say* fakt-**oh**-tum) *noun* a servant or assistant who does all kinds of work. [from Latin *fac* = do, + *totum* = everything]

factual *adjective* based on facts; containing facts. **factually** *adverb*

faculty *noun* (*plural* **faculties**) **1** any of the powers of the body or mind (e.g. sight, speech, understanding). **2** a department teaching a particular subject in a university, *the faculty of music*.

fad *noun* a person's particular like or dislike; a craze. **faddy** *adjective*

fade *verb* (**faded, fading**) **1** lose or cause to lose colour or freshness or strength. **2** disappear gradually. **3** make a sound etc. become gradually weaker (*fade it out*) or stronger (*fade it in* or *up*).

faeces (*say* **fee**-seez) *plural noun* solid waste matter expelled from the anus.

fag *noun* **1** tiring work; drudgery. **2** tiredness, *brain-fag*. **3** (*slang*) a cigarette. **fagged out** tired out; exhausted.

faggot *noun* **1** a meat ball made with chopped liver and baked. **2** a bundle of sticks bound together, especially as firewood.

Fahrenheit *adjective* measuring temperature on a scale where water freezes at 32° and boils at 212°. [named after a German scientist, G.D. Fahrenheit]

fail¹ *verb* **1** try to do something but be unable to do it. **2** become weak or useless; break down, *The brakes failed*. **3** not to do something, *He failed to warn me*. **4** grade a candidate or be graded as not having passed an examination.

fail² *noun* **without fail** for certain; whatever happens.

failing *noun* a weakness; a fault.

failure *noun* **1** not being able to do something. **2** a person or thing that has failed.

faint¹ *adjective* **1** weak; not clear, not distinct. **2** exhausted; nearly unconscious. **faintly** *adverb*, **faintness** *noun*

faint² *verb* become unconscious.

fair¹ *adjective* **1** right or just; according to the rules, *a fair fight*. **2** (of hair or skin) light in colour; (of a person) having fair hair. **3** (*old use*) beautiful. **4** fine; favourable, *fair weather*. **5** moderate; quite good, *a fair number of people*. **fairness** *noun*
fair go (*Australian*) an equal opportunity, a reasonable chance. [from Old English *faeger*]

fair² *adverb* fairly, *Play fair!*

▶▶▶ T H E S A U R U S ◀◀

factory *noun* forge, foundry, mill, plant, refinery, works, workshop.

factual *adjective* accurate, faithful, objective, strict, true, truthful.

faculty *noun* **1** ability, aptitude, bent, capability, capacity, facility, flair, gift, knack, power, skill, talent.

fad *noun* craze, cult, fashion, mania, passion, rage, trend, vogue.

fade *verb* **1** bleach, dim, dull, lighten, pale, wash out, whiten. **2** decline, decrease, die away, diminish, disappear, dwindle, ebb, grow faint, peter out, trail away, vanish, wane, weaken.
fade away die, shrivel, waste away, wither.

fail¹ *verb* **1** abort, backfire, be unsuccessful, bomb out (*informal*), come unstuck (*informal*), fall through, flop (*informal*), flunk (*informal*), founder, miscarry, misfire. **2** break down, conk out (*informal*), decline, deteriorate, dwindle, ebb, fade, malfunction, pack up (*informal*), wane, weaken. **3** forget, neglect, omit.

failing *noun* fault, flaw, foible, imperfection, shortcoming, vice, weakness.

failure *noun* **2** damp squib, disaster, fiasco, fizzer (*Australian informal*), flop (*informal*), non-event, wash-out (*informal*).

faint¹ *adjective* **1** (*a faint picture*) blurred, dim, hazy, indistinct, misty, unclear; (*faint colours*) delicate, faded, light, pale, pastel, soft, subtle; (*faint sounds*) feeble, low, muffled, muted, slight, soft, subdued, weak. **2** dizzy, giddy, light-headed, unsteady, weak, woozy (*informal*).

faint² *verb* black out, collapse, flake out (*informal*), keel over, lose consciousness, pass out (*informal*), swoon.

fair¹ *adjective* **1** above board, disinterested, equitable, even-handed, honest, impartial, just, legitimate, objective, open-minded, proper, reasonable, right, sporting, sportsmanlike, unbiased, unprejudiced. **2** blond, flaxen, golden, light, tow-coloured. **4** bright, clear, cloudless, fine, sunny, unclouded. **5** all right, average, indifferent, mediocre, middling, OK (*informal*), passable, reasonable, satisfactory, so-so (*informal*), tolerable.
fairness *noun* disinterest, equity, even-handedness, impartiality, justice, neutrality, objectivity.

►►DICTIONARY◄◄

fair³ *noun* **1** a group of entertainments such as roundabouts and sideshows. **2** an exhibition. **3** a market. [from Latin *feriae* = holiday]

fairly *adverb* **1** justly; according to the rules. **2** moderately, *It is fairly hard.*

fairy *noun* (*plural* **fairies**) an imaginary very small creature with magic powers. **fairyland** *noun*, **fairy-tale** *noun*
fairy floss a fluffy mass of spun sugar.
fairy penguin a small Australian penguin. [from an old word *fay*, from Latin *fata* = the Fates, three goddesses who were believed to control people's lives]

faith *noun* **1** strong belief; trust. **2** a system of religious belief.
in good faith with honest intentions.

faithful *adjective* **1** loyal and trustworthy. **2** sexually loyal to one partner. **faithfully** *adverb*, **faithfulness** *noun*
Yours faithfully see *yours*.

fake¹ *noun* a thing or person that looks genuine but is not; a forgery. **fake** *adjective*

fake² *verb* (**faked, faking**) **1** make something that looks genuine, so as to deceive people. **2** pretend, *They faked illness.* **faker** *noun*

fakir (*say* **fay**-keer) *noun* a Muslim or Hindu religious beggar regarded as a holy man. [Arabic, = a poor man]

falcon *noun* a kind of hawk often used in the sport of hunting other birds or game. **falconry** *noun*

fall¹ *verb* (**fell, fallen, falling**) **1** come or go down without being pushed or thrown etc. **2** decrease; become lower, *Prices fell.* **3** be captured or overthrown, *The city fell.* **4** die in battle. **5** happen, *Silence fell.* **6** become, *She fell asleep.*
fall back retreat.
fall back on use for support or in an emergency.
fall for (*informal*) be attracted by a person; be taken in by a deception.
fall out quarrel.
fall through fail, *plans fell through.*

fall² *noun* **1** the action of falling. **2** (*American*) autumn.

fallacy (*say* **fal**-a-see) *noun* (*plural* **fallacies**) a false idea or belief. **fallacious** (*say* fal-**ay**-shus) *adjective* [from Latin *fallere* = deceive]

fallible (*say* **fal**-ib-ul) *adjective* liable to make mistakes; not infallible, *All people are fallible.* **fallibility** *noun*

fall-out *noun* particles of radioactive material carried in the air after a nuclear explosion.

fallow *adjective* (of land) ploughed but left without crops in order to restore its fertility.
fallow deer a kind of light-brown deer.

falls *plural noun* a waterfall.

►►THESAURUS◄◄

fair³ *noun* **1** carnival, funfair, show. **2** exhibition, expo, exposition, sale, show. **3** bazaar, fête, gala, market.

fairly *adverb* **1** equitably, honestly, impartially, justly, objectively, properly, reasonably. **2** moderately, pretty, quite, rather, reasonably, somewhat.

fairy *noun* elf, imp, pixie, sprite.

faith *noun* **1** belief, confidence, reliance, trust. **2** belief, church, conviction, creed, doctrine, persuasion, religion.

faithful *adjective* **1** committed, constant, dedicated, dependable, devoted, dutiful, loyal, reliable, stalwart, staunch, steadfast, true, trustworthy, trusty.
faithfulness *noun* SEE FIDELITY.

fake¹ *noun* (*thing*) copy, counterfeit, duplicate, forgery, fraud, hoax, imitation, phoney (*informal*), replica, reproduction, sham; (*person*) charlatan, cheat, con man (*informal*), fraud, humbug, impostor, phoney (*informal*), quack.

fake *adjective* artificial, bogus, counterfeit, false, forged, imitation, phoney (*informal*), pretend (*informal*), pseudo, sham, synthetic.

fake² *verb* **1** copy, counterfeit, fabricate, forge, reproduce. **2** affect, feign, fudge, pretend, simulate.

fall¹ *verb* **1** cascade, collapse, come a buster (*Australian informal*), come a cropper (*informal*), come a gutser (*Australian slang*), crash, descend, founder, nosedive, overbalance, plummet, plunge, slide, slip, spill, stumble, topple, trip, tumble. **2** decline, decrease, diminish, drop, dwindle, reduce, slump. **4** be killed, die, perish. **5** happen, occur, take place.
fall out argue, disagree, fight, quarrel, squabble.
fall through see FAIL¹.

fall² *noun* **1** collapse, crash, decline, decrease, descent, dip, dive, downturn, drop, nosedive, plunge, reduction, slump.

fallacy *noun* delusion, error, inconsistency, misconception, mistake, myth.

falls *plural noun* cascade, cataract, waterfall.

▶▶▶ D I C T I O N A R Y ◀◀◀

false *adjective* **1** untrue; incorrect. **2** not genuine; sham; faked. **3** treacherous; deceitful. **falsely** *adverb*, **falseness** *noun*, **falsity** *noun* [from Latin *falsum* = deceived]

falsehood *noun* **1** a lie. **2** telling lies.

falsetto *noun* (*plural* **falsettos**) a man's voice forced into speaking or singing higher than is natural.

falsify *verb* (**falsified, falsifying**) alter a thing dishonestly. **falsification** *noun*

falsity *noun* falseness.

falter *verb* **1** stumble; go unsteadily. **2** hesitate when you speak. **3** become weaker; begin to give way, *His courage faltered.*

fame *noun* being famous. **famed** *adjective*

familiar *adjective* **1** well-known; often seen or experienced. **2** knowing something well, *Are you familiar with this book?* **3** very friendly. **4** too informal. **familiarly** *adverb*, **familiarity** *noun* [same origin as *family*]

familiarise *verb* (**familiarised, familiarising**) make familiar; accustom. **familiarisation** *noun*

family *noun* (*plural* **families**) **1** parents and their children, sometimes including grand-children and other relations. **2** a person's children. **3** all the descendants of a common ancestor. **4** a group of things that are alike in some way.

family planning birth control.

family tree a diagram showing how people in a family are related. [from Latin *familia* = household]

famine *noun* a very bad shortage of food in an area. [from Latin *fames* = hunger]

famished *adjective* very hungry. **famishing** *adjective* [same origin as *famine*]

famous *adjective* known to very many people.

famously *adverb* (*informal*) very well, *They get on famously.*

fan¹ *noun* a device for making air move about so as to cool people or things.

fan² *verb* (**fanned, fanning**) send a current of air on something.

fan³ *noun* an enthusiast; a great admirer or supporter. [short for *fanatic*]

fanatic *noun* a person who is very enthusiastic or too enthusiastic about something. **fanatical** *adjective*, **fanatically** *adverb*, **fanaticism** *noun*

fanciful *adjective* **1** imagining things. **2** quaint; imaginative, *fanciful designs.*

▶▶▶ T H E S A U R U S ◀◀◀

false *adjective* **1** erroneous, fallacious, faulty, inaccurate, incorrect, invalid, misleading, spurious, unsound, untrue, wrong. **2** artificial, assumed (*name*), bogus, counterfeit, fake, fictitious, imitation, made-up, phoney (*informal*), pretend (*informal*), pseudo, sham, synthetic. **3** deceitful, dishonest, disloyal, duplicitous, faithless, hypocritical, insincere, lying, perfidious, treacherous, two-faced, unfaithful, untruthful.

falsehood *noun* **1** fabrication, fairy story, fairy tale, fib, fiction, lie, myth, porky (*slang*), story, untruth.

falsify *verb* alter, cook (*informal*), doctor, fiddle (*slang*), tamper with.

falter *verb* **1** stagger, stumble, totter. **2** hesitate, pause, stammer, stutter.

fame *noun* celebrity, distinction, eminence, glory, honour, kudos (*informal*), prestige, prominence, recognition, renown, reputation, repute.

familiar *adjective* **1** common, commonplace, customary, everyday, habitual, normal, regular, routine, usual, well-known. **2** (*familiar with*) acquainted with, at home with, conversant with, knowledgeable about, used to, versed in. **3** chummy (*informal*), close, friendly, informal, intimate, matey, pally (*informal*). **4** disrespectful, forward, free and easy, impertinent, impudent, informal, presumptuous.

familiarise *verb* (*familiarise with*) accustom to, acquaint with, inform about, instruct in, teach.

family *noun* **1** clan, flesh and blood, folk, kin, kindred, kinsmen, kinswomen, kith and kin, people, relations, relatives, tribe. **2** brood, children, kids (*informal*), offspring, progeny. **3** ancestry, dynasty, forebears, genealogy, house, line, lineage, parentage, pedigree, roots, stock.

famished *adjective* hungry, peckish (*informal*), ravenous, starving.

famous *adjective* acclaimed, celebrated, distinguished, eminent, famed, great, illustrious, important, legendary, notable, noted, outstanding, pre-eminent, prominent, renowned, well-known.

fan³ *noun* addict, admirer, aficionado, buff (*informal*), devotee, enthusiast, fanatic, follower, lover, nut (*informal*), supporter.

fanatic *noun* enthusiast, extremist, maniac, zealot.

fanciful *adjective* **2** curious, fabulous, fantastic, imaginative, romantic, unrealistic, visionary, whimsical, wild.

▶▶ D I C T I O N A R Y ◀◀

fancy¹ *noun* (*plural* **fancies**) **1** a liking or desire for something. **2** imagination.

fancy² *adjective* decorated; elaborate.

fancy³ *verb* (**fancied, fancying**) **1** believe, *I fancy it's raining*. **2** imagine. **3** have a liking or desire for something. [originally a shortened spelling of *fantasy*]

fanfare *noun* a short piece of loud music played on trumpets.

fang *noun* a long sharp tooth.

fanlight *noun* a window above a door.

fantasia (*say* fan-**tay**-zee-a) *noun* an imaginative piece of music or writing.

fantasise *verb* (**fantasised, fantasising**) imagine in fantasy; daydream.

fantastic *adjective* **1** (*informal*) excellent. **2** designed in a very fanciful way. **fantastically** *adverb*

fantasy *noun* (*plural* **fantasies**) something imaginary or fantastic.

far¹ *adverb* **1** at or to a great distance, *We didn't go far.* **2** much; by a great amount, *This is far better.*

far² *adjective* distant; remote, *On the far side of the river.*

farce *noun* **1** an exaggerated comedy. **2** events that are ridiculous or a pretence. **farcical** *adjective*

fare¹ *noun* **1** the price charged for a passenger to travel. **2** food and drink, *There was only very plain fare.*

fare² *verb* (**fared, faring**) get along; progress, *How did they fare?*

farewell¹ *interjection* & *noun* goodbye.

farewell² *verb* (*Australian*) take leave of someone leaving a job or district, usually with a formal gathering.

farm¹ *noun* an area of land where someone grows crops or keeps animals for food or other use. **farmhouse** *noun*, **farmyard** *noun*

farm² *verb* **1** grow crops or keep animals for food etc. **2** use land for growing crops; cultivate.

farmer *noun* a person who owns or manages a farm.

farrier (*say* **fa**-ree-er) *noun* a smith who shoes horses. **farriery** *noun* [from Latin *ferrum* = iron, an iron horseshoe]

farrow *noun* a litter of pigs.

▶▶ T H E S A U R U S ◀◀

fancy¹ *noun* **1** craving, desire, hunger, liking, longing. **2** delusion, fantasy, illusion, imagination, make-believe, unreality.

fancy² *adjective* complicated, decorated, decorative, detailed, elaborate, intricate, ornamental, ornate, showy.

fancy³ *verb* **1** believe, guess, reckon, suppose, suspect, think. **2** dream, fantasise, imagine, picture. **3** be attracted to, desire, hanker after, like, long for, prefer, want, wish for, yearn for.

fantasise *verb* daydream, dream, imagine.

fantastic *adjective* **1** see EXCELLENT. **2** absurd, amazing, bizarre, extraordinary, fanciful, far-fetched, implausible, incredible, outlandish, preposterous, strange, unbelievable, unreal, unrealistic, weird, whimsical, wild.

fantasy *noun* daydream, delusion, dream, fancy, hallucination, illusion, imagination, invention, make-believe, reverie.

far² *adjective* distant, far-away, far-off, remote.

farce *noun* **2** charade, joke, mockery, sham. **farcical** *adjective* absurd, comical, laughable, ludicrous, nonsensical, preposterous, ridiculous.

fare¹ *noun* **1** charge, cost, fee, payment, price, rate. **2** food, meals, tucker (*Australian informal*).

fare² *verb* do, get on, make out, manage.

farewell¹ *interjection* adieu, au revoir, bye (*informal*), bye-bye (*informal*), cheerio (*informal*), cheers (*informal*), ciao (*informal*), goodbye, hooray (*Australian informal*), see you (*informal*), see you later (*informal*), so long (*informal*).
farewell *noun* departure, goodbye, leave-taking, parting, send-off.

farm¹ *noun* plantation, property, ranch, run (*Australian*), smallholding, station (*Australian*).

farm² *verb* **2** cultivate, till, work.
farming *noun* agribusiness, agriculture, cultivation, husbandry.

farmer *noun* agriculturalist, cocky (*Australian informal*), grazier (*Australian*), pastoralist (*Australian*), peasant, sharefarmer (*Australian*), smallholder.

▶▷ D I C T I O N A R Y ◁◀

farther *adverb* & *adjective* at or to a greater distance; more distant.

> **Usage** *Farther* and *farthest* are used only in connection with distance (e.g. *She lives farther from the school than I do*), but even in such cases many people prefer to use *further*. Only *further* can be used to mean 'additional', e.g. in *We must make further inquiries*. If you are not sure which is right, use *further*.

farthest *adverb* & *adjective* at or to the greatest distance; most distant.

farthing *noun* a former coin worth one-quarter of a penny. [from Old English *feorthing* = one-fourth]

fascinate *verb* (**fascinated**, **fascinating**) be very attractive or interesting to somebody. **fascination** *noun*, **fascinator** *noun* [from Latin, = cast a spell]

Fascist (*say* **fash**-ist) *noun* a person who supports an extreme right-wing dictatorial type of government. **Fascism** *noun* [from Latin *fasces*, the bundle of rods with an axe through it, carried before a magistrate in ancient Rome as a symbol of his power to punish people]

fashion¹ *noun* **1** the style of clothes or other things that most people like at a particular time. **2** a way of doing something, *Continue in the same fashion*. **fashionable** *adjective*, **fashionably** *adverb*

fashion² *verb* make in a particular shape or style.

fast¹ *adjective* **1** moving or done quickly; rapid. **2** allowing fast movement, *a fast road*. **3** showing a time later than the correct time, *Your watch is fast*. **4** firmly fixed or attached. **5** not likely to fade, *fast colours*. **fastness** *noun*

fast² *adverb* **1** quickly, *Run fast!* **2** firmly; securely, *They are fast asleep*.

fast³ *verb* go without food. **fast** *noun*

fasten *verb* fix one thing firmly to another. **fastener** *noun*, **fastening** *noun*

fastidious *adjective* choosing carefully and liking only what is very good. **fastidiously** *adverb*, **fastidiousness** *noun*

fat¹ *noun* **1** the white greasy part of meat. **2** oil or grease used in cooking. **the fat of the land** the best food.

fat² *adjective* (**fatter**, **fattest**) **1** having a very thick round body. **2** thick, *a fat book*. **3** full of fat. **fatness** *noun*

fatal *adjective* causing death or disaster, *a fatal accident*. **fatally** *adverb*

fatalist *noun* a person who accepts whatever happens and thinks it could not have been avoided. **fatalism** *noun*, **fatalistic** *adjective*

fatality (*say* fa-**tal**-it-ee) *noun* (*plural* **fatalities**) a death caused by an accident, war, or other disaster.

▶▷ T H E S A U R U S ◁◀

fascinate *verb* attract, beguile, bewitch, captivate, charm, enchant, enthral, entrance, hold spellbound, hypnotise, mesmerise, rivet.

fashion¹ *noun* **1** craze, fad, mode, rage, style, trend, vogue. **2** manner, method, mode, way. **fashionable** *adjective* chic, classy (*informal*), contemporary, elegant, in, in fashion, latest, modern, smart, stylish, swish (*informal*), trendy (*informal*), up to date, with it (*informal*).

fashion² *verb* carve, construct, create, devise, form, make, manufacture, model, mould, produce, shape, work.

fast¹ *adjective* **1** breakneck, brisk, express, fleet, hasty, high-speed, nippy (*informal*), quick, rapid, rattling, speedy, swift, zippy. **5** fixed, indelible, permanent.

fast² *adverb* **1** at full pelt, at full speed, at the double, briskly, hastily, hell for leather (*informal*), hurriedly, like lightning (*informal*), like mad (*informal*), like the clappers (*in-*

formal), post-haste, quickly, rapidly, speedily, swiftly. **2** firmly, securely, solidly, tightly.

fast³ *verb* go without food, starve.

fasten *verb* adhere, affix, anchor, attach, bind, bolt, bond, buckle, button, chain, clamp, clasp, clip, close, connect, couple, do up, fix, hitch, hook, join, knot, lace, lash, latch, link, lock, moor, nail, peg, pin, rivet, screw, seal, secure, sew, shut, staple, stick, strap, tack, tape, tether, tie, truss, zip up.

fastidious *adjective* choosy (*informal*), finicky, fussy, particular, pernickety (*informal*), picky (*informal*), selective.

fat¹ *noun* **1** blubber, corpulence, flab (*informal*). **2** butter, dripping, grease, lard, margarine, suet.

fat² *adjective* **1** chubby, corpulent, dumpy, flabby, gross, heavy, large, obese, overweight, plump, podgy, portly, roly-poly, rotund, squat, stout, tubby. **2** bulky, thick, weighty.

fatal *adjective* deadly, lethal, mortal, terminal.

fatality *noun* casualty, death.

►►►DICTIONARY◄◄

fate *noun* **1** a power that is thought to make things happen. **2** what will happen or has happened to somebody or something; destiny.

fated *adjective* destined by fate; doomed, *the fated lovers, Romeo and Juliet.*

fateful *adjective* bringing events that are important and usually unpleasant. **fatefully** *adverb*

father¹ *noun* **1** a male parent. **2** the title of certain priests. **fatherly** *adjective*
Father's Day a tribute to fathers, in Australia the first Sunday in September.

father² *verb* be the father of, *He fathered six children.* [from Old English *faeder*]

father-in-law *noun* (*plural* **fathers-in-law**) the father of a married person's husband or wife.

fathom¹ *noun* a unit of 6 feet (about 1.8 metres), used in measuring the depth of water.

fathom² *verb* **1** measure the depth of something. **2** get to the bottom of something; work it out. **fathomless** *adjective*

fatigue *noun* **1** tiredness. **2** weakness in metals, caused by stress. **fatigued** *adjective* [from Latin *fatigare* = tire]

fatten *verb* make or become fat.

fatty *adjective* like fat; containing fat.

fatuous *adjective* silly. **fatuously** *adverb*, **fatuousness** *noun*, **fatuity** *noun*

fault¹ *noun* **1** anything that makes a person or thing imperfect; a flaw or mistake. **2** the responsibility for something wrong, *It wasn't your fault.* **3** a break in a layer of rock.

fault² *verb* **1** find faults in something. **2** form a fault. [from Latin *fallere* = deceive]

faultless *adjective* without a fault. **faultlessly** *adverb*, **faultlessness** *noun*

faulty *adjective* having a fault or faults. **faultily** *adverb*, **faultiness** *noun*

faun *noun* an ancient country-god with a goat's legs, horns, and tail. [from the name of Faunus, an ancient Roman country-god (see *fauna*)]

fauna *noun* the animals of a certain area or period of time. (Compare *flora*.) [from the name of Fauna, an ancient Roman country-goddess, sister of Faunus (see *faun*)]

favour¹ *noun* **1** a kind or helpful act. **2** approval; goodwill. **3** friendly support shown to one person or group but not to another, *without fear or favour.*

favour² *verb* **1** be in favour of something. **2** show favour to a person.

favourable *adjective* **1** helpful. **2** approving; pleasing. **favourably** *adverb*

►►►THESAURUS◄◄

fate *noun* **1** chance, destiny, fortune, luck, predestination, providence. **2** destiny, doom, fortune, karma, kismet, lot, portion.

fated *adjective* destined, doomed, predestined, preordained.

fateful *adjective* decisive, important, momentous, significant; see also DISASTROUS (at DISASTER).

father¹ *noun* **1** patriarch; (*informal terms of address*) dad, daddy, pa, papa, pater, pop.
fatherly *adjective* fatherlike, kindly, paternal, protective, tender.

father² *verb* beget, procreate, sire.

fathom² *verb* **1** measure, plumb, sound. **2** comprehend, get to the bottom of, penetrate, understand, work out.

fatigue *noun* **1** exhaustion, lassitude, lethargy, tiredness, weariness.

fatty *adjective* greasy, oily.

fault¹ *noun* **1** blemish, bug (*informal*), defect, error, failing, flaw, foible, glitch (*informal*), imperfection, lapse, malfunction, misdeed, misdemeanour, mistake, offence, shortcoming, sin, slip-up (*informal*), transgression, trespass

(*old use*), vice, weakness, wrongdoing. **2** blame, responsibility.
at fault culpable, guilty, in the wrong, liable, responsible, to blame.

fault² *verb* **1** censure, criticise, find fault with, knock (*informal*), pick holes in.

faultless *adjective* consummate, correct, exemplary, flawless, ideal, immaculate, perfect, unblemished.

faulty *adjective* defective, imperfect, kaput (*informal*), malfunctioning, on the blink (*informal*), out of order.

fauna *noun* animals, wildlife.

favour¹ *noun* **1** courtesy, good deed, good turn, kindness, service. **2** approval, goodwill, support, sympathy. **3** bias, favouritism, partiality, preference.

favour² *verb* **1** advocate, approve, back, choose, endorse, espouse, opt for, prefer, recommend, select, support. **2** assist, benefit, give an advantage to, help.

favourable *adjective* **1** advantageous, auspicious, beneficial, conducive, helpful, promising, propitious. **2** approving, encouraging, good, positive, reassuring, supportive, sympathetic.

▶▶▶ D I C T I O N A R Y ◀◀

favourite *adjective* liked more than others. **favourite** *noun*

favouritism *noun* unfairly being kinder to one person than to others.

fawn¹ *noun* **1** a young deer. **2** a light-brown colour.

fawn² *verb* try to win a person's favour or affection by flattery and humility.

fax *noun* a system for transmitting facsimiles of documents using telephone networks. **fax** *verb*

faze *verb* (*informal*) disconcert, daunt.

fear¹ *noun* a feeling that something unpleasant may happen.

fear² *verb* feel fear; be afraid of somebody or something.

fearful *adjective* **1** feeling fear; afraid. **2** causing fear or horror, *a fearful monster*. **3** (*informal*) very great or bad. **fearfully** *adverb*

fearless *adjective* without fear. **fearlessly** *adverb*, **fearlessness** *noun*

fearsome *adjective* frightening.

feasible *adjective* able to be done; possible. **feasibly** *adverb*, **feasibility** *noun*

feast *noun* **1** a large splendid meal. **2** a religious festival. **feast** *verb* [from Latin *festus* = joyful]

feat *noun* a brave or clever deed.

feather¹ *noun* one of the very light coverings that grow from a bird's skin. **feathery** *adjective*

feather² *verb* cover or line with feathers.

featherweight *noun* **1** a person who weighs very little. **2** a boxer weighing between 54 and 57 kilograms.

feature¹ *noun* **1** any part of the face (e.g. mouth, nose, eyes). **2** an important or noticeable part; a characteristic. **3** a long or important film, broadcast programme, or newspaper article.

feature² *verb* (**featured, featuring**) make or be a noticeable part of something.

feckless *adjective* feeble and incompetent, irresponsible. [from Scottish *feck* = effect, + *-less* = without]

fed *past tense* of **feed**. **fed up** (*informal*) discontented.

federal *adjective* of a system in which several States are ruled by a central government but are responsible for their own internal affairs. **federation** *noun* [from Latin *foederis* = of a treaty]

▶▶▶ T H E S A U R U S ◀◀

favourite *adjective* chosen, pet, preferred.

favouritism *noun* bias, nepotism (*towards relatives*), partiality, positive discrimination, preference, prejudice.

fawn¹ *noun* **2** beige, buff, camel, khaki, light brown, neutral.

faze *verb* daunt, discomfit, disconcert, fluster, perturb, rattle (*informal*), throw (*informal*), trouble, unnerve, upset, worry.

fear¹ *noun* alarm, anxiety, apprehension, awe, consternation, dismay, dread, foreboding, fright, horror, panic, phobia, terror, trepidation, worry.

fear² *verb* be afraid of, be frightened of, be scared of, dread, worry about.

fearful *adjective* **1** afraid, alarmed, anxious, apprehensive, cowardly, faint-hearted, frightened, nervous, panicky, pusillanimous, scared, terrified, timid, timorous, worried. **2** alarming, appalling, awful, dreadful, fearsome, frightening, frightful, ghastly, horrendous, horrific, scary, shocking, terrible, terrific, terrifying.

fearless *adjective* bold, brave, courageous, daring, dauntless, gallant, game, heroic, intrepid, lion-hearted, plucky, unafraid, undaunted, valiant, valorous. **fearlessness** *noun* boldness, bravery, courage, daring, grit, guts (*informal*), intrepidity, nerve, pluck, valour.

feasible *adjective* achievable, possible, practicable, viable, workable.

feast *noun* **1** banquet, dinner, meal, repast (*formal*), spread. **2** celebration, festival, fête, holiday. **feast** *verb* dine, eat, gorge, tuck in (*informal*).

feat *noun* achievement, act, action, deed, exploit, performance, stunt.

feather¹ *noun* hackle, plume, quill; (*feathers*) down, plumage.

feature¹ *noun* **1** (*features*) countenance, face, lineaments, physiognomy, visage. **2** aspect, attribute, characteristic, detail, facet, point, property, quality, respect, trait.

federation *noun* alliance, association, confederation, league, syndicate, union.

▶▶ D I C T I O N A R Y ◀◀

fee *noun* a charge for something.

feeble *adjective* weak; without strength. **feebly** *adverb*, **feebleness** *noun* [from Latin *flebilis* = wept over]

feed¹ *verb* (**fed**, **feeding**) **1** give food to a person or animal. **2** take food. **3** supply something to a machine etc. **feeder** *noun*

feed² *noun* **1** a meal. **2** food for animals.

feedback *noun* the return of information about an event or thing; a response.

feel¹ *verb* (**felt**, **feeling**) **1** touch something to find out what it is like. **2** be aware of something. **3** have an opinion. **4** give a certain sensation, *It feels warm*.
feel like (*informal*) want.

feel² *noun* the sensation caused by feeling something, *I like the feel of silk*.

feeler *noun* **1** a long thin projection on an insect's or crustacean's body, used for feeling; an antenna. **2** a cautious question or suggestion etc. to test people's reactions.

feeling *noun* **1** the ability to feel things; the sense of touch. **2** what a person feels. **3** an idea or opinion.

feign (*say* fayn) *verb* pretend.

feint¹ (*say* faynt) *noun* a sham attack or blow etc. meant to deceive an opponent.

feint² *verb* make a feint.

felicity *noun* **1** great happiness. **2** a pleasing manner or style, *He expressed himself with great felicity*. **felicitous** *adjective*, **felicitously** *adverb*

feline (*say* **feel**-I'n) *adjective* of cats; cat-like. [from Latin *feles* = cat]

fell¹ *past tense* of **fall**.

fell² *verb* cause to fall; cut or knock down, *They were felling the trees*.

fell³ *noun* a piece of wild hilly country, especially in the north of England.

fellow¹ *noun* **1** a friend or companion; one who belongs to the same group. **2** (*informal*) a man or boy. **3** a member of a learned society.

fellow² *adjective* of the same group or kind, *Her fellow teachers supported her*.

fellowship *noun* **1** friendship. **2** a group of friends; a society.

felon (*say* **fel**-on) *noun* a criminal. [from Latin *fellonis* = of an evil person]

felony (*say* **fel**-on-ee) *noun* (*plural* **felonies**) a serious crime.

felt¹ *past tense* of **feel**.

felt² *noun* a thick fabric made of fibres of wool or fur etc. pressed together.

female¹ *adjective* of the sex that can bear offspring or produce eggs or fruit.

female² *noun* a female person, animal, or plant.

feminine *adjective* of or like women; suitable for women. **femininity** *noun* [from Latin *femina* = woman]

feminist *noun* a person who believes that women should be given the same rights and status as men. **feminism** *noun*

▶▶ T H E S A U R U S ◀◀

fee *noun* brokerage, charge, commission, cost, dues, levy, payment, price, rate, remuneration, subscription, sum, tariff, toll.

feeble *adjective* debilitated, decrepit, delicate, frail, helpless, infirm, listless, poorly, puny, sickly, weak, weedy.

feed¹ *verb* **1** nourish, nurse, suckle. **2** browse, eat, graze; (*feed on*) dine on, live on, subsist on.

feedback *noun* reaction, response.

feel¹ *verb* **1** finger, fumble, grope, handle, manipulate, maul, paw, stroke, touch. **2** be aware of, be conscious of, experience, notice, perceive, sense, suffer, undergo. **3** believe, consider, reckon, think.

feeler *noun* **1** antenna, tentacle.

feeling *noun* **1** awareness, sensation. **2** compassion, concern, emotion, empathy, passion, sensitivity, sympathy, tenderness, understanding. **3** attitude, hunch, idea, impression, inkling, instinct, intuition, notion, opinion, premonition, sense, sentiment, suspicion, thought, view.

feign *verb* affect, fake, pretend, sham, simulate.

fell² *verb* chop down, cut down, knock down.

fellow¹ *noun* **1** associate, colleague, companion, comrade, mate, peer. **2** bloke (*informal*), boy, chap (*informal*), gentleman, guy (*informal*), lad, man.

fellowship *noun* **1** camaraderie, companionship, company, friendship, society. **2** association, brotherhood, club, fraternity, league, sisterhood, society, sorority.

felon *noun* criminal, culprit, lawbreaker, miscreant, offender, outlaw.

female¹ *adjective* see FEMININE.

female² *noun* see GIRL, WOMAN.

feminine *adjective* female, girlish, ladylike, womanly; see also EFFEMINATE.

femur (*say* **fee**-mur) *noun* the thigh-bone.

fen *noun* an area of low-lying marshy or flooded ground.

fence¹ *noun* **1** a barrier made of wood or wire etc. round an area. **2** a structure for a horse to jump over. **3** (*informal*) a person who buys stolen goods and sells them again.

fence² *verb* (**fenced**, **fencing**) **1** put a fence round or along something. **2** fight with long narrow swords (called *foils*) as a sport. **fencer** *noun* [from *defence*]

fend *verb* **fend for** provide things for someone. **fend off** keep a person or thing away from yourself. [from *defend*]

fender *noun* **1** something placed round a fireplace to stop coals from falling into the room. **2** something hung over the side of a boat to protect it from knocks.

fennel *noun* a herb with yellow flowers.

feral *adjective* wild, untamed.

ferment¹ (*say* fer-**ment**) *verb* bubble and change chemically by the action of a substance such as yeast. **fermentation** *noun*

ferment² (*say* **fer**-ment) *noun* **1** fermenting. **2** an excited or agitated condition.

fern *noun* a plant with feathery leaves and no flowers.

ferocious *adjective* fierce; savage. **ferociously** *adverb*, **ferocity** *noun* [from Latin *ferox* = bold, fierce]

ferret¹ *noun* a small animal used in catching rabbits and rats.

ferret² *verb* (**ferreted**, **ferreting**) **1** hunt with a ferret. **2** search; rummage. [from Latin *fur* = thief]

ferric or **ferrous** *adjectives* containing iron. [from Latin *ferrum* = iron]

ferry¹ *verb* (**ferried**, **ferrying**) transport people or things, especially across water.

ferry² *noun* (*plural* **ferries**) a boat or aircraft used in ferrying.

fertile *adjective* **1** producing good crops, *fertile soil*. **2** able to produce offspring. **3** able to produce ideas, *a fertile imagination*. **fertility** *noun*

fertilise *verb* (**fertilised**, **fertilising**) **1** add substances to the soil to make it more fertile. **2** put pollen into a plant or sperm into an egg or female animal so that it develops seed or young. **fertilisation** *noun*, **fertiliser** *noun*

fervent or **fervid** *adjectives* showing warm or strong feeling. **fervently** *adverb*, **fervency** *noun*, **fervour** *noun* [from Latin *fervens* = boiling]

fester *verb* **1** become septic and filled with pus. **2** cause resentment for a long time.

festival *noun* a time when people arrange special celebrations, performances, etc. [same origin as *feast*]

festive *adjective* of a festival; suitable for a festival, joyful. **festively** *adverb*

festivity *noun* (*plural* **festivities**) a festive occasion or celebration.

festoon¹ *noun* a chain of flowers or ribbons etc. hung as a decoration.

fence¹ *noun* **1** barricade, barrier, hoarding, palings, palisade, railing, stockade, wall.

fence² *verb* **1** (*fence in*) box in, close in, confine, coop up, enclose, hedge in, hem in, surround, wall in.

fend *verb* **fend for** look after, shift for, support, take care of.
fend off fight off, hold at bay, keep off, parry, repel, repulse, ward off.

ferocious *adjective* barbarous, bestial, bloodthirsty, brutal, cruel, fierce, ruthless, sadistic, savage, vicious, violent, wild.

ferret² *verb* **2** dig out, discover, forage, fossick (*Australian informal*), hunt, root out, rummage, search, unearth.

ferry¹ *verb* carry, convey, ship, shuttle, take, transfer, transport.

fertile *adjective* **1** fruitful, productive, rich. **3** creative, imaginative, inventive, productive, prolific, rich.

fertilise *verb* **1** compost, dress, feed, manure, top-dress. **2** impregnate, inseminate, pollinate.

fervent or **fervid** *adjective* ardent, devout, eager, earnest, emotional, enthusiastic, fanatical, impassioned, keen, passionate, vehement, warm, zealous.

fester *verb* **1** become infected, discharge, gather, putrefy, suppurate. **2** grow, intensify, rankle, smoulder.

festival *noun* anniversary, carnival, celebration, eisteddfod, fair, fête, fiesta, gala, holiday, jamboree, jubilee, pageant, party, show.

festive *adjective* cheerful, gay, happy, jolly, jovial, joyous, light-hearted, merry.

festivity *noun* celebration, gaiety, jollification, merrymaking, mirth, party, rejoicing, revelry, revels, roistering, wassailing (*old use*).

festoon¹ *noun* garland, wreath.

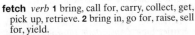

D I C T I O N A R Y

festoon² *verb* decorate with ornaments.

fetch *verb* **1** go for and bring back, *fetch some milk*; *fetch a doctor*. **2** be sold for a particular price, *The chairs fetched $20*.

fête¹ (*say* fayt) *noun* an outdoor fundraising event with stalls and sideshows.

fête² *verb* (**fêted, fêting**) honour a person with celebrations. [same origin as *feast*]

fetish *noun* an object supposed to have magical powers. [from Portuguese *feitiço* = a charm]

fetlock *noun* the part of a horse's leg above and behind the hoof.

fetter¹ *noun* a chain or shackle put round a prisoner's ankle.

fetter² *verb* put fetters on a prisoner.

fettle *noun* condition, *in fine fettle*.

fettler *noun* a railway maintenance worker.

feud (*say* fewd) *noun* a long-lasting quarrel or enmity.

feudal (*say* few-dal) *adjective* of the system used in the Middle Ages in which people could farm land in exchange for work done for the owner. **feudalism** *noun*

fever *noun* **1** an abnormally high body-temperature, usually with an illness. **2** excitement; agitation. **fevered** *adjective*, **feverish** *adjective*, **feverishly** *adverb*

few¹ *adjective* not many. **fewness** *noun*

few² *noun* a small number of people or things.

fez *noun* (*plural* **fezzes**) a high flat-topped red hat with a tassel, worn by Muslim men in some countries. [named after Fez, a town in Morocco]

fiancé (*say* fee-**ahn**-say) *noun* a man who is engaged to be married. [French, = betrothed]

fiancée (*say* fee-**ahn**-say) *noun* a woman who is engaged to be married.

fiasco (*say* fee-as-koh) *noun* (*plural* **fiascos**) a complete failure.

fib *noun* a lie about something unimportant. **fib** *verb*, **fibber** *noun*, **fibbing** *noun*

fibre *noun* **1** a very thin thread. **2** a substance made of thin threads. **3** indigestible material in certain foods that stimulates the action of the intestines. **fibrous** *adjective*

fibreglass *noun* **1** fabric made from glass fibres. **2** plastic containing glass fibres.

fibro *noun* (*Australian*) a building material made from glass fibre, cellulose fibre, etc. and cement, also **fibro-cement**.

fickle *adjective* constantly changing, not loyal to one person or group etc. **fickleness** *noun*

fiction *noun* **1** writings about events that have not really happened; stories and novels. **2** something imagined or untrue. **fictional** *adjective* [from Latin *fictio* = pretending]

fictitious *adjective* imagined; untrue.

fiddle¹ *noun* **1** (*informal*) a violin. **2** (*slang*) a swindle.

T H E S A U R U S

fetch *verb* **1** bring, call for, carry, collect, get, pick up, retrieve. **2** bring in, go for, raise, sell for, yield.

fête¹ *noun* bazaar, fair, gala, jumble sale; see also FESTIVAL.

fetter¹ *noun* (*fetters*) bonds, chains, irons, manacles, shackles.

feud *noun* conflict, dispute, quarrel, row, vendetta.

feverish *adjective* **1** burning, febrile, hot. **2** agitated, excited, frantic, frenetic, frenzied, hectic, restless.

few¹ *adjective* infrequent, rare, scarce, sparse, sporadic.

few² *noun* handful, remnant, sprinkling.

fiancé, fiancée *noun* betrothed, husband-to-be, intended, wife-to-be.

fiasco *noun* catastrophe, disaster, failure, fizzer (*Australian informal*), flop (*informal*), non-event, wash-out (*informal*).

fib *noun* fabrication, fairy story, falsehood, fiction, lie, porky (*slang*), story, untruth, white lie (*informal*).
fib *verb* lie, prevaricate.

fibre *noun* **1** filament, strand, thread.

fickle *adjective* capricious, changeable, erratic, inconsistent, inconstant, mercurial, mutable, temperamental, unfaithful, unpredictable, unreliable, vacillating, variable.

fiction *noun* **1** fable, fairy story, fantasy, legend, myth, novel, romance, story, tale. **2** fabrication, fib, invention, lie, make-believe.

fictitious *adjective* apocryphal, bogus, fabled, false, fanciful, fictional, imaginary, invented, legendary, made-up, mythical, phoney (*informal*), spurious, untrue.

fiddle¹ *noun* **1** violin. **2** fraud, racket, rort (*Australian slang*), scam (*slang*), swindle, swizz (*informal*).

▶▶ D I C T I O N A R Y ◀◀

fiddle² *verb* (**fiddled, fiddling**) **1** (*informal*) play the violin. **2** fidget or tinker with something, using your fingers. **3** (*slang*) swindle; get or change something dishonestly. **fiddler** *noun*

fiddly *adjective* small and awkward to use or do.

fidelity *noun* **1** faithfulness; loyalty. **2** accuracy; the exactness with which sound is reproduced. [from Latin *fidelitas* = faithfulness]

fidget¹ *verb* (**fidgeted, fidgeting**) **1** make small restless movements. **2** worry. **fidgety** *adjective*

fidget² *noun* a person who fidgets. [from a dialect word *fidge* = twitch]

field¹ *noun* **1** a piece of land with grass or crops growing on it. **2** a sportsground, *a football field.* **3** an area or section, *recent advances in the field of science.* **4** a battlefield. **5** those who are taking part in a race or outdoor game etc.

field² *verb* **1** stop or catch the ball in cricket etc. **2** be on the side not batting in cricket etc. **3** put a team into a match etc., *They fielded their best players.* **fielder** *noun*, **fieldsman** *noun*

fieldwork *noun* practical work or research done in various places, not in a library or museum or laboratory etc.

fiend (*say* feend) *noun* **1** an evil spirit; a devil. **2** a very wicked or cruel person. **3** an enthusiast, *a fresh-air fiend.* **fiendish** *adjective*

fierce *adjective* **1** angry and violent or cruel. **2** intense, *fierce heat.* **fiercely** *adverb*, **fierceness** *noun*

fiery *adjective* **1** full of flames or heat. **2** full of emotion. **3** easily made angry.

fife *noun* a small shrill flute.

fifteen *noun* & *adjective* **1** the number 15; one more than fourteen. **2** a team in Rugby Union football. **fifteenth** *adjective* & *noun*

fifth *adjective* & *noun* next after the fourth. **fifthly** *adverb*

fifty *noun* & *adjective* (*plural* **fifties**) the number 50; five times ten. **fiftieth** *adjective* & *noun*

fifty-fifty *adjective* & *adverb* **1** shared equally between two people or groups. **2** evenly balanced, *a fifty-fifty chance.*

fig *noun* a soft fruit full of small seeds.

fight¹ *noun* **1** a struggle against somebody using hands, weapons, etc. **2** an attempt to achieve or overcome something, *the fight against poverty.*

fight² *verb* (**fought, fighting**) **1** have a fight. **2** attempt to achieve something. **3** attempt to overcome something. **fighter** *noun*

▶▶ T H E S A U R U S ◀◀

fiddle² *verb* **2** fidget, finger, jiggle, juggle, mess about, muck around, play, tamper, tinker, toy, twiddle. **3** alter, cook (*informal*), doctor, falsify, fix.

fiddly *adjective* awkward, intricate, messy, ticklish, tricky.

fidelity *noun* **1** allegiance, devotion, faithfulness, loyalty. **2** accuracy, faithfulness, honesty, integrity, truthfulness.

fidget¹ *verb* **1** fiddle, jiggle around, shuffle, squirm, twitch, wriggle.

fidgety *adjective* jittery (*informal*), nervous, restive, restless, twitchy.

field¹ *noun* **1** lea (*poetical*), meadow, paddock, paddy (*for rice*), pasture. **2** arena, ground, oval, pitch, stadium. **3** area, domain, province, sphere, subject.

fiend *noun* **1** demon, devil, evil spirit. **2** beast, brute, monster, ogre. **3** addict, crank, devotee, enthusiast, fanatic, freak (*informal*), maniac, nut (*informal*).

fierce *adjective* **1** bloodthirsty, bloody, brutal, cutthroat, ferocious, merciless, relentless, savage, vicious, violent, wild. **2** extreme, great, intense, severe, strong.

fiery *adjective* **1** blazing, burning, flaming, hot, red-hot. **2** ardent, emotional, fervent, impassioned, intense, passionate, spirited, tempestuous, vehement. **3** hotheaded, impetuous, irascible, pugnacious, violent.

fight¹ *noun* **1** action, affray, aggression, altercation, argument, barney (*informal*), battle, blue (*Australian informal*), brawl, brush, campaign, clash, combat, conflict, confrontation, contest, dispute, duel, dust-up (*informal*), encounter, engagement, feud, fisticuffs, fracas, fray, free-for-all, hostilities, joust, mêlée, punch-up (*informal*), quarrel, row, scrap (*informal*), scrimmage, scuffle, set-to, skirmish, squabble, stoush (*Australian slang*), strife, struggle, tussle, war, wrestle; see also BOUT.

fight² *verb* **1** argue, battle, be at loggerheads, bicker, box, brawl, clash, combat, contend, duel, feud, grapple, joust, quarrel, scrap (*informal*), scuffle, skirmish, spar, squabble, stoush (*Australian slang*), strive, struggle, tussle, war, wrestle. **2** campaign, crusade, strive, struggle, take a stand. **3** defy, oppose, resist.

fighter *noun* aggressor, battler, boxer, campaigner, combatant, duellist, gladiator,

► DICTIONARY ◄

figment *noun* something imagined, *a figment of the imagination.*

figurative *adjective* using a figure of speech (see *figure*); metaphorical, not literal. **figuratively** *adverb*

figure[1] *noun* **1** the symbol of a number. **2** a diagram or illustration. **3** a pattern or shape; the shape of someone's body. **4** a representation of a person or animal in painting, sculpture, etc. **figure of speech** a word or phrase used for dramatic effect and not intended literally, e.g. '*a flood* of letters'.

figure[2] *verb* (**figured, figuring**) **1** imagine. **2** work out. **3** appear or take part in something. [from Latin *figura* = shape]

figurehead *noun* **1** a carved figure decorating the prow of a sailing-ship. **2** a person who is head of a country or organisation but has no real power.

filament *noun* a thread or thin wire. [same origin as *file*[4]]

filch *verb* steal something slyly; pilfer.

file[1] *noun* a metal tool with a rough surface that is rubbed on things to shape them or make them smooth.

file[2] *verb* (**filed, filing**) shape or smooth with a file.

file[3] *noun* **1** a folder or box etc. for keeping papers in order. **2** a set of papers kept in this. **3** a set of data stored under one reference in a computer. **4** a line of people one behind the other.

file[4] *verb* (**filed, filing**) **1** put into a file. **2** walk in a file, *They filed out.* [from Latin *filum* = thread (because a string of wire was put through papers to hold them in order)]

filial (*say* **fil**-ee-al) *adjective* of a son or daughter. [from Latin *filius* = son, *filia* = daughter]

filibuster *verb* try to delay or prevent the passing of a law by making long speeches. **filibuster** *noun*

filigree *noun* ornamental lace-like work of twisted metal wire.

fill[1] *verb* **1** make or become full. **2** block up a hole or cavity. **filler** *noun*

fill[2] *noun* enough to fill a person or thing.

fillet[1] *noun* a piece of fish or meat without bones.

fillet[2] *verb* (**filleted, filleting**) remove the bones from fish or meat.

filling *noun* **1** something used to fill a hole or gap, e.g. in a tooth. **2** something put in pastry to make a pie, or between layers of bread to make a sandwich.

filly *noun* (*plural* **fillies**) a young female horse.

film[1] *noun* **1** a motion picture, such as those shown in cinemas or on television. **2** a rolled strip or sheet of thin plastic coated with material that is sensitive to light, used for taking photographs or making a motion picture. **3** a very thin layer, *a film of grease.*

film[2] *verb* make a film of a story etc.

filmy *adjective* (**filmier, filmiest**) thin and almost transparent. **filminess** *noun*

filter[1] *noun* **1** a device for holding back dirt or other unwanted material from a liquid or gas etc. that passes through it. **2** a system for filtering traffic.

filter[2] *verb* **1** pass through a filter. **2** move gradually, *They filtered into the hall.* **3** move in a particular direction while other traffic is held up. [from *felt*[2], originally used for making filters]

filth *noun* disgusting dirt.

► THESAURUS ◄

guerrilla, marine, mercenary, partisan, pugilist, soldier, warrior, wrestler.

figure[1] *noun* **1** digit, integer, number, numeral. **3** body, build, form, outline, physique, shape. **4** effigy, figurine, image, sculpture, statue.

figure[2] *verb* **2** calculate, compute, work out. **3** appear, feature, play a part.

filament *noun* fibre, strand, thread, wire.

file[2] *verb* rub, shape, smooth.

file[3] *noun* **1** binder, folder, holder, portfolio. **2** dossier, papers, records. **4** column, line, queue, rank, row, string, train.

file[4] *verb* **1** arrange, catalogue, organise, pigeon-hole, put away, store. **2** march, parade, troop.

fill[1] *verb* **1** cram, jam, load up, occupy, pack, stuff. **2** block up, bung up, close, plug, seal, stop up.

filling *noun* **1** contents, padding, stuffing, wadding.

film[1] *noun* **1** feature, flick (*informal*), motion picture, movie, picture, video. **3** coating, covering, layer, sheet, skin.

film[2] *verb* photograph, record, shoot, video.

filter[1] *noun* **1** colander, screen, sieve, strainer.

filter[2] *verb* **1** clarify, purify, refine, sieve, strain. **2** leach, percolate, seep, trickle.

filth *noun* dirt, grime, gunge, gunk (*informal*), muck (*informal*), mud, slime, sludge.

▶▶ DICTIONARY ◀◀

filthy *adjective* (**filthier, filthiest**) **1** disgustingly dirty. **2** obscene. **filthiness** *noun*

fin *noun* **1** a thin flat part projecting from a fish's body, that helps it to swim. **2** a small projection on an aircraft or rocket etc., that helps its balance.

final¹ *adjective* **1** coming at the end, last. **2** that puts an end to an argument etc., *You must go, and that's final!* **finally** *adverb*, **finality** *noun*

final² *noun* the last in a series of contests. [same origin as *finish*]

finale (*say* fin-**ah**-lee) *noun* the final section of a piece of music or a play etc.

finalise *verb* (**finalised, finalising**) put into its final form. **finalisation** *noun*

finalist *noun* competitor in the final.

finance¹ *noun* the use or management of money.
finances *plural noun* money resources; funds.

finance² *verb* (**financed, financing**) provide the money for something. **financier** *noun* [from Old French *finer* = to settle a debt]

financial *adjective* **1** of finance. **2** (*Australian*) financially solvent. **financially** *adverb*

finch *noun* (*plural* **finches**) a small bird with a short stubby bill.

find¹ *verb* (**found, finding**) **1** get or see something by looking for it or by chance. **2** learn by experience, *He found that digging was hard work.*

find² *noun* something found.

fine¹ *adjective* **1** of high quality; excellent. **2** dry and clear; sunny, *fine weather.* **3** very thin; consisting of small particles. **4** in good health; comfortable, *I'm fine.* **finely** *adverb*, **fineness** *noun*

fine² *adverb* **1** finely, *chop it fine.* **2** (*informal*) very well, *That will suit me fine.* [same origin as *finish*]

fine³ *noun* money which has to be paid as a punishment.

fine⁴ *verb* (**fined, fining**) make somebody pay a fine. [from Latin *finis* = end (in the Middle Ages it referred to the sum paid to settle a lawsuit)]

finery *noun* fine clothes or decorations.

finesse (*say* fin-**ess**) *noun* clever management; artfulness. [French, = fineness]

finger¹ *noun* **1** one of the separate parts of the hand. **2** a narrow piece of something, *fish fingers.*

finger² *verb* touch or feel with your fingers.

fingerprint *noun* a mark made by the tiny ridges on the fingertip, used as a way of identifying someone.

fingertip *noun* the tip of a finger.
have something at your fingertips be very familiar with a subject etc.

finicky *adjective* fussy about details; hard to please.

▶▶ THESAURUS ◀◀

filthy *adjective* **1** blackened, dirty, dusty, grimy, grubby, muddy, soiled, squalid. **2** blue, coarse, crude, dirty, foul, improper, indecent, obscene, offensive, rude, smutty, vile, vulgar.

final¹ *adjective* **1** closing, concluding, end, finishing, last, ultimate. **2** conclusive, decisive, definitive, indisputable, irrevocable, unalterable.
finally *adverb* at last, eventually, in the end, lastly, once and for all, ultimately.

finale *noun* SEE ENDING.

finalise *verb* clinch, complete, conclude, finish, settle, sew up (*informal*), wrap up (*informal*).

finance¹ *noun* **finances** assets, capital, cash, funds, means, money, resources.

finance² *verb* back, fund, pay for, sponsor, subsidise, underwrite.

financial *adjective* **1** budgetary, economic, fiscal, monetary, pecuniary. **2** in funds, solvent.

find¹ *verb* **1** bring to light, chance upon, come across, come upon, detect, diagnose, dig up,

discover, identify, light on, locate, recover, regain, retrieve, spot, stumble on, trace, track down, uncover, unearth. **2** discover, learn.

fine¹ *adjective* **1** accomplished, brilliant, consummate, excellent, exceptional, exquisite, fantastic, first-class, first-rate, flawless, great, high-quality, impressive, magnificent, marvellous, masterly, meritorious, meticulous, outstanding, peerless, praiseworthy, prize, sensational, skilful, splendid, sterling, super (*informal*), superb, superior, superlative, top-notch (*informal*), wonderful. **2** balmy, bright, clear, fair, sunny. **3** (*a fine line*) narrow, slender, slim, thin; (*fine material*) delicate, diaphanous, filmy, flimsy, gauzy, gossamer, lacy, light, sheer, thin, transparent. **4** all right, comfortable, OK (*informal*), well.

fine³ *noun* charge, penalty, ticket.

fine⁴ *verb* book, charge, penalise.

finicky *adjective* choosy (*informal*), fastidious, fussy, particular, pernickety (*informal*), picky (*informal*).

▶▶▶ DICTIONARY ◀◀

finish¹ *verb* bring or come to an end.

finish² *noun* (*plural* **finishes**) **1** the last stage of something; the end. **2** the surface or coating on woodwork etc. [from Latin *finis* = end]

finite (*say* **fy**-nyt) *adjective* limited; not infinite, *We have only a finite supply of coal.*
finite verb a verb that agrees with its subject in person and number, '*was*', '*went*', *and* '*says*' *are finite verbs*; '*going*' *and* '*to say*' *are not.* [from Latin *finitum* = ended]

fiord (*say* fee-**ord**) *noun* an inlet of the sea between high cliffs, as in Norway. [a Norwegian word]

fir *noun* an evergreen tree with needle-like leaves, that produces cones.

fire¹ *noun* **1** the process of burning that produces light and heat. **2** destructive burning. **3** coal and wood etc. burning in a grate or furnace to give heat. **4** a device using electricity or gas to heat a room. **5** the shooting of guns, *Hold your fire!*
fire brigade a team of people organised to fight fires.
on fire burning.
set fire to start something burning.

fire² *verb* (**fired**, **firing**) **1** set fire to. **2** bake pottery or bricks etc. in a kiln. **3** shoot a gun; send out a bullet or missile. **4** dismiss someone from a job. **5** excite, *fire them with enthusiasm.* **firer** *noun*

firearm *noun* a small gun; a rifle, pistol, or revolver.

firebrand *noun* a person who stirs up trouble.

fire-engine *noun* a large vehicle that carries firemen and equipment to put out large fires.

fire-escape *noun* a special staircase or apparatus by which people may escape from a burning building etc.

firefly *noun* (*plural* **fireflies**) a kind of beetle that gives off a glowing light.

fireman *noun* (*plural* **firemen**) a member of a fire brigade.

fireplace *noun* an open structure for holding a fire in a room or (*Australian*) at a roadside stop.

fireside *noun* the part of the room near a fireplace.

firestick *noun* a stick used to light a fire, especially a smouldering one carried by Aboriginal people while travelling.

firewood *noun* wood for use as fuel.

firework *noun* a device containing chemicals that burn attractively or noisily.

firing-squad *noun* a group ordered to shoot a condemned person.

firm¹ *noun* a business organisation.

firm² *adjective* **1** not giving way when pressed; hard, solid. **2** steady; not shaking or moving. **3** definite and not likely to change, *a firm belief.* **firmly** *adverb.* **firmness** *noun*

firm³ *adverb* firmly, *Stand firm!*

firm⁴ *verb* make something become firm.

▶▶▶ THESAURUS ◀◀

finish¹ *verb* accomplish, achieve, cease, close, come to an end, complete, conclude, discontinue, end, finalise, get through, halt, round off, stop, terminate, wind up, wrap up (*informal*); see also CONSUME.

finish² *noun* **1** cessation, close, completion, conclusion, culmination, end, ending, finale, termination. **2** coating, exterior, surface, veneer.

finite *adjective* bounded, limited, measurable, restricted.

fire¹ *noun* **1** burning, combustion, flames. **2** blaze, bonfire, bushfire (*Australian*), conflagration, holocaust, inferno. **5** flak, fusillade, gunfire, salvo, shelling, shooting, volley.
on fire ablaze, aflame, alight, blazing, burning, in flames.

fire² *verb* **1** ignite, kindle, light, set ablaze, set fire to, set on fire. **3** open fire, shoot, snipe; (*fire a*

rocket) detonate, discharge, explode, launch, let off, set off. **4** discharge, dismiss, give someone notice, give someone the boot (*informal*), remove, sack (*informal*). **5** animate, excite, inspire, motivate, stimulate.

fireplace *noun* fire, grate, hearth, range.

fireworks *plural noun* crackers, pyrotechnics.

firm¹ *noun* business, company, concern, corporation, enterprise, establishment, organisation, partnership.

firm² *adjective* **1** compact, dense, hard, rigid, set, solid, stiff, unyielding. **2** fixed, secure, stable, steady, strong, sure, tight. **3** (*a firm belief*) adamant, definite, dogged, inflexible, obstinate, persistent, resolute, rigid, settled, staunch, steadfast, stubborn, unalterable, unchangeable, unshakeable, unwavering, unyielding; (*firm friends*) constant, dependable, faithful, loyal, reliable, steadfast.

firm⁴ *verb* compact, harden, jell, set, solidify, stiffen.

firmament *noun* the sky with its clouds and stars.

first¹ *adjective* **1** coming before all others in time or order. **2** coming before all others in importance. **firstly** *adverb*
first aid treatment given to an injured person before a doctor comes.
First Fleet the eleven ships arriving in Australia in 1788.

first² *adverb* before everything else, *Finish this work first.*

first³ *noun* a person or thing that is first.

firth *noun* an estuary or inlet of the sea on the coast of Scotland.

fiscal *adjective* of public finances. [from Latin *fiscus* = treasury]

fish¹ *noun* (*plural* **fish** or **fishes**) an animal that always lives and breathes in water.

fish² *verb* **1** try to catch fish. **2** search for something; try to get something, *He is only fishing for praise.*

fisherman *noun* (*plural* **fishermen**) a person who tries to catch fish.

fishery *noun* (*plural* **fisheries**) **1** the part of the sea where fishing is carried on. **2** the business of fishing.

fishmonger *noun* a shopkeeper who sells fish.

fishy *adjective* (**fishier, fishiest**) **1** smelling or tasting of fish. **2** (*informal*) causing doubt or suspicion, *a fishy excuse.* **fishily** *adverb*, **fishiness** *noun*

fissile *adjective* **1** likely to split. **2** capable of undergoing nuclear fission.

fission *noun* splitting something; splitting the nucleus of an atom so as to release energy.

fissionable *adjective* [from Latin *fissum* = split]

fissure (*say* **fish**-er) *noun* a narrow opening made where something splits.

fist *noun* a tightly closed hand with the fingers bent into the palm.

fisticuffs *noun* fighting with the fists.

fit¹ *adjective* (**fitter, fittest**) **1** suitable; good enough, *a meal fit for a king.* **2** healthy, *Keep fit!* **fitly** *adverb*, **fitness** *noun*

fit² *verb* (**fitted, fitting**) **1** be the right size and shape for something; be suitable. **2** put into place, *Fit a lock on the door.* **3** alter something to make it the right size and shape. **4** make suitable, *His training fits him for the job.* **fitter** *noun*

fit³ *noun* the way something fits, *a good fit.*

fit⁴ *noun* **1** a sudden illness, especially one that makes you move violently or become unconscious. **2** an outburst, *a fit of rage.*

fitful *adjective* happening in short periods, not steadily. **fitfully** *adverb*

fitment *noun* a piece of fixed furniture etc.

fitting *adjective* proper; suitable.

fittings *plural noun* the fixtures and fitments of a building.

five *noun* & *adjective* the number 5; one more than four.

fix¹ *verb* **1** fasten or place firmly. **2** make permanent and unable to change. **3** decide; arrange, *We fixed a date for the party.* **4** repair; put into working condition, *He is fixing my bike.* **fixer** *noun*
fix up arrange, organise.

first¹ *adjective* **1** earliest, initial, introductory, maiden (*voyage*), oldest, opening, original, preliminary. **2** basic, cardinal, chief, foremost, fundamental, greatest, highest, leading, main, major, premier, primary, prime, principal, supreme.

fish² *verb* **1** angle, go fishing, trawl. **2** fossick (*Australian informal*), hunt, look, probe, search, seek.

fishy *adjective* **2** doubtful, dubious, questionable, shady, strange, suspect, suspicious, suss (*informal*).

fissure *noun* cleft, crack, cranny, crevasse, crevice, opening, rift, slit, split.

fit¹ *adjective* **1** appropriate, fitting, proper, right, suitable, worthy. **2** hardy, healthy, in condition, in fine fettle, in training, robust, well.

fit² *verb* **1** belong, conform, correspond, dovetail, go, interlock, join, match, meet,

satisfy, suit. **2** assemble, connect, install, join, put together. **3** adapt, adjust, alter, modify, shape.

fit⁴ *noun* **1** attack, convulsion, paroxysm, seizure, spasm. **2** bout, burst, outbreak, outburst, paroxysm, spell.

fitful *adjective* erratic, haphazard, intermittent, irregular, occasional, spasmodic, sporadic, variable.

fitting *adjective* apposite, appropriate, apt, fit, proper, right, suitable, timely.

fix¹ *verb* **1** anchor, attach, cement, fasten, fit, glue, implant, install, mount, nail, peg, pin, plant, rivet, screw, secure, stick, tape. **3** agree on, appoint, arrange, decide on, establish, organise, set, settle on, specify. **4** correct, cure, mend, put right, rectify, remedy, repair, sort out.

▶▶DICTIONARY◀◀

fix² *noun* (*plural* **fixes**) **1** (*informal*) an awkward situation, *I'm in a fix.* **2** finding the position of something. **3** (*slang*) an addict's dose of a drug.

fixation *noun* **1** fixing something. **2** a strong interest or a concentration on one idea etc.; an obsession.

fixative *noun* a substance used to keep something in position or make it permanent.

fixedly *adverb* in a fixed way.

fixity *noun* a fixed condition; permanence.

fixture *noun* **1** something fixed in its place. **2** a sports event planned for a particular day.

fizz *verb* make a hissing or spluttering sound; produce a lot of small bubbles. **fizzy** *adjective*, **fizziness** *noun*

fizzer *noun* (*Australian*) a failure or fiasco.

fizzle *verb* (**fizzled, fizzling**) make a slight fizzing sound.
fizzle out end feebly or unsuccessfully.

fjord (*say* fee-**ord**) *noun* a fiord.

flabbergast *verb* astonish greatly.

flabby *adjective* fat and soft, not firm. **flabbily** *adverb*, **flabbiness** *noun*

flaccid (*say* **flak**-sid) *adjective* soft and limp. **flaccidly** *adverb*, **flaccidity** *noun*

flag¹ 1 a piece of cloth with a coloured pattern or shape on it, used as a sign or signal. **2** a small piece of paper or plastic that looks like a flag. **flag-pole** *noun*, **flagstaff** *noun*

flag² *verb* (**flagged, flagging**) **1** become weak; droop. **2** signal with a flag or by waving. [from an old word *flag* = drooping]

flag³ *noun* a flagstone. [from Old Norse *flaga* = slab of stone]

flagon *noun* a large bottle or container for wine or cider etc.

flagrant (*say* **flay**-grant) *adjective* very bad and noticeable, *flagrant disobedience*. **flagrantly** *adverb*, **flagrancy** *noun* [from Latin *flagrans* = blazing]

flagship *noun* a ship that carries an admiral and flies his flag.

flagstone *noun* a flat slab of stone used for paving. [from *flag³* + *stone*]

flail¹ *noun* an old-fashioned tool for threshing grain.

flail² *verb* beat as if with a flail; wave about wildly. [from Latin *flagellum* = a whip]

flair *noun* a natural ability, talent. [French, = power to smell things]

flak *noun* shells fired by anti-aircraft guns. [short for German *Fliegerabwehrkanone* = aircraft-defence-cannon]

flake¹ *noun* **1** a very light thin piece of something. **2** a small flat piece of falling snow. **flaky** *adjective*

flake² *verb* (**flaked, flaking**) come off in flakes.

flamboyant *adjective* very showy in appearance or manner. [French, = blazing]

flame¹ *noun* a tongue-shaped portion of fire or burning gas.

flame² *verb* (**flamed, flaming**) **1** produce flames. **2** become bright red.

flamingo *noun* (*plural* **flamingoes**) a wading bird with long legs, a long neck, and pinkish feathers.

▶▶THESAURUS◀◀

fix² *noun* **1** bind (*informal*), catch-22 (*informal*), difficulty, dilemma, hole (*informal*), jam (*informal*), mess, pickle (*informal*), plight, predicament, quandary, spot (*informal*).

fixation *noun* **2** infatuation, mania, obsession, preoccupation, thing (*informal*).

fixture *noun* **1** fitment, fitting. **2** engagement, event, match, meet, meeting.

fizz *verb* bubble, effervesce, fizzle, froth, hiss, sparkle, sputter.
fizzy *adjective* aerated, bubbly, carbonated, effervescent, sparkling.

fizzer *noun* damp squib, disappointment, failure, fiasco, flop (*informal*), non-event.

flabbergasted *adjective* astonished, astounded, confounded, dumbfounded, nonplussed, overwhelmed, speechless, staggered, stunned, surprised, thunderstruck.

flabby *adjective* flaccid, limp, soft, weak.

flag¹ *noun* **1** banner, colours, ensign, jack, pennant, standard, streamer.

flag² *verb* **1** decline, droop, fail, languish, tire, wane, weaken, weary, wilt. **2** hail, signal, wave.

flagrant *adjective* barefaced, blatant, brazen, conspicuous, glaring, gross, obvious, open, patent, scandalous, shameless, undisguised.

flair *noun* ability, aptitude, faculty, gift, knack, talent.

flake¹ *noun* **1** bit, leaf, piece, scale, shaving, sliver.

flamboyant *adjective* bright, colourful, extravagant, flashy, gaudy, lairy (*Australian informal*), ostentatious, showy, theatrical.

flame² *verb* **1** blaze, burn, flare.

▶▶ DICTIONARY ◀◀

flammable *adjective* able to be set on fire. **flammability** *noun*

flan *noun* a pastry or sponge shell with no cover over the filling.

flank¹ *noun* the side of something.

flank² *verb* place or be placed at the side of something or somebody.

flannel *noun* **1** a soft cloth for washing yourself. **2** a soft woollen material.

flap¹ *verb* (**flapped, flapping**) **1** wave about. **2** (*informal*) panic; fuss.

flap² *noun* **1** a part that is fixed at one edge on to something else, often to cover an opening. **2** the action or sound of flapping. **3** (*informal*) a panic or fuss, *in a flap*.

flare¹ *verb* (**flared, flaring**) **1** blaze with a sudden bright flame. **2** become angry suddenly. **3** become gradually wider.

flare² *noun* **1** a sudden bright flame or light. **2** a gradual widening.

flash¹ *noun* (*plural* **flashes**) **1** a sudden bright flame or light. **2** a device for making a sudden bright light for taking photographs. **3** a sudden display of anger, wit, etc. **4** a short item of news. **5** an instant.

flash² *verb* **1** make a flash. **2** appear suddenly; move quickly, *The train flashed past us.*

flashback *noun* going back in a film or story to something that happened earlier.

flashy *adjective* gaudy; showy.

flask *noun* **1** a bottle with a narrow neck. **2** a vacuum flask.

flat¹ *adjective* (**flatter, flattest**) **1** with no curves or bumps; smooth and level. **2** spread out; lying at full length, *Lie flat on the ground.* **3** (of a tyre) with no air inside. **4** (of feet) without the normal arch underneath. **5** absolute, *a flat refusal.* **6** dull; not changing. **7** (of a drink) having lost its fizziness. **8** (of a battery) unable to produce any more electric current. **9** (in music) one semitone lower than the natural note, *E flat.* **flatly** *adverb*, **flatness** *noun*

flat² *adverb* **1** so as to be flat, *Press it flat.* **2** (*informal*) exactly, *in ten seconds flat.* **3** (in music) below the correct pitch. **flat out** as fast as possible.

flat³ *noun* **1** a flat thing or area. **2** a set of rooms for living in, usually on one floor of a building. **3** (in music) a note one semitone lower than the natural note; the sign (♭) that indicates this.

flatten *verb* **1** make or become flat. **2** (*informal*) knock down.

flatter *verb* **1** praise somebody more than he or she deserves. **2** make a person or thing seem better or more attractive than they really are. **flatterer** *noun*, **flattery** *noun* [from Old French *flateri* = smooth down]

▶▶ THESAURUS ◀◀

flammable *adjective* combustible, inflammable.

flan *noun* pie, quiche, tart.

flank¹ *noun* face, side.

flank² *verb* border, edge, line.

flap¹ *verb* **1** flutter, swing, wave.

flap² *noun* **3** bother, flat spin (*informal*), fluster, panic, state, stew (*informal*), tizzy (*informal*).

flare¹ *verb* **1** blaze, burn, flame. **2** blow up, erupt, rage; see also BECOME ANGRY (at ANGRY). **3** broaden, widen.

flash¹ *noun* **1** blaze, flare, gleam, ray, shaft. **3** burst, display, spark. **5** instant, jiffy (*informal*), moment, second, split second, tick (*informal*), trice.

flash² *verb* **1** blink, flicker, gleam, glimmer, glint, sparkle, twinkle, wink.

flashy *adjective* flamboyant, garish, gaudy, jazzy, lairy (*Australian informal*), loud, ostentatious, pretentious, showy, snazzy (*informal*), tacky (*informal*), tasteless, tawdry.

flat¹ *adjective* **1** even, horizontal, level, plane, smooth, unruffled. **5** absolute, categorical, definite, firm, unqualified. **6** boring, dull, lacklustre, lifeless, monotonous, unemotional, uninteresting.

flat³ *noun* **2** apartment, bedsit (*British*), condominium (*American*), home unit (*Australian*), penthouse, tenement, unit (*Australian*).

flatten *verb* **1** compress, iron out, level, pat down, press, roll, smooth. **2** crush, demolish, destroy, knock down, level, raze, run over, squash, trample.

flatter *verb* **1** butter up (*informal*), compliment, crawl to, humour, play up to, praise, suck up to (*informal*), sweet-talk (*informal*). **2** become, do something for, suit.

flattery *noun* adulation, blandishments, cajolery, compliments, obsequiousness, praise, smooth talk, soft soap (*informal*), sweet talk (*informal*), sycophancy.

▶▶▶ DICTIONARY ◀◀◀

flaunt *verb* display something proudly, show it off, *They flaunted the trophy.*

Usage *Flaunt* is often confused with *flout.*

flavour¹ *noun* the taste of something.

flavour² *verb* give something a flavour, season it. **flavouring** *noun*

flaw *noun* something that makes a person or thing imperfect. **flawed** *adjective*

flawless *adjective* without a flaw; perfect. **flawlessly** *adverb*, **flawlessness** *noun*

flax *noun* a plant that produces fibres from which linen is made and seeds from which linseed oil is obtained.

flaxen *adjective* pale-yellow like flax fibres, *flaxen hair.*

flay *verb* strip the skin from an animal.

flea *noun* a small jumping insect that sucks blood.

fleck *noun* 1 a very small patch of colour. 2 a particle; a speck, *flecks of dirt.* **flecked** *adjective*

fledged *adjective* (of young birds) having grown feathers and able to fly. **fully-fledged** *adjective* fully trained, *a fully-fledged engineer.*

fledgeling *noun* a young bird that is just fledged.

flee *verb* (**fled**, **fleeing**) run or hurry away from something.

fleece¹ *noun* the woolly hair of a sheep or similar animal. **fleecy** *adjective*

fleece² *verb* (**fleeced**, **fleecing**) 1 shear the fleece from a sheep. 2 swindle a person out of some money.

fleet¹ *noun* a number of ships, aircraft, or vehicles owned by one country or company. [from Old English *fleot* = ships]

fleet² *adjective* moving swiftly; nimble.

fleeting *adjective* passing quickly; brief.

Flemish *adjective* of Flanders in Belgium or its people or language. **Flemish** *noun*

flesh *noun* 1 the soft substance of the bodies of people and animals, consisting of muscle and fat. 2 the pulpy part of fruits and vegetables. **fleshly** *adjective*

flex¹ *verb* bend or stretch something that is flexible, *flex your muscles.*

flex² *noun* (*plural* **flexes**) flexible insulated wire for carrying electric current. [from Latin *flexum* = bent]

flexible *adjective* 1 easy to bend or stretch. 2 able to be changed or adapted, *Our plans are flexible.* **flexibility** *noun*

flick¹ *noun* a quick light hit or movement.

flick² *verb* hit or move with a flick.

flicker¹ *verb* 1 burn or shine unsteadily. 2 move quickly to and fro or up and down.

flicker² *noun* a flickering light or movement.

flier *noun* a flyer.

▶▶▶ THESAURUS ◀◀◀

flaunt *verb* display, exhibit, parade, show off, sport.

flavour¹ *noun* piquancy, relish, savour, tang, taste.

flavour² *verb* season, spice.

flaw *noun* blemish, bug, defect, error, failing, fault, foible, imperfection, mistake, shortcoming, weakness.

flawless *adjective* faultless, immaculate, impeccable, perfect, spotless, unblemished.

fleck *noun* 1 dot, freckle, patch, speck, speckle, spot.

flee *verb* abscond, beat it (*slang*), bolt, decamp, disappear, do a bunk (*slang*), escape, leave, make tracks (*slang*), retreat, run away, scarper (*slang*), scram (*slang*), shoot through (*Australian informal*), skedaddle (*informal*), take flight, vanish.

fleece¹ *noun* coat, wool.

fleece² *verb* 2 cheat, con (*informal*), defraud, diddle (*informal*), rip off (*informal*), rob, swindle.

fleet¹ *noun* argosy (*poetical*), armada, convoy, flotilla, line, navy, squadron.

fleet² *adjective* fast, nimble, quick, rapid, speedy, swift.

fleeting *adjective* brief, ephemeral, momentary, passing, short-lived, temporary, transient, transitory.

flex² *noun* cable, cord, lead, wire.

flexible *adjective* 1 bendable, elastic, limber, lithe, pliable, resilient, springy, supple. 2 adaptable, adjustable, changeable, open, versatile.

flick² *verb* brush, flip, sweep, whisk. **flick through** flip through, leaf through, skim (through), thumb through.

flicker¹ *verb* 1 blink, glimmer, shimmer, twinkle, wink. 2 flutter, quiver, tremble, waver.

▶▶ DICTIONARY ◀◀

flight[1] *noun* **1** flying. **2** a journey in an aircraft etc. **3** a series of stairs. **4** the feathers or fins on a dart or arrow.

flight[2] *noun* fleeing; an escape.

flighty *adjective* (**flightier, flightiest**) silly and frivolous. **flightiness** *noun*

flimsy *adjective* (**flimsier, flimsiest**) **1** light and thin. **2** fragile; not strong. **flimsily** *adverb*, **flimsiness** *noun*

flinch *verb* move or shrink back because you are afraid; wince. **flinch** *noun*

fling[1] *verb* (**flung, flinging**) throw something violently or carelessly.

fling[2] *noun* **1** the movement of flinging. **2** a vigorous dance, *the Highland fling*. **3** a short time of enjoyment, *have a fling*.

flint *noun* **1** a very hard kind of stone. **2** a piece of flint or hard metal used to produce sparks. **flinty** *adjective*

flip[1] *verb* (**flipped, flipping**) **1** flick. **2** throw something into the air and make it turn over, *flip a coin*. **3** (*slang*) become crazy or very angry.

flip[2] *noun* a flipping movement.

flippant *adjective* not showing proper seriousness. **flippantly** *adverb*, **flippancy** *noun*

flipper *noun* **1** a limb that water-animals use for swimming. **2** a device that you wear on your feet to help you to swim.

flirt[1] *verb* behave lovingly towards somebody to amuse yourself. **flirtation** *noun*

flirt[2] *noun* a person who flirts. **flirtatious** *adjective*, **flirtatiously** *adverb*

flit *verb* (**flitted. flitting**) fly or move lightly and quickly. **flit** *noun*

flitter *verb* flit about. **flitter** *noun*

float[1] *verb* **1** stay or move on the surface of a liquid or in air. **2** make something float. **floater** *noun*

float[2] *noun* **1** a device designed to float. **2** a vehicle with a platform used for carrying a display in a parade etc. **3** a small amount of money kept for paying small bills or giving change etc.

flock[1] *noun* a group of sheep, goats, or birds.

flock[2] *verb* gather or move in a crowd.

flock[3] *noun* a tuft of wool or cotton etc.

floe *noun* a sheet of floating ice. [from Norwegian *flo* = layer]

flog *verb* (**flogged, flogging**) **1** beat hard with a whip or stick as a punishment. **2** (*slang*) sell. **flogging** *noun*

flood[1] *noun* **1** a large amount of water spreading over a place that is usually dry. **2** a great amount, *a flood of requests*. **3** the movement of the tide when it is coming in towards the land.

flood[2] *verb* **1** cover with a flood. **2** come in great amounts, *Letters flooded in*.

floodlight *noun* a lamp that makes a broad bright beam to light up a stage or building etc. **floodlit** *adjective*

▶▶ THESAURUS ◀◀

flight[1] *noun* **2** journey, trip.

flight[2] *noun* departure, escape, exit, exodus, fleeing, getaway, retreat.

flighty *adjective* capricious, changeable, erratic, fickle, frivolous, scatterbrained, scatty (*informal*), temperamental, unpredictable.

flimsy *adjective* **1** delicate, diaphanous, filmy, fine, gossamer, lacy, see-through, sheer, thin. **2** breakable, fragile, frail, gimcrack, jerry-built, ramshackle, rickety, shaky, weak.

flinch *verb* cower, cringe, draw back, duck, quail, recoil, shrink, wince.

fling[1] *verb* cast, catapult, chuck (*informal*), heave, hurl, launch, pitch, shy, sling, throw, toss.

flip[1] *verb* **2** flick, spin, throw, toss.
flip through flick through, leaf through, skim (through), thumb through.

flippant *adjective* cheeky, disrespectful, frivolous, glib, impertinent, jocular, light-hearted, offhand, pert.

flirt[1] *verb* (*flirt with*) chat up, dally with, lead on, philander with, trifle with.

flirt[2] *noun* coquette (*female*), philanderer (*male*), tease.

flit *verb* dart, flitter, flutter, fly.

float[1] *verb* **1** bob, drift, glide, hover, sail, waft.

flock[1] *noun* assembly, band, bevy, brood, bunch, cluster, collection, colony, community, company, congregation, contingent, crowd, drove, flight, gaggle, gathering, herd, horde, mob, multitude, pack, swarm, throng, troop.

flock[2] *verb* assemble, cluster, collect, congregate, converge, crowd, gather, herd, huddle, mass, mob, swarm, throng.

flog *verb* **1** beat, belt (*slang*), birch, cane, chastise, lash, scourge, thrash, whip.

flood[1] *noun* **1** deluge, inundation, spate, torrent. **2** deluge, outpouring, rush, shower, spate, stream, torrent, wave.

flood[2] *verb* **1** cover, deluge, drown, engulf, inundate, overflow, run a banker (*Australian*), submerge, swamp. **2** flow, pour.

▶▶ D I C T I O N A R Y ◀◀

floor¹ *noun* **1** the part of a room that people walk on. **2** a storey of a building; all the rooms at the same level.

floor² *verb* **1** put a floor into a building. **2** knock a person down. **3** baffle somebody.

floorboard *noun* one of the boards forming the floor of a room.

flop¹ *verb* (**flopped, flopping**) **1** fall or sit down clumsily. **2** hang or sway heavily and loosely. **3** (*informal*) be a failure.

flop² *noun* **1** a flopping movement or sound. **2** (*informal*) a failure.

floppy *adjective* hanging loosely; not firm or rigid. **floppiness** *noun*
floppy disk a flexible disc holding data for use in a computer.

flora *noun* the plants of a particular area or period. (Compare *fauna*.) [from the name of Flora, the ancient Roman goddess of flowers (Latin *flores* = flowers)]

floral *adjective* of flowers.

florin *noun* **1** a Dutch guilder. **2** a former coin worth 20 cents.

florist *noun* a shopkeeper who sells flowers.

floss *noun* silky thread or fibres. **flossy** *adjective*

flotation *noun* floating something.

flotilla (*say* flot-**il**-a) *noun* a fleet of boats or small ships. [Spanish, = little fleet]

flotsam *noun* wreckage or cargo found floating after a shipwreck.
flotsam and jetsam odds and ends.

flounce¹ *verb* (**flounced, flouncing**) go in an impatient or annoyed manner, *She flounced out of the room.* **flounce** *noun*

flounce² *noun* a wide frill.

flounder¹ *verb* **1** move clumsily and with difficulty. **2** make mistakes or become confused when trying to do something.

flounder² *noun* the common flat fish.

flour *noun* a fine powder of wheat or other grain, used in cooking. **floury** *adjective* [old spelling of *flower*]

flourish¹ *verb* **1** grow or develop strongly. **2** be successful; prosper. **3** wave something about dramatically.

flourish² *noun* (*plural* **flourishes**) a dramatic sweeping movement, curve, or passage of music. [from Latin *florere* = to flower]

flout *verb* disobey openly and scornfully, *They flouted the rules.*

Usage Do not confuse this word with *flaunt*, which has a different meaning.

flow¹ *verb* **1** move along smoothly or continuously. **2** gush out, *Water flowed from the tap.* **3** hang loosely, *flowing hair.* **4** (of the tide) come in towards the land.

flow² *noun* **1** a flowing movement or mass. **2** the movement of the tide when it is coming in towards the land, *the ebb and flow of the tide.*

flower¹ *noun* **1** the part of a plant from which seed and fruit develop. **2** a blossom and its stem used for decoration, usually in groups. [compare *flora*]

flower² *verb* produce flowers.

flowerpot *noun* a pot in which a plant may be grown.

▶▶ T H E S A U R U S ◀◀

floor¹ *noun* **2** deck, level, storey.

floor² *verb* **2** bowl over, fell, knock down. **3** baffle, bamboozle (*informal*), confound, confuse, dumbfound, flummox (*informal*), nonplus, perplex, stump (*informal*), throw.

flop¹ *verb* **1** collapse, drop, fall, loll, slump, tumble. **2** dangle, droop, hang down, sag.

flop² *noun* **2** disaster, failure, fiasco, fizzer (*Australian informal*), non-event, wash-out (*informal*).

floppy *adjective* baggy, drooping, flaccid, limp, loose, wilting.

flora *noun* botany, plants, vegetation.

flounce¹ *verb* march, stamp, stomp, storm, strut.

flounce² *noun* frill, furbelow, ruffle.

flounder¹ *verb* **1** bumble, fumble, stagger, struggle, stumble, wallow.

flourish¹ *verb* **1** bloom, blossom, burgeon, flower, grow, thrive. **2** be successful, boom, grow, prosper, succeed, thrive. **3** brandish, display, flaunt, wave.

flow¹ *verb* **1** circulate, course, move, proceed, run. **2** discharge, dribble, drip, gush, leak, ooze, pour, run, rush, seep, spill, spout, spurt, squirt, stream, trickle.

flow² *noun* **1** course, current, drift, flood, gush, influx, outflow, outpouring, spate, stream, tide, torrent.

flower¹ *noun* **1** bloom, blossom, bud. **2** (*flowers*) bouquet, corsage, garland, nosegay, posy, spray, wreath.

flower² *verb* bloom, blossom.

▶▶ D I C T I O N A R Y ◀◀

flowery *adjective* **1** full of flowers. **2** full of ornamental phrases.

flu *noun* influenza.

fluctuate *verb* (**fluctuated, fluctuating**) rise and fall; vary, *Prices fluctuated.* **fluctuation** *noun* [from Latin *fluctus* = a wave]

flue *noun* a pipe or tube through which smoke or hot gases are drawn off.

fluent (*say* **floo**-ent) *adjective* skilful at speaking; using a language easily and well. **fluently** *adverb*, **fluency** *noun* [from Latin *fluens* = flowing]

fluff *noun* a fluffy substance.

fluffy *adjective* having a mass of soft fur or fibres. **fluffiness** *noun*

fluid¹ *noun* a substance that is able to flow freely as liquids and gases do.

fluid² *adjective* able to flow freely, not solid or stiff. **fluidity** *noun* [from Latin *fluere* = to flow]

fluke *noun* a piece of good luck that makes you able to do something you thought you could not do.

flummox *verb* (*informal*) baffle.

fluorescent (*say* floo-er-**ess**-ent) *adjective* creating light from radiations. **fluorescence** *noun*

fluoridation *noun* adding fluoride to drinking-water.

fluoride *noun* a chemical substance that is thought to prevent tooth-decay.

flurry *noun* (*plural* **flurries**) **1** a sudden whirling gust of wind, rain, or snow. **2** an excited or flustered disturbance.

flush¹ *verb* **1** blush. **2** clean or remove something with a fast flow of water.

flush² *noun* **1** a blush. **2** a fast flow of water.

flush³ *adjective* **1** level; without projections, *The doors are flush with the walls.* **2** having plenty of money.

fluster *verb* make somebody nervous and confused. **fluster** *noun*

flute *noun* a musical instrument consisting of a long pipe with holes that are stopped by fingers or keys.

flutter¹ *verb* **1** flap wings quickly. **2** move or flap quickly and irregularly.

flutter² *noun* **1** a fluttering movement. **2** a nervously excited condition. **3** (*informal*) a small bet, *Have a flutter!*

flux *noun* continual change or flow.

fly¹ *noun* (*plural* **flies**) **1** a small flying insect with two wings. **2** a real or artificial fly used as bait in fishing.

fly wire a fine mesh to keep out flies.

no flies on (*Australian*) no lack of alertness, *There are no flies on today's young people.*

fly² *verb* (**flew, flown, flying**) **1** move through the air by means of wings or in an aircraft. **2** travel through the air or through space. **3** wave in the air, *Flags were flying.* **4** make something fly, *They flew model aircraft.* **5** move or pass quickly, *Time flies.* **6** flee from, *You must fly the country!* **flyer** *noun*

fly³ *noun* (*plural* **flies**) **1** flying. **2** the front opening of a pair of trousers.

flying doctor (*Australian*) a doctor who visits outback patients by air.

flying saucer a mysterious saucer-shaped object reported to have been seen in the sky.

flying squad a team of police or doctors etc. organised so that they can move rapidly.

▶▶ T H E S A U R U S ◀◀

flowery *adjective* **2** elaborate, embellished, florid, grandiloquent, high-flown, ornate.

fluctuate *verb* alternate, change, oscillate, see-saw, shift, swing, vacillate, vary, waver.

fluent *adjective* articulate, eloquent, smooth-spoken, voluble.

fluff *noun* down, fuzz, lint.

fluffy *adjective* downy, fleecy, furry, fuzzy, woolly.

fluid¹ *noun* gas, liquid, solution.

fluid² *adjective* flowing, gaseous, liquid, molten, runny, sloppy, watery.

fluke *noun* accident, chance, stroke of luck.

flush¹ *verb* **1** blush, colour, glow, redden. **2** clean out, rinse out, wash out.
flushed *adjective* florid, red, rosy, ruddy.

flush³ *adjective* **1** flat, level. **2** rich, wealthy, well in (*Australian informal*), well off.

flustered *adjective* agitated, bothered, confused, disconcerted, fazed (*informal*), in a dither, in a flap (*informal*), in a state, in a tizzy (*informal*), nervous, panicky, rattled (*informal*), ruffled, thrown (*informal*), upset.

flutter¹ *verb* **1** flit, flitter. **2** bat, beat, flap, palpitate, quiver, shake, tremble, vibrate, wave.

flutter² *noun* **2** dither, flap (*informal*), fluster, stir, tizzy (*informal*). **3** bet, gamble, punt, wager.

fly² *verb* **1** flit, flitter, flutter, glide, hover, soar, swoop, wing. **3** flap, flutter, wave. **5** burst, dart, dash, hurry, hurtle, race, run, rush, scoot, shoot, speed, sweep, tear, whiz, zoom.
flying *noun* aeronautics, aviation, flight.

flyleaf *noun* (*plural* **flyleaves**) a blank page at the beginning or end of a book.

flyover *noun* a bridge that carries one road or railway over another.

flywheel *noun* a heavy wheel used to regulate machinery.

foal¹ *noun* a young horse.

foal² *verb* give birth to a foal.

foam¹ *noun* **1** froth. **2** a spongy kind of rubber or plastic. **foamy** *adjective*

foam² *verb* form foam; send out foam.

fob¹ *noun* an ornament hanging from a watch-chain; a tab on a keyring.

fob² *verb* (**fobbed, fobbing**) **fob off** get rid of someone by an excuse or a trick.

focal *adjective* of or at a focus.

focus¹ *noun* (*plural* **focuses** or **foci**) **1** the distance from an eye or lens at which an object appears clearest. **2** the point at which rays etc. seem to meet. **3** something that is a centre of interest or attention etc.
in focus appearing clearly.
out of focus not appearing clearly.

focus² *verb* (**focused, focusing**) **1** use or adjust a lens so that objects appear clearly. **2** concentrate, *She focused her attention on it.* [Latin, = hearth (the central point of a household)]

fodder *noun* food for horses and farm animals.

foe *noun* (*old use*) an enemy.

foetus (*say* **fee**-tus) *noun* (*plural* **foetuses**) a developing embryo, especially an unborn human baby. **foetal** *adjective*

fog *noun* thick mist. **foggy** *adjective*

fogey *noun* (*plural* **fogies**) **old fogey** a person with old-fashioned ideas.

foghorn *noun* a loud horn for warning ships in fog.

foible *noun* a slight peculiarity in someone's character or tastes.

foil¹ *noun* **1** a very thin sheet of metal. **2** a person or thing that makes another look better in contrast.

foil² *noun* a long narrow sword used in the sport of fencing.

foil³ *verb* frustrate, prevent from being successful, *We foiled his evil plan.*

foist *verb* make a person accept something inferior or unwelcome, *They foisted the job on me.* [originally = dishonestly substitute a loaded dice]

fold¹ *verb* bend or move so that one part lies on another part.

fold² *noun* a line where something is folded.

fold³ *noun* an enclosure for sheep.

folder *noun* a folding cover for loose papers.

foliage *noun* the leaves of a tree or plant. [from Latin *folium* = leaf]

folk *noun* **1** people. **2** one's relatives.

folk-dance, folk-song *nouns* a dance or song in the traditional style of a country.

folklore *noun* old beliefs and legends.

follow *verb* **1** go or come after. **2** come next in order or time. **3** take a person or thing as a guide or example. **4** take an interest in the progress of events or a sport or team etc. **5** understand, *Did you follow what he said?* **6** result from something. **follower** *noun*

foal¹ *noun* colt (*male*), filly (*female*).

foam¹ *noun* **1** bubbles, froth, lather, suds. **2** rubber, sponge.

foam² *verb* bubble, effervesce, fizz, froth.

fob² *verb* **fob off** get rid of, offload, palm off (*informal*), pass off, unload.

focus¹ *noun* **3** centre, core, hub.

focus² *verb* **2** centre, concentrate, fix, home in, zero in.

fodder *noun* feed, food, forage, provender, silage.

foe *noun* adversary, antagonist, enemy, opponent, rival.

fog *noun* cloud, haze, mist, murkiness, smog. **foggy** *adjective* hazy, misty, murky.

foible *noun* failing, flaw, idiosyncrasy, peculiarity, quirk, shortcoming, weakness.

foil³ *verb* baffle, baulk, frustrate, hamper, hinder, obstruct, stonker (*Australian slang*), thwart.

fold¹ *verb* bend, crease, crimp, double over, pleat, wrinkle.

fold² *noun* crease, crinkle, gather, pleat, pucker, tuck, wrinkle.

fold³ *noun* compound, enclosure, pen, yard.

folder *noun* binder, cover, file, portfolio, ringbinder.

folk *noun* **2** family, kin, kinsfolk, parents, people, relations, relatives.

folklore *noun* beliefs, legends, lore, myths, traditions.

follow *verb* **1** chase, go after, hound, hunt, pursue, run after, shadow, stalk, tail (*informal*), track, trail. **2** come after, replace, succeed, supersede, supplant. **3** comply with, conform

following *preposition* after, as a result of, *Following the burglary, we had new locks fitted.*

folly *noun* (*plural* **follies**) foolishness, a foolish action etc. [from French *folie* = madness]

foment (*say* fo-**ment**) *verb* arouse or stimulate deliberately, *foment trouble.* [from Latin *fomentum* = poultice]

fomentation *noun* **1** fomenting. **2** hot liquid used to bathe an inflamed or aching part of the body.

fond *adjective* **1** loving. **2** foolishly hopeful, *fond hopes.* **fondly** *adverb,* **fondness** *noun* [from *fon* = a fool]

fondle *verb* (**fondled, fondling**) touch or stroke lovingly.

font *noun* a basin (often of carved stone) in a church, to hold water for baptism. [from Latin *fontis* = of a fountain]

food *noun* any substance that a plant or animal can take into its body to help it to grow and be healthy.

food chain a series of plants and animals each of which serves as food for the one above it in the series.

fool¹ *noun* **1** a stupid person; someone who acts unwisely. **2** a jester or clown, *Stop playing the fool.* **3** a creamy pudding with crushed fruit in it.

fool's paradise happiness that comes only from being mistaken about something.

fool² *verb* **1** behave in a joking way; play about. **2** trick or deceive someone.

foolery *noun* foolish acts or behaviour.

foolhardy *adjective* bold but foolish; reckless. **foolhardiness** *noun*

foolish *adjective* without good sense or judgement; unwise. **foolishly** *adverb,* **foolishness** *noun*

foolproof *adjective* easy to use or do correctly.

to, copy, emulate, heed, imitate, keep, obey, observe. **5** comprehend, cotton on to (*informal*), get (*informal*), grasp, latch on to (*informal*), take in, understand. **6** come next, ensue, result.

follower *noun* adherent, admirer, devotee, disciple, fan, hanger-on, supporter.

folly *noun* foolishness, idiocy, imprudence, insanity, lunacy, madness, recklessness, silliness, stupidity.

fond *adjective* **1** adoring, affectionate, caring, devoted, doting, indulgent, loving, tender, warm. **2** absurd, foolish, naïve, silly, vain.
fondness *noun* affection, attachment, devotion, love, tenderness, warmth.

fondle *verb* caress, cuddle, pat, pet, stroke, touch.

food *noun* chow (*slang*), delicacies, diet, eats (*informal*), fare, feed, fodder, foodstuff, forage, grub (*slang*), nosh (*slang*), nourishment, nutriment, produce, provender, provisions, rations, refreshments, sustenance, tucker (*Australian informal*), victuals.

fool¹ *noun* **1** ass (*informal*), blockhead, bonehead, boofhead (*Australian informal*), chump (*informal*), clot (*informal*), cretin, dill (*Australian informal*), dimwit (*informal*), dingbat (*informal*), dodo (*informal*), dolt, dope (*informal*), drongo (*Australian informal*), duffer, dummy (*informal*), dunce,

fat-head (*informal*), galah (*Australian slang*), gig (*Australian informal*), git (*informal*), goof (*slang*), goon (*slang*), goose (*informal*), half-wit, idiot (*informal*), ignoramus, imbecile, jerk (*slang*), lunatic, moron (*informal*), mug (*informal*), muggins (*informal*), nincompoop, ninny, nitwit (*informal*), nong (*Australian informal*), numskull, nut (*informal*), sap (*informal*), silly (*informal*), silly billy (*informal*), simpleton, sucker (*informal*), thickhead (*informal*), tomfool, twerp (*slang*), twit (*slang*), wally (*slang*). **2** buffoon, clown, comic, entertainer, jester, zany.

fool² *verb* **1** jest, joke, kid (*informal*), tease; (*fool around*) clown around, mess around, monkey about, play around, play the fool. **2** bluff, con (*informal*), deceive, delude, dupe, hoax, hoodwink, mislead, take in, trick.

foolhardy *adjective* bold, daredevil, daring, impetuous, imprudent, irresponsible, madcap, precipitate, rash, reckless, unwise.

foolish *adjective* absurd, barmy (*slang*), crazy, daft (*informal*), dopey (*informal*), fatuous, goofy (*slang*), half-witted, hare-brained, idiotic, illogical, imprudent, inane, insane, irrational, ludicrous, lunatic, mad, madcap, misguided, nonsensical, nutty (*informal*), potty (*informal*), ridiculous, senseless, short-sighted, silly, stupid, unintelligent, unwise, witless.

foolishness *noun* see FOLLY.

▶▶▷ D I C T I O N A R Y ◁◀◀

foot *noun* (*plural* **feet**) **1** the lower part of the leg below the ankle. **2** any similar part, e.g. one used by certain animals to move or attach themselves to things. **3** the lowest part, *the foot of the hill*. **4** a measure of length, 12 inches or about 30 centimetres, *a ten-foot pole*; *it is ten feet long*. **5** a unit of rhythm in a line of poetry, e.g. each of the four divisions in *Jack / and Jill / went up / the hill.*
on foot walking.

football *noun* **1** a game played by two teams which try to kick an inflated leather ball into their opponents' goal. **2** the ball used in this game. **footballer** *noun*

foothill *noun* a low hill near the bottom of a mountain or range of mountains.

foothold *noun* **1** a place to put your foot when climbing. **2** a small but firm position from which you can advance in business etc.

footing *noun* **1** having your feet placed on something; a foothold, *He lost his footing and slipped*. **2** a status, *We are on a friendly footing with that country.*

footlights *plural noun* a row of lights along the front of the floor of a stage.

footman *noun* (*plural* **footmen**) a male servant who opens doors, serves at table, etc.

footnote *noun* a note printed at the bottom of the page.

footpath *noun* a path for pedestrians.

footprint *noun* a mark made by a foot or shoe.

footsore *adjective* having feet that are painful or sore from walking.

footstep *noun* **1** a step taken in walking or running. **2** the sound of this.

footstool *noun* a stool for resting your feet on when you are sitting.

footy *noun* (*Australian informal*) football.

for¹ *preposition* This word is used to show (**1**) purpose or direction (*This letter is for you. We set out for home*), (**2**) distance or time (*Walk for six kilometres or two hours*). (**3**) price or exchange (*We bought it for $2. New lamps for old*). (**4**) cause (*She was fined for speeding*), (**5**) defence or support (*He fought for his country. Are you for us or against us?*), (**6**) reference (*For all her wealth, she is bored*), (**7**) similarity or correspondence (*We took him for a fool*).
for ever for all time; always.

for² *conjunction* because, *They hesitated, for they were afraid.*

for- *prefix* **1** away, off (as in *forgive*). **2** prohibiting (as in *forbid*). **3** abstaining or neglecting (as in *forgo, forsake*).

forage¹ *noun* **1** food for horses and cattle. **2** the action of foraging.

forage² *verb* (**foraged, foraging**) go searching for something; rummage.

foray *noun* a raid.

forbear *verb* (**forbore, forborne, forbearing**) **1** refrain from something, *We forbore to mention it*. **2** be patient or tolerant. **forbearance** *noun*

forbid *verb* (**forbade, forbidden, forbidding**) **1** order someone not to do something. **2** refuse to allow, *We shall forbid the marriage.*

forbidding *adjective* looking stern or unfriendly.

force¹ *noun* **1** strength; power; intense effort. **2** (in science) an influence, which can be measured, that causes something to move. **3** an organised group of police, soldiers, etc.
in or **into force** in or into effectiveness, *The new law comes into force next week.*
the forces a country's armed forces.

▶▶▷ T H E S A U R U S ◁◀◀

foot *noun* **1** hoof, pad, paw, trotter. **3** base, bottom.

foothold *noun* **1** footing, purchase, toehold.

footing *noun* **2** basis, standing, status, terms.

footpath *noun* footway, path, pavement, sidewalk (*American*).

footprint *noun* footmark, footstep, track.

forage¹ *noun* **1** feed, fodder, food, provender.

forage² *verb* fossick (*Australian informal*), hunt, poke around, ransack, rummage, scrounge, search.

foray *noun* assault, attack, incursion, invasion, offensive, raid.

forbearance *noun* indulgence, lenience, mercy, patience, self-control, tolerance.

forbid *verb* ban, bar, outlaw, prohibit, proscribe, veto.

forbidding *adjective* grim, harsh, hostile, inhospitable, menacing, off-putting, ominous, severe, stern, threatening, unfriendly, uninviting.

force¹ *noun* **1** effort, energy, exertion, might, power, pressure, strength, vigour. **3** body, corps, posse, squad, team, unit.
into force into effect, into operation, into play, into use.

▶▶ D I C T I O N A R Y ◀◀

force² *verb* (**forced, forcing**) **1** use force in order to get or do something, or to make somebody obey. **2** break something open by force. **3** cause plants to grow or bloom earlier than is normal, *You can force them in a greenhouse.*

forceful *adjective* strong and vigorous. **forcefully** *adverb*

forceps *noun* (*plural* **forceps**) pincers or tongs used by dentists, surgeons, etc.

forcible *adjective* done by force; forceful. **forcibly** *adverb*

ford¹ *noun* a shallow place where you can walk across a river.

ford² *verb* cross a river at a ford.

fore¹ *adjective* & *adverb* at or towards the front, *fore and aft.*

fore² *noun* the front part.
to the fore to or at the front; in or to a prominent position.

fore- *prefix* before (as in *forecast*); in front (as in *foreleg*).

forearm¹ *noun* the arm from the elbow to the wrist or fingertips.

forearm² *verb* arm or prepare in advance against possible danger.

forebears *plural noun* ancestors.

foreboding *noun* a feeling that trouble is coming.

forecast¹ *noun* a statement that tells in advance what is likely to happen.

forecast² *verb* (**forecast, forecasting**) make a forecast. **forecaster** *noun*

forecastle (*say* **foh**-ksul) *noun* the forward part of certain ships.

forecourt *noun* an enclosed area in front of a building etc.

forefathers *plural noun* ancestors.

forefinger *noun* the finger next to the thumb.

forefoot *noun* (*plural* **forefeet**) an animal's front foot.

forefront *noun* the very front.

foregoing *adjective* preceding; previous.

foregone conclusion a result that can be foreseen easily and with certainty.

foreground *noun* the front part of a scene or view etc.

forehand *noun* a stroke made in tennis etc. with the palm of the hand turned forwards.

forehead (*say* **fo**rrid or **for**-hed) *noun* the part of the face above the eyes.

foreign *adjective* **1** of or in another country; of other countries. **2** not belonging, unnatural, *Lying is foreign to her nature.* [from Latin *foris* = outside, abroad]

foreigner *noun* a person from another country.

foreleg *noun* an animal's front leg.

foreman *noun* (*plural* **foremen**) **1** a worker in charge of a group of other workers. **2** the leader of a jury who speaks on its behalf.

foremost *adjective* & *adverb* first in position or rank; most important.

forensic (*say* fer-**en**-sik) *adjective* of or used in lawcourts.
forensic medicine medical knowledge needed in legal matters.

▶▶ T H E S A U R U S ◀◀

force² *verb* **1** bully, coerce, compel, constrain, dragoon, drive, make, oblige, order, pressure. **2** break open, burst open, prise open, push open, wrench open.

forceful *adjective* aggressive, assertive, dynamic; effective, energetic, masterful, potent, powerful, pushy, strong, vigorous, weighty.

forebears *plural noun* ancestors, forefathers, predecessors, progenitors.

foreboding *noun* apprehension, forewarning, intuition, misgiving, omen, portent, pre- monition, presentiment.

forecast¹ *noun* outlook, prediction, prognosis, projection, prophecy.

forecast² *verb* foretell, forewarn, predict, prophesy.

forefathers *plural noun* ancestors, forebears, predecessors, progenitors.

forefront *noun* cutting edge, fore, lead, van, vanguard.

forehead *noun* brow.

foreign *adjective* **1** alien, exotic, imported, overseas, strange, unfamiliar. **2** alien, outside, uncharacteristic, unnatural.

foreigner *noun* alien, immigrant, new chum (*Australian informal*), newcomer, outsider, stranger, visitor.

foreman *noun* **1** boss, overseer, superintendent, supervisor. **2** spokesman, spokesperson, spokeswoman.

foremost *adjective* best, chief, greatest, leading, main, major, pre-eminent, premier, principal, supreme, top.

►►►DICTIONARY◄◄◄

forerunner *noun* a person or thing that comes before another; a sign of what is to come.

foresee *verb* (**foresaw, foreseen, foreseeing**) realise what is going to happen.

foreseeable *adjective* able to be foreseen.

foreshadow *verb* be a sign of something that is to come.

foreshorten *verb* show an object in a drawing etc. with some lines shortened to give an effect of distance or depth.

foresight *noun* the ability to foresee and prepare for future needs.

forest *noun* trees and undergrowth covering a large area. **forested** *adjective*

forestall *verb* prevent somebody or something by taking action first. [from Old English *foresteall* = ambush]

forestry *noun* planting forests and looking after them. **forester** *noun*

foretaste *noun* an experience of something that is to come in the future.

foretell *verb* (**foretold, foretelling**) forecast; prophesy.

forethought *noun* careful thought and planning for the future.

forever *adverb* continually, persistently.

forewarn *verb* warn someone beforehand.

foreword *noun* a preface.

forfeit[1] (*say* **for**-fit) *verb* pay or give up something as a penalty. **forfeiture** *noun*

forfeit[2] *noun* something forfeited.

forge[1] *noun* a place where metal is heated and shaped; a blacksmith's workshop.

forge[2] *verb* (**forged, forging**) **1** shape metal by heating and hammering. **2** copy something so as to deceive people. **forger** *noun*, **forgery** *noun*

forge[3] *verb* (**forged, forging**) **forge ahead** move forward by a strong effort.

forget *verb* (**forgot, forgotten, forgetting**) **1** fail to remember. **2** stop thinking about, *Forget your troubles.*

forget yourself behave rudely or thoughtlessly.

forgetful *adjective* tending to forget. **forgetfully** *adverb*, **forgetfulness** *noun*

forget-me-not *noun* a plant with small blue flowers.

forgive *verb* (**forgave, forgiven, forgiving**) stop feeling angry with somebody about something. **forgivable** *adjective*, **forgiveness** *noun*

forgo *verb* (**forwent, forgone, forgoing**) give something up; go without.

fork[1] *noun* **1** a small device with prongs for lifting food to your mouth. **2** a large device with prongs used for digging or lifting things. **3** a place where something separates into two or more parts.

►►►THESAURUS◄◄◄

forerunner *noun* ancestor, harbinger, herald, precursor, predecessor, prototype.

foresee *verb* anticipate, envisage, expect, forecast, foretell, predict, prophesy.

foresight *noun* far-sightedness, forethought, prescience, providence, vision.

forest *noun* brush, jungle, plantation, thicket, wood, woodland, woods.

forestall *verb* anticipate, foil, pre-empt, prevent, thwart.

foretaste *noun* preview, sample, token.

foretell *verb* forecast, foresee, predict, prophesy.

forethought *noun* foresight, planning, preparation.

forever *adverb* always, constantly, continually, eternally, everlastingly, incessantly, permanently, perpetually.

foreword *noun* introduction, preamble, preface, prologue.

forfeit[1] *verb* cede, forgo, give up, relinquish, renounce, sacrifice, surrender, waive.

forfeit[2] *noun* fine, penalty.

forge[1] *noun* furnace, smithy, workshop.

forge[2] *verb* **1** fashion, form, hammer out, mould, shape. **2** copy, counterfeit, fake, falsify. **forgery** *noun* copy, counterfeit, dud (*informal*), fake, fraud, imitation, phoney (*informal*), replica, reproduction, sham.

forget *verb* **1** leave behind, leave out, miss, neglect, omit, overlook, pass over, skip.

forgetful *adjective* absent-minded, careless, inattentive, neglectful, negligent, oblivious, remiss, scatterbrained, vague.

forgive *verb* absolve, excuse, exonerate, let off, overlook, pardon, remit. **forgivable** *adjective* excusable, pardonable, venial. **forgiveness** *noun* absolution, amnesty, exoneration, pardon, remission.

forgo *verb* abandon, abstain from, give up, go without, renounce.

fork[1] *noun* **3** bifurcation, Y-junction.

fork² *verb* **1** lift or dig with a fork. **2** form a fork by separating into two branches. **3** follow one of these branches, *Fork left.*
fork out (*slang*) pay out money.

fork-lift truck a truck with two metal bars at the front for lifting and moving heavy loads.

forlorn *adjective* left alone and unhappy.
forlorn hope the only faint hope left.

form¹ *noun* **1** the shape or appearance of something. **2** the way something exists, *Ice is a form of water.* **3** a kind or variety. **4** a class in school. **5** a bench. **6** a piece of paper with spaces to be filled in. **7** (of an athlete, horse, etc.) condition of health and training.

form² *verb* **1** shape or construct something; create. **2** come into existence; develop, *Clouds formed.*

formal *adjective* strictly following the accepted rules or customs; ceremonious.
formally *adverb*

formality *noun* (*plural* **formalities**) **1** formal behaviour. **2** something done to obey a rule or custom.

format *noun* the shape and size of something; the way it is arranged.

formation *noun* **1** the act of forming something. **2** a thing formed. **3** a special arrangement or pattern, *flying in formation.* [from Latin *formare* = to mould]

formative *adjective* forming or developing something.

former *adjective* of an earlier period; of past times. **formerly** *adverb*
the former the first of two people or things just mentioned.

formidable (*say* **for**-mid-a-bul) *adjective* frightening; difficult to deal with or do, *a formidable task.* **formidably** *adverb* [from Latin *formido* = fear]

formula *noun* (*plural* **formulae**) **1** a set of chemical symbols showing what a substance consists of. **2** a rule or statement expressed in symbols or numbers. **3** a list of substances needed for making something. **4** a fixed wording for a ceremony etc. **5** one of the groups into which racing-cars are placed according to the size of their engines. [Latin, = little form]

formulate *verb* (**formulated**, **formulating**) express clearly and exactly. **formulation** *noun* [from *formula*]

forsake *verb* (**forsook**, **forsaken**, **forsaking**) abandon.

fort *noun* a fortified building. [from Latin *fortis* = strong]

forte (*say* **for**-tay) *noun* a person's strong point. [from French *fort* = strong]

fork² *verb* **2** bifurcate, branch, divide, separate, split.

forlorn *adjective* dejected, depressed, desolate, disconsolate, forsaken, heavy-hearted, lonely, melancholy, miserable, sad, unhappy, woe-begone, wretched.

form¹ *noun* **1** appearance, arrangement, composition, configuration, construction, contour, design, figure, format, formation, layout, mould, organisation, outline, pattern, profile, shape, silhouette, structure. **3** brand, breed, class, edition, genre, genus, kind, model, sort, species, style, type, variety, version. **4** class, grade, year. **5** bench, seat. **6** application, coupon, document, paper, questionnaire. **7** condition, fettle, fitness, health, shape, trim.

form² *verb* **1** build, carve, cast, construct, create, establish, fabricate, fashion, forge, found, make, model, mould, produce, sculpt, set up, shape. **2** appear, develop, grow, materialise, take shape.

formal *adjective* (*a formal occasion*) ceremonial, official, solemn, stately; (*a formal manner*) ceremonious, conventional, dignified,

pompous, prim, proper, punctilious, reserved, starchy, stiff, stilted, strait-laced.

formality *noun* **1** ceremoniousness, ceremony, conventionality, decorum, punctiliousness, stiffness. **2** convention, custom, form, procedure, regulation, rite, ritual, rule.

format *noun* arrangement, design, form, layout, organisation, shape, size, structure.

former *adjective* ancient, bygone, earlier, old, olden, past, previous.
formerly *adverb* in the past, once, previously.

formidable *adjective* arduous, challenging, daunting, difficult, herculean, mammoth, onerous, overwhelming, tough.

formula *noun* **2** algorithm, rule, statement, theorem. **3** prescription, recipe.

formulate *verb* articulate, compose, express, form, frame, phrase, work out.

forsake *verb* abandon, desert, leave, reject.

fort *noun* see FORTRESS.

forte *noun* speciality, specialty, strength, strong point.

▶▶ D I C T I O N A R Y ◀◀

forth *adverb* **1** out; into view. **2** onwards; forwards, *from this day forth.*
and so forth and so on.

forthcoming *adjective* **1** about to come forth or happen, *forthcoming events.* **2** made available when needed, *Money for the trip was not forthcoming.* **3** (*informal*) willing to give information.

forthright *adjective* frank; outspoken.

forthwith *adverb* immediately.

fortification *noun* **1** fortifying something. **2** a wall or building constructed to make a place strong against attack.

fortify *verb* (**fortified, fortifying**) **1** make a place strong against attack, especially by building fortifications. **2** strengthen. [same origin as *fort*]

fortissimo *adverb* very loudly. [Italian]

fortitude *noun* courage in bearing pain or trouble. [from Latin *fortis* = strong]

fortnight *noun* a period of two weeks. **fortnightly** *adverb* & *adjective* [from an old word meaning 'fourteen nights']

fortress *noun* (*plural* **fortresses**) a fortified building or town. [same origin as *fort*]

fortuitous (*say* for-**tew**-it-us) *adjective* happening by chance. **fortuitously** *adverb* [from Latin, = accidental]

fortunate *adjective* **1** lucky. **2** favourable. **fortunately** *adverb*

fortune *noun* **1** luck; chance; fate. **2** a great amount of money. **fortune-teller** *noun* [from Latin *fortuna* = luck]

forty *noun* & *adjective* (*plural* **forties**) the number 40; four times ten. **fortieth** *adjective* & *noun*
forty winks a short sleep; a nap.

forum *noun* (*plural* **forums** or **fora**) **1** the public square in an ancient Roman city. **2** a meeting where a public discussion is held. [Latin]

forward¹ *adjective* **1** going forwards. **2** placed in the front. **3** having made more than the normal progress. **4** too eager or bold. **forwardness** *noun*

forward² *adverb* forwards.

forward³ *noun* a player in the front line of a team in football, hockey, etc.

forward⁴ *verb* **1** send on a letter etc. to a new address. **2** help something to improve or make progress.

forwards *adverb* **1** to or towards the front. **2** in the direction you are facing.

fossick *verb* (*Australian*) search or pick about for gold or other desirable things.

▶▶ T H E S A U R U S ◀◀

forthcoming *adjective* **1** coming, future, imminent, impending, prospective, upcoming. **3** communicative, expansive, responsive, talkative.

forthright *adjective* blunt, candid, direct, frank, open, outspoken, plain-spoken, straightforward, truthful, upfront (*informal*).

fortification *noun* **2** bastion, battlement, bulwark, parapet, rampart, stronghold.

fortify *verb* **1** defend, garrison, protect, reinforce, secure, strengthen. **2** boost, invigorate, strengthen, sustain.

fortitude *noun* boldness, bravery, courage, determination, endurance, grit, guts (*informal*), pluck, resoluteness, stoicism.

fortress *noun* acropolis, castle, citadel, fort, fortification, garrison, stronghold.

fortuitous *adjective* accidental, casual, chance, coincidental, random, serendipitous, unexpected, unintentional, unplanned.

fortunate *adjective* **1** blessed, favoured, happy, lucky, prosperous. **2** auspicious, favourable,

lucky, opportune, propitious, providential, timely.

fortune *noun* **1** chance, destiny, fate, luck, providence. **2** big bickies (*Australian informal*), bundle (*informal*), heaps (*informal*), megabucks (*informal*), mint, packet (*informal*), pile (*informal*), pots (*informal*), riches, wealth.
fortune-teller *noun* astrologer, clairvoyant, crystal-gazer, diviner, palmist, prophet, seer, sibyl (*female*), soothsayer.

forward¹ *adjective* **3** advanced, developed, early, precocious, quick. **4** assertive, audacious, bold, brazen, cheeky, fresh (*informal*), impertinent, impudent, pert, presumptuous, pushy, saucy.

forward⁴ *verb* **1** deliver, dispatch, readdress, redirect, send on. **2** advance, assist, foster, further, help, promote, support.

forwards *adverb* ahead, forward, frontwards, onwards.

fossick *verb* ferret, fish, forage, hunt, poke around, rake through, rummage, scavenge, scrounge, search.

▶▶ DICTIONARY ◀◀

fossil *noun* the remains or traces of a prehistoric animal or plant that has been buried in the ground for a very long time and become hardened in rock.
fossil fuel coal, oil, and natural gas.

fossilise *verb* (**fossilised, fossilising**) turn into a fossil. **fossilisation** *noun*

foster *verb* 1 bring up someone else's child as if he or she was your own. 2 help to grow or develop. **foster-child** *noun*, **foster-father** *noun*, **foster-mother** *noun* [from Old English *foster* = food]

foul¹ *adjective* 1 disgusting; filthy; tasting or smelling unpleasant. 2 (of weather) rough; stormy. 3 morally offensive, evil. 4 unfair; breaking the rules of a game. 5 colliding or entangled with something. **foully** *adverb*, **foulness** *noun*
foul play unfair play; a violent crime, especially murder.

foul² *noun* an action that breaks the rules of a game.

foul³ *verb* 1 make or become foul, *Smoke had fouled the air.* 2 commit a foul against a player in a game. 3 entangle or become entangled.

found¹ *past tense* of **find**.

found² *verb* 1 establish; provide money for starting, *They founded a hospital.* 2 base, *This novel is founded on fact.* [from Latin *fundus* = bottom]

foundation *noun* 1 the founding of something. 2 a base or basis. 3 the solid base on which a building is built up. **foundation-stone** *noun*

founder¹ *noun* a person who founds something, *the founder of the hospital.*

founder² *verb* 1 fill with water and sink, *The ship foundered.* 2 stumble; fall. 3 fail completely, *Their plans foundered.* [same origin as *found²*]

foundling *noun* a child found abandoned, whose parents are not known.

foundry *noun* (*plural* **foundries**) a factory or workshop where metal or glass is made.

fount *noun* (in poetry) a fountain.

fountain *noun* a device that makes a jet of water shoot up into the air.

fountain-pen *noun* a pen that can be filled with a supply of ink.

four *noun & adjective* the number 4; one more than three.
on all fours on hands and knees.

fourteen *noun & adjective* the number 14; one more than thirteen. **fourteenth** *adjective & noun*

fourth¹ *adjective* next after the third. **fourthly** *adverb*

fourth² *noun* 1 the fourth person or thing. 2 one of four equal parts; a quarter.

fowl *noun* a bird, especially one kept on a farm etc. for its eggs or meat.

fox¹ *noun* (*plural* **foxes**) a wild animal that looks like a dog with a long furry tail. **foxy** *adjective*

fox² *verb* deceive; puzzle.

foxglove *noun* a tall plant with flowers like the fingers of gloves.

▶▶ THESAURUS ◀◀

fossil *noun* relic, remains.

foster *verb* 2 advance, cultivate, encourage, further, nurture, promote.

foul¹ *adjective* 1 bad, disgusting, horrible, nauseating, noisome (*literary*), objectionable, obnoxious, off (*informal*), offensive, on the nose (*Australian informal*), putrid, rank, revolting, rotten, smelly, stinking, vile. 2 atrocious (*informal*), crook (*Australian informal*), dreadful (*informal*), lousy (*informal*), rough, shocking (*informal*), stormy, terrible (*informal*), wild. 3 (*a foul crime*) abhorrent, abominable, appalling, atrocious, beastly, contemptible, despicable, detestable, evil, loathsome, monstrous, shocking, terrible, vicious, vile, villainous, violent, wicked; (*foul language*) abusive, bad, blasphemous, coarse, crude, dirty, disgusting, filthy, impolite, indecent, obscene, offensive, rude, smutty, vulgar.

foul³ *verb* 1 contaminate, pollute, taint. 3 entangle, snarl, tangle.

found² *verb* 1 begin, create, establish, inaugurate, initiate, institute, originate, pioneer, set up, start. 2 base, build, ground, root.

foundation *noun* 1 establishment, institution, organisation. 2 base, basis, grounds, justification, support. 3 base, footing, substructure.

fountain *noun* fount, jet, shower, spout, spray, spring.

fox¹ *noun* cub (*young*), kit (*young*), vixen (*female*).
foxy *adjective* see CUNNING.

fox² *verb* baffle, bamboozle (*informal*), confound, flummox (*informal*), perplex, puzzle, stump, trick.

▶▶ DICTIONARY ◀◀

foyer *noun* the entrance hall of a theatre, cinema, or hotel. [French, = hearth]

fraction *noun* **1** a number that is not a whole number, e.g. ½, 0.5. **2** a tiny part. **fractional** *adjective*, **fractionally** *adverb* [same origin as *fracture*]

fractious (*say* **frak**-shus) *adjective* irritable. **fractiously** *adverb*, **fractiousness** *noun*

fracture[1] *noun* the breaking of something, especially of a bone.

fracture[2] *verb* (**fractured, fracturing**) break. [from Latin *fractum* = broken]

fragile *adjective* easy to break or damage. **fragilely** *adverb*, **fragility** *noun*

fragment *noun* **1** a small piece broken off. **2** a small part. **fragmentary** *adjective*, **fragmentation** *noun*, **fragmented** *adjective*

fragrant *adjective* having a pleasant smell. **fragrance** *noun*

frail *adjective* **1** (of things) fragile. **2** (of people) not strong; not robust, *a frail old man*. **frailty** *noun*

frame[1] *noun* **1** a holder that fits round the outside of a picture. **2** a rigid structure that supports something. **3** a human or animal body, *He has a small frame.* **4** a single exposure on a cinema film.
frame of mind the way you think or feel for a while.

frame[2] *verb* (**framed, framing**) **1** put a frame on or round. **2** construct, *They framed the question badly.* **3** make an innocent person seem guilty by arranging false evidence. **frame-up** *noun*

framework *noun* **1** a frame supporting something. **2** a basic plan or system.

franc *noun* a unit of money in Switzerland and many other countries.

franchise *noun* **1** the right to vote in elections. **2** a licence to sell a firm's goods or services in a certain area.

frank[1] *adjective* making your thoughts and feelings clear to people; candid. **frankly** *adverb*, **frankness** *noun*

frank[2] *verb* mark a letter etc. automatically in a machine to show that postage has been paid.

frankincense *noun* a sweet-smelling gum burnt as incense.

frantic *adjective* wildly agitated or excited. **frantically** *adverb* [from Greek *phrenetikos* = mad]

fraternal (*say* fra-**tern**-al) *adjective* of a brother or brothers. **fraternally** *adverb* [from Latin *frater* = brother]

fraternise *verb* (**fraternised, fraternising**) associate with other people in a friendly way. **fraternisation** *noun*

fraternity *noun* (*plural* **fraternities**) **1** a brotherly feeling. **2** a group of people who have the same interests or occupation, *the medical fraternity.*

▶▶ THESAURUS ◀◀

foyer *noun* entrance hall, lobby, vestibule.

fraction *noun* **2** bit, fragment, part, piece, portion, section.

fracture[1] *noun* break, cleft, crack, fissure, rift, rupture, split.

fracture[2] *verb* break, crack, rupture, split.

fragile *noun* breakable, brittle, delicate, flimsy, frail, weak.

fragment *noun* bit, chip, crumb, morsel, part, particle, piece, remnant, scrap, shred, sliver, snatch, snippet, speck, splinter; (*fragments*) smithereens.

fragrance *noun* aroma, balm, bouquet, odour, perfume, redolence, scent, smell.

frail *adjective* **1** delicate, flimsy, fragile, rickety, unsound, weak. **2** ailing, decrepit, feeble, infirm, sickly, weak.

frame[1] *noun* **1** border, case, edge, margin, mount, mounting, surround. **2** chassis, frame-work, shell, skeleton, structure, substructure. **3** body, build, figure, physique, skeleton.
frame of mind attitude, disposition, humour, mood, outlook, state, temper.

frame[2] *verb* **1** enclose, mount, surround. **2** compose, construct, devise, draft, formulate.

framework *noun* **1** chassis, frame, shell, skeleton, structure, substructure. **2** outline, plan, structure, system.

franchise *noun* **1** suffrage, right to vote, vote.

frank[1] *adjective* blunt, candid, direct, forthright, honest, open, outspoken, plain-spoken, straightforward, truthful, upfront (*informal*).

frantic *adjective* agitated, anxious, berserk, beside yourself, crazy, desperate, distraught, frenzied, hysterical, overwrought, panic-stricken, worried.

fraternise *verb* associate, consort, hobnob, mingle, mix, socialise.

▶▶ D I C T I O N A R Y ◀◀

fraud *noun* **1** criminal deception; a dishonest trick. **2** an impostor; a person or thing that is not what it pretends to be. **fraudulent** *adjective*, **fraudulently** *adverb*, **fraudulence** *noun*

fraught *adjective* filled; involving, *The situation is fraught with danger.* [from an old use, = loaded with freight]

fray¹ *noun* a fight; a conflict, *ready for the fray.* [same origin as *affray*]

fray² *verb* **1** make or become ragged so that loose threads show. **2** (of tempers or nerves) become strained or upset.

freak *noun* a very strange or abnormal person, animal, or thing. **freakish** *adjective*

freckle *noun* a small brown spot on the skin. **freckled** *adjective*

free¹ *adjective* (**freer**, **freest**) **1** able to do what you want to do or go where you want to go. **2** not costing anything. **3** not fixed, *Leave one end free.* **4** not having or affected by something, *free of responsibilities.* **5** available; not being used or occupied. **6** generous, *She is very free with her money.* **freely** *adverb*

free² *verb* (**freed**, **freeing**) **1** set free. **2** clear, disentangle.

freedom *noun* being free; independence.

freehand *adjective* (of a drawing) done without a ruler or compasses etc.

freehold *noun* possessing land or a house as its absolute owner, not as a tenant renting from a landlord.

Freemason *noun* a member of a certain secret society. **Freemasonry** *noun*

freestyle *adjective* (of a swimming race) in which any stroke may be used, in practice usually the crawl.

freeway *noun* a multi-laned highway for high-speed traffic.

freewheel *verb* ride a bicycle without needing to pedal.

freeze¹ *verb* (**froze, frozen, freezing**) **1** turn into ice; become covered with ice. **2** make or be very cold. **3** keep wages or prices etc. at a fixed level. **4** suddenly stand completely still.

freeze² *noun* **1** a period of freezing weather. **2** the freezing of prices etc.

freezer *noun* a refrigerator in which food can be frozen quickly and stored.

freezing works (*Australian*) an abattoir freezing animal carcasses for export.

freight (*say* frayt) *noun* **1** the transport of goods. **2** goods transported as cargo. **freight** *verb*

freighter (*say* **fray**-ter) *noun* a ship or aircraft carrying mainly cargo.

▶▶ T H E S A U R U S ◀◀

fraud *noun* **1** cheating, deceit, deception, dishonesty, duplicity, fraudulence, rorting (*Australian slang*), swindling, trickery. **2** charlatan, cheat, con man (*informal*), fake, humbug, impostor, phoney (*informal*), quack, sham, swindler, trickster.
fraudulent *adjective* crooked, deceitful, dishonest, false, phoney (*informal*), shady, shonky (*Australian informal*), unscrupulous.

frayed *adjective* ragged, shabby, tattered, tatty (*informal*), threadbare, unravelled, worn.

freak *noun* monster, monstrosity, mutant, oddity, weirdo (*informal*).
freakish *adjective* abnormal, atypical, bizarre, eccentric, exceptional, extraordinary, freak, odd, outlandish, peculiar, queer, strange, unusual, weird.

free¹ *adjective* **1** at liberty, emancipated, liberated, released. **2** complimentary, gratis, on the house (*informal*), unpaid. **3** detached, loose, unattached, untied. **4** exempt (from), immune (from), rid (of), without. **5** available, spare, uncommitted, unoccupied, vacant. **6** bountiful, generous, lavish, liberal, open-handed, unstinting.

free² *verb* **1** deliver, emancipate, excuse, exempt, let loose, let off, let out, liberate, release, relieve, rescue, save, set free, spare, uncage, unchain, unleash. **2** clear, detach, disengage, disentangle, extricate, loosen, untangle.

freedom *noun* **1** autonomy, deliverance, emancipation, independence, liberation, liberty, release, self-determination, self-government. **2** discretion, free hand, free rein, latitude, licence, scope.

freeway *noun* expressway, highway, motorway.

freewheel *verb* coast, drift, glide.

freeze¹ *verb* **1** ice over, turn to ice. **2** chill, cool, refrigerate. **3** fix, hold, peg. **4** halt, petrify, stop.
freezing *adjective* arctic, bitter, chilly, cold, frigid, frosty, ice-cold, icy, nippy (*informal*), perishing (*informal*), subzero.

freight *noun* **1** carriage, cartage, conveyance, haulage, shipment, shipping, transport. **2** cargo, consignment, goods, lading, load.
freight *verb* carry, cart, dispatch, forward, move, send, ship, transport.

▶▶▷ D I C T I O N A R Y ◁◀

French knitting a form of circular knitting in which the yarn is looped over hooks on a hollow reel. Also called *tomboy stitch*.

French window a long window that serves as a door on an outside wall.

frenzy *noun* wild excitement or agitation. **frenzied** *adjective*, **frenziedly** *adverb* [same origin as *frantic*]

frequency *noun* (*plural* **frequencies**) **1** being frequent. **2** how often something happens. **3** the number of oscillations per second of a wave of sound or light etc.

frequent¹ (*say* **freek**-went) *adjective* happening often. **frequently** *adverb*

frequent² (*say* frik-**went**) *verb* be in or go to a place often, *They frequented the club.* [from Latin *frequens* = crowded]

fresco *noun* (*plural* **frescoes**) a picture painted on a wall or ceiling before the plaster is dry. [Italian, = fresh]

fresh *adjective* **1** newly made or produced or arrived; not stale, *fresh bread.* **2** different or new, *a fresh approach.* **3** not tinned, not preserved, *fresh fruit.* **4** cool and clean, *fresh air.* **5** not salty, *fresh water.* **6** alert, not weary. **freshly** *adverb*, **freshness** *noun*

freshen *verb* make or become fresh.

freshwater *adjective* of fresh water not sea water; living in rivers or lakes.

fret¹ *verb* (**fretted, fretting**) worry or be upset about something. **fretful** *adjective*, **fretfully** *adverb*

fret² *noun* a bar or ridge on the fingerboard of a guitar etc.

fretsaw *noun* a very narrow saw used for making fretwork.

fretwork *noun* cutting decorative patterns in wood; wood cut in this way.

friable *adjective* easily crumbled.

friar *noun* a man who is a member of certain Roman Catholic religious orders, who has vowed to live a life of poverty. **friary** *noun* [from Latin *frater* = brother]

friction *noun* **1** rubbing. **2** disagreement, quarrelling. **frictional** *adjective* [from Latin *frictum* = rubbed]

fridge *noun* (*informal*) a refrigerator.

friend *noun* **1** a person you like who likes you. **2** a helpful or kind person.

friendless *adjective* without a friend.

friendly *adjective* behaving like a friend. **friendliness** *noun*

▶▶▷ T H E S A U R U S ◁◀

frenzy *noun* agitation, excitement, fever, hysteria, insanity, madness, mania.
  frenzied *adjective* agitated, berserk, crazy, delirious, demented, distraught, excited, feverish, frantic, frenetic, hectic, hysterical, mad, wild.

frequent¹ *adjective* common, constant, continual, eternal, familiar, habitual, incessant, perpetual, persistent, recurrent, regular, repeated.
  frequently *adverb* again and again, commonly, constantly, continually, habitually, often, regularly, repeatedly.

frequent² *verb* haunt, patronise, visit.

fresh *adjective* **1** latest, new, recent, up to date, up to the minute. **2** alternative, different, innovative, new, newfangled (*derogatory*), novel, original, untried. **4** clean, cool, crisp, pure, refreshing, unpolluted. **6** alert, energetic, invigorated, lively, perky, refreshed, revived.

freshen *verb* air, clean, deodorise, ventilate.

fret¹ *verb* brood, distress yourself, grieve, mope, pine, worry.
  fretful *adjective* anxious, distressed, miserable, peevish, restless, troubled, upset.

friar *noun* brother, monk, religious.

friction *noun* **1** abrasion, chafing, fretting, rubbing. **2** antagonism, conflict, contention, disagreement, discord, dissension, quarrelling, strife.

friend *noun* **1** acquaintance, ally, boyfriend, buddy (*informal*), chum (*informal*), cobber (*Australian informal*), companion, comrade, confidant, confidante, crony, girlfriend, mate, pal (*informal*), partner, penfriend, playmate, steady. **2** backer, benefactor, helper, patron, supporter, sympathiser.

friendly *adjective* affable, affectionate, amiable, amicable, approachable, brotherly, chummy (*informal*), companionable, convivial, cordial, familiar, genial, good-natured, gracious, hospitable, intimate, kind, kind-hearted, kindly, loving, matey, neighbourly, outgoing, pally (*informal*), sisterly, sociable, sympathetic, tender, warm-hearted, welcoming.
  friendliness *noun* affability, affection, amiability, amicability, approachability, camaraderie, conviviality, cordiality, geniality, goodwill, hospitality, kindness, neighbourliness, sociability, warmth.

DICTIONARY

friendship *noun* being friends.

frieze (*say* freez) *noun* a strip of designs or pictures round the top of a wall.

frigate *noun* a small warship.

fright *noun* **1** sudden great fear. **2** a person or thing that looks ridiculous.

frighten *verb* make or become afraid.
be frightened of be afraid of.

frightful *adjective* awful; very great or bad. **frightfully** *adverb*

frigid *adjective* **1** extremely cold. **2** unfriendly; not affectionate. **frigidly** *adverb*, **frigidity** *noun* [from Latin *frigidus* = cold]

frill *noun* **1** a decorative gathered or pleated trimming on a dress, curtain, etc. **2** something extra that is pleasant but unnecessary, *a simple life with no frills.* **frilled** *adjective*, **frilly** *adjective*

fringe *noun* **1** a decorative edging with many threads hanging down loosely. **2** a straight line of short hair hanging down over the forehead. **3** the edge of something. **fringed** *adjective*

frisk *verb* **1** jump or run about playfully. **2** search somebody by running your hands over his or her clothes. **frisky** *adjective*, **friskily** *adverb*, **friskiness** *noun*

fritter[1] *noun* a slice of meat or fruit or potato etc. coated in batter and fried. [from Latin *frictum* = fried]

fritter[2] *verb* waste something gradually; spend money or time on trivial things. [from an old word *fritters* = fragments]

frivolous *adjective* seeking pleasure in a light-hearted way; not serious, not sensible. **frivolously** *adverb*, **frivolity** *noun*

frizz *noun* hair curled into a wiry mass. **frizzy** *adjective*, **frizziness** *noun*

frizzle *verb* (**frizzled, frizzling**) **1** fry with a spluttering noise. **2** shrivel something by burning it.

fro *adverb* **to and fro** backwards and forwards.

frock *noun* a girl's or woman's dress.

frog *noun* a small jumping animal that can live both in water and on land.
a frog in your throat hoarseness.

frogman *noun* (*plural* **frogmen**) a swimmer equipped with a rubber suit, flippers, and breathing-apparatus for swimming and working underwater.

frolic[1] *noun* a lively cheerful game or entertainment. **frolicsome** *adjective*

frolic[2] *verb* (**frolicked, frolicking**) play about in a lively cheerful way.

from *preposition*. This word is used to show (**1**) starting-point in space or time or order (*We flew from Uluru to Perth. We work from 9 to 5 o'clock. Count from one to ten*), (**2**) source or origin (*Get water from the tap*), (**3**) separation or release (*Take the gun from him.*

THESAURUS

friendship *noun* alliance, amity, association, camaraderie, companionship, comradeship, cordiality, friendliness, harmony, mateship, partnership, relationship.

fright *noun* **1** alarm, anxiety, apprehension, consternation, dismay, dread, fear, horror, panic, scare, shock, start, terror, trepidation.

frighten *verb* alarm, cow, daunt, dismay, freak out (*informal*), horrify, intimidate, menace, perturb, petrify, put the wind up (*informal*), rattle (*informal*), scare, shock, startle, terrify, terrorise, unnerve.
frightened *adjective* afraid, alarmed, anxious, apprehensive, chicken (*informal*), faint-hearted, fearful, nervous, panic-stricken, petrified, scared, terrified, terror-stricken.
frightening *adjective* alarming, chilling, creepy, daunting, dreadful, eerie, fearful, fearsome, frightful, hair-raising, horrifying, nightmarish, scary, sinister, spine-chilling, spooky, terrifying.

frightful *adjective* appalling, awful, bad, dreadful, fearful, fearsome, ghastly, grisly,

gruesome, hideous, horrendous, horrible, horrid, horrific, shocking, terrible.

frill *noun* **1** flounce, ruff, ruffle. **2** addition, extra, supplement, trimming.

fringe *noun* **1** border, edge, edging, tassels. **3** borders, edge, limits, margin, outskirts, perimeter, periphery.

frisk *verb* **1** caper, cavort, dance, frolic, gambol, jump, leap, play, prance, romp, skip. **2** check, inspect, search.
frisky *adjective* active, frolicsome, lively, perky, playful, skittish, spirited.

fritter[2] *verb* (*fritter away*) dissipate, misspend, squander, waste.

frivolous *adjective* facetious, flighty, flippant, giddy, inane, irresponsible, light-hearted, petty, ridiculous, shallow, silly, superficial, trivial, unimportant.

frizzy *adjective* Afro, bushy, curly, fuzzy.

frock *noun* dress, gown, robe.

frolic[2] *verb* caper, cavort, frisk, gambol, let off steam, play, romp, skip.

►►DICTIONARY◄◄

She was freed from prison), (**4**) difference (*Can you tell margarine from butter?*), (**5**) cause (*I suffer from headaches*).

frond *noun* a leaf-like part of a fern, palm-tree, etc. [from Latin *frondis* = of a leaf]

front[1] *noun* **1** the part or side that comes first or is the most important or furthest forward. **2** a road or promenade along the seashore. **3** the place where fighting is happening in a war. **frontal** *adjective*

front[2] *adjective* of the front; in front. [from Latin *frontis* = of the forehead]

frontage *noun* the front of a building; the land beside this.

frontier *noun* the boundary between two countries or regions.

frontispiece *noun* an illustration opposite the title-page of a book.

frost[1] *noun* **1** powdery ice that forms on things in freezing weather. **2** weather with a temperature below freezing-point. **frosty** *adjective*

frost[2] *verb* cover with frost or frosting.
frosted glass glass made cloudy so that you cannot see through it.

frostbite *noun* harm done to the body by very cold weather. **frostbitten** *adjective*

frosting *noun* sugar icing for cakes.

froth *noun* a white mass of tiny bubbles on a liquid. **frothy** *adjective*

frown[1] *verb* wrinkle your forehead because you are angry or worried.

frown[2] *noun* a frowning movement or look.

frugal (*say* **froo**-gal) *adjective* **1** very economical and careful. **2** costing very little money; not plentiful, *a frugal meal*. **frugally** *adverb*, **frugality** *noun*

fruit[1] *noun* (*plural* **fruits** or **fruit**) **1** the seed-container that grows on a tree or plant and is often used as food. **2** the result of doing something, *the fruits of his efforts*. **fruity** *adjective*

fruit[2] *verb* produce fruit.

fruitful *adjective* producing good results, *fruitful discussions*. **fruitfully** *adverb*

fruition (*say* froo-**ish**-on) *noun* the achievement of what was hoped or worked for, *Our plans never came to fruition*. [from Latin *frui* = enjoy]

fruitless *adjective* producing no results. **fruitlessly** *adverb*

frustrate *verb* (**frustrated, frustrating**) prevent somebody from doing something; prevent from being successful, *frustrate their wicked plans*. **frustration** *noun* [from Latin *frustra* = in vain]

fry[1] *verb* (**fried, frying**) cook something in very hot fat. **fryer** *noun*

fry[2] *plural noun* very young fishes.

frying-pan *noun* a shallow pan for frying things.

fuchsia (*say* **few**-sha) *noun* an ornamental plant with flowers that hang down.

fudge *noun* a soft sugary sweet.

fuel[1] *noun* something that is burnt to produce heat or power.

fuel[2] *verb* (**fuelled, fuelling**) supply something with fuel.

fug *noun* (*informal*) a stuffy atmosphere. **fuggy** *adjective*, **fugginess** *noun*

fugitive (*say* **few**-jit-iv) *noun* a person who is running away from something. [from Latin *fugere* = flee]

►►THESAURUS◄◄

front[1] *noun* **1** beginning, bow (*of a ship*), façade, face, fore, forefront, frontage, head, start, van, vanguard.

front[2] *adjective* anterior, first, fore, initial, leading.

frontier *noun* border, boundary, limits.

frost[1] *noun* **1** hoar-frost, rime.

froth *noun* bubbles, foam, lather, scum, suds.

frown[1] *verb* glare, glower, grimace, knit your brow, lour, scowl.

frugal *adjective* **1** economical, parsimonious, penny-pinching, provident, sparing, thrifty. **2** meagre, paltry, scanty, skimpy.

fruit[1] *noun* **2** consequence, harvest, outcome, product, result, reward, upshot.

fruitful *adjective* fertile, productive, profitable, rewarding, successful, useful, valuable, worthwhile.

fruitless *adjective* abortive, barren, futile, ineffective, pointless, unproductive, unsuccessful, useless, vain.

frustrate *verb* baffle, baulk, block, check, foil, hamper, hamstring, hinder, impede, prevent, stonker (*Australian slang*), stop, stymie, thwart.

fry[1] *verb* brown, sauté.

fugitive *noun* deserter, escapee, renegade, runaway.

▶▶▶ D I C T I O N A R Y ◀◀◀

fugue (*say* fewg) *noun* a piece of music in which tunes are repeated in a pattern.

fulcrum *noun* the point on which a lever rests.

fulfil *verb* (**fulfilled, fulfilling**) **1** do what is required; satisfy; carry out, *You must fulfil your promises.* **2** make something come true, *It fulfilled an ancient prophecy.* **fulfilment** *noun*

full¹ *adjective* **1** containing as much or as many as possible. **2** having many people or things, *full of ideas.* **3** complete, *the full story.* **4** the greatest possible, *at full speed.* **5** fitting loosely; with many folds, *a full skirt.* **fully** *adverb*, **fullness** *noun*

full moon the moon when you can see its whole disc.

full stop the dot used as a punctuation mark at the end of a sentence or an abbreviation.

full² *adverb* completely; exactly, *It hit him full in the face.*

full-blown *adjective* fully developed.

fully *adverb* completely.

fulsome *adjective* praising something too much or too emotionally.

fumble *verb* (**fumbled, fumbling**) hold or handle something clumsily.

fume¹ *noun* (also **fumes**) strong-smelling smoke or gas.

fume² *verb* (**fumed, fuming**) **1** give off fumes. **2** be very angry. [from Latin *fumus* = smoke]

fumigate (*say* **few**-mig-ayt) *verb* (**fumigated, fumigating**) disinfect something by fumes. **fumigation** *noun*

fun *noun* amusement; enjoyment.
make fun of make people laugh at a person or thing.

function¹ *noun* **1** what somebody or something is there to do, *The function of a knife is to cut things.* **2** an important event or party. **3** a basic operation in a computer.

function² *verb* perform a function; work properly. [from Latin *functum* = performed]

functional *adjective* **1** working properly. **2** practical without being decorative or luxurious. **functionally** *adverb*

fund¹ *noun* **1** money collected or kept for a special purpose. **2** a stock or supply.
funds *plural noun* money resources.

fund² *verb* supply with money.

fundamental *adjective* basic. **fundamentally** *adverb* [from Latin *fundamentum* = foundation]

funeral *noun* the ceremony when a dead person is buried or cremated. [from Latin *funeris* = of a burial]

▶▶▶ T H E S A U R U S ◀◀◀

fulfil *verb* **1** accomplish, achieve, carry out, complete, comply with, conform to, discharge, execute, keep, live up to, meet, perform, satisfy.

full¹ *adjective* **1** brimming, bursting, chock-a-block, chockers (*Australian informal*), chock-full, congested, crammed, crowded, filled, jam-packed, overcrowded, overflowing, packed, stuffed. **2** abounding (in), rich (in), teeming (with). **3** complete, comprehensive, detailed, entire, exhaustive, thorough, total, unabridged, whole.

fumbling *adjective* awkward, bumbling, bungling, clumsy, inept.

fume¹ *noun* **fumes** exhaust, gas, smoke, vapour.

fume² *verb* **1** smoke, smoulder. **2** blow up (*informal*), blow your stack (*informal*), blow your top (*informal*), explode, flare up, lose your temper, rage, seethe, smoulder.

fun *noun* amusement, diversion, enjoyment, entertainment, frivolity, frolic, gaiety, hilarity, joking, jollity, kicks (*informal*), laughter, merriment, merrymaking, mirth, play, pleasure, recreation, relaxation, sport.
make fun of chiack (*Australian informal*), deride, jeer at, joke about, laugh at, mock,

parody, poke borak at (*Australian informal*), poke fun at, rib (*informal*), ridicule, satirise, send up (*informal*), sling off at (*Australian informal*), take the mickey out of (*informal*), taunt, tease.

function¹ *noun* **1** activity, duty, job, purpose, role, task, use. **2** affair (*informal*), ceremony, do (*informal*), event, gathering, occasion, party, reception.

function² *verb* act, behave, go, operate, perform, run, serve, work.

functional *adjective* **1** functioning, going, operational, running, working. **2** practical, serviceable, useful, utilitarian.

fund¹ *noun* **1** kitty, nest egg, pool, reserve. **2** hoard, mine, reserve, reservoir, stock, store, supply.
funds *plural noun* capital, cash, finances, means, money, resources, savings, wealth.

fund² *verb* back, finance, pay for, sponsor, subsidise.

fundamental *adjective* basic, cardinal, central, crucial, elementary, essential, important, key, primary, principal, underlying, vital.

funeral *noun* burial, cremation, interment.

►►DICTIONARY◄◄

funereal (*say* few-**neer**-ee-al) *adjective* dark; dismal.

fungus *noun* (*plural* **fungi**, *say* **fung**-I) a plant without leaves or flowers that grows on other plants or on decayed material, *Mushrooms are fungi.*

funk¹ *noun* (*slang*) **1** fear. **2** a coward.

funk² *verb* (*slang*) be afraid of doing something and avoid it.

funnel *noun* **1** a metal chimney on a ship or steam-engine. **2** a tube that is wide at the top and narrow at the bottom to help you pour things into a narrow opening. [from Latin *fundere* = pour]

funnel-web *noun* a venomous spider.

funny *adjective* (**funnier, funniest**) **1** that makes you laugh or smile. **2** strange; odd, *a funny smell*. **funnily** *adverb*

fur *noun* **1** the soft hair that covers some animals. **2** animal skin with the fur on it, used for clothing; fabric that looks like animal fur.

furbelows *plural noun* showy trimmings, *frills and furbelows.*

furbish *verb* polish or clean; renovate.

furious *adjective* **1** very angry. **2** violent; intense, *furious heat*. **furiously** *adverb*

furl *verb* roll up a sail, flag, or umbrella.

furlong *noun* one-eighth of a mile, about 200 metres.

furlough (*say* **ferl**-oh) *noun* leave of absence from duty; a holiday.

furnace *noun* a device in which great heat can be produced, e.g. for melting metals or making glass.

furnish *verb* **1** provide a place with furniture. **2** provide; supply.

furnishings *plural noun* furniture and fitments, curtains, etc.

furniture *noun* tables, chairs, and other movable things that you need in a house or school or office etc.

furore (*say* few-**ror**-ee) *noun* an excited or angry uproar. [from Latin *furor* = madness]

furphy *noun* (*Australian informal*) a rumour, a false report.

furrow¹ *noun* **1** a long cut in the ground made by a plough or other implement. **2** a groove. **3** a deep wrinkle in the skin.

furrow² *verb* make furrows in something.

furry *adjective* like fur; covered with fur.

further¹ *adverb & adjective* **1** at or to a greater distance; more distant. **2** more; additional, *We made further enquiries.*
further education education beyond secondary school.

further² *verb* help something to progress, *This success will further your career*. **furtherance** *noun*

furthermore *adverb* also; moreover.

furthest *adverb & adjective* at or to the greatest distance; most distant.

furtive *adjective* stealthy; trying not to be seen. **furtively** *adverb*, **furtiveness** *noun* [from Latin *furtivus* = stolen]

►►THESAURUS◄◄

funnel *noun* **1** chimney, smokestack.

funny *adjective* **1** amusing, comical, crazy, droll, entertaining, facetious, farcical, hilarious, humorous, laughable, ludicrous, priceless (*informal*), ridiculous, witty, zany. **2** abnormal, bizarre, curious, extraordinary, odd, peculiar, queer, strange, unusual, weird.

fur *noun* **1** coat, down, fleece, hair. **2** hide, pelt, skin.

furious *adjective* **1** angry, cross, enraged, hopping mad (*informal*), incensed, indignant, infuriated, irate, livid, mad, rabid, ropeable (*Australian informal*), wrathful. **2** fierce, intense, raging, savage, tempestuous, violent, wild.

furnace *noun* boiler, forge, incinerator, kiln, oven.

furnish *verb* **2** arm, equip, fit out, provide, supply.

furniture *noun* effects, furnishings, movables.

furore *noun* commotion, hullabaloo, rumpus, stir, storm, to-do, uproar.

furrow¹ *noun* **1** channel, ditch, drill, rut, trench. **2** channel, corrugation, groove, hollow, rut. **3** crease, line, wrinkle.

furry *adjective* downy, fleecy, fluffy, fuzzy, hairy, woolly.

further¹ *adjective* **2** additional, extra, fresh, more, new, other, supplementary.

further² *verb* advance, aid, assist, boost, champion, forward, help, promote.

furthermore *adverb* also, besides, in addition, moreover, too.

furthest *adjective* extreme, farthest, furthermost, outermost, ultimate, uttermost.

furtive *adjective* clandestine, covert, secretive, shifty, sly, sneaky, stealthy, surreptitious, wily.

fury *noun* wild anger; rage. [from Latin *furia* = rage; an avenging spirit]

furze *noun* gorse.

fuse[1] *noun* a safety device containing a short piece of wire that melts if too much electricity is passed through it.

fuse[2] *verb* (**fused, fusing**) **1** stop working because a fuse has melted. **2** blend together, especially through melting. [from Latin *fusum* = melted]

fuse[3] *noun* a length of material that burns easily, used for setting off an explosive. [from Latin *fusus* = a spindle]

fuselage (*say* **few**-zel-ah*zh*) *noun* the body of an aircraft.

fusillade (*say* few-zil-**ayd**) *noun* a great outburst of firing guns or questions etc. [from French *fusil* = gun]

fusion *noun* **1** the action of blending or uniting things. **2** the uniting of atomic nuclei, usually releasing energy.

fuss[1] *noun* (*plural* **fusses**) **1** unnecessary excitement or bustle. **2** an agitated protest.

fuss[2] *verb* make a fuss about something.

fussy *adjective* (**fussier, fussiest**) **1** fussing; inclined to make a fuss. **2** choosing very carefully; hard to please. **3** full of unnecessary details or decorations. **fussily** *adverb*, **fussiness** *noun*

fusty *adjective* (**fustier, fustiest**) smelling stale or stuffy. **fustiness** *noun*

futile (*say* **few**-tyl) *noun* useless; having no result. **futility** *noun* [from Latin *futilis* = leaking]

future[1] *noun* the time that will come; what is going to happen then.

future[2] *adjective* belonging or referring to the future.

fuzz *noun* something fluffy or frizzy.

fuzzy *adjective* **1** like fuzz; covered with fuzz. **2** blurred; not clear. **fuzzily** *adverb*, **fuzziness** *noun*

fury *noun* anger, exasperation, frenzy, ire, paddy (*informal*), rage, temper, wrath.

fuse[2] *verb* **2** amalgamate, blend, bond, coalesce, combine, consolidate, incorporate, merge, stick, synthesise, unite, weld.

fuss[1] *noun* **1** ado, bother, bustle, commotion, excitement, flurry, fluster, furore, hue and cry, hullabaloo, kerfuffle (*informal*), palaver (*informal*), rumpus, stir, to-do, uproar.

fuss[2] *verb* carry on, complain, create (*slang*), flap (*informal*), fret, niggle, quibble, worry.

fussy *adjective* **2** choosy (*informal*), faddy, fastidious, finicky, hard to please, particular,

pernickety (*informal*), picky (*informal*), selective. **3** busy, cluttered, detailed, elaborate, fancy, intricate, ornate.

futile *adjective* fruitless, ineffective, ineffectual, pointless, senseless, unproductive, unsuccessful, useless, vain, worthless.

future[1] *noun* hereafter, outlook, prospect.

future[2] *adjective* approaching, coming, forthcoming, prospective, subsequent.

fuzzy *adjective* **1** downy, fleecy, fluffy, frizzy, furry, woolly. **2** blurred, dim, hazy, imprecise, indistinct, unclear, vague, woolly.

▶ Gg ◀

gabardine *noun* a strong fabric woven in a slanting pattern.

gabble *verb* (**gabbled**, **gabbling**) talk so quickly that it is difficult to know what is being said.

gable *noun* the pointed part at the top of an outside wall, between two sloping roofs. **gabled** *adjective*

gad *verb* (**gadded**, **gadding**) **gad about** gallivant. **gadabout** *noun*

gadget *noun* any small useful tool. **gadgetry** *noun*

Gaelic (*say* **gay**-lik) *noun* the Celtic languages of Scotland and Ireland.

gaff *noun* a stick with a metal hook for landing large fish.

gag¹ *noun* **1** something put into a person's mouth or tied over it to prevent speaking. **2** a joke.

gag² *verb* (**gagged**, **gagging**) **1** put a gag on a person. **2** prevent from making comments, *We cannot gag the press.* **3** retch.

gaiety *noun* cheerfulness.

gaily *adverb* in a cheerful way.

gain¹ *verb* **1** get something that you did not have before; obtain. **2** (of a clock or watch) become ahead of the correct time. **3** reach; arrive at, *At last we gained the shore.* **gainer** *noun*

gain on come closer to a person or thing in chasing them or in a race.

gain² *noun* something gained; a profit or improvement. **gainful** *adjective*
gains *plural noun* money made from trade etc.

gait *noun* a way of walking or running, *He walked with a shuffling gait.* [from a dialect word *gate* = going]

gaiter *noun* a leather or cloth covering for the lower part of the leg.

gala (*say* **gah**-la) *noun* **1** a celebration with cheerful festivities. **2** a set of sports contests.

galah (*say* ga-**lah**) *noun* (*Australian*) **1** a rose-breasted cockatoo with a grey back. **2** (*slang*) a fool or simpleton.

galaxy *noun* (*plural* **galaxies**) a very large group of stars. **galactic** *adjective*

gale *noun* a very strong wind.

gall¹ (*say* gawl) *noun* **1** bile. **2** bitterness of feeling. **3** (*slang*) impudence.

gall² (*say* gawl) *noun* a sore spot on an animal's skin.

gall³ *verb* **1** rub sore. **2** vex or humiliate someone.

gallant (*say* **gal**-lant) *adjective* **1** brave; chivalrous. **2** fine; stately, *our gallant ship.* **gallantly** *adverb*, **gallantry** *noun*

▶▶▶ THESAURUS ◀◀◀

gabble *verb* babble, chatter, jabber, prattle, yabber (*Australian informal*).

gadget *noun* apparatus, appliance, contraption (*informal*), device, gizmo (*informal*), implement, instrument, machine, tool, utensil.

gag¹ *noun* **2** jest, joke, quip, wisecrack, witticism.

gag² *verb* **1** muzzle. **2** keep quiet, muzzle, silence, stifle. **3** choke, gasp, retch.

gaiety *noun* celebration, cheer, cheerfulness, festivity, fun, glee, happiness, hilarity, jollity, joy, merriment, merrymaking, mirth, revelry.

gain¹ *verb* **1** achieve, acquire, attain, earn, get, obtain, procure, profit, receive, score, secure, win. **3** arrive at, get to, reach.

gain² *noun* advantage, benefit, dividend, improvement, income, increase, jump, profit, return, reward, rise, yield.

gains *plural noun* booty, earnings, income, loot, proceeds, profits, takings, winnings.

gait *noun* carriage, pace, step, stride, tread, walk.

gala *noun* **1** carnival, fair, festival, fête, pageant.

gale *noun* blast, cyclone, gust, hurricane, storm, tempest, tornado, typhoon, wind.

gall¹ *noun* **3** audacity, boldness, cheek, effrontery, hide, impertinence, impudence, nerve, temerity.

gall³ *verb* **1** abrade, chafe, fret, rub.

gallant *adjective* **1** attentive, brave, chivalrous, considerate, courageous, courteous, daring, dauntless, fearless, gentlemanly, gracious, heroic, intrepid, kind, lion-hearted, manly, noble, polite, suave, valiant.

galleon *noun* a large Spanish sailing-ship used in the 16th–17th centuries.

gallery *noun* (*plural* **galleries**) **1** a platform jutting out from the wall in a church or hall. **2** the highest balcony in a cinema or theatre. **3** a long room or passage. **4** a room or building for showing works of art.

galley *noun* (*plural* **galleys**) **1** an ancient type of ship driven by oars. **2** the kitchen in a ship or aircraft.

galling (*say* **gawl**-ing) *adjective* vexing; humiliating.

gallivant *verb* go about in search of pleasure.

gallon *noun* a measure of liquid, 8 pints or about 4¹/₂ litres.

gallop¹ *noun* **1** the fastest pace a horse can go. **2** a fast ride on a horse.

gallop² *verb* (**galloped**, **galloping**) go or ride at a gallop.

gallows *noun* a framework with a noose for hanging criminals.

galore *adverb* in plenty; in great numbers, *bargains galore*.

galoshes *plural noun* a pair of waterproof shoes worn over ordinary shoes.

galvanise *verb* (**galvanised**, **galvanising**) **1** stimulate in sudden activity. **2** coat iron with zinc to protect it from rust. **galvanisation** *noun* [named after an Italian scientist, Luigi Galvani]

galvo *noun* (*Australian informal*) galvanised iron.

gambit *noun* **1** a kind of opening move in chess. **2** an action or remark intended to gain an advantage.

gamble¹ *verb* (**gambled**, **gambling**) **1** bet on the result of a game, race, or other event. **2**

take great risks in the hope of gaining something. **gambler** *noun*

gamble² *noun* **1** gambling. **2** a risky attempt.

gambol *verb* (**gambolled**, **gambolling**) jump or skip about in play.

game¹ *noun* **1** a form of play or sport, especially one with rules. **2** a section of a long game such as tennis or whist. **3** a scheme or plan; a trick. **4** wild animals or birds hunted for sport or food.

game² *adjective* **1** able and willing to do something. *She is game for all kinds of tricks.* **2** brave. **gamely** *adverb*

gamekeeper *noun* a person employed to protect game-birds and animals, especially from poachers.

gaming *noun* gambling.

gamma *noun* the third letter of the Greek alphabet, = g.
gamma rays very short X-rays.

gammon *noun* a kind of ham.

gander *noun* a male goose.

gang *noun* a number of people who do things together.

gangling *adjective* tall, thin, and awkward looking.

gangplank *noun* a plank placed so that people can walk into or out of a boat.

gangrene (*say* **gang**-green) *noun* decay of body tissue in a living person.

gangster *noun* a member of a gang of violent criminals.

gangway *noun* **1** a gap left for people to pass between rows of seats or through a crowd. **2** a movable bridge placed so that people can walk into or out of a ship.

gannet *noun* a large sea-bird.

gallery *noun* **2** balcony, gods (*informal*). **3** arcade, cloister, colonnade, loggia, portico, veranda. **4** hall, museum.

gallop² *verb* bolt, bound, dash, fly, hurry, hurtle, race, run, rush, shoot, speed, sprint, tear, whiz.

gallows *noun* gibbet, scaffold.

gamble¹ *verb* bet, chance, have a flutter (*informal*), punt, risk, stake, venture, wager. **gambler** *noun* better, punter, speculator.

gamble² *noun* **2** chance, lottery, punt, risk, speculation, uncertainty.

game¹ *noun* **1** amusement, diversion, entertainment, pastime, playing, recreation, sport. **2**

bout, competition, event, match, round.

game² *adjective* **1** eager, keen, prepared, ready, willing. **2** bold, brave, courageous, daring, fearless, intrepid, plucky.

gang *noun* band, bunch, crew, group, mob (*informal*), pack, push (*Australian old use*), relay, set, squad, team, troop.

gangling *adjective* gawky, lanky, lean, skinny, tall, thin, ungainly.

gangster *noun* bandit, brigand, criminal, crook (*informal*), desperado, robber, ruffian, thug, tough.

gangway *noun* **1** aisle, gap, passage.

gaol (*say* jayl) *noun* a jail. **gaol** *verb*, **gaoler** *noun*

gap *noun* **1** a break or opening in something continuous such as a hedge or fence. **2** an interval. **3** a wide difference in ideas.

gape *verb* (**gaped, gaping**) **1** have your mouth open. **2** stare with your mouth open. **3** be open wide; split.

garage (*say* ga-rah*zh* or ga-rij) *noun* **1** a building in which a motor vehicle or vehicles may be kept. **2** an establishment where motor vehicles are repaired or serviced.

garb *noun* special clothing. **garb** *verb*

garbage *noun* rubbish.

garble *verb* (**garbled, garbling**) give a confused account of a story or message so that it is misunderstood. **garbled** *adjective*

garbo *noun* (*Australian slang*) a garbage collector.

garden *noun* a piece of ground where flowers, fruit, or vegetables are grown. **gardener** *noun*, **gardening** *noun*

gargantuan (*say* gar-**gan**-tew-an) *adjective* gigantic. [from the name of Gargantua, a giant in a story]

gargle *verb* (**gargled, gargling**) hold a liquid at the back of the mouth and breathe air through it to wash the inside of the throat. **gargle** *noun*

gargoyle *noun* an ugly or comical face or figure carved on a building, especially on a water-spout.

garish (*say* **gair**-ish) *adjective* too bright or highly coloured; gaudy. **garishly** *adverb*

garland *noun* a wreath of flowers worn or hung as a decoration. **garland** *verb*

garlic *noun* a plant rather like an onion, used for flavouring food.

garment *noun* a piece of clothing.

garner *verb* store up, gather; collect.

garnet *noun* a dark-red stone used as a gem.

garnish¹ *verb* decorate.

garnish² *noun* something used to decorate food or give it extra flavour.

garret *noun* an attic.

garrison *noun* **1** troops stationed in a town or fort to defend it. **2** the building they occupy. **garrison** *verb*

garrotte¹ (*say* ga-**rot**) *noun* **1** a metal collar for strangling a person condemned to death, used in Spain. **2** a cord or wire used for strangling a victim.

garrotte² *verb* (**garrotted, garrotting**) strangle with a garrotte.

garrulous (*say* **ga**-rool-us) *adjective* talkative. **garrulousness** *noun*

garter *noun* a band of elastic to hold up a sock or stocking.

gas¹ *noun* (*plural* **gases**) **1** a substance that (like air) can move freely and is not liquid or solid at ordinary temperatures. **2** a flammable gas used for lighting, heating, or cooking.

gas² *verb* (**gassed, gassing**) **1** kill or injure with gas. **2** (*informal*) talk idly for a long time.

gas³ *noun* (*American*) gasoline.

gash¹ *noun* a long deep cut or wound.

gash² *verb* make a gash in something.

gap *noun* **1** aisle, aperture, breach, break, chasm, crack, cranny, crevice, discontinuity, fissure, gangway, hole, opening, space. **2** break, hiatus, interlude, intermission, interval, lull, pause, recess. **3** chasm, difference, disparity, divergence, gulf.

gape *verb* **2** gawp (*informal*), gaze, goggle, stare. **3** come apart, open up, part, split open.

garage *noun* **1** shed. **2** filling station, petrol station, service station.

garbage *noun* debris, junk, litter, refuse, rubbish, scraps, trash, waste.

garbled *adjective* confused, incoherent, jumbled, mixed-up, unclear.

garden *noun* allotment, grounds, lawn, patch, plot, yard.

garish *adjective* bright, flashy, gaudy, lairy (*Australian informal*), loud, showy, vivid.

garland *noun* festoon, lei, wreath.

garment *noun* (*garments*) apparel (*formal*), attire (*formal*), clothes, clothing, costume, dress, garb, gear (*informal*), outfit, raiment (*old use*), vestments, wear.

garnish¹ *verb* decorate, embellish.

garrison *noun* **2** citadel, fort, fortress, stronghold.
garrison *verb* defend, guard, occupy, protect.

garrulous *adjective* chatty, long-winded, loquacious, talkative, verbose, voluble, wordy.

gas¹ *noun* **1** exhaust, fumes, vapour.

gash¹ *noun* cut, laceration, slash, slit, tear, wound.

gash² *verb* cut, lacerate, slash, slit, tear, wound.

▶▶ D I C T I O N A R Y ◀◀

gasket *noun* a flat ring or strip of soft material for sealing a joint between metal surfaces.

gasoline *noun* (*American*) petrol.

gasometer (*say* gas-**om**-it-er) *noun* a large round tank in which gas is stored.

gasp *verb* 1 breathe in suddenly when you are shocked or surprised. 2 struggle to breathe with your mouth open when you are tired or ill. 3 speak in a breathless way. **gasp** *noun*

gassy *adjective* of or like gas.

gastric *adjective* of the stomach. [from Greek *gaster* = stomach]

gastronomy (*say* gas-**tron**-om-ee) *noun* the science of good eating. **gastronomic** *adjective* [from Greek *gaster* = stomach, + *nomia* = management]

gastropod *noun* an animal (e.g. a snail) that moves by means of a fleshy 'foot' on its stomach. [from Greek *gaster* = stomach, + *podos* = of the foot]

gate *noun* 1 a movable barrier, usually on hinges, serving as a door in a wall or fence. 2 the opening it covers. 3 a barrier for controlling the flow of water in a dam or lock. 4 the number of people attending a football match etc.

gateau (*say* **gat**-oh) *noun* a large rich cream cake. [from French *gâteau* = cake]

gatecrash *verb* go to a private party without being invited. **gatecrasher** *noun*

gateway *noun* 1 an opening containing a gate. 2 a way to reach something, *The gateway to success.*

gather *verb* 1 come or bring together. 2 collect; obtain gradually, *gather information.*

3 collect as harvest; pluck, *Gather the corn when it is ripe; gather flowers.* 4 understand; learn, *We gather you have been on holiday.* 5 pull cloth into folds by running a thread through it. 6 (of a sore) swell up and form pus.

gathering *noun* 1 an assembly of people. 2 a swelling that forms pus.

gaudy *adjective* too showy and bright. **gaudily** *adverb*, **gaudiness** *noun* [from Latin *gaudere* = rejoice]

gauge¹ (*say* gayj) *noun* 1 a standard measurement. 2 the distance between a pair of rails on a railway. 3 a measuring instrument.

gauge² *verb* (**gauged, gauging**) 1 measure. 2 estimate; form a judgement.

gaunt *adjective* 1 (of a person) lean and haggard. 2 (of a place) grim or desolate-looking. **gauntness** *noun*

gauntlet¹ *noun* a glove with a wide cuff covering the wrist. [from French *gant* = glove]

gauntlet² *noun* **run the gauntlet** have to suffer continuous severe criticism or risk. [from a former military and naval punishment in which the victim was made to pass between two rows of men who struck him as he passed; the word is from Swedish *gatlopp* = passage]

gauze *noun* 1 thin transparent woven material. 2 fine wire mesh. **gauzy** *adjective* [from Gaza, a town in Israel]

gay *adjective* 1 cheerful. 2 brightly coloured. 3 (*informal*) homosexual. **gayness** *noun*

▶▶ T H E S A U R U S ◀◀

gasp *verb* 2 choke, pant, puff, wheeze.

gate *noun* 1 barrier, door, portcullis, turnstile. 2 entrance, entry, exit, gateway, portal.

gather *verb* 1 assemble, cluster, concentrate, congregate, convene, crowd, flock, herd, marshal, mass, meet, mobilise, muster, rally, rendezvous, round up, swarm, throng. 2 accumulate, amass, collect, hoard, pile up, stack up, stockpile, store. 3 collect, garner, glean, harvest, pick, pluck, reap. 4 conclude, infer, learn, surmise, take it, understand. 5 ruffle, shirr.

gathering *noun* 1 assembly, collection, congregation, congress, convention, crowd, flock, get-together (*informal*), group, meeting, mob, muster, party, rally, reunion, social, swarm, throng.

gaudy *adjective* bright, colourful, flamboyant, flashy, garish, jazzy, lairy (*Australian informal*), loud, lurid, showy, tawdry, vivid.

gauge¹ *noun* 3 guide, indicator, measure, meter, rule, yardstick.

gauge² *verb* 1 calculate, compute, determine, measure, quantify, weigh. 2 assess, estimate, judge.

gaunt *adjective* 1 bony, cadaverous, emaciated, haggard, lanky, lean, scraggy, scrawny, skeletal, skinny, thin.

gauzy *adjective* diaphanous, fine, flimsy, light, see-through, sheer, thin, transparent.

gay *adjective* 1 blithe, bright, carefree, cheerful, happy, jolly, jovial, light-hearted, lively, merry. 2 bright, colourful, gaudy, showy, vivid. 3 homosexual, lesbian (*female*).

▶▶▶ D I C T I O N A R Y ◀◀

gaze¹ *verb* (**gazed**, **gazing**) look at something steadily for a long time.

gaze² *noun* a long steady look.

gazelle *noun* a small antelope.

gazette *noun* **1** a newspaper. **2** an official journal.

gazetteer (*say* gaz-it-**eer**) *noun* a list of place-names.

gear¹ *noun* **1** a cog-wheel, especially one of a set in a motor vehicle that transmit movement from the engine to the wheels when they are connected. **2** equipment; apparatus, *camping gear*. **3** (*informal*) clothing.

gear² *verb* **1** provide with a gear or gears. **2** provide with equipment etc.

gearbox *noun* a case enclosing gears.

gecko *noun* (*plural* **geckos**) a house lizard found in warm climates.

Geiger counter (*say* **gy**-ger) *noun* an instrument that detects and measures radioactivity. [named after the German scientist H. W. Geiger]

gelatine *noun* a clear jelly-like substance made by boiling animal tissue and used to make jellies and other foods and in photographic film. **gelatinous** (*say* jil-**at**-in-us) *adjective* [same origin as *jelly*]

geld *verb* castrate, spay.

gelding *noun* a castrated horse or other male animal.

gelignite (*say* **jel**-ig-nyt) *noun* a kind of explosive. [from *gelatine*, + Latin *ignis* = fire]

gem *noun* **1** a precious stone. **2** an excellent person or thing.

gemfish *noun* (*Australian*) hake.

gender *noun* the group in which a noun is classed in the grammar of some languages (e.g. *masculine, feminine, neuter*). [from Latin *genus* = a kind]

gene (*say* jeen) *noun* one of the factors controlling which characteristics (such as the colour of hair or eyes) are inherited from parents. [from Greek, = born]

genealogy (*say* jeen-ee-**al**-o-jee) *noun* **1** a statement or diagram showing how people are descended from an ancestor; a pedigree. **2** the study of family history and ancestors. **genealogical** (*say* jeen-ee-a-**loj**-ik-al) *adjective* [from Greek *genea* = race of people, + *-logy*]

general¹ *adjective* **1** of all or most people or things, *general approval*. **2** usual. **3** not detailed; not exact, *a general account*. **4** chief; head, *the general secretary*.

general election an election of Members of Parliament for the whole country or State.

general² *noun* a senior army officer.

generalise *verb* (**generalised**, **generalising**) **1** make a statement that is true of most cases. **2** bring into general use. **generalisation** *noun*

generality *noun* (*plural* **generalities**) **1** being general. **2** a general statement without exact details.

generally *adverb* **1** usually. **2** in a general sense; without regard to details, *I was speaking generally.*

generate *verb* (**generated**, **generating**) produce; create.

generation *noun* **1** generating. **2** a single stage in a family, *Three generations were included: children, parents, and grandparents*. **3** all the people born at about the same time.

generator *noun* **1** an apparatus for producing gases or steam. **2** a machine for converting mechanical energy into electricity.

▶▶▶ T H E S A U R U S ◀◀

gaze¹ *verb* (*gaze at*) behold (*old use*), contemplate, eye, gape at, gawp at (*informal*), look at, observe, peer at, stare at, study, survey, view, watch.

gaze² *noun* look, stare.

gear¹ *noun* **2** apparatus, appliances, equipment, implements, instruments, kit, materials, outfit, paraphernalia, rig, stuff, tackle, things, tools. **3** apparel (*formal*), attire (*formal*), clothes, clothing, dress, garments, get-up (*informal*), outfit, rig (*informal*), wear.

geld *verb* castrate, de-sex, doctor, neuter, spay, sterilise.

gem *noun* **1** gemstone, jewel, precious stone.

genealogy *noun* **1** ancestry, family history, lineage, pedigree.

general¹ *adjective* **1** all-round, broad, common, comprehensive, extensive, global, overall, popular, public, sweeping, universal, wholesale, widespread, worldwide. **2** customary, everyday, familiar, habitual, normal, ordinary, regular, standard, typical, usual. **3** broad, imprecise, indefinite, vague. **4** chief, head, principal.

generally *adverb* by and large, for the most part, in general, largely, mainly, mostly, normally, on the whole, usually.

generate *verb* bring about, create, drum up, give rise to, inspire, produce, whip up.

generic (*say* jin-**e**-rik) *adjective* of a whole genus or kind. **generically** *adverb*

generous *adjective* **1** willing to give things or share them. **2** given freely; plentiful, *a generous helping.* **3** kindly and not petty in making judgements. **generously** *adverb*, **generosity** *noun*

genesis *noun* beginning; origin. [Greek, = creation or origin]

genetic (*say* jin-**et**-ik) *adjective* of genes; of characteristics inherited from parents or ancestors. **genetically** *adverb* [from *genesis*]

genial (*say* jee-nee-al) *adjective* kindly and cheerful. **genially** *adverb*, **geniality** (*say* jee-nee-**al**-it-ee) *noun*

genie (*say* **jee**-nee) *noun* (in Arabian tales) a spirit with strange powers. [from Arabic *jinni*]

genital (*say* **jen**-it-al) *adjective* of animal reproduction or reproductive organs.

genitals (*say* **jen**-it-alz) *plural noun* external sexual organs.

genius *noun* (*plural* **geniuses**) **1** an unusually clever person. **2** a very great natural ability. [Latin, = a spirit]

genocide (*say* **jen**-o-syd) *noun* deliberate extermination of a race of people. [from Greek *genos* = a race, + Latin *caedere* = kill]

gent *noun* (*slang*) a gentleman; a man.

genteel (*say* jen-**teel**) *adjective* trying to seem polite and refined. **genteelly** *adverb*, **gentility** (*say* jen-**til**-it-ee) *noun*

gentile *noun* a person who is not Jewish.

gentle *adjective* **1** kind and quiet. **2** not rough or severe. **gently** *adverb*, **gentleness** *noun*

gentlefolk *noun* upper-class people.

gentleman (*plural* **gentlemen**) **1** a well mannered or honourable man. **2** a man of good social position. **3** (in polite use) a man.

gentry *noun* upper-class people.

genuine *adjective* really what it is said to be, not faked or pretending. **genuinely** *adverb*, **genuineness** *noun*

genus (*say* **jee**-nus) *noun* (*plural* **genera**, *say* **jen**-er-a) a group of similar animals or plants, *Lions and tigers belong to the same genus.* [Latin, = family or race]

geo- *prefix* earth. [from Greek *ge* = earth]

geography (*say* jee-**og**-ra-fee) *noun* the study of the earth's surface and of its climate, peoples, and products. **geographer** *noun*, **geographical** *adjective*, **geographically** *adverb* [from *geo-* + *graphy*]

geology (*say* jee-**ol**-o-jee) *noun* the study of the structure of the earth's crust and its layers. **geological** *adjective*, **geologically** *adverb*, **geologist** *noun* [from *geo* + *logy*]

geometry (*say* jee-**om**-it-ree) *noun* the study of lines, angles, surfaces and solids in mathematics. **geometric** *adjective*, **geometrical** *adjective*, **geometrically** *adverb* [from *geo-*, + Greek *-metria* = measurement]

Georgian *adjective* of the time of the kings George I–IV (1714–1830) or George V–VI (1910–52).

geranium *noun* a garden plant with red, pink, or white flowers.

gerbil (*say* **jer**-bil) *noun* a small brown animal with long hind legs.

generous *adjective* **1** benevolent, big-hearted, bountiful, charitable, kind-hearted, lavish, magnanimous, munificent, open-handed, philanthropic, selfless, unselfish, unstinting. **2** abundant, ample, copious, lavish, liberal, plentiful, sizeable.
generosity *noun* benevolence, bounty, charity, largesse, liberality, magnanimity, munificence, philanthropy.

genesis *noun* beginning, birth, commencement, creation, inception, origin, start.

genial *adjective* affable, amiable, convivial, cordial, easygoing, friendly, hospitable, kind, outgoing, pleasant, sociable, warm-hearted.

genius *noun* **1** brain (*informal*), expert, know-all, mastermind, prodigy, virtuoso, whiz-kid (*informal*). **2** ability, aptitude, brains, brilliance, intellect, intelligence, talent.

genteel *adjective* civil, courteous, courtly, gentlemanly, ladylike, mannerly, polite, posh (*informal*), refined, well-bred, well-mannered.

gentle *adjective* **1** benign, compassionate, docile, harmless, humane, kind, kind-hearted, kindly, lenient, meek, merciful, mild, peaceful, placid, quiet, serene, soft-hearted, sympathetic, tame, tender-hearted. **2** (*a gentle voice*) calm, mild, pleasant, quiet, soft, soothing, sweet, tender; (*a gentle breeze*) balmy, faint, light, mild, moderate, soft; (*a gentle slope*) easy, gradual, moderate, slight.

genuine *adjective* actual, authentic, bona fide, dinkum (*Australian informal*), dinky-di (*Australian informal*), honest, honest-to-goodness (*informal*), kosher (*informal*), real, ridgy-didge (*Australian informal*), sincere, true.

▶▶ DICTIONARY ◀◀

geriatric (*say* je-ree-**at**-rik) *adjective* concerned with the care of old people and their health. [from Greek *geras* = old age, + *iatros* = doctor]

germ *noun* **1** a micro-organism, especially one that can cause disease. **2** a tiny living structure from which a plant or animal may develop. **3** part of the seed of a cereal plant.

German measles a disease like mild measles, rubella.

germicide *noun* a substance that kills germs. [from *germ*, + Latin *caedere* = kill]

germinate *verb* (**germinated**, **germinating**) begin to grow and develop; put forth shoots. **germination** *noun*

gesticulate (*say* jes-**tik**-yoo-layt) *verb* (**gesticulated**, **gesticulating**) make expressive movements with hands and arms. **gesticulation** *noun*

gesture (*say* **jes**-cher) *noun* a movement or action that expresses what a person feels. **gesture** *verb*

get *verb* (**got**, **getting**) **1** obtain or receive, *She got first prize.* **2** become, *Don't get angry!* **3** reach a place, *We got there by midnight.* **4** put or move, *I can't get my shoe on.* **5** prepare, *Will you get the tea?* **6** persuade or order, *Get him to wash up.* **7** catch or suffer from an illness. **8** (*informal*) understand, *Do you get what I mean?*
get away escape.

get away with escape with something; avoid being punished for what you have done.
get by (*informal*) manage.
get on make progress; be friendly with somebody.
get out of avoid or escape something.
get over recover from an illness etc.
get up stand up; get out of your bed in the morning; prepare or organise, *We got up a concert.*
get your own back (*informal*) have your revenge.
have got to must.

getaway *noun* an escape after committing a crime.

get-together *noun* (*informal*) a social gathering.

geyser (*say* **gee**-zer or **gy**-zer) *noun* **1** a natural spring that shoots up columns of hot water. **2** a kind of water-heater. [from the name of a hot spring in Iceland (*geysa* = gush)]

ghastly *adjective* **1** very unpleasant or bad. **2** looking pale and ill. **ghastliness** *noun* [related to *aghast* horrified]

gherkin (*say* **ger**-kin) *noun* a small cucumber used for pickling.

ghetto (*say* **get**-oh) *noun* (*plural* **ghettos**) a slum area inhabited by a group of people who are treated unfairly in comparison with others. [from Italian *getto* = foundry (the first ghetto was in Venice, on the site of a foundry)]

▶▶ THESAURUS ◀◀

germ *noun* **1** bacterium, bug (*informal*), microbe, micro-organism, virus.

germinate *verb* come up, grow, shoot, spring up, sprout.

gesture *noun* action, gesticulation, motion, movement, sign, signal.
gesture *verb* beckon, gesticulate, motion, nod, point, signal, wave.

get *verb* **1** acquire, be given, buy, come by, earn, gain, get hold of, land, obtain, procure, purchase, receive, score, take, win; see also FETCH. **2** become, grow, turn. **3** arrive at, reach. **5** fix, make ready, prepare. **6** cause, convince, induce, influence, make, persuade. **7** be afflicted with, catch, come down with, contract, develop, pick up, suffer from. **8** comprehend, cotton on to (*informal*), fathom, follow, grasp, realise, understand.
get away abscond, bolt, break free, decamp, depart, do a bunk (*slang*), escape, flee, leave,

nick off (*Australian slang*), push off (*informal*), scarper, shoot through (*Australian informal*), slip away.

get on cope, fare, get along, make out (*informal*), manage.
get out of avoid, dodge, escape, evade, shirk, wriggle out of.
get over overcome, pull through, recover from, survive.
get up arise (*old use*), rise, surface.
get your own back get even, have your revenge, pay back, retaliate.

getaway *noun* escape, flight, retreat.

get-together *noun* function, gathering, meeting, party, rendezvous, reunion, social.

ghastly *adjective* **1** appalling, awful, dreadful, frightful, gruesome, hideous, horrendous, horrible, repulsive, shocking, terrible. **2** ashen, deathly, ghostly, pale, pallid, pasty, sickly, wan, washed out.

▶▶ DICTIONARY ◀◀

ghost *noun* the spirit of a dead person. **ghostly** *adjective*

ghoulish (*say* **gool**-ish) *adjective* enjoying things that are grisly or unpleasant. **ghoulishly** *adverb*, **ghoulishness** *noun* [from *ghoul* = a demon in Muslim stories]

giant *noun* **1** (in fairy-tales) a human-like creature of very great height and size. **2** a human, animal, or plant that is much larger than the usual size.

giantess *noun* (*plural* **giantesses**) a female giant.

gibber¹ (*say* **jib**-er) *verb* make quick meaningless sounds, especially when shocked or terrified.

gibber² (*say* **gib**-er) *noun* a stone or rock.

gibberish (*say* **jib**-er-ish) *noun* meaningless speech; nonsense.

gibbet (*say* **jib**-it) *noun* **1** a gallows. **2** an upright post with an arm from which a criminal's body was hung after execution.

gibbon *noun* an ape with very long arms.

gibe (*say* jyb) *noun* & *verb* jeer.

giblets (*say* **jib**-lits) *plural noun* the edible parts of the inside of a bird, taken out before it is cooked.

giddy *adjective* having or causing the feeling that everything is spinning round. **giddily** *adverb*, **giddiness** *noun*

gift *noun* **1** a present. **2** a talent, *She has a gift for music.*

gifted *adjective* talented.

gig *noun* (*informal*) a show when a musician or band plays pop music in public.

gigantic *adjective* very large.

giggle¹ *verb* (**giggled, giggling**) laugh in a silly way.

giggle² *noun* **1** a silly laugh. **2** (*informal*) something amusing; a joke.

gild *verb* cover with a thin layer of gold or gold paint.

gilgai *noun* (*Australian*) land with hollows and mounds; one of the hollows.

gills *plural noun* **1** the part of the body through which fishes and certain other water animals breathe while in water. **2** the thin upright parts under the cap of a mushroom.

gilt¹ *noun* a thin gold covering.

gilt² *adjective* gilded; gold coloured.

gimlet *noun* a small tool with a screw-like tip for boring holes.

gimmick *noun* something unusual done or used to attract people's attention.

gin¹ *noun* a colourless alcoholic spirit flavoured with juniper berries. [from the name of Geneva, a city in Switzerland]

gin² *noun* **1** a kind of trap for catching animals. **2** a machine for separating the fibres of the cotton-plant from its seeds.

▶▶ THESAURUS ◀◀

ghost *noun* apparition, phantom, poltergeist, shade, spectre, spirit, spook (*informal*), vision, wraith.
 ghostly *adjective* creepy, eerie, sinister, spooky (*informal*), uncanny, unearthly, weird.

ghoulish *adjective* gruesome, macabre, morbid.

giant *noun* **1** monster, ogre, Titan.

gibberish *noun* babble, double Dutch, drivel, gobbledegook (*informal*), jabber, mumbo-jumbo, nonsense, poppycock (*slang*), rubbish, twaddle.

gibe *verb* (*gibe at*) chiack (*Australian informal*), jeer, make fun of, mock, poke borak at (*Australian informal*), ridicule, scoff at, sling off at (*Australian informal*), sneer at, taunt, tease.

giddy *adjective* dizzy, faint, light-headed, unsteady.
 giddiness *noun* dizziness, light-headedness, unsteadiness, vertigo.

gift *noun* **1** alms, bequest, bonus, contribution, donation, endowment, freebie (*informal*), give-away (*informal*), gratuity, handout, legacy, offering, offertory, present, tip. **2** ability, aptitude, facility, flair, genius, head, knack, talent.

gifted *adjective* able, accomplished, bright, brilliant, capable, clever, intelligent, skilful, skilled, talented.

gig *noun* performance, show.

gigantic *adjective* big, boomer (*Australian informal*), colossal, enormous, extensive, gargantuan, giant, ginormous (*slang*), huge, humungous (*slang*), immeasurable, immense, jumbo-sized, king-sized, large, mammoth, massive, mighty, monstrous, monumental, prodigious, stupendous, tremendous, vast, whopping (*slang*).

giggle¹ *verb* chuckle, laugh, snicker, snigger, titter.

giggle² *noun* **1** chuckle, laugh, snicker, snigger, titter.

gimmick *noun* device, ploy, stratagem, trick.

▶▷ D I C T I O N A R Y ◁◀

gin³ *verb* (**ginned, ginning**) treat cotton in a gin. [from Old French *engin* = engine]

ginger¹ *noun* **1** a flavouring made from the hot-tasting root of a tropical plant. **2** this root. **3** liveliness; energy. **4** reddish-yellow. **ginger** *adjective*

ginger² *verb* make more lively, *This will ginger things up!*

gingerbread *noun* a ginger-flavoured cake or biscuit.

gingerly *adverb* cautiously.

gipsy *noun* (*plural* **gipsies**) a gypsy.

giraffe *noun* an African animal rather like a horse but with a very long neck.

gird *verb* **1** fasten with a belt or band, *He girded on his sword.* **2** prepare for an effort, *gird yourself for action.* **3** encircle.

girder *noun* a metal beam supporting part of a building or a bridge.

girdle¹ *noun* a belt or cord worn round the waist.

girdle² *noun* a griddle.

girl *noun* **1** a female child. **2** a young woman. **girlhood** *noun*, **girlish** *adjective*

girlfriend *noun* a girl that a boy regularly goes out with.

girt *adjective* girded.

girth *noun* **1** the distance round a thing. **2** a band passing under a horse's body to hold the saddle in place.

gist (*say* jist) *noun* the essential points or general sense of a speech etc.

give *verb* (**gave, given, giving**) **1** cause another person to receive something that you have or can provide. **2** deliver a message etc. **3** make or perform an action or effort, *He gave a laugh.* **4** be flexible or springy; bend or collapse when pressed. **giver** *noun*
give away give as a present; (*Australian*) give up, abandon; reveal a secret.
give in acknowledge that you are defeated; yield.
give off send out something.
give up cease (doing something); part with; surrender; abandon hope.

given *adjective* named or stated in advance, *All the people in a given area.*

gizzard *noun* a bird's second stomach, in which food is ground up.

glacé (*say* **glas**-ay) *adjective* iced with sugar; crystallised. [French, = iced]

glacial (*say* **glay**-shal) *adjective* icy; of or from ice. **glacially** *adverb* [from Latin *glacies* = ice]

glacier (*say* **glay**-see-er) *noun* a river of ice that moves very slowly.

glad *adjective* **1** pleased; expressing joy. **2** giving pleasure, *We brought the glad news.* **gladly** *adverb*, **gladness** *noun*
glad of grateful for; pleased with.

gladden *verb* make a person glad.

glade *noun* an open space in a forest.

▶▷ T H E S A U R U S ◁◀

gingerly *adverb* carefully, cautiously, charily, timidly, warily.

gird *verb* **2** brace, prepare, ready, steel. **3** encircle, enclose, encompass, ring, surround.

girl *noun* babe (*informal*), bird (*informal*), chick (*slang*), damsel (*old use*), female, gal (*informal*), lass, lassie (*informal*), maid (*old use*), maiden (*old use*), miss, schoolgirl, sheila (*Australian slang*); see also CHILD, WOMAN.

girlfriend *noun* date (*informal*), female friend, fiancée, steady, sweetheart.

girth *noun* **1** circumference, perimeter.

gist *noun* content, core, drift, essence, meaning, pith, point, substance.

give *verb* **1** allot, allow, award, bestow, confer, contribute, deal out, dish out (*informal*), distribute, dole out, donate, endow with, entrust with, equip with, furnish with, grant, hand out, hand over, offer, pay, present, proffer, provide with, ration out, supply with.

2 communicate, convey, deliver, impart, pass on, report, tell, transmit. **3** emit, let out, utter. **4** break, buckle, collapse, crack, fold up, give way, yield.
give away betray, blab, divulge, leak, let out, make known, reveal.
give back pay back, refund, reimburse, repay, return.
give in capitulate, cave in, concede, give up, submit, succumb, surrender, yield.
give off discharge, emit, exude, give out, release.
give up 1 abandon, cease, chuck in (*informal*), discontinue, give away (*Australian*), leave, quit, resign, retire, stop. **2** cede, forfeit, forgo, part with, relinquish, renounce, sacrifice, waive. **3** capitulate, concede, give in, surrender, throw in the towel, throw up the sponge, yield.

glad *adjective* **1** delighted, gratified, happy, joyful, pleased, thrilled. **2** cheerful, good, happy, joyful, pleasing, welcome.

gladden *verb* brighten, cheer, delight, please.

►► DICTIONARY ◄◄

gladiator (*say* **glad**-ee-ay-ter) *noun* a man trained to fight in public shows in ancient Rome. **gladiatorial** (*say* glad-ee-at-**or**-ee-al) *adjective* [from Latin *gladius* sword]

glamorise *verb* (**glamorised**, **glamorising**) make glamorous or romantic.

glamour *noun* attractiveness, romantic charm. **glamorous** *adjective* [from an old use of *grammar* = magic]

glance *verb* (**glanced**, **glancing**) 1 look at something briefly. 2 strike something at an angle and slide off it, *The ball glanced off his bat*. **glance** *noun*

gland *noun* an organ of the body that separates substances from the blood so that they can be used or expelled. **glandular** *adjective*

glare *verb* (**glared**, **glaring**) 1 shine with an unpleasant dazzling light. 2 stare angrily or fiercely. **glare** *noun*

glaring *adjective* 1 shining dazzlingly. 2 obvious, *a glaring error*.

glass *noun* (*plural* **glasses**) 1 a hard brittle substance that is usually transparent. 2 a container made of glass for drinking from. 3 a mirror. 4 a lens or telescope. **glassy** *adjective*

glasses *plural noun* 1 spectacles. 2 binoculars.

glaze[1] *verb* (**glazed**, **glazing**) 1 fit or cover with glass. 2 give a shiny surface to something. 3 become glassy.

glaze[2] *noun* a shiny surface or coating, especially on pottery. [from *glass*]

glazier (*say* **glay**-zee-er) *noun* a person whose job is to fit glass in windows.

gleam[1] *noun* 1 a beam of soft light, especially one that comes and goes. 2 a small amount of hope, humour, etc.

gleam[2] *verb* send out gleams.

glean *verb* 1 pick up grain left by harvesters. 2 gather bit by bit, *glean some information*. **gleaner** *noun*

glee *noun* lively or triumphant delight. **gleeful** *adjective*, **gleefully** *adverb*

glen *noun* a narrow valley.

glib *adjective* speaking or writing readily but not sincerely or thoughtfully. **glibly** *adverb*, **glibness** *noun* [from an old word *glibbery* = slippery]

glide *verb* (**glided**, **gliding**) 1 fly or move along smoothly. 2 fly without using an engine. **glide** *noun*

glider *noun* an aeroplane that does not use an engine.

glimmer[1] *noun* a faint gleam.

glimmer[2] *verb* gleam faintly.

glimpse[1] *noun* a brief view.

►► THESAURUS ◄◄

glamorous *adjective* attractive, beautiful, bewitching, charming, elegant, exciting, fascinating.

glance *verb* 1 look, peek, peep, scan, skim. **glance** *noun* glimpse, look, peek, peep, squiz (*Australian slang*).

glare *verb* 2 frown, glower, lour, scowl, stare. **glare** *noun* 1 brightness, dazzle, radiance. 2 black look, frown, glower, lour, scowl, stare.

glaring *adjective* 1 blazing, blinding, bright, dazzling, harsh, strong. 2 blatant, conspicuous, flagrant, obvious, patent, plain, unmistakable.

glass *noun* 1 crystal, pane, plate glass. 2 beaker, goblet, tumbler, wineglass. 3 looking-glass, mirror. **glassy** *adjective* glazed, reflective, shiny, smooth, vitreous.

glasses *plural noun* 1 eyeglasses, goggles, lorgnette, pince-nez, specs (*informal*), spectacles, sunglasses. 2 binoculars, field glasses, opera glasses.

glaze[2] *noun* enamel, finish, lustre.

gleam[1] *noun* 1 beam, flash, glimmer, glint, ray, shaft, shimmer, spark.

gleam[2] *verb* flash, glimmer, glisten, shimmer, shine, sparkle.

glean *verb* 1 collect, garner, gather, harvest, obtain, pick up.

glee *noun* cheerfulness, delight, ecstasy, elation, excitement, exhilaration, happiness, joy, jubilation, mirth.

gleeful *adjective* cheerful, chuffed (*slang*), delighted, ecstatic, elated, excited, exhilarated, exuberant, exultant, glad, happy, joyful, jubilant, merry, pleased.

glib *adjective* facile, offhand, pat, ready, slick, smooth.

glide *verb* 1 aquaplane, coast, glissade, skate, skid, skim, slide, slip. 2 drift, float, fly, sail, soar.

glimmer[1] *noun* flash, flicker, gleam, glint, glow, ray, shimmer, sparkle.

glimmer[2] *verb* flicker, gleam, glint, glow, shimmer, shine, twinkle.

glimpse[1] *noun* glance, look, peek, peep, squiz (*Australian slang*), view.

▶▶▶ D I C T I O N A R Y ◀◀

glimpse² *verb* (**glimpsed, glimpsing**) catch a glimpse of.

glint¹ *noun* very brief flash of light.

glint² *verb* send out a glint.

glissade (*say* gliss-**ayd**) *verb* (**glissaded, glissading**) glide or slide skilfully, especially down a steep slope.

glisten (*say* **glis**-en) *verb* shine like something wet or polished.

glitter *verb* & *noun* sparkle.

gloaming *noun* the evening twilight.

gloat *verb* be full of greedy or unkind pleasure.

global *adjective* **1** of the whole world; worldwide. **2** of or in the whole system. **globally** *adverb*

globe *noun* **1** something shaped like a ball, especially one with a map of the whole world on it. **2** the world, *She has travelled all over the globe.* **3** a hollow round glass object.

globular (*say* **glob**-yoo-ler) *adjective* shaped like a globe.

globule (*say* **glob**-yool) *noun* a small rounded drop.

gloom *noun* **1** darkness. **2** depression.

gloomy *adjective* (**gloomier, gloomiest**) **1** almost dark. **2** depressed; depressing; sad. **gloomily** *adverb*, **gloominess** *noun*

glorify *verb* (**glorified, glorifying**) **1** give glory or honour. **2** make a thing seem more splendid than it really is. **glorification** *noun*

glorious *adjective* **1** having glory. **2** splendid. **gloriously** *adverb*

glory¹ *noun* **1** fame and honour. **2** praise. **3** beauty, magnificence.

glory² *verb* (**gloried, glorying**) rejoice; pride yourself, *They gloried in victory.*

gloss¹ *noun* (*plural* **glosses**) the shine on a smooth surface.

gloss² *verb* make a thing glossy. **gloss over** make a fault or mistake etc. seem less serious than it really is.

glossary *noun* (*plural* **glossaries**) a list of difficult words with their meanings explained. [from Greek *glossa* = tongue, language]

glossy *adjective* (**glossier, glossiest**) shiny. **glossily** *adverb*, **glossiness** *noun*

glove *noun* a covering for the hand, usually with separate divisions for each finger and thumb. **gloved** *adjective*

▶▶▶ T H E S A U R U S ◀◀

glimpse² *verb* catch sight of, discern, espy, notice, peep at, see, sight, spot.

glint¹ *noun* flash, gleam, sparkle.

glint² *verb* flash, gleam, glimmer, glisten, glitter, shine, sparkle, twinkle.

glisten *verb* gleam, shimmer, shine, sparkle.

glitter *verb* glimmer, scintillate, shimmer, shine, sparkle, twinkle.

gloat *verb* crow, delight, exult, glory, rejoice, revel; see also BOAST¹.

global *adjective* **1** general, international, universal, widespread, worldwide.

globe *noun* **1** ball, bulb, sphere. **2** earth, world.

gloom *noun* **1** darkness, dimness, dusk, gloaming, semi-darkness, shadows, twilight. **2** dejection, depression, despair, glumness, melancholy, misery, pessimism, sadness, unhappiness, woe.

gloomy *adjective* **1** black, bleak, cheerless, cloudy, dark, depressing, dismal, dreary, dull, murky, overcast. **2** depressed, desolate, dismal, doleful, down-hearted, funereal, glum, heavy-hearted, lugubrious, melancholy, moody, morbid, morose, mournful, pessimistic, sad, saturnine, sombre, sullen, unhappy.

glorify *verb* **1** adore, exalt, extol, hallow, honour, laud (*formal*), magnify (*old use*), praise, revere, venerate, worship.

glorious *adjective* **1** famous, grand, heroic, illustrious, noble. **2** beautiful, brilliant, excellent, fine, gorgeous, grand, impressive, magnificent, majestic, marvellous, spectacular, splendid, stunning, sublime, superb, terrific (*informal*), wonderful.

glory¹ *noun* **1** credit, distinction, esteem, fame, honour, kudos (*informal*), prestige, renown. **2** adoration, exaltation, honour, praise, reverence, veneration, worship. **3** beauty, grandeur, greatness, magnificence, majesty, splendour.

glory² *verb* delight, exult, pride yourself, rejoice, revel, take pride.

gloss¹ *noun* brightness, gleam, lustre, polish, sheen, shine, sparkle.

gloss² *verb* **gloss over** conceal, cover up, hide, make light of, whitewash.

glossy *adjective* gleaming, glistening, lustrous, shining, shiny, sleek.

glove *noun* gauntlet, mitt, mitten.

glow¹ *noun* **1** brightness and warmth without flames. **2** a warm or cheerful feeling. *We felt a glow of pride.*

glow² *verb* produce a glow.

glower (*rhymes with* flower) *verb* stare angrily; scowl.

glow-worm *noun* a kind of beetle whose tail gives out a green light.

glucose *noun* a form of sugar found in fruit-juice. [same origin as *glycerine*]

glue¹ *noun* a sticky substance used for joining things. **gluey** *adjective*

glue² *verb* (**glued, gluing**) **1** stick with glue. **2** attach or hold closely, *His ear was glued to the keyhole.*

glum *adjective* sad and gloomy. **glumly** *adverb*, **glumness** *noun* [from dialect *glum* = to frown]

glut¹ *verb* (**glutted, glutting**) **1** supply with much more than is need. **2** satisfy fully with food.

glut² *noun* an excessive supply. [same origin as *glutton*]

gluten (*say* **gloo**-ten) *noun* a sticky protein substance in flour. [from Latin, = glue]

glutinous (*say* **gloo**-tin-us) *adjective* gluelike, sticky. [same origin as *gluten*]

glutton *noun* a person who eats too much. **gluttonous** *adjective*, **gluttony** *noun* [from Latin *gluttire* = to swallow]

glycerine (*say* **glis**-er-een) *noun* a thick sweet colourless liquid used in ointments and medicines and in explosives. [from Greek *glykys* = sweet]

gnarled (*say* narld) *adjective* twisted and knobbly, like an old tree.

gnash (*say* nash) *verb* grind teeth together.

gnat (*say* nat) *noun* a tiny fly that bites.

gnaw (*say* naw) *verb* keep on biting something hard.

gnome (*say* nohm) *noun* a kind of dwarf in fairy-tales, usually living underground.

gnu (*say* noo) *noun* a large ox-like antelope.

go¹ *verb* (**went, gone, going**) **1** move or begin to move, *Where are you going?* **2** leave, *It was time to go.* **3** extend, lead, *The road goes to Darwin.* **4** work or function, *The car doesn't go.* **5** become, *The milk went sour.* **6** belong in some place or position, *Plates go on that shelf.* **7** proceed, turn out, *Things went well.* **8** (of time) pass, *The time went quickly.* **9** be spent or used up, *The money has all gone.* **10** be sold, *The house went very cheaply.* **11** make a particular movement or sound, *The gun went bang.*

glow¹ *noun* **1** brightness, gleam, heat, incandescence, light, luminosity, radiance, warmth. **2** blush, colour, flush, radiance, redness, rosiness, ruddiness.

glow² *verb* **1** gleam, radiate, shine, smoulder. **2** blush, colour, flush, redden, shine.

glower *verb* frown, glare, lour, scowl, stare.

glue¹ *noun* adhesive, cement, gum, paste. **gluey** *adjective* adhesive, gluggy (*informal*), glutinous, sticky, tacky, viscous.

glue² *verb* **1** affix, attach, cement, fasten, gum, paste, stick.

glum *adjective* cheerless, crestfallen, depressed, despondent, doleful, down-hearted, down in the mouth, forlorn, gloomy, melancholy, miserable, moody, morose, mournful, sad, unhappy, woebegone.

glut¹ *verb* **1** flood, inundate, oversupply, saturate, swamp. **2** cram, gorge, overfill, satiate, stuff.

glut² *noun* excess, overabundance, oversupply, superfluity, surfeit, surplus.

glutton *noun* gormandiser, gourmand, greedy-guts (*informal*), guts (*informal*), guzzler, hog (*informal*), pig (*informal*).

gluttonous *adjective* greedy, gutsy (*slang*), insatiable, voracious.

gnarled *adjective* distorted, knobbly, knotty, lumpy, misshapen, rough, twisted.

gnash *verb* grate, grind.

gnaw *verb* bite, chew, chomp, crunch, eat, munch, nibble.

gnome *noun* dwarf, elf, goblin, troll.

go¹ *verb* **1** head for, journey, make for, nip (*informal*), pop, proceed, set out for, start for, travel, visit, wend your way, zip off; see also ADVANCE². **2** beat it (*slang*), be off, buzz off (*slang*), clear off (*informal*), decamp, depart, disappear, exit, get away, go away, hop it (*slang*), leave, make tracks (*informal*), make yourself scarce, nick off (*Australian slang*), push off (*informal*), retire, retreat, run off, scarper (*informal*), scoot, scram (*informal*), set off, shoot through (*Australian informal*), shove off (*informal*), skedaddle (*informal*), take your leave, take yourself off, vanish, withdraw. **3** extend, lead, reach, run, stretch. **4** function, move, operate, perform, run, work. **5** become, turn. **6** belong, fit. **7** fare, proceed, progress, turn out, work out. **8** elapse, pass, slip by. **9** be spent, be used, dry up, run out.

go along with agree.

go back on fail to keep a promise etc.

go off explode; (of food) become bad or stale.

go on continue.

go through penetrate; experience, undergo; study, inspect.

go² *noun* (*plural* **goes**) **1** a turn or try, *May I have a go?* **2** (*informal*) a success, *They made a go of it.* **3** (*informal*) energy; liveliness. *She is full of go.*

on the go active; always working or moving.

goad¹ *noun* a stick with a pointed end for prodding cattle to move onwards.

goad² *verb* stir into action by being annoying, *He goaded me into fighting.*

go-ahead¹ *noun* a signal to proceed.

go-ahead² *adjective* energetic; willing to try new methods.

goal *noun* **1** the place where a ball must go to score a point in football, hockey, etc. **2** a point scored in this way. **3** an objective. [from an old word *gol* = boundary]

goalkeeper *noun* the player who stands in the goal to try and keep the ball from entering.

goanna *noun* (*Australian*) a large lizard.

goat *noun* a small animal with horns, kept for its milk.

gobble *verb* (**gobbled, gobbling**) eat quickly and greedily.

gobbledegook *noun* (*informal*) pompous language used by officials. [imitation of the sound a turkey-cock makes]

go-between *noun* a person who acts as a messenger or negotiator between others.

goblet *noun* a drinking-glass with a stem and a foot.

goblin *noun* a mischievous ugly elf.

go-cart *noun* a billycart.

God *noun* the creator of the universe in Christian, Jewish, and Muslim belief.

god *noun* a person or thing that is worshipped, *Mars was a Roman god.*

goddess *noun* (*plural* **goddesses**) a female god.

godhead *noun* the divine nature of God.

godly *adjective* (**godlier, godliest**) sincerely religious. **godliness** *noun*

go after chase, follow, pursue, tail (*informal*), track, trail.

go along with agree with, be in sympathy with, concur with, subscribe to.

go back on break, recant, renege on, repudiate.

go before lead, precede.

go off 1 blow up, detonate, explode. **2** decay, deteriorate, go bad, go rotten, perish, rot, spoil.

go on carry on, continue, keep on, persevere, persist, proceed.

go round circle, gyrate, orbit, revolve, rotate, spin, swirl, swivel, turn, twirl, whirl.

go through 1 enter, penetrate, pierce, puncture. **2** bear, endure, experience, suffer, undergo. **3** check, inspect, look through, search, sift through.

go up ascend, climb, escalate, increase, mount, rise, rocket, soar.

go with accompany, escort.

go without be deprived of, deny yourself, do without, forgo, give up, sacrifice.

go² *noun* **1** attempt, bash (*informal*), crack (*informal*), shot, stab (*informal*), try, turn. **3** dash, drive, dynamism, energy, get-up-and-go (*informal*), oomph (*informal*), pep, vigour, vim (*informal*), vivacity, zip.

goad² *verb* drive, egg on, incite, prod, prompt, provoke, sool (*Australian informal*), spur, stimulate, urge.

go-ahead² *adjective* ambitious, dynamic, energetic, enterprising, forward-looking, progressive.

goal *noun* **3** aim, ambition, end, object, objective, purpose, target.

goat *noun* billy goat, he-goat, kid, nanny goat.

gobble *verb* bolt, devour, gulp, guzzle, scoff (*informal*), wolf.

gobbledegook *noun* double Dutch, gibberish, humbug, jargon, mumbo-jumbo, nonsense.

go-between *noun* agent, broker, intermediary, liaison, mediator, messenger, middleman, negotiator.

goblin *noun* bogy, elf, gnome, hobgoblin, imp, leprechaun, sprite.

go-cart *noun* billycart, hill trolley.

God *noun* Allah, the Almighty, the Creator, the Father, Jehovah, the Lord, our Maker, Yahweh.

god *noun* deity, divinity.

goddess *noun* deity, divinity.

godly *adjective* devout, God-fearing, holy, pious, religious, saintly.

▶▶ DICTIONARY ◀◀

godparent *noun* a person at a child's christening who promises to see that it is brought up as a Christian. **godchild** *noun*, **god-daughter** *noun*, **godfather** *noun*, **god-mother** *noun*, **godson** *noun*

godsend *noun* a piece of unexpected good luck.

goggle *verb* (**goggled**, **goggling**) stare with wide-open eyes.

goggles *plural noun* large spectacles for protecting the eyes from wind, water, dust, etc.

going *present participle of* **go**.
be going to do something be ready or likely to do it.

go-kart *noun* a miniature racing car with a skeleton body.

gold *noun* **1** a precious yellow metal. **2** a deep yellow colour. **3** a gold medal, usually given as first prize. **gold** *adjective*

golden *adjective* **1** made of gold. **2** coloured like gold. **3** precious; excellent, *a golden opportunity*.
golden wedding the 50th anniversary of a wedding.

goldfield *noun* a place where gold is found and mined.

goldfinch *noun* (*plural* **goldfinches**) a bird with yellow feathers in its wings.

goldfish *noun* (*plural* **goldfish**) a small red or orange fish, often kept as a pet.

goldsmith *noun* a person who makes things in gold.

golf *noun* an outdoor game played by hitting a small white ball with a club into a series of holes on a specially prepared ground (a **golf-course** or **golf-links**). **golfer** *noun*, **golfing** *noun*

golliwog *noun* a black (male) doll with woolly hair.

gondola (*say* **gond**-ol-a) *noun* a boat with high pointed ends used on the canals in Venice. **gondolier** *noun* [Italian]

gong *noun* a large metal disc that makes an echoing sound when hit.

good¹ *adjective* (**better**, **best**) **1** having the right qualities; of the kind that people like, *a good book*. **2** kind; morally excellent, *It was good of you to help us*. **3** well-behaved, *Be a good boy*. **4** healthy; giving benefit, *Fish is good for you*. **5** competent, skilful. **6** enjoyable, *Have a good time*. **7** thorough, *Give it a good clean*. **8** large; considerable, *It's a good distance from the shops*.
Good Friday the Friday before Easter, when Christians commemorate the Crucifixion of Christ.

good² *noun* **1** something good, *Do good to others*. **2** benefit, *It's for your own good*.
for good for ever.
no good useless.

goodbye *interjection* a word used when you leave somebody or at the end of a phone call. [short for *God be with you*]

▶▶ THESAURUS ◀◀

godsend *noun* blessing, bonanza, boon, windfall.

goggles *plural noun* glasses, spectacles.

gold *adjective* gilded, gilt, golden, gold-plated.

golden *adjective* **2** blond, flaxen, gold, yellow. **3** excellent, favourable, precious, priceless, valuable, wonderful.

good¹ *adjective* **1** acceptable, adequate, admirable, appropriate, commendable, desirable, meritorious, praiseworthy, proper, right, satisfactory, suitable, worthy. **2** benevolent, benign, blameless, considerate, decent, ethical, godly, holy, honest, honourable, innocent, just, kind, law-abiding, moral, noble, righteous, upright, virtuous, well-intentioned, well-meaning, worthy. **3** biddable, courteous, dutiful, helpful, obedient, polite, well-behaved, well-mannered. **4** beneficial, healthy, nutritious, wholesome. **5** able, accomplished, adept, capable, competent, conscientious, dependable, diligent, effective, efficient, expert, first-rate, professional, proficient, reliable, skilful, skilled, sound, thorough. **6** agreeable, cool (*informal*), delightful, enjoyable, excellent, fabulous (*informal*), fantastic (*informal*), fine, great (*informal*), happy, lovely, marvellous, nice, outstanding, pleasant, satisfying, superb, swell (*informal*), terrific (*informal*), tremendous (*informal*), wonderful.

good² *noun* **1** goodness, merit, virtue. **2** advantage, benefit, interest, profit, welfare, well-being.

goodbye *interjection* adieu, au revoir, bon voyage, bye-bye (*informal*), cheerio (*informal*), cheers (*informal*), ciao (*informal*), farewell, hooray (*Australian informal*), see you (*informal*), see you later (*informal*), so long (*informal*), ta-ta (*informal*).

good-looking *adjective* attractive, beautiful, bonny (*Scottish*), comely, fair (*old use*), fetching, handsome, lovely, personable, pretty.

▶▶ DICTIONARY ◀◀

goodness *noun* **1** being good. **2** the good part of something.

goods *plural noun* **1** things that are bought and sold. **2** things that are carried on trains or trucks.

goodwill *noun* a kindly feeling.

goody *noun* (*plural* **goodies**) (*informal*) **1** something good or attractive, especially to eat. **2** a person of good character.

goog *noun* (*Australian slang*) an egg.

goose *noun* (*plural* **geese**) a kind of bird with webbed feet, larger than a duck.

gooseberry *noun* (*plural* **gooseberries**) a small green fruit that grows on a prickly bush.

goose-flesh *noun* (also called **goose-pimples**) skin that has turned rough with small bumps on it because a person is cold or afraid.

gore¹ *verb* (**gored, goring**) wound by piercing with a horn or tusk.

gore² *noun* thickened blood from a cut or wound. [from Old English *gor* = dirt]

gorge¹ *noun* **1** a narrow valley with steep sides. **2** the throat or gullet.

gorge² *verb* (**gorged, gorging**) eat greedily; stuff with food. [French, = throat]

gorgeous *adjective* magnificent; beautiful. **gorgeously** *adverb*

gorilla *noun* a large strong African ape.

gorse *noun* a prickly bush with small yellow flowers.

gory *adjective* **1** covered with blood. **2** with much bloodshed, *a gory battle.*

gosh *interjection* (*slang*) an exclamation of surprise.

gosling *noun* a young goose.

gospel *noun* **1** the teachings of Jesus Christ. **2** something you can safely believe.
the Gospels the first four books of the New Testament, telling of the life and teachings of Jesus Christ. [from Old English *god* = good, + *spel* = news]

gossamer *noun* **1** fine cobwebs made by small spiders. **2** any fine delicate material.

gossip¹ *verb* (**gossiped, gossiping**) talk a lot about other people.

gossip² *noun* **1** gossiping talk. **2** a person who enjoys gossiping. **gossipy** *adjective*

got *past tense* of **get**.
have got possess, *Have you got a car?*
have got to must.

Gothic *adjective* of the style of building common in the 12th–16th centuries, with pointed arches and much carving.

gouge (*say* gowj) *verb* (**gouged, gouging**) scoop or force out by pressing.

goulash (*say* **goo**-lash) *noun* a meat stew seasoned with red pepper. [from Hungarian *gulyashus* = herdsman's meat]

gourd (*say* goord) *noun* the rounded hard-skinned fruit of a climbing plant.

gourmet (*say* **goor**-may) *noun* a person who understands and appreciates good food and drink. [French, = wine-taster]

gout *noun* a disease that causes painful inflammation of the toes, knees, and fingers. **gouty** *adjective*

▶▶ THESAURUS ◀◀

good-natured *adjective* benevolent, big-hearted, compassionate, easygoing, forgiving, friendly, generous, genial, gracious, helpful, kind, kind-hearted, kindly, obliging, sympathetic, tender-hearted, thoughtful, tolerant, unselfish.

goodness *noun* **1** benevolence, generosity, honour, integrity, kindness, merit, morality, probity, rectitude, righteousness, virtue.

goods *plural noun* **1** articles, commodities, merchandise, products, wares. **2** cargo, freight.

good-tempered *adjective* affable, amiable, amicable, cheerful, easygoing, even-tempered, gentle, good-humoured, happy, happy-go-lucky, jovial, mild, pleasant.

goodwill *noun* benevolence, charity, favour, friendliness, grace, kindness.

goose *noun* gander (*male*), gosling (*young*).

gore¹ *verb* pierce, poke, puncture, wound.

gorge¹ *noun* **1** canyon, chasm, gully, pass, ravine, valley.

gorge² *verb* feast, fill, glut, overeat, satiate, stuff.

gorgeous *adjective* beautiful, colourful, exquisite, magnificent, rich, splendid, stunning (*informal*), sumptuous.

gory *adjective* **2** bloody, grisly, gruesome, macabre, sanguinary, violent.

gossip¹ *verb* blab, chat, natter (*informal*), prattle, tattle, tell tales, tittle-tattle.

gossip² *noun* **1** backbiting, chit-chat, hearsay, rumour, scandal, talk, tittle-tattle. **2** busybody, gossip-monger, rumour-monger, scandal-monger, tattler.

gouge *verb* bore, chisel, cut, dig, groove, hollow, incise, scoop.

gourmet *noun* connoisseur, epicure, foodie (*informal*), gastronome.

▶▶ D I C T I O N A R Y ◀◀

govern *verb* be in charge of the public affairs of a country or an organisation.

governess *noun* a woman employed to teach children in a private household.

government *noun* 1 the group of people who govern a country. 2 the process of governing. **governmental** *adjective*

governor *noun* 1 a person who governs a State or a colony etc. 2 the Queen's representative in an Australian State. 3 a member of the governing body of a school or other institution. 4 the person in charge of a prison.

Governor-General *noun* the Queen's representative in the Commonwealth of Australia and in any other Commonwealth country that recognises the Queen as head of State.

gown *noun* a loose flowing garment.

GP *abbreviation* general practitioner.

grab *verb* (**grabbed, grabbing**) take hold of suddenly or greedily.

grace¹ *noun* 1 beauty of movement or manner or design. 2 goodwill; favour. 3 a short prayer of thanks before or after a meal. 4 the title of a duke, duchess, or archbishop, *His Grace the Duke of York.*

grace² *verb* (**graced, gracing**) bring honour or dignity to something.

graceful *adjective* full of grace. **gracefully** *adverb*, **gracefulness** *noun*

gracious *adjective* kind and pleasant. **graciously** *adverb*, **graciousness** *noun*

grade¹ *noun* 1 a step in a scale of quality or value or rank; a standard. 2 a class in school.

grade² *verb* (**graded, grading**) arrange in grades. [from Latin *gradus* = a step]

gradient (*say* **gray**-dee-ent) *noun* a slope.

gradual *adjective* happening slowly but steadily. **gradually** *adverb*

graduate¹ (*say* **grad**-yoo-ayt) *verb* (**graduated, graduating**) 1 get a university degree. 2 divide into graded sections; mark with units of measurement.

graduate² (*say* **grad**-yoo-at) *noun* a person who has a university degree.

graffiti *plural noun* scribblings on a wall, *These graffiti are a problem.* [Italian, = scratchings]

Usage Note that this word is a plural (the singular is *graffito*). It is incorrect to say 'a graffiti' or 'this graffiti'.

---

graft¹ *noun* 1 a shoot from one plant or tree fixed into another to form a new growth. 2 a piece of living tissue transplanted by a surgeon to replace what is diseased or damaged, *a skin graft.*

graft² *verb* insert or transplant as a graft.

grain *noun* 1 a small hard seed or similar particle. 2 cereal plants when they are growing or after being harvested. 3 the pattern of lines made by the fibres in a piece of wood. **grainy** *adjective*

gram *noun* a unit of mass or weight in the metric system.

-gram *suffix* forming nouns meaning something written or drawn etc. (e.g. *diagram*). [from Greek *gramma* = thing written]

grammar *noun* 1 the rules for using words correctly. 2 a book about these rules. [from Greek, = the art of letters]

▶▶ T H E S A U R U S ◀◀

govern *verb* administer, be in charge of, command, control, direct, guide, head, lead, manage, reign over, rule, run, superintend, supervise.

government *noun* 2 administration, command, control, leadership, management, regime, rule.

governor *noun* 1 chief, head, ruler. 2 viceroy.

gown *noun* dress, frock, habit, kimono, robe, vestment.

grab *verb* clasp, clutch, grasp, hold, nab (*informal*), pluck, seize, snatch, swipe (*informal*).

grace¹ *noun* 1 beauty, elegance, gracefulness, smoothness. 2 favour, forbearance, forgiveness, goodness, goodwill, lenience, mercy. 3 benediction, blessing, prayer, thanksgiving.

graceful *adjective* agile, elegant, limber, lissom, lithe, nimble, supple.

gracious *adjective* amiable, benevolent, benign, courteous, friendly, good-natured, hospitable, kind, kindly, merciful, polite, tactful.

grade¹ *noun* 1 category, class, level, quality, rank, rating, standard; (*exam grade*) mark, result, score. 2 class, form, year.

grade² *verb* class, classify, mark, rank, rate, sort.

gradient *noun* grade, hill, incline, slope.

gradual *adjective* gentle, piecemeal, progressive, slow, steady. **gradually** *adverb* bit by bit, by degrees, little by little, progressively, slowly, steadily, step by step.

grain *noun* 1 granule, grist, kernel, seed.

grammatical *adjective* of grammar; according to its rules. **grammatically** *adverb*

gramophone *noun* a record-player. [altered from 'phonogram', from Greek *phone* = a sound, + -*gram*]

grampus *noun* (*plural* **grampuses**) a large dolphin-like sea animal.

granary *noun* (*plural* **granaries**) a storehouse for grain.

grand *adjective* **1** splendid, magnificent. **2** including everything; complete, *The grand total*. **grandly** *adverb*, **grandness** *noun*
grand piano a large piano with the strings fixed horizontally.

grandad (*informal*) grandfather.

grandchild *noun* (*plural* **grandchildren**) the child of a person's son or daughter. **granddaughter** *noun*, **grandson** *noun*

grandeur (*say* **grand**-yer) *noun* grandness; splendour.

grandfather *noun* the father of a person's father or mother.
grandfather clock a clock in a tall wooden case.

grandiose (*say* **grand**-ee-ohss) *adjective* imposing, trying to seem grand.

grandma *noun* (*informal*) grandmother.

grandmother *noun* the mother of a person's father or mother.

grandpa *noun* (*informal*) grandfather.

grandparent *noun* a grandfather or grandmother.

grandstand *noun* a building with a roof and rows of seats for spectators at a racecourse or sports ground.

grange *noun* (*British*) a large country house.

granite *noun* a very hard kind of rock.

granny *noun* (*plural* **grannies**) (*informal*) grandmother.
granny knot a reef-knot with the strings crossed the wrong way.

Granny Smith a green-skinned Australian variety of apple.

grant[1] *verb* **1** give or allow what is asked for, *grant a request*. **2** admit; agree that something is true.
take for granted assume that something is true or will always be available.

grant[2] *noun* something granted, especially a sum of money.

granular *adjective* like grains.

granule *noun* a small grain.

grape *noun* a small green or purple berry that grows in bunches on a vine.

grapefruit *noun* (*plural* **grapefruit**) a large round yellow citrus fruit.

grapevine *noun* **1** a vine on which grapes grow. **2** a way by which news is passed on unofficially.

graph *noun* a diagram showing how two qualities are related.
graph paper paper printed with small squares, used for drawing graphs. [from Greek *graphia* = writing]

-graph *suffix* forming nouns and verbs meaning something written or drawn etc. (e.g. *photograph*). [same origin as *graph*]

graphic *adjective* **1** of drawing or painting, *a graphic artist*. **2** giving a lively description. **graphically** *adverb*

graphics *plural noun* diagrams, lettering, and drawings.

graphite *noun* a soft black form of carbon used for the lead in pencils, as a lubricant, and in nuclear reactors.

-graphy *suffix* forming names of descriptive sciences (e.g. *geography*) or methods of writing or drawing etc. (e.g. *photography*). [same origin as *graph*]

grapnel *noun* a heavy metal device with claws for hooking things.

grand *adjective* **1** elegant, glorious, imposing, impressive, large, luxurious, magnificent, majestic, opulent, palatial, posh (*informal*), splendid, stately, sumptuous, superb. **2** all-inclusive, complete, comprehensive, full.

grandeur *noun* dignity, magnificence, majesty, pomp, splendour.

grandiose *adjective* ambitious, grand, impressive, ostentatious, pretentious.

grant[1] *verb* **1** accord, allocate, allow, award, bestow, donate, give, pay, provide. **2** acknowledge, admit, agree, concede.

grant[2] *noun* allowance, award, bursary, endowment, scholarship, subsidy.

grapevine *noun* **2** bush telegraph, mulga wire, network.

graphic *adjective* **1** diagrammatic, drawn, illustrated, pictorial, visual. **2** colourful, descriptive, detailed, explicit, vivid.

grapple *verb* (**grappled, grappling**) 1 struggle; wrestle. 2 seize or hold firmly.

grasp *verb* 1 seize and hold firmly. 2 understand. **grasp** *noun*

grasping *adjective* greedy for money or possessions.

grass *noun* (*plural* **grasses**) 1 a plant with green blades and stalks that are eaten by animals. 2 ground covered with grass. **grassy** *adjective*

grass roots the ordinary people in a political party or other group.

grasshopper *noun* a jumping insect that makes a shrill noise.

grassland *noun* a wide area covered in grass with few trees.

grate¹ *noun* 1 a metal framework that keeps fuel in a fireplace. 2 a fireplace.

grate² *verb* (**grated, grating**) 1 shred into small pieces by rubbing on a rough surface. 2 make an unpleasant noise by rubbing. 3 sound harshly.

grateful *adjective* feeling or showing that you value what was done for you. **gratefully** *adverb* [from Latin *gratus* = thankful, pleasing]

grater *noun* a device with a jagged surface for grating food.

gratify *verb* (**gratified, gratifying**) 1 give pleasure. 2 satisfy a wish etc., *Please gratify our curiosity.* **gratification** *noun* [from Latin *gratus* = pleasing]

grating¹ *noun* a framework of metal or wooden bars placed across an opening.

grating² *adjective* sounding harsh.

gratis (*say* **grar**-tiss) *adverb & adjective* free of charge, *You can have the leaflet gratis.* [Latin, = out of kindness]

gratitude *noun* being grateful.

gratuitous (*say* gra-**tew**-it-us) *adjective* given or done without payment or without good reason. **gratuitously** *adverb*

gratuity (*say* gra-**tew**-it-ee) *noun* (*plural* **gratuities**) money given in gratitude; a tip.

grave¹ *noun* the place where a corpse is buried. [from Old English *graef* = hole dug out]

grave² *adjective* 1 serious, solemn. 2 important. **gravely** *adverb* [from Latin *gravis* = heavy]

gravel *noun* small stones mixed with coarse sand. **gravelled** *adjective*, **gravelly** *adjective*

graven (*say* **gray**-ven) *adjective* carved.

gravestone *noun* a stone monument over a grave.

graveyard *noun* a burial ground.

gravitate *verb* (**gravitated, gravitating**) move or be attracted towards something.

gravitation *noun* 1 gravitating. 2 the force of gravity. **gravitational** *adjective*

gravity *noun* 1 the force that pulls everything towards the earth. 2 seriousness. [same origin as *grave²*]

grapple *verb* 1 fight, struggle, tackle, tussle, wrestle.

grasp *verb* 1 clasp, clench, cling to, clutch, grab, grip, hang on to, hold, seize, snatch, take, take hold of. 2 apprehend, comprehend, cotton on to (*informal*), fathom, follow, get (*informal*), latch on to (*informal*), see, understand. **grasp** *noun* 1 clasp, clutch, grip, hold. 2 command, comprehension, mastery, understanding.

grasping *adjective* acquisitive, avaricious, covetous, greedy, mercenary.

grass *noun* 2 green, lawn, pasture, sward, turf.

grassland *noun* field, meadow, pampas, pasture, plain, prairie, range, savannah, steppe.

grate¹ *noun* 2 fireplace, hearth.

grate² *verb* 1 grind, mince, shred. 2 grind, rasp, rub, scrape, scratch.

grateful *adjective* appreciative, thankful.

gratify *verb* 1 content, delight, gladden, please. 2 fulfil, indulge, pander to, satisfy.

grating¹ *noun* grate, grid, grille.

grating² *adjective* discordant, harsh, jarring, rasping, raucous, shrill, strident.

gratitude *noun* appreciation, thankfulness, thanks.

gratuity *noun* bonus, gift, present, tip.

grave¹ *noun* burial place, crypt, mausoleum, sepulchre, tomb, vault.

grave² *adjective* 1 earnest, funereal, gloomy, grim, pensive, serious, sober, solemn, sombre, staid, thoughtful. 2 critical, crucial, important, momentous, serious, weighty.

gravel *noun* pebbles, road metal, shingle, stones.

gravestone *noun* headstone, monument, tombstone.

graveyard *noun* burial ground, cemetery, churchyard, necropolis.

►► DICTIONARY ◄◄

gravy *noun* a hot brown liquid served with meat.

graze¹ *verb* (**grazed, grazing**) **1** feed on growing grass. **2** scrape slightly in passing. *I grazed my elbow on the wall.*

graze² *noun* a raw place where skin has been scraped.

grazier *noun* a farmer who raises sheep or cattle.

grease¹ *noun* melted fat; any thick oily substance. **greasy** *adjective*

grease² *verb* (**greased, greasing**) put grease on something.

great *adjective* **1** very large; much above average. **2** above average in intensity. **3** very important or talented, *a great composer.* **4** (*informal*) very good or enjoyable, *It's great to see you again.* **5** older or younger by one generation, *great-grandfather.* **greatly** *adverb*, **greatness** *noun*

grebe (*say* greeb) *noun* a kind of diving bird.

greed *noun* being greedy.

greedy *adjective* wanting more food, money, or other things than you need. **greedily** *adverb*, **greediness** *noun*

green¹ *noun* **1** the colour of growing grass. **2** an area of grass, *the village green.*

green² *adjective* **1** of the colour green. **2** inexperienced and likely to make mistakes. **3** concerned with the natural environment. **greenness** *noun*

green ban a prohibition, especially by a trade union, against a development likely to damage the environment.

green belt an area kept as open land round a city.

greenery *noun* green leaves or plants.

greenfly *noun* (*plural* **greenfly**) a small green insect that sucks the juices from plants.

greengrocer *noun* a person who keeps a shop that sells fruit and vegetables. **greengrocery** *noun*

greenhouse *noun* a glass building where plants are protected from cold.

greenhouse effect the warming up of the earth's surface when radiation from the sun is trapped by the atmosphere.

Greenwich Mean Time (*say* **gren**-ich) the time on the line of longitude which passes through Greenwich in London, used as a basis for calculating time throughout the world.

greet *verb* **1** speak to a person who arrives. **2** receive, *They greeted the song with applause.* **3** present itself to, *A strange sight greeted our eyes.*

►► THESAURUS ◄◄

graze¹ *verb* **1** browse, feed. **2** bark, scrape, scratch, skin.

graze² *noun* abrasion, scrape, scratch.

grazier *noun* cattle farmer, pastoralist (*Australian*), sheep farmer.

grease¹ *noun* dripping, fat, lard, lubricant, oil, suet, tallow.

greasy *adjective* fatty, oily, slick.

grease² *verb* lubricate, oil.

great *adjective* **1** big, colossal, considerable, enormous, extensive, gigantic, huge, humungous (*slang*), immense, immeasurable, large, massive, monumental, phenomenal, prodigious, stupendous, sweeping, vast. **2** acute, deep, extreme, intense, profound, severe, strong. **3** brilliant, celebrated, distinguished, eminent, first-class, gifted, illustrious, important, leading, noted, outstanding, pre-eminent, prominent, remarkable, renowned, superior, talented, well-known. **4** brilliant (*informal*), cool (*informal*), delightful, enjoyable, excellent, fabulous (*informal*), fantastic (*informal*), fine, first-rate, good,

grand (*informal*), lovely, magnificent, marvellous, outstanding, pleasant, splendid, super (*informal*), superb, swell (*informal*), terrific (*informal*), tremendous (*informal*), wonderful.

greatest *adjective* best, chief, highest, main, maximum, paramount, supreme, top, utmost.

greatness *noun* distinction, eminence, grandeur, importance, pre-eminence, stature.

greed *noun* avarice, covetousness, cupidity, gluttony, rapacity, voraciousness.

greedy *adjective* (*for food*) gluttonous, ravenous, voracious; (*for money etc.*) avaricious, covetous, grasping, miserly, money-hungry, on the make (*informal*), rapacious.

green² *adjective* **1** apple green, aquamarine, beryl, bottle green, chartreuse, emerald, jade, lime, olive, pea green, sea green. **2** callow, immature, inexperienced, naïve, raw.

greenhouse *noun* conservatory, glasshouse, hothouse.

greet *verb* **1** address, receive, welcome. **3** appear to, meet, present itself to.

greeting *noun* **1** words or actions used to greet somebody. **2** good wishes.

gregarious (*say* grig-**air**-ee-us) *adjective* **1** fond of company. **2** living in flocks or communities. **gregariously** *adverb*, **gregariousness** *noun* [from Latin *gregis* = of a flock]

grenade (*say* grin-**ayd**) *noun* a small bomb, usually thrown by hand.

grey¹ *noun* the colour between black and white, like ashes.

grey² *adjective* **1** of the colour grey. **2** overcast. **greyness** *noun*

greyhound *noun* a slender dog with smooth hair, used in racing.

grid *noun* **1** a framework of bars. **2** a pattern of lines crossing each other.

griddle *noun* a round iron plate for cooking things on.

gridiron *noun* a framework of bars for cooking on.

grief *noun* deep sorrow.
come to grief suffer a disaster.

grievance *noun* something that people are discontented about.

grieve *verb* (**grieved**, **grieving**) **1** cause a person grief. **2** feel grief.

grievous (*say* **gree**-vus) *adjective* **1** causing grief. **2** serious. **grievously** *adverb*

griffin *noun* a creature in fables, with an eagle's head and wings on a lion's body.

grill¹ *noun* **1** a heated element on a cooker for sending heat downwards. **2** food cooked under this. **3** a grille.

grill² *verb* **1** cook under a grill. **2** question closely and severely, *The police grilled him for an hour.*

grille *noun* a metal grating covering a window or similar opening.

grim *adjective* (**grimmer**, **grimmest**) **1** stern; severe. **2** without cheerfulness; unattractive, *a grim prospect.* **grimly** *adverb*, **grimness** *noun*

grimace¹ (*say* grim-**ayss**) *noun* a twisted expression on the face made in pain or disgust.

grimace² *verb* (**grimaced**, **grimacing**) make a grimace.

grime *noun* dirt clinging to a surface or to the skin. **grimy** *adjective*

grin¹ *noun* a broad smile.

grin² *verb* (**grinned**, **grinning**) smile broadly.

grind *verb* (**ground**, **grinding**) *verb* **1** crush into grains or powder. **2** sharpen or smooth by rubbing on a rough surface. **3** rub harshly together. *He ground his teeth in fury.* **4** move with a harsh grating noise, *The bus ground to a halt.* **grinder** *noun*

grindstone *noun* a thick round rough revolving stone for sharpening or grinding things.

grip¹ *verb* (**gripped**, **gripping**) **1** hold firmly. **2** hold a person's attention.

grip² *noun* **1** a firm hold. **2** understanding. **3** a handle. **4** (*American*) a suitcase or travel-bag.

greeting *noun* **1** reception, salutation, welcome. **2** compliments, congratulations, regards, wishes.

gregarious *adjective* **1** extroverted, friendly, outgoing, sociable, social.

grey² *adjective* **1** charcoal grey, dun, grizzled, grizzly, gunmetal, hoary, mousy, silver, slate, smoky, steely. **2** cloudy, dark, dull, gloomy, heavy, leaden, louring, overcast.

grid *noun* **1** grating, grille. **2** lattice, network.

grief *noun* anguish, desolation, distress, heartache, heartbreak, misery, regret, remorse, sadness, sorrow, suffering, unhappiness, woe.

grievance *noun* beef (*slang*), complaint, gripe (*informal*), objection.

grieve *verb* **1** distress, hurt, pain, sadden, upset. **2** fret, lament, mope, mourn, pine, weep.

grill² *verb* **1** barbecue, broil, brown, toast. **2** cross-examine, interrogate, question.

grim *adjective* **1** dour, forbidding, gloomy, glum, harsh, severe, stern. **2** bleak, desolate, dire, dismal, dreadful, forbidding, frightful, ghastly, gloomy, horrible, unpleasant.

grimace² *verb* frown, pull a face, scowl, wince.

grimy *adjective* blackened, dirty, filthy, grubby, soiled, sooty.

grin² *verb* beam, smile, smirk.

grind *verb* **1** crush, granulate, mill, pound, pulverise. **2** file, polish, rub, sharpen, smooth, whet. **3** gnash, grate.

grip¹ *verb* **1** clasp, clutch, grab, grasp, hang on to, hold, seize, snatch, take hold of. **2** absorb, captivate, engross, enthral, hold spellbound, rivet.

grip² *noun* **1** clasp, clutch, grasp, hold. **2** command, comprehension, grasp, hold, mastery, understanding.

▶▶ D I C T I O N A R Y ◀◀

gripe *verb* (**griped**, **griping**) (*informal*) grumble. **gripe** *noun*

grisly *adjective* (**grislier**, **grisliest**) causing horror or disgust; gruesome.

grist *noun* grain for grinding.

gristle *noun* tough rubbery tissue in meat. **gristly** *adjective*

grit[1] *noun* **1** tiny pieces of stone or sand. **2** courage and endurance. **gritty** *adjective*. **grittiness** *noun*

grit[2] *verb* (**gritted**, **gritting**) **1** spread with grit, *grit the roads*. **2** clench the teeth when in pain or trouble.

grizzle *verb* (**grizzled**, **grizzling**) whimper, whine.

grizzled *adjective* streaked with grey hairs.

grizzly *adjective* grey-haired. **grizzly bear** a large fierce bear.

groan *verb* **1** make a long deep sound in pain or distress or disapproval. **2** creak loudly under a heavy load. **groan** *noun*, **groaner** *noun*

grocer *noun* a person who keeps a shop that sells food and household supplies. **grocery** *noun* (*plural* **groceries**)

grog *noun* **1** a drink of alcoholic spirits, usually rum, mixed with water. **2** (*Australian*) any alcoholic drink.

groggy *adjective* (**groggier**, **groggiest**) weak and unsteady, especially after illness. **groggily** *adverb*, **grogginess** *noun*

groin *noun* the groove where the thigh joins the trunk of the body.

groom[1] *noun* **1** a person whose job is to look after horses. **2** a bridegroom.

groom[2] *verb* **1** clean and brush (an animal). **2** make neat and trim. **3** train a person for a certain job or position.

groove *noun* a long narrow furrow or channel cut in the surface of something. **grooved** *adjective*

grope *verb* (**groped**, **groping**) feel about for something you cannot see.

gross[1] (*say* grohss) *adjective* **1** fat and ugly. **2** having bad manners; vulgar. **3** very obvious or shocking, *gross stupidity*. **4** total; without anything being deducted, *our gross income*. (Compare *net*[3].) **5** (*informal*) disgusting, repulsive. **grossly** *adverb*, **grossness** *noun*

gross[2] *noun* (*plural* **gross**) twelve dozen (144) of something, *ten gross = 1440*.

grotesque (*say* groh-**tesk**) *adjective* very strange, fantastically ugly. **grotesquely** *adverb*, **grotesqueness** *noun*

grotto *noun* (*plural* **grottoes**) a picturesque cave.

▶▶ T H E S A U R U S ◀◀

gripe *verb* beef (*slang*), bitch (*informal*), complain, find fault, grizzle (*informal*), groan, grumble, moan, protest, whine, whinge (*informal*). **gripe** *noun* beef (*slang*), complaint, grievance, grizzle (*informal*), grumble, objection, protest, whine, whinge (*informal*).

grisly *adjective* appalling, dreadful, frightful, ghastly, gory, grim, gruesome, hideous, horrendous, horrible, horrid, macabre, repugnant, repulsive, shocking, vile.

gristly *adjective* leathery, tough.

grit[1] *noun* **1** dirt, dust, sand. **2** backbone, courage, determination, endurance, fortitude, guts (*informal*), mettle, pluck, spirit, spunk (*informal*).

grit[2] *verb* **2** clench, set.

grizzle *verb* cry, fret, moan, whimper, whine, whinge (*informal*); see also COMPLAIN.

groan *verb* **1** bellow, cry, howl, moan, wail.

grog *noun* **2** alcohol, liquor.

groggy *adjective* dazed, dopey (*informal*), shaky, unsteady, wonky (*informal*), woozy (*informal*).

groom[1] *noun* **2** bridegroom, husband.

groom[2] *verb* **1** brush, comb, curry. **2** clean up, preen, spruce up, tidy, wash. **3** prepare, prime, train.

groove *noun* channel, cut, furrow, rut, score, slot.

grope *verb* feel about, fish, fossick (*Australian informal*), fumble, rummage, scrabble, search.

gross[1] *adjective* **1** corpulent, enormous, fat, flabby, huge, obese, overweight, rotund. **2** boorish, coarse, crass, crude, rude, unrefined, vulgar. **3** blatant, clear, flagrant, glaring, manifest, obvious, outrageous. **4** entire, pre-tax, total, whole. **5** see DISGUSTING (at DISGUST[2]).

grotesque *adjective* absurd, bizarre, deformed, distorted, fantastic, freakish, hideous, misshapen, monstrous, odd, ugly, weird.

grotto *noun* cave, cavern.

▶▶ D I C T I O N A R Y ◀◀

grouch *noun* (*informal*) a discontented person. **grouchy** *adjective*

ground¹ *past tense* of **grind**.

ground² *noun* **1** the solid surface of the earth. **2** a sports field.

ground³ *verb* **1** run aground. **2** prevent from flying, *All aircraft are grounded because of the fog.* **3** give a good basic training, *Ground them in the rules of spelling.* **4** base, *This theory is grounded on known facts.*

grounding *noun* basic training.

groundless *adjective* without foundation or reasons, *Your fears are groundless.*

grounds *plural noun* **1** the gardens of a large house. **2** solid particles that sink to the bottom, *coffee grounds.* **3** reasons, *There are grounds for suspicion.*

groundsheet *noun* a piece of waterproof material for spreading on the ground.

groundsman *noun* (*plural* **groundsmen**) a person whose job is to look after a sports ground or school grounds. **groundsperson** *noun*

groundwork *noun* work that lays the basis for something.

group¹ *noun* a number of people, animals, or things that come together or belong together in some way.

group² *verb* **1** put together or come together in a group or groups. **2** classify.

grouse¹ *noun* (*plural* **grouse**) a bird with feathered feet, hunted as game.

grouse² *verb* (**groused**, **grousing**) (*informal*) grumble. **grouse** *noun*, **grouser** *noun*

grove *noun* a group of trees, a small wood.

grovel *verb* (**grovelled**, **grovelling**) **1** crawl on the ground, especially in a show of fear or humility. **2** act in an excessively humble way. **groveller** *noun*

grow *verb* (**grew**, **grown**, **growing**) **1** become bigger or greater. **2** develop; put out shoots. **3** cultivate, plant and look after. *She grows roses.* **4** become, *He grew rich.* **grower** *noun*

growl *verb* make a deep angry sound. **growl** *noun*

▶▶ T H E S A U R U S ◀◀

grouch *noun* crosspatch, grumbler, grump (*informal*), killjoy, malcontent, misery (*informal*), sourpuss (*informal*), spoilsport, wet blanket, whinger (*informal*).
grouchy *adjective* bad-tempered, cantankerous, churlish, crabby, cranky, cross, crotchety, crusty, discontented, disgruntled, fractious, grumpy, irritable, peevish, shirty (*informal*), snaky (*Australian informal*), stroppy (*informal*), sullen, surly, testy, tetchy.

ground² *noun* **1** dirt, earth, land, loam, soil. **2** arena, field, oval, pitch, stadium.

ground³ *verb* **1** beach, run aground, shipwreck, strand. **3** drill, educate, instruct, teach, train. **4** base, establish, found, root.

groundless *adjective* baseless, irrational, unfounded, unjustified, unwarranted.

grounds *plural noun* **1** campus, estate, garden(s), lawn(s), surroundings. **2** deposit, dregs, lees, sediment. **3** basis, cause, evidence, justification, reason.

groundwork *noun* preparation, spadework.

group¹ *noun* alliance, assembly, association, assortment, band, batch, battery, bevy, body, bracket, brigade, brood, bunch, category, circle, clan, class, classification, clique, club, cluster, cohort, collection, colony, combination, community, company, congregation, consortium, constellation (*of stars*), contingent, convoy, corps, crew, crop, crowd, drove, ensemble, faction, family, federation, fleet, flock, flotilla, force, gaggle (*of geese*), galaxy (*of stars*), gang, gathering, genus, herd, host, league, legion, litter, lot, mass, mob, movement, order, organisation, pack, panel, party, phalanx, platoon, pod (*of seals, dolphins, or whales*), posse, pride (*of lions*), rabble, ring, school (*of fish, dolphins, or whales*), series, set, shoal (*of fish*), society, species, squad, subset, swarm (*of bees*), syndicate, team, throng, tribe, troop, troupe (*of actors*), union.

group² *verb* **1** associate, band, cluster, collect, congregate, gather. **2** arrange, class, classify, organise, sort.

grove *noun* orchard, plantation.

grovel *verb* **2** crawl (*informal*), fawn (on), ingratiate yourself (with), kowtow, suck up (*informal*), toady.

grow *verb* **1** become bigger, boom, build up, develop, enlarge, evolve, expand, extend, fill out, flourish, grow up, increase, lengthen, mature, multiply, mushroom, progress, prosper, shoot up, snowball, spread, thrive. **2** burgeon, develop, flourish, germinate, live, shoot, spring up, sprout, thrive. **3** cultivate, produce, propagate, raise. **4** become, get, turn.

growl *verb* snarl.

growth *noun* **1** the process of growing; development. **2** something that has grown. **3** a tumour.

grub[1] *noun* **1** a tiny worm-like creature that will become an insect; a larva. **2** (*slang*) food.

grub[2] *verb* (**grubbed**, **grubbing**) **1** dig up by the roots. **2** rummage.

grubby *adjective* (**grubbier**, **grubbiest**) rather dirty. **grubbiness** *noun*

grudge[1] *noun* a feeling of resentment or ill will.

grudge[2] *verb* (**grudged**, **grudging**) resent having to give or allow something.

gruelling *adjective* exhausting.

gruesome *adjective* causing people to feel horror or disgust.

gruff *adjective* **1** (of a voice) harsh. **2** having a rough unfriendly manner. **gruffly** *adverb*, **gruffness** *noun*

grumble *verb* (**grumbled**, **grumbling**) complain in a bad-tempered way. **grumble** *noun*, **grumbler** *noun*

grumpy *adjective* bad-tempered. **grumpily** *adverb*, **grumpiness** *noun*

grunt *verb* **1** make a pig's gruff snort. **2** speak or say gruffly. **grunt** *noun*

GST *abbreviation* goods and services tax.

guarantee[1] *noun* a formal promise to do something or to repair an object if it breaks or goes wrong.

guarantee[2] *verb* (**guaranteed**, **guaranteeing**) give a guarantee; promise. **guarantor** *noun*

guard[1] *verb* **1** protect; keep safe. **2** watch over and prevent from escaping.

guard[2] *noun* **1** guarding; protection, *Keep the prisoners under close guard*. **2** someone who guards a person or place. **3** a group of soldiers or police officers etc. acting as a guard. **4** a railway official in charge of a train. **5** a protecting device, *a fire-guard*.

guardian *noun* **1** someone who guards. **2** a person who is legally in charge of a child whose parents cannot look after him or her. **guardianship** *noun*

gubba *noun* an Aboriginal name for a white person.

growth *noun* **1** advancement, development, enlargement, expansion, improvement, increase, progress, proliferation. **3** cancer, cyst, lump, polyp, tumour.

grub[1] *noun* **1** caterpillar, larva, maggot.

grubby *adjective* blackened, dirty, dusty, filthy, grimy, soiled.

grudge[1] *noun* animosity, bitterness, grievance, hard feelings, ill will, rancour, resentment.
hold a grudge against have a derry on (*Australian informal*), have a down on (*informal*), have a set on (*Australian informal*).

grudging *adjective* reluctant, resentful, sparing, unwilling.

gruelling *adjective* arduous, demanding, exhausting, hard, laborious, strenuous, tiring, tough.

gruesome *adjective* ghastly, ghoulish, gory, grisly, hideous, horrible, macabre, repulsive, revolting, shocking, sickening.

gruff *adjective* **1** gravelly, guttural, harsh, hoarse, husky, rough, throaty. **2** abrupt, bad-tempered, blunt, brusque, crabby, crusty, curt, grouchy (*informal*), grumpy, sullen, surly, unfriendly.

grumble *verb* beef (*slang*), bitch (*informal*), carp, cavil, complain, find fault with, gripe (*informal*), grizzle (*informal*), groan, moan, object, protest, whine, whinge (*informal*).

grumpy *adjective* bad-tempered, cantankerous, churlish, crabby, cranky, cross, crotchety, grouchy, irritable, peevish, petulant, shirty (*informal*), snaky (*Australian informal*), sullen, surly, testy, tetchy.

guarantee[1] *noun* assurance, pledge, promise, undertaking, warranty, word.

guarantee[2] *verb* certify, ensure, pledge, promise, secure, swear, vow.

guard[1] *verb* **1** defend, keep an eye on, look after, mind, preserve, protect, safeguard, shelter, shield, supervise, watch over.

guard[2] *noun* **2** bodyguard, chaperone, escort, garrison, guardian, guardsman, lookout, minder, patrol, picket, security officer, sentinel, sentry, warder, watchman. **5** protector, screen, shield.
on (your) guard alert, careful, on the watch, prepared, ready, vigilant, wary, watchful.
stand guard guard, keep a lookout, keep nit (*slang*), keep watch, patrol.

guardian *noun* **1** custodian, defender, keeper, preserver, protector, trustee, warden, watchdog.
guardianship *noun* care, charge, custody, keeping, protection.

guernsey noun (*Australian*) a football jumper.
get a guernsey be selected for a team, win recognition or approval.

guerrilla (*say* ger-**il**-a) noun a person who fights by making surprise attacks as one of a small group. [Spanish, = little war]

guess[1] noun (*plural* **guesses**) an opinion given without making careful calculations or without certain knowledge.

guess[2] verb make a guess. **guesser** noun

guest noun 1 a person who is invited to visit or stay at another's house. 2 a person staying at a hotel. 3 a person who takes part in another's show as a visiting performer.

guffaw verb give a noisy laugh. **guffaw** noun

guidance noun 1 guiding. 2 advising or advice on problems.

Guide noun a member of the Guides Association, an organisation for girls.

guide[1] noun 1 a person who shows others the way or points out interesting sights. 2 a book giving information about a place or subject. 3 an adviser.

guide[2] verb (**guided**, **guiding**) act as guide to.

guidebook noun a book of information about a place, for travellers or visitors.

guidelines plural noun statements that give general advice about something.

guild (*say* gild) noun a society of people with similar skills or interests.

guilder (*say* **gild**-er) noun a Dutch coin.

guile (*rhymes with* mile) noun craftiness.

guillotine[1] (*say* **gil**-ot-een) noun 1 a machine with a heavy blade for beheading criminals, used in France. 2 a machine with a long blade for cutting paper or metal. 3 fixing a time for a vote to be taken in Parliament in order to cut short a debate.

guillotine[2] verb (**guillotined**, **guillotining**) cut with a guillotine. [named after Dr Guillotin, who suggested its use in France in 1789]

guilt noun 1 the fact of having committed an offence. 2 a feeling of being to blame for something that has happened.

guilty adjective 1 having done wrong. 2 feeling or showing guilt. **guiltily** adverb

guinea (*say* **gin**-ee) noun 1 a former British gold coin worth about $2. 2 this amount of money.

guinea-pig noun 1 a small furry animal without a tail. 2 a person who is used as the subject of an experiment.

guise (*say as* guys) noun an outward disguise or pretence.

guitar noun a musical instrument played by plucking its strings. **guitarist** noun

gulf noun 1 a large area of the sea that is partly surrounded by land. 2 a wide gap; a great difference.

gull noun a seagull.

gullet noun the tube from the throat to the stomach.

gullible adjective easily deceived. [from an old word *gull* = a fool]

guess[1] noun assumption, conjecture, estimate, guesstimate (*informal*), hunch, hypothesis, prediction, shot in the dark, supposition, surmise, suspicion, theory.

guess[2] verb assume, conjecture, estimate, have a stab at (*informal*), imagine, predict, reckon, speculate, suppose, surmise, suspect, think.

guest noun 1 billet, caller, company, visitor.

guidance noun 2 advice, counselling, direction, help, information, instruction.

guide[1] noun 1 conductor, courier, director, escort, leader, pilot, usher. 3 adviser, counsellor, guru, mentor, teacher.

guide[2] verb conduct, direct, escort, lead, manoeuvre, navigate, pilot, show the way, steer, usher.

guidebook noun directory, guide, handbook, manual.

guidelines plural noun instructions, principles, regulations, requirements, rules, standards.

guild noun association, federation, league, organisation, society, union.

guile noun artifice, craftiness, cunning, deceit, duplicity, slyness, trickery.

guilt noun 1 blame, fault, responsibility. 2 compunction, contrition, disgrace, remorse, self-reproach, shame.

guilty adjective 1 blameworthy, culpable, responsible. 2 ashamed, contrite, hangdog, remorseful, shamefaced, sheepish.

guise noun cover, disguise, masquerade, pretence, show.

gulf noun 1 bay, cove, inlet. 2 chasm, gap, rift.

gullet noun craw, oesophagus, throat.

gullible adjective believing, credulous, green, naïve, trusting, unsuspecting.

▶▶ DICTIONARY ◀◀

gully *noun* (*plural* **gullies**) **1** (*Australian*) a narrow valley. **2** a narrow channel that carries water.

gulp¹ *verb* **1** swallow hastily or greedily. **2** make a loud swallowing noise.

gulp² *noun* **1** the act of gulping. **2** a large mouthful of liquid.

gum¹ *noun* the firm flesh in which teeth are rooted. [from Old English *goma*]

gum² *noun* **1** a sticky substance produced by some trees and shrubs, used as glue. **2** a sweet made with gum or gelatine. **3** chewing-gum. **4** a gum-tree. **gummy** *adjective*.

gum³ *verb* (**gummed**, **gumming**) cover or stick with gum. [from Latin *gummi*]

gumnut *noun* the woody seed-case of a gum-tree.

gum-tree *noun* a eucalyptus.

gumption *noun* (*informal*) common sense.

gun¹ *noun* **1** a weapon that fires shells or bullets from a metal tube. **2** a starting-pistol. **3** a device that forces a substance out of a tube, *a grease-gun.* **gunfire** *noun*, **gunshot** *noun*

gun² *verb* (**gunned**, **gunning**) shoot with a gun, *They gunned him down.*

gunboat *noun* a small warship.

gunman *noun* (*plural* **gunmen**) a criminal with a gun.

gunner *noun* a person who operates a gun.

gunnery *noun* the making or use of guns.

gunpowder *noun* a kind of explosive.

gunwale (*say* **gun**-al) *noun* the upper edge of a small ship's or boat's side. [from *gun* + *wale* = a ridge (because it was formerly used to support guns)]

gurgle *verb* (**gurgled**, **gurgling**) make a low bubbling sound. **gurgle** *noun*

gush *verb* **1** flow suddenly or quickly. **2** talk effusively. **gush** *noun*

gust¹ *noun* **1** a sudden rush of wind. **2** a burst of rain, smoke, or sound. **gusty** *adjective*, **gustily** *adverb*

gust² *verb* blow in gusts.

gusto *noun* great enjoyment; zest.

gut¹ *noun* the lower part of the digestive system; the intestine.

gut² *verb* (**gutted**, **gutting**) **1** remove the guts from a dead fish or other animal. **2** remove or destroy the inside of something, *The fire gutted the factory.*

guts *plural noun* **1** the digestive system; the inside parts of a person or thing. **2** (*informal*) courage.

gutter¹ *noun* a long narrow channel at the side of a street, or along the edge of a roof, for carrying away rainwater.

gutter² *verb* (of a candle) burn unsteadily so that melted wax runs down. [from Latin *gutta* = a drop]

guttersnipe *noun* a poor child who plays in the streets in a slum.

guttural (*say* **gut**-er-al) *adjective* throaty, harsh-sounding, *a guttural voice.* [from Latin *guttur* = throat]

▶▶ THESAURUS ◀◀

gully *noun* **1** gorge, ravine, valley. **2** channel, ditch, drain, gutter.

gulp¹ *verb* **1** bolt, devour, gobble, guzzle, wolf.

gulp² *noun* **2** draught, mouthful, swallow, swig (*informal*).

gum² *noun* **1** adhesive, glue, paste.

gum³ *verb* glue, paste, stick.

gumption *noun* common sense, enterprise, initiative, nous (*informal*), sense, wit.

gun¹ *noun* **1** arm, firearm; (*various guns*) airgun, automatic, blunderbuss, cannon, carbine, flintlock, handgun, howitzer, machine-gun, mortar, musket, pistol, revolver, rifle, semi-automatic, shotgun, sub-machine-gun, tommy-gun.
gunfire *noun* broadside, cannonade, fire, flak, fusillade, salvo, shooting.

gunman *noun* assassin, gunslinger, marksman, sniper.

gurgle *verb & noun* babble, burble.

gush *verb* **1** flow, pour, run, rush, spout, spurt, stream, surge. **2** babble on, get carried away (*informal*), go overboard (*informal*), rave (*informal*).
gush *noun* cascade, flood, jet, outflow, outpouring, rush, spurt, stream, torrent.

gust¹ *noun* **1** blast, puff, rush, squall.
gusty *adjective* blowy, blustery, squally, stormy, windy.

gusto *noun* enjoyment, enthusiasm, relish, spirit, verve, vigour, zeal, zest.

gut¹ *noun* abdomen, bowel, insides (*informal*), intestine.

gut² *verb* **2** destroy, devastate, ravage.

guts *plural noun* **2** boldness, courage, determination, grit (*informal*), nerve, pluck, spunk (*informal*).

gutter¹ *noun* channel, culvert, ditch, drain, gully, sewer, trench, trough.

▶▶ D I C T I O N A R Y ◀◀

gutzer *noun* (*Australian slang*) a bad fall, *he came a gutzer.*

guy[1] *noun* (*informal*) **1** a man. **2** a person. [from Guy Fawkes, a conspirator in the Gunpowder Plot]

guy[2] or **guy-rope** *noun* a rope used to hold something in place.

guzzle *verb* (**guzzled, guzzling**) eat or drink greedily. **guzzler** *noun*

gym (*say* jim) *noun* (*informal*) **1** a gymnasium. **2** gymnastics.

gymkhana (*say* jim-**kah**-na) *noun* a series of horse-riding contests and other sports events.

gymnasium *noun* a place fitted up for gymnastics. [from Greek *gymnos* = naked (because Greek men exercised naked)]

gymnast *noun* an expert in gymnastics.

gymnastics *plural noun* exercises performed to develop the muscles or to show the performer's agility. **gymnastic** *adjective*

gypsy *noun* (*plural* **gypsies**) a member of a people who live in caravans and wander from place to place. [from *Egyptian*, because gypsies were originally thought to have come from Egypt]

gyrate (*say* jy-**rayt**) *verb* (**gyrated, gyrating**) revolve; move in circles or spirals. **gyration** *noun* [from Greek *gyros* = a ring or circle]

gyroscope (*say* **jy**-ro-skohp) *noun* a device that keeps steady because of a heavy wheel spinning inside it. [same origin as *gyrate*]

▶▶ T H E S A U R U S ◀◀

guy *noun* **1** bloke (*informal*), boy, chap (*informal*), fellow (*informal*), gentleman, lad, male, man.

guzzle *verb* bolt, devour, gobble, gulp, scoff (*informal*), wolf.

gymnastics *plural noun* acrobatics, callisthenics.

gypsy *noun* nomad, Romany, traveller, vagabond, wanderer.

gyrate *verb* circle, pirouette, revolve, rotate, spin, spiral, turn, twirl, wheel, whirl.

► Hh ◄

ha *interjection* an exclamation of triumph or surprise.

haberdashery *noun* dress accessories and small articles used in sewing, e.g. ribbons, buttons, thread.

habit *noun* **1** something that you do without thinking because you have done it so often; a settled way of behaving. **2** the long dress worn by a monk or nun.

habitat *noun* where an animal or plant lives naturally.

habitation *noun* **1** a dwelling. **2** inhabiting a place.

habitual *adjective* **1** done as a habit; usual. **2** given to a habit, *a habitual liar*.

hack¹ *verb* **1** chop or cut roughly. **2** (*informal*) access a computer file without authorisation. **hacker** *noun*

hack² *noun* a horse for ordinary riding.

hackles *plural noun* **with their hackles up** angry and ready to fight. [*hackles* are the long feathers on some birds' necks]

hackneyed *adjective* used so often that it is no longer interesting.

hacksaw *noun* a saw for cutting metal.

haddock *noun* (*plural* **haddock**) a North Atlantic seafish like cod but smaller, used as food.

hadn't (*mainly spoken*) had not.

haemoglobin (*say* heem-a-**gloh**-bin) *noun* the red substance that carries oxygen in the blood. [from Greek *haima* = blood]

haemophilia (*say* heem-o-**fil**-ee-a) *noun* a disease that causes people to bleed dangerously from even a slight cut. [from Greek *haima* = blood, + *philia* = loving]

haemorrhage (*say* **hem**-er-ij) *noun* bleeding. [from Greek *haima* = blood, + *rhegnum* = burst]

hag *noun* an ugly old woman.

haggard *adjective* looking ill or very tired.

haggis *noun* (*plural* **haggises**) a Scottish food made from sheep's offal.

haggle *verb* (**haggled**, **haggling**) argue about a price or agreement.

ha ha *interjection* laughter.

haiku (*say* **hy**-koo) *noun* (*plural* **haiku**) a kind of short poem, usually with three lines. [Japanese]

hail¹ *noun* frozen drops of rain. **hail** *verb*, **hailstone** *noun*, **hailstorm** *noun*

hail² *interjection* an exclamation of greeting.

hail³ *verb* call out to somebody. **hail from** come from, *He hails from Ireland.*

hair *noun* **1** a soft covering that grows on the heads and bodies of people and animals. **2** one of the threads that make up this covering. **hairbrush** *noun*, **haircut** *noun* **keep your hair on** (*informal*) do not lose your temper. **split hairs** make petty or unimportant distinctions of meaning. **hair-splitting** *noun*

►►►THESAURUS ◄◄◄

habit *noun* **1** custom, inclination, practice, predisposition, propensity, routine, tendency, way, wont. **2** costume, dress, garb, robe.

habitat *noun* domain, environment, habitation, home, setting, surroundings, territory.

habitual *adjective* **1** accustomed, customary, established, familiar, fixed, normal, regular, routine, set, standard, traditional, usual. **2** addicted, chronic, confirmed, hardened, inveterate.

hack¹ *verb* **1** chop, cut, hew, mutilate, slash.

hackneyed *adjective* banal, clichéd, common, commonplace, conventional, overused, pedestrian, stale, stereotyped, stock, trite.

hag *noun* bag (*slang*), battleaxe (*informal*), crone, witch.

haggard *adjective* careworn, drawn, emaciated, exhausted, gaunt, thin, worn.

haggle *verb* argue, bargain, dispute, negotiate, quarrel, quibble, wrangle.

hail³ *verb* call to, flag down, signal to, wave to. **hail from** be born in, come from, originate from.

hair *noun* **1** curls, locks, ringlets, tresses; (*facial hair*) beard, bristles, fuzz, moustache, sideburns, whiskers; (*an animal's hair*) coat, down, fleece, fur, mane, pelt, wool. **2** bristle, filament, strand.

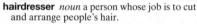

hairdresser *noun* a person whose job is to cut and arrange people's hair.

hairpin *noun* a U-shaped pin for keeping hair in place.

hairpin bend a sharp bend in a road.

hair-raising *adjective* terrifying.

hairy *adjective* **1** with a lot of hair. **2** (*slang*) hair-raising; difficult.

hake *noun* (*plural* **hake**) a sea-fish used as food, also called *gemfish* in Australia.

halal *noun* meat prepared according to Muslim law.

halcyon (*say* **hal**-see-on) *noun* happy and peaceful, *halcyon days*.

hale *adjective* strong and healthy, *hale and hearty*.

half¹ *noun* (*plural* **halves**) one of the two equal parts or amounts into which something is or can be divided.

half² *adverb* partly; not completely, *This meat is only half cooked*.

not half (*slang*) extremely, *Was she cross? Not half!*

half-baked *adjective* (*informal*) not well planned; foolish.

half-brother *noun* a brother to whom you are related by one parent but not by both parents.

half-hearted *adjective* not very enthusiastic.
half-heartedly *adverb*

halfpenny (*say* **hayp**-nee) *noun* (*plural* **halfpennies** for separate coins, **halfpence** for a sum of money) a former coin worth half a penny.

half-sister *noun* a sister to whom you are related by one parent but not by both parents.

half-time *noun* the point or interval halfway through a game.

halfway *adjective* & *adverb* between two others and equally distant from each.

half-witted *adjective* mentally deficient; stupid. **half-wit** *noun*

halibut *noun* (*plural* **halibut**) a large flat fish used as food.

hall *noun* **1** a space or passage into which the front entrance of a house etc. opens. **2** a very large room or building used for meetings, concerts, etc.

hallelujah *interjection* & *noun* alleluia.

hallmark *noun* an official mark made on gold, silver, and platinum to show its quality.

hallo *interjection* a word used to greet somebody or to attract attention.

hallow *verb* **1** make a thing holy. **2** honour something as being holy.

Hallowe'en *noun* 31 October, the eve of All Saints' Day.

hallucination *noun* something you think you can see or hear that is not really there.

halo *noun* (*plural* **haloes**) a circle of light round something, especially round the head of a saint etc. in paintings.

halt¹ *verb* stop.

halt² *noun* **1** a stop, *Work came to a halt*. **2** a small stopping-place on a railway.

halter *noun* a rope or strap put round a horse's head so that it can be led or fastened by this.

hairdresser *noun* barber, haircutter, hair stylist.

hair-raising *adjective* frightening, hairy (*slang*), nerve-racking, scary, spine-chilling, terrifying.

hairy *adjective* **1** bristly, bushy, downy, fleecy, furry, fuzzy, hirsute, shaggy, stubbly, unshaven, whiskery, woolly. **2** dangerous, dicey (*slang*), difficult, frightening, hair-raising, nerve-racking, scary, terrifying.

hale *adjective* fit, healthy, lively, robust, sprightly, spry, strong, vigorous, well.

half² *adverb* partially, partly, slightly.

half-hearted *adjective* apathetic, feeble, indifferent, lackadaisical, lukewarm, un-enthusiastic.

halfway *adjective* intermediate, median, mid, middle, midway.

hall *noun* **1** corridor, entrance hall, foyer, lobby, passage, vestibule. **2** assembly hall, auditorium, chamber, concert hall, room, theatre.

hallmark *noun* badge, brand, characteristic, mark, stamp, trade mark.

hallow *verb* **1** bless, consecrate, make holy, make sacred, sanctify. **2** honour, respect, revere, venerate.

hallucination *noun* apparition, dream, fantasy, illusion, mirage, nightmare, phantasm, vision.

halo *noun* aureole, nimbus.

halt¹ *verb* arrest, block, check, come to a stop, pull up, stem, stop.

halt² *noun* **1** break, close, delay, hiatus, intermission, interruption, pause, recess, shut-down, standstill, stop, stoppage, suspension, termination.

DICTIONARY

halve *verb* (**halved**, **halving**) **1** divide into halves. **2** reduce to half its size.

ham *noun* **1** meat from a pig's leg. **2** (*slang*) an actor or performer who is not very good. **3** (*informal*) someone who operates a radio to send and receive messages as a hobby.

hamburger *noun* a flat round cake of minced beef served fried, often in a bread roll. [named after Hamburg in West Germany (not after *ham*)]

hamlet *noun* a small village.

hammer[1] *noun* a tool with a heavy metal head used for driving nails in, breaking things, etc.

hammer[2] *verb* **1** hit with a hammer. **2** strike loudly. **3** (*informal*) defeat.

hammock *noun* a bed made of a strong net or piece of cloth hung by cords.

hamper[1] *noun* a large box-shaped basket with a lid.

hamper[2] *verb* hinder; prevent from moving or working freely.

hamster *noun* a small furry animal with cheek-pouches for carrying grain.

hand[1] *noun* **1** the end part of the arm below the wrist. **2** a pointer on a clock or dial. **3** a worker; a member of a ship's crew, *All hands on deck!* **4** the cards held by one player in a card-game. **5** side or direction, *on the other hand.* **6** control; care, *You are in good hands.* **7** influence; help, *Give me a hand with these boxes.*

at hand near; about to happen.
by hand using your hand or hands.
hands down winning easily.
in hand in your possession; being dealt with.
on hand available.
out of hand out of control.

hand[2] *verb* give or pass something to somebody, *Hand it over.*

handbag *noun* a small bag for holding a purse and personal articles.

handbook *noun* a small book that gives useful facts about something.

handcuff[1] *noun* one of a pair of metal rings linked by a chain, for fastening wrists together.

handcuff[2] *verb* fasten with handcuffs.

handful *noun* (*plural* **handfuls**) **1** as much as can be carried in one hand. **2** a few people or things. **3** (*informal*) a troublesome person or task.

handicap *noun* **1** a disadvantage. **2** a physical or mental disability. **handicap** *verb*, **handicapped** *adjective*

handicraft *noun* artistic work done with the hands, e.g. woodwork, needlework.

handily *adverb* in a handy way.

handiwork *noun* **1** something made by hand. **2** something done, *Is this mess your handiwork?*

handkerchief *noun* a small square of cloth for wiping the nose or face. [from *hand* + *kerchief*]

THESAURUS

halve *verb* **1** bisect, divide in two. **2** cut by half, reduce to half.

hammer[1] *noun* claw hammer, gavel, mallet, sledgehammer.

hammer[2] *verb* **1** bang, drive, hit, knock, nail, tack. **2** bash, batter, beat, hit, knock, pound, strike, thump.

hamper[1] *noun* basket, pannier.

hamper[2] *verb* check, curb, hinder, impede, inhibit, interfere with, limit, obstruct, restrict.

hand[1] *noun* **1** fist, mitt (*slang*), palm, paw (*informal*). **3** assistant, employee, labourer, worker. **6** authority, care, charge, control, custody, jurisdiction, keeping, possession, power, responsibility. **7** aid, assistance, help, support.
at hand 1 accessible, close, handy, near, nearby. **2** approaching, close, coming, imminent, near, soon.
by hand manually.

hands down easily, effortlessly.
on hand accessible, available, handy, present.
out of hand chaotic, out of control, out of order.

hand[2] *verb* give, pass.
hand in deliver, give, present, submit.
hand out deal out, dish out (*informal*), dispense, distribute, dole out, give out, share out.
hand over deliver, give, pass, present, surrender, turn over.

handbag *noun* bag, purse (*American*).

handbook *noun* guidebook, manual.

handcuffs *plural noun* manacles, shackles.

handful *noun* **2** few, remnant, sprinkling.

handicap *noun* **1** barrier, disadvantage, drawback, hindrance, impediment, limitation, obstacle, stumbling block. **2** disability, impairment.
handicap *verb* disadvantage, hamper, hinder, impede, limit, restrict.

▶▶ D I C T I O N A R Y ◀◀

handle[1] *noun* the part of a thing by which it is carried or controlled.

handle[2] *verb* (**handled, handling**) **1** touch or feel something with your hands. **2** operate something with your hands. **3** deal with; manage, *Will you handle the catering?* **handler** *noun*

handlebar *noun* (also **handlebars**) the bar, with a handle at each end, that steers a bicycle or motor cycle etc.

handrail *noun* a narrow rail for people to hold as a support.

handshake *noun* shaking hands with someone as a greeting etc.

handsome *adjective* **1** good-looking. **2** generous. **handsomely** *adverb*

handstand *noun* balancing on your hands with your feet in the air.

handwriting *noun* writing done by hand. **handwritten** *adjective*

handy *adjective* (**handier, handiest**) **1** convenient, useful. **2** ready to hand. **3** good at using the hands. **handily** *adverb*, **handiness** *noun*

handyman *noun* (*plural* **handymen**) a person who does household repairs or odd jobs.

hang[1] *verb* (**hung, hanging**) **1** fix the top or side of something to a hook or nail etc.; be supported in this way. **2** stick wallpaper to a wall. **3** decorate with drapery or hanging ornaments etc., *The tree was hung with lights.* **4** droop; lean, *People hung over the gate.* **5** (with *past tense & past participle* **hanged**) execute people by hanging them from a rope that tightens round the neck.

hang about loiter; not go away.

hang back hesitate to go forward or to do something.

hang on hold tightly; (*informal*) wait.

hang up end a telephone conversation by putting back the receiver.

hang[2] *noun* the way something hangs.

get the hang of (*informal*) learn how to do or use something.

hangar *noun* a large shed where aircraft are kept.

hanger *noun* a device on which to hang things, *a coat-hanger.*

hang-glider *noun* a framework in which a person can glide through the air. **hang-gliding** *noun*

hangman *noun* (*plural* **hangmen**) a man whose job it is to hang people condemned to death.

hangover *noun* an unpleasant feeling after drinking too much alcohol.

hank *noun* a coil or piece of wool, thread, etc.

hanker *verb* feel a longing for something.

hanky *noun* (*plural* **hankies**) (*informal*) a handkerchief.

Hanukka (*say* **hah**-noo-ka) *noun* an eight-day Jewish festival beginning in December. [Hebrew, = consecration]

haphazard *adjective* done or chosen at random, not by planning. [same origin as *happen,* + *hazard*]

hapless *adjective* having no luck. [same origin as *happen,* + *-less*]

▶▶ T H E S A U R U S ◀◀

handle[1] *noun* grip, haft, helve, hilt, knob, shaft, stock.

handle[2] *verb* **1** feel, finger, pick up, poke, touch. **2** control, drive, manage, manoeuvre, operate, steer. **3** cope with, deal with, look after, manage, tackle, take care of.

handsome *adjective* **1** attractive, beautiful, comely, elegant, fine-looking, good-looking, smart. **2** ample, considerable, generous, large, lavish, liberal, sizeable.

handwriting *noun* calligraphy, copperplate, hand, longhand, scrawl, scribble, script, writing.

handy *adjective* **1** convenient, helpful, practical, useful. **2** accessible, at hand, available, convenient, near, on hand, to hand. **3** adept, adroit, capable, competent, deft, dexterous, expert, good, proficient, skilful.

hang[1] *verb* **1** dangle, drape, string, suspend. **4** bend, bow, dangle, droop, drop, flop, incline, lean.

hang about hang around, hover, linger, loiter, lurk, remain, stay, wait.

hang back hesitate, hold back, wait.

hang on 1 cling, clutch, grasp, grip, hold on. **2** (*informal*) hold on, hold the line, wait.

hang[2] *noun* **get the hang of** come to grips with, comprehend, figure out, get the knack of, grasp, master, understand.

hanker *verb* (**hanker after**) covet, crave, desire, have a yen for, hunger for, long for, thirst for, want, yearn for.

haphazard *adjective* arbitrary, careless, casual, chaotic, disorganised, hit-or-miss, indiscriminate, random, slapdash, unorganised, unplanned, unsystematic.

►► D I C T I O N A R Y ◄◄

happen *verb* **1** take place; occur. **2** do something by chance, *I happened to see him.* [from Old Norse *happ* = luck]

happening *noun* something that happens; an event.

happy *adjective* (**happier, happiest**) **1** pleased; contented. **2** fortunate. **happily** *adverb*, **happiness** *noun* [same origin as *happen*]

harangue (*say* ha-**rang**) *verb* (**harangued, haranguing**) make a long speech to somebody. **harangue** *noun*

harass (*say* **ha**-ras) *verb* trouble or annoy somebody often. **harassment** (*say* **ha**-ras-ment) *noun* [from Old French *harer* = set the dog on someone]

harbour¹ *noun* a place where ships can shelter or unload.

harbour² *verb* **1** give shelter to somebody, *harbouring a criminal.* **2** keep in your mind, *harbouring a grudge.*

hard¹ *adjective* **1** firm; solid; not soft. **2** difficult to do, understand or answer, *hard sums.* **3** severe; stern. **4** causing suffering, *hard luck.* **5** using great effort, *a hard worker.* **hardness** *noun*

hard case (*Australian*) someone who is amusingly unconventional.

hard of hearing slightly deaf.

hard up (*informal*) short of money.

hard water water containing minerals that prevent soap from making much lather.

hard² *adverb* **1** so as to be hard, *The ground froze hard.* **2** with great effort; intensively, *We worked hard. It is raining hard.* **3** with difficulty, *hard-earned.*

hardboard *noun* stiff board made of compressed wood-pulp.

harden *verb* make or become hard or hardy. **hardener** *noun*

hard-hearted *adjective* unsympathetic.

►► T H E S A U R U S ◄◄

happen *verb* **1** arise, come about, come to pass, crop up, ensue, eventuate, occur, result, take place.

happening *noun* episode, event, incident, occasion, occurrence, proceeding.

happy *adjective* **1** blissful, blithe, cheerful, contented, delighted, ecstatic, elated, enraptured, euphoric, exhilarated, glad, gleeful, gratified, joyful, joyous, jubilant, light-hearted, merry, overjoyed, pleased, rapturous, satisfied, thrilled. **2** auspicious, convenient, favourable, fortunate, lucky, opportune, propitious, timely.

happiness *noun* bliss, cheerfulness, contentment, delight, ecstasy, elation, enjoyment, euphoria, exhilaration, exuberance, felicity, gladness, glee, joy, jubilation, light-heartedness, merriment, mirth, pleasure, rapture, satisfaction.

harangue *verb* berate, earbash (*Australian informal*), lecture, nag, scold.

harangue *noun* diatribe, earbashing (*Australian informal*), lecture, sermon, speech, tirade.

harass *verb* annoy, badger, bother, bug (*informal*), disturb, harry, hassle (*informal*), hound, importune, pester, plague, stand over (*Australian*), trouble, worry.

harbour¹ *noun* anchorage, dock, haven, marina, port, shelter.

harbour² *verb* **1** conceal, hide, house, protect, shelter, shield. **2** cling to, foster, hold, maintain, nurse, nurture, retain.

hard¹ *adjective* **1** dense, firm, inflexible, rigid, solid, stiff, tough. **2** (*a hard question*) awkward, baffling, complex, complicated, confusing, cryptic, difficult, knotty, puzzling, thorny, ticklish, tricky; (*a hard job*) arduous, back-breaking, demanding, difficult, exacting, gruelling, heavy, herculean, laborious, onerous, rigorous, strenuous, taxing, tiring, tough. **3** severe, stern, strict, unbending, uncompromising. **4** bad, difficult, grim, harsh, oppressive, painful, rough, severe, tough, unbearable, unpleasant. **5** assiduous, conscientious, diligent, earnest, energetic, indefatigable, industrious, painstaking, sedulous, unflagging, untiring.

hard up broke (*informal*), impecunious, impoverished, penniless, poor, poverty-stricken, skint (*informal*).

hard² *adverb* **2** (*work hard*) assiduously, conscientiously, diligently, doggedly, energetically, indefatigably, industriously, sedulously, strenuously, untiringly, vigorously; (*press hard*) firmly, forcefully, forcibly, heavily, intensely, powerfully, strongly, violently.

harden *verb* firm, set, solidify, stiffen, strengthen, toughen.

hard-hearted *adjective* callous, cold, cruel, hard, harsh, heartless, indifferent, inhuman, insensitive, mean, merciless, pitiless, remorseless, ruthless, stony-hearted, uncaring, unfeeling, unforgiving, unkind, unrepentant, unsympathetic.

▶▶ DICTIONARY ◀◀

hardly *adverb* only just; only with difficulty, *She can hardly walk.*

hardship *noun* difficult conditions that cause discomfort or suffering.

hardware *noun* **1** metal implements and tools etc.; machinery. **2** the machinery of a computer. (Compare *software*.)

hard-wearing *adjective* able to stand a lot of wear.

hardwood *noun* hard heavy wood from deciduous trees, e.g. oak and teak.

hardy *adjective* (**hardier**, **hardiest**) able to endure cold or difficult conditions. **hardiness** *noun*

hare *noun* an animal like a rabbit but larger.

harem (*say* **har**-eem) *noun* the part of a Muslim palace or house where the women live; the women living there. [from Arabic *harim* = forbidden]

hark *verb* listen.
hark back return to an earlier subject.

harlequin *adjective* in mixed colours.

harm[1] *verb* damage; injure.

harm[2] *noun* damage; injury. **harmful** *adjective*, **harmless** *adjective*

harmonic *adjective* of harmony in music.

harmonica *noun* a mouth-organ.

harmonise *verb* (**harmonised**, **harmonising**) make harmonious; produce harmony. **harmonisation** *noun*

harmony *noun* (*plural* **harmonies**) **1** a pleasant combination, especially of musical notes. **2** being friendly to each other and not quarrelling. **harmonious** *adjective*

harness[1] *noun* (*plural* **harnesses**) the straps put round a horse's head and neck for controlling it.

harness[2] *verb* **1** put a harness on a horse. **2** control and use something, *Could we harness the power of the wind?*

harp[1] *noun* a musical instrument made of strings stretched across a frame and plucked by the fingers. **harpist** *noun*

harp[2] *verb* **harp on** keep on talking about something in a tiresome way, *He is always harping on his misfortunes.*

harpoon *noun* a spear attached to a rope, used for catching whales etc. **harpoon** *verb*

harpsichord *noun* an instrument like a piano but with strings that are plucked (not struck) by a mechanism. [from *harp*, + Latin *chorda* = string]

harrow *noun* a heavy device pulled over the ground to break up the soil.

harrowing *adjective* causing horror and distress.

harry *verb* (**harried**, **harrying**) harass.

▶▶ THESAURUS ◀◀

hardly *adverb* barely, scarcely.

hardship *noun* adversity, affliction, deprivation, difficulty, distress, misery, misfortune, need, poverty, privation, strain, suffering, trials, tribulation, woe.

hardware *noun* equipment, implements, instruments, ironmongery, machinery, tools.

hard-wearing *adjective* durable, heavy-duty, long-lasting, stout, strong, tough.

hardy *adjective* drought-resistant, frost-resistant, resilient, robust, strong, sturdy, tough, vigorous.

hare *noun* buck (*male*), doe (*female*), leveret (*young*).

hark *verb* **hark back** go back, return, revert.

harlequin *adjective* motley, multicoloured, variegated.

harm[1] *verb* abuse, damage, destroy, hurt, ill-treat, impair, injure, maltreat, mistreat, molest, ruin, spoil, undermine, wound.

harm[2] *noun* damage, destruction, detriment, hurt, injury, pain, suffering.
harmful *adjective* adverse, bad, damaging, dangerous, deleterious, destructive, detrimental, hurtful, injurious, noxious, pernicious, ruinous, unhealthy.
harmless *adjective* gentle, innocent, innocuous, inoffensive, mild, non-toxic, safe.

harmony *noun* **1** euphony, melodiousness, tunefulness. **2** accord, agreement, compatibility, concord, friendliness, peace, sympathy, unanimity, unity.
harmonious *adjective* **1** dulcet, euphonious, melodious, musical, sweet, tuneful. **2** amicable, compatible, congenial, friendly, pleasant.

harness[2] *verb* **1** bridle, hitch up, yoke. **2** capture, control, exploit, use.

harp[2] *verb* **harp on** dwell on, get on your hobby-horse, go on (*informal*), keep on, nag.

harrowing *adjective* alarming, chilling, distressing, disturbing, horrifying, spine-chilling, terrifying.

▶▶ DICTIONARY ◀◀

harsh *adjective* **1** rough and unpleasant. **2** severe; cruel. **harshly** *adverb*, **harshness** *noun*

hart *noun* a male deer. (Compare *hind²*.)

harvest¹ *noun* **1** the time when farmers gather in the grain, fruit, or vegetables that they have grown. **2** the crop that is gathered in.

harvest² *verb* gather in a crop; reap. **harvester** *noun*

hash *noun* a mixture of small pieces of meat and vegetables, usually fried.
make a hash of (*informal*) make a mess of something; bungle.

hashish *noun* a drug made from hemp.

hasn't (*mainly spoken*) has not.

hassle¹ *noun* (*informal*) trouble.

hassle² *verb* (*informal*) annoy, harass.

hassock *noun* a small thick cushion for kneeling on in church.

haste *noun* a hurry.
make haste act quickly.

hasten *verb* **1** hurry. **2** speed something up.

hasty *adjective* **1** hurried. **2** done too quickly. **hastily** *adverb*, **hastiness** *noun*

hat *noun* a shaped covering for the head.
hat trick getting three goals, wickets, victories, etc. one after the other.
keep it under your hat keep it secret.

hatch¹ *noun* (*plural* **hatches**) an opening in a floor, wall, or door, usually with a covering.

hatch² *verb* **1** break out of an egg. **2** keep an egg warm until a baby bird comes out. **3** plan, *They hatched a plot*.

hatchback *noun* a car with a sloping back hinged at the top.

hatchet *noun* a small axe.

hate¹ *verb* (**hated, hating**) dislike very strongly.

hate² *noun* hatred.

hateful *adjective* arousing hatred.

hatred *noun* strong dislike.

hatter *noun* a person who makes hats.

haughty *adjective* proud of yourself and looking down on other people. **haughtily** *adverb*, **haughtiness** *noun*

▶▶ THESAURUS ◀◀

harsh *adjective* **1** (*a harsh voice*) cacophonous, discordant, grating, gravelly, gruff, guttural, jarring, rasping, raucous, rough, shrill, stern, strident; (*harsh light*) bright, brilliant, dazzling, glaring. **2** (*harsh conditions*) austere, hard, inhospitable, rough, severe, stark, tough, unpleasant; (*harsh treatment*) bitter, brutal, cruel, hard, hostile, hurtful, malicious, mean, merciless, nasty, severe, spiteful, stern, unfeeling, unfriendly, unkind, unsympathetic, vicious, vindictive.

harvest¹ *noun* **2** crop, produce, vintage, yield.

harvest² *verb* collect, garner, gather, glean, pick, reap.

hash *noun* **make a hash of** botch, bungle, make a mess of, mess up, muff (*informal*), ruin, spoil.

hassle¹ *noun* bother, difficulty, inconvenience, problem, trouble, worry.

hassle² *verb* annoy, badger, bother, bug (*informal*), harass, hound, nag, pester, worry.

haste *noun* alacrity, dispatch, promptness, rapidity, speed, swiftness, urgency.

hasten *verb* **1** dash, fly, hurry, make haste, race, rush, scurry, scuttle, speed. **2** accelerate, bring forward, expedite, precipitate, quicken, speed up.

hasty *adjective* **1** fast, hurried, prompt, quick, rapid, speedy, sudden, swift. **2** careless, headlong, hurried, impetuous, impulsive, precipitate, quick, rash, rushed, snap.

hat *noun* (*kinds of hat*) Akubra (*trade mark*), beanie, bearskin, beret, boater, bonnet, bowler hat, busby, cabbage-tree hat (*Australian*), cap, deerstalker, fez, mortarboard, panama, slouch hat, sombrero, sou'wester, stetson, sunhat, tam o'shanter, top hat, trilby.

hatch¹ *noun* aperture, manhole, opening.

hatch² *verb* **2** brood, incubate. **3** conceive, concoct, cook up (*informal*), design, devise, dream up, invent, plan, think up.

hatchet *noun* axe, mogo (*Australian*), tomahawk.

hate¹ *verb* abhor, abominate, despise, detest, dislike, loathe.

hateful *adjective* abhorrent, abominable, atrocious, contemptible, despicable, detestable, disgusting, execrable, horrid, loathsome, nasty, objectionable, obnoxious, odious, offensive, repugnant, repulsive, revolting, vile.

hatred *noun* abhorrence, abomination, animosity, antagonism, antipathy, aversion, bitterness, contempt, detestation, disgust, dislike, enmity, hate, hostility, loathing, malevolence, odium, repugnance, resentment, revulsion.

haughty *adjective* arrogant, conceited, condescending, contemptuous, disdainful, high and mighty, hoity-toity, lofty, lordly, patronising, proud, scornful, self-important, snobbish, snooty (*informal*), stuck-up (*informal*), supercilious, superior.

▶▶▷ DICTIONARY ◁◀◀

haul¹ *verb* pull or drag with great effort. **haulage** *noun*

haul² *noun* **1** hauling. **2** the amount obtained by an effort; booty, *The robbers made a good haul*. **3** a distance to be covered, *a long haul*.

haunch *noun* (*plural* **haunches**) the buttock and top part of the thigh.

haunt *verb* **1** (of ghosts) appear often in a place or to a person. **2** visit a place often. **3** stay in your mind, *Memories haunt me*.

have¹ *verb* (**had, having**) This word has many uses, including (**1**) possess; own, *We have two dogs*. (**2**) contain, *This tin has lollies in it*. (**3**) experience, *He had a shock*. (**4**) be obliged to do something, *We have to go now*. (**5**) allow, *I won't have him bullied*. (**6**) receive; accept, *Will you have a lolly?* (**7**) get something done, *I'm having my watch mended*. (**8**) (*slang*) cheat; deceive, *We've been had!*

have somebody on (*informal*) fool him or her.

have² *auxiliary verb* used to form the past tense of verbs, e.g. *He has gone*.

haven *noun* a refuge.

haven't (*mainly spoken*) have not.

haversack *noun* a strong bag carried on your back or over your shoulder.

havoc *noun* great destruction or disorder.

hawk¹ *noun* a bird of prey with very strong eyesight.

hawk² *verb* carry goods about and try to sell them. **hawker** *noun*

hawthorn *noun* a thorny tree with small red berries (called *haws*).

hay *noun* dried grass for feeding to animals. **hay fever** irritation of the nose, throat, and eyes, caused by pollen or dust.

haystack or **hayrick** *noun* a large neat pile of hay packed for storing.

haywire *adjective* (*informal*) badly disorganised; out of control.

hazard *noun* **1** a danger; a risk. **2** an obstacle. **hazardous** *adjective*

haze *noun* thin mist.

hazel *noun* **1** a bush with small nuts. **2** a light-brown colour. **hazelnut** *noun*

hazy *adjective* **1** misty. **2** vague; uncertain. **hazily** *adverb*, **haziness** *noun*

H-bomb *noun* a hydrogen bomb.

he *pronoun* **1** the male person or animal being talked about. **2** a person (male or female), *He who hesitates is lost*.

head¹ *noun* **1** the part of the body containing the brains, eyes, and mouth. **2** brains; the mind; intelligence, *Use your head!* **3** a talent or ability, *She has a good head for figures*. **4** the side of a coin on which someone's head is shown. **5** a person, *It costs $2 per head*. **6** the top, *a pin-head*; the leading part of something, *at the head of the procession*. **7** the chief; the person in charge; a headteacher. **8** a crisis, *Matters came to a head*.

keep your head stay calm.

▶▶▷ THESAURUS ◁◀◀

haul¹ *verb* drag, draw, heave, hoick (*slang*), lug, pull, tow, tug, wrench, yank (*informal*).

haul² *noun* **2** booty, profit, swag (*informal*), takings. **3** distance, stretch.

haunt *verb* **2** frequent, hang around, loiter around, patronise. **3** linger with, obsess, plague, prey on, stay with.

have¹ *verb* **1** keep, own, possess. **2** contain, hold, include. **3** endure, experience, go through, suffer, undergo. **4** (*have to*) be forced to, be obliged to, must, need to. **5** accept, allow, permit, put up with, stand for (*informal*), take, tolerate. **8** cheat, con (*informal*), deceive, swindle, take for a ride (*informal*), trick. **have on** fool, hoax, kid (*informal*), pull someone's leg, tease.

haven *noun* asylum, hide-out, refuge, retreat, sanctuary, shelter; see also HARBOUR¹.

haversack *noun* backpack, knapsack, pack, rucksack, satchel.

havoc *noun* chaos, confusion, destruction, devastation, disorder, mayhem, ruin, upheaval.

hawker *noun* huckster, pedlar, travelling salesman.

haywire *adjective* awry, chaotic, confused, disorganised, out of control, wrong.

hazard *noun* **1** danger, peril, pitfall, risk, threat. **hazardous** *adjective* chancy, dangerous, dicey (*slang*), hairy (*slang*), perilous, precarious, risky, tricky, uncertain.

haze *noun* cloud, fog, mist, smog.

hazy *adjective* **1** foggy, misty, smoggy. **2** blurred, confused, faint, fuzzy, imprecise, indefinite, indistinct, nebulous, sketchy, unclear, vague.

head¹ *noun* **1** cranium, pate (*old use*), scone (*Australian informal*), skull. **2** brain, intellect, intelligence, loaf (*slang*), mind, nut (*informal*). **3** ability, aptitude, capacity, faculty, gift, intellect, mind, talent. **6** beginning, front, origin, source, top. **7** boss, captain, CEO,

▶▶ D I C T I O N A R Y ◀◀

head² *verb* **1** be at the top or front of something. **2** hit a ball with your head. **3** move in a particular direction, *We headed for the coast.*
head off force someone to turn by getting in front.

headache *noun* **1** a pain in the head. **2** (*informal*) a worrying problem.

headdress *noun* a covering or decoration for the head.

header *noun* **1** heading the ball in soccer. **2** a dive or fall with the head first.

heading *noun* a word or words put at the top of a piece of printing or writing.

headland *noun* a promontory.

headlight *noun* a powerful light at the front of a car, engine, etc.

headline *noun* a heading in a newspaper.
the headlines the main items of news.

headlong *adverb & adjective* **1** head first. **2** in a hasty or thoughtless way.

head-on *adverb & adjective* with the front parts colliding, *a head-on collision.*

headphone *noun* a radio or telephone receiver that fits over the head.

headquarters *noun* or *plural noun* the place from which an organisation is controlled.

headstrong *adjective* determined to do as you want.

headteacher *noun* school principal.

headway *noun* progress, *make headway.*

heal *verb* **1** make or become healthy again, *The wound healed.* **2** (*old use*) cure, *healing the sick.*

health *noun* **1** the condition of a person's body or mind, *His health is bad.* **2** being healthy, *in sickness and in health.*

healthy *adjective* (**healthier, healthiest**) **1** being well; free from illness. **2** producing good health, *Fresh air is healthy.* **healthily** *adverb*, **healthiness** *noun*

heap¹ *noun* a pile, especially if untidy.
heaps *plural noun* (*informal*) a great amount; plenty, *There's heaps of time.*

heap² *verb* **1** make into a heap. **2** put on large amounts, *She heaped the plate with food.*

hear *verb* (**heard, hearing**) **1** take in sounds through the ears. **2** receive news or information etc. **hearer** *noun*
hear! hear! (in a debate) I agree.

▶▶ T H E S A U R U S ◀◀

chairman, chief, commander, director, governor, headmaster, headmistress, head teacher, leader, manager, president, principal, superintendent, supervisor; see also RULER. **8** climax, crisis.

head² *verb* **1** be in charge of, command, control, direct, govern, lead, manage, rule, superintend, supervise. **3** aim for, go, make for, make tracks for (*informal*), proceed, set off for, start for, steer for, turn for.
head off block, cut off, deflect, divert, intercept, turn aside.

headache *noun* **2** bugbear, difficulty, nightmare (*informal*), nuisance, pain (*informal*), problem, worry.

heading *noun* caption, headline, title.

headland *noun* cape, head, promontory.

headline *noun* caption, heading, title.

headlong *adverb* **1** head first, head-on. **2** hastily, impetuously, impulsively, precipitately, rashly, recklessly.

headquarters *plural noun* base, central office, depot, head office.

headstrong *adjective* determined, intractable, obstinate, pigheaded, recalcitrant, refractory, self-willed, strong-willed, stubborn, uncontrollable, wilful.

headteacher *noun* head, headmaster, headmistress, principal.

headway *noun* **make headway** advance, get ahead, get on, have a breakthrough, make inroads, progress.

heal *verb* **1** get better, improve, knit, mend. **2** cure, restore, treat.

health *noun* **1** condition, constitution, fettle, form, shape, state. **2** fitness, healthiness, robustness, vitality, well-being.

healthy *adjective* **1** fit, flourishing, hale, hearty, robust, sound, strapping, strong, thriving, well. **2** beneficial, bracing, health-giving, invigorating, salubrious, wholesome.

heap¹ *noun* accumulation, bundle, mass, mound, mountain, pile, stack, stockpile.
heaps *plural noun* loads (*informal*), lots (*informal*), masses, mountains, oodles (*informal*), piles (*informal*), plenty, stacks (*informal*), tons (*informal*), whips (*Australian informal*).

heap² *verb* **1** accumulate, bank, collect, gather, pile, stack. **2** fill, load, pile.

hear *verb* **1** catch, listen to, overhear, pick up. **2** discover, find out, gather, learn.

▶▶ D I C T I O N A R Y ◀◀

hearing *noun* **1** the ability to hear. **2** a chance to be heard; a trial in a lawcourt.

hearing-aid *noun* a device to help a deaf person to hear.

hearsay *noun* something heard, e.g. in a rumour or gossip.

hearse *noun* a vehicle for taking the coffin to a funeral.

heart *noun* **1** the organ of the body that makes the blood circulate. **2** a person's feelings or emotions; sympathy. **3** enthusiasm; courage, *Take heart.* **4** the middle or most important part. **5** a curved shape representing a heart; a playing card with red heart shapes on it.
break a person's heart make him or her very unhappy. **heartbroken** *adjective*
by heart memorised.
heart attack or **heart failure** a sudden failure of the heart to work properly.

hearten *verb* make a person feel encouraged.

heartfelt *adjective* felt deeply.

hearth *noun* the floor of a fireplace or the area in front of it.

heartland *noun* the central or most important region.

heartless *adjective* without pity or sympathy.

heart-warming *adjective* encouraging; causing people to rejoice.

hearty *adjective* **1** strong; vigorous. **2** enthusiastic; sincere, *hearty congratulations.* **3** (of a meal) large. **heartily** *adverb*, **heartiness** *noun*

heat[1] *noun* **1** hotness or (in scientific use) the form of energy causing this. **2** hot weather. **3** a race or contest to decide who will take part in the final.
heat wave a long period of hot weather.

heat[2] *verb* make or become hot.

heater *noun* a device for heating something; a stove.

heath *noun* flat land with low shrubs.

heathen *noun* a person who does not believe in one of the chief religions.

heather *noun* an evergreen plant with small purple, pink, or white flowers.

heave *verb* (**heaved** (in sense **4 hove**), **heaving**) **1** lift or move something heavy. **2** (*informal*) throw. **3** rise and fall like sea-waves; pant; retch. **4** (of ships) **heave in sight** appear; **heave to** stop without mooring or anchoring, *The ships hove to.*
heave a sigh utter a deep sigh.

heaven *noun* **1** the place where God and angels are thought to live. **2** a very pleasant place or condition.
the heavens the sky.

heavenly *adjective* **1** of heaven. **2** in the sky, *Stars are heavenly bodies.* **3** (*informal*) very pleasing.

▶▶ T H E S A U R U S ◀◀

hearing *noun* **2** inquiry, investigation, trial.

hearsay *noun* gossip, rumour, tittle-tattle.

heart *noun* **1** ticker (*informal*). **2** compassion, consideration, emotions, feelings, humanity, love, pity, sympathy, tenderness. **3** courage, determination, enthusiasm, guts (*informal*), nerve, pluck, spirit, spunk (*informal*). **4** centre, core, crux, essence, hub, middle, nitty-gritty (*informal*), nub, nucleus.
heartbroken *adjective* broken-hearted, desolate, devastated, disconsolate, forlorn, grief-stricken, woebegone, wretched.
by heart by memory, by rote, parrot-fashion.

hearten *verb* buck up (*informal*), buoy up, cheer, comfort, encourage, please.

heartfelt *adjective* deep, earnest, fervent, genuine, profound, sincere, warm.

hearth *noun* fireplace, fireside.

heartless *adjective* callous, cold, cruel, hard-hearted, harsh, merciless, pitiless, ruthless, unfeeling, unkind, unsympathetic.

heart-warming *adjective* cheering, encouraging, heartening, inspiring, pleasing, touching.

hearty *adjective* **1** energetic, hardy, healthy, robust, sprightly, spry, strong, vigorous. **2** effusive, enthusiastic, exuberant, heartfelt, lively, sincere, vigorous, warm, wholehearted. **3** big, large, solid, substantial.

heat[1] *noun* **1** hotness, temperature, warmth. **3** preliminary, round.

heat[2] *verb* reheat, warm up.

heathen *noun* infidel, non-believer, pagan, unbeliever.

heave *verb* **1** drag, draw, haul, hoick (*slang*), hoist, lift, pull, raise, yank (*informal*). **2** cast, chuck (*informal*), fling, hurl, pitch, sling, throw, toss.

heaven *noun* **1** Elysium, hereafter, next world, paradise. **2** bliss, delight, ecstasy, happiness, joy, paradise.
the heavens firmament, sky.

heavenly *adjective* **1** angelic, celestial, divine. **3** beautiful, blissful, delightful, divine (*informal*), exquisite, glorious, sublime, wonderful.

▶▶ D I C T I O N A R Y ◀◀

heavy *adjective* (**heavier, heaviest**) **1** having great weight; difficult to lift or carry. **2** great in amount or force etc., *heavy rain*; *a heavy penalty*. **3** needing much effort, *heavy work*. **4** full of sadness or worry, *with a heavy heart*. **heavily** *adverb*, **heaviness** *noun*

heavy industry industry producing metal, machines, etc.

heavyweight *noun* **1** a heavy person. **2** a boxer of the heaviest weight. **heavyweight** *adjective*

Hebrew *noun* the language of the Jews in ancient Palestine and modern Israel.

heckle *verb* (**heckled, heckling**) harass a speaker with interruptions and questions. **heckler** *noun*

hectare (*say* **hek**-tair) *noun* a unit of area equal to 10,000 square metres or nearly 2½ acres.

hectic *adjective* full of activity.

hecto- *prefix* one hundred (as in *hectogram* = 100 grams). [from Greek *hekaton* = a hundred]

hector *verb* frighten by bullying talk.

hedge¹ *noun* a row of bushes forming a barrier or boundary.

hedge² *verb* (**hedged, hedging**) **1** surround with a hedge or other barrier. **2** make or trim a hedge. **3** avoid giving a definite answer. **hedger** *noun*

hedgehog *noun* a small animal covered with long prickles.

hedgerow *noun* a hedge round a field etc.

heed¹ *verb* pay attention to.

heed² *noun* attention given to something, *take heed*. **heedful** *adjective*, **heedless** *adjective*

hee-haw *noun* a donkey's bray.

heel¹ *noun* **1** the back part of the foot. **2** the part round or under the heel of a sock or shoe etc.

take to your heels run away.

heel² *verb* lean over to one side; tilt.

hefty *adjective* (**heftier, heftiest**) large and strong. **heftily** *adverb*

Hegira (*say* **hej**-ir-a) *noun* the flight of Muhammad from Mecca in AD622. The Muslim era is reckoned from this date. [from Arabic *hijra* = departure from a country]

heifer (*say* **hef**-er) *noun* a young cow.

height *noun* **1** how high something is; the distance from the base to the top or from head to foot. **2** a high place. **3** the highest or most intense part, *at the height of the holiday season*.

heighten *verb* make or become higher or more intense.

heir (*say as* air) *noun* a person who inherits something.

heir apparent an heir whose right to inherit cannot be cancelled.

heir presumptive an heir whose right to inherit will be cancelled if someone with a stronger right is born.

heiress (*say* **air**-ess) *noun* (*plural* **heiresses**) a female heir, especially to great wealth.

▶▶ T H E S A U R U S ◀◀

heavy *adjective* **1** (*a heavy person*) big, burly, fat, hefty, hulking, large, overweight, solid, stocky, stout, sturdy, thickset; (*a heavy object*) bulky, cumbersome, massive, ponderous, unwieldy, weighty. **2** (*heavy rain*) copious, hard, pouring, profuse, torrential; (*heavy drinking*) excessive, immoderate, intemperate, unrestrained; (*heavy fighting*) concentrated, extensive, intense, relentless, severe, unrelenting. **3** arduous, exhausting, hard, laborious, onerous, strenuous, tiring. **4** depressed, downcast, forlorn, gloomy, melancholy, miserable, sad, sorrowful, unhappy.

heckle *verb* harass, harry, interrupt, jeer at, shout down, taunt.

hectic *adjective* active, busy, exciting, frantic, frenzied, lively, wild.

hedge¹ *noun* hedgerow, screen, windbreak.

hedge² *verb* **3** beat about the bush, dodge, equivocate, play for time, stall, temporise

heed¹ *verb* bear in mind, listen to, mark, mind, pay attention to, take notice of.

heed² *noun* attention, notice, regard, thought. **heedless** *adjective* careless, inattentive, negligent, oblivious, rash, reckless, unthinking, unwary.

hefty *adjective* beefy, big, brawny, burly, heavy, huge, husky, large, massive, mighty, muscular, powerful, sizeable, solid, strong, sturdy, substantial, tough, vigorous.

height *noun* **1** altitude, elevation, stature, tallness. **2** cliff, highland, hill, hilltop, peak, pinnacle, rise, summit, top. **3** acme, apex, climax, heyday, peak, pinnacle, zenith.

heighten *verb* grow, increase, intensify.

heir, heiress *noun* beneficiary, inheritor, legatee, successor.

331

heirloom (*say* **air**-loom) *noun* a valued possession that has been handed down in a family for several generations.

helicopter *noun* a kind of aircraft with a large horizontal propeller or rotor. [from *helix* + Greek *pteron* = wing]

heliotrope *noun* a plant with small fragrant purple flowers. [from Greek *helios* = sun, + *trope* = turning (the plant turns its flowers to the sun)]

helium (*say* **hee**-lee-um) *noun* a light colourless gas that does not burn. [from Greek *helios* = sun]

helix (*say* **hee**-liks) *noun* (*plural* **helices**, *say* **hee**-liss-eez) a spiral. [Greek, = coil]

hell *noun* 1 a place where wicked people are thought to be punished after they die. 2 a very unpleasant place or condition. 3 (*informal*) an exclamation of anger.
hell for leather (*informal*) at high speed.

hello *interjection* hallo.

helm *noun* the handle or wheel used to steer a ship. **helmsman** *noun*

helmet *noun* a strong covering worn to protect the head.

help¹ *verb* 1 do part of another person's work for him or her. 2 benefit; make something better or easier, *This will help you to sleep.* 3 avoid, *I can't help coughing.* 4 serve food etc. to somebody. **helper** *noun*, **helpful** *adjective*, **helpfully** *adverb*

help² *noun* 1 helping somebody. 2 a person or thing that helps.

helping *noun* a portion of food.

helpless *adjective* not able to do things. **helplessly** *adverb*, **helplessness** *noun*

helpmate *noun* a helper.

helter-skelter *adverb* in great haste.

hem¹ *noun* the edge of a piece of cloth that is folded over and sewn down.

hem² *verb* (**hemmed, hemming**) put a hem on something.
hem in surround and restrict.

hemisphere *noun* 1 half a sphere. 2 half the earth. **hemispherical** *adjective* [from Greek *hemi-* = half, + *sphere*]

hemlock *noun* a poisonous plant; poison made from it.

hemp *noun* 1 a plant that produces coarse fibres from which cloth and ropes are made. 2 a drug made from this plant. **hempen** *adjective*

hen *noun* 1 a female bird. 2 a female fowl.

hence *adverb* 1 henceforth. 2 therefore. 3 (*old use*) from here.

henceforth *adverb* from now on.

henchman *noun* (*plural* **henchmen**) a trusty supporter.

henna *noun* a reddish-brown dye.

hepta- *prefix* seven. [from Greek *hepta* = seven]

heptagon *noun* a flat shape with seven sides and seven angles. **heptagonal** *adjective* [from *hepta-*, + Greek *gonia* = angle]

her¹ *pronoun* the form of *she* used as the object of a verb or after a preposition.

her² *adjective* belonging to her, *her book.*

hell *noun* 1 Hades, inferno, underworld. 2 agony, misery, torment, torture.

help¹ *verb* 1 abet, aid, assist, back, collaborate, cooperate, lend a hand, serve, support. 2 alleviate, cure, ease, improve, relieve, remedy, soothe. 3 avoid, keep from, prevent, refrain from, resist.
helper *noun* abetter, accessory, accomplice, aid, aide, assistant, auxiliary, collaborator, helpmate, offsider (*Australian*), partner, sidekick (*informal*), supporter.
helpful *adjective* (*a helpful person*) accommodating, considerate, cooperative, kind, neighbourly, obliging, supportive, willing; (*a helpful thing*) constructive, handy, instructive, practical, useful, valuable, worthwhile.

help² *noun* 1 advice, aid, assistance, backing, backup, collaboration, contribution, cooperation, encouragement, succour, support. 2 advantage, asset, benefit, boon.

helping *noun* portion, ration, serving.

helpless *adjective* defenceless, dependent, feeble, impotent, incapable, powerless, vulnerable.

hem² *verb* **hem in** beset, besiege, box in, encircle, enclose, fence in, hedge in, restrict, surround.

hence *adverb* 2 accordingly, consequently, so, therefore, thus.

henchman *noun* attendant, follower, hanger-on, lackey, retainer (*old use*), stooge (*informal*), supporter, yes-man.

▶▶ D I C T I O N A R Y ◀◀

herald¹ *noun* **1** an official in former times who made announcements and carried messages for a king or queen. **2** a person or thing that heralds something.

herald² *verb* show that something is coming.

heraldry *noun* the study of coats of arms. **heraldic** (*say* hir-**al**-dik) *adjective*

herb *noun* a plant used for flavouring or for making medicine. **herbal** *adjective* [from Latin *herba* = grass]

herbaceous (*say* her-**bay**-shus) *adjective* **1** of or like herbs. **2** containing many flowering plants, *a herbaceous border.*

herbivorous (*say* her-**biv**-er-us) *adjective* plant-eating. (Compare *carnivorous*.) **herbivore** *noun* [from Latin *herba* = grass, + *vorare* = devour]

herculean (*say* her-kew-**lee**-an) *adjective* **1** needing great strength or effort, *a herculean task*. **2** as strong as Hercules (a hero in ancient Greek legend).

herd¹ *noun* **1** a group of cattle or other animals that feed together. **2** a mass of people; a mob. **herdsman** *noun*

herd² *verb* **1** gather or move or send in a herd, *We all herded into the dining room*. **2** look after a herd of animals.

here *adverb* in or to this place etc. **here and there** in various places or directions.

hereafter *adverb* from now on; in future.

hereby *adverb* by this act or decree etc.

hereditary *adjective* **1** inherited, *a hereditary disease*. **2** inheriting a position, *The Queen is a hereditary monarch*.

heredity (*say* hir-**ed**-it-ee) *noun* inheriting characteristics from parents or ancestors. [from Latin *heredis* = of an heir]

heresy (*say* **h**erri-see) *noun* (*plural* **heresies**) an opinion that disagrees with the beliefs accepted by the Christian Church or other authority.

heretic (*say* **h**erri-tik) *noun* a person who supports a heresy. **heretical** (*say* hi-**ret**-ik-al) *adjective*

heritage *noun* the things that someone has inherited.

hermetically *adverb* so as to be airtight, *hermetically sealed.*

hermit *noun* a person who lives alone and keeps away from people. [from Greek *eremites* = of the desert]

hermitage *noun* a hermit's home.

hernia *noun* a condition in which an internal part of the body pushes through another part; a rupture.

hero *noun* (*plural* **heroes**) **1** a man or boy who is admired for doing something very brave or great. **2** the chief male character in a story etc. **heroic** *adjective*, **heroically** *adverb*, **heroism** *noun*

heroin *noun* a very strong drug.

heroine *noun* **1** a woman or girl who is admired for doing something very brave or great. **2** the chief female character in a story, play, or poem.

heron *noun* a wading bird with long legs and a long neck.

herring *noun* (*plural* **herring** or **herrings**) a sea-fish used as food.

herringbone *noun* a zigzag pattern.

hers *possessive pronoun* belonging to her, *Those books are hers.*

Usage It is incorrect to write *her's*.

▶▶ T H E S A U R U S ◀◀

herald¹ *noun* **1** announcer, messenger, town crier. **2** forerunner, harbinger, portent, precursor, sign.

herald² *verb* announce, foretell, proclaim, signal, usher in.

herb *noun* flavouring, seasoning, spice.

herd¹ *noun* **1** drove, flock, mob (*Australian*), pack. **2** army, company, crowd, drove, flock, group, horde, host, mass, mob, multitude, swarm, throng.

herd² *verb* **1** assemble, congregate, crowd, flock, gather, group, huddle, mob, muster, throng. **2** drive, guide, lead, round up, shepherd.

hereditary *adjective* **1** genetic, inbred, inherited.

heretic *noun* apostate, dissenter, iconoclast, nonconformist, rebel, renegade.

heritage *noun* background, history, inheritance, legacy, past, tradition.

hermit *noun* loner, recluse, solitary.

hero, heroine *noun* **1** celebrity, champion, idol, legend (*informal*), star, superstar. **2** protagonist.
heroic *adjective* bold, brave, chivalrous, courageous, daring, dauntless, doughty, fearless, gallant, intrepid, lion-hearted, plucky, valiant.

▶▶▷ D I C T I O N A R Y ◁◀◀

herself *pronoun* she or her and nobody else. The word is used to refer back to the subject of a sentence (e.g. *She cut herself*) or for emphasis (e.g. *She herself has said it*).
by herself alone; on her own.

hertz *noun* (*plural* **hertz**) a unit of frequency of electromagnetic waves, = one cycle per second. [named after the German scientist H.R. Hertz]

hesitant *adjective* hesitating. **hesitantly** *adverb*, **hesitancy** *noun*

hesitate *verb* (**hesitated, hesitating**) be slow or uncertain in speaking, moving, etc. **hesitation** *noun* [from Latin *haesitare* = get stuck]

hessian *noun* sackcloth.

hetero- *prefix* other; different. [from Greek *heteros* = other]

heterogeneous (*say* het-er-o-**jeen**-ee-us) *adjective* composed of people or things of different kinds. [from *hetero-*, + Greek *genos* = a kind]

heterosexual *adjective* attracted to people of the opposite sex; not homosexual.

hew *verb* (**hewed, hewn, hewing**) chop or cut with an axe or sword etc.

hexa- *prefix* six. [from Greek *hex* = six]

hexagon *noun* a flat shape with six sides and six angles. **hexagonal** *adjective* [from *hexa-*, + Greek *gonia* = angle]

hey *interjection* an exclamation calling attention or expressing surprise or enquiry.

heyday *noun* the time of a thing's greatest success or prosperity.

hi *interjection* an exclamation calling attention or expressing a greeting.

hiatus (*say* hy-**ay**-tus) *noun* (*plural* **hiatuses**) a gap in something that is otherwise continuous. [Latin, = gaping]

hibernate *verb* (**hibernated, hibernating**) spend the winter in a state like deep sleep. **hibernation** *noun* [from Latin *hibernus* = of winter]

hiccup *noun* 1 a high gulping sound made when your breath is briefly interrupted. 2 a brief hitch. **hiccup** *verb* (**hiccuped, hiccuping**)

hickory *noun* (*plural* **hickories**) a tree rather like the walnut tree.

hide¹ *verb* (**hid, hidden, hiding**) 1 keep a person or thing from being seen; conceal. 2 get into a place where you cannot be seen. 3 keep a thing secret.

hide² *noun* an animal's skin.

hide-and-seek *noun* a game in which one person looks for others who are hiding.

hidebound *adjective* narrow-minded.

hideous *adjective* very ugly or unpleasant. **hideously** *adverb*

hideout *noun* a place where somebody hides.

hiding¹ *noun* being hidden, *She went into hiding*. **hiding-place** *noun*

hiding² *noun* a thrashing; a beating.

hielaman (*say* **heel**-a-man) *noun* a narrow Aboriginal shield made of bark or wood.

hierarchy (*say* **hyr**-ark-ee) *noun* an organisation that ranks people one above another according to the power or authority that they hold. [from Greek *hieros* = sacred, + *archein* = to rule]

hieroglyphics (*say* hyr-o-**glif**-iks) *plural noun* pictures or symbols used in ancient Egypt to represent words. [from Greek *hieros* = sacred, + *glyphe* = carving]

hi-fi *noun* (*informal*) 1 high fidelity. 2 equipment that gives high fidelity.

▶▶▷ T H E S A U R U S ◁◀◀

hesitant *adjective* diffident, dubious, faltering, halting, indecisive, in two minds, irresolute, reluctant, uncertain, unsure.

hesitate *verb* delay, dilly-dally (*informal*), dither, falter, hang back, hum and haw, pause, shilly-shally, vacillate, waver.

hew *verb* chop, cut, fell, hack, saw; see also CARVE.

heyday *noun* height, peak, pinnacle, prime, zenith.

hibernate *verb* be dormant, be inactive, sleep.

hide¹ *verb* 1 bury, conceal, put away, secrete, stash (*informal*). 2 conceal yourself, go into

hiding, go underground, hole up (*informal*), lie low, take cover. 3 bottle up, conceal, cover up, disguise, mask, repress, suppress.

hide² *noun* fell, pelt, skin.

hideous *adjective* abominable, appalling, atrocious, dreadful, frightful, ghastly, grim, grisly, grotesque, gruesome, horrendous, horrible, horrid, monstrous, objectionable, odious, repulsive, revolting, shocking, sickening, ugly, unsightly, vile.

hideout *noun* den, hidey-hole (*informal*), hiding place, lair, refuge, sanctuary.

hiding² *noun* beating, caning, flogging, spanking, thrashing, whipping.

▶▶ D I C T I O N A R Y ◀◀

higgledy-piggledy *adverb* & *adjective* completely mixed up; in great disorder.

high¹ *adjective* **1** reaching a long way upwards, *high hills*. **2** far above the ground or above sea-level, *high clouds*. **3** measuring from top to bottom, *two metres high*. **4** above average level in importance, quality, amount, etc., *high rank; high prices*. **5** (of a sound or voice) having rapid vibrations; shrill. **6** (of meat) beginning to go bad. **7** (*slang*) affected by a drug.

High Court the federal supreme court in Australia.

high explosive a powerful explosive.

high fidelity reproducing sound with very little distortion.

high road the main road.

high school a secondary school.

high time fully time, *It's high time we left.*

high² *adverb* at or to a high level or position etc., *They flew high above us.*

highbrow *adjective* intellectual.

higher *adjective* & *adverb* more high.

higher education education at a university etc., especially to degree level.

highlands *plural noun* mountainous country. **highland** *adjective*, **highlander** *noun*

highlight¹ *noun* **1** a light area in a painting etc. **2** the most interesting part.

highlight² *verb* draw special attention to something.

highly *adverb* **1** extremely, *highly amusing*. **2** very favourably, *We think highly of her.*

Highness *noun* (*plural* **Highnesses**) the title of a prince or princess.

high-rise *adjective* with many storeys.

highway *noun* a main road or route.

highwayman *noun* (*plural* **highwaymen**) a man who robbed travellers on highways in former times.

hijack *verb* seize control of an aircraft or vehicle during a journey. **hijack** *noun*, **hijacker** *noun*

hike *noun* a long walk. **hike** *verb* (**hiked**, **hiking**), **hiker** *noun*

hilarious *adjective* **1** very funny. **2** noisily merry. **hilariously** *adverb*, **hilarity** *noun* [from Greek *hilaros* = cheerful]

hill *noun* a piece of land that is higher than the ground around it. **hillside** *noun*, **hilly** *adjective*

hillock *noun* a small hill; a mound.

hilt *noun* the handle of a sword or dagger etc. **to the hilt** completely.

him *pronoun* the form of *he* used as the object of a verb or after a preposition.

himself *pronoun* he or him and nobody else. (Compare *herself*.)

hind¹ *adjective* at the back, *the hind legs*.

hind² *noun* a female deer. (Compare *hart*.)

▶▶ T H E S A U R U S ◀◀

higgledy-piggledy *adjective* chaotic, confused, disorderly, jumbled, mixed-up, muddled, topsy-turvy.

high¹ *adjective* **1** elevated, high-rise, lofty, soaring, tall, towering. **4** (*high rank*) exalted, important, powerful, prominent, senior, top; (*high quality*) best, first, superior, supreme, top; (*high temperature*) above average, extreme, great, intense; (*high prices*) dear, excessive, exorbitant, expensive, steep (*informal*), stiff (*informal*). **5** high-pitched, piercing, sharp, shrill, soprano, treble. **7** delirious, euphoric, high as a kite (*slang*), spaced out (*slang*); see also INTOXICATED.

highbrow *adjective* cultured, erudite, intellectual, learned, scholarly, sophisticated.

highlands *plural noun* heights, hills, mountains, plateau, ranges, tableland, uplands.

highlight¹ *noun* **2** climax, feature, high point, high spot.

highlight² *verb* accent, accentuate, emphasise, point up, spotlight, stress, underline.

highway *noun* expressway, freeway, main road, motorway, tollway.

highwayman *noun* bandit, brigand, bushranger, robber, thief.

hike *noun* bushwalk, ramble, tramp, trek, walk. **hike** *verb* backpack, ramble, roam, rove, tramp, trek, walk. **hiker** *noun* backpacker, bushwalker, rambler, trekker, walker.

hilarious *adjective* **1** amusing, comical, funny, humorous, witty. **2** boisterous, exuberant, jolly, lively, merry, noisy, riotous, rollicking.

hill *noun* bluff, dune, elevation, fell, foothill, headland, hillock, mesa, mountain, peak, promontory, rise, summit, tor; (*hills*) downs, heights, highlands, ranges, tiers (*Tasmania & early South Australia*). **hillside** *noun* bank, brae (*Scottish*), slope.

hillock *noun* hummock, knoll, mound, rise.

hind¹ *adjective* back, hinder, posterior, rear.

hinder *verb* get in someone's way; make it difficult for a person to do something quickly or for something to happen. **hindrance** *noun*

Hindi *noun* one of the languages of India.

hindmost *adjective* furthest behind.

hindquarters *plural noun* an animal's hind legs and rear parts.

hindsight *noun* looking back on an event with knowledge or understanding that you did not have at the time.

Hindu *noun* (*plural* **Hindus**) a person who believes in Hinduism, which is one of the religions of India.

hinge¹ *noun* a joining device on which a lid or door etc. turns when it opens.

hinge² *verb* (**hinged, hinging**) **1** fix with a hinge. **2** depend, *Everything hinges on this meeting.*

hint¹ *noun* **1** a slight indication or suggestion, *Give me a hint of what you want.* **2** a useful suggestion, *household hints.*

hint² *verb* make a hint.

hinterland *noun* the district behind a coast or port etc.

hip¹ *noun* the bony part at the side of the body between the waist and the thigh.

hip² *interjection* part of a cheer, *Hip, hip, hooray!*

hippie *noun* (*slang*) a young person who joins with others to live in an unconventional way.

hippo *noun* (*plural* **hippos**) (*informal*) a hippopotamus.

hippopotamus *noun* (*plural* **hippopotamuses**) a very large African animal that lives near water. [from Greek *hippos* = horse, + *potamos* = river]

hire¹ *verb* (**hired, hiring**) **1** pay to borrow something. **2** lend for payment, *He hires out bicycles.* **3** employ a person. **hirer** *noun*

hire² *noun* hiring, *for hire.*

hire-purchase *noun* buying something by paying in instalments.

hirsute (*say* **herss**-yoot) *adjective* hairy.

his *adjective* & *possessive pronoun* belonging to him, *That is his book. That book is his.*

hiss *verb* make a sound like an *s*, *The snakes were hissing.* **hiss** *noun*

historian *noun* a person who writes or studies history.

historic *adjective* famous or important in history, *a historic town.*

history *noun* (*plural* **histories**) **1** what happened in the past. **2** study of past events. **3** a description of important events. **historical** *adjective*, **historically** *adverb* [from Greek *historia* = finding out, narrative]

hit¹ *verb* (**hit, hitting**) **1** come forcefully against a person or thing; knock or strike. **2** have a bad effect on, *Famine has hit the poor countries.* **3** reach, *I can't hit that high note.*
hit on discover something by chance.

hinder *verb* block, curb, delay, frustrate, hamper, handicap, hold back, hold up, impede, inhibit, obstruct, prevent, restrict, slow, stonker (*Australian slang*), stop, thwart.
hindrance *noun* barrier, handicap, impediment, obstacle, obstruction, restriction, snag, stumbling block.

hinge¹ *noun* joint, pivot.

hinge² *verb* **2** depend, hang, pivot, rest, revolve (around), turn.

hint¹ *noun* **1** allusion, clue, implication, indication, inkling, innuendo, insinuation, intimation, lead, suggestion. **2** pointer, suggestion, tip, wrinkle (*informal*).

hint² *verb* imply, indicate, insinuate, intimate, suggest.

hire¹ *verb* **1** charter, lease, rent. **3** appoint, employ, engage, take on.

hiss *verb* boo, deride, heckle, hoot, jeer.

historic *adjective* celebrated, famous, important, memorable, momentous, significant.

history *noun* **1** background, past. **3** account, annals, biography, chronicle, memoirs, record, saga, story.
historical *adjective* actual, authentic, documented, factual, real, recorded, true.

hit¹ *verb* **1** bash, batter, beat, belt (*slang*), box, buffet, butt, clip (*informal*), clobber (*slang*), clout (*informal*), club, cuff, dong (*Australian informal*), flog, hammer, job (*informal*), knock, lash, lay into (*informal*), pound, pummel, punch, quilt (*Australian slang*), rap, slap, slog, slug, smack, smite, sock (*slang*), spank, stoush (*Australian slang*), strike, swat, swipe (*informal*), tap, thrash, thump, thwack, trounce, wallop (*slang*), whack, whip; (*of a vehicle, etc.*) bang into, bump into, collide with, crash into, knock, ram into, run into, slam into, smash into, strike. **2** affect, attack, strike, touch.
hit back see RETALIATE.

hit on chance on, come up with, discover, stumble on.

▶▶ DICTIONARY ◀◀

hit² *noun* **1** hitting; a knock or stroke. **2** a shot that hits the target. **3** a success; a successful song, show, etc.

hitch¹ *verb* **1** raise or pull with a slight jerk. **2** fasten with a loop or hook etc. **3** hitchhike.

hitch² *noun* **1** a hitching movement. **2** a knot. **3** a difficulty causing delay.

hitchhike *verb* travel by begging rides in passing vehicles. **hitchhiker** *noun*

hither *adverb* to or towards this place.

hitherto *adverb* until this time.

hive *noun* **1** a beehive. **2** the bees living in a beehive.
hive of industry a place full of people working busily.

ho *interjection* an exclamation of triumph, surprise, etc.

hoard¹ *noun* a carefully saved store of money, treasure, food, etc.

hoard² *verb* store away. **hoarder** *noun*

hoarding *noun* a tall fence covered with advertisements.

hoar-frost *noun* a white frost.

hoarse *adjective* with a rough voice. **hoarsely** *adverb*, **hoarseness** *noun*

hoary *adjective* **1** white or grey from age, *hoary hair.* **2** old, *hoary jokes.*

hoax *verb* deceive somebody as a joke. **hoax** *noun*, **hoaxer** *noun*

hob *noun* a flat surface on a cooker or beside a fireplace, where food etc. can be cooked or kept warm.

hobble *verb* (**hobbled, hobbling**) limp.

hobby *noun* (*plural* **hobbies**) something you do for pleasure in your spare time.

hobby-horse *noun* **1** a stick with a horse's head, used as a toy. **2** a subject that a person likes to talk about.

hobgoblin *noun* a mischievous or evil spirit; a bogy.

hobnob *verb* (**hobnobbed, hobnobbing**) spend time together in a friendly way, *hobnobbing with pop stars.*

hock *noun* the middle joint of an animal's hind leg.

hockey *noun* a game played by two teams with curved sticks and a hard ball.

hoe¹ *noun* a tool for scraping up weeds.

hoe² *verb* (**hoed, hoeing**) scrape or dig with a hoe.

hog¹ *noun* **1** a male pig. **2** (*informal*) a greedy person.
go the whole hog (*slang*) do something completely or thoroughly.

hog² *verb* (**hogged, hogging**) (*slang*) take more than your fair share of something; hoard selfishly.

Hogmanay *noun* New Year's Eve in Scotland.

▶▶ THESAURUS ◀◀

hit² *noun* **1** bash, blow, buffet, bump, clip (*informal*), clout (*informal*), dong (*Australian informal*), king-hit (*Australian informal*), knock, knock-out, punch, slap, slog, slug, smack, stroke, swipe (*informal*), thump, thwack, wallop (*slang*), whack. **3** sell-out, sensation, smash hit (*informal*), success, triumph, winner.

hitch¹ *verb* **1** jerk, pull, tug, yank (*informal*). **2** attach, connect, couple, fasten, harness, join, tie, yoke. **3** hitchhike, thumb a lift.

hitch² *noun* **3** catch, complication, difficulty, hiccup, hold-up, interruption, obstacle, problem, snag, stumbling block.

hitchhike *verb* hitch, thumb a lift.

hive *noun* **1** apiary, beehive.

hoard¹ *noun* cache, fund, reserve, stash (*informal*), stock, stockpile, store, supply, treasure trove.

hoard² *verb* accumulate, amass, collect, gather, hang on to, hold on to, keep, lay up, save, stash away (*informal*), stockpile, store.

hoarding *noun* billboard, fence.

hoarse *adjective* croaky, gravelly, gruff, harsh, husky, rasping, rough, scratchy.

hoax *verb* bluff, con (*informal*), deceive, delude, dupe, fool, have on (*informal*), hoodwink, pull someone's leg, swindle, take in (*informal*), trick.
hoax *noun* con (*informal*), confidence trick, deception, fraud, prank, scam (*slang*), spoof (*informal*), swindle, trick.

hobble *verb* limp, shamble, shuffle, stumble.

hobby *noun* diversion, interest, leisure activity, pastime, recreation, relaxation, sideline.

hobby-horse *noun* **2** fixation, obsession, pet subject, preoccupation.

hobgoblin *noun* bogy, goblin, imp, spirit, sprite.

hog¹ *noun* **2** glutton, greedy-guts (*slang*), pig (*informal*).

▶▶▶ D I C T I O N A R Y ◀◀

hoist *verb* lift; raise something by using ropes and pulleys etc.

hold¹ *verb* (**held, holding**) This word has many uses, including (**1**) have and keep, especially in your hands, (**2**) have room for (*The hall holds 1000 people*), (**3**) support (*This plank won't hold my weight*), (**4**) stay unbroken; continue (*Will the fine weather hold?*), (**5**) believe; consider (*We shall hold you responsible*), (**6**) cause to take place (*hold a meeting*), (**7**) restrain; stop (*Hold everything!*).
hold back prevent a person from doing something.
hold forth make a long speech.
hold off delay; not begin.
hold out stretch forth; last; continue.
hold your tongue (*informal*) stop talking.
hold up hinder; stop and rob somebody by threats or force.
hold with approve of, *We don't hold with bullying.*

hold² *noun* **1** holding something; a grasp. **2** something to hold on to for support. **3** the part of a ship where cargo is stored, below the deck.
get hold of grasp; obtain; make contact with a person.

holdall *noun* a large portable bag or case.

holder *noun* a person or thing that holds something.

hold-up *noun* **1** a delay. **2** a robbery with threats or force.

hole¹ *noun* **1** a hollow place; a gap or opening. **2** a burrow. **3** (*informal*) an unpleasant place. **4** (*slang*) an awkward situation. **holey** *adjective*

hole² *verb* (**holed, holing**) **1** make a hole or holes in something. **2** put into a hole.

holiday *noun* **1** a day or week etc. when people do not go to work or to school. **2** a time when you go away to enjoy yourself. [from *holy* + *day* (because holidays were originally religious festivals)]

holiness *noun* being holy or sacred.
His Holiness the title of the pope.

hollow¹ *adjective* with an empty space inside; not solid. **hollowly** *adverb*

hollow² *adverb* completely, *We beat them hollow.*

hollow³ *noun* **1** a hollow or sunken place. **2** a valley.

hollow⁴ *verb* make a thing hollow.

holly *noun* (*plural* **hollies**) an evergreen bush with shiny prickly leaves and red berries.

hollyhock *noun* a plant with large flowers on a very tall stem.

holocaust *noun* an immense destruction, especially by fire, *the nuclear holocaust*. [from Greek *holos* = whole, + *kaustos* = burnt]

▶▶▶ T H E S A U R U S ◀◀

hoist *verb* haul, heave, hoick (*slang*), lift, pull up, raise, winch.

hold¹ *verb* **1** carry, clasp, clutch, grasp, grip, hang on to, have, keep, maintain, possess, retain, seize, take. **2** accommodate, contain, have a capacity of, house, seat, take. **3** bear, carry, support, sustain, take. **4** carry on, continue, endure, last, persist, stay. **5** believe, consider, deem, judge, regard, think. **6** call, conduct, convene, run. **7** check, control, curb, restrain, stop.
hold back block, check, control, curb, halt, keep back, repress, restrain, stop, suppress, withhold.
hold forth harangue, lecture, preach, sermonise, sound off (*informal*), speak, spout.
hold off defer, delay, postpone, put off, stall.
hold out 1 extend, put out, reach out, stretch out. **2** continue, hang on (*informal*), last, persevere, persist, stick it out (*informal*).
hold up 1 delay, hinder, obstruct, slow down. **2** bail up (*Australian*), mug, rob, stick up (*informal*), waylay.
hold² *noun* **1** clasp, clutch, grasp, grip.

holder *noun* see CONTAINER.

hold-up *noun* **1** delay, jam, snarl, stoppage. **2** burglary, robbery, stick-up (*informal*).

hole¹ *noun* **1** aperture, breach, break, cavity, chink, crabhole (*Australian*), crack, crater, depression, fissure, gap, gash, gilgai (*Australian*), hollow, leak, opening, orifice, perforation, pit, pocket, pothole, puncture, slit, slot, space, split, tear, tunnel. **2** burrow, den, hideout (*informal*), lair, warren.

holiday *noun* **1** feast day, festival. **2** break, furlough, leave, rest, time off, vacation.

hollow¹ *adjective* empty, unfilled, void.

hollow³ *noun* **1** basin, bunker (*Golf*), cave, cavern, cavity, crabhole (*Australian*), crater, depression, ditch, gilgai (*Australian*), hole, pit, pothole, trough. **2** dell, glen, gully (*Australian*), valley.

hollow⁴ *verb* dig, excavate, gouge, scoop.

holocaust *noun* annihilation, carnage, conflagration, destruction, devastation, genocide, massacre, mass murder.

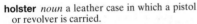

holster *noun* a leather case in which a pistol or revolver is carried.

holy *adjective* (**holier, holiest**) **1** belonging or devoted to God. **2** consecrated, *holy water*. **holiness** *noun*

homage *noun* an act or expression of respect or honour, *We paid homage to his achievements*.

home¹ *noun* **1** the place where you live. **2** the place where you were born or where you feel you belong. **3** a place where those who need help are looked after, *an old people's home*. **4** the place to be reached in a race or in certain games. **5** (*Australian*) a house.
home economics the study of household management.

home² *adjective* **1** of a person's own home or country, *home industries*. **2** played on a team's own ground, *a home match*.

home³ *adverb* **1** to or at home, *Is she home yet?* **2** to the point aimed at, *Push the bolt home*.
bring something home to somebody make him or her realise it.

home⁴ *verb* (**homed, homing**) make for a target, *The missile homed in*.

homeless *adjective* having no home.

homely *adverb* simple and ordinary, *a homely meal*. **homeliness** *noun*

home-made *adjective* made at home, not bought from a shop.

homesick *adjective* sad because you are away from home. **homesickness** *noun*

homestead *noun* a farmhouse, usually with the land and buildings round it.

home unit (*Australian*) a residence which is one of several in a building.

homeward *adjective* & *adverb* going towards home. **homewards** *adverb*

homework *noun* school work that a pupil has to do at home.

homicide *noun* the killing of one person by another. **homicidal** *adjective* [from Latin *homo* = person, + *caedere* = kill]

homily *noun* (*plural* **homilies**) a lecture about behaviour.

homing *adjective* trained to fly home, *a homing pigeon*.

homo- *prefix* same. [from Greek *homos* = same]

homogeneous (*say* hom-o-**jeen**-ee-us) *adjective* composed of people or things of the same kind. [from *homo-*, + Greek *genos* = a kind]

homograph *noun* a word that is spelt like another but has a different meaning or origin, e.g. *bat* (a flying animal) and *bat* (for hitting a ball). [from *homo-* + *-graph*]

homonym (*say* **hom**-o-nim) *noun* a homograph or homophone. [from *homo-*, + Greek *onyma* = name]

homophone *noun* a word with the same sound as another, e.g. *son, sun*. [from *homo-*, + Greek *phone* = sound]

homosexual *adjective* attracted to people of the same sex. **homosexual** *noun*, **homosexuality** *noun*

holy *adjective* **1** blameless, devout, godly, pious, religious, righteous, saintly, virtuous. **2** blessed, consecrated, divine, hallowed, heavenly, sacred, sacrosanct.

homage *noun* honour, obeisance, respect, tribute.

home¹ *noun* **1,5** abode (*old use*), domicile, dwelling, habitation, house, place, residence; see also FLAT³, HOUSE¹. **2** birthplace, fatherland, homeland, mother country, native land. **3** hospice, hostel, institution, nursing home, rest home, retirement home.

home⁴ *verb* **home in on** aim at, concentrate on, focus on, zero in on, zoom in on.

homeless *adjective* abandoned, displaced, evicted, exiled, itinerant, nomadic, outcast, stray, vagabond, vagrant, wandering.

homely *adjective* comfortable, cosy, friendly, informal, liveable, ordinary, plain, simple, unpretentious, welcoming.

homestead *noun* farmhouse, home, house, residence.

home unit apartment, condominium (*American*), flat, unit.

homework *noun* assignment, prep, preparation, study, work.

homicide *noun* assassination, killing, manslaughter, murder, slaying.

homily *noun* address, lecture, sermon, speech.

homogeneous *adjective* consistent, uniform, unvarying.

homosexual *adjective* gay (*informal*), lesbian (*female*).

▶▶ DICTIONARY ◀◀

honest *adjective* **1** not stealing or cheating or telling lies. **2** truthful; sincere. **3** fairly earned. **honestly** *adverb*, **honesty** *noun* [from Latin *honestus* = honourable]

honey *noun* a sweet sticky food made by bees.

honeycomb *noun* a wax structure of small six-sided sections made by bees to hold their honey and eggs.

honeycombed *adjective* with many holes or tunnels.

honeyeater *noun* a bird that feeds on nectar.

honeymoon *noun* a holiday spent together by a newly married couple.

honeysuckle *noun* a climbing plant with fragrant yellow or pink flowers.

honk *noun* a loud sound like that made by an old-fashioned car-horn. **honk** *verb*

honorary *adjective* **1** given or received as an honour, *an honorary degree.* **2** unpaid, *the honorary treasurer.*

honour¹ *noun* **1** great respect. **2** a person or thing that brings honour. **3** honesty and loyalty, *a man of honour.* **4** an award for distinction.

honour² *verb* **1** feel or show honour for a person. **2** acknowledge and pay a cheque etc. **3** keep to the terms of an agreement or promise.

honourable *adjective* deserving honour; honest and loyal. **honourably** *adverb*

hood *noun* **1** a covering of soft material for the head and neck. **2** a folding roof or cover. **hooded** *adjective*

hoodwink *verb* deceive.

hoof *noun* (*plural* **hoofs** or **hooves**) the horny part of the foot of a horse etc.

hook¹ *noun* a bent or curved piece of metal etc. for hanging things on or for catching hold of something.

hook² *verb* **1** catch with a hook. **2** fasten with or on a hook. **3** send a ball in a curving direction.

be hooked on something (*slang*) be addicted to it.

hookah *noun* an oriental tobacco-pipe with a long tube passing through a jar of water.

hooked *adjective* hook-shaped.

hooligan *noun* a rough lawless young person. **hooliganism** *noun*

hoon *noun* (*Australian informal*) a lout.

hoop *noun* a ring made of metal or wood.

hoop-la *noun* a game in which people try to throw hoops round objects.

hooray *interjection* hurray.

hoot *noun* **1** the sound made by an owl or a vehicle's horn or a steam whistle. **2** a cry of scorn or disapproval. **3** laughter; a cause of this. **hoot** *verb*, **hooter** *noun*

▶▶ THESAURUS ◀◀

honest *adjective* **1** honourable, law-abiding, principled, scrupulous, straight, trustworthy, truthful, upright, upstanding, veracious. **2** blunt, candid, direct, forthright, frank, genuine, open, sincere, straightforward, truthful. **3** above board, ethical, fair, lawful, legal, legitimate, proper.

honesty *noun* frankness, genuineness, integrity, openness, probity, rectitude, sincerity, trustworthiness, truthfulness, uprightness, veracity.

honour¹ *noun* **1** acclaim, admiration, credit, distinction, esteem, fame, glory, homage, prestige, recognition, renown, repute, respect, reverence, veneration, worship. **3** decency, fairness, honesty, integrity, morality, principle, probity, rectitude, scruples, virtue.

honour² *verb* **1** admire, esteem, glorify, hallow, pay homage to, pay tribute to, pay your respects to, praise, respect, revere, salute, value, venerate, worship. **3** abide by, keep, stand by, stick to.

honourable *adjective* above board, decent, ethical, high-minded, honest, principled, reputable, respectable, scrupulous, upright.

hoodwink *verb* bamboozle (*informal*), bluff, cheat, con (*informal*), deceive, defraud, dupe, fool, hoax, swindle, trick.

hook¹ *noun* hanger, nail, peg.

hook² *verb* **1** capture, catch, take. **2** fasten, hitch, latch, secure.

be hooked on be addicted to, be dependent on.

hooked *adjective* aquiline (*nose*).

hooligan *noun* delinquent, hoodlum, hoon (*Australian informal*), larrikin (*Australian*), lout, ruffian, tearaway, thug, tough, trouble-maker, vandal, yob (*informal*).

hoop *noun* band, circle, ring.

hoot *noun* **1** (*an owl's hoot*) cry, scream, screech, shriek, whoop. **2** boo, catcall, hiss, jeer. **hoot** *verb* **1** (*hoot a horn*) blast, blow, honk, sound, toot. **2** boo, deride, heckle, hiss, jeer, mock.

hooter *noun* horn, siren, whistle.

DICTIONARY

hop¹ *verb* (**hopped, hopping**) **1** jump on one foot. **2** (of an animal) spring from all feet at once. **3** (*informal*) move quickly, *Here's the car – hop in!*
hop it (*slang*) go away.

hop² *noun* a hopping movement.

hop³ *noun* a climbing plant used to give beer its flavour.

hope¹ *noun* **1** a wish for something to happen. **2** a person or thing that gives hope, *You are our only hope.*

hope² *verb* (**hoped, hoping**) feel hope; want and expect something.

hopeful *adjective* **1** feeling hope. **2** likely to be good or successful. **hopefully** *adverb*

hopeless *adjective* **1** feeling no hope. **2** admitting no hope, *a hopeless case.* **3** very bad at something. **hopelessly** *adverb*, **hopelessness** *noun*

hopper *noun* **1** one who hops. **2** a V-shaped container with an opening at the bottom.

hopscotch *noun* a game of hopping into squares drawn on the ground.

horde *noun* a large group or crowd.

horizon *noun* the line where the earth and the sky seem to meet. [from Greek *horisein* = form a boundary]

horizontal *adjective* level, so as to be parallel to the horizon; going across from left to right. (The opposite is *vertical*.) **horizontally** *adverb*

hormone *noun* a substance that stimulates an organ of the body or of a plant.

horn *noun* **1** a hard substance that grows into a point on the head of a bull, cow, ram, etc. **2** a pointed part. **3** a brass instrument played by blowing. **4** a device for making a warning sound. **horned** *adjective*, **horny** *adjective*

hornet *noun* a large kind of wasp.

hornpipe *noun* a sailors' dance.

horoscope *noun* an astrologer's forecast of future events. [from Greek *hora* = hour (of birth), + *skopos* = observer]

horrendous *adjective* horrifying.

horrible *adjective* **1** horrifying. **2** (*informal*) unpleasant. **horribly** *adverb*

horrid *adjective* horrible. **horridly** *adverb*

horrific *adjective* horrifying. **horrifically** *adverb*

horrify *verb* (**horrified, horrifying**) arouse horror in somebody; shock.

horror *noun* **1** great fear and dislike or dismay. **2** a person or thing causing horror.

horse *noun* **1** a large four-legged animal used for riding on and for pulling carts etc. **2** a framework for hanging clothes on to dry. **3** a vaulting-horse.
on horseback mounted on a horse.

THESAURUS

hop¹ *verb* **2** bob, bounce, bound, jump, leap, skip, spring.

hope¹ *noun* **1** ambition, aspiration, confidence, desire, dream, expectation, faith, longing, optimism, trust, wish.

hope² *verb* aspire, desire, dream, expect, hanker, long, trust, want, wish.

hopeful *adjective* **1** confident, expectant, optimistic, sanguine, trusting. **2** auspicious, encouraging, favourable, heartening, positive, promising, propitious, reassuring.

hopeless *adjective* **1** dejected, demoralised, depressed, despairing, desperate, despondent, downcast, forlorn, pessimistic, wretched. **2** incurable, irredeemable, irreparable, irretrievable, irrevocable. **3** bad, feeble, inadequate, incompetent, poor, useless.

horde *noun* crowd, drove, mass, mob, multitude, swarm, throng.

horizon *noun* skyline.

horizontal *adjective* flat, level, prone, prostrate, supine.

horrible *adjective* **1** abhorrent, abominable, appalling, atrocious, awful, despicable, detestable, dreadful, foul, frightful, ghastly, grisly, gruesome, hideous, horrendous, horrid, horrific, loathsome, monstrous, odious, repugnant, repulsive, revolting, shocking, sickening, terrible, vile. **2** awful, disagreeable, horrid, mean, nasty, objectionable, obnoxious, offensive, unbearable, unkind, unpleasant.

horrify *verb* alarm, appal, disgust, frighten, revolt, scare, shock, terrify.

horror *noun* **1** abhorrence, alarm, antipathy, aversion, consternation, dislike, dismay, dread, fear, hatred, loathing, panic, revulsion, terror, trepidation.

horse *noun* **1** bronco, brumby (*Australian*), carthorse, charger, draughthorse, gee-gee (*informal*), hack, moke (*Australian*), mount, mustang, nag (*informal*), nanto (*Australian old use*), neddy (*informal*), pacer, palfrey (*old use*), pony, racehorse, steed (*poetical*), trotter, yarraman (*Australian*); (*male horses*) colt, gelding, sire, stallion; (*female horses*) filly, mare; (*young horses*) colt, filly, foal.

horse-chestnut *noun* a large tree that produces dark-brown nuts (*conkers*).

horseman *noun* (*plural* **horsemen**) a man who rides a horse, especially a skilled rider. **horsemanship** *noun*

horseplay *noun* rough play.

horsepower *noun* a unit for measuring the power of an engine.

horseshoe *noun* a U-shaped piece of metal nailed to a horse's hoof.

horsewoman *noun* (*plural* **horsewomen**) a woman who rides a horse, especially a skilled rider.

horticulture *noun* the art of cultivating gardens. **horticultural** *adjective* [from Latin *hortus* = garden, + *culture*]

hose¹ *noun* 1 (also **hose-pipe**) a flexible tube for taking water to something. 2 (*old use*) breeches, *doublet and hose*.

hose² *verb* (**hosed, hosing**) water or spray with a hose.

hosiery *noun* (in shops) socks and stockings.

hospice (*say* **hosp**-iss) *noun* 1 a nursing home for people who are very ill. 2 a lodging-house for travellers, especially one kept by a religious institution.

hospitable *adjective* welcoming; liking to give hospitality. **hospitably** *adverb*

hospital *noun* a place providing medical and surgical treatment for people who are ill or injured. [from Latin *hospitium* = hospitality]

hospitality *noun* welcoming people and giving them food and entertainment.

host¹ *noun* 1 a person who has guests and looks after them. 2 a person who introduces the performers in a show. [same origin as *hospital*]

host² *noun* a large number of people or things. [same origin as *hostile*]

host³ *noun* the bread consecrated at Holy Communion. [from Latin *hostia* = sacrifice]

hostage *noun* a person who is held prisoner until the holder gets what he or she wants.

hostel *noun* a lodging-house for travellers, students, or other groups.

hostess *noun* a woman who has guests and looks after them.

hostile *adjective* 1 of an enemy. 2 unfriendly, *a hostile glance*. **hostility** *noun* [from Latin *hostis* = an enemy]

hot¹ *adjective* (**hotter, hottest**) 1 having great heat or a high temperature. 2 giving a burning sensation when tasted. 3 enthusiastic; excitable, *a hot temper*. **hotly** *adverb*, **hotness** *noun*

hot cross bun a fresh spicy bun marked with a cross, to be eaten on Good Friday.

hot dog a hot sausage in a bread roll.

in hot water (*informal*) in trouble or disgrace.

hot² *verb* (**hotted, hotting**) **hot up** (*informal*) make or become hot or hotter or more exciting.

hotel *noun* 1 a building where people pay to have meals and stay for the night. 2 (*Australian*) a pub.

hotfoot *adverb* in eager haste.

horseman, horsewoman *noun* equestrian, horse-rider, jockey, rider.

hospice *noun* 1 home, hospital, institution, nursing home.

hospitable *adjective* amiable, cordial, friendly, generous, genial, gracious, kind, sociable, warm, welcoming.

hospital *noun* clinic, hospice, infirmary, medical centre, nursing home, sanatorium.

host¹ *noun* 2 anchorperson, announcer, compère, disc jockey, DJ, Master of Ceremonies, MC, presenter.

host² *noun* army, crowd, horde, lot, mass, mob, multitude, myriad, swarm, throng; see also GROUP¹.

hostage *noun* captive, prisoner.

hostel *noun* boarding house, guest house, home.

hostile *adjective* 1 attacking, enemy, opposing, warring. 2 aggressive, angry, belligerent, chilly, cold, frosty, icy, spiteful, unfriendly, unkind, vicious.

hostility *noun* aggression, animosity, antagonism, antipathy, belligerence, enmity, friction, opposition, rancour, resentment, unfriendliness; (*hostilities*) see WAR.

hot¹ *adjective* 1 baking, blazing, boiling, burning, fiery, flaming, glowing, piping hot, red-hot, roasting, scalding, scorching, searing, sizzling, steaming, sultry, summery, sweltering, torrid, warm. 2 burning, peppery, piquant, pungent, sharp, spicy. 3 animated, ardent, emotional, excited, fervent, fiery, heated, intense, lively, passionate, stormy.

hot² *verb* **hot up** heat up, reheat, warm up.

hotel *noun* guest house, inn, local (*informal*), motel, pub (*informal*), public house, tavern.

hothead *noun* an impetuous person. **hotheaded** *adjective*

hothouse *noun* a heated greenhouse.

hotplate *noun* a heated surface for cooking food etc. or keeping it hot.

hotpot *noun* a stew.

hound¹ *noun* a dog used in hunting or racing.

hound² *verb* chase; harass.

hour *noun* **1** one twenty-fourth part of a day and night; sixty minutes. **2** a time, *Why are you up at this hour?*
hours *plural noun* a fixed period for work, *Office hours are 9 a.m. to 5 p.m.*

hourglass *noun* a glass container with a very narrow part in the middle through which sand runs from the top half to the bottom half, taking one hour.

hourly *adverb & adjective* every hour.

house¹ (*say* howss) *noun* **1** a building made for people to live in. **2** a building or establishment for a special purpose, *the opera house.* **3** a building for a government assembly; the assembly itself, *the House of Representatives.* **4** each of the divisions of a school for sports competitions etc. **5** a family or dynasty, *the royal house of Tudor.*

house² (*say* howz) *verb* (**housed**, **housing**) provide accommodation or room for someone or something.

houseboat *noun* a barge-like boat for living in.

household *noun* all the people who live together in the same house.

householder *noun* a person who owns or rents a house.

housekeeper *noun* a person employed to look after a household.

housekeeping *noun* **1** looking after a household. **2** (*informal*) the money for a household's food and other necessities.

housemaid *noun* a woman servant in a house, especially one who cleans rooms.

house-proud *adjective* very careful to keep a house clean and tidy.

house-trained *adjective* (of an animal) trained to be clean in the house.

house-warming *noun* a party to celebrate moving into a new home.

housewife *noun* (*plural* **housewives**) a woman who does the housekeeping for her family.

housework *noun* the cleaning and cooking etc. done in housekeeping.

housing *noun* **1** accommodation; houses. **2** a stiff cover or guard for a piece of machinery.
housing estate a set of houses planned and built together in one area.

hove *past tense* of **heave** (when used of ships).

hovel *noun* a small shabby house.

hover *verb* **1** stay in one place in the air. **2** wait about near someone or something; linger.

hovercraft *noun* (*plural* **hovercraft**) a vehicle that travels just above the surface of land or water, supported by a strong current of air sent downwards from its engines.

how *adverb* **1** in what way; by what means, *How did you do it?* **2** to what extent or amount etc., *How high can you jump?* **3** in what condition, *How are you?*
how about would you like, *How about a game of football?*
how do you do? a formal greeting.

hotheaded *adjective* excitable, fiery, impetuous, impulsive, rash, reckless, wild.

hothouse *noun* conservatory, glasshouse, greenhouse.

hotpot *noun* casserole, goulash, ragout, stew.

hound¹ *noun* beagle, bloodhound, dog, foxhound, greyhound, hunting dog, wolfhound.

hound² *verb* badger, chase, dog, harass, hunt, keep at, nag, pester, pursue.

house¹ *noun* **1** abode (*old use*), accommodation, domicile, dwelling, habitation, home, place, residence; (*kinds of house*) bungalow, chalet, cottage, farmhouse, homestead, hut, igloo, maisonette, manor, manse, mansion, presbytery, rectory, shack, shanty, terrace house, town house, vicarage,

villa. **2** auditorium, hall, theatre. **3** assembly, chamber, council, legislative body. **5** dynasty, family, line, lineage.

house² *verb* accommodate, billet, put up, shelter.

householder *noun* occupant, owner, resident, tenant.

housework *noun* cleaning, cooking, home duties, housekeeping.

housing *noun* **1** accommodation, dwellings, homes, houses, lodging(s), quarters, residences, shelter. **2** case, casing, container, cover.

hovel *noun* dump (*informal*), hole (*informal*), hut, shack, shanty, shed.

hover *verb* **1** float, flutter. **2** hang about, linger, wait near.

however *adverb* **1** in whatever way; to whatever extent, *You will never catch him, however hard you try.* **2** all the same; nevertheless, *Later, however, he decided to go.*

howl¹ *noun* a long loud sad-sounding cry or sound, such as that made by a dog or wolf.

howl² *verb* **1** make a howl. **2** weep loudly.

howler *noun* **1** an animal that howls. **2** (*informal*) a foolish mistake.

hub *noun* the central part of a wheel.

hubbub *noun* a loud confused noise of voices.

huddle *verb* (**huddled, huddling**) **1** crowd together into a small space. **2** curl your body closely. **huddle** *noun*

hue¹ *noun* a colour or tint.

hue² *noun* **hue and cry** a general outcry of demand, alarm, or protest.

huff¹ *noun* an annoyed or offended mood, *She went away in a huff.* **huffy** *adjective*

huff² *verb* blow, *huffing and puffing.*

hug¹ *verb* (**hugged, hugging**) **1** clasp tightly in your arms; embrace. **2** keep close to, *The ship hugged the shore.*

hug² *noun* hugging; an embrace.

huge *adjective* extremely large; enormous. **hugely** *adverb*, **hugeness** *noun*

hulk *noun* **1** the body or wreck of an old ship. **2** a large clumsy person or thing. **hulking** *adjective*

hull *noun* the framework of a ship.

hullabaloo *noun* an uproar.

hullo *interjection* hallo.

hum¹ *verb* (**hummed, humming**) **1** sing a tune with your lips closed. **2** make a low continuous sound as some flying insects do.

hum² *noun* a humming sound.

hum³ *verb* (*Australian slang*) cadge. [from *humbug*]

human¹ *adjective* of human beings.
human being a creature distinguished from other animals by its better mental development, power of speech, and upright posture.

human² *noun* a human being.

humane (*say* hew-**mayn**) *adjective* kind-hearted; merciful. **humanely** *adverb*

humanise *verb* (**humanised, humanising**) make human or humane. **humanisation** *noun*

humanist *noun* a humanitarian person.

humanitarian *adjective* concerned with people's welfare and the reduction of suffering. **humanitarian** *noun*

however *adverb* **2** nevertheless, none the less, though.

howl¹ *noun* bay, bellow, cry, groan, scream, shout, shriek, wail, whine, yell, yelp, yowl.

howl² *verb* **1** bawl, bellow, cry, roar, scream, shout, shriek, wail, whine, yell, yelp, yowl. **2** see WEEP.

hub *noun* centre, core, focus, heart, middle.

hubbub *noun* babble, clamour, din, hullabaloo, noise, racket.

huddle *verb* **1** cluster, cram, crowd, flock, herd, jam, pile, press, squash, squeeze, throng. **2** curl up, nestle, snuggle.

hue¹ *noun* colour, shade, tinge, tint, tone.

hue² *noun* **hue and cry** clamour, commotion, furore, fuss, hullabaloo, outcry, protest, to-do, uproar.

huffy *adjective* annoyed, grumpy, in a huff, miffed (*informal*), offended, peevish, petulant, piqued, resentful, shirty (*informal*), sulky, testy, touchy.

hug¹ *verb* **1** clasp, cuddle, embrace, hold, squeeze.

huge *adjective* astronomical, big, colossal, enormous, exorbitant, gargantuan, giant, gigantic, great, humungous (*slang*), immense, jumbo, large, mammoth, massive, mighty, monstrous, staggering, stupendous, sweeping, vast.

hulking *adjective* bulky, burly, heavy, hefty, husky, large, massive.

hull *noun* body, frame, framework, skeleton.

hullabaloo *noun* clamour, commotion, din, fracas, fuss, hubbub, racket, rumpus, uproar.

hum¹ *verb* **2** buzz, drone, purr, vibrate, whirr.

hum² *noun* buzz, drone, purr, vibration, whirr.

human¹ *adjective* **human being** child, human, individual, man, mortal, person, woman.

humane *adjective* benevolent, compassionate, humanitarian, kind, kind-hearted, merciful, sympathetic, understanding.

humanitarian *adjective* benevolent, humane, philanthropic.

humanity *noun* **1** human beings; people. **2** being human. **3** being humane.
humanities *plural noun* arts subjects.

humble¹ *adjective* **1** modest; not proud or showy. **2** of low rank or importance. **humbly** *adverb*, **humbleness** *noun*

humble² *verb* (**humbled, humbling**) make humble. [from Latin *humilis* = lowly]

humbug *noun* **1** deceitful talk or behaviour. **2** a person who tries to win sympathy by deceit. **3** a hard peppermint sweet.

humdrum *adjective* dull and not exciting; commonplace; without variety.

humid (*say* hew-mid) *adjective* (of air) moist. **humidity** *noun*

humiliate *verb* (**humiliated, humiliating**) make a person feel disgraced. **humiliation** *noun*

humility *noun* being humble.

humming-bird *noun* a small tropical bird that makes a humming sound by moving its wings rapidly.

hummock *noun* a hump in the ground.

humorist *noun* a humorous person.

humorous *adjective* full of humour.

humour¹ *noun* **1** being amusing; what makes people laugh. **2** the ability to enjoy comical things, *a sense of humour.* **3** a mood, *in a good humour.*

humour² *verb* keep a person contented by doing what he or she wants.

hump¹ *noun* **1** a rounded projecting part. **2** an abnormal outward curve at the top of a person's back. **humpback** *noun*, **humpbacked** *adjective*

hump² *verb* **1** form a hump. **2** carry something on your back.

humus (*say* hew-mus) *noun* rich earth made by decayed plants.

hunch¹ *noun* (*plural* **hunches**) **1** a hump. **2** a feeling that you can guess what will happen. **hunchback** *noun*

hunch² *verb* bend into a hump, *He hunched his shoulders.*

hundred *noun* & *adjective* the number 100; ten times ten. **hundredth** *adjective* & *noun*

hundredfold *adjective* & *adverb* one hundred times as much or as many.

hundredweight *noun* (*plural* **hundredweight**) a unit of weight, 50.8 kilograms.

hunger *noun* the feeling that you have when you have not eaten for some time; need for food.

hunger strike refusing to eat, as a way of making a protest.

humanity *noun* **1** humankind, human race, man, mankind, people, society. **3** benevolence, compassion, goodness, humaneness, kindness, mercy, sympathy, understanding.

humble¹ *adjective* **1** meek, modest, ordinary, plain, self-effacing, simple, unassertive, unassuming, unpretentious. **2** insignificant, low, lowly, unimportant.

humble² *verb* abase, chasten, disgrace, humiliate, mortify, shame, subdue, take down a peg (*informal*).

humbug *noun* **1** blarney, boloney (*informal*), bull (*slang*), bunkum, claptrap, deceit, deception, fraud, hocus-pocus, lies, mumbo-jumbo, nonsense, pretence, rubbish, rot (*slang*), sham, trickery. **2** charlatan, cheat, con man (*informal*), fake, fraud, phoney (*informal*), quack, sham, swindler, trickster.

humdrum *adjective* boring, commonplace, dreary, dull, monotonous, mundane, ordinary, repetitive, routine, tedious, unexciting, uninteresting, wearisome.

humid *adjective* clammy, close, damp, dank, moist, muggy, steamy, sticky, sultry.

humiliate *verb* abase, chasten, demean, disgrace, embarrass, humble, mortify, put down, shame, take down a peg (*informal*).
humiliation *noun* abasement, disgrace, embarrassment, indignity, mortification, shame.

humility *noun* deference, humbleness, lowliness, meekness, modesty, unpretentiousness.

humorous *adjective* amusing, comic, comical, droll, facetious, farcical, funny, hilarious, laughable, ridiculous, witty.

humour¹ *noun* **1** absurdity, comedy, farcicalness, funniness, ludicrousness, ridiculousness, wittiness. **3** disposition, mood, spirits, temper.

humour² *verb* go along with, indulge, pamper, pander to, play up to.

hump¹ *noun* **1** bulge, bump, hunch, lump, swelling.

hump² *verb* **1** arch, curve, hunch.

hunch¹ *noun* **2** feeling, idea, inkling, intuition, premonition, suspicion.

hunch² *verb* arch, bend, crouch, hump.

hunger *noun* appetite, emptiness, malnutrition, ravenousness, starvation.

▶▶▶ DICTIONARY ◀◀

hungry *adjective* (**hungrier, hungriest**) feeling hunger. **hungrily** *adverb*

hunk *noun* a large or clumsy piece.

hunt¹ *verb* 1 chase and kill animals for food or as a sport. 2 search for something. **hunter** *noun*

hunt² *noun* 1 hunting. 2 a group of hunters.

huntsman *noun* 1 a hunter. 2 a large Australian spider that stalks its prey.

Huon pine a Tasmanian conifer.

hurdle *noun* 1 an upright frame to be jumped over in hurdling. 2 an obstacle.

hurdling *noun* racing in which the runners jump over hurdles. **hurdler** *noun*

hurl *verb* throw something violently.

hurly-burly *noun* a rough bustle of activity.

hurrah or **hurray** *interjection* a shout of joy or approval; a cheer.

hurricane *noun* a storm with violent wind.

hurry¹ *verb* (**hurried, hurrying**) 1 move quickly; do something quickly. 2 try to make somebody or something be quick. **hurried** *adjective*, **hurriedly** *adverb*

hurry² *noun* hurrying; a need to hurry.

hurt¹ *verb* (**hurt, hurting**) 1 cause pain or damage or injury. 2 suffer pain.

hurt² *noun* an injury; harm. **hurtful** *adjective*

hurtle *verb* (**hurtled, hurtling**) move rapidly, *The train hurtled along.*

husband¹ *noun* the man to whom a woman is married.

husband² *verb* manage economically and try to save, *husband your strength.* [from Old English *husbonda* = master of a house (*hus*)]

husbandry *noun* 1 farming. 2 management of resources. [from an old use of *husband* = person who manages things]

hush¹ *verb* make or become silent or quiet.

hush² *noun* silence.

husk *noun* the dry outer covering of some seeds and fruits.

husky¹ *adjective* (**huskier, huskiest**) 1 hoarse. 2 big and strong; burly. **huskily** *adverb*, **huskiness** *noun*

▶▶▶ THESAURUS ◀◀

hungry *adjective* famished, peckish (*informal*), ravenous, starved, starving.

hunk *noun* block, chunk, lump, piece, slab, wedge.

hunt¹ *verb* 1 chase, pursue, stalk, track, trail. 2 ferret out, forage for, fossick for (*Australian informal*), look for, rummage for, search for, seek.

hunter *noun* huntsman, predator, tracker.

hunt² *noun* 1 chase, pursuit, quest, search.

hurdle *noun* 1 barricade, barrier, fence. 2 barrier, difficulty, impediment, obstacle, problem, snag, stumbling block.

hurl *verb* cast, chuck (*informal*), fling, heave, pitch, propel, sling (*informal*), throw, toss.

hurly-burly *noun* activity, bustle, commotion, hubbub, hustle and bustle, tumult.

hurricane *noun* cyclone, tropical cyclone, typhoon; see also STORM¹, WIND¹.

hurry¹ *verb* 1 be quick, bolt, dash, fly, get a move on (*informal*), get cracking (*informal*), get your skates on (*informal*), hasten, hurtle, hustle, make haste, make it snappy (*informal*), race, run, rush, scoot, scurry, scuttle, speed, step on it (*informal*), whiz, zip, zoom. 2 accelerate, expedite, fast-track (*informal*), hasten, push, quicken, speed up.

hurry² *noun* bustle, haste, hurry-scurry, hustle, rush, urgency.

hurt¹ *verb* 1 bruise, cripple, cut, damage, disable, distress, grieve, harm, impair, injure, maim, mutilate, offend, pain, scratch, spoil, sprain, trouble, upset, wound. 2 ache, be painful, be sore, smart, sting, throb.

hurt² *noun* ache, affliction, agony, anguish, damage, discomfort, distress, grief, harm, injury, misery, pain, sadness, soreness, sorrow, suffering, torment, torture.

hurtful *adjective* brutal, cruel, cutting, distressing, malicious, mean, nasty, unkind, upsetting.

hurtle *verb* fly, race, shoot, speed, tear, whiz, zip, zoom.

husband¹ *noun* bridegroom, groom, mate, partner, spouse.

husband² *verb* conserve, hoard, preserve, save.

hush¹ *verb* calm, lull, quieten, shush (*informal*), silence, soothe.

hushed *adjective* low, quiet, soft, subdued.

hush² *noun* quietness, silence, stillness.

husk *noun* case, hull, pod, shell.

husky¹ *adjective* 1 croaking, dry, gravelly, gruff, guttural, harsh, hoarse, rasping, rough, throaty. 2 beefy, brawny, burly, hefty, hulking, muscular, nuggety (*Australian*), solid, stocky, strapping, strong, sturdy, thickset, tough.

▶▶ D I C T I O N A R Y ◀◀

husky² *noun* (*plural* **huskies**) a large dog used in the Arctic and (formerly) in the Antarctic for pulling sledges.

hustle *verb* (**hustled, hustling**) hurry; bustle. **hustle** *noun*, **hustler** *noun*

hut *noun* a small roughly-made house or shelter.

hutch *noun* (*plural* **hutches**) a box-like cage for a pet rabbit etc.

hyacinth *noun* a fragrant flower that grows from a bulb.

hybrid *noun* **1** a plant or animal produced by combining two different species or varieties. **2** something that combines parts or characteristics of two different things.

hydra *noun* a microscopic freshwater animal with a tubular body.

hydrangea (*say* hy-**drayn**-ja) *noun* a shrub with pink, blue, or white flowers growing in large clusters.

hydrant *noun* a special water-tap to which a large hose can be attached for fire-fighting or street-cleaning etc.

hydraulic *adjective* worked by the force of water or other fluid, *hydraulic brakes*. [from *hydro-*, + *aulos* = pipe]

hydro- *prefix* **1** water (as in *hydroelectric*). **2** (in chemical names) containing hydrogen (as in *hydrochloric*). [from Greek *hydor* = water]

hydrochloric acid a colourless acid containing hydrogen and chlorine.

hydroelectric *adjective* using water-power to produce electricity. **hydroelectricity** *noun*

hydrofoil *noun* a boat designed to skim over the surface of water.

hydrogen *noun* a lightweight gas that combines with oxygen to form water. **hydrogen bomb** a very powerful bomb using energy created by the fusion of hydrogen nuclei. [from *hydro-*, + *gen* = producing]

hydrophobia *noun* abnormal fear of water, as in someone suffering from rabies. [from *hydro-* + *phobia*]

hyena *noun* a wild animal that looks like a wolf and makes a shrieking howl.

hygiene (*say* **hy**-jeen) *noun* keeping things clean in order to remain healthy and prevent disease. **hygienic** *adjective*, **hygienically** *adverb* [from Greek *hygieine* = of health]

hymn *noun* a religious song, usually of praise to God.

hymnal *noun* a book of hymns.

hyper- *prefix* over or above; excessive. [from Greek *hyper* = over]

hyperbola (*say* hy-**per**-bol-a) *noun* a kind of curve. [same origin as *hyperbole*]

hyperbole (*say* hy-**per**-bol-ee) *noun* a dramatic exaggeration that is not meant to be taken literally, e.g. 'I've got a stack of work a mile high'. [from *hyper-*, + Greek *bole* = a throw]

hyphen *noun* a short dash used to join words or parts of words together (e.g. in *hymn-book*). [from Greek, = together]

hyphenate *verb* (**hyphenated, hyphenating**) join with a hyphen. **hyphenation** *noun*

hypnosis (*say* hip-**noh**-sis) *noun* a condition like a deep sleep in which a person's actions may be controlled by someone else. [from Greek *hypnos* = sleep]

hypnotise *verb* (**hypnotised, hypnotising**) produce hypnosis in somebody. **hypnotism** *noun*, **hypnotic** *adjective*, **hypnotist** *noun*

hypo- *prefix* below; under. [from Greek *hypo* = under]

hypochondriac (*say* hy-po-**kon**-dree-ak) *noun* a person who constantly imagines that he or she is ill. **hypochondria** *noun*

▶▶ T H E S A U R U S ◀◀

hustle *verb* bustle, hasten, hurry, jostle, pressure, push, rush, shove, thrust. **hustle** *noun* activity, bustle, haste, hurly-burly, hurry, hurry-scurry, rush, tumult.

hut *noun* cabin, chalet, gunyah (*Australian*), house, hovel, humpy (*Australian*), lean-to, mia mia (*Australian*), shack, shanty, shed, shelter, skillion (*Australian*), wurley (*Australian*).

hutch *noun* box, cage, coop, enclosure, pen.

hybrid *noun* blend, cross, cross-breed, half-breed, mixture.

hygienic *adjective* aseptic, clean, disinfected, germ-free, healthy, sanitary, sterile, sterilised.

hymn *noun* anthem, canticle, carol, chorus, introit, psalm, song.

hyperbole *noun* exaggeration, overstatement.

hypnotise *verb* bewitch, enthral, entrance, fascinate, mesmerise. **hypnotic** *adjective* mesmerising, soporific, spellbinding.

▶▶ DICTIONARY ◀◀

hypocrite (*say* **hip**-o-krit) *noun* a person who pretends to be more virtuous than he or she really is. **hypocrisy** (*say* hip-**ok**-riss-ee) *noun*, **hypocritical** *adjective* [from Greek, = acting a part]

hypodermic *adjective* injecting something under the skin, *a hypodermic syringe.* [from *hypo-*, + Greek *derma* = skin]

hypotenuse (*say* hy-**pot**-i-newz) *noun* the side opposite the right angle in a right-angled triangle.

hypothermia *noun* being too cold; the condition in which someone's temperature is below normal. [from *hypo-* + Greek *therme* = heat]

hypothesis (*say* hy-**poth**-i-sis) *noun* (*plural* **hypotheses**) a suggestion or guess that tries to explain something. **hypothetical** *adjective*

hysterectomy (*say* hist-er-**ek**-tom-ee) *noun* surgical removal of the womb. [from Greek *hystera* = womb, + *-ectomy* = cutting out]

hysteria *noun* wild uncontrollable excitement or emotion. **hysterical** *adjective*, **hysterically** *adverb*, **hysterics** *noun* [from Greek *hystera* = womb (once thought to be the cause of hysterics)]

▶▶ THESAURUS ◀◀

hypocrite *noun* deceiver, dissembler, phoney (*informal*), pretender.

hypocrisy *noun* deceit, dishonesty, dissembling, falseness, insincerity.

hypocritical *adjective* false, inconsistent, insincere, pharisaical, two-faced.

hypothesis *noun* assumption, conjecture, idea, proposition, speculation, supposition, theory, thesis.

hypothetical *adjective* academic, conjectural, imaginary, speculative, theoretical.

hysterical *adjective* berserk, crazed, distraught, frantic, frenzied, overwrought, raving, uncontrollable.

I *pronoun* a word used by a person to refer to himself or herself.

ice¹ *noun* 1 frozen water, a brittle transparent solid substance. 2 an ice-cream.
ice rink a place made for skating.

ice² *verb* (**iced**, **icing**) 1 make or become icy. 2 put icing on a cake.

iceberg *noun* 1 a large mass of ice floating in the sea with most of it under water. 2 (*Australian*) a regular winter swimmer.

ice-cream *noun* a sweet creamy frozen food.

icicle *noun* a pointed hanging piece of ice formed when dripping water freezes.

icing *noun* a sugary substance for decorating cakes.

icon (*say* **I**-kon) *noun* a sacred painting or mosaic etc. [from Greek *eikon* = image]

icy *adjective* (**icier**, **iciest**) like ice; very cold.
icily *adverb*, **iciness** *noun*

idea *noun* 1 a plan etc. formed in the mind. 2 an opinion.

ideal¹ *adjective* perfect; completely suitable.
ideally *adverb*

ideal² *noun* a person or thing regarded as perfect or worth trying to achieve.

idealist *noun* a person who has high ideals and wishes to achieve them. **idealism** *noun*, **idealistic** *adjective*

identical *adjective* exactly the same. **identically** *adverb* [same origin as *identity*]

identify *verb* (**identified**, **identifying**) 1 recognise as being a certain person or thing. 2 treat as being identical, *Don't identify wealth with happiness.* 3 think of yourself as sharing someone's feelings etc., *We can identify with the hero of this play.* **identification** *noun*

identity *noun* (*plural* **identities**) 1 who or what a person or thing is. 2 being identical; sameness. 3 distinctive character. [from Latin *idem* = same]

ideology (*say* I-dee-**ol**-o-jee) *noun* (*plural* **ideologies**) a set of beliefs and aims, especially in politics, *a socialist ideology.* **ideological** *adjective* [from *idea* + *-logy*]

ides (*say* I'dz) *plural noun* the ancient Roman name for the 15th day of March, May, July, and October, and the 13th day of other months.

idiocy *noun* 1 being an idiot. 2 stupid behaviour.

idiom *noun* 1 a phrase that means something different from the meanings of the words in it, e.g. *in hot water* (= in disgrace), *hell for leather* (= at high speed). 2 a special way of using words, e.g. *wash up the dishes* but not e.g. *wash up the baby.* **idiomatic** *adjective*, **idiomatically** *adverb* [from Greek *idios* = your own]

▶▶ T H E S A U R U S ◀◀

ice¹ *noun* 1 black ice, floe, frost, glacier, iceberg, icicle, pack ice, rime.

icing *noun* frosting, glaze.

icon *noun* idol, image, statue.

icy *adjective* biting, bitter, chilly, cold, freezing, frigid, frosty, glacial, nippy (*informal*), subzero; (*icy roads*) frozen, glassy, slippery.

idea *noun* 1 brainwave, concept, hunch, hypothesis, impression, notion, plan, proposal, scheme, suggestion, suspicion, theory, thought. 2 attitude, belief, conviction, notion, opinion, thought, view.

ideal¹ *adjective* excellent, exemplary, faultless, model, optimal, optimum, perfect.

idealistic *adjective* impractical, optimistic, romantic, unrealistic, Utopian, visionary.

identical *adjective* alike, duplicate, indistinguishable, matching, same, twin.

identify *verb* 1 diagnose, discover, distinguish, name, pick out, pinpoint, recognise, single out, spot. 3 (*identify with*) empathise with, relate to, respond to, sympathise with.

identity *noun* 3 distinctiveness, individuality, personality, uniqueness.

ideology *noun* beliefs, creed, doctrine, ideas, philosophy, principles, tenets.

idiom *noun* 1 expression, phrase.

▶▶▶ DICTIONARY ◀◀

idiosyncrasy (*say* id-ee-o-**sink**-ra-see) *noun* (*plural* **idiosyncrasies**) one person's own way of behaving or doing something. [from Greek *idios* = your own, + *syn* = with, + *krasis* = mixture]

idiot *noun* **1** a person who is mentally deficient. **2** (*informal*) a very stupid person. **idiocy** *noun*, **idiotic** *adjective*, **idiotically** *adverb* [from Greek *idiotes* = private citizen, uneducated person]

idle[1] *adjective* **1** doing no work; lazy. **2** not in use, *The machines were idle.* **3** useless; with no special purpose, *idle gossip.* **idly** *adverb*, **idleness** *noun*

idle[2] *verb* (**idled, idling**) **1** be idle. **2** (of an engine) work slowly. **idler** *noun*

idol *noun* **1** a statue or image that is worshipped as a god. **2** a person who is idolised. [from Greek *eidolon* = image]

idolatry *noun* **1** worship of idols. **2** idolising someone. **idolatrous** *adjective* [from *idol*, + Greek *latreia* = worship]

idolise *verb* (**idolised, idolising**) admire someone intensely. **idolisation** *noun*

idyll (*say* id-il) *noun* a poem describing a peaceful or romantic scene. **idyllic** (*say* id-**il**-ik) *adjective*

i.e. *abbreviation* id est (Latin, = that is), *The world's highest mountain (i.e. Mount Everest) is in the Himalayas.*

if *conjunction* **1** on condition that; supposing that, *He will do it if you pay him.* **2** even though, *I'll finish this job if it kills me.* **3** whether, *Do you know if dinner is ready?* **if only** I wish, *If only I were rich!*

igloo *noun* an Eskimo's round house built of blocks of hard snow. [from Eskimo, = house]

igneous *adjective* formed by the action of a volcano, *igneous rocks.* [from Latin *igneus* = fiery]

ignite *verb* (**ignited, igniting**) **1** set fire to something. **2** catch fire. [from Latin *ignis* = fire]

ignition *noun* **1** igniting. **2** starting the fuel burning in an engine.

ignoble *adjective* not noble; shameful.

ignominious *adjective* humiliating; with disgrace. **ignominy** *noun*

ignoramus *noun* (*plural* **ignoramuses**) an ignorant person. [Latin, = we do not know]

ignorant *adjective* not knowing about something or about many things; uneducated. **ignorantly** *adverb*, **ignorance** *noun*

ignore *verb* (**ignored, ignoring**) take no notice of a person or thing. [from Latin *ignorare* = not know]

▶▶▶ THESAURUS ◀◀

idiosyncrasy *noun* characteristic, eccentricity, foible, habit, mannerism, peculiarity, quirk, trait.

idiot *noun* **2** ass (*informal*), blockhead, bonehead, chump (*informal*), clot (*informal*), cretin, dill (*Australian informal*), dimwit (*informal*), dodo (*informal*), dolt, dope (*informal*), drongo (*Australian informal*), dummy (*informal*), dunce, fat-head (*informal*), fool, galah (*Australian slang*), half-wit, ignoramus, imbecile, jerk (*slang*), lunatic, moron (*informal*), nincompoop, ninny, nitwit (*informal*), nong (*Australian informal*), numskull, nut (*informal*), simpleton, thickhead (*informal*), twerp (*slang*), twit (*slang*). **idiotic** *adjective* absurd, crazy, dumb (*informal*), foolhardy, foolish, inane, irrational, lunatic, mad, nutty (*informal*), reckless, ridiculous, senseless, silly, stupid, unintelligent, unwise.

idle[1] *adjective* **1** indolent, lazy, shiftless, slothful, sluggish. **2** inactive, out of action, unused. **3** empty, frivolous, pointless, superficial, trivial, useless, worthless.

idle[2] *verb* **1** laze, loaf, potter, slack, take it easy, vegetate. **idler** *noun* bludger (*Australian informal*), good-for-nothing, layabout, lazybones (*informal*), loafer, malingerer, shirker, skiver (*informal*), slacker, slouch (*informal*).

idol *noun* **1** effigy, graven image, icon, image, statue. **2** celebrity, heart-throb (*slang*), hero, heroine, star, superstar.

idolise *verb* adore, deify, dote on, glorify, lionise, look up to, love, revere, venerate, worship.

ignite *verb* **1** fire, kindle, light, set fire to. **2** burn, catch fire, kindle.

ignominious *adjective* degrading, disgraceful, dishonourable, humiliating, infamous, inglorious, shameful.

ignorant *adjective* **1** oblivious (of), unaware (of), unfamiliar (with), uninformed (about). **2** illiterate, uneducated, uninformed, unschooled, untaught.

ignore *verb* brush aside, close your eyes to, cold-shoulder, disregard, neglect, overlook, pass over, send a person to Coventry, shrug off, slight, snub, take no notice of.

iguana (*say* ig-**wah**-na) *noun* a large tree-climbing tropical lizard.

il- *prefix* see **in-**.

ilk *noun* **of that ilk** (*informal*) of that kind.

ill¹ *adjective* **1** unwell; in bad health. **2** bad; harmful, *There were no ill effects.*
ill will unkind feeling.

ill² *adverb* badly, *She was ill-treated.*
ill at ease uncomfortable; embarrassed.

illegal *adjective* not legal; against the law. **illegally** *adverb*, **illegality** *noun*

illegible *adjective* not legible. **illegibly** *adverb*, **illegibility** *noun*

illegitimate *adjective* not legitimate. **illegitimately** *adverb*, **illegitimacy** *noun*

illicit *adjective* unlawful; not allowed. **illicitly** *adverb* [from *il-* = not, + Latin *licitus* = allowed]

illiterate *adjective* unable to read or write; uneducated. **illiterately** *adverb*, **illiteracy** *noun*

illness *noun* (*plural* **illnesses**) being ill; a particular form of bad health.

illogical *adjective* not logical; not reasoning correctly. **illogically** *adverb*, **illogicality** *noun*

illuminate *verb* (**illuminated**, **illuminating**) **1** light something up. **2** decorate streets etc. with lights. **3** decorate a manuscript with coloured designs. **4** clarify or help to explain something. **illumination** *noun* [from *il-* = in, + Latin *lumen* = light]

illusion *noun* something unreal or imaginary; a false impression, *The train went so fast that we had the illusion that it was flying.* (Compare *delusion*.) **illusive** *adjective*, **illusory** *adjective* [from Latin *illudere* = mock]

illusionist *noun* a conjuror.

illustrate *verb* (**illustrated**, **illustrating**) **1** show something by pictures, examples, etc. **2** put illustrations in a book. **illustrator** *noun*

illustration *noun* **1** a picture in a book etc. **2** illustrating something. **3** an example.

illustrious *adjective* famous; distinguished.

illywhacker *noun* (*Australian*) a small-scale confidence trickster.

im- *prefix* see **in-**.

image *noun* **1** a picture or statue of a person or thing. **2** the appearance of something as seen in a mirror or through a lens etc. **3** a person or thing that is very much like another, *He is the image of his father.* **4** reputation.

imagery *noun* **1** a writer's or speaker's use of words to produce effects. **2** images; statues.

imaginable *adjective* able to be imagined.

ill¹ *adjective* **1** ailing, crook (*Australian informal*), diseased, indisposed, infirm, nauseous, off colour, out of sorts, poorly, queasy, rotten, seedy (*informal*), sick, sickly, under the weather, unhealthy, unwell. **2** adverse, bad, damaging, destructive, detrimental, evil, harmful, unfavourable.
ill will animosity, antipathy, hostility, malevolence, malice, rancour, resentment, spite.

illegal *adjective* banned, criminal, forbidden, illegitimate, illicit, outlawed, prohibited, proscribed, unauthorised, unlawful.

illegible *adjective* indecipherable, unreadable.

illegitimate *adjective* illegal, improper, inadmissible, wrong.

illicit *adjective* see ILLEGAL.

illiterate *adjective* ignorant, uneducated, uninformed, unknowledgeable.

illness *noun* affliction, ailment, bug (*informal*), complaint, condition, disease, disorder, indisposition, infection, infirmity, malady, sickness, trouble, wog (*Australian informal*).

illogical *adjective* absurd, irrational, unreasonable, unsound.

illuminate *verb* **1** brighten up, floodlight, light up. **4** clarify, elucidate, explain, shed light on, throw light on.

illusion *noun* deception, hallucination, mirage, trick.
illusory *adjective* deceptive, fancied, illusive, imaginary, imagined, unreal.

illustrate *verb* **1** clarify, demonstrate, depict, draw, elucidate, exemplify, explain, picture, portray, represent, show.

illustration *noun* **1** diagram, drawing, figure, picture, plate. **3** example, instance, sample, specimen.

illustrious *adjective* celebrated, distinguished, eminent, famous, notable, prominent, renowned, well-known.

image *noun* **1** carving, effigy, figure, icon, idol, picture, representation, statue. **2** appearance, likeness, reflection. **3** copy, dead ringer (*informal*), duplicate, replica, spit, spitting image.

▶▶▶ D I C T I O N A R Y ◀◀◀

imaginary *adjective* existing only in the imagination; not real.

imagination *noun* the ability to imagine things, especially in a creative or inventive way. **imaginative** *adjective*

imagine *verb* (**imagined, imagining**) form pictures or ideas in your mind.

imam *noun* a Muslim religious leader. [Arabic, = leader]

imbalance *noun* lack of balance; disproportion.

imbecile (*say* **imb**-i-seel) *noun* an idiot. **imbecile** *adjective*, **imbecility** *noun*

imbibe *verb* (**imbibed, imbibing**) 1 drink. 2 take ideas etc. into the mind.

imitate *verb* (**imitated, imitating**) copy; mimic. **imitator** *noun*, **imitative** *adjective*

imitation *noun* 1 imitating. 2 a copy. **imitation** *adjective*

immaculate *adjective* 1 perfectly clean; spotless. 2 without any fault or blemish. **immaculately** *adverb*, **immaculacy** *noun*

immaterial *adjective* 1 having no material body, *as immaterial as a ghost*. 2 unimportant; not mattering, *It is immaterial whether he goes or stays*.

immature *adjective* not mature. **immaturity** *noun*

immediate *adjective* 1 happening or done without any delay. 2 nearest; with nothing or no one between, *our immediate neighbours*. **immediately** *adverb*, **immediacy** *noun*

immemorial *adjective* existing from before what can be remembered or found in histories, *from time immemorial*.

immense *adjective* exceedingly great; huge. **immensely** *adverb*, **immensity** *noun* [from *im-* = not, + Latin *mensum* = measured]

immerse *verb* (**immersed, immersing**) 1 put something completely into a liquid. 2 absorb or involve deeply, *She was immersed in her work*. **immersion** *noun*

immersion heater a device that heats water by means of an electric element immersed in the water in a tank etc. [from *im-* = in, + Latin *mersum* = dipped]

immigrate *verb* (**immigrated, immigrating**) come into another country to live there. **immigration** *noun*, **immigrant** *noun* [from *im-* = in, + *migrate*]

Usage See the note on *emigrate*.

imminent *adjective* likely to happen at any moment, *an imminent storm*. **imminence** *noun*

▶▶▶ T H E S A U R U S ◀◀◀

imaginary *adjective* fancied, fanciful, fictitious, hypothetical, illusory, invented, legendary, made-up, mythical, mythological, non-existent, pretend (*informal*), unreal.

imagination *noun* creativity, fancy, fantasy, ingenuity, innovation, inspiration, inventiveness, vision.
imaginative *adjective* creative, ingenious, innovative, inspired, inventive, visionary.

imagine *verb* conceive, dream up, envisage, fancy, fantasise, picture, speculate, think up, visualise.

imbalance *noun* disproportion, inequality, unevenness.

imitate *verb* ape, copy, duplicate, echo, emulate, impersonate, mimic, parody, replicate, reproduce, send up (*informal*), simulate, take off.

imitation *noun* 1 burlesque, impersonation, impression, mimicry, parody, send-up (*informal*), spoof (*informal*), take-off. 2 copy, counterfeit, duplicate, fake, forgery, replica, reproduction.
imitation *adjective* artificial, fake, mock, phoney (*informal*), sham, synthetic.

immaculate *adjective* 1 clean, neat, spick and span, spotless, tidy. 2 faultless, flawless, impeccable, perfect, unblemished.

immature *adjective* babyish, callow, childish, green, inexperienced, infantile, juvenile, naïve, puerile, youthful.

immediate *adjective* 1 direct, instant, instantaneous, prompt, speedy, swift, unhesitating. 2 adjacent, closest, nearest, next.
immediately *adverb* at once, directly, forthwith, instantly, on the knocker (*Australian informal*), on the spot, promptly, right away, straight away, then and there.

immense *adjective* astronomical, big, colossal, considerable, enormous, excessive, exorbitant, extensive, gigantic, great, hefty, huge, immeasurable, large, mammoth, massive, monstrous, prodigious, staggering, stupendous, terrific, tremendous, vast.

immerse *verb* 1 dip, drench, dunk, plunge, soak, steep, submerge, wet. 2 absorb, bury, engross, occupy, preoccupy.

immigrant *noun* migrant, newcomer, settler.

imminent *adjective* approaching, close, impending, looming, near, nigh, threatening.

▶▶DICTIONARY◀◀

immobile *adjective* not moving; immovable. **immobility** *noun*

immobilise *verb* (**immobilised, immobilising**) stop a thing from moving or working. **immobilisation** *noun*

immodest *adjective* **1** without modesty; indecent. **2** conceited.

immoral *adjective* morally wrong; wicked. **immorally** *adverb*, **immorality** *noun*

immortal *adjective* **1** living for ever; not mortal. **2** famous for all time. **immortal** *noun*, **immortality** *noun*, **immortalise** *verb*

immovable *adjective* unable to be moved. **immovably** *adverb*

immune *adjective* safe from or protected against something, *immune from* (or *against* or *to*) *infection* etc. **immunity** *noun* [from Latin *immunis* = exempt]

immunise *verb* (**immunised, immunising**) make a person immune from a disease etc., e.g. by vaccination. **immunisation** *noun*

immutable (*say* i-**mewt**-a-bul) *adjective* unchangeable. **immutably** *adverb*

imp *noun* **1** a small devil. **2** a mischievous child. **impish** *adjective*

impact *noun* **1** a collision; the force of a collision. **2** an influence or effect, *the impact of computers on our lives.* [from *im-* = in, + Latin *pactum* = driven]

impair *verb* damage; weaken, *Smoking impairs health.* **impairment** *noun* [from *im-* = in, + Latin *pejor* = worse]

impala (*say* im-**pah**-la) *noun* (*plural* **impala**) a small African antelope. [Zulu]

impale *verb* (**impaled, impaling**) pierce or fix something on a sharp pointed object. **impalement** *noun* [from *im-* = in, + Latin *palus* = a stake]

impart *verb* **1** tell, *She imparted the news to her brother.* **2** give, *Lemon imparts a sharp flavour to drinks.*

impartial *adjective* not favouring one side more than the other; not biased; fair. **impartially** *adverb*, **impartiality** *noun*

impassable *adjective* not able to be travelled along or over, *The roads are impassable because of floods.*

impasse (*say* **im**-pahss) *noun* a deadlock. [French, = impassable place]

impassive *adjective* not feeling or not showing emotion. **impassively** *adverb*

impatient *adjective* not patient. **impatiently** *adverb*, **impatience** *noun*

impeach *verb* bring a person to trial for a serious crime against his or her country. **impeachment** *noun*

impeccable *adjective* faultless. **impeccably** *adverb*, **impeccability** *noun* [from *im-* = not, + Latin *peccare* = to sin]

▶▶THESAURUS◀◀

immobile *adjective* fixed, immobilised, immovable, motionless, paralysed, stationary, still, stuck.

immodest *adjective* **1** brazen, forward, improper, indecent, shameless, wanton. **2** see CONCEITED (at CONCEIT).

immoral *adjective* bad, base, corrupt, degenerate, depraved, evil, iniquitous, shameless, sinful, unethical, unprincipled, unscrupulous, wicked.

immortal *adjective* **1** abiding, enduring, eternal, everlasting, undying.

immovable *adjective* fast, fixed, immobile, immobilised, jammed, stationary, stuck.

immune *adjective* exempt (from), free (from), impervious (to), invulnerable (to), protected (from), resistant (to), safe (from).

immunisation *noun* inoculation, vaccination.

imp *noun* **1** demon, devil, elf, fairy, goblin, hobgoblin, pixie, spirit, sprite. **2** devil, monkey, rascal, scallywag, scamp.

impact *noun* **1** bump, collision, crash, knock, smash. **2** consequence, effect, impression, influence, repercussions.

impair *verb* damage, harm, hurt, injure, ruin, spoil, undermine, weaken.

impart *verb* **1** communicate, convey, disclose, divulge, make known, pass on, report, reveal, tell, transmit. **2** contribute, give.

impartial *adjective* disinterested, even-handed, fair, just, neutral, non-aligned, non-partisan, objective, unbiased.

impasse *noun* deadlock, stalemate, standstill.

impassive *adjective* apathetic, cool, dispassionate, indifferent, phlegmatic, stolid, stony, unemotional, unmoved, unresponsive, wooden.

impatient *adjective* edgy, fidgety, nervous, nervy, restive, restless, toey (*Australian informal*); (*impatient to*) anxious to, eager to, itching to, keen to, raring to.

impeccable *adjective* blameless, exemplary, faultless, flawless, irreproachable, perfect, unimpeachable.

▶▶▶ DICTIONARY ◀◀

impede *verb* (**impeded, impeding**) hinder. [from Latin *impedire* = to shackle the feet (*im-* = in, + *pedis* = of a foot)]

impediment *noun* **1** a hindrance. **2** a defect, *He has an impediment in his speech* (= a lisp or stammer). [same origin as *impede*]

impel *verb* (**impelled, impelling**) **1** urge or drive someone to do something, *Curiosity impelled her to investigate.* **2** drive forward; propel. [from *im-* = towards, + Latin *pellere* = drive]

impending *adjective* imminent. [from *im-* = in, + Latin *pendere* = hang]

impenetrable *adjective* not able to be penetrated.

impenitent *adjective* not penitent; unrepentant.

imperative¹ *adjective* **1** expressing a command. **2** essential, *Speed is imperative.*

imperative² *noun* a command; the form of a verb used in making commands (e.g. 'come' in *Come here!*). [from Latin *imperare* = to command]

imperceptible *adjective* not perceptible; difficult or impossible to see.

imperfect *adjective* not perfect. **imperfectly** *adverb*, **imperfection** *noun*

imperfect tense a tense of a verb showing a continuous action, e.g. *She was singing.*

imperial *adjective* **1** of an empire or its rulers. **2** (of weights and measures) fixed by British law, *an imperial gallon.* **imperially** *adverb* [from Latin *imperium* = supreme power]

imperialism *noun* the policy of extending a country's empire or its influence; colonialism. **imperialist** *noun*

imperious *adjective* commanding; bossy.

impersonal *adjective* **1** not affected by personal feelings; showing no emotion. **2** not referring to a particular person. **impersonally** *adverb*

impersonal verb a verb used only with 'it', e.g. in *It is raining* or *It is hard to find one.*

impersonate *verb* (**impersonated, impersonating**) pretend to be another person. **impersonation** *noun*, **impersonator** *noun*

impertinent *adjective* **1** insolent; not showing proper respect. **2** not pertinent; irrelevant. **impertinently** *adverb*, **impertinence** *noun*

imperturbable *adjective* not excitable; calm. **imperturbably** *adverb*

impervious *adjective* **1** impenetrable, *impervious to water.* **2** not influenced by something, *impervious to criticism.* [from *im-* = not, + Latin *per* = through, *via* = way]

impetuous *adjective* **1** hasty; rash. **2** eager; impulsive.

impetus *noun* force or energy of movement. [Latin, = an attack]

▶▶▶ THESAURUS ◀◀

impede *verb* block, check, curb, delay, hamper, handicap, hinder, hold up, inhibit, obstruct, prevent, restrict, retard, slow, stonker (*Australian slang*), thwart.

impediment *noun* **1** bar, barrier, hindrance, hitch, hurdle, obstacle, obstruction, snag, stumbling block. **2** defect, handicap, lisp, stammer, stutter.

impel *verb* **1** compel, drive, force, make, prompt, urge.

impending *adjective* approaching, coming, forthcoming, imminent, looming, threatening.

impenetrable *adjective* dense, impassable, impervious, inaccessible, thick.

impenitent *adjective* hardened, remorseless, unrepentant.

imperative¹ *adjective* **2** compulsory, essential, mandatory, necessary, obligatory.

imperceptible *adjective* indiscernible, minuscule, minute, negligible, slight, subtle, tiny, unnoticeable.

imperfect *adjective* defective, deficient, faulty, flawed, incomplete, shoddy, substandard, unfinished.

imperfection *noun* blemish, defect, deficiency, fault, flaw, shortcoming, weakness.

imperious *verb* bossy, commanding, dictatorial, domineering, lordly, magisterial, masterful, overbearing, peremptory.

impersonate *verb* ape, imitate, masquerade as, mimic, portray, pose as, pretend to be, take off.

impertinent *adjective* **1** cheeky, disrespectful, forward, impolite, impudent, insolent, presumptuous, rude.

impertinence *noun* cheek, effrontery, gall, hide, impudence, insolence, nerve, presumptuousness, rudeness.

impervious *adjective* **1** impenetrable, impermeable, resistant, waterproof. **2** immune, invulnerable, unaffected (by), unresponsive.

impetuous *adjective* **1** hasty, headlong, impulsive, precipitate, quick, rash, reckless, spontaneous, spur-of-the-moment, sudden, wild. **2** eager, foolhardy, headstrong, hotheaded, impulsive, rash, reckless, spontaneous.

impetus *noun* boost, drive, impulse, incentive, momentum, motivation, push, spur, stimulus.

►►► DICTIONARY ◄◄

impiety *noun* lack of reverence. **impious** (*say* **imp**-ee-us) *adjective*

impinge *verb* (**impinged, impinging**) **1** make an impact. **2** encroach.

implacable *adjective* not able to be placated; relentless. **implacably** *adverb*

implant *verb* insert; fix something in. **implant** *noun,* **implantation** *noun*

implement[1] *noun* a tool.

implement[2] *verb* put into action, *We shall implement these plans next month.* **implementation** *noun*

implicate *verb* (**implicated, implicating**) involve a person in a crime etc.; show that a person is involved, *His evidence implicates his sister.*

implication *noun* **1** implicating. **2** implying; something that is implied.

implicit (*say* im-**pliss**-it) *adjective* **1** implied but not stated openly. (Compare *explicit.*) **2** absolute; unquestioning, *She expects implicit obedience.* **implicitly** *adverb* [from Latin, = folded in]

implore *verb* (**implored, imploring**) beg somebody to do something; entreat. [from *im*- = in, + Latin *plorare* = weep]

imply *verb* (**implied, implying**) suggest something without actually saying it. **implication** *noun* [same origin as *implicate*]

impolite *adjective* not polite.

imponderable *adjective* not able to be estimated.

import[1] *verb* bring in goods etc. from another country.

import[2] *noun* **1** importing; something imported. **2** meaning; importance, *The message was of great import.* [from *im*- = in, + Latin *portare* = carry]

important *adjective* **1** having or able to have a great effect. **2** having great authority or influence. **importantly** *adverb,* **importance** *noun*

impose *verb* (**imposed, imposing**) put; inflict, *It imposes a strain upon us.* **impose on somebody** put an unfair burden on him or her. [from *im*- = on, + Latin *positum* = placed]

imposing *adjective* impressive.

imposition *noun* **1** something imposed; a burden imposed unfairly. **2** imposing something.

impossible *adjective* **1** not possible. **2** (*informal*) very annoying; unbearable, *He really is impossible!* **impossibly** *adverb.* **impossibility** *noun*

►►► THESAURUS ◄◄

impinge *verb* **1** affect, have an effect, have an impact, touch. **2** encroach, infringe, intrude, trespass.

implant *verb* fix, insert, introduce, plant, put, sow.

implement[1] *noun* appliance, device, gadget, instrument, tool, utensil.

implement[2] *verb* accomplish, carry out, effect, enforce, execute, put into effect.

implicate *verb* dob in (*Australian informal*), embroil, grass on (*slang*), incriminate, inform on, involve.

implication *noun* **2** innuendo, insinuation, intimation, overtone, significance.

implicit *adjective* **1** implied, tacit, understood, unsaid, unspoken.

implore *verb* appeal to, ask, beg, beseech, entreat, plead with, request.

imply *verb* hint, indicate, insinuate, intimate, suggest.

impolite *adjective* bad-mannered, boorish, cheeky, churlish, coarse, discourteous, disrespectful, impudent, insolent, insulting, loutish, rude, tactless, uncivil, vulgar.

important *adjective* **1** big, consequential, critical, crucial, fateful, grave, historic, key, life and death, major, momentous, newsworthy, noteworthy, pivotal, pressing, primary, serious, significant, urgent, vital, weighty. **2** celebrated, distinguished, eminent, famed, famous, great, high-ranking, influential, leading, notable, outstanding, powerful, pre-eminent, prominent, renowned, well-known.
   importance *noun* **1** account, consequence, import, moment, significance, weight. **2** distinction, eminence, influence, note, prominence, renown, standing, stature, status.

impose *verb* enforce, exact, inflict, lay, levy, prescribe, put.
   impose on abuse, exploit, presume on, take advantage of.

imposing *adjective* big, grand, impressive, magnificent, majestic, ostentatious, splendid, stately, striking.

impossible *adjective* **1** hopeless, impracticable, inconceivable, insoluble, out of the question, unachievable, unattainable, unthinkable, unworkable.

impostor *noun* a person who dishonestly pretends to be someone else.

imposture *noun* a dishonest pretence.

impotent *adjective* 1 powerless; unable to take action. 2 (of a man) unable to have sexual intercourse. **impotently** *adverb*, **impotence** *noun*

impound *verb* confiscate.

impoverish *verb* 1 make a person poor. 2 make a thing poor in quality, *impoverished soil*. **impoverishment** *noun*

impracticable *adjective* not practicable.

impractical *adjective* not practical; unwise.

imprecise *adjective* not precise.

impregnable *adjective* strong enough to be safe against attack.

impregnate *verb* (**impregnated, impregnating**) 1 fertilise; make pregnant. 2 saturate; fill throughout, *The air was impregnated with the scent*. **impregnation** *noun*

impresario *noun* (*plural* **impresarios**) a person who organises concerts, shows, etc. [Italian]

impress *verb* 1 affect or influence deeply. 2 cause a person to admire or think something is very good. 3 fix firmly in the mind, *He impressed on them the need for secrecy*. 4 press a mark into something.

impression *noun* 1 an effect produced on the mind. 2 a vague idea. 3 an imitation of a person or a sound etc. 4 a reprint of a book.

impressionism *noun* a style of painting that gives the general effect of a scene etc. but without details. **impressionist** *noun*

impressive *adjective* making a strong impression; seeming very good.

imprint *noun* a mark pressed into or on something. **imprint** *verb*

imprison *verb* put into prison; keep in confinement. **imprisonment** *noun*

improbable *adjective* unlikely. **improbably** *adverb*, **improbability** *noun*

impromptu *adjective & adverb* done without any rehearsal or preparation. [from Latin *in promptu* = in readiness]

improper *adjective* 1 incorrect; wrong. 2 indecent. **improperly** *adverb*, **impropriety** (*say* im-pro-**pry**-it-ee) *noun*
improper fraction a fraction that is greater than unity, with the numerator greater than the denominator, e.g. $^5/_3$.

improve *verb* (**improved, improving**) make or become better. **improvement** *noun*

impostor *noun* charlatan, con man (*informal*), fraud, impersonator, phoney (*informal*), pretender.

impotent *adjective* 1 feeble, helpless, ineffective, ineffectual, powerless, unable, weak.

impound *verb* confiscate, seize, take, take possession of.

impoverished *adjective* destitute, down and out, hard up (*informal*), impecunious, needy, penniless, penurious, poor, poverty-stricken.

impractical *adjective* airy-fairy, idealistic, starry-eyed, unrealistic, visionary.

imprecise *adjective* approximate, fuzzy, general, hazy, indefinite, inexact, nebulous, rough, sketchy, vague.

impregnable *adjective* invincible, invulnerable, safe, secure, unassailable, unconquerable.

impregnate *verb* 1 fertilise, inseminate. 2 fill, imbue, permeate, saturate, soak, steep.

impress *verb* 1 affect, influence, move, stir, strike, touch. 3 emphasise, stress, underline.

impression *noun* 1 effect, impact, mark. 2 belief, feeling, hunch, idea, notion, opinion, sense, suspicion. 3 imitation, impersonation, parody, send-up (*informal*), take-off.

impressive *adjective* august, awe-inspiring, grand, great, imposing, magnificent, majestic, memorable, moving, outstanding, remarkable, sensational, spectacular, splendid, stately, striking, superb.

imprint *noun* impression, indentation, mark, print, seal, stamp.
imprint *verb* engrave, etch, impress, stamp.

imprison *verb* confine, detain, incarcerate, intern, jail, lock up, place in custody, shut up.
imprisonment *noun* confinement, custody, detention, incarceration, internment, jail.

improbable *adjective* far-fetched, implausible, incredible, unbelievable, unlikely.

impromptu *adjective* ad lib, extempore, off the cuff, spontaneous, unprepared, unrehearsed, unscripted.

improper *adjective* 2 coarse, crude, inappropriate, indecent, irreverent, obscene, offensive, rude, unbecoming, unseemly, unsuitable, vulgar.

improve *verb* advance, ameliorate, amend, be on the mend, develop, enhance, fix up, get better, lift, look up, perk up, pick up, polish, progress, rally, recover, recuperate, refine, reform, revamp, revise, take a turn for the better, touch up, upgrade.

►►DICTIONARY◄◄

improvident *adjective* not providing or planning for the future; not thrifty.

improvise *verb* (**improvised, improvising**) 1 compose something impromptu. 2 make something quickly with whatever is available. **improvisation** *noun*

imprudent *adjective* unwise.

impudent *adjective* impertinent; cheeky. **impudently** *adverb*, **impudence** *noun*

impulse *noun* 1 a sudden desire to do something. 2 a push; impetus. 3 (in physics) a force acting for a very short time, *electrical impulses*. [same origin as *impel*]

impulsive *adjective* done or doing things on impulse, not after careful thought. **impulsively** *adverb*, **impulsiveness** *noun*

impunity (*say* im-**pewn**-it-ee) *noun* freedom from punishment or injury. [from *im-* = without, + Latin *poena* = penalty]

impure *adjective* not pure. **impurity** *noun*

impute *verb* (**imputed, imputing**) attribute; ascribe. **imputation** *noun*

in¹ *preposition* This word is used to show position or condition, e.g. (**1**) at or inside; within the limits of something (*in a box; in two hours*), (**2**) into (*He fell in a puddle*), (**3**) arranged as; consisting of (*a serial in four parts*), (**4**) occupied with; a member of (*He is in the army*), (**5**) by means of (*We paid in cash*).
in all in total number; altogether.

in² *adverb* (**1**) so as to be in something or inside (*Get in*), (**2**) inwards (*The top caved in*), (**3**) at home; indoors (*Is anybody in?*), (**4**) in action; (in cricket) batting; (of a fire) burning, (**5**) having arrived (*The train is in*).
in for likely to get, *You're in for a shock.*
in on (*informal*) aware of or sharing in, *I want to be in on this project.*

in- *prefix* (changing to **il-** before *l*, **im-** before *b*, *m, p*, **ir-** before *r*) 1 in; into; on; towards (as in *include, invade*). [from Latin *in.*] 2 not (as in *incorrect, indirect*). (Compare the prefixes *an-¹* and *un-*.)

inability *noun* being unable.

inaccessible *adjective* not accessible.

inaccurate *adjective* not accurate.

inactive *adjective* not active. **inaction** *noun*, **inactivity** *noun*

inadequate *adjective* 1 not enough. 2 not capable enough. **inadequately** *adverb*, **inadequacy** *noun*

inadvertent *adjective* unintentional.

inadvisable *adjective* not advisable.

inalienable *adjective* that cannot be taken away, *an inalienable right.*

inane *adjective* silly; without sense. **inanely** *adverb*, **inanity** *noun* [from Latin *inanis* = empty]

inanimate *adjective* 1 not living. 2 not moving.

inappropriate *adjective* not appropriate.

►►THESAURUS◄◄

improvement *noun* advance, amelioration, amendment, development, enhancement, lift, progress, rally, recovery, refinement, reform, revamp, revision, touch-up, upgrade, upturn.

improvise *verb* ad lib (*informal*), extemporise, invent, make up, play by ear.

imprudent *adjective* foolhardy, foolish, ill-advised, impolitic, inadvisable, indiscreet, reckless, short-sighted, unintelligent, unwise.

impudent *adjective* brazen, cheeky, discourteous, disrespectful, fresh (*informal*), impertinent, impolite, insolent, pert, presumptuous, rude, saucy.

impulsive *adjective* (*an impulsive person*) capricious, hotheaded, impetuous, rash, reckless; (*an impulsive action*) automatic, hasty, headlong, impetuous, instinctive, precipitate, rash, reckless, spontaneous, spur-of-the-moment, unplanned.

impure *adjective* adulterated, contaminated, dirty, filthy, foul, polluted, tainted, unclean.

inability *noun* helplessness, impotence, incapacity, powerlessness.

inaccessible *adjective* cut off, isolated, out of reach, remote, unreachable.

inaccurate *adjective* careless, false, imprecise, incorrect, inexact, sloppy, untruthful, wrong.

inactive *adjective* asleep, dormant, hibernating, idle, indolent, inert, lazy, lethargic, listless, passive, resting, sedentary, sleepy, slothful, sluggish, torpid.

inadequate *adjective* 1 deficient, insufficient, scanty, sketchy, skimpy, sparse.

inadvertent *adjective* accidental, involuntary, unconscious, unintentional, unwitting.

inadvisable *adjective* foolish, ill-advised, impolitic, imprudent, unwise.

inane *adjective* see SILLY.

inanimate *adjective* 1 lifeless.

inappropriate *adjective* improper, incongruous, irrelevant, unbecoming, unsatisfactory, unsuitable, wrong.

inarticulate *adjective* **1** not able to speak or express yourself clearly, *inarticulate with rage*. **2** not expressed in words, *an inarticulate cry*.

inattention *noun* not being attentive; not listening. **inattentive** *adjective*

inaudible *adjective* not audible. **inaudibly** *adverb*, **inaudibility** *noun*

inaugurate *verb* (**inaugurated**, **inaugurating**) **1** start or introduce something new and important. **2** install a person in office, *inaugurate a new President*. **inaugural** *adjective*, **inauguration** *noun*, **inaugurator** *noun*

inauspicious *adjective* not auspicious.

inborn *adjective* present in a person or animal from birth, *an inborn ability*.

inbred *adjective* **1** inborn. **2** produced by inbreeding.

inbreeding *noun* breeding from closely related individuals.

incalculable *adjective* not able to be calculated or predicted.

incandescent *adjective* giving out light when heated; shining. **incandescence** *noun* [from Latin, = becoming white]

incantation *noun* a spoken spell or charm; the chanting of this. [from *in-* = in, + Latin *cantare* = sing]

incapable *adjective* not able to do something, *incapable of working alone*.

incapacitate *verb* (**incapacitated**, **incapacitating**) make unable to do something; disable.

incapacity *noun* inability; lack of sufficient strength or power.

incarcerate *verb* (**incarcerated**, **incarcerating**) shut in; imprison. **incarceration** *noun* [from *in-* = in, + Latin *carcer* = prison]

incarnate *adjective* having a body or human form, *a devil incarnate* **incarnation** *noun*

the Incarnation the embodiment of God in human form as Jesus Christ. [from *in-* = in, + Latin *carnis* = of flesh]

incautious *adjective* rash.

incendiary *adcjective* starting or designed to start a fire, *an incendiary bomb*.

incense[1] (*say* **in**-sens) *noun* a substance making a spicy smell when burnt.

incense[2] (*say* in-**sens**) *verb* (**incensed**, **incensing**) make a person angry.

incentive *noun* something that encourages a person to do something or to work harder.

inception *noun* a beginning.

incessant *adjective* unceasing.

incest *noun* sexual intercourse between two people who are so closely related that they cannot marry each other. **incestuous** *adjective*

inch *noun* (*plural* **inches**) a measure of length, about 2.5 centimetres.

incidence *noun* the extent or frequency of something, *Study the incidence of the disease*. [from Latin *incidens* = happening]

incident *noun* an event.

incidental *adjective* happening with something else, *incidental expenses*.

incidentally *adverb* by the way.

incinerate *verb* (**incinerated**, **incinerating**) destroy something by burning. **incineration** *noun* [from *in-* = in, + Latin *cineris* = of ashes]

incinerator *noun* a device for burning rubbish.

incipient (*say* in-**sip**-ee-ent) *adjective* just beginning, *incipient decay*.

incise *verb* (**incised**, **incising**) cut or engrave something into a surface. [from *in-* = into, + Latin *caesum* = cut]

inattentive *adjective* absent-minded, careless, distracted, heedless, incautious, negligent.

inborn *adjective* congenital, hereditary, inbred, inherent, innate, native, natural.

incalculable *adjective* countless, enormous, immeasurable, inestimable, infinite, innumerable.

incapable *adjective* incompetent, ineffective, ineffectual, inept, useless.

incapacitate *verb* cripple, disable, immobilise, lay up, maim.

incense[2] *verb* anger, enrage, exasperate, infuriate, madden, outrage, provoke, rile (*informal*), vex.

incentive *noun* carrot, encouragement, goad, inducement, lure, reward, spur, stimulus.

incessant *adjective* ceaseless, chronic, constant, continual, continuous, endless, eternal, everlasting, interminable, non-stop, permanent, perpetual, persistent, relentless.

incidence *noun* frequency, occurrence, prevalence, rate.

incident *noun* affair, episode, event, experience, happening, occasion, occurrence.

incidental *adjective* ancillary, minor, secondary, subsidiary.

▶▶ D I C T I O N A R Y ◀◀

incision *noun* a cut, especially one made in a surgical operation.

incisive *adjective* clear and sharp, *incisive comments.*

incisor (*say* in-**sy**-zer) *noun* each of the sharp-edged front teeth in the upper and lower jaws.

incite *verb* (**incited, inciting**) urge a person to do something; stir up, *They incited a riot.* **incitement** *noun* [from *in-* = towards, + Latin *citare* = rouse]

incivility *noun* being uncivil; rudeness.

inclement *adjective* (*formal*) cold, wet, or stormy, *inclement weather.*

inclination *noun* 1 a tendency. 2 a liking or preference. 3 a slope or slant.

incline¹ *verb* (**inclined, inclining**) 1 lean; slope. 2 bend the head or body forward, as in a nod or bow. 3 cause or influence, *Her frank manner inclines me to believe her.* **be inclined** have a tendency, *The door is inclined to bang.* [from Latin *inclinare* = to bend]

incline² *noun* a slope.

include *verb* (**included, including**) make or consider something as part of a group of things. [from Latin, = enclose]

inclusive *adjective* including everything.

incognito (*say* in-kog-**neet**-oh or in-**kog**-nit-oh) *adjective & adverb* with your name or identity concealed, *The film star was travelling incognito.* [Italian, = unknown]

incoherent *adjective* not speaking or reasoning in an orderly way.

incombustible *adjective* unable to be set on fire.

income *noun* money received regularly from wages, investments, etc. **income tax** tax charged on income.

incomparable *adjective* without an equal; unsurpassed, *incomparable beauty.*

incompatible *adjective* not compatible.

incompetent *adjective* not competent.

incomplete *adjective* not complete.

incomprehensible *adjective* not able to be understood. **incomprehension** *noun*

inconceivable *adjective* not able to be imagined; most unlikely.

inconclusive *adjective* not conclusive.

incongruous *adjective* unsuitable; not harmonious; out of place. **incongruously** *adverb*, **incongruity** *noun*

inconsiderable *adjective* of small value.

inconsiderate *adjective* not considerate.

▶▶ T H E S A U R U S ◀◀

incision *noun* cut, slit.

incite *verb* arouse, egg on, encourage, excite, goad, provoke, rouse, spur, stimulate, stir up, urge.

inclement *adjective* bad, foul, rough, stormy, wet.

inclination *noun* 1 habit, predisposition, propensity, tendency. 2 fondness, liking, partiality, penchant, predilection, preference. 3 angle, gradient, incline, slant, slope.

incline¹ *verb* 1 cant, pitch, slant, slope. 2 bend, bow, lean, tilt, tip. **be inclined** be apt, be liable, be prone, be wont (*old use*), tend.

incline² *noun* grade, gradient, hill, inclination, pitch, rise, slant, slope.

include *verb* comprise, consist of, contain, count, cover, embrace, encompass, incorporate, subsume, take in.

incoherent *adjective* confused, garbled, illogical, inarticulate, incomprehensible, jumbled, muddled, rambling, unclear, unintelligible.

income *noun* earnings, livelihood, pay, receipts, revenue, salary, stipend, takings, wages.

incomparable *adjective* inimitable, matchless, peerless, superlative, supreme, unequalled, unparalleled, unrivalled, unsurpassed.

incompatible *adjective* conflicting, contradictory, incongruous, inconsistent, irreconcilable, mismatched, unsuited.

incompetent *adjective* clueless (*informal*), hopeless, inadequate, incapable, ineffectual, inefficient, inept, inexpert, unskilful, useless.

incomplete *adjective* abridged, fragmentary, imperfect, partial, sketchy, unfinished.

incomprehensible *adjective* abstruse, bewildering, complicated, inexplicable, inscrutable, unfathomable, unintelligible.

inconceivable *adjective* impossible, improbable, incredible, unbelievable, unimaginable, unthinkable.

incongruous *adjective* absurd, inappropriate, odd, out of keeping, out of place.

inconsiderate *adjective* careless, insensitive, rude, selfish, tactless, thoughtless, uncaring, unthinking.

▶▶▶ D I C T I O N A R Y ◀◀◀

inconsistent *adjective* **1** not consistent; variable. **2** not in keeping. **inconsistently** *adverb*, **inconsistency** *noun*

inconsolable *adjective* not able to be consoled; very sad.

inconspicuous *adjective* not conspicuous. **inconspicuously** *adverb*

incontinent *adjective* not able to control excretion. **incontinence** *noun*

incontrovertible *adjective* indisputable.

inconvenience¹ *noun* being inconvenient.

inconvenience² *verb* (**inconvenienced, inconveniencing**) cause inconvenience or slight difficulty to someone.

inconvenient *adjective* not convenient.

incorporate *verb* (**incorporated, incorporating**) include something as a part. **incorporation** *noun*

incorporated *adjective* (of a business firm) formed into a legal corporation.

incorrect *adjective* not correct. **incorrectly** *adverb*

incorrigible *adjective* not able to be reformed, *an incorrigible liar.*

incorruptible *adjective* **1** not liable to decay. **2** not able to be bribed.

increase¹ *verb* (**increased, increasing**) make or become larger or more.

increase² *noun* increasing; the amount by which a thing increases. [from *in-* = in, + Latin *crescere* = grow]

incredible *adjective* unbelievable. **incredibly** *adverb*, **incredibility** *noun*

incredulous *adjective* not believing somebody; showing disbelief. **incredulously** *adverb*, **incredulity** *noun*

increment (say **in**-krim-ent) *noun* an increase; an added amount.

incriminate *verb* (**incriminated, incriminating**) show a person to have been involved in a crime etc. **incrimination** *noun*

incrustation *noun* encrusting, a crust or deposit formed on a surface.

incubate *verb* (**incubated, incubating**) **1** hatch eggs by keeping them warm. **2** cause bacteria or a disease etc. to develop. **incubation** *noun*

incubator *noun* **1** a device for incubating eggs etc. **2** a device in which a baby born prematurely can be kept warm and supplied with oxygen.

incumbent¹ *adjective* forming an obligation, *It is incumbent on you to warn people of the danger.*

incumbent² *noun* a person who holds a particular office or position. [from *in-* = on, + Latin *-cumbens* = lying]

incur *verb* (**incurred, incurring**) bring something on yourself, *incur expense.* [from *in-* = on, + Latin *currere* = to run]

▶▶▶ T H E S A U R U S ◀◀◀

inconsistent *adjective* **1** capricious, changeable, erratic, fickle, patchy, temperamental, unpredictable, unreliable, variable. **2** at odds, conflicting, contradictory, incompatible, irreconcilable.

inconspicuous *adjective* unnoticeable, unobtrusive, unostentatious.

inconvenience¹ *noun* bother, disruption, disturbance, hassle (*informal*), irritation, nuisance, trouble.

inconvenience² *verb* bother, disrupt, disturb, hassle (*informal*), impose on, put out (*informal*), trouble.

inconvenient *adjective* awkward, bothersome, ill-timed, inopportune, troublesome, unsuitable, untimely.

incorporate *verb* amalgamate, blend, combine, consolidate, integrate, merge, mix, unite; see also INCLUDE.

incorrect *adjective* erroneous, false, inaccurate, mistaken, untrue, wrong.

incorrigible *adjective* hardened, hopeless, incurable, inveterate, unreformable.

increase¹ *verb* add to, advance, appreciate, augment, boost, build up, develop, enlarge, escalate, expand, extend, gain, go up, grow, heighten, improve, intensify, jump, lengthen, lift, magnify, multiply, prolong, protract, raise, skyrocket, soar, step up, strengthen, supplement, swell.

increase² *noun* addition, advance, boost, build-up, development, enlargement, escalation, expansion, explosion, extension, gain, growth, increment, inflation, jump, rise, upsurge.

incredible *adjective* amazing, extraordinary, far-fetched, implausible, improbable, inconceivable, miraculous, unbelievable, unlikely.

incredulous *adjective* disbelieving, distrustful, doubtful, dubious, sceptical, unbelieving.

incriminate *verb* accuse, blame, implicate, inculpate.

incubate *verb* **1** brood, hatch.

▶▶ D I C T I O N A R Y ◀◀

incurable *adjective* not able to be cured.
incurably *adverb*

incurious *adjective* feeling or showing no curiosity about something.

incursion *noun* a raid or brief invasion. [same origin as *incur*]

indebted *adjective* owing money or gratitude to someone.

indecent *adjective* not decent; improper.
indecently *adverb*, **indecency** *noun*

indecipherable *adjective* not able to be deciphered.

indecision *noun* being unable to make up your mind; hesitation.

indecisive *adjective* not decisive.

indeed *adverb* 1 really; truly, *I am indeed surprised*. (used to strengthen a meaning), *very nice indeed*. 2 admittedly, *It is, indeed, his first attempt*.

indefensible *adjective* unable to be defended; unable to be justified.

indefinable *adjective* unable to be defined or described clearly.

indefinite *adjective* not definite; vague.
indefinite article the word 'a' or 'an'.

indefinitely *adverb* for an indefinite or unlimited time.

indelible *adjective* impossible to rub out or remove. **indelibly** *adverb* [from *in-* = not, + Latin *delere* = destroy]

indelicate *adjective* 1 slightly indecent. 2 tactless. **indelicacy** *noun*

indent *verb* 1 make notches or recesses in something. 2 start a line of writing or printing

further in from the margin than other lines, *Always indent the first line of a new paragraph*. 3 place an official order for goods or stores, *Indent for a new office desk*.
indentation *noun*

indenture *noun* (also **indentures**) an agreement binding an apprentice to work for a certain employer. **indentured** *adjective*

independent *adjective* 1 not dependent; not controlled by any other person or thing. 2 (of a country) governing itself. 3 (of a school) non-government. **independently** *adverb*, **independence** *noun*

indescribable *adjective* unable to be described. **indescribably** *adverb*

indestructible *adjective* unable to be destroyed. **indestructibility** *noun*

indeterminate *adjective* not fixed or decided exactly; left vague.

index[1] *noun* 1 (*plural* **indexes**) an alphabetical list of things, especially at the end of a book. 2 a number showing how prices or wages have changed from a previous level. 3 (*plural* **indices**) the exponent of a number.
index finger the forefinger.

index[2] *verb* make an index to a book etc.; put into an index. [Latin, = pointer]

Indian *adjective* 1 of India or its people. 2 of American Indians. **Indian** *noun*
American Indian a member or descendant of the original inhabitants of the continent of America (other than Eskimos).
Indian summer a warm period in late autumn (originally in North America).

▶▶ T H E S A U R U S ◀◀

incurable *adjective* hopeless, inoperable, uncorrectable, untreatable; see also IN-CORRIGIBLE.

indebted *adjective* beholden, grateful, obliged, thankful.

indecent *adjective* blue, coarse, crude, dirty, filthy, foul, improper, indelicate, lewd, obscene, offensive, pornographic, risqué, rude, suggestive, tasteless, unprintable, unseemly, vulgar.

indecisive *adjective* hesitant, in two minds, irresolute, tentative, uncertain, undecided, unsure.

indefinable *adjective* elusive, indescribable, obscure, vague.

indefinite *adjective* confused, equivocal, evasive, fuzzy, general, hazy, imprecise, indeterminate, inexact, non-committal, ob-

scure, open-ended, tentative, uncertain, unspecified, unsure, vague.

indelible *adjective* fast, fixed, lasting, permanent.

indentation *noun* cut, groove, nick, notch, recess, score.

independent *adjective* 1 self-reliant, self-sufficient, self-supporting; see also NEUTRAL. 2 autonomous, free, self-determining, self-governing, self-ruling, sovereign. 3 non-government, private.

indescribable *adjective* ineffable, inexpressible, unspeakable, unutterable.

indestructible *adjective* durable, enduring, eternal, everlasting, lasting, permanent, strong, sturdy, tough, unbreakable, undying.

index[1] *noun* 1 catalogue, concordance, directory, gazetteer, inventory, list, register.

▶▶ DICTIONARY ◀◀

indicate *verb* (**indicated, indicating**) **1** point out; make known. **2** be a sign of. **indication** *noun* [from *in-* = towards, + Latin *dicatum* = proclaimed]

indicative[1] *adjective* giving an indication.

indicative[2] *noun* the form of a verb used in making a statement (e.g. 'he said' or 'he is coming'), not in a command or question etc.

indicator *noun* **1** a thing that indicates or points to something. **2** a flashing light used to signal that a motor vehicle is turning.

indict (*say* ind-**I**'t) *verb* charge a person with having committed a crime. **indictment** *noun*

indifferent *adjective* **1** not caring about something; not interested. **2** not very good, *an indifferent cricketer*. **indifferently** *adverb*, **indifference** *noun*

indigenous (*say* in-**dij**-in-us) *adjective* growing or originating in a particular country; native, *The koala is indigenous to Australia*. [from Latin *indigena* = born in a country]

indigent (*say* **in**-dij-ent) *adjective* needy.

indigestible *adjective* difficult or impossible to digest.

indigestion *noun* pain caused by difficulty in digesting food.

indignant *adjective* angry at something that seems unfair or wicked. **indignantly** *adverb*, **indignation** *noun* [from Latin *indignari* = regard as unworthy]

indignity *noun* (*plural* **indignities**) treatment that makes a person feel undignified or humiliated; an insult.

indigo *noun* a deep-blue colour.

indirect *adjective* not direct. **indirectly** *adverb*

indiscreet *adjective* **1** not discreet; revealing secrets. **2** incautious; unwise. **indiscreetly** *adverb*, **indiscretion** *noun*

indiscriminate *adjective* showing no discrimination; not making a careful choice. **indiscriminately** *adverb*

indispensable *adjective* not able to be dispensed with; essential. **indispensability** *noun*

indisposed *adjective* **1** slightly unwell. **2** unwilling, *They seem indisposed to help us.* **indisposition** *noun*

indisputable *adjective* undeniable.

indistinct *adjective* not distinct. **indistinctly** *adverb*, **indistinctness** *noun*

indistinguishable *adjective* not distinguishable.

individual[1] *adjective* **1** of or for one person. **2** single; separate, *Count each individual word*. **individually** *adverb*

individual[2] *noun* one person, animal, or plant.

individuality *noun* the things that make one person or thing different from another; distinctive identity.

indivisible *adjective* not able to be divided or separated. **indivisibly** *adverb*

▶▶ THESAURUS ◀◀

indicate *verb* **1** make known, point out, reveal, show, signal, specify, tell. **2** be a sign of, denote, imply, mean, show, signify, spell, suggest.
indication *noun* clue, evidence, hint, mark, sign, signal, symptom, token, warning.

indicator *noun* **1** dial, display, gauge, guide, index, meter.

indifferent *adjective* **1** apathetic, blasé, cold, cool, dispassionate, half-hearted, lukewarm, neutral, nonchalant, uncaring, unconcerned, uninterested. **2** fair, mediocre, middling, ordinary, passable, so-so, unexciting, uninspired.

indigenous *adjective* Aboriginal, native, original.

indignant *adjective* angry, cross, disgruntled, infuriated, irate, irritated, livid (*informal*), riled (*informal*), ropeable (*Australian informal*), up in arms (*informal*), vexed.
indignation *noun* anger, displeasure, dudgeon, fury, ire, irritation, outrage, umbrage, wrath.

indirect *adjective* circuitous, devious, meandering, rambling, roundabout, tortuous.

indiscreet *adjective* **2** impolitic, imprudent, injudicious, tactless, thoughtless, untactful, unwise.

indispensable *adjective* essential, key, necessary, required, requisite, vital.

indisposed *adjective* **1** ailing, crook (*Australian informal*), ill, off colour, poorly, sick, unwell.

indisputable *adjective* certain, conclusive, incontestable, incontrovertible, indubitable, irrefutable, undeniable, unquestionable.

indistinct *adjective* blurred, confused, dim, faint, fuzzy, hazy, indefinite, nebulous, obscure, unclear, vague.

individual[1] *adjective* **1** characteristic, distinct, distinctive, exclusive, idiosyncratic, own, particular, peculiar, personal, special, specific, unique. **2** separate, single.

individual[2] *noun* character, fellow, human being, man, person, woman.

▶▶ D I C T I O N A R Y ◀◀

indoctrinate *verb* (**indoctrinated, indoctrinating**) fill a person's mind with particular ideas or beliefs, especially so as to make him or her accept them uncritically. **indoctrination** *noun* [from *in-* = in, + *doctrine*]

indolent *adjective* lazy. **indolently** *adverb*, **indolence** *noun*

indomitable *adjective* not able to be overcome or conquered. [from *in-* = not, + Latin *domitare* = to tame]

indoor *adjective* used or placed or done etc. inside a building, *indoor games*.

indoors *adverb* inside a building.

indubitable (*say* in-**dew**-bit-a-bul) *adjective* not able to be doubted; certain. **indubitably** *adverb* [from *in-* = not, + Latin *dubium* = doubt]

induce *verb* (**induced, inducing**) 1 persuade. 2 produce; cause, *Some substances induce sleep.* **induction** *noun* [from *in-* = in, + Latin *ducere* = to lead]

inducement *noun* an incentive.

indulge *verb* (**indulged, indulging**) allow a person to have or do what he or she wishes. **indulgence** *noun*, **indulgent** *adjective* **indulge in** allow yourself to have or do something that you like.

industrial *adjective* of industry, working or used in industry. **industrially** *adverb* **industrial action** striking or working to rule.

Industrial Revolution the expansion of British industry by the use of machines in the late 18th and early 19th century.

industrialised *adjective* (of a country or district) having many industries. **industrialisation** *noun*

industrialist *noun* a person who owns or manages an industrial business.

industrious *adjective* working hard. **industriously** *adverb*

industry *noun* (*plural* **industries**) 1 making or producing goods etc., especially in factories. 2 being industrious. [from Latin *industria* = hard work]

inebriated *adjective* drunk; drunken.

inedible *adjective* not edible.

ineffective *adjective* 1 not effective. 2 (of a person) inefficient. **ineffectively** *adverb*

ineffectual *adjective* not effectual; not confident, not convincing.

inefficient *adjective* 1 not efficient. 2 (of a person) not capable. **inefficiently** *adverb*, **inefficiency** *noun*

inelegant *adjective* not elegant.

ineligible *adjective* not eligible.

inept *adjective* 1 unsuitable. 2 bungling. **ineptly** *adverb*, **ineptitude** *noun* [from *in-* = not, + Latin *aptus* = suitable]

inequality *noun* (*plural* **inequalities**) not being equal.

inequity *noun* (*plural* **inequities**) unfairness. **inequitable** *adjective*

▶▶ T H E S A U R U S ◀◀

indoctrinate *verb* brainwash; see also TEACH.

indolent *adjective* idle, inactive, inert, lazy, lethargic, slothful, sluggish.

indubitable *adjective* certain, definite, indisputable, undeniable, undoubted, unquestionable.

induce *verb* 1 coax, influence, inspire, motivate, move, persuade, prompt, sway, tempt. 2 bring about, cause, give rise to, lead to, produce, provoke.

inducement *noun* attraction, carrot, enticement, goad, incentive, spur, stimulus.

indulge *verb* (*indulge a person*) cosset, mollycoddle, pamper, pander to, spoil; (*indulge a craving*) cater to, give in to, gratify, satisfy.

indulgent *adjective* easygoing, forbearing, forgiving, kind, lenient, liberal, merciful, permissive, soft, tolerant.

industrious *adjective* assiduous, conscientious, diligent, energetic, hard-working, indefatigable, tireless, unflagging, zealous.

industry *noun* 1 business, commerce, manufacturing, trade.

inedible *adjective* uneatable, unpalatable.

ineffective *adjective* 1 futile, unavailing, unproductive, unsuccessful, useless. 2 feckless, incapable, incompetent, ineffectual, inefficient, useless.

ineffectual *adjective* feckless, feeble, hopeless, impotent, incapable, incompetent, ineffective, weak.

inefficient *adjective* 1 ineffective, uneconomic, unproductive, wasteful. 2 disorganised, incapable, incompetent, ineffective, ineffectual.

inept *adjective* 1 absurd, inappropriate, unsuitable. 2 bungling, clumsy, incompetent, inefficient, inexpert, unskilful.

inequality *noun* bias, difference, discrimination, disparity, imbalance, prejudice.

inert *adjective* not moving; not reacting. **inertly** *adverb* [from Latin *iners* = idle]

inertia (*say* in-**er**-sha) *noun* **1** inactivity; being inert or slow to take action. **2** the tendency for a moving thing to keep moving in a straight line.

inescapable *adjective* unavoidable.

inessential *adjective* not essential.

inestimable *adjective* too great or precious to be able to be estimated.

inevitable *adjective* unavoidable; sure to happen. **inevitably** *adverb*, **inevitability** *noun* [from *in-* = not, + Latin *evitare* = avoid]

inexact *adjective* not exact.

inexcusable *adjective* not excusable.

inexhaustible *adjective* so great that it cannot be used up completely.

inexorable (*say* in-**eks**-er-a-bul) *adjective* relentless; not yielding to requests or entreaties. **inexorably** *adverb*

inexpensive *adjective* not expensive; cheap. **inexpensively** *adverb*

inexperience *noun* lack of experience. **inexperienced** *adjective*

inexpert *adjective* unskilful.

inexplicable *adjective* impossible to explain. **inexplicably** *adverb*

infallible *adjective* never wrong; never failing, *an infallible remedy.* **infallibly** *adverb*, **infallibility** *noun*

infamous (*say* **in**-fam-us) *adjective* having a bad reputation; wicked. **infamously** *adverb*, **infamy** *noun*

infancy *noun* **1** early childhood; babyhood. **2** an early stage of development.

infant *noun* a baby or young child. [from Latin, = person unable to speak]

infantile *adjective* **1** of an infant. **2** very childish.

infantry *noun* soldiers who fight on foot. (Compare *cavalry*.) [from Italian *infante* = a youth]

infatuated *adjective* filled with foolish or unreasoning love. **infatuation** *noun* [from *in-* = in, + Latin *fatuus* = foolish]

infect *verb* pass on a disease or bacteria etc. to a person, animal, or plant. [from Latin *infectum* = tainted]

infection *noun* **1** infecting. **2** an infectious disease or condition.

infectious *adjective* **1** (of a disease) able to be spread by air or water etc. (Compare *contagious*.) **2** quickly spreading to others, *His fear was infectious.*

infer *verb* (**inferred, inferring**) form an opinion by reasoning; conclude, *I infer from your luggage that you are going on holiday.* **inference** *noun*. [from *in-*, + Latin *ferre* = bring]

Usage Do not confuse with *imply*.

inertia *noun* **1** inactivity, indolence, languor, laziness, lethargy, listlessness, passivity, sluggishness, torpor.

inevitable *adjective* certain, fated, inescapable, sure, unavoidable.

inexact *adjective* approximate, imprecise, inaccurate, loose, rough.

inexcusable *adjective* indefensible, unforgivable, unjustifiable, unpardonable.

inexhaustible *adjective* boundless, endless, everlasting, infinite, never-ending, unending, unlimited.

inexpensive *adjective* budget-priced, cheap, economical, low-priced, reasonable.

inexperienced *adjective* callow, green, immature, naïve, raw, unsophisticated, unworldly.

inexplicable *adjective* baffling, enigmatic, incomprehensible, insoluble, mysterious, puzzling, unaccountable, unexplainable, unfathomable.

infallible *adjective* certain, dependable, foolproof, guaranteed, perfect, reliable, sure, unfailing.

infamous *adjective* disgraceful, dishonourable, disreputable, evil, nefarious, notorious, outrageous, scandalous, wicked.

infancy *noun* **1** babyhood, childhood.

infant *noun* babe, baby, bairn (*Scottish*), child, piccaninny, toddler, tot.

infantile *adjective* babyish, childish, immature, juvenile, puerile.

infatuated *adjective* (*infatuated with*) besotted with, crazy about, enamoured of, in love with, keen on, mad about, rapt in. **infatuation** *noun* crush (*informal*), obsession, passion.

infect *verb* contaminate, poison, pollute, taint.

infection *noun* **2** ailment, bug (*informal*), disease, illness, virus, wog (*Australian informal*).

infectious *adjective* catching, communicable, contagious, transmittable.

infer *verb* conclude, deduce, gather, reason, surmise, work out.

inferior *adjective* less good or less important; low or lower in position, quality, etc. **inferiority** *noun* [Latin, = lower]

infernal *adjective* **1** of or like hell, *the infernal regions*. **2** (*informal*) detestable; tiresome. **infernally** *adverb*

inferno *noun* (*plural* **infernos**) a terrifying fire.

infertile *adjective* not fertile. **infertility** *noun*

infest *verb* (of pests) be numerous and troublesome in a place. **infestation** *noun* [from Latin, = hostile]

infidel (*say* **in**-fid-el) *noun* a person who does not believe in a religion. [from *in-* = not, + Latin *fidelis* = faithful]

infidelity *noun* unfaithfulness.

infiltrate *verb* (**infiltrated, infiltrating**) get into a place or organisation gradually and without being noticed. **infiltration** *noun*, **infiltrator** *noun*

infinite *adjective* **1** endless; without a limit. **2** too great to be measured. **infinitely** *adverb*

infinitesimal *adjective* extremely small. **infinitesimally** *adverb*

infinitive *noun* a form of a verb that does not indicate a particular tense or number or person, in English used with or without *to*, e.g. *go* in 'Let him go' or 'Allow him to go'. [from *in-* = not, + Latin *finitivus* = definite]

infinitude *noun* infinity.

infinity *noun* an infinite number or distance or time.

infirm *adjective* weak, especially from old age or illness. **infirmity** *noun*

infirmary *noun* (*plural* **infirmaries**) **1** a hospital. **2** a place where sick people are cared for in a school or monastery etc.

inflame *verb* (**inflamed, inflaming**) **1** arouse strong feelings or anger in people. **2** cause redness, heat, and swelling in a part of the body. **inflammation** *noun*, **inflammatory** *adjective*

inflammable *adjective* able to be set on fire.

Usage This word means the same as *flammable*; its opposite is *non-inflammable*.

inflatable *adjective* able to be inflated.

inflate *verb* (**inflated, inflating**) **1** fill with air or gas and expand. **2** increase too much; raise prices or wages etc. more than is justifiable. [from *in-* = in, + Latin *flatum* = blown]

inflation *noun* **1** inflating. **2** a general rise in prices and fall in the purchasing power of money. **inflationary** *adjective*

inflect *verb* **1** change the ending or form of a word to show its tense or its grammatical relation to other words, e.g. *sing* changes to *sang* or *sung*, *child* changes to *children*. **2** alter the voice in speaking. **inflexion** *noun* [from *in-* = in, + Latin *flectere* = to bend]

inflexible *adjective* **1** not able to be bent. **2** not able to be changed or persuaded. **inflexibly** *adverb*, **inflexibility** *noun*

inflict *verb* make a person suffer something, *She inflicted a severe blow on him*. **infliction** *noun* [from *in-* = on, + Latin *flictum* = struck]

inflow *noun* flowing in; what flows in.

influence[1] *noun* the power to produce an effect; a person or thing with this power.

inferior *adjective* (*inferior rank*) junior, lower, subordinate; (*inferior quality*) cheap, crook (*Australian informal*), faulty, imperfect, inadequate, indifferent, mediocre, poor, second-rate, shoddy, substandard, third-rate.

infertile *adjective* barren, poor, sterile, unproductive.

infest *verb* invade, overrun, swarm, take over.

infidelity *noun* adultery, disloyalty, unfaithfulness.

infinite *adjective* **1** boundless, endless, inexhaustible, interminable, limitless, never-ending, unbounded, unending, unlimited. **2** countless, immeasurable, immense, incalculable, innumerable, myriad.

infinitesimal *adjective* little, microscopic, miniature, minuscule, minute, small, teeny, tiny.

infirm *adjective* ailing, decrepit, feeble, frail, ill, poorly, senile, unwell, weak.

inflame *verb* **1** anger, arouse, enrage, fire up, incense, incite, infuriate, provoke, rouse, stir up.

inflamed *adjective* festering, infected, red, sore, swollen.

inflammable *adjective* combustible, flammable.

inflate *verb* **1** blow up, fill, pump up. **2** increase, raise.

inflexible *adjective* **1** firm, hard, rigid, solid, stiff. **2** adamant, firm, immutable, intractable, intransigent, obstinate, pigheaded, rigid, stubborn, unbending, uncompromising, unyielding.

inflict *verb* administer, deal out, impose, wreak.

influence[1] *noun* authority, clout (*informal*), control, leverage, muscle, power, pressure, sway, weight.

▶▶ D I C T I O N A R Y ◀◀

influence² *verb* (**influenced, influencing**) have influence on a person or thing; affect.

influential *adjective* having influence.

influenza *noun* an infectious disease that causes fever, catarrh, and pain.

influx *noun* a flowing in, especially of people or things coming in.

inform *verb* give information to somebody. **informant** *noun*

informal *adjective* not formal. **informally** *adverb*, **informality** *noun*
informal vote (*Australian*) a vote that is not valid, a spoiled vote.

Usage In this dictionary, words marked *informal* are used in talking but not when you are writing or speaking formally.

---

information *noun* facts told or heard or discovered, or put into a computer etc.

informative *adjective* giving a lot of useful information.

informed *adjective* knowing about something.

informer *noun* a person who gives information against someone.

infra- *prefix* below. [Latin]

infra-red *adjective* below or beyond red in the spectrum.

infrequent *adjective* not frequent.

infringe *verb* (**infringed, infringing**) break a rule or an agreement etc.; violate. **infringement** *noun*

infuriate *verb* (**infuriated, infuriating**) make a person very angry; enrage. **infuriation** *noun*

infuse *verb* (**infused, infusing**) **1** add or inspire with a feeling etc., *infuse them with courage*; *infuse courage into them.* **2** soak or steep tea or herbs etc. in a liquid to extract the flavour. **infusion** *noun* [from Latin *infusum* = poured in]

ingenious *adjective* clever at inventing things; cleverly made. **ingeniously** *adverb*, **ingenuity** *noun* [from Latin *ingenium* = genius]

ingenuous *adjective* naïve. **ingenuously** *adverb*, **ingenuousness** *noun*

ingot *noun* a lump of gold or silver etc. cast in a brick shape.

ingrained *adjective* **1** (of dirt) marking a surface deeply. **2** (of feelings or habits etc.) firmly fixed.

ingratiate *verb* (**ingratiated, ingratiating**) **ingratiate yourself** get yourself into favour. **ingratiation** *noun* [from Latin *in gratiam* = into favour]

ingratitude *noun* lack of gratitude.

▶▶ T H E S A U R U S ◀◀

influence² *verb* affect, bias, change, control, lead, manipulate, motivate, move, persuade, predispose, prejudice, sway.

influential *adjective* authoritative, important, persuasive, powerful, strong.

influx *noun* flood, inflow, inrush, rush, stream.

inform *verb* acquaint, advise, apprise (*formal*), brief, enlighten, fill in (*informal*), instruct, keep posted, notify, tell, warn.
inform on betray, blow the whistle on (*informal*), denounce, dob in (*Australian informal*), grass (on) (*slang*), rat on (*informal*), report, shelf (*Australian slang*), shop (*slang*), sneak on (*informal*), split on (*slang*), tell on.

informal *adjective* casual, easygoing, free and easy, homely, natural, relaxed, unofficial; (*informal language*) colloquial, everyday, slangy, vernacular.

information *noun* advice, communication, data, evidence, facts, info (*informal*), intelligence, knowledge, low-down (*informal*), material, message, news, notice, notification, particulars, report, tidings.

informer *noun* dobber (*Australian informal*), dog (*slang*), grass (*slang*), informant, source,

stool-pigeon, tell-tale, whistle-blower (*informal*).

infrequent *adjective* irregular, occasional, rare, sporadic, uncommon.

infringe *verb* breach, break, contravene, disobey, transgress, violate.
infringement *noun* breach, contravention, transgression, violation.

infuriate *verb* anger, enrage, exasperate, gall, incense, irritate, madden, needle (*informal*), outrage, rile (*informal*), vex.

ingenious *adjective* artful, brilliant, clever, crafty, cunning, imaginative, inventive, neat, nifty (*informal*), resourceful, shrewd, skilful, smart.

ingenuous *adjective* artless, guileless, innocent, naïve, simple, unaffected, unsophisticated.

ingrained *adjective* **2** confirmed, deep-rooted, deep-seated.

ingratiate *verb* **ingratiate yourself with** crawl to, curry favour with, fawn on, grovel to, kowtow to, play up to, suck up to (*informal*), toady to.

ingratitude *noun* thanklessness, unappreciativeness, ungratefulness.

▶▶ D I C T I O N A R Y ◀◀

ingredient *noun* one of the parts of a mixture; one of the things used in a recipe. [from Latin *ingrediens* = going in]

inhabit *verb* (**inhabited, inhabiting**) live in a place. **inhabitant** *noun*

inhale *verb* (**inhaled, inhaling**) breathe in. **inhalation** *noun* [from *in-* = in, + Latin *halare* = breathe]

inharmonious *adjective* not harmonious.

inherent (*say* in-**heer**-ent) *adjective* existing in something as one of its natural or permanent qualities. **inherently** *adverb*, **inherence** *noun* [from *in-* = in, + Latin *haerere* = to stick]

inherit *verb* (**inherited, inheriting**) **1** receive money, property, or a title etc. when its previous owner dies. **2** get certain qualities etc. from parents or predecessors. **inheritance** *noun*, **inheritor** *noun* [from *in-* = in, + Latin *heres* = heir]

inhibit *verb* (**inhibited, inhibiting**) restrain; hinder; repress. **inhibition** *noun*

inhospitable *adjective* **1** not hospitable. **2** (of a place) giving no shelter.

inhuman *adjective* cruel; without pity or kindness. **inhumanity** *noun*

inhumane *adjective* not humane.

inimitable *adjective* impossible to imitate.

iniquitous *adjective* very unjust. **iniquity** *noun* [from *in-* = not, + *equity*]

initial[1] *noun* the first letter of a word or name.

initial[2] *verb* (**initialled, initialling**) mark or sign something with the initials of your names.

initial[3] *adjective* of the beginning, *the initial stages*. **initially** *adverb* [from Latin *initium* = the beginning]

initiate *verb* (**initiated, initiating**) **1** start something. **2** admit a person as a member of a society or group, often with special ceremonies. **initiation** *noun*, **initiator** *noun*

initiative (*say* in-**ish**-a-tiv) *noun* the power or courage to start a new process; enterprising ability.
take the initiative take action to start something happening.

inject *verb* **1** put a medicine or drug into the body by means of a hollow needle. **2** put liquid into something by means of a syringe etc. **3** add a new quality, *Inject some humour into it.* **injection** *noun* [from *in-* = in, + Latin *-jectum* = thrown]

injudicious *adjective* unwise.

injunction *noun* a command given with authority, e.g. by a lawcourt.

injure *verb* (**injured, injuring**) harm; damage; hurt. **injury** *noun*, **injurious** (*say* in-**joor**-ee-us) *adjective*

▶▶ T H E S A U R U S ◀◀

ingredient *noun* component, constituent, element, part.

inhabit *verb* abide in (*old use*), dwell in, live in, occupy, people, populate, reside in, settle in. **inhabitant** *noun* citizen, denizen, dweller, inmate, native, occupant, resident, tenant.

inhale *verb* breathe in, draw in, suck in.

inherent *adjective* essential, inborn, inbred, innate, intrinsic, native, natural.

inheritance *noun* bequest, birthright, estate, heritage, legacy.

inheritor *noun* beneficiary, heir, heiress.

inhibit *verb* block, check, curb, hamper, hinder, hold back, impede, limit, obstruct, prevent, restrain, restrict, retard, stunt.
inhibition *noun* hang-up (*informal*), mental block, reserve, self-consciousness, shyness.

inhospitable *adjective* **1** cool, unfriendly, unsociable, unwelcoming. **2** bleak, desolate, forbidding, uninviting.

inhuman *adjective* barbarous, brutal, cold-hearted, cruel, heartless, inhumane, merciless, ruthless, savage, unfeeling, vicious.

inimitable *adjective* incomparable, matchless, singular, unique.

iniquity *noun* crime, evil, injustice, offence, sin, transgression, trespass, wickedness, wrong, wrongdoing.

initial[3] *adjective* beginning, early, first, introductory, opening, original, preliminary, starting.

initiate *verb* **1** begin, commence, embark on, inaugurate, instigate, institute, kick off (*informal*), launch, open, originate, set in motion, start.

initiative *noun* drive, dynamism, enterprise, resourcefulness.
take the initiative begin, commence, make the first move, start, take the lead.

inject *verb* **3** bring in, infuse, instil, introduce.
injection *noun* booster, immunisation, inoculation, jab (*informal*), shot, vaccination.

injure *verb* bruise, cripple, cut, damage, disable, fracture, harm, hurt, impair, lacerate, maim, mangle, mutilate, scar, sprain, strain, wound.
injurious *adjective* adverse, damaging, deleterious, destructive, detrimental, harmful, hurtful.
injury *noun* abrasion, bruise, contusion, cut, damage, fracture, harm, hurt, laceration, lesion, scrape, scratch, wound.

▶▶ D I C T I O N A R Y ◀◀

injustice *noun* **1** lack of justice. **2** an unjust action or treatment.

ink *noun* a black or coloured liquid used in writing and printing.

inkling *noun* a hint; a slight knowledge or suspicion.

inky *adjective* **1** stained with ink. **2** black like ink, *inky darkness*.

inland *adjective & adverb* in or towards the interior of a country; away from the coast. **inland** *noun*

in-laws *plural noun* (*informal*) relatives by marriage.

inlay *verb* (**inlaid, inlaying**) set pieces of wood or metal etc. into a surface to form a design. **inlay** *noun*

inlet *noun* **1** a strip of water reaching into the land from a sea or lake. **2** a passage that lets something in (e.g. to a tank).

inmate *noun* one of the occupants of a prison, hospital, or other institution.

inmost *adjective* most inward.

inn *noun* a hotel or public house, especially in the country. **innkeeper** *noun*

innate *adjective* inborn. [from *in-* = in, + Latin *natus* = born]

inner *adjective* inside; internal; nearer to the centre. **innermost** *adjective*

innings *noun* (*plural* **innings**) the time when a cricket team or player is batting.

innocent *adjective* **1** not guilty. **2** not wicked. **3** harmless. **4** naïve. **innocently** *adverb*, **innocence** *noun* [from *in-* = not, + Latin *nocens* = doing harm]

innocuous *adjective* harmless.

innovation *noun* **1** introducing new things or new methods. **2** something newly introduced. **innovative** *adjective*, **innovator** *noun* [from *in-* = in, + Latin *novus* = new]

innuendo *noun* (*plural* **innuendoes**) an unpleasant insinuation or hint.

innumerable *adjective* countless.

inoculate *verb* (**inoculated, inoculating**) inject or treat with a vaccine or serum as a protection against a disease. **inoculation** *noun*

inoffensive *adjective* harmless.

inordinate *adjective* excessive. **inordinately** *adverb*

inorganic *adjective* not of living organisms; of mineral origin.

input *noun* what is put into something (e.g. data into a computer). **input** *verb*

inquest *noun* an official inquiry to find out how a person died.

inquire *verb* (**inquired, inquiring**) make an investigation. **inquiry** *noun* [from in- = *into*, + Latin quaerere = seek]

Usage It is best to use *enquire* and *enquiry* of asking something, and *inquire* and *inquiry* of investigating.

▶▶ T H E S A U R U S ◀◀

injustice *noun* **1** bias, discrimination, inequity, prejudice, unfairness, unjustness. **2** abuse, injury, offence, wrong.

inkling *noun* clue, hint, idea, knowledge, suspicion.

inland *noun* backblocks (*Australian*), back of beyond, bush, interior, never-never (*Australian*), outback (*Australian*), sticks (*informal*).

inlet *noun* **1** bay, cove, creek (*British*), estuary, fiord, firth, harbour, sound.

inn *noun* hotel, pub (*informal*), public house, tavern.

innkeeper *noun* hotelier, hotel-keeper, landlady, landlord, proprietor, publican.

innate *adjective* congenital, hereditary, inborn, inbred, inherent, inherited, intrinsic, native, natural.

inner *adjective* central, inside, interior, internal.

innocent *adjective* **1** blameless, guiltless. **2** angelic, moral, pure, righteous, sinless, virtuous. **3** harmless, innocuous, inoffensive. **4** green, gullible, inexperienced, ingenuous, naïve, trusting, unworldly.

innocuous *adjective* harmless, inoffensive, safe.

innovative *adjective* creative, imaginative, new, novel, original.

innuendo *noun* hint, insinuation, intimation, overtone, suggestion.

innumerable *adjective* countless, infinite, myriad, numberless, numerous.

inoculate *verb* immunise, vaccinate.

inoffensive *adjective* bland, harmless, innocuous, safe, unobjectionable, unoffending.

inordinate *adjective* disproportionate, excessive, exorbitant, undue, unreasonable.

inquire *verb* ask, enquire, query, question; (*inquire into*) examine, explore, inspect, investigate, look into, probe, research, study. **inquiry** *noun* **1** hearing, inquest, inquisition, investigation, post-mortem, probe, review, study. **2** enquiry, query, question.

►►► DICTIONARY ◄◄◄

inquisition *noun* a detailed questioning or investigation. **inquisitor** *noun*
  the Inquisition a council of the Roman Catholic Church in the Middle Ages set up to discover and punish heretics.

inquisitive *adjective* always asking questions or trying to look at things; prying. **inquisitively** *adverb*

inroad *noun* an invasion; a raid.
  make inroads on or **into** use up large quantities of stores etc.

inrush *noun* (*plural* **inrushes**) a sudden rush in; an influx.

insane *adjective* not sane; mad. **insanely** *adverb*, **insanity** *noun*

insanitary *adjective* unclean and likely to be harmful to health.

insatiable (*say* in-**say**-sha-bul) *adjective* impossible to satisfy, *an insatiable appetite*.

inscribe *verb* (**inscribed**, **inscribing**) write or carve words etc. on something. [from *in-* = on, + Latin *scribere* = write]

inscription *noun* **1** words or names inscribed on a monument, coin, stone, etc. **2** inscribing.

inscrutable *adjective* enigmatic; impossible to interpret, *an inscrutable smile*.

insect *noun* a small animal with six legs, no backbone, and a body divided into three parts (head, thorax, abdomen).

insecticide *noun* a substance for killing insects. [from *insect*, + Latin *caedere* = kill]

insectivorous *adjective* feeding on insects and other small invertebrate creatures.

insectivore *noun* [from *insect*, + Latin *vorare* = devour]

insecure *adjective* not secure; unsafe. **insecurely** *adverb*, **insecurity** *noun*

inseminate *verb* (**inseminated**, **inseminating**) insert semen into the womb. **insemination** *noun*

insensible *adjective* **1** unconscious. **2** unaware. **3** imperceptible.

insensitive *adjective* not sensitive. **insensitively** *adverb*, **insensitivity** *noun*

inseparable *adjective* **1** not able to be separated. **2** liking to be constantly together, *inseparable friends*. **inseparably** *adverb*

insert *verb* put a thing into something else. **insertion** *noun*

inshore *adverb* & *adjective* near or nearer to the shore.

inside[1] *noun* the inner side, surface, or part.
  inside out with the inside turned to face outwards.
  insides *plural noun* (*informal*) the organs in the abdomen; the stomach and bowels.

inside[2] *adjective* on or coming from the inside; in or nearest to the middle.

inside[3] *adverb* & *preposition* on or to the inside of something; in, *Come inside. It's inside that box*.

insider *noun* a member of a certain group, especially someone with access to private information.

insidious *adjective* inconspicuous but harmful. **insidiously** *adverb*

►►► THESAURUS ◄◄◄

inquisitive *adjective* curious, nosy (*informal*), prying, snoopy (*informal*).

insane *adjective* berserk, crazy, demented, deranged, irrational, lunatic, mad, mental (*informal*), nutty (*informal*), unbalanced, unhinged.

insatiable *adjective* greedy, ravenous, unquenchable, voracious.

inscribe *verb* carve, engrave, etch, write.

inscription *noun* **1** engraving, epitaph, words, writing.

inscrutable *adjective* arcane, baffling, cryptic, enigmatic, impenetrable, incomprehensible, mysterious, puzzling, unfathomable.

insect *noun* bug (*informal*), creepy-crawly (*informal*).

insecure *adjective* dangerous, precarious, rickety, rocky, shaky, unsafe, unsteady, wobbly.

insensible *adjective* **1** comatose, knocked out, senseless, unconscious. **2** oblivious, unaware, unconscious.

insensitive *adjective* callous, cold-hearted, hard-hearted, heartless, indifferent, tactless, thick-skinned, thoughtless, uncaring, unfeeling, unsympathetic.

inseparable *adjective* **2** attached, close, thick as thieves (*informal*).

insert *verb* add, implant, interject, interpolate, interpose, introduce, put in, slip in, stick in, tuck in.

inside[1] *noun* centre, core, heart, interior, middle.
  insides *plural noun* bowels, entrails, guts, innards (*informal*), intestines, stomach, viscera.

inside[2] *adjective* inmost, inner, innermost, interior, internal.

▶▶▶ D I C T I O N A R Y ◀◀◀

insight *noun* being able to perceive the truth about things; understanding.

insignia *plural noun* emblems; a badge.

insignificant *adjective* not important; not influential. **insignificance** *noun*

insincere *adjective* not sincere. **insincerely** *adverb*, **insincerity** *noun*

insinuate *verb* (**insinuated, insinuating**) 1 hint artfully or unpleasantly. 2 insert gradually or craftily. **insinuation** *noun*

insipid *adjective* 1 lacking flavour. 2 not lively or interesting. **insipidity** *noun*

insist *verb* be very firm in saying or asking for something. **insistent** *adjective*, **insistence** *noun* [from Latin *insistere* = stand firm]

insolent *adjective* very impudent; insulting. **insolently** *adverb*, **insolence** *noun*

insoluble *adjective* 1 impossible to solve, *an insoluble problem.* 2 impossible to dissolve. **insolubility** *noun*

insomnia *noun* being unable to sleep. **insomniac** *noun* [from *in-* = without, + Latin *somnus* = sleep]

inspect *verb* examine carefully and critically. **inspection** *noun* [from *in-* = in, + Latin *specere* = to look]

inspector *noun* 1 a person whose job is to inspect or supervise things. 2 a police officer ranking next above a sergeant.

inspiration *noun* 1 a sudden brilliant idea. 2 inspiring; an inspiring influence.

inspire *verb* (**inspired, inspiring**) fill a person with good or useful feelings or ideas, *The applause inspired us with confidence.* [from *in-* = into, + Latin *spirare* = breathe]

instability *noun* lack of stability.

install *verb* 1 put something in position and ready to use, *They installed central heating.* 2 put a person into an important position with a ceremony, *He was installed as pope.* **installation** *noun*

instalment *noun* each of the parts in which something is given or paid for gradually, *an instalment of a serial.*

instance *noun* an example, *for instance.*

instant[1] *adjective* 1 happening immediately, *instant success.* 2 (of food) designed to be prepared quickly and easily, *instant coffee.* **instantly** *adverb*

instant[2] *noun* a moment, *not an instant too soon.* [from Latin *instans* = urgent]

instantaneous *adjective* happening immediately. **instantaneously** *adverb*

▶▶▶ T H E S A U R U S ◀◀◀

insight *noun* acumen, discernment, intuition, judgement, perception, perspicacity, understanding.

insignificant *adjective* inconsequential, little, minor, minute, negligible, paltry, petty, slight, tiny, trifling, trivial, unimportant, useless, worthless.

insincere *adjective* deceitful, dishonest, false, hypocritical, phoney (*informal*), two-faced.

insinuation *noun* hint, implication, innuendo, intimation, suggestion.

insipid *adjective* 1 bland, tasteless, watery, weak, wishy-washy. 2 characterless, colourless, dull, uninteresting, vapid, wishy-washy.

insist *verb* assert, claim, command, contend, declare, demand, emphasise, maintain, put your foot down, require, stipulate, stress.

insolent *adjective* arrogant, brazen, cheeky, contemptuous, disrespectful, impertinent, impolite, impudent, insubordinate, presumptuous, rude.

insolence *noun* arrogance, audacity, backchat (*informal*), cheek, effrontery, impertinence, impudence, insubordination, lip (*slang*), rudeness.

insoluble *adjective* 1 baffling, inexplicable, mysterious, perplexing, puzzling, unanswerable, unfathomable, unsolvable.

inspect *verb* check, examine, investigate, look over, scrutinise, survey, suss out (*informal*), view.

inspection *noun* check, check-up, examination, going-over (*informal*), investigation, once-over (*informal*), review, scrutiny.

inspire *verb* animate, drive, encourage, motivate, move, prompt, provoke, spur, stimulate, stir.

install *verb* 1 establish, fit, fix, mount, place, put, set up. 2 inaugurate, induct, invest, ordain.

instalment *noun* chapter, episode, part, section.

instance *noun* case, example, illustration, sample.

instant[1] *adjective* 1 immediate, instantaneous, prompt, quick, ready, speedy, unhesitating.

instant[2] *noun* flash, jiffy (*informal*), moment, split second, trice, twinkling of an eye.

instantaneous *adjective* immediate, instant, quick, swift.

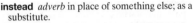

instead *adverb* in place of something else; as a substitute.

instep *noun* the top of the foot between the toes and the ankle.

instigate *verb* (**instigated, instigating**) urge; incite; cause something to be done, *instigate a rebellion.* **instigation** *noun*, **instigator** *noun*

instil *verb* (**instilled, instilling**) put ideas into a person's mind gradually. [from *in-* = in, + Latin *stilla* = a drop]

instinct *noun* a natural tendency or ability, *Birds fly by instinct; He has an instinct for finding a good place.* **instinctive** *adjective*, **instinctively** *adverb*

institute[1] *noun* a society or organisation; the building used by this.

institute[2] *verb* (**instituted, instituting**) establish; found; start an inquiry or custom etc. [from *in-* = in, + Latin *statuere* = set up]

institution *noun* **1** an institute; a public organisation, e.g. a hospital or university. **2** a habit or custom. **3** instituting something. **institutional** *adjective*

instruct *verb* **1** teach a person a subject or skill. **2** inform. **3** tell a person what he or she must do. **instructor** *noun* [same origin as *structure*]

instruction *noun* **1** teaching; education. **2** a statement telling a person what he or she must do; an order. **instructional** *adjective*

instructive *adjective* giving knowledge.

instrument *noun* **1** a device for producing musical sounds. **2** a tool used for delicate or scientific work. **3** a measuring-device.

instrumental *adjective* **1** of or using musical instruments. **2** being the means of doing something, *She was instrumental in getting me a job.*

instrumentalist *noun* a person who plays a musical instrument.

insubordinate *adjective* disobedient; rebellious. **insubordination** *noun*

insufferable *adjective* unbearable.

insufficient *adjective* not sufficient.

insular *adjective* of or like an island.

insulate *verb* (**insulated, insulating**) cover or protect something to prevent heat, cold, or electricity etc. from passing in or out. **insulation** *noun*, **insulator** *noun* [from Latin *insula* = island]

insulin *noun* a substance that controls the amount of sugar in the blood.

insult[1] (*say* in-**sult**) *verb* hurt a person's feelings or pride.

instead *adverb* **instead of** in place of, in lieu of.

instigate *verb* bring about, initiate, prompt, set up, start.

instil *verb* implant, inculcate, infuse.

instinct *noun* aptitude, flair, gift, intuition, knack, sixth sense, skill, talent.
instinctive *adjective* automatic, inborn, innate, intuitive, natural, reflex, spontaneous, subconscious, unlearned.

institute[1] *noun* academy, college, establishment, institution, organisation, school, society.

institute[2] *verb* begin, create, establish, found, inaugurate, initiate, originate, start.

institution *noun* **1** establishment, foundation, institute, organisation, society. **2** convention, custom, habit, practice, ritual, routine, tradition.

instruct *verb* **1** coach, drill, educate, ground, lecture, school, teach, train, tutor. **2** acquaint, advise, apprise (*formal*), brief, enlighten, inform, notify, tell. **3** bid, charge, command, direct, enjoin, order, tell.
instructor *noun* coach, educator, lecturer, mentor, teacher, trainer, tutor.

instruction *noun* **1** education, guidance, lessons, schooling, teaching, training, tuition. **2** command, direction, guideline, order, prescription, recipe.

instructive *adjective* edifying, educational, enlightening, helpful, illuminating, informative.

instrument *noun* **2** apparatus, appliance, device, gadget, implement, machine, tool, utensil; see also EQUIPMENT.

instrumentalist *noun* musician, performer, player.

insubordinate *adjective* contrary, defiant, disobedient, insurgent, mutinous, rebellious, recalcitrant.

insufferable *adjective* intolerable, obnoxious, unbearable, unendurable.

insufficient *adjective* deficient, inadequate, meagre, scant, scanty, scarce, wanting.

insulate *verb* clad, cover, encase, lag, protect, shield, wrap.

insult[1] *verb* abuse, affront, be rude to, disparage, malign, offend, put down, slight, snub.
insulting *adjective* abusive, derogatory, disparaging, offensive, rude, uncomplimentary.

371

▶▶ D I C T I O N A R Y ◀◀

insult[2] (*say* in-sult) *noun* an insulting remark or action.

insuperable *adjective* unable to be overcome, *an insuperable difficulty.*

insurance *noun* an agreement to compensate someone for a loss, damage, or injury etc., in return for a payment (called a *premium*) made in advance.

insure *verb* (**insured, insuring**) protect with insurance.

Usage Do not confuse with *ensure.*

insurgent *noun* a rebel. **insurgent** *adjective* [from *in-* = against, + Latin *surgere* = to rise]

insurmountable *adjective* insuperable.

insurrection *noun* a rebellion.

intact *adjective* not damaged; complete. [from *in-* = not, + Latin *tactum* = touched]

intake *noun* **1** taking something in. **2** the number of people or things taken in.

intangible *adjective* not tangible.

integer *noun* a whole number (e.g. 0, 3, 19), not a fraction. [Latin, = whole]

integral (*say* in-tig-ral) *adjective* **1** (of a part) essential to the whole thing, *An engine is an integral part of a car.* **2** whole; complete.

integrate *verb* (**integrated, integrating**) **1** make parts into a whole; combine. **2** join together harmoniously into a single community. **integration** *noun* [from Latin *integrare* = make whole]

integrity (*say* in-**teg**-rit-ee) *noun* honesty.

intellect *noun* the ability to think (contrasted with *feeling* and *instinct*).

intellectual[1] *adjective* **1** of or using the intellect. **2** having a good intellect and a liking for knowledge. **intellectually** *adverb*

intellectual[2] *noun* an intellectual person.

intelligence *noun* **1** being intelligent. **2** information, especially of military value; the people who collect and study this information.

intelligent *adjective* able to learn and understand things; having great mental ability. **intelligently** *adverb*

intelligentsia *noun* intellectual people regarded as a group.

intelligible *adjective* able to be understood. **intelligibly** *adverb*, **intelligibility** *noun*

intend *verb* have something in mind as what you want to do; plan. [from Latin *intendere* = stretch, aim]

▶▶ T H E S A U R U S ◀◀

insult[2] *noun* abuse, affront, insolence, put-down (*informal*), rudeness, slight, snub.

insuperable *adjective* insurmountable, unconquerable.

insurance *noun* assurance, cover, indemnity, protection.

insurgent *noun* dissident, insurrectionist, mutineer, rebel, revolutionary. **insurgent** *adjective* dissident, insubordinate, mutinous, rebellious, revolutionary, seditious.

insurmountable *adjective* insuperable, overwhelming, unconquerable.

insurrection *noun* mutiny, rebellion, revolt, revolution, riot, rising, uprising.

intact *adjective* complete, entire, perfect, sound, unbroken, undamaged, whole.

intangible *adjective* abstract, elusive, impalpable, subtle.

integral *adjective* **1** basic, constituent, essential, indispensable, necessary, vital.

integrate *verb* **1** amalgamate, blend, combine, consolidate, incorporate, join, merge, mix, unite.

integrity *noun* honesty, honour, morality, probity, rectitude, scrupulousness, trustworthiness, truthfulness, uprightness, veracity, virtue.

intellect *noun* brains, intelligence, mental ability, mind, nous (*informal*), reason, sense, understanding, wits.

intellectual[1] *adjective* **1** academic, mental. **2** academic, bookish, brainy, erudite, highbrow, intelligent, learned, scholarly, studious, thinking.

intellectual[2] *noun* academic, brain (*informal*), highbrow, scholar, thinker.

intelligence *noun* **1** acumen, brains, cleverness, intellect, mental ability, nous (*informal*), reason, sense, understanding, wisdom, wits. **2** advice, information, knowledge, low-down (*informal*), news, notification, report, tidings, word.

intelligent *adjective* astute, brainy, bright, clever, discerning, intellectual, perceptive, perspicacious, quick, reasoning, sagacious, sensible, sharp, shrewd, smart, thinking, wise.

intelligible *adjective* clear, coherent, comprehensible, lucid, plain, understandable.

intend *verb* aim, mean, plan, propose.

▶▶ D I C T I O N A R Y ◀◀

intense *adjective* very strong or great. **intensely** *adverb*, **intensity** *noun*

intensify *verb* (**intensified, intensifying**) make or become more intense. **intensification** *noun*

intensive *adjective* concentrated; thorough; using a lot of effort. **intensively** *adverb*

intent¹ *noun* intention.

intent² *adjective* with concentrated attention; very interested. **intently** *adverb* [same origin as *intend*]

intention *noun* what a person intends; a purpose or plan.

intentional *adjective* intended; deliberate, not accidental. **intentionally** *adverb*

inter *verb* (**interred, interring**) bury. [from *in-* = in, + Latin *terra* = earth]

inter- *prefix* between; among. [from Latin]

interact *verb* have an effect upon one another. **interaction** *noun*

interbreed *verb* (**interbred, interbreeding**) breed with each other; cross-breed.

intercede *verb* (**interceded, interceding**) intervene on behalf of another person or as a peacemaker. **intercession** *noun* [from *inter-*, + Latin *cedere* = go]

intercept *verb* stop or catch a person or thing that is going from one place to another.

interception *noun* [from *inter-*, + Latin *captum* = seized]

interchange¹ *verb* (**interchanged, interchanging**) 1 put each of two things into the other's place. 2 exchange. 3 alternate. **interchangeable** *adjective*

interchange² *noun* 1 interchanging. 2 a road junction where vehicles or passengers can move from one route to another.

intercom *noun* (*informal*) a system of communication between rooms or compartments, operating rather like a telephone. [short for *intercommunication*]

intercourse *noun* 1 communication or dealings between people. 2 sexual intercourse (see *sexual*).

interdependent *adjective* dependent upon each other.

interdict *noun* a prohibition. [from *inter-*, + Latin *dictum* = said]

interest¹ *noun* 1 a feeling of wanting to know about or help with something. 2 a thing that interests somebody, *Science fiction is one of my interests.* 3 advantage, *She looks after her own interests.* 4 money paid regularly in return for money lent or deposited.

interest² *verb* arouse a person's interest. **interested** *adjective*, **interesting** *adjective* [Latin, = it matters]

▶▶ T H E S A U R U S ◀◀

intense *adjective* (*intense pain*) acute, concentrated, excruciating, extreme, great, piercing, raging, severe, sharp, strong, violent; (*intense feeling*) ardent, burning, deep, earnest, fervent, keen, passionate, powerful, profound, strong, vehement.

intensify *verb* aggravate, boost, compound, escalate, exacerbate, heighten, increase, magnify, mount, multiply, reinforce, strengthen.

intensive *adjective* comprehensive, concentrated, in-depth, thorough.

intent¹ *noun* intention, object, objective, plan, purpose.

intent² *adjective* absorbed, concentrated, engrossed, fixed, intense, keen, steadfast, steady, watchful.

intention *noun* aim, ambition, design, end, goal, intent, object, objective, plan, purpose.

intentional *adjective* conscious, deliberate, intended, planned, premeditated, purposeful, wilful.

intentionally *adverb* consciously, deliberately, on purpose, wilfully, wittingly.

inter *verb* bury, entomb, lay to rest.

intercept *verb* ambush, block, cut off, head off, obstruct, stop, waylay.

interchange¹ *verb* **1,2** exchange, substitute, swap, transpose.

interchange² *noun* **2** crossroads, intersection, junction.

interest¹ *noun* **1** concern, curiosity, enthusiasm, fascination. **2** activity, diversion, hobby, pastime, preoccupation, pursuit. **3** advantage, benefit, gain, good.

interest² *verb* absorb, appeal to, attract, concern, engage, engross, excite, fascinate, intrigue, preoccupy.

interested *adjective* absorbed, attentive, concerned, curious, engrossed, enthusiastic, inquisitive, keen.

interesting *adjective* absorbing, engrossing, exciting, fascinating, gripping, intriguing, readable, riveting, stimulating.

►►► DICTIONARY ◄◄

interfere *verb* (**interfered, interfering**) **1** take part in something that has nothing to do with you. **2** get in the way; obstruct. **interference** *noun*

interim[1] *noun* an interval of time between two events.

interim[2] *adjective* of or in the interim; temporary, *an interim arrangement*. [Latin, = meanwhile]

interior[1] *adjective* inner.

interior[2] *noun* the inside of something; the central or inland part of a country. [Latin, = further in]

interject *verb* break in with a remark while someone is speaking. [from *inter-*, + Latin *jactum* = thrown]

interjection *noun* **1** an exclamation such as *oh!* or *good heavens!* **2** interjecting; a remark interjected.

interlock *verb* fit into each other.

interloper *noun* an intruder.

interlude *noun* **1** an interval. **2** something happening in an interval or between other events. [from *inter-*, + Latin *ludus* = game]

intermediary *noun* (*plural* **intermediaries**) a mediator; a go-between.

intermediate *adjective* coming between two things in time, place, or order.

interment *noun* interring; burial.

interminable *adjective* endless; long and boring. **interminably** *adverb* [from *in-* = not, + *terminable*]

intermission *noun* an interval or pause.

intermittent *adjective* happening at intervals; not continuous. **intermittently** *adverb* [from *inter-*, + Latin *mittere* = let go]

intern *verb* imprison in a special camp or area, usually in wartime.

internal *adjective* inside. **internally** *adverb* **internal-combustion engine** an engine that produces power by burning fuel inside the engine itself.

international *adjective* of or belonging to more than one country; agreed between nations. **internationally** *adverb*

Internet *noun* (*trade mark*) an international computer network linking computers from educational institutions, government agencies, industry, etc.

internment *noun* being interned.

interplanetary *adjective* between planets.

interplay *noun* interaction.

interpolate *verb* (**interpolated, interpolating**) **1** interject. **2** insert words; put terms into a mathematical series. **interpolation** *noun*

interpose *verb* (**interposed, interposing**) **1** insert; interject. **2** intervene. [from *inter-*, + Latin *positum* = put]

interpret *verb* **1** explain what something means. **2** translate what someone says into another language orally. **interpretation** *noun*, **interpreter** *noun*

interregnum *noun* an interval between the reign of one ruler and that of his or her successor. [from *inter-*, + Latin *regnum* = reign]

interrogate *verb* (**interrogated, interrogating**) question closely or formally. **interrogation** *noun*, **interrogator** *noun* [from *inter-*, + Latin *rogare* = ask]

interrogative *adjective* questioning; expressing a question. **interrogatory** *adjective*

►►► THESAURUS ◄◄

interfere *verb* **1** butt in, intervene, intrude, meddle, poke your nose in, pry. **2** conflict, get in the way, hamper, hinder, impede, obstruct.

interim[1] *noun* interval, meantime, meanwhile.

interim[2] *adjective* provisional, stopgap, temporary.

interior[1] *adjective* inner, inside, internal.

interior[2] *noun* backblocks (*Australian*), centre, inland, outback (*Australian*).

interlude *noun* **1** break, gap, intermission, interval, pause, recess, rest.

intermediary *noun* agent, go-between, intercessor, mediator, middleman.

intermediate *adjective* halfway, medial, middle, midway, neutral.

interminable *adjective* ceaseless, endless, everlasting, lengthy, long, never-ending, unending.

intermission *noun* break, interlude, interruption, interval, lull, pause, recess, respite, rest.

intermittent *adjective* fitful, occasional, on and off, periodic, spasmodic, sporadic.

intern *verb* confine, detain, imprison, jail, lock up.

internal *adjective* inner, inside, interior.

international *adjective* cosmopolitan, global, universal, worldwide.

interpret *verb* **1** construe, decipher, decode, explain, read, take, translate, understand.

interrogate *verb* cross-examine, examine, grill, question, quiz.

interrogation *noun* cross-examination, examination, inquisition, questioning, third degree.

▶▶ D I C T I O N A R Y ◀◀

interrupt *verb* prevent from continuing; break in on a person's speech etc. by inserting a remark. **interruption** *noun* [from *inter-*, + Latin *ruptum* = broken]

intersect *verb* divide a thing by passing or lying across it; (of lines or roads etc.) cross each other. **intersection** *noun* [from *inter-*, + Latin *sectum* = cut]

intersperse *verb* (**interspersed**, **interspersing**) insert things here and there in something. [from *inter-*, + Latin *sparsum* = scattered]

interstate *adjective and adverb* **1** (*Australian and American*) existing or carried on between states. **2** (*Australian*) to, in, from another state, *My friend has gone interstate. They were married interstate. An interstate visitor.*

interval *noun* **1** a time between two events or parts of a play etc. **2** a space between two things.
at intervals with some time or distance between each one. [from Latin *intervallum* = space between ramparts]

intervene *verb* (**intervened**, **intervening**) **1** come between two events, *in the intervening years.* **2** interrupt a discussion or fight etc. to try and stop it or change its result. **intervention** *noun* [from *inter-*, + Latin *venire* = come]

interview[1] *noun* a formal meeting with someone to ask him or her questions or to obtain information.

interview[2] *verb* hold an interview with someone. **interviewer** *noun*

intestine *noun* the long tube along which food passes while being absorbed by the body, between the stomach and the anus. **intestinal** *adjective*

intimate[1] (*say* **in**-tim-at) *adjective* **1** very friendly with someone. **2** private and personal, *intimate thoughts.* **3** detailed, *an intimate knowledge of the country.* **intimately** *adverb*, **intimacy** *noun*

intimate[2] (*say* **in**-tim-ayt) *verb* (**intimated**, **intimating**) tell or hint. **intimation** *noun*

intimidate *verb* (**intimidated**, **intimidating**) frighten a person by threats into doing something. **intimidation** *noun* [from *in-* = in, + *timidus* = timid]

into *preposition* used to express (**1**) movement to the inside (*Go into the house*), (**2**) change of condition or occupation etc. (*It broke into pieces. She went into politics*), (**3**) (in division) *4 into 20* = 20 divided by four.

intolerable *adjective* unbearable. **intolerably** *adverb*

intolerant *adjective* not tolerant. **intolerantly** *adverb*, **intolerance** *noun*

intonation *noun* **1** the tone or pitch of the voice in speaking. **2** intoning.

intone *verb* (**intoned**, **intoning**) recite in a chanting voice.

intoxicate *verb* (**intoxicated**, **intoxicating**) make a person drunk or very excited. **intoxication** *noun* [from *in-* = in, + Latin *toxicum* = poison]

▶▶ T H E S A U R U S ◀◀

interrupt *verb* barge in, break in, butt in, chip in, cut in, discontinue, disrupt, disturb, halt, hold up, interfere (with), interject, stop, suspend.
interruption *noun* break, disruption, gap, halt, hiatus, pause, stop, stoppage, suspension.

intersect *verb* converge, cross, cut.
intersection *noun* corner, crossing, crossroads, interchange, junction.

interval *noun* **1** break, gap, hiatus, interlude, intermission, interruption, lapse, lull, pause, recess, respite, rest, space, spell. **2** gap, opening, space.

intervene *verb* **2** butt in, intercede, interfere, intrude, meddle, mediate, step in.

interview[1] *noun* conversation, dialogue, discussion, meeting.

intestines *plural noun* bowels, entrails, guts, innards (*informal*), insides (*informal*), viscera.

intimate[1] *adjective* **1** affectionate, bosom, close, familiar. **2** confidential, heart-to-heart, per-

sonal, private. **3** deep, detailed, firsthand, in-depth, thorough.

intimate[2] *verb* hint, imply, indicate, insinuate, make known, suggest.

intimidate *verb* browbeat, bully, coerce, cow, frighten, hector, menace, scare, stand over (*Australian*), terrorise, threaten.

intolerable *adjective* agonising, excruciating, insufferable, insupportable, unbearable.

intolerant *adjective* bigoted, illiberal, narrow-minded, prejudiced.

intoxicated *adjective* drunk, drunken, fuddled, full (*slang*), happy (*informal*), high (*informal*), high as a kite (*informal*), inebriated, merry (*informal*), off one's face (*Australian slang*), plastered (*slang*), shickered (*Australian slang*), smashed (*slang*), sozzled (*slang*), stoned (*slang*), tiddly (*informal*), tipsy, under the influence, under the weather.

intoxicating *adjective* alcoholic, heady, spirituous, strong.

► ► DICTIONARY ◄ ◄

intra- *prefix* within. [from Latin]

intractable *adjective* unmanageable; difficult to deal with or control. **intractability** *noun*

intransigent *adjective* stubborn. **intransigence** *noun*

intransitive *adjective* (of a verb) used without a direct object after it, e.g. *hear* in *we can hear* (but not in *we can hear you*). (Compare *transitive.*) **intransitively** *adverb*

intravenous (*say* in-tra-**veen**-us) *adjective* into a vein.

intrepid *adjective* fearless; brave. **intrepidly** *adverb*, **intrepidity** *noun* [from *in-* = not, + Latin *trepidus* = alarmed]

intricate *adjective* very complicated. **intricately** *adverb*, **intricacy** *noun* [from Latin *intricatum* = entangled]

intrigue¹ (*say* in-**treeg**) *verb* (**intrigued, intriguing**) **1** plot with someone in an underhand way. **2** interest very much, *The subject intrigues me.*

intrigue² *noun* **1** plotting; an underhand plot. **2** (*old use*) a secret love affair. [from Latin *intricare* = to tangle]

intrinsic *adjective* belonging naturally in something; inherent. **intrinsically** *adverb*

intro- *prefix* into; inwards. [from Latin]

introduce *verb* (**introduced, introducing**) **1** make a person known to other people. **2** announce a broadcast, speaker, etc. **3** bring something into use or for consideration. [from *intro-*, + Latin *ducere* = to lead]

introduction *noun* **1** introducing somebody or something. **2** an explanation put at the beginning of a book or speech etc. **introductory** *adjective*

introspective *adjective* examining your own thoughts and feelings. **introspection** *noun* [from *intro-*, + Latin *specere* = to look]

introvert *noun* an introspective person. (The opposite is *extrovert.*) **introverted** *adjective* [from *intro-*, + Latin *vertere* = to turn]

intrude *verb* (**intruded, intruding**) come in or join in without being wanted; interfere. **intrusion** *noun*, **intrusive** *adjective* [from *in-* = in, + Latin *trudere* = to push]

intruder *noun* **1** someone who intrudes. **2** a burglar.

intuition *noun* the power to know or understand things without having to think hard or without being taught. **intuitive** *adjective*, **intuitively** *adverb*

Inuit (*say* **in**-yoo-it) *noun* (in Canada) **1** an Eskimo. **2** the Eskimo language.

inundate *verb* (**inundated, inundating**) flood. **inundation** *noun* [from *in-* = in, + Latin *unda* = a wave]

inure (*say* in-**yoor**) *verb* (**inured, inuring**) accustom, especially to something unpleasant.

invade *verb* (**invaded, invading**) **1** attack and enter a country etc. **2** crowd into a place, *Ants invaded the cat's bowl.* **3** intrude on someone's rights, privacy, etc. **invader** *noun* [from *in-* = into, + Latin *vadere* = go]

► ► ► THESAURUS ◄ ◄

intractable *adjective* headstrong, mulish, obstinate, perverse, rebellious, recalcitrant, refractory, stubborn, uncontrollable, unmanageable, unruly, wayward, wild, wilful.

intrepid *adjective* bold, brave, courageous, daring, fearless, gallant, game, heroic, plucky, valiant.

intricate *adjective* complex, complicated, detailed, elaborate, fancy, involved, ornate.

intrigue¹ *verb* **2** appeal to, fascinate, interest.

intrigue² *noun* **1** conspiracy, machination, plot, scheme.

intrinsic *adjective* basic, essential, inherent, natural.

introduce *verb* **1** acquaint (with), make known, present. **2** announce, present. **3** begin, bring in, establish, inaugurate, initiate, institute, launch, phase in, pioneer, set up, start.

introduction *noun* **2** beginning, foreword, opening, preamble, preface, prelude, prologue.

introductory *adjective* opening, prefatory, preliminary, preparatory.

introverted *adjective* introspective, inward-looking, reserved, shy, unsociable, withdrawn.

intrude *verb* barge in, break in, butt in, encroach, gatecrash, interfere, intervene, muscle in (*slang*), trespass.

intruder *noun* burglar, gatecrasher, housebreaker, interloper, invader, robber, thief, trespasser.

intuition *noun* feeling, hunch, instinct, sixth sense.

intuitive *adjective* automatic, inborn, innate, instinctive, spontaneous, subconscious, unlearned.

inundate *verb* deluge, drown, engulf, flood, overflow, overwhelm, submerge, swamp.

invade *verb* **1** attack, enter, infiltrate, occupy, overrun, penetrate, raid. **3** encroach on, impinge on, infringe upon, intrude on, trespass on, violate.

invalid¹ (*say* **in**-va-lid) *noun* a person who is ill or who is weakened by illness.

invalid² (*say* in-**val**-id) *adjective* not valid, *This passport is invalid.* **invalidity** *noun*

invalidate *verb* (**invalidated, invalidating**) make a thing invalid. **invalidation** *noun*

invaluable *adjective* having a value that is too great to be measured; extremely valuable. [from *in-* = not, + *valuable*]

invariable *adjective* not variable; never changing. **invariably** *adverb*

invasion *noun* invading; being invaded.

invective *noun* abusive words.

inveigle (*say* in-**vay**-gul) *verb* (**inveigled, inveigling**) entice. **inveiglement** *noun*

invent *verb* **1** be the first person to make or think of a particular thing. **2** make up a false story etc., *invent an excuse.* **invention** *noun*, **inventive** *adjective*, **inventor** *noun*

inventory (*say* **in**-ven-ter-ee) *noun* (*plural* **inventories**) a detailed list of goods or furniture.

inverse *adjective* reversed; opposite. **inversely** *adverb* [same origin as *invert*]

invert *verb* turn something upside down. **inversion** *noun*

inverted commas punctuation marks "" or ' ' put round spoken words. [from *in-* = in, + Latin *vertere* = to turn]

invertebrate *noun* an animal without a backbone. **invertebrate** *adjective*

invest *verb* **1** use money to make a profit, e.g. by lending it in return for interest to be paid, or by buying stocks and shares or property. **2** give somebody a rank, medal, etc. in a formal ceremony. **investment** *noun*, **investor** *noun*

investigate *verb* (**investigated, investigating**) find out as much as you can about something; make a systematic inquiry. **investigation** *noun*, **investigator** *noun*, **investigative** *adjective*

investiture *noun* the process of investing someone with an honour etc.

inveterate *adjective* firmly established; habitual, *an inveterate reader.*

invidious *adjective* causing resentment because of unfairness.

invigilate *verb* (**invigilated, invigilating**) supervise candidates at an examination. **invigilation** *noun*, **invigilator** *noun* [from *in-* = on, + Latin *vigilare* = keep watch]

invigorate *verb* (**invigorated, invigorating**) give a person strength or courage. [compare *vigour*]

invincible *adjective* not able to be defeated; unconquerable. **invincibly** *adverb*, **invincibility** *noun* [from *in-* = not, + Latin *vincere* = conquer]

invisible *adjective* not visible; not able to be seen. **invisibly** *adverb*, **invisibility** *noun*

invite *verb* (**invited, inviting**) **1** ask a person to come or do something. **2** be likely to cause something to happen, *You are inviting disaster.* **invitation** *noun*

invalid¹ *noun* patient, sufferer.

invalid² *adjective* expired, illegal, out of date, unusable, useless, void, worthless.

invalidate *verb* annul, cancel, nullify, rescind, revoke, void.

invaluable *adjective* inestimable, precious, useful, valuable.

invariable *adjective* consistent, constant, immutable, predictable, regular, set, unchangeable, unchanging, unfailing, uniform.

invasion *noun* attack, foray, incursion, infiltration, inroad, onslaught, raid.

invent *verb* **1** coin, conceive, contrive, create, design, devise, make, manufacture, mint, originate. **2** concoct, cook up (*informal*), dream up, fabricate, make up, think up.
invention *noun* coinage, contraption, contrivance, creation, device, innovation.
inventive *adjective* clever, creative, enterprising, imaginative, ingenious, innovative, resourceful.

inventor *noun* architect, creator, designer, discoverer, innovator, maker, originator.

invest *verb* **1** devote, expend, lay out, put in, spend.

investigate *verb* check on, examine, explore, go into, inquire into, look into, probe, research, study, suss out (*informal*).
investigation *noun* examination, exploration, inquest, inquiry, inspection, research, review, scrutiny, study, survey.

inveterate *adjective* chronic, confirmed, established, habitual, incorrigible.

invigorate *verb* enliven, pep up (*informal*), perk up, refresh, rejuvenate, stimulate, strengthen.

invincible *adjective* strong, unbeatable, unconquerable, undefeatable, unstoppable.

invisible *adjective* concealed, hidden, imperceptible, inconspicuous, undetectable, unnoticeable, unseen.

invite *verb* **1** ask, bid, call on, request, summon, urge. **2** ask for, attract, court, provoke, tempt.

▶▶ D I C T I O N A R Y ◀◀

inviting *adjective* attractive; tempting. **invitingly** *adverb*

invoice *noun* a list of goods sent or work done, with the prices charged. [from French *envoyer* = send]

invoke *verb* (**invoked, invoking**) **1** call upon a god in prayer asking for help etc. **2** appeal to for help or protection, *invoke the law*. **invocation** *noun* [from *in-* = in, + Latin *vocare* = to call]

involuntary *adjective* not deliberate; unintentional. **involuntarily** *adverb*

involve *verb* (**involved, involving**) **1** have as a part; make a thing necessary, *The job involves hard work*. **2** make someone share in something, *They involved us in their charity work*. **involvement** *noun* [from *in-* = in, + Latin *volvere* = to roll]

involved *adjective* **1** complicated. **2** concerned; sharing in something.

invulnerable *adjective* not vulnerable.

inward¹ *adjective* **1** on the inside. **2** going or facing inwards.

inward² *adverb* inwards.

inwards *adverb* towards the inside.

iodine *noun* a chemical substance used as an antiseptic.

ion *noun* an electrically charged particle.

ionosphere (*say* I-**on**-os-feer) *noun* a region of the upper atmosphere, containing ions.

IQ *abbreviation* intelligence quotient, a number showing how a person's intelligence compares with that of an average person.

ir- *prefix* see **in-**.

IRA *abbreviation* Irish Republican Army.

irascible (*say* ir-**as**-ib-ul) *adjective* easily becoming angry; irritable.

irate (*say* I-**rayt**) *adjective* angry.

iridescent *adjective* showing rainbow-like colours. **iridescence** *noun*

iris *noun* (*plural* **irises**) **1** a plant with long pointed leaves and large flowers. **2** the coloured part of the eyeball. [Greek, = rainbow]

irk *verb* annoy.

irksome *adjective* annoying; tiresome.

iron¹ *noun* **1** a hard grey metal. **2** a device with a flat base that is heated for smoothing clothes or cloth. **3** a tool etc. made of iron. **iron** *adjective*
Iron Age the time when tools and weapons were made of iron.
irons *plural noun* fetters.

iron² *verb* smooth clothes or cloth with an iron.

ironic (*say* I-**ron**-ik) *adjective* using irony; full of irony. **ironical** *adjective*, **ironically** *adverb*

ironmonger *noun* a shopkeeper who sells tools and other metal objects. **ironmongery** *noun*

irony (*say* **I**-ron-ee) *noun* (*plural* **ironies**) **1** saying the opposite of what you mean in order to emphasise it, e.g. saying 'What a lovely day' when it is pouring with rain. **2** an oddly contradictory situation, *The irony of it is that I tripped while telling someone else to be careful*.

irrational *adjective* not rational; illogical. **irrationally** *adverb*

irreducible *adjective* unable to be reduced, *an irreducible minimum*.

irrefutable (*say* ir-**ef**-yoo-ta-bul) *adjective* unable to be refuted.

▶▶ T H E S A U R U S ◀◀

inviting *adjective* appealing, attractive, enticing, tempting.

invoice *noun* account, bill, statement.

involuntary *adjective* automatic, impulsive, instinctive, mechanical, reflex, spontaneous, unconscious, unintentional.

involve *verb* **1** entail, mean, necessitate, require. **2** embroil, entangle, implicate, include, incriminate, mix up.

involved *adjective* **1** complex, complicated, convoluted, elaborate, intricate. **2** caught up in, concerned, embroiled, implicated, interested, mixed up.

inward¹ *adjective* **1** inner, mental, personal, spiritual.

irate *adjective* angry, annoyed, cross, enraged, furious, indignant, infuriated, livid (*informal*), mad, ropeable (*Australian informal*).

irk *verb* annoy, exasperate, gall, irritate, pique, rile (*informal*), vex.

iron¹ *noun* **irons** bonds, chains, fetters, manacles, shackles.

iron² *verb* press, smooth.

ironic *adjective* derisory, mocking, sarcastic, satirical, wry.

irrational *adjective* crazy, illogical, insane, mad, nonsensical, senseless, unreasonable.

irrefutable *adjective* incontrovertible, indisputable, undeniable, watertight.

irregular *adjective* **1** not regular; uneven. **2** not occurring at regular intervals. **3** against the rules or usual custom. **4** (of troops) not in the regular armed forces. **irregularly** *adverb*, **irregularity** *noun*

irrelevant (*say* ir-**el**-iv-ant) *adjective* not relevant. **irrelevantly** *adverb*, **irrelevance** *noun*

irreparable (*say* ir-**ep**-er-a-bul) *adjective* unable to be repaired or replaced. **irreparably** *adverb*

irreplaceable *adjective* unable to be replaced.

irrepressible *adjective* unable to be repressed. **irrepressibly** *adverb*

irreproachable *adjective* blameless; faultless. **irreproachably** *adverb*

irresistible *adjective* unable to be resisted; very attractive. **irresistibly** *adverb*

irresolute *adjective* feeling uncertain; hesitant. **irresolutely** *adverb*

irrespective *adjective* not taking something into account, *Prizes are awarded to winners, irrespective of age.*

irresponsible *adjective* not showing a proper sense of responsibility. **irresponsibly** *adverb*, **irresponsibility** *noun*

irretrievable *adjective* not able to be retrieved. **irretrievably** *adverb*

irreverent *adjective* not reverent; not respectful. **irreverently** *adverb*, **irreverence** *noun*

irrevocable (*say* ir-**ev**-ok-a-bul) *adjective* unable to be revoked or altered. **irrevocably** *adverb*

irrigate *verb* (irrigated, irrigating) supply land with water so that crops etc. can grow. **irrigation** *noun*

irritable *adjective* easily annoyed; bad-tempered. **irritably** *adverb*, **irritability** *noun*

irritate *verb* (irritated, irritating) **1** annoy. **2** cause itching. **irritation** *noun*, **irritant** *adjective* & *noun*

irrupt *verb* enter forcibly or violently. **irruption** *noun* [from *ir-* = into, + Latin *ruptum* = burst]

Islam *noun* the religion of Muslims. **Islamic** *adjective* [Arabic, = submission to God]

island *noun* **1** a piece of land surrounded by water. **2** something resembling an island because it is isolated.

islander *noun* an inhabitant of an island.

irregular *adjective* **1** asymmetric, bumpy, lopsided, lumpy, pitted, rough, rugged, uneven. **2** erratic, haphazard, infrequent, intermittent, occasional, random, spasmodic, sporadic. **3** aberrant, abnormal, anomalous, deviant, eccentric, extraordinary, odd, peculiar, strange, unconventional, unusual.

irrelevant *adjective* beside the point, extraneous, immaterial, inapplicable, neither here nor there, unconnected.

irrepressible *adjective* boisterous, buoyant, ebullient, exuberant, lively, spirited, unrestrained.

irreproachable *adjective* beyond reproach, blameless, faultless, impeccable, unimpeachable.

irresistible *adjective* compelling, overpowering, overwhelming, powerful; see also TEMPTING (at TEMPT).

irresolute *adjective* hesitant, indecisive, spineless, tentative, uncertain, undecided, unsure, vacillating, wavering.

irrespective *adjective* **irrespective of** disregarding, ignoring, regardless of.

irresponsible *adjective* careless, negligent, reckless, thoughtless, unthinking, untrustworthy.

irreverent *adjective* blasphemous, disrespectful, impious, irreligious, profane, sacrilegious, ungodly.

irrevocable *adjective* binding, final, immutable, irreversible, settled, unalterable.

irritable *adjective* bad-tempered, cantankerous, crabby, cranky, cross, crotchety, fractious, grouchy (*informal*), grumpy, irascible, peevish, petulant, prickly, ratty (*informal*), shirty (*informal*), short-tempered, snaky (*Australian informal*), snappy, stroppy (*informal*), surly, testy, tetchy.

irritate *verb* **1** anger, annoy, bother, bug (*informal*), drive someone mad (*informal*), drive someone up the wall (*informal*), exasperate, get on someone's nerves, give someone the pip (*informal*), harass, infuriate, irk, nark (*informal*), needle (*informal*), pester, plague, provoke, rankle, rile (*informal*), rub someone up the wrong way (*informal*), trouble, upset, vex.

irritating *adjective* annoying, bothersome, exasperating, irksome, tiresome, trying, upsetting.

irritation *noun* anger, annoyance, chagrin, displeasure, exasperation, impatience, vexation.

island *noun* **1** isle, islet; (*group of islands*) archipelago.

isle (*say as* I'll) *noun* (*poetic & in names*) an island. [from Latin *insula* = island]

isn't (*mainly spoken*) is not.

iso- *prefix* equal (as in *isobar*). [from Greek *isos* = equal]

isobar (*say* I-so-bar) *noun* a line (on a map) connecting places that have the same atmospheric pressure.

isolate *verb* (**isolated, isolating**) place a person or thing apart or alone; separate. **isolation** *noun* [from Latin *insula* = island]

isosceles (*say* I-**soss**-il-eez) *adjective* having two sides equal, *an isosceles triangle*. [from *iso-*, + Greek *skelos* = leg]

isotope *noun* a form of an element that differs from other forms in its nuclear properties but not in its chemical properties.

issue[1] *verb* (**issued, issuing**) 1 come out; go out; flow out. 2 supply; give out, *We issued one blanket to each refugee.* 3 put out for sale; publish. 4 send out, *They issued a gale warning.* 5 result.

issue[2] *noun* 1 a subject for discussion or concern, *What are the real issues?* 2 a result, *Await the issue of the trial.* 3 something issued, *The Christmas issue of our magazine.* 4 issuing something, *The issue of passports is held up.*

isthmus (*say* **iss**-mus) *noun* (*plural* **isthmuses**) a narrow strip of land connecting two larger pieces of land.

it *pronoun* 1 the thing being talked about. 2 the player who has to catch others in a game. The word is also used (3) in statements about the weather (*It is raining*) or about circumstances etc. (*It is nine kilometres to Gundagai*), (4) as an indefinite object (*Run*

for it!), (5) to refer to a phrase (*It is unlikely that she will fail*).

italic (*say* it-**al**-ik) *adjective* printed with sloping letters (called **italics**) *like this*.

itch[1] *verb* 1 have or feel a tickling sensation in the skin that makes you want to scratch it. 2 long to do something.

itch[2] *noun* (*plural* **itches**) 1 an itching feeling. 2 a longing. **itchy** *adjective*, **itchiness** *noun*

item *noun* 1 one thing in a list or group of things. 2 one piece of news in a newspaper or bulletin.

itemise *verb* (**itemised, itemising**) list item by item.

itinerant (*say* It-**in**-er-ant) *adjective* travelling from place to place, *an itinerant preacher.*

itinerary (*say* I-**tin**-er-ee) *noun* (*plural* **itineraries**) a list of places to be visited on a journey; a route. [from Latin *itineris* = of a journey]

its *possessive pronoun* belonging to it, *The cat hurt its paw.*

Usage Do not put an apostrophe into *its* unless you mean 'it is' or 'it has' (see the next entry).

---

it's (*mainly spoken*) 1 it is, *It's very hot.* 2 it has, *It's broken all records.*

Usage Do not confuse with *its*.

---

itself *pronoun* it and nothing else. (Compare *herself.*)

by itself on its own; alone.

ivory *noun* 1 the hard creamy-white substance that forms elephants' tusks. 2 a creamy-white colour.

ivy *noun* (*plural* **ivies**) a climbing evergreen plant with shiny leaves.

▶▶ T H E S A U R U S ◀◀

isolate *verb* cut off, detach, insulate, quarantine, seclude, segregate, separate, set apart, shut off.

issue[1] *verb* 1 come out, discharge, emanate, emerge, erupt, escape, flow out, gush, pour, stream. 2 distribute, give out, provide, supply. 3 circulate, distribute, publish, put out, release, send out.

issue[2] *noun* 1 affair, matter, point, question, subject, topic. 2 conclusion, consequence, outcome, result. 3 edition, number, publication.

itch[1] *verb* 1 prickle, tickle, tingle. 2 be desperate, be eager, hanker, long, thirst, yearn.

itch[2] *noun* 1 irritation, prickling, tickle, tingling. 2 desire, longing, urge, yearning, yen.

item *noun* 1 article, detail, entry, object, piece, point, product, thing. 2 article, feature, piece, report, story.

itemise *verb* detail, enumerate, list, specify, spell out.

itinerant *adjective* nomadic, peripatetic, roving, travelling, wandering.

► Jj ◄

jab¹ *verb* (**jabbed, jabbing**) poke roughly; push a thing into something.

jab² *noun* **1** a jabbing movement. **2** (*informal*) an injection.

jabber *verb* speak quickly and not clearly; chatter. **jabber** *noun*

jack¹ *noun* **1** a device for lifting something heavy off the ground. **2** a playing card with a picture of a young man. **3** a small white ball aimed at in bowls.
jack of all trades someone who can do many different kinds of work.

jack² *verb* lift with a jack.
jack it in (*slang*) give up or abandon an attempt etc.
jack up (*Australian slang*) refuse to join in, show disapproval.

jack³ *adjective* (*Australian slang*) fed up, tired, *He got jack of the place and cleared out.*

jackal *noun* a wild animal rather like a dog.

jackass *noun* (*plural* **jackasses**) **1** a male donkey. **2** a stupid person. **3** a kookaburra.

jackdaw *noun* a kind of small crow.

jackeroo¹ *noun* (*Australian*) a young person learning the life of a sheep or cattle station by working on it.

jackeroo² *verb* work as a jackeroo.

jacket *noun* **1** a short coat, usually reaching to the hips. **2** a cover to keep the heat in a water-tank etc. **3** a paper wrapper for a book.

4 the skin of a potato that is baked without being peeled.

jack-in-the-box *noun* a toy figure that springs out of a box when the lid is lifted.

jackknife *verb* (**jackknifed, jackknifing**) fold one part against another, like a folding knife.

jackpot *noun* an amount of prize-money that increases until someone wins it.

Jacobean *adjective* of the reign of James I of England (1603–25). [from Latin *Jacobus* = James]

Jacobite *noun* a supporter of the exiled Stuarts after the abdication of James II (1688). [same origin as *Jacobean*]

jade *noun* a green stone that is carved to make ornaments.

jaded *adjective* tired and bored.

jagged (*say* **jag**-id) *adjective* having an uneven edge with sharp points.

jaguar *noun* a large fierce South American animal rather like a leopard.

jail *noun* (also **gaol**) a prison. **jail** *verb*, **jailer** *noun* [from Latin *cavea* = a cage]

Jain (*say as* jine) *noun* a believer in an Indian religion rather like Buddhism.

jam¹ *noun* **1** a sweet food made of fruit boiled with sugar until it is thick. **2** a lot of people, cars, or logs etc. crowded together so that movement is difficult. **3** (*informal*) a difficult situation, *in a jam.*

►►► THESAURUS ◄◄◄

jab¹ *verb* poke, prod, stab, thrust.

jab² *noun* **1** dig, nudge, poke, prod, stab, thrust. **2** immunisation, injection, shot, vaccination.

jabber *verb* babble, blather, chatter, gabble, gibber, prattle, yabber (*Australian informal*); see also TALK¹.

jack² *verb* hoist, lift, raise.

jacket *noun* **1** anorak, blazer, bolero, cagoule, coat, parka, tuxedo, windcheater. **3** cover, dust cover, dust jacket, wrapper.

jaded *adjective* done in (*informal*), fatigued, spent, tired, weary, worn out.

jagged *adjective* broken, chipped, indented, notched, ragged, rough, serrated, uneven.

jail *noun* detention centre, lock-up, nick (*slang*), penitentiary (*American*), prison, remand centre, watch-house.
jail *verb* imprison, incarcerate, intern, lock up, put away, put behind bars, send down.
jailer *noun* keeper, prison officer, warder.

jam¹ *noun* **1** conserve, jelly, marmalade, preserve. **2** bottleneck, build-up, congestion, hold-up, snarl. **3** bind (*informal*), difficulty, fix (*informal*), hole (*informal*), mess, pickle (*informal*), plight, predicament, quandary, spot (*informal*).

▶▶ D I C T I O N A R Y ◀◀

jam² *verb* (**jammed, jamming**) **1** crowd or squeeze into a space. **2** make or become fixed and difficult to move. **3** push something forcibly, *jam the brakes on.* **4** block by crowding or obstructing. **5** block a broadcast by causing interference with the transmission.

jamb (*say* jam) *noun* a side-post of a doorway or window-frame. [from French *jambe* = leg]

jamboree *noun* **1** a large party or celebration. **2** a large gathering of Scouts.

jangle *verb* (**jangled, jangling**) make a loud harsh ringing sound. **jangle** *noun*

janitor *noun* a caretaker. [from Latin *janua* = door]

jar¹ *noun* a container made of glass or pottery. [from Arabic *jarra* = pot]

jar² *verb* (**jarred, jarring**) **1** cause an unpleasant jolt or shock. **2** sound harshly.

jar³ *noun* a jarring effect.

jargon *noun* special words used by a group of people, *scientists' jargon.*

jarrah *noun* a Western Australian eucalypt with durable reddish-brown timber.

jasmine *noun* a shrub with yellow or white flowers.

jaundice *noun* a disease in which the skin becomes yellow. [from French *jaune* = yellow]

jaunt *noun* a short trip. **jaunting** *noun*

jaunty *adjective* (**jauntier, jauntiest**) lively and cheerful. **jauntily** *adverb*, **jauntiness** *noun*

javelin *noun* a lightweight spear.

jaw *noun* **1** either of the two bones that form the framework of the mouth. **2** the lower part of the face. **3** something shaped like the jaws or used for gripping things. **4** (*slang*) talking.

jay *noun* a noisy brightly-coloured bird.

jazz *noun* a kind of music with strong rhythm. **jazzy** *adjective*

jealous *adjective* **1** unhappy or resentful because you feel that someone is your rival or is better or luckier than yourself. **2** careful in keeping something, *He is very jealous of his own rights.* **jealously** *adverb*, **jealousy** *noun*

jeans *plural noun* trousers made of strong cotton fabric.

jeer *verb* laugh or shout at somebody rudely or scornfully. **jeer** *noun*

jelly *noun* (*plural* **jellies**) **1** a soft transparent food. **2** any soft slippery substance. **jellied** *adjective* [from Latin *gelare* = freeze]

jellyfish *noun* (*plural* **jellyfish**) a sea animal with a body like jelly.

jemmy *noun* (*plural* **jemmies**) a burglar's crowbar.

jeopardise (*say* **jep**-er-dyz) *verb* (**jeopardised, jeopardising**) endanger.

jeopardy (*say* **jep**-er-dee) *noun* danger.

jerk¹ *verb* make a sudden sharp movement; pull suddenly; move unevenly.

▶▶ T H E S A U R U S ◀◀

jam² *verb* **1** cram, crowd, fill, jam-pack, pack, push, ram, squash, squeeze, stick, stuff, wedge. **4** block, choke, clog, obstruct.

jamboree *noun* carnival, celebration, convention, festival, gathering, rally.

jangle *verb* clang, clank, clink, jingle, rattle. **jangle** *noun* clang, clangour, clank, clink, jingle, rattle.

janitor *noun* caretaker, concierge, doorkeeper, doorman.

jar¹ *noun* bottle, container, crock, jug, pot, receptacle, vase, vessel.

jar² *verb* **1** jerk, jolt, shake. **2** grate, irritate, jangle.

jarring *adjective* discordant, grating, harsh, irritating, raucous.

jargon *noun* cant, gobbledegook (*informal*), idiom, lingo (*informal*), slang.

jaunt *noun* drive, excursion, expedition, outing, trip.

jaunty *adjective* breezy, bright, cheerful, energetic, lively, perky, sprightly.

jaw *noun* **1** jowl, mandible, maxilla.

jazzy *adjective* flash (*informal*), flashy, gaudy, showy, smart, snazzy (*informal*).

jealous *adjective* **1** covetous, envious, grudging, resentful. **2** protective, vigilant, watchful.

jeer *verb* boo, chiack (*Australian informal*), deride, gibe, heckle, hiss, laugh at, make fun of, mock, poke borak at (*Australian informal*), ridicule, scoff at, sneer at, taunt. **jeer** *noun* boo, catcall, gibe, hiss, scoff, sneer, taunt.

jeopardise *verb* endanger, imperil, put on the line, risk, threaten.

jeopardy *noun* danger, peril, risk, threat.

jerk¹ *verb* bump, jig, jiggle, jolt, lurch, pull, shake, tug, tweak, twist, twitch, wrench, yank.

▶▶ D I C T I O N A R Y ◀◀

jerk² *noun* a jerking movement. **jerky** *adjective*, **jerkily** *adverb*

jerkin *noun* a sleeveless jacket.

jerry-built *adjective* built badly and with poor materials.

jersey *noun* (*plural* **jerseys**) **1** a pullover with sleeves. **2** a plain machine-knitted material used for making clothes.

jest¹ *noun* a joke.

jest² *verb* make jokes.

jester *noun* a professional entertainer at a royal court in the Middle Ages.

Jesuit *noun* a member of the Society of Jesus (a Roman Catholic religious order).

jet¹ *noun* **1** a stream of water, gas, flame, etc. shot out from a narrow opening. **2** a narrow opening from which a jet comes. **3** an aircraft driven by engines that send out a high-speed jet of hot gases at the back.

jet² *verb* (**jetted, jetting**) **1** come or send out in a strong stream. **2** (*informal*) travel in a jet aircraft. [from French *jeter* = to throw]

jet³ *noun* **1** a hard black mineral substance. **2** a deep glossy black colour.

jetsam *noun* goods thrown overboard and washed ashore from a ship in distress. [from *jettison*]

jettison *verb* throw overboard or away; release or drop something from an aircraft or spacecraft in flight. [same origin as *jet²*]

jetty *noun* (*plural* **jetties**) a small landing-stage. [same origin as *jet²*]

Jew *noun* a member of a people descended from the ancient tribes of Israel, or who believes in the religion of this people. **Jewess**

noun, **Jewish** *adjective* [from Hebrew, = of the tribe of Judah]

jewel *noun* a precious stone; an ornament containing precious stones. **jewelled** *adjective*

jeweller *noun* a person who sells or makes jewellery.

jewellery *noun* jewels and similar ornaments for wearing.

jib¹ *noun* **1** a triangular sail stretching forward from a ship's front mast. **2** the projecting arm of a crane.

jib² *verb* (**jibbed, jibbing**) be reluctant or unwilling to do something.

jiffy *noun* (*informal*) a moment.

jig¹ *noun* **1** a lively jumping dance. **2** a device that holds something in place while you work on it with tools.

jig² *verb* (**jigged, jigging**) move up and down quickly and jerkily.

jiggle *verb* (**jiggled, jiggling**) rock or jerk something lightly.

jigsaw *noun* **1** a saw that can cut curved shapes. **2** a jigsaw puzzle.

jigsaw puzzle a picture cut into irregular pieces which are then shuffled and fitted together again for amusement.

jihad *noun* (in Islam) a holy war. [Arabic]

jilt *verb* abandon a boyfriend or girlfriend, especially after promising to marry him or her.

Jindyworobak (*say* jindee-**wor**-o-bak) *noun* a member of a group founded in 1938 to promote Australian values in literature and the arts.

jingle¹ *verb* (**jingled, jingling**) make or cause to make a tinkling sound.

▶▶ T H E S A U R U S ◀◀

jerk² *noun* bump, jig, jiggle, jolt, lurch, pull, shake, tug, tweak, twist, twitch, wrench, yank. **jerky** *adjective* bumpy, disconnected, rough, spasmodic, twitchy, uncoordinated, uneven.

jersey *noun* **1** jumper, pullover, sweater, top.

jest¹ *noun* gag, joke, quip, wisecrack (*informal*), witticism.

jest² *verb* joke, kid (*informal*), pull someone's leg (*informal*), tease.

jester *noun* buffoon, clown, comedian, comic, entertainer, fool, joker, wag, zany.

jet¹ *noun* **1** fountain, gush, spray, spurt, stream. **2** nozzle, spout, sprinkler. **3** jumbo, jumbo jet, plane; see also AIRCRAFT.

jettison *verb* discard, dump, eject, get rid of, throw away, throw overboard, toss out.

jetty *noun* landing stage, pier, quay, wharf.

jewel *noun* gem, gemstone, precious stone.

jewellery *noun* adornments, jewels, ornaments, trinkets; (*kinds of jewellery*) anklet, bangle, beads, bracelet, brooch, chain, charm, cuff link, earring, locket, necklace, pendant, ring, stud, tiepin.

jib² *verb* (**jib at**) baulk at, recoil from, refuse, shrink from.

jiffy *noun* flash, instant, minute, moment, second (*informal*), tick (*informal*), trice.

jig² *verb* bob, bounce, dance, hop, jump.

jiggle *verb* jerk, rock, shake, wiggle.

jilt *verb* abandon, drop (*informal*), dump (*informal*), forsake, reject.

jingle¹ *verb* clink, jangle, rattle, ring, tinkle.

▶▶ D I C T I O N A R Y ◀◀

jingle² *noun* **1** a jingling sound. **2** a very simple verse or tune.

jinx *noun* (*informal*) a person or thing that is thought to bring bad luck. **jinxed** *adjective*

jitters *plural noun* (*informal*) nervousness. **jittery** *adjective*

job *noun* **1** work that someone does regularly to earn a living. **2** a piece of work to be done. **3** (*informal*) a difficult task, *You'll have a job to lift that box.* **4** (*informal*) a thing; a state of affairs, *It's a good job you're here.*

jobless *adjective* without a job.

jockey *noun* (*plural* **jockeys**) a person who rides horses in races.

jocular *adjective* joking. **jocularly** *adverb*, **jocularity** *noun*

jodhpurs (*say* **jod**-perz) *plural noun* trousers for horse-riding, fitting closely from the knee to the ankle. [named after Jodhpur in India]

joey *noun* a baby kangaroo or possum.

jog¹ *verb* (**jogged, jogging**) **1** run or trot slowly, especially for exercise. **2** give something a slight push. **jogger** *noun*

jog someone's memory help him or her to remember something.

jog² *noun* **1** a slow run or trot. **2** a slight knock or push.

joggle *verb* (**joggled, joggling**) shake slightly; move jerkily. **joggle** *noun*

jogtrot *noun* a slow steady trot.

join¹ *verb* **1** put or come together; fasten; unite; connect. **2** do something together with others, *We all joined in the chorus.* **3** become a member of a group or organisation etc., *Join the Navy.*

join up enlist in the armed forces.

join² *noun* a place where things join.

joiner *noun* a person whose job is to make furniture and fitments out of wood. **joinery** *noun*

joint¹ *noun* **1** a join. **2** the place where two bones fit together. **3** a large piece of meat cut ready for cooking.

joint² *adjective* shared or done by two or more people, nations, etc., *a joint project*; combined. **jointly** *adverb*

joist *noun* any of the long beams supporting a floor or ceiling.

joke¹ *noun* something said or done to make people laugh.

joke² *verb* (**joked, joking**) make jokes.

joker *noun* **1** someone who jokes. **2** an extra playing card with a jester on it. **3** (*Australian slang*) a fellow, bloke.

jolly¹ *adjective* (**jollier, jolliest**) cheerful; merry. **jollity** *noun*

jolly² *adverb* (*informal*) very, *jolly good.*

▶▶ T H E S A U R U S ◀◀

jingle² *noun* **1** clink, jangle, rattle, ring, tinkle. **2** chorus, poem, rhyme, song, tune, verse.

jinx *noun* curse, hex, spell.
jinxed *adjective* see UNLUCKY.

jitters *plural noun* butterflies (*informal*), collywobbles (*informal*), heebie-jeebies (*informal*), jim-jams (*informal*), nerves, shakes, willies (*informal*).
jittery *adjective* anxious, apprehensive, frightened, jumpy, nervous, nervy, quaking, quivering, shaky, uneasy.

job *noun* **1** appointment, career, employment, occupation, position, post, profession, situation, trade, vocation, work. **2** activity, assignment, chore, duty, errand, function, piece of work, project, responsibility, role, task.

jobless *adjective* out of work, unemployed.

jockey *noun* hoop (*Australian informal*), horseman, horse-rider, horsewoman, rider.

jocular *adjective* amusing, funny, humorous, jesting, joking, playful, witty.

jog¹ *verb* **1** run, trot. **2** jerk, jolt, knock, nudge, prod, push, shake.

jog someone's memory prompt, remind; see also STIMULATE.

join¹ *verb* **1** add, attach, bind, bracket, cement, combine, come together, connect, converge, couple, dovetail, fasten, fit, fuse, glue, knit, link, meet, merge, put together, solder, splice, stick, tack, tie, unite, weld, yoke. **2** partake, participate, share, take part. **3** enlist in, enrol in, enter, register for, sign up for, volunteer for.

join² *noun* connection, joint, knot, link, seam.

joint² *adjective* collective, combined, common, concerted, cooperative, shared, united.
jointly *adverb* as a team, cooperatively, in partnership, together.

joke¹ *noun* gag, jest, pun, quip, wisecrack (*informal*), witticism; see also PRACTICAL JOKE (at PRACTICAL).

joke² *verb* crack jokes, jest, kid (*informal*), pun, quip, tease.

joker *noun* **1** buffoon, clown, comedian, comic, jester, prankster, wag, wit, zany.

jolly¹ *adjective* bright, cheerful, cheery, exuberant, good-humoured, happy, high-spirited, jocular, jovial, joyful, merry.

jolly³ *verb* (**jollied**, **jollying**) (*informal*) keep someone in a good humour.

jolt¹ *verb* **1** shake or dislodge with a sudden sharp movement. **2** move along jerkily, e.g. on a rough road. **3** give someone a shock.

jolt² *noun* **1** a jolting movement. **2** a shock.

jostle *verb* (**jostled**, **jostling**) push roughly, especially in a crowd.

jot *verb* (**jotted**, **jotting**) write something quickly, *jot it down*.

jotter *noun* a notepad or notebook.

joule (*say* jool) *noun* a unit of work or energy. [named after the English scientist J.P. Joule]

journal *noun* **1** a newspaper or magazine. **2** a diary. [from Latin, = by day]

journalist *noun* a person who writes for a newspaper or magazine. **journalism** *noun*, **journalistic** *adjective*

journey¹ *noun* (*plural* **journeys**) **1** going from one place to another. **2** the distance or time taken to travel somewhere, *two days' journey*.

journey² *verb* make a journey. [from French, = a day's travel (*jour* = day)]

joust (*say* jowst) *verb* fight on horseback with lances.

jovial *adjective* cheerful and good-humoured. **jovially** *adverb*, **joviality** *noun*

jowl *noun* **1** the jaw or cheek. **2** loose skin on the neck.

joy *noun* **1** a feeling of great pleasure; gladness. **2** a thing that causes joy. **joyful** *adjective*, **joyfully** *adverb*, **joyfulness** *noun*, **joyous** *adjective*, **joyously** *adverb*

joy-ride *noun* a car ride taken for pleasure, usually without the owner's permission. **joy-riding** *noun*

joystick *noun* **1** the control lever of an aircraft. **2** a device for moving a cursor etc. on a VDU screen.

JP *abbreviation* Justice of the Peace.

jubilant *adjective* rejoicing; triumphant. **jubilantly** *adverb*, **jubilation** *noun* [from Latin *jubilans* = shouting for joy]

jubilee (*say* **joo**-bil-ee) *noun* a special anniversary, *silver* (25th), *golden* (50th), *and diamond* (60th) *jubilee*.

Judaism (*say* **joo**-day-izm) *noun* the religion of the Jewish people. [same origin as *Jew*]

judder *verb* shake noisily or violently.

judge¹ *noun* **1** a person appointed to hear cases in a lawcourt and decide what should be done. **2** a person deciding who has won a contest or competition. **3** a person who is able to give an authoritative opinion on the value or quality of something.

judge² *verb* (**judged**, **judging**) **1** act as a judge. **2** form and give an opinion. **3** estimate, *He judged the distance carefully.* [from Latin *judex* = judge]

jolt¹ *verb* **1** bump, dislodge, jerk, shake. **2** bounce, bump, jerk, judder, kangaroo, kangaroo-hop, lurch.

jolt² *noun* **1** bounce, bump, jerk, lurch. **2** shock, start, surprise.

jostle *verb* bump, elbow, knock, push, shove.

jot *verb* **jot down** note, record, scribble, take down, write down.

jotter *noun* notebook, notepad, pad, writing pad.

journal *noun* **1** gazette, magazine, newspaper, paper, periodical. **2** chronicle, diary, logbook, record.

journalist *noun* columnist, commentator, correspondent, editor, journo (*Australian informal*), reporter, roundsman (*Australian*), writer.

journey¹ *noun* **1** cruise, drive, excursion, expedition, flight, jaunt, mission, outing, pilgrimage, ride, safari, tour, trek, trip, voyage, walk.

journey² *verb* commute, cruise, fly, go, roam, rove, tour, travel, trek, voyage, wander.

jovial *adjective* breezy, bright, cheerful, convivial, good-humoured, happy, jolly, joyful, lively, merry.

joy *noun* **1** bliss, contentment, delight, ecstasy, elation, euphoria, exultation, gladness, happiness, jubilation, pleasure, rapture.

joyful *adjective* blithe, cheerful, content, delighted, ecstatic, elated, euphoric, exultant, glad, happy, jolly, jovial, joyous, jubilant, merry, overjoyed.

jubilant *adjective* delighted, elated, exultant, gleeful, happy, joyful, overjoyed, rejoicing, triumphant.

jubilation *noun* delight, elation, exultation, glee, happiness, joy, rejoicing, triumph.

jubilee *noun* anniversary, celebration, commemoration, festival.

judge¹ *noun* **1** justice, magistrate. **2** adjudicator, arbiter, arbitrator, referee, umpire. **3** authority, connoisseur, expert.

judge² *verb* **1** adjudicate, arbitrate, referee, umpire; (*judge a case*) decide, hear, try. **3** appraise, assess, estimate, evaluate, gauge, guess, rate, size up (*informal*).

▶▶▶ D I C T I O N A R Y ◀◀

judgement *noun* **1** judging. **2** the decision made by a lawcourt. **3** someone's opinion. **4** the ability to judge wisely. **5** something considered as a punishment from God, *It's a judgement on you!*

judicial *adjective* of lawcourts, judges, or judgements. **judicially** *adverb*

judiciary (*say* joo-**dish**-er-ee) *noun* all the judges in a country.

judicious (*say* joo-**dish**-us) *adjective* having or showing good sense. **judiciously** *adverb*

judo *noun* a Japanese method of self-defence without using weapons. [from Japanese *ju* = gentle, + *do* = way]

jug *noun* a container for holding and pouring liquids, with a handle and a lip.

juggernaut *noun* a huge lorry. [named after a Hindu god whose image was dragged in procession on a huge wheeled vehicle]

juggle *verb* (**juggled, juggling**) **1** toss and keep a number of objects in the air, for entertainment. **2** rearrange or alter things skilfully or in order to deceive people. **juggler** *noun*

jugular *adjective* of or in the throat or neck, *the jugular veins.*

juice *noun* **1** the liquid from fruit, vegetables, or other food. **2** a liquid produced by the body, *the digestive juices.* **juicy** *adjective*

juke-box *noun* a machine that plays a record when you put a coin in.

jumble¹ *verb* (**jumbled, jumbling**) mix things up into a confused mass.

jumble² *noun* a confused mixture of things; a muddle.
jumble sale a sale of second-hand goods.

jumbo *noun* (*plural* **jumbos**) **1** something very large; a jumbo jet. **2** an elephant.
jumbo jet a very large jet aircraft.

jumbuck *noun* (*Australian*) a sheep.

jump¹ *verb* **1** move up suddenly from the ground into the air. **2** go over something by jumping, *jump the fence.* **3** pass over something; miss out part of a book etc. **4** move suddenly in surprise. **5** pass quickly to a different place or level; rise or increase.
jump at (*informal*) accept something eagerly.
jump the gun start before you should.
jump the queue not wait your turn.

jump² *noun* **1** a jumping movement. **2** an obstacle to jump over. **3** a sudden rise or change.

jumper *noun* **1** a person or animal that jumps. **2** a jersey.

jumpy *adjective* nervous.

junction *noun* **1** a join. **2** a place where roads or railway lines meet. [from Latin *junctum* = joined]

juncture *noun* **1** a point of time, especially in a crisis. **2** a join.

jungle *noun* a thick tangled forest, especially in the tropics. [from Hindi *jangal* = forest]

▶▶▶ T H E S A U R U S ◀◀

judgement *noun* **2** adjudication, decision, decree, finding, ruling, sentence, verdict. **3** assessment, belief, mind, opinion, view. **4** acumen, discernment, discretion, discrimination, good sense, insight, sagacity, shrewdness, wisdom.

judicial *adjective* legal.

judicious *adjective* discerning, politic, prudent, sensible, shrewd, sound, wise.

jug *noun* carafe, decanter, ewer, pitcher, vessel.

juggle *verb* **2** cook (*informal*), doctor, falsify, fiddle (*slang*), fix, manipulate, rearrange, rig, tamper with.

juice *noun* **1** drink, extract, liquid, nectar, sap. **2** fluid, secretion.
juicy *adjective* moist, ripe, succulent.

jumble¹ *verb* confuse, disorganise, mix, mix up, muddle.

jumble² *noun* confusion, hotchpotch, mess, mixture, muddle.

jumble sale bazaar, boot sale, bring-and-buy-sale, garage sale, rummage sale.

jump¹ *verb* **1** bounce, bound, hop, leap, pounce, spring. **2** clear, go over, hurdle, pass over, vault. **3** leave out, miss, omit, overlook, pass over, skip. **4** buck, flinch, rear, recoil, shy, start. **5** escalate, increase, rise, shoot up.
jump at grab, leap at, seize, snatch.

jump² *noun* **1** bounce, bound, hop, leap, pounce, spring, vault. **2** fence, gate, hurdle, obstacle. **3** boost, escalation, increase, rise, upturn.

jumper *noun* **2** guernsey, jersey, pullover, skivvy, sweater, top.

jumpy *adjective* anxious, edgy, jittery (*informal*), nervous, nervy, tense, twitchy (*informal*), uneasy, uptight (*informal*).

junction *noun* **2** corner, crossroads, interchange, intersection, meeting point, T-junction, Y-junction.

juncture *noun* **1** point, point in time, stage, time.
jungle *noun* forest, rainforest.

► ► D I C T I O N A R Y ◄ ◄

junior¹ *adjective* **1** younger. **2** for young children, *a junior school*. **3** lower in rank or importance, *junior officers*.

junior² *noun* a junior person. [from Latin, = younger]

juniper *noun* an evergreen shrub.

junk¹ *noun* rubbish; things of no value.
junk food food that is not nourishing.
junk mail unsolicited advertising or promotional material delivered to letter-boxes.

junk² *noun* a Chinese sailing-boat.

jurisdiction *noun* authority; official power, especially to interpret and apply the law. [from Latin *juris* = of the law, + *dictum* = said]

juror *noun* a member of a jury.

jury *noun* (*plural* **juries**) a group of people (usually twelve) appointed to give a verdict about a case in a lawcourt. [from Latin *jurare* = take an oath]

just¹ *adjective* **1** giving proper consideration to everyone's claims. **2** deserved; right in amount etc., *a just reward*. **justly** *adverb*, **justness** *noun*

just² *adverb* **1** exactly, *It's just what I wanted*. **2** only; simply, *They're just good friends*. **3** barely; by only a small amount, *just below the knee*. **4** at this moment or only a little while ago, *She has just gone*. [from Latin *justus* = rightful]

justice *noun* **1** being just; fair treatment. **2** legal proceedings, *a court of justice*. **3** a judge or magistrate.

justify *verb* (**justified**, **justifying**) show that something is fair, just, or reasonable. **justifiable** *adjective*, **justification** *noun*

jut *verb* (**jutted**, **jutting**) stick out. [same origin as *jet²*]

jute *noun* fibre from tropical plants, used for making sacks etc.

juvenile *adjective* **1** of or for young people. **2** immature.
juvenile delinquent a young person who has broken the law. [from Latin *juvenis* = young person]

juxtapose *verb* (**juxtaposed**, **juxtaposing**) put things side by side. **juxtaposition** *noun* [from Latin *juxta* = next, *positum* = put]

► ► T H E S A U R U S ◄ ◄

junior¹ *adjective* **1** younger. **3** inferior, lower, subordinate.

junk¹ *noun* cast-offs, clutter, garbage, odds and ends, rubbish, scrap, trash.

jurisdiction *noun* authority, control, dominion, power, rule.

just¹ *adjective* **1** equitable, even-handed, fair, impartial, neutral, reasonable, unbiased, unprejudiced. **2** appropriate, deserved, due, fair, fitting, merited, right, rightful.

just² *adverb* **1** exactly, precisely, right. **2** merely, no more than, only, simply.

justice *noun* **1** equity, even-handedness, fairness, fair play, impartiality, right. **3** judge, magistrate.

justify *verb* defend, excuse, explain, rationalise, vindicate, warrant.
justifiable *adjective* fair, legitimate, reasonable, valid.
justification *noun* defence, excuse, explanation, grounds, reason.

jut *verb* poke out, project, protrude, stick out.

juvenile *adjective* **1** adolescent, junior, teenage, young, youthful. **2** childish, immature, infantile, puerile.

► Kk ◄

kale *noun* a kind of cabbage.

kaleidoscope (*say* kal-**I**-dos-kohp) *noun* a tube that you look through to see brightly coloured patterns which change as you turn the end of the tube. **kaleidoscopic** *adjective* [from Greek *kalos* = beautiful, + *eidos* = form, + *skopein* = look at]

kangaroo *noun* an Australian animal that jumps along on its strong hind legs. (See *marsupial.*)

kaolin *noun* fine white clay used in making porcelain and in medicine.

karate (*say* ka-**rah**-tee) *noun* a Japanese method of self-defence in which the hands and feet are used as weapons. [from Japanese *kara* = empty, *te* = hand]

kayak *noun* a small canoe with a covering that fits round the canoeist's waist. [Eskimo word]

kebabs *plural noun* small pieces of meat etc. cooked on a skewer.

keel¹ *noun* the long piece of wood or metal along the bottom of a boat.
on an even keel steady.

keel² *verb* tilt; overturn, *The ship keeled over.*

keen¹ *adjective* **1** enthusiastic; very interested in or eager to do something, *a keen swimmer.*
2 sharp, *a keen edge.* **3** piercingly cold, *a keen wind.* **keenly** *adverb*, **keenness** *noun*

keen² *verb* wail, especially in mourning.

keep¹ *verb* (**kept, keeping**) **1** have something and look after it or not get rid of it. **2** stay or cause to stay in the same condition etc., *keep still; keep it hot.* **3** do something continually, *She keeps laughing.* **4** respect and not break, *keep a promise*; *keep the law.* **5** celebrate a feast, *keep the sabbath.* **6** make entries in, *keep a diary.* **7** prevent a person from doing something; detain, *What kept you?* **8** guard or protect a person or place, *keep goal.* **9** own and look after animals, *He keeps chickens.* **10** remain in a good condition, *Margarine keeps for a long time.*
keep up make the same progress as others; continue something.

keep² *noun* **1** maintenance; the food etc. that you need to live, *She earns her keep.* **2** a strong tower in a castle.
for keeps (*informal*) permanently; to keep, *Is this football mine for keeps?*

keeper *noun* a person who looks after an animal, building, etc., *the park keeper.*

keeping *noun* care; looking after something, *in safe keeping.*
in keeping with conforming to; suiting, *Modern furniture is not in keeping with an old house.*

►►THESAURUS◄◄

kangaroo *noun* boomer (*male*), doe (*female*), joey (*young*), old man (*male*), roo (*informal*).
keel¹ *noun* base, bottom, underside.
on an even keel balanced, calm, level, stable, steady.
keel² *verb* **keel over** capsize, collapse, fall over, heel over, overturn, tilt, turn over, upset.
keen¹ *adjective* **1** ardent, avid, eager, enthusiastic, fervent, intense, zealous; (*keen on*) fond of, interested in, mad about, nuts about (*informal*). **2** sharp. **3** biting, bitter, cold, penetrating, piercing, severe.
keep¹ *verb* **1** conserve, hang on to, hold on to, maintain, preserve, put aside, put away, reserve, retain, save, store, withhold. **2** hold, remain, stay. **3** carry on, continue, go on, persevere in, persist in. **4** abide by, comply with, conform to, fulfil, honour, obey, respect,

stick to. **5** celebrate, commemorate, honour, observe. **7** delay, detain, hinder, hold up, impede, obstruct, prevent. **8** defend, guard, protect, shield. **9** care for, look after, own, tend. **10** be usable, last, stay fresh.
keep up carry on with, continue, maintain, sustain.
keep² *noun* **1** board, food, maintenance, subsistence. **2** donjon, stronghold, tower.
for keeps forever, for good, permanently.
keeper *noun* caretaker, curator, custodian, guard, guardian, jailer, ranger, warden, warder, watchman.
keeping *noun* care, charge, custody, guardianship, hands.
in keeping with conforming with, fitting, in harmony with, in line with, in step with, in tune with, suiting.

▶▶DICTIONARY◀◀

keepsake *noun* a gift to be kept in memory of the person who gave it.

keg *noun* a small barrel.

kelp *noun* a large seaweed.

kelpie *noun* an Australian breed of short-haired sheep-dog.

kennel *noun* a shelter for a dog.

kerb *noun* the edge of a pavement.

kerchief *noun* (*old use*) 1 a square scarf worn on the head. 2 a handkerchief.

kernel *noun* the part inside the shell of a nut etc.

kestrel *noun* a small falcon.

ketchup *noun* a thick sauce made from tomatoes and vinegar etc.

kettle *noun* a container with a spout and handle, for boiling water in.

kettledrum *noun* a drum consisting of a large metal bowl with skin or plastic over the top.

key *noun* 1 a piece of metal shaped so that it will open a lock. 2 a device for winding up a clock or clockwork toy etc. 3 a small lever to be pressed by a finger, e.g. on a piano or a typewriter. 4 a system of notes in music, *the key of C major*. 5 a fact or clue that explains or solves something, *the key to the mystery*.

keyboard *noun* the set of keys on a piano, typewriter, etc.

keyhole *noun* the hole through which a key is put into a lock.

keynote *noun* 1 the note on which a key in music is based, *The keynote of C major is C*. 2 the main idea in something said, written, or done; a theme.

keystone *noun* the central wedge-shaped stone in an arch, locking the others together.

khaki *noun* a dull yellowish-brown colour, used for military uniforms. [from Urdu, = dust-coloured]

kibbutz *noun* (*plural* **kibbutzim**) a commune in Israel, especially for farming. [from Hebrew, = gathering]

kick[1] *verb* 1 hit or move a person or thing with your foot. 2 move your legs about vigorously. 3 (of a gun) recoil when fired.
kick out get rid of; dismiss.
kick up (*informal*) make a noise or fuss.

kick[2] *noun* 1 a kicking movement. 2 the recoiling movement of a gun. 3 (*informal*) a thrill. 4 (*informal*) an interest or activity, *He's on a health kick.*

kid[1] *noun* 1 a young goat. 2 fine leather made from goat's skin. 3 (*informal*) a child.

kid[2] *verb* (**kidded**, **kidding**) (*informal*) deceive in fun; tease.

kiddie *noun* (*informal*) a child.

kidnap *verb* (**kidnapped**, **kidnapping**) abduct, especially in order to obtain a ransom.
kidnapper *noun*

kidney *noun* (*plural* **kidneys**) either of the two organs in the body that remove waste products from the blood and excrete urine into the bladder.

kill[1] *verb* 1 make a person or thing die. 2 destroy or put an end to something. **killer** *noun*, **killing** *noun*
kill time occupy time idly while waiting.

▶▶THESAURUS◀◀

keepsake *noun* memento, reminder, souvenir.

keg *noun* barrel, cask, hogshead.

kerb *noun* edge, roadside, verge.

kernel *noun* nut, seed.

key *noun* 1 latchkey, master key, passkey, skeleton key. 5 answer, clue, explanation, guide, interpretation, secret, solution.

kick[1] *verb* 1 boot, punt. 3 recoil, spring back.
kick out dismiss, drive out, evict, expel, fire, oust, sack, throw out.

kick[2] *noun* 1 boot, punt. 3 buzz (*informal*), enjoyment, excitement, fun, pleasure, satisfaction, thrill.

kid[1] *noun* 3 child, youngster.

kid[2] *verb* bluff, deceive, fool, have on (*informal*), hoax, hoodwink, jest, joke, pull someone's leg (*informal*), tease, trick.

kidnap *verb* abduct, carry off, seize, snatch.

kill[1] *verb* 1 annihilate, assassinate, bump off (*slang*), butcher, cull, destroy, dispatch, do in (*slang*), eliminate, execute, exterminate, finish off, knock off (*informal*), liquidate, martyr, massacre, mow down, murder, put down, put to death, put to sleep, slaughter, slay, take someone's life, wipe out, zap (*slang*); (*various ways to kill*) asphyxiate, behead, choke, crucify, decapitate, drown, electrocute, gas, guillotine, gun down, hang, knife, poison, shoot, stab, starve, stifle, stone, strangle, suffocate, throttle. 2 destroy, do away with, end, put an end to, ruin, stop.
killer *noun* assassin, executioner, hit man (*slang*), murderer, slayer.
killing *noun* annihilation, assassination, bloodshed, butchery, carnage, destruction, euthanasia, execution, extermination, genocide, homicide, manslaughter, massacre, murder, pogrom, slaughter, slaying, suicide.

kill² *noun* **1** killing. **2** the animal or animals killed by a hunter.

kiln *noun* an oven for hardening pottery or bricks, for drying hops, or for burning lime. [from Latin *culina* = kitchen]

kilo *noun* (*plural* **kilos**) a kilogram.

kilo- *prefix* one thousand (as in *kilolitre* = 1,000 litres, *kilohertz* = 1,000 hertz). [from Greek *khilioi* = thousand]

kilogram *noun* a unit of mass or weight equal to 1,000 grams (about 2.2 pounds).

kilometre (*say* **kil**-o-meet-er or kil-**om**-it-er) *noun* a unit of length equal to 1,000 metres (about 0.6 miles).

kilowatt *noun* a unit of electrical power equal to 1,000 watts.

kilt *noun* a kind of pleated skirt worn especially by Scotsmen.

kimono *noun* (*plural* **kimonos**) a long loose Japanese robe.

kin *noun* a person's relatives. **kinsman** *noun*, **kinswoman** *noun*
next of kin a person's closest relative.

kina *noun* the unit of money in Papua New Guinea.

kind¹ *noun* a class of similar things or animals; a sort or type.
payment in kind payment in goods not in money.

Usage Correct use is *this kind of thing* or *these kinds of things* (not 'these kind of things').

kind² *adjective* friendly and helpful; considerate. **kind-hearted** *adjective*, **kindness** *noun*

kindergarten *noun* a school or class for very young children. [from German *kinder* = children, + *garten* = garden]

kindle *verb* (**kindled**, **kindling**) **1** start a flame; set light to something. **2** begin burning. **3** stimulate, *kindle interest*.

kindling *noun* small pieces of wood for use in lighting fires.

kindly *adjective* (**kindlier**, **kindliest**) kind, *a kindly smile*. **kindliness** *noun*

kindred¹ *noun* kin.

kindred² *adjective* related; similar, *chemistry and kindred subjects*.

kindy *noun* (*Australian informal*) kindergarten.

kinetic *adjective* of or produced by movement, *kinetic energy*. [from Greek *kinetikos* = moving]

king *noun* **1** a man who is the ruler of a country through inheriting the position. **2** a person or thing regarded as supreme, *the lion is the king of beasts*. **3** the most important piece in chess. **4** a playing card with a picture of a king. **kingly** *adjective*, **kingship** *noun*

kingdom *noun* a country ruled by a king or queen.

kingfisher *noun* a small bird with a long beak that dives to catch fish.

king-hit *noun* (*Australian slang*) a sudden damaging blow, a knock-out blow.

kink *noun* **1** a short twist in a rope, wire, piece of hair, etc. **2** a peculiarity. **kinky** *adjective*

kin *noun* family, kindred, kinsfolk, kith and kin, relations, relatives.

kind¹ *noun* brand, breed, category, class, classification, form, genre, genus, ilk (*informal*), make, nature, order, set, sort, species, strain, style, type, variety.

kind² *adjective* affectionate, altruistic, amiable, attentive, avuncular, benevolent, benign, big-hearted, caring, charitable, compassionate, considerate, fatherly, friendly, generous, genial, gentle, good, good-natured, gracious, helpful, hospitable, humane, kind-hearted, kindly, lenient, loving, merciful, motherly, neighbourly, nice, obliging, philanthropic, soft-hearted, sympathetic, tender-hearted, thoughtful, understanding, unselfish, warm-hearted, well-meaning.

kindergarten *noun* nursery school, preschool.

kindle *verb* **1** fire, ignite, light, set alight, set fire to. **3** arouse, awaken, excite, inspire, spark off, stimulate, stir.

kindred² *adjective* allied, associated, related, similar.

king *noun* **1** monarch, ruler, sovereign; see also RULER.
kingly *adjective* regal, royal.

kingdom *noun* country, domain, dominion, empire, land, monarchy, nation, realm, state, territory.

kink *noun* **1** bend, coil, crinkle, curve, loop, tangle, twist. **2** eccentricity, foible, idiosyncrasy, peculiarity, quirk.
kinky *adjective* abnormal, depraved, deviant, perverted, unnatural, warped.

▶▶ D I C T I O N A R Y ◀◀

kiosk *noun* **1** a small hut or stall where newspapers, sweets, etc. are sold. **2** (*Australian*) a tea room in a park. [from Persian, = pavilion]

kipper *noun* a smoked herring.

kiss¹ *noun* (*plural* **kisses**) touching somebody with your lips as a sign of affection.

kiss² *verb* give somebody a kiss.

kit *noun* **1** equipment or clothes for a particular occupation. **2** a set of parts sold ready to be fitted together.

kitchen *noun* a room in which meals are prepared and cooked.

kitchenette *noun* a small kitchen.

kite *noun* **1** a light framework covered with cloth, paper, etc. and flown in the wind on the end of a long piece of string. **2** a large hawk.

kith and kin friends and relatives.

kitten *noun* a very young cat.

kitty *noun* (*plural* **kitties**) **1** an amount of money that you can win in a card-game. **2** a fund for use by several people.

kiwi (*say* **kee**-wee) *noun* (*plural* **kiwis**) a New Zealand bird that cannot fly.
kiwi fruit a small green-fleshed oval fruit with brown hairy skin.

kleptomania *noun* an uncontrollable tendency to steal things. **kleptomaniac** *noun* [from Greek *kleptes* = thief, + *mania*]

knack *noun* a special skill.

knacker *noun* a person who buys and slaughters horses and sells the meat and hides.

knapsack *noun* a bag carried on the back by soldiers, hikers, etc.

knave *noun* **1** (*old use*) a dishonest man; a rogue. **2** a jack in playing cards.

knead *verb* press and stretch something soft (especially dough) with your hands.

knee *noun* the joint in the middle of the leg.

kneecap *noun* the small bone covering the front of the knee-joint.

kneel *verb* (**knelt, kneeling**) be or get yourself in a position on your knees.

knell *noun* the sound of a bell rung solemnly after death or at a funeral.

knickerbockers *plural noun* loose-fitting short trousers gathered in at the knees.

knickers *plural noun* a woman's or girl's undergarment worn for the lower part of the body.

knick-knack *noun* a small ornament.

knife¹ *noun* (*plural* **knives**) a cutting instrument consisting of a sharp blade set in a handle.

knife² *verb* (**knifed, knifing**) stab with a knife.

knight¹ *noun* **1** a man who has been given the rank that allows him to put 'Sir' before his name. **2** a piece in chess, with a horse's head. **knighthood** *noun*

knight² *verb* make someone a knight.

knit *verb* (**knitted** or **knit, knitting**) **1** make something by looping together wool or other yarn, using long needles or a machine. **2** (of broken bones) become joined; heal. **knitter** *noun*, **knitting-needle** *noun*
knit your brow frown.

knob *noun* **1** the round handle of a door, drawer, etc. **2** a round projecting part. **3** a small lump. **knobbly** *adjective*, **knobby** *adjective*

▶▶ T H E S A U R U S ◀◀

kiosk *noun* **1** booth, stall, stand. **2** café, snack bar, tea room.

kiss¹ *noun* caress, peck, smack, smooch (*informal*).

kit *noun* **1** clothing, equipment, gear, outfit, paraphernalia, rig, tackle, things.

kitchen *noun* galley, kitchenette, scullery.

kitty *noun* **2** fund, pool, reserve.

knack *noun* ability, aptitude, art, expertise, flair, gift, skill, talent, trick.

knapsack *noun* backpack, haversack, pack, rucksack; see also BAG¹.

knave *noun* **1** baddy (*informal*), blackguard, miscreant, rascal, rogue, scoundrel, villain.

kneel *verb* bend, bow, crouch, genuflect, stoop.

knickers *plural noun* briefs, drawers, panties (*informal*), pants (*informal*), underpants, underwear, undies (*informal*).

knick-knack *noun* bagatelle, curio, ornament, trifle, trinket.

knife¹ *noun* blade, cutter; (*kinds of knife*) bowie knife, carving knife, chopper, clasp-knife, cleaver, flick knife, jackknife, lancet, machete, paperknife, penknife, pocket knife, scalpel, sheath knife, switchblade.

knife² *verb* cut, slash, slit, stab.

knit *verb* **2** grow together, heal, join, mend.

knob *noun* **1** handle. **2** bulge, bump, knot, lump, node, nodule, nub, projection, swelling.
knobbly *adjective* gnarled, knotty, lumpy, rough, uneven.

▶▶ D I C T I O N A R Y ◀◀

knock¹ *verb* **1** hit a thing hard or so as to make a noise. **2** produce by hitting, *knock a hole in it.* **3** (*informal*) criticise unfavourably, *Stop knocking Britain!*
knock back (*informal*) eat or drink, especially quickly; refuse.
knock down strike to the ground; demolish; lower the price of.
knock off (*informal*) stop working; deduct something from a price; (*slang*) steal.
knock out make a person unconscious, especially by a blow to the head.

knock² *noun* the act or sound of knocking.

knocker *noun* a hinged metal device for knocking on a door.

knock-out *noun* **1** knocking somebody out. **2** a contest in which the loser in each round has to drop out. **3** (*slang*) an amazing person or thing.

knoll *noun* a small round hill; a mound.

knot¹ *noun* **1** a place where a piece of string rope, or ribbon etc. is twisted about itself or another piece. **2** a tangle; a lump. **3** a round spot on a piece of wood where a branch joined it. **4** a cluster of people or things. **5** a unit for measuring the speed of ships and aircraft, 1,852 metres per hour.

knot² *verb* (**knotted, knotting**) **1** tie or fasten with a knot. **2** entangle.

knotty *adjective* (**knottier, knottiest**) **1** full of knots. **2** difficult; puzzling.

know *verb* (**knew, known, knowing**) **1** have something in your mind that you have learnt or discovered. **2** recognise or be familiar with a person or place, *I've known him for years.* **3** identify; be able to distinguish. **4** understand, *She knows how to please us.*

know-all *noun* a person who behaves as if he or she knows everything.

know-how *noun* skill; ability for a particular job.

knowing *adjective* showing that you know something, *a knowing look.*

knowingly *adverb* **1** in a knowing way. **2** deliberately.

knowledge *noun* **1** knowing. **2** all that a person knows. **3** all that is known.
to my knowledge as far as I know.

knowledgeable *adjective* well-informed.
knowledgeably *adverb*

knuckle¹ *noun* a joint in the finger.

knuckle² *verb* (**knuckled, knuckling**)
knuckle down to buckle down to.
knuckle under be submissive.

koala (*say* koh-**ah**-la) *noun* a furry Australian animal that lives in trees.

▶▶ T H E S A U R U S ◀◀

knock¹ *verb* **1** bang, bash, batter, beat, belt, clip (*informal*), clout (*informal*), dong (*Australian informal*), hammer, hit, kick, pound, pummel, punch, rap, smite, sock (*slang*), strike, tap, thrash, thud, thump, wallop (*slang*), whack. **3** bag (*Australian informal*), belittle, bucket (*Australian informal*), criticise, disparage, find fault with, insult, pan (*informal*), pick holes in, rubbish (*Australian informal*), run down, slam (*informal*), tear to pieces.
knock back SEE REFUSE¹.
knock down 1 demolish, destroy, pull down, raze. **2** bring down, decrease, lower, reduce.
knock off 1 cease, finish, quit, stop. **2** deduct, subtract, take off. **3** nick (*slang*), pinch (*informal*), steal, thieve.

knock² *noun* bang, blow, bump, clip (*informal*), clout (*informal*), dong (*Australian informal*), hit, kick, punch, rap, slap, smack, tap, thud, thump, thwack, wallop (*slang*), whack, wham (*informal*).

knot¹ *noun* **1** bow, hitch, loop, twist. **2** snarl, tangle. **3** knob, lump, node, nodule.

knot² *verb* **1** bind, fasten, hitch, join, lash, loop, tie. **2** entangle, snarl up, tangle.

knotty *adjective* **1** gnarled, knobbly, uneven. **2** baffling, complex, complicated, difficult, intricate, perplexing, puzzling, thorny, tricky.

know *verb* **1** be aware of, be in on (*informal*), comprehend, have learnt, have memorised, perceive, realise, remember, understand. **2** be acquainted with, be a friend of, be familiar with, recognise. **3** discern, discriminate, distinguish, identify, recognise.

know-all *noun* expert, genius, smart alec (*informal*), wise guy (*informal*).

know-how *noun* ability, competence, expertise, knack, knowledge, skill.

knowing *adjective* artful, astute, aware, crafty, cunning, meaningful, perceptive, shrewd, sly, wily.

knowledge *noun* **1** awareness, consciousness, experience, expertise, familiarity, grasp, know-how, perception, realisation, understanding. **3** education, learning, scholarship, science; see also INFORMATION.

knowledgeable *adjective* educated, enlightened, erudite, intelligent, learned, well-informed.

DICTIONARY

kookaburra *noun* a large Australian kingfisher with a cry resembling laughter.

Koori *noun* an Aboriginal Australian.

Koran (*say* kor-**ahn**) *noun* the sacred book of Islam, written in Arabic, believed by Muslims to contain the words of Allah revealed to the prophet Muhammad. [from Arabic *kur'an* = reading]

kosher *adjective* keeping to Jewish laws about food, *kosher meat*. [from Hebrew *kasher* = proper]

kremlin *noun* a citadel in a Russian city. [from Russian *kreml*]

krill *noun* a mass of tiny shrimp-like creatures, the chief food of certain whales. [from Norwegian, = tiny fish]

kudos (*say* **kew**-doss) *noun* honour and glory. [from Greek]

kung fu a Chinese method of self-defence, rather like karate.

THESAURUS

kudos *noun* acclaim, fame, glory, honour, prestige, renown, respect.

► LI ◄

L *abbreviation* learner, a person learning to drive a car.

lab *noun* (*informal*) a laboratory.

label¹ *noun* a small piece of paper, cloth, or metal etc. fixed on or beside something to show what it is or what it costs, or its owner or destination etc.

label² *verb* (**labelled, labelling**) put a label on something.

labial (*say* **lay**-bee-al) *adjective* of the lips. [from Latin *labia* = lips]

Labor *noun* the Australian Labor Party, a political party claiming to represent industrial workers and welfare.

laboratory *noun* (*plural* **laboratories**) a room or building equipped for scientific experiments. [same origin as *labour*]

laborious *adjective* **1** needing or using much hard work. **2** explaining something at great length and with obvious effort. **laboriously** *adverb*

labour¹ *noun* **1** hard work. **2** a task. **3** the contractions of the womb when a baby is being born.

labour² *verb* **1** work hard. **2** explain something laboriously, *Don't labour the point.* [from Latin *labor* = toil]

labourer *noun* a person who does hard manual work, especially outdoors.

Labrador *noun* a large black or light-brown dog. [named after Labrador, a district of Canada]

laburnum *noun* a tree with hanging yellow flowers.

labyrinth *noun* a complicated arrangement of paths etc.

lace¹ *noun* **1** net-like material with decorative patterns of holes in it. **2** a piece of thin cord or leather for fastening a shoe etc. **lacy** *adjective*

lace² *verb* (**laced, lacing**) **1** fasten with a lace. **2** thread a cord etc. through something. **3** add spirits to a drink.

lacerate *verb* (**lacerated, lacerating**) injure flesh by cutting or tearing it; wound. **laceration** *noun*

lachrymal (*say* **lak**-rim-al) *adjective* of tears; producing tears, *lachrymal ducts.* [from Latin *lacrima* = a tear]

lack¹ *noun* being without something.

lack² *verb* be without, *He lacks courage.*

lackadaisical *adjective* lacking vigour or determination; careless.

lackey *noun* (*plural* **lackeys**) a footman.

laconic *adjective* terse, *a laconic reply.* **laconically** *adverb*

lacquer *noun* a hard glossy varnish. **lacquered** *adjective*

►► THESAURUS ◄◄

label¹ *noun* sticker, tag, ticket.

label² *verb* brand, identify, mark, name, stamp, tag.

laborious *adjective* **1** arduous, difficult, exhausting, hard, onerous, strenuous, taxing, tiring. **2** forced, laboured, ponderous, strained, studied.

labour¹ *noun* **1** effort, exertion, industry, slog, toil, work, yakka (*Australian informal*). **3** childbirth, contractions, travail (*old use*).

labour² *verb* **1** exert oneself, grind away, slave, sweat, toil, work. **2** dwell on, elaborate, emphasise, harp on, impress, stress.

labourer *noun* blue-collar worker, hand, manual worker, navvy, unskilled worker, worker, workman.

labyrinth *noun* maze, network, warren.

lace² *verb* **1** do up, fasten, tie. **2** entwine, intertwine, weave. **3** fortify, spike (*informal*).

lacerate *verb* cut, gash, injure, mangle, rip, slash, tear, wound.

lack¹ *noun* absence, dearth, deficiency, insufficiency, need, paucity, scarcity, shortage, want.

lack² *verb* be deficient in, be short of, be without, miss, need, want.

lackadaisical *adjective* apathetic, blasé, careless, casual, half-hearted, indifferent, listless, lukewarm, unconcerned, unenthusiastic.

laconic *adjective* brief, concise, economical, succinct, terse.

lacquer *noun* gloss, varnish.

▶▶ D I C T I O N A R Y ◀◀

lacrosse *noun* a game using a stick with a net on it (a *crosse*) to catch and throw a ball. [from French *la crosse* = the crosse]

lacy *adjective* of or like lace.

lad *noun* a boy; a youth.

ladder[1] *noun* **1** a device with two upright pieces of wood or metal etc. and cross-pieces (*rungs*), for use in climbing. **2** a vertical ladder-like flaw in a stocking etc. where a stitch has become undone.

ladder[2] *verb* cause or have a ladder in a stocking etc.

laden *adjective* carrying a heavy load.

ladle[1] *noun* a large deep spoon with a long handle, used for lifting and pouring liquids.

ladle[2] *verb* (**ladled**, **ladling**) lift and pour with a ladle.

lady *noun* (*plural* **ladies**) **1** a well-mannered woman. **2** a woman of good social position. **3** (in polite use) a woman. **ladylike** *adjective*, **ladyship** *noun*
Lady *noun* the title of a noblewoman.
Lady Chapel a chapel in a large church, dedicated to the Virgin Mary (**Our Lady**). [from Old English *hlæfdige* = a person who makes the bread (compare *lord*)]

ladybird *noun* a small flying beetle, usually red with black spots.

lag[1] *verb* (**lagged**, **lagging**) go too slowly and fail to keep up with others.

lag[2] *noun* lagging; a delay.

lag[3] *verb* (**lagged**, **lagging**) wrap pipes or boilers etc. in insulating material to keep them warm.

lag[4] *noun* a convict, *an old lag.*

lager (*say* **lah**-ger) *noun* a light beer.

laggard *noun* a person who lags behind.

lagoon *noun* **1** a saltwater lake separated from the sea by sandbanks or reefs. **2** (*Australian*) a similar lake of fresh water. [from Latin *lacuna* = a pool]

laid *past tense* of **lay**[1].

lain *past participle* of **lie**[3].

lair[1] *noun* a sheltered place where a wild animal lives.

lair[2] *noun* (*Australian informal*) a flashy show-off. **lairy** *adjective*

laity (*say* **lay**-it-ee) *noun* lay people.

lake *noun* a large area of water entirely surrounded by land.

lama *noun* a Buddhist priest or monk in Tibet and Mongolia. [from Tibetan *blama* = superior]

lamb *noun* **1** a young sheep. **2** meat from a lamb. **lambswool** *noun*

lame *adjective* **1** unable to walk normally. **2** weak; not convincing, *a lame excuse.* **lamely** *adverb*, **lameness** *noun*

lament[1] *noun* a statement, song, or poem expressing grief or regret.

lament[2] *verb* express grief or regret about something. **lamentation** *noun* [from Latin *lamentari* = weep]

lamentable (*say* **lam**-in-ta-bul) *adjective* regrettable; deplorable.

laminated *adjective* made of layers joined together. [from Latin *lamina* = layer]

lamington *noun* (*Australian*) a block of sponge cake dipped in chocolate and coconut.

▶▶ T H E S A U R U S ◀◀

lacy *adjective* delicate, fine, flimsy, net.

lad *noun* boy, child, kid (*informal*), young man, youngster, youth.

ladder[1] *noun* **1** stepladder, steps.

laden *adjective* burdened, encumbered, loaded, weighed down.

ladle[2] *verb* dish out, serve.

lady *noun* **3** see WOMAN.
ladylike *adjective* dignified, genteel, polite, posh (*informal*), proper, refined, respectable.

lag[1] *verb* dawdle, drag the chain (*Australian*), drop back, drop behind, fall behind, go slow, straggle, trail.

lag[3] *verb* encase, insulate, wrap.

lagoon *noun* billabong, lake, pond, pool.

lair[1] *noun* burrow, den, hideout (*informal*), hidey-hole (*informal*), hiding place, hole, home, shelter.

lair[2] *noun* see LARRIKIN, SHOW-OFF (at SHOW[1]).
lairy *adjective* bright, flash (*informal*), flashy, garish, gaudy, loud, showy.

lake *noun* lagoon, loch (*Scottish*), mere (*poetical*), pond, reservoir, sea, tarn.

lame *adjective* **1** crippled, disabled, maimed, paralysed, paraplegic. **2** feeble, flimsy, unconvincing, unsatisfactory, weak.

lament[1] *noun* dirge, elegy, keen, lamentation, requiem.

lament[2] *verb* bewail, grieve over, mourn, regret, wail over, weep over.

lamentable *adjective* deplorable, regrettable, sad, sorry, terrible, unfortunate.

▶▶DICTIONARY◀◀

lamp *noun* a device for producing light from electricity, gas, or oil. **lamplight** *noun*, **lampshade** *noun*

lamppost *noun* a tall post in a street etc., with a lamp at the top.

lamprey *noun* (*plural* **lampreys**) a small eel-like water animal.

lance[1] *noun* a long spear.

lance[2] *verb* (**lanced**, **lancing**) cut open with a surgeon's lancet.

lance-corporal *noun* a soldier ranking between a private and a corporal.

lancet *noun* **1** a pointed two-edged knife used by surgeons. **2** a tall narrow pointed window or arch.

land[1] *noun* **1** the part of the earth's surface not covered by sea. **2** the ground or soil. **3** an area of country, *forest land*. **4** the area occupied by a nation; a country.

land[2] *verb* **1** arrive or put on land from a ship or aircraft etc. **2** reach the ground after jumping or falling. **3** bring a fish out of the water. **4** obtain, *She landed an excellent job*. **5** arrive or cause to arrive at a certain place or position etc., *They landed up in gaol*. **6** present with a problem, *He landed me with this task*.

landed *adjective* **1** owning land. **2** consisting of land, *landed estates*.

landing *noun* **1** bringing or coming to land. **2** a place where people can land. **3** the level area at the top of the stairs.

landing-stage *noun* a platform on which people and goods are landed from a boat.

landlady *noun* (*plural* **landladies**) **1** a woman who lets rooms to lodgers. **2** a female landlord.

landlord *noun* **1** a person who lets a house, room, or land to a tenant. **2** a person who looks after a public house.

landlubber *noun* (*informal*) a person who is not used to the sea.

landmark *noun* **1** an object that is easily seen in a landscape. **2** an important event in the history of something.

landowner *noun* a person who owns a large amount of land.

landscape *noun* the scenery or a picture of the countryside.
landscape gardening laying out a garden to imitate natural scenery.

landslide *noun* **1** a landslip. **2** an overwhelming victory in an election.

landslip *noun* a huge mass of soil and rocks sliding down a slope.

landward *adjective & adverb* towards the land. **landwards** *adverb*

lane *noun* **1** a narrow road. **2** a strip of road for a single line of traffic. **3** a strip of track or water for one runner, swimmer, etc. in a race.

language *noun* **1** words and their use. **2** the words used in a particular country or by a particular group of people. [from Latin *lingua* = tongue]

languid *adjective* slow because of tiredness, weakness, or laziness. **languidly** *adverb*, **languor** *noun*

languish *verb* **1** become weak or listless and depressed; pine. **2** live in miserable conditions; be neglected.

lank *adjective* lanky; long and limp.

▶▶THESAURUS◀◀

lamp *noun* see LIGHT[1].

lance[1] *noun* harpoon, javelin, pike, shaft, spear.

lance[2] *verb* cut open, incise, jab, pierce, prick.

land[1] *noun* **1** ground. **2** earth, ground, soil. **3** area, country, region, terrain, tract. **4** country, empire, nation, state, territory.

land[2] *verb* **1** alight, arrive, berth, disembark, dock, go ashore, put into port, touch down. **4** clinch, get, obtain, secure, win. **5** end up, fetch up (*informal*), find yourself, finish up, wind up. **6** give, present.

landing *noun* **1** arrival, touchdown. **2** jetty, landing stage, pier, quay, wharf.

landlady, landlord *noun* owner, proprietor.

landmark *noun* **1** feature. **2** milestone, turning point, watershed.

landowner *noun* grazier (*Australian*), laird (*Scottish*), landholder, pastoralist (*Australian*), squire.

landscape *noun* panorama, scene, scenery, view, vista.

landslide *noun* **1** avalanche, landslip.

lane *noun* **1** alley, path, road, track.

language *noun* **2** dialect, idiom, jargon, lingo (*informal*), slang, speech, terminology, tongue, vocabulary, words.

languid *adjective* apathetic, drained, inert, lazy, lethargic, listless, sluggish, torpid, weak, weary.

languish *verb* **1** droop, faint, wilt, wither. **2** decline, deteriorate, fail, go downhill, stagnate.

lank *adjective* lifeless, limp, long, straight, thin.

lanky *adjective* (**lankier**, **lankiest**) awkwardly thin and tall. **lankiness** *noun*

lanolin *noun* a kind of ointment, made of fat from sheep's wool.

lantern *noun* a transparent case for holding a light and shielding it from the wind.

lanyard *noun* a short cord for fastening or holding something.

lap¹ *noun* **1** the level place formed by the front of the legs above the knees when a person is sitting down. **2** going once round a race-course. **3** one section of a journey, *the last lap*.

lap² *verb* (**lapped**, **lapping**) **1** fold or wrap round. **2** be a lap ahead of someone in a race.

lap³ *verb* (**lapped**, **lapping**) **1** take up liquid by moving the tongue, as a cat does. **2** make a gentle splash against something, *Waves lapped the shore*.

lapel (*say* la-**pel**) *noun* a flap folded back at the front edge of a coat etc. [from *lap¹*]

lapse¹ *noun* **1** a slight mistake or failure, *a lapse of memory*. **2** a relapse, *a lapse into bad habits*. **3** an amount of time elapsed, *after a lapse of six months*.

lapse² *verb* (**lapsed**, **lapsing**) **1** pass or slip gradually, *He lapsed into unconsciousness*. **2** be no longer valid, through not being renewed, *My insurance policy has lapsed*. [from Latin *lapsum* = slipped]

laptop *noun* a portable microcomputer.

larceny *noun* stealing possessions.

larch *noun* (*plural* **larches**) a tall deciduous tree that bears small cones.

lard *noun* a white greasy substance prepared from pig-fat and used in cooking. **lardy** *adjective*

larder *noun* a cupboard or small room for storing food.

large *adjective* of more than the ordinary or average size; big. **largeness** *noun*
at large free to roam about, not captured, *The escaped prisoners are still at large*; in general, as a whole, *She is respected by the country at large*.

largely *adverb* to a great extent, *You are largely responsible for the accident*.

largesse (*say* lar-**jess**) *noun* money or gifts generously given.

lark¹ *noun* a small sandy-brown bird; the skylark.

lark² *noun* (*informal*) something amusing; a bit of fun, *We did it for a lark*.

lark³ *verb* (*informal*) have fun; play.

larrikin *noun* (*Australian*) a hooligan, a lout.

larva *noun* (*plural* **larvae**) an insect in the first stage of its life, after it comes out of the egg. **larval** *adjective* [from Latin, = ghost, mask]

laryngitis *noun* inflammation of the larynx, causing hoarseness.

larynx (*say* **la**-rinks) *noun* (*plural* **larynxes**) the part of the throat that contains the vocal cords.

laser *noun* a device that makes a very strong narrow beam of light or other electro-magnetic radiation. [from the initials of 'light amplification (by) stimulated emission (of) radiation']

►►►T H E S A U R U S ◄◄◄

lanky *adjective* gangling, gawky, lank, lean, skinny, thin.

lantern *noun* lamp, light.

lap¹ *noun* **2** circuit, orbit, tour. **3** part, section, stage.

lap³ *verb* **1** drink, lick, sip. **2** splash, wash.

lapse¹ *noun* **1** error, fault, mistake, omission, oversight, slip, slip-up. **2** backsliding, decline, deterioration, drop, regression, slip. **3** break, gap, hiatus, interlude, interruption, interval, passage.

lapse² *verb* **1** degenerate, fall, regress, relapse, slip. **2** expire, run out, stop, terminate.

larceny *noun* robbery, stealing, theft.

larder *noun* food cupboard, pantry.

large *adjective* ample, big, broad, bulky, capacious, colossal, commodious, consider-able, copious, enormous, extensive, fat, gargantuan, generous, giant, gigantic, ginormous (*slang*), grand, great, handsome, hefty, huge, hulking (*informal*), humungous (*slang*), immeasurable, immense, infinite, jumbo-sized, king-sized, mammoth, massive, monstrous, outsize, oversized, overweight, prodigious, roomy, sizeable, spacious, stupendous, substantial, tremendous, un-limited, vast, whopping (*slang*), wide.
at large free, loose, unconfined, unrestrained.

largely *adverb* chiefly, in the main, mainly, mostly, primarily, principally.

largesse *noun* benevolence, bounty, generos-ity, liberality, munificence, philanthropy.

lark² *noun* game, joke, prank, tease, trick.

larrikin *noun* hooligan, hoon (*Australian informal*), lair (*Australian informal*), rowdy, ruffian, tearaway.

larva *noun* caterpillar, grub, maggot.

▶▶ D I C T I O N A R Y ◀◀

lash¹ *noun* (*plural* **lashes**) **1** a stroke with a whip etc. **2** the cord or cord-like part of a whip. **3** an eyelash.

lash² *verb* **1** strike with a whip; beat violently. **2** move like a whip. **3** tie with cord etc., *Lash the sticks together.*

lass *noun* (*plural* **lasses**) a girl; a young woman. **lassie** *noun*

lassitude *noun* tiredness; listlessness.

lasso¹ *noun* (*plural* **lassoes**) a rope with a sliding noose at the end, used for catching cattle etc.

lasso² *verb* (**lassoed, lassoing**) catch with a lasso. [from Spanish *lazo* = lace]

last¹ *adjective* & *adverb* **1** coming after all others; final. **2** latest; most recent, *last night.* **3** least likely, *She is the last person I'd have chosen.*
the last straw a final thing that makes problems unbearable.

last² *noun* **1** a person or thing that is last. **2** the end, *He was brave to the last.*
at last or **at long last** finally; after much delay. [originally short for *latest*]

last³ *verb* **1** continue; go on existing or living or being usable. **2** be enough for, *The food will last us for three days.*

last⁴ *noun* a block of wood or metal shaped like a foot, used in making and repairing shoes.

lasting *adjective* able to last for a long time.

lastly *adverb* in the last place; finally.

latch¹ *noun* (*plural* **latches**) a small bar fastening a door or gate, lifted by a lever or spring. **latchkey** *noun*

latch² *verb* fasten with a latch.

late *adjective* & *adverb* **1** after the usual or expected time. **2** near the end, *late in the afternoon.* **3** recent, *the latest news.* **4** who has died recently, *the late king.*
of late recently.

lately *adverb* recently.

latent (*say* **lay**-tent) *adjective* existing but not yet developed or active or visible, *latent heat.*

lateral *adjective* of, at, or towards the side or sides. **laterally** *adverb* [from Latin *lateris* = of a side]

lath *noun* a narrow thin strip of wood.

lathe (*say* layth) *noun* a machine for holding and turning pieces of wood while they are being shaped.

lather¹ *noun* a mass of froth.

lather² *verb* **1** cover with lather. **2** form a lather.

Latin *noun* the language of the ancient Romans. [from Latium, an ancient district of Italy including Rome]

Latin America the parts of Central and South America where the main language is Spanish or Portuguese. (These languages were developed from Latin.)

latitude *noun* **1** the distance of a place from the equator, measured in degrees. **2** freedom from restrictions on what people can do or believe. [from Latin, = breadth]

latrine (*say* la-**treen**) *noun* a lavatory in a camp or barracks etc.

latter *adjective* later, *the latter part of the year.*
the latter the second of two people or things just mentioned. (Compare *former.*)

latterly *adverb* lately; recently.

▶▶ T H E S A U R U S ◀◀

lash¹ *noun* **1** blow, cut, stroke.

lash² *verb* **1** beat, belt, cane, flog, hit, lay into (*informal*), strike, thrash, whip. **3** fasten, secure, tie.

lass *noun* damsel (*old use*), girl, lassie (*informal*), maid (*old use*), maiden (*old use*), young woman.

lassitude *noun* languor, lethargy, listlessness, tiredness, weariness.

lasso¹ *noun* lariat, rope.

last¹ *adjective* **1** closing, concluding, final, ultimate. **2** latest, most recent.

last² *noun* **at last** eventually, finally, in the end, ultimately.

last³ *verb* **1** carry on, continue, endure, go on, keep on, persist. **2** do, suffice.

lasting *adjective* abiding, enduring, everlasting, long-lasting, long-lived, long-term, permanent.

lastly *adverb* finally, in conclusion.

latch¹ *noun* bar, bolt, catch, lock, snib.

latch² *verb* bar, bolt, fasten, lock, secure, snib.

late *adjective* **1** belated, delayed, held up, overdue, tardy. **3** (*latest*) current, freshest, most recent, newest, up to date, up to the minute. **4** dead, deceased, departed.

lately *adverb* latterly, nowadays, of late, recently.

latent *adjective* concealed, dormant, hidden, invisible, potential, undeveloped.

lather¹ *noun* bubbles, foam, froth, suds.

latitude *noun* **2** freedom, independence, leeway, liberty, scope.

▶▶ D I C T I O N A R Y ◀◀

lattice *noun* a framework of crossed laths or bars with spaces between.

laud *verb* (*formal*) praise. **laudatory** (*say* lawdat-er-ee) *adjective* [from Latin *laudare* = to praise]

laudable *adjective* praiseworthy. **laudably** *adverb*

laugh¹ *verb* 1 make the sounds that show you think something is funny. 2 make fun of someone or something.

laugh² *noun* an act or sound of laughing.

laughable *adjective* deserving to be laughed at.

laughter *noun* the act, sound, or manner of laughing.

launch¹ *verb* 1 send a ship from the land into the water. 2 set a thing moving by throwing or pushing it; send a rocket etc. into space. 3 start into action, *launch an attack*.

launch² *noun* (*plural* **launches**) the launching of a ship or spacecraft.

launch³ *noun* (*plural* **launches**) a large motor boat.

launder *verb* wash and iron clothes etc.

laundromat *noun* (*trade mark*) a place fitted with washing-machines that people pay to use.

laundry *noun* (*plural* **laundries**) 1 a place where clothes etc. are laundered for customers. 2 clothes etc. sent to or from a laundry.

laureate (*say* lorri-at) *adjective*
Poet Laureate a person in Britain appointed to write poems for national occasions. [from *laurel*, because a laurel wreath was worn in ancient times as a sign of victory]

laurel *noun* an evergreen shrub with smooth shiny leaves.

lava *noun* molten rock that flows from a volcano; the solid rock formed when it cools.

lavatory *noun* (*plural* **lavatories**) a toilet. [from Latin *lavare* = to wash]

lavender *noun* 1 a shrub with sweet-smelling purple flowers. 2 light-purple colour.

lavish¹ *adjective* 1 generous. 2 plentiful. **lavishly** *adverb*, **lavishness** *noun*

lavish² *verb* give generously, *They lavished praise upon him.* [from Old French *lavasse* = downpour of rain]

law *noun* 1 a rule or set of rules that everyone must obey. 2 (*informal*) the police. 3 a scientific statement of something that always happens, *the law of gravity*.

law-abiding *adjective* obeying the law.

lawbreaker *noun* a person who breaks the law.

lawcourt *noun* a room or building in which a judge or magistrate hears evidence and decides whether someone has broken the law.

lawful *adjective* allowed or accepted by the law. **lawfully** *adverb*

▶▶ T H E S A U R U S ◀◀

lattice *noun* framework, trellis.

laudable *adjective* admirable, commendable, creditable, meritorious, praiseworthy.

laugh¹ *verb* 1 be in stitches (*informal*), cackle, chortle, chuckle, crack up (*informal*), giggle, guffaw, snicker, snigger, split your sides, titter. 2 (*laugh at*) deride, jeer at, joke about, make fun of, mock, poke borak at (*Australian informal*), poke fun at, ridicule, satirise, sling off at (*Australian informal*), take the mickey out of (*informal*), taunt, tease.

laugh² *noun* cackle, chortle, chuckle, giggle, guffaw, snicker, snigger, titter.

laughable *adjective* absurd, derisory, farcical, ludicrous, nonsensical, outrageous, preposterous, ridiculous.

laughter *noun* cackling, chuckling, giggling, glee, hilarity, hysterics, laughing, merriment, mirth, sniggering.

launch¹ *verb* 1 float, set afloat. 2 fire, project, propel, send forth, send off. 3 begin, embark upon, introduce, open, set going, start.

launch² *noun* blast-off, lift-off, take-off.

launder *verb* clean, wash.

lavatory *noun* bathroom, convenience, dunny (*Australian slang*), Gents (*informal*), Ladies, latrine, loo (*informal*), men's, powder room, privy, rest room, toilet, toot (*Australian informal*), urinal, washroom, water closet, WC, women's.

lavish¹ *adjective* 1 extravagant, generous, liberal, unstinting. 2 abundant, bountiful, copious, plentiful, profuse.

lavish² *verb* bestow, heap, pour, shower.

law *noun* 1 act, by-law, commandment, decree, edict, regulation, rule, statute. 3 axiom, formula, principle, rule, theorem.

law-abiding *adjective* honest, obedient, orderly, upstanding.

lawbreaker *noun* criminal, delinquent, felon, miscreant, offender, transgressor, wrongdoer.

lawful *adjective* allowable, authorised, constitutional, legal, legitimate, permissible, permitted, sanctioned, valid.

▶▶DICTIONARY◀◀

lawless *adjective* **1** not obeying the law. **2** without proper laws, *a lawless country.* **lawlessly** *adverb*, **lawlessness** *noun*

lawn¹ *noun* an area of closely-cut grass in a garden or park.

lawn² *noun* very fine cotton material.

lawnmower *noun* a machine for cutting the grass of lawns.

lawsuit *noun* a dispute or claim etc. brought to a lawcourt for judgement.

lawyer *noun* an expert on law.

lax *adjective* slack; not strict, *discipline was lax.* **laxly** *adverb*, **laxity** *noun* [from Latin *laxus* = loose]

laxative *noun* a medicine that stimulates the bowels to empty.

lay¹ *verb* (**laid, laying**) **1** put something down in a particular place or way. **2** arrange things, especially for a meal, *lay the table.* **3** place, *He laid the blame on his sister.* **4** prepare; arrange, *We laid our plans.* **5** produce an egg. **lay off** stop employing somebody for a while; (*informal*) stop doing something. **lay on** supply; provide. **lay out** arrange or prepare; knock a person unconscious; prepare a corpse for burial. [from Old English *lecgan*]

Usage Do not confuse *lay/laid/laying* = 'put down', with *lie/lay/lain/lying* = 'be in a flat position'. Correct uses are as follows: *Go and lie down; she went and lay down; please lay it on the floor.* 'Go and lay down' is incorrect.

lay² *past tense* of **lie³**.

lay³ *noun* (*old use*) a poem meant to be sung; a ballad. [from Old French *lai*]

lay⁴ *adjective* **1** not belonging to the clergy, *a lay preacher.* **2** not professionally qualified, *lay opinion.* [from Greek *laos* = people]

layabout *noun* a loafer; a person who lazily avoids working for a living.

lay-by *noun* (*plural* **lay-bys**) **1** (*Australian*) a way of reserving something in a shop by paying a deposit and instalments. **2** (in Britain) a place where vehicles can stop beside a main road.

layer *noun* a single thickness or coating.

layman *noun* (also **layperson**) a person who does not have specialised knowledge or training (e.g. as a doctor or lawyer), or who is not ordained as a member of the clergy. [from *lay⁴* + *man*]

layout *noun* an arrangement of parts of something according to a plan.

laze *verb* (**lazed, lazing**) spend time in a lazy way.

lazy *adjective* (**lazier, laziest**) not wanting to work; doing little work. **lazily** *adverb*, **laziness**, *noun*

lazybones *noun* (*informal*) a lazy person.

lea *noun* (*poetic*) a meadow.

▶▶THESAURUS◀◀

lawless *adjective* **1** disorderly, insubordinate, rebellious, riotous, rowdy, uncontrolled, unruly, wild. **2** anarchic, chaotic, ungoverned.

lawn¹ *noun* grass, sward, turf.

lawsuit *noun* action, case, legal proceedings, litigation, suit, trial.

lawyer *noun* advocate, attorney, barrister, counsel, legal adviser, QC, Queen's Counsel, solicitor.

lax *adjective* careless, casual, easygoing, indulgent, lenient, permissive, relaxed, remiss, slack.

lay¹ *verb* **1** deposit, leave, place, put, rest, set down. **2** arrange, set, spread. **3** ascribe, assign, attribute, impute, place. **4** concoct, design, devise, formulate, hatch, make. **lay off** stand down, suspend; see also DISMISS. **lay on** provide, supply. **lay out** arrange, design, plan, prepare, set out.

lay⁴ *adjective* **1** non-clerical, non-ordained. **2** non-professional, non-specialist.

layabout *noun* bludger (*Australian informal*), bum (*slang*), good-for-nothing, idler, lazybones (*informal*), loafer, malingerer, shirker, skiver (*informal*), slacker.

layer *noun* coating, film, level, ply, sheet, stratum, thickness, tier.

layman *noun* amateur, layperson, non-professional, non-specialist.

layout *noun* arrangement, composition, design, organisation, plan, structure.

laze *verb* loaf, lounge, put your feet up, relax, rest, take it easy.

lazy *adjective* idle, inactive, indolent, inert, languid, lethargic, listless, shiftless, slack, slothful, sluggish, torpid.

lazybones *noun* couch potato (*informal*), good-for-nothing, idler, layabout, loafer, slacker, sluggard.

►►► D I C T I O N A R Y ◄◄

lead¹ (*say* leed) *verb* (**led**, **leading**) **1** take or guide, especially by going in front. **2** influence a person's actions or opinions. **3** be in charge of something. **4** be winning in a race or contest etc.; be ahead. **5** be a way or route, *This path leads to the beach.* **6** play the first card in a card-game. **7** live or experience, *He leads a dull life.*

lead² (*say* leed) *noun* **1** the action of leading; guidance, *Give us a lead.* **2** a leading place or part or position, *She took the lead.* **3** a strap or cord for leading a dog or other animal. **4** an electrical wire attached to something.

lead³ (*say* led) *noun* **1** a soft heavy grey metal. **2** the writing substance (graphite) in a pencil. **lead** *adjective*

leaden (*say* **led**-en) *adjective* **1** made of lead. **2** heavy and slow. **3** lead-coloured; dark-grey, *leaden skies.*

leader *noun* a person or thing that leads; a chief. **leadership** *noun*

leaf *noun* (*plural* **leaves**) **1** a flat usually green part of a plant, growing out from its stem or a branch. **2** the paper forming one page of a book. **3** a very thin sheet of metal, *gold leaf.* **4** a flap that makes a table larger. **leafy** *adjective*, **leafless** *adjective*
turn over a new leaf make a fresh start and improve your behaviour.

leaflet *noun* **1** a piece of paper printed with information. **2** a small leaf.

league¹ *noun* **1** a group of people or nations who agree to work together. **2** a group of teams who compete against each other for a championship.
in league with working or plotting together.

league² *noun* an old measure of distance, about 3 miles or 5 kilometres.

leak¹ *noun* **1** a hole or crack etc. through which liquid or gas wrongly escapes. **2** the revealing of secret information. **leaky** *adjective*

leak² *verb* **1** get out or let out through a leak. **2** reveal secret information. **leakage** *noun*

lean¹ *adjective* **1** with little or no fat, *lean meat.* **2** thin, *a lean body.*

lean² *verb* (**leaned** or **leant**, **leaning**) **1** bend your body towards or over something. **2** put or be in a sloping position. **3** rest against something.

leaning *noun* a tendency or preference.

leap *verb* (**leaped** or **leapt**, **leaping**) jump vigorously. **leap** *noun*
leap year a year with an extra day in it (29 February).

leap-frog *noun* a game in which each player jumps with legs apart over another who is bending down.

learn *verb* (**learned** or **learnt**, **learning**) **1** get knowledge or skill. **2** find out about something.

learned (*say* **ler**-nid) *adjective* having much knowledge obtained by study.

►►► T H E S A U R U S ◄◄

lead¹ *verb* **1** conduct, escort, guide, pilot, steer, usher. **2** cause, induce, influence, persuade, prompt. **3** be in charge of, command, control, direct, head, spearhead, supervise.

lead² *noun* **1** direction, example, guidance, leadership. **3** leash.

leader *noun* boss, captain, chief, chieftain, commander, conductor, director, governor, head, manager, overseer, premier, president, prime minister, principal, ringleader, ruler, supervisor.

leaf *noun* **1** blade, frond, needle; (*leaves*) foliage, greenery. **2** folio, page, sheet.

leaflet *noun* **1** booklet, brochure, flyer, handout, pamphlet.

league¹ *noun* **1** alliance, association, group, organisation, society, union.

leak¹ *noun* **1** crack, fissure, gash, hole, puncture, split. **2** disclosure, revelation.

leak² *verb* **1** discharge, drip, escape, ooze, seep, trickle. **2** disclose, divulge, let out, reveal.

lean¹ *adjective* **2** angular, bony, emaciated, gaunt, lanky, scraggy, scrawny, skinny, slender, slim, thin, weedy, wiry.

lean² *verb* **2** incline, list, slant, slope, tilt, tip. **3** prop yourself, rest, support yourself.

leaning *noun* bent, inclination, partiality, penchant, predilection, preference, proclivity, tendency.

leap *verb & noun* bounce, bound, jump, pounce, spring, vault.

learn *verb* **1** assimilate, grasp, master, memorise, pick up, study. **2** ascertain, become aware, discover, find out, gather, hear.

learned *adjective* clever, educated, erudite, informed, intellectual, knowledgeable, scholarly, well-informed, well-read.

DICTIONARY

learner *noun* a person who is learning something, especially to drive a car.

learning *noun* knowledge obtained by study.

lease¹ *noun* an agreement to allow someone to use a building or land etc. for a fixed period in return for payment. **leaseholder** *noun*

lease² *verb* (**leased, leasing**) allow or obtain the use of something by lease.

leash *noun* (*plural* **leashes**) a dog's lead.

least¹ *adjective & adverb* very small in amount etc., *the least bit; the least expensive bike.*

least² *noun* the smallest amount etc.

leather *noun* material made from animal skins. **leathery** *adjective*

leave¹ *verb* (**left, leaving**) **1** go away from a person or place. **2** stop belonging to a group or working for an employer. **3** abandon; go away without intending to return. **4** cause or allow something to stay where it is or as it is, *You left the door open.* **5** go away without taking something, *I left my book at home.* **6** put something to be collected or passed on, *leave a message.* **7** give something to a person when you die.
leave off cease.
leave out omit; not include.

leave² *noun* **1** permission. **2** official permission to be away from work; the time for which this permission lasts.

leaven (*say* **lev**-en) *noun* a substance (e.g. yeast) used to make dough rise.

lechery *noun* excessive sexual lust. **lecherous** *adjective*

lectern *noun* a stand to hold a Bible or other large book or notes for reading. [same origin as *lecture*]

lecture¹ *noun* **1** a talk about a subject to an audience or a class. **2** a long serious warning or rebuke.

lecture² *verb* (**lectured, lecturing**) give a lecture. **lecturer** *noun* [from Latin *lectum* = read]

led *past tense* of **lead¹**.

ledge *noun* a narrow shelf or similar projecting part.

ledger *noun* an account-book.

lee *noun* the sheltered side or part of something, away from the wind.

leech *noun* (*plural* **leeches**) a small blood-sucking worm that lives in water.

leek *noun* a white vegetable rather like an onion, with broad leaves.

leer *verb* look at someone in an insulting, sly, or unpleasant way. **leer** *noun*

leeward *adjective* on the lee side.

leeway *noun* **1** drift to leeward or off course. **2** extra space or time available.
make up leeway make up lost time; regain a lost position.

THESAURUS

learner *noun* apprentice, beginner, cadet, novice, pupil, rookie (*informal*), student, trainee.

learning *noun* education, erudition, knowledge, scholarship.

lease² *verb* hire, let, rent.

least¹ *adjective* barest, faintest, littlest, lowest, minimum, scantiest, slightest, smallest, tiniest.

leather *noun* hide, skin, suede.
leathery *adjective* hard, hardened, rugged, tough, weather-beaten.

leave¹ *verb* **1** abscond, beat it (*slang*), buzz off (*slang*), clear off (*informal*), decamp, depart, disappear, do a bunk (*slang*), escape, exit, flee, get away, go away, head off, make off, make yourself scarce, nick off (*Australian slang*), push off (*informal*), quit, rack off (*Australian slang*), retire, retreat, run away, run off, scarper (*informal*), scram (*informal*), set off, shoot through (*Australian informal*), shove off (*informal*), skedaddle (*informal*), slope off (*informal*), take off, take your leave, vanish,

withdraw. **2** chuck in (*informal*), give up, quit, resign, retire from, walk out of. **3** abandon, desert, forsake, leave in the lurch, part from, separate from, will. **7** bequeath, give, hand down, will.

leave off cease, desist, lay off (*informal*), quit, refrain from, stop.

leave out drop, exclude, miss out, omit, skip.

leave² *noun* **1** consent, permission. **2** break, exeat, furlough, holiday, sabbatical, vacation.

lecherous *adjective* lascivious, lewd, lustful, randy.

lecture¹ *noun* **1** address, discourse, lesson, speech, talk. **2** dressing down (*informal*), earbashing (*Australian informal*), reprimand, reproof, scolding, sermon, serve (*Australian informal*), talking-to (*informal*), telling-off (*informal*).

ledge *noun* mantelpiece, projection, shelf, sill.

leer *verb* goggle, ogle, smirk, stare.

leeway *noun* **2** freedom, latitude, margin, play, room, scope.

▶▶DICTIONARY◀◀

left¹ *adjective & adverb* **1** of or on or towards the left-hand side. **2** (of political groups) in favour of socialist reforms.
left hand the hand that most people use less than the other, on the same side of the body as the heart. **left-hand** *adjective*
left-handed *adjective* using the left hand in preference to the right hand.

left² *noun* the left-hand side or part etc. [the word originally meant 'weak']

left³ *past tense* of **leave¹**.
leftovers *plural noun* food not eaten.

leg *noun* **1** each of the projecting parts of a person's or animal's body, on which it stands or moves. **2** the part of a garment covering a leg. **3** each of the projecting supports of a chair or other piece of furniture. **4** one part of a journey. **5** one of a pair of matches between the same teams.

legacy *noun* (*plural* **legacies**) something left to a person in a will.

legal *adjective* **1** lawful. **2** of the law or lawyers. **legally** *adverb*, **legality** *noun* [from Latin *legis* = of a law]

legalise *verb* (**legalised, legalising**) make a thing legal. **legalisation** *noun*

legate *noun* an official representative, especially of the pope.

legend *noun* an old story handed down from the past. **legendary** *adjective* (Compare *myth*.) [from Latin *legenda* = things to be read]

leggings *plural noun* an outer covering for each leg.

legible *adjective* clear enough to read. **legibly** *adverb*, **legibility** *noun* [from Latin *legere* = to read]

legion *noun* **1** a division of the ancient Roman army. **2** a group of soldiers or former soldiers.

legislate *verb* (**legislated, legislating**) make laws. **legislation** *noun*, **legislator** *noun* [from Latin *legis* = of a law, + *latio* = proposing]

legislative *adjective* making laws, *a legislative assembly*.

legislature *noun* a country's legislative assembly.

legitimate *adjective* **1** lawful. **2** born when parents are married to each other. **legitimately** *adverb*, **legitimacy** *noun*

leisure *noun* time that is free from work, when you can do what you like. **leisured** *adjective*, **leisurely** *adjective*
at leisure having leisure; not hurried.
at your leisure when you have time.

lemming *noun* a small mouse-like animal of Arctic regions that migrates in large numbers and is said to run headlong into the sea and drown.

lemon *noun* **1** an oval yellow citrus fruit with a sour taste. **2** pale-yellow colour.

lemonade *noun* a lemon-flavoured drink.

lemur (*say* **lee**-mur) *noun* a monkey-like animal.

lend *verb* (**lent, lending**) **1** allow a person to use something of yours for a short time. **2** provide someone with money that they must repay usually in return for payments (called *interest*). **lender** *noun*
lend a hand help somebody.

length *noun* **1** how long something is. **2** the amount of time that something takes or lasts. **3** a piece of cloth, rope, wire, etc. cut from a larger piece. **4** the amount of thoroughness in an action, *They went to great lengths to make us comfortable.*
at length after a long time; taking a long time; in detail.

▶▶THESAURUS◀◀

left² *noun* larboard (*old use*), port.

leftovers *plural noun* dregs, excess, remainder(s), residue, scraps, surplus.

leg *noun* **1** limb, pin (*informal*), shank. **4** lap, part, section, stage.

legacy *noun* bequest, inheritance.

legal *adjective* **1** allowed, authorised, lawful, legitimate, permissible, permitted, proper, rightful.

legalise *verb* allow, authorise, decriminalise, permit.

legend *noun* folk tale, myth, saga, story, tale.
legendary *adjective* fabled, fictional, fictitious, mythical, traditional; see also FAMOUS.

legible *adjective* clear, neat, plain, readable, tidy.

legislation *noun* act, bill, law, statute.

legislative *adjective* law-making, parliamentary.

legitimate *adjective* **1** lawful, legal, permissible.

leisure *noun* free time, recreation, relaxation, spare time, time off.
leisurely *adjective* calm, easy, gentle, relaxed, restful, slow, unhurried.

lend *verb* **1** advance, loan.

length *noun* **1** distance, extent, measurement, size, span. **2** duration, period, span, term, time.
at length 1 at last, eventually, finally, in the end. **2** fully, in depth, in detail.

lengthen *verb* make or become longer.

lengthways or **lengthwise** *adverb* from end to end; along the longest part.

lengthy *adjective* very long; long and boring. **lengthily** *adverb*

lenient (*say* **lee**-nee-ent) *adjective* merciful; not severe. **leniently** *adverb*, **lenience** *noun* [from Latin *lenis* = gentle]

lens *noun* (*plural* **lenses**) **1** a curved piece of glass or plastic used to focus things. **2** the transparent part of the eye, immediately behind the pupil.

Lent *noun* a time of fasting and penitence observed by Christians for about six weeks before Easter. **Lenten** *adjective*

lent *past tense* of **lend**.

lentil *noun* a kind of small bean.

leopard (*say* **lep**-erd) *noun* a large lion-like spotted wild animal, also called a panther. **leopardess** *noun*

leotard (*say* **lee**-o-tard) *noun* a close-fitting garment worn by acrobats and dancers.

leper *noun* a person who has leprosy.

lepidopterous *adjective* of the group of insects that includes butterflies and moths.

leprechaun (*say* **lep**-rek-awn) *noun* (in Irish folklore) an elf who looks like a little old man. [from Irish, = a small body]

leprosy *noun* an infectious disease that makes parts of the body waste away. **leprous** *adjective*

lesbian *noun* a homosexual woman. **lesbian** *adjective*

less¹ *adjective* & *adverb* smaller in amount; not so much, *Make less noise. It is less important.*

less² *noun* a smaller amount.

less³ *preposition* minus; deducting, *She earned $100, less tax.*

lessen *verb* make or become less.

lesser *adjective* not so great as the other, *the lesser evil.*

lesson *noun* **1** an amount of teaching given at one time. **2** something to be learnt by a pupil. **3** an example or experience from which you should learn, *Let this be a lesson to you!* **4** a passage from the Bible read aloud as part of a church service.

lest *conjunction* so that something should not happen, *Remind us, lest we forget.*

let *verb* (**let, letting**) **1** allow to do something; not prevent; not forbid, *Let me see it.* **2** cause to, *Let us know what happens.* **3** allow or cause to come or go or pass, *Let me out!* **4** allow someone to use a house or building etc. in return for payment (*rent*). **5** leave, *Let it alone.*

let down deflate; disappoint somebody. **let-down** *noun*

let off cause to explode; excuse somebody from a duty or punishment etc.

let on (*informal*) reveal a secret.

let out allow to go, set free; make clothes looser by adjusting seams.

let up (*informal*) relax. **let-up** *noun*

lengthen *verb* draw out, elongate, extend, increase, prolong, protract, spin out, stretch out.

lengthways *adverb* lengthwise, longitudinally, longways, longwise.

lengthy *adjective* drawn-out, extended, interminable, long, long-winded, prolonged, protracted, verbose, wordy.

lenient *adjective* compassionate, easygoing, forbearing, indulgent, merciful, mild, soft, sparing.

leprechaun *noun* elf, fairy, sprite.

lesbian *adjective* gay (*informal*), homosexual.

less¹ *adjective* slighter, smaller.

less³ *preposition* deducting, minus, subtracting, taking away.

lessen *verb* abate, cut down, deaden, decrease, die down, diminish, dwindle, ease, let up, minimise, moderate, reduce, subside, weaken.

lesser *adjective* minor, secondary, slighter, smaller, subsidiary.

lesson *noun* **1** class, period, session. **3** message, moral, principle, rule, warning. **4** passage, reading.

let *verb* **1** agree to, allow, consent to, enable, permit. **4** lease, rent.

let down 1 deflate. **2** disappoint, fail, leave high and dry, leave in the lurch.

let-down *noun* anticlimax, comedown, disappointment, disillusionment.

let off 1 detonate, discharge, explode, set off. **2** excuse, exempt, pardon, release, reprieve, spare.

let on admit, confess, disclose, divulge, give away, let slip, reveal.

let out 1 free, let go, let loose, liberate, release, set free. **2** enlarge, loosen.

let up abate, ease, lessen, relax, slacken, subside.

▶▶ D I C T I O N A R Y ◀◀

lethal (*say* **lee**-thal) *adjective* deadly; causing death. **lethally** *adverb*

lethargy (*say* **leth**-er-jee) *noun* extreme lack of energy or vitality; sluggishness. **lethargic** (*say* lith-**ar**-jik) *adjective*

letter *noun* **1** a symbol representing a sound used in speech. **2** a written message, usually sent by post. [from Latin *littera* = letter of the alphabet]

letterbox *noun* a box or slot through which you can receive letters or a box where you can post letters.

lettering *noun* letters drawn or painted.

lettuce *noun* a garden plant with broad crisp leaves eaten as salad.

leukaemia (*say* lew-**kee**-mee-a) *noun* a disease in which there are too many white corpuscles in the blood. [from Greek *leukos* = white, + *haima* = blood]

level¹ *adjective* **1** flat; horizontal. **2** at the same height or position etc. as others. **3** steady, uniform.
level crossing a place where a road crosses a railway at the same level.

level² *noun* **1** height, depth, position, or value etc., *Fix the shelves at eye level*. **2** a level surface. **3** a device that shows whether something is level. **4** a floor of a building, ship, etc. **on the level** (*informal*) honest.

level³ *verb* (**levelled, levelling**) **1** make or become level. **2** aim a gun or missile. **3** direct an accusation at a person. **4** knock a building down to the ground. [from Latin *libra* = balance]

lever¹ *noun* **1** a bar that turns on a fixed point (the *fulcrum*) in order to lift something or force something open. **2** a bar used as a handle to operate machinery etc., *a gear-lever*.

lever² *verb* lift or move by means of a lever. [from Latin *levare* = raise]

leverage *noun* **1** the action or power of a lever. **2** influence.

leveret *noun* a young hare.

levitation *noun* rising into the air and floating there.

levity *noun* being humorous, especially at an unsuitable time; frivolity. [from Latin *levis* = lightweight]

levy *verb* (**levied, levying**) **1** impose or collect a tax or other payment by the use of authority or force. **2** enrol, *levy an army*. **levy** *noun*

lewd *adjective* indecent; obscene. **lewdly** *adverb*, **lewdness** *noun*

lexicography *noun* the process of writing dictionaries. **lexicographer** *noun* [from Greek *lexis* = word, + *-graphy*]

liability *noun* (*plural* **liabilities**) **1** being liable. **2** a debt or obligation. **3** (*informal*) a disadvantage; a handicap.

liable *adjective* **1** likely to do or get something, *She is liable to colds. The cliff is liable to crumble*. **2** legally responsible for something.

liaise (*say* lee-**ayz**) *verb* (**liaised, liaising**) (*informal*) act as a liaison or go-between.

▶▶ T H E S A U R U S ◀◀

lethal *adjective* deadly, fatal, mortal, poisonous, toxic.

lethargy *noun* indolence, inertia, languor, lassitude, listlessness, sluggishness, torpor, weariness.

letter *noun* **1** character, symbol. **2** communication, dispatch, epistle, message, missive, note; (*letters*) correspondence, mail, post.

letterbox *noun* mailbox, pillar box (*old use*), postbox.

level¹ *adjective* **1** even, flat, horizontal, plane, smooth. **2** equal, even, neck and neck, tied. **3** constant, steady, unchanging, uniform.

level² *noun* **1** altitude, amount, degree, depth, grade, elevation, height, measure, position, rank, rung, stage, standard, value. **4** deck, floor, storey, tier.

level³ *verb* **1** even out, tie. **2** aim, direct, point, train. **4** demolish, flatten, knock down, raze, tear down, topple.

lever¹ *noun* **2** control, handle.

lever² *verb* prise, wrench.

levy *verb* **1** charge, collect, exact, impose.
levy *noun* charge, duty, excise, impost, tariff, tax, toll.

lewd *adjective* bawdy, blue, crude, dirty, indecent, obscene, ribald, salacious, vulgar.

liability *noun* **1** accountability, answerability, responsibility. **2** debt, obligation, responsibility. **3** burden, disadvantage, drawback, encumbrance, handicap, millstone.

liable *adjective* **1** (*liable to colds*) prone, subject, susceptible, vulnerable; (*liable to cry*) apt, inclined, likely, prone. **2** accountable, answerable, responsible.

▶▶ D I C T I O N A R Y ◀◀

liaison (*say* lee-**ay**-zon) *noun* **1** communication and cooperation between people or groups. **2** a person who is a link or go-between. [from French *lier* = bind]

liar *noun* a person who tells lies.

libel¹ (*say* **ly**-bel) *noun* an untrue written, printed, or broadcast statement that damages a person's reputation. (Compare *slander*.) **libellous** *adjective*

libel² *verb* (**libelled**, **libelling**) make a libel against someone. [from Latin *libellus* = little book]

Liberal *noun* a member of the Liberal Party, a political party favouring private enterprise.

liberal *adjective* **1** giving generously. **2** given in large amounts. **3** not strict; tolerant. **liberally** *adverb*, **liberality** *noun* [from Latin *liber* = free]

liberalise *verb* (**liberalised**, **liberalising**) make less strict. **liberalisation** *noun*

liberate *verb* (**liberated**, **liberating**) set free. **liberation** *noun*, **liberator** *noun* [same origin as *liberty*]

liberty *noun* freedom.
take liberties behave too casually; be presumptuous. [from Latin *liber* = free]

librarian *noun* a person in charge of or assisting in a library. **librarianship** *noun*

library (*say* **ly**-bra-ree) *noun* (*plural* **libraries**) **1** a place where books are kept for people to use or borrow. **2** a collection of books, records, films, etc. [from Latin *libri* = books]

libretto *noun* (*plural* **librettos**) the words of an opera or other long musical work. [Italian = little book]

lice *plural* of **louse**.

licence *noun* **1** an official permit to do or use or own something, *a driving-licence*. **2** special freedom to avoid the usual rules or customs. [from Latin *licere* = be allowed]

license *verb* (**licensed**, **licensing**) give a licence to a person; authorise, *We are licensed to sell tobacco.*

licensee *noun* a person who holds a licence, especially to sell alcohol.

licentious (*say* ly-**sen**-shus) *adjective* breaking the rules of conduct; immoral. **licentiousness** *noun*

lichen (*say* **ly**-ken or **lich**-en) *noun* a dry-looking plant that grows on rocks, walls, trees, etc.

lick¹ *verb* **1** pass the tongue over something. **2** (of a wave or flame) move like a tongue; touch lightly. **3** (*informal*) defeat.

lick² *noun* **1** the act of licking. **2** a slight application of paint etc. **3** (*slang*) a fast pace.

lid *noun* **1** a cover for a box or pot etc. **2** an eyelid.

lido (*say* **leed**-oh) *noun* (*plural* **lidos**) a public open-air swimming-pool or pleasure-beach. [from Lido, the name of a beach near Venice]

lie¹ *noun* a statement that the person who makes it knows to be untrue.

lie² *verb* (**lied**, **lying**) tell a lie or lies; be deceptive.

lie³ *verb* (**lay**, **lain**, **lying**) **1** be or get in a flat or resting position, *He lay on the grass. The cat has lain here all night.* **2** be situated, *The island lies near the coast.* **3** remain, *The machinery lay idle.*
lie low keep yourself hidden.

Usage See the note on *lay*¹.

▶▶ T H E S A U R U S ◀◀

liaison *noun* **1** communication, contact, co-operation. **2** contact, coordinator, go-between, link, mediator.

liar *noun* fibber, storyteller (*informal*).

libel¹ *noun* calumny, defamation, denigration, false statement, slander, slur, smear, vilification.

libel² *verb* defame, denigrate, discredit, malign, slander, smear, vilify.

liberal *adjective* **2** abundant, ample, copious, extravagant, generous, lavish, plentiful. **3** broad-minded, enlightened, flexible, lax, open-minded, permissive, tolerant, unbiased, unprejudiced.

liberate *verb* deliver, emancipate, free, let go, release, set free.

liberation *noun* deliverance, emancipation, freedom, liberty, release.

liberty *noun* autonomy, freedom, independence, self-determination, self-rule.

licence *noun* **1** authorisation, franchise, permit, warrant.

license *verb* allow, authorise, permit.

lick¹ *verb* **1** lap, tongue.

lid *noun* **1** cap, cover, top.

lie¹ *noun* falsehood, fib, porky (*slang*), story (*informal*), untruth, whopper (*slang*).

lie² *verb* bluff, deceive, dissemble, fib, perjure yourself, prevaricate.

lie³ *verb* **1** recline, rest, sprawl. **2** be, be found, be located, be situated. **3** be, remain, stay.
lie low go into hiding, go to ground, hide, keep a low profile (*informal*), take cover.

▶▶ DICTIONARY ◀◀

lie⁴ *noun* the way something lies, *the lie of the land*.

liege (*say* leej) *noun* (*old use*) a person entitled to receive feudal service or allegiance (*a liege lord*) or bound to give it (*a liege man*).

lieu (*say* lew) *noun* **in lieu** instead, *He accepted a cheque in lieu of cash.* [French, = place]

lieutenant (*say* lef-**ten**-ant) *noun* **1** an officer in the army or navy. **2** a deputy or chief assistant. [from French *lieu* = place, + *tenant* = holding]

life *noun* (*plural* **lives**) **1** the ability to function and grow; the period between birth and death. **2** living things, *Is there life on Mars?* **3** liveliness, *full of life.* **4** a biography.

lifebelt *noun* a circle of material that will float, used to support someone's body in water.

lifeboat *noun* a boat for rescuing people at sea.

lifebuoy *noun* a device to support someone's body in water.

lifeguard *noun* someone whose job is to rescue swimmers who are in difficulty.

life-jacket *noun* a jacket of material that will float, used to support someone's body in water.

lifeless *adjective* **1** without life. **2** unconscious. **lifelessly** *adverb*

lifelike *adjective* looking exactly like a real person or thing.

lifelong *adjective* continuing for the whole of someone's life.

lifetime *noun* the time for which someone is alive.

lift¹ *verb* **1** raise; pick up. **2** rise; go upwards. **3** (*informal*) steal. **4** remove; abolish, *The ban has been lifted.*

lift² *noun* **1** the act of lifting. **2** a device for taking people or goods from one floor or level to another in a building. **3** a free ride in somebody else's vehicle.

lift-off *noun* the vertical take-off of a rocket or spacecraft.

ligament *noun* a piece of the tough flexible tissue that holds bones etc. together. [from Latin *ligare* = bind]

ligature *noun* a thing used in tying something, especially in surgical operations. [from Latin *ligare* = bind]

light¹ *noun* **1** radiation that stimulates the sense of sight and makes things visible. **2** something that provides light, especially an electric lamp. **3** a flame.
bring or **come to light** make or become known.

light² *adjective* **1** full of light; not dark. **2** pale, *light blue.*

light³ *verb* (**lit** or **lighted, lighting**) **1** start a thing burning; kindle. **2** provide the light.
light up put lights on, especially at dusk; make or become light or bright.

Usage Say *He lit the lamps; the lamps were lit* (not 'lighted'), but *She carried a lighted torch* (not 'a lit torch').

▶▶ THESAURUS ◀◀

lieu *noun* **in lieu of** instead of, in the place of.

lieutenant *noun* **2** assistant, deputy.

life *noun* **1** being, existence, survival. **2** flora and fauna, living things. **3** animation, energy, exuberance, go, liveliness, vigour, vitality, vivacity. **4** autobiography, biography.

lifeless *adjective* **1** dead, deceased, inanimate, inert, non-living. **2** blacked out, comatose, insensible, knocked out, senseless, unconscious.

lifelike *adjective* accurate, authentic, realistic, true to life.

lifelong *adjective* abiding, enduring, lasting, permanent.

lifetime *noun* existence, life, life span.

lift¹ *verb* **1** boost, elevate, hoist, jack up, pick up, push up, raise. **2** ascend, climb, go upwards, mount, rise, soar. **3** see STEAL. **4** cancel, remove, revoke, withdraw.

lift² *noun* **2** elevator.

lift-off *noun* blast-off, launch, take-off.

light¹ *noun* **1** blaze, brightness, brilliance, flash, glare, glow, illumination, incandescence, radiance, reflection. **2** beacon, candle, floodlight, headlight, lamp, lantern, spotlight, torch.
bring to light disclose, expose, reveal, uncover.
come to light appear, become apparent, come out, emerge, transpire.

light² *adjective* **1** bright, illuminated, well-lit. **2** delicate, pale, pastel, soft.

light³ *verb* **1** ignite, kindle, set alight, start.
light up brighten, illuminate, lighten.

light⁴ *adjective* **1** delicate, flimsy, lightweight,

▶▶ D I C T I O N A R Y ◀◀

light⁴ *adjective* **1** having little weight; not heavy. **2** small in amount or force etc., *light rain*; *a light punishment.* **3** needing little effort, *light work.* **4** cheerful, not sad, *with a light heart.* **5** not serious or profound, *light music.* **lightly** *adverb*, **lightness** *noun*
light industry industry producing small or light articles.

light⁵ *adverb* lightly; with only a small load, *We were travelling light.*

lighten¹ *verb* **1** make or become lighter or brighter. **2** producing lighting.

lighten² *verb* make or become lighter or less heavy.

lighter *noun* a device for lighting cigarettes etc.

light-headed *adjective* feeling slightly faint or giddy.

light-hearted *adjective* cheerful; free from worry; not serious.

lighthouse *noun* a tower with a bright light at the top to guide or warn ships.

lighting *noun* lamps, or the light they provide.

lightning *noun* a flash of bright light produced by natural electricity during a thunderstorm.
lightning conductor a metal rod or wire fixed on a building to divert lightning into the earth.
like lightning with very great speed.

lightweight *noun* **1** a person who is not heavy. **2** a boxer weighing between 57 and 60 kg. **lightweight** *adjective*

light-year *noun* the distance that light travels in one year (about 6 million million miles, or 9.5 million million kilometres).

like¹ *verb* (**liked**, **liking**) **1** think a person or thing is pleasant or satisfactory. **2** wish, *I should like to come.*

like² *adjective* similar; having some or all of the qualities of another person or thing, *They are as like as two peas.*

like³ *noun* a similar person or thing, *We shall not see his like again.*

like⁴ *preposition* **1** similar to; in the manner of, *He swims like a fish.* **2** in a suitable state for, *It looks like rain.*

likeable *adjective* easy to like; pleasant.

likelihood *noun* being likely; probability.

likely *adjective* (**likelier**, **likeliest**) **1** probable; expected to happen or be true etc., *Rain is likely.* **2** expected to be successful, *a likely lad.*

liken *verb* compare, *He likened the human heart to a pump.*

likeness *noun* (*plural* **likenesses**) **1** being like; a resemblance. **2** a portrait.

likewise *adverb* similarly.

liking *noun* a feeling that you like something, *She has a liking for ice-cream.*

lilac *noun* **1** a bush with fragrant purple or white flowers. **2** pale purple.

lilly-pilly *noun* a small eastern Australian tree or its edible purplish to white berries.

lilt *noun* a light pleasant rhythm. **lilting** *adjective*

lily *noun* (*plural* **lilies**) a garden plant with trumpet-shaped flowers, growing from a bulb.

▶▶ T H E S A U R U S ◀◀

portable, thin. **2** faint, fine, gentle, low, moderate, slight. **3** easy, effortless, simple, undemanding. **5** entertaining, frivolous, superficial.

lighten¹ *verb* **1** brighten, illuminate, light up.

lighten² *verb* alleviate, ease, lessen, mitigate, reduce, relieve.

light-headed *adjective* dizzy, faint, giddy, woozy (*informal*).

light-hearted *adjective* blithe, bright, carefree, cheerful, gay, happy, jolly, merry.

lighthouse *noun* beacon.

like¹ *verb* **1** admire, appreciate, approve of, be fond of, be keen on, delight in, enjoy, fancy, relish; see also LOVE². **2** care, desire, have a mind to, want, wish.

like² *adjective* corresponding, identical, matching, similar, the same.

likeable *adjective* agreeable, amiable, attractive, charming, congenial, friendly, genial, pleasant, pleasing, winsome.

likelihood *noun* chance, possibility, probability, prospect.

likely *adjective* **1** believable, credible, expected, plausible, probable. **2** appropriate, fitting, promising, qualified, suitable.

liken *verb* compare, draw an analogy between, equate.

likeness *noun* **1** resemblance, sameness, similarity. **2** copy, picture, portrait, replica, representation.

liking *noun* affinity, appetite, appreciation, fondness, partiality, penchant, preference, taste.

▶▶ D I C T I O N A R Y ◀◀

limb *noun* **1** a leg, arm, or wing. **2** a projecting part, e.g. a bough of a tree.
out on a limb isolated; stranded.

limber *verb* **limber up** exercise in preparation for an athletic activity.

limbo *noun* intermediate state where nothing is happening, *Lack of money has left our plans in limbo.* [from the name of a region formerly thought to exist on the border of hell]

lime¹ *noun* a white substance (calcium oxide) used in making cement and as a fertiliser.

lime² *noun* a green fruit like a small round lemon. **lime-juice** *noun*

lime³ *noun* a tree with yellow flowers.

limelight *noun* great publicity. [from *lime¹* which gives a bright light when heated, formerly used to light up the stage of a theatre]

limerick *noun* a type of comical poem with five lines. [named after Limerick, a town in Ireland]

limestone *noun* a kind of rock from which lime (calcium oxide) is obtained.

limit¹ *noun* **1** a line, point, or level where something ends. **2** the greatest amount allowed, *the speed limit.*

limit² *verb* **1** keep within certain limits. **2** be a limit to something. **limitation** *noun* [from Latin *limes* = boundary]

limited *adjective* **1** kept within limits; restricted; small. **2** that is a **limited company** or

limited liability company, a business company whose members would have to pay only some of its debts, *'Ltd.' after the name of a business shows that it is a limited company.*

limousine (*say* lim-oo-**zeen**) *noun* a luxurious car.

limp¹ *verb* walk lamely.

limp² *noun* a limping walk.

limp³ *adjective* **1** not stiff or firm. **2** without strength or energy. **limply** *adverb*, **limpness** *noun*

limpet *noun* a small shellfish that attaches itself firmly to rocks.

limpid *adjective* (of liquids) clear; transparent. **limpidity** *noun*

linchpin *noun* a pin passed through the end of an axle to keep a wheel in position.

line¹ *noun* **1** a long thin mark. **2** a crease or wrinkle in the skin. **3** a limit or boundary. **4** a row or series of people or things; a row of words. **5** a length of rope, string, wire, etc. used for a special purpose, *a fishing-line.* **6** a railway; a line of railway track. **7** a system of ships, aircraft, buses, etc. **8** a way of doing things or behaving. **9** a type of business.
in line forming a straight line; conforming.

line² *verb* (**lined, lining**) **1** mark with lines, *Use lined paper.* **2** form into a line or lines, *Line them up.* [from Latin *linea* = linen thread]

line³ *verb* (**lined, lining**) cover the inside of something. [from *linen* (used for linings)]

lineage (*say* **lin**-ee-ij) *noun* ancestry; a line of descendants from an ancestor.

▶▶ T H E S A U R U S ◀◀

limb *noun* **1** appendage, arm, leg, wing. **2** bough, branch.
out on a limb alone, isolated, stranded.

limber *verb* **limber up** exercise, loosen up, prepare, warm up.

limbo *noun* **in limbo** half-finished, in abeyance, suspended, unfinished, up in the air.

limelight *noun* prominence, public eye, publicity, spotlight.

limit¹ *noun* **1** border, boundary, bounds, confines, edge, end, extent, frontier, perimeter. **2** ceiling, cut-off, limitation, maximum, restriction.

limit² *verb* **1** check, confine, contain, control, curb, restrain, restrict.
limitation *noun* deficiency, shortcoming, weakness.

limited *adjective* **1** minimal, restricted, scanty, small.

limp¹ *verb* falter, hobble, shuffle.

limp³ *adjective* **1** droopy, flaccid, floppy, lifeless, wilted.

line¹ *noun* **1** band, dash, mark, score, slash, streak, strip, stripe, stroke. **2** crease, crow's-foot, furrow, wrinkle. **3** border, borderline, boundary, limit. **4** chain, column, cordon, crocodile, file, procession, queue, row, series. **5** cable, cord, hawser, lead, rope, string, wire. **6** branch, route, track. **7** company, fleet. **8** course, direction, path, tack, tendency, track, trend, way.
in line with conforming with, in accordance with, in agreement with, in keeping with, in step with.

line² *verb* **1** rule. **2** align, form a line, queue up, straighten.

lineage *noun* ancestry, descent, extraction, family, genealogy, line, origins, pedigree.

DICTIONARY

lineal (*say* **lin**-ee-al) *adjective* of or in a line, especially as a descendant.

linear (*say* **lin**-ee-er) *adjective* **1** of a line; of length. **2** arranged in a line.

line-ball *noun* **1** a ball striking the boundary line in tennis. **2** (*Australian*) an indecisive event, a borderline case.

linen *noun* **1** cloth made from flax. **2** shirts, sheets, and tablecloths etc. (which were formerly made of linen). [from Latin *linum* = flax]

liner *noun* a large ship or aircraft on a regular route, usually carrying passengers.

linesman *noun* (*plural* **linesmen**) an official in football or tennis etc. who decides whether the ball has crossed a line.

linger *verb* stay for a long time, as if unwilling to leave; be slow to leave.

lingerie (*say* **lan**-*zh*er-ee) *noun* women's underwear. [from French *linge* = linen]

linguist *noun* an expert in languages. [from Latin *lingua* = language]

linguistics *noun* the study of languages. **linguistic** *adjective*

liniment *noun* a liquid for rubbing on the skin to relieve soreness.

lining *noun* a layer that covers the inside of something. (Compare *line³*.)

link¹ *noun* **1** one ring or loop of a chain. **2** a connection.

link² *verb* join things together; connect. **linkage** *noun*

links *noun* or *plural noun* a golf-course.

linnet *noun* a kind of finch.

lino *noun* linoleum.

linocut *noun* a print made from a design cut into a block of thick linoleum.

linoleum *noun* a stiff shiny floor-covering. [from Latin *linum* = flax, + *oleum* = oil]

linseed *noun* the seed of flax, from which oil is obtained. [from Latin *linum* = flax, + *seed*]

lint *noun* a soft material for covering wounds.

lintel *noun* a horizontal piece of wood or stone etc. above a door or other opening.

lion *noun* a large strong flesh-eating animal found in Africa and India. **lioness** *noun*

lip *noun* **1** either of the two fleshy edges of the mouth. **2** the edge of something hollow, such as a cup or crater. **3** a projecting part at the top of a jug etc., shaped for pouring things.

lip-reading *noun* understanding what a person says by watching the movements of his or her lips, not by hearing.

lip-service *noun* **pay lip-service to something** say that you approve of it but do nothing to support it.

lipstick *noun* a stick of a waxy substance for colouring the lips.

liquefy *verb* (**liquefied, liquefying**) make or become liquid. **liquefaction** *noun*

liqueur (*say* lik-**yoor**) *noun* a strong sweet alcoholic drink. [French, = liquor]

liquid¹ *noun* a substance (such as water or oil) that flows freely but is not a gas.

liquid² *adjective* **1** in the form of a liquid; flowing freely. **2** easily converted into cash, *the firm's liquid assets.* **liquidity** *noun* [from Latin *liquidus* = flowing]

liquidate *verb* (**liquidated, liquidating**) **1** pay off or settle a debt. **2** close down a business and divide its value between its creditors. **3** get rid of, especially by killing. **liquidation** *noun*, **liquidator** *noun*

liquidise *verb* (**liquidised, liquidising**) cause to become liquid; crush into a liquid pulp. **liquidiser** *noun*

liquor *noun* **1** alcoholic drink. **2** juice produced in cooking; liquid in which food has been cooked.

THESAURUS

linen *noun* **2** manchester, napery.

linger *verb* dally, dawdle, delay, dilly-dally, hang about, hang around, loiter, remain, stay, take your time, tarry.

lingerie *noun* corsetry, underclothes, undergarments, underwear, undies (*informal*).

liniment *noun* balm, embrocation, ointment, salve.

lining *noun* backing, facing, interfacing.

link¹ *noun* **1** loop, ring. **2** association, bond, connection, relationship, tie, tie-up.

link² *verb* associate, connect, identify, join, relate, tie up, unite.

lion *noun* cub (*young*), king of beasts, lioness (*female*).

lip *noun* **2** brim, edge, rim.

liquid¹ *noun* fluid, juice, liquor, solution.

liquid² *adjective* **1** flowing, fluid, molten, runny, watery.

liquidate *verb* **1** clear, discharge, pay, settle. **2** close down, dissolve, wind up. **3** do away with, eliminate, exterminate, get rid of, remove; see also KILL¹.

liquidise *verb* crush, liquefy, pulp, purée.

liquor *noun* **1** alcohol, drink, grog (*Australian*), spirits.

▶▷ D I C T I O N A R Y ◁◀

liquorice *noun* **1** a black substance used in medicine and as a sweet. **2** the plant from whose root this substance is obtained. [from Greek *glykys* = sweet, + *rhiza* = root]

lisp *noun* a fault in speech in which *s* and *z* are pronounced like *th*. **lisp** *verb*

list¹ *noun* a number of names, items, or figures etc. written or printed one after another.

list² *verb* make a list of people or things. [from Old English *liste* = border]

list³ *verb* (of a ship) lean over to one side; tilt. **list** *noun* [origin unknown]

listen *verb* pay attention in order to hear something. **listener** *noun*

listless *adjective* too tired to be active or enthusiastic. **listlessly** *adverb*, **listlessness** *noun* [from an old word *list* = desire, + *-less*]

lit *past tense* of **light³**.

litany *noun* (*plural* **litanies**) a formal prayer with fixed responses.

literacy *noun* being literate; the ability to read and write.

literal *adjective* meaning exactly what is said, not metaphorical or exaggerated; precise. **literally** *adverb* [same origin as *letter*]

literary (*say* **lit**-er-er-i) *adjective* of literature; interested in literature.

literate *adjective* able to read and write. [same origin as *letter*]

literature *noun* **1** books and other writings, especially those considered to have been written well. **2** printed material, leaflets, etc. about a subject. [same origin as *letter*]

lithe *adjective* flexible; supple; agile.

litigant *noun* a person who is involved in a lawsuit. [from Latin *litigare* = start a lawsuit]

litigation *noun* a lawsuit; the process of carrying on a lawsuit.

litmus *noun* a blue substance that is turned red by acids and can be turned back to blue by alkalis.
litmus-paper *noun* paper stained with litmus.

litre *noun* a measure of liquid, 1000 millilitres, equivalent to four standard cups.

litter¹ *noun* **1** rubbish or untidy things left lying about. **2** straw etc. put down as bedding for animals. **3** the young animals born to one mother at one time. **4** a kind of stretcher.

litter² *verb* **1** make a place untidy with litter. **2** spread straw etc. for animals.

little¹ *adjective* (**less**, **least**) **1** small in amount or size or intensity etc.; not great or big or much. **2** trivial; unimportant.
little by little gradually; by a small amount at a time.

little² *adverb* not much, *I eat very little*.

liturgy *noun* (*plural* **liturgies**) a fixed form of public worship used in churches. **liturgical** *adjective*

live¹ (rhymes with *give*) *verb* (**lived**, **living**) **1** have life; be alive; stay alive. **2** have your home, *She lives in Denmark*. **3** pass your life in a certain way, *He lived as a hermit*.
live on use something as food; depend on for your living.

▶▷ T H E S A U R U S ◁◀

list¹ *noun* catalogue, directory, index, inventory, register, roll, schedule, series, table.

list² *verb* catalogue, enter, enumerate, index, itemise, note, record, register, write down.

list³ *verb* heel, lean, tilt, tip over.

listen *verb* lend an ear, pay attention, pay heed, take notice, tune in.
listen in bug (*informal*), eavesdrop, overhear, tap.
listener *noun* auditor, hearer; (*listeners*) audience.

listless *adjective* apathetic, languid, lethargic, lifeless, sluggish, tired, torpid, unenthusiastic.

literal *adjective* exact, precise, strict, true, verbatim, word for word.

literate *adjective* educated, well-read.

literature *noun* **1** letters, writings, written works. **2** booklets, brochures, handouts, information, leaflets, material, pamphlets.

lithe *adjective* agile, flexible, limber, lissom, nimble, pliant, supple.

litter¹ *noun* **1** debris, garbage, mess, refuse, rubbish, trash, waste. **3** brood, family, group.

litter² *verb* **1** clutter, mess up, scatter, strew.

little¹ *adjective* **1** baby, brief, compact, concise, diminutive, dwarf, microscopic, midget, miniature, minuscule, minute, petite, pocket-sized, puny, short, slight, small, stunted, tiny, undersized, wee; (*little in amount*) inadequate, meagre, measly (*informal*), scanty, skimpy, small, stingy. **2** insignificant, marginal, minimal, minor, negligible, petty, slight, trivial, unimportant.
little by little bit by bit, by degrees, gradually, progressively, slowly.

live¹ *verb* **1** be, be alive, breathe, continue, endure, exist, keep going, last, persist, remain, stay alive, subsist, survive. **2** abide (*old use*), dwell, reside; see also INHABIT.

►►DICTIONARY◄◄

live² (rhymes with *hive*) *adjective* **1** alive. **2** burning, *live coals.* **3** carrying electricity. **4** broadcast while it is actually happening, not from a recording.
live wire a wire carrying electricity; a forceful energetic person.

livelihood *noun* a living (= *living²* 3).

lively *adjective* (**livelier, liveliest**) full of life or action; vigorous and cheerful. **liveliness** *noun*

liven *verb* make or become lively, *liven things up.*

liver *noun* **1** a large organ of the body, found in the abdomen, that processes digested food and produces bile. **2** an animal's liver used as food.

livery *noun* (*plural* **liveries**) **1** a uniform worn by male servants in a household. **2** the distinctive colours used by a railway or bus company etc.
livery stables a place where horses are kept for their owner or where horses may be hired.

livestock *noun* farm animals.

livid *adjective* **1** bluish-grey, *a livid bruise.* **2** (*informal*) furiously angry.

living¹ *adjective* alive.

living² *noun* **1** being alive. **2** the way that a person lives, *a good standard of living.* **3** a way of earning money or providing enough food to support yourself.

living room a room for general use during the day.

lizard *noun* a reptile with a rough or scaly skin, four legs, and a long tail.

llama (*say* **lah**-ma) *noun* a South American animal with woolly fur, like a camel but with no hump.

lo *interjection* (*old use*) see, behold.

load¹ *noun* **1** something carried; a burden. **2** the quantity that can be carried. **3** the total amount of electric current supplied. **4** (*informal*) a large amount, *It's a load of nonsense.*

load² *verb* **1** put a load in or on something. **2** fill heavily. **3** weight with something heavy, *loaded dice.* **4** put a bullet or shell into a gun; put a film into a camera. **5** enter data etc. into a computer.

loading *noun* (*Australian*) payment in addition to wages for skill, productivity, etc.

loaf¹ *noun* (*plural* **loaves**) **1** a shaped mass of bread baked in one piece. **2** minced or chopped meat etc. moulded into an oblong shape. **3** (*slang*) the head, *Use your loaf.* [from Old English *hlaf*]

loaf² *verb* spend time idly; loiter or stand about. **loafer** *noun*

loam *noun* rich soil containing clay, sand and decayed leaves etc. **loamy** *adjective*

loan¹ *noun* **1** something lent, especially money. **2** lending; being lent, *These books are on loan from the library.*

loan² *verb* lend.

Usage Many people dislike the use of this verb except when it means to lend money. (It is really better to use *lend* in all cases.)

loath (rhymes with *both*) *adjective* unwilling, *I was loath to go.*

►►THESAURUS◄◄

live² *adjective* **1** alive, animate, breathing, living, surviving. **2** burning, glowing, hot.

livelihood *noun* crust (*Australian informal*), income, living, means of support.

lively *adjective* active, animated, boisterous, cheerful, chirpy, energetic, enthusiastic, full of beans (*informal*), irrepressible, perky, spirited, sprightly, spry, vigorous, vivacious.

liven *verb* brighten up, buck up (*informal*), cheer up, perk up.

livestock *noun* animals, stock.

livid *adjective* **2** see ANGRY.

living¹ *adjective* alive, animate, breathing, live, quick (*old use*).

living² *noun* **1** being alive, existence, life. **3** crust (*Australian informal*), income, livelihood, means of support; see also JOB.

living room drawing room, family room, lounge, lounge room, parlour (*old use*), sitting room.

load¹ *noun* **1** burden, cargo, consignment, freight, shipment; see also WEIGHT. **4** see LOT.

load² *verb* **2** fill, pack, pile up.

loading *noun* allowance, margin.

loaf² *verb* idle, laze, lounge, take it easy, veg out (*slang*).
loafer *noun* bludger (*Australian informal*), bum (*slang*), couch potato (*informal*), good-for-nothing, idler, layabout, lazybones (*informal*), shirker, skiver (*informal*), slacker.

loan¹ *noun* advance, credit, mortgage.

loan² *verb* advance, lend.

loath *adjective* disinclined, reluctant, unwilling.

▶▶ D I C T I O N A R Y ◀◀

loathe (rhymes with *clothe*) *verb* (**loathed**, **loathing**) feel great hatred and disgust for something; detest. **loathing** *noun*

loathsome *adjective* arousing a feeling of loathing; detestable.

lob¹ *verb* (**lobbed**, **lobbing**) send a ball in a high curve into the air.

lob² *noun* a lobbed ball.

lobby¹ *noun* (*plural* **lobbies**) **1** an entrance hall. **2** a group who lobby Members of Parliament etc.

lobby² *verb* (**lobbied**, **lobbying**) try to influence a Member of Parliament etc. in favour of a special interest.

lobe *noun* a rounded fairly flat part of a leaf or an organ of the body; the rounded soft part at the bottom of an ear. **lobar** *adjective*, **lobed** *adjective*

lobster *noun* a large crustacean with eight legs and two long claws.

lobster-pot *noun* a basket for catching lobsters.

local¹ *adjective* **1** belonging to a particular place or a small area. **2** of or affecting a particular part. **locally** *adverb*
local anaesthetic an anaesthetic affecting only the part of the body where it is applied.
local government the organisation of the affairs of a town or district etc. by people elected by those who live there.

local² *noun* (*informal*) someone who lives in a particular district. [from Latin *locus* = place]

localise *verb* (**localised**, **localising**) keep something within a particular area. **localisation** *noun*

locality *noun* (*plural* **localities**) a district; a location.

locate *verb* (**located**, **locating**) **1** discover where something is, *locate the electrical fault*. **2** situate something in a particular place, *the cinema is located in Pitt Street*.

location *noun* **1** the place where something is situated. **2** discovering where something is; locating.
on location filmed in natural surroundings, not in a studio.

loch *noun* a lake in Scotland.

lock¹ *noun* **1** a fastening that is opened with a key or other device. **2** a section of a canal or river fitted with gates and sluices so that boats can be raised or lowered to the level beyond each gate. **3** a wrestling-hold that keeps an opponent's arm or leg from moving. **4** the distance that a vehicle's front wheels can be turned by the steering wheel.
lock, stock, and barrel completely.

lock² *verb* **1** fasten or secure by means of a lock. **2** store away securely. **3** become fixed in one place; jam.
lock up imprison.

lock³ *noun* a clump of hair.
locks *plural noun* the hair of the head.

locker *noun* a small cupboard or compartment where things can be stowed safely.

locket *noun* a small ornamental case for holding a portrait or lock of hair etc., worn on a chain round the neck.

locksmith *noun* a person whose job is to make and mend locks.

locomotive¹ *noun* a railway engine.

locomotive² *adjective* of movement or the ability to move, *locomotive power*. **locomotion** *noun* [from Latin *locus* = place, + *motivus* = moving]

▶▶ T H E S A U R U S ◀◀

loathe *verb* abhor, abominate, despise, detest, dislike, hate.

loathsome *adjective* abhorrent, abominable, despicable, detestable, disgusting, hateful, odious, offensive, repugnant, repulsive.

lob¹ *verb* see THROW.

lobby¹ *noun* **1** corridor, entrance hall, foyer, hall, porch, vestibule. **2** force, pressure group.

lobby² *verb* campaign, petition, push.

local¹ *adjective* **1** area, community, district, neighbourhood, provincial, regional. **2** confined, localised, restricted.

local² *noun* inhabitant, native, resident.

localise *verb* confine, contain, limit, restrict.

locality *noun* area, community, district, neighbourhood, region, suburb, vicinity.

locate *verb* **1** detect, discover, find, identify, pinpoint. **2** place, position, put, site, situate.

location *noun* **1** area, locality, place, position, setting, site, spot, whereabouts.

lock¹ *noun* **1** bar, bolt, catch, latch, padlock, snib.

lock² *verb* **1** bar, bolt, fasten, secure, snib.
lock up imprison, incarcerate, intern, jail, put away.

lock³ *noun* tress, tuft.

locker *noun* cabinet, compartment, cupboard.

locomotion *noun* mobility, motion, movement, moving, transport, travel.

▶▶ D I C T I O N A R Y ◀◀

locum *noun* a doctor or member of the clergy who takes the place of another who is temporarily away. [short for Latin *locum tenens* = person holding the place]

locus (*say* **loh**-kus) *noun* (*plural* **loci**, *say* **loh**-sy) **1** the exact place of something. **2** (in geometry) the path traced by a moving point, or made by points placed in a certain way. [Latin, = place]

locust *noun* a kind of grasshopper that travels in large swarms which eat all the plants in an area.

locution *noun* a word or phrase. [from Latin *locutum* = spoken]

lodestone *noun* a kind of stone that can be used as a magnet.

lodge¹ *noun* **1** a small house, especially at the gates of a park. **2** a cabin or hut; a holiday house, *a ski lodge.* **3** a beaver's or otter's lair. **The Lodge** (*Australian*) the official residence of the Prime Minister in Canberra.

lodge² *verb* (**lodged, lodging**) **1** stay somewhere as a lodger. **2** provide a person with somewhere to live temporarily. **3** deposit; be or become fixed, *The ball lodged in the tree.* **4** present formally for attention, *lodge a complaint.*

lodger *noun* a person who pays to live in another person's house.

lodgings *plural noun* a room or rooms (not in a hotel) rented for living in.

loft *noun* a room or storage-space under the roof of a house or barn etc.

lofty *adjective* **1** tall. **2** noble. **3** haughty. **loftily** *adverb*, **loftiness** *noun*

log¹ *noun* **1** a large piece of a tree that has fallen or been cut down; a piece cut off this. **2** a detailed record of a ship's voyage, aircraft's flight, etc. kept in a **logbook**. **log cabin** a hut built of logs.

log² *verb* (**logged, logging**) enter facts in a logbook. **log in** (or **on**), **log out** (or **off**) connect and disconnect a terminal correctly to or from a computer system.

log³ *noun* a logarithm, *log tables.*

loganberry *noun* (*plural* **loganberries**) a dark-red fruit like a blackberry.

logarithm *noun* one of a series of numbers set out in tables which make it possible to do sums by adding and subtracting instead of multiplying and dividing. [from Greek *logos* = reckoning, + *arithmos* = number]

loggerheads *plural noun* **at loggerheads** arguing; quarrelling.

logging *noun* cutting down trees for timber. **logger** *noun*

logic *noun* **1** reasoning; a system of reasoning. **2** the principles used in designing a computer; the circuits involved in this. [from Greek *logos* = word, reason]

logical *adjective* using logic; reasoning or reasoned correctly. **logically** *adverb*, **logicality** *noun*

Logie *noun* (*Australian*) a television award made by the proprietors of *TV Week.* [from John *Logie* Baird, Scottish inventor of television, who died in 1946]

logo (*say* **loh**-goh) *noun* (*plural* **logos**) a printed symbol used by a business company etc. as its emblem.

-logy *suffix* forming nouns meaning a subject of study (e.g. *biology*). [from Greek *-logia* = study]

loin *noun* the side and back of the body between the ribs and the hip-bone.

loincloth *noun* a piece of cloth worn round the hips as a garment.

loiter *verb* linger or stand about idly. **loiterer** *noun*

▶▶ T H E S A U R U S ◀◀

locum *noun* deputy, replacement, stand-in, substitute.

lodge¹ *noun* **1** cottage, gatehouse, home, house, residence. **2** cabin, chalet, hostel, hotel, motel, resort.

lodge² *verb* **1** board, live, reside, stay. **3** become embedded, get stuck, stick. **4** file, lay, make, register, submit.

lodger *noun* boarder, guest, tenant.

lodgings *plural noun* accommodation, billet, digs (*informal*), quarters, residence, room(s).

loft *noun* attic, garret.

lofty *adjective* **1** high, soaring, tall, towering. **2** exalted, high-minded, noble, sublime. **3** arrogant, disdainful, haughty, high and mighty, hoity-toity, proud, scornful, snooty (*informal*), supercilious.

log¹ *noun* **1** block, piece, stump. **2** diary, journal, logbook, record.

logical *adjective* coherent, intelligent, rational, reasonable, reasoned, sensible, sound, valid.

logo *noun* emblem, symbol, trade mark.

loiter *verb* dally, dawdle, hang around, linger, lurk, skulk.

loll *verb* lean lazily against something.

lollipop *noun* a large round hard sweet on a stick.

lolly *noun* (*plural* **lollies**) (*informal*) **1** (*Australian*) a sweet. **2** (*slang*) money.

lone *adjective* solitary. [from *alone*]

lonely *adjective* (**lonelier, loneliest**) **1** sad because you are on your own. **2** solitary. **3** far from inhabited places; not often visited or used, *a lonely road.* **loneliness** *noun* [from *lone*]

lonesome *adjective* lonely.

long¹ *adjective* **1** measuring a lot or a certain amount from one end to the other. **2** taking a lot of time, *a long holiday.* **3** having a certain length, *The line is 5cm long.* **4** lasting, *a long friendship.*
long division dividing one number by another and writing down all the calculations.

long² *adverb* **1** for a long time, *Have you been waiting long?* **2** at a long time before or after, *They left long ago.* **3** throughout a time, *all night long.*
as long as or **so long as** provided that; on condition that.

long³ *verb* feel a strong desire.

longevity (*say* lon-**jev**-it-ee) *noun* long life. [from Latin *longus* = long, + *aevum* = age]

longhand *noun* ordinary writing, contrasted with shorthand or typing.

longing *noun* a strong desire.

longitude *noun* the distance east or west, measured in degrees, from the Greenwich meridian.

longitudinal *adjective* **1** of longitude. **2** of length; measured lengthwise.

long-suffering *adjective* putting up with things patiently.

long-winded *adjective* talking or writing at great length.

loo *noun* (*informal*) a toilet.

loofah *noun* a rough sponge made from a dried gourd. [from Arabic *lufa*]

look¹ *verb* **1** use your eyes; turn your eyes in a particular direction. **2** face in a particular direction. **3** have a certain appearance; seem, *You look sad.*
look after protect; attend to somebody's needs; be in charge of something.
look down on despise.
look forward to be waiting eagerly for something you expect.
look in make a short visit.
look into investigate.
look out be careful.
look up search for information about something; improve in prospects, *Things are looking up.*
look up to admire or respect.

loll *verb* lie, lounge, recline, relax, slump, sprawl.

lolly *noun* **1** candy (*American*), confection, sweet, toffee.

lone *adjective* alone, lonely, single, sole, solitary, unaccompanied.

lonely *adjective* **1** forlorn, forsaken, friendless, lonesome. **2** companionless, isolated, solitary. **3** deserted, isolated, remote, secluded, unfrequented, uninhabited.

long¹ *adjective* **1,2** big, drawn-out, elongated, endless, extended, interminable, lengthy, prolonged, protracted, sustained, unending. **4** abiding, enduring, lasting, long-lasting, long-lived, long-standing, long-term, permanent.

long³ *verb* (*long for*) crave, desire, hanker after, hunger for, pine for, thirst for, want, wish for, yearn for.

longing *noun* appetite, craving, desire, hunger, thirst, urge, wish, yearning, yen.

long-suffering *adjective* forbearing, patient, tolerant.

long-winded *adjective* garrulous, loquacious, rambling, tedious, verbose, wordy.

look¹ *verb* **1** gape, gawp (*informal*), gaze, glance, glare, goggle, leer, ogle, peek, peep, peer, squint, stare; (*look at*) behold (*old use*), consider, contemplate, examine, eye, glimpse, inspect, observe, scrutinise, see, study, survey, view, watch, witness; (*look for*) check for, fossick for (*Australian informal*), hunt for, search for, seek. **2** face. **3** appear, seem.
look after attend to, care for, guard, mind, protect, take care of.
look down on despise, disdain, look down your nose at, patronise, scorn.
look forward to anticipate, await, long for.
look in call in, drop in, visit.
look into check on, examine, explore, go into, inquire into, investigate, probe, research.
look out beware, keep your eyes open, pay attention, take care, watch out.
look up 1 check, hunt for, search for, seek. **2** get better, improve, pick up.
look up to admire, esteem, idolise, respect, revere, worship.

▶▶ D I C T I O N A R Y ◀◀

look² *noun* **1** the act of looking; a gaze or glance. **2** appearance, *I don't like the look of this place.*

looker-on *noun* (*plural* **lookers-on**) a spectator; someone who sees what happens but takes no part in it.

looking-glass *noun* a glass mirror.

lookout *noun* **1** looking out or watching for something. **2** a place from which you can keep watch. **3** a person whose job is to keep watch. **4** a future prospect, *It's a poor lookout for us.* **5** (*informal*) a person's own concern, *If he wastes his money, that's his lookout.*

loom¹ *noun* an apparatus for weaving cloth.

loom² *verb* appear suddenly; seem large or close and threatening, *An iceberg loomed up through the fog.*

loony *adjective* (**loonier**, **looniest**) (*slang*) crazy. [short for *lunatic*]

loop¹ *noun* the shape made by a curve crossing itself; a piece of string, ribbon, wire, etc. made into this shape.

loop² *verb* **1** make into a loop. **2** enclose in a loop.

loophole *noun* **1** a way of avoiding a law or rule or promise etc. without actually breaking it. **2** a narrow opening in the wall of a fort etc.

loose¹ *adjective* **1** not tight; slack; not firmly fixed, *a loose tooth.* **2** not tied up or shut in,

There's a lion loose! **3** not packed in a box or packet etc. **4** not exact, *a loose translation.* **loosely** *adverb*, **looseness** *noun*

at a loose end with nothing to do.

loose² *verb* (**loosed**, **loosing**) **1** loosen. **2** untie; release.

loose-leaf *adjective* with each leaf or page removable, *a loose-leaf notebook.*

loosen *verb* make or become loose or looser.

loot¹ *noun* stolen things; goods taken from an enemy.

loot² *verb* **1** rob a place or an enemy, especially in a time of war or disorder. **2** take as loot. **looter** *noun*

lop *verb* (**lopped**, **lopping**) cut away branches or twigs; cut off.

lope *verb* (**loped**, **loping**) run with a long jumping stride. **lope** *noun*

lop-eared *adjective* with drooping ears.

lopsided *adjective* with one side lower than the other; uneven.

loquacious (*say* lok-**way**-shus) *adjective* talkative. **loquacity** (*say* lok-**wass**-it-ee) *noun* [from Latin *loqui* = speak]

lord¹ *noun* **1** a nobleman, especially one who is allowed to use the title 'Lord' in front of his name. **2** a master or ruler. **lordly** *adjective*, **lordship** *noun*

Lord Mayor the mayor of a large city.

the Lord God, Jesus Christ.

▶▶ T H E S A U R U S ◀◀

look² *noun* **1** gaze, glance, glare, glimpse, peek, peep, squint (*informal*), squiz (*Australian slang*), stare, stickybeak (*Australian informal*); see also SEARCH. **2** appearance, countenance, expression, face.

looker-on *noun* bystander, observer, onlooker, spectator, viewer, witness.

lookout *noun* **3** guard, picket, sentinel, sentry, watchman. **4** future, outlook, prospect.

loom² *verb* appear, menace, rise, soar, stand out, threaten, tower.

loop¹ *noun* circle, circuit, coil, curl, knot, noose, ring, twirl, twist.

loop² *verb* **1** coil, curl, entwine, kink, twist, wind.

loophole *noun* **1** escape, get-out, let-out, way out. **2** aperture, gap, opening, slit.

loose¹ *adjective* **1** detached, rickety, shaky, unattached, unfastened, unsteady, unstuck, wobbly; (*of clothing*) baggy, floppy, slack. **2** at large, free, uncaged, unconfined, unleashed, unrestrained, untethered, untied. **3** bulk, un-

packaged. **4** broad, imprecise, inexact, rough, sloppy, vague.

loose² *verb* **1** ease, loosen, relax, slacken, undo, unfasten, untie. **2** free, let go, let loose, liberate, release, set free, untie.

loosen *verb* ease, free, loose, relax, release, slacken, undo, unfasten, untie.

loot¹ *noun* booty, goods, pillage, plunder, spoils, swag (*informal*), takings.

loot² *verb* **1** pillage, plunder, raid, ransack, rob, sack.

lop *verb* chop, cut, prune.

lopsided *adjective* askew, asymmetrical, awry, crooked, unbalanced, uneven.

lord¹ *noun* **1** aristocrat, noble, nobleman, peer. **2** king, master, monarch, ruler, sovereign.

lordly *adjective* arrogant, bossy, disdainful, haughty, high and mighty, imperious, lofty, overbearing, snobbish, stuck-up (*informal*).

the Lord God, Jehovah, Jesus Christ, Yahweh.

▶▶▷ DICTIONARY ◁◀◀

lord² *verb* domineer; behave in a masterful way, *lording it over the whole club*. [from Old English *hlaford* = person who keeps the bread (compare *lady*)]

lore *noun* a set of traditional facts or beliefs, *gypsy lore*. [from *learn*]

lorgnette (*say* lorn-**yet**) *noun* a pair of spectacles held on a long handle.

lorikeet *noun* a small brightly coloured Australian parrot.

lorry *noun* (*plural* **lorries**) a large strong motor vehicle for carrying heavy goods or troops; a truck.

lose *verb* (**lost, losing**) **1** be without something that you once had, especially because you cannot find it. **2** be deprived of something; fail to keep or obtain, *We lost control*. **3** be defeated in a contest or argument etc. **4** cause the loss of, *That fall lost us the game*. **5** (of a clock or watch) become behind the correct time. **loser** *noun*
be lost or **lose your way** not know where you are or which is the right path.
lose your life be killed.
lost cause an idea or policy etc. that is failing.

loss *noun* (*plural* **losses**) **1** losing something. **2** a person or thing lost.
be at a loss be puzzled; not know what to do or say.

lot *noun* **1** a number of people or things. **2** one of a set of objects used in choosing or deciding something by chance, *We drew lots to see who should go first*. **3** a person's share. **4** a person's fate. **5** something for sale at an auction. **6** a piece of land.
a lot or **lots** (*informal*) a large amount; plenty.
the lot or **the whole lot** everything; all. [from Old English *hlot* = share]

loth *adjective* loath.

lotion *noun* a liquid for putting on the skin.

lottery *noun* (*plural* **lotteries**) a way of raising money by selling numbered tickets and giving prizes to people who hold winning numbers, which are chosen by a method depending on chance (compare *lot* 2).

lotto *noun* a game like bingo.

lotus *noun* (*plural* **lotuses**) a kind of tropical water-lily.

loud *adjective* **1** easily heard; producing much noise. **2** unpleasantly bright; gaudy, *loud colours*. **loudly** *adverb*, **loudness** *noun*

loudspeaker *noun* a device that changes electrical impulses into sound.

lounge¹ *noun* a sitting room.

lounge² *verb* (**lounged, lounging**) sit or stand lazily; loll.

louring (rhymes with *flowering*) *adjective* looking dark and threatening, *a louring sky*.

louse *noun* (*plural* **lice**) a small insect that lives as a parasite on animals or plants.

lousy *adjective* (**lousier, lousiest**) **1** full of lice. **2** (*informal*) very bad.

▶▶▷ THESAURUS ◁◀◀

lore *noun* folklore, legends, myths, traditions.

lorry *noun* pick-up, road train (*Australian*), semi (*Australian informal*), semitrailer, transport, truck, van.

lose *verb* **1** mislay, misplace; (*lost*) gone, mislaid, misplaced, missing, strayed, vanished. **2** forfeit, let slip, miss, pass up (*informal*), waste. **3** be defeated, get beaten.
lose your way miss the way, stray from the way, wander from the way.

loss *noun* **1** bereavement, deprivation, disappearance, forfeiture, impairment, reduction. **2** casualty, death, fatality.
at a loss baffled, mystified, nonplussed, perplexed, puzzled.

lot *noun* **3** allocation, allotment, part, portion, quota, ration, share. **4** destiny, fate, fortune, portion. **5** batch, collection, group, set. **6** allotment, block, plot.
a lot, lots dozens (*informal*), a good deal, a great deal, heaps (*informal*), loads (*informal*), many, masses, oodles (*informal*), piles (*informal*), plenty, scores, stacks (*informal*), a swag (*Australian informal*), tons (*informal*).

lotion *noun* balm, cream, liniment, moisturiser, ointment, salve.

loud *adjective* **1** amplified, blaring, booming, deafening, noisy, penetrating, piercing, raucous, resounding, rowdy, sonorous, stentorian, strident, thundering. **2** bold, bright, flashy, garish, gaudy, lurid, obtrusive, showy. **loudness** *noun* volume.

lounge¹ *noun* drawing room, living room, lounge room, parlour (*old use*), sitting room.

lounge² *verb* laze, lie, loaf, loll, recline, relax, sprawl, veg out (*slang*).

louring *adjective* black, cloudy, dark, gloomy, grey, heavy, leaden, overcast.

lousy *adjective* **2** awful (*informal*), bad, dreadful (*informal*), miserable, nasty, rotten (*informal*), terrible (*informal*); see also BAD.

▶▶▶ D I C T I O N A R Y ◀◀

lout *noun* a bad-mannered man. **loutish** *adjective*

lovable *adjective* easy to love.

love¹ *noun* **1** great liking or affection. **2** sexual affection or passion. **3** a strong liking for a thing. **4** a loved person; a sweetheart. **5** (in games) no score; nil.
in love feeling strong love.

love² *verb* (**loved, loving**) **1** feel love for a person or thing. **2** like very much. **lover** *noun*, **loving** *adjective*, **lovingly** *adverb*

loveless *adjective* without love.

lovelorn *adjective* pining with love, especially when abandoned by a lover.

lovely *adjective* (**lovelier, loveliest**) **1** beautiful. **2** (*informal*) very pleasant or enjoyable. **loveliness** *noun*

lovesick *adjective* languishing with love.

low¹ *adjective* **1** not high or tall. **2** not far above the ground or above sea-level. **3** below average level in importance, quality, etc., *low rank*. **4** of less than normal amount, extent, intensity, etc., *low prices*. **5** (of a sound) not shrill or loud. **6** depressed, *in low spirits*. **7** mean, vulgar. **lowness** *noun*

low² *adverb* at or to a low level or position etc., *The plane was flying low*.

low³ *verb* moo like a cow.

lower¹ *adjective* & *adverb* less high.

lower² *verb* **1** make or become lower. **2** bring something down, *lower the flag*.

lowlands *plural noun* low-lying country. **lowland** *adjective*, **lowlander** *noun*

lowly *adjective* (**lowlier, lowliest**) humble. **lowliness** *noun*

loyal *adjective* always firmly supporting your friends or group or country etc. **loyally** *adverb*, **loyalty** *noun*

loyalist *noun* a person who is loyal to the government during a revolt.

lozenge *noun* **1** a small flavoured tablet, especially as medicine. **2** a diamond shape.

LPG *abbreviation* liquefied petroleum gas.

Ltd. *abbreviation* limited.

lubricant *noun* a lubricating substance.

lubricate *verb* (**lubricated, lubricating**) oil or grease something so that it moves smoothly. **lubrication** *noun* [from Latin *lubricus* = slippery]

▶▶▶ T H E S A U R U S ◀◀

loutish *adjective* boorish, churlish, discourteous, ill-mannered, impolite, rough, rude, uncouth.

lovable *adjective* adorable, appealing, charming, darling, dear, delightful, endearing, likeable, lovely, sweet.

love¹ *noun* **1** adoration, affection, devotion, fondness, tenderness, warmth. **2** ardour, desire, fervour, infatuation, lust, passion. **3** delight, enjoyment, fondness, liking, pleasure, taste. **4** beloved, darling, lover, sweetheart.
in love besotted, devoted, enamoured, infatuated, smitten.

love² *verb* **1** adore, be devoted to, be fond of, care for, cherish, dote on, hold dear, idolise, revere, treasure. **2** appreciate, be fond of, delight in, enjoy, like, relish, treasure.
lover *noun* admirer, beloved, boyfriend, girlfriend, suitor, sweetheart; see also ENTHUSIAST (at ENTHUSIAST).
loving *adjective* adoring, affectionate, amorous, ardent, caring, close, devoted, doting, fond, friendly, kind, kind-hearted, passionate, sympathetic, tender, warm, warm-hearted.

lovely *adjective* **1** adorable, attractive, beautiful, charming, good-looking, gorgeous, pretty, winsome. **2** cool (*informal*), delightful,

enjoyable, excellent, fantastic (*informal*), good, great (*informal*), nice, pleasant, terrific (*informal*), wonderful.

low¹ *adjective* **1** dwarf, little, miniature, short, small, squat, stunted. **3** humble, inferior, junior, lowly, unimportant. **4** budget, cheap, cut-price, inexpensive, modest, reduced. **5** faint, gentle, hushed, muffled, quiet, soft, subdued; (*low-pitched*) bass, deep. **6** blue, dejected, depressed, despondent, down, downcast, forlorn, gloomy, glum, listless, melancholy, miserable, sad.

lower² *verb* **1** (*lower the volume*) quieten, soften, subdue, tone down, turn down; (*lower the price*) cut, decrease, discount, drop, mark down, reduce. **2** bring down, drop, let down, pull down, take down.

lowly *adjective* humble, modest, unassuming, unpretentious.

loyal *adjective* constant, dedicated, dependable, devoted, faithful, patriotic, staunch, steadfast, true, true-blue, trustworthy.
loyalty *noun* allegiance, constancy, devotion, faithfulness, fidelity, steadfastness, trustworthiness.

lozenge *noun* **1** drop, lolly, pastille, sweet, tablet.

lubricate *verb* grease, oil.

lucid *adjective* **1** clear and easy to understand. **2** sane. **lucidly** *adverb*, **lucidity** *noun* [from Latin *lucidus* = bright]

luck *noun* **1** the way things happen without being planned; chance. **2** good fortune, *It will bring you luck.*

luckless *adjective* unlucky.

lucky *adjective* (**luckier, luckiest**) **1** having good luck. **2** bringing good luck. **3** resulting from good luck. **luckily** *adverb*

lucrative (*say* loo-kra-tiv) *adjective* profitable; producing much money.

lucre (*say* **loo**-ker) *noun* (*contemptuous*) money. [from Latin *lucrum* = profit]

Luddite *noun* a person who opposes new kinds of machinery or methods, like the English workers who in 1811–16 destroyed the new machinery because they thought it would take their jobs.

ludicrous *adjective* ridiculous. **ludicrously** *adverb*

ludo *noun* a game played with dice and counters on a board. [Latin, = I play]

lug¹ *verb* (**lugged, lugging**) drag or carry something heavy.

lug² *noun* an ear-like part on an object, by which it may be carried or fixed.

luggage *noun* suitcases and bags etc. holding things for taking on a journey.

lugger *noun* a small sailing-ship.

lugubrious (*say* lug-**oo**-bree-us) *adjective* dismal. **lugubriously** *adverb* [from Latin *lugubris* = mourning]

lukewarm *adjective* **1** only slightly warm; tepid. **2** not very enthusiastic. [from *luke* = tepid, + *warm*]

lull¹ *verb* soothe or calm; send to sleep.

lull² *noun* a short period of quiet or inactivity.

lullaby *noun* (*plural* **lullabies**) a song that is sung to send a baby to sleep.

lumbago *noun* pain in the muscles of the loins. [from Latin *lumbus* = loin]

lumbar *adjective* of the loins.

lumber¹ *noun* **1** unwanted furniture etc.; junk. **2** (*American*) timber.

lumber² *verb* **1** encumber. **2** fill up space with junk. **3** move in a heavy clumsy way.

lumberjack *noun* (*American*) a person whose job is to cut or carry timber.

luminescent *adjective* giving out light. **luminescence** *noun* [from Latin *lumen* = light]

luminous *adjective* glowing in the dark. **luminosity** *noun* [from Latin *lumen* = light]

lump¹ *noun* **1** a solid piece of something. **2** a swelling. **lumpy** *adjective*
lump sum a single payment, especially one covering a number of items.

lump² *verb* put things together as being similar; deal with things together.

lump³ *verb* **lump it** (*informal*) put up with something you dislike.

lucid *adjective* **1** clear, comprehensible, intelligible, straightforward, understandable. **2** all there, rational, sane, sensible.

luck *noun* **1** accident, chance, coincidence, destiny, fate, fluke, fortune, serendipity. **2** good fortune, prosperity, success.

luckless *adjective* doomed, fated, hapless, ill-fated, jinxed, unfortunate, unlucky.

lucky *adjective* **1** blessed, charmed, favoured, fortunate. **3** accidental, chance, fluky, fortuitous, serendipitous.

lucrative *adjective* profitable, remunerative, well-paid.

ludicrous *adjective* absurd, crazy, derisory, farcical, laughable, nonsensical, preposterous, ridiculous.

lug¹ *verb* carry, drag, haul, heave, pull.

luggage *noun* baggage, bags, cases, gear, ports (*Australian*), suitcases, trunks; see also BELONGINGS.

lukewarm *adjective* **1** tepid, warm. **2** apathetic, cool, half-hearted, indifferent, unenthusiastic.

lull¹ *verb* calm, hush, pacify, quieten, relax, soothe.

lull² *noun* break, gap, hiatus, interval, let-up (*informal*), pause, silence.

lumber² *verb* **1** burden, encumber, land, load, saddle. **3** clump, plod, shuffle, trudge, waddle.

luminous *adjective* bright, glowing, luminescent, phosphorescent, radiant, shining.

lump¹ *noun* **1** ball, bit, chunk, cube, hunk, piece, wedge. **2** bulge, bump, growth, protrusion, swelling, tumour.
lumpy *adjective* bumpy, chunky, uneven.

lump² *verb* combine, group, mix.

lump³ *verb* accept, endure, put up with, suffer, tolerate, wear (*informal*).

▶▶▶ D I C T I O N A R Y ◀◀◀

lunacy *noun* (*plural* **lunacies**) **1** insanity. **2** great folly, madness. [from *lunatic*]

lunar *adjective* of the moon.
lunar month the period between new moons; four weeks. [from Latin *luna* = moon]

lunatic *noun* an insane person. **lunatic** *adjective* [from Latin *luna* = moon (because formerly people were thought to be affected by changes of the moon)]

lunch *noun* (*plural* **lunches**) a meal eaten in the middle of the day. **lunch** *verb*

luncheon *noun* (*formal*) lunch.

lung *noun* either of the two parts of the body, in the chest, used in breathing.

lunge *verb* (**lunged, lunging**) thrust the body forward suddenly. **lunge** *noun*

lupin *noun* a garden plant with tall spikes of flowers.

lurch¹ *verb* stagger; lean suddenly to one side. **lurch** *noun*

lurch² *noun* **leave somebody in the lurch** leave somebody in difficulties.

lure *verb* (**lured, luring**) tempt a person or animal into a trap; entice. **lure** *noun*

lurid (*say* **lewr**-id) *adjective* **1** in very bright colours; gaudy. **2** sensational and shocking, *the lurid details of the murder.* **luridly** *adverb*, **luridness** *noun*

lurk¹ *verb* wait where you cannot be seen.

lurk² *noun* (*Australian*) a dodge or stratagem.

luscious (*say* **lush**-us) *adjective* delicious. **lusciously** *adverb*, **lusciousness** *noun*

lush *adjective* **1** growing thickly and strongly, *lush grass.* **2** luxurious. **lushly** *adverb*, **lushness** *noun*

lust *noun* powerful desire. **lustful** *adjective*

lustre *noun* brightness; brilliance. **lustrous** *adjective* [from Latin *lustrare* = illuminate]

lusty *adjective* (**lustier, lustiest**) strong and vigorous. **lustily** *adverb*, **lustiness** *noun*

lute *noun* a musical instrument rather like a guitar.

Lutheran *noun* a member of a Christian religious denomination based on the doctrines of Martin Luther (1483–1546). **Lutheranism** *noun*

luxuriant *adjective* growing abundantly.

luxuriate *verb* (**luxuriated, luxuriating**) enjoy something as a luxury, *luxuriating in the warm sunshine.*

luxury *noun* (*plural* **luxuries**) **1** something expensive that you enjoy but do not really need. **2** expensive and comfortable surroundings, possessions, etc. **luxurious** *adjective*, **luxuriously** *adverb* [from Latin *luxus* = plenty]

▶▶▶ T H E S A U R U S ◀◀◀

lunacy *noun* **1** insanity, madness, mania, mental illness. **2** folly, foolhardiness, foolishness, idiocy, imprudence, madness, recklessness, stupidity.

lunatic *noun* crackpot (*informal*), loony (*informal*), madman, madwoman, maniac, nut (*informal*), nutter (*informal*), psychopath.

lunch *noun* dinner, luncheon (*formal*), midday meal.

lunge *verb* charge, dive, plunge, pounce, rush, thrust.

lurch¹ *verb* flounder, reel, stagger, stumble, sway, totter.

lurch² *noun* **leave in the lurch** abandon, desert, forsake, leave high and dry, leave stranded.

lure *verb* attract, draw, entice, seduce, tempt. **lure** *noun* attraction, bait, decoy, draw, drawcard, enticement.

lurid *adjective* **1** bright, flashy, garish, gaudy, loud, showy. **2** explicit, gory, graphic, horrifying, sensational, shocking, vivid.

lurk¹ *verb* hide, lie in wait, linger, skulk.

lurk² *noun* dodge (*informal*), racket, rort (*Australian slang*), scam (*slang*), scheme, stratagem.

luscious *adjective* delectable, delicious, juicy, rich, succulent, sweet.

lush *adjective* **1** green, luxuriant, profuse, prolific, strong, thick.

lust *noun* appetite, craving, desire, greed, hunger, longing, passion.
lustful *adjective* lascivious, lecherous, lewd, randy.

lustre *noun* brightness, brilliance, gleam, gloss, sheen, shine, sparkle.

luxuriant *adjective* abundant, dense, lush, profuse, strong, thick.

luxuriate *verb* bask, delight, enjoy yourself, indulge yourself, relax, wallow.

luxury *noun* **1** extra, extravagance, indulgence, treat. **2** affluence, comfort, ease, opulence, self-indulgence.
luxurious *adjective* de luxe, elegant, expensive, first-class, grand, opulent, plush, posh (*informal*), sumptuous, swish (*informal*), upmarket.

▶▶ D I C T I O N A R Y ◀◀

lying *present participle* of **lie²** and **lie³**.

lymph (*say* limf) *noun* a colourless fluid from the flesh or organs of the body, containing white blood-cells. **lymphatic** *adjective* [from Latin *lympha* = water]

lynch *verb* join together to execute or punish someone violently without a proper trial. [named after William Lynch, an American judge who allowed this kind of punishment in about 1780]

lynx *noun* (*plural* **lynxes**) a wild animal like a very large cat with thick fur and very sharp sight.

lyre *noun* an ancient musical instrument like a small harp.

lyre-bird *noun* an Australian bird, the male with a lyre-shaped tail display.

lyric (*say* **li**rrik) *noun* **1** a short poem that expresses thoughts and feelings. **2** the words of a song. **lyrical** *adjective*, **lyrically** *adverb* [from *lyre*]

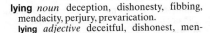

▶▶ T H E S A U R U S ◀◀

lying *noun* deception, dishonesty, fibbing, mendacity, perjury, prevarication.
lying *adjective* deceitful, dishonest, mendacious, untruthful.

lynch *verb* execute, put to death.
lyric *noun* **2** libretto, text, words.
lyrical *adjective* melodic, melodious, musical, poetic, songlike.

▶ Mm ◀

MA *abbreviation* Master of Arts.

ma *noun* (*slang*) mother. [short for *mama*]

ma'am (*say* mam) *noun* madam.

macabre (*say* mak-**ah**br) *adjective* gruesome.

macadam *noun* layers of broken stone rolled flat to make a firm road-surface. **macadamised** *adjective* [named after a Scottish engineer, J. McAdam]

macadamia *noun* **1** a tree providing edible nuts. **2** a nut from this tree. (also called *Queensland nut*). [named after J. Macadam, scientist]

macaroni *noun* flour-paste (*pasta*) formed into tubes.

macaroon *noun* a small sweet cake or biscuit made with ground almonds.

macaw *noun* a brightly coloured parrot.

mace *noun* an ornamental staff carried or placed in front of an official.

mach (*say* mahk) *noun* **mach number** the ratio of the speed of a moving object to the speed of sound, *mach one is the speed of sound.* [named after the Austrian scientist Ernst Mach]

machete (*say* ma-**shet**-ee) *noun* a broad heavy knife used as a tool or weapon.

machiavellian (*say* mak-ee-a-**vel**-ee-an) *adjective* very cunning or deceitful. [named after an unscrupulous Italian statesman, Niccolo dei Machiavelli (1469–1527)]

machinations (*say* mash-in-**ay**-shonz) *plural noun* clever schemes or plots.

machine¹ *noun* something with parts that work together to do a job.

machine² *verb* (**machined**, **machining**) make something with a machine. [from Greek *mechane* = device]

machine-gun *noun* a gun that can keep firing bullets quickly one after another.

machinery *noun* **1** machines. **2** mechanism. **3** an organised system for doing something.

macho (*say* **mach**-oh) *adjective* showing off masculine strength. [Spanish, = male]

mackerel *noun* (*plural* **mackerel**) a seafish used as food.

mackintosh *noun* (*plural* **mackintoshes**) a raincoat. [named after the Scottish inventor of a waterproof material, C. Macintosh]

mad *adjective* (**madder**, **maddest**) **1** having something wrong with the mind; insane. **2** extremely foolish. **3** very keen, *He is mad about football.* **4** (*informal*) very excited or annoyed. **madly** *adverb*, **madness** *noun*, **madman** *noun*, **madwoman** *noun*
like mad (*informal*) with great speed, energy, or enthusiasm.

▶▶THESAURUS◀◀

macabre *adjective* eerie, frightening, ghastly, ghoulish, gory, grim, grisly, gruesome, hideous, horrific, morbid, spooky (*informal*), weird.

machine¹ *noun* apparatus, appliance, computer, contraption, device, engine, gadget, instrument, mechanism, robot, tool.

machinery *noun* **1** equipment, gear, machines, plant.

macho *adjective* manly, masculine, tough, virile.

mad *adjective* **1** bananas (*slang*), barmy (*slang*), batty (*slang*), berserk, bonkers (*slang*), crackers (*slang*), crazy, demented, deranged, dotty (*informal*), flaky (*slang*), frenzied, insane, irrational, loony (*informal*), lunatic, manic, mental (*informal*), nuts (*informal*), nutty (*informal*), off your head, out of your mind, potty (*informal*), psychotic, round the bend (*informal*), screwy (*informal*), troppo (*Australian slang*), unbalanced, unhinged. **2** absurd, crazy, daft (*informal*), foolhardy, foolish, hare-brained, idiotic, illogical, insane, lunatic, nonsensical, preposterous, rash, reckless, silly, stupid, unwise, wild. **3** crazy, enthusiastic, fanatical, infatuated, keen, nuts (*informal*), obsessed, passionate, wild. **4** angry, annoyed, cross, enraged, furious, incensed, infuriated, irate, livid, riled (*informal*), ropeable (*Australian informal*), wild.
madman, madwoman *noun* crackpot (*informal*), loony (*slang*), lunatic, maniac, nut (*informal*), nutcase (*informal*), nutter (*informal*), psychopath.
madness *noun* **1** dementia, derangement, insanity, lunacy, mania, mental illness, psychosis. **2** folly, foolishness, idiocy, lunacy, stupidity.

madam *noun* a word used when speaking politely to a woman, *Can I help you, madam?* [from French *ma dame* = my lady]

madcap *noun* a wildly impulsive person.

madden *verb* make a person mad or angry.

madonna *noun* a picture or statue of the Virgin Mary. [from Old Italian *ma donna* = my lady]

madrigal *noun* a song for several voices singing different parts together.

maelstrom (*say* **mayl**-strom) *noun* a great whirlpool. [from Dutch *malen* = whirl, + *stroom* = stream]

maestro (*say* **my**-stroh) *noun* (*plural* **maestros**) a master, especially a musician. [Italian, = master]

magazine *noun* **1** a paper-covered publication that comes out regularly, with articles or stories etc. by a number of writers. **2** the part of a gun that holds the cartridges. **3** a store for weapons and ammunition or for explosives. **4** a device that holds film for a camera or slides for a projector. [from Arabic *makhazin* = storehouses]

magenta (*say* ma-**jen**-ta) *noun* a colour between bright red and purple. [named after Magenta, a town in north Italy, where Napoleon III won a battle in the year when the dye was discovered (1859)]

maggot *noun* the larva of some kinds of fly. **maggoty** *adjective*

Magi (*say* **mayj**-I) *plural noun* the 'wise men' from the East who brought offerings to the infant Jesus at Bethlehem.

magic *noun* the art or pretended art of making things happen by secret or unusual

powers. **magic** *adjective*, **magical** *adjective*, **magically** *adverb*.

magician *noun* a person who is skilled in magic; a wizard.

magisterial *adjective* **1** of a magistrate. **2** masterful; full of authority; imperious. [same origin as *magistrate*]

magistrate *noun* an official who hears and judges minor cases in a local court. **magistracy** *noun* [from Latin *magister* = master]

magma *noun* a molten substance beneath the earth's crust.

magnanimous (*say* mag-**nan**-im-us) *adjective* generous and forgiving; not petty-minded. **magnanimously** *adverb*, **magnanimity** *noun* [from Latin *magnus* = great, + *animus* = mind]

magnate *noun* a wealthy influential person, especially in business. [from Latin *magnus* = great]

magnesia *noun* a white powder that is a compound of magnesium, used in medicine.

magnesium *noun* a silvery-white metal that burns with a very bright flame.

magnet *noun* a piece of iron or steel etc. that can attract iron and that points north and south when it is hung up. **magnetism** *noun*

magnetic *adjective* **1** having the powers of a magnet. **2** very attractive, *a magnetic personality.* **magnetically** *adverb*
magnetic tape a plastic strip coated with a magnetic substance for recording sound.

magnetise *verb* (**magnetised, magnetising**) **1** make into a magnet. **2** attract like a magnet. **magnetisation** *noun*

madden *verb* anger, annoy, bug (*informal*), drive someone mad, enrage, exasperate, incense, infuriate, irritate, needle (*informal*), rile (*informal*), vex, wind up (*informal*).

maelstrom *noun* eddy, swirl, vortex, whirlpool.

maestro *noun* ace (*informal*), adept, expert, genius, master, virtuoso, whiz (*informal*), wizard; see also MUSICIAN.

magazine *noun* **1** bulletin, journal, newsletter, pamphlet, periodical.

maggot *noun* grub, larva.

magic *noun* black magic, conjuring, divination, illusion, sleight of hand, sorcery, spells, trickery, voodoo, witchcraft, wizardry.

magician *noun* conjuror, enchanter, enchantress, illusionist, medicine man, sorcerer,

sorceress, warlock (*old use*), witch, witch-doctor, wizard.

magisterial *adjective* **2** assertive, authoritative, bossy (*informal*), domineering, high-handed, imperious, lordly, masterful, overbearing, peremptory.

magistrate *noun* beak (*slang*), justice, stipendiary magistrate.

magnanimous *adjective* benevolent, big-hearted, bountiful, charitable, generous, kind, noble.

magnate *noun* baron, big shot (*informal*), bigwig (*informal*), leader, mogul (*informal*), tycoon; see also BUSINESSMAN.

magnetic *adjective* **2** alluring, attractive, captivating, charismatic, charming, enchanting, enthralling, fascinating, irresistible, seductive.

▶▶ DICTIONARY ◀◀

magneto (*say* mag-**neet**-oh) *noun* (*plural* **magnetos**) a small electric generator using magnets. [from *magnet*]

magnificent *adjective* **1** grand or splendid in appearance etc. **2** excellent. **magnificently** *adverb*, **magnificence** *noun* [same origin as *magnify*]

magnify *verb* (**magnified, magnifying**) **1** make something look or seem bigger than it really is. **2** (*old use*) praise, *My soul doth magnify the Lord*. **magnification** *noun*, **magnifier** *noun* **magnifying glass** a lens that magnifies things. [from Latin *magnus* = great, *facere* = make]

magnitude *noun* **1** largeness; size. **2** importance. [from Latin *magnus* = great]

magnolia *noun* a tree with large white or pale-pink flowers.

magnum *noun* a large bottle containing about 1.5 litres of wine or spirits. [Latin, = large thing]

magpie *noun* **1** a noisy bird with black and white feathers. **2** a similar Australian bird with a melodious song.

maharajah *noun* the title of certain Indian princes. [Hindi, = great rajah]

mah-jong *noun* a Chinese game for four people, played with pieces called tiles.

mahogany *noun* a hard brown wood.

maid *noun* **1** a female servant. **2** (*old use*) a girl. **maidservant** *noun*

maiden¹ *noun* (*old use*) a girl. **maidenhood** *noun*

maiden² *adjective* **1** not married, *a maiden aunt*. **2** first, *a maiden voyage*.
maiden name a woman's family name before she married.
maiden over a cricket over in which no runs are scored.

mail¹ *noun* letters or parcels etc. sent by post.
mail order ordering goods by post.

mail² *verb* send by post.

mail³ *noun* armour made of metal rings joined together, *a suit of chain-mail*.

maim *verb* injure a person so that part of his or her body is useless.

main¹ *adjective* principal; most important; largest.

main² *noun* **1** the main pipe or cable in a public system carrying water, gas, or (usually called **mains**) electricity to a building. **2** (*old use*) the mainland; the seas, *Drake sailed the Spanish main*.

mainland *noun* the main part of a country or continent, not the islands round it.

mainly *adverb* chiefly; almost completely.

mainstay *noun* the chief support.

maintain *verb* **1** cause something to continue; keep in existence. **2** keep a thing in good condition. **3** provide money for a person to live on. **4** state that something is true.

maintenance *noun* **1** the process of maintaining or being maintained. **2** money payable to a spouse after separation or divorce.

▶▶ THESAURUS ◀◀

magnificent *adjective* **1** beautiful, brilliant, exquisite, extraordinary, fine, glorious, gorgeous, grand, great, imposing, impressive, majestic, opulent, spectacular, splendid, stately, striking, stunning, sumptuous, superb. **2** see EXCELLENT.

magnify *verb* **1** amplify, blow up (*informal*), enlarge, exaggerate, overstate.

magnitude *noun* **1** extent, largeness, size. **2** consequence, importance, significance.

maid *noun* **1** chambermaid, domestic, help, housemaid, lady's maid, maidservant, parlourmaid, servant.

maiden¹ *noun* damsel (*old use*), girl, lass, lassie (*informal*), maid (*old use*).

maiden² *adjective* **1** spinster, unmarried, un-wed. **2** first, inaugural, initial.

mail¹ *noun* correspondence, letters, packages, parcels, post.

mail² *verb* dispatch, post, send.

maim *verb* cripple, disable, incapacitate, injure, lame, mutilate, wound.

main¹ *adjective* biggest, central, chief, critical, crucial, essential, first, foremost, greatest, head, largest, leading, major, most important, outstanding, paramount, predominant, primary, prime, principal, vital.

mainly *adverb* chiefly, especially, generally, in the main, largely, mostly, predominantly, primarily, principally.

mainstay *noun* anchor, backbone, foundation, linchpin, pillar, support.

maintain *verb* **1** carry on, continue, keep, keep up, perpetuate, preserve, prolong, uphold. **2** care for, keep in good repair, look after, preserve, service, take care of. **3** finance, keep, provide for, support. **4** assert, claim, contend, declare, hold, insist.

maintenance *noun* **1** care, preservation, repairs, running, servicing, upkeep. **2** alimony, allowance.

▶▶ D I C T I O N A R Y ◀◀

maisonette *noun* **1** a small house. **2** part of a house used as a separate dwelling.

maize *noun* a tall kind of corn with large seeds on cobs.

majestic *adjective* stately and dignified; imposing. **majestically** *adverb*

majesty *noun* (*plural* **majesties**) **1** the title of a king or queen, *Her Majesty the Queen.* **2** being majestic.

major[1] *adjective* **1** greater; very important, *major roads.* **2** of the musical scale that has a semitone after the 3rd and 7th notes. (Compare *minor.*) [Latin, = larger, greater]

major[2] *noun* an army officer ranking next above a captain.

majority *noun* (*plural* **majorities**) **1** the greatest part of a group of people or things. (Compare *minority.*) **2** the difference between numbers of votes, *She had a majority of 25 over her opponent.* **3** the age at which a person becomes an adult according to the law (now 18, formerly 21 years of age), *He attained his majority.*

makarrata (*say* mak-a-**rah**-ta) *noun* an Aboriginal ceremonial ritual symbolising peace after a dispute; an agreement.

make[1] *verb* (**made**, **making**) **1** bring something into existence, especially by putting things together. **2** gain or earn, *She makes $30,000 a year.* **3** cause or compel, *Make him repeat it.* **4**

achieve, *The swimmer just made the shore.* **5** reckon, *What do you make the time?* **6** perform an action etc., *make an effort.* **7** arrange for use, *make the beds.* **8** cause to be successful or happy, *Her visit made my day.* **9** compose; draw up, *make a list; make a will.* **10** amount to, *3 and 3 make 6.* **11** decide on, *They made a time for the next meeting.*

make do manage with something that is not what you really want.

make for go towards.

make love embrace a lover; have sexual intercourse.

make off go away quickly.

make out manage to see, hear, or understand something; pretend.

make up build or put together; (of parts) form a whole; invent a story etc.; compensate for something; put on make-up.

make up your mind decide.

make[2] *noun* **1** making; how something is made. **2** a brand of goods; something made by a particular firm.

make-believe *noun* pretending; imagining things.

maker *noun* the person or firm that has made something.

makeshift *adjective* improvised or used because you have nothing better, *We used a box as a makeshift table.*

▶▶ T H E S A U R U S ◀◀

majestic *adjective* august, dignified, glorious, grand, imperial, imposing, impressive, kingly, lordly, magnificent, noble, regal, royal, splendid, stately.

majesty *noun* **2** dignity, glory, grandeur, magnificence, nobility, pomp, royalty, splendour, stateliness.

major[1] *adjective* **1** bigger, chief, crucial, greater, important, key, larger, main, paramount, primary, prime, principal, significant.

majority *noun* **1** bulk, greater part, lion's share, most. **2** margin.

make[1] *verb* **1** assemble, build, carve, concoct, construct, create, erect, fabricate, fashion, forge, form, invent, manufacture, model, mould, produce, put together, sculpture, sew, shape. **2** acquire, earn, gain, get, obtain, realise, win. **3** cause, coerce, compel, force, oblige, order, pressure. **4** accomplish, achieve, arrive at, attain, reach. **6** (*make a bow*) do, execute, perform; (*make a speech*) deliver, give, present, utter. **7** arrange, prepare, straighten, tidy. **9** compile, compose, devise, draw up, establish,

formulate, frame, invent, think up, write. **10** add up to, amount to, come to, equal, total. **11** agree on, arrange, choose, decide on, fix, organise, settle on.

make do get by, improvise, manage.

make for aim for, go towards, head for, proceed towards.

make out 1 discern, distinguish, espy, perceive, see. **2** decipher, figure out, read, understand, work out. **3** allege, assert, claim, imply, pretend.

make up 1 compose, constitute, form. **2** concoct, cook up (*informal*), dream up, fabricate, invent, manufacture, think up. **3** (*make up for*) atone for, compensate for, offset, recompense, redeem.

make up your mind choose, come to a decision, decide, resolve, settle.

make[2] *noun* **2** brand, kind, sort, type.

make-believe *noun* daydreaming, dreaming, fantasy, imagination, play-acting, pretence.

maker *noun* builder, constructor, creator, inventor, manufacturer, producer.

makeshift *adjective* improvised, provisional, stopgap, temporary.

▶▶ D I C T I O N A R Y ◀◀

make-up *noun* **1** cosmetics. **2** the way something is made up. **3** a person's character.

mal- *prefix* bad; badly (as in *malnourished*). [from Latin *male* = badly]

maladjusted *adjective* not fitting well with his or her circumstances.

maladministration *noun* bad administration, especially of business affairs.

malady *noun* (*plural* **maladies**) an illness or disease. [from French *malade* = ill]

malapropism *noun* a comical confusion of words, e.g. using *hooligan* instead of *hurricane*. [named after Mrs Malaprop in Sheridan's play *The Rivals*, who made mistakes of this kind]

malaria *noun* a feverish disease spread by mosquitoes. **malarial** *adjective* [from Italian *mala aria* = bad air, which was once thought to cause the disease]

malcontent *noun* a discontented person.

male¹ *adjective* **1** of the sex that reproduces by fertilising egg-cells produced by the female. **2** of men, *a male voice choir*.

male² *noun* a male person, animal, or plant.

malediction (*say* mal-id-**ik**-shon) *noun* a curse. [from Latin *male* = evilly, + *diction*]

malefactor (*say* **mal**-if-ak-ter) *noun* a wrong-doer. [from Latin *male* = evilly, + *factor* = doer]

malevolent (*say* ma-**lev**-ol-ent) *adjective* wishing to harm people. **malevolently** *adverb*, **malevolence** *noun* [from Latin *male* = evilly, + *volens* = wishing]

malformed *adjective* faultily formed.

malfunction *noun* faulty functioning. **malfunction** *verb*

malice *noun* a desire to harm others or to tease. **malicious** *adjective*, **maliciously** *adverb* [from Latin *malus* = evil]

malign¹ (*say* mal-**I**'n) *adjective* **1** harmful, *a malign influence*. **2** showing malice. **malignity** (*say* mal-**ig**-nit-ee) *noun*

malign² *verb* say unpleasant and untrue things about somebody. [same origin as *malice*]

malignant *adjective* **1** (of a tumour) growing uncontrollably. **2** full of ill will. **malignantly** *adverb*, **malignancy** *noun*

malinger *verb* pretend to be ill in order to avoid work. **malingerer** *noun*

mall (*say* mawl *or* mal) *noun* **1** an area without traffic where people can walk and shop. **2** a shopping centre.

▶▶ T H E S A U R U S ◀◀

make-up *noun* **1** cosmetics, face paint, greasepaint. **3** character, nature, personality, temperament.

maladjusted *adjective* disturbed, mixed-up (*informal*), neurotic, screwed-up (*informal*).

malady *noun* affliction, ailment, complaint, condition, disease, disorder, illness, infirmity, sickness.

malcontent *noun* agitator, complainer, dissenter, grouch (*informal*), grumbler, moaner, rebel, stirrer (*Australian informal*), troublemaker, whinger (*informal*).

male¹ *adjective* masculine.

male² *noun* see BOY, MAN¹.

malefactor *noun* baddy (*informal*), criminal, crook (*informal*), delinquent, evildoer, felon, lawbreaker, miscreant, offender, outlaw, sinner, villain, wrongdoer.

malevolent *adjective* hostile, malicious, malignant, nasty, sinister, spiteful, vicious, vindictive.

malformed *adjective* crooked, deformed, distorted, misshapen, twisted.

malfunction *noun* breakdown, failure, fault, glitch (*informal*), hiccup, hitch.
malfunction *verb* break down, conk out (*informal*), fail, go bung (*Australian slang*), stop working.

malice *noun* animosity, bitterness, enmity, hostility, ill will, malevolence, maliciousness, spite, spitefulness, vindictiveness.
malicious *adjective* bitchy (*informal*), hostile, malevolent, malignant, mean, mischievous, nasty, spiteful, unkind, vicious, vindictive.

malign¹ *adjective* **1** bad, baleful, damaging, deleterious, destructive, evil, harmful, injurious, noxious, pernicious, sinister.

malign² *verb* defame, denigrate, disparage, knock (*informal*), libel, revile, run down, slander, smear, vilify.

malignant *adjective* **1** cancerous, deadly, fatal. **2** destructive, evil, harmful, hostile, malevolent, malicious, pernicious, spiteful, venomous, vicious, vindictive.

malingerer *noun* see SHIRKER (at SHIRK).

mall *noun* **2** arcade, centre, complex, plaza, precinct.

malleable *adjective* **1** able to be pressed or hammered into shape. **2** easy to influence; adaptable. **malleability** *noun* [from Latin *malleare* = to hammer]

mallee *noun* a eucalypt flourishing in dry areas forming **mallee scrub.**

mallet *noun* **1** a large hammer, usually made of wood. **2** an implement with a long handle, used in croquet or polo for striking the ball. [from Latin *malleus* = a hammer]

malnutrition *noun* not having enough food to eat. **malnourished** *adjective*

malpractice *noun* wrongdoing.

malt *noun* dried barley used in brewing, making vinegar, etc. **malted** *adjective*

maltreat *verb* ill-treat. **maltreatment** *noun*

mama or **mamma** *noun* (*old use*) mother.

mammal *noun* any animal of which the female can feed her babies with her own milk. **mammalian** (*say* mam-**ay**-lee-an) *adjective* [from Latin *mamma* = breast]

mammoth¹ *noun* an extinct elephant with a hairy skin and curved tusks.

mammoth² *adjective* huge. [from Russian]

man¹ *noun* (*plural* **men**) **1** a grown-up male human being. **2** an individual person. **3** mankind. **4** a piece used in chess etc. [from Old English *mann*]

man² *verb* (**manned, manning**) supply with people to work something, *Man the pumps!*

manacle¹ *noun* a fetter or handcuff.

manacle² *verb* (**manacled, manacling**) fasten with manacles. [from Latin *manus* = hand]

manage *verb* (**managed, managing**) **1** be able to do something difficult. **2** control. **3** be in charge of a shop, factory, etc. **4** meet your needs with limited resources; cope. **manageable** *adjective* [from Latin *manus* = hand]

management *noun* **1** managing. **2** managers; the people in charge.

manager *noun* a person who manages something. **manageress** *noun*, **managerial** (*say* man-a-**jeer**-ee-al) *adjective*

manchester *noun* household linen. [from *Manchester* in England]

mandarin *noun* **1** an important official. **2** a kind of small orange.

mandate *noun* authority given to someone to carry out a certain task or policy, *An elected government has a mandate to govern the country.* [from Latin *mandatum* = commanded]

mandatory *adjective* obligatory; compulsory.

mandible *noun* **1** a jaw, especially the lower one. **2** either part of a bird's beak or the similar part in insects etc. (Compare *maxilla.*)

mandolin *noun* a musical instrument rather like a guitar.

mane *noun* the long hair on a horse's or lion's neck.

malleable *adjective* **1** plastic, soft, workable. **2** adaptable, biddable, docile, impressionable, manageable, pliable, suggestible, tractable.

malnutrition *noun* emaciation, hunger, starvation, undernourishment.

malpractice *noun* dereliction, misconduct, negligence, wrongdoing.

maltreat *verb* abuse, bully, harm, ill-treat, ill-use, mistreat, oppress.

mammoth² *adjective* colossal, enormous, gargantuan, giant, gigantic, herculean, huge, immense, large, massive, mighty, stupendous, tremendous.

man¹ *noun* **1** bloke (*informal*), chap (*informal*), fellow (*informal*), gentleman, guy (*informal*), lad (*informal*), male. **2** human, human being, individual, mortal, person. **3** human beings, humanity, humankind, human race, humans, mankind, people.

man² *verb* attend, operate, staff.

manage *verb* **1** accomplish, carry out, do, perform, succeed in, undertake. **2** control, cope with, deal with, handle, manipulate, operate, use, wield. **3** administer, be in charge of, command, conduct, control, direct, govern, head, oversee, run, superintend, supervise. **4** cope, get along, get by, make do, make ends meet, survive.

manageable *adjective* biddable, compliant, controllable, docile, governable, pliable, tractable.

management *noun* **1** administration, control, direction, handling, organisation, running, supervision. **2** administrators, bosses, directors, employers, executives, managers.

manager *noun* administrator, boss, chief, director, foreman, head, organiser, overseer, proprietor, superintendent, supervisor.

manchester *noun* bedlinen, linen, napery, table linen.

mandate *noun* approval, authorisation, authority, direction, permission.

▶▶ D I C T I O N A R Y ◀◀

manful *adjective* brave. **manfully** *adverb*

manganese *noun* a hard brittle metal.

mange *noun* a skin disease of dogs etc. **mangy** *adjective*

manger *noun* a trough in a stable etc., for horses or cattle to feed from.

mangle¹ *noun* a wringer. **mangle** *verb*

mangle² *verb* (**mangled, mangling**) damage something by crushing or cutting it roughly.

mango *noun* (*plural* **mangoes**) a tropical fruit with yellow pulp.

mangrove *noun* a tropical tree growing in mud and swamps, with many tangled roots above the ground.

manhandle *verb* (**manhandled, manhandling**) treat or push roughly.

manhole *noun* a space or opening, usually with a cover, by which a person can get into a sewer or boiler etc. to inspect or repair it.

manhood *noun* **1** the condition of being a man. **2** manly qualities.

mania *noun* **1** violent madness. **2** great enthusiasm, *a mania for sport*. **manic** *adjective* [Greek, = madness]

maniac *noun* a person with mania.

manicure *noun* care and treatment of the hands and nails. **manicure** *verb*, **manicurist** *noun* [from Latin *manus* = hand, + *cura* = care]

manifest¹ *adjective* clear and obvious. **manifestly** *adverb*

manifest² *verb* show a thing clearly. **manifestation** *noun*

manifesto *noun* (*plural* **manifestos**) a public statement of a group's or person's policy or principles.

manifold *adjective* of many kinds; very varied. [from *many* + *-fold*]

manioc *noun* cassava; the flour made from this.

manipulate *verb* (**manipulated, manipulating**) **1** handle something skilfully. **2** handle or arrange something cleverly or cunningly. **manipulation** *noun*, **manipulator** *noun* [from Latin *manus* = hand]

mankind *noun* human beings in general.

manly *adjective* **1** suitable for a man. **2** strong, brave. **manliness** *noun*

manner *noun* **1** the way something happens or is done. **2** a person's way of behaving. **3** sort, *all manner of things*.

manners *plural noun* how a person behaves with other people; politeness.

mannerism *noun* a person's habit or way of doing something.

mannish *adjective* like a man.

manoeuvre¹ (*say* man-**oo**-ver) *noun* a difficult or skilful or cunning action.

▶▶ T H E S A U R U S ◀◀

mangle² *verb* crush, cut, damage, disfigure, injure, lacerate, maim, mutilate.

manhole *noun* hatch, opening, trapdoor.

manhood *noun* **1** adulthood, majority, maturity. **2** bravery, courage, machismo, manliness, masculinity, strength, valour, virility.

mania *noun* **1** dementia, derangement, insanity, lunacy, madness, mental illness. **2** craze, enthusiasm, fad, obsession, passion.

maniac *noun* crackpot (*informal*), loony (*slang*), lunatic, madman, madwoman, nut (*informal*), nutcase (*informal*), nutter (*informal*), psychopath.

manifest¹ *adjective* apparent, blatant, clear, conspicuous, evident, obvious, patent, plain, transparent, undisguised, unmistakable, visible.

manifest² *verb* declare, demonstrate, display, exhibit, express, indicate, make known, reveal, show.

manifesto *noun* declaration, platform, policy statement, programme.

manipulate *verb* **1** control, handle, manage, operate, use, wield, work. **2** (*manipulate figures, etc.*) cook (*informal*), falsify, fiddle (*slang*), juggle, massage, rig.

mankind *noun* human beings, humanity, humankind, human race, man, people, society.

manly *adjective* **1** male, mannish, masculine. **2** brave, chivalrous, courageous, fearless, gallant, heroic, macho, manful, valiant.

man-made *adjective* artificial, made, manufactured, synthetic.

manner *noun* **1** fashion, method, procedure, style, technique, way. **2** air, attitude, bearing, demeanour, disposition, mien. **3** category, class, kind, sort, type, variety.

manners *plural noun* **1** behaviour, conduct, form. **2** courtesy, decorum, etiquette, politeness, social graces, tact.

mannerism *noun* habit, idiosyncrasy, peculiarity, quirk, trait.

mannish *adjective* butch (*slang*), masculine.

manoeuvre¹ *noun* device, dodge (*informal*), move, ploy, ruse, scheme, stratagem, tactic, trick.

▶▶ D I C T I O N A R Y ◀◀

manoeuvre² *verb* (**manoeuvred**, **manoeuvring**) make a manoeuvre. **manoeuvrable** *adjective* [from Latin, = work by hand (*manus* = hand, *operari* = to work)]

man-of-war *noun* (*plural* **men-of-war**) a warship.

manor *noun* a large important house (*manor house*) in the country; the land belonging to it. **manorial** *adjective*

manpower *noun* the number of people who are working or needed or available for work on something.

manse *noun* a church minister's house.

mansion *noun* a large stately house.

manslaughter *noun* killing a person unlawfully but without meaning to.

mantelpiece *noun* a shelf above a fireplace.

mantilla *noun* a lace veil worn by Spanish women over the hair and shoulders.

mantle *noun* a cloak.

manual¹ *adjective* of or done with the hands, *manual work*. **manually** *adverb*

manual² *noun* 1 a handbook. 2 an organ keyboard played with the hands. [from Latin *manus* = hand]

manufacture *verb* (**manufactured**, **manufacturing**) make things. **manufacture** *noun*, **manufacturer** *noun* [from Latin *manu* = by hand, + *facere* = make]

manure *noun* fertiliser, especially dung.

manuscript *noun* something written or typed but not printed. [from Latin *manu* = by hand, + *scriptum* = written]

Manx *adjective* of the Isle of Man.

many¹ *adjective* (**more**, **most**) great in number; numerous, *many people*.

many² *noun* many people or things, *Many were found*.

Māori (*say* mah-o-ree) *noun* (*plural* **Māoris**) 1 a member of the indigenous people of New Zealand. 2 their language.

map¹ *noun* a diagram of part or all of the earth's surface or of the sky.

map² *verb* (**mapped**, **mapping**) make a map of an area.
map out plan the details of something.

maple *noun* a tree with broad leaves.

mar *verb* (**marred**, **marring**) spoil.

marathon *noun* a long-distance race for runners. [named after Marathon in Greece, from which a messenger ran to Athens in 490BC to announce that the Greeks had defeated the Persian army]

marauding *adjective* going about in search of plunder or prey. **marauder** *noun* [from French *maraud* = rogue]

marble *noun* 1 a small glass ball used in games. 2 a kind of limestone polished and used in sculpture or building.

march¹ *verb* 1 walk with regular steps. 2 make somebody walk somewhere, *He marched them up the hill*. **marcher** *noun*

▶▶ T H E S A U R U S ◀◀

manoeuvre² *verb* guide, jockey, manipulate, move, negotiate, position, steer.

manpower *noun* employees, hands, human resources, labour, personnel, staff, workers, workforce.

manse *noun* house, rectory, residence.

mansion *noun* castle, château, manor, manor house, palace.

manslaughter *noun* homicide, killing.

mantle *noun* cape, cloak, shawl.

manual¹ *adjective* (*a manual device*) hand-operated; (*manual work*) blue-collar, hand, physical.

manual² *noun* 1 handbook, primer, reference book, textbook.

manufacture *verb* assemble, build, construct, fabricate, make, process, produce.
manufacture *noun* assembly, building, construction, fabrication, making, production.

manure *noun* compost, dung, fertiliser, muck.

manuscript *noun* document, script.

many¹ *adjective* a lot of (*informal*), copious, countless, dozens of (*informal*), heaps of (*informal*), innumerable, lots of (*informal*), myriad, numbers of, numerous, oodles of (*informal*), piles of (*informal*), plenty of, scores of, umpteen (*informal*).

map¹ *noun* chart, diagram, plan, projection.

map² *verb* chart, survey.
map out arrange, devise, organise, plan, plot, prepare.

mar *verb* blemish, damage, deface, disfigure, flaw, ruin, scar, spoil, stain, tarnish.

marauder *noun* bandit, buccaneer, looter, pillager, pirate, plunderer, robber.

march¹ *verb* 1 file, parade, stride, tramp, troop, walk.

▶▶▶ D I C T I O N A R Y ◀◀

march² *noun* (*plural* **marches**) **1** marching. **2** music suitable for marching to. **3** a procession as demonstration. [from Latin *marcus* = hammer]

marchioness *noun* (*plural* **marchionesses**) the wife or widow of a marquis.

mare *noun* a female horse or donkey.

margarine (*say* mar-ja-**reen** or mar-ga-**reen**) *noun* a substance used like butter, made from animal or vegetable fats.

marge *noun* (*informal*) margarine.

margin *noun* **1** an edge or border. **2** the blank space between the edge of a page and the writing or pictures etc. on it. **3** the difference between two scores or prices etc., *She won by a narrow margin.*

marginal *adjective* **1** of or in a margin, *marginal notes.* **2** very slight, *a marginal difference.* **marginally** *adverb*
marginal seat a seat where a Member of Parliament was elected with only a small majority and may be defeated in the next election.

marginalise *verb* (**marginalised, marginalising**) treat as insignificant or less important.

marigold *noun* a yellow or orange garden flower.

marijuana (*say* ma-ri-**hwah**-na) *noun* a drug made from hemp.

marina *noun* a harbour for yachts, motor boats, etc. [same origin as *marine*]

marinade *noun* a flavoured liquid in which meat or fish is soaked before being cooked. **marinade** *verb*

marine¹ (*say* ma-**reen**) *adjective* **1** of or concerned with the sea. **2** of shipping.

marine² *noun* a member of the troops who are trained to serve at sea as well as on land. [from Latin *mare* = sea]

mariner (*say* **ma**-rin-er) *noun* a sailor.

marionette *noun* a puppet worked by strings or wires.

marital *adjective* of marriage. [from Latin *maritus* = husband]

maritime *adjective* **1** of the sea or ships. **2** found near the sea. [same origin as *marine*]

mark¹ *noun* **1** a spot, dot, line, or stain etc. on something. **2** a number or letter etc. put on a piece of work to show its quality. **3** a distinguishing feature. **4** a symbol. **5** a target; the normal standard. **6** the position from which you start a race, *On your marks!*

mark² *verb* **1** put a mark on something. **2** give a mark to a piece of work; correct. **3** pay attention to something, *Mark my words!* **4** keep close to an opposing player in football etc. **marker** *noun*
mark time march on one spot without moving forward; occupy your time without making progress.

marked *adjective* noticeable, *a marked improvement.* **markedly** *adverb*

market¹ *noun* **1** a place where things are bought and sold, usually from stalls in the open air. **2** demand for things; trade. **market-place** *noun*

market² *verb* (**marketed, marketing**) offer things for sale. **marketable** *adjective* [from Latin *merx* = merchandise]

marksman *noun* (*plural* **marksmen**) an expert in shooting at a target. **marksmanship** *noun*, **markswoman** *noun*

▶▶▶ T H E S A U R U S ◀◀

march² *noun* **3** demo (*informal*), demonstration, parade, procession.

margin *noun* **1** border, boundary, edge, frame, fringe. **3** difference, gap.

marginal *adjective* **2** little, minimal, minor, negligible, slight.

marine¹ *adjective* **1** oceanic, salt-water, sea. **2** maritime, nautical, naval, ocean-going, seafaring, seagoing.

mariner *noun* sailor, seafarer, seaman.

marital *adjective* conjugal, married, matrimonial, nuptial, wedded.

maritime *adjective* **1** marine, nautical, naval, seafaring, seagoing, shipping.

mark¹ *noun* **1** blemish, blotch, dot, impression, line, patch, scar, scratch, smear, smudge, spatter, speck, speckle, splash, splotch, spot, stain, streak, trace. **2** assessment, grade, rating, result, score. **3,4** badge, brand, emblem, hallmark, imprint, label, logo, seal, sign, stamp, symbol, token, trade mark. **5** bull's-eye, goal, objective, target.

mark² *verb* **1** blemish, brand, deface, disfigure, label, mar, scar, score, scratch, scuff, smudge, spot, stain. **2** assess, correct, evaluate, grade, judge, rate, score. **3** heed, mind, note, pay attention to, take notice of.

marked *adjective* clear, definite, distinct, noticeable, obvious, pronounced, strong, unmistakable.

market¹ *noun* **1** bazaar, fair, mart, sale.

market² *verb* see SELL¹.

marksman, markswoman *noun* gunman, sharpshooter, shooter, shot, sniper.

►►DICTIONARY◄◄

marmalade *noun* jam made from oranges, lemons, or other citrus fruit.

marmoset *noun* a kind of small monkey.

maroon¹ *verb* abandon or isolate somebody in a deserted place; strand.

maroon² *noun* dark brownish red.

marquee (*say* mar-**kee**) *noun* a large tent used for a party or exhibition etc.

marquis *noun* (*plural* **marquises**) a nobleman ranking next above an earl.

marriage *noun* 1 the state of being married. 2 a wedding.

marrow *noun* 1 a large gourd eaten as a vegetable. 2 the soft substance inside bones.

marry *verb* (**married, marrying**) 1 become a person's husband or wife. 2 unite a man and woman legally for the purpose of living together. [from Latin *maritus* = husband]

marsh *noun* (*plural* **marshes**) an area of very wet ground. **marshy** *adjective*

marshal¹ *noun* 1 an official who supervises a contest or ceremony etc. 2 an officer of very high rank, *a Field Marshal.*

marshal² *verb* (**marshalled, marshalling**) 1 arrange neatly. 2 usher; escort.

marshmallow *noun* a soft spongy sweet.

marsupial (*say* mar-**soo**-pee-al) *noun* an animal such as a kangaroo or wallaby. The female has a pouch on the front of its body in which its babies are carried. [from Greek *marsypion* = pouch]

martial *adjective* 1 of war. 2 warlike.
   martial arts fighting sports, such as judo and karate.
   martial law government of a country by the armed forces during a crisis. [from Latin, = of Mars, the Roman god of war]

martin *noun* a bird rather like a swallow.

martinet *noun* a very strict person.

martyr¹ *noun* a person who is killed or suffers because of his or her beliefs. **martyrdom** *noun*

martyr² *verb* kill or torment someone as a martyr. [from Greek, = witness]

marvel¹ *noun* a wonderful thing.

marvel² *verb* (**marvelled, marvelling**) be filled with wonder.

marvellous *adjective* wonderful.

Marxism *noun* the Communist theories of the German writer Karl Marx (1818–83). **Marxist** *noun*

marzipan *noun* a soft sweet food made of ground almonds and sugar.

mascara *noun* a cosmetic for darkening the eyelashes. [from Italian, = mask]

mascot *noun* a person, animal, or thing that is believed to bring good luck.

masculine *adjective* of or like men; suitable for men. **masculinity** *noun*

mash¹ *verb* crush into a soft mass.

mash² *noun* 1 a soft mixture of cooked grain or bran etc. 2 (*informal*) mashed potatoes.

►►THESAURUS◄◄

maroon¹ *verb* abandon, desert, forsake, isolate, leave, strand.

marriage *noun* 1 matrimony, wedlock. 2 marriage ceremony, wedding.

marry *verb* 1 become husband and wife, become man and wife, get hitched (*informal*), tie the knot (*informal*), wed.

marsh *noun* bog, fen, mire, morass, quagmire, slough, swamp.
   marshy *adjective* boggy, spongy, swampy, waterlogged.

marshal¹ *noun* 1 controller, officer, official, organiser.

marshal² *verb* 1 align, arrange, array, assemble, collect, deploy, dispose, gather, mobilise, muster, organise. 2 conduct, escort, lead, usher.

martial *adjective* 1 military. 2 belligerent, combative, fighting, militant, pugnacious, warlike.

martyr¹ *noun* sufferer, victim.

martyr² *verb* kill, put to death, torment, torture.

marvel¹ *noun* miracle, wonder.

marvel² *verb* (**marvel at**) admire, be amazed by, be astonished by, be staggered by, be surprised by, wonder at.

marvellous *adjective* amazing, astonishing, astounding, breathtaking, brilliant (*informal*), cool (*informal*), excellent, extraordinary, fabulous (*informal*), fantastic (*informal*), fine, first-rate, glorious, grand, great, magnificent, miraculous, outstanding, phenomenal, prodigious, remarkable, sensational, spectacular, splendid, staggering, stunning (*informal*), stupendous, superb, terrific (*informal*), tremendous (*informal*), wonderful.

mascot *noun* charm, emblem, symbol, talisman.

masculine *adjective* macho, male, manly, virile; (*of a woman*) butch (*slang*), mannish.

mash¹ *verb* crush, pound, pulp, purée, squash.

mask¹ *noun* a covering worn over the face to disguise or protect it.

mask² *verb* **1** cover with a mask. **2** disguise; screen; conceal.

masochist (*say* **mas**-ok-ist) *noun* a person who enjoys things that seem painful or tiresome. **masochism** *noun*

Mason *noun* a Freemason.

mason *noun* a person who builds or works with stone.

masonry *noun* **1** the stone parts of a building; stonework. **2** a mason's work.

masquerade¹ *noun* a pretence.

masquerade² *verb* (**masqueraded, masquerading**) pretend to be something, *He masqueraded as a policeman.* [from Spanish *mascára* = mask]

mass¹ *noun* (*plural* **masses**) **1** a large number or amount. **2** a heap, lump, or other collection of matter. **3** (in scientific use) the quantity of matter that a thing contains. In non-scientific use this is called *weight*.
mass production manufacturing goods in large quantities. **mass-produced** *adjective*

mass² *verb* collect into a mass.

Mass³ *noun* (*plural* **Masses**) the Communion service in a Roman Catholic church.

massacre *noun* the killing of a large number of people. **massacre** *verb*

massage (*say* **mas**-ah*z*h) *verb* (**massaged, massaging**) rub and press the body to make it less stiff or less painful. **massage** *noun*, **masseur** *noun*, **masseuse** *noun*

massive *adjective* large and heavy; huge.

mast *noun* a tall pole that holds up a ship's sail or a flag or an aerial.

master¹ *noun* **1** a man who is in charge of something. **2** a male teacher. **3** a great artist, composer, sportsman, etc. **4** something from which copies are made. **5** Master a title put before a boy's name.
Master of Arts a person who has taken the next degree after Bachelor of Arts.

master² *verb* **1** learn a subject or a skill thoroughly. **2** overcome; bring under control. [from Latin *magister* = master]

masterful *adjective* **1** domineering. **2** very skilful. **masterfully** *adverb*

masterly *adjective* very skilful.

mastermind¹ *noun* **1** a very clever person. **2** the person who is planning and organising a scheme etc.

mastermind² *verb* plan and organise a scheme etc.

mask¹ *noun* covering, cover-up, disguise, goggles, shield, visor.

mask² *verb* camouflage, conceal, cover up, disguise, hide, obscure, screen.

mass¹ *noun* **1** congregation, crowd, flock, gathering, herd, horde, host, mob, multitude, sea, swarm, throng. **2** blob, block, body, bundle, chunk, collection, heap, hunk, lump, mound, mountain, pile, quantity, stack.

mass² *verb* assemble, collect, congregate, flock, gather, herd, muster, rally.

Mass³ *noun* Communion, Eucharist, Holy Communion, Lord's Supper.

massacre *noun* bloodbath, carnage, extermination, killing, murder, pogrom, slaughter, slaying.
massacre *verb* butcher, execute, exterminate, kill, murder, slaughter, slay.

massage *noun* kneading, manipulation, rubbing.

massive *adjective* colossal, enormous, extensive, giant, gigantic, heavy, hefty, huge, hulking, immense, large, mammoth, monumental, solid, substantial, vast.

mast *noun* pole, post, spar.

master¹ *noun* **1** boss (*informal*), captain, chief, employer, governor (*slang*), head, leader, lord, overseer, owner, ruler, skipper. **2** schoolmaster, teacher. **3** ace, expert, genius, maestro, past master, professional, virtuoso, wizard. **4** original.

master² *verb* **1** get the hang of (*informal*), get the knack of, grasp, learn, understand. **2** conquer, control, overcome, subdue, tame, vanquish.

masterful *adjective* **1** authoritative, bossy, commanding, controlling, dictatorial, domineering, forceful, imperious, magisterial, overbearing, powerful.

masterly *adjective* accomplished, adept, brilliant, consummate, deft, excellent, expert, skilful, virtuoso.

mastermind¹ *noun* **1** ace, brain (*informal*), expert, genius, master, wizard. **2** architect, creator, designer, engineer, originator, planner.

mastermind² *verb* conceive, devise, direct, engineer, lead, orchestrate, organise, plan.

▶▶▶ D I C T I O N A R Y ◀◀

masterpiece *noun* **1** an excellent piece of work. **2** a person's best piece of work.

mastery *noun* **1** complete control. **2** thorough knowledge or skill in something.

masticate *verb* (**masticated, masticating**) chew food. **mastication** *noun* [from Greek *mastichan* = gnash the teeth]

mastiff *noun* a large kind of dog.

masturbate *verb* (**masturbated, masturbating**) excite yourself by fingering your genitals. **masturbation** *noun*

mat *noun* **1** a small carpet; a doormat. **2** a small piece of material put on a table to protect the surface.

matador *noun* a bullfighter who fights on foot. [from Spanish *matar* = kill]

match¹ *noun* (*plural* **matches**) a small thin stick with a head made of a substance that gives a flame when rubbed on something rough. **matchbox** *noun*, **matchstick** *noun*

match² *noun* (*plural* **matches**) **1** a game or contest between two teams or players. **2** one person or thing that matches another. **3** a marriage.

match³ *verb* **1** be equal or similar to another person or thing. **2** put teams or players to compete against each other. **3** find something that is similar or corresponding.

matchboard *noun* a piece of board that fits into a groove in a similar piece.

mate¹ *noun* **1** a companion or friend. **2** one of a mated pair. **3** an officer on a merchant ship.

mate² *verb* (**mated, mating**) **1** come or put together so as to have offspring. **2** put together as a pair or as corresponding.

mate³ *noun & verb* (in chess) checkmate.

material *noun* **1** anything used for making something else. **2** cloth; fabric. [from Latin *materia* = matter]

materialise *verb* (**materialised, materialising**) **1** become visible; appear, *The ghost didn't materialise.* **2** become a fact; happen, *The trip did not materialise.* **materialisation** *noun*

materialism *noun* regarding possessions as very important. **materialist** *noun*, **materialistic** *adjective*

maternal *adjective* **1** of a mother. **2** motherly. **maternally** *adverb* [from Latin *mater* = mother]

maternity *noun* **1** motherhood. **2** having a baby. [same origin as *maternal*]

mateship *noun* the bond between partners; comradeship as an ideal.

matey *adjective* friendly; sociable.

mathematics *noun* the study of numbers, measurements, and shapes. **mathematical** *adjective*, **mathematically** *adverb*, **mathematician** *noun*

maths *noun* (*informal*) mathematics.

matilda *noun* (*Australian*) a swag. **waltzing matilda** carrying a swag.

matinée *noun* an afternoon performance at a theatre or cinema.

matins *noun* the church service of morning prayer. [from Latin *matutinus* = of morning]

▶▶▶ T H E S A U R U S ◀◀

masterpiece *noun* **1** *chef-d'œuvre*, classic, treasure.

mastery *noun* **1** authority, control, domination, dominion, power, rule, supremacy, sway, the upper hand. **2** ability, command, competence, expertise, grasp, proficiency, skill, understanding.

mat *noun* **1** carpet, doormat, matting, rug.

matador *noun* bullfighter, toreador.

match² *noun* **1** bout, competition, contest, game, rubber, tournament. **2** equal, equivalent, peer, rival.

match³ *verb* **1** agree with, coincide with, coordinate with, correspond with, equal, fit, go with, harmonise with, suit, team with, tone with. **3** connect, couple, fit, join, link, pair, put together, unite.

mate¹ *noun* **1** buddy (*informal*), chum (*informal*), cobber (*Australian informal*), companion, comrade, crony, friend, pal (*informal*).

mate² *verb* **1** breed, copulate, couple, pair up.

material *noun* **1** constituent, element, ingredient, matter, stuff, substance. **2** cloth, fabric, textile.

materialise *verb* **1** appear, emerge, show up (*informal*), turn up. **2** come to pass, eventuate, happen, occur, take place.

materialistic *adjective* acquisitive, greedy, mercenary, worldly.

maternity *noun* **1** motherhood, motherliness. **2** see BIRTH.

mateship *noun* camaraderie, comradeship, friendship.

matey *adjective* chummy (*informal*), familiar, friendly, pally (*informal*), sociable.

▶▶ DICTIONARY ◀◀

matriarch (*say* **may**-tree-ark) *noun* a woman who is head of a family or tribe. (Compare *patriarch*.) **matriarchal** *adjective* **matriarchy** *noun* [from Latin *mater* = mother, + Greek *archein* = to rule]

matrimony *noun* marriage. **matrimonial** *adjective*

matrix (*say* **may**-triks) *noun* (*plural* **matrices**) an array of mathematical quantities etc. in rows and columns.

matron *noun* **1** a mature married woman. **2** a woman in charge of nursing in a school etc. or (formerly) of the nursing staff in a hospital. **matronly** *adjective*

matt *adjective* not shiny, *matt paint.*

matted *adjective* tangled into a mass.

matter¹ *noun* **1** something you can touch or see, not spirit or mind or qualities etc. **2** things of a certain kind, *printed matter.* **3** something to be thought about or done, *It's a serious matter.* **4** a quantity, *in a matter of minutes.*
no matter it does not matter.
what is the matter? what is wrong? [same origin as *material*]

matter² *verb* be important.

matter-of-fact *adjective* keeping to facts; not imaginative or emotional.

matting *noun* rough material for covering floors.

mattress *noun* (*plural* **mattresses**) soft or springy material in a fabric covering, used on or as a bed.

mature¹ *adjective* **1** fully grown or developed; grown-up. **2** ripe. **maturely** *adverb*, **maturity** *noun*

mature² *verb* (**matured, maturing**) make or become mature. [from Latin *maturus* = ripe]

maudlin *adjective* sentimental in a silly or tearful way.

maul *verb* injure by handling or clawing, *He was mauled by a lion.*

Maundy Thursday the day before Good Friday, celebrated by Christians in commemoration of the Last Supper.

mausoleum (*say* maw-sol-**ee**-um) *noun* a magnificent tomb. [named after the tomb of Mausolus, a king in the 4th century BC in what is now Turkey]

mauve *noun* pale purple.

maverick *noun* a person who belongs to a group but often disagrees with its beliefs.

maw *noun* the jaws, mouth, or stomach of a hungry or fierce animal.

maxilla *noun* (*plural* **maxillae**) the upper jaw; a similar part in a bird or insect etc. (Compare *mandible*.)

maxim *noun* a short saying giving a general truth or rule of behaviour, e.g. 'Waste not, want not'.

maximise *verb* (**maximised, maximising**) increase something to a maximum.

maximum *noun* (*plural* **maxima**) the greatest possible number or amount. (The opposite is *minimum*.) **maximum** *adjective* [Latin, = greatest thing]

may¹ *auxiliary verb* (*past tense* **might**) used to express (**1**) permission (*You may go now*), (**2**) possibility (*It may be true*), (**3**) wish (*Long may she reign*), (**4**) uncertainty (*whoever it may be*).

may² *noun* hawthorn blossom.

▶▶ THESAURUS ◀◀

matrimony *noun* marriage, wedlock.

matt *adjective* dull, flat.

matted *adjective* knotted, knotty, tangled, unkempt.

matter¹ *noun* **1** material, stuff, substance, thing. **3** affair, business, concern, issue, question, situation, subject, topic.

matter² *verb* be important, count, signify.

matter-of-fact *adjective* down-to-earth, factual, unemotional.

mature¹ *adjective* **1** adult, developed, fully-fledged, grown, grown-up. **2** aged, mellow, ripe, ripened.
maturity *noun* adulthood, coming of age, majority, manhood, womanhood.

mature² *verb* age, develop, grow up, mellow, ripen.

maudlin *adjective* mawkish, sentimental, soppy (*informal*), tearful, weepy (*informal*).

maul *verb* claw, lacerate, mutilate, savage, tear to pieces.

maverick *noun* dissenter, dissident, eccentric, individualist, law unto yourself, nonconformist, rebel.

maxim *noun* adage, aphorism, axiom, motto, principle, proverb, rule, saying, slogan.

maximise *verb* boost, build up, enhance, improve, increase.

maximum *noun* ceiling, peak, top, upper limit. **maximum** *adjective* extreme, full, greatest, highest, most, top, utmost.

►►► DICTIONARY ◄◄

maybe *adverb* perhaps; possibly.

mayday *noun* an international radio signal calling for help. [from French *m'aider* = (come to) help me]

mayfly *noun* an insect that lives for only a short time, in spring.

mayhem *noun* violent confusion or damage, *The mob caused mayhem.*

mayonnaise *noun* a creamy sauce made from eggs, oil, vinegar, etc.

mayor *noun* the person in charge of the council in a town or city. **mayoral** *adjective*, **mayoress** *noun*

maypole *noun* a decorated pole round which people dance on 1 May.

maze *noun* a network of paths, especially one designed as a puzzle in which to try and find your way.

me *pronoun* the form of *I* used as the object of a verb or after a preposition.

mead *noun* an alcoholic drink made from honey and water.

meadow *noun* a field of grass.

meagre *adjective* scanty in amount.

meal[1] *noun* food served and eaten at one sitting. **mealtime** *noun*

meal[2] *noun* coarsely-ground grain. **mealy** *adjective*

mealy-mouthed *adjective* too polite.

mean[1] *verb* (**meant, meaning**) **1** have as an equivalent, '*Maybe' means 'perhaps'.* **2** have as a purpose; intend, *I mean to win.* **3** indicate, *Dark clouds mean rain.*

mean[2] *adjective* **1** not generous; miserly. **2** unkind; spiteful, *a mean trick.* **3** poor in quality or appearance, *a mean little house.* **meanly** *adverb*, **meanness** *noun*

mean[3] *noun* a middle point or condition.

mean[4] *adjective* average.

meander (*say* mee-**an**-der) *verb* **1** take a winding course. **2** wander. **meander** *noun* [named after the Meander, a river in Turkey]

meaning *noun* what something means. **meaningful** *adjective*, **meaningless** *adjective*

means[1] *noun* a way of achieving something or producing a result, *We transport our goods by means of trucks.*
by all means certainly.
by no means not at all.

means[2] *plural noun* money or other wealth.
means test an inquiry into how much money etc. a person has, in order to decide whether he or she is entitled to get help from public funds. [from *mean*[3]]

meantime *noun* the time between two events or while something else is happening, *in the meantime.* [from *mean*[3] + *time*]

meanwhile *adverb* **1** in the time between two events. **2** while something else is happening. [from *mean*[3] + *while*]

►►► THESAURUS ◄◄

maybe *adverb* perchance (*old use*), perhaps, possibly.

mayhem *noun* bedlam, chaos, commotion, confusion, disorder, havoc, pandemonium, tumult, uproar, violence.

maze *noun* labyrinth, network, warren.

meadow *noun* field, grassland, lea (*poetical*), paddock, pasture.

meagre *adjective* mean, measly (*informal*), mingy (*informal*), paltry, scanty, skimpy, small, stingy.

meal[1] *noun* banquet, breakfast, brunch, dinner, feast, lunch, luncheon, repast (*formal*), spread, supper, tea.

mean[1] *verb* **1,3** communicate, connote, convey, denote, express, imply, indicate, say, signify, stand for, symbolise. **2** aim, intend, plan.

mean[2] *adjective* **1** miserly, niggardly, parsimonious, penny-pinching, stingy, tight-fisted. **2** base, beastly (*informal*), contemptible, cruel, despicable, hard-hearted, lousy (*informal*), low-down, malicious, nasty, spiteful, unkind. **3** humble, inferior, lowly, miserable, poor, shabby, sordid, squalid.

meander *verb* **1** loop, snake, twist, wind, zigzag. **2** ramble, roam, rove, wander.

meaning *noun* drift, gist, implication, import, importance, point, purpose, purport, sense, significance, value.
meaningful *adjective* deep, eloquent, expressive, pointed, significant, telling.
meaningless *adjective* absurd, aimless, empty, hollow, incomprehensible, nonsensical, pointless, senseless, unintelligible, useless, worthless.

means[1] *noun* agency, manner, medium, method, mode, process, way.

means[2] *plural noun* assets, funds, income, money, property, resources, riches, wealth.

meanwhile *adverb* **1** for now, in the interim, in the interval, in the meantime, in the meanwhile, meantime. **2** at the same time, concurrently, simultaneously.

▶▶ D I C T I O N A R Y ◀◀

measles *noun* an infectious disease that causes small red spots on the skin.

measly *adjective* (*informal*) very small.

measure[1] *verb* (**measured, measuring**) **1** find how big or heavy something is by comparing it with a unit of standard size or weight. **2** be a certain size. **measurable** *adjective*, **measurement** *noun*

measure[2] *noun* **1** a unit used for measuring, *A kilometre is a measure of length.* **2** a device used in measuring. **3** the size or quantity of something. **4** the rhythm of poetry; time in music. **5** something done for a particular purpose; a law, *We took measures to stop vandalism.*

meat *noun* animal flesh used as food. **meaty** *adjective*

mechanic *noun* a person who uses or repairs machinery.

mechanical *adjective* **1** of machines; produced or worked by machines. **2** automatic; done or doing things without thought. **mechanically** *adverb* [from Greek *mechane* = machine]

mechanics *noun* **1** the study of movement and force. **2** the study or use of machines.

mechanised *adjective* equipped with machines. **mechanisation** *noun*

mechanism *noun* **1** the moving parts of a machine. **2** the way a machine works.

medal *noun* a piece of metal shaped like a coin, star, or cross, given to a person for bravery or for achieving something.

medallion *noun* a large medal.

medallist *noun* a winner of a medal.

meddle *verb* (**meddled, meddling**) **1** interfere. **2** tinker, *Don't meddle with it.* **meddler** *noun*, **meddlesome** *adjective*

media *plural* of **medium** *noun*
the media newspapers, radio, and television, which convey information and ideas to the public. (See *medium*[2] 2.)

Usage This word is a plural. Say *The media are* (not '*is*') *very influential.* It is incorrect to speak of one of them (e.g. television) as 'this media'.

medial *adjective* in the middle; average. [from Latin *medius* = middle]

median[1] *adjective* in the middle.

median[2] *noun* **1** a median point or line. **2** a median number or position.

mediate *verb* (**mediated, mediating**) negotiate between the opposing sides in a dispute. **mediation** *noun*, **mediator** *noun* [from Latin *medius* = middle]

medical *adjective* connected with the treatment of disease. **medically** *adverb* [from Latin *medicus* = doctor]

▶▶ T H E S A U R U S ◀◀

measly *adjective* meagre, mean, mingy (*informal*), miserable, paltry, stingy.

measure[1] *verb* **1** assess, calculate, compute, determine, estimate, gauge, quantify, weigh; (*measure depth*) fathom, plumb, sound.
measure out apportion, deal out, dispense, distribute, dole out, mete out, ration out.
measure up to come up to, fulfil, meet, pass, reach, satisfy.
measurable *adjective* appreciable, calculable, considerable, determinable, discernible, mensurable, noticeable, perceptible, quantifiable, significant.
measurement *noun* area, breadth, capacity, depth, dimension, extent, height, length, magnitude, mass, size, volume, weight, width.

measure[2] *noun* **1** standard, unit. **2** callipers, gauge, rule, ruler, scale, tape-measure, yardstick. **3** amount, capacity, dimensions, extent, magnitude, mass, measurement, proportions, quantity, size. **5** action, course, law, means, method, procedure, process, step, way.

meat *noun* flesh.
meat-eating *adjective* carnivorous, flesh-eating.

mechanic *noun* repairman, technician, workman.

mechanical *adjective* **1** automated, mechanised. **2** automatic, instinctive, involuntary, reflex, unconscious, unthinking.

mechanism *noun* **1** action, machinery, movement, workings, works.

medal *noun* award, decoration, gong (*slang*), medallion, prize.

medallist *noun* champion, prizewinner, winner.

meddle *verb* **1** butt in, interfere, intervene, intrude, poke your nose in, pry.
meddler *noun* busybody, interloper, intruder, Nosy Parker, stickybeak (*Australian informal*).

median[1] *adjective* mid, middle.

mediate *verb* arbitrate, conciliate, intercede, intervene, liaise, negotiate.
mediator *noun* arbitrator, broker, conciliator, go-between, intercessor, intermediary, middleman, negotiator, referee, umpire.

medicament *noun* a medicine or ointment etc.

medicated *adjective* treated with a medicinal substance. **medication** *noun*

medicine *noun* **1** a substance, usually swallowed, used to try to cure a disease. **2** the study and treatment of diseases. **medicinal** (*say* med-**iss**-in-al) *adjective*, **medicinally** *adverb*

medieval (*say* med-ee-**ee**-val) *adjective* of the Middle Ages. [from Latin *medius* = middle, + *aevum* = age]

mediocre (*say* mee-dee-**oh**-ker) *adjective* not very good; of only medium quality; middling. **mediocrity** *noun*

meditate *verb* (**meditated**, **meditating**) think deeply and quietly. **meditation** *noun*, **meditative** *adjective*

Mediterranean *adjective* of the Mediterranean Sea (which lies between Europe and Africa) or the countries round it. [from Latin, = sea in the middle of the earth (*media* = middle, + *terra* = land)]

medium¹ *adjective* of middle size or degree or quality etc.; moderate.

medium² *noun* (*plural* **media**) **1** a middle size or degree or quality etc. **2** a thing in which something exists, moves, or is expressed, *Air is the medium in which sound travels. Television is used as a medium for advertising.* (See *media*.) **3** (with plural **mediums**) a person who claims to be able to communicate with the dead. [Latin, = middle thing]

medley *noun* (*plural* **medleys**) an assortment or mixture of things.

meek *adjective* quiet and obedient. **meekly** *adverb*, **meekness** *noun*

meet¹ *verb* (**met**, **meeting**) **1** come together from different places; come face to face. **2** make the acquaintance of. **3** come into contact; touch. **4** go to receive an arrival, *We will meet your train.* **5** pay a bill or the cost of something. **6** deal with a problem.

meet² *noun* a gathering of riders and hounds for a hunt.

meet³ *adjective* (*old use*) suitable; proper.

meeting *noun* **1** coming together. **2** a number of people who have come together for a discussion, contest, etc.

mega- *prefix* **1** large; great (as in *megaphone*). **2** one million (as in *megahertz* = one million hertz). [from Greek *megas* = great]

megalomania *noun* an exaggerated idea of your own importance. **megalomaniac** *noun* [from *mega-* + *mania*]

megaphone *noun* a funnel-shaped device for amplifying a person's voice. [from *mega-*, + Greek *phone* = voice]

melamine *noun* a strong kind of plastic.

melancholy¹ *adjective* sad; gloomy.

melancholy² *noun* sadness; gloom. [from Greek *melas* = black, + *chole* = bile]

medication *noun* drug, medicament, medicine.

medicine *noun* **1** capsule, cure, drug, elixir, linctus, medicament, medication, pill, remedy, tablet, treatment.
medicinal *adjective* curative, healing, restorative, therapeutic.

mediocre *adjective* average, fair, indifferent, middling, ordinary, passable, run-of-the-mill, second-rate, so-so (*informal*).

meditate *verb* cogitate, contemplate, deliberate, muse, ponder, reflect, ruminate, think.

medium¹ *adjective* average, intermediate, middle, middling, moderate.

medium² *noun* **1** average, compromise, mean, middle ground. **2** agency, channel, instrument, means, vehicle.

medley *noun* anthology, assortment, collection, miscellany, mixture, pot-pourri.

meek *adjective* compliant, deferential, docile, gentle, humble, mild, obedient, submissive, tame, unassuming.

meet¹ *verb* **1** assemble, come together, congregate, convene, gather, get together, join up, muster, rally, rendezvous; (*meet by chance*) bump into (*informal*), come across, encounter, run into, see. **2** be introduced to, make the acquaintance of. **3** abut, butt, connect, converge, cross, intersect, join, touch. **5** cover, pay, take care of. **6** come up against, confront, deal with, encounter, experience, face, run into.

meeting *noun* **1** appointment, date (*informal*), encounter, engagement, get-together (*informal*), rendezvous. **2** assembly, conference, congregation, congress, convention, council, forum, gathering, rally, summit, synod.

melancholy¹ *adjective* dejected, depressed, despondent, dismal, doleful, down, down in the dumps (*informal*), forlorn, gloomy, glum, heavy-hearted, in the doldrums, in low spirits, miserable, sad.

melancholy² *noun* blues, dejection, depression, despondency, gloom, misery, sadness, woe.

melanoma *noun* a malignant skin tumour.

mêlée (*say* **mel**-ay) *noun* **1** a confused fight. **2** a muddle. [French, = medley]

mellow[1] *adjective* **1** not harsh; soft and rich in flavour, colour, or sound. **2** kindly and genial. **mellowness** *noun*

mellow[2] *verb* make or become mellow.

melodious *adjective* full of melody.

melodrama *noun* a play full of dramatic excitement and emotion. **melodramatic** *adjective* [from Greek *melos* = music, + *drama*]

melody *noun* (*plural* **melodies**) a tune, especially a pleasing tune. [from Greek *melos* = music, + *oide* = song]

melon *noun* a large sweet fruit with a yellow or green skin.

melt *verb* **1** make or become liquid by heating. **2** disappear slowly. **3** soften.

member *noun* **1** a person or thing that belongs to a particular society or group. **2** a part of something. **membership** *noun* [from Latin *membrum* = limb]

membrane *noun* a thin skin or similar covering. **membranous** *adjective*

memento *noun* (*plural* **mementoes**) a souvenir. [Latin, = remember]

memo (*say* **mem**-oh) *noun* (*plural* **memos**) (*informal*) a memorandum.

memoir (*say* **mem**-wahr) *noun* a biography.

memoirs *plural noun* an autobiography.

memorable *adjective* worth remembering; easy to remember. **memorably** *adverb*

memorandum *noun* (*plural* **memoranda**) a written note, especially to remind yourself of something. [from Latin, = thing to be remembered]

memorial *noun* something to remind people of a person or event, *a war memorial*. **memorial** *adjective*

memorise *verb* (**memorised, memorising**) get something into your memory.

memory *noun* (*plural* **memories**) **1** the ability to remember things. **2** something that you remember. **3** the part of a computer where information is stored. [from Latin *memor* = remembering]

menace[1] *noun* **1** a threat or danger. **2** a troublesome person or thing.

menace[2] *verb* (**menaced, menacing**) threaten with harm or danger.

menagerie *noun* a small zoo.

mend[1] *verb* **1** repair. **2** make or become better; improve. **mender** *noun*

mend[2] *noun* a repair.

mendacious (*say* men-**day**-shus) *adjective* untruthful; telling lies. **mendaciously** *adverb*, **mendacity** *noun* [from Latin *mendax* = lying]

mendicant *noun* a beggar. [from Latin *mendicans* = begging]

mellow[1] *adjective* **1** (*mellow fruit*) juicy, luscious, mature, ripe, sweet; (*mellow sounds*) dulcet, rich, smooth, velvety. **2** affable, amiable, easygoing, genial, gentle, kindly, pleasant, sympathetic.

mellow[2] *verb* develop, mature, soften.

melodious *adjective* dulcet, euphonious, harmonious, lyrical, musical, sweet, tuneful.

melodramatic *adjective* exaggerated, histrionic, overdone, sensational, theatrical.

melody *noun* air, strain, theme, tune.

melt *verb* **1** dissolve, liquefy, thaw. **2** (*melt away*) disappear, disperse, evaporate, fade away, vanish. **3** disarm, mollify, soften, touch.

member *noun* **1** associate, fellow, subscriber. **2** component, constituent, element.

membrane *noun* film, integument, lining, sheet, skin, tissue.

memento *noun* keepsake, remembrance, reminder, souvenir.

memoirs *plural noun* autobiography, diary, life story, memories, recollections, reminiscences.

memorable *adjective* historic, impressive, momentous, noteworthy, outstanding, remarkable, significant, striking, unforgettable.

memorial *noun* see MONUMENT.

memorise *verb* commit to memory, learn by heart, learn by rote, remember.

memory *noun* **1** recall, retention. **2** recollection, remembrance, reminder, reminiscence, souvenir.

menace[1] *noun* **1** danger, hazard, risk, threat. **2** nuisance, pest.

menace[2] *verb* bully, frighten, intimidate, terrify, terrorise, threaten. **menacing** *adjective* baleful, black, forbidding, hostile, intimidating, malignant, ominous, sinister, threatening.

mend[1] *verb* **1** fix, patch up, put right, repair, restore. **2** ameliorate, correct, improve, rectify, reform.

►►► DICTIONARY ◄◄

menial¹ (*say* **meen**-ee-al) *adjective* lowly; needing little or no skill, *menial tasks.* **menially** *adverb*

menial² *noun* a person who does menial work; a servant.

meningitis *noun* a disease causing inflammation of the membranes (*meninges*) round the brain and spinal cord.

menopause *noun* the time of life when a woman finally ceases to menstruate. [from Greek *menos* = of a month, + *pause*]

menstruate *verb* (**menstruated, menstruating**) bleed from the womb about once a month, as normally happens to girls and women from their teens until middle age. **menstruation** *noun*, **menstrual** *adjective* [from Latin *menstruus* = monthly]

mental *adjective* **1** of or in the mind. **2** (*informal*) mad. **mentally** *adverb* [from Latin *mentis* = of the mind]

mentality *noun* (*plural* **mentalities**) a person's mental ability or attitude.

menthol *noun* a solid white peppermint-flavoured substance. [from Latin *mentha* = mint]

mention¹ *verb* speak or write about a person or thing briefly; refer to.

mention² *noun* mentioning something.

mentor *noun* a trusted adviser; a counsellor. [from Mentor in Greek legend, who advised Odysseus' son]

menu (*say* **men**-yoo) *noun* **1** a list of the food available in a restaurant or served at a meal. **2** a list of things, shown on a screen, from which you decide what you want a computer to do.

mercantile *adjective* trading; of trade.

mercenary¹ *adjective* working only for money or some other reward.

mercenary² *noun* (*plural* **mercenaries**) a soldier hired to serve in a foreign army.

merchandise *noun* goods for sale.

merchant *noun* a person involved in trade.

merciful *adjective* showing mercy. **mercifully** *adverb*

merciless *adjective* showing no mercy; cruel. **mercilessly** *adverb*

mercurial *adjective* **1** of mercury. **2** having sudden changes of mood.

mercury *noun* a heavy silvery metal (also called *quicksilver*) that is usually liquid, used in thermometers. **mercuric** *adjective* [from the name of the planet Mercury]

mercy *noun* (*plural* **mercies**) **1** kindness or pity shown in not punishing or harming a wrongdoer or enemy etc. **2** something to be thankful for.

mere¹ *adjective* not more than, *He's a mere child.*

mere² *noun* (*poetic*) a lake.

merely *adverb* only; simply.

merest *adjective* very small, *the merest trace of colour.*

merge *verb* (**merged, merging**) combine; blend. [from Latin *mergere* = dip]

merger *noun* the combining of two business companies etc. into one.

►►► THESAURUS ◄◄

menial¹ *adjective* degrading, demeaning, humble, lowly, servile, unskilled.

menial² *noun* dogsbody (*informal*), domestic, drudge, lackey, minion, servant, underling.

mental *adjective* **1** cerebral, intellectual, psychological. **2** see MAD.

mentality *noun* **1** ability, brains, intellect, intelligence, IQ. **2** attitude, disposition, mindset, outlook.

mention¹ *verb* allude to, bring up, comment on, hint at, refer to, speak of, touch on.

mention² *noun* allusion, hint, indication, reference, remark.

mentor *noun* adviser, counsellor, guide, guru, instructor, supervisor, teacher, tutor.

mercenary¹ *adjective* avaricious, grasping, greedy, money-grubbing.

merchandise *noun* commodities, goods, produce, stock, wares.

merchant *noun* dealer, distributor, exporter, importer, salesman, supplier, trader, wholesaler.

merciful *adjective* compassionate, forbearing, forgiving, gentle, humane, kind, lenient, mild, sympathetic, tender-hearted, tolerant.

merciless *adjective* callous, cruel, hard-hearted, harsh, heartless, implacable, inhuman, inhumane, pitiless, relentless, remorseless, ruthless, severe, strict, unforgiving, unsympathetic.

mercy *noun* **1** clemency, compassion, forbearance, forgiveness, grace, kindness, lenience, pity, sympathy, tolerance.

merge *verb* amalgamate, blend, combine, consolidate, converge, join, meet, unite.

▶▶▶ D I C T I O N A R Y ◀◀◀

meridian *noun* a line on a map or globe from the North Pole to the South Pole. The meridian that passes through Greenwich is shown on maps as 0° longitude.

meringue (*say* mer-**ang**) *noun* a crisp cake made from egg-white and sugar.

merino *noun* (*plural* **merinos**) a kind of sheep with fine soft wool.

merit¹ *noun* **1** a quality that deserves praise; excellence. **2** a quality or good point. **meritorious** *adjective*

merit² *verb* (**merited, meriting**) deserve. [from Latin *meritum* = deserved]

mermaid *noun* a mythical sea-creature with a woman's body but with a fish's tail instead of legs. **merman** *noun* [from *mere²* (old word, = sea), + *maid*]

merry *adjective* (**merrier, merriest**) cheerful and lively. **merrily** *adverb*, **merriment** *noun*

merry-go-round *noun* a circular revolving ride at fun-fairs.

mesh¹ *noun* **1** the open spaces in a net, sieve, or other criss-cross structure. **2** material made like a net; network.

mesh² *verb* (of gears) engage.

mesmerise *verb* hypnotise; fascinate or hold a person's attention completely. **mesmerism** *noun*

mess¹ *noun* (*plural* **messes**) **1** a dirty or untidy condition or thing. **2** a difficult or confused situation; trouble. **3** (in the armed forces) a dining room.
make a mess of bungle.

mess² *verb* **1** make a thing dirty or untidy. **2** bungle; spoil by muddling, *They messed up our plans.*
mess about behave stupidly; potter.
mess with interfere or tinker with.

message *noun* **1** a piece of information etc. sent from one person to another. **2** the central theme of a book etc.

messenger *noun* a person who carries a message.

Messiah (*say* mis-**I**-a) *noun* **1** the saviour expected by the Jews. **2** Jesus Christ, who Christians believe was this saviour. **Messianic** *adjective* [from Hebrew, = the anointed one]

Messrs *plural* of **Mr.**

messy *adjective* **1** dirty; untidy. **2** difficult to deal with; awkward. **messily** *adverb*, **messiness** *noun*

metabolism (*say* mit-**ab**-ol-izm) *noun* the process by which food is built up into living material in a plant or animal, or used to supply it with energy. **metabolic** *adjective*, **metabolise** *verb* [from Greek *metabole* = change]

▶▶▶ T H E S A U R U S ◀◀◀

merit¹ *noun* **1** excellence, goodness, quality, value, worth. **2** advantage, good point, strength, virtue.
meritorious *adjective* commendable, creditable, excellent, good, honourable, laudable, praiseworthy.

merit² *verb* be entitled to, be worthy of, deserve, justify, warrant.

merry *adjective* cheerful, convivial, gleeful, happy, high-spirited, jolly, jovial, joyous, light-hearted, lively.
merriment *noun* see MIRTH.

merry-go-round *noun* carousel, roundabout, whirligig.

mesh¹ *noun* **2** lacework, net, netting, network.

mesmerise *verb* bewitch, captivate, enthral, fascinate, hypnotise, magnetise.

mess¹ *noun* **1** chaos, clutter, confusion, disarray, jumble, litter, muddle, shambles, shemozzle (*informal*), untidiness. **2** difficulty, fix (*informal*), hot water (*informal*), pickle (*informal*), plight, predicament, spot (*informal*), trouble. **3** canteen, dining room, refectory.

make a mess of botch, bungle, make a hash of (*informal*), mess up, muddle, muff (*informal*), ruin, spoil.

mess² *verb* **1** clutter up, jumble, litter, muck up, untidy. **2** botch, bungle, muck up (*informal*), ruin, spoil.
mess with fiddle with, interfere with, meddle with, play with, tamper with, tinker with.

message *noun* **1** announcement, bulletin, communication, communiqué, dispatch, letter, memo (*informal*), missive, news, note, notice, report, statement, tidings, word. **2** meaning, moral, point, teaching, theme.
get the message catch on, comprehend, cotton on (*informal*), get it (*informal*), grasp it, latch on (*informal*), twig (*informal*), understand.

messenger *noun* ambassador, courier, envoy, go-between, herald.

messy *adjective* **1** bedraggled, chaotic, cluttered, dirty, dishevelled, disorderly, jumbled, littered, mucked-up, muddled, sloppy, slovenly, topsy-turvy, unkempt, untidy. **2** awkward, complicated, difficult, embarrassing, problematical, sticky (*informal*), ticklish, tricky.

▶▶ D I C T I O N A R Y ◀◀

metal *noun* a hard mineral substance (e.g. gold, silver, copper, iron) that melts when it is heated. **metallic** *adjective*

metallurgy (*say* mit-**al**-er-jee) *noun* the study of metals; the craft of making and using metals. **metallurgical** *adjective*, **metallurgist** *noun* [from *metal*, + Greek *-ourgia* = working]

metamorphic *adjective* formed or changed by heat or pressure, *Marble is a metamorphic rock*. [from Greek *meta-* = change, + *morphe* = form]

metamorphosis (*say* met-a-**mor**-fo-sis) *noun* (*plural* **metamorphoses**) a change of form or character. **metamorphose** *verb* [same origin as *metamorphic*]

metaphor *noun* using a word or phrase in a way that is not literal, e.g. '*The pictures of starving people touched our hearts*'. **metaphorical** *adjective*, **metaphorically** *adverb* [from Greek *metapherein* = transfer]

mete *verb* (**meted, meting**) **mete out** deal out; allot, *mete out punishment*.

meteor (*say* **meet**-ee-er) *noun* a piece of rock or metal that moves through space and burns up when it enters the earth's atmosphere. [from Greek *meteoros* = high in the air]

meteoric (*say* meet-ee-**o**-rik) *adjective* **1** of meteors. **2** like a meteor in brilliance or sudden appearance, *a meteoric career*.

meteorite *noun* a meteor that has landed on the earth.

meteorology *noun* the study of the conditions of the atmosphere, especially in order to forecast the weather. **meteorological** *adjective*, **meteorologist** *noun* [from Greek *meteoros* = high in the air, + *-logy*]

meter *noun* a device for measuring something, e.g. the amount supplied, *a gas meter*. **meter** *verb* [from *mete*]

methane (*say* **mee**-thayn) *noun* an inflammable gas found in marshy areas and in coalmines.

method *noun* **1** a procedure or way of doing something. **2** methodical behaviour; orderliness. [from Greek *methodos* = pursuit of knowledge]

methodical *adjective* doing things in an orderly or systematic way. **methodically** *adverb*

Methodist *noun* a member of a Christian religious group started by John and Charles Wesley in the 18th century. **Methodism** *noun*

meths *noun* (*informal*) methylated spirit.

methylated spirit or **spirits** a liquid fuel made from alcohol.

meticulous *adjective* very careful and exact. **meticulously** *adverb*

metre *noun* **1** a unit of length in the metric system, 100 centimetres. **2** rhythm in poetry. [from Greek *metron* = measure]

metric *adjective* **1** of the metric system. **2** of metre in poetry. **metrically** *adverb* **metric system** a measuring system based on decimal units (the metre, litre, and gram).

metrical *adjective* of or in rhythmic metre, not prose, *metrical psalms*.

metrication *noun* changing to the metric system.

metronome *noun* a device that makes a regular clicking noise to help a person keep in time when practising music. [from Greek *metron* = measure, + *nomos* = law]

metropolis *noun* the chief city of a country or region. **metropolitan** *adjective* [from Greek *meter* = mother, + *polis* = city]

▶▶ T H E S A U R U S ◀◀

metallic *adjective* (*metallic paint*) gleaming, glistening, lustrous, shiny; (*metallic sounds*) brassy, clanging, clanking, clinking, jangling, ringing, tinny.

metamorphosis *noun* change, conversion, mutation, transfiguration, transformation, transmutation.

metaphorical *adjective* figurative, non-literal.

mete *verb* **mete out** allocate, allot, apportion, deal out, dispense, distribute, dole out, measure out.

meteoric *adjective* **2** brilliant, fast, overnight, quick, rapid, speedy, sudden, swift.

meter *noun* clock, dial, gauge, indicator.

method *noun* **1** approach, knack, manner, means, procedure, process, routine, system, technique, way. **2** design, order, orderliness, pattern, plan, structure, system.

methodical *adjective* careful, disciplined, logical, meticulous, orderly, organised, structured, systematic, tidy.

meticulous *adjective* accurate, careful, exact, fastidious, fussy, methodical, orderly, painstaking, precise, punctilious, scrupulous, thorough.

metropolis *noun* capital, city.

mettle *noun* courage; strength of character.
mettlesome *adjective*
be on your mettle be determined to show your courage or ability.

mew *verb* make a cat's cry. **mew** *noun*

miaow *verb* & *noun* mew.

miasma (*say* mee-**az**-ma) *noun* unpleasant or unhealthy air. [Greek, = pollution]

mica *noun* a mineral substance used to make electrical insulators.

mickery *noun* (*Australian*) a depression holding water in a sandy inland riverbed.

micro- *prefix* very small (as in *microfilm*). [from Greek *mikros* = small]

microbe *noun* a micro-organism. [from *micro-*, + Greek *bios* = life]

microchip *noun* a very small piece of silicon etc. made to work like a complex wired electric circuit.

microcomputer *noun* a very small computer.

microcosm *noun* a world in miniature; something regarded as resembling something else on a very small scale. [from Greek *mikros kosmos* = little world]

microfilm *noun* a length of film on which written or printed material is photographed in greatly reduced size.

micro-organism *noun* a microscopic creature, e.g. a bacterium or virus.

microphone *noun* an electrical device that picks up sound waves for recording, amplifying, or broadcasting. [from *micro-*, + Greek *phone* = sound]

microprocessor *noun* a miniature computer (or a unit of this) consisting of one or more microchips.

microscope *noun* an instrument with lenses that magnify tiny objects or details. [from *micro-*, + Greek *skopein* = look at]

microscopic *adjective* 1 extremely small; too small to be seen without the aid of a microscope. 2 of a microscope.

microwave *noun* 1 a very short electro-magnetic wave. 2 a microwave oven.
microwave oven an oven that uses micro-waves to heat food very quickly.

mid *adjective* in the middle of; middle.

midday *noun* the middle of the day; noon.

middle[1] *noun* 1 the place or part of something that is at the same distance from all its sides or edges or from both its ends. 2 someone's waist.

middle[2] *adjective* 1 placed or happening in the middle. 2 moderate in size or rank etc.
Middle Ages the period in history from about AD1000 to 1400.
middle class the class of people between the upper class and the working class, including business and professional people.
Middle East the countries from Egypt to Iran inclusive.

middleman *noun* (*plural* **middlemen**) 1 a trader who buys from a producer and sells to a consumer. 2 an intermediary.

middling *adjective* & *adverb* moderately good; moderately.

midge *noun* a small insect like a gnat.

midget *noun* an extremely small person or thing. **midget** *adjective*

midland *adjective* of the Midlands.
the Midlands central England.

midnight *noun* twelve o'clock at night.

midriff *noun* the front part of the body just above the waist.

midshipman *noun* (*plural* **midshipmen**) a sailor ranking next above a cadet.

midst *noun* the middle of something.
in the midst of among; in the middle of.

▶▶ THESAURUS ◀◀

mettle *noun* boldness, bravery, courage, gameness, grit, guts (*informal*), intrepidity, nerve, pluck, spirit.

microbe *noun* bacterium, bug (*informal*), germ, micro-organism, virus.

microphone *noun* bug (*informal*), mike (*informal*).

microscopic *adjective* 1 little, minuscule, minute, small, tiny.

middle[1] *noun* 1 centre, core, heart, hub, nucleus. 2 midriff, stomach, waist.

middle[2] *adjective* 1 central, halfway, medial, median, mid, midway. 2 average, intermediate, medium, moderate.

middleman *noun* 2 agent, broker, distributor, go-between, intermediary.

middling *adjective* average, fair, indifferent, mediocre, medium, ordinary, so-so (*informal*), unremarkable.

midget *noun* dwarf, lilliputian, pygmy.
midget *adjective* diminutive, little, miniature, minuscule, minute, small, tiny.

midst *noun* **in the midst of** 1 amid, amidst, among, amongst, surrounded by. 2 during, halfway through, in the middle of.

▶▶ D I C T I O N A R Y ◀◀

midsummer *noun* the middle of summer.

midway *adverb* halfway.

midwife *noun* (*plural* **midwives**) a person trained to look after a woman who is giving birth to a baby. **midwifery** *noun*

mien (*say* meen) *noun* a person's manner.

might[1] *noun* great strength or power.

might[2] *auxiliary verb* used (**1**) as the past tense of *may*[1] (*We told her she might go*), (**2**) to express possibility (*It might be true*).

mighty *adjective* very strong or powerful. **mightily** *adverb*, **mightiness** *noun*

mignonette (*say* min-yon-**et**) *noun* **1** a plant with fragrant leaves. **2** a kind of lettuce.

migraine (*say* **my**-grayn) *noun* a severe kind of headache.

migrant *noun* a person or animal that migrates or has migrated.

migrate *verb* (**migrated, migrating**) **1** leave one place or country and settle in another. **2** (of birds or animals) move periodically from one area to another. **migration** *noun*, **migratory** *adjective* [from Latin *migrare* = migrate]

mike *noun* (*informal*) a microphone.

mild *adjective* **1** gentle; not harsh or severe. **2** (of weather) moderately warm. **3** not strongly flavoured. **mildly** *adverb*, **mildness** *noun*

mildew *noun* a tiny fungus that forms a white coating on things kept in damp conditions. **mildewed** *adjective*

mile *noun* a measure of distance, about 1.6 kilometres. [from Latin *mille* = thousand (paces)]

mileage *noun* the number of miles or kilometres travelled.

milestone *noun* **1** a stone of a kind that used to be fixed beside a road to mark the distance between towns. **2** an important event in life or history.

militant *adjective* eager to fight or be aggressive. **militant** *noun*, **militancy** *noun*

militarism *noun* belief in the use of military strength and methods. **militarist** *noun*, **militaristic** *adjective*

military *adjective* of soldiers or the armed forces. [from Latin *miles* = soldier]

militate *verb* (**militated, militating**) have a strong effect or influence, *The weather militated against the success of our plans.*

militia (*say* mil-**ish**-a) *noun* a military force, especially one raised from civilians. [same origin as *military*]

milk[1] *noun* **1** a white liquid that female mammals produce in their bodies to feed their babies. **2** the milk of cows, used as food by human beings. **3** a milky liquid, e.g. that in a coconut.

milk[2] *verb* get the milk from a cow or other animal.

milkman *noun* (*plural* **milkmen**) a person who delivers milk to customers' houses.

milky *adjective* like milk; white.

Milky Way the broad bright band of stars formed by our galaxy.

mill[1] *noun* **1** machinery for grinding corn to make flour; a building containing this machinery. **2** a grinding machine, *a coffee-mill.* **3** a factory for processing certain materials, *a paper-mill.*

mill[2] *verb* **1** grind or crush in a mill. **2** cut markings round the edge of a coin. **3** move in a confused crowd, *The animals were milling around.* **miller** *noun*

millennium *noun* (*plural* **millenniums**) a period of 1,000 years. [from Latin *mille* = thousand, + *annus* = year]

▶▶ T H E S A U R U S ◀◀

mien *noun* air, appearance, bearing, demeanour, expression, look, manner.

might[1] *noun* energy, force, power, strength.

mighty *adjective* indomitable, invincible, powerful, robust, strong, sturdy; see also HUGE.

migrant *noun* emigrant, immigrant, newcomer.

migrate *verb* **1** emigrate, go overseas, immigrate, move, relocate, travel.

mild *adjective* **1** calm, docile, easygoing, gentle, kind, placid, serene, unassuming. **2** balmy, moderate, temperate, warm. **3** bland, delicate, faint, subtle.

mildew *noun* mould.

milestone *noun* **1** distance marker, milepost. **2** landmark, red-letter day, turning point, watershed.

militant *adjective* aggressive, assertive, belligerent, defiant, pugnacious, pushy (*informal*), uncompromising.

military *adjective* armed, army, defence, service.

milky *adjective* cloudy, opaque, white, whitish.

mill[1] *noun* **2** grinder.

mill[2] *verb* **1** crush, granulate, grind, pulverise. **3** congregate, crowd, hover, mass, swarm, throng.

▶▶ DICTIONARY ◀◀

millet *noun* a kind of cereal with tiny seeds.

milli- *prefix* **1** one thousand (as in *millipede*). **2** one-thousandth (as in *milligram*, *millilitre*, *millimetre*). [from Latin *mille* = thousand]

milliner *noun* a person who makes or sells women's hats. **millinery** *noun*

million *noun* & *adjective* one thousand thousand (1,000,000).

millionaire *noun* an extremely rich person.

millipede *noun* a small crawling creature like a centipede, with many legs. [from Latin *mille* = thousand, + *pedes* = feet]

millstone *noun* **1** either of a pair of large circular stones between which corn is ground. **2** a heavy responsibility.

milometer *noun* an instrument for measuring how far a vehicle has travelled. [from *mile* + *meter*]

milt *noun* a male fish's sperm.

mime *noun* acting with movements of the body, not using words. **mime** *verb*

mimic¹ *verb* (**mimicked**, **mimicking**) imitate. **mimicry** *noun*

mimic² *noun* a person who mimics others, especially to amuse people.

mimosa *noun* a tropical tree or shrub with small ball-shaped flowers.

minaret *noun* the tall tower of a mosque. [from Arabic *manara* = lighthouse]

mince¹ *verb* (**minced**, **mincing**) **1** cut into very small pieces in a machine. **2** walk in an affected way. **mincer** *noun*
not to mince matters speak bluntly.

mince² *noun* minced meat.

mincemeat *noun* a sweet mixture of currants, raisins, apple, etc. used in pies.

mince pie a pie containing mincemeat.

mind¹ *noun* **1** the ability to think, feel, understand, and remember, originating in the brain. **2** a person's thoughts and feelings or opinion, *I changed my mind*.
mind-boggling (*informal*) amazing, unbelievable.

mind² *verb* **1** look after, *He was minding the baby*. **2** be careful about, *Mind the step*. **3** be sad or upset about something; object to, *We don't mind waiting*. **minder** *noun*

mindful *adjective* taking thought or care, *He was mindful of his reputation*.

mindless *adjective* **1** without intelligence. **2** not requiring thought or skill, *a mindless job*.

mine¹ *possessive pronoun* belonging to me.

mine² *noun* **1** a place where coal, metal, precious stones, etc. are dug out of the ground. **2** an explosive placed in or on the ground or in the sea etc. to destroy people or things that come close to it.

mine³ *verb* (**mined**, **mining**) **1** dig from a mine. **2** lay explosive mines in a place.

minefield *noun* an area where explosive mines have been laid.

miner *noun* a person who works in a mine.

mineral *noun* a hard inorganic substance found in the ground. [from Latin *minera* = ore]

mineralogy (*say* min-er-**al**-o-jee) *noun* the study of minerals. **mineralogist** *noun* [from *mineral* + -*logy*]

minestrone (*say* mini-**stroh**-nee) *noun* an Italian soup containing vegetables and pasta.

▶▶ THESAURUS ◀◀

millstone *noun* **2** burden, load, responsibility, trouble, worry.

mimic¹ *verb* ape, caricature, copy, imitate, impersonate, parody, send up (*informal*), take off.
mimicry *noun* burlesque, caricature, imitation, impersonation, parody, send-up (*informal*), spoof (*informal*), take-off.

mince¹ *verb* **1** chop, cut, grind, hash.

mind¹ *noun* **1** brain, common sense, head, imagination, intellect, intelligence, mentality, reasoning, sense, understanding, wits. **2** attitude, intention, judgement, opinion, outlook, point of view, position, thoughts, view.
mind-boggling *adjective* amazing, astonishing, astounding, incredible, staggering, startling, unbelievable.

bring to mind recall, recollect, remember.

mind² *verb* **1** babysit, keep an eye on, look after, take care of, tend. **2** be careful of, beware of, look out for, take care with, watch out for. **3** be bothered by, dislike, object to, resent, take exception to.
minder *noun* babysitter, bodyguard, carer, child-minder.

mindful *adjective* alert, attentive, aware, careful, conscious, considerate, heedful, thoughtful, wary, watchful.

mindless *adjective* **2** boring, mechanical, routine, tedious.

mine² *noun* **1** colliery, excavation, pit, quarry, workings.

mine³ *verb* **1** dig for, excavate, extract.

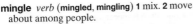

▶▶DICTIONARY◀◀

mingle *verb* (**mingled, mingling**) **1** mix. **2** move about among people.

mingy *adjective* (*informal*) mean; stingy.

mini- *prefix* miniature; very small. [short for *miniature*]

miniature¹ *adjective* very small; copying something on a very small scale.

miniature² *noun* **1** a very small portrait. **2** a small-scale model.

minibus *noun* (*plural* **minibuses**) a very small bus.

minicomputer *noun* a small computer.

minim *noun* a note in music, lasting half as long as a semibreve (written ♩).

minimise *verb* (**minimised, minimising**) reduce something to a minimum.

minimum *noun* (*plural* **minima**) the lowest possible number or amount. (The opposite is *maximum*.) **minimal** *adjective* [Latin, = least thing]

minion *noun* (*contemptuous*) a very obedient assistant or servant.

minister¹ *noun* **1** a person in charge of a government department. **2** a member of the clergy. **ministerial** *adjective*

minister² *verb* attend to people's needs. [Latin, = servant]

ministry *noun* (*plural* **ministries**) **1** (*Australian*) the Prime Minister or Premier with his or her cabinet. **2** the work of the clergy.

mink *noun* **1** an animal rather like a stoat. **2** this animal's valuable brown fur.

minnow *noun* a tiny freshwater fish.

minor¹ *adjective* **1** less important; not very important. **2** of the musical scale that has a semitone after the second note. (Compare *major*.) [Latin, = smaller, lesser]

minor² *noun* a person under the full legal age.

minority *noun* (*plural* **minorities**) **1** the smallest part of a group of people or things. **2** a small group that is different from others. (Compare *majority*.)

minster *noun* a large or important church, York Minster.

minstrel *noun* a travelling singer and musician in the Middle Ages.

mint¹ *noun* **1** a plant with fragrant leaves that are used for flavouring things. **2** peppermint; a sweet flavoured with this. [from Latin *mentha* = mint]

mint² *noun* the place where a country's coins are made.

mint³ *adjective* clean and new or unused.

mint⁴ *verb* make coins. [from Latin *moneta* = money]

minuet *noun* a slow stately dance.

minus¹ *preposition* with the next number or thing subtracted, *Ten minus four equals six* (10–4 = 6).

minus² *adjective* less than zero, *temperatures of minus ten degrees* (–10°). [Latin, = less]

minute¹ (*say* **min**-it) *noun* **1** one-sixtieth of an hour. **2** a very short time; a moment. **3** a particular time, *Come here this minute!* **4** one-sixtieth of a degree (used in measuring angles). **minutes** *plural noun* a written summary of what was said at a meeting.

▶▶THESAURUS◀◀

mingle *verb* **1** blend, combine, intermingle, merge, mix. **2** circulate, mix, socialise.

mingy *adjective* meagre, mean, measly (*informal*), niggardly, paltry, stingy.

miniature¹ *adjective* diminutive, dwarf, little, microscopic, minuscule, minute, pocket-size, small, small-scale, tiny.

minimise *verb* cut, decrease, diminish, keep down, lessen, reduce.

minimum *noun* least, lowest.
minimal *adjective* imperceptible, least, littlest, lowest, marginal, minuscule, minutest, negligible, slightest, smallest, subtle, token.

minister¹ *noun* **2** archbishop, archdeacon, bishop, chaplain, clergyman, clergywoman, cleric, curate, deacon, dean, evangelist, father, padre, parson, pastor, preacher, priest, rector, vicar.

minister² *verb* (*minister to*) attend to, care for, cater to, help, tend.

minor¹ *adjective* **1** inconsequential, insignificant, lesser, petty, slight, small, subordinate, trivial, unimportant.

minor² *noun* adolescent, child, juvenile, teenager, youngster, youth.

minstrel *noun* bard, entertainer, musician, performer, singer, troubadour.

mint⁴ *verb* cast, coin, make, produce, strike.

minute¹ *noun* **2** flash, instant, jiffy (*informal*), moment, tick (*informal*), trice.
minutes *plural noun* account, notes, proceedings, record, summary.

►►► DICTIONARY ◄◄

minute² (*say* my-**newt**) *adjective* **1** very small, *a minute insect.* **2** very detailed, *a minute examination.* **minutely** *adverb* [from Latin *minutus* = little]

minx *noun* (*plural* **minxes**) a cheeky or mischievous girl.

miracle *noun* something wonderful and good that happens, especially something believed to have a supernatural or divine cause. **miraculous** *adjective*, **miraculously** *adverb* [from Latin *mirari* = to wonder]

mirage (*say* **mi**-rah*zh*) *noun* an illusion; something that seems to be there but is not, especially when a lake seems to appear in a desert. [from French *se mirer* = be reflected]

mire *noun* swampy ground; mud.

mirror¹ *noun* a device or surface of reflecting material, usually glass.

mirror² *verb* reflect in or like a mirror. [from Latin *mirare* = look at]

mirth *noun* merriment; laughter. **mirthful** *adjective*, **mirthless** *adjective*

mis- *prefix* badly; wrongly. (Compare *amiss*.)

misadventure *noun* a piece of bad luck.

misanthropy *noun* dislike of people. **misanthropist** *noun*, **misanthropic** *adjective* [from Greek *misos* = hatred, *anthropos* = human being]

misapprehend *verb* misunderstand. **misapprehension** *noun*

misappropriate *verb* take something dishonestly. **misappropriation** *noun*

misbehave *verb* behave badly. **misbehaviour** *noun*

miscalculate *verb* calculate incorrectly. **miscalculation** *noun*

miscarriage *noun* **1** the birth of a baby before it has developed enough to live. **2** failure to achieve the right result, *a miscarriage of justice.*

miscellaneous (*say* mis-el-**ay**-nee-us) *adjective* of various kinds; mixed. **miscellany** (*say* mis-**el**-an-ee) *noun* [from Latin *miscellus* = mixed]

mischance *noun* misfortune.

mischief *noun* **1** naughty or troublesome behaviour. **2** trouble caused by this. **mischievous** *adjective*, **mischievously** *adverb*

misconception *noun* a mistaken idea.

misconduct *noun* **1** bad behaviour. **2** improper or unprofessional behaviour.

misconstrue *verb* (**misconstrued, misconstruing**) misinterpret. **misconstruction** *noun*

miscreant (*say* **mis**-kree-ant) *noun* a wrongdoer; a villain.

misdeed *noun* a wrong or improper action.

misdemeanour *noun* a misdeed; an unlawful act.

►►► THESAURUS ◄◄

minute² *adjective* **1** little, microscopic, minuscule, small, tiny. **2** close, detailed, exhaustive, meticulous, thorough.

miracle *noun* marvel, wonder.
miraculous *adjective* amazing, astonishing, astounding, extraordinary, incredible, marvellous, mysterious, phenomenal, remarkable, supernatural, unbelievable, wonderful.

mirage *noun* hallucination, illusion, phantasm, vision.

mirror¹ *noun* glass, looking-glass.

mirror² *verb* reflect.

mirth *noun* amusement, cheerfulness, festivity, fun, gaiety, glee, happiness, hilarity, jollity, joviality, laughter, merriment, merrymaking, rejoicing, revelry.

misappropriate *verb* embezzle, misuse, steal, take.

misbehaviour *noun* bad manners, delinquency, disobedience, misconduct, naughtiness, playing up (*informal*), rebelliousness, unruliness.

miscalculate *verb* misjudge, overestimate, overvalue, underestimate, undervalue.

miscarriage *noun* **1** spontaneous abortion. **2** breakdown, collapse, error, failure.

miscellaneous *adjective* assorted, different, diverse, mixed, motley, varied, various.

mischief *noun* **1** high jinks, misbehaviour, misconduct, naughtiness, playfulness, playing up (*informal*), pranks, shenanigans (*informal*). **2** damage, harm, hurt, injury, trouble.
mischievous *adjective* devilish, impish, naughty, playful, roguish.

misconduct *noun* **1** misbehaviour, naughtiness, playing up (*informal*), unruliness. **2** impropriety, malpractice, mishandling, mismanagement.

misconstrue *verb* misapprehend, misinterpret, misread, misunderstand.

miscreant *noun* baddy (*informal*), criminal, evildoer, rascal, scoundrel, villain, wretch, wrongdoer.

misdemeanour *noun* crime, misdeed, offence, sin, transgression, wrongdoing.

▶▶▶ D I C T I O N A R Y ◀◀◀

miser *noun* a person who hoards money and spends as little as possible. **miserly** *adjective*, **miserliness** *noun* [same origin as *misery*]

miserable *adjective* **1** full of misery; very unhappy, poor, or uncomfortable. **2** disagreeable; unpleasant, *miserable weather*. **miserably** *adverb*

misery *noun* (*plural* **miseries**) **1** great unhappiness or discomfort or suffering. **2** something causing this. **3** (*informal*) a discontented or disagreeable person. [from Latin *miser* = wretched]

misfire *verb* (**misfired, misfiring**) fail to fire; fail to function correctly or to have the required effect, *The joke misfired.*

misfit *noun* **1** a person who does not fit in well with other people or who is not well suited to his or her work. **2** a garment that does not fit.

misfortune *noun* **1** bad luck. **2** an unlucky event or accident.

misgiving *noun* a feeling of doubt or slight fear or mistrust.

misguided *adjective* mistaken.

mishap (*say* **mis**-hap) *noun* an unlucky accident.

misinterpret *verb* interpret incorrectly. **misinterpretation** *noun*

misjudge *verb* (**misjudged, misjudging**) judge wrongly; form a wrong opinion or estimate. **misjudgement** *noun*

mislay *verb* (**mislaid, mislaying**) lose something for a short time.

mislead *verb* (**misled, misleading**) give somebody a wrong idea; deceive.

mismanagement *noun* bad management.

misnomer *noun* an unsuitable name for something. [from *mis*-, + Latin *nomen* = name]

misogynist (*say* mis-**oj**-in-ist) *noun* a person who hates women. **misogyny** *noun* [from Greek *misos* = hatred, + *gyne* = woman]

misplace *verb* (**misplaced, misplacing**) place wrongly. **misplacement** *noun*

misprint *noun* a mistake in printing.

mispronounce *verb* pronounce incorrectly. **mispronunciation** *noun*

misquote *verb* (**misquoted, misquoting**) quote incorrectly. **misquotation** *noun*

misread *verb* read or interpret incorrectly.

misrepresent *verb* represent in a false or misleading way. **misrepresentation** *noun*

misrule *noun* bad government.

▶▶▶ T H E S A U R U S ◀◀◀

miser *noun* cheapskate (*informal*), hoarder, Scrooge, skinflint, tightwad (*informal*).
miserly *adjective* close-fisted, mean, mingy (*informal*), niggardly, parsimonious, penny-pinching, stingy, tight-fisted.

miserable *adjective* **1** crestfallen, dejected, depressed, desolate, despondent, disconsolate, doleful, downcast, down-hearted, forlorn, gloomy, glum, heavy-hearted, melancholy, sad, sorrowful, unhappy, woebegone, wretched. **2** abysmal (*informal*), appalling (*informal*), atrocious (*informal*), depressing, dismal, dreadful (*informal*), dreary, inclement, lousy (*informal*), terrible (*informal*), unpleasant.

misery *noun* **1** blues, depression, despair, discomfort, distress, gloom, grief, melancholy, sadness, sorrow, suffering, torment, unhappiness, woe, wretchedness. **2** adversity, affliction, deprivation, hardship, misfortune, suffering, trouble. **3** complainer, grouch (*informal*), grumbler, malcontent, moaner, wet blanket, whinger (*informal*).

misfit *noun* **1** fish out of water, maverick, nonconformist, square peg in a round hole.

misfortune *noun* **1** adversity, bad luck, mischance. **2** accident, affliction, blow, calamity, catastrophe, disaster, misadventure, mishap, reverse, setback, trial, tribulation, trouble.

misgiving *noun* anxiety, apprehension, doubt, fear, hesitation, qualm, question, reservation, second thoughts, uncertainty, worry.

misguided *adjective* foolish, misdirected, misinformed, misled, mistaken, unwise.

mishap *noun* see MISFORTUNE.

misinterpret *verb* misapprehend, misconstrue, misread, misunderstand.

misjudge *verb* exaggerate, get wrong, miscalculate, overestimate, underestimate.

mislay *verb* lose, misplace.

mislead *verb* bluff, con (*informal*), deceive, delude, dupe, fool, hoax, hoodwink, kid (*informal*), lead astray, lie, misguide, misinform, take for a ride (*informal*), take in, trick.
misleading *adjective* ambiguous, confusing, deceptive, equivocal.

mismanagement *noun* bungling, maladministration, mishandling.

misplace *verb* lose, mislay.

misrepresent *verb* distort, falsify, misquote, misreport, twist.

▶▶ DICTIONARY ◀◀

Miss *noun* (*plural* **Misses**) a title put before a girl's or unmarried woman's name. [short for *mistress*]

miss¹ *verb* **1** fail to hit, reach, catch, see, hear, or find something. **2** fail to attend an event etc. **3** fail to seize an opportunity etc. **4** be sad because someone or something is not with you. **5** notice that something has gone. **6** avoid. [from Old English *missan*]

miss² *noun* (*plural* **misses**) missing something, *Was that shot a hit or a miss?*

missal *noun* a Roman Catholic prayerbook. [from Latin *missa* = mass (*Mass³*)]

misshapen *adjective* badly shaped.

missile *noun* a weapon or other object for firing or throwing at a target. [from Latin *missum* = sent]

missing *adjective* **1** lost; not in the proper place. **2** absent.

mission *noun* **1** an important job that somebody is sent to do or feels he or she must do. **2** a place or building where missionaries work. [from Latin *missio* = a sending]

missionary *noun* (*plural* **missionaries**) a person who is sent to another country to spread the Christian faith.

mist *noun* **1** damp cloudy air near the ground. **2** condensed water-vapour on a window, mirror, etc.

mistake¹ *noun* something done wrongly; an incorrect opinion.

mistake² *verb* (**mistook, mistaken, mistaking**) **1** misunderstand, *Don't mistake my meaning.* **2** choose or identify wrongly, *We mistook her for her sister.*

mistaken *adjective* incorrect; unwise.

mistime *verb* (**mistimed, mistiming**) do or say something at a wrong time.

mistletoe *noun* a plant with white berries that grows as a parasite on trees.

mistreat *verb* treat badly.

mistress *noun* (*plural* **mistresses**) **1** a woman who is in charge of something. **2** a woman teacher. **3** a woman who is a man's lover but not his wife.

mistrust *verb* feel no trust in somebody or something. **mistrust** *noun*

misty *adjective* full of mist; not clear. **mistily** *adverb*, **mistiness** *noun*

misunderstand *verb* (**misunderstood, misunderstanding**) get a wrong idea or impression of something.

misuse *verb* (**misused, misusing**) **1** use incorrectly. **2** treat badly. **misuse** *noun*

▶▶ THESAURUS ◀◀

miss¹ *verb* **2** absent yourself from, be absent from, forgo, give up, skip. **3** let go, let pass, let slip, lose, pass up. **4** crave for, long for, pine for, want, yearn for. **6** avoid, bypass, dodge, steer clear of.
miss out forget, leave out, omit, overlook, pass over, skip.

misshapen *adjective* contorted, crooked, deformed, distorted, malformed, twisted, warped.

missile *noun* projectile; (*kinds of missile*) arrow, ballistic missile, bomb, boomerang, bullet, dart, grenade, guided missile, harpoon, javelin, rocket, shell, spear, torpedo.

missing *adjective* **1** gone, lost, mislaid, misplaced, removed. **2** absent, disappeared, gone, lost.

mission *noun* **1** assignment, campaign, exercise, expedition, operation, quest, undertaking; (*a mission in life*) calling, purpose, vocation.

missionary *noun* apostle, evangelist, preacher.

mist *noun* cloud, fog, haze, smog, steam, vapour.

mistake¹ *noun* blooper (*informal*), blue (*Australian informal*), blunder, booboo (*slang*), clanger (*informal*), error, faux pas, gaffe, howler (*informal*), miscalculation, misjudgement, misprint, mix-up, oversight, slip, slip-up (*informal*), typo (*informal*).

mistake² *verb* **1** confuse, get wrong, misapprehend, misconstrue, misinterpret, misunderstand. **2** confuse with, mix up with, take for.

mistreat *verb* abuse, harm, hurt, ill-treat, maltreat, manhandle, molest, torment.

mistress *noun* **1** keeper, owner. **2** schoolmistress, teacher. **3** girlfriend, lover.

mistrust *verb* distrust, doubt, have misgivings about, question, suspect.
mistrust *noun* distrust, scepticism, suspicion, wariness.

misty *adjective* foggy, hazy.

misunderstand *verb* get wrong, misapprehend, misconstrue, misinterpret, misjudge, misread, mistake.
misunderstanding *noun* confusion, misapprehension, misconception, misinterpretation, misjudgement, misreading, mistake, mix-up.

misuse *noun* abuse, misappropriation, squandering, waste.

mite *noun* 1 a tiny spider-like creature found in food, *cheese-mites*. 2 a very small amount. 3 a small child.

mitigate *verb* (**mitigated, mitigating**) make a thing less intense or less severe. **mitigation** *noun*

mitigating circumstances facts that may partially excuse wrongdoing. [from Latin *mitigare* = make mild]

mitre[1] *noun* 1 the tall tapering hat worn by a bishop. 2 a mitred join.

mitre[2] *verb* (**mitred, mitring**) join two tapered pieces of wood or cloth etc. so that they form a right angle.

mitt *noun* 1 a mitten. 2 a fielder's glove in baseball or softball. 3 (*slang*) a hand or fist.

mitten *noun* a kind of glove without separate parts for the fingers.

mix[1] *verb* 1 put different things together so that the substances etc. are no longer distinct; blend; combine. 2 (of a person) get together with others. **mixer** *noun*

mix up mix thoroughly; confuse.

mix[2] *noun* (*plural* **mixes**) a mixture.

mixed *adjective* containing two or more kinds of things or people.

mixed blessing something that has disadvantages as well as advantages.

mixture *noun* 1 something made of different things mixed together. 2 the process of mixing.

mizzen-mast *noun* the mast nearest to the stern on a three-masted ship.

mnemonic (*say* nim-**on**-ik) *noun* a verse or saying that helps you to remember something. [from Greek *mnemonikos* = for the memory]

moan *verb* 1 make a long low sound of pain or suffering. 2 grumble. **moan** *noun*

moat *noun* a deep wide ditch round a castle, usually filled with water. **moated** *adjective*

mob[1] *noun* 1 a large disorderly crowd; a rabble. 2 a gang. 3 (*Australian*) a flock or herd. 4 an Aboriginal extended family or community.

mob[2] *verb* (**mobbed, mobbing**) crowd round somebody. [from Latin *mobile vulgus* = excitable crowd]

mobile[1] *adjective* moving easily. **mobility** *noun*

mobile home a large caravan permanently parked and used for living in.

mobile phone a portable radio telephone.

mobile[2] *noun* a decoration for hanging up so that its parts move in currents of air. [from Latin *movere* = move]

mobilise *verb* (**mobilised, mobilising**) assemble people or things for a particular purpose, especially for war. **mobilisation** *noun*

moccasin *noun* a soft leather shoe.

mock[1] *verb* 1 make fun of a person or thing. 2 imitate; mimic.

mitigate *verb* alleviate, appease, assuage, diminish, ease, lessen, lighten, moderate, mollify, palliate, reduce, relieve, soften, soothe, subdue, weaken.

mix[1] *verb* 1 blend, combine, incorporate, integrate, join, merge, mingle, unite. 2 be sociable, fraternise, mingle, socialise.

mix up confuse, jumble up, muddle up, rearrange, shuffle.

mix[2] *noun* see MIXTURE.

mixed *adjective* (*a mixed group*) assorted, diverse, miscellaneous, motley, varied; (*a mixed breed*) cross-bred, hybrid, mongrel.

mixture *noun* 1 alloy, amalgam, assortment, blend, collection, combination, compound, concoction, cross, hash, hotchpotch, hybrid, jumble, medley, mix, patchwork, pot-pourri, rag-bag, variety.

moan *noun* 1 groan, wail, whimper, whine. 2 beef (*slang*), complaint, grievance, gripe (*informal*), grizzle (*informal*), grumble, whine, whinge (*informal*).

moan *verb* 1 groan, wail, whimper, whine. 2 beef (*slang*), complain, gripe (*informal*), grizzle (*informal*), grumble, whine, whinge (*informal*).

mob[1] *noun* 1 bunch, crowd, crush, gathering, herd, horde, lot, mass, multitude, pack, rabble, throng. 3 flock, group, herd.

mob[2] *verb* besiege, crowd round, gather round, surround, swarm round.

mobile[1] *adjective* movable, portable, transportable, travelling.

mobilise *verb* assemble, gather, marshal, muster, organise, rally.

mock[1] *verb* 1 chiack (*Australian informal*), deride, jeer at, make fun of, pay out (*informal*), poke fun at, ridicule, scoff at, scorn, sling off at (*Australian informal*), sneer at, take the mickey out of (*informal*), taunt. 2 ape, caricature, copy, imitate, impersonate, mimic, parody, send up (*informal*), take off.

▶▶ D I C T I O N A R Y ◀◀

mock² *adjective* sham; imitation, not real, *a mock battle.*

mockery *noun* 1 ridicule. 2 a ridiculous representation.

mock-up *noun* a model of something, made in order to test or study it.

mode *noun* 1 the way a thing is done. 2 what is fashionable.

model¹ *noun* 1 a copy of an object, usually on a smaller scale. 2 a particular design. 3 a person who poses for an artist or displays clothes by wearing them. 4 a person or thing that is worth copying.

model² *adjective* 1 miniature. 2 excellent; being an example to others, *a model pupil.*

model³ *verb* (**modelled, modelling**) 1 make a model of something. 2 make according to a model. 3 work as an artist's model or a fashion model.

moderate¹ *adjective* medium; not extremely small or great or hot etc., *a moderate climate.* **moderately** *adverb*

moderate² (*say* **mod**-er-ayt) *verb* (**moderated, moderating**) make or become moderate. **moderation** *noun*
in moderation in moderate amounts.

modern *adjective* of the present or recent times; in fashion now. **modernity** *noun*

modernise *verb* (**modernised, modernising**) make a thing more modern. **modernisation** *noun*

modest *adjective* 1 not vain; not boasting. 2 moderate. 3 not showy or splendid. 4 rather shy; decorous. **modestly** *adverb*, **modesty** *noun* [from Latin, = keeping the proper measure]

modicum *noun* a small amount.

modify *verb* (**modified, modifying**) 1 change something slightly. 2 qualify a word by describing it, *Adjectives modify nouns.* **modification** *noun*

modulate *verb* (**modulated, modulating**) 1 adjust; regulate. 2 vary in pitch or tone etc. **modulation** *noun*

module *noun* 1 an independent part of a spacecraft, building, etc. 2 a unit; a section of a course of study. **modular** *adjective*

moggy *noun* (*slang*) a cat.

mogul (*say* **moh**-gul) *noun* (*informal*) an important or influential person. [the Moguls were the ruling family in India in the 16th–19th centuries]

mohair *noun* fine silky wool from an angora goat. [from Arabic, = special]

moist *adjective* slightly wet; damp. **moistly** *adverb*, **moistness** *noun*

moisten *verb* make or become moist.

▶▶ T H E S A U R U S ◀◀

mock² *adjective* fake, imitation, pretend (*informal*), pretended, sham, simulated.

mockery *noun* 1 derision, disdain, jeering, ridicule, scorn. 2 farce, joke, pretence, travesty.

mode *noun* 1 approach, fashion, form, manner, means, method, practice, procedure, system, technique, way. 2 custom, fashion, style, trend, vogue.

model¹ *noun* 1 archetype, copy, dummy, miniature, mock-up, prototype, replica, representation. 2 design, style, type, version. 3 mannequin. 4 archetype, epitome, exemplar, ideal, paragon.

model² *adjective* 2 excellent, exemplary, ideal, perfect.

model³ *verb* 1 cast, form, make, mould, sculpt (*informal*), shape. 2 (*model on*) base on, copy on, follow.

moderate¹ *adjective* average, fair, intermediate, medium, middling, modest, reasonable; (*of climate*) mild, temperate.
moderately *adverb* fairly, pretty, quite, rather, reasonably, slightly, somewhat.

moderate² *verb* abate, calm down, check, curb, die down, ease, quieten down, restrain, soften, subdue, subside, tame, temper, tone down.

modern *adjective* contemporary, current, fashionable, innovative, new, newfangled (*derogatory*), present, progressive, recent, trendy (*informal*), up to date, with it (*informal*).

modernise *verb* rejuvenate, renovate, update.

modest *adjective* 1 humble, quiet, unassertive, unassuming. 2 moderate, slight, small. 3 humble, lowly, ordinary, simple, unpretentious. 4 bashful, coy, self-conscious, shy.

modify *verb* 1 adapt, adjust, alter, change, refine, revise, transform, vary. 2 limit, qualify, restrict.

modulate *verb* adjust, alter, change, moderate, regulate, temper, tone down, vary.

module *noun* 2 component, part, piece, unit.

moist *adjective* clammy, damp, dank, dewy, humid, muggy, steamy, wet.

moisten *verb* damp, dampen, irrigate, soak, spray, water, wet.

moisture *noun* water in the air or making a thing moist.

molar *noun* any of the wide teeth at the back of the jaw, used in chewing. [from Latin *mola* = millstone]

molasses *noun* syrup from raw sugar.

mole¹ *noun* **1** a small furry animal that burrows under the ground. **2** a person who secretly gives confidential information to an enemy or rival.

mole² *noun* a small dark spot on skin.

mole³ *noun* a stone wall built out into the sea as a breakwater or causeway.

molecule *noun* the smallest part into which a substance can be divided without changing its chemical nature; a group of atoms. **molecular** *adjective* [from Latin, = little mass]

molehill *noun* a small pile of earth thrown up by a burrowing mole.

molest *verb* pester. **molestation** *noun* [from Latin *molestus* = troublesome]

mollify *verb* (**mollified**, **mollifying**) make a person less angry. **mollification** *noun* [from Latin, = soften]

molten *adjective* melted; made liquid by great heat.

moment *noun* **1** a very short time. **2** a particular time, *Call me the moment she arrives.* **3** importance, *These are matters of great moment.*

momentary *adjective* lasting for only a moment. **momentarily** *adverb*

momentous (*say* mo-**ment**-us) *adjective* very important.

momentum *noun* amount or force of movement, *The stone gathered momentum as it rolled downhill.* [Latin, = movement]

monarch *noun* **1** a king, queen, emperor, or empress ruling a country. **2** a large orange and black butterfly. **monarchic** *adjective* [from Greek *monos* = alone, + *archein* = to rule]

monarchy *noun* (*plural* **monarchies**) a country ruled by a monarch. **monarchist** *noun*

monastery *noun* (*plural* **monasteries**) a building where monks live and work. (Compare *nunnery*.) **monastic** *adjective* [from Greek *monazein* = live alone]

monetary *adjective* of money.

money *noun* **1** coins and banknotes. **2** wealth. [same origin as *mint*⁴]

mongoose *noun* (*plural* **mongooses**) a small tropical animal rather like a stoat, that can kill snakes.

mongrel (*say* **mung**-grel) *noun* a dog of mixed breeds. [from *mingle*]

monitor¹ *noun* **1** a device for watching or testing how something is working; a visual display unit. **2** a pupil who is given a special responsibility in a school.

monitor² *verb* watch or test how something is working. [from Latin *monere* = warn]

moisture *noun* condensation, damp, dampness, dew, humidity, liquid, steam, vapour, water, wetness.

molest *verb* abuse, annoy, bother, harass, ill-treat, maltreat, mistreat, persecute, pester, tease, torment.

mollify *verb* appease, calm, pacify, placate, quiet, soothe, subdue.

molten *adjective* liquefied, liquid, melted.

moment *noun* **1** flash, instant, jiffy (*informal*), minute, second, tick (*informal*), trice, two shakes (*informal*). **2** instant, juncture, point, stage. **3** consequence, gravity, import, importance, significance.

momentary *adjective* brief, ephemeral, fleeting, passing, short, short-lived, temporary, transient.

momentous *adjective* crucial, fateful, grave, historic, important, significant, weighty.

momentum *noun* force, impetus, strength.

monarch *noun* **1** emperor, empress, head, king, queen, ruler, sovereign.

monarchy *noun* empire, kingdom, realm. **monarchist** *noun* royalist.

monastery *noun* abbey, cloister, friary, lamasery (*Buddhism*), priory, religious house. **monastic** *adjective* ascetic, austere, cloistered, reclusive, secluded, solitary, spartan.

money *noun* **1** banknotes, cash, coins, currency, dosh (*slang*), dough (*slang*), lucre (*derogatory*), notes, paper money, ready money. **2** assets, capital, finance, funds, means, resources, riches, wealth.

mongrel *noun* bitser (*Australian informal*), cross-breed, hybrid.

monitor¹ *noun* **1** display terminal, screen, VDU, visual display unit. **2** prefect.

monitor² *verb* check, keep an eye on, keep track of, observe, record, watch.

▶▶▶ D I C T I O N A R Y ◀◀

monk *noun* a member of a community of men who live according to the rules of a religious organisation. (Compare *nun*.) [same origin as *mono*-]

monkey *noun* (*plural* **monkeys**) **1** an animal with long arms, hands with thumbs, and often a tail. **2** a mischievous person. [origin unknown]

mono- *prefix* one; single. [from Greek *monos* = alone]

monochrome *adjective* done in one colour or in black and white. [from *mono*-, + Greek *chroma* = colour]

monocle *noun* an eyeglass for one eye. [from *mono*-, + Latin *oculus* = eye]

monogamy *noun* the custom of being married to only one person at a time. (Compare *polygamy*.) **monogamous** *adjective* [from *mono*-, + Greek *gamos* = marriage]

monogram *noun* a design made up of a letter or letters, especially a person's initials. **monogrammed** *adjective* [from *mono*- + -*gram*]

monograph *noun* a scholarly book or article on one particular subject. [from *mono*- + -*graph*]

monolith *noun* a large single upright block of stone. [from *mono*-, + Greek *lithos* = stone]

monolithic *adjective* **1** consisting of monoliths. **2** single and huge.

monologue *noun* a speech by one person. [from *mono*-, + Greek *logos* = word]

monoplane *noun* a type of aeroplane with only one set of wings.

monopolise *verb* (**monopolised, monopolising**) take the whole of something for yourself, *One girl monopolised my attention.* **monopolisation** *noun*

monopoly *noun* (*plural* **monopolies**) complete possession or control of something by one group, *The company had a monopoly in supplying electricity.* [from *mono*-, + Greek *polein* = sell]

monorail *noun* a railway that uses a single rail, not a pair of rails.

monosyllable *noun* a word with only one syllable. **monosyllabic** *adjective*

monotheism (*say* **mon**-oth-ee-izm) *noun* belief that there is only one god. **monotheist** *noun* [from *mono*-, + Greek *theos* = god]

monotone *noun* a level unchanging tone of voice in speaking or singing.

monotonous *adjective* boring because it does not change. **monotonously** *adverb*, **monotony** *noun*

monotreme *noun* an egg-laying mammal, e.g. the platypus and the echidna.

monoxide *noun* an oxide with one atom of oxygen.

monsoon *noun* **1** a strong wind in and near the Indian Ocean, bringing heavy rain in summer. **2** the rainy season brought by this wind. [from Arabic *mausim* = fixed season]

monster[1] *noun* **1** a large frightening creature. **2** a huge thing.

monster[2] *adjective* huge. [from Latin *monstrum* = marvel]

monstrosity *noun* (*plural* **monstrosities**) a monstrous thing.

monstrous *adjective* **1** like a monster. **2** huge. **3** very shocking; outrageous.

month *noun* each of the twelve parts into which a year is divided. [related to *moon* (because time was measured by the changes in the moon's appearance)]

monthly *adjective* & *adverb* happening or done once a month.

▶▶▶ T H E S A U R U S ◀◀

monk *noun* abbot, brother, friar, lama (*Buddhism*), prior, religious.

monkey *noun* **1** simian. **2** devil, imp, rascal, rogue, scallywag, scamp.

monolithic *adjective* **2** colossal, enormous, gigantic, huge, large, massive, monumental.

monologue *noun* address, lecture, oration, sermon, soliloquy, speech.

monopolise *verb* dominate, preoccupy, take over.

monotonous *adjective* (*monotonous work*) boring, dreary, dull, humdrum, mechanical, repetitive, routine, soporific, tedious, un-varying; (*a monotonous voice*) droning, expressionless, flat, singsong, unexpressive.

monster[1] *noun* **1** beast, bogyman, brute, bunyip (*Australian*), demon, devil, dragon, fiend, giant, ogre.

monstrosity *noun* eyesore, horror, monster.

monstrous *adjective* **1** abnormal, freakish, grotesque, misshapen, odd, ugly, unnatural, weird. **2** colossal, enormous, gigantic, huge, immense, massive. **3** abhorrent, appalling, atrocious, brutal, cruel, despicable, detestable, fiendish, ghastly, heinous, hideous, horrible, horrid, outrageous, repulsive, savage, shocking, vile, wicked.

▶▶▶ D I C T I O N A R Y ◀◀◀

monument *noun* a statue, building, or column etc. put up as a memorial of some person or event.

monumental *adjective* **1** of or as a monument. **2** extremely great; huge. **3** (of books etc.) of lasting value.

moo *verb* make the low deep sound of a cow. **moo** *noun*

mood *noun* the way someone feels, *She is in a cheerful mood.*

moody *adjective* **1** gloomy or sullen. **2** likely to become bad-tempered suddenly. **moodily** *adverb*, **moodiness** *noun*

moon¹ *noun* **1** the natural satellite of the earth that can be seen in the sky at night. **2** a satellite of any planet. **moonbeam** *noun*, **moonlight** *noun*, **moonlit** *adjective*

moon² *verb* go about in a dreamy or listless way.

Moor *noun* a member of a Muslim people of north-west Africa. **Moorish** *adjective*

moor¹ *noun* an area of rough land with bushes but no trees.

moor² *verb* fasten a boat etc. to a fixed object by means of a cable.

moorhen *noun* a small water-bird.

moose *noun* (*plural* **moose**) a North American elk.

moot¹ *adjective* debatable; undecided, *That's a moot point.*

moot² *verb* put forward an idea for discussion.

mop¹ *noun* **1** a bunch or pad of soft material fastened on the end of a stick, used for cleaning floors etc. **2** a thick mass of hair.

mop² *verb* (**mopped, mopping**) clean or wipe with a mop etc.; wipe away.

mope *verb* (**moped, moping**) be sad.

moped (*say* **moh**-ped) *noun* a bicycle worked by a motor. [from *motor* + *ped*al]

mopoke (*say* **moh**-poke) *noun* (*Australian*) a boobook.

moraine *noun* a mass of stones and earth etc. carried down by a glacier.

moral¹ *adjective* **1** connected with what is right and wrong in behaviour. **2** virtuous. **morally** *adverb*, **morality** *noun*
a moral certainty probability approaching certainty.
moral support encouragement.

moral² *noun* **1** a lesson in right behaviour taught by a story or event. **2** (*Australian*) a moral certainty.
morals *plural noun* standards of behaviour; virtuousness. [from Latin *mores* = customs]

morale (*say* mor-**ahl**) *noun* confidence; the state of someone's spirits, *Morale was high after the victory.*

moralise *verb* (**moralised, moralising**) talk or write about right and wrong behaviour. **moralist** *noun*

morass *noun* (*plural* **morasses**) **1** a marsh or bog. **2** a confused mass.

moratorium *noun* a temporary ban. [from Latin *morari* = to delay]

morbid *adjective* **1** thinking about gloomy or unpleasant things. **2** unhealthy. **morbidly** *adverb*, **morbidity** *noun* [from Latin *morbus* = disease]

▶▶▶ T H E S A U R U S ◀◀◀

monument *noun* cairn, cenotaph, gravestone, headstone, mausoleum, memorial, obelisk, plaque, shrine, statue, tombstone.

monumental *adjective* **2** colossal, enormous, great, huge, immense, large, massive, monstrous, stupendous, terrific (*informal*), tremendous. **3** classic, enduring, great, impressive, lasting, major.

mood *noun* attitude, disposition, feeling, frame of mind, humour, spirits, state of mind, temper.

moody *adjective* **1** blue, depressed, dismal, gloomy, glum, irritable, melancholy, morose, peevish, sulky, sullen, testy, tetchy, unhappy. **2** changeable, erratic, inconsistent, mercurial, temperamental, unpredictable, volatile.

moor¹ *noun* fell, heath.

moor² *verb* anchor, berth, dock, secure, tie up.

moorings *plural noun* anchorage, berth.

moot¹ *adjective* arguable, controversial, debatable, disputable, undecided, unresolved.

mop² *verb* clean, sponge, wash, wipe.

mope *verb* brood, fret, languish, mooch (*informal*), moon, pine.

moral¹ *adjective* **1** ethical. **2** above board, blameless, decent, ethical, good, honourable, principled, proper, right, righteous, upright, virtuous.
morality *noun* decency, ethics, fairness, goodness, honour, integrity, morals, principles, rectitude, scruples, standards, virtue.

moral² *noun* **1** lesson, message, principle, teaching.

morale *noun* confidence, self-confidence, spirit.

morbid *adjective* **1** ghoulish, grim, gruesome, macabre, sick, unwholesome. **2** diseased, pathological, unhealthy.

▶▶ D I C T I O N A R Y ◀◀

more¹ *adjective* (comparative of **much** and **many**) greater in amount etc.

more² *noun* a greater amount.

more³ *adverb* **1** to a greater extent, *more beautiful.* **2** again, *once more.*
more or less about; approximately.

moreover *adverb* besides; in addition to what has been said.

Moreton Bay a bay in southern Queensland.
Moreton Bay bug a kind of lobster used as food.
Moreton Bay chestnut a hardwood tree.
Moreton Bay fig a massive tree with glossy leaves and smooth bark.

morgue *noun* a mortuary.

Mormon *noun* a member of a religious group founded in the USA.

morn *noun* (*poetic*) morning.

morning *noun* the early part of the day, before noon or before lunchtime.

morocco *noun* a kind of leather originally made in Morocco from goatskins.

moron *noun* (*informal*) a very stupid person. [from Greek *moros* = foolish]

morose *adjective* sullen and gloomy. **morosely** *adverb*, **moroseness** *noun*

morphia or **morphine** (*say* **mor**-feen) *noun* a drug made from opium, used to lessen pain. [named after Morpheus, the Roman god of dreams]

morris dance a traditional English dance performed in costume by men with ribbons and bells. [originally 'Moorish dance']

morrow *noun* (*poetic*) the following day.

Morse code a signalling code using short and long sounds or flashes of light (dots and dashes) to represent letters. [named after its American inventor, S. F. B. Morse]

morsel *noun* a small piece of food; a small amount. [from Latin *morsus* = bite]

mortal¹ *adjective* **1** that can die, *All of us are mortal.* **2** causing death; fatal, *a mortal wound.* **3** deadly, *mortal enemies.* **mortally** *adverb*, **mortality** *noun*

mortal² *noun* a person who is not immortal. [from Latin *mortis* = of death]

mortar *noun* **1** a mixture of sand, cement, and water used in building to stick bricks together. **2** a hard bowl in which substances are pounded with a pestle. **3** a short cannon.

mortarboard *noun* an academic cap with a stiff square top.

mortgage¹ (*say* **mor**-gij) *noun* an arrangement to borrow money to buy a house, with the house as security for the loan.

mortgage² *verb* (**mortgaged, mortgaging**) offer a house etc. as security in return for a loan.

mortify *verb* (**mortified, mortifying**) humiliate a person greatly. **mortification** *noun* [same origin as *mortal*]

mortise *noun* a hole made in a piece of wood for another piece to be joined to it. (Compare *tenon.*)
mortise lock a lock set into a door.

mortuary *noun* a place where dead bodies are kept before being buried. [from Latin *mortuus* = dead]

mosaic (*say* mo-**zay**-ik) *noun* a picture or design made from small coloured pieces of stone or glass.

mosque (*say* mosk) *noun* a building where Muslims worship.

mosquito *noun* (*plural* **mosquitoes**) a kind of gnat that sucks blood. [Spanish, = little fly]

moss *noun* (*plural* **mosses**) a plant that grows in damp places and has no flowers. **mossy** *adjective*

mossie (*say* **moz**-ee) *noun* (*Australian slang*) a mosquito.

most¹ *adjective* (superlative of **much** and **many**) greatest in amount etc., *Most people came by bus.*

▶▶ T H E S A U R U S ◀◀

more¹ *adjective* additional, extra, further, other, reserve, spare, supplementary.

moreover *adverb* also, besides, further, furthermore, in addition.

moron *noun* see IDIOT.

morose *adjective* bad-tempered, churlish, depressed, dismal, dour, gloomy, glum, lugubrious, moody, sour, sulky, sullen, surly, taciturn, unsociable.

morsel *noun* bit, bite, fragment, mouthful, nibble, piece, scrap, sliver, taste, titbit.

mortal¹ *adjective* **1** earthly, ephemeral, human, transient, worldly. **2** deadly, fatal, lethal.

mortal² *noun* human being, man, person, woman.

mortify *verb* abase, abash, chagrin, discomfit, embarrass, humble, humiliate, shame.

mortuary *noun* morgue.

▶▶ D I C T I O N A R Y ◀◀

most² *noun* the greatest amount, *Most of the food was eaten.*

most³ *adverb* **1** to the greatest extent; more than any other, *most beautiful.* **2** very; extremely, *most impressive.*

mostly *adverb* mainly.

motel *noun* a hotel providing accommodation for motorists and their cars. [from *mot*or + ho*tel*]

moth *noun* an insect rather like a butterfly, that usually flies at night.

mother¹ *noun* a female parent. **motherhood** *noun*

mother² *verb* look after someone in a motherly way.
Mother's Day a celebration of mothers, in Australia the second Sunday in May. [from Old English *modor*]

mother-in-law *noun* (*plural* **mothers-in-law**) the mother of a married person's husband or wife.

motherly *adjective* kind and gentle like a mother. **motherliness** *noun*

mother-of-pearl *noun* a pearly substance lining the shells of mussels etc.

motif *noun* a repeated design or theme.

motion¹ *noun* **1** moving; movement. **2** a formal statement to be discussed and voted on at a meeting.

motion² *verb* signal by a gesture, *She motioned him to sit beside her.* [from Latin *motio* = movement]

motionless *adjective* not moving.

motivate *verb* (**motivated, motivating**) give a person a motive or incentive to do something. **motivation** *noun*

motive¹ *noun* what makes a person do something, *a motive for murder.*

motive² *adjective* providing movement, *The engine provides motive power.* [from Latin *motivus* = moving]

motley *adjective* **1** multicoloured. **2** made up of various sorts of things.

motor¹ *noun* a machine providing power to drive machinery etc.; an engine.

motor² *verb* go or take someone in a car. [from Latin *motor* = mover]

motorcade *noun* a procession of cars. [from *motor* + caval*cade*]

motorcycle *noun* a two-wheeled motor vehicle. **motorcyclist** *noun*

motorised *adjective* equipped with a motor or with motor vehicles.

motorist *noun* a person who drives a car.

motorway *noun* a wide road for fast long-distance traffic.

mottled *adjective* marked with spots or patches of colour. [from *motley*]

▶▶ T H E S A U R U S ◀◀

most² *noun* bulk, lion's share, majority.
make the most of capitalise on, exploit, profit by, take advantage of.

most³ *adverb* **2** exceedingly, extremely, highly, very.

mostly *adverb* chiefly, for the most part, generally, in general, largely, mainly, on the whole, predominantly, primarily, principally, usually.

motel *noun* hotel, inn, motor inn.

mother¹ *noun* matriarch; (*informal terms of address*) ma, mama, mamma, mammy, mom (*American*), mum, mummy.

mother² *verb* care for, fuss over, look after, nurse, nurture, protect, raise, rear, tend.

motherly *adjective* caring, gentle, kind, loving, maternal, protective, tender.

motif *noun* decoration, design, feature, idea, leitmotif, pattern, subject, theme.

motion¹ *noun* **1** locomotion, mobility, movement. **2** proposal, recommendation, suggestion.

motion² *verb* beckon, gesticulate, gesture, indicate, nod, signal, wave.

motionless *adjective* at rest, immobile, inert, paralysed, static, stationary, still, stock-still, transfixed.

motivate *verb* actuate, drive, galvanise, induce, influence, inspire, prompt, provoke, stimulate.
motivation *noun* ambition, drive, impetus, inspiration, stimulus.

motive¹ *noun* grounds, motivation, purpose, reason.

motley *adjective* **1** harlequin, mottled, multi-coloured, variegated. **2** assorted, disparate, diverse, heterogeneous, miscellaneous, mixed, varied.

motorcycle *noun* bike (*informal*), motor bike (*informal*).
motorcyclist *noun* biker, bikie (*Australian informal*).

mottled *adjective* blotchy, dappled, flecked, marbled, motley, speckled, spotty, variegated.

▶▶ D I C T I O N A R Y ◀◀

motto *noun* (*plural* **mottoes**) **1** a short saying used as a guide for behaviour, *Their motto is 'Who dares, wins'.* **2** a short verse or riddle etc. found inside a cracker. [Italian, = word]

mould¹ *noun* a hollow container of a particular shape, in which a liquid or soft substance is put to set into this shape.

mould² *verb* make something have a particular shape or character.

mould³ *noun* a fine furry growth of very small fungi. **mouldy** *adjective*

moulder *verb* rot away; decay into dust.

moult *verb* shed feathers, hair, or skin etc. while a new growth forms.

mound *noun* **1** a pile of earth or stones etc. **2** a small hill.

mount¹ *verb* **1** climb or go up; ascend. **2** get on a horse or bicycle etc. **3** increase in amount, *Our costs mounted.* **4** place or fix in position for use or display, *Mount your photos in an album.*

mount² *noun* **1** a mountain, *Mount Everest.* **2** something on which an object is mounted. **3** a horse etc. for riding. [from Latin *mons* = mountain]

mountain *noun* **1** a very high hill. **2** a large heap or pile or quantity. **mountainous** *adjective*

mountaineer *noun* a person who climbs mountains. **mountaineering** *noun*

mounted *adjective* serving on horseback, *mounted police.*

mourn *verb* be sad, especially because someone has died. **mourner** *noun*

mournful *adjective* sad; sorrowful. **mournfully** *adverb*

mouse *noun* (*plural* **mice**) a small animal with a long thin tail and a pointed nose. **mousetrap** *noun*, **mousy** *adjective*

mousse (*say* mooss) *noun* **1** a creamy pudding flavoured with fruit or chocolate. **2** a frothy creamy substance. [French, = froth]

moustache (*say* mus-**tahsh**) *noun* hair allowed to grow on a man's upper lip.

mouth¹ *noun* **1** the opening through which food is taken into the body. **2** the place where a river enters the sea. **3** an opening or outlet. **mouthful** *noun*

mouth² *verb* form words carefully with your lips, especially without saying them aloud.

mouth-organ *noun* a small musical instrument that you play by blowing and sucking while passing it along your lips.

mouthpiece *noun* the part of a musical or other instrument that you put to your mouth.

movable *adjective* able to be moved.

move¹ *verb* (**moved**, **moving**) **1** take or go from one place to another; change a person's or thing's position. **2** make progress. **3** affect a person's feelings, *Their sad story moved us deeply.* **4** put forward a formal statement (*a motion*) to be discussed and voted on at a meeting. **mover** *noun*

▶▶ T H E S A U R U S ◀◀

motto *noun* **1** adage, maxim, proverb, saying, slogan, watchword.

mould² *verb* (*mould a statue*) cast, fashion, forge, form, model, sculpt, shape; (*mould character*) develop, form, influence, make, shape.

mould³ *noun* fungus, mildew.
mouldy *adjective* bad, mildewed, musty, rotten, stale.

mound *noun* **1** cairn, heap, pile, pyramid, stack. **2** hill, hillock, hummock, knoll.

mount¹ *verb* **1** ascend, clamber up, climb, go up. **2** climb on, get astride, get on, straddle. **3** escalate, grow, heighten, increase, rise. **4** fix, install, place, position, put.

mountain *noun* **1** alp, ben (*Scottish*), bluff, elevation, hill, mount, peak, pinnacle, range, tier (*Tasmania & early South Australia*). **2** heap (*informal*), load (*informal*), lot (*informal*), pile

(*informal*), stack (*informal*), swag (*Australian informal*), ton (*informal*).

mourn *verb* grieve, lament, sorrow, weep.

mournful *adjective* dismal, doleful, funereal, gloomy, lugubrious, melancholy, sad, sombre, sorrowful.

mouth¹ *noun* **1** gob (*slang*), jaws, lips, trap (*slang*). **3** entrance, opening, outlet, portal.
mouthful *noun* bit, bite, gulp, morsel, nibble, sip, spoonful, sup, swallow, swig (*informal*).

movable *adjective* mobile, portable, transportable.

move¹ *verb* **1** budge, relocate, remove, shift, swap, switch, transfer, transplant, transport, transpose. **2** advance, go, go on, make headway, proceed, progress. **3** affect, disturb, stir, touch, upset. **4** propose, put forward, recommend, suggest.

moving *adjective* emotional, inspiring, poignant, rousing, stirring, touching.

▶▶ D I C T I O N A R Y ◀◀

move² *noun* **1** moving; a movement. **2** a player's turn to move a piece in chess etc. **3** an action taken to achieve a purpose.
get a move on (*informal*) hurry up.
on the move moving; making progress. [from Latin *movere* = to move]

movement *noun* **1** the action of moving or being moved. **2** a group of people working together to achieve something. **3** one of the main divisions of a symphony or other long musical work. **4** progress; a trend.

movie *noun* (*informal*) a cinema film. [short for *moving picture*]

mow *verb* (**mowed, mown, mowing**) cut down grass etc. **mower** *noun*
mow down knock down and kill.

MP *abbreviation* Member of Parliament.

Mr (*say* **mist**-er) *noun* (*plural* **Messrs**) a title put before a man's name. [short for *mister*]

Mrs (*say* **mis**-iz) *noun* (*plural* **Mrs**) a title put before a married woman's name. [short for *mistress*]

Ms (*say* miz) *noun* a title put before a woman's name. [from *Mrs* and *Miss*]

Mt *abbreviation* mount or mountain.

much¹ *adjective* (**more, most**) existing in a large amount, *much noise*.

much² *noun* a large amount of something.

much³ *adverb* **1** greatly; considerably, *much to my surprise*. **2** approximately, *It is much the same*.

muck¹ *noun* **1** farmyard manure. **2** (*informal*) dirt; filth. **3** (*informal*) a mess. **mucky** *adjective*

muck² *verb* make dirty; mess.
muck about (*slang*) mess about.
muck up (*slang*) mess up; spoil.

mucous (*say* **mew**-kus) *adjective* like mucus; covered with mucus, *a mucous membrane*.

mucus (*say* **mew**-kus) *noun* the moist sticky substance on the inner surface of the throat etc.

mud *noun* wet soft earth. **muddy** *adjective*, **muddiness** *noun*

muddle¹ *verb* (**muddled, muddling**) **1** mix things up. **2** bewilder; confuse. **muddler** *noun*

muddle² *noun* a muddled condition or thing; confusion; disorder.

mudguard *noun* a curved cover over the top part of the wheel of a bicycle etc. to protect the rider from the mud and water thrown up by the wheel.

muesli (*say* **mewz**-lee) *noun* a food made of mixed cereals, dried fruit, nuts, etc.

muff¹ *noun* a short tube-shaped piece of warm material into which the hands are pushed from opposite ends.

muf² *verb* (*informal*) bungle.

muffin *noun* **1** a large cupcake. **2** a kind of spongy cake eaten toasted and buttered.

muffle *verb* (**muffled, muffling**) **1** cover or wrap something to protect it or keep it warm. **2** deaden the sound of something, *a muffled scream*. [from *muff¹*]

muffler *noun* a warm scarf.

mufti *noun* ordinary clothes worn by someone who usually wears a uniform.

▶▶ T H E S A U R U S ◀◀

move² *noun* **1** gesture, motion, movement. **2** chance, go, opportunity, shot (*informal*), turn. **3** act, action, initiative, measure, step, tactic.

movement *noun* **1** action, activity, gesture, manoeuvre, motion, move, step, stroke. **2** faction, group, lobby, organisation, party; see also CAMPAIGN¹. **3** division, part, section. **4** evolution, progress, shift, swing, tendency, trend.

movie *noun* film, flick (*informal*), motion picture, moving picture, picture, video.

mow *verb* clip, cut, trim.

much¹ *adjective* abundant, a lot of (*informal*), ample, copious, plentiful.

much² *noun* a great deal, heaps (*informal*), loads (*informal*), lots (*informal*), plenty, stacks (*informal*), volumes.

much³ *adverb* **1** a great deal, a lot, considerably, decidedly, far, greatly. **2** about, almost, approximately, nearly, virtually.

muck¹ *noun* **1** droppings, dung, manure. **2** dirt, filth, mud.

muck² *verb* **muck up 1** disorganise, jumble, mess up, muddle, turn upside down. **2** botch, bungle, mess up, ruin, spoil.

mud *noun* dirt, filth, mire, muck (*informal*), silt, slime, sludge.
muddy *adjective* boggy, dirty, filthy, mucky, slimy, waterlogged; (*muddy liquid*) cloudy, impure, murky, turbid.

muddle¹ *verb* **1** disorganise, jumble, mess up, mix up, muck up. **2** bewilder, confuse, disorient, fluster, mix up.

muddle² *noun* chaos, clutter, confusion, disarray, jumble, mess, shambles.

muff² *verb* blow (*slang*), botch, bungle, fluff (*slang*), mess up, spoil.

muffle *verb* **1** cover, wrap. **2** dampen, deaden, dull, mute, quieten, silence, soften, stifle, suppress.

▶▶ D I C T I O N A R Y ◀◀

mug¹ *noun* **1** a kind of large cup, usually used without a saucer. **2** (*informal*) a fool; a person who is easily deceived. **3** (*slang*) a person's face.

mug² *verb* (**mugged, mugging**) attack and rob somebody in the street. **mugger** *noun*

muggy *adjective* unpleasantly warm and damp, *muggy weather*. **mugginess** *noun*

mulberry *noun* (*plural* **mulberries**) a purple or white fruit rather like a blackberry.

mule *noun* an animal that is the offspring of a donkey and a mare, known for being stubborn. **mulish** *adjective*

mulga *noun* **1** a scrubby Australian tree. **2** the bush, wild country. **3** a club or shield made of mulga wood.
mulga wire (*slang*) the bush telegraph, news spread by hearsay.

mull¹ *verb* heat wine or beer with sugar and spices, as a drink, *mulled ale*.

mull² *verb* think about something carefully; ponder, *mull it over*.

mullet *noun* a kind of fish used as food.

multi- *prefix* many (as in *multicoloured* = with many colours). [from Latin *multus* = many]

multicultural *adjective* (of a country) with cultural activities from several countries.

multifarious (*say* multi-**fair**-ee-us) *adjective* of many kinds; very varied.

multilateral *adjective* (of an agreement or treaty) made between three or more people or countries etc.

multimillionaire *noun* a person with a fortune of several million dollars.

multinational *adjective* (of a business company) working in several countries.

multiple¹ *adjective* having many parts.

multiple² *noun* a number that contains another number (a *factor*) an exact amount of times without remainder, *8 and 12 are multiples of 4*.

multiplicity *noun* a great variety.

multiply *verb* (**multiplied, multiplying**) **1** take a number a given quantity of times, *Five multiplied by four equals twenty* (5 x 4 = 20). **2** make or become many; increase. **multiplication** *noun*, **multiplier** *noun*

multiracial *adjective* consisting of people of many different races.

multitude *noun* a great number of people or things. **multitudinous** *adjective*

mum¹ *noun* (*informal*) mother.

mum² *adjective* (*informal*) silent, *keep mum*.

mum³ *verb* (**mummed, mumming**) act in a mime. **mummer** *noun*

mumble *verb* (**mumbled, mumbling**) speak indistinctly and not be easy to hear. **mumble** *noun*, **mumbler** *noun*

mumbo-jumbo *noun* talk or ceremony that has no real meaning.

mummy¹ *noun* (*plural* **mummies**) (*informal*) mother.

mummy² *noun* (*plural* **mummies**) a corpse treated with preservatives before being buried, as was the custom in ancient Egypt. **mummify** *verb*

mumps *noun* an infectious disease that causes the neck to swell painfully.

▶▶ T H E S A U R U S ◀◀

mug¹ *noun* **1** beaker, cup, tankard. **2** bunny (*Australian informal*), duffer, dupe, fool, muggins (*informal*), simpleton, soft touch, sucker (*informal*).

mug² *verb* assault, attack, rob.

muggy *adjective* close, humid, oppressive, steamy, sticky, stuffy, sultry.

mulga *noun* **2** backblocks (*Australian*), bush, country, donga (*Australian*), mallee (*Australian*), never-never (*Australian*), outback (*Australian*), scrub, sticks (*informal*).

mull² *verb* (**mull over**) consider, contemplate, deliberate on, dwell on, meditate on, ponder, reflect on, review, think over.

multicoloured *adjective* harlequin, motley, particoloured, pied, variegated.

multicultural *adjective* cosmopolitan, multiracial, pluralist.

multinational *adjective* international, worldwide.

multiple¹ *adjective* manifold, many, numerous, several, sundry, various.

multiply *verb* **2** breed, increase, proliferate, propagate, reproduce.

multitude *noun* crowd, horde, host, lot, mass, mob, myriad, swag (*Australian informal*), swarm, throng.

mumble *verb & noun* babble, murmur, mutter.

mumbo-jumbo *noun* bunkum, double Dutch, gibberish, gobbledegook (*informal*), hocus-pocus, humbug, nonsense, poppycock (*informal*).

▶▶ D I C T I O N A R Y ◀◀

munch *verb* chew vigorously.

mundane *adjective* **1** ordinary, not exciting. **2** concerned with practical matters, not ideals. [from Latin *mundus* = world]

municipal (*say* mew-**nis**-ip-al) *adjective* of a town or city.

municipality *noun* (*plural* **municipalities**) a community with its own local government (see *local*).

munificent *adjective* extremely generous. **munificently** *adverb*, **munificence** *noun* [from Latin *munus* = gift]

munitions *plural noun* military weapons and ammunition etc. [from Latin *munitum* = fortified]

mural¹ *adjective* of or on a wall.

mural² *noun* a wall-painting. [from Latin *murus* = wall]

murder¹ *verb* kill a person unlawfully and deliberately. **murderer** *noun*, **murderess** *noun*

murder² *noun* the murdering of somebody. **murderous** *adjective*

murky *adjective* **1** dark and gloomy. **2** (of liquid) dirty or cloudy. **murk** *noun*, **murkiness** *noun*

murmur *verb* **1** make a low continuous sound. **2** speak in a soft voice. **murmur** *noun*

Murray cod a large Australian river fish. [from river *Murray*]

muscle *noun* **1** a band or bundle of fibrous tissue that can contract and relax and so produce movement in parts of the body. **2** the power of muscles; strength. **muscular** *adjective*, **muscularity** *noun*

muse *verb* (**mused**, **musing**) think deeply about something; ponder; meditate.

museum *noun* a place where interesting objects are displayed for people to see. [from Greek, = place of the Muses (goddesses of the arts and sciences)]

mush *noun* soft pulp. **mushy** *adjective*

mushroom¹ *noun* an edible fungus with a stem and a dome-shaped top.

mushroom² *verb* grow or appear suddenly in large numbers, *Blocks of flats mushroomed in the city.*

music *noun* **1** pleasant or interesting sounds made by instruments or by the voice. **2** printed or written instructions for making music. [from Greek, = of the Muses (see *museum*)]

musical¹ *adjective* **1** of or with music; producing music. **2** melodious; harmonious. **3** good at music; interested in music. **musically** *adverb*

▶▶ T H E S A U R U S ◀◀

munch *verb* bite, chew, chomp, crunch, eat, gnaw.

mundane *adjective* **1** commonplace, dreary, dull, everyday, ordinary, prosaic, routine, unexciting, uninspiring, uninteresting.

municipal *adjective* civic, community, council, district, local.

munificent *adjective* bountiful, generous, lavish, liberal, philanthropic.

munitions *plural noun* ammunition, arms, ordnance, weapons.

mural² *noun* fresco, wall-painting.

murder¹ *verb* assassinate, bump off (*slang*), do in (*slang*), exterminate, kill, massacre, slaughter, slay. **murderer** *noun* assassin, cutthroat, hit man (*slang*), killer, murderess.

murder² *noun* assassination, extermination, genocide, homicide, killing, massacre, slaughter, slaying. **murderous** *adjective* bloodthirsty, brutal, deadly, homicidal, savage, vicious.

murky *adjective* **1** dark, dim, dull, dusky, foggy, gloomy, shadowy. **2** cloudy, dirty, impure, muddy, turbid.

murmur *verb* **1** babble, burble, drone, hum, rumble, sigh. **2** mumble, mutter, whisper. **murmur** *noun* babble, burble, drone, hum, mumble, mutter, rumble, sigh, undercurrent, whisper.

muscle *noun* **2** brawn, might, muscularity, power, strength. **muscular** *adjective* athletic, beefy, brawny, burly, hefty, nuggety (*Australian*), robust, sinewy, strapping, strong, sturdy, thickset.

muse *verb* contemplate, meditate, ponder, reflect, ruminate, speculate, think.

mush *noun* mash, pap, pulp, purée. **mushy** *adjective* mashed, puréed, sloppy, soft, squidgy (*informal*), squishy (*informal*).

mushroom² *verb* burgeon, develop, expand, grow, pop up, proliferate, shoot up, spring up, sprout.

music *noun* **1** harmony, melody. **2** score, soundtrack.

musical¹ *adjective* **2** dulcet, euphonious, harmonious, lyrical, melodic, melodious, sweet, tuneful.

▶▶ DICTIONARY ◀◀

musical² *noun* a play or film containing a lot of songs.

musician *noun* someone who plays a musical instrument.

musk *noun* a strong-smelling substance used in perfumes. **musky** *adjective*

musket *noun* a kind of gun with a long barrel, formerly used by soldiers.

musketeer *noun* a soldier armed with a musket.

Muslim *noun* a person who follows the religious teachings of Muhammad (who lived in about 570–632), set out in the Koran.

muslin *noun* very thin cotton cloth.

mussel *noun* a black shellfish.

must¹ *auxiliary verb* used to express (**1**) necessity or obligation (*You must go*), (**2**) certainty (*You must be joking!*).

must² *noun* (*informal*) a thing that should not be missed.

mustang *noun* a wild horse of Mexico and California.

mustard *noun* a yellow paste or powder used to give food a hot taste.
mustard and cress small green plants eaten in salads.

muster¹ *verb* assemble; gather together; (*Australian*) round up cattle, sheep, etc.

muster² *noun* an assembly of people or things. **pass muster** be up to the required standard.

mustn't (*mainly spoken*) must not.

musty *adjective* smelling or tasting mouldy or stale. **mustiness** *noun*

mutable (*say* **mew**-ta-bul) *adjective* able or likely to change. **mutability** *noun* [from Latin *mutare* = to change]

mutation *noun* a change or alteration in the form of something.

mute¹ *adjective* **1** silent; not speaking; not able to speak. **2** not pronounced, *The g in 'gnat' is mute.* **mutely** *adverb*, **muteness** *noun*

mute² *noun* a person who cannot speak.

mute³ *verb* (**muted, muting**) make a thing quieter or less intense.

mutilate *verb* (**mutilated, mutilating**) damage something by breaking or cutting off part of it. **mutilation** *noun*

mutineer *noun* a person who mutinies.

mutiny¹ *noun* (*plural* **mutinies**) rebellion against authority; refusal by members of the armed forces to obey orders. **mutinous** *adjective*, **mutinously** *adverb*

mutiny² *verb* (**mutinied, mutinying**) take part in a mutiny.

mutter *verb* **1** speak in a low voice. **2** grumble. **mutter** *noun*

mutton *noun* meat from a sheep.

muttonbird *noun* a kind of seabird, breeding especially on Bass Strait islands.

mutual (*say* **mew**-tew-al) *adjective* given to each other; felt by each for the other, *mutual affection.* **mutually** *adverb*

muzzle¹ *noun* **1** an animal's nose and mouth. **2** a cover put over an animal's nose and mouth so that it cannot bite. **3** the open end of a gun.

muzzle² *verb* (**muzzled, muzzling**) **1** put a muzzle on an animal. **2** silence; prevent a person from expressing opinions.

my *adjective* belonging to me.

▶▶ THESAURUS ◀◀

musician *noun* artist, busker, composer, entertainer, instrumentalist, maestro, muso (*slang*), performer, player, soloist, virtuoso, vocalist.

must² *noun* essential, necessity, requirement.

muster¹ *verb* assemble, collect, gather, marshal, mobilise, rally, round up, summon.

musty *adjective* damp, fusty, mildewed, mouldy, stale, stuffy.

mutation *noun* alteration, change, metamorphosis, transformation, variation.

mute¹ *adjective* **1** dumb, mum (*informal*), quiet, silent, speechless, tight-lipped, tongue-tied, uncommunicative.

mute³ *verb* damp, deaden, dull, muffle, quieten, soften, subdue, suppress, tone down.

muted *adjective* pale, pastel, soft, subdued, toned down.

mutilate *verb* damage, destroy, disfigure, dismember, injure, maim, mangle.

mutiny¹ *noun* insurrection, rebellion, revolt, riot, rising, uprising.
mutinous *adjective* defiant, disobedient, insubordinate, rebellious.

mutiny² *verb* rebel, revolt, riot, rise up.

mutter *verb* **1** mumble, murmur. **2** complain, gripe (*informal*), grumble, moan, whine, whinge (*informal*).

mutual *adjective* reciprocal, reciprocated, requited.

muzzle¹ *noun* **1** jaws, mouth, nose, snout.

muzzle² *verb* **2** bridle, control, gag, restrain.

►►► D I C T I O N A R Y ◄◄

myriad (*say* **mi**rri-ad) *adjective* innumerable.

myriads *plural noun* a very great number, *myriads of gnats*. [from Greek *myrioi* = 10,000]

myrrh (*say* mer) *noun* a substance used in perfumes and incense and medicine.

myrtle *noun* an evergreen shrub with dark leaves and white flowers.

myself *pronoun* I or me and nobody else. (Compare *herself*.)

mysterious *adjective* full of mystery; puzzling. **mysteriously** *adverb*

mystery *noun* (*plural* **mysteries**) something that cannot be explained or understood; something puzzling.

mystic[1] *adjective* **1** having a spiritual meaning. **2** mysterious and filling people with wonder. **mystical** *adjective*, **mystically** *adverb*, **mysticism** *noun*

mystic[2] *noun* a person who seeks to obtain spiritual contact with God by deep religious meditation.

mystify *verb* (**mystified**, **mystifying**) puzzle; bewilder. **mystification** *noun*

mystique (*say* mis-**teek**) *noun* an air of mystery or mystical power.

myth (*say* mith) *noun* **1** an old story containing ideas about ancient times or about supernatural beings. (Compare *legend*.) **2** an untrue story or belief. [from Greek *mythos* = story]

mythical *adjective* **1** imaginary. **2** found in myths, *a mythical animal*.

mythology *noun* myths; the study of myths. **mythological** *adjective* [from *myth* + *-logy*]

myxomatosis (*say* miks-om-at-**oh**-sis) *noun* a disease that kills rabbits.

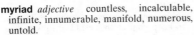

►►► T H E S A U R U S ◄◄

myriad *adjective* countless, incalculable, infinite, innumerable, manifold, numerous, untold.

myriads *plural noun* army, horde, host, millions, multitude, scores, swarm, thousands, throng.

mysterious *adjective* arcane, baffling, bizarre, cryptic, curious, enigmatic, incomprehensible, inexplicable, inscrutable, mystical, mystifying, puzzling, strange, supernatural, uncanny, weird; see also SECRETIVE.

mystery *noun* conundrum, enigma, problem, puzzle, riddle, secret.

mystical *adjective* allegorical, arcane, cryptic, esoteric, hidden, mysterious, mystic, occult, spiritual, supernatural, symbolic, transcendental.

mystify *verb* baffle, bamboozle (*informal*), bewilder, confound, confuse, perplex, puzzle.

myth *noun* **1** fable, legend, narrative, story, tale. **2** delusion, fallacy, falsehood, fantasy, fiction, lie, untruth.

mythical *adjective* **1** fictitious, imaginary, invented, made-up, non-existent. **2** fabled, legendary, mythological.

► Nn ◄

N. *abbreviation* north; northern.

nab *verb* (**nabbed, nabbing**) (*informal*) catch or arrest (a wrongdoer); seize.

nag¹ *verb* (**nagged, nagging**) **1** pester a person by keeping on criticising, complaining, or asking for things. **2** keep on hurting, *a nagging pain.*

nag² *noun* (*informal*) a horse.

nail¹ *noun* **1** the hard covering over the end of a finger or toe. **2** a small sharp piece of metal hammered in to fasten pieces of wood etc. together.

nail² *verb* **1** fasten with a nail or nails. **2** catch; arrest.

naïve (*say* ny-**eev**) *adjective* showing a lack of experience or good judgement; innocent and unsophisticated. **naïvely** *adverb*, **naïvety** *noun*

naked *adjective* without any clothes or coverings on. **nakedly** *adverb*, **nakedness** *noun*
the naked eye the eye when it is not helped by a telescope or microscope etc.

name¹ *noun* **1** the word or words by which a person, animal, place, or thing is known. **2** a reputation.

name² *verb* (**named, naming**) **1** give a name to. **2** state the name or names of.

nameless *adjective* without a name.

namely *adverb* that is to say, *My two favourite subjects are sciences, namely chemistry and biology.*

namesake *noun* a person or thing with the same name as another.

nanna *noun* (*informal*) grandmother.

nanny *noun* (*plural* **nannies**) a nurse who looks after young children.

nanny-goat *noun* a female goat. (Compare *billy-goat.*)

nap¹ *noun* a short sleep.
catch a person napping catch a person unprepared for something or not alert.

nap² *noun* short raised fibres on the surface of cloth or leather.

napalm (*say* **nay**-pahm) *noun* a substance made of petrol, used in some incendiary bombs.

napkin *noun* **1** a piece of cloth or paper used to keep your clothes clean or to wipe your lips or fingers; a serviette, *a table-napkin.* **2** a piece of cloth or other fabric put round a baby's bottom.

nappy *noun* (*plural* **nappies**) a baby's napkin.

narcissus *noun* (*plural* **narcissi**) a garden flower like a daffodil.

►►► THESAURUS ◄◄◄

nab *verb* apprehend, arrest, capture, catch, collar (*informal*), nail, nick (*slang*), seize.

nag¹ *verb* **1** badger, harass, harp on at, hassle (*informal*), henpeck, hound, keep on at, pester, scold.
nagging *adjective* continuous, niggling, persistent.

nail² *verb* **1** attach, fasten, fix, hammer, join, pin, tack.

naïve *adjective* artless, credulous, green, gullible, inexperienced, ingenuous, innocent, simple, unaffected, unsophisticated, unsuspecting, unworldly.

naked *adjective* bare, in the altogether (*informal*), in your birthday suit (*informal*), nude, starkers (*slang*), unclothed, uncovered, undressed.

name¹ *noun* **1** alias, appellation, assumed name, Christian name, false name, family name, first name, given name, label, last name, maiden name, nickname, nom de plume, pen-name, pet name, pseudonym, surname, term, title. **2** see REPUTATION.

name² *verb* **1** baptise, call, christen, dub, entitle, nickname, title. **2** appoint, choose, designate, identify, mention, nominate, pick, select, specify.

nameless *adjective* anonymous, unidentified, unnamed.

nanny *noun* nurse, nursemaid.

nap¹ *noun* catnap, doze, forty winks, kip (*slang*), lie-down, rest, shut-eye (*informal*), siesta, sleep, slumber, snooze.

napkin *noun* **1** serviette.

nappy *noun* diaper (*American*), napkin.

▶▶▷ DICTIONARY ◁◀◀

narcotic *noun* a drug that makes a person sleepy or unconscious. **narcotic** *adjective*, **narcosis** *noun*

narrate *verb* (**narrated, narrating**) tell a story; give an account of something. **narration** *noun*, **narrator** *noun*

narrative *noun* a spoken or written account of something.

narrow¹ *adjective* **1** not wide; not broad. **2** uncomfortably close; with only a small margin of safety, *a narrow escape*. **narrowly** *adverb*

narrow² *verb* make or become narrower.

narrow-minded *adjective* not tolerant of other people's beliefs and ways.

nasal *adjective* **1** of the nose. **2** sounding as if the breath comes out through the nose, *a nasal voice*. **nasally** *adverb* [from Latin *nasus* = nose]

nasturtium (*say* na-**ster**-shum) *noun* a garden plant with round leaves and red, yellow, or orange flowers.

nasty *adjective* **1** unpleasant. **2** unkind. **nastily** *adverb*, **nastiness** *noun*

natal (*say* **nay**-tal) *adjective* of birth; from birth. [from Latin *natus* = born]

nation *noun* a large community of people most of whom have the same ancestors, language, history, and customs, and who usually live in the same part of the world under one government. **national** *adjective & noun*, **nationally** *adverb* [from Latin *natio* = birth; race]

National Party an Australian political party formed to represent rural interests.

nationalise *verb* (**nationalised, nationalising**) put an industry etc. under public ownership. **nationalisation** *noun*

nationalist *noun* **1** a person who is very patriotic. **2** a person who wants his or her country to be independent and not to form part of another country, *Scottish Nationalists*. **nationalism** *noun*, **nationalistic** *adjective*

nationality *noun* (*plural* **nationalities**) the condition of belonging to a particular nation, *What is his nationality?*

native¹ *noun* a person born in a particular place, *He is a native of Sweden*.

native² *adjective* **1** belonging to a person because of the place of his or her birth, *my native country*. **2** born in a place, *a native inhabitant*. **3** natural; belonging to a person by nature, *native ability*. [from Latin *nativus* = born]

native title the right of the indigenous people to own their traditional land.

nativity *noun* a person's birth.

the Nativity the birth of Jesus Christ.

natty *adjective* (**nattier, nattiest**) neat and trim; dapper. **nattily** *adverb*

natural¹ *adjective* **1** produced or done by nature, not by people or machines. **2** normal; not surprising. **3** inborn. **4** without pretence. **5** (of a note in music) neither sharp nor flat. **naturally** *adverb*, **naturalness** *noun*

natural history the study of plants and animals.

▶▶▷ THESAURUS ◁◀◀

narcotic *adjective* anaesthetic, dulling, hypnotic, numbing, sedative, soporific.

narrate *verb* describe, recount, relate, tell.

narrative *noun* account, chronicle, report, saga, story, tale, yarn.

narrow¹ *adjective* **1** fine, slender, slim, thin. **2** close, confined, constricted, cramped, limited, restricted, strait (*old use*), tight.

narrow² *verb* close up, diminish, lessen, reduce.

narrow-minded *adjective* biased, bigoted, blinkered, hidebound, illiberal, inflexible, intolerant, parochial, petty, prejudiced, rigid, small-minded.

nasty *adjective* **1** awful, bad, disagreeable, disgusting, dreadful (*informal*), foul, horrible (*informal*), lousy (*informal*), nauseating, objectionable, obnoxious, offensive, repulsive, revolting, rotten (*informal*), shocking (*informal*), sickening, unpalatable, unpleasant, vile, yucky (*informal*). **2** beastly, ill-tempered,

malevolent, malicious, malignant, mean, spiteful, unkind, vicious, vindictive.

nation *noun* community, country, land, people, race, society, state.

national *adjective* countrywide, general, nationwide.

national *noun* citizen, native, resident, subject.

nationalism *noun* chauvinism, jingoism, patriotism.

native¹ *noun* inhabitant, local, resident.

native² *adjective* **2** aboriginal, indigenous, original. **3** inborn, inherent, innate, natural.

natural¹ *adjective* **1** crude, raw, unprocessed, unrefined. **2** normal, ordinary, predictable, reasonable, understandable. **3** inborn, inherent, innate, instinctive, intuitive, native. **4** artless, authentic, down-to-earth, genuine, spontaneous, unaffected, unpretentious, unsophisticated.

▶▶ DICTIONARY ◀◀

natural² *noun* **1** a person who is naturally good at something. **2** a natural note in music; a sign (♮) that shows this.

naturalise *verb* (**naturalised, naturalising**) **1** give a person full rights as a citizen of a country although they were not born there. **2** cause a plant or animal to grow or live naturally in a country that is not its own. **naturalisation** *noun*

naturalist *noun* an expert in natural history.

nature *noun* **1** everything in the world that was not made by people. **2** the qualities and characteristics of a person or thing, *She has a loving nature.* **3** a kind or sort of thing, *He likes things of that nature.* [from Latin *natus* = born]

naught *noun* (*old use*) nothing.

naughty *adjective* behaving badly; disobedient. **naughtily** *adverb*, **naughtiness** *noun* [from *naught*]

nausea (*say* **naw**-zee-a) *noun* a feeling of sickness or disgust. **nauseous** *adjective*, **nauseating** *adjective* [originally 'seasickness', from Greek *naus* = ship]

nautical *adjective* of ships or sailors. **nautical mile** a measure of distance used in navigating, 2025 yards (1.852 kilometres). [from Greek *nautes* = sailor]

naval *adjective* of a navy.

nave *noun* the main central part of a church (the other parts are the chancel, aisles, and transepts).

navel *noun* the small hollow in the centre of the abdomen, where the umbilical cord was attached.

navigable *adjective* **1** suitable for ships to sail in, *a navigable river.* **2** able to be steered. **navigability** *noun*

navigate *verb* (**navigated, navigating**) **1** sail in or through a river or sea etc., *The ship navigated the Suez Canal.* **2** make sure that a ship, aircraft, or vehicle is going in the right direction. **navigation** *noun*, **navigator** *noun* [from Latin *navis* = ship, + *agere* = to drive]

navvy *noun* (*plural* **navvies**) a labourer digging a road, railway, canal, etc. [short for 'navigator', = person who constructs a 'navigation' (= canal)]

navy *noun* (*plural* **navies**) **1** a country's warships; the people trained to use them. **2** (also **navy blue**) very dark blue, the colour of naval uniform. [from Latin *navis* = ship]

nay *adverb* (*old use*) no.

Nazi (*say* **nah**-tsee) *noun* (*plural* **Nazis**) a member of the National Socialist Party in Germany in Hitler's time, with Fascist beliefs. **Nazism** *noun*

NB *abbreviation* take note that (Latin *nota bene* = note well).

NCO *abbreviation* non-commissioned officer.

NE *abbreviation* north-east; north-eastern.

near¹ *adverb* & *adjective* not far away in space or time.

near² *preposition* not far away from, *near the shops.*

near³ *verb* come near to, *The ship neared the harbour.*

nearby *adjective* & *adverb* near, *a nearby house; He lives nearby.*

▶▶ THESAURUS ◀◀

nature *noun* **2** character, characteristics, disposition, features, make-up, personality, properties, qualities, spirit, temperament. **3** kind, sort, type, variety.

naughty *adjective* bad, contrary, disobedient, impish, incorrigible, mischievous, perverse, undisciplined, unruly, wayward, wilful.

nausea *noun* biliousness, motion-sickness, queasiness, seasickness, sickness, travel-sickness. **nauseous** *adjective* bilious, carsick, queasy, seasick, sick. **nauseating** *adjective* disgusting, foul, objectionable, offensive, repulsive, revolting, sickening.

nautical *adjective* marine, maritime, naval, seafaring, seagoing.

navel *noun* belly button (*informal*), umbilicus.

navigate *verb* **1** cross, sail, traverse. **2** direct, guide, manoeuvre, pilot, sail, steer.

navy *noun* **1** armada, fleet, flotilla.

near¹ *adverb* & *adjective* (*near in space*) alongside, at close quarters, close, nigh, within close range, within cooee (*Australian informal*); (*near in time*) approaching, at hand, close, imminent, impending, in sight, looming.

near² *preposition* adjacent to, around, close to, in the vicinity of.

near³ *verb* approach, draw near to.

nearby *adjective* adjacent, adjoining, close, neighbouring.

▶▶ D I C T I O N A R Y ◀◀

nearly *adjective* **1** almost, *We have nearly finished.* **2** closely, *They are nearly related.*

neat *adjective* **1** simple and clean and tidy. **2** skilful. **3** undiluted, *neat whisky.* **neatly** *adverb*, **neatness** *noun*

neaten *verb* make or become neat.

nebula *noun* (*plural* **nebulae**) a bright or dark patch in the sky, caused by a distant galaxy or a cloud of dust or gas. [Latin, = mist]

nebulous *adjective* indistinct; vague, *nebulous ideas.* [from *nebula*]

necessary *adjective* **1** not able to be done without; essential. **2** unavoidable. **necessarily** *adverb*

necessitate *verb* (**necessitated, necessitating**) make a thing necessary.

necessitous *adjective* needy.

necessity *noun* (*plural* **necessities**) **1** need. **2** something necessary.

neck *noun* **1** the part of the body that joins the head to the shoulders. **2** the part of a garment round the neck. **3** a narrow part of something, especially of a bottle.

neckerchief *noun* a square of cloth worn round the neck.

necklace *noun* an ornament worn round the neck.

necklet *noun* **1** a necklace. **2** a small fur worn round the neck.

necktie *noun* a strip of material worn passing under the collar of a shirt and knotted in front.

nectar *noun* **1** a sweet liquid collected by bees from flowers. **2** a delicious drink.

nectary *noun* (*plural* **nectaries**) the nectar-producing part of a plant.

née (*say* nay) *adjective* born (used in giving a married woman's maiden name), *Mrs Smith, née Jones.* [French]

need¹ *verb* **1** be without something you should have; require, *We need two more chairs.* **2** (as an *auxiliary verb*) have to do something, *You need not answer.*

need² *noun* **1** something needed; a necessary thing. **2** a situation where something is necessary, *There is no need to cry.* **3** great poverty or hardship. **needful** *adjective*, **needless** *adjective*

needle *noun* **1** a very thin pointed piece of steel that can be threaded and used in sewing. **2** something long and thin and sharp, *a knitting-needle.* **3** the pointer of a meter or compass.

needlework *noun* sewing or embroidery.

needy *adjective* very poor; lacking things necessary for life. **neediness** *noun*

ne'er *adverb* (*poetic*) never.

nefarious (*say* nif-**air**-ee-us) *adjective* wicked. [from Latin *nefas* = wrong]

▶▶ T H E S A U R U S ◀◀

nearly *adverb* **1** about, almost, approaching, approximately, around, close to, in the region of, in the vicinity of, nigh on, practically, roughly, virtually.

neat *adjective* **1** clean, dapper, natty (*informal*), orderly, organised, shipshape, smart, spruce, straight, tidy, trim. **2** clever, deft, dexterous, elegant, nifty (*informal*), simple, skilful. **3** pure, straight, unadulterated, undiluted.

nebulous *adjective* fuzzy, hazy, imprecise, indefinite, obscure, uncertain, unclear, vague, woolly.

necessary *adjective* **1** compulsory, essential, indispensable, needed, obligatory, required, requisite, vital. **2** inevitable, inexorable, unavoidable.

necessarily *adverb* automatically, inevitably, naturally, of necessity, perforce.

necessitate *verb* call for, entail, involve, mean, require.

necessity *noun* **1** destitution, hardship, need, poverty, straits, want. **2** essential, must

(*informal*), need, prerequisite, requirement, requisite.

necklace *noun* beads, chain, choker, necklet.

need¹ *verb* **1** be short of, lack, require, want; see also DEPEND ON (at DEPEND). **2** be compelled to, be obliged to, be required to, have to, must.

need² *noun* **1** demand, desire, necessity, requirement, want. **2** call, cause, necessity, reason. **3** crisis, destitution, hardship, poverty, want.

needless *adjective* inessential, pointless, uncalled-for, unjustifiable, unnecessary, useless.

needle *noun* **1** bodkin, crewel, sharp.

needlework *noun* embroidery, sewing.

needy *adjective* deprived, destitute, disadvantaged, down and out, hard up (*informal*), impecunious, impoverished, indigent, penniless, poor, poverty-stricken, skint (*informal*).

nefarious *adjective* abominable, atrocious, base, criminal, despicable, diabolical, evil, heinous, immoral, infamous, iniquitous, odious, vile, villainous, wicked.

negate *verb* (**negated, negating**) **1** make a thing ineffective. **2** disprove. **negation** *noun* [from Latin *negare* = deny]

negative¹ *adjective* **1** that says 'no', *a negative answer*. **2** not definite; not positive. **3** less than nought; minus. **4** of the kind of electric charge carried by electrons. **negatively** *adverb*

Usage The opposite of sense 1 is *affirmative*, and of senses 2, 3, 4 *positive*.

---

negative² *noun* **1** something negative. **2** a photograph on film with the dark parts light and the light parts dark, from which a positive print (with the dark and light or colours correct) can be made. [from Latin *negare* = deny]

neglect¹ *verb* **1** not look after or attend to a person or thing. **2** not do something; forget, *He neglected to lock the door*.

neglect² *noun* neglecting; being neglected. **neglectful** *adjective*

negligence *noun* lack of proper care or attention; carelessness. **negligent** *adjective*, **negligently** *adverb*

negligible *adjective* not big enough or important enough to be worth bothering about.

negotiable *adjective* **1** able to be changed after being discussed, *The salary is negotiable*. **2** (of a cheque) able to be changed for cash or transferred to another person.

negotiate *verb* (**negotiated, negotiating**) **1** bargain or discuss with others in order to reach an agreement. **2** arrange after discussion, *They negotiated a treaty*. **3** get over an obstacle or difficulty. **negotiation** *noun*, **negotiator** *noun* [from Latin *negotium* = business]

Negro *noun* (*plural* **Negroes**) a member of the black-skinned race of people originally from Africa. **Negress** *noun* [from Latin *niger* = black]

neigh *verb* make the high-pitched cry of a horse. **neigh** *noun*

neighbour *noun* a person who lives next door or near to another. **neighbouring** *adjective*, **neighbourly** *adjective* [from Old English *neahgebur* = near dweller]

neighbourhood *noun* the surrounding district or area.

neither¹ (*say* **ny**-*th*er) *adjective & pronoun* not either.

Usage Correct use is *Neither of them likes it. Neither he nor his children like it.* Use a singular verb (e.g. *likes*) unless one of its subjects is plural (e.g. *children*).

---

neither² *adverb & conjunction*
neither...nor not one thing and not the other, *She neither knew nor cared*.

nemesis (*say* **nem**-i-sis) *noun* retribution; justifiable punishment that comes upon somebody who hoped to escape it. [named after Nemesis, goddess of retribution in Greek mythology]

neo- *prefix* new. [from Greek *neos* = new]

neolithic (*say* nee-o-**lith**-ik) *adjective* of the later part of the Stone Age. [from *neo-*, + Greek *lithos* = stone]

neon *noun* a gas that glows when electricity passes through it, used in glass tubes to make illuminated signs.

nephew *noun* the son of a person's brother or sister. [from Latin *nepos*]

negate *verb* **1** annul, cancel, invalidate, nullify, void. **2** contradict, deny, disprove, refute.

negative¹ *adjective* **1** contradictory, dissenting, objecting, opposing, refusing, rejecting. **2** antagonistic, defeatist, gloomy, pessimistic, reluctant, uncooperative, unenthusiastic, unwilling.

neglect¹ *verb* **1** disregard, forget, ignore, let go, let slide, let slip, overlook, shirk. **2** fail, forget, omit.

negligence *noun* carelessness, forgetfulness, inattention, laxity, slackness, thoughtlessness. **negligent** *adjective* careless, heedless, inattentive, neglectful, remiss, slack, thoughtless, unthinking.

negligible *adjective* imperceptible, insignificant, minuscule, minute, small, tiny, trifling, unimportant.

negotiate *verb* **1** bargain, discuss, haggle, talk. **2** agree on, arrange, settle, transact, work out. **3** clear, cross, get over.
negotiator *noun* broker, facilitator, go-between, intermediary, mediator, peacemaker.

neighbourhood *noun* area, community, district, locality, quarter, spot, suburb.

neighbouring *adjective* adjacent, adjoining, close, contiguous, nearby.

neighbourly *adjective* affable, considerate, friendly, helpful, hospitable, kind, kindly, obliging, sociable, thoughtful.

▶▶ D I C T I O N A R Y ◀◀

nepotism (*say* **nep**-ot-izm) *noun* showing favouritism to relatives in appointing them to jobs. [from Latin *nepos* = nephew]

nerve¹ *noun* **1** any of the fibres in the body that carry messages to and from the brain, so that parts of the body can feel and move. **2** courage; calmness in a dangerous situation, *Don't lose your nerve.* **3** (*informal*) impudence, *Oliver Twist had the nerve to ask for more.*
nerves *plural noun* nervousness.

nerve² *verb* (**nerved**, **nerving**) give strength or courage to someone. [from Latin *nervus* = sinew]

nerve-racking *adjective* causing anxiety.

nervous *adjective* **1** easily upset or agitated; excitable. **2** slightly afraid; timid. **3** of the nerves, *a nervous illness.* **nervously** *adverb*, **nervousness** *noun*

nervy *adjective* nervous.

nest¹ *noun* **1** a structure or place in which a bird lays its eggs and feeds its young. **2** a place where some small creatures (e.g. mice, wasps) live. **3** a set of similar things that fit inside each other, *a nest of tables.*

nest² *verb* **1** have or make a nest. **2** fit inside something.

nest-egg *noun* a sum of money saved up for future use.

nestle *verb* (**nestled**, **nestling**) curl up comfortably.

nestling *noun* a bird that is too young to leave the nest.

net¹ *noun* **1** material made of pieces of thread, cord, or wire etc. joined together in a criss-cross pattern with holes between. **2** something made of this.

net² *verb* (**netted**, **netting**) cover or catch with a net.

net³ *adjective* remaining when nothing more is to be deducted, *The net weight, without the box, is 100 grams.* (Compare *gross.*)

net⁴ *verb* (**netted**, **netting**) obtain or produce as net profit.

netball *noun* a game in which two teams try to throw a ball into a high net hanging from a ring.

nether *adjective* lower, *the nether regions.*

netting *noun* a piece of net.

nettle¹ *noun* a wild plant with leaves that sting when they are touched.

nettle² *verb* (**nettled**, **nettling**) annoy or provoke someone.

network *noun* a net-like arrangement of connected lines or parts.

neuralgia (*say* newr-**al**-ja) *noun* pain along a nerve. [from Greek *neuron* = nerve, + *algos* = pain]

neurology *noun* the study of nerves and their diseases. **neurological** *adjective*, **neurologist** *noun* [from Greek *neuron* = nerve, + *-logy*]

neurotic (*say* newr-**ot**-ik) *adjective* always very worried about something.

neuter¹ *adjective* neither masculine nor feminine. [Latin, = neither]

neuter² *verb* make an animal unable to reproduce; castrate or spay.

▶▶ T H E S A U R U S ◀◀

nerve¹ *noun* **2** bravery, coolness, courage, daring, fearlessness, grit, guts (*informal*), intrepidity, mettle, pluck, spunk (*informal*). **3** audacity, boldness, cheek, effrontery, gall (*slang*), hide (*informal*), impertinence, impudence, insolence, presumption, temerity.

nerve-racking *adjective* stressful, tense, testing, trying, unnerving, worrying.

nervous *adjective* **1,2** afraid, agitated, alarmed, anxious, apprehensive, edgy, fidgety, flustered, frightened, highly-strung, jittery (*informal*), jumpy, nervy, neurotic, restive, shaky, tense, timid, timorous, twitchy, uneasy, uptight (*informal*), worried.
nervousness *noun* agitation, anxiety, apprehension, butterflies (*informal*), heebie-jeebies (*informal*), jitters (*informal*), nerves, stage fright, tension, trembling, uneasiness.

nest¹ *noun* **1** eyrie, perch, roost.

nestle *verb* cuddle, curl up, huddle, snuggle.

net¹ *noun* **1** mesh, netting, network, web. **2** dragnet, drift-net, trawl.

net² *verb* capture, catch, ensnare, snare, trap.

net³ *adjective* (*net income*) clear, disposable, take-home.

net⁴ *verb* clear, earn, gain, make, realise.

network *noun* complex, grid, system.

neurotic *adjective* anxious, obsessive, unbalanced.

neuter² *verb* castrate, de-sex, doctor, geld, spay, sterilise.

▶▶▶ DICTIONARY ◀◀

neutral *adjective* **1** not supporting either side in a war or quarrel. **2** not very distinctive, *a neutral colour such as grey.* **neutrally** *adverb*, **neutrality** *noun*
neutral gear a gear that is not connected to the driving parts of an engine. [from Latin *neuter* = neither]

neutralise *verb* (**neutralised, neutralising**) make a thing neutral or ineffective. **neutralisation** *noun*

neutron *noun* a particle with no electric charge. [from *neutral*]

never *adverb* at no time; not ever; not at all.
never-never *noun* (*informal*) hire-purchase; (*Australian*) remote areas especially in Queensland and the Northern Territory. [from *ne* = not, + *ever*]

nevertheless *adverb & conjunction* in spite of this; although this is a fact.

new¹ *adjective* **1** not existing before; just made, invented, discovered, or received etc. **2** unfamiliar. **3** additional. **4** changed or renewed. **newly** *adverb*, **newness** *noun*
New Australian an immigrant especially if without English.
new chum (*Australian*) a newcomer, a novice.
New Year's Day 1 January.

new² *adverb* newly, *new-born*; *new-laid*.

newcomer *noun* **1** a person who has arrived recently. **2** a beginner.

newel *noun* the upright post to which the handrail of a stair is fixed, or that forms the centre pillar of a winding stair.

newfangled *adjective* needlessly new in method or style. [from *new*, + *fang* = seize]

newly *adverb* **1** recently. **2** in a new way.

news *noun* **1** information about recent events; a broadcast report of this. **2** a piece of new information.

newsagent *noun* a shopkeeper who sells newspapers.

newsletter *noun* a printed bulletin of a club etc.

newspaper *noun* **1** a daily or weekly publication on large sheets of paper, containing news reports, articles, etc. **2** the sheets of paper forming a newspaper, *Wrap it in newspaper.*

newsy *adjective* (*informal*) full of news.

newt *noun* a small animal rather like a lizard, that lives near or in water.

next¹ *adjective* **1** nearest. **2** coming immediately after, *on the next day.*
next door in the next house or room.

next² *adverb* **1** in the next place. **2** on the next occasion, *What happens next?*

nib *noun* the pointed metal part of a pen.

nibble *verb* (**nibbled, nibbling**) take small quick or gentle bites. **nibble** *noun*

▶▶▶ THESAURUS ◀◀

neutral *adjective* **1** detached, disinterested, impartial, independent, non-aligned, non-partisan, unbiased, uninvolved. **2** beige, buff, colourless, dull, grey, indefinite, wishy-washy.

neutralise *verb* cancel (out), counteract, counterbalance, offset.

never-ending *adjective* constant, continuous, endless, everlasting, inexhaustible, infinite, limitless, unlimited.

nevertheless *adverb* but, however, none the less, still, yet.

new¹ *adjective* **1** brand-new, fresh, hot, innovative, latest, modern, newfangled (*derogatory*), novel, original, recent, red-hot, trendy (*informal*), unused, up to date. **2** strange, unfamiliar, unheard-of, unknown. **3** additional, another, extra. **4** altered, changed, different, rejuvenated, renovated, restored, transformed.

newcomer *noun* **1** immigrant, migrant, new chum (*Australian informal*), stranger. **2** beginner, novice, probationer, tiro, trainee.

newly *adverb* **1** freshly, just, lately, recently.

news *noun* announcement, bulletin, communication, communiqué, dispatch, information, intelligence, message, press release, report, statement, story, tidings, word.

newsletter *noun* bulletin, magazine, report.

newspaper *noun* broadsheet, daily, gazette, journal, paper, rag (*derogatory*), tabloid, weekly.

newsy *adjective* gossipy, informative, interesting.

next¹ *adjective* **1** adjacent, adjoining, closest, nearest, neighbouring, next-door. **2** following, subsequent, succeeding.

next² *adverb* **2** afterwards, subsequently, then.

nibble *verb* bite, gnaw, munch, peck at, pick at; see also EAT.
nibble *noun* bite, morsel, mouthful, taste, titbit.

▶▶ D I C T I O N A R Y ◀◀

nice *adjective* **1** pleasant; satisfactory. **2** kind; good-natured. **3** precise; careful, *a nice distinction.* **nicely** *adverb,* **niceness** *noun* [the word originally meant 'stupid', from Latin *nescius* = ignorant]

nicety (*say* **ny**-sit-ee) *noun* (*plural* **niceties**) **1** precision. **2** a small detail or difference pointed out.

niche (*say* nich or neesh) *noun* **1** a small recess, especially in a wall, *The vase stood in a niche.* **2** a suitable place or position, *She found her niche in the drama club.* [from Latin *nidus* = nest]

nick¹ *noun* **1** a small cut or notch. **2** (*slang*) a police station or prison. **3** (*slang*) condition, *in good nick.*
in the nick of time only just in time.

nick² *verb* **1** make a nick in something. **2** (*slang*) steal. **3** (*slang*) catch; arrest.
nick off (*Australian slang*) depart quickly.

nickel *noun* **1** a silvery-white metal. **2** (*American*) a 5-cent coin.

nickname *noun* a name given to a person instead of his or her real name. [originally *a nekename,* from *an eke-name* (*eke* = addition, + *name*)]

nicotine *noun* a poisonous substance found in tobacco. [from the name of J. Nicot, who introduced tobacco into France in 1560]

niece *noun* the daughter of a person's brother or sister.

niggardly *adjective* mean; stingy. **niggardliness** *noun*

niggle *verb* (**niggled, niggling**) fuss over details or very small faults.

nigh *adverb* & *preposition* (*old use*) near.

night *noun* **1** the dark hours between sunset and sunrise. **2** a particular night or evening, *the first night of the play.* **nightcap** *noun,* **nightdress** *noun*

nightfall *noun* the coming of darkness at the end of the day.

nightingale *noun* a small brown bird that sings sweetly.

nightly *adjective* & *adverb* happening every night.

nightmare *noun* a frightening dream. **nightmarish** *adjective*

nil *noun* nothing; nought. [from Latin *nihil* = nothing]

nimble *adjective* able to move quickly; agile. **nimbly** *adverb*

nine *noun* & *adjective* the number 9; one more than eight. **ninth** *adjective* & *noun*

ninepins *noun* the game of skittles played with nine objects.

nineteen *noun* & *adjective* the number 19; one more than eighteen. **nineteenth** *adjective* & *noun*

ninety *noun* & *adjective* (*plural* **nineties**) the number 90; nine times ten. **ninetieth** *adjective* & *noun*

nip¹ *verb* (**nipped, nipping**) **1** pinch or bite quickly. **2** (*informal*) go quickly.

nip² *noun* **1** a quick pinch or bite. **2** sharp coldness, *There's a nip in the air.*

▶▶ T H E S A U R U S ◀◀

nice *adjective* **1** agreeable, delightful, enjoyable, fabulous (*informal*), fantastic (*informal*), fine, good, great (*informal*), lovely, marvellous, pleasant, satisfactory, splendid, wonderful; see also EXCELLENT, GOOD¹. **2** agreeable, amiable, amicable, attractive, benevolent, benign, caring, charming, compassionate, congenial, considerate, delightful, friendly, good, good-natured, gracious, kind, kindly, likeable, pleasant, polite, sweet, sympathetic, thoughtful, understanding, winsome. **3** careful, delicate, fine, minute, precise, subtle.

nicety *noun* **2** detail, finer point, refinement, subtlety.

niche *noun* **1** alcove, bay, nook, recess. **2** calling, place, slot, vocation.

nick¹ *noun* **1** cut, gouge, notch, score, scratch, snick. **3** condition, health, trim.

nick² *verb* **1** cut, gash, scratch, snick. **2** knock off (*slang*), lift, pilfer, pinch (*informal*), snatch,

snitch (*slang*), steal, swipe (*informal*), take. **3** arrest, catch, nab (*informal*), pick up.

nickname *noun* alias, pet name, sobriquet.

niggardly *adjective* mean, miserly, parsimonious, penny-pinching, stingy, tight-fisted.

niggle *verb* carp, fuss, nag, nit-pick (*informal*), quibble.
niggling *adjective* annoying, lurking, nagging, persistent, worrying.

night *noun* **1** dark, darkness, dusk, evening, nightfall, night-time.

nightly *adjective* after-dark, evening, night-time, nocturnal.

nightmarish *adjective* dreadful, frightening, horrible, horrifying, scary, terrible, terrifying.

nil *noun* love, none, nothing, nought, zero.

nimble *adjective* active, agile, lithe, lively, nippy (*informal*), quick, sprightly, spry, swift.

nip¹ *verb* **1** bite, nibble, pinch, squeeze, tweak.

▶▶ D I C T I O N A R Y ◀◀

nipper *noun* (*slang*) a young child.
nippers *plural noun* pincers.

nipple *noun* a small projecting part, especially at the front of a person's breast.

nippy *adjective* (**nippier, nippiest**) (*informal*) **1** quick; nimble. **2** cold.

nit *noun* a parasitic insect; its egg.

nit-picking *noun* pointing out very small faults.

nitric acid (*say* **ny**-trik) a very strong colourless acid containing nitrogen.

nitrogen (*say* **ny**-tro-jen) *noun* a gas that makes up about four-fifths of the air.

nitwit *noun* (*informal*) a stupid person.
nitwitted *adjective*

no¹ *adjective* not any, *We have no money.*
no man's land an area that does not belong to anybody.
no one no person; nobody.

no² *adverb* **1** used to deny or refuse something, *Will you come? No.* **2** not at all, *She is no better.*

No. or **no.** *abbreviation* (*plural* **Nos.** or **nos.**) number. [from Latin *numero* = by number]

noble¹ *adjective* **1** of high social rank; aristocratic. **2** having a very good character or qualities, *a noble king.* **3** stately; impressive, *a noble building.* **nobly** *adverb*, **nobility** *noun*

noble² *noun* a person of high social rank.
nobleman *noun*, **noblewoman** *noun*

nobody *pronoun* no person; no one.

nocturnal *adjective* of or in the night; active at night, *nocturnal animals.* [from Latin *noctis* = of night]

nocturne *noun* a piece of music with the quiet dreamy feeling of night.

nod *verb* (**nodded, nodding**) **1** move the head up and down, especially as a way of agreeing with somebody or as a greeting. **2** be drowsy.
nod *noun*

node *noun* a swelling like a small knob.

nodule *noun* a small node.

noise *noun* a sound, especially one that is loud or unpleasant. **noisy** *adjective*, **noisily** *adverb*, **noiseless** *adjective*

noisome (*say* **noi**-sum) *adjective* smelling unpleasant; harmful. [from *annoy*]

nomad *noun* a member of a tribe that moves from place to place looking for pasture for their animals. **nomadic** *adjective*

nominal *adjective* **1** in name, *He is the nominal ruler, but the real power is held by the generals.* **2** small, *We charged them only a nominal fee.* **nominally** *adverb* [from Latin *nomen* = name]

▶▶ T H E S A U R U S ◀◀

nipple *noun* teat.

nippy *adjective* **2** biting, bitter, chilly, cold, freezing, icy.

nit-picking *noun* carping, cavilling, faultfinding, niggling, quibbling.

noble¹ *adjective* **1** aristocratic, blue-blooded, lordly, titled. **2** exalted, generous, high-minded, honourable, lofty, selfless, virtuous, worthy. **3** fine, grand, imposing, impressive, magnificent, majestic, splendid, stately.
nobility *noun* aristocracy, peerage, upper class, upper crust (*informal*).

noble² *noun* aristocrat, grandee, lady, lord, peer, peeress; (*kinds of nobleman*) baron, count, duke, earl, marquess, marquis, viscount; (*kinds of noblewoman*) baroness, countess, duchess, marchioness, marquise, viscountess.

nobody *pronoun* none, no one.

nocturnal *adjective* after-dark, evening, nightly, night-time.

nod *verb* **1** bob, bow, incline; see also SIGNAL². **2** (*nod off*) doze off, drop off, drowse, fall asleep.

node *noun* bump, knob, knot, lump, nodule, protuberance, swelling.

noise *noun* bedlam, clamour, clatter, commotion, din, hubbub, hullabaloo, outcry, pandemonium, racket, row, rumpus, sound, tumult, uproar.
noisy *adjective* (*a noisy crowd*) boisterous, lively, rowdy, tumultuous, turbulent, uproarious, vociferous; (*noisy music*) blaring, booming, deafening, discordant, grating, jarring, loud, piercing, raucous, shrill, strident, thundering.

nomad *noun* gypsy, itinerant, rover, traveller, vagabond, wanderer.
nomadic *adjective* itinerant, migratory, peripatetic, roving, travelling, vagabond, vagrant, wandering.

nominal *adjective* **1** in name only, ostensible, professed, so-called, theoretical. **2** minimal, small, token.

►►►DICTIONARY◄◄

nominate *verb* (**nominated, nominating**) name a person or thing to be appointed or chosen. **nomination** *noun*, **nominator** *noun* [from Latin *nominare* = to name]

nominee *noun* a person who is nominated.

non- *prefix* not. [from Latin *non* = not]

nonagenarian *noun* a person aged between 90 and 99. [from Latin *nonageni* = ninety each]

non-believer *noun* a person who does not believe or who has no faith.

nonchalant (*say* **non**-shal-ant) *adjective* calm and casual; showing no anxiety or excitement. **nonchalantly** *adverb*, **nonchalance** *noun* [from French *non* = not, + *chaloir* = be concerned]

non-commissioned *adjective* not holding a commission, *Non-commissioned officers include corporals and sergeants.*

non-committal *adjective* not committing yourself; not showing what you think.

nonconformist *noun* a person who does not conform to established principles.

nondescript *adjective* having no special or distinctive qualities and therefore difficult to describe.

none¹ *pronoun* **1** not any. **2** no one, *None can tell.*

Usage In sense 1 it is better to use a singular verb (e.g. *None of them is here*), but the plural is not incorrect (e.g. *None of them are here*).

none² *adverb* not at all, *He is none too bright.* [from *not one*]

nonentity (*say* non-**en**-tit-ee) *noun* (*plural* **nonentities**) an unimportant person. [from *non- + entity*]

non-existent *adjective* not existing; unreal.

non-fiction *noun* writings that are not fiction; books about real people and things and true events.

nong *noun* (*Australian slang*) a simpleton.

nonplus *verb* (**nonplussed, nonplussing**) puzzle someone completely. [from Latin *non plus* = not further]

nonsense *noun* **1** words put together in a way that does not mean anything. **2** stupid ideas or behaviour. **nonsensical** (*say* non-**sens**-ik-al) *adjective* [from *non- + sense*]

non-stop *adjective* **1** not stopping, *non-stop chatter.* **2** not stopping between two main stations, *a non-stop train.*

noodles *plural noun* pasta made in narrow strips, used in soups etc.

nook *noun* a sheltered corner; a recess.

►►►THESAURUS◄◄

nominate *verb* appoint, choose, designate, elect, name, pick, propose, put forward, recommend, select, submit, suggest.

non-believer *noun* agnostic, atheist, free-thinker, heathen, infidel, pagan, sceptic, unbeliever.

nonchalant *adjective* apathetic, blasé, calm, carefree, careless, casual, composed, cool, imperturbable, indifferent, laid-back (*informal*), unconcerned, unemotional, unexcited, unflappable (*informal*).

non-committal *adjective* cagey (*informal*), cautious, circumspect, evasive, guarded, indefinite, reserved, temporising, tentative, wary.

nonconformist *noun* dissenter, eccentric, heretic, iconoclast, individualist, maverick, misfit, radical, rebel.

nondescript *adjective* bland, characterless, ordinary, plain, unexceptional, uninteresting, unremarkable.

nonentity *noun* lightweight, nobody, small fry, unknown.

non-existent *adjective* fictitious, hypothetical, imaginary, make-believe, mythical, pretend (*informal*), pretended, unreal.

nonplus *verb* amaze, baffle, bamboozle (*informal*), bewilder, confound, confuse, dumbfound, flummox (*informal*), perplex, puzzle, stun, surprise.

nonsense *noun* balderdash, boloney (*informal*), borak (*Australian*), bunkum, claptrap, codswallop (*slang*), drivel, folly, foolishness, garbage, gibberish, gobbledegook (*informal*), guff (*slang*), hogwash (*informal*), hooey (*informal*), humbug, inanity, kidstakes (*Australian informal*), mumbo-jumbo, piffle (*informal*), poppycock (*slang*), rot (*slang*), rubbish, silliness, stupidity, tommyrot (*slang*), trash, tripe (*informal*), twaddle.

nonsensical *adjective* absurd, crazy, fatuous, foolish, idiotic, inane, laughable, ludicrous, meaningless, preposterous, ridiculous, senseless, silly, stupid.

non-stop *adjective* **1** ceaseless, constant, continuous, endless, incessant, persistent, steady. **2** direct, express, through.

nook *noun* alcove, corner, cubby hole, niche, recess.

▶▶▶ D I C T I O N A R Y ◀◀◀

noon *noun* twelve o'clock at midday.

noose *noun* a loop in a rope that gets smaller when the rope is pulled.

nor *conjunction* and not, *She cannot do it; nor can I.*

norm *noun* a standard or average type, amount, level, etc.

normal *adjective* **1** usual or ordinary. **2** natural and healthy; without a physical or mental illness. **normally** *adverb*, **normality** *noun*

Norman *noun* a member of the people of Normandy in northern France, who conquered England in 1066. **Norman** *adjective*

Norse *noun* the Norwegian language or the Scandinavian group of languages. [from Dutch *noord* = north]

north¹ *noun* **1** the direction to the left of a person who faces east. **2** the northern part of a country, city, etc.

north² *adjective & adverb* towards or in the north. **northerly** *adverb*, **northern** *adjective*, **northerner** *noun*, **northernmost** *adjective*

north-east *noun, adjective, & adverb* midway between north and east. **north-easterly** *adjective*, **north-eastern** *adjective*

northward *adjective & adverb* towards the north. **northwards** *adverb*

north-west *noun, adjective, & adverb* midway between north and west. **north-westerly** *adjective*, **north-western** *adjective*

Nos. or **nos.** *plural* of **No.** or **no.**

nose¹ *noun* **1** the part of the face that is used for breathing and for smelling things. **2** the front end or part.

on the nose (*Australian informal*) offensively smelly; unacceptable.

nose² *verb* (**nosed, nosing**) **1** push the nose into or near something. **2** pry or search, *nosing around.* **3** go forward cautiously, *Ships nosed through the ice.*

nosebag *noun* a bag containing fodder, for hanging on a horse's head.

nosedive *noun* a steep downward dive, especially of an aircraft. **nosedive** *verb*

nosegay *noun* a small bunch of flowers. [from *nose* + *gay* = ornament]

nostalgia (*say* nos-**tal**-ja) *noun* sentimental remembering or longing for the past. **nostalgic** *adjective*, **nostalgically** *adverb* [from Greek *nostos* = return home, + *algos* = pain (= homesickness)]

nostril *noun* either of the two openings in the nose.

nosy *adjective* (**nosier, nosiest**) unduly inquisitive. **nosily** *adverb*, **nosiness** *noun*

not *adverb* used to change the meaning of something to its opposite or absence.

notable *adjective* **1** worth noticing; remarkable. **2** famous. **notably** *adverb*, **notability** *noun*

notation *noun* a system of symbols representing numbers, quantities, musical notes, etc.

notch¹ *noun* (*plural* **notches**) a small V-shape cut into a surface.

notch² *verb* cut a notch or notches in. **notch up** score.

note¹ *noun* **1** something written down as a reminder or as a comment or explanation. **2** a short letter. **3** a banknote, *a $10 note.* **4** a

▶▶▶ T H E S A U R U S ◀◀◀

noon *noun* midday, noonday, twelve o'clock.

norm *noun* average, benchmark, criterion, mean, par, pattern, rule, standard, usual, yardstick.

normal *adjective* **1** average, conventional, customary, habitual, ordinary, regular, routine, standard, typical, usual. **2** balanced, rational, reasonable, sane.

nose¹ *noun* **1** beak (*informal*), conk (*slang*), muzzle, proboscis, snout.

nose² *verb* **1** nudge, nuzzle. **2** poke, prowl, pry, search, snoop (*informal*), stickybeak (*Australian informal*). **3** ease, edge, inch.

nosedive *noun* descent, dive, drop, fall, plunge, swoop.
  nosedive *verb* crash, drop, fall, plummet, plunge.

nostalgia *noun* longing, pining, yearning.
  nostalgic *adjective* homesick, maudlin, sentimental, wistful.

nosy *adjective* curious, inquisitive, meddlesome, prying, snoopy (*informal*).

notable *adjective* **1** conspicuous, important, noticeable, obvious, outstanding, remarkable, significant, striking. **2** celebrated, distinguished, eminent, famous, noted, prominent, renowned, well-known.

notation *noun* code, signs, symbols, system.

notch¹ *noun* blaze, cut, nick, score, snick.

notch² *verb* cut, gouge, nick, score, snick.
  notch up achieve, gain, score.

note¹ *noun* **1** annotation, comment, endnote, explanation, footnote, jotting, minute, record. **2** communication, epistle, letter, memo (*informal*), memorandum, message, missive. **3**

single sound in music. **5** any of the black or white keys on a piano etc. (see *key* 3). **6** a sound or quality that indicates something, *a note of warning*. **7** notice; attention, *Take care*.

note² *verb* (**noted, noting**) **1** make a note about something; write down. **2** notice; pay attention to, *Note what we say*. [from Latin *nota* = a mark]

notebook *noun* a book with blank pages on which to write notes.

noted *adjective* famous; well-known.

notepaper *noun* paper for writing letters.

nothing¹ *noun* **1** no thing; not anything. **2** no amount; nought. **nothingness** *noun*
for nothing without payment, free; without a result.

nothing² *adverb* not at all; in no way, *It's nothing like as good*.

notice¹ *noun* **1** something written or printed and displayed for people to see. **2** attention, *It escaped my notice*. **3** information that something is going to happen; warning that you are about to end an agreement or a person's employment etc., *We gave him a month's notice*.

notice² *verb* (**noticed, noticing**) see; become aware of something. [from Latin *notus* = known]

noticeable *adjective* easily seen or noticed. **noticeably** *adverb*

noticeboard *noun* a board on which notices may be displayed.

notifiable *adjective* that must be reported.

notify *verb* (**notified, notifying**) **1** inform, *Notify the police*. **2** report; make something known. **notification** *noun*

notion *noun* an idea, especially one that is vague or incorrect.

notional *adjective* guessed and not definite. **notionally** *adverb*

notorious *adjective* well-known for something bad. **notoriously** *adverb*, **notoriety** (*say* noh-ter-I-it-ee) *noun* [from Latin *notus* = known]

notwithstanding *preposition* in spite of.

nougat (*say* noo-gah) *noun* a chewy sweet made from nuts, sugar or honey, and egg-white. [French]

nought (*say* nawt) *noun* **1** the figure 0. **2** nothing.

noun *noun* a word that stands for a person, place, or thing. *Common nouns* are words such as *boy*, *dog*, *river*, *sport*, *table*, which are used as a whole kind of people or things; *proper nouns* are words such as *Bruce*, *Yarra*, and *Sydney* which name a particular person or thing. [from Latin *nomen* = name]

nourish *verb* keep a person, animal, or plant alive and well by means of food. **nourishment** *noun*

novel¹ *noun* a story that fills a whole book.

banknote, bill. **6** air, element, feeling, sound, tone. **7** attention, heed, notice.

note² *verb* **1** enter, jot down, record, register, write down. **2** heed, mark, mind, notice, observe, pay attention to, perceive, see.

notebook *noun* exercise book, jotter, journal, logbook, memo book, pocketbook.

noted *adjective* celebrated, distinguished, eminent, famous, notable, prominent, renowned, well-known.

nothing¹ *noun* **2** nil, nought, zero, zilch (*informal*).
nothingness *noun* emptiness, non-existence, nothing, oblivion, vacuum, void.

notice¹ *noun* **1** advertisement, announcement, circular, flyer, leaflet, letter, memo (*informal*), message, note, pamphlet, placard, poster, sign. **2** attention, consideration. **3** advice, notification, warning.

notice² *verb* be aware of, catch sight of, detect, discern, note, observe, perceive, see, spot.

noticeable *adjective* clear, conspicuous, definite, discernible, distinct, manifest, marked, obvious, perceptible, pronounced, striking, visible.

notify *verb* **1** advise, alert, inform, tell, warn. **2** announce, declare, make known, proclaim, publish, report.
notification *noun* advice, announcement, communication, information, notice, warning.

notion *noun* belief, concept, fancy, idea, opinion, thought.

notorious *adjective* disreputable, infamous, scandalous, well-known.

nought *noun* **1** cipher, zero. **2** nil, nothing, zero, zilch (*informal*).

nourish *verb* feed, nurture, provide for.
nourishing *adjective* healthy, nutritious, nutritive, wholesome.

novel¹ *noun* fiction, saga, story, tale.

▶▶ D I C T I O N A R Y ◀◀

novel² *adjective* of a new and unusual kind, *a novel experience*. **novelty** *noun* [from Latin *novus* = new]

novelist *noun* a person who writes novels.

novice *noun* a beginner.

now¹ *adverb* **1** at this time. **2** by this time. **3** immediately, *You must go now*. **4** I insist or I wonder, *Now behave yourself; Now why didn't I think of that?*
now and again or **now and then** sometimes; occasionally.

now² *conjunction* as a result of or at the same time as something, *Now that you have come, we'll start*.

now³ *noun* this moment, *They will be at home by now*.

nowadays *adverb* at the present time, as contrasted with years ago.

nowhere¹ *adverb* not anywhere.

nowhere² *noun* no place, *Nowhere is as beautiful as New Zealand*.

noxious *adjective* unpleasant and harmful. [from Latin *noxius* = harmful]

nozzle *noun* the spout of a hose or pipe etc. [= little nose]

nuance (*say* **new**-ahns) *noun* a slight difference or shade of meaning.

nub *noun* **1** a small knob or lump. **2** the central point of a problem.

nuclear *adjective* **1** of a nucleus. **2** using the energy that is created by reactions in the nuclei of atoms.

nucleus *noun* (*plural* **nuclei**) **1** the part in the centre of something, round which other things are grouped. **2** the central part of an atom or of a seed or a biological cell. [Latin, = kernel]

nude *adjective* not wearing any clothes; naked. **nudity** *noun*

nudge *verb* (**nudged**, **nudging**) **1** poke a person gently with your elbow. **2** push slightly or gradually. **nudge** *noun*

nudist *noun* a person who believes that going naked is enjoyable and good for the health. **nudism** *noun*

nugget *noun* a rough lump of gold or platinum found in the earth.

nuggety *adjective* (*Australian*) stocky, thick-set, *a nuggety man*.

nuisance *noun* an annoying person or thing.

null *adjective* not valid, *null and void*. [from Latin *nullus* = none]

nullify *verb* (**nullified**, **nullifying**) make a thing null. **nullification** *noun*

numb¹ *adjective* unable to feel or move. **numbly** *adverb*, **numbness** *noun*

numb² *verb* make numb.

numbat *noun* a small reddish-brown Australian ant-eater.

▶▶ T H E S A U R U S ◀◀

novel² *adjective* different, innovative, new, original, strange, unfamiliar, unusual.
novelty *noun* newness, originality, strangeness, unfamiliarity, uniqueness; see also TRINKET.

novice *noun* apprentice, beginner, learner, new chum (*Australian informal*), rookie (*informal*), tiro, trainee.

now¹ *adverb* **1** at present, at the moment, at this moment, at this point, at this stage, at this time, currently, nowadays.

noxious *adjective* damaging, deleterious, destructive, harmful, pernicious, poisonous, toxic.

nuance *noun* difference, distinction, nicety, refinement, shade, subtlety.

nub *noun* **2** core, crux, essence, gist, heart, kernel, nitty-gritty (*informal*), substance.

nucleus *noun* **1** basis, centre, core, heart, kernel.

nude *adjective* bare, exposed, naked, stripped, unclothed, undressed.

in the nude in the altogether (*informal*), in the raw, in your birthday suit (*informal*), starkers (*slang*).

nudge *verb* bump, dig in the ribs, elbow, jog, poke, prod, push, shove, touch.

nuggety *adjective* beefy, burly, hefty, husky, stocky, sturdy, thickset.

nuisance *noun* annoyance, bother, drag, hassle (*informal*), inconvenience, irritation, menace, pain (*informal*), pest, problem, trouble.

null *adjective* annulled, invalid, nullified, worthless.

nullify *verb* abolish, annul, cancel, invalidate, negate, neutralise, repeal, rescind, revoke, undo, void.

numb¹ *adjective* asleep, deadened, insensible, paralysed.

numb² *verb* anaesthetise, deaden, dull, paralyse.

▶▶ D I C T I O N A R Y ◀◀

number[1] *noun* **1** a symbol or word indicating how many; a numeral or figure. **2** a numeral given to a thing to identify it, *a telephone number*. **3** a quantity of people or things, *the number of people present*. **4** one issue of a magazine or newspaper. **5** a song or piece of music.

number[2] *verb* **1** mark with numbers. **2** count. **3** amount to, *The crowd numbered 10,000*.

numberless *adjective* too many to count.

numeral *noun* a symbol that represents a certain number; a figure. [from Latin *numerus* = number]

numerate *adjective* having a good basic knowledge of mathematics. **numeracy** *noun* [same origin as *numeral*]

numeration *noun* numbering.

numerator *noun* the number above the line in a fraction, showing how many parts are to be taken, e.g. 2 in ⅔. (Compare *denominator*.)

numerical (*say* new-**merri**-kal) *adjective* of a number or series of numbers, *in numerical order*. **numerically** *adverb*

numerous *adjective* many. [from Latin *numerus* = number]

numismatics (*say* new-miz-**mat**-iks) *noun* the study of coins. **numismatist** *noun* [from Greek *nomisma* = coin]

nun *noun* a member of a community of women who live according to the rules of a religious organisation. (Compare *monk*.) [from Latin *nonna* = nun]

nunnery *noun* (*plural* **nunneries**) a convent for nuns. (Compare *monastery*.)

nuptial *adjective* of marriage; of a wedding. **nuptials** *plural noun* a wedding.

nurse[1] *noun* **1** a person trained to look after people who are ill or injured. **2** a woman employed to look after young children.

nurse[2] *verb* (**nursed, nursing**) **1** look after someone who is ill or injured. **2** hold carefully. **3** feed a baby.
nursing home a small hospital or home for invalids. [same origin as *nourish*]

nursemaid *noun* a young woman employed to look after young children.

nursery *noun* (*plural* **nurseries**) **1** a place where young children are looked after or play. **2** a place where young plants are grown and usually for sale.
nursery rhyme a simple rhyme or song of the kind that young children like.

nurture[1] *verb* (**nurtured, nurturing**) **1** nourish. **2** train and educate; bring up.

nurture[2] *noun* nurturing; nourishment.

nut *noun* **1** a fruit with a hard shell. **2** a kernel. **3** a small piece of metal with a hole in the middle, for screwing on to a bolt. **4** (*slang*) the head. **5** (*slang*) a mad or eccentric person.
nutty *adjective*

nutcrackers *plural noun* pincers for cracking nuts.

nutmeg *noun* the hard seed of a tropical tree, grated and used in cooking.

nutrient (*say* **new**-tree-ent) *noun* a nourishing substance. **nutrient** *adjective* [from Latin *nutrire* = nourish]

nutriment (*say* **new**-trim-ent) *noun* nourishing food.

nutrition (*say* new-**trish**-on) *noun* nourishment; the study of what nourishes people. **nutritional** *adjective*, **nutritionally** *adverb*

▶▶ T H E S A U R U S ◀◀

number[1] *noun* **1** digit, figure, integer, numeral. **3** amount, quantity, sum, total; (*a number of*) see SEVERAL; (*numbers of*) see MANY[1]. **4** copy, edition, issue, publication. **5** item, piece, song.

number[2] *verb* **2** calculate, count, enumerate, reckon, tally, tot up. **3** add up to, amount to, come to, total.

numeral *noun* digit, figure, integer, number.

numerous *adjective* abundant, copious, countless, innumerable, many, myriad, numberless, numbers of, untold.

nun *noun* abbess, prioress, religious, sister.

nunnery *noun* abbey, cloister, convent, priory, religious house.

nurse[2] *verb* **1** care for, look after, minister to, tend. **3** breastfeed, feed, suckle.

nursing home convalescent home, hospice, hospital, hostel, institution, rest home, sanatorium.

nurture[1] *verb* **1** care for, feed, look after, nourish, provide for. **2** bring up, develop, discipline, educate, instruct, raise, rear, school, train.

nurture[2] *noun* care, development, discipline, education, instruction, rearing, training, upbringing.

nut *noun* **2** kernel, seed. **5** crackpot (*informal*), crank, eccentric, fruitcake (*informal*), loony (*informal*), lunatic, madman, madwoman, maniac, nutcase (*informal*), nutter (*informal*), psychopath, weirdo (*informal*).
nutty *adjective* see CRAZY.

▶▶DICTIONARY◀◀

nutritious (*say* new-**trish**-us) *adjective* nourishing; giving good nourishment. **nutritiousness** *noun*

nutritive (*say* **new**-trit-iv) *adjective* nourishing.

nutshell *noun* the shell of a nut.
in a nutshell stated very briefly.

nuzzle *verb* (**nuzzled, nuzzling**) rub gently with the nose.

NW *abbreviation* north-west; north-western.

nylon *noun* a synthetic lightweight very strong cloth or fibre.

nymph (*say* nimf) *noun* (in myths) a young goddess living in the sea or woods etc.

NZ *abbreviation* New Zealand.

▶▶THESAURUS◀◀

nutritious *adjective* healthy, nourishing, nutritive, wholesome.

▶ Oo ◀

O *interjection* oh.

oaf *noun* (*plural* **oafs**) a stupid lout.

oak *noun* a large deciduous tree with seeds called *acorns.* **oaken** *adjective*

oar *noun* a pole with a flat blade at one end, used for rowing a boat. **oarsman** *noun,* **oarsmanship** *noun*

oasis (*say* oh-**ay**-sis) *noun* (*plural* **oases**) a fertile place in a desert, with a spring or well of water.

oath *noun* **1** a solemn promise to do something or that something is true, appealing to God or a holy person as witness. **2** use of the name of God in anger or to emphasise something.

oatmeal *noun* ground oats.

oats *plural noun* a cereal used to make food (*oats* for horses, *oatmeal* for people).

ob- *prefix* (changing to **oc-** before *c*, **of-** before *f*, **op-** before *p*) **1** to; towards (as in *observe*). **2** against (as in *opponent*). **3** in the way; blocking (as in *obstruct*). [from Latin *ob* = towards, against]

obedient *adjective* doing what you are told; willing to obey. **obediently** *adverb,* **obedience** *noun*

obeisance (*say* o-**bay**-sans) *noun* a deep bow or curtsy.

obelisk *noun* a tall pillar set up as a monument. [from Greek, = little rod]

obese (*say* o-**beess**) *adjective* very fat. **obesity** (*say* o-**beess**-it-ee) *noun* [from Latin *obesus* = having overeaten]

obey *verb* do what you are told to do by a person, law, etc.

obituary *noun* (*plural* **obituaries**) a printed notice of a person's death, often with a short account of his or her life.

object¹ (*say* **ob**-jikt) *noun* **1** something that can be seen or touched. **2** a purpose or intention. **3** (in grammar) the word or words naming who or what is acted upon by a verb or by a preposition, e.g. *him* in *the dog bit him* and *against him.*

object² (*say* ob-**jekt**) *verb* say that you are not in favour of something or do not agree; protest. **objector** *noun* [from *ob* = in the way, + Latin *-jectum* = thrown]

objection *noun* **1** objecting to something. **2** a reason for objecting.

objectionable *adjective* unpleasant; not liked. **objectionably** *adverb*

objective¹ *noun* what you are trying to reach or do; an aim.

objective² *adjective* **1** real; actual, *Dreams have no objective existence.* **2** not influenced by personal feelings or opinions, *an objective account of the quarrel.* (Compare *subjective.*) **objectively** *adverb,* **objectivity** *noun*

▶▶THESAURUS◀◀

oath *noun* **1** pledge, promise, vow. **2** blasphemy, curse, expletive, obscenity, profanity, swearword.

obedient *adjective* biddable, compliant, disciplined, docile, dutiful, meek, submissive, tractable.

obese *adjective* see FAT².

obey *verb* abide by, adhere to, comply with, follow, heed, keep to, observe, respect, stick to, submit to.

object¹ *noun* **1** article, body, contraption (*informal*), device, entity, item, thing. **2** aim, goal, intention, objective, point, purpose.

object² *verb* (*object to*) complain about, criticise, disapprove of, dislike, find fault with, grumble at, knock (*informal*), mind, oppose, protest at, take exception to.

objection *noun* **1** disagreement, disapproval, opposition, protest. **2** complaint, criticism, demur, grievance, quibble, reservation.

objectionable *adjective* abhorrent, disagreeable, disgusting, foul, insufferable, intolerable, nasty, nauseating, obnoxious, offensive, on the nose (*Australian informal*), repugnant, repulsive, revolting, unacceptable, unbearable, unpleasant, vile.

objective¹ *noun* aim, design, goal, intention, mission, object, purpose, target.

objective² *adjective* **1** actual, concrete, factual, observable, real. **2** detached, dispassionate, fair, impartial, just, unbiased, unprejudiced.

▶▶ D I C T I O N A R Y ◀◀

obligation *noun* **1** being obliged to do something. **2** what you are obliged to do; a duty.
under an obligation owing gratitude to someone who has helped you.

obligatory (*say* ob-**lig**-a-ter-ee) *adjective* compulsory, not optional.

oblige *verb* (**obliged**, **obliging**) **1** compel. **2** help and please someone, *Can you oblige me with a loan?*
be obliged to someone feel gratitude to a person who has helped you. [from *ob-* = to, + Latin *ligare* = bind]

obliging *adjective* polite and helpful.

oblique (*say* ob-**leek**) *adjective* **1** slanting. **2** not saying something straightforwardly, *an oblique reply.* **obliquely** *adverb*

obliterate *verb* (**obliterated**, **obliterating**) blot out; destroy and remove all traces of something. **obliteration** *noun* [from Latin, = erase (*ob* = over, *littera* = letter)]

oblivion *noun* **1** being forgotten. **2** being oblivious.

oblivious *adjective* unaware of something, *oblivious to the danger.*

oblong *adjective* rectangular in shape and longer than it is wide (like a page of this book). **oblong** *noun*

obnoxious *adjective* very unpleasant; objectionable.

oboe *noun* a high-pitched woodwind instrument. **oboist** *noun* [from French *haut* = high, + *bois* = wood]

obscene (*say* ob-**seen**) *adjective* indecent in a repulsive or very offensive way. **obscenely** *adverb*, **obscenity** *noun*

obscure[1] *adjective* **1** dark, indistinct. **2** difficult to understand; not clear. **3** not famous. **obscurely** *adverb*, **obscurity** *noun*

obscure[2] *verb* (**obscured**, **obscuring**) make a thing obscure; darken or conceal, *Clouds obscured the sun.*

obsequious (*say* ob-**seek**-wee-us) *adjective* respectful in an excessive or sickening way. **obsequiously** *adverb*, **obsequiousness** *noun*

observance *noun* obeying or keeping a law, custom, religious festival, etc.

observant *adjective* quick at observing or noticing things. **observantly** *adverb*

observation *noun* **1** observing; watching. **2** a comment or remark.

observatory *noun* (*plural* **observatories**) a building with telescopes etc. for observation of the stars or weather.

▶▶ T H E S A U R U S ◀◀

obligation *noun* **1** compulsion, constraint, liability, requirement. **2** commitment, duty, onus, requirement, responsibility.

obligatory *adjective* compulsory, mandatory, necessary, required.

oblige *verb* **1** bind, compel, constrain, force, require.

obliging *adjective* accommodating, considerate, cooperative, courteous, helpful, kind, neighbourly.

oblique *adjective* **1** angled, diagonal, slanting, sloping.

obliterate *verb* annihilate, blot out, cancel, destroy, efface, erase, expunge, rub out, wipe out.

oblivious *adjective* forgetful, heedless, insensible, unaware, unconscious, unmindful.

oblong *noun* rectangle.

obnoxious *adjective* abhorrent, despicable, detestable, disagreeable, disgusting, hateful, horrible, insufferable, loathsome, nasty, objectionable, odious, offensive, repugnant, repulsive, unpleasant, vile.

obscene *adjective* blue, crude, dirty, filthy, foul, improper, indecent, lewd, offensive, pornographic, rude, smutty, unprintable, vulgar.
obscenity *noun* **1** immorality, indecency, lewdness, pornography, smuttiness, vulgarity. **2** curse, expletive, profanity, swear-word.

obscure[1] *adjective* **1** dark, dim, faint, fuzzy, hazy, indistinct, misty, murky, shadowy. **2** abstruse, arcane, cryptic, enigmatic, esoteric, hidden, inscrutable, mysterious, uncertain, unclear, vague. **3** forgotten, little-known, unheard-of, unimportant, unknown.

obscure[2] *verb* block out, blot out, blur, cloud, conceal, cover, darken, eclipse, envelop, hide, mask, screen, shroud.

obsequious *adjective* crawling (*informal*), deferential, fawning, grovelling, kowtowing, servile, slimy, smarmy (*informal*), subservient, sycophantic, toadying, truckling.

observant *adjective* alert, attentive, aware, perceptive, sharp-eyed, shrewd, vigilant, watchful, wide awake (*informal*).

observation *noun* **1** surveillance, viewing, watching. **2** comment, remark, statement.

▶▶DICTIONARY◀◀

observe *verb* (**observed, observing**) **1** see and notice; watch carefully. **2** obey a law. **3** keep or celebrate a custom or religious festival etc. **4** make a remark. **observer** *noun* [from *ob-* = towards, + Latin *servare* = to watch]

obsess *verb* occupy a person's thoughts continually. **obsession** *noun*, **obsessive** *adjective*

obsolescent *adjective* becoming obsolete; going out of use or fashion. **obsolescence** *noun*

obsolete *adjective* not used any more; out of date. [from Latin *obsoletus* = worn out]

obstacle *noun* something that stands in the way or obstructs progress. [from *ob* = in the way, + Latin *stare* = to stand]

obstetrics *noun* the branch of medicine and surgery that deals with the birth of babies. [from Latin, = of a midwife]

obstinate *adjective* keeping firmly to your own ideas or ways, even though they may be wrong. **obstinately** *adverb*, **obstinacy** *noun*

obstreperous (*say* ob-**strep**-er-us) *adjective* noisy and unruly.

obstruct *verb* **1** stop a person or thing from getting past. **2** hinder. **obstruction** *noun*, **obstructive** *adjective*

obtain *verb* get; come into possession of something by buying, taking, or being given it. **obtainable** *adjective* [from *ob-* = to, + Latin *tenere* = hold]

obtrude *verb* (**obtruded, obtruding**) force yourself or your ideas on someone; be obtrusive. **obtrusion** *noun* [from *ob-*, + Latin *trudere* = push]

obtrusive *adjective* **1** obtruding. **2** unpleasantly noticeable. **obtrusiveness** *noun*

obtuse *adjective* stupid. **obtusely** *adverb*, **obtuseness** *noun*
obtuse angle an angle of more than 90° but less than 180°. (Compare *acute*.) [from *ob-* = towards, + Latin *tusum* = blunted]

obverse *noun* the side of a coin or medal showing the head or chief design (the other side is the *reverse*). [from *ob-* = towards, + Latin *versum* = turned]

obvious *adjective* easy to see or understand. **obviously** *adverb* [from Latin *ob viam* = in the way]

oc- *prefix* see **ob-**.

▶▶THESAURUS◀◀

observe *verb* **1** contemplate, detect, discover, look at, monitor, note, notice, perceive, see, spot, study, survey, view, watch, witness. **2** abide by, adhere to, comply with, follow, heed, keep, obey. **3** celebrate, commemorate, honour, keep, mark. **4** comment, remark, say, state.
observer *noun* bystander, eyewitness, on-looker, spectator, viewer, witness.

obsess *verb* consume, dominate, grip, haunt, possess, preoccupy.
obsession *noun* fetish, fixation, hobby-horse, infatuation, mania, passion, preoccupation.

obsolescent *adjective* declining, disappearing, dying out, moribund, on the way out (*informal*), waning.

obsolete *adjective* antiquated, archaic, dead, defunct, disused, old-fashioned, outdated, out of date.

obstacle *noun* bar, barrier, blockage, difficulty, hindrance, hurdle, impediment, obstruction, snag, stumbling block.

obstinate *adjective* defiant, dogged, head-strong, inflexible, intractable, intransigent, mulish, perverse, pigheaded, recalcitrant, refractory, resolute, self-willed, stiff-necked, strong-willed, stubborn, uncompromising, unyielding, wilful.

obstreperous *adjective* boisterous, disorderly, irrepressible, noisy, rowdy, stroppy (*informal*), uncontrollable, unmanageable, unruly, wild.

obstruct *verb* **1** block, bung up, choke, clog, jam, plug up, stop up. **2** block, delay, deter, frustrate, halt, hamper, hinder, hold up, impede, inhibit, prevent, retard, slow down, stall, stop, thwart.
obstruction *noun* barricade, barrier, blockage, obstacle.

obtain *verb* achieve, acquire, attain, buy, come by, earn, elicit, extract, gain, gather, get, get hold of, glean, pick up, procure, purchase, receive, secure.

obtrusive *adjective* **1** forward, importunate, interfering, intrusive, meddlesome, nosy (*informal*), pushy. **2** blatant, conspicuous, glaring, noticeable, obvious, prominent.

obtuse *adjective* dense, dim-witted, dopey (*informal*), dumb (*informal*), slow, stupid, thick.

obvious *adjective* apparent, blatant, clear, conspicuous, distinct, evident, glaring, mani-fest, noticeable, palpable, patent, plain, prominent, pronounced, self-evident, un-concealed, unmistakable, visible.

occasion¹ *noun* **1** the time when something happens. **2** a special event. **3** a suitable time; an opportunity.

occasion² *verb* cause.

occasional *adjective* **1** happening at intervals. **2** for special occasions, *occasional music.* **occasionally** *adverb*

Occident (*say* **ok**-sid-ent) *noun* the West as opposed to the Orient. **occidental** *adjective* [from Latin, = sunset]

occult *adjective* **1** mysterious; supernatural, *occult powers.* **2** secret except when people have special knowledge. [from Latin *occultum* = hidden]

occupant *noun* someone who occupies a place. **occupancy** *noun*

occupation *noun* **1** an activity that keeps a person busy; a job. **2** occupying.

occupational *adjective* of or caused by an occupation, *an occupational disease.*

occupational therapy mental or physical activity designed to help people to recover from certain illnesses.

occupy *verb* (**occupied, occupying**) **1** live in a place; inhabit. **2** fill a space or position. **3** capture enemy territory and place troops there. **4** keep somebody busy; fill with activity. **occupier** *noun*

occur *verb* (**occurred, occurring**) **1** happen; come into existence as an event or process. **2** be found to exist, *These plants occur in ponds.* **3** come into a person's mind, *An idea occurred to me.*

occurrence *noun* **1** occurring. **2** an incident or event; a happening.

ocean *noun* the seas that surround the continents of the earth, especially one of the large named areas of this, *the Pacific Ocean.* **oceanic** *adjective* [from Oceanus, the river that the ancient Greeks thought surrounded the world]

ocelot (*say* **oss**-il-ot) *noun* a leopard-like animal of Central and South America.

ochre (*say* **oh**-ker) *noun* **1** a mineral used as a pigment. **2** pale brownish-yellow.

ocker¹ *noun* (*Australian*) an uncultivated Australian male.

ocker² *adjective* aggressively Australian.

o'clock *adverb* by the clock, *Lunch is at one o'clock.* [short for *of the clock*]

octa- or **octo-** *prefix* eight. [from Greek *okto* = eight]

octagon *noun* a flat shape with eight sides and eight angles. **octagonal** *adjective* [from *octa-,* + Greek *gonia* = angle]

octave *noun* the interval of eight steps between one musical note and the next note of the same name above or below it. [from Latin *octavus* = eighth]

octet *noun* a group of eight instruments or singers. [from *octo-*]

octo- *prefix* see **octa-**.

octogenarian *noun* a person aged between 80 and 89. [from Latin *octogeni* = 80 each]

octopus *noun* (*plural* **octopuses**) a sea animal with eight long tentacles. [from *octo-,* + Greek *pous* = foot]

ocular *adjective* of or for the eyes; visual. [from Latin *oculus* = eye]

occasion¹ *noun* **2** ceremony, episode, event, function, happening, incident, occurrence. **3** chance, moment, opportunity, time.

occasional *adjective* **1** fitful, infrequent, intermittent, irregular, odd, random, rare, scattered, spasmodic, sporadic.

occasionally *adverb* at times, every so often, from time to time, now and then, once in a while, on occasion, sometimes.

occult *adjective* arcane, esoteric, hidden, magic, mysterious, mystic, mystical, secret, supernatural.

occupant *noun* dweller, householder, inhabitant, lessee, occupier, resident, tenant.

occupation *noun* **1** business, calling, career, employment, job, profession, trade, vocation, work. **2** capture, conquest, invasion, possession, seizure, takeover.

occupy *verb* **1** dwell in, inhabit, live in, reside in. **2** fill, hold, hold down, take up, use. **3** capture, conquer, invade, seize, take over, take possession of. **4** absorb, employ, engage, engross, involve, keep busy, preoccupy.

occur *verb* **1** befall, come about, come off, come to pass, eventuate, happen, take place. **2** appear, arise, be found, crop up, emerge, exist, manifest itself, show up, surface. **3** (*occur to*) come to, dawn on, enter a person's head, strike, suggest itself to.

occurrence *noun* **2** bout, episode, event, happening, incident, instance, occasion, phenomenon.

ocean *noun* the blue, the briny (*humorous*), the deep, sea.

▶▶DICTIONARY◀◀

oculist *noun* a doctor who treats diseases of the eye. [from Latin *oculus* = eye]

odd *adjective* 1 strange; unusual. 2 not an even number; not able to be divided exactly by 2. 3 left over from a pair or set, *I've got one odd sock*. 4 of various kinds; not regular, *odd jobs*. **oddly** *adverb*, **oddness** *noun*, **oddity** *noun*

oddments *plural noun* small things of various kinds.

odds *plural noun* the chances that a certain thing will happen; a measure of this, *When the odds are 10 to 1, you will win $10 if you bet $1*.
odds and ends oddments.

ode *noun* a poem addressed to a person or thing. [from Greek *oide* = song]

odious (*say* **oh**-dee-us) *adjective* hateful. **odiously** *adverb*, **odiousness** *noun*

odium (*say* **oh**-dee-um) *noun* general hatred or disgust felt towards a person or actions. [Latin, = hatred]

odour *noun* a smell. **odorous** *adjective*, **odourless** *adjective* [Latin *odor* = smell]

odyssey (*say* **od**-iss-ee) *noun* (*plural* **odysseys**) a long adventurous journey. [named after the *Odyssey*, a Greek poem telling of the wanderings of Odysseus]

o'er *preposition & adverb* (*poetic*) over.

oesophagus (*say* ee-**sof**-a-gus) *noun* (*plural* **oesophagi**) the gullet.

of *preposition* (used to indicate relationships) 1 belonging to, *the mother of the child*. 2 concerning; about, *news of the disaster*. 3 made from, *built of stone*. 4 from, *north of the town*.

of- *prefix* see **ob-**.

off[1] *preposition* 1 not on; away or down from, *He fell off the ladder*. 2 not taking or wanting, *She is off her food*. 3 deducted from, *$5 off the price*.

off[2] *adverb* 1 away or down from something, *His hat blew off*. 2 not working; not happening, *The heating is off*. 3 to the end; completely, *Finish it off*. 4 as regards money or supplies, *How are you off for cash?* 5 behind or at the side of a stage, *There were noises off*. 6 (of food) beginning to go bad.

offal *noun* the organs of an animal (e.g. liver, kidneys) that can be used as food.

offbeat *adjective* unconventional, eccentric.

offcut *noun* a piece of timber etc. remaining after cutting.

offence *noun* 1 an illegal action. 2 a feeling of annoyance or resentment.

offend *verb* 1 cause offence to someone; hurt a person's pride. 2 do wrong, *offend against the law*. **offender** *noun*

offensive[1] *adjective* 1 causing offence; insulting. 2 disgusting, *an offensive smell*. 3 used in attacking, *offensive weapons*. **offensively** *adverb*, **offensiveness** *noun*

▶▶THESAURUS◀◀

odd *adjective* 1 aberrant, abnormal, anomalous, bizarre, curious, deviant, eccentric, extraordinary, freakish, funny, incongruous, irregular, offbeat, peculiar, queer, quirky, singular, strange, uncommon, unconventional, unnatural, unusual, weird. 3 leftover, lone, remaining, single, spare, surplus, unpaired. 4 casual, miscellaneous, occasional, random, sporadic, sundry, various.

oddments *plural noun* leftovers, odds and ends, odds and sods (*informal*), remainders, remnants, sundries.

odious *adjective* abhorrent, abominable, contemptible, despicable, detestable, hateful, heinous, horrible, loathsome, monstrous, obnoxious, repugnant, repulsive, vile.

odour *noun* aroma, bouquet, fragrance, perfume, scent, smell; (*a bad odour*) pong (*informal*), reek, stench, stink.

offbeat *adjective* bizarre, eccentric, odd, strange, unconventional, unusual, way-out, weird.

offcuts *plural noun* leftovers, remnants, scraps.

offence *noun* 1 crime, felony (*old use*), misdeed, misdemeanour, sin, transgression, trespass (*old use*), wickedness, wrongdoing. 2 annoyance, indignation, irritation, resentment, umbrage, upset.
take offence be affronted, be offended, resent, take umbrage.

offend *verb* 1 affront, anger, disgust, displease, hurt someone's feelings, insult, outrage, upset. 2 do wrong, sin, transgress, trespass (*old use*). **offender** *noun* criminal, culprit, felon, lawbreaker, malefactor, miscreant, sinner, transgressor, trespasser (*old use*), wrongdoer.

offensive[1] *adjective* 1 abusive, disrespectful, improper, indecent, insolent, insulting, nasty, objectionable, obscene, odious, rude. 2 bad, disgusting, foul, nasty, nauseating, obnoxious, off-putting (*informal*), on the nose (*Australian informal*), repulsive, revolting, sickening, unsavoury, yucky (*informal*). 3 aggressive, attacking.

▶▶ D I C T I O N A R Y ◀◀

offensive² *noun* an attack.
take the offensive be the first to attack.

offer¹ *verb* (**offered, offering**) **1** present something so that people can accept it if they want to. **2** say that you are willing to do or give something or to pay a certain amount. [from *of-* = to, + Latin *ferre* = bring]

offer² *noun* **1** offering something. **2** an amount offered.

offering *noun* what is offered.

offhand *adjective* **1** without preparation. **2** casual; curt. **offhanded** *adjective*

office *noun* **1** a room or building used for business, especially for clerical work or for a special department; the people who work there. **2** a government department, *the Tax Office*. **3** an important job or position.
be in office hold an official position.

officer *noun* **1** a person who is in charge of others, especially in the armed forces. **2** an official. **3** a member of the police.

official¹ *adjective* **1** done or said by someone with authority. **2** of officials. **officially** *adverb*

official² *noun* a person who holds a position of authority.

officiate *verb* (**officiated, officiating**) be in charge of a meeting, event, etc.

officious *adjective* too ready to give orders; bossy. **officiously** *adverb*

offing *noun* **in the offing** not far away; likely to happen.

off-putting *adjective* repellent.

offset *verb* (**offset, offsetting**) counterbalance or make up for something, *Defeats are offset by successes*.

offshoot *noun* **1** a sideshoot on a plant. **2** a by-product.

offshore *adjective* **1** from the land towards the sea, *an offshore breeze*. **2** in the sea some distance from the shore, *an offshore island*. **3** overseas, *an offshore investment*.

offside *adjective & adverb* (of a player in football etc.) in a position where the rules do not allow him or her to play the ball.

offsider *noun* (*Australian*) an assistant.

offspring *noun* (*plural* **offspring**) **1** a person's child or children. **2** the young of an animal.

oft *adverb* (*old use*) often.

often *adverb* many times; in many cases.

ogle *verb* (**ogled, ogling**) stare at someone whom you find attractive.

ogre *noun* **1** a cruel giant in fairy-tales. **2** a terrifying person.

oh *interjection* an exclamation of pain, surprise, delight, etc., or used for emphasis (*Oh yes I will!*).

ohm *noun* a unit of electrical resistance. [named after a German scientist, G. S. Ohm]

▶▶ T H E S A U R U S ◀◀

offensive² *noun* assault, attack, blitz, drive, invasion, onslaught, raid.

offer¹ *verb* **1** give, hand, present, proffer. **2** propose, put forward, submit, suggest, tender, volunteer.

offer² *noun* bid, proposal, proposition, suggestion, tender.

offering *noun* contribution, donation, gift, offertory, present, sacrifice.

offhand *adjective* **1** ad lib, extempore, impromptu, off the cuff, spontaneous, unprepared. **2** brusque, casual, curt, perfunctory, rude, terse, unceremonious, unconcerned.

office *noun* **1** den, study, workroom. **2** agency, bureau, department, secretariat. **3** appointment, duty, function, job, position, post, role.

officer *noun* **2** functionary, official. **3** SEE POLICE.

official¹ *adjective* **1** accredited, approved, authorised, certified, endorsed, formal, legitimate, proper.

official² *noun* bureaucrat, functionary, office-bearer, officer.

officious *adjective* bossy, bumptious, cocky, interfering, intrusive, meddlesome, overbearing, self-important.

off-putting *adjective* disconcerting, disgusting, offensive, repellent, repugnant, repulsive, unpleasant.

offset *verb* balance, cancel out, compensate for, counteract, counterbalance, neutralise, nullify.

offshoot *noun* **1** branch, side shoot. **2** by-product, derivative, development, spin-off.

offsider *noun* assistant, associate, helper, partner, sidekick (*informal*).

offspring *noun* **1** child(ren), descendant(s), family, heir(s), kid(s) (*informal*), progeny. **2** brood, litter, young.

often *adverb* constantly, continually, frequently, regularly, repeatedly.

ogle *verb* eye, gawp at (*informal*), gaze at, leer at, stare at.

ogre *noun* **1** bogyman, giant, monster. **2** beast, brute, bully, fiend, monster, tyrant.

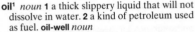

DICTIONARY

oil¹ *noun* **1** a thick slippery liquid that will not dissolve in water. **2** a kind of petroleum used as fuel. **oil-well** *noun*

oil² *verb* put oil on something, especially to make it work smoothly. [from Latin *oleum* = olive oil]

oil-colour *noun* paint made with oil.

oilfield *noun* an area where oil is found.

oil-painting *noun* a painting done with oil-colours.

oilskin *noun* cloth made waterproof by treatment with oil.

oily *adjective* of or like oil; covered or soaked with oil. **oiliness** *noun*

ointment *noun* a cream or slippery paste for putting on sore skin and cuts.

OK *adverb & adjective* (*informal*) all right. [perhaps from the initials of *oll* (or *orl*) *korrect*, a humorous spelling of *all correct*, first used in the USA in 1839]

old *adjective* **1** not new; born or made or existing from a long time ago. **2** of a particular age, *I'm ten years old*. **3** shabby from age or wear. **4** former; original, *in its old place*. **5** (*informal*, used casually or for emphasis), *good old mum!* **oldness** *noun*

olden *adjective* (*old use*) of former times.

old-fashioned *adjective* of the kind that was usual a long time ago.

old hand (*Australian*) an experienced person.

old man kangaroo a fully grown male kangaroo.

olfactory *adjective* of the sense of smell.

oligarchy *noun* (*plural* **oligarchies**) a country ruled by a small group of people. **oligarch**

noun, **oligarchic** *adjective* [from Greek *oligoi* = few, + *archein* = to rule]

olive *noun* **1** an evergreen tree with a small bitter fruit. **2** this fruit, from which an oil (*olive oil*) is made. **3** a shade of green like an unripe olive.

olive branch something done or offered that shows you want to make peace.

Olympic Games or **Olympics** *plural noun* a series of international sports contests held every fourth year in a different part of the world. [from the name of Olympia, a city in Greece where they were held in ancient times]

ombudsman *noun* (*plural*) **ombudsmen**) an official whose job is to investigate complaints against government organisations etc. [from Swedish, = legal representative]

omega (*say* **oh**-meg-a) *noun* the last letter of the Greek alphabet, a long *o*. [from Greek *o mega* = big O]

omelette *noun* eggs beaten together and cooked in a pan, often with a filling.

omen *noun* an event regarded as a sign of what is going to happen.

ominous *adjective* seeming as if trouble is coming. **ominously** *adverb* [from *omen*]

omission *noun* **1** omitting. **2** something that has been omitted or not done.

omit *verb* (**omitted, omitting**) **1** miss something out. **2** fail to do something.

omni- *prefix* all. [from Latin *omnis* = all]

omnibus *noun* (*plural* **omnibuses**) **1** (*formal*) a bus. **2** a book containing several stories or books that were previously published separately. [Latin, = for everybody]

THESAURUS

oil² *verb* grease, lubricate.

oily *adjective* fatty, greasy.

ointment *noun* balm, cream, embrocation, liniment, lotion, oil, salve.

OK *adjective* adequate, all right, fine, passable, reasonable, satisfactory, so-so (*informal*), tolerable.

old *adjective* **1** (*an old person*) aged, elderly, geriatric, mature, retired, senior; (*an old car*) antiquated, antique, archaic, obsolescent, obsolete, outdated, primitive, veteran, vintage; (*an old custom*) age-old, ancient, early, long-standing, time-honoured, traditional. **3** decrepit, dilapidated, ragged, shabby, tatty (*informal*), worn, worn-out. **4** earlier, former, original, previous, prior.

olden *adjective* bygone, earlier, early, former, old.

old-fashioned *adjective* antediluvian (*informal*), antiquated, archaic, behind the times, conservative, conventional, fuddy-duddy (*informal*), obsolete, old hat (*informal*), outdated, outmoded, out-of-date, traditional, unfashionable.

omen *noun* indication, portent, sign, warning.

ominous *adjective* inauspicious, menacing, portentous, sinister, threatening.

omission *noun* **1** exclusion, neglect, negligence, non-inclusion. **2** exclusion, gap, oversight.

omit *verb* **1** drop, exclude, ignore, leave out, miss, overlook, pass over, skip. **2** fail, forget, neglect.

omnipotent *adjective* having unlimited power or very great power. [from *omni-* + *potent*]

omniscient (*say* om-**nis**-ee-ent) *adjective* knowing everything. **omniscience** *noun* [from *omni-*, + Latin *sciens* = knowing]

omnivorous (*say* om-**niv**-er-us) *adjective* feeding on all kinds of food. (Compare *carnivorous, herbivorous*.) [from *omni-*, + Latin *vorare* = devour]

on[1] *preposition* **1** supported by; covering; added or attached to, *the sign on the door*. **2** close to; towards, *The army advanced on Paris*. **3** during; at the time of, *on my birthday*. **4** by reason of, *Arrest him on suspicion*. **5** concerning, *a book on butterflies*. **6** in a state of; using or showing, *The house was on fire*.

on[2] *adverb* **1** so as to be on something, *Put it on*. **2** further forward, *Move on*. **3** working; in action, *Is the heater on?*
on and off not continually.

once[1] *adverb* **1** for one time or on one occasion only, *They came only once*. **2** formerly, *They once lived here*.

once[2] *noun* one time, *Once is enough*.

once[3] *conjunction* as soon as, *You can go once I have taken your names*.

oncoming *adjective* approaching; coming towards you, *oncoming traffic*.

one[1] *adjective* single; individual; united.

one[2] *noun* **1** the smallest whole number, 1. **2** a person or thing alone.
one another each other.

one[3] *pronoun* a person; any person, *One likes to help*. **oneself** *pronoun*

onerous (*say* **oh**-ner-us) *adjective* burdensome. [from Latin *onus* = burden]

one-sided *adjective* unfair, prejudiced.

one-way *adjective* where traffic is allowed to travel in one direction only.

onion *noun* a round vegetable with a strong flavour. **oniony** *adjective*

onlooker *noun* a spectator.

only[1] *adjective* being the one person or thing of a kind; sole, *my only wish*.
only child a child who has no brothers or sisters.

only[2] *adverb* no more than; and that is all, *There are only three cakes left*.

only[3] *conjunction* but then; however, *He makes promises, only he never keeps them*.

onomatopoeia (*say* on-om-at-o-**pee**-a) *noun* the formation of words that imitate what they stand for, e.g. *cuckoo, plop*. **onomatopoeic** *adjective* [from Greek *onoma* = name, + *poiein* = make]

onrush *noun* an onward rush.

onset *noun* **1** a beginning, *the onset of winter*. **2** an attack.

onshore *adjective* from the sea towards the land, *an onshore breeze*.

onslaught *noun* a fierce attack.

onto *preposition* to a position on.

onus (*say* **oh**-nus) *noun* the duty or responsibility of doing something. [Latin, = burden]

onward *adverb* & *adjective* going forward; further on. **onwards** *adverb*

onyx *noun* a stone rather like marble, with different colours in layers.

ooze[1] *verb* (**oozed, oozing**) **1** flow out slowly; trickle. **2** allow something to flow out slowly, *The wound oozed blood*.

ooze[2] *noun* mud at the bottom of a river or sea.

op- *prefix* see **ob-**.

opal *noun* a kind of stone with a rainbow sheen. **opalescent** *adjective*

omnipotent *adjective* all-powerful, almighty, sovereign, supreme.

omniscient *adjective* all-knowing, all-seeing, all-wise.

once[1] *adverb* **2** formerly, hitherto, in days gone by, in the past, previously.

oncoming *adjective* advancing, approaching.

onerous *adjective* arduous, burdensome, difficult, exacting, hard, heavy, herculean, oppressive, taxing, tiring.

one-sided *adjective* biased, unbalanced, unequal, uneven, unfair, prejudiced.

onlooker *noun* bystander, eyewitness, looker-on, observer, spectator, viewer, witness.

only[1] *adjective* lone, one, single, sole, solitary.

only[2] *adverb* just, merely, purely, simply.

onset *noun* **1** beginning, commencement, inception, outbreak, outset, start.

onslaught *noun* aggression, assault, attack, blitz, bombardment, charge, incursion, offensive, raid.

onus *noun* burden, duty, obligation, responsibility.

ooze[1] *verb* **1** discharge, dribble, drip, exude, leak, seep, trickle.

▶▶ D I C T I O N A R Y ◀◀

opaque (*say* o-**payk**) *adjective* not transparent; not translucent.

OPEC *abbreviation* Organisation of Petroleum Exporting Countries.

open[1] *adjective* **1** allowing people or things to go in and out; not closed or covered; not blocked up. **2** spread out; unfolded. **3** not limited; not restricted, *an open championship.* **4** letting in visitors or customers. **5** with wide spaces between solid parts. **6** honest; frank; not secret or secretive, *Be open about the danger.* **7** undisguised, *open hostility.* **8** not decided, *an open mind.* **openness** *noun*
in the open air not inside a house or building.
open-air *adjective*

open[2] *verb* **1** make or become open or more open. **2** begin. **opener** *noun*

open-cut *adjective* (of a mine) worked by removing layers of earth from the surface, not underground.

opening *noun* **1** a space or gap; a place where something opens. **2** the beginning of something. **3** an opportunity.

openly *adverb* without secrecy.

opera[1] *noun* a play in which all or most of the words are sung. **operatic** *adjective*

opera[2] *plural* of **opus**.

operate *verb* (**operated**, **operating**) **1** make something work. **2** be in action; work. **3** perform a surgical operation on somebody. **operable** *adjective* [from Latin *operari* = to work]

operation *noun* **1** operating; working. **2** a piece of work. **3** something done to the body to take away or repair a part of it. **4** a planned military activity. **operational** *adjective*

operative *adjective* **1** working; functioning. **2** of surgical operations.

operator *noun* a person who works something, especially a telephone switchboard or exchange.

operetta *noun* a short light opera.

ophthalmic (*say* off-**thal**-mik) *adjective* of or for the eyes. [from Greek *ophthalmos* = eye]

opinion *noun* what you think of something; a belief or judgement.
opinion poll an estimate of what people think, made by questioning a sample of them. [from Latin *opinari* = believe]

opinionated *adjective* having strong opinions and holding them obstinately.

opium *noun* a drug made from the juice of certain poppies, used in medicine.

opponent *noun* a person or group opposing another in a contest or war. [from Latin *opponere* = set against]

▶▶ T H E S A U R U S ◀◀

opaque *adjective* cloudy, milky, muddy, murky, turbid, unclear.

open[1] *adjective* **1** (*an open door*) ajar, gaping, unbolted, undone, unfastened, unlatched, unlocked; (*open spaces*) broad, clear, empty, exposed, extensive, unbounded, uncluttered, uncrowded, unfenced, unobstructed. **2** outspread, outstretched, spread out, unfolded, unfurled. **3** general, public, unrestricted. **6** candid, communicative, direct, forthright, frank, honest, outspoken, straightforward. **7** blatant, flagrant, obvious, overt, patent, unconcealed, undisguised. **8** undecided, unresolved, unsettled.
open-air *adjective* alfresco, outdoor, outside.
open-minded *adjective* fair, impartial, just, objective, tolerant, unbiased, unprejudiced.

open[2] *verb* **1** unbolt, unclasp, uncork, undo, unfasten, unhook, unlatch, unlock, unroll, unseal, untie, unwrap, unzip. **2** begin, commence, initiate, kick off (*informal*), launch, start.

opening *noun* **1** aperture, breach, break, chink, cleft, crack, cut, fissure, gap, hatch, hole, leak, manhole, mouth, orifice, outlet, passage, rift, slit, slot, space, vent. **2** beginning, commencement, inception, launch, outset, start. **3** break (*informal*), chance, opportunity, position, vacancy.

operate *verb* **1** control, drive, handle, manage, manipulate, use, wield, work. **2** function, go, perform, run, work.

operation *noun* **2** action, business, exercise, job, procedure, process, task, undertaking. **3** op (*informal*), surgery. **4** action, campaign, exercise, manoeuvre.

opinion *noun* belief, comment, conclusion, conviction, creed, feeling, idea, impression, judgement, notion, point of view, sentiment, standpoint, thought, view, viewpoint.
opinion poll Gallup poll, straw poll, poll, survey.

opinionated *adjective* bigoted, cocksure, dogmatic, headstrong, obstinate, self-assertive, stubborn.

opponent *noun* adversary, challenger, competitor, contender, enemy, foe, opposition, rival.

▶▶ D I C T I O N A R Y ◀◀

opportune *adjective* **1** (of time) suitable for a purpose. **2** done or happening at a suitable time. **opportunely** *adverb* [from *op-*, + Latin *portus* = harbour (originally used of wind blowing a ship towards a harbour)]

opportunist *noun* a person who is quick to seize opportunities.

opportunity *noun* (*plural* **opportunities**) a time or set of circumstances that are suitable for doing a particular thing.
opportunity shop (*Australian*) a shop run by a charity to sell donated secondhand clothes etc. [same origin as *opportune*]

oppose *verb* (**opposed, opposing**) **1** argue or fight against; resist. **2** contrast, *'Soft' is opposed to 'hard'*.

opposite¹ *adjective* **1** placed on the other or further side; facing, *on the opposite side of the road*. **2** moving away from or towards each other, *The trains are travelling in opposite directions*. **3** completely different, *opposite characters*.

opposite² *noun* an opposite person or thing.

opposite³ *adverb* in an opposite position or direction, *I'll sit opposite*.

opposite⁴ *preposition* opposite to, *They live opposite the school*. [from Latin *oppositum* = placed against]

opposition *noun* **1** opposing something; resistance. **2** the people who oppose something.
the Opposition the chief political party opposing the one that is in power.

oppress *verb* **1** govern or treat somebody cruelly or unjustly. **2** weigh down with care.

oppression *noun*, **oppressor** *noun* [from *op-* = against, + *press*]

oppressive *adjective* **1** oppressing; harsh or cruel. **2** (of weather) sultry.

op shop an opportunity shop.

opt *verb* choose.
opt out decide not to join in. [from Latin *optare* = wish for]

optic *adjective* of the eye or sight.
optics *noun* the study of sight and of light as connected with this. [from Greek *optos* = seen]

optical *adjective* of sight; aiding sight, *optical instruments*. **optically** *adverb*
optical illusion a deceptive appearance that makes you see something wrongly. [from *optic*]

optician *noun* a person who makes or sells spectacles etc.
ophthalmic optician someone who is qualified to test people's eyesight and prescribe spectacles etc.

optimist *noun* a person who expects that things will turn out well. (Compare *pessimist*.) **optimism** *noun*, **optimistic** *adjective*, **optimistically** *adverb* [from Latin *optimus* = best]

optimum *adjective* best; most favourable. **optimum** *noun*, **optimal** *adjective* [Latin, = best thing]

option *noun* **1** the right or power to choose something. **2** something chosen or that may be chosen. [same origin as *opt*]

▶▶ T H E S A U R U S ◀◀

opportune *adjective* **1** advantageous, appropriate, apt, auspicious, convenient, expedient, favourable, fitting, fortunate, good, lucky, propitious. **2** convenient, timely, well-timed.

opportunity *noun* break (*informal*), chance, moment, occasion, opening, time.

oppose *verb* **1** argue against, buck (*informal*), contest, counter, defy, fight, object to, resist, withstand.

opposite¹ *adjective* **1** facing. **3** conflicting, contradictory, contrary, contrasting, incompatible, opposing.

opposite² *noun* antithesis, contrary, converse, reverse.

opposition *noun* **1** antagonism, disagreement, disapproval, hostility, objection, resistance. **2** competitor, enemy, opponent, rival.

oppress *verb* **1** abuse, bully, crush, exploit, maltreat, persecute, subjugate, tyrannise. **2** afflict, burden, depress, overwhelm, torment, trouble, weigh down, worry.

oppressive *adjective* **1** cruel, despotic, hard, harsh, repressive, severe, tyrannical, unjust. **2** close, humid, muggy, stifling, stuffy, sultry, uncomfortable.

opt *verb* (**opt for**) choose, decide on, go for, pick, select, settle on, vote for.

optical *adjective* see VISUAL.

optimistic *adjective* cheerful, confident, expectant, hopeful, positive, sanguine, upbeat (*informal*).

optimum *adjective* best, ideal, optimal, peak, perfect.

option *noun* **2** alternative, choice, possibility.

optional *adjective* that you can choose, not compulsory. **optionally** *adverb*

optometrist *noun* a person who tests eyesight and supplies lenses to correct defects of vision.

opulent *adjective* **1** wealthy; rich. **2** luxurious. **3** plentiful. **opulently** *adverb*, **opulence** *noun* [from Latin *opes* = wealth]

opus (*say* **oh**-pus) *noun* (*plural* **opera**) a numbered musical composition, *Beethoven opus 15.* [Latin, = work]

or *conjunction* used to show that there is a choice or an alternative, *Do or die.*

oracle *noun* **1** a shrine where the ancient Greeks consulted one of their gods for advice or a prophecy. **2** a wise adviser. **oracular** (*say* or-**ak**-yoo-ler) *adjective* [from Latin *orare* = speak]

oracy (*say* **or**-a-see) *noun* the ability to express yourself well in speaking.

oral *adjective* **1** spoken, not written. **2** of or using the mouth. **orally** *adverb* [from Latin *oris* = of the mouth]

orange *noun* **1** a round juicy citrus fruit with reddish-yellow peel. **2** a reddish-yellow colour. **orange** *adjective* [from Persian *narang*]

orangeade *noun* an orange-flavoured drink.

orang-utan *noun* a large ape of Borneo and Sumatra. [from Malay, = wild man]

oration *noun* a long formal speech. [from Latin *orare* = speak]

orator *noun* a person who makes speeches. **oratory** *noun*, **oratorical** *adjective*

oratorio *noun* (*plural* **oratorios**) a piece of music for voices and an orchestra, usually on a religious subject.

orb *noun* a sphere or globe.

orbit¹ *noun* **1** the curved path taken by something moving round a planet etc. in space. **2** the range of someone's influence or control. **orbital** *adjective*

orbit² *verb* (**orbited, orbiting**) move in an orbit round something, *The spacecraft orbited the earth.* [from Latin *orbis* = circle]

orchard *noun* a piece of ground planted with fruit-trees. [from Latin *hortus* = garden, + *yard*]

orchestra *noun* a large group of people playing various musical instruments together. **orchestral** *adjective* [Greek, = space where the chorus danced during a play]

orchestrate *verb* (**orchestrated, orchestrating**) **1** compose or arrange music for an orchestra. **2** coordinate things deliberately, *They orchestrated their campaigns.* **orchestration** *noun*

orchid *noun* a kind of flower, often with unevenly shaped petals.

ordain *verb* **1** appoint a person ceremonially to perform spiritual duties in the Christian Church. **2** destine. **3** declare authoritatively; decree.

ordeal *noun* something very hard to endure.

order¹ *noun* **1** a command. **2** a request for something to be supplied. **3** the way things are arranged, *in alphabetical order.* **4** a condition in which everything is in its right place; tidiness. **5** the condition or state of something, *in working order.* **6** obedience to rules or laws, *law and order.* **7** a kind or sort, *She showed courage of the highest order.* **8** a special group; a religious organisation, *an order of monks.*

optional *adjective* elective, non-essential, voluntary.

opulent *adjective* **1** affluent, moneyed, prosperous, rich, wealthy, well off. **2** luxurious, plush (*informal*), splendid, sumptuous.

oral *adjective* spoken.

orange *adjective* amber, apricot, carroty, coral, ginger, saffron, salmon, tangerine.

oration *noun* address, discourse, eulogy, homily, lecture, speech.

orbit¹ *noun* **1** circuit, course, path, revolution, track, trajectory.

orbit² *verb* circle, circumnavigate, revolve around.

orchestra *noun* band, ensemble.

orchestrate *verb* **1** arrange, score. **2** coordinate, mastermind, organise, stage-manage.

ordain *verb* **1** appoint, consecrate, induct, install, invest. **3** command, decree, dictate, order, prescribe, rule.

ordeal *noun* affliction, distress, hardship, nightmare, suffering, test, trial, tribulation, trouble.

order¹ *noun* **1** command, decree, dictate, direction, directive, edict, injunction, instruction. **3** arrangement, classification, grouping, layout, organisation, sequence, series, system. **4** neatness, orderliness, tidiness. **5** condition, nick (*informal*), repair, shape, state. **6** calm, control, discipline, harmony, peace, quiet. **7** degree, kind, level, quality, sort, type. **8** association,

▶▶ D I C T I O N A R Y ◀◀

in order that or **in order to** so that; for the purpose of.

order² *verb* **1** command. **2** ask for something to be supplied. **3** put into order; arrange neatly.
order about keep giving somebody commands.

orderly¹ *adjective* **1** arranged neatly or well; methodical. **2** well-behaved; obedient. **orderliness** *noun*

orderly² *noun* (*plural* **orderlies**) **1** a soldier whose job is to assist an officer. **2** an assistant in a hospital.

ordinal numbers numbers showing a thing's position in a series, e.g. *first, fifth, twentieth*. (Compare *cardinal*.) [same origin as *ordinary*]

ordinance *noun* a command; a decree.

ordinary *adjective* normal; usual; not special. **ordinarily** *adverb* [from Latin *ordinis* = of a row or an order]

ordination *noun* ordaining or being ordained as a member of the clergy.

ordnance *noun* military equipment.

ore *noun* rock with metal or other useful substances in it, *iron ore*.

organ *noun* **1** a musical instrument from which sounds are produced by air forced through pipes, played by keys and pedals. **2** a part of the body with a particular function,

the digestive organs. [from Greek *organon* = tool]

organdie *noun* a kind of thin fabric, usually stiffened.

organic *adjective* **1** of organs of the body, *organic diseases*. **2** of or formed from living things, *organic matter*. **organically** *adverb*

organisation *noun* **1** an organised group of people. **2** the organising of something. **3** the way something is organised. **organisational** *adjective*

organise *verb* (**organised, organising**) **1** plan and prepare something, *We organised a picnic*. **2** form people into a group to work together. **3** put things in order. **organiser** *noun* [same origin as *organ*]

organism *noun* a living thing; an individual animal or plant.

organist *noun* a person who plays the organ.

orgasm *noun* the climax of sexual excitement.

orgy *noun* (*plural* **orgies**) **1** a wild party. **2** an extravagant activity, *an orgy of spending*.

Orient *noun* the East; oriental countries. (Compare *Occident*.) [from Latin, = sunrise]

orient *verb* orientate.

oriental *adjective* of the countries east of the Mediterranean Sea, especially China and Japan.

▶▶ T H E S A U R U S ◀◀

brotherhood, community, fraternity, group, sisterhood, society.
out of order broken, bung (*Australian informal*), damaged, inoperative, kaput (*informal*), on the blink (*informal*).

order² *verb* **1** bid, charge, command, decree, direct, enjoin, instruct, prescribe, tell. **2** apply for, book, request, reserve. **3** arrange, classify, dispose, group, lay out, organise, sort.
order about boss around, bully, control, push around, tell someone what to do.

orderly¹ *adjective* **1** methodical, neat, ordered, organised, shipshape, spick and span, straight, systematic, tidy. **2** controlled, disciplined, law-abiding, quiet, well-behaved.

ordinary *adjective* average, common, commonplace, conventional, customary, everyday, familiar, humble, humdrum, mediocre, middling, mundane, nondescript, normal, orthodox, plain, regular, routine, run-of-the-mill, simple, so-so (*informal*), standard, typical, undistinguished, unexceptional, unexciting,

unimpressive, uninspired, uninteresting, unremarkable, usual.

organisation *noun* **1** alliance, association, body, business, club, company, corporation, corps, enterprise, establishment, federation, fellowship, firm, fraternity, group, institution, league, movement, order, party, society, union. **2** administration, arrangement, coordination, management, orchestration, planning, running. **3** arrangement, design, form, format, layout, presentation, structure, system.

organise *verb* **1** arrange, control, coordinate, manage, orchestrate, plan, run, stage-manage. **2** assemble, establish, form, mobilise, put together, set up. **3** arrange, catalogue, classify, group, order, put in order, sort, structure, systematise, tidy.

organism *noun* being, creature, living thing.

orgy *noun* **1** binge (*slang*), party, revelry, spree (*informal*). **2** frenzy, splurge (*informal*), spree (*informal*).

▶▶ DICTIONARY ◀◀

orientate *verb* (**orientated, orientating**) place something or face in a certain direction. **orientation** *noun*

orienteering *noun* the sport of finding your way across rough country with a map and compass.

orifice (*say* o-rif-iss) *noun* an opening. [from Latin *oris* = of the mouth]

origami (*say* o-rig-**ah**-mee) *noun* folding paper into decorative shapes. [from Japanese *ori* = fold, + *kami* = paper]

origin *noun* **1** the start of something; the point or cause from which something began. **2** a person's ancestry. [from Latin *origo* = source]

original *adjective* **1** existing from the start; earliest, *the original inhabitants*. **2** new in its design etc., not a copy. **3** producing new ideas; inventive. **original** *noun*, **originally** *adverb*, **originality** *noun*

originate *verb* (**originated, originating**) **1** cause to begin; create. **2** have its origin, *The quarrel originated in rivalry*. **origination** *noun*, **originator** *noun*

ornament[1] *noun* a decoration. **ornamental** *adjective*

ornament[2] *verb* decorate with things. **ornamentation** *noun* [from Latin *ornare* = adorn]

ornate *adjective* elaborately ornamented. **ornately** *adverb* [from Latin *ornatum* = adorned]

ornithology *noun* the study of birds. **ornithologist** *noun*, **ornithological** *adjective* [from Greek *ornithos* = of a bird, + *-logy*]

orphan *noun* a child whose parents are dead. **orphaned** *adjective*

orphanage *noun* a home for orphans.

ortho- *prefix* right; straight; correct. [from Greek *orthos* = straight]

orthodox *adjective* holding beliefs that are correct or generally accepted. **orthodoxy** *noun*

Orthodox Church the Christian Churches of eastern Europe. [from *ortho-*, + Greek *doxa* = opinion]

orthopaedics (*say* orth-o-**pee**-diks) *noun* the treatment of deformities and injuries to bones and muscles. **orthopaedic** *adjective* [from *ortho-*, + Greek *paideia* = rearing of children (because the treatment was originally of children)]

oscillate *verb* (**oscillated, oscillating**) **1** move to and fro like a pendulum; vibrate. **2** waver; vary. **oscillation** *noun*, **oscillator** *noun*

osier (*say* **oh**-zee-er) *noun* a willow with flexible twigs used in making baskets.

osmosis *noun* the passing of fluid through a porous partition into another more concentrated fluid. [from Greek *osmos* = push]

ostensible *adjective* pretended; used to conceal the true reason, *Their ostensible reason for travelling was to visit friends*. **ostensibly** *adverb* [from Latin *ostendere* = to show]

ostentatious *adjective* making a showy display of something to impress people. **ostentatiously** *adverb*, **ostentation** *noun*

osteopath *noun* a person who treats certain diseases etc. by manipulating a patient's bones and muscles. **osteopathy** *noun*, **osteopathic** *adjective* [from Greek *osteon* = bone, + *-patheia* = suffering]

▶▶ THESAURUS ◀◀

orientate *verb* **orientate yourself 1** find your position, get your bearings, orient yourself. **2** acclimatise, adapt, adjust, familiarise yourself, orient yourself.

origin *noun* **1** basis, beginning, birth, cause, commencement, creation, derivation, emergence, foundation, genesis, inception, root, source, start, starting point. **2** ancestry, birth, descent, extraction, lineage, parentage, pedigree.

original *adjective* **1** Aboriginal, earliest, first, initial, native, primeval. **2** firsthand, fresh, new, novel, unique. **3** creative, imaginative, innovative, inventive, unconventional. **original** *noun* archetype, master, prototype.

originate *verb* **2** arise, begin, commence, date from, emerge, spring up, start.

ornament[1] *noun* adornment, bauble, decoration, embellishment, jewellery, knick-knack, trimming, trinket.

ornate *adjective* baroque, decorated, elaborate, fancy, flamboyant, ornamented, rococo, showy.

orthodox *adjective* accepted, conventional, established, mainstream, official, ordinary, standard, traditional.

oscillate *verb* **1** sway, swing. **2** fluctuate, see-saw, swing, vacillate, vary, waver.

ostensible *adjective* alleged, apparent, declared, outward, pretended, professed, seeming.

ostentatious *adjective* conspicuous, extravagant, flamboyant, flash (*informal*), flashy, grandiose, imposing, pretentious, showy, swanky (*informal*).

▶▶ D I C T I O N A R Y ◀◀

ostracise *verb* (**ostracised, ostracising**) exclude; ignore someone completely. **ostracism** *noun* [from Greek *ostrakon* = piece of pottery (because people voted that a person should be banished by writing his name on this)]

ostrich *noun* (*plural* **ostriches**) a large long-legged African bird that can run very fast but cannot fly. It is said to bury its head in the sand when pursued, believing that it cannot then be seen.

other[1] *adjective* **1** different, *some other time*. **2** remaining, *Try the other shoe*. **3** additional, *my other friends*. **4** just recent or past, *I saw him the other day*.

other[2] *noun & pronoun* the other person or thing, *Where are the others?*

otherwise *adverb* **1** if things happen differently; if you do not, *Write it down, otherwise you'll forget*. **2** in other ways, *It rained, but otherwise the holiday was good*. **3** differently, *We could not do otherwise*.

otter *noun* a fish-eating animal with webbed feet, a flat tail, and thick brown fur, living near water.

ottoman *noun* **1** a long padded seat. **2** a storage box with a padded top.

ought *auxiliary verb* expressing duty (*We ought to feed them*), rightness or advisability (*You ought to take more exercise*), or probability (*At this speed, we ought to be there by noon*).

oughtn't (*mainly spoken*) ought not.

ounce *noun* a unit of weight equal to 1/16 of a pound (about 28 grams).

our *adjective* belonging to us.

ours *possessive pronoun* belonging to us, *These seats are ours*.

Usage It is incorrect to write *our's*.

---

ourselves *pronoun* we or us and nobody else. (Compare *herself*.)

oust *verb* drive out; expel; eject from a position or employment etc.

out *adverb* **1** away from or not in a particular place or position or state etc.; not at home. **2** into the open; into existence or sight etc., *The sun came out*. **3** not in action or use etc.; (of a batsman) having had the innings ended; (of a fire) not burning. **4** to or at an end; completely, *sold out; tired out*. **5** without restraint; boldly; loudly, *Speak out!*

be out for or **out to** be seeking or wanting, *They are out to make trouble*.

out of date old-fashioned; not valid any more.

out of doors in the open air.

out of the way remote; unusual.

out- *prefix* **1** out of; away from (as in *outcast*). **2** external; separate (as in *outhouse*). **3** more than; so as to defeat or exceed (as in *outdo*).

out-and-out *adjective* thorough; complete, *an out-and-out villain*.

outback *noun* the remote inland districts of Australia.

outboard motor a motor fitted to the outside of a boat's stern.

outbreak *noun* the start of a disease or war or anger etc.

outburst *noun* the bursting out of anger or laughter etc.

outcast *noun* a person who has been rejected by family, friends, or society.

outcome *noun* the result of what happens or has happened.

outcrop *noun* a piece of rock from a lower level that sticks out on the surface of the ground.

outcry *noun* (*plural* **outcries**) **1** a loud cry. **2** a strong protest.

▶▶ T H E S A U R U S ◀◀

ostracise *verb* avoid, banish, blackball, blacklist, boycott, cold-shoulder, disown, exclude, reject, send to Coventry, shun, snub.

other[1] *adjective* **1** alternative, different. **3** additional, extra, further, more, supplementary.
other than apart from, aside from, besides, except.

oust *verb* banish, dismiss, drive out, eject, expel, fire, give the boot (*slang*), give the sack (*informal*), kick out (*informal*), sack (*informal*), throw out.

out-and-out *adjective* absolute, arrant, complete, downright, thorough, total, utter.

outback *noun* backblocks (*Australian*), back of beyond, bush, inland, interior, never-never (*Australian*), sticks (*informal*).

outbreak *noun* epidemic, eruption, outburst.

outburst *noun* blaze, burst, eruption, explosion, fit, flood, outbreak, spasm.

outcast *noun* deportee, exile, outlaw, pariah, refugee.

outcome *noun* consequence, effect, end, fruit, result, sequel, upshot.

outcry *noun* clamour, hue and cry, hullabaloo, objection, outburst, protest, uproar.

▶▶▶ D I C T I O N A R Y ◀◀

outdated *adjective* out of date.

outdistance *verb* (**outdistanced, outdistancing**) get far ahead of someone in a race etc.

outdo *verb* (**outdid, outdone, outdoing**) do better than another person etc.

outdoor *adjective* done or used outdoors.

outdoors *adverb* in the open air.

outer *adjective* outside; external; nearer to the outside. **outermost** *adjective*

outfit *noun* 1 a set of clothes worn together. 2 a set of equipment.

outflow *noun* 1 flowing out; what flows out. 2 a pipe for liquid flowing out.

outgoing *adjective* 1 going out, *the outgoing president*. 2 sociable and friendly.
outgoings *plural noun* expenditure.

outgrow *verb* (**outgrew, outgrown, outgrowing**) 1 grow out of clothes or habits etc. 2 grow faster or larger than another person or thing.

outgrowth *noun* 1 something that grows out of another thing, *Feathers are outgrowths on a bird's skin*. 2 a natural development.

outhouse *noun* a small building (e.g. a shed or barn) that belongs to a house but is separate from it.

outing *noun* a journey for pleasure.

outlandish *adjective* looking or sounding strange or foreign.

outlast *verb* last longer than something else.

outlaw[1] *noun* a person who is punished by being excluded from legal rights and the protection of the law.

outlaw[2] *verb* 1 make a person an outlaw. 2 declare something to be illegal; forbid.

outlay *noun* what is spent on something.

outlet *noun* 1 a way for something to get out. 2 a market for goods.

outline[1] *noun* 1 a line round the outside of something, showing its boundary or shape. 2 a summary.

outline[2] *verb* (**outlined, outlining**) 1 make an outline of something. 2 summarise.

outlive *verb* (**outlived, outliving**) live or last longer than another person etc.

outlook *noun* 1 a view on which people look out. 2 a person's mental attitude to something. 3 future prospects.

outlying *adjective* far from a centre; remote, *the outlying districts*.

outmoded *adjective* out of date.

outnumber *verb* be more numerous than another group.

out-patient *noun* a person who visits a hospital for treatment but does not stay there.

outpost *noun* a distant settlement.

▶▶▶ T H E S A U R U S ◀◀

outdated *adjective* antiquated, archaic, obsolete, old, old-fashioned, outmoded, out-of-date, unfashionable.

outdo *verb* beat, defeat, eclipse, exceed, excel, get the better of, outclass, outshine, outstrip, overshadow, surpass, top.

outdoors *adverb* al fresco, in the open air, out of doors, outside.

outer *adjective* exterior, external, outside, superficial, surface; see also OUTLYING.

outfit *noun* 1 clothes, clothing, costume, gear (*informal*), get-up (*informal*). 2 apparatus, equipment, gear, kit.

outgoing *adjective* 1 departing, ex-, former, past, retiring. 2 extroverted, friendly, gregarious, sociable, warm.
outgoings *plural noun* costs, expenditure, expenses.

outgrowth *noun* 1 knob, lump, node, nodule, offshoot, shoot, sprout. 2 by-product, consequence, development, offshoot, outcome, product, result, spin-off, upshot.

outhouse *noun* barn, outbuilding, shed.

outing *noun* drive, excursion, expedition, hike, jaunt, tour, trip.

outlandish *adjective* bizarre, exotic, freakish, odd, outrageous, peculiar, preposterous, strange, unusual, way-out, weird.

outlaw[1] *noun* bandit, brigand, criminal, desperado, fugitive, marauder, outcast.

outlaw[2] *verb* 2 ban, forbid, prohibit, proscribe.

outlay *noun* charge, cost, expenditure, expense.

outlet *noun* 1 channel, duct, escape, exit, hole, opening, overflow, release, vent, way out. 2 shop, store.

outline[1] *noun* 1 contour, profile, shadow, shape, silhouette, tracing. 2 abstract, draft, framework, plan, précis, résumé, run-down, sketch, summary, synopsis.

outlive *verb* outlast, survive.

outlook *noun* 1 aspect, panorama, prospect, scene, sight, view, vista. 2 attitude, frame of mind, perspective, view, viewpoint. 3 forecast, prediction, prognosis, prospect.

outlying *adjective* distant, far-flung, outer, remote.

outnumber *verb* exceed.

▶▶DICTIONARY◀◀

output *noun* the product of a process; the amount produced.

outrage¹ *noun* **1** something that shocks people by being very wicked or cruel. **2** great anger. **outrageous** *adjective*, **outrageously** *adverb*

outrage² *verb* (**outraged, outraging**) shock and anger people greatly.

outrider *noun* a person riding on horseback or on a motor cycle as an escort.

outrigger *noun* a projecting framework attached to a boat, e.g. to prevent a canoe from capsizing.

outright¹ *adverb* **1** completely; entirely. **2** not gradually. **3** frankly, *We told him this outright.*

outright² *adjective* thorough; complete, *an outright fraud.*

outrun *verb* (**outran, outrun, outrunning**) **1** run faster or further than another. **2** go on for longer than it should.

outset *noun* the beginning, *from the outset of his career.*

outside¹ *noun* the outer side, surface, or part.

outside² *adjective* **1** on or coming from the outside, *the outside edge.* **2** greatest possible, *the outside price.* **3** remote; unlikely, *an outside chance.*

outside³ *adverb* on or to the outside; outdoors, *Leave it outside. It's cold outside.*

outside⁴ *preposition* on or to the outside of, *Leave it outside the door.*

outsider *noun* **1** a person who does not belong to a certain group. **2** a horse or person thought to have little chance of winning a race or competition.

outsize *adjective* much larger than average.

outskirts *plural noun* the outer parts or districts, especially of a town.

outsource *verb* contract out part of the work of an industry or office.

outspoken *adjective* speaking or spoken very frankly.

outspread *adjective* spread out.

outstanding *adjective* **1** extremely good or distinguished. **2** conspicuous. **3** not yet paid or dealt with.

outstation *noun* (*Australian*) an outlying sheep or cattle station or Aboriginal settlement.

outstretched *adjective* stretched out.

outstrip *verb* (**outstripped, outstripping**) **1** outrun. **2** surpass.

outvote *verb* (**outvoted, outvoting**) defeat by a majority of votes.

outward *adjective* **1** going outwards. **2** on the outside. **outwardly** *adverb*, **outwards** *adverb*

▶▶THESAURUS◀◀

output *noun* production, yield.

outrage¹ *noun* **1** affront, atrocity, crime, evil, insult, offence, scandal. **2** anger, disgust, fury, indignation, ire, rage, shock.
outrageous *adjective* (*outrageous prices*) absurd, excessive, exorbitant, immoderate, preposterous, shocking, unreasonable; (*outrageous crimes*) atrocious, barbarous, despicable, disgraceful, heinous, infamous, monstrous, notorious, offensive, scandalous, shocking, unspeakable, vile, wicked.

outrage² *verb* affront, anger, enrage, incense, infuriate, insult, offend, scandalise, shock.

outright¹ *adverb* **1** absolutely, altogether, categorically, completely, entirely, utterly. **2** at once, immediately, instantly. **3** directly, frankly, openly, straight.

outright² *adjective* absolute, complete, downright, out-and-out, sheer, thorough, utter.

outset *noun* beginning, commencement, inception, start.

outside¹ *noun* case, coating, cover, covering, crust, exterior, façade, face, shell, skin, surface.

outside² *adjective* **1** exterior, external, outer. **3** distant, faint, remote, slender, slight, slim.

outside³ *adverb* al fresco, in the open air, outdoors, out of doors.

outsider *noun* **1** alien, foreigner, immigrant, intruder, newcomer, odd man out, ring-in (*Australian informal*), stranger, visitor.

outskirts *plural noun* edge, fringe, limits, periphery.

outspoken *adjective* blunt, candid, forthright, frank, open, straightforward, unreserved.

outstanding *adjective* **1** distinguished, eminent, excellent, exceptional, exemplary, extraordinary, great, impressive, memorable, notable, pre-eminent, remarkable, sensational, singular, special, splendid, superior. **3** due, overdue, owing, unpaid.

outstrip *verb* **1** beat, outdistance, outpace, outrun. **2** eclipse, exceed, excel, outclass, outdo, outshine, overshadow, surpass, top.

outward *adjective* **2** exterior, external, observable, outer, outside, superficial, visible.

▶▶▶ D I C T I O N A R Y ◀◀

outweigh *verb* be greater in weight or importance than something else.

outwit *verb* (**outwitted, outwitting**) deceive somebody by being crafty.

ova *plural* of **ovum**.

oval¹ *adjective* shaped like a O, rounded and longer than it is broad. [from Latin *ovum* = egg]

oval² *noun* **1** an oval shape. **2** (*Australian*) a sportsground.

ovary *noun* (*plural* **ovaries**) **1** either of the two organs in which ova or egg-cells are produced in a woman's or female animal's body. **2** part of the pistil in a plant, from which fruit is formed. [from Latin *ovum* = egg]

ovation *noun* enthusiastic applause. [from Latin *ovare* = rejoice]

oven *noun* a closed space in which things are cooked or heated.

over¹ *preposition* **1** above. **2** more than, *It's over an hour ago.* **3** concerning, *They quarrelled over money.* **4** across the top of; on or to the other side of, *They rowed the boat over the lake.* **5** during, *We can talk over dinner.* **6** in superiority or preference to, *their victory over Carlton.*

over² *adverb* **1** out and down from the top or edge; from an upright position, *He fell over.* **2** so that a different side shows, *Turn it over.* **3** at or to a place; across, *Walk over to our house.* **4** remaining, *There is nothing left over.* **5** all through; thoroughly, *Think it over.* **6** at an end, *The lesson is over.*
over and over many times; repeatedly.

over³ *noun* a series of six (or eight) balls bowled in cricket.

over- *prefix* **1** over (as in *overturn*). **2** too much; too (as in *over-anxious*).

overall *adjective* including everything; total, *the overall cost.*

overalls *plural noun* a garment worn over other clothes to protect them.

overarm *adjective* & *adverb* with the arm lifted above shoulder level and coming down in front of the body.

overawe *verb* (**overawed, overawing**) overcome a person with awe.

overbalance *verb* (**overbalanced, overbalancing**) lose balance and fall over; cause to lose balance.

overbearing *adjective* domineering.

overblown *adjective* (of a flower) too fully open; past its best.

overboard *adverb* from in or on a ship into the water, *She jumped overboard.*

overcast *adjective* covered with cloud.

overcoat *noun* a warm outdoor coat.

overcome *verb* (**overcame, overcome, overcoming**) **1** win a victory over somebody; defeat. **2** make a person helpless, *He was overcome by the fumes.* **3** find a way of dealing with a problem etc.

overcrowd *verb* crowd too many people into a place or vehicle etc.

overdo *verb* (**overdid, overdone, overdoing**) **1** do something too much; exaggerate. **2** cook food for too long.

overdose *noun* too large a dose of a drug. **overdose** *verb*

overdraft *noun* the amount by which a bank account is overdrawn.

overdraw *verb* (**overdrew, overdrawn, overdrawing**) draw more money from a bank account than the amount you have in it.

▶▶▶ T H E S A U R U S ◀◀

outweigh *verb* exceed, override, predominate over, surpass.

outwit *verb* dupe, hoodwink, outfox (*informal*), outsmart, trick.

oval¹ *adjective* egg-shaped, elliptical, ovoid.

oval² *noun* **1** ellipse. **2** playing field, sports field, sportsground.

ovation *noun* applause, clap, hand (*informal*).

oven *noun* cooker, furnace, kiln, microwave, range, stove.

overall *adjective* all-inclusive, broad, complete, general, total.

overalls *plural noun* boiler suit, dungarees.

overbearing *adjective* arrogant, autocratic, bossy, domineering, high-handed, imperious, officious, peremptory.

overcast *adjective* cloudy, dull, foggy, gloomy, grey, heavy, leaden, louring, misty.

overcoat *noun* greatcoat, topcoat; see also COAT¹.

overcome *verb* **1** beat, conquer, crush, defeat, lick (*informal*), master, overpower, overthrow, quell, subdue, thrash, triumph over, trounce, vanquish. **3** conquer, rise above, surmount, triumph over.

overdo *verb* **1** exaggerate, lay (it) on a bit thick (*informal*), overstate, pile (it) on (*informal*).

▶▶▶ D I C T I O N A R Y ◀◀

overdue *adjective* late; not paid or arrived etc. by the proper time.

overestimate *verb* (**overestimated, overestimating**) estimate too highly.

overflow *verb* flow over the edge or limits of something. **overflow** *noun*

overgrown *adjective* covered with weeds or unwanted plants.

overhang *verb* (**overhung, overhanging**) jut out over something. **overhang** *noun*

overhaul *verb* **1** examine something thoroughly and repair it if necessary. **2** overtake. **overhaul** *noun*

overhead *adjective & adverb* **1** above the level of your head. **2** in the sky.
overheads *plural noun* the expenses of running a business.

overhear *verb* (**overheard, overhearing**) hear something accidentally or without the speaker intending you to hear it.

overjoyed *adjective* filled with great joy.

overland[1] *adjective & adverb* travelling over the land, not by sea or air.

overland[2] *verb* (*Australian*) drive cattle a long distance over land.

overlap *verb* (**overlapped, overlapping**) **1** lie across something. **2** happen partly at the same time. **overlap** *noun*

overlay[1] *verb* (**overlaid, overlaying**) cover with a layer; lie on top of something.

overlay[2] *noun* a thing laid over another.

overlie *verb* (**overlay, overlain, overlying**) be or lie over something.

overload *verb* load too heavily. **overload** *noun*

overlook *verb* **1** not notice or consider something. **2** not punish an offence. **3** have a view over something.

overlord *noun* a supreme lord.

overnight *adjective & adverb* of or during a night, *an overnight stop in Rome.*

overpower *verb* overcome.

overpowering *adjective* very strong.

overrate *verb* (**overrated, overrating**) have too high an opinion of something.

overreach *verb* **overreach yourself** fail through being too ambitious.

override *verb* (**overrode, overridden, overriding**) **1** overrule. **2** be more important than, *Safety overrides all other considerations.*

overripe *adjective* too ripe.

overrule *verb* (**overruled, overruling**) reject a suggestion etc. by using your authority, *We voted for having a picnic but the principal overruled the idea.*

overrun *verb* (**overran, overrun, overrunning**) **1** spread over and occupy or harm something, *Mice overran the place.* **2** go on for longer than it should, *The broadcast overran its time.*

overseas *adverb & adjective* across or beyond the sea; abroad.

▶▶▶ T H E S A U R U S ◀◀

overdue *adjective* in arrears, late, outstanding, owing.

overeat *verb* binge (*informal*), gorge yourself, overindulge, pig out (*informal*), stuff yourself.

overestimate *verb* exaggerate, overrate, overstate.

overflow *verb* brim over, flood, flow over, pour over, run over, slop over, spill over.
overflow *noun* excess, spillage, surplus.

overgrown *adjective* tangled, uncut, unkempt, untidy, wild.

overhang *verb* jut out over, project over, protrude over, stick out over.

overhaul *verb* **1** recondition, repair, restore, service.

overhear *verb* eavesdrop on, hear, listen in on.

overjoyed *adjective* delighted, ecstatic, elated, euphoric, exuberant, exultant, happy, joyful, joyous, jubilant, over the moon (*informal*), rapt, rapturous, thrilled.

overload *verb* overburden, overtax, weigh down.

overlook *verb* **1** disregard, forget, ignore, leave out, miss, neglect, omit, pass over, skip. **2** condone, disregard, excuse, forgive, ignore, pardon, turn a blind eye to. **3** face, front on to, look out on, look over.

overpower *verb* beat, conquer, defeat, get the better of, overcome, overwhelm, subdue.

overpowering *adjective* irresistible, overwhelming, powerful, uncontrollable.

overrate *verb* exaggerate, overestimate.

override *verb* **1** see OVERRULE. **2** have precedence over, outweigh, prevail over.
overriding *adjective* chief, foremost, main, major, paramount, primary, principal, supreme.

overrule *verb* disallow, invalidate, override, overturn, reject, reverse, revoke, set aside, veto.

overrun *verb* **1** cover, infest, invade, occupy, spread over, swarm over, take over.

overseas *adverb* abroad.
overseas *adjective* foreign, offshore.

oversee *verb* (**oversaw, overseen, overseeing**) superintend. **overseer** *noun*

overshadow *verb* **1** cast a shadow over something. **2** make a person or thing seem unimportant in comparison.

overshoot *verb* (**overshot, overshooting**) go beyond a target or limit, *The plane overshot the runway.*

oversight *noun* a mistake made by not noticing something.

oversleep *verb* (**overslept, oversleeping**) sleep for longer than intended.

overstate *verb* exaggerate. **overstatement** *noun*

overstep *verb* (**overstepped, overstepping**) go beyond a limit.

overt *adjective* done or shown openly, *overt hostility.* **overtly** *adverb*

overtake *verb* (**overtook, overtaken, overtaking**) **1** pass a moving vehicle or person etc. **2** catch up with someone.

overtax *verb* **1** tax too heavily. **2** put too heavy a burden or strain on someone.

overthrow¹ *verb* (**overthrew, overthrown, overthrowing**) cause the downfall of, *They overthrew the king.*

overthrow² *noun* **1** overthrowing; downfall. **2** throwing a ball too far.

overtime *noun* time spent working outside the normal hours; payment for this.

overtone *noun* an extra quality, *There were overtones of envy in his speech.*

overture *noun* **1** a piece of music written as an introduction to an opera, ballet, etc. **2** a friendly attempt to start a discussion, *They made overtures of peace.*

overturn *verb* **1** turn over or upside-down. **2** overthrow.

overview *noun* a general survey.

overweight *adjective* too heavy.

overwhelm *verb* **1** bury or drown beneath a huge mass. **2** overcome completely.

overwork *verb* **1** work or cause to work too hard. **2** use too often, *'Nice' is an overworked word.* **overwork** *noun*

overwrought *adjective* very upset and nervous or worried.

ovoid *adjective* egg-shaped. [from *ovum*]

ovulate *verb* (**ovulated, ovulating**) produce an ovum from an ovary. [from Latin *ovum* = egg]

ovum (*say* **oh**-vum) *noun* (*plural* **ova**) a female cell that can develop into a new individual when fertilised. [Latin, = egg]

oversee *verb* be in charge of, direct, manage, run, superintend, supervise.
  overseer *noun* boss, foreman, forewoman, manager, superintendent, supervisor.

overshadow *verb* **2** dwarf, eclipse, outshine, put in the shade, surpass, tower over.

oversight *noun* blunder, carelessness, error, lapse, mistake, omission, slip-up (*informal*).

overstate *verb* blow up, exaggerate, inflate, magnify.
  overstatement *noun* exaggeration, hyperbole.

overt *adjective* blatant, evident, manifest, obvious, open, patent, plain, unconcealed, visible.

overtake *verb* catch up with, go past, outpace, outstrip, overhaul, pass.

overtax *verb* **2** overburden, overload, overwork, strain, stretch.

overthrow¹ *verb* bring down, defeat, depose, oust, overturn, topple, unseat.

overthrow² *noun* **1** collapse, defeat, downfall, fall.

overtone *noun* connotation, hint, implication, innuendo, insinuation, suggestion, undercurrent.

overture *noun* **1** beginning, introduction, opening, prelude.

overturn *verb* **1** capsize, invert, keel over, knock over, spill, tip over, topple over, turn over, turn turtle, up-end, upset, upturn. **2** see OVERTHROW¹.

overview *noun* outline, sketch, survey.

overweight *adjective* chubby, corpulent, dumpy, fat, gross, heavy, obese, plump, podgy, portly, rotund, stout, tubby.

overwhelm *verb* **1** bury, cover, deluge, drown, engulf, flood, inundate, submerge, swamp. **2** beat, conquer, crush, defeat, overcome, overpower, rout, vanquish.
  overwhelming *adjective* irresistible, overpowering, uncontrollable.

overwrought *adjective* agitated, beside yourself, distressed, frantic, hysterical, nervous, nervy, on edge, overexcited, uptight (*informal*), worked up.

▶▶ D I C T I O N A R Y ◀◀

owe *verb* (**owed, owing**) **1** have a duty to pay or give something to someone, especially money. **2** have something because of the action of another person or thing, *They owed their lives to the pilot's skill.*
owing to because of; caused by.

owl *noun* a bird of prey with large eyes, usually flying at night.

own¹ *adjective* belonging to yourself or itself.
get your own back get revenge.
on your own alone.

own² *verb* **1** possess; have something as your property. **2** acknowledge; admit, *I own that I made a mistake.*
own up (*informal*) confess; admit guilt.

owner *noun* the person who owns something.
ownership *noun*

ox *noun* (*plural* **oxen**) a large animal kept for its meat and for pulling carts.

oxide *noun* a compound of oxygen and one other element.

oxidise *verb* (**oxidised, oxidising**) **1** combine or cause to combine with oxygen. **2** coat with an oxide. **oxidation** *noun*

oxtail *noun* the tail of an ox, used to make soup or stew.

oxygen *noun* a colourless odourless tasteless gas that exists in the air and is essential for living things.

oyster *noun* a kind of shellfish whose shell sometimes contains a pearl.

ozone *noun* a form of oxygen with a sharp smell.
ozone layer a layer of ozone high in the atmosphere, protecting the world from harmful amounts of the sun's rays. [from Greek *ozein* = to smell]

Ozzie alternative spelling of **Aussie**.

▶▶ T H E S A U R U S ◀◀

owe *verb* **1** be beholden to, be indebted to, be in debt to, be under an obligation to.
owing *adjective* due, outstanding, overdue, unpaid.
owing to because of, caused by, on account of, thanks to.

own¹ *adjective* individual, personal, private.
on your own alone, by yourself, independently, single-handed, solo, unaccompanied, unaided, unassisted, unescorted.

own² *verb* **1** be the owner of, have, hold, keep, possess.
own up admit, come clean (*informal*), confess.

owner *noun* holder, landlady, landlord, master, mistress, possessor, proprietor, proprietress.

ox *noun* bull, bullock, steer.

▶ Pp ◀

p. *abbreviation* (*plural* **pp.**) page.

pa *noun* (*slang*) father. [short for *papa*]

pace¹ *noun* **1** one step in walking, marching, or running. **2** speed.

pace² *verb* (**paced, pacing**) **1** walk with slow or regular steps. **2** measure a distance in paces, *pace it out.*

pacemaker *noun* **1** a person who sets the pace for another in a race. **2** an electrical device to keep the heart beating.

pacific (*say* pa-**sif**-ik) *adjective* peaceful; making or loving peace. **pacifically** *adverb* [from Latin *pacis* = of peace]

pacifist (*say* **pas**-if-ist) *noun* a person who believes that war is always wrong. **pacifism** *noun*

pacify *verb* (**pacified, pacifying**) make peaceful or calm. **pacification** *noun* [from Latin *pacis* = of peace]

pack¹ *noun* **1** a bundle, a collection of things wrapped or tied together. **2** a rucksack. **3** a set of playing cards (usually 52). **4** a group of hounds or wolves etc. **5** a group of people; a group of Brownies or Cub Scouts. **6** a large amount, *a pack of lies.* **7** a mass of pieces of ice floating in the sea, *pack-ice.*
go to the pack (*Australian*) deteriorate.

pack² *verb* **1** put things into a suitcase, bag, or box etc. in order to move or store them. **2** crowd together; fill tightly.
pack off send a person away.
send a person packing dismiss him or her.

package *noun* **1** a parcel or packet. **2** a package deal. **packaging** *noun*
package deal a number of things offered or accepted together.
package tour a holiday with everything arranged and included in the price.

packet *noun* a small parcel.

pact *noun* an agreement; a treaty.

pad¹ *noun* **1** a soft thick mass of material, used e.g. to protect or stuff something. **2** a device worn to protect the leg in cricket and other games. **3** a set of sheets of paper fastened together at one edge. **4** the soft fleshy part under an animal's foot or the end of a finger or toe. **5** a flat surface from which spacecraft are launched or where helicopters take off and land. **6** (*Australian*) a path made by animals.

pad² *verb* (**padded, padding**) put a pad on or in something.
pad out make a book etc. longer with unnecessary material.

pad³ *verb* (**padded, padding**) walk softly.

padding *noun* material used to pad things.

▶▶ THESAURUS ◀◀

pace¹ *noun* **1** step, stride. **2** rate, speed, velocity.

pace² *verb* **1** see WALK¹.

pacifist *noun* conscientious objector, dove, peace lover.

pacify *verb* appease, calm, placate, quieten, settle, soothe.

pack¹ *noun* **1** bag, box, bundle, carton, package, packet, parcel. **2** backpack, haversack, kitbag, knapsack, rucksack, satchel; see also SWAG. **5** band, gang, group, mob, push (*Australian*), set. **6** heap, load, lot.
go to the pack see DETERIORATE.

pack² *verb* **1** load, package, parcel, place, put, store, stow, wrap up. **2** compact, compress, cram, crowd, fill, jam, press, ram, squash, squeeze, stuff, tamp.

pack off bundle off, dispatch, send away, send off.

package *noun* **1** bag, bale, box, bundle, carton, container, pack, packet, parcel.

packet *noun* bag, envelope, pack, package, parcel, sachet.

pact *noun* accord, agreement, bargain, compact, contract, covenant, deal, treaty, understanding.

pad¹ *noun* **1** buffer, cushion, padding, pillow, wad. **3** jotter, notepad.

pad² *verb* cushion, fill, line, protect, stuff, upholster.
pad out bulk out, expand, fill out, lengthen, protract, spin out, stretch out.

padding *noun* cushioning, filling, stuffing, wadding.

▶▶ D I C T I O N A R Y ◀◀

paddle¹ *verb* (**paddled, paddling**) walk about in shallow water. **paddle** *noun*

paddle² *noun* a short oar with a broad blade; something shaped like this.

paddle³ *verb* (**paddled, paddling**) move a boat along with a paddle or paddles; row gently.

paddock *noun* **1** (*Australian*) a field. **2** a small field where horses are kept.

paddy *noun* (*plural* **paddies**) a field where rice is grown. **paddy-field** *noun*

padlock *noun* a detachable lock with a metal loop that passes through a ring or chain etc.

padre (*say* **pah**-dray) *noun* a chaplain in the armed forces. [Italian, = father]

paean (*say* **pee**-an) *noun* a song of praise or triumph. [from Greek, = hymn]

paediatrics (*say* peed-ee-**at**-riks) *noun* the study of children's diseases. **paediatric** *adjective*, **paediatrician** *noun* [from Greek *paidos* = of a child, + *iatros* = doctor]

pagan (*say* **pay**-gan) *adjective* & *noun* heathen. [same origin as *peasant*]

page¹ *noun* a piece of paper that is part of a book or newspaper etc.; one side of this. [from Latin *pagina* = page]

page² *noun* a boy or man employed to go on errands or be an attendant. [from Greek *paidion* = small boy]

pageant *noun* **1** a play or entertainment about historical events and people. **2** a procession of people in costume as an entertainment. **pageantry** *noun*

pagoda (*say* pag-**oh**-da) *noun* a Buddhist tower, or a Hindu temple shaped like a pyramid, in India and East Asia.

paid *past tense* of **pay**.

put paid to (*informal*) put an end to someone's activity or hope etc.

pail *noun* a bucket.

pain¹ *noun* **1** an unpleasant feeling caused by injury or disease. **2** suffering in the mind. **painful** *adjective*, **painfully** *adverb*, **painless** *adjective*

take pains make a careful effort with work etc.

painstaking *adjective*

pain² *verb* cause pain to someone. [from Latin *poena* = punishment]

paint¹ *noun* a liquid substance put on something to colour it. **paintbox** *noun*, **paintbrush** *noun*

paint² *verb* **1** put paint on something. **2** make a picture with paints.

painter¹ *noun* a person who paints.

painter² *noun* a rope used to tie up a boat. [from Old French *penteur* = rope]

painting *noun* a painted picture.

pair¹ *noun* **1** a set of two things or people; a couple. **2** something made of two joined parts, *a pair of scissors*.

pair² *verb* put together as a pair. [from Latin *paria* = equal things]

pal *noun* (*informal*) a friend. [from a gypsy word *pal* = brother]

▶▶ T H E S A U R U S ◀◀

paddle¹ *verb* dabble, splash about, wade.

paddle² *noun* oar, scull.

paddle³ *verb* row, scull.

paddock *noun* **1** field, lea (*poetical*), meadow, pasture.

pagan *noun* heathen, infidel, non-believer, unbeliever.

page¹ *noun* folio, leaf, sheet.

pageant *noun* display, parade, procession, show, spectacle, tableau.

pain¹ *noun* **1** ache, affliction, agony, discomfort, distress, hurt, pang, soreness, sting, suffering, throb, torture, twinge. **2** affliction, agony, anguish, distress, grief, heartache, hurt, sadness, sorrow, suffering, torment, torture, woe.

painful *adjective* aching, agonising, distressing, excruciating, hurting, raw, sensitive, smarting, sore, splitting, stabbing, stinging, tender, throbbing, upsetting.

painless *adjective* comfortable, easy, effortless, pain-free, simple.

painstaking *adjective* assiduous, careful, conscientious, diligent, hard-working, meticulous, precise, punctilious, scrupulous, thorough.

pain² *verb* distress, grieve, hurt, sadden, trouble.

paint¹ *noun* colour, colouring, dye, pigment, stain, tint.

paint² *verb* **1** coat, colour, daub, decorate. **2** depict, portray, represent.

painter¹ *noun* artist, decorator.

painting *noun* picture, work of art; (*kinds of painting*) abstract, fresco, landscape, mural, oil painting, portrait, seascape, still life, watercolour.

pair¹ *noun* **1** brace, couple, duo, partnership, twosome.

pair² *verb* match, pair up, put together.

pal *noun* buddy (*informal*), chum (*informal*), cobber (*Australian informal*), comrade, crony, friend, mate.

▶▶▷ DICTIONARY ◁◀◀

palace *noun* a mansion where a king, queen, or other important person lives. [from Palatium, the name of a hill on which the house of the emperor Augustus stood in ancient Rome]

palaeolithic (*say* pal-ee-o-**lith**-ik) *adjective* of the early part of the Stone Age. [from Greek *palaios* = old, + *lithos* = stone]

palatable *adjective* tasting pleasant.

palate *noun* **1** the roof of the mouth. **2** a person's sense of taste.

palatial (*say* pa-**lay**-shal) *adjective* like a palace; large and splendid.

pale¹ *adjective* **1** almost white, *a pale face*. **2** not bright in colour or light, *pale green; the pale moonlight*. **palely** *adverb*, **paleness** *noun* [from Latin *pallidus* = pallid]

pale² *noun* a boundary.
beyond the pale beyond the limits of good taste or behaviour etc. [from Latin *palus* = pointed stick set in the ground]

palette *noun* a board on which an artist mixes colours ready for use.

paling *noun* a fence made of wooden posts or railings; one of its posts.

palisade *noun* a fence of pointed sticks or boards. [same origin as *pale*²]

pall¹ (*say* pawl) *noun* **1** a cloth spread over a coffin. **2** a dark covering, *A pall of smoke lay over the town*. [from Latin *pallium* = cloak]

pall² (*say* pawl) *verb* become uninteresting or boring to someone. [from *appal*]

pallbearer *noun* a person helping to carry the coffin at a funeral.

pallet *noun* **1** a mattress stuffed with straw. **2** a hard narrow bed. **3** a portable wooden platform for transporting and storing loads.

palliate *verb* (**palliated, palliating**) make a thing less serious or less severe. **palliation** *noun*, **palliative** *adjective* & *noun* [same origin as *pall*¹]

pallid *adjective* pale, especially because of illness. **pallor** *noun*

palm¹ *noun* **1** the inner part of the hand, between the fingers and the wrist. **2** a palm-tree.
Palm Sunday the Sunday before Easter, commemorating Jesus Christ's entry into Jerusalem when people spread palm-leaves in his path.

palm² *verb* pick up something secretly and hide it in the palm of your hand.
palm off deceive a person into accepting something.

palmistry *noun* fortune-telling by looking at the creases in the palm of a person's hand. **palmist** *noun*

palm-tree *noun* a tropical tree with large leaves and no branches.

palpable *adjective* **1** able to be touched or felt. **2** obvious, *a palpable lie*. **palpably** *adverb* [from Latin *palpare* = touch]

palpitate *verb* (**palpitated, palpitating**) **1** (of the heart) beat hard and quickly. **2** (of a person) quiver with fear or excitement. **palpitation** *noun*

palsy (*say* **pawl**-zee) *noun* paralysis.

paltry (*say* **pol**-tree) *adjective* very small and almost worthless, *a paltry amount*.

pampas *noun* wide grassy plains in South America.

pampas-grass *noun* a tall ornamental grass with feathery flowers.

pamper *verb* treat very kindly and indulgently; coddle.

pamphlet *noun* a leaflet or booklet giving information on a subject.

pan *noun* **1** a wide container with a flat base, used for cooking etc. **2** something shaped like this. **3** the bowl of a lavatory.

pan- *prefix* **1** all (as in *panorama*). **2** of the whole of a continent or group etc. (as in *pan-African*). [from Greek *pan* = all]

▶▶▷ THESAURUS ◁◀◀

palace *noun* castle, château, mansion.

pale¹ *adjective* **1** anaemic, ashen, colourless, deathly, ghostly, pallid, pasty, peaky, wan, washed out, white. **2** bleached, dim, faint, light, misty, muted, pastel, soft, subdued.
paleness *noun* pallor, pastiness, whiteness.

palpable *adjective* **2** apparent, blatant, clear, distinct, evident, manifest, obvious, patent, plain, tangible, unmistakable.

paltry *adjective* beggarly, meagre, mean, measly (*informal*), minor, negligible, niggardly, pathetic, petty, puny, trifling, trivial, worthless.

pamper *verb* cosset, humour, indulge, mollycoddle, spoil.

pamphlet *noun* booklet, brochure, flyer, handout, leaflet, notice, tract.

pan *noun* **1** billy (*Australian*), casserole, cauldron, Dutch oven, frying pan, frypan, griddle, pot, pressure cooker, saucepan, skillet, wok.

▶▶▶ DICTIONARY ◀◀◀

panacea (*say* pan-a-**see**-a) *noun* a cure for all kinds of diseases or troubles. [from *pan-*, + Greek *akos* = remedy]

panama *noun* a hat made of a fine strawlike material. [from Panama in Central America]

pancake *noun* a thin round cake of batter fried on both sides. [from *pan* + *cake*]

pancreas (*say* **pan**-kree-as) *noun* a gland near the stomach, producing insulin and digestive juices. [from *pan-*, + Greek *kreas* = flesh]

panda *noun* a large bear-like black-and-white animal found in China.

pandemonium *noun* uproar. [from *pan-* + *demon*]

pander *verb* **pander to** indulge someone by providing things, *Don't pander to his taste for sweet things!*

pane *noun* a sheet of glass in a window.

panegyric (*say* pan-i-**ji**rrik) *noun* a piece of praise; a eulogy.

panel *noun* 1 a long flat piece of wood, metal, etc. that is part of a door, wall, piece of furniture, etc. 2 a group of people appointed to discuss or decide something. **panelled** *adjective*, **panelling** *noun*

panel van (*Australian*) a vehicle like a station wagon but with a single row of seats.

pang *noun* a sudden sharp pain.

panic¹ *noun* sudden uncontrollable fear. **panic-stricken** *adjective*, **panicky** *adjective*

panic² *verb* (**panicked, panicking**) fill or be filled with panic. [from the name of Pan, an ancient Greek god thought to be able to cause sudden fear]

pannier *noun* a large bag or basket hung on one side of a bicycle or horse etc. [from Latin *panarium* = bread-basket]

panoply *noun* (*plural* **panoplies**) a splendid array. [from *pan-*, + Greek *hopla* = weapons]

panorama *noun* a view or picture of a wide area. **panoramic** *adjective* [from *pan-*, + Greek *horama* = view]

pansy *noun* (*plural* **pansies**) a small brightly coloured garden flower with velvety petals. [from French *pensée* = thought]

pant *verb* take short quick breaths, usually after running or working hard.

pantaloons *plural noun* wide trousers.

panther *noun* a leopard.

panties *plural noun* (*informal*) short knickers.

pantihose *noun* women's tights usually made of fine material. [from *panties* + *hose* = *hosiery*]

pantile *noun* a curved tile for a roof. [from *pan* + *tile*]

pantomime *noun* 1 a Christmas entertainment based on a fairy-tale. 2 mime. [from *pan-* + *mime* (because in its most ancient form an actor mimed the different parts)]

pantry *noun* (*plural* **pantries**) 1 a room where china, glasses, cutlery, etc. are kept. 2 a larder. [from Latin *panis* = bread]

pants *plural noun* (*informal*) 1 trousers. 2 underpants; knickers. [short for *pantaloons*]

pap *noun* soft food suitable for babies.

papa *noun* (*old use*) father.

papacy (*say* **pay**-pa-see) *noun* the position of pope. [from Latin *papa* = pope]

papal (*say* **pay**-pal) *adjective* of the pope.

▶▶▶ THESAURUS ◀◀◀

pancake *noun* crêpe, flapjack, pikelet.

pandemonium *noun* bedlam, chaos, commotion, confusion, disorder, hubbub, hullabaloo, racket, rumpus, tumult, turmoil, uproar.

pander *verb* **pander to** cater for, gratify, indulge.

panel *noun* 1 insert, piece, section, strip. 2 body, committee, group, jury, team.

pang *noun* ache, pain, spasm, stab, sting, twinge; see also QUALM.

panic¹ *noun* alarm, anxiety, consternation, dismay, dread, fear, fright, horror, hysteria, terror, trepidation.
  panicky *adjective* agitated, flustered, frantic, frightened, jittery (*informal*), nervous, nervy,

panic-stricken, petrified, scared, terrified, terror-stricken.

panic² *verb* drop your bundle (*Australian informal*), freak out (*informal*), get into a flap (*informal*), get into a state, get into a tizzy (*informal*), get the jitters (*informal*), go to pieces, lose your cool (*informal*).

panorama *noun* landscape, prospect, scene, view, vista.

pant *verb* gasp, huff, puff, wheeze.

pantry *noun* 2 cupboard, larder, storeroom.

pants *plural noun* 1 slacks, trousers. 2 boxer shorts, briefs, drawers, jocks (*slang*), knickers, panties (*informal*), trunks, underpants, undies (*informal*).

▶▶ D I C T I O N A R Y ◀◀

paper¹ *noun* **1** a substance made in thin sheets from wood, rags, etc. and used for writing or printing or drawing on or for wrapping things. **2** a newspaper. **3** wallpaper. **4** a document.

paper² *verb* cover with wallpaper. [from *papyrus*]

paperback *noun* a book with a thin flexible cover.

paperbark *noun* an Australian tree with papery bark.

papier mâché (*say* pap-yay **mash**-ay) paper made into pulp and moulded to make models, ornaments, etc. [French, = chewed paper]

paprika (*say* **pap**-rik-a) *noun* red pepper. [Hungarian]

papyrus (*say* pap-**I**-rus) *noun* (*plural* **papyri**) **1** a kind of paper made from the stems of a plant like a reed, used in ancient Egypt. **2** a document written on this paper.

par *noun* an average or normal amount or condition. [from Latin *par* = equal]

para-¹ *prefix* **1** beside (as in *parallel*). **2** beyond (as in *paradox*). [from Greek *para* = beside or past]

para-² *prefix* protecting (as in *parasol*). [from Italian *para* = defend]

parable *noun* a story told to teach people something, especially one of those told by Jesus Christ. [from Greek *parabole* = comparison (same origin as *parabola*)]

parabola (*say* pa-**rab**-ol-a) *noun* a curve like the path of an object thrown into the air and falling down again. **parabolic** *adjective* [from *para-¹* = beside, + Greek *bole* = a throw]

parachute *noun* an expanding device on which people or things can float slowly to the ground from an aircraft. **parachuting** *noun*, **parachutist** *noun* [from *para-²* + *chute*]

parade¹ *noun* **1** a procession that displays people or things. **2** an assembly of troops for inspection, drill, etc.; a ground for this. **3** a public square, promenade or street.

parade² *verb* (**paraded, parading**) **1** move in a parade. **2** assemble for a parade.

paradise *noun* **1** heaven; a heavenly place. **2** the Garden of Eden. [from ancient Persian, = a park or garden]

paradox *noun* (*plural* **paradoxes**) a statement that seems to contradict itself but which contains a truth, e.g. 'More haste, less speed'. **paradoxical** *adjective*, **paradoxically** *adverb* [from *para-¹*, + *doxa* = opinion]

paraffin *noun* a kind of oil used as fuel.

paragon *noun* a person or thing that seems to be perfect.

paragraph *noun* one or more sentences on a single subject, forming a section of a piece of writing and beginning on a new line, usually away from the margin of the page. [from *para-¹* + *-graph*]

parakeet *noun* a kind of small parrot.

parallax *noun* what seems to be a change in the position of something when you look at it from a different place.

parallel¹ *adjective* **1** (of lines etc.) always at the same distance from each other, like the rails on which a train runs. **2** similar; corresponding, *When petrol prices rise there is a parallel rise in bus fares.* **parallelism** *noun*

parallel² *noun* **1** a line etc. that is parallel to another. **2** a line of latitude. **3** something similar or corresponding. **4** a comparison.

parallel³ *verb* (**paralleled, paralleling**) find or be a parallel to something. [from *para-¹*, + Greek *allelos* = each other]

parallelogram *noun* a quadrilateral with its opposite sides equal and parallel. [from *parallel* + *-gram*]

▶▶ T H E S A U R U S ◀◀

paper¹ *noun* **1** card, letterhead, notepaper, papyrus, parchment, stationery, writing paper. **2** broadsheet, daily, gazette, journal, newspaper, rag (*derogatory*), tabloid, weekly. **4** certificate, deed, document, form, record.

par *noun* average, mean, norm, normal, standard.

parable *noun* allegory, fable, story, tale.

parade¹ *noun* **1** cavalcade, march, march-past, motorcade, pageant, procession. **3** avenue, boulevard, road, street.

parade² *verb* **1** file past, march.

paradise *noun* **1** heaven. **2** Eden, Garden of Eden.

paradoxical *adjective* absurd, anomalous, illogical, incongruous, inconsistent, self-contradictory.

paragon *noun* example, exemplar, ideal, model, pattern, quintessence.

parallel¹ *adjective* **2** analogous, comparable, corresponding, like, similar.

parallel² *noun* **3** counterpart, equal, equivalent. **4** analogy, comparison, correspondence, likeness, similarity.

parallel³ *verb* equal, match, rival.

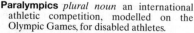

▶▶ D I C T I O N A R Y ◀◀

Paralympics *plural noun* an international athletic competition, modelled on the Olympic Games, for disabled athletes.

paralyse *verb* (**paralysed, paralysing**) **1** cause paralysis in a person etc. **2** make something be unable to move.

paralysis *noun* being unable to move, especially because of a disease or an injury to the nerves. **paralytic** (*say* pa-ra-**lit**-ik) *adjective* [from Greek *para* = on one side, + *lysis* = loosening]

paramedical *adjective* supplementing and supporting medical work. **paramedic** *noun*

parameter (*say* pa-**ram**-it-er) *noun* a quantity or quality etc. that is variable and affects other things (which depend on it) by its changes. [from *para-1* = beside, + Greek *metron* = measure]

paramilitary *adjective* organised like a military force but not part of the armed services. [from *para-1* = beside, + *military*]

paramount *adjective* more important than anything else, *Secrecy is paramount.*

paranoia *noun* an abnormal mental condition in which a person has delusions or suspects and distrusts people. **paranoid** *adjective* [Greek, = distraction]

parapet *noun* a low wall along the edge of a balcony, bridge, roof, etc.

paraphernalia *noun* numerous pieces of equipment, possessions, etc. [from Greek, = personal articles that a woman could keep after her marriage, as opposed to her dowry which went to her husband (Greek *para* = beside, *pherne* = dowry)]

paraphrase *verb* (**paraphrased, paraphrasing**) give the meaning of something by using different words. **paraphrase** *noun* [from *para-1* + *phrase*]

parasite *noun* an animal or plant that lives in or on another, from which it gets its food. **parasitic** *adjective* [from Greek *parasitos* = guest at a meal]

parasol *noun* a lightweight umbrella used to shade yourself from the sun. [from *para-2*, + Italian *sole* = sun]

paratroops *plural noun* troops trained to come down from aircraft by parachute. **paratrooper** *noun* [from *parachute* + *troops*]

parboil *verb* boil food until it is partly cooked.

parcel1 *noun* something wrapped up to be sent by post or carried.

parcel2 *verb* (**parcelled, parcelling**) **1** wrap up as a parcel. **2** divide into portions, *parcel out the work.* [same origin as *particle*]

parched *adjective* very dry or thirsty.

parchment *noun* a kind of heavy paper, originally made from animal skins. [from the city of Pergamum, now in Turkey, where parchment was made in ancient times]

pardon1 *noun* forgiveness.

pardon2 *verb* **1** forgive. **2** excuse somebody for a minor fault. **pardonable** *adjective*, **pardonably** *adverb*

pare (*say* as pair) (**pared, paring**) **1** trim by cutting away the edges; peel. **2** reduce gradually, *We had to pare down our expenses.* [from Latin *parare* = prepare]

parent *noun* **1** a father or mother; a living thing that has produced others of its kind. **2** a source from which others are derived, *the parent company.* **parenthood** *noun*, **parenting**, *noun*, **parental** (*say* pa-**rent**-al) *adjective* [from Latin *parens* = producing offspring]

parentage *noun* descent from parents; lineage; ancestry.

▶▶ T H E S A U R U S ◀◀

paralysed *adjective* crippled, disabled, immobile, incapacitated, lame, numb, paraplegic, quadriplegic.

paramount *adjective* chief, foremost, greatest, highest, main, major, primary, prime, supreme, utmost.

parapet *noun* battlements, rampart.

paraphernalia *noun* accessories, belongings, effects, equipment, gear, materials, odds and ends, possessions, stuff, tackle, things.

paraphrase *verb* rephrase, reword, rewrite.

parasol *noun* sunshade, umbrella.

parcel1 *noun* bale, bundle, pack, package, packet.

parched *adjective* (*parched earth*) arid, baked, bone-dry, dried out, dry, scorched, seared, waterless; (*parched walkers*) dehydrated, dry, thirsty.

pardon1 *noun* absolution, amnesty, exoneration, forbearance, forgiveness, mercy, remission, reprieve.

pardon2 *verb* **1** absolve, acquit, exonerate, forgive, let off, reprieve. **2** condone, excuse, forgive, overlook.

parent *noun* **1** father, mother.

parentage *noun* ancestry, birth, descent, extraction, lineage, origin.

►► D I C T I O N A R Y ◄◄

parenthesis (*say* pa-**ren**-thi-sis) (*plural* **parentheses**) **1** something extra that is inserted in a sentence, usually between brackets or dashes. **2** either of the pair of brackets (like these) used to mark off words from the rest of a sentence. **parenthetical** *adjective* [Greek, = putting in besides]

pariah (*say* pa-**ry**-a) *noun* an outcast.

parish *noun* (*plural* **parishes**) a district with its own church. **parishioner** *noun* [from Greek, = neighbourhood (Greek *para* = beside, *oikein* = dwell)]

parity *noun* equality. [from *par*]

park¹ *noun* **1** a large garden or recreation ground for public use. **2** an area of grassland belonging to a mansion.
car park an area where cars may be parked.

park² *verb* leave a vehicle somewhere for a time.

parka *noun* a warm jacket with a hood attached.

parley *verb* (**parleyed**, **parleying**) hold a discussion with someone. **parley** *noun* [from French *parler* = speak]

parliament *noun* the assembly that makes a country's laws. **parliamentary** *adjective* [same origin as *parley*]

parlour *noun* (*old use*) a sitting room. [from French *parler* = speak]

parochial (*say* per-**oh**-kee-al) *adjective* **1** of a parish. **2** local; interested only in your own area, *a narrow parochial attitude*.

parody¹ *noun* (*plural* **parodies**) an imitation that makes fun of a person or thing.

parody² *verb* (**parodied**, **parodying**) make or be a parody of a person or thing. [from *para-*¹ = beside, + Greek *oide* = song]

parole *noun* the release of a prisoner before the end of his or her sentence on condition of good behaviour, *He was on parole*. [French, = word of honour]

paroxysm (*say* pa-**roks**-izm) *noun* a spasm; a sudden outburst of rage, laughter, etc.

parquet (*say* **par**-kay) *noun* wooden blocks arranged in a pattern to make a floor.

parrot *noun* a brightly-coloured tropical bird that can learn to repeat words etc.

parry *verb* (**parried**, **parrying**) **1** turn aside an opponent's weapon or blow by using your own to block it. **2** avoid an awkward question skilfully.

parse *verb* (**parsed**, **parsing**) state what is the grammatical form and function of a word or words in a sentence. [from Latin *pars* = part (of speech)]

parsimonious *adjective* stingy; very sparing in the use of something. **parsimony** *noun*

parsley *noun* a plant with crinkled green leaves used to flavour and decorate food.

parsnip *noun* a plant with a pointed pale-yellow root used as a vegetable.

parson *noun* a rector or vicar; (*informal*) a member of the clergy.

parsonage *noun* a rectory or vicarage.

part¹ *noun* **1** some but not all of a thing or number of things; anything that belongs to something bigger. **2** a region. **3** the character played by an actor or actress. **4** the words spoken by a character in a play. **5** one side in an agreement or in a dispute or quarrel.
part of speech any of the groups into which words are divided in grammar (noun, pronoun, adjective, verb, adverb, preposition, conjunction, interjection).
take in good part not be offended at something.
take part join in an activity.

►► T H E S A U R U S ◄◄

park¹ *noun* **1** garden(s), parkland(s), playground, recreation ground, reserve.

parka *noun* anorak; see also JACKET.

parlour *noun* drawing room, living room, lounge, salon, sitting room.

parochial *adjective* **2** hidebound, insular, narrow, narrow-minded, petty, provincial, small-minded.

parody¹ *noun* burlesque, imitation, satire, send-up (*informal*), spoof (*informal*), take-off.

parry *verb* **1** avert, beat off, block, deflect, fend off, repel, repulse, ward off. **2** avoid, cir-cumvent, dodge, duck, elude, evade, side-step.

parson *noun* chaplain, clergyman, clergy-woman, minister, padre, pastor, preacher, priest, rector, vicar.

part¹ *noun* **1** bit, chunk, division, fraction, fragment, percentage, piece, portion, pro-portion, section, sector, segment, share, slice, subdivision; (*parts of a serial*) chapter, episode, instalment, issue, section, volume; (*spare parts*) component, constituent, element, ingredient, module, unit. **2** area, district, neighbourhood, region. **3** character, role.
take part be involved, compete, enter, join in, partake, participate, play a part.

▶▶ D I C T I O N A R Y ◀◀

part² *verb* separate; divide.
part up (*Australian*) pay out money.
part with give away or get rid of something.

partake *verb* (**partook, partaken, partaking**) **1** participate. **2** eat or drink something, *We all partook of the food.*

part-exchange *noun* giving something that you own, as part of the price of what you are buying.

Parthian shot a sharp remark made by a person who is just leaving. [named after the horsemen of Parthia (an ancient kingdom in what is now Iran), who were famous for shooting arrows at the enemy while retreating]

partial *adjective* **1** of a part; not complete, not total, *a partial eclipse.* **2** biased; unfair.
partially *adverb*, **partiality** *noun*
be partial to be fond of something.

participate *verb* (**participated, participating**) take part or have a share in something.
participant *noun*, **participation** *noun*, **participator** *noun* [from Latin *pars* = part, + *capere* = take]

participle *noun* a word formed from a verb (e.g. *gone, going*; *guided, guiding*) and used with an auxiliary verb to form certain tenses (e.g. *It has gone. It is going*) or the passive (e.g. *We were guided to our seats*), or as an adjective (e.g. *a guided missile*; *a guiding light*). The **past participle** (e.g. *gone, guided*) describes a completed action or past condition. The **present participle** (which ends in *-ing*) describes a continuing action or condition.

particle *noun* a very small portion or amount. [from Latin, = little part]

particoloured *adjective* partly of one colour and partly of another; variegated.

particular¹ *adjective* **1** of this one and no other; individual, *This particular stamp is very rare.* **2** special, *Take particular care of it.* **3** giving something close attention; choosing carefully, *He is very particular about his clothes.* **particularly** *adverb*

particular² *noun* a single fact; a detail.
in particular especially, *We liked this one in particular*; special, *We did nothing in particular.* [same origin as *particle*]

parting *noun* **1** leaving; separation. **2** a line where hair is combed away in different directions.

partisan *noun* **1** a strong supporter of a party or group etc. **2** a member of an organisation resisting the authorities in a conquered country.

partition¹ *noun* **1** a thin wall that divides a room or space. **2** dividing something into parts.

partition² *verb* **1** divide into parts. **2** divide a room or space by means of a partition.

partly *adverb* to some extent but not completely.

partner¹ *noun* **1** one of a pair of people who do something together, e.g. in business or dancing or playing a game. **2** either member of a married or unmarried couple. **partnership** *noun*

partner² *verb* be a person's partner; put together as partners.

▶▶ T H E S A U R U S ◀◀

part² *verb* break up, divorce, separate, split up.
part with give away, give up, hand over, relinquish, spare, surrender.

partial *adjective* **1** imperfect, incomplete, limited. **2** biased, partisan, prejudiced, unfair.
be partial to be fond of, be keen on, enjoy, like, love.

participate *verb* be active, be involved, join, partake, play a part, share, take part.
participant *noun* contributor, party, player.

particle *noun* atom, bit, crumb, fragment, grain, iota, jot, morsel, scrap, shred, skerrick (*Australian informal*), speck, trace.

particular¹ *adjective* **1** distinct, exact, individual, precise, special, specific. **2** especial, exceptional, special. **3** choosy (*informal*), fastidious, finicky, fussy, pernickety (*informal*), selective.

particular² *noun* (*particulars*) circumstances, details, facts, information.

partisan *noun* **1** adherent, backer, champion, fan, follower, supporter, zealot. **2** freedom fighter, guerrilla.

partition¹ *noun* **1** barrier, divider, panel, room divider, screen, wall.

partition² *verb* **1** break up, divide, separate, split up, subdivide.

partly *adverb* half, in part, partially, semi-.

partner¹ *noun* **1** accessory, accomplice, ally, associate, collaborator, colleague, helper, offsider (*Australian informal*), sidekick (*informal*). **2** companion, consort, husband, mate, spouse, wife.
partnership *noun* alliance, association, collaboration, marriage, relationship, union.

▶▶▷ DICTIONARY ◁◀◀

partook *past tense* of **partake**.

partridge *noun* a game-bird with brown feathers.

part-time *adjective & adverb* working for only some of the normal hours. **part-timer** *noun*

party[1] *noun* (*plural* **parties**) 1 a gathering of people to enjoy themselves, *a birthday party.* 2 a group working or travelling together. 3 an organised group of people with similar political beliefs, *the Labor Party.* 4 a person who is involved in an action or lawsuit etc., *the guilty party.* [from *part*]

party[2] *verb* attend a party; celebrate.

pass[1] *verb* (**passed**, **passing**) 1 go past something. 2 go onwards. 3 cause to move, *Pass the cord through the ring.* 4 give or transfer to another person, *Pass the butter to your father.* 5 be successful in a test or examination. 6 approve or accept, *They passed a law.* 7 occupy time. 8 happen, *We heard what passed when they met.* 9 (of time) go by. 10 disappear. 11 utter, *Pass a remark.* 12 let your turn go by at cards or in a competition etc., *Pass!*
pass away die.
pass out (*informal*) faint.

pass[2] *noun* (*plural* **passes**) 1 passing something. 2 a permit to go in or out of a place. 3 a route through a gap in a range of mountains. 4 a critical state of affairs, *Things have come to a pretty pass!* [from Latin *passus* = pace]

passable *adjective* 1 able to be passed. 2 satisfactory but not especially good. **passably** *adverb*

passage *noun* 1 a way through something; a corridor. 2 a journey by sea or air. 3 a section of a piece of writing or music. 4 passing, *the passage of time.* **passageway** *noun*

passbook *noun* a special notebook in which a bank or building society records how much a customer has paid in or drawn out.

passenger *noun* a person who is driven or carried in a car, train, ship, or aircraft etc.

passer-by *noun* (*plural* **passers-by**) a person who happens to be going past something.

passing *adjective* not lasting long; casual.

passion *noun* 1 strong emotion. 2 great enthusiasm.
the Passion the sufferings of Jesus Christ at the Crucifixion. [from Latin *passia* = suffering]

passionate *adjective* full of passion. **passionately** *adverb*

passive *adjective* 1 acted upon and not active; not resisting or fighting against something. 2 (of a form of a verb) used when the subject of the sentence receives the action, e.g. *was hit* in 'She was hit on the head'. (Compare *active*.) **passively** *adverb*, **passiveness** *noun*, **passivity** *noun*

▶▶▷ THESAURUS ◁◀◀

party[1] *noun* 1 at-home, ball, banquet, bash (*informal*), celebration, do (*informal*), feast, festivity, formal, function, gathering, get-together (*informal*), orgy, rave (*informal*), reception, shindig (*informal*), shivoo (*Australian informal*), social. 2 band, body, crew, force, group, squad, team. 3 camp, faction, league, side.

pass[1] *verb* 1 get ahead of, go by, go past, outstrip, overhaul, overtake. 2 go on, move on, proceed, progress. 4 give, hand over, transfer. 5 get through, qualify, succeed. 6 adopt, approve, authorise, decree, enact, ratify. 7 employ, fill, kill, occupy, spend, take up, use up, while away. 9 elapse, fly, go by, roll by, slip away. 10 blow over, die away, disappear, evaporate, fade, peter out, vanish.
pass away see DIE[1].
pass out black out, collapse, faint, keel over, swoon.

pass[2] *noun* 2 permit, ticket. 3 canyon, defile, gap, gorge, ravine.

passable *adjective* 1 clear, open, traversable. 2 acceptable, adequate, all right, fair, mediocre, middling, OK (*informal*), reasonable, satisfactory, so-so (*informal*), tolerable.

passage *noun* 1 aisle, alley, arcade, corridor, gangway, hall, opening, passageway, shaft, tunnel. 2 crossing, journey, trip, voyage. 3 episode, excerpt, extract, paragraph, piece, portion, quotation, section.

passenger *noun* commuter, traveller.

passing *adjective* brief, casual, cursory, fleeting, hasty, momentary, quick, short, superficial, transient.

passion *noun* 1 ardour, earnestness, emotion, feeling, fervour, fire, intensity, vehemence, zeal. 2 craze, enthusiasm, infatuation, mania, obsession.

passionate *adjective* ardent, burning, eager, earnest, emotional, enthusiastic, fervent, heartfelt, heated, impassioned, intense, vehement, zealous.

passive *adjective* 1 apathetic, compliant, docile, inactive, inert, resigned, submissive, unassertive, unresisting, unresponsive.

▶▶ D I C T I O N A R Y ◀◀

Passover *noun* a Jewish religious festival commemorating the freeing of the Jews from slavery in Egypt. [from *pass over*, because God spared the Jews from the fate which affected the Egyptians]

passport *noun* an official document that entitles the person holding it to travel abroad. [from *pass* + *port*[1]]

password *noun* a secret word or phrase used to distinguish friends from enemies.

past[1] *adjective* of the time before now, *during the past week*.

past[2] *noun* past times or events.

past[3] *preposition* 1 beyond, *Walk past the school.* 2 after, *It is past midnight.*
past it (*slang*) too old to be able to do something.

pasta *noun* an Italian food consisting of a dried paste made from flour and shaped into macaroni, spaghetti, etc. [Italian, = paste]

paste[1] *noun* 1 a soft and moist or gluey substance. 2 a hard glassy substance used to make imitation gems.

paste[2] *verb* (**pasted, pasting**) 1 stick by using paste. 2 coat something with paste. 3 (*slang*) beat or thrash.

pastel *noun* 1 a crayon that is like chalk. 2 a light delicate colour. **pastel** *adjective*

pastern *noun* the part of a horse's foot between the fetlock and the hoof.

pasteurise *verb* (**pasteurised, pasteurising**) purify milk by heating and then cooling it. [named after a French scientist, Louis Pasteur]

pastille *noun* a small flavoured sweet for sucking.

pastime *noun* something done to make time pass pleasantly; a recreation.

pastor *noun* a member of the clergy who is in charge of a church or congregation. [Latin, = shepherd]

pastoral *adjective* 1 of country life, *a pastoral scene.* 2 of a pastor or a pastor's duties. 3 of or used for raising stock, *pastoral district.*

pastoralist *noun* a grazier.

pastry *noun* (*plural* **pastries**) 1 dough made with flour, fat, and water, rolled flat and baked. 2 something made of pastry. [from *paste*]

pasture[1] *noun* land covered with grass etc. that cattle, sheep, or horses can eat.

pasture[2] *verb* (**pastured, pasturing**) put animals to graze in a pasture. [same origin as *pastor*]

pasty[1] (*say* **pas**-tee) *noun* (*plural* **pasties**) pastry with a filling of meat, fruit, or jam etc., baked without a dish to shape it.

pasty[2] (*say* **pay**-stee) *adjective* 1 like paste. 2 looking pale and unhealthy.

pat[1] *verb* (**patted, patting**) tap gently with the open hand or with something flat.

pat[2] *noun* 1 a patting movement or sound. 2 a small piece of butter or other soft substance.
a pat on the back praise.

patch[1] *noun* (*plural* **patches**) 1 a piece of material or metal etc. put over a hole or damaged place. 2 a pad or dressing put over a wound. 3 an area that is different from its surroundings. 4 a piece of ground, *the cabbage patch.* 5 a small area or piece of something, *There are patches of fog.*
not a patch on (*informal*) not nearly as good as.

▶▶▶ T H E S A U R U S ◀◀◀

password *noun* countersign, sign, signal, watchword.

past[1] *adjective* bygone, earlier, former, previous, prior.

past[2] *noun* antiquity, history, old days, olden days, yesterday, yesteryear.

past[3] *preposition* 1 beyond, by, in front of.

paste[1] *noun* 1 adhesive, glue, gum.

paste[2] *verb* 1 glue, gum, stick.

pastel *adjective* delicate, faint, light, muted, pale, soft, subdued.

pastime *noun* activity, amusement, diversion, entertainment, game, hobby, interest, leisure pursuit, recreation, sport.

pastor *noun* chaplain, clergyman, clergy-woman, minister, padre, parson, preacher, priest, rector, vicar.

pastoral *adjective* 1 bucolic, country, rural, rustic. 3 agricultural, farming, grazing, stock-raising.

pastoralist *noun* cattle farmer, grazier (*Australian*), sheep farmer, squatter (*Australian*).

pasture[1] *noun* field, meadow, paddock, run (*Australian*).

pasty[1] *noun* pastry, turnover.

pasty[2] *adjective* 2 anaemic, colourless, pale, pallid, sallow, unhealthy, wan.

pat[1] *verb* caress, dab, slap, stroke, tap, touch.

pat[2] *noun* 1 caress, dab, slap, stroke, tap, touch.

patch[1] *noun* 1 mend, reinforcement, repair. 2 bandage, cover, dressing, pad, plaster. 3 area, blob, blotch, mark, speck, speckle, splash, splotch, spot. 4 area, garden, lot, plot.

patch² *verb* **1** put a patch on something. **2** piece things together.
patch up repair something roughly; settle a quarrel.

patchwork *noun* needlework in which small pieces of different cloth are sewn edge to edge.

patchy *adjective* occurring in patches; uneven. **patchily** *adverb*, **patchiness** *noun*

pate *noun* (*old use*) the head.

pâté (*say* **pat**-ay) *noun* paste made of meat or fish. [French]

patent¹ (*say* **pay**-tent) *noun* the official right given to an inventor to make or sell his or her invention and to prevent other people from copying it.

patent² (*say* **pay**-tent) *adjective* **1** protected by a patent, *patent medicines*. **2** obvious. **patently** *adverb*
patent leather glossy leather.

patent³ *verb* get a patent for something.

patentee (*say* pay-ten-**tee**) *noun* a person who holds a patent.

paternal *adjective* **1** of a father. **2** fatherly. **paternally** *adverb* [from Latin *pater* = father]

paternalistic *adjective* treating people in a paternal way, providing for their needs but giving them no responsibility. **paternalism** *noun*

paternity *noun* **1** fatherhood. **2** being the father of a particular baby. [from Latin *pater* = father]

path *noun* **1** a narrow way along which people or animals can walk. **2** a line along which a person or thing moves.

pathetic *adjective* **1** arousing pity or sadness. **2** miserably inadequate or useless, *a pathetic attempt*. **pathetically** *adverb* [same origin as *pathos*]

pathology *noun* the study of diseases of the body. **pathological** *adjective*, **pathologist** *noun* [from Greek *pathos* = suffering, + *-logy*]

pathos (*say* **pay**-thoss) *noun* a quality that arouses pity or sadness. [Greek, = feeling or suffering]

patience *noun* **1** the ability to wait or put up with annoyances without becoming angry. **2** perseverance. **3** a card game for one person.

patient¹ *adjective* **1** able to wait or put up with annoyances without becoming angry. **2** able to persevere. **patiently** *adverb*

patient² *noun* a person who has treatment from a doctor or dentist etc. [from Latin *patiens* = suffering]

patio *noun* (*plural* **patios**) a paved area beside a house. [Spanish]

patriarch (*say* **pay**-tree-ark) *noun* **1** a man who is head of a family or tribe. **2** a bishop of high rank in certain Churches. **patriarchal** *adjective* [from Greek *patria* = family, + *archein* = to rule]

patrician *noun* an ancient Roman noble. (Compare *plebeian*.) **patrician** *adjective* [from Latin, = having a noble father]

patriot (*say* **pay**-tree-ot *or* **pat**-ree-ot) *noun* a person who loves his or her country and supports it loyally. **patriotic** *adjective*, **patriotically** *adverb*, **patriotism** *noun* [from Greek *patris* = fatherland]

patrol¹ *verb* (**patrolled**, **patrolling**) walk or travel regularly over an area so as to guard it and see that all is well.

patch² *verb* **1** mend, reinforce, repair.
patch up make up, resolve, set right, settle.

patchy *adjective* blotchy, dappled, inconsistent, mottled, speckled, uneven, variable.

patent² *adjective* **2** apparent, blatant, clear, conspicuous, evident, manifest, obvious, plain, unconcealed.

paternal *adjective* **2** fatherlike, fatherly, kindly, protective.

paternity *noun* **1** fatherhood, fathership.

path *noun* **1** aisle, alley, footpath, footway, lane, passage, pathway, pavement, sidewalk (*American*), track, trail, walkway, way. **2** course, line, orbit, route, trajectory, way.

pathetic *adjective* **1** distressing, heartbreaking, heart-rending, moving, piteous, pitiable, pitiful, poignant, sad, touching, tragic, wretched. **2**

meagre, measly (*informal*), miserable, paltry, stingy, woeful.

patience *noun* **1** calmness, endurance, forbearance, restraint, self-control, tolerance. **2** determination, diligence, doggedness, perseverance, persistence, staying power, tenacity.

patient¹ *adjective* **1** calm, forbearing, long-suffering, resigned, stoical, tolerant. **2** determined, diligent, dogged, indefatigable, persistent, tenacious, tireless, unflagging.

patient² *noun* case, client, invalid, sufferer.

patio *noun* courtyard, terrace.

patriotic *adjective* chauvinistic, jingoistic, loyal, nationalistic.

patrol¹ *verb* guard, police, watch.

▶▶ DICTIONARY ◀◀

patrol² *noun* **1** a patrolling group of people, ships, aircraft, etc. **2** a group of Scouts or Guides. [from French *patouiller* = paddle in mud]
on patrol patrolling.

patron (*say* **pay**-tron) *noun* **1** someone who supports a person or cause with money or encouragement. **2** a regular customer.
patronage (*say* **pat**-ron-ij) *noun*
patron saint a saint who is thought to protect a particular place or activity. [from Latin *patronus* = protector]

patronise (*say* **pat**-ron-I'z) *verb* (**patronised**, **patronising**) **1** be a patron or supporter of something. **2** treat someone in a condescending way.

patter¹ *noun* **1** a series of light tapping sounds. **2** the quick talk of a comedian, conjuror, salesman, etc.

patter² *verb* make light tapping sounds.

pattern *noun* **1** an arrangement of lines, shapes, or colours etc. **2** a thing to be copied in order to make something, *a dress pattern.* **3** an excellent example; a model. **4** a regular form, order, or arrangement of parts.

patty *noun* (*plural* **patties**) **1** a small pie or pasty. **2** a small cake of meat, fish, etc.

paucity *noun* scarcity; shortage. [from Latin *pauci* = few]

paunch *noun* a large belly.

pauper *noun* a person who is very poor. [Latin, = poor]

pause¹ *noun* a temporary stop in speaking or doing something.

pause² *verb* (**paused**, **pausing**) make a pause. [from Greek *pauein* = to stop]

pave *verb* (**paved**, **paving**) lay a hard surface on a road or path etc. **paving-stone** *noun*
pave the way prepare for something. [from Latin *pavire* = ram down]

pavement *noun* a paved path along the side of a street.

pavilion *noun* **1** a building for use by players and spectators etc. **2** an ornamental building or shelter used for dances, concerts, exhibitions, etc.

pavlova *noun* (*Australian & NZ*) an open meringue tart filled with cream and fruit.

paw¹ *noun* the foot of an animal that has claws.

paw² *verb* touch with a hand or foot.

pawl *noun* a bar with a catch that fits into the notches of a ratchet.

pawn¹ *noun* **1** any of the least valuable pieces in chess. **2** a person whose actions are controlled by somebody else. [from Latin *pedo* = foot-soldier]

pawn² *verb* leave something with a pawnbroker as security for a loan. [from Old French *pan* = pledge]

pawnbroker *noun* a shopkeeper who lends money to people in return for objects that they leave as security. **pawnshop** *noun*

pawpaw *noun* an orange-coloured tropical fruit used as food.

▶▶ THESAURUS ◀◀

patrol² *noun* **1** guard, lookout, sentinel, sentry, watch, watchman.

patron *noun* **1** backer, benefactor, champion, promoter, sponsor, supporter. **2** client, customer, regular.
patronage *noun* **1** aid, backing, help, promotion, sponsorship, support. **2** business, custom.

patronise *verb* **2** look down on, put down, talk down to.
patronising *adjective* condescending, contemptuous, disdainful, haughty, lofty, supercilious, superior.

patter¹ *noun* **1** beating, pit-a-pat, pitter-patter, tapping. **2** pitch, spiel (*slang*).

patter² *verb* beat, rap, tap.

pattern *noun* **1** decoration, design, figure, marking, motif, ornament. **2** design, guide, model, template. **3** example, exemplar, guide, ideal, model, standard. **4** consistency, formula, order, regularity, system.

patty *noun* **2** cake, croquette, rissole.

paunch *noun* abdomen, belly, pot-belly, stomach, tummy (*informal*).

pause¹ *noun* break, breather, gap, halt, hesitation, hiatus, interlude, interruption, let-up, lull, rest, spell, stop.

pause² *verb* break off, delay, halt, hesitate, rest, stop, wait.

pavement *noun* footpath, path, pathway, sidewalk (*American*).

paw¹ *noun* foot, pad.

pawn¹ *noun* **2** instrument, puppet, stooge (*informal*), tool.

pawn² *verb* hock (*slang*), pledge.

▶▶ D I C T I O N A R Y ◀◀

pay¹ *verb* (**paid, paying**) **1** give money in return for goods or services. **2** give what is owed, *pay your debts; pay the rent.* **3** be profitable or worth while, *It pays to advertise.* **4** give or express, *pay attention; pay them a visit; pay compliments.* **5** suffer a penalty. **6** let out a rope by loosening it gradually. **payer** *noun*
pay back give back money you owe; take revenge on someone.
pay up pay fully; pay what is asked.

pay² *noun* payment; wages. [from Latin *pacare* = appease]

payable *adjective* that must be paid.

payee *noun* a person to whom money is paid or is to be paid.

PAYG *abbreviation* pay as you go.

paymaster *noun* an official who pays troops or workers etc.

payment *noun* **1** paying. **2** money paid.

PC *abbreviation* personal computer.

PE *abbreviation* physical education.

pea *noun* the small round green seed of a climbing plant, growing inside a pod and used as a vegetable.

peace *noun* **1** a condition in which there is no war, violence, or disorder. **2** quietness; calm. **peaceful** *adjective*, **peacefully** *adverb*, **peacefulness** *noun*, **peacemaker** *noun* [from Latin *pax* = peace]

peaceable *adjective* peaceful; not quarrelsome. **peaceably** *adverb*

peach *noun* (*plural* **peaches**) **1** a round soft juicy fruit with a pinkish or yellowish skin and a large stone. **2** (*slang*) a beauty.

peacock *noun* a male bird with a long brightly-coloured tail that it can spread out like a fan. **peahen** *noun*

peak¹ *noun* **1** a pointed top, especially of a mountain. **2** the highest or most intense part of something, *Traffic reaches its peak at 5 p.m.* **3** the part of a cap that sticks out in front. **peaked** *adjective*

peak² *verb* reach its highest point.

peaky *adjective* looking pale and ill.

peal¹ *noun* **1** the loud ringing of a bell or set of bells. **2** a loud burst of thunder or laughter.

peal² *verb* sound in a peal.

peanut *noun* a small round nut that grows in a pod in the ground.
peanut butter roasted peanuts crushed into a paste.

pear *noun* a juicy fruit that gets narrower near the stalk.

pearl *noun* **1** a small shiny white ball found in the shells of some oysters and used as a jewel. **2** something shaped like this. **pearly** *adjective*
pearl barley grains of barley made small by grinding.

peasant *noun* (in some countries) a person who works on a farm. **peasantry** *noun* [from Latin *paganus* = villager]

▶▶ T H E S A U R U S ◀◀

pay¹ *verb* **1** (*pay a person*) compensate, indemnify, recompense, reimburse, remunerate, repay; (*pay an amount*) advance, contribute, cough up (*informal*), expend, fork out (*slang*), give, hand over, outlay, part with, refund, remit, shell out (*informal*), spend. **2** (*pay one's debts*) clear, discharge, honour, meet, pay off, pay up, settle, square. **3** be advantageous, be profitable, be worthwhile, pay off. **4** bestow, extend, give, grant, present. **5** be punished, pay a penalty, pay the price, suffer.
pay back see REPAY, RETALIATE.

pay² *noun* earnings, emolument, fee, income, remuneration, salary, stipend, wages.

payment *noun* **2** advance, allowance, award, benefit, bonus, commission, compensation, contribution, donation, fee, instalment, outlay, pay, pay-off (*informal*), payout, premium, recompense, refund, reimbursement, re-

mittance, remuneration, repayment, reward, royalty, salary, settlement, subscription, surcharge, tip, toll, wage(s).

peace *noun* **1** accord, concord, harmony, order. **2** calm, calmness, quiet, quietness, repose, serenity, silence, stillness, tranquillity.
peaceful *adjective* balmy, calm, quiet, restful, serene, still, tranquil, undisturbed, unruffled, untroubled; see also PEACEABLE.
peacemaker *noun* conciliator, intercessor, mediator, negotiator.
peaceable *adjective* amicable, friendly, gentle, harmonious, mild, non-violent, pacific, peaceful, peace-loving, placid.

peak¹ *noun* **1** apex, crest, pinnacle, summit, tip, top, zenith. **2** acme, apex, climax, culmination, height, heyday, pinnacle, summit, top, zenith.

peal¹ *noun* **1** carillon, chime, knell, ringing, toll. **2** blast, burst, clap, crash, roar, rumble.

peal² *verb* chime, resound, ring, sound, toll.

▶▶ D I C T I O N A R Y ◀◀

peat *noun* rotted plant material that can be dug out of the ground and used as fuel or in gardening. **peaty** *adjective*

pebble *noun* a small round stone. **pebbly** *adjective*

peccadillo *noun* (*plural* **peccadilloes**) an unimportant offence. [Spanish, = little sin]

peck¹ *verb* 1 bite or eat something with the beak. 2 kiss lightly.

peck² *noun* a pecking movement.

peck³ *noun* a measure of grain or fruit etc. (9.09 litres), *4 pecks = 1 bushel*.

peckish *adjective* (*informal*) hungry.

pectin *noun* a substance found in ripe fruits, causing jam to set firmly.

pectoral *adjective* of the chest or breast, *pectoral muscles*. [from Latin *pectoris* = of the breast]

peculiar *adjective* 1 strange; unusual. 2 particular; special, *This point is of peculiar interest.* 3 restricted, *This custom is peculiar to this tribe.* **peculiarly** *adverb*, **peculiarity** *noun* [from Latin *peculium* = private property]

pecuniary *adjective* of money, *pecuniary aid*. [from Latin *pecunia* = money (from *pecu* = cattle, because in early times wealth consisted in cattle and sheep)]

pedagogue (*say* **ped**-a-gog) *noun* a teacher who teaches in a pedantic way. [from Greek, = slave who led a boy to school]

pedal¹ *noun* a lever pressed by the foot to operate a bicycle, car, machine, etc. or in certain musical instruments.

pedal² *verb* (**pedalled, pedalling**) use a pedal; move or work something by means of pedals. [from Latin *pedis* = of a foot]

pedant *noun* a pedantic person.

pedantic *adjective* being very careful and strict about exact meanings and facts etc. in learning. **pedantically** *adverb* [same origin as *pedagogue*]

peddle *verb* (**peddled, peddling**) 1 sell goods as a pedlar. 2 sell drugs illegally. [from *pedlar*]

pedestal *noun* the raised base on which a statue or pillar etc. stands. [from Italian *piede* = foot, + *stall*]

put someone on a pedestal admire him or her greatly.

pedestrian *noun* a person who is walking. [from Latin *pedis* = of a foot]

pedigree *noun* a list of a person's or animal's ancestors, especially to show how well an animal has been bred.

pediment *noun* a wide triangular part decorating the top of a building.

pedlar *noun* a person who goes from house to house selling small things.

peek *verb & noun* peep.

peel¹ *noun* the skin of certain fruits and vegetables.

peel² *verb* 1 remove the peel or covering from something. 2 come off in strips or layers. 3 lose a covering or skin.

peelings *plural noun* strips of skin peeled from potatoes etc.

peep *verb* 1 look quickly or secretly. 2 look through a narrow opening. 3 show slightly or briefly, *The moon peeped out from behind the clouds.* **peep** *noun*, **peep-hole** *noun*

peer¹ *verb* look at something closely or with difficulty. [from *appear*]

▶▶ T H E S A U R U S ◀◀

pebble *noun* (*pebbles*) cobbles, gravel, shingle, stones.

peck¹ *verb* 1 bite, nibble, nip, pick at.

peculiar *adjective* 1 abnormal, bizarre, crazy, curious, eccentric, extraordinary, freakish, funny, odd, offbeat, outlandish, quaint, queer, strange, unconventional, unusual, weird. 2 particular, special. 3 characteristic, distinctive, exclusive, idiosyncratic, individual, particular, personal, special, specific, unique.
peculiarity *noun* characteristic, eccentricity, foible, idiosyncrasy, mannerism, quirk, trait.

pedant *noun* dogmatist, pedagogue, purist, stickler.

pedantic *adjective* exact, fussy, hair-splitting, meticulous, nit-picking, particular, pernickety (*informal*), precise.

pedestrian *noun* hiker, rambler, walker.

pedigree *noun* ancestry, background, family, genealogy, line, lineage, stock.

pedlar *noun* door-to-door salesman, hawker, huckster.

peel¹ *noun* rind, skin, zest.

peel² *verb* 1 flake, pare, remove, scale, skin, strip.

peep *verb* 1 glance, look, peek, peer. 3 appear, come into view, emerge, show.
peep *noun* glance, glimpse, look, peek.

peer¹ *verb* gaze, look, peek, peep, stare.

▶▶▶ D I C T I O N A R Y ◀◀

peer² *noun* **1** a noble. **2** someone who is equal to another in rank or merit etc., or is of the same age, *She had no peer.* **peeress** *noun* [from Latin *par* = equal]

peerage *noun* **1** peers. **2** the rank of peer, *He was raised to the peerage.*

peerless *adjective* without an equal; superb.

peeve *verb* (*slang*) annoy.

peevish *adjective* irritable.

peewit *noun* a kind of plover, named after its cry; a small Australian magpie.

peg¹ *noun* a piece of wood or metal or plastic for fastening things together or for hanging things on.

peg² *verb* (**pegged, pegging**) **1** fix with pegs. **2** keep wages or prices at a fixed level.
peg away work diligently; persevere.
peg out (*slang*) die.

pejorative (*say* pij-**o**rra-tiv) *adjective* disparaging; derogatory; insulting. [from Latin *pejor* = worse]

peke *noun* (*informal*) a Pekingese.

Pekingese *noun* (*plural* **Pekingese**) a small kind of dog with short legs, a flat face, and long silky hair. [from Peking, now Beijing, the capital of China]

pelican *noun* a large bird with a pouch in its long beak.

pellet *noun* a tiny ball of metal, food, paper, etc.

pell-mell *adverb* & *adjective* in a hasty untidy way.

pelmet *noun* an ornamental strip of wood or material etc. above a window, especially to conceal a curtain rail.

pelt¹ *verb* **1** throw a lot of things at someone. **2** run fast. **3** rain very hard.

pelt² *noun* an animal skin, especially with the fur still on it.

pelvis *noun* (*plural* **pelvises**) the round framework of bones at the lower end of the spine.
pelvic *adjective*

pen¹ *noun* a device with a point for writing with ink. [from Latin *penna* = feather (because a pen was originally a sharpened quill)]

pen² *noun* an enclosure for cattle, sheep, hens, or other animals.

pen³ *verb* (**penned, penning**) shut into a pen or other enclosed space.

pen⁴ *noun* a female swan. (Compare *cob*.)

penal (*say* **peen**-al) *adjective* of punishment; used for punishment. [from Latin *poena* = punishment]
penal colony an early Australian colony regarded primarily as a place to send convicts from Britain.

penalise *verb* (**penalised, penalising**) punish; put a penalty on someone. **penalisation** *noun*

penalty *noun* (*plural* **penalties**) **1** a punishment. **2** a point or advantage given to one side in a game when a member of the other side has broken a rule.
penalty rates (*Australian*) rates of pay for employees working overtime or on public holidays.

▶▶▶ T H E S A U R U S ◀◀

peer² *noun* **1** aristocrat, lord, noble, nobleman; (*kinds of peer*) baron, duke, earl, marquess, viscount. **2** contemporary, equal, fellow.
peeress *noun* aristocrat, lady, noblewoman; (*kinds of peeress*) baroness, countess, duchess, marchioness, viscountess.

peerless *adjective* incomparable, inimitable, matchless, superlative, supreme, unequalled, unparalleled, unrivalled, unsurpassed.

peeve *verb* annoy, bug (*informal*), irritate, miff (*informal*), needle, pique, provoke, rile, upset, vex.

peevish *adjective* bad-tempered, crabby, cranky, cross, fractious, grouchy, grumpy, irritable, petulant, querulous, snaky (*Australian informal*), sulky, surly, testy.

peg¹ *noun* hook, pin, spike.

peg² *verb* **1** attach, fasten, pin, secure. **2** control, fix, freeze, limit, set.

pejorative *adjective* derogatory, disparaging, uncomplimentary.

pellet *noun* ball, bead, pill.

pelt¹ *verb* **1** assail, batter, bombard, pepper, shower. **3** bucket, pour, teem.

pelt² *noun* coat, fleece, hide, skin.

pen¹ *noun* ballpoint, Biro (*trade mark*), felt-tipped pen, fountain pen, marker, quill, Texta (*trade mark*).

pen² *noun* cage, compound, coop, corral, enclosure, fold, hutch, pound, run, stall, sty.

pen³ *verb* close in, confine, coop up, enclose, fence in, impound, restrict, shut in.

penalise *verb* fine, handicap, punish.

penalty *noun* **1** fine, forfeit, price, punishment.

penance *noun* something done to show penitence.

pence *plural noun* see **penny**.

pencil[1] *noun* a device for drawing or writing, made of a thin stick of graphite or coloured chalk etc. enclosed in a cylinder of wood or metal.

pencil[2] *verb* (**pencilled, pencilling**) **1** write, draw, or mark with a pencil. **2** arrange provisionally, *Let's pencil in the 29th.*

pendant *noun* an ornament worn hanging on a cord or chain round the neck. [from Latin *pendens* = hanging]

pendent *adjective* hanging.

pending[1] *preposition* **1** until, *Please take charge, pending his return.* **2** during, *pending these discussions.*

pending[2] *adjective* waiting to be decided or settled. [same origin as *pendant*]

pendulous *adjective* hanging down.

pendulum *noun* a weight hung so that it can swing to and fro, especially in the works of a clock.

penetrable *adjective* able to be penetrated.

penetrate *verb* (**penetrated, penetrating**) **1** make or find a way through or into something; pierce. **2** permeate. **penetration** *noun*, **penetrative** *adjective* [from Latin *penitus* = inside]

penfriend *noun* a friend to whom you write without meeting.

penguin *noun* an Antarctic sea-bird that cannot fly but uses its wings as flippers for swimming.

penicillin *noun* an antibiotic obtained from mould. [from the Latin name of the mould used]

peninsula *noun* a piece of land that is almost surrounded by water. **peninsular** *adjective* [from Latin *paene* = almost, + *insula* = island]

penis (*say* **peen**-iss) *noun* (*plural* **penises**) the part of the body with which a male urinates and has sexual intercourse. [Latin, = tail]

penitence *noun* regret for having done wrong. **penitent** *adjective*, **penitently** *adverb*

penknife *noun* (*plural* **penknives**) a small folding knife. [originally used for sharpening quill pens]

pen-name *noun* a false name used by an author.

pennant *noun* a long pointed flag.

penniless *adjective* having no money; very poor.

penny *noun* (*plural* **pennies** for separate coins, **pence** for a sum of money) a bronze or copper coin worth a small amount.

pension[1] *noun* an income consisting of regular payments made by a government or firm to someone who is retired, widowed, or disabled.

pension[2] *verb* pay a pension to someone. [from Latin *pensio* = payment]

pensioner *noun* a person who receives a pension.

pensive *adjective* thinking deeply; thoughtful. **pensively** *adverb* [from Latin *pensare* = consider]

pent *adjective* shut in, *pent in* or *up*. [from *pen[3]*]

penta- *prefix* five. [from Greek *pente* = five]

pentagon *noun* a flat shape with five sides and five angles. **pentagonal** (*say* pent-**ag**-on-al) *adjective* [from *penta-*, + Greek *gonia* = angle]

the Pentagon a five-sided building in Washington, headquarters of the American armed forces.

pentameter *noun* a line of verse with five rhythmic beats. [from *penta-*, + Greek *metron* = measure]

penetrate *verb* **1** break through, drill through, enter, perforate, pierce, prick, probe, puncture, spike. **2** permeate, saturate, seep through, soak through.
   penetrating *adjective* (*a penetrating voice*) harsh, loud, piercing, sharp, shrill; (*a penetrating mind*) astute, discerning, incisive, intelligent, keen, perceptive, sharp, shrewd.

penitent *adjective* apologetic, contrite, regretful, remorseful, repentant, sorry.

pen-name *noun* alias, assumed name, nom de plume, pseudonym.

pennant *noun* banner, ensign, flag, standard.

penniless *adjective* broke, destitute, hard up (*informal*), impecunious, impoverished, needy, poor, poverty-stricken, skint (*informal*).

pension[1] *noun* annuity, benefit, super (*informal*), superannuation.

pensive *adjective* day-dreaming, dreamy, introspective, meditative, reflective, serious, thoughtful.

pent *adjective* (*pent up*) bottled up, held in, repressed, restrained, stifled, suppressed.

▶▶ D I C T I O N A R Y ◀◀

pentathlon *noun* an athletic contest consisting of five events. [from *penta-*, + Greek *athlon* = contest]

Pentecost *noun* **1** the Jewish harvest festival, fifty days after Passover. **2** Whit Sunday. [from Greek, = fiftieth day]

penthouse *noun* a flat at the top of a tall building.

penultimate *adjective* last but one. [from Latin *paene* = almost, + *ultimate*]

penumbra *noun* an area that is partly but not fully shaded, e.g. during an eclipse. [from Latin *paene* = almost, + *umbra* = shade]

penurious (*say* pin-**yoor**-ee-us) *adjective* **1** in great poverty. **2** mean; stingy. **penury** (*say* **pen**-yoor-ee) *noun* [from Latin *penuria* = poverty]

peony *noun* (*plural* **peonies**) a plant with large round red, pink, or white flowers.

people¹ *plural noun* **1** human beings. **2** persons, especially those belonging to a particular country, area, or group etc.

people² *noun* a community or nation, *a warlike people*; *the English-speaking peoples*.

people³ *verb* fill a place with people; populate. [from Latin *populus* = people]

pep *noun* (*informal*) vigour; energy. [from *pepper*]

pepper¹ *noun* **1** a hot-tasting powder used to flavour food. **2** a bright green, red, or yellow vegetable. **peppery** *adjective*

pepper² *verb* **1** sprinkle with pepper. **2** pelt with small objects.

peppercorn *noun* the dried black berry from which pepper is made.

peppermint *noun* **1** a kind of mint used for flavouring. **2** a sweet flavoured with this mint.

per *preposition* for each, *The charge is $10 per person.*

per annum for each year; yearly.

per cent for or in every hundred, *three per cent* (3%). [from Latin, = through]

per- *prefix* **1** through (as in *perforate*). **2** thoroughly (as in *perturb*). **3** away entirely; towards badness (as in *pervert*). [from Latin *per* = through]

perambulate *verb* (**perambulated, perambulating**) walk through or round an area. **perambulation** *noun* [from *per-* + Latin *ambulare* = to walk]

perambulator *noun* a baby's pram.

perceive *verb* (**perceived, perceiving**) **1** see; notice. **2** understand. [from Latin *percipere* = seize, understand]

percentage *noun* the amount per cent (see *per*); a proportion or part.

perceptible *adjective* able to be perceived. **perceptibly** *adverb*, **perceptibility** *noun*

perception *noun* perceiving.

perceptive *adjective* quick to notice things.

perch¹ *noun* (*plural* **perches**) **1** a place where a bird sits or rests. **2** a seat high up.

perch² *verb* rest or place on a perch. [from Latin *pertica* = pole]

perch³ *noun* (*plural* **perch**) an edible fresh-water or sea-fish.

percipient *adjective* perceptive. **percipience** *noun*

percolate *verb* (**percolated, percolating**) flow through small holes or spaces. **percolation** *noun* [from *per-*, + Latin *colum* = strainer]

percolator *noun* a pot for making coffee, in which boiling water percolates through coffee grounds.

▶▶ T H E S A U R U S ◀◀

people¹ *plural noun* **1** human beings, humanity, humans, mankind, men and women, persons. **2** citizens, community, electorate, inhabitants, nation, populace, population, public, residents, society.

people³ *verb* colonise, inhabit, occupy, populate, settle.

pep *noun* dash, energy, go, life, liveliness, spirit, verve, vigour, vim (*informal*), vitality, vivacity.

pepper¹ *noun* **2** capsicum.

pepper² *verb* **2** bombard, pelt, riddle, shower, spray.

perceive *verb* **1** become aware of, detect, discern, notice, observe, recognise, see. **2** apprehend, deduce, feel, gather, grasp, realise, sense, understand.

perceptible *adjective* appreciable, discernible, evident, noticeable, observable, obvious, palpable, tangible, visible.

perceptive *adjective* astute, clever, discerning, keen, observant, percipient, perspicacious, quick, sensitive, sharp, shrewd, understanding.

perch¹ *noun* **1** roost.

perch² *verb* alight, land, rest, roost, settle, sit.

percolate *verb* filter, leach, ooze, permeate, seep, trickle.

▶▶▶ D I C T I O N A R Y ◀◀◀

percussion *noun* the striking of one thing against another. **percussive** *adjective*
percussion instruments musical instruments (e.g. drum, cymbals) played by being struck or shaken. [from Latin *percussum* = hit]

perdition *noun* eternal damnation. [from Latin *perditum* = destroyed]

peregrination *noun* travelling about; a journey. [from Latin *per* = through, + *ager* = field]

peregrine *noun* a kind of falcon.

peremptory *adjective* giving commands; imperious.

perennial¹ *adjective* lasting for many years; keeping on recurring. **perennially** *adverb*

perennial² *noun* a plant that lives for many years. [from *per-*, + Latin *annus* = year]

perfect¹ (*say* **per**-fikt) *adjective* **1** so good that it cannot be made any better. **2** exact; precise. **3** complete, *a perfect stranger.* **perfectly** *adverb*
perfect tense a tense of a verb showing a completed action, e.g. He *has arrived.*

perfect² (*say* per-**fekt**) *verb* make a thing perfect. **perfection** *noun*
to perfection perfectly. [from Latin *perfectum* = completed]

perfectionist *noun* a person who likes everything to be done perfectly.

perfidious *adjective* treacherous; disloyal. **perfidiously** *adverb*, **perfidy** *noun* [from *per-* = becoming bad, + Latin *fides* = faith]

perforate *verb* (**perforated**, **perforating**) **1** make tiny holes in something, especially so that it can be torn off easily. **2** pierce. **perforation** *noun* [from *per-*, + Latin *forare* = bore through]

perforce *adverb* by necessity; unavoidably.

perform *verb* **1** do something in front of an audience, *perform a play; perform in a show.* **2** do something, *perform an operation.* **3** function, *The car performed well.* **performance** *noun*, **performer** *noun*

perfume *noun* **1** a pleasant smell. **2** a liquid for giving something a pleasant smell; scent. **perfume** *verb*, **perfumery** *noun* [from *per-* + *fume* (originally used of smoke from a burning substance)]

perfunctory *adjective* done without much care or interest, *a perfunctory glance.* **perfunctorily** *adverb*

pergola *noun* an arch formed by climbing plants growing over trellis-work.

perhaps *adverb* it may be; possibly.

peri- *prefix* around (as in *perimeter*). [from Greek *peri* = around]

peril *noun* danger. **perilous** *adjective*, **perilously** *adverb* [from Latin *periculum* = danger]

perimeter *noun* **1** the outer edge or boundary of something. **2** the distance round the edge. [from *peri-*, + Greek *metron* = measure]

▶▶▶ T H E S A U R U S ◀◀◀

perennial¹ *adjective* chronic, constant, continuous, eternal, everlasting, lasting, never-ending, permanent, perpetual, persistent, recurring.

perfect¹ *adjective* **1** complete, excellent, exemplary, faultless, flawless, ideal, immaculate, impeccable, in mint condition, model, optimum, spotless, unblemished, undamaged. **2** accurate, correct, exact, precise. **3** absolute, complete, out-and-out, pure, sheer, thorough, total, utter.

perfect² *verb* polish, refine.

perforate *verb* **2** penetrate, pierce, prick, puncture.

perform *verb* **1** act, appear, enact, play, present, put on, stage, star. **2** accomplish, achieve, carry out, complete, discharge, do, execute, fulfil. **3** behave, function, go, operate, run, work.
performance *noun* concert, enactment, gig (*informal*), play, presentation, production, show, showing, staging.

performer *noun* actor, actress, artist, artiste, busker, dancer, entertainer, instrumentalist, musician, player, singer, star, vocalist.

perfume *noun* **1** aroma, bouquet, fragrance, odour, scent, smell.

perfunctory *adjective* brief, careless, casual, cursory, half-hearted, hasty, mechanical, offhand, routine, slapdash, superficial.

perhaps *adverb* maybe, perchance (*old use*), possibly.

peril *noun* danger, hazard, jeopardy, risk, threat.
perilous *adjective* chancy, dangerous, dicey (*slang*), hairy (*slang*), hazardous, precarious, risky, unsafe.

perimeter *noun* **1** border, boundary, circumference, edge, fringe, limits, margin.

▶▶DICTIONARY◀◀

period *noun* **1** a length of time. **2** the time allocated for a lesson in school. **3** the time when a woman menstruates. **4** (in punctuation) a full stop. **periodic** *adjective*

periodical¹ *adjective* periodic; at set times. **periodically** *adverb*

periodical² *noun* a magazine published at regular intervals (e.g. monthly).

peripatetic *adjective* going from place to place. [from *peri-*, + Greek *patein* = to walk]

periphery (*say* per-**if**-er-ee) *noun* the part at the edge or boundary. **peripheral** *adjective* [from Greek, = circumference]

periphrasis (*say* per-**if**-ra-sis) *noun* (*plural* **periphrases**) a roundabout way of saying something; a circumlocution. [from *peri-*, + Greek *phrasis* = speech]

periscope *noun* a device with a tube and mirrors by which a person in a trench or submarine etc. can see things that are otherwise out of sight. [from *peri-*, + Greek *skopein* = look at]

perish *verb* **1** die; be destroyed. **2** rot, *The rubber ring has perished.* **3** (*informal*) make a person etc. feel very cold. **perishable** *adjective*

periwinkle¹ *noun* a trailing plant with blue or white flowers.

periwinkle² *noun* a winkle.

perjure *verb* (**perjured**, **perjuring**) **perjure yourself** commit perjury.

perjury *noun* telling a lie while you are on oath to speak the truth. [from Latin *perjurare* = break an oath]

perk¹ *verb* raise the head quickly or cheerfully. **perk up** make or become more cheerful. [from *perch¹*]

perk² *noun* (*informal*) a perquisite.

perky *adjective* lively and cheerful. **perkily** *adverb*

perm *noun* a permanent wave. **perm** *verb*

permanent *adjective* lasting for always or for a very long time. **permanently** *adverb*, **permanence** *noun*
permanent wave treatment of the hair to give it long-lasting waves. [from *per-*, + Latin *manens* = remaining]

permeable *adjective* able to be permeated by fluids etc. **permeability** *noun*

permeate *verb* (**permeated**, **permeating**) spread into every part of something; pervade, *Smoke had permeated the hall.* **permeation** *noun* [from *per-*, + Latin *meare* = to pass]

permissible *adjective* allowable.

permission *noun* the right to do something, given by someone in authority; authorisation.

permissive *adjective* permitting things; allowing much freedom to do things.

▶▶THESAURUS◀◀

period *noun* **1** age, bout, duration, epoch, era, interval, patch, phase, season, space, span, spell, stage, stint, stretch, term, time, while. **2** class, lesson, session.
periodic *adjective* cyclical, periodical, recurrent, regular, seasonal.

periodical² *noun* journal, magazine, newspaper, paper, serial.

peripatetic *adjective* itinerant, mobile, travelling.

periphery *noun* boundary, edge, fringe, limits, outskirts, perimeter.
peripheral *adjective* incidental, marginal, minor, secondary, subsidiary, tangential.

perish *verb* **1** die, expire, lose your life, pass away. **2** disintegrate, give way, go, rot.

perjure *verb* **perjure yourself** bear false witness, give false testimony, lie.

perk¹ *verb* **perk up** brighten up, buck up, liven up, pep up, revive.

perk² *noun* bonus, extra, fringe benefit, perquisite.

perky *adjective* animated, bright, cheerful, energetic, frisky, lively, sprightly, spry, vivacious.

permanent *adjective* chronic, constant, continual, continuous, durable, enduring, everlasting, fixed, indelible, indestructible, ingrained, lasting, lifelong, long-lasting, never-ending, ongoing, perennial, perpetual, persistent, stable.
permanently *adverb* always, constantly, continuously, eternally, forever, for good, for keeps (*informal*), perpetually, persistently.

permeate *verb* flow through, penetrate, pervade, saturate, soak through, spread through.

permissible *adjective* acceptable, admissible, allowable, authorised, lawful, legal, legitimate, permitted, proper, right, sanctioned, valid.

permission *noun* approval, authorisation, authority, clearance, consent, go-ahead, leave, licence.

permissive *adjective* broad-minded, easygoing, indulgent, lenient, liberal, tolerant.

▶▶ D I C T I O N A R Y ◀◀

permit¹ (*say* per-**mit**) *verb* (**permitted, permitting**) give permission or consent or a chance to do something; allow.

permit² (*say* **per**-mit) *noun* written or printed permission to do something or go somewhere. [from *per*-, + Latin *mittere* = send]

permutation *noun* **1** the order of a set of things. **2** a changed order, *3, 1, 2, is a permutation of 1, 2, 3*. [from *per*-, + Latin *mutare* = to change]

pernicious *adjective* very harmful.

peroration *noun* an elaborate ending to a speech. [from *per*- + *oration*]

perpendicular *adjective* upright; at a right angle (90°) to a line or surface. [from Latin, = plumb-line]

perpetrate *verb* (**perpetrated, perpetrating**) commit or be guilty of, *perpetrate a crime or an error*. **perpetration** *noun*, **perpetrator** *noun*

perpetual *adjective* **1** lasting for a long time. **2** continual. **perpetually** *adverb* [from Latin, = uninterrupted]

perpetuate *verb* (**perpetuated, perpetuating**) make a thing perpetual; cause to be remembered for a long time, *The statue will perpetuate his memory*. **perpetuation** *noun*

perpetuity *noun* being perpetual.
in perpetuity for ever.

perplex *verb* bewilder or puzzle somebody. **perplexity** *noun* [from *per*-, + Latin *plexus* = twisted together]

perquisite (*say* **per**-kwiz-it) *noun* something extra given to a worker, *Use of the firm's car is a perquisite of this job*.

perry *noun* a drink rather like cider, made from pears.

persecute *verb* (**persecuted, persecuting**) be continually cruel to somebody, especially because you disagree with his or her beliefs; harass. **persecution** *noun*, **persecutor** *noun* [from Latin *persecutum* = pursued]

persevere *verb* (**persevered, persevering**) go on doing something even though it is difficult. **perseverance** *noun* [from *per*-, + Latin *severus* = strict]

persist *verb* **1** continue firmly or obstinately, *She persists in breaking the rules*. **2** continue to exist, *The custom persists in some countries*. **persistent** *adjective*, **persistently** *adverb*, **persistence** *noun*, **persistency** *noun* [from *per*-, + Latin *sistere* = to stand]

person *noun* **1** a human being; a man, woman, or child. **2** (in grammar) any of the three groups of personal pronouns and forms taken by verbs. The **first person** (= *I, me, we, us*) refers to the person(s) speaking; the **second person** (= *thou, thee, you*) refers to the person(s) spoken to; the **third person** (= *he, him, she, her, it, they, them*) refers to the person(s) spoken about.
in person being actually present oneself, *She was there in person*. [from Latin *persona* = mask used by an actor]

▶▶ T H E S A U R U S ◀◀

permit¹ *verb* agree to, allow, approve of, authorise, consent to, legalise, license, put up with, sanction, tolerate.

permit² *noun* authorisation, licence, pass, warrant.

perpendicular *adjective* upright, vertical.

perpetual *adjective* **1** abiding, endless, enduring, eternal, everlasting, lasting, never-ending, permanent, unending. **2** ceaseless, constant, continual, endless, incessant, interminable, non-stop, persistent, recurrent, repeated, unceasing.

perplex *verb* baffle, bamboozle (*informal*), bewilder, confuse, mystify, nonplus, puzzle, stump (*informal*), throw (*informal*).

persecute *verb* bully, harass, hassle, intimidate, maltreat, mistreat, oppress, terrorise, torment, torture, tyrannise, victimise.

persevere *verb* battle on, carry on, continue, endure, keep on, persist, plug away, stick at (*informal*).

perseverance *noun* determination, diligence, doggedness, endurance, patience, persistence, pertinacity, stamina, staying power, sticking power, tenacity.

persist *verb* **1** carry on, continue, go on, keep on, persevere, stick at (*informal*). **2** continue, hold, last, live on, remain, survive.
persistent *adjective* (*a persistent person*) assiduous, determined, diligent, dogged, firm, indefatigable, obstinate, patient, pertinacious, relentless, resolute, steadfast, stubborn, tenacious, tireless, unwavering; (*a persistent problem*) chronic, constant, continuous, endless, eternal, everlasting, incessant, interminable, nagging, permanent, perpetual, recurrent, unceasing, unrelenting, unremitting.

person *noun* **1** chap (*informal*), character, creature, fellow (*informal*), human, human being, individual, mortal, sort (*informal*), soul, type (*informal*); see also CHILD, MAN¹, WOMAN.

▶▶ D I C T I O N A R Y ◀◀

personable *adjective* good-looking.

personage *noun* a person; someone important.

personal *adjective* **1** belonging to, done by, or concerning a particular person. **2** private, *a personal diary*. **3** criticising a person, *making personal remarks*. **personally** *adverb*

personality *noun* (*plural* **personalities**) **1** a person's character, *She has a cheerful personality*. **2** a well-known person.

personify *verb* (**personified**, **personifying**) represent a quality or idea etc. as a person. **personification** *noun*

personnel *noun* the people employed by a firm etc. [French, = personal]

perspective *noun* **1** the impression of depth and space in a picture or scene. **2** a view of a scene or of facts or events.
in perspective giving a well-balanced view of things. [from Latin *perspectum* = looked through]

perspicacious *adjective* perceptive. **perspicacity** *noun*

perspire *verb* (**perspired**, **perspiring**) sweat. **perspiration** *noun* [from *per-*, + Latin *spirare* = breathe]

persuade *verb* (**persuaded**, **persuading**) cause a person to believe or agree to do something. **persuasion** *noun*, **persuasive** *adjective* [from *per-*, + Latin *suadere* = induce]

pert *adjective* cheeky. **pertly** *adverb*, **pertness** *noun*

pertain *verb* be relevant to something, *evidence pertaining to the crime*. [from Latin *pertinere* = belong]

pertinacious *adjective* persistent and determined. **pertinaciously** *adverb*, **pertinacity** *noun* [from *per-* + *tenacious*]

pertinent *adjective* pertaining; relevant. **pertinently** *adverb*, **pertinence** *noun*

perturb *verb* worry someone. **perturbation** *noun* [from *per-*, + Latin *turbare* = disturb]

peruse (*say* per-**ooz**) *verb* (**perused**, **perusing**) read something carefully. **perusal** *noun* [from *per-* + *use*]

pervade *verb* (**pervaded**, **pervading**) spread all through something; permeate. **pervasion** *noun*, **pervasive** *adjective* [from *per-*, + Latin *vadere* = go]

perverse *adjective* obstinately doing something different from what is reasonable or required. **perversely** *adverb*, **perversity** *noun* [same origin as *pervert*]

pervert¹ (*say* per-**vert**) *verb* **1** turn something from the right course of action, *By false evidence they perverted the course of justice*. **2** cause a person to behave wickedly or abnormally.

pervert² (*say* **per**-vert) *noun* a person who behaves wickedly or abnormally. [from *per-*, + Latin *vertere* = to turn]

▶▶ T H E S A U R U S ◀◀

personal *adjective* **1** characteristic, distinctive, idiosyncratic, individual, special, unique. **2** confidential, intimate, private, secret.

personality *noun* **1** character, disposition, make-up, nature, temperament. **2** celebrity, identity (*Australian informal*), luminary, star.

personify *verb* embody, epitomise, exemplify, represent, symbolise, typify.

personnel *noun* employees, human resources, staff, workers, workforce.

perspective *noun* **2** angle, outlook, point of view, standpoint, viewpoint.

persuade *verb* cajole, coax, convert, convince, entice, induce, influence, lead, move, prevail on, sway, talk into, tempt, win over.
persuasion *noun* argument, cajolery, coaxing, convincing, influence.
persuasive *adjective* cogent, compelling, convincing, eloquent, forceful, plausible, powerful, strong, telling, weighty.

pertinent *adjective* applicable, apposite, appropriate, apt, germane, material, relevant, suitable.

perturb *verb* agitate, alarm, bother, disconcert, distress, disturb, frighten, scare, trouble, upset, worry.

peruse *verb* examine, inspect, look over, read, scan, scrutinise, study.
perusal *noun* examination, inspection, reading, scanning, scrutiny, study.

pervade *verb* diffuse through, fill, permeate, spread through.

perverse *adjective* contrary, disobedient, headstrong, intractable, obstinate, pigheaded (*informal*), rebellious, recalcitrant, refractory, stroppy (*informal*), stubborn, unreasonable, wayward, wilful.

pervert¹ *verb* **2** bribe, corrupt, lead astray.
perverted *adjective* corrupt, depraved, deviant, kinky (*informal*), sick, twisted, warped.

pervert² *noun* deviant, weirdo (*informal*).

▶▶▷ D I C T I O N A R Y ◁◀◀

pessimist *noun* a person who expects that things will turn out badly. (Compare *optimist*.) **pessimism** *noun*, **pessimistic** *adjective*, **pessimistically** *adverb* [from Latin *pessimus* = worst]

pest *noun* **1** a destructive insect or animal, such as a locust or a mouse. **2** a nuisance. [from Latin *pestis* = plague]

pester *verb* keep annoying someone by frequent questions or requests.

pesticide *noun* a substance for killing harmful insects etc. [from *pest*, + Latin *caedere* = kill]

pestiferous *adjective* troublesome. [from *pest*, + Latin *ferre* = carry]

pestilence *noun* a deadly epidemic. [same origin as *pest*]

pestilential *adjective* troublesome.

pestle *noun* a tool with a heavy rounded end for pounding substances in a mortar.

pet¹ *noun* **1** a tame animal kept for companionship and amusement. **2** a person treated as a favourite, *teacher's pet*.

pet² *adjective* **1** kept as a pet, *a pet wallaby*. **2** favourite, *a pet subject*.

pet³ *verb* (**petted, petting**) treat or fondle affectionately.

petal *noun* any of the separate coloured outer parts of a flower.

peter *verb* **peter out** become gradually less and cease to exist.

petition¹ *noun* a formal request for something, especially a written one signed by many people.

petition² *verb* request by a petition. **petitioner** *noun* [from Latin *petere* = seek]

petrel *noun* a kind of sea-bird.

petrify *verb* (**petrified, petrifying**) **1** paralyse someone with terror, surprise, etc. **2** change into a stony mass. **petrifaction** *noun* [from Greek *petra* = rock]

petrol *noun* a liquid made from petroleum, used as fuel for engines.

petroleum *noun* an oil found underground that is refined to make fuel (e.g. petrol, paraffin) or for use in dry-cleaning etc. [from Greek *petra* = rock, + *oleum* = oil]

petticoat *noun* a woman's or girl's dress-length undergarment. [from *petty* = little, + *coat*]

pettifogging *adjective* & *noun* paying too much attention to unimportant details.

petting *noun* affectionate treatment or fondling.

pettish *adjective* peevish.

petty *adjective* (**pettier, pettiest**) unimportant; trivial, *petty regulations*. **pettily** *adverb*, **pettiness** *noun*
petty cash cash kept by an office for small payments.
petty officer an NCO in the navy. [from French *petit* = small]

petulant *adjective* peevish. **petulantly** *adverb*, **petulance** *noun*

petunia *noun* a garden plant with funnel-shaped flowers.

pew *noun* a long wooden seat, usually fixed in rows, in a church.

pewter *noun* a grey alloy of tin and lead.

phalanx *noun* (*plural* **phalanxes**) a number of people or soldiers in a close formation. [Greek]

▶▶▷ T H E S A U R U S ◁◀◀

pessimistic *adjective* cynical, defeatist, despairing, despondent, fatalistic, gloomy, hopeless, morbid, negative, resigned, unhappy.

pest *noun* **2** annoyance, bother, curse, inconvenience, menace, nuisance, pain (*informal*).

pester *verb* annoy, badger, bother, harass, hassle (*informal*), hound, irritate, keep on at, nag, plague, torment, trouble, worry.

pet¹ *noun* **2** apple of someone's eye, darling, favourite.

pet² *adjective* **1** domestic, domesticated, tame. **2** favourite, special.

pet³ *verb* caress, cuddle, fondle, pat, stroke.

peter *verb* **peter out** diminish, end, fail, give out, run out, stop, taper off.

petition¹ *noun* appeal, entreaty, plea, request, supplication.

petition² *verb* appeal to, ask, beseech, call upon, entreat, plead, pray, request.

petrify *verb* **1** appal, frighten, numb, paralyse, scare stiff (*informal*), terrify.

petrol *noun* fuel, gas (*American informal*), gasoline (*American*).
petrol station filling station, garage, roadhouse, service station, servo (*Australian informal*).

petticoat *noun* slip, underskirt.

petty *adjective* insignificant, minor, paltry, piffling (*informal*), small, trifling, trivial, unimportant.

petulant *adjective* bad-tempered, crabby, cross, grouchy, grumpy, huffy, irritable, peevish, snappy, sulky, sullen, testy, tetchy.

▶▶DICTIONARY◀◀

phantasm *noun* a phantom.

phantom *noun* a ghost; something that is not real. [from Greek, = made visible]

Pharaoh (*say* **fair**-oh) *noun* the title of the king of ancient Egypt. [from ancient Egyptian *pr-ʻo* = great house]

pharmaceutical (*say* farm-as-**yoot**-ik-al) *adjective* of pharmacy; of medicines.

pharmacist *noun* a person who is trained in pharmacy; a pharmaceutical chemist.

pharmacology *noun* the study of medicinal drugs. **pharmacological** *adjective*, **pharmacologist** *noun* [from Greek *pharmakon* = drug, + *-logy*]

pharmacy *noun* (*plural* **pharmacies**) 1 a shop selling medicines; a dispensary. 2 the process of preparing medicines. [from Greek *pharmakon* = drug]

pharynx (*say* **fa**-rinks) *noun* the cavity at the back of the mouth and nose.

phase[1] *noun* a stage in the progress or development of something.

phase[2] *verb* (**phased, phasing**) do something in stages, *a phased withdrawal.*

pheasant (*say* **fez**-ant) *noun* a game-bird with a long tail.

phenomenal *adjective* amazing; remarkable. **phenomenally** *adverb*

phenomenon *noun* (*plural* **phenomena**) an event or fact, especially one that is remarkable. [from Greek, = thing appearing]

Usage Note that *phenomena* is a plural; it is incorrect to say 'this phenomena' or 'these phenomenas'.

phial *noun* a small glass bottle.

phil- *prefix* see **philo-**.

philander *verb* flirt. **philanderer** *noun*

philanthropy *noun* love of mankind, especially as shown by kind and generous acts that benefit large numbers of people. **philanthropist** *noun*, **philanthropic** *adjective* [from *phil-*, + Greek *anthropos* = human being]

philately (*say* fil-**at**-il-ee) *noun* stamp-collecting. **philatelist** *noun* [from *phil-*, + Greek *ateleia* = not needing to pay (because postage has been paid for by buying a stamp)]

philharmonic *adjective* (in names of orchestras etc.) devoted to music.

philistine (*say* **fil**-ist-I'n) *noun* a person who dislikes art, poetry, etc. **philistine** *adjective* [named after the Philistines, who were enemies of the Israelites in the Old Testament]

philo- *prefix* (becoming **phil-** before vowels and *h*) fond of; lover of (as in *philosophy*). [from Greek *philein* = to love]

philology *noun* the study of languages. **philological** *adjective*, **philologist** *noun* [from *philo-*, + Greek *logos* = word]

philosopher *noun* an expert in philosophy.

philosophical *adjective* 1 of philosophy. 2 calm and not upset, *Be philosophical about losing.* **philosophically** *adverb*

philosophy *noun* (*plural* **philosophies**) 1 the study of truths about life, morals, etc. 2 a set of ideas or principles or beliefs. [from *philo-*, + Greek *sophia* = wisdom]

philtre (*say* **fil**-ter) *noun* a magic drink; a love potion.

phlegm (*say* flem) *noun* thick mucus that forms in the throat and lungs when someone has a bad cold.

▶▶THESAURUS◀◀

phantom *noun* apparition, ghost, hallucination, phantasm, poltergeist, spectre, spirit, spook (*informal*), vision, wraith.

pharmacist *noun* apothecary (*old use*), chemist, dispenser, druggist, pharmaceutical chemist.

pharmacy *noun* 1 dispensary, drugstore (*American*).

phase[1] *noun* period, point, stage, step, time.

phenomenal *adjective* amazing, exceptional, extraordinary, fabulous (*informal*), fantastic (*informal*), great, incredible (*informal*), marvellous, miraculous, noteworthy, outstanding, prodigious, rare, remarkable, sensational, singular, stupendous, uncommon, wonderful.

phenomenon *noun* event, experience, happening, occurrence.

philanthropic *adjective* benevolent, charitable, generous, humane, humanitarian, kind-hearted, magnanimous, munificent.

philistine *adjective* boorish, ignorant, lowbrow, uncultivated, uncultured, unrefined.

philosophical *adjective* 2 calm, fatalistic, logical, rational, reasonable, resigned, serene, stoical, unemotional.

philosophy *noun* 2 belief system, convictions, doctrine, ideology, principles, values, view.

▶▶ D I C T I O N A R Y ◀◀

phlegmatic (*say* fleg-**mat**-ik) *adjective* not easily excited or worried; sluggish. **phlegmatically** *adverb*

phobia (*say* **foh**-bee-a) *noun* great or abnormal fear of something. [from Greek *phobos* = fear]

phoenix (*say* **feen**-iks) *noun* (*plural* **phoenixes**) a mythical bird that was said to burn itself to death in a fire and be born again from the ashes.

phone¹ *noun* a telephone.

phone² *verb* (**phoned**, **phoning**) telephone. [short for *telephone*]

phone-in *noun* a broadcast in which people phone the studio and take part.

phonetic (*say* fon-**et**-ik) *adjective* of speech-sounds. **phonetically** *adverb* [from Greek *phonein* = speak]

phoney *adjective* (*informal*) sham; not genuine. [origin unknown]

phosphate *noun* a substance containing phosphorus.

phosphorescent (*say* fos-fer-**ess**-ent) *adjective* luminous. **phosphorescence** *noun*

phosphorus *noun* a chemical substance that glows in the dark. [from Greek *phos* = light, + *-phoros* = bringing]

photo *noun* (*plural* **photos**) a photograph.

photo- *prefix* light (as in *photograph*). [from Greek *photos* = of light]

photocopy *noun* (*plural* **photocopies**) a copy of a document or page etc. made by photographing it on special paper. **photocopy** *verb*, **photocopier** *noun*

photoelectric *adjective* using the electrical effects of light.

photogenic *adjective* looking attractive in photographs.

photograph¹ *noun* a picture made by the effect of light or other radiation on film or special paper.

photograph² *verb* take a photograph of a person or thing. **photographer** *noun* [from *photo-* + *-graph*]

photography *noun* taking photographs. **photographic** *adjective*

photosynthesis *noun* the process by which green plants use sunlight to turn carbon dioxide and water into complex substances, giving off oxygen. [from *photo-* + *synthesis*]

phrase¹ *noun* **1** a group of words that form a unit in a sentence or clause, e.g. *in the garden* 'The Queen was in the garden'. **2** a short section of a tune.

phrase² *verb* (**phrased**, **phrasing**) **1** put something into words. **2** divide music into phrases. [from Greek *phrazein* = declare]

phraseology (*say* fray-zee-**ol**-o-jee) *noun* wording; the way something is worded. [from *phrase* + *-logy*]

physical *adjective* **1** of the body. **2** of things that you can touch or see. **3** of physics. **physically** *adverb*
physical education or **physical training** gymnastics or other exercises done to keep the body healthy. [same origin as *physics*]

physician *noun* a doctor, especially one who is not a surgeon.

physicist (*say* **fiz**-i-sist) *noun* an expert in physics.

physics (*say* **fiz**-iks) *noun* the study of the properties of matter and energy (e.g. heat, light, sound, movement). [from Greek *physikos* = natural]

physiognomy (*say* fiz-ee-**on**-o-mee) *noun* the features of a person's face. [from Greek *physis* = nature, + *gnomon* = indicator]

▶▶ T H E S A U R U S ◀◀

phlegmatic *adjective* apathetic, calm, cool, impassive, indifferent, lethargic, nonchalant, placid, serene, sluggish, stolid, unemotional, unexcitable, unflappable (*informal*).

phobia *noun* aversion, dislike, dread, fear, hang-up (*informal*), horror.

phone¹ *noun* blower (*informal*), telephone.

phone² *verb* call, dial, ring (up), telephone.

phoney *adjective* artificial, bogus, counterfeit, fake, false, forged, imitation, pretend (*informal*), pseudo, sham, synthetic.

photocopy *noun* copy, duplicate.
photocopy *verb* copy, duplicate, reproduce.

photograph¹ *noun* photo, picture, print, shot, snap, snapshot.

photograph² *verb* shoot, snap.

phrase¹ *noun* **1** expression, idiom, term; see also SAYING.

phrase² *verb* **1** couch, express, formulate, frame, put, word.

phraseology *noun* idiom, language, parlance, terminology, vocabulary, wording.

physical *adjective* **1** bodily, corporal. **2** actual, concrete, material, real, solid, tangible.

physician *noun* doctor, medical practitioner.

▶▶▶ D I C T I O N A R Y ◀◀

physiology (*say* fiz-ee-**ol**-o-jee) *noun* the study of the body and its parts and how they function. **physiological** *adjective* **physiologist** *noun* [from Greek *physis* = nature, + *-logy*]

physiotherapy (*say* fiz-ee-o-th'**e**-ra-pee) *noun* the treatment of a disease or weakness by massage, exercises, etc. **physiotherapist** *noun* [from Greek *physis* = nature, + *therapy*]

physique (*say* fiz-**eek**) *noun* a person's build. [French]

pianist *noun* a person who plays the piano.

piano *noun* (*plural* **pianos**) a large musical instrument with a keyboard. [short for *pianoforte*, from Italian *piano* = soft, + *forte* = loud (because it can produce soft notes and loud notes)]

piccaninny *adjective* little.

piccolo *noun* (*plural* **piccolos**) a small high-pitched flute. [Italian, = small]

pick[1] *verb* **1** separate a flower or fruit from its plant, *We picked apples.* **2** choose; select carefully. **3** pull bits off or out of something. **4** open a lock by using something pointed, not with a key.
pick a quarrel deliberately provoke a quarrel with somebody.
pick holes in find fault with.
pick on keep criticising or harassing a particular person.
pick someone's pocket steal from it.
pick up lift, take up; collect; take someone into a vehicle; manage to hear something; get better, recover.

pick[2] *noun* **1** choice. **2** the best of a group.

pick[3] *noun* **1** a pickaxe. **2** a plectrum.

pickaxe *noun* a heavy pointed tool with a long handle, used for breaking up hard ground etc.

picket[1] *noun* **1** a striker or group of strikers who try to persuade other people not to go into a place during a strike. **2** a group of sentries. **3** a pointed post as part of a fence.

picket[2] *verb* (**picketed, picketing**) act as a picket; place people as pickets. [from French *piquet* = pointed post]

pickle[1] *noun* **1** a strong-tasting food made of pickled vegetables. **2** (*informal*) a mess.

pickle[2] *verb* (**pickled, pickling**) preserve in vinegar or salt water.

pickpocket *noun* a thief who picks people's pockets (see *pick*[1]).

pick-up *noun* **1** the part of a record-player holding the stylus. **2** an open truck for carrying small loads.

picnic[1] *noun* a meal eaten in the open air away from home.

picnic[2] *verb* (**picnicked, picnicking**) have a picnic. **picnicker** *noun*

pictorial *adjective* with or using pictures. **pictorially** *adverb*

picture[1] *noun* **1** a representation of a person or thing made by painting, drawing, or photography. **2** a film at the cinema. **3** how something seems; an impression.

picture[2] *verb* (**pictured, picturing**) **1** show in a picture. **2** imagine. [from Latin *pictum* = painted]

picturesque *adjective* **1** forming an attractive scene, *a picturesque village.* **2** vividly described; expressive, *picturesque language.* **picturesquely** *adverb*

▶▶▶ T H E S A U R U S ◀◀

physique *noun* body, build, figure, shape.

pick[1] *verb* **1** collect, cut, gather, harvest, pluck, pull off. **2** choose, decide on, elect, name, nominate, opt for, select, settle on, single out, vote for.
pick on bully, criticise, find fault with, get at (*informal*), harass, nag.
pick up 1 call for, collect, fetch, get. **2** get better, improve, rally, recover.

pick[2] *noun* **1** choice, option, preference, selection. **2** best, choice, cream, elite.

picket[1] *noun* **2** guard, lookout, patrol, sentinel, sentry, watch. **3** paling, post, stake.

pickle[1] *noun* **2** fix (*informal*), jam (*informal*), mess, plight, predicament, spot (*informal*).

pickle[2] *verb* preserve, souse.

picture[1] *noun* **1** cartoon, collage, design, diagram, drawing, engraving, etching, illustration, image, landscape, likeness, mosaic, mural, painting, photo, photograph, plate, portrait, print, representation, reproduction, sketch, snapshot; (*pictures*) graphics. **2** film, flick (*informal*), motion picture, movie (*informal*), moving picture, video.

picture[2] *verb* **1** depict, draw, illustrate, paint, portray, represent, reproduce, sketch. **2** conceive, dream up, envisage, fancy, imagine, see, visualise.

picturesque *adjective* **1** attractive, beautiful, charming, pretty, quaint, scenic. **2** colourful, descriptive, expressive, graphic, imaginative, striking, vivid.

▶▶ D I C T I O N A R Y ◀◀

pidgin *noun* a simplified form of English or another language used between people who speak different languages. [from the Chinese pronunciation of *business* (because it was used by traders)]

pie *noun* a baked dish of meat, fish, or fruit covered with pastry.

piebald *adjective* with patches of black and white, *a piebald donkey*. [from *pie* = magpie, + *bald*]

piece¹ *noun* **1** a part or portion of something; a fragment. **2** a separate thing or example, *a fine piece of work*. **3** something written, composed, or painted etc., *a piece of music*. **4** any of the objects used to play a game on a board, *a chess-piece*.

piece² *verb* (**pieced**, **piecing**) put pieces together to make something.

piecemeal *adjective & adverb* done or made one piece at a time.

pier *noun* **1** a long structure built out into the sea for people to walk on. **2** a pillar supporting a bridge or arch.

pierce *verb* (**pierced**, **piercing**) make a hole through something; penetrate.

piercing *adjective* **1** very loud. **2** penetrating; very strong, *a piercing wind*.

piety *noun* piousness. [from Latin *pietas* = dutiful behaviour]

piffle *noun* (*slang*) nonsense.

pig *noun* **1** a fat animal with short legs and a blunt snout, kept for its meat. **2** (*informal*) someone greedy, dirty, or unpleasant. **piggy** *adjective & noun*

pigeon¹ *noun* a bird with a fat body and a small head. [from Old French *pijon* = young bird]

pigeon² *noun* (*informal*) a person's business or responsibility, *That's your pigeon.* [same origin as *pidgin*]

pigeon-hole *noun* a small compartment above a desk etc., used for holding letters or papers.

piggery *noun* (*plural* **piggeries**) a place where pigs are bred or kept.

piggyback *adverb* carried on somebody else's back or shoulders. **piggyback** *noun* [from *pick-a-back*]

piggy bank a money-box made in the shape of a hollow pig.

pigheaded *adjective* obstinate.

pig-iron *noun* iron that has been processed in a smelting-furnace.

piglet *noun* a young pig.

pigment *noun* a substance that colours something. **pigmented** *adjective*, **pigmentation** *noun* [from Latin *pingere* = to paint]

pigsty *noun* (*plural* **pigsties**) a partly-covered pen for pigs.

pigtail *noun* a plait or bunch of hair worn hanging at the back or side of the head.

pike *noun* **1** a heavy spear. **2** (*plural* **pike**) a large freshwater fish.

pikelet *noun* a small thick pancake.

pilchard *noun* a small sea-fish.

▶▶ T H E S A U R U S ◀◀

pie *noun* flan, quiche, tart.

piebald *adjective* dappled, mottled, pied, skewbald.

piece¹ *noun* **1** amount, bar, bit, bite, block, chip, chunk, component, division, element, fraction, fragment, hunk, length, lump, module, morsel, part, portion, quantity, remnant, scrap, section, segment, share, shred, slab, slice, sliver, snippet, stick, titbit, unit, wedge. **2** example, instance, item, object, sample, specimen, thing. **3** article, composition, creation, item, number, opus, work.

piece² *verb* (*piece together*) assemble, join together, mend, patch up, put together, reassemble.

pier *noun* **1** breakwater, jetty, landing stage, quay, wharf.

pierce *verb* bore through, enter, gore, impale, jab, lance, penetrate, perforate, prick, puncture, skewer, spear, spike, stab, wound.

piercing *adjective* **1** deafening, loud, noisy, penetrating, screeching, sharp, shrill, strident. **2** biting, bitter, cutting, keen.

piety *noun* devotion, devoutness, faith, godliness, holiness, piousness, reverence, saintliness, sanctity.

pig *noun* **1** boar, hog, piglet, porker, sow (*female*), swine. **2** see GLUTTON.

pigeon-hole *noun* compartment, cubby hole, niche.

pigheaded *adjective* headstrong, intractable, mulish, obstinate, refractory, self-willed, stiff-necked, stubborn, wilful.

pigment *noun* colour, colouring, dye, tint.

pikelet *noun* drop scone, flapjack, pancake.

pile¹ *noun* **1** a number of things on top of one another. **2** (*informal*) a large quantity; a lot of money. **3** a tall building.

pile² *verb* (**piled, piling**) put things into a pile; make a pile. [from Latin *pila* = pillar]

pile³ *noun* a heavy beam made of metal, concrete, or timber driven into the ground to support something. [from Latin *pilum* = spear]

pile⁴ *noun* a raised surface on fabric, made of upright threads, *a carpet with a thick pile*. [from Latin *pilus* = hair]

pilfer *verb* steal small things. **pilferer** *noun*, **pilferage** *noun*

pilgrim *noun* a person who travels to a holy place for religious reasons. **pilgrimage** *noun*

pill *noun* a small solid piece of medicinal substance for swallowing.
the pill a contraceptive pill. [from Latin *pila* = ball]

pillage *verb* (**pillaged, pillaging**) plunder. **pillage** *noun*

pillar *noun* a tall stone or wooden post. [from Latin *pila* = pillar]

pillar box *noun* a postbox standing in a street.

pillion *noun* a seat behind the driver on a motor cycle.

pillory¹ *noun* (*plural* **pillories**) a wooden framework with holes for a person's head and hands, in which offenders were formerly made to stand and be ridiculed and scorned by the public as punishment.

pillory² *verb* (**pilloried, pillorying**) **1** put into a pillory. **2** expose a person to public ridicule and scorn, *He was pilloried in the newspapers for what he had done.*

pillow¹ *noun* a cushion for a person's head to rest on, especially in bed.

pillow² *verb* rest the head on a pillow etc.

pillowcase or **pillowslip** *noun* a cloth cover for a pillow.

pilot¹ *noun* **1** a person who works the controls for flying an aircraft. **2** a person qualified to steer a ship in and out of a port or through a difficult stretch of water. **3** a guide.

pilot² *verb* (**piloted, piloting**) **1** be pilot of an aircraft or ship. **2** guide; steer.

pilot³ *adjective* testing on a small scale how something will work, *a pilot scheme*.

pilot-light *noun* **1** a small flame that lights a larger burner on a gas cooker etc. **2** an electric indicator light.

pimpernel (*say* **pimp**-er-nel) *noun* a plant with small red, blue, or white flowers that close in cloudy weather.

pimple *noun* a small round raised spot on the skin. **pimply** *adjective*

PIN *abbreviation* personal identification number.

pin¹ *noun* **1** a short thin piece of metal with a sharp point and a rounded head, used to fasten pieces of cloth or paper etc. together. **2** a pointed device for fixing or marking something.
pins and needles a prickling feeling.

pin² *verb* (**pinned, pinning**) **1** fasten with a pin or pins. **2** make a person or thing unable to move, *He was pinned under the wreckage.* **3** fix, *They pinned the blame on her.*

pile¹ *noun* **1** batch, collection, heap, hoard, mass, mound, mountain, pyramid, stack, stockpile. **2** heap (*informal*), load (*informal*), lot (*informal*), mountain, oodles (*informal*), plenty, stack (*informal*), ton (*informal*).

pile² *verb* accumulate, assemble, collect, gather, heap (up), load, mass, stack (up), stockpile.

pile³ *noun* column, pillar, post, stilt, support, upright.

pile⁴ *noun* nap, surface.

pilfer *verb* filch, help yourself to, lift (*informal*), nick (*slang*), pinch (*informal*), snitch (*slang*), souvenir (*slang*), steal, take.

pill *noun* capsule, lozenge, pellet, tablet.

pillage *verb* loot, maraud, plunder, raid, ransack, ravage, rob, sack.

pillar *noun* column, obelisk, pile, post, prop, shaft, stanchion, standard, support, upright.

pillow¹ *noun* bolster, cushion.

pilot¹ *noun* **1** airman, airwoman, aviator, captain. **2** coxswain, helmsman, navigator, steersman.

pilot² *verb* conduct, escort, fly, guide, lead, navigate, steer.

pilot³ *adjective* experimental, preliminary, test, trial.

pimple *noun* blackhead, pustule, spot, whitehead, zit (*slang*); (*pimples*) acne.

pin¹ *noun* brooch, drawing pin, hairpin, hatpin, nappy pin, safety pin, skewer, spike, split pin, staple, tack, tiepin.

pin² *verb* **1** affix, attach, fasten, fix, nail, secure, spike, staple, stick, tack. **2** hold down, hold fast, immobilise, pinion.

pinafore *noun* an apron. [from *pin* + *afore* = before]

pincer *noun* the claw of a shellfish such as a lobster.
pincers *plural noun* a tool with two parts that are pressed together for gripping and holding things.

pinch¹ *verb* **1** squeeze tightly or painfully between two things, especially between the finger and thumb. **2** (*informal*) steal. **3** (*informal*) arrest.

pinch² *noun* (*plural* **pinches**) **1** a pinching movement. **2** difficulty; stress or pressure of circumstances, *They began to feel the pinch.* **3** the amount that can be held between the tips of the thumb and forefinger, *a pinch of salt.*
at a pinch in time of difficulty.

pincushion *noun* a small pad into which pins are stuck to keep them ready for use.

pine¹ *noun* an evergreen tree with needle-shaped leaves.

pine² *verb* (**pined, pining**) **1** feel an intense longing. **2** become weak through longing for somebody or something.

pineapple *noun* a large tropical fruit with a tough prickly skin and yellow flesh.

ping *noun* a short sharp ringing sound.

ping-pong *noun* table tennis.

pinion¹ *noun* a bird's wing, especially the outer end.

pinion² *verb* **1** clip a bird's wings to prevent it from flying. **2** hold or fasten a person's arms or legs so as to prevent movement.

pinion³ *noun* a small cog-wheel that engages with another or with a rod (called a *rack*).

pink¹ *adjective* pale red. **pinkness** *noun*

pink² *noun* **1** pink colour. **2** a garden plant with fragrant flower, often pink or white.

pink³ *verb* **1** pierce slightly. **2** cut a zigzag edge on cloth.

pinnacle *noun* **1** a pointed ornament on a roof. **2** a peak. **3** the highest point, *the pinnacle of her career.*

pinpoint¹ *adjective* exact; precise, *with pinpoint accuracy.*

pinpoint² *verb* find or identify something precisely.

pinprick *noun* a small annoyance.

pin-stripe *noun* a very narrow stripe. **pin-striped** *adjective*

pint *noun* a measure for liquids, one-eighth of a gallon (about 0.57 litres).

pin-up *noun* (*informal*) a picture of an attractive or famous person for pinning on a wall.

pioneer *noun* one of the first people to go to a place or do or investigate something. **pioneer** *verb* [from French *pionnier* = foot-soldier]

pious *adjective* very religious; devout. **piously** *adverb*, **piousness** *noun* [from Latin *pius* = dutiful]

pip¹ *noun* **1** a small hard seed of an apple, pear, orange, etc. **2** one of the spots on playing cards, dice, or dominoes. **3** a short high-pitched sound, *She heard the six pips of the time-signal on the radio.*

pip² *verb* (**pipped, pipping**) (*informal*) defeat.

pipe¹ *noun* **1** a tube through which water or gas etc. can flow from one place to another. **2** a short narrow tube with a bowl at one end in which tobacco can burn for smoking. **3** a tube forming a musical instrument or part of one.
the pipes bagpipes.

pinch¹ *verb* **1** nip, squeeze, tweak. **2** lift (*informal*), nick (*slang*), pilfer, purloin, snatch, snavel (*Australian informal*), snitch (*slang*), steal, swipe (*informal*), take.

pinch² *noun* **1** nip, squeeze, tweak. **3** bit, smidgen, speck, touch, trace.

pine² *verb* **1** crave for, hanker after, hunger for, long for, thirst for, yearn for. **2** grieve, languish, mope, mourn, waste away.

pink¹ *adjective* coral, flesh-coloured, peach, rose, rosy, salmon-pink, shell-pink, skin-coloured.

pinnacle *noun* **2** apex, cap, crest, peak, summit, tip, top. **3** acme, apex, climax, culmination, height, heyday, peak, summit, top, zenith.

pinpoint² *verb* discover, find, identify, locate, spot.

pioneer *noun* **1** colonist, discoverer, explorer, settler, trailblazer. **2** founder, innovator, trailblazer.
pioneer *verb* create, develop, discover, establish, found, introduce, initiate, originate, start.

pious *adjective* devout, faithful, God-fearing, godly, holy, religious, reverent, saintly.
piousness *noun* see PIETY.

pipe¹ *noun* **1** channel, conduit, drainpipe, duct, hose, main, pipeline, tube.

►►►DICTIONARY◄◄

pipe² *verb* (**piped**, **piping**) **1** send something along pipes. **2** transmit music or other sound by wire or cable. **3** play music on a pipe or the bagpipes. **4** trim or ornament with piping.
  pipe down (*informal*) be quiet.

pipe-dream *noun* an impossible wish.

pipeline *noun* a pipe for carrying oil or water etc. a long distance.
  in the pipeline in the process of being made or organised.

piper *noun* a person who plays a pipe or bagpipes.

pipette *noun* a small glass tube used in a laboratory, usually filled by suction.

piping¹ *noun* **1** pipes; a length of pipe. **2** a long narrow pipe-like fold or line decorating something.

piping² *adjective* shrill, *a piping voice*.
  piping hot very hot.

piquant (*say* **pee**-kant) *adjective* pleasantly sharp and appetising or stimulating, *a piquant smell*. **piquancy** *noun* [same origin as *pique*]

pique (*say* peek) *noun* a feeling of hurt pride.
  pique *verb* [from French *piquer* = to prick]

pirate *noun* **1** a person on a ship who robs other ships at sea or makes a plundering raid on the shore. **2** someone who produces or publishes or broadcasts without authorisation, *a pirate radio station*. **piratical** *adjective*, **piracy** *noun* [from Greek *peiraein* = to attack]

pirouette (*say* pir-oo-**et**) *noun* a spinning movement of the body made while balanced on the point of the toe or on one foot.
  pirouette *verb* [French, = spinning-top]

pistachio *noun* (*plural* **pistachios**) a nut with an edible green kernel.

pistil *noun* the part of a flower that produces the seed, consisting of the ovary, style, and stigma.

pistol *noun* a small hand-gun.

piston *noun* a disc or cylinder that fits inside a tube in which it moves up and down as part of an engine or pump etc.

pit¹ *noun* **1** a deep hole or depression. **2** a coal-mine. **3** the part of a racecourse where racing-cars are refuelled and repaired during a race.

pit² *verb* (**pitted**, **pitting**) **1** make pits or depressions in something, *The ground was pitted with holes*. **2** put somebody in competition with somebody else, *He was pitted against the champion*. [from Latin *puteus* = a well]

pitch¹ *noun* (*plural* **pitches**) **1** a piece of ground marked out for games. **2** the highness or lowness of a voice or a musical note. **3** intensity; strength, *Excitement was at fever pitch*. **4** the steepness of a slope, *the pitch of the roof*.

pitch² *verb* **1** throw; fling. **2** fix a tent etc. **3** fall heavily. **4** move up and down on a rough sea. **5** set something at a particular level, *They pitched their hopes high*. **6** (of a bowled ball in cricket) strike the ground.
  pitched battle a battle between troops in prepared positions.
  pitch in (*informal*) start working or eating vigorously.

pitch³ *noun* a black sticky substance rather like tar.
  pitch-black or **pitch-dark** *adjectives* very black or very dark.

pitchblende *noun* a mineral ore (uranium oxide) from which radium is obtained.

pitcher *noun* a large jug.

pitchfork¹ *noun* a large fork with two prongs, used for lifting hay.

pitchfork² *verb* **1** lift with a pitchfork. **2** put a person somewhere suddenly.

piteous *adjective* causing pity. **piteously** *adverb*

►►►THESAURUS◄◄

piquant *adjective* appetising, flavoursome, pungent, sharp, spicy, tangy, tart.

pique *noun* annoyance, displeasure, humiliation, irritation, mortification, resentment, umbrage.
  pique *verb* affront, annoy, gall, humiliate, hurt, irk, irritate, mortify, needle, nettle, offend, peeve (*informal*), vex, wound.

pirate *noun* **1** buccaneer, corsair, marauder, privateer.

pit¹ *noun* **1** abyss, bunker, cavity, crater, depression, ditch, gully, hole, hollow, trench. **2** coalmine, colliery, mine, quarry, shaft, working.

pit² *verb* **1** dent, gouge, nick, pock-mark, scar. **2** match, oppose, set against.

pitch¹ *noun* **2** highness, lowness. **3** degree, height, intensity, level, point. **4** angle, cant, grade, gradient, incline, slope.

pitch² *verb* **1** bowl, cast, chuck (*informal*), fling, heave, hurl, lob, sling, throw, toss. **2** erect, put up, raise, set up. **4** lurch, plunge, rock, roll, toss about.

pitcher *noun* ewer, jug.

pitfall *noun* an unsuspected danger or difficulty.

pith *noun* the spongy substance in the stems of certain plants or lining the rind of oranges etc.

pithy *adjective* 1 like pith; containing much pith. 2 short and full of meaning, *pithy comments.*

pitiable *adjective* pitiful.

pitiful *adjective* 1 arousing pity. 2 miserably inadequate. **pitifully** *adverb*

pitiless *adjective* showing no pity. **pitilessly** *adverb*

pittance *noun* a very small allowance of money. [same origin as *pity* and *piety* (the word *pittance* originally meant 'pious gift')]

pity¹ *noun* 1 the feeling of being sorry because someone is in pain or trouble. 2 a cause for regret, *It's a pity that you can't come.*
take pity on feel sorry for someone and help them.

pity² *verb* (**pitied**, **pitying**) feel pity for someone. [same origin as *piety*]

pivot¹ *noun* a point or part on which something turns or swings. **pivotal** *adjective*

pivot² *verb* (**pivoted**, **pivoting**) turn or place something to turn on a pivot.

pixie *noun* a small fairy; an elf.

pizza (*say* **peets**-a) *noun* an Italian food consisting of a layer of dough baked with a savoury topping. [Italian, = pie]

pizzicato (*say* pits-i-**kah**-toh) *adjective* & *adverb* plucking the strings of a musical instrument. [Italian]

placard *noun* a poster; a notice.

placate *verb* (**placated**, **placating**) pacify; conciliate. **placatory** *adjective*

place¹ *noun* 1 a particular part of space, especially where something belongs; an area; a position. 2 a particular town, district, etc. 3 a seat, *Save me a place.* 4 a job; employment. 5 a building; a home, *Come round to our place.* 6 a duty or function, *It's not my place to interfere.* 7 a point in a series of things, *In the first place, the date is wrong.*
in place in the right position; suitable.
out of place in the wrong position; unsuitable.

place² *verb* (**placed**, **placing**) put something in a particular place. **placement** *noun* [from Greek *plateia* = broad way]

placenta *noun* a piece of body tissue that forms in the womb during pregnancy and supplies the foetus with nourishment.

placid *adjective* calm and peaceful; not easily made anxious or upset. **placidly** *adverb*, **placidity** *noun* [from Latin *placidus* = gentle]

placket *noun* an opening in a skirt to make it easy to put on and take off.

plagiarise (*say* **play**-jee-er-I'z) *verb* (**plagiarised**, **plagiarising**) copy and use someone else's writings or ideas etc. as if they were your own. **plagiarism** *noun*, **plagiarist** *noun* [from Latin *plagiarius* = kidnapper]

pitfall *noun* danger, difficulty, hazard, peril, snag, snare, trap.

pithy *adjective* 2 brief, concise, meaningful, succinct, terse.

pitiful *adjective* 1 forlorn, heartbreaking, heart-rending, moving, pathetic, poignant, sad, touching, wretched. 2 contemptible, hopeless, miserable, pathetic, poor, sorry, useless, woeful.

pitiless *adjective* brutal, callous, cruel, hard-hearted, heartless, inhuman, merciless, relentless, remorseless, ruthless.

pittance *noun* chicken-feed (*informal*), pea-nuts (*informal*), trifle.

pity¹ *noun* 1 commiseration, compassion, condolence, fellow-feeling, regret, sorrow, sympathy. 2 shame.

pity² *verb* commiserate with, feel for, feel sorry for, sympathise with.

pivot¹ *noun* axis, fulcrum, shaft, spindle.

pivot² *verb* revolve, rotate, spin, swivel, turn, twirl.

placard *noun* advertisement, bill, notice, poster, sign.

placate *verb* appease, calm, conciliate, mollify, pacify, propitiate, soothe.

place¹ *noun* 1 address, area, locality, location, scene, setting, site, situation, spot, venue. 2 area, city, country, district, locality, neighbourhood, region, town, township, village. 3 chair, position, seat, space, spot. 5 dwelling, home, house, premises, residence.
in place of in lieu of, instead of.

place² *verb* arrange, deposit, dump, lay, leave, locate, plant, plonk, position, put, rest, set, situate, stand, station, stick (*informal*).

placid *adjective* calm, easygoing, equable, even-tempered, level-headed, mild, peaceable, peaceful, quiet, sedate, serene, tranquil, unexcitable, unruffled.

plagiarise *verb* appropriate, copy, crib, lift (*informal*), pirate.

►►►DICTIONARY◄◄

plague¹ *noun* **1** a dangerous illness that spreads very quickly. **2** a large number of pests, *a plague of locusts*.

plague² *verb* (**plagued, plaguing**) pester; annoy.

plaice *noun* (*plural* **plaice**) a flat edible seafish.

plaid (*say* plad) *noun* cloth with a tartan or similar pattern.

plain¹ *adjective* **1** not decorated; not elaborate; not flavoured. **2** not beautiful. **3** easy to see or hear or understand. **4** frank; straightforward.
plainly *adverb*, **plainness** *noun*
plain clothes civilian clothes worn instead of a uniform, e.g. by police.

plain² *noun* a large area of flat country. [from Latin *planus* = flat]

plaintiff *noun* the person who brings a complaint against somebody else to a lawcourt. (Compare *defendant*.) [same origin as *complain*]

plaintive *adjective* sounding sad. [same origin as *complain*]

plait¹ (*say* plat) *verb* weave three or more strands to form one length.

plait² *noun* something plaited. [from Latin *plicatum* = folded]

plan¹ *noun* **1** a way of doing something thought out in advance. **2** a drawing showing the arrangement of parts of something. **3** a map of a town or district.

plan² *verb* (**planned, planning**) **1** make a plan for something. **2** intend. **planner** *noun*

plane¹ *noun* **1** an aeroplane. **2** a tool for making wood smooth by scraping its surface. **3** a flat or level surface.

plane² *verb* (**planed, planing**) smooth wood with a plane.

plane³ *adjective* flat; level, *a plane surface*. [same origin as *plain*]

plane⁴ *noun* a tall tree with broad leaves.

planet *noun* any of the heavenly bodies that move in an orbit round the sun, *The main planets are Mercury, Venus, Earth, Mars, Jupiter, Saturn, Uranus, Neptune, and Pluto*.
planetary *adjective* [from Greek *planetes* = wanderer (because it was not a 'fixed star')]

plank *noun* a long flat piece of wood.

plankton *noun* microscopic plants and animals that float in the sea, lakes, etc. [from Greek, = wandering]

plant¹ *noun* **1** a living thing that cannot move and that makes its food from chemical substances, *Flowers, trees, and shrubs are plants*. **2** a small plant, not a tree or shrub. **3** a factory or its equipment. **4** (*slang*) something planted to deceive people (see *plant²*).

plant² *verb* **1** put something in soil for growing. **2** fix firmly in place. **3** place something where it will be found, usually to mislead people or cause trouble. **planter** *noun* [from Latin *planta* = a shoot]

plantation *noun* **1** a large area of land where cotton, tobacco, or tea etc. is planted. **2** a group of planted trees.

►►►THESAURUS◄◄

plague¹ *noun* **1** epidemic, pandemic, pestilence. **2** infestation, invasion, scourge.

plague² *verb* annoy, bother, bug (*informal*), disturb, harass, hassle (*informal*), irritate, pester, torment, trouble, vex, worry.

plain¹ *adjective* **1** austere, basic, bland, homely, insipid, ordinary, simple, unadorned, uncomplicated, undecorated, unembellished, uninteresting, unpatterned. **2** homely (*American*), unattractive, unprepossessing. **3** apparent, certain, clear, comprehensible, evident, explicit, intelligible, manifest, obvious, patent, transparent, unambiguous, understandable, unmistakable. **4** blunt, candid, direct, forthright, frank, honest, open, outspoken, straightforward, unambiguous.

plain² *noun* flat, grassland, pampas, prairie, savannah, steppe, tundra, veld.

plaintive *adjective* doleful, melancholy, mournful, pitiful, sad, sorrowful.

plait¹ *verb* braid, interlace, intertwine, interweave.

plan¹ *noun* **1** aim, formula, intention, method, outline, plot, policy, procedure, programme, project, proposal, schedule, scheme, strategy. **2** blueprint, chart, design, diagram, drawing, layout, map, sketch.

plan² *verb* **1** arrange, contrive, design, devise, draft, draw up, formulate, map out, organise, plot, premeditate, prepare, scheme, think up. **2** aim, intend, mean, propose.

plane¹ *noun* **1** aeroplane, aircraft, jet, jumbo. **3** flat, level.

plane³ *adjective* even, flat, flush, level, smooth.

plank *noun* board, slab, timber.

plant¹ *noun* **1** (*plants*) flora, greenery, vegetation. **3** factory, foundry, mill, works, workshop; see also EQUIPMENT.

plant² *verb* **1** set out, sow, transplant. **2** fix, implant, put. **3** conceal, hide, secrete.

▶▶ D I C T I O N A R Y ◀◀

plaque (*say* plark) *noun* **1** a flat piece of metal or porcelain fixed on a wall as an ornament or memorial. **2** a filmy substance that forms on teeth and gums, where bacteria can live.

plasma *noun* the colourless liquid part of blood, carrying the corpuscles.

plaster¹ *noun* **1** a mixture of lime, sand, and water etc. for covering walls and ceilings. **2** plaster of Paris. **3** a piece of sticking-plaster. **plaster of Paris** a white paste used for making moulds or for casts round a broken limb etc.

plaster² *verb* **1** cover with plaster. **2** cover thickly; daub.

plastic¹ *noun* a strong light synthetic substance that can be moulded into a permanent shape.

plastic² *adjective* **1** made of plastic. **2** soft and easy to mould, *Clay is a plastic substance.* **plasticity** *noun*
plastic surgery surgery to repair deformed or injured parts of the body.

plate¹ *noun* **1** an almost flat usually circular object from which food is eaten or served. **2** a thin flat sheet of metal, glass, or other hard material. **3** an illustration on special paper in a book. **plateful** *noun*

plate² *verb* (**plated, plating**) **1** coat metal with a thin layer of gold, silver, tin, etc. **2** cover with sheets of metal.

plateau (*say* plat-oh) *noun* (*plural* **plateaux**, *say* **plat**-ohz) a flat area of high land. [from French *plat* = flat]

platform *noun* **1** a flat surface that is above the level of the ground or the rest of the floor, e.g. in a hall or beside a railway line at a station. **2** the policy that a political party puts forward when there is an election.

platinum *noun* a valuable silver-coloured metal that does not tarnish. [from Spanish *plata* = silver]

platitude *noun* a very ordinary remark. **platitudinous** *adjective*

platoon *noun* a small group of soldiers.

platter *noun* a flat dish or plate.

platypus *noun* (*plural* **platypuses**) an Australian animal with a beak like that of a duck, that lays eggs like a bird but is a mammal and suckles its young. [from Greek *platys* = broad, + *pous* = foot]

plaudits *plural noun* applause; expressions of approval. [same origin as *applaud*]

plausible *adjective* seeming to be honest or worth believing but perhaps deceptive, *a plausible excuse.* **plausibly** *adverb*, **plausibility** *noun*

play¹ *verb* **1** take part in a game or other amusement. **2** make music or sound with a musical instrument, record-player, etc. **3** perform a part in a play or film. **player** *noun*
play down give people the impression that something is not important.
play for time seek to gain time by delaying.
play up (*informal*) be mischievous or annoying.

play² *noun* **1** a story acted on a stage or on radio or television. **2** playing.

playback *noun* playing back something that has been recorded.

▶▶ T H E S A U R U S ◀◀

plaster¹ *noun* **3** bandage, dressing.

plaster² *verb* **2** coat, cover, daub, smear, spread.

plate¹ *noun* **1** dish, platter. **2** layer, pane, panel, plaque, sheet.

plateau *noun* highland, tableland.

platform *noun* **1** dais, podium, pulpit, rostrum, stage, stand. **2** manifesto, policy, programme.

platitude *noun* banality, cliché, commonplace, truism.

platter *noun* dish, plate, salver, tray.

platypus *noun* duckbill, water mole (*old use*).

plausible *adjective* believable, conceivable, credible, likely, reasonable.

play¹ *verb* **1** amuse yourself, cavort, enjoy yourself, entertain yourself, fool about, frisk, frolic, gambol, have fun, mess about, romp, skylark; (*play a game or sport*) join in, participate in, take part in; (*play the other team*) challenge, compete against, meet, oppose, take on, vie with. **2** perform on. **3** act as, impersonate, perform as, portray, pretend to be, represent, star as.

player *noun* **1** competitor, contestant, participant, sportsperson. **2** artist, artiste, entertainer, musician, performer. **3** actor, actress, performer.

play down downplay, gloss over, make light of, minimise.

play for time delay, hedge, procrastinate, stall, stonewall, temporise.

play up be disobedient, be mischievous, be naughty, misbehave, muck up (*informal*).

play² *noun* **1** drama, entertainment, production, show. **2** amusement, diversion, entertainment, fun, leisure, pleasure, recreation, sport.

►►DICTIONARY◄◄

playful *adjective* **1** wanting to play. **2** full of fun; not serious. **playfully** *adverb*, **playfulness** *noun*

playground *noun* a piece of ground for children to play on.

playgroup *noun* a group of very young children who play together regularly, supervised by adults.

playing card each of a set of cards (usually 52) used for playing games.

playing field a field used for outdoor games.

playlunch *noun* (*Australian*) a snack eaten at playtime.

playmate *noun* a person you play games with.

plaything *noun* a toy.

playtime *noun* the time when young schoolchildren may go out to play.

playwright *noun* a dramatist. [from *play*, + *wright* = maker]

plea *noun* **1** a request; an appeal, *a plea for mercy.* **2** an excuse, *He stayed at home on the plea of a headache.* **3** a formal statement of 'guilty' or 'not guilty' made in a lawcourt by someone accused of a crime. [same origin as *please*]

plead *verb* make a plea.

pleasant *adjective* **1** pleasing; giving pleasure. **2** friendly. **pleasantly** *adverb*, **pleasantness** *noun*

pleasantry *noun* (*plural* **pleasantries**) being humorous; a humorous remark.

please *verb* (**pleased**, **pleasing**) **1** make a person feel satisfied or glad. **2** (used to make a request or an order polite), *Please ring the bell.* **3** like; think suitable, *Do as you please.* [from Latin *placere* = satisfy]

pleasurable *adjective* causing pleasure.

pleasure *noun* **1** a feeling of satisfaction or gladness; enjoyment. **2** something that pleases you.

pleat *noun* a flat fold made by doubling cloth upon itself. **pleated** *adjective* [from *plait*]

plebeian (*say* plib-**ee**-an) *noun* a member of the common people in ancient Rome. (Compare *patrician*.) **plebeian** *adjective* [from Latin *plebs* = the common people]

plebiscite (*say* **pleb**-iss-it) *noun* a referendum. [from Latin *plebs* = the common people, + *scitum* = decree]

plectrum *noun* (*plural* **plectra**) a small piece of metal or bone etc. for plucking the strings of a musical instrument.

pledge¹ *noun* **1** a solemn promise. **2** a thing handed over as security for a loan or contract.

pledge² *verb* (**pledged**, **pledging**) **1** promise solemnly. **2** hand something over as security.

plenary (*say* **pleen**-er-ee) *adjective* attended by all members, *a plenary session of the council.* [from Latin *plenus* = full]

plenipotentiary (*say* plen-i-pot-**en**-sher-ee) *adjective* having full authority to make decisions on behalf of a government, *Our ambassador has plenipotentiary power.* **plenipotentiary** *noun* [from Latin *plenus* = full, + *potentia* = power]

►►THESAURUS◄◄

playful *adjective* **1** active, frisky, high-spirited, lively, mischievous, skittish, spirited, sprightly, vivacious. **2** arch, facetious, humorous, jesting, jocular, light-hearted, teasing, tongue-in-cheek.

playground *noun* park, recreation ground.

plea *noun* **1** appeal, entreaty, petition, request, supplication. **2** excuse, grounds, pretext.

plead *verb* allege, assert, claim.
plead with appeal to, ask, beg, beseech, entreat, implore, petition, request, urge.

pleasant *noun* **1** agreeable, attractive, beautiful, delightful, enjoyable, fine, good, inviting, lovely, mild, nice, peaceful, pleasing, pleasurable, relaxing, satisfying, soothing. **2** affable, agreeable, amiable, amicable, charming, cheerful, congenial, cordial, friendly, genial, good-humoured, hospitable, jolly, jovial, kindly, likeable, nice, sweet, sympathetic, winsome.

please *verb* **1** content, delight, gratify, satisfy, suit. **3** choose, desire, like, prefer, think fit, want, wish.
pleased *adjective* content, contented, delighted, elated, glad, grateful, gratified, happy, joyful, satisfied, thankful.

pleasure *noun* **1** amusement, bliss, contentment, delight, diversion, enjoyment, entertainment, fulfilment, fun, gratification, happiness, joy, kick(s) (*informal*), recreation, satisfaction, thrill. **2** amusement, delight, diversion, entertainment, joy, recreation.

pleat *noun* crease, fold, tuck.

plebiscite *noun* ballot, poll, referendum, vote.

pledge¹ *noun* **1** assurance, commitment, guarantee, oath, promise, vow, word.

pledge² *verb* **1** guarantee, plight (*old use*), promise, swear, vow.

▶▶ DICTIONARY ◀◀

plentiful *adjective* quite enough in amount; abundant. **plentifully** *adverb*

plenty[1] *noun* quite enough; as much as is needed or wanted.

plenty[2] *adverb* (*informal*) quite; fully, *It's plenty big enough.* [from Latin *plenus* = full]

pleurisy (*say* **ploor**-i-see) *noun* inflammation of the membrane round the lungs. [from Greek *pleura* = ribs]

pliable *adjective* **1** easy to bend; flexible. **2** easy to influence. **pliability** *noun* [from French *plier* = to bend]

pliant *adjective* pliable.

pliers *plural noun* pincers that have jaws with flat surfaces for gripping things.

plight[1] *noun* a difficult situation.

plight[2] *verb* (*old use*) pledge.

Plimsoll line a mark on a ship's side showing how deeply it may legally go down in the water when loaded. [named after an English politician, S. Plimsoll, who in the 1870s protested about ships being overloaded]

plinth *noun* a block or slab forming the base of a column or a support for a statue or vase etc.

PLO *abbreviation* Palestine Liberation Organisation.

plod *verb* (**plodded, plodding**) **1** walk slowly and heavily. **2** work slowly but steadily. **plodder** *noun*

plop *noun* the sound of something dropping into water. **plop** *verb*

plot[1] *noun* **1** a secret plan. **2** the story in a play, novel, or film. **3** a small piece of land.

plot[2] *verb* (**plotted, plotting**) **1** make a secret plan. **2** make a chart or graph of something, *We plotted the ship's route on our map.*

plough[1] *noun* a farming implement for turning the soil over.

plough[2] *verb* **1** turn over soil with a plough. **2** go through something with great effort or difficulty, *He ploughed through the book.* **ploughman** *noun*
plough back reinvest profits in the business that produced them.

ploughshare *noun* the cutting-blade of a plough.

plover (*say* **pluv**-er) *noun* a kind of wading bird. [from Latin *pluvia* = rain]

ploy *noun* **1** a cunning manoeuvre to gain an advantage; a ruse. **2** an occupation.

pluck[1] *verb* **1** pick a flower or fruit. **2** pull the feathers off a bird. **3** pull something up or out. **4** pull a string (e.g. on a guitar) and let it go again. **5** pull at something.
pluck up courage summon up courage and overcome fear.

pluck[2] *noun* **1** courage; bravery. **2** plucking; a pull.

plucky *adjective* (**pluckier, pluckiest**) showing pluck; brave. **pluckily** *adverb*

plug[1] *noun* **1** something used to stop up a hole. **2** a device that fits into a socket to connect wires to a supply of electricity. **3** (*informal*) a piece of publicity for something.

▶▶ THESAURUS ◀◀

plentiful *adjective* abundant, ample, bountiful, copious, generous, large, lavish, liberal, profuse, prolific.

plenty[1] *noun* abundance, heaps (*informal*), lashings (*informal*), loads (*informal*), lots (*informal*), masses, much, oodles (*informal*), piles (*informal*), stacks (*informal*), tons (*informal*).

pliable *adjective* **1** bendable, flexible, malleable, plastic, pliant, springy, supple. **2** adaptable, amenable, compliant, flexible, malleable, suggestible, tractable, yielding.

plight[1] *noun* difficulty, dire straits, jam (*informal*), mess, pickle (*informal*), predicament, situation, state.

plod *verb* **1** lumber, plough, slog, traipse (*informal*), tramp, trudge. **2** beaver on, grind away, peg away, persevere, plug away, soldier on.

plot[1] *noun* **1** conspiracy, intrigue, plan, scheme. **2** outline, scenario, story, storyline, synopsis. **3** allotment, block (*Australian*), field, garden, lot, patch.

plot[2] *verb* **1** conspire, plan, scheme. **2** chart, draw, map out, outline, sketch.

ploy *noun* **1** dodge, manoeuvre, ruse, scheme, stratagem, tactic, trick.

pluck[1] *verb* **1** gather, harvest, pick, pull off. **3** pull out, pull up, remove. **5** clutch, grab, pull at, snatch, tug, yank (*informal*).

pluck[2] *noun* **1** bravery, courage, daring, grit, guts (*informal*), mettle, nerve, spunk (*informal*), valour.

plucky *adjective* bold, brave, courageous, daring, fearless, game, hardy, heroic, intrepid, mettlesome, spirited, valiant.

plug[1] *noun* **1** bung, cork, stopper. **3** advertisement, boost, commercial, promotion, publicity.

▶▶ D I C T I O N A R Y ◀◀

plug² *verb* (**plugged, plugging**) **1** stop up a hole. **2** (*informal*) publicise something.
plug in put a plug into an electrical socket.

plum *noun* **1** a soft juicy fruit with a pointed stone in the middle. **2** (*old use*) a dried grape or raisin used in cooking, *plum pudding*. **3** reddish-purple colour. **4** (*informal*) something good, *a plum job*.

plumage (*say* **ploom**-ij) *noun* a bird's feathers. [same origin as *plume*]

plumb¹ *verb* **1** measure how deep something is. **2** get to the bottom of a matter, *We could not plumb the mystery*. **3** fit with a plumbing system.

plumb² *adjective* exactly upright; vertical, *The wall was plumb*.

plumb³ *adverb* (*informal*) exactly, *It fell plumb in the middle*. [from Latin *plumbum* = lead³ (the metal)]

plumber *noun* a person who fits and mends plumbing.

plumbing *noun* **1** the water-pipes, water-tanks, and drainage-pipes in a building. **2** the work of a plumber.

plumb-line *noun* a cord with a weight on the end, used to find how deep something is or whether a wall etc. is vertical.

plume¹ *noun* **1** a large feather. **2** something shaped like a feather, *a plume of smoke*.

plume² *verb* (**plumed, pluming**) preen. [from Latin *pluma* = feather]

plumed *adjective* ornamented with plumes, *a plumed helmet*.

plummet¹ *noun* a plumb-line or the weight on its end.

plummet² *verb* (**plummeted, plummeting**) drop downwards quickly.

plump¹ *adjective* slightly fat; rounded. **plumpness** *noun*

plump² *verb* drop or fall quickly.
plump for (*informal*) choose.

plunder¹ *verb* rob a person or place forcibly or systematically; loot. **plunderer** *noun*

plunder² *noun* **1** plundering. **2** goods etc. that have been plundered; loot.

plunge¹ *verb* (**plunged, plunging**) **1** go or push forcefully into something; dive. **2** fall or go downwards suddenly. **3** go or force into action etc., *They plunged the world into war*. **4** immerse something completely. **plunger** *noun*

plunge² *noun* plunging; a dive.
take the plunge start a bold course of action.

plural *noun* the form of a noun or verb used when it stands for more than one person or thing, *The plural of 'child' is 'children'*. (Compare *singular*.) **plural** *adjective*, **plurality** *noun* [from Latin *pluris* = of more]

plus *preposition* with the next number or thing added, *Two plus two equals four* (2 + 2 = 4). [Latin, = more]

plush *noun* a thick velvety cloth used in furnishings. **plushy** *adjective* [from Latin *pilus* = hair]

plutocrat *noun* a person who is powerful because of wealth. [from Greek *ploutos* = wealth, + -*kratia* = power]

plutonium *noun* a radioactive substance used in nuclear weapons and reactors. [named after the planet Pluto]

ply¹ *noun* **1** a thickness or layer of wood or cloth etc. **2** a strand in yarn, *four-ply wool*. [same origin as *pliable*]

ply² *verb* (**plied, plying**) **1** use or wield a tool or weapon. **2** work at, *Tailors plied their trade*. **3** keep offering, *They plied her with food or with questions*. **4** go regularly, *The boat plies between the two harbours*. **5** drive or wait about looking for custom, *Taxis are allowed to ply for hire*. [from *apply*]

plywood *noun* strong thin board made of layers of wood glued together.

p.m. *abbreviation* post meridiem. [Latin, = after noon]

▶▶ T H E S A U R U S ◀◀

plug² *verb* **1** block up, close up, fill, seal, stop up.

plummet² *verb* crash, drop, fall, nosedive, plunge, take a dive, tumble.

plump¹ *adjective* chubby, corpulent, dumpy, fat, obese, overweight, podgy, portly, roly-poly, rotund, squat, stout, tubby.

plunder¹ *verb* loot, maraud, pillage, raid, ransack, ravage, rob, sack.

plunder² *noun* **2** booty, loot, pillage, spoils, swag (*informal*), takings.

plunge¹ *verb* **1** force, jab, push, stick, thrust. **2** descend, dip, dive, drop, duck, fall, jump, leap, nosedive, plummet, sink, throw yourself, tumble. **4** dip, douse, immerse, lower, submerge.

plunge² *noun* dive, drop, fall, header, jump, leap, nosedive, tumble.

▶▶▶ DICTIONARY ◀◀◀

pneumatic (*say* new-**mat**-ik) *adjective* filled with or worked by compressed air, *a pneumatic drill*. **pneumatically** *adverb* [from Greek *pneuma* = wind]

pneumonia (*say* new-**moh**-nee-a) *noun* inflammation of one or both lungs. [from Greek *pneumon* = lung]

PNG *abbreviation* Papua New Guinea.

poach *verb* **1** cook an egg (removed from its shell) in or over boiling water. **2** cook fish or fruit etc. in a small amount of liquid. **3** steal game or fish from someone else's land or water. **4** take unfairly, *One club was poaching members from another*. **poacher** *noun* [same origin as *pouch*]

pocket¹ *noun* **1** a small bag-shaped part, especially in a garment. **2** a person's supply of money, *The expense is beyond my pocket*. **3** an isolated part or area, *small pockets of rain*. **pocketful** *noun*
be out of pocket have spent more money than you have gained.
pocket money money given to a child to spend as he or she likes.

pocket² *verb* (**pocketed, pocketing**) put something into a pocket. [from Old French *pochet* = little pouch]

pod *noun* a long seed-container of the kind found on a pea or bean plant.

poddy *noun* (*Australian*) a hand-fed calf.

podgy *adjective* (**podgier, podgiest**) short and fat.

podiatry *noun* the treatment of ailments of the feet. **podiatrist** *noun* [from Greek *podos* = foot, + *iatreia* = healing]

podium (*say* **poh**-dee-um) *noun* (*plural* **podia**) a platform or pedestal. [from Greek *podion* = little foot]

poem *noun* a composition in verse. [from Greek *poiema* = thing made]

poet *noun* a person who writes poems. **poetess** *noun*

poetry *noun* poems. **poetic** *adjective*, **poetical** *adjective*, **poetically** *adverb*

pogrom *noun* an organised massacre. [Russian, = destruction]

poignant (*say* **poin**-yant) *adjective* very distressing; affecting the feelings, *poignant memories*. **poignancy** *noun* [from French, = pricking]

point¹ *noun* **1** the narrow or sharp end of something. **2** a dot, *the decimal point*. **3** a particular place, *a meeting point*. **4** a particular time, *At this point she was winning*. **5** a detail; a characteristic, *He has his good points*. **6** the important or essential idea, *Keep to the point!* **7** purpose; value, *There is no point in hurrying*. **8** an electrical socket. **9** a device for changing a train from one track to another.
point of view a way of looking at or thinking of something.
to the point relevant.

point² *verb* **1** aim; direct, *She pointed a gun at me*. **2** show where something is, especially by holding out a finger etc. towards it. **3** fill in the parts between bricks with mortar or cement.
point out draw attention to something. [from Latin *punctum* = pricked]

▶▶▶ THESAURUS ◀◀◀

poach *verb* **1,2** simmer. **3** hunt, steal.

pocket¹ *noun* **1** bag, compartment, envelope, pouch.
pocket knife clasp-knife, jackknife, penknife.
pocket money allowance.

pocket² *verb* appropriate, misappropriate, pilfer, steal, take.

pod *noun* case, hull, husk, shell.

podgy *adjective* chubby, dumpy, fat, overweight, plump, portly, roly-poly, pudgy, rotund, squat, stout, tubby.

podiatry *noun* chiropody.

poem *noun* ballad, clerihew, doggerel, elegy, epic, haiku, idyll, jingle, lay, limerick, lyric, ode, rhyme, sonnet, verse.

poet *noun* bard.

poetry *noun* poems, verse.
poetic *adjective* lyrical, metrical, poetical, rhythmic.

poignant *adjective* distressing, heartbreaking, heart-rending, moving, pathetic, pitiful, stirring, touching.

point¹ *noun* **1** apex, extremity, nib, prong, spike, tine, tip, vertex. **2** dot, spot. **3** location, place, position, site, situation, spot. **4** instant, juncture, moment, stage, time. **5** aspect, attribute, characteristic, detail, feature, item, particular, property, quality, trait. **6** argument, drift, essence, gist, meaning, message, pith, substance, thrust. **7** aim, goal, intention, object, purpose, reason, sense, use, value.
point of view opinion, outlook, perspective, stance, standpoint, viewpoint.
to the point apposite, apropos, apt, germane, pertinent, relevant.

point² *verb* **1** aim, direct, level, train. **2** indicate, show, signal.
point out draw attention to, indicate, show.

▶▶ D I C T I O N A R Y ◀◀

point-blank¹ *adjective* **1** aimed or fired from close to the target. **2** direct; straightforward, *a point-blank refusal.*

point-blank² *adverb* in a point-blank manner, *He refused point-blank.*

point-duty *noun* being stationed at a road junction to control the movement of traffic.

pointed *adjective* **1** with a point at the end. **2** clearly directed at a person, *a pointed remark.* **pointedly** *adverb*

pointer *noun* **1** a stick, rod, or mark etc. used to point at something. **2** a dog that points with its muzzle towards birds that it scents. **3** an indication or hint.

pointless *adjective* without a point; with no purpose. **pointlessly** *adverb*

poise¹ *verb* (**poised, poising**) balance.

poise² *noun* **1** balance; the way something is poised. **2** a dignified self-confident manner.

poison¹ *noun* a substance that can harm or kill a living thing. **poisonous** *adjective*

poison² *verb* **1** give poison to; kill with poison. **2** put poison in something. **3** corrupt; fill with prejudice, *He poisoned their minds.* **poisoner** *noun* [same origin as *potion*]

poke¹ *verb* (**poked, poking**) **1** prod; jab. **2** push out or forward; stick out. **3** search, *I was poking about in the attic.* **poke fun at** ridicule.

poke² *noun* a poking movement; a prod.

poke³ *noun* (*dialect*) a bag. **buy a pig in a poke** buy something without seeing it. [compare *pouch*]

poker¹ *noun* a stiff metal rod for poking a fire.

poker² *noun* a card-game in which players bet on who has the best cards.

poky *adjective* (**pokier, pokiest**) small and cramped, *poky little rooms.* [from *poke¹*]

polar *adjective* **1** of or near the North Pole or South Pole. **2** of either pole of a magnet. **polarity** *noun* **polar bear** a white bear living in Arctic regions.

polarise *verb* (**polarised, polarising**) **1** keep vibrations of light-waves etc. to a single direction. **2** set at opposite extremes of feeling, *Opinions had polarised.* **polarisation** *noun*

pole¹ *noun* a long slender rounded piece of wood or metal. [same origin as *pale²*]

pole² *noun* **1** a point on the earth's surface that is as far north (**North Pole**) or as far south (**South Pole**) as possible. **2** either of the ends of a magnet. **3** either terminal of an electric cell or battery. [from Greek *polos* = axis]

polecat *noun* an animal of the weasel family with an unpleasant smell.

pole-star *noun* the star above the North Pole.

pole-vault *noun* a jump over a high bar done with the help of a long pole.

polemic (*say* pol-**em**-ik) *noun* an attack in words against someone's opinion or actions. **polemical** *adjective* [from Greek *polemos* = war]

▶▶ T H E S A U R U S ◀◀

pointed *adjective* **1** pointy, sharp, tapering. **2** barbed, cutting, incisive, penetrating, sharp, trenchant.

pointer *noun* **3** clue, hint, indication, indicator, lead, recommendation, sign, suggestion, tip, wrinkle (*informal*).

pointless *adjective* aimless, fatuous, futile, irrelevant, meaningless, needless, senseless, unnecessary, unproductive, useless, worthless.

poise¹ *verb* balance, steady.

poise² *noun* **1** balance, equilibrium, steadiness. **2** aplomb, calmness, composure, confidence, coolness, equanimity, self-assurance, self-confidence, self-control.

poison¹ *noun* toxin, venom. **poisonous** *adjective* deadly, fatal, harmful, lethal, toxic, venomous.

poison² *verb* **1** kill. **2** contaminate, infect, pollute, taint. **3** corrupt, defile, pervert, pollute, warp.

poke¹ *verb* **1** butt, dig, elbow, jab, nudge, prod, push, stab, stick, thrust. **2** (*poke out*) jut out, project, protrude, stick out. **3** (*poke about*) forage, fossick (*Australian informal*), rummage, search, snoop (*informal*). **poke fun at** chiack (*Australian informal*), deride, jeer at, laugh at, make fun of, mock, poke borak at (*Australian informal*), rib (*informal*), ridicule, satirise, sling off at (*Australian informal*), take the mickey out of (*informal*), tease.

pole¹ *noun* bar, boom, column, mast, post, rod, shaft, spar, staff, stanchion, standard, stick, stilt, upright.

DICTIONARY

police¹ *noun* the people whose job is to catch criminals and make sure that the law is kept. **policeman** *noun*, **policewoman** *noun*

police² *verb* (**policed, policing**) keep order in a place by means of police.

policy¹ *noun* (*plural* **policies**) the aims or plan of action of a person or group. [same origin as *political*]

policy² *noun* (*plural* **policies**) a document stating the terms of a contract of insurance. [from Greek, = evidence]

polio *noun* poliomyelitis.

poliomyelitis (*say* poh-lee-oh-my-il-**I**-tiss) *noun* a disease that can cause paralysis.

polish¹ *verb* 1 make a thing smooth and shiny by rubbing. 2 make a thing better by making corrections and alterations. **polisher** *noun* **polish off** finish off.

polish² *noun* (*plural* **polishes**) 1 a substance used in polishing. 2 a shine. 3 elegance of manner.

polite *adjective* having good manners. **politely** *adverb*, **politeness** *noun* [from Latin *politus* = polished]

politic (*say* **pol**-it-ik) *adjective* prudent.

political *adjective* connected with the governing of a country, city, or county. **politically** *adverb* [from Greek *politeia* = government]

politician *noun* a person who is involved in politics.

politics *noun* political matters.

polka *noun* a lively dance for couples.

poll¹ (*say as* pole) *noun* 1 voting or votes at an election. 2 an opinion poll (see *opinion*). 3 (*old use*) the head.

poll² *verb* 1 vote at an election. 2 receive a stated number of votes. **polling-booth** *noun*, **polling-station** *noun*

pollarded *adjective* (of trees) with the tops trimmed so that young shoots start to grow thickly there. [from *poll¹* 3]

polled *adjective* (of cattle) with the horns trimmed. [from *poll¹* 3]

pollen *noun* powder produced by the anthers of flowers, containing male cells for fertilising other flowers. [Latin, = fine flour]

pollinate *verb* (**pollinated, pollinating**) fertilise with pollen. **pollination** *noun*

pollster *noun* a person who conducts an opinion poll.

pollute *verb* (**polluted, polluting**) make a place or thing dirty or impure. **pollutant** *noun*, **pollution** *noun*

polo *noun* a game rather like hockey, with players on horseback.
polo neck a high round turned-over collar.

poltergeist *noun* a ghost or spirit that throws things about noisily. [from German *poltern* = make a disturbance, + *geist* = ghost]

poly- *prefix* many (as in *polyhedron*). [from Greek *polys* = much]

polyanthus *noun* (*plural* **polyanthuses**) a kind of cultivated primrose. [from *poly-*, + Greek *anthos* = flower]

polychromatic or **polychrome** *adjective* having many colours. [from *poly-*, + Greek *chroma* = colour]

polyester *noun* a kind of synthetic substance.

polygamy (*say* pol-**ig**-a-mee) *noun* the system of having more than one wife at a time. **polygamous** *adjective* [from *poly-*, + Greek *gamos* = marriage]

THESAURUS

police¹ *noun* constabulary, cops (*slang*), fuzz (*slang*), law (*informal*).
police officer constable, cop (*slang*), copper (*slang*), detective, inspector, officer, policeman, policewoman, sergeant, superintendent.

police² *verb* control, patrol, supervise.

policy¹ *noun* code, guidelines, line, manifesto, plan, platform, principles, procedure, rules, strategy, system, tactics.

polish¹ *verb* 1 buff, burnish, rub, shine, smooth. 2 brush up, improve, perfect, refine, smarten up, touch up.

polish² *noun* 2 brilliance, gloss, lustre, sheen, shine, smoothness, sparkle.

polite *adjective* attentive, chivalrous, civil, civilised, considerate, courteous, diplomatic, gallant, genteel, gentlemanly, ladylike, refined, respectful, suave, tactful, thoughtful, urbane, well-behaved, well-bred, well-mannered.

politic *adjective* advisable, expedient, judicious, prudent, sensible, wise.

politician *noun* Member of Parliament, MP, parliamentarian, polly (*slang*), senator, statesman.

poll¹ *noun* 1 ballot, election, vote. 2 Gallup poll, opinion poll, straw poll, survey.

poll² *verb* 2 gain, get, receive, win.

pollute *verb* contaminate, defile, dirty, foul, infect, poison, soil, taint.

▶▶ D I C T I O N A R Y ◀◀

polyglot *adjective* knowing or using several languages. [from *poly-*, + Greek *glotta* = language]

polygon *noun* a shape with many sides, *Hexagons and octagons are polygons.* **polygonal** *adjective* [from *poly-*, + Greek *gonia* = corner]

polyhedron *noun* a solid shape with many sides. [from *poly-*, + Greek *hedra* = base]

polymer *noun* a substance whose molecule is formed from a large number of simple molecules combined. [from *poly-*, + Greek *meros* = part]

polyp (*say* **pol**-ip) *noun* **1** a tiny creature with a tube-shaped body. **2** a small abnormal growth.

polystyrene *noun* a kind of plastic used for insulating or packing things.

polytheism (*say* **pol**-ith-ee-izm) *noun* belief in more than one god. **polytheist** *noun* [from *poly-*, + Greek *theos* = god]

polythene *noun* a lightweight plastic used to make bags, wrappings, etc.

pom *noun* (*Australian informal*) an immigrant from the British Isles; an English person. **pommy** *noun*

pomegranate *noun* a hard red fruit with many seeds. [from Latin *pomum* = apple, + *granatum* = having many seeds]

pommel *noun* **1** a knob on the handle of a sword. **2** the raised part at the front of a saddle. [from Latin *pomum* = apple]

pomp *noun* stately and splendid ceremonial. [from Greek, = procession]

pompom *noun* a ball of coloured threads used as a decoration.

pompous *adjective* full of great dignity and self-importance. **pompously** *adverb*, **pomposity** *noun* [from *pomp*]

pond *noun* a small lake.

ponder *verb* think deeply and seriously; muse. [from Latin *ponderare* = weight]

ponderous *adjective* **1** heavy and awkward. **2** laborious, *He writes in a ponderous style.* **ponderously** *adverb* [from Latin *ponderis* = of weight]

pontiff *noun* **1** the pope. **2** a bishop; a chief priest. [from Latin *pontifex* = chief priest]

pontifical *adjective* **1** of a pontiff. **2** speaking or writing pompously. **pontifically** *adverb*

pontificate *verb* (**pontificated**, **pontificating**) speak or write pompously. **pontification** *noun*

pontoon[1] *noun* a boat or float used to support a bridge (a **pontoon bridge**) over a river. [from Latin *pontis* = of a bridge]

pontoon[2] *noun* **1** a card game in which players try to get cards whose value totals 21. **2** a score of 21 from two cards in this game. [from French *vingt-et-un* = 21]

pony *noun* (*plural* **ponies**) a small horse.

pony-tail *noun* a bunch of long hair tied at the back of the head.

poodle *noun* a dog with thick curly hair.

pooh *interjection* an exclamation of contempt.

pool[1] *noun* **1** a pond. **2** a puddle. **3** a swimming pool.

pool[2] *noun* **1** the fund of money staked in a gambling game. **2** a group of things shared by several people.
the pools gambling based on the results of football matches.

pool[3] *verb* put money or things together for sharing.

poop *noun* the stern of a ship.

▶▶ T H E S A U R U S ◀◀

pomp *noun* ceremony, display, glory, grandeur, magnificence, ostentation, pageantry, show, solemnity, spectacle, splendour, style.

pompous *adjective* arrogant, bombastic, grandiose, haughty, high and mighty, high-falutin (*informal*), hoity-toity, imperious, overbearing, pretentious, self-important, snobbish, stuck-up (*informal*), supercilious, superior.

pond *noun* dam (*Australian*), lake, pool, waterhole.

ponder *verb* brood, cogitate, consider, contemplate, deliberate, meditate, mull over, muse, reflect, ruminate, study, think.

ponderous *adjective* **1** bulky, cumbersome, heavy, massive, unwieldy, weighty. **2** dull, laborious, laboured, long-winded, stilted, stodgy, tedious, turgid, verbose, wordy.

pool[1] *noun* **1** bogey hole (*Australian*), lagoon, lake, mere (*poetical*), pond, swimming hole, waterhole. **2** puddle. **3** aquatic centre, baths, swimming pool.

pool[2] *noun* **1** bank, fund, jackpot, kitty. **2** reserve, supply.

pool[3] *verb* amalgamate, combine, consolidate, merge, share.

▶▶ DICTIONARY ◀◀

poor *adjective* **1** having very little money or other resources. **2** not good; inadequate, *a poor piece of work*. **3** unfortunate; deserving pity, *Poor fellow!* **poorness** *noun*

poorly *adverb* **1** in a poor way, *She was poorly dressed.* **2** rather ill.

pop¹ *noun* **1** a small explosive sound. **2** a fizzy drink.

pop² *verb* (**popped, popping**) **1** make a pop. **2** (*informal*) put or go quickly, *Pop down to the shop*; *Pop in any time.*

pop³ *noun* modern popular music. [short for *popular*]

popcorn *noun* maize heated to burst and form fluffy balls.

pope *noun* the bishop of Rome, leader of the Roman Catholic Church. [from Greek *papas* = father]

popery *noun* (*contemptuous*) the papal system.

pop-eyed *adjective* with bulging eyes.

popgun *noun* a toy that shoots a cork etc. with a popping sound.

poplar *noun* a tall slender tree.

poplin *noun* a plain woven cotton material.

poppadam *noun* a thin crisp biscuit made of lentil-flour. [from Tamil]

poppy *noun* (*plural* **poppies**) a plant with showy flowers, often red.

populace *noun* the general public.

popular *adjective* **1** liked or enjoyed by many people. **2** of or for the general public. **popularly** *adverb*, **popularity** *noun* [from Latin *populus* = people]

popularise *verb* (**popularised, popularising**) make a thing generally liked or known. **popularisation** *noun*

populate *verb* (**populated, populating**) supply with a population; inhabit.

population *noun* the people who live in a district or country; inhabitants.

porcelain *noun* the finest kind of china.

porch *noun* (*plural* **porches**) a shelter outside the entrance to a building. [from Latin *porticus* (compare *portico*)]

porcupine *noun* a small animal covered with long prickles. [from Latin *porcus* = pig, + *spine*]

pore¹ *noun* a tiny opening on the skin through which moisture can pass in or out. [from Greek *poros* = passage]

pore² *verb* (**pored, poring**) **pore over** study with close attention, *He was poring over his books.* [related to *peer¹*]

pork *noun* meat from a pig. [from Latin *porcus* = pig]

pornography (*say* porn-**og**-ra-fee) *noun* obscene pictures or writings. **pornographic** *adjective* [from Greek *porne* = prostitute, + -*graphy*]

porous *adjective* allowing liquid or air to pass through. **porosity** *noun* [same origin as *pore¹*]

▶▶ THESAURUS ◀◀

poor *adjective* **1** bankrupt, broke (*informal*), destitute, hard up (*informal*), impecunious, impoverished, indigent, needy, penniless, penurious, poverty-stricken, skint (*informal*), stony-broke (*informal*). **2** bad, crummy (*informal*), defective, deficient, faulty, imperfect, inadequate, insufficient, inferior, lacking, mediocre, rotten, rubbishy, secondrate, shoddy, slipshod, substandard, unsatisfactory, useless, wanting. **3** hapless, miserable, pathetic, pitiable, pitiful, sorry, unfortunate, unlucky, wretched.

poorly *adjective* **2** ill, indisposed, off colour, seedy (*informal*), sick, under the weather (*informal*), unwell.

pop¹ *noun* **1** bang, burst, crack, explosion, snap.

pop² *verb* **1** bang, burst, crackle, explode. **2** (*pop in*) call in, drop in, nip in (*informal*), stop by, visit; (*pop up*) appear, come up, crop up, emerge, surface.

pope *noun* Bishop of Rome, Holy Father, pontiff.

populace *noun* masses, mob, multitude, people, population, public.

popular *adjective* **1** admired, celebrated, famous, favourite, renowned, sought-after, well-known, well-liked. **2** common, general, mainstream, prevalent, universal, widely-held, widespread.

populate *verb* colonise, inhabit, occupy, people, settle.

population *noun* citizens, inhabitants, occupants, people, populace, public, residents.

porch *noun* entrance, lobby, portico, vestibule.

pore¹ *noun* hole, opening, orifice.

pore² *verb* **pore over** examine, go over, peruse, read, scrutinise, study.

pornographic *adjective* blue, dirty, erotic, indecent, lewd, obscene, smutty.

porous *adjective* absorbent, permeable, pervious, spongy.

porphyry (*say* por-fir-ee) *noun* a kind of rock containing crystals of minerals. [from Latin, = purple stone]

porpoise (*say* por-pus) *noun* a sea-animal rather like a small whale. [from Latin *porcus* = pig, + *piscis* = fish]

porridge *noun* a food made by boiling oatmeal to a thick paste.

porringer *noun* a small bowl for holding porridge.

port[1] *noun* **1** a harbour. **2** a place where goods pass in and out of a country by ship or aircraft. **3** the left-hand side of a ship or aircraft when you are facing forward. (Compare *starboard*.) [from Latin *portus* = harbour]

port[2] *noun* a strong red Portuguese wine. [from the city of Oporto in Portugal]

port[3] *noun* (*especially north-eastern Australian*) **1** a portmanteau or suitcase. **2** a satchel or shopping-bag.

portable *adjective* able to be carried. [from Latin *portare* = carry]

portal *noun* a doorway or gateway. [from Latin *porta* = gate]

portcullis *noun* (*plural* **portcullises**) a strong heavy vertical grating that can be lowered in grooves to block the gateway to a castle. [from French, = sliding door (*porte* = door)]

portend *verb* foreshadow; be a sign that something will happen, *Dark clouds portend a storm.* [from Latin, *pro-* = forwards, + *tendere* = stretch]

portent *noun* an omen; a sign that something will happen. **portentous** *adjective*

porter[1] *noun* a person whose job is to carry luggage or other goods. [from Latin *portare* = carry]

porter[2] *noun* a person whose job is to look after the entrance to a large building. [from Latin *porta* = gate]

portfolio *noun* (*plural* **portfolios**) **1** a case for holding documents or drawings. **2** a government minister's special responsibility. [from Italian *portare* = carry, + *foglio* = sheet of paper]

porthole *noun* a small window in the side of a ship or aircraft (formerly a hole for pointing a ship's cannon through).

portico *noun* (*plural* **porticoes**) a roof supported on columns, usually forming a porch to a building. [from Latin *porticus* = porch]

portion[1] *noun* a part or share given to somebody.

portion[2] *verb* divide into portions, *Portion it out.*

portly *adjective* (**portlier**, **portliest**) stout and dignified. **portliness** *noun*

portmanteau (*say* port-**mant**-oh) *noun* a trunk that opens into two equal parts for holding clothes etc.
  portmanteau word a word made from the sounds and meanings of two others, e.g. *motel* (from *motor* + *hotel*). [from French *porter* = carry, + *manteau* = coat]

portrait *noun* a picture of a person or animal.

portray *verb* **1** make a picture of a person or scene etc. **2** describe or show, *The play portrays the king as a kindly man.* **3** perform a part in a play or film etc. **portrayal** *noun*

pose[1] *noun* **1** a position or posture of the body, e.g. for a portrait or photograph. **2** a pretence; unnatural behaviour to impress people.

port[1] *noun* **1** anchorage, dock, dockyard, harbour, marina, seaport.

portable *adjective* compact, light, movable, transportable.

portent *noun* harbinger, omen, presage, sign, warning.
  portentous *adjective* menacing, ominous, threatening, warning.

porter[1] *noun* attendant, carrier.

porter[2] *noun* commissionaire, concierge, doorkeeper, doorman, gatekeeper, janitor.

portion[1] *noun* allocation, allotment, bit, cut (*informal*), division, fraction, helping, part, percentage, piece, quantity, quota, ration, section, segment, serving, share, slice.

portion[2] *verb* (*portion out*) allocate, allot, apportion, distribute, divide out, dole out, mete out, parcel out, share.

portly *noun* bulky, corpulent, fat, obese, overweight, rotund, stocky, stout, tubby.

portrait *noun* drawing, image, likeness, painting, photograph, picture, representation, sketch.

portray *verb* **1** depict, picture, represent, show. **2** characterise, depict, describe, represent, show. **3** act as, impersonate, perform as, play, represent.

pose[1] *noun* **1** attitude, position, posture, stance.

▶▶▷ D I C T I O N A R Y ◁◀◀

pose² *verb* (**posed, posing**) **1** take up a pose. **2** put someone into a pose. **3** pretend. **4** put forward, *pose a question*.

poser *noun* **1** a puzzling question or problem. **2** a person who poses.

posh *adjective* (*informal*) very smart; high-class; luxurious.

position¹ *noun* **1** the place where something is or should be. **2** the way a person or thing is placed or arranged, *in a sitting position*. **3** a situation or condition, *I am in no position to help you*. **4** paid employment; a job. **positional** *adjective*

position² *verb* place a person or thing in a certain position. [from Latin *positum* = placed]

positive¹ *adjective* **1** definite; certain, *We have positive proof that he is guilty*. **2** holding an opinion confidently. **3** agreeing; saying 'yes', *We received a positive reply*. **4** greater than nought. **5** constructive and helpful. **6** of the kind of electric charge that lacks electrons. **7** (of an adjective or adverb) in the simple form, not comparative or superlative, *The positive form is 'big', the comparative is 'bigger', the superlative is 'biggest'*. **positively** *adverb*

positive² *noun* a photograph with the light and dark parts or colours as in the thing photographed. (Compare *negative*.)

positron *noun* a particle of matter with a positive electric charge. [from *positive*]

posse (*say* **poss**-ee) *noun* a strong group, especially one that helps a sheriff. [same origin as *possible*]

possess *verb* **1** have or own something. **2** control someone's thoughts or behaviour, *I don't know what possessed you to do such a thing!* **possessor** *noun*

possessed *adjective* seeming to be controlled by strong emotion or an evil spirit, *He fought like a man possessed*.

possession *noun* **1** something you possess or own. **2** possessing.

possessive *adjective* **1** wanting to possess and keep things for yourself. **2** showing that somebody owns something, *a possessive pronoun* (see *pronoun*).

possibility *noun* (*plural* **possibilities**) **1** being possible. **2** something that may exist or happen etc.

possible *adjective* able to exist, happen, be done, or be used. [from Latin *posse* = be able]

possibly *adverb* **1** in any way, *I can't possibly do it*. **2** perhaps.

possie (*say* **poz**-ee) *noun* (*Australian informal*) a position.

possum *noun* a furry long-tailed marsupial that lives in trees.

post¹ *noun* **1** an upright piece of wood, concrete, or metal etc. set in the ground. **2** the starting point or finishing point of a race, *He was left at the post*.

▶▶▷ T H E S A U R U S ◁◀◀

pose² *verb* **1** model, sit. **3** (*pose as*) act as, impersonate, masquerade as, pass yourself off as, pretend to be. **4** ask, present, put forward, raise.

posh *adjective* elegant, grand, luxurious, opulent, smart, stylish, sumptuous, swanky (*informal*), swish (*informal*), upmarket.

position¹ *noun* **1** locality, location, niche, place, point, possie (*Australian informal*), setting, site, situation, slot, spot, whereabouts. **2** pose, posture, stance. **3** circumstances, condition, situation, state. **4** appointment, job, occupation, office, post, situation.

position² *verb* arrange, array, dispose, lay out, line up, mount, place, put, set.

positive¹ *adjective* **1** absolute, categorical, certain, conclusive, definite, firm, incontrovertible, indisputable, irrefutable, sure, undeniable, unequivocal. **2** assured, certain, confident, convinced, definite, sure. **3** affirmative. **5** beneficial, constructive, helpful, practical, useful.

possess *verb* **1** be blessed with, be endowed with, be gifted with, have, hold, own. **2** control, dominate, govern, influence, rule.

possession *noun* (*possessions*) assets, belongings, chattels, effects, gear, goods, property, stuff, things.

possessive *adjective* **1** clinging, domineering, jealous, proprietorial.

possibility *noun* **1** chance, contingency, likelihood, probability, prospect, risk.

possible *adjective* achievable, admissible, attainable, conceivable, credible, feasible, manageable, potential, practicable, reasonable, viable, workable.

possibly *adverb* **2** maybe, perchance, perhaps.

post¹ *noun* **1** bollard, column, newel, pale, paling, picket, pier, pile, pillar, pole, prop, shaft, stake, stanchion, standard, stilt, support, upright.

►►► D I C T I O N A R Y ◄◄

post² *verb* put up a notice or poster etc. to announce something. [from Latin *postis* = post]

post³ *noun* **1** the collecting and delivering of letters, parcels, etc. **2** these letters and parcels etc.
  post office a building or room where postal business is carried on.

post⁴ *verb* put a letter or parcel etc. into a postbox or post office for collection.
  keep someone posted keep him or her informed. [same origin as *position*]

post⁵ *noun* **1** a position of paid employment; a job. **2** the place where someone is on duty, *a sentry-post*. **3** a place occupied by soldiers, traders, etc.
  last post a military bugle-call sounded at sunset and at military funerals etc.

post⁶ *verb* place someone on duty, *We posted sentries*.

post- *prefix* after (as in *post-war*). [from Latin *post* = after]

postage *noun* the charge for sending something by post.
  postage stamp a stamp for sticking on things to be posted, showing the amount paid.

postal *adjective* of or by the post.

postbox *noun* a box into which letters are put for collection.

postcard *noun* a card for sending messages by post without an envelope.

postcode *noun* a group of numbers or letters and numbers included in an address to help in sorting the post.

poster *noun* a large sheet of paper announcing or advertising something, for display in a public place. [from *post¹*]

posterior¹ *adjective* situated at the back of something. (The opposite is *anterior*.)

posterior² *noun* the buttocks. [Latin, = further back]

posterity *noun* future generations of people.

postern *noun* a small entrance at the back or side of a fortress etc.

post-haste *adverb* with great speed or haste. [from *post³* + *haste*]

posthumous (*say* **poss**-tew-mus) *adjective* happening after a person's death. [from Latin *postumus* = last]

postilion (*say* poss-**til**-yon) *noun* a person riding one of the horses pulling a carriage.

postman *noun* (*plural* **postmen**) a person who delivers or collects letters etc.

postmark *noun* an official mark put on something sent by post to show where and when it was posted.

post-mortem *noun* an examination of a dead body to discover the cause of death. [Latin, = after death]

postpone *verb* (**postponed, postponing**) fix a later time for something, *They postponed the meeting for a fortnight*. **postponement** *noun* [from *post-*, + Latin *ponere* = to place]

postscript *noun* something extra added at the end of a letter (after the writer's signature) or at the end of a book. [from *post-*, + Latin *scriptum* = written]

postulant *noun* a person who applies to be admitted to an order of monks or nuns.

postulate¹ *verb* (**postulated, postulating**) assume that something is true and use it in reasoning. **postulation** *noun*

postulate² *noun* something postulated. [from Latin *postulare* = to claim]

posture¹ *noun* the way a person stands, sits, or walks; a pose.

►►► T H E S A U R U S ◄◄

post² *verb* display, paste up, pin up, put up, stick up.

post³ *noun* **2** correspondence, letters, mail, packets.

post⁴ *verb* dispatch, mail, send.
  keep someone posted advise, brief, inform, notify.

post⁵ *noun* **1** appointment, employment, job, occupation, office, position, situation, work. **2** place, point, position, station.

post⁶ *verb* install, place, position, put, set, station.

postbox *noun* letterbox, mailbox, pillar box (*old use*).

poster *noun* advertisement, announcement, bill, notice, placard, sign.

post-mortem *noun* autopsy, necropsy.

postpone *verb* adjourn, defer, delay, hold over, put off, put on ice, shelve.

postscript *noun* addendum, addition, afterthought, epilogue, PS, supplement.

postulate¹ *verb* assume, hypothesise, posit, propose, suppose, theorise.

posture¹ *noun* attitude, bearing, carriage, deportment, pose, position, stance.

▶▶▷ D I C T I O N A R Y ◁◀◀

posture² *verb* (**postured, posturing**) pose, especially to impress people. [same origin as *position*]

post-war *adjective* of the time after a war.

posy *noun* (*plural* **posies**) a small bunch of flowers.

pot¹ *noun* **1** a deep usually round container. **2** (*slang*) a lot of something, *He has got pots of money.*
go to pot (*slang*) lose quality; be ruined.
take pot luck (*informal*) take whatever is available.

pot² *verb* (**potted, potting**) **1** put into a pot. **2** (*informal*) abridge, *a potted version of the story.*

pot³ *noun* (*slang*) marijuana. [short for Spanish *potiguaya* = drink of grief]

potash *noun* potassium carbonate. [from *pot¹* + *ash¹* (because it was first obtained from vegetable ashes washed in a pot)]

potassium *noun* a soft silver-white metal substance that is essential for living things. [from *potash*]

potato *noun* (*plural* **potatoes**) a starchy white tuber growing underground, used as a vegetable. [from South American *batata* (potatoes were first brought to Europe from South America)]

potent (*say* **poh**-tent) *adjective* powerful. **potency** *noun* [from Latin *potens* = able]

potentate (*say* **poh**-ten-tayt) *noun* a powerful monarch or ruler. [from *potent*]

potential¹ (*say* po-**ten**-shal) *adjective* capable of happening or being used or developed, *a potential winner.* **potentially** *adverb*, **potentiality** *noun*

potential² *noun* an ability or resources etc. available for use or development. [from Latin *potentia* = power]

pothole *noun* **1** a deep natural hole in the ground. **2** a hole in a road.

potholing *noun* exploring underground potholes. **potholer** *noun*

potion *noun* a liquid for drinking as a medicine etc. [from Latin *potus* = having drunk something]

pot-pourri (*say* **poh**-poor-ee) *noun* a scented mixture of dried petals and spices. [French, = rotten pot]

potter¹ *noun* a person who makes pottery.

potter² *verb* work or move about in a leisurely way.

pottery *noun* (*plural* **potteries**) **1** cups, plates, ornaments, etc. made of baked clay. **2** a place where a potter works.

potty *adjective* (*slang*) mad.

pouch *noun* (*plural* **pouches**) **1** a small bag. **2** something shaped like a bag. [from French *poche* = bag or pocket]

pouffe (*say* poof) *noun* a low padded stool. [French]

poultice *noun* a soft hot dressing put on a sore or inflamed place.

poultry *noun* birds (e.g. chickens, geese, turkeys) kept for their eggs and meat.

pounce *verb* (**pounced, pouncing**) jump or swoop down quickly on something. **pounce** *noun*

pound¹ *noun* **1** a unit of money (in Britain = 100 pence). **2** a unit of weight equal to 16 ounces or about 454 grams.

pound² *noun* **1** a place where stray animals are taken. **2** a public enclosure for vehicles officially removed.

▶▶▷ T H E S A U R U S ◁◀◀

posture² *verb* pose, put on airs, show off.

posy *noun* bouquet, bunch, corsage, nosegay, spray.

pot¹ *noun* **1** billy, casserole, cauldron, crockpot, dixie, pan, quartpot, saucepan, urn, vessel.

potent *adjective* effective, efficacious, forceful, mighty, overpowering, powerful, strong.
potency *noun* effectiveness, efficacy, force, might, power, strength.

potential¹ *adjective* budding, future, likely, possible, promising.

potential² *noun* ability, aptitude, capability, possibility, promise.

potion *noun* brew, concoction, drink, liquid, mixture, philtre.

pottery *noun* **1** ceramics, china, crockery, earthenware, porcelain, stoneware, terracotta.

pouch *noun* **1** bag, dillybag (*Australian*), holder, pocket, purse, sack, wallet.

poultry *noun* domestic fowls.

pounce *verb* (**pounce on**) ambush, attack, fall upon, jump on, leap on, seize, spring on, swoop down on.
pounce *noun* jump, leap, spring, swoop.

pound² *noun* compound, enclosure, pen, yard.

▶▶▶ D I C T I O N A R Y ◀◀

pound³ *verb* **1** hit something often, especially so as to crush it. **2** run or go heavily, *pounding along.* **3** thump, *My heart was pounding.*

pour *verb* **1** flow; cause to flow. **2** rain heavily, *It poured all day.* **3** come or go in large amounts, *Letters poured in.* **pourer** *noun*

pout *verb* push out your lips when you are annoyed or sulking. **pout** *noun*

poverty *noun* being poor.

powder¹ *noun* **1** a mass of fine dry particles of something. **2** a medicine or cosmetic etc. made as a powder. **3** gunpowder, *Keep your powder dry.* **powdery** *adjective*

powder² *verb* **1** put powder on something. **2** make into powder. [from Latin *pulveris* = of dust]

power *noun* **1** strength; energy; vigour. **2** the ability to do something. **3** authority. **4** a powerful country, person, or organisation. **5** mechanical or electrical energy; the electricity supply, *There was a power failure after the storm.* **6** (in mathematics) the product of a number multiplied by itself a given number of times, *The third power of 2 = 2 x 2 x 2 = 8.* **powered** *adjective*, **powerless** *adjective*

powerful *adjective* **1** having great power or strength. **2** influential. **powerfully** *adverb*

powerhouse *noun* a power station.

power station a building where electricity is produced.

pp. *abbreviation* pages.

practicable *adjective* able to be done.

practical *adjective* **1** able to do useful things, *a practical person.* **2** likely to be useful, *a very practical invention.* **3** actually doing something, *She has had practical experience.*
practicality *noun*
practical joke a trick played on somebody. [from Greek *praktikos* from *prattein* = do]

practically *adverb* **1** in a practical way. **2** almost, *I've practically finished.*

practice *noun* **1** practising, *Have you done your piano practice?* **2** actually doing something; action, not theory, *It works well in practice.* **3** the professional business of a doctor, dentist, lawyer, etc. **4** a habit or custom, *It is his practice to work until midnight.*
out of practice no longer skilful because you have not practised recently.

practise *verb* (**practised, practising**) **1** do something repeatedly in order to become better at it. **2** do something actively or habitually, *Practise what you preach.* **3** work as a doctor, dentist, or lawyer. [same origin as *practical*]

Usage Note the spelling: *practice* is a noun, *practise* is a verb.

practised *adjective* experienced; expert.

practitioner *noun* a professional worker, especially a doctor.

▶▶▶ T H E S A U R U S ◀◀

pound³ *verb* **1** bang, batter, beat, clobber (*slang*), crush, grind, hammer, hit, knock, mash, pulp, pulverise, pummel, squash, thump. **3** beat, palpitate, pulsate, throb, thump.

pour *verb* **1** cascade, discharge, flow, gush, issue, run, spew, spill, spout, spurt, stream. **2** bucket, deluge, pelt, rain cats and dogs (*informal*), teem. **3** flood, rush, stream, swarm, throng.

poverty *noun* beggary, deprivation, destitution, hardship, impoverishment, indigence, need, penury, want.

power *noun* **1** energy, force, might, muscle, potency, strength, vigour. **2** ability, capability, capacity, competence, faculty, skill, talent. **3** authority, clout (*informal*), control, dominance, dominion, influence, leverage, licence, mandate, muscle, right, sway, warrant.
powerless *adjective* defenceless, feeble, helpless, impotent, incapable, weak.

powerful *adjective* **1** dynamic, energetic, hefty, invincible, mighty, potent, robust, strong,

sturdy. **2** authoritative, cogent, compelling, convincing, effective, forceful, influential, persuasive, potent, sound, strong, weighty.

practicable *adjective* achievable, feasible, manageable, possible, practical, realistic, viable, workable.

practical *adjective* **1** businesslike, capable, competent, down-to-earth, hard-headed, pragmatic, proficient, realistic, sensible, skilled. **2** functional, handy, usable, useful, utilitarian. **3** applied, hands-on.
practical joke gag, hoax, prank, trick.

practically *adverb* **2** almost, close to, essentially, nearly, virtually.

practice *noun* **1** drill, exercise, preparation, rehearsal, training. **2** action, effect, operation, use. **4** convention, custom, habit, procedure, ritual, routine, tradition, way, wont.

practise *verb* **1** brush up, drill, exercise, rehearse, train. **2** apply, carry out, do, perform. **3** engage in, pursue, work at.

▶▶ D I C T I O N A R Y ◀◀

pragmatic *adjective* treating things in a practical way, *Take a pragmatic approach to the problem.* **pragmatically** *adverb*, **pragmatism** *noun*, **pragmatist** *noun* [from Greek, = businesslike]

prairie *noun* a large area of flat grass-covered land in North America. [from Latin *pratum* = meadow]

praise¹ *verb* (**praised, praising**) **1** say that somebody or something is very good. **2** honour God in words.

praise² *noun* words that praise somebody or something. **praiseworthy** *adjective* [from Latin *pretium* = value]

pram *noun* a four-wheeled carriage for a baby, pushed by a person walking. [short for *perambulator*]

prance *verb* (**pranced, prancing**) move about in a lively or happy way.

prank *noun* a piece of mischief; a practical joke. **prankster** *noun*

prattle *verb* (**prattled, prattling**) chatter like a young child. **prattle** *noun*

prawn *noun* an edible shellfish like a large shrimp.
come the raw prawn (*slang*) try to trick someone.

pray *verb* **1** talk to God. **2** ask earnestly for something; entreat. **3** (*formal*) please, *Pray be seated.*

prayer *noun* praying; words used in praying.

pre- *prefix* before (as in *prehistoric*). [from Latin *prae* = before]

preach *verb* give a religious or moral talk. **preacher** *noun*

preamble *noun* the introduction to a speech or book or document etc. [from *pre-*, + Latin *ambulare* = go]

prearranged *adjective* arranged beforehand. **prearrangement** *noun*

precarious (*say* pri-**kair**-ee-us) *adjective* not safe or secure. **precariously** *adverb* [from Latin *precarius* = uncertain]

precaution *noun* something done to prevent future trouble or danger. **precautionary** *adjective* [from *pre-* + *caution*]

precede *verb* (**preceded, preceding**) come or go in front of or before a person or thing. [from *pre-*, + Latin *cedere* = go]

precedence (*say* **press**-i-dens) *noun* priority; a first or earlier place.

precedent (*say* **press**-i-dent) *noun* a previous case that is taken as an example to be followed.

precept (*say* **pree**-sept) *noun* a rule for action or conduct; an instruction.

▶▶ T H E S A U R U S ◀◀

praise¹ *verb* **1** acclaim, applaud, commend, compliment, congratulate, honour, pay homage to, pay tribute to. **2** adore, exalt, glorify, hallow, honour, laud (*formal*), magnify (*old use*), revere, venerate, worship.

praise² *noun* acclaim, accolade, applause, bouquet, commendation, compliment, congratulations, eulogy, homage, honour, ovation, tribute.
praiseworthy *adjective* admirable, commendable, creditable, deserving, exemplary, honourable, laudable, meritorious, worthy.

pram *noun* baby buggy, baby carriage, perambulator, pushchair, pusher (*Australian*), stroller.

prance *verb* caper, cavort, dance, frisk, frolic, gambol, jump, leap, romp, skip.

prank *noun* antic, caper, escapade, hoax, lark, practical joke, trick.

prattle *verb* babble, chatter, gabble, natter (*informal*), rabbit on (*informal*), yabber (*Australian informal*).

pray *verb* **2** appeal to, ask, beg, beseech, entreat, implore, plead with, urge.

prayer *noun* benediction, blessing, collect, devotion, entreaty, intercession, litany, petition, request, supplication, thanksgiving.

preach *verb* deliver a sermon, expound, lecture, moralise, pontificate, proclaim, sermonise, teach.
preacher *noun* chaplain, clergyman, clergywoman, curate, evangelist, minister, missionary, padre, parson, pastor, priest, rector, vicar.

prearranged *adjective* fixed, planned, predetermined.

precarious *adjective* chancy, dangerous, delicate, dicey (*slang*), dodgy (*informal*), hazardous, insecure, perilous, risky, rocky, shaky, ticklish, touch-and-go, uncertain, unsafe, unstable, unsteady, vulnerable.

precaution *noun* defence, preventive measure, protection, safeguard, safety measure.

precede *verb* come before, go before, herald, lead into, pave the way for, usher in.

precedent *noun* example, model, pattern, standard, yardstick.

►► D I C T I O N A R Y ◄◄

precinct (*say* **pree**-sinkt) *noun* **1** the area round a place, especially round a cathedral. **2** a part of a town where traffic is not allowed, *a shopping precinct.* [from *pre-*, + Latin *cinctum* = surrounded]

precious[1] *adjective* **1** very valuable. **2** greatly loved. **preciousness** *noun*

precious[2] *adverb* (*informal*) very, *We have precious little time.* [from Latin *pretium* = value]

precipice *noun* a very steep place, such as the face of a cliff. [from Latin *praeceps* = headlong]

precipitate[1] *verb* (**precipitated, precipitating**) **1** make something happen suddenly or soon, *The insult precipitated a quarrel.* **2** throw or send down; cause to fall, *The push precipitated him through the window.* **3** cause a solid substance to separate chemically from a solution. **precipitation** *noun*

precipitate[2] *noun* a substance precipitated from a solution.

precipitate[3] *adjective* hurried; hasty, *a precipitate departure.* [from Latin *praeceps* = headlong]

precipitation *noun* rain, dew or snow; the amount of this.

precipitous *adjective* like a precipice; steep. **precipitously** *adverb*

précis (*say* **pray**-see) *noun* (*plural* **précis**, *say* **pray**-seez) a summary. [French, = precise]

precise *adjective* **1** exact; clearly stated. **2** taking care to be exact. **precisely** *adverb*,

precision *noun* [from Latin *praecisum* = cut short]

preclude *verb* (**precluded, precluding**) prevent. [from *pre-*, + Latin *claudere* = shut]

precocious (*say* prik-**oh**-shus) *adjective* developed or having abilities earlier than is usual, *a precocious child.* **precociously** *adverb*, **precocity** *noun* [from Latin *praecox* = ripe very early]

preconceived *adjective* (of an idea) formed in advance, before full information is available. **preconception** *noun*

precursor *noun* a forerunner.

predator (*say* **pred**-a-ter) *noun* an animal that hunts or preys upon others. **predatory** *adjective* [from Latin, = plunderer]

predecessor (*say* **pree**-dis-ess-er) *noun* an earlier person or thing, e.g. an ancestor or the former holder of a job. [from *pre-*, + Latin *decessor* = person departed]

predestine *verb* (**predestined, predestining**) destine beforehand. **predestination** *noun*

predicament (*say* prid-**ik**-a-ment) *noun* a difficult or unpleasant situation.

predicate *noun* the part of a sentence that says something about the subject, e.g. 'is short' in *life is short.* [from Latin *praedicare* = proclaim]

predicative (*say* prid-**ik**-a-tiv) *adjective* forming part of the predicate, e.g. '*old*' in *The dog is old.* (Compare *attributive.*) **predicatively** *adverb*

►►► T H E S A U R U S ◄◄◄

precious[1] *adjective* **1** costly, dear, expensive, invaluable, priceless, valuable. **2** beloved, cherished, dear, prized, treasured, valuable.

precipice *noun* bluff, cliff, crag, escarpment, rockface, scarp.

precipitate[1] *verb* **1** accelerate, bring on, expedite, hasten, speed up. **2** fling down, hurl down, throw down.

precipitate[3] *adjective* abrupt, hasty, headlong, hurried, impetuous, impulsive, rapid, rash, reckless, speedy, sudden, swift.

precipitation *noun* dew, hail, rain, rainfall, sleet, snow, snowfall.

precipitous *adjective* perpendicular, sheer, steep, vertical.

précis *noun* abstract, outline, résumé, summary, synopsis.

precise *adjective* **1** accurate, clear, correct, definite, exact, explicit, express, minute, particular, specific. **2** careful, fastidious, finicky,

meticulous, painstaking, particular, pernickety (*informal*), punctilious, scrupulous.

preclude *verb* bar, block, debar, exclude, prevent, prohibit, rule out.

precocious *adjective* advanced, bright, forward, gifted, mature, quick.

preconception *noun* assumption, expectation, prejudgement, prejudice, presumption, presupposition.

precursor *noun* ancestor, antecedent, forerunner, predecessor.

predator *noun* hunter, marauder.

predecessor *noun* ancestor, forebear, forefather, progenitor.

predestine *verb* destine, fate, foreordain, intend, mean, preordain.

predicament *noun* difficulty, dilemma, emergency, fix (*informal*), jam (*informal*), mess, pickle (*informal*), plight, quandary, spot (*informal*), trouble.

▶▶ D I C T I O N A R Y ◀◀

predict *verb* forecast; prophesy. **predictable** *adjective*, **prediction** *noun*, **predictor** *noun* [from *pre-*, + Latin *dicere* = to say]

predispose *verb* (**predisposed, predisposing**) cause a tendency; influence in advance, *We are predisposed to pity the refugees.* **predisposition** *noun*

predominate *verb* (**predominated, predominating**) be the largest or most important or most powerful. **predominant** *adjective*, **predominance** *noun*

pre-eminent *adjective* excelling others; outstanding. **pre-eminently** *adverb*, **pre-eminence** *noun*

preen *verb* **1** (of a bird) smooth its feathers with its beak. **2** (of a person) smarten. **preen yourself** congratulate yourself.

prefab *noun* (*informal*) a prefabricated building.

prefabricated *adjective* made in sections ready to be assembled on a site. **prefabrication** *noun*

preface (*say* **pref**-as) *noun* an introduction at the beginning of a book or speech. **preface** *verb*

prefect *noun* **1** a school pupil given authority to help to keep order. **2** a district official in France, Japan, and other countries. [from Latin *praefectus* = overseer]

prefer *verb* (**preferred, preferring**) **1** like one person or thing more than another. **2** put forward, *They preferred charges of forgery against him.* [from Latin *prae* = before, + *ferre* = carry]

preferable (*say* **pref**-er-a-bul) *adjective* liked better; more desirable. **preferably** *adverb*

preference *noun* **1** preferring. **2** something preferred.

preferential (*say* pref-er-**en**-shal) *adjective* being favoured above others, *preferential treatment.*

preferment *noun* promotion.

prefix *noun* (*plural* **prefixes**) a word or syllable joined to the front of a word to change or add to its meaning, as in *dis*order, *out*stretched, *un*happy.

pregnant *adjective* having a baby developing in the womb. **pregnancy** *noun* [from *pre-*, + Latin *gnasci* = be born]

prehensile *adjective* (of an animal's foot or tail etc.) able to grasp things. [from Latin *prehendere* = seize]

prehistoric *adjective* belonging to very ancient times, before written records of events were made. **prehistory** *noun*

prejudice *noun* a fixed opinion formed without examining the facts fairly. **prejudiced** *adjective* [from Latin *prae* = before, + *judicium* = judgement]

prelate (*say* **prel**-at) *noun* an important member of the clergy.

preliminary *adjective* coming before an important action or event and preparing for it. [from *pre-*, + Latin *limen* = threshold]

prelude *noun* **1** a thing that introduces or leads up to something else. **2** a short piece of music. [from *pre-*, + Latin *ludere* = to play]

▶▶ T H E S A U R U S ◀◀

predict *verb* forecast, foretell, prophesy.
predictable *adjective* expected, foreseeable, on the cards, unsurprising.
prediction *noun* forecast, prognosis, prophecy.

predisposition *noun* inclination, proneness, propensity, susceptibility, tendency, vulnerability.

predominate *verb* dominate, preponderate, prevail.
predominant *adjective* chief, dominant, main, major, paramount, prevailing, primary.

pre-eminent *adjective* distinguished, excellent, foremost, leading, outstanding, peerless, superior, supreme, unrivalled, unsurpassed.

preen *verb* clean, groom, neaten, plume, primp, smarten, spruce, tidy.

preface *noun* foreword, introduction, preamble, prologue.

prefer *verb* **1** choose, fancy, favour, like better, opt for, pick out, select.

preference *noun* **1** inclination, leaning, liking, partiality, predilection. **2** choice, option, pick, selection.

pregnant *adjective* expectant, expecting, with child (*literary*).

prehistoric *adjective* ancient, antediluvian, earliest, olden (*old use*), primeval, primitive, primordial.

prejudice *noun* bias, bigotry, discrimination, intolerance, partiality, unfairness.
prejudiced *adjective* biased, bigoted, discriminatory, intolerant, narrow-minded, one-sided, partisan, unfair.

preliminary *adjective* early, first, initial, introductory, opening, prefatory, preparatory.

prelude *noun* **1** beginning, curtain-raiser, introduction, opening, overture, preamble, precursor, preface, prologue, start.

▶▶ D I C T I O N A R Y ◀◀

premature *adjective* too early; coming before the usual or proper time. **prematurely** *adverb*

premeditated *adjective* planned beforehand, *a premeditated crime.*

premier[1] (*say* **prem**-ee-er) *adjective* first in importance, order, or time.

premier[2] *noun* a prime minister; in Australia the leader of a State government. [French, = first]

première (*say* prem-**yair**) *noun* the first public performance of a play or film. [French, = first]

premises *plural noun* a building and its grounds.

premiss or **premise** (*say* **prem**-iss) *noun* (*plural* **premisses**) a statement used as the basis for a piece of reasoning.

premium *noun* **1** an amount or instalment paid to an insurance company. **2** an extra payment; a bonus.
at a premium above the normal price; highly valued. [from Latin *praemium* = reward]

premonition *noun* a presentiment. [from *pre-*, + Latin *monere* = warn]

preoccupied *adjective* having your thoughts completely busy with something. **preoccupation** *noun*

prep *noun* homework. [short for *preparation*]

preparation *noun* **1** preparing. **2** something prepared.

preparatory *adjective* preparing for something.

prepare *verb* (**prepared**, **preparing**) make ready; get ready.
be prepared to be ready and willing to do something. [from *pre-*, + Latin *parare* = make ready]

preponderate *verb* (**preponderated**, **preponderating**) be more than others or more powerful. **preponderance** *noun*, **preponderant** *adjective* [from Latin *praeponderare* = outweigh]

preposition *noun* a word used with a noun or pronoun to show place, position, time, or means, e.g. *at* home, *in* the hall, *on* Sunday, *by* train. [from *pre-*, + Latin *positum* = placed]

prepossessing *adjective* attractive, *Its appearance is not very prepossessing.*

preposterous *adjective* very absurd; outrageous. [from Latin, = back to front (from *prae* = before, + *posterus* = behind)]

prerequisite *noun* something required as a condition or in preparation for something else, *The ability to swim is a prerequisite for learning to sail.* **prerequisite** *adjective*

prerogative *noun* a right or privilege that belongs to one person or group. [from Latin, = people voting first]

Presbyterian (*say* prez-bit-**eer**-ee-an) *noun* a member of a Church that is governed by people called *elders* or *presbyters* who are chosen by the congregation. [from Greek *presbyteros* = elder]

presbytery *noun* **1** a group of presbyters. **2** the house of a Roman Catholic priest.

▶▶ T H E S A U R U S ◀◀

premature *adjective* hasty, precipitate, too early, too soon, untimely.

premeditated *adjective* calculated, deliberate, intended, intentional, planned, wilful.

premises *plural noun* accommodation, building, campus, house, property, site.

premiss or **premise** *noun* assumption, basis, grounds, hypothesis, postulate, presupposition, proposition, supposition.

premonition *noun* feeling, foreboding, hunch, intuition, presentiment, suspicion.

preoccupied *adjective* absent-minded, absorbed, abstracted, engrossed, faraway, immersed, lost in thought, pensive, wrapped up.

preparation *noun* **1** groundwork, homework, organisation, plan, planning, practice, setting up, spadework.

preparatory *adjective* introductory, preliminary.

prepare *verb* (*prepare a lesson*) arrange, design, develop, devise, get ready, lay out, map out, organise, plan, set up; (*prepare someone for a job*) brief, coach, equip, fit, groom, prime, train; (*prepare a meal*) assemble, concoct, cook, make, mix, produce, put together, whip up.
be prepared to be minded to, be ready to, be willing to.

preposterous *adjective* absurd, crazy, farcical, laughable, ludicrous, monstrous, nonsensical, outrageous, ridiculous, unthinkable, weird.

prerequisite *noun* condition, essential, must (*informal*), necessity, pre-condition, requirement, requisite.

prerogative *noun* authority, power, privilege, right.

▶▶ D I C T I O N A R Y ◀◀

preschool[1] *adjective* of the time before a child is old enough to attend school.

preschool[2] *noun* a kindergarten.

prescribe *verb* (**prescribed, prescribing**) 1 advise a person to use a particular medicine or treatment etc. 2 say what should be done. [from *pre-*, + Latin *scribere* = write]

prescription *noun* 1 a doctor's written order for a medicine. 2 the medicine prescribed. 3 prescribing.

presence *noun* being present in a place, *Your presence is required.*
presence of mind the ability to act quickly and sensibly in an emergency.

present[1] *adjective* 1 in a particular place, *No one else was present.* 2 belonging or referring to what is happening now; existing now, *the present Queen.*

present[2] *noun* present times or events. [from Latin *praesens* = being at hand]

present[3] *noun* something given or received without payment; a gift.

present[4] (*say* priz-**ent**) *verb* 1 give, especially with a ceremony, *Who is to present the prizes?* 2 introduce someone to another person or to an audience. 3 put on a play or other entertainment. 4 show. 5 cause, *Writing a dictionary presents many problems.* **presentation** *noun*, **presenter** *noun*

presentable *adjective* fit to be presented to someone; looking good.

presentiment *noun* a feeling that something is about to happen; a foreboding.

presently *adverb* 1 soon, *I shall be with you presently.* 2 now, *the person who is presently in charge.*

preserve[1] *verb* (**preserved, preserving**) 1 keep something safe or in good condition. 2 treat food so that it can be kept for future use. **preserver** *noun*, **preservation** *noun*, **preservative** *adjective* & *noun*

preserve[2] *noun* 1 jam. 2 an activity that belongs to a particular person or group. [from *pre-*, + Latin *servare* = keep]

preside *verb* (**presided, presiding**) be in charge of a meeting etc. [from Latin *prae* = in front, + *-sidere* = sit]

president *noun* 1 the person in charge of a club, society, or council etc. 2 the head of a republic. **presidency** *noun*, **presidential** *adjective* [from *preside*]

press[1] *verb* 1 put weight or force steadily on something; squeeze. 2 make something by pressing. 3 flatten; smooth; iron. 4 urge, *They pressed him to come.* 5 make demands, *They pressed for an increase in wages.*

press[2] *noun* (*plural* **presses**) 1 the action of pressing something. 2 a device for pressing things. 3 a device for printing things. 4 a firm

▶▶ T H E S A U R U S ◀◀

preschool[2] *noun* kindergarten, nursery school.

prescribe *verb* 1 advise, order, recommend, suggest. 2 dictate, impose, lay down, ordain, order, specify, stipulate.

presence *noun* attendance, company, society.

present[1] *adjective* 1 about, at hand, here, in attendance, on the scene, on the spot. 2 contemporary, current, existing, immediate.

present[2] *noun* here and now, now, today.

present[3] *noun* contribution, donation, gift, handout, offering, tip.

present[4] *verb* 1 award, bestow, confer, distribute, donate, give, hand out, hand over. 2 announce, introduce, make known. 3 act, mount, perform, put on, stage. 4 demonstrate, display, exhibit, reveal, show.
present yourself appear, arrive, attend, front up (*informal*), turn up.

presentable *adjective* acceptable, all right, decent, neat, OK (*informal*), passable, respectable, satisfactory, suitable, tidy.

presently *adverb* 1 anon, before long, by and by, directly, in a moment, shortly, soon. 2 at present, currently, now.

preserve[1] *verb* 1 conserve, defend, guard, keep, keep safe, look after, maintain, perpetuate, protect, retain, safeguard, save, secure. 2 bottle, can, corn, cure, dry, freeze, pickle, salt, smoke, tin.

preserve[2] *noun* 1 conserve, jam, jelly.

preside *verb* (*preside over*) be in charge of, chair, conduct, control, direct, officiate at, run.

president *noun* 1 chairman, chairperson, chairwoman, chief, director, head, leader.

press[1] *verb* 1 compress, crush, depress, mash, push, squash, squeeze. 3 flatten, iron, smooth. 4 beg, entreat, implore, lean on (*informal*), persuade, pressure, request, urge. 5 (*press for*) call for, campaign for, demand, insist on, push for.

pressing *adjective* critical, crucial, important, insistent, urgent, vital.

press[2] *noun* 5 newspapers, papers, print media; see also JOURNALIST.

that prints or publishes books etc., *Oxford University Press*. **5** newspapers; journalists.
press conference an interview with a group of journalists. [from Latin *pressum* = squeezed]

press-gang *noun* (in history) a group of men whose job was to force people to serve in the army or navy.

pressure¹ *noun* **1** continuous pressing. **2** the force with which something presses. **3** an influence that persuades or compels you to do something, *under pressure to resign*; *financial pressures*.

pressure² *verb* try to compel a person to do something.

pressurise *verb* (**pressurised, pressurising**) **1** keep a compartment at the same air-pressure all the time. **2** try to compel a person to do something. **pressurisation** *noun*

prestige (*say* pres-**teej**) *noun* good reputation. **prestigious** *adjective* [from Latin, = an illusion]

presumably *adverb* according to what you may presume.

presume *verb* (**presumed, presuming**) **1** suppose; assume something to be true. **2** take the liberty of doing something; venture, *May we presume to advise you?* **presumption** *noun*

presumptive *adjective* presuming something. **heir presumptive** see *heir*.

presumptuous *adjective* too bold or confident. **presumptuously** *adverb*

presuppose *verb* (**presupposed, presupposing**) suppose or assume something beforehand. **presupposition** *noun*

pretence *noun* **1** pretending. **2** a pretext.
false pretences pretending to be something that you are not, in order to deceive people.

pretend *verb* **1** behave as if something is true or real when you know that it is not, either in play or so as to deceive people. **2** put forward a claim (to a right or title). **pretender** *noun* [from Latin *prae* = in front, + *tendere* = offer]

pretension *noun* **1** a doubtful claim. **2** pretentious or showy behaviour.

pretentious *adjective* **1** showy; ostentatious. **2** claiming to have great merit or importance. **pretentiously** *adverb*, **pretentiousness** *noun*

pretext *noun* a reason put forward to conceal the true reason. [from Latin *praetextus* = an outward display]

pretty¹ *adjective* (**prettier, prettiest**) attractive in a delicate way. **prettily** *adverb*, **prettiness** *noun*

pretty² *adverb* quite, *It's pretty cold.*

prevail *verb* **1** be the most frequent or general, *The prevailing wind is from the south-west.* **2** be victorious. [from *pre-*, + Latin *valere* = have power]

pressure¹ *noun* **1** compression, force. **3** burden, constraint, demand, difficulty, hardship, load, oppression, strain, stress, tension.

pressure² *verb* browbeat, bulldoze (*informal*), bully, coerce, compel, constrain, drive, force, lean on (*informal*), persuade, press, pressurise, put pressure on, put the acid on (*Australian slang*), put the screws on (*informal*), railroad.

prestige *noun* celebrity, distinction, fame, glamour, glory, honour, kudos, renown, reputation, respect, status.

presume *verb* **1** assume, believe, guess, imagine, presuppose, suppose, surmise, take for granted, take it. **2** be so bold as, dare, have the audacity, take the liberty, venture.

presumptuous *adjective* arrogant, audacious, bold, cheeky, cocky, forward, impertinent, impudent, overconfident, pushy (*informal*).

presuppose *verb* assume, presume, suppose, take for granted.

pretence *noun* **1** acting, affectation, deception, fabrication, faking, hypocrisy, invention, lying, make-believe, pretending. **2** act, charade,

cover, front, hoax, masquerade, pretext, put-on (*informal*), ruse, sham, show, trick.

pretend *verb* **1** act, affect, bluff, deceive, fake, feign, kid (*informal*), make believe, make out, profess, put on an act, sham; (*pretend to be someone*) act as, impersonate, masquerade as, pass yourself off as, pose as.

pretentious *adjective* affected, arty (*informal*), la-di-da (*informal*), ostentatious, pompous, self-important, showy, snobbish, stuck-up (*informal*), toffee-nosed (*informal*).

pretext *noun* excuse, pretence, ruse.

pretty¹ *adjective* appealing, attractive, beautiful, bonny (*Scottish*), captivating, charming, dainty, fair (*old use*), fetching, good-looking, handsome, lovely, nice, pleasing, sweet (*informal*), winsome.

pretty² *adverb* fairly, moderately, quite, rather, reasonably, somewhat.

prevail *verb* **2** be victorious, rule, triumph, win the day.
prevailing *adjective* chief, common, dominant, main, predominant, usual.

▶▶ D I C T I O N A R Y ◀◀

prevalent (*say* **prev**-a-lent) *adjective* most frequent or common; widespread. **prevalence** *noun* [same origin as *prevail*]

prevaricate *verb* (**prevaricated, prevaricating**) say something that is not actually a lie but is evasive or misleading. **prevarication** *noun* [from Latin, = walk crookedly]

prevent *verb* **1** stop something from happening. **2** stop a person from doing something. **preventable** *adjective*, **prevention** *noun*, **preventive** or **preventative** *adjective* & *noun* [from pre- + Latin *ventum* = come]

preview *noun* a showing of a film or play etc. before it is shown to the general public.

previous *adjective* coming before this; preceding. **previously** *adverb* [from *pre-*, + Latin *via* = way]

prey[1] (*say as* pray) *noun* an animal that is hunted or killed by another for food; a victim.
bird or **beast of prey** one that kills and eats other birds or four-footed animals.

prey[2] *verb* **prey on** hunt or take as prey; cause to worry, *The problem preyed on his mind.* [from Latin *praeda* = booty]

price[1] *noun* **1** the amount of money for which something is bought or sold. **2** what must be given or done in order to achieve something.

price[2] *verb* (**priced, pricing**) decide the price of something.

priceless *adjective* **1** very valuable. **2** (*informal*) very amusing.

prick *verb* **1** make a tiny hole in something. **2** hurt somebody with a pin or needle etc. **prick** *noun*
prick up your ears start listening suddenly.

prickle[1] *noun* **1** a small thorn. **2** a sharp-pointed projection on an echidna or cactus etc. **3** a feeling that something is pricking you. **prickly** *adjective*

prickle[2] *verb* (**prickled, prickling**) feel or cause a pricking feeling.

pride[1] *noun* **1** pleasure or satisfaction with yourself or someone else who has done well. **2** something that makes you feel proud. **3** self-respect. **4** an unduly high opinion of your own merits or importance. **5** a group of lions.
pride of place the most important or most honoured position.

pride[2] *verb* (**prided, priding**) **pride yourself on** be proud of.

priest *noun* **1** a member of the clergy. **2** a person who conducts religious ceremonies. **priestess** *noun*, **priesthood** *noun*, **priestly** *adjective*

prig *noun* a self-righteous person. **priggish** *adjective*

▶▶ T H E S A U R U S ◀◀

prevalent *adjective* common, current, dominant, general, popular, predominant, prevailing, usual, widespread.

prevent *verb* avert, avoid, bar, block, curb, deter, fend off, foil, forestall, halt, hamper, hinder, impede, inhibit, obstruct, preclude, prohibit, stave off, stop, thwart, ward off.

previous *adjective* earlier, former, one-time, past, preceding, prior.
previously *adverb* above (*in a book*), before, earlier, formerly, hitherto, in the past, once.

prey[1] *noun* quarry, victim.

prey[2] *verb* **prey on** devour, eat, feed on, hunt, kill, live off. **2** haunt, oppress, trouble, weigh on, worry.

price[1] *noun* **1** amount, charge, cost, expense, fare, fee, payment, rate, sum, terms, toll, value, worth. **2** consequence, cost, penalty, punishment, sacrifice.

priceless *adjective* **1** costly, dear, expensive, invaluable, irreplaceable, precious, pricey (*informal*), valuable. **2** absurd, amusing, funny, hilarious.

prick *verb* jab, lance, perforate, pierce, puncture, stab.
prick *noun* jab, pinprick, prickle, stab, sting.

prickle[1] *noun* **1,2** barb, needle, spike, spine, thorn.

prickle[2] *verb* itch, smart, sting, tingle.

pride[1] *noun* **1** delight, enjoyment, gratification, happiness, joy, pleasure, satisfaction. **2** delight, joy, pleasure. **3** dignity, honour, self-esteem, self-respect. **4** arrogance, conceit, egotism, hubris, self-importance, self-love, self-satisfaction, smugness, vanity.

pride[2] *verb* **pride yourself on** be proud of, boast about, congratulate yourself on, flatter yourself on.

priest *noun* **1** archdeacon, chaplain, chief priest, clergyman, clergywoman, cleric, father, high priest, minister, padre, parson, pastor, rector, vicar.
priestly *adjective* clerical, ecclesiastical, ministerial, pastoral.

▶▶▷ D I C T I O N A R Y ◁◀◀

prim *adjective* (**primmer, primmest**) formal and correct in manner; disliking anything rough or rude. **primly** *adverb*, **primness** *noun*

primacy (*say* **pry**-ma-see) *noun* being the first or most important.

prima donna (*say* **preem**-a) the chief female singer in an opera. [Italian, = first lady]

primary *adjective* first; most important. (Compare *secondary*.) **primarily** (*say* **pry**-mer-il-ee) *adverb*

primary colours the colours from which all others can be made by mixing (red, yellow, and blue for paint; red, green, and violet for light).

primary industry agriculture, forestry, fishing, etc., as distinct from manufacturing industry.

primary school a school for the first stage of a child's education. [same origin as *prime*]

primate (*say* **pry**-mayt) *noun* **1** an archbishop. **2** an animal of the group that includes human beings, apes, and monkeys.

prime¹ *adjective* **1** chief; most important, *the prime cause*. **2** excellent; first-rate, *prime beef*. **prime minister** the leader of a government, in Australia of the Federal Government.

prime number a number (e.g. 2, 3, 5, 7, 11) that can be divided exactly only by itself and one.

prime² *noun* the best time or stage of something, *in the prime of life*.

prime³ *verb* (**primed, priming**) **1** prepare something for use or action. **2** put a coat of liquid on something to prepare it for painting. **3** equip a person with information. [from Latin *primus* = first]

primer *noun* **1** a liquid for priming a surface. **2** an elementary textbook.

primeval (*say* pry-**mee**-val) *adjective* of the earliest times of the world. [from Latin *primus* = first, + *aevum* = age]

primitive *adjective* of or at an early stage of development or civilisation; not complicated or sophisticated.

primogeniture *noun* being a first-born child; the custom by which an eldest son inherits all his parents' property. [from Latin *primo* = first, + *genitus* = born]

primordial *adjective* primeval.

primrose *noun* a pale-yellow flower that blooms in spring. [from Latin *prima rosa* = first rose]

prince *noun* **1** the son of a king or queen. **2** a man or boy in a royal family. **princely** *adjective* [from Latin *princeps* = chieftain]

princess *noun* (*plural* **princesses**) **1** the daughter of a king or queen. **2** a woman or girl in a royal family. **3** the wife of a prince.

principal¹ *adjective* chief; most important. **principally** *adverb*

principal² *noun* **1** the head of a college or school. **2** a sum of money that is invested or lent, *Interest is paid on the principal*. [same origin as *prince*]

Usage Do not confuse with *principle* (which is never used of a person).

---

principality *noun* a country ruled by a prince.

principle *noun* **1** a general truth, belief, or rule, *She taught me the principles of geometry*. **2** a code of conduct, *Cheating is against his principles*; *a man of principle*.

in principle in general, not in details.

▶▶▷ T H E S A U R U S ◁◀◀

prim *adjective* demure, formal, old-fashioned, precise, prissy, proper, prudish, starchy, strait-laced, stuffy.

primary *adjective* basic, chief, essential, first, fundamental, key, main, major, paramount, prime, principal.
primarily *adverb* basically, chiefly, essentially, firstly, fundamentally, generally, largely, mainly, mostly, predominantly, principally.

prime¹ *adjective* **1** chief, key, leading, main, major, primary, principal. **2** best, excellent, first-class, superior, top-quality.

prime² *noun* best, heyday, peak, zenith.

prime³ *verb* **1** make ready, prepare. **3** brief, coach, equip, fill in (*informal*), forearm, inform, instruct, prepare, train.

primeval *adjective* ancient, early, prehistoric, primal, primitive, primordial.

primitive *adjective* (*primitive tribes*) ancient, barbarian, prehistoric, primeval, primordial, savage, uncivilised; (*primitive methods*) archaic, basic, crude, elementary, obsolete, rough, rudimentary, simple, unsophisticated.

principal¹ *adjective* basic, capital, cardinal, chief, dominant, essential, foremost, fundamental, leading, main, major, outstanding, predominant, primary, prime, supreme.

principal² *noun* **1** head, headmaster, headmistress, head teacher. **2** capital.

principle *noun* **1** assumption, axiom, belief, guideline, law, precept, rule, standard, tenet, truth. **2** conscience, ethics, honesty, honour, integrity, morality, morals, probity, scruples, standards, virtue.

on principle because of your principles of behaviour. [from Latin *principium* = source]

Usage See the note on *principal*.

print¹ *verb* **1** put words or pictures on paper by using a machine. **2** write with letters that are not joined together. **3** press a mark or design etc. on a surface. **4** make a picture from the negative of a photograph. **printer** *noun*

printed circuit an electric circuit made by pressing thin metal strips on to a surface.

print² *noun* **1** printed lettering or words. **2** a mark made by something pressing on a surface. **3** a printed picture, photograph, or design.

printout *noun* information etc. produced in printed form by a computer or teleprinter.

prior¹ *adjective* earlier or more important than something else.

prior² *noun* a monk who is the head of a religious house or order. **prioress** *noun* [Latin, = former, more important]

priority *noun* (*plural* **priorities**) **1** being earlier or more important than something else; precedence. **2** something considered more important than other things, *Safety is a priority*. [from *prior*]

priory *noun* (*plural* **priories**) a religious house governed by a prior or prioress.

prise *verb* (**prised, prising**) lever something out or open, *Prise the lid off the crate*.

prism (*say* prizm) *noun* **1** a solid shape with ends that are triangles or polygons which are equal and parallel. **2** a glass prism that breaks up light into the colours of the rainbow. **prismatic** *adjective*

prison *noun* a place where criminals are kept as a punishment.

prisoner *noun* **1** a person kept in prison. **2** a captive.

pristine *adjective* ancient and unspoilt; original, *in its pristine form*. [from Latin *pristinus* = former]

private¹ *adjective* **1** belonging to a particular person or group, *private property*. **2** confidential. **3** secluded. **4** not holding public office, *a private citizen*. **5** independent; not organised by a government, *private medicine*; *a private detective*. **privately** *adverb*, **privacy** (*say* pry-vas-ee) *noun*

in private where only particular people can see or hear; not in public.

private² *noun* a soldier of the lowest rank.

privation *noun* loss or lack of something; lack of necessities. [from Latin *privatus* = deprived]

privatise *verb* (**privatised, privatising**) transfer a nationalised industry etc. to a private organisation. **privatisation** *noun*

privet *noun* an evergreen shrub with small leaves, used to make hedges.

privilege *noun* a special right or advantage given to one person or group. **privileged** *adjective* [from Latin *privus* = of an individual, + *legis* = of law]

privy *adjective* (*old use*) hidden; secret.

be privy to be sharing in the secret of someone's plans etc. [from Latin, = private]

prize¹ *noun* an award given to the winner of a game or competition etc.

prize² *verb* (**prized, prizing**) value something greatly. [from *price*]

print¹ *verb* **1** produce, reproduce, run off; see also PUBLISH. **3** impress, imprint, stamp.

print² *noun* **1** font, letters, type, typeface. **2** impression, imprint, indentation, mark, stamp. **3** copy, duplicate, facsimile, replica, re-production.

printout *noun* hard copy, output.

prior¹ *adjective* anterior, earlier, pre-existing, previous.
prior *adverb* **prior to** see BEFORE².

priority *noun* **1** precedence, preference.

priory *noun* abbey, cloister, convent, friary, monastery, nunnery, religious house.

prise *verb* force, lever, wrench.

prison *noun* detention centre, dungeon, jail, lock-up, nick (*slang*), penitentiary (*American*), remand centre.

prisoner *noun* captive, convict, detainee, hostage, inmate, internee, jailbird, lag (*slang*).

private¹ *adjective* **1** individual, own, personal. **2** classified, confidential, hush-hush (*informal*), quiet, secret. **3** hidden, isolated, off-limits, quiet, remote, secluded. **5** independent, non-government.

privilege *noun* advantage, benefit, concession, entitlement, exemption, perk (*informal*), prerogative, right.

prize¹ *noun* award, crown, cup, jackpot, laurels, medal, reward, trophy.

prize² *verb* appreciate, cherish, esteem, treasure, value.

pro *noun* (*plural* **pros**) (*informal*) a professional.

pro- *prefix* **1** favouring or supporting (as in *pro-British*). **2** deputising or substituted for (as in *pronoun*). **3** onwards; forwards (as in *proceed*). [from Latin *pro* = for; in front of]

pro and con for and against. [from Latin *pro* = for, + *contra* = against]
pros and cons reasons for and against something.

probable *adjective* likely to happen or be true. **probably** *adverb*, **probability** *noun* [same origin as *prove*]

probate *noun* the official process of proving that a person's will is valid. [from Latin *probatus* = tested, proved]

probation *noun* the testing of a person's character and abilities. **probationary** *adjective* **on probation** being supervised by an official (a **probation officer**) instead of being sent to prison. [same origin as *prove*]

probationer *noun* a person at an early stage of training, e.g. as a nurse.

probe¹ *noun* **1** an instrument for exploring something. **2** an investigation.

probe² *verb* (**probed, probing**) **1** explore with a probe. **2** investigate. [from Latin *probare* = to test]

probity (*say* **proh**-bit-ee) *noun* honesty. [from Latin *probus* = good]

problem *noun* **1** something difficult to deal with or understand. **2** something that has to

be done or answered. **problematic** or **problematical** *adjective* [from Greek, = an exercise]

proboscis (*say* pro-**bohss**-iss) *noun* (*plural* **proboscises**) **1** a long flexible snout. **2** an insect's long mouth-part. [from Greek *pro* = in front, + *boskein* = feed]

procedure *noun* an orderly way of doing something.

proceed *verb* **1** go forward or onward. **2** continue; go on with an action, *She proceeded to explain the plan.* [from *pro-* + Latin *cedere* = go]

proceedings *plural noun* **1** things that happen; activities. **2** a lawsuit.

proceeds *plural noun* the money made from a sale or show etc.; profit.

process¹ (*say* **proh**-sess) *noun* (*plural* **processes**) **1** a series of actions for making or doing something. **2** an outgrowth.

process² *verb* put something through a manufacturing or other process, *processed cheese.* [same origin as *proceed*]

process³ (*say* pro-**sess**) *verb* go in procession. [from *procession*]

procession *noun* a number of people or vehicles etc. moving steadily forward following each other.

processor *noun* a machine that processes things.

proclaim *verb* announce officially or publicly. **proclamation** *noun*

probable *adjective* expected, likely, on the cards, predictable.
probability *noun* chance, likelihood, possibility, prospect.

probationary *adjective* test, testing, trial.

probe¹ *noun* **2** examination, exploration, inquiry, inspection, investigation, study.

probe² *verb* **1** examine, explore, feel around, poke, prod. **2** examine, inquire into, investigate, look into, question, scrutinise, sound out.

problem *noun* **1** burden, complication, concern, difficulty, dilemma, hassle (*informal*), headache, hitch, predicament, setback, snag, strife (*Australian informal*), trouble, worry. **2** conundrum, enigma, mystery, poser, puzzle, question, riddle, sum, teaser.
problematic, problematical *adjective* **1** complicated, difficult, messy, ticklish, tricky, troublesome. **2** debatable, disputable, doubtful, questionable, uncertain.

procedure *noun* approach, method, operation, practice, process, routine, system, technique, way.

proceed *verb* **1** advance, go on, head, make your way, move on, press on, progress, push on. **2** carry on, continue, go on, keep going.

proceedings *plural noun* **1** actions, activities, business, events, goings-on, happenings. **2** action, lawsuit, legal action, litigation.

proceeds *plural noun* earnings, gain, income, profit(s), revenue, takings.

process¹ *noun* **1** course of action, means, method, operation, procedure, system, technique, way.

process² *verb* (*process food*) change, convert, refine, transform, treat; (*process an application*) deal with, handle, take care of.

procession *noun* cavalcade, column, cortège, line, march, motorcade, pageant, parade.

proclaim *verb* advertise, announce, broadcast, circulate, declare, make known, pronounce, publicise, publish, tell, trumpet.

▶▶▷ DICTIONARY ◁◀◀

procrastinate *verb* (**procrastinated, procrastinating**) put off doing something. **procrastination** *noun*, **procrastinator** *noun* [from *pro-*, + Latin *crastinus* = of tomorrow]

procreate *verb* (**procreated, procreating**) produce offspring by the natural process of reproduction. **procreation** *noun*

procure *verb* (**procured, procuring**) obtain; acquire. **procurement** *noun* [from *pro-*, + Latin *curare* = look after]

prod *verb* (**prodded, prodding**) 1 poke. 2 stimulate into action. **prod** *noun*

prodigal *adjective* wasteful; extravagant. **prodigally** *adverb*, **prodigality** *noun* [from Latin *prodigus* = generous]

prodigious *adjective* 1 wonderful. 2 enormous. **prodigiously** *adverb*

prodigy *noun* (*plural* **prodigies**) 1 a person with wonderful abilities. 2 a wonderful thing. [from Latin *prodigium* = good omen]

produce¹ *verb* (**produced, producing**) 1 make or create something; bring into existence. 2 bring out so that it can be seen. 3 organise the performance of a play, making of a film, etc. 4 extend a line further, *Produce the base of the triangle.* **producer** *noun*

produce² (*say* **prod**-yooss) *noun* things produced, especially by farmers. [from *pro-*, + Latin *ducere* = to lead]

product *noun* 1 something produced. 2 the result of multiplying two numbers. (Compare *quotient*.)

production *noun* 1 producing. 2 the thing or amount produced.

productive *adjective* 1 producing a lot of things. 2 profitable; useful. **productivity** *noun*

profane¹ *adjective* irreverent; blasphemous. **profanely** *adverb*, **profanity** *noun*

profane² *verb* (**profaned, profaning**) treat irreverently. [from Latin *profanus* = outside the temple]

profess *verb* 1 declare. 2 claim; pretend, *She professed interest in our work.* **professedly** *adverb*

profession *noun* 1 an occupation that needs special education and training, *The professions include being a doctor, nurse, or lawyer.* 2 a declaration, *They made professions of loyalty.*

▶▶▷ THESAURUS ◁◀◀

procrastinate *verb* dally, delay, dilly-dally (*informal*), dither, drag your feet, hesitate, hold off, play for time, stall.

procure *verb* acquire, buy, come by, find, get, get hold of, lay your hands on, obtain, pick up, secure.

prod *verb* 1 butt, elbow, jab, nudge, poke, push. 2 goad, prompt, push, rouse, spur, stimulate, stir, urge.

prod *noun* 1 butt, elbow, jab, nudge, poke, push. 2 prompt, reminder, spur, stimulus.

prodigal *adjective* extravagant, improvident, profligate, spendthrift, wasteful.

prodigious *adjective* 1 amazing, astonishing, astounding, exceptional, extraordinary, great, marvellous, miraculous, phenomenal, rare, remarkable, stupendous, terrific (*informal*), wonderful. 2 colossal, enormous, gigantic, great, immense, massive, monumental, tremendous, vast.

prodigy *noun* 1 genius, marvel, sensation, virtuoso, whiz-kid (*informal*), wizard.

produce¹ *verb* 1 assemble, build, compose, construct, create, devise, fabricate, form, invent, make, manufacture, think up, write; (*produce offspring*) bear, beget, breed, bring forth, give birth to, raise, rear, reproduce; (*produce crops*) bear, bring forth, grow, yield; (*produce a sensation*) bring about, cause, create, generate, give rise to, provoke, raise. 2 bring forward, bring out, come up with, disclose, display, exhibit, furnish, offer, present, provide, reveal, show, supply.

produce² *noun* crops, foodstuffs, harvest, products, yield.

product *noun* 1 artefact, article, commodity, creation, item, object, production, thing; (*products*) goods, merchandise, output, produce, wares.

productive *adjective* 1 fertile, fruitful, prolific, rich. 2 beneficial, constructive, effective, profitable, rewarding, useful, valuable, worthwhile.

profane¹ *adjective* blasphemous, disrespectful, impious, irreligious, irreverent, sacrilegious.

profane² *verb* abuse, debase, defile, desecrate, misuse, violate.

profess *verb* 1 assert, avow, claim, confess, declare, proclaim, pronounce, state. 2 allege, claim, make out, pretend, purport.

profession *noun* 1 calling, career, employment, job, occupation, vocation.

▶▶ DICTIONARY ◀◀

professional *adjective* **1** of a profession. **2** doing a certain kind of work as a full-time job for payment, not as an amateur, *a professional footballer*. **professional** *noun*, **professionally** *adverb*

professor *noun* a university lecturer of the highest rank. **professorship** *noun*

proffer *verb* & *noun* offer. [from *pro-* + *offer*]

proficient *adjective* doing something properly because of training or practice; skilled. **proficiency** *noun* [from Latin *proficiens* = making progress]

profile *noun* **1** a side view of a person's face. **2** a short description of a person's character or career.
keep a low profile not make yourself noticeable.

profit¹ *noun* **1** the extra money obtained by selling something for more than it cost to buy or make. **2** an advantage gained by doing something. **profitable** *adjective*, **profitably** *noun*

profit² *verb* (**profited, profiting**) get a profit.

profiteer *noun* a person who makes a great profit unfairly. **profiteering** *noun*

profligate *adjective* wasteful; unrestrained. **profligacy** *noun*

profound *adjective* **1** very deep or intense, *We take a profound interest in it.* **2** showing or needing great study. **profoundly** *adverb*,

profundity *noun* [from Latin *profundus* = deep]

profuse *adjective* lavish; plentiful. **profusely** *adverb*, **profuseness** *noun*, **profusion** *noun* [from *pro-*, + Latin *fusum* = poured]

progenitor *noun* an ancestor.

progeny (*say* **proj**-in-ee) *noun* offspring; descendants.

prognosis (*say* prog-**noh**-sis) *noun* (*plural* **prognoses**) a forecast or prediction, especially about a disease. **prognostication** *noun* [from Greek *pro-* = before, + *gnosis* = knowing]

program¹ *noun* a series of coded instructions for a computer to carry out.

program² *verb* (**programmed, programming**) prepare a computer by means of a program. **programmer** *noun*

programme *noun* **1** a list of planned events; a leaflet giving details of a play, concert, etc. **2** a show, play or talk etc. on radio or television. [from Greek *programma* = public notice]

progress¹ (*say* **proh**-gress) *noun* **1** forward movement; an advance. **2** a development or improvement.

progress² (*say* pro-**gress**) *verb* make progress. **progression** *noun* [from *pro-*, + Latin *gressus* = going]

▶▶ THESAURUS ◀◀

professional *adjective* **1** adept, competent, expert, knowledgeable, proficient, qualified, skilful, skilled, trained.
professional *noun* authority, expert, master, pro (*informal*), specialist.

proficient *adjective* able, accomplished, adept, adroit, capable, competent, deft, dexterous, expert, skilful, skilled, trained.
proficiency *noun* ability, aptitude, capability, competence, expertise, mastery, skill.

profile *noun* **1** contour, outline, shape, silhouette. **2** account, biography, character sketch, description.

profit¹ *noun* **1** gain, proceeds, return, surplus. **2** advantage, avail, benefit, gain, good, use, value.
profitable *adjective* advantageous, beneficial, commercial, fruitful, helpful, lucrative, moneymaking, paying, productive, remunerative, rewarding, useful, valuable, worthwhile.

profit² *verb* (*profit from*) be helped by, benefit from, capitalise on, exploit, gain from, make the most of.

profound *adjective* **1** deep, great, heartfelt, intense, sincere. **2** deep, erudite, intellectual, learned, penetrating, serious, thoughtful, wise.

profuse *adjective* abundant, ample, copious, extravagant, lavish, plentiful.

progeny *noun* children, descendants, family, offspring.

prognosis *noun* forecast, prediction.

programme *noun* **1** agenda, calendar, plan, schedule, timetable. **2** broadcast, performance, presentation, production, show, telecast.

progress¹ *noun* **1** advance, headway, march, strides. **2** advance, advancement, development, evolution, expansion, growth, improvement, progression.
in progress going on, happening, proceeding, taking place, under way.

progress² *verb* advance, come along, come on, continue, develop, go ahead, improve, make headway, move ahead, move forward, move on, proceed.
progression *noun* sequence, series, string, succession.

▶▶▶ D I C T I O N A R Y ◀◀◀

progressive *adjective* **1** moving forward. **2** proceeding step by step. **3** favouring rapid progress or reform.

prohibit *verb* (**prohibited, prohibiting**) forbid; ban, *Smoking is prohibited.* **prohibition** *noun* [from Latin, = keep off]

prohibitive *adjective* **1** prohibiting. **2** (of prices) so high that people will not buy things.

project[1] (*say* **proj**-ekt or **proh**-jekt) *noun* **1** a plan or scheme. **2** the task of finding out as much as you can about something and writing about it.

project[2] (*say* pro-**jekt**) *verb* **1** stick out. **2** throw outwards. **3** show a picture on a screen. **4** forecast. **projection** *noun* [from *pro-*, + Latin *-jectum* = thrown]

projectile *noun* a missile.

projectionist *noun* a person who works a projector.

projector *noun* a machine for showing films or photographs on a screen.

proletariat (*say* proh-lit-**air**-ee-at) *noun* working people.

proliferate *verb* (**proliferated, proliferating**) increase rapidly in numbers. **proliferation** *noun* [from Latin *proles* = offspring, + *ferre* = to bear]

prolific *adjective* producing much fruit or many flowers or other things. **prolifically** *adverb*

prologue (*say* **proh**-log) *noun* an introduction to a poem or play etc. [from Greek *pro-* = before, + *logos* = speech]

prolong *verb* make a thing longer or make it last for a long time. **prolongation** *noun*

prom *noun* (*informal*) **1** a promenade. **2** a promenade concert.

promenade (*say* prom-in-**ahd**) *noun* **1** a place suitable for walking, especially beside the seashore. **2** a leisurely walk. **promenade** *verb* **promenade concert** a concert where part of the audience may stand or walk about. [from French *se promener* = to walk]

prominent *adjective* **1** sticking out; projecting. **2** conspicuous. **3** important. **prominently** *adverb*, **prominence** *noun*

promiscuous *adjective* **1** indiscriminate. **2** having many casual sexual relationships. **promiscuously** *adverb*, **promiscuity** *noun*

promise[1] *noun* **1** a statement that you will definitely do or not do something. **2** an indication of future success or good results, *His work shows promise.*

promise[2] *verb* (**promised, promising**) make a promise.

▶▶▶ T H E S A U R U S ◀◀◀

progressive *adjective* **2** continuous, gradual, ongoing, steady. **3** avant-garde, enlightened, enterprising, forward-thinking, go-ahead, innovative, modern, up-and-coming (*informal*).

prohibit *verb* ban, bar, forbid, outlaw, proscribe, veto.

project[1] *noun* **1** enterprise, plan, proposal, scheme, undertaking, venture. **2** assignment, exercise, task.

project[2] *verb* **1** extend, jut out, overhang, protrude, stand out, stick out. **2** cast, fling, hurl, launch, propel, shoot, throw.
projection *noun* **1** ledge, overhang, ridge, shelf. **2** estimate, estimation, extrapolation, forecast, prediction.

projectile *noun* bullet, grenade, missile, rocket, shell, shot.

proletariat *noun* commoners, masses, plebs (*informal*), rank and file, wage earners, workers, working class.

proliferate *verb* burgeon, increase, multiply, mushroom.

prolific *adjective* fertile, fruitful, productive.

prologue *noun* foreword, introduction, preamble, preface, prelude.

prolong *verb* drag out, draw out, extend, lengthen, protract, spin out, stretch out, string out.

promenade *noun* **1** boulevard, esplanade, mall, parade. **2** amble, saunter, stroll, walk.

prominent *adjective* **1** jutting out, projecting, protruding, sticking out. **2** conspicuous, noticeable, obtrusive, obvious, pronounced, salient, striking. **3** celebrated, distinguished, eminent, famous, illustrious, important, notable, outstanding, pre-eminent, renowned, well-known.

promiscuous *adjective* **2** fast, immoral, licentious, loose, wanton.

promise[1] *noun* **1** assurance, commitment, contract, covenant, guarantee, oath, pledge, vow, word, word of honour. **2** aptitude, capability, potential, talent.

promise[2] *verb* agree, assure, commit yourself, give your word, guarantee, pledge, swear, undertake, vow.

▶▶ D I C T I O N A R Y ◀◀

promising *adjective* likely to be good or successful, *a promising pianist.*

promontory *noun* (*plural* **promontories**) a piece of high land that sticks out into a sea or lake.

promote *verb* (**promoted, promoting**) **1** move a person to a higher rank or position. **2** help the progress of something. **3** publicise a product. **promoter** *noun*, **promotion** *noun* [from *pro-*, + Latin *motum* = moved]

prompt¹ *adjective* **1** without delay, *a prompt reply.* **2** punctual. **promptly** *adverb*, **promptness** *noun*, **promptitude** *noun*

prompt² *verb* **1** cause or encourage a person to do something. **2** remind an actor or speaker of words when he or she has forgotten them. **prompter** *noun* [from Latin *promptum* = produced]

promulgate *verb* (**promulgated, promulgating**) make known to the public; proclaim. **promulgation** *noun*

prone *adjective* lying face downwards. (The opposite is *supine*.)
be prone to be likely to do or suffer something, *He is prone to headaches.*

prong *noun* a spike of a fork. **pronged** *adjective*

pronoun *noun* a word used instead of a noun. **demonstrative pronouns** are *this, that, these, those*; **interrogative pronouns** are *who? what? which?*, etc.; **personal pronouns** are *I, me, we,* *us, thou, thee, you, ye, he, him, she, her, it, they, them*; **possessive pronouns** are *mine, yours, theirs*, etc.; **reflexive pronouns** are *myself, yourself*, etc.; **relative pronouns** are *who, what, which, that.*

pronounce *verb* (**pronounced, pronouncing**) **1** say a sound or word in a particular way, '*Two*' is pronounced like '*too*'. **2** declare formally, *I now pronounce you man and wife.* [from *pro-*, + Latin *nuntiare* = announce]

pronounced *adjective* noticeable, *She walks with a pronounced limp.*

pronouncement *noun* a declaration.

pronunciation *noun* **1** the way a word is pronounced. **2** the way a person pronounces words.

proof¹ *noun* **1** a fact or thing that shows something is true. **2** a printed copy of a book or photograph etc. made for checking before other copies are printed.

proof² *adjective* able to resist something or not be penetrated, *a bullet-proof jacket.*

prop¹ *noun* a support, especially one made of a long piece of wood or metal.

prop² *verb* (**propped, propping**) support something by leaning it against something else.

prop³ *noun* (*Australian*) a sudden stop by a horse when galloping. **prop** *verb*

propaganda *noun* publicity intended to make people believe something.

▶▶ T H E S A U R U S ◀◀

promising *adjective* (*a promising start*) auspicious, encouraging, favourable, propitious, reassuring; (*a promising actor*) able, gifted, talented, up-and-coming (*informal*).

promontory *noun* cape, head, headland, point.

promote *verb* **1** advance, elevate, move up, raise, upgrade. **2** advance, boost, encourage, facilitate, foster, further, help, sponsor, support. **3** advertise, hype up (*slang*), make known, market, plug (*informal*), publicise, push.

prompt¹ *adjective* **1** early, expeditious, immediate, instant, instantaneous, quick, speedy, swift. **2** on time, punctual.
promptly *adverb* **1** at once, expeditiously, immediately, instantly, quickly, readily, right away, speedily, straight away, swiftly, without delay. **2** on the dot, on the knocker (*Australian informal*), on time, punctually.

prompt² *verb* **1** egg on, encourage, incite, induce, influence, inspire, motivate, move, spur, stimulate. **2** cue, jog the memory of, remind.

prone *adjective* face down, flat, horizontal, prostrate.
be prone to be inclined to, be liable to, be predisposed to, be subject to, be susceptible to.

prong *noun* point, spike, tine.

pronounce *verb* **1** articulate, enunciate, say, sound, speak, utter, voice. **2** announce, declare, proclaim.

pronounced *adjective* apparent, clear, clear-cut, conspicuous, definite, distinct, evident, marked, noticeable, obvious, prominent, striking, strong, unmistakable.

proof¹ *noun* **1** confirmation, corroboration, demonstration, documentation, evidence, facts, grounds, substantiation, testimony, verification.

prop¹ *noun* brace, buttress, post, reinforcement, stake, stay, strut, support.

prop² *verb* lean, rest, stand.
prop up brace, buttress, hold up, reinforce, shore up, stake, strengthen, support.

prop³ *verb* baulk, jib, pull up, stop.

▶▶▶ DICTIONARY ◀◀◀

propagate *verb* (**propagated, propagating**) **1** breed; reproduce. **2** send out or transmit sound, light, etc. **propagation** *noun*, **propagator** *noun*

propel *verb* (**propelled, propelling**) push something forward. [from *pro-*, + Latin *pellere* = to drive]

propellant *noun* a substance that propels things, *Liquid fuel is the propellant used in these rockets.*

propeller *noun* a device with blades that spin round to drive an aircraft or ship.

propensity *noun* (*plural* **propensities**) a tendency.

proper *adjective* **1** suitable; right, *the proper way to hold a bat.* **2** respectable, *prim and proper.* **3** (*informal*) complete; great, *You're a proper nuisance!* **properly** *adverb*

proper fraction a fraction that is less than unity, with the numerator less than the denominator, e.g. ⅗.

proper noun the name of one person or thing, e.g. *Mary, Darwin, Spain.* [from Latin *proprius* = your own]

property *noun* (*plural* **properties**) **1** a thing or things that belong to somebody. **2** a building or someone's land. **3** a quality or characteristic, *It has the property of becoming soft when heated.* [same origin as *proper*]

prophecy *noun* (*plural* **prophecies**) **1** a statement that prophesies something. **2** the action of prophesying.

prophesy *verb* (**prophesied, prophesying**) forecast; foretell. [from Greek *pro* = before, + *phanai* = speak]

prophet *noun* **1** a person who makes prophecies. **2** a religious teacher who is believed to be inspired by God. **prophetess** *noun*, **prophetic** *adjective*
the Prophet Muhammad, who founded the Muslim faith.

propinquity *noun* nearness.

propitiate (*say* pro-**pish**-ee-ayt) *verb* (**propitiated, propitiating**) win a person's favour or forgiveness. **propitiation** *noun*, **propitiatory** *adjective*

propitious (*say* pro-**pish**-us) *adjective* favourable.

proponent (*say* prop-**oh**-nent) *noun* the person who puts forward a proposal. [from *pro-*, + Latin *ponere* = to place]

proportion *noun* **1** a part or share of a whole thing. **2** a ratio. **3** the correct relationship in size, amount, or importance between two things. **proportional** *adjective*, **proportionally** *adverb*, **proportionate** *adjective*
proportions *plural noun* size, *a ship of large proportions.*
proportional representation a system in which each political party has a number of Members of Parliament in proportion to the number of votes for all its candidates. [from *pro-* + *portion*]

propose *verb* (**proposed, proposing**) **1** suggest an idea or plan etc. **2** ask a person to marry you. **proposal** *noun* [from *pro-*, + Latin *positum* = put]

proposition *noun* **1** a suggestion. **2** a statement. **3** (*informal*) an undertaking; a matter, *a difficult proposition.*

▶▶▶ THESAURUS ◀◀◀

propel *verb* catapult, drive, eject, fling, impel, push, send, shoot, throw, thrust.

propensity *noun* inclination, leaning, penchant, predisposition, proclivity, proneness, tendency.

proper *adjective* **1** accepted, appropriate, apt, conventional, correct, established, fitting, orthodox, right, standard, suitable. **2** courteous, decent, decorous, dignified, formal, polite, prim, respectable, seemly. **3** absolute, complete, real, thorough, utter.

property *noun* **1** assets, belongings, chattels, effects, fortune, gear, goods, possessions, riches, things, wealth. **2** building(s), land, real estate. **3** characteristic, feature, quality, trait.

prophecy *noun* **1** forecast, prediction.

prophesy *verb* forecast, foresee, foretell, predict.

prophet *noun* **1** augur, forecaster, fortune-teller, oracle, prophetess (*female*), seer, sibyl (*female*), soothsayer.

propitious *adjective* advantageous, auspicious, favourable, fortunate, lucky, opportune, timely.

proportion *noun* **1** cut (*informal*), division, fraction, part, percentage, piece, portion, quota, section, share. **2** balance, ratio, relationship.
proportions *plural noun* dimensions, extent, magnitude, measurements, size.

propose *verb* **1** advance, offer, present, proffer, propound, put forward, recommend, submit, suggest, tender.
proposal *noun* bid, offer, plan, project, proposition, recommendation, scheme, submission, suggestion.

▶▶DICTIONARY◀◀

propound *verb* put forward an idea for consideration. [same origin as *propose*]

proprietary (*say* pro-**pry**-it-er-ee) *adjective* **1** made or sold by one firm; branded, *proprietary medicines*. **2** of an owner or ownership. [same origin as *property*]

proprietor *noun* the owner of a shop or business. **proprietress** *noun*

propriety (*say* pro-**pry**-it-ee) *noun* (*plural* **proprieties**) **1** being proper. **2** correct behaviour.

propulsion *noun* propelling something.

prorogue *verb* (**prorogued, proroguing**) stop the meetings of Parliament temporarily without dissolving it. **prorogation** *noun* [from Latin *prorogare* = prolong]

prosaic *adjective* plain or dull and ordinary. **prosaically** *adverb* [from *prose*]

proscribe *verb* (**proscribed, proscribing**) forbid by law. [from Latin *proscribere* = to outlaw]

prose *noun* writing or speech that is not in verse.

prosecute *verb* (**prosecuted, prosecuting**) **1** make someone go to a lawcourt to be tried for a crime. **2** perform; carry on, *prosecuting their trade*. **prosecution** *noun*, **prosecutor** *noun* [from Latin *prosecutus* = pursued]

proselyte *noun* a person who has been converted to the Jewish faith or from one religion, opinion, etc. to another.

prosody (*say* **pross**-od-ee) *noun* the study of verse and its structure.

prospect[1] *noun* **1** a possibility, *There is no prospect of success.* **2** a wide view.

prospect[2] (*say* pro-**spekt**) *verb* explore in search of something, *prospecting for gold.* **prospector** *noun* [from Latin *pro* = forward, + *spectere* = to look]

prospective *adjective* expected to be or to happen; possible, *prospective customers*.

prospectus *noun* (*plural* **prospectuses**) a booklet describing and advertising a school, business company, etc.

prosper *verb* be successful.

prosperous *adjective* successful; rich. **prosperity** *noun*

prostitute *noun* a person who takes part in sexual acts for payment. **prostitution** *noun* [from Latin, = for sale]

prostrate[1] *adjective* lying face downwards.

prostrate[2] *verb* (**prostrated, prostrating**) cause to be prostrate. **prostration** *noun* [from Latin *prostratum* = laid flat]

protagonist *noun* **1** the main character in a play. **2** a person competing against another. [from *proto-*, + Greek *agonistes* = actor]

protect *verb* keep safe from harm or injury. **protection** *noun*, **protective** *adjective*, **protector** *noun* [from *pro-*, + Latin *tectum* = covered]

▶▶THESAURUS◀◀

proprietor *noun* landlady, landlord, manager, owner, proprietress.

propriety *noun* **2** correctness, courtesy, decency, decorum, politeness, respectability, seemliness.

prosaic *adjective* banal, boring, commonplace, dull, humdrum, monotonous, mundane, ordinary, pedestrian, routine, uninspiring, uninteresting, workaday.

proscribe *verb* ban, bar, forbid, outlaw, prohibit.

prosecute *verb* **1** accuse, bring to trial, charge, indict, sue, take to court, try.

prospect[1] *noun* **1** chance, hope, likelihood, odds, outlook, possibility, probability. **2** outlook, panorama, scene, sight, view, vista.

prospect[2] *verb* explore, fossick (*Australian informal*), look, search.

prospective *adjective* future, likely, possible, potential, would-be.

prosper *verb* boom, do well, flourish, grow, make money, succeed, thrive.

prosperous *adjective* affluent, flourishing, moneyed, rich, successful, thriving, wealthy, well-heeled (*informal*), well off, well-to-do. **prosperity** *noun* affluence, fortune, plenty, riches, success, wealth.

prostitute *noun* call-girl, courtesan (*old use*), harlot (*old use*), hooker (*slang*), sex worker, whore.

prostrate[1] *adjective* face down, flat, horizontal, procumbent, prone.

prostrate[2] *verb* (*prostrate yourself*) bow, kneel, kowtow, throw yourself down.

protect *verb* care for, cherish, cover, defend, guard, insulate, keep safe, look after, mind, preserve, safeguard, screen, secure, shelter, shield, take care of, tend, watch over. **protection** *noun* armour, barrier, buffer, cover, defence, immunity, refuge, safeguard, screen, security, shelter, shield. **protective** *adjective* (*a protective person*) possessive, solicitous, vigilant, watchful; (*protective clothing*) covering, fireproof, insulating, protecting, waterproof.

▶▶▶ D I C T I O N A R Y ◀◀

protectorate *noun* a country that is under the official protection of a stronger country.

protégé (*say* **prot**-e*zh*-ay) *noun* a person who is given helpful protection or encouragement by another. [French, = protected]

protein *noun* a substance that is found in all living things and is an essential part of the food of animals.

protest[1] (*say* **proh**-test) *noun* a statement or action showing that you disapprove of something.

protest[2] (*say* pro-**test**) *verb* 1 make a protest. 2 declare firmly, *They protested their innocence.* **protestation** *noun*, **protester** *noun* [from *pro-*, + Latin *testari* = say on oath]

Protestant *noun* a member of any of the Western Christian Churches separated from the Roman Catholic Church. [because in the 16th century many people protested (= declared firmly) their opposition to the Catholic Church]

proto- *prefix* first. [from Greek *protos* = first or earliest]

protocol *noun* etiquette connected with people's rank.

proton *noun* a particle of matter with a positive electric charge.

prototype *noun* the first model of something, from which others are copied or developed. [from *proto-* + *type*]

protract *verb* prolong in time; lengthen. **protraction** *noun* [from *pro-*, + Latin *tractum* = drawn out]

protractor *noun* a device for measuring angles, usually a semicircle marked off in degrees.

protrude *verb* (**protruded, protruding**) project; stick out. **protrusion** *noun* [from *pro-*, + Latin *trudere* = push]

protuberance *noun* a protuberant part.

protuberant *adjective* sticking out from a surface. [from *pro-*, + Latin *tuber* = a swelling]

proud *adjective* 1 very pleased with yourself or with someone else who has done well. 2 causing pride, *This is a proud moment for us.* 3 full of self-respect and independence, *They were too proud to ask for help.* 4 having an unduly high opinion of your own merits or importance. **proudly** *adverb* [from Old French *prud* = brave]

prove *verb* (**proved, proving**) 1 show that something is true. 2 turn out, *The forecast proved to be correct.* **provable** *adjective* [from Latin *probare* = to test]

proven (*say* **proo**-ven) *adjective* proved, *a man of proven ability.*

provender *noun* fodder; food.

proverb *noun* a short well-known saying that states a truth, e.g. 'Many hands make light work'. [from *pro-*, + Latin *verbum* = word]

proverbial *adjective* 1 of or in a proverb. 2 well-known.

provide *verb* (**provided, providing**) 1 make something available; supply. 2 prepare for something, *Try to provide against emergencies.* **provider** *noun* [from Latin *providere* = foresee]

provided *conjunction* on condition, *You can stay provided that you help.*

providence *noun* 1 being provident. 2 God's or nature's care and protection.

▶▶▶ T H E S A U R U S ◀◀

protest[1] *noun* beef (*slang*), complaint, demur, grumble, hue and cry, objection, outcry; see also DEMONSTRATION.

protest[2] *verb* 1 beef (*slang*), be up in arms, complain, demonstrate, demur, grumble, moan, object, remonstrate, squeal (*informal*). 2 affirm, assert, avow, declare, insist on, maintain, profess.
protester *noun* agitator, complainer, demonstrator, dissident, objector.

prototype *noun* archetype, original, sample, trial model.

protract *verb* drag out, draw out, extend, lengthen, prolong, spin out, stretch out.

protrude *verb* bulge, jut out, poke out, project, stand out, stick out.

proud *adjective* 1 delighted, gratified, happy, pleased, satisfied. 3 dignified, independent, self-respecting. 4 arrogant, boastful, cocky, conceited, disdainful, egotistic(al), haughty, high and mighty, hoity-toity, self-satisfied, smug, snobbish, snooty (*informal*), stuck-up (*informal*), supercilious, superior, vain.

prove *verb* 1 bear out, confirm, corroborate, demonstrate, document, establish, show, substantiate, verify. 2 be found, turn out.

proverb *noun* adage, axiom, catchphrase, dictum, maxim, motto, saying, slogan.

provide *verb* 1 allot, arm, contribute, donate, endow, equip, furnish, give, grant, offer, present, supply. 2 (*provide for*) allow for, anticipate, cater for, make provision for, plan for, prepare for.

▶▶ D I C T I O N A R Y ◀◀

provident *adjective* wisely providing for the future; thrifty. [same origin as *provide*]

providential *adjective* happening very luckily. **providentially** *adverb*

providing *conjunction* provided.

province *noun* 1 a section of a country. 2 the area of a person's special knowledge or responsibility, *Teaching you to swim is not my province.* **provincial** *adjective*
    the provinces the parts of a country outside its capital city.

provision *noun* 1 providing something. 2 a statement in a document, *the provisions of the treaty.*
    provisions *plural noun* supplies of food and drink.

provisional *adjective* arranged or agreed upon temporarily but possibly to be altered later. **provisionally** *adverb*

proviso (*say* prov-**I**-zoh) *noun* (*plural* **provisos**) a requirement before agreeing to something.

provoke *verb* (**provoked, provoking**) 1 make a person angry. 2 arouse; stimulate, *The joke provoked laughter.* **provocation** *noun,* **provocative** *adjective* [from *pro-,* + Latin *vocare* = summon]

prow *noun* the front end of a ship.

prowess *noun* 1 great ability. 2 daring.

prowl *verb* move about quietly or cautiously. **prowl** *noun,* **prowler** *noun*

proximity *noun* 1 nearness. 2 the part near something, *in the proximity of the station.* [from Latin *proximus* = nearest]

proxy *noun* (*plural* **proxies**) a person authorised to represent or act for another person.

prude *noun* a person who is easily shocked. **prudish** *adjective,* **prudery** *noun*

prudent *adjective* careful, not rash or reckless. **prudently** *adverb,* **prudence** *noun,* **prudential** *adjective* [same origin as *provide*]

prune¹ *noun* a dried plum.

prune² *verb* (**pruned, pruning**) cut off unwanted parts of a tree or bush etc.

pry *verb* (**pried, prying**) look or ask inquisitively.

PS *abbreviation* postscript.

psalm (*say* sahm) *noun* a religious song, especially one from the Book of Psalms in the Bible. **psalmist** *noun* [from Greek, = song sung to the harp]

pseudo- (*say* s'**yood**-oh) *prefix* false; pretended. [Greek, = false]

pseudonym *noun* a false name used by an author. [from *pseudo-,* + Greek *onyma* = name]

▶▶ T H E S A U R U S ◀◀

providential *adjective* fortunate, heaven-sent, lucky, opportune, timely.

province *noun* 1 area, district, region, state, territory. 2 area, domain, field, responsibility, sphere.
    provincial *adjective* country, district, local, regional, rural.

provision *noun* 1 arrangement, plan, preparation. 2 clause, condition, proviso, requirement, specification, stipulation, term.
    provisions *plural noun* food, groceries, rations, stores, supplies.

provisional *adjective* interim, stopgap, temporary.

proviso *noun* condition, provision, qualification, requirement, rider, stipulation.

provoke *verb* 1 anger, annoy, enrage, exasperate, incense, infuriate, irritate, madden, needle (*informal*), outrage, rile (*informal*), upset, vex, wind up (*informal*). 2 arouse, cause, draw, elicit, evoke, generate, inspire, produce, prompt, spark, stimulate, trigger.
    provocative *adjective* (*a provocative dress*) alluring, inviting, seductive, sexy, tantalising,

tempting; (*a provocative comment*) annoying, exasperating, infuriating, irritating, maddening.

prow *noun* bow, front, nose.

prowess *noun* 1 ability, aptitude, competence, expertise, genius, proficiency, skill, talent. 2 boldness, bravery, courage, daring, grit, guts (*informal*), heroism, mettle, valour.

prowl *verb* lurk, roam, skulk, slink, sneak, steal.

prudent *adjective* careful, cautious, far-sighted, judicious, politic, sage, sensible, shrewd, smart, wise.

prudish *adjective* demure, narrow-minded, old-fashioned, prim, prissy, puritanical, strait-laced.

prune² *verb* chop, cut back, lop, remove, snip off, trim.

pry *verb* delve, inquire, interfere, intrude, meddle, poke about, probe, snoop (*informal*), stickybeak (*Australian informal*).

pseudonym *noun* alias, assumed name, false name, nom de plume, pen-name.

▶▶▶ D I C T I O N A R Y ◀◀◀

psychiatrist (*say* sy-**ky**-a-trist) *noun* a doctor who treats mental illnesses. **psychiatry** *noun*, **psychiatric** *adjective* [from *psycho-*, + Greek *iatreia* = healing]

psychic (*say* **sy**-kik) *adjective* 1 of powers or events that seem to be supernatural. 2 of the mind or soul. **psychical** *adjective* [same origin as *psycho-*]

psycho- *prefix* of the mind. [from Greek *psyche* = life or soul]

psychoanalysis *noun* investigation of a person's mental processes, especially in psychotherapy.

psychology *noun* the study of the mind and how it works. **psychological** *adjective*, **psychologist** *noun* [from *psycho-* + *-logy*]

psychotherapy *noun* treatment of mental illness by psychological methods.

PT *abbreviation* physical training.

ptarmigan (*say* **tar**-mig-an) *noun* a bird of the grouse family.

pterodactyl (*say* te-ro-**dak**-til) *noun* an extinct reptile with wings. [from Greek *pteron* = wing, + *daktylos* = finger]

PTO *abbreviation* please turn over.

pub *noun* (*informal*) a place licensed to serve alcoholic drinks to the public.

puberty (*say* **pew**-ber-tee) *noun* the time when a young person is developing physically into an adult.

pubic (*say* **pew**-bik) *adjective* of the lower front part of the abdomen.

public[1] *adjective* belonging to or known by everyone, not private. **publicly** *adverb*
public school a school run by the State.
public service people employed by the government in various departments other than the armed forces.

public[2] *noun* all the people.
in public openly, not in private. [from Latin *publicus* = of the people]

publican *noun* the person in charge of a pub; a hotel-keeper.

publication *noun* 1 publishing. 2 a published book or newspaper etc.

publicise *verb* (**publicised, publicising**) bring something to people's attention; advertise.

publicity *noun* 1 public attention. 2 doing things (e.g. advertising) to draw people's attention to something.

publish *verb* 1 have something printed and sold to the public. 2 announce something in public. **publisher** *noun* [from *public*]

puce *noun* brownish-purple colour. [French, = flea-colour]

puck *noun* a hard rubber disc used in ice hockey.

pucker *verb* wrinkle. **pucker** *noun*

pudding *noun* 1 a food made in a soft mass, especially in a mixture of flour and other ingredients. 2 the sweet course of a meal.

puddle *noun* a shallow patch of liquid, especially of rainwater on a road.

pudgy *adjective* podgy.

▶▶▶ T H E S A U R U S ◀◀◀

psychic *adjective* 1 clairvoyant, extrasensory, occult, paranormal, supernatural, telepathic.

psychological *adjective* emotional, mental.

pub *noun* bar, hotel (*Australian*), inn, local (*informal*), public house, saloon (*American*), tavern.

puberty *noun* adolescence, pubescence, teens.

public[1] *adjective* civic, civil, common, community, council, general, government, municipal, national, popular, state; (*public information*) disclosed, familiar, known, open, published, unconcealed.
public servant bureaucrat, civil servant (*British & American*), functionary, government employee, official.

public[2] *noun* citizens, community, country, electorate, nation, people, populace, population, society, voters.
in public openly, publicly.

publican *noun* hotelier, hotel-keeper, innkeeper, landlady, landlord, licensee, proprietor, proprietress.

publicise *verb* advertise, announce, hype up (*slang*), make known, plug (*informal*), promote, publish, push.

publicity *noun* 1 attention, fame, limelight, notice. 2 advertising, build-up, hype (*slang*), marketing, plug (*informal*), promotion, propaganda.

publish *verb* 1 bring out, issue, release; see also PRINT[1]. 2 advertise, announce, broadcast, disclose, disseminate, make known, make public, proclaim, promulgate, publicise, report, reveal.

pucker *verb* contract, crinkle, furrow, gather, screw up, wrinkle.
pucker *noun* crease, crinkle, fold, gather, pleat, tuck, wrinkle.

puddle *noun* pool.

puerile (say **pew**-er-I'll) adjective silly and childish. **puerility** noun [from Latin puer = boy]

puff¹ noun **1** a short blowing of breath, wind, or smoke etc. **2** a soft pad for putting powder on the skin. **3** a cake of very light pastry filled with cream.

puff² verb **1** blow out puffs of smoke etc. **2** breathe with difficulty; pant. **3** inflate or swell something, He puffed out his chest.

puffin noun a sea-bird with a large striped beak.

puffy adjective puffed out; swollen. **puffiness** noun

pug noun a small dog with a flat face like a bulldog.

pugilist (say **pew**-jil-ist) noun a boxer.

pugnacious adjective wanting to fight; aggressive. **pugnaciously** adverb, **pugnacity** noun [from Latin pugnare = to fight]

pull verb **1** make a thing come towards or after you by using force on it. **2** move by a driving force, The car pulled out into the road. **3** damage a muscle by abnormal strain. **pull** noun

pull a face make a strange face.

pull off achieve something.

pull somebody's leg deceive him or her playfully.

pull through recover from an illness.

pull up stop.

pull yourself together become calm or sensible.

pullet noun a young hen.

pulley noun (plural **pulleys**) a wheel with a rope, chain, or belt over it, used for lifting or moving heavy things.

pullover noun a knitted garment (with no fastenings) for the top half of the body.

pulmonary (say **pul**-mon-er-ee) adjective of the lungs. [from Latin pulmo = lung]

pulp noun **1** the soft moist part of fruit. **2** any soft moist mass. **pulpy** adjective

pulpit noun a small enclosed platform for the preacher in a church or chapel.

pulsate verb (**pulsated, pulsating**) expand and contract rhythmically; vibrate. **pulsation** noun

pulse¹ noun **1** the rhythmical movement of the arteries as blood is pumped through them by the beating of the heart, The pulse can be felt in a person's wrists. **2** a throb.

pulse² verb (**pulsed, pulsing**) throb. [from Latin pulsum = driven, beaten]

pulse³ noun the edible seed of peas, beans, lentils, etc.

pulverise verb (**pulverised, pulverising**) crush into powder. **pulverisation** noun [from Latin pulveris = of dust]

puma (say **pew**-ma) noun a large brown animal of western America, also called a cougar or mountain lion.

pumice noun a kind of porous volcanic rock used for rubbing stains from the skin or as powder for polishing things.

pummel verb (**pummelled, pummelling**) keep on hitting something.

pump¹ noun a device that pushes air or liquid into or out of something, or along pipes.

puerile adjective childish, foolish, immature, infantile, juvenile, silly.

puff¹ noun **1** blast, breath, draught, gust.

puff² verb **2** blow, exhale, gasp, heave, huff, pant, wheeze. **3** (puff up) bloat, blow up, distend, expand, inflate, swell.

puffy adjective puffed up, swollen.

pugnacious adjective aggressive, argumentative, bellicose, belligerent, combative, hostile, hot-tempered, militant, quarrelsome.

pull verb **1** drag, draw, haul, heave, jerk, lug, tow, trail, tug, wrench, yank (informal). **3** sprain, strain, stretch, tear, wrench.

pull down demolish, destroy, dismantle, knock down, level, raze, remove, take down, tear down.

pull off accomplish, achieve, carry off, do, manage, succeed in.

pull out draw, extract, remove, take out, withdraw.

pull somebody's leg have on (informal), kid (informal), tease, trick.

pull through get better, rally, recover, survive.

pull up draw up, halt, stop.

pullover noun jersey, jumper, sweater.

pulp noun **1** flesh. **2** mash, mush, purée.

pulsate verb beat, palpitate, pound, pulse, quiver, throb, thump, vibrate.

pulse¹ noun **2** beat, pulsation, rhythm, throb, vibration.

pulverise verb crush, grind, mill, pound.

pummel verb hit, pound, punch.

pump² *verb* **1** move air or liquid with a pump. **2** (*informal*) question a person to obtain information.
pump up inflate.

pump³ *noun* a lightweight shoe.

pumpkin *noun* a very large rounded vegetable with a hard skin.

pun *noun* a joking use of a word sounding the same as another, e.g. 'Deciding where to bury him was a *grave* decision'.

punch¹ *verb* **1** hit with a fist. **2** make a hole in something.

punch² *noun* (*plural* **punches**) **1** a hit with a fist. **2** a device for making holes in paper, metal, leather, etc. **3** vigour.
punch line words that give the climax of a joke or story. [same origin as *puncture*]

punch³ *noun* a drink made by mixing wine or spirits and fruit-juice in a bowl.

punch-up *noun* (*informal*) a fight.

punctilious *adjective* very careful about details; conscientious. **punctiliously** *adverb*, **punctiliousness** *noun* [from Latin *punctillum* = little point]

punctual *adjective* doing things exactly at the time arranged; not late. **punctually** *adverb*, **punctuality** *noun*

punctuate *verb* (**punctuated, punctuating**) **1** put punctuation marks into something. **2** put in at intervals, *His speech was punctuated with cheers.* [from Latin *punctum* = a point]

punctuation *noun* **1** marks such as commas, full stops, and brackets put into a piece of writing to make it easier to read. **2** the action of punctuating.

puncture¹ *noun* a small hole made by something sharp, especially in a tyre.

puncture² *verb* (**punctured, puncturing**) make a puncture in something. [from Latin *punctum* = pricked]

pundit *noun* a person who is an authority on something. [from Hindi *pandit* = learned (person)]

pungent (*say* **pun**-jent) *adjective* **1** having a strong taste or smell. **2** (of remarks) sharp. **pungently** *adverb*, **pungency** *noun* [from Latin *pungens* = pricking]

punish *verb* make a person suffer because he or she has done something wrong. **punishable** *adjective*, **punishment** *noun* [from Latin *poena* = penalty]

punitive (*say* **pew**-nit-iv) *adjective* inflicting punishment.

punnet *noun* a small container for soft fruit such as strawberries.

punt¹ *noun* a flat-bottomed boat, usually moved by pushing a pole against the bottom of a river while standing in the punt.

punt² *verb* move a punt with a pole.

punt³ *verb* kick a football after dropping it from your hands and before it touches the ground.

punt⁴ *verb* gamble; bet on a horse race. **punter** *noun*

puny (*say* **pew**-nee) *adjective* small or undersized; feeble.

pup *noun* **1** a puppy. **2** a young seal.

pupa (*say* **pew**-pa) *noun* (*plural* **pupae**) a chrysalis.

pupate (*say* pew-**payt**) *verb* (**pupated, pupating**) become a pupa. **pupation** *noun*

▶▶▶ T H E S A U R U S ◀◀

pump² *verb* **1** (*pump out*) drain, empty; (*pump up*) blow up, fill, inflate. **2** grill, interrogate, probe, question, quiz.

pun *noun* play on words.

punch¹ *verb* **1** bash, box, clout (*informal*), cuff, dong (*Australian informal*), hit, pummel, quilt (*Australian slang*), slog, slug, sock (*slang*), stoush (*Australian slang*), strike, thump.

punch² *noun* **1** blow, box, clout (*informal*), hit, slog, slug, sock (*slang*), thump. **3** force, forcefulness, power, vigour.

punctual *adjective* on schedule, on the dot, on the knocker (*Australian informal*), on time, prompt.

punctuate *verb* **2** break, dot, interrupt, intersperse, pepper.

puncture¹ *noun* hole, leak, perforation, rupture, slit, tear.

puncture² *verb* penetrate, perforate, pierce, prick.

pundit *noun* authority, expert, sage.

pungent *adjective* **1** acid, acrid, aromatic, hot, piquant, sharp, spicy, strong, tangy, tart.

punish *verb* castigate, chastise, discipline, make to suffer, penalise, scold, sentence.
punishment *noun* castigation, chastisement, discipline, fine, imposition, penalty, sentence.

punt⁴ *verb* bet, gamble, risk, speculate, stake, wager.

puny *adjective* feeble, frail, sickly, skinny, small, tiny, undersized, weak, weedy.

pup *noun* **1** puppy, whelp.

▶▶▶ D I C T I O N A R Y ◀◀◀

pupil *noun* **1** someone who is being taught by another person. **2** the opening in the centre of the eye. [from Latin *pupilla* = little girl or doll (the use of sense 2 refers to the tiny images of people and things that can be seen in the eye)]

puppet *noun* **1** a kind of doll that can be made to move by fitting it over your hand or working it by strings or wires. **2** a person whose actions are controlled by someone else. **puppetry** *noun*

puppy *noun* (*plural* **puppies**) a young dog.

purchase¹ *verb* (**purchased, purchasing**) buy. **purchaser** *noun*

purchase² *noun* **1** something bought. **2** buying. **3** a firm hold to pull or raise something.

purdah *noun* the Muslim or Hindu custom of keeping women from the sight of men or strangers. [Urdu, = veil]

pure *adjective* **1** not mixed with anything else; clean. **2** free from evil or sin. **3** mere; nothing but, *pure nonsense.* **purely** *adverb*, **pureness** *noun*

purée (*say* **pewr**-ay) *noun* fruit or vegetables made into pulp. [French, = squeezed]

purgative *noun* a strong laxative.

purgatory *noun* (in Roman Catholic belief) a place or condition in which souls are purified by punishment. [same origin as *purge*]

purge¹ *verb* (**purged, purging**) get rid of unwanted people or things.

purge² *noun* **1** purging. **2** a purgative. [from Latin *purgare* = make pure]

purify *verb* (**purified, purifying**) make a thing pure. **purification** *noun*, **purifier** *noun*

purist *noun* a person who likes things to be exactly right, especially in people's use of words.

Puritan *noun* a Protestant in the 16th and 17th centuries who wanted simpler religious ceremonies and strictly moral behaviour.

puritan *noun* a person with very strict morals. **puritanical** *adjective* [from Latin *puritas* = purity]

purity *noun* pureness.

purl¹ *noun* a knitting-stitch that makes a ridge towards the knitter. **purl** *verb* [from Scottish *pirl* = twist]

purl² *verb* (of a stream) ripple with a murmuring sound.

purloin *verb* take something without permission.

purple *noun* deep reddish-blue colour. **purple** *adjective*

purport¹ (*say* per-**port**) *verb* claim, *The letter purports to be from the council.* **purportedly** *adverb*

purport² (*say* **per**-port) *noun* meaning.

purpose *noun* **1** what you intend to do; a plan or aim. **2** determination. **purposeful** *adjective*, **purposefully** *adverb*, **purposeless** *adjective* **on purpose** by intention, not by accident. [same origin as *propose*]

▶▶▶ T H E S A U R U S ◀◀◀

pupil *noun* **1** apprentice, disciple, learner, scholar, schoolboy, schoolchild, schoolgirl, student.

puppet *noun* **1** doll, finger puppet, glove puppet, marionette, string puppet.

purchase¹ *verb* acquire, buy, get, obtain, pay for.
purchaser *noun* buyer, customer.

purchase² *noun* **1** acquisition, buy.

pure *adjective* **1** clean, clear, fresh, solid, straight, unadulterated, unalloyed, uncontaminated, undiluted, unmixed, unpolluted, untainted. **2** blameless, chaste, decent, good, guiltless, innocent, modest, moral, sinless, uncorrupted, upright, virtuous. **3** absolute, complete, downright, perfect, sheer, thorough, total, utter.

purée *noun* mash, mush, pulp.

purgative *noun* enema, laxative, purge.

purge¹ *verb* clear out, dismiss, eliminate, eradicate, expel, get rid of, remove, weed out.

purify *verb* clean, disinfect, distil, filter, refine, sterilise.

purist *noun* dogmatist, pedant, stickler.

puritanical *adjective* ascetic, austere, moralistic, prim, prudish, strait-laced, strict, wowserish (*Australian*).

purple *adjective* amethyst, hyacinth, jacaranda, lavender, lilac, mauve, mulberry, plum, violet.

purport¹ *verb* allege, claim, pretend, profess.

purport² *noun* drift, gist, meaning, substance, thrust.

purpose *noun* **1** aim, function, goal, intent, intention, justification, motivation, motive, object, objective, point, use, value. **2** determination, resolution, resolve, single-mindedness.
purposeless *adjective* aimless, meaningless, pointless, senseless, useless.
on purpose consciously, deliberately, intentionally, knowingly, purposely, wittingly.

▶▶ D I C T I O N A R Y ◀◀

purposely *adverb* on purpose.

purr *verb* make the low murmuring sound that a cat does when it is pleased. **purr** *noun*

purse¹ *noun* a small pouch for carrying money.

purse² *verb* (**pursed, pursing**) draw into folds, *She pursed her lips.* [from Latin *bursa* = a bag]

purser *noun* a ship's officer in charge of accounts. [from *purse*]

pursuance *noun* performing or carrying out an intention etc., *in pursuance of my duties.*

pursue *verb* (**pursued, pursuing**) 1 chase in order to catch or kill. 2 continue with something; work at, *We are pursuing our enquiries.* **pursuer** *noun*

pursuit *noun* 1 the action of pursuing. 2 a regular activity.

purvey *verb* (**purveyed, purveying**) supply food etc. as a trade. **purveyor** *noun* [same origin as *provide*]

pus *noun* a thick yellowish substance produced in inflamed or infected tissue, e.g. in an abscess or boil.

push¹ *verb* 1 make a thing go away from you by using force on it. 2 move yourself by using force, *He pushed in front of me.* 3 try to force someone to do or use something; urge.
push off (*slang*) go away.

push² *noun* (*plural* **pushes**) 1 a pushing movement or effort. 2 (*Australian*) a gang or set.
at a push if necessary but only with difficulty.

pushchair *noun* a folding chair on wheels, in which a child can be pushed along.

pusher *noun* 1 a seller of illegal drugs. 2 (*Australian*) a pushchair, a stroller.

pushover *noun* (*informal*) 1 something that is easily done. 2 a person who is easily convinced or defeated.

pushy *adjective* unpleasantly self-confident and eager to do things.

pusillanimous (*say* pew-sil-**an**-im-us) *adjective* timid; cowardly. [from Latin *pusillus* = small, + *animus* = mind]

puss *noun* (*informal*) a cat.

pussy *noun* (*plural* **pussies**) (*informal*) a cat.

pustule *noun* a pimple containing pus.

put *verb* (**put, putting**) This word has many uses, including (1) move a person or thing to a place or position (*Put the lamp on the table*), (2) cause a person or thing to do or experience something or be in a certain condition (*Put the light on. Put her in a good mood*). (3) express in words (*She put it tactfully*).
be hard put have difficulty in doing something.
put by save for future use.
put down suppress; snub; kill an old or sick animal.
put forward suggest, propose.

▶▶ T H E S A U R U S ◀◀

purse¹ *noun* pouch, wallet.

purse² *verb* press together, pucker, squeeze.

pursue *verb* 1 chase, follow, go after, hound, hunt, run after, shadow, stalk, tail (*informal*), track down, trail. 2 carry on, conduct, continue, engage in, follow, work at.

pursuit *noun* 1 chase, hunt, stalking, tracking. 2 activity, hobby, interest, occupation, pastime, recreation.

push¹ *verb* 1 drive, move, propel, shove, thrust. 2 advance, butt, elbow, force, forge, jostle, nudge, press, ram, shoulder, shove, squeeze, thrust. 3 bully, coerce, compel, dragoon, drive, egg on, encourage, force, goad, hound, press, pressure, spur, urge.

pusher *noun* 1 dealer, peddler, seller. 2 pushchair, stroller.

pushover *noun* 1 bludge (*Australian informal*), breeze (*informal*), child's play, cinch (*informal*), doddle (*informal*), piece of cake

(*informal*), snack (*Australian informal*), snap (*informal*), walkover. 2 dupe, easy prey, mug (*informal*), sitter (*informal*), sitting duck (*informal*), soft touch, sucker (*informal*).

pushy *adjective* aggressive, assertive, bumptious, forceful, forward, self-assertive.

put *verb* 1 arrange, bung (*informal*), deposit, dump, fit, hang, implant, insert, install, lay, leave, locate, mount, place, plant, plonk, pop, position, rest, set down, settle, situate, slap, stand, station, stick. 3 express, formulate, phrase, say, state, word.
put by put aside, reserve, save, set aside, stash (*informal*).
put down 1 crush, quash, quell, stop, subdue, suppress. 2 belittle, denigrate, disparage, humiliate, slight, snub. 3 destroy, kill, put to sleep.
put forward advance, nominate, offer, present, propose, propound, put up, recommend, submit, suggest.

▶▶ DICTIONARY ◀◀

put off postpone; dissuade; stop someone wanting something, *The smell puts me off.*

put on clothe yourself with; assume; pretend to have; increase; stage a play etc.

put out stop a fire from burning or a light from shining; annoy or inconvenience, *Our lateness has put her out.*

put up build; raise; give someone a place to sleep; provide, *Who will put up the money?*

put up with endure; tolerate.

putrefy (*say* **pew**-trif-I) *verb* (**putrefied, putrefying**) decay; rot. **putrefaction** *noun* [from Latin *puter* = rotten]

putrid (*say* **pew**-trid) *adjective* 1 decomposed; rotting. 2 smelling bad.

putt *verb* hit a golf-ball gently towards the hole. **putt** *noun*, **putter** *noun*, **putting-green** *noun*

putty *noun* a soft paste that sets hard, used for fitting the glass into a window-frame.

puzzle¹ *noun* 1 a difficult question; a problem. 2 a game or toy that sets a problem or difficult task. 3 a jigsaw puzzle.

puzzle² *verb* (**puzzled, puzzling**) 1 give someone a problem so that they have to think hard. 2 think patiently about how to solve something. **puzzlement** *noun*

pygmy (*say* **pig**-mee) *noun* (*plural* **pygmies**) 1 a very small person or thing. 2 a member of a Black people in Central Africa who are very short. **pygmy** *adjective*

pyjamas *plural noun* a loose jacket and trousers worn in bed. [from Urdu *pay jama* = leg-clothes]

pylon *noun* 1 a tall framework made of steel, supporting electricity cables. 2 a monumental gate-tower. [from Greek *pyle* = gate]

pyramid *noun* 1 a structure with a square base and with sloping sides that meet in a point at the top. 2 an ancient Egyptian tomb shaped like this. **pyramidal** (*say* pir-**am**-id-al) *adjective*

pyre *noun* a pile of wood etc. for burning a dead body as part of a funeral ceremony. [from Greek *pyr* = fire]

python *noun* a large snake that squeezes its prey so as to suffocate it.

▶▶ THESAURUS ◀◀

put off 1 defer, delay, hold off, postpone, reschedule, shelve. 2 deter from, discourage from, dissuade from, talk out of. 3 disgust, repel, revolt, sicken.

put on 1 change into, don, dress in, slip into, wear. 2 adopt, affect, assume, fake, feign, pretend. 3 gain, increase. 4 mount, perform, present, produce, stage.

put out 1 douse, extinguish, quench, snuff out. 2 annoy, bother, inconvenience, irritate, trouble.

put together assemble, build, construct, join, make.

put up 1 build, construct, erect, pitch (*a tent*), set up. 2 boost, bump up (*informal*), increase, jack up (*informal*), raise. 3 accommodate, billet, house, lodge, take in. 4 contribute, donate, pay, provide, supply.

put up with abide, accept, bear, brook, endure, stand for, suffer, take, tolerate.

putrid *adjective* 1 bad, decayed, decomposed, rotten. 2 foul, rank, smelly, stinking.

puzzle¹ *noun* 1 brainteaser, conundrum, dilemma, enigma, mystery, paradox, problem, question, riddle.

puzzle² *verb* 1 baffle, bamboozle (*informal*), bewilder, confound, confuse, flummox (*informal*), mystify, nonplus, perplex, stump (*informal*), throw (*informal*). 2 brood, muse, ponder, rack your brains, wonder.
puzzling *adjective* abstruse, baffling, difficult, enigmatic, inexplicable, inscrutable, insoluble, mysterious, perplexing, strange, unfathomable.

pygmy *noun* 1 dwarf, lilliputian, midget.
pygmy *adjective* dwarf, miniature, small, tiny, undersized.

► Qq ◄

QC *abbreviation* Queen's Counsel.

QED *abbreviation* quod erat demonstrandum (Latin, = which was the thing that had to be proved).

quack¹ *verb* make the harsh cry of a duck. **quack** *noun* [imitation of the sound]

quack² *noun* **1** a person who falsely claims to have medical skill or have remedies to cure diseases. **2** (*slang*) a doctor. [from Dutch *quacken* = to boast]

quad (*say* kwod) *noun* **1** a quadrangle. **2** a quadruplet.

quadrangle *noun* a rectangular courtyard with large buildings round it. [from *quadri-* + *angle*]

quadrant *noun* **1** a quarter of a circle. **2** an instrument for measuring angles, especially altitudes.

quadri- *prefix* four. [from Latin *quattuor* = four]

quadrilateral *noun* a flat geometric shape with four sides. [from *quadri-* + *lateral*]

quadrille *noun* a square dance for four couples.

quadruped *noun* an animal with four feet. [from *quadri-*, + Latin *pedis* = of a foot]

quadruple¹ *adjective* **1** four times as much or as many. **2** having four parts.

quadruple² *verb* (**quadrupled**, **quadrupling**) make or become four times as much or as many. [from *quadri-*]

quadruplet *noun* each of four children born to the same mother at one time.

quaff (*say* kwof) *verb* drink.

quagmire *noun* a bog or marsh.

quail¹ *noun* (*plural* **quail** or **quails**) a bird related to the partridge.

quail² *verb* flinch; feel or show fear.

quaint *adjective* attractive through being unusual or old-fashioned. **quaintly** *adverb*, **quaintness** *noun*

quake *verb* (**quaked**, **quaking**) tremble; shake with fear.

Quaker *noun* a member of a religious group called the Society of Friends, founded by George Fox in the 17th century.

qualify *verb* (**qualified**, **qualifying**) **1** make or become able to do something through having certain qualities or training, or by passing a test. **2** make a statement less extreme, limit its meaning. **3** (of an adjective) add meaning to a noun. **qualification** *noun*

quality *noun* (*plural* **qualities**) **1** how good or bad something is. **2** excellence. **3** a characteristic; something that is special in a person or thing. [from Latin *qualis* = of what kind]

qualm (*say* kwahm) *noun* a misgiving; a scruple.

quandary *noun* (*plural* **quandaries**) a difficult situation where you are uncertain what to do.

►►►THESAURUS◄◄◄

quack² *noun* **1** charlatan, fake, impostor, phoney (*informal*). **2** see DOCTOR.

quadrangle *noun* courtyard, quad.

quaff *verb* drink, gulp, guzzle, swallow, swig (*informal*).

quagmire *noun* bog, fen, marsh, mire, morass, slough, swamp.

quail² *verb* cower, cringe, flinch, recoil, shrink, wince.

quaint *adjective* attractive, charming, curious, odd, old-fashioned, picturesque, twee, unusual.

quake *verb* quaver, quiver, shake, shiver, shudder, tremble.

qualify *verb* **1** allow, authorise, entitle, equip, fit, licence, make eligible, permit, prepare, train. **2** limit, modify, restrict.

qualification *noun* **1** ability, aptitude, attribute, competence, competency, credentials, eligibility, experience, knowledge, prerequisite, quality, skill, training. **2** condition, limitation, modification, proviso, reservation, restriction, stipulation.

quality *noun* **1** calibre, class, grade, level, standard, value, worth. **2** excellence, merit, value, worth. **3** attribute, characteristic, feature, trait.

qualm *noun* compunction, misgiving, pang of conscience, scruple.

quandary *noun* difficulty, dilemma, predicament.

in a quandary confused, perplexed, uncertain, unsure.

▶▶ D I C T I O N A R Y ◀◀

quandong *noun* an Australian tree, especially one with red fruit containing an edible kernel.

quantity *noun* (*plural* **quantities**) **1** how much there is of something; how many things there are of one sort. **2** a large amount. [from Latin *quantus* = how much]

quantum *noun* (*plural* **quanta**) a quantity or amount.

quarantine *noun* keeping a person or animal isolated in case they have a disease which could spread to others. [from Italian *quaranta* = forty (the original period of isolation was 40 days)]

quarrel[1] *noun* an angry disagreement.

quarrel[2] *verb* (**quarrelled, quarrelling**) have a quarrel. **quarrelsome** *adjective* [from Latin *querela* = complaint]

quarry[1] *noun* (*plural* **quarries**) an open place where stone or slate is dug or cut out of the ground.

quarry[2] *verb* (**quarried, quarrying**) dig or cut from a quarry.

quarry[3] *noun* (*plural* **quarries**) an animal etc. being hunted or pursued.

quart *noun* a liquid measure equal to a quarter of a gallon.

quarter[1] *noun* **1** each of four equal parts into which a thing is or can be divided. **2** three months, one-fourth of a year. **3** a district or region, *People came from every quarter.* **4** mercy towards an enemy, *They gave no quarter.*

quarters *plural noun* lodgings. **at close quarters** very close together.

quarter[2] *verb* **1** divide something into quarters. **2** put soldiers etc. into lodgings. [from Latin *quartus* = fourth]

quarterdeck *noun* the part of a ship's upper deck nearest the stern, usually reserved for the officers.

quarterly[1] *adjective* & *adverb* happening or produced once in every three months.

quarterly[2] *noun* (*plural* **quarterlies**) a quarterly magazine etc.

quartet *noun* **1** a group of four musicians. **2** a piece of music for four musicians. **3** a set of four people or things.

quartz *noun* a hard mineral.

quash *verb* cancel or annul something, *The judges quashed his conviction.*

quasi- (*say* **kwayz**-I) *prefix* seeming to be something but not really so, *a quasi-scientific explanation.* [from Latin *quasi* = as if]

quatrain *noun* a stanza with four lines. [from French *quatre* = four]

quaver[1] *verb* tremble; quiver.

quaver[2] *noun* **1** a quavering sound. **2** a note in music (♪) lasting half as long as a crotchet.

quay (*say* kee) *noun* a landing place where ships can be tied up for loading and unloading; a wharf. **quayside** *noun*

queasy *adjective* feeling slightly sick. **queasily** *adverb*, **queasiness** *noun*

▶▶ T H E S A U R U S ◀◀

quantity *noun* **1** amount, dose, extent, load, lot, mass, measure, number, portion, quantum, sum, volume, weight.

quarantine *noun* isolation, segregation.

quarrel[1] *noun* altercation, argument, barney (*informal*), clash, conflict, controversy, difference, disagreement, dispute, feud, fight, row, spat (*informal*), squabble, tiff, wrangle.

quarrel[2] *verb* argue, be at loggerheads, bicker, brawl, differ, fall out, fight, row (*informal*), scrap, squabble, wrangle.
quarrelsome *adjective* argumentative, belligerent, cantankerous, contentious, contrary, cross, disputatious, irritable, petulant, pugnacious, truculent.

quarry[1] *noun* excavation, mine, pit, working.
quarry[3] *noun* prey, victim.

quarter[1] *noun* **3** area, district, locality, neighbourhood, region.
quarters *plural noun* accommodation, barracks, billet, digs (*informal*), housing, lodgings.

quarter[2] *verb* **2** accommodate, billet, house, lodge, put up, station.

quash *verb* annul, invalidate, nullify, overrule, overturn, rescind, reverse, revoke.

quaver[1] *verb* quiver, shake, tremble, vibrate, waver.

quaver[2] *noun* **1** quiver, shaking, trembling, tremor, vibration, wavering.

quay *noun* berth, dock, jetty, landing stage, pier, wharf.

queasy *adjective* bilious, ill, nauseous, off colour, sick, unwell.

queen *noun* **1** a woman who is the ruler of a country through inheriting the position. **2** the wife of a king. **3** a female bee or ant that produces eggs. **4** an important piece in chess. **5** a playing card with a picture of a queen on it. **queenly** *adjective*
Queen's Counsel a senior barrister.

queer[1] *adjective* **1** strange; eccentric. **2** slightly ill or faint. **queerly** *adverb*, **queerness** *noun*

queer[2] *verb* **queer someone's pitch** spoil his or her chances beforehand.

quell *verb* suppress; subdue.

quench *verb* **1** satisfy your thirst by drinking. **2** put out a fire or flame.

quern *noun* a hand-operated device for grinding corn or pepper.

querulous (*say* **kwe**-rew-lus) *adjective* complaining peevishly. **querulously** *adverb* [same origin as *quarrel*]

query[1] (*say* **kweer**-ee) *noun* (*plural* **queries**) **1** a question. **2** a question mark. [from Latin *quaere* = ask]

query[2] *verb* ask a question about something.

quest *noun* a search, *the quest for gold.*

question[1] *noun* **1** a sentence asking something. **2** a matter to be discussed, *Parliament debated the question of immigration.* **3** a problem to be solved. **4** doubt, *Whether we shall win is open to question.*
in question being discussed or disputed, *His honesty is not in question.*
out of the question impossible.
question mark the punctuation mark ? placed after a question.

question[2] *verb* **1** ask someone questions. **2** say that you are doubtful about something. **questioner** *noun* [from Latin *quaesitum* = sought for]

questionable *adjective* causing doubt; not certainly true or honest or advisable.

questionnaire *noun* a list of questions.

queue[1] (*say* kew) *noun* a line of people or vehicles waiting for something.

queue[2] *verb* (**queued, queuing**) wait in a queue. [from Latin *cauda* = tail]

quibble[1] *noun* a petty objection.

quibble[2] *verb* (**quibbled, quibbling**) make petty objections.

quiche (*say* keesh) *noun* an open tart with a savoury filling. [French]

quick *adjective* **1** taking only a short time to do something. **2** done in a short time. **3** able to notice or learn or think quickly. **4** nimble; agile. **5** (*old use*) alive, *the quick and the dead.*
quickly *adverb*, **quickness** *noun*

queen *noun* **1** monarch, ruler, sovereign.
queenly *adjective* majestic, regal, royal.

queer[1] *adjective* **1** abnormal, bizarre, curious, eccentric, funny, odd, offbeat, peculiar, singular, strange, unconventional, unusual, weird. **2** dizzy, faint, giddy, ill, off colour, out of sorts, poorly, queasy, unwell.

quell *verb* (*quell a rebellion*) crush, defeat, overcome, put down, quash, subdue, suppress; (*quell fears*) allay, alleviate, assuage, calm, quieten, soothe, subdue.

quench *verb* **1** satisfy, slake. **2** douse, extinguish, put out, smother.

query[1] **1** *noun* enquiry, inquiry, question.

query[2] *verb* challenge, dispute, doubt, question.

quest *noun* hunt, pursuit, search.

question[1] *noun* **2** issue, matter, point, problem. **3** conundrum, enquiry, inquiry, poser, problem, puzzle, query, riddle. **4** argument, controversy, debate, dispute, doubt, uncertainty.
out of the question impossible, inconceivable, unthinkable.

question[2] *verb* **1** ask, cross-examine, enquire of, examine, grill, inquire of, interrogate, interview, probe, pump, quiz, sound out. **2** call into question, cast doubt on, challenge, dispute, doubt, query.

questionable *adjective* doubtful, dubious, suspect, suss (*informal*), uncertain.

questionnaire *noun* set of questions, survey.

queue[1] *noun* chain, column, file, line, line-up, row, string.

queue[2] *verb* line up.

quibble[1] *noun* complaint, objection, protest.

quibble[2] *verb* argue, carp, cavil, find fault, niggle, nit-pick (*informal*), object, protest, quarrel, split hairs.

quiche *noun* flan, pie, tart.

quick *adjective* **1** brisk, express, fast, fleet, rapid, speedy, swift, zippy. **2** (*a quick look*) brief, cursory, fleeting, hasty, hurried, perfunctory, short; (*a quick response*) expeditious, immediate, instant, instantaneous, prompt, speedy, swift. **3** able, alert, astute, bright, clever, intelligent, perceptive, sharp, shrewd, smart. **4** agile, lively, nimble, nippy (*informal*), sprightly, spry.

▶▷ D I C T I O N A R Y ◁◀

quicken *verb* **1** make or become quicker. **2** stimulate; make or become livelier.

quicksand *noun* an area of loose wet sand which is so deep that heavy objects sink into it.

quicksilver *noun* mercury.

quid *noun* (*plural* **quid**) (*slang*) one English pound.
not the full quid (*Australian slang*) mentally defective, not all there.

quiescent (*say* kwee-**ess**-ent) *adjective* inactive; quiet. **quiescence** *noun* [from Latin *quiescens* = becoming quiet]

quiet¹ *adjective* **1** silent, *Be quiet!* **2** with little sound; not loud or noisy. **3** calm; without disturbance; peaceful, *a quiet life.* **4** shy; reserved. **5** (of colours) not bright. **quietly** *adverb*, **quietness** *noun*

quiet² *noun* quietness. [from Latin *quietus* = calm]

quieten *verb* make or become quiet.

quiff *noun* an upright tuft of hair.

quill *noun* **1** a large feather. **2** a pen made from a large feather. **3** one of the spines on a hedgehog.

quilt¹ *noun* a padded bed-cover.

quilt² *verb* line material with padding and fix it with lines of stitching.

quin *noun* a quintuplet.

quince *noun* a hard pear-shaped fruit used for making jam.

quincentenary *noun* the 500th anniversary of something. [from Latin *quinque* = five, + *centenary*]

quinine (*say* kwin-**een**) *noun* a bitter-tasting medicine used to cure malaria.

quintessence *noun* **1** the essence of something. **2** a perfect example of a quality.

quintet *noun* **1** a group of five musicians. **2** a piece of music for five musicians. [from Latin *quintus* = fifth]

quintuplet *noun* each of five children born to the same mother at one time. [from Latin *quintus* = fifth]

quip *noun* a witty remark.

quirk *noun* **1** a peculiarity of a person's behaviour. **2** a trick of fate.

quit *verb* (**quitted** or **quit**, **quitting**) **1** leave. **2** abandon. **3** (*informal*) stop doing something. **quitter** *noun*

quite *adverb* **1** completely; entirely, *I am quite all right.* **2** somewhat; rather, *She is quite a good swimmer.* **3** really, *It's quite a change.*

quits *adjective* even or equal after retaliating or paying someone.

quiver¹ *noun* a container for arrows.

quiver² *verb* tremble. **quiver** *noun*

quixotic (*say* kwiks-**ot**-ik) *adjective* very chivalrous and unselfish, often to an impractical extent. **quixotically** *adverb* [named after Don Quixote, hero of a Spanish story]

▶▷ T H E S A U R U S ◁◀

quickly *adverb* apace, at full pelt, at speed, at the double, briskly, expeditiously, fast, hastily, hell for leather (*informal*), hurriedly, immediately, in a flash, in a jiffy (*informal*), in no time, instantly, like greased lightning (*informal*), post-haste, promptly, rapidly, speedily, swiftly.

quicken *verb* **1** accelerate, hasten, hurry, speed up. **2** arouse, enliven, inspire, kindle, stimulate.

quiet¹ *adjective* **1** noiseless, silent, soundless, still. **2** gentle, hushed, inaudible, low, soft. **3** calm, gentle, mild, peaceful, placid, restful, sedate, serene, tranquil, undisturbed. **4** introverted, reserved, reticent, retiring, shy, silent, taciturn, uncommunicative. **5** muted, soft, subdued, subtle, unobtrusive.
quietness *noun* calm, hush, peace, quiet, serenity, silence, stillness, tranquillity.

quieten *verb* calm, hush, pacify, quiet, restrain, shush (*informal*), silence, soothe, subdue.

quilt¹ *noun* continental quilt, coverlet, Doona (*trade mark*), duvet, eiderdown.

quip *noun* jest, joke, sally, wisecrack, witticism.

quirk *noun* **1** eccentricity, foible, idiosyncrasy, oddity, peculiarity. **2** aberration, fluke, trick, twist, vagary.

quit *verb* **1** depart from, desert, go away from, leave, vacate. **2** abandon, abdicate, chuck in (*informal*), forsake, give up, jack in (*slang*), leave, pack in (*informal*), relinquish, resign, retire, toss in (*informal*). **3** cease, desist from, discontinue, leave off, stop.

quite *adverb* **1** absolutely, altogether, completely, entirely, fully, perfectly, positively, totally, utterly. **2** comparatively, fairly, moderately, pretty, rather, reasonably, relatively, somewhat.

quiver² *verb* pulsate, quake, quaver, shake, shiver, shudder, tremble, vibrate.

quiz¹ *noun* (*plural* **quizzes**) a series of questions, especially as an entertainment or competition.

quiz² *verb* (**quizzed, quizzing**) question someone closely.

quizzical *adjective* **1** in a questioning way. **2** gently amused. **quizzically** *adverb* [from *quiz*]

quoit (*say* koit) *noun* a ring thrown at a peg in the game of **quoits**.

quoll *noun* a small predatory Australian marsupial, also called *native cat*.

quorum *noun* the smallest number of people needed to make a meeting of a committee etc. valid. [Latin, = of which people]

quota *noun* **1** a fixed share that must be given or received or done. **2** a limited amount. [from Latin *quot* = how many]

quotation *noun* **1** quoting. **2** something quoted. **3** a statement of the price. **quotation marks** inverted commas (see *invert*).

quote *verb* (**quoted, quoting**) **1** repeat words that were first written or spoken by someone else. **2** mention something as proof. **3** state the price of goods or services that you can supply.

quoth *verb* (*old use*) said.

quotient (*say* **kwoh**-shent) *noun* the result of dividing one number by another. (Compare *product*.) [from Latin, = how many times]

quiz¹ *noun* competition, exam, examination, questionnaire, test.

quiz² *verb* ask, examine, grill, interrogate, question, test.

quota *noun* **1** allocation, allowance, cut (*informal*), lot, part, portion, proportion, ration, share.

quotation *noun* **2** citation, excerpt, extract, passage, quote (*informal*), reference. **3** estimate, quote (*informal*), tender.

quote *verb* **1** recite, repeat. **2** call up, cite, instance, mention, name, refer to. **3** estimate, tender.

► Rr ◄

rabbi (*say* **rab**-I) *noun* (*plural* **rabbis**) a Jewish religious leader. [Hebrew, = my master]

rabbit *noun* a furry animal with long ears that digs burrows.

rabble *noun* a disorderly crowd; a mob.

rabid (*say* **rab**-id) *adjective* **1** fanatical, *a rabid tennis fan*. **2** suffering from rabies. [from Latin *rabidus* = raving]

rabies (*say* **ray**-beez) *noun* a fatal disease that affects dogs, cats, etc. and can infect people.

raccoon *noun* an American animal with a bushy tail.

race¹ *noun* **1** a competition to be the first to reach a particular place or to do something. **2** a strong fast current of water, *the tidal race*.

race² *verb* (**raced**, **racing**) **1** compete in a race. **2** move very fast. **racer** *noun*

race³ *noun* a very large group of people thought to have the same ancestors and with physical characteristics (e.g. colour of skin and hair, shape of eyes and nose) that differ from those of other groups. **racial** *adjective* **race relations** relationships between people of different races in the same country.

race⁴ *noun* (*Australian*) a fenced passageway for drafting sheep or cattle.

racecourse *noun* a place where horse races are run.

racetrack *noun* **1** a racecourse. **2** a track for motor racing.

racialism (*say* **ray**-shal-izm) *noun* racism. **racialist** *noun*

racism (*say* **ray**-sizm) *noun* **1** belief that a particular race of people is better than others. **2** hostility towards people of other races. **racist** *noun*

rack¹ *noun* **1** a framework used as a shelf or container. **2** a bar or rail with cogs into which the cogs of a gear or wheel etc. fit. **3** an ancient device for torturing people by stretching them.

rack² *verb* torment, *He was racked with pain.* **rack your brains** think hard in trying to solve a problem.

rack³ *noun* destruction, *The place has gone to rack and ruin.*

racket¹ *noun* see **racquet.**

racket² *noun* **1** a loud noise; a din. **2** dishonest business; a swindle.

racketeer *noun* a person involved in a dishonest business. **racketeering** *noun*

racquet *noun* a bat with strings stretched across a frame used in tennis and similar games. [from Arabic *rahat* = palm of the hand]

racy *adjective* lively in style, *She gave a racy account of her travels.*

radar *noun* a system or apparatus that uses radio waves to show on a screen etc. the position of objects that cannot be seen because of darkness, fog, distance, etc. [from the initial letters of *radio detection and ranging*]

radial *adjective* **1** of rays or radii. **2** having spokes or lines that radiate from a central point. **radially** *adverb*

►►THESAURUS◄◄

rabbit *noun* buck (*male*), bunny (*informal*), doe (*female*), kitten (*young*).

rabble *noun* crowd, horde, mob, swarm, throng.

race¹ *noun* **1** chase, competition, contest, heat, marathon, rally, relay.

race² *verb* **1** compete. **2** career, dart, dash, fly, hurry, hurtle, run, rush, shoot, speed, sprint, sweep, tear, whiz, zip, zoom.

race³ *noun* ethnic group, nation, people, tribe. **racial** *adjective* ethnic, national, tribal.

racetrack *noun* **2** circuit, course, racecourse, speedway, track.

racism *noun* racial discrimination, racial intolerance, racialism, racial prejudice.

rack¹ *noun* **1** framework, holder, shelf, stand, support.

racket² *noun* **1** clamour, commotion, din, disturbance, hubbub, hullabaloo, noise, pandemonium, row, ruckus, rumpus, tumult, uproar. **2** dodge (*informal*), lurk (*Australian informal*), rort (*Australian slang*), scam (*slang*), scheme, swindle.

racy *adjective* animated, exciting, juicy (*informal*), lively, spicy, spirited, stimulating.

radiant *adjective* **1** radiating light or heat etc.; radiated. **2** looking very bright and happy. **radiantly** *adverb*, **radiance** *noun*

radiate *verb* (**radiated, radiating**) **1** send out light, heat, or other energy in rays. **2** spread out from a central point like the spokes of a wheel. [from Latin *radius* = ray]

radiation *noun* **1** the process of radiating. **2** light, heat, or other energy radiated. **3** radioactivity.

radiator *noun* **1** a device that gives out heat, especially a metal case that is heated electrically or through which steam or hot water flows. **2** a device that cools the engine of a motor vehicle.

radical¹ *adjective* **1** basic; thorough, *radical changes.* **2** wanting to make great reforms, *a radical politician.* **radically** *adverb*

radical² *noun* a person who wants to make great reforms. [from Latin *radicis* = of a root]

radicle *noun* a root that forms in the seed of a plant. [from Latin, = little root]

radio *noun* (*plural* **radios**) (also called *wireless*) **1** the process of sending and receiving sound or pictures by means of electromagnetic waves without a connecting wire. **2** an apparatus for receiving sound (a *receiver*) or sending it out (a *transmitter*) in this way. **3** sound-broadcasting. [from Latin *radius* = ray]

radio- *prefix* **1** of rays or radiation. **2** of radio.

radioactive *adjective* having atoms that break up and send out radiation which produces electrical and chemical effects and penetrates things. **radioactivity** *noun*

radiography *noun* the production of X-ray photographs. **radiographer** *noun* [from *radio-* + *-graphy*]

radiology *noun* the study of X-rays and similar radiation. **radiologist** *noun* [from *radio-* + *-logy*]

radish *noun* (*plural* **radishes**) a small hard round red vegetable, eaten raw in salads. [from Latin *radix* = root]

radium *noun* a radioactive substance found in pitchblende. [from Latin *radius* = ray]

radius *noun* (*plural* **radii**) **1** a straight line from the centre of a circle or sphere to the circumference; the length of this line. **2** a range or distance from a central point, *The school takes pupils living within a radius of ten kilometres.* [from Latin *radius* = a spoke or ray]

Rafferty's rules (*Australian slang*) no rules at all.

raffia *noun* soft fibre from the leaves of a kind of palm-tree.

raffish *adjective* looking disreputable.

raffle¹ *noun* a kind of lottery, usually to raise money for a charity.

raffle² *verb* (**raffled, raffling**) offer something as a prize in a raffle.

raft *noun* a flat floating structure made of wood etc., used as a boat.

rafter *noun* any of the long sloping pieces of wood that hold up a roof.

rag¹ *noun* **1** an old or torn piece of cloth. **2** a piece of ragtime music.

rag² *verb* (**ragged, ragging**) (*slang*) tease.

ragamuffin *noun* a person in ragged dirty clothes.

rage¹ *noun* **1** great or violent anger. **2** a craze, *Skateboarding was all the rage.* **3** (*Australian slang*) a lively party.

rage² *verb* (**raged, raging**) **1** be very angry. **2** be violent or noisy, *A storm was raging.* **3** (*Australian slang*) have a good time, revel.

radiant *adjective* **1** bright, brilliant, dazzling, gleaming, glowing, incandescent, luminous, shining. **2** beaming, beautiful, blissful, ecstatic, glowing, happy, joyful, overjoyed.

radiate *verb* **1** diffuse, emit, give off, give out, send out, shed, transmit. **2** branch out, diverge, issue, spread out.

radical¹ *adjective* **1** basic, complete, drastic, far-reaching, fundamental, profound, sweeping, thorough. **2** extreme, extremist, immoderate, revolutionary.

radio *noun* **2** receiver, set, transistor, tuner, wireless.

raffle¹ *noun* art union (*Australian*), draw, lottery, sweep, sweepstake.

rag¹ *noun* **1** cloth, fragment, remnant, scrap.

ragamuffin *noun* guttersnipe, urchin, waif.

rage¹ *noun* **1** anger, exasperation, frenzy, fury, ire, paddy (*informal*), tantrum, temper, wrath. **2** craze, fashion, mode, trend, vogue.

rage² *verb* **1** be angry, be beside yourself, be furious, blow your stack (*informal*), blow your top (*informal*), do your block (*Australian informal*), flare up, fly off the handle (*informal*), fume, go off the deep end (*informal*), let off steam, lose your cool

ragged *adjective* **1** torn or frayed. **2** wearing torn clothes. **3** jagged. **4** irregular; uneven, *a ragged performance.*

raglan *noun* a sleeve joined to a garment by sloping seams. [named after Lord Raglan, British military commander (died 1855)]

ragtime *noun* a kind of jazz music.

raid¹ *noun* **1** a sudden attack. **2** a surprise visit by police etc. to arrest people or seize illegal goods.

raid² *verb* **1** make a raid on a place. **2** plunder.
raider *noun*

rail¹ *noun* **1** a level or sloping bar for hanging things on or forming part of a fence, banisters, etc. **2** a long metal bar forming part of a railway track.
by rail on a train.

rail² *verb* protest angrily.

railings *plural noun* a fence made of metal bars.

railway *noun* **1** the parallel metal bars that trains travel on. **2** a system of transport using rails.

raiment *noun* (*old use*) clothing.

rain¹ *noun* drops of water that fall from the sky. **rainy** *adjective*

rain² *verb* **1** fall as rain or like rain. **2** send down like rain, *They rained blows on him.*

rainbow *noun* a curved band of colours seen in the sky when the sun shines through rain.

rainbow serpent the great snake of the Dreamtime which is associated with rain and water.

raincoat *noun* a waterproof coat.

raindrop *noun* a single drop of rain.

rainfall *noun* the amount of rain that falls in a particular place or time.

raise¹ *verb* (**raised, raising**) **1** move something to a higher place or an upright position. **2** increase the amount or level of something. **3** collect; manage to obtain, *They raised $500 for charity.* **4** bring up young children or animals, *raise a family.* **5** rouse; cause, *She raised a laugh with her joke.* **6** put forward, *We raised objections.* **7** end a siege.

raise² *noun* an increase in wages.

raisin *noun* a dried grape.

raj (*say* rahj) *noun* the period of Indian history when the country was ruled by Britain. [Hindi, = reign]

rajah *noun* an Indian king or prince. (Compare *ranee.*) [Hindi]

rake¹ *noun* a gardening tool with a row of short spikes fixed to a long handle.

rake² *verb* (**raked, raking**) **1** gather or smooth with a rake. **2** search. **3** gather; collect, *raking it in.*
rake up collect; remind people of an old scandal etc., *Don't rake that up.*

rake³ *noun* a man who lives an irresponsible and immoral life.

(*informal*), lose your temper, rail, rant, rave, seethe.

ragged *adjective* **1** dilapidated, frayed, holey, scruffy, shabby, tattered, tatty (*informal*), threadbare, torn, worn-out. **3** irregular, jagged, rough, uneven.

raid¹ *noun* **1** assault, attack, blitz, foray, incursion, invasion, offensive, onslaught, sortie, swoop. **2** bust (*informal*), search.

raid² *verb* **1** attack, descend on, invade, storm, swoop on. **2** loot, pillage, plunder, ransack, rifle, rob.

rail¹ *noun* **1** banisters, bar, handrail, railing.

rail² *verb* complain, declaim, inveigh, lash out, protest, rage, vociferate.

railings *plural noun* balustrade, barrier, fence, rails.

railway *noun* **2** rail, railroad (*American*), train.

rain¹ *noun* cloudburst, deluge, downpour, drizzle, precipitation, rainfall, shower, storm, thunderstorm.
rainy *adjective* damp, drizzly, showery, wet.

rain² *verb* **1** bucket down, drizzle, pelt, pour, rain cats and dogs (*informal*), spit, sprinkle, teem.

raincoat *noun* anorak, mac (*informal*), mackintosh, oilskin, trench coat, waterproof.

rainfall *noun* precipitation.

raise¹ *verb* **1** elevate, heave, hoist, jack, lift, pick up. **2** boost, build up, bump up (*informal*), heighten, increase, inflate, jack up (*informal*), mark up, put up. **3** accumulate, amass, collect, gather, get, obtain. **4** (*raise children*) bring up, educate, nurture, rear; (*raise crops*) breed, cultivate, farm, grow, produce, propagate. **5** arouse, awaken, cause, encourage, kindle, provoke, rouse, stimulate. **6** bring up, broach, initiate, introduce, pose, put forward.
raise from the dead restore to life, resurrect, resuscitate, revive.

raise² *noun* increase, rise.

rake² *verb* **1** collect, gather, sweep up. **2** comb, forage, fossick (*Australian informal*), rummage, scour, search.

rally¹ *noun* (*plural* **rallies**) **1** a large meeting to support something or share an interest. **2** a competition to test skill in driving, *the Monte Carlo Rally*. **3** a series of strokes in tennis before a point is scored. **4** a recovery.

rally² *verb* (**rallied, rallying**) **1** bring or come together for a united effort, *They rallied support. People rallied round.* **2** revive; recover strength.

RAM *abbreviation* random-access memory (in a computer), with contents that can be retrieved or stored directly without having to read through items already stored.

ram¹ *noun* **1** a male sheep. **2** a device for ramming things.

ram² *verb* (**rammed, ramming**) **1** push one thing hard against another. **2** crash into something.

Ramadan *noun* the ninth month of the Muslim year, when Muslims fast between sunrise and sunset.

ramble¹ *noun* a long walk in the country.

ramble² *verb* (**rambled, rambling**) **1** go for a ramble; wander. **2** talk or write a lot without keeping to the subject. **rambler** *noun*

ramifications *plural noun* **1** the branches of a structure. **2** the many effects of a plan or action. [from Latin *ramus* = branch]

ramp¹ *noun* a slope or grid joining two different levels.

ramp² *noun* a swindle.

rampage *verb* (**rampaged, rampaging**) rush about wildly or destructively. **rampage** *noun*

rampant *adjective* **1** growing or increasing unrestrained, *Disease was rampant in the poorer districts.* **2** (of an animal on coats of arms) standing upright on a hind leg, *a lion rampant.* [from *ramp¹*]

rampart *noun* a wide bank of earth built as a fortification; a wall on top of this.

ramrod *noun* a straight rod formerly used for ramming an explosive into a gun.

ramshackle *adjective* badly made and rickety, *a ramshackle hut.*

ranch *noun* (*plural* **ranches**) a large cattle-farm in America.

rancid *adjective* smelling or tasting unpleasant like stale fat.

rancour (*say* **rank**-er) *noun* bitter resentment or ill will. **rancorous** *adjective*

random¹ *noun* **at random** using no particular order or method, *In bingo, numbers are chosen at random.*

random² *adjective* done or taken at random, *a random sample.*

ranee (*say* **rah**-nee) *noun* a rajah's wife or widow. [Hindi]

range¹ *noun* **1** a line or series of things, *a range of mountains.* **2** the limits between which things exist or are available; an extent, *a wide range of goods.* **3** the distance that a gun can shoot, an aircraft can travel, a sound

►►► THESAURUS ◄◄

rally¹ *noun* **1** assembly, convention, demo (*informal*), demonstration, jamboree, gathering, meeting. **2** competition, race.

rally² *verb* **1** assemble, come together, convene, gather, marshal, mobilise, muster, round up, summon, unite. **2** get better, improve, pull through, recover, revive.

ram² *verb* **1** compress, cram, drive, force, hammer, jam, pack, push, squeeze, stuff, tamp. **2** bump into, collide with, crash into, hit, run into, slam into, smash into.

ramble¹ *noun* hike, roam, stroll, trek, walk.

ramble² *verb* **1** amble, hike, roam, rove, saunter, stroll, traipse, tramp, trek, walk, wander. **2** digress, go off at a tangent, waffle (*informal*), wander, witter on (*informal*).

ramification *noun* **2** complication, consequence, implication, offshoot.

ramp¹ *noun* incline, slope.

rampage *verb* go berserk, go wild, run amok, run riot.

rampant *adjective* **1** epidemic, flourishing, out of control, prevalent, rife, unchecked, uncurbed, unrestrained, widespread.

rampart *noun* bulwark, earthwork, embankment, fortification, parapet, wall.

ramshackle *adjective* decrepit, derelict, dilapidated, rickety, run-down, tumbledown.

ranch *noun* farm, stud.

rancid *adjective* bad, high, off, on the nose (*Australian informal*), rank, rotten, sour, stale.

rancour *noun* acrimony, animosity, bitterness, grudge, hatred, hostility, ill will, malice, resentment, spite, venom.

random² *adjective* accidental, arbitrary, chance, fortuitous, haphazard, hit-or-miss, indiscriminate, unplanned.

range¹ *noun* **1** chain, line, row, series. **2** area, bounds, compass, domain, extent, field, gamut, limits, orbit, scope, span, spectrum, sphere, spread; see also ASSORTMENT (at ASSORTED). **6** cooker, fireplace, oven, stove.

►► D I C T I O N A R Y ◄◄

can be heard, etc. **4** a place with targets for shooting-practice. **5** a large open area of grazing-land or hunting-ground. **6** a kitchen fireplace with ovens.

range² *verb* (**ranged, ranging**) **1** exist between two limits; extend, *Prices ranged from $1 to $50*. **2** arrange. **3** move over a wide area; wander.

Ranger *noun* a senior Guide.

ranger *noun* someone who looks after or patrols a park, forest, etc.

rank¹ *noun* **1** a line of people or things. **2** a place where taxis stand to await customers. **3** a position in a series of different levels, *He holds the rank of sergeant*.
the rank and file ordinary people.

rank² *verb* **1** arrange in a rank or ranks. **2** have a certain rank or place, *She ranks among the greatest novelists*.

rank³ *adjective* **1** growing too thickly and coarsely. **2** smelling very unpleasant. **3** complete; unmistakably bad, *rank injustice*.
rankly *adverb*, **rankness** *noun*

rankle *verb* (**rankled, rankling**) cause lasting annoyance or resentment.

ransack *verb* **1** search thoroughly or roughly. **2** rob or pillage a place.

ransom¹ *noun* money that has to be paid for a prisoner to be set free.
hold to ransom hold someone captive or in your power and demand ransom.

ransom² *verb* **1** free someone by paying a ransom. **2** get a ransom for someone. [same origin as *redeem*]

rant *verb* speak loudly and violently.

rap¹ *verb* (**rapped, rapping**) **1** knock loudly. **2** (*informal*) reprimand. **3** (*slang*) chat. **4** speak rhymes with a backing of rock music. **5** (*Australian*) praise extravagantly.

rap² *noun* **1** a rapping movement or sound. **2** (*informal*) blame; punishment, *take the rap*. **3** (*slang*) a chat. **4** rhymes spoken with a backing of rock music. **5** (*Australian*) extravagant praise.

rapacious (*say* ra-**pay**-shus) *adjective* greedy; plundering. **rapaciously** *adverb*, **rapacity** *noun* [from Latin *rapax* = grasping]

rape¹ *noun* the act of having sexual intercourse with a person without her or his consent.

rape² *verb* (**raped, raping**) commit rape on a person. **rapist** *noun* [from Latin *rapere* = seize]

rape³ *noun* a plant grown as food for sheep and for its seed from which oil is obtained.

rapid *adjective* quick; swift. **rapidly** *adverb*, **rapidity** *noun*

rapids *plural noun* part of a river where the water flows very quickly.

rapier *noun* a thin lightweight sword.

rapt *adjective* very intent and absorbed; enraptured. **raptly** *adverb* [from Latin *raptum* = seized]

rapture *noun* very great delight. **rapturous** *adjective*, **rapturously** *adverb*

►► T H E S A U R U S ◄◄

range² *verb* **1** differ, extend, fluctuate, go, vary. **3** ramble, roam, rove, stray, travel, wander.

ranger *noun* curator, keeper, warden.

rank¹ *noun* **1** column, file, line, queue, row. **3** class, degree, grade, level, position, standing, station, status.

rank² *verb* **1** arrange, class, grade, order, place, rate.

rank³ *adjective* **1** dense, lush, luxuriant, overgrown, profuse, thick. **2** bad, foul, off, offensive, on the nose (*Australian informal*), rancid, smelly, stinking, strong. **3** absolute, complete, downright, flagrant, glaring, gross, obvious, out-and-out, sheer, total, utter.

ransack *verb* **1** comb, fossick in (*Australian informal*), rake through, rummage in, scour, search. **2** loot, pillage, plunder, raid, rob, sack.

rant *verb* bluster, declaim, hold forth, rave, sound off (*informal*), spout, vociferate.

rap¹ *verb* **1** hit, knock, strike, tap.

rap² *noun* **1** blow, hit, knock, tap, whack. **2** blame, censure, punishment.

rape² *verb* assault sexually, ravish, violate.

rapid *adjective* brisk, expeditious, fast, hasty, high-speed, meteoric, precipitate, prompt, quick, speedy, sudden, swift, whirlwind.
rapidity *noun* alacrity, dispatch, haste, promptness, quickness, speed, swiftness.
rapidly *adverb* see QUICKLY (at QUICK).

rapt *adjective* absorbed, captivated, engrossed, enraptured, enthralled, entranced, intent, spellbound.

rapture *noun* bliss, delight, ecstasy, elation, euphoria, happiness, joy.

▶▶ D I C T I O N A R Y ◀◀

rare¹ *adjective* **1** unusual; not often found or happening. **2** (of air) thin; below normal pressure. **rarely** *adverb*, **rareness** *noun*, **rarity** *noun*

rare² *adjective* (of meat) cooked so that the inside is still red.

rarefied *adjective* **1** (of air) thin; rare. **2** (of an idea etc.) very subtle.

rascal *noun* **1** a dishonest person; a rogue. **2** a mischievous person. **rascally** *adjective*

rash¹ *adjective* doing something or done without thinking of the possible risks or effects. **rashly** *adverb*, **rashness** *noun*

rash² *noun* (*plural* **rashes**) an outbreak of spots or patches on the skin.

rasher *noun* a slice of bacon.

rasp¹ *noun* **1** a file with sharp points on its surface. **2** a rough grating sound.

rasp² *verb* **1** scrape roughly. **2** make a rough grating sound or effect.

raspberry *noun* (*plural* **raspberries**) a small soft red fruit.

rat *noun* **1** an animal like a large mouse. **2** an unpleasant or treacherous person.
rat race a continuous struggle for success in a career, business, etc.

ratbag *noun* (*Australian slang*) someone who is unpleasant or eccentric.

ratchet *noun* a row of notches on a bar or wheel in which a device (a *pawl*) catches to prevent it running backwards.

rate¹ *noun* **1** speed, *The train travelled at a great rate.* **2** a measure of cost, value, etc., *Postage rates went up.* **3** quality; standard, *first-rate.* **4** a tax paid by householders to the local council.
at any rate anyway.

rate² *verb* (**rated**, **rating**) **1** put a value on something. **2** regard as, *He rated me among his friends.* [from Latin *ratum* = reckoned]

rather *adverb* **1** slightly; somewhat, *It's rather dark.* **2** more willingly; preferably, *I would rather not go.* **3** more exactly, *He is lazy rather than stupid.* **4** (*informal*) definitely; yes, '*Will you come?*' '*Rather!*'

ratify *verb* (**ratified**, **ratifying**) confirm or agree to something officially, *They ratified the treaty.* **ratification** *noun*

rating *noun* **1** the way something is rated. **2** a sailor who is not an officer.

ratio (*say* **ray**-shee-oh) *noun* (*plural* **ratios**) **1** the relationship between two numbers, given by the quotient, *The ratio of 2 to 10 = 2:10 = ²⁄₁₀ = ⅕.* **2** proportion, *Mix flour and butter in the ratio of two to one* (= two measures of flour to one measure of butter). [from Latin, = reckoning]

ration¹ *noun* an amount allowed to one person.

ration² *verb* share something out in fixed amounts. [same origin as *ratio*]

rational *adjective* **1** reasonable; sane. **2** able to reason, *Plants are not rational.* **rationally** *adverb*, **rationality** *noun*

▶▶ T H E S A U R U S ◀◀

rare¹ *adjective* **1** abnormal, infrequent, occasional, odd, scarce, strange, uncommon, unfamiliar, unusual.
rarely *adverb* infrequently, occasionally, once in a blue moon, seldom.

rare² *adjective* undercooked, underdone.

rarefied *adjective* **1** rare, thin.

rascal *noun* **1** blackguard, knave (*old use*), miscreant, rogue, scoundrel, villain, wretch. **2** devil, imp, monkey, scallywag, scamp.

rash¹ *adjective* foolhardy, hare-brained, hasty, headlong, heedless, hotheaded, impetuous, imprudent, impulsive, madcap, precipitate, reckless.

rash² *noun* dermatitis, eczema, eruption, hives, spots.

rate¹ *noun* **1** pace, speed, velocity. **2** charge, cost, fare, fee, price, tariff. **4** levy, tax, taxation.

rate² *verb* **1** assess, class, estimate, evaluate, gauge, judge, measure, rank, reckon, value. **2** class, consider, count, deem, reckon, regard.

rather *adverb* **1** comparatively, fairly, moderately, pretty, quite, relatively, slightly, somewhat.

ratify *verb* agree to, approve, assent to, confirm, consent to, countersign, endorse, sign, validate.

ratio *noun* proportion, relationship.

ration¹ *noun* allocation, allowance, helping, portion, quota, share.

ration² *verb* (*ration out*) allocate, apportion, distribute, dole out, mete out, share out.

rational *adjective* **1** intelligent, logical, lucid, normal, reasonable, sane, sensible, sound, well-balanced.

▶▶ D I C T I O N A R Y ◀◀

rationalise *verb* (**rationalised, rationalising**) **1** make a thing logical and consistent, *Attempts to rationalise English spelling have failed.* **2** invent a reasonable explanation of something, *She rationalised her meanness by calling it economy.* **3** make an industry etc. more efficient by reorganising it. **rationalisation** *noun*

rattle[1] *verb* (**rattled, rattling**) **1** make a series of short sharp hard sounds. **2** say something quickly, *She rattled off the poem.* **3** (*informal*) make a person nervous or flustered.

rattle[2] *noun* **1** a rattling sound. **2** a device or baby's toy that rattles.

rattlesnake *noun* a poisonous American snake with a tail that rattles.

rattling *adjective* **1** that rattles. **2** vigorous; brisk, *a rattling pace.*

ratty *adjective* (*slang*) angry.

raucous (*say* **raw**-kus) *adjective* loud and harsh, *a raucous voice.*

ravage *verb* (**ravaged, ravaging**) do great damage to something; devastate. **ravages** *plural noun*

rave *verb* (**raved, raving**) **1** talk wildly or angrily or madly. **2** talk rapturously about something. **rave** *noun*

ravel *verb* (**ravelled, ravelling**) tangle.

raven *noun* a large black bird.

ravenous *adjective* very hungry. **ravenously** *adverb*

ravine (*say* ra-**veen**) *noun* a deep narrow gorge or valley.

ravish *verb* **1** rape. **2** enrapture.

ravishing *adjective* very beautiful.

raw *adjective* **1** not cooked. **2** in the natural state; not yet processed, *raw materials.* **3** without experience, *raw recruits.* **4** with the skin removed, *a raw wound.* **5** cold and damp, *a raw morning.* **rawness** *noun*
raw deal (*informal*) unfair treatment.

ray[1] *noun* **1** a thin line of light, heat, or other radiation. **2** each of a set of lines or parts extending from a centre. [from Latin *radius* = ray]

ray[2] *noun* a large sea-fish.

rayon *noun* a synthetic fibre or cloth made from cellulose.

raze *verb* (**razed, razing**) destroy a building or town completely, *raze it to the ground.* [from Latin *rasum* = scraped]

razoo (*say* ra-**zoo**) *noun* (*Australian*) an imaginary very small coin, *I haven't got a brass razoo.*

razor *noun* a device with a very sharp blade, especially one used for shaving. [from *raze*]

razzamatazz *noun* (*informal*) showy publicity.

RC *abbreviation* Roman Catholic.

re- *prefix* **1** again (as in *rebuild*). **2** back again, to an earlier condition (as in *reopen*). **3** in return; to each other (as in *react*). **4** against (as in *rebel*). **5** away or down (as in *recede*). [Latin]

reach[1] *verb* **1** go as far as; arrive at a place or thing. **2** stretch out your hand to get or touch something. **reachable** *adjective*

▶▶ T H E S A U R U S ◀◀

rationalise *verb* **2** account for, excuse, explain away, justify. **3** make efficient, reorganise, restructure, streamline.

rattle[1] *verb* **1** clank, clatter, clink, jangle, shake. **2** (*rattle off*) recite, recount, reel off, relate. **3** agitate, alarm, disconcert, disturb, faze (*informal*), fluster, frighten, perturb, shake, throw, unnerve, upset, worry.

raucous *adjective* grating, harsh, hoarse, jarring, loud, noisy, piercing, rasping, shrill, strident.

ravage *verb* damage, destroy, devastate, lay waste, loot, pillage, plunder, raid, ransack, raze, ruin, sack, wreck.
ravages *plural noun* damage, depredation, destruction, devastation.

rave *verb* **1** carry on (*informal*), go on (*informal*), rant, sound off (*informal*); see also

BE ANGRY (at ANGRY). **2** be effusive, be enthusiastic, go overboard (*informal*), go wild, gush, wax lyrical (*informal*).

ravenous *adjective* famished, hungry, starving.

ravine *noun* canyon, defile, gorge, gully, valley.

raw *adjective* **1** uncooked. **2** crude, natural, unprocessed, unrefined, untreated. **3** callow, fresh, green, inexperienced, new, untrained. **4** grazed, scratched, skinned.

ray[1] *noun* **1** beam, shaft, streak, stream.

raze *verb* bulldoze, demolish, destroy, flatten, knock down, level, tear down, wreck.

reach[1] *verb* **1** achieve, arrive at, attain, come to, get to, go as far as, hit, make. **2** extend, hold out, put out, stick out, stretch out.

reach[2] *noun* **1** capability, capacity, compass, grasp, range, scope. **3** part, section, stretch.

▶▶ D I C T I O N A R Y ◀◀

reach² *noun* (*plural* **reaches**) **1** the distance a person or thing can reach. **2** a distance you can easily travel, *We live within reach of the sea.* **3** a straight stretch of a river or canal.

react *verb* have a reaction.

reaction *noun* **1** an effect or feeling etc. produced in one person or thing by another. **2** a chemical change caused when substances act upon each other.

reactionary *adjective* wanting to undo progress or reform.

reactor *noun* an apparatus for producing nuclear power in a controlled way.

read *verb* (**read** (*say as* red), **reading**) **1** look at something written or printed and understand it or say it aloud. **2** (of a computer) copy, search, or extract data. **3** indicate; register, *The thermometer reads 20° Celsius.* **readable** *adjective*

reader *noun* **1** a person who reads. **2** a book that helps you learn to read.

readily (*say* **red**-il-ee) *adverb* **1** willingly. **2** easily; without any difficulty.

ready¹ *adjective* (**readier**, **readiest**) **1** able to do something or be used immediately; prepared. **2** willing. **3** quick; prompt, *a ready answer.* **4** within reach, *Have a blanket ready.* **readiness** *noun*

at the ready ready for use or action.

ready² *adverb* beforehand, *This meat is ready cooked.* **ready-made** *adjective*

real *adjective* **1** existing; true; not imaginary. **2** genuine; not an imitation, *real pearls.*

realise *verb* (**realised**, **realising**) **1** be fully aware of something; accept something as true. **2** make a hope or plan etc. happen, *She realised her ambition to become a racing driver.* **3** convert into money; be sold for; produce as profit. **realisation** *noun*

realism *noun* seeing or showing things as they really are. **realist** *noun*

realistic *adjective* **1** showing things as they really are, *a realistic painting.* **2** facing facts; based on facts rather than ideals, *a realistic proposal.* **realistically** *adverb*

reality *noun* (*plural* **realities**) what is real; something real.

really *adverb* truly; certainly; in fact.

realm (*say* relm) *noun* **1** a kingdom. **2** an area of knowledge, interest, etc., *in the realms of science.*

ream *noun* 500 (originally 480) sheets of paper.

reams *plural noun* a large quantity of writing.

reap *verb* **1** cut down and gather corn when it is ripe. **2** obtain as the result of something done, *They reaped great benefit from their training.* **reaper** *noun*

reappear *verb* appear again.

▶▶ T H E S A U R U S ◀◀

react *verb* act, behave, respond.

reaction *noun* **1** answer, feedback, reply, response.

read *verb* **1** (*read a book*) browse through, dip into, glance at, peruse, pore through, scan, skim, study, wade through; (*read someone's writing*) decipher, interpret, make out, understand. **3** indicate, register, show.
    readable *adjective* (*a readable book*) absorbing, enjoyable, entertaining, interesting; (*readable handwriting*) clear, decipherable, legible, neat, plain, understandable.

ready¹ *adjective* **1** equipped, fit, geared up, organised, prepared, primed, set. **2** disposed, eager, game, glad, happy, inclined, keen, willing. **3** immediate, instant, pat, prompt, quick, rapid, speedy. **4** accessible, available, convenient, handy, on hand.

real *adjective* **1** actual, existent, factual, historical, true. **2** authentic, dinkum (*Australian informal*), dinky-di (*Australian informal*), genuine, honest-to-goodness (*informal*), natural, proper, true; (*of feelings*) heartfelt, honest, sincere, unaffected.

realise *verb* **1** appreciate, apprehend, become aware of, catch on to (*informal*), comprehend, cotton on to (*informal*), grasp, jerry to (*Australian informal*), know, latch on to (*informal*), perceive, sense, suss out (*informal*), twig (*informal*), understand, wake up to. **2** accomplish, achieve, attain, fulfil.
    realisation *noun* appreciation, awareness, consciousness, knowledge, perception, recognition, understanding.

realistic *adjective* **1** accurate, authentic, faithful, lifelike, natural, true-to-life. **2** feasible, practicable, practical, pragmatic, viable, workable.

really *adverb* actually, certainly, definitely, genuinely, honestly, indeed, in fact, positively, sincerely, surely, truly.

realm *noun* **1** country, domain, dominion, empire, kingdom, monarchy, territory. **2** area, domain, field, province, sphere, world.

reap *verb* **1** cut, gather in, harvest. **2** gain, obtain, realise, receive.

▶▶▶ DICTIONARY ◀◀◀

rear¹ *noun* the back part.

rear² *adjective* placed at the rear.

rear³ *verb* **1** bring up young children or animals. **2** rise up; raise itself on hind legs, *The horse reared in fright.* **3** build or set up a monument etc.

rearguard *noun* troops protecting the rear of an army.

rearrange *verb* (**rearranged, rearranging**) arrange in a different way or order. **rearrangement** *noun*

reason¹ *noun* **1** a cause or explanation of something. **2** reasoning; common sense, *Listen to reason.*

Usage Do not use the phrase *the reason is* with the word *because* (which means the same thing). Correct usage is *We cannot come. The reason is that we both have flu* (not 'The reason is because . . .').

reason² *verb* **1** use your ability to think and draw conclusions. **2** try to persuade someone by giving reasons, *We reasoned with the rebels.*

reasonable *adjective* **1** ready to use or listen to reason; sensible; logical. **2** fair; moderate; not expensive, *reasonable prices.* **reasonably** *adverb*

reassure *verb* (**reassured, reassuring**) restore someone's confidence by removing doubts and fears. **reassurance** *noun*

rebate *noun* a reduction in the amount to be paid; a partial refund. [from *re-* + *abate*]

rebel¹ (*say* rib-**el**) *verb* (**rebelled, rebelling**) refuse to obey someone in authority, especially the government; fight against the rulers of your own country.

rebel² (*say* **reb**-el) *noun* someone who rebels. **rebellion** *noun*, **rebellious** *adjective* [from *re-*, + Latin *bellare* = fight]

rebirth *noun* a return to life or activity; a revival of something.

rebound *verb* bounce back after hitting something. **rebound** *noun*

rebuff *noun* an unkind refusal; a snub. **rebuff** *verb*

rebuild *verb* (**rebuilt, rebuilding**) build something again after it has been destroyed.

rebuke *verb* (**rebuked, rebuking**) speak severely to a person who has done wrong. **rebuke** *noun*

▶▶▶ THESAURUS ◀◀◀

rear¹ *noun* back, end, stern, tail.

rear² *adjective* back, hind.

rear³ *verb* **1** (*rear children*) bring up, care for, look after, nurture, raise; (*rear animals*) breed, keep, produce, raise.

rearrange *verb* change, interchange, juggle, reorder, reorganise, reshuffle, shift, shuffle, swap, switch, transpose.

reason¹ *noun* **1** cause, excuse, explanation, grounds, justification, motive, pretext, rationale. **2** common sense, good sense, logic, reasoning, sense, wisdom.

reason² *verb* **1** conclude, deduce, figure out, infer, solve, think through, work out, work through. **2** argue, debate, discuss, plead, remonstrate.

reasonable *adjective* **1** (*a reasonable person*) intelligent, logical, rational, sane, sensible, thinking; (*a reasonable explanation*) logical, plausible, rational, reasoned, sensible, sound, tenable, valid. **2** equitable, fair, just, justifiable, moderate.

reassure *verb* assure, comfort, encourage, set someone's mind at rest. **reassuring** *adjective* comforting, encouraging, favourable, hopeful, promising.

rebel¹ *verb* buck (*informal*), disobey, mutiny, resist, revolt, rise up.

rebel² *noun* dissenter, insurgent, malcontent, mutineer, nonconformist, revolutionary. **rebellion** *noun* insurgence, insurrection, mutiny, resistance, revolt, revolution, rising, uprising. **rebellious** *adjective* defiant, disobedient, insubordinate, insurgent, intractable, mutinous, recalcitrant, refractory, unmanageable, unruly, wild.

rebound *verb* bounce back, ricochet, spring back.

rebuff *noun* brush-off, knock-back (*informal*), refusal, rejection, snub. **rebuff** *verb* brush off, decline, knock back (*informal*), refuse, reject, snub, spurn, turn down.

rebuild *verb* reconstruct, remake, renew, restore.

rebuke *verb* admonish, berate, castigate, censure, chide (*old use*), reprimand, reproach, reprove, scold, tell off (*informal*), tick off (*informal*), upbraid. **rebuke** *noun* admonition, censure, dressing down (*informal*), lecture, rap over the knuckles, reprimand, reproach, reproof, scolding, serve (*Australian informal*).

▶▶ D I C T I O N A R Y ◀◀

rebut *verb* (**rebutted, rebutting**) refute; disprove. **rebuttal** *noun* [from re- + *butt*]

recalcitrant *adjective* disobedient. **recalcitrance** *noun* [from Latin, = kicking back]

recall[1] *verb* **1** ask a person to come back. **2** bring back into the mind; remember.

recall[2] *noun* recalling.

recant *verb* withdraw something you have said. **recantation** *noun* [from re-, + Latin *cantare* = sing]

recap *verb* (**recapped, recapping**) (*informal*) recapitulate. **recap** *noun*

recapitulate *verb* (**recapitulated, recapitulating**) state again the main points of what has been said. **recapitulation** *noun* [from re-, + Latin *capitulum* = chapter]

recapture *verb* (**recaptured, recapturing**) capture again; recover. **recapture** *noun*

recede *verb* (**receded, receding**) go back from a certain point, *The floods receded.* [from re-, + Latin *cedere* = go]

receipt (*say* ris-**eet**) *noun* **1** a written statement that money has been paid or something has been received. **2** receiving something.

receive *verb* (**received, receiving**) **1** take or get something that is given or sent. **2** greet a guest. [from re- = back again, + Latin *capere* = take]

receiver *noun* **1** a person or thing that receives something. **2** a person who buys and sells stolen goods. **3** an official who takes charge of a bankrupt person's property. **4** a radio or television set that receives broadcasts. **5** the part of a telephone that receives the sound and is held to a person's ear.

recent *adjective* not long past; happening or made a short time ago. **recently** *adverb*, **recency** *noun*

receptacle *noun* something for holding or containing what is put into it.

reception *noun* **1** the way a person or thing is received. **2** a formal party to receive guests, *a wedding reception*. **3** a place in a hotel or office etc. where visitors are received and registered. **4** a first class at school.

receptionist *noun* a person whose job is to receive and direct visitors, patients, etc.

receptive *adjective* quick or willing to receive ideas etc.

recess (*say* ris-**ess**) *noun* (*plural* **recesses**) **1** an alcove. **2** a time when work or business is stopped for a while. **3** the mid-morning break between classes at school, a snack eaten during this break. [same origin as *recede*]

recession *noun* **1** receding from a point. **2** a reduction in trade or prosperity.

recharge *verb* (**recharged, recharging**) charge again. **rechargeable** *adjective*

recipe (*say* **ress**-ip-ee) *noun* instructions for preparing or cooking food. [Latin, = take]

recipient *noun* a person who receives something.

reciprocal[1] (*say* ris-**ip**-rok-al) *adjective* given and received; mutual, *reciprocal help*. **reciprocally** *adverb*, **reciprocity** *noun*

reciprocal[2] *noun* a reversed fraction, ³⁄₂ *is the reciprocal of* ²⁄₃. [from Latin, = moving backwards and forwards]

reciprocate *verb* (**reciprocated, reciprocating**) give and receive; do the same thing in return, *She did not reciprocate his love.* **reciprocation** *noun*

▶▶ T H E S A U R U S ◀◀

rebut *verb* counter, disprove, invalidate, negate, refute.

recalcitrant *adjective* defiant, disobedient, headstrong, intractable, obstinate, perverse, refractory, stubborn, wayward, wilful.

recall[1] **2** *verb* call to mind, recollect, remember.

recap *verb* go over, recapitulate, reiterate, repeat, restate, summarise, sum up. **recap** *noun* recapitulation, résumé, summary, summing up.

recede *verb* ebb, go back, move back, retreat, subside.

receipt *noun* **1** docket, proof of purchase.

receive *verb* **1** accept, acquire, collect, earn, gain, get, land, obtain, take, win. **2** greet, meet, welcome.

recent *adjective* contemporary, current, fresh, latest, new, up to date.

receptacle *noun* carrier, container, holder, repository, vessel.

reception *noun* **1** greeting, welcome. **2** do (*informal*), function, gathering, party.

receptive *adjective* amenable, open, open-minded, responsive.

recess *noun* **1** alcove, bay, niche, nook. **3** break, little lunch, morning tea, playlunch, playtime.

recession *noun* **2** decline, depression, downturn, slump.

recipe *noun* directions, formula, instructions.

reciprocal[1] *adjective* mutual, reciprocated, requited, returned.

▶▶ D I C T I O N A R Y ◀◀

recital *noun* **1** reciting something. **2** a musical entertainment given by one performer or group.

recitative (*say* res-it-a-**teev**) *noun* a speech sung to music in an oratorio or opera.

recite *verb* (**recited, reciting**) say a poem etc. aloud from memory. **recitation** *noun* [from Latin, = read aloud]

reckless *adjective* rash; heedless. **recklessly** *adverb*, **recklessness** *noun* [from *reck* = heed, + *-less* = without]

reckon *verb* **1** calculate; count up. **2** have as an opinion; feel confident, *I reckon we shall win*.

reclaim *verb* **1** claim or get something back. **2** make a thing usable again, *reclaimed land*. **reclamation** *noun*

recline *verb* (**reclined, reclining**) lean or lie back. [from *re-*, + Latin *-clinare* = to lean]

recluse *noun* a person who lives alone and avoids mixing with people. [from *re-* = away, + Latin *clausum* = shut]

recognise *verb* (**recognised, recognising**) **1** know who someone is or what something is because you have seen that person or thing before. **2** realise, *We recognise the truth of what you said*. **3** accept something as genuine, welcome, or lawful etc., *Nine countries recognised the island's new government*. **recognition** *noun*, **recognisable** *adjective* [from *re-*, + Latin *cognoscere* = know]

recoil *verb* **1** spring back suddenly. **2** draw back in fear or disgust.

recollect *verb* remember. **recollection** *noun*

recommend *verb* **1** say that a person or thing would be a good one to do a job or achieve something. **2** advise doing something. **recommendation** *noun*

recompense *verb* (**recompensed, recompensing**) repay or reward someone; compensate. **recompense** *noun*

reconcile *verb* (**reconciled, reconciling**) **1** make people who have quarrelled become friendly again. **2** persuade a person to put up with something, *New frames reconciled him to wearing glasses*. **3** make things agree, *I cannot reconcile what you say with what you do*. **reconciliation** *noun* [from *re-* + *conciliate*]

recondition *verb* overhaul and repair.

reconnaissance (*say* rik-**on**-i-sans) *noun* an exploration of an area, especially in order to gather information about it for military purposes. [French, = recognition]

reconnoitre *verb* (**reconnoitred, reconnoitring**) make a reconnaissance of an area.

reconsider *verb* consider something again and perhaps change an earlier decision. **reconsideration** *noun*

reconstitute *verb* (**reconstituted, reconstituting**) put together again; reconstruct; reorganise.

reconstruct *verb* **1** construct or build something again. **2** create or act past events again, *Police reconstructed the robbery*. **reconstruction** *noun*

▶▶ T H E S A U R U S ◀◀

recital *noun* **2** concert, performance.

recite *verb* deliver, narrate, perform, rattle off, reel off, repeat, say, tell.

reckless *adjective* careless, daredevil, foolhardy, hare-brained, heedless, hotheaded, impetuous, imprudent, impulsive, incautious, irresponsible, mad, madcap, negligent, rash, unthinking, wild.

reckon *verb* **1** add up, assess, calculate, compute, count, figure out, tally, total, tot up (*informal*), work out. **2** believe, consider, fancy, judge, think.

recline *verb* lean back, lie, loll, lounge, repose, rest, sprawl, stretch out. **reclining** *adjective* horizontal, leaning, lying, recumbent.

recluse *noun* hermit, loner, solitary.

recognise *verb* **1** identify, know, pick out, place, recall, recollect, remember. **2** accept, acknowledge, admit, appreciate, be aware of, concede, grant, perceive, realise, see, understand.

recoil *verb* **1** kick, kick back, spring back. **2** cower, cringe, draw back, flinch, jump back, quail, shrink, shy away, start, wince.

recollect *verb* call to mind, recall, remember.

recommend *verb* **1** approve of, commend, endorse, laud (*formal*), praise, speak well of. **2** advise, advocate, counsel, prescribe, propose, suggest, urge.

reconcile *verb* **1** bring together, conciliate, placate, reunite.

recondition *verb* overhaul, rebuild, renovate, repair, restore.

reconnaissance *noun* exploration, inspection, investigation, observation, recce (*informal*), spying, survey.

reconsider *verb* consider again, reassess, rethink, review, think again.

reconstruct *verb* **1** reassemble, rebuild, remake, repair, restore. **2** re-create, re-enact.

▶▶ D I C T I O N A R Y ◀◀

record¹ (*say* **rek**-ord) *noun* **1** information kept in a permanent form, e.g. written or printed. **2** a disc on which sound has been recorded. **3** facts known about a person's past life or career etc., *She has a good school record.* **4** the best performance in a sport etc., or the most remarkable event of its kind, *He holds the record for the high jump.*

record² (*say* rik-**ord**) *verb* **1** put something down in writing or other permanent form. **2** store sounds or scenes (e.g. television pictures) on a disc or magnetic tape etc. so that you can play or show them later.

recorder *noun* **1** a kind of flute held downwards from the player's mouth. **2** a person or thing that records something.

record-player *noun* a device for reproducing sound from records.

recount *verb* give an account of, *We recounted our adventures.* [from Old French *reconter* = tell]

re-count *verb* count something again.

recoup (*say* ri-**koop**) *verb* recover the cost of an investment etc. or of a loss.

recourse *noun* a source of help.
have recourse to go to a person or thing for help.

recover *verb* **1** get something back again after losing it; regain. **2** get well again after being ill or weak. **recovery** *noun*

recreation *noun* **1** refreshing your mind or body after work through an enjoyable pastime. **2** a game or hobby etc. that is an enjoyable pastime. **recreational** *adjective* [from re- + creation]

recrimination *noun* an angry retort or accusation made against a person who has criticised or blamed you. [from *re-*, + Latin *criminare* = accuse]

recrudescence (*say* rek-roo-**dess**-ens) *noun* a fresh outbreak of a disease or trouble etc. [from *re-*, + Latin *crudescens* = becoming raw]

recruit¹ *noun* **1** a person who has just joined the armed forces. **2** a new member of a society or group etc.

recruit² *verb* enlist recruits. **recruitment** *noun*

rectangle *noun* a shape with four sides and four right angles. **rectangular** *adjective* [from Latin *rectus* = straight or right, + *angle*]

rectify *verb* (**rectified, rectifying**) correct or put something right. **rectification** *noun* [from Latin *rectus* = right]

rectilinear *adjective* with straight lines, *Squares and triangles are rectilinear figures.* [from Latin *rectus* = straight, + *linear*]

rectitude *noun* moral goodness; rightness of behaviour or procedure. [from Latin *rectus* = right]

rector *noun* a member of the clergy in charge of a parish. [Latin, = ruler]

rectory *noun* (*plural* **rectories**) the house of a rector.

rectum *noun* the last part of the large intestine, ending at the anus. [Latin, = straight (intestine)]

recumbent *adjective* lying down. [from *re-*, + Latin *cumbens* = lying]

recuperate *verb* (**recuperated, recuperating**) get better after an illness. **recuperation** *noun*

▶▶ T H E S A U R U S ◀◀

record¹ *noun* **1** account, annals, archives, chronicle, diary, document, dossier, history, journal, log, memorandum, minutes, narrative, note, register, report, transcription. **2** album, disc, recording, release. **3** background, curriculum vitae, CV, experience, history.

record² *verb* **1** chronicle, document, enter, jot down, list, log, minute, note, register, take down, transcribe, write down. **2** film, tape, tape-record, video.

recount *verb* describe, detail, narrate, recite, relate, report, tell.

recoup *verb* get back, recover, redeem, regain, retrieve, win back.

recover *verb* **1** find, get back, reclaim, recoup, redeem, regain, retrieve, salvage, track down.

2 convalesce, get better, heal, improve, mend, pick up, pull through, rally, recuperate.

recreation *noun* **1** amusement, diversion, enjoyment, entertainment, fun, leisure, play, pleasure, relaxation. **2** game, hobby, pastime, sport.

recruit¹ *noun* **2** apprentice, beginner, newcomer, novice, rookie (*informal*), tiro, trainee.

recruit² *verb* engage, enlist, sign on, take on.

rectangle *noun* oblong, square.

rectify *verb* correct, cure, fix, mend, put right, redress, remedy, repair.

recuperate *verb* convalesce, get better, improve, mend, recover, regain health.

recur *verb* (**recurred, recurring**) happen again; keep on happening. **recurrent** *adjective*, **recurrence** *noun* [from *re-*, + Latin *currere* = to run]

recycle *verb* (**recycled, recycling**) convert waste material into a form in which it can be reused.

red[1] *adjective* (**redder, reddest**) of the colour of blood or a colour rather like this. **redness** *noun*

red herring something that draws attention away from the main subject; a misleading clue.

red tape use of too many rules and forms in official business.

red[2] *noun* red colour.

in the red in debt (debts were entered in red in account-books).

red-back *noun* a small venomous Australian spider with a distinctive red or orange-red stripe on the female.

redden *verb* make or become red.

redeem *verb* **1** buy something back; pay off a debt. **2** save a person from damnation, *Christians believe that Christ redeemed us all.* **3** make up for faults, *His one redeeming feature is his kindness.* **redeemer** *noun*, **redemption** *noun* [from *re-*, + Latin *emere* = buy]

redevelop *verb* (**redeveloped, redeveloping**) develop land etc. in a different way. **redevelopment** *noun*

redfin *noun* a fish, the European perch, introduced to Australia.

redfish *noun* a native Australian fish also called *nannygai*.

red-handed *adjective* while actually committing a crime, *He was caught red-handed.*

redhead *noun* a person with reddish hair.

Red Indian a North American Indian.

redolent (*say* **red**-ol-ent) *adjective* **1** having a strong smell, *redolent of onions.* **2** full of memories, *a castle redolent of romance.* [from *re-*, + Latin *olens* = smelling]

redoubtable *adjective* formidable. [from French *redouter* = to fear]

redound *verb* come back as an advantage or disadvantage, *This will redound to our credit.* [from Latin *redundare* = overflow]

redress[1] *verb* set right; rectify, *redress the balance.*

redress[2] *noun* redressing; compensation, *You should seek redress for this damage.*

reduce *verb* (**reduced, reducing**) **1** make or become smaller or less. **2** force someone into a condition or situation, *He was reduced to borrowing the money.* **reduction** *noun* [from *re-*, + Latin *ducere* = bring]

redundant *adjective* not needed, especially for a particular job. **redundancy** *noun* [same origin as *redound*]

re-echo *verb* (**re-echoed, re-echoing**) echo; go on echoing.

reed *noun* **1** a tall plant that grows in water or marshy ground. **2** a thin strip that vibrates to make the sound in a clarinet, saxophone, oboe, etc.

reedy *adjective* **1** full of reeds. **2** (of a voice) having a thin high tone like a reed instrument. **reediness** *noun*

reef[1] *noun* a ridge of rock or sand etc., especially one near the surface of the sea.

recur *verb* be repeated, happen again, re-appear, repeat itself, resurface, return.
recurrent *adjective* continual, cyclical, frequent, perennial, periodic, perpetual, recurring, regular, repeated.

recycle *verb* reprocess, reuse, salvage, use again.

red[1] *adjective* blood-red, brick-red, burgundy, cardinal, carmine, cerise, cherry, claret, cochineal, crimson, flame, garnet, maroon, ruby, russet, scarlet, vermilion; (*of hair*) auburn, carroty, ginger, sandy; (*of the face*) florid, flushed, rubicund, ruddy; (*of the eyes*) bloodshot.

redden *verb* blush, colour, flush, glow.

redeem *verb* **1** buy back, reclaim, recover, repurchase. **2** atone for, ransom, rescue, save, set free.

redress[1] *verb* compensate for, make amends for, make up for, put right, rectify, remedy, repair.

redress[2] *noun* compensation, recompense, reparation, restitution.

reduce *verb* **1** abbreviate, abridge, condense, contract, curtail, cut, cut back, cut down, decline, decrease, diminish, dwindle, ease, lessen, lighten, lower, minimise, moderate, pare down, prune, scale down, shorten, shrink, slash, trim, whittle down.

redundant *adjective* excess, superfluous, surplus, unnecessary, unwanted.

▶▶▶ D I C T I O N A R Y ◀◀◀

reef² *verb* shorten a sail by drawing in a strip (called a *reef*) at the top or bottom to reduce the area exposed to the wind.

reef-knot *noun* a symmetrical double knot that is very secure.

reek *verb* smell strongly or unpleasantly. **reek** *noun*

reel¹ *noun* **1** a spool. **2** a lively Scottish dance.

reel² *verb* **1** wind something on to or off a reel. **2** stagger.
reel off say something quickly.

re-elect *verb* elect again.

re-enter *verb* enter again.

re-examine *verb* examine again.

ref *noun* (*informal*) a referee.

refectory *noun* (*plural* **refectories**) the dining-room of a monastery etc. [from Latin *refectum* = refreshed]

refer *verb* (**referred, referring**) pass a problem etc. to someone else, *My doctor referred me to a specialist.* **referral** *noun*
refer to mention; speak about, *I wasn't referring to you*; look in a book etc. for information, *We referred to our dictionary.* [from *re-* = back, + Latin *ferre* = bring]

referee¹ *noun* someone appointed to see that people keep to the rules of a game.

referee² *verb* (**refereed, refereeing**) act as a referee; umpire.

reference *noun* **1** referring to something, *There was no reference to recent events.* **2** a direction to a book or page or file etc. where information can be found. **3** a testimonial.
in or **with reference to** concerning; about.
reference book a book (such as a dictionary or encyclopedia) that gives information systematically.

reference library a library where books can be used but not taken away.

referendum *noun* (*plural* **referendums**) voting by all the people of a country (not by Parliament) to decide whether something shall be done. It is also called a *plebiscite.* [Latin, = referring]

refill *verb* fill again. **refill** *noun*

refine *verb* (**refined, refining**) **1** purify. **2** improve something, especially by making small changes.

refined *adjective* **1** purified. **2** cultured; with good manners.

refinement *noun* **1** the action of refining. **2** being refined. **3** something added to improve a thing.

refinery *noun* (*plural* **refineries**) a factory for refining something, *an oil refinery.*

reflect *verb* **1** send back light, heat, or sound etc. from a surface. **2** form an image of something as a mirror does. **3** think something over; consider. **4** show; be influenced by something, *Prices reflect the cost of producing things.* **reflection** *noun*, **reflective** *adjective*, **reflector** *noun* [from *re-*, + Latin *flectere* = to bend]

reflex *noun* (*plural* **reflexes**) a movement or action done without any conscious thought.
reflex angle an angle of more than 180°. [from *reflect*]

reflexive *adjective* referring back.
reflexive pronoun any of the pronouns *myself, herself, himself,* etc. (as in 'She cut *herself*'), which refer back to the subject of the verb.
reflexive verb a verb where the subject and the object are the same person or thing, as in *The child behaved himself.*

▶▶▶ T H E S A U R U S ◀◀◀

reek *verb* pong (*informal*), smell, stink.

reel¹ *noun* **1** bobbin, spindle, spool.

reel² *verb* **2** lurch, rock, stagger, stumble, sway, teeter, totter, wobble.
reel off rattle off, recite.

refer *verb* direct, pass, send.
refer to 1 allude to, bring up, cite, comment on, mention, speak of, touch on. **2** consult, look up in, turn to.

referee¹ *noun* adjudicator, ref (*informal*), umpire.

reference *noun* **1** allusion, hint, mention. **2** citation, example, quotation. **3** testimonial.

referendum *noun* ballot, plebiscite, poll, vote.

refill *verb* replenish, restock, top up.

refine *verb* **1** clarify, distil, filter, process, purify.

refined *adjective* **2** civilised, cultivated, cultured, dignified, elegant, genteel, gentlemanly, ladylike, polished, polite, sophisticated, urbane, well-bred, well-mannered.

reflect *verb* **1** mirror. **3** brood, cogitate, consider, contemplate, deliberate, meditate, mull over, muse, ponder, ruminate, think. **4** demonstrate, display, exhibit, indicate, reveal, show.
reflection *noun* image, likeness.

reform¹ *verb* make or become better by removing faults. **reformer** *noun*, **reformative** *adjective*, **reformatory** *adjective*

reform² *noun* **1** reforming. **2** a change made in order to improve something.

reformation *noun* reforming.
the Reformation a religious movement in Europe in the 16th century to reform certain teachings and practices of the Church, which resulted in the establishment of the Reformed or Protestant Churches.

refract *verb* bend a ray of light at the point where it enters water or glass etc. at an angle. **refraction** *noun*, **refractor** *noun*, **refractive** *adjective* [from *re-*, + Latin *fractum* = broken]

refractory *adjective* **1** difficult to control; stubborn. **2** (of substances) resistant to heat.

refrain¹ *verb* stop yourself from doing something, *Refrain from talking.*

refrain² *noun* the chorus of a song.

refresh *verb* make a tired person etc. feel fresh and strong again.

refreshment *noun* refreshing.
refreshments *plural noun* drinks and snacks.

refrigerate *verb* (**refrigerated, refrigerating**) make a thing extremely cold, especially in order to preserve it and keep it fresh. **refrigeration** *noun* [from *re-*, + Latin *frigus* = cold]

refrigerator *noun* a cabinet or room in which food is stored at a very low temperature.

refuel *verb* (**refuelled, refuelling**) supply a ship or aircraft with more fuel.

refuge *noun* **1** shelter from pursuit or danger. **2** a place where a person is safe from pursuit or danger. [from *re-*, + Latin *fugere* = flee]

refugee *noun* a person who has had to leave home and seek refuge somewhere, e.g. because of war or persecution or famine.

refund¹ *verb* pay money back.

refund² *noun* money paid back.

refurbish *verb* freshen something up; redecorate.

refuse¹ (*say* re-**fewz**) *verb* (**refused, refusing**) say that you are unwilling to do or give or accept something. **refusal** *noun*

refuse² (*say* **ref**-yooss) *noun* waste material, *Trucks collected the refuse.*

refute *verb* (**refuted, refuting**) prove that a person or statement etc. is wrong. **refutation** *noun*

regain *verb* **1** get something back after losing it. **2** reach a place again.

regal (*say* **ree**-gal) *adjective* of or by a monarch; fit for a king or queen. [from Latin *regis* = of a king]

regale (*say* rig-**ayl**) *verb* (**regaled, regaling**) feed or entertain well, *They regaled us with stories.*

regalia *plural noun* the emblems of royalty or rank, *The royal regalia include the crown, sceptre, and orb.*

reform¹ *verb* **1** ameliorate, amend, change, correct, improve, mend, rectify, revise, revolutionise, transform. **2** go straight, mend your ways, turn over a new leaf.

refractory *adjective* **1** disobedient, headstrong, intractable, obstinate, perverse, pigheaded, rebellious, recalcitrant, stubborn, uncontrollable, unmanageable, wayward, wilful.

refrain¹ *verb* (*refrain from*) abstain from, avoid, desist from, forbear from, stop.

refrain² *noun* chorus.

refresh *verb* freshen, invigorate, perk up (*informal*), rejuvenate, restore, revive.

refreshments *plural noun* drinks, eats (*informal*), food, nibbles (*informal*), snacks.

refrigerate *verb* chill, cool, freeze.

refuge *noun* **1** asylum, cover, protection, safety, sanctuary, shelter. **2** haven, hideout (*informal*), hidey-hole (*informal*), hiding place, retreat, sanctuary, shelter.

refugee *noun* asylum seeker, displaced person, exile, fugitive, runaway.

refund¹ *verb* give back, pay back, reimburse, repay, return.

refund² *noun* reimbursement, repayment.

refurbish *verb* clean up, do up (*informal*), redecorate, remodel, renovate, restore, revamp, spruce up.

refuse¹ *verb* (*refuse an offer*) decline, knock back (*informal*), pass up (*informal*), rebuff, reject, scorn, spurn, turn down; (*refuse permission*) deny, withhold.
refusal *noun* knock-back (*informal*), rebuff, rejection, veto.

refuse² *noun* debris, garbage, junk, litter, rubbish, scrap, trash, waste.

refute *verb* disprove, negate, rebut.

regain *verb* **1** get back, recoup, recover, retrieve, win back.

regal *adjective* kingly, lordly, majestic, princely, queenly, royal, stately.

▶▶▶ D I C T I O N A R Y ◀◀

regard¹ *verb* **1** look or gaze at. **2** think of in a certain way; consider to be, *We regard the matter as serious.*

regard² *noun* **1** a gaze. **2** consideration; heed, *You acted without regard to people's safety.* **3** respect, *We have a great regard for her.*
regards *plural noun* kind wishes sent in a message, *Give him my regards.*
with regard to concerning.

regarding *preposition* concerning, *There are laws regarding drugs.*

regardless *adverb* without considering something, *Do it, regardless of the cost.*

regatta *noun* a meeting for boat or yacht races. [from Italian]

regency *noun* being a regent.

regenerate *verb* (**regenerated, regenerating**) give new life or strength to something. **regeneration** *noun*

regent *noun* a person appointed to rule a country while the monarch is too young or unable to rule. [from Latin *regens* = ruling]

reggae (*say* **reg**-ay) *noun* a West Indian style of music with a strong beat.

regime (*say* ray-*zh***eem**) *noun* a system of government or organisation, *a Communist regime.*

regiment *noun* an army unit, usually divided into battalions or companies. **regimental** *adjective*

region *noun* an area; a part of a country or of the world, *in tropical regions.* **regional** *adjective*, **regionally** *adverb*
in the region of near, *The cost will be in the region of $100.*

register¹ *noun* **1** an official list of things or names etc. **2** a book in which items are recorded for reference. **3** a device that records the amount of something automatically, *a cash register.* **4** the range of a voice or musical instrument.

register² *verb* **1** list something in a register. **2** indicate; show, *The thermometer registered 100°.* **3** make an impression on someone's mind. **4** pay extra for a letter or parcel to be sent with special care. **registration** *noun*

registrar *noun* an official whose job is to keep written records or registers.

registry *noun* (*plural* **registries**) a place where registers are kept.
registry office an office where marriages are performed and records of births, marriages, and deaths are kept.

rego *noun* (*Australian informal*) motor vehicle registration.

regression *noun* **1** a backward movement. **2** reversion; returning to an earlier condition. **regressive** *adjective* [from *re-*, + Latin *gressus* = gone]

regret¹ *noun* a feeling of sorrow or disappointment about something that has happened or been done. **regretful** *adjective*, **regretfully** *adverb*

regret² *verb* (**regretted, regretting**) feel regret about something. **regrettable** *adjective*, **regrettably** *adverb*

regular *adjective* **1** always happening or doing something at certain times. **2** even; symmetrical, *regular teeth.* **3** normal; standard; correct, *the regular procedure.* **4** of a

▶▶▶ T H E S A U R U S ◀◀

regard¹ *verb* **1** behold (*old use*), contemplate, eye, gaze at, look at, observe, scrutinise, stare at, view, watch. **2** consider, deem, judge, look upon, reckon, view.

regard² *noun* **2** attention, care, concern, consideration, heed, notice, thought. **3** admiration, approval, esteem, favour, honour, respect.

regarding *preposition* about, apropos, concerning, in regard to, with reference to, with regard to, with respect to.

regardless *adverb* anyhow, anyway, heedlessly, nevertheless, nonetheless.
regardless of despite, disregarding, in spite of, irrespective of, notwithstanding.

region *noun* area, district, land, locality, neighbourhood, part, place, province, spot, territory, tract, vicinity, zone.
regional *adjective* district, local, provincial.

in the region of about, approximately, around, in the neighbourhood of, in the vicinity of, nearly, roughly.

register¹ *noun* **1** catalogue, directory, index, list, record, roll.

register² *verb* **1** catalogue, enter, file, list, place on record, record, write down; see also ENROL. **2** indicate, read, record, show.

regret¹ *noun* compunction, disappointment, penitence, remorse, repentance, sorrow.
regretful *adjective* apologetic, contrite, penitent, remorseful, repentant, rueful, sorry.

regret² *verb* bemoan, be sad about, be sorry about, deplore, lament, repent, rue.
regrettable *adjective* deplorable, lamentable, reprehensible, sad, shameful, unfortunate.

regular *adjective* **1** consistent, fixed, periodic, predictable, repeated, routine, set, systematic, unchanging, unvarying. **2** (*regular footsteps*)

▶▶▶ D I C T I O N A R Y ◀◀

country's permanent armed forces, *a regular soldier*. **regularly** *adverb*, **regularity** *noun* [from Latin *regula* = a rule]

regulate *verb* (**regulated, regulating**) 1 adjust. 2 control. **regulator** *noun*

regulation *noun* 1 regulating. 2 a rule or law. [same origin as *regular*]

regurgitate *verb* (**regurgitated, regurgitating**) bring swallowed food up again into the mouth. **regurgitation** *noun*

rehabilitation *noun* restoring a person to a normal life or a building etc. to a good condition. **rehabilitate** *verb*

rehash *verb* (*informal*) repeat something without changing it very much.

rehearse *verb* (**rehearsed, rehearsing**) practise something before performing to an audience. **rehearsal** *noun*

reign[1] *verb* 1 rule a country as king or queen. 2 be supreme; be the strongest influence, *Silence reigned*.

reign[2] *noun* the time when someone reigns. [from Latin *regnum* = royal authority]

reimburse *verb* (**reimbursed, reimbursing**) repay. **reimbursement** *noun*

rein *noun* a strap used to guide a horse. [same origin as *retain*]

reincarnation *noun* being born again into a new body.

reindeer *noun* (*plural* **reindeer**) a kind of deer that lives in Arctic regions.

reinforce *verb* (**reinforced, reinforcing**) strengthen by adding extra people or supports etc.

reinforcement *noun* 1 reinforcing. 2 something that reinforces.

reinforcements *plural noun* extra troops or ships etc. sent to strengthen a force.

reinstate *verb* (**reinstated, reinstating**) put a person or thing back into a former position. **reinstatement** *noun*

reiterate *verb* (**reiterated, reiterating**) say something again and again. **reiteration** *noun* [from re-, + Latin *iterum* = again]

reject *verb* 1 refuse to accept a person or thing. 2 throw away; discard. **rejection** *noun* [from *re-* = away, + Latin *-jectum* = thrown]

rejoice *verb* (**rejoiced, rejoicing**) feel or show great joy.

rejoin *verb* 1 join again. 2 answer; retort.

rejuvenate *verb* (**rejuvenated, rejuvenating**) make a person seem young again. **rejuvenation** *noun* [from *re-*, + Latin *juvenis* = young]

relapse *verb* (**relapsed, relapsing**) return to a previous condition; become worse after improving. **relapse** *noun* [from *re-*, + Latin *lapsum* = slipped]

relate *verb* (**related, relating**) 1 narrate. 2 connect or compare one thing with another. 3 behave happily towards people or animals, *some people cannot relate to animals*.

▶▶▶ T H E S A U R U S ◀◀

even, measured, rhythmic, steady, uniform; (*a regular shape*) even, symmetrical. 3 conventional, correct, customary, established, habitual, normal, official, ordinary, orthodox, proper, routine, standard, traditional, typical, usual.

regulate *verb* 1 adjust, alter, change, moderate, modulate, vary. 2 control, direct, govern, manage, oversee, supervise.

regulation *noun* 2 by-law, decree, directive, law, ordinance, rule, statute.

rehearse *verb* go over, practise, prepare, run through.

reign[1] *verb* 1 be on the throne, govern, rule.

reign[2] *noun* kingship, rule, sovereignty.

reimburse *verb* indemnify, pay back, recompense, refund, repay.

reinforce *verb* bolster, brace, buttress, fortify, prop up, shore up, strengthen, support, toughen.

reject *verb* 1 (*reject a person*) brush off, disown, ditch (*informal*), drop, dump, forsake, jilt,

rebuff, renounce, repudiate, snub; (*reject an offer*) decline, dismiss, knock back (*informal*), pass up (*informal*), refuse, spurn, turn down, turn your nose up at. 2 discard, get rid of, jettison, scrap, send back, throw away, throw out.

rejection *noun* brush-off, knock-back (*informal*), rebuff, refusal, snub, thumbs down, veto.

rejoice *verb* be happy, be joyful, be overjoyed, celebrate, crow, delight, exult, revel.

rejuvenate *verb* refresh, reinvigorate, renew, restore, revitalise, revive.

relapse *verb* backslide, degenerate, fall back, lapse, regress, retrogress, revert, slip back. **relapse** *noun* deterioration, regression, setback.

relate *verb* 1 describe, narrate, recite, recount, report, spin, tell. 2 (*relate to*) apply to, belong to, be relevant to, concern, connect with, have a bearing on, pertain to, refer to. 3 (*relate to*) empathise with, get on with, identify with, interact with, understand.

related *adjective* **1** belonging to the same family. **2** connected.

relation *noun* **1** a relative. **2** the way one thing is related to another.

relationship *noun* **1** how people or things are related. **2** how people get on with each other.

relative¹ *noun* a person who is related to another.

relative² *adjective* connected or compared with something; compared with the average, *They live in relative comfort.* **relatively** *adverb* **relative pronoun** see *pronoun*.

relax *verb* **1** make or become less tight or stiff. **2** make or become less strict, *relax the rules.* **3** stop working; rest. **relaxation** *noun* [from *re-* = back, + Latin *laxus* = loose]

relay¹ *verb* pass on a message or broadcast.

relay² *noun* **1** a fresh group taking the place of another, *The firemen worked in relays.* **2** a relay race. **3** a device for relaying a broadcast. **relay race** a race between teams in which each person covers part of the distance.

release¹ *verb* (**released, releasing**) **1** set free; unfasten. **2** let a thing fall or fly or go out. **3** make a film or record etc. available to the public.

release² *noun* **1** being released. **2** something released. **3** a device that unfastens something.

relegate *verb* (**relegated, relegating**) **1** put into a less important place. **2** put a sports team into a lower division of a league. **relegation** *noun* [from *re-* = back, + Latin *legatum* = sent]

relent *verb* become less severe or more merciful. [from *re-* = back, + Latin *lentus* = flexible]

relentless *adjective* **1** not relenting; pitiless. **2** unceasing. **relentlessly** *adverb*

relevant *adjective* connected with what is being discussed or dealt with. (The opposite is *irrelevant.*) **relevance** *noun*

reliable *adjective* able to be relied on; trustworthy. **reliably** *adverb*, **reliability** *noun*

reliance *noun* relying; trust. **reliant** *adjective*

relic *noun* something that has survived from an earlier time. [same origin as *relinquish*]

relief *noun* **1** the ending or lessening of pain, trouble, boredom, etc. **2** something that gives relief or help. **3** a person who takes over a turn of duty when another finishes. **4** a method of making a design etc. that stands out from a surface.
relief map a map that shows hills and valleys by shading or moulding. [from *re-*, + Latin *levis* = lightweight]

related *adjective* **2** allied, associated, connected, interconnected, interrelated.

relation *noun* **1** see RELATIVE¹. **2** association, connection, correlation, correspondence, link, relationship, tie-in.

relationship *noun* **1** affinity, association, attachment, bond, connection, link, rapport, tie.

relative¹ *noun* kinsman, kinswoman, relation; (*relatives*) clan, family, flesh and blood, folk, kin, kindred, kith and kin.

relative² *adjective* comparative.

relax *verb* **1** ease off, loosen, slacken, weaken. **2** ease, liberalise, moderate, soften, stretch. **3** calm down, laze, lounge, rest, take it easy, unwind, veg out (*slang*).
relaxation *noun* diversion, enjoyment, fun, hobby, leisure, pastime, pleasure, recreation, rest.
relaxed *adjective* calm, carefree, casual, easygoing, informal, laid-back (*informal*), nonchalant, serene, slack.

relay¹ *verb* communicate, pass on, send on, transmit.

release¹ *verb* **1** deliver, discharge, emancipate, free, let go, let loose, let out, liberate, set free, unbuckle, undo, unfasten, untie. **3** circulate, distribute, issue, launch, publish.

relent *verb* be merciful, capitulate, give in, have pity, soften, yield.

relentless *adjective* **1** cruel, harsh, implacable, inexorable, merciless, pitiless, remorseless, ruthless, severe, unyielding. **2** constant, continuous, endless, incessant, persistent, unceasing, unrelenting, unremitting.

relevant *adjective* applicable, apposite, appropriate, apropos, apt, connected, germane, pertinent, related, to the point.

reliable *adjective* constant, dependable, faithful, loyal, staunch, steadfast, steady, sure, true, trusted, trustworthy, trusty (*old use*).

relic *noun* antique, heirloom, keepsake, memento, reminder, remnant, souvenir, survival, vestige.

relief *noun* **1** alleviation, comfort, ease, let-up, palliation, remission, respite, rest, solace. **2** aid, assistance, help, succour, support.

▶▶ D I C T I O N A R Y ◀◀

relieve *verb* (**relieved, relieving**) **1** end or lessen a person's pain, trouble, boredom, etc. **2** release a person from a duty by acting as or providing a replacement.
relieve of take something from a person, *The thief relieved him of his wallet.*

religion *noun* what people believe about God or gods, and how they worship. [from Latin *religio* = reverence]

religious *adjective* **1** of religion. **2** believing firmly in a religion and taking part in its customs. **religiously** *adverb*

relinquish *verb* give up; let go. **relinquishment** *noun* [from *re-* = behind, + Latin *linquere* = leave]

relish¹ *noun* **1** great enjoyment. **2** something tasty that adds flavour to plainer food.

relish² *verb* enjoy greatly.

reluctant *adjective* unwilling; not keen. **reluctantly** *adverb*, **reluctance** *noun* [from Latin, = struggling against something]

rely *verb* (**relied, relying**) **rely on** trust a person or thing to help or support you.

remain *verb* **1** be there after other parts have gone or been dealt with; be left over. **2** continue to be in the same place or condition; stay. [from *re-* = behind, + Latin *manere* = stay]

remainder *noun* **1** the remaining part of people or things. **2** the number left after subtraction or division.

remains *plural noun* **1** all that is left over after other parts have been removed or destroyed. **2** ancient ruins or objects; relics. **3** a dead body.

remand *verb* send back a prisoner into custody while further evidence is sought. **remand** *noun* [from *re-*, + Latin *mandare* = entrust]

remark¹ *noun* something said; a comment.

remark² *verb* **1** make a remark; say. **2** notice.

remarkable *adjective* unusual; extraordinary. **remarkably** *adverb*

remedial *adjective* helping to cure an illness or deficiency.

remedy¹ *noun* (*plural* **remedies**) **1** something that cures or relieves a disease etc. **2** something that puts a matter right.

remedy² *verb* (**remedied, remedying**) be a remedy for something; put right. [from *re-*, + Latin *mederi* = heal]

▶▶ T H E S A U R U S ◀◀

relieve *verb* **1** alleviate, assuage, ease, help, lessen, lighten, mitigate, palliate, reduce, soothe, subdue. **2** cover for, fill in for, replace, stand in for, substitute for, take the place of.

religion *noun* belief, creed, cult, denomination, faith, sect.

religious *adjective* **1** devotional, divine, doctrinal, holy, sacred, scriptural, spiritual, theological. **2** devout, God-fearing, godly, pious, spiritual.

relinquish *verb* abandon, abdicate, cede, forgo, forsake, give up, renounce, resign, surrender, waive.

relish¹ *noun* **1** delight, enthusiasm, gusto, keenness, pleasure, zest.

relish² *verb* delight in, enjoy, fancy, like, love, revel in, savour.

reluctant *adjective* averse, disinclined, hesitant, loath, unwilling.

rely *verb* **rely on** bank on, count on, depend on, reckon on, trust.

remain *verb* **1** be left (over). **2** continue, endure, hang around, keep on, linger, live on, persist, prevail, stay, stick around (*informal*), survive, tarry, wait.

remainder *noun* **1** balance, excess, leftovers, remnant, residue, rest, surplus.

remains *plural noun* **1** dregs, leftovers, remnants, scraps. **2** relics, ruins, wreckage. **3** body, carcass, corpse.

remark¹ *noun* comment, observation, opinion, statement, word.

remark² *verb* **1** comment, mention, note, observe, reflect, say.

remarkable *adjective* amazing, astounding, conspicuous, exceptional, extraordinary, impressive, marvellous, memorable, notable, noteworthy, outstanding, phenomenal, sensational, signal, significant, singular, special, startling, striking, surprising, uncommon, unusual, wonderful.

remedial *adjective* corrective, curative, therapeutic.

remedy¹ *noun* **1** antidote, cure, medication, medicine, panacea, therapy, treatment. **2** answer, corrective, cure, solution.

remedy² *verb* correct, cure, fix, mend, put right, rectify, redress, repair, solve.

▶▶▶ D I C T I O N A R Y ◀◀

remember *verb* **1** keep something in your mind. **2** bring something back into your mind. **remembrance** *noun* [from *re-*, + Latin *memor* = mindful]

remind *verb* help or cause a person to remember something. **reminder** *noun*

reminisce (*say* rem-in-**iss**) *verb* (**reminisced, reminiscing**) think or talk about things that you remember. **reminiscence** *noun*

reminiscent *adjective* reminding of something.

remiss *adjective* negligent; careless about doing what you ought to do.

remit *verb* (**remitted, remitting**) **1** send, especially money. **2** forgive; reduce or cancel a punishment etc. **3** make or become less intense; slacken, *We must not remit our efforts.* **remission** *noun* [from *re-* = back, + Latin *mittere* = send]

remittance *noun* **1** sending money. **2** the money sent.

remnant *noun* a part or piece left over from something. (Compare *remain.*)

remonstrate *verb* (**remonstrated, remonstrating**) make a protest, *We remonstrated with him about his behaviour.* [from *re-* = against, + Latin *monstrare* = to show]

remorse *noun* deep regret for having done wrong. **remorseful** *adjective*, **remorsefully** *adverb* [from *re-* = back, + Latin *morsum* = bitten]

remorseless *adjective* relentless.

remote *adjective* **1** far away. **2** some but very little; unlikely, *a remote chance.* **remotely** *adverb*, **remoteness** *noun*

remote control controlling something from a distance, usually by electricity or radio. [from Latin *remotum* = removed]

removable *adjective* able to be removed.

removal *noun* removing or moving something.

removalist *noun* (*Australian*) a person or firm that moves household or office furniture.

remove *verb* (**removed, removing**) **1** take something away or off. **2** move or take to another place. **3** dismiss a person from a job. **4** get rid of, *remove graffiti.*

remunerate *verb* (**remunerated, remunerating**) pay or reward someone. **remuneration** *noun*, **remunerative** *adjective* [from *re-*, + Latin *muneris* = of a gift]

Renaissance (*say* ren-**ay**-sans) *noun* the revival of classical styles of art and literature in Europe in the 14th–16th centuries. [French, = rebirth]

renal (*say* **reen**-al) *adjective* of the kidneys.

rend *verb* (**rent, rending**) rip; tear.

render *verb* **1** give or perform something, *render help to the victims.* **2** cause to become, *The shock rendered us speechless.* [from Latin *reddere* = give back]

rendezvous (*say* **rond**-ay-voo) *noun* (*plural* **rendezvous**, *say* **rond**-ay-vooz) a meeting with somebody; a place arranged for this. [from French *rendezvous* = present yourselves]

▶▶▶ T H E S A U R U S ◀◀

remember *verb* **1** keep in mind, memorise, recall, recollect, retain. **2** call to mind, look back on, recall, recollect, reflect on, reminisce about, think back on.

remembrance *noun* commemoration, memory, recollection.

remind *verb* jog someone's memory, prompt, refresh someone's memory.

reminder *noun* keepsake, memento, remembrance, souvenir.

reminiscences *plural noun* memoirs, memories, recollections.

remiss *adjective* careless, forgetful, lax, neglectful, negligent, slack, slipshod, sloppy.

remnant *noun* fragment, leftover, offcut, piece, remainder, remains, residue, scrap.

remorse *noun* compunction, contrition, guilt, penitence, regret, repentance, shame, sorrow.

remote *adjective* **1** distant, far-away, far-flung, inaccessible, isolated, lonely, outlying, out of the way, secluded, solitary. **2** faint, outside, slender, slight, slim, unlikely.

remove *verb* **1** (*remove clothing*) doff (*a hat*), peel off, pull off, shed, strip off, take off; (*remove a branch*) chop off, cut off, lop off, prune; (*remove a tooth*) extract, pull out, take out. **2** carry away, cart off, convey, move, relocate, shift, take away, transfer, transport. **3** depose, dismiss, drive out, eject, evict, expel, fire, get rid of, kick out (*informal*), oust, sack (*informal*), throw out, turn out. **4** delete, efface, eliminate, eradicate, erase, expunge, get rid of, obliterate, rub out, wash off, wipe out.

remuneration *noun* pay, payment, recompense, reward, salary, wages.

render *verb* **1** do, give, perform, provide, supply. **2** make.

rendezvous *noun* appointment, assignation, date (*informal*), engagement, meeting.

▶▶DICTIONARY◀◀

renegade (say **ren**-ig-ayd) *noun* a person who deserts a group or religion etc. [from *re-* = back, + Latin *negare* = deny]

renew *verb* 1 restore something to its original condition or replace it with something new. 2 begin or make or give again, *We renewed our request.* **renewal** *noun*

renewable *adjective* able to be renewed.

rennet *noun* a substance used to curdle milk in making cheese or junket.

renounce *verb* (**renounced, renouncing**) give up; reject. **renunciation** *noun* [from *re-* = back, + Latin *nuntiare* = announce]

renovate *verb* (**renovated, renovating**) repair a thing and make it look new. **renovation** *noun* [from *re-*, + Latin *novus* = new]

renown *noun* fame. **renowned** *adjective*

rent¹ *noun* a regular payment for the use of something especially a house that belongs to another person.

rent² *verb* have or allow the use of something in return for rent.

rent³ *past tense* of **rend**.

rent⁴ *noun* a torn place; a split.

rental *noun* rent (= *rent¹*).

renunciation *noun* renouncing something.

reorganise *verb* organise again or in a new way. **reorganisation** *noun*

repair¹ *verb* put something into good condition after it has been damaged or broken etc. **repairable** *adjective*

repair² *noun* repairing; being repaired. [from *re-*, + Latin *parare* = make ready]

repair³ *verb* (*formal*) go, *The guests repaired to the dining room.* [same origin as *repatriate*]

reparation *noun* compensation; amends.

repartee *noun* quick retorts.

repast *noun* (*formal*) a meal.

repatriate *verb* (**repatriated, repatriating**) send a person back to his or her own country. **repatriation** *noun* [from *re-*, + Latin *patria* = native country]

repay *verb* (**repaid, repaying**) 1 pay back, especially money. 2 give in return, *repay their kindness.* **repayable** *adjective*, **repayment** *noun*

repeal *verb* cancel a law officially. **repeal** *noun*

repeat¹ *verb* say or do the same thing again. **repeatedly** *adverb*

repeat² *noun* 1 the action of repeating. 2 something that is repeated. [from *re-*, + Latin *petere* = seek]

repel *verb* (**repelled, repelling**) 1 drive away; repulse, *repel the attack.* 2 disgust somebody. **repellent** *adjective* & *noun* [from *re-*, + Latin *pellere* = to drive]

▶▶THESAURUS◀◀

renegade *noun* apostate, defector, deserter, traitor, turncoat.

renew *verb* 1 change, refresh, reinvigorate, rejuvenate, renovate, replace, restore, revive. 2 (*renew their requests*) begin again, begin anew, reiterate, repeat, restate; (*renew a friendship*) pick up again, re-establish, resume, resurrect, revive.

renounce *verb* abandon, abdicate, discard, disown, forgo, forsake, forswear, give up, reject, relinquish, repudiate, surrender, waive.

renovate *verb* do up (*informal*), modernise, redecorate, refurbish, rejuvenate, remodel, restore, revamp, update.

renown *noun* distinction, fame, importance, note, prestige, reputation, repute.
renowned *adjective* celebrated, distinguished, eminent, famed, famous, illustrious, notable, noted, prominent, well-known.

rent² *verb* charter, hire, lease, let.

reorganise *verb* change, rationalise, rearrange, reshuffle, restructure, transform.
reorganisation *noun* change, rationalisation, rearrangement, reshuffle, restructuring, shake-up, transformation.

repair¹ *verb* darn, fix, mend, overhaul, patch (up), recondition, restore, service.

reparation *noun* atonement, compensation, damages, indemnity, redress, restitution.

repay *verb* 1 pay back, recompense, refund, reimburse, remunerate. 2 pay back, reciprocate, requite, return, reward.

repeal *verb* abrogate, annul, cancel, nullify, rescind, revoke, withdraw.

repeat¹ *verb* do again, duplicate, echo, quote, recite, redo, reiterate, reproduce, retell, say again, tell again.
repeatedly *adverb* again and again, continually, frequently, often, over and over, time and time again.

repeat² *noun* 2 rebroadcast, replay, rerun.

repel *verb* 1 drive away, fend off, force back, keep at bay, parry, repulse, stave off, ward off. 2 disgust, nauseate, offend, put off, revolt, sicken.
repellent *adjective* disgusting, distasteful, horrible, loathsome, nauseating, offensive, off-putting, repugnant, repulsive, revolting, sickening.

▶▶ D I C T I O N A R Y ◀◀

repent *verb* be sorry for what you have done. **repentance** *noun*, **repentant** *adjective* [from *re-* + *penitent*]

repercussion *noun* a result or reaction produced indirectly by something.

repertoire (*say* **rep**-er-twahr) *noun* a stock of songs or plays etc. that a person or company knows and can perform.

repertory *noun* a repertoire.
repertory company or **theatre** a company or theatre giving performances of various plays for short periods.

repetition *noun* repeating; something repeated. **repetitious** *adjective*

repetitive *adjective* full of repetitions. **repetitively** *adverb*

replace *verb* (**replaced**, **replacing**) **1** put a thing back in its place. **2** take the place of another person or thing. **3** put a new or different thing in place of something. **replacement** *noun*

replay *verb* play a sports match or a recording again. **replay** *noun*

replenish *verb* fill again; add a new supply of something. **replenishment** *noun* [from *re-*, + Latin *plenus* = full]

replete *adjective* **1** well supplied. **2** feeling full after eating. [from *re-*, + Latin *-pletum* = filled]

replica *noun* an exact copy.

reply[1] *noun* (*plural* **replies**) something said or written to deal with a question, letter, etc.; an answer.

reply[2] *verb* (**replied**, **replying**) give a reply to; answer.

report[1] *verb* **1** describe something that has happened or that you have done or studied. **2** make a complaint or accusation against somebody. **3** go and tell somebody that you have arrived or are ready for work.

report[2] *noun* **1** a description or account of something. **2** a regular statement of how someone has worked or behaved, e.g. at school. **3** an explosive sound. [from *re-* = back, + Latin *portare* = carry]

reporter *noun* a person whose job is to collect and report news for a newspaper, radio or television programme, etc.

repose[1] *noun* rest; sleep.

repose[2] *verb* (**reposing**, **reposing**) rest or lie somewhere.

repository *noun* (*plural* **repositories**) a place where things are stored.

reprehensible *adjective* deserving blame or rebuke.

represent *verb* **1** show a person or thing in a picture or play etc. **2** symbolise; stand for, *In Roman numerals, V represents 5.* **3** be an

▶▶ T H E S A U R U S ◀◀

repent *verb* be sorry, bewail, feel remorse, lament, regret, rue.
repentant *adjective* apologetic, contrite, penitent, regretful, remorseful, rueful, sorry.

repercussion *noun* after-effect, backlash, consequence, effect, knock-on effect, result, side effect.

repetitive *adjective* boring, humdrum, monotonous, repetitious, tedious, unchanging, unvaried.

replace *verb* **1** put back, restore, return. **2** come after, follow, oust, substitute for, succeed, supersede, supplant, take the place of. **3** change, renew, replenish.
replacement *noun* deputy, locum, proxy, ring-in (*Australian informal*), stand-in, substitute, successor, surrogate.

replica *noun* copy, duplicate, facsimile, imitation, likeness, model, reproduction.

reply[1] *noun* acknowledgement, answer, comeback (*informal*), rejoinder, response, retort, riposte.

reply[2] *verb* answer, counter, rejoin, respond, retort.

report[1] *verb* **1** announce, communicate, declare, disclose, divulge, document, notify, publish, record, say, state, tell, write up. **2** denounce, dob in (*Australian informal*), grass (on) (*slang*), inform on, shop (*slang*), tell on. **3** front up (*informal*), introduce yourself, present yourself.

report[2] *noun* **1** account, announcement, article, bulletin, communiqué, description, narrative, news, paper, proceedings, record, statement, story, write-up. **3** bang, blast, boom, detonation, explosion, noise.

reporter *noun* correspondent, journalist, writer.

repose[1] *noun* rest, sleep, slumber.

repose[2] *verb* lie, recline, relax, rest, stretch out; see also SLEEP[2].

reprehensible *adjective* blameworthy, culpable, deplorable, despicable, inexcusable, shameful, unworthy, wicked, wrong.

represent *verb* **1** depict, describe, illustrate, picture, portray, present, show. **2** correspond to, denote, express, indicate, mean, signify, stand

▶▶DICTIONARY◀◀

example or equivalent of something. **4** help someone by speaking or doing something on their behalf. **representation** *noun*

representative[1] *noun* a person or thing that represents another or others.

representative[2] *adjective* **1** representing others. **2** typical of a group.

repress *verb* keep down; restrain; suppress. **repression** *noun*, **repressive** *adjective*

reprieve[1] *noun* postponement or cancellation of a punishment etc., especially the death penalty.

reprieve[2] *verb* (**reprieved, reprieving**) give a reprieve to.

reprimand[1] *noun* a rebuke, especially a formal or official one.

reprimand[2] *verb* give someone a reprimand.

reprisal *noun* an act of revenge.

reproach *verb* rebuke. **reproach** *noun*, **reproachful** *adjective*, **reproachfully** *adverb*

reproduce *verb* (**reproduced, reproducing**) **1** cause to be seen or heard or happen again. **2** make a copy of something. **3** produce offspring. **reproduction** *noun*, **reproductive** *adjective*

reprove *verb* (**reproved, reproving**) rebuke; reproach. **reproof** *noun*

reptile *noun* a cold-blooded animal that has a backbone and very short legs or no legs at all, e.g. a snake, lizard, crocodile, or tortoise. [from Latin *reptilis* = crawling]

republic *noun* a country that has a president, especially one who is elected. (Compare *monarchy*.) **republican** *adjective* [from Latin *res publica* = public affairs]

repudiate *verb* (**repudiated, repudiating**) reject; deny. **repudiation** *noun*

repugnant *adjective* distasteful; objectionable. **repugnance** *noun* [from *re-* = against, + Latin *pugnans* = fighting]

repulse *verb* (**repulsed, repulsing**) **1** drive away; repel. **2** reject an offer etc.; rebuff. [same origin as *repel*]

repulsion *noun* **1** repelling; repulsing. **2** a feeling of disgust. (The opposite is *attraction*.)

repulsive *adjective* **1** disgusting. **2** repelling things. (The opposite is *attractive*.) **repulsively** *adverb*, **repulsiveness** *noun*

▶▶THESAURUS◀◀

for, symbolise. **4** act for, act on behalf of, speak for.

representative[1] *noun* agent, ambassador, delegate, deputy, emissary, envoy, mouthpiece, proxy, spokesperson, stand-in, substitute.

representative[2] *adjective* **2** archetypal, characteristic, illustrative, typical.

repress *verb* bottle up, check, control, crush, curb, hold back, inhibit, keep down, oppress, put down, quash, quell, restrain, stifle, subdue, subjugate, suppress.

reprieve[1] *noun* pardon, postponement, remission, stay of execution.

reprieve[2] *verb* let off, pardon, spare.

reprimand[1] *noun* admonition, castigation, dressing down (*informal*), lecture, rebuke, reproach, reproof, rocket (*slang*), scolding, serve (*Australian informal*), talking-to (*informal*), wigging (*informal*).

reprimand[2] *verb* admonish, berate, castigate, censure, chastise, chide (*old use*), go crook at (*Australian informal*), haul over the coals, lecture, rap over the knuckles, rebuke, reproach, reprove, rouse on (*Australian informal*), scold, take to task, tell off (*informal*), tick off (*informal*), upbraid.

reprisal *noun* retaliation, retribution, revenge, vengeance.

reproach *verb* admonish, blame, castigate, censure, chide (*old use*), criticise, rebuke, reprimand, reprove, scold, upbraid. **reproach** *noun* condemnation, discredit, disgrace, disrepute, humiliation, ignominy, rebuke, shame.

reproduce *verb* **1** mimic, recreate, repeat, replicate. **2** copy, duplicate, fax, photocopy, print. **3** breed, multiply, procreate, proliferate, propagate. **reproduction** *noun* **1** breeding, procreation, proliferation, propagation. **2** copy, duplicate, facsimile, imitation, print, replica.

repudiate *verb* deny, disclaim, disown, reject.

repugnant *adjective* abhorrent, abominable, detestable, disgusting, distasteful, hateful, hideous, horrible, loathsome, nasty, nauseating, objectionable, obnoxious, odious, offensive, off-putting, repulsive, revolting, vile.

repulse *verb* **1** drive back, fend off, force back, repel, ward off.

repulsive *adjective* **1** abominable, disgusting, distasteful, foul, gross (*informal*), hideous, horrible, loathsome, nasty, nauseating, objectionable, obnoxious, odious, offensive, off-putting, repellent, repugnant, revolting, sickening, ugly, vile, yucky (*informal*).

▶▶ DICTIONARY ◀◀

reputable (*say* **rep**-yoo-ta-bul) *adjective* having a good reputation; respected. **reputably** *adverb*

reputation *noun* what people say about a person or things. [from Latin *reputare* = consider]

repute *noun* reputation.

reputed *adjective* said or thought to be something, *This is reputed to be the best hotel.* **reputedly** *adverb*

request¹ *verb* 1 ask for a thing. 2 ask a person to do something.

request² *noun* 1 asking for something. 2 a thing asked for. [same origin as *require*]

requiem (*say* **rek**-wee-em) *noun* a special Mass for someone who has died; music for the words of this. [Latin, = rest]

require *verb* (**required, requiring**) 1 need. 2 make somebody do something; oblige, *Drivers are required to pass a test.* [from *re-*, + Latin *quaerere* = seek]

requirement *noun* what is required; a need.

requisite¹ (*say* **rek**-wiz-it) *adjective* required; needed.

requisite² *noun* a thing needed for something. [same origin as *require*]

requisition *verb* take something over for official use.

rescue¹ *verb* (**rescued, rescuing**) save from danger, harm, etc.; bring away from captivity. **rescuer** *noun*

rescue² *noun* the action of rescuing.

research¹ (*say* ri-**serch**) *noun* careful study or investigation to discover facts or information.

research² (*say* ri-**serch**) *verb* do research into something.

resemblance *noun* likeness.

resemble *verb* (**resembled, resembling**) be like another person or thing. [from *re-*, + Latin *similis* = like]

resent *verb* feel indignant about or insulted by something. **resentful** *adjective*, **resentfully** *adverb*, **resentment** *noun* [from *re-* = against, + Latin *sentire* = feel]

reservation *noun* 1 reserving. 2 something reserved. 3 an area of land kept for a special purpose. 4 a limit on how far you agree with something, *I believe most of his story, but I have some reservations.*

reserve¹ *verb* (**reserved, reserving**) 1 keep something for a particular person or a special use. 2 order a place in a theatre, hotel, etc. in advance. 3 postpone, *reserve judgement.*

▶▶ THESAURUS ◀◀

reputable *adjective* above board, honest, honourable, reliable, respectable, respected, trustworthy.

reputation *noun* fame, name, prestige, renown, repute, standing.

reputed *adjective* alleged, putative, supposed.

request¹ *verb* 1 apply for, ask for, beg for, petition for, plead for, seek, solicit. 2 appeal to, ask, beseech, entreat, implore.

request² *noun* appeal, application, entreaty, petition, plea, supplication.

require *verb* 1 call for, demand, depend on, necessitate, need, rely on. 2 command, compel, direct, oblige, order.
required *adjective* compulsory, essential, mandatory, necessary, obligatory, prescribed, requisite, set.

requirement *noun* essential, must, necessity, prerequisite, requisite, specification, stipulation.

rescue¹ *verb* deliver, free, liberate, recover, release, retrieve, salvage, save.

rescue² *noun* deliverance, liberation, recovery, release, retrieval, salvage, saving.

research¹ *noun* experimentation, exploration, inquiry, investigation, study.

research² *verb* delve into, explore, inquire into, investigate, study.

resemblance *noun* affinity, correspondence, likeness, similarity.

resemble *verb* be like, be similar to, look like, take after.

resent *verb* begrudge, dislike, mind, object to, take exception to, take umbrage at.
resentful *adjective* aggrieved, angry, bitter, discontented, disgruntled, envious, grudging, huffy, indignant, jealous, piqued, rancorous, sullen.
resentment *noun* anger, animosity, bitterness, discontent, envy, grudge, hatred, hostility, ill will, indignation, jealousy, pique, rancour.

reservation *noun* 1,2 arrangement, booking. 4 condition, doubt, hesitation, limitation, misgiving, objection, proviso, qualification, qualm, scruple.

reserve¹ *verb* 1 hoard, hold back, keep, keep back, preserve, put aside, retain, save, spare, withhold. 2 book, order, prearrange, secure. 3 defer, delay, postpone, suspend, withhold.

▶▶▶ D I C T I O N A R Y ◀◀◀

reserve² *noun* **1** something kept ready to be used if necessary. **2** an extra player chosen as a substitute in a team. **3** an area of land kept for a special purpose, *a nature reserve, an Aboriginal reserve*. **4** shyness; keeping your thoughts and feelings private. [from *re-* = back, + Latin *servare* = keep]

Reserve Bank (*Australian*) a central bank administering government monetary policy.

reserved *adjective* (of a person) showing reserve of manner (see *reserve²* 4).

reservoir (*say* **rez**-er-vwar) *noun* a place where water is stored, especially an artificial lake.

reshuffle *noun* a rearrangement, especially an exchange of jobs between members of a group, *a Cabinet reshuffle*. **reshuffle** *verb*

reside *verb* (**resided, residing**) live in a particular place; dwell. [from *re-*, + Latin *-sidere* = sit]

residence *noun* **1** a place where a person lives. **2** residing.

resident *noun* **1** a person living or residing in a particular place. **2** a guest staying in a hotel. **resident** *adjective* [from *re-*, + Latin *-sidens* = sitting]

residential *adjective* containing people's homes, *a residential area*.

residue *noun* what is left over. **residual** *adjective*

resign *verb* give up your job or position. **resignation** *noun*

be resigned or **resign yourself to something** accept that you must put up with it. [from Latin *resignare* = unseal]

resilient *adjective* **1** springy. **2** recovering quickly from illness or trouble. **resilience** *noun* [from *re-* = back, + Latin *-siliens* = jumping]

resin *noun* a sticky substance that comes from plants or is manufactured, used in varnish, plastics, etc. **resinous** *adjective*

resist *verb* oppose; fight or act against something. **resistance** *noun*, **resistant** *adjective* [from *re-* = against, + Latin *sistere* = stand firmly]

resistor *noun* a device that increases the resistance to an electric current.

resolute *adjective* showing great determination. **resolutely** *adverb* [same origin as *resolve*]

resolution *noun* **1** being resolute. **2** something you have resolved to do, *New Year resolutions*. **3** a formal decision made by a committee etc. **4** the solving of a problem etc.

resolve¹ *verb* (**resolved, resolving**) **1** decide firmly or formally. **2** solve a problem etc. **3** overcome doubts or disagreements.

resolve² *noun* **1** something you have decided to do; a resolution. **2** great determination. [from *re-*, + Latin *solvere* = loosen]

▶▶▶ T H E S A U R U S ◀◀◀

reserve² *noun* **1** cache, fund, hoard, kitty, pool, reservoir, stock, stockpile, store, supply. **2** backup, deputy, stand-by, stand-in, substitute, understudy. **3** conservation park, game park, preserve, safari park, sanctuary, wildlife park.

reserved *adjective* aloof, bashful, distant, remote, restrained, reticent, shy, stand-offish, taciturn, uncommunicative, undemonstrative, unemotional, withdrawn.

reservoir *noun* dam, lake, pond.

reshuffle *noun* rearrangement, reorganisation, shake-up, spill (*Australian informal*).

reside *verb* (*reside in*) dwell in, hang out in (*informal*), inhabit, live in, lodge in, occupy, stay in.

residence *noun* **1** abode (*old use*), domicile, dwelling, habitation, home, house, place.

resident *noun* **1** citizen, denizen, householder, inhabitant, local, native. **2** guest, inmate, lodger, occupant, visitor.

residue *noun* balance, dregs, lees, leftovers, remainder, remains, remnant, rest.

resign *verb* abdicate, give up, leave, quit, relinquish, stand down from, step down from, vacate.
resign yourself to accept, reconcile yourself to.

resist *verb* battle against, confront, defy, fight (against), oppose, stand up to, withstand.
resistant *adjective* immune, impervious, proof, unaffected.

resolute *adjective* adamant, determined, dogged, firm, persistent, purposeful, resolved, staunch, steadfast, tenacious, unwavering.

resolution *noun* **1** determination, doggedness, persistence, purpose, resolve, tenacity, willpower. **2** commitment, decision, intention, pledge, promise, resolve. **3** decision, motion, proposition. **4** resolving, settlement, solution, solving, sorting out, working out.

resolve¹ *verb* **1** decide, determine. **2,3** clear up, fix, overcome, remedy, settle, solve, sort out, work out.

resolve² *noun* **1** intention, pledge, promise, resolution. **2** determination, doggedness, purpose, resolution, steadfastness, will-power.

▶▶ DICTIONARY ◀◀

resonant *adjective* resounding; echoing. **resonance** *adjective* [from *re-*, + Latin *sonans* = sounding]

resort¹ *verb* turn to or make use of something, *They resorted to violence.*

resort² *noun* 1 a place where people go for relaxation or holidays. 2 resorting, *without resort to cheating.*
the last resort something to be tried when everything else has failed.

resound *verb* fill a place with sound; echo.

resounding *adjective* very great; outstanding, *a resounding victory.*

resource *noun* 1 something that can be used; an asset, *The country's natural resources include coal and oil.* 2 an ability; ingenuity.

resourceful *adjective* clever at finding ways of doing things. **resourcefully** *adverb*, **resourcefulness** *noun*

respect¹ *noun* 1 admiration for a person's or thing's good qualities. 2 politeness; consideration, *Have respect for people's feelings.* 3 a detail or aspect, *In this respect he is like his sister.* 4 reference, *The rules with respect to bullying are quite clear.*

respect² *verb* have respect for a person or thing. [from *re-* = back, + Latin *specere* = to look]

respectable *adjective* 1 having good manners and character etc. 2 fairly good, *a respectable score.* **respectably** *adverb*, **respectability** *noun*

respectful *adjective* showing respect. **respectfully** *adverb*

respecting *preposition* concerning.

respective *adjective* of or for each individual, *We went to our respective rooms.* **respectively** *adverb*

respiration *noun* breathing. **respiratory** *adjective*

respirator *noun* 1 a device that fits over a person's nose and mouth to purify air before it is breathed. 2 an apparatus for giving artificial respiration.

respire *verb* (**respired, respiring**) breathe. [from *re-*, + Latin *spirare* = breathe]

respite *noun* an interval of rest, relief, or delay.

resplendent *adjective* brilliant with colour or decorations. [from *re-*, + Latin *splendens* = glittering]

respond *verb* 1 reply. 2 react. [from *re-*, + Latin *spondere* = promise]

respondent *noun* the person answering.

response *noun* 1 a reply. 2 a reaction.

responsibility *noun* (*plural* **responsibilities**) 1 being responsible. 2 something for which a person is responsible.

▶▶ THESAURUS ◀◀

resonant *adjective* booming, echoing, full, resounding, reverberating, rich, sonorous, stentorian, vibrant.

resort¹ *verb* (*resort to*) adopt, fall back on, have recourse to, turn to, use, utilise.

resort² *noun* 1 centre, haunt, holiday centre, retreat, spot.

resound *verb* echo, resonate, reverberate, ring.

resounding *adjective* enormous, great, marked, notable, outstanding, remarkable, striking, tremendous (*informal*).

resource *noun* 1 (*resources*) assets, capital, funds, materials, means, money, reserves, riches, wealth.

resourceful *adjective* clever, creative, enterprising, ingenious, innovative, inventive, shrewd.

respect¹ *noun* 1 admiration, awe, esteem, honour, regard, reverence, veneration. 2 consideration, courtesy, deference, politeness, regard. 3 aspect, detail, facet, feature,

particular, point, regard, way. 4 reference, regard, relation.

respect² *verb* admire, esteem, honour, look up to, revere, value, venerate.

respectable *adjective* 1 decent, honest, honourable, law-abiding, presentable, proper, reputable, upright, worthy. 2 acceptable, adequate, fair, passable, reasonable, satisfactory.

respectful *adjective* civil, considerate, courteous, deferential, polite, well-mannered.

respite *noun* break, breather, intermission, let-up, lull, pause, relief, reprieve, rest, spell (*Australian*).

respond *verb* 1 answer, counter, rejoin, reply, retort. 2 act in response, react.

response *noun* 1 answer, comeback, rejoinder, reply, retort, riposte. 2 acknowledgement, feedback, reaction.

responsibility *noun* 1 blame, culpability, fault, guilt, liability. 2 burden, duty, job, obligation, onus, task.

▶▶▶ D I C T I O N A R Y ◀◀

responsible *adjective* **1** looking after a person or thing and having to take the blame if something goes wrong. **2** reliable; trustworthy. **3** with important duties, *a responsible job.* **4** causing something, *His carelessness was responsible for their deaths.*
responsibly *adverb*

responsive *adjective* responding well.

rest¹ *noun* **1** a time of sleep or freedom from work as a way of regaining strength. **2** a support, *an arm-rest.* **3** an interval of silence between notes in music.

rest² *verb* **1** have a rest; be still. **2** allow to rest, *Sit down and rest your feet.* **3** be supported. **4** be left without further investigation etc., *And there the matter rests.* [from Old English *raest* = bed]

rest³ *noun* **the rest** the remaining part; the others.

rest⁴ *verb* remain, *Rest assured, it will be a success.*
rest with be left to someone to deal with, *It rests with you to suggest a date.* [from Latin *restare* = stay behind]

restaurant *noun* a place where you can buy a meal and eat it.

restful *adjective* giving rest or a feeling of rest.

restitution *noun* **1** restoring something. **2** compensation. [from *re-*, + Latin *statutum* = established]

restive *adjective* restless or impatient because of delay, boredom, etc.

restless *adjective* unable to rest or keep still.
restlessly *adverb*

restore *verb* (**restored, restoring**) **1** bring something back to its original condition. **2** put something back in its original place.
restoration *noun*

restrain *verb* hold a person or thing back; keep under control. **restraint** *noun*

restrict *verb* limit. **restriction** *noun*, **restrictive** *adjective*

result¹ *noun* **1** something produced by an action or condition etc.; an effect or consequence. **2** the score or situation at the end of a game, competition, or race etc. **3** the answer to a sum or calculation.

▶▶▶ T H E S A U R U S ◀◀

responsible *adjective* **1** accountable, answerable, in charge (of), liable. **2** conscientious, dependable, dutiful, honest, law-abiding, level-headed, mature, reliable, sensible, trustworthy. **3** executive, important, managerial, senior, supervisory. **4** at fault, culpable, guilty, to blame.

responsive *adjective* alert, alive, awake, impressionable, interested, quick, receptive, sensitive, sympathetic.

rest¹ *noun* **1** ease, idleness, inactivity, leisure, relaxation, repose, respite; (*a rest on the sofa*) doze, forty winks, kip (*slang*), lie-down, nap, repose, siesta, sleep, snooze; (*a rest from work*) break, breather, holiday, interlude, intermission, interval, pause, recess, smoko (*Australian informal*), spell (*Australian*), time off, vacation. **2** base, holder, prop, stand, support, tripod.
at rest inactive, inert, motionless, still.

rest² *verb* **1** doze, idle, laze, lie down, pause, relax, sleep, slumber, snooze, take it easy. **3** lean, perch, place, prop, stand, support.

rest³ *noun* balance, excess, leftovers, others, remainder, remnant, residue, surplus.

restaurant *noun* bistro, brasserie, buffet, café, cafeteria, canteen, diner (*American*), eatery (*informal*).

restitution *noun* **2** compensation, indemnification, recompense, redress, reparation.

restless *adjective* agitated, disturbed, edgy, excitable, fidgety, frisky, impatient, lively, nervous, restive, skittish, sleepless, toey (*Australian informal*), unsettled, wakeful.

restore *verb* **1** do up (*informal*), fix, mend, rebuild, recondition, reconstruct, refurbish, rehabilitate, remodel, renovate, repair, resurrect. **2** bring back, give back, hand back, put back, re-establish, reinstate, reintroduce, replace, return.

restrain *verb* bind, bridle, chain, check, contain, control, curb, curtail, fetter, harness, hold back, keep a tight rein on, keep in check, limit, moderate, muzzle, pinion, rein in, repress, restrict, shackle, strait-jacket, suppress, tie up.
restraint *noun* control, moderation, self-control, self-discipline, self-restraint.

restrict *verb* bound, check, circumscribe, confine, cramp, curb, enclose, hamper, handicap, hem in, hinder, impede, limit.
restriction *noun* condition, constraint, control, limitation, proviso, qualification, stipulation.

result¹ *noun* **1** consequence, effect, fruit, outcome, output, repercussion, upshot. **2** grade, mark, score. **3** answer, finding, solution.

result² *verb* **1** arise, come about, ensue, follow, happen, occur, originate, spring, stem. **2** (*result in*) bring about, cause, culminate in, end in, finish in, give rise to, lead to.

result² *verb* **1** happen as a result. **2** have a particular result. **resultant** *adjective*

resume *verb* (**resumed, resuming**) **1** begin again after stopping for a while. **2** take or occupy again, *After the interval we resumed our seats.* **resumption** *noun* [from *re-*, + Latin *sumere* = take up]

résumé (*say* **rez**-yoo-may) *noun* a summary. [French, = summed up]

resurgence *noun* a rise or revival of something, *a resurgence of interest in grammar.* [from *re-*, + Latin *surgens* = rising]

resurrect *verb* bring back into use or existence, *resurrect an old custom.*

resurrection *noun* **1** coming back to life after being dead. **2** the revival of something. [same origin as *resurgence*]

resuscitate *verb* (**resuscitated, resuscitating**) revive a person from unconsciousness or a custom etc. from disuse. **resuscitation** *noun*

retail¹ *verb* **1** sell goods to the general public. **2** tell what happened; recount; relate. **retailer** *noun*

retail² *noun* selling to the general public. (Compare *wholesale*.)

retain *verb* **1** continue to have something; keep in your possession. **2** keep in your memory. **3** hold something in place. [from *re-*, + Latin *tenere* = to hold]

retainer *noun* (*old use*) an attendant of a person of high rank.

retaliate *verb* (**retaliated, retaliating**) repay an injury or insult etc. with a similar one; counter-attack. **retaliation** *noun* [from *re-*, + Latin *talis* = the same kind]

retard *verb* slow down or delay the progress or development of something. **retarded** *adjective*, **retardation** *noun* [from *re-*, + Latin *tardus* = slow]

retch *verb* strain your throat as if being sick.

retention *noun* retaining; keeping. **retentive** *adjective*

reticent (*say* **ret**-i-sent) *adjective* not telling people what you feel or think; discreet. **reticence** *noun*

retina *noun* a layer of membrane at the back of the eyeball, sensitive to light.

retinue *noun* a group of people accompanying an important person.

retire *verb* (**retired, retiring**) **1** give up your regular work because you are getting old. **2** retreat. **3** go to bed or to your private room. **retirement** *noun* [from French *retirer* = draw back]

retiring *adjective* shy; avoiding company.

retort¹ *noun* **1** a quick or witty or angry reply. **2** a glass bottle with a long downward-bent neck, used in distilling liquids. **3** a receptacle used in making steel etc.

retort² *verb* make a quick, witty, or angry reply. [from *re-*, + Latin *tortum* = twisted]

retrace *verb* (**retraced, retracing**) go back over something, *We retraced our steps and returned to the ferry.*

retract *verb* **1** pull back or in, *The snail retracts its horns.* **2** withdraw, *She refused to retract her threat.* **retraction** *noun*, **retractable** *adjective*, **retractile** *adjective* [from *re-*, + Latin *tractum* = pulled]

resume *verb* **1** begin again, carry on, continue, recommence, restart. **2** reoccupy, return to, take again.

résumé *noun* abstract, outline, précis, summary, synopsis.

resurrect *verb* bring back, reactivate, re-introduce, restore, resuscitate, revive.

retain *verb* **1** hang on to, hold on to, keep, reserve, save. **2** learn, memorise, recall, recollect, remember.

retaliate *verb* counter-attack, get even, get your own back (*informal*), hit back, pay back, reciprocate, seek retribution, take reprisals, take revenge.
retaliation *noun* counter-attack, reprisal, retribution, revenge, vengeance, vindictiveness.

retard *verb* delay, hamper, handicap, hinder, impede, inhibit, obstruct, slow down, stunt.

reticent *adjective* diffident, discreet, quiet, reserved, secretive, shy, silent, taciturn, tight-lipped, uncommunicative, unforthcoming.

retire *verb* **1** give up work, leave work, quit work, stop working. **2** retreat, withdraw. **3** go to bed, hit the hay (*informal*), hit the sack (*informal*), turn in (*informal*).

retiring *adjective* bashful, diffident, meek, modest, reserved, shy, timid, uncommunicative, withdrawn.

retort¹ *noun* **1** answer, comeback, rejoinder, reply, response, riposte.

retort² *verb* answer, counter, react, rejoin, reply, respond.

retrace *verb* **retrace your steps** backtrack, go back, return.

retract *verb* **1** draw in, pull in. **2** cancel, disclaim, recant, rescind, revoke, take back, withdraw.

▶▶DICTIONARY◀◀

retreat[1] *verb* go back after being defeated or to avoid danger or difficulty etc.; withdraw.

retreat[2] *noun* **1** retreating. **2** a quiet place to which someone can withdraw. [same origin as *retract*]

retrench *verb* **1** reduce the amount of something; economise. **2** dismiss staff in order to reduce costs. **retrenchment** *noun*

retribution *noun* a deserved punishment. [from *re-*, + Latin *tributum* = assigned]

retrieve *verb* (**retrieved, retrieving**) get something back; rescue. **retrievable** *adjective*, **retrieval** *noun* [from Old French *retrover* = find again]

retriever *noun* a kind of dog that is often trained to retrieve game.

retro- *prefix* back; backward (as in *retrograde*). [from Latin *retro* = backwards]

retrograde *adjective* **1** going backwards. **2** becoming less good.

retrogress *verb* **1** move backwards. **2** deteriorate. **retrogression** *noun*, **retrogressive** *adjective* [from *retro-* + *progress*]

retrospect *noun* a survey of past events. **in retrospect** when you look back at what has happened. [from *retro-* + *prospect*]

retrospective *adjective* **1** looking back on the past. **2** applying to the past as well as the future, *The law could not be made retrospective*. **retrospection** *noun*

return[1] *verb* **1** come back or go back. **2** bring, give, put, or send back.

returned serviceman (*Australian*) one who has served in wars overseas.

return[2] *noun* **1** returning. **2** something returned. **3** profit, *He gets a good return on his savings.* **4** a return ticket.

return match a second match played between the same teams.

return ticket a ticket for a journey to a place and back again.

reunion *noun* **1** reuniting. **2** a meeting of people who have not met for some time.

reunite *verb* (**reunited, reuniting**) unite again after being separated.

reuse[1] *verb* (**reused, reusing**) use again. **reusable** *adjective*

reuse[2] *noun* using again.

rev[1] *verb* (**revved, revving**) (*informal*) make an engine run quickly, especially when starting.

rev[2] *noun* (*informal*) a revolution of an engine. [short for *revolution*]

Rev. *abbreviation* Reverend.

reveal *verb* **1** let something be seen. **2** make known. [from Latin *revelare* = unveil]

reveille (*say* riv-**al**-ee) *noun* a military waking-signal sounded on a bugle or drums. [from French *réveillez* = wake up!]

revel *verb* (**revelled, revelling**) **1** take great delight in something. **2** hold revels. **reveller** *noun*

revels *plural noun* noisy festivities.

revelation *noun* **1** revealing. **2** something revealed, especially something surprising.

revelry *noun* revelling; revels.

▶▶THESAURUS◀◀

retreat[1] *verb* back away, bolt, depart, escape, flee, go away, leave, retire, run away, shrink back, take flight, withdraw.

retreat[2] *noun* **1** departure, escape, exit, flight, getaway, withdrawal. **2** asylum, haven, hideout (*informal*), hiding-place, refuge, resort, sanctuary, shelter.

retrench *verb* **1** cut back, downsize, economise, rationalise, tighten your belt. **2** dismiss, get rid of, lay off, make redundant, sack (*informal*), shed.

retribution *noun* just deserts, justice, nemesis, punishment, recompense, revenge, vengeance.

retrieve *verb* bring back, fetch, find, get back, recapture, recover, regain, rescue, salvage, track down.

return[1] *verb* **1** backtrack, come back, go back, reappear, recur, resurface, revert. **2** bring back, give back, hand back, pay back, put back, reciprocate, repay, replace, requite, restore, send back, take back.

return[2] *noun* **1** arrival, homecoming, reappearance. **3** earnings, gain, income, interest, profit, revenue, yield.

reunion *noun* **2** gathering, get-together.

reuse[1] *verb* recycle, use again.

reveal *verb* **1** bare, display, expose, show, uncover, unmask, unveil. **2** admit, air, betray, bring to light, confess, declare, disclose, divulge, expose, leak, let out, let slip, make known, proclaim, publish, tell, voice.

revel *verb* **1** (*revel in*) bask in, delight in, enjoy, glory in, luxuriate in, rejoice in, relish, savour, wallow in.

revelation *noun* **2** admission, confession, disclosure, discovery, eye-opener, leak.

revelry *noun* carousing, celebration, festivities, high jinks, jollification, merrymaking, orgy, party, revels, roistering, spree, wassailing (*old use*).

▶▶ DICTIONARY ◀◀

revenge¹ *noun* harming somebody in return for harm that they have caused.

revenge² *verb* (**revenged, revenging**) avenge; take vengeance.

revenue *noun* a country's income from taxes etc., used for paying public expenses. [French, = returned]

reverberate *verb* (**reverberated, reverberating**) resound; re-echo. **reverberation** *noun* [from *re-*, + Latin *verberare* = to lash]

revere (*say* riv-**eer**) *verb* (**revered, revering**) respect deeply or with reverence.

reverence *noun* a feeling of awe and deep or religious respect.

Reverend *noun* the title of a member of the clergy, *the Reverend John Smith.* [from Latin, = person to be revered]

reverent *adjective* feeling or showing reverence. **reverently** *adverb* [from Latin, = revering]

reverie (*say* **rev**-er-ee) *noun* a daydream.

revers (*say* riv-**eer**) *noun* (*plural* **revers**, *say* riv-**eerz**) a folded-back part of a garment, as in a lapel.

reversal *noun* reversing.

reverse¹ *adjective* opposite in direction, order, or manner, etc.

reverse gear a gear that allows a vehicle to be driven backwards.

reverse² *noun* **1** the reverse side. **2** the opposite or contrary. **3** a piece of misfortune, *They suffered several reverses.*

in reverse the opposite way round.

reverse³ *verb* (**reversed, reversing**) **1** turn in the opposite direction or order etc.; turn something inside out or upside down. **2** move backwards. **3** cancel a decision or decree. **reversible** *adjective* [same origin as *revert*]

revert *verb* return to a former condition, habit, or subject etc. **reversion** *noun* [from *re-* = back, + Latin *vertere* = to turn]

review¹ *noun* **1** an inspection or survey. **2** a published description and opinion of a book, film, play, etc.

review² *verb* **1** make a review of something. **2** write a review of a book, film, play, etc. **reviewer** *noun*

revile *verb* (**reviled, reviling**) criticise angrily. **revilement** *noun*

revise *verb* (**revised, revising**) **1** go over work that you have already done, especially in preparing for an examination. **2** alter or correct something. **revision** *noun* [from *re-*, + Latin *visere* = examine]

revive *verb* (**revived, reviving**) **1** come or bring back to life, strength, etc. **2** come or bring back into use, activity etc. **revival** *noun* [from *re-*, + Latin *vivere* = to live]

▶▶ THESAURUS ◀◀

revenge¹ *noun* reprisal, retaliation, retribution, vengeance.

take revenge avenge yourself, get even, get your own back, pay back, retaliate, take reprisals.

revenue *noun* income, proceeds, receipts, return, takings.

reverberate *verb* boom, echo, resonate, resound, ring, thunder.

revere *verb* admire, adore, esteem, glorify, hold in awe, honour, idolise, look up to, respect, reverence, venerate, worship.

reverence *noun* admiration, adoration, awe, devotion, esteem, homage, honour, respect, veneration.

reversal *noun* about-face, about-turn, backflip, change, turn-about, turn-around, U-turn.

reverse² *noun* **1** back, flip side (*informal*), other side, underside, verso. **2** antithesis, contrary, converse, opposite.

reverse³ *verb* **1** invert, transpose, turn round, turn upside down. **2** back, drive backwards. **3**
countermand, do a backflip on (*informal*), override, overrule, overturn, revoke, undo.

revert *verb* backslide, go back, lapse, regress, retrogress, return.

review¹ *noun* **1** analysis, assessment, examination, inspection, reappraisal, reassessment, reconsideration, re-examination, stocktaking, study, survey. **2** criticism, critique, notice, write-up.

review² *verb* **1** analyse, assess, examine, go over, inspect, reappraise, reassess, reconsider, re-examine, scrutinise, study, survey, take stock of, think over. **2** appraise, assess, comment on, criticise, evaluate, judge.

revise *verb* **1** brush up on, cram, go over, learn, study, swot (*informal*). **2** alter, amend, change, edit, modify, revamp, rework, rewrite, update.

revive *verb* **1** bring round, come round, rally, recover, regain consciousness, resuscitate. **2** bring back, re-establish, reintroduce, restore, resurrect.

revival *noun* reawakening, rebirth, renaissance, renewal, restoration, resurgence, resurrection.

▶▶DICTIONARY◀◀

revoke *verb* (**revoked**, **revoking**) withdraw or cancel a decree or licence etc. [from *re-*, + Latin *vocare* = to call]

revolt[1] *verb* **1** rebel. **2** disgust somebody.

revolt[2] *noun* **1** a rebellion. **2** a feeling of disgust. [same origin as *revolve*]

revolting *adjective* disgusting.

revolution *noun* **1** a rebellion that overthrows the government. **2** a complete change. **3** revolving; rotation; one complete turn of a wheel, engine, etc. [same origin as *revolve*]

revolutionary *adjective* **1** involving a great change. **2** of a political revolution.

revolutionise *verb* (**revolutionised**, **revolutionising**) make a great change in something.

revolve *verb* (**revolved**, **revolving**) turn or keep on turning round. [from *re-*, + Latin *volvere* = to roll]

revolver *noun* a pistol with a revolving mechanism that makes it possible to fire it a number of times without reloading.

revue *noun* an entertainment consisting of a number of items. [French]

revulsion *noun* **1** strong disgust. **2** a sudden violent change of feeling.

reward[1] *noun* something given in return for a useful action or merit.

reward[2] *verb* give a reward to someone.

rewrite *verb* (**rewrote**, **rewritten**, **rewriting**) write something again or differently.

rhapsody (*say* **rap**-so-dee) *noun* (*plural* **rhapsodies**) **1** a statement of great delight about something. **2** a romantic piece of music.

rhapsodise *verb* [from Greek *rhapsoidos* = one who stitches songs together]

rhetoric (*say* **ret**-er-ik) *noun* **1** the art of using words impressively, especially in public speaking. **2** affected or exaggerated expressions used because they sound impressive. **rhetorical** *adjective*, **rhetorically** *adverb*
rhetorical question something put as a question so that it sounds dramatic, not to get an answer, e.g. 'Who cares?' (= nobody cares). [from Greek *rhetor* = orator]

rheumatism *noun* a disease that causes pain and stiffness in joints and muscles. **rheumatic** *adjective*, **rheumatoid** *adjective*

rhinoceros *noun* (*plural* **rhinoceroses**) a large heavy animal with a horn or two horns on its nose. [from Greek *rhinos* = of the nose, + *keras* = horn]

rhododendron *noun* an evergreen shrub with large trumpet-shaped flowers. [from Greek *rhodon* = rose, + *dendron* = tree]

rhombus *noun* (*plural* **rhombuses**) a quadrilateral with equal sides but no right angles, like the diamond on playing cards.

rhubarb *noun* a plant with thick reddish stalks that are used as fruit.

rhyme[1] *noun* **1** a similar sound in the endings of words, e.g. *bat/fat/mat, batter/fatter/matter*. **2** a poem with rhymes. **3** a word that rhymes with another.

rhyme[2] *verb* (**rhymed**, **rhyming**) form a rhyme; have rhymes.

rhythm *noun* a regular pattern of beats, sounds, or movements. **rhythmic** *adjective*, **rhythmical** *adjective*, **rhythmically** *adverb*

▶▶THESAURUS◀◀

revoke *verb* abrogate, annul, cancel, nullify, quash, repeal, rescind, retract, take back, withdraw.

revolt[1] *verb* **1** disobey, mutiny, rebel, rise up. **2** appal, disgust, horrify, nauseate, offend, repel, shock, sicken.

revolt[2] *noun* **1** insurrection, mutiny, rebellion, revolution, rising, uprising.

revolting *adjective* abhorrent, abominable, detestable, disgusting, distasteful, foul, gross (*informal*), gruesome, hateful, hideous, horrible, loathsome, nasty, nauseating, objectionable, obnoxious, obscene, odious, offensive, off-putting, repellent, repugnant, repulsive, vile, yucky (*informal*).

revolution *noun* **1** coup, coup d'état, insurrection, mutiny, rebellion, revolt, rising, uprising. **2** change, reformation, shift, transformation, upheaval. **3** circuit, orbit, rotation, spin, turn.

revolve *verb* circle, go round, orbit.

reward[1] *noun* award, bounty, compensation, payment, prize, recompense, remuneration.

reward[2] *verb* compensate, pay, recompense, remunerate, repay.
rewarding *adjective* fulfilling, gratifying, profitable, satisfying, worthwhile.

rewrite *verb* adapt, edit, paraphrase, revamp, revise, rework.

rhetoric *noun* **1** elocution, eloquence, oratory. **2** bombast, grandiloquence.

rhyme[1] *noun* **2** jingle, poem, verse.

rhythm *noun* beat, cadence, lilt, metre, pattern, pulse.
rhythmic *adjective* metrical, regular, rhythmical, steady.

▶▶ DICTIONARY ◀◀

rib *noun* **1** each of the curved bones round the chest. **2** a curved part that looks like a rib or supports something, *the ribs of an umbrella*. **ribbed** *adjective*

ribald (*say* **rib**-ald) *adjective* funny in a vulgar or disrespectful way. **ribaldry** *noun*

riband *noun* a ribbon.

ribbon *noun* **1** a narrow strip of silk or nylon etc. used for decoration or for tying something. **2** a long narrow strip of inked material used in a typewriter etc.

rice *noun* the white seeds of a plant that is grown in marshes in hot countries, used as food.

rich *adjective* **1** having a lot of money or property or resources etc.; wealthy. **2** having a large amount of something, *rich in minerals*. **3** costly; luxurious. **4** (of colours, sounds, etc.) deep; strong. **richly** *adverb*, **richness** *noun*

riches *plural noun* wealth.

rick¹ *noun* a large neat stack of hay or straw.

rick² *verb* sprain; wrench.

rickets *noun* a disease caused by lack of vitamin D, causing deformed bones.

rickety *adjective* unsteady.

rickshaw *noun* a two-wheeled carriage pulled by one or more people, used in Asian countries. [from Japanese *jin-riki-sha* = person-power-vehicle]

ricochet (*say* **rik**-osh-ay) *verb* (**ricocheted, ricocheting**) bounce off something; rebound, *The bullets ricocheted off the wall*. **ricochet** *noun*

rid *verb* (**rid, ridding**) make a person or place free from something unwanted, *He rid the town of rats*. **riddance** *noun*
get rid of cause to go away.

riddle¹ *noun* a puzzling question, especially as a joke.

riddle² *noun* a coarse sieve.

riddle³ *verb* (**riddled, riddling**) **1** pass gravel etc. through a riddle. **2** pierce with many holes, *They riddled the target with bullets*.

ride¹ *verb* (**rode, ridden, riding**) **1** sit on a horse, bicycle, etc. and be carried along on it. **2** travel in a car, bus, train, etc. **3** float or be supported on something, *The ship rode the waves*.

ride² *noun* riding; a journey on a horse, bicycle, etc. or in a vehicle.

rider *noun* **1** someone who rides. **2** an extra comment or statement.

ridge *noun* a long narrow part higher than the rest of something. **ridged** *adjective*

ridicule *verb* (**ridiculed, ridiculing**) make fun of a person or thing. **ridicule** *noun* [from Latin *ridere* = to laugh]

▶▶ THESAURUS ◀◀

ribbon *noun* **1** band, braid, strip, tape.

rich *adjective* **1** affluent, flush (*informal*), loaded (*informal*), moneyed, prosperous, wealthy, well-heeled (*informal*), well off, well-to-do. **2** abounding, abundant, well endowed, well supplied. **3** costly, expensive, grand, lavish, luxurious, magnificent, opulent, precious, splendid, sumptuous, valuable. **4** deep, full, intense, strong, vibrant, vivid.

riches *plural noun* affluence, assets, fortune, means, money, opulence, property, prosperity, resources, wealth.

rickety *adjective* decrepit, dilapidated, flimsy, ramshackle, shaky, tumbledown, unstable, unsteady, weak, wobbly.

ricochet *verb* bounce, rebound.

rid *verb* cleanse, clear, free, purge, relieve.
get rid of chuck out (*informal*), discard, dispense with, dispose of, ditch (*informal*), drive out, dump, eject, eliminate, eradicate, evict, expel, exterminate, remove, scrap, throw away, throw out, weed out.

riddle¹ *noun* brainteaser, conundrum, enigma, mystery, poser, problem, puzzle, teaser.

ride¹ *verb* **1** control, handle, manage. **2** go, journey, travel.

ride² *noun* drive, journey, lift, outing, spin (*informal*), trip.

rider *noun* **1** (*a horse-rider*) equestrian, hoop (*Australian slang*), horseman, horsewoman, jockey; (*a bicycle or motorcycle rider*) bicyclist, biker, bikie (*Australian informal*), cyclist, motorcyclist.

ridge *noun* brow, crest, hilltop, saddle.

ridicule *verb* caricature, chiack (*Australian informal*), deride, gibe at, jeer at, lampoon, laugh at, make fun of, mock, parody, pillory, poke borak at (*Australian informal*), poke fun at, satirise, scoff at, send up (*informal*), sling off at (*Australian informal*), sneer at, take off, take the mickey out of (*informal*), taunt, tease.
ridicule *noun* banter, derision, mockery, sarcasm, satire, scorn.

ridiculous *adjective* so silly that it makes people laugh or despise it. **ridiculously** *adverb*

rife *adjective* widespread; happening frequently, *Crime was rife in the town.*

riff-raff *noun* the rabble; disreputable people.

rifle¹ *noun* a long gun with spiral grooves (called *rifling*) inside the barrel that make the bullet spin and so travel more accurately.

rifle² *verb* (**rifled**, **rifling**) search and rob, *They rifled his desk.*

rift *noun* **1** a crack or split. **2** a disagreement that separates friends.

rift-valley *noun* a steep-sided valley formed where the land has sunk.

rig¹ *verb* (**rigged**, **rigging**) **1** provide a ship with ropes, spars, sails, etc. **2** set something up quickly or out of makeshift materials.
rig out provide with clothes or equipment.
rig-out *noun*

rig² *noun* **1** a framework supporting the machinery for drilling an oil-well. **2** the way a ship's masts and sails etc. are arranged. **3** (*informal*) an outfit of clothes.

rigging *noun* the ropes etc. that support a ship's mast and sails.

right¹ *adjective* **1** of the right-hand side. **2** correct; true, *the right answer.* **3** morally good; fair; just, *Is it right to cheat?* **4** most suitable, *the right person for the job.* **5** (of political groups) not in favour of socialist reforms.
rightly *adverb*, **rightness** *noun*

right angle an angle of 90°.

right hand the hand that a majority of people use more than the left, on the side of the body opposite the left hand. **right-hand** *adjective*

right-handed *adjective* using the right hand in preference to the left hand.

right² *adverb* **1** on or towards the right-hand side, *Turn right.* **2** straight, *Go right on.* **3** completely, *Go right round it.* **4** exactly, *right in the middle.* **5** rightly, *You did right to tell me.*
right away immediately.

right³ *noun* **1** the right-hand side or part etc. **2** what is morally good or fair or just. **3** something that people are allowed to do or have, *People over 18 have the right to vote in elections.*

right⁴ *verb* make a thing right or upright, *They righted the boat.*

righteous *adjective* doing what is right; virtuous. **righteously** *adverb*, **righteousness** *noun*

rightful *adjective* deserved; proper, *in her rightful place.* **rightfully** *adverb*

rigid *adjective* **1** stiff; firm; not bending, *a rigid support.* **2** strict, *rigid rules.* **rigidly** *adverb*, **rigidity** *noun*

rigmarole *noun* **1** a long rambling statement. **2** a complicated procedure.

rigorous *adjective* strict; severe. **rigorously** *adverb*

ridiculous *adjective* absurd, comical, crazy, derisory, droll, farcical, foolish, funny, harebrained, hilarious, idiotic, laughable, ludicrous, mad, nonsensical, outrageous, preposterous, silly, stupid, zany.

rife *adjective* common, prevalent, rampant, widespread.

rift *noun* **1** break, chink, cleft, crack, crevasse, crevice, fissure, fracture, opening, slit, split. **2** breach, disagreement, division, estrangement, schism, split.

rig¹ *verb* **rig out** dress, equip, fit out, kit out, outfit.

rig² *noun* **1** installation, platform. **3** clothes, gear (*informal*), get-up (*informal*), kit, outfit, rig-out (*informal*).

right¹ *adjective* **2** accurate, correct, exact, perfect, precise, proper, true, valid. **3** decent, ethical, fair, good, honest, honourable, just, lawful, legal, moral, proper, upright, virtuous. **4** appropriate, apt, fitting, proper, suitable.

right³ *noun* **1** starboard. **3** authority, entitlement, licence, permission, power, prerogative, privilege.

right⁴ *verb* correct, put right, rectify, redress, repair, set right, set upright, stand upright, straighten up.

righteous *adjective* blameless, ethical, good, holy, honest, honourable, just, law-abiding, moral, upright, virtuous.

rightful *adjective* lawful, legal, legitimate, proper, true.

rigid *adjective* **1** firm, hard, inflexible, stiff, unbending. **2** (*rigid rules*) cut and dried, firm, hard and fast, inflexible, rigorous, strict, stringent; (*a rigid master*) harsh, intransigent, stern, strict, stubborn, uncompromising, unyielding.

rigorous *adjective* austere, harsh, rigid, severe, stern, strict, stringent, tough, uncompromising.

▶▶ D I C T I O N A R Y ◀◀

rigour *noun* **1** strictness; severity. **2** harshness of weather or conditions, *the rigours of winter*.

rile *verb* (**riled, riling**) (*informal*) annoy.

rill *noun* a very small stream.

rim *noun* the outer edge of a cup, wheel, or other round object.

rimmed *adjective* edged.

rind *noun* the tough skin on bacon, cheese, or fruit.

ring¹ *noun* **1** a circle. **2** a thin circular piece of metal worn on a finger. **3** the space where a circus performs. **4** a square area in which a boxing-match or wrestling-match takes place.

ring² *verb* put a ring round something; encircle.

ring³ *verb* (**rang, rung, ringing**) **1** cause a bell to sound. **2** make a loud clear sound like that of a bell. **3** be filled with sound, *The hall rang with cheers*. **4** telephone, *Please ring me tomorrow*.

ring⁴ *noun* **1** the act or sound of ringing. **2** a telephone call.

ringbark *verb* (*Australian*) kill a tree by cutting a ring of bark from around the trunk.

ringbinder *noun* a loose-leaf binder with ring-shaped clasps.

ringer *noun* (*Australian*) someone or something that is very good.

ring-in *noun* (*Australian*) a replacement, especially a dishonest one.

ringleader *noun* a person who leads others in rebellion, mischief, crime, etc.

ringlet *noun* a tube-shaped curl.

ringmaster *noun* the person in charge of a performance in a circus ring.

rink *noun* a place made for skating.

rinse *verb* (**rinsed, rinsing**) **1** wash something lightly. **2** wash in clean water to remove soap. **rinse** *noun*

riot¹ *noun* wild or violent behaviour by a crowd of people.

riot² *verb* (**rioted, rioting**) take part in a riot.

riotous *adjective* **1** disorderly; unruly. **2** boisterous, *riotous laughter*.

rip¹ *verb* (**ripped, ripping**) **1** tear roughly. **2** rush. **rip off** (*slang*) swindle. **rip-off** *noun*

rip² *noun* **1** a torn place. **2** rough water with strong currents.

ripe *adjective* **1** ready to be harvested or eaten. **2** ready and suitable, *The time is ripe for revolution*. **3** mature; advanced, *She lived to a ripe old age*. **ripeness** *noun*

ripen *verb* make or become ripe.

riposte (*say* rip-**ost**) *noun* **1** a quick counterstroke in fencing. **2** a quick retort.

ripple¹ *noun* a small wave or series of waves.

ripple² *verb* (**rippled, rippling**) form ripples.

▶▶ T H E S A U R U S ◀◀

rile *verb* anger, annoy, exasperate, infuriate, irk, irritate, madden, nark (*informal*), provoke, vex.

rim *noun* border, brim, brink, circumference, edge, lip, perimeter, verge.

rind *noun* crust, husk, peel, skin.

ring¹ *noun* **1** band, circle, disc, halo, hoop, loop. **3** arena, enclosure.

ring² *verb* circle, encircle, enclose, encompass, hem in, surround.

ring³ *verb* **2** chime, clang, ding, dong, jingle, peal, tinkle, toll. **3** echo, resonate, resound, reverberate. **4** call, phone, ring up, telephone.

ring⁴ *noun* **1** chime, clang, jingle, knell, peal, tinkle, toll. **2** bell (*informal*), buzz (*informal*), call, phone call.

ring-in *noun* impostor, phoney (*informal*), replacement, substitute, swap.

rinse *verb* **1** clean, swill, wash.

riot¹ *noun* brawl, commotion, disorder, disturbance, fracas, mêlée, mutiny, pandemonium, revolt, rising, tumult, turmoil, uprising, uproar.

riot² *verb* mutiny, rampage, rebel, revolt, run amok, run riot.

riotous *adjective* **1** anarchic, boisterous, disorderly, lawless, mutinous, rebellious, rowdy, unruly, wild.

rip¹ *verb* **1** gash, lacerate, rupture, sever, slash, slit, split, tear. **rip off** cheat, con (*informal*), defraud, diddle (*informal*), fleece, rob, rook, swindle, take for a ride (*informal*). **rip-off** *noun* con (*informal*), swindle, swizz (*informal*).

rip² *noun* **1** gash, laceration, rupture, slash, slit, split, tear.

ripe *adjective* **1** in season, mature, mellow, ready. **3** advanced, mature, old.

ripen *verb* age, develop, mature, mellow.

ripple¹ *noun* wave, wavelet.

ripple² *verb* agitate, disturb, ruffle, stir.

rise¹ *verb* (**rose, risen, rising**) **1** go upwards. **2** get up from lying, sitting, or kneeling; get out of bed. **3** come to life again after death, *Christ is risen.* **4** rebel, *They rose in revolt against the tyrant.* **5** (of a river) begin its course. **6** (of the wind) begin to blow more strongly. **7** increase in number, size, intensity, etc.

rise² *noun* **1** the action of rising; an upward movement. **2** an increase in amount etc. or in wages. **3** an upward slope.
give rise to cause.

rising *noun* a revolt.

risk¹ *noun* a chance of danger or loss.

risk² *verb* take the chance of damaging or losing something.

risky *adjective* (**riskier, riskiest**) full of risk.

rissole *noun* a fried cake of minced meat or fish.

rite *noun* a religious ceremony; a solemn ritual.

ritual *noun* the series of actions used in a religious or other ceremony. **ritual** *adjective*, **ritually** *adverb*

rival¹ *noun* a person or thing that competes with another or tries to do the same thing. **rivalry** *noun*

rival² *verb* (**rivalled, rivalling**) be a rival of a person or thing. [from Latin *rivalis* = person using the same stream (*rivus* = stream)]

riven *adjective* split; torn apart.

river *noun* a large stream of water flowing in a natural channel. [from Latin *ripa* = bank]

rivet¹ *noun* a strong nail or bolt for holding pieces of metal together. The end opposite the head is flattened to form another head when it is in place.

rivet² *verb* (**riveted, riveting**) **1** fasten with rivets. **2** hold firmly, *He stood riveted to the spot.* **3** fascinate, *The concert was riveting.* **riveter** *noun*

rivulet *noun* a small stream.

road *noun* **1** a level way with a hard surface made for traffic to travel on. **2** a way or course, *the road to success.* **roadside** *noun*, **roadway** *noun*
road train (*Australian*) a truck pulling two or three long trailers.

roadworthy *adjective* safe to be used on roads.

roam *verb* wander. **roam** *noun*

roan *adjective* (of a horse) brown or black with many white hairs.

roar¹ *noun* **1** a loud deep sound like that made by a lion. **2** a loud laugh.

roar² *verb* make a roar.
a roaring trade brisk selling of something.

roast¹ *verb* **1** cook meat etc. in an oven or by exposing it to heat. **2** make or be very hot.

rise¹ *verb* **1** ascend, climb, go up, lift, mount, soar. **2** arise (*old use*), get up, stand up. **4** mutiny, rebel, revolt, take up arms. **5** begin, commence, flow from, originate, spring from, start. **7** appreciate, escalate, go up, grow, increase, jump, rocket, shoot up, skyrocket, soar, swell.

rise² *noun* **1** ascent, climb. **2** gain, increase, increment, raise. **3** elevation, hill, hillock, incline, slope.

risk¹ *noun* chance, danger, possibility.
at risk in danger, in jeopardy, in peril.

risk² *verb* chance, endanger, gamble, hazard, imperil, jeopardise, stake, venture.

risky *adjective* chancy, dangerous, dicey (*slang*), dodgy (*informal*), hairy (*slang*), hazardous, perilous, precarious, tricky, uncertain, unsafe.

ritual *noun* ceremony, practice, procedure, rite, routine, service, tradition.

rival¹ *noun* adversary, antagonist, challenger, competitor, contender, enemy, foe, opponent.

rival² *verb* compare with, compete with, contend with, contest, equal, match, measure up to, oppose, vie with.

river *noun* brook, creek, rill, rivulet, stream, tributary, watercourse, waterway.

road *noun* **1** alley, avenue, boulevard, bypass, byway, causeway, clearway, close, crescent, cul-de-sac, dead end, drive, expressway, freeway, highway, lane, motorway, orbital, parade, ring road, route, street, thoroughfare, tollway, track, turnpike (*historical & American*), way. **2** path, route, way.
roadside *noun* edge, kerb, verge, wayside.
roadway *noun* carriageway, road.
road train juggernaut (*informal*), lorry, semi (*Australian informal*), semitrailer, truck.

roam *verb* meander, ramble, range, rove, saunter, stroll, tootle around (*informal*), travel, wander.

roar¹ *noun* **1** bellow, howl, shout, rumble, thunder, yell. **2** guffaw, hoot (*informal*), howl, scream, shout, shriek.

roar² *verb* **1** bawl, bellow, howl, rumble, scream, shout, thunder, yell. **2** guffaw, laugh.

roast¹ *verb* **1** bake.

▶▶▶ DICTIONARY ◀◀◀

roast² *adjective* roasted, *roast beef.*

roast³ *noun* meat for roasting; roast meat.

rob *verb* (**robbed, robbing**) take or steal from somebody, *He robbed me of my watch.* **robber** *noun*, **robbery** *noun* [from Old French *robe* = booty]

robe¹ *noun* a long loose garment.

robe² *verb* (**robed, robing**) dress in a robe or ceremonial robes.

robin *noun* a small bird with a red breast.

robot *noun* **1** a machine that looks and acts like a person. **2** a machine operated by remote control. [from Czech *robota* = compulsory labour]

robust *adjective* strong; vigorous. **robustly** *adverb*, **robustness** *noun* [from Latin *robur* = strength]

rock¹ *noun* **1** a large stone or boulder. **2** the hard part of the earth's crust, under the soil. **rock lobster** (*Australian*) a marine crayfish. **rockmelon** a cantaloupe.

rock² *verb* **1** move gently backwards and forwards while supported on something. **2** shake violently, *The earthquake rocked the city.*

rock³ *noun* **1** a rocking movement. **2** rock music.
rock music popular music with a heavy beat.

rocker *noun* **1** a thing that rocks something or is rocked. **2** a rocking-chair.
off your rocker (*slang*) mad.

rockery *noun* (*plural* **rockeries**) a mound or bank in a garden, where plants are made to grow between large rocks.

rocket¹ *noun* **1** a firework that shoots high into the air. **2** a structure that flies by expelling burning gases, used to send up a missile or a spacecraft. **rocketry** *noun*

rocket² *verb* (**rocketed, rocketing**) move quickly upwards or away.

rocking-chair *noun* a chair that can be rocked by a person sitting in it.

rocking-horse *noun* a model of a horse that can be rocked by a child sitting on it.

rocky¹ *adjective* (**rockier, rockiest**) like rock; full of rocks.

rocky² *adjective* (**rockier, rockiest**) unsteady. **rockiness** *noun*

rod *noun* **1** a long thin stick or bar. **2** a stick with a line attached for fishing.

rodent *noun* an animal that has large front teeth for gnawing things, *Rats, mice, and squirrels are rodents.* [from Latin *rodens* = gnawing]

rodeo (*say* roh-**day**-oh) *noun* (*plural* **rodeos**) a display of cowboys' skill in riding, controlling horses, etc.

roe¹ *noun* a mass of eggs or reproductive cells in a fish's body.

roe² *noun* (*plural* **roes** or **roe**) a kind of small deer. The male is called a **roebuck**.

rogaine *noun* a marathon orienteering event usually taking 24 hours to complete. **rogainer** *noun*, **rogaining** *noun*

rogue *noun* **1** a dishonest person. **2** a mischievous person. **roguery** *noun*

roguish *adjective* playful.

roister *verb* make merry noisily.

▶▶▶ THESAURUS ◀◀◀

rob *verb* burgle, hold up, loot, mug, pilfer from, plunder, ransack, steal from, stick up (*informal*); see also SWINDLE.
robber *noun* bandit, brigand, buccaneer, burglar, bushranger, crook (*informal*), highwayman, housebreaker, looter, marauder, mugger, pickpocket, pilferer, pirate, plunderer, shoplifter, thief.
robbery *noun* burglary, heist (*informal*), hold-up, larceny, looting, mugging, pillage, plunder, stealing, stick-up (*informal*), theft.
robe¹ *noun* bathrobe, cassock, dress, dressing gown, gown, habit, kimono, vestment.
robot *noun* android, automaton, machine.
robust *adjective* brawny, hardy, healthy, muscular, powerful, strapping, strong, sturdy, tough, vigorous.

rock¹ *noun* **1** boulder, crag, outcrop, pebble, stone.
rock² *verb* **1** move to and fro, sway, swing. **2** lurch, pitch, reel, roll, shake, toss, totter, wobble.
rocky¹ *adjective* craggy, gravelly, pebbly, rugged, stony.
rocky² *adjective* precarious, shaky, uncertain, unstable, unsteady.
rod *noun* **1** bar, baton, cane, cue, dowel, mace, poker, pole, sceptre, staff, stick, wand.
rogue *noun* **1** blackguard, con man (*informal*), crook (*informal*), good-for-nothing, knave (*old use*), miscreant, rascal, rotter, scoundrel, villain, wretch. **2** devil, imp, monkey, rascal, scallywag, scamp, wag.

▶▶DICTIONARY◀◀

role *noun* **1** a performer's part in a play or film etc. **2** a person's or thing's function.

roll¹ *verb* **1** move along by turning over and over, like a ball or wheel. **2** form something into the shape of a cylinder or ball. **3** flatten something by rolling a rounded object over it. **4** rock from side to side. **5** pass steadily, *The years rolled on.* **6** make a long vibrating sound, *The thunder rolled.*
roll up (*Australian*) arrive.

roll² *noun* **1** a cylinder made by rolling something up. **2** a small individual portion of bread baked in a rounded shape. **3** an official list of names. **4** a long vibrating sound, *a drum roll.* [from Latin *rotula* = little wheel]

roll-call *noun* the calling of a list of names to check that everyone is present.

roller *noun* **1** a cylinder for rolling over things, or on which something is wound. **2** a long swelling sea-wave.

Rollerblade *noun* (*trade mark*) a roller skate with the four wheels one behind the other.
rollerblade *verb*

roller coaster a switchback at a fair etc.

roller skate a framework with wheels, fitted under a shoe so that the wearer can roll smoothly over the ground. **roller skating** *noun*

rollicking *adjective* boisterous and full of fun. [from *romp* + *frolic*]

rolling-pin *noun* a heavy cylinder for rolling over pastry in the kitchen.

rolling-stock *noun* railway engines and carriages and wagons etc.

roly-poly *noun* **1** a pudding of pastry covered with jam, rolled up and boiled. **2** a bushy Australian plant that breaks free and is rolled about by the wind.

ROM *abbreviation* read-only memory (in a computer), with contents that can be searched or copied but not changed.

Roman *adjective* **1** of ancient or modern Rome or its people. **2** Roman Catholic.
Roman *noun*
Roman candle a tubular firework that sends out coloured fire-balls.
Roman Catholic of the Church that has the pope (bishop of Rome) as its leader; a member of this Church.
Roman numerals letters that represent numbers ($I = 1$, $V = 5$, $X = 10$, etc.), used by the ancient Romans.

romance (*say* ro-**manss**) *noun* **1** tender feelings, experiences, and qualities connected with love. **2** a love story. **3** a love affair. **4** an imaginative story about the adventures of heroes, *a romance of King Arthur's court.*
romantic *adjective*, **romantically** *adverb*

Romany *noun* (*plural* **Romanies**) **1** a gypsy. **2** the language of gypsies. [from a Romany word *rom* = man]

romp *verb* play in a lively way. **romp** *noun*

rompers *plural noun* a young child's garment covering the trunk of the body.

rondo *noun* (*plural* **rondos**) a piece of music whose first part recurs several times.

roo *noun* (*Australian informal*) a kangaroo.
roo bar a bullbar.

rood *noun* a crucifix in a church, especially one placed on top of a screen (the **rood-screen**) separating the nave from the chancel.

roof *noun* (*plural* **roofs**) **1** the part that covers the top of a building, shelter, or vehicle. **2** the upper part of the mouth.

rook¹ *noun* a black crow that nests in large groups. [from Old English *hroc*]

rook² *verb* (*informal*) swindle; charge people an unnecessarily high price.

rook³ *noun* a chess piece shaped like a castle. [from Arabic *rukk*]

rookery *noun* (*plural* **rookeries**) a place where many rooks nest.

▶▶THESAURUS◀◀

role *noun* **1** character, part. **2** function, job, part, place.

roll¹ *verb* **1** go round, revolve, rotate, somersault, spin, trundle, tumble, turn, twirl, wheel, whirl. **2** coil, curl, furl, twist, wind, wrap. **3** flatten, level, smooth. **4** lurch, pitch, reel, rock, sway, toss, totter.

roll² *noun* **1** cylinder, reel, spool. **2** bagel, bap, bun. **3** list, register. **4** boom, reverberation, rumble, thunder.

roller coaster big dipper, switchback.

romance *noun* **2** love story. **3** affair, courtship, liaison, love affair, relationship.
romantic *adjective* **1** amorous, emotional, loving, mushy, nostalgic, passionate, sentimental, sloppy, soppy (*informal*), tender. **2** idealistic, impractical, quixotic, starry-eyed, unrealistic, Utopian, visionary.

romp *verb* caper, dance, frisk, frolic, gambol, jump, play, prance, run, skip.

rook² *verb* cheat, defraud, diddle (*informal*), have (*slang*), overcharge, rip off (*informal*), swindle.

▶▶ D I C T I O N A R Y ◀◀

room *noun* **1** a part of a building with its own walls and ceiling. **2** enough space, *Is there room for me?* **roomful** *noun*

roomy *adjective* (**roomier, roomiest**) containing plenty of room; spacious.

roost¹ *noun* a place where birds perch or settle for sleep.

roost² *verb* perch; settle for sleep.

rooster *noun* a cockerel.

root¹ *noun* **1** that part of a plant that grows under the ground and absorbs water and nourishment from the soil. **2** a source or basis, *The love of money is the root of all evil.* **3** a number in relation to the number it produces when multiplied by itself, *9 is the square root of 81 (9 x 9 = 81).*
take root grow roots; become established.

root² *verb* **1** take root; cause something to take root. **2** fix firmly, *Fear rooted us to the spot.*
root out get rid of something.

root³ *verb* rummage; (of an animal) turn up ground in search of food.

rope¹ *noun* a strong thick cord made of twisted strands of fibre.
show someone the ropes show him or her how to do something.

rope² *verb* (**roped, roping**) fasten with a rope.
rope in persuade a person to take part in something.

ropeable *adjective* (*Australian informal*) angry.

rort¹ *noun* (*Australian slang*) **1** a wild party. **2** a dishonest trick.

rort² *verb* (*Australian slang*) engage in trickery; rig a ballot.

rosary *noun* (*plural* **rosaries**) a string of beads for keeping count of a set of prayers as they are said.

rose¹ *noun* **1** a shrub that has showy flowers often with thorny stems. **2** deep pink colour. **3** a sprinkling-nozzle with many holes, e.g. on a watering-can or hose-pipe.

rose² *past tense* of **rise**.

roseate *adjective* deep pink; rosy.

rosebud *noun* the bud of a rose.

rosella¹ *noun* a brightly coloured Australian parakeet.

rosella² *noun* an Australian shrub with fruit used in making **rosella jam**.

rosemary *noun* an evergreen shrub with fragrant leaves.

rosette *noun* a large circular badge or ornament. [French, = little rose]

Ross River virus a virus carried by mosquitoes causing a rash and joint and muscle pain. [from the name of a river in Queensland]

roster¹ *noun* a list showing people's turns to be on duty etc.

roster² *verb* place on a roster.

rostrum *noun* (*plural* **rostra**) a platform for one person.

rosy *adjective* (**rosier, rosiest**) **1** deep pink. **2** hopeful; cheerful, *a rosy future.* **rosiness** *noun*

rot¹ *verb* (**rotted, rotting**) go soft or bad and become useless; decay.

rot² *noun* **1** rotting; decay. **2** (*slang*) nonsense.

rota (*say* **roh**-ta) *noun* a list of people to do things or of things to be done in turn. [Latin, = wheel]

▶▶ T H E S A U R U S ◀◀

room *noun* **1** cell, chamber (*old use*), office. **2** area, elbow room, space.

roomy *adjective* ample, big, capacious, commodious, huge, large, spacious, vast.

roost² *verb* nest, perch, settle, sleep.

rooster *noun* cock, cockerel.

root¹ *noun* **1** radicle, rhizome, rootlet, tuber. **2** basis, bottom, cause, foundation, origin, source.
take root become established, catch on, take hold.

root² *verb* **1** grow roots, take root. **2** anchor, fix, stick.
root out eliminate, eradicate, get rid of, remove, weed out.

rope¹ *noun* cable, cord, guy, hawser, lanyard, lariat, lasso, line, noose, painter, stay, tether.

rope² *verb* attach, bind, fasten, hitch, secure, tie.

rort¹ *noun* **2** dodge (*informal*), lurk (*Australian informal*), racket, scam (*slang*), scheme, swindle.

roster¹ *noun* list, rota.

rostrum *noun* dais, platform, podium, stage, stand.

rosy *adjective* **1** blushing, florid, flushed, glowing, pink, red, rose, rubicund, ruddy. **2** auspicious, bright, cheerful, encouraging, hopeful, optimistic, promising.

rot¹ *verb* decay, decompose, disintegrate, fester, go bad, go off, moulder, perish, putrefy, spoil.

rot² *noun* **1** decay, decomposition, disintegration, mould, putrefaction. **2** see NONSENSE.

rotate *verb* (**rotated, rotating**) **1** go round like a wheel; revolve. **2** arrange or happen in a series; take turns at doing something. **rotation** *noun*, **rotary** *adjective*, **rotatory** *adjective* [same origin as *rota*]

rote *noun* **by rote** from memory or by routine, without full understanding of the meaning, *We used to learn French songs by rote.*

rotor *noun* a rotating part of a machine or helicopter.

rotten *adjective* **1** rotted, *rotten apples.* **2** (*informal*) worthless; unpleasant; ill. **rottenness** *noun*

rotter *noun* (*slang*) a dishonourable person.

rotund *adjective* rounded; plump. **rotundity** *noun* [from Latin, = round]

rouble (*say* **roo**-bul) *noun* the unit of money in Russia.

rouge (*say* roo*zh*) *noun* a reddish cosmetic for colouring the cheeks. [French, = red]

rough¹ *adjective* **1** not smooth; uneven. **2** not gentle or careful; violent, *a rough push.* **3** made or done quickly; lacking finish, *a rough job.* **4** not exact, *a rough guess.* **roughly** *adverb*, **roughness** *noun*

rough² *verb*
rough it do without ordinary comforts.
rough out draw or plan something roughly.
rough up (*slang*) treat a person violently.

roughage *noun* fibre in food, which helps digestion.

roughen *verb* make or become rough.

roulette (*say* roo-**let**) *noun* a gambling game where players bet on where the ball in a rotating disc will come to rest. [French, = little wheel]

round¹ *adjective* **1** shaped like a circle or ball or cylinder; curved. **2** full; complete, *a round dozen.* **3** returning to the start, *a round trip.* **roundness** *noun*
in round figures approximately, without giving exact units.

round² *adverb* **1** in a circle or curve; round something, *Go round to the back of the house.* **2** in every direction, *Hand the cakes round.* **3** in a new direction, *Turn your chair round.* **4** to someone's house or office etc., *Go round after dinner.* **5** into being conscious again, *Has she come round from the anaesthetic yet?*
round about near by; approximately.

round³ *preposition* **1** on all sides of, *Put a fence round the pool.* **2** in a curve or circle at an even distance from, *The earth moves round the sun.* **3** to all parts of, *Show them round the house.* **4** on the further side of, *The shop is round the corner.*

round⁴ *noun* **1** a round object. **2** a series of visits made by a doctor, postman, etc. **3** one section or stage in a competition, *Winners go on to the next round.* **4** a shot or volley of shots from a gun; ammunition for this. **5** a song in which people sing the same words but start at different times.

rotate *verb* **1** go round, gyrate, revolve, spin, swivel, turn, twirl, whirl. **2** alternate, swap, take turns at.

rotten *adjective* **1** bad, crumbling, decayed, decomposed, disintegrating, mouldy, off, perished, putrid, rancid, rank, stinking. **2** (*a rotten thing to do*) beastly, contemptible, despicable, lousy (*informal*), low-down, mean, nasty, unkind; (*rotten weather*) abysmal (*informal*), appalling (*informal*), atrocious (*informal*), bad, dreadful (*informal*), foul, shocking (*informal*), terrible (*informal*); (*feeling rotten*) ill, miserable, poorly, seedy (*informal*), sick, unwell, wretched.

rotund *adjective* chubby, corpulent, fat, obese, overweight, plump, podgy, portly, stout, tubby.

rough¹ *adjective* **1** (*a rough surface*) broken, bumpy, coarse, craggy, irregular, jagged, knobbly, pitted, ragged, rocky, rugged, stony, uneven; (*rough skin*) bristly, calloused, chapped, hard, leathery, scaly, unshaven. **2** (*a rough voice*) grating, gruff, harsh, hoarse, husky, rasping, raucous, strident; (*rough play*) boisterous, lively, rowdy, unrestrained, wild; (*rough weather*) blustery, inclement, squally, stormy, tempestuous, turbulent, violent, wild. **3** careless, clumsy, crude, hasty, imperfect, makeshift, patchy, rough-and-ready, rudimentary, unfinished. **4** approximate, ballpark (*informal*), general, hazy, imprecise, inexact, sketchy, vague.
roughly *adverb* about, approximately, around, close to, in the vicinity of, nearly, round about.

round¹ *adjective* **1** bulbous, circular, curved, globular, rotund, spherical. **2** complete, entire, full, whole.

round⁴ *noun* **2** course, cycle, series, succession. **3** bout, division, game, heat, section, stage.

▶▶▶ D I C T I O N A R Y ◀◀

round⁵ *verb* **1** make or become round. **2** travel round, *The car rounded the corner.*
round off finish something.
round up gather people or animals together.
round-up *noun*

roundabout¹ *noun* **1** a road junction where traffic has to pass round a circular structure in the road. **2** a merry-go-round.

roundabout² *adjective* indirect; not using the shortest way of going or of saying or doing something, *I heard the news in a roundabout way.*

rounders *noun* a game in which players try to hit a ball and run round a circuit.

roundly *adverb* **1** thoroughly; severely, *We were roundly told off for being late.* **2** in a rounded shape.

rouse *verb* (**roused, rousing**) **1** make or become awake. **2** cause to become active or excited.

rouseabout *noun* (*Australian*) a general hand on a rural property or in a shearing shed.

rousing *adjective* exciting, stirring, *a rousing speech.*

rout *verb* defeat and chase away an enemy.
rout *noun*

route (*say as* root) *noun* the way taken to get to a place.

routine (*say* roo-**teen**) *noun* a regular way of doing things. **routine** *adjective*, **routinely** *adverb*

rove *verb* (**roved, roving**) roam. **rover** *noun*

row¹ (*rhymes with* go) *noun* a line of people or things.

row² (*rhymes with* go) *verb* make a boat move by using oars. **rower** *noun*, **rowing-boat** *noun*

row³ (*rhymes with* cow) *noun* (*informal*) **1** a loud noise. **2** a quarrel. **3** a scolding.

rowan (*say* **roh**-an) *noun* a tree that bears hanging bunches of red berries.

rowdy *adjective* (**rowdier, rowdiest**) noisy and disorderly. **rowdiness** *noun*

rowlock (*say* **rol**-ok) *noun* a device on the side of a boat, keeping an oar in place.

royal *adjective* of or connected with a king or queen. **royally** *adverb* [from Latin *regalis* = regal]

royalty *noun* (*plural* **royalties**) **1** being royal. **2** a royal person or persons, *in the presence of royalty.* **3** a payment made to an author or composer etc. for each copy of a work sold or for each performance.

RSVP *abbreviation* répondez s'il vous plaît (French, = please reply).

▶▶▶ T H E S A U R U S ◀◀

round⁵ *verb* **2** go round, turn.
round off bring to a close, close, complete, conclude, end, finish, terminate.
round up assemble, collect, gather, herd, muster.

roundabout¹ *noun* **2** carousel, merry-go-round, whirligig.

roundabout² *adjective* circuitous, circumlocutory, devious, indirect, meandering, oblique, tortuous.

rouse *verb* **1** arouse, awaken, stir, waken, wake up. **2** excite, incite, move, provoke, stimulate, stir.

rouseabout *noun* blue tongue (*Australian informal*), handyman, knockabout (*Australian*), loppy (*Australian*), odd-job man.

rousing *adjective* exciting, inspiring, moving, powerful, provoking, stirring.

rout *verb* beat, conquer, crush, defeat, overpower, overthrow, put to flight, scatter, thrash, trounce, vanquish.

route *noun* course, itinerary, path, road, way.

routine *noun* custom, habit, method, pattern, practice, procedure, ritual, system, way.

routine *adjective* customary, familiar, habitual, humdrum, mechanical, monotonous, normal, ordinary, predictable, regular, scheduled, standard, usual.

rove *verb* prowl, ramble, roam, stray, wander.
rover *noun* gypsy, itinerant, nomad, traveller, vagabond, wanderer, wayfarer.

row¹ *noun* chain, column, file, line, queue, rank, sequence, series, string, tier.

row² *verb* paddle, propel, scull.

row³ *noun* **1** clamour, commotion, din, disturbance, fuss, hubbub, hullabaloo, noise, racket, ruckus, rumpus, shindy (*informal*), tumult, uproar. **2** altercation, argument, barney (*informal*), blue (*Australian informal*), bust-up (*informal*), disagreement, dispute, fight, fracas, quarrel, run-in, scrap (*informal*), squabble, tiff, wrangle.

rowdy *adjective* boisterous, disorderly, lawless, noisy, obstreperous, riotous, rough, unruly, wild.

royal *adjective* kingly, monarchic, queenly, regal, sovereign.

rub *verb* (**rubbed, rubbing**) **1** move something backwards and forwards while pressing it on something else. **2** apply polish, ointment, etc. by rubbing. **3** polish or clean by rubbing. **4** make sore or bare by rubbing. **rub** *noun* **rub out** remove something by rubbing.

rubber *noun* **1** a strong elastic substance used for making tyres, balls, hoses, etc. **2** a piece of rubber for rubbing out pencil or ink marks. **rubbery** *adjective*

rubbish¹ *noun* **1** things that are worthless or not wanted. **2** nonsense.

rubbish² *verb* (*Australian*) belittle, disparage.

rubble *noun* broken pieces of brick or stone.

rubella (*say* roo-**bel**-a) *noun* German measles.

rubicund *adjective* ruddy; red-faced. [same origin as *ruby*]

ruby *noun* (*plural* **rubies**) a red jewel. [from Latin *rubeus* = red]

ruck *noun* a dense crowd.

rucksack *noun* a bag on straps for carrying on the back. [from German *rücken* = back, + *sack*]

ructions *plural noun* (*informal*) protests and noisy argument.

rudder *noun* a hinged upright piece at the back of a ship or aircraft, used for steering.

ruddy *adjective* red and healthy-looking, *a ruddy complexion*.

rude *adjective* **1** impolite. **2** indecent; improper. **3** roughly made; crude, *a rude shelter*. **4** vigorous; hearty, *in rude health*. **rudely** *adverb*, **rudeness** *noun* [from Latin *rudis* = raw, wild]

rudimentary *adjective* **1** of rudiments; elementary. **2** not fully developed, *Penguins have rudimentary wings*.

rudiments (*say* **rood**-i-ments) *plural noun* the elementary principles of a subject, *Learn the rudiments of chemistry*.

rue *verb* (**rued, ruing**) regret, *I rue the day I started this!*

rueful *adjective* regretful. **ruefully** *adverb*

ruff *noun* **1** a starched pleated frill worn round the neck in the 16th century. **2** a collar-like ring of feathers or fur round a bird's or animal's neck.

ruffian *noun* a violent lawless person. **ruffianly** *adjective*

ruffle¹ *verb* (**ruffled, ruffling**) **1** disturb the smoothness of a thing. **2** upset or annoy someone.

rub *verb* **1** caress, massage, pat, stroke. **2** apply, smear, spread, wipe, work in. **3** buff, burnish, polish, shine, wipe. **4** abrade, chafe, gall, wear away.
rub out blot out, cancel, delete, efface, erase, expunge, obliterate, remove, wipe out.

rubbish¹ *noun* **1** debris, detritus, dross, garbage, junk, litter, muck (*informal*), mullock (*Australian*), refuse, rubble, scrap, trash, waste. **2** balderdash, boloney (*informal*), bunkum, claptrap, cobblers (*slang*), codswallop (*slang*), drivel, garbage, gibberish, gobbledegook (*informal*), guff (*slang*), hogwash (*informal*), humbug, nonsense, piffle (*informal*), poppycock (*slang*), rot (*slang*), stuff and nonsense (*informal*), tommyrot (*slang*), tripe (*informal*), twaddle.

rubbish² *verb* bag (*Australian informal*), belittle, criticise, disparage, knock (*informal*), pan (*informal*), pick holes in, pooh-pooh, run down, scoff at, slate (*informal*), tear to pieces.

rubble *noun* debris.

rucksack *noun* backpack, haversack, knapsack, pack.

ruddy *adjective* florid, flushed, red, rosy, rubicund.

rude *adjective* **1** abrupt, abusive, bad-mannered, boorish, brazen, brusque, cheeky, churlish, curt, discourteous, disrespectful, foul-mouthed, ill-mannered, impertinent, impolite, impudent, inconsiderate, insolent, insulting, loutish, offensive, offhand, rough, saucy, surly, uncivil, uncouth, vulgar. **2** blue, coarse, crude, dirty, filthy, foul, improper, indecent, lewd, obscene, offensive, pornographic, smutty, tasteless, unprintable, vulgar. **3** crude, makeshift, primitive, rough, simple.

rudimentary *adjective* **1** basic, elementary, fundamental, primary. **2** immature, incomplete, undeveloped, vestigial.

rudiments *plural noun* ABC, basics, elements, essentials, fundamentals.

rue *verb* lament, mourn, regret, repent.

rueful *adjective* apologetic, contrite, penitent, regretful, remorseful, repentant, sorrowful, sorry.

ruffian *noun* bully, gangster, hood (*informal*), hoodlum, hooligan, hoon (*Australian informal*), larrikin (*Australian*), lout, mugger, rogue, rough, scoundrel, thug, tough, villain.

ruffle¹ *verb* **1** disturb, ripple, stir. **2** agitate, disconcert, disturb, faze (*informal*), fluster, perturb, rattle (*informal*), unsettle, upset.

▶▶ D I C T I O N A R Y ◀◀

ruffle² *noun* a gathered ornamental frill.

rug *noun* **1** a thick mat for the floor. **2** a piece of thick fabric used as a blanket.

Rugby *noun* (also **Rugby football**) a kind of football game using an oval ball that players may carry or kick. [named after Rugby School in England, where it was first played]

rugged *adjective* **1** having an uneven surface or outline; craggy. **2** sturdy.

ruin¹ *noun* **1** severe damage or destruction to something. **2** a building that has fallen down.

ruin² *verb* damage a thing so severely that it is useless; destroy. **ruination** *noun* [from Latin *ruere* = to fall]

ruinous *adjective* **1** causing ruin. **2** in ruins; ruined.

rule¹ *noun* **1** something that people have to obey. **2** the customary or normal state of things. **3** ruling; governing, *under French rule.* **4** a carpenter's ruler.
as a rule usually; more often than not.

rule² *verb* (**ruled, ruling**) **1** govern; reign. **2** make a decision, *The referee ruled that it was a foul.* **3** draw a straight line with a ruler or other straight edge. [from Latin *regula* = rule]

ruler *noun* **1** a person who governs. **2** a strip of wood, metal, or plastic with straight edges, used for measuring and drawing straight lines.

ruling *noun* a judgement.

rum *noun* a strong alcoholic drink made from sugar or molasses.

rumble *verb* (**rumbled, rumbling**) make a deep heavy continuous sound like thunder. **rumble** *noun*

ruminant¹ *adjective* ruminating.

ruminant² *noun* an animal that chews the cud (see *cud*).

ruminate *verb* (**ruminated, ruminating**) **1** chew the cud. **2** meditate; ponder. **rumination** *noun*, **ruminative** *adjective*

rummage *verb* (**rummaged, rummaging**) turn things over or move them about while looking for something. **rummage** *noun*

rummy *noun* a card game in which players try to form sets or sequences of cards.

rumour¹ *noun* information that spreads to a lot of people but may not be true.

rumour² *verb* **be rumoured** be spread as a rumour. [from Latin *rumor* = noise]

rump *noun* the hind part of an animal.

rumple *verb* (**rumpled, rumpling**) crumple; make a thing untidy.

rumpus *noun* (*plural* **rumpuses**) (*slang*) an uproar; an angry protest.

▶▶ T H E S A U R U S ◀◀

ruffle² *noun* flounce, frill, ruff.

ruffled *adjective* dishevelled, messed up, rumpled, tangled, tousled, untidy.

rug *noun* **1** mat. **2** blanket, coverlet.

rugged *adjective* **1** bumpy, craggy, irregular, jagged, rocky, rough, stony, uneven, wild. **2** beefy, brawny, burly, hardy, husky, muscular, nuggety (*Australian*), robust, strong, sturdy, tough, vigorous.

ruin¹ *noun* **1** collapse, decay, destruction, devastation, dilapidation, disrepair, downfall, failure, fall, rack and ruin, ruination, undoing. **2** (*ruins*) debris, remains, rubble, shell, wreck, wreckage.

ruin² *verb* damage, demolish, destroy, devastate, mess up, muck up, sabotage, scupper (*informal*), shatter, spoil, undermine, vandalise, wreck.

rule¹ *noun* **1** by-law, code, commandment, convention, decree, formula, guideline, instruction, law, order, ordinance, policy, precept, principle, protocol, regulation, ruling, statute. **2** convention, custom, norm, practice, routine, standard. **3** authority, command, control, dominion, government, jurisdiction, leadership, regime, reign, sovereignty.
as a rule for the most part, generally, normally, ordinarily, usually.

rule² *verb* **1** administer, command, control, direct, govern, lead, manage, reign over, run. **2** adjudicate, decide, decree, determine, find, judge, pronounce.

ruler *noun* **1** chief, commander, emir, emperor, empress, governor, head, head of state, king, leader, lord, monarch, overlord, potentate, president, prince, princess, queen, sovereign, sultan. **2** measure, rule, yardstick.

rumble *verb* & *noun* boom, roar, thunder.

rummage *verb* comb, ferret, forage, fossick (*Australian informal*), hunt, ransack, rifle, scour, search.

rumour¹ *noun* bush telegraph, furphy (*Australian informal*), gossip, hearsay, mulga wire (*Australian informal*), tale, whisper.

rumour² *verb* bandy about, gossip, put about, report, say, spread about, whisper.

rumpus *noun* commotion, din, disturbance, fuss, hullabaloo, pandemonium, protest, racket, row, ruckus, shindy (*informal*), storm, to-do, uproar.

▶▶▶ D I C T I O N A R Y ◀◀

run¹ *verb* (**ran, run, running**) **1** move with quick steps so that both or all feet leave the ground at each stride. **2** go or travel; flow, *Tears ran down his cheeks*. **3** produce a flow of liquid, *Run some water into it*. **4** work or function, *The engine was running smoothly*. **5** manage; organise, *She runs a grocery shop*. **6** compete in a contest, *He ran for President*. **7** extend, *A fence runs round the estate*. **8** go or take in a vehicle, *I'll run you to the station*.
run away leave a place secretly or quickly.
run down criticise.
run into collide with; happen to meet.
run out have used up your stock of something; knock over the wicket of a running batsman.
run over overflow; knock down or crush with a moving vehicle; study or repeat quickly.

run² *noun* **1** the action of running; a time spent running, *Go for a run*. **2** a short trip or journey. **3** a point scored in cricket or baseball. **4** a continuous series of events, etc., *She had a run of good luck*. **5** an enclosure for animals, *a chicken run*. **6** (*Australian*) a sheep or cattle station. **7** a track, *a ski-run*.
on the run running away from pursuit or capture.

runaway¹ *noun* someone who has run away.

runaway² *adjective* **1** having run away or out of control. **2** won easily, *a runaway victory*.

run-down *noun* a summary or analysis.

rung¹ *noun* a cross-piece in a ladder.

rung² *past participle* of **ring³**.

runner *noun* **1** a person or animal that runs, especially in a race. **2** a stem that grows away from a plant and roots itself. **3** a groove, rod, or roller for a thing to move on; each of the long strips under a sledge. **4** a long narrow strip of carpet or covering.
runner bean a kind of climbing bean.

runner-up *noun* (*plural* **runners-up**) someone who comes second in a competition.

running¹ *noun* **in the running** competing and with a chance of winning.

running² *adjective* continuous; consecutive; without an interval, *It rained for four days running*.

runny *adjective* flowing like liquid; producing a flow of liquid.

runway *noun* a long hard surface on which aircraft take off and land.

rupiah (*say* roo-**pee**-a) *noun* the unit of money in Indonesia.

rupture *verb* (**ruptured, rupturing**) break; burst.
rupture *noun* [from Latin *ruptum* = broken]

rural *adjective* of or like the countryside. [from Latin *ruris* = of the country]

ruse *noun* a deception or trick.

▶▶▶ T H E S A U R U S ◀◀

run¹ *verb* **1** bound, dart, dash, fly, gallop, hasten, hurry, hurtle, jog, race, rush, scamper, scoot, scurry, scuttle, shoot, speed, sprint, spurt, stampede, streak, sweep, tear, trot, whiz, zip. **2** cascade, drip, flow, gush, issue, leak, pour, roll, spurt, stream, trickle. **4** behave, function, go, operate, perform, work. **5** administer, carry on, conduct, control, direct, govern, look after, maintain, manage, organise, oversee, supervise. **8** convey, drive, take, transport.
run after chase, follow, pursue.
run away abscond, beat it (*slang*), bolt, clear off (*informal*), decamp, depart, disappear, do a runner (*slang*), escape, flee, go away, hightail it (*informal*), leave, make off, nick off (*Australian slang*), retreat, run off, scarper (*informal*), scoot, scram (*informal*), shoot through (*Australian informal*), skedaddle (*informal*), take flight, take off, take to your heels, withdraw.
run down bag (*Australian informal*), belittle, criticise, disparage, knock (*informal*), malign, pan (*informal*), revile, rubbish, slate (*informal*).
run into 1 bump into, career into, collide with, crash into, hit, knock into, ram, smash into,

strike. **2** bump into, come across, meet, run across.
run over 1 brim over, overflow, spill over. **2** hit, knock down, run down. **3** go over, practise, rehearse, run through.

run² *noun* **2** drive, excursion, jaunt, outing, ride, spin (*informal*), trip. **4** sequence, series, spate, string, succession. **5** compound, coop, enclosure, pen. **6** farm, property, station (*Australian*).

runaway¹ *noun* absconder, bolter, deserter, escapee, fugitive.

run-down *noun* outline, recap (*informal*), report, review, round-up, summary, survey.

runny *adjective* fluid, liquid, sloppy, thin, watery.

runway *noun* airstrip, landing strip.

rupture *verb* break, burst, split, tear.

rural *adjective* bucolic, country, pastoral, rustic.

ruse *noun* artifice, deception, dodge (*informal*), hoax, manoeuvre, ploy (*informal*), stratagem, subterfuge, trick, wile.

rush¹ *verb* **1** hurry. **2** move or flow quickly. **3** attack or capture by rushing.

rush² *noun* (*plural* **rushes**) **1** a hurry. **2** a sudden movement towards something. **3** a sudden great demand for something.

rush³ *noun* (*plural* **rushes**) a plant with a thin stem that grows in marshy places.

rush-hour *noun* the time when traffic is busiest.

rusk *noun* a kind of biscuit, especially for feeding babies.

russet *noun* reddish-brown colour. [from Latin *russus* = red]

rust¹ *noun* **1** a red or brown substance that forms on iron or steel exposed to damp and corrodes it. **2** reddish-brown colour.

rust² *verb* make or become rusty.

rustic *adjective* **1** rural. **2** made of rough timber or branches, *a rustic bridge*.

rusticate *verb* (**rusticated, rusticating**) settle in the country. **rustication** *noun* [from *rustic*]

rustle *verb* (**rustled, rustling**) **1** make a sound like paper being crumpled. **2** (*American*) steal horses or cattle, *cattle rustling*. (Compare *duff.*) **rustle** *noun*, **rustler** *noun*
rustle up (*informal*) produce, *rustle up a meal.*

rusty *adjective* (**rustier, rustiest**) **1** coated with rust. **2** weakened by lack of use or practice, *My French is a bit rusty*. **rustiness** *noun*

rut *noun* **1** a deep track made by wheels in soft ground. **2** a settled and usually dull way of life, *We are getting into a rut*. **rutted** *adjective*

ruthless *adjective* pitiless; merciless; cruel. **ruthlessly** *adverb*, **ruthlessness** *noun* [from *ruth* = pity]

rye *noun* a cereal used to make bread, biscuits, etc.

rush¹ *verb* **1,2** charge, dash, fly, gallop, hasten, hurry, hustle, race, run, scoot, scramble, scurry, shoot off, speed, sprint, storm, tear, whiz, zip, zoom. **3** attack, capture, charge, seize, storm.

rush² *noun* **1** haste, hurry, hustle, race. **2** charge, dash, run, scramble, stampede.

rust² *verb* corrode, oxidise, rot.

rustic *adjective* **1** bucolic, country, pastoral, rural.

rustle *verb & noun* **1** swish, whisper.

rut *noun* **1** channel, furrow, groove, track. **2** grind, habit, routine.

ruthless *adjective* brutal, callous, cruel, ferocious, harsh, heartless, merciless, pitiless, relentless, remorseless, savage, vicious.

▶ Ss ◀

S. *abbreviation* south; southern.

sabbath *noun* a weekly day for rest and prayer, Saturday for Jews, Sunday for Christians. [from Hebrew, = rest]

sable *noun* **1** a kind of dark fur. **2** (*poetic*) black.

sabotage *noun* deliberate damage or disruption to hinder an enemy, employer, etc. **sabotage** *verb*, **saboteur** *noun*

sabre *noun* **1** a heavy sword with a curved blade. **2** a light fencing-sword.

sac *noun* a bag-shaped part in an animal or plant.

saccharin (*say* **sak**-er-in) *noun* a very sweet substance used as a substitute for sugar. [from Greek *saccharon* = sugar]

saccharine (*say* **sak**-er-een) *adjective* unpleasantly sweet, *a saccharine smile*.

sachet (*say* **sash**-ay) *noun* a small sealed bag or packet holding a scented substance or a single portion of something. [French, = little sack]

sack¹ *noun* a large bag made of strong material. **sacking** *noun*
the sack (*informal*) dismissal from a job, *He got the sack.*

sack² *verb* (*informal*) dismiss someone from a job.

sack³ *verb* plunder a captured town in a violent destructive way. **sack** *noun*

sacrament *noun* an important Christian religious ceremony such as baptism or Holy Communion. [same origin as *sacred*]

sacred *adjective* holy; of God or a god.
sacred site a place of spiritual significance, especially to Aboriginal people. [from Latin *sacer* = holy]

sacrifice¹ *noun* **1** giving something that you think will please a god. **2** giving up a thing you value, so that something good may happen. **3** a thing sacrificed. **sacrificial** *adjective*

sacrifice² *verb* (**sacrificed, sacrificing**) give something as a sacrifice. [from Latin, = make a thing sacred]

sacrilege (*say* **sak**-ril-ij) *noun* disrespect or damage to something people regard as sacred. **sacrilegious** *adjective* [from Latin *sacer* = sacred, + *legere* = take away]

sacrosanct *adjective* sacred or respected and therefore not to be harmed. [from Latin *sacro* = by a sacred rite, + *sanctus* = holy]

sad *adjective* (**sadder, saddest**) **1** unhappy; showing sorrow. **2** causing sorrow. **sadly** *adverb*, **sadness** *noun*

▶▶▶ THESAURUS ◀◀◀

sabotage *noun* damage, destruction, disruption, vandalism.
sabotage *verb* destroy, disrupt, ruin, spoil, undermine, wreck.

sachet *noun* bag, pack, packet.

sack¹ *noun* bag, pack, package.

sack² *verb* discharge, dismiss, fire, give notice to, give someone the boot (*slang*), lay off, make redundant.

sack³ *verb* destroy, lay waste, loot, pillage, plunder, raid, ransack, ravage.

sacred *adjective* blessed, consecrated, divine, hallowed, holy, religious, revered, sacrosanct, sanctified, spiritual, venerated.

sacrifice¹ *noun* **3** oblation, offering.

sacrifice² *verb* forfeit, forgo, give up, offer, renounce, surrender.

sacrilege *noun* desecration, disrespect, irreverence, profanation, profanity, violation.
sacrilegious *adjective* disrespectful, impious, irreverent, profane; see also BLASPHEMOUS (at BLASPHEMY).

sacrosanct *adjective* inviolable, protected, respected, sacred.

sad *adjective* **1** blue, broken-hearted, dejected, depressed, desolate, despondent, disconsolate, discontented, dismal, distressed, doleful, downcast, gloomy, glum, heartbroken, heavy-hearted, lugubrious, melancholy, miserable, mournful, rueful, sorrowful, unhappy, woebegone, wretched. **2** dismal, distressing, gloomy, heartbreaking, pessimistic, touching, tragic, upsetting.
sadness *noun* dejection, depression, desolation, despondency, discontent, distress, gloom, glumness, melancholy, misery, sorrow, unhappiness, woe, wretchedness.

▶▶ D I C T I O N A R Y ◀◀

sadden *verb* make a person sad.

saddle¹ *noun* 1 a seat for putting on the back of a horse or other animal. 2 the seat of a bicycle. 3 a ridge of high land between two peaks.

saddle² *verb* (**saddled**, **saddling**) put a saddle on a horse etc.

sadist (*say* **say**-dist) *noun* a person who enjoys hurting other people. **sadism** *noun*, **sadistic** *adjective* [named after a French novelist, the Marquis de Sade, noted for his crimes]

safari *noun* (*plural* **safaris**) an expedition to see or hunt wild animals.
safari park a park where wild animals are kept to be seen by visitors. [from Arabic *safara* = travel]

safe¹ *adjective* 1 free from risk or danger; not dangerous. 2 providing protection, *a safe place*. 3 reliable, certain, *a safe method*. 4 unharmed. **safely** *adverb*, **safeness** *noun*, **safety** *noun*

safe² *noun* a strong cupboard or box in which valuables can be locked safely. [from Latin *salvus* = uninjured]

safeguard¹ *noun* a protection.

safeguard² *verb* protect.

safety-pin *noun* a U-shaped pin with a clip fastening over the point.

saffron *noun* 1 deep yellow colour. 2 a kind of crocus with orange-coloured stigmas. 3 these stigmas dried and used to colour or flavour food.

sag *verb* (**sagged**, **sagging**) go down in the middle because something heavy is pressing on it; droop. **sag** *noun*

saga (*say* **sah**-ga) *noun* a long story with many episodes.

sagacious (*say* sa-**gay**-shus) *adjective* shrewd and wise. **sagaciously** *adverb*, **sagacity** *noun* [from Latin *sagax* = wise]

sage¹ *noun* a kind of herb.

sage² *adjective* wise. **sagely** *adverb*

sage³ *noun* a wise and respected person.

sago *noun* a starchy white food used to make puddings.

sail¹ *noun* 1 a large piece of strong cloth attached to a mast etc. to catch the wind and make a ship or boat move. 2 a short voyage. 3 an arm of a windmill.

sail² *verb* 1 travel in a ship or boat. 2 start a voyage, *We sail at noon.* 3 control a ship or boat. 4 move quickly and smoothly. **sailing-ship** *noun*

sailor *noun* a person who sails; a member of a ship's crew or of a navy.

saint *noun* a holy or very good person. **saintly** *adverb*, **saintliness** *noun* [from Latin *sanctus* = holy]

sake *noun* **for the sake of** so as to help or please a person, get a thing, etc.

salaam *noun* a low bow with the right hand on the forehead. [from Arabic *salam* = peace]

salad *noun* a mixture of vegetables eaten raw or cold.

salamander *noun* a lizard-like animal formerly thought to live in fire.

salami *noun* a spiced sausage.

▶▶ T H E S A U R U S ◀◀

sadden *verb* depress, dishearten, dismay, distress, grieve, upset.

sadistic *adjective* brutal, cruel, inhuman, monstrous, vicious.

safari *noun* expedition, tour, trip.

safe¹ *adjective* 1 harmless, innocuous, non-toxic. 2 defended, impregnable, protected, secure, sheltered. 3 certain, dependable, reliable, sound, sure. 4 all right, OK (*informal*), safe and sound, unharmed, uninjured, unscathed.
safety *noun* protection, security.

safe² *noun* strongbox, vault.

safeguard¹ *noun* defence, precaution, protection, security.

safeguard² *verb* defend, guard, look after, preserve, protect.

sag *verb* bow, droop, flop, sink, slump, subside.

saga *noun* chronicle, epic, history, legend, romance, story, tale.

sage² *adjective* judicious, prudent, sagacious, sensible, shrewd, wise.

sage³ *noun* authority, expert, guru, philosopher, pundit, scholar, wise man.

sail¹ *noun* 1 cruise. 2 journey, trip, voyage.

sail² *verb* 2 cruise, embark, put to sea, set out, set sail, weigh anchor. 3 navigate, pilot, skipper, steer. 4 drift, float, glide, scud, sweep, waft.

sailor *noun* mariner, navigator, seafarer, seaman, yachtsman, yachtswoman.

saintly *adjective* blameless, blessed, God-fearing, godly, holy, innocent, pious, righteous, upright, virtuous.

salary *noun* (*plural* **salaries**) a regular wage, usually for a year's work, paid in monthly instalments. **salaried** *adjective* [from Latin *salarium* = salt-money, money given to Roman soldiers to buy salt]

sale *noun* **1** selling. **2** a time when things are sold at reduced prices.

salesman, salesperson, saleswoman *nouns* a person employed to sell goods.

salient[1] (*say* **say**-lee-ent) *adjective* **1** projecting. **2** most noticeable, *the salient features of the plan.*

salient[2] *noun* a part of a fortification or battle-line that juts out. [from Latin *saliens* = leaping]

saline *adjective* containing salt.

saliva *noun* the natural liquid in a person's or animal's mouth. **salivary** *adjective*

salivate (*say* **sal**-iv-ayt) *verb* (**salivated, salivating**) form saliva. **salivation** *noun*

sallow *adjective* slightly yellow, *a sallow complexion.* **sallowness** *noun*

sally[1] *noun* (*plural* **sallies**) **1** a sudden rush forward. **2** an excursion. **3** a lively or witty remark.

sally[2] *verb* (**sallied, sallying**) make a sudden attack or an excursion. [same origin as *salient*]

sally[3] *noun* a eucalypt resembling a willow.

salmon (*say* **sam**-on) *noun* (*plural* **salmon**) a large edible fish with pink flesh.

salmonella (*say* sal-mon-**el**-a) *noun* a bacterium that can cause food-poisoning and various diseases.

salon *noun* **1** a large elegant room. **2** a room or shop where a hairdresser etc. receives customers.

saloon *noun* **1** a car with a hard roof. **2** a room where people can sit, drink, etc.

salt[1] *noun* **1** sodium chloride, the white substance that gives sea-water its taste and is used for flavouring food. **2** a chemical compound formed by a metal and an acid. **salty** *adjective*

salts *plural noun* a substance that looks like salt, especially a laxative.

salt[2] *verb* flavour or preserve food with salt.

saltbush *noun* an Australian plant growing in saline areas especially in desert country.

salt-cellar *noun* a small dish or perforated pot holding salt for use at meals.

salubrious *adjective* good for people's health. **salubrity** *noun* [from Latin *salus* = health]

salutary *adjective* beneficial; having a good effect, *She gave us some salutary advice.* [from Latin *salus* = health]

salutation *noun* a greeting.

salute[1] *verb* (**saluted, saluting**) **1** raise your right hand to your forehead as a sign of respect. **2** greet. **3** say that you respect or admire something, *We salute this achievement.*

salute[2] *noun* **1** the act of saluting. **2** the firing of guns as a sign of greeting or respect. [from Latin *salus* = health]

salvage *verb* (**salvaged, salvaging**) save or rescue something so that it can be used again. **salvage** *noun* [from Latin *salvare* = save]

salvation *noun* **1** saving from loss or damage etc. **2** (in Christian teaching) saving the soul from sin and its consequences.

salve[1] *noun* **1** a soothing ointment. **2** something that soothes.

salve[2] *verb* (**salved, salving**) soothe a person's conscience or wounded pride.

salver *noun* a small tray, usually of metal.

salvo *noun* (*plural* **salvoes**) a volley of shots or of applause.

salary *noun* earnings, emolument, income, pay, remuneration, stipend.

sale *noun* **1** selling, vending. **2** auction, clearance, sell-out.

salesperson *noun* sales assistant, salesman, saleswoman, shop assistant.

salient[1] *adjective* **2** conspicuous, noticeable, outstanding, prominent, striking.

saline *adjective* brackish, briny, salt, salty.

saliva *noun* dribble, spit, spittle, sputum.

sallow *adjective* pale, pallid, sickly, wan, yellowish.

salon *noun* **2** establishment, parlour, shop.

salty *adjective* brackish, briny, saline, salt.

salute[1] *verb* **2** acknowledge, greet, nod to. **3** applaud, commend, congratulate, honour, pay tribute to.

salute[2] *noun* **1** greeting, salutation, welcome.

salvage *verb* preserve, recover, recycle, rescue, retrieve, save. **salvage** *noun* recovery, rescue, retrieval.

salvation *noun* **2** deliverance, redemption, rescue, saving.

salve[1] *noun* **1** balm, lotion, ointment.

salve[2] *verb* appease, ease, relieve, soothe.

salvo *noun* firing, report, salute, volley.

▶▶ D I C T I O N A R Y ◀◀

same *adjective* **1** of one kind, exactly alike or equal; not different. **2** not changing. **sameness** *noun*

samovar *noun* a Russian tea-urn. [Russian, = self-boiler]

sampan *noun* a small flat-bottomed boat used in China. [from Chinese *sanpan* (*san* = three, *pan* = boards)]

sample¹ *noun* a small amount that shows what something is like; a specimen.

sample² *verb* (**sampled**, **sampling**) take a sample of something.

sampler *noun* a piece of embroidery worked in various stitches to show skill in needlework.

sanatorium *noun* a hospital for treating chronic diseases (e.g. tuberculosis) or convalescents. [from Latin *sanara* = heal]

sanctify *verb* (**sanctified**, **sanctifying**) make holy or sacred. **sanctification** *noun* [from Latin *sanctus* = holy]

sanctimonious *adjective* making a show of being virtuous or pious.

sanction¹ *noun* **1** permission; authorisation. **2** action taken against a nation that is considered to have broken an international law etc., *Sanctions against that country include refusing to trade with it.*

sanction² *verb* permit; authorise. [from Latin *sancire* = make holy]

sanctity *noun* being sacred; holiness.

sanctuary *noun* (*plural* **sanctuaries**) **1** a safe place; a refuge. **2** a sacred place; the part of a church where the altar stands. **3** a place where wildlife is protected. [from Latin *sanctus* = holy]

sanctum *noun* a person's private room. [Latin, = holy thing]

sand¹ *noun* the tiny particles that cover the ground in deserts, sea-shores, etc. **sands** *plural noun* a sandy area.

sand² *verb* smooth or polish with sandpaper or some other rough material. **sander** *noun*

sandal *noun* a lightweight shoe with straps over the foot. **sandalled** *adjective*

sandalwood *noun* a scented wood from a tropical tree.

sandbag *noun* a bag filled with sand, used to build defences.

sandbank *noun* a bank of sand under water.

sandpaper *noun* strong paper coated with sand or a similar substance, rubbed on rough surfaces to make them smooth.

sandstone *noun* rock made of compressed sand.

sandwich¹ *noun* (*plural* **sandwiches**) two or more slices of bread with jam, meat, or cheese etc., between them. [invented by the Earl of Sandwich (1718–92) so that he could eat while gambling]

sandwich² *verb* put a thing between two other things.

sandy *adjective* **1** like sand; covered with sand. **2** yellowish-red, *sandy hair.* **sandiness** *noun*

sane *adjective* **1** having a healthy mind; not mad. **2** sensible. **sanely** *adverb*, **sanity** *noun* [from Latin *sanus* = healthy]

sanger *noun* (*Australian slang*) a sandwich.

sanguinary *adjective* bloodthirsty. [from Latin *sanguis* = blood]

▶▶ T H E S A U R U S ◀◀

same *adjective* **1** alike, identical, indistinguishable, selfsame. **2** constant, unchanged, unchanging, uniform, unvarying.
sameness *noun* evenness, monotony, similarity, uniformity.

sample¹ *noun* example, foretaste, instance, model, specimen, taste.

sample² *verb* taste, test, try.

sanatorium *noun* clinic, convalescent home, hospital, nursing home.

sanctify *verb* bless, consecrate, hallow.

sanctimonious *adjective* holier-than-thou, hypocritical, pharisaical, pious, self-righteous.

sanction¹ *noun* **1** approval, authorisation, blessing, consent, go-ahead, OK (*informal*), permission, support. **2** ban, boycott, embargo, penalty.

sanction² *verb* allow, approve, authorise, consent to, legalise, permit, support.

sanctity *noun* holiness, inviolability, sacredness.

sanctuary *noun* **1** asylum, haven, protection, refuge, retreat, safety, shelter. **2** chapel, church, sanctum, shrine, temple. **3** conservation park, preserve, reservation, reserve, wildlife park.

sand² *verb* polish, sandpaper, smooth.

sandbank *noun* reef, sandbar, shoal.

sandwich¹ *noun* sambo (*Australian slang*), sanger (*Australian slang*).

sandwich² *verb* jam, squash, squeeze, wedge.

sane *adjective* **1** all there (*informal*), lucid, normal, of sound mind, rational. **2** logical, rational, reasonable, sensible, sound.

sanguine (*say* **sang**-gwin) *adjective* hopeful; optimistic.

sanitary *adjective* **1** free from germs and dirt; hygienic. **2** of sanitation. [from Latin *sanus* = healthy]

sanitary towel an absorbent pad worn during menstruation.

sanitation *noun* arrangements for drainage and the disposal of sewage.

sanity *noun* being sane.

Sanskrit *noun* the ancient language of the Hindus in India.

sap¹ *noun* the liquid inside a plant, carrying food to all its parts.

sap² *verb* (**sapped, sapping**) take away a person's strength gradually.

sapling *noun* a young tree. [from *sap*]

sapphire *noun* a bright-blue jewel.

Saracen *noun* an Arab or Muslim of the time of the Crusades.

sarcastic *adjective* saying amusing or contemptuous things that hurt someone's feelings; using irony. **sarcastically** *adverb*, **sarcasm** *noun* [from Greek *sarkazein* = tear the flesh]

sarcophagus *noun* (*plural* **sarcophagi**) a stone coffin, often decorated with carvings. [from Greek *sarkos* = of flesh, + *phagos* = eating]

sardine *noun* a small sea-fish, usually sold in tins, packed tightly in oil.

sardonic *adjective* funny in a grim or sarcastic way. **sardonically** *adverb*

sari *noun* (*plural* **saris**) a length of cloth worn wrapped round the body as a garment, especially by Indian women and girls. [Hindi]

sarong *noun* a skirt-like garment consisting of a strip of cloth wrapped round the body and tucked at the waist or under the armpits.

sartorial *adjective* of clothes. [from Latin *sartor* = tailor]

sash *noun* (*plural* **sashes**) a strip of cloth worn round the waist or over one shoulder. [from Arabic *shash* = turban]

sash window a window that slides up and down. [from French *châssis* = frame]

satanic (*say* sa-**tan**-ik) *adjective* of or like Satan. [from *Satan*, the Devil in Jewish and Christian teaching]

satchel *noun* a bag worn on the shoulder or over the back, especially for carrying books to and from school. [from Latin *saccellus* = little sack]

sate *verb* (**sated, sating**) satiate.

sateen *noun* a cotton material that looks like satin.

satellite *noun* **1** a heavenly body or spacecraft etc. that moves in an orbit round a planet, *The moon is a satellite of the earth.* **2** a country that is under the influence of a more powerful country; a hanger-on. [from Latin *satelles* = guard]

satiate (*say* **say**-shee-ayt) *verb* (**satiated, satiating**) satisfy an appetite or desire etc. fully; glut. [from Latin *satis* = enough (compare *satisfaction*)]

satiety (*say* sat-**I**-it-ee) *noun* being or feeling satiated.

satin *noun* a silky material that is shiny on one side. **satin** *adjective*, **satiny** *adjective*

satire *noun* **1** using humour or exaggeration to make fun of a person or thing. **2** a play or poem etc. that does this. **satirical** *adjective*, **satirically** *adverb*, **satirise** *verb*, **satirist** *noun*

sanguine *adjective* confident, hopeful, optimistic, positive.

sanitary *adjective* **1** antiseptic, aseptic, clean, disinfected, germ-free, healthy, hygienic, sanitised, sterile, sterilised.

sanity *noun* normality, rationality, reason, saneness, sense, soundness.

sap¹ *noun* juice, lifeblood.

sap² *verb* deplete, drain, exhaust, rob, weaken.

sarcastic *adjective* derisive, ironic, mocking, sardonic, satirical, scornful, sneering, taunting.

sardonic *adjective* cynical, derisive, mocking, sarcastic, scornful, sneering, wry.

sash *noun* cummerbund, girdle, obi, tie.

satanic *adjective* demonic, devilish, diabolic, diabolical, evil, fiendish, hellish, infernal, wicked.

satchel *noun* backpack, bag, pack, schoolbag.

satellite *noun* **1** moon, space station, sputnik.

satin *adjective* glossy, shiny, smooth.

satire *noun* **1** irony, mockery, ridicule, sarcasm. **2** burlesque, caricature, lampoon, parody, send-up (*informal*), skit, spoof (*informal*), take-off.

satirical *adjective* derisive, ironic, mocking, sarcastic.

satirise *verb* caricature, deride, lampoon, make fun of, parody, ridicule, send up (*informal*), take off.

▶▶ D I C T I O N A R Y ◀◀

satisfaction *noun* **1** satisfying. **2** being satisfied and pleased because of this. **3** something that satisfies a desire etc. [from Latin *satis* = enough, + *facere* = make]

satisfactory *adjective* good enough; sufficient. **satisfactorily** *adverb*

satisfy *verb* (**satisfied**, **satisfying**) **1** give a person etc. what is needed or wanted. **2** make someone feel certain; convince, *The firemen were satisfied that the fire was out*. [same origin as *satisfaction*]

saturate *verb* (**saturated**, **saturating**) **1** make a thing very wet. **2** make something take in as much as possible of a substance or goods etc. **saturation** *noun*

saturnine *adjective* looking gloomy and forbidding, *a saturnine face*.

satyr (*say* **sat**-er) *noun* (in Greek myths) a woodland god with a man's body and a goat's ears, tail, and legs.

sauce *noun* **1** a thick liquid served with food to add flavour. **2** (*informal*) being cheeky; impudence.

saucepan *noun* a metal cooking-pan with a handle at the side.

saucer *noun* a small shallow dish on which a cup etc. is placed.

saucy *adjective* (**saucier**, **sauciest**) cheeky; impudent. **saucily** *adverb*, **sauciness** *noun*

sauna *noun* a room or compartment filled with steam, used as a kind of bath (originally in Finland). [Finnish]

saunter *verb* walk slowly and casually. **saunter** *noun*

sausage *noun* a tube of skin or plastic stuffed with minced meat and other filling.

savage¹ *adjective* **1** wild; primitive. **2** fierce; cruel. **savagely** *adverb*, **savageness** *noun*, **savagery** *noun*

savage² *noun* a primitive or savage person. [from Latin *silvaticus* = of the woods, wild]

savannah *noun* a grassy plain in a hot country, with few or no trees.

save¹ *verb* (**saved**, **saving**) **1** keep safe; free a person or thing from danger or harm. **2** keep something, especially money so that it can be used later. **3** avoid wasting something, *This will save time*. **4** (in sports) prevent an opponent from scoring. **save** *noun*, **saver** *noun*

save² *preposition* except, *All the trains save one were late*. [from Latin *salvus* = safe]

savings *plural noun* money saved.

saviour *noun* a person who saves someone. **our Saviour** Jesus Christ as the saviour of mankind.

savour¹ *noun* the taste or smell of something.

savour² *verb* **1** taste or smell. **2** enjoy; relish. [from Latin *sapor* = flavour]

▶▶ T H E S A U R U S ◀◀

satisfaction *noun* **2** contentment, delight, fulfilment, gratification, happiness, pleasure, pride.

satisfactory *adjective* acceptable, adequate, all right, enough, fair, fine, OK (*informal*), passable, sufficient, tolerable, up to scratch.

satisfy *verb* **1** (*satisfy a person*) content, fulfil, gratify, please; (*satisfy thirst*) appease, assuage, quench, sate, satiate, slake; (*satisfy requirements*) answer, comply with, fill, fulfil, meet, supply. **2** assure, convince, persuade, reassure. **satisfying** *adjective* enjoyable, fulfilling, gratifying, pleasing, rewarding.

saturate *verb* **1** drench, soak, souse, wet through.

sauce *noun* **1** condiment, dressing, gravy, relish.

saucepan *noun* cauldron, pan, pot.

saucy *adjective* bold, brazen, cheeky, forward, fresh, impertinent, impudent, insolent, pert, presumptuous.

saunter *verb* amble, mosey (*slang*), ramble, roam, stroll, wander.

sausage *noun* banger (*slang*), snag (*Australian slang*).

savage¹ *adjective* **1** barbaric, feral, primitive, uncivilised, untamed, wild. **2** brutal, callous, cruel, ferocious, fierce, harsh, inhuman, merciless, ruthless, vicious, violent.

save¹ *verb* **1** deliver, guard, keep safe, liberate, preserve, protect, ransom, redeem, release, rescue, set free, spare. **2** collect, conserve, hoard, hold on to, invest, keep, lay by, preserve, put aside, put by, reserve, retain, salvage, set aside, stockpile, store. **3** be sparing with, economise on, use sparingly.

savings *plural noun* capital, funds, investments, nest egg, reserves.

saviour *noun* deliverer, liberator, protector, redeemer, rescuer. **our Saviour** Christ, Jesus, Messiah.

savour¹ *noun* aroma, flavour, smell, taste.

savour² *verb* **2** appreciate, delight in, enjoy, relish.

►► DICTIONARY ◄◄

savoury¹ *adjective* **1** tasty but not sweet. **2** having an appetising taste or smell.

savoury² *noun* (*plural* **savouries**) a savoury dish.

savoy *noun* a kind of cabbage.

saw¹ *noun* a tool with a zigzag edge for cutting wood or metal etc.

saw² *verb* (**sawed, sawn, sawing**) **1** cut with a saw. **2** move to and fro as a saw does.

saw³ *past tense* of **see**.

sawdust *noun* powder that comes from wood cut by a saw.

sawmill *noun* a mill where timber is cut into planks etc. by machinery.

sawyer *noun* a person whose job is to saw timber.

Saxon *noun* a member of a people who came from Europe and occupied parts of England in the 5th–6th centuries.

saxophone *noun* a brass wind instrument with a reed in the mouthpiece. **saxophonist** *noun* [from the name of A. Sax, its Belgian inventor]

say¹ *verb* (**said, saying**) **1** speak or express something in words. **2** give an opinion. **3** convey information.

say² *noun* the power to decide something, *I have no say in the matter.*

saying *noun* a well-known phrase or proverb or other statement.

scab *noun* **1** a hard crust that forms over a cut or graze while it is healing. **2** (*informal*) a blackleg. **scabby** *adjective*

scabbard *noun* the sheath of a sword or dagger.

scabies (*say* **skay**-beez) *noun* a contagious skin-disease that causes itching.

scaffold *noun* **1** a platform on which criminals are executed. **2** scaffolding.

scaffolding *noun* a structure of poles or tubes and planks making platforms for workers to stand on while building or repairing a house etc.

scald *verb* **1** burn yourself with very hot liquid or steam. **2** heat milk until it is nearly boiling. **3** clean pans etc. with boiling water. **scald** *noun*

scale¹ *noun* **1** a series of units, degrees, or qualities etc. for measuring something. **2** a series of musical notes going up or down in a fixed pattern. **3** proportion; ratio, *The scale of this map is one centimetre to the kilometre.* **4** the relative size or importance of something, *They entertain friends on a large scale.*

scale² *verb* (**scaled, scaling**) **1** climb, *She scaled the ladder.* **2** alter or arrange something in proportion to something else, *Scale your spending according to your income!* [from Latin *scala* = ladder]

scale³ *noun* **1** each of the thin overlapping parts on the outside of fish, snakes, etc.; a thin flake or part like this. **2** a hard substance formed in a kettle or boiler by hard water, or on teeth. **scaly** *adjective*

scale⁴ *verb* (**scaled, scaling**) remove scales or scale from something. [from Old French *escale* = flake, from an old Germanic word *skalo*]

scale⁵ *noun* the pan of a balance.
  scales *plural noun* a device for weighing things. [from Old Norse *skal* = bowl, from *skalo* (see *scale⁴*)]

scallop *noun* **1** a shellfish with two hinged fan-shaped shells. **2** each curve in an ornamental wavy border. **scalloped** *adjective*

►► THESAURUS ◄◄

savoury¹ *adjective* **1** piquant, salty. **2** appetising, delectable, delicious, mouth-watering, scrumptious (*informal*), tasty.

saw¹ *noun* (*kinds of saw*) chainsaw, circular saw, fretsaw, hacksaw, jigsaw.

say¹ *verb* **1** affirm, allege, announce, answer, articulate, assert, bellow, blurt out, call out, comment, cry, declare, exclaim, moan, mumble, murmur, mutter, pronounce, recite, remark, repeat, reply, respond, scream, shout, shriek, snap, snarl, speak, splutter, squawk, squeal, stammer, state, stutter, tell, utter, voice, whisper, yell. **3** communicate, convey, disclose, divulge, express, impart, indicate, mention, refer to, report, reveal, speak of, tell.

say² *noun* input, opinion, voice, vote.

saying *noun* adage, aphorism, axiom, byword, catchphrase, cliché, dictum, epigram, maxim, motto, proverb, quotation, slogan.

scaffold *noun* **1** gallows, gibbet.

scaffolding *noun* frame, framework, gantry, platform.

scale¹ *noun* **1** hierarchy, ladder, progression, range, sequence, series, spectrum. **3** proportion, ratio. **4** dimensions, extent, level, scope, size.

scale² *verb* **1** ascend, clamber up, climb, mount.

scale³ *noun* **1** flake, lamina, plate. **2** coating, crust, deposit, encrustation.
  scaly *adjective* flaky, peeling, rough, scurfy.

scale⁵ *noun* **scales** balance, weighing machine.

▶▶ D I C T I O N A R Y ◀◀

scallywag *noun* a rascal.

scalp¹ *noun* the skin on the top of the head.

scalp² *verb* cut or tear the scalp from.

scalpel *noun* a small straight knife used by a surgeon or artist.

scamp¹ *noun* a rascal.

scamp² *verb* do work hastily and without proper care.

scamper *verb* run hurriedly. **scamper** *noun*

scampi *plural noun* large prawns. [Italian]

scan *verb* (**scanned, scanning**) **1** look at every part of something. **2** glance at something. **3** count the beats of a line of poetry; be correct in rhythm, *This line doesn't scan.* **4** sweep a radar or electronic beam over an area in search of something. **scan** *noun*, **scanner** *noun*

scandal *noun* **1** something shameful or disgraceful. **2** gossip about people's faults and wrongdoing. **scandalous** *adjective* [from Greek, = stumbling-block]

scandalise *verb* (**scandalised, scandalising**) shock a person by something considered shameful or disgraceful.

scandalmonger *noun* a person who invents or gossips about scandal.

Scandinavian *adjective* of Scandinavia (= Norway, Sweden, and Denmark; sometimes also Finland and Iceland). **Scandinavian** *noun*

scansion *noun* the scanning of verse.

scant *adjective* scanty.

scanty *adjective* (**scantier, scantiest**) small in amount or extent; meagre, *a scanty harvest.* **scantily** *adverb*, **scantiness** *noun*

scapegoat *noun* a person who is made to bear the blame or punishment for what others have done. [named after the *goat* which the ancient Jews allowed to *escape* into the desert after the priest had symbolically laid the people's sins upon it]

scar¹ *noun* the mark left by a cut or burn etc. after it has healed.

scar² *verb* (**scarred, scarring**) make a scar or scars on skin etc.

scarab *noun* an ancient Egyptian ornament or symbol carved in the shape of a beetle.

scarce *adjective* not enough to supply people; rare. **scarcity** *noun*

make yourself scarce (*informal*) go away; keep out of the way.

scarcely *adverb* only just; only with difficulty, *She could scarcely walk.*

scare¹ *verb* (**scared, scaring**) frighten.

scare² *noun* a fright; alarm. **scary** *adjective*

scarecrow *noun* a figure of a person dressed in old clothes, set up to frighten birds away from crops.

scarf *noun* (*plural* **scarves**) a strip of material worn round the neck or head.

scarlet *adjective* & *noun* bright red.

scarlet fever an infectious fever producing a scarlet rash.

▶▶ T H E S A U R U S ◀◀

scallywag *noun* devil, imp, knave, miscreant, rascal, rogue, scamp, wretch.

scamper *verb* dash, hurry, race, run, rush, scoot, scurry, scuttle, skip.

scan *verb* **1** examine, look at, scrutinise, study, survey. **2** flick through, flip through, glance at, leaf through, skim.

scandal *noun* **1** crime, disgrace, outrage, shame, sin. **2** gossip, rumour, tattle, tittle-tattle.

scandalous *adjective* disgraceful, improper, outrageous, shameful, shocking, unseemly, wicked.

scandalise *verb* affront, appal, offend, outrage, shock.

scandalmonger *noun* gossip, muckraker (*informal*), mud-slinger (*informal*), rumour-monger, tittle-tat.

scanty *adjective* inadequate, insufficient, limited, little, meagre, minimal, scant, skimpy, sparse.

scapegoat *noun* bunny (*Australian informal*), fall guy (*slang*), victim, whipping boy.

scar¹ *noun* cicatrice, mark, scratch, wound.

scar² *verb* damage, disfigure, mark, scratch, wound.

scarce *adjective* in short supply, insufficient, rare, scanty.

scarcity *noun* dearth, lack, paucity, shortage.

scarcely *adverb* barely, hardly, only just.

scare¹ *verb* alarm, dismay, frighten, intimidate, panic, shock, startle, terrify, terrorise, unnerve.

scared *adjective* afraid, alarmed, fearful, frightened, intimidated, nervous, panic-stricken, petrified, terrified.

scare² *noun* alarm, fright, shock, start.

scary *adjective* alarming, creepy, eerie, frightening, hair-raising, spine-chilling, spooky (*informal*), terrifying.

scarf *noun* bandanna, headscarf, kerchief, muffler, neckerchief.

▶▶▷ D I C T I O N A R Y ◁◀◀

scarp *noun* a steep slope on a hill.

scarper *verb* (*slang*) run away.

scathing (*say* **skay**th-ing) *adjective* severely criticising a person or thing.

scatter *verb* throw or send or move in various directions.

scatterbrain *noun* a careless forgetful person. **scatterbrained** *adjective*

scavenge *verb* (**scavenged**, **scavenging**) 1 search for useful things amongst rubbish. 2 (of a bird or animal) search for decaying flesh as food. **scavenger** *noun*

scenario *noun* (*plural* **scenarios**) a summary of the plot of a play etc. [Italian]

scene *noun* 1 the place where something happens, *the scene of the crime.* 2 a part of a play or film. 3 a view as seen by a spectator. 4 an angry or noisy outburst, *He made a scene about the money.* 5 stage scenery. [from Greek *skene* = stage]

scenery *noun* 1 the natural features of a landscape. 2 things put on a stage to make it look like a place.

scenic *adjective* having fine natural scenery, *a scenic road along the coast.*

scent¹ *noun* 1 a pleasant smell. 2 a liquid perfume. 3 an animal's smell that other animals can detect.

scent² *verb* 1 discover something by its scent; detect. 2 put scent on something; make fragrant. **scented** *adjective* [from Latin *sentire* = perceive]

sceptic (*say* **skep**-tik) *noun* a sceptical person.

sceptical (*say* **skep**-tik-al) *adjective* not believing things. **sceptically** *adverb*. **scepticism** *noun* [from Greek *skeptikos* = thoughtful]

sceptre *noun* a rod carried by a king or queen as a symbol of sovereignty.

schedule¹ (*say* **shed**-yool) *noun* a programme or timetable of planned events or work.

schedule² *verb* (**scheduled**, **scheduling**) put into a schedule; plan. [from Latin *scedula* = little piece of paper]

schematic (*say* ske-**mat**-ik) *adjective* in the form of a diagram or chart.

scheme¹ *noun* 1 a plan of action. 2 a secret plan. 3 an orderly pattern or arrangement, *a colour scheme.*

scheme² *verb* (**schemed**, **scheming**) make plans; plot. **schemer** *noun* [from Greek *schema* = form]

scherzo (*say* **skairts**-oh) *noun* (*plural* **scherzos**) a lively piece of music. [Italian, = joke]

schism (*say* sizm or skizm) *noun* the splitting of a group into two opposing sections because they disagree about something important. [from Greek *schisma* = split]

schizophrenia (*say* skid-zo-**free**-nee-a) *noun* a kind of mental illness. **schizophrenic** *adjective* & *noun* [from Greek *schizein* = to split, + *phren* = mind]

▶▶▷ T H E S A U R U S ◁◀◀

scarp *noun* bluff, cliff, escarpment, precipice, slope.

scathing *adjective* biting, caustic, harsh, savage, severe, withering.

scatter *verb* broadcast, disperse, disseminate, spread, sprinkle, strew, throw about.

scatterbrained *adjective* absent-minded, disorganised, dreamy, forgetful, hare-brained, muddle-headed, scatty (*informal*), silly, vague.

scavenge *verb* 1 forage, fossick (*Australian informal*), look, rummage, scrounge, search.

scenario *noun* outline, plot, script, storyline, summary, synopsis.

scene *noun* 1 locale, locality, location, place, setting, site, spot. 3 landscape, outlook, panorama, prospect, scenery, sight, view, vista. 4 exhibition, fuss, incident, outburst, spectacle.

scenery *noun* 1 landscape, panorama, view, vista. 2 backdrop, set.

scenic *adjective* beautiful, panoramic, picturesque, pretty.

scent¹ *noun* 1 aroma, bouquet, fragrance, odour, perfume, redolence, smell, whiff. 3 spoor, track, trail.

sceptical *adjective* disbelieving, distrustful, doubting, dubious, incredulous, mistrustful, questioning, suspicious. **scepticism** *noun* disbelief, distrust, doubt, mistrust, suspicion.

schedule¹ *noun* agenda, diary, itinerary, plan, programme, timetable.

schedule² *verb* appoint, arrange, book, list, plan, programme, timetable.

scheme¹ *noun* 1 plan, programme, project, strategy. 2 conspiracy, dodge (*informal*), lurk (*Australian informal*), plot, ploy, racket, rort (*Australian slang*), ruse, scam (*slang*), stratagem. 3 arrangement, design, system.

scheme² *verb* collude, conspire, intrigue, plan, plot.

►►► DICTIONARY ◄◄

scholar *noun* **1** a person who has studied a subject thoroughly. **2** a person who has been awarded a scholarship. **scholarly** *adjective* [same origin as *school²*]

scholarship *noun* **1** a grant of money given to someone to help to pay for his or her education. **2** scholars' knowledge or methods; advanced study.

scholastic *adjective* of schools or education; academic.

school¹ *noun* **1** a place where teaching is done, especially of pupils aged 5–18. **2** the pupils in a school. **3** the time when teaching takes place in a school, *School begins at 9 a.m.* **4** a group of people who have the same beliefs or style of work etc. **schoolboy** *noun*, **schoolchild** *noun*, **schoolgirl** *noun*, **schoolmaster** *noun*, **schoolmistress** *noun*, **schoolroom** *noun*, **schoolteacher** *noun*
School of the Air (*Australian*) education by two-way radio for outback children.

school² *verb* train, *She was schooling her horse for the competition.* [from Greek *schole* = leisure, lecture-place]

school³ *noun* a shoal of fish or whales etc. [from an old word *scolu* = troop]

schooling *noun* training; education, especially in a school.

schooner (*say* **skoon**-er) *noun* a sailing-ship with two or more masts and with sails rigged along its length, not crosswise.

sciatica (*say* sy-**at**-ik-a) *noun* pain in the sciatic nerve (a large nerve in the hip and thigh).

science *noun* the study of chemistry, physics, plants and animals, etc.
science fiction stories about imaginary scientific discoveries or space travel and life on other planets. [from Latin *scientia* = knowledge]

scientific *adjective* **1** of science or scientists. **2** studying things systematically and testing ideas carefully. **scientifically** *adverb*

scientist *noun* an expert in science; someone who studies science.

scimitar *noun* a curved oriental sword.

scintillate *verb* (**scintillated**, **scintillating**) sparkle; be brilliant. **scintillation** *noun* [from Latin *scintilla* = spark]

scion (*say* **sy**-on) *noun* a descendant, especially of a noble family. [from Old French *cion* = a twig]

scissors *plural noun* a cutting-instrument used with one hand, with two blades pivoted so that they can close against each other. [from Latin *scissum* = cut]

scoff *verb* jeer; speak contemptuously. **scoffer** *noun*

scold *verb* rebuke; find fault with someone angrily. **scolding** *noun*

scone (*say* skon) *noun* a soft flat cake, usually eaten with butter.

►►► THESAURUS ◄◄

scholar *noun* **1** academic, expert, highbrow, intellectual, pundit.
scholarly *adjective* academic, bookish, erudite, highbrow, intellectual, learned, studious.

scholarship *noun* **1** award, bursary, fellowship, grant. **2** erudition, learning, research.

scholastic *adjective* academic, educational.

school¹ *noun* **1** academy, college, educational institution, seminary. **4** circle, group, movement, set.
schoolchild *noun* collegian, pupil, scholar, schoolboy, schoolgirl, student.
schoolteacher *noun* chalkie (*Australian slang*), master, mistress, pedagogue (*old use*), schoolie (*Australian informal*), schoolmaster, schoolmistress, teacher.

school² *verb* discipline, educate, instruct, teach, train.

schooling *noun* education, instruction, learning, training, tuition.

scientific *adjective* **2** analytical, methodical, precise, rigorous, systematic.

scintillating *adjective* animated, brilliant, lively, sparkling, stimulating, witty.

scissors *plural noun* clippers, cutters, secateurs, shears, snips.

scoff *verb* (*scoff at*) belittle, chiack (*Australian informal*), deride, disparage, gibe at, jeer at, knock (*informal*), make fun of, mock, ridicule, rubbish (*Australian informal*), scorn, sling off at (*Australian informal*), sneer at.

scold *verb* admonish, berate, castigate, censure, chastise, chide (*old use*), go crook at (*Australian informal*), haul over the coals, rap over the knuckles, rebuke, reprimand, reproach, reprove, rouse on (*Australian informal*), tell off (*informal*), tick off (*informal*), upbraid.
scolding *noun* dressing down (*informal*), lecture, rap over the knuckles, rebuke, reprimand, reproof, talking-to (*informal*), wigging (*informal*).

▶▶ D I C T I O N A R Y ◀◀

scoop[1] *noun* **1** a kind of deep spoon for serving ice-cream etc. **2** a deep shovel for lifting grain, sugar, etc. **3** a scooping movement. **4** an important piece of news published by only one newspaper.

scoop[2] *verb* lift or hollow something out with a scoop.

scoot *verb* run or go away quickly.

scooter *noun* **1** a kind of lightweight motor cycle. **2** a board for riding on, with wheels and a long handle.

scope *noun* **1** opportunity to work, *This job gives scope for your musical abilities.* **2** the range or extent of a subject. [from Greek *skopos* = target]

scorch *verb* make something go brown by burning it slightly.

scorching *adjective* (*informal*) very hot.

score[1] *noun* **1** the number of points or goals made in a game; a result. **2** twenty, *'Three score years and ten' means 3 x 20 + 10 = 70 years.* **3** written or printed music.

score[2] *verb* (**scored, scoring**) **1** get a point or goal in a game. **2** keep a count of the score. **3** mark with lines or cuts. **4** write out a musical score; arrange music for instruments. **scorer** *noun*

scorn[1] *noun* contempt. **scornful** *adjective*, **scornfully** *adverb*

scorn[2] *verb* treat or refuse scornfully.

scorpion *noun* an animal that looks like a tiny lobster, with a poisonous sting.

scotch *verb* put an end to an idea or rumour etc.

scot-free *adjective* **1** without harm or punishment. **2** free of charge. [from *scot* = tax, + *free*]

scoundrel *noun* a dishonest person.

scour[1] *verb* **1** rub something until it is clean and bright. **2** clear a channel or pipe by the force of water flowing through it. **scourer** *noun*

scour[2] *verb* search thoroughly.

scourge[1] (*say* skerj) *noun* **1** a whip for flogging people. **2** something that inflicts suffering or punishment.

scourge[2] *verb* (**scourged, scourging**) **1** flog with a whip. **2** cause suffering or punishment.

Scout *noun* a member of the Scout Association, an international youth organisation.

scout[1] *noun* someone sent out to collect information.

scout[2] *verb* act as a scout; search an area thoroughly.

scowl[1] *noun* a bad-tempered frown.

scowl[2] *verb* make a scowl.

Scrabble *noun* (*trade mark*) a game played on a board, in which words are built up from single letters.

scrabble *verb* (**scrabbled, scrabbling**) **1** scratch or claw at something with the hands or feet. **2** grope or struggle to get something.

scraggy *adjective* thin and bony.

scram *verb* (*slang*) go away. [from *scramble*]

▶▶ T H E S A U R U S ◀◀

scoop[1] *noun* **1,2** ladle, shovel, spoon.

scoop[2] *verb* dig, excavate, gouge, hollow.

scoot *verb* dart, dash, go, hurry, run, rush.

scope *noun* **1** capacity, latitude, opportunity, outlet, room. **2** area, bounds, compass, extent, limits, orbit, range.

scorch *verb* brown, burn, discolour, sear, singe.

score[1] *noun* **1** grade, mark, points, result, tally.

score[2] *verb* **1** achieve, gain, get, make, notch up, win. **3** cut, gash, gouge, groove, incise, notch, scratch. **4** arrange, orchestrate, write.

scorn[1] *noun* contempt, derision, disdain, ridicule.
scornful *adjective* contemptuous, derisive, disdainful, jeering, mocking, sarcastic, scathing, scoffing, sneering, snide (*informal*).

scorn[2] *verb* despise, disdain, rebuff, refuse, reject, shun, snub, spurn, turn your nose up at.

scoundrel *noun* blackguard, cad, crook (*informal*), knave (*old use*), miscreant, rascal, rogue, villain.

scour[1] *verb* **1** clean, cleanse, polish, rub, scrub.

scour[2] *verb* comb, rake through, ransack, search.

scourge[1] *noun* **1** lash, whip. **2** affliction, bane, curse, plague, suffering.

scourge[2] *verb* **1** beat, flog, lash, thrash, whip.

scout[1] *noun* lookout, spy, vanguard.

scout[2] *verb* ferret, fossick (*Australian informal*), hunt, look, search, snoop (*informal*).

scowl[2] *verb* frown, glare, glower, lour.

scraggy *adjective* bony, emaciated, gaunt, lean, scrawny, skinny, thin.

▶▶ D I C T I O N A R Y ◀◀

scramble¹ *verb* (**scrambled, scrambling**) **1** move quickly and awkwardly. **2** struggle to do or get something. **3** (of aircraft or their crew) hurry and take off quickly. **4** cook eggs by mixing them up and heating them in a pan. **5** mix things together. **6** alter a telephone signal so that it cannot be used without a special receiver. **scrambler** *noun*

scramble² *noun* **1** a climb or walk over rough ground. **2** a struggle to do or get something. **3** a motorcycle race over rough ground.

scrap¹ *noun* **1** a small piece. **2** rubbish; waste material, especially metal that is suitable for reprocessing.

scrap² *verb* (**scrapped, scrapping**) get rid of something that is useless or unwanted.

scrap³ *noun* (*informal*) a fight.

scrap⁴ *verb* (**scrapped, scrapping**) (*informal*) fight.

scrape¹ *verb* (**scraped, scraping**) **1** clean or smooth something by passing something hard over it. **2** damage by scraping. **3** remove by scraping, *Scrape the mud off your shoes.* **4** pass with difficulty, *We scraped through.* **5** get something by great effort or care, *They scraped together enough money for a holiday.* **scraper** *noun*

scrape² *noun* **1** a scraping movement or sound. **2** a mark etc. made by scraping. **3** an awkward situation caused by mischief or foolishness.

scrappy *adjective* made of scraps or bits or disconnected things. **scrappiness** *noun*

scratch¹ *verb* **1** mark or cut the surface of a thing with something sharp. **2** rub the skin with fingernails or claws because it itches. **3** withdraw from a race or competition.

scratch² *noun* (*plural* **scratches**) **1** a mark made by scratching. **2** the action of scratching. **scratchy** *adjective*

start from scratch start from the beginning or with nothing prepared.

up to scratch up to the proper standard.

scrawl¹ *noun* untidy handwriting.

scrawl² *verb* write in a scrawl.

scrawny *adjective* scraggy.

scream¹ *noun* **1** a loud piercing cry of pain, fear, anger, or excitement. **2** (*slang*) a very amusing person or thing.

scream² *verb* make a scream.

scree *noun* a mass of loose stones on the side of a mountain.

screech *noun* a harsh high-pitched scream or sound. **screech** *verb*

screed *noun* a very long piece of writing.

screen¹ *noun* **1** a thing that protects, hides, or divides something. **2** a surface on which films or television pictures etc. are shown. **3** a windscreen.

screen door (*Australian*) a door fitted with fly wire, to keep flies out.

screen² *verb* **1** protect, hide, or divide with a screen. **2** show a film or television pictures on a screen. **3** examine carefully, e.g. to check whether a person is suitable for a job or

▶▶ T H E S A U R U S ◀◀

scramble¹ *verb* **1** clamber, climb, crawl, dash, hurry, race, run, rush, scurry, struggle.

scramble² *noun* **2** race, run, rush, scrimmage, struggle, tussle.

scrap¹ *noun* **1** bit, fragment, piece, rag, remnant, shred, tatter. **2** junk, refuse, rubbish, salvage, trash, waste; (*scraps*) crumbs, leftovers, scrapings.

scrap² *verb* abandon, discard, ditch (*informal*), do away with, drop, get rid of, give up, jettison.

scrap³ *noun* altercation, argument, barney (*informal*), dispute, fight, quarrel, row, squabble, tiff.

scrape¹ *verb* **1** clean, rub, scrub. **2** abrade, bark, grate, graze, rasp, scratch, scuff, skin.

scrape² *noun* **2** abrasion, cut, graze, injury, laceration, scratch. **3** difficulty, plight, predicament, trouble.

scrappy *adjective* bitty, disjointed, fragmentary.

scratch¹ *verb* **1** abrade, cut, gouge, graze, lacerate, mark, score, scrape, scuff, skin. **3** remove, withdraw.

scratch² *noun* **1** abrasion, gouge, graze, laceration, mark, score, scrape, scuff, wound.

scrawl² *verb* scribble; see also WRITE.

scrawny *adjective* bony, emaciated, gaunt, lanky, lean, puny, scraggy, skinny, thin.

scream¹ *noun* **1** cry, howl, screech, shriek, squawk, squeal, yell, yowl. **2** hoot (*informal*), laugh, riot (*informal*).

scream² *verb* bawl, cry out, howl, screech, shriek, squawk, squeal, wail, yell, yowl.

screen¹ *noun* **1** barrier, blind, cover, curtain, divider, partition, protection, shelter, shield. **2** monitor, VDU, visual display unit.

screen² *verb* **1** camouflage, conceal, hide, protect, shelter, shield. **2** broadcast, present, show. **3** check, examine, investigate, test, vet. **4** filter, riddle, sieve, sift, strain.

whether a substance is present in something. **4** sift gravel etc.

screw¹ *noun* **1** a metal pin with a spiral ridge (the *thread*) round it, holding things together by being twisted in. **2** a twisting movement. **3** something twisted. **4** a propeller, especially for a ship or motor boat.

screw² *verb* **1** fasten with a screw or screws. **2** twist.

screwdriver *noun* a tool for turning screws.

scribble *verb* (**scribbled, scribbling**) **1** write quickly or untidily or carelessly. **2** make meaningless marks. **scribble** *noun* [same origin as *scribe*]

scribe *noun* **1** a person who made copies of writings before printing was invented. **2** (in biblical times) a professional religious scholar. **scribal** *adjective* [from Latin *scribere* = write]

scrimmage *noun* a confused struggle.

scrimp *verb* skimp, *scrimp and save*.

script *noun* **1** handwriting. **2** a manuscript. **3** the text of a play, film, broadcast talk, etc. [from Latin *scriptum* = written]

scripture *noun* sacred writings, especially the Bible. [same origin as *script*]

scroll *noun* **1** a roll of paper or parchment used for writing on. **2** a spiral design.

scrotum (*say* **skroh**-tum) *noun* the pouch of skin behind the penis, containing the testicles. **scrotal** *adjective*

scrounge *verb* (**scrounged, scrounging**) cadge. **scrounger** *noun*

scrub¹ *verb* (**scrubbed, scrubbing**) **1** rub with a hard brush, especially to clean something. **2** (*informal*) cancel. **scrub** *noun*

scrub² *noun* low trees and bushes; land covered with these.

scrubby *adjective* undersized and shabby or wretched. [from *scrub²*]

scruff *noun* the back of the neck.

scruffy *adjective* shabby and untidy. **scruffily** *adverb*, **scruffiness** *noun*

scrum *noun* **1** (also **scrummage**) a group of players from each side in Rugby football who push against each other and try to heel out the ball which is thrown between them. **2** a crowd pushing against each other.

scrumptious *adjective* delicious.

scrunch *verb* crunch.

scruple¹ *noun* a feeling of doubt or hesitation when your conscience tells you that an action would be wrong.

scruple² *verb* (**scrupled, scrupling**) have scruples, *He would not scruple to betray us.*

scrupulous *adjective* **1** very careful and conscientious. **2** strictly honest or honourable. **scrupulously** *adverb*

scrutinise *verb* (**scrutinised, scrutinising**) examine or look at something carefully. **scrutiny** *noun*

scud *verb* (**scudded, scudding**) move fast, *Clouds scudded across the sky.*

scuff *verb* **1** drag your feet while walking. **2** scrape with your foot; mark or damage something by doing this.

screw² *verb* **2** rotate, turn, twist.

scribble *verb* doodle, scrawl.

scrimp *verb* economise, save, skimp, stint, tighten your belt.

script *noun* **1** handwriting, writing. **3** lines, screenplay, text, words.

scripture *noun* sacred writings. **Scripture** the Bible, the Word of God.

scrounge *verb* beg, bludge (*Australian informal*), borrow, cadge, scab (*Australian slang*), sponge.

scrub¹ *verb* **1** clean, scour, wash. **2** abandon, call off, cancel, drop, forget, scrap.

scrub² *noun* bush, mallee, mulga.

scrubby *adjective* low, small, stunted.

scruffy *adjective* bedraggled, dishevelled, messy, shabby, slovenly, tatty (*informal*), unkempt, untidy.

scrumptious *adjective* appetising, delectable, delicious, luscious, mouth-watering, tasty, yummy (*informal*).

scrunch *verb* crumple, crunch, crush, screw up, squash.

scruple¹ *noun* compunction, doubt, hesitation, misgiving, qualm, twinge of conscience.

scrupulous *adjective* **1** careful, conscientious, fastidious, meticulous, painstaking, particular, punctilious, rigorous, thorough. **2** ethical, honest, honourable, moral, principled, upright.

scrutinise *verb* examine, inspect, look over, peruse, study, survey. **scrutiny** *noun* examination, inspection, investigation, perusal, study.

scud *verb* fly, race, speed, sweep.

scuff *verb* **2** mark, rub, scrape, wear away.

scuffle¹ *noun* a confused fight or struggle.

scuffle² *verb* (**scuffled, scuffling**) take part in a scuffle.

scull¹ *noun* a small or lightweight oar.

scull² *verb* row with sculls.

scullery *noun* (*plural* **sculleries**) a room where dishes etc. are washed up.

sculptor *noun* a person who makes sculptures.

sculpture *noun* making shapes by carving wood or stone or casting metal; a shape made in this way. **sculpture** *verb* [from Latin *sculptere* = carve]

scum *noun* 1 froth or dirt on top of a liquid. 2 worthless people.

scungy *adjective* (*Australian slang*) disagreeable, sordid.

scupper¹ *noun* an opening in a ship's side to let water drain away.

scupper² *verb* 1 sink a ship deliberately. 2 (*informal*) wreck, *It scuppered our plans*.

scurf *noun* flakes of dry skin. **scurfy** *adjective*

scurrilous *adjective* 1 very insulting. 2 vulgar. **scurrilously** *adverb*

scurry *verb* (**scurried, scurrying**) run with short steps; hurry.

scurvy *noun* a disease caused by lack of vitamin C in food.

scutter *verb* scurry.

scuttle¹ *noun* a bucket or container for coal in a house. [from Latin *scutella* = dish]

scuttle² *verb* (**scuttled, scuttling**) scurry; hurry away. [from *scud*]

scuttle³ *noun* a small opening with a lid in a ship's deck or side.

scuttle⁴ *verb* (**scuttled, scuttling**) sink a ship deliberately by letting water into it. [from Spanish *escotar* = cut out]

scythe¹ *noun* a tool with a long curved blade for cutting grass or corn.

scythe² *verb* (**scythed, scything**) cut with a scythe.

SE *abbreviation* south-east; south-eastern.

se- *prefix* 1 apart; aside (as in *secluded*). 2 without (as in *secure*). [Latin]

sea *noun* 1 the salt water that covers most of the earth's surface; a part of this. 2 a large lake, *the Sea of Galilee*. 3 a large area of something, *a sea of faces*.
at sea on the sea; not knowing what to do.
sea anemone a sea-creature with short tentacles round its mouth.
sea change a dramatic change.

seaboard *noun* the coast.

seafaring *adjective* & *noun* working or travelling on the sea. **seafarer** *noun*

seafood *noun* fish or shellfish from the sea eaten as food.

seagull *noun* a sea-bird with long wings.

sea-horse *noun* a small fish with a head rather like a horse's head.

seal¹ *noun* a sea-animal with thick fur or bristles, that eats fish.

seal² *noun* 1 a piece of metal with an engraved design for pressing on a soft substance to leave an impression. 2 this impression. 3 something designed to close an opening and prevent air or liquid etc. from getting in or out.

seal³ *verb* 1 close something by sticking two parts together. 2 close securely; stop up. 3 press a seal on something. 4 coat (road) with tar.
seal off prevent people getting to an area.

scuffle¹ *noun* brawl, fight, fisticuffs, scrap (*informal*), scrimmage, skirmish, stoush (*Australian slang*), struggle, tussle.

sculpture *noun* bust, carving, cast, figure, figurine, statue, statuette.
sculpture *verb* carve, chisel, form, hew, make, model, sculpt (*informal*), shape.

scum *noun* 1 film, foam, froth.

scupper² *verb* 1 scuttle, sink. 2 foil, ruin, spoil, stonker (*Australian slang*), thwart, wreck.

scurrilous *adjective* 1 abusive, defamatory, insulting, low, offensive, vilifying.

scurry *verb* flit, hurry, run, rush, scamper, scoot, scramble, scutter, scuttle.

scuttle¹ *noun* bucket, pail.

scuttle⁴ *verb* scupper, sink.

sea *noun* 1 the blue, the deep, the main (*old use*), ocean. 3 expanse, mass.
at sea baffled, bewildered, confused, perplexed, puzzled, uncertain.

seafaring *adjective* maritime, nautical, naval, sailing, seagoing.
seafarer *noun* mariner, sailor, seaman.

seal² *noun* 2 crest, emblem, imprint, insignia, stamp, symbol.

seal³ *verb* 1 close, fasten, secure, stick down. 4 bituminise, macadamise, surface, tar, tarmac, tar-seal (*Australian*).
seal off block off, close off, cordon off.

▶▶ D I C T I O N A R Y ◀◀

sea-level *noun* the level of the sea halfway between high and low tide.

sealing-wax *noun* a substance that is soft when heated but hardens when cooled, used for sealing documents or for marking with a seal.

sea-lion *noun* a kind of large seal.

seam *noun* 1 the line where two edges of cloth or wood etc. join. 2 a layer of coal in the ground.

seaman *noun* (*plural* **seamen**) a sailor.

seamanship *noun* skill in seafaring.

seamy *adjective* **seamy side** the less attractive side or part, *Police see a lot of the seamy side of life.*

seance (*say* **say**-ahns) *noun* a spiritualist meeting. [French, = a sitting]

seaplane *noun* an aeroplane that can land on and take off from water.

seaport *noun* a port on the coast.

sear *verb* scorch or burn the surface of something.

search *verb* look very carefully in a place etc. in order to find something. **search** *noun*, **searcher** *noun*

searchlight *noun* a light with a strong beam that can be turned in any direction.

seascape *noun* a picture or view of the sea. (Compare *landscape*.)

seasick *adjective* sick because of the movement of a ship. **seasickness** *noun*

seaside *noun* a place by the sea where people go for holidays.

season¹ *noun* 1 each of the four main parts of the year (spring, summer, autumn, winter). 2 the time of year when something happens, *the football season.*

in season available and ready for eating, *Apples are in season in the autumn.*

season ticket a ticket that can be used as often as you like throughout a period of time.

season² *verb* 1 give extra flavour to food by adding salt, pepper, or other strong-tasting substances. 2 dry and treat timber etc. to make it ready for use.

seasonable *adjective* suitable for the season, *Hot weather is seasonable in summer.* **seasonably** *adverb*

seasonal *adjective* of or for a season; happening in a particular season, *Fruit-picking is seasonal work.* **seasonally** *adverb*

seasoning *noun* a substance used to season food.

seat¹ *noun* 1 a thing made or used for sitting on. 2 the right to be a member of a council, committee, parliament, etc., *She won the seat ten years ago.* 3 the buttocks; the part of a skirt or trousers covering them. 4 the place where something is based or located, *Canberra is the seat of our government.*

seat² *verb* 1 place in or on a seat. 2 have seats for, *The theatre seats 3,000 people.*

seat-belt *noun* a strap to hold a person securely in a seat.

sea-urchin *noun* a sea-animal with a shell covered in sharp spikes.

seaward *adjective* & *adverb* towards the sea. **seawards** *adverb*

seaweed *noun* a plant or plants that grow in the sea.

seaworthy *adjective* (of a ship) fit for a sea voyage. **seaworthiness** *noun*

secateurs *plural noun* clippers held in the hand for pruning plants. [from Latin *secare* = to cut]

▶▶ T H E S A U R U S ◀◀

seam *noun* 1 join, stitching. 2 layer, lode, stratum, vein.

seaman *noun* mariner, sailor, seafarer.

seamy *adjective* sordid, squalid, unattractive, unpleasant, unsavoury.

sear *verb* brown, burn, scorch, singe.

search *verb* check, comb, examine, explore, ferret, forage, fossick (*Australian informal*), frisk, hunt, inspect, look, look over, look through, probe, ransack, rummage, scour, seek. **search** *noun* examination, exploration, hunt, inspection, look, probe, quest.

seasick *adjective* nauseous, queasy, sick.

seaside *noun* beach, coast.

season¹ *noun* 2 period, time. **in season** available, ready, ripe.

season² *verb* 1 flavour, pepper, salt, spice. 2 age, condition, dry, harden, mature.

seasoning *noun* condiment, flavour, herb, relish, spice.

seat¹ *noun* 1 armchair, bench, chair, couch, form, lounge, pew, place, settee, settle, sofa, stall, stool, throne. 3 backside (*informal*), behind (*informal*), bottom, bum (*slang*), buttocks, rump.

seat² *verb* 1 place, position, put, situate. 2 accommodate, hold, take.

secateurs *plural noun* clippers, cutters, pruning shears.

secede (*say* sis-**seed**) *verb* (**seceded**, **seceding**) withdraw from being a member of an organisation. **secession** *noun* [from *se-* = aside, + Latin *cedere* = go]

secluded *adjective* screened or sheltered from view. **seclusion** *noun* [from *se-* = aside, + Latin *claudere* = shut]

second[1] *adjective* **1** next after the first. **2** another, *a second chance*. **3** less good, *second quality*. **secondly** *adverb*

second nature behaviour that has become automatic or a habit, *Lying is second nature to him.*

second sight the ability to foresee the future.

second[2] *noun* **1** a person or thing that is second. **2** an attendant of a fighter in a boxing-match, duel, etc. **3** a thing that is of second (not the best) quality. **4** one-sixtieth of a minute (of time or of a degree used in measuring angles). **5** a very short time.

second[3] *verb* **1** assist someone. **2** support a proposal, motion, etc. **seconder** *noun* [from Latin *secundus* = next]

second[4] (*say* sik-**ond**) *verb* transfer a person temporarily to another job or department etc. **secondment** *noun*

secondary *adjective* **1** coming after or from something. **2** less important. **3** (of education etc.) for children of more than about 11 years old, *a secondary school*. (Compare *primary*.) **secondary colours** colours made by mixing two primary colours.

second-hand *adjective* **1** bought or used after someone else has owned it. **2** selling used goods, *a second-hand shop*.

secret[1] *adjective* **1** that must not be told or shown to other people. **2** not known by everybody. **3** working secretly. **secretly** *adverb*, **secrecy** *noun*

secret[2] *noun* **1** something secret. **2** a mystery. **3** a method for achieving something, *the secret of her success*. [from Latin *secretum* = set apart]

secretariat *noun* an administrative department of a large organisation such as the United Nations.

secretary (*say* **sek**-rit-ree) *noun* (*plural* **secretaries**) **1** a person whose job is to help with letters, answer the telephone, and make business arrangements for a person or organisation. **2** the chief assistant of a government minister or ambassador. **secretarial** *adjective*

secrete (*say* sik-**reet**) *verb* (**secreted**, **secreting**) **1** hide something. **2** produce a substance in the body, *Saliva is secreted in the mouth*. **secretion** *noun* [from *secret*]

secretive (*say* **seek**-rit-iv) *adjective* liking or trying to keep things secret. **secretively** *adverb*, **secretiveness** *noun*

sect *noun* a group whose beliefs differ from those of others in the same religion; a faction.

sectarian (*say* sekt-**air**-ee-an) *adjective* belonging to or supporting a sect.

section *noun* **1** a part of something. **2** a cross-section. **sectional** *adjective* [from Latin *sectum* = cut]

sector *noun* **1** one part of an area. **2** a part of something, *the private sector of industry*.

secede *verb* break away, leave, pull out, quit, separate, split, withdraw.

secluded *adjective* hidden, isolated, lonely, private, remote, sheltered, solitary.

second[1] *adjective* **1** following, next, subsequent. **2** additional, alternative, backup, extra, other, substitute, supplementary.

second[2] *noun* **5** flash, instant, jiffy (*informal*), minute, moment, tick (*informal*).

second[3] *verb* **2** back, endorse, support.

secondary *adjective* **1** derivative, derived. **2** lesser, minor, subordinate, subsidiary.

second-hand *adjective* **1** hand-me-down, pre-loved, pre-owned, recycled, used, worn.

secret[1] *adjective* **1** classified, concealed, confidential, hidden, hushed up, hush-hush (*informal*), private, under wraps, undisclosed. **2** arcane, cryptic, mysterious, occult. **3** clandestine, covert, private, stealthy, surreptitious, undercover.

secrecy *noun* confidentiality, furtiveness, mystery, privacy, stealth.

secret[2] *noun* **1** confidence. **2** enigma, mystery, puzzle, riddle. **3** formula, key, recipe.

secrete *verb* **1** conceal, hide, stash. **2** discharge, emit, excrete, exude, give off, ooze, produce.

secretive *adjective* cagey (*informal*), enigmatic, evasive, furtive, mysterious, reticent, tight-lipped, uncommunicative.

sect *noun* cult, denomination, faction, party.

section *noun* **1** bit, branch, chapter, compartment, department, division, fraction, instalment, part, piece, portion, sector, segment, slice, stage, subdivision.

sector *noun* **1** area, district, division, part, quarter, region, section, zone.

▶▶ D I C T I O N A R Y ◀◀

secular *adjective* of worldly affairs, not of spiritual or religious matters.

secure[1] *adjective* **1** safe, especially against attack. **2** certain not to slip or fail. **3** reliable. **securely** *adverb*

secure[2] *verb* (**secured**, **securing**) **1** make a thing secure. **2** obtain, *We secured two tickets for the show.* [from Latin, = free from worry (*se-* = apart, *cura* = care)]

security *noun* (*plural* **securities**) **1** being secure; safety. **2** precautions against theft or spying etc. **3** something given as a guarantee that a promise will be kept or a debt repaid. **4** investments such as stocks and shares.

sedan *noun* an enclosed car seating four or more people.

sedan-chair *noun* an enclosed chair for one person, mounted on two horizontal poles and carried by two men, used in the 17th–18th centuries.

sedate *adjective* calm and dignified. **sedately** *adverb*, **sedateness** *noun* [from Latin *sedatum* = made calm]

sedative (*say* sed-a-tiv) *noun* a medicine that makes a person calm. **sedation** *noun*

sedentary (*say* sed-en-ter-ee) *adjective* done sitting down, *sedentary work.* [from Latin *sedens* = sitting]

sedge *noun* a grass-like plant growing in marshes or near water.

sediment *noun* fine particles of solid matter that float in liquid or sink to the bottom of it. [from Latin *sedere* = sit]

sedimentary *adjective* formed from particles that have settled on a surface, *sedimentary rocks.*

sedition *noun* inciting people to rebel against the authority of the State. **seditious** *adjective*

seduce *verb* (**seduced**, **seducing**) **1** persuade a person to have sexual intercourse. **2** attract or lead astray by offering temptations. **seducer** *noun*, **seduction** *noun*, **seductive** *adjective* [from *se-* = aside, + Latin *ducere* = to lead]

sedulous *adjective* diligent and persevering. **sedulously** *adverb*

see *verb* (**saw**, **seen**, **seeing**) **1** perceive with the eyes. **2** meet or visit somebody, *See a doctor about your cough.* **3** understand, *She saw what I meant.* **4** imagine, *Can you see yourself as a teacher?* **5** consider, *I will see what can be done.* **6** make sure, *See that the windows are shut.* **7** discover, *See who is at the door.* **8** escort, *See her to the door.*
see through not be deceived by something.
see to attend to.

seed[1] *noun* (*plural* **seeds** or **seed**) **1** a fertilised part of a plant, capable of growing into a new plant. **2** (*old use*) descendants. **3** a seeded player.

▶▶ T H E S A U R U S ◀◀

secular *adjective* earthly, lay, temporal, worldly.

secure[1] *adjective* **1** defended, impregnable, protected, safe, sheltered, unassailable. **2** firm, safe, solid, sound, steady, strong. **3** assured, certain, guaranteed, reliable, safe, sure.

secure[2] *verb* **1** batten down, bolt, defend, fasten, fortify, guard, lock, make safe, protect, safeguard. **2** acquire, come by, get, obtain, procure.

security *noun* **1** assurance, certainty, confidence, protection, safety. **3** guarantee, pledge, surety.

sedate *adjective* calm, collected, composed, decorous, dignified, peaceful, placid, serious, sober, staid, tranquil.

sedative *noun* narcotic, opiate, sleeping pill, tranquilliser.

sedentary *adjective* inactive, seated, sitting, stationary.

sediment *noun* deposit, dregs, grounds, lees, precipitate, residue.

seditious *adjective* insurrectionist, mutinous, rabble-rousing, subversive, treasonous.

seduce *verb* **2** beguile, corrupt, entice, lead astray, lure, persuade, tempt.
seductive *adjective* alluring, attractive, enticing, inviting, provocative, sexy, tempting.

see *verb* **1** behold (*old use*), discern, distinguish, espy, glimpse, identify, look at, make out, notice, observe, perceive, recognise, regard, spot, view, watch. **2** bump into, call on, chance upon, confer with, consult, encounter, meet (with), run into, speak to, talk to, visit. **3** appreciate, comprehend, get (*informal*), grasp, perceive, realise, understand. **4** conceive, envisage, foresee, imagine, picture, visualise. **5** consider, decide, ponder, reflect on, think about. **6** ensure, make sure, mind, take care. **7** ascertain, determine, discover, find out, investigate, learn. **8** accompany, conduct, escort, lead, show, take, usher.
see to attend to, deal with, look after, sort out, take care of.

seed[1] *noun* **1** germ, grain, ovule, pip, spore, stone.

seed² *verb* **1** plant or sprinkle seeds in something. **2** name the best players and arrange for them not to play against each other in the early rounds of a tournament.

seedling *noun* a very young plant growing from a seed.

seedy *adjective* (**seedier**, **seediest**) **1** full of seeds. **2** shabby and disreputable. **3** (*informal*) unwell. **seediness** *noun*

seeing *conjunction* considering, *Seeing that we have all finished, let's go.*

seek *verb* (**sought**, **seeking**) search for; try to find or obtain.

seem *verb* give the impression of being something, *She seems worried about her work.* **seemingly** *adverb*

seemly *adjective* (of behaviour etc.) proper; suitable. **seemliness** *noun*

seep *verb* ooze slowly out or through something. **seepage** *noun*

seer *noun* a prophet. [from *see*]

seersucker *noun* fabric woven with a puckered surface. [from Persian, = milk and sugar, or a striped garment]

see-saw *noun* a plank balanced in the middle so that two people can sit, one on each end, and make it go up and down.

seethe *verb* (**seethed**, **seething**) **1** bubble and surge like water boiling. **2** be very angry or excited.

segment *noun* a part that is cut off or separates naturally from other parts, *the segments of an orange.* **segmented** *adjective*

segregate *verb* (**segregated**, **segregating**) **1** separate people of different religions, races, etc. **2** isolate a person or thing. **segregation** *noun* [from *se-* = apart, + Latin *-gregatum* = herded]

seismic (*say* **sy**-zmik) *adjective* of earthquakes or other vibrations of the earth.

seismograph (*say* **sy**-zmo-grahf) *noun* an instrument for measuring the strength of earthquakes. [from Greek *seismos* = earthquake, + *-graph*]

seize *verb* (**seized**, **seizing**) **1** take hold of a person or thing suddenly or forcibly. **2** arrest a person. **3** take possession of goods etc. **4** take eagerly, *Seize your chance!* **5** have a sudden effect on, *Panic seized us.*
seize up become jammed, especially because of friction or overheating.

seizure *noun* **1** seizing. **2** a sudden fit, as in epilepsy or a heart attack.

seldom *adverb* rarely; not often.

select¹ *verb* choose a person or thing. **selection** *noun*, **selector** *noun*

select² *adjective* **1** carefully chosen, *a select group of students.* **2** (of a club etc.) choosing its members carefully; exclusive. [from *se-* = apart, + Latin *legere* = pick]

selective *adjective* choosing or chosen carefully. **selectively** *adverb*, **selectivity** *noun*

seedy *adjective* **2** disreputable, scruffy, shabby, untidy. **3** ill, off colour, poorly, queasy, sick, under the weather, unwell.

seek *verb* ask for, look for, pursue, request, search for, solicit; see also AIM¹.

seem *verb* appear, feel, look, sound.

seemly *adjective* appropriate, becoming, befitting, decorous, fitting, proper, right, suitable.

seep *verb* dribble, exude, filter, flow, leak, ooze, percolate, trickle.

seer *noun* augur, clairvoyant, diviner, prophet, sibyl (*female*), soothsayer, visionary.

seethe *verb* **1** boil, bubble, churn, foam, surge. **2** be furious, be livid, get steamed up (*informal*), boil, fume.

segment *noun* division, part, piece, portion, section, slice, wedge.

segregate *verb* isolate, keep apart, separate.
segregation *noun* apartheid, isolation, separation.

seize *verb* **1** clutch, grab, grasp, pluck, snatch, take hold of. **2** apprehend, arrest, capture, catch, collar (*informal*), nab (*informal*), nick (*slang*). **3** commandeer, confiscate, impound, take away, take possession of. **4** grab, jump at, make use of, take advantage of, use, utilise.
seize up become stuck, jam, lock up.

seizure *noun* **2** apoplexy, attack, convulsion, fit, stroke.

seldom *adverb* hardly ever, infrequently, once in a blue moon, rarely.

select¹ *verb* appoint, choose, elect, nominate, pick.
selection *noun* **1** choice, decision, option, pick. **2** assortment, collection, mixture, range, variety.

select² *adjective* **1** choice, chosen, hand-picked. **2** closed, elite, exclusive, restricted.

selective *adjective* careful, choosy (*informal*), discriminating, fussy, particular, picky (*informal*).

▶▶DICTIONARY◀◀

self *noun* (*plural* **selves**) **1** a person as an individual. **2** a person's particular nature, *She has recovered and is her old self again.* **3** a person's own advantage, *He always puts self first.*

self- *prefix* **1** of or to or done by yourself or itself. **2** automatic (as in *self-loading*).

self-addressed addressed to yourself.

self-assured self-confident.

self-catering catered for yourself (instead of having meals provided).

self-centred selfish.

self-confident confident of your own abilities.

self-conscious embarrassed or unnatural because you know that people are watching you.

self-contained complete in itself.

self-control the ability to control your own behaviour.

self-controlled having self-control.

self-defence defending yourself.

self-denial deliberately going without things you would like to have.

self-employed working independently, not for an employer.

self-evident obvious and not needing proof or explanation.

self-important pompous.

self-interest your own advantage.

self-possessed calm and dignified.

self-raising (of flour) making cakes rise without needing to have baking-powder etc. added.

self-respect your own proper respect for yourself.

self-righteous smugly sure that you are behaving virtuously.

self-satisfied very pleased with yourself.

self-seeking selfishly trying to benefit yourself.

self-service where customers help themselves to things and pay a cashier for what they have taken.

self-sufficient able to provide what you need without help from others.

self-willed obstinately doing what you want; stubborn.

selfish *adjective* doing what you want and not thinking of other people; keeping things for yourself. **selfishly** *adverb*, **selfishness** *noun*

selfless *adjective* unselfish.

selfsame *adjective* the very same.

sell¹ *verb* (**sold, selling**) exchange something for money. **seller** *noun*

sell out sell all your stock of something; (*informal*) betray someone.

sell² *noun* **1** the manner of selling something. **2** (*informal*) a deception.

selvedge *noun* an edge of cloth woven so that it does not unravel. [from *self* + *edge*]

selves *plural* of **self**.

semaphore *noun* a system of signalling by holding the arms in positions that indicate letters of the alphabet. [from Greek *sema* = sign, + *phoros* = carrying]

▶▶THESAURUS◀◀

self- *prefix*

self-centred *adjective* egocentric, egotistic, self-absorbed, selfish, self-seeking, wrapped up in yourself.

self-confident *adjective* assured, bold, confident, poised, self-assured.

self-conscious *adjective* awkward, bashful, diffident, embarrassed, insecure, shy, uncomfortable.

self-control *noun* restraint, self-discipline, self-restraint, will-power.

self-denial *noun* abstemiousness, asceticism, selflessness, self-sacrifice.

self-important *adjective* arrogant, bumptious, conceited, egocentric, egotistic, high and mighty, pompous, self-centred, self-satisfied, snobbish, snooty (*informal*), stuck-up (*informal*), vain.

self-possessed *adjective* calm, collected, composed, confident, cool, dignified, sedate, self-assured, self-confident, self-controlled, unflappable (*informal*).

self-respect *noun* dignity, pride, self-esteem.

self-righteous *adjective* holier-than-thou, pompous, priggish, sanctimonious, self-satisfied, smug.

self-satisfied *adjective* cocky, complacent, conceited, proud, self-important, smug.

self-sufficient *adjective* independent, self-contained, self-reliant, self-supporting.

self-willed *adjective* determined, headstrong, intractable, obstinate, pigheaded, refractory, stubborn, wilful.

selfish *adjective* egocentric, greedy, inconsiderate, mean, miserly, self-centred, self-seeking, stingy, thoughtless, wrapped up in yourself.

selfless *adjective* altruistic, generous, kind, self-denying, self-sacrificing, unselfish.

sell¹ *verb* auction, barter, deal in, flog (*slang*), handle, hawk, market, peddle, retail, stock, trade in, traffic in, vend.

seller *noun* dealer, hawker, merchant, peddler, pedlar, pusher, retailer, salesman, salesperson, saleswoman, shopkeeper, stockist, supplier, trader, trafficker, vendor, wholesaler.

▶▶▶ D I C T I O N A R Y ◀◀

semblance *noun* an outward appearance.

semen (*say* **seem**-en) *noun* a white liquid produced by males and containing sperm. [Latin, = seed]

semi- *prefix* half; partly. [Latin, = half]

semibreve *noun* the longest musical note normally used (𝅝), equal to two minims in length.

semicircle *noun* half a circle. **semicircular** *adjective*

semicolon *noun* a punctuation mark (;) used to mark a break that is more than that marked by a comma.

semiconductor *noun* a substance that can conduct electricity but not as well as most metals do.

semi-detached *adjective* (of a house) joined to another house on one side only.

semifinal *noun* a match or round whose winner will take part in the final.

seminar *noun* a meeting for advanced discussion and research on a subject.

seminary *noun* (*plural* **seminaries**) a training college for priests or rabbis.

semiquaver *noun* a note in music (𝅘𝅥𝅯), equal to half a quaver in length.

Semitic (*say* sim-**it**-ik) *adjective* of the Semites, the group of people that includes the Jews and Arabs. **Semite** (*say* **see**-my't) *noun*

semitone *noun* half a tone in music.

semitrailer *noun* an articulated vehicle consisting of a driver's cabin and a detachable trailer.

semolina *noun* hard round grains of wheat used to make milk puddings and pasta. [from Italian *semola* = bran]

senate *noun* **1** the governing council in ancient Rome. **2** the upper house of the parliament of the United States, France, Australia, and certain other countries. **senator** *noun* [from Latin *senatus* = council of elders]

send *verb* (**sent**, **sending**) **1** make a person or thing go somewhere. **2** cause to become, *It sent them mad.* **sender** *noun*

send for order a person or thing to come or be brought to you.

send up (*informal*) make fun of something by imitating it. **send-up** *noun*

senile (*say* **seen**-I'll) *adjective* suffering from weakness of the body or mind because of old age. **senility** *noun* [from Latin *senilis* = old]

senior[1] *adjective* **1** older in age. **2** higher in rank. **3** for older children, *a senior school.* **seniority** *noun*

senior[2] *noun* **1** a person who is older or higher in rank than you are, *He is my senior.* **2** a member of a senior school. [Latin, = older]

senna *noun* the dried pods of a tropical tree, used as a laxative.

sensation *noun* **1** a feeling, *a sensation of warmth.* **2** a very excited condition; something causing this, *The news caused a great sensation.* **sensational** *adjective*, **sensationally** *adverb* [same origin as *sense*]

sensationalism *noun* deliberate use of dramatic words or style etc. to arouse excitement. **sensationalist** *noun*

sense[1] *noun* **1** the ability to see, hear, smell, touch, or taste things. **2** the ability to feel or appreciate something; awareness, *a sense of humour.* **3** the power to think or make wise decisions, *He hasn't got the sense to come in out of the rain.* **4** meaning, *The word 'run' has many senses.*

▶▶▶ T H E S A U R U S ◀◀

semblance *noun* air, appearance, façade, pretence, show.

seminar *noun* class, discussion group, tutorial.

semitrailer *noun* articulated vehicle, lorry, road train (*Australian*), semi (*Australian informal*), transport, truck.

send *verb* **1** (*send a message, package, etc.*) consign, convey, direct, dispatch, email, fax, forward, pass on, post, relay, remit, ship, transmit, write; (*send a rocket*) discharge, fire, launch, propel, release, shoot.
send away see DISMISS.
send for ask for, call, order, summon.
send up caricature, lampoon, make fun of, mimic, parody, satirise, take off.
send-up *noun* burlesque, caricature, lampoon, parody, satire, spoof (*informal*), take-off.

senile *adjective* decrepit, doddery, feeble-minded, infirm.

senior[1] *adjective* **1** elder, older. **2** higher-ranking, superior.

sensation *noun* **1** awareness, consciousness, feeling, perception, sense. **2** commotion, excitement, stir.
sensational *adjective* dramatic, electrifying, exciting, lurid, scandalous, shocking, spectacular, startling, striking, stunning, thrilling.

sense[1] *noun* **1** faculty, perception, power, sensation. **2** awareness, consciousness, perception, recognition. **3** brains (*informal*), common sense, gumption, intelligence, judgement, nous (*informal*), reason, sagacity, wisdom, wit. **4** denotation, import, meaning, signification.

▶▶ DICTIONARY ◀◀

senses *plural noun* sanity, *bring him to his senses*.

make sense have a meaning; be a sensible idea.

sense² *verb* (**sensed, sensing**) **1** feel; get an impression, *I sensed that she did not like me.* **2** detect something, *This device senses radioactivity.* **sensor** *noun*

senseless *adjective* **1** stupid; not showing good sense. **2** unconscious.

sensibility *noun* (*plural* **sensibilities**) sensitiveness; feeling, *The criticism hurt the artist's sensibilities.*

sensible *adjective* **1** wise; having or showing good sense. **2** aware, *We are sensible of the honour you have done us.* **3** (of clothing etc.) practical. **sensibly** *adverb*

sensitise *verb* (**sensitised, sensitising**) make a thing sensitive to something.

sensitive *adjective* **1** receiving impressions quickly and easily, *sensitive fingers.* **2** easily hurt or offended, *She is very sensitive about her height.* **3** affected by something, *Photographic paper is sensitive to light.* **4** considerate of other people's feelings. **sensitively** *adverb*, **sensitivity** *noun*

sensory *adjective* of the senses; receiving sensations, *sensory nerves.*

sensual *adjective* of the senses; pleasing the body, *sensual pleasures.*

sensuous *adjective* giving pleasure to the senses, especially by being beautiful or delicate.

sentence¹ *noun* **1** a group of words that express a complete thought and form a statement, question, exclamation, or command. **2** the punishment announced to a convicted person in a lawcourt.

sentence² *verb* (**sentenced, sentencing**) give someone a sentence in a lawcourt, *The judge sentenced him to a year in prison.* [from Latin *sententia* = opinion]

sententious *adjective* giving moral advice in a pompous way.

sentient *adjective* capable of feeling and perceiving things, *sentient beings.* [from Latin *sentiens* = feeling]

sentiment *noun* **1** an opinion. **2** sentimentality. [from Latin *sentire* = feel]

sentimental *adjective* showing or arousing tenderness or romantic feelings or foolish emotion. **sentimentally** *adverb*, **sentimentality** *noun*

sentinel *noun* a sentry.

sentry *noun* (*plural* **sentries**) a soldier guarding something.

sepal *noun* each of the leaves forming the calyx of a bud.

separable *adjective* able to be separated.

separate¹ *adjective* not joined to anything; on its own; not shared. **separately** *adverb*

▶▶ THESAURUS ◀◀

sense² *verb* **1** be aware, detect, discern, feel, perceive, realise, suspect, twig (*informal*).

senseless *adjective* **1** absurd, foolish, inane, mad, meaningless, nonsensical, pointless, silly, stupid. **2** cold (*informal*), insensible, out, unconscious.

sensibility *noun* sensitiveness, sensitivity; (*sensibilities*) emotions, feelings, susceptibilities.

sensible *adjective* **1** intelligent, judicious, level-headed, logical, prudent, rational, realistic, reasonable, sagacious, sage, shrewd, thoughtful, wise. **3** functional, practical, serviceable.

sensitive *adjective* **2** delicate, hypersensitive, reactive, tender, thin-skinned, touchy. **3** affected by, responsive to, susceptible to. **4** considerate, empathetic, perceptive, sympathetic, understanding.

sensual *adjective* bodily, carnal, fleshly, physical, sexual.

sensuous *adjective* appealing, attractive, beautiful, exquisite.

sentence¹ *noun* **2** decision, judgement, penalty, punishment.

sentence² *verb* condemn, penalise, punish.

sentiment *noun* **1** attitude, belief, feeling, opinion, thought, view. **2** emotion, feeling, sentimentality.

sentimental *adjective* corny (*informal*), emotional, maudlin, mawkish, mushy, nostalgic, romantic, schmaltzy, soppy (*informal*), weepy (*informal*).

sentry *noun* guard, lookout, sentinel, watchman.

separable *adjective* discrete, distinct.

separate¹ *adjective* autonomous, detached, discrete, distinct, free-standing, independent, individual, single, unconnected, unrelated.

▶▶▶ D I C T I O N A R Y ◀◀

separate² *verb* (**separated, separating**) **1** make or keep separate; divide. **2** become separate. **3** stop living together as a married couple. **separation** *noun*, **separator** *noun* [from *se-* = apart, + Latin *parare* = make ready]

sepia *noun* reddish-brown. [from Greek, = cuttlefish (from which the dye was originally obtained)]

sepsis *noun* a septic condition.

septet *noun* **1** a group of seven musicians. **2** a piece of music for seven musicians. [from Latin *septem* = seven]

septic *adjective* infected with harmful bacteria that cause pus to form. [from Greek *septikos* = made rotten]

sepulchral (*say* sep-**ul**-kral) *adjective* **1** of a sepulchre. **2** (of a voice) sounding deep and hollow.

sepulchre (*say* **sep**-ul-ker) *noun* a tomb. [from Latin *sepultum* = buried]

sequel *noun* **1** a book or film etc. that continues the story of an earlier one. **2** something that follows or results from an earlier event.

sequence *noun* **1** the following of one thing after another; the order in which things happen. **2** a series of things. [from Latin *sequens* = following]

sequestrate *verb* (**sequestrated, sequestrating**) confiscate. **sequestration** *noun*

sequin *noun* a tiny bright disc sewn on clothes etc. to decorate them. **sequinned** *adjective*

seraph *noun* (*plural* **seraphim** or **seraphs**) a kind of angel.

seraphic (*say* ser-**af**-ik) *adjective* angelic, *a seraphic smile.* **seraphically** *adverb*

serenade¹ *noun* a song or tune played by a lover to his lady.

serenade² *verb* (**serenaded, serenading**) sing or play a serenade to someone.

serene *adjective* calm and cheerful. **serenely** *adverb*, **serenity** *noun*

serf *noun* a farm labourer who worked for a landowner in the Middle Ages. **serfdom** *noun* [same origin as *servant*]

serge *noun* a kind of strong woven fabric.

sergeant (*say* **sar**-jent) *noun* a soldier or police officer who is in charge of others.

sergeant-major *noun* a soldier who is one rank higher than a sergeant.

serial *noun* a story or film etc. that is presented in separate parts.

serialise *verb* (**serialised, serialising**) produce a story or film etc. as a serial. **serialisation** *noun*

series *noun* (*plural* **series**) a number of things following or connected with each other. [Latin, = row or chain]

serious *adjective* **1** solemn and thoughtful; not smiling. **2** sincere; not casual; not light-hearted, *a serious attempt.* **3** causing anxiety, not trivial, *a serious accident.* **4** important, *a serious decision.* **seriously** *adverb*, **seriousness** *noun*

sermon *noun* a talk given by a preacher, especially as part of a religious service.

serpent *noun* a snake. [from Latin *serpens* = creeping]

serpentine *adjective* twisting and curving like a snake, *a serpentine road.*

serrated *adjective* having a notched edge. [from Latin *serratum* = sawn]

serried *adjective* arranged in rows close together, *serried ranks of troops.*

▶▶▶ T H E S A U R U S ◀◀

separate² *verb* **1** break, break apart, detach, disconnect, dissociate, divide, part, segregate, sever, sort, split, sunder, take apart. **3** break up, divorce, part, split up.
separation *noun* **1** break, detachment, disconnection, dissociation, division, partition, segregation, split. **2** break-up, divorce, parting, split-up.

sequel *noun* continuation, development, follow-up.

sequence *noun* chain, course, order, progression, series, succession, train.

serene *adjective* calm, composed, peaceful, placid, quiet, tranquil, unperturbed, unruffled.

series *noun* chain, cycle, group, line, order, progression, row, sequence, set, string, succession, train.

serious *adjective* **1** earnest, grave, long-faced, pensive, sedate, sober, solemn, staid, steady, thoughtful. **2** determined, earnest, genuine, keen, resolute, sincere. **3** bad, critical, dangerous, grave, life-threatening, major, severe. **4** crucial, important, momentous, vital, weighty.

sermon *noun* address, homily, talk.

serpentine *adjective* corkscrew, curving, sinuous, tortuous, twisting, winding.

serum (*say* **seer**-um) *noun* the thin pale-yellow liquid that remains from blood when the rest has clotted; this fluid used medically. [Latin, = whey]

servant *noun* a person whose job is to work or serve in someone else's house. [from Latin *servus* = slave]

serve¹ *verb* (**served, serving**) **1** work for a person or organisation or country etc. **2** sell things to people in a shop. **3** give out food to people at a meal. **4** spend time in something; undergo, *He served a prison sentence.* **5** be suitable for something, *This box will serve as a table.* **6** start play in tennis etc. by hitting the ball. **server** *noun*
it serves you right you deserve it.

serve² *noun* a service in tennis etc.

service¹ *noun* **1** working for a person or organisation or country etc. **2** use, assistance, *be of service.* **3** something that helps people or supplies what they want, *a bus service.* **4** the army, navy, or air force, *the armed services.* **5** a religious ceremony. **6** providing people with goods, food, etc., *quick service.* **7** a set of dishes and plates etc. for a meal, *a dinner service.* **8** the servicing of a vehicle or machine etc. **9** the action of serving in tennis etc.

service² *verb* (**serviced, servicing**) **1** repair or keep a vehicle or machine etc. in working order. **2** supply with services.

serviceable *adjective* **1** usable. **2** suitable for ordinary use or wear.

serviceman *noun* (*plural* **servicemen**), **servicewoman** *noun* (*plural* **servicewomen**) a member of the armed services.

serviette *noun* a piece of cloth or paper used to keep your clothes or hands clean at a meal.

servile *adjective* of or like a slave; slavish. **servility** *noun* [same origin as *servant*]

servitude *noun* the condition of being obliged to work for someone else and having no independence; slavery.

session *noun* **1** a meeting or series of meetings, *The Governor will open the next session of Parliament.* **2** a time spent doing one thing, *a recording session.* [from Latin *sessio* = sitting]

set¹ *verb* (**set, setting**) This word has many uses, including (**1**) put or place (*Set the vase on the table*), (**2**) fix in position (*Set the post in concrete*), (**3**) adjust the hands of a clock etc. to show the right time, (**4**) arrange (*Set the table for dinner*), (**5**) fix or appoint (*Set a date for the wedding*), (**6**) make or become firm or hard (*Leave the jelly to set*), (**7**) give someone a task (*This sets us a problem*), (**8**) put into a condition (*Set them free*), (**9**) go down below the horizon (*The sun was setting*).
set about start doing something; (*informal*) attack somebody.
set back stop or slow the progress of something.

servant *noun* attendant, butler, domestic, factotum, footman, help, housekeeper, lackey, maid, maidservant, manservant, menial, minion (*derogatory*), page, retainer, slave, valet, vassal.

serve¹ *verb* **1** help, work for. **2** assist, attend to, look after, wait on. **3** dish up, distribute, dole out, give, hand, present. **4** complete, discharge, go through, undergo. **5** act, be suitable, do, function.

service¹ *noun* **1** employment, labour, work. **2** aid, assistance, benefit, help, use. **3** facility, provision, set-up, supply, system, utility. **4** (*services*) air force, armed forces, armed services, army, defence forces, forces, marines, military, navy, troops. **5** ceremony, rite, ritual, sacrament. **8** maintenance, overhaul, repair.

service² *verb* **1** check, fix, maintain, overhaul, repair, tune.

serviceable *adjective* **1** functioning, operative, usable, working. **2** durable, functional, hard-wearing, practical, strong, tough.

serviette *noun* napkin, table napkin.

servile *adjective* abject, fawning, grovelling, humble, lowly, menial, obsequious, slavish, submissive, subservient, sycophantic.

servitude *noun* bondage, enslavement, slavery, subjection.

session *noun* **1** meeting, sitting. **2** period, spell, time.

set¹ *verb* **1** bung (*informal*), deposit, dump, install, lay, leave, park (*informal*), place, plonk, position, put, rest, stand. **2** embed, fix, install, lodge, mount, stick. **3** adjust, regulate. **4** arrange, lay, prepare. **5** appoint, choose, decide on, determine, establish, fix, name, settle on, specify. **6** congeal, firm, gel, jell, solidify, stiffen. **7** allot, assign, give, prescribe.
set about begin, commence, start.
set back delay, hamper, hinder, hold back, impede, slow.

▶▶ D I C T I O N A R Y ◀◀

set off begin a journey; start something happening; cause to explode.

set out begin a journey; display or make known.

set sail begin a voyage.

set to begin doing something vigorously; begin fighting or arguing.

set up place in position; organise; establish, *set up house*; cause or start, *set up a din*.

set² *noun* **1** a group of people or things that belong together. **2** a radio or television receiver. **3** the way something is placed, *the set of his jaw*. **4** a badger's burrow. **5** the scenery or stage for a play or film. **6** a group of games in a tennis match. **7** (*Australian*) a grudge, *The authorities had a set on the local youth*.

setback *noun* something that stops progress or slows it down.

set-square *noun* a device shaped like a right-angled triangle, used in drawing lines parallel to each other etc.

settee *noun* a long soft seat with a back and arms.

setter *noun* a dog of a long-haired breed that can be trained to stand rigid when it scents game.

setting *noun* **1** the way or place in which something is set. **2** music for the words of a song etc.

settle¹ *verb* (**settled, settling**) **1** arrange, *They settled on a time*; decide or solve something,

That settles the problem. **2** make or become calm or comfortable or orderly; stop being restless, *Stop chattering and settle down!* **3** go and live somewhere, *They settled in Canada.* **4** sink; come to rest on something, *Dust had settled on his books.* **5** pay a bill or debt. **settler** *noun*

settle² *noun* a long wooden seat with a high back and arms.

settlement *noun* **1** settling something. **2** the way something is settled. **3** a small number of people or houses established in a new area.

set-up *noun* (*informal*) the way something is organised or arranged.

seven *noun & adjective* the number 7; one more than six. **seventh** *adjective & noun*

seventeen *noun & adjective* the number 17; one more than sixteen. **seventeenth** *adjective & noun*

seventy *noun & adjective* (*plural* **seventies**) the number 70; seven times ten. **seventieth** *adjective & noun*

sever *verb* (**severed, severing**) cut or break off. **severance** *noun*

several *adjective & noun* more than two but not many.

severally *adverb* separately.

severe *adjective* **1** strict; not gentle or kind. **2** intense; forceful, *severe gales*. **3** very plain, *a severe style of dress*. **severely** *adverb*, **severity** *noun*

▶▶ T H E S A U R U S ◀◀

set off 1 depart, leave, set forth, set out, start. **2** cause, spark, start, stimulate, touch off, trigger. **3** detonate, explode, ignite, let off.

set out 1 begin, depart, embark, leave, set forth, set off, start. **2** declare, detail, make known, present, state.

set sail depart, leave, put to sea, sail.

set up 1 arrange, organise, prepare. **2** begin, create, develop, establish, found, institute, start.

set² *noun* **1** assortment, batch, bunch, class, collection, group, series. **2** apparatus, receiver. **5** backdrop, scene, scenery, setting.

setback *noun* blow, complication, hiccup, hitch, obstacle, problem, reverse, snag.

settee *noun* couch, lounge, sofa.

setting *noun* **1** background, context, environment, locale, locality, place, scene, site, surroundings.

settle¹ *verb* **1** (*settle on a time etc.*) agree, arrange, choose, decide, determine, fix; (*settle a problem etc.*) clear up, deal with, reconcile,

resolve, sort out, straighten out, work out. **2** calm, pacify, quieten, relax, soothe. **3** establish yourself, immigrate, move, put down roots; see also POPULATE. **4** come to rest, descend, fall, land, sink, subside. **5** clear, discharge, liquidate, pay.

settler *noun* colonist, immigrant, pioneer.

settlement *noun* **2** agreement, arrangement, reconciliation, resolution. **3** colony, community, outpost, township.

set-up *noun* arrangement, format, organisation, structure, system.

several *adjective* a few, a good many, a number of, some.

severe *adjective* **1** cold, cruel, dour, Draconian, forbidding, grim, hard, harsh, merciless, pitiless, rigorous, ruthless, stern, strict, stringent, tough, unsmiling, unsympathetic. **2** acute, bad, critical, dangerous, drastic, extreme, fierce, forceful, grave, intense, serious, strong, violent. **3** austere, plain, simple, spartan, unadorned.

▶▶▷ DICTIONARY ◁◀◀

sew *verb* (**sewed**, **sewn** or **sewed**, **sewing**) **1** join things together by using a needle and thread. **2** work with a needle and thread or with a sewing-machine.

sewage (*say* **soo**-ij) *noun* liquid waste matter carried away in drains.

sewer (*say* **soo**-er) *noun* a drain for carrying away sewage.

sewing-machine *noun* a machine for sewing things.

sex *noun* (*plural* **sexes**) **1** each of the two groups (*male* and *female*) into which living things are placed according to their functions in the process of reproduction. **2** the instinct that causes members of the two sexes to be attracted to one another. **3** sexual intercourse. [from Latin *secus* = division]

sexism *noun* discrimination against people of a particular sex, especially women. **sexist** *adjective* & *noun*

sextant *noun* an instrument for measuring the angle of the sun and stars, used for finding your position when navigating. [from Latin *sextus* = sixth (because early sextants contained 60°, one-sixth of a circle)]

sextet *noun* **1** a group of six musicians. **2** a piece of music for six musicians. [from Latin *sextus* = sixth]

sexton *noun* a person whose job is to take care of a church and churchyard.

sextuplet *noun* each of six children born to the same mother at one time. [from Latin *sextus* = sixth]

sexual *adjective* **1** of sex or the sexes. **2** (of reproduction) happening by the fusion of male and female cells. **sexually** *adverb*, **sexuality** *noun*
sexual intercourse the coming together of two people to make love, by the male putting his penis into the female's vagina.

sexy *adjective* (**sexier**, **sexiest**) (*informal*) **1** sexually attractive. **2** concerned with sex.

SF *abbreviation* science fiction.

shabby *adjective* (**shabbier**, **shabbiest**) **1** in a poor or worn-out condition; dilapidated. **2** poorly dressed. **3** unfair; dishonourable, *a shabby trick*. **shabbily** *adverb*, **shabbiness** *noun*

shack *noun* a roughly-built hut.

shackle[1] *noun* an iron ring for fastening a prisoner's wrist or ankle to something.

shackle[2] *verb* (**shackled**, **shackling**) put shackles on a prisoner.

shade[1] *noun* **1** slight darkness produced where something blocks the sun's light. **2** a device that reduces or shuts out bright light. **3** a colour; how light or dark a colour is. **4** a slight difference, *The word had several shades of meaning.* **5** a ghost.

shade[2] *verb* (**shaded**, **shading**) **1** shelter something from bright light. **2** make part of a drawing darker than the rest.

shadow[1] *noun* **1** the dark shape that falls on a surface when something is between the surface and a light. **2** an area of shade. **shadowy** *adjective*
Shadow Cabinet members of the Opposition in Parliament who comment on important matters.

▶▶▷ THESAURUS ◁◀◀

sew *verb* baste, darn, embroider, mend, smock, stitch, tack.

sewage *noun* effluent, waste.

sex *noun* **1** gender. **3** coitus, copulation, intercourse, love-making, mating, sexual intercourse.

sexism *noun* male chauvinism, sexual discrimination; see also PREJUDICE.

sexual *adjective* **1** (*sexual organs*) genital, reproductive, sex; (*sexual attraction*) carnal, erotic, physical, sensual.

sexy *adjective* **1** alluring, attractive, erotic, flirtatious, seductive, sensual.

shabby *adjective* **1** (*shabby clothes*) frayed, ragged, scruffy, tattered, tatty (*informal*), threadbare, worn; (*shabby buildings*) dilapidated, dingy, drab, neglected, ramshackle, run-down, seedy, squalid, tumbledown. **3** contemptible, despicable, dirty, dishonourable, low-down, mean, unfair.

shack *noun* cabin, hovel, hut, shanty, weekender (*Australian*).

shackle[1] *noun* (*shackles*) bonds, chains, fetters, handcuffs, irons, manacles.

shackle[2] *verb* bind, chain, fetter, handcuff, manacle, restrain.

shade[1] *noun* **1** semi-darkness, shadow. **2** blind, cover, screen, shield. **3** colour, degree, hue, intensity, tinge, tint, tone. **4** degree, difference, gradation, nuance, variation.

shade[2] *verb* **1** cast shadow on, screen, shelter. **2** darken, hatch.

shadow[1] *noun* **1** outline, shape, silhouette. **2** darkness, dimness, gloom, semi-darkness, shade.

▶▶ D I C T I O N A R Y ◀◀

shadow² *verb* **1** cast a shadow on something. **2** follow a person secretly.

shady *adjective* (**shadier**, **shadiest**) **1** giving shade, *a shady tree*. **2** in the shade, *a shady place*. **3** not completely honest; disreputable, *a shady deal*.

shaft *noun* **1** a long slender rod or straight part, *the shaft of an arrow*. **2** a ray of light. **3** a deep narrow hole, *a mine-shaft*.

shaggy *adjective* (**shaggier**, **shaggiest**) **1** having long rough hair or fibre. **2** rough, thick, and untidy, *shaggy hair*.

shah *noun* the former ruler of Iran. [Persian, = king]

shake¹ *verb* (**shook**, **shaken**, **shaking**) **1** move quickly up and down or from side to side. **2** disturb; shock; upset, *The news shook us*. **3** tremble; be unsteady, *His voice was shaking*. **shaker** *noun*
shake hands clasp a person's right hand with yours in greeting or parting or as a sign of agreement.

shake² *noun* **1** shaking; a shaking movement. **2** (*informal*) a moment, *I'll be there in two shakes*. **shaky** *adjective*, **shakily** *adverb*

shale *noun* a kind of stone that splits easily into layers. [same origin as *scale⁴*]

shall *auxiliary verb* **1** used with *I* and *we* to express the ordinary future tense, e.g. *I shall arrive tomorrow*, and in questions, e.g. *Shall I shut the door?* (but *will* is used with other

words, e.g. *they will arrive*; *will you shut the door?*) **2** used with words other than *I* and *we* in promises, e.g. *Cinderella, you shall go to the ball!* (but *I will go* = I promise or intend to go).

Usage If you want to be strictly correct, keep to the rules given here, but nowadays many people use *will* after *I* and *we* and it is not usually regarded as wrong.

shallot *noun* a kind of small onion.

shallow *adjective* **1** not deep, *shallow water*. **2** not showing deep thought; not capable of deep feelings. **shallowness** *noun*

shallows *plural noun* a shallow part of a stretch of water.

sham¹ *noun* something that is not genuine; a pretence. **sham** *adjective*

sham² *verb* (**shammed**, **shamming**) pretend.

shamble *verb* (**shambled**, **shambling**) walk or run in a lazy or awkward way.

shambles *noun* a scene of great disorder or bloodshed. [the word originally meant 'slaughterhouse']

shame¹ *noun* **1** a feeling of great sorrow or guilt because you have done wrong. **2** something you regret, *It's a shame that it rained*. **shameful** *adjective*, **shamefully** *adverb*

shame² *verb* (**shamed**, **shaming**) make a person feel ashamed.

shamefaced *adjective* looking ashamed.

▶▶ T H E S A U R U S ◀◀

shadow² *verb* **2** follow, pursue, stalk, tail (*informal*), track, trail.

shady *adjective* **2** cool, dark, dim, shaded, shadowy. **3** crooked, dishonest, dubious, fishy (*informal*), questionable, shonky (*Australian informal*), suspect, suspicious.

shaft *noun* **1** handle, pole, rod, shank, stem, stick. **2** beam, bolt (*of lightning*), ray, streak. **3** opening, passage, tunnel, well.

shaggy *adjective* **1** hairy, hirsute, long-haired, unshorn. **2** bushy, messy, rough, thick, tousled, unkempt, untidy, woolly.

shake¹ *verb* **1** brandish, jiggle, rock, sway, swing, vibrate, wag, waggle, wave, wiggle, wobble. **2** agitate, disconcert, distress, disturb, jolt, perturb, rattle (*informal*), ruffle, shock, stun, unnerve, unsettle, upset. **3** quake, quaver, quiver, shiver, shudder, tremble, wobble.

shaky *adjective* doddery, quivery, rocky, trembling, tremulous, unsteady, weak, wobbly.

shallow *adjective* **2** empty, frivolous, glib, skin-deep, superficial, trivial.

sham¹ *noun* act, charade, counterfeit, fake, fraud, hoax, imitation, phoney (*informal*), pretence, put-on (*informal*).
sham *adjective* artificial, counterfeit, fake, false, imitation, phoney (*informal*), pseudo, synthetic.

sham² *verb* counterfeit, fake, feign, pretend, simulate.

shambles *noun* disaster area (*informal*), mess, muddle, pigsty, shemozzle (*informal*).

shame¹ *noun* **1** embarrassment, guilt, humiliation, ignominy, mortification, regret, remorse. **2** disappointment, pity.
shameful *adjective* contemptible, deplorable, disgraceful, dishonourable, ignominious, reprehensible, scandalous, shocking, unbecoming.

shame² *verb* disgrace, embarrass, humble, humiliate, mortify.

shamefaced *adjective* abashed, ashamed, embarrassed, hangdog, humiliated, mortified, sheepish.

►►► D I C T I O N A R Y ◄◄

shameless *adjective* not feeling or looking ashamed. **shamelessly** *adverb*

shampoo[1] *noun* **1** a liquid substance for washing the hair. **2** a substance for cleaning a carpet etc. or washing a car.

shampoo[2] *verb* wash or clean with a shampoo. [from Hindi *champo* = press]

shamrock *noun* a plant rather like clover.

shandy *noun* (*plural* **shandies**) a mixture of beer and lemonade or some other soft drink.

shanghai *noun* (*Australian*) a catapult.

shank *noun* **1** the leg, especially the part from knee to ankle. **2** a long narrow part, *the shank of a pin.*

shan't (*mainly spoken*) shall not.

shantung *noun* soft Chinese silk. [from Shantung, a province of China]

shanty[1] *noun* (*plural* **shanties**) a shack.
shanty town a settlement consisting of shanties.

shanty[2] *noun* (*plural* **shanties**) a sailors' song with a chorus. [from French *chantez* = sing]

shape[1] *noun* **1** a thing's outline; the appearance an outline produces. **2** proper form or condition, *Get it into shape.*

shape[2] *verb* (**shaped, shaping**) **1** make into a particular shape. **2** develop, *It's shaping up nicely.* **3** adapt.

shapeless *adjective* having no definite shape.

shapely *adjective* (**shapelier, shapeliest**) having an attractive shape.

share[1] *noun* **1** a part given to one person or thing out of something that is being divided. **2** each of the equal parts forming a business company's capital, giving the person who holds it the right to receive a portion (*a dividend*) of the company's profits. **shareholder** *noun*

share[2] *verb* (**shared, sharing**) **1** give portions of something to two or more people. **2** have or use or experience something that others have too, *share a room*; *share the responsibility.*

shark *noun* a large sea-fish with sharp teeth.

sharp[1] *adjective* **1** with an edge or point that can cut or make holes. **2** quick at noticing or learning things, *sharp eyes.* **3** steep or pointed; not gradual, *a sharp bend.* **4** intense; severe, *sharp pain.* **5** distinct, *a sharp image.* **6** loud and shrill, *a sharp cry.* **7** slightly sour. **8** (in music) one semitone higher than the natural note, *C sharp.* **9** (of words) harsh. **sharply** *adverb*, **sharpness** *noun*
sharp practice dishonest or barely honest dealings in business.

sharp[2] *adverb* **1** sharply, *turn sharp right.* **2** punctually, *at six o'clock sharp.* **3** (in music) above the correct pitch, *You were singing sharp.*

sharp[3] *noun* (in music) a note one semitone higher than the natural note; the sign (♯) that indicates this.

sharpen *verb* make or become sharp. **sharpener** *noun*

sharpshooter *noun* a skilled marksman.

shatter *verb* **1** break violently into small pieces. **2** destroy, *It shattered our hopes.* **3** upset greatly, *We were shattered by the news.*

►►► T H E S A U R U S ◄◄

shameless *adjective* bold, brazen, cheeky, immodest, impudent, unashamed, unseemly.

shanghai *noun* catapult, ging (*Australian informal*), sling, slingshot.

shanty[1] *noun* hovel, hut, shack.

shape[1] *noun* **1** build, contour, figure, form, outline, profile, silhouette. **2** condition, fettle, form, health, state, trim.

shape[2] *verb* **1** construct, fashion, form, frame, make, model, mould, sculpt, sculpture. **2** develop, evolve, progress, take shape. **3** adapt, adjust, fit, modify, tailor.

shapeless *adjective* amorphous, formless, nebulous, unstructured, vague.

share[1] *noun* **1** allocation, allotment, allowance, bit, cut (*informal*), division, fraction, helping, part, portion, quota, ration, whack (*slang*).

share[2] *verb* **1** allocate, allot, apportion, deal out, distribute, divide.

sharp[1] *adjective* **1** cutting, keen, pointed. **2** alert, astute, bright, clever, intelligent, knowing, perceptive, quick, shrewd, smart. **3** (*a sharp slope*) abrupt, precipitous, sheer, steep, vertical; (*a sharp bend*) acute, hairpin, sudden. **4** acute, excruciating, intense, severe, shooting, stabbing. **5** clear, distinct, well-defined. **6** high-pitched, penetrating, piercing, shrill, strident. **7** acid, acrid, bitter, piquant, pungent, sour, strong, tangy, tart, vinegary. **9** acrimonious, angry, bitter, caustic, cutting, harsh, stinging, unkind.

sharp[2] *adverb* **2** exactly, on the dot, on the knocker (*Australian informal*), precisely, promptly, punctually.

sharpen *verb* grind, hone, strop, whet.

shatter *verb* **1** break, burst, crack, explode, smash, splinter. **2** dash, destroy. **3** crush, devastate, disturb, upset.

▶▶ D I C T I O N A R Y ◀◀

shave¹ *verb* (**shaved**, **shaving**) **1** scrape growing hair off the skin. **2** cut or scrape a thin slice off something. **shaver** *noun*

shave² *noun* the act of shaving the face. **close shave** (*informal*) a narrow escape.

shavings *plural noun* thin strips shaved off a piece of wood or metal.

shawl *noun* a large piece of material worn round the shoulders or head or wrapped round a baby.

she *pronoun* **1** the female person or animal being talked about. **2** (*Australian informal*) a thing, material or not, *she's a hot day*. **she's apples** everything is all right.

sheaf *noun* (*plural* **sheaves**) **1** a bundle of corn-stalks tied together. **2** a bundle of arrows, papers, etc. held together.

shear *verb* (**sheared**, **shorn** or **sheared**, **shearing**) cut or trim; cut the wool off a sheep. **shearer** *noun*

shears *plural noun* a shearing, clipping or cutting tool shaped like a very large pair of scissors.

sheath *noun* a close-fitting cover; a cover for the blade of a knife or sword etc.

sheathe *verb* (**sheathed**, **sheathing**) **1** put into a sheath, *He sheathed his sword*. **2** put a close covering on something.

shed¹ *noun* a simply-made building used for storing things or sheltering animals, or as a workshop.

shed² *verb* (**shed**, **shedding**) **1** let something fall or flow, *The tree shed its leaves. We shed tears. The snake shed its skin.* **2** give off, *A heater sheds warmth.*

sheen *noun* a shine; a gloss.

sheep *noun* (*plural* **sheep**) an animal that eats grass and has a thick fleecy coat, kept in flocks for its wool and its meat.

sheepdog *noun* a dog trained to guard and herd sheep.

sheepish *adjective* bashful; embarrassed. **sheepishly** *adverb*, **sheepishness** *noun*

sheepshank *noun* a knot used to shorten a rope.

sheer¹ *adjective* **1** complete; thorough, *sheer stupidity*. **2** vertical, with almost no slope, *a sheer drop*. **3** (of material) very thin; transparent.

sheer² *verb* swerve; move sharply away.

sheet¹ *noun* **1** a large piece of lightweight material used on a bed in pairs for a person to sleep between. **2** a whole flat piece of paper, glass, or metal. **3** a wide area of water, ice, flame, etc. **4** a layer or covering.

sheet² *noun* a rope or chain fastening a sail.

sheikh (*say* shayk) *noun* the leader of an Arab tribe or village. [Arabic, = old man]

sheila *noun* (*Australian slang*) a girl.

shelf *noun* (*plural* **shelves**) **1** a flat piece of wood, metal, or glass etc. fixed to a wall or in a piece of furniture so that things can be placed on it. **2** a flat level surface that sticks out; a ledge.

shell¹ *noun* **1** the hard outer covering of a nut, egg, snail, tortoise, etc. **2** the walls or framework of a building, ship, etc. **3** a metal case filled with explosive, fired from a large gun. [from Old English *sciell*, which has the same origin as *scale*⁴]

▶▶ T H E S A U R U S ◀◀

shave¹ *verb* **1** cut off, snip off, trim. **2** pare, plane, scrape, slice, trim, whittle.

shave² *noun* **close shave** close call (*informal*), narrow escape.

shawl *noun* scarf, stole.

sheaf *noun* bunch, bundle.

shear *verb* clip, crop, cut, strip, trim.

shears *plural noun* clippers, cutters, scissors.

sheath *noun* case, cover, scabbard, sleeve.

shed¹ *noun* barn, garage, hut, lean-to, outbuilding, outhouse, shelter, workshop.

shed² *verb* **1** cast, cast off, discard, drop, lose, moult, slough, spill, throw off.

sheen *noun* brightness, gleam, gloss, lustre, polish, shine.

sheep *noun* ewe (*female*), jumbuck (*Australian*), lamb, ram (*male*), wether (*male*).

sheepish *adjective* abashed, ashamed, bashful, coy, embarrassed, hangdog, self-conscious, shamefaced, shy, timid.

sheer¹ *adjective* **1** absolute, complete, pure, total, utter. **2** abrupt, perpendicular, precipitous, sharp, steep, vertical. **3** diaphanous, fine, flimsy, gauzy, see-through, thin, transparent.

sheer² *verb* slew, swerve, turn, veer.

sheet¹ *noun* **2** (*of paper*) folio, leaf, page; (*of glass*) pane, panel, plate. **3** area, expanse, stretch. **4** coating, cover, covering, film, layer, overlay, veneer.

shelf *noun* **2** ledge, mantelpiece, sill.

shell¹ *noun* **1** carapace, case, cover, covering, exterior, hull, husk, outside, pod. **2** body, chassis, frame, framework, hull.

shell² *verb* **1** take something out of its shell. **2** fire explosive shells at something.
shell out (*slang*) pay out money.

shellfish *noun* (*plural* **shellfish**) an aquatic animal that has a shell.

shelter¹ *noun* **1** something that protects people from rain, wind, danger, etc. **2** protection, *Seek shelter from the rain.*
shelter-shed *noun* a roofed partly enclosed shed giving shelter from wet weather.

shelter² *verb* **1** provide with shelter. **2** protect. **3** find a shelter, *They sheltered under the trees.*

shelve *verb* (**shelved, shelving**) **1** put things on a shelf or shelves. **2** fit a wall or cupboard etc. with shelves. **3** postpone or reject a plan etc. **4** slope, *The bed of the river shelves steeply.*

she-oak *noun* a casuarina.

shepherd¹ *noun* a person whose job is to look after sheep. **shepherdess** *noun*

shepherd² *verb* guide or direct people. [from *sheep* + *herd*]

sherbet *noun* a fizzy sweet powder or drink. [from Arabic *sharab* = a drink]

sheriff *noun* the chief law officer of a county, whose duties vary in different countries. [from *shire* + *reeve* = officer]

sherry *noun* (*plural* **sherries**) a kind of strong wine. [from *Jerez* in Spain]

shickered *adjective* (*Australian slang*) drunk.

shield¹ *noun* **1** a large piece of metal, wood, etc. carried to protect the body. **2** a model of a triangular shield used as a trophy. **3** a protection.

shield² *verb* protect from harm or from being discovered.

shift¹ *verb* **1** move; change. **2** manage, *Learn to shift for yourself.*

shift² *noun* **1** a change of position or condition etc. **2** a group of workers who start work as another group finishes; the time when they work, *the night shift.* **3** a straight dress.

shifty *adjective* evasive, not straightforward; untrustworthy. **shiftily** *adverb*, **shiftiness** *noun*

shilling *noun* a former coin, = 10c.

shilly-shally *verb* (**shilly-shallied, shilly-shallying**) be unable to make up your mind. [from *shall I? shall I?*]

shimmer *verb* shine with a quivering light, *The sea shimmered in the moonlight.* **shimmer** *noun*

shin¹ *noun* the front of the leg between the knee and the ankle.

shin² *verb* (**shinned, shinning**) climb by using the arms and legs, not on a ladder.

shindy *noun* (*plural* **shindies**) (*informal*) a din; a brawl.

shine¹ *verb* (**shone** (in sense 4 **shined**), **shining**) **1** give out or reflect light; be bright. **2** be excellent, *He doesn't shine in maths.* **3** aim a light, *Shine a torch on it.* **4** polish, *Have you shined your shoes?*

shine² *noun* **1** brightness. **2** a polish.

shell² *verb* **2** bomb, bombard, fire on.

shelter¹ *noun* **1** bunker, haven, hut, refuge, sanctuary, shed. **2** asylum, cover, protection, refuge, safety, sanctuary.

shelter² *verb* **1,2** conceal, cover, give refuge to, harbour, hide, protect, screen, shield. **3** take cover, take refuge.

shelve *verb* **3** defer, postpone, put aside, put on the back burner (*informal*), put on hold, suspend.

shield¹ *noun* **1** buckler, escutcheon, hielaman (*Australian*). **3** barrier, defence, guard, protection, refuge, safeguard, screen, shelter.

shield² *verb* defend, guard, preserve, protect, safeguard, screen, shelter.

shift¹ *verb* **1** change, move, rearrange, relocate, switch, transfer.

shift² *noun* **1** alteration, change, move, relocation, switch, transfer, transposition, variation.

shifty *adjective* deceitful, dodgy (*informal*), evasive, shonky (*Australian informal*), slippery, sly, sneaky, underhand, untrustworthy, wily.

shilly-shally *verb* hesitate, hum and haw, vacillate, waver.

shimmer *verb* flicker, gleam, glimmer, glisten, sparkle, twinkle.

shindy *noun* brawl, din, disturbance, fight, fracas, row, rumpus, uproar.

shine¹ *verb* **1** beam, blaze, dazzle, flash, flicker, gleam, glimmer, glint, glisten, glitter, glow, radiate, reflect, scintillate, shimmer, sparkle, twinkle. **2** do well, excel, stand out. **4** buff, burnish, clean, polish.

shine² *noun* brightness, gleam, glint, gloss, glow, lustre, polish, radiance, sheen, shimmer, sparkle.

►► DICTIONARY ◄◄

shingle *noun* **1** pebbles on a beach. **2** rectangular wooden tile used on roofs etc.

shiny *adjective* (**shinier**, **shiniest**) shining; glossy.

ship¹ *noun* a large boat, especially one that goes to sea.

ship² *verb* (**shipped**, **shipping**) send goods etc. by ship; transport.

shipment *noun* **1** the process of shipping goods. **2** the amount shipped.

shipping *noun* **1** ships. **2** transporting goods by ship.

shipshape *adjective* in good order; tidy.

shipwreck *noun* the wrecking of a ship.
shipwrecked *adjective*

shipyard *noun* a ship-building yard; a dock.

shire *noun* a rural municipality.

shirk *verb* avoid a duty or work etc. selfishly or unfairly. **shirker** *noun*

shirr *verb* gather cloth into folds by rows of threads run through it.

shirt *noun* a loose-fitting garment of cotton or silk etc. for the top half of the body.
in your shirt-sleeves not wearing a jacket over your shirt.

shirty *adjective* (*informal*) annoyed.

shiver¹ *verb* tremble with cold or fear. **shiver** *noun*, **shivery** *adjective*

shiver² *verb* shatter into pieces.

shivoo *noun* (*Australian slang*) a celebration, a boisterous party.

shoal¹ *noun* a large number of fish swimming together.

shoal² *noun* a shallow place; an underwater sandbank.

shock¹ *noun* **1** a sudden unpleasant surprise. **2** great weakness caused by pain or injury etc. **3** the effect of a violent shake or knock. **4** an effect caused by electric current passing through the body.

shock² *verb* **1** give someone a shock; surprise or upset a person greatly. **2** seem very improper or scandalous to a person.

shock³ *noun* a bushy mass of hair.

shod *past tense of* **shoe²**.

shoddy *adjective* (**shoddier**, **shoddiest**) of poor quality; badly made or done, *shoddy work*.
shoddily *adverb*, **shoddiness** *noun*

shoe¹ *noun* **1** a strong covering for the foot. **2** a horseshoe. **3** something shaped or used like a shoe. **shoelace** *noun*, **shoemaker** *noun*
be in somebody's shoes be in his or her situation.
on a shoe-string with only a small amount of money.

shoe² *verb* (**shod**, **shoeing**) fit with a shoe or shoes.

shoehorn *noun* a curved piece of stiff material for easing your heel into the back of a shoe.

►► THESAURUS ◄◄

shiny *adjective* bright, burnished, gleaming, glistening, glossy, lustrous, polished, satin, shimmering.

ship¹ *noun* vessel; (*various ships*) aircraft carrier, battleship, brig, clipper, container ship, corvette, cruiser, destroyer, flagship, freighter, frigate, galleon, galley, gunboat, ice-breaker, liner, man-of-war, merchant ship, mine-sweeper, sailing ship, steamship, submarine, tanker, warship, windjammer; see also BOAT.

ship² *verb* consign, convey, dispatch, export, freight, send, transport.

shipment *noun* **2** cargo, consignment, load.

shirk *verb* avoid, dodge, duck, evade, get out of, shun, shy away from.
shirker *noun* bludger (*Australian informal*), idler, layabout, loafer, malingerer, skiver (*informal*), slacker.

shirty *adjective* angry, annoyed, mad, rude, stroppy (*informal*).

shiver¹ *verb* quake, quaver, quiver, shake, shudder, tremble.

shoal¹ *noun* school.

shock¹ *noun* **1** blow, bolt from the blue, bombshell, surprise. **2** trauma. **3** impact, jolt, quake, shake, tremor.

shock² *verb* **1** amaze, astonish, astound, dumbfound, stagger, stun, surprise, take aback, traumatise, upset. **2** appal, disgust, horrify, offend, outrage, scandalise.
shocking *adjective* abominable, appalling, atrocious, disgusting, disturbing, dreadful, foul, hideous, horrible, horrific, horrifying, monstrous, outrageous, scandalous, terrible.

shoddy *adjective* bad, careless, gimcrack, inferior, poor, second-rate, slipshod, sloppy, sub-standard.

shoe¹ *noun* **1** (*kinds of shoe*) boot, brogue, clog, court shoe, Loafer (*trade mark*), moccasin, pump, sandal, sandshoe, slipper, sneaker, thong, trainer.
shoemaker *noun* bootmaker, cobbler, shoe repairer.

▶▶▷ D I C T I O N A R Y ◁◀◀

shonky *adjective* (*Australian informal*) unreliable, dishonest.

shoo *interjection* a word used to frighten animals away. **shoo** *verb*

shoot[1] *verb* (**shot**, **shooting**) **1** fire a gun or missile etc. **2** hurt or kill by shooting. **3** move or send very quickly, *The car shot past us*. **4** kick or hit a ball at a goal. **5** (of a plant) put out buds or shoots. **6** slide the bolt of a door into or out of its fastening. **7** film or photograph something, *They shot the film in Africa*.
shooting star a meteor.
shoot through (*Australian informal*) depart, especially suddenly.

shoot[2] *noun* **1** a young branch or new growth of a plant. **2** an expedition for shooting animals.

shop[1] *noun* **1** a building or room where goods or services are on sale to the public. **2** a workshop. **3** talk that is about your own work or job, *She is always talking shop*.
shop steward a trade-union official who represents his or her fellow workers.

shop[2] *verb* (**shopped**, **shopping**) go and buy things at shops. **shopper** *noun*

shopkeeper *noun* a person who owns or manages a shop.

shoplifter *noun* a person who steals goods from a shop after entering as a customer. **shoplifting** *noun*

shopping *noun* **1** buying goods in shops. **2** the goods bought.

shore[1] *noun* the land along the edge of a sea or of a lake.

shore[2] *verb* (**shored**, **shoring**) prop something up with a piece of wood etc.

shorn *past participle* of **shear**.

short[1] *adjective* **1** not long; occupying a small distance or time, *a short walk*. **2** not tall, *a short person*. **3** not enough; not having enough of something, *We are short of water*. **4** concise. **5** curt. **6** (of pastry) rich and crumbly because it contains a lot of fat. **shortness** *noun*
for short as an abbreviation, *Raymond is called Ray for short*.
short circuit a fault in an electrical circuit in which current flows along a shorter route than the normal one.
short cut a route or method that is quicker than the usual one.
short division dividing one number by another without writing down the calculations.
short for an abbreviation of, *'Ray' is short for Raymond*.

short[2] *adverb* suddenly, *She stopped short*.

shortage *noun* lack or scarcity of something; insufficiency.

shortbread *noun* a rich sweet biscuit.

shortcoming *noun* a fault or failure to reach a good standard.

shorten *verb* make or become shorter.

shorthand *noun* a set of special signs for writing words down as quickly as people say them.

▶▶▷ T H E S A U R U S ◁◀◀

shonky *adjective* crooked, dishonest, dodgy (*informal*), shady (*informal*), underhand, unreliable, untrustworthy.

shoot[1] *verb* **1** discharge, fire, launch, project, propel. **2** gun down, hit, kill, snipe at, wound. **3** bolt, charge, dash, fly, race, rush, speed, streak, tear. **5** bud, germinate, grow, sprout. **7** film, photograph.
shoot through see LEAVE[1].

shoot[2] *noun* **1** branch, bud, offshoot, sprig, sprout, sucker, tendril.

shop[1] *noun* **1** boutique, department store, emporium, mart, megastore, retailer, salon, store, supermarket.

shore[1] *noun* beach, coast, foreshore, seashore, seaside, strand (*poetical*).

shore[2] *verb* brace, buttress, prop, support.

short[1] *adjective* **1** brief, fleeting, momentary, passing, quick, short-lived. **2** diminutive, dwarf, little, miniature, petite, pygmy, small, squat, stubby, stumpy, stunted, tiny, undersized, wee. **3** deficient, insufficient, lacking, light on (*Australian informal*), limited, low, scanty, scarce, wanting. **4** brief, concise, laconic, pithy, succinct, terse, to the point. **5** abrupt, blunt, brusque, curt, gruff, impatient, sharp, snappy, terse.

short[2] *adverb* abruptly, suddenly, unexpectedly.

shortage *noun* dearth, deficiency, deficit, famine, insufficiency, lack, paucity, scarcity, shortfall, want.

shortcoming *noun* defect, deficiency, failing, fault, flaw, foible, imperfection, limitation, vice, weakness.

shorten *verb* abbreviate, abridge, compress, condense, curtail, cut down, diminish, prune, reduce, truncate.

shortly *adverb* **1** in a short time; soon, *They will arrive shortly.* **2** in a few words. **3** curtly.

shorts *plural noun* trousers reaching to the knee and higher.

short-sighted *adjective* unable to see distant things clearly.

short-tempered *adjective* easily becoming angry.

shot[1] *past tense* of **shoot[1]**.

shot[2] *noun* **1** the firing of a gun or missile etc.; the sound of this. **2** something fired from a gun; lead pellets for firing from small guns. **3** a person judged by skill in shooting, *He's a good shot.* **4** a heavy metal ball thrown as a sport. **5** a stroke in tennis, cricket, billiards, etc. **6** a photograph; a filmed scene. **7** an attempt, *Have a shot at the crossword.* **8** an injection.

shot[3] *adjective* (of fabric) woven so that different colours show at different angles, *shot silk.*

shotgun *noun* a gun for firing small shot at close range.

should *auxiliary verb* used to express (**1**) obligation or duty, = ought to (*You should have told me*), (**2**) something expected (*They should be here by ten o'clock*), (**3**) a possible event (*if you should happen to see him*), (**4**) with *I* and *we* to make a polite statement (*I should like to come*) or in a conditional clause (*If they had supported us we should have won*).

Usage In sense 4, although *should* is strictly correct, many people nowadays use *would* and this is not regarded as wrong.

shoulder[1] *noun* **1** the part of the body between the neck and the arm, foreleg, or wing. **2** a side that juts out, *the shoulder of the bottle.*

shoulder[2] *verb* **1** take something on your shoulder or shoulders. **2** push with your shoulder. **3** accept responsibility or blame.

shoulder-blade *noun* either of the two large flat bones at the top of your back.

shouldn't (*mainly spoken*) should not.

shout[1] *noun* a loud cry or call.

shout[2] *verb* **1** give a shout; call loudly. **2** (*Australian informal*) pay for a round of drinks.

shove *verb* (**shoved, shoving**) push roughly. **shove** *noun*
shove off (*informal*) go away.

shovel[1] *noun* a tool like a spade with the sides turned up, used for lifting coal, earth, snow, etc.

shovel[2] *verb* (**shovelled, shovelling**) **1** move or clear with a shovel. **2** scoop or push roughly, *He was shovelling food into his mouth.*

show[1] *verb* (**showed, shown, showing**) **1** allow or cause something to be seen, *Show me your new bike.* **2** indicate your feelings etc. **3** make a person understand; demonstrate, *Show me how to use it.* **4** guide, *Show him in a certain way, She showed us much kindness.* **6** be visible, *That scratch won't show.* **7** prove your ability to someone, *We'll show them!*
show off show something proudly; try to impress people. **show-off** *noun*
show up make or be clearly visible; reveal a fault etc.; (*informal*) arrive.

shortly *adverb* **1** before long, directly, presently, soon. **3** abruptly, brusquely, curtly, gruffly, impatiently, sharply, tersely.

short-sighted *adjective* myopic, near-sighted.

short-tempered *adjective* cross, grumpy, hot-tempered, impatient, irascible, irritable, quick-tempered, snappy, testy, tetchy.

shot[2] *noun* **1** bang, blast, discharge, explosion, report. **2** bullet, pellet, slug. **3** archer, marksman, sharpshooter, shooter, sniper. **6** photo, photograph, picture, snapshot. **7** attempt, chance, go, try. **8** immunisation, injection, jab (*informal*), vaccination.

shoulder[2] *verb* **2** elbow, jostle, push, shove. **3** assume, bear, carry, take on, take upon yourself.

shout[1] *noun* bellow, cry, outcry, roar, scream, screech, shriek, yell.

shout[2] *verb* **1** bawl, bellow, call, cry out, roar, scream, screech, shriek, thunder, yell. **2** pay for, stand, treat.

shove *verb* elbow, jostle, push, shoulder, thrust.

shovel[2] *verb* **1** dig, excavate, scoop, shift.

show[1] *verb* **1** display, exhibit, present. **2** disclose, express, indicate, manifest, reveal. **3** demonstrate, describe, explain, illustrate, instruct, point out, teach. **4** conduct, direct, escort, guide, lead, usher. **6** be visible, stick out.
show off 1 display, flaunt, parade. **2** boast, brag, skite (*Australian informal*), swagger, swank (*informal*).
show-off *noun* boaster, braggart, exhibitionist, lair (*Australian informal*), skite (*Australian informal*).
show up 1 expose, highlight, reveal. **2** appear, arrive, be present, come, front up (*informal*), materialise, turn up.

▶▶ D I C T I O N A R Y ◀◀

show² *noun* **1** a display or exhibition, *a flower show*. **2** an entertainment. **3** (*informal*) something that happens or is done, *He runs the whole show*.
give the show away reveal a secret.
good show! well done!

showdown *noun* a final test or confrontation.

shower¹ *noun* **1** a brief fall of rain or snow. **2** a lot of small things coming or falling like rain, *a shower of stones*. **3** a device or cabinet for spraying water to wash a person's body; a wash in this.

shower² *verb* **1** fall or send things in a shower. **2** wash under a shower.

showery *adjective* (of weather) with many showers.

show-jumping *noun* a competition in which riders make their horses jump over fences and other obstacles. **show-jumper** *noun*

showman *noun* (*plural* **showmen**) **1** a person who presents entertainments. **2** someone who is good at attracting attention. **showmanship** *noun*

showroom *noun* a room where goods are displayed for people to look at.

showy *adjective* (**showier**, **showiest**) likely to attract attention; brightly or highly decorated. **showily** *adverb*, **showiness** *noun*

shrapnel *noun* pieces of metal scattered from an exploding shell. [named after H. Shrapnel, the British officer who invented it in about 1806]

shred¹ *noun* **1** a tiny piece torn or cut off something. **2** a small amount, *There is not a shred of evidence*.

shred² *verb* (**shredded**, **shredding**) cut into shreds. **shredder** *noun*

shrew *noun* **1** a small mouse-like animal. **2** a bad-tempered woman who is constantly scolding people. **shrewish** *adjective*

shrewd *adjective* having common sense and good judgement; clever. **shrewdly** *adverb*, **shrewdness** *noun*

shriek¹ *noun* a shrill cry or scream.

shriek² *verb* give a shriek.

shrift *noun* **short shrift** curt treatment.

shrill *adjective* sounding very high and piercing. **shrilly** *adverb*, **shrillness** *noun*

shrimp *noun* **1** a small shellfish, pink when boiled. **2** (*informal*) a small person.

shrine *noun* an altar, chapel, or other sacred place.

shrink *verb* (**shrank**, **shrunk**, **shrinking**) **1** make or become smaller. **2** move back to avoid something. **3** avoid doing something because of fear, conscience, embarrassment, etc. **shrinkage** *noun*

shrive *verb* (**shrove**, **shriven**, **shriving**) (*old use*) (of a priest) hear a person's confession and give absolution.

shrivel *verb* (**shrivelled**, **shrivelling**) make or become dry and wrinkled.

shroud¹ *noun* **1** a cloth in which a dead body is wrapped. **2** each of a set of ropes supporting a ship's mast.

▶▶ T H E S A U R U S ◀◀

show² *noun* **1** display, exhibition, expo (*informal*), exposition, fair, pageant, presentation. **2** entertainment, gig (*informal*), performance, play, production. **3** business, enterprise, operation, undertaking.

showdown *noun* clash, confrontation, crisis, moment of truth.

shower¹ *noun* **1** drizzle, rain, sprinkle.

shower² *verb* **1** deluge, flood, inundate, overwhelm, spatter, spray, sprinkle.

showy *adjective* bright, brilliant, conspicuous, flamboyant, flashy, garish, gaudy, lairy (*Australian informal*), ostentatious, striking.

shred¹ *noun* **1** bit, fragment, piece, scrap, strip; (*shreds*) rags, tatters. **2** bit, iota, jot, particle, scrap, skerrick (*Australian informal*), trace.

shred² *verb* cut up, destroy, rip up, tear up.

shrew *noun* **2** battleaxe (*informal*), nag, scold (*old use*), termagant, virago.

shrewd *adjective* astute, canny, clever, crafty, cunning, far-sighted, ingenious, intelligent, knowing, perceptive, sagacious, savvy (*informal*), sharp, sly, smart, wily, wise.

shriek¹ *noun* cry, howl, scream, screech, squeal, yell.

shriek² *verb* cry (out), howl, scream, screech, squeal, yell.

shrill *adjective* high-pitched, penetrating, piercing, screeching, sharp.

shrine *noun* altar, cenotaph, chapel, church, memorial, monument, mosque, sanctuary, temple.

shrink *verb* **1** contract, decline, diminish, dwindle, reduce. **2** back away, draw back, flinch, recoil, retire, retreat, shy away, withdraw.

shrivel *verb* dehydrate, dry up, shrink, wilt, wither, wrinkle.

shroud¹ *noun* **1** winding-sheet.

shroud² *verb* **1** wrap in a shroud. **2** cover or conceal, *The town was shrouded in mist.*

shrove *past tense* of **shrive**.
Shrove Tuesday the day before Ash Wednesday, when it was formerly the custom to be shriven.

shrub *noun* a woody plant smaller than a tree; a bush. **shrubby** *adjective*

shrubbery *noun* (*plural* **shrubberies**) an area planted with shrubs.

shrug *verb* (**shrugged, shrugging**) raise your shoulders as a sign that you do not care, do not know, etc. **shrug** *noun*
shrug off dismiss something as unimportant.

shrunken *adjective* having shrunk.

shudder *verb* **1** shiver violently with horror, fear, or cold. **2** make a strong shaking movement. **shudder** *noun*

shuffle *verb* (**shuffled, shuffling**) **1** walk without lifting the feet from the ground. **2** slide playing cards over each other to get them into random order. **3** shift; rearrange. **shuffle** *noun*

shun *verb* (**shunned, shunning**) avoid.

shunt *verb* move a train or wagons on to another track; divert. **shunt** *noun*, **shunter** *noun*

shut *verb* (**shut, shutting**) **1** move a door, lid, or cover etc. so that it blocks an opening; make or become closed. **2** bring or fold parts together, *Shut the book.*
shut down stop work; stop business.
shut up shut securely; imprison; (*informal*) stop talking or making a noise.

shutter *noun* **1** a panel or screen that can be closed over a window. **2** the device in a camera that opens and closes to let light fall on the film. **shuttered** *adjective* [from *shut*]

shuttle¹ *noun* **1** a holder carrying the weft-thread across a loom in weaving. **2** a train, bus, or aircraft that makes frequent short journeys between two points. **3** a space shuttle (see *space*).

shuttle² *verb* (**shuttled, shuttling**) move, travel, or send backwards and forwards.

shuttlecock *noun* a small rounded piece of cork or plastic with a crown of feathers, struck to and fro by players in badminton etc.

shy¹ *adjective* (**shyer, shyest**) afraid to meet or talk to other people; timid. **shyly** *adverb*, **shyness** *noun*

shy² *verb* (**shied, shying**) move suddenly in alarm, *The horse shied at the sound.*

shy³ *verb* (**shied, shying**) throw a stone etc.

shy⁴ *noun* (*plural* **shies**) a throw.

SI *abbreviation* Système International d'Unités (French, = International System of Units).

Siamese *adjective* of Siam (now called Thailand) or its people. **Siamese** *noun*
Siamese cat a cat with short pale fur with darker face, ears, tail, and feet.
Siamese twins twins who are born with their bodies joined together.

sibilant¹ *adjective* having a hissing sound, *a sibilant whisper.*

sibilant² *noun* a speech-sound that sounds like hissing, e.g. *s, sh.* [from Latin *sibilans* = hissing]

sibling *noun* a brother or sister.

sibyl *noun* a prophetess in ancient Greece or Rome.

shroud² *verb* **1** cover, swathe, wrap. **2** cloak, clothe, conceal, cover, envelop, hide, veil.

shrub *noun* bush, plant.

shrug *verb* **shrug off** dismiss, disregard, ignore, laugh off, make light of, play down.

shudder *verb* **1** quake, quaver, quiver, shake, shiver, tremble. **2** judder, rock, shake, vibrate. **shudder** *noun* convulsion, quake, quiver, shake, shiver, spasm, tremble, tremor, vibration.

shuffle *verb* **1** drag your feet, hobble, scrape your feet, scuff your feet, shamble. **2,3** jumble, mix, rearrange, reorganise, scramble, shift.

shun *verb* avoid, dodge, evade, keep away from, recoil from, shy away from, steer clear of.

shunt *verb* divert, sidetrack.

shut *verb* **1** bolt, close, fasten, latch, lock, secure. **shut out** bar, exclude, keep out, leave out, lock out.
shut up 1 confine, imprison, incarcerate, intern, jail, lock up, put away (*informal*). **2** be quiet, be silent, stop talking.

shy¹ *adjective* bashful, coy, diffident, hesitant, nervous, reserved, reticent, retiring, self-conscious, timid, timorous.

shy² *verb* buck, jump, recoil, start.
shy away from avoid, back away from, flinch from, recoil from, shrink from, shun.

shy³ *verb* cast, fling, hurl, pitch, throw, toss.

sick *adjective* **1** ill; physically or mentally unwell. **2** vomiting or likely to vomit, *I feel sick.* **3** distressed; disgusted.
sick of tired of.

sicken *verb* **1** begin to be ill. **2** make or become distressed or disgusted, *Vandalism sickens us all.* **sickening** *adjective*

sickie *noun* (*Australian informal*) a day's sick leave, especially if without medical evidence.

sickle *noun* **1** a tool with a narrow curved blade, used for cutting corn etc. **2** something shaped like this blade, e.g. the crescent moon.

sickly *adjective* **1** often ill; unhealthy. **2** making people feel sick, *a sickly smell.* **3** weak, *a sickly smile.*

sickness *noun* **1** illness. **2** a disease. **3** vomiting.

side¹ *noun* **1** a surface, especially one joining the top and bottom of something. **2** a line that forms part of the boundary of a triangle, square, etc. **3** either of the two halves into which something can be divided by a line down its centre. **4** the part near the edge and away from the centre. **5** the place or region next to a person or things, *He stood at my side.* **6** one aspect or view of something, *Study all sides of the problem.* **7** one of two groups or teams etc. who oppose each other.
on the side as a sideline.
side by side next to each other.

side² *adjective* at or on a side, *the side door.*

side³ *verb* (**sided**, **siding**) take a person's side in an argument, *He sided with his son.*

sideboard *noun* a long piece of furniture with drawers and cupboards for china etc. and a flat top.

sidecar *noun* a small compartment for a passenger, fixed to the side of a motorcycle.

sideline *noun* **1** something done in addition to the main work or activity. **2** a line at the side of a football field etc.; the area just outside this.

sidelong *adjective* towards one side; sideways, *a sidelong glance.*

sidereal (*say* sy-**deer**-ee-al) *adjective* of or measured by the stars. [from Latin *sideris* = of a star]

sideshow *noun* a small entertainment forming part of a large one, e.g. at a fair.

sidestep *verb* avoid by stepping sideways; evade a problem etc.

sideways *adverb* & *adjective* **1** to or from one side, *Move it sideways.* **2** with one side facing forwards, *We sat sideways in the bus.*

siding *noun* a short railway line by the side of a main line.

sidle *verb* (**sidled**, **sidling**) walk in a shy or nervous manner. [from *sidelong*]

siege *noun* the besieging of a place.
lay siege to begin besieging.

sienna *noun* a kind of clay used in making brownish paints. [from Siena, a town in Italy]

sierra *noun* a range of mountains with sharp peaks, in Spain or parts of America. [from Latin *serra* = a saw]

sick *adjective* **1** ailing, bedridden, crook (*Australian informal*), diseased, ill, indisposed, infirm, poorly, sickly, unwell. **2** bilious, nauseous, queasy. **3** angry, annoyed, disgusted, distressed, mad, sickened, upset.
be sick barf (*slang*), chuck (*informal*), chunder (*Australian slang*), heave, puke (*informal*), retch, sick up (*informal*), spew, throw up, vomit.
sick of bored with, fed up with (*informal*), jack of (*Australian slang*), tired of, weary of.

sicken *verb* **2** appal, disgust, distress, horrify, nauseate, offend, repel, revolt, shock, upset.

sickly *adjective* **1** ailing, delicate, frail, ill, sick, unhealthy, unwell, weak; (*looking sickly*) ashen, green, grey, pale, pallid, peaky, wan, yellow. **2** cloying, nauseating, over-sweet, saccharine, sugary, syrupy. **3** faint, feeble, weak.

sickness *noun* **1** ill health, illness, infirmity. **2** affliction, ailment, bug (*informal*), complaint,

disease, disorder, illness, malady. **3** biliousness, nausea, queasiness, vomiting.

side¹ *noun* **1** face, facet, flank, slope, surface. **4** boundary, brink, edge, fringe, limit, margin, perimeter, periphery, rim, verge. **6** aspect, facet, perspective, position, slant, standpoint, view, viewpoint. **7** camp, faction, party, squad, team.

side² *adjective* lateral.

side³ *verb* (*side with*) ally with, back, defend, go along with, stand up for, stick up for (*informal*), support.

sideboard *noun* buffet, cabinet, cupboard, dresser.

sidestep *verb* avoid, bypass, circumvent, dodge, duck, evade, skirt round.

sideways *adjective* indirect, oblique, sidelong.

sidle *verb* creep, cringe, edge, slink.

siege *noun* blockade.
lay siege to beleaguer, besiege, blockade, encircle, surround.

▶▶▶ DICTIONARY ◀◀◀

siesta (*say* see-**est**-a) *noun* an afternoon rest. [Spanish, from Latin *sexta* = sixth (hour)]

sieve¹ (*say* siv) *noun* a device made of mesh or perforated metal or plastic, used to separate the smaller or soft parts of something from the larger or hard parts.

sieve² *verb* (**sieved**, **sieving**) put something through a sieve.

sift *verb* 1 sieve. 2 examine and analyse facts or evidence etc. carefully. **sifter** *noun*

sigh¹ *noun* a sound made by breathing out heavily when you are sad, tired, relieved, etc.

sigh² *verb* make a sigh.

sight¹ *noun* 1 the ability to see. 2 a thing that can be seen or is worth seeing, *Our roses are a wonderful sight.* 3 an unsightly thing, *You do look a sight in those clothes!* 4 a device looked through to help aim a gun or telescope etc.
at sight or **on sight** as soon as a person or thing has been seen.
in sight visible; clearly near, *Victory was in sight.*

sight² *verb* 1 see or observe something. 2 aim a gun or telescope etc.

sightless *adjective* blind.

sight-reading *noun* playing or singing music at sight, without preparation.

sightseeing *noun* visiting interesting places in a town etc. **sightseer** *noun*

sign¹ *noun* 1 something that shows that a thing exists, *There are signs of decay.* 2 a symbol, *a dollar sign.* 3 a board etc. displaying information. 4 an action or movement giving information or a command etc. 5 any of the twelve divisions of the zodiac, represented by a symbol.

sign² *verb* 1 make a sign or signal. 2 write your signature on something; accept a contract etc. by doing this. [from Latin *signum* = a mark]
sign up enlist in the armed forces; enrol.

signal¹ *noun* 1 a device, gesture, or sound etc. that gives information or a command; a message made up of such things. 2 a sequence of electrical impulses or radio waves.

signal² *verb* (**signalled**, **signalling**) make a signal to somebody. **signaller** *noun*

signal³ *adjective* remarkable, *a signal success.* **signally** *adverb* [same origin as *sign*]

signal-box *noun* a building from which railway signals are controlled.

signalman *noun* (*plural* **signalmen**) a person who controls railway signals.

signatory *noun* (*plural* **signatories**) a person who signs an agreement etc.

signature *noun* a person's name written by himself or herself.
signature tune a special tune always used to announce a particular programme, performer, etc. [same origin as *sign*]

signet *noun* a seal with an engraved design, especially one set in a person's ring (a **signet-ring**). [same origin as *sign*]

significant *adjective* 1 having a meaning; full of meaning. 2 important, *a significant event.* **significantly** *adverb*, **significance** *noun*

▶▶▶ THESAURUS ◀◀◀

siesta *noun* catnap, forty winks, kip, nap, rest, sleep, snooze.

sieve¹ *noun* colander, filter, riddle, screen, sifter, strainer.

sieve² *verb* filter, riddle, screen, sift, strain.

sift *verb* 1 filter, riddle, screen, sieve, strain. 2 analyse, examine, investigate, review, sort through, study.

sight¹ *noun* 1 eyesight, vision. 2 display, scene, spectacle.
in sight 1 in view, visible. 2 approaching, at hand, close, imminent, near.

sight² *verb* 1 behold (*old use*), catch sight of, espy, glimpse, make out, observe, see, spot, spy.

sightless *adjective* blind, visually impaired.

sightseer *noun* holidaymaker, tourist, traveller, visitor.

sign¹ *noun* 1 clue, evidence, forewarning, hint, indication, manifestation, omen, pointer, portent, proof, symptom, token, trace, warning. 2 mark, symbol; see also BADGE. 3 notice, placard, plaque, poster, signboard, signpost. 4 cue, gesture, motion, nod, signal, wave.

sign² *verb* 1 beckon, gesture, indicate, motion, nod, signal, wave. 2 autograph, countersign, endorse, undersign.
sign up enlist, enrol, join up, register, sign on, volunteer.

signal¹ *noun* 1 cue, gesture, indication, nod, semaphore, sign, tip-off, warning, wave.

signal² *verb* beckon, gesture, indicate, motion, nod, sign, wave.

significant *adjective* 1 eloquent, expressive, knowing, meaningful, pregnant, telling. 2 considerable, great, important, momentous, noteworthy, outstanding, remarkable.
significance *noun* 1 implication, import, meaning, point, purport, sense, signification. 2 consequence, importance, moment.

signification *noun* meaning.

signify *verb* (**signified**, **signifying**) **1** be a sign or symbol of; mean. **2** indicate, *She signified her approval.* **3** be important; matter. [from Latin *signum* = sign]

signpost *noun* a sign at a road junction etc. showing the names and distances of places down each road.

Sikh (*say as* seek) *noun* a member of an Indian religion believing in one God and accepting some Hindu and some Islamic beliefs. **Sikhism** *noun* [Hindi, = disciple]

silage *noun* fodder made from green crops stored in a silo.

silence[1] *noun* absence of sound or talk.

silence[2] *verb* (**silenced**, **silencing**) make a person or thing silent. [from Latin *silere* = to be silent]

silencer *noun* a device for reducing the sound made by a gun or a vehicle's exhaust system etc.

silent *adjective* **1** without any sound. **2** not speaking. **silently** *adverb*

silhouette (*say* sil-oo-**et**) *noun* a dark shadow seen against a light background. **silhouette** *verb* [named after a French author, E. de Silhouette, who made paper cut-outs of people's profiles from their shadows]

silica *noun* a hard white mineral that is a compound of silicon. [from Latin *silicis* = of flint]

silicon *noun* a substance found in many rocks, used in making transistors, chips for microprocessors, etc.

silicone *noun* a compound of silicon used in paints, varnish, and lubricants.

silk *noun* a fine soft thread or cloth made from the fibre produced by silkworms for making their cocoons. **silken** *adjective*, **silky** *adjective*

silkworm *noun* the caterpillar of a kind of moth, which feeds on mulberry leaves and spins itself a cocoon.

sill *noun* a strip of stone, wood, or metal underneath a window or door.

silly *adjective* (**sillier**, **silliest**) foolish; unwise. **silliness** *noun* [the word originally meant 'feeble' (from an older word *seely* = happy or fortunate)]

silo (*say* sy-loh) *noun* (*plural* **silos**) **1** a pit or tower for storing green crops (see *silage*) or corn or cement etc. **2** an underground place for storing a missile ready for firing.

silt[1] *noun* sand or mud laid down by a river or sea etc.

silt[2] *verb* block or clog or become blocked with silt, *The harbour had silted up.*

silver[1] *noun* **1** a shiny white precious metal. **2** the colour of silver. **3** coins or objects made of silver or silver-coloured metal. **4** a silver medal, usually given as second prize. **silvery** *adjective*

silver[2] *adjective* **1** made of silver. **2** coloured like silver.

silver wedding the 25th anniversary of a wedding.

silver[3] *verb* make or become silvery.

simian *adjective* like a monkey. [from Latin *simia* = monkey]

similar *adjective* nearly the same as another person or thing; of the same kind. **similarly** *adverb*, **similarity** *noun* [from Latin *similis* = like]

signify *verb* **1** be a sign of, betoken, denote, imply, indicate, mean, represent, stand for, symbolise. **2** communicate, convey, demonstrate, express, indicate, intimate, make known, show.

silence[1] *noun* calm, hush, peace, quietness, stillness, tranquillity.

silence[2] *verb* gag, hush, muzzle, quieten.

silent *adjective* **1** calm, hushed, peaceful, quiet, soundless, still, tranquil. **2** dumb, mum (*informal*), mute, quiet, reserved, reticent, speechless, taciturn, tight-lipped, tongue-tied, uncommunicative, unforthcoming, voiceless.

silhouette *noun* contour, form, outline, profile, shadow, shape.

silky *adjective* fine, satiny, sleek, smooth, soft.

sill *noun* ledge.

silly *adjective* absurd, asinine, barmy (*slang*), childish, crazy, daft (*informal*), dopey (*informal*), dotty (*informal*), fatuous, foolhardy, foolish, goofy (*slang*), hare-brained, idiotic, illogical, immature, inane, insane, ludicrous, mad, mindless, naïve, pointless, potty (*informal*), reckless, ridiculous, scatty (*informal*), senseless, stupid, unwise.

silt[2] *verb* (*silt up*) become obstructed, block up, clog up.

similar *adjective* akin, alike, analogous, comparable, equivalent, kindred, like, parallel. **similarity** *noun* affinity, closeness, correspondence, likeness, resemblance, similitude.

▶▶ DICTIONARY ◀◀

simile (*say* **sim**-il-ee) *noun* a comparison of one thing with another, e.g. *He is as strong as a horse. We ran like the wind.* [from Latin *similis* = like]

similitude *noun* similarity.

simmer *verb* boil very gently.
simmer down calm down.

simper *verb* smile in a silly affected way.
simper *noun*

simple *adjective* **1** easy, *a simple question.* **2** not complicated or elaborate; plain, not showy, *a simple cottage.* **3** without much sense or intelligence. **4** not of high rank; ordinary, *a simple countryman.* **simplicity** *noun*

simpleton *noun* a foolish person.

simplify *verb* (**simplified, simplifying**) make a thing simple or easy to understand. **simplification** *noun*

simply *adverb* **1** in a simple way, *Explain it simply.* **2** without doubt; completely, *It's simply marvellous.* **3** only; merely, *It's simply a question of time.*

simulate *verb* (**simulated, simulating**) **1** reproduce the appearance or conditions of something; imitate, *This device simulates a space flight.* **2** pretend, *They simulated fear.* **simulation** *noun*, **simulator** *noun* [from Latin *similis* = like]

simultaneous (*say* sim-ul-**tay**-nee-us) *adjective* happening at the same time. **simultaneously** *adverb*

sin¹ *noun* **1** the breaking of a religious or moral law. **2** a very bad action.

sin² *verb* (**sinned, sinning**) commit a sin. **sinner** *noun*

since¹ *conjunction* **1** from the time when, *Where have you been since I last saw you?* **2** because, *Since we have missed the bus we must walk home.*

since² *preposition* from a certain time, *She has been here since Christmas.*

since³ *adverb* between then and now, *He ran away and hasn't been seen since.*

sincere *adjective* without pretence; truly felt or meant, *my sincere thanks.* **sincerely** *adverb*, **sincerity** *noun* [from Latin *sincerus* = pure]
Yours sincerely see *yours.*

sine *verb* (in a right-angled triangle) the ratio of the length of a side opposite one of the acute angles to the length of the hypotenuse. (Compare *cosine.*)

sinecure (*say* **sy**-nik-yoor) *noun* a paid job that requires no work. [from Latin *sine cura* = without care]

sinew *noun* **1** a tendon. **2** strength; muscular power. **sinewy** *adjective*

sinful *adjective* guilty of sin; wicked. **sinfully** *adverb*, **sinfulness** *noun*

sing *verb* (**sang, sung, singing**) **1** make musical sounds with the voice. **2** perform a song. **3** make a humming or whistling sound. **singer** *noun*

▶▶ THESAURUS ◀◀

simmer *verb* boil, bubble, stew.

simple *adjective* **1** basic, easy, elementary, rudimentary, straightforward. **2** austere, modest, natural, ordinary, plain, unadorned, uncomplicated, unpretentious, unsophisticated. **3** backward, childish, dumb (*informal*), feeble-minded, naïve, obtuse, simple-minded, slow, stupid.

simpleton *noun* ass (*informal*), blockhead, bonehead, clot (*informal*), cretin, dill (*Australian informal*), dimwit (*informal*), dodo (*informal*), dolt, dope (*informal*), drip (*informal*), drongo (*Australian informal*), dunce, fool, half-wit, idiot, imbecile, moron (*informal*), mug (*informal*), muggins (*informal*), nincompoop, ninny, nitwit (*informal*), nong (*Australian informal*), sap (*informal*), twit (*slang*).

simulate *verb* **2** act, fake, feign, imitate, pretend, sham.

simultaneous *adjective* coexistent, coincident, concurrent, contemporaneous, parallel.

sin¹ *noun* **1** corruption, crime, evil, immorality, iniquity, sinfulness, ungodliness, unrighteousness, vice, wickedness, wrongdoing. **2** crime, error, fault, iniquity, misdeed, misdemeanour, offence, peccadillo, transgression, trespass (*old use*), vice, wrong, wrongdoing.

sin² *verb* do wrong, err, go astray, offend, transgress, trespass (*old use*).

sinner *noun* evildoer, malefactor, miscreant, offender, transgressor, trespasser (*old use*), wrongdoer.

sincere *adjective* artless, authentic, dinkum (*Australian informal*), dinky-di (*Australian informal*), earnest, frank, genuine, guileless, heartfelt, honest, natural, open, real, true.

sinful *adjective* bad, blasphemous, corrupt, depraved, evil, immoral, impious, iniquitous, sacrilegious, ungodly, unrighteous, wicked, wrong.

sing *verb* **1,2** carol, chant, croon, serenade, trill, yodel; (*of birds*) chirp, chirrup, tweet, twitter, warble.

singer *noun* chorister, crooner, diva, minstrel, prima donna, songster, troubadour, vocalist.

►►DICTIONARY◄◄

singe (*say* sinj) *verb* (**singed, singeing**) burn something slightly.

single¹ *adjective* **1** one only; not double or multiple. **2** suitable for one person, *single beds.* **3** separate, *We sold every single thing.* **4** not married. **5** for the journey to a place but not back again, *a single ticket.* **singly** *adverb*
single file a line of people one behind the other.

single² *noun* **1** a single person or thing. **2** a single ticket.

single³ *verb* (**singled, singling**) **single out** pick out or distinguish from other people or things.

single-handed *adjective* without help.

single-minded *adjective* with your mind set on one purpose only.

singlet *noun* a garment worn under or instead of a shirt; a vest.

singsong¹ *adjective* having a monotonous tone or rhythm, *a singsong voice.*

singsong² *noun* **1** informal singing by a gathering of people. **2** a singsong tone.

singular¹ *noun* the form of a noun or verb used when it stands for only one person or thing, *The singular is 'man', the plural is 'men'.*

singular² *adjective* **1** of the singular. **2** uncommon; extraordinary, *a woman of singular courage.* **singularly** *adverb,* **singularity** *noun*

sinister *adjective* **1** looking evil or harmful. **2** wicked. [from Latin, = on the left (which was thought to be unlucky)]

sink¹ *verb* (**sank, sunk, sinking**) **1** go or cause to go under the surface or to the bottom of the sea etc., *The ship sank. They sank the ship.* **2** go or fall slowly downwards, *He sank to his* knees. **3** dig or drill, *They sank a well.* **4** invest money in something.
sink in become understood.

sink² *noun* a fixed basin with a drainpipe and usually a tap or taps to supply water.

sinuous *adjective* with many bends or curves. [same origin as *sinus*]

sinus (*say* **sy**-nus) *noun* (*plural* **sinuses**) a hollow part in the bones of the skull, connected with the nose, *My sinuses are blocked.* [Latin, = curve]

sip *verb* (**sipped, sipping**) drink in small mouthfuls. **sip** *noun*

siphon¹ *noun* **1** a pipe or tube in the form of an upside-down U, arranged so that liquid is forced up it and down to a lower level. **2** a bottle containing soda-water which is released through a tube.

siphon² *verb* flow or draw out through a siphon. [Greek, = pipe]

sir *noun* **1** a word used when speaking politely to a man, *Please sir, may I go?* **2 Sir** the title given to a knight or baronet, *Sir Henry Parkes.* [from *sire*]

sire *noun* **1** the male parent of a horse or dog etc. (Compare *dam³*.) **2** a word formerly used when speaking to a king. [same origin as *senior*]

siren *noun* **1** a device that makes a long loud sound as a signal. **2** a dangerously attractive woman. [named after the Sirens in Greek legend, women who by their sweet singing lured seafarers to shipwreck on the rocks]

sirloin *noun* beef from the upper part of the loin. [from *sur-* = over, + *loin*]

sirocco *noun* a hot dry wind that reaches Italy from Africa. [from Arabic *saruk* = east wind]

►►THESAURUS◄◄

singe *verb* burn, scorch, sear.

single¹ *adjective* **1** isolated, lone, odd, one, sole, solitary, unique. **3** individual, separate. **4** unattached, unmarried.

single³ *verb* **single out** choose, earmark, pick out, select.

single-handed *adjective* alone, independent, solo, unaided, unassisted.

single-minded *adjective* determined, dogged, obsessive, purposeful, resolute, unswerving, unwavering.

singular² *adjective* **2** exceptional, extraordinary, outstanding, rare, remarkable, uncommon, unique, unusual; see also STRANGE.

sinister *adjective* **1** alarming, disturbing, forbidding, frightening, menacing, ominous, threatening. **2** bad, criminal, diabolical, evil, malevolent, malignant, vile, villainous, wicked.

sink¹ *verb* **1** founder, go down, scupper, scuttle, submerge. **2** descend, dip, droop, drop, fall, go down, slump, subside. **3** bore, dig, drill, excavate.
sink in be absorbed, go in, penetrate, register.

sink² *noun* basin, washbasin.

sip *verb* drink, sup, taste.
sip *noun* drink, drop, mouthful, sup, swallow, swig (*informal*), taste.

siren *noun* **1** alarm, signal, tocsin, warning. **2** enchantress, seductress, temptress.

▶▶ DICTIONARY ◀◀

sisal (*say* **sy**-sal) *noun* fibre from a tropical plant, used for making ropes.

sissy *noun* (*plural* **sissies**) a timid or cowardly person. [from *sis* = sister]

sister *noun* **1** a daughter of the same parents as another person. **2** a woman who is a fellow member of an association etc. **3** a nun. **4** a hospital nurse in charge of others. **sisterhood** *noun*, **sisterly** *adjective*

sister-in-law *noun* (*plural* **sisters-in-law**) the sister of a married person's husband or wife; the wife of a person's brother.

sit *verb* (**sat**, **sitting**) **1** rest with the body supported on the buttocks; occupy a seat, *We were sitting in the front row.* **2** seat; cause someone to sit. **3** (of birds) perch; stay on the nest to hatch eggs. **4** be a candidate for an examination. **5** be situated; stay. **6** (of Parliament or a lawcourt etc.) be assembled for business. **sitter** *noun*

sitar *noun* an Indian musical instrument that is like a guitar. [Hindi, = three-stringed]

site[1] *noun* the place where something happens or happened or is built etc., *a camping-site.*

site[2] *verb* (**sited**, **siting**) provide with a site; locate. [from Latin *situs* = position]

sitting room a room with comfortable chairs for sitting in.

situated *adjective* in a particular place or situation.

situation *noun* **1** a position, with its surroundings. **2** a state of affairs at a certain time, *The police faced a difficult situation.* **3** a job. [same origin as *site*]

six *noun* (*plural* **sixes**) & *adjective* the number 6; one more than five. **sixth** *adjective* & *noun* **at sixes and sevens** in disorder.

sixteen *noun* & *adjective* the number 16; one more than fifteen. **sixteenth** *adjective* & *noun*

sixty *noun* & *adjective* (*plural* **sixties**) the number 60; six times ten. **sixtieth** *adjective* & *noun*

size[1] *noun* **1** the measurements or extent of something. **2** any of the series of standard measurements in which certain things are made, *a size eight shoe.*

size[2] *verb* (**sized**, **sizing**) arrange things according to their size.
   size up estimate the size of something; (*informal*) form an opinion or judgement about a person or thing.

size[3] *noun* a gluey substance used to glaze paper or stiffen cloth etc.

size[4] *verb* (**sized**, **sizing**) treat with size.

sizeable *adjective* large; fairly large.

sizzle *verb* (**sizzled**, **sizzling**) make a crackling or hissing sound.

skate[1] *noun* **1** a boot with a steel blade attached to the sole, used for sliding smoothly over ice. **2** a roller skate.

skate[2] *verb* (**skated**, **skating**) move on skates. **skater** *noun*

skate[3] *noun* (*plural* **skate**) a large flat edible sea-fish.

skateboard *noun* a small board with wheels, used for riding on (as a sport) while standing. **skateboarding** *noun*

skein *noun* a coil of yarn or thread.

skeleton *noun* **1** the framework of bones of the body. **2** the shell or other hard part of a crab etc. **3** a framework, e.g. of a building. **skeletal** *adjective* [from Greek *skeletos* = dried-up]

skerrick *noun* (*Australian informal*) slightest amount, *not a skerrick left.*

▶▶ THESAURUS ◀◀

sissy *noun* coward, cry-baby, sook (*Australian informal*), wimp (*informal*), wuss (*slang*).

sit *verb* **1** be seated, perch yourself, rest, settle, squat. **5** lie, remain, stand, stay. **6** assemble, be in session, convene, meet.

site[1] *noun* location, place, position, setting, spot, venue.

site[2] *verb* locate, place, position, situate.

sitting room drawing room, living room, lounge, parlour (*old use*).

situation *noun* **1** locality, location, place, position, setting, site, spot. **2** circumstances, plight, position, predicament, state of affairs. **3** employment, job, position, post.

size[1] *noun* **1** amount, area, bulk, capacity, dimensions, extent, magnitude, measurements, proportions, scale, scope.

size[2] *verb* **size up** appraise, assess, gauge, judge, weigh up (*informal*).

sizeable *adjective* ample, big, considerable, generous, handsome, hefty, large, substantial.

sizzle *verb* hiss, sputter.

skate[2] *verb* glide, skid, skim, slide.

skeleton *noun* **1** bones, frame. **3** framework, shell, structure.

skerrick *noun* bit, crumb, fragment, jot, particle, scrap, shred, trace.

▶▶ D I C T I O N A R Y ◀◀

sketch¹ *noun* (*plural* **sketches**) **1** a rough drawing or painting. **2** a short account of something. **3** a short amusing play.

sketch² *verb* make a sketch. [from Greek *schedios* = impromptu]

sketchy *adjective* rough and not detailed or careful.

skew¹ *adjective* askew; slanting.

skew² *verb* make a thing askew.

skewer *noun* a long pin pushed through meat to hold it together while it is being cooked. **skewer** *verb*

ski¹ (*say* skee) *noun* (*plural* **skis**) each of a pair of long narrow strips of wood, metal, or plastic fixed under the feet for moving quickly over snow.

ski² *verb* (**ski'd**, **skiing**) travel on skis. **skier** *noun* [Norwegian]

skid¹ *verb* (**skidded**, **skidding**) slide accidentally.

skid² *noun* **1** a skidding movement. **2** a runner on a helicopter, for use in landing.

skilful *adjective* having or showing great skill. **skilfully** *adverb*

skill *noun* the ability to do something well. **skilled** *adjective*

skillion *noun* (*Australian*) a lean-to, especially for sheep waiting to be shorn.

skim *verb* (**skimmed**, **skimming**) **1** remove something from the surface of a liquid; take the cream off milk. **2** move quickly over a surface or through the air. **3** read something quickly.

skimp *verb* supply or use less than is needed, *Don't skimp on the food.*

skimpy *adjective* (**skimpier**, **skimpiest**) scanty; too small.

skin¹ *noun* **1** the flexible outer covering of a person's or animal's body. **2** an outer layer or covering, e.g. of a fruit. **3** a skin-like film formed on the surface of a liquid.

skin² *verb* (**skinned**, **skinning**) take the skin off something.

skin-diving *noun* swimming under water with flippers and breathing-apparatus but without a diving-suit. **skin-diver** *noun*

skinflint *noun* a miserly person.

skinhead *noun* a youth with very closely cropped hair.

skinny *adjective* (**skinnier**, **skinniest**) very thin.

skip¹ (**skipped**, **skipping**) **1** move along lightly, especially by hopping on each foot in turn. **2** jump with a skipping-rope. **3** go quickly from one subject to another. **4** miss something out, *You can skip chapter six.* **5** (*informal*) not attend something, *He skipped his maths lesson.*

skip² *noun* a skipping movement.

skip³ *noun* a large metal container for taking away builders' rubbish etc.

skipper *noun* a captain.

skipping-rope *noun* a rope, usually with a handle at each end, that is swung over your head and under your feet as you jump.

skirmish *noun* (*plural* **skirmishes**) a small fight or conflict. **skirmish** *verb*

▶▶ T H E S A U R U S ◀◀

sketch¹ *noun* **1** design, diagram, drawing, picture. **2** abstract, draft, outline, plan, précis, summary, synopsis. **3** play, skit.

sketchy *adjective* cursory, incomplete, patchy, rough, superficial, vague.

skew¹ *adjective* askew, oblique, slanting.

skid¹ *verb* aquaplane, glide, slide, slip.

skilful *adjective* able, accomplished, adept, adroit, brilliant, capable, clever, competent, consummate, deft, dexterous, expert, gifted, ingenious, masterly, professional, proficient, skilled, talented.

skill *noun* ability, adroitness, aptitude, art, capability, cleverness, competence, dexterity, expertise, ingenuity, knack, know-how, mastery, proficiency, prowess, talent.

skim *verb* **1** remove, scrape. **2** fly, glide, sail, sweep. **3** flick, flip, glance, leaf, scan, thumb.

skimp *verb* economise, save, scrimp, stint.

skimpy *adjective* brief, inadequate, insufficient, meagre, scanty, small, tiny.

skin¹ *noun* **1** dermis, epidermis; (*an animal's skin*) coat, fur, hide, pelt. **2** casing, coating, covering, exterior, husk, jacket (*of a potato*), membrane, peel, rind, shell. **3** film, membrane.

skin² *verb* abrade, bark, graze, scrape, scratch.

skinflint *noun* cheapskate (*informal*), miser, niggard, Scrooge.

skinny *adjective* bony, emaciated, gaunt, lanky, lean, scraggy, scrawny, slender, thin.

skip¹ *verb* **1** bob, bound, caper, cavort, dance, frisk, gambol, hop, leap, prance, romp, run, trip. **3** flit, jump, pass. **4** leave out, miss, neglect, omit, overlook, pass over. **5** absent yourself from, cut (*informal*), miss, play truant from, wag (*informal*).

skirmish *noun* altercation, argument, brush, clash, conflict, confrontation, fight, scrap (*informal*), scrimmage, scuffle, struggle, tussle.

▶▶ D I C T I O N A R Y ◀◀

skirt[1] *noun* a woman's or girl's garment that hangs down from the waist.

skirt[2] *verb* **1** go round the edge of something. **2** avoid dealing with an issue etc.

skirting *noun* (also **skirting-board**) a narrow board round the wall of a room, close to the floor.

skit *noun* a parody, *He wrote a skit on 'Hamlet'.*

skite[1] *verb* (*Australian informal*) boast.

skite[2] *noun* (*Australian informal*) **1** a boaster. **2** boasting.

skittish *adjective* frisky.

skittle *noun* a wooden pin that people try to knock down by bowling a ball in the game of **skittles**.

skive *verb* (**skived, skiving**) (*slang*) dodge work etc. **skiver** *noun*

skivvy *noun* a thin high-necked long-sleeved garment.

skulk *verb* loiter stealthily.

skull *noun* the framework of bones of the head.

skunk *noun* a black furry American animal that can spray a bad-smelling fluid.

sky *noun* (*plural* **skies**) the space above the earth, appearing blue in daylight on fine days.

skylark *noun* a lark that sings while it hovers high in the air.

skylight *noun* a window in a roof.

skyline *noun* **1** the horizon, where earth and sky appear to meet. **2** the outline of buildings etc. against the sky.

skyscraper *noun* a very tall building.

slab *noun* a thick flat piece.

slack[1] *adjective* **1** not pulled tight. **2** not busy. **3** not working hard; careless. **slackly** *adverb*, **slackness** *noun*

slack[2] *verb* avoid work. **slacker** *noun*

slacken *verb* make or become slack.

slacks *plural noun* trousers for informal occasions.

slag *noun* waste material separated from metal in smelting.

slag-heap *noun* a mound of waste matter from a mine etc.

slain *past participle* of **slay**.

slake *verb* (**slaked, slaking**) quench, *slake your thirst.*

slam *verb* (**slammed, slamming**) **1** shut loudly. **2** hit violently. **slam** *noun*

slander[1] *noun* a spoken statement that damages a person's reputation and is untrue. (Compare *libel*.) **slanderous** *adjective*

slander[2] *verb* make a slander against someone. **slanderer** *noun*

slang[1] *noun* words that are used very informally to add vividness or humour to what is said. **slangy** *adjective*

slang[2] *verb* speak insultingly to somebody.

▶▶ T H E S A U R U S ◀◀

skirt[2] *verb* **1** border, bound, circle, edge, encircle, fringe, surround. **2** avoid, bypass, circumvent, dodge, evade, sidestep.

skit *noun* burlesque, parody, satire, send-up (*informal*), sketch, spoof (*informal*), take-off.

skite[1] *verb* blow your own trumpet, boast, brag, congratulate yourself, crow, show off, vaunt.

skite[2] *noun* **1** boaster, braggart, show-off.

skittish *adjective* excitable, fidgety, frisky, jumpy, lively, nervous, playful, restive, restless.

skulk *verb* creep, hide, loiter, lurk, prowl.

sky *noun* air, atmosphere, ether, firmament, heavens, stratosphere.

slab *noun* block, chunk, hunk, piece, slice, wedge.

slack[1] *adjective* **1** floppy, limp, loose, relaxed. **2** inactive, quiet, slow, sluggish. **3** careless, casual, lackadaisical, lax, lazy, negligent, offhand, remiss, slapdash, slipshod, sloppy.

slack[2] *verb* be lazy, ease off, idle, let up, take it easy.

slacken *verb* decrease, drop off, ease (off), lessen, let up, loosen, reduce, relax, release, slack, slow down.

slam *verb* **1** bang, close, shut. **2** bump, crash, knock, ram, run, smash.

slander[1] *noun* calumny, defamation, denigration, libel, misrepresentation, vilification. **slanderous** *adjective* defamatory, denigratory, libellous, malicious, scurrilous, untrue.

slander[2] *verb* defame, denigrate, libel, malign, misrepresent, slur, smear, vilify.

slang[1] *noun* argot, cant, jargon, lingo (*informal*).

▶▶DICTIONARY◀◀

slant *verb* **1** slope. **2** present news or information etc. from a particular point of view. **slant** *noun*

slap *verb* (**slapped**, **slapping**) **1** hit with the palm of the hand or with something flat. **2** put forcefully or carelessly, *We slapped paint on the walls.* **slap** *noun*

slapdash *adjective* hasty and careless.

slapstick *noun* comedy with people hitting each other, falling over, etc.

slash¹ *verb* **1** make large cuts in something; cut or strike with a long sweeping movement. **2** reduce greatly, *Prices were slashed.*

slash² *noun* (*plural* **slashes**) **1** a slashing cut. **2** an oblique stroke.

slat *noun* each of the thin strips of wood or metal or plastic arranged so that they overlap and form a screen, e.g. in a venetian blind.

slate¹ *noun* **1** a kind of grey rock that is easily split into flat plates. **2** a piece of this rock used in covering a roof or (formerly) for writing on. **slaty** *adjective*

slate² *verb* (**slated**, **slating**) **1** cover a roof with slates. **2** (*informal*) criticise severely; reprimand.

slather *noun* **open slather** without restraint, no holds barred.

slattern *noun* a slovenly woman. **slatternly** *adjective*

slaughter *verb* **1** kill an animal for food. **2** kill people or animals ruthlessly or in great numbers. **slaughter** *noun*

slaughterhouse *noun* a place where animals are killed for food.

slave¹ *noun* a person who is owned by another and obliged to work for him or her without being paid. **slavery** *noun*

slave² *verb* (**slaved**, **slaving**) work very hard.

slave-driver *noun* a person who makes others work very hard.

slaver (*say* **slav**-er or **slay**-ver) *verb* have saliva flowing from the mouth, *a slavering dog.*

slavish *adjective* **1** like a slave. **2** showing no independence or originality.

slay *verb* (**slew**, **slain**, **slaying**) kill.

sled *noun* (*American*) a sledge.

sledge *noun* a vehicle for travelling over snow, with strips of metal or wood instead of wheels. **sledging** *noun*

sledgehammer *noun* a very large heavy hammer.

sleek *adjective* smooth and shiny.

sleep¹ *noun* the condition or time of rest in which the eyes are closed, the body relaxed, and the mind unconscious. **sleepy** *adjective*, **sleepily** *adverb*, **sleepiness** *noun*

sleep² *verb* (**slept**, **sleeping**) have a sleep.

▶▶THESAURUS◀◀

slant *verb* **1** incline, lean, list, slope, tilt. **2** angle, bias, distort.
slant *noun* **1** angle, incline, list, slope, tilt. **2** angle, attitude, bias, perspective, prejudice, view.

slap *verb* **1** cuff, hit, smack, spank, strike, whack. **slap** *noun* blow, cuff, hit, smack, whack.

slapdash *adjective* careless, haphazard, hasty, perfunctory, slipshod, sloppy.

slash¹ *verb* **1** cut, gash, hack, rip, slice, slit, tear. **2** cut, drop, lower, reduce.

slash² *noun* **1** cut, gash, incision, laceration, rip, slit. **2** line, oblique, stroke.

slaughter *verb* **1** butcher, destroy, kill. **2** annihilate, butcher, execute, exterminate, kill, massacre, murder, slay.
slaughter *noun* bloodbath, bloodshed, butchery, carnage, killing, massacre, murder, pogrom, slaying.

slave¹ *noun* serf, servant, vassal.
slavery *noun* bondage, captivity, enslavement, serfdom, servitude, thraldom, thrall.

slave² *verb* drudge, grind away, labour, slog, sweat, toil, work hard.

slave-driver *noun* despot, oppressor, taskmaster, tyrant.

slavish *adjective* **1** obsequious, servile, submissive, subservient. **2** unimaginative, unoriginal.

slay *verb* assassinate, execute, kill, massacre, murder, put to death, slaughter.

sledge *noun* bob-sled, bob-sleigh, luge, sled, sleigh, toboggan.

sleek *adjective* glossy, lustrous, shiny, silky, smooth.

sleep¹ *noun* catnap, dormancy, doze, forty winks, hibernation, kip (*slang*), nap, repose, rest, shut-eye (*informal*), siesta, slumber, snooze.
sleepy *adjective* dopey (*informal*), dormant, drowsy, inactive, lethargic, peaceful, quiet, somnolent, tired, torpid, weary.

sleep² *verb* catnap, doze, drop off, kip (*slang*), nap, nod off, rest, slumber, snooze.

sleeper *noun* **1** someone who is asleep. **2** each of the wooden or concrete beams on which the rails of a railway rest. **3** a railway carriage with beds or berths for passengers to sleep in; a place in this.

sleepless *adjective* unable to sleep.

sleep-out *noun* (*Australian*) part of a veranda closed off as a bedroom.

sleepwalker *noun* a person who walks about while asleep. **sleepwalking** *noun*

sleet *noun* a mixture of rain and snow or hail.

sleeve *noun* **1** the part of a garment that covers the arm. **2** the cover of a record.
up your sleeve hidden but ready for you to use.

sleeveless *adjective* without sleeves.

sleigh (*say as* slay) *noun* a sledge, especially a large one pulled by horses. **sleighing** *noun*

sleight (*say as* slight) *noun* **sleight of hand** skill in using the hands to do conjuring tricks etc. [from Norse *slægth* = slyness]

slender *adjective* **1** slim. **2** small, *a slender hope*. **slenderness** *noun*

sleuth (*say* slooth) *noun* a detective.

slew *past tense* of **slay**.

slice¹ *noun* **1** a thin piece cut off something. **2** a portion.

slice² *verb* (**sliced, slicing**) **1** cut into slices. **2** cut from a larger piece, *Slice the top off the egg.* **3** cut cleanly, *The knife sliced through the apple.*

slick¹ *adjective* **1** quick and clever or cunning. **2** slippery.

slick² *noun* **1** a large patch of oil floating on water. **2** a slippery place.

slide¹ *verb* (**slid, sliding**) **1** move or cause to move smoothly on a surface. **2** move quietly or secretly, *The thief slid behind a bush.*

slide² *noun* **1** a sliding movement. **2** a smooth surface or structure on which people or things can slide. **3** a photograph that can be projected on a screen. **4** a small glass plate on which things are placed to be examined under a microscope. **5** a fastener to keep hair tidy.

slight¹ *adjective* very small; not serious or important. **slightly** *adverb*, **slightness** *noun*

slight² *verb* insult a person by treating him or her without respect.

slim¹ *adjective* (**slimmer, slimmest**) **1** thin and graceful. **2** small, *a slim chance.* **slimness** *noun*

slim² *verb* (**slimmed, slimming**) make yourself thinner. **slimmer** *noun*

slime *noun* unpleasant wet slippery stuff. **slimy** *adjective*, **sliminess** *noun*

sling¹ *noun* **1** a loop or band placed round something to support or lift it. **2** a looped strap used to throw a stone etc.

sling² *verb* (**slung, slinging**) **1** support or lift with a sling. **2** (*informal*) throw. **sling off at** (*Australian slang*) mock, ridicule.

sleepless *adjective* disturbed, insomniac, restless, wakeful.

sleepwalker *noun* noctambulist, somnambulist.

sleeve *noun* **2** case, casing, cover, sheath.

sleight *noun* **sleight of hand** conjuring, dexterity, legerdemain, trickery.

slender *adjective* **1** lean, slight, slim, svelte, thin. **2** faint, feeble, remote, slight, slim, small, weak.

sleuth *noun* detective, investigator, private eye (*informal*).

slice¹ *noun* **1** chunk, piece, portion, segment, sliver, wedge. **2** cut, part, portion, proportion, share.

slice² *verb* **1** carve, cut, divide. **2** pare, peel, shave, trim, whittle.

slick¹ *adjective* **1** clever, cunning, glib, sly, smarmy (*informal*), smooth.

slide¹ *verb* **1** coast, glide, glissade, skate, skid, slip, slither.

slide² *noun* **2** chute, ramp, slippery dip (*Australian*), slope.

slight¹ *adjective* imperceptible, infinitesimal, insignificant, little, minor, minute, negligible, small, subtle, superficial, tiny, trivial.

slight² *verb* affront, ignore, insult, rebuff, scorn, snub.

slim¹ *adjective* **1** lean, slender, slight, svelte, thin. **2** faint, feeble, remote, slender, slight, small.

slim² *verb* diet, lose weight, reduce.

slime *noun* goo (*informal*), gunge (*informal*), gunk (*informal*), muck, mud, ooze, sludge.
slimy *adjective* gooey (*informal*), gungy (*informal*), mucky, muddy, oozy, slippery, sludgy, viscous; (*a slimy person*) crawling, obsequious, oily, slick, smarmy (*informal*), smooth, unctuous.

sling¹ *noun* **1** bandage, belt, strap, support. **2** catapult, shanghai (*Australian*), slingshot.

sling² *verb* **1** dangle, hang, suspend, swing. **2** cast, chuck (*informal*), fling, hurl, throw, toss.
sling off at deride, disparage, gibe at, make fun of, mock, poke borak at (*Australian informal*), poke fun at, ridicule.

▶▶ D I C T I O N A R Y ◀◀

slink *verb* (**slunk**, **slinking**) move in a stealthy or guilty way. **slinky** *adjective*

slip[1] *verb* (**slipped**, **slipping**) 1 slide accidentally; lose your balance by sliding. 2 move or put quickly and quietly, *Slip it in your pocket. We slipped away from the party.* 3 escape from, *The dog slipped its leash. It slipped my memory.*
slip up make a mistake.

slip[2] *noun* 1 an accidental slide or fall. 2 a mistake. 3 a small piece of paper. 4 a petticoat. 5 a pillowcase.
give someone the slip escape or avoid him or her skilfully.

slipper *noun* a soft comfortable shoe to wear indoors.

slippery *adjective* smooth or wet so that it is difficult to stand on or hold. **slipperiness** *noun*

slip-rail *noun* (*Australian*) a movable rail in a fence making a gateway.

slipshod *adjective* careless; not systematic.

slit[1] *noun* a narrow straight cut or opening.

slit[2] *verb* (**slitted**, **slitting**) make a slit or slits in something.

slither *verb* slip or slide unsteadily.

sliver (*say* **sliv**-er) *noun* a thin strip of wood or glass etc.

slobber *verb* slaver; dribble.

slog *verb* (**slogged**, **slogging**) 1 hit hard. 2 work hard and steadily. 3 walk with effort.
slog *noun*, **slogger** *noun*

slogan *noun* a phrase used to advertise something or to sum up the aims of a campaign etc., *Their slogan was 'Ban the bomb!'*

sloop *noun* a small sailing-ship with one mast.

slop *verb* (**slopped**, **slopping**) spill liquid over the edge of its container.
slops *plural noun* slopped liquid; liquid waste matter.

slope[1] *verb* (**sloped**, **sloping**) lie or turn at an angle; slant.
slope off (*slang*) go away.

slope[2] *noun* 1 a sloping surface. 2 the amount by which something slopes.

sloppy *adjective* (**sloppier**, **sloppiest**) 1 liquid and splashing easily. 2 careless; slipshod, *sloppy work.* 3 weakly sentimental, *a sloppy story.* **sloppily** *adverb*, **sloppiness** *noun*

slosh *verb* (*informal*) 1 splash; slop; pour liquid carelessly. 2 hit.

slot *noun* a narrow opening to put things in. **slotted** *adjective*

sloth (*rhymes with* both) *noun* 1 laziness. 2 a South American animal that lives in trees and moves very slowly. **slothful** *adjective*

slot-machine *noun* a machine worked by putting a coin in the slot.

▶▶ T H E S A U R U S ◀◀

slink *verb* creep, edge, skulk, slip, sneak, steal.

slip[1] *verb* 1 fall, glide, skid, slide, slither. 2 creep, skulk, slink, sneak, steal. 3 detach, release.
slip up blunder, err, goof (*slang*), make a mistake.

slip[2] *noun* 1 fall, glide, skid, slide. 2 blue (*Australian informal*), blunder, booboo (*slang*), error, lapse, mistake, slip-up (*informal*). 3 piece, scrap, sheet, strip. 5 case, cover, pillowcase, pillowslip.
give someone the slip avoid, dodge, elude, escape, evade, lose.

slippery *adjective* greasy, oily, slick, slithery, smooth, wet.

slipshod *adjective* careless, lax, messy, shoddy, slapdash, sloppy, slovenly, unmethodical.

slit[1] *noun* crack, cut, fissure, gash, hole, incision, opening, rip, slash, slot, split, tear.

slit[2] *verb* cut, gash, rip, slash, split, tear.

slither *verb* slide, slink, slip.

sliver *noun* flake, fragment, piece, shaving, slice, strip.

slobber *verb* dribble, drool, salivate, slaver.

slog *verb* 1 hit, strike, thump, whack. 2 grind, labour, plod, plough, toil, work. 3 plod, tramp, trek, trudge.

slogan *noun* catchphrase, catchword, jingle, motto.

slop *verb* slosh (*informal*), spill, splash, splatter.
slops *plural noun* dregs, refuse, swill, waste.

slope[1] *verb* ascend, bank, descend, drop, incline, rise, slant, tilt, tip.

slope[2] *noun* angle, ascent, bank, descent, escarpment, grade, gradient, hill, hillside, inclination, incline, pitch, rake, ramp, rise, scarp, slant, tilt.

sloppy *adjective* 1 gooey (*informal*), liquid, runny, watery. 2 careless, lax, messy, shoddy, slapdash, slipshod, slovenly, unmethodical, untidy. 3 mushy, romantic, sentimental, soppy (*informal*).

slot *noun* groove, hole, opening, slit.

slothful *adjective* idle, inactive, indolent, lazy, slack, sluggish.

▶▶▶ D I C T I O N A R Y ◀◀

slouch *verb* stand, sit, or move in a lazy awkward way, not with an upright posture. **slouch** *noun*
slouch hat a hat with a wide flexible brim, especially with left brim turned up, associated with the Australian army.

slough¹ (*rhymes with* cow) *noun* a swamp or marshy place.

slough² (*say* sluf) *verb* shed, *A snake sloughs its skin periodically.*

slovenly (*say* **sluv**-en-lee) *adjective* careless; untidy. **slovenliness** *noun*

slow¹ *adjective* **1** not quick; taking more time than is usual. **2** showing a time earlier than the correct time, *Your watch is slow.* **3** not quick to learn or understand. **slowly** *adverb*, **slowness** *noun*

slow² *adverb* slowly, *Go slow.*

slow³ *verb* go more slowly; cause to go more slowly, *The storm slowed us down.*

slowcoach *noun* (*informal*) a slow person.

sludge *noun* thick mud.

slug *noun* **1** a small slimy animal like a snail without a shell. **2** a pellet for firing from a gun.

sluggard *noun* a slow or lazy person.

sluggish *adjective* slow-moving; not alert or lively.

sluice¹ (*say* slooss) *noun* **1** a sliding barrier for controlling a flow of water. **2** a channel carrying off water.

sluice² *verb* (**sluiced**, **sluicing**) **1** wash with a flow of water. **2** let out water.

slum *noun* an area of dirty overcrowded houses.

slumber *noun* & *verb* sleep. **slumberer** *noun*, **slumberous** or **slumbrous** *adjective*

slump¹ *verb* fall heavily or suddenly.

slump² *noun* a sudden great fall in prices or trade.

slur¹ *verb* (**slurred**, **slurring**) **1** pronounce words indistinctly by running the sounds together. **2** mark with a slur in music.

slur² *noun* **1** a slurred sound. **2** discredit, *It casts a slur on his reputation.* **3** a curved line placed over notes in music to show that they are to be sung or played smoothly without a break.

slush *noun* partly melted snow on the ground; watery mud.

slushy *noun* (*Australian*) a cook's assistant.

sly *adjective* (**slyer**, **slyest**) **1** unpleasantly cunning or secret. **2** mischievous, *a sly smile.* **slyly** *adverb*, **slyness** *noun*

smack¹ *noun* a slap; a hard hit.

smack² *verb* slap; hit hard.
smack your lips close and then part them noisily in enjoyment.

smack³ *adverb* (*informal*) with a smack; directly, *The ball went smack through the window.*

▶▶▶ T H E S A U R U S ◀◀

slouch *verb* droop, hunch, loll, sag, slump, stoop.

slovenly *adjective* careless, dirty, disreputable, messy, scruffy, slatternly, unkempt, untidy; see also SLOPPY.

slow¹ *adjective* **1** (*a slow pace*) dawdling, deliberate, leisurely, measured, plodding, sluggish, steady, unhurried; (*a slow process*) drawn-out, endless, gradual, interminable, long, painstaking, prolonged, protracted, time-consuming; (*a slow response*) delayed, dilatory, late, tardy. **3** dense, dim, dull, dumb (*informal*), obtuse, stupid, thick (*informal*).
slowly *adverb* at a snail's pace, gradually, leisurely, sluggishly, steadily, unhurriedly.

slow³ *verb* brake, decelerate, delay, hinder, hold back, impede, reduce speed, retard.

slowcoach *noun* dawdler, laggard, sluggard, straggler.

sludge *noun* goo (*informal*), mire, muck, mud, silt, slime, slush.

sluggish *adjective* inactive, indolent, inert, lazy, lethargic, listless, phlegmatic, slack, slothful, slow, torpid.

slumber *noun* repose, rest, sleep.
slumber *verb* doze, nap, rest, sleep, snooze.

slump¹ *verb* collapse, crash, decline, drop, fall, flop, nosedive, plummet, plunge, sink, tumble.

slump² *noun* collapse, crash, decline, depression, downturn, drop, fall, recession, setback, tumble.

slur¹ *verb* **1** mumble, mutter.

slur² *noun* **2** aspersion, blot, insult, libel, slander, slight, smear, stain, stigma.

sly *adjective* **1** artful, crafty, cunning, devious, foxy, furtive, secretive, shifty, shrewd, sneaky, underhand, wily. **2** arch, knowing, mischievous, playful, roguish.

smack¹ *noun* blow, hit, rap, slap, spanking, whack.

smack² *verb* belt (*slang*), hit, rap, slap, spank, strike, wallop (*slang*), whack.

smack³ *adverb* bang, directly, slap, straight.

▶▶ DICTIONARY ◀◀

smack⁴ *noun* a slight flavour of something; a trace.

smack⁵ *verb* have a slight flavour or trace, *His manner smacks of conceit.*

smack⁶ *noun* a small sailing-boat used for fishing etc.

small *adjective* **1** not large; less than the usual size. **2** insignificant. **smallness** *noun*
the small of the back the smallest part of the back (at the waist).

smallgoods *plural noun* (*Australian*) delicatessen meats.

small-minded *adjective* selfish; petty.

smallpox *noun* a former contagious disease with spots that often left bad scars on the skin.

smart¹ *adjective* **1** neat and elegant; dressed well. **2** clever. **3** forceful; brisk, *She ran at a smart pace.* **smartly** *adverb*, **smartness** *noun*

smart² *verb* feel a stinging pain. **smart** *noun*

smarten *verb* make or become smarter.

smash¹ *verb* **1** break noisily into pieces. **2** hit hard. **3** move with great force. **4** destroy or defeat completely.

smash² *noun* (*plural* **smashes**) **1** the action or sound of smashing. **2** a collision. **3** a disaster.
smash hit (*slang*) something very successful.

smashing *adjective* (*informal*) excellent; beautiful.

smattering *noun* a slight knowledge of a subject or a foreign language.

smear *verb* **1** rub something greasy or sticky or dirty on a surface. **2** try to damage someone's reputation. **smear** *noun*, **smeary** *adjective*

smell¹ *verb* (**smelt, smelling**) **1** be aware of something by means of the sense-organs of the nose, *I can smell smoke.* **2** give out a smell.

smell² *noun* **1** something you can smell; a quality in something that makes people able to smell it. **2** an unpleasant quality of this kind. **3** the ability to smell things. **smelly** *adjective*

smelt *verb* melt ore to get the metal it contains.

smile¹ *noun* an expression on the face that shows pleasure or amusement with the lips stretched and turning upwards at the ends.

smile² *verb* (**smiled, smiling**) give a smile.

smirch *verb* **1** soil. **2** disgrace or dishonour a reputation. **smirch** *noun*

smirk¹ *noun* a self-satisfied smile.

smirk² *verb* give a smirk.

▶▶ THESAURUS ◀◀

smack⁵ *verb* savour, suggest.

small *adjective* **1** baby, compact, diminutive, dwarf, infinitesimal, little, meagre, measly (*informal*), microscopic, miniature, minuscule, minute, petite, pocket-sized, poky, puny, scant, scanty, short, slender, slight, stunted, teeny (*informal*), tiny, undersized, wee, weeny (*informal*). **2** insignificant, minimal, negligible, paltry, petty, trifling, trivial, unimportant.

small-minded *adjective* bigoted, hidebound, intolerant, narrow-minded, petty, prejudiced, selfish, ungenerous.

smart¹ *adjective* **1** chic, dapper, dolled up (*informal*), elegant, fashionable, natty (*informal*), neat, posh (*informal*), snappy (*informal*), snazzy (*informal*), spruce, stylish, swanky (*informal*), swish (*informal*), trim. **2** able, astute, brainy, bright, capable, clever, ingenious, intelligent, prudent, sensible, sharp, shrewd, wise. **3** brisk, cracking (*slang*), energetic, fast, jaunty, quick, swift, vigorous.

smart² *verb* hurt, sting, throb.

smash¹ *verb* **1** break, crash, shatter, shiver, splinter. **2** bash, batter, break, hammer, hit,

knock, pound, strike. **3** (*smash into*) bang into, bump into, collide with, crash into, hit, knock into, ram into, run into, slam into.

smash² *noun* **2** accident, bingle (*Australian informal*), collision, crash, pile-up (*informal*), prang (*slang*).
smash hit hit, success, triumph, winner.

smear *verb* **1** coat, cover, daub, plaster, rub, spread. **2** blacken, defame, denigrate, malign, slander, slur, smirch, sully, vilify.
smear *noun* blotch, mark, smudge, splotch, stain, streak.

smell¹ *verb* **1** nose, scent, sniff. **2** pong (*informal*), reek, stink.

smell² *noun* **1** aroma, bouquet, fragrance, odour, perfume, redolence, scent, whiff. **2** pong (*informal*), reek, stench, stink.
smelly *adjective* foul-smelling, high, malodorous, noisome (*literary*), on the nose (*Australian informal*), pongy (*informal*), putrid, rancid, rank, reeking, stinking.

smile¹ *noun* grin, simper, smirk.

smile² *verb* beam, grin, simper, smirk.

smirk *noun & verb* grin, simper, smile, sneer.

▶▶ D I C T I O N A R Y ◀◀

smite *verb* (**smote**, **smitten**, **smiting**) hit hard. **be smitten with** be affected by a disease or desire or fascination etc.

smith *noun* a person who makes things out of metal; a blacksmith.

smithereens *plural noun* (*informal*) small fragments.

smithy *noun* a blacksmith's workshop.

smitten *past participle* of **smite**.

smock[1] *noun* an overall shaped like a very long shirt.

smock[2] *verb* stitch into close gathers with embroidery. **smocking** *noun*

smog *noun* a mixture of smoke and fog. [from *smoke* + *fog*]

smoke[1] *noun* **1** the mixture of gas and solid particles given off by a burning substance. **2** a period of smoking tobacco, *He wanted a smoke*. **smoky** *adjective*

smoke[2] *verb* (**smoked**, **smoking**) **1** give out smoke. **2** have a lighted cigarette, cigar, or pipe between your lips and draw its smoke into your mouth; do this as a habit. **3** preserve meat or fish by treating it with smoke, *smoked salmon*. **smoker** *noun*

smokeless *adjective* without smoke.

smokescreen *noun* **1** a mass of smoke used to hide the movement of troops. **2** something that conceals what is happening.

smoko *noun* (*Australian*) a break from work for a cup of tea and a smoke.

smoodge *verb* **1** caress, fondle. **2** behave ingratiatingly, toady.

smooth[1] *adjective* **1** having a surface without any lumps, wrinkles, roughness, etc. **2** moving without bumps or jolts etc. **3** not harsh, *a smooth flavour*. **4** pleasantly polite but perhaps insincere. **smoothly** *adverb*, **smoothness** *noun*

smooth[2] *verb* make a thing smooth.

smote *past tense* of **smite**.

smother *verb* **1** suffocate. **2** put out a fire by covering it. **3** cover thickly, *The buns were smothered in sugar*. **4** restrain; conceal, *She smothered a smile*.

smoulder *verb* **1** burn slowly without a flame. **2** continue to exist inwardly, *Their anger smouldered*.

smudge[1] *noun* a dirty mark made by rubbing something. **smudgy** *adjective*

smudge[2] *verb* (**smudged**, **smudging**) make a smudge on something; become smudged.

smug *adjective* self-satisfied. **smugly** *adverb*, **smugness** *noun*

smuggle *verb* (**smuggled**, **smuggling**) bring something into a country etc. secretly or illegally. **smuggler** *noun*, **smuggling** *noun*

smut *noun* **1** a small piece of soot or dirt. **2** indecent talk or pictures etc. **smutty** *adjective*

snack *noun* **1** a small meal; food eaten between meals. **2** (*Australian slang*) an easy task.

▶▶ T H E S A U R U S ◀◀

smite *verb* SEE STRIKE[1]. **be smitten with** be besotted with, be bowled over by, be captivated by, be enchanted by, be enthralled by, be infatuated with.

smithereens *plural noun* bits, fragments, pieces.

smoke[1] *noun* **1** exhaust, fumes, smog.

smoke[2] *verb* **1** fume, smoulder.

smoko *noun* coffee break, rest, spell (*Australian*), tea break.

smooth[1] *adjective* **1** (*a smooth surface*) even, flat, flush, level, unbroken; (*smooth hair*) glossy, shiny, silky, sleek, soft, velvety; (*a smooth batter*) creamy, flowing, runny; (*smooth seas*) calm, even, flat, peaceful, still, unruffled. **2** flowing, orderly, steady, well-regulated. **3** dulcet, mellow, pleasant, soothing, sweet. **4** facile, glib, persuasive, plausible, slick, smarmy (*informal*), suave, unctuous. **smoothly** *adverb* easily, straightforwardly, well, without a hitch.

smooth[2] *verb* even, flatten, iron, level, plane, press, sand, sandpaper.

smother *verb* **1** asphyxiate, choke, stifle, suffocate. **2** extinguish, put out, quench, snuff. **3** cover. **4** conceal, hide, hold back, repress, restrain, stifle, suppress.

smoulder *verb* **1** burn, smoke.

smudge[1] *noun* blot, blotch, mark, smear, splash, splotch, spot, stain, streak.

smudge[2] *verb* blot, smear, stain, streak.

smug *adjective* complacent, conceited, self-righteous, self-satisfied, supercilious, superior.

smuggling *noun* bootlegging, contraband, drug running, gunrunning.

snack *noun* **1** playlunch, recess, refreshments. **2** bludge (*Australian informal*), breeze (*informal*), cinch (*informal*), doddle (*informal*), piece of cake (*informal*), pushover (*informal*).

▶▶ D I C T I O N A R Y ◀◀

snag *noun* **1** a difficulty. **2** a sharp projection. **3** a tear in material that has been caught on something sharp.

snail *noun* a small animal with a soft body and a shell.
snail's pace a very slow pace.

snake *noun* a reptile with a long narrow body and no legs.

snaky *adjective* (*Australian informal*) irritable, angry.

snap¹ *verb* (**snapped, snapping**) **1** break suddenly or with a sharp sound. **2** bite suddenly or quickly. **3** say something quickly and angrily. **4** take something or move quickly. **5** take a snapshot of something.

snap² *noun* **1** the action or sound of snapping. **2** a snapshot. **3** Snap a card game in which players shout 'Snap!' when they see two similar cards.

snap³ *adjective* sudden, *a snap decision*.

snapdragon *noun* a plant with flowers that have a mouth-like opening.

snappy *adjective* **1** snapping at people. **2** quick; lively. **snappily** *adverb*

snapshot *noun* an informal photograph.

snare¹ *noun* a trap for catching birds or animals.

snare² *verb* (**snared, snaring**) catch in a snare.

snarl¹ *verb* **1** growl angrily. **2** speak in a bad-tempered way. **snarl** *noun*

snarl² *verb* make or become tangled or jammed, *Traffic was snarled up*. **snarl** *noun*

snatch *verb* seize; take quickly.

sneak¹ *verb* **1** move quietly and secretly. **2** (*informal*) take secretly, *He sneaked a biscuit from the tin*. **3** (*informal*) tell tales.

sneak² *noun* (*informal*) a tell-tale. **sneaky** *adjective*, **sneakily** *adverb*

sneer *verb* speak or behave in a scornful way. **sneer** *noun*

sneeze *verb* (**sneezed, sneezing**) send out air suddenly and uncontrollably through the nose and mouth in order to get rid of something irritating the nostrils. **sneeze** *noun*
not to be sneezed at (*informal*) worth having.

sniff *verb* **1** make a sound by drawing in air through the nose. **2** smell something. **sniff** *noun*, **sniffer** *noun*

sniffle *verb* (**sniffled, sniffling**) sniff slightly; keep on sniffing. **sniffle** *noun*

snig *verb* drag (a log) by one end using a rope or **snigging chain**.

snigger *verb* giggle slyly. **snigger** *noun*

snip *verb* (**snipped, snipping**) cut with scissors or shears in small quick cuts. **snip** *noun*

▶▶ T H E S A U R U S ◀◀

snag *noun* **1** catch, difficulty, hitch, impediment, obstacle, obstruction, problem, stumbling block. **3** hole, ladder, rip, run, tear.

snake *noun* serpent.

snaky *adjective* angry, annoyed, bad-tempered, crabby, irritable, shirty (*informal*).

snap¹ *verb* **1** break, crack, fracture, give way, split. **2** bite, nip. **3** bark, growl, snarl. **4** (*snap up*) accept, grab, nab (*informal*), seize, snatch, take. **5** photograph, shoot.

snap² *noun* **1** click, crack, crackle, fracture, pop. **2** photo, photograph, picture, snapshot.

snap³ *adjective* hasty, precipitate, quick, sudden.

snappy *adjective* **1** crabby, cross, crotchety, grumpy, irascible, irritable, short-tempered, testy, tetchy. **2** brisk, energetic, fast, lively, vigorous, zippy.

snare¹ *noun* gin, net, noose, trap.

snare² *verb* capture, catch, ensnare, entrap, trap.

snarl¹ *verb* **1** bare your teeth, growl.

snarl² *verb* entangle, entwine, knot, tangle, twist.

snarl *noun* blockage, hold-up, jam, obstruction, tangle.

snatch *verb* grab, nab (*informal*), pluck, seize, snitch (*slang*), steal, swipe (*informal*), take.

sneak¹ *verb* **1** creep, slink, slip, steal, tiptoe. **2** smuggle, snitch (*informal*), steal. **3** betray, dob (*Australian informal*), grass (*slang*), inform, rat (*informal*), report, shop (*slang*), split (*slang*), tell, tell tales.

sneak² *noun* dobber (*Australian informal*), grass (*slang*), informer, pimp (*Australian slang*), tale-bearer, tell-tale.

sneaky *adjective* crafty, cunning, deceitful, devious, furtive, secretive, shifty, slippery, sly, stealthy, treacherous, underhand, wily.

sneer *verb* (*sneer at*) deride, disdain, gibe at, jeer at, laugh at, mock, ridicule, scoff at, scorn, snigger at.

sniff *verb* **1** sniffle, snivel, snuffle. **2** nose, smell.

sniffle *verb & noun* sniff, snivel, snuffle.

snigger *verb & noun* chuckle, giggle, simper, snicker, titter.

snip *verb* clip, crop, cut, lop, prune, trim.

▶▶ D I C T I O N A R Y ◀◀

snipe *verb* (**sniped, sniping**) **1** shoot at people from a hiding-place. **2** make a sly critical attack. **sniper** *noun*

snippet *noun* a small piece of news, information, etc. [from *snip*]

snivel *verb* (**snivelled, snivelling**) cry or complain in a whining way.

snob *noun* a person who despises those who have not got wealth, power, or particular tastes or interests. **snobbery** *noun*, **snobbish** *adjective*

snooker *noun* a game played with cues and 21 balls on a special cloth-covered table.

snoop *verb* (*informal*) pry. **snooper** *noun*

snooze *noun* a nap. **snooze** *verb*

snore *verb* (**snored, snoring**) breathe very noisily while sleeping. **snore** *noun*

snorkel *noun* a tube through which a person swimming under water can take in air. **snorkelling** *noun*

snort *verb* make a rough sound by breathing forcefully through the nose. **snort** *noun*

snout *noun* an animal's projecting nose, or nose and jaws.

snow¹ *noun* frozen drops of water that fall from the sky in small white flakes. **snowy** *adjective*

snow² *verb* send down snow.
be snowed under be overwhelmed with a mass of letters or work etc.

snowdrop *noun* a small white flower that blooms in early spring.

snowman *noun* (*plural* **snowmen**) a figure made of snow.

snow-plough *noun* a vehicle or device for clearing a road or railway track etc. by pushing snow aside.

snow-white *adjective* pure white.

snub *verb* treat someone in a scornful or unfriendly way. **snub** *noun*

snub-nosed *adjective* having a short thick nose.

snuff¹ *noun* powdered tobacco for taking into the nose by sniffing.

snuff² *verb* put out a candle by covering or pinching the flame. **snuffer** *noun*

snuffle *verb* (**snuffled, snuffling**) sniff in a noisy way. **snuffle** *noun*

snug *adjective* (**snugger, snuggest**) cosy. **snugly** *adverb*, **snugness** *noun*

snuggle *verb* (**snuggled. snuggling**) press closely and comfortably; nestle.

so¹ *adverb* **1** in this way; to such an extent, *Why are you so cross?* **2** very, *Cricket is so boring.* **3** also, *I was wrong but so were you.*
or so or about that number.
so far up to now.
so long! (*informal*) goodbye.
so what? (*informal*) that is not important.

so² *conjunction* for that reason, *They threw me out, so I came here.*

soak *verb* make a person or thing very wet. **soak** *noun*
soak up take in a liquid in the way that a sponge does.

so-and-so *noun* (*plural* **so-and-so's**) a person or thing that need not be named.

soap¹ *noun* a substance used with water for washing and cleaning things. **soapy** *adjective*

soap² *verb* put soap on something.

soar *verb* **1** rise high in the air. **2** rise very high, *Prices were soaring.*

sob *verb* (**sobbed, sobbing**) make a gasping sound when crying. **sob** *noun*

▶▶ T H E S A U R U S ◀◀

snipe *verb* **1** fire, shoot.

snippet *noun* bit, extract, fragment, part, snatch.

snivel *verb* blubber, cry, sob, weep, whimper, whine; see also SNIFFLE.

snobbish *adjective* condescending, disdainful, haughty, patronising, pompous, pretentious, snooty (*informal*), stuck-up (*informal*), supercilious, superior, toffee-nosed (*informal*).

snoop *verb* nose about, poke your nose in, pry, spy, stickybeak (*Australian informal*).

snooze *noun* catnap, doze, forty winks, kip (*slang*), nap, rest, siesta, sleep.
snooze *verb* catnap, doze, kip (*slang*), nap, rest, sleep.

snub *verb* cold-shoulder, give someone the brush-off, humiliate, ignore, insult, rebuff, reject, scorn.

snuffle *verb & noun* sniff, sniffle, snivel.

snug *adjective* comfortable, comfy (*informal*), cosy, secure, warm.

snuggle *verb* cuddle, curl up, huddle, nestle.

soak *verb* drench, immerse, saturate, souse, steep, submerge, wet.
soak through penetrate, permeate, seep through.
soak up absorb, sop up, take up.

soar *verb* **1** ascend, fly, rise. **2** climb, escalate, increase, mount, rise, rocket.

sob *verb* bawl, blubber, cry, snivel, wail, weep.

▶▶▶ D I C T I O N A R Y ◀◀◀

sober[1] *adjective* **1** not intoxicated. **2** serious and calm. **3** (of colour) not bright. **soberly** *adverb*, **sobriety** (*say* so-**bry**-it-ee) *noun*

sober[2] *verb* make or become sober.

so-called *adjective* named in what may be the wrong way, *This so-called gentleman slammed the door.*

soccer *noun* a kind of football game played by sides of eleven with a round ball.

Socceroos the Australian international soccer team.

sociable *adjective* liking to be with other people; friendly. **sociably** *adverb*, **sociability** *noun*

social *adjective* **1** living in a community, not alone, *Bees are social insects.* **2** of life in a community, *social science.* **3** concerned with people's welfare, *social worker.* **4** helping people to meet each other, *a social club.* **5** sociable. **socially** *adverb*

social security money and other assistance provided by the government for those in need through being ill, disabled, unemployed, etc.

social services welfare services provided by the government, including schools, hospitals, and pensions. [from Latin *socius* = companion]

socialism *noun* a political system where wealth is shared equally between people, and the main industries and trade etc. are controlled by the government. (Compare *capitalism*.)

socialist *noun* a person who believes in socialism.

society *noun* (*plural* **societies**) **1** a community; people living together in a group or nation. **2** a group of people organised for a particular purpose, *the school dramatic society*. **3** company; companionship, *We enjoy the society of our friends*. [same origin as *social*]

sociology (*say* soh-see-**ol**-o-jee) *noun* the study of human society and social behaviour. **sociological** *adjective*, **sociologist** *noun* [from *socio-* = of society, + *-logy*]

sock[1] *noun* a short stocking reaching only to the ankle or below the knee.

sock[2] *verb* (*slang*) hit hard; punch, *He socked me on the jaw*. **sock** *noun*

socket *noun* **1** a hollow into which something fits, *a tooth-socket*. **2** a device into which an electric plug or bulb is put to make a connection.

sod *noun* a piece of turf.

soda *noun* **1** a compound of sodium used in washing, cooking, etc. **2** soda-water.

soda-water *noun* water made fizzy with carbon dioxide, used in drinks.

sodden *adjective* made very wet.

sodium *noun* a soft white metal.

sofa *noun* a kind of settee.

soft *adjective* **1** not hard or firm; easily pressed. **2** smooth, not rough or stiff. **3** gentle; not loud. **4** (of colours) not harsh or bright. **5** lenient; sympathetic. **6** (*informal*) easy, *a soft job*. **softly** *adverb*, **softness** *noun*

soft drink a drink that is not alcoholic.

softball *noun* a modified form of baseball.

soften *verb* make or become soft or softer. **softener** *noun*

▶▶▶ T H E S A U R U S ◀◀◀

sober[1] *adjective* **1** abstemious, abstinent, clear-headed, lucid, on the wagon (*informal*), teetotal, temperate. **2** calm, earnest, grave, level-headed, restrained, sedate, self-controlled, sensible, serious, solemn, staid. **3** drab, dreary, dull, inconspicuous, sombre, subdued.

sociable *adjective* affable, communicative, companionable, convivial, extroverted, friendly, gregarious, outgoing, social.

social *adjective* **1** gregarious, interdependent. **2** community, public. **5** see SOCIABLE.

society *noun* **1** civilisation, community, culture, humanity, mankind, nation, people, the public. **2** association, body, club, group, guild, organisation, union. **3** companionship, company, fellowship, presence.

socket *noun* **1** hole, hollow.

sodden *adjective* drenched, saturated, soaked, soggy, sopping, waterlogged, wet.

sofa *noun* couch, settee.

soft *adjective* **1** flabby, flaccid, flexible, floppy, limp, malleable, pliable, spongy, springy, squashy, supple. **2** fleecy, satiny, silky, sleek, smooth, velvety. **3** faint, gentle, hushed, inaudible, low, mellow, muted, quiet, subdued. **4** delicate, light, pale, pastel, restful, subdued. **5** easygoing, indulgent, lax, lenient, merciful, permissive, tolerant; see also SOFT-HEARTED. **6** comfortable, cosy, cushy (*informal*), easy, undemanding.

soften *verb* buffer, cushion, dampen, deaden, lessen, lower, moderate, quieten, reduce, subdue, tone down.

▶▶▷ D I C T I O N A R Y ◁◀◀

soft-hearted *adjective* compassionate, tender.

software *noun* computer programs, tapes, etc. (Compare *hardware*.)

soggy *adjective* (**soggier, soggiest**) very wet and heavy, *soggy ground*.

soil¹ *noun* **1** the loose earth in which plants grow. **2** territory, *on native soil*.

soil² *verb* make a thing dirty.

sojourn¹ (*say* **soj**-ern) *verb* stay at a place temporarily.

sojourn² *noun* a temporary stay.

solace (*say* **sol**-as) *verb* (**solaced, solacing**) comfort someone who is unhappy or disappointed. **solace** *noun* [from Latin *solari* = to console]

solar *adjective* of or from the sun. [from Latin *sol* = sun]
solar system the sun and the planets that revolve round it.

solder *noun* a soft alloy that is melted to join pieces of metal together. **solder** *verb* [from Latin *solidare* = make firm or solid]

soldier *noun* a member of an army.

sole¹ *noun* **1** the bottom surface of a foot or shoe. **2** an edible flat-fish.

sole² *verb* (**soled, soling**) put a sole on a shoe.

sole³ *adjective* single; only, *She was the sole survivor*. **solely** *adverb*

solemn *adjective* **1** not smiling; not cheerful. **2** dignified; formal. **solemnly** *adverb*, **solemnity** *noun*

solemnise *verb* (**solemnised, solemnising**) celebrate a festival; perform a marriage ceremony. **solemnisation** *noun*

solenoid *noun* a coil of wire that becomes magnetic when an electric current is passed through it.

sol-fa *noun* a system of syllables (*doh, ray, me, fah, soh, la, te*) used to represent the notes of the musical scale.

solicit *verb* (**solicited, soliciting**) ask for; try to obtain, *solicit votes* or *solicit for votes*. **solicitation** *noun*

solicitor *noun* a lawyer who advises clients, prepares legal documents, etc.

solicitous *adjective* anxious and concerned about a person's comfort, welfare, etc. **solicitously** *adverb*, **solicitude** *noun* [from Latin *sollicitus* = worrying]

solid¹ *adjective* **1** not hollow; with no space inside. **2** keeping its shape; not liquid or gas. **3** continuous, *for two solid hours*. **4** firm or strongly made; not flimsy, *a solid foundation*. **5** showing solidarity; unanimous. **solidly** *adverb*, **solidity** *noun*

solid² *noun* **1** a solid thing; solid food. **2** a shape that has three dimensions (length, width, and height or depth).

solidarity *noun* **1** being solid. **2** unity and support for each other because of agreement in opinions, interests, etc.

solidify *verb* (**solidified, solidifying**) make or become solid.

soliloquy (*say* sol-**il**-ok-wee) *noun* (*plural* **soliloquies**) a speech in which a person speaks his or her thoughts aloud without addressing anyone. **soliloquise** *verb* [from Latin *solus* = alone, + *loqui* = speak]

▶▶▷ T H E S A U R U S ◁◀◀

soft-hearted *adjective* caring, compassionate, generous, gentle, kind, merciful, mild, soft, sympathetic, tender-hearted, understanding, warm-hearted.

soggy *adjective* drenched, moist, saturated, soaked, sodden, sopping, waterlogged, wet.

soil¹ *noun* **1** dirt, earth, ground, loam. **2** country, ground, land, territory.

soil² *verb* blacken, dirty, stain.

solace *noun* comfort, consolation, relief.

soldier *noun* commando, conscript, fighter, GI (*American*), marine, mercenary, NCO, private, regular, serviceman, servicewoman, trooper, warrior.

sole³ *adjective* exclusive, lone, only, single, solitary.

solemn *adjective* **1** earnest, glum, grave, sad, sedate, serious, sober, sombre, staid, unsmiling. **2** awesome, ceremonial, ceremonious, dignified, formal, grand, important, impressive, stately.

solicit *verb* appeal for, ask for, beg for, request, seek.

solicitous *adjective* anxious, concerned, considerate, thoughtful, troubled, worried.

solid¹ *adjective* **1** compact, dense, firm, hard, rigid, stable. **3** continuous, unbroken, uninterrupted. **4** durable, firm, robust, sound, stout, strong, sturdy, substantial. **5** unanimous, undivided, united.

solidarity *noun* **2** agreement, harmony, like-mindedness, unanimity, unity.

solidify *verb* congeal, gel, harden, jell, set.

soliloquy *noun* monologue; see also SPEECH.

▶▶▶ D I C T I O N A R Y ◀◀

solitaire *noun* **1** a game for one person. **2** a diamond or other precious stone set by itself.

solitary *adjective* **1** alone, without companions. **2** single, *a solitary example*. **3** lonely, *a solitary valley*. [from Latin *solus* = alone]

solitude *noun* being solitary.

solo *noun* (*plural* **solos**) something sung, played, danced, or done by one person. **solo** *adjective* & *adverb*, **soloist** *noun* [Italian, = alone]

solstice (*say* **sol**-stiss) *noun* either of the two times in each year when the sun is at its furthest point north or south of the equator. [from Latin *sol* = sun, + *sistere* = stand still]

soluble *adjective* **1** able to be dissolved. **2** able to be solved. **solubility** *noun* [same origin as *solve*]

solution *noun* **1** a liquid in which something is dissolved. **2** the answer to a problem or puzzle. [same origin as *solve*]

solve *verb* (**solved, solving**) find the answer to a problem or puzzle. [from Latin *solvere* = unfasten]

solvent[1] *adjective* **1** having enough money to pay all your debts. **2** able to dissolve another substance. **solvency** *noun*

solvent[2] *noun* a liquid used for dissolving something.

sombre *adjective* dark and gloomy. [from Latin *sub* = under, + *umbra* = shade]

sombrero (*say* som-**brair**-oh) *noun* (*plural* **sombreros**) a hat with a very wide brim. [from Spanish *sombra* = shade (same origin as *sombre*)]

some[1] *adjective* **1** a few; a little, *some apples*; *some sugar*. **2** an unknown person or thing, *Some fool left the door open*. **3** about, *We waited some 20 minutes*.

some[2] *pronoun* a certain number or amount that is less than the whole, *Some of them were late*.

somebody *pronoun* some person.

somehow *adverb* in some way.

someone *pronoun* somebody.

somersault *noun* a movement in which you turn head over heels before landing on your feet. **somersault** *verb* [from Latin *supra* = above, + *saltus* = a leap]

something *noun* some thing.
something like rather like, *It's something like a rabbit*; approximately, *It cost something like $10*.

sometime *adjective* former, *her sometime friend*.

sometimes *adverb* at some times but not always, *We sometimes walk to school*.

somewhat *adverb* to some extent, *He was somewhat annoyed*.

somewhere *adverb* in or to some place.

somnambulist *noun* a sleepwalker. [from Latin *somnus* = sleep, + *ambulare* = to walk]

somnolent *adjective* sleeping; sleepy. **somnolence** *noun* [from Latin *somnus* = sleep]

son *noun* a boy or man who is someone's child.

son-in-law *noun* (*plural* **sons-in-law**) a daughter's husband.

sonar *noun* a device for finding objects under water by the reflection of sound-waves. [from *so*und *n*avigation and *r*anging]

sonata *noun* a musical composition for one instrument or two, in several movements. [from Italian *sonare* = to sound]

song *noun* **1** a tune for singing. **2** singing, *He burst into song*.
a song and dance (*informal*) a great fuss.
for a song bought or sold very cheaply.

▶▶▶ T H E S A U R U S ◀◀

solitary *adjective* **1** alone, lone, single, sole, solo, unaccompanied. **2** isolated, one and only, single, sole. **3** deserted, desolate, empty, isolated, lonely, remote, secluded, unfrequented.

solo *adjective* & *adverb* alone, independent, individual, on your own, single-handed, unaccompanied.

solution *noun* **1** blend, mixture. **2** answer, explanation, key, remedy, resolution, result.

solve *verb* answer, crack, decipher, figure out, resolve, work out.

sombre *adjective* dark, dismal, drab, dreary, dull, funereal, gloomy, grave, melancholy, sad, serious, sober, solemn.

sometime *adjective* erstwhile, former, onetime.

sometimes *adverb* every so often, from time to time, now and then, occasionally, on and off.

somnolent *adjective* dopey (*informal*), drowsy, lethargic, sleepy, tired, torpid, weary.

song *noun* **1** air, anthem, aria, ballad, canticle, carol, chant, chorus, ditty, hymn, jingle, lay (*old use*), lied, lullaby, madrigal, number, psalm, serenade, shanty.

▶▶▶ D I C T I O N A R Y ◀◀

songbird *noun* a bird that sings sweetly.

songster *noun* **1** a singer. **2** a songbird.

sonic *adjective* of sound or sound-waves. [from Latin *sonus* = sound]

sonnet *noun* a kind of poem with 14 lines.

sonny *noun* (*informal*) boy, young man, *Come on, sonny!*

sonorous (*say* **sonn**-er-us) *adjective* giving a loud deep sound; resonant. [from Latin *sonor* = sound]

sook *noun* (*Australian informal*) a cry-baby, a timid child. **sooky** *adjective*

sool *verb* (*Australian informal*) urge a dog to attack, harass. **sooler** *noun*

soon *adverb* **1** in a short time from now. **2** not long after something.
as soon as willingly, *I'd just as soon stay here.*
as soon as at the moment that.
sooner or later at some time in the future.

soot *noun* the black powder left by smoke in a chimney or on a building etc. **sooty** *adjective*

soothe *verb* (**soothed, soothing**) calm; ease pain or distress. **soothingly** *adverb*

soothsayer *noun* a prophet. [from an old word *sooth* = truth, + *say*]

sop *noun* **1** a piece of bread dipped in liquid before being eaten or cooked. **2** something unimportant given to pacify or bribe a troublesome person.

sophisticated *adjective* **1** of or accustomed to fashionable life and its ways. **2** complicated, *a sophisticated machine.* **sophistication** *noun*

sophistry (*say* **sof**-ist-ree) *noun* (*plural* **sophistries**) a piece of reasoning that is clever but false or misleading. [from Greek *sophos* = wise]

soporific *adjective* causing sleep. [from Latin *sopor* = sleep, + *facere* = make]

sopping *adjective* very wet; drenched.

soppy *adjective* **1** very wet. **2** (*informal*) sentimental in a sickly way.

soprano *noun* (*plural* **sopranos**) a woman, girl, or boy with a high singing voice. [from Italian *sopra* = above]

sorcerer *noun* a wizard. **sorceress** *noun*, **sorcery** *noun*

sordid *adjective* **1** dirty; squalid. **2** dishonourable; selfish and mercenary, *sordid motives.* **sordidly** *adverb*, **sordidness** *noun*

sore[1] *adjective* **1** painful, smarting. **2** (*informal*) annoyed; offended. **3** serious; distressing, *in sore need.* **soreness** *noun*

sore[2] *noun* a sore place.

sorely *adverb* seriously; very, *I was sorely tempted to run away.*

sorrel[1] *noun* a herb with sharp-tasting leaves.

sorrel[2] *noun* a reddish-brown horse.

sorrow[1] *noun* unhappiness or regret caused by loss or disappointment. **sorrowful** *adjective*, **sorrowfully** *adverb*

▶▶▶ T H E S A U R U S ◀◀

sonorous *adjective* deep, loud, powerful, resonant, resounding, reverberant, rich.

sook *noun* baby, coward, cry-baby, sissy, softie (*informal*), wimp (*informal*), wuss (*slang*).

sool *verb* egg on, goad, incite, urge.

soon *adverb* **1** anon (*old use*), before long, by and by, presently, shortly.

soot *noun* dirt, grime.
sooty *adjective* black, blackish, charcoal, dirty, grimy.

soothe *verb* alleviate, appease, assuage, calm, ease, mitigate, mollify, pacify, palliate, placate, reduce, relieve.

sophisticated *adjective* **1** cosmopolitan, cultivated, cultured, experienced, knowledgeable, refined, urbane, worldly, worldly-wise. **2** advanced, complex, complicated, elaborate, intricate.

sopping *adjective* drenched, dripping, saturated, soaked, sodden, wet.

sorcerer *noun* enchanter, magician, warlock, wizard.

sorceress *noun* enchantress, magician, witch.

sorcery *noun* black magic, enchantment, magic, witchcraft, wizardry.

sordid *adjective* **1** dirty, filthy, foul, putrid, seamy, seedy, sleazy, squalid. **2** base, dishonourable, mean, mercenary, shabby, vile.

sore[1] *adjective* **1** aching, bruised, chafed, grazed, hurting, inflamed, injured, painful, sensitive, smarting, stinging, tender, uncomfortable. **2** aggrieved, angry, annoyed, distressed, irritated, peeved (*informal*), touchy, upset, vexed.

sore[2] *noun* abrasion, abscess, blister, boil, burn, graze, inflammation, laceration, scratch, ulcer, wound.

sorrow[1] *noun* affliction, anguish, distress, grief, hardship, heartache, misery, misfortune, regret, sadness, suffering, trial, tribulation, trouble, unhappiness, woe.
sorrowful *adjective* blue, broken-hearted, dejected, depressed, desolate, despondent, disconsolate, discontented, dismal, distressed,

▶▶ D I C T I O N A R Y ◀◀

sorrow² *verb* feel sorrow; grieve.

sorry *adjective* (**sorrier**, **sorriest**) **1** feeling regret. **2** feeling pity or sympathy. **3** wretched, *His clothes were in a sorry state.*

sort¹ *noun* **1** a group of things or people that are similar; a kind or variety. **2** (*informal*) a person, *He's quite a good sort.*
out of sorts slightly unwell or depressed.
sort of (*informal*) rather; to some extent, *I sort of expected it.*

sort² *verb* arrange things in groups according to their size, kind, etc. **sorter** *noun*
sort out disentangle; select; resolve a problem etc.; (*slang*) deal with and punish someone.

sortie *noun* **1** an attack by troops coming out of a besieged place. **2** an attacking expedition by a military aircraft. [from French *sortir* = go out]

SOS *noun* (*plural* **SOSs**) an urgent appeal for help. [the international Morse code-signal of extreme distress]

soul *noun* **1** the invisible part of a person that is believed to go on living after the body has died. **2** a person's mind and emotions etc. **3** a person, *There isn't a soul about.*

soulful *adjective* having or showing deep feeling. **soulfully** *adverb*

sound¹ *noun* **1** vibrations that travel through the air and can be detected by the ear; the sensation they produce. **2** sound reproduced in a film etc. **3** a mental impression, *We don't like the sound of his plans.*
sound barrier the resistance of the air to objects moving at nearly supersonic speed.

sound² *verb* **1** produce or cause to produce a sound. **2** give an impression when heard, *He sounds angry.* **3** test by noting the sounds heard, *A doctor sounds a patient's lungs with a stethoscope.* [from Latin *sonus* = a sound]

sound³ *verb* test the depth of water beneath a ship.
sound out try to find out what a person thinks or feels about something. [from Latin *sub* = under, + *unda* = wave]

sound⁴ *adjective* **1** in good condition; not damaged. **2** healthy; not diseased. **3** reasonable; correct, *His ideas are sound.* **4** reliable; secure, *a sound investment.* **5** thorough; deep, *a sound sleep.* **soundly** *adverb*, **soundness** *noun* [from Old English *gesund* = healthy]

sound⁵ *noun* a strait; an inlet, *Milford Sound.* [from Old English *sund* = swimming or sea]

soundtrack *noun* the sound that goes with a cinema film.

soup *noun* liquid food made from stewed bones, meat, fish, vegetables, etc.
in the soup (*slang*) in trouble.

sour¹ *adjective* **1** tasting sharp like unripe fruit. **2** stale and unpleasant, not fresh, *sour milk.* **3** bad-tempered. **sourly** *adverb*, **sourness** *noun*

▶▶ T H E S A U R U S ◀◀

doleful, downcast, gloomy, glum, heartbroken, heavy-hearted, lugubrious, melancholy, miserable, mournful, rueful, sad, sorry, unhappy, woebegone, wretched.

sorry *adjective* **1** apologetic, contrite, penitent, regretful, remorseful, repentant, rueful, sad, sorrowful. **2** compassionate, pitying, sympathetic, understanding. **3** bad, deplorable, dreadful, lamentable, miserable, pitiful, terrible, woeful, wretched.

sort¹ *noun* **1** brand, breed, category, class, form, genus, group, kind, make, species, style, type, variety.

sort² *verb* arrange, categorise, class, classify, divide, grade, group, organise, separate.
sort out 1 disentangle, organise, straighten out, tidy. **2** pick out, segregate, select, separate, sift. **3** attend to, clear up, deal with, handle, resolve, solve.

soul *noun* **1,2** psyche, spirit. **3** creature, individual, person.

soulful *adjective* emotional, expressive, inspiring, moving, passionate, profound, stirring.

sound¹ *noun* **1** noise.

sound² *verb* **1** enunciate, pronounce, speak, utter, voice. **2** appear, seem.

sound³ *verb* fathom, measure, plumb, probe, test.
sound out see QUESTION².

sound⁴ *adjective* **1** intact, solid, strong, sturdy, undamaged, well-built. **2** fit, healthy, robust, well. **3** cogent, coherent, logical, rational, reasonable, solid, well-founded. **4** reliable, safe, secure, solid. **5** continuous, deep, thorough, unbroken, uninterrupted.

soup *noun* bisque, broth, chowder, consommé.

sour¹ *adjective* **1** acid, acidic, astringent, mouth-puckering, sharp, tangy, tart, vinegary. **2** bad, curdled, fermented, off, rancid, stale. **3** bad-tempered, bitter, crabby, disagreeable, embittered, grouchy (*informal*), irritable, nasty, peevish, sullen, surly, testy, tetchy, unpleasant.

▶▶DICTIONARY◀◀

sour² *verb* make or become sour.

source *noun* **1** the place from which something comes. **2** a person or book etc. providing information.

soursob *noun* (*Australian*) a garden weed of the *Oxalis* genus.

souse *verb* (**soused, sousing**) **1** soak; drench. **2** soak fish in pickle.

south¹ *noun* **1** the direction to the right of a person who faces east. **2** the southern part of a country, city, etc.

south² *adjective* & *adverb* towards or in the south. **southerly** (*say* **su**th-er-lee) *adjective*, **southern** *adjective*, **southerner** *noun*, **southernmost** *adjective*

south-east *noun*, *adjective*, & *adverb* midway between south and east. **south-easterly** *adjective*, **south-eastern** *adjective*

southward *adjective* & *adverb* towards the south. **southwards** *adverb*

south-west *noun*, *adjective*, & *adverb* midway between south and west. **south-westerly** *adjective*, **south-western** *adjective*

souvenir (*say* soo-ven-**eer**) *noun* something that you keep to remind you of a person, place, or event. [from French *se souvenir* = remember]

sou'wester *noun* a waterproof hat.

sovereign¹ *noun* **1** a king or queen who is the ruler of a country; a monarch. **2** an old British gold coin. **sovereignty** *noun*

sovereign² *adjective* **1** supreme, *sovereign power*. **2** having sovereign power; independent, *sovereign states*. [from Latin *super* = over]

sow¹ (*rhymes with* go) *verb* (**sowed, sown** or **sowed, sowing**) put seeds into the ground so that they will grow into plants. **sower** *noun*

sow² (*rhymes with* cow) *noun* a female pig.

soya bean a kind of bean from which edible oil and flour are made.

spa *noun* a health resort where there is a spring of water containing mineral salts. [from Spa, a town in Belgium with a mineral spring]

space¹ *noun* **1** the whole area outside the earth, where the stars and planets are. **2** an area or volume, *This table takes too much space*. **3** an empty area; a gap. **4** an interval of time, *within the space of an hour*.
  space shuttle a spacecraft for repeated use to and from outer space.

space² *verb* (**spaced, spacing**) arrange things with spaces between, *Space them out*. [from Latin *spatium* = a space]

spacecraft *noun* (*plural* **spacecraft**) a vehicle for travelling in outer space.

spaceman *noun* (*plural* **spacemen**) an astronaut. **spacewoman** *noun* (*plural* **spacewomen**)

spaceship *noun* a spacecraft.

spacious *adjective* providing a lot of space; roomy. **spaciousness** *noun*

spade¹ *noun* a tool with a long handle and a wide blade for digging. [from Old English *spadu*]

spade² *noun* a playing card with black shapes like upside-down hearts on it, each with a short stem. [from Italian *spada* = sword]

spaghetti *noun* pasta made in long thin sticks. [from Italian, = little strings]

span¹ *noun* **1** the length from end to end or across something. **2** the distance from the tip of the thumb to the tip of the little finger when the hand is spread out. **3** the part between two uprights of an arch or bridge. **4** the length of a period of time.

▶▶THESAURUS◀◀

source *noun* **1** beginning, cause, derivation, head, origin, root, spring, start. **2** authority, informant.

souvenir *noun* keepsake, memento, reminder.

sovereign¹ *noun* **1** emperor, empress, king, monarch, potentate, queen, ruler, sultan.

sovereign² *adjective* **1** absolute, paramount, supreme, unlimited. **2** autonomous, independent, self-governing, self-ruling.

sow¹ *verb* broadcast, disseminate, plant, scatter, spread, strew.

space¹ *noun* **1** the heavens, outer space, the universe. **2** area, capacity, room, volume. **3** blank, break, distance, gap, hiatus, hole,

interval, opening. **4** duration, interval, period, span, stretch.
  space traveller astronaut, cosmonaut.

space² *verb* arrange, place, position, separate, spread.

spacecraft *noun* space probe, spaceship, space shuttle.

spacious *adjective* big, capacious, commodious, enormous, extensive, large, roomy, sizeable, vast.

span¹ *noun* **1** breadth, distance, extent, length, measure, reach, spread, stretch. **4** duration, interval, length, period, space, spell, stretch, term.

▶▶ D I C T I O N A R Y ◀◀

span² *verb* (**spanned, spanning**) reach across, *A bridge spans the river.*

spangle *noun* a small piece of glittering material. **spangled** *adjective*

spaniel *noun* a kind of dog with long ears and silky fur. [from French, = Spanish dog]

spank *verb* smack a person on the bottom as a punishment.

spanking *adjective* (*informal*) brisk; lively, *at a spanking pace.*

spanner *noun* a tool for gripping and turning the nut on a bolt etc.

spar¹ *noun* a strong pole used for a mast or boom etc. on a ship.

spar² *verb* (**sparred, sparring**) **1** practise boxing. **2** quarrel or argue.

spare¹ *verb* (**spared, sparing**) **1** afford to give something, *Can you spare a moment?* **2** be merciful towards someone; not hurt or harm a person or thing. **3** use or treat economically, *No expense will be spared. Spare the rod and spoil the child!*

spare² *adjective* **1** not used but kept ready in case it is needed; extra, *a spare wheel.* **2** thin; lean. **sparely** *adverb,* **spareness** *noun*
spare time time not needed for work.

sparing (*say* **spair**-ing) *adjective* economical; grudging. **sparingly** *adverb*

spark¹ *noun* **1** a tiny glowing particle. **2** a flash produced electrically.

spark² *verb* give off a spark or sparks.
spark off start something happening.

sparkle *verb* (**sparkled, sparkling**) **1** shine with tiny flashes of light. **2** show brilliant wit or liveliness.

sparkler *noun* a sparkling firework.

sparkling *adjective* (of a liquid) giving off bubbles of gas; fizzy.

spark plug a device that makes a spark to ignite the fuel in an engine.

sparrow *noun* a small brown bird.

sparse *adjective* thinly scattered; not numerous, *a sparse population.* **sparsely** *adverb,* **sparseness** *noun* [from Latin *sparsum* = scattered]

spartan *adjective* simple and without comfort or luxuries. [named after the people of Sparta in ancient Greece, famous for their hardiness]

spasm *noun* **1** a sudden involuntary movement of a muscle. **2** a sudden brief spell of activity etc.

spasmodic *adjective* in spasms, happening or done at irregular intervals. **spasmodically** *adverb*

spastic *adjective* suffering from spasms of the muscles and jerky movements, especially caused by a condition called *cerebral palsy.*

spat¹ *past tense* of **spit¹**.

spat² *noun* a short gaiter.

spate *noun* a sudden flood or rush.

spathe (*rhymes with* bathe) *noun* a large petal-like part of a flower, round a central spike.

spatial *adjective* of or in space. [same origin as *space*]

spatter *verb* scatter in small drops; splash. **spatter** *noun*

▶▶ T H E S A U R U S ◀◀

span² *verb* bridge, cross, extend across, straddle, stretch across, traverse.

spank *verb* hit, slap, smack.

spar² *verb* **1** box, fight. **2** argue, be at loggerheads, bicker, fight, quarrel, squabble, wrangle.

spare¹ *verb* **1** afford, give, grant, part with. **2** protect from, relieve of, save, shield from.

spare² *adjective* **1** additional, available, extra, free, in reserve, leftover, surplus, unoccupied. **2** lanky, lean, skinny, slim, thin, weedy, wiry.

sparing *adjective* careful, economical, frugal, miserly, niggardly, parsimonious, penny-pinching, stingy, thrifty.

spark¹ *noun* flash, flicker, glimmer, glint, sparkle.

spark² *verb* **spark off** provoke, set off, start, stimulate, touch off, trigger off.

sparkle *verb* **1** flash, gleam, glint, glitter, scintillate, shimmer, shine, twinkle.

sparkling *adjective* aerated, bubbly, carbonated, effervescent, fizzy.

sparse *adjective* meagre, scanty, scarce, scattered, sporadic, thin.

spartan *adjective* ascetic, austere, frugal, hard, harsh, severe, simple, strict.

spasm *noun* **1** contraction, convulsion, cramp, fit, jerk, seizure, shudder, tic, twitch. **2** attack, bout, burst, fit, outburst, spell, spurt.

spasmodic *adjective* erratic, fitful, intermittent, irregular, occasional, sporadic.

spate *noun* deluge, flood, inundation, run, rush, torrent.

spatter *verb* shower, splash, splatter, spot, spray, sprinkle, stain.

spatula *noun* a tool like a knife with a broad blunt flexible blade, used for spreading things.

spawn¹ *noun* **1** the eggs of fish, frogs, toads, or shellfish. **2** the thread-like matter from which fungi grow.

spawn² *verb* **1** put out spawn; produce from spawn. **2** produce something in great quantities.

spay *verb* sterilise a female animal by removing the ovaries.

speak *verb* (**spoke, spoken, speaking**) **1** say something; talk. **2** hold a conversation. **3** give a speech. **4** talk or be able to talk in a foreign language, *Do you speak French?*
speak up speak more loudly; give your opinion.

speaker *noun* **1** a person who is speaking; someone who makes a speech. **2** a loudspeaker.
the Speaker the person who controls the debates in a parliament.

spear¹ *noun* a weapon for throwing or stabbing, with a long shaft and a pointed tip.

spear² *verb* pierce with a spear or with something pointed.

spearmint *noun* mint used in cookery and for flavouring chewing-gum.

special *adjective* **1** of a particular kind; for some purpose, not general, *special training*. **2** exceptional, *Take special care of it.*

specialise *verb* (**specialised, specialising**) give particular attention or study to one subject or thing, *She specialised in biology.* **specialisation** *noun*

specialist *noun* an expert in one subject, *a skin specialist.*

speciality *noun* (*plural* **specialities**) a special quality or product; something in which a person specialises.

specially *adverb* in a special way; for a special purpose.

species (*say* spee-shiz) *noun* (*plural* **species**) **1** a group of animals or plants that are very similar. **2** a kind or sort, *a species of sledge.* [Latin, = appearance]

specific *adjective* **1** definite; precise. **2** of or for a particular thing, *The money was given for a specific purpose.* **specifically** *adverb*
specific gravity the weight of something as compared with the same volume of water or air.

specify *verb* (**specified, specifying**) name or list things precisely, *The recipe specified cream, not milk.* **specification** *noun*

specimen *noun* **1** a sample. **2** an example, *a fine specimen of an oak-tree.*

specious (*say* spee-shus) *adjective* seeming good but lacking real merit, *specious reasoning.* [from Latin *speciosus* = attractive]

speck *noun* a small spot or particle.

speckle *noun* a small spot or mark. **speckled** *adjective*

spawn² *verb* **2** beget, bring about, engender, generate, give rise to, produce, yield.

spay *verb* de-sex, doctor, neuter, sterilise.

speak *verb* **1** articulate, communicate, declare, enunciate, express, pronounce, say, state, talk, utter, vocalise, voice. **2** chat, communicate, confer, converse, talk. **3** address, hold forth, lecture, preach, talk.
speak of allude to, discuss, mention, refer to, talk about.
speak out be outspoken, sound off (*informal*), speak up, speak your mind.

speaker *noun* **1** lecturer, orator, preacher, spokesman, spokesperson, spokeswoman, talker.

spear¹ *noun* harpoon, javelin, lance, pike, trident.

spear² *verb* harpoon, impale, lance, pierce, stab.

special *adjective* **1** certain, characteristic, distinctive, individual, particular, specific, unique. **2** exceptional, extraordinary, out-standing, rare, remarkable, singular, uncommon, unusual.

specialist *noun* authority, connoisseur, consultant, expert, master, professional.

speciality *noun* forte, line, specialty, strength, strong point, talent, thing (*informal*).

species *noun* **1** breed, class, classification, strain. **2** see SORT¹.

specific *adjective* **1** definite, exact, explicit, express, precise, unambiguous. **2** individual, particular, special, unique.

specify *verb* detail, identify, itemise, list, mention, name, spell out, state, stipulate.

specimen *noun* example, instance, model, representative, sample.

specious *adjective* deceptive, misleading, plausible.

speck *noun* bit, fleck, grain, particle, skerrick (*Australian informal*), speckle, spot, trace.

speckled *adjective* brindled, dotted, flecked, freckled, mottled, spotted.

specs *plural noun* (*informal*) spectacles.

spectacle *noun* **1** an impressive sight or display. **2** a public show. **3** a ridiculous sight.

spectacles *plural noun* a pair of lenses set in a frame, worn in front of the eyes to help the wearer to see clearly.

spectacled *adjective* [from Latin *spectare* = look at]

spectacular *adjective* impressive.

spectator *noun* a person who watches a game, show, incident, etc.

spectre *noun* a ghost. **spectral** *adjective* [same origin as *spectrum*]

spectrum *noun* (*plural* **spectra**) **1** the bands of colours seen in a rainbow. **2** a wide range of things, ideas, etc. [Latin, = image]

speculate *verb* (**speculated, speculating**) **1** form opinions without having any definite evidence. **2** make investments in the hope of making a profit but risking a loss. **speculation** *noun*, **speculator** *noun*, **speculative** *adjective* [from Latin *speculari* = spy out]

sped *past tense of* **speed²**.

speech *noun* (*plural* **speeches**) **1** the action or power of speaking. **2** words spoken; a talk to an audience.

speechless *adjective* unable to speak because of great emotion.

speed¹ *noun* **1** a measure of the time in which something moves or happens. **2** quickness; swiftness.
at speed quickly.

speed² *verb* (**sped** (in senses 3 and 4 **speeded**), **speeding**) **1** go quickly, *The train sped by.* **2** send quickly, *to speed you on your way.* **3** travel too fast. **4** make or become quicker, *This will speed things up.*

speedboat *noun* a fast motor-boat.

speedometer *noun* a device in a vehicle, showing its speed. [from *speed* + *meter*]

speedway *noun* a track for motorcycle racing.

speedwell *noun* a wild plant with small blue flowers.

speedy *adjective* (**speedier, speediest**) quick; swift. **speedily** *adverb*

speleology (*say* spel-ee-**ol**-o-jee) *noun* the exploration and study of caves. [from Greek *spelaion* = cave, + *-logy*]

spell¹ *noun* a saying or action etc. supposed to have magical power.

spell² *noun* **1** a period of time. **2** a period of a certain work or activity etc. **3** (*Australian*) a rest from work.

spectacle *noun* **1** display, scene, sight. **2** exhibition, exposition, extravaganza, pageant, show, spectacular.
spectacles *plural noun* eyeglasses, glasses, specs (*informal*).

spectacular *adjective* amazing, breathtaking, dramatic, electrifying, exciting, impressive, magnificent, marvellous, sensational, splendid, stunning, thrilling.

spectator *noun* bystander, eyewitness, looker-on, observer, onlooker, viewer, witness; (*spectators*) audience, crowd.

spectre *noun* apparition, ghost, phantom, poltergeist, spirit, spook (*informal*), vision, wraith.

spectrum *noun* **2** compass, gamut, range, span, spread.

speculate *verb* **1** conjecture, guess, hypothesise, surmise, theorise, wonder.
speculative *adjective* **1** conjectural, hypothetical, suppositional, theoretical. **2** dicey (*slang*), dodgy (*informal*), hazardous, risky, uncertain, unreliable.

speech *noun* **1** articulation, communication, diction, elocution, enunciation, language, pronunciation, speaking, talking, utterance. **2** address, discourse, harangue, homily, lecture, monologue, sermon, soliloquy, spiel (*slang*), talk, tirade.

speechless *adjective* dumb, dumbfounded, inarticulate, mute, silent, thunderstruck, tongue-tied.

speed¹ *noun* **1** pace, rate, velocity. **2** alacrity, briskness, dispatch, haste, promptness, quickness, rapidity, swiftness.

speed² *verb* **1** bolt, dash, fly, gallop, hasten, hurry, race, run, rush, scoot, scurry, shoot, streak, tear, zip, zoom. **4** (*speed up*) accelerate, expedite, fast-track (*informal*), get a move on (*informal*), hasten, hurry along, hurry up, quicken, step on it (*informal*).

speedy *adjective* expeditious, express, fast, immediate, prompt, quick, rapid, swift.

spell¹ *noun* charm, curse, hex, incantation.

spell² *noun* **1** interval, period, time, while. **2** bout, period, session, shift, stint, stretch, term, turn. **3** break, breather, pause, rest, smoko (*Australian informal*).

▶▶▷ D I C T I O N A R Y ◁◀

spell³ *verb* (**spelt, spelling**) **1** put letters in the right order to make a word or words. **2** have as a result, *Drought spells ruin for crops.* **speller** *noun*
spell out explain in detail.

spellbound *adjective* entranced as if by a magic spell.

spend *verb* (**spent, spending**) **1** use money to pay for things. **2** use up, *Don't spend too much time on it.* **3** pass time, *We spent a holiday in Bali.*

spendthrift *noun* a person who spends money extravagantly and wastefully.

sperm *noun* (*plural* **sperms** or **sperm**) the male cell that fuses with an ovum. [from Greek *sperma* = seed]

spew *verb* **1** vomit. **2** cast out in a stream, *The volcano spewed out lava.*

sphere *noun* **1** a perfectly round solid shape; the shape of a ball. **2** a field of action or interest etc., *That country is in Russia's sphere of influence.* **spherical** *adjective* [from Greek *sphaira* = ball]

spheroid *noun* a sphere-like but not perfectly spherical solid.

sphinx *noun* (*plural* **sphinxes**) a stone statue with the body of a lion and a human head, especially the huge one (almost 5,000 years old) in Egypt.

spice *noun* a substance used to flavour food, often made from dried parts of plants. **spicy** *adjective*

spick and span neat and clean.

spider *noun* **1** a small animal with eight legs that spins webs to catch insects on which it feeds. **2** (*Australian*) a soft drink with a scoop of ice-cream in it. **spidery** *adjective*

spike¹ *noun* **1** a pointed piece of metal; a sharp point. **2** a long narrow projecting part. **spiky** *adjective*

spike² *verb* (**spiked, spiking**) **1** put spikes on something. **2** pierce with a spike.
spike a person's guns spoil his or her plans.

spill¹ *verb* (**spilt** or **spilled, spilling**) **1** let something fall out of a container. **2** become spilt, *The coins came spilling out.* **spillage** *noun*

spill² *noun* **1** spilling. **2** a fall.

spill³ *noun* a thin strip of wood or rolled paper used to carry a flame, e.g. to light a pipe.

spin¹ *verb* (**spun, spinning**) **1** turn round and round quickly. **2** make raw wool or cotton into threads by pulling and twisting its fibres. **3** (of a spider or silkworm) make a web or cocoon out of threads from its body. **4** tell a story etc., *spin a yarn.*
spin out cause to last a long time.

spin² *noun* **1** a spinning movement. **2** a short excursion in a vehicle.

spinach *noun* a vegetable with dark-green leaves.

spinal *adjective* of the spine.

▶▶▷ T H E S A U R U S ◁◀

spell³ *verb* **2** mean, portend, result in, signal, signify.
spell out detail, explain, set out, specify.

spellbound *adjective* bewitched, captivated, charmed, enchanted, enraptured, enthralled, entranced, fascinated, hypnotised, mesmerised, rapt, riveted.

spend *verb* **1** blow (*slang*), consume, cough up (*slang*), fork out (*slang*), lash out, outlay, pay out, shell out (*informal*), splash out, splurge, squander, use up. **2,3** devote, fill, occupy, pass, use (up), while away.

spendthrift *noun* prodigal, profligate, squanderer, wastrel.

spew *verb* **1** barf (*slang*), be sick, chuck (*informal*), chunder (*Australian slang*), puke (*informal*), sick up (*informal*), throw up, vomit. **2** discharge, disgorge, eject, expel, spit out, spurt.

sphere *noun* **1** ball, globe, orb. **2** area, circle, domain, field, range, scope.
spherical *adjective* globular, round.

spice *noun* condiment, flavouring, herb, seasoning.
spicy *adjective* aromatic, fragrant, hot, piquant, pungent, sharp, strong.

spick and span clean, neat, orderly, shipshape, smart, tidy.

spike¹ *noun* **1** barb, point, prong, spine, stake, thorn.

spike² *verb* **2** impale, pierce, skewer, spear, stab.

spill¹ *verb* **1** knock over, overturn, slop, tip over, upset. **2** brim over, fall out, overflow, pour, run over, slop.

spin¹ *verb* **1** gyrate, pirouette, revolve, rotate, swirl, turn, twirl, twist, wheel, whirl. **4** concoct, invent, make up, narrate, relate, tell.
spin out drag out, draw out, extend, prolong, protract.

spin² *noun* **2** drive, ride, run, trip.

▶▶DICTIONARY◀◀

spindle *noun* **1** a thin rod on which thread is wound. **2** a pin or bar that turns round or on which something turns.

spindly *adjective* thin and long or tall.

spin-drier *noun* a machine in which washed clothes are spun round and round to dry them.

spindrift *noun* spray blown along the surface of the sea.

spine *noun* **1** the line of bones down the middle of the back. **2** a thorn or prickle. **3** the back part of a book where the pages are joined together.

spine-chilling *adjective* frightening.

spineless *adjective* **1** without a backbone. **2** lacking in determination or strength of character.

spinet *noun* a small harpsichord.

spinifex *noun* a coarse grass with spiny leaves found in inland Australia.

spinney *noun* (*plural* **spinneys**) a small wood; a thicket.

spinning-wheel *noun* a household device for spinning fibre into thread.

spin-off *noun* (*plural* **spin-offs**) a by-product; an extra benefit from a process.

spinster *noun* a woman who has not married. [the original meaning was 'one who spins']

spiny *adjective* full of spines; prickly.

spiral¹ *adjective* going round and round a central point and becoming gradually closer to it or further from it; twisting continually round a central line or cylinder etc. **spirally** *adverb*

spiral² *noun* a spiral line or course.

spiral³ *verb* (**spiralled, spiralling**) move in a spiral.

spire *noun* a tall pointed part on top of a church tower.

spirit¹ *noun* **1** the soul. **2** a person's mood or mind and feelings, *He was in good spirits.* **3** a ghost; a supernatural being. **4** courage; liveliness, *She answered with spirit.* **5** a kind of quality in something, *the romantic spirit of the book.* **6** a person's nature. **7** a strong distilled alcoholic drink.

spirit² *verb* carry off quickly and secretly, *They spirited her away.* [from Latin *spiritus* = breath]

spirited *adjective* brave; lively.

spiritual¹ *adjective* **1** of the human soul; not physical. **2** of the Church or religion. **spiritually** *adverb*, **spirituality** *noun*

spiritual² *noun* a religious folk-song, especially of Black people in America.

spiritualism *noun* the belief that the spirits of dead people communicate with living people. **spiritualist** *noun*

spirituous *adjective* containing a lot of alcohol; distilled, *spirituous liquors.*

spit¹ *verb* (**spat** or **spit, spitting**) **1** send out drops of liquid etc. forcibly from the mouth, *He spat at me.* **2** fall lightly, *It's spitting with rain.*

spit² *noun* saliva; spittle.

dead spit or **spitting image** an exact likeness.

▶▶THESAURUS◀◀

spindle *noun* **2** axle, pin, rod, shaft.

spindly *adjective* lanky, long, skinny, thin.

spine *noun* **1** backbone, spinal column, vertebral column. **2** barb, bristle, needle, prickle, quill, spike, thorn.

spine-chilling *adjective* blood-curdling, chilling, frightening, hair-raising, horrifying, scary, terrifying.

spineless *adjective* **2** chicken (*informal*), cowardly, fearful, gutless (*informal*), irresolute, lily-livered, pusillanimous, timid, timorous, weak.

spin-off *noun* by-product, offshoot, side benefit.

spiral² *noun* coil, corkscrew, helix, twist, whorl.

spirit¹ *noun* **1** mind, psyche, soul. **2** (*spirits*) feelings, frame of mind, humour, mood, morale, temper. **3** apparition, bogy, genie, ghost, gremlin (*informal*), phantom, poltergeist, spectre, spook (*informal*), sprite. **4** animation, courage, dash, determination, drive, endurance, energy, enthusiasm, fearlessness, grit, gusto, guts (*informal*), liveliness, mettle, passion, pluck, spunk (*informal*), verve, vigour, vivacity, will, zeal, zest. **5** atmosphere, attitude, feeling, mood. **6** character, disposition, heart, make-up, nature, temperament.

spirited *adjective* animated, ardent, bold, brave, courageous, daring, determined, energetic, fearless, feisty (*informal*), fervent, intrepid, lively, mettlesome, passionate, plucky, vigorous.

spiritual¹ *adjective* **1** emotional, inner, mental, psychic, psychological. **2** divine, ecclesiastical, religious, sacred.

spit² *noun* saliva, slag (*Australian slang*), spittle, sputum.

dead spit double, image, likeness, look-alike, ringer (*informal*), spitting image.

spit³ *noun* **1** a long thin metal spike put through meat to hold it while it is being roasted. **2** a narrow strip of land sticking out into the sea.

spite *noun* a desire to hurt or annoy somebody. **spiteful** *adjective*, **spitefully** *adverb*, **spitefulness** *noun*
in spite of not being prevented by, *We went out in spite of the rain.*

spitfire *noun* a fiery-tempered person.

spittle *noun* saliva, especially that spat out.

spittoon *noun* a receptacle for people to spit into.

splash¹ *verb* **1** make liquid fly about in drops. **2** (of liquid) be splashed. **3** wet by splashing, *The bus splashed us.*

splash² *noun* (*plural* **splashes**) **1** the action or sound of splashing. **2** a mark made by splashing. **3** a striking display or effect.

splatter *verb* splash noisily.

splay *verb* spread or slope apart.

spleen *noun* **1** an organ of the body, close to the stomach, that helps to keep the blood in good condition. **2** bad temper; spite, *He vented his spleen on us.*

splendid *adjective* **1** magnificent; full of splendour. **2** excellent. **splendidly** *adverb* [from Latin *splendidus* = shining]

splendour *noun* a brilliant display or appearance.

splice *verb* (**spliced, splicing**) **1** join pieces of rope etc. by twisting their strands together. **2** join pieces of film or wood etc. by overlapping the ends.

splint¹ *noun* a straight piece of wood or metal etc. tied to a broken arm or leg to hold it firm.

splint² *verb* hold with a splint.

splinter¹ *noun* a thin sharp piece of wood, glass, stone, etc. broken off a larger piece.

splinter² *verb* break into splinters.

split¹ *verb* (**split, splitting**) **1** break into parts. **2** divide. **3** (*slang*) reveal a secret.
split up (of a couple) separate.

split² *noun* **1** the splitting or dividing of something. **2** a place where something has split.
the splits an acrobatic position in which the legs are stretched widely in opposite directions.

splutter *verb* **1** make a quick series of spitting sounds. **2** speak quickly but not clearly. **splutter** *noun*

spit³ *noun* **2** peninsula, point, promontory.

spite *noun* animosity, bitterness, hatred, hostility, ill will, malevolence, malice, rancour, resentment, revenge, spleen, vengeance, vindictiveness.
spiteful *adjective* bitchy (*informal*), bitter, catty, malevolent, malicious, nasty, rancorous, resentful, revengeful, unkind, vengeful, venomous, vindictive.
in spite of despite, notwithstanding, regardless of.

splash¹ *verb* **1** shower, slosh (*informal*), spatter, splatter, spray.

splash² *noun* **2** blob, blotch, mark, smear, smudge, splotch, stain, streak.

spleen *noun* **2** anger, animosity, bitterness, gall, hostility, irritability, malice, rancour, spite, wrath.

splendid *adjective* **1** beautiful, brilliant, dazzling, fine, glittering, glorious, gorgeous, grand, imposing, impressive, lavish, magnificent, resplendent, rich, showy, spectacular, sumptuous, superb. **2** brilliant, excellent,

exceptional, fabulous (*informal*), fantastic (*informal*), first-rate, great, marvellous, outstanding, remarkable, stupendous, super (*informal*), superb, terrific (*informal*), wonderful.

splendour *noun* beauty, brilliance, glory, grandeur, greatness, magnificence, majesty, resplendence, richness, show, sumptuousness.

splice *verb* **1** braid, intertwine, interweave, join, plait.

splinter¹ *noun* fragment, shard, shiver, sliver.

splinter² *verb* fracture, shatter, split.

split¹ *verb* **1** break, burst, chop, cleave, come apart, crack, fracture, hew, rip, splinter, tear. **2** allocate, apportion, carve up, distribute, divide, dole out, share.
split up break up, divorce, part, separate.

split² *noun* **1** breach, division, rift, rupture, schism. **2** breach, break, cleft, crack, fissure, fracture, slit.

splutter *verb* **1** hiss, sizzle, spit, sputter. **2** mumble, stammer, stutter.

▶▶▶ D I C T I O N A R Y ◀◀

spoil¹ *verb* (**spoilt** or **spoiled**, **spoiling**) **1** damage something and make it useless or unsatisfactory. **2** make someone selfish by always letting them have what they want. **3** (of food) go bad.

spoil² *noun* (also **spoils**) plunder or other things gained by a victor, *the spoils of war.* [from Latin *spolium* = plunder]

spoilsport *noun* a person who spoils other people's enjoyment of things.

spoke¹ *noun* each of the bars or rods that go from the centre of a wheel to its rim.

spoke² *past tense* of **speak**.

spoken *past participle* of **speak**.

spokesman *noun* (*plural* **spokesmen**) a person (man or woman) who speaks for a group of people. **spokeswoman** *noun* (*plural* **spokeswomen**), **spokesperson** *noun*

spoliation *noun* pillaging.

sponge¹ *noun* **1** a sea-creature with a soft porous body. **2** the skeleton of this creature, or a piece of a similar substance, used for washing or padding things. **3** a soft lightweight cake or pudding. **spongy** *adjective*

sponge² *verb* (**sponged**, **sponging**) **1** wipe or wash something with a sponge. **2** (*informal*) live off the generosity of other people, *He sponged on his friends.* **sponger** *noun*

sponsor¹ *noun* someone who provides money or help etc. for a person or thing, or who gives money to a charity in return for something achieved by another person. **sponsorship** *noun*

sponsor² *verb* be a sponsor for a person or thing. [from Latin *sponsum* = promised]

spontaneous (*say* spon-**tay**-nee-us) *adjective* happening or done naturally; not forced or suggested by someone else. **spontaneously** *adverb*, **spontaneity** *noun* [from Latin *sponte* = of your own accord]

spoof *noun* (*informal*) a hoax; a parody.

spook *noun* (*informal*) a ghost. **spooky** *adjective*, **spookiness** *noun*

spool *noun* a rod or cylinder on which something is wound.

spoon¹ *noun* a small device with a rounded bowl on a handle, used for lifting things to the mouth or for stirring or measuring things. **spoonful** *noun* (*plural* **spoonfuls**)

spoon² *verb* take or lift something with a spoon.

spoonerism *noun* an accidental exchange of the initial letters of two words, e.g. by saying *a boiled sprat* instead of *a spoiled brat.* [named after Canon Spooner (1844–1930), who made mistakes of this kind]

spoor *noun* the track left by an animal.

sporadic *adjective* happening or found at irregular intervals; scattered. **sporadically** *adverb* [from Greek *sporas* = scattered]

spore *noun* a tiny reproductive cell of a plant such as a fungus or fern. [from Greek *spora* = seed]

sporran *noun* a pouch worn in front of a kilt.

▶▶▶ T H E S A U R U S ◀◀

spoil¹ *verb* **1** blight, botch, bungle, damage, destroy, harm, mar, mess up, ruin, undo, upset, wreck. **2** cosset, indulge, lavish, mollycoddle, overindulge, pamper. **3** decay, decompose, deteriorate, go bad, go off, perish, putrefy, rot.

spoil² *noun* booty, loot, pillage, plunder, prizes, spoils, swag (*informal*).

spoilsport *noun* damper, killjoy, nark (*Australian informal*), party-pooper (*informal*), wet blanket (*informal*), wowser (*Australian informal*).

spoken *adjective* oral, unwritten, verbal.

spokesperson *noun* delegate, mouthpiece, representative, speaker, spokesman, spokeswoman.

sponge² *verb* **1** clean, mop, wash, wipe. **2** (*sponge off, on*) bludge on (*Australian informal*), cadge from, impose on, live off, scrounge from.

sponger *noun* bludger (*Australian informal*), cadger, freeloader (*informal*), hanger-on, parasite, scrounger.

spongy *adjective* absorbent, boggy, marshy, porous, soft, springy, swampy.

sponsor¹ *noun* backer, benefactor, financier, patron, promoter, supporter.

sponsor² *verb* back, finance, fund, promote, subsidise, support.

spontaneous *adjective* ad lib, automatic, extempore, impetuous, impromptu, impulsive, instinctive, involuntary, natural, off-the-cuff, reflex, unconscious, unforced, unplanned, unprepared, unrehearsed, voluntary.

spooky *adjective* creepy, eerie, frightening, ghostly, scary, uncanny, weird.

spool *noun* bobbin, reel.

sporadic *adjective* fitful, infrequent, intermittent, irregular, isolated, occasional, random, scattered, spasmodic.

sport¹ *noun* **1** an athletic activity; a game or pastime, especially outdoors. **2** games of this kind, *Are you keen on sport?* **3** (*informal*) a person who behaves fairly and generously, *Come on, be a sport!*
sports car an open low-built fast car.
sports coat or **jacket** a man's jacket for informal wear (not part of a suit).

sport² *verb* **1** play; amuse yourself. **2** wear, *He sported a gold tie-pin.*

sporting *adjective* **1** connected with sport; interested in sport. **2** behaving fairly and generously.
a sporting chance a reasonable chance of success.

sportive *adjective* playful.

sportsground *noun* a piece of land for sports.

sportsman *noun* (*plural* **sportsmen**) a sporting man.

sportsmanship *noun* being generous in victory or defeat in sports.

sportswoman *noun* (*plural* **sportswomen**) a sporting woman.

spot¹ *noun* **1** a small round mark. **2** a pimple; a blemish. **3** a small amount, *We had a spot of trouble.* **4** a place. **5** a drop, *a few spots of rain.*
on the spot without delay or change of place; under pressure to take action, *This really puts him on the spot!*

spot² *verb* (**spotted**, **spotting**) **1** mark with spots. **2** (*informal*) notice, *We spotted her in the crowd.* **3** watch for and take note of, *trainspotting.* **spotter** *noun*

spotless *adjective* perfectly clean.

spotlight *noun* a strong light that can shine on one small area.

spotty *adjective* marked with spots.

spouse *noun* a person's husband or wife. [from Latin *sponsus* = betrothed]

spout¹ *noun* **1** a pipe or similar opening from which liquid can pour. **2** a jet of liquid.

spout² *verb* **1** come or send out as a jet of liquid. **2** (*informal*) speak for a long time.

sprain *verb* injure a joint by twisting it. **sprain** *noun*

sprat *noun* a small edible fish.

sprawl *verb* **1** sit or lie with the arms and legs spread out loosely. **2** spread out loosely or untidily. **sprawl** *noun*

spray¹ *verb* scatter tiny drops of liquid over something.

spray² *noun* **1** tiny drops of liquid sprayed. **2** a device for spraying liquid.

spray³ *noun* **1** a single shoot with its leaves and flowers. **2** a small bunch of flowers.

sport¹ *noun* **1** diversion, game, pastime, physical activity, recreation. **3** sportsman, sportswoman.

sporting *adjective* **2** considerate, decent, fair, generous, sportsmanlike.

sportsground *noun* arena, field, ground, oval, pitch, playing field, stadium.

sportsman, sportswoman *noun* contestant, participant, player, sportsperson.

spot¹ *noun* **1** blot, blotch, dot, fleck, mark, patch, smudge, speck, speckle, splash, splotch, stain. **2** birthmark, blackhead, blemish, freckle, mole, pimple, whitehead, zit (*informal*); (*spots*) rash. **4** area, district, locality, location, neighbourhood, place, position, region, setting, site, situation. **5** bead, blob, drop.
on the spot at the scene, immediately, right away, straight away, then and there.

spot² *verb* **1** dot, mark, smudge, soil, spatter, speckle, splash, splotch, spray, stain. **2** catch sight of, detect, discover, distinguish, espy, find, identify, locate, notice, pick out, recognise, see.

spotless *adjective* clean, faultless, flawless, immaculate, impeccable, perfect, unblemished, unstained, untarnished.

spotty *adjective* blotchy, brindled, dappled, dotted, flecked, freckled, mottled, pimply, speckled, splotchy, spotted.

spouse *noun* consort, husband, mate (*informal*), partner, wife.

spout¹ *noun* **1** jet, nozzle, outlet.

spout² *verb* **1** flow, gush, jet, spray, spurt, squirt, stream. **2** carry on (*informal*), declaim, go on (*informal*), hold forth, pontificate, rant, rave, sermonise.

sprain *verb* twist, wrench.

sprawl *verb* **1** flop, lie spread-eagled, loll, lounge, recline, slouch, slump, spread yourself out, stretch out.

spray¹ *verb* shower, spatter, splash, sprinkle, wet.

spray² *noun* **1** drizzle, droplets, mist, shower, vapour. **2** aerosol, atomiser, vaporiser.

spray³ *noun* **2** bouquet, bunch, corsage, nosegay, posy, sprig.

spread¹ *verb* (**spread**, **spreading**) **1** open or stretch something out to its full size, *The bird spread its wings*. **2** make something cover a surface, *We spread jam on the bread*. **3** become longer or wider, *The stain was spreading*. **4** make or become more widely known or felt or distributed etc., *We spread the news. Panic spread.*

spread² *noun* **1** the action or result of spreading. **2** a thing's breadth or extent. **3** a paste for spreading on bread. **4** (*informal*) a huge meal.

spread-eagle *verb* (**spread-eagled**, **spread-eagling**) spread out a person's body with arms and legs stretched out.

spree *noun* (*informal*) a lively outing or bout of activity.

sprig *noun* a small branch; a shoot.

sprightly *adjective* (**sprightlier**, **sprightliest**) lively; full of energy.

spring¹ *verb* (**sprang**, **sprung**, **springing**) **1** jump; move quickly or suddenly, *He sprang to his feet*. **2** originate; arise, *The trouble has sprung from carelessness*. **3** present or produce suddenly, *They sprang a surprise on us*. **4** appear suddenly.

spring² *noun* **1** a springy coil or bent piece of metal. **2** a springing movement. **3** a place where water comes up naturally from the ground. **4** the season when most plants begin to grow.

springboard *noun* a springy board from which people jump in diving and gymnastics.

springbok *noun* a South African gazelle.

spring-clean *verb* clean a house thoroughly in springtime.

springy *adjective* (**springier**, **springiest**) able to spring back easily after being bent or squeezed. **springiness** *noun*

sprinkle *verb* (**sprinkled**, **sprinkling**) make tiny drops or pieces fall on something. **sprinkler** *noun*

sprinkling *noun* a few here and there.

sprint *verb* run very fast for a short distance. **sprint** *noun*, **sprinter** *noun*

sprite *noun* an elf, fairy, or goblin.

sprocket *noun* each of the row of teeth round a wheel, fitting into links on a chain.

sprout¹ *verb* start to grow; put out shoots.

sprout² *noun* **1** a shoot of a plant. **2** a Brussels sprout.

spruce¹ *noun* a kind of fir-tree.

spruce² *adjective* neat and trim; smart.

spruce³ *verb* (**spruced**, **sprucing**) smarten, *Spruce yourself up*.

spruik (*say* sprook) *verb* (*Australian*) hold forth in public, especially to advertise a show or sideshow. **spruiker** *noun*

spread¹ *verb* **1** lay out, open out, stretch out, unfold, unfurl, unroll. **2** apply, coat, lay on, paste, plaster, smear. **3** enlarge, expand, extend, grow, increase, multiply, permeate, pervade, proliferate, sprawl, widen. **4** broadcast, circulate, diffuse, disperse, disseminate, distribute, promulgate, publicise, scatter, sprinkle, strew, transmit.

spread² *noun* **1** advance, enlargement, expansion, extension, growth, increase, proliferation. **2** breadth, compass, coverage, expanse, extent, range, reach, scope, span, stretch, sweep, width. **4** banquet, feast, meal.

spree *noun* bender (*slang*), binge (*slang*), field day, fling, orgy, outing, revel, splurge.

sprig *noun* branch, shoot, spray.

sprightly *adjective* active, agile, dynamic, energetic, hale, lively, nimble, perky, spry, vivacious.

spring¹ *verb* **1** bounce, bound, dart, hop, jump, leap, pounce, shoot out, vault. **2** arise, derive, emanate, flow, originate, proceed, stem. **4** appear, burst forth, come up, emerge, grow, shoot up, sprout.

spring back bounce back, fly back, rebound, recoil.

spring² *noun* **2** bound, hop, jump, leap, vault. **3** fountain, geyser, spa, well-spring.

springy *adjective* bouncy, elastic, resilient, spongy.
springiness *noun* bounce, elasticity, resilience, spring.

sprinkle *verb* dust, scatter, shower, spatter, splash, spray, strew.

sprinkling *noun* few, handful.

sprint *verb* dash, race, run, rush, speed, tear.

sprite *noun* elf, fairy, goblin, hobgoblin, imp, leprechaun, pixie, spirit.

sprout¹ *verb* bud, develop, germinate, grow, shoot.

spruce² *adjective* chic, dapper, neat, smart, tidy, trim, well-groomed.

spruce³ *verb* clean up, groom, neaten, smarten, tidy, titivate (*informal*).

spruiker *noun* barker, tout.

spry *adjective* (**spryer**, **spryest**) active; nimble; lively.

spud *noun* (*slang*) a potato.

spume *noun* froth; foam.

spur¹ *noun* **1** a sharp device worn on the heel of a rider's boot to urge a horse to go faster. **2** a stimulus or incentive. **3** a projecting part. **on the spur of the moment** on an impulse; without planning.

spur² *verb* (**spurred**, **spurring**) urge on; encourage.

spurious *adjective* not genuine.

spurn *verb* reject scornfully.

spurt¹ *verb* **1** gush out. **2** increase your speed suddenly.

spurt² *noun* **1** a sudden gush. **2** a sudden increase in speed or effort.

sputter *verb* splutter. **sputter** *noun*

spy¹ *noun* (*plural* **spies**) someone who works secretly to find out things about another country, person, etc.

spy² *verb* (**spied**, **spying**) **1** be a spy; keep watch secretly. **2** see; notice, *She spied a house.* **3** pry.

squabble *verb* (**squabbled**, **squabbling**) quarrel; bicker. **squabble** *noun*

squad *noun* a small group of people working or being trained together.

squadron *noun* part of an army, navy, or air force.

squalid *adjective* dirty and unpleasant. **squalidly** *adverb*, **squalor** *noun* [from Latin *squalidus* = rough, dirty]

squall¹ *noun* **1** a sudden storm or gust of wind. **2** a baby's loud cry.

squall² *verb* (of a baby) cry loudly.

squander *verb* spend money or time etc. wastefully.

square¹ *noun* **1** a flat shape with four equal sides and four right angles. **2** an area surrounded by buildings, *Chifley Square.* **3** the number produced by multiplying something by itself, *9 is the square of 3 (9 = 3 x 3).* **4** (*informal*) an old-fashioned or conventional person.

square² *adjective* **1** having the shape of a square. **2** forming a right angle, *The desk has square corners.* **3** equal; even, *The teams are all square with six points each.* **4** honest; fair, *a square deal.* **5** (*informal*) old-fashioned. **squarely** *adverb*, **squareness** *noun*
square meal a satisfying meal.
square metre the area of a surface with sides that are one metre long.
square root the number that gives a particular number if it is multiplied by itself, *3 is the square root of 9 (3 x 3 = 9).*

spry *adjective* active, agile, dynamic, energetic, hale, lively, nimble, sprightly.

spur² *verb* egg on, encourage, goad, motivate, prompt, stimulate, urge.

spurious *adjective* bogus, counterfeit, fake, false, phoney (*informal*).

spurn *verb* disdain, rebuff, refuse, reject, repudiate, scorn, turn your nose up at.

spurt¹ *verb* **1** burst, flow, gush, jet, shoot, spout, spray, squirt, stream, surge. **2** dash, race, shoot, speed, sprint, tear.

spurt² *noun* **1** burst, gush, jet, rush, spray, squirt, stream, surge.

sputter *verb* hiss, sizzle, spit, splutter.

spy¹ *noun* double agent, informer, intelligence agent, mole, secret agent, undercover agent.

spy² *verb* **1** (*spy on*) keep under surveillance, keep watch on, observe, peep on, shadow, snoop on (*informal*), tail (*informal*), watch. **2** catch sight of, discern, discover, espy, make out, notice, observe, perceive, see, spot.

spying *noun* espionage, intelligence, surveillance.

squabble *verb* argue, bicker, fight, quarrel, scrap (*informal*), wrangle.
squabble *noun* altercation, argument, barney (*informal*), dispute, fight, quarrel, row, scrap (*informal*), tiff, wrangle.

squad *noun* band, force, gang, group, team, unit.

squalid *adjective* dilapidated, dirty, filthy, rundown, seedy, shabby, sordid, wretched.

squall¹ *noun* **1** gust, storm, wind.

squander *verb* blow (*slang*), dissipate, fritter away, throw away, waste.

square¹ *noun* **4** conservative, fuddy-duddy (*informal*), old fogy, stick-in-the-mud (*informal*).

square² *adjective* **3** equal, even, level, tied. **4** above board, decent, equitable, fair, honest, just, straight. **5** conservative, conventional, old-fashioned, out of date, out of touch.

► D I C T I O N A R Y ◄

square³ *verb* (**squared, squaring**) **1** make a thing square. **2** multiply a number by itself, *5 squared is 25.* **3** match; make or be consistent, *His story doesn't square with yours.* **4** (*informal*) bribe. [from Latin *quadra* = square]

square-rigged *adjective* with the sails set across the ship, not lengthways.

squash¹ *verb* **1** press something so that it loses its shape; crush. **2** pack tightly. **3** suppress; quash.

squash² *noun* (*plural* **squashes**) **1** a crowded condition. **2** a fruit-flavoured soft drink. **3** a game played with racquets and a soft ball in a special indoor court.

squash³ *noun* (*plural* **squashes**) a kind of gourd used as a vegetable.

squat¹ *verb* (**squatted, squatting**) **1** sit on your heels; crouch. **2** use an unoccupied house for living in without permission. **squat** *noun*

squat² *adjective* short and fat.

squatter *noun* **1** someone who squats. **2** (*Australian*) a grazier.

squaw *noun* a North American Indian woman or wife.

squawk *verb* make a loud harsh cry. **squawk** *noun*

squeak *verb* make a short high-pitched cry or sound. **squeak** *noun*, **squeaky** *adjective*, **squeakily** *adverb*

squeal *verb* make a long shrill cry or sound. **squeal** *noun*

squeamish *adjective* easily disgusted or shocked. **squeamishness** *noun*

squeeze¹ *verb* (**squeezed, squeezing**) **1** press from opposite sides; press something so as to get liquid out of it. **2** force into or through a place, *We squeezed through a gap in the hedge.* **squeezer** *noun*

squeeze² *noun* **1** the action of squeezing. **2** a drop of liquid squeezed out, *Add a squeeze of lemon.* **3** a time when money is difficult to get or borrow. **4** a clasp or hug.

squelch *verb* make a sound like someone treading in thick mud. **squelch** *noun*

squib *noun* a small firework that hisses and then explodes.

squid *noun* a sea-animal with eight short tentacles and two long ones.

squiggle *noun* a short curly line.

squint *verb* **1** be cross-eyed. **2** peer; look with half-shut eyes at something. **squint** *noun*

squire *noun* (*British*) the man who owns most of the land in a country parish or district.

squirm *verb* wriggle.

squirrel *noun* a small animal with a bushy tail and red or grey fur, living in trees.

squirt *verb* send or come out in a jet of liquid.

squiz *noun* (*Australian slang*) a look.

St. *abbreviation* **1** Saint. **2** Street.

stab¹ *verb* (**stabbed, stabbing**) pierce or wound with something sharp.

stab² *noun* **1** the action of stabbing. **2** a sudden sharp pain, *She felt a stab of fear.* **3** (*informal*) an attempt, *I'll have a stab at it.*

stabilise *verb* (**stabilised, stabilising**) make or become stable. **stabilisation** *noun*, **stabiliser** *noun*

stability *noun* being stable.

► T H E S A U R U S ◄

square³ *verb* **3** agree, be consistent, correspond, fit, match, tally.

squash¹ *verb* **1** compress, crush, flatten, mangle, mash, press, pulp, smash, squeeze. **2** cram, crowd, crush, jam, pack, squeeze. **3** crush, put down, quash, quell, suppress.

squat¹ *verb* **1** crouch.

squat² *adjective* dumpy, nuggety (*Australian*), short, stocky, stubby, thickset.

squatter *noun* **2** grazier, pastoralist, sheep farmer.

squawk *verb & noun* cry, scream, screech.

squeak *verb & noun* cheep, chirp, cry, peep, screech, shriek, squeal, yelp.

squeal *verb & noun* cry, scream, screech, shriek, wail, yell.

squeamish *adjective* easily nauseated, queasy.

squeeze¹ *verb* **1** compact, compress, crush, press, squash, wring. **2** cram, crowd, force, jam, pack, pile, push, squash.

squeeze² *noun* **4** clasp, cuddle, embrace, hug.

squirm *verb* fidget, twist, wiggle, wriggle, writhe.

squirt *verb* gush, shoot, shower, spatter, splash, splatter, spray, sprinkle, spurt, syringe.

stab¹ *verb* jab, knife, lance, pierce, spear, spike, wound.

stab² *noun* **2** jab, pang, prick, tweak, twinge. **3** attempt, bash (*informal*), crack (*informal*), go (*Australian informal*), shot (*informal*), try.

▶▶ D I C T I O N A R Y ◀◀

stable¹ *adjective* steady; firmly fixed. **stably** *adverb* [from Latin *stabilis* = standing firm]

stable² *noun* a building where horses are kept.

stable³ *verb* (**stabled**, **stabling**) put or keep in a stable.

staccato *adverb* & *adjective* (in music) played with each note short and separate. [Italian, = detached]

stack¹ *noun* **1** a neat pile. **2** a haystack. **3** (*informal*) a large amount, *a stack of work.* **4** a single tall chimney; a group of chimneys.

stack² *verb* pile things up.

stadium *noun* a sportsground surrounded by seats for spectators.

staff¹ *noun* **1** the people who work in an office, shop, etc. **2** the teachers in a school or college. **3** a stick or pole used as a weapon or support or as a symbol of authority. **4** (*plural* **staves**) a set of five horizontal lines on which music is written.

staff² *verb* provide with a staff of people.

stag *noun* a male deer.

stage¹ *noun* **1** a platform for performances in a theatre or hall. **2** a point or part of a process, journey, etc., *the final stage.*

stage² *verb* (**staged**, **staging**) **1** present a performance on a stage. **2** organise, *We decided to stage a protest.*

stagecoach *noun* a horse-drawn coach that formerly ran regularly from one point to another along the same route.

stagger *verb* **1** walk unsteadily. **2** shock deeply; amaze, *We were staggered at the price.* **3** arrange things so that they do not coincide, *Please stagger your holidays so that there is always someone here.* **stagger** *noun*

stagnant *adjective* not flowing or not changing, *a pool of stagnant water.*

stagnate *verb* (**stagnated**, **stagnating**) **1** be stagnant. **2** be dull through lack of activity or variety. **stagnation** *noun* [from Latin *stagnum* = a pool]

staid *adjective* steady and serious in manner; sedate.

stain¹ *noun* **1** a dirty mark on something. **2** a blemish on someone's character or past record. **3** a liquid used for staining things.

stain² *verb* **1** make a stain on something. **2** colour with a liquid that sinks into the surface.

stainless *adjective* without a stain. **stainless steel** steel that does not rust easily.

stair *noun* a fixed step in a series that leads from one level or floor to another in a building.

staircase *noun* a flight of stairs.

▶▶ T H E S A U R U S ◀◀

stable¹ *adjective* anchored, balanced, constant, enduring, established, firm, fixed, lasting, permanent, reliable, secure, solid, sound, steady, strong, sturdy, unchanged.

stable² *noun* stall.

stack¹ *noun* **1** bundle, heap, load, mound, mountain, pile. **2** cock, haycock, hayrick, haystack, rick. **3** heap, load, lot (*informal*), mass, mountain, pile (*informal*), plenty, ton (*informal*).

stack² *verb* collect, heap, pile.

stadium *noun* amphitheatre, arena, ground, sportsground.

staff¹ *noun* **1** crew, employees, manpower, personnel, team, workers, workforce. **3** baton, cane, crook, crosier, crutch, mace, pole, rod, sceptre, stick, truncheon.

staff² *verb* man, run, service.

stage¹ *noun* **1** dais, platform, podium, rostrum. **2** juncture, leg, part, period, phase, point, section.

stage² *verb* **1** mount, perform, present, produce, put on. **2** arrange, carry out, hold, organise, plan.

stagger *verb* **1** falter, lurch, reel, stumble, teeter, totter. **2** astonish, astound, confound, dumbfound, flabbergast, nonplus, overwhelm, shake, shock, startle, stun, surprise, take aback.

stagnant *adjective* motionless, sluggish, stale, standing, static, still.

stagnate *verb* **2** become stale, idle, languish, mark time, vegetate.

staid *adjective* dignified, earnest, grave, restrained, sedate, serious, settled, sober, steady.

stain¹ *noun* **1** blotch, discoloration, mark, smudge, speck, splotch, spot. **2** blemish, blot, flaw, stigma, taint, tarnish. **3** dye, tint.

stain² *verb* **1** discolour, mark, smear, smudge, soil, spot.

▶▶▶ DICTIONARY ◀◀◀

stake¹ *noun* **1** a thick pointed stick to be driven into the ground. **2** the post to which people used to be tied for execution by being burnt alive. **3** an amount of money bet on something. **4** an investment that gives a person a share or interest in an enterprise.
at stake being risked.

stake² *verb* (**staked, staking**) **1** fasten, support, or mark out with stakes. **2** bet or risk money etc. on an event.
stake a claim claim or obtain a right to something.

stalactite *noun* a stony spike hanging like an icicle from the roof of a cave. [from Greek *stalaktos* = dripping]

stalagmite *noun* a stony spike standing like a pillar on the floor of a cave. [from Greek *stalagma* = a drop]

stale *adjective* not fresh. **staleness** *noun*

stalemate *noun* **1** a drawn position in chess when a player cannot make a move without putting his or her king in check. **2** a deadlock; a draw in a contest that was held to decide something.

stalk¹ *noun* a stem of a plant etc.

stalk² *verb* **1** track or hunt stealthily. **2** walk in a stiff or dignified way.

stall¹ *noun* **1** a stand from which things are sold. **2** a place for one animal in a stable or shed. **3** a seat in the part of a theatre (*the stalls*) nearest the stage.

stall² *verb* **1** stop suddenly, *The car engine stalled*. **2** put an animal into a stall.

stall³ *verb* delay things deliberately so as to avoid having to take action. [from *stall* = pickpocket's helper]

stallion *noun* a male horse.

stalwart *adjective* sturdy; strong and faithful, *my stalwart supporters*.

stamen *noun* the part of a flower bearing pollen.

stamina *noun* strength and ability to endure things for a long time.

stammer *verb* keep repeating the same syllables when you speak. **stammer** *noun*

stamp¹ *noun* **1** a postage stamp; a small piece of gummed paper with a special design on it. **2** a small device for pressing words or marks on something; the words or marks made by this. **3** a distinctive characteristic, *His story bears the stamp of truth.*

stamp² *verb* **1** bang a foot heavily on the ground; crush or flatten in this way. **2** walk with loud heavy steps. **3** stick a stamp on something. **4** press a mark or design etc. on something.
stamp out put out a fire etc. by stamping; stop something, *stamp out cruelty*.

stampede *noun* a sudden rush by animals or people. **stampede** *verb*

stance *noun* **1** the way a person or animal stands. **2** an attitude.

stanchion *noun* an upright bar or post forming a support.

▶▶▶ THESAURUS ◀◀◀

stake¹ *noun* **1** picket, pole, post, spike, stick. **3** bet, wager. **4** concern, interest, investment, share.

stake² *verb* **1** brace, prop, support. **2** bet, chance, gamble, hazard, risk, wager.

stale *adjective* (*stale bread*) dry, hard, mouldy, old; (*stale air*) close, fusty, musty, stuffy.

stalemate *noun* **2** deadlock, impasse, stand-off, standstill.

stalk¹ *noun* shoot, stem.

stalk² *verb* **1** follow, hound, hunt, prowl after, pursue, shadow, tail (*informal*), track, trail. **2** march, stride, strut.

stall¹ *noun* **1** booth, counter, kiosk, stand, table. **2** compartment, cubicle, enclosure, pen.

stall³ *verb* block, delay, hedge, obstruct, play for time, procrastinate, put off, stave off, temporise.

stalwart *adjective* dependable, faithful, firm, loyal, reliable, staunch, steadfast, strong.

stamina *noun* endurance, energy, fortitude, perseverance, staying power, strength, vigour.

stammer *verb* falter, splutter, stumble, stutter.

stamp¹ *noun* **2** brand, hallmark, imprint, logo, mark, seal, trade mark. **3** characteristic, hallmark, mark.
stamp-collecting *noun* philately.

stamp² *verb* **1** crush, flatten, squash, step, stomp, tramp, trample, tread. **4** brand, emboss, engrave, imprint, inscribe, print.
stamp out abolish, eliminate, eradicate, put an end to, stop.

stampede *noun* charge, dash, race, run, rush.
stampede *verb* bolt, charge, dash, race, rush.

stance *noun* **1** bearing, carriage, deportment, position, posture. **2** attitude, line, opinion, position, stand, standpoint, viewpoint.

▶▶ D I C T I O N A R Y ◀◀

stand¹ *verb* (**stood**, **standing**) **1** be on your feet without moving, *We were standing at the back of the hall.* **2** set or be upright; place, *We stood the vase on the table.* **3** stay the same, *My offer still stands.* **4** be a candidate for election, *She stood for Parliament.* **5** tolerate; endure, *I can't stand that noise.* **6** provide and pay for, *I'll stand you a drink.*
it stands to reason it is reasonable or obvious.
stand by be ready for action.
stand down withdraw from a position etc.; suspend an employee.
stand for represent; tolerate.
stand in for act in place of another. **stand-in** *noun*
stand out stick out; be noticeable.
stand up for support; defend.
stand up to resist bravely; stay in good condition in hard use.

stand² *noun* **1** something made for putting things on, *a music-stand.* **2** a stall where things are sold or displayed. **3** a grandstand. **4** a stationary condition or position, *He took his stand near the door.* **5** resistance to attack, *We made a stand.*

standard¹ *noun* **1** how good something is, *a high standard of work.* **2** a thing used to measure or judge something else. **3** a special flag, *the royal standard.* **4** an upright support.

standard lamp a lamp on an upright pole that stands on the floor.
standard² *adjective* **1** of the usual or average quality or kind. **2** regarded as the best and widely used, *the standard book on spiders.*
standardise *verb* (**standardised**, **standardising**) make things be of a standard size, quality, etc. **standardisation** *noun*
standover *adjective* (*Australian*) threatening, intimidating, *standover tactics.*
standpoint *noun* a point of view.
standstill *noun* a stop; an end to movement or activity.
stanza *noun* a verse of poetry.
staple¹ *noun* **1** a small piece of metal pushed through papers and clenched to fasten them together. **2** a U-shaped nail. **staple** *verb*, **stapler** *noun*
staple² *adjective* main; usual, *Rice is their staple food.* **staple** *noun*
star¹ *noun* **1** a heavenly body that is seen as a speck of light in the sky at night. **2** a shape with rays from it; an asterisk; a mark of this shape showing that something is good, *a five-star hotel.* **3** a famous performer; one of the chief performers in a play or show etc.
star² *verb* (**starred**, **starring**) **1** perform or present as a star in a show etc. **2** mark with an asterisk or star symbol.

▶▶ T H E S A U R U S ◀◀

stand¹ *verb* **1** get up, rise. **2** deposit, place, position, put, set. **3** continue, remain, stay. **5** abide, bear, cope with, endure, face, handle, put up with, stomach, suffer, take, tolerate, undergo, weather, withstand. **6** pay for, provide, shout (*Australian informal*), treat to.
stand down 1 resign, step down, withdraw. **2** lay off, stand off, suspend.
stand for 1 be short for, denote, indicate, mean, represent, signify, symbolise. **2** brook, endure, put up with, suffer, take, tolerate.
stand in for cover for, deputise for, fill in for, relieve, replace, substitute for, take the place of.
stand-in *noun* deputy, locum, relief, replacement, reserve, stand-by, substitute, surrogate.
stand out be conspicuous, be noticeable, be prominent, stick out.
stand up for defend, speak up for, stand by, stick up for, support.
stand up to 1 challenge, confront, defy, face up to, oppose, resist. **2** endure, last through, resist, survive, withstand.
stand² *noun* **1** base, pedestal, rack, shelf, support, tripod. **2** booth, counter, kiosk, stall. **4** place, position.

standard¹ *noun* **1** grade, level, quality. **2** benchmark, criterion, guideline, requirement, specification, touchstone, yardstick. **3** banner, ensign, flag, pennant.
standard² *adjective* **1** common, conventional, customary, normal, ordinary, orthodox, regular, routine, set, stock, usual. **2** accepted, approved, authoritative, classic, definitive, established, official, prescribed, recognised.
standover *adjective* bullying, intimidating, threatening.
standpoint *noun* angle, attitude, opinion, point of view, position, stance, stand, viewpoint.
standstill *noun* halt, impasse, stop.
staple² *adjective* basic, chief, essential, main, primary, principal, standard.
star¹ *noun* **1** celestial body, heavenly body; (*group of stars*) constellation, galaxy. **2** asterisk, pentagram. **3** celebrity, idol, megastar (*informal*), superstar.
star² *verb* **1** act, appear, feature, perform, play.

▶▶ D I C T I O N A R Y ◀◀

starboard *noun* the right-hand side of a ship or aircraft when you are facing forward. (Compare *port¹*.)

starch¹ *noun* (*plural* **starches**) **1** a white carbohydrate in bread, potatoes, etc. **2** this or a similar substance used to stiffen clothes. **starchy** *adjective*

starch² *verb* stiffen with starch.

stardom *noun* being a star performer.

stare *verb* (**stared, staring**) look at something fixedly. **stare** *noun*

starfish *noun* (*plural* **starfish** or **starfishes**) a sea-animal shaped like a star with five or more points.

stark¹ *adjective* **1** complete; unmistakable, *stark nonsense*. **2** desolate; without cheerfulness, *the stark lunar landscape*. **starkly** *adverb*, **starkness** *noun*

stark² *adverb* completely, *stark naked*.

starlight *noun* light from the stars.

starling *noun* a noisy black bird with speckled feathers.

starry *adjective* full of stars.

start¹ *verb* **1** begin or cause to begin. **2** establish or found, *start a company*. **3** begin a journey. **4** make a sudden movement of pain or surprise. **starter** *noun*

start² *noun* **1** the beginning; the place where a race starts. **2** an advantage that someone starts with, *We gave the younger ones ten minutes' start*. **3** a sudden movement.

startle *verb* (**startled, startling**) surprise or alarm someone.

starve *verb* (**starved, starving**) suffer or die from lack of food; cause to do this. **starvation** *noun*

state¹ *noun* **1** the quality of a person's or thing's characteristics or circumstances; condition. **2** a grand style, *She arrived in state*. **3** an organised community under one government (*the State of Israel*) or forming part of a federation (*the 50 States of the USA*). **4** a country's government, *Help for the earthquake victims was provided by the State*. **5** (*informal*) an excited or upset condition, *Don't get into a state about the robbery*. **state school** a public school.

state² *verb* (**stated, stating**) express something in spoken or written words. [same origin as *status*]

stately *adjective* (**statelier, stateliest**) dignified; imposing; grand. **stateliness** *noun*

statement *noun* **1** words stating something. **2** a formal account of facts, *The witness made a statement to the police*. **3** a written report of a financial account, *a bank statement*.

▶▶ T H E S A U R U S ◀◀

stare *verb* gape, gawk (*informal*), gawp (*informal*), gaze, glare, goggle, look, peer, watch.
  stare *noun* gape, gaze, glare, look.

stark¹ *adjective* **1** absolute, complete, downright, pure, sheer, total, utter. **2** austere, bare, bleak, desolate, grim, harsh, plain, severe, simple, spartan.

stark² *adverb* absolutely, altogether, completely, quite, totally, utterly, wholly.

start¹ *verb* **1** activate, begin, commence, embark on, enter upon, switch on, take up, turn on. **2** create, establish, found, inaugurate, initiate, institute, launch, originate, pioneer, set up. **3** depart, get going, leave, set off, set out. **4** blench, flinch, jump, leap, recoil, spring, twitch, wince.

start² *noun* **1** beginning, birth, commencement, dawn, genesis, inauguration, inception, kick-off (*informal*), launch, onset, opening, origin, outset. **2** advantage, break (*informal*), chance, edge, head start, lead, opening, opportunity. **3** jolt, jump, shock, surprise.

starting point base, basis, beginning, foundation, premise.

startle *verb* alarm, disturb, frighten, scare, shake, surprise, unsettle, upset.
  startling *adjective* alarming, astonishing, disturbing, dramatic, remarkable, shocking, staggering, surprising, unexpected.

starvation *noun* famine, hunger, malnutrition, undernourishment.

starving *adjective* famished, hungry, ravenous.

state¹ *noun* **1** circumstances, condition, frame of mind, health, mood, shape, situation. **3** country, kingdom, land, nation, principality, republic. **4** government. **5** dither, flap (*informal*), fluster, panic, stew (*informal*), tizzy (*informal*).

state² *verb* affirm, announce, assert, declare, express, proclaim, report, say, voice.

stately *adjective* dignified, grand, imposing, impressive, magnificent, majestic.

statement *noun* **1,2** account, affidavit, affirmation, announcement, assertion, comment, communication, communiqué, confession, declaration, proclamation, remark, report, utterance. **3** account, bill, invoice.

statesman *noun* (*plural* **statesmen**) a person who is important or skilled in governing a country. **statesmanship** *noun*, **stateswoman** *noun*

static *adjective* not moving; not changing.
static electricity electricity that is present in something, not flowing as current. [from Greek *statikos* = standing]

station¹ *noun* **1** a place where a person or thing stands or is stationed; a position. **2** a stopping-place on a railway with buildings for passengers and goods. **3** a building equipped for people who serve the public or for certain activities, *the police station*. **4** a broadcasting establishment with its own frequency. **5** (*Australian*) a large sheep or cattle farm.
station wagon (*Australian*) a car with a door or doors at the back and rear seats that can be removed or folded away.

station² *verb* put someone in a certain place for a purpose, *He was stationed at the door to take the tickets.* [from Latin *statio* = a standing]

stationary *adjective* not moving, *The car was stationary when the van hit it.*

Usage Do not confuse with *stationery*.

stationer *noun* a shopkeeper who sells stationery.

stationery *noun* paper, envelopes, and other articles used in writing or typing.

statistic *noun* a piece of information expressed as a number, *These statistics show that the population has doubled.* **statistical** *adjective*, **statistically** *adverb*
statistics *noun* the study of information based on the numbers of things.

statistician (*say* stat-is-**tish**-an) *noun* an expert in statistics.

statuary *noun* statues.

statue *noun* a model made of stone or metal etc. to look like a person or animal.

statuesque (*say* stat-yoo-**esk**) *adjective* like a statue in stillness or dignity.

statuette *noun* a small statue.

stature *noun* **1** the natural height of the body. **2** greatness because of ability or achievement.

status (*say* **stay**-tus) *noun* (*plural* **statuses**) **1** a person's or thing's position or rank in relation to others. **2** high rank or prestige. [from Latin *status* = a standing]

statute *noun* a law passed by a parliament. **statutory** *adjective* [from Latin *statutum* = set up]

staunch *adjective* firm and loyal, *our staunch supporters*. **staunchly** *adverb*

stave¹ *noun* **1** each of the curved strips of wood forming the side of a cask or tub. **2** a staff in music (see *staff¹* 4).

stave² *verb* (**staved**, or **stove**, **staving**) dent or break a hole in something, *The collision stove in the front of the ship.*
stave off keep something away, *We staved off the disaster.*

stay¹ *verb* **1** continue to be in the same place or condition; remain. **2** spend time in a place as a visitor. **3** satisfy temporarily, *We stayed our hunger with a sandwich*. **4** pause. **5** show endurance in a race or task.
stay put (*informal*) remain in place.

stay² *noun* **1** a time spent somewhere, *We had a short stay in Rome*. **2** a postponement, *a stay of execution.*

static *adjective* constant, fixed, frozen, pegged, stable, stationary, steady, unchanging, unvarying.

station¹ *noun* **1** location, place, position, post, site. **2** depot, stop, terminal, terminus. **4** broadcaster, channel. **5** estate, property, ranch (*American*), run (*Australian*).

station² *verb* assign, base, locate, place, position, post.

stationary *adjective* immobile, motionless, parked, standing, static, still, unmoving.

statue *noun* bust, carving, cast, figurine, sculpture, statuette.

stature *noun* **1** height, size, tallness. **2** calibre, eminence, greatness, importance, prominence, standing.

status *noun* **1** level, position, rank, standing, station. **2** distinction, importance, prestige, recognition.

statute *noun* act, law, regulation, rule.

staunch *adjective* dependable, faithful, firm, loyal, reliable, steadfast, strong, trustworthy.

stave² *verb* **stave off** avert, defer, fend off, prevent, ward off.

stay¹ *verb* **1** continue, hang around, keep on, linger, remain, stick around (*informal*), tarry, wait. **2** dwell, live, lodge, reside, sleep, sleep over, sojourn, visit.

stay² *noun* **1** holiday, sojourn, stop, stopover, time, visit. **2** deferment, postponement, reprieve.

▶▶ D I C T I O N A R Y ◀◀

stay³ *noun* a support, especially a rope or wire holding up a mast etc.

stead *noun*
in a person's or thing's stead instead of this person or thing.
stand a person in good stead be very useful to him or her.

steadfast *adjective* firm and not changing, *a steadfast refusal.*

steady¹ *adjective* (**steadier, steadiest**) **1** not shaking or moving; firm. **2** regular; continuing the same, *a steady pace.* **steadily** *adverb*, **steadiness** *noun*

steady² *verb* make or become steady.

steak *noun* a thick slice of meat or fish.

steal *verb* (**stole, stolen, stealing**) **1** take and keep something that does not belong to you; take secretly or dishonestly. **2** move secretly or without being noticed, *He stole out of the room.*

stealthy (*say* **stel**th-ee) *adjective* (**stealthier, stealthiest**) quiet and secret, so as not to be noticed. **stealth** *noun*, **stealthily** *adverb*, **stealthiness** *noun*

steam¹ *noun* **1** the gas or vapour that comes from boiling water; this used to drive machinery. **2** energy, *He ran out of steam.* **steamy** *adjective*

steam² *verb* **1** give out steam. **2** cook or treat by steam, *a steamed pudding.* **3** move by the power of steam, *The ship steamed down the river.*

steam-engine *noun* an engine driven by steam.

steamer *noun* **1** a steamship. **2** a container in which things are steamed.

steamroller *noun* a heavy vehicle with a large roller used to flatten surfaces when making roads.

steamship *noun* a ship driven by steam.

steed *noun* (*poetical*) a horse.

steel *noun* **1** a strong metal made from iron and carbon. **2** a steel rod for sharpening knives. **steely** *adjective*
steel band a band of musicians with instruments usually made from oil-drums.

steep¹ *adjective* **1** sloping very sharply, not gradually. **2** (*informal*) unreasonably high, *a steep price.* **steeply** *adverb*, **steepness** *noun*

steep² *verb* soak thoroughly; saturate.

steepen *verb* make or become steeper.

steeple *noun* a church tower with a spire on top.

steeplechase *noun* a race across country or over hedges or fences. [so called because the race originally had a distant church steeple in view as its goal]

steeplejack *noun* a person who climbs tall chimneys or steeples to do repairs.

steer¹ *verb* make a car, ship, or bicycle etc. go in the direction you want; guide. **steersman** *noun*

steer² *noun* a young bull kept for its beef.

steering-wheel *noun* a wheel for steering a car, boat, etc.

stellar *adjective* of a star or stars. [from Latin *stella* = star]

▶▶ T H E S A U R U S ◀◀

stay³ *noun* brace, line, prop, rope, support.

steadfast *adjective* constant, determined, firm, persistent, resolute, staunch, steady, sure, unchanging, unshakeable.

steady¹ *adjective* **1** balanced, firm, immovable, secure, stable. **2** consistent, constant, continuous, even, invariable, regular, unchanging, uniform.

steady² *verb* balance, control, secure, stabilise, support.

steal *verb* **1** appropriate, duff (*Australian*), embezzle, filch, help yourself to, knock off (*slang*), lift (*informal*), make off with, misappropriate, nick (*slang*), pilfer, pinch (*informal*), poach, pocket, purloin, seize, snaffle (*informal*), snatch, snavel (*Australian*

informal), snitch (*slang*), souvenir (*slang*), swipe (*informal*), take, thieve. **2** creep, flit, skulk, slink, slip, sneak, tiptoe.
stealing *noun* see THEFT.

stealthy *adjective* covert, furtive, secret, secretive, sly, sneaky, surreptitious, undercover, unobtrusive.

steam¹ *noun* **1** mist, vapour. **2** energy, momentum, power, puff (*informal*), stamina.

steep¹ *adjective* **1** abrupt, precipitous, sharp, sheer, vertical. **2** dear, excessive, exorbitant, expensive, extortionate, high.

steep² *verb* immerse, impregnate, marinade, saturate, soak, souse, submerge.

steer¹ *verb* conduct, direct, guide, lead, navigate, pilot.

▶▶ D I C T I O N A R Y ◀◀

stem¹ *noun* **1** the main central part of a tree, shrub, or plant. **2** a thin part on which a leaf, flower, or fruit is supported. **3** a thin upright part; the thin part of a wineglass between the bowl and the foot. **4** the main part of a verb or other word, to which endings are attached. **5** the front part of a ship, *from stem to stern*.

stem² *verb* (**stemmed, stemming**) **stem from** arise from; have as its source.

stem³ *verb* (**stemmed, stemming**) stop the flow of something.

stench *noun* (*plural* **stenches**) a very unpleasant smell.

stencil¹ *noun* a piece of card, metal, or plastic with pieces cut out of it, used to produce a picture, design, etc.

stencil² *verb* (**stencilled, stencilling**) produce or decorate with a stencil.

stentorian *adjective* very loud, *a stentorian voice*. [from the name of Stentor, a herald in ancient Greek legend]

step¹ *noun* **1** a movement made by lifting the foot and setting it down. **2** the sound or rhythm of stepping. **3** a level surface for placing the foot on in climbing up or down. **4** each of a series of things done in some process or action, *The first step is to find somewhere to practise*.
steps *plural noun* a stepladder.
in step stepping in time with others in marching or dancing; in agreement.
watch your step be careful.

step² *verb* (**stepped, stepping**) tread; walk.
step in intervene.
step on it (*slang*) hurry.
step up increase something.

step- *prefix* related through remarriage of one parent.

stepchild *noun* (*plural* **stepchildren**) a child that a person's husband or wife has from an earlier marriage. **stepbrother, stepdaughter, stepsister, stepson** *nouns*

stepfather *noun* a man who is married to your mother but was not your natural father.

stepladder *noun* a folding ladder with flat treads.

stepmother *noun* a woman who is married to your father but was not your natural mother.

steppe *noun* a grassy plain with few trees, in south-east Europe or Asia.

stepping-stone *noun* each of a line of stones put into a shallow stream so that people can walk across.

stereo¹ *adjective* stereophonic.

stereo² *noun* (*plural* **stereos**) **1** stereophonic sound or recording. **2** a stereophonic record-player, radio, etc.

stereophonic *adjective* using sound that comes from two different directions so as to give a natural effect. [from Greek *stereos* = solid, + *phone* = sound]

stereoscopic *adjective* giving the effect of being three-dimensional, e.g. in photographs. [from Greek *stereos* = solid, + *skopein* = look at]

stereotype *noun* a standardised character; a fixed idea etc., *The stereotype of a hero is one who is tall, strong, brave, and good-looking.* [from Greek *stereos* = solid, + *type* (= fixed type formerly used in printing)]

sterile *adjective* **1** not fertile; barren. **2** free from germs. **sterility** *noun*

sterilise *verb* (**sterilised, sterilising**) **1** make a thing free from germs, e.g. by heating it. **2** make a person or animal unable to reproduce. **sterilisation** *noun*, **steriliser** *noun*

sterling¹ *noun* British money. [from *steorling* = Norman coin with a star on it]

sterling² *adjective* **1** genuine, *sterling silver*. **2** excellent; of great worth, *her sterling qualities*.

▶▶ T H E S A U R U S ◀◀

stem¹ *noun* **1** cane, stalk, stock, trunk.

stem² *verb* arise, derive, issue, originate, result, spring.

stem³ *verb* check, curb, halt, hold back, stanch, stop.

stench *noun* pong (*informal*), reek, stink.

step¹ *noun* **1** pace, stride. **2** footstep, gait, tread, walk. **3** rung, stair, tread. **4** action, initiative, measure, move.
steps *plural noun* ladder, staircase, stairs, stepladder.

step² *verb* trample, tread, walk.
step in intercede, interfere, intervene.

step on it see HURRY¹.
step up boost, build up, increase, raise.

stereotyped *adjective* clichéd, conventional, hackneyed, standardised, typecast.

sterile *adjective* **1** arid, bare, barren, desert, fruitless, infertile, unfruitful, unproductive, waste. **2** antiseptic, aseptic, clean, disinfected, germ-free, hygienic, sanitary, sterilised.

sterilise *verb* **1** clean, disinfect, fumigate, pasteurise, purify, sanitise. **2** castrate, de-sex, doctor, geld, neuter, spay.

sterling² *adjective* **1** genuine, pure, real. **2** see EXCELLENT.

▶▶▶ D I C T I O N A R Y ◀◀

stern¹ *adjective* strict and severe, not lenient or kindly. **sternly** *adverb*, **sternness** *noun*

stern² *noun* the back part of a ship.

steroid *noun* a substance of a kind that includes certain hormones and other natural secretions.

stethoscope *noun* a device used for listening to sounds in a person's body, e.g. heart-beats and breathing. [from Greek *stethos* = breast, + *skopein* = look at]

stevedore *noun* a person employed in loading and unloading ships.

stew¹ *verb* cook slowly in liquid.

stew² *noun* a dish of stewed food, especially meat and vegetables.
in a stew (*informal*) very worried or agitated.

steward *noun* 1 a person whose job is to look after the passengers on a ship or aircraft. 2 an official who looks after something. **stewardess** *noun*

stick¹ *noun* 1 a long thin piece of wood. 2 a walking-stick. 3 the implement used to hit the ball in hockey, polo, etc. 4 a long thin piece of something, *a stick of liquorice*.
the sticks (*informal*) a remote rural area.

stick² *verb* (**stuck**, **sticking**) 1 push a thing into something, *Stick a pin in it.* 2 fix or be fixed by glue or as if by this, *Stick stamps on the parcel.* 3 become fixed and unable to move, *The boat stuck on a sandbank.* 4 (*informal*) stay, *We must stick together.* 5 (*informal*) endure; tolerate, *I can't stick that noise!* 6 (*informal*) impose a task on someone, *We were stuck with the clearing up.*
stick at (*informal*) persevere.
stick out come or push out from a surface; stand out from the surrounding area; be very noticeable.
stick to remain faithful to a friend or promise etc.; keep to and not alter, *He stuck to his story.*
stick up for (*informal*) stand up for.

sticker *noun* an adhesive label or sign for sticking to something.

sticking-plaster *noun* a strip of adhesive material for covering cuts.

stickleback *noun* a small fish with sharp spines on its back.

stickler *noun* a person who insists on something, *a stickler for punctuality.*

sticky *adjective* (**stickier**, **stickiest**) 1 able or likely to stick to things. 2 (of weather) hot and humid, causing perspiration. 3 (*informal*) difficult, awkward, *a sticky problem.* **stickily** *adverb*, **stickiness** *noun*

stickybeak *noun* (*Australian informal*) an inquisitive person.

▶▶▶ T H E S A U R U S ◀◀

stern¹ *adjective* austere, authoritarian, dour, forbidding, grim, hard, harsh, inflexible, rigid, severe, strict, tyrannical.

stern² *noun* back, poop, rear.

stevedore *noun* docker, watersider (*Australian*), waterside worker, wharfie (*Australian informal*), wharf labourer.

stew¹ *verb* braise, casserole.

stew² *noun* casserole, fricassee, goulash, hotpot, ragout.
in a stew in a dither, in a flap (*informal*), in a fluster, in a panic, in a state, in a tizzy (*informal*).

steward *noun* 1 attendant. 2 agent, bailiff, manager.

stick¹ *noun* 1 baton, bludgeon, cane, club, cudgel, pole, rod, stake, truncheon, twig, waddy (*Australian*), wand. 2 cane, crook, staff, walking-stick. 3 bat, club, cue.
the sticks the backblocks (*Australian*), the back of beyond, the backwoods, the bush, the country, the outback (*Australian*), Woop Woop (*Australian informal*).

stick² *verb* 1 insert, jab, poke, push, thrust. 2 adhere, affix, attach, bind, bond, cement, fasten, fix, fuse, glue, gum, join, paste, seal, tape, weld. 3 become immobilised, become trapped, become wedged, catch, jam, lodge. 4 keep, remain, stay.
stick at continue, keep at, last at, persevere with, persist at.
stick out 1 extend, jut out, poke out, project, protrude, stand out. 2 be conspicuous, be noticeable, stand out.
stick to abide by, adhere to, follow, keep to.
stick up for back, back up, defend, side with, stand by, stand up for, support.

sticker *noun* label, notice, seal, sign.

sticky *adjective* 1 adhesive, glued, gluey, glutinous, gooey (*informal*), gummed, tacky, viscous. 2 clammy, close, humid, muggy, steamy, sultry. 3 awkward, delicate, difficult, ticklish, tricky.

stickybeak *noun* busybody, Nosy Parker (*informal*), snooper (*informal*).

stiff *adjective* **1** not bending or moving or changing its shape easily. **2** not fluid; hard to stir, *a stiff dough.* **3** difficult, *a stiff examination.* **4** formal in manner; not friendly. **5** strong, *a stiff breeze.* **6** severe, *a stiff sentence.* **stiffly** *adverb*, **stiffness** *noun*

stiffen *verb* make or become stiff. **stiffener** *noun*

stifle *verb* (**stifled, stifling**) **1** suffocate. **2** suppress, *She stifled a yawn.*

stigma *noun* **1** a mark of disgrace; a stain on a reputation. **2** the part of a pistil that receives the pollen in pollination. [Greek, = a mark]

stigmatise *verb* (**stigmatised, stigmatising**) brand as something disgraceful, *He was stigmatised as a coward.*

stile *noun* an arrangement of steps or bars for people to climb over a fence.

stiletto *noun* (*plural* **stilettos**) a dagger with a narrow blade.
stiletto heel a high pointed shoe-heel. [Italian, = little dagger]

still[1] *adjective* **1** not moving, *still water.* **2** silent. **3** not fizzy. **stillness** *noun*

still[2] *adverb* **1** without moving, *Stand still.* **2** up to this or that time, *He was still there.* **3** in a greater amount or degree, *You can do still better.* **4** nevertheless, *They've lost. Still, they tried, and that was good.*
still life a painting of lifeless things such as ornaments and fruit.

still[3] *verb* make or become still; quieten.

still[4] *noun* an apparatus for distilling alcohol or other liquid. [from *distil*]

stillborn *adjective* born dead.

stilted *adjective* stiffly formal.

stilts *plural noun* **1** a pair of poles with supports for the feet so that the user can walk high above the ground. **2** posts for supporting a house etc. above marshy or flood-prone ground.

stimulant *noun* something that stimulates.

stimulate *verb* (**stimulated, stimulating**) make more lively or active; excite or interest. **stimulation** *noun*

stimulus *noun* (*plural* **stimuli**) something that stimulates or produces a reaction. [Latin, = goad]

sting[1] *noun* **1** a sharp-pointed part of an animal or plant that can cause a wound. **2** a painful wound caused by this part.

sting[2] *verb* (**stung, stinging**) **1** wound or hurt with a sting. **2** feel a sharp pain. **3** stimulate sharply, *I was stung into answering rudely.* **4** (*slang*) cheat a person by overcharging; extort money from someone.

stingy (*say* **stin**-jee) *adjective* (**stingier, stingiest**) mean, not generous; giving or given in small amounts. **stingily** *adverb*, **stinginess** *noun*

stink[1] *noun* **1** an unpleasant smell. **2** (*slang*) an unpleasant fuss or protest.

stiff *adjective* **1** firm, hard, inflexible, rigid, taut, tense, tight. **2** dense, firm, heavy, solid, thick. **3** arduous, challenging, difficult, exacting, formidable, hard, rigorous, tough. **4** aloof, austere, cold, cool, formal, prim, reserved, stand-offish, starchy, stilted, strait-laced, unfriendly, wooden. **5** brisk, keen, potent, powerful, strong. **6** Draconian, drastic, hard, harsh, merciless, severe, tough.

stiffen *verb* coagulate, congeal, firm up, harden, jell (*informal*), set, solidify, thicken.

stifle *verb* **1** asphyxiate, smother, suffocate. **2** hold back, restrain, smother, suppress.

stigmatise *verb* brand, condemn, denounce, label.

still[1] *adjective* **1** calm, immobile, inert, motionless, static, stagnant, stationary, stock-still, undisturbed. **2** calm, noiseless, peaceful, quiet, silent, soundless, tranquil.
stillness *noun* calm, peace, quietness, silence, tranquillity.

still[3] *verb* allay, appease, calm, lull, pacify, quieten, settle, soothe, subdue.

stilted *adjective* artificial, awkward, forced, formal, laboured, pompous, stiff, unnatural.

stilts *plural noun* **2** blocks, piles, pillars, posts.

stimulate *verb* activate, arouse, awaken, encourage, excite, inspire, kindle, prompt, provoke, rouse, spur, stir up, whet.

stimulus *noun* encouragement, goad, incentive, inducement, shot in the arm, spur.

sting[1] *noun* **2** bite, prick, tingle, wound.

sting[2] *verb* **1** bite, nip, prick, wound. **2** burn, hurt, smart, tingle. **3** goad, incite, provoke, spur, stimulate, stir.

stingy *adjective* (*a stingy person*) close-fisted, mean, mingy (*informal*), miserly, niggardly, parsimonious, penny-pinching, tight, tight-fisted; (*a stingy amount*) beggarly, inadequate, insufficient, meagre, measly (*informal*), paltry, scanty, skimpy, small.

stink[1] *noun* **1** pong (*informal*), reek, stench.

▶▶ D I C T I O N A R Y ◀◀

stink² *verb* (**stank** or **stunk, stinking**) have an unpleasant smell.

stint¹ *noun* **1** a fixed amount of work to be done. **2** limitation of a supply or effort, *They gave help without stint.*

stint² *verb* limit; be niggardly, *Don't stint them of food.*

stipend (say **sty**-pend) *noun* a salary. [from Latin *stips* = wages, + *pendere* = to pay]

stipple *verb* (**stippled, stippling**) paint, draw, or engrave in small dots.

stipulate *verb* (**stipulated, stipulating**) insist on something as part of an agreement. **stipulation** *noun*

stir¹ *verb* (**stirred, stirring**) **1** mix a liquid or soft mixture by moving a spoon etc. round and round in it. **2** move slightly; start to move. **3** excite; stimulate, *They stirred up trouble.*

stir² *noun* **1** the action of stirring. **2** a disturbance; excitement, *The news caused a stir.*

stirrup *noun* a metal part that hangs from each side of a horse's saddle, for a rider to put his or her foot in.

stitch¹ *noun* (*plural* **stitches**) **1** a loop of thread made in sewing or knitting. **2** a method of arranging the threads, *cross-stitch.* **3** a sudden sharp pain in the side of the body, caused by running.

stitch² *verb* sew or fasten with stitches.

stoat *noun* a kind of weasel also called an ermine.

stock¹ *noun* **1** a number of things kept ready to be sold or used. **2** livestock. **3** a line of ancestors, *a man of Irish stock.* **4** liquid made by stewing meat, fish, or vegetables, used for making soup etc. **5** a garden flower with a sweet smell. **6** shares in a business company's capital (see *share¹* 2). **7** the main stem of a tree or plant. **8** the base, holder, or handle of an implement etc. **9** a kind of cravat.
Stock Exchange a place where stocks and shares are bought and sold.

stock² *verb* **1** keep goods in stock. **2** provide a place with a stock of something.

stockade *noun* a fence made of stakes.

stockbroker *noun* a broker who deals in stocks and shares.

stock-car *noun* an ordinary car strengthened for use in races where deliberate bumping is allowed.

stocking *noun* a garment covering the foot and part or all of the leg.

stockist *noun* a shopkeeper who stocks a certain kind of goods.

stockman *noun* a person employed to look after livestock.

stockpile *noun* a large stock of things kept in reserve. **stockpile** *verb*

stocks *plural noun* a wooden framework with holes for a seated person's legs, used like the pillory.

stock-still *adjective* quite still.

stocky *adjective* (**stockier, stockiest**) short and solidly built, *a stocky man.*

stodge *noun* stodgy food.

▶▶ T H E S A U R U S ◀◀

stink² *verb* pong (*informal*), reek.
    stinking *adjective* see SMELLY (at SMELL²).

stint¹ *noun* **1** period, quota, shift, spell, stretch, term, turn.

stint² *verb* be niggardly, be stingy, economise, pinch, skimp.

stipend *noun* allowance, emolument, income, pay, salary.

stipulate *verb* demand, designate, insist on, lay down, specify, state.
    stipulation *noun* condition, demand, proviso, requirement, specification.

stir¹ *verb* **1** agitate, beat, blend, mix, whip, whisk. **2** flutter, move, quiver, rustle, twitch. **3** arouse, awaken, excite, inspire, kindle, provoke, quicken, rouse, stimulate.
    stirring *adjective* exciting, inspiring, moving, provocative, rousing, stimulating.

stir² *noun* **2** commotion, disturbance, excitement, fuss, kerfuffle (*informal*), sensation, to-do.

stitch² *verb* baste, darn, embroider, mend, sew, tack.

stock¹ *noun* **1** accumulation, cache, hoard, quantity, reserve, stockpile, store, supply. **2** animals, beasts, livestock. **3** ancestry, background, blood, descent, extraction, lineage. **4** bouillon, broth.

stock² *verb* **1** carry, handle, have, keep, sell.
    stock up on accumulate, amass, buy up, hoard, lay in, stockpile.

stocking *noun* (*stockings*) hosiery, pantihose, tights.

stockman *noun* drover (*Australian*), herdsman, stockrider (*Australian*).

stocky *adjective* burly, dumpy, nuggety (*Australian*), solid, stout, sturdy, thickset.

▶▶ DICTIONARY ◀◀

stodgy *adjective* (**stodgier, stodgiest**) **1** (of food) heavy and filling. **2** dull and boring, *a stodgy book*. **stodginess** *noun*

stoical (*say* **stoh**-ik-al) *adjective* bearing pain or difficulties etc. calmly without complaining. **stoically** *adverb*, **stoicism** *noun* [named after ancient Greek philosophers called *Stoics*]

stoke *verb* (**stoked, stoking**) put fuel in a furnace or on a fire. **stoker** *noun*

stole[1] *noun* a wide piece of material worn round the shoulders.

stole[2] *past tense* of **steal**.

stolid *adjective* not excitable; not feeling or showing emotion. **stolidly** *adverb*, **stolidity** *noun*

stomach[1] *noun* **1** the part of the body where foods starts to be digested. **2** the abdomen.

stomach[2] *verb* endure; tolerate.

stone[1] *noun* **1** a piece of rock. **2** stones or rock as material, e.g. for building. **3** a jewel. **4** the hard case round the kernel of plums, cherries, etc. **5** a unit of weight equal to 6.35 kg.
Stone Age the time when tools and weapons were made of stone.

stone[2] *verb* (**stoned, stoning**) **1** throw stones at somebody. **2** remove the stones from fruit.

stone- *prefix* completely, *stone-cold*.

stoned *adjective* (*slang*) very drunk or drugged.

stonker *verb* (*Australian slang*) tire out, overcome, thwart.

stony *adjective* **1** full of stones. **2** like stone; hard. **3** cold; unfeeling, *a stony silence*.

stony-broke *adjective* (*slang*) having spent all your money.

stooge *noun* (*informal*) **1** a comedian's assistant, used as a target for jokes. **2** an assistant who does dull or routine work.

stool *noun* a movable seat without arms or a back; a footstool.

stoop *verb* **1** bend your body forwards and down. **2** lower yourself, *He would not stoop to cheating*. **stoop** *noun*

stop[1] *verb* (**stopped, stopping**) **1** bring or come to an end; not continue working or moving. **2** stay. **3** prevent or obstruct something. **4** fill a hole, especially in a tooth. **stoppage** *noun*

stop[2] *noun* **1** stopping; a pause or end. **2** a place where a bus or train etc. regularly stops. **3** a punctuation mark, especially a full stop. **4** a lever or knob that controls pitch in a wind instrument or allows organ-pipes to sound.

stopcock *noun* a valve controlling the flow of liquid or gas in a pipe.

stopgap *noun* a temporary substitute.

▶▶ THESAURUS ◀◀

stodgy *adjective* **1** heavy, indigestible, starchy. **2** boring, dreary, dull, tedious, uninteresting.

stoical *adjective* calm, fatalistic, impassive, patient, philosophical, resigned, self-controlled, uncomplaining.

stole[1] *noun* scarf, shawl, wrap.

stolid *adjective* apathetic, dull, impassive, indifferent, phlegmatic, unemotional, unexcitable, uninterested.

stomach[1] *noun* **2** abdomen, belly, gut, insides (*informal*), paunch, tummy (*informal*).

stomach[2] *verb* abide, bear, endure, put up with, stand, take, tolerate.

stone[1] *noun* **1** boulder, cobble, gibber (*Australian*), pebble, rock; (*stones*) gravel, scree, shingle. **3** gem, jewel. **4** pip, pit, seed.

stoned *adjective* see INTOXICATED.

stonker *verb* beat, defeat, euchre, get the better of, outwit, thwart.

stony *adjective* **1** cobbled, gravelly, pebbly, rocky, rough, rugged, shingly. **3** blank, chilly, cold, fixed, frosty, hard, icy, indifferent, unfeeling, unresponsive, unsympathetic.

stooge *noun* **1** butt, fall guy (*slang*), foil, straight man.

stoop *verb* **1** bend down, crouch, duck, kneel, lean over. **2** demean yourself, descend, fall, lower yourself, resort, sink.
stoop *noun* droop, hunch, slouch.

stop[1] *verb* **1** abandon, break off, cease, come to an end, conclude, desist, discontinue, end, expire, finish, give up, halt, interrupt, knock off (*informal*), leave off, pause, peter out, pull up, put an end to, quit, refrain from, run out, stall, switch off, terminate, turn off. **2** put up, rest, sojourn, stay, stop off, stop over. **3** arrest, bar, block, check, curb, halt, hamper, hinder, immobilise, impede, interrupt, obstruct, preclude, prevent, stanch, stem. **4** block, bung, close, fill, plug, seal.
stoppage *noun* interruption, shut-down, strike, walk-out.

stop[2] *noun* **1** break, cessation, close, conclusion, end, finish, halt, interlude, intermission, pause, recess, rest, standstill, suspension, termination.

stopgap *noun* fill-in, relief, stand-in (*informal*), substitute, temporary.

stopper *noun* a plug for closing a bottle etc.

stop-press *noun* late news put into a newspaper after printing has started.

stopwatch *noun* a watch that can be started and stopped when you wish, used for timing races etc.

storage *noun* the storing of things.

store[1] *noun* 1 a stock of things kept for future use. 2 a place where these are kept. 3 a shop, especially a large one.
in store being stored; going to happen, *There's a surprise in store for you.*
set store by something value it greatly.

store[2] *verb* (**stored, storing**) keep things until they are needed.

storey *noun* (*plural* **storeys**) one whole floor of a building.

stork *noun* a large bird with long legs and a long beak.

storm[1] *noun* 1 a very strong wind usually with rain, snow, etc. 2 a violent attack or outburst, *a storm of protest.* **stormy** *adjective*
storm in a teacup a great fuss over something unimportant.

storm[2] *verb* 1 move or behave violently or angrily, *He stormed out of the room.* 2 attack or capture by a sudden assault, *They stormed the castle.*

story *noun* (*plural* **stories**) 1 an account of a real or imaginary event. 2 the plot of a play or novel etc. 3 (*informal*) a lie, *Don't tell stories!* [same origin as *history*]

stoush[1] *verb* (*Australian slang*) thrash, punch.

stoush[2] *noun* (*Australian slang*) a fight, fighting.

stout[1] *adjective* 1 rather fat. 2 thick and strong. 3 brave. **stoutly** *adverb*, **stoutness** *noun*

stout[2] *noun* a kind of dark beer.

stove[1] *noun* 1 a device containing an oven or ovens. 2 a device for heating a room.

stove[2] *past tense* of **stave**[2].

stow *verb* pack or store something away. **stowage** *noun*
stow away hide on a ship or aircraft so as to travel without paying. **stowaway** *noun* [from *bestow*]

straddle *verb* (**straddled, straddling**) be astride; sit or stand across something, *A long bridge straddles the river.*

straggle *verb* (**straggled, straggling**) 1 grow or spread in an untidy way. 2 lag behind; wander on your own. **straggler** *noun*, **straggly** *adjective*

straight[1] *adjective* 1 going continuously in one direction; not curving or bending. 2 tidy; in proper order. 3 honest; frank, *a straight answer.* **straightness** *noun*

stopper *noun* bung, cork, plug.

store[1] *noun* 1 accumulation, cache, collection, hoard, pile, reserve, stock, stockpile, supply. 2 depot, storehouse, warehouse. 3 department store, emporium, general store, megastore, retailer, shop.

store[2] *verb* accumulate, collect, hoard, keep, lay up, preserve, put aside, put away, reserve, save, stash (*informal*), stockpile, stow.

storey *noun* floor, level.

storm[1] *noun* 1 blizzard, cloudburst, cyclone, deluge, downpour, dust storm, gale, hailstorm, hurricane, rainstorm, sandstorm, snowstorm, squall, tempest, thunderstorm, tornado, typhoon, willy willy (*Australian*). 2 commotion, furore, fuss, outcry, row, rumpus, stir, to-do, uproar.
stormy *adjective* blustery, foul, gusty, inclement, squally, tempestuous, turbulent, violent, wild, windy.

storm[2] *verb* 1 charge, rush, stamp, stomp, tear. 2 attack, charge, invade, raid, rush, take by storm, take over.

story *noun* 1 account, allegory, anecdote, chronicle, fable, legend, myth, narrative, novel, parable, record, report, statement, tale, version, yarn. 2 plot, scenario, storyline. 3 falsehood, fib, fiction, furphy (*Australian informal*), lie, untruth.

stout[1] *adjective* 1 burly, corpulent, fat, obese, overweight, plump, portly, rotund, stocky, tubby. 2 fat, solid, strong, sturdy, thick. 3 bold, brave, courageous, determined, fearless, resolute, valiant.

stow *verb* load, pack, put, stash (*informal*), store, stuff.

straggle *verb* 2 dawdle, lag, loiter, stray, trail.
straggler *noun* dawdler, laggard, loiterer, slowcoach, stray.
straggly *adjective* lank, loose, unkempt, untidy.

straight[1] *adjective* 1 direct, unbending, unswerving. 2 aligned, level, neat, orderly, shipshape, square, tidy. 3 candid, direct, frank, honest, straightforward, truthful, upfront (*informal*).

▶▶ D I C T I O N A R Y ◀◀

straight² *adverb* **1** in a straight line or manner. **2** directly; without delay, *Go straight home.* **straight away** immediately.

straighten *verb* make or become straight.

straightforward *adjective* **1** easy, not complicated. **2** honest; frank.

strain¹ *verb* **1** stretch tightly. **2** injure or weaken something by stretching or working it too hard. **3** make a great effort. **4** put something through a sieve or filter to separate liquid from solid matter.

strain² *noun* **1** straining; the force of straining. **2** an injury caused by straining. **3** something that uses up strength, patience, resources, etc. **4** exhaustion. **5** a part of a tune.

strain³ *noun* **1** a breed or variety of animals, plants, etc.; a line of descent. **2** an inherited characteristic, *There's an artistic strain in the family.*

strainer *noun* a device for straining liquids, *a tea-strainer.*

strait *noun* a narrow stretch of water connecting two seas, *Bass Strait.* **straits** *plural noun* **1** a strait, *the Straits of Dover.* **2** a difficult condition, *We were in dire straits when we lost our money.*

straitened *adjective* restricted; made narrow. **in straitened circumstances** short of money.

straitjacket *noun* a strong jacket-like garment put round a violent person to restrain his or her arms.

strait-laced *adjective* very prim and proper.

strand¹ *noun* **1** each of the threads or wires etc. twisted together to form a rope, yarn, or cable. **2** a single thread. **3** a lock of hair.

strand² *noun* a shore.

strand³ *verb* **1** run or cause to run on to sand or rocks in shallow water. **2** leave in a difficult or helpless position, *We were stranded when our car broke down.*

strange *adjective* **1** unusual. **2** not known or seen or experienced before. **strangely** *adverb*, **strangeness** *noun*

stranger *noun* **1** a person you do not know. **2** a person who is in a place or company that he or she does not know.

strangle *verb* (**strangled, strangling**) kill by squeezing the throat to prevent breathing. **strangler** *noun* [from Greek *strangale* = a halter]

strangulate *verb* (**strangulated, strangulating**) strangle; squeeze so that nothing can pass through. **strangulation** *noun*

strap¹ *noun* a flat strip of leather or cloth etc. for fastening things or holding them in place.

strap² *verb* (**strapped, strapping**) fasten with a strap or straps; bind.

▶▶ T H E S A U R U S ◀◀

straight² *adverb* **1** candidly, directly, frankly, honestly, without beating about the bush. **straight away** at once, directly, immediately, instantly, on the spot, right away, without delay.

straightforward *adjective* **1** easy, simple, uncomplicated. **2** candid, direct, frank, honest, open, straight, truthful.

strain¹ *verb* **1** pull, stretch, tauten, tense, tighten. **2** damage, injure, overtax, overwork, pull, rick, sprain, tax, wrench. **3** exert yourself, heave, push, strive, struggle, try. **4** filter, percolate, riddle, screen, sieve, sift.

strain² *noun* **2** injury, pull, rick, sprain, wrench. **3** burden, drag, effort, exertion, pressure, stress, struggle, tax, tension, worry. **5** air, melody, song, tune.

strain³ *noun* **1** breed, kind, type, variety.

strainer *noun* colander, filter, sieve, sifter.

strait *noun* channel, narrows, passage, sound. **in dire straits** in a mess, in a predicament, in a spot (*informal*), in difficulties, in distress, in

need, in strife (*Australian informal*), in trouble.

strait-laced *adjective* old-fashioned, prim, proper, prudish, puritanical, stuffy.

strand¹ *noun* **1,2** fibre, filament, thread.

strand³ *verb* **stranded** *adjective* **1** beached, grounded, shipwrecked. **2** abandoned, deserted, high and dry, in the lurch, marooned.

strange *adjective* **1** abnormal, bizarre, curious, eccentric, extraordinary, funny, odd, outlandish, peculiar, queer, singular, surprising, uncanny, unconventional, unusual, way-out (*informal*), weird, zany. **2** alien, exotic, foreign, new, novel, unfamiliar, unknown.

stranger *noun* alien, foreigner, newcomer, outsider, visitor.

strangle *verb* asphyxiate, choke, garrotte, suffocate, throttle.

strap¹ *noun* band, belt, bowyang (*Australian*), cord, thong, tie.

strap² *verb* attach, bind, fasten, lash, secure, tie, truss.

▶▶▶ D I C T I O N A R Y ◀◀

strapping *adjective* tall and healthy-looking, *a strapping lad.*

strata *plural* of **stratum**.

stratagem *noun* a cunning method of achieving something; a trick.

strategic *adjective* **1** of strategy. **2** giving an advantage. **strategical** *adjective*, **strategically** *adverb*

strategist *noun* an expert in strategy.

strategy *noun* (*plural* **strategies**) **1** a plan or policy to achieve something, *our economic strategy.* **2** the planning of a war or campaign. (Compare *tactics.*) [from Greek *strategos* = a general]

stratified *adjective* arrange in strata. **stratification** *noun*

stratosphere *noun* a layer of the atmosphere between about 10 and 60 kilometres above the earth's surface. [from *stratum* + *sphere*]

stratum (*say* **strah**-tum or **stray**-tum) *noun* (*plural* **strata**) **1** a layer, especially of rock. **2** a social level or class. [Latin, = thing spread]

Usage The word *strata* is a plural. It is incorrect to say 'a strata' or 'this strata'; correct use is *this stratum* or *these strata.*

straw *noun* **1** dry cut stalks of corn. **2** a narrow tube for drinking through.

strawberry *noun* (*plural* **strawberries**) a small red juicy fruit.

stray¹ *verb* leave a group or proper place and wander; get lost.

stray² *adjective* that has strayed, *a stray cat.* **stray** *noun*

streak¹ *noun* **1** a long thin line or mark. **2** a trace, *a streak of cruelty.* **streaky** *adjective*

streak² *verb* **1** mark with streaks. **2** move very quickly.

stream¹ *noun* **1** water flowing in a channel; a creek or river. **2** a flow of liquid or of things or people. **3** a group in which children of similar ability are placed in a school.

stream² *verb* **1** move in or like a stream. **2** produce a stream of liquid. **3** arrange schoolchildren in streams according to their ability.

streamer *noun* a long narrow ribbon or strip of paper etc.

streamline *verb* (**streamlined**, **streamlining**) **1** give something a smooth shape that helps it to move easily through air or water. **2** organise something so that it works more efficiently. **streamlined** *adjective*

street *noun* a road with houses beside it in a city or town. [from Latin *strata via* = paved way]

strength *noun* **1** how strong a person or thing is; being strong. **2** a good quality of a person or thing.

strengthen *verb* make or become stronger.

▶▶▶ T H E S A U R U S ◀◀

strapping *adjective* healthy, husky, robust, strong, sturdy, tall, vigorous.

stratagem *noun* artifice, dodge, manoeuvre, plan, ploy (*informal*), ruse, scheme, subterfuge, tactic, trick.

strategic *adjective* calculated, planned, politic, tactical.

strategy *noun* **1** approach, method, plan, policy, scheme, tactics.

stratum *noun* **1** layer, lode, seam, vein. **2** class, echelon, level, rank, station.

stray¹ *verb* deviate, digress, diverge, drift, go astray, roam, rove, straggle, wander.

stray² *adjective* abandoned, homeless, lost, roaming, wandering.

streak¹ *noun* **1** band, line, strip, stripe. **2** element, side, strain, vein.

streak² *verb* **1** mark, smear, stain, stripe. **2** dart, dash, run, rush, speed, tear, whiz, zoom.

stream¹ *noun* **1** brook, creek, rill, river, rivulet, tributary, watercourse. **2** current, flood, flow, gush, jet, rush, surge, tide, torrent.

stream² *verb* **1** flood, gush, issue, pour, run, rush, shoot, spill, spout, spurt, surge.

streamer *noun* bunting, flag, pennant, ribbon.

streamlined *adjective* **1** aerodynamic, sleek, smooth. **2** efficient, rationalised, simplified, smooth.

street *noun* alley, avenue, boulevard, close, crescent, cul-de-sac, drive, highway, lane, place, road, terrace, thoroughfare.

strength *noun* **1** brawn, endurance, force, intensity, might, muscle, potency, power, robustness, stamina, toughness, vigour. **2** asset, forte, strong point.

strengthen *verb* bolster, boost, brace, build up, buttress, enhance, fortify, heighten, increase, intensify, prop up, reinforce, shore up, support, toughen.

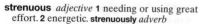

strenuous *adjective* **1** needing or using great effort. **2** energetic. **strenuously** *adverb*

stress¹ *noun* (*plural* **stresses**) **1** a force that acts on something, e.g. by pressing, pulling, or twisting it; strain. **2** emphasis, especially the extra force with which you pronounce part of a word or phrase. **stressful** *adjective*

stress² *verb* lay stress on something; emphasise. [from *distress*]

stretch¹ *verb* **1** pull something or be pulled so that it becomes longer or wider or larger. **2** be continuous, *The wall stretches right round the estate.* **3** push out your arms and legs etc.

stretch² *noun* (*plural* **stretches**) **1** the action of stretching. **2** the ability to be stretched, *The elastic has lost its stretch.* **3** a continuous period of time or area of land or water.

stretcher *noun* **1** a framework for carrying a sick or injured person. **2** (*Australian*) a collapsible single bed.

strew *verb* (**strewed**, **strewn** or **strewed**, **strewing**) scatter things over a surface.

striated (*say* stry-**ay**-tid) *adjective* marked with lines or ridges. **striation** *noun*

stricken *adjective* overcome or strongly affected by an illness, grief, fear, etc.

strict *adjective* **1** demanding obedience and good behaviour, *a strict teacher.* **2** complete; exact, *the strict truth*; *a strict translation.* **strictly** *adverb*, **strictness** *noun*

stricture *noun* **1** criticism. **2** constriction.

stride¹ *verb* (**strode**, **stridden**, **striding**) **1** walk with long steps. **2** stand astride something.

stride² *noun* **1** a long step when walking or running. **2** progress.
get into your stride settle into a fast and steady pace of working.

strident (*say* **stry**-dent) *adjective* loud and harsh. **stridently** *adverb*, **stridency** *noun* [from Latin *stridens* = creaking]

strife *noun* **1** a conflict; fighting or quarrelling. **2** (*Australian informal*) trouble of any kind, *You'll be in strife if you don't get your homework finished.*

strike¹ *verb* (**struck**, **striking**) **1** hit. **2** attack suddenly. **3** produce by pressing or stamping something, *They are striking some special coins.* **4** light a match by rubbing it against a rough surface. **5** sound, *The clock struck ten.* **6** make an impression on someone's mind, *She strikes me as truthful.* **7** find gold or oil etc. by digging or drilling. **8** stop work until the people in charge agree to improve wages or conditions etc. **9** go in a certain direction, *We struck north through the forest.*

strenuous *adjective* **1** arduous, demanding, difficult, exhausting, hard, herculean, laborious, taxing, tough, uphill. **2** dynamic, energetic, enthusiastic, hard-working, indefatigable, industrious, persistent, sedulous, tenacious, untiring.

stress¹ *noun* **1** anxiety, pressure, strain, tension, worry. **2** accent, beat, emphasis, force, importance, priority, value, weight.
stressful *adjective* demanding, difficult, draining, exhausting, onerous, pressured, taxing, tense, trying, worrying.

stress² *verb* accentuate, dwell on, emphasise, highlight, impress, insist on, labour, underline.

stretch¹ *verb* **1** broaden, distend, draw out, elongate, expand, extend, inflate, lengthen, pull out, widen. **2** continue, cover, extend, reach, spread.

stretch² *noun* **2** elasticity, give, stretchiness. **3** (*a stretch of time*) period, spell, stint, term; (*a stretch of land*) area, distance, expanse, length, section, tract.

stretcher *noun* **2** camp bed, camp stretcher, folding bed.

stricken *adjective* affected, afflicted, smitten, struck down.

strict *adjective* **1** (*a strict teacher*) authoritarian, firm, inflexible, rigid, severe, stern, tough, uncompromising; (*strict rules*) absolute, binding, firm, hard and fast, inflexible, rigid, stringent. **2** close, exact, faithful, literal, meticulous, precise, scrupulous.

stride¹ *verb* **1** march, pace, stalk, walk.

stride² *noun* **1** pace, step.

strident *adjective* discordant, grating, harsh, loud, rasping, raucous.

strife *noun* **1** conflict, disagreement, discord, dissension, friction, trouble, unrest.
in strife in a mess, in difficulties, in hot water (*informal*), in the soup (*slang*), in trouble.

strike¹ *verb* **1** bash, batter, beat, belt (*slang*), box, clobber (*slang*), clout (*informal*), cuff, dong (*Australian informal*), flog, hit, job (*informal*), knock, lash, punch, quilt (*Australian slang*), rap, slap, smack, smite, sock (*slang*), spank, stoush (*Australian slang*), swipe (*informal*), tap, thrash, thump, thwack, trounce, wallop (*slang*), whack, whip; (*of a vehicle, etc.*) bump into, collide with, crash into,

▶▶▶ D I C T I O N A R Y ◀◀

strike off or **out** cross out.

strike up begin playing or singing; start (a friendship etc.)

strike² *noun* **1** a hit. **2** an attack. **3** a stoppage of work, as a way of making a protest (see sense 8 of the verb). **4** a sudden discovery of gold or oil etc.

on strike (of workers) striking.

striker *noun* **1** a person or thing that strikes something. **2** a worker who is on strike. **3** a hockey or soccer player whose function is to try to score goals.

striking *adjective* **1** that strikes. **2** noticeable. **strikingly** *adverb*

strine *noun* a jocular imitation of Australian speech.

string¹ *noun* **1** cord used to fasten or tie things; a piece of this or similar material. **2** a piece of wire or cord etc. stretched and vibrated to produce sounds in a musical instrument. **3** a line or series of things, *a string of buses*.

strings *plural noun* stringed instruments.

string² *verb* (**strung, stringing**) **1** fit or fasten with string. **2** thread on a string. **3** remove the tough fibre from beans.

string out spread out in a line; cause something to last a long time.

stringed *adjective* (of musical instruments) having strings.

stringent (*say* **strin**-jent) *adjective* strict, *There are stringent rules*. **stringently** *adverb*, **stringency** *noun*

stringy *adjective* **1** like string. **2** containing tough fibres.

stringybark *noun* an Australian eucalypt with tough fibrous bark.

strip¹ *verb* (**stripped, stripping**) **1** take a covering or layer off something. **2** undress. **3** deprive a person of something. **stripper** *noun*

strip² *noun* a long narrow piece or area.

strip cartoon a comic strip (see *comic*).

stripe *noun* **1** a long narrow band of colour. **2** a strip of cloth worn on the sleeve of a uniform to show the wearer's rank. **striped** *adjective*, **stripy** *adjective*

stripling *noun* a youth.

striptease *noun* an entertainment in which a person slowly undresses.

strive *verb* (**strove, striven, striving**) **1** try hard to do something. **2** carry on a conflict.

strobe *noun* (short for **stroboscope**) a light that flashes on and off continuously. [from Greek *strobos* = whirling]

stroke¹ *noun* **1** a hit; a movement or action. **2** the sound made by a clock striking. **3** a sudden illness that often causes paralysis.

stroke² *verb* (**stroked, stroking**) move your hand gently along something. **stroke** *noun*

stroll *verb* walk in a leisurely way. **stroll** *noun*

stroller *noun* **1** a person who strolls. **2** a pushchair.

▶▶▶ T H E S A U R U S ◀◀

hit, knock into, ram into, run into, smash into. **2** affect, afflict, assail, assault, attack, hit. **5** chime, peal, sound, toll. **6** appear to, come across (*informal*), impress, seem to. **7** come upon, discover, find, reach, stumble on. **8** down tools (*informal*), go on strike, stop work, take industrial action, walk out.

strike² *noun* **2** assault, attack, blitz, bombardment, offensive, onslaught, raid. **3** industrial action, stoppage, walk-out.

striking *adjective* **2** amazing, astounding, conspicuous, extraordinary, impressive, noticeable, obvious, remarkable.

string¹ *noun* **1** cord, rope, strand, twine. **3** chain, column, file, line, queue, row, sequence, series, succession.

string² *verb* **1** fasten, hang, sling, stretch, suspend, tie. **2** lace, thread.

stringent *adjective* firm, inflexible, rigid, rigorous, strict, tough, uncompromising.

strip¹ *verb* **1** peel off, remove, shave off, take off. **2** disrobe, expose yourself, undress.

strip² *noun* band, bar, belt, ribbon, stripe.

stripe *noun* **1** band, bar, chevron, line, strip. **striped** *adjective* banded, lined, striated, stripy.

strive *verb* **1** aim, attempt, endeavour, make an effort, try. **2** battle, contend, fight, struggle.

stroke¹ *noun* **1** blow, hit, lash, whack. **3** apoplexy, brain attack, cerebrovascular accident, seizure.

stroke² *verb* caress, massage, pat, rub, touch.

stroll *verb* amble, promenade, ramble, saunter, walk, wander.

stroller *noun* **2** pushchair, pusher (*Australian*).

▶▶ DICTIONARY ◀◀

strong¹ *adjective* **1** having great power, energy, effect, etc. **2** not easy to break, damage, or defeat. **3** firmly held; deeply felt, *a strong faith*. **4** having a lot of flavour, smell, etc.; (of colours) vivid. **5** having a certain number of members, *an army 5,000 strong*. **strongly** *adverb*

strong² *adverb* strongly, *going strong*.

stronghold *noun* a fortified place.

strontium *noun* a soft silvery metal.

strop¹ *noun* a strip of leather or canvas on which a razor is sharpened.

strop² *verb* (**stropped, stropping**) sharpen on a strop.

stroppy *adjective* (*informal*) bad-tempered; awkward to deal with.

strove *past tense* of **strive**.

structure *noun* **1** something that has been constructed or built. **2** the way something is constructed or organised. **structural** *adjective*, **structurally** *adverb*, **structure** *verb* [from Latin *structura* = thing built]

struggle¹ *verb* (**struggled, struggling**) **1** move your arms, legs, etc. in trying to get free. **2** make strong efforts to do something. **3** try to overcome an opponent or a problem etc.

struggle² *noun* **1** the action of struggling. **2** a fight.

strum *verb* (**strummed, strumming**) **1** sound a guitar by running your fingers across its strings. **2** play badly or casually on a musical instrument.

strut¹ *verb* (**strutted, strutting**) walk proudly or stiffly.

strut² *noun* **1** a bar of wood or metal strengthening a framework. **2** a strutting walk.

strychnine (*say* **strik**-neen) *noun* a bitter poisonous substance.

stub¹ *noun* **1** a short stump left when the rest has been used or worn down. **2** a counterfoil.

stub² *verb* (**stubbed, stubbing**) bump your toe painfully.
stub out put out a cigarette by pressing it against something hard.

stubble *noun* **1** the short stalks of wheat, etc. left in the ground after the harvest is cut. **2** short hairs growing after shaving.

stubborn *adjective* obstinate. **stubbornly** *adverb*, **stubbornness** *noun*

stubby *adjective* short and thick.

▶▶ THESAURUS ◀◀

strong¹ *adjective* **1** (*a strong man*) brawny, burly, hardy, hefty, mighty, muscular, powerful, robust, sinewy, stalwart, sturdy, tough; (*a strong argument*) cogent, compelling, convincing, forceful, irrefutable, persuasive, powerful, solid, sound, weighty; (*a strong wind*) destructive, mighty, powerful, violent; (*strong measures*) drastic, extreme, firm, harsh, severe, stiff, stringent. **2** (*strong furniture*) durable, hard-wearing, heavy-duty, indestructible, sound, stout, sturdy, tough, unbreakable; (*a strong opponent*) formidable, invincible, powerful, unbeatable, unconquerable. **3** (*a strong faith*) ardent, earnest, fervent, firm, intense, keen, passionate, powerful, steadfast, unshakeable. **4** (*a strong flavour*) aromatic, hot, piquant, pungent, sharp, spicy; (*a strong drink*) alcoholic, concentrated, fortified, heady, intoxicating, potent, stiff; (*strong colours*) bold, bright, dark, deep, intense, loud, solid, vivid; (*a strong accent*) clear, definite, distinct, marked, noticeable, obvious, pronounced, unmistakable.
strong point asset, forte, speciality, strength.

stronghold *noun* bastion, castle, citadel, fort, fortification, fortress.

stroppy *adjective* bad-tempered, difficult, irritable, obstreperous, perverse, snaky (*Australian informal*), uncooperative.

structure *noun* **1** building, construction, edifice. **2** arrangement, composition, configuration, constitution, design, form, framework, layout, make-up, organisation, shape.
structure *verb* arrange, design, construct, organise, put together.

struggle¹ *verb* **2** endeavour, labour, strain, strive, toil, try, work hard. **3** battle, contend, fight, grapple, scuffle, spar, tussle, vie, wrestle.

struggle² *noun* **1** effort, exertion, grind, hassle (*informal*), strain, trial. **2** battle, conflict, confrontation, contest, fight, scuffle, skirmish, tussle.

strut¹ *verb* flounce, parade, prance, stride, swagger.

stub¹ *noun* **1** butt, end, remains, remnant, stump. **2** butt, counterfoil.

stub² *verb* bump, hit, knock, strike.
stub out extinguish, put out, snuff.

stubborn *adjective* adamant, defiant, dogged, headstrong, inflexible, intractable, intransigent, obstinate, pigheaded, recalcitrant, refractory, strong-minded, uncompromising, unyielding.

▶▶DICTIONARY◀◀

stucco *noun* plaster or cement used for coating walls and ceilings, often moulded into decorations. **stuccoed** *adjective* [from Italian]

stuck-up *adjective* (*informal*) conceited; snobbish.

stud[1] *noun* **1** a small curved lump or knob. **2** a device like a button on a stalk, used to fasten a detachable collar to a shirt.

stud[2] *verb* (**studded, studding**) set or decorate with studs etc., *The necklace was studded with jewels.*

stud[3] *noun* horses kept for breeding.

student *noun* a person who studies a subject, especially at a college or university. [from Latin *studens* = studying]

studio *noun* (*plural* **studios**) **1** the room where a painter or photographer etc. works. **2** a place where cinema films are made. **3** a room from which radio or television broadcasts are made or recorded. [same origin as *study*]

studious *adjective* **1** keen on studying. **2** deliberate, *with studious politeness.* **studiously** *adverb*, **studiousness** *noun*

study[1] *verb* (**studied, studying**) **1** spend time learning about something. **2** look at something carefully.

study[2] *noun* (*plural* **studies**) **1** the process of studying. **2** a subject studied; a piece of research. **3** a room where someone studies. **4**

a piece of music for playing as an exercise. [from Latin *studium* = zeal]

stuff[1] *noun* **1** a substance or material. **2** things, *Leave your stuff outside.* **3** (*slang*) valueless matter, *stuff and nonsense!*

stuff[2] *verb* **1** fill tightly. **2** fill with stuffing. **3** push a thing into something, *He stuffed the catapult into his pocket.* **4** (*informal*) eat greedily.

stuffing *noun* **1** material used to fill the inside of something; padding. **2** a savoury mixture put into meat or poultry etc. before cooking.

stuffy *adjective* (**stuffier, stuffiest**) **1** badly ventilated; without fresh air. **2** with blocked breathing passages, *a stuffy nose.* **3** formal; boring. **stuffily** *adverb*, **stuffiness** *noun*

stultify *verb* (**stultified, stultifying**) prevent from being effective, *Their stubbornness stultified the discussions.* **stultification** *noun* [from Latin *stultus* = foolish]

stumble *verb* (**stumbled, stumbling**) **1** trip and lose your balance. **2** speak or do something hesitantly or uncertainly. **stumble** *noun* **stumble across** or **on** find accidentally.

stumbling block an obstacle; something that causes difficulty.

stump[1] *noun* **1** the bottom of a tree-trunk left in the ground when the rest has fallen or been cut down. **2** something left when the main part is cut off or worn down. **3** each of the three upright sticks of a wicket in cricket.

▶▶THESAURUS◀◀

stuck-up *adjective* arrogant, conceited, condescending, haughty, high and mighty, hoity-toity, patronising, pretentious, proud, snobbish, snooty (*informal*), toffee-nosed (*informal*), uppity (*informal*).

student *noun* apprentice, learner, postgraduate, pupil, scholar, schoolboy, schoolchild, schoolgirl, trainee, undergraduate.

studio *noun* **1** workroom, workshop.

studious *adjective* **1** academic, bookish, diligent, intellectual, scholarly.

study[1] *verb* **1** cram, learn, memorise, revise, swot (*informal*). **2** analyse, examine, inquire into, investigate, look at, research, survey.

study[2] *noun* **1** education, instruction, learning, research, scholarship, training. **2** analysis, examination, inquiry, investigation, review, survey. **3** den, office, studio, workroom.

stuff[1] *noun* **1** material, matter, substance. **2** belongings, bits and pieces, effects, gear, goods, junk (*informal*), odds and ends, paraphernalia, possessions, things.

stuff[2] *verb* **1** cram, jam, pack, ram, squash, squeeze. **2** fill, pack, pad, wad. **3** push, put, shove (*informal*), stash (*informal*), stick (*informal*), stow, thrust. **4** fill, gorge, sate, satiate.

stuffing *noun* **1** filling, padding, wadding. **2** filling, seasoning.

stuffy *adjective* **1** airless, close, fusty, humid, muggy, musty, oppressive, stale, stifling, suffocating, sultry, unventilated. **2** blocked up, clogged up, congested, stuffed up. **3** conventional, dreary, dull, narrow-minded, old-fashioned, priggish, prim, staid, straitlaced.

stumble *verb* **1** fall, falter, flounder, lurch, reel, sprawl, stagger, topple, totter, trip. **2** blunder, falter, flounder.
stumble on chance on, come across, discover, find, happen on, hit on.

stumbling block difficulty, hindrance, hitch, hurdle, impediment, obstacle, snag.

stump[1] *noun* **2** base, butt, end, remnant, stub.

▶▶▶ D I C T I O N A R Y ◀◀

stump² *verb* **1** walk stiffly or noisily. **2** put a batsman out by knocking the bails off the stumps while he or she is out of the crease. **3** (*informal*) be too difficult for somebody, *The question stumped me*.
stump up (*slang*) produce the money to pay for something.

stumpy *adjective* short and thick. **stumpiness** *noun*

stun *verb* (**stunned**, **stunning**) **1** knock a person unconscious. **2** daze or shock, *She was stunned by the news*.

stunt¹ *verb* prevent a thing from growing or developing normally, *a stunted tree*.

stunt² *noun* something unusual or difficult done as a performance or to attract attention.

stupefy *verb* (**stupefied**, **stupefying**) make a person dazed. **stupefaction** *noun* [from Latin *stupere* = be amazed]

stupendous *adjective* amazing; tremendous. **stupendously** *adverb*

stupid *adjective* not clever or thoughtful; without reason or common sense. **stupidly** *adverb*, **stupidity** *noun* [from Latin *stupidus* = dazed]

stupor (*say* **stew**-per) *noun* a dazed condition. [same origin as *stupefy*]

sturdy *adjective* (**sturdier**, **sturdiest**) **1** strong and vigorous. **2** solid; strongly built. **sturdily** *adverb*, **sturdiness** *noun*

sturgeon *noun* (*plural* **sturgeon**) a large edible fish.

stutter *verb* & *noun* stammer.

sty¹ *noun* (*plural* **sties**) a pigsty.

sty² or **stye** *noun* (*plural* **sties** or **styes**) a sore swelling on an eyelid.

style¹ *noun* **1** the way something is done, made, said, or written etc. **2** a shape or design. **3** elegance. **4** the part of a pistil that supports the stigma in a plant. **stylistic** *adjective*

style² *verb* (**styled**, **styling**) design or arrange something, especially in a fashionable style. **stylist** *noun* [same origin as *stylus*]

stylish *adjective* in a fashionable style.

stylus *noun* (*plural* **styluses**) the device like a needle that travels in the grooves of a record to produce the sound. [from Latin *stilus* = pointed writing-instrument]

suave (*say* swahv) *adjective* smoothly polite. **suavely** *adverb*, **suavity** *noun* [from Latin *suavis* = agreeable]

sub *noun* (*informal*) **1** a submarine. **2** a subscription. **3** a substitute.

sub- *prefix* (often changing to **suc-**, **suf-**, **sum-**, **sup-**, **sur-**, **sus-** before certain consonants) **1**

▶▶▶ T H E S A U R U S ◀◀

stump² *verb* **3** baffle, bewilder, confound, mystify, perplex, puzzle, throw (*informal*).

stun *verb* **1** daze, knock out, stupefy. **2** amaze, astonish, astound, bewilder, bowl over, daze, dumbfound, flabbergast, floor, overwhelm, shock, stagger, stupefy, surprise.

stunt¹ *verb* check, curb, hamper, hinder, impede, inhibit, restrict, retard.

stunt² *noun* act, exploit, feat, performance, trick.

stupefy *verb* amaze, astonish, astound, bewilder, confound, daze, flabbergast, numb, overwhelm, shock, stagger, stun, surprise.

stupendous *adjective* amazing, astonishing, astounding, colossal, enormous, exciting, extraordinary, great, huge, immense, incredible, marvellous, phenomenal, prodigious, sensational (*informal*), spectacular, stunning (*informal*), terrific (*informal*), tremendous (*informal*), unbelievable, unreal (*slang*), wonderful.

stupid *adjective* (*a stupid person*) asinine, bovine, brainless, clueless (*informal*), dense, dim (*informal*), dim-witted, dopey (*informal*), dull, dumb (*informal*), feeble-minded, foolish, half-witted, idiotic, obtuse, simple-minded, slow, thick, unintelligent; (*a stupid thing to do*) absurd, crazy, foolhardy, foolish, idiotic, imprudent, inane, irrational, ludicrous, mad, mindless, nonsensical, reckless, senseless, silly, unwise.

sturdy *adjective* **1** brawny, burly, hardy, hefty, husky, mighty, muscular, nuggety (*Australian*), robust, stalwart, stout, strapping, strong, tough, vigorous. **2** durable, indestructible, solid, sound, strong, tough, unbreakable.

stutter *verb* falter, stammer, stumble.

style¹ *noun* **1** (*a style of painting*) approach, genre, manner, method, mode, technique, way; (*a style of writing*) expression, language, phraseology, wording. **2** design, fashion, kind, pattern, shape, sort, type, version. **3** chic, class, elegance, flair, panache, polish, sophistication.

style² *verb* arrange, cut, design, shape.

stylish *adjective* chic, classy (*informal*), elegant, fashionable, smart, snazzy (*informal*), trendy (*informal*), up to date, with it (*informal*).

suave *adjective* bland, charming, debonair, diplomatic, gracious, polite, smooth, sophisticated, urbane.

▶▶▶ D I C T I O N A R Y ◀◀

under (as in *submarine*). **2** subordinate, secondary (as in *subsection*). [from Latin *sub* = under]

subaltern *noun* an army officer ranking below a captain.

subconscious *adjective* of our own mental activities of which we are not fully aware. **subconscious** *noun*

subcontinent *noun* a large mass of land not large enough to be called a continent, *the Indian subcontinent.*

subdivide *verb* (**subdivided, subdividing**) divide again or into smaller parts. **subdivision** *noun*

subdue *verb* (**subdued, subduing**) **1** overcome; bring under control. **2** make quieter or gentler.

subject¹ *noun* **1** the person or thing being talked about or written about etc. **2** something that is studied. **3** (in grammar) the word or words naming who or what does the action of a verb, e.g. '*the cat*' in *the cat caught a mouse.* **4** someone who is ruled by a particular king, government, etc.

subject² *adjective* ruled by a king or government etc.; not independent. **subject to** having to obey; liable to, *She is subject to hay fever*; depending upon, *Our decision is subject to your approval.*

subject³ (*say* sub-**jekt**) *verb* **1** make a person or thing undergo something, *They subjected him to torture.* **2** bring a country under your control. **subjection** *noun* [from *sub-*, + Latin *-jectum* = thrown]

subjective *adjective* **1** existing in a person's mind and not produced by things outside it. **2** depending on a person's own taste or opinions etc. (Compare *objective.*)

subjugate *verb* (**subjugated, subjugating**) bring under your control; conquer. **subjugation** *noun* [from Latin *sub* = under, + *jugum* = a yoke]

subjunctive *noun* the form of a verb used to indicate what is imagined or wished or possible. There are only a few cases where it is commonly used in English, e.g. '*were*' in *if I were you* and '*save*' in *God save the Queen.* [from *sub-*, + Latin *junctum* = joined]

sublet *verb* (**sublet, subletting**) let to another person a house etc. that is let to you by a landlord.

sublime *adjective* **1** noble; impressive. **2** extreme; not caring about the consequences, *with sublime carelessness.*

submarine¹ *adjective* under the sea, *We laid a submarine cable.*

submarine² *noun* a ship that can travel under water.

submerge *verb* (**submerged, submerging**) go under or put under water or other liquid. **submergence** *noun*, **submersion** *noun* [from *sub-*, + Latin *mergere* = dip]

submissive *adjective* willing to obey.

submit *verb* (**submitted, submitting**) **1** let someone have authority over you; surrender. **2** put forward for consideration, etc., *Submit your plans to the committee.* **submission** *noun* [from *sub-* + Latin *mittere* = send]

▶▶▶ T H E S A U R U S ◀◀

subconscious *adjective* instinctive, intuitive, unconscious.

subdue *verb* **1** control, defeat, overcome, overpower, quell, repress, restrain, suppress. **2** hush, lower, moderate, mute, quieten, soften, tone down.

subject¹ *noun* **1** issue, matter, substance, theme, topic. **2** course, discipline, field. **4** citizen, national, subordinate, vassal.

subject² *adjective* **subject to 1** accountable to, amenable to, answerable to, bound by. **2** liable to, prone to, susceptible to, vulnerable to. **3** conditional upon, contingent on, dependent upon.

subject³ *verb* **1** expose, put through, submit, treat.

subjective *adjective* **2** biased, idiosyncratic, individual, personal, prejudiced.

subjugate *verb* conquer, overpower, quell, subdue, subject, vanquish.

sublime *adjective* **1** awe-inspiring, elevated, exalted, glorious, grand, lofty, magnificent, majestic, noble, wonderful. **2** complete, extreme, supreme, total, utter.

submerge *verb* cover, dip, dive, drown, duck, dunk, engulf, flood, go under, immerse, inundate, plunge, sink, soak, souse, steep, swamp.

submissive *adjective* accommodating, acquiescent, compliant, deferential, docile, humble, meek, obedient, passive, servile, tractable, unassertive, yielding.

submit *verb* **1** bow, capitulate, give in, succumb, surrender, throw in the towel, yield. **2** give in, hand in, offer, present, proffer, propose, put forward, tender.

submission *noun* **1** capitulation, compliance, deference, humility, meekness, obedience, passivity, surrender. **2** entry, presentation, proposal, suggestion, tender.

▶▶▶ D I C T I O N A R Y ◀◀

subnormal *adjective* below normal.

subordinate[1] *adjective* **1** less important. **2** lower in rank.
subordinate clause a clause that is not the main clause in a sentence.

subordinate[2] *verb* (**subordinated, subordinating**) treat as being less important than another person or thing. **subordination** *noun* [from *sub-*, + Latin *ordinare* = arrange]

sub-plot *noun* a secondary plot in a play etc.

subpoena[1] (*say* sub-**peen**-a) *noun* an official document ordering a person to appear in a lawcourt.

subpoena[2] *verb* (**subpoenaed, subpoenaing**) summon by a subpoena. [from Latin *sub poena* = under a penalty (because there is a punishment for not obeying)]

subscribe *verb* (**subscribed, subscribing**) **1** contribute money; pay regularly so as to be a member of a society, get a periodical, have the use of a telephone, etc. **2** sign, *subscribe your name.* **3** say that you agree, *We cannot subscribe to this theory.* **subscriber** *noun*, **subscription** *noun* [from *sub-*, + Latin *scribere* = write]

subsequent *adjective* coming after in time or order; later. **subsequently** *adverb* [from *sub-*, + Latin *sequens* = following]

subservient *adjective* under someone's power; submissive. **subservience** *noun* [from *sub-*, + Latin *serviens* = serving]

subset *noun* a group that is part of a larger group.

subside *verb* (**subsided, subsiding**) **1** sink. **2** become less intense, *Her fear subsided.*

subsidence *noun* [from *sub-*, + Latin *sidere* = settle]

subsidiary *adjective* **1** less important; secondary. **2** (of a business) controlled by another, *a subsidiary company.* [same origin as *subsidy*]

subsidise *verb* (**subsidised, subsidising**) pay a subsidy to a person or firm etc.

subsidy *noun* (*plural* **subsidies**) money paid to an industry etc. that needs help, or to keep down the price at which its goods etc. are sold to the public. [from Latin *subsidium* = assistance]

subsist *verb* exist; keep yourself alive, *We subsisted on nuts.* **subsistence** *noun* [from Latin *subsistere* = stand firm]

subsoil *noun* soil lying just below the surface layer.

subsonic *adjective* not as fast as the speed of sound. (Compare *supersonic.*)

substance *noun* **1** matter of a particular kind. **2** the main or essential part of something, *We agree with the substance of your report but not with all its details.* [from Latin *substantia* = essence]

substantial *adjective* **1** of great size, value, or importance, *a substantial fee.* **2** solidly built, *substantial houses.* **3** actually existing. **substantially** *adverb*

substantiate *verb* (**substantiated, substantiating**) produce evidence to prove something. **substantiation** *noun*

substation *noun* a subsidiary station for distributing electric current.

substitute[1] *noun* a person or thing that acts or is used instead of another.

▶▶▶ T H E S A U R U S ◀◀

subordinate[1] *adjective* **1** lesser, secondary, subsidiary. **2** inferior, junior, lower.

subpoena[1] *noun* order, summons, writ.

subscribe *verb* **1** (*subscribe to*) contribute to, donate to, give to, help, support. **3** (*subscribe to*) accept, agree with, approve of, believe in, endorse, go along with, hold with (*informal*), support.

subscription *noun* contribution, dues, fee, membership fee, sub (*informal*).

subsequent *adjective* ensuing, following, later, succeeding.

subservient *adjective* deferential, fawning, obsequious, servile, slavish, submissive, sycophantic, toadying, truckling.

subside *verb* **1** cave in, collapse, drop, settle, sink. **2** abate, decrease, die down, diminish, ebb, lessen, let up, moderate, recede, wane, weaken.

subsidiary *adjective* **1** additional, extra, lesser, minor, secondary, subordinate, supplementary.

subsidise *verb* back, contribute to, finance, fund, sponsor, support, underwrite.

subsidy *noun* assistance, contribution, grant.

subsist *verb* exist, live, survive.

substance *noun* **1** material, matter, stuff. **2** essence, gist, heart, nub, pith, thrust.

substantial *adjective* **1** big, considerable, large, significant, sizeable, tidy (*informal*). **2** solid, strong, well-built.

substantiate *verb* authenticate, back up, confirm, corroborate, prove, support, validate, verify.

substitute[1] *noun* deputy, fill-in, locum, proxy, relief, replacement, reserve, ring-in (*Australian informal*), stand-in, stopgap, sub (*informal*), surrogate, understudy.

substitute² *verb* (**substituted, substituting**) put or use a person or thing as a substitute. **substitution** *noun* [from *sub-*, + Latin *statuere* = to set up]

subterfuge *noun* a deception.

subterranean *adjective* underground. [from *sub-*, + Latin *terra* = ground]

subtitle *noun* **1** a subordinate title. **2** words shown on the screen during a film, e.g. to translate a foreign language.

subtle (*say* sut-el) *adjective* **1** slight, *a subtle difference*. **2** delicate, *a subtle perfume*. **3** ingenious; not immediately obvious, *a subtle joke*. **subtly** *adverb*, **subtlety** *noun*

subtotal *noun* the total of part of a group of figures.

subtract *verb* deduct; take away a part, quantity, or number from a greater one. **subtraction** *noun* [from *sub-*, + Latin *tractum* = pulled]

subtropical *adjective* of regions that border on the tropics.

suburb *noun* a district with houses that is outside the central part of a city. **suburban** *adjective*, **suburbia** *noun* [from *sub-*, + Latin *urbs* = city]

subvert *verb* get people to be disloyal to their government, religion, standards of behaviour, etc.; overthrow a government etc. in this way. **subversion** *noun*, **subversive** *adjective* [from *sub-*, + Latin *vertere* = to turn]

subway *noun* an underground passage.

suc- *prefix* see **sub-**.

succeed *verb* **1** be successful. **2** come after another person or thing; become the next king or queen, *She succeeded to the throne; Edward VII succeeded Queen Victoria.* [from *suc-*, + Latin *cedere* = go]

success *noun* (*plural* **successes**) **1** doing or getting what you wanted or intended. **2** a person or thing that does well, *The show was a great success.*

successful *adjective* having success; being a success. **successfully** *adverb*

succession *noun* **1** a series of people or things. **2** the process of following in order. **3** succeeding to the throne; the right of doing this.

successive *adjective* following one after another, *on five successive days.* **successively** *adverb*

successor *noun* a person or thing that succeeds another.

succinct (*say* suk-**sinkt**) *adjective* concise. **succinctly** *adverb* [from Latin *succinctum* = tucked up]

succour (*say* suk-er) *noun* & *verb* help. [from Latin *succurrere* = run to a person's aid]

succulent *adjective* juicy.

substitute² *verb* exchange, interchange, replace, swap, switch; (*substitute for*) cover for, deputise for, fill in for, relieve for, replace, stand in for.

subterfuge *noun* artifice, deception, dodge (*informal*), lurk (*Australian informal*), plan, ploy, pretext, ruse, scheme, stratagem, trick, wile.

subtle *adjective* **1** fine, imperceptible, minor, slight, tiny. **2** delicate, faint, gentle, mild, understated. **3** clever, cunning, devious, ingenious, sly, sneaky, wily.

subtract *verb* deduct, remove, take away, take off.

suburb *noun* area, community, district, neighbourhood.

subvert *verb* destroy, overthrow, overturn, sabotage, topple, undermine.

subway *noun* tunnel, underpass.

succeed *verb* **1** achieve success, bear fruit, be effective, be successful, do well, make good,

make it, prosper, work. **2** come after, follow, replace, supplant, take over from.

success *noun* **1** achievement, attainment, prosperity, triumph, victory. **2** hit, sell-out (*informal*), sensation, smash hit (*informal*), triumph, winner.

successful *adjective* booming, effective, flourishing, fruitful, productive, profitable, prosperous, thriving, triumphant, victorious, winning.

succession *noun* **1** chain, cycle, line, round, run, sequence, series, string, train.
in succession consecutively, in a row, one after the other, running, successively.

successive *adjective* consecutive, straight, uninterrupted.

succinct *adjective* brief, concise, condensed, laconic, pithy, terse.

succour *noun* aid, assistance, help, relief.
succour *verb* aid, assist, help, minister to, relieve.

succulent *adjective* juicy, luscious, moist, tasty.

▶▶ D I C T I O N A R Y ◀◀

succumb (*say* suk-**um**) *verb* give way to something overpowering. [from *suc-*, + Latin *cumbere* = to lie]

such *adjective* **1** of the same kind; similar, *Cakes, biscuits and all such foods are fattening.* **2** of the kind described, *There's no such person.* **3** so great or intense, *It gave me such a fright!*

such-and-such *adjective* particular but not now named, *He promises to come at such-and-such a time but is always late.*

suchlike *adjective* (*informal*) of that kind.

suck *verb* **1** take in liquid or air through almost-closed lips. **2** squeeze something in your mouth by using your tongue, *sucking a toffee.* **3** draw in, *The canoe was sucked into the whirlpool.* **suck** *noun*
suck up to (*slang*) flatter someone in the hope of winning favour.

sucker *noun* **1** a thing that sucks something. **2** something that can stick to a surface by suction. **3** a shoot coming up from a root or underground stem. **4** (*informal*) a person who is easily deceived.

suckle *verb* (**suckled, suckling**) feed on milk at the mother's breast or udder.

suckling *noun* a child or animal that has not yet been weaned.

suction *noun* **1** sucking. **2** producing a vacuum so that things are sucked into the empty space, *Vacuum cleaners work by suction.*

sudden *adjective* happening or done quickly or without warning. **suddenly** *adverb*, **suddenness** *noun*

suds *plural noun* froth on soapy water.

sue *verb* (**sued, suing**) start a lawsuit to claim money from somebody.

suede (*say* swayd) *noun* leather with one side rubbed to make it velvety. [from *Suède*, the French name for Sweden, where it was first made]

suet *noun* hard fat from cattle and sheep, used in cooking.

suf- *prefix* see **sub-**.

suffer *verb* **1** feel pain or sadness. **2** experience something bad, *suffer damage.* **3** (*old use*) allow; tolerate. **sufferer** *noun*, **suffering** *noun* [from *suf-*, + Latin *ferre* = to bear]

sufferance *noun* **on sufferance** allowed but only reluctantly.

suffice *verb* (**sufficed, sufficing**) be enough for someone's needs.

sufficient *adjective* enough. **sufficiently** *adverb*, **sufficiency** *noun*

suffix *noun* (*plural* **suffixes**) a letter or set of letters joined to the end of a word to make another word (e.g. in forget*ful*, lion*ess*, rust*y*) or a form of a verb (e.g. sing*ing*, wait*ed*). [from *suf-* + *fix*]

suffocate *verb* (**suffocated, suffocating**) **1** make it difficult or impossible for someone to breathe. **2** suffer or die because breathing is prevented. **suffocation** *noun* [from *suf-*, + Latin *fauces* = throat]

suffrage *noun* the right to vote in political elections. [from Latin, = vote]

suffragette *noun* a woman who campaigned in the early 20th century for women to have the right to vote.

suffuse *verb* (**suffused, suffusing**) spread through or over something, *A blush suffused her cheeks.* [from *suf-*, + Latin *fusum* = poured]

▶▶ T H E S A U R U S ◀◀

succumb *verb* bow, capitulate, give in, give way, submit, surrender, yield.

suck *verb* **suck up to** crawl to (*informal*), fawn on, flatter, grovel to, kowtow to, play up to, toady to.

sucker *noun* **4** dupe, mug (*informal*), muggins (*informal*), pushover (*informal*), sap (*informal*).

suckle *verb* breastfeed, feed, nurse.

sudden *adjective* abrupt, hasty, impetuous, instant, precipitate, quick, rapid, rash, snap, surprise, swift, unexpected, whirlwind.
all of a sudden abruptly, all at once, in an instant, in the twinkling of an eye, out of the blue, quickly, suddenly, unexpectedly, without warning.

suds *plural noun* bubbles, foam, froth, lather.

suffer *verb* **1** be in pain, feel pain, hurt. **2** bear, cope with, endure, experience, feel, go through, put up with, undergo. **3** allow, permit, put up with, stand, take, tolerate.
suffering *noun* affliction, agony, anguish, discomfort, distress, grief, hardship, heartache, hurt, misery, pain, sorrow, torment, torture, tribulation, woe.

suffice *verb* answer, be adequate, be ample, be enough, be sufficient, do, satisfy, serve.

sufficient *adjective* adequate, ample, enough.

suffocate *verb* **1** asphyxiate, choke, smother, stifle, strangle, throttle.

►►DICTIONARY◄◄

sugar *noun* a sweet food obtained from the juices of various plants (e.g. sugar-cane, sugar-beet). **sugar** *verb*, **sugary** *adjective* [from Arabic *sukkar*]
sugar-bag *noun* (*Australian*) a nest of wild honey.

suggest *verb* **1** give somebody an idea that you think is useful. **2** cause an idea or possibility to come into the mind. **suggestion** *noun*, **suggestive** *adjective*

suggestible *adjective* easily influenced by people's suggestions.

suicide *noun* **1** killing yourself deliberately, *commit suicide*. **2** a person who deliberately kills himself or herself. **suicidal** *adjective* [from Latin *sui* = of yourself, + *caedere* = kill]

suit[1] *noun* **1** a matching jacket and trousers, or a jacket and skirt, that are meant to be worn together. **2** clothing for a particular activity, *a diving-suit*. **3** any of the four sets of cards (clubs, hearts, diamonds, spades) in a pack of playing cards. **4** a lawsuit.

suit[2] *verb* **1** be suitable or convenient for a person or thing. **2** make a person look attractive.

suitable *adjective* satisfactory or right for a particular person, purpose, or occasion etc. **suitably** *adverb*, **suitability** *noun*

suitcase *noun* a rectangular container for carrying clothes, usually with a hinged lid and a handle.

suite (*say as* sweet) *noun* **1** a set of furniture. **2** a set of rooms. **3** a set of attendants. **4** a set of short pieces of music.

suitor *noun* a man who is courting a woman. [from Latin *secutor* = follower]

sulk *verb* be silent and bad-tempered because you are not pleased. **sulks** *plural noun*, **sulky** *adjective*, **sulkily** *adverb*, **sulkiness** *noun*

sullen *adjective* sulking and gloomy. **sullenly** *adverb*, **sullenness** *noun*

sully *verb* (**sullied, sullying**) soil or stain something; blemish, *The scandal sullied his reputation*.

sulphur *noun* a yellow chemical used in industry and in medicine. **sulphurous** *adjective*

sulphuric acid a strong colourless acid containing sulphur.

sultan *noun* the ruler of certain Muslim countries. [from Arabic, = ruler]

sultana *noun* a raisin without seeds.

sultry *adjective* hot and humid, *sultry weather*. **sultriness** *noun*

sum[1] *noun* **1** a total. **2** a problem in arithmetic. **3** an amount of money.

sum[2] *verb* (**summed, summing**) **sum up** summarise, especially at the end of a talk etc.; form an opinion of a person, *sum him up*. [from Latin *summa* = main thing]

sum- *prefix* see **sub-**.

summarise *verb* (**summarised, summarising**) make or give a summary of something.

►►THESAURUS◄◄

sugary *adjective* cloying, saccharine, sickly, sweet.

suggest *verb* **1** advise, advocate, propose, put forward, recommend. **2** hint, imply, indicate, insinuate, intimate.
suggestion *noun* advice, proposal, recommendation, tip.

suicidal *adjective* self-destructive.

suit[1] *noun* **1** costume, ensemble, outfit. **4** action, case, lawsuit, proceedings.

suit[2] *verb* **1** be acceptable to, be convenient for, be right for, be suitable for, fit in with, please. **2** become, look good on.

suitable *adjective* acceptable, apposite, appropriate, apt, becoming, befitting, convenient, fitting, meet (*old use*), pertinent, proper, relevant, right, satisfactory, seemly, timely.

suitcase *noun* bag, case, grip, port (*Australian*), portmanteau, trunk, valise.

suitor *noun* admirer, beau, boyfriend, lover, swain (*old use*), sweetheart.

sulky *adjective* bad-tempered, brooding, disgruntled, moody, peevish, petulant, pouting, resentful, scowling, sullen.

sullen *adjective* bad-tempered, brooding, dismal, gloomy, grouchy (*informal*), grumpy, melancholy, moody, morose, resentful, sour, sulky, surly, unsociable.

sully *verb* blemish, disgrace, smirch, soil, spoil, stain, taint, tarnish.

sultry *adjective* close, hot, humid, muggy, oppressive, sticky, stifling, stuffy, suffocating.

sum[1] *noun* **1** addition, aggregate, subtotal, total. **2** calculation, problem. **3** amount, quantity.

sum[2] *verb* **sum up 1** précis, recap (*informal*), recapitulate, review, summarise. **2** assess, judge, size up.

summarise *verb* précis, recap (*informal*), recapitulate, review, sum up.

▶▶ D I C T I O N A R Y ◀◀

summary¹ *noun* (*plural* **summaries**) a statement of the main points of something said or written.

summary² *adjective* **1** brief. **2** done or given hastily, without delay, *summary punishment*. **summarily** *adverb* [same origin as *sum*]

summer *noun* the warm season between spring and autumn. **summery** *adjective*

summer-house *noun* a small building providing shade in a garden or park.

summit *noun* **1** the top of a mountain or hill. **2** a meeting between the leaders of powerful countries, *a summit conference*. [from Latin *summus* = highest]

summon *verb* **1** order someone to come or appear. **2** request firmly, *He summoned the rebels to surrender*.
summon up gather or prepare, *Can you summon up the energy to get out of bed?* [from *sum-*, + Latin *monere* = warn]

summons *noun* (*plural* **summonses**) a command to appear in a lawcourt.

sump *noun* a metal case that holds oil round an engine.

sumptuous *adjective* splendid and expensive-looking. **sumptuously** *adverb* [from Latin *sumptus* = cost]

sun¹ *noun* **1** the large ball of fire round which the earth travels. **2** light and warmth from the sun, *Go and sit in the sun*.

sun² *verb* (**sunned, sunning**) warm something in the sun, *sunning ourselves on the beach*.

sunbathe *verb* (**sunbathed, sunbathing**) expose your body to the sun.

sunbeam *noun* a ray of sun.

sunburn *noun* redness of the skin caused by the sun. **sunburnt** *adjective*

sundae (*say* **sun**-day) *noun* a mixture of ice-cream and fruit, nuts, cream, etc.

sunder *verb* (*poetical*) break apart; sever.

sundial *noun* a device that shows the time by a shadow on a dial.

sundown *noun* sunset.

sundowner *noun* (*Australian*) a swagman arriving at sundown, too late to work for his meal.

sundries *plural noun* various small things.

sundry *adjective* various; several.
all and sundry everyone.

sunflower *noun* a very tall flower with golden petals round a dark centre.

sunglasses *plural noun* dark glasses to protect your eyes from strong sunlight.

sunken *adjective* sunk deeply into a surface, *Their cheeks were pale and sunken*.

sunlight *noun* light from the sun. **sunlit** *adjective*

sunny *adjective* (**sunnier, sunniest**) **1** full of sunshine. **2** cheerful, *She was in a sunny mood*. **sunnily** *adverb*

sunrise *noun* the rising of the sun; dawn.

sunset *noun* the setting of the sun.

sunshade *noun* a parasol or other device to protect people from the sun.

sunshine *noun* sunlight with no cloud between the sun and the earth.

sunspot *noun* **1** a dark place on the sun's surface. **2** (*informal*) a sunny place.

sunstroke *noun* illness caused by being in the sun too long.

suntan *noun* brownish skin colour caused by exposure to the sun.

▶▶ T H E S A U R U S ◀◀

summary¹ *noun* abstract, digest, outline, précis, recap (*informal*), recapitulation, résumé, synopsis.

summary² *adjective* **1** brief, concise, condensed, short, succinct. **2** hasty, instant, instantaneous, prompt.

summit *noun* **1** apex, crest, crown, peak, pinnacle, top, zenith.

summon *verb* **1** call, command, order, send for, subpoena, summons.
summon up call on, draw on, gather, invoke, muster.

summons *noun* command, demand, order, subpoena, writ.

sumptuous *adjective* costly, expensive, extravagant, grand, lavish, luxurious, magnificent, opulent, posh (*informal*), splendid.

sunbathe *verb* bask, sunbake, sun yourself.

sundry *adjective* assorted, diverse, miscellaneous, several, various.

sunny *adjective* **1** bright, clear, cloudless, fair, fine, sunlit. **2** blithe, bright, buoyant, cheerful, gay, genial, happy, jovial, joyful, light-hearted, smiling.

sunrise *noun* cock-crow, dawn, daybreak, first light, sun-up.

sunset *noun* dusk, evening, gloaming, nightfall, sundown, twilight.

sunshade *noun* awning, canopy, parasol.

sup *verb* (**supped, supping**) **1** drink liquid in sips or spoonfuls. **2** eat supper.

sup- *prefix* see **sub-**.

super *adjective* (*slang*) excellent; superb.

super- *prefix* **1** over; on top (as in *super-structure*). **2** of greater size or quality etc. (as in *supermarket*). **3** extremely (as in *superabundant*). **4** beyond (as in *super-natural*). [from Latin *super* = over]

superannuation *noun* regular payments made by an employee towards his or her pension. [from *super-*, + Latin *annus* = a year]

superb *adjective* magnificent; excellent. **superbly** *adverb* [from Latin *superbus* = proud]

supercilious *adjective* haughty and scornful. **superciliously** *adverb* [from Latin *supercilium* = eyebrow]

superficial *adjective* **1** on the surface; not deep. **2** hasty; not thorough. **superficially** *adverb*, **superficiality** *noun* [from *super-*, + Latin *facies* = face]

superfluous *adjective* more than is needed. **superfluity** *noun* [from *super-*, + Latin *fluere* = flow]

superhuman *adjective* **1** beyond ordinary human ability, *superhuman strength*. **2** higher than human; divine.

superimpose *verb* (**superimposed, superimposing**) place a thing on top of something else. **superimposition** *noun*

superintend *verb* supervise. **superintendent** *noun*

superior¹ *adjective* **1** higher in position or rank, *She is your superior officer.* **2** better than another person or thing. **3** conceited. **superiority** *noun*

superior² *noun* a person or thing that is superior to another. [Latin, = higher]

superlative¹ *adjective* of the highest degree or quality, *superlative skill.* **superlatively** *adverb*

superlative² *noun* the form of an adjective or adverb that expresses 'most', *The superlative of 'great' is 'greatest'.* (Compare *positive* and *comparative*.) [from Latin *superlatum* = carried above]

superman *noun* (*plural* **supermen**) a man with superhuman powers.

supermarket *noun* a large self-service shop that sells food and other goods.

supernatural *adjective* not belonging to the natural world, *supernatural beings such as ghosts.*

superpower *noun* one of the most powerful nations in the world.

supersede *verb* (**superseded, superseding**) take the place of something, *Cars superseded horse-drawn carriages.* [from *super-*, + Latin *sedere* = sit]

superb *adjective* brilliant (*informal*), cool (*informal*), excellent, exceptional, fabulous (*informal*), fantastic (*informal*), fine, first-class, first-rate, grand, great, impressive, magnificent, marvellous, outstanding, remarkable, splendid, stupendous, super (*informal*), superlative, terrific (*informal*), top-notch (*informal*), wonderful.

supercilious *adjective* arrogant, condescending, disdainful, haughty, hoity-toity, lofty, lordly, patronising, proud, scornful, self-important, snobbish, stuck-up (*informal*), superior.

superficial *adjective* **1** exterior, external, shallow, skin-deep, slight, surface. **2** cursory, hasty, hurried, perfunctory, quick, sketchy.

superfluous *adjective* excess, extra, redundant, spare, surplus, unnecessary, unneeded.

superhuman *adjective* divine, miraculous, prodigious, supernatural.

superintend *verb* administer, control, direct, manage, organise, oversee, preside over, run, supervise.

superintendent *noun* administrator, boss, chief, foreman, head, manager, overseer, supervisor, warden.

superior¹ *adjective* **1** higher, senior. **2** better, excellent, first-class, greater, outstanding, super (*informal*), top, unequalled. **3** arrogant, condescending, disdainful, haughty, high and mighty, hoity-toity, lofty, patronising, self-important, smug, snobbish, stuck-up (*informal*), supercilious.

superlative¹ *adjective* consummate, excellent, first-class, incomparable, magnificent, matchless, outstanding, superb, supreme, unparalleled, unsurpassed.

supernatural *adjective* extraordinary, metaphysical, miraculous, mysterious, mystic, occult, paranormal, psychic, unearthly.

supersede *verb* displace, oust, replace, supplant, take the place of.

▶▶ DICTIONARY ◀◀

supersonic *adjective* faster than the speed of sound. (Compare *subsonic*.)

superstition *noun* a belief or action that is not based on reason or evidence, e.g. the belief that it is unlucky to walk under a ladder. **superstitious** *adjective*

superstructure *noun* a structure that rests on something else; a building as distinct from its foundations.

supertanker *noun* a very large tanker.

supervene *verb* (**supervened, supervening**) happen and interrupt or change something, *The country was prosperous until an earthquake supervened.* [from *super-*, + Latin *venire* = come]

supervise *verb* (**supervised, supervising**) be in charge of a person or thing and inspect what is done. **supervision** *noun*, **supervisor** *noun*, **supervisory** *adjective* [from *super-*, + Latin *visum* = seen]

supine (*say* **soop**-I'n) *adjective* **1** lying face upwards. (The opposite is *prone*.) **2** not taking action.

supper *noun* a meal eaten in the evening.

supplant *verb* take the place of a person or thing that has been ousted.

supple *adjective* bending easily; flexible. **supplely** *adverb*, **suppleness** *noun*

supplejack *noun* a climbing or twining shrub.

supplement¹ *noun* **1** something added as an extra. **2** an extra section added to a book or newspaper, *the colour supplement.* **supplementary** *adjective*

supplement² *verb* add to something, *She supplements her pocket money by working on Saturdays.* [same origin as *supply*]

suppliant (*say* **sup**-lee-ant) *noun* a person who asks humbly for something.

supplicate *verb* (**supplicated, supplicating**) beg humbly; beseech. **supplication** *noun* [from Latin, = kneel]

supply¹ *verb* (**supplied, supplying**) give or sell or provide what is needed or wanted. **supplier** *noun*

supply² *noun* (*plural* **supplies**) **1** an amount of something that is available for use when needed. **2** the action of supplying something; the thing supplied. [from *sup-*, + Latin *-plere* = fill]

support¹ *verb* **1** keep a person or thing from falling or sinking. **2** give strength, help, or encouragement to someone, *Support your local team.* **3** provide with the necessities of life, *She has two children to support.* **4** help to confirm a statement etc. **supporter** *noun*, **supportive** *adjective*

▶▶ THESAURUS ◀◀

supervise *verb* administer, control, direct, head, manage, organise, oversee, preside over, run, stage-manage, superintend, watch over.

supervision *noun* administration, control, direction, management, observation, organisation, oversight, scrutiny, surveillance, watch.

supervisor *noun* administrator, boss, chief, director, foreman, head, manager, overseer, superintendent, superior.

supine *adjective* **1** face upwards, flat on your back; see also HORIZONTAL.

supplant *verb* displace, oust, replace, supersede, take the place of.

supple *adjective* flexible, limber, lithe, pliable.

supplement¹ *noun* **1** addition, additive, add-on, extra, surcharge. **2** addendum, addition, appendix, codicil, insert, postscript, rider. **supplementary** *adjective* additional, extra.

supplement² *verb* add to, augment, boost, increase, top up.

supplication *noun* appeal, entreaty, petition, plea, prayer, request.

supply¹ *verb* equip, furnish, give, provide. **supplier** *noun* dealer, distributor, merchant, retailer, seller, shopkeeper, stockist, vendor, wholesaler.

supply² *noun* **1** hoard, reserve, stock, stockpile, store. **2** delivery, provision.

support¹ *verb* **1** bear, bolster, brace, buttress, carry, hold up, prop up, reinforce, shore up. **2** assist, back, barrack for (*Australian*), champion, comfort, contribute to, defend, encourage, finance, help, patronise, side with, sponsor, stand by, stand up for, stick by, stick up for, subsidise, succour, sustain. **3** finance, fund, keep, maintain, provide for. **4** back up, confirm, corroborate, endorse, substantiate, uphold, verify. **supporter** *noun* ally, backer, benefactor, champion, fan, follower, helper, patron, well-wisher.

supportive *adjective* caring, encouraging, helpful, sympathetic, understanding.

▶▶▷ D I C T I O N A R Y ◁◀◀

support² *noun* **1** the action of supporting. **2** a person or thing that supports. [from *sup-*, + Latin *portare* = carry]

suppose *verb* (**supposed, supposing**) think that something is likely to happen or be true. **supposedly** *adverb*, **supposition** *noun*
be supposed to be expected to do something; have as a duty.

suppress *verb* **1** put an end to something forcibly or by authority, *Troops suppressed the rebellion*. **2** keep something from being known or seen, *They suppressed the truth*. **suppression** *noun*, **suppressor** *noun*

supreme *adjective* **1** highest in rank; most important. **2** greatest, *supreme courage*. **supremely** *adverb*, **supremacy** *noun* [from Latin *supremus* = highest]

sur-¹ *prefix* see **sub-**.

sur-² *prefix* = super- (as in *surcharge, surface*).

surcharge *noun* an extra charge.

sure¹ *adjective* **1** convinced; feeling no doubt. **2** certain to happen or do something, *Our team is sure to win*. **3** reliable. **4** undoubtedly true. **sureness** *noun*
for sure definitely.
make sure find out exactly; make something happen or be true, *Make sure the door is locked*.

sure² *adverb* (*informal*) surely. [from Latin *securus* = secure]
sure enough certainly; in fact.

surely *adverb* **1** in a sure way; certainly; securely. **2** it must be true; I feel sure, *Surely we met last year?*

surety *noun* (*plural* **sureties**) **1** a guarantee. **2** a person who promises to pay a debt or fulfil a contract etc. if another person fails to do so.

surf¹ *noun* the white foam of waves breaking on a rock or shore.

surf² *verb* ride waves on a board or by streamlining your body and letting it be carried by the waves. **surfer** *noun*, **surfie** *noun* (*informal*), **surfing** *noun*

surface¹ *noun* **1** the outside of something. **2** any of the sides of an object, especially the top part. **3** an outward appearance, *On the surface he was a kindly man*.

surface² *verb* (**surfaced, surfacing**) **1** put a surface on a road, path, etc. **2** come up to the surface from under water.

surfboard *noun* a board used in surfing.

surfeit (*say* ser-fit) *noun* too much of something. **surfeited** *adjective*

surge *verb* (**surged, surging**) move forwards or upwards like waves. **surge** *noun* [from Latin *surgere* = rise]

surgeon *noun* a doctor who treats disease or injury by cutting or repairing the affected parts of the body.

surgery *noun* (*plural* **surgeries**) **1** the place where a doctor or dentist etc. regularly gives advice and treatment to patients. **2** the time when patients can visit the doctor etc. **3** the work of a surgeon. **surgical** *adjective*, **surgically** *adverb* [from Greek, = handiwork]

surly *adjective* (**surlier, surliest**) bad-tempered and unfriendly. **surliness** *noun*

▶▶▷ T H E S A U R U S ◁◀◀

support² *noun* **1** aid, assistance, backing, help, patronage, sponsorship. **2** bolster, brace, bracket, buttress, calliper, column, crutch, foundation, joist, pillar, post, prop, stanchion, stay, stilt, strut.

suppose *verb* assume, believe, expect, fancy, guess, imagine, presume, surmise, think.
supposition *noun* assumption, conjecture, guess, hypothesis, opinion, presumption, speculation, surmise, theory.
be supposed to be expected to, be meant to, be obliged to.

suppress *verb* **1** crush, overcome, overpower, put an end to, quash, quell, squash, stop. **2** bottle up, censor, conceal, contain, control, cover up, hide, keep in check, keep secret, repress, restrain, silence, stifle, withhold.

supreme *adjective* **1** chief, highest, leading, paramount, principal, sovereign. **2** consummate, extreme, greatest, highest, utmost, uttermost.

sure¹ *adjective* **1** assured, certain, confident, convinced, persuaded, positive. **2** bound, certain, guaranteed. **3** certain, dependable, fail-safe, infallible, reliable, sure-fire (*informal*), trustworthy, unfailing. **4** certain, clear, definite, indisputable, true, undeniable.
make sure ascertain, check, confirm, double-check, make certain, verify.

surf¹ *noun* foam, spume; see also WAVE¹.

surface¹ *noun* **1** coating, covering, exterior, façade, finish, outside, shell, skin, top, veneer.

surface² *verb* **2** come up, emerge, rise.

surge *verb* billow, heave, push, roll, rush, stream, swell.
surge *noun* flow, gush, rush, stream, upsurge, wave.

surly *adjective* bad-tempered, churlish, crabby, crotchety, crusty, grouchy (*informal*), gruff, grumpy, rude, snaky (*Australian informal*), sullen, testy, unfriendly.

▶▶ D I C T I O N A R Y ◀◀

surmise *noun* a guess. **surmise** *verb*

surmount *verb* **1** overcome a difficulty. **2** get over an obstacle. **3** be on top of something.

surname *noun* the name held by all members of a family.

surpass *verb* do or be better than all others; excel.

surplice *noun* a loose white garment worn over a cassock by clergy and choir at a religious service.

surplus *noun* (*plural* **surpluses**) an amount left over after spending or using all that was needed.

surprise¹ *noun* **1** something unexpected. **2** the feeling caused by something that was not expected.

surprise² *verb* (**surprised, surprising**) **1** be a surprise to somebody. **2** come upon or attack somebody unexpectedly. **surprisingly** *adverb*

surrealism *noun* a style of painting that shows strange shapes like those seen in dreams and fantasies. **surrealist** *noun*, **surrealistic** *adjective* [from *sur-²* + *real*]

surrender *verb* **1** give yourself up to an enemy. **2** hand something over to another person, especially when compelled to do so. **surrender** *noun* [from *sur-²* + *render*]

surreptitious (*say* su-rep-**tish**-us) *adjective* stealthy. **surreptitiously** *adverb* [from Latin, = seized secretly]

surrogate (*say* **su**-rog-at) *noun* a deputy, a substitute.

surround *verb* come or be all round a person or thing; encircle.

surroundings *plural noun* the things or conditions round a person or thing.

surveillance (*say* ser-**vay**-lans) *noun* a close watch kept on a person or thing, *Police kept him under surveillance.*

survey¹ (*say* **ser**-vay) *noun* **1** a general look at something. **2** an inspection of an area, building, etc.

survey² (*say* ser-**vay**) *verb* **1** make a survey of something; inspect. **2** measure and map out an area. **surveyor** *noun* [from *sur-²*, + Latin *videre* = see]

survive *verb* (**survived, surviving**) **1** stay alive. **2** go on living or existing after someone has died or after a disaster. **survival** *noun*, **survivor** *noun* [from *sur-²*, + Latin *vivere* = to live]

sus- *prefix* see **sub-**.

susceptible (*say* sus-**ept**-ib-ul) *adjective* likely to be affected by something, *She is susceptible to colds.* **susceptibility** *noun* [from Latin *susceptum* = caught up]

▶▶ T H E S A U R U S ◀◀

surmise *verb* assume, conjecture, guess, infer, presume, speculate, suppose, suspect.

surmount *verb* **1** conquer, get over, overcome, prevail over, triumph over. **3** cap, crown, top.

surname *noun* family name, last name.

surpass *verb* beat, do better than, eclipse, exceed, excel, go beyond, outclass, outdo, outshine, outstrip, overshadow, top, transcend.

surplus *noun* excess, glut, residue, surfeit.

surprise¹ *noun* **1** bolt from the blue, bombshell, shock. **2** amazement, astonishment, incredulity, shock, wonder.

surprise² *verb* **1** amaze, astonish, astound, confound, dumbfound, flabbergast, nonplus, shock, stagger, startle, stun, take aback. **2** catch, catch red-handed, discover, spring (*Australian informal*), take unawares.

surprising *adjective* amazing, astonishing, astounding, incredible, mind-boggling (*informal*), staggering, startling, unexpected, unforeseen.

surrender *verb* **1** capitulate, give in, give yourself up, submit, throw in the towel, yield. **2** give, hand over, part with, relinquish.

surreptitious *adjective* clandestine, covert, furtive, secret, secretive, sly, stealthy, sneaky, underhand.

surround *verb* beset, besiege, encircle, enclose, encompass, envelop, hem in, ring, skirt.

surroundings *plural noun* environment, environs, milieu, setting.

surveillance *noun* observation, scrutiny, supervision, watch.

survey¹ *noun* **1** examination, inquiry, inspection, investigation, overview, poll, review, study.

survey² *verb* **1** consider, contemplate, examine, explore, inspect, investigate, look at, look over, observe, review, scrutinise, study, view. **2** map out, measure, plot.

survive *verb* **1** continue, endure, exist, keep on, last, live (on), persist, subsist. **2** come through, live through, outlast, outlive, weather.
survival *noun* existence, life, subsistence.

susceptible *adjective* (*susceptible to*) inclined to, liable to, open to, predisposed to, prone to, receptive to, responsive to, sensitive to, subject to, vulnerable to.

►►DICTIONARY◄◄

suspect¹ (*say* sus-**pekt**) *verb* **1** think that a person is not to be trusted or has committed a crime; distrust. **2** have a feeling that something is likely or possible.

suspect² (*say* **sus**-pekt) *noun* a person who is suspected of a crime etc. **suspect** *adjective*

suspend *verb* **1** hang something up. **2** postpone; stop something temporarily. **3** deprive a person of a job or position etc. for a time. [from *sus*-, + Latin *pendere* = hang]

suspender *noun* a fastener to hold up a sock or stocking by its top.

suspense *noun* an anxious or uncertain feeling while waiting for something to happen or become known.

suspension *noun* suspending.
  suspension bridge a bridge supported by cables.

suspicion *noun* **1** suspecting a person or thing; being suspected; distrust. **2** a slight belief.

suspicious *adjective* **1** feeling suspicion. **2** causing suspicion. **suspiciously** *adverb*

sustain *verb* **1** support. **2** keep someone alive. **3** keep something happening. **4** undergo; suffer, *We sustained a defeat.* [from *sus*-, + Latin *tenere* = hold]

sustenance *noun* food; nourishment.

suture (*say* **soo**-cher) *noun* surgical stitching of a cut. [from Latin *sutura* = sewing]

suzerainty (*say* **soo**zer-en-tee) *noun* **1** the partial control of a weaker country by a stronger one. **2** the power of an overlord in feudal times.

svelte *adjective* slim and graceful.

SW *abbreviation* south-west; south-western.

swab¹ (*say* swob) *noun* a mop or pad for cleaning or wiping something.

swab² *verb* (**swabbed**, **swabbing**) clean or wipe with a swab.

swaddle *verb* (**swaddled**, **swaddling**) wrap in warm clothes or blankets etc.

swag *noun* **1** loot. **2** (*Australian*) a tramp's bundle of belongings. **3** (*Australian*) a large quantity, *a swag of letters to answer.*

swagger *verb* walk or behave in a conceited way; strut. **swagger** *noun*

swagman *noun* (*plural* **swagmen**) (*Australian*) a tramp.

swain *noun* (*old use*) **1** a country lad. **2** a suitor.

swallow¹ *verb* **1** make something go down your throat. **2** believe something that ought not to be believed. **swallow** *noun*
  swallow up take in and cover; engulf, *She was swallowed up in the crowd.*

swallow² *noun* a small bird with a forked tail and pointed wings.

swamp¹ *noun* a marsh. **swampy** *adjective*

swamp² *verb* **1** flood. **2** overwhelm with a great mass or number of things.

►►THESAURUS◄◄

suspect¹ *verb* **1** distrust, doubt, have misgivings about, mistrust, question. **2** believe, fancy, guess, have a feeling, have a hunch, imagine, suppose, surmise, think.

suspend *verb* **1** dangle, hang, sling. **2** adjourn, defer, delay, discontinue, interrupt, postpone, put off, shelve. **3** lay off, stand down.

suspense *noun* anticipation, expectation, tension, uncertainty, waiting.

suspicion *noun* **1** distrust, doubt, misgiving, mistrust, scepticism. **2** feeling, hunch, idea, notion.

suspicious *adjective* **1** disbelieving, distrustful, doubting, incredulous, mistrustful, sceptical, wary. **2** dubious, fishy (*informal*), questionable, shady, suspect, untrustworthy.

sustain *verb* **1** bear, carry, hold, support, take. **2** keep alive, keep going, nourish. **3** continue, keep up, maintain, prolong. **4** experience, suffer, undergo.

swag *noun* **1** booty, loot, plunder, spoils, takings. **2** bluey (*Australian*), drum (*Australian*), matilda (*Australian*), shiralee (*Australian*). **3** heap (*informal*), lot, masses, mountain, pile (*informal*).

swagger *verb* parade, prance, strut.

swagman *noun* bagman (*Australian*), sundowner (*Australian*), swaggie (*Australian*), tramp.

swallow¹ *verb* **1** consume, devour, down (*informal*), eat, gobble, gulp, guzzle, imbibe, ingest, quaff, scoff (*informal*), swig (*informal*), swill. **2** accept, believe, buy (*slang*), fall for (*informal*).
  swallow up absorb, assimilate, engulf, swamp.

swamp¹ *noun* bog, fen, marsh, morass, quagmire, slough.

swamp² *verb* **1** deluge, engulf, fill, flood, inundate, submerge. **2** deluge, flood, inundate, overwhelm, snow under.

►►D I C T I O N A R Y◄◄

swan *noun* a large black or white swimming bird with a long neck.

swank[1] *verb* (*informal*) boast; swagger.

swank[2] *noun* (*informal*) 1 swanking; boasting. 2 a boastful person.

swansong *noun* a person's last performance or work. [from the old belief that a swan sang sweetly when about to die]

swap *verb* (**swapped, swapping**) (*informal*) exchange. **swap** *noun*

swarm[1] *noun* a large number of insects or birds etc. flying or moving about together.

swarm[2] *verb* 1 gather or move in a swarm. 2 be crowded or overrun with insects, people, etc.

swarthy *adjective* having a dark complexion. **swarthiness** *noun*

swashbuckling *adjective* swaggering aggressively.

swastika *noun* an ancient symbol formed by a cross with its ends bent at right angles, adopted by the Nazis as their sign.

swat *verb* (**swatted, swatting**) hit or crush a fly etc. **swatter** *noun*

swathe *verb* (**swathed, swathing**) wrap in layers of bandages, paper, or clothes etc.

sway *verb* 1 swing gently; move from side to side. 2 influence, *His speech swayed the crowd.* **sway** *noun*

swear *verb* (**swore, sworn, swearing**) 1 make a solemn promise, *She swore to tell the truth.* 2 make a person take an oath, *We swore him to secrecy.* 3 use curses or coarse words in anger or surprise etc. **swear-word** *noun*
swear by have great confidence in something.

sweat[1] (*say* swet) *noun* moisture given off by the body through the pores of the skin; perspiration. **sweaty** *adjective*

sweat[2] *verb* give off sweat; perspire.

sweater *noun* a jersey or pullover.

swede *noun* a large yellow kind of turnip.

sweep[1] *verb* (**swept, sweeping**) 1 clean or clear with a broom or brush etc. 2 move or remove quickly, *The floods swept away the bridge.* 3 go smoothly, quickly, or proudly, *She swept out of the room.* **sweeper** *noun*

sweep[2] *noun* 1 the process of sweeping, *Give this room a good sweep.* 2 a chimney-sweep. 3 a sweepstake.

sweeping *adjective* general; wide-ranging, *He made sweeping changes.*

sweepstake *noun* a kind of lottery used in gambling on the result of a horse-race etc.

sweet[1] *adjective* 1 tasting as if it contains sugar; not bitter. 2 very pleasant, *a sweet smell.* 3 melodious. 4 (*informal*) charming. **sweetly** *adverb*, **sweetness** *noun*
sweet corn the seeds of maize.
sweet pea a climbing plant with fragrant flowers.

►►T H E S A U R U S◄◄

swan *noun* cob (*male*), cygnet (*young*), pen (*female*).

swap *verb* barter, exchange, interchange, substitute, switch, trade.
swap *noun* exchange, substitution.

swarm[1] *noun* army, cluster, crowd, drove, flock, herd, host, mass, mob, multitude, myriad, throng.

swarm[2] *verb* 1 cluster, congregate, crowd, flock, herd, mass, mob, pour, stream, surge, throng. 2 (*swarm with*) be alive with, be crowded with, be overflowing with, be overrun by, crawl with, teem with.

swarthy *adjective* dark, tanned.

swathe *verb* bandage, bind up, cover, envelop, swaddle, wrap.

sway *verb* 1 lurch, reel, rock, stagger, swing, totter, wobble. 2 influence, move, persuade, win over.

swear *verb* 1 pledge, promise, vow. 3 blaspheme, curse.

swear-word *noun* blasphemy, expletive, four-letter word (*informal*), obscenity, profanity.

sweat[1] *noun* lather, perspiration.

sweat[2] *verb* perspire.

sweater *noun* jersey, jumper, pullover, skivvy (*Australian*), sweatshirt, top, windcheater.

sweep[1] *verb* 1 brush, clean, clear. 3 belt (*slang*), charge, dash, fly, race, rush, sail, speed, tear, zoom.

sweeping *adjective* broad, comprehensive, extensive, far-reaching, general, huge, massive, radical, wholesale, wide-ranging.

sweet[1] *adjective* 1 cloying, luscious, saccharine, sickly, sugary, syrupy. 2 balmy, fragrant, perfumed, scented. 3 dulcet, euphonious, harmonious, mellifluous, mellow, melodious, pleasant, tuneful. 4 amiable, appealing, charming, considerate, dear, delightful, endearing, generous, gentle, good-natured, kind, likeable, lovable, lovely, nice, pleasant, thoughtful.

▶▶▷ D I C T I O N A R Y ◁◀◀

sweet² *noun* **1** a small shaped piece of sweet food made with sugar, chocolate, etc. **2** the sweet course in a meal. **3** a beloved person.

sweetbread *noun* an animal's pancreas or thymus used as food.

sweeten *verb* make or become sweet. **sweetener** *noun*

sweetheart *noun* a person you love very much.

sweetmeat *noun* a sweet.

swell¹ *verb* (**swelled, swollen** or **swelled, swelling**) make or become larger in size or amount or force. **swelled head** (*slang*) conceit.

swell² *noun* **1** the process of swelling. **2** the rise and fall of the sea's surface.

swell³ *adjective* (*American informal*) very good.

swelling *noun* a swollen place.

swelter *verb* feel uncomfortably hot. **sweltering** *adjective*

swerve *verb* (**swerved, swerving**) turn to one side suddenly. **swerve** *noun*

swift¹ *adjective* quick; rapid. **swiftly** *adverb*, **swiftness** *noun*

swift² *noun* a small bird rather like a swallow.

swig *verb* (**swigged, swigging**) (*informal*) drink; swallow. **swig** *noun*

swill¹ *verb* pour water over or through something; wash or rinse.

swill² *noun* **1** the process of swilling, *Give it a swill.* **2** a sloppy mixture of waste food given to pigs.

swim¹ *verb* (**swam, swum, swimming**) **1** move the body through the water; be in the water for pleasure. **2** cross by swimming, *She swam the Channel.* **3** float. **4** be covered with or full of liquid, *Our eyes were swimming in tears.* **5** feel dizzy, *His head swam.* **swimmer** *noun*

swimming costume a garment worn for swimming.

swimming pool an artificial pool for swimming in.

swim² *noun* the action of swimming, *We went for a swim.* **swimsuit** *noun*

swimmers *plural noun* (*Australian*) a swimming costume.

swindle *verb* (**swindled, swindling**) cheat a person in business etc. **swindle** *noun*, **swindler** *noun*

swine *noun* (*plural* **swine**) **1** a pig. **2** a very unpleasant person or thing.

swing¹ *verb* (**swung, swinging**) **1** move to and fro while hanging; move or turn in a curve, *The door swung open.* **2** change from one opinion or mood etc. to another.

swinging voter a person who does not support any political party permanently.

▶▶▷ T H E S A U R U S ◁◀◀

sweet² *noun* **1** candy (*American*), confection, lolly (*Australian*), toffee. **2** afters (*informal*), dessert, pudding (*British*).

sweetheart *noun* beloved, boyfriend, darling, dear, fiancé, fiancée, girlfriend, love, lover.

swell¹ *verb* augment, balloon, billow, bloat, blow up, boost, build up, bulge, distend, expand, grow, grow louder, heighten, increase, inflate, intensify, mount, multiply, puff up, rise, surge.

swell² *noun* **1** increase, rise, surge, upsurge. **2** billows, surge, waves.

swelling *noun* blister, boil, bulge, bump, inflammation, lump, protuberance.

sweltering *adjective* boiling, hot, scorching, stifling, sultry, torrid.

swerve *verb* deviate, sheer, turn, veer.

swift¹ *adjective* brisk, expeditious, fast, fleet, nimble, nippy (*informal*), prompt, quick, rapid, speedy.

swig *verb* drink, gulp, guzzle, quaff, swallow, swill. **swig** *noun* draught, gulp, mouthful.

swill¹ *verb* clean, rinse, wash.

swill² *noun* **2** pigswill, slop.

swim¹ *verb* **1** bathe, bogey (*Australian*), have a dip.

swimming costume bathers (*Australian*), bathing suit, bikini, cossie (*Australian informal*), swimmers (*Australian*), swimsuit, togs (*Australian informal*), trunks.

swimming pool aquatic centre, baths, pool.

swindle *verb* cheat, con (*informal*), deceive, defraud, diddle (*informal*), dupe, fleece, hoax, hoodwink, rip off (*informal*), rook, trick. **swindle** *noun* con (*informal*), confidence trick, deception, fraud, hoax, racket, rip-off (*informal*), rort (*Australian slang*), scam (*slang*), swizz (*informal*), trick. **swindler** *noun* charlatan, cheat, con man (*informal*), crook (*informal*), fraud, racketeer, rogue, shark, sharper, shicer (*Australian slang*), shyster (*informal*), trickster.

swing¹ *verb* **1** be suspended, dangle, flap, oscillate, rock, rotate, see-saw, spin, sway, swivel, turn. **2** alter, change, fluctuate, oscillate, shift, switch, vary, waver.

▶▶ D I C T I O N A R Y ◀◀

swing² *noun* **1** a swinging movement. **2** a seat hung on chains or ropes etc. so that it can be moved backwards and forwards. **3** the amount by which votes or opinions etc. change from one side to another. **4** a kind of jazz music.

in full swing full of activity; working fully.

swingeing (*say* **swin**-jing) *adjective* **1** (of a blow) very powerful. **2** huge in amount, *a swingeing increase in taxes*.

swipe *verb* (**swiped, swiping**) (*informal*) **1** hit hard. **2** steal something. **swipe** *noun*

swirl *verb* move round quickly in circles; whirl. **swirl** *noun*

swish¹ *verb* move with a hissing sound. **swish** *noun*

swish² *adjective* (*informal*) smart; fashionable.

Swiss roll a thin sponge-cake spread with jam or cream and rolled up.

switch¹ *noun* (*plural* **switches**) **1** a device that is pressed or turned to start or stop something working, especially by electricity. **2** a change of opinion, policy, or methods. **3** mechanism for moving the points on a railway track. **4** a flexible rod or whip.

switch² *verb* **1** turn something on or off by means of a switch. **2** change or transfer or divert something.

switchback *noun* a railway at a fun-fair, with steep slopes up and down alternately.

switchboard *noun* a panel with switches etc. for making telephone connections or operating electric circuits.

swivel *verb* (**swivelled, swivelling**) turn round.

swollen *past participle* of **swell**.

swoon *verb* faint. **swoon** *noun*

swoop *verb* **1** come down with a rushing movement. **2** make a sudden attack. **swoop** *noun*

swop *verb* (**swopped, swopping**) swap.

sword (*say* sord) *noun* a weapon with a long pointed blade fixed in a handle or hilt. **swordsman** *noun*

swot *verb* (**swotted, swotting**) (*slang*) study hard. **swot** *noun* [a dialect word for *sweat*]

sycamore *noun* a kind of maple-tree.

sycophant (*say* **sik**-o-fant) *noun* a person who tries to win people's favour by flattering them. **sycophantic** *adjective*, **sycophantically** *adverb*, **sycophancy** *noun*

syl- *prefix* see **syn-**.

syllable *noun* a word or part of a word that has one sound when you say it, '*Cat*' has one syllable, '*el-e-phant*' has three syllables. **syllabic** *adjective* [from *syl-*, + Greek *lambenein* = take]

syllabus *noun* (*plural* **syllabuses**) a summary of the things to be studied by a class or for an examination etc.

sylph *noun* a slender and graceful girl or woman.

sym- *prefix* see **syn-**.

symbol *noun* **1** a thing that suggests something, *The cross is a symbol of Christianity*. **2** a mark or sign with a special meaning (e.g. +, −, and ÷ in mathematics). **symbolic** *adjective*, **symbolical** *adjective*, **symbolically** *adverb* [from Greek *symbolon* = token]

symbolise *verb* (**symbolised, symbolising**) make or be a symbol of something.

▶▶ T H E S A U R U S ◀◀

swing² *noun* **1** stroke, sweep, swipe (*informal*). **3** change, movement, shift, turnaround.

swipe *verb* **1** belt (*slang*), hit, strike, swing at, whack. **2** grab, nab (*informal*), nick (*slang*), pinch (*informal*), seize, snatch, snitch (*slang*), steal.
swipe *noun* hit, stroke, swing.

swirl *verb* eddy, revolve, spin, spiral, twirl, twist, whirl.

swish² *adjective* elegant, fashionable, posh (*informal*), smart, snazzy (*informal*), swanky (*informal*).

switch¹ *noun* **2** about-face, change, changeover, shift, U-turn, variation. **4** lash, rod, stick, whip.

switch² *verb* **1** flick, turn. **2** change, exchange, interchange, substitute, swap.

swivel *verb* pivot, revolve, rotate, spin, turn, twirl, whirl.

swollen *adjective* bloated, bulging, distended, inflated, puffed-up, puffy.

swoop *verb* **1** descend, dive, plunge, pounce, spring. **2** (*swoop on*) attack, descend on, raid, rush, storm.

sword *noun* blade, broadsword, claymore, cutlass, foil, rapier, sabre, scimitar, steel (*literary*).

sycophant *noun* crawler (*informal*), fawner, flatterer, lackey, toady, truckler, yes-man.

symbol *noun* **1** badge, emblem, insignia, logo, sign, token, trade mark. **2** character, figure, ideogram, letter, mark, pictogram, sign.

symbolic *adjective* allegorical, figurative, metaphorical.

symbolise *verb* betoken, denote, express, indicate, mean, represent, signify, stand for.

▶▶ D I C T I O N A R Y ◀◀

symbolism *noun* the use of symbols to represent things.

symmetrical *adjective* able to be divided into two halves which are exactly the same but the opposite way round, *Wheels and butterflies are symmetrical.* **symmetrically** *adverb*, **symmetry** *noun* [from *sym-* + *metrical*]

sympathise *verb* (**sympathised, sympathising**) **1** show or feel sympathy. **2** agree. **sympathiser** *noun*

sympathy *noun* (*plural* **sympathies**) **1** the sharing or understanding of other people's feelings, opinions, etc. **2** a feeling of pity or tenderness towards someone who is hurt, sad, or in trouble. **sympathetic** *adjective*, **sympathetically** *adverb* [from *sym-*, + Greek *pathos* = feeling]

symphony *noun* (*plural* **symphonies**) a long piece of music for an orchestra. **symphonic** *adjective* [from *sym-*, + Greek *phone* = sound]

symptom *noun* a sign that a disease or condition exists, *Red spots are a symptom of measles.* **symptomatic** *adjective*

syn- *prefix* (changing to **syl-** or **sym-** before certain consonants) **1** with, together (as in *synchronise*). **2** alike (as in *synonym*). [from Greek *syn* = with]

synagogue (*say* **sin**-a-gog) *noun* a place where Jews meet for worship. [from Greek, = assembly]

synchronise (*say* **sink**-ron-I'z) *verb* (**synchronised, synchronising**) **1** make things happen at the same time. **2** make watches or clocks show the same time. **3** happen at the same time. **synchronisation** *noun* [from *syn-*, + Greek *chronos* = time]

syncopate (*say* **sink**-o-payt) *verb* (**syncopated, syncopating**) change the strength of beats in a piece of music. **syncopation** *noun*

syndicate *noun* a group of people or firms who work together in business.

syndrome *noun* a group of concurrent symptoms of a disease.

synod (*say* **sin**-od) *noun* a council of senior members of the clergy. [from Greek, = meeting]

synonym (*say* **sin**-o-nim) *noun* a word that means the same or almost the same as another word, '*Large*' *and* '*great*' *are synonyms of* '*big*'. **synonymous** (*say* sin-**on**-im-us) *adjective* [from *syn-*, + Greek *onyma* = name]

synopsis (*say* sin-**op**-sis) *noun* (*plural* **synopses**) a summary. [from *syn-*, + Greek *opsis* = seeing]

syntax (*say* **sin**-taks) *noun* the way words are arranged to make phrases or sentences. **syntactic** *adjective*, **syntactically** *adverb* [from *syn-*, + Greek *taxis* = arrangement]

synthesis (*say* **sin**-thi-sis) *noun* (*plural* **syntheses**) combining different things to make something. **synthesise** *verb* [from *syn-*, + Greek *thesis* = placing]

synthesiser *noun* an electronic musical instrument that can make a large variety of sounds.

synthetic *adjective* artificially made; not natural. **synthetically** *adverb*

syringe *noun* a device for sucking in a liquid and squirting it out.

syrup *noun* a thick sweet liquid. **syrupy** *adjective* [from Arabic *sharab* = a drink]

▶▶ T H E S A U R U S ◀◀

symmetrical *adjective* balanced, even, regular. **symmetry** *noun* balance, evenness, harmony, regularity.

sympathise *verb* **1** (*sympathise with*) commiserate with, empathise with, feel compassion for, feel for, feel sorry for, identify with, offer condolences to, pity, relate to, understand. **2** (*sympathise with*) agree with, approve of, go along with, side with, support. **sympathiser** *noun* comrade, fellow-traveller, supporter.

sympathy *noun* commiseration, compassion, concern, condolences, empathy, feeling, pity, tenderness, understanding. **sympathetic** *adjective* caring, compassionate, concerned, humane, kind, kindly, merciful, supportive, tender-hearted, understanding, warm-hearted.

symptom *noun* feature, indication, mark, pointer (*informal*), sign, signal.

syndicate *noun* alliance, association, cartel, consortium, federation, group, league.

synopsis *noun* abstract, outline, précis, résumé, summary.

synthesis *noun* amalgamation, blend, combination, fusion, mixture, union.

synthetic *adjective* artificial, fake, imitation, man-made, manufactured.

syringe *noun* hypodermic, needle.

►►DICTIONARY◄◄

system *noun* **1** a set of parts, things, or ideas that are organised to work together. **2** a way of doing something, *a new system of training drivers*. [from Greek, = setting up]

systematic *adjective* methodical; carefully planned. **systematically** *adverb*

►►THESAURUS◄◄

system *noun* **1** arrangement, network, organisation, set-up, structure. **2** approach, method, methodology, order, plan, procedure, routine, scheme, structure, technique, way.

systematic *adjective* businesslike, efficient, logical, methodical, ordered, orderly, organised, planned, scientific.

▶ **Tt** ◀

tab *noun* a small flap or strip that sticks out.

tabard *noun* a kind of tunic decorated with a coat of arms.

tabby *noun* (*plural* **tabbies**) a grey or brown cat with dark stripes.

tabernacle *noun* (in the Bible) the portable shrine used by the ancient Jews during their wanderings in the desert.

table¹ *noun* **1** a piece of furniture with a flat top supported on legs. **2** a list of facts or figures arranged in order; a list of the results of multiplying a number by other numbers, *multiplication tables*.

table² *verb* (**tabled, tabling**) put forward a proposal etc. for discussion in Parliament. [from Latin *tabula* = plank]

tableau (*say* **tab**-loh) *noun* (*plural* **tableaux**, *say* **tab**-lohz) a dramatic or picturesque scene, especially one posed on a stage by a group of people who do not speak or move. [French, = little table]

tablecloth *noun* a cloth for covering a table, especially at meals.

tableland *noun* an extensive high area of flat land.

tablespoon *noun* a large spoon for serving food. **tablespoonful** *noun*

tablet *noun* **1** a pill. **2** a solid piece of soap. **3** a flat piece of stone or wood etc. with words carved or written on it.

tabloid *noun* a newspaper with pages that are half the size of larger newspapers.

taboo *adjective* not to be touched or done or used. **taboo** *noun*

tabor (*say* **tay**-ber) *noun* a small drum.

tabular *adjective* arranged in a table or in columns.

tabulate *verb* (**tabulated, tabulating**) arrange information or figures in a table or list. **tabulation** *noun*

tabulator *noun* a device on a typewriter or computer that automatically sets the positions for columns.

tachograph (*say* **tak**-o-grahf) *noun* a device that automatically records the speed and travelling-time of a motor vehicle in which it is fitted. [from Greek *tachos* = speed, + -*graph*]

tacit (*say* **tas**-it) *adjective* implied or understood without being put into words; silent, *tacit approval*. [from Latin *tacitus* = not speaking]

taciturn (*say* **tas**-i-tern) *adjective* saying very little. **taciturnity** *noun*

tack¹ *noun* **1** a short nail with a flat top. **2** a tacking stitch. **3** (in sailing) direction taken when tacking. **4** a course of action.

tack² *verb* **1** nail down with tacks. **2** fasten material together with long stitches. **3** sail a zigzag course so as to use what wind there is. **tack on** (*informal*) add an extra thing.

tack³ *noun* harness, saddles, etc. [from *tackle* = equipment]

tackle¹ *verb* (**tackled, tackling**) **1** try to do something that needs doing. **2** try to get the ball from someone else in a game of football or hockey.

tackle² *noun* **1** equipment, especially for fishing. **2** a set of ropes and pulleys. **3** the action of tackling someone.

▶▶ T H E S A U R U S ◀◀

table¹ *noun* **1** altar, bar, bench, buffet, counter, desk, lectern, stand. **2** chart, list, tabulation.

tableland *noun* highland, plateau.

tablet *noun* **1** capsule, lozenge, pill. **3** panel, plaque, plate, slab.

taboo *adjective* banned, forbidden, prohibited, proscribed, unacceptable, unmentionable.

tacit *adjective* implicit, implied, silent, unspoken, unstated.

taciturn *adjective* quiet, reserved, reticent, silent, uncommunicative, unforthcoming.

tack¹ *noun* **1** drawing pin, nail, pin, staple. **4** approach, course, direction, method, policy, strategy, tactic.

tack² *verb* **1** fasten, fix, nail, pin, staple. **2** baste, sew, stitch.

tack on add, annex, append, attach, tag on.

tackle¹ *verb* **1** address, approach, attack, deal with, grapple with, handle, manage, set about. **2** attack, challenge, intercept, take on.

tackle² *noun* **1** apparatus, equipment, gear, kit, rig.

▶▶ D I C T I O N A R Y ◀◀

tacky *adjective* **1** sticky, not quite dry, *The paint is still tacky.* **2** (*informal*) cheap and of poor quality. **tackiness** *noun*

tact *noun* skill in not offending people. **tactful** *adjective*, **tactfully** *adverb*, **tactless** *adjective*, **tactlessly** *adverb* [from Latin *tactus* = sense of touch]

tactics *noun* the method of arranging troops etc. skilfully for a battle, or of doing things to achieve something. **tactic** *noun*, **tactical** *adjective*, **tactically** *adverb*, **tactician** *noun* [from Greek *taktika* = things arranged]

Usage *Strategy* is a general plan for a whole campaign, *tactics* is for one part of this.

tactile *adjective* of or using the sense of touch. [from Latin *tactum* = touched]

tadpole *noun* a young frog or toad that has developed from the egg and lives entirely in water. [from old words *tad* = toad, + *poll* = head]

TAFE *abbreviation* Technical and Further Education.

taffeta *noun* a stiff silky material.

tag¹ *noun* **1** a label tied on or stuck into something. **2** a metal or plastic point at the end of a shoelace.

tag² *verb* (**tagged, tagging**) **1** label something with a tag. **2** add as an extra thing, *A postscript was tagged on to her letter.* **3** (*informal*) go with other people, *Her sister tagged along.*

tag³ *noun* a game in which one person chases the others.

tail¹ *noun* **1** the part that sticks out from the rear end of the body of a bird, fish, or animal. **2** the part at the end or rear of something. **3** the side of a coin opposite the head, *Heads or tails?*

tail² *verb* **1** remove stalks etc. from fruit or vegetables, *top and tail beans.* **2** follow a person or thing or (*Australian*) cattle.
tail off become fewer, smaller, or slighter etc.; cease gradually.

tailless *adjective* without a tail.

tailor¹ *noun* a person who makes men's clothes.

tailor² *verb* **1** make or fit clothes. **2** adapt or make something for a special purpose.

taint¹ *noun* a small amount of decay, pollution, or a bad quality that spoils something.

taint² *verb* give something a taint. [same origin as *tint*]

taipan (*say* ty-pan) *noun* a large venomous Australian snake.

take *verb* (**took, taken, taking**) **1** get something into your hands, *He took the cup.* **2** get possession of something; win, receive, *She took all the prizes.* **3** capture, *They took many prisoners.* **4** make use of; indulge in, *He takes the bus; Let's take a holiday.* **5** carry or convey, *Take this parcel to the post; Take the man to the station.* **6** remove; steal, *Who took my watch?* **7** perform or deal with, *When do you take your music exam?* **8** study or teach a subject, *Who takes you for maths?* **9** make an effort, *take trouble.* **10** experience a feeling, *Don't take offence.* **11** accept; endure, *I'll take*

▶▶ T H E S A U R U S ◀◀

tacky *adjective* **1** sticky, wet. **2** cheap, kitsch, shabby, tasteless, tawdry.

tact *noun* courtesy, delicacy, diplomacy, discretion, sensitivity.
tactful *adjective* considerate, courteous, diplomatic, discreet, polite, politic, sensitive, thoughtful.
tactless *adjective* impolite, impolitic, inconsiderate, indiscreet, insensitive, thoughtless, undiplomatic.

tactic *noun* approach, manoeuvre, plan, ploy (*informal*), policy, scheme, strategy, tack.

tag¹ *noun* **1** label, sticker, tab, ticket.

tag² *verb* **1** identify, label, mark, ticket. **2** add, append, attach, tack. **3** (*tag along with*) accompany, come with, follow, go with, trail after.

tail¹ *noun* **1** brush, dock, scut. **2** back, end, rear.

tail² *verb* **2** dog, follow, pursue, shadow, stalk, track, trail.

tailor¹ *noun* clothier, couturier, dressmaker, outfitter.

taint² *verb* (*taint the water*) contaminate, infect, poison, pollute, spoil; (*taint a reputation*) blacken, blemish, blot, stain, sully, tarnish.

take *verb* **1** clasp, clutch, grab, grasp, hold, pluck, seize, snatch. **2** acquire, gain, get, obtain, receive, scoop up, secure, win. **3** abduct, capture, carry off, catch, detain, seize. **4** catch, travel by, use. **5** accompany, bring, carry, conduct, convey, deliver, escort, guide, lead, run, transport. **6** appropriate, help yourself to, lift (*informal*), make off with, nick (*slang*), pilfer, pinch (*informal*), poach, pocket, purloin, remove, snaffle (*informal*), snatch, snavel (*Australian informal*), snitch (*slang*), souvenir (*slang*), steal, swipe (*informal*). **8** (*of a student*) learn, read, study; (*of a teacher*) instruct in, lecture in, teach, tutor in. **10** be affected by, experience, feel, get. **11** accept, bear, endure,

▶▶ D I C T I O N A R Y ◀◀

a risk. **12** require, *It takes a strong man to lift this.* **13** write down, *take notes.* **14** make a photograph. **15** subtract, *take 4 from 10.* **16** assume, *I take it that you agree.* **taker** *noun*
take after be like a parent etc.
take away remove something; subtract.
take back withdraw something you have said.
take in understand; deceive somebody.
take leave of say goodbye to.
take off remove clothes; (of an aircraft) leave the ground and become airborne; mimic satirically. **take-off** *noun*
take on begin to employ someone; play or fight against someone; agree to do something.
take out remove something; escort someone on an outing.
take over take control. **take-over** *noun*
take place happen; occur.
take up start something; occupy space or time etc.; accept an offer.
take-away *noun* a place that sells cooked meals for customers to take away; a meal from this.

takings *plural noun* money received.

talcum powder a scented powder put on the skin to make it feel smooth and dry.

tale *noun* a story.

talent *noun* a special or very great ability. **talented** *adjective* [from Greek *talanton* = sum of money]

talisman *noun* (*plural* **talismans**) an object supposed to bring good luck. [from Greek *telesma* = consecrated object]

talk[1] *verb* speak; have a conversation. **talker** *noun*
talk down to speak to someone in a way which shows that you feel superior.
talk into persuade by talking.
talk out of dissuade by talking.

talk[2] *noun* **1** talking; a conversation. **2** an informal lecture. **3** rumour or gossip.

talkative *adjective* talking a lot.

▶▶ T H E S A U R U S ◀◀

put up with, stand, stomach, suffer, tolerate, undergo, withstand. **12** call for, demand, need, require. **15** deduct, subtract. **16** assume, conclude, construe, gather, infer, interpret, suppose, understand.
take after be the (spitting) image of, look like, resemble.
take away 1 appropriate, commandeer, confiscate, deprive someone of, impound, remove, seize. **2** deduct, subtract.
take back recant, retract, revoke, withdraw.
take in 1 absorb, assimilate, comprehend, digest, grasp, realise, understand. **2** cheat, con (*informal*), deceive, dupe, fool, have on (*informal*), hoodwink, mislead, trick.
take off 1 doff, peel off, remove, shed, strip off. **2** caricature, imitate, lampoon, mimic, parody, send up (*informal*).
take-off *noun* caricature, imitation, lampoon, parody, send-up (*informal*), spoof (*informal*).
take on 1 appoint, employ, engage, hire, recruit. **2** accept, assume, shoulder, undertake.
take out draw out, extract, pull out, remove.
take place befall, come about, come to pass, happen, occur.
take up 1 begin, commence, embark on, start. **2** consume, eat up, fill, make inroads into, occupy, use up.

takings *plural noun* earnings, income, proceeds, receipts, revenue.

tale *noun* account, anecdote, fable, fairy tale, legend, myth, narrative, saga, story, yarn (*informal*).
talent *noun* ability, accomplishment, aptitude, bent, capacity, flair, genius, gift, knack, know-how, prowess, skill.
talk[1] *verb* babble, chat, chatter, communicate, confer, converse, gabble, gossip, jabber, lecture, mag (*Australian informal*), natter (*informal*), prattle, preach, rabbit on (*informal*), speak, unburden yourself, verbalise, vocalise, yabber (*Australian informal*), yak (*informal*).
talker *noun* chatterbox, conversationalist, gasbag (*informal*), orator, speaker, windbag (*informal*).
talk down to condescend to, patronise.
talk into cajole into, coax into, convince to, persuade to.
talk out of deter from, discourage from, dissuade from, stop.
talk[2] *noun* **1** chat, chinwag (*informal*), confabulation, conference, consultation, conversation, dialogue, discussion, gossip, natter (*informal*), tête-à-tête, yabber (*Australian informal*), yak (*informal*). **2** address, discourse, lecture, oration, presentation, sermon, speech. **3** gossip, hearsay, report, rumour.
talkative *adjective* chatty, communicative, garrulous, loquacious, voluble.

► ► D I C T I O N A R Y ◄ ◄

tall *adjective* **1** higher than the average, *a tall tree*. **2** measured from the bottom to the top, *It is 10 metres tall*. **tallness** *noun*
tall story (*informal*) a story that is hard to believe. [the original meaning was 'swift']

tallow *noun* animal fat used to make candles, soap, lubricants, etc.

tally¹ *noun* (*plural* **tallies**) the total amount of a debt or score.

tally² *verb* (**tallied, tallying**) correspond or agree with something else, *Does your list tally with mine?*

talon *noun* a strong claw.

tambourine *noun* a circular musical instrument with metal discs round it, tapped or shaken to make it jingle.

tame¹ *adjective* **1** (of animals) gentle and not afraid of people; not wild or dangerous. **2** not exciting; dull. **tamely** *adverb*, **tameness** *noun*

tame² *verb* (**tamed, taming**) make an animal become tame. **tamer** *noun*

Tamil *noun* **1** a member of a people of southern India and Sri Lanka. **2** their language.

tammar *noun* a **tammar wallaby**, a small wallaby in coastal western and southern Australia.

tam-o'-shanter *noun* a beret with a wide top. [named after Tam o'Shanter, hero of a poem by the Scottish poet Robert Burns]

tamp *verb* pack or ram down tightly.

tamper *verb* meddle or interfere with something.

tampon *noun* a plug of absorbent material especially to absorb menstrual blood.

tan¹ *noun* **1** light-brown colour. **2** brown colour in skin that has been exposed to sun.

tan² *adjective* light-brown.

tan³ *verb* (**tanned, tanning**) **1** make or become brown by exposing skin to the sun. **2** make an animal's skin into leather by treating it with chemicals.

tandem *noun* a bicycle for two riders, one behind the other. [Latin, = at length]

tandoori *noun* food cooked in a clay oven (a *tandoor*).

tang *noun* a strong flavour or smell.

tangent *noun* a straight line that touches the outside of a curve or circle. [from Latin *tangens* = touching]

tangerine *noun* a kind of small orange from Tangier in Morocco. [named after *Tangier*]

tangible *adjective* able to be touched; real. **tangibly** *adverb*, **tangibility** *noun* [from Latin *tangere* = touch]

tangle *verb* (**tangled, tangling**) make or become twisted into a confused mass. **tangle** *noun*, **tangled** *adjective*

tango *noun* (*plural* **tangos**) a ballroom dance with gliding steps.

tank *noun* **1** a large container for a liquid or gas. **2** a heavy armoured vehicle used in war. **3** (*Australian*) a reservoir formed by excavation and a dam.

tankard *noun* a large mug for drinking from, usually made of silver or pewter.

tanker *noun* **1** a large ship for carrying oil. **2** a large truck for carrying a liquid.

tanner *noun* a person who tans animal skins into leather. **tannery** *noun*

tannin *noun* a substance obtained from the bark or fruit of various trees (also found in tea), used in tanning and dyeing things.

► ► T H E S A U R U S ◄ ◄

tall *adjective* **1** (*a tall person*) gangling, gigantic, lanky, leggy; (*a tall building*) high, lofty, multi-storey, towering.

tally¹ *noun* account, count, reckoning, record, score, total.

tally² *verb* accord, agree, coincide, concur, conform, correspond, match, square.

tame¹ *adjective* **1** docile, domestic, domesticated, gentle. **2** bland, boring, dull, flat, unexciting, uninteresting.

tame² *verb* break in, domesticate, subdue, train.

tamper *verb* *tamper with* fiddle with, interfere with, meddle with, muck around with, play with, tinker with.

tan² *adjective* bronze, brownish-yellow, khaki, tawny, yellowish-brown.

tan³ *verb* **1** bronze, brown, suntan.

tang *noun* bite, piquancy, pungency, savour, sharpness, spiciness.

tangible *adjective* concrete, definite, objective, palpable, real, solid, substantial.

tangle *verb* confuse, entangle, entwine, knot, ravel, snarl, twist.
tangle *noun* confusion, jumble, jungle, knot, maze, muddle, snarl, web.
tangled *adjective* dishevelled, knotted, knotty, matted, ruffled, tousled, unkempt.

tank *noun* **1** cistern, reservoir, vat.

►►► D I C T I O N A R Y ◄◄

tantalise *verb* (**tantalised, tantalising**) tease or torment a person by showing him or her something good but keeping it out of reach. [from the name of Tantalus in Greek mythology, who was punished by being made to stand near water and fruit which moved away when he tried to reach them]

tantamount *adjective* equivalent, *The Queen's request was tantamount to a command.* [from Italian *tanto montare* = amount to so much]

tantrum *noun* an outburst of bad temper.

tap[1] *noun* a device for letting out liquid or gas in a controlled flow.

tap[2] *verb* (**tapped, tapping**) **1** take liquid out of something, especially through a tap. **2** obtain supplies or information etc. from a source. **3** fix a device to a telephone cable etc. so that you can overhear conversations on it.

tap[3] *noun* **1** a quick light hit; the sound of this. **2** tap-dancing.

tap[4] *verb* (**tapped, tapping**) hit a person or thing quickly and lightly.

tap-dancing *noun* dancing with shoes that make elaborate tapping sounds on the floor. **tap-dance** *noun*, **tap-dancer** *noun*

tape[1] *noun* **1** a narrow strip of cloth, paper, plastic, etc. **2** a narrow plastic strip coated with a magnetic substance and used for making recordings. **3** a tape-recording. **4** a tape-measure.

tape[2] *verb* (**taped, taping**) **1** fix, cover, or surround something with tape. **2** record something on magnetic tape.
get or **have something taped** (*slang*) know or understand it; be able to deal with it.

tape-measure *noun* a long strip of tape or flexible metal marked in centimetres or inches for measuring things.

taper[1] *verb* make or become narrower gradually.

taper[2] *noun* a very thin candle.

tape-recorder *noun* a device for recording sounds or computer data on magnetic tape and reproducing them. **tape-recording** *noun*

tapestry *noun* (*plural* **tapestries**) a piece of strong cloth with pictures or patterns woven or embroidered on it. [from French *tapis* = carpet]

tapeworm *noun* a long flat worm that can live as a parasite in the intestines of people and animals.

tapioca *noun* a starchy substance in hard white grains obtained from cassava, used for making puddings.

tapir (*say* **tay**-per) *noun* a pig-like animal with a long flexible snout.

tar[1] *noun* a thick black liquid made from coal or wood etc. and used in making roads.

tar[2] *verb* (**tarred, tarring**) coat something with tar.

tarantula *noun* **1** a large kind of spider found in southern Europe and in tropical countries. **2** (*Australian*) a huntsman spider.

tardy *adjective* (**tardier, tardiest**) slow; late. **tardily** *adverb*, **tardiness** *noun* [from Latin *tardus* = slow]

target[1] *noun* **1** something aimed at; a thing that someone tries to hit or reach. **2** a person or thing that people criticise, ridicule, etc.

target[2] *verb* (**targeted, targeting**) aim at or have as a target.

tariff *noun* a list of prices or charges.

tarmac *noun* an area surfaced with tar macadam, especially on an airfield. [*Tarmac* is a trade mark]

tar macadam a mixture of tar and broken stone, used for making a hard surface on roads, paths, etc.

tarnish *verb* **1** make or become less shiny, *The silver had tarnished.* **2** spoil; blemish, *The scandal tarnished his reputation.* **tarnish** *noun*

►►► T H E S A U R U S ◄◄

tantalise *verb* entice, lead on, tease, tempt, torment.

tantamount *adjective* as good as, equal, equivalent, the same as.

tantrum *noun* fit of temper, hysterics, outburst, paddy (*informal*), rage.

tap[1] *noun* faucet, stopcock, valve.

tap[2] *verb* **1** drain, draw off, extract, siphon off. **2** draw on, exploit, make use of, milk, use.

tap[3] *noun* **1** knock, patter, pit-a-pat, rap.

tap[4] *verb* beat, drum, hit, knock, patter, rap, strike.

tape[1] *noun* **1** binding, ribbon, strip. **2** audiotape, cassette, video, videotape.

tape[2] *verb* **1** bind, fasten, fix, seal, sellotape, stick. **2** record, tape-record, video, videotape.

taper[1] *verb* narrow, thin.

target[1] *noun* **1** aim, goal, object, objective. **2** butt, object, scapegoat, victim.

tariff *noun* charges, fees, prices, rates.

tarnish *verb* **1** blacken, discolour, dull, stain. **2** besmirch, blacken, blemish, mar, smirch, spoil, stain, sully, taint.

DICTIONARY

tarpaulin *noun* a large sheet of waterproof canvas. [from *tar* + *pall*[1]]

tarragon *noun* a plant with leaves that are used to flavour salads etc.

tarry[1] (*say* **tar**-ee) *adjective* of or like tar.

tarry[2] (*say* **ta**-ree) *verb* (**tarried, tarrying**) (*old use*) linger.

tart[1] *noun* a pastry case containing fruit, jam etc.

tart[2] *adjective* 1 sour. 2 sharp in manner, *a tart reply*. **tartly** *adverb*, **tartness** *noun*

tartan *noun* a pattern with coloured stripes crossing each other, especially one associated with a Scottish clan.

tartar[1] *noun* a person who is fierce or difficult to deal with. [named after the Tartars, warriors from central Asia in the 13th century]

tartar[2] *noun* a hard chalky deposit that forms on teeth. [medieval Latin from Greek]

tartlet *noun* a small pastry tart.

task *noun* a piece of work to be done.
take a person to task rebuke him or her.
task force a group specially organised for a particular task.

taskmaster *noun* a person imposing tasks on others, *a hard taskmaster*.

tassel *noun* a bundle of threads tied together at the top and used to decorate something. **tasselled** *adjective*

taste[1] *verb* (**tasted, tasting**) 1 take a small amount of food or drink to try its flavour. 2 be able to perceive flavours. 3 have a certain flavour.

taste[2] *noun* 1 the feeling caused in the tongue by something placed on it. 2 the ability to taste things. 3 the ability to enjoy beautiful things or to choose what is suitable, *Her choice of clothes shows her good taste*. 4 a liking, *He always had a taste for camping*. 5 a very small amount of food or drink.

tasteful *adjective* showing good taste. **tastefully** *adverb*, **tastefulness** *noun*

tasteless *adjective* 1 having no flavour. 2 showing poor taste. **tastelessly** *adverb*, **tastelessness** *noun*

tasty *adjective* (**tastier, tastiest**) having a strong pleasant taste.

tattered *adjective* badly torn; ragged.

tatters *plural noun* rags; badly torn pieces, *My coat was in tatters*.

tatting *noun* a kind of hand-made lace.

tattle *verb* (**tattled, tattling**) gossip. **tattle** *noun*

tattoo[1] *verb* mark a person's skin with a picture or pattern by using a needle and some dye.

tattoo[2] *noun* a tattooed mark.

tattoo[3] *noun* 1 a drumming or tapping sound. 2 an entertainment consisting of military music, marching, etc.

tatty *adjective* 1 ragged; shabby and untidy. 2 cheap and gaudy. **tattily** *adverb*, **tattiness** *noun*

THESAURUS

tart[1] *noun* flan, pastry, pie, quiche, tartlet.

tart[2] *adjective* 1 acid, acidic, astringent, piquant, pungent, sharp, sour, tangy. 2 acid, biting, caustic, cutting, sharp, trenchant.

task *noun* assignment, charge, chore, commission, duty, errand, function, job, mission, work.
take to task admonish, castigate, censure, chastise, chide (*old use*), criticise, rebuke, reprimand, reproach, reprove, scold, tell off (*informal*), tick off (*informal*), upbraid.

taskmaster *noun* boss, disciplinarian, martinet, slave-driver, tyrant.

taste[1] *verb* 1 sample, savour, sip, test, try.

taste[2] *noun* 1 flavour, savour, tang. 3 discernment, discrimination, judgement, refinement, style. 4 appetite, fondness, inclination, liking, love, partiality, penchant, predilection. 5 bit, bite, morsel, mouthful, nibble, piece, sample, sip, swallow, titbit.

tasteful *adjective* aesthetic, artistic, attractive, elegant, graceful, handsome, refined, stylish.

tasteless *adjective* 1 bland, flavourless, insipid, weak, wishy-washy. 2 cheap, coarse, crude, garish, gaudy, improper, indelicate, inelegant, kitsch, offensive, rude, showy, tacky (*informal*), tawdry, unattractive, unseemly, vulgar.

tasty *adjective* appetising, delectable, delicious, flavoursome, luscious, mouth-watering, palatable, piquant, savoury, scrumptious (*informal*), yummy (*informal*).

tattered *adjective* frayed, holey, ragged, ripped, tatty (*informal*), threadbare, torn, worn-out.

tatters *plural noun* rags, shreds.

tatty *adjective* 1 frayed, holey, moth-eaten, old, patched, ragged, scruffy, shabby, tattered, untidy, worn.

taunt *verb* jeer at or insult someone. **taunt** *noun* [from French *tant pour tant* = tit for tat]

taut *adjective* stretched tightly. **tautly** *adverb*, **tautness** *noun*

tauten *verb* make or become taut.

tautology *noun* (*plural* **tautologies**) saying the same thing again in different words, e.g. *You can get the book free for nothing* (where *free* and *for nothing* mean the same). [from Greek *tauto* = the same, + *logos* = word]

tavern *noun* (*old use*) an inn or public house. [from Latin *taberna* = hut]

tawdry *adjective* cheap and gaudy. **tawdriness** *noun* [from *St. Audrey's lace* (cheap finery formerly sold at St. Audrey's fair at Ely in England)]

tawny *adjective* brownish-yellow.

tax¹ *noun* (*plural* **taxes**) **1** money that people or business firms have to pay to the government, to be used for public purposes. **2** a strain or burden, *The long walk was a tax on his strength.*

tax² *verb* **1** put a tax on something. **2** charge someone a tax. **3** put a strain or burden on a person or thing, *Will it tax your strength?* **4** accuse, *I taxed him with leaving the door open.* **taxable** *adjective*, **taxation** *noun*, **taxing** *adjective* [from Latin *taxare* = calculate]

taxi¹ *noun* (*plural* **taxis**) a car that carries passengers for payment, usually with a meter (*taximeter*) to record the fare payable. **taxi-cab** *noun* [short for *taximeter cab*]

taxi² *verb* (**taxied, taxiing**) (of an aircraft) move along the ground or water, especially before or after flying.

taxidermist *noun* a person who prepares and stuffs the skins of animals in a lifelike form. **taxidermy** *noun* [from Greek *taxis* = arrangement, + *derma* = skin]

taxpayer *noun* a person who pays tax.

TB *abbreviation* tuberculosis.

tea *noun* **1** a drink made by pouring hot water on the dried leaves of an evergreen shrub (the *tea-plant*). **2** these dried leaves. **3** a meal in the afternoon or evening at which tea is served (often the main evening meal). **teacup** *noun*, **tea-leaf** *noun*, **teatime** *noun* [from Chinese *t'e*]

tea-bag *noun* a small bag holding about a teaspoonful of tea.

teacake *noun* a kind of bun usually served toasted and buttered.

teach *verb* (**taught, teaching**) **1** give a person knowledge or skill; train. **2** give lessons, especially in a particular subject. **3** show someone what to do or avoid, *That will teach you not to meddle!*

teachable *adjective* able to be taught.

teacher *noun* a person who teaches others, especially in a school.

teaching *noun* **1** the profession of a teacher. **2** what is taught, *the Church's teachings.*

teak *noun* the hard strong wood of an evergreen Asian tree.

teal *noun* (*plural* **teal**) a kind of duck.

taunt *verb* chiack (*Australian informal*), deride, gibe, jeer at, make fun of, mock, poke borak at (*Australian informal*), poke fun at, ridicule, scoff at, sling off at (*Australian informal*), sneer at, take the mickey out of (*informal*), tease, torment.
taunt *noun* barb, dig, gibe, insult, jeer, sneer.

taut *adjective* stretched, tense, tight.

tawdry *adjective* cheap, flashy, garish, gaudy, kitsch, showy, tacky (*informal*), tasteless, tatty (*informal*).

tax¹ *noun* **1** charge, customs, duty, excise, impost, levy, rates, slug (*Australian informal*), tariff, taxation, tithe (*historical*), toll, tribute (*historical*).

tax² *verb* **3** burden, challenge, exhaust, overload, overwork, strain, stretch, tire.

taxing *adjective* challenging, demanding, difficult, draining, exacting, exhausting, hard, onerous, strenuous, stressful, tiring, tough.

taxi¹ *noun* cab, taxi-cab.

teach *verb* **1** coach, drill, edify, educate, enlighten, implant, inculcate, indoctrinate, inform, instil, instruct, lecture, school, train, tutor.

teacher *noun* chalkie (*Australian slang*), coach, educator, governess, guide, guru, headmaster, headmistress, instructor, lecturer, master, mentor, mistress, pedagogue (*old use*), preacher, principal, professor, rabbi, schoolie (*Australian slang*), schoolmaster, schoolmistress, schoolteacher, trainer, tutor.

teaching *noun* **1** education, instruction, training, tuition. **2** doctrine, dogma, precept, principle, tenet.

▶▶ D I C T I O N A R Y ◀◀

team¹ *noun* **1** a set of players forming one side in certain games and sports. **2** a set of people working together. **3** two or more animals harnessed to pull a vehicle or a plough etc. **teamwork** *noun*

team² *verb* put together in a team; combine.

teapot *noun* a pot with a lid and a handle, for making and pouring tea.

tear¹ (*say* teer) *noun* a drop of the water that comes from the eyes when a person cries. **tear-drop** *noun*
in tears crying.

tear² (*say* tair) *verb* (**tore, torn, tearing**) **1** pull something apart or into pieces. **2** become torn, *Newspaper tears easily.* **3** run or travel hurriedly. **4** pull something away.

tear³ *noun* a split made by tearing.

tearful *adjective* in tears; crying easily. **tearfully** *adverb*

tear-gas *noun* a gas that makes people's eyes water painfully.

tease¹ *verb* (**teased, teasing**) **1** amuse yourself by deliberately annoying or making fun of someone. **2** pick threads apart into separate strands.

tease² *noun* a person who often teases others.

teasel *noun* a plant with bristly heads formerly used to brush up the surface of cloth. [from *tease¹* 2]

teaser *noun* a difficult problem.

teaspoon *noun* a small spoon for stirring tea etc. **teaspoonful** *noun*

teat *noun* **1** a nipple through which a baby sucks milk. **2** the cap of a baby's feeding-bottle.

tea-towel *noun* a cloth for drying washed dishes, cutlery, etc.

tea-tree *noun* **1** a shrub producing tea. **2** any of various Australian shrubs resembling this.

technical *adjective* **1** concerned with technology. **2** of a particular subject and its methods, *the technical terms of chemistry.* **technically** *adverb* [from Greek *technikos* = skilful]

technicality *noun* (*plural* **technicalities**) **1** being technical. **2** a technical word or phrase; a special detail.

technician *noun* a skilled mechanic.

technique *noun* the method of doing something skilfully.

technology *noun* (*plural* **technologies**) the study of machinery, engineering, and how things work. **technological** *adjective*, **technologist** *noun* [from Greek *techne* = skill, + *-logy*]

teddy-bear *noun* a soft furry toy bear. [named after US President Theodore ('Teddy') Roosevelt in about 1906]

tedious *adjective* annoyingly slow or long; boring. **tediously** *adverb*, **tediousness** *noun*, **tedium** *noun* [from Latin *taedium* = tiredness]

tee *noun* **1** the flat area from which golfers strike the ball at the start of play for each hole. **2** a small piece of wood or plastic on which the ball is placed for being struck.

teem *verb* **1** be full of something, *The river was teeming with fish.* **2** rain very hard; pour.

▶▶ T H E S A U R U S ◀◀

team¹ *noun* **1** club, line-up, side, squad. **2** band, corps, crew, force, gang, group, staff, unit. **teamwork** *noun* collaboration, cooperation.

team² *verb* (**team up**) band together, collaborate, combine, cooperate, join forces, unite.

tear² *verb* **1** gash, lacerate, ladder, mangle, mutilate, rend, rip, rupture, shred, slash, slit, snag, split. **3** bolt, dart, dash, fly, gallop, hurry, hurtle, race, rip, run, rush, shoot, speed, sprint, spurt, streak, sweep, whiz, zip. **4** grab, pluck, pull, rip, seize, snatch.

tear³ *noun* gash, hole, laceration, rent, rip, rupture, slash, slit, split.

tearful *adjective* crying, emotional, lachrymose, maudlin, sobbing, teary (*informal*), upset, weepy (*informal*).

tease¹ *verb* **1** annoy, bait, bother, chaff, chiack (*Australian informal*), gibe, make fun of, molest, needle, pay out, pester, poke borak at (*Australian informal*), poke fun at, provoke, rag, rib (*informal*), ridicule, sling off at (*Australian informal*), stir (*informal*), take the mickey out of (*informal*), tantalise, taunt, torment.

teat *noun* **1** dug, nipple.

technical *adjective* **1** applied, mechanical, practical. **2** scientific, specialised, specialist.

technique *noun* approach, art, craft, knack, manner, method, procedure, skill, system, trick, way.

tedious *adjective* boring, dreary, dull, humdrum, laborious, long-winded, monotonous, stodgy, tiresome, tiring, unexciting, uninteresting, wearisome.

teem *verb* **1** abound, be full (of), be overrun, brim, overflow, seethe, swarm. **2** bucket down, pelt, pour, rain, rain cats and dogs (*informal*).

▶▶ D I C T I O N A R Y ◀◀

teenage *adjective* of teenagers.

teenaged *adjective* in your teens.

teenager *noun* a person in his or her teens.

teens *plural noun* the time of life from 13 to 19 years of age.

teeny *adjective* (**teenier**, **teeniest**) (*informal*) tiny.

teeter *verb* stand or move unsteadily.

teething *noun* (of a baby) having its first teeth beginning to grow through the gums.

teetotal *adjective* never drinking alcohol. **teetotaller** *noun*

tele- *prefix* far; at a distance (as in *telescope*). [from Greek *tele* = far off]

telecommunications *plural noun* communications over a long distance, e.g. by telephone, telegraph, radio, satellite, or television.

telegram *noun* a message sent by telegraph. [from *tele-* + *-gram*]

telegraph *noun* a way of sending messages by using electric current along wires or by radio. **telegraphic** *adjective*, **telegraphy** *noun* [from *tele-* + *-graph*]

telepathy (*say* til-**ep**-ath-ee) *noun* communication of thoughts from one person's mind to another without speaking, writing, or gestures. **telepathic** *adjective* [from *tele-*, + Greek *pathos* = feeling]

telephone¹ *noun* a device or system using electric wires or radio etc. to enable one person to speak to another who is some distance away.

telephone² *verb* (**telephoned**, **telephoning**) speak to a person on the telephone. [from *tele-*, + Greek *phone* = voice]

telephonist (*say* til-**ef**-on-ist) *noun* a person who operates a telephone switchboard.

telescope¹ *noun* an instrument using lenses to magnify distant objects. **telescopic** *adjective* [from *tele-*, + Greek *skopein* = look at]

telescope² *verb* (**telescoped**, **telescoping**) **1** make or become shorter by sliding overlapping sections into each other. **2** compress or condense so as to take less space or time.

televise *verb* (**televised**, **televising**) broadcast something by television.

television *noun* **1** a system using radio waves to reproduce a view of scenes, events, or plays etc. on a screen. **2** an apparatus for receiving these pictures. **3** televised programmes. [from *tele-* + *vision*]

telex *noun* a system for sending printed messages by telegraphy. **telex** *verb*

tell *verb* (**told**, **telling**) **1** make a thing known to someone, especially by words. **2** speak, *Tell the truth.* **3** order, *Tell them to wait.* **4** reveal a secret, *Promise you won't tell; We won't tell on you.* **5** decide; distinguish, *Can you tell the difference between butter and margarine?* **6** produce an effect, *The strain began to tell on him.* **7** count, *There are ten of them, all told.* **tell off** (*informal*) reprimand. **tell tales** report what someone has done.

telling *adjective* having a strong effect, *a very telling reply.*

▶▶ T H E S A U R U S ◀◀

teenager *noun* adolescent, juvenile, minor, youth.

teeter *verb* lurch, reel, stagger, sway, totter, wobble.

teetotal *adjective* abstinent, non-drinking, temperate.
  teetotaller *noun* abstainer, non-drinker, wowser (*Australian*).

telepathic *adjective* psychic.

telephone¹ *noun* blower (*informal*), phone.

telephone² *verb* call, dial, give someone a bell (*informal*), give someone a buzz (*informal*), give someone a call, phone, ring (up).

televise *verb* broadcast, screen, telecast, transmit.

television *noun* **2** television receiver, television set, telly (*informal*), the box (*informal*), TV.

tell *verb* **1** acquaint (with), advise, announce, apprise (*formal*), broadcast, chronicle, communicate, confess, describe, disclose, divulge, explain, impart, inform, make known, mention, narrate, notify, proclaim, recite, recount, relate, report, reveal, state, warn. **2** say, speak, utter. **3** bid, command, direct, instruct, order. **4** blab, give the show away, let the cat out of the bag, spill the beans (*slang*), squeal (*slang*), talk, tittle-tattle; (*tell on*) betray, blow the whistle on (*informal*), dob in (*Australian informal*), grass (on) (*slang*), inform on, rat on (*slang*), report, shop (*slang*), sneak on (*slang*), split on (*slang*). **5** determine, discern, discover, distinguish, identify, make out, recognise.
  tell off admonish, blast (*informal*), castigate, censure, chastise, go crook at (*Australian informal*), lecture, rebuke, reprimand, reproach, rouse on (*Australian informal*), scold, tick off (*informal*).

telling *adjective* effective, forceful, powerful, significant, strong, weighty.

tell-tale¹ *noun* a person who tells tales.

tell-tale² *adjective* revealing or indicating something, *There was a tell-tale spot of jam on his chin.*

telly *noun* (*plural* **tellies**) (*informal*) **1** television. **2** a television set.

temerity (*say* tim-**e**rri-tee) *noun* rashness; boldness.

temper¹ *noun* **1** a person's mood, *He is in a good temper.* **2** an angry mood, *She was in a temper.*

lose your temper lose your calmness and become angry.

temper² *verb* **1** harden or strengthen metal etc. by heating and cooling it. **2** moderate or soften the effects of something, *tempering justice with mercy.* [from Latin *temperare* = mix]

temperament *noun* a person's nature as shown in the way he or she usually behaves, *a nervous temperament.*

temperamental *adjective* **1** of a person's temperament. **2** likely to become excitable or moody suddenly. **temperamentally** *adverb*

temperance *noun* **1** moderation; self-restraint. **2** drinking little or no alcohol.

temperate *adjective* neither extremely hot nor extremely cold, *Tasmania has a temperate climate.*

temperature *noun* **1** how hot or cold a person or thing is. **2** an abnormally high temperature of the body.

tempest *noun* a violent storm. [from Latin *tempestas* = weather]

tempestuous *adjective* stormy; full of commotion.

temple¹ *noun* a building where a god is worshipped. [from Latin *templum* = consecrated place]

temple² *noun* the part of the head between the forehead and the ear. [from Latin *tempora* = sides of the head]

tempo *noun* (*plural* **tempos**) the speed or rhythm of something, especially of a piece of music. [Italian, from Latin *tempus* = time]

temporary *adjective* lasting for a limited time only; not permanent. **temporarily** (*say* **tem**-per-er-il-ee) *adverb* [from Latin *temporis* = of a time]

temporise *verb* (**temporised**, **temporising**) avoid giving a definite answer, in order to postpone something.

tempt *verb* try to persuade or attract someone, especially into doing something wrong or unwise. **temptation** *noun*, **tempter** *noun*, **temptress** *noun*, **tempting** *adjective* [from Latin *temptare* = test]

ten *noun* & *adjective* the number 10; one more than nine.

tenable *adjective* able to be held, *a tenable theory; the job is tenable for one year only.* [from Latin *tenere* = to hold]

tell-tale¹ *noun* blabbermouth, dobber (*Australian informal*), grass (*slang*), informer, sneak (*informal*), tale-bearer.

tell-tale² *adjective* give-away (*informal*), indicative, meaningful, revealing, significant.

temerity *noun* audacity, boldness, cheek, effrontery, gall, hide, impertinence, impudence, nerve, presumption, rashness.

temper¹ *noun* **1** disposition, frame of mind, humour, mood. **2** anger, fury, hotheadedness, irascibility, ire, irritation, paddy (*informal*), peevishness, petulance, pique, rage, tantrum, wrath.

temper² *verb* **2** mitigate, moderate, palliate, soften, tone down.

temperament *noun* character, disposition, make-up, nature, personality, spirit, temper.

temperamental *adjective* **2** capricious, changeable, emotional, erratic, excitable, fickle, highly-strung, hotheaded, mercurial, moody, touchy, unpredictable, volatile.

temperate *adjective* gentle, mild, moderate.

tempest *noun* cyclone, gale, hurricane, storm, tornado, typhoon.

tempestuous *adjective* blustery, rough, squally, stormy, turbulent, violent, wild, windy.

temple¹ *noun* church, gurdwara, mosque, pagoda, sanctuary, shrine, stupa, synagogue, tabernacle.

tempo *noun* pace, rate, speed.

temporary *adjective* brief, ephemeral, fleeting, impermanent, interim, makeshift, momentary, passing, provisional, short-lived, short-term, stopgap, transient, transitory.

tempt *verb* allure, attract, bait, coax, entice, inveigle, lure, seduce, tantalise.

temptation *noun* attraction, bait, draw, enticement, incentive, inducement, lure.

tempting *adjective* alluring, appealing, attractive, enticing, inviting, irresistible, seductive.

tenable *adjective* arguable, defensible, plausible, reasonable, supportable.

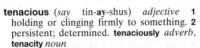

tenacious (*say* tin-**ay**-shus) *adjective* **1** holding or clinging firmly to something. **2** persistent; determined. **tenaciously** *adverb*, **tenacity** *noun*

tenant *noun* a person who rents a house, building, or land etc. from a landlord. **tenancy** *noun* [from Latin *tenens* = holding]

tend[1] *verb* have a certain tendency, *Prices tend to rise.* [from Latin *tendere* = stretch]

tend[2] *verb* look after, *Shepherds were tending their sheep.* [from *attend*]

tendency *noun* (*plural* **tendencies**) the way a person or thing is likely to behave, *She has a tendency to be lazy.*

tender[1] *adjective* **1** easy to chew; not tough or hard. **2** easily hurt or damaged; sensitive; delicate, *tender plants.* **3** gentle and loving, *a tender smile.* **tenderly** *adverb*, **tenderness** *noun* [from Latin *tener* = soft]

tender[2] *verb* offer something formally, *He tendered his resignation.*

tender[3] *noun* a formal offer to supply goods or carry out work at a stated price, *The council asked for tenders to build a school.* [same origin as *tend*[1]]
legal tender kinds of money that are legal for making payments, *Are two-cent coins still legal tender?*

tender[4] *noun* **1** a truck attached to a steam locomotive to carry its coal and water. **2** a small boat carrying stores or passengers to and from a larger one. [from *tend*[2]]

tender-hearted *adjective* compassionate.

tendon *noun* a strong strip of tissue that joins muscle to bone.

tendril *noun* **1** a thread-like part by which a climbing plant clings to a support. **2** a thin curl of hair etc.

tenement *noun* a large house or building divided into flats or rooms that are let to separate tenants.

tenet (*say* **ten**-it) *noun* a firm belief held by a person or group. [Latin, = he or she holds]

tennis *noun* a game played with racquets and a ball on a court with a net across the middle. [from French *tenez!* = receive (called by the person serving)]

tenon *noun* a projecting piece of wood etc. shaped to fit into a mortise.

tenor *noun* a male singer with a high voice.

tense[1] *noun* the form of a verb that shows when something happens, e.g. he *came* (**past tense**), he *comes* or *is coming* (**present tense**), he *will come* (**future tense**). [from Latin *tempus* = time]

tense[2] *adjective* **1** tightly stretched. **2** with muscles tight because you are nervous or excited. **3** causing tenseness. **tensely** *adverb*, **tenseness** *noun*

tense[3] *verb* (**tensed**, **tensing**) make or become tense. [from Latin *tensum* = stretched]

tensile *adjective* **1** of tension. **2** able to be stretched.

tension *noun* **1** pulling so as to stretch something; being stretched. **2** tenseness; the condition when feelings are tense. **3** voltage, *high-tension cables.*

tenacious *adjective* **1** firm, iron, powerful, strong, tight. **2** determined, dogged, obstinate, persistent, resolute, staunch, stubborn, unyielding.

tenant *noun* inhabitant, lessee, occupant, resident.

tend[1] *verb* be apt, be disposed, be inclined, be liable, be prone.

tend[2] *verb* attend to, care for, cherish, keep an eye on, keep watch over, look after, mind, nurse, take care of, watch.

tendency *noun* disposition, inclination, penchant, predilection, predisposition, proclivity, propensity, readiness.

tender[1] *adjective* **1** edible, soft, succulent. **2** delicate, fragile, frail, sensitive, vulnerable. **3** affectionate, compassionate, fond, gentle, kind, loving.

tender[2] *verb* give, hand in, offer, present, proffer, submit.

tender[3] *noun* bid, offer, proposal, quotation, quote (*informal*).

tender-hearted *adjective* caring, compassionate, humane, kind, kind-hearted, kindly, merciful, soft-hearted, sympathetic, warm-hearted.

tenet *noun* belief, creed, doctrine, dogma, precept, principle, teaching.

tense[2] *adjective* **1** stiff, strained, stretched, taut, tight. **2** anxious, apprehensive, edgy, highly-strung, jumpy, keyed up, nervous, nervy, uneasy, uptight (*informal*). **3** explosive, fraught, nerve-racking, strained, stressful, uneasy, volatile.

tension *noun* **1** stiffness, tautness, tightness. **2** anxiety, apprehension, strain, stress, suspense, uneasiness.

tent *noun* a shelter made of canvas or other material. [same origin as *tense*³]

tentacle *noun* a long flexible part of the body of certain animals (e.g. octopuses), used for feeling or grasping things or for moving.

tentative *adjective* cautious; trying something out, *a tentative suggestion.* **tentatively** *adverb* [same origin as *tempt*]

tenterhooks *plural noun* **on tenterhooks** tense and anxious. [from *tenter* = a machine with hooks for stretching cloth to dry]

tenth *adjective & noun* next after the ninth.

tenuous *adjective* very slight or thin, *tenuous threads.* [from Latin *tenuis* = thin]

tenure (*say* **ten**-yoor) *noun* the holding of office or of land, accommodation, etc.

tepee (*say* **tee**-pee) *noun* a wigwam.

tepid *adjective* only slightly warm; lukewarm, *tepid water.*

term¹ *noun* **1** the period of weeks when a school or college is open. **2** a definite period, *a term of imprisonment.* **3** a word or expression, *technical terms.*

terms *plural noun* a relationship between people, *They are on friendly terms*; conditions offered or accepted, *peace terms*; charges, prices.

term² *verb* name; call by a certain term, *This music is termed jazz.* [from Latin *terminus* = boundary]

termagant *noun* a shrewish bullying woman.

terminable *adjective* able to be terminated.

terminal¹ *noun* **1** the place where something ends; a terminus. **2** a building where air passengers arrive or depart. **3** a place where a

wire is connected in an electric circuit or battery etc. **4** a device for sending information to a computer, or for receiving it.

terminal² *adjective* **1** of or at the end or boundary of something. **2** of or in the last stage of a fatal disease, *terminal cancer.* **terminally** *adverb*

terminate *verb* (**terminated, terminating**) end; stop finally. **termination** *noun* [same origin as *terminus*]

terminology *noun* the technical terms of a subject. **terminological** *adjective* [from *term* + *-logy*]

terminus *noun* (*plural* **termini**) the end of something; the last station on a railway or bus route. [Latin, = the end]

termite *noun* a small insect that is very destructive to timber.

tern *noun* a sea-bird with long wings.

terrace *noun* **1** a level area on a slope or hillside. **2** a paved area beside a house. **3** a row of houses joined together. **terraced** *adjective* [from Latin *terra* = earth]

terracotta *noun* **1** a kind of pottery. **2** the brownish-red colour of flowerpots. [Italian, = baked earth]

terrain *noun* a stretch of land, *hilly terrain.* [from Latin *terra* = earth]

terrapin *noun* an edible freshwater turtle of North America.

terrestrial *adjective* **1** of the earth. **2** of land; living on land. [from Latin *terra* = earth]

terrible *adjective* very bad; distressing. **terribly** *adverb* [from Latin *terrere* = frighten]

terrier *noun* a kind of small lively dog.

tent *noun* big top, marquee, tepee, wigwam.

tentative *adjective* cautious, experimental, hesitant, provisional, trial, unconfirmed.

term¹ *noun* **1** semester, trimester. **2** course, duration, period, session, spell, stint, stretch, time. **3** expression, name, phrase, word.

terms *plural noun* **1** footing, relations, standing. **2** conditions, provisions, specifications, stipulations. **3** charges, fees, prices, rates.

term² *verb* call, designate, label, name.

terminal¹ *noun* **1** depot, station, terminus.

terminal² *adjective* **2** deadly, fatal, incurable, mortal.

terminate *verb* cease, close, come to an end, conclude, cut off, end, finish, round off, stop, wind up.

terminology *noun* jargon, language, lingo (*informal*), nomenclature, phraseology, terms, vocabulary, words.

terminus *noun* depot, last stop, station, terminal.

terrain *noun* country, ground, land, landscape, region, territory.

terrible *adjective* abominable, abysmal, appalling, atrocious, awful, bad, catastrophic, disastrous, distressing, dreadful, excruciating, frightful, ghastly, gruesome, hideous, horrendous, horrible, horrific, intolerable, lousy (*informal*), miserable, nasty, rotten (*informal*), shocking, terrifying, unbearable, woeful.

▶▶ D I C T I O N A R Y ◀◀

terrific *adjective* (*informal*) **1** very great, *a terrific storm.* **2** excellent. **terrifically** *adverb*

terrify *verb* (**terrified, terrifying**) fill someone with terror.

territory *noun* (*plural* **territories**) an area of land, especially one that belongs to a country or person. **territorial** *adjective* [from Latin *terra* = earth]

terror *noun* **1** very great fear. **2** a terrifying person or thing. [from Latin *terrere* = frighten]

terrorise *verb* (**terrorised, terrorising**) fill someone with terror; control or compel someone by frightening them. **terrorisation** *noun*

terrorist *noun* a person who uses violence for political purposes. **terrorism** *noun*

terse *adjective* concise; curt. **tersely** *adverb*, **terseness** *noun* [from Latin *tersum* = polished]

tertiary (*say* **ter**-sher-ee) *adjective* of the third stage of something; coming after secondary. [from Latin *tertius* = third]

tessellate *verb* (**tessellated, tessellating**) fit shapes into a pattern without overlapping. **tessellation** *noun*

test¹ *noun* **1** a short examination; a way of discovering the qualities or abilities etc. of a person or thing. **2** (*informal*) a test match.

test match a cricket or Rugby match between teams from different countries.

test² *verb* make a test of a person or thing. **tester** *noun*

testament *noun* **1** a written statement. **2** either of the two main parts of the Bible, the Old Testament or the New Testament. [from Latin *testis* = witness]

testator *noun* a person who has made a will.

testicle *noun* either of the two glands in the scrotum where semen is produced.

testify *verb* (**testified, testifying**) give evidence; swear that something is true. [from Latin *testis* = witness]

testimonial *noun* **1** a letter describing someone's abilities, character, etc. **2** a gift presented to someone as a mark of respect.

testimony *noun* (*plural* **testimonies**) **1** what someone testifies. **2** evidence in support of something.

test-tube *noun* a tube of thin glass with one end closed, used for experiments in chemistry etc.

testy *adjective* easily annoyed; irritable.

tetanus *noun* a disease that makes the muscles become stiff, caused by bacteria. [from Greek *tetanos* = a spasm]

tether¹ *verb* tie an animal so that it cannot move far.

▶▶ T H E S A U R U S ◀◀

terrific *adjective* **1** astronomical, colossal, enormous, excessive, exorbitant, extravagant, extreme, fierce, huge, intense, large, mighty, monumental, severe, staggering, stupendous, tremendous. **2** admirable, brilliant, excellent, extraordinary, fabulous (*informal*), fantastic (*informal*), fine, first-class, great, incredible, magnificent, marvellous, outstanding, phenomenal, remarkable, sensational, spectacular, splendid, super (*informal*), superb, unbelievable, wonderful.

terrify *verb* alarm, appal, dismay, freak out (*informal*), frighten, horrify, petrify, scare, terrorise.
terrifying *adjective* alarming, frightening, hair-raising, horrifying, nightmarish, scary, spine-chilling.

territory *noun* area, country, district, domain, land, province, region, state, terrain, tract, zone.

terror *noun* **1** alarm, consternation, dismay, dread, fear, fright, horror, panic, trepidation.

terrorise *verb* bully, frighten, intimidate, menace, persecute, terrify, torment.

terse *adjective* abrupt, brief, brusque, compact, concise, crisp, curt, laconic, pithy, short, snappy (*informal*), succinct.

test¹ *noun* **1** analysis, appraisal, assessment, audition, check, evaluation, exam (*informal*), examination, experiment, quiz, trial, try-out.

test² *verb* appraise, assess, audition, check, evaluate, examine, experiment with, question, quiz, sample, screen, trial, try out.

testify *verb* affirm, attest, bear witness, declare, give evidence, state under oath, swear.

testimony *noun* **1** affidavit, declaration, deposition, evidence, statement. **2** demonstration, evidence, indication, manifestation, proof.

testy *adjective* bad-tempered, cranky, cross, crotchety, grouchy (*informal*), grumpy, irritable, peevish, petulant, prickly, querulous, shirty (*informal*), short-tempered, snaky (*Australian informal*), stroppy (*informal*), surly, tetchy, touchy.

tether¹ *verb* chain up, secure, tie up.

▶▷ D I C T I O N A R Y ◁◀

tether² *noun* a rope for tethering an animal.
at the end of your tether unable to endure something any more.

tetra- *prefix* four. [Greek, = four]

tetrahedron *noun* a solid with four sides (e.g. a pyramid with a triangular base). [from *tetra-*, + Greek *hedra* = base]

text *noun* **1** the words of something written or printed. **2** a sentence from the Bible used as the subject of a sermon etc. [from Latin *textus* = literary style]

textbook *noun* a book that teaches you about a subject.

textiles *plural noun* kinds of cloth; fabrics. [from Latin *textum* = woven]

texture *noun* the way that the surface of something feels.

thalidomide *noun* a medicinal drug that was found (in 1961) to cause babies to be born with deformed arms and legs. [from its chemical name]

than *conjunction* compared with another person or thing, *His brother is taller than he is* or *taller than him.*

thank *verb* tell someone that you are grateful to him or her.
thank you I thank you.

thankful *adjective* grateful. **thankfully** *adverb*

thankless *adjective* not likely to win thanks from people, *a thankless task.*

thanks *plural noun* **1** statements of gratitude. **2** (*informal*) thank you.
thanks to as a result of; because of, *Thanks to your help, we succeeded.*

thanksgiving *noun* an expression of gratitude, especially to God.

that¹ *adjective & pronoun* (*plural* **those**) the one there, *That book is mine. Whose is that?*

that² *adverb* to such an extent, *I'll come that far but no further.*

that³ *relative pronoun* which, who, or whom, *This is the record that I wanted. We liked the people that we met on holiday.*

that⁴ *conjunction* used to introduce a wish, reason, result, etc., *I hope that you are well. The puzzle was so hard that no one could solve it.*

thatch *noun* straw or reeds used to make a roof. **thatch** *verb*

thaw¹ *verb* melt; stop being frozen.

thaw² *noun* the process of thawing; weather that thaws ice.

the *adjective* (called the *definite article*) a particular one; that or those.

theatre *noun* **1** a building where plays etc. are performed to an audience. **2** a special room where surgical operations are done, *the operating-theatre.* [from Greek *theatron* = place for seeing things]

theatrical *adjective* of plays or acting. **theatrically** *adverb*

theatricals *plural noun* performances of plays etc.

thee *pronoun* (*old use*) the form of *thou* used as the object of a verb or after a preposition.

theft *noun* stealing.

their *adjective* **1** belonging to them, *Their coats are over there.* **2** (*informal*) belonging to a person, *Somebody has left their coat on the bus.*

theirs *possessive pronoun* belonging to them, *These coats are theirs.*

Usage It is incorrect to write *their's.*

them *pronoun* the form of *they* used as the object of a verb or after a preposition, *We saw them.*

▶▷ T H E S A U R U S ◁◀

tether² *noun* chain, halter, lead, leash, rope.
at the end of your tether at the end of your patience, at your wits' end, desperate.

text *noun* **1** content, matter, script, transcript, wording, words. **2** passage, quotation, sentence, verse.

textbook *noun* manual, primer, schoolbook, text.

textiles *plural noun* cloths, fabrics, materials.

texture *noun* appearance, composition, consistency, feel, grain, structure, weave.

thank *verb* acknowledge, express appreciation to, express gratitude to.

thankful *adjective* appreciative, grateful, indebted, obliged, pleased.

thankless *adjective* unappreciated, unrewarding, useless, vain.

thanks *plural noun* **1** acknowledgement, appreciation, gratefulness, gratitude, thankfulness.

thaw¹ *verb* defrost, liquefy, melt, soften, unfreeze.

theatre *noun* **1** auditorium, hall, playhouse.

theatrical *adjective* dramatic, stage.

theft *noun* burglary, embezzlement, larceny, misappropriation, pilfering, poaching, robbery, shoplifting, stealing, thieving.

►►D I C T I O N A R Y◄◄

theme *noun* **1** the subject about which a person speaks, writes, or thinks. **2** a melody.

themselves *pronoun* they or them and nobody else. (Compare *herself.*)

then *adverb* **1** at that time, *We were younger then.* **2** after that; next, *Make the tea, then pour it out.* **3** in that case, *If this is yours, then this must be mine.*

thence *adverb* from that place.

theology *noun* the study of religion. **theological** *adjective*, **theologian** *noun* [from Greek *theos* = a god, + *-logy*]

theorem *noun* a mathematical statement that can be proved by reasoning. [from Greek *theorema* = theory]

theoretical *adjective* based on theory not on experience. **theoretically** *adverb*

theorise *verb* (**theorised, theorising**) form a theory or theories.

theory *noun* (*plural* **theories**) **1** an idea or set of ideas put forward to explain something. **2** ideas (contrasted with *practice*). **3** the principles of a subject.

therapeutic (*say* therra-**pew**-tik) *adjective* treating or curing a disease etc.

therapy *noun* treatment to cure a disease etc. [from Greek *therapeia* = healing]

there *adverb* **1** in or to that place etc. **2** used to call attention to something (*There's a good boy!*) or to introduce a sentence where the verb comes before its subject (*There was plenty to eat*).

thereabouts *adverb* near there.

thereafter *adverb* from then or there onwards.

thereby *adverb* by that means; because of that.

therefore *adverb* for that reason.

therm *noun* a unit for measuring heat, especially from gas. [from Greek *therme* = heat]

thermal *adjective* **1** of heat; worked by heat. **2** hot, *thermal springs.*

thermo- *prefix* heat.

thermodynamics *noun* the science dealing with the relation between heat and other forms of energy.

thermometer *noun* a device for measuring temperature. [from *thermo-* + *meter*]

Thermos *noun* (*trade mark*) a kind of vacuum flask.

thermostat *noun* a device that automatically keeps the temperature of a room or device steady. **thermostatic** *adjective*, **thermostatically** *adverb* [from *thermo-*, + Greek *statos* = standing]

thesaurus (*say* thi-**sor**-us) *noun* (*plural* **thesauruses**) a kind of dictionary containing sets of words grouped according to their meaning. [from Greek, = treasury]

these *plural* of **this**.

thesis *noun* (*plural* **theses**) a theory put forward, especially a long essay written by a candidate for a university degree. [from Greek, = placing]

thews *plural noun* (*literary*) muscles; muscular strength.

they *pronoun* **1** the people or things being talked about. **2** people in general, *They say the show is a great success.* **3** (*informal*) he or she; a person, *I am never angry with anyone unless they deserve it.*

they're (*mainly spoken*) they are.

thick *adjective* **1** measuring a lot or a certain amount between opposite surfaces. **2** (of a line) broad, not fine. **3** crowded with things; dense, *a thick forest; thick fog.* **4** fairly stiff, *thick cream.* **5** (*informal*) stupid. **thickly** *adverb*, **thickness** *noun*

►►T H E S A U R U S◄◄

theme *noun* **1** argument, keynote, matter, subject, topic. **2** air, melody, motif, tune.

theology *noun* divinity, religion.

theoretical *adjective* abstract, academic, conjectural, hypothetical, notional, unproven, untested.

theory *noun* **1** argument, assumption, conjecture, explanation, hypothesis, idea, notion, supposition, surmise, thesis, view. **3** laws, principles, rules, science, system.

therapeutic *adjective* curative, healing, medicinal, remedial, restorative.

therapy *noun* cure, healing, remedy, treatment.

therefore *adverb* accordingly, consequently, hence, so, thus.

thick *adjective* **1** broad, bulky, chunky, deep, fat, solid, squat, stout, stubby, stumpy, wide. **2** broad, fat, wide. **3** abundant, bushy, dense, impenetrable, lush, luxuriant, profuse, rank. **4** concentrated, condensed, heavy, solid, stiff, viscous. **5** dense, dim (*informal*), dull, dumb (*informal*), half-witted, obtuse, slow, stupid, unintelligent.

thickness *noun* **1** breadth, depth, diameter, width. **2** layer, ply.

thicken *verb* make or become thicker.

thicket *noun* a number of shrubs and small trees etc. growing close together.

thickset *adjective* **1** with parts placed or growing close together. **2** having a stocky or burly body.

thief *noun* (*plural* **thieves**) a person who steals things. **thievish** *adjective*, **thievery** *noun*, **thieving** *noun*

thigh *noun* the part of the leg between the hip and the knee.

thimble *noun* a small metal or plastic cap worn on the end of the finger to push the needle in sewing.

thin¹ *adjective* (**thinner**, **thinnest**) **1** not thick; not fat. **2** made of thin material, *thin curtains*. **3** lean; not plump. **4** not dense or plentiful, *thin hair*. **5** runny, *thin soup*. **6** feeble, *a thin excuse*. **thinly** *adverb*, **thinness** *noun*

thin² *verb* (**thinned**, **thinning**) make or become less thick. **thinner** *noun*

thine *adjective* & *possessive pronoun* (*old use*) belonging to thee.

thing *noun* **1** an object; that which can be seen, touched, thought about, etc. **2** an act, fact, idea, event, etc., *a funny thing to happen*; *things to discuss*.
things *plural noun* personal belongings; circumstances or conditions.

think *verb* (**thought**, **thinking**) **1** use your mind; form connected ideas. **2** have as an idea or opinion, *We think we shall win*. **thinker** *noun*

third¹ *adjective* next after the second. **thirdly** *adverb*

third² *noun* **1** the third person or thing. **2** one of three equal parts of something.

Third World the poorest and under-developed countries of Asia, Africa, and South America (originally called 'third' because they were not considered to be politically connected with either the USA or the USSR).

thirst *noun* **1** a feeling of dryness in the mouth and throat, causing a desire to drink. **2** a strong desire, *a thirst for adventure*. **thirsty** *adjective*, **thirstily** *adverb*

thirteen *noun* & *adjective* the number 13; one more than twelve. **thirteenth** *adjective* & *noun*

thirty *noun* & *adjective* (*plural* **thirties**) the number 30; three times ten. **thirtieth** *adjective* & *noun*

this¹ *adjective* & *pronoun* (*plural* **these**) the one here, *This house is ours. Whose is this?*

this² *adverb* to such an extent, *I'm surprised he got this far.*

thistle *noun* a prickly wild plant with purple, white, or yellow flowers.

thistledown *noun* the very light fluff on thistle seeds.

thither *adverb* (*old use*) to that place.

thicken *verb* clot, coagulate, concentrate, condense, congeal, reduce, set, solidify, stiffen.

thicket *noun* bushes, copse, grove, spinney, wood.

thickset *adjective* **2** beefy, brawny, burly, heavy, husky, nuggety (*Australian*), solid, stocky, sturdy.

thief *noun* bandit, brigand, burglar, bushranger, crook (*informal*), highwayman, housebreaker, kleptomaniac, looter, mugger, pickpocket, pilferer, robber, shoplifter.

thin¹ *adjective* **1** fine, narrow. **2** delicate, diaphanous, fine, flimsy, fragile, light, see-through, sheer, transparent. **3** bony, emaciated, gangling, gaunt, lanky, lean, puny, scraggy, scrawny, skinny, slender, slight, slim, spare, spindly, weedy, wiry. **4** light, meagre, scant, scanty, sparse, wispy. **5** dilute, runny, watery. **6** feeble, flimsy, inadequate, lame.

thin² *verb* dilute, water down, weaken.

thing *noun* **1** article, commodity, device, item, object, product. **2** (*a thing to happen, do, etc.*)

act, affair, business, deed, doing, event, feat, happening, incident, occurrence, phenomenon; (*a thing to discuss*) aspect, concern, detail, fact, feature, item, matter, particular, point.
things *plural noun* **1** belongings, bits and pieces, chattels, clothes, effects, equipment, gear, goods, paraphernalia, possessions, property, stuff. **2** circumstances, conditions, matters, the situation.

think *verb* **1** brood, cogitate, consider, contemplate, deliberate, meditate, mull over, muse, ponder, rack your brains, reason, reflect, ruminate. **2** assume, believe, conjecture, consider, deem, expect, hold, imagine, judge, reckon, regard, suppose, surmise.
think up conceive, concoct, create, devise, dream up, invent, make up.

thirst *noun* **2** appetite, craving, desire, fancy, hankering, hunger, longing, lust, passion, yearning.
thirsty *adjective* dehydrated, dry, parched.

▶▶ D I C T I O N A R Y ◀◀

thong *noun* **1** a narrow strip of leather etc. used for fastening things. **2** (*Australian*) a light backless sandal with a thong between the big toe and the other toes.

thorax *noun* (*plural* **thoraxes**) the part of the body between the head or neck and the abdomen. **thoracic** *adjective* [Greek, = breastplate]

thorn *noun* a small pointed growth on the stem of a plant.

thorny *adjective* (**thornier, thorniest**) **1** having many thorns. **2** like a thorn. **3** difficult, *a thorny problem.*

thorough *adjective* **1** done or doing things carefully and in detail. **2** complete in every way, *a thorough mess.* **thoroughly** *adverb*, **thoroughness** *noun*

thoroughbred *adjective* bred of pure or pedigree stock. **thoroughbred** *noun*

thoroughfare *noun* a public road or path that is open at both ends.

those *plural* of **that**.

thou *pronoun* (*old use*, in speaking to one person) you.

though¹ *conjunction* in spite of the fact that; even if, *We must look for it, though we probably shan't find it.*

though² *adverb* however, *She's right, though.*

thought¹ *noun* **1** something that you think; an idea or opinion. **2** the process of thinking, *She was deep in thought.*

thought² *past tense* of **think**.

thoughtful *adjective* **1** thinking a lot. **2** showing thought for other people's needs; considerate. **thoughtfully** *adverb*, **thoughtfulness** *noun*

thoughtless *adjective* **1** careless, not thinking of what may happen. **2** inconsiderate. **thoughtlessly** *adverb*, **thoughtlessness** *noun*

thousand *noun* & *adjective* the number 1,000; ten hundred. **thousandth** *adjective* & *noun*

Usage Say *a few thousand* (not 'a few thousands').

thrall *noun* slavery; servitude, *in thrall.*

thrash *verb* **1** beat with a stick or whip; keep hitting very hard. **2** defeat someone thoroughly. **3** move violently, *The crocodile thrashed its tail.*

thread¹ *noun* **1** a thin length of any substance. **2** a length of spun cotton, wool, or nylon etc. used for making cloth or in sewing or knitting. **3** the spiral ridge round a screw.

thread² *verb* **1** put a thread through the eye of a needle. **2** pass a strip of film etc. through or round something. **3** put beads on a thread.

threadbare *adjective* (of cloth) with the surface worn away so that the threads show.

threat *noun* **1** a warning that you will punish, hurt, or harm a person or thing. **2** a sign of something undesirable. **3** a person or thing causing danger.

▶▶ T H E S A U R U S ◀◀

thong *noun* **1** belt, lash, strap, strip.

thorn *noun* barb, needle, prickle, spike, spine.

thorny *adjective* **1** barbed, prickly, spiky, spiny. **3** complicated, difficult, hard, intricate, knotty, problematic, ticklish, troublesome.

thorough *adjective* **1** (*a thorough account*) blow-by-blow, close, complete, comprehensive, detailed, exhaustive, extensive, full, in-depth, minute; (*a thorough worker*) careful, conscientious, diligent, methodical, meticulous, painstaking, punctilious, rigorous, scrupulous, systematic. **2** absolute, complete, downright, out-and-out, outright, total, utter.

thoroughbred *adjective* pedigree, pure-bred.

thought¹ *noun* **1** belief, concept, idea, notion, opinion, sentiment, view. **2** contemplation, daydreaming, deliberation, introspection, meditation, reasoning, reflection, reverie, rumination, thinking.

thoughtful *adjective* **1** absorbed, broody, contemplative, introspective, pensive, reflective, serious, wistful. **2** attentive, caring, concerned, considerate, helpful, kind, obliging, solicitous.

thoughtless *adjective* **1** absent-minded, careless, forgetful, heedless, negligent, scatterbrained, unthinking. **2** inconsiderate, indiscreet, insensitive, rude, selfish, tactless, unfeeling.

thrash *verb* **1** beat, belt (*slang*), cane, flog, hit, lash, lay into (*informal*), quilt (*Australian slang*), scourge, tan (*slang*), wallop (*slang*), whack, whip. **2** beat, clobber (*slang*), defeat, drub, lick (*informal*), overwhelm, paste (*slang*), pulverise, rout, slaughter, trounce.

thread¹ *noun* **1** fibre, filament, strand, yarn.

threadbare *adjective* frayed, holey, ragged, shabby, tattered, tatty (*informal*), thin, worn.

threat *noun* **1** intimidation, menace, warning. **3** danger, hazard, menace, risk.

threaten *verb* **1** make threats against someone. **2** be a threat or danger to a person or thing.

three *noun* & *adjective* the number 3; one more than two.

three-dimensional *adjective* having three dimensions (length, width, and height or depth).

thresh *verb* beat wheat etc. so as to separate the grain from the husks.

threshold *noun* **1** a slab of stone or board etc. forming the bottom of a doorway; the entrance. **2** the beginning, *We are on the threshold of a great discovery*.

thrice *adverb* (*old use*) three times.

thrift *noun* **1** being economical with money or resources. **2** a plant with pink flowers. **thrifty** *adjective*, **thriftily** *adverb* [same origin as *thrive*]

thrill¹ *noun* a feeling of excitement.

thrill² *verb* feel or cause someone to feel a thrill. **thrilling** *adjective*

thriller *noun* an exciting story, play, or film, usually about crime.

thrive *verb* (**thrived**, or **throve**, **thriving**) grow strongly; prosper or be successful. [from Old Norse *thrifask* = prosper]

throat *noun* **1** the tube in the neck that takes food and drink down into the body. **2** the front of the neck.

throaty *adjective* **1** produced deep in the throat, *a throaty chuckle*. **2** hoarse. **throatily** *adverb*

throb *verb* (**throbbed**, **throbbing**) beat or vibrate with a strong rhythm, *My heart throbbed*. **throb** *noun*

throes *plural noun* severe pangs of pain.
in the throes of (*informal*) struggling with, *We are in the throes of exams*.

thrombosis *noun* the formation of a clot of blood in the body. [from Greek *thrombos* = lump]

throne *noun* a special chair for a king, queen, or bishop at ceremonies. [from Greek *thronos* = high seat]

throng¹ *noun* a crowd of people.

throng² *verb* crowd, *People thronged the streets*.

throttle¹ *noun* a device controlling the flow of fuel to an engine; an accelerator.

throttle² *verb* (**throttled**, **throttling**) strangle.
throttle back or **down** reduce the speed of an engine by partially closing the throttle.

through¹ *preposition* **1** from one end or side to the other end or side of, *Climb through the window*. **2** by means of; because of, *We lost it through carelessness*. **3** at the end of; having finished successfully, *He is through his exam*.

through² *adverb* **1** through something, *We squeezed through*. **2** with a telephone connection made, *I'll put you through to the president*. **3** finished, *Wait till I'm through with these papers*.

through³ *adjective* **1** going through something, *No through road*. **2** going all the way to a destination, *a through train*.

throughout *preposition* & *adverb* all the way through.

throve *past tense* of **thrive**.

throw *verb* (**threw**, **thrown**, **throwing**) **1** send a person or thing through the air. **2** put carelessly or hastily. **3** move part of your

threaten *verb* **1** bully, intimidate, menace, terrorise. **2** endanger, imperil, jeopardise, put at risk.

threshold *noun* **1** doorstep, doorway, entrance. **2** beginning, brink, dawn, outset, start, verge.

thrifty *adjective* economical, frugal, provident, sparing.

thrill¹ *noun* buzz (*informal*), enjoyment, excitement, flutter, kick (*informal*), pleasure, quiver, shiver, tingle.

thrill² *verb* delight, electrify, excite, rouse, stir, wow (*slang*).
thrilling *adjective* electrifying, exciting, exhilarating, heady, rousing, sensational, stirring.

thrive *verb* boom, burgeon, do well, flourish, grow, prosper, succeed.

throat *noun* **1** gullet, oesophagus, trachea, windpipe.

throaty *adjective* deep, gruff, guttural, hoarse, husky, rasping.

throb *verb* beat, palpitate, pound, pulsate, pulse, thump, vibrate.

throng¹ *noun* crowd, gathering, herd, horde, host, mass, mob, multitude, swarm.

throng² *verb* congregate, crowd, flock, gather, herd, mill, press, swarm.

throttle² *verb* choke, garrotte, strangle, suffocate.

throw *verb* **1** bowl, cast, chuck (*informal*), fling, heave, hurl, launch, lob, pelt, pitch, project, propel, shy, sling, toss. **2** bung (*informal*), chuck (*informal*), dump, plonk, slam, toss.

body quickly, *He threw his head back.* **4** cause to be in a certain condition etc., *It threw us into confusion.* **5** move a switch or lever so as to operate it. **6** shape a pot on a potter's wheel. **throw** *noun*, **thrower** *noun*

throw away put something out as being useless or unwanted; waste, *You threw away an opportunity.*

throw up (*informal*) vomit.

thrum *verb* (**thrummed, thrumming**) sound monotonously; strum. **thrum** *noun*

thrush¹ *noun* (*plural* **thrushes**) a song-bird with a speckled breast.

thrush² *noun* a disease causing tiny white patches in the mouth and throat.

thrust *verb* (**thrust, thrusting**) push hard. **thrust** *noun*

thud *verb* (**thudded, thudding**) make the dull sound of a heavy knock or fall. **thud** *noun*

thug *noun* a violent ruffian. **thuggery** *noun* [the Thugs were robbers in India in the 17th–19th centuries]

thumb¹ *noun* the short thick finger set apart from the other four.

be under a person's thumb be completely under his or her influence.

thumb² *verb* turn the pages of a book etc. quickly with your thumb.

thumb a lift hitchhike.

thumbscrew *noun* a former instrument of torture for squeezing the thumb.

thump *verb* **1** hit or knock something heavily. **2** punch. **3** thud. **thump** *noun*

thunder¹ *noun* **1** the loud noise that goes with lightning. **2** a similar noise, *thunder of applause.* **thunderous** *adjective*, **thunderstorm** *noun*, **thundery** *adjective*

thunder² *verb* **1** sound with thunder. **2** make a noise like thunder; speak loudly.

thunderbolt *noun* a lightning-flash thought of as a destructive missile.

thunderstruck *adjective* amazed.

thus *adverb* **1** in this way, *Hold the wheel thus.* **2** therefore.

thwart *verb* frustrate.

thy *adjective* (*old use*) belonging to thee.

thyme (*say as* time) *noun* a herb with fragrant leaves. [from Greek *thymon*]

thyroid gland a large gland at the front of the neck. [from Greek *thyreos* = shield]

thyself *pronoun* (*old use*) thou or thee and nobody else. (Compare *herself*.)

tiara (*say* tee-**ar**-a) *noun* a woman's jewelled crescent-shaped ornament worn like a crown.

tic *noun* an unintentional twitch of a muscle, especially of the face. [French]

tick¹ *noun* **1** a small mark (usually ✓) put by something to show that it is correct or has been checked. **2** a regular clicking sound, especially that made by a clock or watch. **3** (*informal*) a moment.

tick² *verb* **1** put a tick by something. **2** make the sound of a tick.

tick off (*informal*) reprimand someone.

tick³ *noun* a blood-sucking insect.

throw *noun* delivery, fling, hurl, launch, lob, pitch, shot, shy, toss.

throw away 1 cast off, chuck out (*informal*), discard, dispose of, ditch (*slang*), dump, get rid of, jettison, reject, scrap, throw out. **2** blow (*informal*), squander, waste.

throw up barf (*slang*), be ill, be sick, chuck (*informal*), chunder (*Australian slang*), puke (*informal*), sick up (*informal*), spew, vomit.

thrust *verb* **1** drive, elbow, force, jostle, propel, push, ram, shoulder, shove. **2** jab, lunge, pierce, plunge, poke, stab, stick.

thud *verb & noun* bump, clunk, crash, thump.

thug *noun* bully, delinquent, gangster, hoodlum, hooligan, mugger, rough, ruffian, tough.

thumb² *verb* browse, flick, flip, leaf, skim.

thump *verb* **1,2** bash, batter, beat, clobber (*slang*), clout (*informal*), hammer, hit, knock, pound, punch, quilt (*Australian slang*), slog, slug, sock (*slang*), stoush (*Australian slang*), strike, thwack, wallop (*slang*), whack. **3** bang, bump, clunk, crash, thud.

thunder¹ *noun* boom, roar, roll, rumble.

thus *adverb* **2** accordingly, consequently, hence, so, therefore.

thwart *verb* baulk, block, foil, frustrate, hamper, hinder, obstruct, prevent, stonker (*Australian slang*), stymie (*informal*).

tic *noun* spasm, twitch.

tick¹ *noun* **3** flash, instant, jiffy, minute, moment, second, trice.

tick² *verb* **tick off** admonish, castigate, censure, chastise, chide (*old use*), lecture, rap over the knuckles, rebuke, reprimand, reproach, scold, tell off (*informal*), upbraid.

▶▶ D I C T I O N A R Y ◀◀

ticket *noun* **1** a printed piece of paper or card that allows a person to travel on a bus or train, see a show, etc. **2** a label showing a thing's price.

tickle *verb* (**tickled, tickling**) **1** touch a person's skin lightly so as to cause a slight tingling feeling. **2** (of a part of the body) have a slight tingling or itching feeling. **3** amuse or please somebody.

ticklish *adjective* **1** likely to laugh or wriggle when tickled. **2** awkward; difficult, *a ticklish situation.*

tidal *adjective* of or affected by tides.
   tidal wave a huge sea-wave.

tiddler *noun* (*informal*) a very small fish.

tiddly-wink *noun* a small counter flicked into a cup by pressing with another counter in the game of **tiddly-winks.**

tide¹ *noun* **1** the regular rise and fall in the level of the sea which usually happens twice a day. **2** (*old use*) a time or season, *Christmas-tide.*

tide² *verb* (**tided, tiding**) **tide a person over** provide him or her with what is needed, for a short time.

tidings *plural noun* news.

tidy¹ *adjective* (**tidier, tidiest**) **1** with everything in its right place; orderly. **2** (*informal*) fairly large, *It costs a tidy amount.* **tidily** *adverb*, **tidiness** *noun*

tidy² *verb* (**tidied, tidying**) make a thing tidy.

tie¹ *verb* (**tied, tying**) **1** fasten with string, ribbon, etc. **2** arrange something into a knot or bow. **3** make the same score as another competitor.

tie² *noun* **1** a necktie. **2** a result when two or more competitors have equal scores.

tier (*say* teer) *noun* each of a series of rows or levels etc. placed one above the other. **tiered** *adjective*

tiff *noun* a slight quarrel.

tiger *noun* a large wild animal of the cat family, with yellow and black stripes.
   tiger snake a very venomous Australian snake.

tight *adjective* **1** fitting very closely. **2** firmly fastened. **3** fully stretched; tense. **4** in short supply, *Money is tight at the moment.* **5** stingy, *He is very tight with his money.* **6** (*slang*) drunk. **tightly** *adverb*, **tightness** *noun*

tighten *verb* make or become tighter.

tightrope *noun* a tightly stretched rope high above the ground, on which acrobats perform.

tights *plural noun* a garment that fits tightly over the feet, legs, and lower part of the body.

tigress *noun* a female tiger.

tile *noun* a thin piece of baked clay or other hard material, used in rows for covering roofs, walls, or floors. **tiled** *adjective*

till¹ *preposition* & *conjunction* until. [from Old English *til* = to]

Usage It is better to use *until* rather than *till* when the word stands first in a sentence (e.g. *Until last year we had never been abroad*) or when you are speaking or writing formally.

till² *noun* a drawer or box for money in a shop; a cash register. [origin unknown]

▶▶ T H E S A U R U S ◀◀

ticket *noun* **1** coupon, pass, permit, token, voucher. **2** label, tab, tag.

tickle *verb* **1** stroke, touch. **2** itch, tingle. **3** amuse, delight, divert, entertain, please, titillate.

ticklish *adjective* **2** awkward, delicate, difficult, knotty, problematic, thorny, tricky.

tide¹ *noun* **1** current, ebb and flow.

tidy¹ *adjective* **1** methodical, neat, orderly, presentable, shipshape, smart, spick and span, spruce, straight, systematic, trim, uncluttered, well-groomed. **2** considerable, goodly, handsome, sizeable, substantial.

tidy² *verb* arrange, clean up, groom, neaten, organise, smarten up, sort out, spruce up, straighten, titivate (*informal*).

tie¹ *verb* **1** attach, bind, connect, couple, fasten, hitch, join, knot, lace, lash, link, moor, secure, strap, tether, truss, unite, yoke. **3** be equal, be even, be level, be neck and neck, draw.

tie² *noun* **1** bow tie, cravat, necktie. **2** dead heat, draw, stalemate.

tier *noun* bank, layer, level, line, rank, row.

tiff *noun* altercation, argument, barney (*informal*), blue (*Australian informal*), disagreement, quarrel, row, squabble.

tight *adjective* **1** close-fitting, skintight, snug. **2** fast, firm, fixed, secure. **3** stiff, stretched, taut, tense. **5** mean, miserly, niggardly, parsimonious, penny-pinching, stingy, tight-fisted.

tighten *verb* constrict, contract, narrow, stiffen, stretch, tauten, tense.

till² *noun* cash drawer, cash register, peter (*Australian slang*).

▶▶ D I C T I O N A R Y ◀◀

till³ *verb* cultivate land. [from Old English *tilian* = try]

tiller *noun* a handle used to turn a boat's rudder.

tilt¹ *verb* move into a sloping position.

tilt² *noun* a sloping position.
at full tilt at full speed or force.

timber *noun* **1** wood for building or making things. **2** a wooden beam.

timbered *adjective* made of wood or with a wooden framework, *timbered houses*.

timbre (*say* tambr) *noun* the quality of a voice or musical sound. [French]

time¹ *noun* **1** all the years of the past, present, and future; the continuous existence of the universe. **2** a particular portion of time; a period in the past. **3** a particular point of time. **4** an occasion, *the first time I saw him*. **5** a period suitable or available for something, *Is there time for a cup of tea?* **6** a system of measuring time, *Greenwich Mean Time*. **7** (in music) rhythm depending on the number and accentuation of beats in the bar. **8** (in mathematics) **times** multiplied by, *Five times three is 15* (5 x 3 = 15).
in time not late; eventually.
on time punctual.

time² *verb* (**timed, timing**) **1** measure how long something takes. **2** arrange when something is to happen. **timer** *noun*

timeless *adjective* not affected by the passage of time; eternal.

time limit a fixed amount of time within which something must be done.

timely *adjective* happening at a suitable or useful time, *a timely warning*.

timetable *noun* a list showing the times when things will happen, e.g. when buses or trains will arrive and depart, or when school lessons will take place.

timid *adjective* easily frightened. **timidly** *adverb*, **timidity** *noun* [from Latin *timidus* = nervous]

timing *noun* the way something is timed.

timorous *adjective* timid. [from Latin *timor* = fear]

timpani *plural noun* kettledrums. [Italian]

tin¹ *noun* **1** a silvery-white metal. **2** a metal container for food.

tin² *verb* (**tinned, tinning**) seal food in a tin to preserve it.

tincture *noun* **1** a solution of medicine in alcohol. **2** a slight trace of something. [same origin as *tint*]

tinder *noun* any dry substance that catches fire easily.

tine *noun* a point or prong of a fork, harrow, or antler.

tinge *verb* (**tinged, tingeing**) colour something slightly; tint. **tinge** *noun* [same origin as *tint*]

tingle *verb* (**tingled, tingling**) have a slight pricking or stinging feeling. **tingle** *noun*

tinker¹ *noun* (*old use*) a person travelling about to mend pots and pans etc.

tinker² *verb* work at something casually, trying to improve or mend it.

tinkle *verb* (**tinkled, tinkling**) make a gentle ringing sound. **tinkle** *noun*

tinny *adjective* of tin; like tin.

tinsel *noun* strips of glittering material used for decoration.

▶▶ T H E S A U R U S ◀◀

till³ *verb* cultivate, farm, plough, work.

tilt¹ *verb* bank, cant, heel over, incline, keel over, lean, list, slope, sway, tip.

tilt² *noun* cant, incline, rake, slant, slope.

timber *noun* **1** beams, boards, logs, lumber, planks, wood.

time¹ *noun* **2** age, days, epoch, era, period. **3** date, day, hour, instant, juncture, moment, point, stage. **4** moment, occasion, opportunity. **5** duration, interval, period, phase, season, session, span, spell, stretch, term, while.
on time on schedule, on the dot, on the knocker (*Australian informal*), punctually.

timeless *adjective* abiding, ageless, enduring, eternal, everlasting, immutable, indestructible, permanent, unchanging.

timely *adjective* opportune, seasonable, well-timed.

timetable *noun* programme, schedule.

timid *adjective* bashful, chicken (*informal*), cowardly, coy, diffident, faint-hearted, fearful, frightened, mousy, nervous, pusillanimous, sheepish, shy, sooky (*Australian informal*), timorous, underconfident, unheroic, wussy (*slang*).

tin¹ *noun* **2** can, canister.

tinge *verb* colour, dye, shade, stain, tint.
tinge *noun* colour, shade, tincture, tint; (*a tinge of sadness, etc.*) hint, suggestion, touch, trace.

tingle *verb* prickle, sting, tickle.

tinker² *verb* fiddle, mess about, play, potter, toy.

tinkle *verb & noun* chime, ding, jingle, peal, ring.

tint¹ *noun* a shade of colour, especially a pale one.

tint² *verb* colour something slightly. [from Latin *tinctum* = stained]

tiny *adjective* (**tinier, tiniest**) very small.

tip¹ *noun* the part right at the top or end of something.

tip² *verb* (**tipped, tipping**) put a tip on something.

tip³ *noun* 1 a small present of money given to someone who has helped you. 2 a small but useful piece of advice; a hint.

tip⁴ *verb* (**tipped, tipping**) 1 give a person a tip. 2 name as a likely winner, *Which team would you tip to win the championship?* **tipper** *noun*

tip⁵ *verb* (**tipped, tipping**) 1 tilt; topple. 2 empty rubbish somewhere.

tip⁶ *noun* 1 a slight tilt or push. 2 a place where rubbish etc. is tipped.

tipple *verb* (**tippled, tippling**) drink alcohol. **tipple** *noun*, **tippler** *noun*

tipsy *adjective* drunk. [from *tip⁵*]

tiptoe *verb* (**tiptoed, tiptoeing**) walk on your toes very quietly or carefully. **on tiptoe** walking or standing on your toes.

tiptop *adjective* (*informal*) excellent; very best, *in tiptop condition*. [from *tip¹*]

tirade (*say* ty-**rayd**) *noun* a long angry or violent speech.

tire *verb* (**tired, tiring**) make or become tired.

tired *adjective* feeling that you need to sleep or rest. **tiredness** *noun*
tired of having had enough of something and impatient or bored with it.

tireless *adjective* not tiring easily; energetic.

tiresome *adjective* annoying.

tiro *noun* (*plural* **tiros**) a beginner. [Latin, = recruit]

tissue *noun* 1 tissue-paper. 2 a paper handkerchief. 3 the substance forming any part of the body of an animal or plant, *bone-tissue*.

tissue-paper *noun* very thin soft paper used for wrapping and packing things.

tit¹ *noun* a kind of small bird.

tit² *noun* **tit for tat** something equal given in return; retaliation.

titanic (*say* ty-**tan**-ik) *adjective* huge. [from the Titans, gods and goddesses in Greek mythology]

titbit *noun* a nice little piece of something, e.g. of food, gossip, or information.

tithe *noun* one-tenth of a year's output from a farm etc., formerly paid as tax to support the clergy and church. [from Old English *teotha* = tenth]

tint¹ *noun* colour, dye, hue, pigment, shade, stain, tincture, tinge, tone.

tiny *adjective* baby, compact, diminutive, dwarf, imperceptible, infinitesimal, insignificant, little, microscopic, midget, miniature, minuscule, minute, negligible, piccaninny, pocket-sized, pygmy, skimpy, small, teeny (*informal*), trifling, undersized, wee (*informal*), weeny (*informal*).

tip¹ *noun* apex, cap, crest, crown, end, extremity, peak, pinnacle, point, summit, top.

tip³ *noun* 1 gift, gratuity, present. 2 advice, clue, hint, pointer, suggestion, warning, wrinkle (*informal*).

tip⁵ *verb* 1 cant, heel over, incline, lean, list, tilt.
tip over capsize, keel over, knock over, overturn, spill, topple over, up-end, upset, upturn.

tip⁶ *noun* 2 dump, garbage dump, refuse dump, rubbish dump.

tipsy *adjective* inebriated, intoxicated, jolly, merry (*informal*), slightly drunk, tiddly (*informal*).

tirade *noun* denunciation, diatribe, harangue, lecture.

tire *verb* drain, exhaust, fatigue, wear out, weary.

tiring *adjective* arduous, exacting, exhausting, hard, laborious, onerous, strenuous, taxing, tiresome, wearing, wearisome, wearying.

tired *adjective* all in (*informal*), beat (*slang*), bushed (*informal*), dog-tired, done in (*informal*), drained, drowsy, exhausted, fagged (*informal*), fatigued, jaded, languid, listless, pooped (*informal*), sapped, sleepy, weary, whacked (*informal*), worn out, zapped (*slang*), zonked (*slang*).
tiredness *noun* drowsiness, exhaustion, fatigue, languor, lassitude, lethargy, listlessness, sleepiness, weariness.
tired of bored of, browned off with (*slang*), fed up with, jack of (*Australian slang*), sick of.

tireless *adjective* energetic, hard-working, indefatigable, industrious, unflagging, untiring.

tiresome *adjective* annoying, boring, bothersome, dreary, dull, exasperating, irksome, irritating, tedious, troublesome, uninteresting, wearisome.

titbit *noun* bit, delicacy, morsel, nibble, snack.

▶▶ D I C T I O N A R Y ◀◀

titillate *verb* (**titillated, titillating**) stimulate something pleasantly. **titillation** *noun*

titivate *verb* (**titivated, titivating**) put the finishing touches to something; smarten up. **titivation** *noun*

title *noun* **1** the name of a book, film, song, etc. **2** a word used to show a person's rank or position, e.g. *Dr, Lord, Mrs*. **3** a championship in sport, *the world heavyweight title*. **4** a legal right to something. [from Latin *titulus* = title]

titled *adjective* having a title as a noble.

titter *verb* & *noun* giggle.

tizzy¹ *noun* anxiety, worry, panic, *She gets into a tizzy when things go wrong*.

tizzy² *verb* (**tizzied, tizzying**) (*Australian*) titivate, adorn, *she got all tizzied up for the end-of-year ball*.

TNT *abbreviation* *tri*nitro*t*oluene, a powerful explosive.

to¹ *preposition* This word is used to show (**1**) direction or arrival at a position (*We walked to school. He rose to power*), (**2**) limit (*from noon to two o'clock*), (**3**) comparison (*We won by six goals to three*), (**4**) receiving or being affected by something (*Give it to me. Be kind to animals*).

to² used before a verb to form an infinitive (*I want to see him*) or to show purpose etc. (*He does that to annoy us*), or alone when the verb is understood (*We meant to go but forgot to*).

to³ *adverb* **1** to or in the proper or closed position or condition, *Push the door to*. **2** into a state of activity, *We set to and cleaned the kitchen*.

to and fro backwards and forwards.

toad *noun* a frog-like animal that lives chiefly on land.

toadstool *noun* a fungus (usually poisonous) with a round top on a stalk.

toady *verb* (**toadied, toadying**) flatter someone so as to make them want to like or help you. **toady** *noun*

toast¹ *verb* **1** heat bread etc., to make it brown and crisp. **2** warm something in front of a fire etc. **3** drink in honour of someone.

toast² *noun* **1** toasted bread. **2** the call to drink in honour of someone; the person honoured in this way. [from Latin *tostum* = dried up]

toaster *noun* an electrical device for toasting bread.

tobacco *noun* the dried leaves of certain plants prepared for smoking or making snuff.

tobacconist *noun* a shopkeeper who sells cigarettes, cigars, etc.

toboggan *noun* a small sledge used for sliding downhill. **tobogganing** *noun*

tocsin *noun* a bell rung as an alarm-signal.

today¹ *noun* this present day, *Today is Monday*.

today² *adverb* on this day, *Have you seen him today?*

toddler *noun* a young child who has only recently learnt to walk. **toddle** *verb*

toddy *noun* a sweetened drink made with spirits and hot water.

to-do *noun* a fuss; a commotion.

toe *noun* **1** any of the separate parts (five in humans) at the end of each foot. **2** the part of a shoe or sock etc. that covers the toes.

toey *adjective* (*Australian*) restless, touchy.

toffee *noun* a sticky sweet made from heated butter and sugar.

toga (*say* **toh**-ga) *noun* a long loose garment worn by men in ancient Rome.

together *adverb* **1** with another person or thing; with each other, *They went to the party together*. **2** at the same time. [from *to* + *gather*]

▶▶ T H E S A U R U S ◀◀

titillate *verb* arouse, excite, stimulate, tantalise, tickle, turn on (*informal*).

title *noun* **1** caption, heading, inscription, name. **2** appellation, designation, position, rank, status.

titter *verb* & *noun* chuckle, giggle, snicker, snigger.

toady *verb* crawl (*informal*), curry favour (with), fawn (on), grovel, kowtow, play up, suck up (*informal*), truckle.
 toady *noun* crawler (*informal*), flatterer, flunkey, hanger-on, lackey, parasite, sycophant, truckler, yes-man.

toast¹ *verb* **1** brown, cook, grill. **3** drink to, raise your glass to, salute.

toboggan *noun* luge, sled, sledge.

toddler *noun* baby, child, infant, preschooler.

to-do *noun* bother, commotion, disturbance, excitement, furore, fuss, hue and cry, hullabaloo, kerfuffle (*informal*), outcry, palaver (*informal*), rumpus, stir, storm, turmoil, uproar.

toey *adjective* agitated, anxious, impatient, nervous, restive, restless, uneasy.

together *adverb* **1** closely, cooperatively, in collaboration, jointly, side by side. **2** as one, in chorus, in unison, simultaneously.

►►DICTIONARY◄◄

toggle *noun* a short piece of wood or metal etc. used like a button.

togs *plural noun* **1** (*slang*) clothing. **2** (*Australian*) a swimming costume.

toil¹ *verb* **1** work hard. **2** move slowly and with difficulty. **toiler** *noun*

toil² *noun* hard work.

toilet *noun* **1** a bowl-like fitment in which the body can get rid of its waste matter. **2** a room containing a toilet. **3** the process of washing, dressing, and tidying yourself.

toilet-paper *noun* paper for use in a toilet.

token *noun* **1** a piece of metal or plastic bought for use instead of money, *milk tokens*. **2** a voucher or coupon that can be exchanged for goods. **3** a sign or signal of something, *a token of our friendship*.

tolerable *adjective* **1** able to be tolerated. **2** fairly good. **tolerably** *adverb*

tolerant *adjective* tolerating things, especially other people's behaviour, beliefs, etc. **tolerantly** *adverb*, **tolerance** *noun*

tolerate *verb* (**tolerated**, **tolerating**) allow something without protesting or interfering. **toleration** *noun* [from Latin *tolerare* = endure]

toll¹ (*rhymes with* hole) *noun* **1** a charge made for using a road, bridge, etc. **2** loss or damage caused, *The death toll in the earthquake is rising.* [from Greek *telos* = tax]

toll² (*rhymes with* hole) *verb* ring a bell slowly. **toll** *noun*

tom *noun* a male cat. **tomcat** *noun* [short for *Thomas*, a man's name]

tomahawk *noun* **1** a small axe used by American Indians. **2** (*Australian*) a hatchet. [from an American Indian word, = he cuts]

tomato *noun* (*plural* **tomatoes**) a soft round red or yellow fruit eaten as a vegetable.

tomb (*say* toom) *noun* a place where someone is buried; a monument built over this.

tombola *noun* a kind of lottery.

tomboy *noun* a girl who enjoys rough noisy games etc.
tomboy stitch French knitting.

tombstone *noun* a memorial stone set up over a grave.

tome *noun* a large heavy book.

tommy-gun *noun* a small machine-gun. [from the name of its American inventor, J.T. Thompson (died 1940)]

tomorrow *noun* & *adverb* the day after today.

tom-tom *noun* a drum with a low sound; a small drum beaten with the hands.

ton *noun* **1** a unit of weight equal to about 1,016 kilograms. **2** a large amount, *there's tons of room*. **3** (*slang*) a speed of 100 kilometres per hour.
metric ton a tonne, 1,000 kilograms.

tone¹ *noun* **1** a sound in music or of the voice. **2** each of the five larger intervals between notes in a musical scale (the smaller intervals are *semitones*). **3** a shade of a colour. **4** the quality or character of something, *a cheerful tone*. **tonal** *adjective*, **tonally** *adverb*

►►THESAURUS◄◄

toil¹ *verb* **1** beaver away, drudge, labour, slave, slog, strive, sweat, work.

toil² *noun* drudgery, effort, exertion, grind, industry, labour, slog, sweat (*informal*), travail (*old use*), work, yakka (*Australian informal*).

toilet *noun* **1,2** bathroom, convenience, dunny (*Australian slang*), Gents (*informal*), Ladies, latrine, lavatory, loo (*informal*), men's, powder room, privy, rest room, toot (*Australian informal*), urinal, washroom, water closet, WC, women's.

token *noun* **1** counter, disc. **2** coupon, voucher. **3** evidence, expression, indication, keepsake, mark, memento, sign, symbol.

tolerable *adjective* **1** bearable, endurable. **2** acceptable, adequate, fair, OK (*informal*), passable, reasonable, satisfactory, so-so (*informal*).

tolerant *adjective* broad-minded, charitable, easygoing, forbearing, forgiving, indulgent, lenient, liberal, long-suffering, open-minded, patient, permissive, understanding.

tolerate *verb* abide, accept, admit, allow, bear, brook, condone, cope with, endure, permit, put up with, sanction, stand, stomach, suffer, take.

toll¹ *noun* **1** charge, fee, levy, payment, tax. **2** cost, damage, loss.

toll² *verb* chime, peal, ring, sound, strike.

tomb *noun* crypt, grave, mausoleum, sepulchre, vault.

tombstone *noun* gravestone, headstone, monument.

tone¹ *noun* **1** inflection, intonation, modulation, note, pitch, sound, timbre. **3** colour, hue, shade, tinge, tint. **4** atmosphere, character, expression, feeling, manner, mood, note, quality, spirit, style, vein.

▶▶ D I C T I O N A R Y ◀◀

tone² *verb* (**toned, toning**) **1** give a particular tone or quality to something. **2** be harmonious in colour.
tone down make a thing quieter or less bright or less harsh.
tone up make a thing brighter or stronger. [from Greek *tonos* = tension]

tongs *plural noun* a tool with two arms joined at one end, used to pick up or hold things.

tongue *noun* **1** the long soft muscular part that moves about inside the mouth. **2** a language. **3** a projecting strip or flap. **4** a pointed flame.

tongue-tied *adjective* too shy to speak.

tongue-twister *noun* something that is difficult to say quickly and correctly, e.g. 'She sells sea shells'.

tonic *noun* **1** a medicine etc. that makes a person healthier or stronger. **2** a keynote in music. **tonic** *adjective* [same origin as *tone*]

tonight *noun & adverb* this evening or night.

tonnage *noun* the amount a ship or ships can carry, expressed in tons.

tonne *noun* a metric unit of weight equal to 1,000 kilograms.

tonsil *noun* either of two small masses of soft tissue at the sides of the throat.

tonsillitis *noun* inflammation of the tonsils.

too *adverb* **1** also, *Take the others too.* **2** more than is wanted or allowed etc., *That's too much sugar for me; She is too generous.*

tool *noun* an object that helps you to do a particular job, *A saw is a tool for cutting wood or metal.*

toot¹ (*rhymes with* boot) *noun* a short sound produced by a horn. **toot** *verb*

toot² (*rhymes with* foot) (*Australian informal*) *noun* a toilet.

tooth *noun* (*plural* **teeth**) **1** any of the hard white bony parts that are rooted in the gums, used for biting and chewing things. **2** each of a row of sharp parts or projections, *the teeth of a saw.* **toothache** *noun*, **toothbrush** *noun*, **toothed** *adjective*
fight tooth and nail fight very fiercely.

toothpaste *noun* a paste for cleaning your teeth.

toothpick *noun* a small pointed piece of wood etc. for removing bits of food from between your teeth.

toothy *adjective* having large teeth.

top¹ *noun* **1** the highest part of something. **2** the upper surface. **3** the covering or stopper of a bottle, jar, etc. **4** a garment for the upper part of the body.
on top of in addition to something.

top² *adjective* highest in position, degree, or importance, *at top speed; the top designer.*
Top End the northern part of the Northern Territory in Australia.
top hat a man's tall stiff black or grey hat worn with formal clothes.

top³ *verb* (**topped, topping**) **1** put a top on something. **2** be at the top of something, *She tops the list.* **3** remove the top of something.
top up fill up something that is half empty.

top⁴ *noun* a toy that can be made to spin on its point.

topaz *noun* a kind of gem, often yellow.

Top-Ender *noun* a resident of the north part of the Northern Territory in Australia.

top-heavy *adjective* too heavy at the top and likely to overbalance.

topic *noun* a subject to write, learn, or talk about. [from Greek *topos* = place]

topical *adjective* connected with things that are happening now, *a topical film.* **topically** *adverb*, **topicality** *noun*

▶▶ T H E S A U R U S ◀◀

tone² *verb* **2** blend, harmonise, match.
tone down moderate, modulate, play down, soften, subdue, temper.

tongue-tied *adjective* dumb, inarticulate, mute, silent, speechless.

too *adverb* **1** also, as well, besides, furthermore, in addition. **2** excessively, extremely, overly, unduly.

tool *noun* apparatus, appliance, contraption, device, gadget, implement, instrument, machine, utensil; (*tools*) equipment, gear, hardware.

toot¹ *noun & verb* beep, blast, honk, hoot, sound.

top¹ *noun* **1** apex, brow, crest, crown, head, peak, pinnacle, summit, tip, vertex, zenith. **3** cap, cover, covering, lid, stopper.

top² *adjective* (*the top level*) highest, maximum, supreme, topmost, uppermost; (*the top designers, etc.*) best, foremost, greatest, leading, outstanding, pre-eminent.

top³ *verb* **1** cap, cover, crown, finish, garnish. **2** (*top the list*) head, lead; (*top their score*) beat, better, exceed, improve on, outdo, surpass.

topic *noun* issue, matter, point, subject, theme.

topical *adjective* contemporary, current, live, up to date, up to the minute.

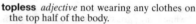

topless *adjective* not wearing any clothes on the top half of the body.

topmost *adjective* highest.

topography (*say* top-**og**-ra-fee) *noun* the position of the rivers, mountains, roads, buildings, etc. in a place. **topographical** *adjective* [from Greek *topos* = place, + -*graphy*]

topple *verb* (**toppled, toppling**) **1** fall over; totter and fall. **2** cause to fall; overthrow. [from *top*¹]

topsy-turvy *adverb* & *adjective* upside-down; muddled.

torch *noun* (*plural* **torches**) **1** a small electric lamp for carrying in the hand. **2** a stick with burning material on the end, used as a light.

toreador (*say* **to**rree-a-dor) *noun* a bull-fighter. [from Spanish *toro* = bull]

torment¹ *verb* **1** cause a person to suffer greatly. **2** tease; keep annoying someone. **tormentor** *noun*

torment² *noun* great suffering. [from Latin *tortum* = twisted]

torn *past participle* of **tear**².

tornado (*say* tor-**nay**-doh) *noun* (*plural* **tornadoes**) a violent storm or whirlwind. [from Spanish, = thunderstorm]

torpedo¹ *noun* (*plural* **torpedoes**) a long tubular missile that can be sent under water to destroy ships. [Latin, = large sea-fish that can give an electric shock which causes numbness]

torpedo² *verb* (**torpedoed, torpedoing**) attack or destroy with a torpedo.

torpid *adjective* slow-moving, not lively. **torpidly** *adverb*, **torpidity** *noun*, **torpor** *noun* [from Latin *torpidus* = numb]

torrent *noun* **1** a rushing stream; a great flow. **2** a great downpour. **torrential** *adjective*

torrid *adjective* very hot and dry. [from Latin *torridus* = parched]

torsion *noun* twisting, especially of one end of a thing while the other is held in a fixed position. [same origin as *torture*]

torso *noun* (*plural* **torsos**) the trunk of the human body. [Italian, = stump]

tortoise *noun* a slow-moving animal with a shell over its body.

tortoiseshell (*say* **tort**-a-shell) *noun* **1** the mottled brown and yellow shell of certain turtles, used for making combs etc. **2** a cat or butterfly with mottled brown colouring.

tortuous *adjective* full of twists and turns. **tortuosity** *noun* [from Latin *tortum* = twisted]

torture *verb* (**tortured, torturing**) make a person feel great pain or worry. **torture** *noun*, **torturer** *noun* [from Latin *tortum* = twisted]

Tory *noun* (*plural* **Tories**) (*especially British*) a Conservative. **Tory** *adjective* [originally used of Irish outlaws]

toss *verb* **1** throw, especially up into the air. **2** spin a coin to decide something according to which side of it is upwards after it falls. **3** move restlessly or unevenly from side to side. **toss** *noun*

toss-up *noun* **1** the tossing of a coin. **2** an even chance.

topple *verb* **1** collapse, crash, fall, stumble, tip over, totter, tumble. **2** bring down, oust, overthrow, overturn, unseat.

topsy-turvy *adjective* chaotic, confused, disorderly, higgledy-piggledy, messy, mixed-up, muddled, upside-down.

torch *noun* **1** flashlight.

toreador *noun* bullfighter, matador, picador.

torment¹ *verb* **1** afflict, bedevil, distress, haunt, plague, rack, torture, trouble, worry. **2** annoy, bait, harass, intimidate, molest, oppress, persecute, pester, plague, provoke, tease, victimise.

torment² *noun* agony, anguish, distress, hell, misery, pain, suffering, torture.

torn *adjective* holey, ragged, rent, ripped, slit, split, tattered, tatty (*informal*).

tornado *noun* twister (*American*), whirlwind; see also STORM¹.

torpor *noun* drowsiness, inertia, languor, lassitude, lethargy, listlessness, sleepiness, sluggishness, somnolence.

torrent *noun* **1** cascade, deluge, flood, rush, spate, stream. **2** deluge, downpour.

tortuous *adjective* circuitous, convoluted, crooked, serpentine, sinuous, twisting, winding, zigzag.

torture *verb* abuse, afflict, distress, maltreat, mistreat, persecute, plague, punish, rack, torment, trouble, worry. **torture** *noun* agony, anguish, pain, suffering, torment.

toss *verb* **1** bowl, cast, chuck (*informal*), fling, heave, hurl, launch, lob, pitch, propel, shy, sling, throw. **3** bob, heave, lurch, pitch, reel, rock, roll, squirm, thrash, welter, wriggle, writhe. **toss** *noun* delivery, fling, hurl, launch, lob, pitch, throw.

▶▷ D I C T I O N A R Y ◁◀

tot¹ *noun* **1** a small child. **2** (*informal*) a small amount of spirits, *a tot of rum*.

tot² *verb* (**totted, totting**) **tot up** (*informal*) add up. [short for *total*]

total¹ *adjective* **1** including everything, *the total amount*. **2** complete, *total darkness*. **totally** *adverb*

total² *noun* the amount you get by adding everything together.

total³ *verb* (**totalled, totalling**) **1** reckon up the total. **2** amount to something. [from Latin *totum* = the whole]

totalitarian *adjective* using a form of government where people are not allowed to form rival political parties.

totality *noun* **1** being total. **2** a total.

totem-pole *noun* a pole carved or painted by North American Indians with the emblems (*totems*) of their tribes or families.

totter *verb* walk unsteadily; wobble. **tottery** *adjective*

toucan (*say* **too**-kan) *noun* a tropical American bird with a huge beak.

touch¹ *verb* **1** put your hand or fingers etc. on something lightly. **2** be or come together so that there is no space between. **3** hit gently. **4** move or meddle with something. **5** reach, *The thermometer touched 40° Celsius.* **6** arouse sympathy etc. in someone, *The sad story touched our hearts.* **7** (*slang*) persuade someone to give or lend money.

touch-and-go *adjective* uncertain; risky.

touch down (of an aircraft) land; (in Rugby football) touch the ball on the ground behind the goal-line.

touch up improve something by making small additions or changes.

touch² *noun* (*plural* **touches**) **1** the action of touching. **2** the ability to feel things by touching them. **3** a small amount; a small thing done, *the finishing touches.* **4** a special skill or style of workmanship, *She hasn't lost her touch.* **5** communication with someone, *We lost touch with him.* **6** the part of a football field outside the playing area.

touchable *adjective* able to be touched.

touchdown *noun* the action of touching down.

touching *adjective* arousing kindly feelings such as pity or sympathy.

touchstone *noun* a test by which the quality of something is judged. [formerly, a kind of stone against which gold and silver were rubbed to test their purity]

touchy *adjective* (**touchier, touchiest**) easily offended. **touchily** *adverb*, **touchiness** *noun*

tough *adjective* **1** strong; difficult to break or damage. **2** difficult to chew. **3** (of a person) strong, hardy. **4** firm; stubborn; rough or violent, *tough criminals.* **5** difficult, *a tough job.* **toughly** *adverb*, **toughness** *noun*

toughen *verb* make or become tough.

▶▷ T H E S A U R U S ◁◀

total¹ *adjective* **1** aggregate, combined, complete, cumulative, entire, full, overall, whole. **2** absolute, complete, outright, perfect, pure, sheer, thorough, utter.

totally *adverb* absolutely, completely, entirely, fully, to the hilt, utterly, wholly.

total² *noun* aggregate, amount, sum, sum total, whole.

total³ *verb* **1** add up, calculate, compute, sum, tot up (*informal*), work out. **2** add up to, amount to, come to, make, tot up to (*informal*).

totter *verb* dodder, falter, reel, rock, shake, stagger, stumble, sway, teeter, wobble.

touch¹ *verb* **1** be in contact with, brush, caress, dab, feel, finger, fondle, graze, handle, manipulate, massage, maul, nudge, pat, paw, poke, press, prod, rub, strike, stroke, tap, tickle. **4** fiddle with, interfere with, meddle with, play with, tamper with, tinker with. **6** affect, impress, move, stir.

touch-and-go *adjective* chancy, dicey (*slang*), doubtful, iffy (*informal*), precarious, risky, uncertain.

touch down arrive, land.

touch up enhance, fix up, improve, repair.

touch² *noun* **3** dash, hint, pinch, soupçon, suggestion, suspicion, tinge, trace, whiff. **4** ability, dexterity, finesse, flair, knack, skill, technique. **5** contact, communication, correspondence.

touching *adjective* emotional, moving, poignant, rousing, stirring.

touchy *adjective* over-sensitive, prickly, sensitive, thin-skinned.

tough *adjective* **1** durable, hard-wearing, hardy, heavy-duty, indestructible, resistant, serviceable, strong, sturdy, unbreakable. **2** chewy, gristly, leathery. **3** beefy, brawny, burly, fit, hardy, robust, rugged, strapping, strong, sturdy. **4** firm, inflexible, merciless, rigid, strict, stubborn, uncompromising. **5** arduous, challenging, demanding, difficult, exacting, formidable, gruelling, hard, laborious, onerous, stiff, strenuous, taxing, uphill.

toughen *verb* fortify, harden, reinforce, strengthen.

▶▶ D I C T I O N A R Y ◀◀

tour¹ *noun* a journey visiting several places.

tour² *verb* make a tour. [same origin as *turn*]

tourist *noun* a person who makes a tour or visits a place for pleasure. **tourism** *noun*

tournament *noun* a series of contests.

tourniquet (*say* **toor**-nik-ay) *noun* a strip of material etc. pulled tightly round an arm or leg to stop bleeding from an artery.

tousle (*rhymes with* **how**-zel) *verb* (**tousled, tousling**) ruffle someone's hair.

tout¹ (*rhymes with* scout) *verb* try to obtain orders for goods or services etc.

tout² *noun* a person who touts things, *ticket touts.*

tow¹ (*rhymes with* go) *verb* pull something along behind you. **tow** *noun*

tow² (*rhymes with* go) *noun* short light-coloured fibres of flax or hemp.

toward *preposition* towards.

towards *preposition* **1** in the direction of, *She walked towards the sea.* **2** in relation to; regarding, *He behaved kindly towards his children.* **3** as a contribution to, *Put the money towards a new bicycle.* **4** near, *towards four o'clock.*

towel¹ *noun* a piece of absorbent cloth for drying things. **towelling** *noun*

towel² *verb* **towel up** (*Australian informal*) beat, thrash.

tower¹ *noun* a tall narrow building.

tower² *verb* be very high; be taller than others, *Skyscrapers towered over the city.* [from Latin *turris* = tower]

town *noun* a place with many houses, shops, offices, and other buildings.

town hall a building with offices for the local council and usually a hall for public events. [from Old English *tun* = enclosure]

township *noun* (*Australian*) a small town.

toxic *adjective* poisonous; caused by poison. **toxicity** *noun* [from Greek, = poison for arrows (*toxa* = arrows)]

toxicology *noun* the study of poisons. **toxicologist** *noun* [from *toxic* + *-logy*]

toxin *noun* a poisonous substance, especially one formed in the body by germs. [from *toxic*]

toy¹ *noun* a thing to play with.

toy² *adjective* **1** made as a toy. **2** (of a dog) of a very small breed kept as a pet, *a toy poodle.*

toy³ *verb* **toy with** handle a thing or consider an idea casually.

toyshop *noun* a shop that sells toys.

trace¹ *noun* **1** a mark left by a person or thing; a sign, *There was no trace of the thief.* **2** a very small amount.

trace² *verb* (**traced, tracing**) **1** copy a picture or map etc. by drawing over it on transparent paper. **2** follow the traces of a person or thing; find. **tracer** *noun*

trace³ *noun* each of the two straps or ropes etc. by which a horse pulls a cart. **kick over the traces** (of a person) become disobedient or reckless.

traceable *adjective* able to be traced.

tracery *noun* a decorative pattern of holes in stone, e.g. in a church window. [from *trace¹*]

track¹ *noun* **1** a mark or marks left by a moving person or thing. **2** a rough path made by being used. **3** a road or area of ground specially prepared for something (e.g. racing). **4** a set of rails for trains or trams etc.

▶▶ T H E S A U R U S ◀◀

tour¹ *noun* excursion, expedition, jaunt, journey, outing, trip.

tour² *verb* explore, go round, holiday in, travel round, visit.

tourist *noun* globe-trotter, holidaymaker, sightseer, traveller, tripper, visitor.

tournament *noun* championship, competition, contest, event, series.

tow¹ *verb* drag, draw, haul, pull, tug.

tower¹ *noun* belfry, keep, minaret, pagoda, skyscraper, steeple, turret.

tower² *verb* loom, rise, soar, stand out, stick up.

town *noun* big smoke (*informal*), city, community, metropolis, settlement, township.

toxic *adjective* deadly, lethal, noxious, poisonous.

toy¹ *noun* game, plaything.

toy³ *verb* **toy with** fiddle with, flirt with, play with, trifle with, twiddle with.

trace¹ *noun* **1** evidence, indication, mark, sign, track, trail. **2** bit, dash, drop, element, hint, overtone, pinch, shade, shadow, suggestion, suspicion, tinge, touch.

trace² *verb* **1** copy, draw over. **2** discover, find, follow, hunt down, locate, pursue, recover, retrieve, track down.

track¹ *noun* **1** footprint, mark, print, scent, spoor, trace, trail. **2** lane, path, road, trail, way. **3** circuit, course, racecourse, racetrack. **4** line, rails, railway line.

►►►DICTIONARY◄◄◄

5 a section of a record or along the length of a magnetic tape etc. **6** a continuous band round the wheels of a tank or tractor etc.

keep track of keep yourself informed about where something is or what someone is doing.

track suit a warm loose suit of the kind worn by athletes etc. before and after contests or for jogging.

track² *verb* **1** follow the tracks left by a person or animal. **2** follow or observe something as it moves. **tracker** *noun*

track down find by searching.

tract¹ *noun* **1** an area of land. **2** a series of connected parts along which something passes, *the digestive tract.*

tract² *noun* a pamphlet containing a short essay, especially about religion.

traction *noun* pulling a load. [from Latin *tractum* = pulled]

traction-engine *noun* a steam or diesel engine for pulling a heavy load along a road or across a field etc.

tractor *noun* a motor vehicle for pulling farm machinery or other heavy loads. [same origin as *traction*]

trade¹ *noun* **1** buying, selling, or exchanging goods. **2** business of a particular kind; the people working in this. **3** an occupation, especially a skilled craft.

trade mark a firm's registered emblem or name used to distinguish its goods etc. from those of other firms.

trade union (*plural* **trade unions**) a group of workers organised to help and protect workers in their own trade.

trade² *verb* (**traded**, **trading**) buy, sell, or exchange things. **trader** *noun*

trade in give a thing as part of the payment for something new, *He traded in his motor cycle for a car.*

tradesman,   **tradesperson**,   **tradeswoman** *nouns* a person engaged in or skilled in a trade.

tradition *noun* **1** the passing down of beliefs or customs etc. from one generation to another. **2** something passed on in this way. **traditional** *adjective*, **traditionally** *adverb* [from Latin *traditum* = handed on]

traffic¹ *noun* **1** vehicles, ships, or aircraft moving along a route. **2** trading, especially when it is illegal or wrong, *drug traffic.*

traffic warden an official who assists police to control the movement and parking of vehicles.

traffic² *verb* (**trafficked**, **trafficking**) trade. **trafficker** *noun*

traffic-lights *plural noun* coloured lights used as a signal to traffic at road junctions etc.

tragedian (*say* tra-**jee**-dee-an) *noun* **1** a person who writes tragedies. **2** an actor in tragedies.

tragedy *noun* (*plural* **tragedies**) **1** a play with unhappy events or a sad ending. **2** a very sad event. [from Greek *tragos* = goat, + *oide* = song]

tragic *adjective* **1** very sad; causing sadness. **2** of tragedies, *a great tragic actor.* **tragically** *adverb*

trail¹ *noun* **1** a track, scent, or other sign left where something has passed. **2** a path or track made through a wild region.

►►►THESAURUS◄◄◄

track² *verb* follow, hunt, pursue, shadow, stalk, tail (*informal*), trail.

track down discover, find, locate, recover, retrieve, trace.

tract¹ *noun* **1** area, expanse, region, stretch, zone.

trade¹ *noun* **1** barter, business, buying and selling, commerce, dealing, exchange, traffic, transactions. **2** business, field, industry. **3** calling, career, craft, employment, job, occupation, vocation, work.

trade mark brand, crest, emblem, hallmark, logo, name, proprietary name, symbol.

trade² *verb* barter, buy and sell, deal, do business, exchange, market, swap, traffic. **trader** *noun* dealer, merchant, retailer, seller, shopkeeper, supplier, vendor.

tradesman *noun* artisan, craftsman, workman.

tradition *noun* **2** convention, custom, habit, institution, practice, ritual.

traditional *adjective* classical, conventional, customary, established, habitual, orthodox, set, standard, time-honoured.

traffic² *verb* deal, peddle, push (*informal*), sell, trade.

tragedy *noun* **2** calamity, catastrophe, disaster, misfortune.

tragic *adjective* **1** appalling, calamitous, catastrophic, dire, disastrous, distressing, ghastly, heartbreaking, pathetic, pitiful, sad, terrible, unfortunate, wretched.

trail¹ *noun* **1** footmarks, footprints, marks, scent, spoor, traces, track, wake. **2** lane, path, track.

trail² *verb* **1** follow the trail of something; track. **2** drag or be dragged along behind. **3** lag behind. **4** hang down or float loosely. [from Latin *tragula* = net for dragging a river]

trailer *noun* **1** a truck or other container pulled along by a vehicle. **2** a short piece from a film or television programme, shown in advance to advertise it.

train¹ *noun* **1** a railway engine pulling a line of carriages or trucks that are linked together. **2** a number of people or animals moving in a line, *a camel train*. **3** a series of things, *a train of events*. **4** part of a long dress or robe that trails on the ground at the back.

train² *verb* **1** give a person instruction or practice so that he or she becomes skilled. **2** practise, *She was training for the race*. **3** make something grow in a particular direction. **4** aim a gun etc., *Train that gun on the bridge*. [same origin as *traction*]

trainee *noun* a person being trained.

trainer *noun* a person who trains people or animals.

traipse *verb* (**traipsed, traipsing**) trudge.

trait (*say as* tray) *noun* a characteristic. [from French]

traitor *noun* a person who betrays his or her country or friends. **traitorous** *adjective* [same origin as *tradition*]

trajectory *noun* (*plural* **trajectories**) the path taken by a moving object such as a bullet or rocket. [from *trans-*, + Latin *-jectum* = thrown]

tram *noun* a public passenger vehicle running on rails in the road.

tramlines *plural noun* **1** rails for a tram. **2** the pair of parallel lines at the side of a tennis court.

tramp¹ *noun* **1** a person without a home or job who walks from place to place. **2** a long walk. **3** the sound of heavy footsteps.

tramp² *verb* **1** walk with heavy footsteps. **2** walk for a long distance.

trample *verb* (**trampled, trampling**) tread heavily on something; crush something by treading on it.

trampoline *noun* a large piece of canvas joined to a frame by springs, used for jumping on in acrobatics. [from Italian *trampoli* = stilts]

trance *noun* a dreamy or unconscious condition rather like sleep. [same origin as *transit*]

tranquil *adjective* calm and quiet. **tranquilly** *adverb*, **tranquillity** *noun*

tranquilliser *noun* a medicine used to make a person feel calm.

trans- *prefix* across; through; beyond. [from Latin *trans* = across]

transact *verb* carry out business. **transaction** *noun*

transatlantic *adjective* across or on the other side of the Atlantic Ocean.

trail² *verb* **1** follow, hound, pursue, shadow, stalk, tail (*informal*), track. **2** drag, draw, haul, pull, tow. **3** dally, dawdle, drop behind, fall behind, lag, straggle. **4** dangle, drag, hang, sweep.

trailer *noun* **2** advertisement, clip, extract, preview.

train¹ *noun* **2** caravan, cavalcade, column, convoy, cortège, file, line, motorcade, procession. **3** chain, sequence, series, set, string, succession.

train² *verb* **1** coach, condition, discipline, drill, educate, instruct, teach. **2** exercise, practise, prepare, work out. **4** aim, direct, focus, level, point.

trainee *noun* apprentice, beginner, cadet, learner, novice, student.

trainer *noun* coach, instructor, teacher, tutor.

traipse *verb* plod, tramp, trek, trudge, walk.

trait *noun* attribute, characteristic, feature, idiosyncrasy, peculiarity, quality.

traitor *noun* betrayer, collaborator, deserter, informer, Judas, quisling, renegade, snake in the grass, turncoat.

tramp¹ *noun* **1** beggar, down-and-out, hobo, sundowner (*Australian*), swagman (*Australian*), vagabond, vagrant.

tramp² *verb* **1** clomp, clump, stamp, stomp, stride. **2** hike, march, plod, ramble, slog, traipse (*informal*), trek, trudge, walk.

trample *verb* crush, flatten, squash, stamp on, step on, tramp on, tread on, walk on.

tranquil *adjective* calm, collected, composed, peaceful, placid, quiet, restful, sedate, serene, still, undisturbed, unflappable (*informal*), untroubled.

transact *verb* carry out, conduct, execute, handle, manage, negotiate, perform. **transaction** *noun* deal, dealing, negotiation, undertaking.

transcend *verb* go beyond something; surpass. [from *trans-*, + Latin *scandere* = climb]

transcribe *verb* (**transcribed**, **transcribing**) copy or write something out. **transcription** *noun* [from *trans-*, + Latin *scribere* = write]

transcript *noun* a written copy.

transept *noun* the part that is at right angles to the nave in a cross-shaped church. [from *trans-*, + Latin *septum* = partition]

transfer¹ *verb* (**transferred**, **transferring**) **1** move a person or thing to another place. **2** hand over. **transferable** *adjective*, **transference** *noun*

transfer² *noun* **1** the transferring of a person or thing. **2** a picture or design that can be transferred on to another surface. [from *trans-*, + Latin *ferre* = carry]

transfigure *verb* (**transfigured**, **transfiguring**) change the appearance of something greatly. **transfiguration** *noun*

transfix *verb* **1** pierce and fix with something pointed. **2** make a person or animal unable to move because of fear or surprise etc.

transform *verb* change the form or appearance or character of a person or thing. **transformation** *noun*

transformer *noun* a device used to change the voltage of an electric current.

transfusion *noun* putting blood taken from one person into another person's body. **transfuse** *verb* [from *trans-*, + Latin *fusum* = poured]

transgress *verb* **1** break a rule or law etc. **2** sin. **transgression** *noun* [from *trans-*, + Latin *gressus* = gone]

transient *adjective* passing away quickly; not lasting. **transience** *noun* [from *trans-*, + Latin *iens* = going]

transistor *noun* **1** a tiny semiconductor device controlling a flow of electricity. **2** (also **transistor radio**) a radio receiver using transistors. **transistorised** *adjective* [from *trans*fer + re*sistor*]

transit *noun* the process of travelling across or through. [from *trans-*, + Latin *itum* = gone]

transition *noun* the process of changing from one condition or style etc. to another. **transitional** *adjective*

transitive *adjective* (of a verb) used with a direct object after it, e.g. *change* in *change your shoes* (but not in *change into dry shoes*). (Compare *intransitive*.) **transitively** *adverb*

transitory *adjective* existing for a time but not lasting.

translate *verb* (**translated**, **translating**) put something into another language. **translatable** *adjective*, **translation** *noun*, **translator** *noun* [from *trans-*, + Latin *latum* = carried]

transliterate *verb* (**transliterated**, **transliterating**) put letters or words into letters of a different alphabet. **transliteration** *noun* [from *trans-*, + Latin *littera* = letter]

translucent (*say* tranz-**loo**-sent) *adjective* allowing light to shine through but not transparent. [from *trans-*, + Latin *lucens* = shining]

transmigration *noun* **1** migration. **2** the passing of a person's soul into another body after his or her death.

transmission *noun* **1** transmitting something. **2** a broadcast. **3** the gears by which power is transmitted from the engine to the wheels of a vehicle.

transcend *verb* eclipse, exceed, go beyond, outshine, outstrip, overshadow, surpass.

transfer¹ *verb* **1** carry, convey, deliver, move, relocate, remove, shift, shunt, switch, take, transplant, transport.

transfix *verb* **1** impale, pierce, skewer, spike, stab. **2** freeze, paralyse, petrify, rivet, root to the spot.

transform *verb* alter, change, convert, metamorphose, modify, remodel, turn. **transformation** *noun* alteration, change, conversion, facelift, makeover, metamorphosis, revolution.

transgress *verb* **1** breach, break, contravene, infringe, offend against, violate. **2** do wrong, err, go astray, sin, trespass (*old use*).

transient *adjective* brief, ephemeral, fleeting, impermanent, momentary, passing, short-lived, temporary, transitory.

transit *noun* conveyance, movement, passage, shipment, transfer, transport, transportation.

transition *noun* change, changeover, conversion, development, evolution, metamorphosis, move, progression, shift, switch, transformation.

translate *verb* change, convert, decipher, decode, interpret, paraphrase, render, rephrase, reword.

▶▶DICTIONARY◀◀

transmit *verb* (**transmitted, transmitting**) **1** send or pass on from one person or place to another. **2** send out a signal or broadcast etc. **transmitter** *noun* [from *trans*-, + Latin *mittere* = send]

transmutation *noun* the process of changing or being changed from one form or substance into another.

transom *noun* **1** a horizontal bar of wood or stone dividing a window or separating a door from a window above it. **2** a small window above a door.

transparency *noun* (*plural* **transparencies**) **1** being transparent. **2** a transparent photograph that can be projected on to a screen.

transparent *adjective* able to be seen through. [from *trans*-, + Latin *parens* = appearing]

transpire *verb* (**transpired, transpiring**) **1** (of information) become known; leak out. **2** (of plants) give off watery vapour from leaves etc. **transpiration** *noun* [from *trans*-, + Latin *spirare* = breathe]

transplant¹ *verb* **1** remove a plant and put it to grow somewhere else. **2** transfer a part of the body to another person or animal. **transplantation** *noun*

transplant² *noun* **1** the process of transplanting. **2** something transplanted.

transport¹ *verb* **1** take a person, animal, or thing from one place to another. **2** (*old use*) send a prisoner to a penal settlement. **transportable** *adjective*, **transportation** *noun*, **transporter** *noun*

transport² *noun* **1** the action of transporting people, animals, or things. **2** the means of transporting people, animals, or things. [from *trans*-, + Latin *portare* = carry]

transpose *verb* (**transposed, transposing**) **1** change the position or order of something. **2** put a piece of music into a different key. **transposition** *noun* [from *trans*-, + Latin *positum* = placed]

transverse *adjective* lying across something. **transversely** *adverb* [from *trans*-, + Latin *versum* = turned]

trap¹ *noun* **1** a device for catching and holding animals. **2** an arrangement for capturing, detecting, or cheating someone. **3** a device for collecting water etc. or preventing it from passing. **4** a two-wheeled carriage pulled by a horse.

trap² *verb* (**trapped, trapping**) **1** catch or hold in a trap. **2** catch or catch out a person by means of a trick, etc. **trapper** *noun*

trapdoor *noun* a door in a floor, ceiling, or roof.

trapeze *noun* a bar hanging from two ropes as a swing for acrobats.

trapezium *noun* a quadrilateral in which two opposite sides are parallel and the other two are not. [from Greek *trapeza* = table]

trapezoid *noun* a quadrilateral in which no sides are parallel.

trappings *plural noun* **1** ornamental accessories or equipment etc., e.g. for officials. **2** ornamental harness for a horse.

trash *noun* rubbish; nonsense. **trashy** *adjective*

trauma (*say* **traw**-ma) *noun* a shock that produces a lasting effect on a person's mind. **traumatic** *adjective*, **traumatise** *verb* [Greek, = a wound]

travail *noun* (*old use*) hard or laborious work. **travail** *verb*

▶▶THESAURUS◀◀

transmit *verb* **1** carry, communicate, convey, dispatch, forward, pass on, relay, send, spread, transfer. **2** broadcast, relay, send out.

transparent *adjective* clear, crystal-clear, diaphanous, filmy, gauzy, limpid, see-through, sheer.

transpire *verb* **1** become known, be disclosed, be revealed, come to light, emerge, leak out.

transplant¹ *verb* **1** move, relocate, shift, transfer.

transport¹ *verb* **1** bear, bring, carry, cart, convey, deliver, ferry, fetch, forward, freight, haul, move, shift, ship, take, transfer. **2** banish, deport, exile, expatriate.
transportable *adjective* demountable, mobile, portable.

transport² *noun* **1** carriage, conveyance, freight, haulage, shipping, transportation. **2** conveyance, transportation, vehicle, wheels (*slang*).

transpose *verb* **1** interchange, reverse, switch.

trap¹ *noun* **1** gin, net, noose, pitfall, snare. **2** ambush, booby trap, pitfall, snare, trick.

trap² *verb* **1** capture, catch, corner, ensnare, snare. **2** catch (out), deceive, dupe, set up (*informal*), trick.

trash *noun* garbage, junk, litter, refuse, rubbish, scraps, waste; see also NONSENSE.

traumatic *adjective* distressing, disturbing, painful, shocking, upsetting.

▶▶DICTIONARY◀◀

travel *verb* (**travelled, travelling**) move from place to place. **travel** *noun*, **traveller** *noun* [the original meaning was *travail*]

traverse *verb* (**traversed, traversing**) go across something. **traversal** *noun* [same origin as *transverse*]

travesty *noun* (*plural* **travesties**) a bad or ridiculous form of something, *His story is a travesty of the truth*. [from French *travesti* = having changed clothes]

trawl *verb* fish by dragging a large net along the sea-bed.

trawler *noun* a boat used in trawling.

tray *noun* **1** a flat piece of wood, metal, or plastic, usually with raised edges, for carrying cups, plates, food, etc. **2** an open container for holding letters etc. in an office. **3** (*Australian*) the flat open part of a truck on which goods are carried.

treacherous *adjective* **1** betraying someone; disloyal. **2** not to be trusted, *treacherous roads*. **treacherously** *adverb*, **treachery** *noun*

treacle *noun* a thick sticky liquid produced when sugar is purified. **treacly** *adjective*

tread¹ *verb* (**trod, trodden, treading**) walk or put your foot on something.

tread² *noun* **1** a sound or way of walking. **2** the top surface of a stair; the part you put your foot on. **3** the part of a tyre that touches the ground.

treadle *noun* a lever that you press with your foot to turn a wheel that works a machine.

treadmill *noun* a wide mill-wheel turned by the weight of people or animals treading on steps fixed round its edge.

treason *noun* the action of betraying your country. **treasonable** *adjective*, **treasonous** *adjective* [same origin as *tradition*]

treasure¹ *noun* **1** a store of precious metals or jewels. **2** a precious thing or person.
treasure trove gold or silver etc. found hidden and with no known owner.

treasure² *verb* (**treasured, treasuring**) value greatly something that you have. [from Greek *thesauros* = treasury]

treasure-hunt *noun* a game in which people try to find a hidden object.

treasurer *noun* a person in charge of the money of a club, society, etc.

treasury *noun* (*plural* **treasuries**) a place where money and valuables are kept.
the Treasury the government department in charge of a country's income.

treat¹ *verb* **1** behave in a certain way towards a person or thing. **2** deal with a subject etc. **3** give medical care in order to cure a person or animal. **4** put something through a chemical or other process, *The fabric has been treated to make it waterproof*. **5** pay for someone else's food, drink, or entertainment, *I'll treat you to an ice-cream*. (Compare *shout*.)

treat² *noun* **1** something special that gives pleasure. **2** the process of treating someone to food, drink, or entertainment. [from Latin *tractare* = to handle]

▶▶THESAURUS◀◀

travel *verb* commute, cross, go, journey, move, progress, roam, rove, tour, trek, voyage, wander.
travels *plural noun* excursion, expedition, exploration, globe-trotting, journey, peregrination, pilgrimage, tour, trip, voyage, wandering.
traveller *noun* backpacker, commuter, explorer, globe-trotter, gypsy, holidaymaker, nomad, passenger, sightseer, tourist, tripper, vagabond, visitor, voyager, wanderer, wayfarer.
travelling *adjective* itinerant, peripatetic, roving, touring, vagabond, wandering.

traverse *verb* bridge, cross, extend across, go across, pass over, span.

travesty *noun* burlesque, misrepresentation, mockery, parody, perversion.

treacherous *adjective* **1** deceitful, disloyal, duplicitous, false, perfidious, sneaky, traitorous, two-faced, untrustworthy. **2** dangerous, hazardous, perilous, precarious, unsafe.
treachery *noun* betrayal, disloyalty, duplicity, perfidy, treason.

tread¹ *verb* stamp, step, tramp, trample, walk.

treason *noun* betrayal, disloyalty, high treason, traitorousness, treachery.

treasure¹ *noun* **1** cache, fortune, hoard, riches, valuables, wealth.

treasure² *verb* appreciate, cherish, esteem, love, prize, value.

treat¹ *verb* **1** behave towards, consider, deal with, handle, look upon, manage, regard, view. **2** deal with, discuss, handle, present, tackle. **3** attend to, care for, look after, minister to, nurse, tend. **4** coat, dress, impregnate, process. **5** buy for, pay for, shout (*Australian informal*), stand.

treat² *noun* **1** delight, joy, luxury, pleasure, thrill. **2** gift, present, shout (*Australian informal*).

▶▶ DICTIONARY ◀◀

treatise *noun* a book or long essay on a subject. [same origin as *treat*]

treatment *noun* the process or manner of dealing with a person, animal, or thing.

treaty *noun* (*plural* **treaties**) a formal agreement between two or more countries. [same origin as *treat*]

treble[1] *adjective* three times as much or as many.

treble[2] *noun* 1 a treble amount. 2 a person with a high-pitched or soprano voice.

treble[3] *verb* (**trebled, trebling**) make or become three times as much or as many. [same origin as *triple*]

tree *noun* a tall plant with a single very thick hard stem or trunk that is usually without branches for some distance above the ground.

trefoil *noun* a plant with three small leaves (e.g. clover). [from Latin *tres* = three, + *folium* = leaf]

trek[1] *noun* a long walk or ride.

trek[2] *verb* (**trekked, trekking**) make a trek. [from Dutch *trekken* = pull]

trellis *noun* (*plural* **trellises**) a framework with crossing bars of wood or metal etc. to support climbing plants.

tremble *verb* (**trembled, trembling**) shake gently, especially with fear. **tremble** *noun*

tremendous *adjective* 1 very large; huge. 2 (*informal*) excellent. **tremendously** *adverb* [from Latin, = causing people to tremble]

tremor *noun* a shaking or trembling movement.

tremulous *adjective* trembling from nervousness or weakness. **tremulously** *adverb* [from Latin *tremulus* = trembling]

trench[1] *noun* (*plural* **trenches**) a long narrow hole cut in the ground.

trench[2] *verb* dig a trench or trenches.

trenchant *adjective* strong and effective, *trenchant criticism*.

trend *noun* 1 the general direction in which something is going. 2 a fashion.

trendy *adjective* (*informal*) fashionable; following the latest trends. **trendily** *adverb*, **trendiness** *noun*

trepidation *noun* fear and anxiety; nervousness. [from Latin *trepidare* = be afraid]

trespass[1] *verb* 1 go on someone's land or property unlawfully. 2 (*old use*) do wrong; sin. **trespasser** *noun*

trespass[2] *noun* (*plural* **trespasses**) (*old use*) wrongdoing; sin. [from Old French *trespasser* = pass over (same origin as *trans-* + *pass*)]

tress *noun* (*plural* **tresses**) a lock of hair.

trestle *noun* each of a set of supports on which a board is rested to form a table. **trestle-table** *noun*

▶▶ THESAURUS ◀◀

treatise *noun* article, discourse, dissertation, essay, monograph, paper, study, thesis.

treatment *noun* care, cure, medication, remedy, therapy.

treaty *noun* agreement, alliance, armistice, compact, convention, covenant, deal, pact.

trek[1] *noun* excursion, expedition, hike, journey, tramp, walk.

trek[2] *verb* hike, journey, slog, traipse (*informal*), tramp, trudge, walk.

trellis *noun* frame, grid, grille, lattice.

tremble *verb* quake, quaver, quiver, shake, shiver, shudder, vibrate, wobble.
tremble *noun* quaver, quiver, shake, shiver, shudder, tremor, vibration, wobble.

tremendous *adjective* 1 big, colossal, enormous, gigantic, huge, immense, large, mammoth, massive, terrific (*informal*), vast. 2 excellent, exceptional, fabulous (*informal*), fantastic (*informal*), fine, great, impressive, magnificent, marvellous, remarkable, stupendous, superb, terrific (*informal*), wonderful.

tremor *noun* quaver, quiver, shake, shiver, shudder, tremble, vibration, wobble; (*earth tremor*) earthquake, quake (*informal*), shock.

tremulous *adjective* nervous, quavering, quivering, shaky, shivering, timid, trembling.

trench[1] *noun* ditch, furrow, sap.

trend *noun* 1 direction, drift, inclination, movement, shift, tendency. 2 craze, fad, fashion, mode, style, vogue.

trendy *adjective* contemporary, cool (*informal*), fashionable, in, modern, stylish, up to date, with it (*informal*).

trepidation *noun* alarm, anxiety, apprehension, consternation, dismay, dread, fear, nervousness, panic, uneasiness.

trespass[1] *verb* 1 encroach, intrude, invade. 2 err, offend, sin, transgress.

trespass[2] *noun* iniquity, misdeed, offence, sin, transgression, wrong, wrongdoing.

tri- *prefix* three (as in *triangle*). [from Latin *tres* or Greek *treis* = three]

trial *noun* **1** testing a thing to see how good it is. **2** a test of qualities or ability. **3** the trying of a person in a lawcourt. **4** an annoying person or thing; a hardship. **trial** *adjective* **on trial** being tried. [from *try*]

triangle *noun* **1** a flat shape with three sides and three angles. **2** a percussion instrument made from a metal rod bent into a triangle. **triangular** *adjective* [from *tri-* + *angle*]

triantelope (*say* try-**ant**-elope) *noun* a huntsman spider. [from *tarantula*]

triathlon *noun* an athletic contest in which competitors take part in three events (usually swimming, cycling and running).

tribe *noun* **1** a group of families living in one area as a community, ruled by a chief. **2** a set of people. **tribal** *adjective*, **tribally** *adverb*, **tribesman** *noun*

tribulation *noun* great troubles.

tribunal (*say* try-**bew**-nal) *noun* a committee appointed to hear evidence and give judgements when there is a dispute.

tribune *noun* an official chosen by the people in ancient Rome.

tributary *noun* (*plural* **tributaries**) a river or stream that flows into a larger one or into a lake.

tribute *noun* **1** something said, done, or given to show respect or admiration. **2** payment that one country or ruler was formerly obliged to pay to a more powerful one. [from Latin *tributum* = assigned]

trice *noun* (*old use*) **in a trice** in a moment.

trick[1] *noun* **1** a crafty or deceitful action. **2** a practical joke. **3** a special technique for doing things. **4** a skilful action, especially one done for entertainment. **5** one round of a card game such as whist.

trick[2] *verb* **1** deceive or cheat someone by a trick. **2** decorate, *The building was tricked out with little flags.*

trickery *noun* the use of tricks.

trickle *verb* flow or move slowly. **trickle** *noun*

trickster *noun* a person who tricks or cheats people.

tricky *adjective* (**trickier**, **trickiest**) **1** difficult; needing skill, *a tricky job.* **2** cunning; deceitful. **trickiness** *noun*

tricolour (*say* **trik**-ol-er) *noun* a flag with three coloured stripes, e.g. the national flag of France or Ireland. [from *tri-* + *colour*]

tricycle *noun* a vehicle like a bicycle but with three wheels.

trident *noun* a spear with three prongs for spearing fish, carried by Neptune and Britannia as a symbol of their power over the sea. [from *tri-*, + Latin *dens* = tooth]

trial *noun* **2** check, evaluation, experiment, test, try-out. **3** case, examination, hearing, inquiry. **4** adversity, affliction, hardship, ordeal, suffering, tribulation, trouble, woe.
trial *adjective* experimental, pilot, probationary, testing.

tribe *noun* **1** clan, community, family, people, race.

tribulation *noun* adversity, affliction, anxiety, distress, hardship, misery, misfortune, ordeal, suffering, trial, trouble, woe, worry.

tribunal *noun* board, committee, court, forum.

tributary *noun* branch, creek, rivulet.

tribute *noun* **1** accolade, commendation, compliment, eulogy, panegyric, testimonial. **pay tribute to** commend, compliment, honour, laud (*formal*), pay homage to, praise, salute.

trick[1] *noun* **1** bluff, con (*informal*), confidence trick, deception, dodge (*informal*), fraud, hoax, lurk (*Australian informal*), manoeuvre, ploy, ruse, stratagem, subterfuge, wile. **2** gag, hoax,

joke, practical joke, prank. **3** art, knack, method, secret, skill, technique, way. **4** illusion, legerdemain, magic, sleight of hand.

trick[2] *verb* **1** bluff, cheat, con (*informal*), deceive, defraud, dupe, fool, have on (*informal*), hoax, hoodwink, kid (*informal*), mislead, outwit, pull someone's leg, swindle, take in.

trickery *noun* artifice, cheating, chicanery, craftiness, cunning, deceit, deceitfulness, deception, fraud, hocus-pocus, pretence, skulduggery, sleight of hand, wiliness.

trickle *verb* dribble, drip, leak, ooze, percolate, seep.

trickster *noun* charlatan, cheat, con man (*informal*), crook (*informal*), fraud, racketeer, rogue, shark, sharp (*informal*), shicer (*Australian slang*), swindler.

tricky *adjective* **1** awkward, complicated, dangerous, delicate, difficult, hard, knotty, problematical, risky, ticklish. **2** artful, crafty, cunning, deceitful, foxy, shifty, slippery, sly, underhand, wily.

▶▶ DICTIONARY ◀◀

triennial (say try-**en**-ee-al) adjective happening every third year. [from tri-, + Latin annus = year]

trier noun a person who tries hard.

trifle¹ noun **1** a dessert made of sponge cake covered in custard, fruit, cream, etc. **2** a very small amount. **3** something that has very little importance or value.

trifle² verb (**trifled**, **trifling**) behave frivolously; toy with something.

trifling adjective trivial.

trigger¹ noun a lever that is pulled to fire a gun.

trigger² verb **trigger off** start something happening.

trigonometry (say trig-on-**om**-it-ree) noun the calculation of distances and angles by using triangles. [from Greek trigonon = triangle, + metria = measurement]

trilateral adjective having three sides. [from tri- + lateral]

trilby noun (plural **trilbies**) a man's soft felt hat.

trill verb make a quivering musical sound. **trill** noun

trillion noun **1** a million million. **2** (now less often) a million million million. [from tri- + million]

trilogy noun (plural **trilogies**) a group of three stories, poems, or plays etc. about the same people or things. [from tri-, + Greek -logia = writings]

trim¹ adjective neat and orderly. **trimly** adverb, **trimness** noun

trim² verb (**trimmed**, **trimming**) **1** cut the edges or unwanted parts off something. **2** ornament a piece of clothing etc. **3** arrange sails to suit the wind. **4** balance a boat or aircraft evenly by arranging the people or cargo in it.

trim³ noun **1** condition, in good trim. **2** cutting or trimming, Your beard needs a trim. **3** ornamentation. **4** the balance of a boat or aircraft.

Trinity noun God regarded as three persons (Father, Son, and Holy Spirit).

trinket noun a small ornament or piece of jewellery.

trio noun (plural **trios**) **1** a group of three people or things. **2** a group of three musicians or singers. **3** a piece of music for three musicians. [from Latin tres = three]

trip¹ verb (**tripped**, **tripping**) **1** catch your foot on something and fall; cause a person to do this. **2** move with quick light steps. **3** operate a switch. **trip up** stumble; make a slip or blunder; cause a person to do this.

trip² noun **1** a journey or excursion. **2** the action of tripping; a stumble.

tripartite adjective having three parts; involving three groups, tripartite talks.

tripe noun **1** part of an ox's stomach used as food. **2** (informal) nonsense.

triple¹ adjective **1** consisting of three parts. **2** involving three people or groups, a triple alliance. **3** three times as much or as many. **triply** adverb

triple² verb (**tripled**, **tripling**) treble. [from Latin triplus = three times as much]

triplet noun each of three children or animals born to the same mother at one time. [from triple]

triplicate noun in triplicate as three identical copies. [from Latin triplex = triple]

tripod (say **try**-pod) noun a stand with three legs, e.g. to support a camera. [from tri-, + Greek podos = of a foot]

▶▶ THESAURUS ◀◀

trifle¹ noun **3** bagatelle, inessential, little thing, nothing, triviality.

trifle² verb dally, flirt, play, toy.

trifling adjective inconsequential, insignificant, little, minor, negligible, paltry, petty, small, superficial, trivial, unimportant.

trigger² verb **trigger off** initiate, provoke, set off, spark off, start, touch off.

trim¹ adjective neat, orderly, shipshape, spick and span, spruce, tidy.

trim² verb **1** bob, clip, crop, cut, shear, snip. **2** adorn, deck, decorate, ornament.

trim³ noun **1** condition, fettle, form, health, shape. **3** decoration, ornamentation, trimming.

trinket noun bric-à-brac, jewellery, knick-knack, novelty, ornament, trifle.

trio noun **1** threesome, triad, trilogy, trinity, triplets, triumvirate.

trip¹ verb **1** fall over, slip, sprawl, stumble. **2** caper, dance, frolic, gambol, prance, skip. **trip up** blunder, bungle, err, slip up (informal), stumble.

trip² noun **1** cruise, drive, excursion, expedition, flight, holiday, jaunt, journey, outing, run, tour, trek, visit, voyage.

triple¹ adjective **1,2** tripartite. **3** threefold, treble.

▶▶DICTIONARY◀◀

tripper *noun* a person who is making a pleasure-trip.

trireme (*say* **try**-reem) *noun* an ancient warship with three banks of oars. [from *tri*-, + Latin *remus* = oar]

trisect *verb* divide into three equal parts. **trisection** *noun* [from *tri*-, + Latin *sectum* = cut]

trite (*rhymes with* kite) *adjective* commonplace; hackneyed, *a few trite remarks.* [from Latin *tritum* = worn by use]

triumph¹ *noun* **1** a great success or victory; a feeling of joy at this. **2** a celebration of a victory. **triumphal** *adjective*, **triumphant** *adjective*, **triumphantly** *adverb*

triumph² *verb* **1** be successful or victorious. **2** rejoice in success or victory.

triumvirate *noun* a ruling group of three people. [from Latin *trium virorum* = of three men]

trivet *noun* an iron stand for a pot or kettle etc., placed over a fire. [from Latin, = three-footed (compare *tripod*)]

trivial *adjective* of only small value or importance. **trivially** *adverb*, **triviality** *noun* [from Latin, = commonplace]

troglodyte *noun* a person living in a cave in ancient times. [from Greek *trogle* = hole]

troll (*rhymes with* hole) *noun* (in Scandinavian mythology) a supernatural being, either a giant or a friendly but mischievous dwarf.

trolley *noun* (*plural* **trolleys**) **1** a small table on wheels or castors. **2** a small cart or truck.

trolley-bus *noun* (*plural* **trolley-buses**) a bus powered by electricity from an overhead wire to which it is connected.

trombone *noun* a large brass musical instrument with a sliding tube. [from Italian *tromba* = trumpet]

troop¹ *noun* **1** an organised group of soldiers, Scouts, etc. **2** a number of people moving along together.
troops *plural noun* armed forces.

troop² *verb* move along as a group or in large numbers, *They all trooped in.*

trooper *noun* a soldier in the cavalry or in an armoured unit.

trophy *noun* (*plural* **trophies**) a prize or souvenir for a victory or other success.

tropic *noun* a line of latitude about 23½° north of the equator (**tropic of Cancer**) or 23½° south of the equator (**tropic of Capricorn**). **tropical** *adjective*
the tropics the region between these two latitudes. [from Greek *trope* = turning (because the sun seems to turn back when it reaches these points)]

troposphere *noun* the layer of the atmosphere extending about 10 kilometres upwards from the earth's surface. [from Greek *tropos* = turning, + *sphere*]

trot¹ *verb* (**trotted**, **trotting**) (of a horse) run, going faster than when walking but more slowly than when cantering.
trot out (*informal*) produce, *He trotted out the usual excuses.*

trot² *noun* a trotting run.
on the trot (*informal*) one after the other without a break, *She worked for ten days on the trot.*

troth (*rhymes with* both) *noun* (*old use*) loyalty; a solemn promise. [from *truth*]

trotter *noun* an animal's foot as food, *pigs' trotters.*

troubadour (*say* **troo**-bad-oor) *noun* a poet and singer in southern France in the 11th–13th centuries.

▶▶THESAURUS◀◀

trite *adjective* banal, clichéd, commonplace, corny, hackneyed, platitudinous, stereotyped, stock, unoriginal.

triumph¹ *noun* **1** accomplishment, achievement, conquest, feat, hit (*informal*), smash hit (*informal*), success, victory, winner.
triumphant *adjective* successful, victorious, winning; see EXULTANT (at EXULT).

triumph² *verb* **1** be successful, be victorious, conquer, prevail, succeed, win; (*triumph over*) beat, conquer, defeat, overcome, overpower, vanquish.

trivial *adjective* inconsequential, insignificant, little, minor, negligible, paltry, petty, small, superficial, trifling, unimportant.

troop¹ *noun* band, company, crew, flock, gang, group, horde, mob, pack.
troops *plural noun* armed forces, army, military, servicemen, servicewomen, soldiers.

troop² *verb* file, march, parade.

trophy *noun* award, cup, medal, prize, shield.

trouble¹ *noun* **1** difficulty, inconvenience, or distress. **2** a cause of any of these. **3** conflict; public disturbance.
take trouble take great care in doing something.

trouble² *verb* (**troubled, troubling**) **1** cause trouble to someone. **2** give yourself trouble or inconvenience etc., *Don't trouble to reply.* [same origin as *turbid*]

troublemaker *noun* a person who habitually causes trouble.

troublesome *adjective* causing trouble or annoyance.

trough (*say* trof) *noun* **1** a long narrow open container, especially one holding water or food for animals. **2** a channel for liquid. **3** the low part between two waves or ridges. **4** a long region of low air-pressure.

trounce *verb* (**trounced, trouncing**) **1** thrash. **2** defeat someone heavily.

troupe (*say* troop) *noun* a company of actors or other performers.

trousers *plural noun* a garment worn over the lower half of the body, with a separate part for each leg.

trousseau (*say* **troo**-soh) *noun* a bride's collection of clothing etc. to begin married life. [from French, = bundle]

trout *noun* (*plural* **trout**) a freshwater fish that is caught as a sport and for food.

trowel *noun* **1** a small garden tool with a curved blade for lifting plants or scooping things. **2** a small tool with a flat blade for spreading mortar etc. [from Latin *trulla* = scoop]

troy weight a system of weights used for precious metals and gems, in which 1 pound = 12 ounces. [said to be from a weight used at Troyes in France]

truant *noun* a child who stays away from school without permission. **truancy** *noun*
play truant be a truant. [the word originally meant 'idle rogue', from a Celtic word related to Welsh *truan* = miserable]

truce *noun* an agreement to stop fighting for a while.

truck¹ *noun* **1** a large strong motor vehicle for transporting goods etc.; a lorry. **2** an open container on wheels for transporting loads; an open railway-wagon.

trouble¹ *noun* **1** adversity, anxiety, bother, burden, concern, difficulty, distress, hardship, hassle (*informal*), inconvenience, irritation, misfortune, nuisance, problem, sorrow, suffering, trial, tribulation, vexation, woe, worry. **2** affliction, ailment, breakdown, defect, disease, disorder, fault, illness, malfunction, pain, problem. **3** commotion, conflict, discord, disorder, disturbance, fuss, mischief, row, strife, turmoil, unrest.
in trouble in a fix, in a jam (*informal*), in a mess, in a pickle (*informal*), in a plight, in a predicament, in a scrape, in a spot (*informal*), in difficulties, in dire straits, in hot water (*informal*), in strife (*Australian informal*), in the soup (*informal*), up the creek (*informal*).
take trouble bother, exert yourself, make an effort, take care, take pains.

trouble² *verb* **1** afflict, agitate, ail, annoy, bother, bug (*informal*), concern, distress, disturb, hassle (*informal*), hurt, inconvenience, irritate, oppress, perturb, pester, plague, prey on, put out, upset, vex, weigh down, worry. **2** bother, make the effort, take the time, take the trouble.

troublemaker *noun* agitator, culprit, delinquent, firebrand, hooligan, mischief-maker, rabble-rouser, ratbag (*Australian informal*), ringleader, ruffian, stirrer (*Australian*).

troublesome *adjective* annoying, bothersome, difficult, distressing, inconvenient, irritating, pesky (*informal*), pestilential, recalcitrant, tiresome, trying, uncooperative, unmanageable, unruly, vexing, worrying.

trough *noun* **2** channel, conduit, culvert, depression, ditch, furrow, gully, gutter, trench.

trounce *verb* **1** beat, belt (*slang*), cane, flog, hit, lash, lay into (*informal*), quilt (*Australian slang*), scourge, tan (*slang*), thrash, wallop (*slang*), whack, whip. **2** beat, clobber (*slang*), defeat, drub, lick (*informal*), overpower, paste (*slang*), rout, slaughter, thrash, vanquish.

troupe *noun* band, company, group.

trousers *plural noun* (*kinds of trousers*) bell-bottoms, breeches, chinos, cords, flares, hipsters, jeans, jodhpurs, knickerbockers, moleskins, pantaloons, pants (*informal*), plus fours, slacks, strides (*informal*).

truant *noun* absentee, malingerer, skiver (*informal*), wag (*informal*).
play truant absent yourself, bludge (*Australian informal*), play hookey (*informal*), skive (*informal*), stay away, wag (*informal*).

truce *noun* armistice, ceasefire, moratorium, peace.

truck¹ *noun* **1** juggernaut, lorry, pick-up, road train (*Australian*), semi (*Australian informal*), semitrailer, van.

▶▶ D I C T I O N A R Y ◀◀

truck² *noun* dealings, *I'll have no truck with fortune-tellers!*

truckie *noun* (*Australian*) a long-distance truck-driver.

truculent (*say* **truk**-yoo-lent) *adjective* defiant and aggressive. **truculently** *adverb*, **truculence** *noun*

trudge *verb* (**trudged**, **trudging**) walk slowly and heavily.

true *adjective* (**truer**, **truest**) **1** representing what has happened or exists, *a true story*. **2** genuine, not false, *He was the true heir.* **3** accurate. **4** loyal; faithful, *Be true to your friends*. **trueness** *noun*

truffle *noun* **1** a soft sweet made with chocolate. **2** a fungus that grows underground and is valued as food because of its rich flavour.

truism *noun* a statement that is obviously true, especially one that is hackneyed, e.g. 'Nothing lasts for ever'.

truly *adverb* **1** truthfully. **2** sincerely; genuinely, *We are truly grateful.* **3** accurately. **4** loyally; faithfully.
Yours truly see *yours*.

trump¹ *noun* a playing card of a suit that ranks above the others for one game.

trump² *verb* defeat a card by playing a trump. **trump up** invent an excuse or an accusation etc. [from *triumph*]

trump³ *noun* (*old use*) the sound of a trumpet.

trumpery *adjective* showy but worthless, *trumpery ornaments.* [from French *tromper* = deceive]

trumpet¹ *noun* **1** a metal wind instrument with a narrow tube that widens near the end. **2** something shaped like this.

trumpet² *verb* (**trumpeted**, **trumpeting**) **1** blow a trumpet. **2** (of an elephant) make a loud sound with its trunk. **3** shout or announce something loudly. **trumpeter** *noun*

truncate *verb* (**truncated**, **truncating**) shorten something by cutting off its top or end. **truncation** *noun*

truncheon *noun* a short thick stick carried as a weapon, especially by police. [from Latin *truncus* = tree-trunk]

trundle *verb* (**trundled**, **trundling**) roll along heavily, *He was trundling a wheelbarrow. A bus trundled up.*

trunk *noun* **1** the main stem of a tree. **2** an elephant's long flexible nose. **3** a large box with a hinged lid for transporting or storing clothes etc. **4** the human body except for the head, arms, and legs.
trunks *plural noun* shorts worn by men and boys for swimming, boxing, etc.

truss¹ *noun* (*plural* **trusses**) **1** a framework of beams or bars supporting a roof or bridge etc. **2** a bundle of hay etc.

truss² *verb* **1** tie up a person or thing securely. **2** support a roof or bridge etc. with trusses.

trust¹ *verb* **1** believe that a person or thing is good, truthful, or strong. **2** entrust. **3** hope, *I trust that you are well.* **trusting** *adjective*
trust to rely on, *trusting to luck.*

trust² *noun* **1** the belief that a person or thing can be trusted. **2** responsibility; being trusted, *Being a prefect is a position of trust.* **3** money legally entrusted to a person with instructions about how to use it. **trustful** *adjective*, **trustfully** *adverb*, **trustworthy** *adjective* [from Norse *traustr* = strong]

trustee *noun* a person who looks after money entrusted to him or her.

▶▶ T H E S A U R U S ◀◀

trudge *verb* lumber, plod, slog, traipse (*informal*), tramp, trek.

true *adjective* **1** accurate, actual, authentic, correct, exact, factual, faithful, genuine, honest, precise, reliable, right, strict, truthful, veracious. **2** authorised, genuine, legal, legitimate, proper, rightful. **3** accurate, correct, exact, faithful, precise, right, strict. **4** constant, dependable, dinkum (*Australian informal*), dinky-di (*Australian informal*), faithful, loyal, real, reliable, sincere, staunch, true-blue, trustworthy.

trunk *noun* **1** bole, stem, stock. **2** proboscis, snout. **3** box, case, chest, coffer. **4** body, torso.

trunks *plural noun* bathers (*Australian*), costume, shorts, swimmers (*Australian*), togs (*Australian informal*).

truss² *verb* **1** bind, secure, tie up.

trust¹ *verb* **1** believe in, depend on, have confidence in, have faith in, rely on. **2** assign, commend, commit, consign, delegate, entrust, hand over. **3** assume, expect, hope, presume, take it.
trusting *adjective* credulous, gullible, naïve, trustful, unsuspecting, unsuspicious.

trust² *noun* **1** belief, confidence, conviction, credence, faith, reliance. **2** responsibility.
trustworthy *adjective* dependable, faithful, honest, loyal, reliable, responsible, staunch, steadfast, steady, sure, true, trusty (*old use*).

▶▶▷ D I C T I O N A R Y ◁◀◀

trusty *adjective* (*old use*) trustworthy; reliable, *my trusty sword*.

truth *noun* **1** something that is true. **2** the quality of being true.

truthful *adjective* **1** telling the truth, *a truthful boy*. **2** true, *a truthful account of what happened*. **truthfully** *adverb*, **truthfulness** *noun*

try¹ *verb* (**tried, trying**) **1** attempt. **2** test something by using or doing it, *Try sleeping on your back*. **3** examine the accusations against someone in a lawcourt. **4** be a strain on, *Very small print tries your eyes*.

try on put on clothes etc. to see if they fit.

try² *noun* (*plural* **tries**) **1** an attempt. **2** (in Rugby football) putting the ball down behind the opponents' goal-line so as to score points. [the original meaning was 'to separate or distinguish things']

trying *adjective* putting a strain on someone's patience; annoying.

tsar (*say* zar) *noun* the title of the former ruler of Russia. [Russian, from Latin *Caesar*]

tsetse fly (*say* **tset**-see) a tropical African fly that can transmit sleeping sickness to people whom it bites.

T-shirt *noun* a short-sleeved shirt shaped like a T.

tub *noun* a round open container holding liquid, ice-cream, soil for plants, etc.

tuba (*say* **tew**-ba) *noun* a large brass wind instrument with a deep tone. [Latin, = trumpet]

tubby *adjective* (**tubbier, tubbiest**) short and fat. **tubbiness** *noun* [from *tub*]

tube *noun* **1** a long hollow piece of metal, plastic, rubber, glass, etc., especially for liquids or air etc. to pass along. **2** a container

made of flexible material with a screw-cap, *a tube of toothpaste*.

tuber *noun* a short thick rounded root (e.g. of a dahlia) or underground stem (e.g. of a potato) that produces buds from which new plants will grow. [Latin, = a swelling]

tuberculosis *noun* a disease of people and animals, producing small swellings in the parts affected by it, especially in the lungs. **tubercular** *adjective* [from Latin *tuberculum* = little swelling]

tubing *noun* tubes; a length of tube.

tubular *adjective* shaped like a tube.

tuck¹ *verb* **1** push a loose edge into something so that it is hidden or held in place. **2** put something away in a small space, *Tuck this in your pocket*.

tuck in (*informal*) eat heartily.

tuck² *noun* **1** a flat fold stitched in a garment. **2** (*British slang*) food, especially sweets and cakes. **tuckshop** *noun*

tucker *noun* (*Australian slang*) food.

tuft *noun* a bunch of threads, grass, hair, or feathers etc. growing close together. **tufted** *adjective*

tug¹ *verb* (**tugged, tugging**) **1** pull hard or suddenly. **2** tow.

tug² *noun* **1** a hard or sudden pull. **2** a small powerful boat used for towing others.

tug of war a contest between two teams pulling a rope from opposite ends.

tuition *noun* teaching. [from Latin *tuitio* = looking after something]

tulip *noun* a large cup-shaped flower on a tall stem growing from a bulb. [from old Turkish *tuliband* = turban (because the flowers are this shape)]

▶▶▷ T H E S A U R U S ◁◀◀

truth *noun* **1** axiom, fact, law, maxim, principle, reality, truism. **2** accuracy, authenticity, genuineness, reliability, truthfulness, veracity.

truthful *adjective* **1** frank, honest, open, sincere, straight, trustworthy, veracious. **2** accurate, correct, factual, faithful, honest, reliable, true.

try¹ *verb* **1** aim, attempt, endeavour, strive, struggle. **2** check out, experiment with, sample, taste, test, try out. **3** adjudicate, examine, hear, judge. **4** strain, tax, test.

try² *noun* **1** attempt, bash (*informal*), crack (*informal*), go, shot (*informal*), stab (*informal*), whack (*informal*).

trying *adjective* annoying, demanding, difficult, exasperating, frustrating, irritating, stressful, taxing, tiresome, troublesome, vexing.

tub *noun* barrel, bath, butt, cask, drum, pot.

tubby *adjective* chubby, dumpy, fat, obese, plump, podgy, portly, rotund, stout.

tube *noun* **1** conduit, duct, hose, pipe.

tuberculosis *noun* consumption (*old use*), TB (*informal*).

tuck¹ *verb* **2** insert, push, shove, stick, stuff.

tuck² *noun* **1** fold, pin-tuck, pleat.

tuft *noun* bunch, clump, tussock.

tug¹ *verb* **1** jerk, pluck, pull, wrench, yank. **2** drag, draw, haul, pull, tow.

tuition *noun* coaching, education, instruction, lessons, teaching, training.

▶▶DICTIONARY◀◀

tulle (*say* tewl) *noun* a very fine silky net material used for veils, wedding-dresses, etc.

tumble *verb* (**tumbled, tumbling**) **1** fall. **2** cause to fall. **3** move or push quickly and carelessly. **tumble** *noun*
tumble to (*informal*) realise what something means.

tumbledown *adjective* falling into ruins.

tumbler *noun* **1** a drinking-glass with no stem or handle. **2** a part of a lock that is lifted when a key is turned to open it.

tumbrel or **tumbril** *noun* (*old use*) an open cart of the kind used to carry condemned people to the guillotine during the French Revolution.

tummy *noun* (*plural* **tummies**) (*informal*) the stomach.

tumour (*say* **tew**-mer) *noun* an abnormal lump growing on or in the body.

tumult (*say* **tew**-mult) *noun* an uproar; a state of confusion and agitation.

tumultuous (*say* tew-**mul**-tew-us) *adjective* making a tumult; noisy.

tun *noun* a large cask or barrel.

tuna (*say* **tew**-na) *noun* (*plural* **tuna**) a large edible sea-fish with pink flesh.

tundra *noun* the vast level Arctic regions of Europe, Asia, and America where there are no trees and the subsoil is always frozen.

tune¹ *noun* a short piece of music; a pleasant series of musical notes. **tuneful** *adjective*, **tunefully** *adverb*
in tune at the correct musical pitch.

tune² *verb* (**tuned, tuning**) **1** put a musical instrument in tune. **2** adjust a radio or television set to receive a certain channel. **3** adjust an engine so that it runs smoothly. **tuner** *noun*

tungsten *noun* a grey metal used to make a kind of steel. [from Swedish *tung* = heavy, + *sten* = stone]

tunic *noun* **1** a jacket worn as part of a uniform. **2** a garment reaching from the shoulders to the hips or knees.

tunnel¹ *noun* an underground passage.

tunnel² *verb* (**tunnelled, tunnelling**) make a tunnel.

tunny *noun* (*plural* **tunnies**) a tuna.

turban *noun* a covering for the head made by wrapping a strip of cloth round a cap. [from old Turkish *tuliband* (Compare *tulip*.)]

turbid *adjective* (of water, etc.) muddy, not clear. **turbidly** *adverb*, **turbidity** *noun* [from Latin *turba* = crowd, disturbance]

turbine *noun* a machine or motor driven by a flow of water, steam, or gas. [from Latin *turbinis* = of a whirlwind]

turbo-jet *noun* a jet engine or aircraft with turbines.

turbot *noun* (*plural* **turbot**) a large flat edible sea-fish.

turbulent *adjective* **1** moving violently and unevenly, *turbulent seas*. **2** unruly. **turbulently** *adverb*, **turbulence** *noun* [same origin as *turbid*]

tureen *noun* a deep dish with a lid, from which soup is served at the table.

turf¹ *noun* short grass and the earth round its roots.

turf² *verb* cover ground with turf.
turf out (*slang*) throw out.

turgid (*say* **ter**-jid) *adjective* **1** swollen and not flexible. **2** (of language) pompous, bombastic.

turkey *noun* (*plural* **turkeys**) a large bird kept for its meat. [the name was originally used of a kind of fowl imported through Turkey in the 16th century]

▶▶THESAURUS◀◀

tumble *verb* **1** collapse, drop, fall, nosedive, plummet, plunge, roll, stumble, topple.

tumbledown *adjective* decrepit, derelict, dilapidated, ramshackle, rickety.

tumour *noun* cancer, carcinoma, growth, lump.

tumult *noun* bedlam, chaos, commotion, confusion, din, disturbance, fracas, hubbub, hullabaloo, kerfuffle (*informal*), mayhem, noise, pandemonium, racket, riot, row, ruckus, rumpus, shindy (*informal*), turmoil, uproar.

tumultuous *adjective* boisterous, excited, noisy, rowdy, uproarious, wild.

tune¹ *noun* air, melody, strain, theme.
tuneful *adjective* catchy, harmonious, melodious, musical, pleasant.

tune² *verb* adjust, regulate, set.

tunnel¹ *noun* adit, burrow, hole, mine, passage, shaft, subway, underpass.

tunnel² *verb* burrow, dig, excavate.

turbulent *adjective* **1** blustery, gusty, rough, stormy, tempestuous, violent, wild, windy. **2** boisterous, disorderly, obstreperous, restless, riotous, rough, rowdy, unruly, violent, wild.

turf¹ *noun* grass, lawn, sod, sward.

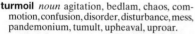

▶▶▶ DICTIONARY ◀◀◀

turmoil *noun* a disturbance; confusion.

turn¹ *verb* **1** move round; move to a new direction. **2** change in position so that a different side becomes uppermost or outermost. **3** change in appearance etc.; become, *He turned pale.* **4** make something change, *You can turn milk into butter.* **5** move a switch or tap etc. to control something, *Turn that radio off.* **6** pass a certain time, *It has turned midnight.* **7** shape something on a lathe.
  turn down fold down; reduce the flow or sound of something; reject, *We offered her a job but she turned it down.*
  turn out send out, expel; empty something, especially to search or clean it; happen; prove to be, *The visitor turned out to be my uncle.*
  turn up appear or arrive; increase the flow or sound of something.

turn² *noun* **1** the action of turning; a turning movement. **2** a change. **3** the point where something turns. **4** an opportunity or duty etc. that comes to each person etc. in succession, *It's your turn to wash up.* **5** a short performance in an entertainment. **6** (*informal*) an attack of illness; a nervous shock, *It gave me a nasty turn.*
  good turn a helpful action.
  in turn in succession; one after another. [from Greek *tornos* = lathe]

turncoat *noun* a person who changes his or her principles or beliefs.

turner *noun* a person who makes things on a lathe. **turnery** *noun*

turning *noun* a place where one road meets another, forming a corner.

turning point a point where an important change takes place.

turnip *noun* a plant with a large round white root used as a vegetable.

turnover *noun* **1** a small pie made by folding pastry over fruit, jam, etc. **2** the amount of money received by a firm selling things. **3** the rate at which goods are sold or workers leave and are replaced.

turnpike *noun* **1** (*old use*) a toll-gate; a road with toll-gates. **2** (*American*) a motorway on which a toll is charged.

turnstile *noun* a revolving gate that admits one person at a time.

turntable *noun* a circular revolving platform or support, e.g. for the record in a record-player.

turpentine *noun* a kind of oil used for thinning paint, cleaning paintbrushes, etc.

turpitude *noun* wickedness. [from Latin *turpis* = shameful]

turps *noun* (*informal*) turpentine.

turquoise *noun* **1** a sky-blue or greenish-blue colour. **2** a blue jewel. [French, = Turkish stone]

turret *noun* **1** a small tower on a castle or other building. **2** a revolving structure containing a gun. **turreted** *adjective* [from French *tour* = tower]

turtle *noun* a sea-animal that looks like a tortoise.
  turn turtle capsize.

turtle-dove *noun* a wild dove.

tusk *noun* a long pointed tooth projecting outside the mouth of an elephant, walrus, etc.

tussle¹ *noun* a struggle; a conflict.

▶▶▶ THESAURUS ◀◀◀

turmoil *noun* agitation, bedlam, chaos, commotion, confusion, disorder, disturbance, mess, pandemonium, tumult, upheaval, uproar.

turn¹ *verb* **1** circle, go round, gyrate, pivot, revolve, rotate, spin, spin round, swing round, swivel, twirl, twist round, veer, wheel round, whirl. **2** flip over, invert, reverse, roll over. **3** become, be transformed, change, metamorphose. **4** adapt, change, convert, make, modify, transform. **5** (*turn off*) cut off, disconnect, switch off; (*turn on*) plug in, put on, start, switch on.
  turn down decline, knock back (*informal*), pass up (*informal*), rebuff, refuse, reject, spurn.
  turn out 1 chuck out (*informal*), eject, evict, expel, kick out (*informal*), remove, throw out, turf out (*informal*). **2** end up, happen, pan out, work out.

turn up appear, arrive, come, front (up) (*informal*), lob in (*Australian informal*), roll up (*informal*), show up.

turn² *noun* **1** revolution, rotation, twist, wind. **2** alteration, change, shift. **3** angle, bend, corner, curve, hairpin bend, loop, turning, twist, wind. **4** chance, go, innings, move, opportunity, shot, spell, stint. **6** fright, scare, shock, start, surprise.

turncoat *noun* apostate, defector, deserter, renegade, traitor.

turning point breakthrough, crisis, crossroads, watershed.

tussle¹ *noun* battle, brawl, clash, conflict, fight, fracas, scrap (*informal*), scuffle, set-to, skirmish, squabble, struggle, wrestle.

DICTIONARY

tussle² *verb* (**tussled, tussling**) take part in a tussle.

tussock *noun* a tuft or clump of grass.

tutor *noun* **1** a private teacher. **2** a teacher directing the studies of a small group of students, especially in a university. **tutor** *verb* [Latin, = guardian]

tutorial *noun* a period of tuition and discussion led by a tutor.

tutu (*say* **too**-too) *noun* a ballet-dancer's short stiff frilled skirt. [French]

tuxedo *noun* (*plural* **tuxedos** or **tuxedoes**) a dinner jacket; a suit including this.

TV *abbreviation* television.

twaddle *noun* nonsense.

twain *noun & adjective* (*old use*) two.

twang *verb* **1** play a guitar etc. by plucking its string. **2** make a sharp sound like that of a wire when plucked. **twang** *noun*

tweak *verb* pinch and twist or pull something sharply. **tweak** *noun*

tweed *noun* thick woollen twill, often woven of mixed colours. [originally a mistake; the Scottish word *tweel* (= twill) was wrongly read as *tweed* by being confused with the River Tweed]

tweet *noun* the chirping sound made by a small bird. **tweet** *verb*

tweezers *plural noun* small pincers for picking up or pulling very small things.

twelve *noun & adjective* the number 12; one more than eleven. **twelfth** *adjective & noun*

twenty *noun & adjective* (*plural* **twenties**) the number 20; two times ten. **twentieth** *adjective & noun*

twice *adverb* **1** two times; on two occasions. **2** double the amount.

twiddle *verb* (**twiddled, twiddling**) twirl or finger something in an idle way; twist something quickly to and fro. **twiddle** *noun*, **twiddly** *adjective* [from *twirl* and *fiddle*]

twig¹ *noun* a small shoot or branch on a tree or shrub.

twig² *verb* (**twigged, twigging**) (*informal*) realise what something means.

twilight *noun* dim light from the sky just after sunset or just before sunrise.

twill *noun* material woven so that there is a pattern of diagonal lines.

twin¹ *noun* **1** either of two children or animals born to the same mother at one time. **2** either of two things that are exactly alike.

twin² *verb* (**twinned, twinning**) put things together as a pair. [from Old English *twinn* = double]

twine¹ *noun* strong thin string.

twine² *verb* (**twined, twining**) twist or wind together or round something.

twinge *noun* a sudden pain; a pang.

twinkle *verb* (**twinkled, twinkling**) sparkle. **twinkle** *noun*

twirl *verb* twist quickly. **twirl** *noun*

twist¹ *verb* **1** pass threads or strands round something or round each other. **2** turn the ends of something in opposite directions. **3** turn round or from side to side, *The road twisted through the hills.* **4** bend something out of its proper shape. **5** (*informal*) swindle somebody. **twister** *noun*

twist² *noun* a twisting movement or action. **twisty** *adjective*

THESAURUS

tussock *noun* clump, tuffet, tuft.

tutor *noun* coach, educator, instructor, mentor, teacher.
   tutor *verb* coach, instruct, school, teach.

tutorial *noun* class, discussion group, seminar.

tweak *verb* jerk, pinch, pull, tug, twist, yank.

tweet *verb* cheep, chirp, chirrup, peep, twitter.

twiddle *verb* fiddle with, fidget with, play with, twirl.

twig¹ *noun* offshoot, shoot, stalk, stem, stick.

twilight *noun* dusk, evening, gloaming, gloom, nightfall, sundown, sunset.

twin¹ *noun* **2** clone, double, look-alike, ringer (*informal*), spitting image.

twin² *verb* couple, link, match, pair.

twine¹ *noun* cord, string, thread.

twine² *verb* coil, entwine, twist, weave, wind.

twinge *noun* ache, cramp, pain, pang, spasm, stitch, throb.

twinkle *verb* blink, flash, flicker, glimmer, glitter, shimmer, shine, sparkle.

twirl *verb* gyrate, loop, pirouette, revolve, rotate, spin, twist, whirl, wind.

twist¹ *verb* **1** braid, coil, curl, entwine, intertwine, interweave, plait, twine, twirl, weave, wind. **3** (*of a road*) bend, curve, kink, loop, meander, turn, wind, worm, zigzag; (*of a person*) squirm, wriggle, writhe. **4** bend, buckle, contort, crumple, distort, screw up, warp; (*twist an ankle*) rick, sprain, turn, wrench.

twist² *noun* bend, coil, convolution, corkscrew, curve, kink, knot, loop, snarl, tangle, turn, wind, zigzag.
   twisty *adjective* crooked, curved, serpentine, sinuous, tortuous, winding, zigzag.

►►DICTIONARY◄◄

twit¹ *verb* (**twitted**, **twitting**) taunt.

twit² *noun* (*slang*) a silly person.

twitch *verb* pull or move with a slight jerk.
twitch *noun*

twitter *verb* make quick chirping sounds.
twitter *noun*

two *noun* & *adjective* (*plural* **twos**) the number 2; one more than one.
be in two minds be undecided about something.

two-faced *adjective* insincere; deceitful.

tycoon *noun* a rich and influential business person. [from Japanese *taikun* = great prince]

tying *present participle* of **tie**.

type¹ *noun* **1** a kind or sort. **2** letters or figures etc. designed for use in printing.

type² *verb* (**typed**, **typing**) write something by using a typewriter. [from Greek *typos* = impression]

typescript *noun* a typewritten document.

typewriter *noun* a machine with keys that are pressed to print letters or figures etc. on a piece of paper. **typewritten** *adjective* [the word *typewriter* at first meant the person using the machine, as well as the machine itself]

typhoid fever a serious infectious disease with fever, caused by harmful bacteria in food or water etc. [from *typhus*]

typhoon *noun* a violent hurricane in the western Pacific or East Asian seas. [from Chinese *tai fung* = great wind]

typhus *noun* an infectious disease causing fever, weakness, and a rash. [from Greek *typhos* = vapour]

typical *adjective* **1** having the qualities of a particular type of person or thing, *a typical school playground*. **2** usual in a particular person or thing, *He worked with typical carefulness*. **typically** *adverb* [same origin as *type*]

typify (*say* **tip**-if-I) *verb* (**typified**, **typifying**) be a typical example of something.

typist *noun* a person who types.

typography (*say* ty-**pog**-ra-fee) *noun* the style or appearance of the letters and figures etc. in printed material. [from *type* + -*graphy*]

tyrannise (*say* **ti**rran-I'z) *verb* (**tyrannised**, **tyrannising**) rule or behave like a tyrant.

tyranny (*say* **ti**rran-ee) *noun* (*plural* **tyrannies**) **1** government by a tyrant. **2** the way a tyrant behaves towards people. **tyrannical** *adjective*, **tyrannous** *adjective*

tyrant (*say* **ty**-rant) *noun* a person who rules cruelly and unjustly; someone who insists on being obeyed. [from Greek *tyrannos* = ruler with full power]

tyre *noun* a covering of rubber fitted round a wheel to make it grip the road and run more smoothly.

►►THESAURUS◄◄

twit² *noun* see FOOL¹.

twitch *verb* fidget, flinch, jerk, jump, quiver, start, wince, wriggle.
twitch *noun* blink, jerk, spasm, tic.

twitter *verb* cheep, chirp, chirrup, peep, tweet.

two-faced *adjective* deceitful, dishonest, double-dealing, duplicitous, false, hypocritical, insincere.

tycoon *noun* baron, magnate, mogul (*informal*).

type¹ *noun* **1** breed, category, class, form, genus, group, kind, make, model, order, sort, species,

strain, style, variety, version. **2** characters, font, print, typeface.

typhoon *noun* hurricane, tropical cyclone; see also STORM¹.

typical *adjective* **1** average, normal, ordinary, regular, representative, standard. **2** characteristic, customary, distinctive, usual.

typify *verb* epitomise, exemplify, represent.

tyrannical *adjective* autocratic, cruel, despotic, dictatorial, domineering, harsh, imperious, oppressive, severe, tyrannous, unjust.

tyrant *noun* autocrat, bully, despot, dictator, martinet, slave-driver.

▶ Uu ◀

ubiquitous (*say* yoo-**bik**-wit-us) *adjective* found everywhere, *The ubiquitous television aerials spoil the view.* **ubiquity** *noun* [from Latin *ubique* = everywhere]

U-boat *noun* a German submarine of the kind used in the Second World War. [short for German *Unterseeboot* = under-sea boat]

udder *noun* the bag-like part of a cow, ewe, female goat, etc. from which milk is taken.

uey (*say* **yoo**-ee) *noun* (*Australian slang*) a U-turn.

UFO *abbreviation* unidentified flying object. **ufo** *noun* (*plural* **ufos**)

ugly *adjective* (**uglier, ugliest**) **1** unpleasant to look at; not beautiful. **2** hostile and threatening, *The crowd was in an ugly mood.* **ugliness** *noun*
ugly duckling someone without early promise but blossoming later. [from Old Norse *uggligr* = frightening]

UHF *abbreviation* ultra-high frequency (between 300 and 3000 megahertz).

UK *abbreviation* United Kingdom.

ukulele (*say* yoo-kul-**ay**-lee) *noun* a small guitar with four strings.

ulcer *noun* an open sore. **ulcerated** *adjective*, **ulceration** *noun*

ulterior *adjective* beyond what is obvious or stated, *an ulterior motive.* [Latin, = further (compare *ultra-*)]

ultimate *adjective* **1** furthest in a series of things; final, *Our ultimate destination is London.* **2** basic, fundamental, *the ultimate cause.* **ultimately** *adverb* [from Latin *ultimus* = last]

ultimatum (*say* ul-tim-**ay**-tum) *noun* a final demand; a statement that unless something is done by a certain time action will be taken or war will be declared. [same origin as *ultimate*]

ultra- *prefix* **1** beyond (as in *ultraviolet*). **2** extremely; excessively (as in *ultra-modern*). [from Latin *ultra* = beyond]

ultramarine *noun* deep bright blue.

ultrasonic *adjective* (of sound) beyond the range of human hearing.

ultraviolet *adjective* (of light-rays) beyond the violet end of the spectrum.

umber *noun* a kind of brown pigment.

umbilical (*say* um-**bil**-ik-al) *adjective* of the navel.
umbilical cord the tube through which a baby receives nourishment before it is born, connecting its body with the mother's womb.

umbrage *noun* **take umbrage** take offence. [from Latin *umbra* = shadow]

umbrella *noun* **1** a circular piece of material stretched over a folding frame with a central stick used as a handle, or a central pole, opened to protect the user from rain or sun. **2** a general protection. [from Italian *ombrella* = a little shade]

umpire[1] *noun* a referee in cricket, tennis, and some other games.

umpire[2] *verb* (**umpired, umpiring**) act as an umpire.

UN *abbreviation* United Nations.

un- *prefix* **1** not (as in *uncertain*). **2** (before a verb) reversing the action (as in *unlock* = release from being locked).
NOTE Many words beginning with this prefix are not listed here if their meaning is obvious.

▶▶ T H E S A U R U S ◀◀

ugly *adjective* **1** frightful, ghastly, grotesque, hideous, horrible, monstrous, repulsive, shocking, unattractive, unsightly. **2** belligerent, hostile, menacing, nasty, threatening, unpleasant.

ulterior *adjective* covert, hidden, secret, undisclosed.

ultimate *adjective* **1** concluding, end, final, last. **2** basic, fundamental, primary, root, underlying.

ultimately *adverb* eventually, finally, in the end, in the long run.

umbrella *noun* **1** brolly (*informal*), parasol, sunshade.

umpire[1] *noun* adjudicator, arbiter, arbitrator, judge, moderator, ref (*informal*), referee.

umpire[2] *verb* adjudicate, arbitrate, judge, moderate, referee.

▶▶▷ D I C T I O N A R Y ◁◀

unable *adjective* not able to do something.

unaccountable *adjective* **1** unable to be explained. **2** not accountable for what you do. **unaccountably** *adverb*

unadulterated *adjective* pure; not mixed with things that are less good.

unaided *adjective* without help.

unanimous (*say* yoo-**nan**-im-us) *adjective* with everyone agreeing, *a unanimous decision*. **unanimously** *adverb*, **unanimity** (*say* yoo-nan-**im**-it-ee) *noun* [from Latin *unus* = one, + *animus* = mind]

unassuming *adjective* modest; not arrogant or pretentious.

unavoidable *adjective* not able to be avoided.

unaware *adjective* not aware.

unawares *adverb* unexpectedly; without noticing.

unbalanced *adjective* **1** not balanced; uneven. **2** biased. **3** emotionally unstable.

unbearable *adjective* not able to be endured. **unbearably** *adverb*

unbeatable *adjective* unable to be defeated or surpassed.

unbeaten *adjective* not defeated; not surpassed.

unbecoming *adjective* **1** not making a person look attractive. **2** not suitable; improper.

unbeknown *adjective* (*informal*) without someone knowing about it, *Unbeknown to us, they were working for our enemies.*

unbelievable *adjective* not able to be believed; incredible. **unbelievably** *adverb*

unbend *verb* (**unbent, unbending**) **1** change or become changed from a bent position. **2** relax and become friendly.

unbiased *adjective* not biased.

unbidden *adjective* not commanded; not invited.

unblock *verb* remove an obstruction from something.

unborn *adjective* not yet born.

unbridled *adjective* unrestrained.

unbroken *adjective* not broken; not interrupted.

unburden *verb* remove a burden from the person etc. carrying it.
unburden yourself tell someone what you know.

uncalled-for *adjective* not justified; impertinent.

▶▶▷ T H E S A U R U S ◁◀

unacceptable *adjective* improper, inadmissible, intolerable, objectionable, offensive, taboo, unsatisfactory, unseemly, unsuitable.

unafraid *adjective* bold, brave, courageous, dauntless, fearless, game, intrepid, plucky, undaunted, valiant.

unanimity *noun* accord, agreement, consensus, solidarity, unity.

unassuming *adjective* diffident, modest, quiet, retiring, self-effacing, unassertive, unpretentious.

unattractive *adjective* drab, hideous, inelegant, plain, repulsive, tasteless, ugly, unappealing, unbecoming, unsightly.

unauthorised *adjective* illegal, illicit, pirated, unofficial, unsanctioned.

unavoidable *adjective* **1** certain, destined, fated, inescapable, inevitable, predestined. **2** compulsory, mandatory, necessary, obligatory.

unaware *adjective* ignorant, oblivious, unconscious, uninformed.

unawares *adverb* by surprise, off guard, unexpectedly.

unbalanced *adjective* **1** asymmetrical, lopsided, uneven. **2** biased, one-sided, partisan,

prejudiced, unfair. **3** crazy, demented, deranged, insane, mad, unhinged, unsound, unstable.

unbearable *adjective* excruciating, insufferable, intolerable, unendurable.

unbeatable *adjective* invincible, unconquerable, undefeatable, unstoppable.

unbecoming *adjective* **1** unattractive, unflattering, unsuitable. **2** improper, inappropriate, indecorous, ungentlemanly, unladylike, unseemly, unsuitable.

unbelievable *adjective* amazing, astounding, extraordinary, far-fetched, implausible, improbable, incredible, unconvincing.

unbiased *adjective* disinterested, even-handed, fair, impartial, just, neutral, non-partisan, objective, open-minded, unprejudiced.

unblock *verb* clear, free, unclog, unstop.

unbreakable *adjective* indestructible, solid, strong, sturdy, tough.

unbroken *adjective* complete, continuous, entire, intact, uninterrupted, whole.

uncalled-for *adjective* gratuitous, needless, unjustified, unnecessary, unsolicited, unwarranted, unwelcome.

▶▶ D I C T I O N A R Y ◀◀

uncanny *adjective* (**uncannier, uncanniest**) **1** strange and rather frightening. **2** extraordinary, *They forecast the exam results with uncanny accuracy.* **uncannily** *adverb*, **uncanniness** *noun*

unceremonious *adjective* without proper formality or dignity.

uncertain *adjective* **1** not certain. **2** not reliable, *His aim is rather uncertain.* **uncertainly** *adverb*, **uncertainty** *noun* **in no uncertain terms** clearly and forcefully.

uncharitable *adjective* making unkind judgements of people or actions. **uncharitably** *adverb*

uncivilised *adjective* **1** not civilised. **2** rough, uncultured.

uncle *noun* the brother of your father or mother; your aunt's husband. [from Latin *avunculus* = uncle]

unclothed *adjective* naked.

uncomfortable *adjective* not comfortable. **uncomfortably** *adverb*

uncommon *adjective* not common; unusual.

uncompromising (*say* un-**komp**-rom-**I**-zing) *adjective* not allowing a compromise; inflexible.

unconcerned *adjective* **1** not caring about something; not worried. **2** not involved, not taking part in something.

unconditional *adjective* without any conditions; absolute, *unconditional surrender.* **unconditionally** *adverb*

unconscious *adjective* **1** not conscious. **2** not aware of things. **3** not intentional. **unconsciously** *adverb*, **unconsciousness** *noun*

uncontrollable *adjective* unable to be controlled or stopped. **uncontrollably** *adverb*

uncooperative *adjective* not cooperative.

uncouple *verb* (**uncoupled, uncoupling**) disconnect.

▶▶ T H E S A U R U S ◀◀

uncanny *adjective* **1** creepy, eerie, frightening, mysterious, scary, spooky (*informal*), strange, unearthly, weird. **2** astonishing, extraordinary, incredible, remarkable, striking, unbelievable.

uncaring *adjective* callous, cold, hard-hearted, heartless, indifferent, insensitive, unfeeling, unsympathetic.

uncertain *adjective* **1** ambivalent, doubtful, dubious, hesitant, indecisive, in two minds, irresolute, undecided, unsure. **2** changeable, erratic, unpredictable, unreliable, variable.

unchangeable *adjective* changeless, consistent, constant, dependable, immutable, invariable, reliable, unvarying.

uncharitable *adjective* mean, unchristian, unfair, ungenerous, unkind.

uncivilised *adjective* **1** barbarian, barbaric, barbarous, primitive, savage, wild. **2** antisocial, boorish, philistine, rude, uncouth, uncultured, vulgar.

uncomfortable *adjective* anxious, apprehensive, awkward, disturbed, embarrassed, nervous, painful, troubled, uneasy, worried.

uncommon *adjective* abnormal, curious, exceptional, extraordinary, infrequent, odd, peculiar, rare, remarkable, singular, special, strange, striking, unfamiliar, unusual.

uncommunicative *adjective* quiet, reserved, reticent, retiring, secretive, silent, taciturn, tight-lipped, unforthcoming, unsociable.

uncomplimentary *adjective* critical, derogatory, disparaging, insulting, pejorative, rude, unkind.

uncompromising *adjective* hard-line, inflexible, intransigent, rigid, strict, stubborn, unbending, unyielding.

unconcerned *adjective* **1** apathetic, carefree, indifferent, lackadaisical, nonchalant, oblivious, unperturbed, untroubled.

unconditional *adjective* absolute, complete, unlimited, unqualified, unreserved.

unconnected *adjective* independent, separate, unrelated.

unconscious *adjective* **1** blacked out, comatose, insensible, knocked out, senseless. **2** oblivious, unaware. **3** automatic, instinctive, involuntary, mechanical, reflex, unintentional, unthinking, unwitting.

uncontrollable *adjective* (*an uncontrollable person*) headstrong, intractable, irrepressible, obstreperous, rebellious, refractory, undisciplined, unmanageable, unruly, wayward, wilful; (*an uncontrollable urge*) compulsive, irresistible, overwhelming.

unconventional *adjective* abnormal, eccentric, odd, offbeat, original, peculiar, singular, strange, unorthodox, unusual, way-out, weird.

unconvincing *adjective* feeble, flimsy, implausible, lame, unbelievable, unsatisfactory, weak.

uncooperative *adjective* difficult, obstructive, perverse, rebellious, recalcitrant, stroppy (*informal*), unhelpful.

uncouth (*say* un-**koo**th) *adjective* rude and awkward in manner; boorish. [from *un-* + Old English *cuth* = known]

uncover *verb* **1** remove the covering from something. **2** reveal; expose, *They uncovered a plot to kill the president.*

unction *noun* **1** anointing with oil, especially in a religious ceremony. **2** unctuousness. [from Latin *unctum* = oiled]

unctuous (*say* **unk**-tew-us) *adjective* having an oily manner, polite in an exaggerated way. **unctuously** *adverb*, **unctuousness** *noun* [same origin as *unction* and *unguent*)]

undecided *adjective* **1** not yet settled, not certain. **2** not having made up your mind yet.

undeniable *adjective* impossible to deny; undoubtedly true. **undeniably** *adverb*

under¹ *preposition* **1** below; beneath, *Hide it under the desk.* **2** less than, *under 5 years old.* **3** inferior to; of lower rank than. **4** governed or controlled by, *The country prospered under his rule.* **5** in the process of; undergoing, *The road is under repair.* **6** using, *He writes under the name of 'Lewis Carroll'.* **7** according to the rules of, *This is permitted under our agreement.*
under way moving on water; in progress.

under² *adverb* in or to a lower place or level or condition, *Slowly the diver went under.*

under³ *adjective* lower, *the under layers.*

under- *prefix* **1** below, beneath (as in *underwear*). **2** lower; subordinate (as in *undermanager*). **3** not enough; incompletely (as in *undercooked*).

underarm *adjective* or *adverb* **1** moving the hand and arm forward and upwards. **2** in or for the armpit.

undercarriage *noun* an aircraft's landing-wheels and their supports.

underclothes *plural noun* underwear. **underclothing** *noun*

undercover *adjective* done or doing things secretly, *an undercover agent.*

undercurrent *noun* **1** a current that is below the surface or below another current. **2** an underlying feeling or influence, *an undercurrent of fear.*

undercut *verb* (**undercut, undercutting**) **1** cut away the part below something. **2** sell something for a lower price than someone else sells it.

underdog *noun* a person or team etc. that is expected to lose a contest or struggle.

underdone *adjective* not thoroughly done; undercooked.

underestimate *verb* (**underestimated, underestimating**) make too low an estimate of a person or thing.

underfoot *adverb* on the ground; under your feet.

undergarment *noun* a piece of underwear.

undergo *verb* (**underwent, undergone, undergoing**) experience or endure something; be subjected to, *The new aircraft underwent intensive tests.*

undergraduate *noun* a student at a university who has not yet taken a degree.

underground¹ *adjective* & *adverb* **1** under the ground. **2** done or working in secret.

underground² *noun* a railway that runs through tunnels under the ground.

undergrowth *noun* bushes and other plants growing closely, especially under trees.

uncouth *adjective* bad-mannered, boorish, coarse, loutish, rough, rude, uncivil, unrefined, vulgar.

uncover *verb* **1** bare, dig up, lay bare, strip, unearth, unwrap. **2** dig up, disclose, discover, expose, reveal, unearth.

uncultivated *adjective* fallow, unused, virgin, waste, wild.

undecided *adjective* **2** ambivalent, in two minds, irresolute, open-minded, uncertain, unsure, vacillating.

undeniable *adjective* certain, incontrovertible, indisputable, indubitable, irrefutable, positive, sure, unquestionable.

under¹ *preposition* **1** below, beneath, underneath. **2** below, less than, lower than. **3** below, junior to, subordinate to.

undercurrent *noun* **1** undertow. **2** atmosphere, feeling, hint, undertone, vibes (*informal*).

underdone *adjective* rare, undercooked.

underestimate *verb* misjudge, underrate, undervalue.

undergo *verb* bear, be subjected to, brave, endure, experience, go through, put up with, submit to, weather.

underground¹ *adjective* **1** subterranean. **2** clandestine, covert, secret, undercover.

undergrowth *noun* brush, bushes, ground cover, shrubs.

▶▶ D I C T I O N A R Y ◀◀

underhand *adjective* done or doing things in a sly or secret way.

underlie *verb* (**underlay, underlain, underlying**) **1** be or lie under something. **2** be the basis or explanation of something.

underline *verb* (**underlined, underlining**) **1** draw a line under a word etc. **2** emphasise something.

underling *noun* a subordinate.

underlying *adjective* **1** lying under something, *the underlying rocks*. **2** forming the basis or explanation of something, *the underlying causes of the trouble*.

undermine *verb* (**undermined, undermining**) **1** make a hollow or tunnel beneath something, especially one causing weakness at the base. **2** weaken something gradually.

underneath *preposition* & *adverb* below; beneath; under.

underpants *plural noun* an undergarment covering the lower part of the body.

underpass *noun* (*plural* **underpasses**) a road that goes underneath another.

underpay *verb* (**underpaid, underpaying**) pay someone too little.

underprivileged *adjective* having less than the normal standard of living or rights in a community.

underrate *verb* (**underrated, underrating**) have too low an opinion of a person or thing.

undersell *verb* (**undersold, underselling**) sell at a lower price than another person.

underside *noun* the side or surface underneath.

undersigned *adjective* who has or have signed at the bottom of this document, *We, the undersigned, wish to protest*.

undersized *adjective* of less than the normal size.

understand *verb* (**understood, understanding**) **1** know what something means or how it works or why it exists. **2** know and tolerate a person's ways. **3** have been told. **4** take something for granted, *Your expenses will be paid, that's understood*. **understandable** *adjective*, **understandably** *adverb*

understanding¹ *noun* **1** the power to understand or think; intelligence. **2** a person's perception of a situation etc. **3** sympathy; tolerance. **4** agreement in opinion or feeling, *a better understanding between nations*; an agreement.

understanding² *adjective* sympathetic and tolerant.

▶▶ T H E S A U R U S ◀◀

underhand *adjective* crafty, crooked (*informal*), cunning, deceitful, devious, dishonest, fraudulent, shonky (*Australian informal*), sly, sneaky, unscrupulous.

underline *verb* **2** emphasise, highlight, point up, stress.

underling *noun* flunkey, menial, minion, servant, subordinate.

undermine *verb* **2** destroy, erode, ruin, sabotage, sap, subvert, weaken.

underneath *preposition* below, beneath, under.

underpants *plural noun* boxer shorts, briefs, drawers, jocks (*slang*), knickers, panties (*informal*), pants, undies (*informal*).

underpass *noun* subway, tunnel.

underprivileged *adjective* deprived, disadvantaged, needy, poor.

underrate *verb* sell short, underestimate, undervalue.

underside *noun* back, bottom, reverse, underneath, wrong side.

undersized *adjective* diminutive, dwarf, little, midget, puny, pygmy, short, small, stunted, tiny, underdeveloped.

understand *verb* **1** appreciate, apprehend, comprehend, cotton on to (*informal*), decipher, decode, fathom, follow, get (*informal*), grasp, interpret, jerry to (*Australian informal*), make head or tail of, make out, know, perceive, realise, recognise, see, take in, tumble to (*informal*), twig (*informal*). **2** accept, appreciate, empathise with, sympathise with, tolerate. **3** believe, gather, have been told, hear.

understanding¹ *noun* **1** intellect, intelligence, knowledge, mentality, perception, wisdom. **2** appreciation, apprehension, awareness, comprehension, conception, insight, perception, realisation. **3** compassion, consideration, empathy, feeling, sensitivity, sympathy, tolerance. **4** accord, agreement, arrangement, bargain, compromise, deal, entente, pact, settlement.

understanding² *adjective* compassionate, considerate, forbearing, perceptive, sensitive, sympathetic, tolerant.

▶▶ D I C T I O N A R Y ◀◀

understatement *noun* an incomplete or very restrained statement of facts or truth, *To say they disagreed is an understatement; they had a violent quarrel.*

understudy[1] *noun* (*plural* **understudies**) an actor who studies a part in order to be able to play it if the usual performer is absent.

understudy[2] *verb* (**understudied, understudying**) be an understudy for an actor or part.

undertake *verb* (**undertook, undertaken, undertaking**) agree or promise to do something.

undertaker *noun* a person whose job is to arrange funerals and burials or cremations.

undertaking *noun* **1** work etc. undertaken. **2** a promise or guarantee. **3** the business of an undertaker.

undertone *noun* **1** a low or quiet tone, *They spoke in undertones.* **2** an underlying quality or feeling etc., *His letter has a threatening undertone.*

undertow *noun* a current below that of the surface of the sea and moving in the opposite direction.

underwater *adjective & adverb* placed, used, or done beneath the surface of water.

underwear *noun* clothes worn next to the skin, under other clothing.

underweight *adjective* not heavy enough.

underwent *past tense* of **undergo**.

underworld *noun* **1** (in myths and legends) the place for the spirits of the dead, under the earth. **2** the people who are regularly engaged in crime.

underwrite *verb* (**underwrote, underwritten, underwriting**) guarantee to finance something, or to pay for any loss or damage etc. **underwriter** *noun*

undesirable *adjective* not desirable; objectionable. **undesirably** *adverb*

undignified *adjective* not dignified.

undo *verb* (**undid, undone, undoing**) **1** unfasten; unwrap. **2** cancel the effect of something, *He has undone all our careful work.*

undoubted *adjective* certain; not regarded as doubtful. **undoubtedly** *adverb*

undress *verb* take clothes off.

undue *adjective* excessive; too great. **unduly** *adverb*

undulate *verb* (**undulated, undulating**) move like a wave or waves; have a wavy appearance. **undulation** *noun* [from Latin *unda* = a wave]

undying *adjective* everlasting.

▶▶ T H E S A U R U S ◀◀

undertake *verb* accept, agree to, assume, commit yourself to, consent to, embark on, enter upon, promise to, tackle, take on.

undertaker *noun* funeral director, mortician (*American*).

undertaking *noun* **1** endeavour, enterprise, job, project, task, venture, work. **2** assurance, commitment, guarantee, pledge, promise, vow.

undertone *noun* **1** murmur, whisper. **2** atmosphere, hint, suggestion, trace, undercurrent.

underwater *adjective* subaquatic, submarine, submerged, undersea.

underwear *noun* lingerie, underclothes, undergarments, undies (*informal*).

underworld *noun* **1** Hades, hell.

undeserved *adjective* unearned, unjustified, unmerited, unwarranted.

undesirable *adjective* objectionable, offensive, repugnant, unacceptable, unsatisfactory.

undeveloped *adjective* embryonic, immature, primitive, rudimentary.

undisciplined *adjective* disobedient, disorderly, naughty, obstreperous, recalcitrant,

refractory, uncontrolled, unruly, wayward, wild, wilful.

undistinguished *adjective* mediocre, ordinary, unexceptional, unimpressive, unremarkable.

undivided *adjective* complete, exclusive, full, total, wholehearted.

undo *verb* **1** detach, disconnect, loosen, open, release, unbuckle, unbutton, unclasp, unfasten, unhook, unpick, unravel, unscrew, untie, unwrap, unzip. **2** cancel, counteract, destroy, nullify, reverse, ruin, spoil, wreck.

undoubted *adjective* certain, clear, clear-cut, indisputable, sure, undisputed.

undress *verb* disrobe, peel off, strip, uncover yourself.
undressed *adjective* bare, naked, nude, unclothed.

undue *adjective* disproportionate, excessive, inordinate, unjustified, unnecessary, unreasonable.

undying *adjective* abiding, constant, endless, eternal, everlasting, immortal, infinite, never-ending, permanent, perpetual, unending.

▶▶DICTIONARY◀◀

unearth *verb* **1** dig something up; uncover by digging. **2** find something by searching.

unearthly *adjective* **1** not earthly; supernatural; strange and frightening. **2** (*informal*) very early or inconvenient, *We had to get up at an unearthly hour.*

uneasy *adjective* **1** uncomfortable. **2** worried; worrying about something. **uneasily** *adverb*, **uneasiness** *noun*

uneatable *adjective* not fit to be eaten.

uneconomic *adjective* not profitable.

unemployed *adjective* without a job. **unemployment** *noun*

unending *adjective* not coming to an end.

unequal *adjective* **1** not equal. **2** not fair or balanced. **unequalled** *adjective*, **unequally** *adverb*

unerring (*say* un-**er**-ing) *adjective* making no mistake, *unerring accuracy.*

uneven *adjective* **1** not level; not regular. **2** unequal. **3** of variable quality. **unevenly** *adverb*, **unevenness** *noun*

unexampled *adjective* unprecedented; exceptional, *an unexampled opportunity.*

unexceptionable *adjective* not in any way objectionable.

unexceptional *adjective* not exceptional; quite ordinary.

unexpected *adjective* not expected. **unexpectedly** *adverb*, **unexpectedness** *noun*

unfair *adjective* not fair; unjust. **unfairly** *adverb*, **unfairness** *noun*

unfaithful *adjective* not faithful; disloyal. **unfaithfulness** *noun*

unfamiliar *adjective* not familiar. **unfamiliarity** *noun*

unfasten *verb* open the fastenings of something.

unfavourable *adjective* not favourable. **unfavourably** *adverb*

▶▶THESAURUS◀◀

unearth *verb* **1** dig up, discover, disinter, excavate, exhume, uncover. **2** dig up, discover, find, uncover.

unearthly *adjective* **1** creepy, eerie, ghostly, spooky (*informal*), supernatural, uncanny, weird.

uneasy *adjective* anxious, apprehensive, edgy, ill at ease, jittery (*informal*), nervous, nervy, tense, uncomfortable, worried.

uneatable *adjective* inedible.

uneconomic *adjective* non-paying, unprofitable, unviable.

uneducated *adjective* ignorant, illiterate, unschooled, untaught.

unemployed *adjective* jobless, laid off, on the dole (*informal*), out of work, redundant.

unequal *adjective* **1** different, disparate, dissimilar, uneven. **2** biased, inequitable, one-sided, unbalanced, uneven, unfair.

unethical *adjective* dishonest, dishonourable, immoral, shady, shonky (*Australian informal*), underhand, unprincipled, unscrupulous, wrong.

uneven *adjective* **1** bumpy, crooked, irregular, jagged, lumpy, ragged, rough, rugged, undulating, wavy. **2** inequitable, one-sided, unbalanced, unequal, unfair. **3** erratic, inconsistent, patchy, variable.

unexcitable *adjective* calm, cool, impassive, listless, nonchalant, phlegmatic, serene, stolid, unemotional, unflappable (*informal*).

unexciting *adjective* boring, dreary, dull, humdrum, monotonous, mundane, ordinary, run-of-the-mill, tame, tedious, uneventful, uninteresting.

unexpected *adjective* accidental, chance, fortuitous, startling, surprising, undreamed-of, unforeseen, unlooked-for.

unfailing *adjective* constant, dependable, infallible, reliable.

unfair *adjective* biased, inequitable, one-sided, partial, partisan, prejudiced, unjust, unreasonable.

unfaithful *adjective* adulterous, disloyal, false, fickle, inconstant, perfidious, traitorous, treacherous, two-timing (*informal*), untrue. **unfaithfulness** *noun* adultery, disloyalty, inconstancy, infidelity, perfidy, treachery, treason.

unfamiliar *adjective* alien, exotic, foreign, new, novel, strange, unheard-of, unknown.

unfashionable *adjective* dated, obsolete, old-fashioned, outdated, outmoded, out-of-date.

unfasten *verb* detach, disconnect, loosen, open, release, unbolt, unbuckle, unbutton, unclasp, undo, unhook, unlatch, unlock, unscrew, untie, unzip.

unfavourable *adjective* adverse, contrary, critical, disadvantageous, discouraging, hostile, inauspicious, negative, unhelpful, unpropitious.

► ► ► D I C T I O N A R Y ◄ ◄

unfeeling *adjective* **1** not able to feel things. **2** not caring about other people's feelings; unsympathetic.

unfit¹ *adjective* **1** unsuitable. **2** not in perfect health.

unfit² *verb* (**unfitted, unfitting**) make a person or thing unsuitable.

unflappable *adjective* (*informal*) remaining calm in a crisis.

unfold *verb* **1** open; spread out. **2** make or become known slowly, *as the story unfolds.*

unforeseen *adjective* not foreseen; unexpected.

unforgettable *adjective* not able to be forgotten.

unforgivable *adjective* not able to be forgiven.

unfortunate *adjective* **1** unlucky. **2** unsuitable; regrettable, *an unfortunate remark.* **unfortunately** *adverb*

unfounded *adjective* not based on facts.

unfreeze *verb* (**unfroze, unfrozen, unfreezing**) thaw; cause something to thaw.

unfriendly *adjective* not friendly. **unfriendliness** *noun*

unfrock *verb* dismiss a person from being a priest.

unfurl *verb* unroll; spread out.

unfurnished *adjective* without furniture.

ungainly *adjective* awkward-looking; clumsy; ungraceful. **ungainliness** *noun* [from *un-*, + *gainly* = graceful]

ungodly *adjective* **1** not giving reverence to God; not religious. **2** (*informal*) outrageous; very inconvenient, *She woke me at an ungodly hour.* **ungodliness** *noun*

ungovernable *adjective* uncontrollable.

ungracious *adjective* not kindly; not courteous. **ungraciously** *adverb*

ungrateful *adjective* not grateful. **ungratefully** *adverb*, **ungratefulness** *noun*

unguarded *adjective* **1** not guarded. **2** without thought or caution; indiscreet, *He said this in an unguarded moment.*

unhappy *adjective* **1** not happy; sad. **2** unfortunate; unsuitable. **unhappily** *adverb*, **unhappiness** *noun*

unhealthy *adjective* **1** not in good health. **2** harmful to health. **unhealthiness** *noun*

unheard-of *adjective* never known or done before; extraordinary.

► ► ► T H E S A U R U S ◄ ◄

unfeeling *adjective* callous, clinical, cold, cold-hearted, cruel, hard, hard-hearted, harsh, heartless, inhuman, insensitive, merciless, pitiless, ruthless, uncaring, unsympathetic.

unfit¹ *adjective* **1** inadequate, inappropriate, incapable, incompetent, unqualified, unsuitable, unsuited, unusable, useless. **2** out of condition, out of form, out of training, unhealthy.

unflappable *adjective* calm, collected, composed, cool, easygoing, imperturbable, nonchalant, phlegmatic, placid, unexcitable.

unfold *verb* **1** open out, spread out, unfurl. **2** develop, emerge, evolve.

unforgettable *adjective* impressive, memorable, noteworthy, remarkable, striking.

unforgivable *adjective* indefensible, inexcusable, unjustifiable, unpardonable.

unforgiving *adjective* hard-hearted, implacable, merciless, pitiless, remorseless, vengeful, vindictive.

unfortunate *adjective* **1** hapless, ill-fated, jinxed (*informal*), luckless, unlucky, wretched. **2** inappropriate, lamentable, regrettable, tactless, unsuitable.

unfounded *adjective* baseless, groundless, needless, unjustified, unwarranted.

unfriendly *adjective* aloof, antagonistic, antisocial, clinical, cool, distant, hostile, icy, inhospitable, stand-offish, surly, uncaring, unfeeling, unkind, unneighbourly, unsociable.

ungainly *adjective* awkward, clumsy, gangling, gawky, inelegant, ungraceful.

ungodly *adjective* **1** evil, godless, immoral, impious, iniquitous, irreligious, sinful, unholy, wicked.

ungrateful *adjective* unappreciative, unthankful.

ungratefulness *noun* ingratitude.

unhappy *adjective* **1** blue, dejected, depressed, despondent, disconsolate, discontented, dismal, dispirited, distressed, doleful, downcast, down-hearted, fed up (*informal*), gloomy, glum, heartbroken, heavy-hearted, melancholy, miserable, mournful, pessimistic, sad, sorrowful, woebegone, wretched. **2** bad, inappropriate, poor, regrettable, unfortunate, unlucky, unsatisfactory, unsuitable.

unharmed *adjective* safe, safe and sound, undamaged, unhurt, uninjured, unscathed.

unhealthy *adjective* **1** ailing, diseased, poorly, sick, sickly, unsound, unwell. **2** deleterious, detrimental, harmful, insalubrious, insanitary, unhygienic, unwholesome.

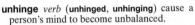

DICTIONARY

unhinge *verb* (**unhinged**, **unhinging**) cause a person's mind to become unbalanced.

uni *noun* (*Australian informal*) a university.

uni- *prefix* one; single (as in *unicorn*). [from Latin *unus* = one]

unicorn *noun* (in legends) an animal that is like a horse with one long straight horn growing from its forehead. [from *uni-*, + Latin *cornu* = horn]

uniform¹ *noun* special clothes showing that the wearer is a member of a certain organisation, school, etc.

uniform² *adjective* always the same; not varying, *The desks are of uniform size.* **uniformly** *adverb*, **uniformity** *noun* [from *uni-* + *form*]

uniformed *adjective* wearing a uniform.

unify *verb* (**unified**, **unifying**) make into one thing; unite. **unification** *noun*

unilateral *adjective* of or done by one person or group or country etc. [from *uni-* + *lateral*]

uninhabitable *adjective* not suitable for habitation.

uninhabited *adjective* not inhabited.

uninhibited *adjective* not inhibited; having no inhibitions.

uninterested *adjective* not interested; showing or feeling no concern.

Usage See the note on *disinterested*.

union *noun* 1 the joining of things together; uniting. 2 a trade union (see *trade*). [from Latin *unio* = unity]

unionist *noun* 1 a member of a trade union. 2 a person who wishes to unite one country with another.

unique (*say* yoo-**neek**) *adjective* being the only one of its kind, *This vase is unique.* **uniquely** *adverb* [from Latin *unus* = one]

unison *noun* **in unison** with all sounding or singing the same tune etc. together, or speaking in chorus; in agreement. [from *uni-*, + Latin *sonus* = sound]

unit *noun* 1 an amount used as a standard in measuring or counting things, *Centimetres are units of length*; *yen are units of money.* 2 a group, device, piece of furniture, etc. regarded as a single thing but forming part of a larger group or whole, *an army unit*; *a home unit*; *a sink unit.* [from Latin *unus* = one]

THESAURUS

unhelpful *adjective* obstructive, stroppy (*informal*), uncooperative.

unidentified *adjective* anonymous, incognito, nameless, unknown, unnamed.

uniform¹ *noun* habit, livery, regalia.

uniform² *adjective* consistent, constant, even, identical, invariable, regular, same, stable, steady, unchanging.

unify *verb* amalgamate, bind, bring together, combine, consolidate, federate, incorporate, integrate, join, merge, tie, unite.

unimaginative *adjective* colourless, dull, hackneyed, ordinary, pedestrian, prosaic, unexciting, uninspired, unoriginal.

unimportant *adjective* inconsequential, insignificant, irrelevant, minor, obscure, peripheral, petty, trivial.

uninhabited *adjective* deserted, empty, unoccupied, vacant.

uninhibited *adjective* free, reckless, spontaneous, unrepressed, unrestrained, unselfconscious.

unintelligible *adjective* confused, incoherent, incomprehensible, indecipherable, meaningless.

unintentional *adjective* accidental, chance, fortuitous, inadvertent, unforeseen, unintended, unplanned, unpremeditated; see also INVOLUNTARY.

uninterested *adjective* apathetic, blasé, bored, detached, indifferent, unconcerned.

uninteresting *adjective* banal, boring, commonplace, dreary, dull, humdrum, monotonous, mundane, ordinary, pedestrian, prosaic, stodgy, tedious, tiresome, uneventful, unexciting, unimaginative, uninspiring, vapid.

uninterrupted *adjective* continuous, non-stop, solid, sound, unbroken, undisturbed.

uninvited *adjective* unasked, unwanted, unwelcome.

uninviting *adjective* inhospitable, unappealing, unattractive, unenticing, unwelcoming.

union *noun* 1 alliance, amalgamation, association, coalition, combination, federation, merger, synthesis, unification. 2 guild, trade union.

unique *adjective* distinctive, inimitable, matchless, one-off, peculiar, singular.

unit *noun* 1 measure, measurement, quantity. 2 component, constituent, element, item, module, part, piece, section; (*a research unit*) group, squad, team; (*a home unit*) apartment, condominium (*American*), flat.

unite *verb* (**united, uniting**) join together; make or become one thing.
Uniting Church in Australia a church formed in 1977 from members of the Methodist, Presbyterian and Congregational churches in Australia.

unity *noun* **1** being united; being in agreement. **2** something whole that is made up of parts. **3** the number one.

universal *adjective* of or including or done by everyone or everything. **universally** *adverb*

universe *noun* everything that exists, including the earth and living things and all the heavenly bodies. [from Latin *universus* = combined into one]

university *noun* (*plural* **universities**) a place where people go to study at an advanced level after leaving school.

unjust *adjective* not fair; not just.

unkempt *adjective* looking untidy or neglected. [from *un-*, + an old word *kempt* = combed]

unkind *adjective* not kind. **unkindly** *adverb*, **unkindness** *noun*

unknown *adjective* not known.

unleash *verb* set free from a leash; let loose.

unleavened (*say* un-**lev**-end) *adjective* (of bread) made without yeast or other substances that would make it rise.

unless *conjunction* except when; if . . . not, *We cannot go unless we are invited.*

unlike[1] *preposition* not like, *Unlike me, she enjoys cricket.*

unlike[2] *adjective* not alike; different, *The two children are very unlike.*

unlikely *adjective* (**unlikelier, unlikeliest**) not likely to happen or be true.

unlimited *adjective* not limited; very great or very many.

unload *verb* remove the load of things carried by a ship, aircraft, vehicle, etc.

unlock *verb* open something by undoing a lock.

unlucky *adjective* not lucky; having or bringing bad luck. **unluckily** *adverb*

unmanageable *adjective* unable to be managed.

unmarried *adjective* not married.

unmask *verb* **1** remove a person's mask. **2** reveal what a person or thing really is.

unmentionable *adjective* too bad to be spoken of.

unite *verb* amalgamate, band together, bind, bring together, collaborate, combine, consolidate, cooperate, federate, incorporate, integrate, join, join forces, link, merge, team up, tie, unify.

unity *noun* **1** accord, agreement, cohesion, concord, consensus, harmony, oneness, solidarity, unanimity.

universal *adjective* general, global, international, ubiquitous, widespread, worldwide.

universe *noun* cosmos, Creation, world.

unjust *adjective* biased, inequitable, one-sided, partial, prejudiced, unfair, unjustified, unreasonable, wrong.

unkempt *adjective* bedraggled, dishevelled, messy, scruffy, tousled, untidy.

unkind *adjective* beastly (*informal*), callous, cold-hearted, cruel, hard-hearted, harsh, heartless, hurtful, inconsiderate, inhuman, inhumane, malicious, mean, merciless, nasty, pitiless, ruthless, sadistic, spiteful, stern, thoughtless, uncaring, uncharitable, unfeeling, unfriendly, unneighbourly, unsympathetic, vicious.

unknown *adjective* anonymous, nameless, obscure, undistinguished, unheard-of, unidentified, unnamed.

unlikely *adjective* far-fetched, implausible, improbable, incredible, unbelievable.

unlimited *adjective* absolute, boundless, complete, endless, everlasting, full, inexhaustible, infinite, limitless, never-ending, unconditional, unqualified, unrestricted, vast.

unload *verb* discharge, drop off, dump, empty, offload, remove, unpack.

unlock *verb* open, unbolt, undo, unfasten, unlatch.

unlucky *adjective* accident-prone, hapless, ill-fated, jinxed (*informal*), luckless, unfortunate, wretched.

unmanageable *adjective* (*an unmanageable load*) awkward, cumbersome, unwieldy; (*an unmanageable person*) difficult, intractable, obstreperous, refractory, stroppy (*informal*), uncontrollable, undisciplined, unruly, wayward.

unmarried *adjective* maiden, single, unattached, unwed.

unmentionable *adjective* forbidden, obscene, rude, shocking, taboo, unprintable.

▶▶ D I C T I O N A R Y ◀◀

unmistakable *adjective* not able to be mistaken for another person or thing. **unmistakably** *adverb*

unmitigated *adjective* absolute, *an unmitigated disaster.*

unnatural *adjective* 1 not natural; not normal. 2 artificial; affected. **unnaturally** *adverb*

unnecessary *adjective* not necessary; more than is necessary.

unnerve *verb* (**unnerved**, **unnerving**) cause someone to lose courage or determination.

unoccupied *adjective* not occupied.

unofficial *adjective* not official. **unofficially** *adverb*

unpack *verb* take things out of a suitcase, bag, box, etc.

unpaid *adjective* 1 (of a debt) not yet paid. 2 not receiving payment for work etc.

unparalleled *adjective* having no parallel or equal.

unparliamentary *adjective* impolite; abusive, *unparliamentary language.*

unpick *verb* undo the stitching of something.

unpleasant *adjective* not pleasant. **unpleasantly** *adverb*, **unpleasantness** *noun*

unpopular *adjective* not popular.

unprecedented (*say* un-**press**-id-en-tid) *adjective* that has never happened before.

unprejudiced *adjective* impartial.

unprepared *adjective* not prepared beforehand; not ready, not equipped.

unprepossessing *adjective* not attractive; not making a good impression.

unprincipled *adjective* without good moral principles; unscrupulous.

unprintable *adjective* too rude or indecent to be printed.

unprofessional *adjective* 1 not professional. 2 not worthy of a member of a profession.

unprofitable *adjective* not producing a profit or advantage. **unprofitably** *adverb*

▶▶ T H E S A U R U S ◀◀

unmistakable *adjective* apparent, blatant, clear, conspicuous, distinct, evident, glaring, manifest, noticeable, obvious, patent, plain, pronounced.

unnatural *adjective* 1 abnormal, bizarre, freakish, odd, peculiar, strange, supernatural, unusual, weird. 2 affected, artificial, contrived, forced, mannered, phoney (*informal*), stilted, studied, theatrical.

unnecessary *adjective* dispensable, excessive, expendable, inessential, needless, nonessential, redundant, superfluous, uncalled-for, unwanted.

unnerve *verb* agitate, disconcert, fluster, frighten, perturb, rattle (*informal*), unsettle, upset.

unoccupied *adjective* deserted, empty, uninhabited, unlived-in, vacant.

unorthodox *adjective* heretical, irregular, nonstandard, unconventional.

unpaid *adjective* 1 outstanding, overdue, owing. 2 honorary, unsalaried, unwaged, voluntary.

unparalleled *adjective* incomparable, inimitable, matchless, peerless, supreme, unequalled, unrivalled, unsurpassed.

unplanned *adjective* accidental, chance, fortuitous, unintended, unintentional, unpremeditated, unscheduled.

unpleasant *adjective* abominable, annoying, appalling, atrocious, awful, bad-tempered, beastly (*informal*), diabolical, disagreeable, disgusting, distasteful, dreadful, foul, frightful,

ghastly, harsh, hateful, hideous, horrible, horrid, irksome, loathsome, nasty, nauseating, objectionable, obnoxious, offensive, off-putting, repugnant, repulsive, revolting, sickening, sordid, squalid, terrible, troublesome, unattractive, unfriendly, unlikeable, unpalatable, unsightly, upsetting, vile.

unpopular *adjective* disliked, friendless, on the outer (*Australian informal*), shunned, unloved.

unprecedented *adjective* exceptional, extraordinary, unheard-of, unparalleled, unusual.

unpredictable *adjective* capricious, changeable, erratic, fickle, inconstant, mercurial, moody, temperamental, unreliable, volatile.

unprejudiced *adjective* disinterested, fair, impartial, objective, open-minded, unbiased.

unprepared *adjective* ad lib, extempore, impromptu, off the cuff, spontaneous, unrehearsed.

unpretentious *adjective* homely, humble, lowly, modest, plain, simple, unimposing, unostentatious.

unproductive *adjective* barren, fruitless, futile, infertile, sterile, unprofitable, unrewarding, useless, vain.

unprofessional *adjective* 1 amateurish, incompetent, inexpert, shoddy. 2 improper, irresponsible, negligent, unethical, unprincipled.

unprofitable *adjective* fruitless, uncommercial, uneconomic, unproductive, useless, worthless.

▶▶ D I C T I O N A R Y ◀◀

unqualified *adjective* **1** not officially qualified to do something. **2** not limited, *We gave it our unqualified approval.*

unravel *verb* (**unravelled, unravelling**) **1** disentangle. **2** undo something that is knitted. **3** investigate and solve a mystery etc.

unreal *adjective* not real, existing in the imagination only. **unreality** *noun*

unreasonable *adjective* **1** not reasonable. **2** excessive; unjust. **unreasonably** *adverb*

unreel *verb* unwind from a reel.

unrelieved *adjective* without anything to vary it, *unrelieved gloom.*

unremitting *adjective* not stopping, not relaxing; persistent.

unrequited (*say* un-ri-**kwy**-tid) *adjective* (of love) not returned or rewarded. [from *un-* + *requited* = paid back]

unreserved *adjective* **1** not reserved. **2** without restriction; complete, *unreserved loyalty.* **unreservedly** *adverb*

unrest *noun* restlessness; trouble caused because people are dissatisfied.

unripe *adjective* not yet ripe.

unrivalled *adjective* having no equal; better than all others.

unroll *verb* open something that has been rolled up.

unruly *adjective* difficult to control; disorderly. **unruliness** *noun* [from *un-* + *rule*]

unsavoury *adjective* unpleasant; disgusting.

unscathed *adjective* uninjured. [from *un-*, + an old word *scathed* = harmed]

unscrew *verb* undo something that has been screwed up.

unscrupulous *adjective* having no scruples about wrongdoing.

unseat *verb* throw a person from horseback or from a seat on a bicycle etc.

unseemly *adjective* not seemly; improper.

unseen[1] *adjective* not seen; invisible.

unseen[2] *noun* a passage for translation without previous preparation.

unselfish *adjective* not selfish.

▶▶ T H E S A U R U S ◀◀

unquestionable *adjective* certain, definite, incontrovertible, indisputable, indubitable, irrefutable, sure, undeniable, undisputed.

unravel *verb* **1** disentangle, untangle, untwist.

unreadable *adjective* illegible, indecipherable.

unreal *adjective* artificial, fabulous, false, fantastic, fictitious, hypothetical, illusory, imaginary, make-believe, mythical, non-existent.

unrealistic *adjective* idealistic, impracticable, impractical, unreasonable, unworkable.

unreasonable *adjective* **1** headstrong, illogical, irrational, obstinate, opinionated, perverse, pigheaded, stubborn, wilful. **2** absurd, excessive, exorbitant, extortionate, immoderate, ludicrous, outrageous, preposterous, steep (*informal*), undue, unjust.

unreliable *adjective* chancy, dicey (*slang*), dodgy (*informal*), erratic, fickle, iffy (*informal*), irresponsible, risky, shonky (*Australian informal*), uncertain, undependable, unsound, unsure, untrustworthy.

unrepentant *adjective* hardened, impenitent, remorseless, unashamed.

unreservedly *adverb* absolutely, completely, totally, unconditionally, utterly, wholeheartedly, without reservation.

unrest *noun* agitation, disquiet, dissatisfaction, rebellion, rioting, strife, trouble, turbulence, turmoil, unease, uprising.

unrivalled *adjective* incomparable, matchless, peerless, unequalled, unparalleled, unsurpassed.

unroll *verb* open out, spread out, unfurl.

unruly *adjective* boisterous, disobedient, disorderly, lawless, obstreperous, riotous, rowdy, uncontrollable, undisciplined, unmanageable, wayward, wild.

unsafe *adjective* dangerous, hazardous, perilous, precarious, risky, treacherous.

unsatisfactory *adjective* defective, deficient, disappointing, faulty, inadequate, insufficient, substandard, unacceptable.

unscathed *adjective* safe, safe and sound, undamaged, unharmed, unhurt, uninjured.

unscrupulous *adjective* corrupt, crooked, deceitful, dishonest, dishonourable, immoral, shady, shonky (*Australian informal*), unethical, unprincipled.

unseemly *adjective* improper, inappropriate, indecent, indecorous, offensive, tasteless, unbecoming, unfitting.

unseen[1] *adjective* concealed, hidden, invisible, out of sight, unnoticed.

unselfish *adjective* altruistic, considerate, generous, kind, magnanimous, open-handed, philanthropic, selfless, thoughtful, unstinting.

▶▶▶ D I C T I O N A R Y ◀◀

unsettled *adjective* **1** not settled; not calm. **2** likely to change.

unshakeable *adjective* not able to be shaken; firm.

unsightly *adjective* not pleasant to look at; ugly. **unsightliness** *noun*

unskilled *adjective* not having or not needing special skill or training.

unsociable *adjective* not sociable.

unsolicited *adjective* not asked for.

unsound *adjective* not sound; damaged, unhealthy, unreasonable, or unreliable. [from *un-* + *sound⁴*]

unspeakable *adjective* too bad to be described; very objectionable.

unstable *adjective* not stable; likely to change or become unbalanced.

unsteady *adjective* not steady.

unstinted *adjective* given generously.

unstuck *adjective* **come unstuck** cease to stick; (*informal*) fail, go wrong.

unsuccessful *adjective* not successful.

unsuitable *adjective* not suitable.

unsure *adjective* not sure.

untenable *adjective* not tenable.

unthinkable *adjective* too bad or too unlikely to be worth considering.

unthinking *adjective* thoughtless.

untidy *adjective* (**untidier, untidiest**) not tidy. **untidily** *adverb*, **untidiness** *noun*

untie *verb* (**untied, untying**) undo something that has been tied.

until *preposition* & *conjunction* up to a particular time or event.

untimely *adjective* happening too soon or at an unsuitable time.

unto *preposition* (*old use*) to.

untold *adjective* **1** not told. **2** too much or too many to be counted, *untold wealth* or *wealth untold*.

untoward *adjective* inconvenient; awkward, *if nothing untoward happens*.

untraceable *adjective* unable to be traced.

untrue *adjective* **1** not true. **2** not faithful or loyal.

untruth *noun* an untrue statement; a lie. **untruthful** *adjective*, **untruthfully** *adverb*

▶▶▶ T H E S A U R U S ◀◀

unsettled *adjective* **1** agitated, disconcerted, disturbed, edgy, flustered, perturbed, rattled (*informal*), restless, ruffled, troubled, uneasy, unnerved, upset. **2** changeable, erratic, patchy, unpredictable, unstable, variable.

unshakeable *adjective* firm, resolute, staunch, steadfast, unwavering.

unsociable *adjective* aloof, antisocial, reclusive, retiring, stand-offish, unfriendly, withdrawn.

unsophisticated *adjective* artless, ingenuous, naïve, natural, simple, unaffected, unpretentious, unrefined, unworldly.

unstable *adjective* changeable, explosive, fluctuating, fluid, unpredictable, volatile.

unsteady *adjective* precarious, rickety, rocky, shaky, unstable, wobbly, wonky (*informal*).

unsuccessful *adjective* abortive, failed, fruitless, futile, ineffective, ineffectual, unavailing, vain.

unsuitable *adjective* inappropriate, out of place, unbecoming, unfitting, unseemly, wrong.

unsure *adjective* see UNCERTAIN.

unsuspecting *adjective* credulous, gullible, ingenuous, naïve, trusting, unsuspicious, unwary.

unsympathetic *adjective* callous, cold, hard-hearted, heartless, indifferent, insensitive, uncaring, uncompassionate, unfeeling.

untamed *adjective* feral, savage, unbroken, undomesticated, warrigal (*Australian*), wild.

untangle *verb* disentangle, unravel, unsnarl, untwist.

unthinkable *adjective* inconceivable, incredible, unbelievable, unimaginable.

unthinking *adjective* careless, heedless, inconsiderate, mindless, negligent, short-sighted, tactless, thoughtless.

untidy *adjective* (*an untidy place*) chaotic, cluttered, disorderly, disorganised, higgledy-piggledy, jumbled, littered, messy, muddled, topsy-turvy; (*an untidy person*) bedraggled, dishevelled, ruffled, rumpled, scruffy, shabby, shaggy, slatternly, sloppy, slovenly, straggly, tatty (*informal*), tousled, unkempt.

untie *verb* detach, disconnect, loosen, release, undo, unfasten, unknot.

untold *adjective* **2** countless, immeasurable, incalculable, indescribable, innumerable, myriad, numberless, numerous.

untrue *adjective* **1** apocryphal, erroneous, false, fictitious, invented, made-up, untruthful, wrong. **2** disloyal, fickle, perfidious, treacherous, unfaithful.

untruth *noun* fabrication, fairy story, falsehood, fib, fiction, lie, story.
untruthful *adjective* deceitful, dishonest, false, lying, mendacious.

▶▶ DICTIONARY ◀◀

unused *adjective* **1** (*say* un-**yoozd**) not yet used, *an unused stamp*. **2** (*say* un-**yoost**) not accustomed, *He is unused to eating meat.*

unusual *adjective* not usual; exceptional; strange. **unusually** *adverb*

unutterable *adjective* too great to be described, *unutterable joy.*

unvarnished *adjective* **1** not varnished. **2** plain and straightforward, *the unvarnished truth.*

unveil *verb* **1** remove a veil or covering from something. **2** reveal.

unwanted *adjective* not wanted.

unwarrantable *adjective* not justifiable. **unwarrantably** *adverb*

unwarranted *adjective* not justified; not authorised.

unwary *adjective* not cautious. **unwarily** *adverb*, **unwariness** *noun*

unwell *adjective* not in good health.

unwholesome *adjective* not wholesome.

unwieldy *adjective* awkward to move or control because of its size, shape, or weight. **unwieldiness** *noun*

unwilling *adjective* not willing. **unwillingly** *adverb*

unwind *verb* (**unwound, unwinding**) **1** unroll. **2** (*informal*) relax after a time of work or strain.

unwise *adjective* not wise; foolish. **unwisely** *adverb*

unwitting *adjective* **1** unaware. **2** unintentional. **unwittingly** *adverb*

unwonted (*say* un-**wohn**-tid) *adjective* not customary; not usual, *She spoke with unwonted rudeness.* **unwontedly** *adverb* [from *un-* + *wont*]

unworn *adjective* not yet worn.

unworthy *adjective* not worthy.

unwrap *verb* (**unwrapped, unwrapping**) open something that is wrapped.

up¹ *adverb* **1** to or in a higher place or position or level, *Prices went up.* **2** so as to be upright, *Stand up.* **3** out of bed, *It's time to get up.* **4** completely, *Eat up your carrots.* **5** finished, *Your time is up.* **6** (*informal*) happening, *Something is up.*

up against close to; (*informal*) faced with difficulties, dangers, etc.

up front in advance, *pay up front.*

ups and downs ascents and descents; alternate good and bad luck.

▶▶ THESAURUS ◀◀

unused *adjective* **1** blank, clean, empty, fresh, new, untouched. **2** inexperienced (at), unaccustomed, unfamiliar (with).

unusual *adjective* abnormal, atypical, bizarre, curious, different, eccentric, exceptional, exotic, extraordinary, freakish, irregular, odd, offbeat, outlandish, peculiar, phenomenal, queer, rare, remarkable, singular, special, strange, surprising, uncommon, unfamiliar, unorthodox, way-out (*informal*), weird.

unwanted *adjective* excluded, on the outer (*Australian*), rejected, shunned, unpopular, unwelcome; see also UNNECESSARY.

unwarranted *adjective* groundless, indefensible, inexcusable, uncalled-for, unjustified, unnecessary, unreasonable.

unwary *adjective* imprudent, incautious, unguarded, unsuspecting, unsuspicious.

unwell *adjective* ailing, bilious, crook (*Australian informal*), funny (*informal*), ill, indisposed, infirm, nauseous, off colour, out of sorts, poorly, queasy, rotten, seedy (*informal*), sick, sickly, under the weather, unhealthy.

unwholesome *adjective* deleterious, detrimental, harmful, insalubrious, insanitary, unhealthy, unhygienic.

unwieldy *adjective* awkward, bulky, clumsy, cumbersome, heavy, hefty.

unwilling *adjective* averse, disinclined, hesitant, loath, reluctant.

unwind *verb* **1** undo, unravel, unroll. **2** calm down, ease off, relax, take it easy.

unwise *adjective* crazy, foolish, impolitic, imprudent, inadvisable, injudicious, silly, stupid, unintelligent.

unworldly *adjective* callow, green, inexperienced, innocent, naïve, unsophisticated.

unworthy *adjective* **1** undeserving. **2** inappropriate, unbecoming, unbefitting, unfitting, unsuitable.

unwritten *adjective* implicit, oral, spoken, tacit, unstated.

unyielding *adjective* adamant, firm, inflexible, intransigent, obstinate, relentless, steadfast, stubborn, tenacious, tough, unbending, uncompromising.

up¹ *adverb* **up to date** contemporary, current, fashionable, latest, modern, modernised, new, trendy (*informal*), up to the minute, with it (*informal*).

▶▶DICTIONARY◀◀

up to until; busy with or doing something; capable of; needed from, *It's up to us to help her.*

up to date modern; fashionable; giving recent information etc.

Usage Use hyphens when this is used as an adjective before a noun, e.g. *up-to-date information* (but *The information is up to date*).

---

up² *preposition* upwards through or along or into, *Water came up the pipes.*

upbraid *verb* (*formal*) reproach.

upbringing *noun* the way someone is trained during childhood.

update *verb* (**updated, updating**) bring a thing up to date.

upfront *adjective* **1** frank, open. **2** made in advance, *upfront fees.*

upgrade *verb* raise in rank; improve (equipment etc.).

upheaval *noun* a sudden violent change or disturbance.

uphill¹ *adverb* up a slope.

uphill² *adjective* **1** going up a slope. **2** difficult, *It was uphill work.*

uphold *verb* (**upheld, upholding**) **1** support, keep something from falling. **2** support a decision or belief etc.

upholster *verb* put covers, padding, and springs etc. on furniture. **upholstery** *noun* [from *uphold* = maintain and repair]

upkeep *noun* keeping something in good condition; the cost of this.

uplands *plural noun* the higher parts of a country or region. **upland** *adjective*

uplift *verb* raise, *uplift their spirits.*

upmarket *adjective & adverb* of or towards the dearer end of the market.

upon *preposition* on.

upper *adjective* higher in place or rank etc.

uppermost¹ *adjective* highest.

uppermost² *adverb* on or to the top or the highest place, *Keep the painted side uppermost.*

upright¹ *adjective* **1** vertical; erect. **2** strictly honest or honourable.

upright² *noun* a post or rod etc. placed upright, especially as a support.

uprising *noun* a rebellion; a revolt.

uproar *noun* an outburst of noise or excitement or anger.

uproarious *adjective* very noisy.

uproot *verb* **1** remove a plant and its roots from the ground. **2** make someone leave the place where he or she has lived for a long time.

▶▶THESAURUS◀◀

upbraid *verb* admonish, berate, castigate, censure, chastise, chide (*old use*), rebuke, reprimand, reproach, reprove, scold, tell off (*informal*), tick off (*informal*).

upbringing *noun* education, nurture, raising, rearing, training.

update *verb* modernise, refurbish, remodel, renovate.

upfront *adjective* **1** direct, forthright, frank, honest, open.

upgrade *verb* enhance, improve.

upheaval *noun* change, chaos, disruption, disturbance, havoc, turbulence, turmoil.

uphill² *adjective* **2** arduous, demanding, difficult, exacting, gruelling, hard, laborious, strenuous, tough.

uphold *verb* **2** confirm, endorse, maintain, stand by, support, sustain.

upkeep *noun* maintenance, repairs, running.

uplift *verb* buoy up, encourage, inspire, lift, raise.

upmarket *adjective* classy (*informal*), de luxe, expensive, luxurious, superior.

upper *adjective* higher, raised, superior.

uppermost¹ *adjective* highest, top, topmost.

upright¹ *adjective* **1** erect, perpendicular, standing, vertical. **2** ethical, good, honest, honourable, just, moral, principled, righteous, trustworthy, upstanding, virtuous.

uprising *noun* insurrection, mutiny, rebellion, revolt, revolution, rising.

uproar *noun* bedlam, chaos, clamour, commotion, confusion, disorder, fracas, furore, hullabaloo, kerfuffle (*informal*), mayhem, outcry, pandemonium, protest, riot, row, ruckus, rumpus, stir, storm, to-do, tumult, turmoil.

uproarious *adjective* boisterous, disorderly, noisy, obstreperous, rowdy, tumultuous, unruly.

uproot *verb* **1** dig up, eradicate, get rid of, pull up, remove, root out.

▶▶▶ D I C T I O N A R Y ◀◀◀

upset¹ *verb* (**upset**, **upsetting**) **1** overturn; knock something over. **2** make a person unhappy. **3** disturb the normal working of something.

upset² *noun* upsetting something; being upset, *a stomach upset.*

upshot *noun* an outcome.

upside-down *adverb & adjective* **1** with the upper part underneath instead of on top. **2** in great disorder; very untidy.

upstairs *adverb & adjective* to or on a higher floor.

upstart *noun* a person who has risen suddenly to a high position, especially one who then behaves arrogantly.

upstream *adjective & adverb* in the direction from which a stream flows.

uptake *noun* (*informal*) understanding, *She is quick on the uptake.*

uptight *adjective* (*informal*) tense and nervous or annoyed.

upward *adjective & adverb* going towards what is higher. **upwards** *adverb*

uranium *noun* a heavy radioactive grey metal used as a source of nuclear energy. [named after the planet Uranus]

urban *adjective* of a town or city. [from Latin *urbis* = of a city]

urbane *adjective* having smoothly polite manners. **urbanely** *adverb*, **urbanity** *noun* [same origin as *urban*]

urbanise *verb* (**urbanised**, **urbanising**) change a place into a town-like area. **urbanisation** *noun*

urchin *noun* **1** a poorly dressed or mischievous boy. **2** a sea-urchin. [from Latin *ericius* = hedgehog]

Urdu (*say* **oor**-doo) *noun* a language related to Hindi.

urge¹ *verb* (**urged**, **urging**) **1** try to persuade a person to do something. **2** drive people or animals onward.

urge² *noun* a strong desire.

urgent *adjective* needing to be done or dealt with immediately. **urgently** *adverb*, **urgency** *noun* [from Latin *urgens* = urging]

urinate (*say* **yoor**-in-ayt) *verb* (**urinated**, **urinating**) pass urine out of your body. **urination** *noun*

urine (*say* **yoor**-in) *noun* waste liquid that collects in the bladder and is passed out of the body. **urinary** *adjective*

urn *noun* **1** a large metal container with a tap, in which water is heated. **2** a container shaped like a vase, usually with a foot; a container for holding the ashes of a cremated person.

US *abbreviation* United States (of America).

us *pronoun* the form of *we* used when it is the object of a verb or after a preposition.

USA *abbreviation* United States of America.

usable *adjective* able to be used.

usage *noun* **1** use; the way something is used. **2** a habitual or customary practice, *modern Australian English usage.*

use¹ (*say* yooz) *verb* (**used**, **using**) perform an action or job with something, *Use soap for washing.* **user** *noun*

▶▶▶ T H E S A U R U S ◀◀◀

upset¹ *verb* **1** knock over, overturn, spill, tip up, topple, up-end, upturn. **2** agitate, alarm, anger, annoy, bother, distress, disturb, fluster, frighten, grieve, hurt, offend, perturb, provoke, rattle (*informal*), trouble, vex, worry. **3** affect, disrupt, interfere with, mess up.

upset² *noun* ailment, bug (*informal*), complaint, disorder, malady.

upshot *noun* consequence, effect, outcome, result.

upside-down *adverb & adjective* **1** inverted, topsy-turvy, upturned.

uptight *adjective* anxious, apprehensive, edgy, jittery (*informal*), keyed up, nervous, tense, uneasy, worried.

urban *adjective* city, metropolitan, town.

urge¹ *verb* **1** beseech, coax, encourage, entreat, exhort, implore, plead with, press, prompt, push, recommend. **2** drive, egg on, force, goad, impel, prod, spur.

urge² *noun* compulsion, desire, drive, fancy, impulse, itch, longing, wish, yearning, yen.

urgent *adjective* compelling, desperate, dire, immediate, imperative, important, necessary, pressing, vital.

urinate *verb* excrete, pass water, relieve yourself, void.

usable *adjective* available, functional, operational, working.

usage *noun* **1** handling, treatment, use. **2** convention, custom, habit, practice, use.

use¹ *verb* apply, consume, employ, exercise, exert, expend, exploit, handle, make use of, manipulate, operate, ply, utilise, wield, work. **user** *noun* consumer, operator.

▶▶ D I C T I O N A R Y ◀◀

used to accustomed to, *He is not used to the climate*; was or were accustomed to, *We used to go by train.*
use up use all of something.

use² (*say* yooss) *noun* **1** the action of using something; being used. **2** the purpose for which something is used. **3** the quality of being useful.

used *adjective* not new; second-hand.

useful *adjective* able to be used a lot or to do something that needs doing. **usefully** *adverb*, **usefulness** *noun*

useless *adjective* not useful; producing no effect, *Their efforts were useless.* **uselessly** *adverb*, **uselessness** *noun*

usher¹ *noun* a person who shows people to their seats in a public hall or church etc.

usher² *verb* lead in or out; escort someone as an usher.

usual *adjective* such as happens or is done or used etc. always or most of the time. **usually** *adverb* [from Latin *usum* = used]

usurp (*say* yoo-**zerp**) *verb* take power or a position or right etc. wrongfully or by force. **usurpation** *noun*, **usurper** *noun*

usury (*say* **yoo**-*zh*er-ee) *noun* the lending of money at an excessively high rate of interest. **usurer** *noun*

utensil (*say* yoo-**ten**-sil) *noun* a device or container, especially one for use in the house, *cooking utensils.*

uterus (*say* **yoo**-ter-us) *noun* the womb. [Latin, = womb]

utilise *verb* (**utilised, utilising**) use; find a use for something. **utilisation** *noun*

utilitarian *adjective* designed to be useful rather than decorative or luxurious; practical. [from *utility*]

utility *noun* (*plural* **utilities**) **1** usefulness. **2** a useful thing. [from Latin *utilis* = useful]

utmost *adjective* extreme; greatest, *Look after it with the utmost care.* **utmost** *noun* [from Old English, = furthest out]

Utopia (*say* yoo-**toh**-pee-a) *noun* an imaginary place or state of things where everything is perfect. **Utopian** *adjective* [named after *Utopia*, the title of a book by Sir Thomas More (1516), meaning 'Nowhere']

utter¹ *verb* say or speak; make a sound with your mouth. **utterance** *noun*

utter² *adjective* complete; absolute, *utter misery.* **utterly** *adverb*

uttermost *adjective* & *noun* utmost.

U-turn *noun* **1** a U-shaped turn made in a vehicle so that it then travels in the opposite direction. **2** a complete change of policy.

UV *abbreviation* ultraviolet.

▶▶ T H E S A U R U S ◀◀

used to acclimatised to, accustomed to, familiar with.
use up blow (*slang*), consume, deplete, exhaust, expend, fritter away, go through, spend.

use² *noun* **1** handling, usage. **2** application, function. **3** advantage, benefit, good, point, purpose, usefulness, utility, value.

used *adjective* cast-off, hand-me-down, old, recycled, second-hand, worn.

useful *adjective* advantageous, beneficial, constructive, convenient, effective, efficient, functional, handy, helpful, invaluable, positive, practical, productive, profitable, serviceable, usable, utilitarian, valuable, worthwhile.

useless *adjective* (*useless efforts*) fruitless, futile, hopeless, ineffective, ineffectual, pointless, unavailing, unproductive, vain; (*a useless gadget*) bung (*Australian informal*), dud (*informal*), impractical, unusable, worthless.

usher¹ *noun* attendant, escort, guide, sidesman.

usher² *verb* conduct, escort, guide, lead, show.

usual *adjective* accustomed, common, conventional, customary, established, everyday, familiar, general, habitual, normal, ordinary, orthodox, regular, routine, set, standard, stock, traditional, typical.

utensil *noun* appliance, device, gadget, implement, instrument, machine, tool.

utilise *verb* see USE¹.

utilitarian *adjective* functional, practical, serviceable, useful.

utility *noun* **1** convenience, practicality, service, serviceability, use, usefulness.

utmost *adjective* extreme, greatest, highest, maximum, paramount, supreme.

utter¹ *verb* come out with, emit, express, let out, pronounce, say, speak, voice.

utter² *adjective* absolute, arrant, complete, downright, out-and-out, perfect, positive, pure, sheer, thorough, total, unmitigated.

U-turn *noun* **2** about-face, about-turn, backflip, reversal.

Vv

vacant *adjective* **1** empty; not filled or occupied. **2** without expression; blank, *a vacant stare*. **vacantly** *adverb*, **vacancy** *noun* [from Latin *vacans* = being empty]

vacate *verb* (**vacated**, **vacating**) leave or give up a place or position. [from Latin *vacare* = be empty or free from work]

vacation (*say* vak-**ay**-shon) *noun* **1** a holiday, especially between the terms at a university. **2** vacating a place etc. [same origin as *vacate*]

vaccinate (*say* **vak**-sin-ayt) *verb* (**vaccinated**, **vaccinating**) inoculate someone with a vaccine. **vaccination** *noun*

vaccine (*say* **vak**-seen) *noun* a substance used to immunise a person against a disease. [from Latin *vacca* = cow (because serum from cows was used to protect people from smallpox)]

vacillate (*say* **vass**-il-ayt) *verb* (**vacillated**, **vacillating**) keep changing your mind; waver. **vacillation** *noun* [from Latin *vacillare* = sway]

vacuous (*say* **vak**-yoo-us) *adjective* empty-headed; without expression, *a vacuous stare*. **vacuously** *adverb*, **vacuousness** *noun*, **vacuity** *noun* [same origin as *vacuum*]

vacuum *noun* **1** a completely empty space; a space without any air in it. **2** (*informal*) a vacuum cleaner. **vacuum** *verb*
vacuum cleaner an electrical device that sucks up dust and dirt etc.
vacuum flask a container with double walls that have a vacuum between them, used for keeping liquids hot or cold. [from Latin *vacuus* = empty]

vagabond *noun* a wanderer; a vagrant. [from Latin *vagari* = wander]

vagary (*say* **vay**-ger-ee) *noun* (*plural* **vagaries**) an impulsive change or whim, *the vagaries of fashion*. [from Latin *vagari* = wander]

vagina (*say* va-**jy**-na) *noun* the passage that leads from the vulva to the womb. [from Latin *vagina* = sheath]

vagrant (*say* **vay**-grant) *noun* a person with no settled home or regular work; a tramp. **vagrancy** *noun* [from Latin *vagans* = wandering]

vague *adjective* not definite; not clear. **vaguely** *adverb*, **vagueness** *noun* [from Latin *vagus* = wandering]

vain *adjective* **1** conceited, especially about your appearance. **2** useless, *They made vain attempts to save her*. **vainly** *adverb*
in vain with no result; uselessly. [from Latin *vanus* = empty]

valance *noun* a short curtain round the frame of a bed or above a window.

vale *noun* a valley. [from Latin *vallis* = valley]

valediction (*say* val-id-**ik**-shon) *noun* saying farewell. **valedictory** *adjective* [from Latin *vale* = farewell, + *dicere* = say (compare *benediction*)]

▶▶▶ T H E S A U R U S ◀◀◀

vacant *adjective* **1** available, clear, deserted, empty, free, spare, unfilled, uninhabited, unoccupied, untenanted, unused, void. **2** absent-minded, blank, deadpan, empty, expressionless, vacuous.
vacancy *noun* job, opening, position, post, situation.

vacate *verb* abandon, depart from, evacuate, leave, quit.

vacation *noun* **1** break, furlough, holiday, leave, time off.

vaccination *noun* booster, immunisation, injection, inoculation, jab (*informal*), shot.

vacillate *verb* dither, fluctuate, hesitate, hum and haw, shilly-shally, swing, waver.

vacuum *noun* **1** emptiness, nothingness, void.

vagabond *noun* beachcomber, gypsy, hobo, itinerant, nomad, rover, swagman (*Australian*), tramp, traveller, vagrant, wanderer, wayfarer.

vagrant *noun* beggar, hobo, homeless person, itinerant, rover, tramp, vagabond.

vague *adjective* ambiguous, amorphous, blurred, dim, equivocal, fuzzy, general, hazy, imprecise, indefinite, indistinct, inexplicit, loose, nebulous, sketchy, uncertain, unclear, woolly.

vain *adjective* **1** arrogant, boastful, cocky, conceited, egotistical, narcissistic, proud, stuck-up (*informal*). **2** abortive, fruitless, futile, hopeless, unavailing, unsuccessful, useless.

valedictory *adjective* farewell, leave-taking, parting.

valentine *noun* **1** a card sent on St. Valentine's day (14 February) to the person you love. **2** the person to whom you send this card.

valet (*say* **val**-ay *or* **val**-it) *noun* a man's servant who looks after his clothes etc.

valetudinarian *noun* a person who is excessively concerned about keeping healthy. [from Latin *valetudo* = health]

valiant *adjective* brave; courageous. **valiantly** *adverb* [same origin as *value*]

valid *adjective* **1** legally able to be used or accepted, *This passport is out of date and not valid*. **2** (of reasoning) sound and logical. **validity** *noun* [from Latin *validus* = strong]

valley *noun* (*plural* **valleys**) **1** a long low area between hills. **2** an area through which a river flows, *the Nile valley*. [same origin as *vale*]

valour *noun* bravery. **valorous** *adjective* [from Latin *valor* = strength]

valuable *adjective* worth a lot of money; of great value. **valuably** *adverb*
valuables *plural noun* valuable things.

value¹ *noun* **1** the amount of money etc. that is considered to be the equivalent of something, or for which it can be exchanged. **2** how useful or important something is, *They learnt the value of regular exercise.*

value² *verb* (**valued, valuing**) **1** think that something is valuable. **2** estimate the value of a thing. **valuation** *noun*, **valuer** *noun* [from Latin *valere* = be strong]

valueless *adjective* having no value.

valve *noun* **1** a device for controlling the flow of gas or liquid through a pipe or tube. **2** a thermionic valve. **3** each piece of the shell of oysters etc. **valvular** *adjective* [from Latin *valva* = section of a folding door]

vamp¹ *noun* the front part of a shoe that goes over the foot.

vamp² *verb* **1** make from odds and ends, *We'll vamp something up*. **2** improvise a musical accompaniment.

vampire *noun* a ghost or revived corpse supposed to leave a grave at night and suck blood from living people.

van¹ *noun* **1** a covered vehicle for carrying goods etc. or prisoners. **2** a railway carriage for luggage or goods, or for the use of the guard. **3** a caravan. [short for *caravan*]

van² *noun* the vanguard; the forefront.

vandal *noun* a person who deliberately breaks or damages things. **vandalism** *noun* [named after the Vandals, a Germanic tribe who invaded the Roman Empire in the 5th century, destroying many books and works of art]

vandalise *verb* (**vandalised, vandalising**) damage things as a vandal.

vane *noun* **1** a weather-vane. **2** the blade of a propeller, sail of a windmill, or other device that acts on or is moved by wind or water.

vanguard *noun* **1** the leading part of an army or fleet. **2** the first people to adopt a fashion or idea etc. [from French *avant* = before, + *garde* = guard]

vanilla *noun* a flavouring obtained from the pods of a tropical plant. [from Spanish *vainilla* = little pod]

vanish *verb* disappear completely.

vanity *noun* conceit; being vain.

valiant *adjective* bold, brave, courageous, daring, dauntless, doughty, fearless, gallant, heroic, intrepid, lion-hearted, plucky, spirited, stout-hearted, undaunted, valorous.

valid *adjective* **1** lawful, legal, legitimate, official. **2** acceptable, allowable, cogent, logical, permissible, proper, reasonable, sound.

valley *noun* basin, canyon, dale, dell, glen, gorge, gully (*Australian*), hollow, pass, ravine, vale.

valour *noun* bravery, courage, daring, gallantry, heroism, intrepidity, pluck.

valuable *adjective* (*valuable jewellery*) costly, expensive, precious, priceless, prized, treasured; (*a valuable lesson*) beneficial, constructive, helpful, important, invaluable, profitable, useful, worthwhile.

value¹ *noun* **1** price, worth. **2** advantage, benefit, importance, merit, profit, use, usefulness, worth.

value² *verb* **1** appreciate, cherish, esteem, prize, respect, set store by, treasure. **2** appraise, assess, estimate, evaluate, price.

van¹ *noun* **1** lorry, panel van (*Australian*), truck, wagon. **3** campervan, caravan.

vandal *noun* delinquent, hoodlum, hooligan, ruffian, thug.

vanguard *noun* **1** advance guard, front line, spearhead, van. **2** avant-garde, cutting edge, forefront, leaders, pioneers, trailblazers, trendsetters.

vanish *verb* become invisible, disappear, evaporate, fade away, go away.

vanity *noun* conceit, egotism, narcissism, pride, self-admiration, self-love.

▶▶DICTIONARY◀◀

vanquish *verb* conquer. [from Latin *vincere* = conquer]

vantage-point *noun* a place from which you have a good view of something. [from *vantage* = advantage]

vapid *adjective* not lively; not interesting.

vaporise *verb* (**vaporised, vaporising**) change or be changed into vapour. **vaporisation** *noun*, **vaporiser** *noun*

vapour *noun* a visible gas to which some substances can be converted by heat; steam or mist. [from Latin *vapor* = steam]

variable¹ *adjective* varying; changeable. **variably** *adverb*, **variability** *noun*

variable² *noun* something that varies or can vary; a variable quantity.

variance *noun* the amount by which things differ.
at variance differing; conflicting.

variant *adjective* differing from something, *'Gipsy' is a variant spelling of 'gypsy'*. **variant** *noun*

variation *noun* **1** varying; the amount by which something varies. **2** a different form of something.

varicose *adjective* (of veins) permanently swollen.

varied *adjective* of different sorts; full of variety.

variegated (*say* **vair**-ig-ay-tid) *adjective* with patches of different colours. **variegation** *noun* [same origin as *various*]

variety *adjective* (*plural* **varieties**) **1** a quantity of different kinds of things. **2** the quality of

not always being the same; variation. **3** a particular kind of something, *There are several varieties of spaniel.* **4** an entertainment that includes short performances of various kinds.

various *adjective* **1** of several kinds; unlike one another, *for various reasons.* **2** several, *We met various people.* **variously** *adverb* [from Latin *varius* = changing]

varnish¹ *noun* (*plural* **varnishes**) a liquid that dries to form a hard shiny usually transparent coating.

varnish² *verb* coat something with varnish.

vary *verb* (**varied, varying**) **1** make or become different; change. **2** be different.

vascular *adjective* consisting of tubes or similar vessels for circulating blood, sap, or water in animals or plants, *the vascular system.* [from Latin *vasculum* = little vessel]

vase *noun* an open usually tall container used for holding cut flowers or as an ornament. [from Latin *vas* = vessel]

Vaseline *noun* (*trade mark*) petroleum jelly for use as an ointment. [from German *Wasser* = water, + Greek *elaion* = oil]

vassal *noun* a humble servant or subordinate.

vast *adjective* very great, especially in area, *a vast expanse of water.* **vastly** *adverb*, **vastness** *noun* [from Latin *vastus* = unoccupied, desert]

vat *noun* a very large container for holding liquid.

vaudeville (*say* **vawd**-vil) *noun* a kind of variety entertainment.

▶▶THESAURUS◀◀

vanquish *verb* beat, conquer, defeat, overcome, overpower, overthrow, rout, subdue, subjugate, thrash, triumph over, trounce.

vapour *noun* fog, fumes, gas, haze, mist, smoke, steam.

variable¹ *adjective* changeable, erratic, fickle, fitful, fluctuating, inconsistent, mutable, patchy, shifting, temperamental, unpredictable, unreliable.

variant *adjective* alternative, different.

variation *noun* **1** alteration, change, deviation, difference, divergence, fluctuation, modification, permutation, shift.

variegated *adjective* harlequin, marbled, motley, mottled, multicoloured, particoloured.

variety *noun* **1** array, assortment, collection, combination, miscellany, mixture, range. **2**

change, contrast, difference, diversity, variation. **3** breed, class, form, kind, sort, strain, type.

various *adjective* **1** assorted, different, disparate, diverse, heterogeneous, miscellaneous, varied. **2** many, numerous, several, sundry.

varnish¹ *noun* coating, glaze, gloss, lacquer.

vary *verb* **1** adjust, alter, change, fluctuate, modify, modulate. **2** be at odds, conflict, differ, diverge.

vast *adjective* big, boundless, broad, colossal, enormous, expansive, extensive, gigantic, great, huge, immense, large, massive, sizeable, spacious, stupendous, substantial, tremendous, wide.

vat *noun* barrel, tank.

vault¹ *verb* jump over something, especially while supporting yourself on your hands or with the help of a pole.

vault² *noun* **1** a vaulting jump. **2** an arched roof. **3** an underground room used to store things. **4** a room for storing money or valuables. **5** a burial chamber. [from Latin *volvere* = to roll]

vaulted *adjective* having an arched roof.

vaulting-horse *noun* a padded structure for vaulting over in gymnastics.

vaunt *verb* & *noun* (*old use* or *poetical*) boast. [from Latin *vanus* = vain]

VDU *abbreviation* visual display unit.

veal *noun* calf's flesh used as food. [from Latin *vitulus* = calf]

vector *noun* (in mathematics) a quantity that has size and direction (e.g. velocity = speed in a certain direction). **vectorial** *adjective*

Veda (*say* **vay**-da or **vee**-da) *noun* the most ancient and sacred literature of the Hindus. **Vedic** *adjective* [Sanskrit, = sacred knowledge]

veer *verb* change direction; swerve.

vegan (*say* **vee**-gan) *noun* a vegetarian who eats no animal products (e.g. eggs) at all.

vegetable *noun* a plant that can be used as food.

vegetarian *noun* a person who does not eat meat. **vegetarianism** *noun*

vegetate *verb* (**vegetated**, **vegetating**) live a dull or inactive life.

vegetation *noun* **1** plants that are growing. **2** vegetating.

vehement (*say* **vee**-im-ent) *adjective* showing strong feeling, *a vehement refusal*. **vehemently** *adverb*, **vehemence** *noun*

vehicle *noun* a device for transporting people or goods on land or in space. [from Latin *vehere* = carry]

veil¹ *noun* **1** a piece of thin material worn to cover the face or head. **2** a thing that conceals.
take the veil become a nun.

veil² *verb* cover with a veil or as if with a veil; conceal partially.

vein *noun* **1** any of the tubes that carry blood from all parts of the body to the heart. (Compare *artery*.) **2** a line or streak on a leaf, rock, insect's wing, etc. **3** a long deposit of mineral or ore in the middle of a rock. **4** a mood or manner, *She spoke in a serious vein*. [from Latin *vena* = vein]

veld (*say* velt) *noun* an area of open grassland in South Africa. [Afrikaans, = field]

vellum *noun* smooth parchment or writing-paper. [same origin as *veal* (because parchment was made from animals' skins)]

velocity *noun* (*plural* **velocities**) speed. [from Latin *velox* = swift]

velodrome (*say* **vel**-o-drohm) *noun* a place or building with a track for cycle racing.

velour (*say* vil-**oor**) *noun* a thick velvety material. [from French *velours* = velvet]

velvet *noun* a woven material with very short soft furry fibres on one side. **velvety** *adjective* [from Latin *villus* = soft fur]

venal (*say* **veen**-al) *adjective* able to be bribed. **venality** *noun* [from Latin *venalis* = for sale]

vend *verb* offer something for sale. [from Latin *vendere* = sell]

vendetta *noun* a feud. [Italian, from Latin *vindicta* = vengeance]

vending-machine *noun* a slot-machine where small articles can be obtained.

vendor *noun* a seller. [from *vend*]

veneer *noun* **1** a thin layer of good wood covering the surface of a cheaper wood in furniture etc. **2** an outward show of some good quality, *a veneer of politeness*.

vault¹ *verb* bound over, clear, hurdle, jump over, leap over, spring over.

vault² *noun* **1** bound, jump, leap, spring. **3** basement, cellar, crypt. **4** strongroom.

veer *verb* bear, diverge, sheer, swerve, swing, turn, wheel.

vegetate *verb* do nothing, idle, stagnate, veg (*informal*).

vegetation *noun* **1** flora, greenery, growth, plants.

vehement *adjective* ardent, fervent, fierce, fiery, heated, impassioned, intense, passionate, vigorous, violent.

vehicle *noun* conveyance; (*various vehicles*) bus, car, caravan, carriage, coach, cycle, tractor, trailer, train, tram, truck, van, wagon.

veil¹ *noun* **1** mantilla, yashmak. **2** cloak, cloud, cover, mantle, mask, screen, shroud.

veil² *verb* conceal, cover, disguise, hide, mask, obscure, screen, shroud.

velocity *noun* pace, rate, speed.

vendetta *noun* conflict, dispute, feud, quarrel.

vendor *noun* see SELLER (at SELL¹).

veneer *noun* **1** coating, covering, exterior, finish, overlay, surface. **2** façade, front, mask, pretence, show.

venerable *adjective* worthy of being venerated, especially because of great age.

venerate *verb* (**venerated, venerating**) honour with great respect or reverence. **veneration** *noun* [from Latin *venerari* = revere]

venereal (*say* vin-**eer**-ee-al) *adjective* **1** of sexual intercourse. **2** caused by sexual intercourse with an infected person, *venereal diseases*. [from *Venus*, the Roman goddess of love]

venetian blind a window blind consisting of horizontal strips that can be adjusted to let light in or shut it out. [from Latin *Venetia* = Venice]

vengeance *noun* revenge.
with a vengeance very strongly or effectively. [same origin as *vindictive*]

vengeful *adjective* seeking vengeance. **vengefully** *adverb*, **vengefulness** *noun*

venial (*say* **veen**-ee-al) *adjective* (of sins or faults) pardonable, not serious. [from Latin *venia* = forgiveness]

venison *noun* deer's flesh as food. [from Latin *venatio* = hunting]

venom *noun* **1** the poisonous fluid produced by snakes, scorpions, etc. **2** very bitter feeling towards somebody; hatred. **venomous** *adjective* [from Latin *venenum* = poison]

vent¹ *noun* an opening in something, especially to let out smoke or gas etc.
give vent to express your feelings etc. openly.

vent² *verb* **1** make a vent in something. **2** give vent to feelings. [from Latin *ventus* = wind]

ventilate *verb* (**ventilated, ventilating**) let air move freely in and out of a room etc. **ventilation** *noun*, **ventilator** *noun* [same origin as *vent*]

ventral *adjective* of or on the abdomen, *This fish has a ventral fin.* [from Latin *venter* = abdomen]

ventriloquist *noun* an entertainer who makes his or her voice sound as if it comes from another source. **ventriloquism** *noun* [from Latin *venter* = abdomen, + *loqui* = speak]

venture¹ *noun* something you decide to do that is risky.

venture² *verb* (**ventured, venturing**) **1** dare to do or say something or to go somewhere, *She did not venture to stop them*; *He ventured an opinion*; *We ventured out into the snow.* **2** risk. [Compare *adventure*]

Venture Scout a member of a senior branch of the Scout Association.

venturesome *adjective* ready to take risks; daring.

venue (*say* ven-**yoo**) *noun* the place where a meeting, sports match, etc. is held. [from French *venir* = come]

veracity (*say* ver-**as**-it-ee) *noun* truth. **veracious** (*say* ver-**ay**-shus) *adjective* [from Latin *verus* = true]

veranda *noun* a terrace with a roof along the side of a house. [from Hindi *varanda*]

verb *noun* a word that shows what a person or thing is doing, e.g. *bring, came, sing, were.* [from Latin *verbum* = word]

verbal *adjective* **1** of or in words. **2** spoken, not written, *a verbal statement.* **3** of verbs. **verbally** *adverb* [same origin as *verb*]

verbatim (*say* ver-**bay**-tim) *adverb & adjective* in exactly the same words, *He copied his friend's essay verbatim.*

venerable *adjective* aged, ancient, august, esteemed, honoured, old, respected, revered, venerated.

venerate *verb* adore, esteem, hallow, honour, look up to, respect, revere, worship.

vengeance *noun* reprisal, retaliation, retribution, revenge.

venial *adjective* excusable, forgivable, minor, pardonable, slight.

venom *noun* **1** poison, toxin.
venomous *adjective* (*venomous snakes*) deadly, fatal, lethal, poisonous, toxic; (*venomous words*) bitter, hostile, malevolent, malicious, malignant, rancorous, spiteful, vicious, virulent.

vent¹ *noun* aperture, duct, hole, opening, outlet, slit.

vent² *verb* **2** air, express, give vent to, release.

ventilate *verb* air, freshen.

venture¹ *noun* endeavour, enterprise, project, undertaking.

venture² *verb* **1** be so bold as, dare, presume, take the liberty; (*venture an opinion etc.*) advance, offer, proffer, put forward, volunteer. **2** chance, gamble, hazard, risk, stake, wager.

venue *noun* location, meeting place, place, site.

verbal *adjective* **1** lexical, linguistic. **2** oral, said, spoken, unwritten.

▶▶ D I C T I O N A R Y ◀◀

verbose *adjective* using more words than are needed. **verbosely** *adverb*, **verbosity** (*say* ver-**boss**-it-ee) *noun*

verdant *adjective* (of grass or fields) green. [Compare *verdure*]

verdict *noun* a judgement or decision made after considering something, especially that made by a jury. [from Latin *verus* = true, + *dictum* = said]

verdigris (*say* **verd**-i-grees) *noun* green rust on copper or brass. [from French, = green (*vert*) of Greece]

verdure *noun* green vegetation; its greenness. [from Old French *verd* = green]

verge[1] *noun* 1 the extreme edge or brink of something. 2 a strip of grass along the edge of a road or path etc.

verge[2] *verb* (**verged, verging**) **verge on** border on something; be close to.

verger *noun* a person who is caretaker and attendant in a church.

verify *verb* (**verified, verifying**) check or show that something is true or correct. **verifiable** *adjective*, **verification** *noun* [from Latin *verus* = true]

verisimilitude *noun* an appearance of being true or lifelike. [from Latin *verus* = true, + *similis* = like]

veritable *adjective* real; rightly named, *a veritable villain*. **veritably** *adverb* [same origin as *verity*]

verity *noun* (*plural* **verities**) truth. [from Latin *veritas* = truth]

vermicelli (*say* verm-i-**sel**-ee) *noun* pasta made in long thin threads. [Italian, = little worms]

vermilion *noun* & *adjective* bright red. [from Latin *vermiculus* = little worm]

vermin *plural noun* 1 pests (e.g. foxes, rats, mice) regarded as harmful to domestic animals, crops, or food. 2 unpleasant or parasitic insects, e.g. lice. **verminous** *adjective* [from Latin *vermis* = worm]

vernacular (*say* ver-**nak**-yoo-ler) *noun* the language of a country or district, as distinct from an official or formal language. [from Latin *vernaculus* = domestic]

vernal *adjective* of the season of spring. [from Latin *ver* = spring]

verruca (*say* ver-**oo**-ka) *noun* a kind of wart on the sole of the foot.

versatile *adjective* able to do or be used for many different things. **versatility** *noun* [from Latin *versare* = to turn]

verse *noun* 1 writing arranged in short lines, usually with a particular rhythm and often with rhymes. 2 a group of lines forming a unit in a poem or hymn. 3 each of the short numbered sections of a chapter in the Bible. [from Latin *versus* = line of writing]

versed *adjective* **versed in** experienced or skilled in something. [from Latin *versatus* = engaged in something]

version *noun* 1 a particular person's account of something that happened. 2 a translation, *modern versions of the Bible*. 3 a special or different form of something, *the latest version of this car*. [from Latin *versum* = turned]

versus *preposition* against; competing with, *Carlton versus Essendon*. [Latin, = against]

vertebra *noun* (*plural* **vertebrae**) each of the bones that form the backbone.

vertebrate *noun* an animal that has a backbone. (The opposite is *invertebrate*.) [from *vertebra*]

vertex *noun* (*plural* **vertices**, *say* **ver**-tis-eez) the highest point (*apex*) of a cone or triangle, or of a hill etc. [from Latin *vertex* = top of the head]

▶▶ T H E S A U R U S ◀◀

verbose *adjective* circumlocutory, lengthy, long-winded, ponderous, tautological, wordy. **verbosity** *noun* long-windedness, loquacity, verbiage, wordiness.

verdict *noun* adjudication, conclusion, decision, finding, judgement, opinion.

verge[1] *noun* 1 border, brink, edge, margin, perimeter, rim, side, threshold.

verge[2] *verb* **verge on** approach, border on, come close to.

verify *verb* authenticate, check, confirm, corroborate, prove, substantiate, support, uphold, validate.

vernacular *noun* dialect, idiom, jargon, language, lingo (*informal*), parlance, patois, phraseology, speech, tongue.

versatile *adjective* adaptable, all-round, flexible, handy, multi-skilled.

verse *noun* 1 poems, poetry; see also POEM. 2 stanza.

version *noun* 1 account, description, narrative, rendition, report, side, story. 2 edition, interpretation, paraphrase, reading, rendering, translation. 3 design, form, model, style, type, variant, variation.

vertex *noun* acme, apex, pinnacle, summit, top, zenith.

vertical *adjective* at right angles to something horizontal; upright. **vertically** *adverb* [from *vertex*]

vertigo *noun* a feeling of dizziness and loss of balance, especially when you are very high up. [Latin, = whirling (*vertere* = to turn)]

verve (*say* verv) *noun* enthusiasm; liveliness.

very[1] *adverb* **1** to a great amount or intensity; extremely, *It was very cold.* **2** (used to emphasise something), *on the very next day; the very last drop.*

very[2] *adjective* **1** exact; actual, *It's the very thing we need.* **2** extreme, *at the very end.* [from Latin *verus* = true]

vespers *plural noun* a church service held in the evening. [from Latin *vesper* = evening]

vessel *noun* **1** a ship or boat. **2** a container, especially for liquid. **3** a tube carrying blood or other liquid in the body of an animal or plant. [same origin as *vase*]

vest[1] *noun* an undergarment covering the trunk of the body, a singlet.

vest[2] *verb* **1** confer something as a right, *The power to make laws is vested in Parliament.* **2** (*old use*) to clothe.
vested interest a right that benefits a person or group and is securely held by them. [from Latin *vestis* = garment]

vestibule *noun* an entrance hall or lobby.

vestige *noun* a trace; a very small amount, especially of something that formerly existed. **vestigial** *adjective* [from Latin *vestigium* = footprint]

vestment *noun* a ceremonial garment, especially one worn by clergy or choir at a service. [same origin as *vest*]

vestry *noun* (*plural* **vestries**) a room in a church where vestments are kept and where clergy and choir put these on.

vet[1] *noun* a person trained to give medical and surgical treatment to animals. [short for *veterinary surgeon*]

vet[2] *verb* (**vetted, vetting**) check a thing to see if it has any mistakes or faults.

vetch *noun* a plant of the pea family.

veteran *noun* **1** a person who has had long service or experience in something. **2** an ex-serviceman or servicewoman. **veteran** *adjective*
veteran car a car made before 1916. [from Latin *vetus* = old]

veterinary (*say* vet-rin-ree) *adjective* of the medical and surgical treatment of animals, *a veterinary surgeon.* [from Latin *veterinae* = cattle]

veto[1] (*say* vee-toh) *noun* (*plural* **vetoes**) **1** a refusal to let something happen. **2** the right to prohibit something.

veto[2] *verb* (**vetoed, vetoing**) refuse or prohibit something. [Latin, = I forbid]

vex *verb* annoy; cause somebody worry. **vexation** *noun*, **vexatious** *adjective*
vexed question a problem that is difficult or much discussed. [from Latin *vexare* = to shake]

VHF *abbreviation* very high frequency.

vertical *adjective* erect, perpendicular, standing, upright; see also PRECIPITOUS.

vertigo *noun* dizziness, giddiness, light-headedness, unsteadiness.

verve *noun* animation, dash, energy, enthusiasm, gusto, liveliness, spirit, vigour, vim (*informal*), vitality, vivacity, zeal, zing (*informal*), zip.

very[1] *adverb* **1** awfully, dreadfully (*informal*), especially, exceedingly, exceptionally, extraordinarily, extremely, frightfully, highly, immensely, jolly (*informal*), mightily, most, particularly, really, terribly, thoroughly, tremendously (*informal*), truly.

very[2] *adjective* **1** actual, exact, precise, selfsame.

vessel *noun* **1** boat, craft, ship; see BOAT, SHIP[1]. **2** container, holder, receptacle, utensil; (*various vessels*) crock, ewer, flask, jar, jug, pitcher, pot, urn, vase.

vestibule *noun* antechamber, ante-room, entrance hall, foyer, hall, porch, lobby.

vestige *noun* relic, remains, remnant, residue, trace.

vet[1] *noun* veterinarian, veterinary surgeon.

vet[2] *verb* check out, examine, investigate, screen.

veteran *noun* **2** ex-serviceman, ex-service-woman, returned serviceman, returned ser-vicewoman, vet (*informal*).
veteran *adjective* experienced, long-serving, old, seasoned.

veto[1] *noun* **1** prohibition, refusal, rejection.

veto[2] *verb* ban, bar, block, disallow, forbid, give the thumbs down to, prohibit, reject, rule out.

vex *verb* anger, annoy, bother, bug (*informal*), displease, disturb, exasperate, harass, hassle (*informal*), infuriate, irk, irritate, nark (*informal*), needle, peeve (*informal*), perturb, pique, plague, provoke, put out, rile (*informal*), trouble, try, upset, worry.

▶▶ DICTIONARY ◀◀

via (*say* **vy**-a) *preposition* by way of; through, *The plane goes from Adelaide to Auckland via Melbourne.* [Latin, = by way]

viable *adjective* able to exist successfully; practicable. **viability** *noun* [from French *vie* = life]

viaduct *noun* a long bridge, usually with many arches, carrying a road or railway over a valley or low ground. [from Latin *via* = way, + *ducere* = to lead (compare *aqueduct*)]

vial *noun* a small glass bottle.

viands (*say* **vy**-andz) *plural noun* food.

vibrant *adjective* **1** vibrating. **2** lively. **3** (of colours) bright and strong.

vibraphone *noun* a musical instrument like a xylophone with metal bars under which there are tiny electric fans making a vibrating effect. [from *vibrate*, + Greek *phone* = voice]

vibrate *verb* (**vibrated, vibrating**) **1** shake very quickly to and fro. **2** make a throbbing sound. **vibration** *noun* [from Latin *vibrare* = shake]

vicar *noun* a member of the clergy who is in charge of a parish.

vicarage *noun* the house of a vicar.

vicarious (*say* vik-**air**-ee-us) *adjective* felt by imagining you share someone else's activities, *We felt a vicarious thrill by watching people skiing.* [from Latin *vicarius* = substitute]

vice[1] *noun* **1** evil; wickedness. **2** an evil or bad habit; a bad fault. [from Latin *vitium* = fault]

vice[2] *noun* a device for gripping something and holding it firmly while you work on it. [from Latin *vitis* = vine]

vice- *prefix* **1** authorised to act as a deputy or substitute (as in *vice-captain, vice-president*). **2** next in rank to someone (as in *vice-admiral*). [from Latin *vice* = by a change]

vicinity *noun* the area near or round something.

vicious *adjective* evil; brutal; dangerously wicked or strong. **viciously** *adverb*, **viciousness** *noun*
vicious circle a situation where a problem produces an effect which itself produces the original problem or makes it worse. [same origin as *vice*[1]]

vicissitude (*say* viss-**iss**-i-tewd) *noun* a change of circumstances. [from Latin *vicissim* = in turn]

victim *noun* **1** someone who is injured, killed, robbed, etc. **2** someone who is tricked or deceived.

victimise *verb* (**victimised, victimising**) make a victim of someone; punish a person unfairly. **victimisation** *noun*

victor *noun* the winner.

Victorian *adjective* **1** of the time of Queen Victoria (1837–1901). **2** of the State of Victoria. **Victorian** *noun*

victory *noun* (*plural* **victories**) success won against an opponent in a battle, contest, or game. **victorious** *adjective* [from Latin *victum* = conquered]

victualler (*say* **vit**-ler) *noun* a person who supplies victuals.
licensed victualler a person who holds the licence of a public house.

▶▶ THESAURUS ◀◀

viable *adjective* feasible, possible, practicable, practical, realistic, workable.

vibrant *adjective* **2** animated, dynamic, energetic, enthusiastic, lively, sparkling, spirited, vivacious. **3** bold, bright, brilliant, intense, radiant, striking, strong, vivid.

vibrate *verb* **1** oscillate, pulsate, quake, quiver, rattle, shake, shudder, throb, tremble, wobble. **vibration** *noun* oscillation, quaver, quiver, rattle, shaking, shudder, tremor.

vice[1] *noun* **1** corruption, depravity, evil, immorality, iniquity, sin, wickedness, wrongdoing. **2** defect, failing, fault, flaw, imperfection, shortcoming, weakness.

vice[2] *noun* clamp.

vicinity *noun* area, district, environs, locality, neighbourhood, precincts, proximity, region, zone.

vicious *adjective* atrocious, barbaric, beastly, brutal, callous, cruel, dangerous, depraved, evil, ferocious, fiendish, fierce, heinous, hostile, immoral, inhuman, malevolent, malicious, mean, monstrous, nasty, nefarious, ruthless, sadistic, savage, spiteful, vile, villainous, vindictive, violent, wicked, wild.

victim *noun* **1** casualty, fatality, martyr, prey, quarry, sacrifice, scapegoat, sufferer. **2** bunny (*Australian informal*), dupe, fall guy (*slang*), mug (*informal*), sucker (*informal*).

victimise *verb* bully, cheat, exploit, oppress, persecute, pick on, torment, use.

victor *noun* champion, conqueror, vanquisher, winner.

victory *noun* conquest, success, triumph, walkover, win.
victorious *adjective* conquering, successful, triumphant, winning.

►►►DICTIONARY◄◄◄

victuals (*say* **vit**-alz) *plural noun* food; provisions. [from Latin *victus* = food]

video *noun* (*plural* **videos**) **1** recorded or broadcast pictures. **2** a video recorder or recording. **3** a visual display unit.
video recorder a device for recording a television programme etc. on magnetic tape for playing back later. [Latin, = I see]

videotape *noun* magnetic tape suitable for recording television programmes.

vie *verb* (**vied**, **vying**) compete; carry on a rivalry, *vying with each other.*

view¹ *noun* **1** what can be seen from one place; beautiful scenery. **2** sight; range of vision, *The ship sailed into view.* **3** an opinion, *She has strong views about politics.*
in view of because of.
on view displayed for inspection.
with a view to with the hope or intention of.

view² *verb* **1** look at something. **2** consider.
viewer *noun*

viewpoint *noun* a point of view.

vigil (*say* **vij**-il) *noun* staying awake to keep watch or to pray, *a long vigil.* [from Latin *vigil* = wakeful]

vigilant (*say* **vij**-il-ant) *adjective* watchful.
vigilantly *adverb*, **vigilance** *noun* [from Latin *vigilans* = keeping watch]

vigilante (*say* vij-il-**an**-tee) *noun* a member of a group who organise themselves, without authority, to try to prevent crime and disorder in a small area. [Spanish, = vigilant]

vigoro *noun* (*Australian*) a women's game with elements of baseball and cricket.

vigorous *adjective* full of vigour. **vigorously** *adverb*

vigour *noun* strength; energy; liveliness. [from Latin *vigor* = strength]

Viking, *noun* a Scandinavian trader and pirate in the 8th–10th centuries.

vile *adjective* **1** extremely disgusting. **2** very bad or wicked. **vilely** *adverb*, **vileness** *noun* [from Latin *vilis* = cheap, unworthy]

vilify (*say* **vil**-if-I) *verb* (**vilified**, **vilifying**) say unpleasant things about a person or thing.
vilification *noun* [same origin as *vile*]

villa *noun* a house. [Latin, = country house]

village *noun* **1** a settlement smaller than a town in a country district. **2** (*Australian*) a suburban shopping centre. **villager** *noun* [from *villa*]

villain *noun* a wicked person; a criminal.
villainous *adjective*, **villainy** *noun*

villein (*say* **vil**-in) *noun* a tenant in feudal ·times.

vim *noun* (*informal*) vigour.

vindicate *verb* (**vindicated**, **vindicating**) **1** clear a person of blame or suspicion etc. **2** prove something to be true or worth while.
vindication *noun* [from Latin *vindicare* = set free]

►►►THESAURUS◄◄◄

vie *verb* compete, contend, contest, rival, strive.

view¹ *noun* **1** landscape, outlook, panorama, prospect, scene, scenery, spectacle, vista. **2** sight, vision. **3** attitude, belief, conviction, idea, notion, opinion, sentiment, thought; see also VIEWPOINT. ·

view² *verb* **1** behold (*old use*), contemplate, examine, eye, gaze at, inspect, look at, observe, scrutinise, stare at, survey, take in, watch, witness. **2** consider, deem, judge, look upon, regard, see.
viewer *noun* observer, onlooker, spectator, watcher.

viewpoint *noun* angle, attitude, opinion, outlook, perspective, point of view, position, side, slant, stance, stand, standpoint, view.

vigilant *adjective* alert, attentive, awake, careful, observant, on the lookout, on your guard, wary, watchful.

vigorous *adjective* active, dynamic, energetic, fit, forceful, hardy, hearty, intense, keen, lively, robust, spirited, strapping, strenuous, strong, vital, vivacious, zealous.

vigour *noun* animation, dash, drive, dynamism, energy, enthusiasm, gusto, liveliness, pep, power, spirit, stamina, strength, verve, vim (*informal*), vitality, vivacity, zeal, zest, zip.

vile *adjective* **1** disgusting, foul, ghastly, horrible, nasty, nauseating, objectionable, obnoxious, offensive, repugnant, repulsive, revolting, unpleasant. **2** abominable, base, contemptible, depraved, despicable, evil, foul, hateful, heinous, hideous, horrible, ignoble, immoral, loathsome, low, nasty, odious, outrageous, shameful, shocking, sinful, sordid, wicked.

vilify *verb* blacken, defame, denigrate, libel, malign, revile, slander, smear.

village *noun* **1** community, hamlet, settlement, township.

villain *noun* baddy (*informal*), blackguard, criminal, crook (*informal*), knave (*old use*), malefactor, miscreant, rascal, rogue, scoundrel, wrongdoer.

vindicate *verb* **1** absolve, acquit, clear, exculpate, exonerate. **2** defend, justify, support, uphold.

vindictive *adjective* showing a desire for revenge. **vindictively** *adverb*, **vindictiveness** *noun* [from Latin *vindicta* = vengeance]

vine *noun* a climbing or trailing plant whose fruit is the grape. [from Latin *vinum* = wine]

vinegar *noun* a sour liquid used to flavour food or in pickling. [from Latin *vinum* = wine, + *acer* = sour]

vineyard (*say* **vin**-yard) *noun* a plantation of vines producing grapes for making wine.

vintage *noun* **1** the harvest of a season's grapes; the wine made from this. **2** the period from which something comes.
vintage car a car made between 1917 and 1930.

vinyl *noun* a kind of plastic.

viola[1] (*say* vee-**oh**-la) *noun* a musical instrument like a violin but slightly larger and with a lower pitch.

viola[2] (*say* **vy**-ol-a) *noun* a plant of the kind that includes violets and pansies.

violate *verb* (**violated**, **violating**) **1** break a promise, law, or treaty etc. **2** break into somewhere; treat a person or place without respect. **violation** *noun*, **violator** *noun* [from Latin *violare* = treat violently]

violence *noun* force that does harm or damage. **violent** *adjective*, **violently** *adverb*

violet *noun* **1** a small plant that often has purple flowers. **2** purple.

violin *noun* a musical instrument with four strings, played with a bow. **violinist** *noun*

VIP *abbreviation* very important person.

viper *noun* a small poisonous snake.

virago (*say* vir-**ah**-goh) *noun* (*plural* **viragos**) a fierce or bullying woman. [Latin, = female soldier]

virgin[1] *noun* a person, especially a girl or woman, who has never had sexual intercourse. **virginal** *adjective*, **virginity** *noun*

virgin[2] *adjective* **1** of a virgin. **2** spotless. **3** not yet touched, *virgin snow*.

virginals *plural noun* an instrument rather like a harpsichord, used in the 16th–17th centuries.

virile (*say* **vir**-I'l) *adjective* having masculine strength or vigour. **virility** *noun* [from Latin *vir* = man]

virology *noun* the study of viruses. **virological** *adjective*, **virologist** *noun* [from *virus* + *-logy*]

virtual *adjective* being something in effect though not in form, *His silence was a virtual admission of guilt*. **virtually** *adverb*

virtue *noun* **1** moral goodness; a particular form of this, *Honesty is a virtue*. **2** a good quality; an advantage. **virtuous** *adjective*, **virtuously** *adverb*
by virtue of because of. [from Latin *virtus* = worth]

virtuoso (*say* ver-tew-**oh**-soh) *noun* (*plural* **virtuosos** or **virtuosi**) a person with outstanding skill, especially in singing or playing music. **virtuosity** *noun* [Italian, = skilful]

virulent (*say* **vir**-oo-lent) *adjective* **1** strongly poisonous or harmful, *a virulent disease*. **2** bitterly hostile, *virulent criticism*. **virulence** *noun* [same origin as *virus*]

vindictive *adjective* revengeful, spiteful, unforgiving, vengeful.

vintage *noun* **1** grape gathering, grape harvest. **2** date, era, period, year.

violate *verb* **1** break, contravene, defy, disobey, disregard, ignore, infringe, transgress. **2** defile, desecrate, dishonour, profane.
violation *noun* abuse, breach, contravention, disregard, infringement, transgression.

violent *adjective* (*a violent person, assault, etc.*) berserk, bloodthirsty, brutal, cruel, desperate, destructive, ferocious, fierce, frenzied, hotheaded, maniacal, murderous, savage, uncontrollable, vicious, wild; (*a violent argument*) fierce, furious, heated, impassioned, intense, passionate, stormy, tempestuous, vehement; (*a violent storm*) destructive, fierce, intense, mighty, powerful, raging, severe, tempestuous, turbulent, wild.

violin *noun* fiddle (*informal*).

VIP *abbreviation* big shot (*informal*), bigwig (*informal*), celebrity, dignitary.

virgin[2] *adjective* **2** clean, fresh, immaculate, new, pristine, pure, spotless, unblemished. **3** uncultivated, unspoilt, untouched, unused.

virile *adjective* macho, manly, masculine, red-blooded, robust, strong.

virtually *adverb* almost, effectively, essentially, more or less, nearly, practically.

virtue *noun* **1** decency, goodness, honesty, honour, integrity, morality, principle, probity, rectitude, righteousness. **2** advantage, asset, good point, merit, plus, strength, strong point.
virtuous *adjective* blameless, chaste, decent, ethical, good, honest, honourable, moral, pure, righteous, saintly, upright.

virtuoso *noun* expert, genius, maestro, master.

virus *noun* (*plural* **viruses**) **1** a very tiny living thing, smaller than a bacterium, that can cause disease. **2** a hidden code in a computer program, designed to sabotage a computer system or destroy data stored in it. [Latin, = poison]

visa (*say* **vee**-za) *noun* an official mark put on someone's passport by officials of a foreign country to show that the holder has permission to enter that country. [Latin, = things seen]

visage (*say* **viz**-ij) *noun* a person's face. [from Latin *visus* = sight]

viscera (*say* **vis**-er-a) *plural noun* the intestines and other internal organs of the body. [Latin, = soft parts]

viscid (*say* **vis**-id) *adjective* thick and gluey. **viscidity** *noun*

viscose (*say* **vis**-kohs) *noun* fabric made from viscous cellulose.

viscount (*say* **vy**-kownt) *noun* a nobleman ranking below an earl and above a baron. **viscountess** *noun* [from *vice-* + *count*³]

viscous (*say* **visk**-us) *adjective* thick and gluey, not pouring easily. **viscosity** *noun*

visible *adjective* able to be seen or noticed, *The ship was visible on the horizon.* **visibly** *adverb*, **visibility** *noun* [same origin as *vision*]

vision *noun* **1** the ability to see; sight. **2** something seen in a person's imagination or in a dream. **3** a supernatural apparition. **4** foresight and wisdom in planning things. **5** a person or thing that is beautiful to see. [from Latin *visum* = seen]

visionary¹ *adjective* imaginary; fanciful.

visionary² *noun* (*plural* **visionaries**) a person with visionary ideas.

visit¹ *verb* **1** go to see a person or place. **2** stay somewhere for a while. **visitor** *noun*

visit² *noun* the action of visiting. [from Latin *visitare* = go to see]

visitant *noun* **1** a visitor, especially a supernatural one. **2** a bird that is a visitor to an area while migrating.

visitation *noun* an official visit, especially to inspect something.

visor (*say* **vy**-zer) *noun* **1** the part of a helmet that covers the face. **2** a shield to protect the eyes from bright light or sunshine. [same origin as *visage*]

vista *noun* a long view. [Italian, = view]

visual *adjective* of or used in seeing; of sight. **visually** *adverb*

visual aids pictures and films etc. used as an aid in teaching.

visual display unit a device that looks like a television screen and displays data being received from a computer or fed into it. [same origin as *vision*]

visualise *verb* (**visualised**, **visualising**) form a mental picture of something. **visualisation** *noun*

vital *adjective* **1** connected with life; necessary for life to continue, *vital functions such as breathing.* **2** essential; very important. **vitally** *adverb* [from Latin *vita* = life]

vitalise *verb* (**vitalised**, **vitalising**) put life or vitality into something.

vitality *noun* liveliness; energy.

vitamin (*say* **vy**-ta-min or **vit**-a-min) *noun* any of a number of substances that are present in various foods and are essential to keep people and animals healthy. [same origin as *vital*]

virus *noun* **1** bug (*informal*), germ, microbe, micro-organism.

viscous *adjective* gluey, glutinous, sticky, thick, viscid.

visible *adjective* apparent, clear, conspicuous, discernible, evident, in sight, in view, manifest, noticeable, observable, obvious, outward, palpable, patent, plain, unmistakable.

vision *noun* **1** eyesight, sight. **2** conception, dream, idea, mental picture, plan. **3** apparition, ghost, hallucination, illusion, phantom, spectre, spirit, wraith. **4** far-sightedness, foresight, imagination, insight.

visit¹ *verb* **1** call in on, drop in on, go to see, look in on, look up, pop in on, stop by. **2** sojourn, stay.

visitor *noun* blow-in (*Australian informal*), caller, company, guest, holidaymaker, non-resident, sightseer, tourist, traveller.

visit² *noun* call, sojourn, stay, stop, visitation.

vista *noun* landscape, outlook, panorama, prospect, scene, scenery, view.

visual *adjective* ocular, ophthalmic, optic, optical, sight.

visualise *verb* conceive, envisage, imagine, picture, see.

vital *adjective* **2** basic, critical, crucial, essential, fundamental, important, indispensable, key, necessary, significant.

vitality *noun* animation, dynamism, energy, exuberance, go, gusto, liveliness, pep, strength, verve, vigour, vim (*informal*), vivacity, zeal, zest, zing (*informal*), zip.

vitiate (*say* **vish**-ee-ayt) *verb* (**vitiated, vitiating**) spoil something by making it imperfect. **vitiation** *noun* [from Latin *vitium* = fault]

vitreous (*say* **vit**-ree-us) *adjective* like glass in being hard, transparent, or brittle, *vitreous enamel*. [from Latin *vitrum* = glass]

vitriol (*say* **vit**-ree-ol) *noun* **1** sulphuric acid or one of its compounds. **2** savage criticism. **vitriolic** *adjective*

vituperation *noun* abusive words.

vivacious (*say* viv-**ay**-shus) *adjective* happy and lively. **vivaciously** *adverb*, **vivacity** *noun* [from Latin *vivere* = to live]

vivid *adjective* **1** bright and strong or clear, *vivid colours*; *a vivid description*. **2** active and lively, *a vivid imagination*. **vividly** *adverb*, **vividness** *noun* [from Latin *vividus* = full of life]

vivisection *noun* doing surgical experiments on live animals. [from Latin *vivus* = alive, + *dissection*]

vixen *noun* a female fox.

vizier (*say* viz-**eer**) *noun* (in former times) an important Muslim official. [from Arabic *wazir* = chief counsellor]

vocabulary *noun* (*plural* **vocabularies**) **1** a list of words with their meanings. **2** the words known to a person or used in a particular book or subject etc. [from Latin *vocabulum* = name]

vocal *adjective* of or producing or using the voice. **vocally** *adverb*

vocal cords two strap-like membranes in the throat that can be made to vibrate and produce sounds. [from Latin *vocis* = of the voice]

vocalist *noun* a singer, especially in a pop group.

vocation *noun* **1** a person's job or occupation. **2** a strong desire to do a particular kind of work, or feeling of being called by God to do something. **vocational** *adjective* [from Latin *vocare* = to call]

vociferate (*say* vo-**sif**-er-ayt) *verb* (**vociferated, vociferating**) say something loudly or noisily. **vociferation** *noun* [from Latin *vocis* = of the voice, + *ferre* = carry]

vociferous (*say* vo-**sif**-er-us) *adjective* making an outcry; shouting.

vodka *noun* a strong alcoholic drink very popular in Russia. [from Russian *voda* = water]

vogue *noun* the current fashion.

voice¹ *noun* **1** sounds formed by the vocal cords and uttered by the mouth, especially in speaking, singing, etc. **2** the ability to speak or sing, *She has lost her voice*. **3** an opinion expressed. **4** the right to express an opinion or desire, *I have no voice in this matter*.

voice² *verb* (**voiced, voicing**) say something, *We voiced our opinions*. [from Latin *vox* = voice]

void¹ *adjective* **1** empty. **2** having no legal validity.

void² *noun* an empty space.

voile (*say* voil) *noun* a very thin almost transparent material. [French, = veil]

vitriolic *adjective* abusive, acrimonious, bitter, caustic, cutting, hostile, savage, scathing, spiteful, stinging, venomous, virulent.

vivacious *adjective* animated, bubbly, exuberant, high-spirited, lively, perky, sparkling, spirited, vital.
vivacity *noun* see VITALITY.

vivid *adjective* **1** (*vivid colours*) bold, bright, brilliant, colourful, deep, garish, gaudy, gay, intense, loud, rich, striking, strong, vibrant; (*a vivid description*) clear, detailed, graphic, lifelike, lively, realistic.

vocabulary *noun* **1** dictionary, glossary, lexicon, word list.

vocal *adjective* oral, spoken, sung.

vocalist *noun* chorister, diva, minstrel, prima donna, singer, songster, troubadour.

vocation *noun* **1** career, job, line of work, occupation, profession, trade. **2** call, calling, mission.

vociferous *adjective* clamorous, insistent, loud, noisy, outspoken, vocal.

vogue *noun* craze, fashion, mode, rage, style, trend.
in vogue fashionable, in, in fashion, popular, trendy (*informal*).

voice¹ *noun* **4** say, vote.

voice² *verb* air, articulate, communicate, declare, enunciate, express, speak, state, utter, ventilate.

void¹ *adjective* **1** bare, empty, unoccupied, vacant. **2** invalid, null and void.

void² *noun* blank, emptiness, gap, hole, space, vacuum.

▶▷ DICTIONARY ◁◀

volatile (*say* **vol**-a-tyl) *adjective* **1** evaporating quickly, *a volatile liquid*. **2** changing quickly from one mood or interest to another. **volatility** *noun* [from Latin *volatilis* = flying]

volcano *noun* (*plural* **volcanoes**) a mountain with an opening at the top from which lava and hot gases etc. flow. **volcanic** *adjective* [from the name of Vulcan, the ancient Roman god of fire]

volition *noun* using your own will in choosing to do something, *She left of her own volition*. [from Latin *volo* = I wish]

volley[1] *noun* (*plural* **volleys**) **1** a number of bullets or shells etc. fired at the same time. **2** hitting back the ball in tennis etc. before it touches the ground.

volley[2] *verb* send or hit something in a volley or volleys. [from Latin *volare* = to fly]

volleyball *noun* a game in which two teams hit a large ball to and fro over a net with their hands.

volt *noun* a unit for measuring electric force. [named after an Italian scientist, Alessandro Volta]

voltage *noun* electric force measured in volts.

voluble *adjective* talking very much. **volubly** *adverb*, **volubility** *noun* [from Latin *volubilis* = rolling]

volume *noun* **1** the amount of space filled by something. **2** an amount or quantity, *The volume of work has increased*. **3** the strength or power of sound. **4** a book, especially one of a set. [from Latin *volumen* = a roll (because ancient books were made in a rolled form)]

voluminous (*say* vol-**yoo**-min-us) *adjective* **1** bulky; large and full, *a voluminous skirt*. **2** numerous; filling many volumes, *a voluminous writer*.

voluntary[1] *adjective* **1** done or doing something willingly, not by being compelled. **2** unpaid. **voluntarily** *adverb*

voluntary[2] *noun* (*plural* **voluntaries**) an organ solo, often improvised, played before or after a church service. [from Latin *voluntas* = the will]

volunteer[1] *verb* give or offer something of your own accord.

volunteer[2] *noun* a person who volunteers to do something, e.g. to serve in the armed forces.

voluptuous *adjective* giving a luxurious feeling, *voluptuous furnishings*. [from Latin *voluptas* = pleasure]

vomit *verb* bring up food etc. from the stomach and out through the mouth; be sick. **vomit** *noun*

voodoo *noun* a form of witchcraft and magical rites, especially in the West Indies.

voracious (*say* vor-**ay**-shus) *adjective* **1** greedy; devouring things eagerly. **2** eager in some activity, *a voracious reader*. **voraciously** *adverb*, **voracity** *noun* [from Latin *vorare* = devour]

vortex *noun* (*plural* **vortices**) a whirlpool or whirlwind. [Latin]

vote[1] *verb* (**voted, voting**) show which person or thing you prefer by putting up your hand, making a mark on a paper, etc. **voter** *noun*

▶▷ THESAURUS ◁◀

volatile *adjective* **2** (*a volatile person*) capricious, changeable, erratic, fickle, inconstant, mercurial, unpredictable, unstable; (*a volatile situation*) charged, explosive, tense, unstable.

volition *noun* **of your own volition** by choice, freely, of your own accord, of your own free will, voluntarily, willingly.

volley[1] *noun* **1** barrage, bombardment, fusillade, hail, salvo, shower.

voluble *adjective* chatty, fluent, garrulous, glib, loquacious, talkative.

volume *noun* **1** capacity, dimensions, measure, size. **2** amount, bulk, mass, quantity. **3** loudness, sound. **4** book, part, tome.

voluminous *adjective* **1** ample, big, billowing, bulky, full, large, roomy, vast.

voluntary[1] *adjective* **1** non-compulsory, optional, unforced. **2** honorary, unpaid, unsalaried.

voluntarily *adverb* by choice, freely, of your own accord, of your own free will, of your own volition, willingly.

volunteer[1] *verb* nominate yourself, offer, step forward; see also ENLIST.

vomit *verb* barf (*slang*), be sick, bring up, chuck (*informal*), chunder (*Australian slang*), puke (*informal*), sick up (*informal*), spew, throw up.

voracious *adjective* **1** greedy, insatiable, ravenous. **2** avid, compulsive, eager, insatiable, keen.

vortex *noun* eddy, maelstrom, spiral, whirlpool, whirlwind.

vote[1] *verb* (*vote for*) choose, elect, opt for, pick, select.

► DICTIONARY ◄

vote² *noun* **1** the action of voting. **2** the right to vote. [from Latin *votum* = a wish or vow]

votive *adjective* given in fulfilment of a vow, *votive offerings at the shrine.*

vouch *verb* **vouch for** guarantee that something is true or certain, *I will vouch for his honesty.*

voucher *noun* a piece of paper that can be exchanged for certain goods or services; a receipt.

vouchsafe *verb* (**vouchsafed, vouchsafing**) grant something in a gracious or condescending way, *She did not vouchsafe a reply.*

vow¹ *noun* a solemn promise, especially to God or a saint.

vow² *verb* make a vow.

vowel *noun* any of the letters a, e, i, o, u, and sometimes y, which represent sounds in which breath comes out freely. (Compare *consonant.*) [from Latin *vocalis littera* = vocal letter]

voyage¹ *noun* a long journey on water or in space.

voyage² *verb* (**voyaged, voyaging**) make a voyage. **voyager** *noun*

vulcanise *verb* (**vulcanised, vulcanising**) treat rubber with sulphur to strengthen it. **vulcanisation** *noun* [same origin as *volcano*]

vulgar *adjective* rude; without good manners. **vulgarly** *adverb*, **vulgarity** *noun*

vulgar fraction a fraction shown by numbers above and below a line (e.g. $\frac{2}{3}$, $\frac{5}{8}$), not a decimal fraction. [from Latin *vulgus* = the ordinary people]

vulnerable *adjective* able to be hurt or harmed or attacked. **vulnerability** *noun* [from Latin *vulnus* = wound]

vulture *noun* a large bird that feeds on dead animals.

vulva *noun* the outer parts of the female genitals. [Latin]

vying *present participle* of **vie**.

► THESAURUS ◄

vote² *noun* **1** ballot, election, plebiscite, poll, referendum. **2** franchise, right to vote, suffrage.

vouch *verb* **vouch for** answer for, attest to, confirm, guarantee, swear to.

voucher *noun* coupon, token.

vow¹ *noun* oath, pledge, promise.

vow² *verb* declare, give your word, pledge, promise, swear, take an oath.

voyage¹ *noun* crossing, cruise, journey, passage, sail, trip.

voyage² *verb* cruise, journey, sail, travel.

vulgar *adjective* bad-mannered, boorish, coarse, common, crude, dirty, ill-mannered, impolite, indecent, lewd, obscene, offensive, risqué, rough, rude, smutty, tasteless, uncouth.

vulnerable *adjective* defenceless, exposed, insecure, precarious, sensitive, susceptible, unguarded, unprotected, weak.

► Ww ◄

W. *abbreviation* west; western.

wad¹ (*say* wod) *noun* a pad or bundle of soft material or pieces of paper etc.

wad² *verb* (**wadded, wadding**) pad something with soft material.

waddle *verb* (**waddled, waddling**) walk with short steps, swaying from side to side. **waddle** *noun*

waddy *noun* an Aboriginal club or bludgeon.

wade *verb* (**waded, wading**) walk through water or mud etc. **wader** *noun*

wafer *noun* a kind of thin biscuit.

waffle¹ (*say* **wof**-el) *noun* a small cake made of batter and eaten hot.

waffle² (*say* **wof**-el) *noun* (*informal*) vague wordy talk or writing. **waffle** *verb* [from a dialect word *waff* = yelp]

waft (*say* woft) *verb* carry or float gently through the air or over water.

wag¹ *verb* (**wagged, wagging**) **1** move quickly to and fro. **2** (*informal*) be absent from school without permission. **wag** *noun*

wag² *noun* a person who makes jokes.

wage¹ *noun* or **wages** *plural noun* a regular payment to someone in return for his or her work.

wage² *verb* (**waged, waging**) carry on a war or campaign.

wager (*say* **way**-jer) *noun* & *verb* bet.

waggle *verb* (**waggled, waggling**) wag. **waggle** *noun*

wagon *noun* **1** a cart with four wheels, pulled by a horse or an ox. **2** an open railway truck, e.g. for coal. **3** a trolley for carrying food etc.

wagtail *noun* **1** a small bird with a long tail that it moves up and down. **2** a willy wagtail.

waif *noun* a homeless and helpless person, especially a child.

wail *verb* make a long sad cry. **wail** *noun*

wainscoting *noun* wooden panelling on the wall of a room.

waist *noun* the narrow part in the middle of the body.

waistcoat *noun* a short close-fitting jacket without sleeves, worn over a shirt and under a jacket.

wait¹ *verb* **1** stay somewhere or postpone an action until something happens; pause. **2** be postponed, *This question must wait until our next meeting.* **3** wait on people.
wait on hand food and drink to people at a meal; be an attendant to someone.

►►THESAURUS◄◄

wad¹ *noun* bundle, hunk, lump, mass, pad, plug, roll.

wad² *verb* fill, line, pad, stuff.

waddle *verb* shuffle, toddle, wobble.

waddy *noun* bludgeon, club, war club.

wade *verb* paddle, plod, splash, trek, trudge.

waffle² *noun* hot air (*slang*), padding, verbiage. **waffle** *verb* prattle, rabbit (*informal*), ramble, witter (*informal*).

waft *verb* drift, float, stream.

wag¹ *verb* **1** shake, waggle, wave, wiggle. **2** absent yourself from, bludge (*Australian informal*), play hookey from (*informal*), play truant from, skive off (*informal*), stay away from.

wag² *noun* clown, comedian, jester, joker, wit.

wage¹ *noun* earnings, income, pay, payment, remuneration, wages.

wage² *verb* carry on, conduct, engage in, fight, pursue.

wager *noun* bet, flutter (*informal*), gamble, punt, speculation, stake.
wager *verb* bet, gamble, hazard, punt (*informal*), risk, stake.

wagon *noun* **1** cart, dray, wain (*old use*).

waif *noun* foundling, homeless person, orphan, stray.

wail *verb* bawl, caterwaul, cry, groan, howl, moan, shriek, sob, weep, whine, yowl.

waist *noun* middle, midriff, waistline.

waistcoat *noun* jerkin, vest.

wait¹ *verb* **1** bide your time, dally, delay, hang around, hang on, hold on, linger, mark time, pause, remain, rest, sit tight (*informal*), stand by, stay, stop, tarry. **2** be deferred, be delayed, be postponed, be put off, be shelved.
wait on attend to, serve.

▶▶ D I C T I O N A R Y ◀◀

wait² *noun* an act or time of waiting, *We had a long wait for the train.*

waiter *noun* a man employed to serve people with food.

waiting-list *noun* a list of people waiting for something to become available.

waiting-room *noun* a room provided for people who are waiting for something.

waitress *noun* a woman employed to serve people with food.

waive *verb* (**waived, waiving**) not insist on having something, *She waived her right to compensation.* [from Old French, = abandon (compare *waif*)]

wake¹ *verb* (**woke, woken, waking**) **1** stop sleeping, *Wake up! I woke when I heard the bell.* **2** cause someone to stop sleeping, *You have woken the baby.*

wake² *noun* festivities held in connection with a funeral.

wake³ *noun* **1** the track left on the water by a moving ship. **2** currents of air left behind a moving aircraft.
in the wake of following.

wakeful *adjective* unable to sleep.

waken *verb* wake.

walk¹ *verb* move along on your feet at an ordinary speed. **walker** *noun*
walk out leave angrily or suddenly; go on strike.
walk out on desert.

walk² *noun* **1** a journey on foot. **2** the manner of walking. **3** a path or route for walking.
walk of life a person's occupation or social level.

walkabout *noun* **1** an Aboriginal's period of journeying in the bush. **2** an informal stroll among a crowd by an important visitor.

walkie-talkie *noun* (*informal*) a small portable radio transmitter and receiver.

walking stick a stick for use as a support while walking.

walkover *noun* an easy victory.

wall¹ *noun* **1** a continuous upright structure, usually made of brick or stone, forming one of the sides of a building or room or supporting something or enclosing an area. **2** the outside part of something.

wall² *verb* enclose or block with a wall.

wallaby *noun* (*plural* **wallabies**) a kind of small kangaroo.

wallaroo *noun* a large kangaroo living in rocky or hilly areas.

wallet *noun* a small flat folding case for holding banknotes, documents, etc.

wallflower *noun* a garden plant with fragrant flowers, blooming in spring.

wallop *verb* (**walloped, walloping**) (*slang*) thrash. **wallop** *noun*

wallow *verb* **1** roll about in water, mud, etc. **2** get great pleasure by being surrounded by something, *wallowing in luxury.* **wallow** *noun*

▶▶ T H E S A U R U S ◀◀

wait² *noun* adjournment, delay, hold-up, interval, pause, postponement, stay.

waive *verb* abandon, dispense with, forgo, forsake, give up, relinquish, renounce, set aside, surrender, yield.

wake¹ *verb* **1** awake, get up, stir, surface (*informal*), wake up. **2** awaken, disturb, rouse, waken, wake up.

wake² *noun* vigil, watch.

wake³ *noun* **1** backwash, track, trail, wash.
in the wake of after, behind, following, subsequent to.

wakeful *adjective* awake, insomniac, restless, sleepless.

walk¹ *verb* amble, bushwalk (*Australian*), creep, foot it, go on foot, hike, hobble, limp, march, pace, parade, perambulate, plod, promenade, prowl, ramble, saunter, shamble, shuffle, slink, slog, stagger, stalk, stamp, step, stride, stroll, strut, swagger, tiptoe, toddle, totter, traipse (*informal*), tramp, trample, tread, trek, troop, trudge, waddle, wade.

walker *noun* bushwalker, hiker, pedestrian, rambler.

walk out 1 depart, flounce out, leave, storm out. **2** down tools, go on strike, stop work, strike, take industrial action, walk off the job.
walk out on abandon, desert, forsake, leave, leave in the lurch.

walk² *noun* **1** amble, bushwalk (*Australian*), constitutional, hike, promenade, ramble, saunter, stroll, tramp, trek, walkabout, wander. **2** gait, pace, step, stride. **3** path, pathway, route, track, trail.

walkover *noun* breeze (*informal*), child's play, cinch (*informal*), doddle (*informal*), piece of cake (*informal*), pushover (*informal*), snack (*Australian informal*), snap (*informal*).

wall¹ *noun* **1** barricade, barrier, battlements, bulkhead, bulwark, dyke, embankment, fence, parapet, partition, rampart, stockade.

wallet *noun* notecase, pocketbook, purse.

wallow *verb* **1** flounder, roll about, splash about. **2** bask, delight, indulge, luxuriate, revel.

wallpaper *noun* paper used to cover the inside walls of rooms.

walnut *noun* an edible nut with a wrinkled surface.

walrus *noun* (*plural* **walruses**) a large Arctic sea-animal with two long tusks.

waltz¹ *noun* (*plural* **waltzes**) a dance with three beats to a bar.

waltz² *verb* dance a waltz. [from German *walzen* = revolve]

wan (*say* wonn) *adjective* pale from being ill or tired. **wanly** *adverb*, **wanness** *noun*

wand *noun* a thin rod, especially one used by a magician.

wander *verb* 1 go about without trying to reach a particular place. 2 leave the right path or direction; stray. **wander** *noun*

wanderer *noun* 1 someone who wanders. 2 a monarch butterfly.

wanderlust *noun* a strong desire to travel.

wane *verb* (**waned**, **waning**) 1 (of the moon) show a bright area that becomes gradually smaller after being full. (The opposite is *wax*.) 2 become less or smaller, *His popularity waned*. **wane** *noun* [from Old English *wanian* = reduce]

wangle *verb* (**wangled**, **wangling**) (*slang*) get or arrange something by using trickery, special influence, etc. **wangle** *noun*

want¹ *verb* 1 wish to have something. 2 need, *Your hair wants cutting*. 3 be without something; lack. 4 be without the necessaries of life, *Waste not, want not*.

want² *noun* 1 a wish to have something. 2 lack or need of something. [same origin as *wane*]

wanted *adjective* (of a suspected criminal) that the police wish to find or arrest.

wanton (*say* **wonn**-ton) *adjective* irresponsible; without a motive, *wanton damage*.

war *noun* 1 fighting between nations or groups, especially using armed forces. 2 a serious struggle or effort against crime, disease, poverty, etc.
at war engaged in a war.

waratah *noun* an Australian shrub with bright red flowers.

warble *verb* (**warbled**, **warbling**) sing with a trilling sound, as some birds do. **warble** *noun*

warbler *noun* a kind of small bird.

ward¹ *noun* 1 a room with beds for patients in a hospital. 2 a child looked after by a guardian. 3 an area electing a councillor to represent it.

ward² *verb* **ward off** keep something away. [from Old English *weard* = guard]

warden *noun* an official who is in charge of a hostel, college, etc., or who supervises something.

warder *noun* an official in charge of prisoners in a prison.

wardrobe *noun* 1 a cupboard to hang clothes in. 2 a stock of clothes or costumes. [from *guard* + *robe*]

wan *adjective* pale, pallid, pasty, peaky, sickly, washed out, waxen.

wand *noun* baton, cane, rod, staff, stick.

wander *verb* 1 meander, mooch (*informal*), mosey (*slang*), prowl, ramble, range, roam, rove, saunter, stroll, tootle (*informal*), traipse (*informal*), travel, walk. 2 deviate, digress, drift, stray.

wanderer *noun* 1 drifter, gypsy, hobo, itinerant, nomad, rambler, rover, swagman (*Australian*), traveller, vagabond, vagrant, wayfarer.

wane *verb* 2 decline, decrease, diminish, dwindle, ebb, fade, lessen, subside, taper off, weaken.

wangle *verb* contrive, engineer, fix (*informal*), get, pull off, swing (*informal*).

want¹ *verb* 1 covet, crave, desire, fancy, hanker after, hunger for, long for, pine for, wish for, yearn for. 2 need, require. 3 be short of, lack, miss.

want² *noun* 1 desire, need, requirement, wish. 2 absence, dearth, deficiency, insufficiency, lack, paucity, scarcity, shortage.

wanton *adjective* arbitrary, groundless, irresponsible, malicious, motiveless, reckless, senseless, unprovoked, wilful.

war *noun* 1 battle, combat, conflict, fighting, hostilities, strife, warfare. 2 attack, battle, blitz, campaign, crusade, fight, struggle.

ward¹ *noun* 2 charge, dependant, protégé(e). 3 area, district, division, section.

ward² *verb* **ward off** avert, beat off, deflect, fend off, keep at bay, parry, repel, repulse, stave off, thwart.

warden *noun* superintendent, supervisor; (*churchwarden*) attendant, sexton, sidesman, steward, verger.

warder *noun* guard, jailer, keeper, prison officer.

wardrobe *noun* 1 closet, cupboard.

▶▶ D I C T I O N A R Y ◀◀

ware *noun* manufactured goods of a certain kind, *hardware; silverware*.
wares *plural noun* goods offered for sale.

warehouse *noun* a large building where goods are stored. [from *ware + house*]

warfare *noun* war; fighting.

warhead *noun* the head of a missile or torpedo etc., containing explosives.

warlike *adjective* **1** fond of making war. **2** of or for war.

warm[1] *adjective* **1** fairly hot; not cold or cool. **2** (of clothes) keeping the body warm. **3** loving; enthusiastic, *a warm welcome*. **warmly** *adverb*, **warmness** *noun*, **warmth** *noun*

warm[2] *verb* make or become warm.

warm-blooded *adjective* having blood that remains warm permanently.

warm-hearted *adjective* kind, friendly.

warn *verb* tell someone about a danger etc. that may affect them, or about what they should do, *I warned you to take your umbrella*. **warning** *noun*

warp[1] (*say* worp) *verb* **1** bend out of shape, e.g. by dampness. **2** distort a person's ideas etc., *Jealousy warped his mind*.

warp[2] *noun* **1** a warped condition. **2** the lengthwise threads in weaving, crossed by the weft.

warrant[1] *noun* a document that authorises a person to do something (e.g. to search a place) or to receive something.

warrant[2] *verb* **1** justify, *Nothing can warrant such rudeness*. **2** guarantee.

warranty *noun* a guarantee.

warren *noun* **1** a piece of ground where there are many burrows in which rabbits live and breed. **2** a building or place with many winding passages.

warrigal[1] *noun* **1** a dingo. **2** an untamed horse.

warrigal[2] *adjective* wild; untamed.

warring *adjective* occupied in war.

warrior *noun* a person who fights in battle; a soldier.

warship *noun* a ship for use in war.

wart *noun* a small hard lump on the skin, caused by a virus.

wartime *noun* a time of war.

wary (*say* **wair**-ee) *adjective* cautious; looking carefully for possible danger or difficulty. **warily** *adverb*, **wariness** *noun* [compare *aware*]

wash[1] *verb* **1** clean something with water or other liquid. **2** be washable, *Cotton washes easily*. **3** flow against or over something, *Waves washed over the deck*. **4** carry along by a moving liquid, *A wave washed him over-*

▶▶ T H E S A U R U S ◀◀

ware *noun* **wares** commodities, goods, merchandise, products, stock.

warehouse *noun* depot, store, storehouse.

warlike *adjective* **1** aggressive, bellicose, belligerent, combative, hostile, militant, militaristic, pugnacious. **2** martial, military.

warm[1] *adjective* **1** (*warm food*) heated, lukewarm, tepid; (*warm weather*) balmy, mild, sunny. **2** cosy, thermal, thick, woolly. **3** cordial, enthusiastic, friendly, hearty, hospitable, rousing, sincere.

warm[2] *verb* heat, heat up, hot up (*informal*), reheat, scald, warm up.

warm-hearted *adjective* affectionate, amiable, caring, compassionate, friendly, genial, kind, kind-hearted, kindly, loving, sympathetic, tender-hearted, warm.

warn *verb* admonish, advise, alert, apprise (*formal*), caution, counsel, forewarn, inform, make aware, notify, remind, tell, tip off.
warning *noun* admonition, advice, caution, caveat, counsel, forewarning, hint, indication, notice, notification, omen, sign, signal, threat, tip-off.

warp[1] *verb* **1** bend, bow, buckle, contort, curve, distort, twist. **2** corrupt, pervert, twist.

warrant[1] *noun* authorisation, authority, entitlement, licence, permit.

warrant[2] *verb* **1** authorise, call for, excuse, justify, permit, sanction.

warrigal[2] *adjective* feral, unbroken, untamed, wild.

warrior *noun* brave, combatant, fighter, gladiator, soldier.

warship *noun* aircraft carrier, battleship, corvette, cruiser, destroyer, frigate, gunboat, man-of-war, submarine, torpedo boat, trireme (*historical*).

wary *adjective* alert, careful, cautious, chary, circumspect, distrustful, guarded, observant, on the lookout, on your guard, suspicious, vigilant, watchful.

wash[1] *verb* **1** clean, cleanse, douse, drench, flush, launder, mop, rinse, scour, scrub, shampoo, sluice, soak, soap, sponge, swab, swill, wipe; (*wash yourself*) bathe, bathe, clean yourself, perform your ablutions, shower. **3** break, flow, splash, sweep. **4** carry, sweep, transport. **5** be accepted, hold water, stand up.

▶▶▶ D I C T I O N A R Y ◀◀◀

board. **5** (*informal*) be accepted or believed, *That excuse won't wash.*

wash out (*informal*) cancel something.

wash up wash dishes and cutlery etc. after use. **washing-up** *noun*

wash² *noun* (*plural* **washes**) **1** the action of washing. **2** clothes etc. being washed. **3** the disturbed water or air behind a moving ship or aircraft. **4** a thin coating of colour.

washable *adjective* able to be washed without becoming damaged.

washbasin *noun* a small sink for washing your hands etc.

washer *noun* **1** a small ring of rubber or metal etc. placed between two surfaces (e.g. under a bolt or screw) to fit them tightly together. **2** a washing-machine. **3** (*Australian*) a face-cloth.

washing *noun* clothes etc. being washed.

washing-machine *noun* a machine for washing clothes etc.

wash-out *noun* (*informal*) a complete failure.

wasn't (*mainly spoken*) was not.

wasp *noun* a stinging insect with black and yellow stripes round its body.

wassail (*say* **woss**-al) *noun* (*old use*) spiced ale drunk especially at Christmas. **wassailing** *noun* [from Norse *ves heill* = be in good health]

wastage *noun* loss of something by waste.

waste¹ *verb* (**wasted**, **wasting**) **1** use something in an extravagant way or without getting enough results. **2** fail to use some-

thing, *You wasted an opportunity.* **3** make or become gradually weaker or useless.

waste² *adjective* **1** left over or thrown away because it is not wanted. **2** not used; not usable, *waste land.*

lay waste destroy the crops and buildings etc. of a district.

waste³ *noun* **1** the action of wasting a thing, not using it well, *a waste of time.* **2** things that are not wanted or not used. **3** an area of waste land, *the wastes of the Sahara Desert.* **wasteful** *adjective,* **wastefully** *noun,* **wastefulness** *noun* [from Latin *vastus* = empty]

wastrel (*say* **way**-strel) *noun* a person who wastes his or her life and does nothing useful.

watch¹ *verb* **1** look at a person or thing for some time. **2** keep under observation. **3** be on guard or ready for something to happen, *Watch for the traffic-lights to turn green.* **4** take care of something. **watcher** *noun*

watch² *noun* (*plural* **watches**) **1** the action of watching. **2** a turn of being on duty on a ship. **3** a device like a small clock, usually worn on the wrist.

watchful *adjective* watching closely; alert. **watchfully** *adverb,* **watchfulness** *noun*

watchman *noun* (*plural* **watchmen**) a person employed to look after an empty building etc., especially at night.

watchword *noun* a word or phrase that sums up a group's policy; a slogan, *Our watchword is 'safety first'.*

▶▶▶ T H E S A U R U S ◀◀◀

wash² *noun* **1** bath, scrub, shower. **3** backwash, wake.

washing *noun* clothes, laundry, wash.

wash-out *noun* damp squib, disaster, failure, fiasco, fizzer (*Australian informal*), flop (*informal*).

waste¹ *verb* **1** blow (*slang*), dissipate, fritter away, misspend, misuse, squander. **2** let slip, miss, throw away. **3** (*waste away*) become emaciated, fade away, grow thin, pine, shrivel, wither.

waste² *adjective* **1** discarded, leftover, superfluous, unwanted, useless. **2** arid, barren, desert, uncultivated, unusable, wild.

waste³ *noun* **1** misuse, squandering. **2** debris, dregs, dross, effluent, garbage, junk, litter, refuse, rubbish, scraps, sewage, trash. **3** desert, wasteland, wilderness.

wasteful *adjective* extravagant, improvident, prodigal, profligate, uneconomical.

watch¹ *verb* **1** attend to, behold (*old use*), concentrate on, contemplate, eye, gaze at, keep your eyes on, look at, mark, monitor, note, notice, observe, pay attention to, peep at, peer at, regard, scrutinise, stare at, survey, take notice of, view. **2** keep an eye on, keep under observation, keep under surveillance, spy on. **3** be on guard, be on the lookout, be vigilant, be wary, be watchful, keep your eyes open, watch out. **4** guard, keep an eye on, look after, mind, protect, supervise, take care of, tend.

watch² *noun* **3** chronometer, pocket watch, stopwatch, timepiece, wristwatch.

watchful *adjective* alert, attentive, careful, eagle-eyed, observant, vigilant, wary.

watchman *noun* guard, nightwatchman, patrol, security guard.

watchword *noun* byword, catchphrase, catchword, maxim, motto, slogan.

▶▶▶ D I C T I O N A R Y ◀◀

water¹ *noun* **1** a colourless odourless tasteless liquid that is a compound of hydrogen and oxygen. **2** a lake, sea, river, etc. **3** the tide, *at high water.* **4** urine; sweat; saliva.

water² *verb* **1** sprinkle or supply something with water. **2** produce tears or saliva, *It makes my mouth water.*
water down dilute.

water closet a toilet with a pan that is flushed by water.

watercolour *noun* **1** paint made with pigment and water (not oil). **2** a painting done with this kind of paint.

watercress *noun* a kind of cress that grows in water.

waterfall *noun* a stream flowing over the edge of a cliff or large rock.

waterhole *noun* **1** a pond. **2** a hole in which water collects, especially in the bed of an otherwise dry river.

watering-can *noun* a container with a long spout, for watering plants.

water lily a plant that grows in water, with broad floating leaves and large flowers.

waterlogged *adjective* completely soaked or swamped in water.

watermark *noun* **1** a mark showing how high a river or tide rises or how low it falls. **2** a design that can be seen in some kinds of paper when they are held up to the light.

waterproof *adjective* that keeps out water.
waterproof *verb*

watershed *noun* **1** a line of high land from which streams flow down on each side. **2** a turning point in the course of events.

water-skiing *noun* skimming over the surface of water on a pair of flat boards (**water-skis**) while being towed by a motor boat.

waterspout *noun* a column of water formed when a whirlwind draws up a whirling mass of water from the sea.

water table the level below which the ground is saturated with water.

watertight *adjective* **1** made or fastened so that water cannot get in or out. **2** that cannot be changed or set aside or proved to be untrue, *a watertight excuse.*

waterway *noun* a river or canal that ships can travel on.

waterworks *noun* a place with pumping machinery etc. for supplying water to a district.

watery *adjective* **1** of or like water. **2** full of water, *watery eyes.* **3** containing too much water.

watt *noun* a unit of electric power. [named after James Watt, a Scottish engineer]

wattage *noun* electric power measured in watts.

wattle¹ *noun* **1** sticks and twigs woven together to make fences, walls, etc. **2** an Australian tree with golden flowers.

wattle² *noun* a red fold of skin hanging from the throat of turkeys and some other birds.

wave¹ *noun* **1** a ridge moving along the surface of the sea etc. or breaking on the shore. **2** a wave-like curve, e.g. in hair. **3** the wave-like movement by which heat, light, sound, or electricity etc. travels. **4** the action of waving. **5** a sudden increase of a condition, emotion, etc., *a wave of anger; a crime wave.*

wave² *verb* (**waved, waving**) **1** move loosely to and fro or up and down. **2** move your hand to and fro as a signal or greeting etc. **3** make a thing wavy. **4** be wavy.

▶▶▶ T H E S A U R U S ◀◀

water¹ *noun* **2** creek, dam, lake, ocean, pond, pool, reservoir, river, sea, stream.

water² *verb* **1** dampen, flood, hose, irrigate, moisten, soak, spray, sprinkle, wet. **2** run, stream, weep.
water down adulterate, dilute, thin, weaken.

waterfall *noun* cascade, cataract, falls.

waterhole *noun* **1** pond, pool. **2** claypan (*Australian*), gilgai (*Australian*), gnamma hole (*Australian*), mickery (*Australian*), rockhole, soak, watering hole.

waterlogged *adjective* boggy, marshy, saturated, soaked, sodden, swampy.

waterproof *adjective* impermeable, impervious, showerproof, water-repellent, water-resistant, watertight, weatherproof.

watershed *noun* **2** crossroads, turning point.

watertight *adjective* **1** sealed, waterproof. **2** irrefutable, sound, unassailable.

waterway *noun* canal, channel, river, stream, watercourse.

watery *adjective* **1** aqueous, fluid, liquid. **2** bleary, damp, lachrymose, moist, streaming, tearful, teary, weepy, wet. **3** diluted, runny, thin, watered down, weak, wishy-washy.

wave¹ *noun* **1** billow, boomer, breaker, comber, dumper (*Australian*), ripple, roller, surf, swell, wavelet. **4** gesticulation, gesture, salutation, signal. **5** outbreak, rush, spate, surge, upsurge.

wave² *verb* **1** brandish, flap, flourish, flutter, shake, swing, wag, wiggle. **2** gesticulate, gesture, signal. **3** coil, curl, kink, twirl.

▶▶ D I C T I O N A R Y ◀◀

waveband *noun* the wavelengths between certain limits.

wavelength *noun* the size of a sound wave or electromagnetic wave.

wavelet *noun* a small wave.

waver *verb* **1** be unsteady; move unsteadily. **2** hesitate; be uncertain.

wavy *adjective* full of waves or curves. **wavily** *adverb*, **waviness** *noun*

wax¹ *noun* (*plural* **waxes**) **1** a soft substance that melts easily, used to make candles, crayons, and polish. **2** beeswax. **waxy** *adjective*

wax² *verb* coat or polish something with wax.

wax³ *verb* **1** (of the moon) show a bright area that becomes gradually larger. (The opposite is *wane*.) **2** become larger, stronger or more important.

waxen *adjective* **1** made of wax. **2** like wax.

waxwork *noun* a model of a person etc. made in wax.

way¹ *noun* **1** a line of communication between places, e.g. a path or road. **2** a route or direction. **3** a distance to be travelled. **4** how something is done; a method or style. **5** a respect, *It's a good idea in some ways.* **6** a condition or state, *Things were in a bad way.* **get** or **have your own way** make people let you do what you want.

give way collapse; let somebody else move first; yield.

in the way forming an obstacle or hindrance.

no way (*informal*) that is impossible!

under way see *under.*

way² *adverb* (*informal*) far, *That is way beyond what we can afford.*

wayfarer *noun* a traveller, especially someone who is walking.

waylay *verb* (**waylaid, waylaying**) lie in wait for a person or people, especially so as to talk to them or rob them.

wayside *noun* the land beside a road or path.

wayward *adjective* disobedient; wilfully doing what you want.

WC *abbreviation* water closet.

we *pronoun* a word used by a person to refer to himself or herself and another or others.

weak *adjective* **1** not strong; easy to break, bend, defeat, etc. **2** lacking vigour; sickly, feeble. **3** lacking in determination or strength of character. **4** not convincing, *a weak excuse.* **5** dilute, watery.

weaken *verb* make or become weaker.

weakling *noun* a weak person or animal.

weakly¹ *adverb* in a weak manner.

weakly² *adjective* sickly; not strong.

▶▶ T H E S A U R U S ◀◀

waver *verb* **1** falter, flicker, quiver, shake, teeter, totter, tremble, wobble. **2** dither, hesitate, hover, oscillate, shilly-shally, swing, vacillate.

wavy *adjective* crimped, curly, curving, kinky, rippled, squiggly, undulating.

wax³ *verb* **2** enlarge, grow, increase.

way¹ *noun* **1,2** course, direction, path, road, route, track, trail. **3** distance, haul, journey. **4** approach, fashion, manner, means, method, mode, procedure, process, style, system, technique; see also PRACTICE. **5** aspect, detail, feature, particular, respect, sense. **6** condition, shape, state.

give way 1 break, buckle, cave in, collapse, crack, crumble, give, snap. **2** back down, capitulate, concede, give in, submit, succumb, surrender, yield.

wayfarer *noun* gypsy, rover, traveller, vagabond, walker, wanderer.

waylay *verb* accost, ambush, assail, bail up (*Australian*), buttonhole, corner, detain, hold up, intercept, lie in wait for, pounce on, set upon.

wayward *adjective* contrary, disobedient, headstrong, incorrigible, intractable, naughty, obstinate, perverse, rebellious, recalcitrant, refractory, self-willed, stroppy (*informal*), stubborn, unmanageable, unruly, wilful.

weak *adjective* **1** decrepit, delicate, feeble, flimsy, fragile, rickety, shaky, unsteady. **2** debilitated, delicate, exhausted, feeble, frail, infirm, listless, puny, sickly, weedy. **3** cowardly, feckless, impotent, ineffective, ineffectual, namby-pamby, powerless, pusillanimous, soft, spineless, timorous, unassertive. **4** flimsy, implausible, lame, pathetic, thin, unconvincing, unsatisfactory. **5** dilute, insipid, tasteless, thin, watery, wishy-washy.

weaken *verb* debilitate, decline, decrease, dilute, diminish, dwindle, ebb, enervate, enfeeble, erode, exhaust, fade, impair, lessen, reduce, sap, undermine, wane, water down.

weakling *noun* coward, drip (*informal*), milksop, runt, sissy, softie (*informal*), sook (*Australian informal*), weed, wimp (*informal*), wuss (*slang*).

weakness *noun* **1** being weak. **2** a weak point; a defect. **3** an inability to resist something; a liking.

weal *noun* a ridge raised on the flesh by a cane or whip etc.

wealth *noun* **1** much money or property; riches. **2** a large quantity, *The book has a wealth of illustrations.* [from *well[1]*]

wealthy *adjective* (**wealthier, wealthiest**) having wealth; rich. **wealthiness** *noun*

wean *verb* make a baby take food other than its mother's milk.

weapon *noun* something used to do harm in a battle or fight. **weaponry** *noun*

wear[1] *verb* (**wore, worn, wearing**) **1** have something on your body as clothes, ornaments, etc. **2** damage something by rubbing or using it often; become damaged in this way, *The carpet has worn thin.* **3** last while in use, *It has worn well.* **wearable** *adjective*, **wearer** *noun*
wear off be removed by wear or use; become less intense.
wear on pass gradually, *The night wore on.*
wear out use or be used until it becomes weak or useless; exhaust.

wear[2] *noun* **1** clothes, *formal wear.* **2** damage resulting from ordinary use, *wear and tear.*

wearisome *adjective* causing weariness.

weary[1] *adjective* (**wearier, weariest**) **1** tired. **2** tiring, *It's weary work.* **wearily** *adverb*, **weariness** *noun*

weary[2] *verb* (**wearied, wearying**) tire.

weasel *noun* a small fierce animal with a slender body and reddish-brown fur.

weather[1] *noun* the rain, snow, wind, sunshine etc. at a particular time or place.
under the weather feeling ill or depressed; drunk.

weather[2] *verb* **1** expose something to the effects of the weather. **2** come through something successfully, *The ship weathered the storm.*

weatherboard *noun* a sloping board for keeping out rain; one of a series of horizontal boards with overlapping edges covering a wall of a house.

weathercock or **weathervane** *noun* a pointer, often shaped like a cockerel, that turns in the wind and shows from which direction the wind is blowing.

weave[1] *verb* (**wove, woven, weaving**) **1** make material or baskets etc. by passing crosswise threads or strips under and over lengthwise ones. **2** put a story together, *She wove a thrilling tale.* **3** (*past tense & past participle* **weaved**) twist and turn, *He weaved through the traffic.* **weaver** *noun*

weakness *noun* **1** debility, decrepitude, feebleness, fragility, frailty. **2** defect, deficiency, failing, fault, flaw, foible, imperfection, shortcoming, weak point. **3** fondness, liking, partiality, passion, penchant, predilection, soft spot.

wealth *noun* **1** affluence, assets, capital, fortune, means, money, opulence, property, prosperity, riches. **2** abundance, fund, mine, profusion, store.

wealthy *adjective* affluent, flush (*informal*), loaded (*informal*), moneyed, opulent, prosperous, rich, well-heeled (*informal*), well in (*Australian informal*), well off, well-to-do.

weapon *noun* (**weapons**) armaments, arms, munitions, weaponry.

wear[1] *verb* **1** be attired in, clothe yourself in, don, dress in, have on, put on, sport. **2** abrade, corrode, eat away, erode, grind down, rub away, scuff, wear away, wear down. **3** endure, last, stand up, survive.
wear off decrease, diminish, dwindle, fade, lessen, subside.
wear out 1 become shabby, become threadbare, fray, wear thin. **2** drain, exhaust, fatigue, tire out, weary.

wear[2] *noun* **1** apparel (*formal*), attire (*formal*), clobber (*slang*), clothes, clothing, dress, garb, garments, gear (*informal*), raiment (*old use*). **2** damage, deterioration, disrepair, wear and tear.

weary[1] *adjective* **1** all in (*informal*), beat (*slang*), dog-tired, done in (*informal*), drained, drowsy, exhausted, fagged out (*informal*), fatigued, jaded, knackered (*slang*), pooped (*informal*), sleepy, spent, tired, whacked (*informal*), worn out, zonked (*slang*).
weariness *noun* exhaustion, fatigue, languor, lassitude, lethargy, listlessness, tiredness.

weary[2] *verb* drain, exhaust, fatigue, sap, tire, wear out.

weather[1] *noun* climate, the elements.

weather[2] *verb* **1** season. **2** brave, come through, endure, ride out, stand up to, survive, withstand.

weave[1] *verb* **1** braid, entwine, interlace, intertwine, interweave, plait. **2** compose, create, put together, spin. **3** meander, wind, zigzag.

▶▶ DICTIONARY ◀◀

weave² *noun* a style of weaving, *a loose weave.*

web *noun* **1** a cobweb. **2** a network.

webbed or **web-footed** *adjective* having toes joined by pieces of skin, *Ducks have webbed feet; they are web-footed.*

wed *verb* (**wedded, wedding**) **1** marry. **2** unite two different things.

wedding *noun* the ceremony when a man and woman get married.

wedge¹ *noun* **1** a piece of wood or metal etc. that is thick at one end and thin at the other. It is pushed between things to force them apart or prevent something from moving. **2** a wedge-shaped thing.

wedge² *verb* (**wedged, wedging**) **1** keep something in place with a wedge. **2** pack tightly together, *Ten of us were wedged in the lift.*

wedlock *noun* the condition of being married; matrimony. [from Old English, = marriage vow]

wee *adjective* (*Scottish*) little.

weed¹ *noun* a wild plant that grows where it is not wanted.

weed² *verb* remove weeds from the ground.

weeds *plural noun* the black clothes formerly worn by a widow in mourning.

weedy *adjective* (**weedier, weediest**) **1** full of weeds. **2** thin and weak.

week *noun* a period of seven days, especially from Sunday to the following Saturday.

weekday *noun* a day other than Saturday or Sunday.

weekend *noun* Saturday and Sunday.

weekender *noun* (*Australian*) a cottage or shack used for weekend visits.

weekly *adjective* & *adverb* happening or done once a week.

weeny *adjective* (*informal*) tiny.

weep *verb* (**wept, weeping**) **1** shed tears; cry. **2** ooze moisture in drops. **weep** *noun*, **weepy** *adjective*

weeping *adjective* (of a tree) having drooping branches, *a weeping willow.*

weevil *noun* a kind of small beetle.

weft *noun* the crosswise threads in weaving, passing through the warp.

weigh *verb* **1** measure the weight of something. **2** have a certain weight. **3** be important; have influence, *Her evidence weighed with the jury.*
weigh anchor raise the anchor and start a voyage.
weigh down keep something down by its weight; depress or trouble somebody.
weigh up estimate; assess.

weight¹ *noun* **1** how heavy something is; an object's mass expressed as a number according to a scale of units. (Compare *mass*¹ 3.) **2** a piece of metal of known weight, especially one used on scales to weigh things. **3** a heavy object. **4** load, burden, *a weight off his mind.* **5** importance; influence.

weight² *verb* put a weight on something.

weighty *adjective* **1** heavy. **2** important, *weighty issues.* **weightiness** *noun*

weir (*say* weer) *noun* a small dam across a river or canal to control the flow of water.

▶▶ THESAURUS ◀◀

web *noun* **1** cobweb, gossamer. **2** mesh, net, network.

wed *verb* **1** get hitched (*informal*), marry, tie the knot (*informal*).
wedded *adjective* conjugal, marital, married, matrimonial, nuptial.

wedding *noun* marriage, nuptials.

wedge¹ *noun* **1** block, chock. **2** chunk, hunk, piece, slab, slice.

wedge² *verb* **2** jam, pack, ram, sandwich, squeeze, stick, stuff.

wedlock *noun* marriage, matrimony.

weed² *verb* (*weed out*) eliminate, eradicate, get rid of, remove, root out.

weedy *adjective* **1** overgrown, rank, wild. **2** delicate, frail, puny, scrawny, thin, undersized, weak.

weep *verb* **1** bawl, blubber, break down, cry, howl, shed tears, snivel, sob, wail. **2** ooze, seep.
weepy *adjective* crying, lachrymose, maudlin, tearful, teary.

weigh *verb* **2** measure, tip the scales at. **3** important, carry weight, count, have an influence, matter.
weigh down burden, depress, encumber, load, oppress, overload, saddle, trouble.
weigh up assess, balance, compare, consider, evaluate.

weight¹ *noun* **1** heaviness, mass. **4** burden, load, millstone, onus, pressure, strain. **5** authority, clout (*informal*), force, importance, influence, power.

weighty *adjective* **1** burdensome, cumbersome, heavy, hefty, massive, ponderous. **2** grave, important, momentous, pressing, serious.

weir *noun* barrage, dam.

weird *adjective* **1** very strange. **2** uncanny. **weirdly** *adverb*, **weirdness** *noun*

weirdo *noun* (*informal*) an odd or eccentric person.

welcome[1] *noun* a greeting or reception, especially a kindly one.

welcome[2] *adjective* **1** that you are glad to receive or see, *a welcome gift*. **2** gladly allowed, *You are welcome to come.*

welcome[3] *verb* (**welcomed, welcoming**) show that you are pleased when a person or thing arrives. [from *well*[3] + *come*]

weld *verb* **1** join pieces of metal or plastic by heating and pressing or hammering them together. **2** unite people or things into a whole.

welfare *noun* people's health, happiness, and comfort. [from *well*[3] + *fare*]
Welfare State a country that looks after the welfare of its people by social services run by the government.

well[1] *noun* **1** a deep hole dug to bring up water or oil from underground. **2** a deep space, e.g. containing a staircase.

well[2] *verb* rise or flow up, *Tears welled up in our eyes.* [from Old English *wella* = spring of water]

well[3] *adverb* (**better, best**) **1** in a good or suitable way, *She swims well.* **2** thoroughly, *Polish it well.* **3** easily; probably, *This may well be our last chance.*
well off fairly rich; in a good situation.

well[4] *adjective* **1** in good health, *He is not well.* **2** satisfactory, *All is well.* [from Old English *wel* = prosperously]

well-being *noun* good health, happiness, and comfort.

wellingtons *plural noun* (*British*) rubber or plastic waterproof boots. **wellies** *plural noun* (*informal*) [named after the first Duke of Wellington]

well-known *adjective* **1** known to many people. **2** known thoroughly.

well-mannered *adjective* having good manners.

wellnigh *adverb* almost.

well-read *adjective* having read much literature.

well-to-do *adjective* fairly rich.

welsh *verb* cheat someone by avoiding paying what you owe them or by breaking an agreement. **welsher** *noun*

welt *noun* **1** a strip or border. **2** a weal.

welter[1] *verb* (of a ship) be tossed to and fro by waves.

welter[2] *noun* a confused mixture.

wench *noun* (*plural* **wenches**) (*old use*) a girl or young woman.

wend *verb* **wend your way** go.

weird *adjective* **1** abnormal, bizarre, curious, eccentric, freakish, funny, kinky (*informal*), odd, offbeat, outlandish, peculiar, queer, strange, unconventional, unusual, wacky (*slang*), way-out (*informal*), zany. **2** creepy, eerie, extraordinary, mysterious, peculiar, queer, spooky (*informal*), strange, supernatural, uncanny, unnatural.

weirdo *noun* crackpot (*informal*), crank, dingbat (*informal*), eccentric, freak, fruitcake (*informal*), nut (*informal*), nutcase (*informal*), oddball (*informal*).

welcome[1] *noun* greeting, reception, salutation.

welcome[2] *adjective* **1** appreciated, gratifying, pleasing.

welcome[3] *verb* accept, admit, greet, hail, let in, meet, receive.

welfare *noun* good, happiness, health, security, well-being.

well[1] *noun* **1** bore, shaft.

well[3] *adverb* **1** ably, commendably, competently, correctly, effectively, fairly, justly, nicely, proficiently, properly, satisfactorily, skilfully, splendidly. **2** carefully, completely, conscientiously, meticulously, scrupulously, thoroughly.

well off affluent, comfortable, loaded (*informal*), moneyed, prosperous, rich, wealthy, well-heeled (*informal*), well in (*Australian informal*), well-to-do.

well[4] *adjective* **1** fit, hale and hearty, healthy, robust, sound, strong. **2** all right, fine, OK (*informal*), satisfactory.

well-being *noun* good, happiness, health, welfare.

well-known *adjective* **1** eminent, famous, illustrious, notable, noted, notorious, prominent, renowned. **2** everyday, familiar, household, proverbial.

well-mannered *adjective* civil, correct, courteous, genteel, polite, refined, respectful, suave, thoughtful, urbane, well-behaved, well-bred.

welt *noun* **2** ridge, scar, stripe, weal.

▶▶ D I C T I O N A R Y ◀◀

weren't (*mainly spoken*) were not.

werewolf *noun* (*plural* **werewolves**) (in legends) a person who sometimes changes into a wolf. [from Old English *wer* = man, + *wolf*]

west[1] *noun* **1** the direction where the sun sets, opposite east. **2** the western part of a country, city, etc.

west[2] *adjective* **1** situated in the west, *the west coast*. **2** coming from the west, *a west wind*.

west[3] *adverb* towards the west, *We sailed west.*

westerly *adjective* to or from the west.

western[1] *adjective* of or in the west.

western[2] *noun* a film or story about cowboys or American Indians in western North America.

westward *adjective & adverb* towards the west. **westwards** *adverb*

wet[1] *adjective* (**wetter, wettest**) **1** soaked or covered in water or other liquid. **2** not yet dry, *wet paint*. **3** rainy, *wet weather*. **wetly** *adverb*, **wetness** *noun*

wet[2] *verb* (**wetted, wetting**) make a thing wet. [from Old English *wæt* = wet]

wet[3] *noun* **1** moisture. **2 the wet** the rainy season.

whack *verb* hit hard, especially with a stick. **whack** *noun*

whale *noun* a very large sea-animal.
a whale of a (*informal*) very good or great, *We had a whale of a time.*

whaler *noun* a person or ship that hunts whales. **whaling** *noun*

wharf (*say* worf) *noun* a quay where ships are loaded and unloaded.

wharfie *noun* (*Australian informal*) a wharf labourer.

what[1] *adjective* used to ask the amount or kind of something (*What kind of bike have you got?*) or to say how strange or great a person or thing is (*What a fool you are!*).

what[2] *pronoun* **1** what thing or things, *What did you say?* **2** the thing that, *This is what you must do.*
what's what (*informal*) which things are important or useful.

whatever[1] *pronoun* **1** anything or everything, *Do whatever you like.* **2** no matter what, *Keep calm, whatever happens.*

whatever[2] *adjective* of any kind or amount, *Take whatever books you need. There is no doubt whatever.*

wheat *noun* a cereal plant from which flour is made. **wheaten** *adjective*

wheedle *verb* (**wheedled, wheedling**) coax.

wheel[1] *noun* **1** a round device that turns on a shaft that passes through its centre. **2** a horizontal revolving disc on which clay is made into a pot.

wheel[2] *verb* **1** push a bicycle or trolley etc. along on its wheels. **2** move in a curve or circle; change direction and face another way, *He wheeled round in astonishment.*

wheelbarrow *noun* a small cart with one wheel at the front and legs at the back, pushed by handles.

wheelchair *noun* a chair on wheels for a person who cannot walk.

wheeze *verb* (**wheezed, wheezing**) make a hoarse whistling sound as you breathe. **wheeze** *noun*, **wheezy** *adjective*

whelk *noun* a shellfish that looks like a snail.

whelp *noun* a young dog; a pup.

when[1] *adverb* at what time; at which time, *When can you come to tea?*

when[2] *conjunction* **1** at the time that, *The bird flew away when I moved.* **2** although; considering that, *Why do you smoke when you know it's dangerous?*

whence *adverb & conjunction* from where; from which.

whenever *conjunction* at whatever time; every time, *whenever I see it, I smile.*

▶▶ T H E S A U R U S ◀◀

wet[1] *adjective* **1** boggy, clammy, damp, dank, dewy, drenched, dripping, humid, moist, muddy, saturated, soaked, sodden, soggy, sopping, waterlogged. **2** sticky, tacky. **3** drizzly, rainy, showery, stormy.
wetness *noun* clamminess, condensation, damp, dampness, humidity, liquid, moisture, perspiration, sweat.

wet[2] *verb* dampen, douse, drench, immerse, moisten, saturate, soak, splash, spray, sprinkle, squirt, water.

wharf *noun* dock, jetty, landing stage, pier, quay.

wharfie *noun* docker, longshoreman, stevedore, watersider (*Australian*), waterside worker (*Australian*), wharf labourer.

wheel[1] *noun* **1** castor, circle, disc, ring, roller.

wheel[2] *verb* **1** push, trundle. **2** circle, gyrate, pivot, revolve, rotate, spin, swing, swivel, turn, veer, whirl.

wheeze *verb & noun* gasp, pant, puff.

▶▶▶ D I C T I O N A R Y ◀◀

where¹ *adverb & conjunction* in or to what place or that place, *where did you put it? Leave it where it is.*

where² *pronoun* what place, *Where does she come from?*

whereabouts *adverb* in or near what place. **whereabouts** *plural noun*

whereas *conjunction* but in contrast, *Some people enjoy sport, whereas others hate it.*

whereby *adverb* by which.

wherefore *adverb* (*old use*) why.

whereupon *conjunction* after which; and then.

wherever *adverb* in or to whatever place.

whet *verb* (**whetted, whetting**) **1** sharpen. **2** stimulate, *whet your appetite.* [from Old English *hwettan* = sharpen]

whether *conjunction* as one possibility; if, *I don't know whether to believe her or not.*

whetstone *noun* a shaped stone for sharpening tools. [from *whet* = sharpen, + *stone*]

whey (*say as* way) *noun* the watery liquid left when milk forms curds.

which¹ *adjective* what particular, *Which way did he go?*

which² *pronoun* **1** what person or thing, *Which is your desk?* **2** the person or thing referred to, *The film, which is a western, will be shown on Saturday.*

whichever *pronoun & adjective* no matter which; any which, *Take whichever you like.*

whiff *noun* **1** a puff of smoke, gas, etc. **2** a smell.

while¹ *conjunction* **1** during the time that; as long as, *Whistle while you work.* **2** although; but, *She is dark, while her sister is fair.*

while² *noun* a period of time; the time spent on something, *a long while.*

while³ *verb* (**whiled, whiling**) **while away** pass time, *We whiled away the afternoon on the river.*

whilst *conjunction* while.

whim *noun* a sudden wish to do or have something.

whimper *verb* cry or whine softly. **whimper** *noun*

whimsical *adjective* impulsive and playful. **whimsically** *adverb*, **whimsicality** *noun*

whine *verb* (**whined, whining**) **1** make a long high miserable cry or a shrill sound. **2** complain in a petty or feeble way. **whine** *noun*

whinge *verb* (**whinged, whinging**) (*informal*) whine; grumble persistently. **whinge** *noun*, **whinger** *noun*

whinny *verb* (**whinnied, whinnying**) neigh gently or happily. **whinny** *noun*

whip¹ *noun* **1** a cord or strip of leather fixed to a handle and used for hitting people or animals. **2** an official of a political party in Parliament. **3** a dessert made of whipped cream and fruit or flavouring.

whip² *verb* (**whipped, whipping**) **1** hit with a whip. **2** beat cream until it becomes thick. **3** move or take suddenly, *He whipped out a gun.* **4** (*informal*) steal something. **whip up** arouse people's feelings etc., *She whipped up support for her plans.*

whiplash *noun* **whiplash injury** a neck injury caused by a sudden jerk of the head, especially in a car accident.

whippet *noun* a small dog rather like a greyhound, used for racing.

whirl *verb* turn or spin very quickly. **whirl** *noun*

whirlpool *noun* a whirling current of water.

whirlwind *noun* a strong wind that whirls round a central point.

▶▶▶ T H E S A U R U S ◀◀

whereabouts *plural noun* location, position, situation.

whet *verb* **1** grind, hone, sharpen, strop. **2** arouse, awaken, excite, kindle, stimulate, stir.

whiff *noun* **1** breath, puff. **2** aroma, fragrance, odour, smell, stink.

while² *noun* period, spell, time.

while³ *verb* **while away** fill, occupy, pass, spend.

whim *noun* caprice, desire, fancy, impulse, urge.

whimper *verb* cry, grizzle (*informal*), moan, snivel, wail, whine.

whine *verb* **1** cry, grizzle (*informal*), moan, wail, whimper, whinge (*informal*).

whinge *verb* beef (*slang*), complain, gripe (*informal*), grizzle (*informal*), grumble, moan, whine.

whip¹ *noun* **1** birch, crop, lash, rawhide, scourge, strap, switch.

whip² *verb* **1** beat, birch, flog, lash, scourge, tan (*slang*), thrash. **2** beat, mix, whisk. **3** pull, seize, snatch, swipe, whisk.

whirl *verb* gyrate, reel, revolve, rotate, spin, swirl, swivel, turn, twirl.

whirlpool *noun* eddy, maelstrom, vortex.

whirlwind *noun* tornado, twister (*American*), vortex, willy willy (*Australian*).

▶▶DICTIONARY◀◀

whirr *verb* make a continuous buzzing sound.
whirr *noun*

whisk¹ *verb* **1** move or brush away quickly
and lightly. **2** beat eggs etc. until they are
frothy.

whisk² *noun* **1** a device for whisking things.
2 a whisking movement.

whisker *noun* **1** a hair of those growing on a
man's face, forming a beard or moustache if
not shaved off. **2** a long bristle growing near
the mouth of a cat etc. **whiskery** *adjective*

whisky *noun* (*plural* **whiskies**) a strong
alcoholic drink.

whisper *verb* **1** speak very softly. **2** talk
secretly. **whisper** *noun*

whist *noun* a card game usually for four
people.

whistle¹ *verb* (**whistled, whistling**) make a
shrill or musical sound, especially by blowing
through your lips. **whistler** *noun*

whistle² *noun* **1** a whistling sound. **2** a device
that makes a shrill sound when air or steam is
blown through it.

whit *noun* the least possible amount, *not a
whit better*. [from an old word *wight* = an
amount]

White *noun* a person with a light-coloured
skin. **White** *adjective*

white¹ *noun* **1** the very lightest colour, like
snow or salt. **2** the transparent substance
(*albumen*) round the yolk of an egg, turning
white when cooked.

white² *adjective* **1** of the colour white. **2** very
pale from the effects of illness or fear etc.
whiteness *noun*
white ant a termite.
white coffee coffee with milk.
white elephant a useless possession.

whitebait *noun* (*plural* **whitebait**) a small
silvery-white fish.

white-hot *adjective* extremely hot; so hot that
heated metal looks white.

whiten *verb* make or become whiter.

whitewash *noun* a white liquid containing
lime or powdered chalk, used for painting
walls and ceilings etc. **whitewash** *verb*

whither *adverb* & *conjunction* (*old use*) to
what place.

whiting *noun* (*plural* **whiting**) a small edible
sea-fish with white flesh.

Whitsun *noun* Whit Sunday and the days
close to it. [from *Whit Sunday*]

Whit Sunday the seventh Sunday after
Easter. [from Old English *hwit* = white,
because people used to be baptised on that
day and wore white clothes]

whittle *verb* (**whittled, whittling**) **1** shape wood
by trimming thin slices off the surface. **2**
reduce something by removing various
things from it, *whittle down the cost*.

whiz *verb* (**whizzed, whizzing**) **1** move very
quickly. **2** sound like something rushing
through the air.

whiz-kid *noun* (*informal*) a brilliant or very
successful young person.

who *pronoun* which person or people; the
particular person or people, *This is the boy
who stole the apples*.

whoa *interjection* a command to a horse to
stop or stand still.

whoever *pronoun* **1** any or every person who.
2 no matter who.

whole¹ *adjective* complete; not injured or
broken.
whole number a number without fractions.

whole² *noun* **1** the full amount. **2** a complete
thing.
on the whole considering everything; mainly.

▶▶THESAURUS◀◀

whirr *verb* buzz, drone, hum.

whisk¹ *verb* **1** brush, sweep. **2** beat, mix, whip.

whisker *noun* **1** (*whiskers*) beard, bristles, facial
hair, moustache, sideburns, stubble.
whiskery *adjective* bristly, hairy, hirsute,
stubbly, unshaven, whiskered.

whisper *verb* **1** breathe, murmur, mutter, say
under your breath.
whisper *noun* hushed tone, murmur,
undertone; see also RUMOUR¹.

whistle² *noun* **1** catcall, hoot. **2** hooter, pipe,
siren.

white² *adjective* **1** chalky, cream, hoary, ivory,
lily-white, milky, off-white, platinum, silvery,
snow-white, snowy. **2** anaemic, ashen,
bloodless, colourless, pale, pallid, pasty, wan,
waxen.

whiten *verb* blanch, bleach, fade, lighten, pale.

whiz *verb* **1** dash, fly, hurry, hurtle, race, shoot,
speed, tear, zip, zoom.

whiz-kid *noun* expert, genius, prodigy, virtuoso,
wizard.

whole¹ *adjective* complete, entire, full, intact,
total, unabridged, unbroken, uncut, undamaged, uninjured.

whole² *noun* **on the whole** all in all, altogether,
by and large, for the most part, generally, in
general, in the main.

wholehearted *adjective* complete and without reservations, *wholehearted support.*

wholemeal *adjective* made from the whole grain of wheat etc.

wholesale[1] *noun* selling goods in large quantities to be resold by others. (Compare *retail*.) **wholesaler** *noun*

wholesale[2] *adjective & adverb* **1** on a large scale; including everybody or everything, *wholesale destruction.* **2** in the wholesale trade.

wholesome *adjective* good for health; healthy, *wholesome food.* **wholesomeness** *noun*

wholly *noun* completely; entirely.

whom *pronoun* the form of *who* used when it is the object of a verb or comes after a preposition, as in *the boy whom I saw* or *to whom we spoke.*

whoop (*say* woop) *noun* a loud cry of excitement. **whoop** *verb*

whoopee *interjection* a cry of joy.

whooping cough (*say* **hoop**-ing) an infectious disease that causes spasms of coughing and gasping for breath.

whopper *noun* (*slang*) something very large.

whopping *adjective* (*slang*) very large or remarkable, *a whopping lie.*

whorl *noun* **1** a coil or curved shape. **2** a ring of leaves or petals.

who's (*mainly spoken*) who is; who has.

whose *pronoun* belonging to what person or persons; of whom; of which, *Whose house is that?*

why *adverb* for what reason or purpose; the particular reason on account of which, *This is why I came.*

wick *noun* **1** the string that goes through the middle of a candle and is lit. **2** the strip of material that you light in a lamp or heater etc. that uses oil.

wicked *adjective* **1** morally bad or cruel. **2** very bad; severe, *a wicked blow.* **3** mischievous, *a wicked smile.* **wickedly** *adverb*, **wickedness** *noun*

wicker *noun* thin canes or osiers woven together to make baskets or furniture etc. **wickerwork** *noun*

wicket *noun* **1** a set of three stumps and two bails used in cricket. **2** the part of a cricket ground between or near the wickets.

wicketkeeper *noun* the fielder in cricket who stands behind the batsman's wicket.

wide[1] *adjective* **1** measuring a lot from side to side; not narrow. **2** measuring from side to side, *The cloth is one metre wide.* **3** covering a great range, *a wide knowledge of birds.* **4** fully open, *staring with wide eyes.* **5** far from the target, *The shot was wide of the mark.* **widely** *adverb*, **wideness** *noun*

wide[2] *adverb* **1** widely. **2** completely; fully, *wide awake.* **3** far from the target, *The shot went wide.*

widen *verb* make or become wider.

widespread *adjective* existing in many places or over a wide area.

widgeon *noun* a kind of wild duck.

widow *noun* a woman whose husband has died. **widowed** *adjective*

widower *noun* a man whose wife has died.

width *noun* how wide something is; wideness. [from *wide*]

wholehearted *adjective* complete, dedicated, devoted, earnest, enthusiastic, full, hearty, sincere, total, unconditional, unreserved.

wholesale[2] *adjective* **1** comprehensive, extensive, general, large-scale, mass, sweeping, universal, widespread.

wholesome *adjective* healthy, nourishing, nutritious.

wicked *adjective* **1** atrocious, bad, base, beastly, contemptible, corrupt, degenerate, depraved, despicable, devilish, diabolical, evil, fiendish, foul, heinous, immoral, incorrigible, infamous, iniquitous, lawless, malicious, monstrous, nefarious, satanic, shameful, sinful, sinister, spiteful, ungodly, unholy, vicious, vile, villainous. **3** arch, devilish, impish, mischievous, naughty, roguish.

wickedness *noun* depravity, evil, immorality, iniquity, sin, sinfulness, turpitude, ungodliness, unrighteousness, vice, villainy, wrongdoing.

wide[1] *adjective* **1** big, broad, expansive, extensive, immense, large, open, spacious, vast, yawning. **3** big, broad, comprehensive, extensive, far-reaching, global, sweeping, vast, wide-ranging.

widen *verb* broaden, dilate, enlarge, expand, open out, spread.

widespread *adjective* common, extensive, general, pervasive, prevalent, rife, ubiquitous, universal, wholesale.

width *noun* breadth, diameter, girth, span, thickness.

▶▶ D I C T I O N A R Y ◀◀

wield *verb* hold something and use it.

wife *noun* (*plural* **wives**) the woman to whom a man is married.

wig *noun* a covering made of real or artificial hair, worn on the head.

wiggle *verb* (**wiggled, wiggling**) move from side to side; wriggle. **wiggle** *noun*

wigwam *noun* a tent formerly used by American Indians, made by fastening skins or mats over poles. [American Indian word, = their house]

wild *adjective* **1** living or growing in its natural state, not looked after by people. **2** not cultivated, *a wild landscape*. **3** not civilised, *the Wild West*. **4** not controlled; very violent or excited. **5** stormy; tempestuous. **6** very foolish or unreasonable, *these wild ideas*. **wildly** *adverb*, **wildness** *noun*

wilderness *noun* (*plural* **wildernesses**) a wild uncultivated area; a desert.

wildlife *noun* wild animals.

wile *noun* a piece of trickery.

wilful *adjective* **1** obstinately determined, *a wilful child*. **2** deliberate, *wilful murder*. **wilfully** *adverb*, **wilfulness** *noun* [from *will²* + *-ful*]

will¹ *auxiliary verb* used to express the future tense, questions, or promises.

Usage See the entry for *shall*.

will² *noun* **1** the mental power to decide and control what you do. **2** a desire; a chosen decision, *I went to the party against my will*. **3** determination, *They set to work with a will*. **4** a person's attitude towards others, *full of good will*. **5** a written statement of how a person's possessions are to be disposed of after his or her death.
at will as you like, *You can come and go at will*.

will³ *verb* **1** use your will-power; influence something by doing this, *I was willing you to win!* **2** bequeath by a will.

willing *adjective* ready and happy to do what is wanted. **willingly** *adverb*, **willingness** *noun*

will-o'-the-wisp *noun* **1** a flickering spot of light seen on marshy ground. **2** an elusive person or hope.

willow *noun* a tree or shrub with flexible branches, usually growing near water.

will-power *noun* strength of mind to control what you do.

willy-nilly *adverb* whether you want to or not. [from *will I*, *nill* (= will not) *I*]

willy wagtail a small truculent Australian bird with a swaying tail when at rest.

▶▶ T H E S A U R U S ◀◀

wield *verb* (*wield a weapon*) handle, hold, manage, manipulate, ply, swing, use; (*wield power*) command, exercise, exert, use.

wife *noun* bride, consort, partner, spouse.

wig *noun* hairpiece, switch, toupee.

wiggle *verb* shake, sway, twitch, wag, waggle, wobble, wriggle.

wigwam *noun* hut, tent, tepee.

wild *adjective* **1** feral, free, myall (*Australian*), natural, savage, unbroken, uncultivated, undomesticated, untamed, warrigal (*Australian*). **2** bleak, desolate, rough, rugged, uncultivated, uninhabited, waste. **3** barbarian, barbaric, barbarous, primitive, uncivilised. **4** berserk, boisterous, crazy, disorderly, excited, frenzied, hysterical, lawless, obstreperous, rebellious, reckless, riotous, rowdy, uncontrolled, undisciplined, unrestrained, unruly, violent. **5** blustery, rough, squally, stormy, tempestuous, turbulent, violent, windy. **6** absurd, crazy, foolish, hare-brained, impracticable, mad, madcap, rash, ridiculous, silly, unreasonable.

wilderness *noun* bush, desert, wasteland, wilds.

wilful *adjective* **1** determined, dogged, headstrong, intractable, mulish, obstinate, perverse, pigheaded, recalcitrant, refractory, self-willed, strong-willed, stubborn, wayward. **2** calculated, deliberate, intentional, premeditated.

will² *noun* **1** will-power. **2** choice, desire, inclination, intention, volition, wish(es). **3** commitment, determination, resolution, resolve. **5** testament.

will³ *verb* **2** bequeath, hand down, leave, pass on.

willing *adjective* amenable, consenting, co-operative, disposed, eager, enthusiastic, game, happy, inclined, keen, obliging, prepared, ready.
willingly *adverb* eagerly, happily, like a shot, of your own accord, of your own free will, of your own volition, readily, voluntarily.

will-power *noun* commitment, determination, resolution, resolve, self-control, self-discipline, will.

▶▶ D I C T I O N A R Y ◀◀

wilt *verb* lose freshness or strength; droop.

wily (*say* **wy**-lee) *adjective* cunning; crafty. **wiliness** *noun* [from *wile*]

wimp *noun* (*informal*) a feeble and cowardly person.

wimple *noun* a piece of cloth folded round the head and neck, worn by women in the Middle Ages.

win¹ *verb* (**won**, **winning**) **1** be victorious in a battle, game or contest. **2** get or achieve something by a victory or by using effort or skill etc., *She won the prize.*

win² *noun* a victory.

wince *verb* (**winced**, **wincing**) make a slight movement because of pain or embarrassment etc.

winch¹ *noun* (*plural* **winches**) a device for lifting or pulling things, using a rope or cable etc. that winds on to a revolving drum or wheel.

winch² *verb* lift or pull with a winch.

wind¹ (*rhymes with* tinned) *noun* **1** a current of air. **2** gas in the stomach or intestines that makes you feel uncomfortable. **3** breath used for a purpose, e.g. for running or speaking. **4** the wind instruments of an orchestra. **get** or **have the wind up** (*slang*) feel frightened. **wind instrument** a musical instrument played by blowing, e.g. a trumpet.

wind² *verb* cause a person to be out of breath, *The climb had winded us.*

wind³ (*rhymes with* find) *verb* (**wound**, **winding**) **1** go or turn something in twists, curves, or circles. **2** twist or wrap something round and round upon itself. **3** wind up a watch or clock etc. **winder** *noun* **wind up** make a clock or watch work by tightening its spring; close a business; (*informal*) end up in a place or condition, *He wound up in gaol.*

windbag *noun* (*informal*) a person who talks at great length.

windfall *noun* **1** a fruit blown off a tree by the wind. **2** a piece of unexpected good luck, especially a sum of money.

windlass *noun* (*plural* **windlasses**) a device for pulling or lifting things (e.g. a bucket from a well), with a rope or cable that is wound round an axle by turning a handle.

windmill *noun* a mill worked by the wind that turns projecting parts (*sails*).

window *noun* **1** an opening in a wall or roof etc. to let in light and often air, usually filled with glass. **2** the glass in this opening.

windpipe *noun* the tube by which air passes from the throat to the lungs.

windscreen *noun* the window at the front of a motor vehicle.

windsurfing *noun* surfing on a board that has a sail fixed to it.

windward *adjective* facing the wind, *the windward side of the ship.*

windy *adjective* with much wind.

▶▶ T H E S A U R U S ◀◀

wilt *verb* become limp, deteriorate, droop, flop, languish, shrivel, wither.

wily *adjective* artful, astute, clever, crafty, cunning, devious, foxy, knowing, scheming, shrewd, sly, tricky, underhand.

wimp *noun* baby, coward, milksop, sissy, sook (*Australian informal*), wuss (*slang*).

win¹ *verb* **1** be victorious, come first, come top, prevail, succeed, triumph. **2** attain, earn, gain, get, land, obtain, pick up, receive, secure, walk away with (*informal*). **win over** convert, convince, persuade, sway, talk round.

win² *noun* conquest, success, triumph, victory.

wince *verb* blench, cringe, flinch, grimace, recoil, start.

winch² *verb* hoist, lift, pull.

wind¹ *noun* **1** air current, blast, breeze, draught, gale, gust, squall, zephyr; (*various winds*) cyclone, doctor (*Australian*), hurricane, mistral, monsoon, sirocco, southerly buster (*Australian*), tornado, typhoon, whirlwind, willy willy (*Australian*). **2** flatulence, gas. **3** air, breath, puff.

wind³ *verb* **1** bend, curl, curve, loop, meander, snake, turn, twist, wander, zigzag. **2** coil, loop, roll, twine, twirl, twist, wrap. **wind up 1** close down, dissolve, liquidate. **2** end up, finish up, land.

windfall *noun* **2** bonanza, godsend.

window *noun* **1** aperture, opening; (*kinds of window*) bay window, bow window, casement, dormer window, fanlight, French window, oriel window, porthole, quarterlight, skylight, transom, windscreen. **2** glass, pane.

windy *adjective* blowy, blustery, breezy, gusty, squally, stormy, tempestuous.

wine *noun* **1** an alcoholic drink made from grapes or other plants. **2** dark red colour. [from Latin *vinum* = wine (compare *vine*)]

wing¹ *noun* **1** each of a pair of projecting parts of a bird, bat, or insect, used in flying. **2** each of a pair of long flat projecting parts that support an aircraft while it flies. **3** a projecting part at one end or side of something. **4** the part of a motor vehicle's body above a wheel. **5** a player at either end of the forward line in football or hockey etc. **6** a section of a political party, with more extreme opinions than the others.
on the wing flying.
take wing fly away.
the wings the sides of a theatre stage out of sight of the audience.

wing² *verb* **1** fly; travel by means of wings, *The bird winged its way home.* **2** wound a bird in the wing or a person in the arm.

winged *adjective* having wings.

wingless *adjective* without wings.

wink¹ *verb* **1** close and open your eye quickly, especially as a signal to someone. **2** (of a light) flicker; twinkle.

wink² *noun* **1** the action of winking. **2** a very short period of sleep, *I didn't sleep a wink.*

winkle¹ *noun* a kind of edible shellfish.

winkle² *verb* (**winkled, winkling**)
winkle out extract; prise a thing out.

winner *noun* **1** a person or animal etc. that wins. **2** something very successful, *Her latest book is a winner.*

winnings *plural noun* money won.

winnow *verb* toss or fan grain etc. so that the loose dry outer part is blown away.

winsome *adjective* charming.

winter¹ *noun* the coldest season of the year, between autumn and spring. **wintry** *adjective*

winter² *verb* spend the winter somewhere.

wipe *verb* (**wiped, wiping**) **1** dry or clean something by rubbing it. **2** spread something over a surface by rubbing. **3** remove data from a magnetic tape or disk. **wiper** *noun*
wipe out cancel, *wipe out the debt*; destroy something completely.

wire¹ *noun* **1** a strand or thin flexible rod of metal. **2** a fence etc. made from wire. **3** a piece of wire used to carry electric current.

wire² *verb* (**wired, wiring**) **1** fasten or strengthen with wire. **2** fit or connect with wires to carry electric current.

wireless *noun* (*plural* **wirelesses**) **1** radio. **2** a radio set.

wiry *adjective* **1** like wire. **2** lean and strong.

wisdom *noun* **1** being wise. **2** wise sayings.
wisdom tooth a molar tooth that may grow at the back of the jaw of a person aged about 20 or more.

wise¹ *adjective* knowing or understanding many things; judging well. **wisely** *adverb*

wise² *noun* (*old use* or as a *suffix*) manner or direction, *It is in no wise better*; *otherwise*; *clockwise*; *crosswise*.

wish¹ *verb* **1** feel or say that you would like to have or do something or would like something to happen. **2** say that you hope someone will get something, *Wish me luck!*

wish² *noun* (*plural* **wishes**) **1** something you wish for; a desire. **2** the action of wishing, *Make a wish when you blow out the candles.*

wine *noun* **1** (*informal terms*) booze, grog, plonk, vino.

wing¹ *noun* **1** pinion. **6** branch, faction, section.

wink¹ *verb* **1** bat an eyelid, blink. **2** blink, flash, flicker, sparkle, twinkle.

winner *noun* **1** champion, conqueror, victor. **2** hit, knockout (*informal*), smash hit (*informal*), success.

wipe *verb* **1** clean, dry, dust, mop, polish, rub, sponge, towel. **2** apply, rub, smear, spread. **3** erase, scrub (*informal*); see also DELETE.
wipe out 1 cancel, erase, expunge, get rid of, remove. **2** annihilate, destroy, eliminate, exterminate, kill, obliterate.

wire¹ *noun* **3** cable, flex, lead.

wiry *adjective* **2** lean, muscular, sinewy, strong, thin, tough.

wisdom *noun* **1** astuteness, discernment, insight, intellect, intelligence, judgement, nous (*informal*), prudence, reason, sagacity, sense, shrewdness, understanding.

wise¹ *adjective* (*a wise person*) astute, discerning, intelligent, knowing, perceptive, prudent, sagacious, sage, savvy (*informal*), sensible, shrewd, smart, understanding; (*a wise decision*) advisable, appropriate, judicious, politic, prudent, sensible, shrewd, smart, sound.

wish¹ *verb* **1** aspire, crave, desire, fancy, hanker, hope, long, want, yearn.

wish² *noun* **1** ambition, aspiration, craving, desire, fancy, hope, longing, objective, request, want, whim, yearning, yen.

wishbone *noun* a forked bone between the neck and breast of a bird (sometimes pulled apart by two people; the person who gets the bigger part can make a wish).

wishful *adjective* desiring something.
wishful thinking believing something because you want it to be true.

wisp *noun* **1** a few strands of hair or bits of straw etc. **2** a small streak of smoke or cloud etc. **wispy** *adjective*

wisteria (*say* wist-**eer**-ee-a) *noun* a climbing plant with hanging blue, purple, or white flowers.

wistful *adjective* sadly longing for something.
wistfully *adverb*, **wistfulness** *noun*

wit *noun* **1** intelligence; cleverness, *Use your wits.* **2** a clever kind of humour. **3** a witty person.
at your wits' end not knowing what to do.

witch *noun* (*plural* **witches**) a person, especially a woman, who uses magic to do things. **witchcraft** *noun*

witchdoctor *noun* a magician in a primitive tribe whose job is to use magic, cure people, etc.

witchetty *noun* **witchetty grub** the edible larva of various Australian beetles and moths.

with *preposition* used to indicate (**1**) being in the company or care etc. of (*Come with me*), (**2**) having (*a man with a beard*), (**3**) using (*Hit it with a hammer*), (**4**) because of (*shaking with laughter*), (**5**) feeling or showing (*We heard it with pleasure*), (**6**) towards, concerning (*I was angry with him*), (**7**) in opposition to; against (*Don't argue with your father*), (**8**) being separated from (*We had to part with it*).

withdraw *verb* (**withdrew, withdrawn, withdrawing**) **1** take back or away; remove, *She withdrew money from the bank.* **2** go away from a place or people, *The troops withdrew from the frontier.* **3** cancel a statement, offer, etc. **withdrawal** *noun*

withdrawn *adjective* shy and unsociable.

wither *verb* **1** shrivel; wilt. **2** cause to shrivel or wilt. **3** make a person feel subdued or snubbed. [from *weather*]

withers *plural noun* the ridge between a horse's shoulder-blades.

withhold *verb* (**withheld, withholding**) refuse to give or allow something (e.g. information or permission). [from *with-* = away, + *hold*]

within *preposition* & *adverb* inside; not beyond something.

without[1] *preposition* **1** not having, *without food.* **2** free from, *without fear.* **3** (*old use*) outside, *without the city wall.*

without[2] *adverb* outside, *We looked at the house from within and without.*

withstand *verb* (**withstood, withstanding**) endure something successfully; resist.

withy *noun* (*plural* **withies**) a thin flexible branch for tying bundles etc.

witness[1] *noun* (*plural* **witnesses**) **1** a person who sees or hears something happen, *There were no witnesses to the accident.* **2** a person who gives evidence in a lawcourt.

witness[2] *verb* **1** be a witness of something. **2** sign a document to confirm that it is genuine. [from *wit*]

witted *adjective* having wits of a certain kind, *quick-witted.*

witticism *noun* a witty remark.

wistful *adjective* doleful, forlorn, longing, melancholy, nostalgic, pensive, pining, sad, yearning.

wit *noun* **1** brains, common sense, intellect, intelligence, judgement, nous (*informal*), sense, understanding, wisdom. **2** banter, humour, jokes, puns, repartee. **3** comedian, comic, humorist, jester, joker, punster, wag.

witch *noun* enchantress, magician, sorceress.
witchcraft *noun* black magic, magic, the occult, sorcery, voodoo, witchery, wizardry.

witchdoctor *noun* medicine man, shaman.

withdraw *verb* **1** extract, pull out, recall, remove, take away, take back, take out. **2** back off, depart, go, go away, leave, pull out, retire, retreat. **3** cancel, recant, rescind, retract, revoke, take back.

withdrawn *adjective* antisocial, detached, introverted, reclusive, reserved, retiring, shy, unsociable.

wither *verb* **1** dehydrate, droop, dry out, dry up, shrivel, wilt.

withhold *verb* (*withhold permission*) deny, refuse; (*withhold information*) conceal, hide, hold back, keep back, suppress.

withstand *verb* bear, cope with, endure, oppose, resist, stand up to, survive, tolerate, weather.

witness[1] *noun* **1** bystander, eyewitness, looker-on, observer, onlooker, spectator, viewer.

witness[2] *verb* **1** behold (*old use*), be present at, observe, see, view, watch. **2** countersign, endorse, validate.

wittingly *adverb* intentionally. [from *wit*]

witty *adjective* (**wittier, wittiest**) clever and amusing; full of wit. **wittily** *adverb*, **wittiness** *noun*

wizard *noun* **1** a male witch; a magician. **2** a person with amazing abilities. **wizardry** *noun* [from *wise* (originally = *wise man*)]

wizened (*say* **wiz**-end) *adjective* full of wrinkles, *a wizened face.*

woad *noun* a kind of blue dye formerly made from a plant.

wobble *verb* (**wobbled, wobbling**) stand or move unsteadily; shake slightly. **wobble** *noun*, **wobbly** *adjective*

woe *noun* **1** sorrow. **2** misfortune. **woeful** *adjective*, **woefully** *adverb*

woebegone *adjective* looking unhappy.

woggle *noun* a neckerchief ring of leather etc. used by Scouts and Guides.

wok *noun* a Chinese cooking-pan shaped like a large bowl.

wolf¹ *noun* (*plural* **wolves**) a fierce wild animal of the dog family.

wolf² *verb* eat something greedily.

woman *noun* (*plural* **women**) a grown-up female human being. **womanhood** *noun*, **womanish** *adjective*, **womanly** *adjective*

womb (*say* woom) *noun* (also called the *uterus*) the hollow organ in a female's body where babies develop before they are born.

wombat *noun* an Australian burrowing animal rather like a small bear.

wonder¹ *noun* **1** a feeling of surprise and admiration or curiosity. **2** something that causes this feeling; a marvel.
no wonder it is not surprising.

wonder² *verb* **1** feel that you want to know; try to form an opinion, *We are still wondering what to do next.* **2** feel wonder.

wonderful *adjective* marvellous; surprisingly good, excellent. **wonderfully** *adverb*

wonderment *noun* a feeling of wonder.

wondrous *adjective* (*old use*) wonderful.

wont¹ (*say* wohnt) *adjective* (*old use*) accustomed, *He was wont to dress in rags.*

wont² *noun* a habit or custom, *He was dressed in rags, as was his wont.*

won't (*mainly spoken*) will not.

woo *verb* **1** (*old use*) court a woman. **2** seek someone's favour. **wooer** *noun*

wood *noun* **1** the substance of which trees are made. **2** many trees growing close together.

witty *adjective* amusing, clever, droll, funny, humorous, quick-witted, scintillating, sharp-witted.

wizard *noun* **1** magician, medicine man, sorcerer, warlock (*old use*), witchdoctor. **2** expert, genius, maestro, master, virtuoso, whiz (*informal*).

wobble *verb* quake, quaver, quiver, reel, rock, shake, stagger, sway, teeter, totter, tremble, waver.
wobbly *adjective* loose, rickety, rocky, shaky, unbalanced, unstable, unsteady, wonky (*informal*).

woe *noun* **1** anguish, distress, grief, hardship, heartache, misery, misfortune, pain, sorrow, suffering, unhappiness. **2** adversity, affliction, burden, misfortune, problem, trial, tribulation, trouble.

woman *noun* bird (*informal*), chick (*slang*), dame (*old use* or *American slang*), damsel (*old use*), female, girl, lady, lass, maid (*old use*), maiden (*old use*), matron, sheila (*Australian slang*).
womanish *adjective* effeminate, sissy, unmanly, unmasculine.
womanly *adjective* feminine, ladylike.

wonder¹ *noun* **1** admiration, amazement, astonishment, awe, bewilderment, fascination, surprise, wonderment. **2** curiosity, marvel, miracle, phenomenon, rarity.

wonder² *verb* **1** ask yourself, be curious, conjecture, muse, ponder, puzzle, question, speculate, think. **2** be amazed, be stunned, be surprised, marvel.

wonderful *adjective* admirable, amazing, astonishing, astounding, awe-inspiring, awesome, breathtaking, brilliant (*informal*), excellent, extraordinary, fabulous (*informal*), fantastic (*informal*), fine, first-class, impressive, incredible, magnificent, marvellous, miraculous, outstanding, phenomenal, prodigious, remarkable, sensational, spectacular, splendid, staggering, stunning, stupendous, superb, terrific (*informal*), tremendous (*informal*), unbelievable, unreal (*slang*), wondrous (*old use*).

woo *verb* **1** court, pursue, seek the hand of. **2** attract, seek, seek to win.

wood *noun* **1** see TIMBER **2** bush, copse, forest, grove, jungle, scrub, spinney, thicket, woodland, woods.

▶▶ D I C T I O N A R Y ◀◀

woodcut *noun* an engraving made on wood; a print made from this.

wooded *adjective* covered with growing trees.

wooden *adjective* **1** made of wood. **2** stiff and clumsy. **3** showing no expression or liveliness. **woodenly** *adverb*

woodland *noun* wooded country.

woodlouse *noun* (*plural* **woodlice**) a small crawling creature with seven pairs of legs, living in rotten wood or damp soil etc.

woodpecker *noun* a bird that taps tree-trunks with its beak to find insects.

woodwind *noun* wind instruments that are usually made of wood, e.g. the clarinet and oboe.

woodwork *noun* **1** making things out of wood. **2** things made out of wood.

woodworm *noun* the larva of a kind of beetle that bores into wooden furniture etc.

woody *adjective* **1** like wood; consisting of wood. **2** full of trees.

wool *noun* **1** the thick soft hair of sheep and goats etc. **2** thread or cloth made from this.

woollen *adjective* made of wool.

woollens *plural noun* woollen clothes.

woolly *adjective* **1** covered with wool or wool-like hair. **2** like wool; woollen. **3** not thinking clearly; vague or confused, *woolly ideas*. **woolliness** *noun*

woolshed *noun* (*Australian*) a shed for shearing and packing wool.

woomera *noun* an Aboriginal throwing stick used to propel a spear.

Woop Woop (*Australian*) an imaginary remote town or district.

word[1] *noun* **1** a set of sounds or letters that has a meaning, and when written or printed has no spaces between the letters. **2** a promise, *He kept his word*. **3** a command or spoken signal, *Run when I give the word*. **4** a message; information, *We sent word of our safe arrival*.
word for word in exactly the same words.
word of honour a solemn promise.
word processor a kind of computer used for editing and printing words typed into it.

word[2] *verb* express something in words, *Word the question carefully*.

wording *noun* the way something is worded.

word-perfect *adjective* having memorised every word perfectly.

wordy *adjective* using too many words; not concise.

work[1] *noun* **1** the use of effort or energy to do something (contrasted with *play* or *recreation*). **2** something you have to do that needs effort or energy. **3** a job; employment. **4** something produced by work, *The teacher marked our work*; *literary works*.
at work working.
out of work having no work; unable to find paid employment.
work of art a fine picture, building, etc.

▶▶ T H E S A U R U S ◀◀

woodcutter *noun* logger, lumberjack (*American*), sawyer, splitter, tree-feller.

wooded *adjective* forested, silvan, timbered, tree-covered.

wooden *adjective* **1** timber, wood. **2** clumsy, leaden, rigid, stiff. **3** blank, deadpan (*informal*), empty, expressionless, glassy, impassive, poker-faced, vacant, vacuous.

woodwork *noun* **1** cabinetmaking, carpentry, joinery.

wool *noun* **1** fleece, hair. **2** yarn.

woolly *adjective* **1** fleecy, fluffy, furry, fuzzy, hairy, shaggy. **2** wool, woollen. **3** fuzzy, hazy, imprecise, indefinite, muddled, unclear, vague.

word[1] *noun* **1** appellation, expression, name, term. **2** assurance, guarantee, pledge, promise, undertaking, vow, word of honour. **3** command, direction, instruction, order. **4** advice, information, intelligence, message, news, report, tidings.

word for word accurately, exactly, faithfully, literally, precisely, verbatim.

word[2] *verb* couch, express, formulate, phrase, put.

wording *noun* expression, language, phraseology, phrasing.

wordy *adjective* diffuse, garrulous, long-winded, loquacious, rambling, talkative, verbose, voluble.

work[1] *noun* **1** drudgery, effort, elbow grease, exertion, graft (*slang*), grind, industry, labour, slog, sweat (*informal*), toil, travail (*old use*), yakka (*Australian informal*). **2** assignment, chore, duty, homework, job, project, task, undertaking. **3** business, career, employment, job, occupation, profession, trade, vocation. **4** (*a literary work*) book, composition, creation, opus, piece, writing.

▶▶▶ D I C T I O N A R Y ◀◀◀

work² *verb* **1** do work. **2** have a job; be employed, *She works in a bank.* **3** act or operate correctly or successfully, *Is the lift working?* **4** make something act; operate, *Can you work the lift?* **5** shape or press etc., *Work the mixture into a paste.* **6** make a way; pass, *The grub works its way into timber.* **7** bring about, *He works miracles.*

working class people who work for wages, especially in manual or industrial work.

work out find an answer by thinking or calculating; have a particular result.

work up make people become excited; arouse.

workable *adjective* usable; practicable.

worker *noun* **1** a person who works. **2** a member of the working class. **3** a bee or ant etc. that does the work in a hive or colony but does not produce eggs.

workman *noun* (*plural* **workmen**) a man employed to do manual labour; a worker.

workmanship *noun* a person's skill in working; the result of this.

workshop *noun* **1** a place where things are made or mended. **2** a meeting for discussion or group activity.

work-shy *adjective* avoiding work; lazy.

world *noun* **1** the earth with all its countries and peoples. **2** the universe. **3** the people or things belonging to a certain activity, *the world of sport.* **4** a very great amount, *It will do him a world of good.*

worldly *adjective* **1** of life on earth, not spiritual. **2** interested only in money, pleasure, etc. **worldliness** *noun*

worldwide *adjective* & *adverb* throughout the world.

worm¹ *noun* **1** an animal with a long small soft rounded or flat body and no backbone or limbs. **2** an unimportant or unpleasant person. **wormy** *adjective*

worm² *verb* move by wriggling or crawling.

wormwood *noun* a woody plant with a bitter taste.

worn¹ *past participle* of **wear¹**.

worn² *adjective* **1** damaged by use or wear. **2** looking tired and exhausted.

worried *adjective* feeling or showing worry.

worry¹ *verb* (**worried**, **worrying**) **1** be troublesome to someone; make a person feel slightly afraid. **2** feel anxious. **3** hold something in the teeth and shake it, *The dog was worrying a rat.* **worrier** *noun*

▶▶▶ T H E S A U R U S ◀◀◀

work² *verb* **1** apply yourself, beaver away, be busy, drudge, exert yourself, graft (*slang*), grind away, labour, peg away, plug away, slave, slog, strive, sweat, toil. **2** be employed, have a job. **3** act, function, go, operate, perform, run. **4** control, handle, manage, manipulate, operate, use, wield. **7** accomplish, achieve, bring about, effect, execute, perform.

work out 1 calculate, compute, deduce, fathom, figure out, infer, reason, solve. **2** develop, evolve, go, pan out, turn out.

work up agitate, arouse, excite, get someone het up (*informal*), get someone hot under the collar, incite, stir up, upset.

workable *adjective* feasible, practicable, practical, viable.

worker *noun* **1** artisan, breadwinner, craftsman, craftswoman, employee, hand, labourer, operative, operator, tradesman, tradeswoman, wage-earner, workman; (*workers*) human resources, manpower, personnel, staff, workforce.

workman *noun* handyman, labourer, navvy, tradesman, worker.

workmanship *noun* craftsmanship, handiwork, skill, technique.

workshop *noun* **1** factory, laboratory, mill, plant, workroom, works.

world *noun* **1** earth, globe, planet. **2** cosmos, Creation, universe. **3** area, circle, domain, field, realm, sphere.

worldly *adjective* **1** earthly, material, mundane, secular, temporal. **2** acquisitive, materialistic, mercenary.

worldwide *adjective* global, international, universal.

worm² *verb* crawl, slither, squirm, twist, wriggle, writhe.

worn² *adjective* **1** dilapidated, frayed, holey, ragged, shabby, tattered, tatty (*informal*), thin, threadbare. **2** careworn, drawn, exhausted, haggard, jaded, tired, weary, worn out.

worried *adjective* afraid, agitated, anxious, apprehensive, concerned, distraught, distressed, fearful, fretful, frightened, nervous, perturbed, troubled, uneasy.

worry¹ *verb* **1** alarm, annoy, bother, distress, disturb, harass, hassle, irritate, perturb, pester, plague, trouble, upset, vex. **2** be agitated, be anxious, be uneasy, brood, fret.

▶▶▶ D I C T I O N A R Y ◀◀

worry² *noun* (*plural* **worries**) **1** the condition of worrying; being uneasy. **2** something that makes a person worry. [the verb originally meant 'to strangle']

worse *adjective* & *adverb* more bad or more badly; less good or less well.

worsen *adjective* make or become worse.

worship¹ *verb* (**worshipped, worshipping**) **1** give praise or respect to God or a god. **2** love or respect a person or thing greatly. **worshipper** *noun*

worship² *noun* **1** worshipping; religious ceremonies. **2** a title of respect for a mayor or certain magistrates. [from *worth*]

worst *adjective* & *adverb* most bad or most badly; least good or least well.

worsted *noun* a kind of woollen material.

worth¹ *adjective* **1** having a certain value, *This stamp is worth $100.* **2** deserving something; good or important enough for something, *That book is worth reading.*
worth while worth the time or effort needed, *The job was not worth while.*

Usage Use *worthwhile* when it comes before the noun (e.g. *a worthwhile job*).

worth² *noun* value; usefulness.

worthless *adjective* having no value; useless. **worthlessness** *noun*

worthwhile *adjective* important or good enough to do; useful, *a worthwhile job.*

Usage See *worth* for the use of *worth while*.

worthy *adjective* having great merit; deserving respect or support, *a worthy cause.* **worthiness** *noun*
worthy of deserving, *This charity is worthy of your support.*

would *auxiliary verb* used (**1**) as the past tense of *will¹* (*We said we would do it*), in questions (*Would you like to come?*), and polite requests (*Would you come in, please?*), (**2**) with *I* and *we* and the verbs *like, prefer, be glad,* etc. (e.g. *I would like to come, we would be glad to help*), where the strictly correct use is *should.* (**3**) of something to be expected (*That's just what he would do!*).

would-be *adjective* wanting or pretending to be, *a would-be comedian.*

wouldn't (*mainly spoken*) would not.

wound¹ (*say* woond) *noun* **1** an injury done by a cut, stab, or hit. **2** a hurt to a person's feelings.

wound² *verb* **1** cause a wound to a person or animal. **2** hurt a person's feelings.

wound³ (*say* wownd) *past tense* of **wind³**.

wowser *noun* (*Australian*) a person with very strict morals; a spoilsport.

wraith *noun* a ghost.

▶▶▶ T H E S A U R U S ◀◀

worry² *noun* **1** anguish, anxiety, apprehension, bother, concern, disquiet, distress, stress, trouble, uneasiness. **2** bugbear, burden, concern, hassle (*informal*), headache, menace, nightmare (*informal*), problem, trial, trouble, vexation.

worsen *verb* (*make worse*) aggravate, exacerbate; (*become worse*) decline, degenerate, deteriorate, go backwards, go downhill (*informal*), go to the pack (*Australian informal*), retrogress.

worship¹ *verb* admire, adore, deify, dote on, exalt, extol, glorify, hallow, honour, idolise, laud (*informal*), look up to, love, magnify, praise, respect, revere, venerate.

worship² *noun* **1** adoration, deification, devotion, exaltation, glorification, homage, honour, praise, respect, reverence, veneration.

worth¹ *adjective* **be worth 1** be priced at, be valued at, cost, sell at. **2** be worthy of, deserve, justify, merit.

worth² *noun* benefit, good, importance, merit, use, usefulness, value.

worthless *adjective* futile, insignificant, meaningless, pointless, unimportant, unproductive, unprofitable, useless, vain, valueless.

worthwhile *adjective* advantageous, beneficial, important, productive, profitable, rewarding, useful, valuable.

worthy *adjective* admirable, commendable, creditable, deserving, estimable, good, honourable, meritorious, praiseworthy, respectable, worthwhile.

wound¹ *noun* **1** cut, gash, graze, incision, injury, laceration, lesion, scratch, sore. **2** blow, damage, distress, hurt, injury, pain, trauma.

wound² *verb* **1** cut, damage, gash, graze, harm, hurt, injure, knife, lacerate, maim, mutilate, shoot, stab. **2** hurt, mortify, offend, pain, sting.

wowser *noun* killjoy, party pooper (*slang*), puritan, spoilsport, teetotaller, wet blanket.

►►► DICTIONARY ◄◄

wrangle *verb* (**wrangled, wrangling**) have a noisy argument or quarrel. **wrangle** *noun*, **wrangler** *noun*

wrap[1] *verb* (**wrapped, wrapping**) put paper or cloth etc. round something as a covering.

wrap[2] *noun* a shawl, coat, or cloak etc. worn for warmth.

wrapper *noun* a piece of paper etc. wrapped round something.

wrath (*rhymes with* cloth) *noun* anger. **wrathful** *adjective*, **wrathfully** *adverb*

wreak (*say* reek) *verb* inflict, *Rain wreaked havoc with the building work.* [from Old English *wrecan* = avenge]

wreath (*say* reeth) *noun* **1** flowers or leaves etc. fastened into a circle, *wreaths of holly.* **2** a curving line of mist or smoke. [compare *writhe*]

wreathe (*say* reethe) *verb* (**wreathed, wreathing**) **1** surround or decorate with a wreath. **2** cover, *Their faces were wreathed in smiles.* **3** move in a curve, *Smoke wreathed upwards.*

wreck[1] *verb* **1** damage something, especially a ship, so badly that it cannot be used again. **2** completely ruin chances, hopes, etc.

wreck[2] *noun* **1** a wrecked ship or building or car etc. **2** a person who is left very weak, *a nervous wreck.* **3** the wrecking of something. [same origin as *wreak*]

wreckage *noun* the pieces of a wreck.

wren *noun* a very small bird with an erect tail.

wrench[1] *verb* twist or pull something violently.

wrench[2] *noun* (*plural* **wrenches**) **1** a wrenching movement. **2** pain caused by parting, *Leaving home was a great wrench.* **3** an adjustable tool rather like a spanner, used for gripping and turning bolts, nuts, etc.

wrest *verb* force or wrench something away, *We wrested his sword from him.*

wrestle *verb* (**wrestled, wrestling**) **1** fight by grasping your opponent and trying to throw him or her to the ground. **2** struggle with a problem etc. **wrestle** *noun*, **wrestler** *noun*

wretch *noun* (*plural* **wretches**) **1** a person who is very unfortunate. **2** a person who is disliked; a rascal.

wretched *adjective* **1** miserable; unhappy. **2** shabby. **3** not satisfactory; causing a nuisance, *This wretched car won't start.* **wretchedly** *adverb*, **wretchedness** *noun*

wriggle *verb* (**wriggled, wriggling**) move with short twisting movements. **wriggle** *noun*, **wriggly** *adjective*

wriggle out of avoid work or blame etc. cunningly.

wring *verb* (**wrung, wringing**) **1** twist and squeeze a wet thing to get water etc. out of it. **2** squeeze firmly or forcibly. **3** get something by a great effort, *We wrung a promise out of him.* **wring** *noun*

wringing wet so wet that water can be squeezed out of it.

►►► THESAURUS ◄◄

wrangle *verb* argue, bicker, debate, disagree, dispute, fight, haggle, quarrel, quibble, squabble.

wrangle *noun* altercation, argument, barney (*informal*), brawl, clash, controversy, disagreement, dispute, quarrel, row, squabble, tiff.

wrap[1] *verb* bind, cocoon, cover, encase, enclose, enfold, envelop, insulate, lag, muffle, pack, package, parcel up, shroud, surround, swaddle, swathe.

wrap[2] *noun* cape, cloak, coat, mantle, poncho, shawl, stole.

wrapper *noun* case, casing, cover, envelope, jacket, packet, sleeve.

wrath *noun* anger, displeasure, exasperation, fury, indignation, ire, rage, temper.

wreath *noun* **1** chaplet, festoon, garland, lei.

wreck[1] *verb* **1** break up, dash, demolish, destroy, devastate, ruin, scupper, scuttle, shatter, shipwreck, smash, trash (*informal*), vandalise. **2** dash, destroy, muck up, ruin, sabotage, shatter, spoil, undermine, undo.

wreckage *noun* debris, flotsam, remains, remnants, rubble, ruins, wreck.

wrench[1] *verb* force, jerk, lever, prise, pull, tear, tug, twist, wrest, yank (*informal*).

wrestle *verb* **1** battle, contend, fight, grapple, scuffle, struggle, tussle. **2** contend, grapple, struggle.

wretch *noun* **1** beggar, down-and-out, unfortunate. **2** blackguard, miscreant, rascal, ratbag (*informal*), rogue, rotter (*slang*), scoundrel, swine (*informal*), villain.

wretched *adjective* **1** dejected, depressed, despondent, disconsolate, dismal, forlorn, hapless, hopeless, miserable, pathetic, pitiful, sad, sorrowful, sorry, unfortunate, unhappy, woebegone.

wriggle *verb* crawl, slither, squirm, twist, wiggle, worm your way, writhe.

wriggle out of avoid, back out of, escape, evade, extricate yourself from, get out of.

wring *verb* **1** mangle, press, squeeze, twist. **3** extort, extract, force, obtain, screw, wrest.

wringer *noun* a device with a pair of rollers for squeezing water out of washed clothes etc.

wrinkle¹ *noun* a small crease; a small furrow or ridge in the skin.

wrinkle² *verb* (**wrinkled, wrinkling**) make wrinkles in something; form wrinkles.

wrist *noun* the joint that connects the hand and arm.

wristwatch *noun* a watch for wearing on the wrist.

writ (*say* rit) *noun* a formal written command issued by a lawcourt etc.
Holy Writ the Bible.

write *verb* (**wrote, written, writing**) **1** put letters or words etc. on paper or another surface. **2** be the author or composer of something, *write books* or *music*. **3** send a letter to somebody. **writer** *noun*, **writing** *noun*
write down put into writing.
write off cancel a debt etc.; damage a vehicle so badly that it cannot be repaired.

writhe *verb* (**writhed, writhing**) **1** twist your body because of pain. **2** wriggle. **3** suffer because of great shame.

wrong¹ *adjective* **1** incorrect; not true, *the wrong answer*. **2** morally bad; unfair; unjust, *It is wrong to cheat*. **3** not working properly, *There's something wrong with the engine*. **wrongly** *adverb*, **wrongness** *noun*

wrong² *adverb* wrongly, *You guessed wrong*.

wrong³ *noun* something morally wrong; a wrong action; an injustice.
in the wrong having done or said something wrong.

wrong⁴ *verb* do wrong to someone; treat a person unfairly.

wrongdoer *noun* a person who does wrong. **wrongdoing** *noun*

wrongful *adjective* unfair; unjust; illegal. **wrongfully** *adverb*

wrought *adjective* (of metal) worked by being beaten out or shaped by hammering or rolling etc., *wrought iron*.

wry *adjective* (**wryer, wryest**) **1** twisted or bent out of shape. (Compare *awry*.) **2** showing disgust or disappointment or mockery, *a wry grin*. **wryly** *adverb*, **wryness** *noun*

wurley *noun* (*plural* **wurlies**) an Aboriginal hut or shelter.

wrinkle¹ *noun* corrugation, crease, crinkle, crow's-foot, crumple, fold, furrow, line, pleat, pucker, ridge.

wrinkle² *verb* crease, crinkle, crumple, pucker, rumple, screw up.

write *verb* **1** inscribe, pen, pencil, print, scrawl, scribble, sign. **2** compose, create, produce. **3** correspond, drop a line, send a letter.
writer *noun* author, columnist, correspondent, dramatist, essayist, journalist, novelist, playwright, poet, screenwriter, scribe, scriptwriter.
writing *noun* **1** calligraphy, copperplate, graffiti, hand, handwriting, hieroglyphics, inscription, longhand, printing, scrawl, scribble, script, shorthand. **2** article, book, composition, diary, document, essay, journal, letter, literature, novel, poem, prose, publication, story, text, work.
write down document, jot down, list, make a note of, note, record, register, take down, transcribe.
write off 1 cancel, erase, forget about, wipe out. **2** destroy, ruin, wreck.

writhe *verb* **2** squirm, twist, wriggle.

wrong¹ *adjective* **1** erroneous, fallacious, false, imprecise, inaccurate, incorrect, inexact, mistaken, untrue. **2** bad, corrupt, criminal, crooked, dishonest, evil, illegal, illicit, immoral, improper, iniquitous, naughty, reprehensible, sinful, unethical, unfair, unjust, unlawful, wicked. **3** amiss, awry, defective, faulty, kaput (*informal*), out of order, wonky (*informal*).

wrong³ *noun* abuse, crime, evil, immorality, iniquity, injustice, misdeed, misdemeanour, offence, sin, sinfulness, transgression, trespass (*old use*), vice, wickedness, wrongdoing.

wrong⁴ *verb* abuse, harm, ill-treat, maltreat, misrepresent, mistreat.

wrongdoer *noun* baddy (*informal*), criminal, crook (*informal*), culprit, delinquent, evildoer, felon, lawbreaker, malefactor, miscreant, offender, sinner, transgressor, villain.

wry *adjective* **1** askew, contorted, crooked, distorted, twisted.

Xx ◄

xenophobia (*say* zen-o-**foh**-bee-a) *noun* strong dislike of foreigners. [from Greek *xenos* = foreigner, + *phobia*]

Xerox (*say* **zeer**-oks) *noun* (*trade mark*) a photocopy made by a special process. **xerox** *verb*

Xmas *noun* Christmas. [the X is short for *Christ*; it represents the Greek letter (= ch) which is the first letter of *Christos* = Christ]

X-ray[1] *noun* a photograph or examination of the inside of something, especially a part of the body, made by a kind of radiation (called *X-rays*) that can penetrate solid things.

X-ray[2] *verb* make an X-ray of something.

xylophone (*say* **zy**-lo-fohn) *noun* a musical instrument made of wooden bars that you hit with small hammers. [from Greek *xylon* = wood, + *phone* = sound]

▶ Yy ◀

yabby *noun* (*plural* **yabbies**) **1** a small Australian freshwater crayfish. **2** an Australian saltwater prawn used as bait.

yacht (*say* yot) *noun* **1** a sailing-boat used for racing or cruising. **2** a private ship. **yachting** *noun*, **yachtsman** *noun*, **yachtswoman** *noun* [from Dutch *jaghtschip* = fast pirate ship]

yak *noun* an ox with long hair, found in central Asia. [from Tibetan]

yakka *noun* (*Australian informal*) work.

yam *noun* the edible starchy tuber of a tropical plant.

Yank *noun* (*informal*) a Yankee.

yank *verb* (*informal*) pull something strongly and suddenly. **yank** *noun*

Yankee *noun* an American, especially of the northern USA.

yap *verb* (**yapped**, **yapping**) bark shrilly. **yap** *noun*

yard¹ *noun* **1** a measure of length, 36 inches or about 91 centimetres. **2** a long pole stretched out from a mast to support a sail.

yard² *noun* an enclosed area beside a building or used for a certain kind of work, *a timber yard*; the garden of a house.

yardstick *noun* a standard by which something is measured.

yarn *noun* **1** thread spun by twisting fibres together, used in knitting etc. **2** (*informal*) a tale or story.

yashmak *noun* a veil worn in public by Muslim women in some countries.

yawl *noun* a kind of sailing-boat or fishing-boat.

yawn *verb* **1** open the mouth wide and breathe in deeply when feeling sleepy or bored. **2** form a wide opening, *A pit yawned in front of us.* **yawn** *noun*

ye *pronoun* (*old use*, in speaking to two or more people) you.

yea (*say* yay) *adverb* (*old use*) yes.

year *noun* **1** the time the earth takes to go right round the sun, about 365¼ days. **2** the time from 1 January to 31 December. **3** an academic level or grade. **yearly** *adjective* & *adverb*

yearling *noun* an animal between one and two years old.

yearn *verb* long for something.

yeast *noun* a substance that causes alcohol and carbon dioxide to form as it develops, used in making beer and wine and in baking bread etc.

yell *verb* give a loud cry; shout. **yell** *noun*

yellow¹ *noun* the colour of butter, egg-yolk, or ripe lemons.

yellow² *adjective* **1** of yellow colour. **2** (*informal*) cowardly. **yellowness** *noun*

yellowcake *noun* uranium ore, concentrated uranium oxide.

yelp *verb* give a shrill bark or cry. **yelp** *noun*

yen¹ *noun* (*plural* **yen**) a unit of money in Japan. [from Chinese *yuan* = round thing]

yen² *noun* a longing. [probably from Cantonese]

yes *adverb* used to agree to something (= the statement is correct) or as an answer (= I am here).

▶▶▶ THESAURUS ◀◀◀

yakka *noun* effort, exertion, graft (*slang*), grind, labour, slog, sweat, toil, work.

yank *verb* & *noun* jerk, pull, tug, wrench.

yap *verb* & *noun* bark, yelp.

yard² *noun* backyard, courtyard, garden, quad (*informal*), quadrangle.

yardstick *noun* benchmark, criterion, gauge, guide, measure, standard, touchstone.

yarn *noun* **1** fibre, strand, thread. **2** anecdote, narrative, story, tale.

year *noun* **3** class, form, grade, level. **yearly** *adjective* annual.

yearn *verb* crave, hanker, have a yen, hunger, long, pine, thirst; see also DESIRE².

yell *verb* bawl, bellow, call, cry, holler (*American*), howl, roar, scream, screech, shout, shriek. **yell** *noun* bellow, cry, howl, roar, scream, screech, shout, shriek.

yellow² *adjective* **1** amber, buttercup, canary, daffodil, gold, golden, jaundiced, lemon, mustard, primrose, saffron.

yelp *verb* & *noun* bark, cry, howl, squeal.

yen² *noun* craving, desire, fancy, hankering, hunger, longing, thirst, yearning.

▶▶ DICTIONARY ◀◀

yesterday *noun* & *adverb* the day before today.

yet¹ *adverb* **1** up to this time; by this time, *The post hasn't come yet.* **2** eventually, *I'll get even with him yet!* **3** in addition; even, *She became yet more excited.*

yet² *conjunction* nevertheless, *It is strange, yet it is true.*

yeti *noun* (*plural* **yetis**) a very large animal thought to live in the Himalayas, sometimes called the 'Abominable Snowman'. [from Tibetan]

yew *noun* an evergreen tree with dark-green needle-like leaves and red berries.

yield¹ *verb* **1** surrender; do what is asked or ordered; give way, *He yielded to persuasion.* **2** produce as a crop or as profit etc.

yield² *noun* the amount yielded or produced, *What is the yield of wheat per hectare?* [from Old English, = pay]

yob or **yobbo** *noun* (*plural* **yobbos**) (*informal*) a lout or hooligan.

yodel *verb* (**yodelled**, **yodelling**) sing or shout with the voice continually going from a low note to a high note and back again. **yodeller** *noun*

yoga (*say* **yoh**-ga) *noun* a Hindu system of meditation and self-control.

yoghurt (*say* **yoh**-gert) *noun* milk thickened by the action of certain bacteria, giving it a sharp taste. [Turkish]

yoke¹ *noun* **1** a curved piece of wood put across the necks of animals pulling a cart or plough etc. **2** a shaped piece of wood fitted across a person's shoulders, with a pail or load hung at each end. **3** a close-fitting upper part of a garment, from which the rest hangs.

yoke² *verb* (**yoked**, **yoking**) harness or join by means of a yoke.

yokel (*say* **yoh**-kel) *noun* a simple country fellow.

yolk (*rhymes with* coke) *noun* the round yellow part inside an egg.

Yom Kippur (*say* yom kip-**oor**) the Day of Atonement, a solemn Jewish religious festival, a day of fasting and repentance. [Hebrew]

yon *adjective* & *adverb* (*dialect*) yonder.

yonder *adjective* & *adverb* over there.

yore *noun* **of yore** of long ago, *in days of yore.*

Yorkshire pudding baked batter, usually eaten with roast beef.

you *pronoun* **1** the person or people being spoken to, *Who are you?* **2** anyone; everyone; one, *You can't tell what will happen next.*

young¹ *adjective* having lived or existed for only a short time; not old.

young² *noun* children or young animals or birds, *The dove was feeding its young.*

youngster *noun* a young person; a child.

your *adjective* belonging to you.

you're (*mainly spoken*) you are.

yours *possessive pronoun* belonging to you. **Yours faithfully, Yours sincerely, Yours truly** ways of ending a letter before you sign it. (*Yours faithfully* and *Yours truly* are more formal than *Yours sincerely.*)

Usage It is incorrect to write *your's.*

yourself *pronoun* (*plural* **yourselves**) you and nobody else. (Compare *herself.*)

youth *noun* **1** being young; the time when you are young. **2** a young man. **3** young people. **youthful** *adjective*, **youthfulness** *noun*

yowl *verb* & *noun* wail; howl.

▶▶ THESAURUS ◀◀

yield¹ *verb* **1** bow, capitulate, cave in, give in, give way, submit, succumb, surrender. **2** bear, bring forth (*old use*), bring in, earn, generate, net, pay, produce, return.

yield² *noun* crop, harvest, output, return.

yob or **yobbo** *noun* hooligan, hoon (*Australian informal*), larrikin (*Australian*), lout, ruffian, thug.

yokel *noun* bushie (*Australian informal*), country bumpkin, countryman, country-woman, hick (*informal*), hill-billy (*American informal*), rustic.

young¹ *adjective* adolescent, baby, developing, fledgeling, growing, junior, juvenile, new, newborn, undeveloped, youthful.

young² *noun* babies, brood, family, litter, offspring, progeny.

youngster *noun* adolescent, boy, child, girl, juvenile, kid (*informal*), lad, lass, teenager, youth.

youth *noun* **1** adolescence, teenage years, teens, young days. **2** adolescent, boy, fellow, juvenile, kid (*informal*), lad, teenager, young man, youngster. **3** kids (*informal*), the young, young people.

youthful *adjective* active, energetic, sprightly, spry, vigorous, young, young-looking.

▶▶ D I C T I O N A R Y ◀◀

yo-yo *noun* (*plural* **yo-yos**) (*trade mark*) a round toy that can be made to rise and fall on a string that winds round it.

yuan (*say* yoo-**ahn**) *noun* the unit of money in China.

yucky *adjective* (*informal*) disgusting, repulsive.

yule *noun* (*old use*) the Christmas festival, also called **yule-tide**.

yummy *adjective* (*informal*) tasty, delicious.

▶▶ T H E S A U R U S ◀◀

yucky *adjective* disgusting, gross (*informal*), repulsive, revolting, sickening.

yummy *adjective* appetising, delectable, delicious, mouth-watering, scrumptious (*informal*), tasty.

► Zz

zany *adjective* crazily funny.

zap *verb* (**zapped, zapping**) (*slang*) **1** attack or destroy something forcefully. **2** change quickly from one section of a videotape etc. to another.

zeal *noun* enthusiasm; keenness. **zealous** (*say* zel-us) *adjective*, **zealously** *adverb*

zealot (*say* zel-ot) *noun* a zealous person; a fanatic.

zebra (*say* zeb-ra) *noun* an African animal of the horse family, with black and white stripes all over its body.
zebra crossing a place for pedestrians to cross a road safely, marked with broad white stripes.

zebu (*say* zee-bew) *noun* an ox with a humped back, found in India, East Asia, and Africa.

zenith *noun* **1** the part of the sky directly above you. **2** the highest point, *His power was at its zenith*. [from Arabic *samt ar-ras* = path over the head]

zephyr (*say* zef-er) *noun* a soft gentle wind. [from Greek *Zephyros* = god of the west wind]

zero *noun* (*plural* **zeros**) **1** nought; the figure 0; nothing. **2** the point marked 0 on a thermometer etc.
zero hour the time when something is planned to start. [from Arabic *sifr* = cipher]

zest *noun* great enjoyment or interest. **zestful** *adjective*, **zestfully** *adverb*

ziff *noun* (*Australian slang*) a beard.

zigzag[1] *noun* a line or route that turns sharply from side to side.

zigzag[2] *verb* (**zigzagged, zigzagging**) move in a zigzag.

zilch *noun* (*slang*) nothing.

zinc *noun* a white metal.

zip[1] *noun* **1** a zip-fastener. **2** a sharp sound like a bullet going through the air. **3** liveliness; vigour. **zippy** *adjective*

zip[2] *verb* (**zipped, zipping**) **1** fasten with a zip-fastener. **2** move quickly with a sharp sound.

zip-fastener or **zipper** *noun* a fastener consisting of two strips of material, each with rows of small teeth that interlock when a sliding tab brings them together.

zit *noun* (*informal*) a pimple.

zither *noun* a musical instrument with many strings stretched over a shallow box-like body.

zodiac (*say* zoh-dee-ak) *noun* a strip of sky where the sun, moon, and main planets are found, divided into twelve equal parts (called **signs of the zodiac**), each named after a constellation. [from Greek *zoidion* = image of an animal]

zombie *noun* **1** (in voodoo) a corpse said to have been revived by witchcraft. **2** (*informal*) a person who seems to have no mind or will. [from West African *zumbi* = fetish]

zone *noun* an area of a special kind or for a particular purpose. [Greek, = girdle]

►►►THESAURUS◄◄◄

zany *adjective* absurd, bizarre, comical, crazy, eccentric, funny, idiotic, mad, odd, offbeat, peculiar, unconventional, unusual, wacky (*slang*), weird.

zeal *noun* ardour, dedication, devotion, diligence, eagerness, earnestness, energy, enthusiasm, fanaticism, fervour, gusto, keenness, passion, verve, vigour, zest.
zealous *adjective* ardent, conscientious, devoted, diligent, eager, earnest, energetic, enthusiastic, fanatical, fervent, keen, passionate.

zealot *noun* bigot, crank, enthusiast, extremist, fanatic.

zenith *noun* **2** acme, apex, climax, height, peak, pinnacle, prime, summit, top.

zero *noun* **1** cipher, duck (*Cricket*), love (*Tennis*), nil, nothing, nought, zilch (*slang*).

zest *noun* eagerness, energy, enjoyment, enthusiasm, excitement, gusto, interest, keenness, liveliness, oomph (*informal*), pleasure, relish, sparkle, spirit, vigour, zeal, zing (*informal*).

zigzag[2] *verb* curve, meander, snake, twist, wind.

zip[1] *noun* **3** energy, go, gusto, life, liveliness, oomph (*informal*), pep, vigour, vim (*informal*), vitality, zest, zing (*informal*).

zip[2] *verb* **2** race, rush, speed, tear, whiz.

zone *noun* area, belt, district, locality, place, region, sector, territory.

zoo *noun* (*plural* **zoos**) a place where wild animals are kept so that people can look at them or study them. [short for *zoological gardens*]

zoology (*say* zoh-**ol**-o-jee) *noun* the study of animals. **zoological** *adjective*, **zoologist** *noun* [from Greek *zoion* = animal, + *-logy*]

zoom *verb* **1** move very quickly, especially with a buzzing sound. **2** rise quickly, *Prices had zoomed*. **zoom** *noun*

zoom lens a camera lens that can be adjusted continuously to focus on things that are close up or far away.

zucchini (*say* zoo-**kee**-nee) *noun* (*plural* **zucchini** *or* **zucchinis**) a kind of small vegetable marrow. [from Italian, plural of *zucchino* from *zucca* = gourd]

Zulu *noun* (*plural* **Zulus**) a member of a Black people in South Africa.

▶▶ THESAURUS ◀◀

zoo *noun* conservation park, menagerie, safari park, sanctuary, wildlife park, zoological gardens.

zoom *verb* **1** dash, fly, hurry, race, rush, speed, tear, whiz, zip.